WORLD
Population Growth
and
Aging

WORLD
Population Growth
and
Aging

Demographic Trends in the Late Twentieth Century

N A T H A N   K E Y F I T Z
and
W I L H E L M   F L I E G E R

THE UNIVERSITY OF CHICAGO PRESS

Chicago and London

NATHAN KEYFITZ is leader of the Populations Program at the
International Institute for Applied Systems Analysis in Laxenburg, Austria.
WILHELM FLIEGER is director of the Office of Population Studies at
the University of San Carlos in the Philippines.

This book is a sequel to *World Population: An Analysis of Vital Data*
by Nathan Keyfitz and Wilhelm Flieger, published by
the University of Chicago Press in 1968.

The University of Chicago Press, Chicago 60637
The University of Chicago Press, Ltd., London

© 1990 by The University of Chicago
All rights reserved. Published 1990
Printed in the United States of America

99 98 97 96 95 94 93 92 91 90   54321

Library of Congress Cataloging-in-Publication Data

Keyfitz, Nathan, 1913–
    World population growth and aging : demographic trends in the late
twentieth century / Nathan Keyfitz and Wilhelm Flieger.
        p. cm.
    Sequel to: World population.
    Includes bibliographical references and index.
    ISBN 0-226-43237-8 (cloth)
    1. Population forecasting—Statistics.   2. Aging—Statistics.
3. Population—Statistics.   I. Flieger, Wilhelm.   II. Title.
HA155.K49 1990
304.6′09′045021—dc20   90-11015
                                                                    CIP

Preface

The present volume was prepared as part of our work at the International Institute for Applied Systems Analysis (IIASA) in Laxenburg, Austria, and the Office of Population Studies (OPS) of the University of San Carlos in the city of Cebu in the Philippines. We are grateful to the authorities of those institutions for their encouragement. To the Ford Foundation, which provided financial assistance and, through Gary Sick, first suggested to us the idea of producing a sequel to our works on world population of some twenty years ago, we want to express our sincere appreciation. One of our incentives to accept the Ford Foundation's suggestion was the permission of the United Nations Population Division to incorporate into the proposed book data and estimates from its 1988 round of global demographic assessments covering virtually all national populations extant in 1985. The inclusion of this information makes our claim of offering a compendium on "world population" true in the full sense of the word. Because of the UN's contribution, part of the credit for what is produced here has to go to its Population Division, particularly to Jean-Claude Chasteland, Shiro Horiuchi, Yeun-Chung Yu, and Shunichi Inoue, for both providing the data tape and answering our queries at various stages of the preparatory work. Similar acknowledgments are owed to our sixty correspondents in as many national statistical agencies all over the world who shared with us their countries' most up-to-date demographic information, on which the majority of our Detailed Country Tabulations is based. To the World Bank, which, through its publisher, Oxford University Press, allowed us the use of some of its socioeconomic data and estimates, and to Hammond Incorporated of New Jersey for permission to reprint, from the *Hammond Ambassador World Atlas*, the areal data for countries and territories with small populations, we express equal gratitude.

A book of this kind can be produced only through the labor of many. The work of collecting, keying into the computer, and documenting primary data was begun in Austria by Claire Doeblin and Zbigniew Kolodziej and continued in the Philippines by Vivencia Tan, Nenita Tan Chinseng, and Azucena Derecho. In many hours of extra work, the latter three also collated the socioeconomic data reproduced here and computerized selected information from two earlier world-population volumes of the authors that has been incorporated in our Summary Table. Martina Joestl-Segalla of IIASA rewrote most of our old computer programs in Microsoft Fortran to make them usable for the PC, and Edwin Dy of OPS streamlined and combined them with other newly created ones in an easy-to-use demographic software package. Edwin Dy, in addition, created all computer routines that ultimately produced the master copies of the more than 500 pages of printed tabular materials collected in this compendium, a task for which he postponed the assumption of a new job in the United States by a number of weeks. The first version of the more than 700 graphs illustrating the UN-based tabulations in this book was developed by Beatrice Keyfitz. She generously shared her acquired expertise later on with those who produced the final version by teaching them many a timesaving technique mechanizing parts of the graphing process. Likewise generous assistance in the creation of the three-dimensional graphs was received from Wolfgang Lutz of IIASA, and Charles Calhoon of the Urban Institute in Washington, D.C., provided valuable advice on graduation techniques. All maps included in this volume are the work of Roman Kintanar of OPS and Richard Jaime of the Water Resources Center of the University of San Carlos. The latter center deserves additional thanks for making available to us its mapping equipment. Domingo Camocamo of the same center labeled the maps and pasted the more than 800 illustrations contained in this book onto the master copies of the individual pages, a painstaking labor extending over a good number of months.

Of special importance for the shaping of the book were the continuously growing interest and indefatigable work of IIASA's Babette Wils, who contributed her energies and considerable skills to every phase of the preparatory work in both Austria and the Philippines. Her contributions range from the decoding of the original UN data tape and the transfer of the data to PC-readable media over the production of seemingly endless numbers of graphs to significant additions and improvements of the explanatory chapter. For her enthusiastic cooperation, constructive criticisms, and valuable ideas, she deserves special recognition and gratitude.

The work on this volume, simultaneously performed on different halves of the globe, could hardly have succeeded without the able liaison work of Susan Stock in Laxenburg and Carmen Su in Cebu. During many hours behind the keyboard or of traveling to and from mailing and telegraph offices, both combined efficiency and good humor in the face of often unreasonable demands by the authors.

NATHAN KEYFITZ
WILHELM FLIEGER

Contents

Introduction

This book continues work started at the University of Chicago in the mid-1960s. Like two earlier books of the authors, it assembles data from official sources intended to show the larger outlines of what has been happening to population; the countries with populations of 300,000 or more in 1985 and regions recognized by the United Nations are all represented. The earlier volumes summarized what national data were available to us going as far back as the 18th century; the present work deals with the period since 1950, and especially with the 1970s and 1980s.

For better understanding of the evolution of population over this recent period we have included charts, more than 800 in number, that help visualize the changes over time of births, deaths, age distributions, urbanization, and other features.

Minimum Information for 182 UN-Recognized Countries and Regions

In addition to the direct use of national sources, obtained in correspondence and from publications, to which the earlier volumes were confined, we have now some data from the United Nations. Its estimates and projections at five-year intervals from 1950 to 2020 are reproduced for 152 countries and for certain groupings of countries, 30 in all.

Estimates and Projections

The distinction between estimates made from data, applying up to 1985, and those that are projections going beyond the data, for the years 1990 to 2020, would appear to be clear. We have printed the numbers after 1985 in italics, to signify that what falls beyond is projection. Yet in fact the distinction between data and projections, between before and after 1985, is not sharp. The majority of the less developed countries of the world do not have acceptably complete vital statistics, and inferences on their past birth and death rates have to be made by indirect means whose accuracy is lower than that of the vital statistics of advanced countries, perhaps lower than that of the projections for some countries. Fortunately, at least census-taking is nearly universal, and censuses have been supplemented by sample surveys, in particular those taken under the auspices of the World Fertility Survey.

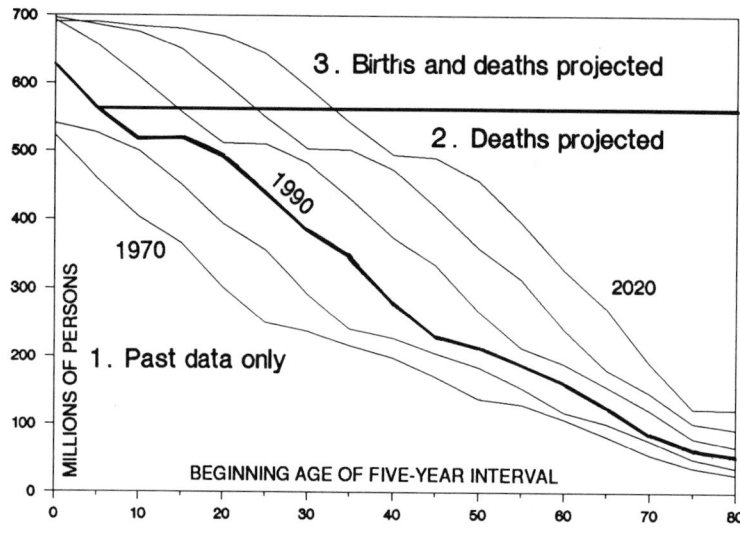

Fig. A. UN Estimates and Projections of the Population of
the World 1970–2020: Three Levels of Precision

Three Levels of Accuracy.

While the years up to 1985 are not always given with factual accuracy, the future is reasonably well projected for the next few years for those countries that have good data of the past.

Projections by age are divisible into three parts as far as accuracy is concerned (Fig. A). We have first the part below and to the left of the line drawn for 1990, and numbered 1, based on counts and estimates for the past. The area above and to the right of that line rests on the projection of deaths. The part of this area corresponding to the persons born after about 1985 rests on the projection of births as well as of deaths. Thus the areas of the figure denoted 1, 2, and 3 are numbered in decreasing order of accuracy.

No Absolute Distinction Between Accuracy of Past and of Future.

Once again, the distinction between past and future as far as accuracy is concerned is not absolute; we cannot assert that all numbers up to 1985 are exact and those later are mere guesses. Recent censuses in the less developed countries have been better than those taken just after the war, so we may speculate that the curve of accuracy with time starts low, rises to a peak in the 1980s, then gradually declines with projections further into the future. The curve of course is different for different countries, and for different age groups, and drawing it empirically is still a distant ideal.

The Problem of Objectivity in the Use of Numbers

Putting these pages together has reminded us of a peculiar hazard of empirical work that has always existed but is intensified with the advent of masses of data and computers to handle them. That is the matter of selection to prove a point. The selection might be among countries; it is easy to select a number of countries to demonstrate that rapid population growth, or urbanization or some other variable, is associated with poverty, and equally easy to select another group of countries to show that there is no relation. Selection of data is one of two hazards to empirical work; the other is the manner of calculation and presentation.

Beyond Selection of Data is Choice of Calculation

Proving Overpopulation. The manner of presentation can give the impression of impending explosion or impending extinction. If one wants to show that population is increasing fast and out of control, one can confine oneself to the absolute numbers, perhaps of population, perhaps of births, citing figures to demonstrate that world population is going up, that it will still be rising by the end of the table in 2020, and that annual increase at that time will be as great as it is now (Table A). It is the absolute numbers of people, not their rates of growth, that affect the environment. The birth figures for the world as a whole suggest that it will be well into the second quarter of the 21st century before the absolute number of births will come down even to the high levels of today, while the population curve continues to slope upward to the end of the projection there shown and beyond. If one stays with the LDC (less developed countries) populations, the impression of increase is stronger yet.

Proving No Danger from Population. On the other hand, if one wants to show that there is really no problem of rapid population growth one points to the rates rather than to absolute numbers, and finds that rates of natural increase in the world have passed their peak, that they now are lower than they were a decade ago and that their decline will continue. The left-hand panel in Table A is for the world, the right-hand one for the

TABLE A.
Population, Births, and Rates of Increase: World and Less Developed Countries, 1950–2020

YEAR	WORLD			LESS DEVELOPED COUNTRIES		
	Population (in thousands)	Births (in thousands)	Rate of Natural Increase*	Population (in thousands)	Births (in thousands)	Rate of Natural Increase*
ESTIMATES BASED ON DATA						
1950	2,515,312	94,138	17.74	1,682,887	75,053	20.27
1955	2,751,559	97,873	18.37	1,864,135	78,391	21.16
1960	3,019,376	106,342	19.76	2,074,525	86,906	23.58
1965	3,335,927	112,948	20.52	2,333,126	94,352	25.39
1970	3,697,918	116,429	19.31	2,648,645	98,296	23.83
1975	4,079,753	115,796	17.31	2,984,140	98,265	21.26
1980	4,450,210	123,151	17.24	3,313,804	105,333	21.07
1985	4,853,848	131,549	17.22	3,680,188	113,832	21.02
PROJECTED						
1990	5,292,178	139,370	17.07	4,086,985	121,952	20.68
1995	5,765,861	142,820	16.09	4,531,294	125,666	19.27
2000	6,251,055	143,312	14.66	4,988,573	126,390	17.43
2005	6,728,575	142,545	13.23	5,441,844	125,843	15.64
2010	7,190,763	142,320	12.06	5,883,294	125,844	14.17
2015	7,639,547	140,270	10.72	6,314,261	123,981	12.55
2020	8,062,274	140,348	9.74	6,722,211	124,166	11.37

*Per 1,000 population.
Source: United Nations, 1988.

LDCs; either of them shows how one can choose a *rising* trend or a *falling* trend according to the point one is trying to prove. Whatever support there is for working with rates as against totals rests on their somehow reflecting individual or average behavior in a way that totals do not. This is patently true among countries; one can compare rates, but hardly total births, for China, say, with those for Fiji, and something like this is also true over time. Yet on the other side, it is not rates that crowd and pollute, but absolute numbers of people.

The Difficulty is Everywhere. An analogous difficulty applies to the larger collection of variables on which the expression of alarm or satisfaction regarding population is usually made to rest. If deforestation continues at the present rate . . . ; if the spread of deserts continues . . . ; then these things, combined with increasing population, will bring disaster. There are many options in projecting the nonpopulation as well as population variables. Ascetically refusing to project either population or the other variables is no protection, for without projection statistical data can make no contribution to policy.

Objectivity a Distant Goal. All this is to say that here as elsewhere objectivity is not to be taken for granted, but is a never-quite-reachable goal. It cannot be attained by merely saying nothing and letting numbers and models speak for themselves, for the way numbers are selected and variables organized into models inevitably causes data to point one way or another.

Accuracy and Significant Figures

The world population as here presented is unlikely to be correct even to within one or two percent. Individual countries included within this total vary enormously in the completeness of their enumerations; there are countries with a well-established statistical tradition that come within one part in a hundred of the true number; for some countries new to census-taking, with mobile populations and inadequate maps, accuracy of 5 percent is not easily attained.

Given that condition, why do we show all populations, past and prospective, to the nearest thousand? For the world as a whole that is four or five orders of magnitude more than the accuracy of the numbers justifies. Partly because the figures are official, whether of the United Nations or national sources, we wanted to change them as little as possible. It seemed an advantage, moreover, to retain the original consistency within the set that we here show—countries adding to regions, for example. But the right way to see these tables in relation to the reality that they represent is to take the first two or three digits only, and regard the remaining digits as what they are: emanations of the computers that make the tables in our offices and in those of the national agencies and the United Nations.

Variants

In recognition that projections are uncertain, the United Nations provides various alternatives to the medium projection that is a best guess. Table B and Figure B give the

TABLE B.
Alternative Population Projections for the World
and the Less Developed Countries: 1985–2025
(totals, thousands of persons)

YEAR	WORLD		LESS DEVELOPED COUNTRIES	
	High	Low	High	Low
1985	4,853,848	4,853,848	3,680,188	3,680,188
1990	5,328,367	5,260,410	4,119,287	4,058,682
1995	5,854,986	5,679,685	4,609,769	4,454,715
2000	6,410,707	6,088,505	5,127,915	4,844,469
2005	6,978,753	6,463,211	5,659,396	5,206,291
2010	7,561,301	6,805,064	6,207,240	5,540,802
2015	8,167,357	7,109,735	6,779,531	5,842,768
2020	8,791,431	7,368,994	7,370,126	6,104,050
2025	9,422,748	7,589,731	7,967,886	6,331,388

Source: United Nations, 1988.

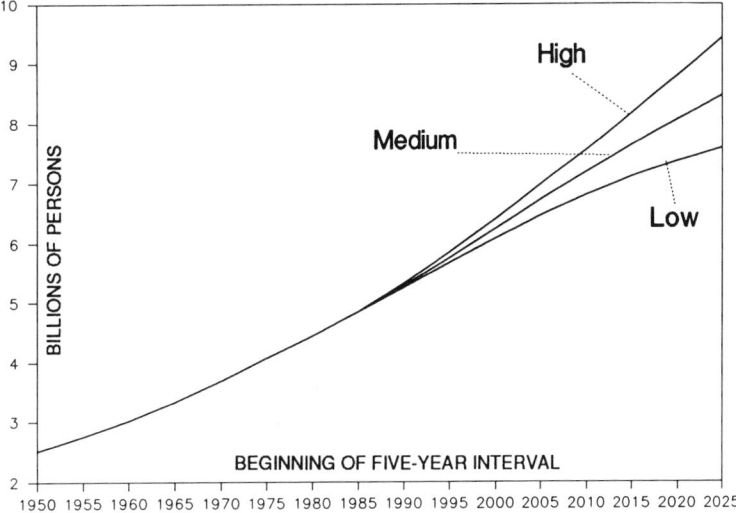

Fig. B. UN Estimates and Projections of the Population of
the World 1950–2025: Three Variants

high and low up to 2025, between which it is expected the performance will fall. Needless to say, most of the numbers are not significant, but they are shown here as they come off the tape. For the less developed countries, the high shows more than doubling and the low somewhat less than doubling, both in relation to 1985. For the world as a whole, the proportional population increase expected over the four decades indicated is only slightly smaller.

The medium projection, used throughout this volume, was arrived at after careful examination of the fluctuations of the birth and death rates since the 1950s as well as the number of women in the reproductive ages. If future fertility does not decline as fast as past developments seem to suggest, population growth over the next couple of decades will move in the general direction bounded by the high variant; in case the opposite holds, the low variant will become a better guess.

Printed and Electronic Versions

Readers of the earlier books keyed the numbers into institutional computers in order to make further calculations. With the abundance these days of personal computers, that effort is not any longer necessary. We are able to provide any of the numbers here contained on diskettes at the cost of copying.

Demographic Data and Parameters

The tabular materials assembled in this compendium are arranged in three sections:

Part I: Summary Table;
Part II: Tabulations Based on United Nations Data and Estimates;
Part III: Detailed Country Tabulations.

The Summary Table consolidates in one place the most commonly used demographic information for every population represented in this book that otherwise is scattered over hundreds of different tables in Parts II and III of the tabular materials. Because of its dependence on the subsequent parts, the Summary Table is discussed last in this explanatory chapter.

1. Tabulations Based on United Nations Data and Estimates

a. Origin and Quality of UN Data and Estimates

All tabulations presented in Part II of the Demographic Data and Parameters section of this volume are based on information collected and estimates prepared by the Population Division of the United Nations Department of Social and Economic Affairs in the course of its eleventh round of Global Demographic Assessments, undertaken around 1988. A data tape containing the principal results of this assessment was made available to the International Institute for Applied Systems Analysis (IIASA) and the authors of this volume in 1988.

The procedures used by the United Nations in the preparation of its demographic estimates are briefly described in one of its publications of the results of the eleventh round of demographic assessments.[1] With respect to the origin and quality of the information, this publication states: "The data used in the 1988 revision were obtained mostly from official national sources, including population censuses, demographic surveys, civil registration records and other administrative records" (p. 12). These data have been evaluated and adjusted whenever it was deemed necessary. If retrospective estimates of the total population and its age and sex structures were not available or not acceptable for any of various reasons, estimates were prepared by the Population Divi-

---

1. *World Population Prospects 1988*. Population Studies, No. 106 (New York: United Nations, 1989), 10–12.

sion, utilizing available information on fertility, mortality, and international migration (cf. p. 10). In the preparation of this volume, no further adjustments on the data or estimates were made; they are reproduced or are used in calculations as given by the United Nations.

b. Geographical Coverage

In the course of the eleventh round of Global Demographic Assessments, the United Nations Population Division prepared extensive demographic estimates for 152 national or administratively separate population units of the world, some three-fourths of all such units extant at that time. The populations of another 57 countries or territories, all but two of them with less than 300,000 inhabitants in 1985, have been combined into or included with populations of larger geographical units. Information for more than one-half of these smaller populations scattered over numerous islands and island chains is combined with tabulations for the Caribbean, Melanesia, Micronesia, and Polynesia. For the remaining others, it is included in tabulations for the larger geographical regions of which they are a part; e.g., data for Brunei are included in tabulations for Southeastern Asia, for Liechtenstein in Western Europe, etc. A listing of the countries and territories with small populations together with information on their land areas and estimated numbers of inhabitants in 1985 can be found in Appendix B.

To permit demographic comparisons between not only individual countries but also larger geographical regions of the world, the UN Population Division has provided additional estimates for groups of countries and/or territories such as continents and subcontinental regions. The demographic estimates of these groups are the weighted sums of the derived figures for individual countries and areas that make up the particular grouping.

Part II of the tabular materials contains information for 30 of such groupings. Three of them are global in nature, viz., Total World Population and population of the More Developed Regions and Less Developed Regions of the world. The latter two are defined in terms of various demographic, economic, and social indicators (United Nations, pp. 4–5). All other country combinations, with the exception of the European Community, represent contiguous geographical areas: four continental (Africa, Asia, Europe, Oceania) and two subcontinental (Latin and Northern America) groupings, which, in turn, are divided into 20 continental regions, five of them in Africa, three in Latin America, and four each in Asia, Europe, and Oceania. The European Community, aside from not forming a contiguous geographical area, is exceptional also in that its (cumulative) demographic estimates were prepared not by the United Nations Population Division but by the authors on the basis of the UN data for its member countries.

In Appendix A, all country/territory groupings represented in this volume are defined with respect to their country composition. For a few of the smaller populations not individually represented but included in tabulations for larger areal units only, more detailed information derived from other data sources can be found in Part III: Detailed Country Tabulations, viz., St. Christopher and Nevis, Greenland, and Guam.

c. Substantive Coverage

For each region, country, or territory included in Part II of this volume, selected information either directly taken from or based on the UN data tape is assembled in five tables. All of these tables depict the *current* (1985) population, its *past* development since the middle of this century (1950), and its possible or probable *future* course until the year 2020. The information for the past and the present has been extracted from actual data, that of the future is estimated on the basis of projections taking into account a population's recent demographic performance and a number of assumptions about anticipated developments. The projected figures, printed in *italics* to distinguish them from factual information, are not meant as unfailing predictions but as reasonable guesses. How reasonable they actually are, only the future can tell.

In projecting the demographic future of countries, the UN assumed "that orderly progress will be made and . . . that catastrophes such as wars, famines or epidemics will not occur" (United Nations, p. 13). The projection method used for all countries/ territories with a population of more than 300,000 in 1985 was the *cohort-component method,* considering changes in fertility, mortality, and whenever such information was available, migration (cf. United Nations, op. cit.).[2] With respect to future changes in vital rates, the UN provides three variants, the first assuming high fertility and medium mortality (*high variant*), the second medium fertility and mortality (*medium variant*), and the third low fertility and medium mortality (*low variant;* cf. United Nations, op. cit.). In this volume, the medium variant is used exclusively.

The first of the five tables shown for every region, country, or territory and entitled OBSERVED AND *PROJECTED* POPULATION DATA provides information on population size and the number of births and deaths as well as the number and percent of urban population. In instances in which the projected population has a size of 10 million or more by the year 2020 (as in Bolivia, to which the sample tables below refer), all absolute figures shown are in thousands, as indicated in the table heading. For all smaller populations, the printed figures indicate the actual or estimated numbers.

OBSERVED AND *PROJECTED* POPULATION DATA (000's)

YEAR	MID-YEAR POPULATION	NO. OF BIRTHS	NO. OF DEATHS	URBAN POPULATION		POPULATION 1985	
				NUMBER	PERCENT	AGE	NUMBER
1950	2766	130	67	1045	37.8	0	1107
1955	3072	143	70	1183	38.5	5	909
1960	3428	158	74	1346	39.3	10	771
1965	3841	175	78	1536	40.0	15	655
1970	4325	196	82	1762	40.8	20	552
1975	4894	219	86	2032	41.5	25	464
1980	5570	245	88	2468	44.3	30	392
1985	6371	273	90	3046	47.8	35	334
1990	*7314*	*302*	*89*	*3759*	*51.4*	40	272
1995	*8421*	*333*	*84*	*4631*	*55.0*	45	226
2000	*9724*	*366*	*85*	*5687*	*58.5*	50	194
2005	*11195*	*397*	*86*	*6919*	*61.8*	55	164
2010	*12820*	*425*	*91*	*8321*	*64.9*	60	126
2015	*14565*	*449*	*96*	*9873*	*67.8*	65	90
2020	*16401*	*468*	*102*	*11555*	*70.5*	70+	114

The numbers of births and deaths presented in the first table are not identical with those contained on the data tape supplied by the United Nations but were derived by multiplying the population for a given year with the corresponding crude birth and death rates shown in the third and fourth tables. Since the latter are annual averages for five-year periods, the births and deaths shown here are not the enumerated or estimated numbers of vital events for the years under which they are listed but *average* annual figures for the five-year periods beginning with the calendar years indicated in the first column of the table.

---

2. For smaller populations, projections were made by applying an assumed rate of growth to the total population.

To precisely define urban population, which is tabulated in column 5, is not possible in this context. The meaning of *urban* varies almost from one country to the next, a fact which is amply demonstrated in the long list of definitions found in the various editions of the United Nations *Demographic Yearbooks*. The definition of urban implied in the UN-based figures is that customary in the particular country or territory described.[3]

The last column in Table 1 presents, in five-year age intervals, the age distribution of the population of both sexes combined for the year 1985. Age distributions for the same year but separate for each sex likewise provided by the United Nations were used to create the second graph on the page, the 1985 Population Pyramid. At the top of this graph, the total number of males and females in the 1985 population can be found.

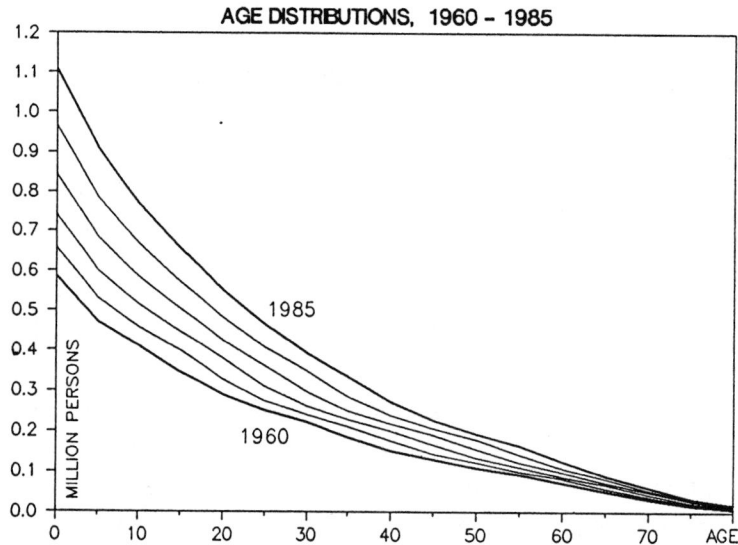

The kind of graphic presentation placed first on each country page differs depending on whether the country belongs to the group of rapidly growing third-world nations or to the aging populations of the developed world. For all countries classified as developing by the UN, the uppermost graph on each page depicts the magnitude of population growth between 1960 and 1985, with the area under a curve representing the absolute

3. It is in the nature of human settlements that their definition cannot easily be made uniform across countries. Cities, towns, and villages differ greatly in their nature as well as in the degree of their separation from the surrounding countryside. The economic activities carried out by the urban inhabitants are not always clearly distinguishable from those of the rural inhabitants. In some places, the urban density is not very different from the rural density, and even if there is a considerable difference at the center of the urban place, there may be, and usually is, a gradation of density with increasing distance from the center so that the stopping point where the urban area ends and the rural begins is arbitrary. When such a stopping point is agreed on, the statistical data to apply it may be lacking. Beyond all of that, national cultures and traditions differ in their perceptions of what constitutes an urban place as against a rural one of the same population.

The numbers of urban people in various countries presented in this volume in the tabulations based on United Nations data and estimates are simply those given by the United Nations, and all of them have been assembled in accordance with national definitions. A few examples will suffice to demonstrate their variety.

The *Philippines* classifies as urban places all administrative centers with a population of at least 2,500 inhabitants along with those municipalities and cities with a density of at least 500 persons per square kilometer; for *Peru*, urban areas are all population centers with 100 or more occupied dwellings; in *Paraguay,* all cities, towns, and administrative centers of departments and districts are considered urban; *Pakistan* defines as urban municipalities plus all other contiguous collections of houses inhabited by not less than 5,000 persons and having urban characteristics; for *Portugal*, it is agglomerations with 10,000 or more inhabitants that are urban places. One can continue through the list—so far, a sample of countries beginning with the letter P has been used—and find a similar variety of definitions at every point.

The United Nations has recommended a uniform definition of *urban* but, after more than 40 years of trying, has succeeded to only a small extent in persuading countries to adopt such a standard. At present, the United Nations has no alternative to accepting the counts of urban people made in individual countries according to their own definitions.

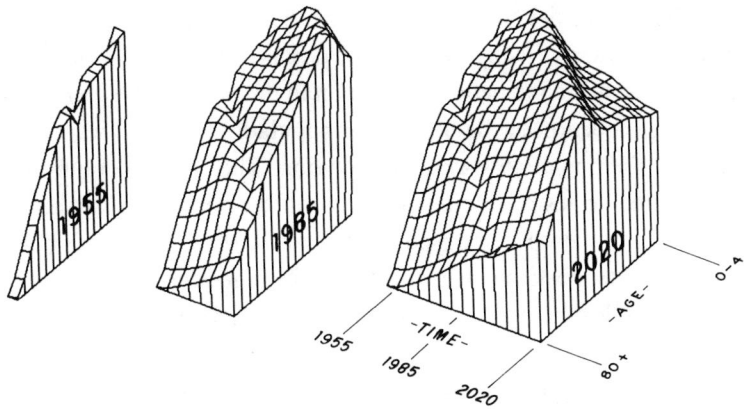

Fig. C. The Changing Age Distribution of the European Community:
1950–2020

population size at a given point in time and the space between two adjacent curves the increment in the absolute number of people during a given five-year interval. The lowest curve always refers to the year 1960, and the uppermost one to the year 1985. The not-labeled curves in between mark the years 1965, 1970, 1975, and 1980.

For developed countries, a three-dimensional graph illustrates, among other things, how present age structures, characterized more often than not by troughs and peaks, have evolved since 1950 as a result of various historical events such as wars before the middle of the century and decreasing fertility after then and what the age structure approximately will be like in the next three decades. The graph represents the age structure of a population (of both sexes) at succeeding points in time between 1950 and 2020, stacked one after the other. Figure C illustrates the changes in the age distribution of the population of the European Community. The high wave running diagonally across the surface of the structure signifies the relatively large number of people born during the baby boom in the first years following World War II. Over time, as the baby-boom cohort grows older, this wave is moving out of the structure, and is replaced by a downward-sloped area representing the steady fertility decline that began in the 1960s.

To bring out the temporal changes in the age composition more clearly, the three-dimensional structure in Fig. C has been cut at two points in time: 1955 and 1985. A comparison of these two time sections and the last one for the year 2020 demonstrates in an easily discernible fashion how the fertility decline following the postwar baby boom has continuously diminished the proportion of young people in the EC and increased that of the old.[4]

The second table on each country page, POPULATION RATIOS, concretizes and further amplifies the demographic situation, past and future, that is implied in the first table and first two graphs. The first four columns quantify changes over time in the age structure by showing what proportions of the population are in four socially important

4. It has to be noted that the age distributions portrayed by the three time sections in Figure C are not complete; they lack their base since the computer program used to create the three-dimensional structure produces only its surface. In doing so, it sets the lowest point of the starting age distribution (that for the year 1950 in our case) equal to zero and then records the deviations from this lowest point across the ages and across years. Since the lowest point of a population age structure is usually represented by the oldest age group (here 80 and older), the age structures shown have to be extended at the bottom by the number of persons 80 years and older in 1950.

age categories: the young dependents under 15; the population in the main working ages 15–64; and the elderly, using two cut-off points: 65 and older and 70 and older. Column 5 shows the resulting dependency burden in the form of the *Dependency Ratio,* an indicator of the proportion of the dependent population (under 15 and 65 and older) that is supported by the potential working population. The last two columns of the table present projected time series of one determinant of the population birth rate, the proportion of the total population composed of *Women in the Childbearing Ages,* and of one indicator of fertility performance, the *Child/Woman Ratio,* which is the average number of children under the age of 5 per female of childbearing age (15–49).

POPULATION RATIOS

YEAR	AGE DISTRIBUTION				DEPENDENCY RATIO	WOMEN 15-49	CHILD-WOMAN RATIO
	UNDER 15	15-64	65 & OLDER	70 & OLDER			
1950	0.420	0.549	0.031	0.016	0.823	0.234	0.736
1955	0.425	0.544	0.031	0.016	0.839	0.232	0.735
1960	0.429	0.540	0.032	0.017	0.853	0.232	0.738
1965	0.428	0.539	0.033	0.017	0.855	0.233	0.734
1970	0.430	0.537	0.033	0.018	0.862	0.234	0.733
1975	0.432	0.535	0.033	0.018	0.868	0.233	0.738
1980	0.435	0.533	0.033	0.018	0.877	0.233	0.746
1985	0.438	0.530	0.032	0.018	0.885	0.232	0.749
1990	0.439	0.529	0.032	0.018	0.891	0.232	0.743
2000	0.435	0.532	0.032	0.018	0.878	0.235	0.715
2010	0.418	0.549	0.032	0.019	0.820	0.241	0.644
2020	0.386	0.579	0.035	0.020	0.728	0.253	0.547

The tables entitled MORTALITY MEASURES and FERTILITY MEASURES together with the third graph describe and illustrate the trends of experienced as well as anticipated mortality and fertility that underlie past and assumed future demographic

MORTALITY MEASURES (Annual Averages)

PERIOD	CRUDE DEATH RATE	INFANT MORT. RATE	LIFE EXPECTANCY AT BIRTH (years)			
			MALE	FEMALE	BOTH SEXES	DIFFERENCE FEMALE-MALE
1950-55	24.09	176.00	38.49	42.49	40.44	4.00
1955-60	22.76	170.00	39.90	44.02	41.91	4.12
1960-65	21.46	164.00	41.39	45.61	43.45	4.22
1965-70	20.19	157.00	42.95	47.27	45.06	4.32
1970-75	18.95	151.00	44.58	49.01	46.74	4.43
1975-80	17.49	138.00	46.46	50.92	48.64	4.46
1980-85	15.87	124.00	48.55	53.03	50.74	4.48
1985-90	14.11	110.00	50.85	55.41	53.07	4.56
1990-95	12.15	93.00	53.57	58.34	55.90	4.77
2000-05	8.71	64.00	59.11	64.25	61.62	5.14
2010-15	7.07	49.00	62.25	67.55	64.83	5.30
2020-25	6.24	40.00	64.50	70.00	67.18	5.50

developments. The *Crude Death Rate,* the simplest mortality indicator, expresses the number of annual deaths per 1,000 population. The *Infant Mortality Rate* in column 3 of the third table is the number of children under one year of age who die in a given period divided by the number of all live births multiplied by 1,000 (cf. United Nations, p. 39). The *Life Expectancy at Birth* for males and females listed in columns 4 and 5 of the same table represents the average length of life a newborn can expect to live under prevailing mortality conditions. These figures were either taken from official national life tables or, in cases where no reliable mortality information was available, estimated with the help of UN or Coale and Demeny model life tables (cf. United Nations, p. 9 and p. 41). The last column in the mortality table, showing differences between female and male life expectancies at birth expressed in number of years, documents the by now well-known phenomenon that the gap between life expectancies of men and women tends to become wider (in favor of women) with the rise of average life expectancy for persons of both sexes. The table immediately above shows that in Bolivia, where average life expectancy at birth for persons of both sexes combined around 1985 was only a little higher than 50 years, the female-male difference amounted to 4.5 years. The Austrian population at the same time had a life expectancy at birth some 20 years longer than Bolivians but with a female-male gap of more than seven years.

The *Crude Birth Rate* in the fourth table is analogous to the crude death rate appearing in the preceding table. It represents the annual number of births (both boys and girls) per 1,000 population. The *Rate of Natural Increase* listed in the last column of the table is the difference between the crude birth and death rates and measures population growth exclusively in terms of the two vital events. The *General Fertility Rate* is similar to the crude birth rate; it differs from it in the denominator, which includes only women of reproductive ages from 15–49 instead of the total population. Accordingly, the rate expresses the number of annual live births per 1,000 women of childbearing age. The *Total Fertility* and *Gross* and *Net Reproduction Rates* are most readily interpreted as prospective fertility measures for individual women. All of them presuppose that a woman just born will bear, throughout her fertile years, children at the observed age-specific birth rates. Under this stipulation, the total fertility rate is defined as the

FERTILITY MEASURES (Annual Averages)

PERIOD	CRUDE BIRTH RATE	FERTILITY RATES GENERAL	TOTAL	REPRODUCTION RATES GROSS	NET	RATE OF NATUR. INCR.
1950-55	47.14	202.21	6.750	3.290	2.003	23.04
1955-60	46.62	200.99	6.690	3.260	2.053	23.86
1960-65	46.06	198.38	6.629	3.230	2.103	24.60
1965-70	45.64	195.75	6.560	3.200	2.150	25.45
1970-75	45.42	194.49	6.500	3.170	2.203	26.46
1975-80	44.84	192.47	6.390	3.120	2.252	27.36
1980-85	44.02	189.50	6.250	3.050	2.294	28.16
1985-90	42.85	184.44	6.060	2.950	2.322	28.74
1990-95	41.34	177.35	5.810	2.830	2.335	29.18
2000-05	37.60	159.22	5.137	2.510	2.239	28.89
2010-15	33.14	135.75	4.305	2.100	1.945	26.07
2020-25	28.52	111.56	3.497	1.710	1.614	22.29

number of *all* children a woman will bear in the course of her lifetime, and the gross reproduction rate as the number of all *girl* children. The net reproduction rate measures the same as the gross reproduction rate except that it takes into account that not all women live through their entire reproductive years. (The two previous rates assume no female mortality before the end of reproduction.) The difference between the gross and net reproduction rates is the result of female mortality prevailing at the time to which the rates refer.

In the third graph on each country page, in which time series of selected mortality and fertility indicators are plotted, the trend lines of past and projected crude birth and death rates are emphasized. This is done to provide a visual impression of the status of the *demographic transition,* i.e., the transition from high birth and death rates to low ones. No attempt is being made here to explain why such a transition has taken place in the developed countries but not or only partially in the developing world. So far, many of the developing nations have seen a significant reduction in their mortality rates but no concomitant shifts in their fertility. What the graph illustrates is the extent to which a transition of this kind has occurred in a given population.[5] The gap between the trend

5. The factual statement that a demographic transition, i.e., a shift from high birth and death rates to low ones, has or has not taken place is to be distinguished from an endorsement of the *Theory of Demographic Transition,* which tries to explain why such a change did or did not occur. For a brief statement of the Theory of Demographic Transition, see, e.g., Ansley J. Coale and Edgar M. Hoover, *Population Growth and Economic Development in Low-Income Countries* (Princeton, N.J.: Princeton University Press, 1958), 11–12.

lines of the crude birth and death rates indicates the magnitude of the population's rate of natural increase during the time period shown.

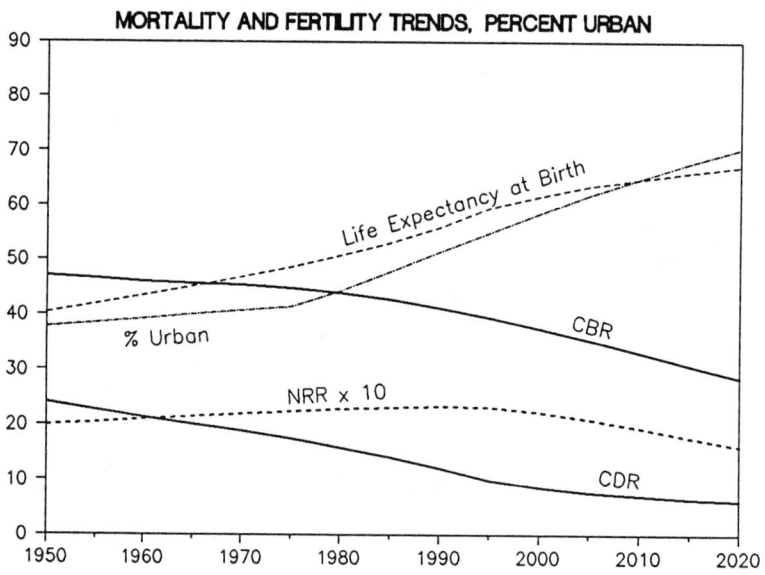

The table labeled AGING MEASURES together with the graph at the bottom of each country page call attention to the aging process populations undergo primarily as a result of fertility reduction. Rapid population aging is a rather recent phenomenon in demographic history, with far-reaching social and economic implications, not all of which are as yet fully understood or appreciated. We have included the graph to give the reader an immediate visual impression of the magnitude that this phenomenon already has assumed or may assume shortly in the developed world.

AGING MEASURES

YEAR	POPULATION AGE RATIOS				POPULATION	
	60+/20-59	65+/20-64	70+/20-69	75+/20-74	MEAN AGE	MEDIAN AGE
1950	0.1219	0.0698	0.0355	0.0150	23.40	18.89
1960	0.1268	0.0726	0.0370	0.0156	23.30	18.55
1970	0.1290	0.0767	0.0396	0.0171	23.19	18.42
1980	0.1269	0.0761	0.0407	0.0187	22.99	18.19
1990	0.1278	0.0752	0.0401	0.0186	22.77	17.94
2000	0.1230	0.0754	0.0417	0.0193	22.78	18.06
2010	0.1212	0.0730	0.0408	0.0201	23.31	18.81
2020	0.1229	0.0750	0.0420	0.0203	24.47	20.35

The most easily understood illustrations of the population aging process are provided by the time series of the population median and mean ages shown in the last two columns of the table. One drawback of these particular averages is that they include people of all ages, the old as well as the young, and thereby partly obscure the point to be made: the demonstration of the rise in the proportion of the elderly. This point is brought out more clearly by the age ratios presented in the first columns of the table, which indicate the sizes of the population groups defined as elderly (60 and older, 65 and older, 70 and older, and 75 and older) relative to the population composed of all people at least 20 years of age who are not yet old.

The lower age limit of 20 for the not-yet-old included in the denominators of the various age ratios is chosen instead of 15, as in the definition of the Dependency Ratio, because in most western countries currently experiencing rapid population aging, large proportions of the teenagers still undergo schooling and, therefore, are economically dependent. Age ratios with varying numerators are shown to illustrate the effect different retirement ages have on the size of the population sector made up of the largely economically inactive elderly.

d. Definition of Variables

Observed and *Projected* Population Data

Midyear Population	Enumerated or estimated number of persons in population around the middle of the calendar year shown. Expressed in 000s for large populations (10 million or more by the year 2020).
Number of Births	Average annual number of estimated live births during five-year period beginning with calendar year shown. In 000s for large populations.
Number of Deaths	Average annual number of estimated deaths during five-year period beginning with calendar year shown. In 000s for large populations.
Number and Percent of Urban Population	Enumerated or estimated number and percent of persons residing in areas classified as *urban* according to country-specific definition. In 000s for large populations.
Population 1985	Number of persons of both sexes in 1985 population, in five-year age groups beginning with age shown. In 000s for large populations. The numbers of total males and females in the 1985 population are shown at the top of the graph: 1985 Age Structure.

Population Ratios

Proportion of Population Aged: Under 15 15–64 65 & older 70 & older	Proportion population of indicated age is of total population.
Dependency Ratio	Proportion of population under 15 plus proportion of population 65 and older divided by proportion of population aged 15–64.
Women 15–49	Proportion of women of reproductive ages (15–49) in the total population.
Child-Woman Ratio	Average number of children under age 5 per woman of reproductive age (15–49).

Mortality Measures (Annual Averages)

Crude Death Rate	Estimated average number of annual deaths during five-year period shown divided by average population during that period, multiplied by 1,000.
Infant Mortality Rate	Estimated number of deaths of children under age 1 during period shown divided by the total number of live births during that period, multiplied by 1,000.
Life Expectancy at Birth	Average number of years a person born during the period shown can expect to live under mortality conditions prevailing at time of birth.

Difference Female–Male	Difference in average life expectancy at birth between females and males, expressed in number of years.

Fertility Measures (Annual Averages)

Crude Birth Rate	Estimated average number of annual live births during five-year period shown divided by average population during that period, multiplied by 1,000.
General Fertility Rate	Estimated number of live births during five-year period shown divided by the average number of women of childbearing age (15–49) during that period, multiplied by 1,000.
Total Fertility Rate	Total number of children a female just born would bear at the prevailing age-specific fertility rates if she survived to the end of her reproductive life.
Gross Reproduction Rate	Same as Total Fertility Rate but for female children only.
Net Reproduction Rate	Same as Gross Reproduction Rate but taking into account that not all females survive to the end of reproduction. Discounts lost fertility of women dying at the prevailing age-specific death rates before reaching the end of reproductive life.
Rate of Natural Increase	Crude Birth Rate minus Crude Death Rate.

Aging Measures

Population Age Ratio:
  60+/20–59
  65+/20–64
  70+/20–69
  75+/20–74
	Population 60 and older (or 65+, 70+, 75+) divided by population aged 20 to 59 (or 20–64, 20–69, 20–74).

Mean Age	Sum of ages of all persons in population divided by number of persons in population.
Median Age	Age above and below which 50 percent of all persons in population fall.

2. Detailed Country Tabulations

a. Purpose

The Detailed Country Tabulations in Part III of the Demographic Data and Parameters section are, in form as well as substance, very similar to those presented in the authors' previous two volumes on world population, viz., *World Population: An Analysis of Vital Data,* Chicago: University of Chicago Press, 1968, and *Population: Facts and Methods of Demography,* San Francisco: W. H. Freeman and Company, 1971. They are meant to continue the time series of demographic country data and parameters begun there.

The purpose of the Detailed Tabulations is not to provide alternatives to the UN-based information in Part II but to complement it. The main theme of the time series of parameters derived from the UN data is the past and future processes of population growth and aging. The tabulations in this section, which are not as extensive as those based on the UN data in terms of geographical areas and time periods covered, are more focused. They zoom in, as it were, on the most recent demographic conditions of individual countries and provide a close-up picture of the forces of mortality and fertility operating in them as well as of the interplay of these forces with the age structure. While the tabulations of Part II highlight demographic trends, those in Part III provide information on the vital forces underlying them.

b. Populations Covered

The Detailed Country Tabulations include information on 60 population units at various points in time. The earliest data refer to the year 1970, and the latest to 1987. The reason for making 1970 the starting point for the present collection is that the earlier two volumes on world population mentioned above cover information reaching into the late 1960s. Our original aim for this volume had been to provide tabulations for every national population in the developed world as well as for all countries with reliable demographic information in the developing regions for the period 1970 through 1985 in intervals of five years. However, in late 1987, data for the year 1985 were not yet available for a number of European countries, so that figures for earlier years had to be substituted. In four instances, national statistical agencies provided us with data for the year 1986 or 1987, and these were given preference over those of 1985. Pertinent parameters for the latter year, though, are included in the Summary Table. With respect to the developing countries for which any data at all could be obtained, we had to be satisfied with whatever was available regardless of date.

The tabulations assembled in Part III of the Demographic Data and Parameters section cover, with a very few exceptions, all national population of the world defined as *more developed* by the United Nations. From among the European nations, only Albania is missing together with a number of smaller countries such as Monaco and San Marino. For the *less developed* regions of the world, detailed demographic information was obtained from or for 22 countries or territories, two of them located in Africa, 10 in Latin America, eight in Asia, and two in Oceania. This rather small number of third-world countries is attributable to our policy of including in this collection only those populations with data sets that are documented as reliable and fit reasonably well into the time series of country data provided by the United Nations Population Division.

The majority of the Detailed Country Tabulations pertains to national population units or populations of independently administered territories, as the section name implies. Added are a few tabulations for supranational and subnational populations, all of which are of considerable current interest. The supranational units are the European Community and its East European counterpart—the countries belonging to the Council of Mutual Economic Assistance, COMECON—both initially established as "common markets" in divided postwar Europe. The European Community presently includes about two-thirds of the entire European population of half a billion living in 12 countries. The COMECON countries, with almost one-fourth of all of Europe's people, are identical with the six nations comprising the Eastern European Region.

Tabulations for England and Wales, Scotland and Northern Ireland, constituent parts of the United Kingdom of Great Britain and Northern Ireland, have been included not only because separate data sets were made available by the Central Statistical Office of the U.K. but because they help document demographic differences between peoples with divergent histories and dissimilar political and social problems at present. In the case of the Republic of South Africa, the tabulations had to be restricted to the white and colored populations because reliable data for the blacks, who constitute the country's majority, were not available.

c. Data Origin and Quality

The bulk of the data on which the Detailed Country Tabulations are based were made available in late 1987 and early 1988 by national statistical agencies. Whenever such data could not be obtained, the United Nations *Demographic Yearbooks* served as secondary source. The exact origins of all data sets used for analysis are described in Appendix C.

The data qualifications appended to the source notes are either those that were given to us by the statistical agencies providing the data or, when the notes were taken from the *Demographic Yearbooks,* those that appear in the footnotes to the data tables. No claim is or can be made that the annotations listed in Appendix C mention all the qualifications actually applying to the data.

Together with the origins of the data, Appendix C also lists the adjustments that had to be made on some data sets either to bring them into the desired form or to eliminate apparent inconsistencies in them. All population figures reproduced in the tables refer to midyear. When such figures could not be extracted directly from the sources, estimates were obtained through straight-line interpolations between two corresponding data sets straddling the desired midyear or, if such pairs of data sets were not to be found either, through an adjustment to midyear by means of the approximate rate of natural increase.

In all instances in which population and death distributions found in the sources did not conform to the desired age groupings, e.g., when age groups Under 1 and 1–4 were lumped together or the distributions ended before age 85, the needed estimates were made by following age patterns indicated in available data for the same population dated a few years earlier or later. All persons or vital events listed in the age-not-stated category were distributed proportionally over the entire age range, and the sums of all age-specific population, birth, and death figures that differed on account of rounding from the totals shown in the sources were adjusted to exactly agree with one another.

d. A Comparison of Detailed Country Tabulations with UN-Based Tabulations

A comparison of data and parameters presented in the Detailed Country Tabulations with corresponding ones in the Tabulations Based on United Nations Data and Estimates will, in most instances, show no exact agreement but reasonable closeness. In Table C, direct comparisons can be made for only two items: total population figures and dependency ratios for the years 1970 and 1980, i.e., those variables that refer to individual calendar years and for which the United Nations relied on actual data. The minor discrepancies that do exist between these figures arise from differences in the particular country sources consulted, the time at which the data were collected, and the manner in which data adjustments of the type exemplified in the previous paragraphs were made.

TABLE C.
A Comparison Between UN-Based and Detailed Country Tabulations:
Canada and Mexico

COUNTRY/INDICATOR	1970		1980	
	UN-Based Tabulations	Detailed Tabulations	UN-Based Tabulations	Detailed Tabulations
CANADA				
Total Population (in 000s)	21,324	21,298	23,941	24,043
Dependency Ratio × 100	61.44	61.99	47.49	48.13
Crude Birth Rate × 1000	17.22	17.47	15.34	15.42
Crude Death Rate × 1000	7.42	7.32	7.14	7.13
Infant Mortality Rate × 1000	18.86	18.82	10.51	10.44
Female Life Expectancy at Birth	76.03	76.31	78.85	78.83
Total Fertility Rate	2.24	2.36	1.71	1.75
MEXICO				
Total Population (in 000s)	52,770	51,176	70,416	69,655
Dependency Ratio × 100	101.25	100.63	90.84	90.66
Crude Birth Rate × 1000	43.57	41.67	33.05	34.85
Crude Death Rate × 100	9.58	9.49	6.75	6.24
Infant Mortality Rate × 1000	74.00	68.47	56.50	39.53
Female Life Expectancy at Birth	63.58	63.61	69.44	69.78
Total Fertility Rate	6.53	6.46	4.55	4.88

For all other data and parameters appearing in both Part II and Part III tabulations, slight discrepancies ought to exist because they differ in their time reference. The mortality and fertility rates listed in the third and fourth tables of the country pages in Part II represent five-year averages, while those shown in the Detailed Country Tabulations refer to the single calendar year indicated. Both types of figures are "correct"; which one to use depends on the purpose they are to serve. If trends over time are to be illustrated, as the UN figures essay to do, averages over a number of years are preferable to single-year figures because they smooth out annual chance fluctuations as well as minimize errors that annual birth and death figures may contain. On the other hand, if the focus is a population at a particular point in time, the time-specific parameter is the more appropriate one. In Table C, the rates derived from data provided by the United Nations represent averages for two adjoining five-year periods preceding and following the reference year of the corresponding detailed tabulation figure. If trends are declining, as generally is the case with fertility and mortality at present, the averaged vital rates will be slightly higher than the single-year ones; if trends are increasing, they will tend to be somewhat lower.

e. Substantive Coverage

For the majority of populations included in this section, sets of demographic tables are displayed for 1970, 1975, 1980, and 1985, or neighboring years. The full set of seven tables is shown for the first and the last years; for intermediate years, only the first four tables are presented. The first four tables, containing the data on which subsequent tabulations are based as well as the most commonly used demographic parameters, describe the makeup of the population at the time of observation. Tables 5 and 6 portray the population's growth potential at the time of observation: how its size, age structure, and vital rates will change in the immediate future and what they ultimately will be like if the existing forces of mortality and fertility continue to operate unchanged. Table 7 spells out in more detail what the observed forces of fertility are and how they interact with mortality, what both of these forces imply for future reproduction, and how the configuration of the present age structure, brought about by past trends and historical events, will affect future population growth. For all national populations, an eighth table is appended to the data set of the first year shown. This table contains a selection of social and demographic indicators for various years between 1970 and 1985, most of them prepared by the World Bank. They are meant to provide a glimpse at the social context within which the demographic forces of a given population are operating.

Two graphs, shown for most populations represented in Part III, illustrate the changes in fertility and mortality these populations have undergone during the latter half of this century. They highlight, as it were, the central theme around which the demographic data and parameters in this volume are organized. In most developing countries, it is the substantial decline of mortality and the absence of a matching reduction in fertility that is keeping their growth rates high and their age structures young; in developed countries with their already low mortality levels, the drastic fertility decline of the recent past signals the opposite: diminishing numbers of people and rapid population aging.

In the following description of the detailed country tables, their purpose is briefly indicated and the parameters they contain are defined. For the reader not familiar with demographic techniques, examples taken from the Austrian population of 1985 are added to aid in the reading of the tables. Those interested in details of the theories and methods that have been applied to the calculations are referred to their rather lengthy expositions in Nathan Keyfitz, *Introduction to the Mathematics of Population*, Reading, Massachusetts: Addison-Wesley Publishing Company, 1968, and Keyfitz and Flieger, *Population: Facts and Methods of Demography*, or other demographic literature.

Table 1: Data. The first table reproduces the population, birth, and death figures on which all parameters assembled in the six following tables are based. For the majority of the countries or territories represented in this section, the population figures by sex and age at last birthday are the official counts or estimates issued by the national authorities. All of them pertain to midyear or near midyear, the latter, for example, in the case of Singapore, where censuses were taken in June of 1970 and 1980. The age distributions for males and females, expressed in percent and shown side by side with the actual population figures, facilitate quick comparisons between the sexes and make existing indentations in the age and sex structure caused by events such as wars, periods of exceptionally high or low fertility, or substantial migration easily detectable.

Unless otherwise indicated in the annotations to the data (Appendix C), the birth and death figures represent registered events for residents of the country during the year indicated. The births refer in all cases to live births. The two figures appearing close to the bottom of the table in the column labeled *Births by Age of Mother and Sex* and marked with an M (male) or F (female) represent the total number of live births of the specified sex for the year. The ages under which the events are listed are ideally those of the mothers at the time of childbirth or of the decedents at the time of death. Unfortu-

AGE AT LAST BIRTHDAY	ESTIMATED MID-YEAR POPULATION					BIRTHS BY AGE OF MOTHER AND SEX	DEATHS			AGE AT LAST BIRTHDAY
	BOTH SEXES	MALES Number	Percent	FEMALES Number	Percent		BOTH SEXES	MALES	FEMALES	
0	96988	49427	1.4	47561	1.2		977	591	386	0
1-4	355687	181341	5.1	174346	4.4		195	113	82	1-4
5-9	427026	218507	6.1	208519	5.2		81	46	35	5-9
10-14	498419	254542	7.1	243877	6.1		128	83	45	10-14
15-19	619233	316536	8.8	302697	7.6	7507	500	387	113	15-19
20-24	658900	332423	9.3	326477	8.2	32632	695	550	145	20-24
25-29	588151	293771	8.2	294380	7.4	28771	544	411	133	25-29
30-34	503952	251627	7.0	252325	6.3	12984	553	389	164	30-34
35-39	502811	253689	7.1	249122	6.3	4559	819	552	267	35-39
40-44	518740	259794	7.3	258946	6.5	927	1428	965	463	40-44
45-49	456250	228529	6.4	227721	5.7	60	1760	1192	568	45-49
50-54	400378	197908	5.5	202470	5.1		2592	1797	795	50-54
55-59	423066	198345	5.5	224721	5.7		4109	2751	1358	55-59
60-64	427295	169025	4.7	258270	6.5		6071	3532	2539	60-64
65-69	257330	98880	2.8	158450	4.0		5530	3104	2426	65-69
70-74	321964	119475	3.3	202489	5.1		11921	6130	5791	70-74
75-79	260350	89423	2.5	170927	4.3		16910	7698	9212	75-79
80-84	157659	48982	1.4	108677	2.7	45054 M	17515	6698	10817	80-84
85+	83468	21098	0.6	62370	1.6	42386 F	17250	4884	12366	85+
TOTAL	7557667	3583322		3974345		87440	89578	41873	47705	TOTAL

nately, the recording of vital events did or still does vary across countries: in the German Democratic Republic, for example, births used to be tabulated by age of mother at the beginning of the year during which the mother gave birth, and in Switzerland, the age at death or childbirth is still calculated as the difference between the year of the event and year of birth of the persons concerned. The most common variation, practiced most often but not exclusively in developing countries, is to tabulate vital events by date of registration rather than occurrence. Whenever information was available to adjust for such or other peculiarities, this was done; however, in most instances, we could do nothing aside from documenting the available figures.

Tables 2 and 3: Life Tables. The two life tables presented as Tables 2 and 3 and composed of nine columns each refer to the male and female populations shown in Table 1. A *life table* is a mathematical model used to portray the mortality conditions prevailing in a population during a given time period, which, in the context of this volume, is defined as one calendar year. In a life table, the probabilities of persons exactly x years old dying while passing through age interval x to $x + n$, calculated from observed age-specific death rates that are assumed to continue unchanged into the future, are applied to a hypothetical cohort of 100,000 just born. The mortality parameters of this hypothetical cohort or, by way of extension, *stationary* population in which every year 100,000 are born and the same number die, are then, in turn, used to describe the mortality situation in the observed population.

x	$_nM_x$	$_nq_x$	l_x	$_nd_x$	$_nL_x$	$_nm_x$	$_na_x$	T_x	$\overset{\circ}{e}_x$	x
0	0.011957	0.011828	100000	1183	98924	0.011957	0.090	7050021	70.500	0
1	0.000623	0.002489	98817	246	394654	0.000623	1.500	6951097	70.343	1
5	0.000211	0.001052	98571	104	492597	0.000211	2.500	6556443	66.515	5
10	0.000326	0.001629	98468	160	492040	0.000326	3.143	6063846	61.582	10
15	0.001223	0.006096	98307	599	490172	0.001223	2.724	5571806	56.678	15
20	0.001655	0.008239	97708	805	486542	0.001655	2.520	5081635	52.008	20
25	0.001399	0.006966	96903	675	482813	0.001398	2.481	4595092	47.420	25
30	0.001546	0.007714	96228	742	479358	0.001549	2.601	4112279	42.735	30
35	0.002176	0.010825	95485	1034	475051	0.002176	2.701	3632921	38.047	35
40	0.003714	0.018417	94452	1740	468194	0.003715	2.663	3157870	33.434	40
45	0.005216	0.025866	92712	2398	458042	0.005236	2.698	2689676	29.011	45
50	0.009080	0.044544	90314	4023	442221	0.009097	2.676	2231635	24.710	50
55	0.013870	0.067156	86291	5795	417810	0.013870	2.645	1789414	20.737	55
60	0.020896	0.100178	80496	8064	383322	0.021037	2.624	1371604	17.039	60
65	0.031392	0.146316	72432	10598	336928	0.031455	2.619	988282	13.644	65
70	0.051308	0.228343	61834	14119	275191	0.051308	2.593	651354	10.534	70
75	0.086085	0.354706	47715	16925	196564	0.086103	2.518	376164	7.884	75
80	0.136744	0.505568	30790	15566	113837	0.136744	2.423	179600	5.833	80
85	0.231491	1.000000	15224	15224	65763	0.169945	4.320	65763	4.320	85

$_nM_x$ **Age-specific death rate.** Death rates specific for age constitute the basic information needed for the construction of a life table. They are the ratios of the number of deaths of persons of a given age during a given time period (in our case one calendar year) to the average number of persons (midyear population is used here) of that age present in the population during the same period. The subscript *x,* which is affixed to all life-table variables, indicates the starting age of the age interval to which the variable applies, and *n* the length of that interval. In the *abbreviated* life tables presented in this volume, *x* = 0, 1, 5, 10 . . . 85, and *n* = 1 for *x* = 0, *n* = 4 for *x* = 1, *n* = 5 for all other age groups except the last one (*x* = 85), which is open-ended.[6] Thus, $_5M_{10}$ denotes the age-specific death rate of persons between the exact ages of 10 and 15. The tables above show that this rate is 83 ÷ 254,542 = 0.000326 for the Austrian male population of 1985. When multiplied by 1,000, the figure tells us that approximately one out of every 3,000 Austrian boys between the ages of 10 and 15 had died in 1985.

$_nq_x$ **Probability of dying.** It indicates, under the mortality conditions implied in the age-specific death rates, the chance of a person exactly *x* years old dying before reaching age *x* + *n*, i.e., the next age group. This probability is commonly approximated as

$$_nq_x = \frac{n \; _nM_x}{1 + n/2 \; _nM_x} \; .$$

Since in the last age group everybody dies, the chance of dying in this age group is always equal to 1. For an Austrian man exactly 70 years old in 1985, the chance of dying before his 75th birthday ($_5q_{70}$) was 0.228343, or almost one in four; for a boy born in 1985, the chance of dying before his first birthday (q_0) was 0.011828, or close to one in 85.[7] The chance of dying during the first year of life is often also referred to as the *Infant Mortality Rate.*[8]

The $_nM_x$ and $_nq_x$ values of the life table are the only ones bearing a direct relationship to the actual mortality in the population under consideration. The remaining seven life-table columns simulate how a hypothetical birth cohort of 100,000 persons (l_0) will die off under the mortality conditions implied in the observed $_nq_x$ values.

l_x **Number of survivors to exact age** *x* of the cohort of 100,000 if the probabilities of dying ($_nq_x$) remain unchanged during the entire lifetime of the co-

6. In contrast to *complete* life tables containing mortality parameters for populations grouped in single-year age categories, *abbreviated* life tables are calculated for populations classified in age groups larger than 1 year. Most commonly, as in our case, five-year age groups are used.

7. Because of the particular method of life-table construction used in this volume (cf. footnote 9), the $_nq_x$ values appearing in Tables 2 and 3 differ slightly from those one would obtain by using the formula quoted in the text. Using the formula shown, the probability of Austrian males dying before age 1 would be 0.011886 instead of 0.011828, as mentioned in the text, and the probability of an Austrian male dying between ages 70 and 75 would be 0.227375 instead of 0.228343. The difference arises from the fact that the above formula assumes deaths to be evenly distributed over the age intervals which, in reality, is not the case. During the first year of life, deaths are concentrated in the first days of life; in the older age groups, the majority of deaths occurs toward the end of the age intervals. The method used for producing the life tables published here takes this uneven distribution of deaths into account.

8. In the UN-based tabulations and the Summary Table, the Infant Mortality Rate is defined in a different manner: number of deaths to infants under 1 year of age divided by the number of live births during that year, times 1,000.

hort. l_0 represents the original birth cohort of 100,000, the survivors of this cohort to the following ages x are obtained as

$$l_x = l_{x-n}(1 - {}_nq_{x-n}).$$

Under the mortality conditions prevailing in Austria in 1985, 98,817 males out of such a birth cohort of 100,000 would survive their first year of life (l_1), 97,708 would reach age 20 (l_{20}), and 15,224 age 85 (l_{85}).

The l_x can also be interpreted as the probability of surviving from birth to any given age x. For example, the probability of a member of a birth cohort of 100,000 just born surviving to at least age 10 is l_{10}/l_0. Under Austrian mortality conditions for males in 1985, this probability is 0.98468. The l_x can likewise be used for calculating the probability of survival from any given age x to any other age: under the 1985 mortality conditions of Austrian males, the chance of surviving from age 20 to age 65 is l_{65}/l_{20}, or $72,432 \div 97,708 = 0.741311$.

$_nd_x$ **Number of deaths between ages x and $x + n$** in a cohort of 100,000 under the observed mortality conditions, calculated as

$$_nd_x = l_x \, {}_nq_x.$$

Of 100,000 men born under 1985 Austrian conditions, 1,183 will die before reaching age 1 (d_0), and 4,023 while between 50 and 55 years old ($_5d_{50}$). Analogous to the interpretation of l_x as the probability of surviving from birth to any given age x, the $_nd_x$ can be interpreted as the probability of a person just born dying between the ages of x and $x + n$. For example, the chance of a newly born boy in the hypothetical cohort dying when he will be between 50 and 55 years of age is $_5d_{50}/l_0$ or, in terms of the Austrian figures, $4,023 \div 100,000 = 0.04023$.

$_nL_x$ **Number of years lived per 100,000 born during age interval x to $x + n$.** The variable represents the area under the l_x curve bounded by ages x and $x + n$. In discrete form, it is calculated as ½ times the number of persons in the stationary population who enter age group x to $x + n$ (l_x) plus the number of people who leave the age group, i.e., move into the next group (l_{x+n}), times n, the length of the age interval:

$$_nL_x = n/2 \, (l_x + l_{x+n}).$$

For the terminal age group, $_\infty L_x$ is usually calculated as $l_x/_\infty M_x$. 100,000 boys born under 1985 Austrian mortality conditions could expect to live a total of 98,924 years before their first birthdays (L_0), and 442,221 years while 50 to 54 years of age ($_5L_{50}$).

When we extend the concept of the hypothetical cohort to that of a *stationary population* in which every year 100,000 are born and the same number die according to the probabilities of dying implied in the observed $_nq_x$ values, i.e., a population whose size remains stationary at every point in time, the $_nL_x$ values represent the age distribution of this stationary population. Under 1985 Austrian male mortality conditions, such a population would have, at any time, 98,924 baby boys (L_0), 442,221 men aged 50 to 54 ($_5L_{50}$), and 65,763 males aged 85 and over ($_\infty L_{85}$).

$_nm_x$ **Age-specific death rate of the stationary population** This parameter, which is analogous to $_nM_x$, the age-specific death rate of the observed population, is the ratio of the number of deaths in a given age group of the stationary population ($_nd_x$) to the number of persons in that same age group ($_nL_x$). In the stationary population with 1985 Austrian mortality conditions, the rate for males aged 65–69 ($_5m_{65}$) is 0.031455. This figure is slightly higher than the corresponding rate $_5M_{65}$ of the observed Austrian population, which is 0.031392.[9]

$_na_x$ **Average number of years lived in age group x to $x + n$ by those who die in that age interval, defined as**

$$_na_x = \frac{_nL_x - n\, l_{x+n}}{_nd_x}.$$

In the Austrian example, each of the 160 boys in the stationary population dying between the ages of 10 and 15 ($_5d_{10}$) would live an average of 3.143 years ($_5a_{10}$) after his tenth birthday. In all life tables in this volume, $_4a_1$ is set to 1.5 years, and $_5a_5$ to 2.5 years.

T_x **Total number of years lived beyond age x by those of the original cohort of 100,000 reaching age x.** The T_x is calculated as the sum of the $_nL_x$ values (numbers of years lived in age group x to $x + n$) from age x to the end of the life table ($_\infty L_x$), i.e.,

$$T_x = \sum_x^\infty {}_nL_x.$$

In the stationary population based on Austrian male data, the 100,000 members of a birth cohort have a combined total of 7,050,021 life years ahead of them (T_0); their survivors to age 50 will live another combined total of

---

9. The procedure used for the construction of the life tables in this volume is an *iterative* one devised by the senior author (Keyfitz, "A Life Table That Agrees with the Data." *Journal of the American Statistical Association*, 61, pt.1 (June, 1966): 305–12). It attempts to arrive at a life table that *agrees with the data*. The intended agreement is one between the age-specific death rates of the stationary population ($_nm_x$) and those of the observed population ($_nM_x$), on which the life table is built. The stationary population which, by definition, excludes population increase, differs from the observed population in that it is weighted in favor of older people in all those age groups that, in the observed population, are increasing in size. In consequence, the $_nm_x$ values for these age groups are larger than the corresponding $_nM_x$ values. The iterative life table procedure adjusts for this weighting.

Agreement between the two types of death rates does not mean identity. The iterative procedure takes into account the specific rate of increase of every individual age group in the observed population and adjusts all life-table variables accordingly, beginning with the l_x values. Only in instances in which the rate of increase of a given age group in the observed population is equal or close to zero will the two types of death rates converge. As protection against error, the computer program used for the life tables sets the rate of increase of the observed population aged x to $x+n$ equal to zero whenever it turns out to be negative. A zero rate of increase is also used for the first three age groups in the life tables. For the calculation of $_\infty m_{85}$, the computer program stipulates that all persons will be dead by age 90.

In the life table for Austrian males, we find that the corresponding $_nM_x$ and $_nm_x$ values for all age groups below 25 are identical, but not for most of the older age groups. This reflects the decrease in the proportions of younger Austrians as a result of declining fertility and the swelling of the older age groups by the larger and longer surviving cohorts of earlier years.

Because of these adjustments as well as others built into the computational procedures used in this volume, the reader trying to exactly duplicate all figures in the printed life tables will not always succeed. However, the discrepancies will not be large and oftentimes affect only the not significant digits of the parameters.

2,231,635 years after their 50th birthdays (T_{50}), and the survivors to age 85 still can expect another combined total of 65,763 years of life until all will have died (T_{85}).

$\overset{\circ}{e}_x$ **Expectation of life at exact age** x, the average number of years still to be lived after age x by those in the stationary population reaching this age. It is calculated as

$$\overset{\circ}{e}_x = \frac{T_x}{l_x}.$$

In the stationary male population based on Austrian data, boys just born have an average life expectancy of 70.5 years, and males exactly 65 years old can look forward to a retirement period that will last an average of 13.6 years.

Table 4: Observed Vital Rates and Ratios. Table 4 summarizes the vital measurements of the population as it presented itself at the time of observation. It is divided into three panels: in the first, crude vital rates together with age-structural measures are assembled; the second provides a comparison of the country's fertility and mortality with that of others by means of birth and death rates standardized by age and sex, and in the third, a number of specific fertility and age-structure parameters are listed.

CRUDE RATES				RATES STANDARDIZED ON USA 1980				VITAL STATISTICS	
Per Thousand	BOTH SEXES	MALES	FEMALES	Per Thousand	BOTH SEXES	MALES	FEMALES	GFR x 1000	45.740
BIRTH RATE	11.57	12.57	10.66	BIRTH RATE	12.77		12.04	TFR	1.480
DEATH RATE	11.85	11.69	12.00	DEATH RATE	9.42	10.02	8.85	GRR	0.718
RATE OF INCREASE	-0.28	0.89	-1.34	RATE OF INCREASE	3.35		3.18	NRR	0.706
								μ	26.644
PERCENT OF POPULATION IN AGE GROUP				RATES STANDARDIZED ON MEXICO 1980				σ^2	29.638
								GENERATION	26.836
UNDER 15	18.23	19.64	16.97	BIRTH RATE	11.48		11.21	POP. SEX RATIO	1.109
15 - 64	67.46	69.81	65.35	DEATH RATE	3.57	4.36	2.77	SEX RATIO AT BIRTH	1.063
65 AND OLDER	14.30	10.54	17.69	RATE OF INCREASE	7.90		8.44	DEP. RATIO x 100	48.225

Crude birth and *crude death rates* are most commonly used for measuring a population's fertility, mortality, and natural growth. The crude birth and death rates are calculated by dividing the number of vital events occurring in a given period (here one calendar year) by the average population present during that period (here midyear population). Normally, the rates are multiplied by 1,000 to express the number of births or deaths per 1,000 persons during the specified time interval. The label *crude* is applied to these rates because they do not take into account a population's age structure, which, as shown below, exercises a strong influence on their magnitudes.

The Austrian crude rates for males indicate that, during 1985, some 12.57 baby boys were born for every 1,000 males present in the population and that, out of every 1,000 males during the year, 11.69 had died. The *rate of natural increase,* which is calculated as the difference between the crude birth and death rates, tells us that the Austrian male population grew by just 0.89 males per every 1,000 during calendar year 1985, which is less than one-tenth of one percent. During the same time period, the female population actually declined by 1.34 per 1,000 women.

The second half of the first panel in Table 4 describes the age composition of the population employing broad age groupings. The three particular age groups shown are commonly used because they approximately separate the children (under 15) and the aged (65 and older) from the population in the working ages (15–64).

The center panel of Table 4 provides two sets of *directly standardized* vital rates permitting comparisons of the fertility and mortality situation in the country shown with that in others. The *standard populations* chosen for comparisons are the 1980 United States and 1980 Mexico populations.

The importance of standardization is easily understood when we compare, for example, the crude death rate of Austrians of both sexes in 1985 (11.85 deaths per 1,000 population) with the corresponding rate of Venezuelans (4.56 deaths per 1,000 population; cf. pp. 90 and 78). The latter is about 60 percent lower than the Austrian rate. If mortality is strongly influenced by a population's living standard, one would expect the death rate of Venezuela, which in 1985 had a per capita GNP of US $ 3,080 compared to Austria's $ 9,120 (cf. pp. 332 and 404), to be higher than that of Austria.

The answer to the question as to which of the two populations had higher mortality can be found through an examination of their age compositions. In Table D, the populations of Austria and Venezuela are decomposed into four age groups. A comparison of the proportions of people in these age categories between the two populations reveals a preponderance of older persons in Austria, and of younger ones in Venezuela. We likewise find that in Austria the age-specific death rates, with the exception of the one for the oldest age group, were lower than the corresponding Venezuelan rates. Because of the increase in age-specific mortality with age and the relatively old age structure of Austria, larger proportions of Austrians compared to Venezuelans are exposed to high mortality risks resulting in a greater number of deaths overall and, consequently, more deaths per 1,000 population. If Austria in 1985 had had the same age structure as Venezuela, its crude death rate would have been lower than the Venezuelan rate on account of its lower age-specific rates: 3.87 deaths per 1,000 population. This latter rate is calculated by multiplying the age-specific rates of Austria (*given population*) with the Venezuelan population of the corresponding age groups, summing up the resultant deaths over all ages and dividing the sum by the total population of Venezuela. It is the age-standardized death rate of Austria, with the population of Venezuela serving as *standard*.

The definitions of the crude and standardized rates in terms of their age-specific components illustrate the similarities and differences between them:

TABLE D.
Percent of Population in Selected Age Groups and Age-Specific Death Rates:
Austria and Venezuela, 1985

AGE GROUP	AUSTRIA 1985		VENEZUELA 1985	
	Percent of Population	Age-Specific Death Rate	Percent of Population	Age-Specific Death Rate
Under 15	18.23	0.001002	39.49	0.002662
15–49	50.91	0.001637	49.74	0.001832
50–64	16.56	0.010212	7.36	0.010601
65 and Older	14.30	0.063960	3.41	0.053301
All Ages	100.00	0.011853	100.00	0.004553

$$\text{CRUDE DEATH RATE} = \frac{D}{P} = \frac{\Sigma P_x M_x}{P},$$

$$\text{STANDARDIZED DEATH RATE} = \frac{\Sigma P_x^s M_x}{P^s},$$

where:

P = total given population,
D = total deaths in given population,
P_x = given population in age group beginning with age x,
M_x = age-specific death rate for age group beginning with age x in given population,
P_x^s = standard population in age group beginning with age x,
P^s = total standard population.

The standardized rate taken by itself is of no particular interest because it is dependent upon the standard chosen. What is of interest is its magnitude relative to the crude rates of the given and standard populations. For example, when we divide the standardized rate of Austria by the crude rate of Venezuela, the standard population, the resulting ratio of 0.85 tells us that Austrian mortality in 1985 was indeed lower than Venezuelan mortality. By subtracting the crude rate of the standard population (Venezuela) from the standardized rate of Austria–a difference which is not affected by the age-structural variations because both rates incorporate the identical age composition, viz.,

$$\frac{\Sigma P_x^s M_x}{P^s} - \frac{\Sigma P_x^s M_x^s}{P^s},$$

we obtain a measure of the amount by which the crude death rates of the populations being compared differ on account of mortality *alone*. In the case of Austria and Venezuela, this difference is $3.87 - 4.55 = -0.68$. The figure indicates that Austrian mortality, with everything in Austria being the same as in Venezuela, would have resulted in 0.68 deaths per 1,000 population less than Venezuelan mortality. It furthermore implies that the total difference in crude death rates between the two countries ($11.85 - 4.55 = 7.30$), which, if taken at face value, suggests higher Austrian than Venezuelan mortality, is exclusively the result of the Austrian age structure, which is heavily weighted in favor of older people. The difference in the crude death rates between the two countries brought about by age-structural variations is actually even larger than the 7.30 shown; it is $7.30 + 0.68 = 7.98$, the difference between Austria's crude and standardized death rates, which differ in their age compositional components but not in their mortality components, as shown above.

Direct standardization can be applied to all kinds of population characteristics, such as civil status, education, occupation, income, and the like, and to more than one characteristic simultaneously. In the case of the male and female birth and death rates appearing in the center panel of Table 4, the death rates for the total population shown are standardized on both age and sex, as are the total population birth rates. The latter, however, represent special cases: they are *female dominant*. To arrive at true age-sex standardized birth rates for the population of both sexes combined, age-specific male birth rates by age of father would be required together with age-specific female birth rates by age of mother. Because of the unavailability of male-specific information, male and female births had to be lumped together and attributed exclusively to mothers. For the same reason, directly standardized male birth rates are omitted from the tabulations.

The birth and death rates of all populations included in the Detailed Country Tabulations are standardized on the same two standard populations: the 1980 United States and 1980 Mexico populations, the first that of a country with a relatively old age structure, and the other of a country with a relatively young age structure. The main reason for providing two sets of standardized rates is to give the reader a choice when making comparisons. In order to minimize ambiguities arising from extreme differences in the age-structural and age-specific rate weights incorporated in the crude rates of the populations being compared, it is preferable to choose a standard population whose age composition and levels of age-specific rates are similar to those of the population for which it is to serve as standard. For developing countries with their generally low crude death rates, resulting from their young age structures despite their high age-specific rates, Mexico is a more appropriate standard than the United States, whose population and rates are weighted in the opposite direction. Vice versa, the United States is the more appropriate standard for developed countries with age compositions and vital rate levels similar to its own. The basic consideration behind the use of the same standards for all populations has been to make comparisons possible across all countries included in these tabulations as well as comparisons over time for populations featured repeatedly in this volume.

In the third panel of Table 4, seven fertility measures and three indicators of the population's sex and age composition are assembled. The fertility parameters, in contrast to the crude birth rates in the first panel of the table, take into account the age-sex structure of the population and, in some instances, mortality.

GFR   **General Fertility Rate.** This measure of fertility is similar to the crude birth rate for both sexes. It differs from the latter in its denominator, which, instead of the total population, includes only the female population of reproductive age, here defined as women aged 15–49. Because of the exclusion of males as well as of females in infertile ages, it is not influenced by the population's sex structure and determined to a lesser extent than the crude birth rate by the age composition of the female population, both features that make it a superior measure of fertility compared to the crude birth rate. As shown in the table, 1,000 women of fertile age in Austria bore 45.47 children in 1985.

TFR   **Total Fertility Rate.** The *TFR* is calculated as the sum of the age-specific birth rates (B_x) over the reproductive ages multiplied by n, the length of the age groups to which the age-specific rates apply:

$$TFR = n \sum_{15}^{50} B_x.$$

The total fertility rate represents the total number of children a woman just born will have if she survives to the end of reproductive life and bears children at the age-specific rates prevailing at the time of observation. The *TFR*, a synthetic estimate based on cross-sectional data, is often taken as an indicator of *average family size*. Under the conditions specified, an Austrian girl born in 1985 would bear, in the course of her lifetime, a total of 1.48 children.

The definition of *reproductive life* varies. In populations in which childbearing starts relatively early, 10 would be an appropriate lower age limit; in developed countries, in which childbirth tends to start late and terminate early, the age range 15–44 is commonly used. In the Detailed Country Tabulations, we follow the example of the United Nations and define reproductive life as the ages 15–49.

GRR **Gross Reproduction Rate.** The *GRR* is the same as the *TFR* but restricted to the birth of baby girls. When information on age-specific female births or birth rates is unavailable, the *GRR* can be approximated by multiplying the *TFR* by the ratio of the total number of female births to the number of all births during the period of observation. In 1985 Austria, where 42,386 out of 87,440 births were girls, this sex ratio at birth is 0.4847. Correspondingly, the *GRR* is equal to *TFR* × 0.4847, which is 0.718.

NRR **Net Reproduction Rate.** The *NRR* is closely related to the *GRR*, measuring the average number of girl children a woman will bear in her lifetime under the given regime of age-specific female birth rates (F_x). But unlike the *GRR*, it does not stipulate that all women live through their entire reproductive lives. It takes account of deaths to women who die before completing their fertile years by including in its calculation the probabilities for women to live from birth to any fertile age group x to $x + n$. A woman's probability of survival from birth to a specific fertile age group is taken from the stationary (life table) population of the same period or year and defined as $_nL_x/100000$. Thus,

$$NRR = n \sum_{15}^{50} F_x \left(_nL_x/100000\right).$$

When mortality levels are relatively low, as in 1985 Austria, the *NRR* does not differ much from the *GRR*: 0.706 compared to 0.718. In Venezuela, where mortality in 1985 was considerably higher, as pointed out above, the difference between the two measures is more appreciable: 1.678 against 1.750 (cf. p. 332).

The *NRR* can also be interpreted as the ratio of the number of women in one generation to that of the following generation, which, for one woman, would be *NRR*/1. If the Austrian fertility and mortality conditions persist into the future, the Austrian female generation succeeding the one born in 1985 will be only 0.706 times as large as the 1985 generation, or 30 percent smaller.

The products of the $F_x {}_nL_x$ values over all reproductive ages used for the calculation of the *NRR* constitute the *net maternity function*. This function, when plotted over the reproductive ages, portrays, among other things, how women in a population space their girl children throughout their reproductive life spans. The shape of the net maternity function and its change over time is illustrated for most populations included in the Detailed Country Tabulations in the graph entitled CHANGES IN FERTILITY.

μ **Mean Age at Childbearing.** One way of summarizing the net maternity function is to calculate its mean, which represents the average age (μ) at which women bear their girl children. With $F_x {}_n L_x$ births in every fertile age group and assuming every woman to be $x + n/2$ years old, μ is obtained as

$$\mu = \frac{\sum_{15}^{50} (x + n/2) F_x {}_n L_x}{\sum_{15}^{50} F_x {}_n L_x} .$$

In developed countries, mean ages at childbearing are usually lower than in developing ones. For example, in 1985 Austria μ was 26.6 years. In Guatemala at the same time it was 2.5 years higher (cf. p. 310). The main reason underlying this difference is the tendency of western women to have their few children early in life, while in the developing world women need more time to space the large number of children they on the average still bear, thereby pushing the mean age at childbirth upward.

σ^2 **Variance around the Mean Age of Childbirth.** While μ tells us around which particular age women concentrate their childbirth, σ^2 measures the spread of births around this point of concentration. It is defined as

$$\sigma^2 = \frac{\sum_{15}^{50} (x + n/2 - \mu)^2 F_x {}_n L_x}{\sum_{15}^{50} F_x {}_n L_x} .$$

For assessing the spread of births, we use the standard deviation of μ, which is σ. The small σ of 5.44 (years) of Austrian women in 1985 together with a μ of 26 reveals that they delivered most of their baby girls in a relatively narrow time span not longer than 11 years centering around age 26. By contrast, Guatemalan women, with an average number of girl children about four times as large as that of their Austrian contemporaries, (had to) spread their baby girls over a time interval 40 percent longer ($\sigma = 7.60$) around a mean age at childbirth of 29 years.

GENER-   **Mean Length of a Generation** (*T*). For an individual, a generation is the
ATION   time needed to replace herself or himself by a daughter or a son. If we consider a population, for example one composed of females of reproductive ages, the length of its generation can similarly be described as the *average* time between the births of its members and those of their daughters.[10]

---

10. The reproductive life spans of males differ from those of females, and husbands and wives are virtually always of different ages when they have their sons and daughters. As a result, the length of a male generation is not identical with that of a female generation.

The net reproduction rate (*NRR*) is defined above as "the ratio of the number of women in one generation to that in the preceding one." According to this definition, the *NRR* represents the *generational* growth rate of the population. The time needed by the population to achieve a growth equivalent to *NRR*, which is one generation, is commonly designated as *T*.

The definition of the *NRR* stipulates that the members of the mother generation survive their reproductive years in accordance with the schedule of age-specific death rates in force at the time of observation and bear girl children according to the age-specific birth rates operating at the same time. Neither schedule of rates is subject to change. In 1925, Dublin and Lotka were the first to demonstrate that any population exposed to unchanging regimes of mortality and fertility and unaffected by migration over an indefinite period of time will ultimately settle on a constant annual rate of natural increase, which they called the *intrinsic growth rate*.[11] Since the net reproduction rate presupposes fixed schedules of age-specific birth and death rates in the course of at least one generation, it may be said to result from a growth pattern similar to that displayed by a population growing for a prolonged period of time at a constant annual rate. When this constant annual rate is compounded instantaneously, the factor by which the population increases or decreases is equal to e^r for one year, and e^{rt} for *t* years. Under the assumption that these conditions hold for the *NRR*, the generational growth rate, the latter can be defined in terms of *r* and *t* as

$$NRR = e^{rt}. \qquad \text{From this, we obtain} \qquad T = \frac{\ln NRR}{r}.$$

To solve for *T*, we use Dublin and Lotka's intrinsic rate *r* as the best approximation to the constant annual population growth rate during the time period covered by *T*.

The intrinsic growth rate is explored in more detail on the following pages. For 1985 Austrian females, it is equal to -0.01297 (cf. p. 405). Accordingly, the length of their generation is $\ln 0.70562 \div -0.01297 = 26.8$ years. This figure is close to 26.6, the mean age of the 1985 Austrian women at the time of the births of their girl children (μ). This correspondence is not surprising considering the dependence of *T* on the age at childbirth. Generally, *T* is slightly smaller than μ in increasing populations, while in decreasing populations like that of 1985 Austria the opposite holds.

POP. SEX RATIO The **Population Sex Ratio** is defined as the number of females in a population per one male. The figure is often multiplied by 100 to express the number of females per 100 males. In 1985, Austria had approximately 1.11 females for every male or 11 percent more females than males, as Table E shows. A preponderance of females is the usual situation in most reasonably large populations under normal growth conditions because of higher male than female mortality. However, this preponderance does not hold for all age

11. Louis I. Dublin and Alfred J. Lotka. "On the True Rate of Natural Increase." *Journal of the American Statistical Association*, 20(150): 305–39, September, 1925.

TABLE E.
Age-Specific Sex Ratios: Austria 1985

AGE GROUP	FEMALES PER 100 MALES	AGE GROUP	FEMALES PER 100 MALES	AGE GROUP	FEMALES PER 100 MALES
0	98.2	30–34	100.3	65–69	160.2
1–4	96.2	35–39	98.2	70–74	169.5
5–9	95.4	40–44	99.7	75–79	191.1
10–14	95.8	45–49	99.6	80–84	221.9
15–19	95.6	50–54	102.3	85+	295.6
20–24	98.2	55–59	113.3		
25–29	100.2	60–64	152.8	All Ages	110.9

groups within populations. The number of male births exceeds that of female births almost everywhere and, for that reason, males tend to outnumber females in the younger age groups. It is only around age 50 that the balance begins to shift significantly in favor of females, as the Austrian example in Table E illustrates.

SEX RATIO AT BIRTH   The **Sex Ratio at Birth** is the number of baby boys born per every baby girl, usually multiplied by 100 to indicate the number of male births per 100 female births. With generally higher male than female mortality, the usual excess of male over female births assures an approximate equal number of males and females in the marriageable ages. Austrian women in 1985 bore 106 baby boys for every 100 baby girls.

DEP. RATIO   The **Dependency Ratio** is a measure of the age composition: the ratio of the number of children and aged persons in a population to the number of persons in the intermediate ages. It is defined as

$$\frac{\text{CHILDREN (under 15)} + \text{AGED (65 \& older)}}{\text{PERSONS 15--64}} \times 100.$$

In high-fertility countries, the dependency ratio often approaches or exceeds 100 because of the large proportion of children; in low-fertility populations, it is usually much smaller but may be on the rise as a result of the increasing proportion of elderly people. Since population aging is caused primarily by fertility reduction, the proportion of children declines at the same time as the proportion of old people increases. The net effect of these two opposing trends on the dependency ratio itself may be close to zero. Austria, for example, had a dependency ratio of 48.2 in 1985; 34 years earlier, the rate was not very different: 50.4.

A more revealing way of examining changes in a population's age structure by means of the dependency ratio is to decompose the latter into its *youth* and *old age* components, as it is done in the Summary Table. The 1951–85 trends of these two dependency components in the Austrian population clearly indicate the extent to which the Austrian age structure changed during that period: youth dependency declined from 34.5 to 27.0, and old-age dependency increased from 15.9 to 21.2.

The *age* dependency ratio is often used as an approximation of the *economic* dependency ratio, which is the ratio of the economically inactive to the economically active population. For any individual country, age and economic dependency ratios may be significantly different depending on who is considered part of the work force and who is not. But because the definition of economically active varies considerably from country to country, the age dependency ratio as defined here is the best available *comparative* measure, albeit only an approximate one, of economic dependency.

The demographic data and parameters presented in Tables 1 through 4 describe the observed population as it appeared at a given point in time and provide measurements of the dynamics—the forces of mortality and fertility—that were operating in it at the time of observation. But the data and the measures derived from them can do more than make explicit what a population is or was like at a particular moment in history. Barring unforeseen major environmental or social occurrences, they also give us clues as to the direction in which the population not necessarily will but *can* develop in the future. What actually will happen depends upon two types of factors: the demographic potential inherent in the existing population and the environmental and social factors molding individual and communal behavior that is brought to bear on this potential. While the latter type of factors determines how the given potential ultimately will be realized, the former sets the limits within which the nondemographic forces can operate. How many births there will be 20 or 30 years from now depends not only on the fertility behavior in the early years of the next millennium but also on the number of baby girls born right now, and it is today's fertility pattern that largely predetermines what configuration the population's age structure will assume in the foreseeable future. The information provided by the figures in the subsequent tables relates to this demographic *potential*, not to its realization.

Table 5: Population Projected with Fixed Age-Specific Birth and Death Rates. One way of assessing the demographic potential of a population is to project it into the future assuming that its observed regimes of mortality and fertility will remain unchanged. Table 5 provides such projections of the population in five-year age groups for two successive five-year periods. The projection method used is the *component method.*

AGE GROUP	PROJECTED POPULATION						STABLE EQUIVALENT TO ORIGINAL POPULATION				AGE GROUP
	1990			1995			MALES		FEMALES		
	BOTH SEXES	MALES	FEMALES	BOTH SEXES	MALES	FEMALES	Number	Percent	Number	Percent	
0-4	436	224	212	422	217	205	235	4.3	222	3.7	0-4
5-9	452	230	222	435	224	211	251	4.5	237	4.0	5-9
10-14	426	218	208	451	230	221	267	4.8	252	4.2	10-14
15-19	498	254	244	425	217	208	284	5.1	269	4.5	15-19
20-24	616	314	302	495	252	243	301	5.4	286	4.8	20-24
25-29	656	330	326	613	312	301	318	5.8	305	5.1	25-29
30-34	586	292	294	653	328	325	337	6.1	325	5.5	30-34
35-39	500	249	251	581	289	292	357	6.5	345	5.8	35-39
40-44	497	250	247	495	246	249	375	6.8	365	6.1	40-44
45-49	510	254	256	490	245	245	391	7.1	386	6.5	45-49
50-54	445	221	224	497	245	252	403	7.3	405	6.8	50-54
55-59	385	187	198	427	208	219	407	7.4	422	7.1	55-59
60-64	398	182	216	362	172	190	398	7.2	433	7.3	60-64
65-69	392	149	243	363	160	203	373	6.8	434	7.3	65-69
70-74	223	81	142	339	121	218	325	5.9	417	7.0	70-74
75-79	251	85	166	175	58	117	248	4.5	364	6.1	75-79
80-84	170	52	118	163	49	114	153	2.8	268	4.5	80-84
85+	110	28	82	119	30	89	94	1.7	215	3.6	85+
TOTAL	7551	3600	3951	7505	3603	3902	5517		5950		TOTAL

A population projection by means of the component method involves two tasks: the survival of present persons from one age group into the next, and the estimation of the number of new entrants (births) into the population during the projection period. Since the age groups into which the population is classified cover five years, the projection period, i.e., the time to survive from one age group into the next, extends likewise over five years. Migration is explicitly excluded. For solving the first task, we stipulate that the observed population aged x to $x + 4$ survives the five years of the projection period, at the end of which the survivors will be exactly five years older, at the ratio at which the corresponding stationary (life table) population survives, i.e., $_nL_{x+n}/_nL_x$. The stationary population is chosen to provide the survival ratio because its attrition results exclusively from mortality. Under the specified conditions, the population $_5P_x$ *will diminish to*

$$_5P_x \left(\frac{_5L_{x+5}}{_5L_x} \right)$$

five years later. The 1985 Austrian population, for example, had 251,627 males 30–34 years old. The corresponding stationary population ($_5L_{30}$) is 479,358, of which, under 1985 mortality conditions, $_5L_{35}$ or 475,051 survive to ages 35–39. The implied survival ratio is 475,051 ÷ 479,358 = 0.991015. Applying this ratio to the 251,627 Austrian males aged 30–34 in 1985 yields 249,366 survivors aged 35–39 in 1990 or, expressed in thousands as in the above table, 249. Through the use of this procedure, age group by age group, the population alive at the starting date is projected five years into the future or, if the entire process is repeated n times, $n \times 5$ years into the future.

The second task of the projection process is the estimation of the number of persons who will be 0–4 years old at the end of the five-year projection period, which is equal to the survivors after five years among those born during the period. Because of the availability of information on births by age of mother only, the projection of births is *female dominant:* all births are attributed to mothers. The total number of births is calculated as the sum of the woman-years of exposure to childbirth in each of the fertile age groups x to $x + n$ multiplied by the corresponding age-specific birth rates B_x. The person-years of exposure to childbirth among women aged x to $x + n$, in turn, are obtained as the arithmetic mean of the number of women present in the age group at the beginning ($_5P_x^0$) and at the end of the projection period ($_5P_x^1$), times 5, the length of that period. Thus, the total number of expected births during the five-year projection period is equal to

$$\sum_{15}^{50} [\tfrac{5}{2} (_5P_x^0 + _5P_x^1) B_x].$$

The number of women x to $x + n$ years old at the beginning ($_5P_x^0$) is indicated in the data (or the last projected population if the projection goes beyond the first five-year cycle); the number of those who will be x to $x + n$ years old after 5 years, the end of the projection period ($_5P_x^1$), is equal to the women $x - n$ to x years old at the beginning (the women in the preceding age group) who survive the projection period. When we look once again at Austria in 1985, we find, for example, 294,380 women 25–29 years old;

in the preceding age group, the number is 326,477. At the end of the projection period of five years, in 1990, the survivors of these latter women will be 25–29 years old. How many of them will survive from ages 20–24 to 25–29 is calculated in the same manner described for task 1 of the projection process: by means of the survival ratio taken from the stationary population. By using this procedure, we obtain:

$$326,477 \, (491,618 \div 492,708) = 325,754,$$

which is the same number shown in the table above for the projected female population aged 25–29 in 1990. The mean number of women present during the projection period, multiplied by 5, the length of the period, gives us

$$5 \times [(294,380 + 325,754) \div 2] = 1,550,335,$$

an approximation of the number of woman-years females 25–29 will be exposed to the risk of childbirth during the five years of the projection period. The number of children expected to be borne by these women according to 1985 fertility is then obtained by multiplying the years of exposure by the age-specific birth rate B_x:

$$1,550,335 \times (28,771 \div 294,380) = 151,521.$$

If we continue our earlier example of projecting the Austrian male population, it is not total births but male births that we want. To obtain these, we multiply the number of projected births to women 25–29 for the 1985–90 period by the 1985 male sex ratio at birth, i.e., 1985 male births ÷ 1985 total births:

$$151,521 \times (45,054 \div 87,440) = 78,072.$$

Repeating the birth projection procedure for all age groups containing women of reproductive age and summing the number of male births over all these ages gives us the total number of baby boys expected to be born during the five-year projection period: 226,930.

The final step in the projection process is the estimation of the number of all those born during the projection period who survive to its end. In terms of our example, this is the Austrian baby boys born between 1985 and 1990 who will still be alive in 1990. The step is accomplished by multiplying the number of male births by the probability of males to survive from birth until the end of the projection period. This probability, taken once again from the stationary population, is defined as $_5L_0/5l_0$. For Austrian males, this survival ratio is $493,578 \div 500,000 = 0.98716$. Correspondingly, the projected male population aged 0–4 in 1990 is $226,930 \times 0.98716 = 224,015$, shown as 224 thousands in the projection table.

For the projection of the female population, the sex ratio at birth to be applied to obtain female births is the total number of female births divided by the number of births of both sexes, and the survival ratio from birth to the end of the projection period, $_5L_0/5l_0$, is to be taken from the female life table.

Even though the projection model applied is artificial because it provides neither for changes in vital rates nor for migration, the projected figures are not entirely without practical use As the age composition of the observed population mirrors past changes— especially in fertility behavior and other events with violent impact on the age structure (the current population structures of Germany and the USSR, both heavily affected by

World War II, are good examples)—so do the projected age structures show the effects of these changes and events as they work themselves through and, eventually, out of the age structure. In Austria, the school-age population will continue to decline at least over the next ten years as a result of fertility reduction during the past two decades, requiring adjustments on the current educational structure, and the large cohorts born during the baby boom following World War II will swell the ranks of the retired in another 25 to 30 years, exactly at a time when the small birth cohorts of today will have to pay the social-security bills of the country.

How relatively accurate projections with fixed mortality and fertility schedules and the exclusion of migration can be in the short run is illustrated in Table F, in which the projected Austrian populations for the years 1980 and 1985, derived from the 1975 observed population, are compared with the official population counts or estimates for the same years. Disparities between official and projected population figures tend to increase with the distance of the projection date from the base year and are largest for the youngest and the oldest age groups. In Austria that is so because both fertility and mortality between 1975 and 1985 declined substantially, mortality especially among the older people. As a result, the number of younger people in the projected populations of 1980 and 1985 is overestimated, and that of older ones underestimated.

The figures in the right-hand panel of Table 5 under the heading *Stable Equivalent to Observed Population* were obtained through a projection of the observed population 500 years into the future. Their meaning relates entirely to the population potential.

TABLE F.
A Comparison Between Official and Projected Population Counts:
Austria 1980 and 1985 (population in thousands)

AGE GROUP	1975 BASE POPULATION	1980 POPULATION				1985 POPULATION			
		Official		Projected		Official		Projected	
		No.	%	No.	%	No.	%	No.	%
0–4	501	433	5.8	473	6.3	452	6.0	502	6.7
5–9	609	498	6.6	499	6.6	427	5.6	471	6.3
10–14	643	608	8.1	608	8.1	498	6.6	498	6.6
15–19	574	647	8.7	641	8.6	619	8.2	605	8.1
20–24	512	578	7.7	570	7.7	659	8.7	637	8.6
25–29	511	508	6.8	508	6.8	588	7.8	567	7.5
30–34	527	509	6.8	508	6.8	504	6.7	505	6.7
35–39	466	523	7.0	522	6.9	503	6.7	504	6.7
40–44	417	461	6.1	460	6.1	519	6.9	515	6.8
45–49	452	408	5.4	408	5.4	456	6.0	451	6.0
50–54	470	438	5.8	439	5.8	400	5.3	396	5.3
55–59	299	451	6.0	451	6.0	423	5.6	420	5.6
60–64	415	281	3.7	280	3.7	427	5.6	421	5.6
65–69	400	375	5.0	372	5.0	257	3.4	251	3.3
70–74	331	337	4.5	333	4.4	322	4.3	309	4.1
75–79	219	247	3.3	242	3.2	260	3.4	244	3.2
80–84	115	134	1.8	131	1.7	158	2.1	146	1.9
85+	60	69	0.9	69	0.9	83	1.1	78	1.0
TOTAL	7,520	7,505		7,514		7,558		7,520	

In any long-term population projection applying fixed age-specific birth and death rates, initially existing age-structural irregularities will disappear and the projected population ultimately settle on a stable sex-age structure and stable birth, death, and growth rates. The major purpose of such a long-term projection is to find out what these ultimate stable rates and the age structure solely depending on them are.[12]

To find the stable rates and age structure, the projection is carried forward in time until the ratio of population increase from one projection cycle to the next settles on a stable value. The computer program used to create Table 5 projects all populations for 500 years, a time period sufficient for any known larger population to reach the stable state. The percent distributions shown side by side with the population figures of the stable equivalent describe the stable age structure that the population will ultimately attain if 1985 mortality and fertility rates continue to operate unchanged.

In the strict sense of the word, the attribute *stable* applies to the female population only since the projection model used is *female dominant*, i.e., all births are attributed to mothers and the number of male births is simply a multiple of the number of female births. To obtain a *true* stable male population, information on male births by age of father is required. Because such data are unavailable, the subsequent discussion will concentrate on the female population.

A stable population can be projected further into the future by simply multiplying the (total or age-specific) population figures by the stable ratio of population increase from one projection cycle to the next (customarily designated as λ). In the same manner, it can be projected backward by successively dividing the stable population by λ, or by λ^n, where n represents the number of five-year projection cycles used in the projection process. The *stable equivalent* of the observed population is the stable population projected backward to the base year. Since the stable population is determined exclusively by the age-specific birth and death rates, the stable equivalent of the observed population represents that portion of the latter that can be explained by the regimes of mortality and fertility in force at the time of observation. Any discrepancies between the age distributions of the observed population and its stable equivalent are the result of either demographic changes, or extraneous events in the past, or both. A comparison of the two kinds of population tells us whether the observed population, at the time of observation, is favorable or unfavorable to overall mortality and fertility.

Figure D represents such a comparison in graphic form: the shaded area indicates the age-sex structure of the observed 1985 Austrian population, the area outlined in white its stable equivalent. Among other things, the graph shows more females 15–24 years old in the observed population than in its stable equivalent. These females belong to the cohort born during the baby boom in the 1960s. Because this relatively large cohort is presently in its early years of childbearing, the number of children under age 5 in the observed population, representing the survivors of the 1980–85 births, is larger than the number of children five years older despite rapidly falling fertility prior to 1985 (the total fertility rate between 1980 and 1985 declined by 12 percent). Expressed differently, the current (1985) Austrian age structure favors overall fertility by keeping the crude birth rate temporarily higher than it would be under stable conditions. This can be

---

12. For another method of obtaining the same information, see Leslie Matrix and Its Analysis, pp. 39–41.

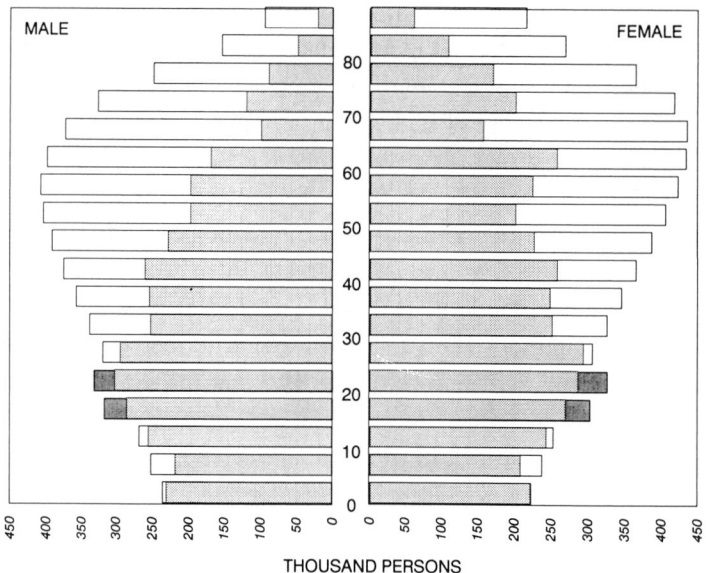

Fig. D. The Age Distribution of 1985 Austria
and Its Stable Equivalent

verified by checking the sex-specific crude birth rates of the 1985 population against those of the stable population shown in Table 6: the 1985 crude birth rates of Austrian males is 12.57 per 1,000, that of females 10.66; the corresponding rates of the stable population are 8.36 and 7.29, respectively.

A comparison of the crude death rate of the 1985 population with that of the stable equivalent reveals the same: in the near future, the 1985 age structure is keeping this rate below the level it would attain in the stable situation. Figure D reveals why this is so. Because age-specific fertility in 1985 was considerably lower than it had been in years prior, and mortality also, increasingly larger portions of people will be shifted into the older age groups if the 1985 regimes of age-specific mortality and fertility continue to operate unchanged, resulting eventually (in the case of Austria) in an *inverted* age pyramid in which the majority of all people will be old. (The same will happen at an even greater pace should Austrian age-specific birth and death rates continue to decline.) Since older persons are exposed to a higher risk of dying than younger ones are, overall mortality as measured by the crude death rate will, in consequence, be higher in the future.

Table 6: Projected Vital Rates and Ratios (female dominant). The information assembled in this table, which pertains to the projected and stable populations in Table 5, is analogous to that shown for the observed population in Table 4. The vital rates are calculated by applying the observed age-specific birth and death rates to the projected populations; the age-structural measures are obtained directly from the projected age distributions.

Of special interest are the vital rates of the stable population appearing in the right-side panel of Table 6. These rates, known as *intrinsic* rates, are the crude rates as they

	VITAL RATES OF PROJECTED POPULATION						VITAL RATES OF STABLE POPULATION		
	1990			1995					
Per Thousand	BOTH SEXES	MALES	FEMALES	BOTH SEXES	MALES	FEMALES	Per Thousand	MALES	FEMALES
BIRTH RATE	11.75	12.70	10.89	10.92	11.72	10.17	BIRTH RATE	8.36	7.29
DEATH RATE	12.56	12.09	12.99	12.66	12.17	13.12	DEATH RATE	21.21	20.27
RATE OF INCREASE	-0.81	0.61	-2.10	-1.75	-0.45	-2.94	RATE OF INCREASE		-12.97

	AGE STRUCTURE OF PROJECTED POPULATION						STABLE AGE STRUCTURE		
% UNDER 15	17.41	18.68	16.24	17.43	18.62	16.33	% UNDER 15	13.65	11.96
% 15-64	67.42	70.35	64.75	67.12	69.77	64.68	% 15-64	64.72	59.51
% 65 AND OLDER	15.17	10.97	19.01	15.45	11.61	18.99	% 65 AND OLDER	21.64	28.53
DEPEND. RATIO x 100	48.32	42.15	54.44	48.98	43.33	54.61	DEPEND. RATIO x 100	54.52	68.05

would ultimately stand if the observed age-specific rates remain fixed over time. If we were to follow the projections of the 1985 Austrian females, we would find, in accordance with Dublin and Lotka (cf. p. 31), that the crude rates of birth, death, and natural increase will begin to converge at stable levels in less than a hundred years and settle at such levels in about 200 years.

The specification *female dominant* in the table heading emphasizes that the projections presented in this volume are essentially those of *females*. The number of future males is obtained simply by multiplying the projected female births by the observed ratio of males to females at birth, implying that the male population is growing at the intrinsic rate of increase of females. For this reason, it is only the stable female rates that are intrinsic rates in the true sense of the word.

Table 7: Leslie Matrix and Its Analysis (females). An alternative method of projecting a population into the future keeping its age-specific vital rates constant was devised by H. P. Leslie, who arranged the projection process as the multiplication of a vector composed of the number of people at the various ages $\{P_0\}$ by a matrix operator, **M,** incorporating the observed regimes of mortality and fertility. The purpose of including the Leslie matrix here is not to provide an alternative to the projection in Table 5; the primary aim is to examine the effects of the age-specific birth and death rates separately from those of the age structure on which they operate. The matrix operator, **M,** which incorporates only these rates, makes such a separate analysis possible. Because fertility data by age of father are unavailable, the matrices shown in this volume are restricted to female populations.

AGE GROUP	FEMALE BIRTH RATES	NET MATERNITY FUNCTION	COEFF. OF MATRIX EQUATION	ORIGINAL MATRIX SUB-DIAGONAL	ORIGINAL MATRIX FIRST ROW	STABLE MATRIX FISHER VALUES	STABLE MATRIX REPRODUCTIVE VALUES	MATRIX PARAMETERS	
0-4	0.0000	0.0000	0.0000	0.99850	0.00000	0.977	216729	λ_1	0.93720
5-9	0.0000	0.0000	0.0000	0.99916	0.00000	0.917	191149	λ_2	0.33133+0.70313ι
10-14	0.0000	0.0000	0.0297	0.99862	0.02975	0.860	209698	λ_4	-0.31872+0.33581ι
15-19	0.0120	0.0594	0.1490	0.99792	0.14959	0.778	235460	λ_6	-0.09462+0.40051ι
20-24	0.0485	0.2387	0.2358	0.99779	0.23719	0.584	190706	r_1	-0.01297
25-29	0.0474	0.2329	0.1776	0.99733	0.17903	0.316	93170	r_2	-0.05039+0.22609ι
30-34	0.0249	0.1223	0.0828	0.99580	0.08370	0.122	30807	r_4	-0.15401+0.46602ι
35-39	0.0089	0.0433	0.0259	0.99294	0.02625	0.033	8176	r_6	-0.17757+0.36056ι
40-44	0.0017	0.0084	0.0045	0.98947	0.00461	0.005	1335	c_1	59497
45-49	0.0001	0.0006	0.0003	0.98433	0.00032	0.000	75	$2\pi/\gamma$	27.7909
50-54	0.0000	0.0000	0.0000	0.00000	0.00000	0.000	0	Δ	15.5263

The basic data needed for the Leslie matrix are the annual female birth rates by age of mother, $F_x/{}_nP_x$, i.e., the average number of baby girls born to women x to $x + n$ years of age in the course of one year, divided by the average number of women of corresponding age in the population during the same year, and the stationary (life table) population of females, $_nL_x$. The female birth rates, representing the chance of a woman bearing a girl child during one year, are listed in the first column of Table 7; the $_nL_x$ values, the average number of years a woman exactly x years old can expect to live in the following five years, are easily obtainable from Table 3. The matrix procedure described here uses, as all previous analyses, population data in five-year age groups, making $n = 5$. Accordingly, our Leslie matrix requires, aside from five-year probabilities of surviving provided by Table 3, also probabilities of women bearing a girl child over a five-year period. This probability, taking into account observed mortality patterns, is $F_x\,_nL_x$, the net maternity function, shown in the second column of Table 7. One other factor to be considered when projecting future births is that almost all women aged x to $x + 4$ at the beginning of a five-year projection cycle will move into the next older age group in the course of the projection cycle. On the average, a woman will spend 2.5 years in the age group in which she is found at the beginning of a fixed five-year period, and the other 2.5 years in the next older one, making her chance of giving birth to a baby girl in five years' time equal to

$$\tfrac{1}{2}\left(F_x\,_5L_x + F_{x+5}\,_5L_{x+5}\right).$$

This particular fertility function, which will reappear at a later stage in the matrix analysis, is found in the third column of Table 7 under the heading *Coefficients of Matrix Equation*.

The Leslie matrix itself contains all zeros except in its first row and subdiagonal. The subdiagonal incorporates the force of mortality in the form of life-table survival ratios, $_nL_{x+n}/_nL_x$. The positive number shown in the second row of the first column of the matrix represents the probability of surviving from age group 0–4 to 5–9, i.e., $_5L_5/_5L_0$; the number in the third row of the second column $_5L_{10}/_5L_5$, etc. The survival rates for all age groups up to the end of the childbearing ages are displayed in the fourth column of Table 7.

The population's fertility is built into the first row of the projection matrix in the form

$$\frac{1}{2}\left(F_x + \frac{_5L_{x+5}}{_5L_x}F_{x+5}\right) {}_5L_0,$$

as defined by Leslie. This formulation of a woman's chance of giving birth to a baby girl within five years, when applied in the matrix projection process, yields the same results as the procedure of projecting females 0–4 years old five years hence employed in the component projection. A comparison of the age-specific values of Leslie's fertility function listed in Table 7 under *First Row* of *Original Matrix* with the corresponding values of the fertility function shown in the third column of the same table under *Coefficients of Matrix Equation* will reveal that both are almost identical.

The matrix used and shown in this volume is an *abbreviated* one, covering the female population only to the end of reproduction. Such a truncated matrix, as the one for 1985 Austrian females replicated below, suffices for the purposes at hand because it embodies all factors that ultimately determine the demographic future of the population. Age-specific mortality for persons beyond reproduction does not affect the number of future births nor, consequently, the population's intrinsic or stable growth rate.

$$\mathbf{M} \qquad\qquad \{P_0\}$$

$$
\begin{bmatrix}
0.0000 & 0.0000 & 0.0298 & 0.1496 & 0.2372 & 0.1790 & 0.0837 & 0.0263 & 0.0046 & 0.0003 \\
0.9985 & 0.0 & 0.0 & 0.0 & 0.0 & 0.0 & 0.0 & 0.0 & 0.0 & 0.0 \\
0.0 & 0.9992 & 0.0 & 0.0 & 0.0 & 0.0 & 0.0 & 0.0 & 0.0 & 0.0 \\
0.0 & 0.0 & 0.9986 & 0.0 & 0.0 & 0.0 & 0.0 & 0.0 & 0.0 & 0.0 \\
0.0 & 0.0 & 0.0 & 0.9979 & 0.0 & 0.0 & 0.0 & 0.0 & 0.0 & 0.0 \\
0.0 & 0.0 & 0.0 & 0.0 & 0.9978 & 0.0 & 0.0 & 0.0 & 0.0 & 0.0 \\
0.0 & 0.0 & 0.0 & 0.0 & 0.0 & 0.9973 & 0.0 & 0.0 & 0.0 & 0.0 \\
0.0 & 0.0 & 0.0 & 0.0 & 0.0 & 0.0 & 0.9958 & 0.0 & 0.0 & 0.0 \\
0.0 & 0.0 & 0.0 & 0.0 & 0.0 & 0.0 & 0.0 & 0.9929 & 0.0 & 0.0 \\
0.0 & 0.0 & 0.0 & 0.0 & 0.0 & 0.0 & 0.0 & 0.0 & 0.9895 & 0.0 \\
\end{bmatrix}
\times
\begin{bmatrix}
221907 \\
208519 \\
243877 \\
302697 \\
326477 \\
294380 \\
252325 \\
249122 \\
258946 \\
227721 \\
\end{bmatrix}
$$

For Austria, premultiplication of $\{P_0\}$ by $\mathbf{M}$ gives us the female population up to ages 45–49 five years hence, i.e., $\mathbf{M}\{P_{1985}\} = P_{1990}$. For a projection further into the future, say k five-year cycles, we simply raise $\mathbf{M}$ to the kth power and premultiply $\{P_0\}$ by $\mathbf{M}^k$.

The computer program used in the production of this volume squares the original matrix $\mathbf{M}$ seven times, providing the 128th power. In the process of successively raising $\mathbf{M}$ to higher powers, the matrix itself approaches stability. This means that the ratio of any element of $\mathbf{M}^k$ to the corresponding element of $\mathbf{M}$ raised to the power $k - 1$ will tend toward a stable value that, once reached, no longer changes with the increase of k.

The high-power stable matrix possesses a number of properties of demographic interest. The first among these is that the stable ratio of increase in the absolute value of corresponding matrix elements from one projection cycle to the next just described is identical to λ, the stable rate of increase over an n-year period obtained through a long-term component projection (cf. p. 37). The stable matrix ratio represents the *dominant root* of the matrix and is commonly labeled λ_1. From this dominant root, we can obtain the stable *annual* (intrinsic) growth rate of the population, r_1. If the latter is compounded instantaneously, then

$$\lambda_1 = e^{5r_1}, \qquad \text{and} \qquad r_1 = \frac{\ln \lambda_1}{5}.$$

Both λ_1 and r_1 are presented in Table 7 under the subheading *Matrix Parameters*. A comparison of r_1 with the intrinsic rate of increase of the female population in Table 5, the latter obtained from the total female population projected for 500 years, reveals agreement up to the last decimal shown.

A second property of the stable matrix is that the elements in each of its columns are distributed in identical proportions. These proportions are the same as those in which the stable population is distributed over the entire age range. Had we used a *complete* projection matrix covering all age groups from 0–4 through 85+ and raised it to a power at which stability is attained, this fact could easily be verified. Since the age distribution of the stable population is already shown in Table 5, expressed in percent, it is omitted here. What is shown in Table 7 under *Matrix Parameters* is c_1, the stable equivalent of the total observed female population, calculated with the help of a complete (18×18) and decomposed projection matrix and the population vector $\{P_0\}$. (For more details on obtaining c_1 from the projection matrix, see p. 46 below.) The same parameter, obtained through component projection, appears in Table 5. The only difference between the two figures save for minor rounding errors in some instances is the division of c_1 by 100 in Table 7, and by 1,000 in Table 5.

While the distribution of column elements in the stable projection matrix provides information on the stable age structure, the proportional distribution of row elements, identical for all rows, provides prospective fertility information, which Fisher called a woman's *Reproductive Value*. This parameter answers the question: For how many prospective girl children will a woman born now be good at any given age x of her life if the observed regimes of fertility and mortality persist? We can rephrase this question by asking: If we consider the birth of a woman as the loaning to her of one life and her giving birth to girl children as the repayment of this loan, how many births will this woman owe at any particular age in her life? The answer evidently depends on the *interest rate* applied to the loan and the *repayment schedule* imposed on the woman. For stable populations Fisher proved that, if the debt of a woman is equal to one at the time of her own birth and zero at the end of her reproductive life and the repayment schedule is fixed at the observed net maternity function, then the rate of interest which the woman is charged and at which her repayments are discounted is equal to the intrinsic rate of population growth r_1.[13]

The column labeled *Fisher Values* in Table 7 contains the average reproductive values (or reproductive debts) of women x to $x + n$ years of age. The use of discrete data covering five-year age intervals stipulates that women aged x to $x + n$ make their repayments in lump sums at the age of $x + n/2$. In any given age group, the *average* reproductive debt of a woman is equal to her probability of living to and through that age group times the rate of interest applied to her lifetime minus the partial repayments already made, discounted at the prevailing interest rate from the time they are being made. Since the repayments owed are calculated prospectively, the reciprocals of the life-table survival ratios are applied: $_nL_x/_nL_{x+n}$. Under the assumption of stability, the reproductive value ($_nV_x$) of a girl aged 0–4 can be calculated as

$$_5V_0 = \frac{_5l_0}{_5L_0} e^{2.5r_1}.$$

Austrian girls under the age of five in 1985, who were charged a *negative* annual interest rate of -1.297 percent, owed an average reproductive debt of

$$1.008931 \times 0.968095 = 0.976741 \text{ baby girls.}$$

In age group 5–9, the average debt, with zero fertility, will be

$$_5V_5 = \frac{_5L_0}{_5L_5}\left(\frac{_5l_0}{_5L_0} e^{2.5r_1}\right) e^{5r_1} = \frac{_5l_0}{_5L_5} e^{7.5r_1},$$

and ten years later, after repayments will have started,

$$_5V_{15} = \frac{_5l_0}{_5L_{15}} e^{17.5r_1} - \frac{_5L_{10}}{_5L_{15}} \frac{_5l_0}{_5L_0} m_{10} e^{2.5r_1}.$$

The variable m_{10} represents the first-row element of the original projection matrix corresponding to age group 10–14. It can be found in Table 7 in the *First Row* column

13. R. A. Fisher, *The Genetical Theory of Natural Selection*. First publ. 1930. New York: Dover Publications, 1958.

under *Original Matrix*. For succeeding age groups, the formula is expanded by further subtractions of the form shown above for women 10–14 years of age to take account of the repayments made at those ages. A computationally simpler procedure, which considers a woman's previous reproductive value five years earlier and subtracts from it the latest repayment, produces the general formula

$$_{n}V_{x} = \frac{_{n}L_{x-n}}{_{n}L_{x}} \left(_{n}V_{x-n}\, e^{5r_1} - \frac{5l_0}{_{5}L_0}\, m_{x-n}\, e^{2.5r_1} \right)$$

The only exception to this general formulation is $_{5}V_0$, for which the previous reproductive value (at birth) is arbitrarily set to 1 (see above).

In the stable projection matrix, the elements in every row are distributed proportionally to the average reproductive values of women x to $x + n$ years of age, e.g.,

$$\frac{_{n}V_{x}}{_{n}V_{x+n}} = \frac{m_x}{m_{x+n}}$$

With $_{5}V_0$ initially defined as $5l_0/_{5}L_0\, e^{2.5r_1}$, we can obtain all other $_{n}V_x$ values by applying to $_{5}V_0$ the appropriate row-element ratios of the stable matrix.[14]

In populations with positive intrinsic growth (interest) rates, the reproductive debt of a woman necessarily increases from the time of birth until the first repayment is made. In female populations like that of 1985 Austria with *negative* intrinsic growth rates and net reproduction rates below unity, the reproductive value declines either immediately, as in 1985 Austria, or shortly after birth (see, e.g., Iceland 1985, p. 468) to the level around the net reproduction rate by the time reproductive life begins.

The column next to Fisher Values in Table 7, entitled *Reproductive Values,* shows the total number of girl children all women aged x to $x + n$ in the observed population are still good for under the existing regimes of fertility and mortality and the prevailing interest rate r_1. The figures are obtained by multiplying the Fisher Value, the average reproductive value of an individual woman x to $x + n$ years old, by the number of all women of the same age in the observed population. The sum of all figures in this column gives us the Total Reproductive Value of the observed female population, the reproductive potential of all women under the current fertility and mortality regimes, discounted by r_1. For all populations included in Part III of the Tabular Materials in this volume, the Total Reproductive Value can be found in column 5 of the Summary Table.

The demographic information provided by the Leslie projection matrix described to this point is derived from ratios of various elements of the stable matrix. All of it, viz., the stable growth rate, the stable age structure, and the reproductive value, applies to populations having achieved stability. In the following section, we look at the path along which a population moves when approaching stability.

A population that in its recent past has experienced noticeable fluctuations in its birth and death rates or demographically disruptive events such as, e.g., wars or massive migration, displays their effects in its present age structure. If such disturbances cease and the population moves forward in time for an extended period with unchanging fertility and mortality, the traces of the past will work themselves out of the age structure and the latter approach a stable configuration. To better understand the pro-

14. For a precise mathematical treatment of the reproductive value, see Keyfitz, *Introduction to the Mathematics of Population*, pp. 52–55.

cess of a population approaching stability, we can compare the projected population at successive future points in time with its corresponding stable equivalent. The stable equivalent, as earlier pointed out, is obtained by projecting a population with unchanging vital rates until its age structure and growth rate have attained stability and then projecting it backward to the base year using the stable (intrinsic) growth rate r_1 (see p. 42). It represents that part of the observed population attributable to the stable growth rate. The deviation of the observed population from its stable equivalent is the result of the past fluctuations and other events just mentioned. For the Austrian population of 1985, this deviation is illustrated in Figure D (p. 38).

A comparison of the projected population with its stable equivalent for successive future points in time will reveal that the difference between them, whether measured in terms of total population, age structure, or growth rate, will be reduced over time and ultimately vanish once the population starts to move toward the stable state. This continuous reduction is demonstrated in Figure E, using again the 1985 Austrian female population as example. The graph was produced by first projecting the Austrian females in successive 5-year cycles to the year 2135 and then calculating, for every fifth year, the corresponding stable equivalent. Plotted in the graph is the difference over time between the total number of women in the projected population and its stable equivalent, c_1, expressed in absolute terms. As clearly shown, the sizable difference between observed and stable population extant in 1985 will approach the zero level in about 50 years and then hover around that level with continuously diminishing deviations from it for the other 100 years indicated.

The trend line of the monotonically decreasing difference between the projected Austrian female populations and their stable equivalents seems to suggest that the difference itself is the result of a single underlying factor or a number of factors decreasing in influence in a coordinated manner. Further analysis of the matrix will show that the

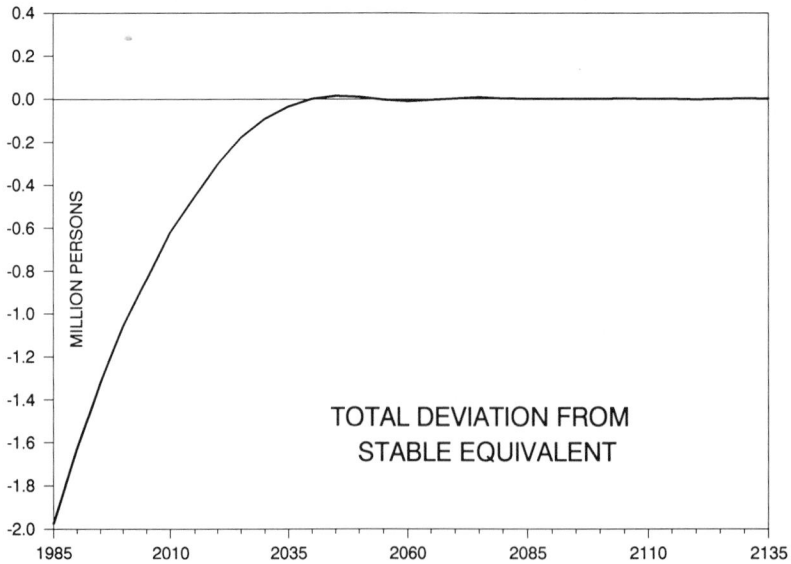

Fig. E. Deviation of 1985 and Projected Austrian Female
Population from Corresponding Stable Equivalents

trend line reflects the *net* effect of a number of diverse factors not necessarily operating in unison.

Built into the projection matrix are the fertility and mortality patterns at work in the observed population. The dominant root λ_1 of the matrix summarizes the largest part of these patterns, more precisely that part that will endure to and through the stable state. The forces not described by λ_1 and necessarily temporary in nature are nevertheless reflected in the projection matrix. For example, effects caused by the concentration of the net maternity function in certain age groups and the thereon depending average age at childbirth are largely summarized in a subsequent root. It turns out that this new root is a pair of complex numbers identical with one another except for the sign of the imaginary components. The first of this pair of complex numbers is referred to as λ_2, and the second as λ_3, each representing a distinct root of the matrix. There are other complex roots in the matrix—as many as the latter has rows or columns—usually coming in pairs of complex conjugates. The next following pair, λ_4 and λ_5, describes a part of what is left in the stable matrix after the effects of λ_1 through λ_3 have been subtracted from it. The succeeding pair, λ_6 and λ_7, partly describes the remainder of the matrix after the effects of λ_4 and λ_5 have likewise been removed, etc. This particular method of obtaining the roots of a matrix is known as *spectral decomposition* and derives from basic matrix algebra.

The spectral decomposition of a matrix involves four steps. When applied to the Leslie projection matrix, we first raise $\mathbf{M}$ to a stable power, $\mathbf{M}^k$. In the second step, we obtain the dominant root, λ_1, as the ratio of any element of the stable matrix $\mathbf{M}^k$ to the corresponding element of $\mathbf{M}^{k-1}$. Third, we find the contribution of λ_1 to the original matrix $\mathbf{M}$ by dividing $\mathbf{M}^k$ by λ_1^k, obtaining a new matrix $\mathbf{Z}_1$, the first *spectral component* of $\mathbf{M}$, a matrix whose columns and rows, like those of $\mathbf{M}^k$, are proportional to the stable age structure and the reproductive values. Note that dividing $\mathbf{M}^k$ by λ_1^k is analogous to dividing the stable population after k n-year projection cycles by the stable rate of increase raised to the power k (cf. p. 37). The fourth and final step is to remove the contribution of λ_1 to $\mathbf{M}$ from the latter, accomplished by subtracting $\mathbf{Z}_1$ from $\mathbf{M}$. The result is the first deflated matrix $\mathbf{N}_1$. To find the other roots of the projection matrix, the same four-step cycle is repeated for each of them, replacing $\mathbf{M}$, the starting point in the first decomposition cycle, by the further deflated matrix, e.g.,

$$\mathbf{N}_i = \mathbf{M} - \mathbf{Z}_1 - \mathbf{Z}_2 - \ldots - \mathbf{Z}_i.$$

Successive λs are complex; those that are conjugates of each other can be obtained in one cycle. The only procedural difference between the first and following decomposition cycles is in the calculation of the λs from the appropriate stabilized matrices.[15]

With the exception of the first (*principal*) pair of complex roots, λ_2 and λ_3, the exact demographic meaning of the complex roots is not known. What is known about λ_4 and higher roots is that their effects of whatever kind on the population move through

---

15. For a mathematical treatment of spectral decomposition and its application to demography, see Keyfitz, *Introduction to the Mathematics of Population*, pp. 41–73.

The method of finding the complex roots of the projection matrix used in the preparation of this volume is a different one, employing an iterative process for solving the polynomial equation

$$\Phi(\lambda) = l_0\lambda^{n-1} - \tfrac{1}{2}(F_{15}\,_5L_{15})\lambda^{n-3} - \tfrac{1}{2}\,(F_{15}\,_5L_{15} + F_{20}\,_5L_{20})\lambda^{n-4} - \ldots - \tfrac{1}{2}(F_{50}\,_5L_{50}) = 0,$$

here arranged to fit the 1985 Austrian data. The coefficients of λ appearing in the polynomial are the COEFFICIENTS OF MATRIX EQUATION listed in Table 7. For details, see Keyfitz and Flieger, *Population: Facts and Methods of Demography*, pp. 201–4.

time in the form of waves varying in amplitude, length, and frequency. Likewise known is that successive roots decrease in absolute magnitude and, consequently, influence on the population. The time needed for the temporary disturbances represented by individual roots to work themselves out of the population moving toward stability becomes shorter from one root to the next higher one.[16]

The decreasing magnitude of successive roots is documented in the last column of Table 7, which, aside from the dominant root, λ_1, also indicates the first three pairs of complex roots of the projection matrix, λ_2, λ_4, and λ_6, together with their corresponding annual values of r. Actually printed are only three quantities each; the omitted ones, conjugates of those shown, can easily be found by reversing the sign of the imaginary component. Thus, for 1985 Austria, λ_2, as printed, is equal to $0.33133 + 0.70313i$; λ_3, its conjugate, is $0.33133 - 0.70313i$.

The temporary influences exerted by the complex roots on a population and the manner in which they diminish over time as the population approaches the stable state is illustrated in the two graphs of Figure F. Shown in the first is the combined effect of λ_2 and λ_3, calculated for the observed Austrian female population of 1985 and its projections to successive points in time five years apart up to the year 2135. The second graph depicts the trend of the same kind of vanishing effect emanating from all other roots of the matrix, λ_4 through λ_{10}. The particular effect illustrated is that of the complex roots on the total number of persons in the population. Earlier, we defined the dominant root's effect on the observed population total as c_1. In terms of matrix algebra, this is

$$\frac{\Sigma \{z_{1,j}\} \{P_0\}}{\Sigma \{z_{1,j}\} \{z_{i,1}\}},$$

where $\{z_{1,j}\}$ represents the first-row vector of the first spectral component of the projection matrix $[\mathbf{Z}_1]$; $\{z_{i,1}\}$, the first column vector of the same matrix, normalized to add to unity; and $\{P_0\}$, the original population vector. The contributions of the complex roots to the observed population total, which we will call c_i, can be obtained in a parallel fashion by replacing $[\mathbf{Z}_1]$ in the above definition with the $[\mathbf{Z}_i]$ corresponding to the particular c_i we wish to calculate.[17]

If the total difference between an observed population and its stable equivalent is $\mathbf{M} - \mathbf{Z}_1$, and $\mathbf{M} - \mathbf{Z}_1 - \ldots - \mathbf{Z}_i = 0$, then $\mathbf{Z}_2$ and all higher $\mathbf{Z}$s represent parts of this total difference. In terms of our example, the two graphs in Figure F decompose the total difference in the number of all persons between the observed and projected populations and their corresponding stable equivalents into *partial* differences stemming from the first pair of complex roots and all other remaining roots combined. The partial difference caused by λ_4 through λ_{10} was obtained simply as residual, i.e.,

Total Observed Population $- c_1 - (c_2 + c_3)$.

An inspection of the first graph in Figure F shows that the deviation of the observed from the stable population attributable to the principal pair of complex roots will move through time in the form of an attenuating sine wave. The residual deviation, depicted

---

16. See Ansley J. Coale, "Convergence of a Human Population to a Stable Form." Annual Meeting of the Population Association of America, 1967.

17. The calculation of c requires an extension of the abbreviated projection matrix to a complete one, incorporating the entire age range of the population, 0–85+ in our example. Normalization of the column vector of Z is necessary only for the calculation of c_1.

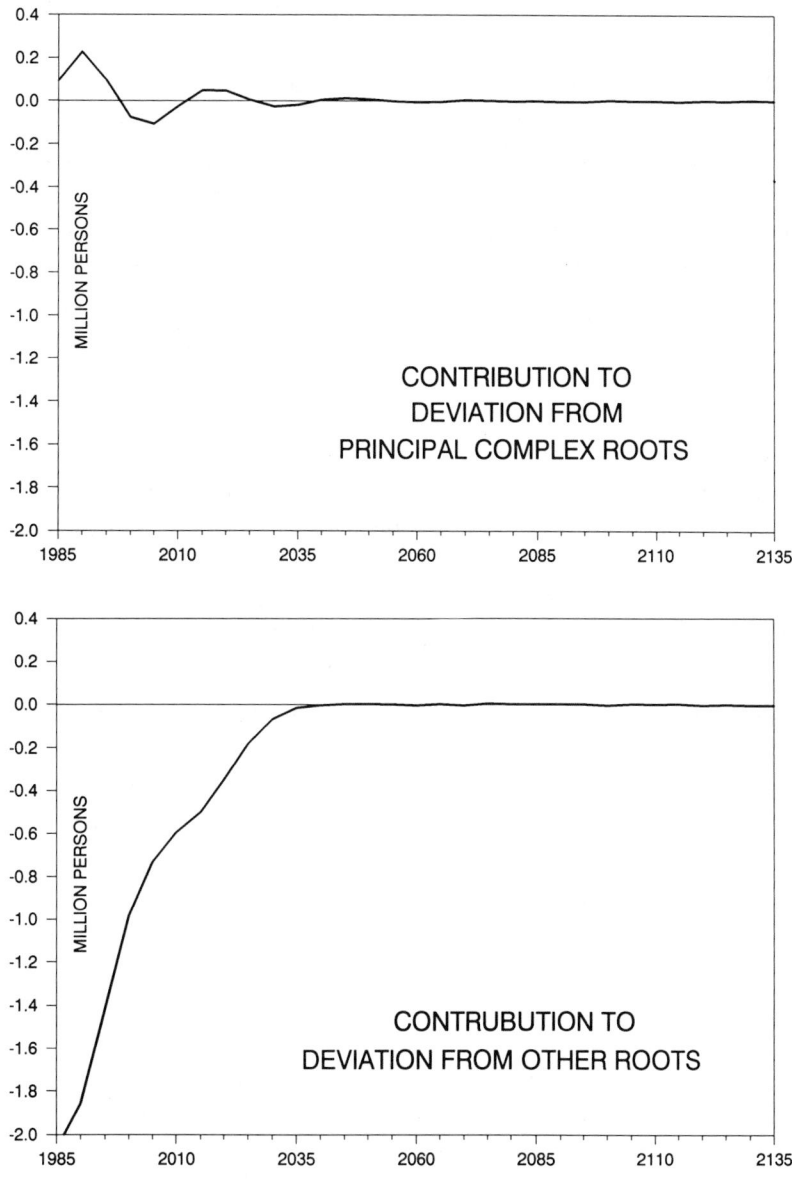

Fig. F. Contributions of Complex Roots to Deviation of
1985 and Projected Austrian Female Population
from Corresponding Stable Equivalents

in the second graph of Figure F, still disappears in a monotonic fashion similar to the total deviation between observed and stable population illustrated in Figure E. However, the removal of the influences coming from λ_2 and λ_3 from the trend line of the total deviation is clearly noticeable, suggesting a non-monotonic movement through time of the disturbances caused by individual complex roots.

Demographic disturbances with future echo effects as described by an attenuating sine curve are typically caused by fertility fluctuations. The Austrian female population offers an excellent example for this. During World War II and the years immediately thereafter, Austrian fertility levels were relatively low. After the war, this low was compensated through a baby boom extending from the late 1950s into the 1960s and resulting in a broad base of the population's age pyramid of those years. After fertility had begun to decline anew, narrowing the population base again in the process, the many births of the baby-boom period relative to those in the preceding and following years appeared in the age structure as a bulge. By 1985, the members of the large baby-boom cohort had reached the age of reproduction and begun to bear more children than the preceding older and numerically smaller cohort a few years earlier despite identical regimes of age-specific fertility. This created an effect mirrored in the positive phase of the wave appearing in the first graph of Figure F. Under the assumption of continuing stable fertility, some 25 to 30 years later, when the children born between 1990 and 2000 will have reached the age of reproduction, the positive wave of "excess" babies will reappear, though in a dampened form.

Figure G provides an enlarged view of the attenuating sine curve. In the context of describing the stabilization process of a population, we are primarily interested in the time intervals in which the disturbances represented by the first pair of complex roots are particularly in evidence and the speed at which the disturbances will diminish and ultimately disappear. The first of these two characteristics can be assessed in terms of the length of the wave, here defined as the time the latter needs to complete one full motion. The second is measured by the rate at which the amplitude of the curve is being reduced while moving through time. Without having to go into the details of trigonometry, we can obtain these measurements from the complex roots themselves or, more precisely, from their annual values r, in which they are reflected.

The complex rs are of the form $x + iy$, where i is the square root of -1 and x and y are real. A curve of the exponential e^{x+iy} takes the form of an attenuating wave whose length is given by the expression $2\pi/y$. For the Austrian female population, $2\pi/y$ is equal to $2(3.14159) \div 0.22609 = 27.79090$ (years), as shown in the last column of

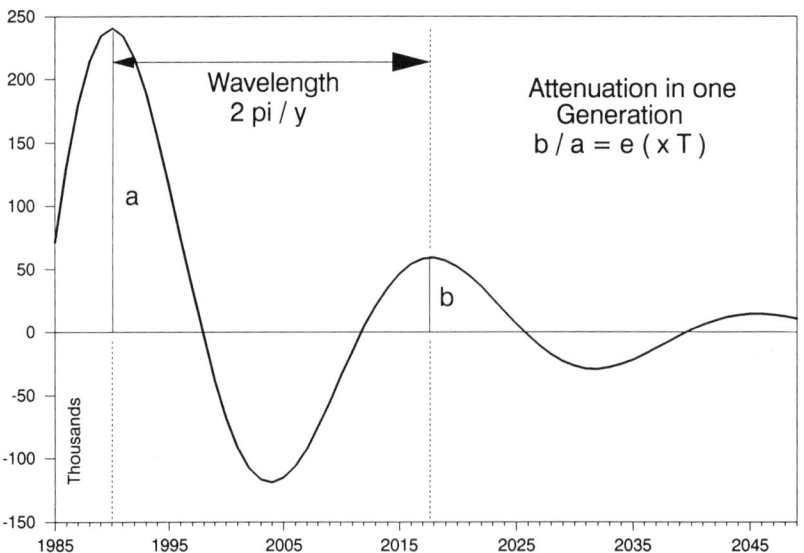

Fig. G. Disturbance Caused by Principal Pair of Complex
Roots on 1985 and Projected Austrian Female Population

Table 7. In terms of our baby-boom example, this means a peak number of births in Austria every 27.8 years for some time to come if the 1985 fertility regime remains in force. The value of $2\pi/y$ is close to that of a generation, 26.8 years for the Austrian females. This closeness is not surprising in view of the earlier referred to statement that the principal pair of complex roots describes the conditions of the net maternity function, which, in turn, determines the length of a population's generation.

The number x, the first part of r_2, is always negative and provides an expression of the attenuation rate of the wave e^{x+iy}. If we define $T = 2\pi/y$, the time needed by the wave to complete one full motion, then e^{xT} tells us by how much the amplitude of the wave will be reduced every 27.8 years. This is equal to b/a, the ratio of two amplitudes of the wave measured one full wavelength apart as indicated above in Figure G. In our example, $e^{xT} = e^{-0.05039(27.79090)} = 0.24650$, or $b = (0.24650)a$. The result implies a reduction of the disturbance caused by λ_2 and λ_3 to practical insignificance in about four generations, after which the amplitude of the wave will be only 0.4 percent as large as it is around the year 1990.

The last measure appearing in Table 7 is Δ, the *Index of Dissimilarity* between an observed age distribution and its stable component. Δ is obtained as the sum of the positive (or negative) percentage-point differences between the two age distributions, calculated age group for age group. It measures, in an approximate manner, how far a given population is from stability. The Austrian Δ of 15.5 is relatively high and, in its magnitude, characteristic for the populations of Europe, whose present-day age structures display the effects of successive periods of high and low fertility and two wars that had marked the first half of this century. Until about 15 to 20 years ago, before fertility began to fall almost everywhere in the world, extremely small Δs were typical for most developing countries, Mexico 1970, with a Δ of 1.7, being a case in point. Since then and as the result of declining fertility, this difference between developing and western countries has largely disappeared. From a technical perspective, Δ provides a clue as to how appropriate is the application of demographic techniques for estimating *current* mortality and fertility parameters of a given population based on stable population theory.

Table 8: Socioeconomic Indicators. For all *national* populations included in the Detailed Country Tabulations of this volume, Table 8 provides selected socioeconomic information. The table appears always on the second page of a set of tabulations for a given country regardless of the number of years for which the country is covered. In most instances, it is appended to the data and parameters for the calendar year 1970. The primary source of the information in Table 8 is the *World Development Report 1987*, prepared by the World Bank and published by Oxford University Press for the World Bank. All figures shown here are reprinted with the express permission of Oxford University Press, New York. Other information sources used in a few instances are listed in Appendix C.

The indicators shown represent the most recent found at the time this volume was in preparation. They are not meant to refer to the same calendar year as the demographic information appearing on the same page but to fit into the time period 1970–85 covered in the detailed tabulations. Their main purpose is to give the reader a general impression of the social and economic context within which the demographic development of a population as reflected in the demographic data and parameters took place. The information presented covers four broad areas: *Education, Labor Force, GNP & Household Income,* and *Health & Nutrition.* Precise definitions of the indicators shown as well as their exact time references, if not indicated in Table 8 itself, can be found in Appendix C.

Changes in Female Mortality and Changes in Fertility (no table number). Appended to the last data set of every population covered in this section for more than one calendar year are two illustrations showing the trends of mortality and fertility from the middle of the twentieth century on or, when mid-century data were not to be had, from the earliest date for which information was available. All data going back to before 1970 and used in the production of the graphs can be found in our already mentioned earlier world-population volumes.

Graphic representations of demographic data or, for that matter, most data do more than just repeat in visual form what has been said before by the figures on which they are based. They give us an immediate feel for entire distributions and do not limit us to summary measures that often hide as much as they reveal; they bring to the fore or emphasize features or patterns as well as shifts in features and patterns implied in the data but not, or not easily, detectable by simply looking at numbers. The two graphs shown, illustrating the two vital population processes, offer numerous examples of this. In recent history, mortality has declined almost everywhere. Has it declined steadily over time? Has it declined proportionally for all age groups in the population or favored the young or the old? Are there age-related patterns common for specific groups of populations? The painstaking work previously needed to find the answers to these and related questions is significantly reduced by the computer and its graphing capabilities. Furthermore, all mortality and fertility graphs reproduced in this volume are of the same scale, making possible immediate visual comparisons among different populations. A glance at the area under the 1985 fertility curves of Malaysia and Austria, for example, indicating the average number of girl children born per woman, instantly demonstrates the fertility gap between the two countries.

Graphic representations of demographic parameters also serve as indicators of the quality of the data on which they are based. Mortality and fertility curves of the type shown here usually display smooth features and smooth changes in these features over time if they represent reasonably large populations unaffected by major recent demographic disturbances. For countries or territories with comparatively small populations such as, for example, Greenland, Saint Christopher Nevis, and Guam, we "corrected" the fertility curves for, as we assumed, random fluctuations. Whenever this was done, it is indicated in the graph itself. In all other cases, we used the data as given by the national statistical agencies or the United Nations without attempting to outguess them.

To illustrate how mortality changes during recent decades have affected people of different ages, the l_x life-table functions of females, pertaining to various points in time from the middle of the current century onward, are plotted in the first of the two figures. This function indicates the percent of women reaching a given age x, with the vertical axis of the graph showing the percent, and the horizontal the ages. The graph for Austrian women reproduced on the left reveals an uneven mortality reduction in terms of time as well as age. During the postwar "recuperation" period of the 1950s, mortality declined significantly for women of all ages. Mortality gains made in the following decade were considerably smaller and accruing primarily to younger women. This trend was reversed in the 1970s, when most improvements made benefited the elderly. For the countries of northwestern Europe, the change patterns are quite similar, as a country-by-country comparison will reveal. By contrast, East European patterns are different, showing a rather rapid mortality reduction during the first or the first two postwar decades and a very slow progress thereafter.

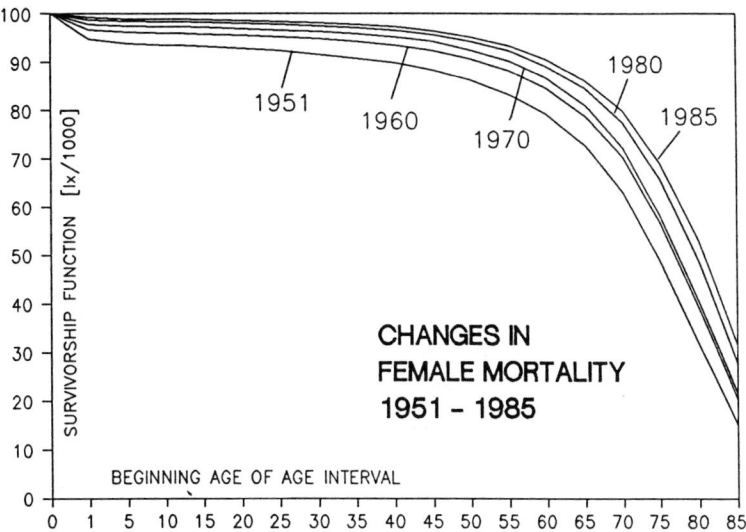

Fertility changes in populations during the post-World War II years are illustrated in the second figure. Displayed are plots of the net maternity function measured at the same points in time as the survivorship function in the mortality graph. The relatively smooth curves shown, embodying both age-specific fertility and mortality, were produced by graduating the net maternity functions originally defined in terms of five-year values. The graphic form of the function makes four fertility-related facts immediately apparent: the ages at which women, on the average, start and terminate their childbearing activities, the manner in which they space their girl children over the childbearing

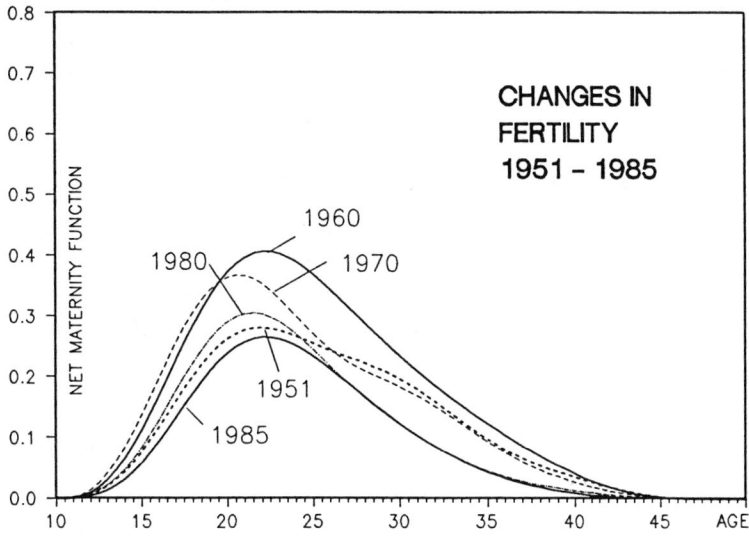

years, the mean age of childbirth, and the total number of girl children they bear, the latter indicated by the area under the curve. A comparison of the 1951 net maternity function of Austrian women with that for the year 1960, both represented in the graph shown, indicates that the postwar baby boom was created primarily by younger women. Ever since, fertility has consistently declined, a development brought about first by women of older childbearing ages, and by the younger ones in more recent times.

3. Summary Table

a. Purpose and Arrangement

To facilitate quick comparisons among countries and points of time, the Summary Table presents, for almost every country and major geographical region in the world and for a number of successive points in time beginning with 1950, a selection of frequently used demographic indicators. The majority of these indicators are extracted from the region- and country-specific tables assembled in this compendium. Added are corresponding figures from tabulations for the years 1950 to 1968 published in the authors' two previous books on world population: *World Population: An Analysis of Vital Data* and *Population: Facts and Methods of Demography.*

For the sake of comparability, the Summary Table is fashioned after similar ones appearing in the earlier volumes. It differs from them in that it incorporates information from the United Nations-Based Tabulations. The latter are less comprehensive than the Detailed Country Tabulations and yield fewer variables for the Summary Table: 13 instead of 23. This smaller number of variables makes the information provided by the UN easily recognizable in the table.

In the present Summary Table, the *General Fertility Rate* (column 19) differs from its predecessors. In the previously published tables, this parameter was calculated as 1,000 times the number of births during a year divided by the number of women aged 15–44. The *GFR* in the present table includes in its denominator women aged 15–49. This adjustment was made to make our *GFR*s comparable to those contained in the UN-based tabulations.

The birth and death rates directly standardized for age and sex, presented in columns 11 and 12 of the Summary Table, continue the time series of such rates begun in the previous world-population volumes. To maintain comparability with those earlier published rates, the standard population used in this volume is again the 1960 United States of America. The rates for the years 1970 and onward appearing in the Summary Table are not identical with the US-standardized rates found in the Detailed Country Tabulations, for which the 1980 population of the United States is used as standard.

The sources of the Summary Table information extracted from the regional and country tabulations assembled in this volume are listed in Appendix C. For the sources of information dating back to before 1970 and taken from the authors' earlier volumes, the reader is referred to those volumes.

The Summary Table is arranged like the tabulations in Parts II and III. The continents are listed in alphabetical order. Immediately following the information for a given continent is that for continental regions and subregions. Then follow the countries located on that continent, ordered alphabetically. This particular arrangement was chosen to make it easy for the reader who does not exactly know in which continental region or subregion a country is situated to locate it in the table. Following common practice, the Americas are treated as two continents: Latin America and Northern America, and information for the Soviet Union is placed at the end of the table.

b. Coverage

The Summary Table combines information for 3 global population groupings, 27 geographical regions and subregions, 158 countries or administratively separate territories, and 5 subnational population units, 193 population units in all.[18] With seven exceptions, information for each of them is given for at least five points in time.[19] Territorial units included in the UN-Based but not the Detailed Country Tabulations are covered for the years 1950, 1960, 1970, 1980, and 1985. Information for all developed countries except Albania is provided for as many years as detailed country tabulations for them are available from either this volume or the authors' previous books. For countries with detailed information for only a few scattered years since 1950, UN information is used to augment their time series so as to make them as comparable as possible to those presented for the other populations.

For a number of countries, two different times series of data and parameters are provided differing in terms of either geographical or racial coverage. The older data for Israel cover the Jewish population in the original State of Israel, while the more recent ones include Jewish settlers in Israeli-occupied territories. The UN data for Malaysia include Sabah and Sarawak, both located in Borneo (East Malaysia) and not part of Peninsular Malaysia covered in the Detailed Country Tabulations. For the Republic of South Africa, the UN data refer to the entire population, while the Detailed Country Tabulations omit the black population of the country. The time series for Australia is likewise divided into two parts, one ending with the year 1970, and the other beginning with 1971. The two partial series are not comparable because of different population estimation procedures employed in obtaining them. Summary-Table footnotes call attention to these and other peculiarities of the data base.

In substantive terms, the Summary Table contains information on *population size* and *density, population age structure, vital rates* in the form of crude and age-sex standardized birth and death and female intrinsic birth, death, and growth rates, and on *mortality* and *fertility*.

c. Definition of Variables

All but one of the variables included in the Summary Table are defined and explained in the introductory sections to the UN-Based Tabulations and Detailed Country Tabulations. The following listing of the Summary-Table variables repeats only their basic definitions or descriptions without going into details of calculation. This is done to

18. Additional limited information for 59 small populations not explicitly covered in the Summary Table, the majority of them island populations in the Caribbean and the Pacific Basin, can be found in Appendix B.
19. The exceptions are the Republic of South Africa (excl. blacks), Grenada, St. Christopher and Nevis, St. Lucia, Peninsular Malaysia, the European Community, and Guam.

make the definitions and descriptions applicable to both United Nations-based and detailed country tabulation parameters which, though using identical labels, have been obtained in a different manner in a number of instances. The reader interested in details of the general descriptions summarized here is referred to the more extensive explanations of the variables previously given.

Population

Col. 3	Midyear Population	Enumerated or estimated population around the middle of the calendar year. Shown in thousands.	cf. p. 15; p. 20
Col. 4	Population Density	Number of persons per square kilometer. Shown in thousands.	

Age Structure

Col. 5	Total Reproductive Value	Index of the replacement potential of the female population under existing fertility and mortality conditions. Defined as the expected number of girl children who will be born to the existing female population on the observed regimes of mortality and fertility, discounted at the intrinsic rate of natural increase.	cf. p. 42
Col. 6	Youth Dependency Ratio	Ratio of population under age 15 to population 15–64, multiplied by 100.	cf. p. 32
Col. 7	Old Age Dependency Ratio	Ratio of population 65 and older to population 15–64, multiplied by 100.	cf. p. 32
Col. 8	Departure from Stability	Index of Dissimilarity between the observed age distribution and its stable component. When both age structures are expressed as percentages, the index is the sum of either the positive or negative differences.	cf. p. 49

Vital Rates

Col. 9	Crude Birth Rate	Number of annual live births of both sexes divided by total midyear population, multiplied by 1,000.	cf. p. 13; p. 25
Col. 10	Crude Death Rate	Number of annual deaths of persons of both sexes divided by total midyear population, multiplied by 1,000.	cf. p. 12; p. 25
Col. 11	Standardized Birth Rate (1960 U.S.)	Directly standardized birth rate obtained through application of given age-specific birth rates to 1960 United States female age distribution. The rate is the number of expected births divided by the total	

		1960 U.S. population, multiplied by 1,000.	cf. p. 26
Col. 12	Standardized Death Rate (1960 U.S.)	Directly standardized death rate obtained through application of given age-sex specific death rates to the 1960 United States male and female age distributions. The rate is the number of expected deaths of both sexes divided by the total 1960 U.S. population, multiplied by 1,000.	cf. p. 26
Col. 13	Intrinsic Birth Rate (female)	Stable birth rate the female population ultimately would obtain if the observed regimes of age-specific mortality and fertility continue unchanged into the future. Here calculated by projecting the female population with fixed mortality and fertility for 500 years. Multiplied by 1,000.	cf. p. 37
Col. 14	Intrinsic Death Rate (female)	Stable female death rate corresponding to stable female birth rate in col. 13.	cf. p. 37
Col. 15	Intrinsic Rate of Increase (female)	Ultimate stable growth rate of female population, obtained through projection of females with constant stable age-specific birth and death rates for 500 years. Multiplied by 1,000.	cf. p. 31; p. 37; p. 41

Mortality

Col. 16	Infant Mortality Rate	Number of deaths to children under 1 during a year divided by the total number of births during the same year, multiplied by 1,000.	cf. p. 12; p. 22
Col. 17	Male Life Expectancy at Birth	Average number of years a male just born can expect to live under the mortality conditions prevailing at the time of his birth.	cf. p. 12; p. 25
Col. 18	Female Life Expectancy at Birth	Average number of years a female just born can expect to live under the mortality conditions prevailing at the time of her birth.	cf. p. 12; p. 25

Fertility

Col. 19	General Fertility Rate	Number of live births during calendar year divided by the midyear population of women of childbearing ages 15–49. Multiplied by 1,000.	cf. p. 13; p. 28
Col. 20	Total Fertility Rate	Measure of completed family size, defined as the total number of children of both sexes a female just born would bear	

	at the prevailing age-specific birth rates if she survives to the end of her reproductive life.	cf. p. 13; p. 28
Col. 21 Gross Reproduction Rate	Same as Total Fertility Rate, but for female children only.	cf. p. 13; p. 29
Col. 22 Net Reproduction Rate	Same as Gross Reproduction Rate but taking into account that not all females survive to the end of reproduction. Discounts lost fertility of women dying at the prevailing age-specific death rates before reaching the end of reproductive life. The *NRR* is equal to the ratio of the number of women in one generation to that in the preceding generation if mortality and fertility remain constant.	cf. p. 13; p. 29
Col. 23 Mean of Net Maternity Function (μ)	Indicator of the mean age of (female) childbirth, expressed in years.	cf. p. 30
Col. 24 Variance of Net Maternity Function (σ^2)	Variance around the mean age of (female) childbirth, expressed in years. Indicator of the spread of girl births over a woman's reproductive years.	cf. p. 30
Col. 25 Generation	In general terms, a generation represents the average number of years between the births of mothers and their daughters. More specifically, it is the number of years needed by the observed female population growing at the intrinsic rate to increase by a ratio equal to the net reproduction rate.	cf. p. 30

4. Tabulation Guide

Region/Country/Territory	Summary Table	UN-Based Tabulations	Detailed Tabulations	Appendix B
1 TOTAL WORLD POPULATION	64	105		
2 MORE DEVELOPED REGIONS	64	106		
3 LESS DEVELOPED REGIONS	64	107		
4 AFRICA	64	109		
5 CENTRAL AFRICA	64	110		
6 EASTERN AFRICA	64	111		
7 NORTHERN AFRICA	64	112		
8 SOUTHERN AFRICA	64	113		
9 WESTERN AFRICA	64	114		
10 Algeria	64	115		
11 Angola	64	116		
12 Benin	64	117		

Region/Country/Territory	Summary Table	UN-Based Tabulations	Detailed Tabulations	Appendix B
13 Botswana	66	118		
14 British Indian Ocean Territories				589
15 Burkina Faso	66	119		
16 Burundi	66	120		
17 Cameroon	66	121		
18 Cape Verde	66	122		
19 Central African Republic	66	123		
20 Chad	66	124		
21 Comoros	66	125		
22 Congo	66	126		
23 Djibouti	66	127		
24 Egypt	66	128		
25 Equatorial Guinea	66	129		
26 Ethiopia	66	130		
27 Gabon	68	131		
28 Gambia	68	132		
29 Ghana	68	133		
30 Guinea	68	134		
31 Guinea-Bissau	68	135		
32 Ivory Coast	68	136		
33 Kenya	68	137		
34 Lesotho	68	138		
35 Liberia	68	139		
36 Libya	68	140		
37 Madagascar	68	141		
38 Malawi	68	142		
39 Mali	70	143		
40 Mauritania	70	144		
41 Mauritius	70	145	294–97	
42 Morocco	70	146		
43 Mozambique	70	147		
44 Namibia	70	148		
45 Niger	70	149		
46 Nigeria	70	150		
47 Réunion	70	151		
48 Rwanda	70	152		
49 São Tomé and Principe				589
50 Senegal	70	153		
51 Seychelles				589
52 Sierra Leone	70	154		
53 Somalia	72	155		
54 South Africa, Republic of	72	156	298–301	
55 St. Helena with Ascension and Tristan da Cunha				589
56 Sudan	72	157		
57 Swaziland	72	158		
58 Tanzania	72	159		
59 Togo	72	160		
60 Tunisia	72	161		
61 Uganda	72	162		
62 Western Sahara				589
63 Zaire	72	163		
64 Zambia	72	164		
65 Zimbabwe	72	165		

Region/Country/Territory	Summary Table	UN-Based Tabulations	Detailed Tabulations	Appendix B
66 LATIN AMERICA	74	167		
67 CARIBBEAN	74	168		
68 CENTRAL AMERICA	74	169		
69 SOUTH AMERICA	74	170		
70 Anguilla				589
71 Antigua and Barbuda				589
72 Argentina	74	171	302–3	
73 Bahamas				589
74 Barbados	74	172	304–5	
75 Belize				589
76 Bolivia	74	173		
77 Brazil	74	174		
78 British Virgin Islands				589
79 Cayman Islands				589
80 Chile	74	175	306–9	
81 Colombia	74	176		
82 Costa Rica	74	177		
83 Cuba	76	178		
84 Dominica				589
85 Dominican Republic	76	179		
86 El Salvador	76	181		
87 Ecuador	76	180		
88 Falkland Islands				589
89 French Guiana				589
90 Grenada	76			589
91 Guadeloupe	76	182		
92 Guatemala	76	183	310–11	
93 Guyana	76	184		
94 Haiti	76	185		
95 Honduras	76	186		
96 Jamaica	76	187		
97 Martinique	76	188		
98 Mexico	78	189	312–15	
99 Montserrat				589
100 Netherlands Antilles				589
101 Nicaragua	78	190		
102 Panama	78	191	316–19	
103 Paraguay	78	192		
104 Peru	78	193		
105 Puerto Rico	78	194	320–23	
106 St. Christopher and Nevis	78		324–27	589
107 St. Lucia	78			589
108 St. Vincent and the Grenadines				589
109 Suriname	78	195		
110 Trinidad and Tobago	78	196	328–29	
111 Turks and Caicos Islands				589
112 Uruguay	78	197		
113 United States Virgin Islands				589
114 Venezuela	78	198	330–33	
115 NORTHERN AMERICA	80	199		
116 Bermuda				589
117 Canada	80	200	334–39	
118 Greenland	80		340–43	589

Region/Country/Territory	Summary Table	UN-Based Tabulations	Detailed Tabulations	Appendix B
119 St. Pierre and Miquelon				589
120 United States of America	80	201	344–49	
121 ASIA	80	203		
122 EASTERN ASIA	80	204		
123 SOUTHEASTERN ASIA	80	205		
124 SOUTHERN ASIA	80	206		
125 WESTERN ASIA	80	207		
126 Afghanistan	80	208		
127 Bahrain	82	209		
128 Bangladesh	82	210		
129 Bhutan	82	211		
130 Brunei				589
131 Burma	82	212		
132 China, People's Republic	82	213	350–51	
133 China, Republic of (Taiwan)	82		352–57	589
134 Cyprus	82	214	358–61	
135 East Timor	82	215		
136 Gaza Strip (Palestine)				590
137 Hong Kong	82	216	362–65	
138 India	82	217		
139 Indonesia	82	218		
140 Iran	84	219		
141 Iraq	84	220		
142 Israel	84	221	366–71	
143 Japan	84	222	372–75	
144 Jordan	84	223		
145 Kampuchea	84	224		
146 Korea, Democratic People's Republic	84	225		
147 Korea, Republic of	84	226		
148 Kuwait	84	227	376–79	
149 Laos	84	228		
150 Lebanon	86	229		
151 Macao				589
152 Malaysia	86	230		
153 Malaysia (Peninsular)	86		380–85	
154 Maldives				590
155 Mongolia	86	231		
156 Nepal	86	232		
157 Oman	86	233		
158 Pakistan	86	234		
159 Philippines	86	235		
160 Qatar	86	236		
161 Saudi Arabia	86	237		
162 Singapore	86	238	386–91	
163 Sri Lanka	86	239		
164 Syria	88	240		
165 Thailand	88	241		
166 Turkey	88	242		
167 United Arab Emirates	88	243		
168 Vietnam	88	244		
169 Yemen	88	245		
170 Yemen, Democratic	88	246		

Region/Country/Territory	Summary Table	UN-Based Tabulations	Detailed Tabulations	Appendix B
171 EUROPE	88	249		
172 EASTERN EUROPE (COMECON)	88	250	392–95	
173 NORTHERN EUROPE	88	251		
174 SOUTHERN EUROPE	88	252		
175 WESTERN EUROPE	88	253		
176 EUROPEAN COMMUNITY	90	254	396–99	
177 Albania	90	255		
178 Andorra				590
179 Austria	90	256	400–405	
180 Belgium	90	257	406–11	
181 Bulgaria	90	258	412–17	
182 Channel Islands				590
183 Czechoslovakia	90	259	418–23	
184 Denmark	90	260	424–29	
185 England and Wales	98		542–45	
186 Faeroe Islands				590
187 Finland	92	261	430–35	
188 France	92	262	436–41	
189 German Democratic Republic	92	263	442–47	
190 Germany, Federal Republic	92	264	448–53	
191 Gibraltar				590
192 Greece	92	265	454–59	
193 Hungary	92	266	460–65	
194 Iceland	94	267	466–69	
195 Ireland	94	268	470–75	
196 Isle of Man				590
197 Italy	94	269	476–81	
198 Liechtenstein				590
199 Luxembourg	94	270	482–85	
200 Malta	94	271	486–89	
201 Monaco				590
202 Netherlands	94	272	490–95	
203 Northern Ireland	98		546–49	
204 Norway	96	273	496–501	
205 Poland	96	274	502–7	
206 Portugal	96	275	508–13	
207 Romania	96	276	514–17	
208 San Marino				590
209 Scotland	98		550–53	
210 Spain	96	277	518–23	
211 Sweden	96	278	524–29	
212 Switzerland	98	279	530–35	
213 United Kingdom of Great Britain and Northern Ireland	98	280	536–41	
214 Vatican State				590
215 Yugoslavia	98	281	554–59	
216 OCEANIA	98	283		
217 AUSTRALIA–NEW ZEALAND	98	284		
218 MELANESIA	100	285		
219 MICRONESIA	100	286		
220 POLYNESIA	100	287		
221 American Samoa				590
222 Australia	100	288	560–65	

Region/Country/Territory	Summary Table	UN-Based Tabulations	Detailed Tabulations	Appendix B
223 Cook Islands				590
224 Fiji	100	289	566–69	
225 French Polynesia	100			590
226 Guam	100		570–73	590
227 Johnston Island				590
228 Kiribati with Canton and Enderbury Islands				590
229 Midway Islands				590
230 Nauru				590
231 New Caledonia				590
232 New Zealand	100	290	574–79	
233 Niue				590
234 Pacific Islands				590
235 Papua New Guinea	100	291		
236 Pitcairn Islands				590
237 Samoa				590
238 Solomon Islands				590
239 Tokelau				590
240 Tonga				590
241 Tuvalu				590
242 Vanuatu				590
243 Wake Islands				590
244 Wallis and Futuna Islands				590
245 UNION OF SOVIET SOCIALIST REPUBLICS	100	292	580–83	

Summary Table

SUMMARY TABLE

64

SERIAL NO.	REGION/ COUNTRY	YEAR	POPULATION ESTIMATED AS OF MID-YEAR (in 000's)	POPULATION DENSITY (per km²)	AGE STRUCTURE TOTAL REPRODUCTIVE VALUE (in 000's)	AGE STRUCTURE DEPENDENCY RATIO YOUTH < 15 (x 100)	AGE STRUCTURE DEPENDENCY RATIO OLD AGE ≥ 65 (x 100)	DEPARTURE FROM STABILITY (Percent)	CRUDE RATES (Both Sexes) BIRTH (x 1000)	CRUDE RATES (Both Sexes) DEATH (x 1000)	VITAL STANDARDIZED RATES Standard: USA 1960 BIRTH (x 1000)	VITAL STANDARDIZED RATES Standard: USA 1960 DEATH (x 1000)
	1	2	3	4	5	6	7	8	9	10	11	12
1	TOTAL WORLD	1950	2515312	19		57.3	8.4		37.43	19.68		
2	POPULATION	1960	3019376	22		64.1	9.2		35.22	15.46		
3		1970	3697918	27		65.7	9.5		31.49	12.18		
4		1980	4450210	33		59.9	10.1		27.67	10.44		
5		1985	4853848	36		55.4	9.9		27.10	9.88		
6	MORE DEVELOPED	1950	832425	15		43.0	11.8		22.64	10.11		
7	REGIONS	1960	944851	17		45.4	13.5		20.12	9.02		
8		1970	1049273	18		41.7	15.1		16.71	9.27		
9		1980	1136406	20		35.4	17.6		15.22	9.59		
10		1985	1173660	21		33.4	17.3		14.60	9.78		
11	LESS DEVELOPED	1950	1682887	21		65.1	6.5		44.60	24.33		
12	REGIONS	1960	2074525	26		73.8	6.9		41.89	18.31		
13		1970	2648644	34		76.8	6.9		37.11	13.28		
14		1980	3313804	42		69.5	7.1		31.79	10.72		
15		1985	3680188	47		63.4	7.2		30.93	9.91		
16	AFRICA	1950	224075	7		78.2	6.1		48.89	27.00		
17		1960	281076	9		82.0	5.7		48.48	22.99		
18		1970	362788	12		86.0	6.0		46.72	19.37		
19		1980	481034	16		86.5	5.9		45.53	16.37		
20		1985	557441	18		87.6	6.0		44.71	14.90		
21	CENTRAL AFRICA	1950	26841	4		74.0	6.9		46.65	27.58		
22		1960	32668	5		77.0	5.7		46.13	24.28		
23		1970	39427	6		79.3	5.8		45.52	20.79		
24		1980	52269	8		84.4	5.8		44.99	17.79		
25		1985	60147	9		85.5	5.9		44.82	15.98		
26	EASTERN AFRICA	1950	64978	10		81.8	5.7		50.29	28.20		
27		1960	82310	13		84.6	5.4		49.87	23.82		
28		1970	108193	17		88.3	5.4		49.00	20.22		
29		1980	144040	23		90.8	5.4		47.80	18.26		
30		1985	166926	26		94.2	6.2		47.78	17.02		
31	NORTHERN	1950	51798	6		74.8	6.3		48.88	24.70		
32	AFRICA	1960	65115	8		81.7	6.1		47.49	20.64		
33		1970	83158	10		86.5	7.6		42.99	16.59		
34		1980	107811	13		80.2	7.0		40.84	12.32		
35		1985	124419	15		79.3	6.7		38.03	10.67		
36	SOUTHERN	1950	15736	6		68.1	6.3		43.71	20.98		
37	AFRICA	1960	19895	7		74.9	6.9		42.45	17.31		
38		1970	25609	10		75.7	6.8		37.33	13.95		
39		1980	32458	12		69.4	6.9		34.69	11.42		
40		1985	36473	14		67.8	7.0		33.39	10.14		
41	WESTERN AFRICA	1950	64722	11		82.0	6.1		49.67	28.88		
42		1960	81088	13		83.5	5.3		50.25	24.93		
43		1970	106402	17		88.5	5.1		49.95	21.41		
44		1980	144455	24		92.4	5.2		49.32	18.08		
45		1985	169477	28		93.4	5.2		48.87	16.51		
46	Algeria	1950	8753	4		72.3	7.9		51.00	23.90		
47		1960	10800	5		83.5	7.4		50.40	19.40		
48		1970	13746	6		101.8	8.7		48.00	15.40		
49		1980	18666	8		93.8	7.9		42.51	10.74		
50		1985	21699	9		90.1	7.2		40.21	9.06		
51	Angola	1950	4131	3		73.9	5.4		49.77	34.80		
52		1960	4816	4		75.4	5.0		49.44	30.19		
53		1970	5588	4		78.9	5.3		47.96	25.43		
54		1980	7723	6		83.6	5.6		47.26	22.23		
55		1985	8754	7		85.1	5.7		47.17	20.18		
56	Benin	1950	2046	18		65.8	16.1		44.15	37.04		
57		1960	2251	20		78.3	13.9		48.26	31.91		
58		1970	2708	24		84.6	8.4		49.83	26.57		
59		1980	3494	31		90.1	6.0		50.73	21.23		
60		1985	4050	36		92.8	5.7		50.47	19.02		

RATES			MORTALITY			FERTILITY							
INTRINSIC RATES (Female)			INFANT MORTALITY RATE (x 1000)	LIFE EXPECTANCY AT BIRTH		GENERAL FERTILITY RATE (x 1000)	TOTAL FERTILITY RATE	GROSS REPRODUCTION RATE	NET MATERNITY FUNCTION				SERIAL NO.
BIRTH (x 1000)	DEATH (x 1000)	INCREASE (x 1000)		MALE (Years)	FEMALE (Years)				TOTAL (NRR)	MEAN μ	VARIANCE σ^2	GENER-ATION (Years)	
13	14	15	16	17	18	19	20	21	22	23	24	25	
			155.26	44.8	47.1	153.01	5.00	2.44	1.65				1
			117.90	50.4	52.6	151.93	4.97	2.42	1.79				2
			93.62	55.6	57.8	135.30	4.45	2.17	1.74				3
			79.29	58.2	61.1	114.35	3.61	1.76	1.46				4
			71.24	60.0	63.0	109.59	3.44	1.68	1.43				5
			55.95	63.0	68.7	85.34	2.84	1.38	1.27				6
			31.56	66.6	72.8	81.32	2.69	1.31	1.23				7
			21.66	67.4	74.6	66.48	2.20	1.07	1.03				8
			16.41	68.5	76.3	60.42	1.93	0.94	0.92				9
			14.76	69.8	77.2	58.09	1.90	0.93	0.90				10
			179.70	40.3	41.9	190.12	6.18	3.01	1.86				11
			136.23	47.0	48.3	186.26	6.08	2.96	2.07				12
			105.96	53.6	54.9	164.49	5.41	2.64	2.04				13
			89.23	56.6	58.7	133.15	4.20	2.05	1.65				14
			79.40	58.6	61.0	125.70	3.92	1.91	1.59				15
			187.26	36.6	39.4	208.79	6.61	3.25	1.90				16
			164.32	40.7	43.7	211.07	6.74	3.32	2.11				17
			140.45	44.5	47.7	206.18	6.60	3.24	2.22				18
			116.37	48.3	51.5	201.30	6.37	3.13	2.28				19
			106.33	50.3	53.6	198.14	6.23	3.06	2.31				20
			182.86	35.3	38.6	189.40	5.92	2.92	1.68				21
			161.04	38.3	41.6	191.78	5.94	2.93	1.80				22
			136.10	42.0	45.3	193.28	6.04	2.98	1.96				23
			116.91	45.9	49.3	195.63	6.09	3.00	2.13				24
			107.07	48.3	51.8	196.16	6.03	2.97	2.19				25
			178.67	35.0	38.0	217.35	6.71	3.31	1.86				26
			155.08	39.4	42.5	217.88	6.85	3.37	2.09				27
			137.88	43.5	46.7	217.87	6.93	3.41	2.29				28
			125.48	46.2	49.4	214.42	6.73	3.31	2.33				29
			116.13	48.2	51.4	215.54	6.74	3.32	2.41				30
			189.35	40.8	43.0	209.73	6.83	3.33	2.12				31
			165.09	45.3	47.6	212.86	7.08	3.45	2.35				32
			137.70	49.7	52.2	192.40	6.36	3.10	2.27				33
			99.17	55.4	58.1	178.48	5.79	2.82	2.25				34
			85.92	57.6	60.4	165.27	5.32	2.60	2.14				35
			152.61	43.0	45.3	183.57	6.45	3.17	2.06				36
			131.47	47.1	51.2	183.03	6.47	3.18	2.28				37
			112.29	50.3	56.2	158.36	5.58	2.74	2.12				38
			87.28	54.4	60.3	141.70	4.95	2.43	2.00				39
			76.85	56.9	62.7	135.22	4.68	2.30	1.95				40
			203.51	34.1	37.2	214.25	6.69	3.30	1.84				41
			181.07	38.0	41.1	217.67	6.78	3.34	2.03				42
			151.25	41.9	45.0	221.73	6.91	3.40	2.23				43
			122.46	45.7	49.0	222.19	6.90	3.40	2.39				44
			112.41	47.8	51.2	221.27	6.84	3.37	2.46				45
			185.00	42.1	44.2	226.87	7.28	3.55	2.30				46
			160.00	47.3	49.4	226.83	7.38	3.60	2.56				47
			132.00	52.5	54.5	225.23	7.38	3.60	2.78				48
			87.98	58.5	61.6	193.52	6.66	3.25	2.69				49
			73.75	61.0	64.1	179.48	6.05	2.95	2.52				50
			230.86	28.6	31.5	205.03	6.39	3.15	1.52				51
			200.01	32.5	35.5	206.59	6.38	3.14	1.69				52
			172.80	36.5	39.6	204.94	6.39	3.15	1.86				53
			148.55	40.4	43.6	206.45	6.39	3.15	2.02				54
			137.00	42.9	46.1	207.18	6.39	3.15	2.12				55
			209.90	31.1	34.0	213.94	6.74	3.32	1.72				56
			175.90	34.5	37.5	218.70	6.81	3.36	1.87				57
			150.90	38.5	41.6	220.76	6.85	3.37	2.03				58
			120.13	42.4	45.6	226.69	7.00	3.45	2.29				59
			110.00	44.9	48.1	227.57	7.00	3.45	2.40				60

SERIAL NO.	REGION/ COUNTRY	YEAR	POPULATION		AGE STRUCTURE				VITAL			
			ESTIMATED AS OF MID-YEAR (in 000's)	DENSITY (per km²)	TOTAL REPRODUCTIVE VALUE (in 000's)	DEPENDENCY RATIO YOUTH < 15 (x 100)	OLD AGE ≥ 65 (x 100)	DEPARTURE FROM STABILITY (Percent)	CRUDE RATES (Both Sexes) BIRTH (x 1000)	DEATH (x 1000)	STANDARDIZED RATES Standard: USA 1960 BIRTH (x 1000)	DEATH (x 1000)
	1	2	3	4	5	6	7	8	9	10	11	12
61	Botswana	1950	389	1		92.5	7.9		48.93	22.65		
62		1960	481	1		96.7	6.9		52.59	19.64		
63		1970	623	1		112.1	5.5		52.10	16.84		
64		1980	902	2		99.5	10.8		49.23	14.34		
65		1985	1078	2		100.9	8.1		47.33	11.65		
66	Burkina Faso	1950	3731	14		81.3	5.6		51.60	32.31		
67		1960	4528	17		77.5	4.3		51.57	28.52		
68		1970	5593	20		80.7	5.1		50.20	25.57		
69		1980	6959	25		82.2	5.3		47.15	19.92		
70		1985	7882	29		82.0	5.4		47.18	18.51		
71	Burundi	1950	2456	88		73.2	5.8		44.00	26.52		
72		1960	2927	105		71.5	5.3		45.61	25.32		
73		1970	3456	124		75.3	5.7		46.24	23.71		
74		1980	4100	147		82.3	6.2		47.16	19.00		
75		1985	4721	170		86.3	6.4		45.72	17.01		
76	Cameroon	1950	4526	10		64.6	6.0		45.97	26.63		
77		1960	5501	12		71.5	5.4		42.82	22.72		
78		1970	6761	14		75.1	6.5		42.58	19.67		
79		1980	8623	18		78.8	7.2		44.27	17.29		
80		1985	9873	21		82.1	7.4		41.64	15.65		
81	Cape Verde	1950	148	37		55.5	6.6		45.42	23.04		
82		1960	200	50		82.8	8.9		43.52	12.36		
83		1970	271	67		100.1	10.7		32.94	11.30		
84		1980	296	73		96.0	12.8		33.28	11.59		
85		1985	330	82		78.5	9.6		38.39	10.33		
86	Central	1950	1417	2		61.0	8.2		43.90	32.28		
87	African	1960	1605	3		67.2	7.2		43.46	28.65		
88	Republic	1970	1875	3		71.8	7.1		43.56	25.05		
89		1980	2298	4		76.4	7.2		44.58	21.82		
90		1985	2576	4		79.3	7.2		44.28	19.73		
91	Chad	1950	2658	2		64.8	7.4		45.08	31.98		
92		1960	3064	2		69.7	6.5		45.54	28.64		
93		1970	3652	3		75.1	6.5		44.61	24.92		
94		1980	4477	3		76.9	6.6		44.23	21.42		
95		1985	5018	4		78.2	6.6		44.18	19.49		
96	Comoros	1950	173	80		82.0	6.5		47.33	24.24		
97		1960	215	99		83.7	5.7		48.15	21.24		
98		1970	271	125		86.2	5.5		46.84	18.32		
99		1980	381	176		88.8	5.5		46.41	15.93		
100		1985	444	205		90.2	5.6		45.59	14.51		
101	Congo	1950	812	2		72.6	6.5		44.36	26.76		
102		1960	972	3		73.3	5.8		45.24	22.42		
103		1970	1201	4		77.2	5.9		45.37	18.63		
104		1980	1529	4		80.8	6.2		44.48	15.41		
105		1985	1740	5		82.3	6.3		44.40	17.17		
106	Djibouti	1950	60	3		73.5	4.6		49.43	30.45		
107		1960	80	4		78.4	5.1		49.10	24.90		
108		1970	167	8		81.7	4.2		49.49	21.19		
109		1980	300	14		85.9	4.1		47.91	19.15		
110		1985	350	16		87.8	4.3		47.28	17.71		
111	Egypt	1950	20330	20		69.2	5.2		48.60	24.00		
112		1960	25922	26		78.3	6.0		45.40	20.40		
113		1970	33053	33		76.2	8.0		38.40	16.30		
114		1980	41520	41		71.5	7.3		39.73	11.87		
115		1985	47578	48		72.8	7.0		35.96	10.07		
116	Equatorial	1950	226	8		56.9	9.4		42.30	31.72		
117	Guinea	1960	252	9		65.2	8.6		41.27	27.98		
118		1970	291	10		69.9	7.9		42.30	24.47		
119		1980	352	13		74.0	7.6		42.49	20.97		
120		1985	392	14		76.1	7.6		42.37	19.00		
121	Ethiopia	1950	19573	16		83.7	5.7		52.34	31.91		
122		1960	24191	20		84.1	4.8		49.87	26.82		
123		1970	30623	25		83.8	4.7		48.04	22.87		

SUMMARY TABLE

RATES			MORTALITY			FERTILITY							
INTRINSIC RATES (Female)			INFANT MORTALITY RATE	LIFE EXPECTANCY AT BIRTH		GENERAL FERTILITY RATE	TOTAL FERTILITY RATE	GROSS REPRODUCTION RATE	NET MATERNITY FUNCTION				SERIAL NO.
BIRTH (x 1000)	DEATH (x 1000)	INCREASE (x 1000)	(x 1000)	MALE (Years)	FEMALE (Years)	(x 1000)			TOTAL (NRR)	MEAN μ	VARIANCE σ^2	GENERATION (Years)	
13	14	15	16	17	18	19	20	21	22	23	24	25	
			130.00	41.0	44.0	213.60	6.50	3.20	2.05				61
			115.00	45.0	48.0	215.27	6.90	3.40	2.30				62
			95.00	49.0	53.0	220.14	6.90	3.40	2.44				63
			76.00	53.0	59.0	216.89	6.50	3.20	2.62				64
			67.00	55.5	61.5	208.10	6.25	3.08	2.60				65
			225.94	31.7	34.7	219.55	6.88	3.39	1.75				66
			198.17	35.7	38.8	215.81	6.74	3.32	1.89				67
			173.14	39.7	42.8	215.84	6.74	3.32	2.06				68
			149.37	43.7	46.8	204.41	6.50	3.20	2.15				69
			137.62	45.6	48.9	205.39	6.50	3.20	2.22				70
			172.00	38.5	41.6	174.53	5.44	2.68	1.53				71
			145.00	41.4	44.6	182.68	5.68	2.80	1.66				72
			135.00	43.0	46.2	192.73	5.93	2.92	1.82				73
			124.14	44.9	48.1	206.14	6.44	3.17	2.21				74
			111.88	47.4	50.7	203.72	6.31	3.11	2.26				75
			190.00	35.0	39.0	180.53	5.81	2.86	1.66				76
			153.90	39.0	43.0	179.84	5.82	2.87	1.81				77
			119.10	43.0	47.0	182.06	5.88	2.89	1.96				78
			103.15	47.0	51.0	194.31	6.19	3.05	2.22				79
			94.00	49.0	53.0	183.90	5.79	2.85	2.14				80
			165.00	41.2	44.1	166.35	6.50	3.20	2.04				81
			135.00	46.0	49.0	195.40	6.29	3.10	2.17				82
			103.00	51.7	54.0	155.48	5.58	2.75	2.09				83
			74.76	57.3	60.8	137.47	5.18	2.55	2.14				84
			65.56	59.3	62.8	152.74	5.18	2.55	2.20				85
			197.20	32.5	35.5	173.14	5.52	2.72	1.41				86
			178.40	36.5	39.6	177.28	5.66	2.79	1.56				87
			148.00	39.5	42.6	180.74	5.72	2.82	1.70				88
			142.00	41.4	44.6	189.58	5.89	2.90	1.90				89
			132.00	43.9	47.1	190.31	5.89	2.90	1.98				90
			211.15	31.0	34.0	182.87	5.77	2.84	1.48				91
			189.43	34.0	37.0	190.09	6.00	2.96	1.65				92
			166.49	37.5	40.6	190.02	5.99	2.95	1.78				93
			142.81	41.4	44.6	190.01	5.89	2.90	1.90				94
			132.00	43.9	47.1	191.00	5.89	2.90	1.98				95
			140.00	38.5	41.6	204.68	6.27	3.09	1.91				96
			124.00	41.9	45.1	208.61	6.32	3.12	2.06				97
			105.89	44.9	48.1	205.59	6.29	3.10	2.16				98
			88.25	48.3	51.7	206.39	6.29	3.10	2.29				99
			79.83	50.3	53.8	203.45	6.19	3.05	2.33				100
			170.00	34.5	37.5	182.66	5.69	2.80	1.59				101
			131.42	37.5	40.6	188.30	5.87	2.89	1.75				102
			89.53	40.9	44.1	193.55	6.04	2.97	1.93				103
			81.06	44.9	48.1	193.33	5.99	2.95	2.06				104
			73.00	46.9	50.2	194.25	5.99	2.95	2.13				105
			207.34	31.5	34.5	208.62	6.60	3.25	1.70				106
			179.36	35.5	38.6	212.51	6.60	3.25	1.88				107
			154.28	39.4	42.6	216.38	6.60	3.25	2.04				108
			131.95	43.4	46.6	213.94	6.60	3.25	2.20				109
			121.63	45.4	48.7	212.45	6.60	3.25	2.28				110
			200.00	41.2	43.6	201.59	6.56	3.20	2.07				111
			175.00	46.2	48.6	205.60	7.07	3.45	2.35				112
			150.00	50.8	53.4	167.34	5.54	2.70	2.00				113
			100.04	56.8	59.5	170.46	5.27	2.57	2.09				114
			85.14	59.3	62.0	155.18	4.82	2.35	1.98				115
			203.54	32.0	35.0	172.43	5.50	2.71	1.44				116
			182.65	35.0	38.0	172.73	5.53	2.72	1.56				117
			160.36	38.5	41.6	178.36	5.66	2.79	1.72				118
			137.31	42.4	45.6	182.20	5.66	2.79	1.86				119
			127.00	44.9	48.1	182.77	5.66	2.79	1.94				120
			190.00	31.4	34.4	227.47	6.70	3.30	1.72				121
			170.00	35.4	38.5	216.26	6.70	3.30	1.90				122
			155.00	39.5	42.6	208.20	6.80	3.35	2.10				123

SERIAL NO.	REGION/ COUNTRY	YEAR	POPULATION		AGE STRUCTURE				VITAL			
			ESTIMATED AS OF MID-YEAR (in 000's)	DENSITY (per km²)	TOTAL REPRODUCTIVE VALUE (in 000's)	DEPENDENCY RATIO		DEPARTURE FROM STABILITY (Percent)	CRUDE RATES (Both Sexes)		STANDARDIZED RATES Standard: USA 1960	
						YOUTH < 15 (x 100)	OLD AGE ≥ 65 (x 100)		BIRTH (x 1000)	DEATH (x 1000)	BIRTH (x 1000)	DEATH (x 1000)
	1	2	3	4	5	6	7	8	9	10	11	12
124	Ethiopia	1980	38750	32		84.0	5.0		43.00	23.50		
125	(cont'd.)	1985	42271	35		93.0	8.2		43.72	23.63		
126	Gabon	1950	469	2		51.1	13.1		30.10	27.10		
127		1960	486	2		52.6	10.4		30.70	22.90		
128		1970	504	2		52.4	9.7		30.90	20.20		
129		1980	806	3		53.1	9.6		33.80	18.05		
130		1985	985	4		57.3	9.8		38.75	16.38		
131	Gambia	1950	294	26		68.6	5.3		47.05	34.15		
132		1960	353	31		69.3	5.3		50.48	31.21		
133		1970	464	41		75.4	5.3		49.18	26.71		
134		1980	641	57		78.2	5.2		48.16	23.06		
135		1985	745	66		80.8	5.3		46.76	21.27		
136	Ghana	1950	4900	21		86.0	4.7		48.28	21.65		
137		1960	6774	28		87.9	4.9		47.58	18.70		
138		1970	8611	36		88.0	5.1		45.77	15.77		
139		1980	10734	45		85.7	5.3		45.22	14.25		
140		1985	12839	54		87.2	5.4		44.30	13.12		
141	Guinea	1950	3245	13		74.7	13.2		47.50	37.21		
142		1960	3660	15		76.5	7.9		48.16	31.36		
143		1970	4388	18		77.8	5.1		46.89	26.79		
144		1980	5407	22		79.0	5.3		46.84	23.55		
145		1985	6075	25		79.7	5.4		46.63	21.90		
146	Guinea-Bissau	1950	505	14		62.9	6.3		41.22	29.60		
147		1960	540	15		63.3	5.9		41.38	27.43		
148		1970	526	15		66.0	7.4		38.48	23.16		
149		1980	809	22		72.2	7.6		40.73	21.66		
150		1985	889	25		74.0	7.7		40.80	19.99		
151	Ivory Coast	1950	2775	9		78.9	4.2		52.67	27.70		
152		1960	3779	12		85.6	4.4		52.51	23.73		
153		1970	5510	17		93.8	4.6		51.19	19.26		
154		1980	8327	26		97.7	4.6		50.99	15.58		
155		1985	10252	32		100.0	4.6		50.90	14.25		
156	Kenya	1950	6265	11		70.6	7.0		52.79	25.29		
157		1960	8332	14		90.6	8.2		52.77	21.41		
158		1970	11498	20		100.9	8.3		52.89	17.34		
159		1980	16632	29		107.7	7.3		53.90	13.65		
160		1985	20353	35		111.9	6.7		53.87	11.86		
161	Lesotho	1950	734	24		74.1	8.1		42.33	26.63		
162		1960	870	29		72.9	7.1		42.88	22.77		
163		1970	1064	35		75.1	6.5		42.41	19.30		
164		1980	1339	44		77.0	6.6		41.63	13.91		
165		1985	1538	51		79.3	6.8		40.85	12.43		
166	Liberia	1950	824	7		74.7	5.4		46.12	25.96		
167		1960	1037	9		76.2	5.6		46.07	21.62		
168		1970	1369	12		80.6	5.8		45.69	17.88		
169		1980	1856	17		85.0	6.1		44.98	14.47		
170		1985	2178	20		87.0	6.2		45.02	13.27		
171	Libya	1950	1029	1		78.5	8.8		48.00	22.50		
172		1960	1349	1		82.1	7.6		49.00	18.30		
173		1970	1986	1		85.9	5.3		49.00	14.80		
174		1980	3043	2		91.3	4.4		45.64	10.85		
175		1985	3786	2		90.5	4.5		43.94	9.41		
176	Madagascar	1950	4230	7		75.3	4.9		48.32	26.51		
177		1960	5309	9		76.2	5.1		47.83	22.87		
178		1970	6742	11		80.7	5.4		45.99	18.94		
179		1980	8777	15		83.2	5.6		45.76	15.36		
180		1985	10221	17		84.6	5.7		45.71	14.02		
181	Malawi	1950	2881	24		89.2	6.0		52.30	30.89		
182		1960	3529	30		88.4	5.0		53.58	27.47		
183		1970	4518	38		91.5	4.6		53.00	23.46		
184		1980	6091	51		90.9	4.5		53.14	21.42		
185		1985	7141	60		89.6	5.0		53.03	19.97		

RATES			MORTALITY			FERTILITY							
INTRINSIC RATES (Female)			INFANT MORTALITY RATE (x 1000)	LIFE EXPECTANCY AT BIRTH		GENERAL FERTILITY RATE (x 1000)	TOTAL FERTI-LITY RATE	GROSS REPRO-DUCTION RATE	NET MATERNITY FUNCTION				SERIAL NO.
BIRTH (x 1000)	DEATH (x 1000)	INCREASE (x 1000)		MALE (Years)	FEMALE (Years)				TOTAL (NRR)	MEAN μ	VARIANCE σ²	GENER-ATION (Years)	
13	14	15	16	17	18	19	20	21	22	23	24	25	
			159.00	38.4	41.6	191.20	6.00	2.96	1.82				124
			154.28	39.4	42.6	195.42	6.15	3.03	1.91				125
			194.00	36.5	39.6	122.34	4.06	2.00	1.18				126
			163.00	39.9	43.1	123.05	4.06	2.00	1.27				127
			131.95	43.4	46.6	122.45	4.26	2.10	1.36				128
			111.88	47.4	50.7	137.03	4.51	2.22	1.61				129
			103.00	49.9	53.2	155.97	4.99	2.46	1.86				130
			230.86	28.6	31.5	192.87	6.09	3.00	1.45				131
			207.34	31.5	34.5	207.27	6.50	3.20	1.68				132
			179.36	35.5	38.6	206.15	6.50	3.20	1.85				133
			154.28	39.4	42.6	205.20	6.50	3.20	2.01				134
			142.81	41.4	44.6	202.43	6.39	3.15	2.06				135
			148.55	40.4	43.6	209.25	6.90	3.40	2.14				136
			126.65	44.4	47.6	208.94	6.90	3.40	2.31				137
			107.28	48.3	51.7	200.84	6.64	3.27	2.38				138
			98.27	50.3	53.8	197.38	6.50	3.20	2.41				139
			89.53	52.2	55.8	194.37	6.39	3.15	2.44				140
			225.07	29.3	32.2	211.58	6.58	3.24	1.60				141
			202.13	32.2	35.2	206.01	6.39	3.15	1.68				142
			181.33	35.2	38.3	199.53	6.19	3.05	1.75				143
			159.14	38.7	41.8	199.74	6.19	3.05	1.89				144
			147.40	40.6	43.8	200.03	6.19	3.05	1.96				145
			203.54	32.0	35.0	162.11	5.05	2.49	1.33				146
			182.65	35.0	38.1	166.62	5.07	2.50	1.43				147
			163.42	38.0	41.1	158.92	5.32	2.62	1.60				148
			142.81	41.4	44.6	171.86	5.38	2.65	1.74				149
			131.95	43.4	46.6	172.66	5.38	2.65	1.80				150
			186.06	34.5	37.5	223.22	6.90	3.40	1.92				151
			157.46	38.9	42.1	236.53	7.31	3.60	2.24				152
			129.40	43.9	47.1	239.57	7.41	3.65	2.49				153
			105.09	48.8	52.2	243.31	7.41	3.65	2.71				154
			96.14	50.8	54.2	244.54	7.41	3.65	2.80				155
			150.00	39.0	43.0	238.33	7.51	3.70	2.23				156
			118.00	44.0	48.0	258.80	8.12	4.00	2.65				157
			98.00	49.0	53.0	260.02	8.12	4.00	2.90				158
			80.00	54.0	58.0	268.26	8.12	4.00	3.14				159
			72.00	56.5	60.5	270.13	8.12	4.00	3.25				160
			160.00	34.0	41.0	174.15	5.84	2.88	1.69				161
			145.00	39.0	47.0	173.86	5.81	2.86	1.83				162.
			130.00	44.0	53.0	172.89	5.74	2.83	1.94				163
			111.00	49.0	58.0	172.84	5.79	2.85	2.28				164
			100.00	51.5	60.5	172.75	5.79	2.85	2.36				165
			176.20	36.0	39.0	193.13	6.09	3.00	1.74				166
			145.76	41.0	44.0	199.62	6.29	3.10	2.00				167
			119.18	46.0	49.0	206.03	6.50	3.20	2.25				168
			96.05	51.0	54.0	207.66	6.50	3.20	2.44				169
			87.40	53.0	56.0	208.89	6.50	3.20	2.51				170
			185.00	41.9	43.9	212.41	6.87	3.35	2.17				171
			150.00	46.7	49.2	221.89	7.18	3.50	2.49				172
			117.00	51.4	54.5	234.95	7.59	3.70	2.87				173
			96.50	56.6	60.0	223.01	7.18	3.50	2.86				174
			82.06	59.1	62.5	210.78	6.87	3.35	2.83				175
			244.86	36.3	39.1	199.92	6.60	3.25	1.88				176
			211.06	40.3	43.2	199.83	6.60	3.25	2.05				177
			172.00	45.0	48.0	198.58	6.60	3.25	2.25				178
			130.00	50.0	53.0	199.60	6.60	3.25	2.44				179
			120.00	52.0	55.0	200.94	6.60	3.25	2.52				180
			212.00	35.8	36.7	226.15	6.78	3.34	1.80				181
			203.50	37.8	39.1	226.50	6.86	3.38	1.96				182
			190.52	40.3	41.7	229.77	6.92	3.41	2.15				183
			163.00	44.4	45.7	229.69	7.00	3.45	2.19				184
			150.46	46.3	47.7	230.02	7.00	3.45	2.28				185

SERIAL NO.	REGION/ COUNTRY	YEAR	POPULATION		AGE STRUCTURE				VITAL			
			ESTIMATED AS OF MID-YEAR (in 000's)	DENSITY (per km²)	TOTAL REPRODUCTIVE VALUE (in 000's)	DEPENDENCY RATIO		DEPARTURE FROM STABILITY (Percent)	CRUDE RATES (Both Sexes)		STANDARDIZED RATES Standard: USA 1960	
						YOUTH < 15 (x 100)	OLD AGE ≥ 65 (x 100)		BIRTH (x 1000)	DEATH (x 1000)	BIRTH (x 1000)	DEATH (x 1000)
	1	2	3	4	5	6	7	8	9	10	11	12
186	Mali	1950	3850	3		82.7	5.9		48.95	31.74		
187		1960	4636	4		80.4	4.9		50.93	28.58		
188		1970	5685	5		84.4	5.0		51.19	25.88		
189		1980	7023	6		89.7	5.4		50.57	22.52		
190		1985	8082	7		90.7	5.3		50.12	20.78		
191	Mauritania	1950	825	1		75.1	4.9		48.34	30.69		
192		1960	991	1		76.5	5.1		47.68	27.54		
193		1970	1221	1		79.0	5.4		46.98	23.83		
194		1980	1551	2		82.1	5.7		46.47	20.51		
195		1985	1766	2		83.7	5.8		46.24	18.97		
196	Mauritius	1950	487	238		87.0	5.7		47.31	15.64		
197		1960	639	312	329	84.2	5.9	4.0	39.31	10.70	37.43	17.71
198		1962	682	333	358	88.0	6.3	5.7	38.00	9.28	38.32	14.91
199		1964	722	353	387	88.1	6.4	5.7	37.93	8.56	38.94	14.49
200		1970	811	397	355	75.0	6.8	11.4	25.97	7.78	24.45	14.11
201		1975	857	419	339	64.5	6.6	13.3	25.11	8.13	20.76	14.96
202		1980	927	453	333	54.8	6.9	14.4	26.40	7.21	18.78	13.47
203		1985	1036	507		46.5	5.3		18.49	5.44		
204	Morocco	1950	8953	20		84.2	5.4		50.40	25.70		
205		1960	11626	26		85.2	4.9		50.10	19.60		
206		1970	15310	34		98.6	8.7		45.60	15.70		
207		1980	19382	43		82.0	7.7		38.25	11.53		
208		1985	22120	50		78.2	7.2		35.29	9.74		
209	Mozambique	1950	6198	8		75.1	4.9		45.96	29.58		
210		1960	7461	9		74.5	5.2		47.00	25.07		
211		1970	9398	12		80.1	5.6		45.67	21.72		
212		1980	12100	15		81.3	5.9		45.73	20.10		
213		1985	13720	17		82.2	6.0		44.96	18.51		
214	Namibia	1950	666	1		74.3	6.7		45.30	25.29		
215		1960	821	1		77.8	6.1		45.81	22.55		
216		1970	1042	1		81.5	6.1		45.09	18.24		
217		1980	1371	2		84.9	6.2		44.41	13.68		
218		1985	1599	2		87.4	6.3		43.98	12.15		
219	Niger	1950	2868	2		62.5	11.9		45.46	35.01		
220		1960	3234	3		78.5	10.8		45.84	29.53		
221		1970	4146	3		84.2	8.9		50.38	26.80		
222		1980	5311	4		91.3	7.5		51.02	22.88		
223		1985	6115	5		93.4	6.5		50.94	20.87		
224	Nigeria	1950	32935	36		88.0	4.6		50.96	27.20		
225		1960	42305	46		86.9	4.4		51.57	23.56		
226		1970	57221	62		92.8	4.6		51.28	20.21		
227		1980	80555	87		97.3	4.9		50.43	17.10		
228		1985	95198	103		97.8	4.9		49.85	15.62		
229	Reunion	1950	257	102		71.9	3.7		39.43	13.26		
230		1960	339	135		82.3	4.7		39.80	10.32		
231		1970	441	176		83.2	5.8		30.72	6.98		
232		1980	508	202		66.1	7.6		24.05	5.84		
233		1985	546	218		53.7	7.6		22.78	5.63		
234	Rwanda	1950	2120	80		88.5	4.4		47.30	23.25		
235		1960	2742	104		86.1	4.5		51.24	21.42		
236		1970	3728	142		93.7	4.8		52.85	20.51		
237		1980	5163	196		99.8	4.9		52.19	18.84		
238		1985	6102	232		100.6	4.9		51.03	17.14		
239	Senegal	1950	2500	13		75.7	6.3		48.35	29.49		
240		1960	3041	16		78.3	5.5		47.19	26.18		
241		1970	4008	20		81.0	5.4		46.64	23.29		
242		1980	5672	29		83.4	5.5		46.43	20.95		
243		1985	6444	33		84.2	5.6		45.73	18.92		
244	Sierra Leone	1950	1944	27		68.5	5.3		47.92	34.32		
245		1960	2241	31		71.6	5.4		48.31	32.27		
246		1970	2656	37		75.9	5.7		48.88	29.19		
247		1980	3263	45		80.6	5.9		48.38	25.19		
248		1985	3665	51		82.8	5.9		48.23	23.35		

RATES			MORTALITY			FERTILITY							
INTRINSIC RATES (Female)			INFANT MORTALITY RATE	LIFE EXPECTANCY AT BIRTH		GENERAL FERTILITY RATE	TOTAL FERTILITY RATE	GROSS REPRODUCTION RATE	NET MATERNITY FUNCTION				SERIAL NO.
BIRTH (x 1000)	DEATH (x 1000)	INCREASE (x 1000)	(x 1000)	MALE (Years)	FEMALE (Years)	(x 1000)			TOTAL (NRR)	MEAN μ	VARIANCE σ^2	GENER-ATION (Years)	
13	14	15	16	17	18	19	20	21	22	23	24	25	
			213.30	31.0	34.0	205.57	6.36	3.13	1.63				186
			208.20	34.0	37.0	211.49	6.46	3.18	1.78				187
			203.10	37.0	40.1	217.04	6.60	3.25	1.95				188
			179.50	40.4	43.6	217.31	6.70	3.30	2.12				189
			169.00	42.4	45.6	218.42	6.70	3.30	2.20				190
			207.34	31.5	34.5	201.63	6.50	3.20	1.66				191
			185.93	34.5	37.5	201.48	6.50	3.20	1.79				192
			160.36	38.5	41.6	201.38	6.50	3.20	1.95				193
			137.31	42.4	45.6	202.20	6.50	3.20	2.11				194
			126.65	44.4	47.6	202.58	6.50	3.20	2.19				195
			99.30	49.7	52.4	209.21	6.28	3.07	2.32				196
41.19	9.78	31.40	72.42	56.2	59.1	178.83	5.71	2.80	2.37	28.22	46.53	27.47	197
41.46	8.38	33.08	67.28	58.8	62.4	178.84	5.86	2.87	2.50	28.46	45.25	27.70	198
41.99	7.70	34.28	59.35	60.1	63.7	178.10	5.96	2.94	2.60	28.63	43.86	27.87	199
27.06	9.45	17.62	58.47	60.9	65.8	111.58	3.75	1.82	1.65	28.71	45.82	28.30	200
23.29	10.04	13.24	48.64	59.6	67.2	101.92	3.19	1.57	1.44	28.09	44.04	27.79	201
20.79	10.07	10.72	33.04	62.3	70.1	98.92	2.89	1.42	1.34	27.40	41.86	27.17	202
			23.01	66.3	71.7	64.69	1.94	0.95	0.90				203
			180.00	41.9	43.9	220.20	7.18	3.50	2.27				204
			155.00	46.7	49.2	222.11	7.15	3.49	2.49				205
			122.00	51.4	54.5	209.62	6.89	3.36	2.52				206
			96.50	56.6	60.0	164.18	5.43	2.65	2.16				207
			82.06	59.1	62.5	148.29	4.82	2.35	1.98				208
			205.00	32.0	35.0	188.47	6.19	3.05	1.59				209
			185.00	37.0	40.1	194.48	6.39	3.15	1.85				210
			168.00	40.9	44.1	196.86	6.50	3.20	2.04				211
			153.47	42.9	46.1	197.43	6.50	3.20	2.12				212
			141.47	44.9	48.1	195.37	6.39	3.15	2.16				213
			168.32	37.5	40.0	189.84	5.87	2.89	1.74				214
			150.27	42.5	45.0	194.49	6.03	2.97	1.90				215
			133.56	47.5	50.0	195.04	6.06	2.98	2.01				216
			116.00	52.5	55.0	197.85	6.09	3.00	2.33				217
			106.00	55.0	57.5	198.57	6.09	3.00	2.41				218
			207.34	31.5	34.5	205.30	6.86	3.38	1.77				219
			185.93	34.5	37.5	213.78	7.06	3.48	1.96				220
			166.49	37.5	40.6	230.55	7.10	3.50	2.11				221
			145.68	40.9	44.1	232.67	7.11	3.50	2.27				222
			134.63	42.9	46.1	232.33	7.11	3.50	2.35				223
			206.70	35.0	38.0	220.22	6.77	3.34	1.90				224
			184.60	39.0	42.1	223.65	6.87	3.39	2.11				225
			147.95	42.9	46.1	230.24	7.11	3.50	2.35				226
			114.18	46.9	50.2	230.73	7.11	3.50	2.52				227
			104.97	48.8	52.2	228.81	7.00	3.45	2.57				228
			141.10	49.7	55.6	186.62	5.65	2.80	2.30				229
			87.16	54.4	61.0	186.56	5.65	2.80	2.44				230
			41.18	60.4	68.1	133.63	3.93	1.95	1.82				231
			16.05	65.5	74.0	91.74	2.82	1.40	1.36				232
			13.75	67.0	75.5	82.85	2.42	1.20	1.17				233
			160.00	38.5	41.6	204.82	7.08	3.50	2.09				234
			142.00	41.4	44.6	222.15	7.68	3.80	2.41				235
			140.00	43.0	46.2	240.38	8.29	4.10	2.69				236
			131.95	44.9	48.1	241.86	8.49	4.20	2.85				237
			121.63	46.9	50.2	236.23	8.29	4.10	2.88				238
			191.20	33.2	36.2	205.76	6.64	3.27	1.76				239
			175.80	35.8	38.9	203.63	6.66	3.28	1.88				240
			161.50	38.5	41.6	202.49	6.74	3.32	2.02				241
			142.24	41.7	44.9	202.51	6.50	3.20	2.08				242
			127.67	44.2	47.4	199.71	6.39	3.15	2.14				243
			230.86	28.6	31.5	193.87	6.09	3.00	1.45				244
			214.96	30.6	33.5	200.15	6.29	3.10	1.59				245
			192.96	33.5	36.5	207.25	6.50	3.20	1.77				246
			166.49	37.5	40.6	209.62	6.50	3.20	1.94				247
			154.28	39.4	42.6	210.62	6.50	3.20	2.02				248

SUMMARY TABLE

SERIAL NO.	REGION/ COUNTRY	YEAR	POPULATION ESTIMATED AS OF MID-YEAR (in 000's)	DENSITY (per km²)	AGE STRUCTURE TOTAL REPRODUCTIVE VALUE (in 000's)	DEPENDENCY RATIO YOUTH < 15 (x 100)	OLD AGE ≥ 65 (x 100)	DEPARTURE FROM STABILITY (Percent)	VITAL CRUDE RATES (Both Sexes) BIRTH (x 1000)	DEATH (x 1000)	STANDARDIZED RATES Standard: USA 1960 BIRTH (x 1000)	DEATH (x 1000)
			1	2	3	4	5	6	7	8	9	10	11	12
249	Somalia	1950	2423	4		73.4	4.6		49.34	30.94		
250		1960	2935	5		78.4	5.4		48.33	26.92		
251		1970	3668	6		82.2	5.8		48.26	23.33		
252		1980	5352	8		81.2	5.4		53.92	22.26		
253		1985	6398	10		89.3	5.3		50.81	20.17		
254	South Africa,	1950	13683	11		66.7	6.2		43.44	20.29		
255	Republic of	1960	17396	14		74.2	7.0		41.88	16.63		
256		1970	22459	18		74.4	6.9		36.11	13.34		
257		1980	28283	23		67.2	6.9		33.14	11.03		
258		1985	31593	26		65.0	7.0		31.69	9.81		
259	South Africa,	1970	6454		2635	63.9	8.7	3.5	28.57	10.50	24.75	14.16
260	Republic of	1980	7994		2426	52.2	9.6	14.0	20.95	8.32	16.23	11.55
261	(excl. Blacks)*	1985	8223		2468	48.0	9.7	11.5	22.37	7.90	16.65	10.70
262	Sudan	1950	9190	4		82.8	6.3		47.00	27.10		
263		1960	11165	4		84.0	5.6		47.00	24.80		
264		1970	13859	6		84.0	5.1		47.00	21.20		
265		1980	18681	7		85.6	5.2		45.87	17.26		
266		1985	21818	9		86.9	5.3		44.55	15.82		
267	Swaziland	1950	264	15		79.2	4.9		50.03	28.34		
268		1960	326	19		82.9	5.1		48.57	22.58		
269		1970	420	24		86.8	5.4		47.52	18.03		
270		1980	564	32		90.6	5.7		47.05	14.11		
271		1985	665	38		93.1	5.9		46.80	12.55		
272	Tanzania	1950	7886	8		93.5	6.8		49.37	27.40		
273		1960	10026	11		89.8	5.6		51.70	22.83		
274		1970	13513	14		93.3	4.7		51.17	18.70		
275		1980	18867	20		98.1	4.7		50.62	15.26		
276		1985	22751	24		98.9	4.7		50.51	13.95		
277	Togo	1950	1329	23		75.9	8.0		47.28	29.10		
278		1960	1514	27		78.6	6.6		47.71	24.37		
279		1970	2020	36		82.0	5.9		45.64	20.20		
280		1980	2554	45		84.6	6.1		45.18	15.72		
281		1985	2960	52		86.1	6.1		44.92	14.09		
282	Tunisia	1950	3530	22		70.2	10.3		46.40	22.60		
283		1960	4221	26		82.6	7.9		46.50	17.90		
284		1970	5127	31		92.5	7.5		37.10	12.30		
285		1980	6384	39		76.2	6.9		33.70	8.44		
286		1985	7261	44		70.0	6.8		30.32	7.36		
287	Uganda	1950	4762	20		84.3	5.7		51.36	24.49		
288		1960	6562	28		91.6	5.2		48.73	20.12		
289		1970	9806	42		93.2	5.1		50.26	18.52		
290		1980	13119	56		96.2	5.1		50.25	16.82		
291		1985	15491	66		97.3	5.1		50.14	15.36		
292	Zaire	1950	12542	5		83.2	7.2		47.33	24.18		
293		1960	15908	7		83.5	5.6		47.25	21.88		
294		1970	19481	8		83.6	5.4		46.63	18.76		
295		1980	26377	11		90.1	4.9		45.13	15.80		
296		1985	30712	13		89.9	4.9		45.56	13.91		
297	Zambia	1950	2440	3		85.8	5.2		50.14	26.06		
298		1960	3141	4		86.3	4.5		49.38	21.38		
299		1970	4189	6		89.6	4.8		49.06	17.97		
300		1980	5738	8		102.4	5.0		50.85	14.90		
301		1985	7007	9		99.3	4.8		51.18	13.70		
302	Zimbabwe	1950	2730	7		85.6	5.8		51.89	23.09		
303		1960	3816	10		91.9	5.6		51.68	19.28		
304		1970	5270	13		102.0	5.6		48.64	15.09		
305		1980	7138	18		96.5	5.2		42.50	11.66		
306		1985	8304	21		90.6	5.3		41.67	10.25		

*
1970 - including Transkei, Bophuthatswana, Venda and Ciskei
1980 - excluding Transkei, Bophuthatswana and Venda
1985 - excluding Transkei, Bophuthatswana, Venda and Ciskei

RATES			MORTALITY			FERTILITY							
INTRINSIC RATES (Female)			INFANT MORTALITY RATE (x 1000)	LIFE EXPECTANCY AT BIRTH		GENERAL FERTILITY RATE (x 1000)	TOTAL FERTILITY RATE	GROSS REPRODUCTION RATE	NET MATERNITY FUNCTION				SERIAL NO.
BIRTH (x 1000)	DEATH (x 1000)	INCREASE (x 1000)		MALE (Years)	FEMALE (Years)				TOTAL (NRR)	MEAN μ	VARIANCE σ^2	GENER- ATION (Years)	
13	14	15	16	17	18	19	20	21	22	23	24	25	
			190.00	31.5	34.5	208.29	6.60	3.25	1.70				249
			170.00	35.5	38.6	209.93	6.60	3.25	1.88				250
			155.00	39.4	42.6	212.24	6.60	3.25	2.04				251
			142.92	41.4	44.6	216.65	6.60	3.25	2.12				252
			132.05	43.4	46.6	212.47	6.60	3.25	2.20				253
			152.00	44.0	46.0	182.46	6.51	3.20	2.10				254
			130.00	48.0	52.0	181.53	6.51	3.20	2.33				255
			110.00	51.0	57.0	153.25	5.49	2.70	2.12				256
			83.27	55.0	61.0	134.14	4.78	2.35	1.95				257
			72.46	57.5	63.5	126.72	4.48	2.20	1.88				258
28.25	9.72	18.53	68.11	57.7	64.8	119.72	3.82	1.88	1.67	28.13	42.64	27.74	259
17.35	12.12	5.23	35.20	62.1	69.9	81.44	2.51	1.23	1.15	27.06	37.86	26.96	260
17.99	11.15	6.84	24.33	64.3	71.4	83.23	2.57	1.26	1.20	27.21	36.31	27.09	261
			185.00	36.1	38.3	205.57	6.67	3.26	1.85				262
			165.00	38.1	40.3	204.56	6.67	3.26	1.93				263
			145.00	41.4	43.9	204.85	6.67	3.26	2.08				264
			117.58	46.6	49.0	203.20	6.59	3.22	2.25				265
			108.12	48.6	51.0	198.66	6.44	3.15	2.28				266
			160.00	34.2	37.0	209.46	6.50	3.20	1.78				267
			150.00	39.7	43.5	208.77	6.50	3.20	2.05				268
			144.00	45.1	49.6	209.31	6.50	3.20	2.28				269
			129.00	51.2	54.8	211.48	6.50	3.20	2.48				270
			118.00	53.7	57.3	212.39	6.50	3.20	2.56				271
			160.00	35.5	38.6	219.97	6.74	3.32	1.92				272
			143.00	40.1	43.3	224.21	6.86	3.38	2.15				273
			130.00	44.9	48.2	228.47	7.00	3.45	2.40				274
			115.00	49.3	52.7	230.79	7.11	3.50	2.62				275
			105.57	51.3	54.7	231.79	7.11	3.50	2.70				276
			203.54	34.5	37.5	200.89	6.15	3.03	1.71				277
			170.17	39.0	42.1	203.04	6.15	3.03	1.89				278
			121.13	43.9	47.1	197.27	6.09	3.00	2.02				279
			102.27	48.8	52.2	198.13	6.09	3.00	2.24				280
			93.83	51.3	54.8	198.89	6.09	3.00	2.32				281
			175.00	44.1	45.1	201.05	6.87	3.35	2.21				282
			155.00	49.1	50.1	215.57	7.18	3.50	2.52				283
			120.00	55.1	56.1	168.63	6.15	3.00	2.36				284
			70.91	62.6	63.6	142.29	4.88	2.38	2.06				285
			58.68	64.6	66.1	124.73	4.10	2.00	1.79				286
			160.00	38.5	41.6	226.03	6.91	3.40	2.10				287
			125.00	42.4	45.6	217.92	6.91	3.40	2.27				288
			116.00	45.4	48.7	226.74	6.90	3.40	2.39				289
			112.00	47.4	50.7	229.69	6.90	3.40	2.47				290
			102.71	49.4	52.7	229.70	6.90	3.40	2.55				291
			157.30	39.0	42.1	194.05	5.98	2.94	1.84				292
			145.68	40.9	44.1	195.86	5.94	2.93	1.90				293
			126.65	44.4	47.6	197.80	6.09	3.00	2.07				294
			107.28	48.3	51.7	196.70	6.09	3.00	2.22				295
			98.00	50.8	54.2	199.95	6.09	3.00	2.30				296
			150.00	36.3	39.4	213.69	6.59	3.25	1.91				297
			130.00	41.2	44.4	213.61	6.62	3.26	2.12				298
			100.00	45.7	49.0	218.22	6.90	3.40	2.40				299
			88.00	50.4	52.5	226.27	7.20	3.55	2.63				300
			79.83	52.4	54.5	227.62	7.20	3.55	2.72				301
			119.93	39.9	43.1	231.08	7.20	3.56	2.26				302
			105.99	44.9	48.1	240.87	7.50	3.71	2.58				303
			92.90	49.8	53.2	230.41	7.20	3.56	2.69				304
			80.24	54.0	57.6	190.50	6.19	3.07	2.45				305
			72.06	56.5	60.1	180.56	5.79	2.87	2.37				306

SERIAL NO.	REGION/ COUNTRY	YEAR	POPULATION ESTIMATED AS OF MID-YEAR (in 000's)	DENSITY (per km²)	AGE STRUCTURE TOTAL REPRODUCTIVE VALUE (in 000's)	DEPENDENCY RATIO YOUTH < 15 (x 100)	OLD AGE ≥ 65 (x 100)	DEPARTURE FROM STABILITY (Percent)	VITAL CRUDE RATES (Both Sexes) BIRTH (x 1000)	DEATH (x 1000)	STANDARDIZED RATES Standard: USA 1960 BIRTH (x 1000)	DEATH (x 1000)
			3	4	5	6	7	8	9	10	11	12
307	LATIN AMERICA	1950	165365	8		72.5	5.8		42.50	15.33		
308		1960	217649	11		78.6	6.5		41.18	12.16		
309		1970	285127	14		79.2	7.2		35.28	9.67		
310		1980	361756	18		69.4	7.6		30.86	8.01		
311		1985	403646	20		64.8	7.8		29.05	7.49		
312	CARIBBEAN	1950	16878	71		69.0	7.2		37.47	15.20		
313		1960	20353	85		71.1	7.8		39.09	11.94		
314		1970	24881	104		75.9	9.1		31.20	9.26		
315		1980	29260	123		62.5	9.8		25.12	8.11		
316		1985	31288	131		54.4	9.8		24.69	7.84		
317	CENTRAL	1950	37241	15		82.1	6.0		47.30	17.07		
318	AMERICA	1960	50456	20		88.6	6.2		46.04	12.34		
319		1970	69665	28		93.7	6.5		42.69	9.55		
320		1980	92677	37		84.8	6.6		33.49	7.01		
321		1985	104746	42		76.3	6.4		31.07	6.29		
322	SOUTH AMERICA	1950	111245	6		69.9	5.6		41.64	14.76		
323		1960	146840	8		76.5	6.5		39.77	12.13		
324		1970	190580	11		74.9	7.2		33.04	9.77		
325		1980	239820	13		64.8	7.8		30.53	8.39		
326		1985	267611	15		61.8	8.0		28.76	7.92		
327	Argentina	1950	17150	6		46.8	6.4		25.39	9.11		
328		1960	20616	7		48.3	8.7		23.21	8.83		
329		1961	21097	8	6448	46.0	8.0	8.6	22.54	8.36	18.54	11.86
330		1970	23962	9	7428	46.0	10.9	4.1	22.72	9.27	19.70	10.97
331		1980	28237	10		48.6	13.2		23.02	8.71		
332		1985	30331	11		50.0	14.1		21.35	8.65		
333	Barbados	1950	211	490		54.3	9.3		32.80	13.20		
334		1960	234	543	98	68.3	11.1	6.8	30.86	9.42	28.35	11.56
335		1970	236	548	83	67.8	15.2	8.6	20.70	8.75	19.79	10.25
336		1980	249	578		49.5	17.6		17.79	8.67		
337		1985	253	587		43.6	17.1		18.54	8.42		
338	Bolivia	1950	2766	3		76.6	5.7		47.14	24.10		
339		1960	3428	3		79.4	5.9		46.06	21.46		
340		1970	4325	4		80.0	6.2		45.42	18.96		
341		1980	5570	5		81.6	6.1		44.02	15.87		
342		1985	6371	6		82.5	6.0		42.85	14.11		
343	Brazil	1950	53444	6		75.7	4.4		44.64	15.07		
344		1960	72595	9		81.5	5.4		42.08	12.26		
345		1970	95847	11		77.8	6.3		33.65	9.74		
346		1980	121286	14		64.8	6.9		30.60	8.36		
347		1985	135564	16		61.4	7.3		28.58	7.87		
348	Chile	1950	6082	8		62.2	7.2		37.20	14.37		
349		1960	7736	10	3788	71.1	7.5	2.3	33.79	12.12	30.61	15.85
350		1962	8145	11	3955	71.1	7.6	2.3	33.69	11.65	30.42	15.10
351		1964	8391	11	3976	70.8	7.8	3.0	32.81	11.21	29.05	14.68
352		1966	8922	12	4012	72.0	8.0	4.8	30.06	10.21	27.20	13.34
353		1967	9137	12	3949	71.5	8.0	6.3	28.43	9.50	25.51	12.70
354		1970	9456	12	3840	70.2	9.0	10.9	25.24	8.78	21.99	12.21
355		1980	11104	15	3382	52.5	8.8	16.0	21.13	6.67	16.11	9.68
356		1985	12121	16		50.2	9.3		23.83	6.41		
357	Colombia	1950	11597	10		81.2	6.7		47.58	16.48		
358		1960	15538	14		91.5	6.1		44.58	12.18		
359		1965	17993	16	10297	92.6	6.0	4.1	38.39	9.91	36.37	13.32
360		1970	20803	18		87.8	5.8		33.34	9.02		
361		1980	25793	23		69.1	6.1		31.01	7.74		
362		1985	28713	25		62.9	6.4		29.23	7.38		
363	Costa Rica	1950	862	17		81.9	7.1		47.33	12.64		
364		1960	1236	24		95.9	6.5		45.31	9.18		
365		1964	1396	28	865	97.2	6.5	3.2	46.87	8.79	46.90	11.37
366		1966	1541	30	898	99.3	6.5	2.3	41.75	7.39	42.40	10.36
367		1970	1731	34		90.8	6.3		31.50	5.83		
368		1980	2285	45		67.4	6.3		30.19	4.13		
369		1985	2642	52		62.1	6.6		28.31	3.96		

RATES			MORTALITY			FERTILITY							
INTRINSIC RATES (Female)			INFANT MORTALITY RATE (x 1000)	LIFE EXPECTANCY AT BIRTH		GENERAL FERTILITY RATE (x 1000)	TOTAL FERTILITY RATE	GROSS REPRODUCTION RATE	NET MATERNITY FUNCTION				SERIAL NO.
BIRTH (x 1000)	DEATH (x 1000)	INCREASE (x 1000)		MALE (Years)	FEMALE (Years)				TOTAL (NRR)	MEAN μ	VARIANCE σ²	GENERATION (Years)	
13	14	15	16	17	18	19	20	21	22	23	24	25	
			125.71	49.6	52.9	179.94	5.87	2.86	2.15				307
			99.81	54.9	58.6	181.66	5.95	2.91	2.35				308
			80.28	58.7	63.2	153.35	5.00	2.44	2.09				309
			62.65	61.9	67.2	126.53	3.98	1.94	1.73				310
			55.78	63.4	68.8	116.13	3.61	1.76	1.60				311
			123.91	50.4	53.7	157.78	5.15	2.51	1.88				312
			94.29	56.8	60.4	168.11	5.43	2.65	2.18				313
			76.83	60.8	64.6	136.62	4.39	2.14	1.85				314
			63.93	63.0	67.1	100.08	3.13	1.53	1.36				315
			57.27	64.3	68.6	94.71	2.92	1.43	1.29				316
			122.73	47.9	50.8	208.76	6.76	3.30	2.38				317
			94.06	55.2	58.3	211.09	6.79	3.31	2.67				318
			74.43	59.2	63.5	195.78	6.33	3.09	2.64				319
			56.75	62.6	68.8	143.21	4.47	2.18	1.97				320
			49.61	64.6	70.6	126.43	3.91	1.91	1.75				321
			127.08	50.1	53.6	174.03	5.69	2.78	2.11				322
			102.86	54.5	58.5	173.78	5.75	2.81	2.27				323
			83.53	58.1	62.9	140.74	4.62	2.26	1.92				324
			65.05	61.5	66.6	123.59	3.90	1.90	1.69				325
			58.26	62.7	68.0	114.71	3.58	1.75	1.58				326
			64.00	60.4	65.1	97.65	3.15	1.55	1.37				327
			60.00	62.5	68.6	92.71	3.09	1.51	1.38				328
19.85	11.43	8.41	61.43	62.5	68.2	86.71	2.84	1.39	1.26	28.16	45.36	27.97	329
21.25	10.30	10.94	59.42	62.5	69.8	89.90	3.02	1.49	1.35	28.06	48.56	27.79	330
			36.00	66.4	73.1	97.04	3.15	1.54	1.46				331
			32.00	67.3	74.0	90.32	2.96	1.44	1.38				332
			132.00	55.0	59.5	126.00	4.69	2.30	1.92				333
31.83	8.16	23.67	76.16	62.9	67.4	128.74	4.30	2.11	1.90	27.63	47.11	27.06	334
22.40	9.26	13.14	46.69	64.9	71.0	93.36	3.02	1.52	1.42	27.10	48.25	26.78	335
			11.00	70.0	75.4	68.47	1.94	0.95	0.92				336
			11.00	71.0	77.0	68.09	2.00	0.98	0.96				337
			176.00	38.5	42.5	202.21	6.75	3.29	2.00				338
			164.00	41.4	45.6	198.38	6.63	3.23	2.10				339
			151.00	44.6	49.0	194.50	6.50	3.17	2.20				340
			124.00	48.6	53.0	189.50	6.25	3.05	2.29				341
			110.00	50.9	55.4	184.44	6.06	2.95	2.32				342
			135.00	49.3	52.8	187.07	6.15	3.00	2.27				343
			109.00	54.0	57.8	184.69	6.15	3.00	2.41				344
			91.00	57.6	62.2	142.28	4.70	2.29	1.95				345
			71.00	61.0	66.0	121.57	3.81	1.86	1.65				346
			63.00	62.3	67.6	111.83	3.46	1.69	1.52				347
			126.00	51.9	55.7	153.75	5.10	2.39	1.96				348
33.53	11.73	21.80	135.43	54.2	59.2	140.45	4.67	2.30	1.87	29.30	47.25	28.78	349
33.23	11.26	21.97	129.99	54.8	60.4	139.87	4.64	2.28	1.88	29.26	46.95	28.73	350
31.99	10.94	21.05	119.28	55.7	61.3	135.99	4.43	2.18	1.82	29.08	48.62	28.55	351
29.96	10.00	19.96	108.30	58.3	64.3	126.62	4.15	2.04	1.76	28.89	48.95	28.39	352
28.08	9.69	18.39	99.92	59.2	66.2	119.45	3.89	1.91	1.68	28.72	49.45	28.25	353
24.12	10.78	13.34	86.68	59.9	65.9	104.74	3.37	1.65	1.45	28.35	50.46	28.01	354
16.75	11.45	5.30	34.76	66.4	72.9	80.94	2.47	1.21	1.15	27.08	44.37	26.97	355
			20.00	68.1	75.1	89.63	2.73	1.33	1.30				356
			123.00	48.8	52.6	207.99	6.72	3.28	2.44				357
			84.00	54.2	58.4	203.31	6.72	3.28	2.66				358
38.82	9.88	28.95	80.12	58.2	61.7	169.42	5.56	2.75	2.31	29.61	50.93	28.86	359
			65.00	58.2	62.7	146.30	4.78	2.33	1.98				360
			50.00	61.4	66.0	124.25	3.93	1.92	1.71				361
			46.00	62.6	67.2	114.49	3.58	1.75	1.58				362
			94.00	56.0	58.6	211.81	6.72	3.28	2.69				363
			81.00	61.6	64.5	214.83	6.95	3.39	2.94				364
47.38	8.20	39.18	76.14	62.4	65.3	220.00	7.15	3.49	3.03	29.25	49.30	28.27	365
43.44	6.84	36.60	64.01	65.0	67.7	198.02	6.45	3.15	2.82	29.30	50.51	28.36	366
			51.00	66.1	70.2	138.84	4.34	2.12	1.95				367
			20.00	71.3	75.8	119.92	3.50	1.71	1.65				368
			18.00	72.4	77.0	111.17	3.26	1.59	1.55				369

SERIAL NO.	REGION/ COUNTRY	YEAR	POPULATION ESTIMATED AS OF MID-YEAR (in 000's)	DENSITY (per km²)	AGE STRUCTURE TOTAL REPRODUCTIVE VALUE (in 000's)	DEPENDENCY RATIO YOUTH < 15 (x 100)	OLD AGE ≥ 65 (x 100)	DEPARTURE FROM STABILITY (Percent)	CRUDE RATES (Both Sexes) BIRTH (x 1000)	DEATH (x 1000)	STANDARDIZED RATES Standard: USA 1960 BIRTH (x 1000)	DEATH (x 1000)
			3	4	5	6	7	8	9	10	11	12
			1	**2**								
370	**Cuba**	1950	5858	53		61.0	7.5		29.69	11.03		
371		1960	7028	63		56.5	7.9		35.26	8.85		
372		1970	8571	77		65.3	10.4		25.78	6.41		
373		1980	9732	88		51.0	11.9		15.01	6.38		
374		1985	9946	90		38.7	12.0		15.96	6.77		
375	**Dominican**	1950	2353	48		85.2	6.2		50.52	20.32		
376	**Republic**	1960	3231	66		92.7	6.0		49.38	14.77		
377		1970	4423	91		95.2	6.0		38.81	9.86		
378		1980	5697	117		77.4	5.7		33.59	7.52		
379		1985	6416	132		69.5	5.7		31.30	6.81		
380	**El Salvador**	1950	1940	92		78.9	5.6		48.30	19.98		
381		1960	2570	122		87.5	5.0		47.80	14.85		
382		1970	3588	171		91.7	5.5		42.81	10.94		
383		1980	4525	215		90.3	6.0		37.96	11.09		
384		1985	4767	227		91.0	6.7		36.33	8.52		
385	**Ecuador**	1950	3310	12		78.3	8.6		46.76	18.87		
386		1960	4413	16		87.5	7.8		45.63	14.32		
387		1970	6051	21		89.1	7.3		41.23	11.15		
388		1980	8123	29		81.7	6.8		36.76	8.09		
389		1985	9378	33		76.7	6.8		35.40	7.55		
390	**Grenada**	1960	89	286	52	101.1	11.0	9.0	44.97	11.56	43.83	12.59
391		1961	92	296	54	101.2	11.0	8.8	44.60	11.07	44.13	12.26
392	**Guadeloupe**	1950	210	118		70.3	7.6		39.00	13.11		
393		1960	275	155		83.1	9.8		36.82	8.45		
394		1970	320	180		81.8	9.1		28.93	7.46		
395		1980	327	184		51.6	12.1		20.88	7.09		
396		1985	334	188		43.7	12.7		19.50	7.27		
397	**Guatemala**	1950	2969	27		82.6	4.8		51.27	22.38		
398		1960	3964	36		89.7	5.2		47.81	18.29		
399		1970	5246	48		89.6	5.5		44.55	13.45		
400		1980	6916	64		89.5	5.6		42.69	10.52		
401		1985	7963	73	4440	89.7	5.7	1.6	41.04	8.72	39.22	12.49
402	**Guyana**	1950	423	2		75.5	8.3		48.10	13.50		
403		1955	467	2	237	80.2	6.4	7.0	43.22	11.90	39.06	18.83
404		1956	480	2	248	82.2	6.3	7.0	43.15	11.20	39.42	18.06
405		1960	569	3		100.5	6.9		40.40	8.60		
406		1970	709	3		97.5	7.1		32.50	7.60		
407		1980	865	4		69.3	6.6		28.49	5.90		
408		1985	953	4		62.5	6.6		24.79	5.41		
409	**Haiti**	1950	3097	112		70.0	7.2		43.67	26.38		
410		1960	3675	132		71.6	7.1		43.15	21.40		
411		1970	4500	162		77.1	7.0		39.46	17.11		
412		1980	5413	195		75.5	6.9		35.37	13.89		
413		1985	5922	213		71.7	6.8		34.33	12.68		
414	**Honduras**	1950	1401	13		83.8	3.6		51.38	22.21		
415		1960	1935	17		86.0	4.3		51.15	18.10		
416		1970	2627	23		94.1	5.1		48.67	13.68		
417		1980	3662	33		95.9	6.0		42.30	8.97		
418		1985	4383	39		92.0	6.4		39.80	8.07		
419	**Jamaica**	1951	1430	130	597	60.2	6.3	3.5	33.87	12.05	26.61	17.89
420		1952	1457	133	601	60.2	6.3	3.5	33.27	11.47	26.27	17.41
421		1956	1564	143	688	65.4	6.7	5.8	37.21	9.38	31.31	14.95
422		1960	1632	149	815	78.3	8.0	7.0	41.91	8.77	36.86	11.07
423		1970	1869	170		99.0	11.7		32.50	7.40		
424		1980	2173	198		75.7	10.8		28.12	5.63		
425		1985	2336	213		64.1	10.7		26.04	5.53		
426	**Martinique**	1950	222	201		65.1	9.1		39.90	12.60		
427		1960	282	256		79.7	8.4		35.70	8.40		
428		1963	308	279	154	79.7	9.4	4.3	33.20	8.17	33.36	11.16
429		1970	326	295		77.5	9.8		24.90	7.30		
430		1980	326	296		45.2	13.3		17.88	7.51		
431		1985	328	298		36.7	13.8		18.57	7.71		

RATES — INTRINSIC RATES (Female)			MORTALITY			FERTILITY			NET MATERNITY FUNCTION				
BIRTH (x 1000)	DEATH (x 1000)	INCREASE (x 1000)	INFANT MORTALITY RATE (x 1000)	LIFE EXPECTANCY AT BIRTH MALE (Years)	FEMALE (Years)	GENERAL FERTILITY RATE (x 1000)	TOTAL FERTILITY RATE	GROSS REPRODUCTION RATE	TOTAL (NRR)	MEAN μ	VARIANCE σ²	GENERATION (Years)	SERIAL NO.
13	14	15	16	17	18	19	20	21	22	23	24	25	
			82.00	56.7	61.0	124.09	4.01	1.95	1.64				370
			56.00	63.3	67.1	148.08	4.67	2.27	2.03				371
			36.00	69.3	72.6	113.19	3.47	1.69	1.59				372
			17.00	71.8	75.2	57.81	1.75	0.85	0.82				373
			15.00	72.2	75.8	57.87	1.71	0.83	0.81				374
			149.00	44.7	47.3	233.56	7.40	3.61	2.45				375
			117.00	52.1	55.2	232.02	7.32	3.57	2.75				376
			94.00	58.1	61.8	177.57	5.63	2.74	2.30				377
			75.00	62.2	66.1	139.63	4.21	2.05	1.82				378
			65.00	63.9	68.1	126.08	3.75	1.83	1.65				379
			175.00	44.1	46.5	206.31	6.46	3.15	2.16				380
			131.00	50.8	54.0	216.34	6.85	3.34	2.54				381
			97.00	56.6	61.1	194.19	6.10	2.93	2.46				382
			70.00	50.7	63.9	168.64	5.21	2.54	2.19				383
			59.00	58.0	66.5	158.95	4.86	2.37	2.09				384
			149.00	47.1	49.6	210.23	6.90	3.37	2.40				385
			119.00	53.4	56.1	211.59	6.90	3.37	2.60				386
			95.00	57.4	60.5	187.46	6.05	2.95	2.43				387
			70.00	62.3	66.4	157.82	5.00	2.44	2.14				388
			63.00	63.4	67.6	148.24	4.65	2.27	2.02				389
47.48	8.33	39.15	81.92	58.7	65.1	210.11	6.68	3.33	2.87	27.87	45.78	26.97	390
46.66	8.17	38.50	64.61	60.5	65.0	208.96	6.70	3.29	2.85	28.19	49.01	27.25	391
			67.60	55.0	58.1	162.56	5.61	2.75	2.27				392
			44.70	62.5	66.8	167.22	5.61	2.75	2.51				393
			42.40	64.7	70.9	131.66	4.49	2.20	2.07				394
			13.90	68.9	76.1	79.86	2.55	1.25	1.21				395
			12.00	70.1	76.7	72.48	2.24	1.10	1.07				396
			141.00	41.9	42.4	226.44	7.09	3.46	2.16				397
			119.00	46.2	47.9	217.68	6.85	3.34	2.30				398
			95.00	52.6	55.5	201.08	6.45	3.15	2.44				399
			70.00	56.8	61.3	195.18	6.12	2.99	2.49				400
41.06	7.94	33.12	55.96	60.6	64.4	188.12	5.96	2.91	2.53	29.06	57.68	28.11	401
			92.60	53.5	57.0	214.20	6.68	3.26	2.69				402
44.07	9.22	34.86	75.38	56.0	58.8	210.99	5.95	2.91	2.51	27.21	44.57	26.43	403
44.77	8.70	36.07	73.19	56.6	60.2	213.46	6.01	2.98	2.59	27.20	43.64	26.40	404
			60.90	59.1	63.3	192.63	6.05	2.95	2.63				405
			55.70	61.9	66.4	146.78	4.55	2.22	2.01				406
			36.18	65.8	70.8	112.33	3.26	1.59	1.50				407
			29.69	67.3	72.3	94.35	2.75	1.34	1.28				408
			220.00	36.3	38.9	177.76	6.15	3.00	1.67				409
			188.00	42.3	44.9	177.85	6.15	3.00	1.94				410
			155.00	47.1	50.0	167.13	5.76	2.81	2.02				411
			128.00	51.2	54.4	146.12	5.05	2.46	1.93				412
			117.00	53.1	56.4	138.88	4.74	2.31	1.87				413
			169.00	40.9	43.8	220.54	7.05	3.44	2.18				414
			136.00	46.3	49.7	228.47	7.36	3.59	2.54				415
			110.00	52.2	55.8	227.69	7.38	3.60	2.82				416
			82.00	60.0	64.0	195.58	6.16	3.00	2.59				417
			69.00	61.9	66.1	178.34	5.55	2.71	2.38				418
31.25	11.99	19.25	87.91	55.2	58.1	115.99	4.07	2.02	1.67	27.15	45.13	26.70	419
30.53	11.45	19.08	79.52	58.2	59.6	125.83	4.02	1.99	1.67	27.23	45.68	26.78	420
35.96	8.14	27.82	59.19	61.1	64.7	147.96	4.79	2.35	2.09	27.18	43.90	26.56	421
41.17	6.53	34.65	51.57	63.4	67.9	176.32	5.61	2.78	2.53	27.62	47.52	26.79	422
			36.20	66.0	69.7	160.94	5.41	2.65	2.49				423
			21.02	70.3	75.7	118.21	3.37	1.65	1.60				424
			18.00	71.3	76.7	102.83	2.86	1.40	1.37				425
			64.70	55.0	58.1	162.17	5.71	2.80	2.31				426
			47.70	62.8	66.9	161.04	5.45	2.67	2.44				427
35.01	6.72	28.29	38.76	63.6	68.8	146.20	5.08	2.53	2.33	30.56	44.12	29.81	428
			34.70	66.7	71.0	110.48	4.08	2.00	1.89				429
			14.06	71.0	75.5	66.50	2.14	1.05	1.02				430
			13.00	72.0	76.5	67.89	2.08	1.02	0.99				431

SERIAL NO.	REGION/ COUNTRY	YEAR	POPULATION ESTIMATED AS OF MID-YEAR (in 000's)	DENSITY (per km²)	AGE STRUCTURE TOTAL REPRODUCTIVE VALUE (in 000's)	DEPENDENCY RATIO YOUTH < 15 (x 100)	OLD AGE ≥ 65 (x 100)	DEPARTURE FROM STABILITY (Percent)	CRUDE RATES (Both Sexes) BIRTH (x 1000)	DEATH (x 1000)	STANDARDIZED RATES Standard: USA 1960 BIRTH (x 1000)	DEATH (x 1000)
			1									
	1	2	3	4	5	6	7	8	9	10	11	12
432	Mexico	1950	28012	14		82.4	6.2		46.56	16.09		
433		1960	34997	18	20814	85.2	6.6	2.5	46.14	11.32	42.33	15.12
434		1962	38543	20	22343	90.1	6.4	1.5	44.25	10.46	41.99	14.29
435		1970	51176	26	30464	93.6	7.0	1.7	41.67	9.49	42.26	12.92
436		1980	69655	35	35190	84.3	6.3	5.8	34.85	6.24	31.88	10.54
437		1983	74625	38	36287	76.2	6.2	6.4	34.96	5.54	30.17	9.56
438	Nicaragua	1950	1098	8		84.2	4.7		54.13	22.66		
439		1960	1493	11		96.6	4.7		50.33	17.06		
440		1970	2053	16		98.1	4.8		46.79	12.67		
441		1980	2771	21		94.6	4.8		44.21	9.72		
442		1985	3272	25		92.1	5.0		41.80	7.99		
443	Panama	1950	893	12		74.4	7.0		40.30	13.18		
444		1960	1148	15		82.8	7.7		40.84	9.58		
445		1970	1434	19	705	82.2	7.0	2.4	37.16	7.13	33.23	10.14
446		1980	1837	24	728	71.1	7.5	10.5	28.65	4.33	23.85	7.08
447		1985	2180	28		64.8	7.7		26.68	5.16		
448	Paraguay	1950	1351	3		79.7	5.9		47.31	9.35		
449		1960	1774	4		97.2	6.7		42.33	8.11		
450		1970	2351	6		92.5	6.8		36.59	7.18		
451		1980	3147	8		77.3	6.3		35.77	6.74		
452		1985	3693	9		73.8	6.3		34.85	6.57		
453	Peru	1950	7632	6		75.6	6.3		47.08	21.58		
454		1960	9931	8		81.4	6.5		46.27	17.56		
455		1970	13193	10		83.8	6.6		40.52	12.75		
456		1980	17295	13		76.5	6.6		36.71	10.74		
457		1985	19698	15		72.3	6.4		34.31	9.24		
458	Puerto Rico	1950	2219	249		81.9	7.2		36.60	9.00		
459		1960	2362	265	1084	81.2	10.0	4.1	32.31	6.69	30.05	8.61
460		1965	2626	295	1044	69.6	10.4	2.8	30.32	6.74	25.73	8.29
461		1970	2716	305	970	64.2	11.5	9.5	24.83	6.66	20.48	7.95
462		1980	3207	360	969	51.9	13.3	8.8	22.78	6.39	18.10	6.89
463		1985	3283	369	842	44.9	16.1	9.8	19.38	7.07	15.74	6.52
464	St.Christopher	1970	45	172	22	110.0	15.9	16.4	25.66	10.83	33.66	13.68
465	and Nevis	1980	43	165	17	70.2	18.0	13.4	26.96	11.36	22.12	12.56
466	St. Lucia	1960	87	144	52	86.9	9.4	7.8	48.89	14.77	45.23	14.21
467	Suriname	1950	215	1		74.1	11.2		43.80	12.60		
468		1960	290	2		98.6	8.6		44.40	10.30		
469		1970	372	2		101.2	8.1		34.60	7.50		
470		1980	355	2		71.3	8.0		28.81	6.85		
471		1985	375	2		63.6	7.3		25.85	6.12		
472	Trinidad and	1950	636	124		72.6	7.1		38.20	11.30		
473	Tobago	1955	721	141	346	75.7	6.9	8.8	41.92	10.35	37.00	15.27
474		1957	765	149	357	78.2	6.6	5.8	37.46	9.46	34.68	15.35
475		1960	843	164		81.2	7.5		38.00	7.70		
476		1970	955	186	405	78.7	8.3	9.8	26.34	7.28	23.77	12.27
477		1980	1095	213		57.4	9.2		25.40	7.00		
478		1985	1185	231		53.4	8.8		23.97	6.45		
479	Uruguay	1950	2239	13		43.6	12.9		21.23	10.51		
480		1960	2538	14		43.6	12.7		21.91	9.56		
481		1970	2808	16		44.1	14.0		21.14	10.06		
482		1980	2908	17		43.3	16.7		19.50	10.23		
483		1985	3012	17		43.1	17.2		18.87	10.24		
484	Venezuela	1950	5009	5		80.0	3.4		47.03	12.28		
485		1960	7502	8		89.6	4.7		44.18	9.14		
486		1963	8144	9	4459	86.9	5.5	3.1	43.41	7.18	41.14	10.80
487		1965	8722	10	4817	88.0	5.8	3.4	43.51	7.06	41.82	10.97
488		1970	10604	12	5518	88.1	4.8	3.1	37.02	6.46	35.05	10.81
489		1980	15024	16	6656	73.8	5.7	7.8	32.81	5.13	27.06	9.07
490		1985	17317	19	7004	69.2	6.0	11.2	29.01	4.56	23.47	8.16

RATES			MORTALITY			FERTILITY							
INTRINSIC RATES (Female)			INFANT MORTALITY RATE (x 1000)	LIFE EXPECTANCY AT BIRTH		GENERAL FERTILITY RATE (x 1000)	TOTAL FERTILITY RATE	GROSS REPRODUCTION RATE	NET MATERNITY FUNCTION				SERIAL NO.
BIRTH (x 1000)	DEATH (x 1000)	INCREASE (x 1000)		MALE (Years)	FEMALE (Years)				TOTAL (NRR)	MEAN μ	VARIANCE σ²	GENERATION (Years)	
13	14	15	16	17	18	19	20	21	22	23	24	25	
			114.00	49.2	52.4	206.11	6.75	3.29	2.43				432
44.11	11.01	33.10	73.03	55.7	58.7	201.95	6.45	3.14	2.54	29.06	48.34	28.26	433
43.26	9.61	33.65	76.70	58.3	61.1	198.38	6.40	3.10	2.59	29.14	46.48	28.34	434
43.44	8.38	35.06	68.47	59.2	63.6	192.74	6.46	3.22	2.76	30.02	59.75	28.98	435
34.51	6.47	28.04	39.53	63.6	69.8	153.39	4.88	2.40	2.21	29.20	64.23	28.30	436
33.12	5.99	27.12	30.62	65.9	71.6	146.98	4.62	2.29	2.14	28.95	61.64	28.12	437
			167.00	40.9	43.7	234.79	7.33	3.58	2.33				438
			131.00	47.3	49.8	231.89	7.33	3.58	2.58				439
			100.00	53.7	55.8	213.84	6.71	3.27	2.58				440
			76.00	58.7	61.0	197.77	5.94	2.90	2.43				441
			62.00	62.0	64.6	184.55	5.50	2.68	2.33				442
			93.04	54.4	56.2	182.57	5.68	2.77	2.22				443
			62.69	60.9	63.1	188.17	5.92	2.89	2.49				444
37.10	7.04	30.06	40.91	65.2	67.9	166.29	5.06	2.49	2.24	27.66	49.72	26.91	445
26.34	6.51	19.83	22.08	71.0	75.9	122.45	3.63	1.78	1.69	27.13	49.95	26.63	446
			23.00	70.2	74.1	106.31	3.14	1.53	1.46				447
			106.00	60.7	64.7	205.15	6.80	3.32	2.89				448
			81.00	62.5	66.4	202.08	6.80	3.32	2.95				449
			53.00	63.7	67.6	166.13	5.65	2.76	2.49				450
			45.00	64.4	68.6	151.66	4.82	2.35	2.14				451
			42.00	64.8	69.1	145.25	4.58	2.23	2.04				452
			159.00	42.9	45.0	206.68	6.85	3.35	2.15				453
			136.00	47.8	50.5	209.23	6.85	3.35	2.37				454
			110.00	53.9	57.3	180.58	6.00	2.93	2.30				455
			99.00	56.8	60.5	155.60	5.00	2.44	2.00				456
			88.00	59.5	63.4	142.44	4.49	2.19	1.86				457
			63.23	63.0	66.7	160.67	5.02	2.45	2.24				458
33.46	6.20	27.26	43.75	67.4	72.0	141.66	4.61	2.26	2.10	27.86	47.20	27.21	459
28.93	6.53	22.40	42.82	68.0	73.7	125.51	3.94	1.92	1.81	26.98	45.56	26.46	460
22.50	7.93	14.57	28.72	68.6	74.9	101.84	3.15	1.54	1.48	27.06	41.48	26.76	461
19.14	8.58	10.57	18.53	70.4	77.8	88.26	2.79	1.36	1.32	26.36	35.72	26.17	462
15.71	10.33	5.38	14.90	71.2	78.8	75.00	2.42	1.18	1.15	26.30	34.68	26.20	463
37.03	8.64	28.39	51.04	59.9	61.9	147.47	5.11	2.42	2.13	27.31	47.59	26.64	464
25.63	9.04	16.59	52.99	60.1	68.2	122.21	3.34	1.68	1.54	26.67	49.86	26.25	465
47.77	12.61	35.16	107.07	54.3	58.0	212.96	6.89	3.37	2.63	28.34	49.93	27.46	466
			89.23	54.4	57.7	197.74	6.56	3.20	2.62				467
			63.46	59.7	63.4	214.65	6.56	3.20	2.81				468
			48.84	62.7	67.3	165.40	5.29	2.58	2.38				469
			36.18	65.6	70.6	115.58	3.59	1.75	1.65				470
			30.53	67.1	72.1	99.76	2.97	1.45	1.39				471
			78.60	56.4	59.4	165.09	5.30	2.60	2.18				472
42.94	7.69	35.25	68.40	59.1	62.4	181.15	5.78	2.82	2.52	27.00	45.43	26.20	473
39.98	7.63	32.35	64.90	60.1	63.2	165.02	5.29	2.59	2.34	26.99	43.21	26.28	474
			43.80	62.8	67.0	166.74	5.00	2.45	2.24				475
27.31	8.44	18.87	34.43	63.2	67.6	115.22	3.64	1.79	1.67	27.70	46.00	27.26	476
			24.03	66.2	71.3	96.92	2.86	1.40	1.37				477
			20.00	67.7	72.8	89.55	2.68	1.30	1.28				478
			57.00	63.3	69.4	84.37	2.73	1.33	1.23				479
			48.00	65.4	71.6	87.81	2.90	1.41	1.33				480
			47.00	65.6	72.2	87.32	3.00	1.46	1.38				481
			30.00	67.1	73.7	83.24	2.76	1.35	1.29				482
			27.00	67.8	74.4	80.51	2.61	1.27	1.22				483
			106.00	53.8	56.6	205.25	6.46	3.15	2.56				484
			73.00	59.3	62.8	204.09	6.46	3.15	2.73				485
43.54	6.84	36.70	55.58	63.3	67.1	198.26	6.28	3.07	2.75	28.50	49.11	27.60	486
43.96	6.36	37.59	47.68	63.9	67.7	200.32	6.38	3.13	2.83	28.63	49.42	27.70	487
38.03	6.45	31.58	49.30	64.3	68.3	167.19	5.35	2.62	2.40	28.56	51.35	27.75	488
30.17	6.23	23.95	31.64	67.1	72.6	137.09	4.13	2.03	1.92	27.95	52.94	27.32	489
25.69	6.86	18.82	26.09	69.4	74.5	118.14	3.58	1.75	1.68	28.03	51.23	27.55	490

SERIAL NO.	REGION/ COUNTRY	YEAR	POPULATION ESTIMATED AS OF MID-YEAR (in 000's)	POPULATION DENSITY (per km²)	AGE STRUCTURE TOTAL REPRODUCTIVE VALUE (in 000's)	DEPENDENCY RATIO YOUTH < 15 (x 100)	DEPENDENCY RATIO OLD AGE ≥ 65 (x 100)	DEPARTURE FROM STABILITY (Percent)	VITAL CRUDE RATES (Both Sexes) BIRTH (x 1000)	VITAL CRUDE RATES (Both Sexes) DEATH (x 1000)	STANDARDIZED RATES Standard: USA 1960 BIRTH (x 1000)	STANDARDIZED RATES Standard: USA 1960 DEATH (x 1000)
	1	2	3	4	5	6	7	8	9	10	11	12
491	NORTHERN	1950	166075	8		41.9	12.5		24.58	9.43		
492	AMERICA	1960	198663	9		52.4	15.2		22.18	9.25		
493		1970	226480	11		45.9	15.5		15.75	9.04		
494		1980	251808	12		34.0	16.8		15.62	8.46		
495		1985	264777	12		32.6	17.7		14.99	8.65		
496	Canada	1951	13657	1	4469	48.6	12.6	4.5	27.24	8.94	22.93	10.06
497		1961	17769	2	6019	57.6	13.1	5.1	25.76	7.77	24.77	8.67
498		1963	18402	2	6167	57.4	13.1	4.0	24.38	7.82	23.84	8.65
499		1964	18771	2	6182	56.7	13.0	3.7	23.35	7.61	22.86	8.41
500		1965	19100	2	5995	55.8	13.0	5.1	21.14	7.63	20.64	8.44
501		1967	19933	2	5685	53.3	12.9	9.6	18.11	7.43	16.84	8.23
502		1970	21298	2	5709	49.1	12.9	12.6	17.47	7.32	15.27	7.90
503		1975	22698	2	5184	40.7	13.1	19.5	15.83	7.37	12.26	7.53
504		1980	24043	2	4964	34.0	14.1	21.8	15.42	7.13	11.22	6.77
505		1985	25358	3	4837	31.6	15.3	22.0	14.82	7.15	10.75	6.20
506	Greenland	1960	32	.015	18	82.5	3.9	5.8	48.85	7.85	44.65	14.89
507		1970	46	.021	17	81.8	5.0	14.3	24.87	6.15	23.22	13.26
508		1975	50	.023	15	61.9	5.2	19.3	17.51	6.31	15.23	13.12
509		1980	50	.023	14	43.7	5.3	20.4	20.47	7.63	15.66	12.78
510		1985	53	.024	13	34.5	5.1	20.2	21.44	8.20	14.64	13.07
511	United States	1950	151345	16	40655	41.7	12.6	6.0	23.93	9.64	20.08	10.45
512	of America	1955	164301	18	47890	48.1	13.9	9.8	25.16	9.28	23.37	9.68
513		1960	179990	19	53999	52.3	15.5	9.7	23.65	9.39	23.65	9.39
514		1962	185888	20	55621	52.7	15.7	8.3	22.66	9.45	22.74	9.38
515		1963	188656	20	55738	52.4	15.6	6.7	21.95	9.61	21.82	9.54
516		1964	191369	20	56001	52.2	15.7	5.3	21.27	9.40	21.00	9.29
517		1965	193818	21	54607	51.8	15.7	4.3	19.61	9.43	19.20	9.30
518		1966	195857	21	53196	51.2	15.7	5.2	18.41	9.51	17.77	9.33
519		1967	197863	21	52115	50.4	15.8	6.2	17.79	9.36	16.71	9.12
520		1970	203665	22	51596	46.2	16.0	6.6	18.32	9.43	16.05	8.88
521		1975	213032	23	44067	39.1	16.4	18.0	14.76	8.89	11.70	7.98
522		1980	226951	24	45307	34.3	17.1	16.7	15.92	8.77	11.93	7.36
523		1985	238742	25	45589	32.8	18.0	16.1	15.75	8.74	12.00	6.89
524	ASIA	1950	1374552	50		61.9	6.7		42.89	24.09		
525		1960	1666801	60		70.1	7.3		39.52	17.72		
526		1970	2101102	76		72.4	7.2		34.81	12.39		
527		1980	2582836	94		64.9	7.6		28.43	9.82		
528		1985	2834226	103		57.6	7.7		27.59	9.13		
529	EASTERN ASIA	1950	671392	57		55.6	7.3		40.83	23.31		
530		1960	791292	67		66.6	8.5		35.48	15.70		
531		1970	986255	84		66.7	8.0		29.40	8.48		
532		1980	1176115	100		56.6	8.4		18.66	6.59		
533		1985	1249474	106		44.6	8.8		19.74	6.65		
534	SOUTHEASTERN	1950	182033	40		68.9	6.5		44.05	24.38		
535	ASIA	1960	224605	50		74.9	6.0		42.53	18.83		
536		1970	286709	64		81.4	6.1		37.36	14.44		
537		1980	360063	80		73.5	6.6		32.86	11.00		
538		1985	400558	89		67.6	6.4		28.91	9.68		
539	SOUTHERN ASIA	1950	478695	71		67.9	6.0		44.92	25.13		
540		1960	595049	88		72.4	6.2		43.21	19.96		
541		1970	754468	111		76.1	6.5		40.38	16.57		
542		1980	948413	140		71.5	6.8		37.64	13.28		
543		1985	1070282	158		69.6	6.9		35.19	11.81		
544	WESTERN ASIA	1950	42432	9		71.1	6.4		47.46	23.39		
545		1960	55856	12		77.9	6.5		44.65	17.80		
546		1970	73670	16		80.6	7.5		39.69	13.44		
547		1980	98244	22		78.0	7.5		36.63	9.55		
548		1985	113913	25		73.9	6.7		35.35	8.43		
549	Afghanistan	1950	8958	14		89.8	3.7		48.28	31.66		
550		1960	10775	17		76.5	3.8		52.62	29.93		
551		1970	13623	21		78.4	4.0		51.56	26.00		
552		1980	16063	25		78.9	4.7		48.87	23.00		
553		1985	14519	22		75.3	4.8		49.27	23.04		

RATES			MORTALITY			FERTILITY							
INTRINSIC RATES (Female)			INFANT MORTALITY RATE	LIFE EXPECTANCY AT BIRTH		GENERAL FERTILITY RATE	TOTAL FERTILITY RATE	GROSS REPRODUCTION RATE	NET MATERNITY FUNCTION				SERIAL NO.
BIRTH (x 1000)	DEATH (x 1000)	INCREASE (x 1000)	(x 1000)	MALE (Years)	FEMALE (Years)	(x 1000)			TOTAL (NRR)	MEAN μ	VARIANCE σ^2	GENERATION (Years)	
13	14	15	16	17	18	19	20	21	22	23	24	25	
			28.56	66.3	72.0	99.35	3.47	1.69	1.61				491
			25.32	66.9	73.5	96.01	3.34	1.63	1.57				492
			17.91	67.7	75.4	64.45	1.97	0.96	0.95				493
			11.15	71.0	78.4	59.85	1.80	0.88	0.86				494
			9.55	72.1	79.1	56.92	1.81	0.88	0.87				495
25.15	8.16	16.98	38.76	66.2	70.8	109.98	3.53	1.71	1.61	28.41	41.40	28.06	496
27.58	6.32	21.26	27.28	68.4	74.3	111.00	3.83	1.86	1.79	27.79	37.47	27.38	497
26.54	6.57	19.97	25.90	68.5	74.4	105.33	3.68	1.79	1.73	27.76	36.61	27.39	498
25.23	6.84	18.39	24.55	68.6	75.0	100.65	3.53	1.72	1.66	27.80	36.60	27.45	499
22.47	7.81	14.67	22.50	68.8	75.0	90.84	3.19	1.55	1.50	27.75	37.09	27.47	500
17.52	10.12	7.40	21.81	68.9	75.5	76.29	2.60	1.27	1.22	27.46	36.61	27.32	501
15.28	11.35	3.93	18.82	69.3	76.3	72.00	2.36	1.15	1.11	27.14	35.69	27.07	502
11.04	14.84	-3.79	13.66	69.8	77.3	62.13	1.91	0.93	0.90	26.68	29.91	26.73	503
9.47	16.25	-6.78	10.44	71.4	78.8	57.95	1.75	0.85	0.83	26.92	27.65	27.01	504
8.74	16.92	-8.18	7.94	72.9	79.9	55.18	1.67	0.81	0.80	27.41	27.87	27.53	505
44.41	6.83	37.59	64.31	60.2	64.9	215.14	6.83	3.20	2.90	29.28	51.73	28.31	506
24.76	9.05	15.71	47.20	60.7	68.0	117.15	3.54	1.62	1.52	26.92	49.46	26.53	507
17.56	13.18	4.38	39.17	62.0	66.4	77.22	2.34	1.19	1.12	26.14	39.53	26.05	508
15.84	13.29	2.55	32.10	59.1	69.5	80.18	2.40	1.14	1.07	26.83	40.24	26.78	509
14.66	15.34	-0.68	24.56	61.3	66.5	78.62	2.23	1.05	0.98	26.34	40.96	26.36	510
22.57	9.01	13.56	29.67	65.3	70.9	93.33	3.08	1.50	1.43	26.55	39.15	26.29	511
26.86	6.98	19.88	29.73	66.5	72.6	102.21	3.60	1.75	1.68	26.47	36.03	26.10	512
27.31	6.56	20.75	25.92	66.9	73.4	102.13	3.65	1.78	1.71	26.37	36.60	25.99	513
26.15	6.91	19.24	25.36	66.9	73.5	97.30	3.51	1.71	1.65	26.42	34.26	26.07	514
24.85	7.36	17.50	25.27	66.7	73.4	94.18	3.37	1.64	1.58	26.48	34.23	26.17	515
23.77	7.67	16.10	24.64	66.9	73.7	91.18	3.24	1.58	1.53	26.53	34.39	26.25	516
21.29	8.64	12.65	24.08	66.9	73.8	83.92	2.96	1.45	1.39	26.52	35.12	26.29	517
19.30	9.60	9.70	23.72	66.8	73.9	79.28	2.74	1.34	1.29	26.35	35.19	26.17	518
17.75	10.36	7.38	22.45	67.0	74.2	76.10	2.57	1.25	1.21	26.28	34.85	26.15	519
16.72	10.82	5.90	20.02	67.1	74.8	76.44	2.47	1.20	1.17	26.00	34.60	25.90	520
10.07	16.21	-6.15	16.07	68.7	76.6	59.12	1.80	0.88	0.85	25.75	33.55	25.85	521
10.36	15.50	-5.14	12.61	70.0	77.7	61.60	1.84	0.89	0.87	25.97	32.78	26.06	522
10.40	15.21	-4.81	10.65	71.3	78.4	59.95	1.84	0.90	0.88	26.31	34.38	26.39	523
			180.63	40.5	41.8	181.83	5.92	2.88	1.78				524
			132.76	47.6	48.4	174.29	5.71	2.78	1.95				525
			98.94	55.5	56.1	153.08	5.06	2.46	1.94				526
			83.43	58.6	60.0	117.84	3.72	1.81	1.49				527
			72.93	60.9	62.6	110.36	3.45	1.68	1.43				528
			181.14	41.2	44.3	172.15	5.72	2.78	1.79				529
			112.34	50.0	52.0	157.53	5.35	2.60	1.94				530
			56.93	62.9	64.8	128.78	4.40	2.14	1.90				531
			36.46	67.1	69.8	74.37	2.33	1.13	1.05				532
			30.47	68.3	71.6	74.02	2.31	1.12	1.06				533
			151.86	40.1	42.3	182.41	6.00	2.92	1.85				534
			121.16	45.4	48.1	182.52	5.89	2.87	2.03				535
			100.44	50.0	53.2	160.46	5.26	2.56	1.96				536
			78.29	55.5	58.9	134.22	4.28	2.08	1.72				537
			67.83	57.9	61.4	114.36	3.58	1.74	1.48				538
			188.54	39.6	38.0	193.21	6.11	2.98	1.69				539
			156.79	45.7	44.2	190.28	6.03	2.94	1.90				540
			136.29	50.4	48.7	179.79	5.76	2.81	1.95				541
			113.14	54.5	54.4	163.59	5.14	2.51	1.90				542
			101.83	56.9	57.0	151.36	4.72	2.30	1.81				543
			203.03	42.2	44.7	205.75	6.79	3.31	2.17				544
			156.88	49.1	51.7	204.00	6.48	3.16	2.26				545
			117.98	54.8	58.0	178.13	5.90	2.88	2.21				546
			83.14	59.5	62.6	163.26	5.21	2.54	2.18				547
			70.43	61.6	64.7	155.76	4.92	2.40	2.11				548
			227.13	31.3	31.8	213.72	6.70	3.25	1.55				549
			210.87	34.0	34.0	222.60	7.01	3.40	1.74				550
			193.77	38.0	38.0	227.92	7.14	3.47	1.95				551
			183.00	40.0	41.0	214.43	6.90	3.35	2.00				552
			172.10	41.0	42.0	215.20	6.90	3.35	2.05				553

SERIAL NO.	REGION/ COUNTRY	YEAR	POPULATION ESTIMATED AS OF MID-YEAR (in 000's)	DENSITY (per km²)	AGE STRUCTURE TOTAL REPRODUCTIVE VALUE (in 000's)	DEPENDENCY RATIO YOUTH < 15 (x 100)	OLD AGE ≥ 65 (x 100)	DEPARTURE FROM STABILITY (Percent)	VITAL CRUDE RATES (Both Sexes) BIRTH (x 1000)	DEATH (x 1000)	STANDARDIZED RATES Standard: USA 1960 BIRTH (x 1000)	DEATH (x 1000)
	1	2	3	4	5	6	7	8	9	10	11	12
554	Bahrain	1950	116	186		77.2	5.2		45.10	16.40		
555		1960	156	251		79.5	5.0		47.00	13.80		
556		1970	220	353		89.2	4.8		36.00	7.50		
557		1980	347	558		54.8	3.3		30.98	4.50		
558		1985	430	691		51.5	3.0		28.16	3.90		
559	Bangladesh	1950	41783	290		64.0	6.2		47.00	24.24		
560		1960	51419	357		74.1	6.7		46.69	22.00		
561		1970	66671	463		88.9	6.9		48.49	20.82		
562		1980	88219	613		91.6	6.8		44.78	17.47		
563		1985	101147	702		89.4	6.0		42.16	15.50		
564	Bhutan	1950	734	16		70.3	6.3		43.46	27.24		
565		1960	868	18		71.0	5.7		42.22	24.12		
566		1970	1045	22		71.2	5.6		41.00	21.32		
567		1980	1245	26		71.6	5.7		39.00	18.14		
568		1985	1362	29		70.7	5.8		38.27	16.83		
569	Burma	1950	17832	26		64.1	5.5		42.22	23.72		
570		1960	21746	32		74.2	6.2		40.60	19.50		
571		1970	27102	40		74.8	6.8		37.63	14.24		
572		1980	33821	50		70.3	7.1		34.30	11.03		
573		1985	37544	55		68.9	6.7		30.60	9.74		
574	China	1950	554760	58		54.1	7.2		43.60	25.00		
575		1960	657492	69		69.1	8.6		37.80	17.10		
576		1970	830675	87		71.0	7.7		30.60	8.70		
577		1981	987166	103	328391	56.5	7.9	16.9	20.96	6.36	17.00	10.58
578		1985	1059522	110		45.8	8.1		20.51	6.66		
579	Republic of	1956	9368	260	5359	82.8	4.6	4.0	44.20	7.91	42.16	14.72
580	China	1960	10612	295	5650	86.1	4.7	3.8	39.62	6.96	37.66	13.45
581	(Taiwan)	1962	11330	315	5805	89.0	4.8	3.7	37.37	6.44	35.58	12.94
582		1963	11698	325	5910	89.0	4.9	4.2	36.27	6.13	34.66	12.51
583		1964	12070	336	5912	88.1	5.0	4.8	34.54	5.74	32.90	11.87
584		1965	12443	346	5888	86.5	5.0	5.3	32.68	5.46	31.06	11.33
585		1966	13021	362	6029	81.4	4.9	4.5	31.88	5.36	30.95	11.37
586		1970	14505	403	6000	70.3	5.0	7.9	27.16	4.90	25.63	10.56
587		1975	16001	445	5407	58.8	5.6	16.6	22.98	4.69	18.06	9.54
588		1980	17642	491	5304	51.1	6.6	19.5	23.35	4.76	15.96	8.43
589		1985	19135	532	4715	45.8	7.6	28.7	17.92	4.80	11.94	7.68
590	Cyprus	1950	494	53		58.0	10.1		27.40	10.50		
591		1960	573	62		63.9	10.3		25.20	10.50		
592		1970	615	66		52.8	17.1		18.00	9.70		
593		1980	627	68	151	37.5	15.0	11.5	20.40	9.27	14.75	8.89
594		1985	665	72	156	39.5	16.6	8.9	19.53	8.50	15.30	7.43
595	East Timor	1950	433	29		72.2	6.0		47.43	34.50		
596		1960	501	34		74.1	4.7		46.76	28.25		
597		1970	605	41		75.8	4.9		44.31	23.02		
598		1980	581	39		54.0	3.7		47.96	22.99		
599		1985	659	44		55.3	4.2		43.84	21.45		
600	Hong Kong	1950	1974	1889		45.2	3.7		37.70	8.90		
601		1961	3161	3025	1326	72.2	5.0	9.6	34.40	5.93	32.26	11.22
602		1966	3732	3571	1529	71.8	5.8	7.3	25.84	5.01	28.85	10.74
603		1970	3959	3789	1455	63.4	7.4	9.6	19.99	5.24	22.57	8.91
604		1975	4462	4270	1394	49.7	8.4	14.6	17.88	4.84	17.13	7.22
605		1980	5024	4808	1309	37.4	9.5	21.9	16.98	4.98	13.26	6.72
606		1985	5456	5221		33.3	10.9		15.91	5.82		
607	India	1950	357561	109		67.4	5.8		44.08	24.97		
608		1960	442346	135		70.0	6.0		41.96	19.43		
609		1970	554911	169		72.3	6.5		38.19	15.80		
610		1980	688856	210		67.2	7.1		34.70	12.66		
611		1985	769183	234		64.8	7.3		32.05	11.29		
612	Indonesia	1950	79538	42		68.9	7.0		43.02	26.13		
613		1960	96194	51		71.1	5.9		42.85	21.51		
614		1970	120280	63		77.4	5.6		38.20	17.33		
615		1980	150958	79		73.7	6.0		32.19	12.65		
616		1985	166464	87		66.8	6.2		27.35	11.15		

RATES			MORTALITY			FERTILITY							
INTRINSIC RATES (Female)			INFANT MORTALITY RATE	LIFE EXPECTANCY AT BIRTH		GENERAL FERTILITY RATE	TOTAL FERTILITY RATE	GROSS REPRODUCTION RATE	NET MATERNITY FUNCTION				SERIAL NO.
BIRTH (x 1000)	DEATH (x 1000)	INCREASE (x 1000)	(x 1000)	MALE (Years)	FEMALE (Years)	(x 1000)			TOTAL (NRR)	MEAN μ	VARIANCE σ^2	GENERATION (Years)	
13	14	15	16	17	18	19	20	21	22	23	24	25	
			175.00	49.6	52.5	217.68	6.97	3.40	2.49				554
			110.00	55.3	58.8	227.44	7.18	3.50	2.81				555
			55.00	61.7	65.4	178.45	5.95	2.90	2.52				556
			31.59	67.1	71.4	146.98	4.63	2.26	2.14				557
			26.17	68.6	72.9	133.48	4.14	2.02	1.93				558
			179.50	38.3	34.9	212.86	6.66	3.25	1.94				559
			150.00	41.7	39.5	221.26	6.68	3.26	2.12				560
			140.00	45.6	44.1	233.54	7.02	3.42	2.27				561
			128.20	49.1	48.1	208.56	6.15	3.00	2.11				562
			119.17	51.1	50.4	189.67	5.54	2.70	1.95				563
			197.10	37.0	35.5	179.93	6.02	2.94	1.57				564
			182.10	39.8	38.3	176.90	5.92	2.89	1.65				565
			152.90	43.0	41.5	174.42	5.74	2.80	1.70				566
			138.70	46.6	45.1	168.09	5.54	2.70	1.78				567
			128.20	48.6	47.1	165.03	5.54	2.70	1.84				568
			183.00	38.7	41.4	173.59	5.64	2.75	1.70				569
			140.00	43.6	46.5	176.05	5.95	2.90	1.98				570
			100.00	51.0	54.1	163.70	5.43	2.65	2.05				571
			80.00	55.8	59.3	143.19	4.61	2.25	1.87				572
			70.23	58.3	61.8	123.94	4.02	1.96	1.68				573
			195.00	39.3	42.3	186.44	6.24	3.03	1.89				574
			120.71	48.7	50.4	173.65	5.93	2.88	2.10				575
			61.10	62.5	63.9	138.08	4.76	2.31	2.04				576
18.09	11.93	6.16	32.97	66.3	69.2	85.67	2.68	1.29	1.19	28.06	26.64	27.98	577
			32.45	68.0	70.9	76.54	2.37	1.15	1.08				578
41.94	6.94	34.99	33.11	60.1	64.8	193.98	6.45	3.14	2.80	30.36	47.61	29.53	579
38.93	6.72	32.21	31.50	61.9	66.4	180.22	5.79	2.81	2.54	29.73	43.76	29.03	580
37.59	6.53	31.06	31.27	62.8	67.4	174.48	5.49	2.66	2.44	29.30	39.53	28.68	581
36.85	6.37	30.49	28.43	63.5	68.0	169.89	5.35	2.59	2.39	29.25	38.82	48.64	582
35.47	6.18	29.29	25.53	64.1	69.0	161.56	5.10	2.47	2.30	28.96	36.73	28.41	583
34.13	6.15	27.98	23.66	64.8	69.7	151.86	4.83	2.34	2.19	28.52	34.67	28.02	584
34.48	6.00	28.48	20.19	65.2	69.8	148.59	4.82	2.34	2.20	28.23	33.83	27.73	585
29.19	6.44	22.75	15.65	66.6	71.5	120.29	4.00	1.94	1.86	27.58	31.47	27.22	586
20.10	9.26	10.84	12.51	68.2	73.3	94.13	2.83	1.38	1.33	·26.62	27.42	26.47	587
17.12	10.56	6.56	10.09	69.6	74.6	91.10	2.51	1.22	1.19	26.17	22.67	26.09	588
11.07	15.30	-4.23	6.99	71.1	76.0	67.96	1.88	0.91	0.89	26.42	20.97	26.46	589
			53.28	65.1	69.0	109.69	3.69	1.79	1.67				590
			29.01	67.5	71.0	105.62	3.42	1.66	1.57				591
			28.50	70.0	72.9	72.69	2.23	1.08	1.04				592
14.72	12.29	2.43	19.15	70.9	74.5	77.25	2.30	1.09	1.07	26.73	28.71	26.69	593
15.16	11.34	3.81	12.01	73.0	76.4	76.11	2.38	1.13	1.11	26.90	29.35	26.85	594
			264.30	29.6	30.4	202.89	6.44	3.14	1.49				595
			220.63	34.4	35.6	198.84	6.37	3.11	1.69				596
			183.25	39.2	40.7	189.78	6.15	3.00	1.83				597
			183.25	39.2	40.7	180.89	5.84	2.85	1.74				598
			165.59	41.7	43.4	168.41	5.41	2.64	1.70				599
			78.54	57.2	64.9	140.26	4.43	2.15	1.90				600
34.13	6.55	27.58	37.72	63.0	70.3	155.32	4.97	2.40	2.21	29.36	38.82	28.81	601
31.20	5.80	25.41	23.83	65.9	72.7	116.91	4.46	2.16	2.07	29.09	34.43	28.63	602
23.94	7.19	16.75	19.20	67.3	75.3	88.85	3.49	1.69	1.63	29.34	35.61	29.04	603
17.22	9.67	7.55	14.94	70.9	77.7	74.95	2.66	1.28	1.24	28.79	32.54	28.67	604
12.25	13.13	-0.88	11.21	72.1	78.7	66.51	2.06	1.00	0.98	28.66	28.02	28.68	605
			8.27	73.4	79.1	59.47	1.70	0.82	0.81				606
			190.00	39.4	38.0	187.15	5.97	2.91	1.63				607
			157.00	46.2	44.7	181.56	5.81	2.83	1.82				608
			135.00	51.2	49.3	167.39	5.43	2.65	1.85				609
			110.25	55.6	55.2	148.90	4.75	2.32	1.78				610
			98.79	57.8	57.9	136.01	4.31	2.10	1.67				611
			160.00	36.9	38.1	176.05	5.49	2.68	1.56				612
			133.00	41.7	43.4	178.05	5.42	2.64	1.72				613
			114.00	46.4	48.7	160.85	5.10	2.49	1.76				614
			95.00	52.2	54.9	131.39	4.10	2.00	1.56				615
			84.00	54.6	57.4	107.40	3.30	1.61	1.30				616

SERIAL NO.	REGION/ COUNTRY	YEAR	POPULATION ESTIMATED AS OF MID-YEAR (in 000's)	DENSITY (per km²)	AGE STRUCTURE TOTAL REPRODUCTIVE VALUE (in 000's)	DEPENDENCY RATIO YOUTH < 15 (x 100)	OLD AGE ≥ 65 (x 100)	DEPARTURE FROM STABILITY (Percent)	VITAL CRUDE RATES (Both Sexes) BIRTH (x 1000)	DEATH (x 1000)	STANDARDIZED RATES Standard: USA 1960 BIRTH (x 1000)	DEATH (x 1000)
			3	4	5	6	7	8	9	10	11	12
617	Iraq	1950	5158	12		88.7	5.3		49.40	21.90		
618		1960	6847	16		89.7	4.7		49.30	18.80		
619		1970	9356	22		91.5	4.8		47.40	14.60		
620		1980	13291	31		93.3	5.1		44.44	8.71		
621		1985	15898	37		93.1	5.3		42.56	7.85		
622	Iran	1950	14206	9		79.7	2.3		48.00	24.50		
623		1960	20301	12		92.6	4.1		46.50	19.60		
624		1970	28397	17		91.2	6.1		44.10	14.50		
625		1980	38900	24		85.1	6.4		41.90	9.70		
626		1985	47624	29		80.6	6.1		42.36	7.96		
627	Israel	1951	1304	63	454	46.3	6.1	9.3	31.89	6.44	25.56	10.15
628	(Jewish	1954	1505	72	504	51.6	7.1	7.6	28.30	6.18	24.10	9.85
629	Population)	1957	1715	83	569	56.7	7.5	6.7	25.48	6.01	22.94	9.57
630		1960	1885	91	624	57.9	8.2	6.7	23.86	5.52	22.60	8.32
631		1963	2115	102	688	55.6	9.1	5.9	21.93	6.02	21.52	8.71
632		1965	2269	109	755	53.4	9.9	6.3	22.61	6.38	22.32	8.52
633		1966	2323	112	768	51.9	10.4	6.0	22.38	6.33	21.85	8.23
634		1967	2363	114	761	50.5	10.6	5.7	21.45	6.63	20.62	8.49
635	Israel	1970	2974		1116	54.7	11.0	5.6	27.18	6.85	25.47	8.69
636	(incl. Jewish	1975	3455		1246	55.3	13.1	4.7	27.68	7.12	23.87	8.30
637	pop. in occu-	1980	3922		1277	57.1	14.8	6.3	24.05	6.70	20.05	7.45
638	pied territ.)	1985	4233		1372	55.5	15.0	5.2	23.48	6.64	20.13	6.87
639	Japan	1951	84260	226	32647	58.7	8.2	7.3	25.64	9.93	21.32	14.33
640		1954	87982	236	28985	55.8	8.5	15.1	20.34	8.29	16.15	12.58
641		1957	90860	244	26405	51.0	8.6	19.1	17.92	7.93	13.59	11.99
642		1960	93224	250	24950	47.1	8.9	19.8	17.24	7.48	12.77	10.98
643		1962	94958	255	24237	44.2	9.0	19.8	17.05	7.48	12.40	10.88
644		1963	95912	258	24333	42.0	9.1	19.2	17.30	6.99	12.56	9.96
645		1964	96916	260	24503	39.4	9.2	17.9	17.71	6.94	12.84	9.73
646		1965	98003	263	25183	38.0	9.2	15.3	18.61	7.15	13.54	9.97
647		1970	104360	280	24739	34.9	10.3	15.2	18.53	6.83	13.13	8.74
648		1975	111640	300	23561	35.9	11.7	16.4	17.03	6.29	12.19	7.34
649		1980	116703	313	22223	35.0	13.4	18.6	13.51	6.19	10.98	6.38
650		1985	120754	320		31.6	15.1		11.41	6.98		
651	Jordan	1950	1237	13		92.4	9.8		46.70	26.00		
652		1960	1695	17		86.2	7.9		52.50	22.00		
653		1970	2299	24		89.9	6.1		50.00	14.40		
654		1980	2923	30		104.1	6.6		44.19	7.91		
655		1985	3506	36		97.7	5.6		45.91	6.62		
656	Kampuchea	1950	4346	24		76.7	4.9		45.35	23.82		
657		1960	5433	30		77.5	4.9		44.87	20.38		
658		1970	6938	38		80.1	5.2		39.91	22.54		
659		1980	6400	35		51.0	3.9		45.50	19.65		
660		1985	7284	40		50.2	4.1		41.39	16.62		
661	Korea,	1950	9740	81		75.3	5.5		37.00	32.00		
662	Democratic	1960	10526	87		82.5	6.3		39.50	12.20		
663	People's	1970	13892	115		83.4	6.6		35.71	9.36		
664	Republic	1980	18025	150		71.8	6.3		30.54	5.97		
665	(North)	1985	20385	169		67.0	6.2		28.94	5.37		
666	Korea,	1950	20357	207		75.3	5.5		37.00	32.00		
667	Republic of	1960	25003	254		76.6	6.1		39.57	12.52		
668	(South)	1970	31923	324		77.0	6.0		28.84	8.85		
669		1980	38124	387		54.7	6.1		21.28	6.25		
670		1985	41056	417		45.6	6.5		18.82	6.17		
671	Kuwait	1950	152	9		59.3	4.8		45.20	11.20		
672		1960	278	16		55.4	3.6		44.50	9.00		
673		1970	744	42	403	78.6	3.1	7.5	45.46	5.02	44.06	9.17
674		1975	1002	56	525	81.9	2.9	6.5	43.36	4.77	39.61	10.67
675		1980	1366	77	645	68.7	2.2	6.9	37.41	3.61	35.64	10.13
676		1985	1710	96		68.2	2.2		32.34	2.78		
677	Laos	1950	1755	7		75.7	5.1		45.73	25.26		
678		1960	2177	9		75.7	4.4		44.87	22.73		
679		1970	2713	11		76.8	4.6		44.40	22.67		
680		1980	3205	14		76.2	5.1		44.72	18.67		
681		1985	3594	15		78.3	5.3		41.28	16.42		

RATES			MORTALITY			FERTILITY							
INTRINSIC RATES (Female)			INFANT MORTALITY RATE (x 1000)	LIFE EXPECTANCY AT BIRTH		GENERAL FERTILITY RATE (x 1000)	TOTAL FERTI-LITY RATE	GROSS REPRO-DUCTION RATE	NET MATERNITY FUNCTION				SERIAL NO.
BIRTH (x 1000)	DEATH (x 1000)	INCREASE (x 1000)		MALE (Years)	FEMALE (Years)				TOTAL (NRR)	MEAN μ	VARIANCE σ^2	GENER-ATION (Years)	
13	14	15	16	17	18	19	20	21	22	23	24	25	
			165.00	43.1	44.9	224.27	7.18	3.50	2.20				617
			130.00	49.1	50.9	224.55	7.18	3.50	2.42				618
			96.00	56.1	57.9	216.80	7.11	3.47	2.61				619
			77.03	61.5	63.3	205.89	6.66	3.25	2.77				620
			68.63	63.0	64.8	196.57	6.36	3.10	2.69				621
			190.00	46.1	46.1	210.77	7.13	3.48	2.23				622
			163.00	50.9	50.6	221.59	7.26	3.54	2.46				623
			122.00	56.2	55.5	203.64	6.54	3.19	2.41				624
			78.00	59.4	63.0	182.56	5.64	2.75	2.31				625
			63.00	65.0	65.5	182.51	5.64	2.75	2.38				626
28.28	7.78	20.50	46.09	66.6	69.6	118.73	3.92	1.90	1.76	27.92	40.98	27.49	627
27.07	7.48	19.59	35.13	68.0	70.8	110.75	3.71	1.80	1.70	27.53	38.93	27.14	628
25.70	7.65	18.04	32.76	68.5	71.5	104.86	3.54	1.72	1.63	27.60	36.87	27.25	629
25.30	7.28	18.02	27.90	70.5	73.3	102.29	3.50	1.71	1.64	27.79	35.74	27.46	630
23.84	7.77	16.08	22.91	70.7	72.8	94.12	3.34	1.61	1.56	27.86	33.31	27.58	631
24.83	7.21	17.63	22.78	71.0	73.7	96.81	3.47	1.68	1.63	27.93	32.51	27.64	632
24.30	7.27	17.03	21.60	71.3	74.3	94.99	3.39	1.66	1.60	27.94	32.33	27.65	633
22.62	7.92	14.69	20.76	70.6	74.1	89.93	3.20	1.55	1.51	28.10	32.04	27.85	634
27.82	6.30	21.52	21.83	70.0	73.3	114.40	3.93	1.90	1.84	28.70	37.31	28.30	635
26.36	6.60	19.76	22.94	70.3	74.1	117.32	3.68	1.80	1.73	28.26	37.09	27.90	636
21.66	7.72	13.94	15.12	72.3	76.0	103.04	3.10	1.51	1.47	28.07	35.74	27.82	637
21.59	7.50	14.09	11.91	73.5	77.0	99.55	3.12	1.52	1.49	28.52	33.69	28.28	638
23.34	11.99	11.35	55.95	59.4	62.8	99.97	3.30	1.60	1.39	29.42	31.27	29.23	639
17.06	13.60	3.46	44.56	62.5	66.5	78.44	2.51	1.22	1.10	28.98	27.44	28.93	640
13.83	15.37	-1.54	38.36	63.8	68.2	67.35	2.13	1.03	0.96	28.43	23.41	28.45	641
12.71	15.60	-2.89	31.01	65.5	70.3	63.76	2.01	0.98	0.92	27.88	19.69	27.91	642
12.23	15.77	-3.54	26.44	66.3	71.2	62.30	1.96	0.95	0.91	27.74	17.56	27.77	643
12.38	15.15	-2.77	23.79	67.3	72.4	62.45	1.98	0.96	0.93	27.78	16.96	27.80	644
12.74	14.61	-1.87	20.36	67.7	72.9	63.00	2.03	0.99	0.95	27.76	16.53	27.78	645
13.85	13.58	0.27	18.50	67.8	73.0	65.59	2.14	1.04	1.01	27.68	16.47	27.68	646
12.89	13.78	-0.89	13.15	69.5	74.9	65.10	2.07	1.00	0.98	27.83	18.14	27.84	647
11.44	14.51	-3.07	10.05	71.9	77.1	62.65	1.93	0.94	0.92	27.38	17.58	27.40	648
9.52	16.17	-6.65	7.51	73.5	79.0	51.65	1.74	0.84	0.83	27.77	16.52	27.83	649
			5.00	75.4	81.1	44.76	1.70	0.83	0.82				650
			160.00	42.2	44.3	227.78	7.38	3.60	2.28				651
			125.00	46.9	49.5	241.14	8.00	3.90	2.79				652
			82.00	54.9	58.3	234.40	7.79	3.80	3.11				653
			54.09	61.9	65.5	215.81	7.28	3.55	3.18				654
			44.42	64.2	67.8	220.30	7.18	3.50	3.21				655
			165.05	38.1	40.8	191.46	6.29	3.07	1.85				656
			139.53	42.0	44.9	191.28	6.29	3.07	2.01				657
			180.85	39.0	41.7	169.65	5.54	2.70	1.68				658
			159.94	42.0	44.9	160.74	5.13	2.50	1.65				659
			129.73	47.0	49.9	149.95	4.72	2.30	1.66				660
			115.00	46.0	49.0	156.30	5.18	2.51	1.78				661
			70.00	53.6	56.9	170.68	5.60	2.72	2.19				662
			46.60	59.2	64.0	152.49	5.24	2.54	2.20				663
			29.66	64.6	71.0	123.12	4.02	1.95	1.83				664
			24.48	66.2	72.7	114.53	3.61	1.75	1.67				665
			115.00	46.0	49.0	154.50	5.18	2.51	1.79				666
			70.00	53.6	56.9	170.26	5.40	2.62	2.11				667
			46.60	59.2	64.0	120.15	4.11	1.99	1.73				668
			29.66	64.6	71.0	79.33	2.40	1.17	1.10				669
			24.78	66.2	72.5	67.69	2.00	0.97	0.93				670
			125.00	54.1	57.5	243.79	7.28	3.55	2.93				671
			77.00	59.1	62.5	252.41	7.38	3.60	3.15				672
45.48	5.36	40.12	41.25	66.6	71.6	234.59	6.71	3.31	3.03	28.73	48.23	27.76	673
42.39	5.02	37.38	39.60	66.2	70.3	207.90	6.06	2.97	2.78	28.28	47.24	27.40	674
38.15	4.69	33.46	27.91	67.8	72.1	181.52	5.46	2.69	2.56	28.95	47.04	28.17	675
			19.14	70.7	75.0	154.62	4.82	2.35	2.28				676
			180.14	36.5	39.2	192.86	6.15	3.00	1.77				677
			149.97	39.1	41.8	191.29	6.15	3.00	1.87				678
			144.98	39.1	41.8	189.70	6.15	3.00	1.87				679
			122.50	44.5	47.5	191.89	6.15	3.00	2.09				680
			109.99	47.0	50.0	178.16	5.74	2.80	2.03				681

SERIAL NO.	REGION/ COUNTRY	YEAR	POPULATION		AGE STRUCTURE				VITAL			
			ESTIMATED AS OF MID-YEAR (in 000's)	DENSITY (per km²)	TOTAL REPRODUCTIVE VALUE (in 000's)	DEPENDENCY RATIO YOUTH < 15 (x 100)	OLD AGE ≥ 65 (x 100)	DEPARTURE FROM STABILITY (Percent)	CRUDE RATES (Both Sexes) BIRTH (x 1000)	DEATH (x 1000)	STANDARDIZED RATES Standard: USA 1960 BIRTH (x 1000)	DEATH (x 1000)
	1	2	3	4	5	6	7	8	9	10	11	12
682	Lebanon	1950	1443	139		58.5	12.4		41.00	18.70		
683		1960	1857	179		76.3	10.9		42.70	13.30		
684		1970	2469	237		85.7	9.6		32.10	9.30		
685		1980	2669	257		73.6	9.9		29.29	8.80		
686		1985	2668	257		65.3	8.9		28.92	7.79		
687	Malaysia	1950	6110	19		75.7	9.4		45.19	19.89		
688	(incl. Sabah	1960	8140	25		88.2	6.6		43.19	13.28		
689	and Sarawak)	1970	10853	33		85.8	6.6		34.70	8.80		
690		1980	13763	42		69.0	6.4		29.50	6.00		
691		1985	15448	47		64.6	6.5		28.63	5.56		
692	Malaysia	1970	9147	71	4612	84.0	6.5	5.6	32.49	6.99	31.82	11.49
693	(Peninsular)	1975	10251	80	4793	75.4	6.8	8.0	30.56	6.25	27.42	10.73
694		1980	11442	89	5064	67.9	6.6	9.0	30.29	5.55	25.21	9.98
695		1985	12981	101	5653	63.8	6.7	7.6	31.34	5.27	25.27	9.42
696	Mongolia	1950	747	0.5		78.0	9.8		39.96	20.54		
697		1960	931	0.6		76.6	7.4		41.21	13.45		
698		1970	1248	0.8		82.5	6.1		41.00	9.35		
699		1980	1663	1.1		80.2	5.9		39.50	8.49		
700		1985	1908	1.2		75.5	5.9		38.90	8.02		
701	Nepal	1950	8182	58		69.5	7.9		45.50	27.01		
702		1960	9404	67		66.5	6.8		45.80	25.03		
703		1970	11488	82		74.2	5.4		47.10	21.00		
704		1980	14858	106		73.9	5.4		42.91	17.00		
705		1985	16915	120		77.2	5.5		39.55	14.84		
706	Oman	1950	413	2		77.4	5.5		50.90	31.90		
707		1960	505	2		80.2	5.1		50.40	26.10		
708		1970	654	3		83.0	5.0		49.60	20.60		
709		1980	984	5		82.5	4.9		47.67	14.58		
710		1985	1242	6		83.3	4.7		46.00	12.69		
711	Pakistan	1950	39513	50		66.9	9.4		49.49	28.51		
712		1960	49955	63		84.3	8.0		48.38	21.85		
713		1970	65706	83		91.6	6.3		47.50	18.34		
714		1980	85299	107		84.1	5.5		50.33	14.35		
715		1985	103241	130		84.9	5.3		46.95	12.56		
716	Philippines	1950	20988	70		82.5	6.8		49.29	19.50		
717		1960	27561	92		85.2	5.8		43.55	13.06		
718		1970	37540	125		87.7	5.2		36.90	10.48		
719		1980	48317	161		77.1	6.2		35.62	8.54		
720		1985	55120	184		74.1	6.1		33.22	7.74		
721	Qatar	1950	25	2		77.8	6.3		46.30	22.20		
722		1960	45	4		66.8	4.6		40.80	16.70		
723		1970	111	10		59.5	2.7		31.30	11.60		
724		1980	229	21		48.6	1.7		34.59	4.55		
725		1985	299	27		52.5	2.5		30.79	4.30		
726	Saudi Arabia	1950	3201	1		76.9	6.1		49.00	25.90		
727		1960	4075	2		81.1	6.3		48.90	21.30		
728		1970	5745	3		85.0	6.1		47.60	16.90		
729		1980	9372	4		83.3	5.3		43.23	8.92		
730		1985	11595	5		85.4	5.0		42.01	7.57		
731	Singapore	1950	1022	1759		70.8	4.2		44.40	10.56		
732		1957	1450	2496	772	78.0	3.9	4.8	43.22	7.38	42.73	14.13
733		1962	1714	2950	843	88.7	4.3	4.6	34.42	5.94	35.35	15.67
734		1967	1956	3367	855	78.7	5.2	9.4	25.99	5.45	26.31	13.39
735		1970	2075	3571	800	67.1	5.8	15.3	22.14	5.16	20.05	10.76
736		1975	2263	3895	683	52.3	6.4	26.5	17.66	5.06	13.38	10.00
737		1980	2414	4155	615	39.7	6.9	30.7	17.07	5.18	11.16	9.13
738		1985	2558	4403	577	34.6	7.4	30.9	16.61	5.22	10.43	8.46
739	Sri Lanka	1950	7678	117		73.4	7.1		38.50	11.50		
740		1953	8162	124	4098	69.9	6.2	4.7	39.35	10.90	34.41	14.32
741		1960	9889	151		77.4	6.7		34.70	8.50		
742		1963	10585	161	5238	76.4	6.6	3.9	34.56	8.66	32.65	12.65
743		1970	12514	191		76.9	6.7		28.90	8.10		
744		1980	14819	226		58.4	7.2		26.87	6.33		
745		1985	16108	246		55.7	7.7		22.47	5.97		

RATES			MORTALITY			FERTILITY							
INTRINSIC RATES (Female)			INFANT MORTALITY RATE	LIFE EXPECTANCY AT BIRTH		GENERAL FERTILITY RATE	TOTAL FERTI-LITY RATE	GROSS REPRO-DUCTION RATE	NET MATERNITY FUNCTION				SERIAL NO.
BIRTH (x 1000)	DEATH (x 1000)	INCREASE (x 1000)	(x 1000)	MALE (Years)	FEMALE (Years)	(x 1000)			TOTAL (NRR)	MEAN μ	VARIANCE σ^2	GENER-ATION (Years)	
13	14	15	16	17	18	19	20	21	22	23	24	25	
			87.00	54.3	57.7	176.13	5.74	2.80	2.15				682
			62.00	58.9	62.6	200.75	6.36	3.10	2.55				683
			48.00	63.1	67.0	145.75	4.92	2.40	2.08				684
			48.00	63.1	67.0	119.92	3.79	1.85	1.69				685
			40.06	65.1	69.0	112.19	3.38	1.65	1.54				686
			98.80	47.0	50.0	202.43	6.83	3.32	2.39				687
			62.70	54.2	57.4	201.57	6.72	3.26	2.64				688
			42.40	61.4	64.7	152.36	5.15	2.50	2.22				689
			28.00	66.0	70.0	117.56	3.91	1.90	1.76				690
			24.07	67.5	71.6	111.69	3.50	1.70	1.61				691
34.11	7.14	26.97	40.87	63.2	67.7	145.62	4.88	2.38	2.17	29.43	46.91	28.80	692
29.76	7.11	22.65	33.11	65.0	69.9	128.88	4.21	2.05	1.92	29.31	44.76	28.80	693
27.28	7.17	20.11	24.04	66.7	71.5	121.37	3.88	1.88	1.79	29.30	40.66	28.89	694
27.12	6.64	20.48	17.01	67.9	72.9	122.56	3.88	1.89	1.82	29.77	38.56	29.37	695
			149.83	43.6	46.5	176.10	5.75	2.80	1.91				696
			96.84	52.9	56.2	176.65	5.72	2.79	2.22				697
			71.00	59.1	62.3	179.77	5.56	2.71	2.34				698
			53.00	60.0	64.1	168.81	5.45	2.66	2.38				699
			45.00	61.5	65.6	164.67	5.40	2.63	2.36				700
			197.10	36.8	35.8	188.56	5.64	2.75	1.37				701
			182.10	39.6	38.6	186.47	5.86	2.86	1.58				702
			152.90	44.0	42.5	201.87	6.52	3.18	1.98				703
			138.70	49.0	47.5	181.96	6.25	3.05	2.07				704
			128.20	51.5	50.3	171.16	5.95	2.90	2.07				705
			231.00	35.8	37.0	220.58	7.18	3.50	1.82				706
			207.00	40.5	42.3	221.08	7.18	3.50	2.06				707
			160.00	45.2	47.6	220.79	7.18	3.50	2.29				708
			117.20	51.0	53.7	224.40	7.18	3.50	2.63				709
			100.20	54.1	56.8	221.45	7.18	3.50	2.75				710
			190.00	40.2	37.6	223.86	6.50	3.17	1.83				711
			155.00	45.7	43.1	229.97	7.00	3.42	2.21				712
			140.00	50.0	48.0	222.67	7.00	3.42	2.40				713
			120.00	54.0	54.0	230.86	7.00	3.42	2.60				714
			108.90	56.5	56.5	217.17	6.50	3.17	2.50				715
			99.58	46.0	49.1	216.74	7.29	3.54	2.51				716
			75.89	52.9	56.2	195.80	6.61	3.21	2.55				717
			63.70	56.4	59.4	159.55	5.29	2.57	2.23				718
			50.58	60.2	63.7	147.18	4.74	2.30	2.02				719
			45.11	61.6	65.4	135.51	4.33	2.10	1.88				720
			180.00	46.7	49.3	216.42	6.97	3.40	2.13				721
			130.00	53.5	56.6	222.58	6.97	3.40	2.35				722
			57.00	60.7	64.4	214.85	6.77	3.30	2.52				723
			37.80	65.4	69.8	188.64	5.95	2.90	2.71				724
			31.26	66.9	71.8	173.77	5.64	2.75	2.62				725
			200.00	39.1	40.7	218.49	7.18	3.50	2.02				726
			160.00	44.8	47.1	222.45	7.26	3.54	2.31				727
			120.00	52.4	55.5	225.94	7.30	3.56	2.57				728
			85.00	59.2	62.7	223.13	7.28	3.55	3.08				729
			70.88	61.7	65.2	219.41	7.18	3.50	3.12				730
			66.03	58.8	62.1	193.47	6.41	3.09	2.66				731
43.61	6.22	37.39	44.49	60.2	66.5	199.54	6.55	3.17	2.90	29.34	43.33	28.52	732
37.27	5.56	31.71	27.25	63.1	68.4	169.96	5.43	2.63	2.49	29.45	42.36	28.76	733
28.97	6.78	22.19	24.77	64.5	70.4	119.82	4.06	1.98	1.89	29.17	38.88	28.72	734
21.73	8.89	12.85	20.62	65.9	72.1	93.07	3.10	1.51	1.45	29.03	37.73	28.79	735
13.18	13.85	-0.67	13.97	67.3	73.9	66.79	2.08	1.01	0.98	28.27	30.49	28.28	736
10.07	17.16	-7.09	11.74	68.9	74.3	59.33	1.74	0.84	0.82	28.25	26.92	28.34	737
8.95	18.27	-9.32	9.28	70.2	75.6	56.35	1.62	0.78	0.76	28.67	26.41	28.79	738
			90.70	57.6	55.5	176.84	5.74	2.80	2.21				739
37.47	11.83	25.64	86.70	59.0	58.2	172.33	5.28	2.58	2.06	28.69	38.68	28.17	740
			65.00	63.3	63.7	155.14	5.16	2.52	2.20				741
35.14	9.04	26.09	55.80	63.0	63.4	154.55	5.00	2.45	2.12	29.29	39.34	28.76	742
			56.00	64.0	66.0	126.73	4.00	1.95	1.72				743
			39.38	67.0	71.0	104.29	3.25	1.59	1.48				744
			33.09	68.3	72.5	85.69	2.67	1.30	1.23				745

SERIAL NO.	REGION/ COUNTRY	YEAR	POPULATION		AGE STRUCTURE				VITAL			
			ESTIMATED AS OF MID-YEAR (in 000's)	DENSITY (per km²)	TOTAL REPRODUCTIVE VALUE (in 000's)	DEPENDENCY RATIO YOUTH < 15 (x 100)	OLD AGE ≥ 65 (x 100)	DEPARTURE FROM STABILITY (Percent)	CRUDE RATES (Both Sexes) BIRTH (x 1000)	DEATH (x 1000)	STANDARDIZED RATES Standard: USA 1960 BIRTH (x 1000)	DEATH (x 1000)
	1	2	3	4	5	6	7	8	9	10	11	12
746	Syria	1950	3495	19		76.5	8.1		46.60	21.40		
747		1960	4561	25		85.7	7.3		47.40	16.60		
748		1970	6258	34		104.6	9.5		46.60	12.10		
749		1980	8800	48		96.4	6.5		45.51	8.62		
750		1985	10458	56		97.9	5.6		44.13	7.01		
751	Thailand	1950	20010	39		78.1	5.6		46.58	19.21		
752		1960	26392	51		85.0	5.2		43.49	13.37		
753		1970	35745	70		91.0	5.9		35.12	9.30		
754		1980	46718	91		70.9	6.3		27.83	7.95		
755		1985	51604	100		60.9	6.1		22.29	7.02		
756	Turkey	1950	20809	27		65.7	5.6		48.20	23.50		
757		1960	27509	35		74.7	6.4		42.90	16.40		
758		1970	35321	45		75.5	8.1		34.50	11.60		
759		1980	44438	57		70.0	8.4		30.20	9.40		
760		1985	50345	64		61.2	7.1		28.39	8.37		
761	United Arab	1950	70	1		77.8	6.3		47.80	22.80		
762	Emirates	1960	90	1		82.4	6.4		43.60	17.30		
763		1970	223	3		55.7	3.8		33.00	9.90		
764		1980	1015	12		40.8	1.8		26.61	3.59		
765		1985	1350	16		45.8	2.2		22.62	3.63		
766	Vietnam	1950	29954	91		55.4	6.3		41.80	28.53		
767		1960	34743	105		67.7	7.4		40.91	21.22		
768		1970	42729	130		84.5	8.3		37.65	14.29		
769		1980	53700	163		80.8	9.1		34.80	11.15		
770		1985	60059	182		74.0	8.1		31.88	9.52		
771	Yemen	1950	3324	17		77.1	7.4		50.50	32.00		
772		1960	4039	21		78.0	5.9		49.30	28.10		
773		1970	4835	25		79.8	5.8		48.70	26.30		
774		1980	5995	31		96.2	6.6		48.60	17.83		
775		1985	6888	35		98.5	6.6		47.87	15.74		
776	Yemen,	1950	992	3		84.0	7.2		50.50	32.00		
777	Democratic	1960	1208	4		85.5	5.5		50.30	27.90		
778		1970	1497	4		87.5	5.1		48.20	23.10		
779		1980	1861	6		89.5	5.3		46.98	17.41		
780		1985	2137	6		86.5	5.4		47.26	15.81		
781	EUROPE	1950	392523	81		38.5	13.2		19.83	11.01		
782		1960	425070	87		40.0	15.0		18.69	10.25		
783		1970	460132	94		39.2	17.9		15.75	10.39		
784		1980	484436	99		34.7	20.2		13.44	10.49		
785		1985	492177	101		31.2	19.1		12.98	10.73		
786	EASTERN EUROPE	1950	88500	89		40.3	10.6		23.62	11.28		
787	(COMECON)	1960	96713	98		43.8	12.9		17.52	9.37		
788		1970	102998	104	23123	38.0	16.0	5.2	16.79	10.33	14.83	10.20
789		1975	106180	107	22668	35.6	17.4	4.7	17.63	10.60	14.53	9.76
790		1980	109400	110	22083	36.7	18.3	4.7	17.03	11.42	14.07	10.04
791		1985	111681	113		35.8	16.3		14.61	11.25		
792	NORTHERN	1950	72477	46		35.5	15.6		16.73	11.09		
793	EUROPE	1960	75647	48		37.4	17.5		17.89	11.21		
794		1970	80457	51		38.2	20.1		14.76	11.22		
795		1980	82494	52		33.1	23.1		12.92	11.23		
796		1985	83180	53		29.9	23.0		13.15	11.56		
797	SOUTHERN	1950	109014	83		42.9	11.4		21.21	10.35		
798	EUROPE	1960	118197	90		41.9	12.9		20.68	9.42		
799		1970	128339	98		41.7	15.6		17.81	9.15		
800		1980	138806	106		38.0	17.9		13.16	8.87		
801		1985	142342	108		33.1	17.7		12.63	9.51		
802	WESTERN EUROPE	1950	122532	123		35.2	15.2		17.65	11.35		
803		1960	134513	135		37.1	17.1		18.24	11.05		
804		1970	148209	149		38.4	20.3		13.75	11.11		
805		1980	153740	155		31.1	22.1		12.07	11.06		
806		1985	154974	156		27.1	20.2		12.04	11.01		

RATES			MORTALITY			FERTILITY							
INTRINSIC RATES (Female)			INFANT MORTALITY RATE (x 1000)	LIFE EXPECTANCY AT BIRTH		GENERAL FERTILITY RATE (x 1000)	TOTAL FERTILITY RATE	GROSS REPRODUCTION RATE	NET MATERNITY FUNCTION				SERIAL NO.
BIRTH (x 1000)	DEATH (x 1000)	INCREASE (x 1000)		MALE (Years)	FEMALE (Years)				TOTAL (NRR)	MEAN μ	VARIANCE σ^2	GENERATION (Years)	
13	14	15	16	17	18	19	20	21	22	23	24	25	
			160.00	44.8	47.2	209.78	7.09	3.46	2.32				746
			125.00	49.7	52.4	227.92	7.46	3.64	2.66				747
			88.00	55.4	58.7	230.83	7.69	3.75	3.09				748
			58.83	60.8	64.4	216.48	7.17	3.50	3.09				749
			48.45	63.2	66.9	208.04	6.76	3.30	2.99				750
			132.00	45.0	49.1	197.87	6.62	3.23	2.29				751
			95.00	51.9	56.2	195.60	6.42	3.13	2.49				752
			65.10	57.7	61.6	155.52	5.01	2.44	2.09				753
			47.51	60.7	64.8	110.82	3.52	1.72	1.52				754
			38.97	63.0	67.1	84.38	2.60	1.27	1.15				755
			233.00	42.0	45.2	203.61	6.85	3.34	2.29				756
			176.00	50.5	53.7	196.23	6.11	2.98	2.21				757
			138.00	55.9	60.0	150.86	5.04	2.46	1.94				758
			92.09	60.0	63.3	127.20	3.90	1.90	1.66				759
			75.63	62.5	65.8	116.44	3.55	1.70	1.53				760
			180.00	46.7	49.3	213.26	6.97	3.40	2.13				761
			130.00	53.5	56.6	214.13	6.87	3.35	2.33				762
			57.00	60.7	64.4	216.04	6.36	3.10	2.50				763
			31.59	67.1	71.4	179.07	5.23	2.55	2.42				764
			26.17	68.6	72.9	152.25	4.82	2.35	2.25				765
			180.14	39.1	41.8	165.44	6.05	2.95	1.84				766
			147.65	43.5	47.4	174.05	6.05	2.95	2.07				767
			119.61	47.7	53.1	164.49	5.85	2.85	2.16				768
			75.75	56.7	61.1	146.90	4.82	2.35	2.00				769
			64.29	59.2	63.6	130.29	4.10	2.00	1.75				770
			231.00	32.9	33.9	223.41	6.97	3.40	1.68				771
			207.00	37.7	39.1	215.78	6.97	3.40	1.85				772
			168.00	42.5	44.3	205.51	6.97	3.40	1.91				773
			129.94	46.9	49.9	210.22	7.07	3.45	2.49				774
			115.67	49.5	52.4	209.96	6.97	3.40	2.56				775
			231.00	32.9	33.9	228.30	6.97	3.40	1.68				776
			207.00	37.7	39.1	224.48	6.97	3.40	1.87				777
			168.00	42.5	44.3	215.58	6.97	3.40	2.08				778
			134.94	46.9	49.9	204.17	6.77	3.30	2.32				779
			120.41	49.4	52.4	203.70	6.66	3.25	2.39				780
			62.45	63.2	67.6	76.59	2.59	1.26	1.13				781
			36.96	67.1	72.4	77.67	2.63	1.28	1.19				782
			24.22	68.4	74.5	65.29	2.20	1.07	1.02				783
			14.60	70.0	76.7	54.91	1.81	0.88	0.86				784
			12.72	70.9	77.6	52.48	1.74	0.85	0.83				785
			83.13	60.9	65.5	88.44	2.95	1.43	1.18				786
			43.82	66.5	71.3	72.10	2.33	1.13	0.99				787
15.18	12.70	2.48	33.49	66.6	72.4	66.08	2.30	1.12	1.07	26.21	33.50	26.17	788
14.79	12.64	2.15	26.30	67.3	73.4	69.55	2.26	1.10	1.06	25.81	31.16	25.78	789
14.26	12.97	1.28	21.53	66.8	73.7	69.07	2.19	1.06	1.03	25.38	28.56	25.36	790
			17.39	67.9	74.8	59.94	2.02	0.98	0.96				791
			28.43	67.1	71.8	67.76	2.32	1.13	1.08				792
			20.87	68.4	73.9	77.05	2.78	1.36	1.32				793
			15.80	69.4	75.5	65.41	2.07	1.01	0.98				794
			9.61	71.3	77.5	54.23	1.79	0.87	0.86				795
			8.44	72.5	78.4	53.62	1.78	0.87	0.85				796
			78.85	61.3	64.9	80.09	2.69	1.30	1.17				797
			52.45	66.2	70.4	81.80	2.72	1.32	1.20				798
			30.73	68.6	74.1	72.23	2.52	1.22	1.15				799
			17.82	70.8	76.9	53.72	1.81	0.88	0.85				800
			15.29	71.8	78.0	51.01	1.67	0.81	0.79				801
			43.67	65.3	70.1	69.33	2.39	1.17	1.09				802
			25.76	67.8	73.8	78.25	2.69	1.31	1.26				803
			18.16	68.5	75.3	58.24	1.94	0.94	0.92				804
			9.79	70.9	78.2	48.73	1.58	0.77	0.76				805
			8.62	71.9	79.1	47.98	1.58	0.77	0.76				806

SERIAL NO.	REGION/ COUNTRY	YEAR	POPULATION ESTIMATED AS OF MID-YEAR (in 000's)	DENSITY (per km²)	AGE STRUCTURE TOTAL REPRODUCTIVE VALUE (in 000's)	DEPENDENCY RATIO YOUTH < 15 (x 100)	OLD AGE ≥ 65 (x 100)	DEPARTURE FROM STABILITY (Percent)	VITAL CRUDE RATES (Both Sexes) BIRTH (x 1000)	DEATH (x 1000)	STANDARDIZED RATES Standard: USA 1960 BIRTH (x 1000)	DEATH (x 1000)
	1	2	3	4	5	6	7	8	9	10	11	12
807	EUROPEAN	1970	302964	134	69732	39.3	19.0	3.2	16.39	10.63	15.62	8.90
808	COMMUNITY	1975	312218	138	63845	37.9	20.4	7.6	13.78	10.66	12.79	8.47
809		1980	318018	141	60085	33.8	21.2	10.7	13.00	10.30	11.62	7.64
810	Albania	1950	1230	43		71.9	12.9		38.23	14.21		
811		1960	1611	56		76.6	9.7		39.91	9.66		
812		1970	2138	74		79.7	8.4		31.94	6.87		
813		1980	2671	93		60.8	8.9		26.73	6.08		
814		1985	2962	103		57.3	8.7		24.00	5.75		
815	Austria	1951	6933	83	1450	34.5	15.9	6.8	15.08	12.37	13.47	12.10
816		1954	6940	83	1443	34.7	17.1	6.8	15.15	12.15	14.05	11.21
817		1957	6966	83	1540	32.7	17.6	7.5	16.95	12.54	16.42	10.92
818		1960	7048	84	1594	33.5	18.6	10.4	18.06	12.45	17.63	10.35
819		1962	7130	85	1641	34.9	19.5	10.4	18.69	12.74	18.15	10.29
820		1963	7172	86	1664	35.3	19.8	11.1	18.80	12.77	18.23	10.22
821		1964	7215	86	1665	35.9	20.3	10.8	18.55	12.35	17.97	9.77
822		1965	7255	87	1647	36.6	20.8	10.0	17.91	12.99	17.44	10.18
823		1967	7323	87	1629	38.2	21.8	8.1	17.39	12.88	17.12	9.95
824		1970	7467	89	1555	39.6	22.9	5.6	15.04	13.23	14.92	10.10
825		1975	7520	90	1390	37.7	24.2	7.8	12.47	12.77	11.93	9.33
826		1980	7505	90	1275	32.1	24.2	10.8	12.11	12.32	10.82	8.45
827		1985	7558	90	1177	27.0	21.2	15.5	11.57	11.85	9.51	7.63
828	Belgium	1950	8647	283	1909	30.8	16.3	5.4	16.78	12.36	15.36	11.17
829		1955	8827	289	1922	32.3	17.1	4.5	16.78	12.09	15.44	10.45
830		1960	9153	300	2025	36.5	18.6	6.3	17.00	11.80	16.51	9.62
831		1964	9378	307	2146	37.4	19.6	7.1	17.15	11.74	17.34	9.33
832		1965	9464	310	2123	37.6	19.9	6.0	16.43	12.16	16.71	9.56
833		1966	9525	312	2106	37.7	20.3	4.5	15.86	12.14	16.09	9.49
834		1970	9649	316	2026	37.4	21.2	4.0	14.73	12.30	14.48	9.45
835		1975	9801	321	1768	34.8	21.8	10.9	12.21	12.19	11.15	8.96
836		1980	9853	323	1701	30.8	21.9	12.1	12.62	11.54	10.79	8.06
837		1984	9857	323	1578	28.3	20.1	15.5	11.73	11.22	9.78	7.41
838	Bulgaria	1951	7284	66	2027	40.2	10.1	11.4	22.39	10.79	16.93	12.84
839		1954	7468	67	1878	39.8	10.4	13.7	20.27	9.12	15.40	11.01
840		1957	7651	69	1787	40.0	11.0	11.9	18.61	8.61	14.75	10.38
841		1960	7867	71	1729	39.3	11.3	10.7	17.58	8.48	14.73	9.84
842		1962	8013	72	1705	38.1	11.8	9.8	16.74	8.69	14.36	9.71
843		1963	8078	73	1687	37.5	12.0	10.8	16.36	8.18	14.15	9.03
844		1964	8144	73	1665	36.7	12.1	11.6	16.08	7.92	14.02	8.61
845		1965	8200	74	1618	35.3	12.7	12.5	15.34	8.17	13.40	8.61
846		1967	8310	75	1617	34.6	13.1	10.3	15.61	8.63	13.64	8.98
847		1970	8490	77	1633	33.8	14.2	8.4	16.34	9.08	14.07	8.96
848		1975	8721	79	1634	33.3	16.2	5.3	16.59	10.32	14.43	9.52
849		1980	8862	80	1511	33.5	18.0	6.7	14.47	11.05	13.31	9.39
850		1985	8960	81	1447	31.5	16.8	6.1	13.28	12.00	12.80	9.67
851	Czechoslovakia	1951	12532	98	3404	39.4	12.1	6.5	22.75	11.19	19.54	12.51
852		1954	12952	101	3351	42.2	12.7	6.5	20.68	10.17	18.43	11.25
853		1957	13358	104	3310	43.4	13.1	5.4	18.71	9.65	17.55	10.40
854		1960	13654	107	3096	42.6	13.8	7.0	15.93	9.35	15.39	9.73
855		1962	13860	108	3102	41.2	14.1	6.1	15.69	10.01	15.03	10.44
856		1963	13952	109	3223	40.3	14.4	6.1	16.92	9.54	16.06	9.78
857		1964	14058	110	3253	39.7	14.7	6.4	17.16	9.59	16.12	9.63
858		1965	14150	111	3187	39.1	15.1	6.1	16.37	9.96	15.21	9.88
859		1966	14240	111	3077	38.2	15.5	6.7	15.63	9.98	14.26	9.75
860		1967	14305	112	2963	37.3	15.9	8.1	15.10	10.10	13.40	9.70
861		1970	14334	112	2902	35.3	17.0	7.1	15.94	11.55	13.30	10.58
862		1975	14802	116	3202	36.2	18.8	5.4	19.55	11.46	15.77	10.07
863		1980	15311	120	3012	38.3	19.7	6.0	16.26	12.16	13.78	10.31
864		1985	15499	121	2918	37.8	17.1	7.0	14.58	11.88	13.20	9.87
865	Denmark	1951	4304	100	1039	41.0	14.3	5.4	18.05	9.02	16.44	9.33
866		1954	4407	102	1051	41.6	15.1	4.8	17.51	8.93	16.59	8.86
867		1960	4581	106	1059	39.3	16.5	4.8	16.48	9.40	16.25	8.47
868		1962	4647	108	1073	37.5	16.9	4.5	16.74	9.76	16.33	8.53
869		1963	4684	109	1096	36.9	17.1	5.0	17.60	9.77	16.94	8.43
870		1964	4720	110	1091	36.7	17.3	4.6	17.66	9.92	16.75	8.44
871		1965	4758	110	1103	36.7	17.6	4.8	18.03	10.06	16.85	8.47
872		1966	4797	111	1108	36.8	17.8	4.8	18.41	10.29	16.91	8.56
873		1967	4839	112	1056	37.0	18.1	4.1	16.82	9.89	15.21	8.14
874		1970	4929	114	977	36.1	19.0	9.0	14.37	9.79	12.63	7.76
875		1975	5060	117	957	35.3	20.9	9.4	14.24	10.06	12.29	7.39

RATES			MORTALITY			FERTILITY							
INTRINSIC RATES (Female)			INFANT MORTALITY RATE	LIFE EXPECTANCY AT BIRTH		GENERAL FERTILITY RATE	TOTAL FERTI-LITY RATE	GROSS REPRO-DUCTION RATE	NET MATERNITY FUNCTION				SERIAL NO.
BIRTH (x 1000)	DEATH (x 1000)	INCREASE (x 1000)	(x 1000)	MALE (Years)	FEMALE (Years)	(x 1000)			TOTAL (NRR)	MEAN μ	VARIANCE σ^2	GENER-ATION (Years)	
13	14	15	16	17	18	19	20	21	22	23	24	25	
15.95	11.38	4.57	23.74	68.4	74.7	69.38	2.42	1.18	1.13	27.77	36.48	27.69	807
11.99	14.37	-2.38	18.71	69.2	75.8	58.57	1.99	0.96	0.94	27.39	34.22	27.43	808
10.27	15.78	-5.50	12.74	70.5	77.3	53.90	1.81	0.88	0.86	27.32	30.47	27.40	809
			145.00	54.4	56.1	169.41	5.60	2.70	2.16				810
			99.00	63.7	66.0	180.48	5.76	2.78	2.40				811
			58.00	66.0	69.5	139.23	4.66	2.25	2.04				812
			44.76	68.0	73.0	111.01	3.40	1.64	1.53				813
			38.83	69.2	74.2	97.55	3.00	1.45	1.37				814
13.17	16.02	-2.84	63.37	62.8	68.1	57.85	2.07	1.00	0.92	27.97	38.68	28.03	815
14.01	14.53	-0.52	50.71	64.5	70.0	60.34	2.17	1.05	0.99	27.87	37.37	27.88	816
17.28	11.80	5.48	44.58	64.8	70.8	68.34	2.54	1.24	1.16	27.79	35.99	27.68	817
18.73	10.52	8.21	38.44	65.7	72.1	75.25	2.72	1.32	1.25	27.53	36.87	27.37	818
19.56	9.90	9.67	34.00	66.3	72.5	79.91	2.80	1.36	1.30	27.45	37.00	27.26	819
19.83	9.70	10.13	32.32	66.4	72.7	81.07	2.81	1.38	1.32	27.39	36.51	27.20	820
19.37	9.75	9.62	29.45	66.8	73.3	80.74	2.77	1.35	1.30	27.39	36.89	27.21	821
18.71	10.17	8.55	28.54	66.6	73.0	78.40	2.68	1.31	1.26	27.28	37.13	27.12	822
18.16	10.34	7.82	26.69	66.6	73.4	75.87	2.63	1.28	1.23	26.89	37.73	26.74	823
15.04	12.42	2.63	25.89	66.5	73.5	65.54	2.29	1.11	1.07	26.64	39.51	26.59	824
10.76	16.11	-5.35	20.54	67.6	74.7	54.52	1.84	0.90	0.87	26.24	37.21	26.34	825
9.11	17.78	-8.67	14.34	69.0	76.1	50.55	1.68	0.81	0.80	26.20	31.38	26.34	826
7.29	20.27	-12.97	11.17	70.5	77.5	45.74	1.48	0.72	0.71	26.64	29.64	26.84	827
15.80	13.27	2.53	45.35	64.5	69.5	66.81	2.37	1.15	1.07	28.72	35.88	28.68	828
15.92	12.46	3.46	38.24	66.3	71.5	69.55	2.39	1.16	1.10	28.49	34.32	28.43	829
17.34	10.84	6.50	25.60	67.7	73.4	75.31	2.56	1.24	1.20	28.01	33.57	27.89	830
18.48	10.02	8.47	25.35	67.7	73.9	76.47	2.69	1.31	1.26	27.74	33.02	27.59	831
17.67	10.52	7.15	23.69	67.6	73.8	73.27	2.60	1.26	1.22	27.58	32.06	27.46	832
16.90	11.00	5.90	24.73	67.7	73.8	70.25	2.50	1.22	1.17	27.47	32.13	27.37	833
14.64	12.49	2.15	21.09	67.8	74.2	63.11	2.25	1.09	1.06	27.13	32.94	27.09	834
9.85	17.07	-7.21	16.14	68.8	75.3	51.77	1.74	0.85	0.82	26.58	29.46	26.69	835
9.29	17.28	-7.98	12.14	69.9	76.7	52.29	1.69	0.83	0.81	26.66	25.38	26.77	836
7.82	19.11	-11.29	10.00	71.0	78.0	48.39	1.54	0.75	0.74	27.00	24.06	27.13	837
17.44	15.04	2.40	103.94	58.8	62.7	82.77	2.62	1.27	1.07	26.67	35.98	26.63	838
15.38	14.77	0.60	88.58	62.7	66.6	75.98	2.38	1.15	1.02	26.19	35.05	26.17	839
14.76	14.40	0.36	66.09	65.1	68.7	71.73	2.28	1.11	1.01	25.65	32.28	25.64	840
14.91	13.62	1.29	47.80	66.9	70.4	68.86	2.28	1.11	1.03	25.09	29.95	25.07	841
14.50	13.57	0.93	37.89	67.8	71.5	65.91	2.22	1.08	1.02	25.13	29.49	25.12	842
14.06	13.68	0.37	36.44	68.7	72.2	64.31	2.19	1.06	1.01	25.03	28.44	25.03	843
13.70	13.61	0.09	33.61	69.3	73.3	63.09	2.17	1.05	1.00	24.87	28.14	24.87	844
12.77	14.31	-1.55	31.73	69.4	73.7	60.15	2.07	1.00	0.96	24.91	28.06	24.93	845
13.28	14.09	-0.81	31.09	68.9	72.9	60.58	2.11	1.02	0.98	24.68	26.22	24.69	846
13.89	13.35	0.54	27.30	69.1	73.5	62.84	2.18	1.05	1.01	24.64	27.31	24.64	847
14.74	12.66	2.07	23.05	68.5	73.4	66.18	2.24	1.09	1.05	24.44	25.73	24.41	848
12.83	14.15	-1.32	20.24	68.6	74.0	59.91	2.06	1.00	0.97	23.87	24.24	23.88	849
12.16	14.76	-2.60	15.39	68.2	74.2	56.19	1.98	0.96	0.94	23.95	24.66	23.98	850
21.42	11.23	10.19	74.30	62.0	66.6	88.17	3.02	1.46	1.32	27.38	37.30	27.18	851
20.21	10.40	9.81	40.13	65.3	70.0	84.02	2.85	1.38	1.30	27.20	35.85	27.01	852
19.16	10.36	8.80	31.40	66.7	71.6	78.65	2.72	1.32	1.26	26.69	33.24	26.54	853
16.18	11.74	4.44	24.51	67.6	73.0	68.24	2.40	1.16	1.12	26.00	29.56	25.93	854
15.83	12.03	3.80	23.17	67.1	72.8	67.25	2.34	1.14	1.10	25.87	28.17	25.81	855
17.22	10.90	6.32	23.42	67.5	73.4	72.36	2.50	1.22	1.18	25.94	27.87	25.85	856
17.25	10.80	6.45	22.08	67.7	73.7	73.41	2.51	1.22	1.18	26.03	28.09	25.93	857
15.96	11.82	4.13	25.44	67.3	73.2	69.66	2.37	1.15	1.11	25.99	28.31	25.93	858
14.53	12.76	1.78	23.79	67.3	73.7	65.59	2.22	1.08	1.05	25.82	27.82	25.79	859
13.16	13.91	-0.75	22.86	67.4	73.8	62.24	2.09	1.01	0.98	25.65	27.41	25.66	860
13.26	14.10	-0.83	22.14	66.2	73.0	63.51	2.07	1.01	0.98	25.45	27.96	25.46	861
17.03	10.80	6.23	20.82	66.9	74.0	79.88	2.46	1.20	1.17	25.36	26.57	25.28	862
13.90	13.15	0.75	18.40	66.8	74.1	67.89	2.15	1.04	1.02	24.96	24.82	24.95	863
13.05	13.67	-0.62	14.00	67.3	74.8	60.75	2.06	1.00	0.98	24.77	23.96	24.78	864
17.33	11.31	6.01	30.09	69.4	72.0	73.02	2.54	1.23	1.18	27.65	36.28	27.54	865
17.49	10.89	6.60	26.97	70.1	72.9	72.45	2.57	1.24	1.20	27.38	34.67	27.26	866
17.22	10.68	6.54	22.25	70.6	74.1	69.59	2.52	1.23	1.19	26.95	31.69	26.84	867
17.35	10.48	6.87	20.26	70.3	74.5	70.36	2.54	1.24	1.20	26.88	31.21	26.77	868
18.16	9.96	8.20	19.84	70.4	74.5	73.94	2.63	1.28	1.24	26.85	31.23	26.71	869
17.73	10.12	7.61	18.98	70.3	74.8	74.39	2.60	1.26	1.22	26.73	31.02	26.61	870
17.94	10.04	7.90	18.72	70.2	74.7	76.16	2.61	1.27	1.23	26.72	30.97	26.59	871
18.10	9.90	8.20	16.95	70.2	74.8	77.86	2.62	1.27	1.24	26.58	30.48	26.45	872
15.67	11.30	4.38	15.81	70.7	75.4	71.55	2.36	1.15	1.12	26.45	30.26	26.38	873
11.88	14.39	-2.51	14.19	70.9	76.0	61.43	1.97	0.96	0.94	26.67	29.78	26.71	874
11.47	14.44	-2.97	10.35	71.3	77.1	61.29	1.92	0.94	0.92	26.45	25.72	26.49	875

SUMMARY TABLE

SERIAL NO.	REGION/ COUNTRY	YEAR	POPULATION ESTIMATED AS OF MID-YEAR (in 000's)	DENSITY (per km²)	AGE STRUCTURE TOTAL REPRODUCTIVE VALUE (in 000's)	DEPENDENCY RATIO YOUTH <15 (x100)	OLD AGE ≥65 (x100)	DEPARTURE FROM STABILITY (Percent)	VITAL CRUDE RATES (Both Sexes) BIRTH (x1000)	DEATH (x1000)	STANDARDIZED RATES Standard: USA 1960 BIRTH (x1000)	DEATH (x1000)
			3	4	5	6	7	8	9	10	11	12
876	Denmark	1980	5123	119	845	32.2	22.3	16.8	11.18	10.92	9.83	7.44
877	(cont'd.)	1985	5114	119	795	27.7	22.7	17.7	10.51	11.42	9.22	7.25
878	Finland	1951	4047	12	1272	47.7	10.5	4.5	23.51	9.89	19.99	12.78
879		1954	4187	12	1264	48.8	11.0	4.6	21.53	9.35	19.07	12.22
880		1957	4324	13	1257	49.3	11.3	4.3	19.81	9.12	18.23	11.54
881		1960	4430	13	1248	48.8	11.7	4.9	18.62	8.97	17.60	11.01
882		1962	4505	13	1239	45.8	11.8	4.6	18.08	9.52	17.01	11.56
883		1963	4543	13	1246	44.3	11.9	4.8	18.11	9.25	17.02	11.09
884		1964	4580	14	1227	42.9	12.1	5.2	17.56	9.28	16.36	10.89
885		1970	4606	14	977	37.2	13.8	12.8	14.02	9.58	11.79	10.36
886		1975	4711	14	896	32.7	15.8	15.5	13.95	9.30	10.86	9.12
887		1980	4780	14	859	30.0	17.7	15.6	13.19	9.29	10.51	8.09
888		1985	4902	15	862	28.5	18.3	14.2	12.81	9.83	10.60	7.66
889	France	1951	42056	77	10594	35.3	17.5	8.2	19.83	13.01	18.46	11.62
890		1956	43843	80	10697	39.3	18.2	6.4	18.40	11.88	17.38	10.30
891		1961	46163	84	11445	42.7	18.9	6.8	18.07	11.32	18.03	9.39
892		1966	49164	90	12048	40.8	19.7	6.3	17.50	10.69	17.84	8.68
893		1967	49548	91	11890	40.6	20.1	4.9	16.90	10.90	17.00	8.77
894		1970	50772	93	11788	39.8	20.7	4.6	16.75	10.63	15.97	8.38
895		1975	52699	96	10636	38.2	21.5	10.8	14.14	10.63	12.44	8.06
896		1980	53880	98	10622	35.1	21.9	10.7	14.85	10.15	12.47	7.24
897		1985	55170	101	10379	32.2	19.7	13.0	13.93	10.01	11.67	6.68
898	German	1952	18328	169	4008	33.3	17.0	8.3	16.70	12.09	15.42	11.34
899	Democratic	1954	18059	167	3850	32.2	17.9	8.7	16.35	11.93	15.23	10.68
900	Republic	1957	17517	162	3527	30.9	19.5	7.5	15.72	12.54	14.55	10.35
901		1960	17241	159	3491	32.3	21.0	8.9	17.13	13.27	15.53	10.27
902		1962	17102	158	3463	35.5	22.3	9.4	17.42	13.68	16.05	10.21
903		1963	17155	159	3513	36.7	22.8	9.6	17.57	12.94	16.29	9.62
904		1964	16992	157	3499	38.1	23.3	9.8	17.18	13.31	16.21	9.76
905		1965	17032	157	3465	38.8	23.7	9.0	16.50	13.52	15.76	9.84
906		1966	17064	158	3440	38.8	24.1	8.0	15.70	13.22	15.34	9.55
907		1967	17082	158	3309	38.9	24.6	6.8	14.80	13.29	14.87	9.51
908		1970	17058	158	3251	38.2	25.4	6.5	13.89	14.12	14.08	9.94
909		1975	16850	156	2594	34.8	26.1	12.5	10.79	14.27	9.99	9.73
910		1980	16737	155	2806	30.5	24.7	6.2	14.65	14.23	12.52	9.53
911		1985	16644	154	2606	28.7	20.2	8.7	13.68	13.54	11.24	8.99
912	Germany,	1950*	49786	202	11221	34.6	14.0	9.0	15.96	10.44	13.64	11.19
913	Federal	1960	55585	224	12587	31.5	16.0	7.1	17.43	11.57	15.55	10.51
914	Republic	1961	56175	226	12720	32.3	16.5	7.4	18.03	11.17	16.11	9.93
915		1962	56938	229	12727	32.8	16.9	6.4	17.89	11.32	15.94	9.92
916		1964	58266	234	13160	34.0	17.7	7.7	18.29	11.05	16.43	9.45
917		1965	59012	237	13124	34.4	18.2	7.3	17.70	11.48	16.13	9.69
918		1966	59638	240	13250	35.0	18.7	7.1	17.61	11.51	16.33	9.63
919		1967	59873	241	13147	35.7	19.3	6.0	17.03	11.48	16.01	9.49
920		1970	60651	244	11737	36.4	20.7	5.9	13.37	12.12	13.05	9.77
921		1975	61829	249	9973	33.5	22.6	15.0	9.71	12.12	9.32	9.24
922		1980	61566	248	9504	27.4	23.4	14.3	10.08	11.60	9.34	8.03
923		1985	61024	245	8621	21.6	21.2	17.3	9.61	11.54	8.32	7.21
924	Greece	1950	7566	57		44.4	10.5		19.44	7.16		
925		1957	8096	61	2179	39.7	11.7	12.7	19.33	7.38	14.70	8.51
926		1960	8327	63	2100	39.7	12.3	12.8	18.74	7.42	14.24	8.35
927		1962	8451	64	2089	39.1	13.1	12.5	18.01	7.88	14.12	7.96
928		1963	8480	64	2066	39.0	13.2	13.2	17.48	7.88	13.86	8.12
929		1964	8510	64	2081	39.1	13.6	10.6	17.99	8.16	14.52	8.33
930		1965	8550	65	2057	39.1	13.8	10.4	17.71	7.87	14.50	7.99
931		1967	8716	66	2098	38.6	14.4	7.8	18.27	8.15	15.29	8.00
932		1970	8793	67	1983	38.3	17.2	5.9	16.48	8.76	15.48	7.61
933		1975	9047	69	1930	37.4	19.1	5.2	15.73	9.46	14.98	7.57
934		1980	9643	73	1902	35.6	20.5	5.3	15.36	9.80	14.37	7.28
935		1985	9924	75	1633	31.6	20.3	13.4	11.74	10.20	10.81	7.01
936	Hungary	1951	9423	101	2382	37.3	11.8	5.6	20.24	11.47	16.52	13.23
937		1954	9706	104	2545	38.4	12.3	5.9	22.00	10.87	18.43	12.34
938		1957	9839	106	2265	39.6	13.0	5.3	17.56	10.36	15.32	11.39
939		1960	9984	107	2047	38.6	13.8	10.3	14.62	10.08	13.02	10.76
940		1963	10088	108	1921	36.9	14.8	13.0	13.12	9.90	11.72	10.15
941		1964	10120	109	1889	36.0	15.2	13.2	13.06	9.96	11.62	9.98

* Excluding the Saarland.

RATES — INTRINSIC RATES (Female)			MORTALITY			FERTILITY			NET MATERNITY FUNCTION				
BIRTH (x 1000)	DEATH (x 1000)	INCREASE (x 1000)	INFANT MORTALITY RATE (x 1000)	LIFE EXPECTANCY AT BIRTH MALE (Years)	FEMALE (Years)	GENERAL FERTILITY RATE (x 1000)	TOTAL FERTILITY RATE	GROSS REPRODUCTION RATE	TOTAL (NRR)	MEAN μ	VARIANCE σ^2	GENERATION (Years)	SERIAL NO.
13	14	15	16	17	18	19	20	21	22	23	24	25	
7.96	19.11	-11.14	8.45	71.2	77.3	46.75	1.54	0.75	0.74	26.83	24.65	26.97	876
7.23	20.29	-13.05	7.94	71.5	77.6	42.17	1.44	0.71	0.69	27.73	24.13	27.89	877
21.64	10.11	11.53	37.76	62.3	68.8	90.21	3.08	1.50	1.40	29.32	41.26	29.07	878
20.72	9.96	10.76	32.29	63.7	70.3	84.78	2.94	1.43	1.36	28.94	40.57	28.72	879
19.74	10.16	9.58	25.97	64.7	71.2	80.24	2.82	1.37	1.31	28.59	39.74	28.39	880
19.02	10.18	8.85	22.54	65.4	72.2	77.29	2.72	1.33	1.28	28.33	38.33	28.16	881
18.34	10.53	7.81	20.82	65.1	72.3	74.28	2.64	1.29	1.24	28.16	37.15	28.01	882
18.29	10.42	7.87	18.61	65.5	72.7	73.84	2.64	1.29	1.25	28.11	37.27	27.96	883
17.40	10.93	6.47	17.44	65.6	72.8	71.11	2.53	1.23	1.20	28.05	37.74	27.93	884
10.97	16.01	-5.04	13.23	66.1	74.4	55.65	1.83	0.89	0.87	27.10	36.04	27.19	885
9.37	17.41	-8.04	9.59	67.4	76.2	54.61	1.69	0.82	0.80	27.00	31.84	27.13	886
8.83	17.55	-8.72	7.63	69.2	78.0	51.75	1.63	0.80	0.78	27.69	30.96	27.82	887
9.02	17.02	-8.00	6.12	70.1	78.6	50.08	1.64	0.81	0.80	28.41	30.00	28.53	888
19.94	10.75	9.20	47.94	63.9	69.6	81.48	2.86	1.39	1.30	28.55	34.44	28.38	889
18.52	10.50	8.02	32.47	66.0	72.4	80.36	2.69	1.32	1.25	28.40	33.72	28.26	890
19.39	9.42	9.97	23.23	67.5	74.2	82.73	2.80	1.37	1.32	28.10	33.30	27.92	891
19.21	9.14	10.07	18.01	68.1	75.5	77.44	2.77	1.35	1.31	27.30	32.50	27.13	892
18.04	9.78	8.25	17.13	68.0	75.5	73.74	2.64	1.29	1.25	27.30	32.36	27.16	893
16.50	10.53	5.97	15.10	68.6	76.1	71.15	2.48	1.21	1.18	27.12	34.20	27.01	894
11.45	14.53	-3.09	13.79	69.0	77.0	59.94	1.93	0.94	0.92	26.65	32.06	26.70	895
11.40	14.07	-2.66	10.01	70.2	78.5	61.76	1.95	0.95	0.93	26.83	27.36	26.87	896
10.20	15.09	-4.90	8.31	71.3	79.6	57.07	1.83	0.89	0.87	27.48	26.96	27.54	897
15.91	13.68	2.23	61.76	64.3	68.3	62.75	2.39	1.15	1.06	27.17	34.02	27.13	898
15.58	13.34	2.23	52.73	65.7	69.8	62.39	2.36	1.14	1.06	26.95	33.95	26.91	899
14.65	13.70	0.95	46.70	66.2	70.8	62.12	2.25	1.09	1.03	26.67	32.64	26.65	900
16.14	12.31	3.83	39.21	66.7	71.5	71.36	2.40	1.16	1.11	26.30	33.23	26.24	901
16.93	11.55	5.38	32.21	67.3	72.1	76.12	2.48	1.20	1.15	26.02	33.25	25.93	902
17.19	11.21	5.98	32.09	67.7	72.7	78.03	2.51	1.22	1.17	26.00	33.08	25.90	903
17.17	11.16	6.01	28.89	67.8	72.8	78.28	2.50	1.22	1.17	26.13	32.70	26.03	904
16.44	11.57	4.87	24.76	68.0	73.0	75.71	2.44	1.18	1.14	26.20	32.15	26.12	905
16.02	11.74	4.28	22.89	68.4	73.3	70.57	2.38	1.16	1.12	26.10	30.66	26.03	906
15.28	12.20	3.08	21.36	68.5	73.6	66.07	2.30	1.11	1.08	25.40	29.59	25.35	907
14.30	13.04	1.26	18.50	68.1	73.4	59.97	2.18	1.06	1.03	25.48	30.13	25.46	908
8.00	20.42	-12.42	15.87	68.6	74.1	45.27	1.55	0.75	0.74	24.56	25.49	24.72	909
11.98	14.79	-2.81	12.07	68.7	74.6	59.00	1.95	0.95	0.93	24.54	22.71	24.57	910
9.89	17.00	-7.11	9.55	69.5	75.5	54.40	1.76	0.85	0.84	24.80	22.95	24.88	911
13.32	15.69	-2.38	55.52	64.6	68.5	58.38	2.10	1.01	0.93	28.98	37.85	29.03	912
16.05	12.24	3.81	35.08	66.5	71.8	69.04	2.41	1.17	1.12	28.83	33.44	28.76	913
16.74	11.57	5.18	33.48	66.9	72.4	72.86	2.50	1.21	1.16	28.65	33.36	28.56	914
16.52	11.59	4.93	30.14	67.1	72.8	73.55	2.47	1.20	1.15	28.54	32.87	28.45	915
17.08	10.96	6.12	26.00	67.6	73.6	77.49	2.55	1.24	1.19	28.54	32.42	28.44	916
16.74	11.21	5.54	24.17	67.6	73.4	75.73	2.50	1.21	1.17	28.47	32.89	28.37	917
17.03	10.99	6.04	23.61	67.6	73.6	75.45	2.53	1.23	1.19	28.28	33.06	28.18	918
16.60	11.18	5.43	22.86	67.7	73.8	72.62	2.48	1.21	1.16	28.14	33.35	28.04	919
12.53	14.57	-2.03	23.64	67.3	73.6	56.95	2.01	0.98	0.95	27.36	38.43	27.39	920
7.35	21.22	-13.87	19.77	68.1	74.7	41.17	1.45	0.70	0.68	27.23	32.55	27.46	921
7.31	20.50	-13.19	12.60	69.9	76.7	41.01	1.46	0.71	0.69	27.53	27.72	27.72	922
6.02	22.62	-16.60	8.95	71.5	78.2	37.51	1.30	0.63	0.62	28.35	26.35	28.57	923
			60.00	64.3	67.5	71.05	2.29	1.10	1.02				924
14.24	13.41	0.83	41.04	69.5	72.6	80.33	2.27	1.09	1.02	29.20	33.37	29.18	925
13.69	13.59	0.10	39.67	70.1	73.3	70.43	2.20	1.06	1.00	28.73	31.47	28.73	926
13.60	13.53	0.07	40.64	70.1	73.7	77.98	2.19	1.06	1.00	28.59	31.49	28.59	927
13.20	13.89	-0.69	38.55	70.2	73.7	66.81	2.15	1.04	0.98	28.47	31.63	28.48	928
14.24	12.99	1.25	36.32	69.9	73.8	69.11	2.25	1.09	1.04	28.21	31.55	28.19	929
14.15	12.87	1.28	34.04	70.6	74.3	68.46	2.25	1.09	1.04	28.09	32.16	28.07	930
15.22	11.98	3.24	34.26	70.7	74.5	70.89	2.37	1.14	1.09	27.82	31.63	27.76	931
15.34	11.67	3.67	37.78	70.7	75.2	66.76	2.40	1.16	1.11	27.41	34.27	27.34	932
14.84	11.88	2.96	29.45	71.0	75.7	64.07	2.32	1.12	1.08	26.80	34.72	26.75	933
13.95	12.27	1.68	20.50	72.0	76.6	63.54	2.23	1.07	1.04	26.12	32.88	26.09	934
8.79	17.73	-8.94	16.15	72.4	77.5	49.13	1.68	0.81	0.79	26.24	31.46	26.38	935
17.43	13.96	3.47	80.03	60.6	65.1	75.49	2.55	1.23	1.10	27.11	37.97	27.04	936
20.06	11.50	8.56	63.76	63.5	67.4	84.45	2.85	1.37	1.26	27.20	36.88	27.03	937
15.75	13.60	2.15	60.30	64.3	68.8	69.21	2.37	1.14	1.06	26.28	34.50	26.25	938
12.42	15.89	-3.47	49.17	65.9	70.3	58.71	2.01	0.97	0.91	25.78	32.30	25.84	939
10.52	17.63	-7.11	42.91	66.6	71.3	53.40	1.82	0.88	0.83	25.80	30.00	25.92	940
10.36	17.64	-7.28	41.30	67.0	71.9	53.24	1.80	0.87	0.83	25.73	28.78	25.85	941

SERIAL NO.	REGION/ COUNTRY	YEAR	POPULATION		AGE STRUCTURE				VITAL			
			ESTIMATED AS OF MID-YEAR (in 000's)	DENSITY (per km²)	TOTAL REPRODUCTIVE VALUE (in 000's)	DEPENDENCY RATIO YOUTH < 15 (x 100)	DEPENDENCY RATIO OLD AGE ≥ 65 (x 100)	DEPARTURE FROM STABILITY (Percent)	CRUDE RATES (Both Sexes) BIRTH (x 1000)	CRUDE RATES (Both Sexes) DEATH (x 1000)	STANDARDIZED RATES Standard: USA 1960 BIRTH (x 1000)	STANDARDIZED RATES Standard: USA 1960 DEATH (x 1000)
	1	2	3	4	5	6	7	8	9	10	11	12
942	Hungary	1965	10148	109	1872	35.1	15.6	12.0	13.11	10.65	11.63	10.47
943	(cont'd.)	1966	10179	109	1887	34.2	16.0	10.6	13.61	10.02	12.10	9.69
944		1967	10215	110	1943	33.4	16.3	7.5	14.58	10.72	12.97	10.14
945		1970	10338	111	1895	30.8	17.1	7.3	14.69	11.63	12.70	10.42
946		1975	10541	113	2041	30.3	18.8	5.5	18.43	12.44	15.41	10.36
947		1980	10711	115	1799	33.9	20.8	5.8	13.88	13.57	12.47	10.78
948		1985	10649	114	1730	32.5	18.7	6.9	12.23	13.86	11.81	10.67
949	Iceland	1950	143	1	49	49.4	12.2	4.4	28.69	7.86	25.30	8.43
950		1955	158	2	55	56.1	12.8	6.1	28.48	6.95	26.29	7.41
951		1960	176	2	63	60.9	14.1	6.8	27.93	6.63	27.60	7.14
952		1962	182	2	64	61.6	14.6	4.9	25.82	6.77	25.99	7.25
953		1965	192	2	67	60.5	14.8	3.9	24.55	6.71	24.29	7.17
954		1970	204	2	60	55.8	15.0	8.2	19.71	7.14	18.41	7.37
955		1975	218	2	62	49.5	15.1	10.1	20.11	6.48	17.23	6.35
956		1980	228	2	60	43.9	15.7	10.8	19.85	6.74	16.18	5.90
957		1985	241	2	56	41.2	15.9	17.8	15.97	6.86	12.62	5.63
958	Ireland	1951	2958	42	949	47.9	17.7	4.3	21.26	14.33	21.48	13.22
959		1956	2895	41	946	51.0	18.6	6.1	21.14	12.09	22.69	10.71
960		1961	2815	40	955	54.1	19.4	10.1	21.59	11.99	25.40	10.02
961		1966	2884	41	997	54.2	19.5	10.2	21.57	12.18	25.84	10.24
962		1967	2899	41	992	54.4	19.5	9.1	21.15	10.83	25.12	9.17
963		1968	2910	41	987	54.6	19.5	8.8	20.97	11.40	24.66	9.63
964		1970	2944	42	1010	54.2	19.6	9.6	21.87	11.44	25.17	9.67
965		1971	2978	42	1043	54.2	19.2	9.9	22.68	10.71	25.90	9.10
966		1975	3127	44	1048	53.9	19.3	6.6	21.48	10.61	22.89	9.02
967		1980	3406	48	1105	51.7	18.2	4.3	21.84	9.74	21.05	8.73
968		1981	3443	49	1098	51.4	18.2	4.1	20.96	9.56	20.00	8.58
969		1986	3541	50	999	48.1	18.0	9.3	17.35	9.50	15.90	8.31
970	Italy	1951	47043	156	13157	40.3	12.6	9.1	18.59	9.98	15.63	11.43
971		1955	48782	162	12726	38.9	13.5	7.5	17.82	9.16	15.17	9.82
972		1961	50521	168	12745	37.7	14.3	5.5	18.32	9.62	15.71	9.75
973		1964	52130	173	13783	36.7	14.7	4.2	19.49	9.40	16.99	9.12
974		1965	52686	175	13087	36.9	15.1	4.5	18.80	9.83	16.60	9.33
975		1966	53128	176	13076	37.1	15.4	4.7	18.44	9.30	16.42	8.71
976		1970	53822	179	12499	38.1	16.9	4.9	16.75	9.68	15.39	8.60
977		1975	55441	184	11831	38.0	18.9	5.9	14.93	10.00	13.99	8.31
978		1980	56434	187	10172	34.5	20.4	14.5	11.35	9.83	10.52	7.66
979		1983	56836	189	9615	30.7	19.4	16.9	10.59	9.93	9.58	7.33
980	Luxembourg	1950	297	115	60	27.3	13.7	8.4	14.80	11.97	12.82	12.21
981		1955	309	119	60	27.3	14.5	6.8	15.90	11.91	13.64	11.06
982		1960	318	123	62	30.2	15.6	5.7	15.80	11.63	14.38	10.30
983		1963	330	128	64	31.4	16.1	4.7	15.50	11.91	14.85	10.33
984		1966	334	129	70	34.3	17.8	4.6	15.54	12.12	15.07	10.29
985		1970	339	131	64	33.6	19.2	5.0	13.01	12.25	12.63	10.02
986		1975	358	138	59	30.1	19.5	13.0	11.12	12.21	9.97	9.66
987		1980	364	141	59	27.8	20.0	14.3	11.45	11.30	9.55	8.56
988		1985	367	142	55	24.7	19.0	18.1	11.19	10.98	8.90	7.86
989	Malta	1950	312	987		58.9	9.7		29.32	10.15		
990		1960	329	1041	124	65.3	12.9	3.8	25.10	8.72	22.61	11.00
991		1962	329	1041	118	61.4	12.8	5.4	22.84	8.63	20.95	10.87
992		1963	328	1038	111	59.2	13.0	8.1	20.33	9.09	18.78	11.43
993		1964	324	1025	108	57.3	13.2	8.2	19.76	8.52	18.04	10.47
994		1965	319	1009	100	56.5	15.3	10.4	17.63	9.40	15.99	10.83
995		1966	317	1003	94	53.7	13.6	12.8	16.82	9.02	15.05	10.86
996		1970	326	1032	86	43.7	14.3	15.5	16.32	9.43	13.08	10.15
997		1986*	345	1092	72	36.5	15.0	14.9	15.22	8.20	12.33	7.56
998	Netherlands	1950	10114	248	3304	46.5	12.3	4.0	23.23	7.56	20.77	8.83
999		1955	10751	263	3337	48.4	13.6	3.7	21.43	7.60	19.89	8.33
1000		1960	11487	281	3529	49.2	14.8	3.8	21.07	7.64	20.43	7.85
1001		1963	11966	293	3649	46.5	15.1	3.7	20.88	8.00	20.56	7.93
1002		1964	12127	297	3665	45.9	15.2	3.7	20.69	7.70	20.35	7.56
1003		1965	12295	301	3620	45.5	15.4	3.3	19.94	7.97	19.56	7.73
1004		1966	12456	305	3565	45.0	15.5	3.0	19.24	8.07	18.65	7.75
1005		1967	12598	308	3521	44.7	15.7	3.6	18.95	7.92	17.98	7.53
1006		1970	13039	319	3464	43.6	16.3	5.0	18.32	8.41	16.61	7.75

* Maltese population only.

RATES			MORTALITY			FERTILITY							
INTRINSIC RATES (Female)			INFANT MORTALITY RATE (x 1000)	LIFE EXPECTANCY AT BIRTH		GENERAL FERTILITY RATE (x 1000)	TOTAL FERTI-LITY RATE	GROSS REPRO-DUCTION RATE	NET MATERNITY FUNCTION				SERIAL NO.
BIRTH (x 1000)	DEATH (x 1000)	INCREASE (x 1000)		MALE (Years)	FEMALE (Years)				TOTAL (NRR)	MEAN μ	VARIANCE σ^2	GENER-ATION (Years)	
13	14	15	16	17	18	19	20	21	22	23	24	25	
10.51	17.59	-7.08	40.37	66.7	71.6	53.20	1.81	0.88	0.83	25.65	28.13	25.76	942
11.01	16.71	-5.70	38.38	67.5	72.2	61.41	1.88	0.91	0.86	25.57	28.11	25.66	943
12.38	15.32	-2.94	36.99	66.9	72.0	57.70	2.01	0.97	0.93	25.55	27.59	25.60	944
12.04	15.60	-3.57	35.89	66.4	72.2	56.65	1.97	0.95	0.91	25.47	29.55	25.52	945
16.14	11.96	4.17	32.85	66.3	72.5	72.86	2.38	1.16	1.11	25.24	29.56	25.18	946
11.85	15.59	-3.74	23.16	65.6	72.8	57.73	1.92	0.94	0.91	24.63	28.21	24.69	947
10.89	16.54	-5.65	20.36	65.1	73.2	51.00	1.83	0.89	0.87	25.04	27.02	25.12	948
26.72	6.77	19.95	22.40	68.7	73.8	118.28	3.87	1.83	1.76	28.69	44.23	28.24	949
29.02	5.48	23.54	23.19	70.8	76.3	124.33	4.02	1.97	1.91	27.98	43.66	27.45	950
30.04	4.98	25.06	13.02	72.5	75.9	126.22	4.22	2.04	1.99	28.03	46.80	27.44	951
28.61	5.39	23.22	17.24	71.5	76.5	117.65	3.98	1.94	1.89	28.02	44.21	27.50	952
27.63	5.67	21.96	15.04	71.4	76.6	111.17	3.71	1.87	1.82	27.75	45.48	27.24	953
19.34	8.47	10.86	13.17	70.7	77.3	86.87	2.82	1.37	1.34	27.22	44.64	26.98	954
17.70	9.00	8.70	12.55	72.4	79.0	85.08	2.65	1.29	1.26	26.94	39.41	26.77	955
16.23	9.47	6.76	7.73	73.5	80.4	81.48	2.48	1.21	1.20	27.11	37.11	26.99	956
11.95	12.91	-0.96	5.71	74.9	80.4	64.23	1.95	0.99	0.97	27.42	34.84	27.43	957
22.59	10.62	11.97	45.37	63.6	66.2	94.08	3.27	1.59	1.45	31.48	34.15	31.26	958
23.61	8.76	14.85	35.88	67.1	70.2	95.83	3.45	1.68	1.59	31.46	34.68	31.19	959
26.34	7.23	19.11	28.64	68.1	71.9	101.98	3.87	1.89	1.80	31.23	34.42	30.88	960
26.84	6.85	20.00	24.95	68.1	72.4	102.53	3.95	1.91	1.84	30.80	35.26	30.43	961
26.09	6.83	19.26	24.43	69.1	73.5	100.72	3.84	1.86	1.79	30.73	35.98	30.36	962
25.83	6.94	18.89	20.98	68.7	73.2	100.04	3.78	1.83	1.77	30.53	35.67	30.18	963
26.54	6.67	19.88	19.49	68.6	73.2	104.41	3.86	1.87	1.81	30.29	37.62	29.92	964
27.30	6.19	21.11	17.97	69.2	74.0	107.82	3.98	1.93	1.87	30.16	37.53	29.77	965
24.36	7.05	17.32	17.51	69.2	74.4	100.60	3.52	1.71	1.66	29.80	37.89	29.47	966
22.02	7.59	14.43	11.25	69.7	75.7	97.26	3.23	1.56	1.53	29.64	36.98	29.37	967
20.97	8.05	12.92	10.34	70.1	75.8	92.51	3.07	1.49	1.46	29.73	36.41	29.49	968
15.79	10.86	4.93	8.69	70.8	76.5	73.17	2.44	1.18	1.16	29.94	34.71	29.85	969
15.78	14.13	1.65	68.22	63.8	67.4	70.36	2.40	1.17	1.05	29.77	38.07	29.74	970
15.17	13.32	1.85	50.91	66.4	70.8	69.16	2.34	1.14	1.06	29.44	35.59	29.40	971
15.91	12.31	3.60	43.54	66.8	72.1	72.82	2.42	1.18	1.11	29.14	35.05	29.07	972
17.37	10.98	6.39	36.09	67.7	73.2	78.09	2.62	1.27	1.21	29.85	34.64	29.73	973
17.03	11.16	5.87	36.02	67.7	73.2	76.03	2.55	1.24	1.18	28.56	37.09	28.45	974
16.65	11.08	5.58	34.91	68.4	74.2	74.86	2.52	1.23	1.17	28.58	37.38	28.47	975
15.47	11.74	3.73	29.55	68.8	74.6	68.10	2.38	1.16	1.11	28.26	36.49	28.20	976
13.58	12.81	0.77	21.17	69.6	75.9	62.39	2.17	1.05	1.02	27.62	35.92	27.60	977
8.67	17.97	-9.30	14.55	70.7	77.3	46.93	1.64	0.79	0.77	27.49	31.49	27.64	978
7.47	19.74	-12.27	12.29	71.4	78.0	43.06	1.49	0.72	0.71	27.79	30.24	27.97	979
12.75	17.02	-4.27	55.67	62.5	66.5	55.84	1.98	0.98	0.88	28.70	33.18	28.77	980
13.70	14.80	-1.09	43.42	64.8	70.0	63.12	2.12	1.03	0.97	28.16	31.37	28.19	981
14.71	13.23	1.48	33.12	66.4	71.9	65.59	2.24	1.09	1.04	27.62	30.31	27.60	982
14.98	12.98	1.99	28.76	66.9	72.0	67.09	2.31	1.10	1.06	27.42	29.60	27.41	983
16.11	11.92	4.19	26.76	66.3	72.6	66.46	2.35	1.16	1.12	27.26	29.94	27.20	984
12.44	14.86	-2.42	24.94	66.5	73.1	54.65	1.96	0.97	0.94	27.13	33.59	27.17	985
8.44	19.52	-11.08	14.82	67.3	74.4	45.54	1.56	0.76	0.74	27.00	29.34	27.17	986
8.08	19.66	-11.58	11.51	70.0	75.4	45.54	1.49	0.75	0.73	27.40	27.37	27.55	987
6.67	21.59	-14.92	9.02	70.2	77.1	43.65	1.39	0.67	0.66	27.84	25.75	28.03	988
			74.65	64.2	67.7	123.18	4.18	2.01	1.85				989
24.74	8.00	16.74	34.43	66.7	71.0	109.89	3.49	1.70	1.63	29.35	40.05	29.00	990
22.56	8.92	13.64	35.77	67.1	70.9	103.30	3.24	1.55	1.48	29.15	39.30	28.87	991
20.02	10.06	9.96	33.60	66.8	70.9	82.07	2.90	1.39	1.33	28.98	38.92	28.78	992
19.35	10.37	8.98	34.62	68.0	71.2	78.66	2.79	1.36	1.30	29.09	38.70	28.91	993
16.75	11.97	4.79	33.80	67.7	71.1	69.66	2.47	1.20	1.15	29.39	38.65	29.29	994
15.15	13.11	2.04	30.15	68.0	71.2	65.59	2.33	1.11	1.06	29.20	42.15	29.16	995
12.51	14.89	-2.37	27.85	67.9	72.9	60.79	2.02	0.96	0.93	28.95	36.19	28.99	996
10.92	15.17	-4.25	10.10	72.4	76.9	59.08	1.91	0.90	0.88	28.82	30.75	28.88	997
21.41	8.95	12.46	26.61	70.1	72.5	92.98	3.17	1.54	1.47	30.94	36.31	30.70	998
20.64	8.81	11.83	20.42	71.0	74.0	89.39	3.05	1.48	1.43	30.41	35.46	30.19	999
21.53	7.99	13.54	16.72	71.4	75.4	90.56	3.15	1.53	1.49	29.75	34.07	29.50	1000
21.78	7.77	14.01	16.13	71.0	75.8	88.67	3.18	1.54	1.50	29.36	33.36	29.11	1001
21.52	7.77	13.75	15.07	71.3	76.3	87.82	3.15	1.53	1.49	29.21	32.96	28.97	1002
20.68	8.16	12.52	14.48	71.1	76.2	84.70	3.03	1.47	1.43	28.98	32.82	28.76	1003
19.73	8.64	11.09	14.70	71.1	76.1	81.69	2.89	1.41	1.37	28.75	32.52	28.56	1004
18.87	8.96	9.91	13.37	71.2	76.6	80.34	2.79	1.36	1.32	28.55	32.09	28.39	1005
17.30	9.86	7.44	12.75	70.8	76.6	77.34	2.58	1.26	1.23	28.16	32.13	28.04	1006

SERIAL NO.	REGION/ COUNTRY	YEAR	POPULATION ESTIMATED AS OF MID-YEAR (in 000's)	DENSITY (per km²)	AGE STRUCTURE TOTAL REPRODUCTIVE VALUE (in 000's)	DEPENDENCY RATIO YOUTH < 15 (x 100)	OLD AGE ≥ 65 (x 100)	DEPARTURE FROM STABILITY (Percent)	VITAL CRUDE RATES (Both Sexes) BIRTH (x 1000)	DEATH (x 1000)	STANDARDIZED RATES Standard: USA 1960 BIRTH (x 1000)	DEATH (x 1000)
			1	2	3	4	5	6	7	8	9	10	11	12
1007	Netherlands	1975	13666	335	2796	39.7	16.9	19.8	13.02	8.32	10.62	7.32
1008	(cont'd.)	1980	14150	346	2702	33.7	17.4	21.1	12.81	8.08	10.18	6.60
1009		1985	14492	355	2577	28.4	17.6	21.6	12.29	8.47	9.67	6.38
1010	Norway	1951	3296	10	807	37.4	14.7	7.3	18.76	8.68	16.40	8.07
1011		1954	3394	10	829	39.5	15.6	6.4	18.59	8.51	17.48	7.66
1012		1957	3492	11	862	41.3	16.5	6.4	18.16	8.80	18.48	7.66
1013		1960	3581	11	883	41.1	17.5	7.1	17.45	9.09	18.71	7.61
1014		1962	3639	11	890	39.9	18.1	7.1	17.11	9.43	18.63	7.73
1015		1964	3694	11	914	39.2	18.6	7.9	17.75	9.52	19.12	7.66
1016		1965	3723	11	917	39.1	18.9	7.7	17.80	9.49	18.94	7.55
1017		1966	3753	12	916	39.1	19.3	7.2	17.87	9.60	18.68	7.52
1018		1967	3784	12	911	39.2	19.6	6.5	17.65	9.57	18.08	7.44
1019		1970	3877	12	875	39.0	20.6	4.7	16.65	9.99	16.21	7.46
1020		1975	4007	12	793	38.1	21.9	9.2	14.06	10.00	12.81	7.06
1021		1980	4086	13	737	35.1	23.4	14.5	12.49	10.12	11.06	6.59
1022		1985	4159	13	720	30.8	24.7	14.9	12.29	10.67	10.71	6.44
1023	Poland	1950	24824	79		44.9	8.0		30.14	10.88		
1024		1960	29577	95	9036	55.5	9.8	7.5	22.35	7.58	19.30	10.22
1025		1962	30324	97	8759	54.5	10.1	8.7	19.77	7.89	17.46	10.78
1026		1965	31182	100	8497	50.7	10.8	9.3	17.52	7.45	16.16	9.90
1027		1970	32526	104	8110	41.6	12.7	10.6	16.79	8.20	14.46	9.97
1028		1975	34022	109	8109	36.2	14.4	9.2	18.92	8.73	14.56	9.27
1029		1980	35578	114	8067	37.0	15.4	7.9	19.47	9.84	14.56	9.76
1030		1985	37203	119	8261	39.3	14.5	6.7	18.21	10.25	14.92	9.77
1031	Portugal	1951	8459	92	3071	46.4	11.1	5.1	24.60	12.17	20.91	14.94
1032		1954	8570	93	3004	46.4	11.6	4.6	23.71	11.36	20.18	13.69
1033		1957	8680	94	2988	46.4	12.1	2.9	24.06	11.54	20.45	13.64
1034		1960	8865	96	3008	46.4	12.6	2.7	24.23	10.99	20.69	12.64
1035		1962	9008	98	3031	46.4	12.9	2.4	24.44	10.75	20.98	12.14
1036		1963	9074	99	2979	46.4	13.1	2.6	23.38	10.80	20.18	12.20
1037		1964	9143	99	3003	46.4	13.3	2.6	23.75	10.60	20.58	11.78
1038		1965	9234	100	2942	46.4	13.5	2.9	22.77	10.31	19.84	11.37
1039		1967	9415	102	2859	46.2	13.8	3.6	21.38	10.29	18.82	10.89
1040		1970	8545	93	2568	45.5	15.6	3.1	20.23	10.89	18.80	11.77
1041		1975	9449	103	2605	44.3	16.5	3.8	19.01	10.36	16.98	10.41
1042		1980	9884	107	2291	40.7	16.5	11.0	16.02	9.61	13.32	9.51
1043		1985	10157	110	1978	36.5	18.6	15.6	12.85	9.58	11.00	7.95
1044	Romania	1950	16311	69		42.9	8.0		24.94	12.00		
1045		1957	17824	75	5117	42.3	10.0	7.3	22.89	9.60	17.79	12.29
1046		1960	18407	78	4617	43.2	10.6	11.6	18.93	9.23	15.02	11.58
1047		1962	18691	79	4257	43.0	11.2	14.4	16.16	9.23	13.24	11.65
1048		1963	18813	79	4171	42.4	11.3	15.1	15.67	8.28	13.05	10.25
1049		1964	18927	80	4088	41.4	11.6	16.0	15.18	8.06	12.73	9.79
1050		1965	19027	80	4064	40.0	12.0	14.9	14.63	8.59	12.36	10.26
1051		1970	20253	85	5271	39.6	13.1	6.1	21.09	9.54	18.73	10.51
1052		1975	21245	89	5063	38.7	14.7	5.9	19.68	9.30	16.99	9.69
1053		1980	22201	93	4941	42.3	16.3	5.4	17.97	10.44	15.85	10.51
1054		1985	22725	96		37.4	14.4		15.53	10.77		
1055	Spain	1950	27849	55	8617	39.4	10.9	10.6	20.07	10.93	16.07	13.41
1056		1960	30401	60	8907	42.4	12.7	4.2	21.53	8.63	18.02	9.52
1057		1962	30895	61	8983	43.1	13.2	3.3	21.03	8.78	18.02	9.48
1058		1963	31160	62	9179	43.4	13.5	2.9	21.26	8.84	18.44	9.44
1059		1966	32102	64	9369	44.2	14.3	3.3	20.61	8.40	18.50	8.58
1060		1970	33853	67	9628	44.4	15.5	3.2	19.53	8.42	18.65	8.30
1061		1975	35515	70	9647	43.5	16.5	3.1	18.83	8.37	17.99	7.87
1062		1980	37386	74	8731	40.9	17.2	9.0	15.26	7.71	14.09	6.83
1063		1983	38172	75	7951	37.9	18.1	15.2	12.71	7.93	11.58	6.38
1064	Sweden	1950	7017	16	1506	35.0	15.3	6.7	16.64	9.85	15.05	9.12
1065		1955	7262	16	1488	36.4	16.7	6.1	14.81	9.65	14.58	8.52
1066		1960	7480	17	1499	34.0	17.9	5.5	14.02	9.82	14.39	8.01
1067		1965	7734	17	1587	31.5	19.1	5.8	15.88	10.11	15.63	7.63
1068		1967	7868	17	1557	31.8	19.8	5.0	15.42	10.14	14.75	7.45
1069		1970	8043	18	1467	31.8	20.9	7.4	13.70	9.95	12.48	7.08
1070		1975	8193	18	1386	32.2	23.5	9.8	12.65	10.77	11.42	6.99
1071		1980	8310	18	1364	30.6	25.4	11.7	11.68	11.05	10.75	6.61
1072		1985	8350	19	1377	28.1	26.7	10.0	11.79	11.26	11.14	6.13

RATES			MORTALITY			FERTILITY							
INTRINSIC RATES (Female)			INFANT MORTALITY RATE	LIFE EXPECTANCY AT BIRTH		GENERAL FERTILITY RATE	TOTAL FERTI- LITY RATE	GROSS REPRO- DUCTION RATE	NET MATERNITY FUNCTION				SERIAL NO.
BIRTH (x 1000)	DEATH (x 1000)	INCREASE (x 1000)	(x 1000)	MALE (Years)	FEMALE (Years)	(x 1000)			TOTAL (NRR)	MEAN μ	VARIANCE σ^2	GENER- ATION (Years)	
13	14	15	16	17	18	19	20	21	22	23	24	25	
9.06	17.22	-8.15	10.65	71.5	77.8	53.91	1.67	0.81	0.80	27.38	25.18	27.48	1007
8.28	17.81	-9.53	8.59	72.5	79.4	50.83	1.60	0.78	0.77	27.73	22.67	27.84	1008
7.59	18.80	-11.21	8.03	73.1	79.8	46.87	1.51	0.74	0.73	28.42	22.41	28.55	1009
16.43	11.28	5.15	26.57	70.6	74.0	75.03	2.52	1.22	1.16	29.65	39.36	29.54	1010
18.08	9.87	8.20	21.82	71.4	75.1	77.53	2.70	1.31	1.27	29.03	38.41	28.86	1011
19.49	8.98	10.51	20.93	71.3	75.5	78.53	2.86	1.39	1.35	28.59	37.20	28.38	1012
19.83	8.68	11.15	18.86	71.3	75.9	76.76	2.90	1.41	1.37	28.27	35.88	28.07	1013
19.95	8.57	11.38	17.96	71.0	76.0	75.19	2.89	1.41	1.37	27.83	34.92	27.62	1014
20.35	8.36	11.99	16.97	71.3	76.1	78.27	2.96	1.43	1.39	27.73	34.35	27.52	1015
20.08	8.38	11.71	16.79	71.1	76.5	78.81	2.93	1.41	1.38	27.68	34.78	27.47	1016
19.82	8.46	11.36	14.55	71.4	76.6	79.49	2.89	1.40	1.36	27.55	34.47	27.34	1017
19.15	8.74	10.41	14.75	71.4	76.9	78.90	2.80	1.36	1.33	27.43	34.21	27.25	1018
16.64	10.04	6.60	12.75	71.0	77.4	75.37	2.51	1.22	1.19	26.95	34.51	26.83	1019
11.88	13.69	-1.81	11.09	71.7	78.2	64.08	1.99	0.97	0.95	26.41	30.84	26.44	1020
9.22	16.46	-7.24	8.05	72.4	79.3	55.16	1.72	0.83	0.82	26.92	28.60	27.02	1021
8.80	16.94	-8.13	8.49	72.6	79.6	51.04	1.67	0.81	0.80	27.48	27.26	27.59	1022
			95.04	58.6	64.2	110.76	3.62	1.76	1.52				1023
20.77	10.10	10.67	60.87	64.9	70.7	92.82	2.99	1.44	1.34	27.47	37.38	27.26	1024
18.50	11.18	7.32	54.85	64.6	70.7	82.83	2.71	1.30	1.22	27.33	35.59	27.19	1025
16.85	11.57	5.28	41.75	66.4	72.3	72.81	2.51	1.21	1.15	27.21	34.36	27.11	1026
14.53	12.99	1.54	33.19	66.4	73.0	64.43	2.25	1.09	1.04	26.97	34.31	26.94	1027
14.60	12.42	2.18	24.86	67.1	74.5	71.30	2.27	1.10	1.06	26.81	32.69	26.77	1028
14.91	12.14	2.78	21.27	66.1	74.6	76.12	2.28	1.11	1.08	26.45	30.33	26.41	1029
15.43	11.67	3.76	18.48	66.5	74.8	74.08	2.33	1.13	1.10	26.41	30.07	26.35	1030
21.54	13.87	7.67	109.97	55.9	61.0	93.16	3.21	1.55	1.26	30.38	43.13	30.21	1031
20.90	13.03	7.87	103.05	58.3	63.5	90.78	3.10	1.50	1.27	30.19	42.79	30.01	1032
21.51	12.51	9.00	99.44	58.9	64.1	93.19	3.14	1.53	1.30	29.72	42.58	29.52	1033
21.64	11.88	9.76	97.67	60.2	65.6	94.99	3.18	1.54	1.33	29.57	41.58	29.35	1034
21.89	11.31	10.58	90.81	61.0	66.7	96.49	3.22	1.56	1.36	29.55	42.18	29.32	1035
21.02	11.33	9.69	80.68	61.7	67.4	92.74	3.10	1.50	1.33	29.66	42.36	29.44	1036
21.40	11.05	10.35	77.17	62.1	67.7	94.68	3.16	1.52	1.36	29.65	42.74	29.42	1037
20.64	10.86	9.77	69.50	63.1	69.0	91.41	3.05	1.47	1.33	29.61	43.05	29.39	1038
19.46	11.10	8.35	61.72	64.0	69.7	86.82	2.89	1.40	1.28	29.45	45.17	29.26	1039
19.59	11.12	8.47	58.04	60.2	69.5	81.85	2.90	1.40	1.28	29.01	41.95	28.83	1040
17.40	11.09	6.31	38.91	65.3	72.7	76.15	2.62	1.26	1.19	28.37	42.43	28.23	1041
12.65	14.12	-1.47	24.33	67.4	74.6	62.76	2.06	1.00	0.96	27.22	40.86	27.25	1042
9.24	17.38	-8.14	17.83	69.5	76.6	52.40	1.70	0.82	0.80	27.16	36.90	27.31	1043
			100.93	59.4	62.8	91.21	2.87	1.40	1.27				1044
19.04	12.82	6.23	81.10	62.1	65.7	85.95	2.74	1.33	1.18	27.21	38.94	27.09	1045
15.12	14.75	0.38	76.36	63.3	67.1	73.20	2.31	1.12	1.01	26.43	38.54	26.43	1046
12.81	16.29	-3.48	60.80	64.4	68.2	63.55	2.04	0.99	0.91	26.06	36.91	26.13	1047
12.30	16.20	-3.90	55.98	65.9	69.7	61.98	2.01	0.97	0.90	25.92	36.78	26.00	1048
11.82	16.34	-4.52	49.42	66.7	70.7	59.97	1.96	0.95	0.89	25.90	35.26	25.99	1049
11.96	16.24	-4.28	44.62	66.6	70.6	57.32	1.91	0.95	0.89	25.99	34.80	26.07	1050
20.50	10.20	10.29	49.43	65.8	70.4	81.24	2.89	1.40	1.31	26.63	37.95	26.43	1051
18.21	10.81	7.40	34.92	67.4	72.1	77.51	2.62	1.28	1.21	25.94	35.55	25.81	1052
16.86	11.67	5.20	29.53	66.6	71.9	74.86	2.45	1.19	1.14	25.27	31.64	25.18	1053
			22.47	67.5	73.0	64.16	2.15	1.04	1.01				1054
16.12	15.52	0.60	87.88	58.7	63.4	72.13	2.47	1.20	1.02	30.63	36.58	30.62	1055
18.60	10.51	8.09	36.99	67.9	72.4	83.89	2.78	1.35	1.27	29.97	33.27	29.83	1056
18.64	10.33	8.31	32.86	68.2	72.8	82.48	2.78	1.35	1.28	29.88	33.04	29.74	1057
19.14	9.97	9.17	32.45	68.1	73.0	83.66	2.84	1.38	1.31	30.01	32.09	29.85	1058
19.13	9.55	9.58	28.08	69.3	74.4	82.00	2.85	1.39	1.33	29.92	33.54	29.75	1059
19.41	9.25	10.15	28.13	69.4	74.9	80.78	2.89	1.40	1.35	29.45	35.45	29.27	1060
18.57	9.25	9.31	18.89	70.4	76.2	78.81	2.79	1.34	1.31	28.83	35.98	28.66	1061
13.29	12.30	0.99	12.34	72.3	78.3	64.19	2.18	1.05	1.03	28.23	36.41	28.21	1062
9.84	15.68	-5.83	10.89	72.9	79.2	53.43	1.79	0.86	0.85	28.39	35.00	28.49	1063
15.23	12.51	2.71	18.92	70.0	72.8	66.62	2.31	1.12	1.08	28.16	39.77	28.10	1064
14.58	12.54	2.04	16.27	70.9	74.2	61.86	2.25	1.09	1.06	27.66	36.86	27.62	1065
14.29	12.43	1.85	15.57	71.6	75.2	59.56	2.23	1.08	1.05	27.45	33.87	27.42	1066
16.01	10.83	5.17	13.51	71.8	76.1	67.90	2.41	1.18	1.15	27.08	33.03	26.99	1067
14.61	11.73	2.88	12.85	71.9	76.6	66.55	2.28	1.10	1.08	26.92	32.52	26.87	1068
11.47	14.39	-2.91	11.00	72.3	77.3	59.65	1.94	0.94	0.92	26.92	31.69	26.96	1069
9.93	15.95	-6.02	8.63	72.2	78.1	56.37	1.78	0.87	0.85	26.71	28.39	26.79	1070
9.03	16.87	-7.84	6.91	72.8	79.0	51.04	1.68	0.82	0.80	27.58	27.47	27.69	1071
9.41	16.03	-6.61	6.76	73.8	79.8	49.92	1.73	0.84	0.83	28.35	27.11	28.44	1072

SUMMARY TABLE

SERIAL NO.	REGION/ COUNTRY	YEAR	POPULATION ESTIMATED AS OF MID-YEAR (in 000's)	DENSITY (per km²)	AGE STRUCTURE TOTAL REPRODUCTIVE VALUE (in 000's)	DEPENDENCY RATIO YOUTH <15 (x 100)	OLD AGE ≥ 65 (x 100)	DEPARTURE FROM STABILITY (Percent)	VITAL CRUDE RATES (Both Sexes) BIRTH (x 1000)	DEATH (x 1000)	STANDARDIZED RATES Standard: USA 1960 BIRTH (x 1000)	DEATH (x 1000)
			3	4	5	6	7	8	9	10	11	12
		1	2									
1073	Switzerland	1951	4749	115	1122	35.2	14.2	5.3	17.56	10.18	15.45	10.39
1074		1954	4927	119	1155	36.5	14.8	5.2	17.06	10.09	14.88	9.99
1075		1957	5117	124	1204	36.7	15.1	4.5	17.60	9.90	15.10	9.52
1076		1960	5429	131	1294	35.4	15.4	3.4	17.60	9.40	15.83	8.80
1077		1962	5584	135	1350	34.7	15.7	3.3	18.68	9.87	16.56	9.26
1078		1965	5852	142	1434	34.6	16.1	3.8	19.11	9.49	16.53	8.53
1079		1966	5917	143	1441	35.4	16.5	3.4	18.55	9.43	15.92	8.44
1080		1967	5990	145	1431	35.6	16.9	4.0	17.93	9.21	15.27	8.15
1081		1970	6181	150	1349	35.4	18.2	7.6	16.05	9.24	13.60	8.02
1082		1975	6339	154	1158	33.2	20.0	17.0	12.38	8.82	10.37	6.99
1083		1980	6319	153	1073	28.3	21.4	16.7	11.66	9.35	9.95	6.52
1084		1985	6470	157	1049	24.7	21.2	17.0	11.54	9.21	9.73	5.82
1085		1986	6504	158	1053	24.3	21.5	16.6	11.73	9.24	9.85	5.71
1086	U.K. of Great	1950	50616	207		33.4	16.0		15.88	11.68		
1087	Britain and	1960	52372	215		35.8	18.0		18.20	11.78		
1088	North. Ireland	1966	54601	223	12627	36.4	18.9	8.2	17.94	11.79	17.96	9.44
1089		1970	55629	227	12036	38.3	20.7	4.5	16.25	11.78	15.79	9.03
1090		1975	56226	230	10348	37.3	22.5	9.5	12.41	11.78	11.66	8.55
1091		1980	56330	230	10441	32.8	23.3	7.4	13.38	11.74	12.16	7.99
1092		1985	56618	231	10039	29.3	23.0	9.2	13.26	11.85	11.58	7.49
1093	U.K. England	1951	43800	287	9008	33.3	16.5	4.8	15.59	11.85	13.99	10.84
1094	& Wales	1956	44667	293	9235	34.7	17.6	4.6	15.61	11.60	15.11	9.87
1095		1961	46166	303	10305	35.2	18.4	9.3	17.58	11.81	17.88	9.59
1096		1963	47028	308	10766	34.6	18.3	9.8	18.16	12.18	18.33	9.84
1097		1964	47401	311	10946	34.8	18.5	9.8	18.48	11.28	18.63	9.05
1098		1965	47763	313	10900	35.1	18.8	9.0	18.06	11.50	18.14	9.13
1099		1966	47985	315	10830	35.6	19.0	8.1	17.71	11.75	17.70	9.29
1100		1967	48301	317	10712	36.1	19.4	6.6	17.26	11.61	17.03	9.08
1101		1968	48593	319	10605	36.6	19.7	5.5	16.86	11.87	16.45	9.25
1102		1970	48891	321	10347	37.6	20.9	4.5	16.05	11.76	15.55	8.90
1103		1975	49470	324	8916	36.7	22.7	9.9	12.20	11.78	11.43	8.44
1104		1980	49603	325	9047	32.3	23.6	7.6	13.23	11.72	12.02	7.86
1105		1985	49924	327	8750	29.0	23.3	9.3	13.15	11.83	11.52	7.38
1106	U.K. Northern	1966	1425	105	480	47.4	16.6	9.2	23.44	11.54	25.15	10.63
1107	Ireland	1970	1524	112	460	50.6	18.1	6.6	21.05	10.86	21.20	9.78
1108		1975	1524	112	405	49.5	19.1	5.1	17.15	10.84	17.25	9.47
1109		1980	1533	113	421	44.8	19.3	5.3	18.65	10.97	17.95	9.32
1110		1985	1558	115	393	41.0	19.2	4.5	17.74	10.24	15.87	8.21
1111	U.K. Scotland	1951	5100	65	1240	37.7	15.3	2.9	17.88	12.50	15.63	12.30
1112		1956	5145	65	1261	38.7	15.8	3.9	18.52	11.96	16.96	11.21
1113		1961	5184	66	1322	40.3	16.5	8.0	19.73	12.15	18.96	10.93
1114		1963	5205	66	1345	40.2	16.8	9.3	19.73	12.59	19.40	11.20
1115		1964	5206	66	1357	40.3	17.1	9.6	20.04	11.72	19.80	10.33
1116		1965	5203	66	1334	40.8	17.5	8.7	19.35	12.08	19.23	10.55
1117		1966	5190	66	1309	41.1	17.9	7.8	18.60	12.27	18.58	10.62
1118		1970	5214	66	1210	42.0	19.7	5.0	16.75	12.21	16.55	10.08
1119		1975	5232	66	1029	39.6	21.4	8.6	12.99	12.06	12.21	9.47
1120		1980	5194	66	978	33.8	22.1	8.6	13.26	12.19	11.82	8.92
1121		1985	5137	65	899	29.4	21.7	10.4	12.98	12.45	11.01	8.46
1122	Yugoslavia	1951	16477	64	6419	48.6	8.9	7.0	29.08	13.00	23.21	15.81
1123		1954	17267	68	6524	51.5	9.5	6.3	27.95	11.52	22.05	14.00
1124		1957	18005	70	5847	47.5	9.6	10.0	24.43	10.29	18.56	12.88
1125		1961	18582	73	5626	49.9	9.9	9.5	22.72	9.01	18.03	11.29
1126		1965	19507	76	5548	46.7	10.5	9.0	20.92	8.74	17.36	10.94
1127		1970	20371	80	5046	41.6	12.0	11.6	17.83	8.93	14.82	10.78
1128		1975	21352	83	5005	39.1	13.3	10.2	18.17	8.66	14.73	9.88
1129		1980	22304	87	4802	36.8	14.2	10.4	17.13	8.85	13.80	9.41
1130		1985	23124	90	4695	35.2	12.5	10.2	15.85	9.21	13.17	9.20
1131	OCEANIA	1950	12647	1		47.4	11.9		27.63	12.41		
1132		1960	15782	2		55.2	12.5		26.71	10.59		
1133		1970	19329	2		53.1	12.0		23.85	9.68		
1134		1980	22794	3		46.7	12.8		20.56	8.09		
1135		1985	24634	3		43.6	13.3		20.09	8.04		
1136	AUSTRALIA-	1950	10127	1		41.7	12.8		23.52	9.37		
1137	NEW ZEALAND	1960	12687	2		50.3	14.0		22.60	8.72		
1138		1970	15371	2		47.2	13.4		19.78	8.51		
1139		1980	17808	2		39.4	14.9		15.67	7.48		
1140		1985	19005	2		35.9	15.4		15.08	7.58		

RATES			MORTALITY			FERTILITY							
INTRINSIC RATES (Female)			INFANT MORTALITY RATE	LIFE EXPECTANCY AT BIRTH		GENERAL FERTILITY RATE	TOTAL FERTILITY RATE	GROSS REPRODUCTION RATE	NET MATERNITY FUNCTION				SERIAL NO.
BIRTH (x 1000)	DEATH (x 1000)	INCREASE (x 1000)	(x 1000)	MALE (Years)	FEMALE (Years)	(x 1000)			TOTAL (NRR)	MEAN μ	VARIANCE σ^2	GENERATION (Years)	
13	14	15	16	17	18	19	20	21	22	23	24	25	
15.87	12.59	3.28	30.98	66.8	71.2	68.64	2.39	1.16	1.10	29.30	33.15	29.24	1073
15.17	12.79	2.38	28.75	67.4	72.2	67.38	2.30	1.12	1.07	29.15	33.11	29.11	1074
15.37	12.27	3.11	24.33	68.0	73.2	70.38	2.34	1.14	1.09	28.95	33.33	28.89	1075
16.34	11.20	5.14	23.91	68.8	74.3	72.18	2.46	1.20	1.16	28.68	31.54	28.60	1076
17.35	10.67	6.68	24.76	68.4	73.9	76.36	2.57	1.25	1.21	28.45	31.83	28.34	1077
17.09	10.45	6.65	17.85	69.6	75.1	77.52	2.57	1.24	1.21	28.34	31.14	28.23	1078
16.31	10.89	5.42	17.09	69.6	75.3	74.96	2.47	1.20	1.16	28.35	31.11	28.26	1079
15.46	11.32	4.14	17.48	69.7	75.9	72.40	2.37	1.16	1.12	28.28	31.39	28.21	1080
12.92	13.41	-0.49	13.03	69.5	75.9	64.96	2.11	1.02	0.99	28.27	32.98	28.27	1081
8.43	18.03	-9.60	9.47	71.2	78.0	49.80	1.62	0.79	0.76	28.04	28.33	28.18	1082
7.92	18.49	-10.57	8.09	72.1	79.0	46.03	1.55	0.76	0.74	28.38	25.10	28.51	1083
7.60	18.47	-10.86	5.86	73.6	80.5	44.81	1.52	0.75	0.73	28.86	23.33	28.99	1084
7.70	18.25	-10.55	5.74	73.8	80.6	45.50	1.53	0.75	0.74	28.98	23.09	29.10	1085
			28.48	66.7	71.8	63.95	2.18	1.06	1.02				1086
			21.55	67.9	73.8	78.48	2.82	1.37	1.34				1087
19.35	9.33	10.02	19.63	68.2	74.4	78.47	2.78	1.35	1.31	27.26	35.08	27.08	1088
16.40	10.93	5.46	18.49	68.7	75.0	72.32	2.45	1.19	1.16	26.76	33.71	26.67	1089
10.41	16.16	-5.75	16.04	69.5	75.8	55.53	1.81	0.88	0.86	26.50	30.58	26.58	1090
11.21	14.91	-3.71	12.14	70.5	76.6	57.21	1.89	0.92	0.90	26.93	29.15	26.98	1091
10.28	15.75	-5.47	9.36	71.7	77.4	54.40	1.80	0.87	0.86	27.30	30.27	27.38	1092
14.10	13.88	0.22	29.47	66.4	71.5	61.49	2.17	1.05	1.01	28.09	33.28	28.09	1093
15.54	12.10	3.45	24.56	67.7	73.3	64.77	2.35	1.14	1.10	27.67	32.17	27.61	1094
19.28	9.51	9.77	22.38	68.1	74.0	75.79	2.78	1.35	1.30	27.42	31.91	27.25	1095
20.00	9.16	10.85	21.68	67.9	73.9	78.25	2.85	1.38	1.34	27.36	31.64	27.18	1096
20.18	8.86	11.32	19.91	68.5	74.7	80.23	2.89	1.40	1.36	27.35	31.85	27.16	1097
19.62	9.10	10.52	19.00	68.5	74.8	78.92	2.81	1.37	1.33	27.24	32.35	27.06	1098
19.03	9.44	9.59	19.00	68.4	74.7	77.50	2.74	1.33	1.29	27.08	32.40	26.91	1099
18.08	9.90	8.18	18.55	68.7	74.9	75.82	2.64	1.28	1.25	27.03	32.56	26.89	1100
17.33	10.37	6.95	18.29	68.6	74.8	74.09	2.55	1.24	1.20	26.93	34.46	26.81	1101
16.05	11.11	4.94	18.19	68.9	75.2	71.43	2.41	1.17	1.14	26.68	33.41	26.60	1102
10.07	16.52	-6.44	15.72	69.8	76.0	54.66	1.78	0.86	0.84	26.46	30.30	26.55	1103
11.00	15.08	-4.09	12.04	70.8	76.8	56.64	1.87	0.91	0.90	26.90	29.02	26.96	1104
10.15	15.84	-5.69	9.36	71.9	77.6	53.99	1.79	0.87	0.86	27.30	30.23	27.38	1105
25.04	7.56	17.49	25.42	67.0	72.2	100.99	3.70	1.79	1.72	31.23	33.14	30.92	1106
23.02	7.87	15.15	22.88	67.7	73.5	94.40	3.26	1.58	1.53	28.52	39.88	28.22	1107
18.21	10.06	8.15	20.44	67.6	74.1	78.92	2.67	1.29	1.25	27.85	35.77	27.70	1108
19.17	9.23	9.94	14.59	68.1	75.0	81.36	2.78	1.35	1.32	28.17	32.75	28.00	1109
16.22	10.57	5.66	9.59	70.3	76.5	74.21	2.45	1.19	1.17	28.23	33.20	28.13	1110
16.44	13.12	3.31	38.75	64.4	68.7	69.42	2.42	1.17	1.10	28.60	34.12	28.54	1111
18.27	11.01	7.25	30.32	65.9	71.1	74.84	2.63	1.28	1.22	28.08	32.72	27.95	1112
20.92	9.31	11.61	27.71	66.1	71.9	83.47	2.94	1.43	1.38	27.72	32.39	27.53	1113
21.63	8.97	12.67	26.32	65.8	71.9	84.36	3.01	1.47	1.41	27.63	31.42	27.42	1114
21.90	8.62	13.28	24.03	66.7	72.8	86.33	3.07	1.49	1.44	27.63	31.96	27.41	1115
21.11	8.99	12.12	23.12	66.6	72.7	83.95	2.98	1.44	1.39	27.53	32.28	27.32	1116
20.34	9.39	10.95	23.19	66.6	72.5	81.10	2.88	1.39	1.35	27.40	32.75	27.21	1117
17.67	10.59	7.09	19.63	67.1	73.4	74.31	2.57	1.24	1.21	26.82	33.08	26.70	1118
11.38	15.49	-4.11	17.19	67.9	74.5	57.07	1.90	0.92	0.90	26.35	30.22	26.41	1119
10.89	15.76	-4.87	12.06	69.0	75.3	55.66	1.84	0.90	0.88	26.70	28.16	26.77	1120
9.71	17.05	-7.34	9.36	70.1	75.9	52.56	1.71	0.83	0.82	26.94	29.12	27.05	1121
25.17	13.81	11.36	117.68	55.3	58.2	107.59	3.58	1.73	1.38	28.92	44.79	28.66	1122
24.00	12.82	11.18	109.62	58.8	61.1	106.75	3.40	1.64	1.37	28.63	43.56	28.38	1123
19.69	13.66	6.03	103.25	60.5	63.1	92.92	2.87	1.39	1.18	27.99	42.07	27.86	1124
19.22	12.35	6.87	83.71	63.6	66.8	90.43	2.79	1.35	1.21	27.43	42.39	27.28	1125
18.37	12.33	6.05	71.88	64.4	68.0	82.52	2.69	1.30	1.18	27.02	37.90	26.90	1126
14.88	13.87	1.01	55.55	65.1	69.8	66.44	2.29	1.11	1.03	26.56	38.32	26.54	1127
14.77	13.21	1.56	39.75	67.0	71.9	68.52	2.28	1.10	1.04	26.26	35.87	26.23	1128
13.46	13.82	-0.36	31.46	67.8	73.3	66.08	2.14	1.03	0.99	26.11	33.51	26.12	1129
12.61	14.40	-1.79	28.26	68.1	73.9	63.33	2.05	0.99	0.95	26.04	31.17	26.07	1130
			67.27	58.9	62.7	116.71	3.83	1.86	1.58				1131
			54.13	61.6	66.1	116.80	3.94	1.92	1.70				1132
			39.74	63.1	68.0	101.60	3.19	1.55	1.39				1133
			30.53	65.6	70.5	83.05	2.64	1.28	1.17				1134
			25.79	66.4	71.3	79.32	2.57	1.25	1.17				1135
			24.15	67.0	72.3	97.95	3.25	1.58	1.51				1136
			19.80	67.9	74.1	97.93	3.37	1.64	1.59				1137
			16.49	68.5	75.1	83.10	2.58	1.26	1.22				1138
			10.32	71.7	78.3	61.86	1.94	0.94	0.93				1139
			8.78	72.7	79.2	57.86	1.86	0.90	0.89				1140

SERIAL NO.	REGION/ COUNTRY	YEAR	POPULATION		AGE STRUCTURE				VITAL			
			ESTIMATED AS OF MID-YEAR (in 000's)	DENSITY (per km²)	TOTAL REPRODUCTIVE VALUE (in 000's)	DEPENDENCY RATIO YOUTH < 15 (x 100)	OLD AGE ≥ 65 (x 100)	DEPARTURE FROM STABILITY (Percent)	CRUDE RATES (Both Sexes) BIRTH (x 1000)	DEATH (x 1000)	STANDARDIZED RATES Standard: USA 1960 BIRTH (x 1000)	DEATH (x 1000)
	1	2	3	4	5	6	7	8	9	10	11	12
1141	MELANESIA	1950	2119	4		73.1	7.3		44.10	26.03		
1142		1960	2583	5		75.6	5.4		43.22	19.03		
1143		1970	3300	6		78.2	5.5		39.53	14.99		
1144		1980	4196	8		76.1	3.4		37.80	11.09		
1145		1985	4767	9		73.6	4.7		37.00	10.30		
1146	MICRONESIA	1950	156	42		72.0	7.5		38.81	16.65		
1147		1960	194	52		83.8	5.5		38.98	12.39		
1148		1970	252	67		78.5	6.9		35.94	8.95		
1149		1980	316	85		74.7	6.2		34.68	6.19		
1150		1985	348	93		73.2	6.5		32.08	5.59		
1151	POLYNESIA	1950	245	9		85.4	8.9		49.34	19.22		
1152		1960	317	12		92.3	7.7		47.31	14.55		
1153		1970	407	15		94.5	6.0		40.89	10.42		
1154		1980	473	18		88.7	6.0		36.92	5.24		
1155		1985	514	19		84.7	6.8		34.24	4.98		
1156	Australia	1951	8422	1	2313	41.7	12.4	6.0	23.18	9.56	19.97	10.57
1157		1954	8987	1	2513	45.1	13.1	6.0	22.71	9.05	20.78	9.90
1158		1957	9640	1	2769	47.7	13.6	6.9	22.65	8.81	21.84	9.68
1159		1960	10275	1	3042	49.0	13.8	7.3	22.62	8.65	22.44	9.52
1160		1962	10705	1	3184	48.7	13.8	6.2	22.15	8.70	22.04	9.32
1161		1963	10916	1	3222	48.4	13.8	5.4	21.59	8.69	21.48	9.30
1162		1964	11136	1	3207	48.1	13.6	3.6	20.58	9.03	20.30	9.69
1163		1965	11360	1	3186	47.6	13.6	3.5	19.62	8.78	19.13	9.46
1164		1966	11550	2	3197	47.3	13.8	3.8	19.27	9.00	18.60	9.54
1165		1967	11810	2	3265	47.1	13.6	3.8	19.42	8.70	18.37	9.24
1166		1970	12552	2	3489	45.9	13.3	3.6	20.52	9.01	18.44	9.62
1167	Australia*	1971	13067	2	3634	45.5	13.2	3.2	21.15	8.47	18.49	8.99
1168		1975	13893	2	3289	43.1	13.7	13.1	16.77	7.85	13.83	8.12
1169		1980	14695	2	3206	38.8	14.8	17.9	15.35	7.40	12.17	7.15
1170		1985	15788	2	3368	35.7	15.5	16.3	15.67	7.53	12.38	6.70
1171	Guam	1970	86	277	37	67.7	3.0	6.2	33.58	4.15	30.65	9.91
1172		1980	107	344	37	56.0	4.5	14.1	28.16	3.96	20.71	8.26
1173	Fiji	1950	289	16		92.5	5.5		44.30	14.10		
1174		1960	394	22		96.9	5.1		39.40	9.20		
1175		1970	520	28		80.5	4.5		31.50	6.50		
1176		1975	573	31	232	67.1	4.8	12.9	28.79	6.89	22.17	12.52
1177		1980	634	35	256	64.5	5.1	12.6	29.67	6.40	22.13	11.25
1178		1985	691	38		62.8	5.9		27.35	5.03		
1179	New Zealand	1951	1833	7	534	46.0	15.4	7.2	24.36	9.55	21.96	9.73
1180		1952	1876	7	560	47.2	15.6	8.2	24.77	9.28	22.77	9.40
1181		1954	1966	7	594	49.4	15.7	8.5	24.53	8.92	23.27	8.97
1182		1957	2089	8	656	51.2	15.7	10.2	24.90	9.07	24.90	9.11
1183		1959	2181	8	703	52.9	15.5	10.9	25.10	9.09	25.75	8.98
1184		1961	2260	8	747	53.9	15.4	11.6	25.53	9.03	26.49	8.90
1185		1963	2543	9	850	56.1	14.3	8.7	25.43	8.81	25.91	9.18
1186		1965	2635	10	842	55.3	14.1	4.5	22.83	8.72	22.71	9.14
1187		1967	2729	10	854	55.1	14.0	4.2	22.43	8.70	21.69	9.19
1188		1970	2829	11	858	53.7	14.2	3.9	21.99	8.78	20.36	10.64
1189		1975	3100	12	806	49.1	14.3	11.2	18.27	8.10	15.25	8.52
1190		1980	3131	12	731	43.0	15.3	15.3	16.14	8.52	13.14	8.34
1191		1985	3279	12	719	37.8	15.8	16.6	15.80	8.38	12.39	7.58
1192	Papua New	1950	1613	3		69.6	7.3		44.43	28.82		
1193	Guinea	1960	1920	4		71.5	5.1		43.71	21.31		
1194		1970	2422	5		76.5	5.5		40.62	17.07		
1195		1980	3086	7		77.4	2.8		38.84	13.07		
1196		1985	3511	8		74.2	4.4		38.72	12.13		
1197	UNION OF	1950	180075	8		47.1	9.5		26.30	9.20		
1198	SOVIET	1959	208827	9	65171	46.0	9.7	8.9	25.21	7.39	23.38	11.00
1199	SOCIALIST	1960	214335	10		49.0	10.8		22.10	7.18		
1200	REPUBLICS	1970	241720	11	63171	45.8	12.2	8.3	17.48	8.74	20.48	12.51
1201		1979	262085	12	61706	37.7	14.6	7.6	18.19	10.05	19.55	12.41
1202		1987	281338	13	66976	38.9	13.8	5.7	19.92	9.85	21.83	11.16

* Time series 1951-70 and 1971-85 based on different population estimation procedures.

RATES — INTRINSIC RATES (Female)			MORTALITY			FERTILITY			NET MATERNITY FUNCTION				
BIRTH (x 1000)	DEATH (x 1000)	INCREASE (x 1000)	INFANT MORTALITY RATE (x 1000)	LIFE EXPECTANCY AT BIRTH MALE (Years)	FEMALE (Years)	GENERAL FERTILITY RATE (x 1000)	TOTAL FERTILITY RATE	GROSS REPRODUCTION RATE	TOTAL (NRR)	MEAN μ	VARIANCE σ^2	GENERATION (Years)	SERIAL NO.
13	14	15	16	17	18	19	20	21	22	23	24	25	
			170.75	39.6	39.5	195.95	6.31	3.06	1.80				1141
			137.94	46.6	47.0	193.94	6.27	3.05	2.08				1142
			91.59	51.2	52.0	176.83	5.64	2.74	2.01				1143
			64.66	54.9	57.0	165.00	5.34	2.59	2.07				1144
			52.19	56.4	58.7	160.84	5.26	2.55	2.21				1145
			102.00	45.9	49.5	184.61	5.94	2.90	2.23				1146
			77.00	50.9	54.5	187.13	6.21	3.03	2.51				1147
			54.00	55.9	59.5	164.67	5.60	2.73	2.39				1148
			35.83	65.9	70.3	154.50	4.98	2.43	2.28				1149
			29.97	67.4	72.0	139.27	4.53	2.21	2.10				1150
			110.00	54.3	57.6	233.45	7.38	3.56	2.56				1151
			67.00	60.3	63.6	227.63	7.29	3.51	2.74				1152
			44.00	64.8	69.2	191.75	6.42	3.10	2.58				1153
			29.95	67.5	72.0	170.33	5.60	2.70	2.57				1154
			25.55	68.6	73.4	154.24	5.08	2.45	2.36				1155
21.99	8.94	13.05	25.07	66.3	71.7	94.80	3.09	1.50	1.44	28.02	35.32	27.78	1156
23.13	8.15	14.98	23.68	67.1	72.7	95.35	3.22	1.57	1.51	27.77	34.42	27.50	1157
24.40	7.46	16.94	21.92	67.5	73.4	96.94	3.39	1.65	1.59	27.59	33.52	27.29	1158
25.28	7.01	18.27	21.10	67.7	73.9	97.65	3.48	1.70	1.64	27.49	32.79	27.18	1159
24.74	7.10	17.64	20.66	67.8	74.2	95.38	3.42	1.67	1.62	27.51	32.54	27.21	1160
24.03	7.36	16.67	19.96	67.9	74.2	92.91	3.33	1.63	1.57	27.49	32.94	27.21	1161
22.38	8.09	14.29	19.07	67.5	73.8	88.43	3.14	1.52	1.48	27.51	33.40	27.26	1162
20.94	8.64	12.29	18.62	67.8	74.1	84.12	2.96	1.44	1.40	27.39	33.31	27.17	1163
20.23	8.99	11.24	18.17	67.6	74.1	82.42	2.88	1.40	1.36	27.29	33.37	27.10	1164
19.96	9.02	10.94	18.26	67.8	74.5	82.83	2.85	1.39	1.34	27.26	32.80	27.07	1165
20.20	8.96	11.24	17.88	67.4	74.2	86.50	2.86	1.39	1.35	27.08	33.67	26.90	1166
20.30	8.76	11.54	17.29	68.2	74.8	88.45	2.87	1.40	1.36	26.92	33.56	26.72	1167
13.48	12.72	0.75	14.27	69.4	76.5	69.33	2.15	1.04	1.02	26.68	30.35	26.67	1168
10.92	14.68	-3.76	10.72	71.0	78.3	61.49	1.90	0.92	0.90	27.14	28.32	27.20	1169
11.22	14.19	-2.97	9.92	72.2	78.7	61.04	1.93	0.94	0.92	27.69	27.68	27.73	1170
33.94	4.81	29.13	21.57	65.1	74.2	155.80	4.72	2.28	2.19	27.62	43.65	26.99	1171
22.79	7.46	15.34	16.32	68.9	75.3	110.21	3.18	1.55	1.51	27.19	42.38	26.87	1172
			88.00	53.8	56.7	203.58	6.63	3.22	2.77				1173
			66.00	58.8	61.7	180.07	5.95	2.89	2.64				1174
			45.00	63.6	66.7	129.49	3.71	1.80	1.70				1175
24.77	9.50	15.27	41.27	60.9	67.6	113.46	3.44	1.66	1.52	27.84	43.77	27.50	1176
25.01	8.87	16.14	38.59	63.0	69.6	114.96	3.43	1.67	1.55	27.49	39.28	27.18	1177
			27.26	68.2	72.7	106.28	3.19	1.55	1.49				1178
24.19	7.81	16.38	23.72	67.9	72.3	102.45	3.40	1.65	1.58	28.30	33.08	28.02	1179
25.37	7.34	18.04	22.68	68.5	72.6	105.11	3.53	1.72	1.65	28.26	33.24	27.94	1180
25.82	6.90	18.91	20.77	68.9	73.6	105.71	3.61	1.75	1.69	28.16	32.56	27.84	1181
27.94	6.15	21.80	20.28	68.9	74.0	109.15	3.87	1.88	1.82	27.85	31.77	27.49	1182
29.09	5.83	23.26	20.41	69.0	74.1	111.85	4.00	1.95	1.89	27.68	31.43	27.30	1183
29.99	5.50	24.49	19.13	69.1	74.4	107.08	4.12	2.01	1.95	27.65	31.93	27.25	1184
29.18	5.78	23.39	19.88	68.5	74.1	114.36	3.99	1.93	1.87	27.28	36.43	26.84	1185
25.42	6.87	18.55	19.51	68.2	74.2	101.69	3.52	1.70	1.65	27.23	34.48	26.90	1186
24.62	7.08	17.55	18.13	68.2	74.3	99.96	3.36	1.64	1.59	26.85	33.50	26.54	1187
22.97	7.77	15.21	16.72	68.0	73.9	97.01	3.16	1.54	1.49	26.62	33.83	26.37	1188
15.85	11.17	4.69	15.96	69.0	75.5	77.74	2.37	1.16	1.13	26.14	31.01	26.07	1189
12.66	13.76	-1.10	12.86	69.9	75.6	65.90	2.05	1.00	0.97	26.51	28.62	26.52	1190
11.45	14.57	-3.12	10.81	71.0	76.9	61.35	1.93	0.94	0.92	27.10	28.05	27.15	1191
			190.00	35.6	34.5	193.34	6.24	3.03	1.60				1192
			155.00	43.0	42.4	194.09	6.29	3.05	1.93				1193
			105.00	47.7	47.6	183.65	5.95	2.89	2.01				1194
			74.40	51.2	52.7	172.92	5.67	2.75	2.08				1195
			58.80	53.2	54.8	171.06	5.67	2.75	2.31				1196
			73.00	60.0	68.5	87.64	2.82	1.38	1.28				1197
19.05	10.65	8.41	38.11	64.4	71.7	88.94	2.82	1.37	1.27	28.43	42.48	28.26	1198
			31.56	65.5	73.0	83.69	2.54	1.24	1.15				1199
16.27	12.17	4.10	25.60	63.7	71.7	66.83	2.42	1.18	1.12	27.46	40.22	27.38	1200
14.83	12.87	1.95	25.55	62.3	72.7	69.69	2.27	1.11	1.05	26.49	34.50	26.45	1201
17.13	10.86	6.28	22.64	65.0	74.0	79.68	2.53	1.23	1.18	26.42	31.98	26.32	1202

Tabulations Based on
United Nations Data
and Estimates

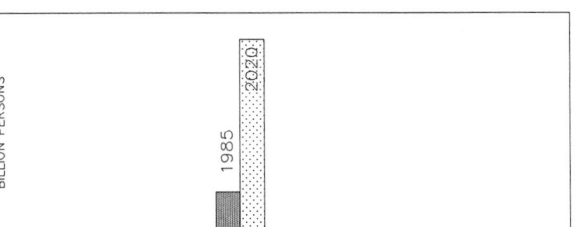

WORLD POPULATION, BY CONTINENT: 1950, 1985, 2020

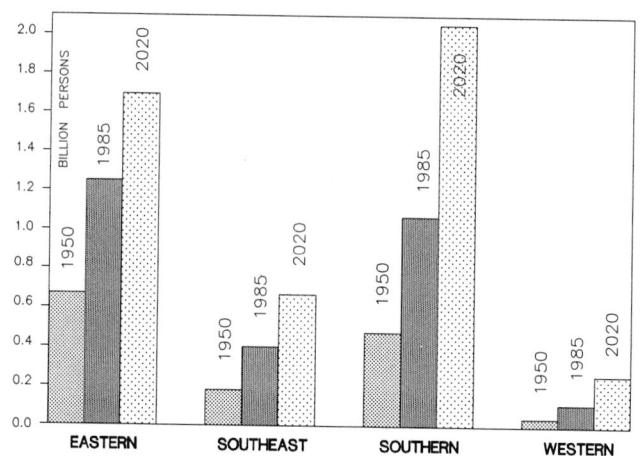

POPULATION OF ASIA, BY REGION: 1950, 1985, 2020

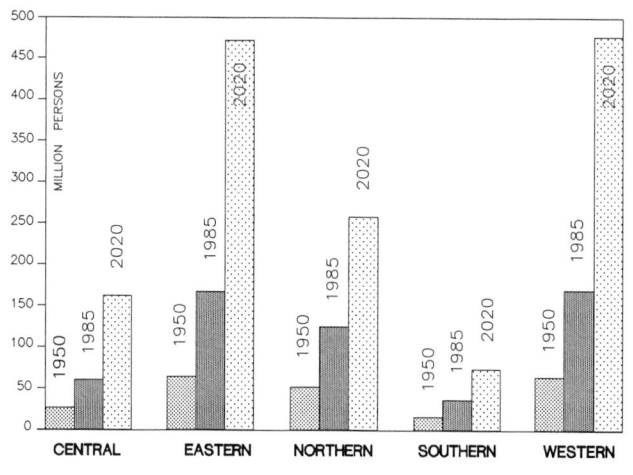

POPULATION OF AFRICA, BY REGION: 1950, 1985, 2020

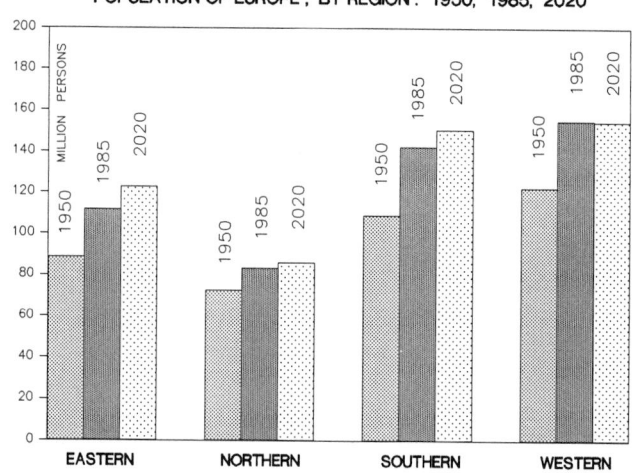

POPULATION OF EUROPE, BY REGION: 1950, 1985, 2020

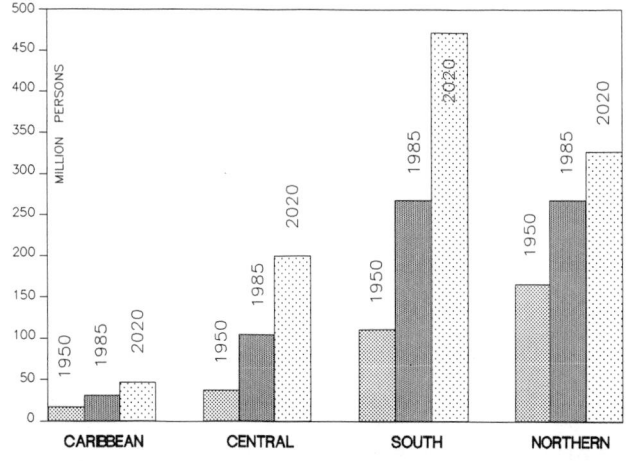

POPULATION OF THE AMERICAS, BY REGION: 1950, 1985, 2020

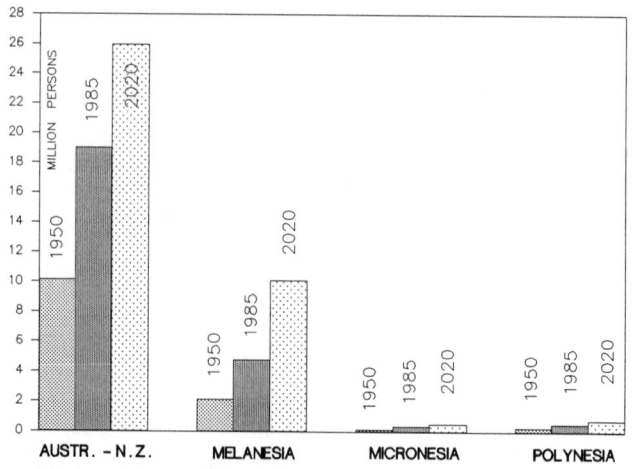

POPULATION OF OCEANIA, BY REGION: 1950, 1985, 2020

OBSERVED AND *PROJECTED* POPULATION DATA (000's)

YEAR	MID-YEAR POPULATION	NO. OF BIRTHS	NO. OF DEATHS	URBAN POPULATION NUMBER	URBAN POPULATION PERCENT	POPULATION 1985 AGE	POPULATION 1985 NUMBER
1950	2515312	94138	49509	732454	29.1	0	581657
1955	2751559	97873	47341	858177	31.2	5	523097
1960	3019376	106342	46683	1030251	34.1	10	522870
1965	3335927	112948	44481	1195213	35.8	15	496343
1970	3697918	116429	45022	1373890	37.2	20	445165
1975	4079753	115796	45200	1568599	38.4	25	388851
1980	4450210	123151	46451	1769654	39.8	30	350717
1985	4853848	131549	47966	1997104	41.1	35	285323
1990	*5292178*	*139370*	*49032*	*2259738*	*42.7*	40	236109
1995	*5765861*	*142820*	*50036*	*2566528*	*44.5*	45	220684
2000	*6251055*	*143312*	*51652*	*2915622*	*46.6*	50	197411
2005	*6728575*	*142545*	*53512*	*3306586*	*49.1*	55	173892
2010	*7190763*	*142320*	*55628*	*3735628*	*52.0*	60	141443
2015	*7639547*	*140270*	*58366*	*4187178*	*54.8*	65	104218
2020	*8062274*	*140348*	*61846*	*4648087*	*57.7*	70+	186066

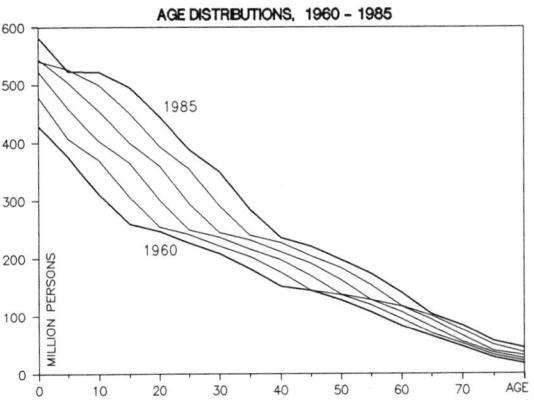

POPULATION RATIOS

YEAR	AGE DISTRIBUTION UNDER 15	AGE DISTRIBUTION 15-64	AGE DISTRIBUTION 65 & OLDER	AGE DISTRIBUTION 70 & OLDER	DEPENDENCY RATIO	WOMEN 15-49	CHILD-WOMAN RATIO
1950	0.346	0.604	0.051	0.029	0.657	0.248	0.547
1955	0.357	0.592	0.052	0.030	0.690	0.242	0.601
1960	0.370	0.577	0.053	0.031	0.732	0.234	0.608
1965	0.376	0.570	0.053	0.032	0.753	0.230	0.624
1970	0.375	0.571	0.054	0.032	0.751	0.232	0.610
1975	0.369	0.574	0.057	0.034	0.741	0.233	0.572
1980	0.352	0.588	0.059	0.037	0.699	0.239	0.509
1985	0.335	0.605	0.060	0.038	0.653	0.245	0.489
1990	*0.323*	*0.615*	*0.062*	*0.038*	*0.627*	*0.249*	*0.476*
2000	*0.313*	*0.619*	*0.068*	*0.043*	*0.615*	*0.251*	*0.441*
2010	*0.286*	*0.641*	*0.073*	*0.047*	*0.559*	*0.252*	*0.384*
2020	*0.256*	*0.657*	*0.088*	*0.054*	*0.523*	*0.250*	*0.342*

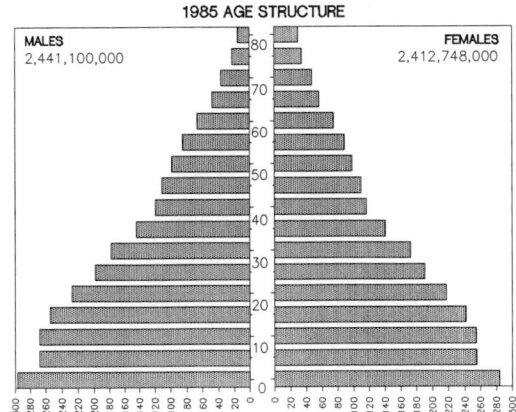

MORTALITY MEASURES (Annual Averages)

PERIOD	CRUDE DEATH RATE	INFANT MORT. RATE	LIFE EXPECTANCY AT BIRTH (years) MALE	FEMALE	BOTH SEXES	DIFFERENCE FEMALE-MALE
1950-55	19.68	155.26	44.76	47.14	45.92	2.38
1955-60	17.20	139.11	47.82	50.15	48.96	2.33
1960-65	15.46	117.90	50.41	52.55	51.46	2.15
1965-70	13.33	102.98	53.82	55.98	54.87	2.16
1970-75	12.18	93.62	55.62	57.80	56.68	2.18
1975-80	11.08	85.86	56.90	59.38	58.11	2.48
1980-85	10.44	79.29	58.21	61.11	59.62	2.90
1985-90	*9.88*	*71.24*	*60.01*	*63.01*	*61.48*	*3.00*
1990-95	*9.27*	*64.60*	*61.51*	*64.64*	*63.04*	*3.13*
2000-05	*8.26*	*52.37*	*64.22*	*67.62*	*65.88*	*3.40*
2010-15	*7.74*	*40.69*	*66.81*	*70.64*	*68.68*	*3.83*
2020-25	*7.67*	*30.37*	*69.31*	*73.48*	*71.35*	*4.16*

FERTILITY MEASURES (Annual Averages)

PERIOD	CRUDE BIRTH RATE	FERTILITY RATES GENERAL	FERTILITY RATES TOTAL	REPRODUCTION RATES GROSS	REPRODUCTION RATES NET	RATE OF NATUR. INCR.
1950-55	37.43	153.01	4.996	2.435	1.652	17.74
1955-60	35.57	149.65	4.880	2.378	1.693	18.36
1960-65	35.22	151.93	4.970	2.422	1.794	19.76
1965-70	33.86	146.59	4.877	2.377	1.862	20.52
1970-75	31.49	135.30	4.451	2.169	1.737	19.31
1975-80	28.38	120.19	3.841	1.872	1.532	17.31
1980-85	27.67	114.35	3.610	1.759	1.463	17.24
1985-90	*27.10*	*109.59*	*3.439*	*1.678*	*1.427*	*17.22*
1990-95	*26.33*	*105.35*	*3.293*	*1.607*	*1.392*	*17.07*
2000-05	*22.93*	*91.41*	*2.960*	*1.445*	*1.294*	*14.66*
2010-15	*19.79*	*78.56*	*2.577*	*1.258*	*1.159*	*12.06*
2020-25	*17.41*	*69.85*	*2.271*	*1.108*	*1.043*	*9.74*

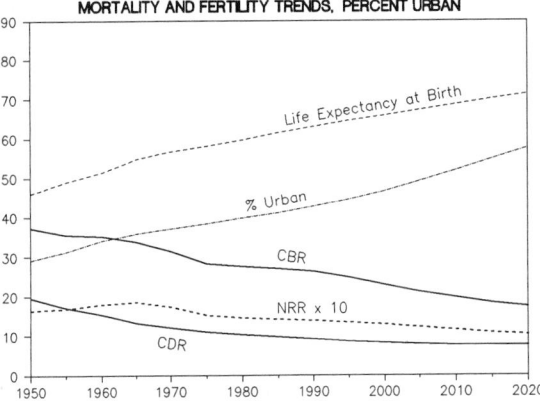

AGING MEASURES

YEAR	POPULATION AGE RATIOS 60+/20-59	65+/20-64	70+/20-69	75+/20-74	POPULATION MEAN AGE	POPULATION MEDIAN AGE
1950	0.1658	0.0996	0.0543	0.0253	27.25	23.37
1960	0.1741	0.1076	0.0605	0.0291	26.79	22.69
1970	0.1879	0.1146	0.0644	0.0331	26.51	21.61
1980	0.1863	0.1218	0.0716	0.0367	27.19	22.62
1990	*0.1896*	*0.1197*	*0.0705*	*0.0392*	*28.12*	*24.22*
2000	*0.1960*	*0.1277*	*0.0769*	*0.0408*	*29.15*	*25.97*
2010	*0.2051*	*0.1319*	*0.0823*	*0.0455*	*30.70*	*27.60*
2020	*0.2410*	*0.1530*	*0.0891*	*0.0482*	*32.60*	*29.81*

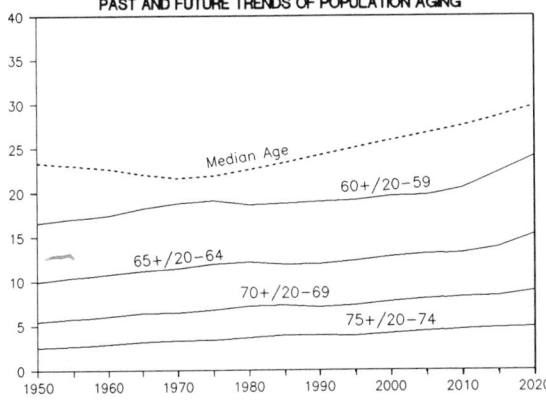

OBSERVED AND *PROJECTED* POPULATION DATA (000's)

YEAR	MID-YEAR POPULATION	NO. OF BIRTHS	NO. OF DEATHS	URBAN POPULATION NUMBER	URBAN POPULATION PERCENT	POPULATION 1985 AGE	POPULATION 1985 NUMBER
1950	832425	18843	8414	447610	53.8	0	86408
1955	887423	19199	8236	505420	57.0	5	85434
1960	944851	19009	8521	571325	60.5	10	88163
1965	1002801	17928	9191	637180	63.5	15	90819
1970	1049273	17531	9725	698838	66.6	20	95996
1975	1095613	17044	10313	753930	68.8	25	95426
1980	1136406	17297	10899	798161	70.2	30	90820
1985	1173660	17135	11482	839519	71.5	35	81689
1990	*1205193*	*16823*	*11606*	*875637*	*72.7*	40	69155
1995	*1234567*	*16633*	*11704*	*911379*	*73.8*	45	71103
2000	*1262482*	*16496*	*12284*	*944639*	*74.8*	50	65305
2005	*1286730*	*16361*	*12839*	*976171*	*75.9*	55	64213
2010	*1307469*	*16196*	*13250*	*1003696*	*76.8*	60	54554
2015	*1325286*	*16080*	*13737*	*1028792*	*77.6*	65	39305
2020	*1340064*	*16004*	*14206*	*1049991*	*78.4*	70+	95269

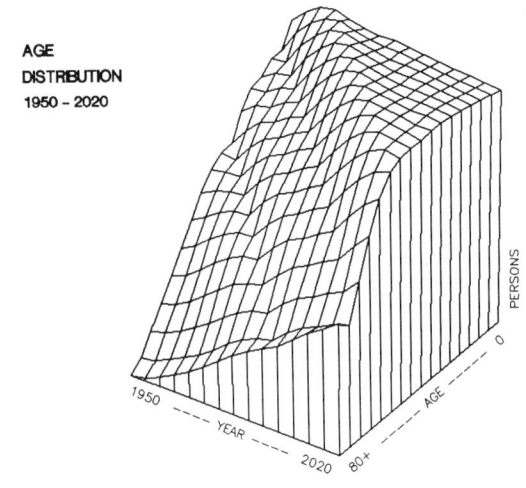

AGE DISTRIBUTION 1950 – 2020

POPULATION RATIOS

YEAR	AGE DISTRIBUTION UNDER 15	15-64	65 & OLDER	70 & OLDER	DEPENDENCY RATIO	WOMEN 15-49	CHILD-WOMAN RATIO
1950	0.278	0.646	0.076	0.046	0.548	0.269	0.381
1955	0.277	0.642	0.081	0.050	0.557	0.262	0.392
1960	0.286	0.630	0.085	0.053	0.589	0.249	0.400
1965	0.278	0.631	0.090	0.056	0.584	0.246	0.382
1970	0.266	0.638	0.096	0.059	0.568	0.251	0.337
1975	0.248	0.645	0.107	0.067	0.551	0.252	0.315
1980	0.231	0.653	0.115	0.077	0.530	0.252	0.300
1985	0.222	0.664	0.115	0.081	0.506	0.252	0.292
1990	*0.214*	*0.666*	*0.121*	*0.079*	*0.502*	*0.251*	*0.283*
2000	*0.201*	*0.663*	*0.137*	*0.093*	*0.509*	*0.246*	*0.268*
2010	*0.190*	*0.662*	*0.148*	*0.104*	*0.510*	*0.232*	*0.271*
2020	*0.182*	*0.644*	*0.173*	*0.117*	*0.552*	*0.219*	*0.274*

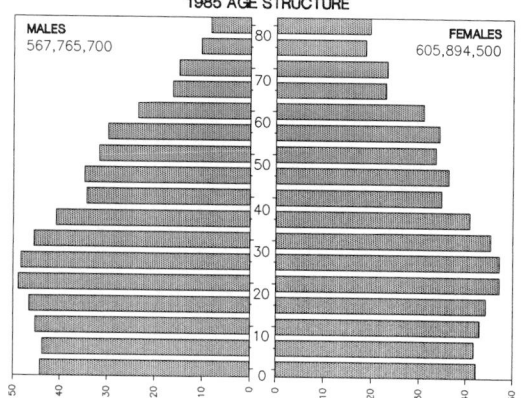

1985 AGE STRUCTURE

MALES 567,765,700

FEMALES 605,894,500

MORTALITY MEASURES (Annual Averages)

PERIOD	CRUDE DEATH RATE	INFANT MORT. RATE	LIFE EXPECTANCY AT BIRTH (years) MALE	FEMALE	BOTH SEXES	DIFFERENCE FEMALE-MALE
1950-55	10.11	55.94	62.98	68.65	65.74	5.67
1955-60	9.28	40.88	65.41	71.14	68.19	5.73
1960-65	9.02	31.56	66.62	72.77	69.61	6.15
1965-70	9.16	25.75	67.12	73.71	70.33	6.59
1970-75	9.27	21.66	67.40	74.64	70.92	7.23
1975-80	9.41	19.16	67.93	75.56	71.65	7.63
1980-85	9.59	16.41	68.55	76.26	72.31	7.72
1985-90	*9.78*	*14.76*	*69.83*	*77.23*	*73.43*	*7.40*
1990-95	*9.63*	*12.32*	*71.00*	*78.21*	*74.51*	*7.21*
2000-05	*9.73*	*9.33*	*72.87*	*79.62*	*76.16*	*6.75*
2010-15	*10.13*	*7.41*	*74.34*	*80.87*	*77.52*	*6.54*
2020-25	*10.60*	*6.10*	*75.63*	*81.96*	*78.71*	*6.33*

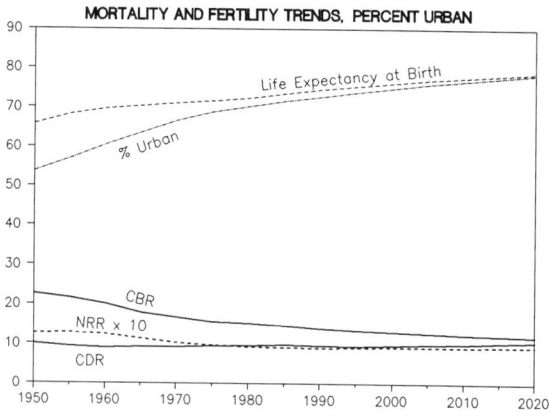

MORTALITY AND FERTILITY TRENDS, PERCENT URBAN

Life Expectancy at Birth

% Urban

CBR

NRR x 10

CDR

FERTILITY MEASURES (Annual Averages)

PERIOD	CRUDE BIRTH RATE	FERTILITY RATES GENERAL	FERTILITY RATES TOTAL	REPRODUCTION RATES GROSS	REPRODUCTION RATES NET	RATE OF NATUR. INCR.
1950-55	22.64	85.34	2.836	1.381	1.271	12.53
1955-60	21.64	84.72	2.819	1.372	1.279	12.35
1960-65	20.12	81.32	2.689	1.309	1.234	11.10
1965-70	17.88	71.97	2.439	1.187	1.134	8.71
1970-75	16.71	66.48	2.198	1.070	1.029	7.44
1975-80	15.56	61.81	2.034	0.990	0.964	6.14
1980-85	15.22	60.42	1.931	0.940	0.921	5.63
1985-90	*14.60*	*58.09*	*1.902*	*0.926*	*0.903*	*4.82*
1990-95	*13.96*	*55.71*	*1.893*	*0.922*	*0.902*	*4.33*
2000-05	*13.07*	*53.79*	*1.915*	*0.932*	*0.917*	*3.34*
2010-15	*12.39*	*54.34*	*1.930*	*0.940*	*0.927*	*2.25*
2020-25	*11.94*	*54.97*	*1.939*	*0.944*	*0.933*	*1.34*

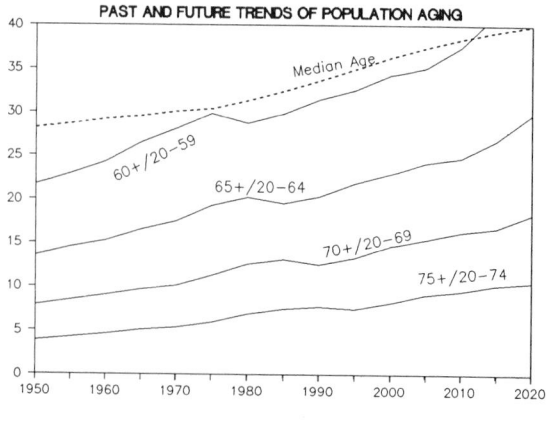

PAST AND FUTURE TRENDS OF POPULATION AGING

Median Age

60+/20-59

65+/20-64

70+/20-69

75+/20-74

AGING MEASURES

YEAR	POPULATION AGE RATIOS 60+/20-59	65+/20-64	70+/20-69	75+/20-74	POPULATION MEAN AGE	POPULATION MEDIAN AGE
1950	0.2169	0.1360	0.0786	0.0386	31.25	28.21
1960	0.2432	0.1527	0.0902	0.0463	31.85	29.23
1970	0.2806	0.1747	0.1009	0.0533	32.79	30.06
1980	0.2872	0.2023	0.1260	0.0688	34.38	31.37
1990	*0.3148*	*0.2036*	*0.1253*	*0.0773*	*35.76*	*33.67*
2000	*0.3432*	*0.2299*	*0.1468*	*0.0821*	*37.29*	*36.35*
2010	*0.3754*	*0.2475*	*0.1626*	*0.0953*	*38.78*	*38.46*
2020	*0.4572*	*0.2976*	*0.1833*	*0.1053*	*40.15*	*39.98*

OBSERVED AND *PROJECTED* POPULATION DATA (000's)

YEAR	MID-YEAR POPULATION	NO. OF BIRTHS	NO. OF DEATHS	URBAN POPULATION NUMBER	URBAN POPULATION PERCENT	POPULATION 1985 AGE	POPULATION 1985 NUMBER
1950	1682887	75053	40936	284845	16.9	0	495250
1955	1864135	78391	38944	352757	18.9	5	437663
1960	2074525	86906	37980	458926	22.1	10	434707
1965	2333126	94352	35116	558033	23.9	15	405525
1970	2648645	98296	35179	675052	25.5	20	349168
1975	2984140	98265	34822	814669	27.3	25	293425
1980	3313804	105333	35517	971493	29.3	30	259897
1985	3680188	113832	36482	1157585	31.5	35	203634
1990	*4086985*	*121952*	*37445*	*1384101*	*33.9*	40	166954
1995	*4531294*	*125666*	*38371*	*1655148*	*36.5*	45	149582
2000	*4988573*	*126390*	*39430*	*1970982*	*39.5*	50	132105
2005	*5441844*	*125843*	*40754*	*2330415*	*42.8*	55	109679
2010	*5883294*	*125844*	*42466*	*2731932*	*46.4*	60	86890
2015	*6314261*	*123981*	*44724*	*3158386*	*50.0*	65	64913
2020	*6722211*	*124166*	*47734*	*3598095*	*53.5*	70+	90796

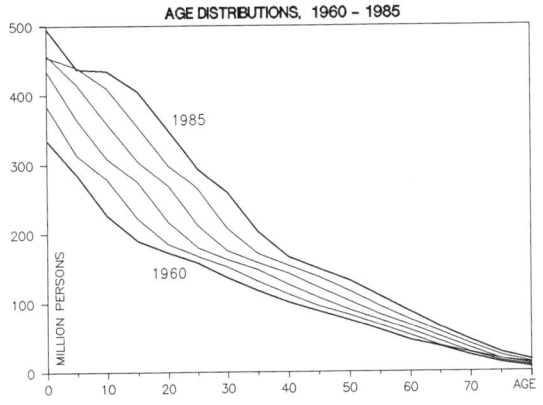

AGE DISTRIBUTIONS, 1960 - 1985

POPULATION RATIOS

YEAR	AGE DISTRIBUTION UNDER 15	AGE DISTRIBUTION 15-64	AGE DISTRIBUTION 65 & OLDER	AGE DISTRIBUTION 70 & OLDER	DEPENDENCY RATIO	WOMEN 15-49	CHILD-WOMAN RATIO
1950	0.379	0.583	0.038	0.020	0.716	0.237	0.640
1955	0.395	0.567	0.038	0.021	0.762	0.232	0.713
1960	0.408	0.554	0.038	0.021	0.807	0.227	0.711
1965	0.419	0.544	0.037	0.021	0.838	0.223	0.739
1970	0.418	0.544	0.037	0.021	0.837	0.224	0.730
1975	0.413	0.549	0.038	0.021	0.822	0.227	0.677
1980	0.394	0.566	0.040	0.023	0.766	0.234	0.586
1985	0.372	0.586	0.042	0.025	0.706	0.243	0.554
1990	*0.356*	*0.600*	*0.044*	*0.026*	*0.667*	*0.249*	*0.533*
2000	*0.342*	*0.608*	*0.050*	*0.030*	*0.644*	*0.252*	*0.484*
2010	*0.307*	*0.637*	*0.056*	*0.035*	*0.571*	*0.257*	*0.407*
2020	*0.271*	*0.659*	*0.070*	*0.041*	*0.517*	*0.257*	*0.353*

MORTALITY MEASURES (Annual Averages)

PERIOD	CRUDE DEATH RATE	INFANT MORT. RATE	LIFE EXPECTANCY AT BIRTH (years) MALE	LIFE EXPECTANCY AT BIRTH (years) FEMALE	LIFE EXPECTANCY AT BIRTH (years) BOTH SEXES	DIFFERENCE FEMALE-MALE
1950-55	24.33	179.70	40.26	41.85	41.04	1.59
1955-60	20.89	162.62	43.60	45.13	44.35	1.53
1960-65	18.31	136.23	46.96	48.27	47.60	1.31
1965-70	15.05	117.04	51.39	52.76	52.06	1.36
1970-75	13.28	105.96	53.60	54.92	54.24	1.33
1975-80	11.67	97.02	55.05	56.67	55.84	1.62
1980-85	10.72	89.23	56.57	58.72	57.61	2.15
1985-90	*9.91*	*79.40*	*58.59*	*60.96*	*59.75*	*2.38*
1990-95	*9.16*	*71.53*	*60.25*	*62.85*	*61.52*	*2.60*
2000-05	*7.90*	*57.79*	*63.13*	*66.12*	*64.59*	*2.99*
2010-15	*7.22*	*44.85*	*65.87*	*69.37*	*67.58*	*3.50*
2020-25	*7.10*	*33.42*	*68.52*	*72.41*	*70.42*	*3.90*

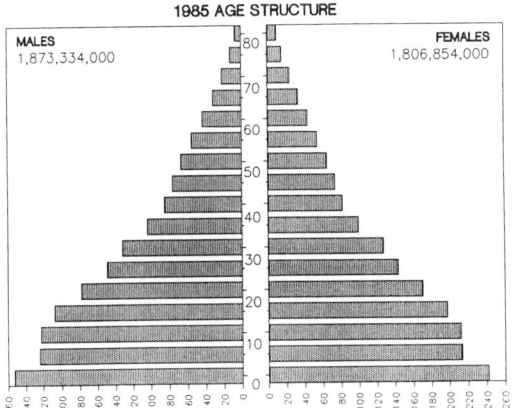

1985 AGE STRUCTURE

MALES 1,873,334,000   FEMALES 1,806,854,000

FERTILITY MEASURES (Annual Averages)

PERIOD	CRUDE BIRTH RATE	FERTILITY RATES GENERAL	FERTILITY RATES TOTAL	REPRODUCTION RATES GROSS	REPRODUCTION RATES NET	RATE OF NATUR. INCR.
1950-55	44.60	190.12	6.180	3.013	1.862	20.27
1955-60	42.05	183.27	5.947	2.899	1.908	21.16
1960-65	41.89	186.26	6.079	2.964	2.067	23.58
1965-70	40.44	180.70	5.991	2.921	2.195	25.39
1970-75	37.11	164.49	5.406	2.636	2.037	23.83
1975-80	32.93	142.78	4.540	2.213	1.752	21.26
1980-85	31.79	133.15	4.195	2.045	1.652	21.07
1985-90	*30.93*	*125.70*	*3.920*	*1.914*	*1.591*	*21.02*
1990-95	*29.84*	*119.45*	*3.690*	*1.802*	*1.531*	*20.68*
2000-05	*25.34*	*100.24*	*3.206*	*1.565*	*1.383*	*17.43*
2010-15	*21.39*	*83.19*	*2.701*	*1.319*	*1.203*	*14.17*
2020-25	*18.47*	*72.31*	*2.326*	*1.135*	*1.062*	*11.37*

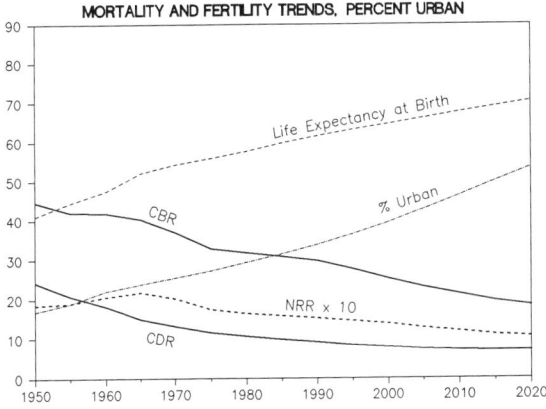

MORTALITY AND FERTILITY TRENDS, PERCENT URBAN

Life Expectancy at Birth   % Urban   CBR   NRR x 10   CDR

AGING MEASURES

YEAR	POPULATION AGE RATIOS 60+/20-59	POPULATION AGE RATIOS 65+/20-64	POPULATION AGE RATIOS 70+/20-69	POPULATION AGE RATIOS 75+/20-74	POPULATION MEAN AGE	POPULATION MEDIAN AGE
1950	0.1368	0.0786	0.0402	0.0174	25.27	21.14
1960	0.1371	0.0829	0.0438	0.0194	24.48	20.00
1970	0.1435	0.0848	0.0457	0.0226	24.02	18.95
1980	0.1441	0.0876	0.0479	0.0223	24.73	19.96
1990	*0.1470*	*0.0900*	*0.0506*	*0.0251*	*25.86*	*21.98*
2000	*0.1546*	*0.0978*	*0.0559*	*0.0279*	*27.09*	*23.75*
2010	*0.1650*	*0.1035*	*0.0619*	*0.0324*	*28.91*	*25.56*
2020	*0.1992*	*0.1235*	*0.0690*	*0.0357*	*31.10*	*28.22*

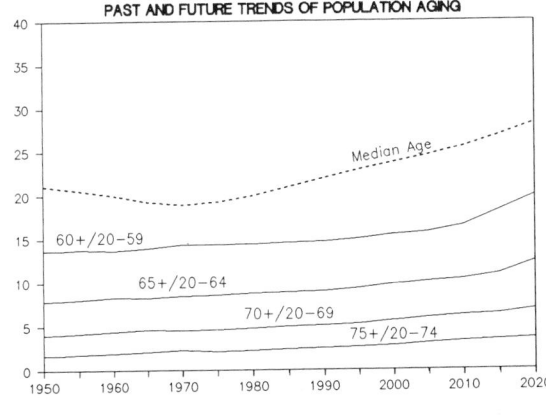

PAST AND FUTURE TRENDS OF POPULATION AGING

Median Age   60+/20-59   65+/20-64   70+/20-69   75+/20-74

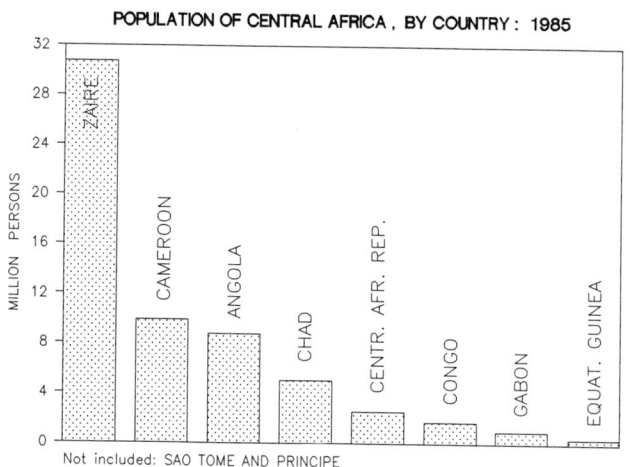

POPULATION OF CENTRAL AFRICA, BY COUNTRY : 1985

Not included: SAO TOME AND PRINCIPE

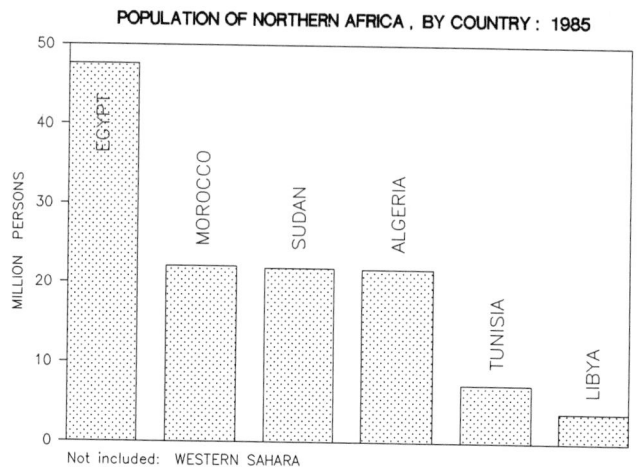

POPULATION OF NORTHERN AFRICA, BY COUNTRY : 1985

Not included: WESTERN SAHARA

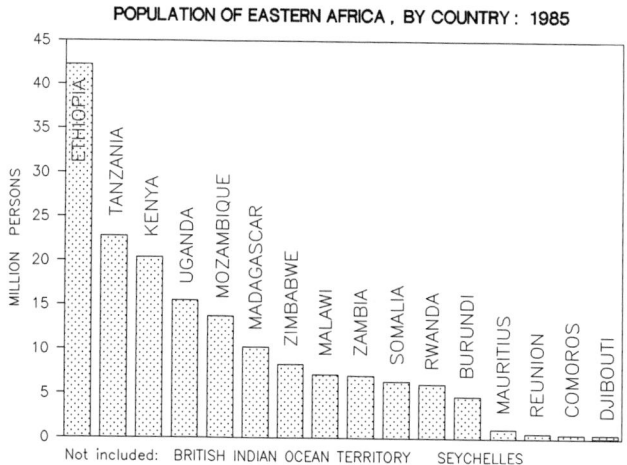

POPULATION OF EASTERN AFRICA, BY COUNTRY : 1985

Not included: BRITISH INDIAN OCEAN TERRITORY   SEYCHELLES

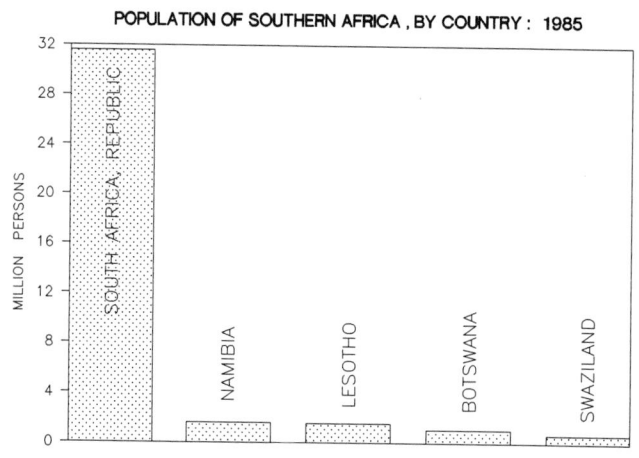

POPULATION OF SOUTHERN AFRICA, BY COUNTRY : 1985

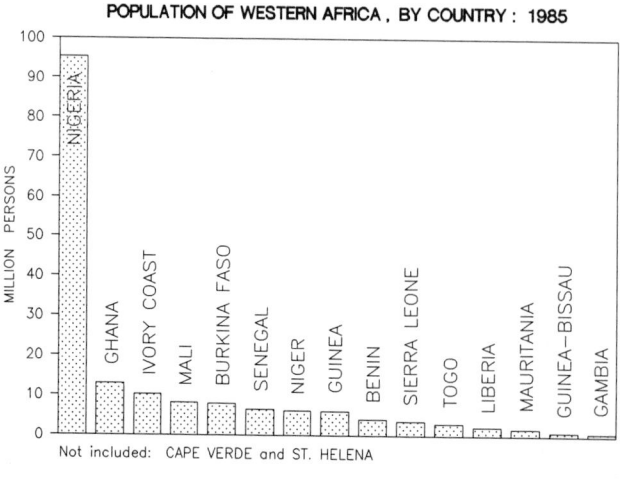

POPULATION OF WESTERN AFRICA, BY COUNTRY : 1985

Not included: CAPE VERDE and ST. HELENA

OBSERVED AND *PROJECTED* POPULATION DATA (000's)

YEAR	MID-YEAR POPULATION	NO. OF BIRTHS	NO. OF DEATHS	URBAN POPULATION NUMBER	URBAN POPULATION PERCENT	POPULATION 1985 AGE	POPULATION 1985 NUMBER
1950	224075	10954	6051	32535	14.5	0	101814
1955	249878	12142	6192	40769	16.3	5	82364
1960	281076	13625	6463	51426	18.3	10	68067
1965	318150	15171	6721	65523	20.6	15	57230
1970	362788	16948	7026	82946	22.9	20	48014
1975	415108	19261	7321	105024	25.3	25	40593
1980	481034	21900	7875	134885	28.0	30	33752
1985	557441	24923	8306	173574	31.1	35	27582
1990	*647518*	*28053*	*8658*	*223315*	*34.5*	40	22538
1995	*752626*	*31163*	*9013*	*285348*	*37.9*	45	19180
2000	*872234*	*34056*	*9330*	*360508*	*41.3*	50	16008
2005	*1005284*	*36325*	*9585*	*449469*	*44.7*	55	12942
2010	*1148497*	*37513*	*9773*	*552189*	*48.1*	60	10003
2015	*1296112*	*37410*	*9914*	*666175*	*51.4*	65	7363
2020	*1441285*	*36724*	*10075*	*787617*	*54.6*	70+	9992

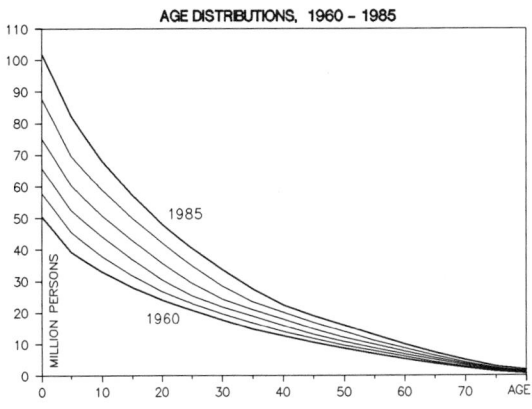

AGE DISTRIBUTIONS, 1960 – 1985

POPULATION RATIOS

YEAR	AGE DISTRIBUTION UNDER 15	15-64	65 & OLDER	70 & OLDER	DEPENDENCY RATIO	WOMEN 15-49	CHILD-WOMAN RATIO
1950	0.424	0.542	0.033	0.018	0.844	0.235	0.741
1955	0.430	0.539	0.031	0.017	0.856	0.234	0.754
1960	0.437	0.533	0.030	0.017	0.877	0.231	0.776
1965	0.444	0.525	0.030	0.017	0.904	0.228	0.796
1970	0.448	0.521	0.031	0.017	0.919	0.227	0.799
1975	0.449	0.520	0.031	0.017	0.922	0.226	0.800
1980	0.450	0.520	0.030	0.017	0.924	0.227	0.803
1985	0.453	0.516	0.031	0.018	0.937	0.226	0.810
1990	*0.453*	*0.517*	*0.030*	*0.017*	*0.935*	*0.226*	*0.801*
2000	*0.443*	*0.526*	*0.031*	*0.018*	*0.901*	*0.230*	*0.748*
2010	*0.418*	*0.550*	*0.032*	*0.019*	*0.819*	*0.239*	*0.649*
2020	*0.372*	*0.591*	*0.037*	*0.021*	*0.691*	*0.255*	*0.502*

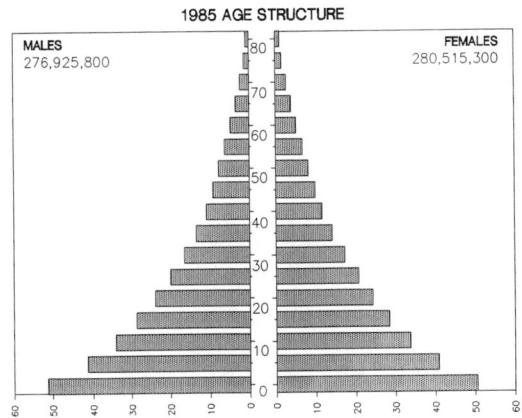

1985 AGE STRUCTURE

MALES 276,925,800   FEMALES 280,515,300

MORTALITY MEASURES (Annual Averages)

PERIOD	CRUDE DEATH RATE	INFANT MORT. RATE	LIFE EXPECTANCY AT BIRTH (years) MALE	FEMALE	BOTH SEXES	DIFFERENCE FEMALE-MALE
1950-55	27.00	187.26	36.65	39.42	38.02	2.78
1955-60	24.78	174.98	38.67	41.54	40.09	2.88
1960-65	22.99	164.32	40.68	43.65	42.15	2.98
1965-70	21.12	154.15	42.61	45.70	44.13	3.09
1970-75	19.37	140.45	44.51	47.71	46.08	3.20
1975-80	17.64	126.28	46.48	49.73	48.08	3.25
1980-85	16.37	116.36	48.28	51.55	49.89	3.27
1985-90	*14.90*	*106.33*	*50.28*	*53.60*	*51.91*	*3.32*
1990-95	*13.37*	*96.96*	*52.17*	*55.52*	*53.81*	*3.35*
2000-05	*10.70*	*79.08*	*55.92*	*59.41*	*57.64*	*3.49*
2010-15	*8.51*	*62.90*	*59.70*	*63.29*	*61.47*	*3.59*
2020-25	*6.99*	*48.42*	*63.46*	*67.06*	*65.23*	*3.60*

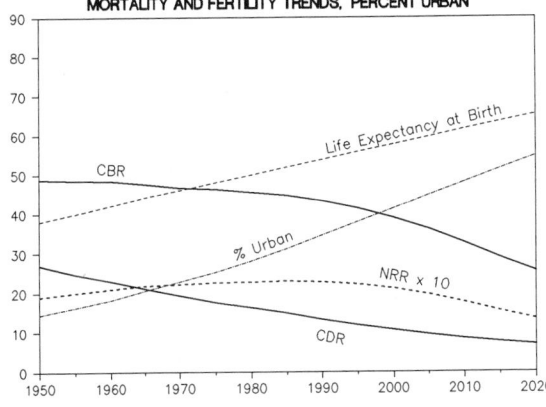

MORTALITY AND FERTILITY TRENDS, PERCENT URBAN

FERTILITY MEASURES (Annual Averages)

PERIOD	CRUDE BIRTH RATE	FERTILITY RATES GENERAL	FERTILITY RATES TOTAL	REPRODUCTION RATES GROSS	REPRODUCTION RATES NET	RATE OF NATUR. INCR.
1950-55	48.89	208.79	6.613	3.251	1.903	21.88
1955-60	48.59	208.93	6.693	3.290	2.016	23.81
1960-65	48.47	211.07	6.744	3.315	2.108	25.48
1965-70	47.69	209.76	6.712	3.299	2.182	26.56
1970-75	46.72	206.18	6.596	3.242	2.220	27.35
1975-80	46.40	204.70	6.524	3.207	2.270	28.76
1980-85	45.53	201.30	6.368	3.130	2.283	29.16
1985-90	*44.71*	*198.13*	*6.226*	*3.062*	*2.306*	*29.81*
1990-95	*43.32*	*191.11*	*5.997*	*2.949*	*2.287*	*29.95*
2000-05	*39.04*	*168.23*	*5.250*	*2.582*	*2.114*	*28.35*
2010-15	*32.66*	*134.51*	*4.180*	*2.056*	*1.765*	*24.16*
2020-25	*25.48*	*97.95*	*3.050*	*1.500*	*1.342*	*18.49*

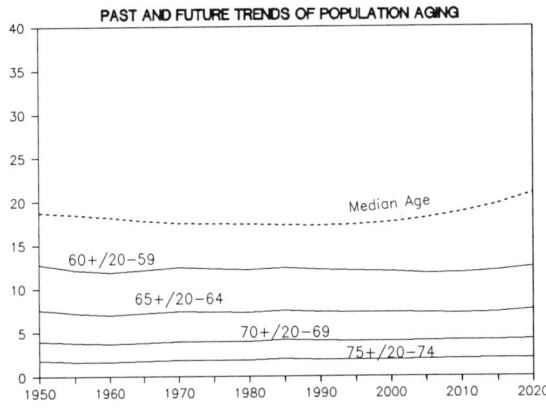

PAST AND FUTURE TRENDS OF POPULATION AGING

AGING MEASURES

YEAR	POPULATION AGE RATIOS 60+/20-59	65+/20-64	70+/20-69	75+/20-74	POPULATION MEAN AGE	POPULATION MEDIAN AGE
1950	0.1276	0.0755	0.0401	0.0179	23.34	18.74
1960	0.1186	0.0700	0.0373	0.0166	22.82	18.17
1970	0.1250	0.0741	0.0398	0.0184	22.53	17.56
1980	0.1222	0.0732	0.0398	0.0187	22.27	17.43
1990	*0.1221*	*0.0735*	*0.0406*	*0.0196*	*22.15*	*17.28*
2000	*0.1197*	*0.0731*	*0.0405*	*0.0193*	*22.38*	*17.67*
2010	*0.1181*	*0.0722*	*0.0412*	*0.0202*	*23.23*	*18.78*
2020	*0.1252*	*0.0762*	*0.0426*	*0.0210*	*24.98*	*21.00*

OBSERVED AND *PROJECTED* POPULATION DATA (000's)

YEAR	MID-YEAR POPULATION	NO. OF BIRTHS	NO. OF DEATHS	URBAN POPULATION NUMBER	URBAN POPULATION PERCENT	POPULATION 1985 AGE	POPULATION 1985 NUMBER
1950	26841	1252	740	3839	14.3	0	10814
1955	29506	1367	759	4734	16.0	5	8795
1960	32668	1507	793	5871	18.0	10	7260
1965	35764	1638	810	7550	21.1	15	6094
1970	39427	1795	819	9775	24.8	20	5179
1975	44976	2054	867	12581	28.0	25	4397
1980	52269	2351	930	16515	31.6	30	3711
1985	60147	2696	961	21386	35.6	35	3008
1990	*69564*	*3072*	*1015*	*27563*	*39.6*	40	2557
1995	*80710*	*3431*	*1064*	*35242*	*43.7*	45	2148
2000	*93498*	*3872*	*1113*	*44496*	*47.6*	50	1779
2005	*108390*	*4263*	*1155*	*55639*	*51.3*	55	1438
2010	*125128*	*4586*	*1188*	*68743*	*54.9*	60	1125
2015	*143353*	*4664*	*1203*	*83686*	*58.4*	65	826
2020	*161769*	*4597*	*1209*	*99703*	*61.6*	70+	1017

AGE DISTRIBUTIONS, 1960 - 1985

POPULATION RATIOS

YEAR	AGE DISTRIBUTION UNDER 15	AGE DISTRIBUTION 15-64	AGE DISTRIBUTION 65 & OLDER	AGE DISTRIBUTION 70 & OLDER	DEPENDENCY RATIO	WOMEN 15-49	CHILD-WOMAN RATIO
1950	0.409	0.553	0.038	0.023	0.809	0.247	0.667
1955	0.416	0.551	0.033	0.019	0.816	0.245	0.699
1960	0.421	0.547	0.031	0.017	0.828	0.242	0.711
1965	0.427	0.542	0.031	0.017	0.845	0.239	0.721
1970	0.428	0.540	0.032	0.017	0.852	0.237	0.731
1975	0.432	0.536	0.032	0.017	0.866	0.234	0.754
1980	0.444	0.526	0.030	0.017	0.902	0.231	0.787
1985	0.447	0.523	0.031	0.017	0.913	0.229	0.785
1990	*0.448*	*0.521*	*0.031*	*0.017*	*0.920*	*0.228*	*0.791*
2000	*0.447*	*0.522*	*0.031*	*0.018*	*0.916*	*0.228*	*0.770*
2010	*0.435*	*0.533*	*0.032*	*0.018*	*0.877*	*0.233*	*0.718*
2020	*0.403*	*0.563*	*0.035*	*0.020*	*0.778*	*0.245*	*0.583*

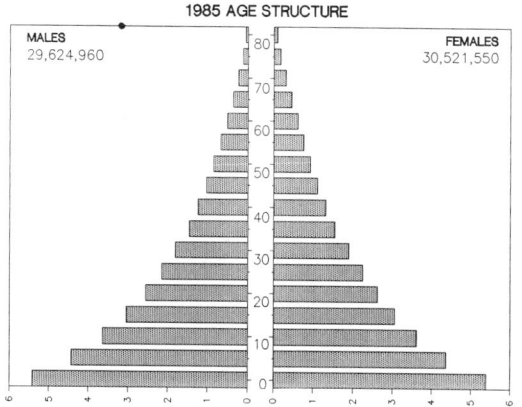

1985 AGE STRUCTURE

MALES 29,624,960   FEMALES 30,521,550

MORTALITY MEASURES (Annual Averages)

PERIOD	CRUDE DEATH RATE	INFANT MORT. RATE	LIFE EXPECTANCY AT BIRTH (years) MALE	LIFE EXPECTANCY AT BIRTH (years) FEMALE	LIFE EXPECTANCY AT BIRTH (years) BOTH SEXES	DIFFERENCE FEMALE-MALE
1950-55	27.58	182.86	35.34	38.55	36.92	3.21
1955-60	25.73	171.83	36.84	40.08	38.43	3.24
1960-65	24.28	161.04	38.31	41.57	39.92	3.26
1965-70	22.66	149.01	40.01	43.30	41.63	3.29
1970-75	20.78	136.10	41.99	45.30	43.62	3.32
1975-80	19.28	126.15	43.94	47.30	45.60	3.36
1980-85	17.78	116.91	45.88	49.30	47.56	3.42
1985-90	*15.98*	*107.07*	*48.33*	*51.76*	*50.02*	*3.42*
1990-95	*14.59*	*98.38*	*50.37*	*53.79*	*52.05*	*3.42*
2000-05	*11.91*	*80.55*	*54.42*	*57.84*	*56.10*	*3.43*
2010-15	*9.50*	*64.28*	*58.47*	*61.89*	*60.16*	*3.42*
2020-25	*7.48*	*49.64*	*62.51*	*65.88*	*64.17*	*3.36*

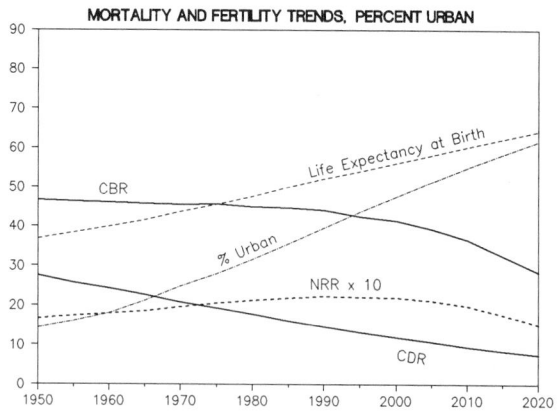

MORTALITY AND FERTILITY TRENDS, PERCENT URBAN

FERTILITY MEASURES (Annual Averages)

PERIOD	CRUDE BIRTH RATE	FERTILITY RATES GENERAL	FERTILITY RATES TOTAL	REPRODUCTION RATES GROSS	REPRODUCTION RATES NET	RATE OF NATUR. INCR.
1950-55	46.65	189.40	5.920	2.916	1.678	19.07
1955-60	46.31	189.97	5.938	2.925	1.741	20.59
1960-65	46.13	191.78	5.943	2.928	1.797	21.85
1965-70	45.81	192.61	5.973	2.943	1.868	23.15
1970-75	45.52	193.27	6.039	2.975	1.962	24.74
1975-80	45.68	196.46	6.124	3.017	2.064	26.40
1980-85	44.99	195.63	6.092	3.001	2.129	27.20
1985-90	*44.82*	*196.16*	*6.033*	*2.972*	*2.194*	*28.84*
1990-95	*44.16*	*193.86*	*5.955*	*2.934*	*2.234*	*29.58*
2000-05	*41.41*	*180.75*	*5.538*	*2.728*	*2.199*	*29.51*
2010-15	*36.65*	*155.90*	*4.769*	*2.349*	*1.992*	*27.15*
2020-25	*28.42*	*113.48*	*3.462*	*1.705*	*1.513*	*20.94*

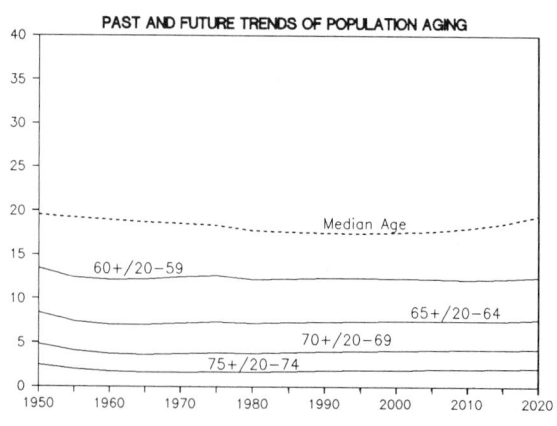

PAST AND FUTURE TRENDS OF POPULATION AGING

AGING MEASURES

YEAR	POPULATION AGE RATIOS 60+/20-59	POPULATION AGE RATIOS 65+/20-64	POPULATION AGE RATIOS 70+/20-69	POPULATION AGE RATIOS 75+/20-74	POPULATION MEAN AGE	POPULATION MEDIAN AGE
1950	0.1348	0.0841	0.0483	0.0245	24.07	19.55
1960	0.1211	0.0701	0.0373	0.0173	23.47	18.97
1970	0.1240	0.0719	0.0373	0.0162	23.25	18.53
1980	0.1218	0.0718	0.0380	0.0170	22.54	17.77
1990	*0.1232*	*0.0737*	*0.0398*	*0.0183*	*22.37*	*17.51*
2000	*0.1226*	*0.0743*	*0.0408*	*0.0192*	*22.35*	*17.55*
2010	*0.1211*	*0.0746*	*0.0418*	*0.0201*	*22.69*	*18.02*
2020	*0.1242*	*0.0761*	*0.0425*	*0.0211*	*23.85*	*19.44*

OBSERVED AND *PROJECTED* POPULATION DATA (000's)

YEAR	MID-YEAR POPULATION	NO. OF BIRTHS	NO. OF DEATHS	URBAN POPULATION NUMBER	PERCENT	POPULATION 1985 AGE	NUMBER
1950	64978	3268	1832	3415	5.3	0	31914
1955	72759	3657	1887	4509	6.2	5	25749
1960	82310	4105	1960	6011	7.3	10	20810
1965	94185	4644	2058	8163	8.7	15	16751
1970	108193	5302	2187	11150	10.3	20	13829
1975	123732	6087	2316	15295	12.4	25	11557
1980	144040	6885	2629	21843	15.2	30	9634
1985	166926	7975	2840	31060	18.6	35	8177
1990	*194823*	*9206*	*2964*	*43734*	*22.4*	40	6698
1995	*228947*	*10497*	*3098*	*60314*	*26.3*	45	5508
2000	*269185*	*11675*	*3198*	*81134*	*30.1*	50	4603
2005	*315182*	*12639*	*3257*	*106153*	*33.7*	55	3659
2010	*365851*	*13183*	*3286*	*136236*	*37.2*	60	2910
2015	*418914*	*13244*	*3300*	*171074*	*40.8*	65	2081
2020	*471764*	*13048*	*3323*	*209642*	*44.4*	70+	3044

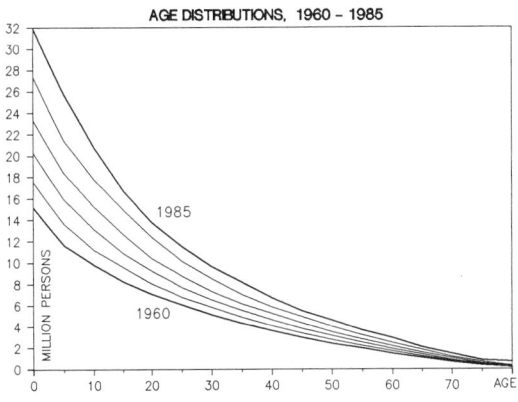

POPULATION RATIOS

YEAR	AGE DISTRIBUTION UNDER 15	15-64	65 & OLDER	70 & OLDER	DEPENDENCY RATIO	WOMEN 15-49	CHILD-WOMAN RATIO
1950	0.436	0.533	0.031	0.016	0.875	0.232	0.784
1955	0.440	0.531	0.029	0.016	0.883	0.231	0.783
1960	0.445	0.527	0.028	0.015	0.899	0.230	0.803
1965	0.450	0.522	0.028	0.015	0.914	0.228	0.817
1970	0.456	0.516	0.028	0.015	0.936	0.226	0.830
1975	0.460	0.512	0.028	0.015	0.953	0.224	0.840
1980	0.463	0.510	0.027	0.015	0.961	0.225	0.846
1985	0.470	0.499	0.031	0.018	1.003	0.221	0.864
1990	*0.471*	*0.500*	*0.029*	*0.016*	*0.999*	*0.222*	*.856*
2000	*0.467*	*0.505*	*0.028*	*0.016*	*0.979*	*0.224*	*0.837*
2010	*0.449*	*0.523*	*0.028*	*0.016*	*0.911*	*0.231*	*0.734*
2020	*0.399*	*0.569*	*0.031*	*0.018*	*0.756*	*0.251*	*0.554*

MORTALITY MEASURES (Annual Averages)

PERIOD	CRUDE DEATH RATE	INFANT MORT. RATE	LIFE EXPECTANCY AT BIRTH (years) MALE	FEMALE	BOTH SEXES	DIFFERENCE FEMALE-MALE
1950-55	28.20	178.67	35.01	38.03	36.53	3.02
1955-60	25.93	165.99	37.21	40.28	38.74	3.08
1960-65	23.82	155.08	39.39	42.52	40.95	3.13
1965-70	21.85	146.17	41.49	44.67	43.07	3.18
1970-75	20.22	137.88	43.47	46.69	45.06	3.23
1975-80	18.72	130.36	45.06	48.34	46.68	3.27
1980-85	18.25	125.48	46.18	49.40	47.77	3.22
1985-90	*17.02*	*116.13*	*48.20*	*51.44*	*49.80*	*3.24*
1990-95	*15.22*	*106.55*	*50.24*	*53.49*	*51.84*	*3.25*
2000-05	*11.88*	*86.40*	*54.65*	*57.99*	*56.29*	*3.34*
2010-15	*8.98*	*67.66*	*58.95*	*62.39*	*60.65*	*3.44*
2020-25	*7.04*	*52.01*	*62.86*	*66.32*	*64.57*	*3.46*

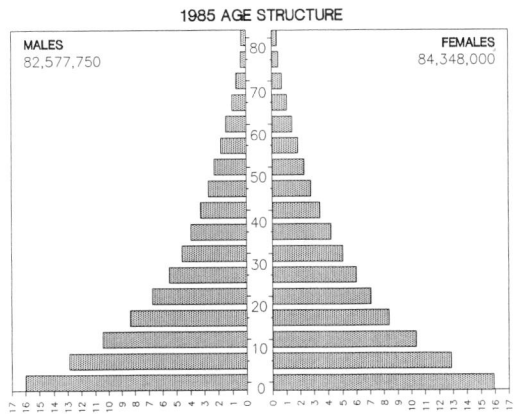

FERTILITY MEASURES (Annual Averages)

PERIOD	CRUDE BIRTH RATE	FERTILITY RATES GENERAL	TOTAL	REPRODUCTION RATES GROSS	NET	RATE OF NATUR. INCR.
1950-55	50.29	217.35	6.708	3.306	1.860	22.09
1955-60	50.26	218.09	6.782	3.342	1.976	24.33
1960-65	49.87	217.88	6.847	3.374	2.089	26.05
1965-70	49.31	217.33	6.872	3.386	2.185	27.46
1970-75	49.00	217.87	6.926	3.413	2.289	28.78
1975-80	49.19	219.16	7.011	3.455	2.380	30.47
1980-85	47.80	214.42	6.725	3.314	2.326	29.54
1985-90	*47.78*	*215.54*	*6.742*	*3.322*	*2.411*	*30.76*
1990-95	*47.25*	*212.18*	*6.629*	*3.267*	*2.448*	*32.04*
2000-05	*43.37*	*192.77*	*5.956*	*2.935*	*2.351*	*31.49*
2010-15	*36.03*	*152.95*	*4.721*	*2.326*	*1.972*	*27.05*
2020-25	*27.66*	*107.71*	*3.327*	*1.639*	*1.454*	*20.61*

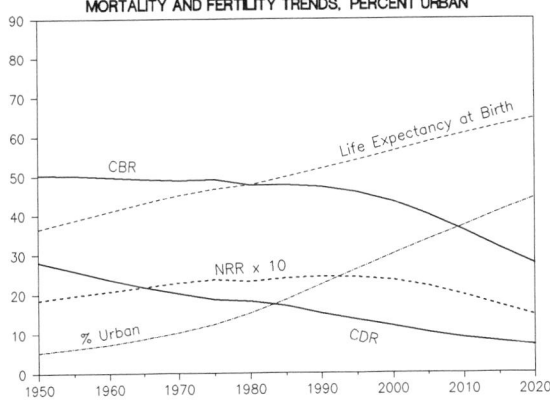

AGING MEASURES

YEAR	POPULATION AGE RATIOS 60+/20-59	65+/20-64	70+/20-69	75+/20-74	POPULATION MEAN AGE	MEDIAN AGE
1950	0.1206	0.0709	0.0368	0.0160	22.75	18.13
1960	0.1128	0.0665	0.0351	0.0156	22.38	17.73
1970	0.1136	0.0666	0.0348	0.0158	22.03	17.19
1980	0.1143	0.0674	0.0359	0.0164	21.69	16.79
1990	*0.1201*	*0.0729*	*0.0401*	*0.0197*	*21.52*	*16.39*
2000	*0.1134*	*0.0690*	*0.0379*	*0.0181*	*21.39*	*16.56*
2010	*0.1116*	*0.0676*	*0.0377*	*0.0183*	*21.96*	*17.35*
2020	*0.1115*	*0.0684*	*0.0386*	*0.0188*	*23.59*	*19.45*

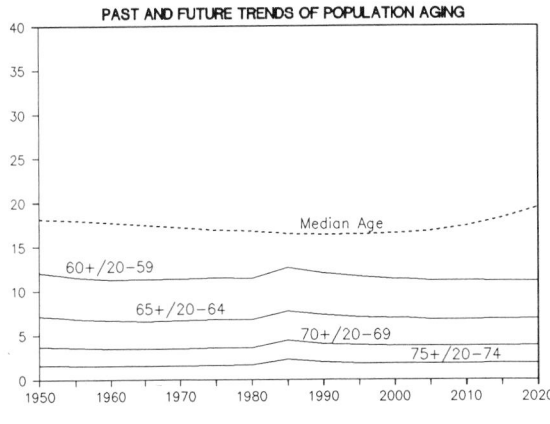

OBSERVED AND *PROJECTED* POPULATION DATA (000's)

YEAR	MID-YEAR POPULATION	NO. OF BIRTHS	NO. OF DEATHS	URBAN POPULATION NUMBER	URBAN POPULATION PERCENT	POPULATION 1985 AGE	POPULATION 1985 NUMBER
1950	51798	2532	1279	12667	24.5	0	20889
1955	57994	2747	1284	15693	27.1	5	17512
1960	65115	3092	1344	19507	30.0	10	14657
1965	73297	3323	1361	24585	33.5	15	13001
1970	83158	3575	1379	29926	36.0	20	11190
1975	93799	3964	1334	35671	38.0	25	9863
1980	107811	4403	1328	43056	39.9	30	8191
1985	124419	4732	1327	52155	41.9	35	6167
1990	*142649*	*4906*	*1306*	*63181*	*44.3*	40	4690
1995	*161832*	*4996*	*1293*	*76023*	*47.0*	45	4387
2000	*181481*	*5022*	*1299*	*90629*	*49.9*	50	3785
2005	*201106*	*5060*	*1332*	*106932*	*53.2*	55	3197
2010	*220655*	*5031*	*1385*	*124433*	*56.4*	60	2402
2015	*239672*	*4918*	*1457*	*142576*	*59.5*	65	1848
2020	*257629*	*4920*	*1556*	*160893*	*62.5*	70+	2641

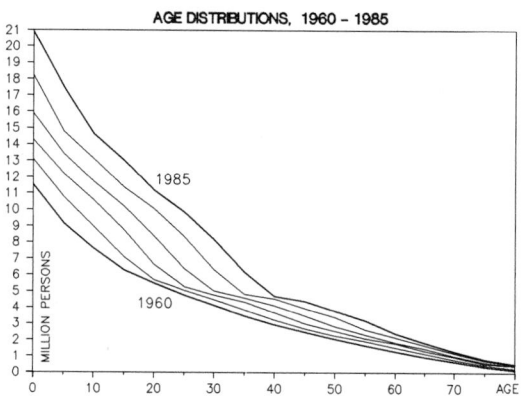
AGE DISTRIBUTIONS, 1960 - 1985

POPULATION RATIOS

YEAR	AGE DISTRIBUTION UNDER 15	AGE DISTRIBUTION 15-64	AGE DISTRIBUTION 65 & OLDER	AGE DISTRIBUTION 70 & OLDER	DEPENDENCY RATIO	WOMEN 15-49	CHILD-WOMAN RATIO
1950	0.413	0.552	0.035	0.019	0.810	0.234	0.716
1955	0.422	0.545	0.033	0.018	0.835	0.232	0.747
1960	0.435	0.532	0.033	0.018	0.878	0.227	0.779
1965	0.448	0.516	0.036	0.020	0.937	0.220	0.813
1970	0.446	0.515	0.039	0.023	0.941	0.221	0.776
1975	0.438	0.525	0.038	0.022	0.906	0.225	0.752
1980	0.428	0.534	0.038	0.022	0.872	0.228	0.741
1985	0.426	0.537	0.036	0.021	0.861	0.229	0.732
1990	*0.422*	*0.542*	*0.035*	*0.021*	*0.844*	*0.231*	*0.691*
2000	*0.384*	*0.578*	*0.038*	*0.022*	*0.731*	*0.247*	*0.546*
2010	*0.332*	*0.627*	*0.041*	*0.025*	*0.595*	*0.261*	*0.435*
2020	*0.286*	*0.661*	*0.053*	*0.030*	*0.514*	*0.268*	*0.354*

MORTALITY MEASURES (Annual Averages)

PERIOD	CRUDE DEATH RATE	INFANT MORT. RATE	LIFE EXPECTANCY AT BIRTH (years) MALE	LIFE EXPECTANCY AT BIRTH (years) FEMALE	LIFE EXPECTANCY AT BIRTH (years) BOTH SEXES	DIFFERENCE FEMALE-MALE
1950-55	24.70	189.35	40.82	42.96	41.86	2.14
1955-60	22.13	176.19	43.06	45.26	44.13	2.19
1960-65	20.64	165.09	45.32	47.56	46.41	2.24
1965-70	18.57	154.88	47.62	49.99	48.78	2.37
1970-75	16.58	137.70	49.75	52.24	50.96	2.49
1975-80	14.22	116.91	52.67	55.26	53.94	2.60
1980-85	12.32	99.17	55.37	58.10	56.71	2.73
1985-90	*10.67*	*85.92*	*57.59*	*60.39*	*58.96*	*2.80*
1990-95	*9.15*	*73.80*	*59.75*	*62.59*	*61.13*	*2.84*
2000-05	*7.16*	*54.06*	*63.20*	*66.46*	*64.79*	*3.26*
2010-15	*6.28*	*40.30*	*66.10*	*69.73*	*67.87*	*3.63*
2020-25	*6.04*	*29.41*	*68.88*	*72.63*	*70.71*	*3.75*

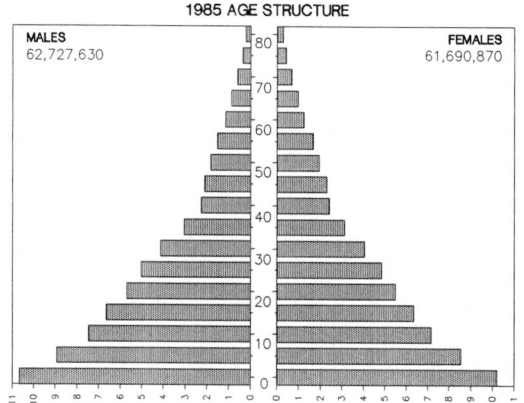
1985 AGE STRUCTURE

MALES 62,727,630   FEMALES 61,690,870

FERTILITY MEASURES (Annual Averages)

PERIOD	CRUDE BIRTH RATE	FERTILITY RATES GENERAL	FERTILITY RATES TOTAL	REPRODUCTION RATES GROSS	REPRODUCTION RATES NET	RATE OF NATUR. INCR.
1950-55	48.88	209.73	6.826	3.331	2.115	24.17
1955-60	47.37	206.46	7.004	3.418	2.266	25.24
1960-65	47.49	212.86	7.075	3.453	2.350	26.85
1965-70	45.34	205.65	6.861	3.348	2.383	26.77
1970-75	42.99	192.40	6.356	3.102	2.274	26.40
1975-80	42.26	186.21	6.013	2.935	2.254	28.04
1980-85	40.84	178.48	5.785	2.823	2.248	28.52
1985-90	*38.03*	*165.27*	*5.322*	*2.597*	*2.135*	*27.36*
1990-95	*34.39*	*146.47*	*4.759*	*2.322*	*1.965*	*25.24*
2000-05	*27.67*	*110.12*	*3.606*	*1.760*	*1.562*	*20.52*
2010-15	*22.80*	*86.57*	*2.789*	*1.361*	*1.249*	*16.52*
2020-25	*19.10*	*70.99*	*2.301*	*1.123*	*1.059*	*13.06*

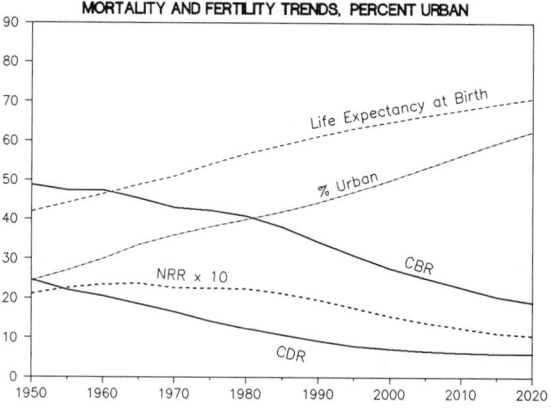
MORTALITY AND FERTILITY TRENDS, PERCENT URBAN

Life Expectancy at Birth; % Urban; NRR x 10; CBR; CDR

AGING MEASURES

YEAR	POPULATION AGE RATIOS 60+/20-59	POPULATION AGE RATIOS 65+/20-64	POPULATION AGE RATIOS 70+/20-69	POPULATION AGE RATIOS 75+/20-74	POPULATION MEAN AGE	POPULATION MEDIAN AGE
1950	0.1304	0.0771	0.0407	0.0179	23.80	19.29
1960	0.1264	0.0749	0.0398	0.0171	23.13	18.37
1970	0.1565	0.0955	0.0538	0.0260	23.14	17.59
1980	0.1409	0.0876	0.0499	0.0248	23.20	18.41
1990	*0.1328*	*0.0801*	*0.0457*	*0.0226*	*23.36*	*18.82*
2000	*0.1302*	*0.0813*	*0.0460*	*0.0221*	*24.62*	*20.34*
2010	*0.1273*	*0.0782*	*0.0471*	*0.0239*	*26.70*	*23.24*
2020	*0.1574*	*0.0936*	*0.0503*	*0.0248*	*29.28*	*26.61*

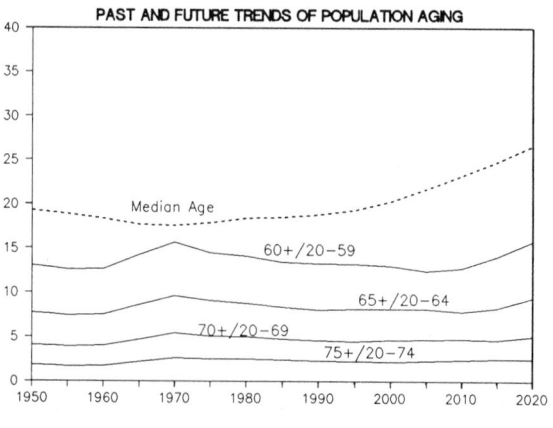
PAST AND FUTURE TRENDS OF POPULATION AGING

Median Age; 60+/20-59; 65+/20-64; 70+/20-69; 75+/20-74

OBSERVED AND *PROJECTED* POPULATION DATA (000's)

YEAR	MID-YEAR POPULATION	NO. OF BIRTHS	NO. OF DEATHS	URBAN POPULATION NUMBER	URBAN POPULATION PERCENT	POPULATION 1985 AGE	POPULATION 1985 NUMBER
1950	15736	688	330	6012	38.2	0	5332
1955	17639	758	332	7067	40.1	5	4633
1960	19895	845	344	8355	42.0	10	4181
1965	22635	885	350	9736	43.0	15	3747
1970	25609	956	357	11287	44.1	20	3440
1975	28912	1033	363	13538	46.8	25	2941
1980	32458	1126	371	16092	49.6	30	2523
1985	36473	1218	370	19155	52.5	35	2062
1990	*40972*	*1296*	*367*	*22770*	*55.6*	40	1741
1995	*45889*	*1367*	*367*	*26918*	*58.7*	45	1451
2000	*51172*	*1423*	*370*	*31563*	*61.7*	50	1216
2005	*56723*	*1462*	*383*	*36618*	*64.6*	55	980
2010	*62385*	*1470*	*401*	*41929*	*67.2*	60	767
2015	*67967*	*1442*	*428*	*47376*	*69.7*	65	594
2020	*73235*	*1388*	*460*	*52764*	*72.0*	70+	866

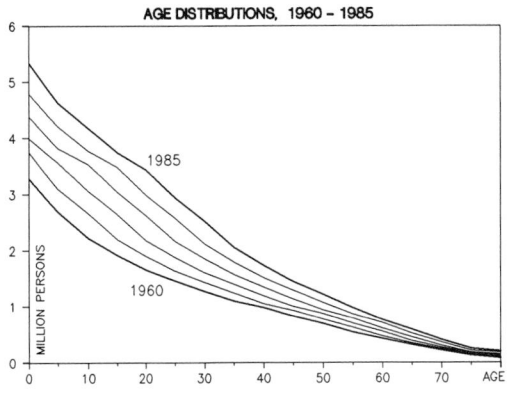

AGE DISTRIBUTIONS, 1960 - 1985

POPULATION RATIOS

YEAR	AGE DISTRIBUTION UNDER 15	AGE DISTRIBUTION 15-64	AGE DISTRIBUTION 65 & OLDER	AGE DISTRIBUTION 70 & OLDER	DEPENDENCY RATIO	WOMEN 15-49	CHILD-WOMAN RATIO
1950	0.390	0.573	0.036	0.019	0.744	0.240	0.645
1955	0.402	0.561	0.038	0.021	0.783	0.237	0.690
1960	0.412	0.550	0.038	0.022	0.818	0.233	0.707
1965	0.420	0.542	0.038	0.022	0.844	0.231	0.718
1970	0.415	0.548	0.037	0.022	0.825	0.233	0.669
1975	0.406	0.557	0.038	0.022	0.797	0.238	0.637
1980	0.394	0.567	0.039	0.023	0.764	0.243	0.606
1985	0.388	0.572	0.040	0.024	0.748	0.246	0.594
1990	*0.382*	*0.577*	*0.040*	*0.024*	*0.732*	*0.248*	*0.578*
2000	*0.366*	*0.591*	*0.043*	*0.026*	*0.692*	*0.251*	*0.526*
2010	*0.337*	*0.614*	*0.049*	*0.030*	*0.629*	*0.256*	*0.459*
2020	*0.299*	*0.641*	*0.060*	*0.036*	*0.559*	*0.262*	*0.378*

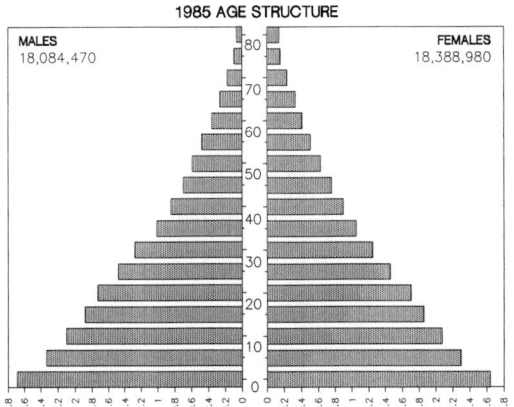

1985 AGE STRUCTURE

MALES 18,084,470   FEMALES 18,388,980

MORTALITY MEASURES (Annual Averages)

PERIOD	CRUDE DEATH RATE	INFANT MORT. RATE	LIFE EXPECTANCY AT BIRTH (years) MALE	LIFE EXPECTANCY AT BIRTH (years) FEMALE	LIFE EXPECTANCY AT BIRTH (years) BOTH SEXES	DIFFERENCE FEMALE-MALE
1950-55	20.98	152.61	43.00	45.31	44.14	2.31
1955-60	18.83	141.12	45.49	48.67	47.05	3.18
1960-65	17.31	131.47	47.12	51.19	49.12	4.07
1965-70	15.46	122.15	48.70	53.68	51.15	4.98
1970-75	13.95	112.29	50.30	56.17	53.19	5.87
1975-80	12.56	98.10	52.33	58.26	55.24	5.92
1980-85	11.42	87.28	54.39	60.26	57.28	5.87
1985-90	*10.14*	*76.85*	*56.86*	*62.72*	*59.74*	*5.86*
1990-95	*8.96*	*66.82*	*59.33*	*65.15*	*62.19*	*5.82*
2000-05	*7.24*	*48.31*	*63.74*	*69.38*	*66.51*	*5.64*
2010-15	*6.43*	*35.49*	*67.05*	*72.49*	*69.73*	*5.44*
2020-25	*6.29*	*26.13*	*69.55*	*74.91*	*72.18*	*5.36*

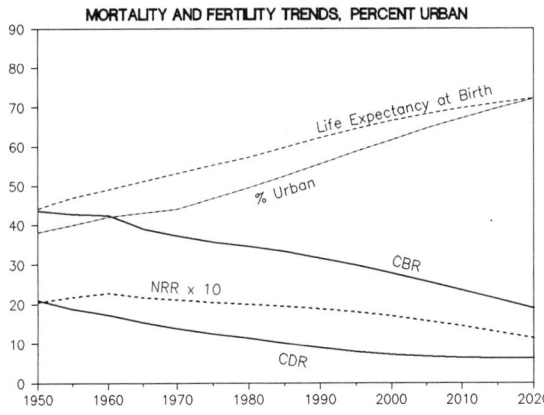

MORTALITY AND FERTILITY TRENDS, PERCENT URBAN

FERTILITY MEASURES (Annual Averages)

PERIOD	CRUDE BIRTH RATE	FERTILITY RATES GENERAL	FERTILITY RATES TOTAL	REPRODUCTION RATES GROSS	REPRODUCTION RATES NET	RATE OF NATUR. INCR.
1950-55	43.71	183.57	6.453	3.172	2.057	22.73
1955-60	42.95	182.99	6.463	3.177	2.184	24.11
1960-65	42.45	183.02	6.469	3.180	2.279	25.14
1965-70	39.10	168.46	5.935	2.918	2.173	23.64
1970-75	37.33	158.36	5.579	2.743	2.118	23.38
1975-80	35.72	148.32	5.219	2.565	2.045	23.16
1980-85	34.69	141.70	4.949	2.433	2.001	23.27
1985-90	*33.39*	*135.22*	*4.679*	*2.300*	*1.952*	*23.25*
1990-95	*31.62*	*127.31*	*4.388*	*2.157*	*1.884*	*22.66*
2000-05	*27.81*	*110.17*	*3.798*	*1.867*	*1.707*	*20.58*
2010-15	*23.56*	*91.56*	*3.137*	*1.542*	*1.448*	*17.13*
2020-25	*18.95*	*71.83*	*2.439*	*1.199*	*1.145*	*12.66*

AGING MEASURES

YEAR	POPULATION AGE RATIOS 60+/20-59	POPULATION AGE RATIOS 65+/20-64	POPULATION AGE RATIOS 70+/20-69	POPULATION AGE RATIOS 75+/20-74	POPULATION MEAN AGE	POPULATION MEDIAN AGE
1950	0.1324	0.0763	0.0397	0.0171	24.84	20.65
1960	0.1384	0.0841	0.0465	0.0223	24.23	19.55
1970	0.1383	0.0836	0.0479	0.0245	24.00	19.12
1980	0.1392	0.0856	0.0490	0.0252	24.47	19.95
1990	*0.1361*	*0.0850*	*0.0497*	*0.0257*	*24.99*	*20.91*
2000	*0.1412*	*0.0883*	*0.0512*	*0.0270*	*25.90*	*21.91*
2010	*0.1529*	*0.0952*	*0.0555*	*0.0294*	*27.30*	*23.52*
2020	*0.1781*	*0.1101*	*0.0633*	*0.0335*	*29.28*	*25.95*

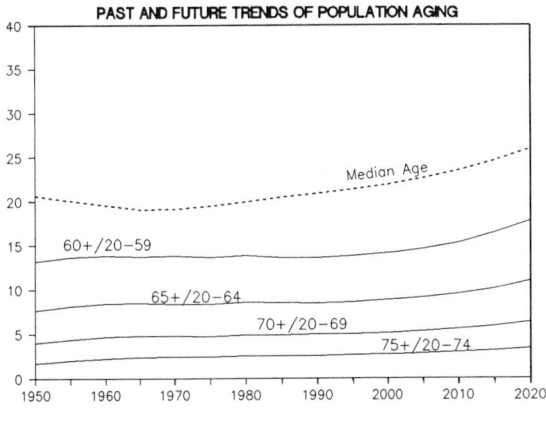

PAST AND FUTURE TRENDS OF POPULATION AGING

OBSERVED AND *PROJECTED* POPULATION DATA (000's)

YEAR	MID-YEAR POPULATION	NO. OF BIRTHS	NO. OF DEATHS	URBAN POPULATION NUMBER	URBAN POPULATION PERCENT	POPULATION 1985 AGE	POPULATION 1985 NUMBER
1950	64722	3215	1869	6602	10.2	0	32864
1955	71981	3613	1930	8765	12.2	5	25674
1960	81088	4074	2021	11682	14.4	10	21159
1965	92268	4676	2139	15489	16.8	15	17637
1970	106402	5314	2278	20808	19.6	20	14376
1975	123690	6114	2435	27940	22.6	25	11835
1980	144455	7124	2612	37377	25.9	30	9694
1985	169477	8283	2798	49817	29.4	35	8169
1990	*199511*	*9536*	*2990*	*66067*	*33.1*	40	6852
1995	*235247*	*10815*	*3171*	*86851*	*36.9*	45	5686
2000	*276898*	*11989*	*3327*	*112687*	*40.7*	50	4625
2005	*323883*	*12824*	*3437*	*144127*	*44.5*	55	3668
2010	*374479*	*13173*	*3496*	*180848*	*48.3*	60	2799
2015	*426206*	*13082*	*3515*	*221464*	*52.0*	65	2015
2020	*476887*	*12730*	*3520*	*264615*	*55.5*	70+	2424

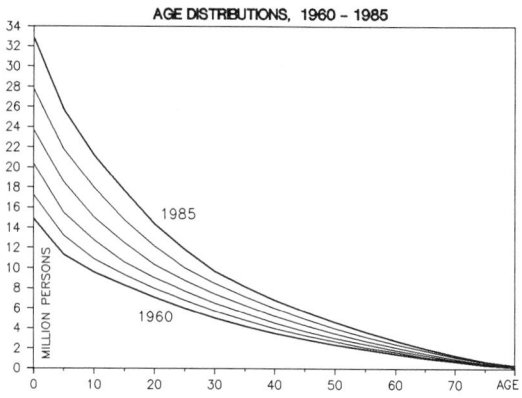

AGE DISTRIBUTIONS, 1960 - 1985

POPULATION RATIOS

YEAR	AGE DISTRIBUTION UNDER 15	AGE DISTRIBUTION 15-64	AGE DISTRIBUTION 65 & OLDER	AGE DISTRIBUTION 70 & OLDER	DEPENDENCY RATIO	WOMEN 15-49	CHILD-WOMAN RATIO
1950	0.436	0.532	0.032	0.017	0.881	0.231	0.775
1955	0.438	0.532	0.030	0.016	0.880	0.232	0.771
1960	0.442	0.530	0.028	0.015	0.888	0.232	0.793
1965	0.448	0.525	0.027	0.015	0.905	0.230	0.813
1970	0.457	0.517	0.027	0.014	0.936	0.226	0.844
1975	0.463	0.511	0.026	0.014	0.958	0.224	0.855
1980	0.468	0.506	0.026	0.014	0.976	0.223	0.864
1985	0.470	0.504	0.026	0.014	0.986	0.221	0.876
1990	*0.473*	*0.501*	*0.026*	*0.014*	*0.998*	*0.220*	*0.883*
2000	*0.472*	*0.501*	*0.026*	*0.015*	*0.994*	*0.222*	*0.848*
2010	*0.447*	*0.525*	*0.028*	*0.016*	*0.905*	*0.233*	*0.718*
2020	*0.392*	*0.578*	*0.031*	*0.018*	*0.731*	*0.255*	*0.528*

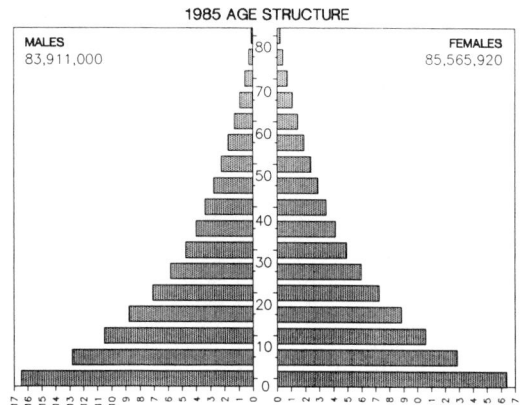

1985 AGE STRUCTURE

MALES 83,911,000   FEMALES 85,565,920

MORTALITY MEASURES (Annual Averages)

PERIOD	CRUDE DEATH RATE	INFANT MORT. RATE	LIFE EXPECTANCY AT BIRTH (years) MALE	LIFE EXPECTANCY AT BIRTH (years) FEMALE	LIFE EXPECTANCY AT BIRTH (years) BOTH SEXES	DIFFERENCE FEMALE-MALE
1950-55	28.88	203.51	34.13	37.15	35.62	3.03
1955-60	26.82	191.46	36.03	39.10	37.54	3.07
1960-65	24.92	181.07	37.96	41.08	39.50	3.11
1965-70	23.19	169.28	39.91	43.06	41.46	3.16
1970-75	21.41	151.25	41.86	45.05	43.43	3.19
1975-80	19.69	132.96	43.75	46.99	45.34	3.23
1980-85	18.08	122.46	45.75	49.03	47.36	3.28
1985-90	*16.51*	*112.41*	*47.79*	*51.16*	*49.45*	*3.37*
1990-95	*14.99*	*102.94*	*49.79*	*53.23*	*51.48*	*3.44*
2000-05	*12.01*	*85.21*	*53.76*	*57.31*	*55.51*	*3.55*
2010-15	*9.34*	*69.05*	*57.68*	*61.30*	*59.47*	*3.62*
2020-25	*7.38*	*53.90*	*61.68*	*65.30*	*63.46*	*3.63*

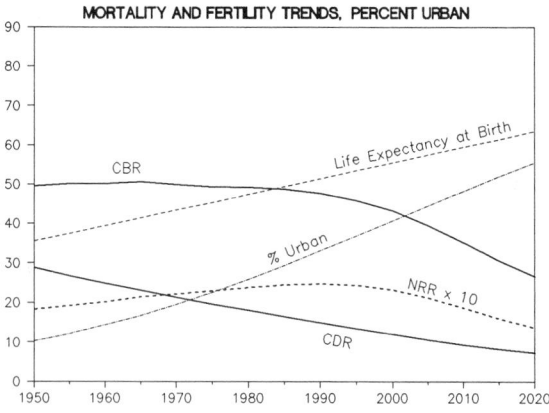

MORTALITY AND FERTILITY TRENDS, PERCENT URBAN

FERTILITY MEASURES (Annual Averages)

PERIOD	CRUDE BIRTH RATE	FERTILITY RATES GENERAL	FERTILITY RATES TOTAL	REPRODUCTION RATES GROSS	REPRODUCTION RATES NET	RATE OF NATUR. INCR.
1950-55	49.67	214.25	6.691	3.296	1.836	20.79
1955-60	50.19	216.21	6.738	3.319	1.932	23.37
1960-65	50.24	217.67	6.781	3.340	2.028	25.32
1965-70	50.67	222.19	6.920	3.409	2.153	27.49
1970-75	49.95	221.73	6.910	3.404	2.232	28.53
1975-80	49.43	221.36	6.893	3.395	2.305	29.74
1980-85	49.32	222.19	6.899	3.398	2.393	31.24
1985-90	*48.87*	*221.27*	*6.836*	*3.367*	*2.457*	*32.36*
1990-95	*47.80*	*217.08*	*6.674*	*3.288*	*2.477*	*32.81*
2000-05	*43.30*	*193.21*	*5.924*	*2.918*	*2.332*	*31.28*
2010-15	*35.18*	*147.58*	*4.523*	*2.228*	*1.874*	*25.84*
2020-25	*26.69*	*102.09*	*3.144*	*1.549*	*1.363*	*19.31*

AGING MEASURES

YEAR	POPULATION AGE RATIOS 60+/20-59	POPULATION AGE RATIOS 65+/20-64	POPULATION AGE RATIOS 70+/20-69	POPULATION AGE RATIOS 75+/20-74	POPULATION MEAN AGE	POPULATION MEDIAN AGE
1950	0.1279	0.0749	0.0393	0.0171	22.88	18.16
1960	0.1121	0.0659	0.0351	0.0152	22.41	17.83
1970	0.1097	0.0636	0.0328	0.0145	21.93	17.17
1980	0.1112	0.0651	0.0341	0.0151	21.57	16.59
1990	*0.1116*	*0.0658*	*0.0351*	*0.0160*	*21.25*	*16.28*
2000	*0.1117*	*0.0668*	*0.0361*	*0.0167*	*21.22*	*16.32*
2010	*0.1095*	*0.0667*	*0.0369*	*0.0175*	*21.92*	*17.37*
2020	*0.1086*	*0.0663*	*0.0374*	*0.0183*	*23.74*	*19.73*

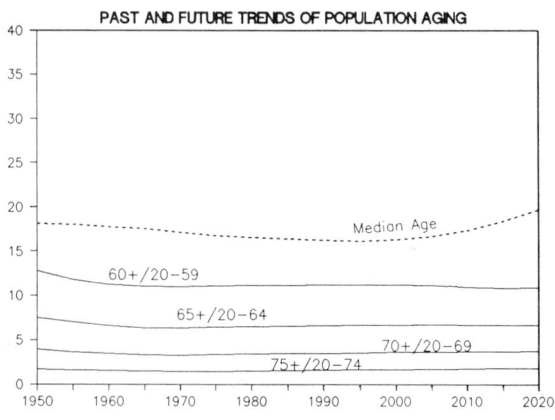

PAST AND FUTURE TRENDS OF POPULATION AGING

OBSERVED AND *PROJECTED* POPULATION DATA (000's)

YEAR	MID-YEAR POPULATION	NO. OF BIRTHS	NO. OF DEATHS	URBAN POPULATION NUMBER	URBAN POPULATION PERCENT	POPULATION AGE	1985 NUMBER
1950	8753	446	209	1948	22.3	0	3820
1955	9715	494	206	2540	26.1	5	3250
1960	10800	544	210	3288	30.4	10	2835
1965	11923	594	207	4486	37.6	15	2430
1970	13746	660	212	5430	39.5	20	1985
1975	16018	721	215	6460	40.3	25	1554
1980	18666	793	200	7684	41.2	30	1289
1985	21699	872	197	9251	42.6	35	923
1990	*25364*	*922*	*190*	*11344*	*44.7*	40	669
1995	*29306*	*923*	*184*	*13896*	*47.4*	45	684
2000	*33247*	*904*	*184*	*16845*	*50.7*	50	614
2005	*37055*	*880*	*188*	*20153*	*54.4*	55	480
2010	*40685*	*866*	*198*	*23568*	*57.9*	60	372
2015	*44169*	*853*	*211*	*27064*	*61.3*	65	300
2020	*47502*	*826*	*227*	*30595*	*64.4*	70+	495

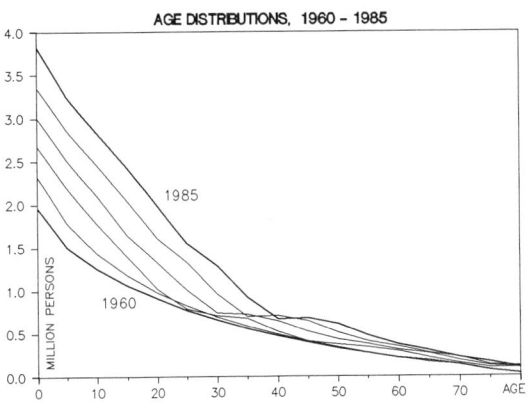

AGE DISTRIBUTIONS, 1960 - 1985

POPULATION RATIOS

YEAR	AGE DISTRIBUTION UNDER 15	15-64	65 & OLDER	70 & OLDER	DEPENDENCY RATIO	WOMEN 15-49	CHILD-WOMAN RATIO
1950	0.401	0.555	0.044	0.025	0.802	0.223	0.712
1955	0.413	0.546	0.041	0.023	0.832	0.226	0.740
1960	0.438	0.524	0.039	0.022	0.909	0.225	0.806
1965	0.465	0.502	0.033	0.019	0.993	0.219	0.889
1970	0.484	0.475	0.041	0.025	1.105	0.213	0.915
1975	0.476	0.482	0.042	0.025	1.074	0.214	0.878
1980	0.465	0.496	0.039	0.025	1.017	0.218	0.824
1985	0.456	0.507	0.037	0.023	0.973	0.221	0.796
1990	*0.444*	*0.521*	*0.034*	*0.021*	*0.918*	*0.227*	*0.750*
2000	*0.403*	*0.561*	*0.036*	*0.021*	*0.782*	*0.246*	*0.567*
2010	*0.332*	*0.630*	*0.037*	*0.025*	*0.586*	*0.270*	*0.403*
2020	*0.274*	*0.677*	*0.048*	*0.027*	*0.476*	*0.279*	*0.324*

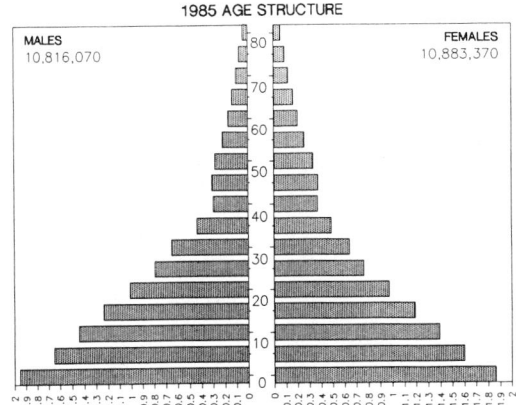

1985 AGE STRUCTURE

MALES 10,816,070 — FEMALES 10,883,370

MORTALITY MEASURES (Annual Averages)

PERIOD	CRUDE DEATH RATE	INFANT MORT. RATE	LIFE EXPECTANCY AT BIRTH (years) MALE	FEMALE	BOTH SEXES	DIFFERENCE FEMALE-MALE
1950-55	23.90	185.00	42.10	44.20	43.12	2.10
1955-60	21.20	175.00	44.70	46.80	45.72	2.10
1960-65	19.40	160.00	47.30	49.40	48.32	2.10
1965-70	17.40	150.00	50.40	52.50	51.42	2.10
1970-75	15.40	132.00	52.50	54.50	53.48	2.00
1975-80	13.40	112.00	55.00	57.10	56.02	2.10
1980-85	10.73	87.98	58.52	61.62	60.03	3.10
1985-90	*9.06*	*73.75*	*60.95*	*64.12*	*62.50*	*3.17*
1990-95	*7.49*	*60.81*	*63.33*	*66.61*	*64.93*	*3.28*
2000-05	*5.52*	*40.67*	*66.80*	*70.90*	*68.80*	*4.11*
2010-15	*4.87*	*28.11*	*69.54*	*73.88*	*71.66*	*4.34*
2020-25	*4.78*	*19.60*	*71.73*	*76.12*	*73.87*	*4.38*

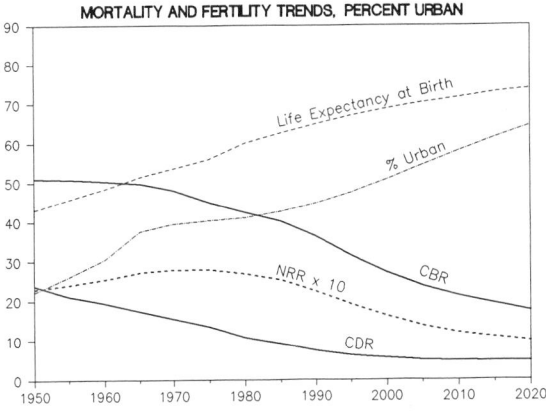

MORTALITY AND FERTILITY TRENDS, PERCENT URBAN

Life Expectancy at Birth — % Urban — NRR x 10 — CBR — CDR

FERTILITY MEASURES (Annual Averages)

PERIOD	CRUDE BIRTH RATE	FERTILITY RATES GENERAL	TOTAL	REPRODUCTION RATES GROSS	NET	RATE OF NATUR. INCR.
1950-55	51.00	226.87	7.277	3.550	2.300	27.10
1955-60	50.80	225.02	7.277	3.550	2.410	29.60
1960-65	50.40	226.82	7.380	3.600	2.560	31.00
1965-70	49.80	230.86	7.482	3.650	2.730	32.40
1970-75	48.00	225.23	7.380	3.600	2.780	32.60
1975-80	45.00	208.33	7.175	3.500	2.790	31.60
1980-85	42.51	193.52	6.662	3.250	2.691	31.77
1985-90	*40.21*	*179.48*	*6.047*	*2.950*	*2.523*	*31.15*
1990-95	*36.33*	*157.03*	*5.227*	*2.550*	*2.249*	*28.84*
2000-05	*27.19*	*107.69*	*3.587*	*1.750*	*1.618*	*21.67*
2010-15	*21.29*	*77.72*	*2.583*	*1.260*	*1.196*	*16.42*
2020-25	*17.38*	*62.41*	*2.070*	*1.010*	*0.975*	*12.60*

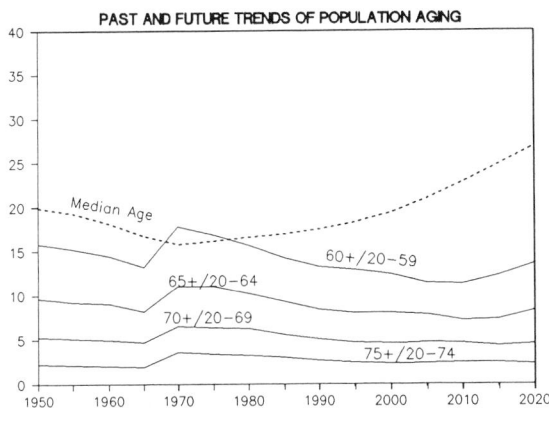

PAST AND FUTURE TRENDS OF POPULATION AGING

Median Age — 60+/20-59 — 65+/20-64 — 70+/20-69 — 75+/20-74

AGING MEASURES

YEAR	POPULATION AGE RATIOS 60+/20-59	65+/20-64	70+/20-69	75+/20-74	POPULATION MEAN AGE	MEDIAN AGE
1950	0.1583	0.0962	0.0523	0.0223	24.76	19.93
1960	0.1446	0.0905	0.0492	0.0205	23.17	18.17
1970	0.1777	0.1105	0.0652	0.0357	22.08	15.81
1980	0.1564	0.1018	0.0625	0.0318	22.10	16.60
1990	*0.1322*	*0.0838*	*0.0504*	*0.0263*	*22.18*	*17.51*
2000	*0.1241*	*0.0799*	*0.0457*	*0.0232*	*23.54*	*19.37*
2010	*0.1126*	*0.0719*	*0.0463*	*0.0245*	*26.14*	*22.78*
2020	*0.1355*	*0.0824*	*0.0452*	*0.0231*	*29.26*	*26.90*

OBSERVED AND *PROJECTED* POPULATION DATA (000's)

YEAR	MID-YEAR POPULATION	NO. OF BIRTHS	NO. OF DEATHS	URBAN POPULATION NUMBER	URBAN POPULATION PERCENT	POPULATION 1985 AGE	POPULATION 1985 NUMBER
1950	4131	206	144	313	7.6	0	1580
1955	4437	220	143	395	8.9	5	1269
1960	4816	238	145	503	10.4	10	1055
1965	5180	254	146	648	12.5	15	876
1970	5588	268	142	836	15.0	20	743
1975	6520	310	154	1160	17.8	25	629
1980	7723	365	172	1621	21.0	30	528
1985	8754	413	177	2147	24.5	35	449
1990	*10020*	*467*	*186*	*2836*	*28.3*	40	381
1995	*11531*	*524*	*196*	*3716*	*32.2*	45	322
2000	*13295*	*581*	*205*	*4809*	*36.2*	50	269
2005	*15317*	*631*	*212*	*6153*	*40.2*	55	219
2010	*17561*	*675*	*218*	*7758*	*44.2*	60	170
2015	*20004*	*679*	*220*	*9624*	*48.1*	65	123
2020	*22438*	*656*	*219*	*11652*	*51.9*	70+	141

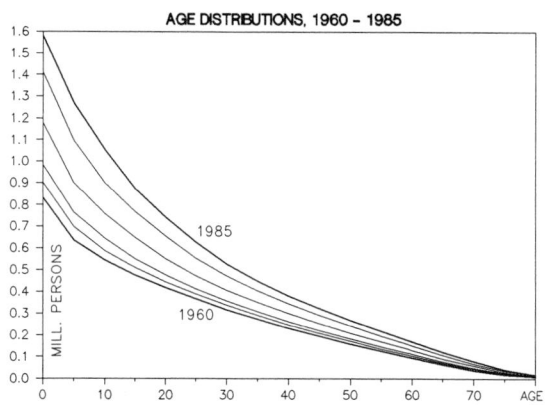

AGE DISTRIBUTIONS, 1960 - 1985

POPULATION RATIOS

YEAR	AGE DISTRIBUTION UNDER 15	AGE DISTRIBUTION 15-64	AGE DISTRIBUTION 65 & OLDER	AGE DISTRIBUTION 70 & OLDER	DEPENDENCY RATIO	WOMEN 15-49	CHILD-WOMAN RATIO
1950	0.412	0.558	0.030	0.016	0.793	0.243	0.698
1955	0.414	0.558	0.028	0.015	0.792	0.243	0.702
1960	0.418	0.554	0.028	0.014	0.804	0.241	0.718
1965	0.423	0.549	0.028	0.014	0.822	0.238	0.733
1970	0.428	0.543	0.029	0.015	0.842	0.236	0.747
1975	0.435	0.536	0.029	0.015	0.867	0.233	0.777
1980	0.442	0.529	0.030	0.016	0.892	0.230	0.795
1985	0.446	0.524	0.030	0.016	0.909	0.228	0.791
1990	*0.449*	*0.521*	*0.030*	*0.017*	*0.921*	*0.227*	*0.806*
2000	*0.452*	*0.517*	*0.031*	*0.017*	*0.934*	*0.227*	*0.800*
2010	*0.441*	*0.528*	*0.031*	*0.017*	*0.893*	*0.232*	*0.731*
2020	*0.406*	*0.561*	*0.032*	*0.019*	*0.782*	*0.246*	*0.589*

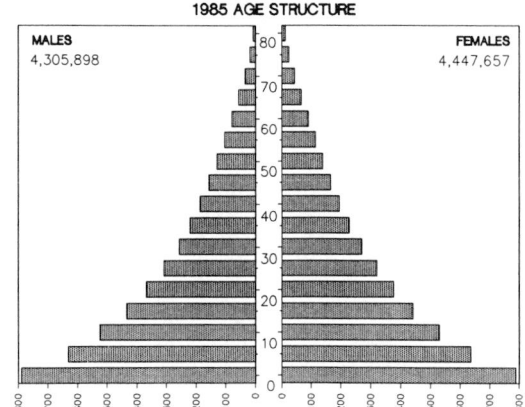

1985 AGE STRUCTURE

MALES 4,305,898   FEMALES 4,447,657

MORTALITY MEASURES (Annual Averages)

PERIOD	CRUDE DEATH RATE	INFANT MORT. RATE	LIFE EXPECTANCY AT BIRTH (years) MALE	LIFE EXPECTANCY AT BIRTH (years) FEMALE	LIFE EXPECTANCY AT BIRTH (years) BOTH SEXES	DIFFERENCE FEMALE-MALE
1950-55	34.80	230.86	28.58	31.46	30.00	2.88
1955-60	32.24	214.96	30.55	33.49	32.00	2.94
1960-65	30.19	200.01	32.53	35.52	34.00	2.99
1965-70	28.12	185.93	34.50	37.54	36.00	3.04
1970-75	25.43	172.80	36.48	39.57	38.00	3.09
1975-80	23.58	160.36	38.46	41.59	40.00	3.13
1980-85	22.23	148.54	40.44	43.61	42.00	3.17
1985-90	*20.18*	*137.00*	*42.94*	*46.11*	*44.50*	*3.17*
1990-95	*18.60*	*127.00*	*44.94*	*48.11*	*46.50*	*3.17*
2000-05	*15.41*	*107.00*	*48.94*	*52.11*	*50.50*	*3.17*
2010-15	*12.43*	*90.00*	*52.94*	*56.11*	*54.50*	*3.17*
2020-25	*9.78*	*73.00*	*56.94*	*60.11*	*58.50*	*3.17*

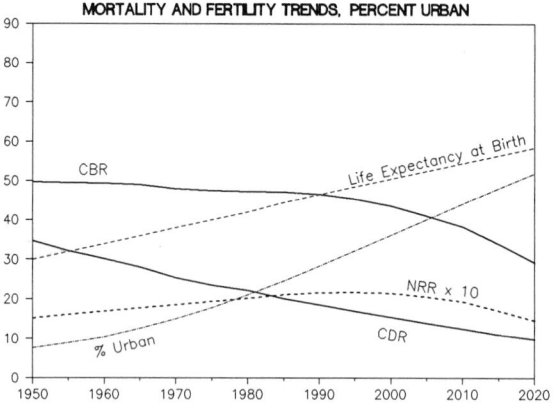

MORTALITY AND FERTILITY TRENDS, PERCENT URBAN

FERTILITY MEASURES (Annual Averages)

PERIOD	CRUDE BIRTH RATE	FERTILITY RATES GENERAL	FERTILITY RATES TOTAL	REPRODUCTION RATES GROSS	REPRODUCTION RATES NET	RATE OF NATUR. INCR.
1950-55	49.76	205.03	6.388	3.147	1.521	14.96
1955-60	49.51	204.96	6.386	3.146	1.609	17.27
1960-65	49.44	206.59	6.380	3.143	1.693	19.25
1965-70	49.07	207.24	6.384	3.145	1.778	20.95
1970-75	47.96	204.94	6.394	3.150	1.863	22.53
1975-80	47.53	205.62	6.394	3.150	1.943	23.95
1980-85	47.26	206.45	6.394	3.150	2.021	25.03
1985-90	*47.17*	*207.18*	*6.394*	*3.150*	*2.116*	*26.99*
1990-95	*46.64*	*205.30*	*6.313*	*3.110*	*2.163*	*28.04*
2000-05	*43.67*	*191.82*	*5.867*	*2.890*	*2.148*	*28.26*
2010-15	*38.44*	*163.52*	*4.994*	*2.460*	*1.940*	*26.01*
2020-25	*29.22*	*115.99*	*3.552*	*1.750*	*1.455*	*19.45*

AGING MEASURES

YEAR	POPULATION AGE RATIOS 60+/20-59	POPULATION AGE RATIOS 65+/20-64	POPULATION AGE RATIOS 70+/20-69	POPULATION AGE RATIOS 75+/20-74	POPULATION MEAN AGE	POPULATION MEDIAN AGE
1950	0.1119	0.0660	0.0342	0.0143	23.61	19.39
1960	0.1095	0.0608	0.0294	0.0126	23.39	19.13
1970	0.1151	0.0649	0.0323	0.0132	23.16	18.63
1980	0.1205	0.0692	0.0353	0.0150	22.72	17.92
1990	*0.1240*	*0.0727*	*0.0382*	*0.0168*	*22.42*	*17.49*
2000	*0.1230*	*0.0737*	*0.0397*	*0.0181*	*22.19*	*17.32*
2010	*0.1198*	*0.0727*	*0.0401*	*0.0189*	*22.45*	*17.75*
2020	*0.1177*	*0.0716*	*0.0399*	*0.0192*	*23.55*	*19.24*

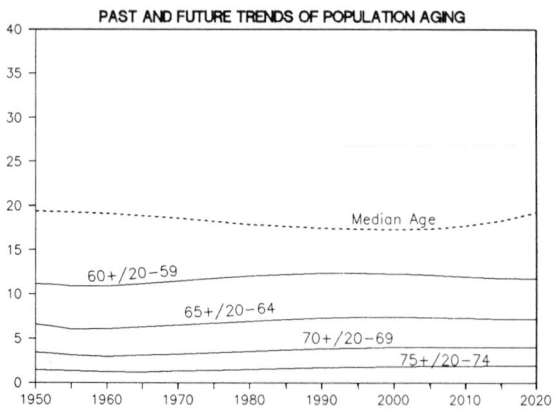

PAST AND FUTURE TRENDS OF POPULATION AGING

OBSERVED AND *PROJECTED* POPULATION DATA (000's)

YEAR	MID-YEAR POPULATION	NO. OF BIRTHS	NO. OF DEATHS	URBAN POPULATION NUMBER	URBAN POPULATION PERCENT	POPULATION 1985 AGE	POPULATION 1985 NUMBER
1950	2046	90	76	136	6.6	0	790
1955	2120	98	73	169	8.0	5	613
1960	2251	109	72	215	9.5	10	490
1965	2443	121	71	278	11.4	15	410
1970	2708	135	72	433	16.0	20	340
1975	3042	155	75	653	21.5	25	282
1980	3494	177	74	985	28.2	30	235
1985	4050	204	77	1427	35.2	35	199
1990	*4741*	*235*	*82*	*1991*	*42.0*	40	163
1995	*5573*	*269*	*87*	*2673*	*48.0*	45	139
2000	*6561*	*303*	*92*	*3467*	*52.8*	50	112
2005	*7708*	*333*	*96*	*4351*	*56.5*	55	91
2010	*8987*	*351*	*99*	*5382*	*59.9*	60	70
2015	*10341*	*353*	*100*	*6526*	*63.1*	65	52
2020	*11691*	*345*	*100*	*7730*	*66.1*	70+	64

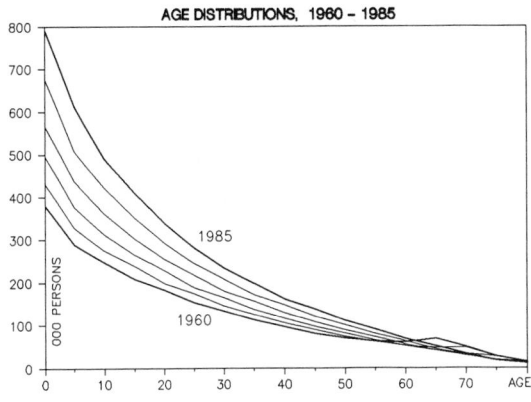

AGE DISTRIBUTIONS, 1960 - 1985

POPULATION RATIOS

YEAR	AGE DISTRIBUTION UNDER 15	AGE DISTRIBUTION 15-64	AGE DISTRIBUTION 65 & OLDER	AGE DISTRIBUTION 70 & OLDER	DEPENDENCY RATIO	WOMEN 15-49	CHILD-WOMAN RATIO
1950	0.362	0.550	0.088	0.050	0.818	0.202	0.748
1955	0.385	0.534	0.080	0.046	0.871	0.211	0.755
1960	0.407	0.520	0.072	0.041	0.923	0.218	0.775
1965	0.424	0.520	0.057	0.037	0.924	0.223	0.790
1970	0.438	0.518	0.043	0.028	0.930	0.225	0.812
1975	0.449	0.516	0.035	0.021	0.936	0.226	0.822
1980	0.459	0.510	0.030	0.018	0.960	0.225	0.860
1985	0.468	0.504	0.029	0.016	0.985	0.223	0.875
1990	*0.475*	*0.497*	*0.028*	*0.015*	*1.012*	*0.221*	*0.893*
2000	*0.478*	*0.495*	*0.026*	*0.015*	*1.020*	*0.220*	*0.879*
2010	*0.463*	*0.511*	*0.026*	*0.015*	*0.958*	*0.228*	*0.785*
2020	*0.417*	*0.555*	*0.028*	*0.016*	*0.803*	*0.247*	*0.596*

MORTALITY MEASURES (Annual Averages)

PERIOD	CRUDE DEATH RATE	INFANT MORT. RATE	LIFE EXPECTANCY AT BIRTH (years) MALE	LIFE EXPECTANCY AT BIRTH (years) FEMALE	LIFE EXPECTANCY AT BIRTH (years) BOTH SEXES	DIFFERENCE FEMALE-MALE
1950-55	37.04	209.90	31.05	34.00	32.50	2.95
1955-60	34.46	192.80	32.53	35.52	34.00	2.99
1960-65	31.91	175.90	34.50	37.54	36.00	3.04
1965-70	28.92	160.00	36.48	39.57	38.00	3.09
1970-75	26.57	150.90	38.46	41.59	40.00	3.13
1975-80	24.63	130.35	40.44	43.61	42.00	3.17
1980-85	21.23	120.13	42.42	45.63	44.00	3.21
1985-90	*19.02*	*110.00*	*44.90*	*48.15*	*46.50*	*3.24*
1990-95	*17.29*	*101.00*	*46.88*	*50.17*	*48.50*	*3.29*
2000-05	*14.05*	*84.00*	*50.77*	*54.28*	*52.50*	*3.51*
2010-15	*11.01*	*68.00*	*54.71*	*58.34*	*56.50*	*3.63*
2020-25	*8.54*	*53.00*	*58.69*	*62.37*	*60.50*	*3.68*

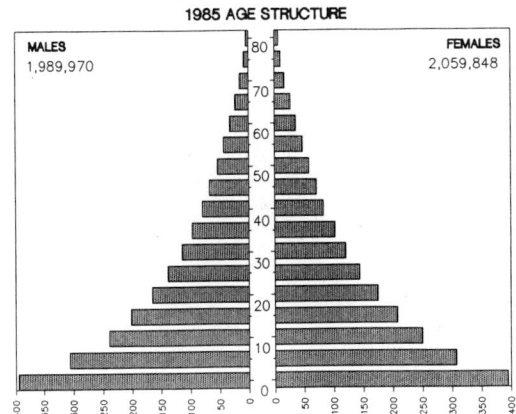

1985 AGE STRUCTURE

MALES 1,989,970   FEMALES 2,059,848

FERTILITY MEASURES (Annual Averages)

PERIOD	CRUDE BIRTH RATE	FERTILITY RATES GENERAL	FERTILITY RATES TOTAL	REPRODUCTION RATES GROSS	REPRODUCTION RATES NET	RATE OF NATUR. INCR.
1950-55	44.15	213.94	6.736	3.318	1.715	7.11
1955-60	46.47	216.74	6.762	3.331	1.790	12.01
1960-65	48.26	218.70	6.811	3.355	1.870	16.36
1965-70	49.49	220.49	6.857	3.378	1.971	20.57
1970-75	49.83	220.76	6.849	3.374	2.034	23.26
1975-80	51.05	226.53	7.003	3.450	2.145	26.42
1980-85	50.73	226.68	7.003	3.450	2.294	29.50
1985-90	*50.47*	*227.57*	*7.003*	*3.450*	*2.397*	*31.45*
1990-95	*49.57*	*224.85*	*6.902*	*3.400*	*2.445*	*32.28*
2000-05	*46.18*	*208.22*	*6.354*	*3.130*	*2.401*	*32.13*
2010-15	*39.03*	*168.22*	*5.116*	*2.520*	*2.046*	*28.01*
2020-25	*29.55*	*116.43*	*3.552*	*1.750*	*1.493*	*21.01*

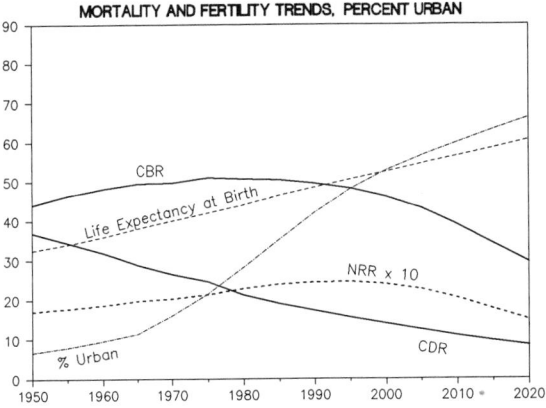

MORTALITY AND FERTILITY TRENDS, PERCENT URBAN

AGING MEASURES

YEAR	POPULATION AGE RATIOS 60+/20-59	POPULATION AGE RATIOS 65+/20-64	POPULATION AGE RATIOS 70+/20-69	POPULATION AGE RATIOS 75+/20-74	POPULATION MEAN AGE	POPULATION MEDIAN AGE
1950	0.3250	0.1895	0.0987	0.0436	29.24	23.66
1960	0.2492	0.1693	0.0901	0.0403	25.71	20.00
1970	0.1565	0.1033	0.0647	0.0355	23.32	18.14
1980	0.1238	0.0743	0.0417	0.0208	22.05	17.02
1990	*0.1171*	*0.0695*	*0.0376*	*0.0172*	*21.36*	*16.22*
2000	*0.1140*	*0.0679*	*0.0370*	*0.0171*	*21.06*	*16.02*
2010	*0.1092*	*0.0658*	*0.0365*	*0.0171*	*21.38*	*16.69*
2020	*0.1060*	*0.0646*	*0.0361*	*0.0172*	*22.81*	*18.63*

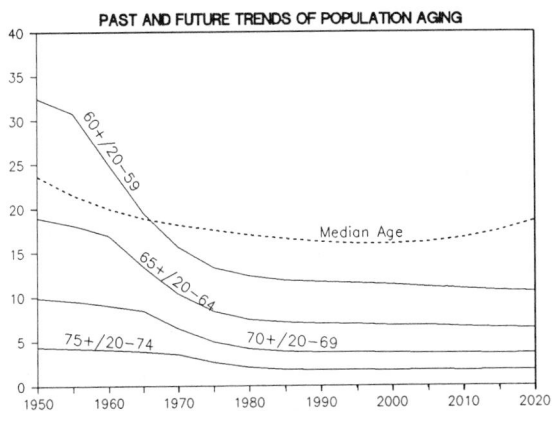

PAST AND FUTURE TRENDS OF POPULATION AGING

OBSERVED AND *PROJECTED* POPULATION DATA

YEAR	MID-YEAR POPULATION	NO. OF BIRTHS	NO. OF DEATHS	URBAN POPULATION NUMBER	URBAN POPULATION PERCENT	POPULATION 1985 AGE	POPULATION 1985 NUMBER
1950	389374	19053	8818	1349	.3	0	219369
1955	433445	22118	9232	3391	.8	5	159309
1960	481444	25321	9455	8460	1.8	10	141668
1965	549188	29496	9961	21415	3.9	15	114472
1970	623472	32483	10499	52554	8.4	20	88413
1975	755070	38168	11734	90725	12.0	25	74762
1980	901517	44383	12925	137657	15.3	30	59622
1985	1078190	51030	12563	207145	19.2	35	43764
1990	*1285253*	*57396*	*12368*	*303107*	*23.6*	40	35237
1995	*1527901*	*63522*	*12188*	*430972*	*28.2*	45	31472
2000	*1804009*	*69386*	*12121*	*592734*	*32.9*	50	26912
2005	*2115017*	*72725*	*12130*	*788755*	*37.3*	55	21916
2010	*2441371*	*72421*	*12390*	*1008331*	*41.3*	60	19263
2015	*2761185*	*70993*	*12881*	*1250510*	*45.3*	65	14285
2020	*3067883*	*70129*	*13726*	*1509290*	*49.2*	70+	27728

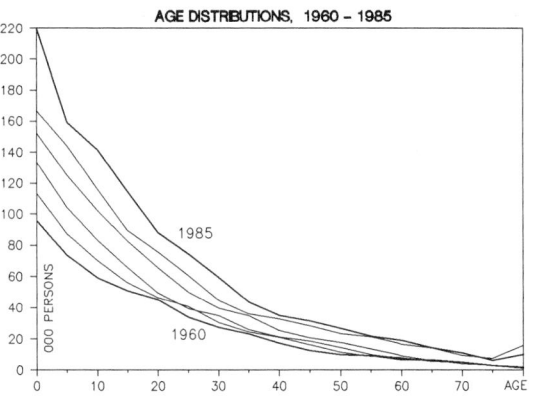

AGE DISTRIBUTIONS, 1960 - 1985

POPULATION RATIOS

YEAR	UNDER 15	15-64	65 & OLDER	70 & OLDER	DEPENDENCY RATIO	WOMEN 15-49	CHILD-WOMAN RATIO
1950	0.461	0.499	0.040	0.022	1.004	0.223	0.801
1955	0.458	0.505	0.037	0.021	0.980	0.234	0.805
1960	0.475	0.491	0.034	0.020	1.036	0.242	0.822
1965	0.494	0.478	0.028	0.018	1.092	0.246	0.840
1970	0.515	0.460	0.025	0.015	1.175	0.238	0.899
1975	0.503	0.476	0.021	0.013	1.103	0.235	0.858
1980	0.473	0.475	0.051	0.036	1.103	0.227	0.815
1985	0.483	0.478	0.039	0.026	1.090	0.227	0.896
1990	*0.485*	*0.481*	*0.034*	*0.021*	*1.077*	*0.228*	*0.872*
2000	*0.473*	*0.498*	*0.029*	*0.018*	*1.007*	*0.234*	*0.769*
2010	*0.427*	*0.545*	*0.028*	*0.017*	*0.835*	*0.247*	*0.620*
2020	*0.359*	*0.608*	*0.033*	*0.019*	*0.643*	*0.271*	*0.437*

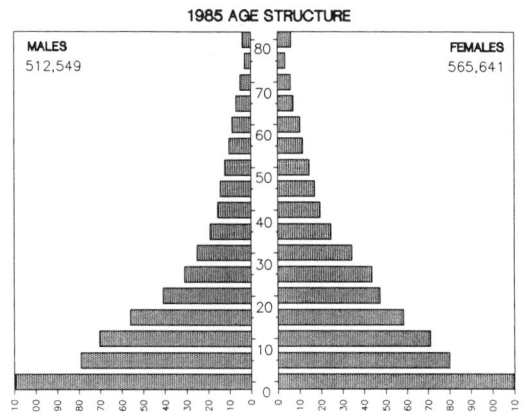

1985 AGE STRUCTURE

MALES 512,549   FEMALES 565,641

MORTALITY MEASURES (Annual Averages)

PERIOD	CRUDE DEATH RATE	INFANT MORT. RATE	LIFE EXPECTANCY AT BIRTH (years) MALE	FEMALE	BOTH SEXES	DIFFERENCE FEMALE-MALE
1950-55	22.65	130.00	41.00	44.00	42.50	3.00
1955-60	21.30	122.00	43.00	46.00	44.50	3.00
1960-65	19.64	115.00	45.00	48.00	46.50	3.00
1965-70	18.14	110.00	47.00	50.50	48.75	3.50
1970-75	16.84	95.00	49.00	53.00	51.00	4.00
1975-80	15.54	82.00	51.00	56.00	53.50	5.00
1980-85	14.34	76.00	53.00	59.00	55.96	6.00
1985-90	*11.65*	*67.00*	*55.50*	*61.50*	*58.46*	*6.00*
1990-95	*9.62*	*58.00*	*58.00*	*64.00*	*60.96*	*6.00*
2000-05	*6.72*	*41.00*	*62.78*	*68.58*	*65.64*	*5.80*
2010-15	*5.07*	*29.00*	*66.38*	*71.98*	*69.14*	*5.60*
2020-25	*4.47*	*22.00*	*69.02*	*74.50*	*71.72*	*5.48*

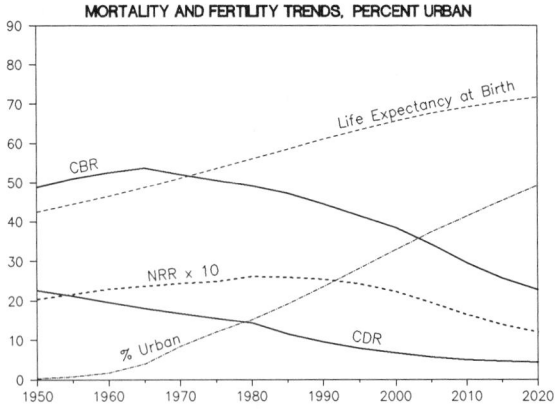

MORTALITY AND FERTILITY TRENDS, PERCENT URBAN

Life Expectancy at Birth
CBR
NRR x 10
% Urban
CDR

FERTILITY MEASURES (Annual Averages)

PERIOD	CRUDE BIRTH RATE	FERTILITY RATES GENERAL	FERTILITY RATES TOTAL	REPRODUCTION RATES GROSS	REPRODUCTION RATES NET	RATE OF NATUR. INCR.
1950-55	48.93	213.60	6.496	3.200	2.050	26.29
1955-60	51.03	213.92	6.699	3.300	2.175	29.73
1960-65	52.59	215.27	6.902	3.400	2.300	32.95
1965-70	53.71	222.06	6.902	3.400	2.370	35.57
1970-75	52.10	220.14	6.902	3.400	2.440	35.26
1975-80	50.55	219.08	6.699	3.300	2.490	35.01
1980-85	49.23	216.88	6.496	3.200	2.621	34.90
1985-90	*47.33*	*208.10*	*6.252*	*3.080*	*2.602*	*35.68*
1990-95	*44.66*	*196.59*	*5.948*	*2.930*	*2.547*	*35.03*
2000-05	*38.46*	*162.16*	*4.973*	*2.450*	*2.234*	*31.74*
2010-15	*29.66*	*117.17*	*3.552*	*1.750*	*1.648*	*24.59*
2020-25	*22.86*	*82.86*	*2.558*	*1.260*	*1.208*	*18.39*

AGING MEASURES

YEAR	POPULATION AGE RATIOS 60+/20-59	65+/20-64	70+/20-69	75+/20-74	POPULATION MEAN AGE	POPULATION MEDIAN AGE
1950	0.1661	0.1016	0.0552	0.0256	22.09	16.77
1960	0.1281	0.0877	0.0510	0.0242	21.01	16.19
1970	0.1074	0.0710	0.0409	0.0224	19.75	14.43
1980	0.1951	0.1367	0.0919	0.0642	22.61	16.35
1990	*0.1384*	*0.0910*	*0.0541*	*0.0303*	*20.92*	*15.70*
2000	*0.1177*	*0.0756*	*0.0447*	*0.0239*	*21.06*	*16.20*
2010	*0.1015*	*0.0649*	*0.0394*	*0.0207*	*22.36*	*18.18*
2020	*0.1098*	*0.0666*	*0.0371*	*0.0193*	*24.91*	*21.37*

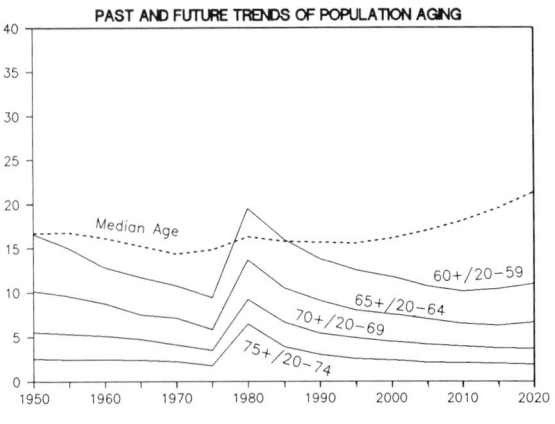

PAST AND FUTURE TRENDS OF POPULATION AGING

Median Age
60+/20-59
65+/20-64
70+/20-69
75+/20-74

OBSERVED AND *PROJECTED* POPULATION DATA (000's)

YEAR	MID-YEAR POPULATION	NO. OF BIRTHS	NO. OF DEATHS	URBAN POPULATION NUMBER	URBAN POPULATION PERCENT	POPULATION 1985 AGE	POPULATION 1985 NUMBER
1950	3731	192	121	143	3.8	0	1390
1955	4090	211	123	174	4.2	5	1093
1960	4528	234	129	213	4.7	10	967
1965	5025	256	135	261	5.2	15	817
1970	5593	281	143	321	5.7	20	683
1975	6202	293	134	394	6.3	25	564
1980	6959	328	139	487	7.0	30	465
1985	7882	372	146	621	7.9	35	419
1990	*9007*	*418*	*153*	*812*	*9.0*	40	358
1995	*10382*	*467*	*161*	*1089*	*10.5*	45	301
2000	*12025*	*518*	*168*	*1487*	*12.4*	50	249
2005	*13910*	*563*	*174*	*2051*	*14.7*	55	196
2010	*16001*	*600*	*179*	*2790*	*17.4*	60	152
2015	*18254*	*606*	*180*	*3733*	*20.4*	65	107
2020	*20520*	*588*	*178*	*4873*	*23.7*	70+	121

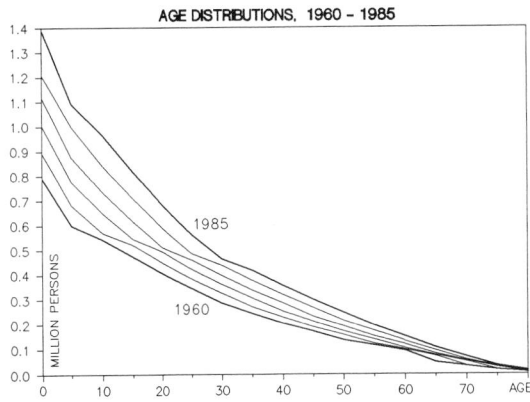

POPULATION RATIOS

YEAR	AGE DISTRIBUTION UNDER 15	AGE DISTRIBUTION 15-64	AGE DISTRIBUTION 65 & OLDER	AGE DISTRIBUTION 70 & OLDER	DEPENDENCY RATIO	WOMEN 15-49	CHILD-WOMAN RATIO
1950	0.435	0.535	0.030	0.016	0.869	0.233	0.767
1955	0.429	0.545	0.026	0.014	0.836	0.237	0.716
1960	0.426	0.550	0.024	0.013	0.818	0.239	0.728
1965	0.427	0.547	0.026	0.012	0.828	0.239	0.744
1970	0.434	0.538	0.027	0.014	0.857	0.234	0.765
1975	0.440	0.533	0.028	0.015	0.877	0.231	0.779
1980	0.438	0.533	0.028	0.015	0.875	0.231	0.751
1985	0.438	0.533	0.029	0.015	0.875	0.230	0.765
1990	*0.438*	*0.532*	*0.030*	*0.016*	*0.880*	*0.229*	*0.783*
2000	*0.446*	*0.523*	*0.031*	*0.017*	*0.913*	*0.225*	*0.789*
2010	*0.435*	*0.533*	*0.033*	*0.018*	*0.877*	*0.232*	*0.715*
2020	*0.399*	*0.567*	*0.034*	*0.020*	*0.764*	*0.246*	*0.575*

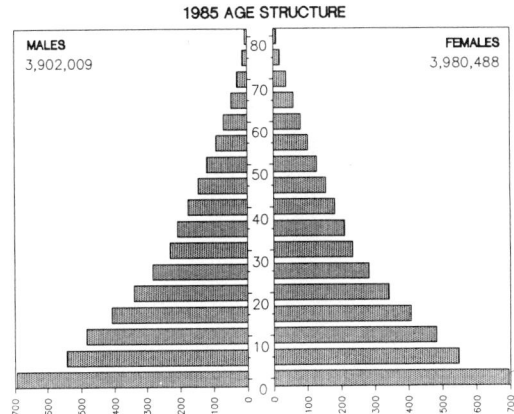

MORTALITY MEASURES (Annual Averages)

PERIOD	CRUDE DEATH RATE	INFANT MORT. RATE	LIFE EXPECTANCY AT BIRTH (years) MALE	LIFE EXPECTANCY AT BIRTH (years) FEMALE	LIFE EXPECTANCY AT BIRTH (years) BOTH SEXES	DIFFERENCE FEMALE-MALE
1950-55	32.31	225.94	31.69	34.68	33.20	2.98
1955-60	30.06	211.67	33.71	36.72	35.20	3.02
1960-65	28.52	198.17	35.71	38.76	37.20	3.04
1965-70	26.83	185.38	37.65	40.78	39.20	3.13
1970-75	25.57	173.14	39.66	42.81	41.22	3.15
1975-80	21.53	161.72	41.63	44.88	43.22	3.25
1980-85	19.92	149.37	43.65	46.84	45.22	3.19
1985-90	*18.51*	*137.62*	*45.60*	*48.90*	*47.22*	*3.30*
1990-95	*17.02*	*126.53*	*47.60*	*50.87*	*49.22*	*3.26*
2000-05	*13.98*	*105.87*	*51.47*	*55.00*	*53.22*	*3.53*
2010-15	*11.18*	*86.61*	*55.41*	*59.03*	*57.22*	*3.62*
2020-25	*8.70*	*68.62*	*59.38*	*63.11*	*61.22*	*3.73*

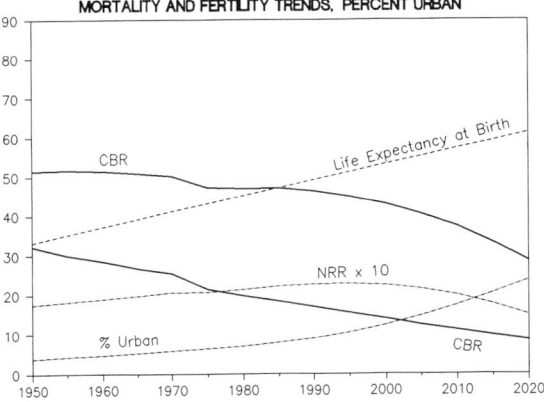

FERTILITY MEASURES (Annual Averages)

PERIOD	CRUDE BIRTH RATE	FERTILITY RATES GENERAL	FERTILITY RATES TOTAL	REPRODUCTION RATES GROSS	REPRODUCTION RATES NET	RATE OF NATUR. INCR.
1950-55	51.60	219.55	6.878	3.388	1.751	19.28
1955-60	51.70	216.93	6.787	3.343	1.818	21.65
1960-65	51.57	215.81	6.736	3.318	1.892	23.05
1965-70	50.95	215.55	6.720	3.310	1.973	24.12
1970-75	50.20	215.84	6.739	3.320	2.062	24.63
1975-80	47.25	204.57	6.496	3.200	2.069	25.73
1980-85	47.15	204.41	6.496	3.200	2.145	27.23
1985-90	*47.18*	*205.38*	*6.496*	*3.200*	*2.224*	*28.67*
1990-95	*46.38*	*203.77*	*6.394*	*3.150*	*2.264*	*29.36*
2000-05	*43.04*	*189.88*	*5.948*	*2.930*	*2.248*	*29.06*
2010-15	*37.49*	*159.43*	*4.994*	*2.460*	*1.997*	*26.32*
2020-25	*28.67*	*113.87*	*3.552*	*1.750*	*1.495*	*19.97*

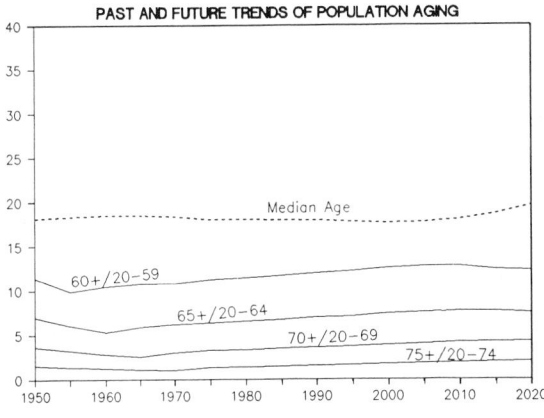

AGING MEASURES

YEAR	POPULATION AGE RATIOS 60+/20-59	POPULATION AGE RATIOS 65+/20-64	POPULATION AGE RATIOS 70+/20-69	POPULATION AGE RATIOS 75+/20-74	POPULATION MEAN AGE	POPULATION MEDIAN AGE
1950	0.1138	0.0694	0.0366	0.0156	22.72	18.14
1960	0.1044	0.0531	0.0282	0.0123	22.81	18.51
1970	0.1083	0.0620	0.0301	0.0104	22.75	18.37
1980	0.1145	0.0657	0.0330	0.0141	22.77	18.02
1990	*0.1194*	*0.0694*	*0.0357*	*0.0154*	*22.67*	*17.95*
2000	*0.1254*	*0.0736*	*0.0385*	*0.0171*	*22.53*	*17.64*
2010	*0.1271*	*0.0765*	*0.0413*	*0.0188*	*22.83*	*18.07*
2020	*0.1229*	*0.0750*	*0.0426*	*0.0202*	*23.97*	*19.61*

OBSERVED AND *PROJECTED* POPULATION DATA (000's)

YEAR	MID-YEAR POPULATION	NO. OF BIRTHS	NO. OF DEATHS	URBAN POPULATION NUMBER	URBAN POPULATION PERCENT	POPULATION AGE	1985 NUMBER
1950	2456	108	65	54	2.2	0	877
1955	2681	116	68	59	2.2	5	691
1960	2927	134	74	64	2.2	10	546
1965	3214	149	80	71	2.2	15	462
1970	3456	160	82	76	2.2	20	393
1975	3747	180	77	111	3.0	25	319
1980	4100	193	78	169	4.1	30	280
1985	4721	216	80	263	5.6	35	243
1990	*5451*	*242*	*84*	*398*	*7.3*	40	209
1995	*6299*	*271*	*88*	*585*	*9.3*	45	178
2000	*7283*	*298*	*92*	*834*	*11.5*	50	149
2005	*8394*	*319*	*94*	*1150*	*13.7*	55	122
2010	*9598*	*326*	*95*	*1560*	*16.3*	60	96
2015	*10825*	*317*	*95*	*2071*	*19.1*	65	71
2020	*11998*	*305*	*94*	*2677*	*22.3*	70+	86

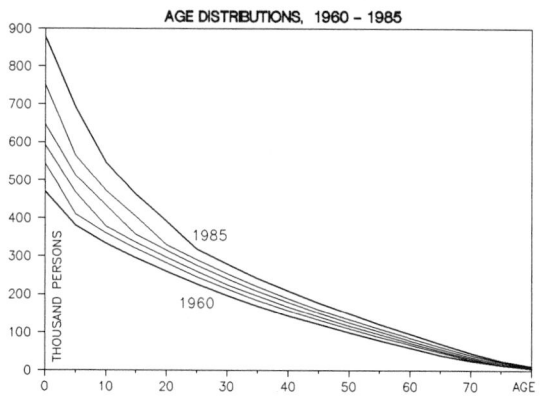

AGE DISTRIBUTIONS, 1960 - 1985

POPULATION RATIOS

YEAR	AGE DISTRIBUTION UNDER 15	15-64	65 & OLDER	70 & OLDER	DEPENDENCY RATIO	WOMEN 15-49	CHILD-WOMAN RATIO
1950	0.409	0.559	0.032	0.018	0.790	0.252	0.648
1955	0.407	0.562	0.031	0.017	0.779	0.252	0.643
1960	0.404	0.566	0.030	0.016	0.768	0.252	0.637
1965	0.409	0.561	0.030	0.016	0.784	0.248	0.682
1970	0.416	0.553	0.031	0.016	0.810	0.243	0.707
1975	0.425	0.543	0.032	0.017	0.843	0.237	0.727
1980	0.436	0.531	0.033	0.018	0.885	0.232	0.792
1985	0.448	0.519	0.033	0.018	0.927	0.226	0.820
1990	*0.456*	*0.511*	*0.033*	*0.019*	*0.959*	*0.223*	*0.823*
2000	*0.450*	*0.517*	*0.033*	*0.019*	*0.936*	*0.226*	*0.782*
2010	*0.430*	*0.536*	*0.034*	*0.020*	*0.866*	*0.237*	*0.682*
2020	*0.380*	*0.584*	*0.036*	*0.021*	*0.714*	*0.257*	*0.503*

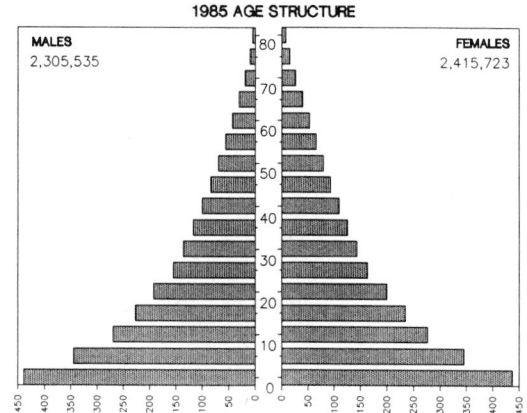

1985 AGE STRUCTURE

MALES 2,305,535   FEMALES 2,415,723

MORTALITY MEASURES (Annual Averages)

PERIOD	CRUDE DEATH RATE	INFANT MORT. RATE	LIFE EXPECTANCY AT BIRTH (years) MALE	FEMALE	BOTH SEXES	DIFFERENCE FEMALE-MALE
1950-55	26.52	172.00	38.46	41.59	40.00	3.13
1955-60	25.54	160.00	39.94	43.10	41.50	3.16
1960-65	25.32	145.00	41.43	44.62	43.00	3.19
1965-70	25.03	140.00	42.52	45.73	44.10	3.21
1970-80	23.71	135.00	43.02	46.23	44.60	3.21
1975-80	20.48	130.00	43.41	46.63	45.00	3.22
1980-85	19.00	124.14	44.90	48.15	46.50	3.24
1985-90	*17.00*	*111.88*	*47.36*	*50.69*	*49.00*	*3.32*
1990-95	*15.44*	*102.71*	*49.31*	*52.75*	*51.00*	*3.44*
2000-05	*12.58*	*85.27*	*53.23*	*56.82*	*55.00*	*3.59*
2010-15	*9.92*	*68.94*	*57.19*	*60.86*	*59.00*	*3.67*
2020-25	*7.87*	*53.77*	*61.19*	*64.86*	*63.00*	*3.67*

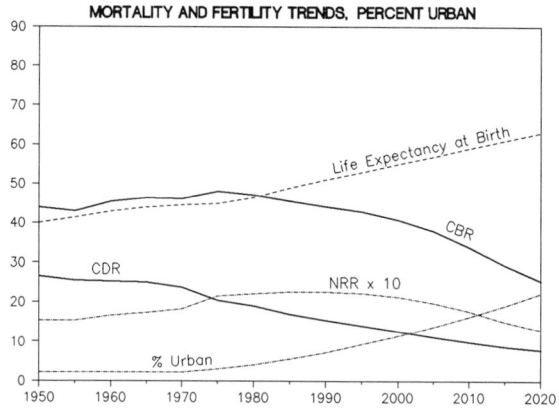

MORTALITY AND FERTILITY TRENDS, PERCENT URBAN

Life Expectancy at Birth, CBR, CDR, NRR x 10, % Urban

FERTILITY MEASURES (Annual Averages)

PERIOD	CRUDE BIRTH RATE	FERTILITY RATES GENERAL	TOTAL	REPRODUCTION RATES GROSS	NET	RATE OF NATUR. INCR.
1950-55	44.00	174.53	5.440	2.680	1.530	17.48
1955-60	43.13	171.26	5.339	2.630	1.530	17.59
1960-65	45.61	182.68	5.684	2.800	1.660	20.29
1965-70	46.46	189.51	5.826	2.870	1.730	21.43
1970-80	46.24	192.73	5.928	2.920	1.820	22.53
1975-80	48.16	205.46	6.435	3.170	2.151	27.68
1980-85	47.16	206.14	6.435	3.170	2.208	28.17
1985-90	*45.72*	*203.72*	*6.313*	*3.110*	*2.260*	*28.71*
1990-95	*44.31*	*198.61*	*6.110*	*3.010*	*2.261*	*28.87*
2000-05	*40.90*	*179.03*	*5.420*	*2.670*	*2.127*	*28.33*
2010-15	*33.94*	*140.83*	*4.263*	*2.100*	*1.762*	*24.02*
2020-25	*25.43*	*96.64*	*2.964*	*1.460*	*1.282*	*17.57*

AGING MEASURES

YEAR	POPULATION AGE RATIOS 60+/20-59	65+/20-64	70+/20-69	75+/20-74	POPULATION MEAN AGE	MEDIAN AGE
1950	0.1187	0.0708	0.0372	0.0164	23.75	19.50
1960	0.1138	0.0645	0.0343	0.0153	23.94	19.74
1970	0.1212	0.0691	0.0350	0.0147	23.70	19.31
1980	0.1309	0.0763	0.0397	0.0173	23.16	18.22
1990	*0.1358*	*0.0811*	*0.0436*	*0.0198*	*22.53*	*17.25*
2000	*0.1339*	*0.0814*	*0.0448*	*0.0211*	*22.36*	*17.33*
2010	*0.1271*	*0.0786*	*0.0443*	*0.0214*	*22.82*	*18.23*
2020	*0.1206*	*0.0761*	*0.0438*	*0.0218*	*24.47*	*20.40*

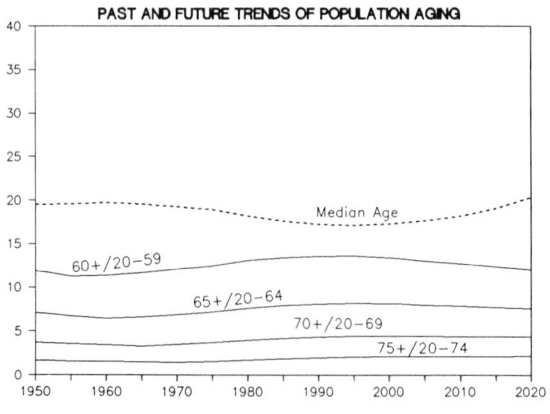

PAST AND FUTURE TRENDS OF POPULATION AGING

Median Age, 60+/20-59, 65+/20-64, 70+/20-69, 75+/20-74

OBSERVED AND *PROJECTED* POPULATION DATA (000's)

YEAR	MID-YEAR POPULATION	NO. OF BIRTHS	NO. OF DEATHS	URBAN POPULATION NUMBER	URBAN POPULATION PERCENT	POPULATION 1985 AGE	POPULATION 1985 NUMBER
1950	4526	208	121	443	9.8	0	1727
1955	4986	221	123	582	11.7	5	1401
1960	5501	236	125	763	13.9	10	1148
1965	6084	256	128	998	16.4	15	961
1970	6761	288	133	1373	20.3	20	830
1975	7582	351	143	2038	26.9	25	727
1980	8623	382	149	2988	34.7	30	633
1985	9873	411	154	4185	42.4	35	469
1990	*11245*	*464*	*160*	*5559*	*49.4*	40	417
1995	*12875*	*523*	*167*	*7126*	*55.3*	45	365
2000	*14787*	*574*	*172*	*8861*	*59.9*	50	318
2005	*16946*	*613*	*175*	*10700*	*63.1*	55	271
2010	*19286*	*633*	*177*	*12758*	*66.1*	60	220
2015	*21710*	*614*	*176*	*14966*	*68.9*	65	167
2020	*24016*	*590*	*176*	*17176*	*71.5*	70+	219

POPULATION RATIOS

YEAR	AGE DISTRIBUTION UNDER 15	15-64	65 & OLDER	70 & OLDER	DEPENDENCY RATIO	WOMEN 15-49	CHILD-WOMAN RATIO
1950	0.379	0.586	0.035	0.019	0.706	0.259	0.570
1955	0.392	0.576	0.032	0.018	0.737	0.251	0.675
1960	0.404	0.565	0.031	0.017	0.769	0.243	0.688
1965	0.417	0.551	0.033	0.017	0.816	0.234	0.700
1970	0.414	0.551	0.036	0.018	0.816	0.234	0.698
1975	0.415	0.547	0.038	0.020	0.828	0.233	0.718
1980	0.424	0.538	0.039	0.022	0.860	0.230	0.754
1985	0.433	0.528	0.039	0.022	0.895	0.226	0.773
1990	*0.436*	*0.525*	*0.039*	*0.022*	*0.903*	*0.227*	*0.752*
2000	*0.432*	*0.531*	*0.037*	*0.022*	*0.883*	*0.233*	*0.730*
2010	*0.418*	*0.546*	*0.036*	*0.021*	*0.832*	*0.238*	*0.655*
2020	*0.373*	*0.588*	*0.039*	*0.022*	*0.700*	*0.256*	*0.493*

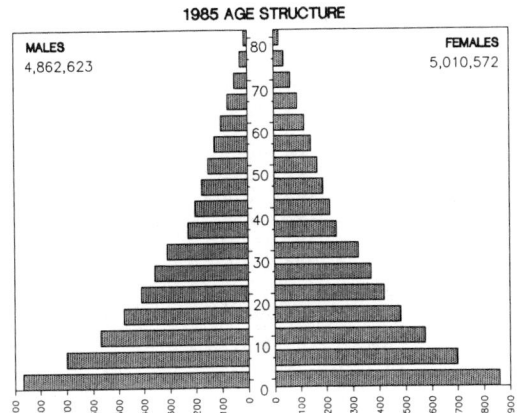

MORTALITY MEASURES (Annual Averages)

PERIOD	CRUDE DEATH RATE	INFANT MORT. RATE	LIFE EXPECTANCY AT BIRTH (years) MALE	FEMALE	BOTH SEXES	DIFFERENCE FEMALE-MALE
1950-55	26.63	190.00	35.00	39.00	36.97	4.00
1955-60	24.72	172.20	37.00	41.00	38.97	4.00
1960-65	22.72	153.90	39.00	43.00	40.97	4.00
1965-70	21.01	136.10	41.00	45.00	42.97	4.00
1970-75	19.67	119.10	43.00	47.00	44.97	4.00
1975-80	18.85	111.10	45.00	49.00	46.97	4.00
1980-85	17.29	103.15	47.00	51.00	48.97	4.00
1985-90	*15.65*	*94.00*	*49.00*	*53.00*	*50.97*	*4.00*
1990-95	*14.27*	*86.00*	*51.00*	*55.00*	*52.97*	*4.00*
2000-05	*11.63*	*69.00*	*55.00*	*59.00*	*56.97*	*4.00*
2010-15	*9.17*	*54.00*	*59.00*	*63.00*	*60.97*	*4.00*
2020-25	*7.32*	*40.00*	*63.00*	*67.00*	*64.97*	*4.00*

FERTILITY MEASURES (Annual Averages)

PERIOD	CRUDE BIRTH RATE	FERTILITY RATES GENERAL	TOTAL	REPRODUCTION RATES GROSS	NET	RATE OF NATUR. INCR.
1950-55	45.97	180.53	5.814	2.864	1.660	19.34
1955-60	44.37	180.01	5.816	2.865	1.733	19.65
1960-65	42.82	179.84	5.820	2.867	1.806	20.10
1965-70	42.10	179.74	5.832	2.873	1.881	21.09
1970-75	42.58	182.06	5.875	2.894	1.963	22.91
1975-80	46.29	199.96	6.394	3.150	2.212	27.44
1980-85	44.27	194.31	6.191	3.050	2.215	26.98
1985-90	*41.64*	*183.90*	*5.785*	*2.850*	*2.138*	*25.99*
1990-95	*41.29*	*181.07*	*5.704*	*2.810*	*2.172*	*27.03*
2000-05	*38.84*	*166.45*	*5.237*	*2.580*	*2.107*	*27.21*
2010-15	*32.81*	*135.92*	*4.263*	*2.100*	*1.801*	*23.64*
2020-25	*24.55*	*93.84*	*2.964*	*1.460*	*1.308*	*17.23*

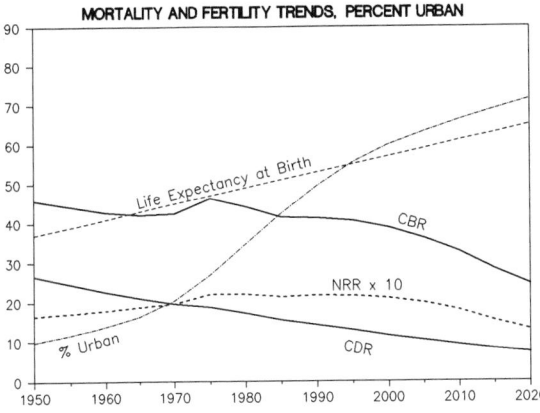

AGING MEASURES

YEAR	POPULATION AGE RATIOS 60+/20-59	65+/20-64	70+/20-69	75+/20-74	POPULATION MEAN AGE	POPULATION MEDIAN AGE
1950	0.1176	0.0719	0.0385	0.0173	24.87	21.18
1960	0.1175	0.0647	0.0353	0.0163	24.35	20.21
1970	0.1400	0.0794	0.0395	0.0160	24.25	19.19
1980	0.1487	0.0887	0.0471	0.0209	23.79	18.88
1990	*0.1493*	*0.0912*	*0.0504*	*0.0238*	*23.32*	*18.21*
2000	*0.1394*	*0.0874*	*0.0497*	*0.0241*	*23.11*	*18.25*
2010	*0.1275*	*0.0813*	*0.0472*	*0.0238*	*23.52*	*18.88*
2020	*0.1339*	*0.0820*	*0.0448*	*0.0231*	*25.08*	*20.93*

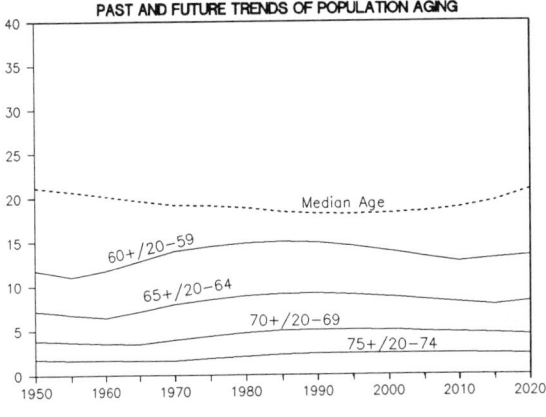

OBSERVED AND *PROJECTED* POPULATION DATA

YEAR	MID-YEAR POPULATION	NO. OF BIRTHS	NO. OF DEATHS	URBAN POPULATION NUMBER	URBAN POPULATION PERCENT	POPULATION 1985 AGE	POPULATION 1985 NUMBER
1950	148330	6737	3418	11718	7.9	0	47553
1955	172197	8190	2462	12487	7.3	5	48789
1960	199902	8700	2471	13298	6.7	10	41164
1965	232751	9189	2588	25752	11.1	15	43890
1970	270999	8927	3062	50998	18.8	20	39618
1975	283082	9302	2752	85388	30.2	25	26164
1980	295713	9840	3428	125410	42.4	30	14721
1985	329614	12652	3406	175650	53.3	35	7324
1990	*379335*	*15215*	*3353*	*233261*	*61.5*	40	7651
1995	*443675*	*16990*	*3249*	*296426*	*66.8*	45	11112
2000	*518149*	*17769*	*3122*	*360389*	*69.6*	50	10389
2005	*596952*	*17461*	*3157*	*430311*	*72.1*	55	9039
2010	*673031*	*17324*	*3222*	*500835*	*74.4*	60	5345
2015	*747443*	*16797*	*3369*	*572202*	*76.6*	65	5351
2020	*817738*	*16733*	*3605*	*642054*	*78.5*	70+	11504

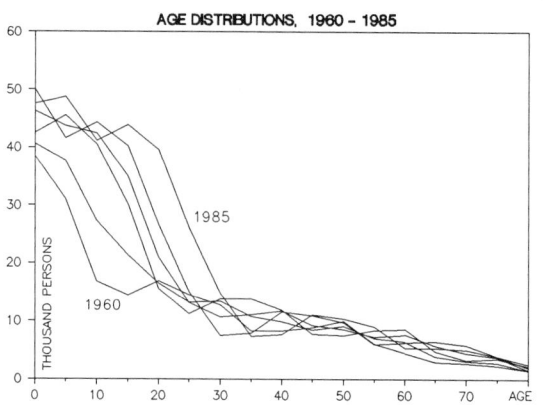

AGE DISTRIBUTIONS, 1960 - 1985

POPULATION RATIOS

YEAR	AGE DISTRIBUTION UNDER 15	AGE DISTRIBUTION 15-64	AGE DISTRIBUTION 65 & OLDER	AGE DISTRIBUTION 70 & OLDER	DEPENDENCY RATIO	WOMEN 15-49	CHILD-WOMAN RATIO
1950	0.342	0.617	0.041	0.025	0.620	0.290	0.365
1955	0.388	0.569	0.044	0.028	0.758	0.259	0.576
1960	0.432	0.522	0.046	0.032	0.917	0.230	0.838
1965	0.454	0.498	0.048	0.031	1.007	0.217	0.804
1970	0.475	0.474	0.051	0.033	1.108	0.205	0.766
1975	0.468	0.478	0.054	0.034	1.093	0.218	0.749
1980	0.460	0.479	0.061	0.039	1.087	0.231	0.731
1985	0.417	0.532	0.051	0.035	0.881	0.252	0.573
1990	*0.416*	*0.544*	*0.040*	*0.028*	*0.839*	*0.251*	*0.661*
2000	*0.434*	*0.530*	*0.036*	*0.021*	*0.888*	*0.253*	*0.665*
2010	*0.396*	*0.575*	*0.029*	*0.021*	*0.739*	*0.258*	*0.515*
2020	*0.321*	*0.651*	*0.028*	*0.015*	*0.535*	*0.268*	*0.390*

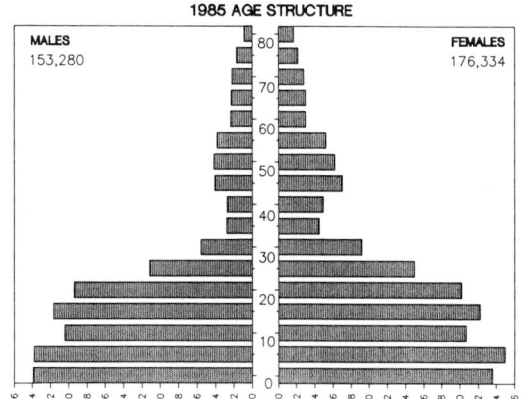

1985 AGE STRUCTURE

MALES 153,280 — FEMALES 176,334

MORTALITY MEASURES (Annual Averages)

PERIOD	CRUDE DEATH RATE	INFANT MORT. RATE	LIFE EXPECTANCY AT BIRTH (years) MALE	LIFE EXPECTANCY AT BIRTH (years) FEMALE	LIFE EXPECTANCY AT BIRTH (years) BOTH SEXES	DIFFERENCE FEMALE-MALE
1950-55	23.04	165.00	41.23	44.10	42.64	2.87
1955-60	14.30	150.00	43.52	46.48	44.98	2.96
1960-65	12.36	135.00	46.03	48.98	47.48	2.95
1965-70	11.12	120.00	48.68	51.63	50.13	2.95
1970-75	11.30	103.00	51.73	54.03	52.86	2.30
1975-80	9.72	86.60	54.85	58.28	56.54	3.43
1980-85	11.59	74.76	57.30	60.80	59.02	3.50
1985-90	*10.33*	*65.56*	*59.30*	*62.80*	*61.02*	*3.50*
1990-95	*8.84*	*56.74*	*61.30*	*64.80*	*63.02*	*3.50*
2000-05	*6.03*	*39.91*	*65.30*	*68.80*	*67.02*	*3.50*
2010-15	*4.79*	*28.91*	*68.30*	*71.50*	*69.88*	*3.20*
2020-25	*4.41*	*21.96*	*70.30*	*73.70*	*71.97*	*3.40*

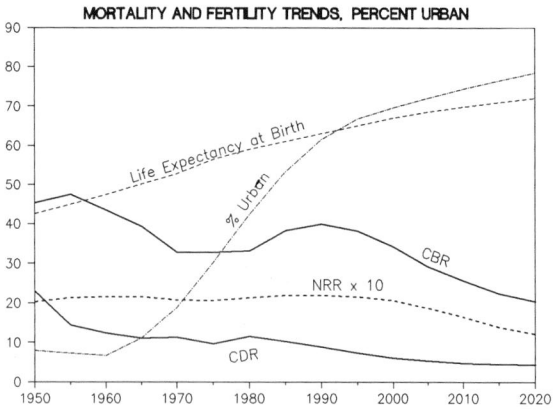

MORTALITY AND FERTILITY TRENDS, PERCENT URBAN

Life Expectancy at Birth — % Urban — CBR — NRR x 10 — CDR

FERTILITY MEASURES (Annual Averages)

PERIOD	CRUDE BIRTH RATE	FERTILITY RATES GENERAL	FERTILITY RATES TOTAL	REPRODUCTION RATES GROSS	REPRODUCTION RATES NET	RATE OF NATUR. INCR.
1950-55	45.42	166.35	6.496	3.200	2.040	22.38
1955-60	47.56	195.67	6.496	3.200	2.140	33.26
1960-65	43.52	195.40	6.293	3.100	2.170	31.16
1965-70	39.48	187.55	5.988	2.950	2.160	28.36
1970-75	32.94	155.48	5.582	2.750	2.090	21.64
1975-80	32.86	146.02	5.176	2.550	2.070	23.14
1980-85	33.28	137.47	5.176	2.550	2.141	21.68
1985-90	*38.38*	*152.74*	*5.176*	*2.550*	*2.197*	*28.05*
1990-95	*40.11*	*157.96*	*5.075*	*2.500*	*2.206*	*31.27*
2000-05	*34.29*	*135.42*	*4.567*	*2.250*	*2.075*	*28.27*
2010-15	*25.74*	*98.79*	*3.552*	*1.750*	*1.655*	*20.95*
2020-25	*20.46*	*75.41*	*2.558*	*1.260*	*1.211*	*16.05*

AGING MEASURES

YEAR	POPULATION AGE RATIOS 60+/20-59	POPULATION AGE RATIOS 65+/20-64	POPULATION AGE RATIOS 70+/20-69	POPULATION AGE RATIOS 75+/20-74	POPULATION MEAN AGE	POPULATION MEDIAN AGE
1950	0.1409	0.0829	0.0500	0.0248	26.04	21.38
1960	0.1603	0.1032	0.0690	0.0393	24.48	19.74
1970	0.2494	0.1400	0.0871	0.0537	23.62	16.13
1980	0.2563	0.1785	0.1080	0.0518	23.07	16.48
1990	*0.1481*	*0.0914*	*0.0620*	*0.0362*	*22.80*	*18.89*
2000	*0.1268*	*0.0816*	*0.0463*	*0.0216*	*22.56*	*18.70*
2010	*0.0840*	*0.0636*	*0.0451*	*0.0237*	*24.01*	*19.64*
2020	*0.1030*	*0.0509*	*0.0264*	*0.0166*	*26.73*	*23.29*

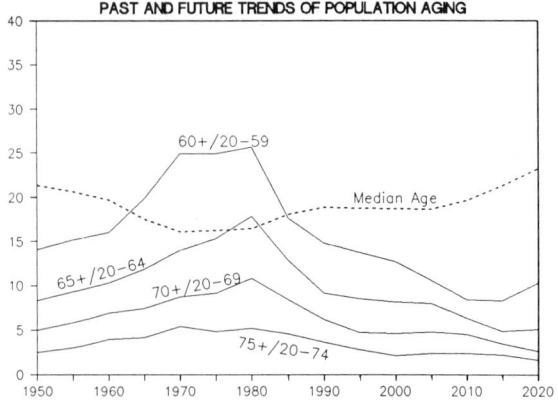

PAST AND FUTURE TRENDS OF POPULATION AGING

60+/20-59 — Median Age — 65+/20-64 — 70+/20-69 — 75+/20-74

OBSERVED AND *PROJECTED* POPULATION DATA

YEAR	MID-YEAR POPULATION	NO. OF BIRTHS	NO. OF DEATHS	URBAN POPULATION NUMBER	URBAN POPULATION PERCENT	POPULATION 1985 AGE	POPULATION 1985 NUMBER
1950	1416734	62195	45731	226285	16.0	0	444786
1955	1501514	65820	45802	286795	19.1	5	358221
1960	1605057	69749	45982	363960	22.7	10	292465
1965	1728468	74715	46586	461494	26.7	15	249073
1970	1875086	81669	46969	569722	30.4	20	216450
1975	2057000	92384	48364	703612	34.2	25	188825
1980	2298450	102458	50150	879027	38.2	30	163497
1985	2575765	114045	50828	1092444	42.4	35	130057
1990	*2912515*	*126400*	*52661*	*1357003*	*46.6*	40	114905
1995	*3306125*	*140312*	*54538*	*1674935*	*50.7*	45	100442
2000	*3764746*	*154460*	*56328*	*2052139*	*54.5*	50	86604
2005	*4289596*	*167972*	*57884*	*2489586*	*58.0*	55	72954
2010	*4877783*	*179366*	*59099*	*2994216*	*61.4*	60	58540
2015	*5518600*	*185745*	*59816*	*3560114*	*64.5*	65	44013
2020	*6186327*	*179236*	*59611*	*4170907*	*67.4*	70+	55094

AGE DISTRIBUTIONS, 1960 - 1985

POPULATION RATIOS

YEAR	AGE DISTRIBUTION UNDER 15	AGE DISTRIBUTION 15-64	AGE DISTRIBUTION 65 & OLDER	AGE DISTRIBUTION 70 & OLDER	DEPENDENCY RATIO	WOMEN 15-49	CHILD-WOMAN RATIO
1950	0.361	0.591	0.048	0.027	0.692	0.255	0.558
1955	0.373	0.582	0.045	0.025	0.718	0.252	0.622
1960	0.385	0.573	0.041	0.023	0.745	0.248	0.640
1965	0.398	0.562	0.040	0.022	0.780	0.243	0.657
1970	0.401	0.559	0.040	0.021	0.789	0.242	0.665
1975	0.406	0.555	0.039	0.021	0.803	0.240	0.684
1980	0.416	0.545	0.039	0.021	0.835	0.237	0.729
1985	0.425	0.536	0.038	0.021	0.865	0.234	0.739
1990	*0.433*	*0.529*	*0.038*	*0.021*	*0.890*	*0.232*	*0.753*
2000	*0.435*	*0.529*	*0.037*	*0.021*	*0.892*	*0.233*	*0.739*
2010	*0.425*	*0.539*	*0.035*	*0.021*	*0.854*	*0.236*	*0.692*
2020	*0.399*	*0.565*	*0.036*	*0.021*	*0.770*	*0.246*	*0.588*

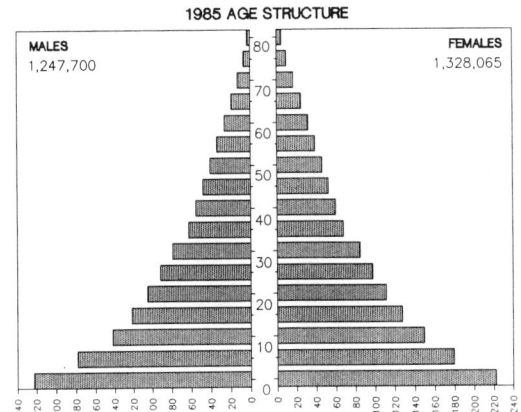

1985 AGE STRUCTURE

MALES 1,247,700   FEMALES 1,328,065

MORTALITY MEASURES (Annual Averages)

PERIOD	CRUDE DEATH RATE	INFANT MORT. RATE	LIFE EXPECTANCY AT BIRTH (years) MALE	FEMALE	BOTH SEXES	DIFFERENCE FEMALE-MALE
1950-55	32.28	197.20	32.53	35.52	34.00	2.99
1955-60	30.50	187.70	34.50	37.54	36.00	3.04
1960-65	28.65	178.40	36.48	39.57	38.00	3.09
1965-70	26.95	160.00	38.46	41.59	40.00	3.13
1970-75	25.05	148.00	39.45	42.60	41.00	3.15
1975-80	23.51	145.00	40.44	43.61	42.00	3.17
1980-85	21.82	142.00	41.43	44.62	43.00	3.19
1985-90	*19.73*	*132.00*	*43.93*	*47.12*	*45.50*	*3.19*
1990-95	*18.08*	*122.00*	*45.93*	*49.12*	*47.50*	*3.19*
2000-05	*14.96*	*103.00*	*49.93*	*53.12*	*51.50*	*3.19*
2010-15	*12.12*	*85.00*	*53.93*	*57.12*	*55.50*	*3.19*
2020-25	*9.64*	*69.00*	*57.93*	*61.12*	*59.50*	*3.19*

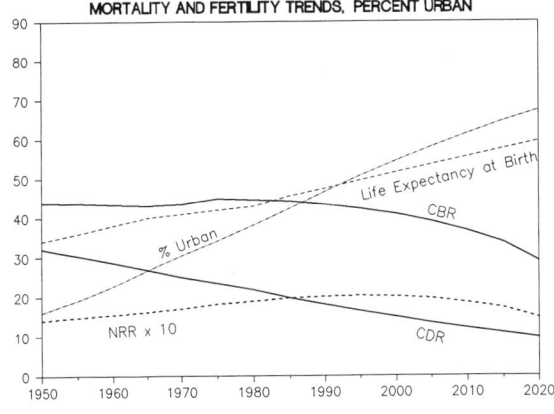

MORTALITY AND FERTILITY TRENDS, PERCENT URBAN

FERTILITY MEASURES (Annual Averages)

PERIOD	CRUDE BIRTH RATE	FERTILITY RATES GENERAL	FERTILITY RATES TOTAL	REPRODUCTION RATES GROSS	REPRODUCTION RATES NET	RATE OF NATUR. INCR.
1950-55	43.90	173.14	5.516	2.717	1.410	11.62
1955-60	43.84	175.39	5.595	2.756	1.486	13.33
1960-65	43.46	177.28	5.656	2.786	1.559	14.81
1965-70	43.23	178.54	5.690	2.803	1.623	16.27
1970-75	43.56	180.74	5.719	2.817	1.704	18.51
1975-80	44.91	188.36	5.887	2.900	1.827	21.40
1980-85	44.58	189.58	5.887	2.900	1.898	22.76
1985-90	*44.28*	*190.31*	*5.887*	*2.900*	*1.984*	*24.54*
1990-95	*43.40*	*187.27*	*5.785*	*2.850*	*2.018*	*25.32*
2000-05	*41.03*	*175.98*	*5.420*	*2.670*	*2.017*	*26.07*
2010-15	*36.77*	*154.53*	*4.730*	*2.330*	*1.864*	*24.66*
2020-25	*28.97*	*115.49*	*3.552*	*1.750*	*1.473*	*19.34*

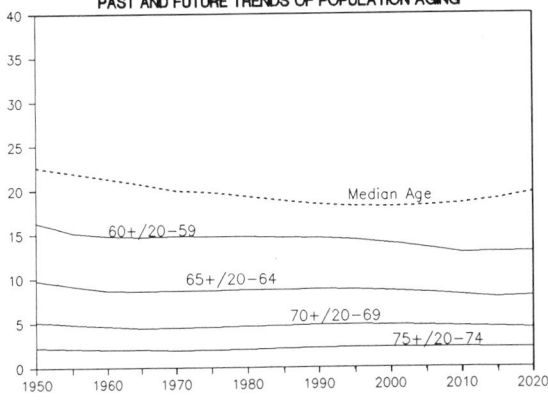

PAST AND FUTURE TRENDS OF POPULATION AGING

AGING MEASURES

YEAR	POPULATION AGE RATIOS 60+/20-59	65+/20-64	70+/20-69	75+/20-74	POPULATION MEAN AGE	MEDIAN AGE
1950	0.1633	0.0976	0.0512	0.0224	26.58	22.63
1960	0.1483	0.0861	0.0462	0.0205	25.51	21.35
1970	0.1482	0.0862	0.0447	0.0192	24.87	20.01
1980	0.1476	0.0873	0.0462	0.0205	24.13	19.31
1990	*0.1462*	*0.0879*	*0.0476*	*0.0218*	*23.47*	*18.43*
2000	*0.1398*	*0.0857*	*0.0475*	*0.0224*	*23.12*	*18.18*
2010	*0.1293*	*0.0808*	*0.0458*	*0.0222*	*23.25*	*18.55*
2020	*0.1301*	*0.0793*	*0.0436*	*0.0217*	*24.13*	*19.74*

OBSERVED AND *PROJECTED* POPULATION DATA (000's)

YEAR	MID-YEAR POPULATION	NO. OF BIRTHS	NO. OF DEATHS	URBAN POPULATION NUMBER	URBAN POPULATION PERCENT	POPULATION 1985 AGE	POPULATION 1985 NUMBER
1950	2658	120	85	112	4.2	0	860
1955	2838	130	86	154	5.4	5	681
1960	3064	140	88	214	7.0	10	582
1965	3334	151	90	298	8.9	15	504
1970	3652	163	91	415	11.4	20	435
1975	4030	178	93	613	15.2	25	373
1980	4477	198	96	931	20.8	30	315
1985	5018	222	98	1355	27.0	35	255
1990	*5678*	*246*	*102*	*1893*	*33.3*	40	225
1995	*6447*	*272*	*105*	*2530*	*39.2*	45	195
2000	*7337*	*299*	*109*	*3251*	*44.3*	50	166
2005	*8352*	*325*	*112*	*4029*	*48.2*	55	138
2010	*9491*	*347*	*115*	*4941*	*52.1*	60	110
2015	*10728*	*359*	*116*	*5977*	*55.7*	65	81
2020	*12013*	*351*	*116*	*7110*	*59.2*	70+	99

AGE DISTRIBUTIONS, 1960 - 1985

POPULATION RATIOS

YEAR	AGE DISTRIBUTION UNDER 15	15-64	65 & OLDER	70 & OLDER	DEPENDENCY RATIO	WOMEN 15-49	CHILD-WOMAN RATIO
1950	0.376	0.581	0.043	0.023	0.723	0.247	0.604
1955	0.385	0.575	0.040	0.022	0.739	0.246	0.652
1960	0.396	0.567	0.037	0.020	0.762	0.242	0.679
1965	0.408	0.555	0.036	0.019	0.800	0.237	0.701
1970	0.414	0.551	0.036	0.019	0.816	0.235	0.710
1975	0.417	0.547	0.036	0.019	0.827	0.234	0.716
1980	0.419	0.545	0.036	0.020	0.835	0.233	0.721
1985	0.423	0.541	0.036	0.020	0.848	0.232	0.738
1990	*0.428*	*0.536*	*0.036*	*0.020*	*0.866*	*0.231*	*0.755*
2000	*0.433*	*0.531*	*0.035*	*0.020*	*0.882*	*0.231*	*0.740*
2010	*0.423*	*0.542*	*0.035*	*0.020*	*0.846*	*0.235*	*0.690*
2020	*0.397*	*0.567*	*0.036*	*0.021*	*0.764*	*0.245*	*0.586*

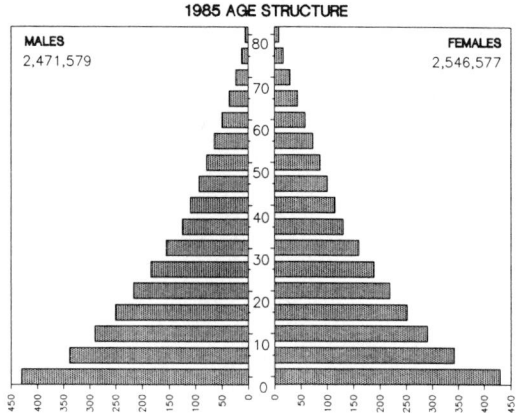

1985 AGE STRUCTURE

MALES 2,471,579 — FEMALES 2,546,577

MORTALITY MEASURES (Annual Averages)

PERIOD	CRUDE DEATH RATE	INFANT MORT. RATE	LIFE EXPECTANCY AT BIRTH (years) MALE	FEMALE	BOTH SEXES	DIFFERENCE FEMALE-MALE
1950-55	31.98	211.15	31.05	34.00	32.50	2.95
1955-60	30.36	200.01	32.53	35.52	34.00	2.99
1960-65	28.64	189.43	34.01	37.04	35.50	3.03
1965-70	26.98	179.36	35.49	38.56	37.00	3.06
1970-75	24.92	166.49	37.47	40.58	39.00	3.11
1975-80	23.06	154.28	39.45	42.60	41.00	3.15
1980-85	21.42	142.81	41.43	44.62	43.00	3.19
1985-90	*19.49*	*132.00*	*43.93*	*47.12*	*45.50*	*3.19*
1990-95	*17.91*	*122.00*	*45.93*	*49.12*	*47.50*	*3.19*
2000-05	*14.87*	*103.00*	*49.93*	*53.12*	*51.50*	*3.19*
2010-15	*12.10*	*85.00*	*53.93*	*57.12*	*55.50*	*3.19*
2020-25	*9.68*	*69.00*	*57.93*	*61.12*	*59.50*	*3.19*

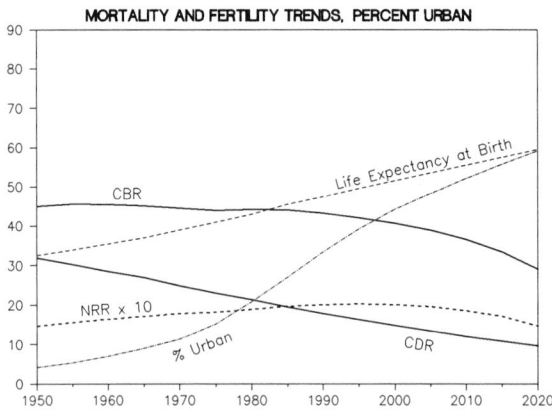

MORTALITY AND FERTILITY TRENDS, PERCENT URBAN

FERTILITY MEASURES (Annual Averages)

PERIOD	CRUDE BIRTH RATE	FERTILITY RATES GENERAL	FERTILITY RATES TOTAL	REPRODUCTION RATES GROSS	REPRODUCTION RATES NET	RATE OF NATUR. INCR.
1950-55	45.08	182.87	5.769	2.842	1.475	13.10
1955-60	45.66	187.21	5.905	2.909	1.569	15.30
1960-65	45.54	190.09	5.999	2.955	1.653	16.90
1965-70	45.20	191.32	6.045	2.978	1.724	18.22
1970-75	44.61	190.02	5.986	2.949	1.783	19.68
1975-80	44.06	188.46	5.887	2.900	1.827	21.01
1980-85	44.23	190.01	5.887	2.900	1.898	22.81
1985-90	*44.18*	*191.00*	*5.887*	*2.900*	*1.984*	*24.69*
1990-95	*43.27*	*188.03*	*5.785*	*2.850*	*2.018*	*25.36*
2000-05	*40.76*	*175.84*	*5.420*	*2.670*	*2.017*	*25.89*
2010-15	*36.58*	*154.14*	*4.730*	*2.330*	*1.864*	*24.48*
2020-25	*29.19*	*116.80*	*3.552*	*1.750*	*1.475*	*19.51*

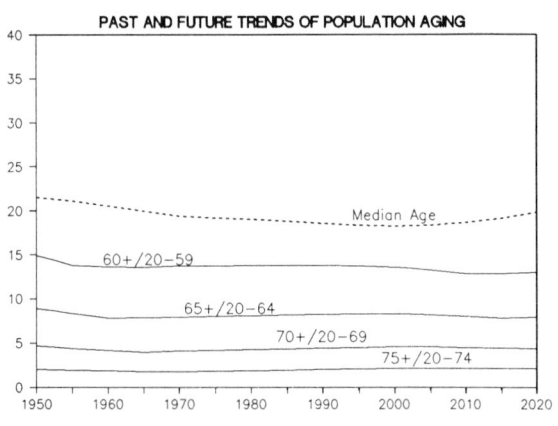

PAST AND FUTURE TRENDS OF POPULATION AGING

AGING MEASURES

YEAR	POPULATION AGE RATIOS 60+/20-59	65+/20-64	70+/20-69	75+/20-74	POPULATION MEAN AGE	POPULATION MEDIAN AGE
1950	0.1492	0.0890	0.0466	0.0203	25.64	21.54
1960	0.1363	0.0778	0.0416	0.0184	24.80	20.57
1970	0.1372	0.0792	0.0410	0.0172	24.21	19.42
1980	0.1378	0.0807	0.0424	0.0186	23.82	19.03
1990	*0.1379*	*0.0823*	*0.0441*	*0.0199*	*23.39*	*18.59*
2000	*0.1356*	*0.0826*	*0.0453*	*0.0212*	*23.16*	*18.28*
2010	*0.1285*	*0.0799*	*0.0449*	*0.0216*	*23.35*	*18.65*
2020	*0.1302*	*0.0789*	*0.0436*	*0.0216*	*24.24*	*19.83*

OBSERVED AND *PROJECTED* POPULATION DATA

YEAR	MID-YEAR POPULATION	NO. OF BIRTHS	NO. OF DEATHS	URBAN POPULATION NUMBER	URBAN POPULATION PERCENT	POPULATION 1985 AGE	POPULATION 1985 NUMBER
1950	172691	8174	4186	5699	3.3	0	82871
1955	193850	9286	4380	7149	3.7	5	66559
1960	214707	10339	4561	8844	4.1	10	55175
1965	240319	11336	4762	11050	4.6	15	45290
1970	271306	12709	4970	30661	11.3	20	38333
1975	321593	14979	5539	68582	21.3	25	31618
1980	381167	17688	6072	88505	23.2	30	26194
1985	444032	20244	6442	112017	25.2	35	21977
1990	518853	23119	6826	143457	27.6	40	18269
1995	607261	26091	7192	185219	30.5	45	15045
2000	709731	28839	7505	239744	33.8	50	12463
2005	825067	31109	7752	309030	37.5	55	9959
2010	950745	32132	7893	394074	41.5	60	7684
2015	1080186	31537	7929	490935	45.4	65	5620
2020	1205055	30507	7956	594723	49.4	70+	6975

AGE DISTRIBUTIONS, 1960 - 1985

POPULATION RATIOS

YEAR	AGE DISTRIBUTION UNDER 15	AGE DISTRIBUTION 15-64	AGE DISTRIBUTION 65 & OLDER	AGE DISTRIBUTION 70 & OLDER	DEPENDENCY RATIO	WOMEN 15-49	CHILD-WOMAN RATIO
1950	0.435	0.530	0.034	0.019	0.885	0.231	0.771
1955	0.438	0.530	0.032	0.018	0.887	0.231	0.770
1960	0.442	0.528	0.030	0.017	0.893	0.231	0.781
1965	0.446	0.525	0.029	0.016	0.906	0.230	0.797
1970	0.450	0.522	0.029	0.016	0.916	0.229	0.797
1975	0.454	0.518	0.028	0.016	0.932	0.227	0.822
1980	0.457	0.515	0.028	0.016	0.943	0.226	0.828
1985	0.461	0.511	0.028	0.016	0.958	0.224	0.833
1990	0.461	0.510	0.028	0.016	0.960	0.224	0.828
2000	0.456	0.515	0.029	0.016	0.942	0.227	0.792
2010	0.434	0.536	0.030	0.018	0.867	0.236	0.688
2020	0.383	0.582	0.034	0.020	0.717	0.255	0.510

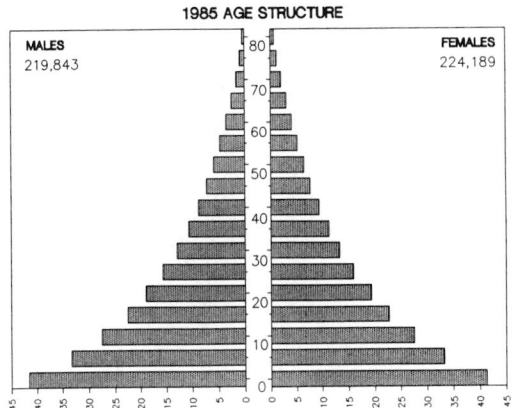

1985 AGE STRUCTURE

MALES 219,843   FEMALES 224,189

MORTALITY MEASURES (Annual Averages)

PERIOD	CRUDE DEATH RATE	INFANT MORT. RATE	LIFE EXPECTANCY AT BIRTH (years) MALE	LIFE EXPECTANCY AT BIRTH (years) FEMALE	LIFE EXPECTANCY AT BIRTH (years) BOTH SEXES	DIFFERENCE FEMALE-MALE
1950-55	24.24	140.00	38.46	41.59	40.00	3.13
1955-60	22.59	132.00	40.44	43.61	42.00	3.17
1960-65	21.24	124.00	41.92	45.12	43.50	3.20
1965-70	19.82	115.12	43.41	46.63	45.00	3.22
1970-75	18.32	105.89	44.90	48.15	46.50	3.24
1975-80	17.22	96.94	46.39	49.66	48.00	3.27
1980-85	15.93	88.25	48.33	51.72	50.00	3.38
1985-90	14.51	79.83	50.28	53.77	52.00	3.49
1990-95	13.15	71.67	52.24	55.81	54.00	3.56
2000-05	10.57	56.37	56.20	59.86	58.00	3.66
2010-15	8.30	42.23	60.19	63.86	62.00	3.67
2020-25	6.60	31.45	64.21	67.85	66.00	3.64

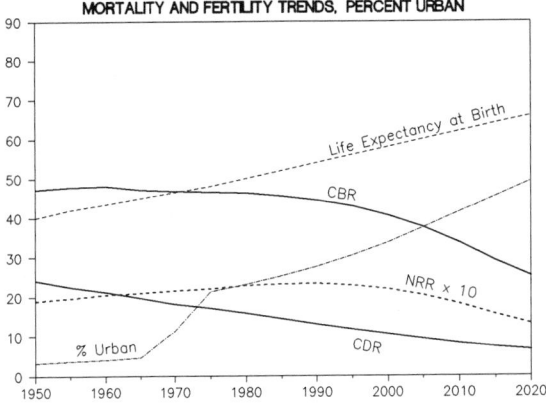

MORTALITY AND FERTILITY TRENDS, PERCENT URBAN

FERTILITY MEASURES (Annual Averages)

PERIOD	CRUDE BIRTH RATE	FERTILITY RATES GENERAL	FERTILITY RATES TOTAL	REPRODUCTION RATES GROSS	REPRODUCTION RATES NET	RATE OF NATUR. INCR.
1950-55	47.33	204.68	6.267	3.087	1.906	23.09
1955-60	47.90	207.02	6.265	3.086	1.982	25.31
1960-65	48.15	208.61	6.323	3.115	2.059	26.91
1965-70	47.17	205.45	6.293	3.100	2.104	27.35
1970-75	46.84	205.59	6.293	3.100	2.159	28.53
1975-80	46.58	205.80	6.293	3.100	2.216	29.35
1980-85	46.41	206.39	6.293	3.100	2.291	30.48
1985-90	45.59	203.45	6.191	3.050	2.327	31.08
1990-95	44.56	198.49	6.029	2.970	2.334	31.40
2000-05	40.63	177.84	5.379	2.650	2.197	30.06
2010-15	33.80	140.74	4.263	2.100	1.824	25.49
2020-25	25.32	96.90	2.964	1.460	1.323	18.71

AGING MEASURES

YEAR	POPULATION AGE RATIOS 60+/20-59	POPULATION AGE RATIOS 65+/20-64	POPULATION AGE RATIOS 70+/20-69	POPULATION AGE RATIOS 75+/20-74	POPULATION MEAN AGE	POPULATION MEDIAN AGE
1950	0.1312	0.0805	0.0438	0.0199	22.94	18.18
1960	0.1180	0.0704	0.0382	0.0179	22.53	17.85
1970	0.1151	0.0681	0.0363	0.0166	22.25	17.49
1980	0.1162	0.0687	0.0368	0.0168	21.95	17.08
1990	0.1175	0.0702	0.0380	0.0176	21.79	16.85
2000	0.1170	0.0711	0.0391	0.0184	21.88	17.07
2010	0.1168	0.0714	0.0399	0.0194	22.58	18.03
2020	0.1188	0.0731	0.0415	0.0205	24.36	20.26

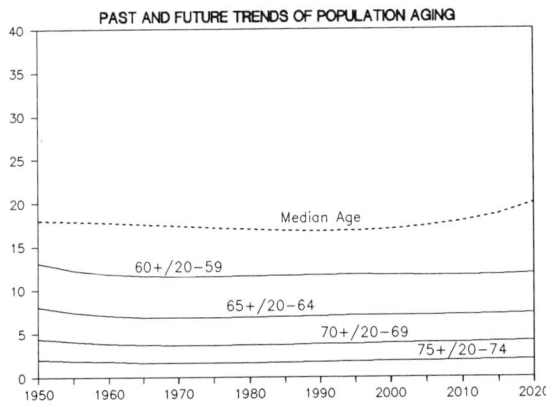

PAST AND FUTURE TRENDS OF POPULATION AGING

OBSERVED AND *PROJECTED* POPULATION DATA

YEAR	MID-YEAR POPULATION	NO. OF BIRTHS	NO. OF DEATHS	URBAN POPULATION NUMBER	URBAN POPULATION PERCENT	POPULATION 1985 AGE	POPULATION 1985 NUMBER
1950	812286	36029	21737	253950	31.3	0	306326
1955	883846	39756	21663	284052	32.1	5	244954
1960	971701	43956	21786	320908	33.0	10	207911
1965	1076964	48603	22035	365359	33.9	15	174694
1970	1200983	54484	22374	418376	34.8	20	148396
1975	1351761	60364	22885	483371	35.8	25	125086
1980	1528521	67990	23555	570101	37.3	30	104808
1985	1740011	77256	29874	686626	39.5	35	90110
1990	*1994224*	*86250*	*31283*	*842444*	*42.2*	40	77333
1995	*2289394*	*96988*	*32731*	*1044367*	*45.6*	45	65843
2000	*2634930*	*107408*	*34070*	*1304718*	*49.5*	50	55231
2005	*3029042*	*118157*	*35276*	*1613982*	*53.3*	55	45190
2010	*3473875*	*127189*	*36229*	*1976054*	*56.9*	60	35591
2015	*3960527*	*132523*	*36821*	*2387798*	*60.3*	65	26228
2020	*4469804*	*130572*	*36965*	*2837792*	*63.5*	70+	32310

AGE DISTRIBUTIONS, 1960 - 1985

POPULATION RATIOS

YEAR	AGE DISTRIBUTION UNDER 15	AGE DISTRIBUTION 15-64	AGE DISTRIBUTION 65 & OLDER	AGE DISTRIBUTION 70 & OLDER	DEPENDENCY RATIO	WOMEN 15-49	CHILD-WOMAN RATIO
1950	0.405	0.559	0.036	0.020	0.790	0.243	0.671
1955	0.406	0.560	0.034	0.019	0.786	0.243	0.670
1960	0.409	0.558	0.032	0.018	0.791	0.242	0.691
1965	0.415	0.553	0.032	0.017	0.809	0.239	0.710
1970	0.422	0.546	0.032	0.017	0.832	0.236	0.726
1975	0.428	0.539	0.033	0.018	0.854	0.233	0.749
1980	0.432	0.535	0.033	0.018	0.870	0.231	0.755
1985	0.436	0.530	0.034	0.019	0.887	0.229	0.768
1990	*0.440*	*0.527*	*0.034*	*0.019*	*0.899*	*0.228*	*0.780*
2000	*0.442*	*0.525*	*0.034*	*0.019*	*0.906*	*0.228*	*0.763*
2010	*0.430*	*0.536*	*0.034*	*0.020*	*0.867*	*0.234*	*0.704*
2020	*0.402*	*0.562*	*0.035*	*0.021*	*0.779*	*0.245*	*0.595*

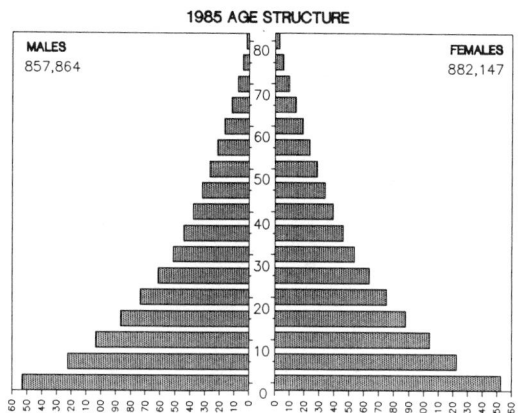

1985 AGE STRUCTURE

MALES 857,864   FEMALES 882,147

MORTALITY MEASURES (Annual Averages)

PERIOD	CRUDE DEATH RATE	INFANT MORT. RATE	LIFE EXPECTANCY AT BIRTH (years) MALE	LIFE EXPECTANCY AT BIRTH (years) FEMALE	LIFE EXPECTANCY AT BIRTH (years) BOTH SEXES	DIFFERENCE FEMALE-MALE
1950-55	26.76	170.00	34.50	37.54	36.00	3.04
1955-60	24.51	153.71	35.98	39.06	37.50	3.08
1960-65	22.42	131.42	37.47	40.58	39.00	3.11
1965-70	20.46	110.50	38.95	42.09	40.50	3.14
1970-75	18.63	89.53	40.93	44.12	42.50	3.18
1975-80	16.93	85.27	42.92	46.13	44.50	3.21
1980-85	15.41	81.06	44.90	48.15	46.50	3.24
1985-90	*17.17*	*73.00*	*46.88*	*50.17*	*48.50*	*3.29*
1990-95	*15.69*	*65.00*	*48.82*	*52.23*	*50.50*	*3.41*
2000-05	*12.93*	*50.00*	*52.74*	*56.31*	*54.50*	*3.58*
2010-15	*10.43*	*37.00*	*56.70*	*60.36*	*58.50*	*3.66*
2020-25	*8.27*	*28.00*	*60.69*	*64.36*	*62.50*	*3.67*

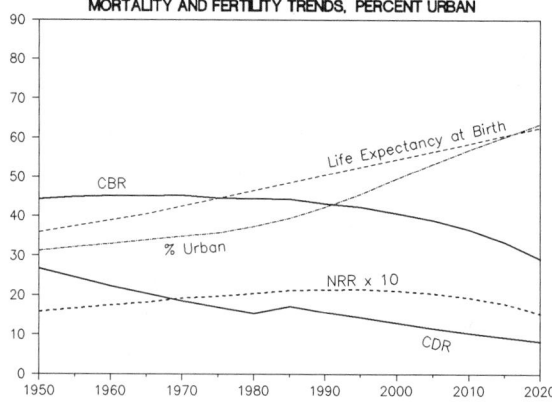

MORTALITY AND FERTILITY TRENDS, PERCENT URBAN

Life Expectancy at Birth / CBR / % Urban / NRR x 10 / CDR

FERTILITY MEASURES (Annual Averages)

PERIOD	CRUDE BIRTH RATE	FERTILITY RATES GENERAL	FERTILITY RATES TOTAL	REPRODUCTION RATES GROSS	REPRODUCTION RATES NET	RATE OF NATUR. INCR.
1950-55	44.35	182.66	5.688	2.802	1.586	17.59
1955-60	44.98	185.62	5.781	2.848	1.668	20.47
1960-65	45.24	188.30	5.869	2.891	1.748	22.82
1965-70	45.13	190.13	5.930	2.921	1.822	24.67
1970-75	45.37	193.55	6.035	2.973	1.928	26.74
1975-80	44.66	192.50	5.988	2.950	1.984	27.73
1980-85	44.48	193.33	5.988	2.950	2.055	29.07
1985-90	*44.40*	*194.25*	*5.988*	*2.950*	*2.126*	*27.23*
1990-95	*43.25*	*189.84*	*5.826*	*2.870*	*2.139*	*27.56*
2000-05	*40.76*	*177.38*	*5.420*	*2.670*	*2.112*	*27.83*
2010-15	*36.61*	*154.78*	*4.730*	*2.330*	*1.943*	*26.18*
2020-25	*29.21*	*117.05*	*3.552*	*1.750*	*1.531*	*20.94*

AGING MEASURES

YEAR	POPULATION AGE RATIOS 60+/20-59	POPULATION AGE RATIOS 65+/20-64	POPULATION AGE RATIOS 70+/20-69	POPULATION AGE RATIOS 75+/20-74	POPULATION MEAN AGE	POPULATION MEDIAN AGE
1950	0.1313	0.0786	0.0420	0.0185	24.12	19.73
1960	0.1215	0.0700	0.0376	0.0169	23.89	19.55
1970	0.1251	0.0723	0.0373	0.0160	23.60	19.02
1980	0.1304	0.0767	0.0405	0.0179	23.25	18.40
1990	*0.1332*	*0.0795*	*0.0428*	*0.0196*	*22.90*	*17.96*
2000	*0.1322*	*0.0802*	*0.0441*	*0.0207*	*22.74*	*17.83*
2010	*0.1283*	*0.0791*	*0.0444*	*0.0214*	*23.00*	*18.31*
2020	*0.1265*	*0.0780*	*0.0445*	*0.0220*	*23.95*	*19.55*

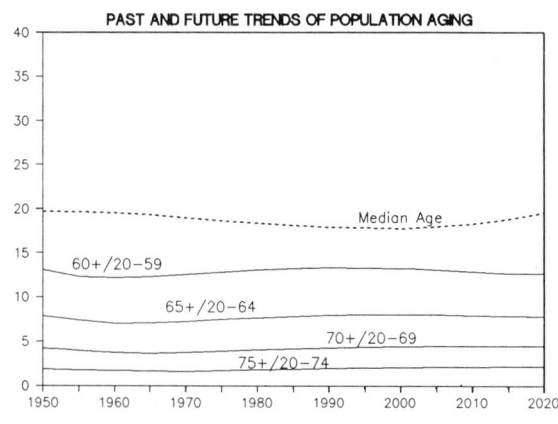

PAST AND FUTURE TRENDS OF POPULATION AGING

Median Age / 60+/20-59 / 65+/20-64 / 70+/20-69 / 75+/20-74

OBSERVED AND *PROJECTED* POPULATION DATA

YEAR	MID-YEAR POPULATION	NO. OF BIRTHS	NO. OF DEATHS	URBAN POPULATION NUMBER	URBAN POPULATION PERCENT	POPULATION 1985 AGE	POPULATION 1985 NUMBER
1950	59976	2965	1826	24565	41.0	0	65284
1955	68943	3382	1961	31187	45.2	5	51978
1960	80054	3930	1993	39694	49.6	10	42881
1965	113774	5630	2596	62638	55.1	15	34917
1970	167032	8266	3539	103564	62.0	20	29461
1975	240092	11729	4888	164441	68.5	25	25773
1980	300302	14387	5750	221336	73.7	30	22853
1985	350485	16570	6207	272396	77.7	35	19210
1990	*406433*	*18906*	*6622*	*327997*	*80.7*	40	15297
1995	*472872*	*21648*	*7068*	*391673*	*82.8*	45	12388
2000	*551858*	*24511*	*7515*	*464967*	*84.3*	50	9656
2005	*643924*	*26894*	*7892*	*550931*	*85.6*	55	7418
2010	*746505*	*28611*	*8165*	*647591*	*86.7*	60	5512
2015	*856250*	*28850*	*8294*	*752120*	*87.8*	65	3730
2020	*965588*	*28103*	*8321*	*857777*	*88.8*	70+	4125

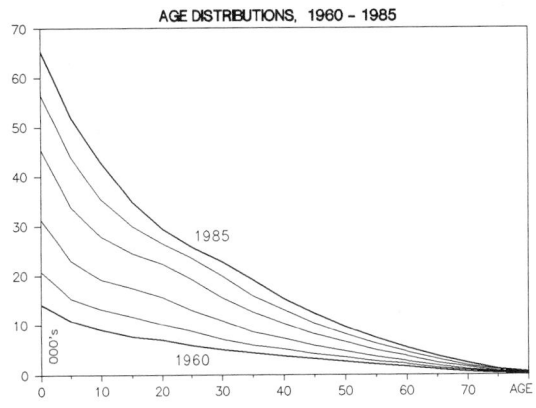

AGE DISTRIBUTIONS, 1960 - 1985

POPULATION RATIOS

YEAR	AGE DISTRIBUTION UNDER 15	AGE DISTRIBUTION 15-64	AGE DISTRIBUTION 65 & OLDER	AGE DISTRIBUTION 70 & OLDER	DEPENDENCY RATIO	WOMEN 15-49	CHILD-WOMAN RATIO
1950	0.413	0.562	0.026	0.012	0.780	0.238	0.722
1955	0.417	0.556	0.027	0.013	0.799	0.236	0.743
1960	0.427	0.545	0.028	0.014	0.835	0.232	0.765
1965	0.434	0.541	0.025	0.013	0.849	0.230	0.794
1970	0.439	0.538	0.023	0.012	0.859	0.230	0.814
1975	0.446	0.533	0.021	0.011	0.877	0.228	0.831
1980	0.452	0.526	0.022	0.011	0.900	0.225	0.835
1985	0.457	0.521	0.022	0.012	0.921	0.223	0.836
1990	*0.458*	*0.518*	*0.024*	*0.012*	*0.930*	*0.222*	*0.838*
2000	*0.459*	*0.515*	*0.026*	*0.014*	*0.941*	*0.222*	*0.834*
2010	*0.451*	*0.521*	*0.029*	*0.016*	*0.921*	*0.226*	*0.768*
2020	*0.412*	*0.555*	*0.033*	*0.019*	*0.801*	*0.245*	*0.595*

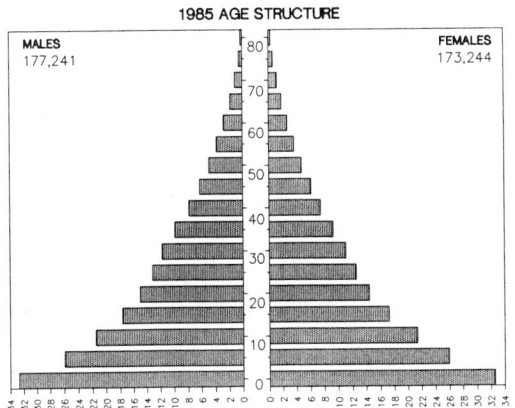

1985 AGE STRUCTURE
MALES 177,241   FEMALES 173,244

MORTALITY MEASURES (Annual Averages)

PERIOD	CRUDE DEATH RATE	INFANT MORT. RATE	LIFE EXPECTANCY AT BIRTH (years) MALE	LIFE EXPECTANCY AT BIRTH (years) FEMALE	LIFE EXPECTANCY AT BIRTH (years) BOTH SEXES	DIFFERENCE FEMALE-MALE
1950-55	30.45	207.34	31.54	34.51	33.00	2.97
1955-60	28.44	192.96	33.51	36.53	35.00	3.02
1960-65	24.90	179.36	35.49	38.56	37.00	3.06
1965-70	22.82	166.49	37.47	40.58	39.00	3.11
1970-75	21.19	154.28	39.45	42.60	41.00	3.15
1975-80	20.36	142.81	41.43	44.62	43.00	3.19
1980-85	19.15	131.95	43.41	46.63	45.00	3.22
1985-90	*17.71*	*121.63*	*45.40*	*48.65*	*47.00*	*3.25*
1990-95	*16.29*	*111.88*	*47.36*	*50.69*	*49.00*	*3.32*
2000-05	*13.62*	*93.83*	*51.26*	*54.79*	*53.00*	*3.53*
2010-15	*10.94*	*76.97*	*55.21*	*58.85*	*57.00*	*3.64*
2020-25	*8.62*	*61.20*	*59.19*	*62.87*	*61.00*	*3.68*

FERTILITY MEASURES (Annual Averages)

PERIOD	CRUDE BIRTH RATE	FERTILITY RATES GENERAL	FERTILITY RATES TOTAL	REPRODUCTION RATES GROSS	REPRODUCTION RATES NET	RATE OF NATUR. INCR.
1950-55	49.43	208.62	6.597	3.250	1.703	18.98
1955-60	49.06	209.84	6.597	3.250	1.790	20.62
1960-65	49.10	212.51	6.597	3.250	1.876	24.20
1965-70	49.49	215.00	6.597	3.250	1.960	26.67
1970-75	49.49	216.38	6.597	3.250	2.042	28.29
1975-80	48.85	215.85	6.597	3.250	2.122	28.50
1980-85	47.91	213.94	6.597	3.250	2.200	28.76
1985-90	*47.28*	*212.45*	*6.597*	*3.250*	*2.278*	*29.57*
1990-95	*46.52*	*209.25*	*6.496*	*3.200*	*2.321*	*30.22*
2000-05	*44.42*	*199.67*	*6.110*	*3.010*	*2.327*	*30.80*
2010-15	*38.33*	*166.39*	*5.075*	*2.500*	*2.043*	*27.39*
2020-25	*29.10*	*115.84*	*3.552*	*1.750*	*1.502*	*20.49*

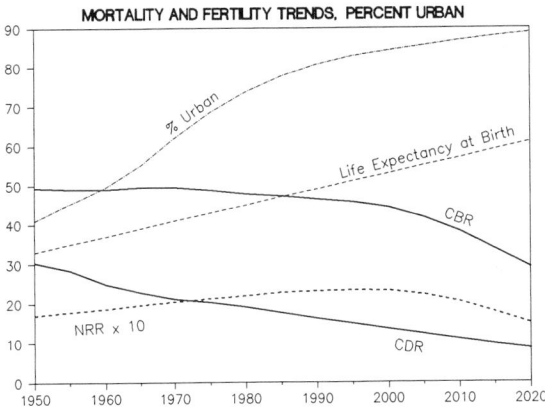

MORTALITY AND FERTILITY TRENDS, PERCENT URBAN

AGING MEASURES

YEAR	POPULATION AGE RATIOS 60+/20-59	POPULATION AGE RATIOS 65+/20-64	POPULATION AGE RATIOS 70+/20-69	POPULATION AGE RATIOS 75+/20-74	POPULATION MEAN AGE	POPULATION MEDIAN AGE
1950	0.1042	0.0558	0.0255	0.0092	23.66	19.54
1960	0.1115	0.0618	0.0298	0.0118	23.15	18.77
1970	0.0937	0.0527	0.0265	0.0112	21.97	17.91
1980	0.0888	0.0505	0.0254	0.0109	21.64	17.40
1990	*0.0997*	*0.0571*	*0.0292*	*0.0127*	*21.78*	*17.03*
2000	*0.1094*	*0.0631*	*0.0331*	*0.0147*	*21.82*	*16.98*
2010	*0.1186*	*0.0693*	*0.0371*	*0.0168*	*22.11*	*17.32*
2020	*0.1210*	*0.0746*	*0.0410*	*0.0190*	*23.33*	*18.93*

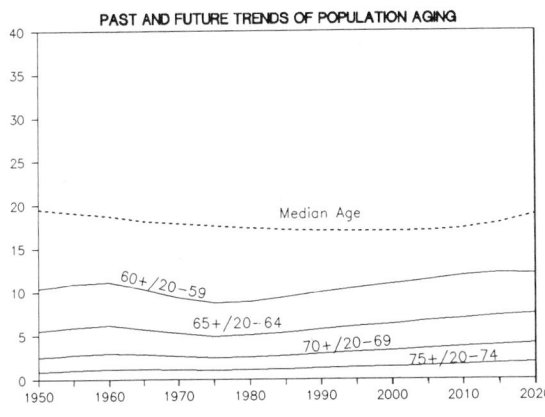

PAST AND FUTURE TRENDS OF POPULATION AGING

OBSERVED AND *PROJECTED* POPULATION DATA (000's)

YEAR	MID-YEAR POPULATION	NO. OF BIRTHS	NO. OF DEATHS	URBAN POPULATION NUMBER	URBAN POPULATION PERCENT	POPULATION 1985 AGE	POPULATION 1985 NUMBER
1950	20330	988	488	6491	31.9	0	7778
1955	22990	1030	483	8009	34.8	5	6405
1960	25922	1177	529	9815	37.9	10	5082
1965	29389	1228	538	11956	40.7	15	4755
1970	33053	1269	539	13951	42.2	20	4240
1975	36289	1481	494	15768	43.5	25	3999
1980	41520	1650	493	18561	44.7	30	3423
1985	47578	1711	479	22121	46.5	35	2553
1990	*54059*	*1673*	*453*	*26381*	*48.8*	40	1896
1995	*60470*	*1621*	*434*	*31194*	*51.6*	45	1711
2000	*66710*	*1565*	*426*	*36547*	*54.8*	50	1537
2005	*72658*	*1550*	*435*	*42365*	*58.3*	55	1301
2010	*78456*	*1530*	*459*	*48352*	*61.6*	60	1044
2015	*83999*	*1471*	*495*	*54381*	*64.7*	65	761
2020	*89025*	*1508*	*545*	*60211*	*67.6*	70+	1095

AGE DISTRIBUTIONS, 1960 - 1985

POPULATION RATIOS

YEAR	AGE DISTRIBUTION UNDER 15	AGE DISTRIBUTION 15-64	AGE DISTRIBUTION 65 & OLDER	AGE DISTRIBUTION 70 & OLDER	DEPENDENCY RATIO	WOMEN 15-49	CHILD-WOMAN RATIO
1950	0.397	0.574	0.030	0.015	0.744	0.245	0.661
1955	0.409	0.561	0.030	0.015	0.783	0.238	0.722
1960	0.425	0.543	0.033	0.017	0.843	0.227	0.752
1965	0.435	0.523	0.041	0.023	0.912	0.215	0.776
1970	0.414	0.543	0.043	0.024	0.842	0.226	0.672
1975	0.400	0.558	0.042	0.025	0.793	0.233	0.637
1980	0.400	0.559	0.041	0.024	0.788	0.234	0.686
1985	0.405	0.556	0.039	0.023	0.798	0.232	0.703
1990	*0.409*	*0.552*	*0.039*	*0.022*	*0.810*	*0.231*	*0.656*
2000	*0.358*	*0.600*	*0.042*	*0.025*	*0.667*	*0.252*	*0.473*
2010	*0.296*	*0.659*	*0.046*	*0.028*	*0.518*	*0.266*	*0.370*
2020	*0.254*	*0.683*	*0.063*	*0.035*	*0.464*	*0.270*	*0.305*

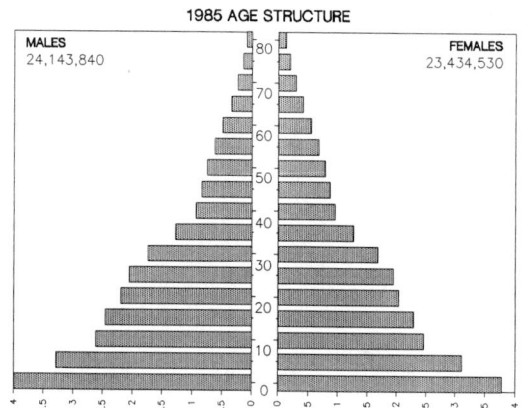

1985 AGE STRUCTURE

MALES 24,143,840   FEMALES 23,434,530

MORTALITY MEASURES (Annual Averages)

PERIOD	CRUDE DEATH RATE	INFANT MORT. RATE	LIFE EXPECTANCY AT BIRTH (years) MALE	LIFE EXPECTANCY AT BIRTH (years) FEMALE	LIFE EXPECTANCY AT BIRTH (years) BOTH SEXES	DIFFERENCE FEMALE-MALE
1950-55	24.00	200.00	41.20	43.60	42.37	2.40
1955-60	21.00	183.00	43.70	46.10	44.87	2.40
1960-65	20.40	175.00	46.20	48.60	47.37	2.40
1965-70	18.30	170.00	48.50	51.00	49.72	2.50
1970-75	16.30	150.00	50.80	53.40	52.07	2.60
1975-80	13.60	120.00	54.30	57.00	55.62	2.70
1980-85	11.87	100.04	56.85	59.45	58.12	2.61
1985-90	*10.07*	*85.14*	*59.29*	*61.97*	*60.60*	*2.68*
1990-95	*8.38*	*70.97*	*61.83*	*64.51*	*63.14*	*2.69*
2000-05	*6.39*	*46.40*	*66.07*	*69.34*	*67.67*	*3.27*
2010-15	*5.85*	*31.82*	*68.81*	*72.82*	*70.76*	*4.01*
2020-25	*6.12*	*22.44*	*71.04*	*75.17*	*73.06*	*4.12*

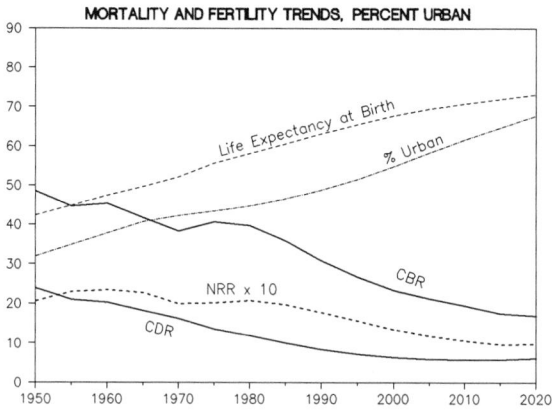

MORTALITY AND FERTILITY TRENDS, PERCENT URBAN

FERTILITY MEASURES (Annual Averages)

PERIOD	CRUDE BIRTH RATE	FERTILITY RATES GENERAL	FERTILITY RATES TOTAL	REPRODUCTION RATES GROSS	REPRODUCTION RATES NET	RATE OF NATUR. INCR.
1950-55	48.60	201.59	6.560	3.200	2.070	24.60
1955-60	44.80	192.85	6.970	3.400	2.300	23.80
1960-65	45.40	205.60	7.072	3.450	2.350	25.00
1965-70	41.80	189.43	6.560	3.200	2.280	23.50
1970-75	38.40	167.34	5.535	2.700	2.000	22.10
1975-80	40.80	174.77	5.268	2.570	2.020	27.20
1980-85	39.73	170.46	5.268	2.570	2.088	27.86
1985-90	*35.96*	*155.18*	*4.817*	*2.350*	*1.976*	*25.90*
1990-95	*30.94*	*131.21*	*4.202*	*2.050*	*1.780*	*22.56*
2000-05	*23.46*	*91.52*	*2.993*	*1.460*	*1.341*	*17.07*
2010-15	*19.50*	*72.91*	*2.296*	*1.120*	*1.062*	*13.65*
2020-25	*16.94*	*62.70*	*2.070*	*1.010*	*0.975*	*10.82*

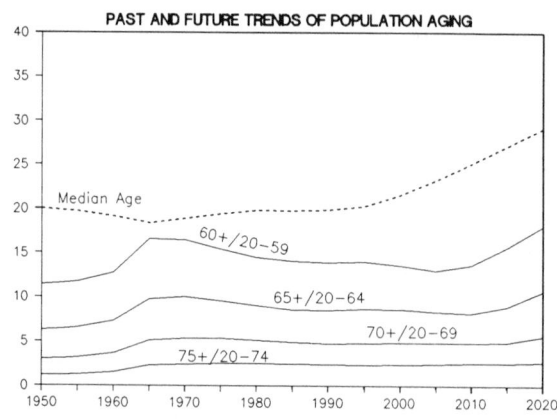

PAST AND FUTURE TRENDS OF POPULATION AGING

AGING MEASURES

YEAR	POPULATION AGE RATIOS 60+/20-59	POPULATION AGE RATIOS 65+/20-64	POPULATION AGE RATIOS 70+/20-69	POPULATION AGE RATIOS 75+/20-74	POPULATION MEAN AGE	POPULATION MEDIAN AGE
1950	0.1144	0.0629	0.0301	0.0116	24.14	20.05
1960	0.1275	0.0727	0.0364	0.0148	23.75	19.14
1970	0.1646	0.0999	0.0533	0.0239	24.33	18.89
1980	0.1444	0.0900	0.0509	0.0249	24.22	19.84
1990	*0.1391*	*0.0846*	*0.0470*	*0.0236*	*24.23*	*19.89*
2000	*0.1358*	*0.0857*	*0.0485*	*0.0239*	*25.83*	*21.59*
2010	*0.1365*	*0.0816*	*0.0483*	*0.0251*	*28.32*	*25.13*
2020	*0.1798*	*0.1059*	*0.0554*	*0.0266*	*31.16*	*29.15*

OBSERVED AND *PROJECTED* POPULATION DATA

YEAR	MID-YEAR POPULATION	NO. OF BIRTHS	NO. OF DEATHS	URBAN POPULATION NUMBER	URBAN POPULATION PERCENT	POPULATION 1985 AGE	POPULATION 1985 NUMBER
1950	225536	9539	7154	34929	15.5	0	65230
1955	237787	9923	7116	47628	20.0	5	52539
1960	252252	10409	7059	64331	25.5	10	44546
1965	269579	11302	7111	85928	31.9	15	38234
1970	291380	12326	7130	113655	39.0	20	32810
1975	318570	13551	7228	148580	46.6	25	28984
1980	351830	14948	7379	188764	53.7	30	25642
1985	391826	16601	7446	233811	59.7	35	19765
1990	*440442*	*18309*	*7672*	*284246*	*64.5*	40	17571
1995	*497046*	*19982*	*7878*	*339196*	*68.2*	45	15519
2000	*561488*	*21609*	*8053*	*397958*	*70.9*	50	13744
2005	*633620*	*23554*	*8234*	*464460*	*73.3*	55	11568
2010	*715149*	*25489*	*8407*	*540180*	*75.5*	60	9401
2015	*805980*	*25878*	*8461*	*625285*	*77.6*	65	7199
2020	*898035*	*26074*	*8485*	*713538*	*79.5*	70+	9074

AGE DISTRIBUTIONS, 1960 – 1985

POPULATION RATIOS

YEAR	AGE DISTRIBUTION UNDER 15	AGE DISTRIBUTION 15-64	AGE DISTRIBUTION 65 & OLDER	AGE DISTRIBUTION 70 & OLDER	DEPENDENCY RATIO	WOMEN 15-49	CHILD-WOMAN RATIO
1950	0.342	0.601	0.056	0.031	0.663	0.247	0.542
1955	0.360	0.588	0.052	0.029	0.701	0.244	0.628
1960	0.375	0.576	0.049	0.028	0.737	0.241	0.636
1965	0.390	0.563	0.047	0.026	0.775	0.237	0.648
1970	0.393	0.562	0.045	0.025	0.778	0.238	0.663
1975	0.399	0.558	0.043	0.024	0.792	0.237	0.682
1980	0.407	0.551	0.042	0.023	0.816	0.234	0.702
1985	0.414	0.544	0.042	0.023	0.838	0.232	0.717
1990	*0.420*	*0.539*	*0.041*	*0.023*	*0.856*	*0.231*	*0.729*
2000	*0.423*	*0.537*	*0.040*	*0.023*	*0.861*	*0.234*	*0.705*
2010	*0.410*	*0.552*	*0.038*	*0.022*	*0.812*	*0.238*	*0.656*
2020	*0.388*	*0.573*	*0.040*	*0.022*	*0.746*	*0.247*	*0.564*

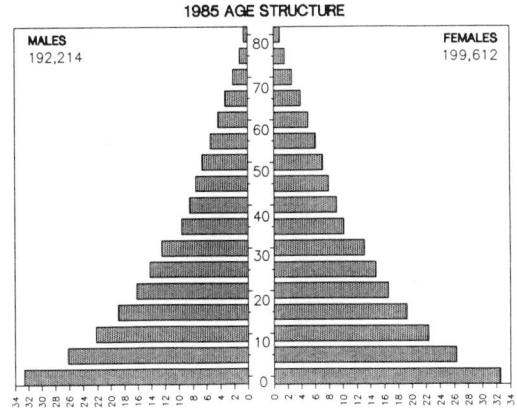

1985 AGE STRUCTURE

MALES 192,214   FEMALES 199,612

MORTALITY MEASURES (Annual Averages)

PERIOD	CRUDE DEATH RATE	INFANT MORT. RATE	LIFE EXPECTANCY AT BIRTH (years) MALE	LIFE EXPECTANCY AT BIRTH (years) FEMALE	LIFE EXPECTANCY AT BIRTH (years) BOTH SEXES	DIFFERENCE FEMALE-MALE
1950-55	31.72	203.54	32.03	35.01	33.50	2.98
1955-60	29.92	192.96	33.51	36.53	35.00	3.02
1960-65	27.98	182.65	35.00	38.05	36.50	3.05
1965-70	26.38	172.80	36.48	39.57	38.00	3.09
1970-75	24.47	160.36	38.46	41.59	40.00	3.13
1975-80	22.69	148.54	40.44	43.61	42.00	3.17
1980-85	20.97	137.31	42.42	45.63	44.00	3.21
1985-90	*19.00*	*127.00*	*44.90*	*48.13*	*46.49*	*3.23*
1990-95	*17.42*	*117.00*	*46.90*	*50.13*	*48.49*	*3.23*
2000-05	*14.34*	*98.00*	*50.90*	*54.13*	*52.49*	*3.23*
2010-15	*11.76*	*81.00*	*54.90*	*58.13*	*56.49*	*3.23*
2020-25	*9.45*	*65.00*	*58.90*	*62.13*	*60.49*	*3.23*

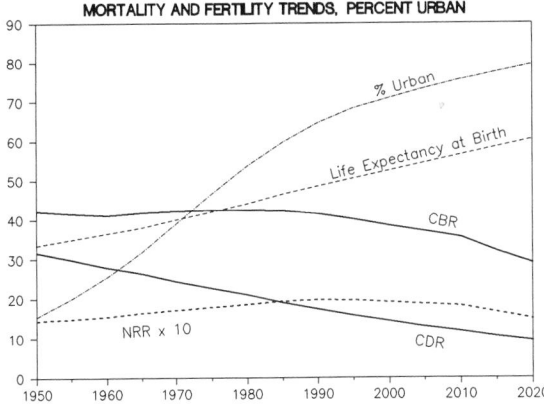

MORTALITY AND FERTILITY TRENDS, PERCENT URBAN

% Urban

Life Expectancy at Birth

CBR

NRR x 10

CDR

FERTILITY MEASURES (Annual Averages)

PERIOD	CRUDE BIRTH RATE	FERTILITY RATES GENERAL	FERTILITY RATES TOTAL	REPRODUCTION RATES GROSS	REPRODUCTION RATES NET	RATE OF NATUR. INCR.
1950-55	42.30	172.43	5.501	2.710	1.444	10.58
1955-60	41.73	172.20	5.499	2.709	1.497	11.81
1960-65	41.26	172.73	5.530	2.724	1.560	13.28
1965-70	41.92	176.60	5.658	2.787	1.650	15.55
1970-75	42.30	178.36	5.664	2.790	1.722	17.83
1975-80	42.54	180.76	5.664	2.790	1.792	19.85
1980-85	42.49	182.20	5.664	2.790	1.860	21.51
1985-90	*42.37*	*182.77*	*5.664*	*2.790*	*1.943*	*23.37*
1990-95	*41.57*	*179.61*	*5.562*	*2.740*	*1.974*	*24.15*
2000-05	*38.49*	*164.08*	*5.075*	*2.500*	*1.917*	*24.14*
2010-15	*35.64*	*148.35*	*4.567*	*2.250*	*1.824*	*23.89*
2020-25	*29.03*	*115.91*	*3.552*	*1.750*	*1.493*	*19.59*

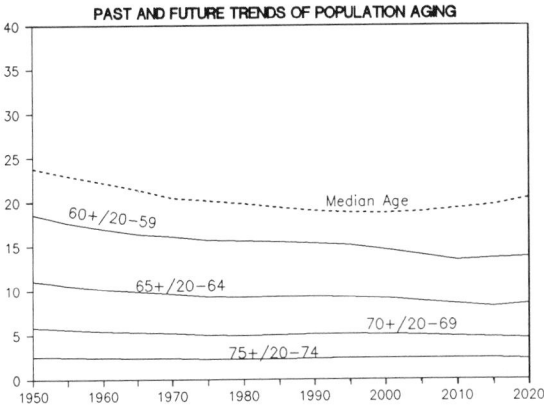

PAST AND FUTURE TRENDS OF POPULATION AGING

Median Age

60+/20-59

65+/20-64

70+/20-69

75+/20-74

AGING MEASURES

YEAR	POPULATION AGE RATIOS 60+/20-59	POPULATION AGE RATIOS 65+/20-64	POPULATION AGE RATIOS 70+/20-69	POPULATION AGE RATIOS 75+/20-74	POPULATION MEAN AGE	POPULATION MEDIAN AGE
1950	0.1858	0.1108	0.0582	0.0256	27.74	23.84
1960	0.1698	0.1015	0.0542	0.0242	26.30	22.21
1970	0.1611	0.0962	0.0520	0.0235	25.42	20.49
1980	0.1559	0.0923	0.0495	0.0226	24.64	19.81
1990	*0.1537*	*0.0931*	*0.0508*	*0.0233*	*24.00*	*19.04*
2000	*0.1463*	*0.0909*	*0.0506*	*0.0241*	*23.70*	*18.78*
2010	*0.1342*	*0.0846*	*0.0485*	*0.0240*	*23.92*	*19.27*
2020	*0.1378*	*0.0844*	*0.0460*	*0.0232*	*24.76*	*20.45*

OBSERVED AND *PROJECTED* POPULATION DATA (000's)

YEAR	MID-YEAR POPULATION	NO. OF BIRTHS	NO. OF DEATHS	URBAN POPULATION NUMBER	URBAN POPULATION PERCENT	POPULATION 1985 AGE	POPULATION 1985 NUMBER
1950	19573	1024	624	893	4.6	0	7509
1955	21680	1108	634	1174	5.4	5	6736
1960	24191	1206	649	1551	6.4	10	5300
1965	27150	1322	669	2058	7.6	15	3804
1970	30623	1471	700	2634	8.6	20	3066
1975	34309	1656	738	3260	9.5	25	2750
1980	38750	1666	911	4062	10.5	30	2534
1985	42271	1848	999	4884	11.6	35	2278
1990	*46743*	*2171*	*1004*	*6044*	*12.9*	40	1914
1995	*53383*	*2495*	*1037*	*7833*	*14.7*	45	1534
2000	*61206*	*2705*	*1044*	*10310*	*16.8*	50	1267
2005	*70116*	*2867*	*1025*	*13680*	*19.5*	55	1000
2010	*79974*	*3009*	*1002*	*18175*	*22.7*	60	862
2015	*90684*	*3055*	*991*	*23768*	*26.2*	65	571
2020	*101631*	*3004*	*982*	*30405*	*29.9*	70+	1146

POPULATION RATIOS

YEAR	AGE DISTRIBUTION UNDER 15	AGE DISTRIBUTION 15-64	AGE DISTRIBUTION 65 & OLDER	AGE DISTRIBUTION 70 & OLDER	DEPENDENCY RATIO	WOMEN 15-49	CHILD-WOMAN RATIO
1950	0.442	0.528	0.030	0.016	0.894	0.230	0.800
1955	0.444	0.528	0.027	0.015	0.892	0.230	0.798
1960	0.445	0.529	0.025	0.014	0.889	0.231	0.794
1965	0.445	0.531	0.024	0.013	0.884	0.231	0.789
1970	0.445	0.530	0.025	0.013	0.886	0.231	0.784
1975	0.444	0.530	0.026	0.014	0.887	0.231	0.783
1980	0.444	0.529	0.026	0.014	0.890	0.230	0.788
1985	0.462	0.497	0.041	0.027	1.012	0.220	0.808
1990	*0.449*	*0.516*	*0.035*	*0.020*	*0.939*	*0.227*	*0.737*
2000	*0.437*	*0.533*	*0.030*	*0.017*	*0.877*	*0.233*	*0.784*
2010	*0.440*	*0.529*	*0.031*	*0.017*	*0.890*	*0.231*	*0.725*
2020	*0.402*	*0.564*	*0.034*	*0.020*	*0.774*	*0.249*	*0.578*

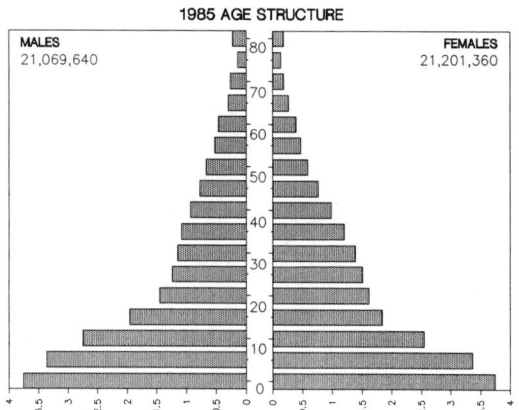

MORTALITY MEASURES (Annual Averages)

PERIOD	CRUDE DEATH RATE	INFANT MORT. RATE	LIFE EXPECTANCY AT BIRTH (years) MALE	LIFE EXPECTANCY AT BIRTH (years) FEMALE	LIFE EXPECTANCY AT BIRTH (years) BOTH SEXES	DIFFERENCE FEMALE-MALE
1950-55	31.91	190.00	31.44	34.40	33.00	2.96
1955-60	29.23	180.00	33.44	36.46	35.00	3.02
1960-65	26.82	170.00	35.44	38.50	37.00	3.06
1965-70	24.65	162.00	37.41	40.52	39.00	3.11
1970-75	22.87	155.00	39.45	42.60	41.00	3.15
1975-80	21.50	149.00	40.43	43.60	42.00	3.17
1980-85	23.50	159.00	38.43	41.56	40.00	3.13
1985-90	*23.63*	*154.28*	*39.45*	*42.60*	*41.00*	*3.15*
1990-95	*21.48*	*142.81*	*41.43*	*44.62*	*43.00*	*3.19*
2000-05	*17.06*	*115.37*	*46.63*	*49.91*	*48.25*	*3.28*
2010-15	*12.52*	*88.46*	*52.49*	*56.06*	*54.25*	*3.57*
2020-25	*9.67*	*68.94*	*57.19*	*60.86*	*59.00*	*3.67*

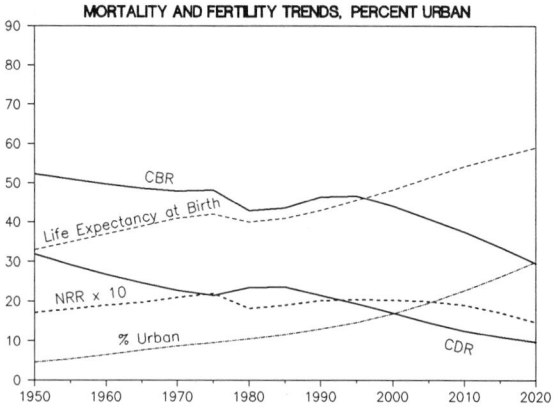

FERTILITY MEASURES (Annual Averages)

PERIOD	CRUDE BIRTH RATE	FERTILITY RATES GENERAL	FERTILITY RATES TOTAL	REPRODUCTION RATES GROSS	REPRODUCTION RATES NET	RATE OF NATUR. INCR.
1950-55	52.34	227.46	6.699	3.300	1.720	20.43
1955-60	51.12	221.89	6.699	3.300	1.810	21.90
1960-65	49.87	216.26	6.699	3.300	1.900	23.06
1965-70	48.69	211.03	6.699	3.300	1.980	24.04
1970-75	48.04	208.20	6.800	3.350	2.101	25.17
1975-80	48.28	209.43	7.003	3.450	2.201	26.78
1980-85	43.00	191.20	6.001	2.956	1.818	19.50
1985-90	*43.72*	*195.42*	*6.151*	*3.030*	*1.908*	*20.10*
1990-95	*46.45*	*200.18*	*6.293*	*3.100*	*2.027*	*24.97*
2000-05	*44.20*	*191.67*	*5.765*	*2.840*	*2.038*	*27.14*
2010-15	*37.63*	*159.93*	*4.892*	*2.410*	*1.900*	*25.10*
2020-25	*29.56*	*116.45*	*3.552*	*1.750*	*1.471*	*19.89*

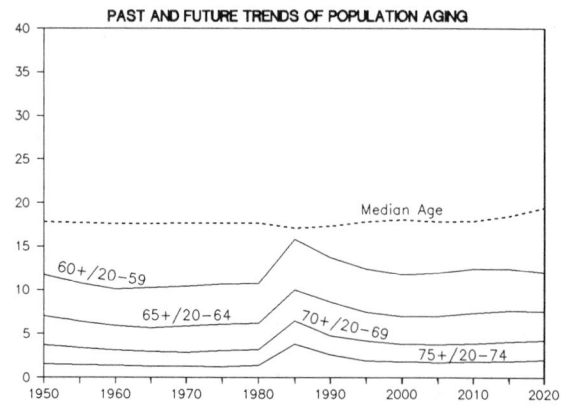

AGING MEASURES

YEAR	POPULATION AGE RATIOS 60+/20-59	POPULATION AGE RATIOS 65+/20-64	POPULATION AGE RATIOS 70+/20-69	POPULATION AGE RATIOS 75+/20-74	POPULATION MEAN AGE	POPULATION MEDIAN AGE
1950	0.1180	0.0704	0.0368	0.0158	22.46	17.86
1960	0.1008	0.0596	0.0314	0.0139	22.17	17.67
1970	0.1043	0.0589	0.0288	0.0127	22.19	17.68
1980	0.1075	0.0621	0.0319	0.0137	22.23	17.69
1990	*0.1375*	*0.0860*	*0.0478*	*0.0264*	*22.83*	*17.30*
2000	*0.1177*	*0.0700*	*0.0379*	*0.0182*	*22.39*	*18.04*
2010	*0.1245*	*0.0735*	*0.0389*	*0.0179*	*22.64*	*17.91*
2020	*0.1197*	*0.0756*	*0.0425*	*0.0199*	*23.77*	*19.43*

OBSERVED AND *PROJECTED* POPULATION DATA

YEAR	MID-YEAR POPULATION	NO. OF BIRTHS	NO. OF DEATHS	URBAN POPULATION NUMBER	URBAN POPULATION PERCENT	POPULATION 1985 AGE	POPULATION 1985 NUMBER
1950	469001	14117	12710	53470	11.4	0	139526
1955	476699	14539	11627	67385	14.1	5	104132
1960	486000	14920	11129	84553	17.4	10	94182
1965	494900	15292	10708	105050	21.2	15	85272
1970	504000	15574	10181	129207	25.6	20	79889
1975	637300	19693	12049	195054	30.6	25	74594
1980	806000	27243	14548	288193	35.8	30	67797
1985	985002	38172	16131	402410	40.9	35	61051
1990	*1170609*	*50406*	*18343*	*534630*	*45.7*	40	55862
1995	*1380253*	*61511*	*20145*	*690382*	*50.0*	45	50568
2000	*1620018*	*63364*	*20749*	*871014*	*53.8*	50	45282
2005	*1848087*	*65189*	*20697*	*1059717*	*57.3*	55	38144
2010	*2084791*	*70157*	*20723*	*1265912*	*60.7*	60	30854
2015	*2347545*	*75683*	*20745*	*1499880*	*63.9*	65	24870
2020	*2639301*	*75025*	*20452*	*1764260*	*66.8*	70+	32979

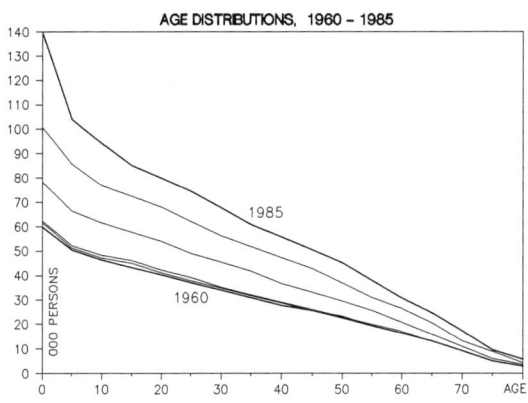

AGE DISTRIBUTIONS, 1960 - 1985

POPULATION RATIOS

YEAR	AGE DISTRIBUTION UNDER 15	AGE DISTRIBUTION 15-64	AGE DISTRIBUTION 65 & OLDER	AGE DISTRIBUTION 70 & OLDER	DEPENDENCY RATIO	WOMEN 15-49	CHILD-WOMAN RATIO
1950	0.311	0.609	0.080	0.050	0.642	0.245	0.495
1955	0.318	0.613	0.069	0.041	0.631	0.247	0.487
1960	0.323	0.614	0.064	0.036	0.630	0.249	0.495
1965	0.323	0.615	0.062	0.035	0.626	0.250	0.497
1970	0.323	0.617	0.060	0.034	0.621	0.251	0.493
1975	0.324	0.619	0.058	0.033	0.617	0.253	0.484
1980	0.327	0.615	0.059	0.033	0.627	0.251	0.497
1985	0.343	0.598	0.059	0.033	0.671	0.243	0.582
1990	*0.322*	*0.619*	*0.058*	*0.035*	*0.615*	*0.253*	*0.540*
2000	*0.403*	*0.542*	*0.055*	*0.032*	*0.844*	*0.222*	*0.821*
2010	*0.429*	*0.519*	*0.051*	*0.032*	*0.926*	*0.222*	*0.689*
2020	*0.387*	*0.568*	*0.045*	*0.030*	*0.762*	*0.246*	*0.582*

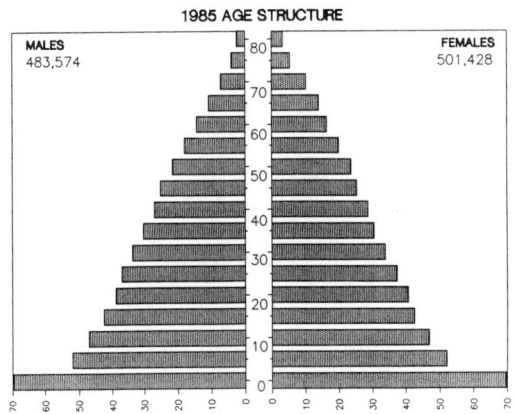

1985 AGE STRUCTURE

MALES 483,574   FEMALES 501,428

MORTALITY MEASURES (Annual Averages)

PERIOD	CRUDE DEATH RATE	INFANT MORT. RATE	LIFE EXPECTANCY AT BIRTH (years) MALE	LIFE EXPECTANCY AT BIRTH (years) FEMALE	LIFE EXPECTANCY AT BIRTH (years) BOTH SEXES	DIFFERENCE FEMALE-MALE
1950-55	27.10	194.00	36.48	39.57	38.00	3.09
1955-60	24.39	178.50	38.46	41.59	40.00	3.13
1960-65	22.90	163.00	39.94	43.10	41.50	3.16
1965-70	21.64	147.40	41.43	44.62	43.00	3.19
1970-75	20.20	131.95	43.41	46.63	45.00	3.22
1975-80	18.91	121.63	45.40	48.65	47.00	3.25
1980-85	18.05	111.88	47.36	50.69	49.00	3.32
1985-90	*16.38*	*103.00*	*49.86*	*53.18*	*51.49*	*3.32*
1990-95	*15.67*	*94.00*	*51.86*	*55.18*	*53.49*	*3.32*
2000-05	*12.81*	*77.00*	*55.86*	*59.18*	*57.49*	*3.32*
2010-15	*9.94*	*61.00*	*59.86*	*63.18*	*61.49*	*3.32*
2020-25	*7.75*	*47.00*	*63.86*	*67.18*	*65.50*	*3.32*

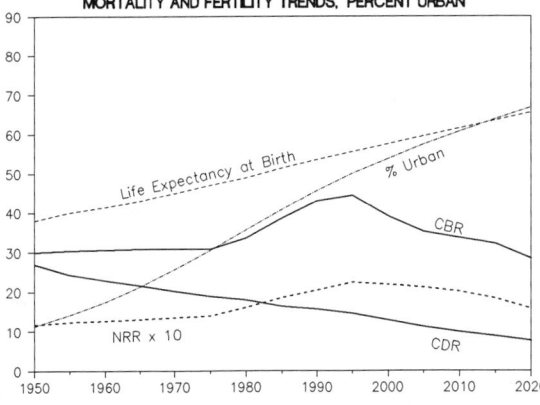

MORTALITY AND FERTILITY TRENDS, PERCENT URBAN

FERTILITY MEASURES (Annual Averages)

PERIOD	CRUDE BIRTH RATE	FERTILITY RATES GENERAL	FERTILITY RATES TOTAL	REPRODUCTION RATES GROSS	REPRODUCTION RATES NET	RATE OF NATUR. INCR.
1950-55	30.10	122.34	4.060	2.000	1.183	3.00
1955-60	30.50	122.87	4.060	2.000	1.236	6.11
1960-65	30.70	123.05	4.060	2.000	1.272	7.80
1965-70	30.90	123.35	4.161	2.050	1.310	9.26
1970-75	30.90	122.45	4.263	2.100	1.355	10.70
1975-80	30.90	122.62	4.385	2.160	1.404	11.99
1980-85	33.80	137.03	4.507	2.220	1.612	15.75
1985-90	*38.75*	*155.96*	*4.994*	*2.460*	*1.858*	*22.38*
1990-95	*43.06*	*175.11*	*5.339*	*2.630*	*2.047*	*27.39*
2000-05	*39.11*	*180.81*	*5.420*	*2.670*	*2.193*	*26.31*
2010-15	*33.65*	*145.46*	*4.730*	*2.330*	*2.008*	*23.71*
2020-25	*28.43*	*115.98*	*3.552*	*1.750*	*1.574*	*20.68*

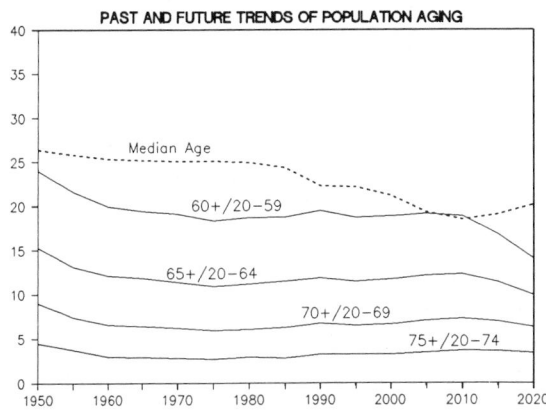

PAST AND FUTURE TRENDS OF POPULATION AGING

AGING MEASURES

YEAR	POPULATION AGE RATIOS 60+/20-59	POPULATION AGE RATIOS 65+/20-64	POPULATION AGE RATIOS 70+/20-69	POPULATION AGE RATIOS 75+/20-74	POPULATION MEAN AGE	POPULATION MEDIAN AGE
1950	0.2400	0.1529	0.0899	0.0450	30.07	26.40
1960	0.1990	0.1214	0.0653	0.0297	28.92	25.34
1970	0.1910	0.1140	0.0616	0.0281	28.66	25.06
1980	0.1865	0.1119	0.0600	0.0291	28.52	24.94
1990	*0.1943*	*0.1186*	*0.0669*	*0.0318*	*27.42*	*22.27*
2000	*0.1880*	*0.1173*	*0.0660*	*0.0323*	*24.99*	*21.17*
2010	*0.1881*	*0.1230*	*0.0723*	*0.0365*	*24.42*	*18.48*
2020	*0.1407*	*0.0992*	*0.0627*	*0.0338*	*24.85*	*20.12*

OBSERVED AND *PROJECTED* POPULATION DATA

YEAR	MID-YEAR POPULATION	NO. OF BIRTHS	NO. OF DEATHS	URBAN POPULATION NUMBER	URBAN POPULATION PERCENT	POPULATION 1985 AGE	POPULATION 1985 NUMBER
1950	293700	13819	10028	31028	10.6	0	135277
1955	313288	15296	10174	35917	11.5	5	104138
1960	352503	17793	11002	43818	12.4	10	83929
1965	403929	20087	11726	54926	13.6	15	69928
1970	463831	22809	12387	69753	15.0	20	61405
1975	547653	26748	13608	90659	16.6	25	53504
1980	640947	30871	14779	116162	18.1	30	46922
1985	744933	34835	15842	149582	20.1	35	42012
1990	*858112*	*38890*	*16781*	*192805*	*22.5*	40	36877
1995	*982681*	*42596*	*17585*	*248878*	*25.3*	45	31061
2000	*1116234*	*45836*	*18172*	*320062*	*28.7*	50	24909
2005	*1263684*	*48193*	*18612*	*410680*	*32.5*	55	19263
2010	*1420787*	*48092*	*18743*	*517837*	*36.4*	60	14389
2015	*1575526*	*46040*	*18599*	*637339*	*40.5*	65	10032
2020	*1718973*	*43660*	*18372*	*764070*	*44.4*	70+	11289

AGE DISTRIBUTIONS, 1960 - 1985

POPULATION RATIOS

YEAR	AGE DISTRIBUTION UNDER 15	15-64	65 & OLDER	70 & OLDER	DEPENDENCY RATIO	WOMEN 15-49	CHILD-WOMAN RATIO
1950	0.395	0.575	0.030	0.015	0.739	0.244	0.656
1955	0.397	0.573	0.031	0.015	0.746	0.243	0.666
1960	0.397	0.573	0.030	0.015	0.745	0.245	0.692
1965	0.405	0.565	0.030	0.015	0.770	0.242	0.730
1970	0.417	0.553	0.029	0.015	0.807	0.238	0.746
1975	0.421	0.550	0.029	0.015	0.817	0.239	0.749
1980	0.426	0.545	0.029	0.015	0.834	0.237	0.763
1985	0.434	0.537	0.029	0.015	0.861	0.233	0.780
1990	*0.439*	*0.531*	*0.029*	*0.016*	*0.882*	*0.229*	*0.783*
2000	*0.438*	*0.530*	*0.032*	*0.017*	*0.887*	*0.229*	*0.754*
2010	*0.418*	*0.546*	*0.035*	*0.020*	*0.831*	*0.238*	*0.660*
2020	*0.370*	*0.592*	*0.038*	*0.022*	*0.690*	*0.259*	*0.485*

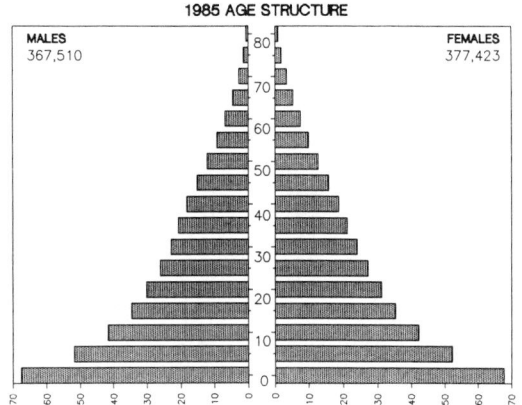

1985 AGE STRUCTURE

MALES 367,510   FEMALES 377,423

MORTALITY MEASURES (Annual Averages)

PERIOD	CRUDE DEATH RATE	INFANT MORT. RATE	LIFE EXPECTANCY AT BIRTH (years) MALE	FEMALE	BOTH SEXES	DIFFERENCE FEMALE-MALE
1950-55	34.15	230.86	28.58	31.46	30.00	2.88
1955-60	32.47	218.77	30.06	32.98	31.50	2.92
1960-65	31.21	207.34	31.54	34.51	33.00	2.97
1965-70	29.03	192.96	33.51	36.53	35.00	3.02
1970-75	26.70	179.36	35.49	38.56	37.00	3.06
1975-80	24.85	166.49	37.47	40.58	39.00	3.11
1980-85	23.06	154.28	39.45	42.60	41.00	3.15
1985-90	*21.27*	*142.81*	*41.43*	*44.62*	*43.00*	*3.19*
1990-95	*19.56*	*131.95*	*43.41*	*46.63*	*45.00*	*3.22*
2000-05	*16.28*	*111.88*	*47.36*	*50.69*	*49.00*	*3.32*
2010-15	*13.19*	*93.83*	*51.26*	*54.79*	*53.00*	*3.53*
2020-25	*10.69*	*76.97*	*55.21*	*58.85*	*57.00*	*3.64*

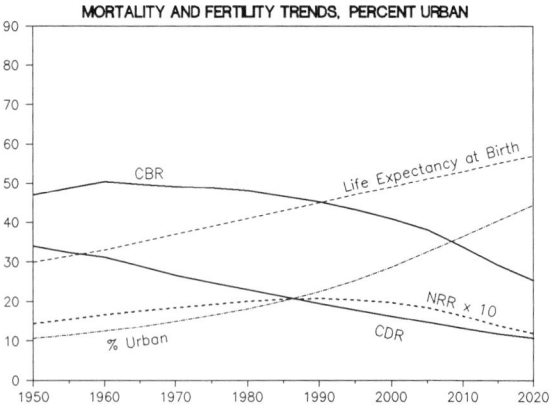

MORTALITY AND FERTILITY TRENDS, PERCENT URBAN

FERTILITY MEASURES (Annual Averages)

PERIOD	CRUDE BIRTH RATE	FERTILITY RATES GENERAL	TOTAL	REPRODUCTION RATES GROSS	NET	RATE OF NATUR. INCR.
1950-55	47.05	192.87	6.090	3.000	1.448	12.91
1955-60	48.82	199.95	6.293	3.100	1.561	16.35
1960-65	50.47	207.27	6.496	3.200	1.678	19.26
1965-70	49.73	206.95	6.496	3.200	1.764	20.70
1970-75	49.18	206.15	6.496	3.200	1.848	22.47
1975-80	48.84	205.51	6.496	3.200	1.931	23.99
1980-85	48.16	205.20	6.496	3.200	2.012	25.11
1985-90	*46.76*	*202.43*	*6.394*	*3.150*	*2.058*	*25.50*
1990-95	*45.32*	*198.29*	*6.232*	*3.070*	*2.079*	*25.76*
2000-05	*41.06*	*178.15*	*5.522*	*2.720*	*1.974*	*24.78*
2010-15	*33.85*	*139.62*	*4.283*	*2.110*	*1.632*	*20.66*
2020-25	*25.40*	*95.74*	*2.964*	*1.460*	*1.193*	*14.71*

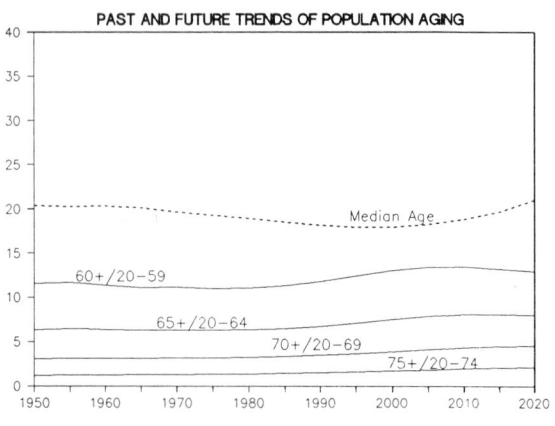

PAST AND FUTURE TRENDS OF POPULATION AGING

AGING MEASURES

YEAR	POPULATION AGE RATIOS 60+/20-59	65+/20-64	70+/20-69	75+/20-74	POPULATION MEAN AGE	POPULATION MEDIAN AGE
1950	0.1154	0.0636	0.0305	0.0116	24.37	20.38
1960	0.1136	0.0635	0.0312	0.0125	24.18	20.35
1970	0.1112	0.0628	0.0315	0.0131	23.66	19.67
1980	0.1105	0.0632	0.0323	0.0138	23.32	18.93
1990	*0.1177*	*0.0673*	*0.0346*	*0.0151*	*23.00*	*18.13*
2000	*0.1302*	*0.0748*	*0.0387*	*0.0170*	*22.96*	*17.98*
2010	*0.1339*	*0.0807*	*0.0433*	*0.0195*	*23.44*	*18.80*
2020	*0.1293*	*0.0799*	*0.0451*	*0.0216*	*25.02*	*21.03*

OBSERVED AND *PROJECTED* POPULATION DATA (000's)

YEAR	MID-YEAR POPULATION	NO. OF BIRTHS	NO. OF DEATHS	URBAN POPULATION NUMBER	URBAN POPULATION PERCENT	POPULATION 1985 AGE	POPULATION 1985 NUMBER
1950	4900	237	106	709	14.5	0	2392
1955	5760	276	116	1067	18.5	5	1834
1960	6774	322	127	1575	23.3	10	1588
1965	7829	366	137	2041	26.1	15	1325
1970	8611	394	136	2493	29.0	20	1141
1975	9831	443	151	2929	29.8	25	952
1980	10734	485	153	3290	30.7	30	784
1985	12839	569	168	4048	31.5	35	647
1990	*15020*	*643*	*178*	*4958*	*33.0*	40	527
1995	*17543*	*717*	*186*	*6161*	*35.1*	45	433
2000	*20418*	*788*	*193*	*7733*	*37.9*	50	354
2005	*23626*	*841*	*199*	*9750*	*41.3*	55	283
2010	*27071*	*857*	*202*	*12252*	*45.3*	60	219
2015	*30558*	*835*	*203*	*15024*	*49.2*	65	159
2020	*33888*	*806*	*205*	*17942*	*52.9*	70+	201

POPULATION RATIOS

YEAR	AGE DISTRIBUTION UNDER 15	AGE DISTRIBUTION 15-64	AGE DISTRIBUTION 65 & OLDER	AGE DISTRIBUTION 70 & OLDER	DEPENDENCY RATIO	WOMEN 15-49	CHILD-WOMAN RATIO
1950	0.451	0.524	0.025	0.013	0.907	0.231	0.802
1955	0.453	0.522	0.025	0.013	0.916	0.230	0.809
1960	0.456	0.519	0.025	0.014	0.928	0.228	0.819
1965	0.457	0.517	0.026	0.014	0.936	0.227	0.820
1970	0.456	0.518	0.027	0.014	0.931	0.228	0.796
1975	0.454	0.519	0.027	0.015	0.927	0.228	0.801
1980	0.449	0.523	0.028	0.015	0.910	0.230	0.771
1985	0.453	0.519	0.028	0.016	0.926	0.228	0.816
1990	*0.454*	*0.518*	*0.028*	*0.016*	*0.930*	*0.228*	*0.803*
2000	*0.448*	*0.523*	*0.029*	*0.017*	*0.912*	*0.230*	*0.755*
2010	*0.421*	*0.547*	*0.032*	*0.018*	*0.827*	*0.239*	*0.649*
2020	*0.368*	*0.594*	*0.038*	*0.022*	*0.682*	*0.258*	*0.478*

MORTALITY MEASURES (Annual Averages)

PERIOD	CRUDE DEATH RATE	INFANT MORT. RATE	LIFE EXPECTANCY AT BIRTH (years) MALE	FEMALE	BOTH SEXES	DIFFERENCE FEMALE-MALE
1950-55	21.65	148.54	40.44	43.61	42.00	3.17
1955-60	20.08	137.31	42.42	45.63	44.00	3.21
1960-65	18.70	126.64	44.41	47.64	46.00	3.23
1965-70	17.48	116.62	46.39	49.66	48.00	3.27
1970-75	15.77	107.28	48.33	51.72	50.00	3.38
1975-80	15.33	102.71	49.31	52.75	51.00	3.44
1980-85	14.24	98.27	50.28	53.77	52.00	3.49
1985-90	*13.12*	*89.53*	*52.24*	*55.81*	*54.00*	*3.56*
1990-95	*11.83*	*81.06*	*54.22*	*57.83*	*56.00*	*3.62*
2000-05	*9.47*	*65.03*	*58.19*	*61.87*	*60.00*	*3.68*
2010-15	*7.46*	*50.22*	*62.20*	*65.86*	*64.00*	*3.66*
2020-25	*6.06*	*36.56*	*66.22*	*69.83*	*68.00*	*3.60*

FERTILITY MEASURES (Annual Averages)

PERIOD	CRUDE BIRTH RATE	FERTILITY RATES GENERAL	FERTILITY RATES TOTAL	REPRODUCTION RATES GROSS	REPRODUCTION RATES NET	RATE OF NATUR. INCR.
1950-55	48.28	209.25	6.902	3.400	2.138	26.63
1955-60	47.93	209.16	6.902	3.400	2.223	27.85
1960-65	47.58	208.94	6.902	3.400	2.306	28.88
1965-70	46.79	205.70	6.800	3.350	2.354	29.31
1970-75	45.77	200.84	6.638	3.270	2.379	30.00
1975-80	45.11	196.82	6.496	3.200	2.368	29.78
1980-85	45.22	197.38	6.496	3.200	2.406	30.97
1985-90	*44.30*	*194.37*	*6.394*	*3.150*	*2.443*	*31.18*
1990-95	*42.82*	*188.63*	*6.212*	*3.060*	*2.443*	*30.99*
2000-05	*38.61*	*166.66*	*5.522*	*2.720*	*2.288*	*29.14*
2010-15	*31.66*	*130.16*	*4.283*	*2.110*	*1.859*	*24.20*
2020-25	*23.78*	*90.18*	*2.964*	*1.460*	*1.341*	*17.73*

AGING MEASURES

YEAR	POPULATION AGE RATIOS 60+/20-59	65+/20-64	70+/20-69	75+/20-74	POPULATION MEAN AGE	POPULATION MEDIAN AGE
1950	0.1020	0.0587	0.0302	0.0130	21.88	17.36
1960	0.1058	0.0612	0.0318	0.0140	21.84	17.15
1970	0.1099	0.0643	0.0338	0.0149	21.89	17.13
1980	0.1123	0.0667	0.0357	0.0161	22.05	17.41
1990	*0.1142*	*0.0685*	*0.0373*	*0.0174*	*21.95*	*17.23*
2000	*0.1170*	*0.0710*	*0.0393*	*0.0187*	*22.24*	*17.44*
2010	*0.1193*	*0.0726*	*0.0408*	*0.0199*	*23.13*	*18.63*
2020	*0.1269*	*0.0777*	*0.0438*	*0.0216*	*25.07*	*21.10*

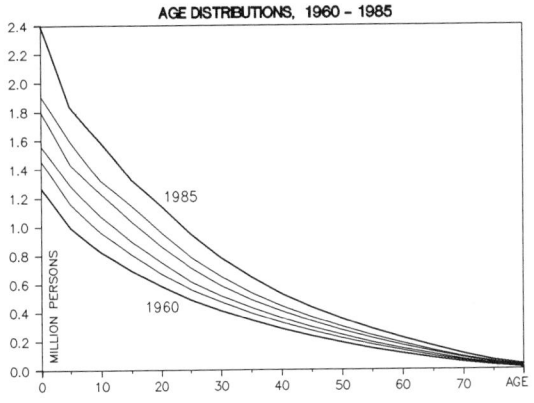

AGE DISTRIBUTIONS, 1960 - 1985

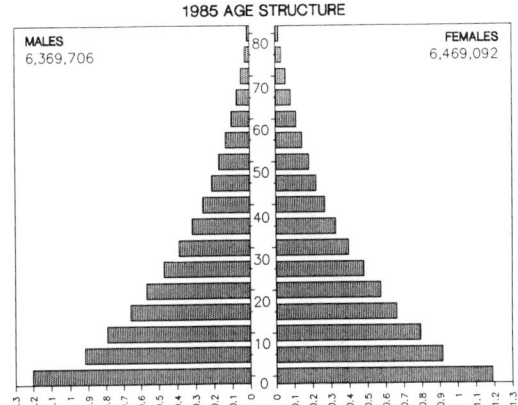

1985 AGE STRUCTURE

MALES 6,369,706

FEMALES 6,469,092

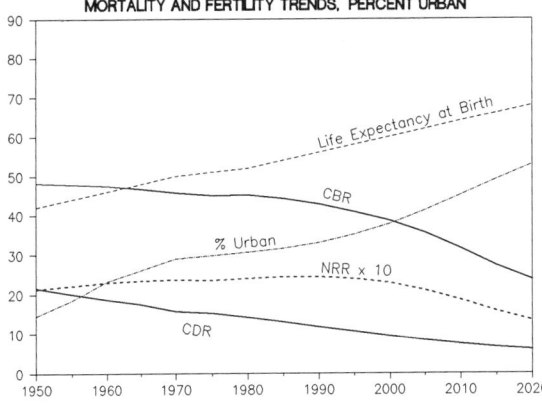

MORTALITY AND FERTILITY TRENDS, PERCENT URBAN

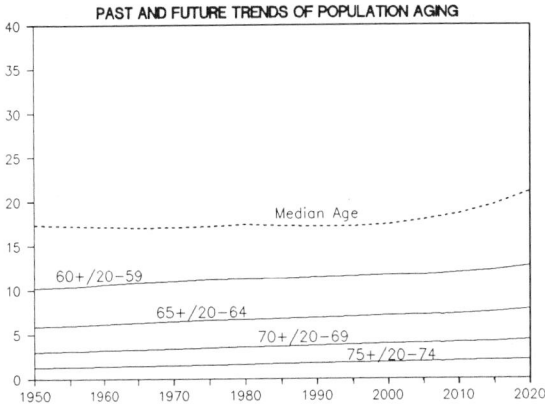

PAST AND FUTURE TRENDS OF POPULATION AGING

OBSERVED AND *PROJECTED* POPULATION DATA (000's)

YEAR	MID-YEAR POPULATION	NO. OF BIRTHS	NO. OF DEATHS	URBAN POPULATION NUMBER	URBAN POPULATION PERCENT	POPULATION 1985 AGE	POPULATION 1985 NUMBER
1950	3245	154	121	178	5.5	0	1073
1955	3416	164	117	286	8.4	5	839
1960	3660	176	115	362	9.9	10	704
1965	3981	193	116	467	11.7	15	622
1970	4388	206	118	608	13.8	20	526
1975	4852	228	123	790	16.3	25	447
1980	5407	253	127	1031	19.1	30	381
1985	6075	283	133	1348	22.2	35	328
1990	*6876*	*313*	*139*	*1763*	*25.6*	40	279
1995	*7807*	*345*	*145*	*2291*	*29.3*	45	234
2000	*8879*	*379*	*150*	*2947*	*33.2*	50	193
2005	*10100*	*408*	*155*	*3753*	*37.2*	55	154
2010	*11451*	*430*	*159*	*4713*	*41.2*	60	118
2015	*12893*	*437*	*160*	*5822*	*45.2*	65	84
2020	*14353*	*419*	*159*	*7042*	*49.1*	70+	94

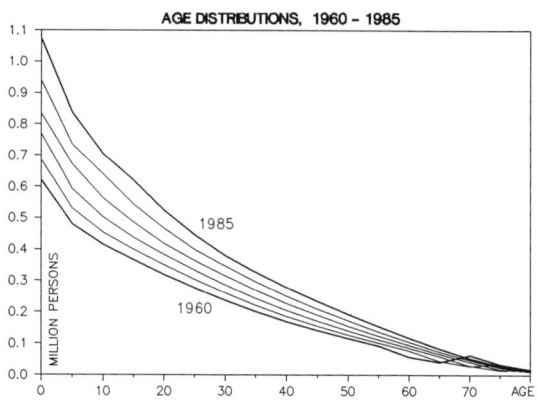

POPULATION RATIOS

YEAR	AGE DISTRIBUTION UNDER 15	AGE DISTRIBUTION 15-64	AGE DISTRIBUTION 65 & OLDER	AGE DISTRIBUTION 70 & OLDER	DEPENDENCY RATIO	WOMEN 15-49	CHILD-WOMAN RATIO
1950	0.397	0.532	0.070	0.039	0.879	0.221	0.737
1955	0.408	0.529	0.063	0.035	0.891	0.228	0.729
1960	0.415	0.542	0.043	0.032	0.844	0.233	0.729
1965	0.420	0.549	0.031	0.020	0.822	0.235	0.733
1970	0.425	0.547	0.028	0.015	0.830	0.235	0.747
1975	0.427	0.545	0.028	0.014	0.835	0.235	0.732
1980	0.429	0.542	0.029	0.015	0.843	0.235	0.742
1985	0.431	0.540	0.029	0.015	0.852	0.234	0.754
1990	*0.436*	*0.534*	*0.030*	*0.016*	*0.873*	*0.232*	*0.769*
2000	*0.439*	*0.530*	*0.031*	*0.017*	*0.888*	*0.231*	*0.757*
2010	*0.428*	*0.539*	*0.033*	*0.018*	*0.854*	*0.236*	*0.700*
2020	*0.397*	*0.568*	*0.035*	*0.020*	*0.761*	*0.247*	*0.578*

MORTALITY MEASURES (Annual Averages)

PERIOD	CRUDE DEATH RATE	INFANT MORT. RATE	LIFE EXPECTANCY AT BIRTH (years) MALE	LIFE EXPECTANCY AT BIRTH (years) FEMALE	LIFE EXPECTANCY AT BIRTH (years) BOTH SEXES	DIFFERENCE FEMALE-MALE
1950-55	37.21	225.07	29.27	32.17	30.70	2.90
1955-60	34.14	213.43	30.75	33.69	32.20	2.94
1960-65	31.36	202.13	32.23	35.22	33.70	2.99
1965-70	29.09	191.55	33.71	36.73	35.20	3.02
1970-75	26.79	181.33	35.19	38.25	36.70	3.06
1975-80	25.25	171.48	36.68	39.77	38.20	3.09
1980-85	23.55	159.14	38.65	41.79	40.20	3.14
1985-90	*21.90*	*147.40*	*40.63*	*43.81*	*42.20*	*3.18*
1990-95	*20.19*	*136.24*	*42.62*	*45.83*	*44.20*	*3.21*
2000-05	*16.91*	*115.62*	*46.59*	*49.86*	*48.20*	*3.28*
2010-15	*13.86*	*97.38*	*50.48*	*53.97*	*52.20*	*3.49*
2020-25	*11.11*	*80.24*	*54.42*	*58.04*	*56.20*	*3.62*

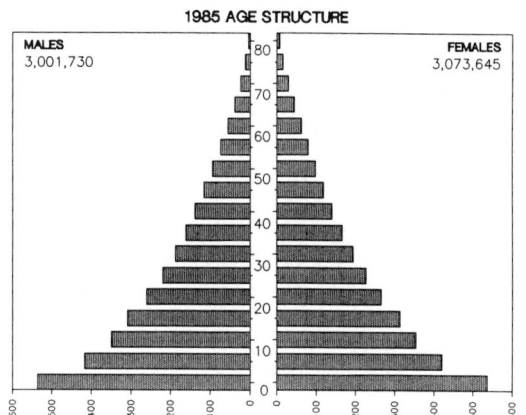

FERTILITY MEASURES (Annual Averages)

PERIOD	CRUDE BIRTH RATE	FERTILITY RATES GENERAL	FERTILITY RATES TOTAL	REPRODUCTION RATES GROSS	REPRODUCTION RATES NET	RATE OF NATUR. INCR.
1950-55	47.50	211.58	6.575	3.239	1.598	10.29
1955-60	47.93	208.13	6.461	3.183	1.636	13.79
1960-65	48.16	206.01	6.392	3.149	1.684	16.80
1965-70	48.53	206.59	6.407	3.156	1.750	19.43
1970-75	46.89	199.53	6.191	3.050	1.750	20.10
1975-80	46.89	199.61	6.191	3.050	1.810	21.64
1980-85	46.84	199.74	6.191	3.050	1.887	23.29
1985-90	*46.63*	*200.03*	*6.185*	*3.050*	*1.962*	*24.73*
1990-95	*45.55*	*196.89*	*6.084*	*3.000*	*2.003*	*25.36*
2000-05	*42.65*	*184.05*	*5.678*	*2.800*	*2.004*	*25.73*
2010-15	*37.57*	*157.80*	*4.847*	*2.390*	*1.825*	*23.71*
2020-25	*29.17*	*115.35*	*3.549*	*1.750*	*1.415*	*18.06*

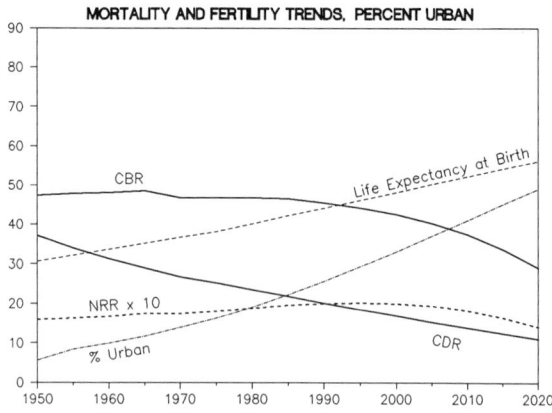

AGING MEASURES

YEAR	POPULATION AGE RATIOS 60+/20-59	POPULATION AGE RATIOS 65+/20-64	POPULATION AGE RATIOS 70+/20-69	POPULATION AGE RATIOS 75+/20-74	POPULATION MEAN AGE	POPULATION MEDIAN AGE
1950	0.2779	0.1611	0.0837	0.0359	25.94	20.44
1960	0.1382	0.0973	0.0697	0.0305	23.92	19.24
1970	0.1110	0.0628	0.0316	0.0164	23.12	18.74
1980	0.1141	0.0652	0.0330	0.0138	23.06	18.53
1990	*0.1187*	*0.0686*	*0.0355*	*0.0154*	*22.85*	*18.20*
2000	*0.1236*	*0.0727*	*0.0385*	*0.0171*	*22.78*	*17.97*
2010	*0.1248*	*0.0749*	*0.0405*	*0.0186*	*23.06*	*18.41*
2020	*0.1246*	*0.0756*	*0.0419*	*0.0198*	*24.08*	*19.75*

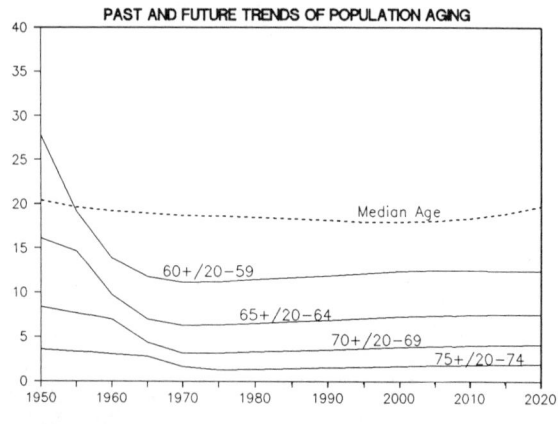

OBSERVED AND *PROJECTED* POPULATION DATA

YEAR	MID-YEAR POPULATION	NO. OF BIRTHS	NO. OF DEATHS	URBAN POPULATION NUMBER	URBAN POPULATION PERCENT	POPULATION 1985 AGE	POPULATION 1985 NUMBER
1950	504776	20804	14941	50549	10.0	0	141580
1955	520140	21209	14577	60797	11.7	5	123708
1960	539524	22327	14799	73379	13.6	10	96889
1965	524640	21629	13724	82475	15.7	15	84590
1970	526228	20248	12185	95252	18.1	20	73710
1975	628454	25678	13771	130425	20.8	25	64226
1980	808513	32932	17509	192112	23.8	30	55881
1985	889491	36289	17782	241131	27.1	35	48732
1990	*987107*	*40526*	*18290*	*303563*	*30.8*	40	42471
1995	*1104921*	*45083*	*18873*	*382510*	*34.6*	45	37458
2000	*1244229*	*49779*	*19432*	*480349*	*38.6*	50	32515
2005	*1405815*	*51949*	*19700*	*599084*	*42.6*	55	27506
2010	*1576872*	*55843*	*19987*	*734533*	*46.6*	60	22299
2015	*1766962*	*59068*	*20253*	*891469*	*50.5*	65	16846
2020	*1972313*	*56887*	*20149*	*1068625*	*54.2*	70+	21080

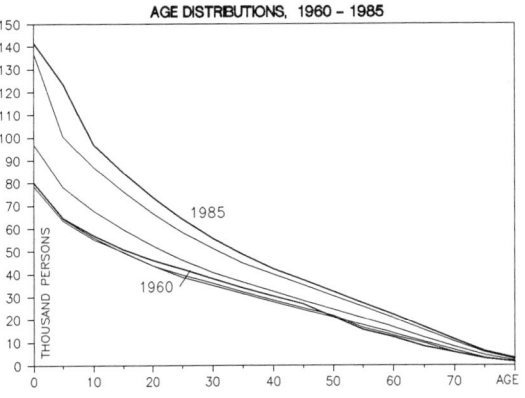

AGE DISTRIBUTIONS, 1960 - 1985

POPULATION RATIOS

YEAR	AGE DISTRIBUTION UNDER 15	AGE DISTRIBUTION 15-64	AGE DISTRIBUTION 65 & OLDER	AGE DISTRIBUTION 70 & OLDER	DEPENDENCY RATIO	WOMEN 15-49	CHILD-WOMAN RATIO
1950	0.372	0.591	0.037	0.020	0.692	0.254	0.580
1955	0.372	0.592	0.036	0.020	0.689	0.254	0.582
1960	0.374	0.591	0.035	0.020	0.693	0.251	0.591
1965	0.376	0.585	0.039	0.021	0.710	0.245	0.610
1970	0.381	0.577	0.042	0.023	0.734	0.243	0.627
1975	0.387	0.571	0.043	0.023	0.753	0.242	0.638
1980	0.401	0.556	0.043	0.023	0.798	0.237	0.713
1985	0.407	0.550	0.043	0.024	0.818	0.237	0.672
1990	*0.413*	*0.544*	*0.043*	*0.024*	*0.838*	*0.236*	*0.684*
2000	*0.416*	*0.543*	*0.041*	*0.024*	*0.842*	*0.237*	*0.699*
2010	*0.413*	*0.547*	*0.040*	*0.024*	*0.827*	*0.238*	*0.649*
2020	*0.388*	*0.572*	*0.040*	*0.024*	*0.749*	*0.248*	*0.579*

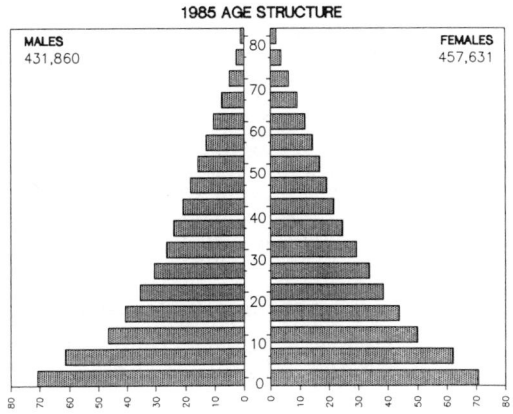

1985 AGE STRUCTURE

MALES 431,860   FEMALES 457,631

MORTALITY MEASURES (Annual Averages)

PERIOD	CRUDE DEATH RATE	INFANT MORT. RATE	LIFE EXPECTANCY AT BIRTH (years) MALE	LIFE EXPECTANCY AT BIRTH (years) FEMALE	LIFE EXPECTANCY AT BIRTH (years) BOTH SEXES	DIFFERENCE FEMALE-MALE
1950-55	29.60	203.54	32.03	35.01	33.50	2.98
1955-60	28.02	192.96	33.51	36.53	35.00	3.02
1960-65	27.43	182.65	35.00	38.05	36.50	3.05
1965-70	26.16	172.80	36.48	39.57	38.00	3.09
1970-75	23.16	163.42	37.96	41.08	39.50	3.12
1975-80	21.91	154.28	39.45	42.60	41.00	3.15
1980-85	21.66	142.81	41.43	44.62	43.00	3.19
1985-90	*19.99*	*131.95*	*43.41*	*46.63*	*45.00*	*3.22*
1990-95	*18.53*	*121.63*	*45.40*	*48.65*	*47.00*	*3.25*
2000-05	*15.62*	*102.71*	*49.31*	*52.75*	*51.00*	*3.44*
2010-15	*12.68*	*85.27*	*53.23*	*56.82*	*55.00*	*3.59*
2020-25	*10.22*	*68.94*	*57.19*	*60.86*	*59.00*	*3.67*

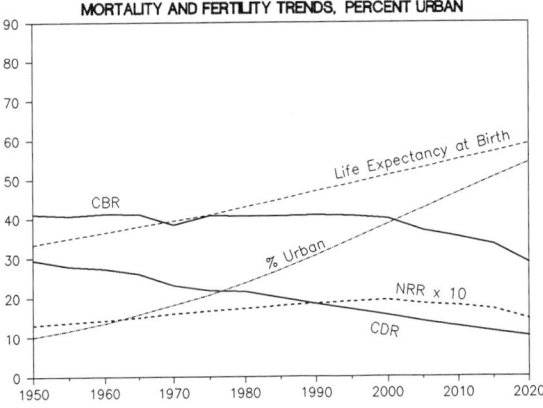

MORTALITY AND FERTILITY TRENDS, PERCENT URBAN

FERTILITY MEASURES (Annual Averages)

PERIOD	CRUDE BIRTH RATE	FERTILITY RATES GENERAL	FERTILITY RATES TOTAL	REPRODUCTION RATES GROSS	REPRODUCTION RATES NET	RATE OF NATUR. INCR.
1950-55	41.22	162.11	5.049	2.487	1.325	11.62
1955-60	40.78	161.28	5.077	2.501	1.382	12.75
1960-65	41.38	166.62	5.065	2.495	1.429	13.95
1965-70	41.23	169.02	5.193	2.558	1.514	15.07
1970-75	38.48	158.91	5.315	2.618	1.600	15.32
1975-80	40.86	170.76	5.379	2.650	1.670	18.95
1980-85	40.73	171.86	5.379	2.650	1.735	19.08
1985-90	*40.80*	*172.66*	*5.379*	*2.650*	*1.798*	*20.81*
1990-95	*41.06*	*173.01*	*5.379*	*2.650*	*1.862*	*22.53*
2000-05	*40.01*	*169.38*	*5.237*	*2.580*	*1.938*	*24.39*
2010-15	*35.41*	*147.47*	*4.567*	*2.250*	*1.793*	*22.74*
2020-25	*28.84*	*114.80*	*3.552*	*1.750*	*1.468*	*18.63*

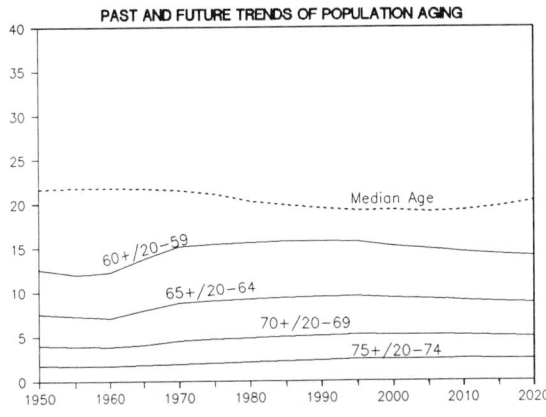

PAST AND FUTURE TRENDS OF POPULATION AGING

AGING MEASURES

YEAR	POPULATION AGE RATIOS 60+/20-59	POPULATION AGE RATIOS 65+/20-64	POPULATION AGE RATIOS 70+/20-69	POPULATION AGE RATIOS 75+/20-74	POPULATION MEAN AGE	POPULATION MEDIAN AGE
1950	0.1259	0.0756	0.0397	0.0173	25.26	21.69
1960	0.1227	0.0707	0.0382	0.0170	25.48	21.83
1970	0.1516	0.0880	0.0452	0.0191	25.77	21.52
1980	0.1562	0.0921	0.0486	0.0215	24.97	20.26
1990	*0.1578*	*0.0948*	*0.0512*	*0.0234*	*24.55*	*19.53*
2000	*0.1519*	*0.0931*	*0.0516*	*0.0243*	*24.07*	*19.27*
2010	*0.1453*	*0.0900*	*0.0510*	*0.0247*	*24.08*	*19.26*
2020	*0.1407*	*0.0872*	*0.0495*	*0.0244*	*24.72*	*20.27*

OBSERVED AND *PROJECTED* POPULATION DATA (000's)

YEAR	MID-YEAR POPULATION	NO. OF BIRTHS	NO. OF DEATHS	URBAN POPULATION NUMBER	URBAN POPULATION PERCENT	POPULATION 1985 AGE	POPULATION 1985 NUMBER
1950	2775	146	77	365	13.2	0	2110
1955	3219	171	84	515	16.0	5	1622
1960	3779	198	90	729	19.3	10	1277
1965	4500	233	96	1040	23.1	15	1032
1970	5510	282	106	1510	27.4	20	849
1975	6754	345	117	2173	32.2	25	713
1980	8327	425	130	3088	37.1	30	596
1985	10252	522	146	4302	42.0	35	466
1990	12596	633	163	5870	46.6	40	398
1995	15315	752	178	7786	50.8	45	332
2000	18547	869	191	10118	54.6	50	267
2005	22276	971	201	12940	58.1	55	206
2010	26486	1023	207	16269	61.4	60	152
2015	30908	1048	210	19950	64.5	65	106
2020	35406	1046	211	23883	67.5	70+	124

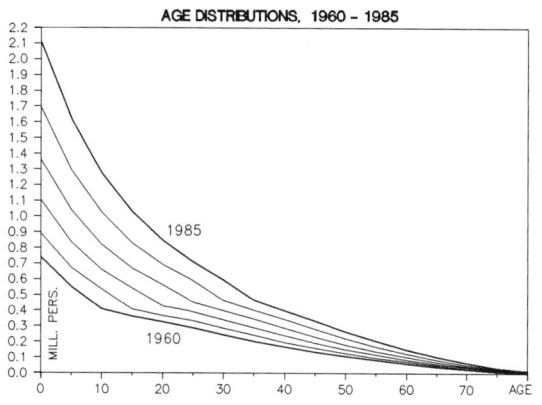

AGE DISTRIBUTIONS, 1960 – 1985

POPULATION RATIOS

YEAR	AGE DISTRIBUTION UNDER 15	15-64	65 & OLDER	70 & OLDER	DEPENDENCY RATIO	WOMEN 15-49	CHILD-WOMAN RATIO
1950	0.431	0.546	0.023	0.012	0.831	0.238	0.723
1955	0.437	0.540	0.023	0.012	0.853	0.234	0.819
1960	0.451	0.526	0.023	0.012	0.900	0.227	0.864
1965	0.468	0.509	0.023	0.012	0.965	0.218	0.911
1970	0.473	0.504	0.023	0.012	0.984	0.215	0.934
1975	0.478	0.500	0.023	0.012	1.002	0.213	0.948
1980	0.483	0.494	0.023	0.012	1.022	0.211	0.969
1985	0.489	0.489	0.022	0.012	1.045	0.209	0.986
1990	0.494	0.483	0.022	0.012	1.069	0.208	0.997
2000	0.498	0.479	0.023	0.013	1.089	0.210	0.965
2010	0.480	0.496	0.024	0.014	1.018	0.220	0.842
2020	0.427	0.547	0.027	0.015	0.829	0.243	0.615

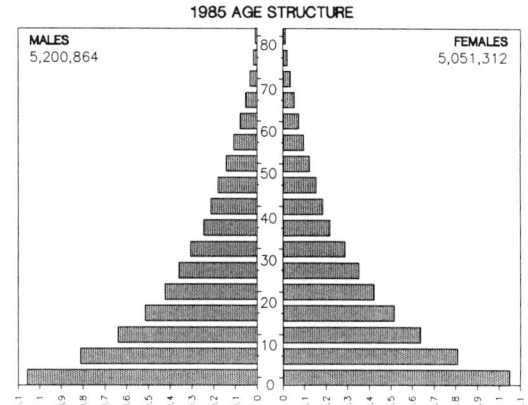

1985 AGE STRUCTURE

MALES 5,200,864   FEMALES 5,051,312

MORTALITY MEASURES (Annual Averages)

PERIOD	CRUDE DEATH RATE	INFANT MORT. RATE	LIFE EXPECTANCY AT BIRTH (years) MALE	FEMALE	BOTH SEXES	DIFFERENCE FEMALE-MALE
1950-55	27.70	186.06	34.50	37.50	35.98	3.00
1955-60	26.10	172.92	36.50	39.50	37.98	3.00
1960-65	23.73	157.46	38.90	42.10	40.48	3.20
1965-70	21.31	142.95	41.40	44.60	42.98	3.20
1970-75	19.26	129.40	43.90	47.10	45.48	3.20
1975-80	17.31	116.50	46.40	49.70	48.03	3.30
1980-85	15.58	105.09	48.80	52.20	50.47	3.40
1985-90	14.25	96.14	50.80	54.20	52.47	3.40
1990-95	12.94	87.48	52.80	56.20	54.47	3.40
2000-05	10.32	70.95	56.80	60.20	58.47	3.40
2010-15	7.82	55.69	60.80	64.20	62.47	3.40
2020-25	5.95	41.62	64.80	68.20	66.47	3.40

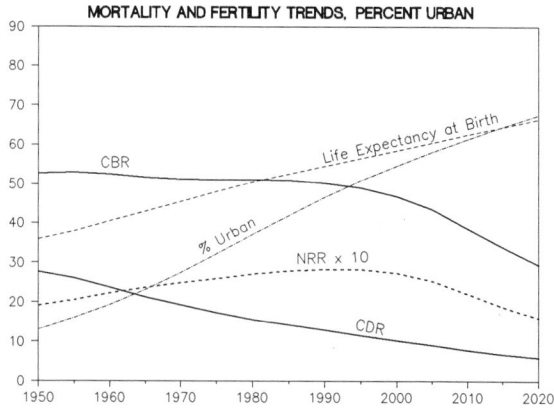

MORTALITY AND FERTILITY TRENDS, PERCENT URBAN

FERTILITY MEASURES (Annual Averages)

PERIOD	CRUDE BIRTH RATE	FERTILITY RATES GENERAL	FERTILITY RATES TOTAL	REPRODUCTION RATES GROSS	REPRODUCTION RATES NET	RATE OF NATUR. INCR.
1950-55	52.67	223.22	6.902	3.400	1.916	24.97
1955-60	52.97	230.21	7.105	3.500	2.062	26.87
1960-65	52.51	236.53	7.308	3.600	2.239	28.77
1965-70	51.68	238.98	7.409	3.650	2.382	30.38
1970-75	51.19	239.57	7.409	3.650	2.491	31.93
1975-80	51.08	241.53	7.409	3.650	2.604	33.77
1980-85	50.99	243.31	7.409	3.650	2.713	35.41
1985-90	50.90	244.54	7.409	3.650	2.797	36.65
1990-95	50.22	241.56	7.308	3.600	2.839	37.28
2000-05	46.86	220.67	6.679	3.290	2.735	36.54
2010-15	38.64	171.29	5.156	2.540	2.212	30.82
2020-25	29.53	117.54	3.552	1.750	1.589	23.58

AGING MEASURES

YEAR	POPULATION AGE RATIOS 60+/20-59	65+/20-64	70+/20-69	75+/20-74	POPULATION MEAN AGE	POPULATION MEDIAN AGE
1950	0.0946	0.0526	0.0261	0.0109	22.48	18.29
1960	0.0962	0.0538	0.0266	0.0110	21.89	17.57
1970	0.0995	0.0567	0.0288	0.0123	21.33	16.37
1980	0.0991	0.0572	0.0298	0.0131	20.87	15.85
1990	0.1014	0.0588	0.0310	0.0140	20.44	15.28
2000	0.1052	0.0623	0.0333	0.0152	20.24	15.10
2010	0.1020	0.0628	0.0350	0.0165	20.67	15.89
2020	0.1023	0.0623	0.0344	0.0172	22.29	18.13

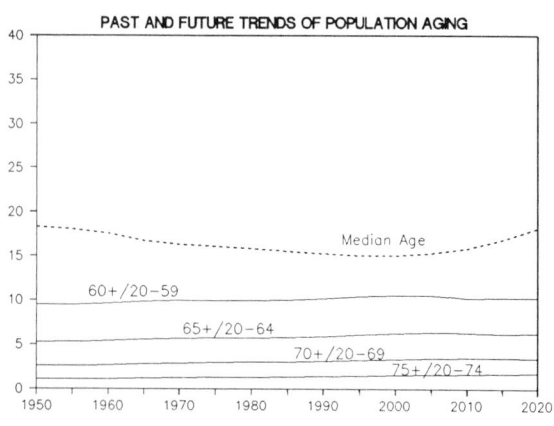

PAST AND FUTURE TRENDS OF POPULATION AGING

OBSERVED AND *PROJECTED* POPULATION DATA (000's)

YEAR	MID-YEAR POPULATION	NO. OF BIRTHS	NO. OF DEATHS	URBAN POPULATION NUMBER	URBAN POPULATION PERCENT	POPULATION 1985 AGE	POPULATION 1985 NUMBER
1950	6265	331	158	350	5.6	0	4420
1955	7189	381	169	462	6.4	5	3373
1960	8332	440	178	613	7.4	10	2627
1965	9749	509	188	839	8.6	15	2074
1970	11498	608	199	1184	10.3	20	1681
1975	13741	736	213	1775	12.9	25	1353
1980	16632	896	227	2675	16.1	30	1085
1985	20353	1096	241	4002	19.7	35	813
1990	25130	1276	250	5923	23.6	40	584
1995	30844	1469	254	8531	27.7	45	534
2000	37581	1642	256	11937	31.8	50	489
2005	45218	1770	258	16140	35.7	55	393
2010	53466	1789	265	21222	39.7	60	306
2015	61671	1769	273	26948	43.7	65	237
2020	69635	1799	289	33175	47.6	70+	384

AGE DISTRIBUTIONS, 1960 – 1985

POPULATION RATIOS

YEAR	AGE DISTRIBUTION UNDER 15	AGE DISTRIBUTION 15-64	AGE DISTRIBUTION 65 & OLDER	AGE DISTRIBUTION 70 & OLDER	DEPENDENCY RATIO	WOMEN 15-49	CHILD-WOMAN RATIO
1950	0.398	0.563	0.039	0.022	0.776	0.226	0.768
1955	0.423	0.537	0.041	0.023	0.863	0.217	0.880
1960	0.456	0.503	0.041	0.024	0.988	0.206	0.952
1965	0.474	0.485	0.041	0.024	1.063	0.202	0.987
1970	0.482	0.478	0.039	0.024	1.092	0.203	0.991
1975	0.491	0.472	0.037	0.023	1.120	0.204	1.018
1980	0.501	0.465	0.034	0.021	1.150	0.202	1.053
1985	0.512	0.458	0.031	0.019	1.186	0.200	1.087
1990	0.521	0.452	0.028	0.017	1.215	0.199	1.104
2000	0.512	0.463	0.025	0.015	1.160	0.208	0.969
2010	0.468	0.510	0.023	0.015	0.962	0.228	0.756
2020	0.392	0.581	0.027	0.015	0.721	0.258	0.506

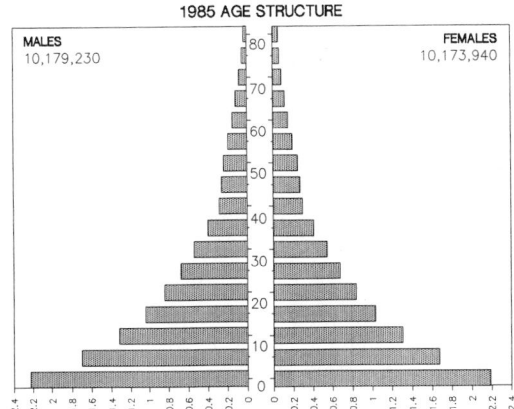

1985 AGE STRUCTURE

MALES 10,179,230   FEMALES 10,173,940

MORTALITY MEASURES (Annual Averages)

PERIOD	CRUDE DEATH RATE	INFANT MORT. RATE	LIFE EXPECTANCY AT BIRTH (years) MALE	LIFE EXPECTANCY AT BIRTH (years) FEMALE	LIFE EXPECTANCY AT BIRTH (years) BOTH SEXES	DIFFERENCE FEMALE-MALE
1950-55	25.29	150.00	39.00	43.02	40.98	4.02
1955-60	23.50	130.00	41.50	45.45	43.45	3.95
1960-65	21.41	118.00	44.04	47.98	45.98	3.94
1965-70	19.31	108.00	46.47	50.47	48.44	3.99
1970-75	17.34	98.00	49.03	53.02	51.00	3.99
1975-80	15.52	88.00	51.46	55.49	53.45	4.03
1980-85	13.65	80.00	54.04	58.01	56.00	3.97
1985-90	11.86	72.00	56.50	60.46	58.45	3.96
1990-95	9.94	64.00	59.00	62.97	60.96	3.97
2000-05	6.81	47.00	63.60	67.83	65.68	4.23
2010-15	4.95	33.00	66.98	71.38	69.15	4.40
2020-25	4.15	23.00	69.47	73.99	71.70	4.52

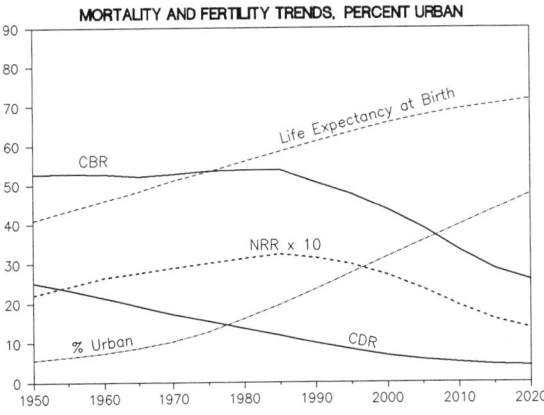

MORTALITY AND FERTILITY TRENDS, PERCENT URBAN

FERTILITY MEASURES (Annual Averages)

PERIOD	CRUDE BIRTH RATE	FERTILITY RATES GENERAL	FERTILITY RATES TOTAL	REPRODUCTION RATES GROSS	REPRODUCTION RATES NET	RATE OF NATUR. INCR.
1950-55	52.79	238.33	7.511	3.700	2.227	27.50
1955-60	52.93	250.61	7.815	3.850	2.434	29.44
1960-65	52.77	258.80	8.120	4.000	2.653	31.36
1965-70	52.22	257.58	8.120	4.000	2.775	32.92
1970-75	52.89	260.02	8.120	4.000	2.901	35.55
1975-80	53.59	264.17	8.120	4.000	3.019	38.07
1980-85	53.90	268.26	8.120	4.000	3.137	40.25
1985-90	53.87	270.13	8.120	4.000	3.248	42.01
1990-95	50.77	252.36	7.612	3.750	3.148	40.83
2000-05	43.70	205.02	6.191	3.050	2.715	36.89
2010-15	33.45	142.02	4.263	2.100	1.939	28.50
2020-25	25.83	97.28	2.964	1.460	1.377	21.68

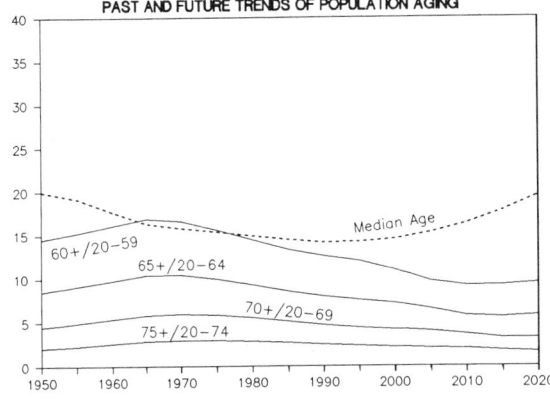

PAST AND FUTURE TRENDS OF POPULATION AGING

AGING MEASURES

YEAR	POPULATION AGE RATIOS 60+/20-59	POPULATION AGE RATIOS 65+/20-64	POPULATION AGE RATIOS 70+/20-69	POPULATION AGE RATIOS 75+/20-74	POPULATION MEAN AGE	POPULATION MEDIAN AGE
1950	0.1451	0.0852	0.0450	0.0208	24.65	19.99
1960	0.1614	0.0977	0.0541	0.0258	23.24	17.70
1970	0.1665	0.1048	0.0600	0.0297	21.93	15.86
1980	0.1445	0.0932	0.0556	0.0290	20.66	14.96
1990	0.1264	0.0798	0.0474	0.0252	19.64	14.22
2000	0.1098	0.0721	0.0420	0.0217	19.63	14.59
2010	0.0922	0.0580	0.0365	0.0201	20.73	16.39
2020	0.0950	0.0581	0.0325	0.0166	23.23	19.53

OBSERVED AND *PROJECTED* POPULATION DATA

YEAR	MID-YEAR POPULATION	NO. OF BIRTHS	NO. OF DEATHS	URBAN POPULATION NUMBER	URBAN POPULATION PERCENT	POPULATION 1985 AGE	POPULATION 1985 NUMBER
1950	733945	31067	19543	7009	1.0	0	264880
1955	793916	34138	19545	14397	1.8	5	212306
1960	870397	37323	19822	29737	3.4	10	178620
1965	962534	41077	20088	61076	6.3	15	152194
1970	1064334	45142	20543	91013	8.6	20	131215
1975	1187249	49771	19590	128282	10.8	25	111501
1980	1339040	55738	18622	181636	13.6	30	93113
1985	1538439	62842	19121	257467	16.7	35	83256
1990	1773761	69709	19444	359325	20.3	40	71740
1995	2044246	77191	19666	491113	24.0	45	61019
2000	2353639	85301	19884	656375	27.9	50	50121
2005	2705150	93008	20170	856955	31.7	55	40225
2010	3095625	98091	20660	1102248	35.6	60	32437
2015	3508613	96041	21199	1389603	39.6	65	24036
2020	3903898	92538	22162	1702460	43.6	70+	31775

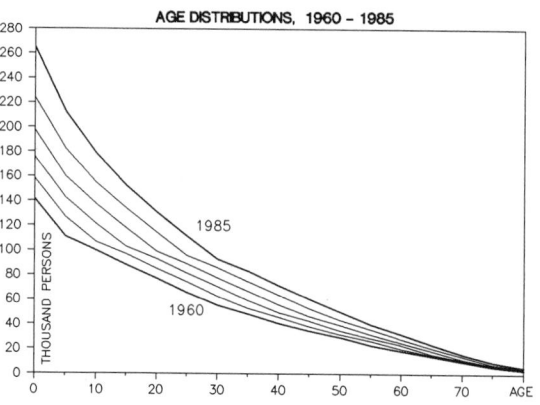

POPULATION RATIOS

YEAR	AGE DISTRIBUTION UNDER 15	AGE DISTRIBUTION 15-64	AGE DISTRIBUTION 65 & OLDER	AGE DISTRIBUTION 70 & OLDER	DEPENDENCY RATIO	WOMEN 15-49	CHILD-WOMAN RATIO
1950	0.407	0.549	0.045	0.025	0.823	0.241	0.674
1955	0.405	0.554	0.042	0.024	0.806	0.245	0.645
1960	0.405	0.556	0.039	0.022	0.800	0.246	0.660
1965	0.407	0.556	0.037	0.021	0.799	0.247	0.666
1970	0.413	0.551	0.036	0.020	0.816	0.246	0.672
1975	0.417	0.547	0.036	0.020	0.828	0.245	0.681
1980	0.420	0.545	0.036	0.020	0.836	0.243	0.688
1985	0.426	0.537	0.036	0.021	0.861	0.239	0.722
1990	0.431	0.532	0.037	0.021	0.881	0.235	0.730
2000	0.427	0.535	0.038	0.022	0.870	0.236	0.691
2010	0.409	0.550	0.041	0.025	0.818	0.244	0.624
2020	0.370	0.585	0.045	0.028	0.709	0.259	0.483

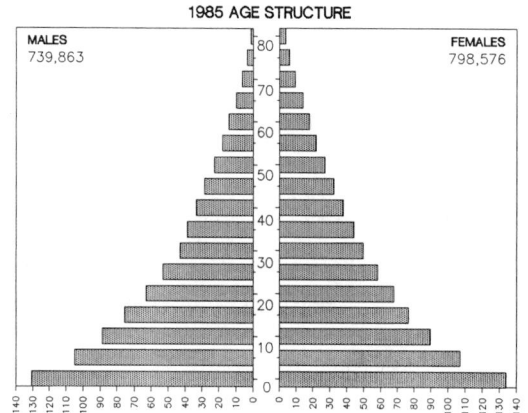

MORTALITY MEASURES (Annual Averages)

PERIOD	CRUDE DEATH RATE	INFANT MORT. RATE	LIFE EXPECTANCY AT BIRTH (years) MALE	LIFE EXPECTANCY AT BIRTH (years) FEMALE	LIFE EXPECTANCY AT BIRTH (years) BOTH SEXES	DIFFERENCE FEMALE-MALE
1950-55	26.63	160.00	34.00	41.00	37.45	7.00
1955-60	24.62	152.00	36.50	44.00	40.19	7.50
1960-65	22.77	145.00	39.00	47.00	42.94	8.00
1965-70	20.87	140.00	41.50	50.00	45.69	8.50
1970-75	19.30	130.00	44.00	53.00	48.43	9.00
1975-80	16.50	122.73	46.50	55.50	50.93	9.00
1980-85	13.91	111.00	49.00	58.00	53.43	9.00
1985-90	12.43	100.00	51.50	60.50	55.93	9.00
1990-95	10.96	89.00	54.00	63.00	58.43	9.00
2000-05	8.45	69.00	59.00	67.78	63.33	8.78
2010-15	6.67	51.00	63.58	71.38	67.42	7.80
2020-25	5.68	35.00	66.98	74.02	70.45	7.04

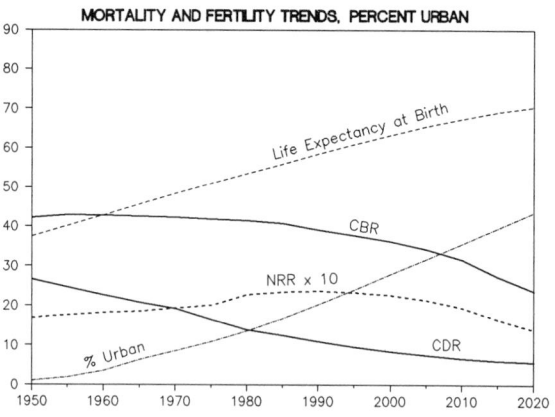

FERTILITY MEASURES (Annual Averages)

PERIOD	CRUDE BIRTH RATE	FERTILITY RATES GENERAL	FERTILITY RATES TOTAL	REPRODUCTION RATES GROSS	REPRODUCTION RATES NET	RATE OF NATUR. INCR.
1950-55	42.33	174.15	5.844	2.879	1.693	15.70
1955-60	43.00	175.16	5.865	2.889	1.772	18.38
1960-65	42.88	173.86	5.806	2.860	1.825	20.11
1965-70	42.68	173.20	5.708	2.812	1.863	21.81
1970-75	42.41	172.89	5.743	2.829	1.943	23.11
1975-80	41.92	171.73	5.743	2.829	2.012	25.42
1980-85	41.63	172.84	5.785	2.850	2.281	27.72
1985-90	40.85	172.75	5.785	2.850	2.358	28.42
1990-95	39.30	167.99	5.643	2.780	2.372	28.34
2000-05	36.24	152.15	5.116	2.520	2.267	27.79
2010-15	31.69	128.30	4.243	2.090	1.949	25.01
2020-25	23.70	89.55	2.964	1.460	1.391	18.03

AGING MEASURES

YEAR	POPULATION AGE RATIOS 60+/20-59	POPULATION AGE RATIOS 65+/20-64	POPULATION AGE RATIOS 70+/20-69	POPULATION AGE RATIOS 75+/20-74	POPULATION MEAN AGE	POPULATION MEDIAN AGE
1950	0.1624	0.0990	0.0532	0.0242	24.68	19.78
1960	0.1414	0.0868	0.0476	0.0222	24.26	19.68
1970	0.1330	0.0789	0.0436	0.0207	23.96	19.48
1980	0.1340	0.0804	0.0438	0.0201	23.75	19.02
1990	0.1396	0.0854	0.0472	0.0225	23.44	18.45
2000	0.1459	0.0893	0.0503	0.0249	23.54	18.49
2010	0.1474	0.0927	0.0534	0.0267	24.06	19.34
2020	0.1467	0.0933	0.0559	0.0290	25.50	21.24

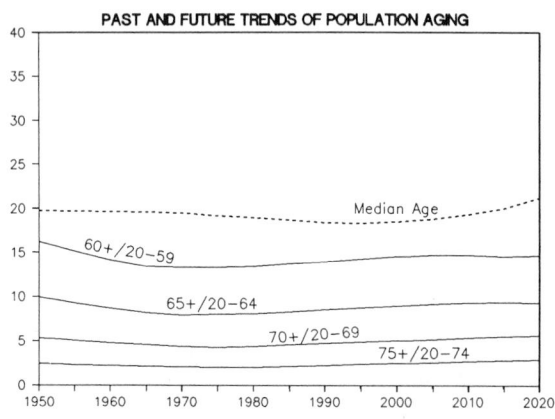

OBSERVED AND *PROJECTED* POPULATION DATA

YEAR	MID-YEAR POPULATION	NO. OF BIRTHS	NO. OF DEATHS	URBAN POPULATION		POPULATION 1985	
				NUMBER	PERCENT	AGE	NUMBER
1950	823900	38001	21390	106866	13.0	0	399912
1955	911361	42192	21576	142110	15.6	5	318428
1960	1036523	47754	22411	193128	18.6	10	262667
1965	1187465	54369	23379	262533	22.1	15	217319
1970	1369284	62565	24481	356372	26.0	20	182095
1975	1590054	71859	25624	482854	30.4	25	152913
1980	1855528	83469	26849	647977	34.9	30	128289
1985	2178235	98060	28912	861077	39.5	35	109407
1990	*2553780*	*113733*	*30745*	*1124298*	*44.0*	40	94757
1995	*3005411*	*131147*	*32531*	*1449916*	*48.2*	45	80829
2000	*3542558*	*149531*	*34196*	*1844209*	*52.1*	50	66784
2005	*4170336*	*167139*	*35590*	*2323586*	*55.7*	55	53633
2010	*4884394*	*180859*	*36521*	*2891045*	*59.2*	60	41688
2015	*5663660*	*186737*	*36887*	*3537378*	*62.5*	65	30575
2020	*6465991*	*184242*	*38033*	*4235968*	*65.5*	70+	38937

AGE DISTRIBUTIONS, 1960 - 1985

POPULATION RATIOS

YEAR	AGE DISTRIBUTION				DEPENDENCY RATIO	WOMEN 15-49	CHILD-WOMAN RATIO
	UNDER 15	15-64	65 & OLDER	70 & OLDER			
1950	0.415	0.555	0.030	0.016	0.802	0.240	0.700
1955	0.418	0.552	0.030	0.016	0.811	0.238	0.717
1960	0.419	0.550	0.031	0.016	0.818	0.234	0.743
1965	0.425	0.544	0.031	0.017	0.839	0.228	0.772
1970	0.432	0.536	0.031	0.017	0.864	0.224	0.797
1975	0.439	0.529	0.032	0.017	0.889	0.220	0.822
1980	0.445	0.523	0.032	0.018	0.911	0.218	0.836
1985	0.450	0.518	0.032	0.018	0.932	0.216	0.851
1990	*0.457*	*0.511*	*0.032*	*0.018*	*0.957*	*0.215*	*0.864*
2000	*0.463*	*0.505*	*0.032*	*0.019*	*0.980*	*0.218*	*0.847*
2010	*0.451*	*0.516*	*0.033*	*0.019*	*0.938*	*0.225*	*0.769*
2020	*0.414*	*0.552*	*0.034*	*0.020*	*0.813*	*0.241*	*0.609*

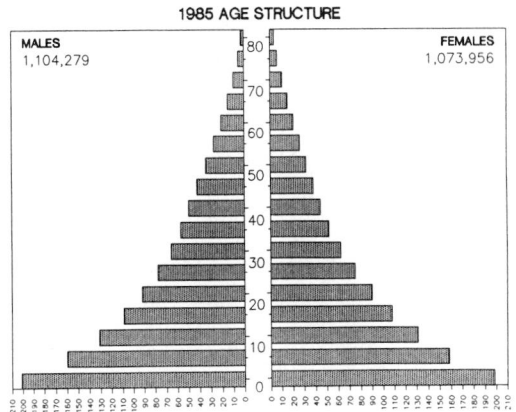

1985 AGE STRUCTURE

MALES 1,104,279   FEMALES 1,073,956

MORTALITY MEASURES (Annual Averages)

PERIOD	CRUDE DEATH RATE	INFANT MORT. RATE	LIFE EXPECTANCY AT BIRTH (years)			
			MALE	FEMALE	BOTH SEXES	DIFFERENCE FEMALE-MALE
1950-55	25.96	176.20	36.00	39.00	37.48	3.00
1955-60	23.67	160.47	38.50	41.50	39.98	3.00
1960-65	21.62	145.76	41.00	44.00	42.48	3.00
1965-70	19.69	132.03	43.50	46.50	44.98	3.00
1970-75	17.88	119.18	46.00	49.00	47.48	3.00
1975-80	16.11	107.30	48.50	51.50	49.98	3.00
1980-85	14.47	96.05	51.00	54.00	52.48	3.00
1985-90	*13.27*	*87.39*	*53.00*	*56.00*	*54.48*	*3.00*
1990-95	*12.04*	*79.01*	*55.00*	*58.00*	*56.48*	*3.00*
2000-05	*9.65*	*63.09*	*59.00*	*62.00*	*60.48*	*3.00*
2010-15	*7.48*	*48.45*	*63.00*	*66.00*	*64.48*	*3.00*
2020-25	*5.88*	*36.58*	*66.50*	*69.50*	*67.98*	*3.00*

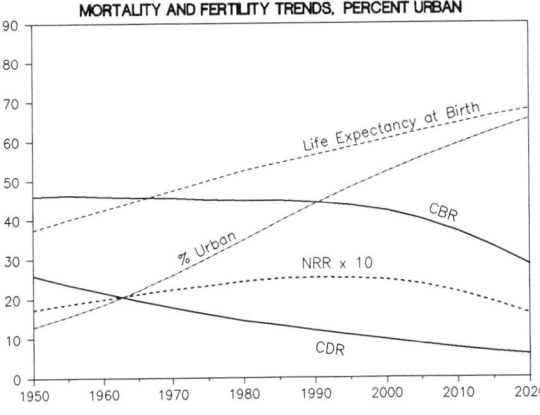

MORTALITY AND FERTILITY TRENDS, PERCENT URBAN

FERTILITY MEASURES (Annual Averages)

PERIOD	CRUDE BIRTH RATE	FERTILITY RATES		REPRODUCTION RATES		RATE OF NATUR. INCR.
		GENERAL	TOTAL	GROSS	NET	
1950-55	46.12	193.13	6.090	3.000	1.743	20.16
1955-60	46.30	196.39	6.191	3.050	1.869	22.62
1960-65	46.07	199.62	6.293	3.100	1.995	24.45
1965-70	45.79	202.74	6.394	3.150	2.122	26.10
1970-75	45.69	206.03	6.496	3.200	2.252	27.81
1975-80	45.19	206.60	6.496	3.200	2.347	29.08
1980-85	44.98	207.66	6.496	3.200	2.441	30.51
1985-90	*45.02*	*208.89*	*6.496*	*3.200*	*2.513*	*31.75*
1990-95	*44.53*	*206.67*	*6.394*	*3.150*	*2.542*	*32.50*
2000-05	*42.21*	*192.49*	*5.928*	*2.920*	*2.478*	*32.56*
2010-15	*37.03*	*161.73*	*4.973*	*2.450*	*2.174*	*29.55*
2020-25	*28.49*	*115.01*	*3.552*	*1.750*	*1.609*	*22.61*

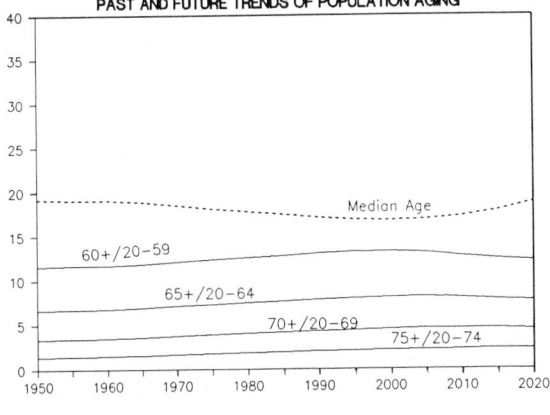

PAST AND FUTURE TRENDS OF POPULATION AGING

AGING MEASURES

YEAR	POPULATION AGE RATIOS				POPULATION	
	60+/20-59	65+/20-64	70+/20-69	75+/20-74	MEAN AGE	MEDIAN AGE
1950	0.1161	0.0663	0.0337	0.0142	23.55	19.22
1960	0.1174	0.0677	0.0348	0.0150	23.41	19.08
1970	0.1213	0.0711	0.0374	0.0166	23.15	18.52
1980	0.1261	0.0749	0.0402	0.0184	22.76	17.79
1990	*0.1305*	*0.0782*	*0.0427*	*0.0200*	*22.29*	*17.12*
2000	*0.1326*	*0.0807*	*0.0447*	*0.0214*	*21.96*	*16.80*
2010	*0.1275*	*0.0800*	*0.0457*	*0.0224*	*22.14*	*17.26*
2020	*0.1224*	*0.0768*	*0.0448*	*0.0230*	*23.28*	*18.84*

OBSERVED AND *PROJECTED* POPULATION DATA (000's)

YEAR	MID-YEAR POPULATION	NO. OF BIRTHS	NO. OF DEATHS	URBAN POPULATION NUMBER	URBAN POPULATION PERCENT	POPULATION AGE	1985 NUMBER
1950	1029	49	23	191	18.6	0	703
1955	1126	55	22	232	20.6	5	571
1960	1349	66	25	307	22.7	10	483
1965	1623	80	27	425	26.2	15	386
1970	1986	97	29	712	35.8	20	296
1975	2446	116	31	1145	46.8	25	264
1980	3043	139	33	1723	56.6	30	238
1985	3786	166	36	2440	64.5	35	206
1990	*4544*	*197*	*37*	*3189*	*70.2*	40	168
1995	*5445*	*229*	*38*	*4027*	*73.9*	45	136
2000	*6500*	*258*	*39*	*4948*	*76.1*	50	108
2005	*7695*	*277*	*40*	*6012*	*78.1*	55	81
2010	*8977*	*285*	*42*	*7178*	*80.0*	60	59
2015	*10278*	*289*	*45*	*8390*	*81.6*	65	40
2020	*11571*	*291*	*49*	*9622*	*83.2*	70+	47

POPULATION RATIOS

YEAR	AGE DISTRIBUTION UNDER 15	15-64	65 & OLDER	70 & OLDER	DEPENDENCY RATIO	WOMEN 15-49	CHILD-WOMAN RATIO
1950	0.419	0.534	0.047	0.027	0.874	0.225	0.746
1955	0.430	0.527	0.043	0.025	0.899	0.227	0.768
1960	0.433	0.527	0.040	0.023	0.897	0.225	0.785
1965	0.434	0.530	0.036	0.022	0.886	0.218	0.826
1970	0.449	0.523	0.027	0.016	0.911	0.212	0.898
1975	0.460	0.517	0.023	0.012	0.933	0.206	0.956
1980	0.467	0.511	0.022	0.012	0.957	0.203	0.926
1985	0.464	0.513	0.023	0.013	0.950	0.206	0.902
1990	*0.458*	*0.517*	*0.024*	*0.013*	*0.934*	*0.211*	*0.866*
2000	*0.457*	*0.515*	*0.028*	*0.015*	*0.942*	*0.215*	*0.841*
2010	*0.437*	*0.531*	*0.033*	*0.018*	*0.885*	*0.226*	*0.709*
2020	*0.379*	*0.583*	*0.039*	*0.023*	*0.717*	*0.251*	*0.513*

MORTALITY MEASURES (Annual Averages)

PERIOD	CRUDE DEATH RATE	INFANT MORT. RATE	LIFE EXPECTANCY AT BIRTH (years) MALE	FEMALE	BOTH SEXES	DIFFERENCE FEMALE-MALE
1950-55	22.50	185.00	41.90	43.90	42.88	2.00
1955-60	19.90	170.00	44.30	46.60	45.42	2.30
1960-65	18.30	150.00	46.70	49.20	47.92	2.50
1965-70	16.80	130.00	49.00	51.80	50.37	2.80
1970-75	14.80	117.00	51.40	54.50	52.91	3.10
1975-80	12.70	107.00	54.10	57.50	55.76	3.40
1980-85	10.85	96.50	56.60	60.00	58.26	3.40
1985-90	*9.41*	*82.06*	*59.05*	*62.46*	*60.71*	*3.41*
1990-95	*8.15*	*68.33*	*61.58*	*65.00*	*63.25*	*3.42*
2000-05	*6.00*	*44.57*	*65.91*	*69.76*	*67.79*	*3.85*
2010-15	*4.72*	*30.00*	*68.91*	*73.30*	*71.05*	*4.38*
2020-25	*4.24*	*21.04*	*71.08*	*75.69*	*73.33*	*4.61*

FERTILITY MEASURES (Annual Averages)

PERIOD	CRUDE BIRTH RATE	FERTILITY RATES GENERAL	TOTAL	REPRODUCTION RATES GROSS	NET	RATE OF NATUR. INCR.
1950-55	48.00	212.41	6.867	3.350	2.170	25.50
1955-60	48.50	214.79	6.970	3.400	2.320	28.60
1960-65	49.00	221.89	7.175	3.500	2.490	30.70
1965-70	49.50	230.81	7.482	3.650	2.720	32.70
1970-75	49.00	234.95	7.585	3.700	2.870	34.20
1975-80	47.30	231.36	7.380	3.600	2.900	34.60
1980-85	45.64	223.01	7.175	3.500	2.857	34.79
1985-90	*43.94*	*210.78*	*6.867*	*3.350*	*2.827*	*34.53*
1990-95	*43.43*	*204.85*	*6.662*	*3.250*	*2.832*	*35.28*
2000-05	*39.69*	*183.08*	*5.842*	*2.850*	*2.623*	*33.69*
2010-15	*31.74*	*136.63*	*4.346*	*2.120*	*2.014*	*27.02*
2020-25	*25.13*	*97.96*	*2.993*	*1.460*	*1.413*	*20.89*

AGING MEASURES

YEAR	POPULATION AGE RATIOS 60+/20-59	65+/20-64	70+/20-69	75+/20-74	POPULATION MEAN AGE	MEDIAN AGE
1950	0.1776	0.1089	0.0604	0.0263	24.27	19.05
1960	0.1455	0.0938	0.0518	0.0218	23.24	18.35
1970	0.1091	0.0651	0.0363	0.0180	22.08	17.51
1980	0.0923	0.0538	0.0283	0.0127	21.53	16.79
1990	*0.1034*	*0.0595*	*0.0311*	*0.0140*	*21.84*	*16.96*
2000	*0.1174*	*0.0687*	*0.0360*	*0.0163*	*22.00*	*17.07*
2010	*0.1296*	*0.0775*	*0.0422*	*0.0198*	*22.72*	*17.91*
2020	*0.1300*	*0.0829*	*0.0472*	*0.0228*	*24.58*	*20.39*

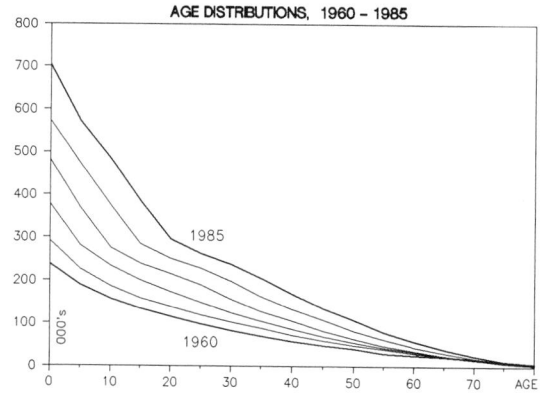

AGE DISTRIBUTIONS, 1960 - 1985

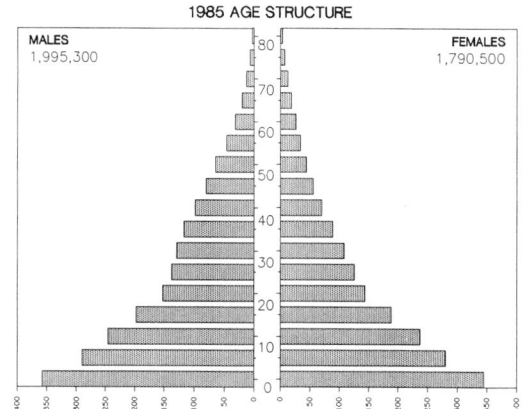

1985 AGE STRUCTURE

MALES 1,995,300   FEMALES 1,790,500

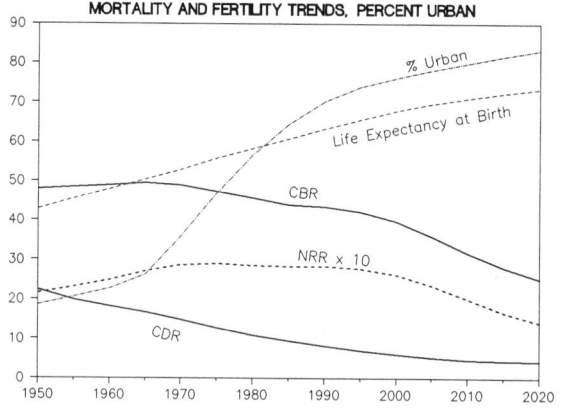

MORTALITY AND FERTILITY TRENDS, PERCENT URBAN

% Urban
Life Expectancy at Birth
CBR
NRR x 10
CDR

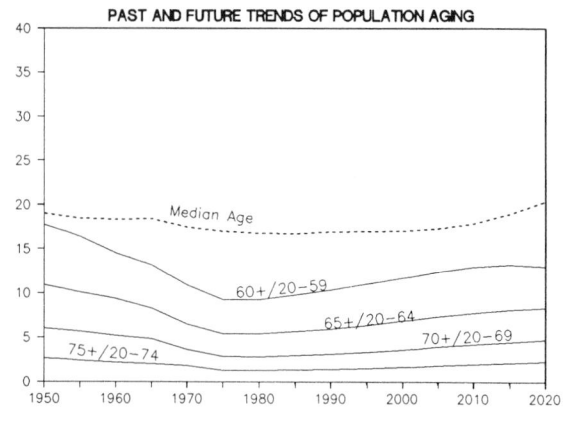

PAST AND FUTURE TRENDS OF POPULATION AGING

Median Age
60+/20-59
65+/20-64
70+/20-69
75+/20-74

OBSERVED AND *PROJECTED* POPULATION DATA (000's)

YEAR	MID-YEAR POPULATION	NO. OF BIRTHS	NO. OF DEATHS	URBAN POPULATION NUMBER	URBAN POPULATION PERCENT	POPULATION AGE	1985 NUMBER
1950	4230	204	112	330	7.8	0	1833
1955	4718	227	116	429	9.1	5	1477
1960	5309	254	121	562	10.6	10	1233
1965	6016	283	128	740	12.3	15	1059
1970	6742	310	128	951	14.1	20	905
1975	7593	346	127	1238	16.3	25	747
1980	8777	402	135	1655	18.9	30	604
1985	10221	467	143	2225	21.8	35	508
1990	*11980*	*536*	*151*	*2999*	*25.0*	40	430
1995	*14074*	*616*	*159*	*4027*	*28.6*	45	367
2000	*16562*	*688*	*165*	*5372*	*32.4*	50	308
2005	*19407*	*758*	*169*	*7060*	*36.4*	55	249
2010	*22594*	*815*	*171*	*9124*	*40.4*	60	195
2015	*26062*	*831*	*170*	*11567*	*44.4*	65	141
2020	*29588*	*812*	*169*	*14295*	*48.3*	70+	165

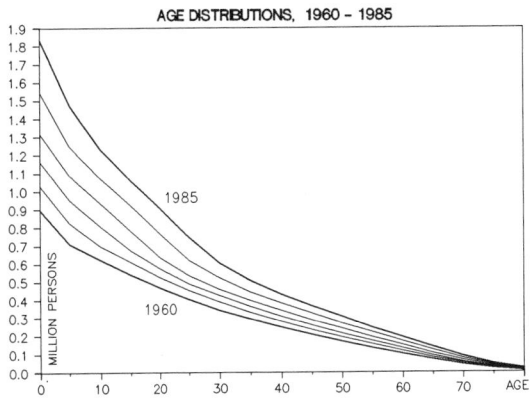

AGE DISTRIBUTIONS, 1960 - 1985

POPULATION RATIOS

YEAR	AGE DISTRIBUTION UNDER 15	15-64	65 & OLDER	70 & OLDER	DEPENDENCY RATIO	WOMEN 15-49	CHILD-WOMAN RATIO
1950	0.418	0.554	0.027	0.014	0.805	0.242	0.689
1955	0.418	0.555	0.028	0.014	0.803	0.242	0.684
1960	0.420	0.552	0.028	0.014	0.813	0.240	0.701
1965	0.424	0.547	0.028	0.015	0.827	0.238	0.717
1970	0.434	0.537	0.029	0.015	0.861	0.233	0.738
1975	0.440	0.530	0.030	0.016	0.885	0.230	0.754
1980	0.441	0.529	0.030	0.016	0.889	0.230	0.766
1985	0.445	0.526	0.030	0.016	0.903	0.229	0.784
1990	*0.451*	*0.519*	*0.030*	*0.016*	*0.925*	*0.226*	*0.803*
2000	*0.455*	*0.515*	*0.029*	*0.016*	*0.940*	*0.226*	*0.796*
2010	*0.440*	*0.531*	*0.029*	*0.016*	*0.884*	*0.232*	*0.714*
2020	*0.401*	*0.568*	*0.031*	*0.017*	*0.761*	*0.246*	*0.571*

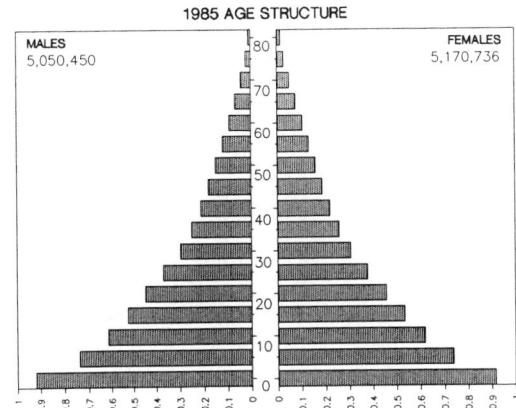

1985 AGE STRUCTURE

MALES 5,050,450   FEMALES 5,170,736

MORTALITY MEASURES (Annual Averages)

PERIOD	CRUDE DEATH RATE	INFANT MORT. RATE	LIFE EXPECTANCY AT BIRTH (years) MALE	FEMALE	BOTH SEXES	DIFFERENCE FEMALE-MALE
1950-55	26.50	244.86	36.33	39.11	37.70	2.78
1955-60	24.59	227.54	38.30	41.14	39.70	2.84
1960-65	22.87	211.06	40.28	43.17	41.70	2.89
1965-70	21.22	195.45	42.25	45.19	43.70	2.94
1970-75	18.94	172.00	45.00	48.00	46.48	3.00
1975-80	16.68	150.00	48.00	51.00	49.48	3.00
1980-85	15.36	130.00	50.00	53.00	51.48	3.00
1985-90	*14.02*	*120.00*	*52.00*	*55.00*	*53.48*	*3.00*
1990-95	*12.63*	*110.00*	*54.00*	*57.00*	*55.48*	*3.00*
2000-05	*9.94*	*90.00*	*58.00*	*61.00*	*59.48*	*3.00*
2010-15	*7.56*	*67.71*	*62.00*	*65.00*	*63.48*	*3.00*
2020-25	*5.72*	*46.75*	*66.00*	*69.00*	*67.48*	*3.00*

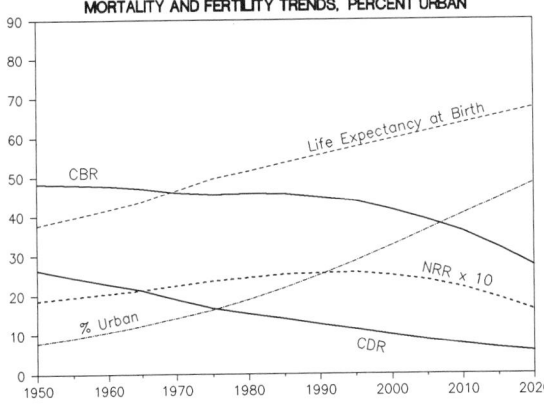

MORTALITY AND FERTILITY TRENDS, PERCENT URBAN

FERTILITY MEASURES (Annual Averages)

PERIOD	CRUDE BIRTH RATE	FERTILITY RATES GENERAL	TOTAL	REPRODUCTION RATES GROSS	NET	RATE OF NATUR. INCR.
1950-55	48.32	199.91	6.597	3.250	1.878	21.81
1955-60	48.19	199.92	6.597	3.250	1.963	23.59
1960-65	47.83	199.83	6.597	3.250	2.048	24.96
1965-70	47.03	199.44	6.597	3.250	2.132	25.81
1970-75	45.99	198.58	6.597	3.250	2.247	27.04
1975-80	45.62	198.40	6.597	3.250	2.367	28.93
1980-85	45.76	199.60	6.597	3.250	2.444	30.40
1985-90	*45.71*	*200.94*	*6.597*	*3.250*	*2.521*	*31.69*
1990-95	*44.78*	*198.22*	*6.496*	*3.200*	*2.554*	*32.15*
2000-05	*41.57*	*182.89*	*6.029*	*2.970*	*2.500*	*31.63*
2010-15	*36.07*	*153.23*	*5.034*	*2.480*	*2.191*	*28.51*
2020-25	*27.43*	*108.73*	*3.552*	*1.750*	*1.613*	*21.71*

AGING MEASURES

YEAR	POPULATION AGE RATIOS 60+/20-59	65+/20-64	70+/20-69	75+/20-74	POPULATION MEAN AGE	MEDIAN AGE
1950	0.1086	0.0608	0.0301	0.0124	23.28	19.01
1960	0.1106	0.0623	0.0310	0.0128	23.26	18.91
1970	0.1163	0.0662	0.0335	0.0140	23.00	18.32
1980	0.1219	0.0705	0.0363	0.0157	22.67	17.82
1990	*0.1209*	*0.0713*	*0.0376*	*0.0167*	*22.23*	*17.41*
2000	*0.1183*	*0.0709*	*0.0381*	*0.0174*	*22.01*	*17.14*
2010	*0.1130*	*0.0684*	*0.0377*	*0.0177*	*22.39*	*17.77*
2020	*0.1132*	*0.0673*	*0.0371*	*0.0177*	*23.67*	*19.46*

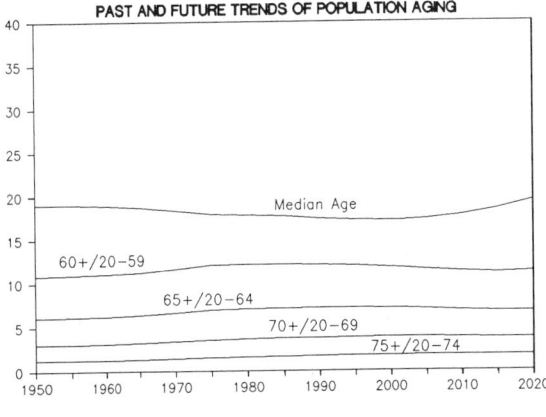

PAST AND FUTURE TRENDS OF POPULATION AGING

OBSERVED AND *PROJECTED* POPULATION DATA (000's)

YEAR	MID-YEAR POPULATION	NO. OF BIRTHS	NO. OF DEATHS	URBAN POPULATION NUMBER	URBAN POPULATION PERCENT	POPULATION 1985 AGE	POPULATION 1985 NUMBER
1950	2881	151	89	101	3.5	0	1369
1955	3169	169	92	124	3.9	5	1025
1960	3529	189	97	155	4.4	10	893
1965	3975	213	101	194	4.9	15	757
1970	4518	239	106	273	6.0	20	618
1975	5244	278	121	402	7.7	25	508
1980	6091	324	130	589	9.7	30	415
1985	7141	379	143	860	12.0	35	365
1990	8428	434	154	1244	14.8	40	299
1995	9950	487	165	1769	17.8	45	243
2000	11706	548	174	2461	21.0	50	196
2005	13735	595	181	3348	24.4	55	153
2010	15972	620	185	4468	28.0	60	116
2015	18303	618	185	5814	31.8	65	91
2020	20605	601	183	7355	35.7	70+	92

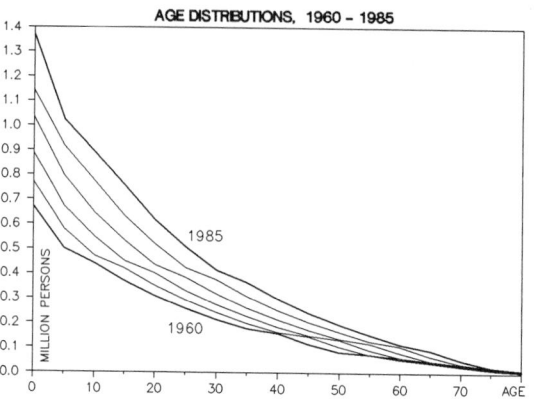

AGE DISTRIBUTIONS, 1960 - 1985

POPULATION RATIOS

YEAR	AGE DISTRIBUTION UNDER 15	15-64	65 & OLDER	70 & OLDER	DEPENDENCY RATIO	WOMEN 15-49	CHILD-WOMAN RATIO
1950	0.457	0.512	0.031	0.017	0.952	0.229	0.841
1955	0.456	0.516	0.028	0.015	0.939	0.233	0.793
1960	0.457	0.517	0.026	0.014	0.934	0.236	0.804
1965	0.458	0.518	0.024	0.013	0.931	0.237	0.817
1970	0.467	0.510	0.023	0.012	0.960	0.232	0.847
1975	0.472	0.506	0.022	0.012	0.976	0.229	0.860
1980	0.465	0.512	0.023	0.012	0.954	0.231	0.812
1985	0.460	0.514	0.026	0.013	0.945	0.232	0.828
1990	0.461	0.513	0.027	0.015	0.951	0.230	0.850
2000	0.466	0.506	0.028	0.016	0.976	0.222	0.848
2010	0.448	0.522	0.030	0.017	0.917	0.227	0.764
2020	0.402	0.564	0.034	0.020	0.773	0.243	0.584

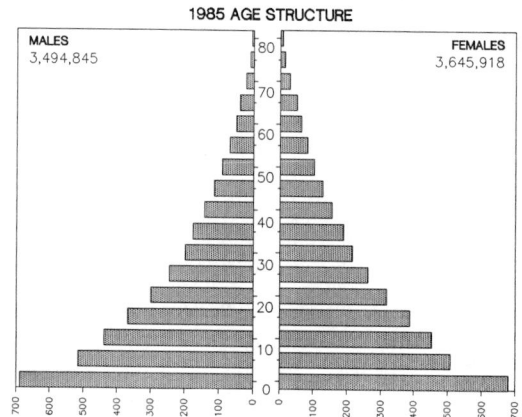

1985 AGE STRUCTURE

MALES 3,494,845   FEMALES 3,645,918

MORTALITY MEASURES (Annual Averages)

PERIOD	CRUDE DEATH RATE	INFANT MORT. RATE	LIFE EXPECTANCY AT BIRTH (years) MALE	FEMALE	BOTH SEXES	DIFFERENCE FEMALE-MALE
1950-55	30.89	212.00	35.83	36.67	36.24	0.84
1955-60	29.07	208.52	36.73	37.59	37.15	0.86
1960-65	27.47	203.50	37.78	39.12	38.44	1.34
1965-70	25.46	197.38	38.92	40.19	39.55	1.27
1970-75	23.46	190.52	40.33	41.67	40.99	1.34
1975-80	23.08	177.00	42.36	43.67	43.01	1.30
1980-85	21.42	163.00	44.38	45.65	45.01	1.28
1985-90	19.97	150.46	46.30	47.71	46.99	1.41
1990-95	18.31	138.34	48.36	49.66	49.00	1.31
2000-05	14.88	117.12	52.38	53.65	53.01	1.28
2010-15	11.59	98.71	56.29	57.67	56.97	1.38
2020-25	8.88	81.47	60.29	61.69	60.98	1.40

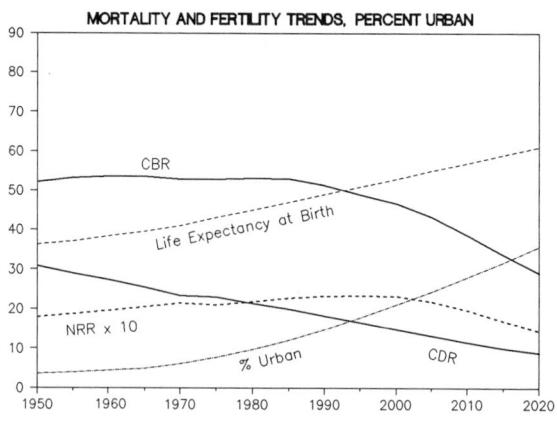

MORTALITY AND FERTILITY TRENDS, PERCENT URBAN

FERTILITY MEASURES (Annual Averages)

PERIOD	CRUDE BIRTH RATE	FERTILITY RATES GENERAL	TOTAL	REPRODUCTION RATES GROSS	NET	RATE OF NATUR. INCR.
1950-55	52.30	226.15	6.780	3.340	1.800	21.41
1955-60	53.22	226.71	6.841	3.370	1.880	24.15
1960-65	53.58	226.50	6.861	3.380	1.960	26.11
1965-70	53.63	228.93	6.922	3.410	2.060	28.17
1970-75	53.00	229.77	6.922	3.410	2.150	29.54
1975-80	52.98	230.06	7.003	3.450	2.110	29.90
1980-85	53.14	229.69	7.003	3.450	2.194	31.72
1985-90	53.03	230.02	7.003	3.450	2.279	33.06
1990-95	51.46	227.09	6.902	3.400	2.328	33.14
2000-05	46.79	210.26	6.435	3.170	2.324	31.91
2010-15	38.80	168.56	5.136	2.530	1.972	27.20
2020-25	29.15	117.16	3.552	1.750	1.441	20.27

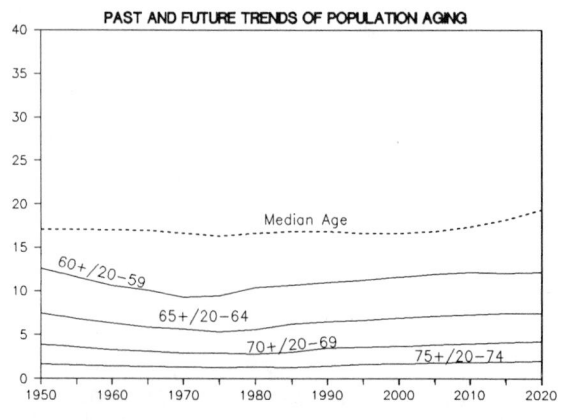

PAST AND FUTURE TRENDS OF POPULATION AGING

AGING MEASURES

YEAR	POPULATION AGE RATIOS 60+/20-59	65+/20-64	70+/20-69	75+/20-74	POPULATION MEAN AGE	POPULATION MEDIAN AGE
1950	0.1257	0.0745	0.0389	0.0167	21.98	17.12
1960	0.1062	0.0633	0.0333	0.0146	21.65	17.05
1970	0.0929	0.0567	0.0295	0.0132	21.29	16.68
1980	0.1038	0.0564	0.0283	0.0133	21.47	16.68
1990	0.1098	0.0649	0.0348	0.0144	21.60	16.88
2000	0.1164	0.0692	0.0373	0.0172	21.70	16.67
2010	0.1218	0.0731	0.0400	0.0187	22.22	17.41
2020	0.1218	0.0749	0.0428	0.0205	23.74	19.37

OBSERVED AND *PROJECTED* POPULATION DATA (000's)

YEAR	MID-YEAR POPULATION	NO. OF BIRTHS	NO. OF DEATHS	URBAN POPULATION NUMBER	URBAN POPULATION PERCENT	POPULATION AGE	1985 NUMBER
1950	3850	188	122	327	8.5	0	1550
1955	4196	209	125	407	9.7	5	1195
1960	4636	236	132	513	11.1	10	994
1965	5105	263	139	643	12.6	15	842
1970	5685	291	147	814	14.3	20	684
1975	6293	320	154	1020	16.2	25	550
1980	7023	355	158	1214	17.3	30	450
1985	8082	405	168	1453	18.0	35	411
1990	*9362*	*459*	*178*	*1793*	*19.2*	40	342
1995	*10878*	*517*	*188*	*2269*	*20.9*	45	282
2000	*12658*	*577*	*198*	*2932*	*23.2*	50	231
2005	*14706*	*631*	*207*	*3843*	*26.1*	55	186
2010	*16992*	*668*	*213*	*5069*	*29.8*	60	145
2015	*19435*	*670*	*214*	*6550*	*33.7*	65	102
2020	*21855*	*648*	*214*	*8234*	*37.7*	70+	119

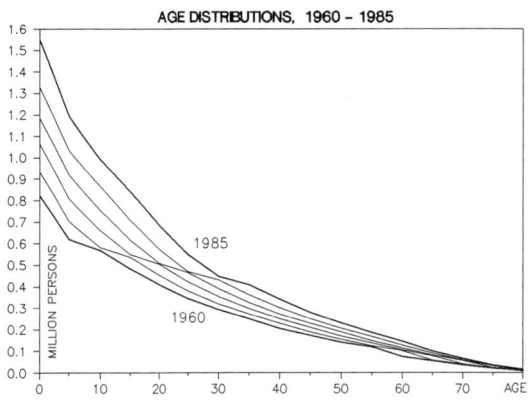

AGE DISTRIBUTIONS, 1960 - 1985

POPULATION RATIOS

YEAR	AGE DISTRIBUTION UNDER 15	AGE DISTRIBUTION 15-64	AGE DISTRIBUTION 65 & OLDER	AGE DISTRIBUTION 70 & OLDER	DEPENDENCY RATIO	WOMEN 15-49	CHILD-WOMAN RATIO
1950	0.439	0.530	0.031	0.017	0.886	0.237	0.775
1955	0.436	0.536	0.029	0.016	0.867	0.239	0.722
1960	0.434	0.540	0.026	0.014	0.852	0.240	0.737
1965	0.434	0.541	0.025	0.013	0.849	0.241	0.758
1970	0.446	0.528	0.026	0.013	0.894	0.237	0.790
1975	0.454	0.518	0.027	0.014	0.929	0.235	0.801
1980	0.460	0.513	0.028	0.015	0.951	0.234	0.808
1985	0.463	0.510	0.027	0.015	0.960	0.231	0.829
1990	*0.466*	*0.506*	*0.027*	*0.015*	*0.975*	*0.228*	*0.846*
2000	*0.468*	*0.505*	*0.027*	*0.015*	*0.979*	*0.225*	*0.838*
2010	*0.453*	*0.519*	*0.028*	*0.015*	*0.927*	*0.231*	*0.759*
2020	*0.413*	*0.558*	*0.029*	*0.017*	*0.792*	*0.247*	*0.594*

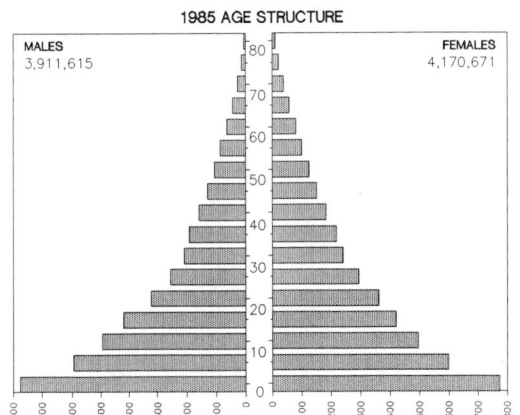

1985 AGE STRUCTURE

MALES 3,911,615   FEMALES 4,170,671

MORTALITY MEASURES (Annual Averages)

PERIOD	CRUDE DEATH RATE	INFANT MORT. RATE	LIFE EXPECTANCY AT BIRTH (years) MALE	LIFE EXPECTANCY AT BIRTH (years) FEMALE	LIFE EXPECTANCY AT BIRTH (years) BOTH SEXES	DIFFERENCE FEMALE-MALE
1950-55	31.74	213.30	31.05	34.00	32.50	2.95
1955-60	29.82	210.70	32.53	35.52	34.00	2.99
1960-65	28.58	208.20	34.01	37.04	35.50	3.03
1965-70	27.27	205.70	35.49	38.56	37.00	3.06
1970-75	25.88	203.10	36.97	40.07	38.50	3.10
1975-80	24.46	191.00	38.46	41.59	40.00	3.13
1980-85	22.52	179.50	40.44	43.61	42.00	3.17
1985-90	*20.78*	*169.00*	*42.42*	*45.63*	*44.00*	*3.21*
1990-95	*19.03*	*159.00*	*44.41*	*47.64*	*46.00*	*3.23*
2000-05	*15.67*	*138.00*	*48.33*	*51.72*	*50.00*	*3.38*
2010-15	*12.51*	*117.00*	*52.24*	*55.81*	*54.00*	*3.56*
2020-25	*9.77*	*98.00*	*56.20*	*59.86*	*58.00*	*3.66*

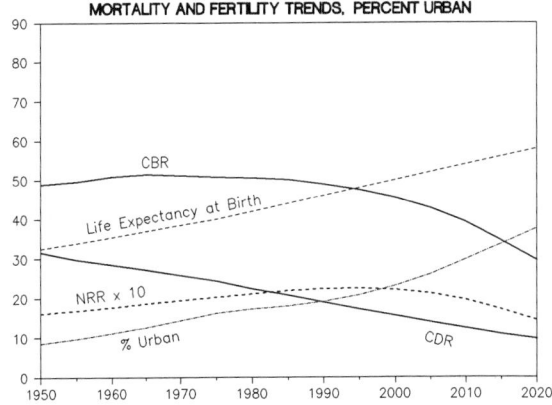

MORTALITY AND FERTILITY TRENDS, PERCENT URBAN

FERTILITY MEASURES (Annual Averages)

PERIOD	CRUDE BIRTH RATE	FERTILITY RATES GENERAL	FERTILITY RATES TOTAL	REPRODUCTION RATES GROSS	REPRODUCTION RATES NET	RATE OF NATUR. INCR.
1950-55	48.95	205.57	6.358	3.132	1.625	17.22
1955-60	49.72	207.47	6.390	3.148	1.698	19.90
1960-65	50.93	211.49	6.455	3.180	1.778	22.36
1965-70	51.57	215.71	6.575	3.239	1.875	24.30
1970-75	51.19	217.04	6.597	3.250	1.945	25.31
1975-80	50.88	216.91	6.699	3.300	2.037	26.43
1980-85	50.57	217.31	6.699	3.300	2.119	28.05
1985-90	*50.12*	*218.42*	*6.699*	*3.300*	*2.199*	*29.34*
1990-95	*48.99*	*216.07*	*6.597*	*3.250*	*2.244*	*29.96*
2000-05	*45.61*	*201.41*	*6.110*	*3.010*	*2.224*	*29.94*
2010-15	*39.33*	*167.71*	*5.075*	*2.500*	*1.964*	*26.83*
2020-25	*29.66*	*117.07*	*3.552*	*1.750*	*1.450*	*19.89*

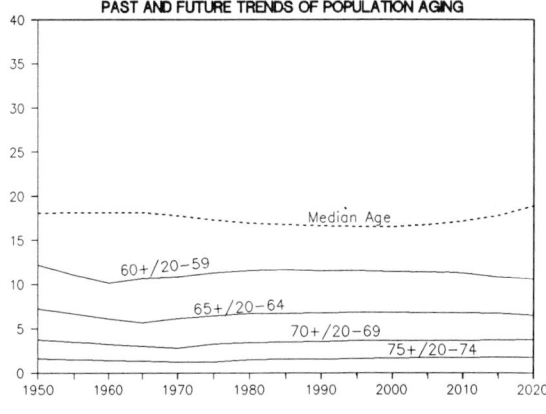

PAST AND FUTURE TRENDS OF POPULATION AGING

AGING MEASURES

YEAR	POPULATION AGE RATIOS 60+/20-59	POPULATION AGE RATIOS 65+/20-64	POPULATION AGE RATIOS 70+/20-69	POPULATION AGE RATIOS 75+/20-74	POPULATION MEAN AGE	POPULATION MEDIAN AGE
1950	0.1218	0.0723	0.0374	0.0161	22.69	18.08
1960	0.1014	0.0607	0.0323	0.0142	22.63	18.17
1970	0.1082	0.0613	0.0284	0.0126	22.32	17.81
1980	0.1153	0.0669	0.0344	0.0148	22.03	16.99
1990	*0.1158*	*0.0678*	*0.0353*	*0.0157*	*21.60*	*16.64*
2000	*0.1145*	*0.0681*	*0.0365*	*0.0166*	*21.44*	*16.55*
2010	*0.1125*	*0.0674*	*0.0366*	*0.0170*	*21.78*	*17.16*
2020	*0.1062*	*0.0649*	*0.0372*	*0.0176*	*23.08*	*18.87*

OBSERVED AND *PROJECTED* POPULATION DATA

YEAR	MID-YEAR POPULATION	NO. OF BIRTHS	NO. OF DEATHS	URBAN POPULATION NUMBER	URBAN POPULATION PERCENT	1985 AGE	1985 NUMBER
1950	824700	39863	25313	25083	3.0	0	318209
1955	900802	43293	26199	40670	4.5	5	251499
1960	990527	47224	27274	65902	6.7	10	210279
1965	1095569	51819	28067	106284	9.7	15	178147
1970	1221133	57371	29093	170192	13.9	20	150738
1975	1371211	64056	30345	269044	19.6	25	127701
1980	1550810	72066	31813	417137	26.9	30	107971
1985	1766038	81662	33507	611738	34.6	35	91750
1990	*2024432*	*91851*	*35260*	*851646*	*42.1*	40	77260
1995	*2328639*	*103331*	*37058*	*1129996*	*48.5*	45	65350
2000	*2685387*	*115157*	*38782*	*1439817*	*53.6*	50	54385
2005	*3096481*	*123757*	*40072*	*1771182*	*57.2*	55	44121
2010	*3545234*	*131191*	*41008*	*2147990*	*60.6*	60	34271
2015	*4026763*	*132134*	*41371*	*2567743*	*63.8*	65	24968
2020	*4507684*	*127824*	*41304*	*3007979*	*66.7*	70+	29388

POPULATION RATIOS

YEAR	AGE DISTRIBUTION UNDER 15	15-64	65 & OLDER	70 & OLDER	DEPENDENCY RATIO	WOMEN 15-49	CHILD-WOMAN RATIO
1950	0.417	0.556	0.027	0.014	0.799	0.240	0.711
1955	0.418	0.554	0.028	0.014	0.805	0.239	0.715
1960	0.421	0.551	0.028	0.014	0.816	0.238	0.727
1965	0.424	0.547	0.029	0.015	0.828	0.236	0.736
1970	0.428	0.542	0.029	0.015	0.844	0.234	0.748
1975	0.433	0.537	0.030	0.016	0.861	0.233	0.761
1980	0.437	0.532	0.030	0.016	0.878	0.231	0.774
1985	0.442	0.528	0.031	0.017	0.896	0.229	0.787
1990	*0.446*	*0.523*	*0.031*	*0.017*	*0.912*	*0.228*	*0.798*
2000	*0.449*	*0.520*	*0.031*	*0.017*	*0.924*	*0.227*	*0.789*
2010	*0.437*	*0.531*	*0.032*	*0.018*	*0.883*	*0.233*	*0.715*
2020	*0.399*	*0.567*	*0.034*	*0.020*	*0.764*	*0.248*	*0.570*

MORTALITY MEASURES (Annual Averages)

PERIOD	CRUDE DEATH RATE	INFANT MORT. RATE	LIFE EXPECTANCY AT BIRTH (years) MALE	FEMALE	BOTH SEXES	DIFFERENCE FEMALE-MALE
1950-55	30.69	207.34	31.54	34.51	33.00	2.97
1955-60	29.08	196.49	33.02	36.02	34.50	3.00
1960-65	27.53	185.93	34.50	37.54	36.00	3.04
1965-70	25.62	172.80	36.48	39.57	38.00	3.09
1970-75	23.83	160.36	38.46	41.59	40.00	3.13
1975-80	22.13	148.54	40.44	43.61	42.00	3.17
1980-85	20.51	137.31	42.42	45.63	44.00	3.21
1985-90	*18.97*	*126.64*	*44.41*	*47.64*	*46.00*	*3.23*
1990-95	*17.42*	*116.62*	*46.39*	*49.66*	*48.00*	*3.27*
2000-05	*14.44*	*98.27*	*50.28*	*53.77*	*52.00*	*3.49*
2010-15	*11.57*	*81.06*	*54.22*	*57.83*	*56.00*	*3.62*
2020-25	*9.16*	*65.03*	*58.19*	*61.87*	*60.00*	*3.68*

FERTILITY MEASURES (Annual Averages)

PERIOD	CRUDE BIRTH RATE	FERTILITY RATES GENERAL	TOTAL	REPRODUCTION RATES GROSS	NET	RATE OF NATUR. INCR.
1950-55	48.34	201.63	6.496	3.200	1.656	17.64
1955-60	48.06	201.62	6.496	3.200	1.721	18.98
1960-65	47.68	201.48	6.496	3.200	1.786	20.14
1965-70	47.30	201.32	6.496	3.200	1.869	21.68
1970-75	46.98	201.38	6.496	3.200	1.951	23.16
1975-80	46.72	201.74	6.496	3.200	2.032	24.59
1980-85	46.47	202.20	6.496	3.200	2.111	25.96
1985-90	*46.24*	*202.58*	*6.496*	*3.200*	*2.188*	*27.27*
1990-95	*45.37*	*199.65*	*6.394*	*3.150*	*2.231*	*27.95*
2000-05	*42.88*	*187.99*	*6.009*	*2.960*	*2.240*	*28.44*
2010-15	*37.01*	*156.76*	*4.994*	*2.460*	*1.974*	*25.44*
2020-25	*28.36*	*111.63*	*3.552*	*1.750*	*1.478*	*19.19*

AGING MEASURES

YEAR	POPULATION AGE RATIOS 60+/20-59	65+/20-64	70+/20-69	75+/20-74	POPULATION MEAN AGE	MEDIAN AGE
1950	0.1079	0.0597	0.0295	0.0120	23.33	19.11
1960	0.1113	0.0623	0.0308	0.0124	23.28	18.95
1970	0.1163	0.0663	0.0335	0.0139	23.13	18.59
1980	0.1213	0.0703	0.0364	0.0157	22.87	18.13
1990	*0.1247*	*0.0736*	*0.0391*	*0.0174*	*22.55*	*17.67*
2000	*0.1249*	*0.0750*	*0.0407*	*0.0187*	*22.37*	*17.47*
2010	*0.1225*	*0.0744*	*0.0412*	*0.0195*	*22.65*	*17.94*
2020	*0.1214*	*0.0742*	*0.0415*	*0.0201*	*23.85*	*19.54*

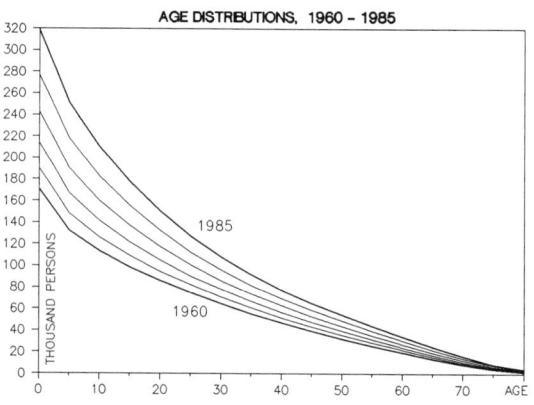

AGE DISTRIBUTIONS, 1960 - 1985

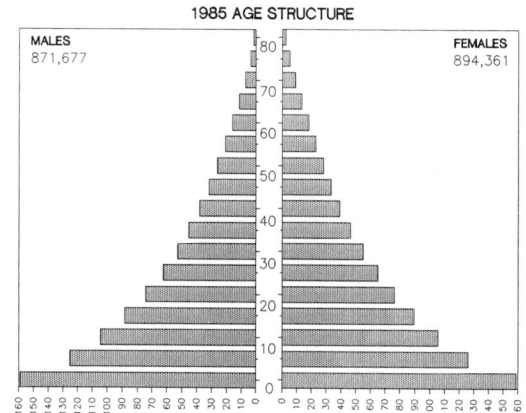

1985 AGE STRUCTURE

MALES 871,677 | FEMALES 894,361

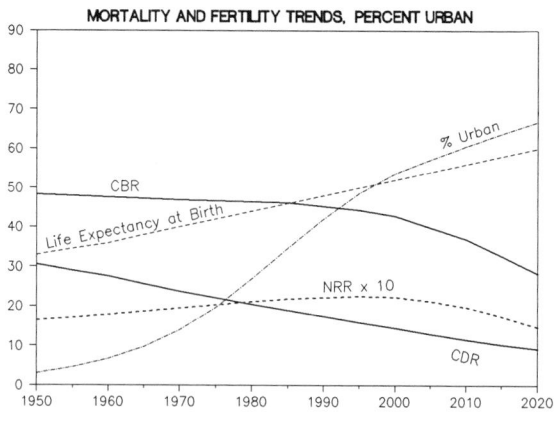

MORTALITY AND FERTILITY TRENDS, PERCENT URBAN

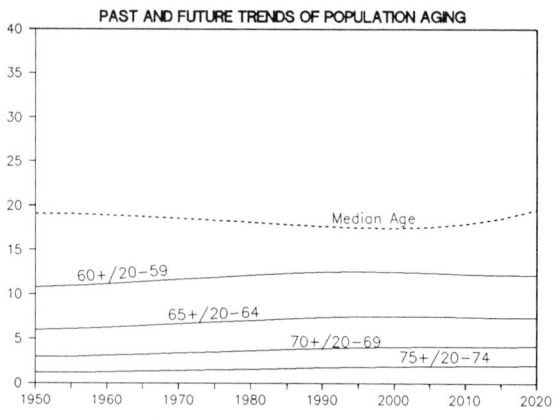

PAST AND FUTURE TRENDS OF POPULATION AGING

OBSERVED AND *PROJECTED* POPULATION DATA

YEAR	MID-YEAR POPULATION	NO. OF BIRTHS	NO. OF DEATHS	URBAN POPULATION NUMBER	PERCENT	POPULATION 1985 AGE	NUMBER
1950	487400	23059	7621	140160	28.8	0	106340
1955	563937	25192	5991	174389	30.9	5	113127
1960	660763	28067	6026	219225	33.2	10	97821
1965	774657	24916	6042	286632	37.0	15	112699
1970	848918	22158	5976	356839	42.0	20	127617
1975	869736	23176	5536	379627	43.6	25	97842
1980	956793	21494	5652	410452	42.9	30	78221
1985	1036332	19164	5636	436837	42.2	35	67732
1990	*1103189*	*19823*	*6164*	*467125*	*42.3*	40	57052
1995	*1171878*	*20040*	*6806*	*509439*	*43.5*	45	46557
2000	*1239966*	*19813*	*7540*	*564588*	*45.5*	50	39682
2005	*1302884*	*19279*	*8444*	*631881*	*48.5*	55	31251
2010	*1358207*	*18909*	*9507*	*710405*	*52.3*	60	23885
2015	*1406038*	*18721*	*10637*	*786698*	*56.0*	65	16703
2020	*1447047*	*18605*	*12094*	*859703*	*59.4*	70+	19805

POPULATION RATIOS

YEAR	AGE DISTRIBUTION UNDER 15	15-64	65 & OLDER	70 & OLDER	DEPENDENCY RATIO	WOMEN 15-49	CHILD-WOMAN RATIO
1950	0.452	0.519	0.030	0.017	0.928	0.227	0.797
1955	0.460	0.513	0.027	0.015	0.950	0.226	0.830
1960	0.466	0.509	0.025	0.014	0.964	0.224	0.830
1965	0.465	0.510	0.025	0.014	0.960	0.224	0.803
1970	0.438	0.536	0.026	0.014	0.864	0.233	0.598
1975	0.397	0.576	0.028	0.015	0.738	0.253	0.453
1980	0.341	0.628	0.031	0.017	0.592	0.276	0.433
1985	0.306	0.659	0.035	0.019	0.518	0.285	0.360
1990	*0.284*	*0.674*	*0.041*	*0.023*	*0.483*	*0.287*	*0.301*
2000	*0.237*	*0.707*	*0.057*	*0.032*	*0.415*	*0.288*	*0.281*
2010	*0.218*	*0.706*	*0.076*	*0.045*	*0.417*	*0.268*	*0.266*
2020	*0.197*	*0.698*	*0.105*	*0.063*	*0.433*	*0.238*	*0.273*

MORTALITY MEASURES (Annual Averages)

PERIOD	CRUDE DEATH RATE	INFANT MORT. RATE	LIFE EXPECTANCY AT BIRTH (years) MALE	FEMALE	BOTH SEXES	DIFFERENCE FEMALE-MALE
1950-55	15.64	99.30	49.74	52.37	51.03	2.63
1955-60	10.62	79.20	56.22	60.09	58.11	3.87
1960-65	9.12	60.96	58.68	61.90	60.26	3.23
1965-70	7.80	67.09	59.67	63.54	61.56	3.87
1970-75	7.04	55.42	60.68	65.31	62.94	4.63
1975-80	6.36	38.32	62.60	67.35	64.92	4.75
1980-85	5.91	28.38	64.29	69.20	66.69	4.91
1985-90	*5.44*	*23.01*	*66.35*	*71.73*	*68.98*	*5.38*
1990-95	*5.59*	*19.58*	*67.86*	*72.64*	*70.20*	*4.78*
2000-05	*6.08*	*14.50*	*70.22*	*75.03*	*72.57*	*4.81*
2010-15	*7.00*	*10.94*	*72.23*	*77.09*	*74.61*	*4.85*
2020-25	*8.36*	*8.49*	*74.06*	*78.86*	*76.41*	*4.80*

FERTILITY MEASURES (Annual Averages)

PERIOD	CRUDE BIRTH RATE	FERTILITY RATES GENERAL	TOTAL	REPRODUCTION RATES GROSS	NET	RATE OF NATUR. INCR.
1950-55	47.31	209.21	6.278	3.070	2.318	31.67
1955-60	44.67	198.75	5.980	2.924	2.460	34.05
1960-65	42.48	189.85	5.726	2.800	2.409	33.36
1965-70	32.16	140.61	4.247	2.077	1.821	24.36
1970-75	26.10	107.19	3.252	1.590	1.422	19.06
1975-80	26.65	100.54	3.067	1.500	1.371	20.28
1980-85	22.47	80.08	2.413	1.180	1.098	16.56
1985-90	*18.49*	*64.69*	*1.943*	*0.950*	*0.903*	*13.06*
1990-95	*17.97*	*62.20*	*1.943*	*0.950*	*0.909*	*12.38*
2000-05	*15.98*	*56.44*	*1.943*	*0.950*	*0.923*	*9.90*
2010-15	*13.92*	*53.90*	*1.943*	*0.950*	*0.933*	*6.92*
2020-25	*12.86*	*54.67*	*1.943*	*0.950*	*0.940*	*4.50*

AGING MEASURES

YEAR	POPULATION AGE RATIOS 60+/20-59	65+/20-64	70+/20-69	75+/20-74	POPULATION MEAN AGE	MEDIAN AGE
1950	0.1182	0.0716	0.0396	0.0192	22.12	17.33
1960	0.1049	0.0619	0.0335	0.0157	21.53	16.67
1970	0.1037	0.0605	0.0321	0.0148	22.55	17.81
1980	0.1080	0.0621	0.0332	0.0152	25.16	21.18
1990	*0.1202*	*0.0708*	*0.0376*	*0.0173*	*28.37*	*26.17*
2000	*0.1505*	*0.0912*	*0.0496*	*0.0236*	*31.48*	*30.60*
2010	*0.2009*	*0.1205*	*0.0670*	*0.0332*	*34.41*	*33.83*
2020	*0.2866*	*0.1673*	*0.0942*	*0.0466*	*37.11*	*37.24*

AGE DISTRIBUTIONS, 1960 - 1985

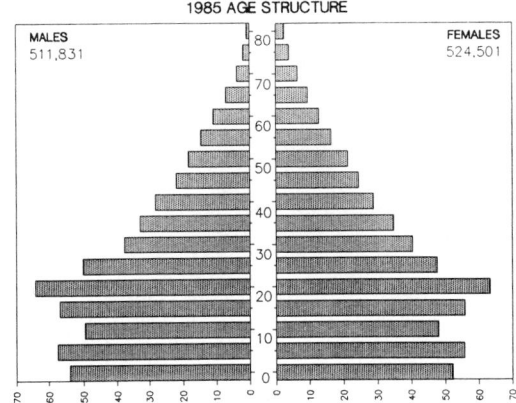

1985 AGE STRUCTURE

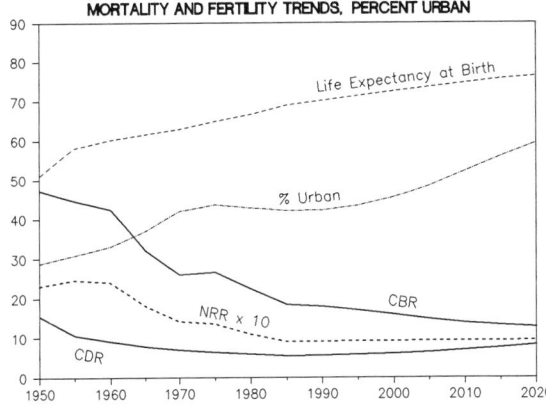

MORTALITY AND FERTILITY TRENDS, PERCENT URBAN

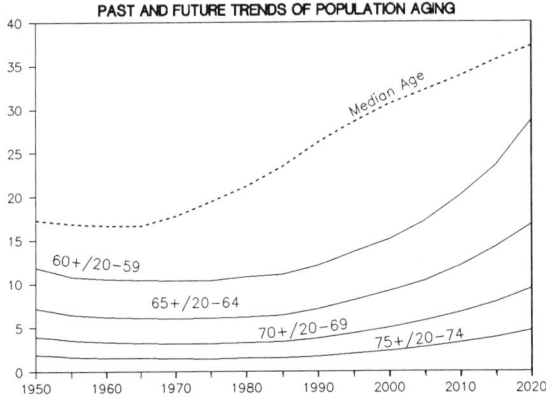

PAST AND FUTURE TRENDS OF POPULATION AGING

OBSERVED AND *PROJECTED* POPULATION DATA (000's)

YEAR	MID-YEAR POPULATION	NO. OF BIRTHS	NO. OF DEATHS	URBAN POPULATION NUMBER	URBAN POPULATION PERCENT	POPULATION AGE	1985 NUMBER
1950	8953	451	230	2345	26.2	0	3507
1955	10132	511	230	2809	27.7	5	3085
1960	11626	582	228	3409	29.3	10	2736
1965	13323	642	232	4251	31.9	15	2386
1970	15310	698	240	5300	34.6	20	2048
1975	17305	682	225	6547	37.8	25	1825
1980	19382	741	223	8000	41.3	30	1418
1985	22120	781	215	9910	44.8	35	1045
1990	*25139*	*797*	*207*	*12180*	*48.5*	40	765
1995	*28274*	*785*	*198*	*14740*	*52.1*	45	797
2000	*31366*	*745*	*193*	*17488*	*55.8*	50	640
2005	*34254*	*722*	*198*	*20290*	*59.2*	55	623
2010	*36977*	*706*	*205*	*23110*	*62.5*	60	383
2015	*39568*	*683*	*220*	*25937*	*65.6*	65	354
2020	*41953*	*710*	*240*	*28690*	*68.4*	70+	507

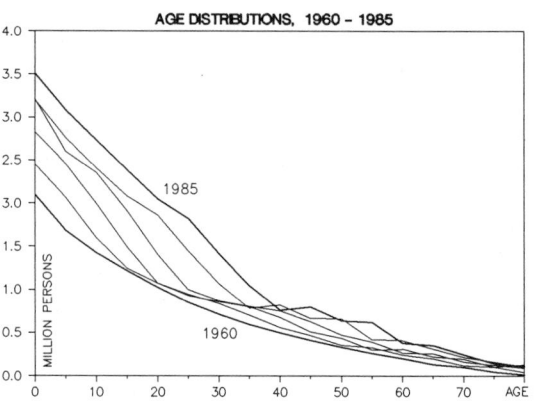

AGE DISTRIBUTIONS, 1960 – 1985

POPULATION RATIOS

YEAR	AGE DISTRIBUTION UNDER 15	15-64	65 & OLDER	70 & OLDER	DEPENDENCY RATIO	WOMEN 15-49	CHILD-WOMAN RATIO
1950	0.444	0.527	0.029	0.016	0.896	0.229	0.779
1955	0.446	0.527	0.027	0.015	0.899	0.229	0.783
1960	0.448	0.526	0.026	0.014	0.901	0.228	0.790
1965	0.459	0.506	0.035	0.020	0.975	0.223	0.825
1970	0.476	0.483	0.042	0.028	1.072	0.216	0.857
1975	0.472	0.492	0.037	0.022	1.034	0.219	0.845
1980	0.432	0.527	0.041	0.025	0.897	0.230	0.718
1985	0.422	0.539	0.039	0.023	0.854	0.236	0.673
1990	*0.407*	*0.557*	*0.036*	*0.023*	*0.795*	*0.240*	*0.623*
2000	*0.362*	*0.598*	*0.040*	*0.024*	*0.673*	*0.259*	*0.475*
2010	*0.299*	*0.657*	*0.044*	*0.028*	*0.522*	*0.274*	*0.355*
2020	*0.250*	*0.692*	*0.058*	*0.033*	*0.445*	*0.276*	*0.295*

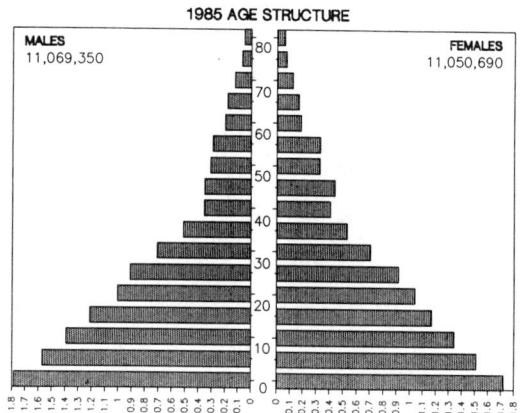

1985 AGE STRUCTURE

MALES 11,069,350   FEMALES 11,050,690

MORTALITY MEASURES (Annual Averages)

PERIOD	CRUDE DEATH RATE	INFANT MORT. RATE	LIFE EXPECTANCY AT BIRTH (years) MALE	FEMALE	BOTH SEXES	DIFFERENCE FEMALE-MALE
1950-55	25.70	180.00	41.90	43.90	42.88	2.00
1955-60	22.70	170.00	44.30	46.60	45.42	2.30
1960-65	19.60	155.00	46.70	49.20	47.92	2.50
1965-70	17.40	138.00	49.00	51.80	50.37	2.80
1970-75	15.70	122.00	51.40	54.50	52.91	3.10
1975-80	13.00	110.00	54.10	57.50	55.76	3.40
1980-85	11.53	96.50	56.60	60.00	58.26	3.40
1985-90	*9.74*	*82.06*	*59.05*	*62.46*	*60.71*	*3.41*
1990-95	*8.22*	*68.33*	*61.58*	*65.00*	*63.25*	*3.42*
2000-05	*6.16*	*44.57*	*65.91*	*69.76*	*67.79*	*3.85*
2010-15	*5.54*	*30.00*	*68.91*	*73.30*	*71.05*	*4.38*
2020-25	*5.73*	*21.04*	*71.08*	*75.69*	*73.33*	*4.61*

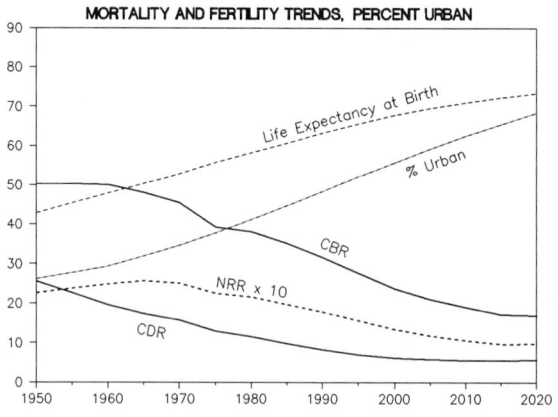

MORTALITY AND FERTILITY TRENDS, PERCENT URBAN

FERTILITY MEASURES (Annual Averages)

PERIOD	CRUDE BIRTH RATE	FERTILITY RATES GENERAL	TOTAL	REPRODUCTION RATES GROSS	NET	RATE OF NATUR. INCR.
1950-55	50.40	220.20	7.175	3.500	2.270	24.70
1955-60	50.40	220.69	7.175	3.500	2.390	27.70
1960-65	50.10	222.11	7.154	3.490	2.490	30.50
1965-70	48.20	219.89	7.093	3.460	2.580	30.80
1970-75	45.60	209.62	6.888	3.360	2.520	29.90
1975-80	39.40	175.16	5.904	2.880	2.260	26.40
1980-85	38.25	164.18	5.433	2.650	2.158	26.72
1985-90	*35.29*	*148.29*	*4.818*	*2.350*	*1.979*	*25.55*
1990-95	*31.70*	*129.29*	*4.203*	*2.050*	*1.783*	*23.48*
2000-05	*23.76*	*89.99*	*2.993*	*1.460*	*1.342*	*17.60*
2010-15	*19.08*	*69.27*	*2.296*	*1.120*	*1.063*	*13.54*
2020-25	*16.92*	*61.83*	*2.071*	*1.010*	*0.975*	*11.19*

AGING MEASURES

YEAR	POPULATION AGE RATIOS 60+/20-59	65+/20-64	70+/20-69	75+/20-74	POPULATION MEAN AGE	MEDIAN AGE
1950	0.1125	0.0677	0.0362	0.0143	22.33	17.70
1960	0.1072	0.0614	0.0331	0.0128	22.09	17.48
1970	0.1700	0.1084	0.0691	0.0359	22.47	16.25
1980	0.1551	0.0973	0.0568	0.0307	23.20	18.17
1990	*0.1380*	*0.0801*	*0.0489*	*0.0240*	*23.71*	*19.31*
2000	*0.1321*	*0.0819*	*0.0479*	*0.0211*	*25.36*	*21.59*
2010	*0.1271*	*0.0791*	*0.0493*	*0.0244*	*28.05*	*25.00*
2020	*0.1664*	*0.0963*	*0.0516*	*0.0255*	*31.15*	*29.09*

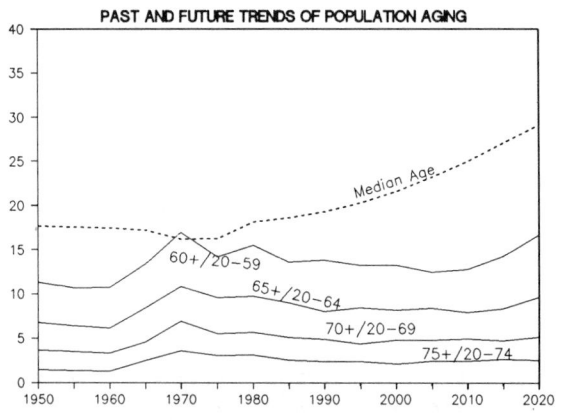

PAST AND FUTURE TRENDS OF POPULATION AGING

OBSERVED AND *PROJECTED* POPULATION DATA (000's)

YEAR	MID-YEAR POPULATION	NO. OF BIRTHS	NO. OF DEATHS	URBAN POPULATION NUMBER	URBAN POPULATION PERCENT	POPULATION 1985 AGE	POPULATION 1985 NUMBER
1950	6198	285	183	147	2.4	0	2446
1955	6744	315	183	199	2.9	5	1931
1960	7461	351	187	274	3.7	10	1619
1965	8339	391	192	381	4.6	15	1411
1970	9398	429	204	534	5.7	20	1196
1975	10502	477	217	905	8.6	25	997
1980	12100	553	243	1586	13.1	30	811
1985	13720	617	254	2667	19.4	35	715
1990	*15663*	*685*	*265*	*4190*	*26.8*	40	602
1995	*17913*	*748*	*275*	*6135*	*34.2*	45	512
2000	*20445*	*807*	*284*	*8397*	*41.1*	50	428
2005	*23241*	*845*	*289*	*10827*	*46.6*	55	347
2010	*26198*	*846*	*291*	*13218*	*50.5*	60	271
2015	*29127*	*811*	*289*	*15782*	*54.2*	65	197
2020	*31856*	*771*	*288*	*18393*	*57.7*	70+	237

AGE DISTRIBUTIONS, 1960 - 1985

POPULATION RATIOS

YEAR	AGE DISTRIBUTION UNDER 15	AGE DISTRIBUTION 15-64	AGE DISTRIBUTION 65 & OLDER	AGE DISTRIBUTION 70 & OLDER	DEPENDENCY RATIO	WOMEN 15-49	CHILD-WOMAN RATIO
1950	0.417	0.556	0.027	0.014	0.800	0.243	0.702
1955	0.413	0.559	0.028	0.014	0.789	0.244	0.671
1960	0.415	0.557	0.029	0.015	0.797	0.243	0.700
1965	0.420	0.551	0.030	0.015	0.816	0.240	0.728
1970	0.431	0.538	0.030	0.016	0.857	0.234	0.759
1975	0.438	0.530	0.031	0.017	0.885	0.230	0.765
1980	0.434	0.534	0.031	0.017	0.871	0.232	0.755
1985	0.437	0.531	0.032	0.017	0.882	0.231	0.772
1990	*0.440*	*0.528*	*0.032*	*0.018*	*0.895*	*0.229*	*0.775*
2000	*0.437*	*0.530*	*0.033*	*0.018*	*0.885*	*0.231*	*0.735*
2010	*0.414*	*0.553*	*0.034*	*0.019*	*0.810*	*0.242*	*0.633*
2020	*0.362*	*0.600*	*0.037*	*0.022*	*0.665*	*0.260*	*0.467*

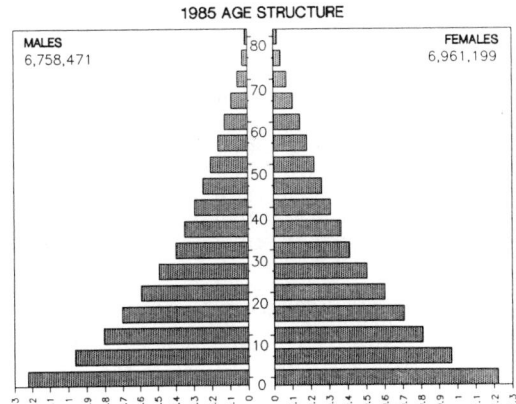

1985 AGE STRUCTURE

MALES 6,758,471   FEMALES 6,961,199

MORTALITY MEASURES (Annual Averages)

PERIOD	CRUDE DEATH RATE	INFANT MORT. RATE	LIFE EXPECTANCY AT BIRTH (years) MALE	LIFE EXPECTANCY AT BIRTH (years) FEMALE	LIFE EXPECTANCY AT BIRTH (years) BOTH SEXES	DIFFERENCE FEMALE-MALE
1950-55	29.58	205.00	32.03	35.01	33.50	2.98
1955-60	27.18	195.00	34.50	37.54	36.00	3.04
1960-65	25.07	185.00	36.97	40.07	38.50	3.10
1965-70	22.99	175.00	39.45	42.60	41.00	3.15
1970-75	21.72	168.00	40.93	44.12	42.50	3.18
1975-80	20.69	160.00	41.92	45.12	43.50	3.20
1980-85	20.10	153.47	42.92	46.13	44.50	3.21
1985-90	*18.51*	*141.47*	*44.90*	*48.15*	*46.50*	*3.24*
1990-95	*16.92*	*130.07*	*46.88*	*50.17*	*48.50*	*3.29*
2000-05	*13.87*	*109.32*	*50.77*	*54.28*	*52.50*	*3.51*
2010-15	*11.11*	*89.83*	*54.71*	*58.34*	*56.50*	*3.63*
2020-25	*9.03*	*71.59*	*58.69*	*62.37*	*60.50*	*3.68*

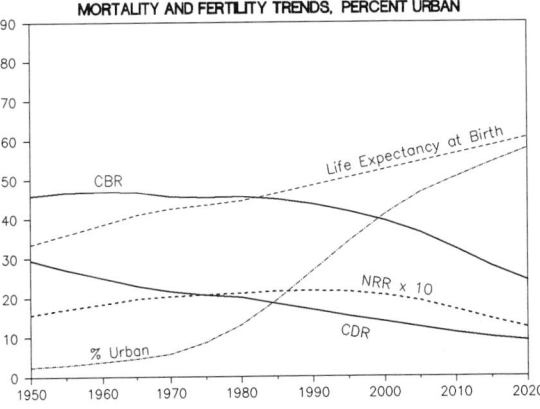

MORTALITY AND FERTILITY TRENDS, PERCENT URBAN

FERTILITY MEASURES (Annual Averages)

PERIOD	CRUDE BIRTH RATE	FERTILITY RATES GENERAL	FERTILITY RATES TOTAL	REPRODUCTION RATES GROSS	REPRODUCTION RATES NET	RATE OF NATUR. INCR.
1950-55	45.96	188.47	6.191	3.050	1.585	16.37
1955-60	46.71	191.60	6.293	3.100	1.715	19.53
1960-65	47.00	194.48	6.394	3.150	1.846	21.93
1965-70	46.84	197.59	6.496	3.200	1.978	23.85
1970-75	45.67	196.85	6.496	3.200	2.037	23.95
1975-80	45.43	196.47	6.496	3.200	2.078	24.74
1980-85	45.73	197.43	6.496	3.200	2.116	25.63
1985-90	*44.96*	*195.37*	*6.394*	*3.150*	*2.160*	*26.46*
1990-95	*43.73*	*190.68*	*6.232*	*3.070*	*2.181*	*26.81*
2000-05	*39.47*	*168.83*	*5.522*	*2.720*	*2.065*	*25.60*
2010-15	*32.29*	*131.25*	*4.283*	*2.110*	*1.698*	*21.18*
2020-25	*24.20*	*90.82*	*2.964*	*1.460*	*1.237*	*15.18*

AGING MEASURES

YEAR	POPULATION AGE RATIOS 60+/20-59	POPULATION AGE RATIOS 65+/20-64	POPULATION AGE RATIOS 70+/20-69	POPULATION AGE RATIOS 75+/20-74	POPULATION MEAN AGE	POPULATION MEDIAN AGE
1950	0.1082	0.0601	0.0293	0.0118	23.34	19.11
1960	0.1120	0.0632	0.0314	0.0129	23.50	19.26
1970	0.1192	0.0685	0.0351	0.0149	23.19	18.63
1980	0.1246	0.0728	0.0381	0.0168	23.01	18.20
1990	*0.1264*	*0.0748*	*0.0399*	*0.0180*	*22.74*	*17.95*
2000	*0.1270*	*0.0765*	*0.0416*	*0.0192*	*22.80*	*18.01*
2010	*0.1248*	*0.0760*	*0.0423*	*0.0201*	*23.49*	*19.00*
2020	*0.1248*	*0.0758*	*0.0432*	*0.0209*	*25.30*	*21.42*

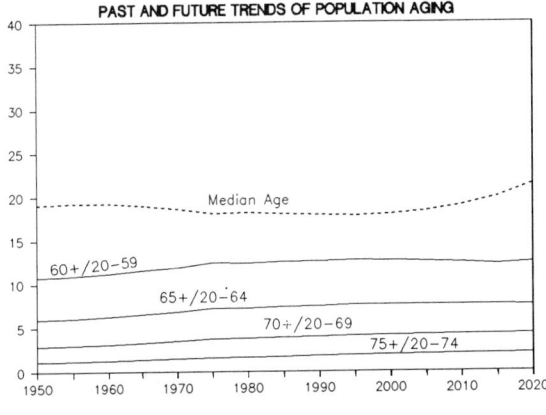

PAST AND FUTURE TRENDS OF POPULATION AGING

OBSERVED AND *PROJECTED* POPULATION DATA

YEAR	MID-YEAR POPULATION	NO. OF BIRTHS	NO. OF DEATHS	URBAN POPULATION NUMBER	PERCENT	POPULATION 1985 AGE	NUMBER
1950	665562	30153	16832	102651	15.4	0	292822
1955	735673	33631	17586	140267	19.1	5	237402
1960	820523	37590	18503	191453	23.3	10	191234
1965	921850	42125	19573	259387	28.1	15	160689
1970	1041955	46979	19005	349011	33.5	20	135278
1975	1181771	53092	18046	463166	39.2	25	113660
1980	1371038	60884	18759	619638	45.2	30	95016
1985	1599185	70332	19436	821024	51.3	35	79664
1990	*1875668*	*77945*	*19837*	*1068472*	*57.0*	40	65918
1995	*2190598*	*89617*	*20259*	*1355519*	*61.9*	45	57229
2000	*2567200*	*100372*	*20594*	*1694198*	*66.0*	50	47691
2005	*2999696*	*109720*	*20935*	*2078917*	*69.3*	55	39719
2010	*3479095*	*114497*	*21351*	*2499912*	*71.9*	60	30650
2015	*3978220*	*114923*	*21996*	*2951996*	*74.2*	65	22831
2020	*4471668*	*113625*	*23029*	*3414613*	*76.4*	70+	29381

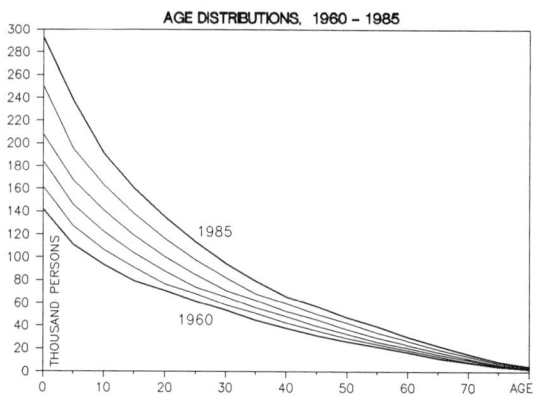

AGE DISTRIBUTIONS, 1960 - 1985

POPULATION RATIOS

YEAR	AGE DISTRIBUTION UNDER 15	15-64	65 & OLDER	70 & OLDER	DEPENDENCY RATIO	WOMEN 15-49	CHILD-WOMAN RATIO
1950	0.411	0.552	0.037	0.021	0.810	0.239	0.698
1955	0.415	0.550	0.035	0.019	0.817	0.239	0.712
1960	0.423	0.544	0.033	0.019	0.838	0.237	0.730
1965	0.429	0.538	0.033	0.018	0.858	0.234	0.748
1970	0.435	0.533	0.032	0.018	0.876	0.232	0.762
1975	0.437	0.530	0.032	0.018	0.885	0.231	0.764
1980	0.444	0.523	0.032	0.018	0.911	0.226	0.808
1985	0.451	0.516	0.033	0.018	0.937	0.223	0.821
1990	*0.457*	*0.510*	*0.033*	*0.019*	*0.961*	*0.220*	*0.834*
2000	*0.450*	*0.517*	*0.034*	*0.020*	*0.936*	*0.224*	*0.784*
2010	*0.432*	*0.534*	*0.034*	*0.021*	*0.872*	*0.232*	*0.697*
2020	*0.385*	*0.577*	*0.038*	*0.023*	*0.732*	*0.250*	*0.526*

MORTALITY MEASURES (Annual Averages)

PERIOD	CRUDE DEATH RATE	INFANT MORT. RATE	LIFE EXPECTANCY AT BIRTH (years) MALE	FEMALE	BOTH SEXES	DIFFERENCE FEMALE-MALE
1950-55	25.29	168.32	37.50	40.00	38.70	2.50
1955-60	23.91	159.14	40.00	42.50	41.20	2.50
1960-65	22.55	150.27	42.50	45.00	43.70	2.50
1965-70	21.23	141.66	45.00	47.50	46.20	2.50
1970-75	18.24	133.56	47.50	50.00	48.70	2.50
1975-80	15.27	126.00	50.00	52.50	51.23	2.50
1980-85	13.68	116.00	52.50	55.00	53.73	2.50
1985-90	*12.15*	*106.00*	*55.00*	*57.50*	*56.23*	*2.50*
1990-95	*10.58*	*97.00*	*57.50*	*60.00*	*58.73*	*2.50*
2000-05	*8.02*	*80.00*	*62.32*	*65.00*	*63.64*	*2.68*
2010-15	*6.14*	*64.00*	*66.08*	*69.38*	*67.71*	*3.30*
2020-25	*5.15*	*50.00*	*68.78*	*72.58*	*70.65*	*3.80*

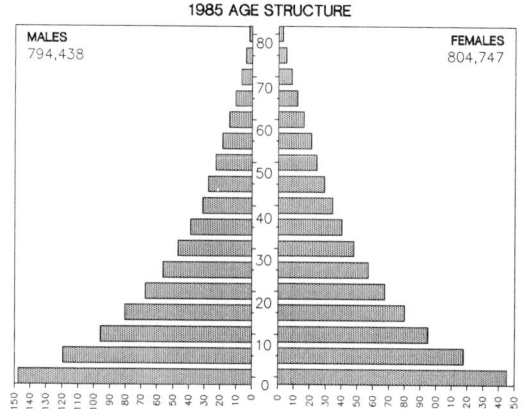

1985 AGE STRUCTURE

MALES 794,438   FEMALES 804,747

FERTILITY MEASURES (Annual Averages)

PERIOD	CRUDE BIRTH RATE	FERTILITY RATES GENERAL	TOTAL	REPRODUCTION RATES GROSS	NET	RATE OF NATUR. INCR.
1950-55	45.30	189.84	5.867	2.890	1.737	20.01
1955-60	45.72	192.34	5.950	2.931	1.817	21.81
1960-65	45.81	194.49	6.027	2.969	1.896	23.26
1965-70	45.70	196.09	6.086	2.998	1.970	24.46
1970-75	45.09	195.04	6.055	2.983	2.013	26.85
1975-80	44.93	196.88	6.090	3.000	2.245	29.66
1980-85	44.41	197.85	6.090	3.000	2.330	30.73
1985-90	*43.98*	*198.57*	*6.090*	*3.000*	*2.413*	*31.83*
1990-95	*41.56*	*187.92*	*5.745*	*2.830*	*2.350*	*30.98*
2000-05	*39.10*	*172.78*	*5.237*	*2.580*	*2.270*	*31.08*
2010-15	*32.91*	*139.48*	*4.243*	*2.090*	*1.921*	*26.77*
2020-25	*25.41*	*99.16*	*2.964*	*1.460*	*1.385*	*20.26*

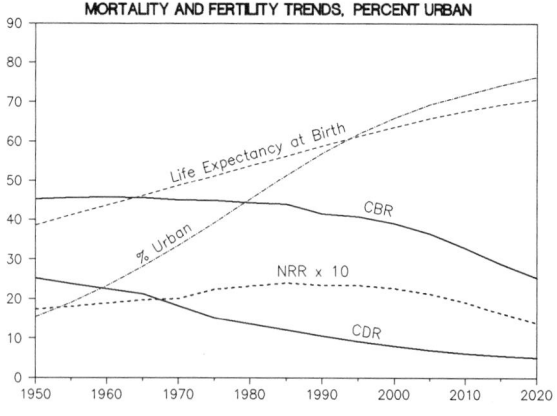

MORTALITY AND FERTILITY TRENDS, PERCENT URBAN

AGING MEASURES

YEAR	POPULATION AGE RATIOS 60+/20-59	65+/20-64	70+/20-69	75+/20-74	POPULATION MEAN AGE	MEDIAN AGE
1950	0.1362	0.0818	0.0441	0.0198	23.99	19.46
1960	0.1261	0.0740	0.0402	0.0183	23.49	18.97
1970	0.1264	0.0745	0.0394	0.0175	23.09	18.28
1980	0.1288	0.0767	0.0416	0.0191	22.70	17.76
1990	*0.1332*	*0.0800*	*0.0441*	*0.0208*	*22.29*	*17.13*
2000	*0.1325*	*0.0820*	*0.0465*	*0.0224*	*22.35*	*17.36*
2010	*0.1277*	*0.0801*	*0.0468*	*0.0236*	*22.89*	*18.23*
2020	*0.1291*	*0.0810*	*0.0471*	*0.0242*	*24.50*	*20.22*

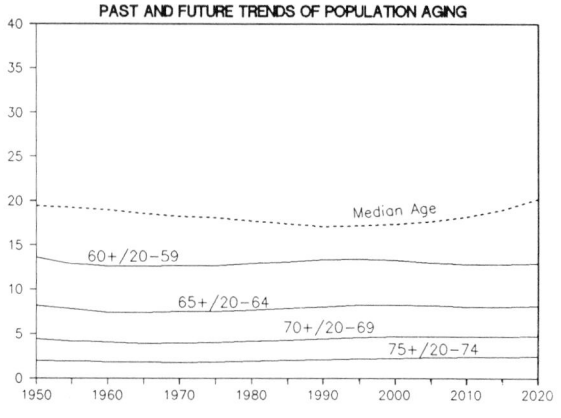

PAST AND FUTURE TRENDS OF POPULATION AGING

OBSERVED AND *PROJECTED* POPULATION DATA (000's)

YEAR	MID-YEAR POPULATION	NO. OF BIRTHS	NO. OF DEATHS	URBAN POPULATION NUMBER	URBAN POPULATION PERCENT	POPULATION 1985 AGE	POPULATION 1985 NUMBER
1950	2868	130	100	139	4.9	0	1188
1955	3022	140	99	160	5.3	5	917
1960	3234	148	96	187	5.8	10	751
1965	3736	184	107	254	6.8	15	623
1970	4146	209	111	353	8.5	20	512
1975	4665	238	117	496	10.6	25	431
1980	5311	271	122	701	13.2	30	365
1985	6115	312	128	989	16.2	35	316
1990	*7109*	*357*	*135*	*1385*	*19.5*	40	228
1995	*8313*	*407*	*142*	*1917*	*23.1*	45	194
2000	*9750*	*456*	*149*	*2613*	*26.8*	50	162
2005	*11415*	*498*	*156*	*3485*	*30.5*	55	131
2010	*13266*	*521*	*160*	*4567*	*34.4*	60	97
2015	*15201*	*521*	*161*	*5839*	*38.4*	65	79
2020	*17114*	*508*	*161*	*7260*	*42.4*	70+	121

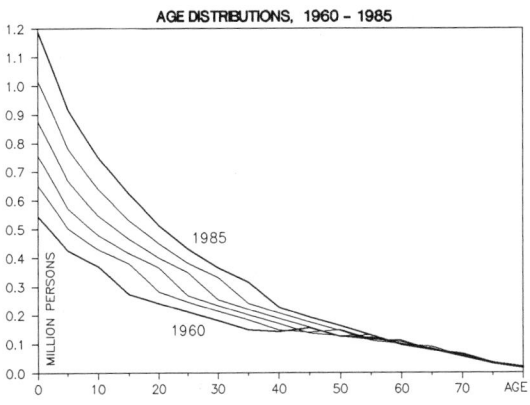

POPULATION RATIOS

YEAR	AGE DISTRIBUTION UNDER 15	AGE DISTRIBUTION 15-64	AGE DISTRIBUTION 65 & OLDER	AGE DISTRIBUTION 70 & OLDER	DEPENDENCY RATIO	WOMEN 15-49	CHILD-WOMAN RATIO
1950	0.358	0.573	0.068	0.038	0.744	0.225	0.714
1955	0.388	0.549	0.063	0.035	0.820	0.218	0.751
1960	0.415	0.528	0.057	0.032	0.893	0.213	0.789
1965	0.424	0.526	0.050	0.028	0.902	0.215	0.810
1970	0.436	0.518	0.046	0.026	0.931	0.218	0.839
1975	0.448	0.511	0.040	0.024	0.956	0.219	0.855
1980	0.459	0.503	0.038	0.021	0.988	0.219	0.873
1985	0.467	0.500	0.033	0.020	0.999	0.219	.886
1990	*0.473*	*0.499*	*0.028*	*0.017*	*1.005*	*0.219*	*0.896*
2000	*0.477*	*0.498*	*0.025*	*0.014*	*1.008*	*0.220*	*0.882*
2010	*0.462*	*0.514*	*0.024*	*0.014*	*0.947*	*0.227*	*0.787*
2020	*0.415*	*0.557*	*0.028*	*0.016*	*0.796*	*0.247*	*0.591*

MORTALITY MEASURES (Annual Averages)

PERIOD	CRUDE DEATH RATE	INFANT MORT. RATE	LIFE EXPECTANCY AT BIRTH (years) MALE	LIFE EXPECTANCY AT BIRTH (years) FEMALE	LIFE EXPECTANCY AT BIRTH (years) BOTH SEXES	DIFFERENCE FEMALE-MALE
1950-55	35.01	207.34	31.54	34.51	33.00	2.97
1955-60	32.66	196.49	33.02	36.02	34.50	3.00
1960-65	29.53	185.93	34.50	37.54	36.00	3.04
1965-70	28.58	176.08	35.98	39.06	37.50	3.08
1970-75	26.80	166.49	37.47	40.58	39.00	3.11
1975-80	25.02	157.30	38.95	42.09	40.50	3.14
1980-85	22.88	145.68	40.93	44.12	42.50	3.18
1985-90	*20.87*	*134.63*	*42.92*	*46.13*	*44.50*	*3.21*
1990-95	*18.95*	*124.14*	*44.90*	*48.15*	*46.50*	*3.24*
2000-05	*15.32*	*104.97*	*48.82*	*52.23*	*50.50*	*3.41*
2010-15	*12.05*	*87.40*	*52.74*	*56.31*	*54.50*	*3.58*
2020-25	*9.42*	*70.89*	*56.70*	*60.36*	*58.50*	*3.66*

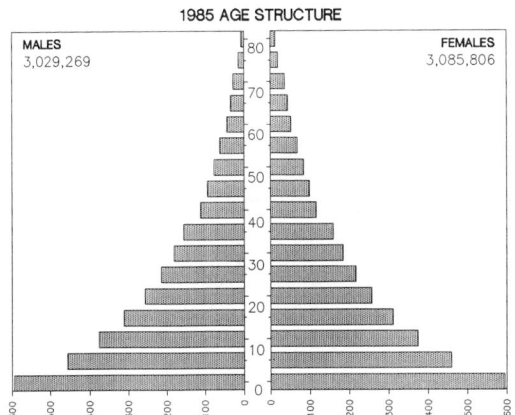

FERTILITY MEASURES (Annual Averages)

PERIOD	CRUDE BIRTH RATE	FERTILITY RATES GENERAL	FERTILITY RATES TOTAL	REPRODUCTION RATES GROSS	REPRODUCTION RATES NET	RATE OF NATUR. INCR.
1950-55	45.46	205.30	6.859	3.379	1.772	10.45
1955-60	46.23	214.55	7.036	3.466	1.887	13.57
1960-65	45.83	213.78	7.058	3.477	1.963	16.30
1965-70	49.38	228.07	7.103	3.499	2.044	20.80
1970-75	50.38	230.55	7.095	3.495	2.108	23.58
1975-80	50.92	232.15	7.105	3.500	2.178	25.90
1980-85	51.02	232.67	7.105	3.500	2.265	28.14
1985-90	*50.94*	*232.33*	*7.105*	*3.500*	*2.349*	*30.07*
1990-95	*50.17*	*228.19*	*7.003*	*3.450*	*2.399*	*31.21*
2000-05	*46.79*	*211.47*	*6.435*	*3.170*	*2.359*	*31.47*
2010-15	*39.25*	*169.39*	*5.136*	*2.530*	*1.999*	*27.19*
2020-25	*29.68*	*116.67*	*3.552*	*1.750*	*1.458*	*20.26*

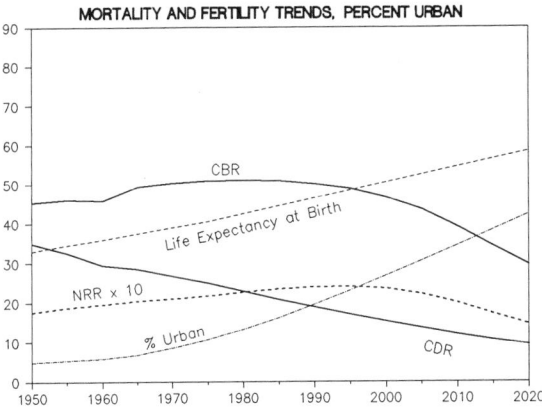

AGING MEASURES

YEAR	POPULATION AGE RATIOS 60+/20-59	POPULATION AGE RATIOS 65+/20-64	POPULATION AGE RATIOS 70+/20-69	POPULATION AGE RATIOS 75+/20-74	POPULATION MEAN AGE	POPULATION MEDIAN AGE
1950	0.2350	0.1392	0.0730	0.0322	28.54	24.19
1960	0.2126	0.1288	0.0690	0.0309	25.82	20.03
1970	0.1766	0.1097	0.0584	0.0270	23.64	18.19
1980	0.1458	0.0936	0.0498	0.0240	22.20	17.04
1990	*0.1170*	*0.0717*	*0.0421*	*0.0214*	*21.34*	*16.32*
2000	*0.1062*	*0.0642*	*0.0349*	*0.0163*	*21.02*	*16.10*
2010	*0.1052*	*0.0602*	*0.0335*	*0.0159*	*21.40*	*16.74*
2020	*0.1057*	*0.0640*	*0.0349*	*0.0154*	*22.88*	*18.72*

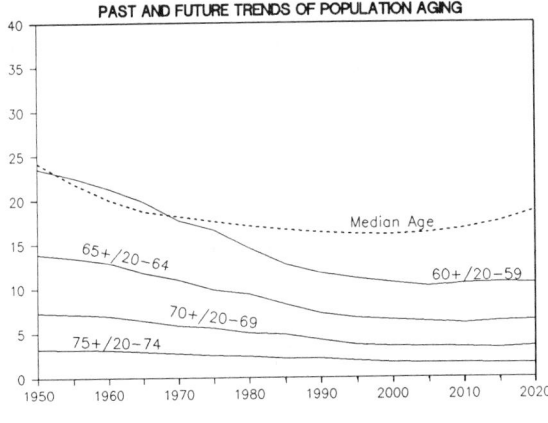

OBSERVED AND PROJECTED POPULATION DATA (000's)

YEAR	MID-YEAR POPULATION	NO. OF BIRTHS	NO. OF DEATHS	URBAN POPULATION NUMBER	URBAN POPULATION PERCENT	POPULATION AGE	1985 NUMBER
1950	32935	1678	896	3340	10.1	0	18971
1955	37094	1913	939	4489	12.1	5	14844
1960	42305	2182	997	6085	14.4	10	12126
1965	48676	2548	1069	8280	17.0	15	10049
1970	57221	2934	1156	11447	20.0	20	8013
1975	67672	3425	1255	15821	23.4	25	6522
1980	80555	4062	1377	21818	27.1	30	5263
1985	95198	4745	1487	29556	31.0	35	4418
1990	113016	5499	1600	39732	35.2	40	3732
1995	134351	6244	1704	52777	39.3	45	3065
2000	159149	6893	1789	68893	43.3	50	2468
2005	186894	7283	1842	88293	47.2	55	1944
2010	216235	7369	1864	110479	51.1	60	1477
2015	245634	7254	1870	134592	54.8	65	1055
2020	274114	7058	1876	159853	58.3	70+	1251

AGE DISTRIBUTIONS, 1960 - 1985

POPULATION RATIOS

YEAR	AGE DISTRIBUTION UNDER 15	15-64	65 & OLDER	70 & OLDER	DEPENDENCY RATIO	WOMEN 15-49	CHILD-WOMAN RATIO
1950	0.457	0.519	0.024	0.013	0.925	0.230	0.811
1955	0.454	0.523	0.023	0.012	0.911	0.232	0.797
1960	0.454	0.523	0.023	0.012	0.913	0.232	0.819
1965	0.459	0.517	0.023	0.012	0.933	0.229	0.841
1970	0.470	0.507	0.023	0.012	0.974	0.224	0.887
1975	0.476	0.500	0.024	0.013	1.001	0.221	0.897
1980	0.481	0.495	0.024	0.013	1.021	0.219	0.908
1985	0.483	0.493	0.024	0.013	1.028	0.218	0.913
1990	0.484	0.491	0.024	0.013	1.036	0.218	0.917
2000	0.480	0.495	0.025	0.014	1.021	0.220	0.869
2010	0.449	0.524	0.026	0.015	0.907	0.234	0.708
2020	0.385	0.585	0.030	0.017	0.709	0.259	0.504

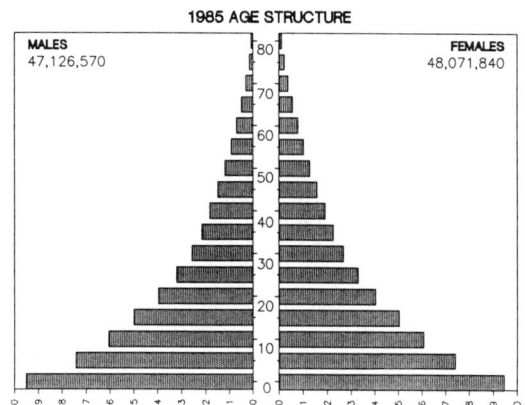

1985 AGE STRUCTURE

MALES 47,126,570   FEMALES 48,071,840

MORTALITY MEASURES (Annual Averages)

PERIOD	CRUDE DEATH RATE	INFANT MORT. RATE	LIFE EXPECTANCY AT BIRTH (years) MALE	FEMALE	BOTH SEXES	DIFFERENCE FEMALE-MALE
1950-55	27.20	206.70	35.00	38.05	36.50	3.05
1955-60	25.31	194.00	36.97	40.07	38.50	3.10
1960-65	23.56	184.60	38.95	42.09	40.50	3.14
1965-70	21.95	172.20	40.93	44.12	42.50	3.18
1970-75	20.20	147.95	42.92	46.13	44.50	3.21
1975-80	18.54	124.14	44.90	48.15	46.50	3.24
1980-85	17.10	114.18	46.88	50.17	48.50	3.29
1985-90	15.62	104.97	48.82	52.23	50.50	3.41
1990-95	14.15	96.05	50.77	54.28	52.50	3.51
2000-05	11.24	79.02	54.71	58.34	56.50	3.63
2010-15	8.62	63.08	58.69	62.37	60.50	3.68
2020-25	6.84	48.45	62.70	66.36	64.50	3.66

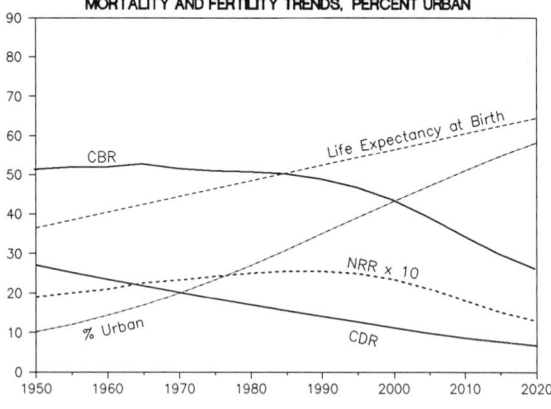

MORTALITY AND FERTILITY TRENDS, PERCENT URBAN

CBR, Life Expectancy at Birth, NRR x 10, % Urban, CDR

FERTILITY MEASURES (Annual Averages)

PERIOD	CRUDE BIRTH RATE	FERTILITY RATES GENERAL	TOTAL	REPRODUCTION RATES GROSS	NET	RATE OF NATUR. INCR.
1950-55	50.96	220.22	6.770	3.335	1.903	23.76
1955-60	51.56	222.11	6.825	3.362	2.006	26.25
1960-65	51.57	223.65	6.872	3.385	2.105	28.01
1965-70	52.34	230.90	7.105	3.500	2.263	30.39
1970-75	51.28	230.24	7.105	3.500	2.348	31.07
1975-80	50.61	230.09	7.105	3.500	2.432	32.07
1980-85	50.43	230.73	7.105	3.500	2.517	33.33
1985-90	49.85	228.81	7.003	3.450	2.566	34.23
1990-95	48.65	223.61	6.800	3.350	2.570	34.50
2000-05	43.31	194.21	5.887	2.900	2.354	32.07
2010-15	34.08	141.68	4.304	2.120	1.809	25.46
2020-25	25.75	96.81	2.964	1.460	1.301	18.91

AGING MEASURES

YEAR	POPULATION AGE RATIOS 60+/20-59	65+/20-64	70+/20-69	75+/20-74	POPULATION MEAN AGE	MEDIAN AGE
1950	0.0995	0.0572	0.0300	0.0132	21.62	17.06
1960	0.0972	0.0552	0.0280	0.0119	21.61	17.18
1970	0.1005	0.0577	0.0295	0.0127	21.29	16.51
1980	0.1053	0.0612	0.0320	0.0141	21.00	15.92
1990	0.1071	0.0631	0.0336	0.0152	20.74	15.74
2000	0.1071	0.0639	0.0346	0.0160	20.79	15.91
2010	0.1045	0.0640	0.0354	0.0168	21.70	17.24
2020	0.1032	0.0630	0.0358	0.0176	23.80	19.94

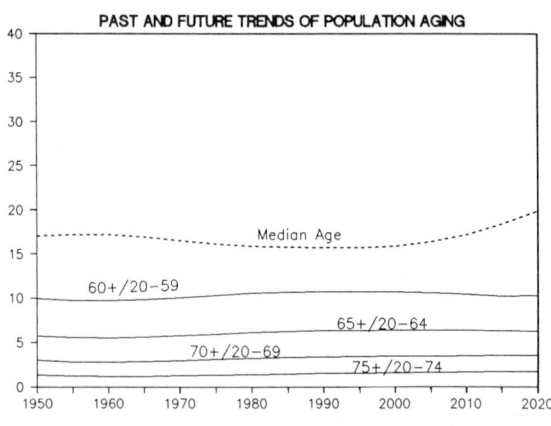

PAST AND FUTURE TRENDS OF POPULATION AGING

Median Age, 60+/20-59, 65+/20-64, 70+/20-69, 75+/20-74

OBSERVED AND *PROJECTED* POPULATION DATA

YEAR	MID-YEAR POPULATION	NO. OF BIRTHS	NO. OF DEATHS	URBAN POPULATION NUMBER	URBAN POPULATION PERCENT	POPULATION 1985 AGE	POPULATION 1985 NUMBER
1950	257203	10141	3411	60429	23.5	0	61652
1955	293213	12019	3494	81889	27.9	5	60974
1960	339179	13498	3502	111382	32.8	10	59189
1965	393140	13827	3427	150005	38.2	15	70976
1970	441326	13558	3080	193179	43.8	20	64718
1975	484260	12565	3036	239968	49.6	25	48731
1980	507808	12212	2967	279002	54.9	30	32961
1985	546054	12439	3073	326280	59.8	35	25027
1990	*594983*	*12148*	*3332*	*380057*	*63.9*	40	23938
1995	*640756*	*12106*	*3577*	*431118*	*67.3*	45	22680
2000	*684868*	*12169*	*3911*	*479331*	*70.0*	50	18817
2005	*727441*	*12177*	*4269*	*527294*	*72.5*	55	16475
2010	*768091*	*12213*	*4670*	*574408*	*74.8*	60	14220
2015	*806758*	*12249*	*5199*	*620341*	*76.9*	65	9602
2020	*842798*	*12277*	*5899*	*664343*	*78.8*	70+	16093

AGE DISTRIBUTIONS, 1960 – 1985

POPULATION RATIOS

YEAR	AGE DISTRIBUTION UNDER 15	AGE DISTRIBUTION 15-64	AGE DISTRIBUTION 65 & OLDER	AGE DISTRIBUTION 70 & OLDER	DEPENDENCY RATIO	WOMEN 15-49	CHILD-WOMAN RATIO
1950	0.409	0.570	0.021	0.011	0.756	0.210	0.758
1955	0.423	0.553	0.023	0.012	0.808	0.212	0.809
1960	0.440	0.535	0.025	0.014	0.869	0.212	0.843
1965	0.451	0.522	0.027	0.015	0.917	0.214	0.819
1970	0.440	0.529	0.030	0.017	0.890	0.224	0.700
1975	0.420	0.542	0.038	0.023	0.846	0.236	0.530
1980	0.380	0.576	0.044	0.026	0.737	0.252	0.481
1985	0.333	0.620	0.047	0.029	0.613	0.272	0.415
1990	*0.313*	*0.634*	*0.052*	*0.031*	*0.577*	*0.278*	*0.388*
2000	*0.274*	*0.665*	*0.060*	*0.039*	*0.503*	*0.291*	*0.311*
2010	*0.242*	*0.689*	*0.069*	*0.045*	*0.451*	*0.284*	*0.284*
2020	*0.221*	*0.699*	*0.081*	*0.051*	*0.431*	*0.252*	*0.293*

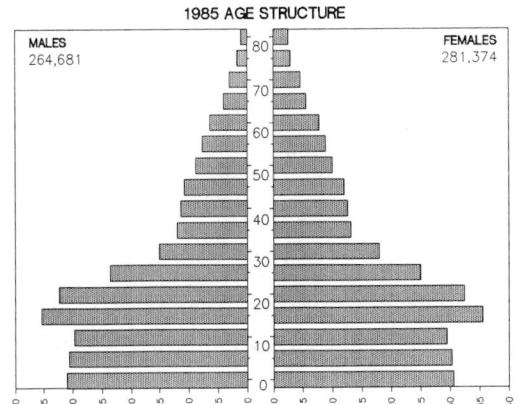

1985 AGE STRUCTURE

MALES 264,681   FEMALES 281,374

MORTALITY MEASURES (Annual Averages)

PERIOD	CRUDE DEATH RATE	INFANT MORT. RATE	LIFE EXPECTANCY AT BIRTH (years) MALE	LIFE EXPECTANCY AT BIRTH (years) FEMALE	LIFE EXPECTANCY AT BIRTH (years) BOTH SEXES	DIFFERENCE FEMALE-MALE
1950-55	13.26	141.10	49.70	55.60	52.61	5.90
1955-60	11.92	109.52	51.80	58.30	55.00	6.50
1960-65	10.32	87.16	54.35	60.95	57.60	6.60
1965-70	8.72	73.29	57.05	64.05	60.50	7.00
1970-75	6.98	41.18	60.40	68.10	64.19	7.70
1975-80	6.27	19.14	63.50	72.48	67.96	8.98
1980-85	5.84	16.05	65.48	74.00	69.71	8.52
1985-90	*5.63*	*13.75*	*66.98*	*75.46*	*71.19*	*8.49*
1990-95	*5.60*	*12.05*	*68.13*	*76.21*	*72.14*	*8.08*
2000-05	*5.71*	*9.39*	*70.09*	*77.98*	*74.00*	*7.90*
2010-15	*6.08*	*7.68*	*71.55*	*79.39*	*75.44*	*7.84*
2020-25	*7.00*	*6.66*	*72.66*	*80.22*	*76.41*	*7.55*

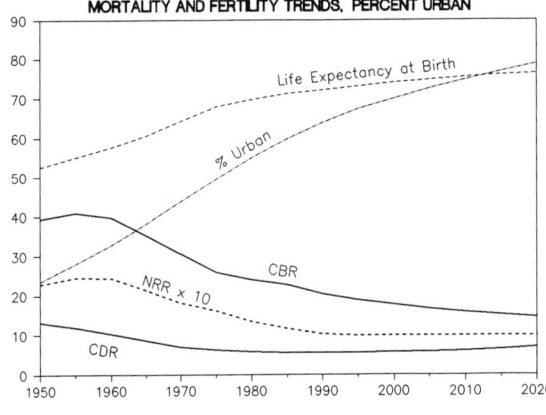

MORTALITY AND FERTILITY TRENDS, PERCENT URBAN

Life Expectancy at Birth / % Urban / CBR / NRR x 10 / CDR

FERTILITY MEASURES (Annual Averages)

PERIOD	CRUDE BIRTH RATE	FERTILITY RATES GENERAL	FERTILITY RATES TOTAL	REPRODUCTION RATES GROSS	REPRODUCTION RATES NET	RATE OF NATUR. INCR.
1950-55	39.43	186.62	5.649	2.802	2.295	26.17
1955-60	40.99	193.12	5.848	2.901	2.452	29.08
1960-65	39.80	186.56	5.649	2.802	2.440	29.47
1965-70	35.17	160.51	4.816	2.389	2.146	26.45
1970-75	30.72	133.63	3.931	1.950	1.818	23.74
1975-80	25.95	106.44	3.407	1.690	1.626	19.68
1980-85	24.05	91.74	2.822	1.400	1.357	18.21
1985-90	*22.78*	*82.85*	*2.419*	*1.200*	*1.170*	*17.15*
1990-95	*20.42*	*72.61*	*2.117*	*1.050*	*1.027*	*14.82*
2000-05	*17.77*	*60.95*	*2.036*	*1.010*	*0.993*	*12.06*
2010-15	*15.90*	*57.54*	*2.036*	*1.010*	*0.996*	*9.82*
2020-25	*14.57*	*58.72*	*2.036*	*1.010*	*0.998*	*7.57*

AGING MEASURES

YEAR	POPULATION AGE RATIOS 60+/20-59	POPULATION AGE RATIOS 65+/20-64	POPULATION AGE RATIOS 70+/20-69	POPULATION AGE RATIOS 75+/20-74	POPULATION MEAN AGE	POPULATION MEDIAN AGE
1950	0.0824	0.0451	0.0229	0.0105	23.28	19.45
1960	0.1039	0.0573	0.0307	0.0146	22.63	18.03
1970	0.1220	0.0723	0.0383	0.0181	22.71	17.77
1980	0.1559	0.0991	0.0555	0.0289	24.98	19.54
1990	*0.1525*	*0.0979*	*0.0564*	*0.0314*	*27.05*	*23.68*
2000	*0.1608*	*0.1044*	*0.0649*	*0.0362*	*29.59*	*27.78*
2010	*0.1650*	*0.1133*	*0.0720*	*0.0403*	*32.25*	*30.97*
2020	*0.2233*	*0.1288*	*0.0774*	*0.0463*	*34.88*	*33.96*

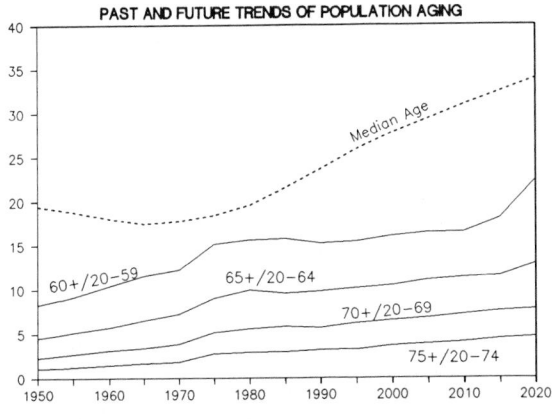

PAST AND FUTURE TRENDS OF POPULATION AGING

Median Age / 60+/20-59 / 65+/20-64 / 70+/20-69 / 75+/20-74

OBSERVED AND *PROJECTED* POPULATION DATA (000's)

YEAR	MID-YEAR POPULATION	NO. OF BIRTHS	NO. OF DEATHS	URBAN POPULATION NUMBER	URBAN POPULATION PERCENT	POPULATION 1985 AGE	POPULATION 1985 NUMBER
1950	2120	100	49	38	1.8	0	1239
1955	2391	119	53	50	2.1	5	964
1960	2742	140	59	66	2.4	10	785
1965	3183	167	66	88	2.8	15	642
1970	3728	197	76	119	3.2	20	516
1975	4384	231	88	175	4.0	25	408
1980	5163	269	97	258	5.0	30	321
1985	6102	311	105	380	6.2	35	286
1990	*7232*	*359*	*112*	*555*	*7.7*	40	234
1995	*8582*	*406*	*119*	*805*	*9.4*	45	192
2000	*10144*	*439*	*125*	*1152*	*11.4*	50	155
2005	*11849*	*445*	*127*	*1610*	*13.6*	55	122
2010	*13556*	*423*	*126*	*2188*	*16.1*	60	93
2015	*15128*	*412*	*125*	*2874*	*19.0*	65	66
2020	*16633*	*403*	*126*	*3687*	*22.2*	70+	78

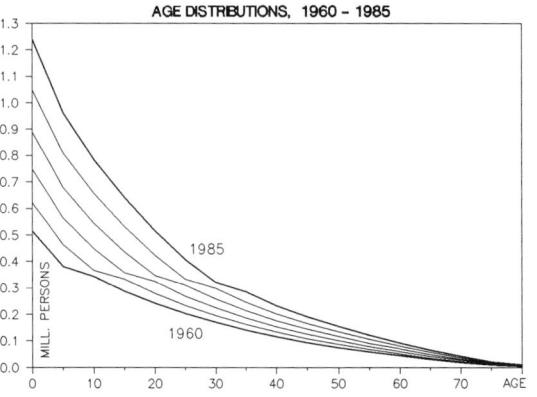

AGE DISTRIBUTIONS, 1960 - 1985

POPULATION RATIOS

YEAR	AGE DISTRIBUTION UNDER 15	AGE DISTRIBUTION 15-64	AGE DISTRIBUTION 65 & OLDER	AGE DISTRIBUTION 70 & OLDER	DEPENDENCY RATIO	WOMEN 15-49	CHILD-WOMAN RATIO
1950	0.459	0.518	0.023	0.012	0.930	0.229	0.826
1955	0.452	0.525	0.023	0.012	0.905	0.232	0.765
1960	0.452	0.524	0.024	0.013	0.907	0.232	0.808
1965	0.456	0.520	0.024	0.013	0.925	0.230	0.850
1970	0.472	0.504	0.024	0.013	0.985	0.222	0.902
1975	0.482	0.494	0.024	0.013	1.026	0.218	0.932
1980	0.488	0.488	0.024	0.013	1.047	0.216	0.941
1985	0.490	0.487	0.024	0.013	1.055	0.216	0.941
1990	*0.490*	*0.487*	*0.024*	*0.013*	*1.055*	*0.216*	*0.931*
2000	*0.482*	*0.494*	*0.024*	*0.013*	*1.024*	*0.221*	*0.871*
2010	*0.443*	*0.531*	*0.025*	*0.014*	*0.882*	*0.239*	*0.665*
2020	*0.362*	*0.608*	*0.029*	*0.017*	*0.644*	*0.271*	*0.442*

MORTALITY MEASURES (Annual Averages)

PERIOD	CRUDE DEATH RATE	INFANT MORT. RATE	LIFE EXPECTANCY AT BIRTH (years) MALE	LIFE EXPECTANCY AT BIRTH (years) FEMALE	LIFE EXPECTANCY AT BIRTH (years) BOTH SEXES	DIFFERENCE FEMALE-MALE
1950-55	23.25	160.00	38.45	41.58	40.00	3.13
1955-60	22.26	150.00	39.94	43.10	41.50	3.16
1960-65	21.42	142.00	41.42	44.61	43.00	3.19
1965-70	20.80	140.00	42.51	45.72	44.10	3.21
1970-75	20.51	140.00	43.01	46.22	44.60	3.22
1975-80	20.16	140.00	43.41	46.63	45.00	3.22
1980-85	18.84	131.95	44.90	48.14	46.50	3.24
1985-90	*17.14*	*121.63*	*46.87*	*50.16*	*48.50*	*3.29*
1990-95	*15.52*	*111.88*	*48.81*	*52.22*	*50.50*	*3.41*
2000-05	*12.30*	*93.83*	*52.73*	*56.31*	*54.50*	*3.58*
2010-15	*9.28*	*76.97*	*56.69*	*60.35*	*58.50*	*3.66*
2020-25	*7.57*	*61.20*	*60.68*	*64.36*	*62.50*	*3.67*

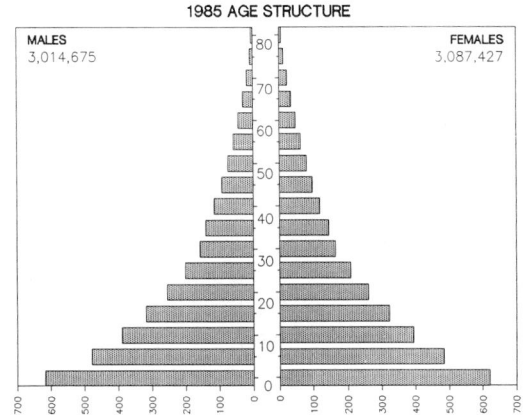

1985 AGE STRUCTURE
MALES 3,014,675 — FEMALES 3,087,427

FERTILITY MEASURES (Annual Averages)

PERIOD	CRUDE BIRTH RATE	FERTILITY RATES GENERAL	FERTILITY RATES TOTAL	REPRODUCTION RATES GROSS	REPRODUCTION RATES NET	RATE OF NATUR. INCR.
1950-55	47.30	204.82	7.077	3.500	2.089	24.05
1955-60	49.56	213.57	7.380	3.650	2.249	27.31
1960-65	51.24	222.15	7.684	3.800	2.413	29.82
1965-70	52.35	232.02	7.987	3.950	2.562	31.55
1970-75	52.85	240.38	8.290	4.100	2.685	32.34
1975-80	52.78	243.44	8.492	4.200	2.771	32.62
1980-85	52.19	241.86	8.492	4.200	2.849	33.35
1985-90	*51.03*	*236.23*	*8.290*	*4.100*	*2.884*	*33.89*
1990-95	*49.67*	*228.83*	*7.987*	*3.950*	*2.878*	*34.14*
2000-05	*43.30*	*192.75*	*6.673*	*3.300*	*2.562*	*31.00*
2010-15	*31.19*	*125.93*	*4.347*	*2.150*	*1.766*	*21.91*
2020-25	*24.24*	*87.22*	*2.952*	*1.460*	*1.260*	*16.67*

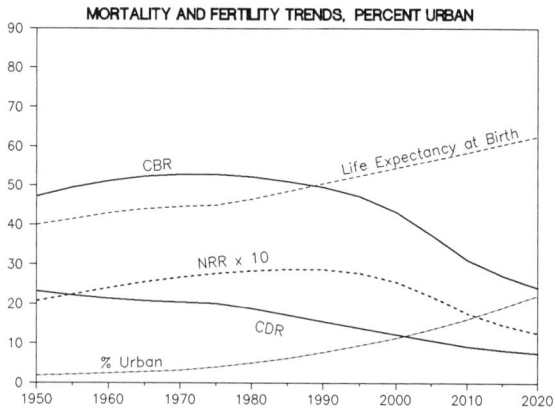

MORTALITY AND FERTILITY TRENDS, PERCENT URBAN

AGING MEASURES

YEAR	POPULATION AGE RATIOS 60+/20-59	POPULATION AGE RATIOS 65+/20-64	POPULATION AGE RATIOS 70+/20-69	POPULATION AGE RATIOS 75+/20-74	POPULATION MEAN AGE	POPULATION MEDIAN AGE
1950	0.0973	0.0554	0.0282	0.0121	21.51	16.97
1960	0.0993	0.0569	0.0291	0.0124	21.77	17.30
1970	0.1024	0.0592	0.0307	0.0134	21.30	16.46
1980	0.1064	0.0619	0.0324	0.0143	20.79	15.60
1990	*0.1058*	*0.0622*	*0.0330*	*0.0148*	*20.52*	*15.49*
2000	*0.1036*	*0.0617*	*0.0333*	*0.0153*	*20.62*	*15.82*
2010	*0.1014*	*0.0610*	*0.0335*	*0.0158*	*21.79*	*17.47*
2020	*0.0983*	*0.0597*	*0.0343*	*0.0165*	*24.41*	*20.88*

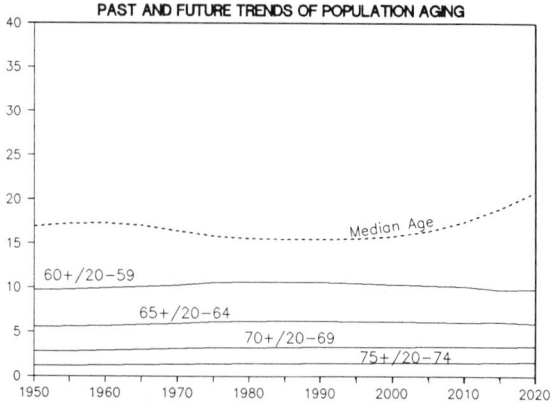

PAST AND FUTURE TRENDS OF POPULATION AGING

OBSERVED AND *PROJECTED* POPULATION DATA (000's)

YEAR	MID-YEAR POPULATION	NO. OF BIRTHS	NO. OF DEATHS	URBAN POPULATION NUMBER	URBAN POPULATION PERCENT	POPULATION 1985 AGE	POPULATION 1985 NUMBER
1950	2500	121	74	762	30.5	0	1155
1955	2747	133	77	857	31.2	5	926
1960	3041	143	80	971	31.9	10	778
1965	3469	162	86	1133	32.7	15	654
1970	4008	187	93	1340	33.4	20	556
1975	4771	221	106	1631	34.2	25	473
1980	5672	263	119	1982	34.9	30	397
1985	6444	295	122	2343	36.4	35	328
1990	*7369*	*329*	*128*	*2831*	*38.4*	40	277
1995	*8448*	*361*	*133*	*3476*	*41.1*	45	236
2000	*9668*	*389*	*138*	*4301*	*44.5*	50	195
2005	*11011*	*407*	*141*	*5332*	*48.4*	55	158
2010	*12431*	*408*	*142*	*6492*	*52.2*	60	121
2015	*13840*	*392*	*141*	*7734*	*55.9*	65	88
2020	*15155*	*373*	*140*	*8993*	*59.3*	70+	103

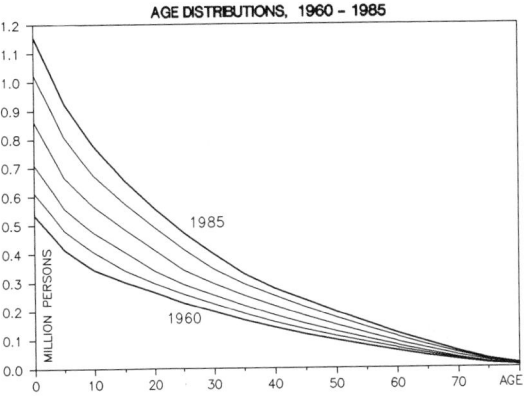

AGE DISTRIBUTIONS, 1960 – 1985

POPULATION RATIOS

YEAR	AGE DISTRIBUTION UNDER 15	AGE DISTRIBUTION 15-64	AGE DISTRIBUTION 65 & OLDER	AGE DISTRIBUTION 70 & OLDER	DEPENDENCY RATIO	WOMEN 15-49	CHILD-WOMAN RATIO
1950	0.416	0.550	0.034	0.019	0.819	0.235	0.718
1955	0.420	0.548	0.032	0.018	0.825	0.235	0.741
1960	0.426	0.544	0.030	0.016	0.838	0.233	0.755
1965	0.432	0.539	0.029	0.016	0.855	0.231	0.764
1970	0.434	0.536	0.029	0.015	0.864	0.231	0.767
1975	0.438	0.533	0.029	0.016	0.878	0.230	0.784
1980	0.441	0.529	0.029	0.016	0.889	0.230	0.786
1985	0.444	0.527	0.030	0.016	0.898	0.229	0.782
1990	*0.444*	*0.526*	*0.030*	*0.016*	*0.903*	*0.229*	*0.785*
2000	*0.441*	*0.528*	*0.031*	*0.017*	*0.894*	*0.232*	*0.747*
2010	*0.418*	*0.550*	*0.032*	*0.018*	*0.818*	*0.241*	*0.643*
2020	*0.366*	*0.598*	*0.036*	*0.021*	*0.672*	*0.260*	*0.473*

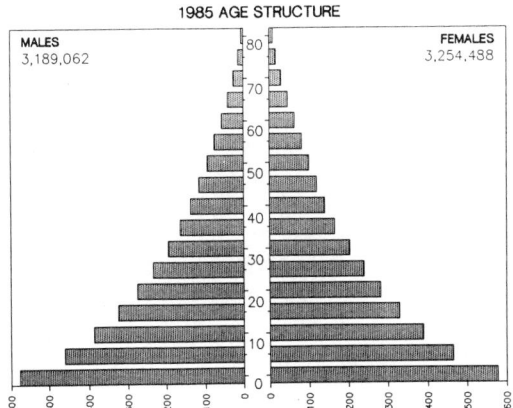

1985 AGE STRUCTURE

MALES 3,189,062   FEMALES 3,254,488

MORTALITY MEASURES (Annual Averages)

PERIOD	CRUDE DEATH RATE	INFANT MORT. RATE	LIFE EXPECTANCY AT BIRTH (years) MALE	LIFE EXPECTANCY AT BIRTH (years) FEMALE	LIFE EXPECTANCY AT BIRTH (years) BOTH SEXES	DIFFERENCE FEMALE-MALE
1950-55	29.49	191.20	33.22	36.23	34.70	3.01
1955-60	28.00	183.50	34.50	37.54	36.00	3.04
1960-65	26.18	175.80	35.79	38.86	37.30	3.07
1965-70	24.65	168.30	37.17	40.28	38.70	3.11
1970-75	23.29	161.50	38.46	41.59	40.00	3.13
1975-80	22.20	153.60	39.74	42.90	41.30	3.16
1980-85	20.94	142.24	41.72	44.92	43.30	3.20
1985-90	*18.92*	*127.67*	*44.21*	*47.44*	*45.80*	*3.23*
1990-95	*17.36*	*117.62*	*46.19*	*49.46*	*47.80*	*3.27*
2000-05	*14.24*	*99.16*	*50.09*	*53.56*	*51.80*	*3.48*
2010-15	*11.39*	*81.88*	*54.02*	*57.63*	*55.80*	*3.61*
2020-25	*9.26*	*65.81*	*57.99*	*61.66*	*59.80*	*3.67*

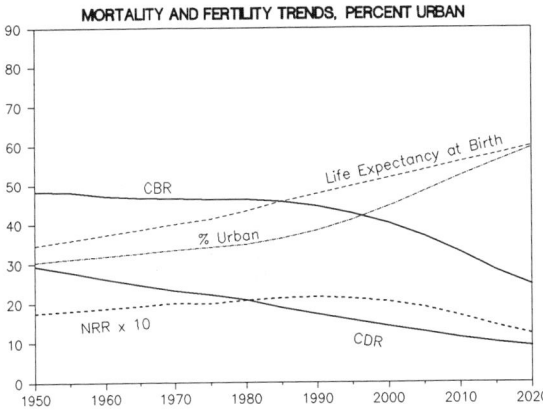

MORTALITY AND FERTILITY TRENDS, PERCENT URBAN

FERTILITY MEASURES (Annual Averages)

PERIOD	CRUDE BIRTH RATE	FERTILITY RATES GENERAL	FERTILITY RATES TOTAL	REPRODUCTION RATES GROSS	REPRODUCTION RATES NET	RATE OF NATUR. INCR.
1950-55	48.35	205.76	6.640	3.271	1.764	18.87
1955-60	48.31	206.55	6.660	3.281	1.827	20.30
1960-65	47.19	203.63	6.656	3.279	1.881	21.00
1965-70	46.69	202.42	6.656	3.279	1.941	22.05
1970-75	46.63	202.49	6.736	3.318	2.019	23.34
1975-80	46.36	201.78	6.496	3.200	2.000	24.16
1980-85	46.43	202.51	6.496	3.200	2.080	25.49
1985-90	*45.73*	*199.71*	*6.394*	*3.150*	*2.142*	*26.81*
1990-95	*44.65*	*194.66*	*6.232*	*3.070*	*2.163*	*27.29*
2000-05	*40.23*	*172.38*	*5.522*	*2.720*	*2.049*	*25.99*
2010-15	*32.85*	*133.90*	*4.283*	*2.110*	*1.687*	*21.46*
2020-25	*24.61*	*92.36*	*2.964*	*1.460*	*1.229*	*15.35*

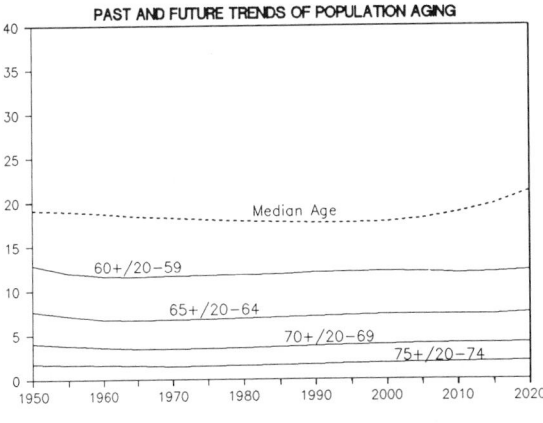

PAST AND FUTURE TRENDS OF POPULATION AGING

AGING MEASURES

YEAR	POPULATION AGE RATIOS 60+/20-59	POPULATION AGE RATIOS 65+/20-64	POPULATION AGE RATIOS 70+/20-69	POPULATION AGE RATIOS 75+/20-74	POPULATION MEAN AGE	POPULATION MEDIAN AGE
1950	0.1285	0.0767	0.0403	0.0174	23.65	19.16
1960	0.1161	0.0673	0.0357	0.0159	23.16	18.73
1970	0.1165	0.0670	0.0343	0.0147	22.90	18.24
1980	0.1179	0.0684	0.0353	0.0154	22.61	17.89
1990	*0.1206*	*0.0708*	*0.0375*	*0.0167*	*22.48*	*17.69*
2000	*0.1215*	*0.0726*	*0.0392*	*0.0179*	*22.56*	*17.83*
2010	*0.1198*	*0.0729*	*0.0404*	*0.0190*	*23.28*	*18.80*
2020	*0.1230*	*0.0745*	*0.0411*	*0.0199*	*25.10*	*21.21*

OBSERVED AND *PROJECTED* POPULATION DATA

YEAR	MID-YEAR POPULATION	NO. OF BIRTHS	NO. OF DEATHS	URBAN POPULATION NUMBER	URBAN POPULATION PERCENT	POPULATION 1985 AGE	POPULATION 1985 NUMBER
1950	1943900	93146	66720	179210	9.2	0	661248
1955	2080678	100268	69312	228409	11.0	5	515035
1960	2241446	108273	72327	291916	13.0	10	431504
1965	2428690	117772	74422	373650	15.4	15	364653
1970	2655557	129804	77508	480264	18.1	20	309861
1975	2930577	142449	79536	619559	21.1	25	264551
1980	3262989	157867	82198	800967	24.5	30	225232
1985	3664616	176744	85583	1035356	28.3	35	188796
1990	4150652	196944	89359	1335481	32.2	40	162012
1995	4725857	219062	93322	1710882	36.2	45	138737
2000	5399357	239872	96935	2170881	40.2	50	117018
2005	6164687	258837	99942	2725122	44.2	55	95822
2010	7013900	271143	101884	3376482	48.1	60	74914
2015	7914561	271580	102296	4112306	52.0	65	54117
2020	8808814	260292	101398	4899608	55.6	70+	61116

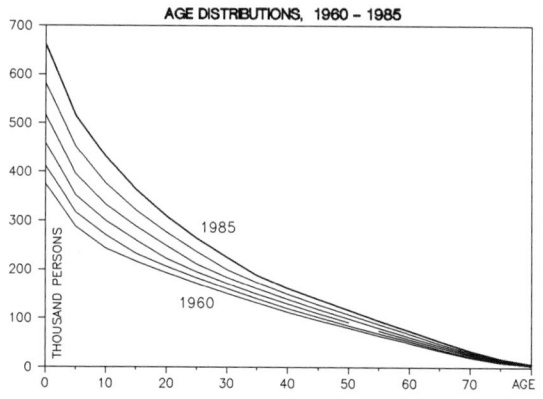

AGE DISTRIBUTIONS, 1960 - 1985

POPULATION RATIOS

YEAR	AGE DISTRIBUTION UNDER 15	15-64	65 & OLDER	70 & OLDER	DEPENDENCY RATIO	WOMEN 15-49	CHILD-WOMAN RATIO
1950	0.394	0.576	0.030	0.015	0.737	0.248	0.645
1955	0.398	0.571	0.030	0.015	0.750	0.246	0.669
1960	0.404	0.565	0.031	0.015	0.770	0.243	0.689
1965	0.412	0.557	0.031	0.016	0.794	0.240	0.707
1970	0.418	0.551	0.031	0.016	0.816	0.237	0.728
1975	0.425	0.544	0.031	0.016	0.840	0.235	0.751
1980	0.432	0.536	0.031	0.016	0.864	0.232	0.769
1985	0.439	0.530	0.031	0.017	0.887	0.230	0.785
1990	0.444	0.524	0.031	0.017	0.907	0.228	0.800
2000	0.449	0.520	0.031	0.017	0.924	0.228	0.793
2010	0.438	0.531	0.031	0.017	0.883	0.234	0.726
2020	0.403	0.565	0.032	0.018	0.770	0.248	0.580

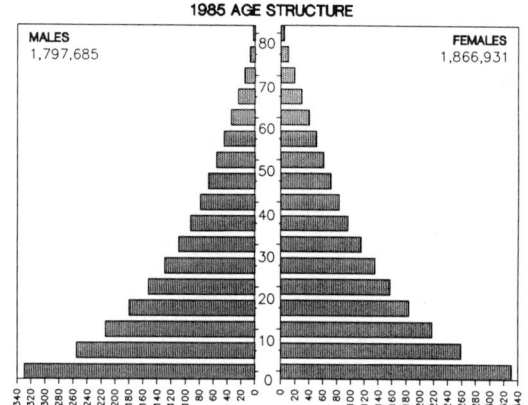

1985 AGE STRUCTURE

MALES 1,797,685

FEMALES 1,866,931

MORTALITY MEASURES (Annual Averages)

PERIOD	CRUDE DEATH RATE	INFANT MORT. RATE	LIFE EXPECTANCY AT BIRTH (years) MALE	FEMALE	BOTH SEXES	DIFFERENCE FEMALE-MALE
1950-55	34.32	230.86	28.58	31.46	30.00	2.88
1955-60	33.31	222.59	29.57	32.48	31.00	2.91
1960-65	32.27	214.96	30.55	33.49	32.00	2.94
1965-70	30.64	203.54	32.03	35.01	33.50	2.98
1970-75	29.19	192.96	33.51	36.53	35.00	3.02
1975-80	27.14	179.36	35.49	38.56	37.00	3.06
1980-85	25.19	166.49	37.47	40.58	39.00	3.11
1985-90	23.35	154.28	39.45	42.60	41.00	3.15
1990-95	21.53	142.81	41.43	44.62	43.00	3.19
2000-05	17.95	121.63	45.40	48.65	47.00	3.25
2010-15	14.53	102.71	49.31	52.75	51.00	3.44
2020-25	11.51	85.27	53.23	56.82	55.00	3.59

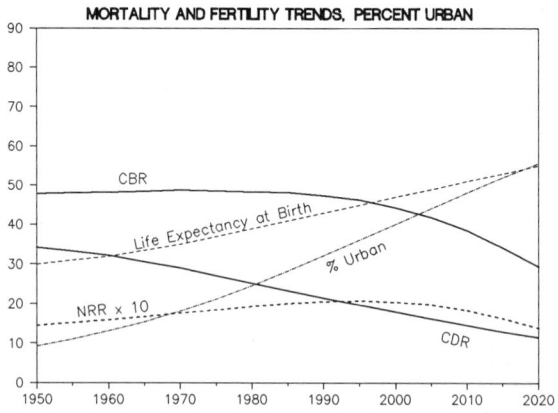

MORTALITY AND FERTILITY TRENDS, PERCENT URBAN

FERTILITY MEASURES (Annual Averages)

PERIOD	CRUDE BIRTH RATE	FERTILITY RATES GENERAL	TOTAL	REPRODUCTION RATES GROSS	NET	RATE OF NATUR. INCR.
1950-55	47.92	193.87	6.090	3.000	1.452	13.59
1955-60	48.19	197.02	6.191	3.050	1.520	14.88
1960-65	48.31	200.15	6.293	3.100	1.587	16.04
1965-70	48.49	203.40	6.394	3.150	1.678	17.85
1970-75	48.88	207.25	6.496	3.200	1.768	19.69
1975-80	48.61	208.44	6.496	3.200	1.852	21.47
1980-85	48.38	209.62	6.496	3.200	1.935	23.19
1985-90	48.23	210.62	6.496	3.200	2.016	24.88
1990-95	47.45	208.12	6.394	3.150	2.061	25.92
2000-05	44.43	193.85	5.928	2.920	2.051	26.47
2010-15	38.66	163.27	4.973	2.450	1.840	24.13
2020-25	29.55	116.23	3.552	1.750	1.394	18.04

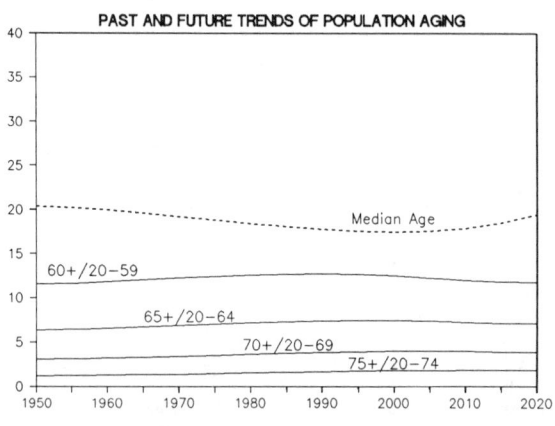

PAST AND FUTURE TRENDS OF POPULATION AGING

AGING MEASURES

YEAR	POPULATION AGE RATIOS 60+/20-59	65+/20-64	70+/20-69	75+/20-74	POPULATION MEAN AGE	POPULATION MEDIAN AGE
1950	0.1152	0.0636	0.0306	0.0121	24.40	20.40
1960	0.1180	0.0656	0.0319	0.0127	24.12	19.95
1970	0.1223	0.0688	0.0340	0.0138	23.72	19.18
1980	0.1254	0.0717	0.0363	0.0152	23.19	18.43
1990	0.1269	0.0741	0.0385	0.0167	22.66	17.77
2000	0.1247	0.0744	0.0397	0.0179	22.36	17.48
2010	0.1195	0.0724	0.0397	0.0184	22.57	17.91
2020	0.1176	0.0710	0.0389	0.0185	23.70	19.43

OBSERVED AND *PROJECTED* POPULATION DATA (000's)

YEAR	MID-YEAR POPULATION	NO. OF BIRTHS	NO. OF DEATHS	URBAN POPULATION NUMBER	URBAN POPULATION PERCENT	POPULATION 1985 AGE	POPULATION 1985 NUMBER
1950	2423	120	75	308	12.7	0	1306
1955	2657	130	77	395	14.9	5	952
1960	2935	142	79	508	17.3	10	677
1965	3267	157	82	652	20.0	15	576
1970	3668	177	86	832	22.7	20	537
1975	4156	217	93	1066	25.6	25	499
1980	5352	289	119	1549	28.9	30	425
1985	6398	325	129	2082	32.5	35	343
1990	*7555*	*352*	*137*	*2748*	*36.4*	40	266
1995	*8505*	*379*	*138*	*3431*	*40.3*	45	223
2000	*9803*	*444*	*146*	*4347*	*44.3*	50	172
2005	*11412*	*494*	*155*	*5509*	*48.3*	55	139
2010	*13247*	*522*	*160*	*6900*	*52.1*	60	108
2015	*15194*	*518*	*161*	*8469*	*55.7*	65	79
2020	*17086*	*507*	*161*	*10117*	*59.2*	70+	96

POPULATION RATIOS

YEAR	AGE DISTRIBUTION UNDER 15	AGE DISTRIBUTION 15-64	AGE DISTRIBUTION 65 & OLDER	AGE DISTRIBUTION 70 & OLDER	DEPENDENCY RATIO	WOMEN 15-49	CHILD-WOMAN RATIO
1950	0.412	0.562	0.026	0.012	0.781	0.238	0.722
1955	0.417	0.556	0.028	0.014	0.800	0.236	0.739
1960	0.427	0.544	0.029	0.015	0.838	0.231	0.760
1965	0.432	0.538	0.030	0.016	0.860	0.229	0.774
1970	0.437	0.532	0.031	0.016	0.880	0.228	0.788
1975	0.443	0.526	0.031	0.017	0.902	0.227	0.806
1980	0.435	0.536	0.029	0.016	0.865	0.254	0.772
1985	0.459	0.514	0.027	0.015	0.946	0.245	0.835
1990	*0.476*	*0.497*	*0.026*	*0.015*	*1.012*	*0.235*	*0.837*
2000	*0.462*	*0.511*	*0.027*	*0.015*	*0.956*	*0.229*	*0.781*
2010	*0.449*	*0.524*	*0.028*	*0.016*	*0.910*	*0.228*	*0.780*
2020	*0.416*	*0.552*	*0.032*	*0.018*	*0.812*	*0.244*	*0.598*

MORTALITY MEASURES (Annual Averages)

PERIOD	CRUDE DEATH RATE	INFANT MORT. RATE	LIFE EXPECTANCY AT BIRTH (years) MALE	LIFE EXPECTANCY AT BIRTH (years) FEMALE	LIFE EXPECTANCY AT BIRTH (years) BOTH SEXES	DIFFERENCE FEMALE-MALE
1950-55	30.94	190.00	31.54	34.51	33.00	2.97
1955-60	28.90	180.00	33.51	36.53	35.00	3.02
1960-65	26.92	170.00	35.49	38.56	37.00	3.06
1965-70	25.07	162.00	37.47	40.58	39.00	3.11
1970-75	23.33	155.00	39.45	42.60	41.00	3.15
1975-80	22.37	148.54	40.44	43.61	42.00	3.17
1980-85	22.26	142.91	41.41	44.60	42.98	3.19
1985-90	*20.17*	*132.05*	*43.41*	*46.60*	*44.98*	*3.19*
1990-95	*18.13*	*121.71*	*45.41*	*48.60*	*46.98*	*3.19*
2000-05	*14.93*	*102.75*	*49.41*	*52.60*	*50.98*	*3.19*
2010-15	*12.06*	*85.28*	*53.41*	*56.60*	*54.98*	*3.19*
2020-25	*9.45*	*68.94*	*57.41*	*60.60*	*58.98*	*3.19*

FERTILITY MEASURES (Annual Averages)

PERIOD	CRUDE BIRTH RATE	FERTILITY RATES GENERAL	FERTILITY RATES TOTAL	REPRODUCTION RATES GROSS	REPRODUCTION RATES NET	RATE OF NATUR. INCR.
1950-55	49.34	208.29	6.597	3.250	1.703	18.40
1955-60	48.80	208.90	6.597	3.250	1.790	19.90
1960-65	48.33	209.93	6.597	3.250	1.876	21.41
1965-70	48.19	210.85	6.597	3.250	1.960	23.12
1970-75	48.26	212.24	6.597	3.250	2.042	24.92
1975-80	52.32	216.12	6.597	3.250	2.082	29.95
1980-85	53.92	216.65	6.597	3.250	2.121	31.66
1985-90	*50.81*	*212.47*	*6.597*	*3.250*	*2.199*	*30.64*
1990-95	*46.64*	*203.58*	*6.496*	*3.200*	*2.242*	*28.52*
2000-05	*45.26*	*197.23*	*6.110*	*3.010*	*2.256*	*30.33*
2010-15	*39.44*	*171.68*	*5.075*	*2.500*	*1.986*	*27.38*
2020-25	*29.65*	*117.64*	*3.552*	*1.750*	*1.466*	*20.20*

AGING MEASURES

YEAR	POPULATION AGE RATIOS 60+/20-59	POPULATION AGE RATIOS 65+/20-64	POPULATION AGE RATIOS 70+/20-69	POPULATION AGE RATIOS 75+/20-74	POPULATION MEAN AGE	POPULATION MEDIAN AGE
1950	0.1042	0.0558	0.0255	0.0093	23.65	19.55
1960	0.1173	0.0651	0.0313	0.0123	23.39	18.87
1970	0.1253	0.0717	0.0363	0.0152	22.97	18.13
1980	0.1118	0.0658	0.0345	0.0152	22.39	18.26
1990	*0.1089*	*0.0648*	*0.0347*	*0.0157*	*21.59*	*16.33*
2000	*0.1152*	*0.0671*	*0.0364*	*0.0168*	*21.75*	*16.65*
2010	*0.1142*	*0.0664*	*0.0361*	*0.0164*	*21.93*	*17.43*
2020	*0.1231*	*0.0738*	*0.0394*	*0.0180*	*23.16*	*18.76*

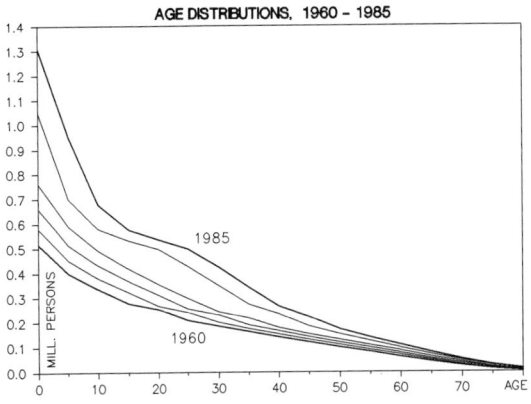

AGE DISTRIBUTIONS, 1960 - 1985

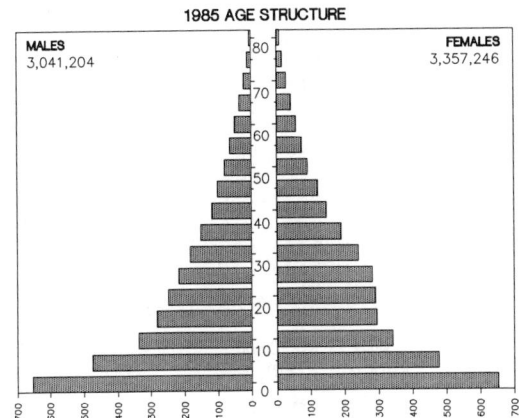

1985 AGE STRUCTURE

MALES 3,041,204

FEMALES 3,357,246

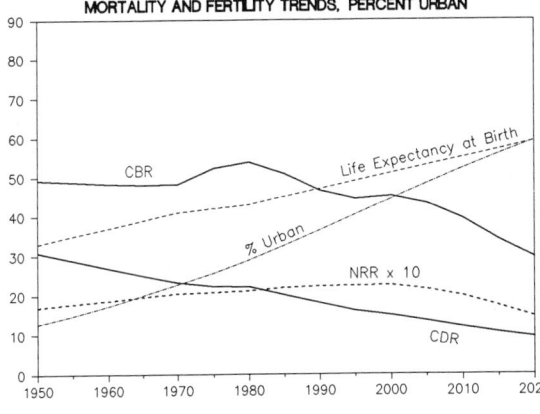

MORTALITY AND FERTILITY TRENDS, PERCENT URBAN

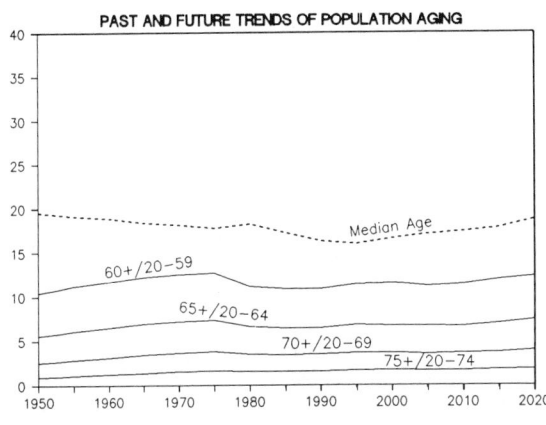

PAST AND FUTURE TRENDS OF POPULATION AGING

OBSERVED AND *PROJECTED* POPULATION DATA (000's)

YEAR	MID-YEAR POPULATION	NO. OF BIRTHS	NO. OF DEATHS	URBAN POPULATION NUMBER	URBAN POPULATION PERCENT	POPULATION 1985 AGE	POPULATION 1985 NUMBER
1950	13683	594	278	5898	43.1	0	4428
1955	15385	653	279	6902	44.9	5	3923
1960	17396	728	289	8113	46.6	10	3587
1965	19832	755	293	9370	47.2	15	3252
1970	22459	811	300	10754	47.9	20	3029
1975	25306	868	306	12788	50.5	25	2594
1980	28283	937	312	15042	53.2	30	2237
1985	31593	1001	310	17694	56.0	35	1823
1990	35248	1053	307	20778	58.9	40	1542
1995	39189	1092	306	24272	61.9	45	1279
2000	43332	1119	308	28123	64.9	50	1073
2005	47584	1133	321	32254	67.8	55	863
2010	51827	1130	337	36512	70.5	60	673
2015	55950	1107	363	40794	72.9	65	524
2020	59799	1059	392	44954	75.2	70+	766

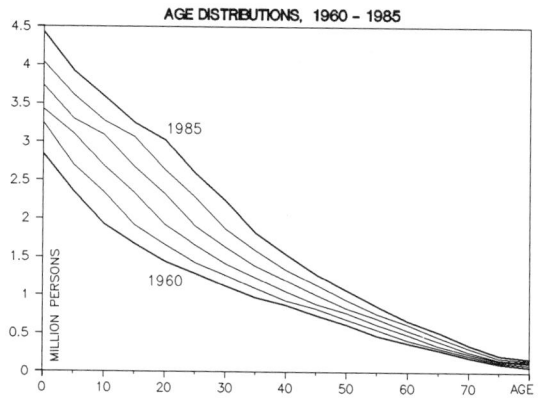

AGE DISTRIBUTIONS, 1960 - 1985

POPULATION RATIOS

YEAR	AGE DISTRIBUTION UNDER 15	AGE DISTRIBUTION 15-64	AGE DISTRIBUTION 65 & OLDER	AGE DISTRIBUTION 70 & OLDER	DEPENDENCY RATIO	WOMEN 15-49	CHILD-WOMAN RATIO
1950	0.386	0.578	0.036	0.019	0.729	0.240	0.635
1955	0.399	0.564	0.038	0.021	0.774	0.236	0.687
1960	0.409	0.552	0.039	0.022	0.812	0.232	0.704
1965	0.418	0.544	0.038	0.023	0.839	0.230	0.714
1970	0.410	0.552	0.038	0.023	0.813	0.233	0.656
1975	0.400	0.561	0.039	0.023	0.781	0.238	0.619
1980	0.386	0.574	0.040	0.023	0.741	0.245	0.582
1985	0.378	0.581	0.041	0.024	0.720	0.249	0.563
1990	0.370	0.588	0.042	0.025	0.699	0.251	0.543
2000	0.350	0.605	0.045	0.027	0.654	0.255	0.488
2010	0.319	0.629	0.052	0.031	0.590	0.260	0.422
2020	0.281	0.654	0.065	0.039	0.530	0.263	0.354

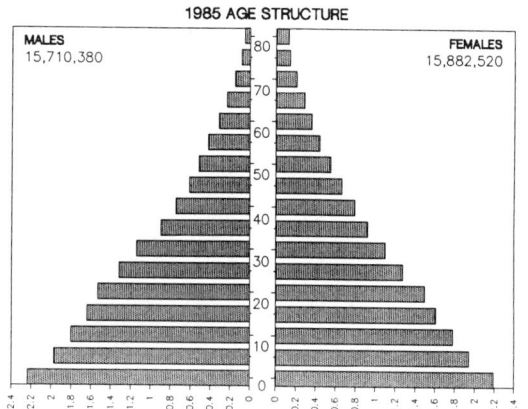

1985 AGE STRUCTURE

MALES 15,710,380

FEMALES 15,882,520

MORTALITY MEASURES (Annual Averages)

PERIOD	CRUDE DEATH RATE	INFANT MORT. RATE	LIFE EXPECTANCY AT BIRTH (years) MALE	LIFE EXPECTANCY AT BIRTH (years) FEMALE	LIFE EXPECTANCY AT BIRTH (years) BOTH SEXES	DIFFERENCE FEMALE-MALE
1950-55	20.29	152.00	43.99	46.03	44.99	2.04
1955-60	18.11	140.00	46.50	49.50	47.97	3.00
1960-65	16.63	130.00	47.99	52.00	49.96	4.00
1965-70	14.77	120.00	49.51	54.52	51.97	5.01
1970-75	13.34	110.00	51.00	57.01	53.95	6.01
1975-80	12.09	94.55	53.00	59.04	55.97	6.04
1980-85	11.03	83.27	55.00	60.97	57.94	5.97
1985-90	9.81	72.46	57.51	63.48	60.44	5.97
1990-95	8.70	62.12	60.01	65.94	62.93	5.93
2000-05	7.12	42.56	64.42	70.16	67.24	5.74
2010-15	6.51	30.03	67.59	73.11	70.30	5.52
2020-25	6.55	21.78	69.96	75.39	72.63	5.43

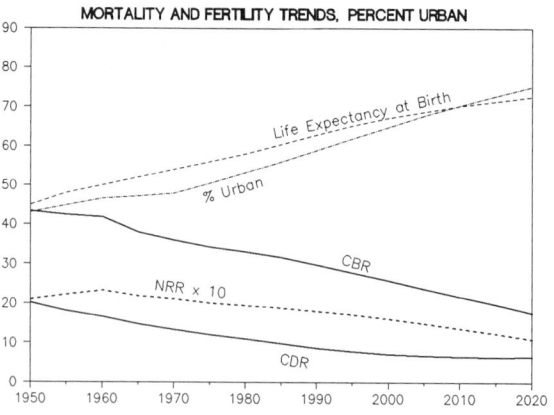

MORTALITY AND FERTILITY TRENDS, PERCENT URBAN

FERTILITY MEASURES (Annual Averages)

PERIOD	CRUDE BIRTH RATE	FERTILITY RATES GENERAL	FERTILITY RATES TOTAL	REPRODUCTION RATES GROSS	REPRODUCTION RATES NET	RATE OF NATUR. INCR.
1950-55	43.44	182.46	6.512	3.200	2.097	23.15
1955-60	42.47	181.58	6.512	3.200	2.229	24.36
1960-65	41.88	181.53	6.512	3.200	2.325	25.24
1965-70	38.06	164.62	5.901	2.900	2.193	23.29
1970-75	36.10	153.25	5.494	2.700	2.119	22.77
1975-80	34.31	141.82	5.087	2.500	2.018	22.22
1980-85	33.14	134.14	4.782	2.350	1.946	22.11
1985-90	31.69	126.72	4.477	2.200	1.879	21.87
1990-95	29.88	118.52	4.172	2.050	1.802	21.18
2000-05	25.83	100.76	3.561	1.750	1.609	18.71
2010-15	21.81	83.81	2.951	1.450	1.366	15.30
2020-25	17.72	67.16	2.340	1.150	1.099	11.16

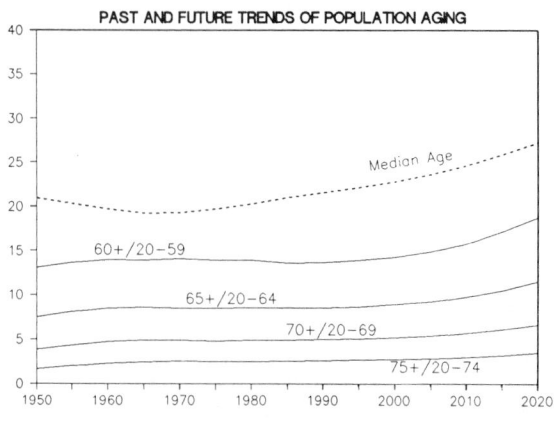

PAST AND FUTURE TRENDS OF POPULATION AGING

AGING MEASURES

YEAR	POPULATION AGE RATIOS 60+/20-59	POPULATION AGE RATIOS 65+/20-64	POPULATION AGE RATIOS 70+/20-69	POPULATION AGE RATIOS 75+/20-74	POPULATION MEAN AGE	POPULATION MEDIAN AGE
1950	0.1304	0.0746	0.0386	0.0165	25.01	20.94
1960	0.1396	0.0848	0.0469	0.0226	24.38	19.70
1970	0.1402	0.0848	0.0488	0.0252	24.19	19.31
1980	0.1388	0.0851	0.0487	0.0248	24.70	20.29
1990	0.1363	0.0852	0.0501	0.0261	25.44	21.58
2000	0.1426	0.0892	0.0519	0.0276	26.56	22.85
2010	0.1574	0.0978	0.0570	0.0303	28.17	24.65
2020	0.1878	0.1158	0.0664	0.0353	30.29	27.29

OBSERVED AND *PROJECTED* POPULATION DATA (000's)

YEAR	MID-YEAR POPULATION	NO. OF BIRTHS	NO. OF DEATHS	URBAN POPULATION NUMBER	URBAN POPULATION PERCENT	POPULATION 1985 AGE	POPULATION 1985 NUMBER
1950	9190	432	249	579	6.3	0	3998
1955	10150	477	264	820	8.1	5	3226
1960	11165	525	277	1150	10.3	10	2637
1965	12359	581	284	1612	13.0	15	2217
1970	13859	651	294	2271	16.4	20	1879
1975	16012	753	311	3023	18.9	25	1588
1980	18681	857	322	3688	19.7	30	1338
1985	21818	972	345	4502	20.6	35	1121
1990	*25195*	*1090*	*363*	*5548*	*22.0*	40	933
1995	*29116*	*1215*	*380*	*6974*	*24.0*	45	770
2000	*33610*	*1331*	*396*	*8902*	*26.5*	50	626
2005	*38633*	*1413*	*408*	*11462*	*29.7*	55	498
2010	*44007*	*1431*	*413*	*14758*	*33.5*	60	384
2015	*49407*	*1406*	*416*	*18530*	*37.5*	65	275
2020	*54618*	*1370*	*418*	*22674*	*41.5*	70+	331

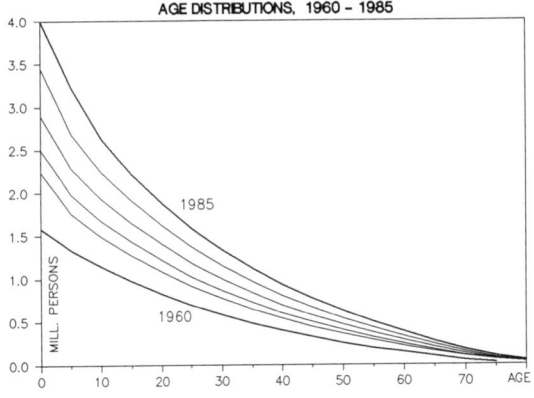

AGE DISTRIBUTIONS, 1960 - 1985

POPULATION RATIOS

YEAR	AGE DISTRIBUTION UNDER 15	AGE DISTRIBUTION 15-64	AGE DISTRIBUTION 65 & OLDER	AGE DISTRIBUTION 70 & OLDER	DEPENDENCY RATIO	WOMEN 15-49	CHILD-WOMAN RATIO
1950	0.438	0.529	0.033	0.018	0.891	0.228	0.789
1955	0.441	0.528	0.031	0.017	0.895	0.229	0.789
1960	0.443	0.527	0.029	0.016	0.896	0.230	0.789
1965	0.444	0.528	0.028	0.015	0.892	0.230	0.787
1970	0.444	0.529	0.027	0.015	0.890	0.230	0.785
1975	0.444	0.528	0.027	0.015	0.893	0.229	0.790
1980	0.449	0.524	0.027	0.015	0.908	0.227	0.815
1985	0.452	0.520	0.028	0.015	0.922	0.225	0.815
1990	*0.452*	*0.519*	*0.028*	*0.016*	*0.925*	*0.224*	*0.803*
2000	*0.442*	*0.528*	*0.030*	*0.017*	*0.894*	*0.227*	*0.760*
2010	*0.421*	*0.547*	*0.032*	*0.018*	*0.828*	*0.235*	*0.664*
2020	*0.371*	*0.592*	*0.037*	*0.021*	*0.688*	*0.254*	*0.496*

MORTALITY MEASURES (Annual Averages)

PERIOD	CRUDE DEATH RATE	INFANT MORT. RATE	LIFE EXPECTANCY AT BIRTH (years) MALE	LIFE EXPECTANCY AT BIRTH (years) FEMALE	LIFE EXPECTANCY AT BIRTH (years) BOTH SEXES	DIFFERENCE FEMALE-MALE
1950-55	27.10	185.00	36.10	38.30	37.17	2.20
1955-60	26.00	175.00	37.10	39.30	38.17	2.20
1960-65	24.80	165.00	38.10	40.30	39.17	2.20
1965-70	23.00	156.00	39.80	42.10	40.92	2.30
1970-75	21.20	145.00	41.40	43.90	42.62	2.50
1975-80	19.40	131.00	43.90	46.40	45.12	2.50
1980-85	17.26	117.58	46.60	49.00	47.77	2.40
1985-90	*15.82*	*108.12*	*48.60*	*51.00*	*49.77*	*2.40*
1990-95	*14.40*	*99.07*	*50.60*	*53.00*	*51.77*	*2.40*
2000-05	*11.79*	*81.83*	*54.60*	*57.00*	*55.77*	*2.40*
2010-15	*9.39*	*65.72*	*58.60*	*61.00*	*59.77*	*2.40*
2020-25	*7.66*	*50.85*	*62.60*	*65.00*	*63.77*	*2.40*

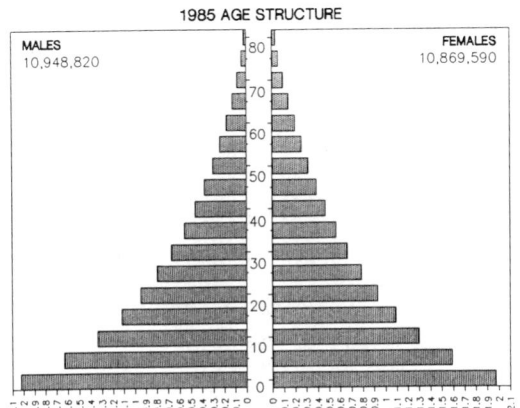

1985 AGE STRUCTURE

MALES 10,948,820   FEMALES 10,869,590

FERTILITY MEASURES (Annual Averages)

PERIOD	CRUDE BIRTH RATE	FERTILITY RATES GENERAL	FERTILITY RATES TOTAL	REPRODUCTION RATES GROSS	REPRODUCTION RATES NET	RATE OF NATUR. INCR.
1950-55	47.00	205.57	6.667	3.260	1.850	19.90
1955-60	47.00	204.88	6.667	3.260	1.890	21.00
1960-65	47.00	204.56	6.667	3.260	1.930	22.20
1965-70	47.00	204.48	6.667	3.260	2.010	24.00
1970-75	47.00	204.85	6.667	3.260	2.080	25.80
1975-80	47.05	206.44	6.667	3.260	2.170	27.65
1980-85	45.87	203.20	6.585	3.220	2.252	28.61
1985-90	*44.55*	*198.66*	*6.442*	*3.150*	*2.279*	*28.73*
1990-95	*43.28*	*192.67*	*6.258*	*3.060*	*2.287*	*28.87*
2000-05	*39.60*	*172.91*	*5.562*	*2.720*	*2.158*	*27.81*
2010-15	*32.52*	*135.71*	*4.315*	*2.110*	*1.766*	*23.13*
2020-25	*25.08*	*96.67*	*2.986*	*1.460*	*1.285*	*17.43*

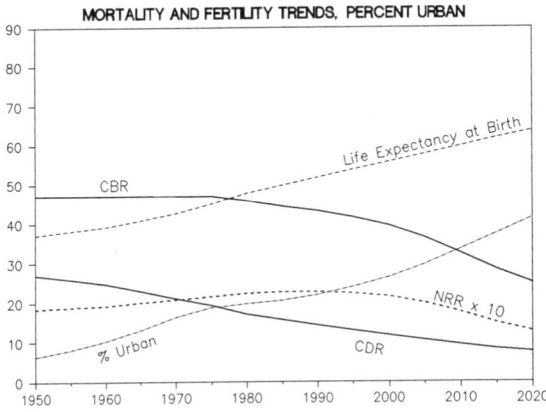

MORTALITY AND FERTILITY TRENDS, PERCENT URBAN

AGING MEASURES

YEAR	POPULATION AGE RATIOS 60+/20-59	POPULATION AGE RATIOS 65+/20-64	POPULATION AGE RATIOS 70+/20-69	POPULATION AGE RATIOS 75+/20-74	POPULATION MEAN AGE	POPULATION MEDIAN AGE
1950	0.1314	0.0779	0.0413	0.0181	22.84	18.07
1960	0.1150	0.0693	0.0370	0.0165	22.41	17.77
1970	0.1088	0.0631	0.0333	0.0152	22.28	17.71
1980	0.1107	0.0647	0.0339	0.0149	22.16	17.51
1990	*0.1152*	*0.0681*	*0.0363*	*0.0165*	*22.16*	*17.33*
2000	*0.1180*	*0.0706*	*0.0384*	*0.0178*	*22.41*	*17.71*
2010	*0.1206*	*0.0730*	*0.0403*	*0.0191*	*23.17*	*18.69*
2020	*0.1249*	*0.0766*	*0.0430*	*0.0209*	*24.96*	*20.97*

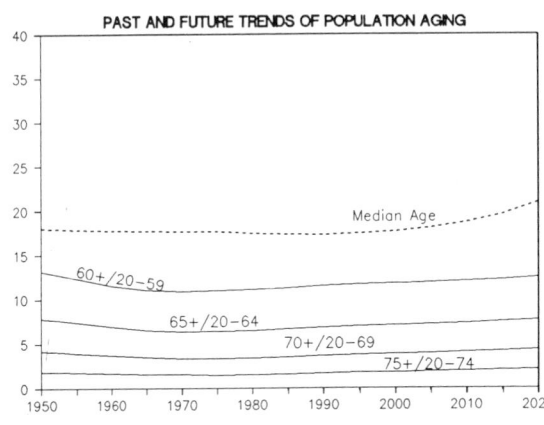

PAST AND FUTURE TRENDS OF POPULATION AGING

OBSERVED AND *PROJECTED* POPULATION DATA

YEAR	MID-YEAR POPULATION	NO. OF BIRTHS	NO. OF DEATHS	URBAN POPULATION NUMBER	URBAN POPULATION PERCENT	POPULATION 1985 AGE	POPULATION 1985 NUMBER
1950	263741	13196	7475	3642	1.4	0	127638
1955	291204	14382	7347	6793	2.3	5	101057
1960	326413	15852	7371	12775	3.9	10	82328
1965	370078	17734	7500	24038	6.5	15	67783
1970	419725	19946	7567	40742	9.7	20	56344
1975	482200	22799	7787	67542	14.0	25	46608
1980	563602	26515	7953	111563	19.8	30	38340
1985	664736	31111	8342	175115	26.3	35	31749
1990	*789244*	*35762*	*8656*	*260934*	*33.1*	40	26099
1995	*937502*	*41462*	*8930*	*368438*	*39.3*	45	22053
2000	*1115615*	*46359*	*9082*	*496873*	*44.5*	50	18408
2005	*1318984*	*50295*	*9167*	*639241*	*48.5*	55	14936
2010	*1542012*	*51674*	*9237*	*806038*	*52.3*	60	11727
2015	*1769882*	*51273*	*9458*	*989722*	*55.9*	65	8730
2020	*1992086*	*50452*	*9851*	*1182929*	*59.4*	70+	10935

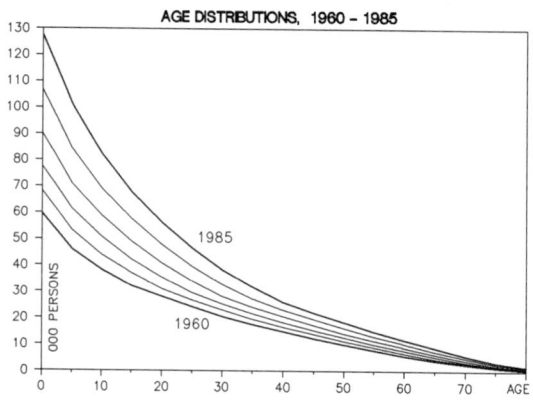

AGE DISTRIBUTIONS, 1960 - 1985

POPULATION RATIOS

YEAR	AGE DISTRIBUTION UNDER 15	15-64	65 & OLDER	70 & OLDER	DEPENDENCY RATIO	WOMEN 15-49	CHILD-WOMAN RATIO
1950	0.430	0.543	0.027	0.013	0.841	0.240	0.744
1955	0.434	0.539	0.027	0.014	0.855	0.238	0.756
1960	0.441	0.532	0.027	0.014	0.880	0.234	0.779
1965	0.447	0.526	0.027	0.015	0.901	0.231	0.797
1970	0.452	0.520	0.028	0.015	0.922	0.228	0.810
1975	0.456	0.515	0.029	0.016	0.941	0.226	0.828
1980	0.462	0.509	0.029	0.016	0.964	0.224	0.847
1985	0.468	0.503	0.030	0.016	0.990	0.221	0.868
1990	*0.473*	*0.497*	*0.030*	*0.017*	*1.012*	*0.220*	*0.881*
2000	*0.473*	*0.498*	*0.029*	*0.017*	*1.008*	*0.221*	*0.850*
2010	*0.449*	*0.521*	*0.030*	*0.018*	*0.920*	*0.231*	*0.725*
2020	*0.390*	*0.577*	*0.033*	*0.020*	*0.734*	*0.254*	*0.518*

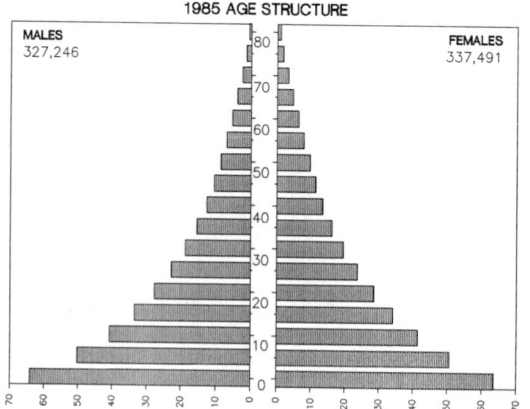

1985 AGE STRUCTURE

MALES 327,246   FEMALES 337,491

MORTALITY MEASURES (Annual Averages)

PERIOD	CRUDE DEATH RATE	INFANT MORT. RATE	LIFE EXPECTANCY AT BIRTH (years) MALE	FEMALE	BOTH SEXES	DIFFERENCE FEMALE-MALE
1950-55	28.34	160.00	34.20	37.00	35.58	2.80
1955-60	25.23	154.00	37.00	40.40	38.67	3.40
1960-65	22.58	150.00	39.70	43.50	41.57	3.80
1965-70	20.26	147.00	42.40	46.50	44.42	4.10
1970-75	18.03	144.00	45.10	49.60	47.32	4.50
1975-80	16.15	140.00	47.60	52.30	49.92	4.70
1980-85	14.11	129.00	51.20	54.80	52.97	3.60
1985-90	*12.55*	*118.00*	*53.70*	*57.30*	*55.47*	*3.60*
1990-95	*10.97*	*107.00*	*56.20*	*59.80*	*57.97*	*3.60*
2000-05	*8.14*	*87.00*	*61.12*	*64.80*	*62.93*	*3.68*
2010-15	*5.99*	*68.00*	*65.36*	*69.20*	*67.25*	*3.84*
2020-25	*4.95*	*51.00*	*68.24*	*72.50*	*70.34*	*4.26*

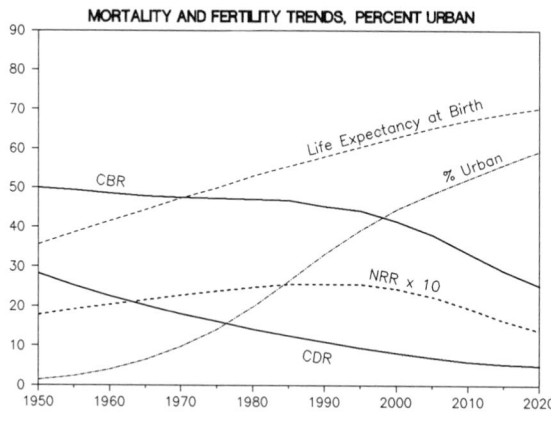

MORTALITY AND FERTILITY TRENDS, PERCENT URBAN

FERTILITY MEASURES (Annual Averages)

PERIOD	CRUDE BIRTH RATE	FERTILITY RATES GENERAL	TOTAL	REPRODUCTION RATES GROSS	NET	RATE OF NATUR. INCR.
1950-55	50.03	209.46	6.496	3.200	1.784	21.69
1955-60	49.39	209.17	6.496	3.200	1.924	24.16
1960-65	48.56	208.77	6.496	3.200	2.047	25.98
1965-70	47.92	208.76	6.496	3.200	2.162	27.66
1970-75	47.52	209.31	6.496	3.200	2.281	29.49
1975-80	47.28	210.29	6.496	3.200	2.384	31.14
1980-85	47.04	211.48	6.496	3.200	2.475	32.93
1985-90	*46.80*	*212.38*	*6.496*	*3.200*	*2.563*	*34.25*
1990-95	*45.31*	*206.22*	*6.293*	*3.100*	*2.565*	*34.34*
2000-05	*41.56*	*186.27*	*5.664*	*2.790*	*2.447*	*33.41*
2010-15	*33.51*	*141.84*	*4.304*	*2.120*	*1.945*	*27.52*
2020-25	*25.33*	*97.00*	*2.964*	*1.460*	*1.381*	*20.38*

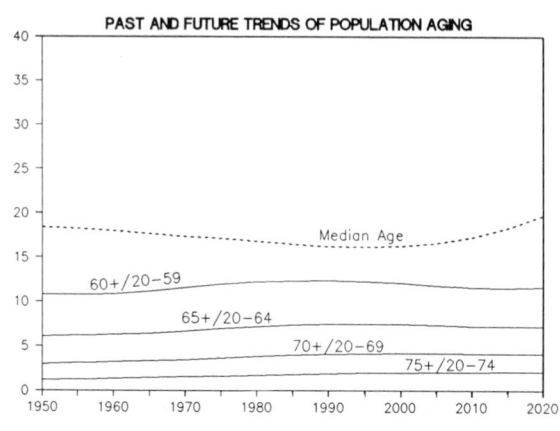

PAST AND FUTURE TRENDS OF POPULATION AGING

AGING MEASURES

YEAR	POPULATION AGE RATIOS 60+/20-59	65+/20-64	70+/20-69	75+/20-74	POPULATION MEAN AGE	POPULATION MEDIAN AGE
1950	0.1079	0.0607	0.0294	0.0117	22.76	18.43
1960	0.1082	0.0626	0.0321	0.0135	22.54	17.99
1970	0.1154	0.0666	0.0344	0.0152	22.28	17.39
1980	0.1221	0.0719	0.0382	0.0171	21.91	16.88
1990	*0.1236*	*0.0748*	*0.0411*	*0.0191*	*21.45*	*16.30*
2000	*0.1209*	*0.0747*	*0.0420*	*0.0204*	*21.34*	*16.29*
2010	*0.1162*	*0.0723*	*0.0418*	*0.0210*	*21.99*	*17.31*
2020	*0.1163*	*0.0724*	*0.0418*	*0.0212*	*23.91*	*19.78*

OBSERVED AND *PROJECTED* POPULATION DATA (000's)

YEAR	MID-YEAR POPULATION	NO. OF BIRTHS	NO. OF DEATHS	URBAN POPULATION NUMBER	URBAN POPULATION PERCENT	POPULATION 1985 AGE	POPULATION 1985 NUMBER
1950	7886	389	216	299	3.8	0	4603
1955	8803	449	220	372	4.2	5	3570
1960	10026	518	229	473	4.7	10	2878
1965	11586	596	240	608	5.3	15	2357
1970	13513	691	253	904	6.7	20	1939
1975	15900	809	267	1602	10.1	25	1555
1980	18867	955	288	3110	16.5	30	1230
1985	22751	1149	317	5554	24.4	35	1115
1990	*27328*	*1355*	*345*	*8971*	*32.8*	40	901
1995	*32892*	*1584*	*371*	*13319*	*40.5*	45	723
2000	*39572*	*1822*	*396*	*18395*	*46.5*	50	573
2005	*47405*	*2038*	*417*	*23873*	*50.4*	55	446
2010	*56271*	*2179*	*430*	*30438*	*54.1*	60	336
2015	*65755*	*2227*	*435*	*37908*	*57.7*	65	238
2020	*75368*	*2213*	*440*	*45984*	*61.0*	70+	286

POPULATION RATIOS

YEAR	AGE DISTRIBUTION UNDER 15	AGE DISTRIBUTION 15-64	AGE DISTRIBUTION 65 & OLDER	AGE DISTRIBUTION 70 & OLDER	DEPENDENCY RATIO	WOMEN 15-49	CHILD-WOMAN RATIO
1950	0.467	0.499	0.034	0.019	1.002	0.222	0.888
1955	0.462	0.508	0.031	0.017	0.970	0.227	0.797
1960	0.460	0.512	0.029	0.016	0.954	0.230	0.824
1965	0.459	0.515	0.026	0.015	0.942	0.231	0.844
1970	0.471	0.505	0.024	0.013	0.980	0.226	0.873
1975	0.479	0.498	0.023	0.013	1.007	0.222	0.897
1980	0.484	0.493	0.023	0.013	1.028	0.220	0.918
1985	0.486	0.491	0.023	0.013	1.036	0.219	0.923
1990	*0.491*	*0.485*	*0.023*	*0.013*	*1.060*	*0.217*	*0.943*
2000	*0.494*	*0.483*	*0.024*	*0.013*	*1.072*	*0.215*	*0.930*
2010	*0.475*	*0.500*	*0.025*	*0.014*	*1.002*	*0.224*	*0.820*
2020	*0.426*	*0.547*	*0.027*	*0.016*	*0.829*	*0.244*	*0.615*

MORTALITY MEASURES (Annual Averages)

PERIOD	CRUDE DEATH RATE	INFANT MORT. RATE	LIFE EXPECTANCY AT BIRTH (years) MALE	LIFE EXPECTANCY AT BIRTH (years) FEMALE	LIFE EXPECTANCY AT BIRTH (years) BOTH SEXES	DIFFERENCE FEMALE-MALE
1950-55	27.40	160.00	35.49	38.56	37.00	3.06
1955-60	24.98	150.00	37.76	40.88	39.30	3.12
1960-65	22.83	143.00	40.14	43.31	41.70	3.17
1965-70	20.70	135.00	42.52	45.73	44.10	3.21
1970-75	18.70	130.00	44.90	48.15	46.50	3.25
1975-80	16.77	125.00	47.30	50.70	48.97	3.40
1980-85	15.26	115.00	49.30	52.70	50.97	3.40
1985-90	*13.95*	*105.57*	*51.30*	*54.70*	*52.97*	*3.40*
1990-95	*12.61*	*96.63*	*53.30*	*56.70*	*54.97*	*3.40*
2000-05	*10.02*	*79.55*	*57.30*	*60.70*	*58.97*	*3.40*
2010-15	*7.64*	*63.59*	*61.30*	*64.70*	*62.97*	*3.40*
2020-25	*5.84*	*49.00*	*65.30*	*68.50*	*66.88*	*3.20*

FERTILITY MEASURES (Annual Averages)

PERIOD	CRUDE BIRTH RATE	FERTILITY RATES GENERAL	FERTILITY RATES TOTAL	REPRODUCTION RATES GROSS	REPRODUCTION RATES NET	RATE OF NATUR. INCR.
1950-55	49.37	219.97	6.744	3.322	1.917	21.97
1955-60	50.96	222.94	6.825	3.362	2.039	25.98
1960-65	51.70	224.21	6.857	3.378	2.151	28.87
1965-70	51.41	225.11	6.874	3.386	2.255	30.71
1970-75	51.17	228.47	7.001	3.449	2.396	32.47
1975-80	50.90	230.53	7.105	3.500	2.539	34.14
1980-85	50.62	230.79	7.105	3.500	2.622	35.36
1985-90	*50.51*	*231.79*	*7.105*	*3.500*	*2.702*	*36.56*
1990-95	*49.57*	*229.66*	*7.003*	*3.450*	*2.740*	*36.96*
2000-05	*46.04*	*212.48*	*6.435*	*3.170*	*2.651*	*36.02*
2010-15	*38.73*	*169.79*	*5.136*	*2.530*	*2.216*	*31.09*
2020-25	*29.36*	*117.07*	*3.552*	*1.750*	*1.594*	*23.52*

AGING MEASURES

YEAR	POPULATION AGE RATIOS 60+/20-59	POPULATION AGE RATIOS 65+/20-64	POPULATION AGE RATIOS 70+/20-69	POPULATION AGE RATIOS 75+/20-74	POPULATION MEAN AGE	POPULATION MEDIAN AGE
1950	0.1404	0.0848	0.0454	0.0203	21.86	16.64
1960	0.1131	0.0708	0.0382	0.0175	21.57	16.88
1970	0.0987	0.0589	0.0322	0.0156	21.14	16.49
1980	0.1010	0.0591	0.0314	0.0144	20.80	15.78
1990	*0.1031*	*0.0607*	*0.0324*	*0.0148*	*20.51*	*15.42*
2000	*0.1058*	*0.0629*	*0.0341*	*0.0159*	*20.39*	*15.30*
2010	*0.1071*	*0.0644*	*0.0354*	*0.0168*	*20.84*	*16.11*
2020	*0.1023*	*0.0632*	*0.0370*	*0.0180*	*22.38*	*18.19*

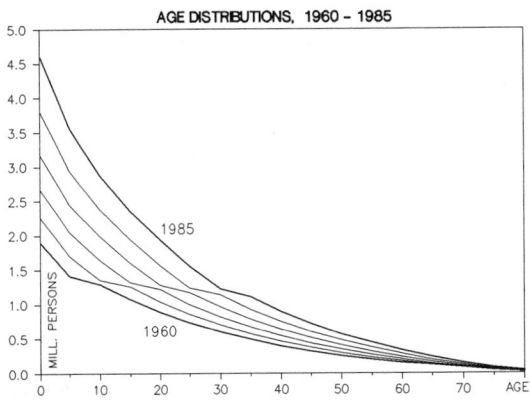

AGE DISTRIBUTIONS, 1960 - 1985

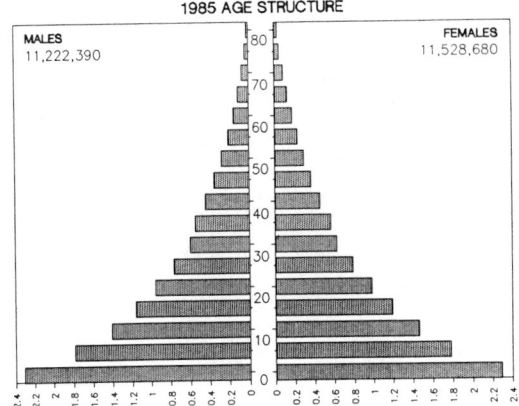

1985 AGE STRUCTURE

MALES 11,222,390   FEMALES 11,528,680

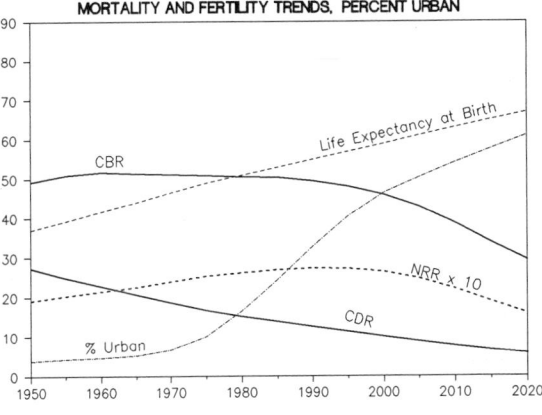

MORTALITY AND FERTILITY TRENDS, PERCENT URBAN

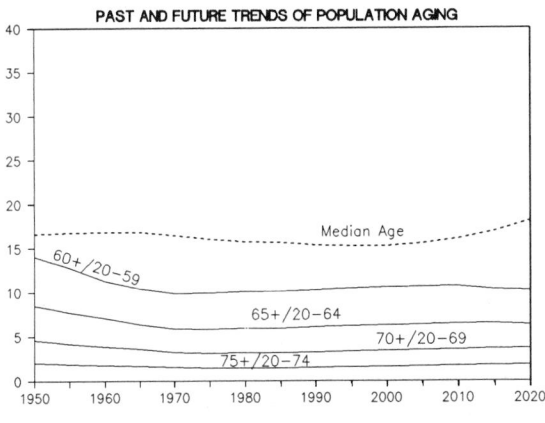

PAST AND FUTURE TRENDS OF POPULATION AGING

OBSERVED AND *PROJECTED* POPULATION DATA

YEAR	MID-YEAR POPULATION	NO. OF BIRTHS	NO. OF DEATHS	URBAN POPULATION NUMBER	URBAN POPULATION PERCENT	POPULATION 1985 AGE	POPULATION 1985 NUMBER
1950	1329007	62829	38679	96165	7.2	0	541113
1955	1413593	66874	37884	119043	8.4	5	429000
1960	1513672	72217	36894	148045	9.8	10	355555
1965	1626892	71894	33867	184358	11.3	15	303469
1970	2020000	92201	40808	265064	13.1	20	253636
1975	2251696	102511	41848	354894	15.8	25	210616
1980	2554007	115395	40144	479360	18.8	30	176998
1985	2960172	132980	41718	654688	22.1	35	149576
1990	*3454595*	*151805*	*44167*	*889250*	*25.7*	40	126166
1995	*4038265*	*173439*	*46541*	*1193112*	*29.5*	45	105599
2000	*4726869*	*196387*	*48786*	*1578999*	*33.4*	50	87476
2005	*5527360*	*218016*	*50691*	*2065706*	*37.4*	55	70916
2010	*6432481*	*237725*	*52212*	*2661848*	*41.4*	60	55660
2015	*7432124*	*249563*	*53162*	*3371759*	*45.4*	65	41582
2020	*8483585*	*245218*	*53379*	*4180102*	*49.3*	70+	52810

POPULATION RATIOS

YEAR	AGE DISTRIBUTION UNDER 15	15-64	65 & OLDER	70 & OLDER	DEPENDENCY RATIO	WOMEN 15-49	CHILD-WOMAN RATIO
1950	0.413	0.544	0.043	0.024	0.839	0.234	0.719
1955	0.419	0.541	0.040	0.022	0.848	0.236	0.722
1960	0.424	0.540	0.036	0.021	0.852	0.236	0.733
1965	0.431	0.536	0.033	0.019	0.864	0.234	0.756
1970	0.436	0.532	0.031	0.018	0.879	0.232	0.770
1975	0.440	0.529	0.031	0.017	0.889	0.231	0.764
1980	0.444	0.525	0.032	0.017	0.906	0.229	0.784
1985	0.448	0.520	0.032	0.018	0.922	0.227	0.804
1990	*0.454*	*0.514*	*0.032*	*0.018*	*0.944*	*0.225*	*0.820*
2000	*0.456*	*0.513*	*0.032*	*0.018*	*0.951*	*0.224*	*0.804*
2010	*0.443*	*0.525*	*0.032*	*0.019*	*0.906*	*0.230*	*0.738*
2020	*0.412*	*0.554*	*0.034*	*0.020*	*0.805*	*0.242*	*0.614*

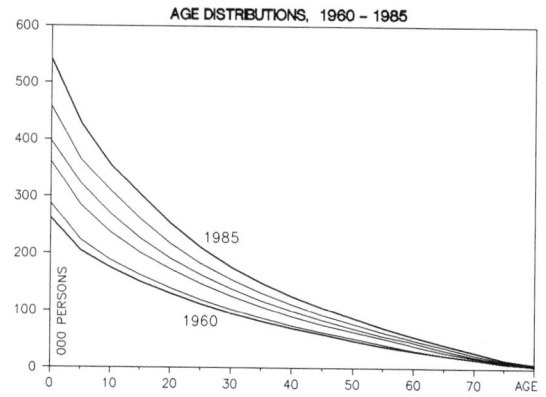

AGE DISTRIBUTIONS, 1960 - 1985

MORTALITY MEASURES (Annual Averages)

PERIOD	CRUDE DEATH RATE	INFANT MORT. RATE	LIFE EXPECTANCY AT BIRTH (years) MALE	FEMALE	BOTH SEXES	DIFFERENCE FEMALE-MALE
1950-55	29.10	203.54	34.50	37.54	36.00	3.04
1955-60	26.80	192.96	36.48	39.57	38.00	3.09
1960-65	24.37	170.17	38.96	42.09	40.50	3.13
1965-70	20.82	140.52	41.43	44.62	43.00	3.19
1970-75	20.20	121.13	43.91	47.14	45.50	3.23
1975-80	18.58	111.42	46.39	49.66	48.00	3.27
1980-85	15.72	102.27	48.82	52.23	50.50	3.41
1985-90	*14.09*	*93.83*	*51.26*	*54.79*	*53.00*	*3.53*
1990-95	*12.78*	*85.27*	*53.23*	*56.82*	*55.00*	*3.59*
2000-05	*10.32*	*68.94*	*57.19*	*60.86*	*59.00*	*3.67*
2010-15	*8.12*	*53.77*	*61.19*	*64.86*	*63.00*	*3.67*
2020-25	*6.29*	*39.90*	*65.21*	*68.84*	*67.00*	*3.62*

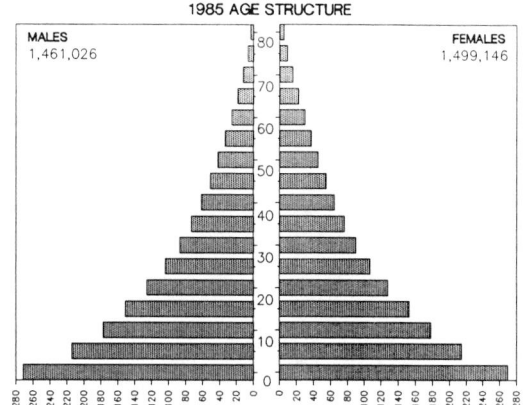

1985 AGE STRUCTURE

MALES 1,461,026   FEMALES 1,499,146

FERTILITY MEASURES (Annual Averages)

PERIOD	CRUDE BIRTH RATE	FERTILITY RATES GENERAL	TOTAL	REPRODUCTION RATES GROSS	NET	RATE OF NATUR. INCR.
1950-55	47.28	200.88	6.145	3.027	1.713	18.17
1955-60	47.31	200.37	6.114	3.012	1.783	20.51
1960-65	47.71	203.04	6.153	3.031	1.891	23.34
1965-70	44.19	189.74	6.171	3.040	1.974	23.37
1970-75	45.64	197.27	6.090	3.000	2.020	25.44
1975-80	45.53	198.08	6.090	3.000	2.091	26.94
1980-85	45.18	198.13	6.090	3.000	2.235	29.46
1985-90	*44.92*	*198.89*	*6.090*	*3.000*	*2.323*	*30.83*
1990-95	*43.94*	*196.05*	*5.988*	*2.950*	*2.350*	*31.16*
2000-05	*41.55*	*184.12*	*5.603*	*2.760*	*2.316*	*31.23*
2010-15	*36.96*	*158.71*	*4.811*	*2.370*	*2.082*	*28.84*
2020-25	*28.91*	*116.69*	*3.552*	*1.750*	*1.600*	*22.61*

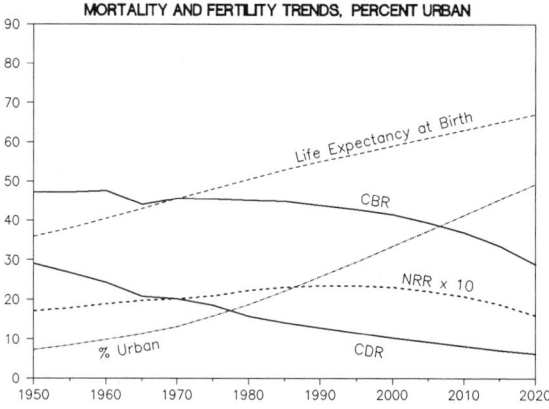

MORTALITY AND FERTILITY TRENDS, PERCENT URBAN

AGING MEASURES

YEAR	POPULATION AGE RATIOS 60+/20-59	65+/20-64	70+/20-69	75+/20-74	POPULATION MEAN AGE	POPULATION MEDIAN AGE
1950	0.1612	0.0971	0.0519	0.0230	24.30	19.44
1960	0.1323	0.0814	0.0454	0.0207	23.47	18.78
1970	0.1229	0.0725	0.0393	0.0185	22.93	18.18
1980	0.1265	0.0751	0.0397	0.0180	22.67	17.77
1990	*0.1271*	*0.0768*	*0.0422*	*0.0197*	*22.27*	*17.29*
2000	*0.1266*	*0.0773*	*0.0431*	*0.0207*	*22.12*	*17.11*
2010	*0.1241*	*0.0767*	*0.0434*	*0.0213*	*22.42*	*17.65*
2020	*0.1233*	*0.0767*	*0.0441*	*0.0221*	*23.46*	*19.02*

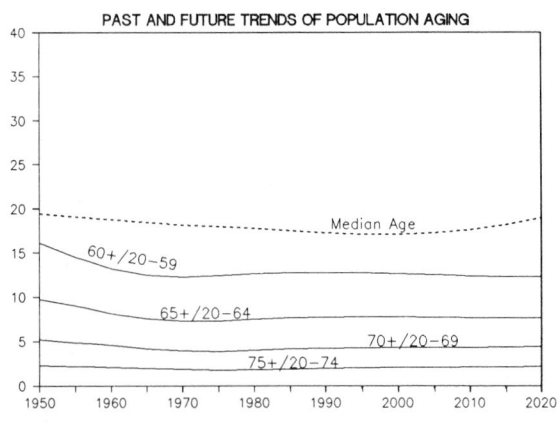

PAST AND FUTURE TRENDS OF POPULATION AGING

OBSERVED AND *PROJECTED* POPULATION DATA (000's)

YEAR	MID-YEAR POPULATION	NO. OF BIRTHS	NO. OF DEATHS	URBAN POPULATION NUMBER	URBAN POPULATION PERCENT	POPULATION 1985 AGE	POPULATION 1985 NUMBER
1950	3530	164	80	1102	31.2	0	1057
1955	3860	180	78	1270	32.9	5	954
1960	4221	196	76	1521	36.0	10	865
1965	4630	194	72	1829	39.5	15	811
1970	5127	190	63	2229	43.5	20	728
1975	5611	204	56	2673	47.6	25	622
1980	6384	215	54	3334	52.2	30	475
1985	7261	220	53	3848	53.0	35	311
1990	8169	214	53	4439	54.3	40	253
1995	9019	207	53	5071	56.2	45	284
2000	9821	197	55	5755	58.6	50	256
2005	10557	197	59	6482	61.4	55	210
2010	11273	193	63	7274	64.5	60	157
2015	11943	200	67	8054	67.4	65	116
2020	12625	202	74	8854	70.1	70+	163

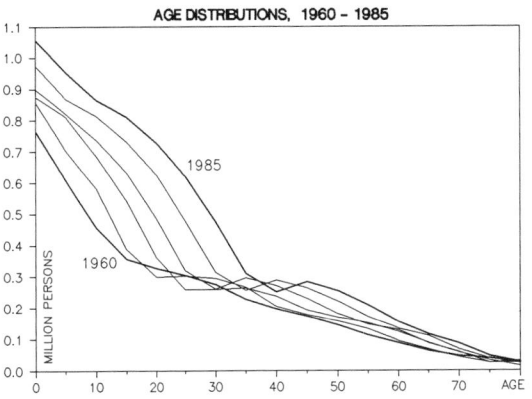

AGE DISTRIBUTIONS, 1960 - 1985

POPULATION RATIOS

YEAR	AGE DISTRIBUTION UNDER 15	AGE DISTRIBUTION 15-64	AGE DISTRIBUTION 65 & OLDER	AGE DISTRIBUTION 70 & OLDER	DEPENDENCY RATIO	WOMEN 15-49	CHILD-WOMAN RATIO
1950	0.389	0.554	0.057	0.038	0.805	0.231	0.706
1955	0.409	0.545	0.046	0.029	0.834	0.230	0.716
1960	0.434	0.525	0.042	0.027	0.906	0.221	0.818
1965	0.463	0.501	0.036	0.021	0.995	0.211	0.879
1970	0.462	0.500	0.038	0.020	1.000	0.214	0.798
1975	0.438	0.527	0.035	0.020	0.898	0.226	0.709
1980	0.416	0.546	0.038	0.020	0.832	0.233	0.654
1985	0.396	0.565	0.038	0.022	0.768	0.240	0.607
1990	0.378	0.582	0.040	0.023	0.718	0.246	0.545
2000	0.323	0.629	0.048	0.028	0.589	0.271	0.389
2010	0.265	0.683	0.052	0.035	0.465	0.279	0.314
2020	0.234	0.700	0.066	0.036	0.428	0.268	0.298

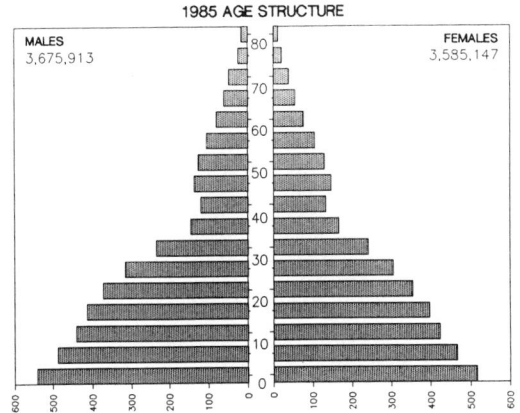

1985 AGE STRUCTURE

MALES 3,675,913   FEMALES 3,585,147

MORTALITY MEASURES (Annual Averages)

PERIOD	CRUDE DEATH RATE	INFANT MORT. RATE	LIFE EXPECTANCY AT BIRTH (years) MALE	LIFE EXPECTANCY AT BIRTH (years) FEMALE	LIFE EXPECTANCY AT BIRTH (years) BOTH SEXES	DIFFERENCE FEMALE-MALE
1950-55	22.60	175.00	44.10	45.10	44.59	1.00
1955-60	20.30	163.00	46.60	47.60	47.09	1.00
1960-65	17.90	155.00	49.10	50.10	49.59	1.00
1965-70	15.50	138.00	51.60	52.60	52.09	1.00
1970-75	12.30	120.00	55.10	56.10	55.59	1.00
1975-80	10.04	87.99	59.57	60.59	60.07	1.03
1980-85	8.44	70.91	62.58	63.61	63.08	1.03
1985-90	7.36	58.68	64.55	66.11	65.31	1.56
1990-95	6.47	47.33	66.56	68.39	67.45	1.83
2000-05	5.64	32.76	69.33	71.92	70.60	2.59
2010-15	5.59	22.74	71.46	74.58	72.98	3.12
2020-25	5.87	15.62	73.30	76.83	75.02	3.53

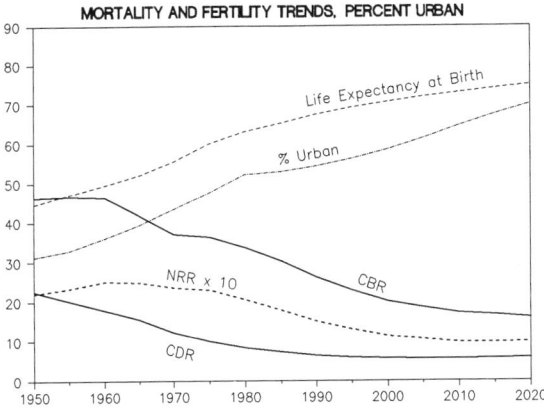

MORTALITY AND FERTILITY TRENDS, PERCENT URBAN

FERTILITY MEASURES (Annual Averages)

PERIOD	CRUDE BIRTH RATE	FERTILITY RATES GENERAL	FERTILITY RATES TOTAL	REPRODUCTION RATES GROSS	REPRODUCTION RATES NET	RATE OF NATUR. INCR.
1950-55	46.40	201.05	6.867	3.350	2.210	23.80
1955-60	46.70	206.98	6.970	3.400	2.340	26.40
1960-65	46.50	215.57	7.175	3.500	2.520	28.60
1965-70	41.80	196.98	6.826	3.330	2.500	26.30
1970-75	37.10	168.63	6.150	3.000	2.360	24.80
1975-80	36.35	158.15	5.658	2.760	2.300	26.31
1980-85	33.70	142.29	4.879	2.380	2.062	25.26
1985-90	30.32	124.73	4.100	2.000	1.785	22.96
1990-95	26.26	104.10	3.382	1.650	1.511	19.78
2000-05	20.08	73.13	2.460	1.200	1.137	14.44
2010-15	17.14	61.76	2.070	1.010	0.976	11.55
2020-25	16.03	60.88	2.070	1.010	0.990	10.16

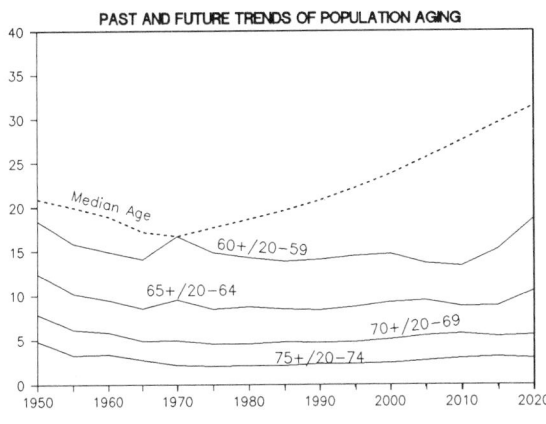

PAST AND FUTURE TRENDS OF POPULATION AGING

AGING MEASURES

YEAR	POPULATION AGE RATIOS 60+/20-59	POPULATION AGE RATIOS 65+/20-64	POPULATION AGE RATIOS 70+/20-69	POPULATION AGE RATIOS 75+/20-74	POPULATION MEAN AGE	POPULATION MEDIAN AGE
1950	0.1843	0.1246	0.0787	0.0486	25.61	20.93
1960	0.1493	0.0947	0.0583	0.0335	23.94	18.92
1970	0.1667	0.0953	0.0493	0.0217	23.10	16.77
1980	0.1431	0.0875	0.0453	0.0212	23.65	18.65
1990	0.1408	0.0839	0.0470	0.0234	24.80	20.84
2000	0.1472	0.0923	0.0512	0.0244	27.04	23.76
2010	0.1338	0.0882	0.0571	0.0294	29.91	27.56
2020	0.1865	0.1054	0.0554	0.0296	32.81	31.49

OBSERVED AND *PROJECTED* POPULATION DATA (000's)

YEAR	MID-YEAR POPULATION	NO. OF BIRTHS	NO. OF DEATHS	URBAN POPULATION NUMBER	URBAN POPULATION PERCENT	POPULATION 1985 AGE	POPULATION 1985 NUMBER
1950	4762	245	117	147	3.1	0	3085
1955	5556	279	124	220	4.0	5	2411
1960	6562	320	132	333	5.1	10	1953
1965	8047	395	150	521	6.5	15	1626
1970	9806	493	182	781	8.0	20	1321
1975	11182	562	197	933	8.3	25	1088
1980	13119	659	221	1146	8.7	30	898
1985	15491	777	238	1458	9.4	35	723
1990	18442	907	256	1923	10.4	40	589
1995	22012	1054	275	2608	11.8	45	443
2000	26285	1204	293	3623	13.8	50	399
2005	31272	1345	307	5114	16.4	55	320
2010	36932	1445	317	7107	19.2	60	246
2015	43036	1472	321	9654	22.4	65	176
2020	49203	1453	323	12741	25.9	70+	212

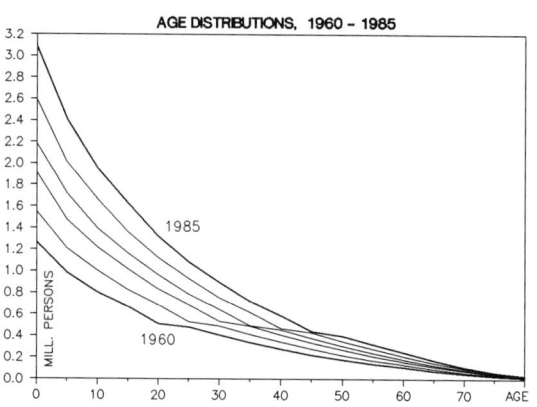

AGE DISTRIBUTIONS, 1960 - 1985

POPULATION RATIOS

YEAR	AGE DISTRIBUTION UNDER 15	15-64	65 & OLDER	70 & OLDER	DEPENDENCY RATIO	WOMEN 15-49	CHILD-WOMAN RATIO
1950	0.444	0.526	0.030	0.017	0.901	0.231	0.821
1955	0.461	0.511	0.028	0.016	0.957	0.224	0.861
1960	0.466	0.508	0.026	0.015	0.968	0.224	0.861
1965	0.468	0.506	0.026	0.014	0.975	0.224	0.861
1970	0.470	0.504	0.026	0.014	0.984	0.223	0.877
1975	0.474	0.501	0.025	0.014	0.996	0.221	0.883
1980	0.478	0.497	0.025	0.014	1.013	0.219	0.903
1985	0.481	0.494	0.025	0.014	1.024	0.218	0.912
1990	0.485	0.490	0.025	0.014	1.043	0.218	0.922
2000	0.487	0.488	0.025	0.014	1.048	0.218	0.903
2010	0.470	0.506	0.024	0.014	0.978	0.225	0.809
2020	0.425	0.548	0.027	0.015	0.825	0.243	0.617

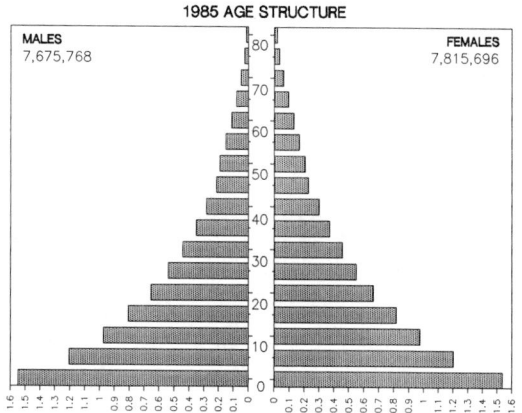

1985 AGE STRUCTURE

MALES 7,675,768   FEMALES 7,815,696

MORTALITY MEASURES (Annual Averages)

PERIOD	CRUDE DEATH RATE	INFANT MORT. RATE	LIFE EXPECTANCY AT BIRTH (years) MALE	FEMALE	BOTH SEXES	DIFFERENCE FEMALE-MALE
1950-55	24.49	160.00	38.46	41.59	40.00	3.13
1955-60	22.35	140.00	40.44	43.61	42.00	3.17
1960-65	20.12	125.00	42.42	45.63	44.00	3.21
1965-70	18.69	118.00	44.41	47.64	46.00	3.23
1970-75	18.52	116.00	45.40	48.65	47.00	3.25
1975-80	17.58	114.00	46.39	49.66	48.00	3.27
1980-85	16.82	112.00	47.36	50.69	49.00	3.33
1985-90	15.36	102.71	49.36	52.69	51.00	3.33
1990-95	13.91	93.83	51.36	54.69	53.00	3.33
2000-05	11.14	77.00	55.36	58.69	57.00	3.33
2010-15	8.58	61.20	59.36	62.69	61.00	3.33
2020-25	6.57	47.00	63.36	66.69	65.00	3.33

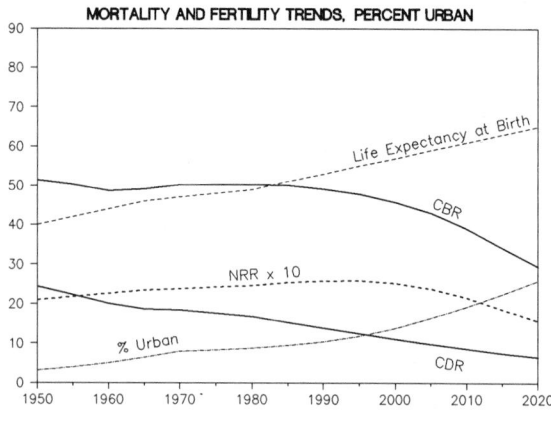

MORTALITY AND FERTILITY TRENDS, PERCENT URBAN

Life Expectancy at Birth, CBR, NRR x 10, % Urban, CDR

FERTILITY MEASURES (Annual Averages)

PERIOD	CRUDE BIRTH RATE	FERTILITY RATES GENERAL	FERTILITY RATES TOTAL	REPRODUCTION RATES GROSS	REPRODUCTION RATES NET	RATE OF NATUR. INCR.
1950-55	51.36	226.03	6.910	3.404	2.101	26.88
1955-60	50.29	224.42	6.941	3.419	2.196	27.93
1960-65	48.73	217.92	6.906	3.402	2.268	28.61
1965-70	49.14	220.41	6.912	3.405	2.351	30.46
1970-75	50.26	226.74	6.902	3.400	2.388	31.74
1975-80	50.26	228.50	6.902	3.400	2.430	32.68
1980-85	50.25	229.69	6.902	3.400	2.471	33.43
1985-90	50.14	229.70	6.902	3.400	2.552	34.78
1990-95	49.21	225.96	6.800	3.350	2.590	35.30
2000-05	45.79	208.82	6.273	3.090	2.523	34.66
2010-15	39.12	170.85	5.116	2.520	2.161	30.53
2020-25	29.54	118.14	3.552	1.750	1.567	22.97

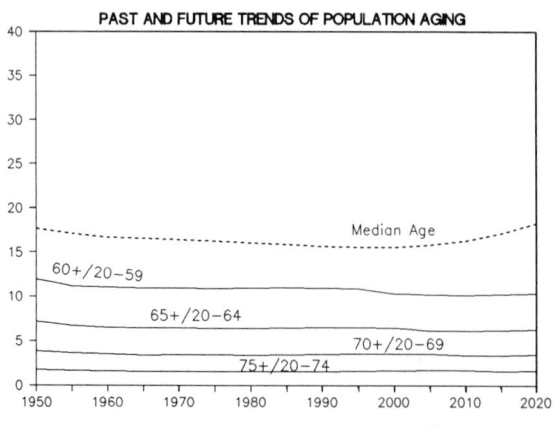

PAST AND FUTURE TRENDS OF POPULATION AGING

Median Age, 60+/20-59, 65+/20-64, 70+/20-69, 75+/20-74

AGING MEASURES

YEAR	POPULATION AGE RATIOS 60+/20-59	65+/20-64	70+/20-69	75+/20-74	POPULATION MEAN AGE	POPULATION MEDIAN AGE
1950	0.1191	0.0718	0.0387	0.0175	22.19	17.69
1960	0.1104	0.0649	0.0353	0.0162	21.64	16.69
1970	0.1093	0.0645	0.0343	0.0154	21.40	16.44
1980	0.1090	0.0638	0.0340	0.0156	21.04	16.06
1990	0.1094	0.0649	0.0346	0.0157	20.70	15.70
2000	0.1030	0.0648	0.0355	0.0166	20.58	15.61
2010	0.1015	0.0611	0.0334	0.0169	21.03	16.35
2020	0.1037	0.0630	0.0348	0.0167	22.51	18.29

OBSERVED AND *PROJECTED* POPULATION DATA (000's)

YEAR	MID-YEAR POPULATION	NO. OF BIRTHS	NO. OF DEATHS	URBAN POPULATION NUMBER	URBAN POPULATION PERCENT	POPULATION 1985 AGE	POPULATION 1985 NUMBER
1950	12542	594	303	2396	19.1	0	5675
1955	14083	663	320	2909	20.7	5	4670
1960	15908	752	348	3548	22.3	10	3824
1965	17529	824	360	4576	26.1	15	3197
1970	19481	908	365	5903	30.3	20	2686
1975	22399	1026	386	7217	32.2	25	2244
1980	26377	1191	417	9021	34.2	30	1866
1985	30712	1399	427	11248	36.6	35	1528
1990	*35990*	*1608*	*455*	*14209*	*39.5*	40	1264
1995	*42255*	*1789*	*480*	*18061*	*42.7*	45	1029
2000	*49349*	*2065*	*507*	*22875*	*46.4*	50	822
2005	*57803*	*2311*	*532*	*29035*	*50.2*	55	641
2010	*67440*	*2520*	*553*	*36396*	*54.0*	60	489
2015	*78052*	*2584*	*564*	*44906*	*57.5*	65	351
2020	*88854*	*2582*	*571*	*54114*	*60.9*	70+	427

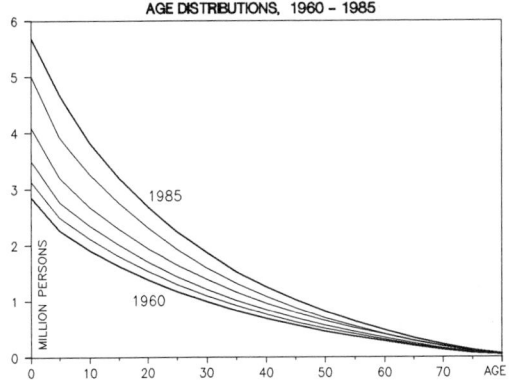

POPULATION RATIOS

YEAR	AGE DISTRIBUTION UNDER 15	AGE DISTRIBUTION 15-64	AGE DISTRIBUTION 65 & OLDER	AGE DISTRIBUTION 70 & OLDER	DEPENDENCY RATIO	WOMEN 15-49	CHILD-WOMAN RATIO
1950	0.437	0.525	0.038	0.024	0.904	0.244	0.729
1955	0.440	0.528	0.032	0.019	0.894	0.244	0.735
1960	0.442	0.529	0.029	0.016	0.891	0.242	0.740
1965	0.442	0.530	0.029	0.016	0.888	0.240	0.743
1970	0.443	0.529	0.028	0.016	0.890	0.238	0.756
1975	0.446	0.526	0.028	0.016	0.902	0.234	0.782
1980	0.462	0.513	0.025	0.014	0.950	0.230	0.823
1985	0.461	0.513	0.025	0.014	0.948	0.229	0.807
1990	*0.461*	*0.513*	*0.026*	*0.014*	*0.950*	*0.227*	*0.819*
2000	*0.455*	*0.517*	*0.027*	*0.015*	*0.933*	*0.227*	*0.781*
2010	*0.442*	*0.528*	*0.029*	*0.017*	*0.892*	*0.231*	*0.742*
2020	*0.412*	*0.555*	*0.033*	*0.019*	*0.802*	*0.242*	*0.606*

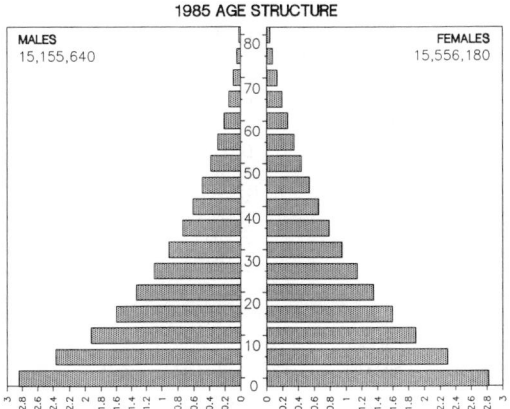

MORTALITY MEASURES (Annual Averages)

PERIOD	CRUDE DEATH RATE	INFANT MORT. RATE	LIFE EXPECTANCY AT BIRTH (years) MALE	LIFE EXPECTANCY AT BIRTH (years) FEMALE	LIFE EXPECTANCY AT BIRTH (years) BOTH SEXES	DIFFERENCE FEMALE-MALE
1950-55	24.18	157.30	38.95	42.09	40.50	3.14
1955-60	22.71	151.41	39.94	43.10	41.50	3.16
1960-65	21.88	145.68	40.93	44.12	42.50	3.18
1965-70	20.52	137.31	42.42	45.63	44.00	3.21
1970-75	18.76	126.64	44.41	47.64	46.00	3.23
1975-80	17.24	116.62	46.39	49.66	48.00	3.27
1980-85	15.80	107.28	48.33	51.72	50.00	3.38
1985-90	*13.90*	*98.00*	*50.83*	*54.22*	*52.50*	*3.39*
1990-95	*12.65*	*90.00*	*52.83*	*56.22*	*54.50*	*3.39*
2000-05	*10.28*	*73.00*	*56.83*	*60.22*	*58.50*	*3.39*
2010-15	*8.20*	*57.00*	*60.83*	*64.22*	*62.50*	*3.39*
2020-25	*6.43*	*43.00*	*64.83*	*68.12*	*66.45*	*3.29*

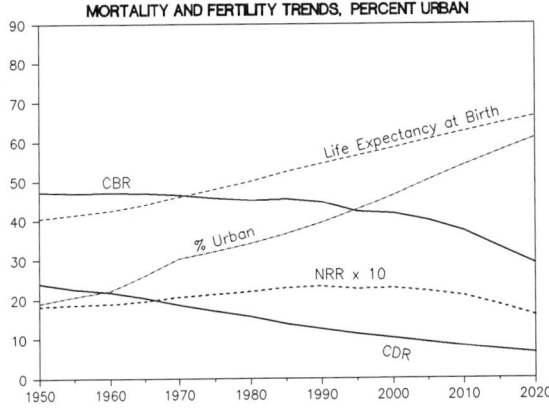

FERTILITY MEASURES (Annual Averages)

PERIOD	CRUDE BIRTH RATE	FERTILITY RATES GENERAL	FERTILITY RATES TOTAL	REPRODUCTION RATES GROSS	REPRODUCTION RATES NET	RATE OF NATUR. INCR.
1950-55	47.33	194.05	5.976	2.944	1.836	23.15
1955-60	47.06	193.76	5.966	2.939	1.870	24.34
1960-65	47.25	195.86	5.942	2.927	1.898	25.36
1965-70	47.03	196.76	5.976	2.944	1.962	26.51
1970-75	46.63	197.80	6.090	3.000	2.071	27.87
1975-80	45.82	197.61	6.090	3.000	2.144	28.58
1980-85	45.13	196.70	6.090	3.000	2.217	29.33
1985-90	*45.56*	*199.95*	*6.090*	*3.000*	*2.304*	*31.65*
1990-95	*44.68*	*197.18*	*6.009*	*2.960*	*2.339*	*32.03*
2000-05	*41.84*	*183.59*	*5.582*	*2.750*	*2.290*	*31.56*
2010-15	*37.37*	*160.56*	*4.872*	*2.400*	*2.093*	*29.18*
2020-25	*29.06*	*117.51*	*3.552*	*1.750*	*1.591*	*22.63*

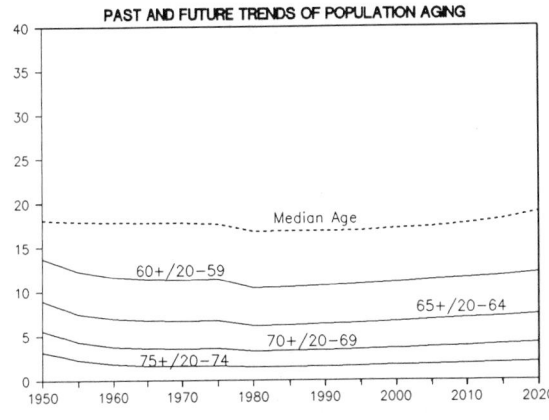

AGING MEASURES

YEAR	POPULATION AGE RATIOS 60+/20-59	POPULATION AGE RATIOS 65+/20-64	POPULATION AGE RATIOS 70+/20-69	POPULATION AGE RATIOS 75+/20-74	POPULATION MEAN AGE	POPULATION MEDIAN AGE
1950	0.1374	0.0893	0.0556	0.0317	23.03	18.11
1960	0.1161	0.0692	0.0372	0.0181	22.49	17.84
1970	0.1130	0.0665	0.0354	0.0161	22.40	17.79
1980	0.1039	0.0613	0.0328	0.0150	21.48	16.81
1990	*0.1065*	*0.0632*	*0.0339*	*0.0156*	*21.60*	*16.85*
2000	*0.1108*	*0.0661*	*0.0359*	*0.0168*	*21.87*	*17.14*
2010	*0.1152*	*0.0699*	*0.0386*	*0.0184*	*22.31*	*17.69*
2020	*0.1210*	*0.0741*	*0.0416*	*0.0204*	*23.48*	*19.02*

OBSERVED AND *PROJECTED* POPULATION DATA (000's)

YEAR	MID-YEAR POPULATION	NO. OF BIRTHS	NO. OF DEATHS	URBAN POPULATION NUMBER	URBAN POPULATION PERCENT	POPULATION 1985 AGE	POPULATION 1985 NUMBER
1950	2440	122	64	216	8.9	0	1424
1955	2753	137	65	343	12.5	5	1075
1960	3141	155	67	541	17.2	10	909
1965	3614	177	70	843	23.3	15	762
1970	4189	206	75	1272	30.4	20	616
1975	4841	250	80	1760	36.3	25	492
1980	5738	292	86	2455	42.8	30	393
1985	7007	359	96	3466	49.5	35	311
1990	*8456*	*415*	*104*	*4700*	*55.6*	40	250
1995	*10174*	*478*	*110*	*6195*	*60.9*	45	207
2000	*12197*	*543*	*117*	*7962*	*65.3*	50	171
2005	*14531*	*603*	*122*	*9990*	*68.7*	55	131
2010	*17152*	*641*	*125*	*12236*	*71.3*	60	101
2015	*19938*	*651*	*127*	*14700*	*73.7*	65	73
2020	*22743*	*643*	*129*	*17268*	*75.9*	70+	91

POPULATION RATIOS

YEAR	AGE DISTRIBUTION UNDER 15	AGE DISTRIBUTION 15-64	AGE DISTRIBUTION 65 & OLDER	AGE DISTRIBUTION 70 & OLDER	DEPENDENCY RATIO	WOMEN 15-49	CHILD-WOMAN RATIO
1950	0.449	0.524	0.027	0.015	0.909	0.235	0.789
1955	0.449	0.525	0.025	0.014	0.904	0.235	0.786
1960	0.452	0.524	0.024	0.013	0.908	0.233	0.804
1965	0.456	0.520	0.024	0.013	0.923	0.230	0.821
1970	0.461	0.514	0.025	0.013	0.944	0.227	0.838
1975	0.465	0.509	0.026	0.014	0.965	0.223	0.860
1980	0.494	0.482	0.024	0.013	1.074	0.223	0.893
1985	0.487	0.490	0.023	0.013	1.041	0.226	0.898
1990	*0.491*	*0.486*	*0.023*	*0.013*	*1.059*	*0.224*	*0.927*
2000	*0.492*	*0.485*	*0.023*	*0.013*	*1.064*	*0.220*	*0.892*
2010	*0.466*	*0.511*	*0.024*	*0.014*	*0.958*	*0.228*	*0.780*
2020	*0.415*	*0.558*	*0.027*	*0.015*	*0.792*	*0.245*	*0.592*

AGE DISTRIBUTIONS, 1960 - 1985

MORTALITY MEASURES (Annual Averages)

PERIOD	CRUDE DEATH RATE	INFANT MORT. RATE	LIFE EXPECTANCY AT BIRTH (years) MALE	FEMALE	BOTH SEXES	DIFFERENCE FEMALE-MALE
1950-55	26.06	150.00	36.28	39.37	37.80	3.09
1955-60	23.60	140.00	38.75	41.89	40.30	3.14
1960-65	21.38	130.00	41.23	44.42	42.80	3.19
1965-70	19.34	115.00	43.71	46.94	45.30	3.22
1970-75	17.97	100.00	45.69	48.95	47.30	3.26
1975-80	16.48	94.00	47.65	50.99	49.30	3.34
1980-85	14.90	88.00	50.40	52.50	51.43	2.10
1985-90	*13.69*	*79.83*	*52.40*	*54.50*	*53.43*	*2.10*
1990-95	*12.25*	*71.67*	*54.40*	*56.50*	*55.43*	*2.10*
2000-05	*9.57*	*56.37*	*58.40*	*60.50*	*59.43*	*2.10*
2010-15	*7.31*	*42.23*	*62.40*	*64.50*	*63.43*	*2.10*
2020-25	*5.69*	*31.45*	*66.10*	*68.30*	*67.18*	*2.20*

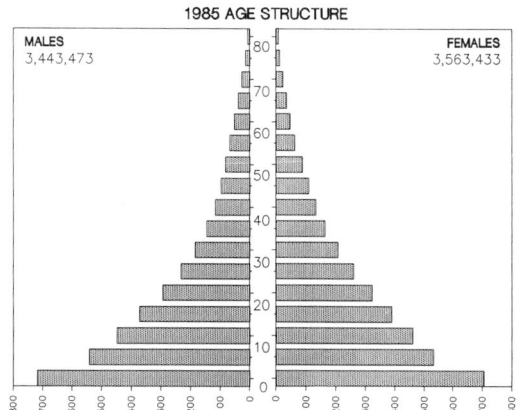

1985 AGE STRUCTURE

MALES 3,443,473   FEMALES 3,563,433

FERTILITY MEASURES (Annual Averages)

PERIOD	CRUDE BIRTH RATE	FERTILITY RATES GENERAL	FERTILITY RATES TOTAL	REPRODUCTION RATES GROSS	REPRODUCTION RATES NET	RATE OF NATUR. INCR.
1950-55	50.14	213.69	6.587	3.245	1.905	24.08
1955-60	49.91	213.62	6.597	3.250	2.012	26.31
1960-65	49.38	213.61	6.616	3.259	2.118	28.00
1965-70	48.87	214.29	6.654	3.278	2.229	29.52
1970-75	49.06	218.22	6.902	3.400	2.395	31.09
1975-80	51.59	231.34	7.200	3.547	2.584	35.11
1980-85	50.85	226.27	7.200	3.547	2.633	35.94
1985-90	*51.18*	*227.62*	*7.200*	*3.547*	*2.715*	*37.48*
1990-95	*49.13*	*222.00*	*7.003*	*3.450*	*2.718*	*36.89*
2000-05	*44.51*	*200.85*	*6.435*	*3.170*	*2.634*	*34.94*
2010-15	*37.35*	*161.16*	*5.136*	*2.530*	*2.204*	*30.04*
2020-25	*28.28*	*112.40*	*3.552*	*1.750*	*1.587*	*22.59*

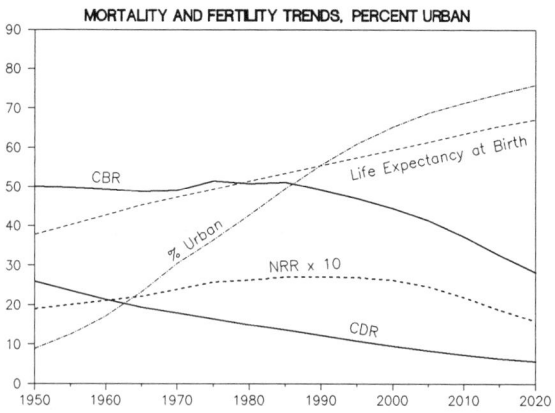

MORTALITY AND FERTILITY TRENDS, PERCENT URBAN

AGING MEASURES

YEAR	POPULATION AGE RATIOS 60+/20-59	65+/20-64	70+/20-69	75+/20-74	POPULATION MEAN AGE	POPULATION MEDIAN AGE
1950	0.1074	0.0647	0.0345	0.0152	21.97	17.46
1960	0.0987	0.0561	0.0304	0.0138	21.85	17.33
1970	0.1054	0.0603	0.0308	0.0131	21.71	16.93
1980	0.1077	0.0636	0.0335	0.0152	20.48	15.29
1990	*0.1011*	*0.0607*	*0.0330*	*0.0153*	*20.25*	*15.41*
2000	*0.1006*	*0.0609*	*0.0331*	*0.0157*	*20.33*	*15.35*
2010	*0.0973*	*0.0593*	*0.0334*	*0.0162*	*21.06*	*16.54*
2020	*0.1010*	*0.0609*	*0.0338*	*0.0166*	*22.79*	*18.70*

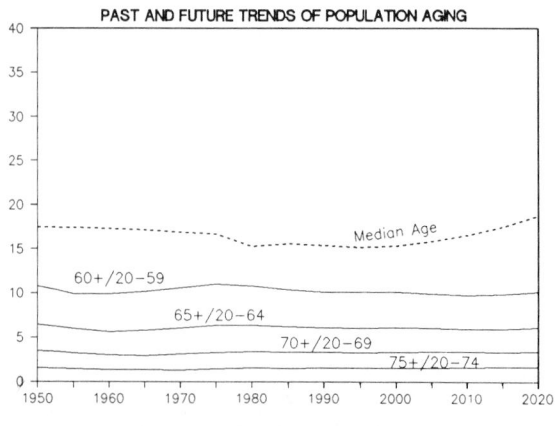

PAST AND FUTURE TRENDS OF POPULATION AGING

OBSERVED AND *PROJECTED* POPULATION DATA (000's)

YEAR	MID-YEAR POPULATION	NO. OF BIRTHS	NO. OF DEATHS	URBAN POPULATION NUMBER	URBAN POPULATION PERCENT	POPULATION 1985 AGE	POPULATION 1985 NUMBER
1950	2730	142	63	291	10.6	0	1474
1955	3258	175	70	378	11.6	5	1241
1960	3816	197	74	481	12.6	10	1125
1965	4473	225	76	645	14.4	15	949
1970	5270	256	80	892	16.9	20	776
1975	6155	272	80	1197	19.4	25	632
1980	7138	303	83	1563	21.9	30	476
1985	8304	346	85	2039	24.6	35	339
1990	*9721*	*388*	*87*	*2680*	*27.6*	40	303
1995	*11352*	*418*	*87*	*3511*	*30.9*	45	254
2000	*13135*	*440*	*87*	*4543*	*34.6*	50	213
2005	*15023*	*457*	*89*	*5779*	*38.5*	55	168
2010	*16984*	*466*	*92*	*7214*	*42.5*	60	127
2015	*18959*	*462*	*97*	*8805*	*46.4*	65	103
2020	*20876*	*440*	*105*	*10504*	*50.3*	70+	124

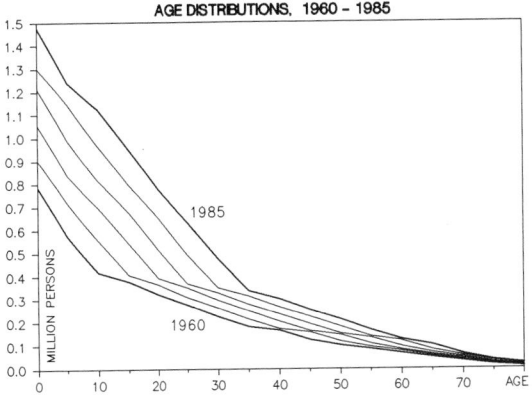

AGE DISTRIBUTIONS, 1960 - 1985

POPULATION RATIOS

YEAR	AGE DISTRIBUTION UNDER 15	15-64	65 & OLDER	70 & OLDER	DEPENDENCY RATIO	WOMEN 15-49	CHILD-WOMAN RATIO
1950	0.447	0.522	0.030	0.016	0.914	0.224	0.790
1955	0.447	0.523	0.029	0.016	0.911	0.225	0.862
1960	0.465	0.506	0.029	0.016	0.976	0.219	0.936
1965	0.486	0.486	0.028	0.015	1.058	0.211	0.956
1970	0.491	0.482	0.027	0.015	1.076	0.210	0.955
1975	0.490	0.484	0.026	0.015	1.066	0.212	0.926
1980	0.478	0.496	0.026	0.015	1.017	0.219	0.832
1985	0.462	0.510	0.027	0.015	0.960	0.227	0.783
1990	*0.448*	*0.525*	*0.027*	*0.016*	*0.906*	*0.234*	*0.753*
2000	*0.431*	*0.540*	*0.029*	*0.017*	*0.851*	*0.243*	*0.662*
2010	*0.388*	*0.580*	*0.032*	*0.019*	*0.725*	*0.256*	*0.535*
2020	*0.335*	*0.626*	*0.039*	*0.022*	*0.597*	*0.268*	*0.421*

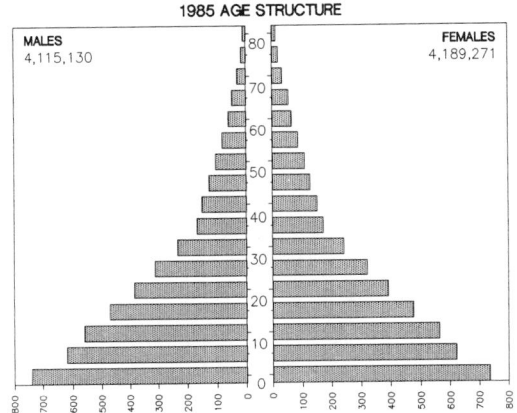

1985 AGE STRUCTURE

MALES 4,115,130   FEMALES 4,189,271

MORTALITY MEASURES (Annual Averages)

PERIOD	CRUDE DEATH RATE	INFANT MORT. RATE	LIFE EXPECTANCY AT BIRTH (years) MALE	FEMALE	BOTH SEXES	DIFFERENCE FEMALE-MALE
1950-55	23.09	119.93	39.94	43.10	41.50	3.16
1955-60	21.54	112.71	42.41	45.62	44.00	3.21
1960-65	19.28	105.99	44.90	48.14	46.50	3.24
1965-70	17.09	100.53	47.36	50.68	49.00	3.32
1970-75	15.09	92.90	49.79	53.25	51.50	3.46
1975-80	13.07	85.57	52.04	55.60	53.80	3.56
1980-85	11.66	80.24	54.02	57.63	55.81	3.61
1985-90	*10.24*	*72.06*	*56.52*	*60.13*	*58.31*	*3.61*
1990-95	*8.92*	*64.25*	*59.02*	*62.63*	*60.81*	*3.61*
2000-05	*6.66*	*49.51*	*63.58*	*67.43*	*65.49*	*3.85*
2010-15	*5.44*	*36.71*	*66.98*	*71.19*	*69.06*	*4.21*
2020-25	*5.02*	*27.82*	*69.50*	*73.89*	*71.67*	*4.39*

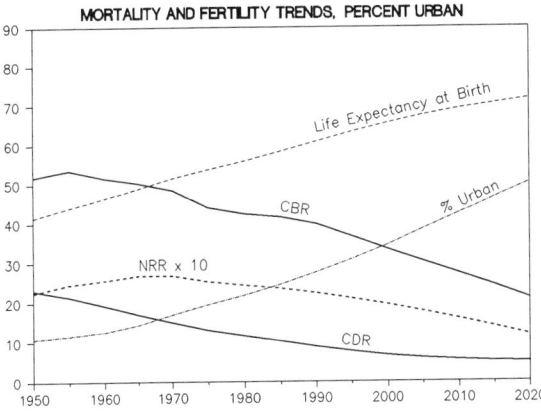

MORTALITY AND FERTILITY TRENDS, PERCENT URBAN

FERTILITY MEASURES (Annual Averages)

PERIOD	CRUDE BIRTH RATE	FERTILITY RATES GENERAL	FERTILITY RATES TOTAL	REPRODUCTION RATES GROSS	REPRODUCTION RATES NET	RATE OF NATUR. INCR.
1950-55	51.88	231.08	7.200	3.564	2.255	28.80
1955-60	53.61	241.59	7.500	3.713	2.463	32.06
1960-65	51.68	240.87	7.500	3.713	2.575	32.40
1965-70	50.40	239.89	7.500	3.713	2.688	33.31
1970-75	48.64	230.41	7.200	3.564	2.688	33.55
1975-80	44.14	204.44	6.600	3.267	2.539	31.07
1980-85	42.50	190.50	6.194	3.069	2.447	30.84
1985-90	*41.67*	*180.56*	*5.794*	*2.871*	*2.366*	*31.43*
1990-95	*39.88*	*168.92*	*5.325*	*2.639*	*2.245*	*30.96*
2000-05	*33.47*	*135.85*	*4.386*	*2.173*	*1.950*	*26.81*
2010-15	*27.42*	*105.76*	*3.447*	*1.708*	*1.591*	*21.98*
2020-25	*21.07*	*77.91*	*2.497*	*1.238*	*1.179*	*16.05*

AGING MEASURES

YEAR	POPULATION AGE RATIOS 60+/20-59	65+/20-64	70+/20-69	75+/20-74	POPULATION MEAN AGE	POPULATION MEDIAN AGE
1950	0.1254	0.0725	0.0375	0.0162	22.57	17.58
1960	0.1182	0.0703	0.0371	0.0164	21.59	16.75
1970	0.1168	0.0709	0.0387	0.0179	20.94	15.41
1980	0.1164	0.0677	0.0372	0.0178	20.98	15.97
1990	*0.1090*	*0.0664*	*0.0378*	*0.0173*	*21.58*	*17.27*
2000	*0.1083*	*0.0672*	*0.0377*	*0.0184*	*22.50*	*18.29*
2010	*0.1070*	*0.0691*	*0.0402*	*0.0204*	*24.20*	*20.11*
2020	*0.1263*	*0.0743*	*0.0412*	*0.0220*	*26.56*	*23.11*

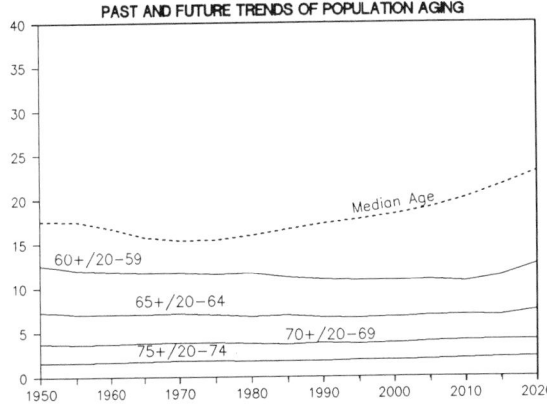

PAST AND FUTURE TRENDS OF POPULATION AGING

POPULATION OF THE CARIBBEAN, BY COUNTRY / TERRITORY : 1985

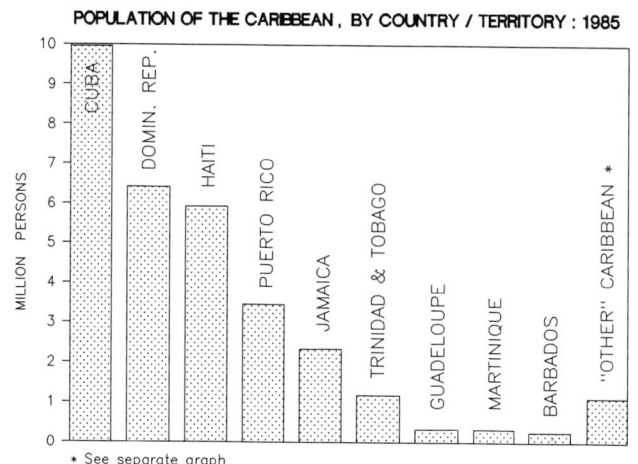

* See separate graph

POPULATION OF "OTHER CARIBBEAN", BY COUNTRY / TERRITORY : 1980

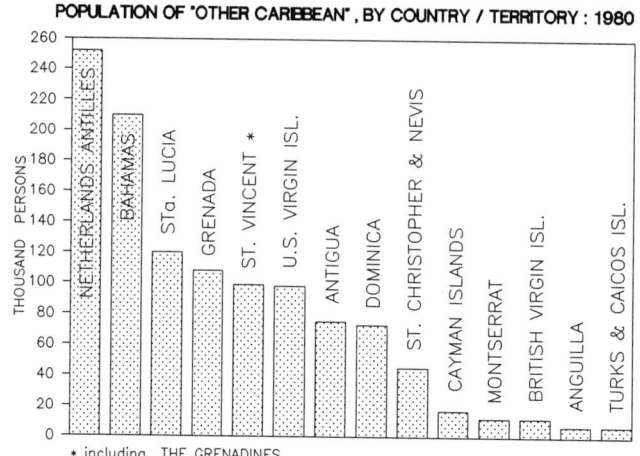

* including THE GRENADINES

POPULATION OF CENTRAL AMERICA, BY COUNTRY : 1985

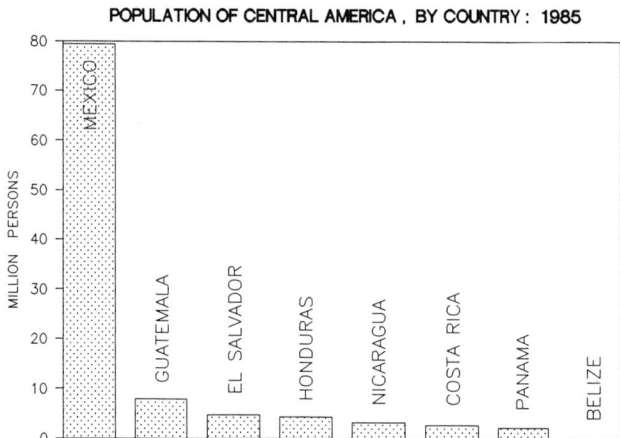

POPULATION OF SOUTH AMERICA, BY COUNTRY : 1985

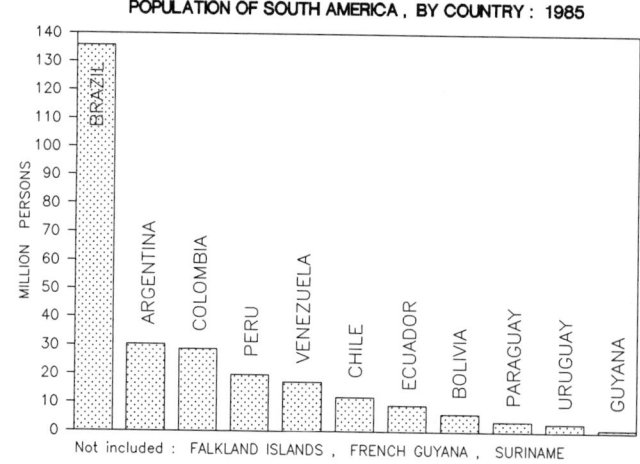

Not included : FALKLAND ISLANDS , FRENCH GUYANA , SURINAME

POPULATION OF NORTHERN AMERICA, BY COUNTRY : 1985

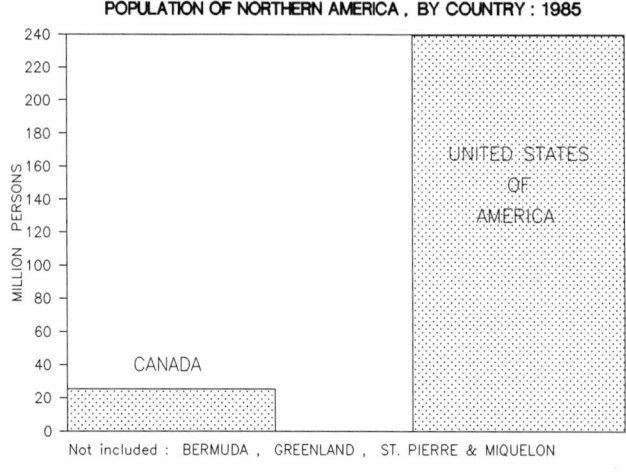

Not included : BERMUDA , GREENLAND , ST. PIERRE & MIQUELON

OBSERVED AND *PROJECTED* POPULATION DATA (000's)

YEAR	MID-YEAR POPULATION	NO. OF BIRTHS	NO. OF DEATHS	URBAN POPULATION NUMBER	PERCENT	POPULATION 1985 AGE	NUMBER
1950	165365	7029	2534	68616	41.5	0	54781
1955	189618	7916	2576	86001	45.4	5	49806
1960	217649	8962	2647	107269	49.3	10	46974
1965	250390	9492	2723	133561	53.3	15	43039
1970	285127	10059	2757	163251	57.3	20	39254
1975	322748	10457	2795	198144	61.4	25	32991
1980	361756	11165	2898	236665	65.4	30	27809
1985	403646	11727	3022	279080	69.1	35	22467
1990	*448096*	*12078*	*3153*	*324021*	*72.3*	40	18514
1995	*493802*	*12296*	*3313*	*370225*	*75.0*	45	15767
2000	*539697*	*12516*	*3536*	*416650*	*77.2*	50	13411
2005	*585443*	*12755*	*3814*	*462876*	*79.1*	55	11485
2010	*630855*	*12984*	*4145*	*508773*	*80.6*	60	9208
2015	*675624*	*13154*	*4557*	*554839*	*82.1*	65	6957
2020	*719032*	*13278*	*5061*	*600331*	*83.5*	70+	11184

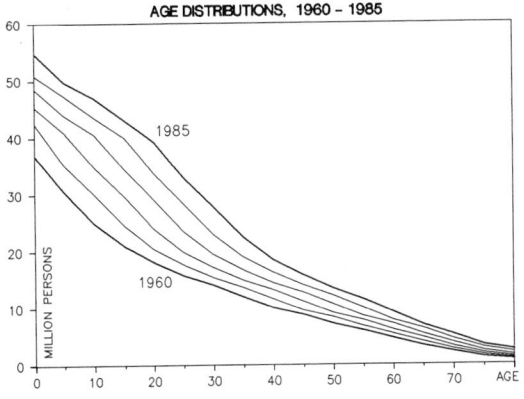

AGE DISTRIBUTIONS, 1960 – 1985

POPULATION RATIOS

YEAR	AGE DISTRIBUTION UNDER 15	15-64	65 & OLDER	70 & OLDER	DEPENDENCY RATIO	WOMEN 15-49	CHILD-WOMAN RATIO
1950	0.406	0.561	0.033	0.019	0.783	0.239	0.677
1955	0.415	0.551	0.034	0.019	0.814	0.234	0.722
1960	0.425	0.540	0.035	0.020	0.851	0.229	0.740
1965	0.431	0.532	0.037	0.021	0.878	0.225	0.753
1970	0.425	0.536	0.039	0.022	0.865	0.227	0.698
1975	0.412	0.547	0.041	0.024	0.827	0.232	0.647
1980	0.392	0.565	0.043	0.026	0.770	0.241	0.584
1985	0.375	0.580	0.045	0.028	0.725	0.247	0.549
1990	*0.360*	*0.593*	*0.047*	*0.029*	*0.687*	*0.253*	*0.511*
2000	*0.328*	*0.619*	*0.053*	*0.034*	*0.616*	*0.262*	*0.433*
2010	*0.294*	*0.645*	*0.061*	*0.038*	*0.550*	*0.264*	*0.382*
2020	*0.268*	*0.657*	*0.075*	*0.046*	*0.523*	*0.258*	*0.354*

MORTALITY MEASURES (Annual Averages)

PERIOD	CRUDE DEATH RATE	INFANT MORT. RATE	LIFE EXPECTANCY AT BIRTH (years) MALE	FEMALE	BOTH SEXES	DIFFERENCE FEMALE-MALE
1950-55	15.32	125.71	49.57	52.90	51.19	3.33
1955-60	13.58	112.25	52.35	55.93	54.10	3.58
1960-65	12.16	99.81	54.87	58.62	56.70	3.75
1965-70	10.87	90.58	56.74	60.75	58.70	4.01
1970-75	9.67	80.28	58.67	63.19	60.88	4.52
1975-80	8.66	70.29	60.37	65.34	62.80	4.97
1980-85	8.01	62.65	61.87	67.22	64.49	5.35
1985-90	*7.49*	*55.78*	*63.35*	*68.78*	*66.00*	*5.42*
1990-95	*7.04*	*49.60*	*64.78*	*70.28*	*67.46*	*5.50*
2000-05	*6.55*	*39.35*	*67.04*	*72.72*	*69.81*	*5.69*
2010-15	*6.57*	*32.15*	*68.70*	*74.55*	*71.56*	*5.85*
2020-25	*7.04*	*26.97*	*69.92*	*75.84*	*72.81*	*5.92*

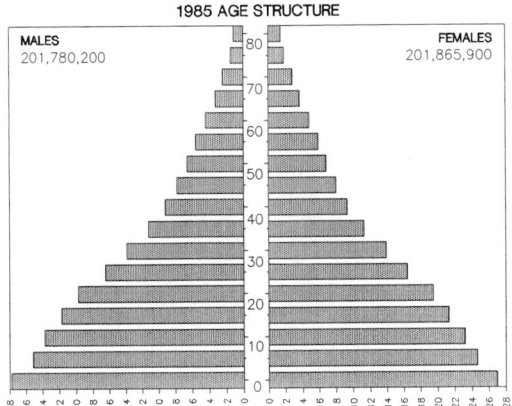

1985 AGE STRUCTURE

MALES 201,780,200   FEMALES 201,865,900

FERTILITY MEASURES (Annual Averages)

PERIOD	CRUDE BIRTH RATE	FERTILITY RATES GENERAL	TOTAL	REPRODUCTION RATES GROSS	NET	RATE OF NATUR. INCR.
1950-55	42.50	179.94	5.865	2.862	2.146	27.18
1955-60	41.75	180.66	5.903	2.881	2.250	28.17
1960-65	41.18	181.66	5.953	2.905	2.350	29.01
1965-70	37.91	167.57	5.505	2.687	2.229	27.04
1970-75	35.28	153.35	5.002	2.441	2.087	25.61
1975-80	32.40	136.89	4.376	2.136	1.874	23.74
1980-85	30.86	126.53	3.976	1.940	1.733	22.85
1985-90	*29.05*	*116.13*	*3.613*	*1.763*	*1.599*	*21.57*
1990-95	*26.95*	*105.52*	*3.297*	*1.609*	*1.480*	*19.92*
2000-05	*23.19*	*88.14*	*2.837*	*1.384*	*1.300*	*16.64*
2010-15	*20.58*	*78.29*	*2.563*	*1.251*	*1.188*	*14.01*
2020-25	*18.47*	*72.01*	*2.391*	*1.167*	*1.121*	*11.43*

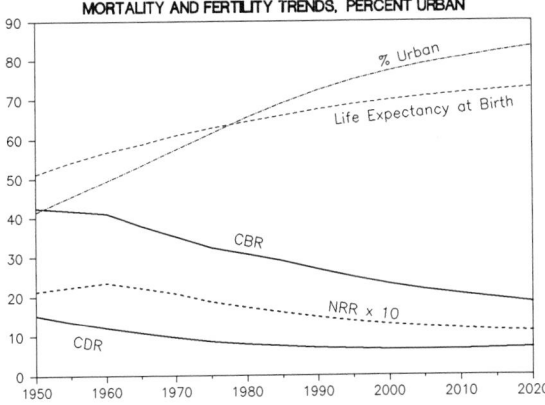

MORTALITY AND FERTILITY TRENDS, PERCENT URBAN

AGING MEASURES

YEAR	POPULATION AGE RATIOS 60+/20-59	65+/20-64	70+/20-69	75+/20-74	POPULATION MEAN AGE	MEDIAN AGE
1950	0.1207	0.0712	0.0393	0.0191	23.96	19.67
1960	0.1331	0.0794	0.0436	0.0207	23.70	18.91
1970	0.1465	0.0899	0.0501	0.0247	23.76	18.61
1980	0.1499	0.0951	0.0547	0.0281	24.66	19.89
1990	*0.1529*	*0.0970*	*0.0573*	*0.0307*	*25.90*	*21.93*
2000	*0.1582*	*0.1026*	*0.0622*	*0.0333*	*27.57*	*24.10*
2010	*0.1727*	*0.1101*	*0.0670*	*0.0369*	*29.55*	*26.50*
2020	*0.2112*	*0.1318*	*0.0772*	*0.0418*	*31.59*	*29.01*

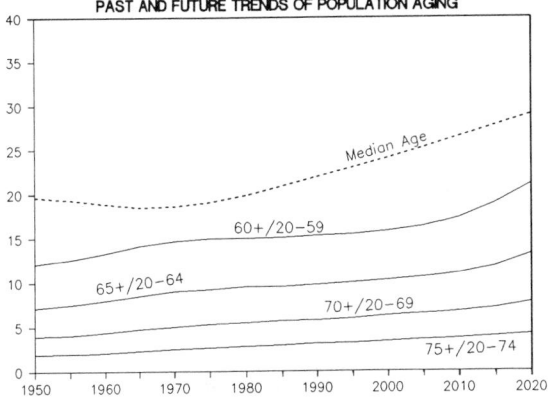

PAST AND FUTURE TRENDS OF POPULATION AGING

OBSERVED AND *PROJECTED* POPULATION DATA (000's)

YEAR	MID-YEAR POPULATION	NO. OF BIRTHS	NO. OF DEATHS	URBAN POPULATION NUMBER	URBAN POPULATION PERCENT	POPULATION 1985 AGE	POPULATION 1985 NUMBER
1950	16878	632	257	5698	33.8	0	3527
1955	18473	684	244	6634	35.9	5	3303
1960	20353	796	243	7774	38.2	10	3530
1965	22632	813	237	9461	41.8	15	3547
1970	24881	776	230	11288	45.4	20	3277
1975	27308	719	230	13436	49.2	25	2481
1980	29260	735	237	15460	52.8	30	2058
1985	31288	773	245	17595	56.2	35	1825
1990	*33640*	*786*	*254*	*19996*	*59.4*	40	1566
1995	*36137*	*780*	*265*	*22551*	*62.4*	45	1352
2000	*38566*	*767*	*277*	*25091*	*65.1*	50	1133
2005	*40861*	*762*	*295*	*27557*	*67.4*	55	1005
2010	*43022*	*766*	*317*	*29945*	*69.6*	60	814
2015	*45092*	*768*	*345*	*32312*	*71.7*	65	684
2020	*47021*	*763*	*379*	*34606*	*73.6*	70+	1188

AGE DISTRIBUTIONS, 1960 - 1985

POPULATION RATIOS

YEAR	AGE DISTRIBUTION UNDER 15	15-64	65 & OLDER	70 & OLDER	DEPENDENCY RATIO	WOMEN 15-49	CHILD-WOMAN RATIO
1950	0.392	0.567	0.041	0.024	0.762	0.238	0.636
1955	0.393	0.565	0.042	0.025	0.769	0.237	0.636
1960	0.397	0.559	0.043	0.026	0.788	0.235	0.650
1965	0.404	0.551	0.045	0.027	0.815	0.231	0.709
1970	0.410	0.540	0.049	0.028	0.850	0.226	0.678
1975	0.398	0.550	0.052	0.031	0.818	0.231	0.585
1980	0.363	0.580	0.057	0.035	0.724	0.244	0.474
1985	0.331	0.609	0.060	0.038	0.642	0.257	0.438
1990	*0.311*	*0.628*	*0.061*	*0.040*	*0.594*	*0.264*	*0.423*
2000	*0.293*	*0.641*	*0.066*	*0.043*	*0.560*	*0.264*	*0.376*
2010	*0.261*	*0.662*	*0.076*	*0.049*	*0.510*	*0.265*	*0.329*
2020	*0.239*	*0.669*	*0.092*	*0.059*	*0.494*	*0.248*	*0.325*

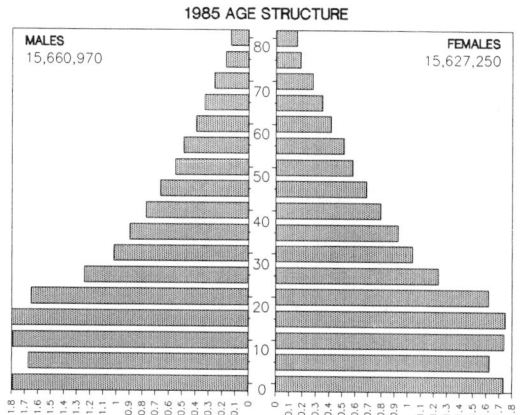

1985 AGE STRUCTURE

MALES 15,660,970 — FEMALES 15,627,250

MORTALITY MEASURES (Annual Averages)

PERIOD	CRUDE DEATH RATE	INFANT MORT. RATE	LIFE EXPECTANCY AT BIRTH (years) MALE	FEMALE	BOTH SEXES	DIFFERENCE FEMALE-MALE
1950-55	15.20	123.90	50.42	53.71	52.03	3.30
1955-60	13.23	110.18	53.58	57.01	55.26	3.43
1960-65	11.94	94.29	56.79	60.40	58.55	3.60
1965-70	10.45	86.63	59.14	62.63	60.84	3.49
1970-75	9.26	76.83	60.84	64.59	62.67	3.75
1975-80	8.41	69.66	61.71	65.59	63.60	3.87
1980-85	8.11	63.93	62.97	67.12	65.00	4.15
1985-90	*7.84*	*57.27*	*64.30*	*68.56*	*66.38*	*4.26*
1990-95	*7.56*	*52.01*	*65.51*	*69.82*	*67.61*	*4.31*
2000-05	*7.18*	*42.83*	*67.53*	*72.00*	*69.71*	*4.47*
2010-15	*7.36*	*34.78*	*69.33*	*74.03*	*71.63*	*4.70*
2020-25	*8.05*	*27.10*	*70.80*	*75.68*	*73.18*	*4.89*

FERTILITY MEASURES (Annual Averages)

PERIOD	CRUDE BIRTH RATE	FERTILITY RATES GENERAL	TOTAL	REPRODUCTION RATES GROSS	NET	RATE OF NATUR. INCR.
1950-55	37.47	157.78	5.148	2.511	1.882	22.27
1955-60	37.01	157.13	5.126	2.500	1.967	23.79
1960-65	39.09	168.11	5.427	2.647	2.177	27.16
1965-70	35.92	157.47	5.027	2.452	2.067	25.47
1970-75	31.20	136.62	4.393	2.142	1.853	21.94
1975-80	26.31	110.65	3.509	1.711	1.501	17.91
1980-85	25.12	100.08	3.130	1.526	1.359	17.02
1985-90	*24.69*	*94.71*	*2.924*	*1.426*	*1.289*	*16.85*
1990-95	*23.38*	*88.61*	*2.756*	*1.344*	*1.230*	*15.82*
2000-05	*19.89*	*75.19*	*2.516*	*1.228*	*1.151*	*12.71*
2010-15	*17.82*	*68.34*	*2.353*	*1.148*	*1.091*	*10.45*
2020-25	*16.23*	*66.27*	*2.250*	*1.098*	*1.055*	*8.18*

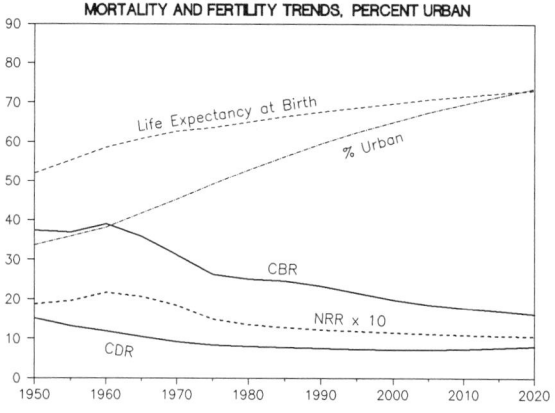

MORTALITY AND FERTILITY TRENDS, PERCENT URBAN

AGING MEASURES

YEAR	POPULATION AGE RATIOS 60+/20-59	65+/20-64	70+/20-69	75+/20-74	POPULATION MEAN AGE	POPULATION MEDIAN AGE
1950	0.1399	0.0863	0.0489	0.0236	25.05	20.71
1960	0.1540	0.0943	0.0534	0.0268	25.20	20.26
1970	0.1802	0.1115	0.0609	0.0312	24.99	19.63
1980	0.1906	0.1229	0.0724	0.0379	26.43	21.18
1990	*0.1789*	*0.1167*	*0.0726*	*0.0399*	*28.01*	*24.19*
2000	*0.1837*	*0.1197*	*0.0744*	*0.0410*	*29.74*	*27.22*
2010	*0.2062*	*0.1328*	*0.0808*	*0.0446*	*31.88*	*29.61*
2020	*0.2450*	*0.1552*	*0.0948*	*0.0520*	*33.99*	*32.00*

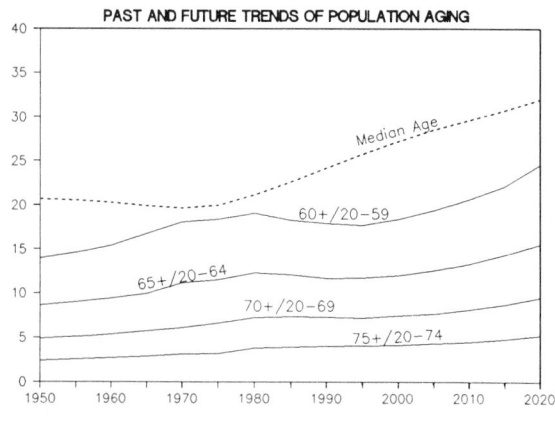

PAST AND FUTURE TRENDS OF POPULATION AGING

OBSERVED AND *PROJECTED* POPULATION DATA (000's)

YEAR	MID-YEAR POPULATION	NO. OF BIRTHS	NO. OF DEATHS	URBAN POPULATION NUMBER	URBAN POPULATION PERCENT	POPULATION AGE	1985 NUMBER
1950	37241	1762	636	14838	39.8	0	15449
1955	43093	2019	618	18645	43.3	5	14176
1960	50456	2323	623	23595	46.8	10	14126
1965	59285	2651	653	29869	50.4	15	12121
1970	69665	2974	665	37632	54.0	20	10030
1975	81361	2935	646	46703	57.4	25	8172
1980	92677	3104	649	56172	60.6	30	6614
1985	104746	3255	659	66627	63.6	35	5067
1990	*117670*	*3393*	*677*	*78085*	*66.4*	40	4372
1995	*131273*	*3483*	*711*	*90394*	*68.9*	45	3591
2000	*145125*	*3554*	*764*	*103239*	*71.1*	50	2995
2005	*159045*	*3621*	*834*	*116447*	*73.2*	55	2432
2010	*172925*	*3693*	*926*	*130073*	*75.2*	60	1918
2015	*186676*	*3762*	*1044*	*143914*	*77.1*	65	1367
2020	*200157*	*3827*	*1192*	*157809*	*78.8*	70+	2315

AGE DISTRIBUTIONS, 1960 - 1985

POPULATION RATIOS

YEAR	AGE DISTRIBUTION UNDER 15	15-64	65 & OLDER	70 & OLDER	DEPENDENCY RATIO	WOMEN 15-49	CHILD-WOMAN RATIO
1950	0.437	0.532	0.032	0.018	0.881	0.229	0.755
1955	0.446	0.523	0.031	0.018	0.913	0.225	0.825
1960	0.455	0.513	0.032	0.018	0.947	0.221	0.851
1965	0.467	0.501	0.032	0.019	0.996	0.216	0.873
1970	0.468	0.499	0.033	0.019	1.003	0.217	0.855
1975	0.463	0.504	0.033	0.020	0.985	0.219	0.821
1980	0.443	0.523	0.034	0.021	0.914	0.228	0.684
1985	0.418	0.547	0.035	0.022	0.828	0.239	0.617
1990	*0.387*	*0.575*	*0.038*	*0.023*	*0.738*	*0.252*	*0.551*
2000	*0.348*	*0.609*	*0.044*	*0.027*	*0.643*	*0.264*	*0.458*
2010	*0.309*	*0.639*	*0.053*	*0.033*	*0.566*	*0.269*	*0.394*
2020	*0.278*	*0.657*	*0.065*	*0.040*	*0.522*	*0.263*	*0.361*

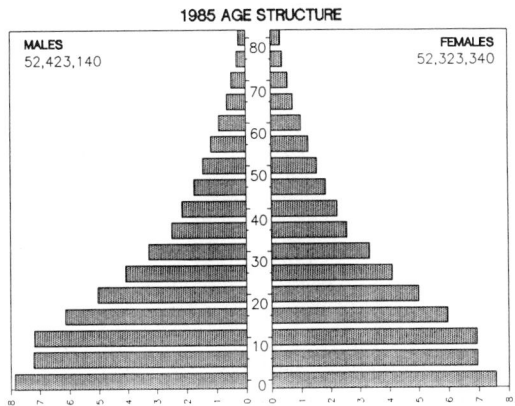

1985 AGE STRUCTURE

MALES 52,423,140　　　FEMALES 52,323,340

MORTALITY MEASURES (Annual Averages)

PERIOD	CRUDE DEATH RATE	INFANT MORT. RATE	LIFE EXPECTANCY AT BIRTH (years) MALE	FEMALE	BOTH SEXES	DIFFERENCE FEMALE-MALE
1950-55	17.07	122.73	47.94	50.77	49.32	2.83
1955-60	14.34	106.94	52.10	55.06	53.54	2.95
1960-65	12.34	94.06	55.22	58.33	56.74	3.11
1965-70	11.01	85.20	57.09	60.60	58.80	3.51
1970-75	9.55	74.43	59.22	63.46	61.29	4.24
1975-80	7.94	64.99	60.92	66.35	63.57	5.43
1980-85	7.01	56.75	62.60	68.80	65.63	6.20
1985-90	*6.29*	*49.61*	*64.55*	*70.65*	*67.53*	*6.09*
1990-95	*5.76*	*42.57*	*66.32*	*72.34*	*69.26*	*6.01*
2000-05	*5.26*	*33.08*	*68.77*	*74.90*	*71.76*	*6.13*
2010-15	*5.35*	*26.98*	*70.39*	*76.60*	*73.42*	*6.20*
2020-25	*5.95*	*22.82*	*71.28*	*77.53*	*74.33*	*6.26*

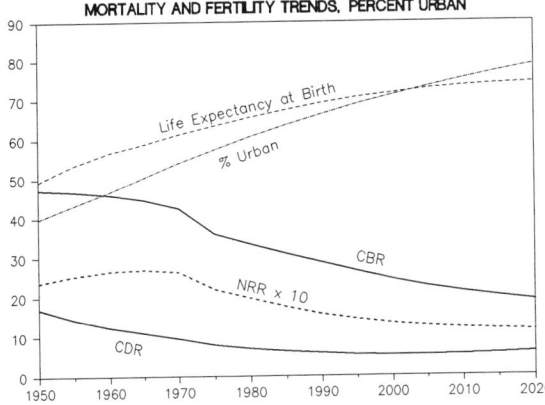

MORTALITY AND FERTILITY TRENDS, PERCENT URBAN

FERTILITY MEASURES (Annual Averages)

PERIOD	CRUDE BIRTH RATE	FERTILITY RATES GENERAL	TOTAL	REPRODUCTION RATES GROSS	NET	RATE OF NATUR. INCR.
1950-55	47.30	208.76	6.762	3.298	2.379	30.24
1955-60	46.85	210.34	6.786	3.310	2.550	32.51
1960-65	46.04	211.09	6.786	3.310	2.668	33.70
1965-70	44.72	206.80	6.684	3.261	2.704	33.71
1970-75	42.69	195.78	6.327	3.086	2.643	33.14
1975-80	36.07	161.09	5.111	2.493	2.198	28.13
1980-85	33.49	143.21	4.474	2.182	1.972	26.48
1985-90	*31.07*	*126.43*	*3.906*	*1.905*	*1.748*	*24.78*
1990-95	*28.84*	*112.98*	*3.454*	*1.685*	*1.568*	*23.08*
2000-05	*24.49*	*91.98*	*2.881*	*1.405*	*1.334*	*19.23*
2010-15	*21.35*	*79.59*	*2.600*	*1.268*	*1.217*	*16.00*
2020-25	*19.12*	*73.65*	*2.447*	*1.194*	*1.154*	*13.17*

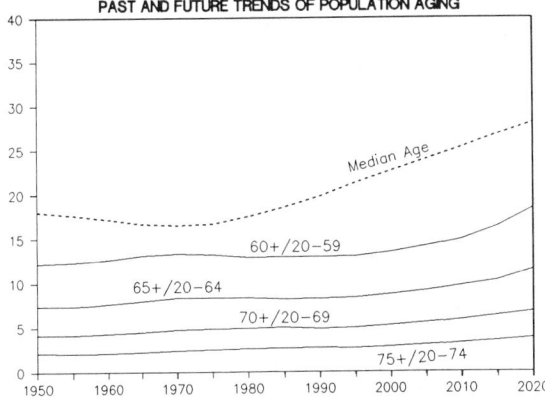

PAST AND FUTURE TRENDS OF POPULATION AGING

AGING MEASURES

YEAR	POPULATION AGE RATIOS 60+/20-59	65+/20-64	70+/20-69	75+/20-74	POPULATION MEAN AGE	MEDIAN AGE
1950	0.1216	0.0740	0.0419	0.0212	22.83	18.06
1960	0.1266	0.0767	0.0429	0.0215	22.21	17.22
1970	0.1330	0.0829	0.0470	0.0239	21.84	16.52
1980	0.1289	0.0834	0.0491	0.0260	22.49	17.54
1990	*0.1296*	*0.0821*	*0.0485*	*0.0270*	*24.06*	*19.77*
2000	*0.1348*	*0.0869*	*0.0522*	*0.0282*	*26.05*	*22.65*
2010	*0.1487*	*0.0968*	*0.0585*	*0.0323*	*28.35*	*25.30*
2020	*0.1844*	*0.1148*	*0.0676*	*0.0378*	*30.71*	*28.09*

OBSERVED AND *PROJECTED* POPULATION DATA (000's)

YEAR	MID-YEAR POPULATION	NO. OF BIRTHS	NO. OF DEATHS	URBAN POPULATION		POPULATION 1985	
				NUMBER	PERCENT	AGE	NUMBER
1950	111245	4632	1642	48080	43.2	0	35805
1955	128052	5210	1713	60721	47.4	5	32327
1960	146840	5839	1782	75901	51.7	10	29319
1965	168474	6019	1833	94231	55.9	15	27371
1970	190580	6297	1862	114331	60.0	20	25947
1975	214078	6797	1920	138005	64.5	25	22338
1980	239820	7321	2012	165033	68.8	30	19137
1985	267611	7696	2118	194858	72.8	35	15575
1990	*296787*	*7895*	*2222*	*225940*	*76.1*	40	12576
1995	*326393*	*8030*	*2339*	*257280*	*78.8*	45	10824
2000	*356007*	*8192*	*2497*	*288319*	*81.0*	50	9283
2005	*385536*	*8370*	*2687*	*318872*	*82.7*	55	8047
2010	*414907*	*8523*	*2904*	*348755*	*84.1*	60	6476
2015	*443855*	*8622*	*3169*	*378613*	*85.3*	65	4906
2020	*471854*	*8687*	*3492*	*407915*	*86.4*	70+	7680

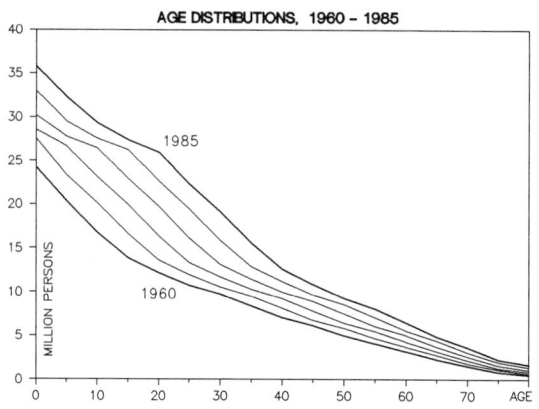

AGE DISTRIBUTIONS, 1960 - 1985

POPULATION RATIOS

YEAR	AGE DISTRIBUTION				DEPENDENCY RATIO	WOMEN 15-49	CHILD-WOMAN RATIO
	UNDER 15	15-64	65 & OLDER	70 & OLDER			
1950	0.398	0.570	0.032	0.018	0.756	0.242	0.658
1955	0.408	0.559	0.034	0.018	0.790	0.237	0.701
1960	0.418	0.547	0.035	0.020	0.829	0.230	0.716
1965	0.422	0.541	0.037	0.021	0.849	0.227	0.719
1970	0.411	0.549	0.040	0.023	0.821	0.231	0.647
1975	0.394	0.563	0.042	0.025	0.775	0.238	0.593
1980	0.376	0.579	0.045	0.027	0.726	0.245	0.562
1985	0.364	0.589	0.047	0.029	0.698	0.249	0.537
1990	*0.354*	*0.596*	*0.050*	*0.030*	*0.678*	*0.252*	*0.505*
2000	*0.324*	*0.620*	*0.056*	*0.035*	*0.612*	*0.261*	*0.428*
2010	*0.291*	*0.646*	*0.063*	*0.040*	*0.548*	*0.262*	*0.382*
2020	*0.267*	*0.655*	*0.078*	*0.048*	*0.527*	*0.257*	*0.353*

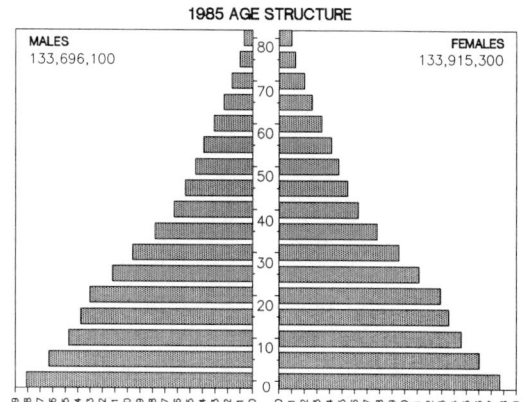

1985 AGE STRUCTURE

MALES 133,696,100   FEMALES 133,915,300

MORTALITY MEASURES (Annual Averages)

PERIOD	CRUDE DEATH RATE	INFANT MORT. RATE	LIFE EXPECTANCY AT BIRTH (years)			
			MALE	FEMALE	BOTH SEXES	DIFFERENCE FEMALE-MALE
1950-55	14.76	127.08	50.08	53.60	51.80	3.51
1955-60	13.38	114.60	52.28	56.14	54.17	3.85
1960-65	12.13	102.86	54.46	58.49	56.43	4.03
1965-70	10.88	93.53	56.27	60.57	58.37	4.30
1970-75	9.77	83.53	58.15	62.89	60.46	4.74
1975-80	8.97	72.66	60.00	64.87	62.38	4.88
1980-85	8.39	65.05	61.45	66.56	63.95	5.11
1985-90	*7.92*	*58.26*	*62.75*	*68.00*	*65.31*	*5.25*
1990-95	*7.49*	*52.41*	*64.04*	*69.43*	*66.67*	*5.40*
2000-05	*7.01*	*41.77*	*66.24*	*71.84*	*68.97*	*5.61*
2010-15	*7.00*	*34.17*	*67.91*	*73.71*	*70.74*	*5.80*
2020-25	*7.40*	*28.79*	*69.24*	*75.10*	*72.10*	*5.86*

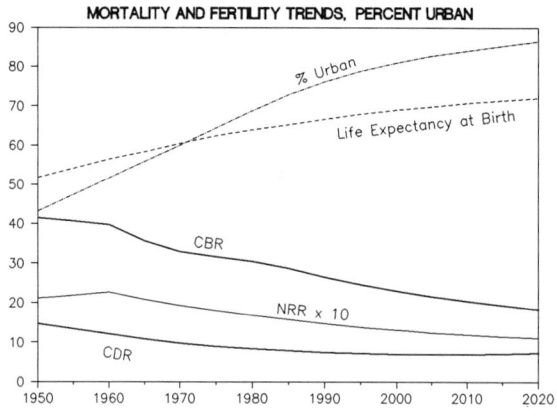

MORTALITY AND FERTILITY TRENDS, PERCENT URBAN

% Urban
Life Expectancy at Birth
CBR
NRR x 10
CDR

FERTILITY MEASURES (Annual Averages)

PERIOD	CRUDE BIRTH RATE	FERTILITY RATES		REPRODUCTION RATES		RATE OF NATUR. INCR.
		GENERAL	TOTAL	GROSS	NET	
1950-55	41.64	174.02	5.685	2.775	2.111	26.88
1955-60	40.68	174.38	5.727	2.796	2.194	27.31
1960-65	39.77	173.78	5.749	2.806	2.268	27.63
1965-70	35.73	155.63	5.169	2.523	2.089	24.85
1970-75	33.04	140.74	4.620	2.255	1.924	23.27
1975-80	31.75	131.50	4.221	2.061	1.804	22.78
1980-85	30.53	123.59	3.895	1.901	1.690	22.14
1985-90	*28.76*	*114.71*	*3.582*	*1.748*	*1.578*	*20.84*
1990-95	*26.60*	*104.49*	*3.296*	*1.609*	*1.474*	*19.11*
2000-05	*23.01*	*87.94*	*2.853*	*1.393*	*1.302*	*16.00*
2010-15	*20.54*	*78.75*	*2.568*	*1.253*	*1.186*	*13.54*
2020-25	*18.41*	*71.85*	*2.380*	*1.161*	*1.113*	*11.01*

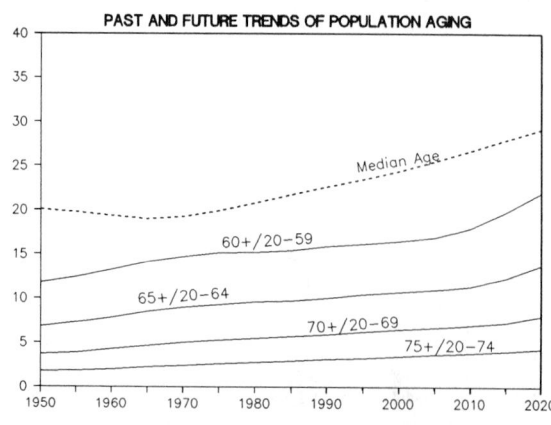

PAST AND FUTURE TRENDS OF POPULATION AGING

Median Age
60+/20-59
65+/20-64
70+/20-69
75+/20-74

AGING MEASURES

YEAR	POPULATION AGE RATIOS				POPULATION	
	60+/20-59	65+/20-64	70+/20-69	75+/20-74	MEAN AGE	MEDIAN AGE
1950	0.1175	0.0681	0.0371	0.0178	24.18	20.09
1960	0.1322	0.0781	0.0425	0.0196	24.00	19.35
1970	0.1466	0.0894	0.0497	0.0240	24.31	19.25
1980	0.1521	0.0956	0.0545	0.0276	25.28	20.79
1990	*0.1584*	*0.1000*	*0.0586*	*0.0310*	*26.39*	*22.60*
2000	*0.1646*	*0.1068*	*0.0647*	*0.0344*	*27.96*	*24.40*
2010	*0.1790*	*0.1131*	*0.0689*	*0.0379*	*29.80*	*26.70*
2020	*0.2191*	*0.1366*	*0.0794*	*0.0424*	*31.73*	*29.14*

OBSERVED AND *PROJECTED* POPULATION DATA (000's)

YEAR	MID-YEAR POPULATION	NO. OF BIRTHS	NO. OF DEATHS	URBAN POPULATION NUMBER	URBAN POPULATION PERCENT	POPULATION 1985 AGE	POPULATION 1985 NUMBER
1950	17150	435	156	11206	65.3	0	3240
1955	18928	460	164	13181	69.6	5	3224
1960	20616	479	182	15176	73.6	10	2777
1965	22283	503	203	16961	76.1	15	2447
1970	23963	560	215	18785	78.4	20	2323
1975	26052	650	231	21004	80.6	25	2257
1980	28237	650	246	23346	82.7	30	2162
1985	30331	648	262	25648	84.6	35	1949
1990	*32322*	*656*	*278*	*27856*	*86.2*	40	1710
1995	*34264*	*679*	*295*	*30007*	*87.6*	45	1558
2000	*36238*	*703*	*314*	*32163*	*88.8*	50	1483
2005	*38235*	*714*	*332*	*34316*	*89.8*	55	1394
2010	*40193*	*715*	*349*	*36408*	*90.6*	60	1196
2015	*42063*	*715*	*367*	*38423*	*91.3*	65	957
2020	*43837*	*718*	*391*	*40350*	*92.0*	70+	1654

POPULATION RATIOS

YEAR	AGE DISTRIBUTION UNDER 15	15-64	65 & OLDER	70 & OLDER	DEPENDENCY RATIO	WOMEN 15-49	CHILD-WOMAN RATIO
1950	0.305	0.653	0.042	0.023	0.532	0.262	0.433
1955	0.308	0.644	0.048	0.026	0.553	0.258	0.442
1960	0.308	0.637	0.055	0.032	0.570	0.252	0.436
1965	0.302	0.636	0.062	0.036	0.573	0.249	0.422
1970	0.294	0.637	0.070	0.041	0.570	0.249	0.413
1975	0.292	0.632	0.076	0.045	0.583	0.246	0.437
1980	0.300	0.618	0.082	0.050	0.618	0.239	0.480
1985	0.305	0.609	0.086	0.055	0.641	0.235	0.454
1990	*0.299*	*0.610*	*0.091*	*0.058*	*0.640*	*0.237*	*0.421*
2000	*0.272*	*0.629*	*0.098*	*0.065*	*0.589*	*0.247*	*0.379*
2010	*0.260*	*0.640*	*0.100*	*0.067*	*0.563*	*0.247*	*0.360*
2020	*0.244*	*0.646*	*0.110*	*0.072*	*0.548*	*0.250*	*0.327*

MORTALITY MEASURES (Annual Averages)

PERIOD	CRUDE DEATH RATE	INFANT MORT. RATE	LIFE EXPECTANCY AT BIRTH (years) MALE	FEMALE	BOTH SEXES	DIFFERENCE FEMALE-MALE
1950-55	9.11	64.00	60.42	65.14	62.73	4.72
1955-60	8.65	62.00	62.14	67.44	64.74	5.30
1960-65	8.83	60.00	62.47	68.62	65.49	6.15
1965-70	9.11	56.00	62.75	69.33	65.97	6.58
1970-75	8.99	49.00	64.07	70.70	67.32	6.63
1975-80	8.85	41.00	65.43	72.12	68.71	6.69
1980-85	8.71	36.00	66.42	73.13	69.71	6.71
1985-90	*8.65*	*32.00*	*67.28*	*74.01*	*70.58*	*6.73*
1990-95	*8.62*	*29.00*	*68.05*	*74.79*	*71.35*	*6.74*
2000-05	*8.66*	*24.00*	*69.24*	*76.00*	*72.55*	*6.76*
2010-15	*8.68*	*20.00*	*70.10*	*76.88*	*73.42*	*6.78*
2020-25	*8.91*	*18.00*	*70.71*	*77.51*	*74.04*	*6.80*

FERTILITY MEASURES (Annual Averages)

PERIOD	CRUDE BIRTH RATE	FERTILITY RATES GENERAL	TOTAL	REPRODUCTION RATES GROSS	NET	RATE OF NATUR. INCR.
1950-55	25.39	97.65	3.154	1.550	1.368	16.27
1955-60	24.31	95.44	3.126	1.530	1.380	15.66
1960-65	23.21	92.71	3.089	1.510	1.376	14.38
1965-70	22.55	90.58	3.049	1.490	1.367	13.44
1970-75	23.38	94.47	3.145	1.540	1.429	14.39
1975-80	24.95	102.89	3.360	1.650	1.546	16.10
1980-85	23.01	97.04	3.150	1.540	1.460	14.30
1985-90	*21.35*	*90.32*	*2.958*	*1.440*	*1.380*	*12.71*
1990-95	*20.28*	*84.19*	*2.788*	*1.360*	*1.308*	*11.67*
2000-05	*19.39*	*78.39*	*2.528*	*1.230*	*1.195*	*10.73*
2010-15	*17.78*	*71.80*	*2.348*	*1.150*	*1.116*	*9.10*
2020-25	*16.38*	*65.67*	*2.238*	*1.090*	*1.068*	*7.47*

AGING MEASURES

YEAR	POPULATION AGE RATIOS 60+/20-59	65+/20-64	70+/20-69	75+/20-74	POPULATION MEAN AGE	POPULATION MEDIAN AGE
1950	0.1321	0.0749	0.0394	0.0188	28.28	25.66
1960	0.1699	0.1004	0.0547	0.0255	29.40	26.84
1970	0.2109	0.1272	0.0704	0.0342	30.50	27.35
1980	0.2404	0.1527	0.0886	0.0447	30.72	27.36
1990	*0.2714*	*0.1738*	*0.1038*	*0.0560*	*31.27*	*27.79*
2000	*0.2693*	*0.1819*	*0.1139*	*0.0623*	*32.09*	*28.38*
2010	*0.2724*	*0.1792*	*0.1135*	*0.0660*	*32.93*	*30.03*
2020	*0.2926*	*0.1941*	*0.1193*	*0.0668*	*34.06*	*31.80*

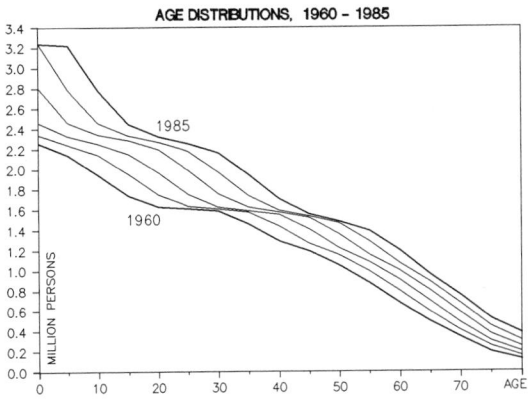

AGE DISTRIBUTIONS, 1960 - 1985

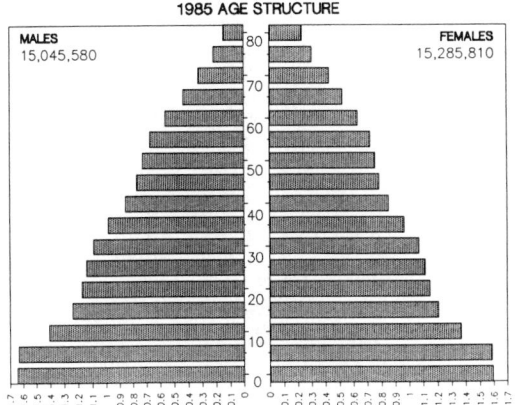

1985 AGE STRUCTURE

MALES 15,045,580   FEMALES 15,285,810

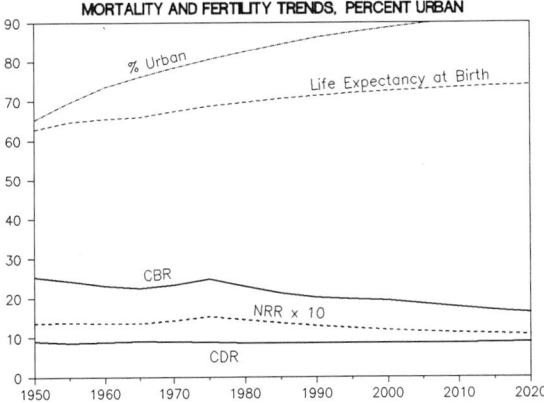

MORTALITY AND FERTILITY TRENDS, PERCENT URBAN

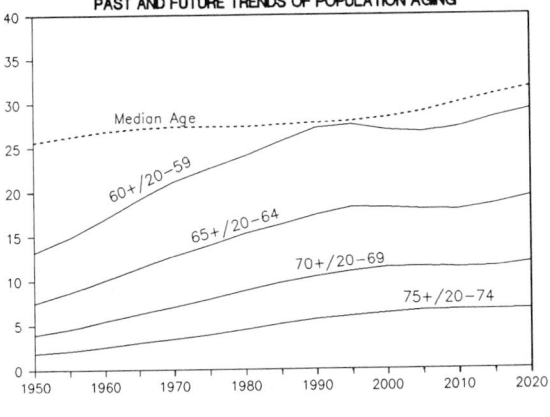

PAST AND FUTURE TRENDS OF POPULATION AGING

OBSERVED AND *PROJECTED* POPULATION DATA

YEAR	MID-YEAR POPULATION	NO. OF BIRTHS	NO. OF DEATHS	URBAN POPULATION NUMBER	URBAN POPULATION PERCENT	POPULATION 1985 AGE	POPULATION 1985 NUMBER
1950	211000	6921	2785	71462	33.9	0	21757
1955	227300	7228	2341	78756	34.6	5	21363
1960	230660	6712	2122	81739	35.4	10	25533
1965	235204	5598	1999	85223	36.2	15	25253
1970	238756	4961	2087	88509	37.1	20	26552
1975	245588	4347	2124	94786	38.6	25	24383
1980	249042	4430	2159	99973	40.1	30	19850
1985	252989	4690	2131	106747	42.2	35	15397
1990	*261001*	*4731*	*2099*	*116757*	*44.7*	40	10437
1995	*271941*	*4650*	*2039*	*129796*	*47.7*	45	9424
2000	*285317*	*4527*	*2004*	*145854*	*51.1*	50	8647
2005	*298215*	*4507*	*2031*	*163483*	*54.8*	55	9381
2010	*310859*	*4563*	*2091*	*181360*	*58.3*	60	8068
2015	*323470*	*4622*	*2249*	*199457*	*61.7*	65	8170
2020	*335557*	*4642*	*2504*	*217339*	*64.8*	70+	18774

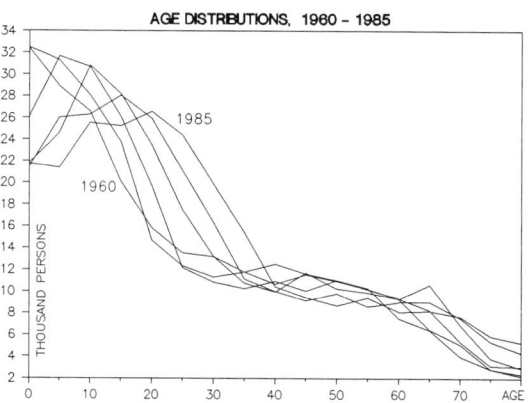

AGE DISTRIBUTIONS, 1960 - 1985

POPULATION RATIOS

YEAR	AGE DISTRIBUTION UNDER 15	AGE DISTRIBUTION 15-64	AGE DISTRIBUTION 65 & OLDER	AGE DISTRIBUTION 70 & OLDER	DEPENDENCY RATIO	WOMEN 15-49	CHILD-WOMAN RATIO
1950	0.332	0.611	0.057	0.038	0.636	0.270	0.456
1955	0.348	0.584	0.068	0.045	0.713	0.251	0.541
1960	0.381	0.552	0.067	0.039	0.812	0.238	0.590
1965	0.391	0.538	0.071	0.044	0.858	0.222	0.621
1970	0.371	0.546	0.083	0.048	0.830	0.222	0.493
1975	0.315	0.587	0.099	0.055	0.704	0.246	0.362
1980	0.296	0.598	0.105	0.069	0.671	0.253	0.341
1985	0.271	0.622	0.107	0.074	0.607	0.267	0.323
1990	*0.253*	*0.645*	*0.102*	*0.074*	*0.550*	*0.278*	*0.322*
2000	*0.247*	*0.660*	*0.093*	*0.067*	*0.515*	*0.276*	*0.299*
2010	*0.222*	*0.688*	*0.089*	*0.062*	*0.453*	*0.257*	*0.285*
2020	*0.206*	*0.672*	*0.122*	*0.074*	*0.488*	*0.233*	*0.298*

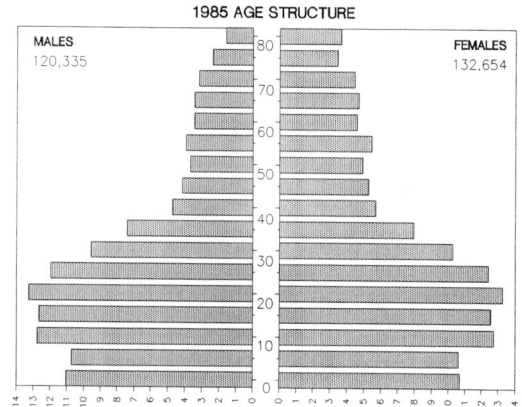

1985 AGE STRUCTURE

MALES 120,335 — FEMALES 132.654

MORTALITY MEASURES (Annual Averages)

PERIOD	CRUDE DEATH RATE	INFANT MORT. RATE	LIFE EXPECTANCY AT BIRTH (years) MALE	LIFE EXPECTANCY AT BIRTH (years) FEMALE	LIFE EXPECTANCY AT BIRTH (years) BOTH SEXES	DIFFERENCE FEMALE-MALE
1950-55	13.20	132.00	55.00	59.50	57.22	4.50
1955-60	10.30	61.00	60.20	65.00	62.57	4.80
1960-65	9.20	46.00	63.50	68.30	65.87	4.80
1965-70	8.50	33.00	65.20	70.10	67.62	4.90
1970-75	8.74	27.00	66.90	72.00	69.42	5.10
1975-80	8.65	14.00	68.70	73.90	71.27	5.20
1980-85	8.67	11.00	70.00	75.45	72.67	5.44
1985-90	*8.42*	*11.00*	*71.00*	*77.01*	*73.94*	*6.01*
1990-95	*8.04*	*10.00*	*72.02*	*77.89*	*74.89*	*5.87*
2000-05	*7.03*	*8.00*	*73.74*	*79.50*	*76.56*	*5.77*
2010-15	*6.73*	*6.00*	*75.28*	*80.71*	*77.94*	*5.44*
2020-25	*7.46*	*6.00*	*76.21*	*81.73*	*78.92*	*5.51*

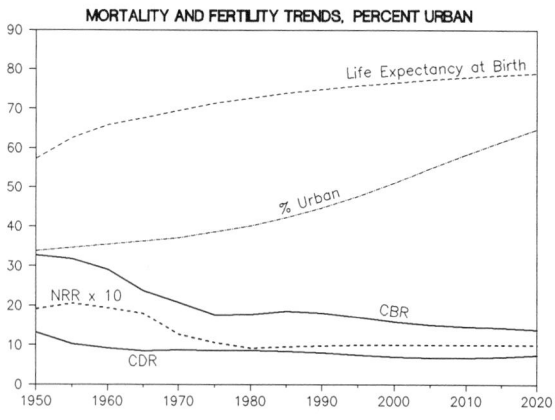

MORTALITY AND FERTILITY TRENDS, PERCENT URBAN

Life Expectancy at Birth / % Urban / NRR x 10 / CBR / CDR

FERTILITY MEASURES (Annual Averages)

PERIOD	CRUDE BIRTH RATE	FERTILITY RATES GENERAL	FERTILITY RATES TOTAL	REPRODUCTION RATES GROSS	REPRODUCTION RATES NET	RATE OF NATUR. INCR.
1950-55	32.80	126.00	4.692	2.300	1.920	19.60
1955-60	31.80	130.03	4.692	2.300	2.060	21.50
1960-65	29.10	126.45	4.284	2.100	1.940	19.90
1965-70	23.80	107.17	3.468	1.700	1.800	15.30
1970-75	20.78	88.84	2.754	1.350	1.270	12.04
1975-80	17.70	70.99	2.244	1.100	1.060	9.05
1980-85	17.79	68.47	1.938	0.950	0.924	9.12
1985-90	*18.54*	*68.09*	*1.999*	*0.980*	*0.959*	*10.12*
1990-95	*18.13*	*65.00*	*2.040*	*1.000*	*0.981*	*10.08*
2000-05	*15.87*	*58.23*	*2.081*	*1.020*	*1.005*	*8.84*
2010-15	*14.68*	*58.63*	*2.081*	*1.020*	*1.007*	*7.95*
2020-25	*13.84*	*60.62*	*2.081*	*1.020*	*1.008*	*6.37*

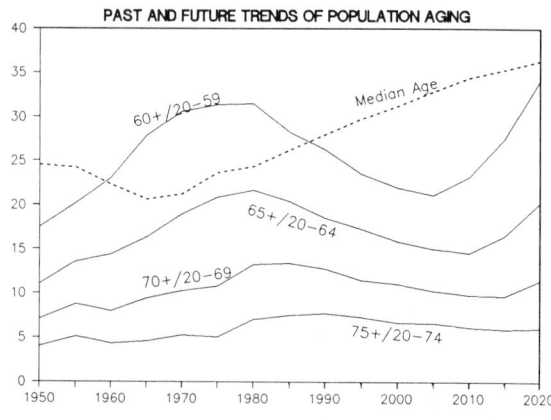

PAST AND FUTURE TRENDS OF POPULATION AGING

Median Age / 60+/20-59 / 65+/20-64 / 70+/20-69 / 75+/20-74

AGING MEASURES

YEAR	POPULATION AGE RATIOS 60+/20-59	POPULATION AGE RATIOS 65+/20-64	POPULATION AGE RATIOS 70+/20-69	POPULATION AGE RATIOS 75+/20-74	POPULATION MEAN AGE	POPULATION MEDIAN AGE
1950	0.1748	0.1101	0.0708	0.0400	28.11	24.56
1960	0.2303	0.1442	0.0798	0.0430	27.86	22.32
1970	0.3059	0.1895	0.1025	0.0524	28.40	21.21
1980	0.3146	0.2164	0.1322	0.0703	30.25	24.37
1990	*0.2629*	*0.1850*	*0.1272*	*0.0770*	*31.59*	*28.02*
2000	*0.2195*	*0.1588*	*0.1103*	*0.0668*	*32.88*	*31.25*
2010	*0.2312*	*0.1458*	*0.0975*	*0.0611*	*34.94*	*34.42*
2020	*0.3399*	*0.2016*	*0.1137*	*0.0603*	*37.19*	*36.36*

OBSERVED AND *PROJECTED* POPULATION DATA (000's)

YEAR	MID-YEAR POPULATION	NO. OF BIRTHS	NO. OF DEATHS	URBAN POPULATION NUMBER	URBAN POPULATION PERCENT	POPULATION 1985 AGE	POPULATION 1985 NUMBER
1950	2766	130	67	1045	37.8	0	1107
1955	3072	143	70	1183	38.5	5	909
1960	3428	158	74	1346	39.3	10	771
1965	3841	175	78	1536	40.0	15	655
1970	4325	196	82	1762	40.8	20	552
1975	4894	219	86	2032	41.5	25	464
1980	5570	245	88	2468	44.3	30	392
1985	6371	273	90	3046	47.8	35	334
1990	7314	302	89	3759	51.4	40	272
1995	8421	333	84	4631	55.0	45	226
2000	9724	366	85	5687	58.5	50	194
2005	11195	397	86	6919	61.8	55	164
2010	12820	425	91	8321	64.9	60	126
2015	14565	449	96	9873	67.8	65	90
2020	16401	468	102	11555	70.5	70+	114

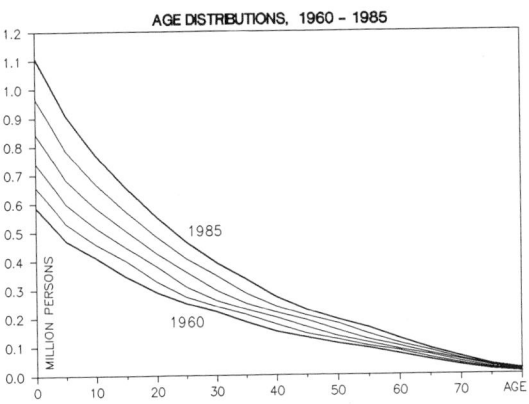

AGE DISTRIBUTIONS, 1960 - 1985

POPULATION RATIOS

YEAR	AGE DISTRIBUTION UNDER 15	AGE DISTRIBUTION 15-64	AGE DISTRIBUTION 65 & OLDER	AGE DISTRIBUTION 70 & OLDER	DEPENDENCY RATIO	WOMEN 15-49	CHILD-WOMAN RATIO
1950	0.420	0.549	0.031	0.016	0.823	0.234	0.736
1955	0.425	0.544	0.031	0.016	0.839	0.232	0.735
1960	0.429	0.540	0.032	0.017	0.853	0.232	0.738
1965	0.428	0.539	0.033	0.017	0.855	0.233	0.734
1970	0.430	0.537	0.033	0.018	0.862	0.234	0.733
1975	0.432	0.535	0.033	0.018	0.868	0.233	0.738
1980	0.435	0.533	0.033	0.018	0.877	0.233	0.746
1985	0.438	0.530	0.032	0.018	0.885	0.232	0.749
1990	0.439	0.529	0.032	0.018	0.891	0.232	0.743
2000	0.435	0.532	0.032	0.018	0.878	0.235	0.715
2010	0.418	0.549	0.032	0.019	0.820	0.241	0.644
2020	0.386	0.579	0.035	0.020	0.728	0.253	0.547

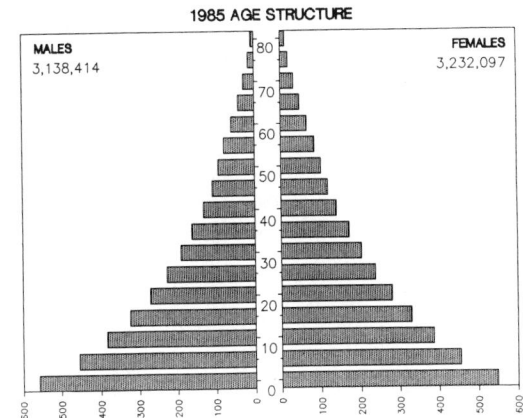

1985 AGE STRUCTURE

MALES 3,138,414   FEMALES 3,232,097

MORTALITY MEASURES (Annual Averages)

PERIOD	CRUDE DEATH RATE	INFANT MORT. RATE	LIFE EXPECTANCY AT BIRTH (years) MALE	LIFE EXPECTANCY AT BIRTH (years) FEMALE	LIFE EXPECTANCY AT BIRTH (years) BOTH SEXES	DIFFERENCE FEMALE-MALE
1950-55	24.09	176.00	38.49	42.49	40.44	4.00
1955-60	22.76	170.00	39.90	44.02	41.91	4.12
1960-65	21.46	164.00	41.39	45.61	43.45	4.22
1965-70	20.19	157.00	42.95	47.27	45.06	4.32
1970-75	18.95	151.00	44.58	49.01	46.74	4.43
1975-80	17.49	138.00	46.46	50.92	48.64	4.46
1980-85	15.87	124.00	48.55	53.03	50.74	4.48
1985-90	14.11	110.00	50.85	55.41	53.07	4.56
1990-95	12.15	93.00	53.57	58.34	55.90	4.77
2000-05	8.71	64.00	59.11	64.25	61.62	5.14
2010-15	7.07	49.00	62.25	67.55	64.83	5.30
2020-25	6.24	40.00	64.50	70.00	67.18	5.50

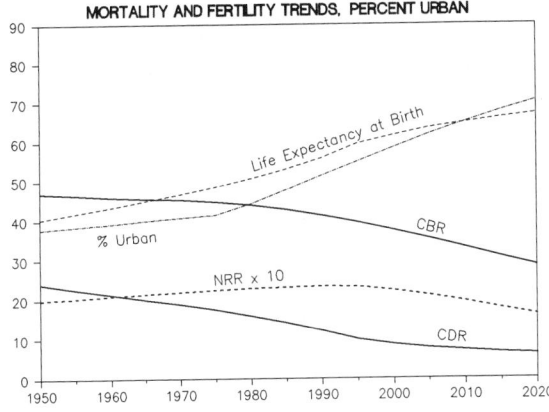

MORTALITY AND FERTILITY TRENDS, PERCENT URBAN

FERTILITY MEASURES (Annual Averages)

PERIOD	CRUDE BIRTH RATE	FERTILITY RATES GENERAL	FERTILITY RATES TOTAL	REPRODUCTION RATES GROSS	REPRODUCTION RATES NET	RATE OF NATUR. INCR.
1950-55	47.14	202.21	6.750	3.290	2.003	23.04
1955-60	46.62	200.99	6.690	3.260	2.053	23.86
1960-65	46.06	198.38	6.629	3.230	2.103	24.60
1965-70	45.64	195.75	6.560	3.200	2.150	25.45
1970-75	45.42	194.49	6.500	3.170	2.203	26.46
1975-80	44.84	192.47	6.390	3.120	2.252	27.36
1980-85	44.02	189.50	6.250	3.050	2.294	28.16
1985-90	42.85	184.44	6.060	2.950	2.322	28.74
1990-95	41.34	177.35	5.810	2.830	2.335	29.18
2000-05	37.60	159.22	5.137	2.510	2.239	28.89
2010-15	33.14	135.75	4.305	2.100	1.945	26.07
2020-25	28.52	111.56	3.497	1.710	1.614	22.29

AGING MEASURES

YEAR	POPULATION AGE RATIOS 60+/20-59	POPULATION AGE RATIOS 65+/20-64	POPULATION AGE RATIOS 70+/20-69	POPULATION AGE RATIOS 75+/20-74	POPULATION MEAN AGE	POPULATION MEDIAN AGE
1950	0.1219	0.0698	0.0355	0.0150	23.40	18.89
1960	0.1268	0.0726	0.0370	0.0156	23.30	18.55
1970	0.1290	0.0767	0.0396	0.0171	23.19	18.42
1980	0.1269	0.0761	0.0407	0.0187	22.99	18.19
1990	0.1278	0.0752	0.0401	0.0186	22.77	17.94
2000	0.1230	0.0754	0.0417	0.0193	22.78	18.06
2010	0.1212	0.0730	0.0408	0.0201	23.31	18.81
2020	0.1229	0.0750	0.0420	0.0203	24.47	20.35

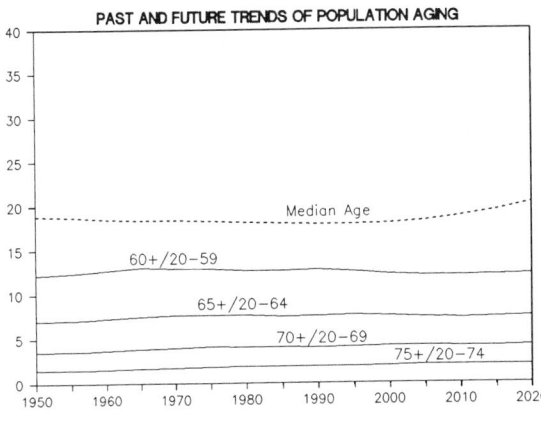

PAST AND FUTURE TRENDS OF POPULATION AGING

OBSERVED AND *PROJECTED* POPULATION DATA (000's)

YEAR	MID-YEAR POPULATION	NO. OF BIRTHS	NO. OF DEATHS	URBAN POPULATION NUMBER	URBAN POPULATION PERCENT	POPULATION 1985 AGE	POPULATION 1985 NUMBER
1950	53444	2386	805	19216	36.0	0	18072
1955	62569	2710	853	25258	40.4	5	16368
1960	72595	3055	890	32627	44.9	10	14926
1965	84292	3072	909	42460	50.4	15	13933
1970	95847	3225	934	53500	55.8	20	13633
1975	108032	3459	961	66793	61.8	25	11663
1980	121286	3711	1014	81888	67.5	30	9883
1985	135564	3875	1067	98599	72.7	35	7955
1990	*150368*	*3931*	*1125*	*115674*	*76.9*	40	6299
1995	*165083*	*3949*	*1189*	*132394*	*80.2*	45	5460
2000	*179487*	*3988*	*1271*	*148397*	*82.7*	50	4539
2005	*193603*	*4042*	*1368*	*163599*	*84.5*	55	3909
2010	*207454*	*4092*	*1475*	*177963*	*85.8*	60	3098
2015	*220960*	*4110*	*1611*	*192140*	*87.0*	65	2283
2020	*233817*	*4116*	*1778*	*205824*	*88.0*	70+	3545

POPULATION RATIOS

YEAR	AGE DISTRIBUTION UNDER 15	15-64	65 & OLDER	70 & OLDER	DEPENDENCY RATIO	WOMEN 15-49	CHILD-WOMAN RATIO
1950	0.420	0.555	0.025	0.014	0.801	0.242	0.701
1955	0.426	0.547	0.027	0.014	0.828	0.236	0.741
1960	0.436	0.535	0.029	0.016	0.869	0.230	0.755
1965	0.438	0.530	0.032	0.018	0.886	0.226	0.756
1970	0.422	0.543	0.034	0.020	0.841	0.232	0.652
1975	0.401	0.562	0.037	0.022	0.779	0.240	0.592
1980	0.377	0.582	0.040	0.024	0.717	0.249	0.553
1985	0.364	0.593	0.043	0.026	0.687	0.254	0.525
1990	*0.352*	*0.601*	*0.047*	*0.028*	*0.664*	*0.257*	*0.490*
2000	*0.318*	*0.628*	*0.054*	*0.034*	*0.591*	*0.266*	*0.407*
2010	*0.282*	*0.655*	*0.063*	*0.040*	*0.526*	*0.267*	*0.361*
2020	*0.257*	*0.662*	*0.081*	*0.050*	*0.511*	*0.259*	*0.336*

MORTALITY MEASURES (Annual Averages)

PERIOD	CRUDE DEATH RATE	INFANT MORT. RATE	LIFE EXPECTANCY AT BIRTH (years) MALE	FEMALE	BOTH SEXES	DIFFERENCE FEMALE-MALE
1950-55	15.07	135.00	49.32	52.75	50.99	3.43
1955-60	13.64	122.00	51.60	55.38	53.44	3.78
1960-65	12.26	109.00	54.02	57.82	55.87	3.80
1965-70	10.79	100.00	55.94	59.95	57.90	4.01
1970-75	9.74	91.00	57.57	62.17	59.81	4.60
1975-80	8.90	79.00	59.54	64.25	61.84	4.71
1980-85	8.36	71.00	60.95	66.00	63.41	5.05
1985-90	*7.87*	*63.00*	*62.30*	*67.60*	*64.89*	*5.30*
1990-95	*7.48*	*57.00*	*63.54*	*69.10*	*66.25*	*5.56*
2000-05	*7.08*	*45.00*	*65.74*	*71.60*	*68.60*	*5.86*
2010-15	*7.11*	*36.00*	*67.59*	*73.75*	*70.60*	*6.16*
2020-25	*7.60*	*30.00*	*69.05*	*75.26*	*72.08*	*6.21*

FERTILITY MEASURES (Annual Averages)

PERIOD	CRUDE BIRTH RATE	FERTILITY RATES GENERAL	FERTILITY RATES TOTAL	REPRODUCTION RATES GROSS	REPRODUCTION RATES NET	RATE OF NATUR. INCR.
1950-55	44.64	187.07	6.150	3.000	2.267	29.57
1955-60	43.31	186.30	6.150	3.000	2.341	29.67
1960-65	42.08	184.69	6.150	3.000	2.410	29.82
1965-70	36.44	158.78	5.310	2.590	2.131	25.66
1970-75	33.65	142.28	4.699	2.290	1.947	23.91
1975-80	32.02	130.66	4.210	2.050	1.795	23.12
1980-85	30.60	121.57	3.809	1.860	1.651	22.24
1985-90	*28.58*	*111.83*	*3.459*	*1.690*	*1.521*	*20.71*
1990-95	*26.14*	*100.65*	*3.159*	*1.540*	*1.407*	*18.66*
2000-05	*22.22*	*83.21*	*2.709*	*1.320*	*1.230*	*15.14*
2010-15	*19.72*	*74.59*	*2.430*	*1.190*	*1.121*	*12.61*
2020-25	*17.60*	*68.32*	*2.280*	*1.110*	*1.062*	*10.00*

AGING MEASURES

YEAR	POPULATION AGE RATIOS 60+/20-59	65+/20-64	70+/20-69	75+/20-74	POPULATION MEAN AGE	POPULATION MEDIAN AGE
1950	0.0973	0.0542	0.0295	0.0143	22.88	18.87
1960	0.1139	0.0660	0.0356	0.0157	22.92	18.34
1970	0.1291	0.0791	0.0439	0.0209	23.53	18.61
1980	0.1376	0.0862	0.0485	0.0249	24.82	20.48
1990	*0.1476*	*0.0926*	*0.0540*	*0.0287*	*26.21*	*22.66*
2000	*0.1585*	*0.1021*	*0.0620*	*0.0330*	*28.09*	*24.72*
2010	*0.1772*	*0.1116*	*0.0683*	*0.0375*	*30.21*	*27.31*
2020	*0.2251*	*0.1396*	*0.0812*	*0.0435*	*32.33*	*29.98*

AGE DISTRIBUTIONS, 1960 - 1985

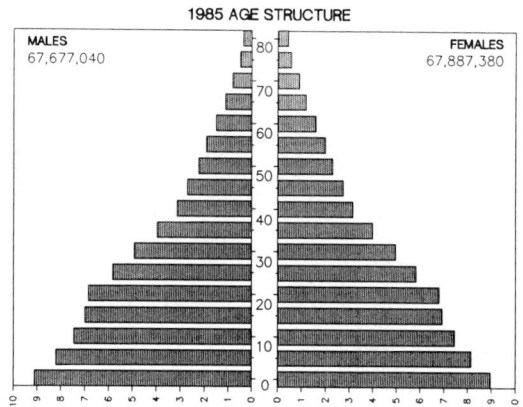

1985 AGE STRUCTURE

MALES 67,677,040   FEMALES 67,887,380

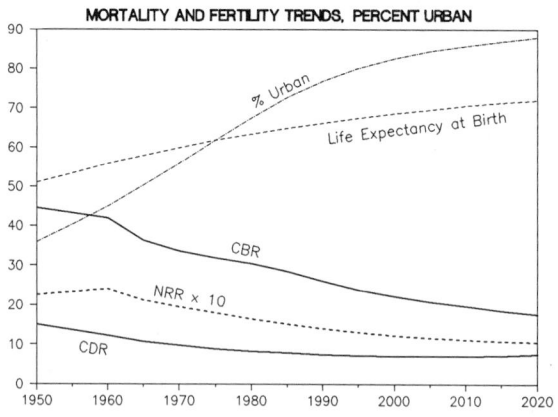

MORTALITY AND FERTILITY TRENDS, PERCENT URBAN

% Urban

Life Expectancy at Birth

CBR

NRR x 10

CDR

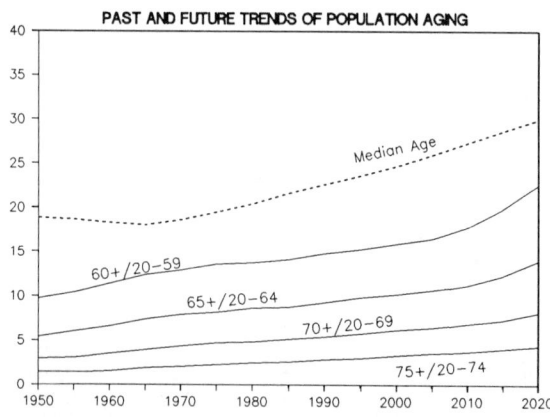

PAST AND FUTURE TRENDS OF POPULATION AGING

Median Age

60+/20-59

65+/20-64

70+/20-69

75+/20-74

OBSERVED AND *PROJECTED* POPULATION DATA (000's)

YEAR	MID-YEAR POPULATION	NO. OF BIRTHS	NO. OF DEATHS	URBAN POPULATION NUMBER	URBAN POPULATION PERCENT	POPULATION 1985 AGE	POPULATION 1985 NUMBER
1950	6082	226	87	3553	58.4	0	1368
1955	6776	254	89	4286	63.3	5	1203
1960	7614	280	92	5165	67.8	10	1243
1965	8579	271	89	6151	71.7	15	1251
1970	9504	262	85	7150	75.2	20	1244
1975	10350	246	77	8103	78.3	25	1080
1980	11145	269	71	9035	81.1	30	918
1985	12121	289	78	10130	83.6	35	751
1990	*13173*	*297*	*85*	*11280*	*85.6*	40	646
1995	*14237*	*298*	*92*	*12429*	*87.3*	45	520
2000	*15272*	*296*	*101*	*13538*	*88.6*	50	465
2005	*16245*	*300*	*112*	*14574*	*89.7*	55	405
2010	*17182*	*309*	*124*	*15558*	*90.5*	60	321
2015	*18100*	*314*	*137*	*16528*	*91.3*	65	259
2020	*18973*	*316*	*153*	*17458*	*92.0*	70+	448

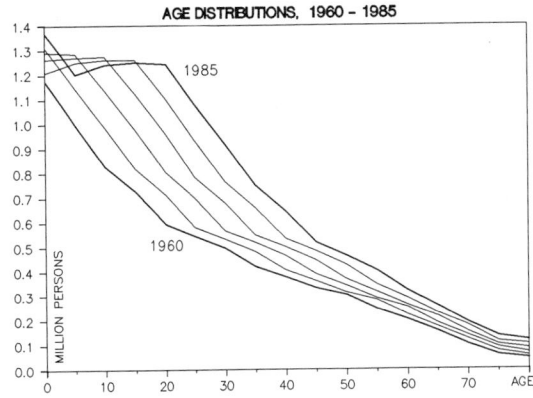

AGE DISTRIBUTIONS, 1960 - 1985

POPULATION RATIOS

YEAR	AGE DISTRIBUTION UNDER 15	15-64	65 & OLDER	70 & OLDER	DEPENDENCY RATIO	WOMEN 15-49	CHILD-WOMAN RATIO
1950	0.367	0.590	0.043	0.025	0.694	0.247	0.578
1955	0.384	0.572	0.044	0.025	0.750	0.238	0.637
1960	0.394	0.559	0.047	0.027	0.790	0.232	0.664
1965	0.401	0.549	0.049	0.029	0.821	0.229	0.667
1970	0.391	0.558	0.051	0.031	0.791	0.235	0.579
1975	0.368	0.578	0.054	0.033	0.729	0.245	0.498
1980	0.334	0.610	0.056	0.035	0.639	0.258	0.420
1985	0.315	0.627	0.058	0.037	0.595	0.265	0.426
1990	*0.306*	*0.634*	*0.060*	*0.038*	*0.578*	*0.267*	*0.420*
2000	*0.294*	*0.639*	*0.067*	*0.043*	*0.565*	*0.262*	*0.378*
2010	*0.263*	*0.660*	*0.077*	*0.049*	*0.516*	*0.258*	*0.342*
2020	*0.245*	*0.659*	*0.096*	*0.060*	*0.517*	*0.247*	*0.339*

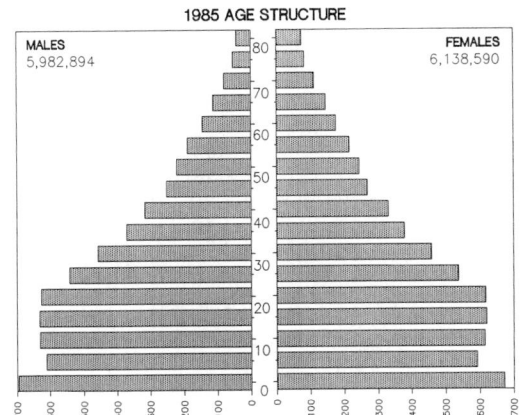

1985 AGE STRUCTURE

MALES 5,982,894   FEMALES 6,138,590

MORTALITY MEASURES (Annual Averages)

PERIOD	CRUDE DEATH RATE	INFANT MORT. RATE	LIFE EXPECTANCY AT BIRTH (years) MALE	FEMALE	BOTH SEXES	DIFFERENCE FEMALE-MALE
1950-55	14.37	126.00	51.85	55.72	53.75	3.87
1955-60	13.14	117.00	53.81	58.69	56.20	4.88
1960-65	12.13	111.00	55.27	60.95	58.05	5.68
1965-70	10.39	95.00	57.64	63.75	60.63	6.11
1970-75	8.91	70.00	60.46	66.80	63.57	6.34
1975-80	7.46	46.00	63.94	70.57	67.19	6.63
1980-85	6.33	23.00	67.55	74.55	70.98	7.00
1985-90	*6.41*	*20.00*	*68.05*	*75.05*	*71.48*	*7.00*
1990-95	*6.41*	*19.00*	*68.54*	*75.59*	*72.00*	*7.05*
2000-05	*6.65*	*17.00*	*69.44*	*76.57*	*72.93*	*7.13*
2010-15	*7.22*	*16.00*	*70.26*	*77.44*	*73.78*	*7.18*
2020-25	*8.07*	*14.00*	*70.99*	*78.20*	*74.52*	*7.21*

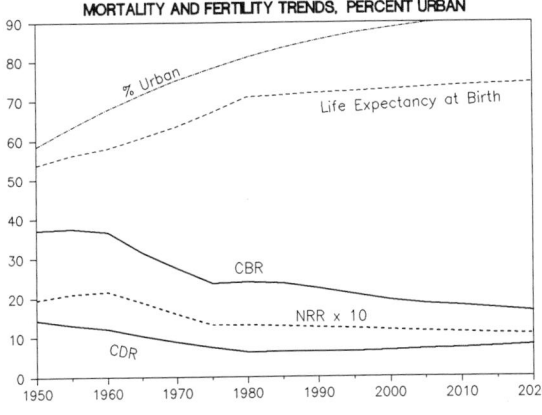

MORTALITY AND FERTILITY TRENDS, PERCENT URBAN

% Urban; Life Expectancy at Birth; CBR; NRR x 10; CDR

FERTILITY MEASURES (Annual Averages)

PERIOD	CRUDE BIRTH RATE	FERTILITY RATES GENERAL	FERTILITY RATES TOTAL	REPRODUCTION RATES GROSS	REPRODUCTION RATES NET	RATE OF NATUR. INCR.
1950-55	37.20	153.74	5.100	2.390	1.960	22.83
1955-60	37.56	159.98	5.301	2.590	2.108	24.42
1960-65	36.77	159.51	5.280	2.580	2.163	24.64
1965-70	31.59	136.17	4.440	2.170	1.894	21.20
1970-75	27.56	114.79	3.630	1.790	1.603	18.65
1975-80	23.73	94.14	2.900	1.410	1.325	16.27
1980-85	24.16	92.28	2.798	1.370	1.320	17.83
1985-90	*23.83*	*89.63*	*2.728*	*1.330*	*1.296*	*17.42*
1990-95	*22.52*	*85.06*	*2.658*	*1.300*	*1.266*	*16.11*
2000-05	*19.38*	*73.97*	*2.498*	*1.220*	*1.194*	*12.74*
2010-15	*17.97*	*70.43*	*2.347*	*1.150*	*1.126*	*10.75*
2020-25	*16.65*	*67.99*	*2.249*	*1.100*	*1.082*	*8.57*

AGING MEASURES

YEAR	POPULATION AGE RATIOS 60+/20-59	65+/20-64	70+/20-69	75+/20-74	POPULATION MEAN AGE	POPULATION MEDIAN AGE
1950	0.1459	0.0859	0.0481	0.0224	26.21	22.20
1960	0.1702	0.1025	0.0557	0.0272	25.59	20.67
1970	0.1803	0.1115	0.0652	0.0337	25.59	20.36
1980	0.1740	0.1126	0.0683	0.0362	27.09	22.67
1990	*0.1734*	*0.1115*	*0.0684*	*0.0379*	*28.47*	*25.34*
2000	*0.1847*	*0.1222*	*0.0750*	*0.0411*	*30.05*	*27.57*
2010	*0.2110*	*0.1347*	*0.0809*	*0.0464*	*31.97*	*29.25*
2020	*0.2660*	*0.1648*	*0.0969*	*0.0535*	*33.73*	*31.37*

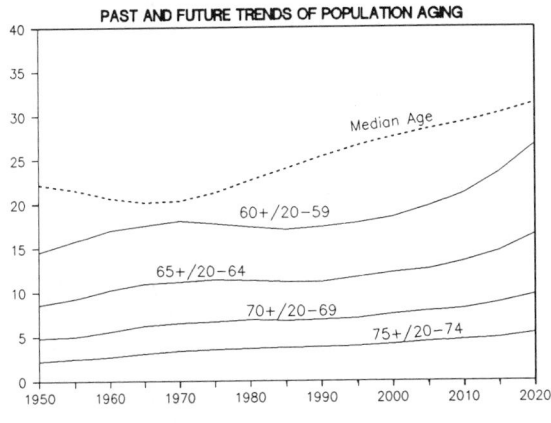

PAST AND FUTURE TRENDS OF POPULATION AGING

Median Age; 60+/20-59; 65+/20-64; 70+/20-69; 75+/20-74

OBSERVED AND *PROJECTED* POPULATION DATA (000's)

YEAR	MID-YEAR POPULATION	NO. OF BIRTHS	NO. OF DEATHS	URBAN POPULATION NUMBER	URBAN POPULATION PERCENT	POPULATION 1985 AGE	POPULATION 1985 NUMBER
1950	11597	552	191	4301	37.1	0	3938
1955	13390	615	190	5697	42.5	5	3531
1960	15538	693	189	7489	48.2	10	3199
1965	18114	718	189	9694	53.5	15	3252
1970	20803	694	188	11899	57.2	20	3009
1975	23176	743	191	14092	60.8	25	2486
1980	25793	800	200	16568	64.2	30	2062
1985	28713	839	212	19357	67.4	35	1606
1990	*31819*	*849*	*225*	*22371*	*70.3*	40	1270
1995	*34939*	*850*	*240*	*25467*	*72.9*	45	1045
2000	*37998*	*851*	*257*	*28557*	*75.2*	50	880
2005	*40962*	*857*	*277*	*31636*	*77.2*	55	741
2010	*43840*	*864*	*301*	*34693*	*79.1*	60	609
2015	*46619*	*869*	*332*	*37705*	*80.9*	65	467
2020	*49259*	*873*	*368*	*40625*	*82.5*	70+	617

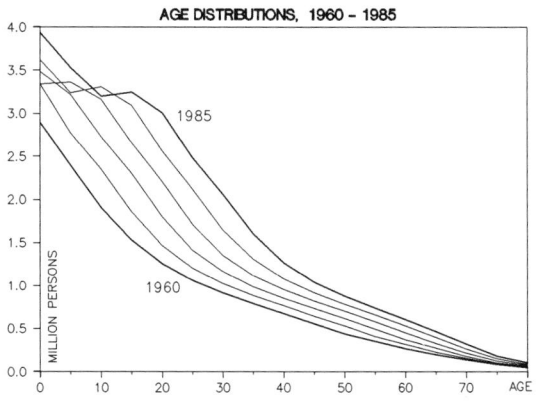

AGE DISTRIBUTIONS, 1960 – 1985

POPULATION RATIOS

YEAR	AGE DISTRIBUTION UNDER 15	AGE DISTRIBUTION 15-64	AGE DISTRIBUTION 65 & OLDER	AGE DISTRIBUTION 70 & OLDER	DEPENDENCY RATIO	WOMEN 15-49	CHILD-WOMAN RATIO
1950	0.432	0.532	0.035	0.020	0.879	0.232	0.766
1955	0.450	0.517	0.033	0.019	0.934	0.226	0.832
1960	0.463	0.506	0.031	0.018	0.975	0.221	0.843
1965	0.468	0.503	0.029	0.017	0.988	0.218	0.848
1970	0.454	0.517	0.030	0.017	0.936	0.223	0.752
1975	0.426	0.542	0.032	0.018	0.844	0.233	0.620
1980	0.394	0.571	0.035	0.019	0.752	0.245	0.573
1985	0.372	0.591	0.038	0.021	0.693	0.254	0.540
1990	*0.362*	*0.598*	*0.040*	*0.023*	*0.672*	*0.257*	*0.509*
2000	*0.327*	*0.628*	*0.045*	*0.027*	*0.592*	*0.266*	*0.417*
2010	*0.287*	*0.661*	*0.052*	*0.031*	*0.514*	*0.268*	*0.363*
2020	*0.260*	*0.670*	*0.070*	*0.040*	*0.492*	*0.259*	*0.339*

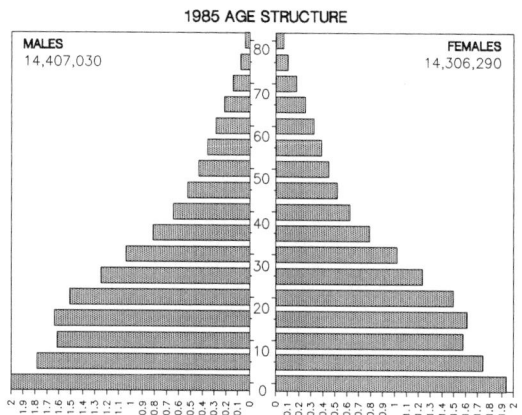

1985 AGE STRUCTURE

MALES 14,407,030   FEMALES 14,306,290

MORTALITY MEASURES (Annual Averages)

PERIOD	CRUDE DEATH RATE	INFANT MORT. RATE	LIFE EXPECTANCY AT BIRTH (years) MALE	LIFE EXPECTANCY AT BIRTH (years) FEMALE	LIFE EXPECTANCY AT BIRTH (years) BOTH SEXES	DIFFERENCE FEMALE-MALE
1950-55	16.48	123.00	48.77	52.62	50.65	3.85
1955-60	14.18	102.00	51.52	55.59	53.51	4.07
1960-65	12.18	84.00	54.15	58.39	56.22	4.24
1965-70	10.44	74.00	56.29	60.66	58.42	4.37
1970-75	9.02	65.00	58.22	62.71	60.41	4.49
1975-80	8.23	55.00	59.96	64.48	62.17	4.52
1980-85	7.74	50.00	61.41	65.96	63.63	4.55
1985-90	*7.38*	*46.00*	*62.58*	*67.16*	*64.81*	*4.58*
1990-95	*7.07*	*42.00*	*63.65*	*68.26*	*65.90*	*4.61*
2000-05	*6.75*	*36.00*	*65.61*	*70.28*	*67.89*	*4.67*
2010-15	*6.88*	*31.00*	*67.39*	*72.12*	*69.70*	*4.73*
2020-25	*7.48*	*26.00*	*69.01*	*73.80*	*71.35*	*4.79*

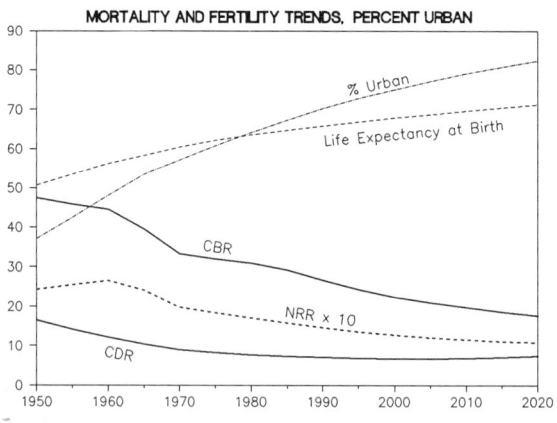

MORTALITY AND FERTILITY TRENDS, PERCENT URBAN

% Urban
Life Expectancy at Birth
CBR
NRR x 10
CDR

FERTILITY MEASURES (Annual Averages)

PERIOD	CRUDE BIRTH RATE	FERTILITY RATES GENERAL	FERTILITY RATES TOTAL	REPRODUCTION RATES GROSS	REPRODUCTION RATES NET	RATE OF NATUR. INCR.
1950-55	47.58	207.99	6.720	3.280	2.436	31.10
1955-60	45.95	205.80	6.720	3.280	2.554	31.77
1960-65	44.58	203.31	6.720	3.280	2.659	32.40
1965-70	39.62	179.75	5.950	2.900	2.418	29.18
1970-75	33.34	146.29	4.780	2.330	1.983	24.32
1975-80	32.06	134.14	4.310	2.100	1.833	23.83
1980-85	31.01	124.25	3.930	1.920	1.706	23.26
1985-90	*29.23*	*114.49*	*3.580*	*1.750*	*1.578*	*21.84*
1990-95	*26.67*	*102.98*	*3.260*	*1.590*	*1.456*	*19.59*
2000-05	*22.40*	*83.80*	*2.779*	*1.360*	*1.268*	*15.65*
2010-15	*19.72*	*74.21*	*2.480*	*1.210*	*1.151*	*12.84*
2020-25	*17.72*	*68.79*	*2.310*	*1.130*	*1.086*	*10.24*

AGING MEASURES

YEAR	POPULATION AGE RATIOS 60+/20-59	POPULATION AGE RATIOS 65+/20-64	POPULATION AGE RATIOS 70+/20-69	POPULATION AGE RATIOS 75+/20-74	POPULATION MEAN AGE	POPULATION MEDIAN AGE
1950	0.1322	0.0824	0.0448	0.0218	22.94	18.32
1960	0.1229	0.0753	0.0424	0.0206	22.08	16.88
1970	0.1228	0.0733	0.0397	0.0188	22.20	17.09
1980	0.1291	0.0774	0.0417	0.0195	23.83	19.40
1990	*0.1295*	*0.0809*	*0.0455*	*0.0218*	*25.34*	*21.97*
2000	*0.1348*	*0.0852*	*0.0496*	*0.0250*	*27.27*	*24.10*
2010	*0.1523*	*0.0924*	*0.0531*	*0.0272*	*29.53*	*26.74*
2020	*0.2007*	*0.1194*	*0.0652*	*0.0321*	*31.80*	*29.56*

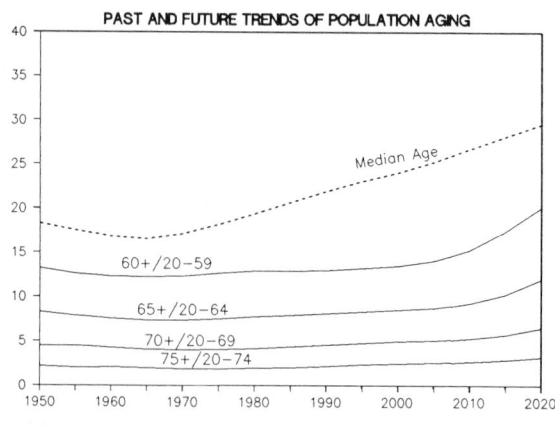

PAST AND FUTURE TRENDS OF POPULATION AGING

Median Age
60+/20-59
65+/20-64
70+/20-69
75+/20-74

OBSERVED AND *PROJECTED* POPULATION DATA

YEAR	MID-YEAR POPULATION	NO. OF BIRTHS	NO. OF DEATHS	URBAN POPULATION NUMBER	PERCENT	POPULATION 1985 AGE	NUMBER
1950	861780	40790	10891	288980	33.5	0	364424
1955	1025471	49453	11260	359208	35.0	5	327464
1960	1236050	56005	11346	451829	36.6	10	280451
1965	1481520	56767	10784	564569	38.1	15	289994
1970	1730778	54523	10085	686864	39.7	20	281136
1975	1968214	62377	9672	830373	42.2	25	241897
1980	2284597	68961	9431	1050284	46.0	30	192020
1985	2642247	74791	10450	1315908	49.8	35	148602
1990	3014785	76922	12095	1616523	53.6	40	114491
1995	3374185	78160	14047	1934328	57.3	45	94953
2000	3710748	79503	16320	2257578	60.8	50	82057
2005	4040705	81651	19052	2589582	64.1	55	67860
2010	4366318	82964	22259	2926647	67.0	60	53530
2015	4680771	83472	25983	3264986	69.8	65	40980
2020	4977320	83719	30611	3597061	72.3	70+	62386

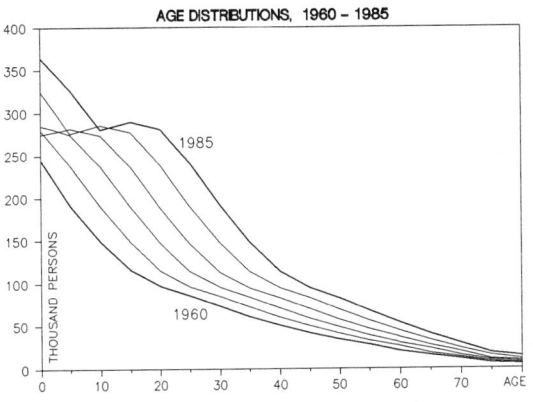

AGE DISTRIBUTIONS, 1960 – 1985

POPULATION RATIOS

YEAR	UNDER 15	15-64	65 & OLDER	70 & OLDER	DEPENDENCY RATIO	WOMEN 15-49	CHILD-WOMAN RATIO
1950	0.433	0.529	0.037	0.023	0.889	0.228	0.797
1955	0.453	0.512	0.034	0.020	0.953	0.220	0.876
1960	0.474	0.494	0.032	0.019	1.024	0.212	0.933
1965	0.478	0.491	0.031	0.019	1.038	0.210	0.897
1970	0.461	0.507	0.032	0.019	0.971	0.218	0.754
1975	0.422	0.544	0.034	0.020	0.838	0.235	0.595
1980	0.388	0.576	0.036	0.022	0.737	0.248	0.573
1985	0.368	0.593	0.039	0.024	0.687	0.255	0.542
1990	0.362	0.596	0.042	0.026	0.678	0.255	0.513
2000	0.323	0.626	0.051	0.032	0.596	0.263	0.414
2010	0.282	0.658	0.060	0.038	0.519	0.262	0.366
2020	0.255	0.665	0.081	0.049	0.504	0.252	0.339

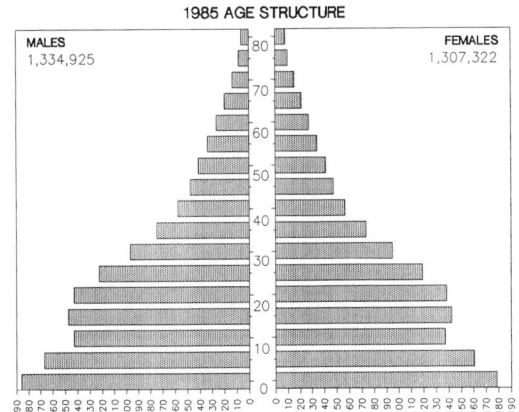

1985 AGE STRUCTURE

MALES 1,334,925   FEMALES 1,307,322

MORTALITY MEASURES (Annual Averages)

PERIOD	CRUDE DEATH RATE	INFANT MORT. RATE	MALE	FEMALE	BOTH SEXES	DIFFERENCE FEMALE-MALE
1950-55	12.64	94.00	56.04	58.55	57.26	2.51
1955-60	10.98	87.00	58.82	61.54	60.15	2.72
1960-65	9.18	81.00	61.59	64.53	63.02	2.94
1965-70	7.28	66.00	63.91	67.46	65.64	3.55
1970-75	5.83	51.00	66.05	70.22	68.08	4.17
1975-80	4.91	30.00	68.63	73.08	70.80	4.45
1980-85	4.13	20.00	71.33	75.85	73.54	4.52
1985-90	3.95	18.00	72.41	77.04	74.67	4.63
1990-95	4.01	17.00	72.89	77.60	75.19	4.71
2000-05	4.40	16.00	73.52	78.39	75.90	4.87
2010-15	5.10	15.00	73.85	78.82	76.27	4.97
2020-25	6.15	14.00	74.00	79.09	76.48	5.09

(LIFE EXPECTANCY AT BIRTH (years))

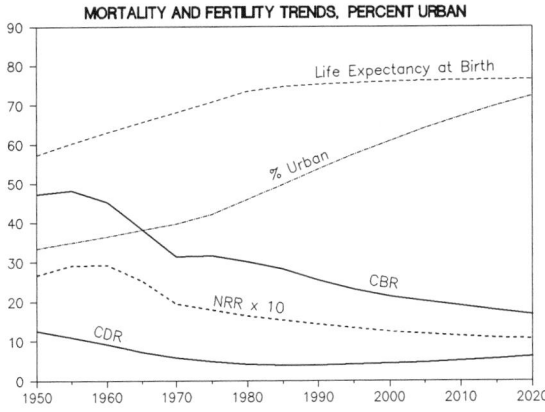

MORTALITY AND FERTILITY TRENDS, PERCENT URBAN

FERTILITY MEASURES (Annual Averages)

PERIOD	CRUDE BIRTH RATE	FERTILITY RATES GENERAL	TOTAL	REPRODUCTION RATES GROSS	NET	RATE OF NATUR. INCR.
1950-55	47.33	211.81	6.723	3.280	2.685	34.69
1955-60	48.22	223.74	7.113	3.470	2.928	37.25
1960-65	45.31	214.83	6.949	3.390	2.942	36.13
1965-70	38.32	178.72	5.801	2.830	2.534	31.04
1970-75	31.50	138.84	4.335	2.120	1.951	25.68
1975-80	31.69	130.96	3.886	1.900	1.793	26.78
1980-85	30.18	119.92	3.501	1.710	1.649	26.06
1985-90	28.31	111.17	3.260	1.590	1.546	24.35
1990-95	25.51	99.34	3.019	1.470	1.436	21.50
2000-05	21.42	81.12	2.620	1.280	1.252	17.03
2010-15	19.00	73.30	2.360	1.150	1.130	13.90
2020-25	16.82	66.85	2.210	1.080	1.060	10.67

AGING MEASURES

YEAR	60+/20-59	65+/20-64	70+/20-69	75+/20-74	MEAN AGE	MEDIAN AGE
1950	0.1404	0.0877	0.0532	0.0274	23.07	18.26
1960	0.1279	0.0807	0.0468	0.0237	21.83	16.40
1970	0.1304	0.0809	0.0456	0.0240	22.12	16.80
1980	0.1275	0.0797	0.0462	0.0240	23.88	19.61
1990	0.1334	0.0846	0.0500	0.0263	25.53	22.27
2000	0.1476	0.0964	0.0581	0.0312	27.73	24.39
2010	0.1693	0.1062	0.0648	0.0362	30.15	27.23
2020	0.2294	0.1381	0.0789	0.0418	32.54	30.23

(POPULATION AGE RATIOS / POPULATION)

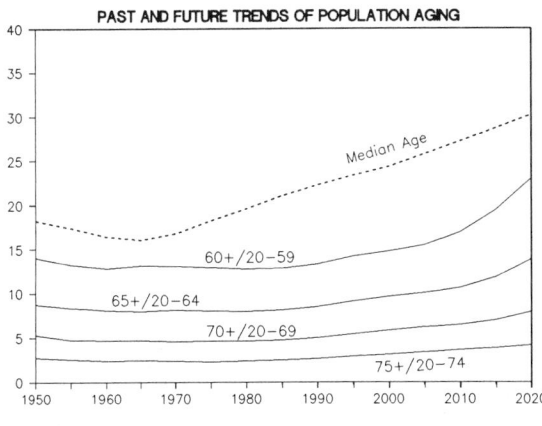

PAST AND FUTURE TRENDS OF POPULATION AGING

OBSERVED AND *PROJECTED* POPULATION DATA (000's)

YEAR	MID-YEAR POPULATION	NO. OF BIRTHS	NO. OF DEATHS	URBAN POPULATION NUMBER	URBAN POPULATION PERCENT	POPULATION 1985 AGE	POPULATION 1985 NUMBER
1950	5858	174	65	2893	49.4	0	715
1955	6426	181	62	3350	52.1	5	769
1960	7028	248	62	3855	54.9	10	1070
1965	7807	250	58	4493	57.6	15	1152
1970	8571	221	55	5160	60.2	20	1099
1975	9331	158	55	5993	64.2	25	737
1980	9732	146	62	6628	68.1	30	697
1985	9946	159	67	7136	71.8	35	665
1990	10324	164	73	7736	74.9	40	604
1995	10788	158	80	8376	77.6	45	526
2000	11189	147	87	8942	79.9	50	420
2005	11493	139	96	9400	81.8	55	381
2010	11710	137	106	9755	83.3	60	318
2015	11868	136	119	10051	84.7	65	279
2020	11958	133	131	10279	86.0	70+	514

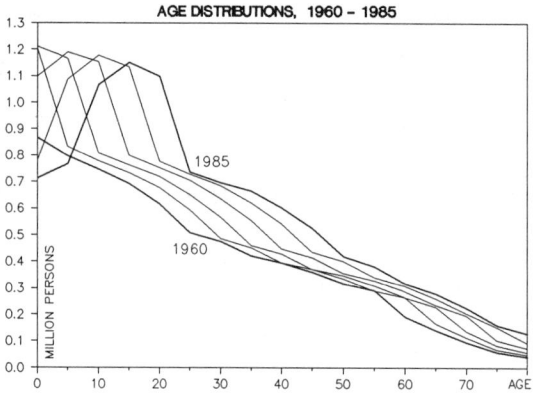

AGE DISTRIBUTIONS, 1960 - 1985

POPULATION RATIOS

YEAR	AGE DISTRIBUTION UNDER 15	15-64	65 & OLDER	70 & OLDER	DEPENDENCY RATIO	WOMEN 15-49	CHILD-WOMAN RATIO
1950	0.362	0.593	0.045	0.027	0.685	0.239	0.558
1955	0.355	0.600	0.045	0.027	0.667	0.240	0.534
1960	0.344	0.608	0.048	0.028	0.644	0.243	0.509
1965	0.360	0.589	0.050	0.029	0.697	0.234	0.658
1970	0.372	0.569	0.059	0.032	0.756	0.228	0.621
1975	0.369	0.566	0.065	0.040	0.767	0.228	0.518
1980	0.313	0.614	0.073	0.046	0.629	0.249	0.323
1985	0.257	0.664	0.080	0.052	0.507	0.270	0.266
1990	0.218	0.698	0.084	0.056	0.434	0.281	0.271
2000	0.214	0.693	0.094	0.062	0.444	0.267	0.265
2010	0.188	0.695	0.117	0.075	0.438	0.262	0.224
2020	0.170	0.689	0.141	0.094	0.451	0.228	0.246

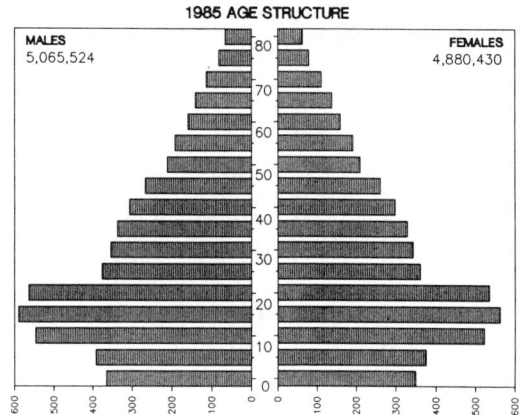

1985 AGE STRUCTURE

MALES 5,065,524 — FEMALES 4,880,430

MORTALITY MEASURES (Annual Averages)

PERIOD	CRUDE DEATH RATE	INFANT MORT. RATE	LIFE EXPECTANCY AT BIRTH (years) MALE	FEMALE	BOTH SEXES	DIFFERENCE FEMALE-MALE
1950-55	11.03	82.00	56.69	61.01	58.79	4.32
1955-60	9.64	68.00	59.81	63.88	61.79	4.07
1960-65	8.85	56.00	63.26	67.05	65.10	3.79
1965-70	7.40	49.00	66.80	70.30	68.50	3.50
1970-75	6.41	36.00	69.33	72.63	70.93	3.30
1975-80	5.95	23.00	71.15	74.45	72.75	3.30
1980-85	6.38	17.00	71.78	75.21	73.45	3.43
1985-90	6.76	15.00	72.21	75.83	73.97	3.62
1990-95	7.07	13.00	73.09	76.83	74.91	3.74
2000-05	7.75	10.00	74.69	78.59	76.59	3.90
2010-15	9.04	9.00	75.81	80.13	77.91	4.32
2020-25	10.98	8.00	76.81	81.13	78.91	4.32

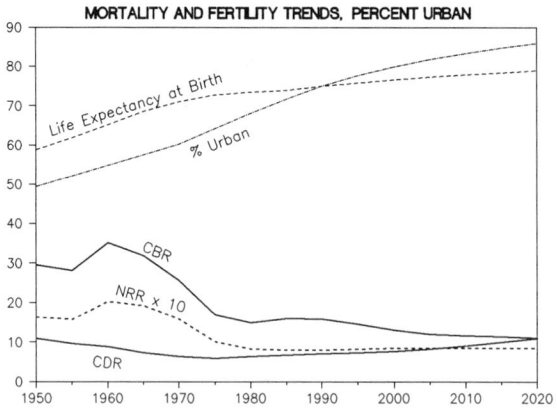

MORTALITY AND FERTILITY TRENDS, PERCENT URBAN

FERTILITY MEASURES (Annual Averages)

PERIOD	CRUDE BIRTH RATE	FERTILITY RATES GENERAL	TOTAL	REPRODUCTION RATES GROSS	NET	RATE OF NATUR. INCR.
1950-55	29.69	124.09	4.010	1.950	1.636	18.66
1955-60	28.19	116.86	3.759	1.830	1.584	18.55
1960-65	35.26	148.08	4.670	2.270	2.034	26.41
1965-70	31.97	138.58	4.291	2.090	1.924	24.56
1970-75	25.78	113.19	3.470	1.690	1.593	19.37
1975-80	16.99	71.19	2.178	1.060	1.018	11.04
1980-85	15.01	57.81	1.749	0.850	0.822	8.63
1985-90	15.95	57.87	1.707	0.830	0.807	9.19
1990-95	15.86	57.03	1.707	0.830	0.810	8.79
2000-05	13.11	49.49	1.789	0.870	0.853	5.36
2010-15	11.72	46.16	1.789	0.870	0.855	2.68
2020-25	11.15	50.49	1.789	0.870	0.856	0.17

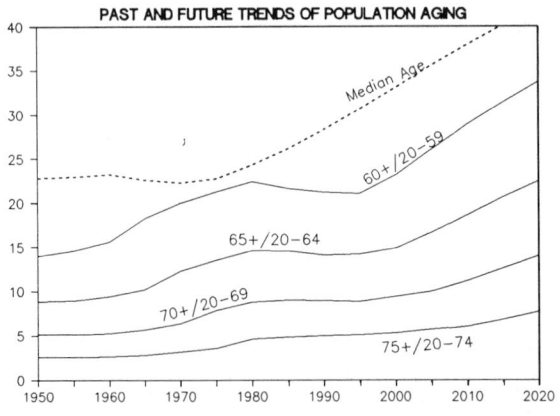

PAST AND FUTURE TRENDS OF POPULATION AGING

AGING MEASURES

YEAR	POPULATION AGE RATIOS 60+/20-59	65+/20-64	70+/20-69	75+/20-74	POPULATION MEAN AGE	MEDIAN AGE
1950	0.1399	0.0885	0.0514	0.0258	26.50	22.85
1960	0.1560	0.0940	0.0526	0.0265	27.41	23.27
1970	0.1995	0.1228	0.0636	0.0314	26.80	22.34
1980	0.2242	0.1464	0.0879	0.0461	29.09	24.38
1990	0.2121	0.1410	0.0895	0.0499	32.16	28.31
2000	0.2312	0.1489	0.0940	0.0527	34.59	33.08
2010	0.2887	0.1864	0.1118	0.0603	37.36	37.93
2020	0.3371	0.2244	0.1398	0.0771	39.81	41.09

OBSERVED AND *PROJECTED* POPULATION DATA (000's)

YEAR	MID-YEAR POPULATION	NO. OF BIRTHS	NO. OF DEATHS	URBAN POPULATION NUMBER	URBAN POPULATION PERCENT	POPULATION 1985 AGE	POPULATION 1985 NUMBER
1950	2353	119	48	559	23.7	0	931
1955	2737	138	48	735	26.9	5	828
1960	3231	160	48	977	30.2	10	786
1965	3806	171	46	1335	35.1	15	751
1970	4423	172	44	1781	40.3	20	665
1975	5048	176	42	2289	45.3	25	536
1980	5697	191	43	2877	50.5	30	420
1985	6416	201	44	3571	55.7	35	338
1990	7170	203	45	4329	60.4	40	269
1995	7915	199	46	5110	64.6	45	226
2000	8621	196	49	5875	68.1	50	188
2005	9282	194	53	6602	71.1	55	163
2010	9902	193	58	7282	73.5	60	107
2015	10480	190	64	7938	75.7	65	85
2020	11001	185	72	8556	77.8	70+	123

POPULATION RATIOS

YEAR	AGE DISTRIBUTION UNDER 15	15-64	65 & OLDER	70 & OLDER	DEPENDENCY RATIO	WOMEN 15-49	CHILD-WOMAN RATIO
1950	0.445	0.523	0.032	0.018	0.914	0.217	0.859
1955	0.455	0.514	0.031	0.017	0.945	0.216	0.876
1960	0.466	0.503	0.030	0.017	0.988	0.214	0.905
1965	0.475	0.495	0.030	0.017	1.021	0.212	0.917
1970	0.473	0.497	0.030	0.017	1.012	0.213	0.850
1975	0.453	0.516	0.030	0.018	0.936	0.223	0.724
1980	0.422	0.546	0.031	0.018	0.831	0.235	0.630
1985	0.397	0.571	0.032	0.019	0.752	0.245	0.591
1990	0.379	0.587	0.034	0.020	0.702	0.251	0.547
2000	0.339	0.619	0.043	0.026	0.617	0.261	0.435
2010	0.289	0.658	0.053	0.033	0.520	0.267	0.362
2020	0.255	0.674	0.071	0.043	0.484	0.257	0.330

MORTALITY MEASURES (Annual Averages)

PERIOD	CRUDE DEATH RATE	INFANT MORT. RATE	LIFE EXPECTANCY AT BIRTH (years) MALE	FEMALE	BOTH SEXES	DIFFERENCE FEMALE-MALE
1950-55	20.32	149.00	44.74	47.31	45.99	2.57
1955-60	17.38	132.00	48.56	51.41	49.95	2.85
1960-65	14.77	117.00	52.14	55.22	53.64	3.08
1965-70	12.17	105.00	55.39	58.67	56.99	3.28
1970-75	9.86	94.00	58.13	61.77	59.91	3.64
1975-80	8.42	84.00	60.27	63.97	62.08	3.70
1980-85	7.52	75.00	62.19	66.11	64.10	3.92
1985-90	6.80	65.00	63.86	68.06	65.91	4.20
1990-95	6.22	57.00	65.42	69.81	67.56	4.39
2000-05	5.63	43.00	67.96	72.71	70.28	4.75
2010-15	5.82	34.00	69.87	74.81	72.28	4.94
2020-25	6.52	28.00	71.16	76.26	73.65	5.10

FERTILITY MEASURES (Annual Averages)

PERIOD	CRUDE BIRTH RATE	FERTILITY RATES GENERAL	FERTILITY RATES TOTAL	REPRODUCTION RATES GROSS	REPRODUCTION RATES NET	RATE OF NATUR. INCR.
1950-55	50.52	233.56	7.400	3.610	2.453	30.20
1955-60	50.50	235.02	7.400	3.610	2.623	33.12
1960-65	49.38	232.02	7.323	3.570	2.745	34.61
1965-70	44.87	210.98	6.675	3.260	2.623	32.69
1970-75	38.81	177.57	5.627	2.740	2.303	28.95
1975-80	34.86	151.88	4.700	2.290	1.980	26.45
1980-85	33.59	139.63	4.209	2.050	1.815	26.07
1985-90	31.30	126.08	3.750	1.830	1.645	24.50
1990-95	28.30	111.79	3.340	1.630	1.487	22.08
2000-05	22.70	86.11	2.729	1.330	1.242	17.08
2010-15	19.47	73.50	2.379	1.160	1.099	13.65
2020-25	16.79	66.00	2.190	1.070	1.022	10.27

AGING MEASURES

YEAR	POPULATION AGE RATIOS 60+/20-59	65+/20-64	70+/20-69	75+/20-74	POPULATION MEAN AGE	POPULATION MEDIAN AGE
1950	0.1290	0.0764	0.0406	0.0181	22.60	17.71
1960	0.1259	0.0752	0.0408	0.0191	21.83	16.70
1970	0.1234	0.0761	0.0423	0.0203	21.54	16.28
1980	0.1182	0.0734	0.0412	0.0205	22.78	18.23
1990	0.1187	0.0701	0.0414	0.0210	24.32	20.67
2000	0.1313	0.0829	0.0483	0.0231	26.55	23.24
2010	0.1513	0.0945	0.0564	0.0300	29.27	26.35
2020	0.1997	0.1208	0.0698	0.0366	32.05	29.85

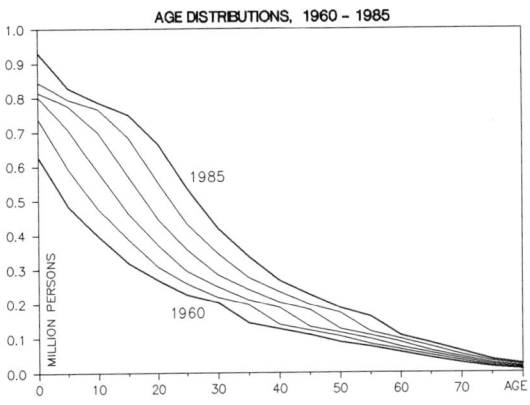

AGE DISTRIBUTIONS, 1960 - 1985

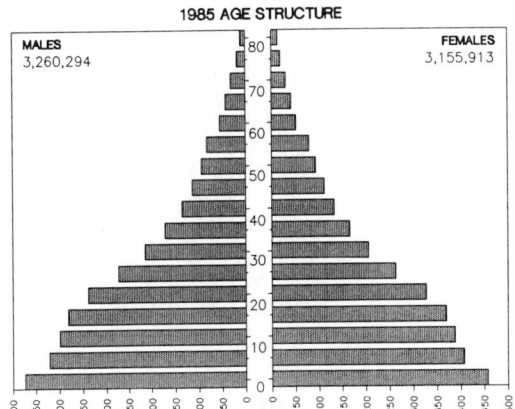

1985 AGE STRUCTURE
MALES 3,260,294
FEMALES 3,155,913

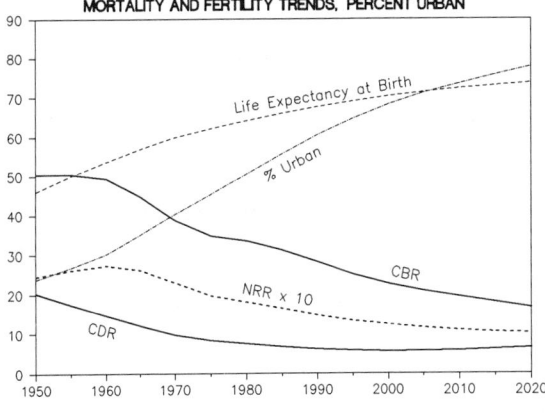

MORTALITY AND FERTILITY TRENDS, PERCENT URBAN

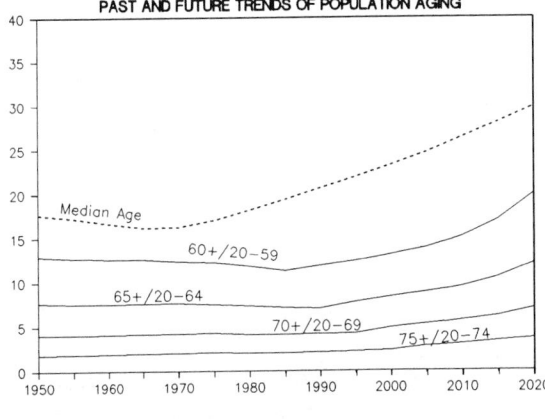

PAST AND FUTURE TRENDS OF POPULATION AGING

OBSERVED AND *PROJECTED* POPULATION DATA (000's)

YEAR	MID-YEAR POPULATION	NO. OF BIRTHS	NO. OF DEATHS	URBAN POPULATION NUMBER	URBAN POPULATION PERCENT	POPULATION 1985 AGE	POPULATION 1985 NUMBER
1950	3310	155	62	935	28.3	0	1480
1955	3806	175	63	1190	31.3	5	1283
1960	4413	201	63	1519	34.4	10	1157
1965	5162	230	66	1920	37.2	15	1037
1970	6051	249	67	2392	39.5	20	876
1975	7035	269	67	2984	42.4	25	732
1980	8123	299	66	3844	47.3	30	617
1985	9378	332	71	4901	52.3	35	486
1990	*10782*	*362*	*76*	*6136*	*56.9*	40	388
1995	*12314*	*386*	*81*	*7529*	*61.1*	45	327
2000	*13939*	*408*	*87*	*9042*	*64.9*	50	263
2005	*15640*	*427*	*94*	*10643*	*68.0*	55	216
2010	*17403*	*447*	*102*	*12303*	*70.7*	60	171
2015	*19219*	*464*	*112*	*14056*	*73.1*	65	135
2020	*21064*	*477*	*124*	*15879*	*75.4*	70+	210

AGE DISTRIBUTIONS, 1960 – 1985

POPULATION RATIOS

YEAR	AGE DISTRIBUTION UNDER 15	AGE DISTRIBUTION 15-64	AGE DISTRIBUTION 65 & OLDER	AGE DISTRIBUTION 70 & OLDER	DEPENDENCY RATIO	WOMEN 15-49	CHILD-WOMAN RATIO
1950	0.419	0.535	0.046	0.026	0.869	0.225	0.762
1955	0.435	0.522	0.043	0.025	0.914	0.220	0.827
1960	0.448	0.512	0.040	0.024	0.954	0.216	0.838
1965	0.455	0.507	0.039	0.023	0.974	0.215	0.845
1970	0.453	0.509	0.037	0.022	0.964	0.217	0.829
1975	0.447	0.517	0.036	0.022	0.935	0.222	0.767
1980	0.433	0.530	0.036	0.022	0.885	0.229	0.704
1985	0.418	0.545	0.037	0.022	0.834	0.236	0.668
1990	*0.406*	*0.557*	*0.037*	*0.023*	*0.797*	*0.241*	*0.637*
2000	*0.383*	*0.578*	*0.040*	*0.025*	*0.731*	*0.248*	*0.560*
2010	*0.349*	*0.606*	*0.045*	*0.028*	*0.649*	*0.254*	*0.485*
2020	*0.317*	*0.627*	*0.056*	*0.034*	*0.595*	*0.256*	*0.434*

MORTALITY MEASURES (Annual Averages)

PERIOD	CRUDE DEATH RATE	INFANT MORT. RATE	LIFE EXPECTANCY AT BIRTH (years) MALE	LIFE EXPECTANCY AT BIRTH (years) FEMALE	LIFE EXPECTANCY AT BIRTH (years) BOTH SEXES	DIFFERENCE FEMALE-MALE
1950-55	18.87	149.00	47.13	49.63	48.35	2.50
1955-60	16.52	129.00	50.13	52.70	51.38	2.57
1960-65	14.32	119.00	53.43	56.06	54.71	2.63
1965-70	12.82	107.00	55.36	58.22	56.76	2.86
1970-75	11.15	95.00	57.36	60.46	58.87	3.10
1975-80	9.51	82.00	59.68	63.23	61.41	3.55
1980-85	8.09	70.00	62.25	66.39	64.27	4.14
1985-90	*7.55*	*63.00*	*63.39*	*67.59*	*65.44*	*4.20*
1990-95	*7.05*	*57.00*	*64.50*	*68.78*	*66.59*	*4.28*
2000-05	*6.24*	*47.00*	*66.57*	*71.06*	*68.76*	*4.49*
2010-15	*5.85*	*37.00*	*68.42*	*73.15*	*70.73*	*4.73*
2020-25	*5.87*	*29.00*	*70.00*	*75.00*	*72.44*	*5.00*

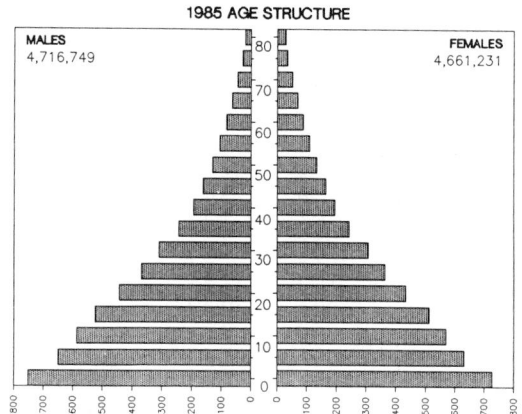

1985 AGE STRUCTURE

MALES 4,716,749   FEMALES 4,661,231

FERTILITY MEASURES (Annual Averages)

PERIOD	CRUDE BIRTH RATE	FERTILITY RATES GENERAL	FERTILITY RATES TOTAL	REPRODUCTION RATES GROSS	REPRODUCTION RATES NET	RATE OF NATUR. INCR.
1950-55	46.76	210.23	6.900	3.370	2.395	27.89
1955-60	46.05	210.99	6.900	3.370	2.498	29.53
1960-65	45.63	211.59	6.900	3.370	2.604	31.31
1965-70	44.51	205.78	6.700	3.270	2.610	31.68
1970-75	41.23	187.46	6.050	2.950	2.434	30.08
1975-80	38.24	169.32	5.400	2.630	2.242	28.73
1980-85	36.76	157.82	5.000	2.440	2.141	28.67
1985-90	*35.40*	*148.24*	*4.650*	*2.270*	*2.015*	*27.85*
1990-95	*33.59*	*138.35*	*4.320*	*2.110*	*1.893*	*26.54*
2000-05	*29.24*	*117.14*	*3.709*	*1.810*	*1.659*	*23.00*
2010-15	*25.69*	*100.78*	*3.209*	*1.570*	*1.461*	*19.83*
2020-25	*22.66*	*88.73*	*2.839*	*1.390*	*1.311*	*16.79*

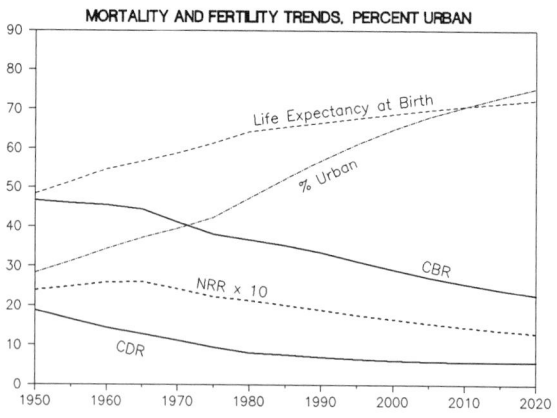

MORTALITY AND FERTILITY TRENDS, PERCENT URBAN

AGING MEASURES

YEAR	POPULATION AGE RATIOS 60+/20-59	POPULATION AGE RATIOS 65+/20-64	POPULATION AGE RATIOS 70+/20-69	POPULATION AGE RATIOS 75+/20-74	POPULATION MEAN AGE	POPULATION MEDIAN AGE
1950	0.1697	0.1046	0.0574	0.0268	24.41	19.25
1960	0.1547	0.0964	0.0557	0.0273	23.08	17.70
1970	0.1473	0.0926	0.0537	0.0272	22.51	17.20
1980	0.1361	0.0860	0.0504	0.0261	22.88	18.07
1990	*0.1296*	*0.0828*	*0.0495*	*0.0262*	*23.70*	*19.39*
2000	*0.1320*	*0.0836*	*0.0500*	*0.0268*	*24.90*	*20.80*
2010	*0.1424*	*0.0895*	*0.0536*	*0.0287*	*26.54*	*22.72*
2020	*0.1685*	*0.1053*	*0.0609*	*0.0325*	*28.38*	*24.90*

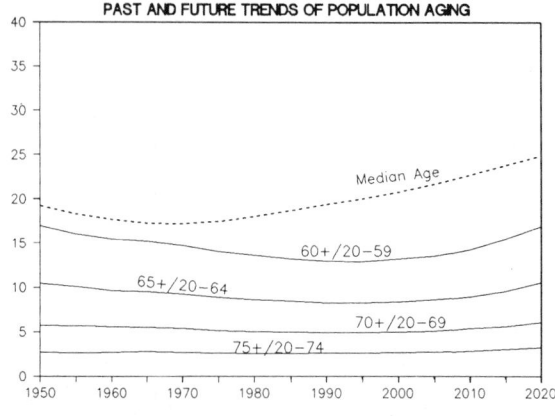

PAST AND FUTURE TRENDS OF POPULATION AGING

OBSERVED AND *PROJECTED* POPULATION DATA (000's)

YEAR	MID-YEAR POPULATION	NO. OF BIRTHS	NO. OF DEATHS	URBAN POPULATION NUMBER	URBAN POPULATION PERCENT	POPULATION 1985 AGE	POPULATION 1985 NUMBER
1950	1940	94	39	708	36.5	0	788
1955	2214	109	39	828	37.4	5	748
1960	2570	123	38	985	38.3	10	659
1965	3006	137	38	1170	38.9	15	546
1970	3588	154	39	1414	39.4	20	394
1975	4085	169	46	1651	40.4	25	302
1980	4525	172	50	1880	41.5	30	256
1985	4767	173	41	2035	42.7	35	210
1990	5252	189	36	2332	44.4	40	195
1995	5943	207	38	2774	46.7	45	164
2000	6739	218	40	3333	49.5	50	138
2005	7600	224	42	4006	52.7	55	115
2010	8491	231	45	4784	56.3	60	91
2015	9409	238	50	5624	59.8	65	69
2020	10348	245	56	6520	63.0	70+	91

AGE DISTRIBUTIONS, 1960 - 1985

POPULATION RATIOS

YEAR	UNDER 15	15-64	65 & OLDER	70 & OLDER	DEPENDENCY RATIO	WOMEN 15-49	CHILD-WOMAN RATIO
1950	0.428	0.542	0.031	0.019	0.846	0.237	0.707
1955	0.442	0.531	0.027	0.015	0.882	0.231	0.801
1960	0.455	0.519	0.026	0.014	0.925	0.225	0.848
1965	0.468	0.506	0.026	0.014	0.978	0.218	0.867
1970	0.465	0.507	0.028	0.015	0.972	0.218	0.837
1975	0.459	0.512	0.029	0.016	0.951	0.223	0.791
1980	0.460	0.509	0.031	0.017	0.963	0.227	0.771
1985	0.460	0.506	0.034	0.019	0.976	0.224	0.739
1990	0.444	0.519	0.037	0.021	0.928	0.233	0.687
2000	0.415	0.543	0.042	0.026	0.841	0.246	0.634
2010	0.385	0.569	0.046	0.029	0.757	0.255	0.528
2020	0.339	0.613	0.049	0.031	0.632	0.265	0.443

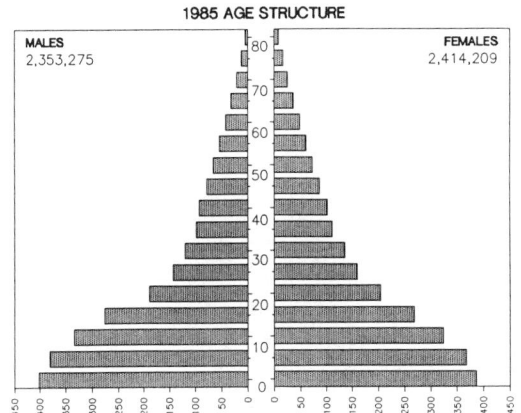

1985 AGE STRUCTURE

MALES 2,353,275 FEMALES 2,414,209

MORTALITY MEASURES (Annual Averages)

PERIOD	CRUDE DEATH RATE	INFANT MORT. RATE	LIFE EXPECTANCY AT BIRTH (years) MALE	FEMALE	BOTH SEXES	DIFFERENCE FEMALE-MALE
1950-55	19.98	175.00	44.10	46.47	45.26	2.37
1955-60	17.49	154.00	47.26	49.95	48.57	2.69
1960-65	14.85	131.00	50.76	54.00	52.34	3.24
1965-70	12.48	112.00	54.12	57.82	55.92	3.70
1970-75	10.94	97.00	56.55	61.05	58.74	4.50
1975-80	11.15	82.00	52.44	62.64	57.42	10.20
1980-85	11.09	70.00	50.74	63.89	57.15	13.15
1985-90	8.52	59.00	58.00	66.50	62.15	8.50
1990-95	6.86	48.00	64.01	68.91	66.40	4.90
2000-05	5.90	34.00	67.01	72.11	69.50	5.10
2010-15	5.34	27.00	69.01	74.31	71.60	5.30
2020-25	5.38	24.00	69.82	75.32	72.50	5.50

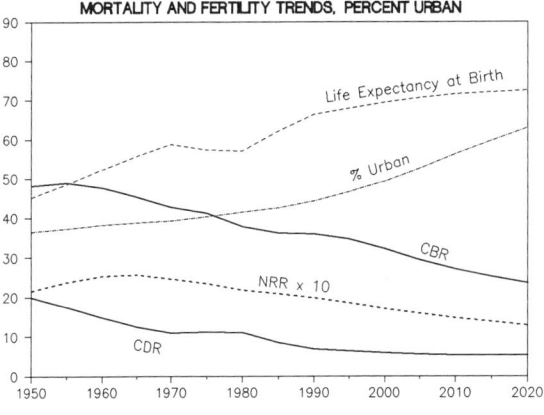

MORTALITY AND FERTILITY TRENDS, PERCENT URBAN

FERTILITY MEASURES (Annual Averages)

PERIOD	CRUDE BIRTH RATE	FERTILITY RATES GENERAL	FERTILITY RATES TOTAL	REPRODUCTION RATES GROSS	REPRODUCTION RATES NET	RATE OF NATUR. INCR.
1950-55	48.30	206.31	6.457	3.150	2.157	28.32
1955-60	49.11	215.66	6.806	3.320	2.394	31.62
1960-65	47.80	216.34	6.847	3.340	2.543	32.95
1965-70	45.46	208.67	6.621	3.230	2.577	32.98
1970-75	42.81	194.19	6.099	2.930	2.464	31.87
1975-80	41.37	184.10	5.700	2.810	2.356	30.22
1980-85	37.96	168.64	5.207	2.540	2.189	26.87
1985-90	36.33	158.95	4.859	2.370	2.094	27.81
1990-95	36.04	151.79	4.510	2.200	1.986	29.18
2000-05	32.36	130.79	3.819	1.870	1.726	26.46
2010-15	27.19	105.12	3.240	1.580	1.489	21.85
2020-25	23.69	89.49	2.800	1.370	1.296	18.31

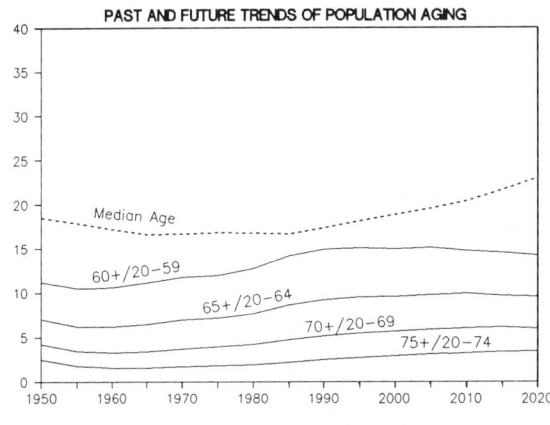

PAST AND FUTURE TRENDS OF POPULATION AGING

AGING MEASURES

YEAR	POPULATION AGE RATIOS 60+/20-59	65+/20-64	70+/20-69	75+/20-74	POPULATION MEAN AGE	POPULATION MEDIAN AGE
1950	0.1119	0.0698	0.0421	0.0248	22.93	18.50
1960	0.1062	0.0616	0.0327	0.0154	21.95	17.24
1970	0.1178	0.0696	0.0369	0.0169	21.82	16.67
1980	0.1272	0.0766	0.0420	0.0192	21.96	16.82
1990	0.1495	0.0920	0.0516	0.0247	22.66	17.35
2000	0.1497	0.0959	0.0566	0.0290	23.45	18.90
2010	0.1478	0.0995	0.0602	0.0324	24.81	20.41
2020	0.1427	0.0959	0.0597	0.0343	26.73	22.96

OBSERVED AND *PROJECTED* POPULATION DATA

YEAR	MID-YEAR POPULATION	NO. OF BIRTHS	NO. OF DEATHS	URBAN POPULATION NUMBER	URBAN POPULATION PERCENT	POPULATION 1985 AGE	POPULATION 1985 NUMBER
1950	210000	8190	2753	88345	42.1	0	33623
1955	236000	9126	2405	95836	40.6	5	24961
1960	275100	10129	2325	107742	39.2	10	34772
1965	300300	9817	2423	118929	39.6	15	39132
1970	320000	9258	2387	130207	40.7	20	36283
1975	328500	6425	2257	137265	41.8	25	27341
1980	326592	6819	2314	141940	43.5	30	21503
1985	334384	6520	2430	152836	45.7	35	20238
1990	*340055*	*6239*	*2512*	*164902*	*48.5*	40	17414
1995	*346398*	*5633*	*2597*	*179310*	*51.8*	45	14716
2000	*354272*	*5320*	*2676*	*196394*	*55.4*	50	13719
2005	*367742*	*5485*	*2796*	*216687*	*58.9*	55	12157
2010	*381436*	*5760*	*2955*	*237285*	*62.2*	60	11290
2015	*395720*	*5866*	*3150*	*258323*	*65.3*	65	9480
2020	*409539*	*5786*	*3425*	*279036*	*68.1*	70+	17755

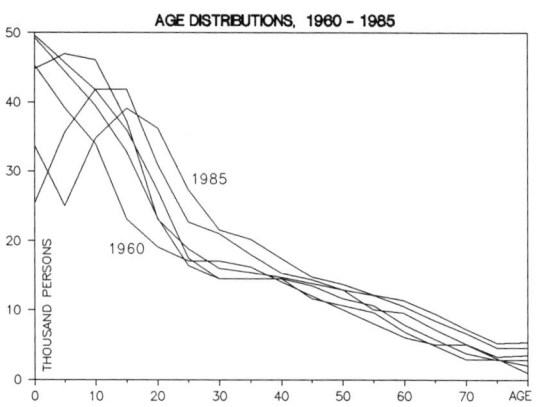

AGE DISTRIBUTIONS, 1960 - 1985

POPULATION RATIOS

YEAR	UNDER 15	15-64	65 & OLDER	70 & OLDER	DEPENDENCY RATIO	WOMEN 15-49	CHILD-WOMAN RATIO
1950	0.395	0.562	0.043	0.029	0.780	0.248	0.692
1955	0.411	0.542	0.047	0.025	0.844	0.233	0.709
1960	0.431	0.518	0.051	0.033	0.929	0.222	0.741
1965	0.444	0.514	0.042	0.026	0.944	0.218	0.752
1970	0.428	0.524	0.047	0.029	0.908	0.223	0.696
1975	0.420	0.522	0.058	0.036	0.915	0.217	0.629
1980	0.315	0.611	0.074	0.048	0.637	0.255	0.305
1985	0.279	0.639	0.081	0.053	0.564	0.268	0.376
1990	*0.263*	*0.648*	*0.089*	*0.059*	*0.544*	*0.270*	*0.349*
2000	*0.254*	*0.646*	*0.101*	*0.069*	*0.549*	*0.258*	*0.307*
2010	*0.216*	*0.673*	*0.111*	*0.075*	*0.485*	*0.259*	*0.280*
2020	*0.210*	*0.660*	*0.130*	*0.089*	*0.516*	*0.230*	*0.314*

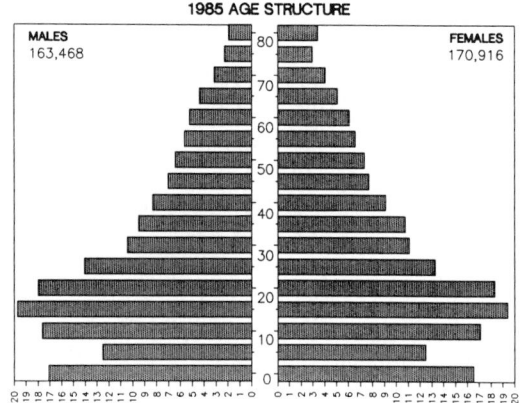

1985 AGE STRUCTURE

MALES 163,468   FEMALES 170,916

MORTALITY MEASURES (Annual Averages)

PERIOD	CRUDE DEATH RATE	INFANT MORT. RATE	LIFE EXPECTANCY AT BIRTH (years) MALE	FEMALE	BOTH SEXES	DIFFERENCE FEMALE-MALE
1950-55	13.11	67.60	55.00	58.10	56.53	3.10
1955-60	10.19	54.40	59.50	63.70	61.57	4.20
1960-65	8.45	44.70	62.50	66.80	64.62	4.30
1965-70	8.07	50.00	63.20	68.50	65.82	5.30
1970-75	7.46	42.40	64.70	70.90	67.76	6.20
1975-80	6.87	25.25	66.40	73.40	69.86	7.00
1980-85	7.09	13.90	68.90	76.12	72.44	7.22
1985-90	*7.27*	*12.00*	*70.11*	*76.66*	*73.32*	*6.55*
1990-95	*7.39*	*11.00*	*71.12*	*77.60*	*74.30*	*6.49*
2000-05	*7.55*	*8.00*	*73.04*	*79.27*	*76.09*	*6.23*
2010-15	*7.75*	*7.00*	*74.60*	*80.51*	*77.50*	*5.91*
2020-25	*8.36*	*6.00*	*75.76*	*81.54*	*78.59*	*5.78*

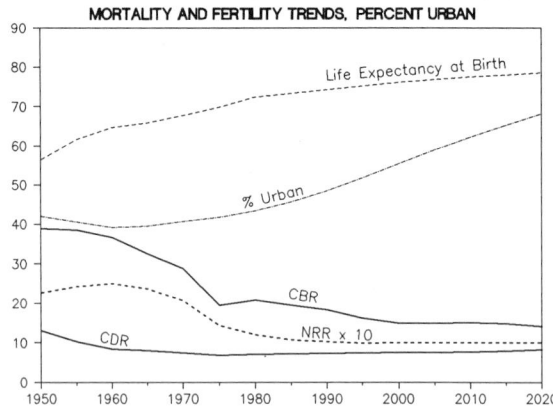

MORTALITY AND FERTILITY TRENDS, PERCENT URBAN

FERTILITY MEASURES (Annual Averages)

PERIOD	CRUDE BIRTH RATE	FERTILITY RATES GENERAL	FERTILITY RATES TOTAL	REPRODUCTION RATES GROSS	REPRODUCTION RATES NET	RATE OF NATUR. INCR.
1950-55	39.00	162.56	5.610	2.750	2.270	25.89
1955-60	38.67	170.24	5.610	2.750	2.430	28.48
1960-65	36.82	167.22	5.610	2.750	2.510	28.37
1965-70	32.69	148.12	5.222	2.560	2.370	24.62
1970-75	28.93	131.66	4.488	2.200	2.070	21.47
1975-80	19.56	82.93	3.060	1.500	1.430	12.69
1980-85	20.88	79.86	2.550	1.250	1.207	13.80
1985-90	*19.50*	*72.48*	*2.244*	*1.100*	*1.065*	*12.23*
1990-95	*18.35*	*69.48*	*2.142*	*1.050*	*1.021*	*10.96*
2000-05	*15.02*	*57.79*	*2.081*	*1.020*	*0.999*	*7.46*
2010-15	*15.10*	*60.06*	*2.081*	*1.020*	*1.002*	*7.35*
2020-25	*14.13*	*62.15*	*2.081*	*1.020*	*1.003*	*5.77*

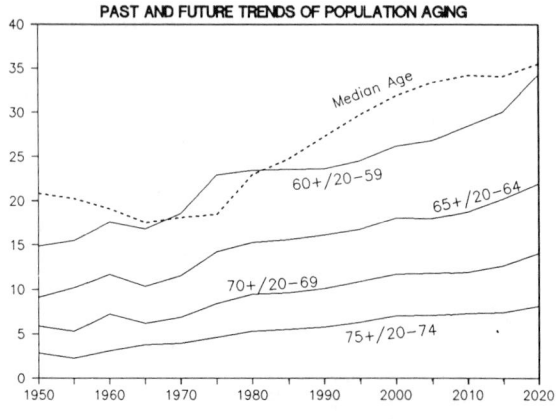

PAST AND FUTURE TRENDS OF POPULATION AGING

AGING MEASURES

YEAR	60+/20-59	65+/20-64	70+/20-69	75+/20-74	MEAN AGE	MEDIAN AGE
1950	0.1489	0.0909	0.0588	0.0286	25.07	20.88
1960	0.1762	0.1172	0.0723	0.0309	24.86	19.12
1970	0.1856	0.1154	0.0684	0.0396	24.39	18.18
1980	0.2348	0.1531	0.0946	0.0529	28.78	23.00
1990	*0.2363*	*0.1615*	*0.1012*	*0.0577*	*31.03*	*27.28*
2000	*0.2619*	*0.1807*	*0.1169*	*0.0702*	*33.40*	*31.90*
2010	*0.2839*	*0.1870*	*0.1190*	*0.0725*	*35.47*	*34.25*
2020	*0.3424*	*0.2188*	*0.1403*	*0.0811*	*37.19*	*35.52*

OBSERVED AND *PROJECTED* POPULATION DATA (000's)

YEAR	MID-YEAR POPULATION	NO. OF BIRTHS	NO. OF DEATHS	URBAN POPULATION NUMBER	URBAN POPULATION PERCENT	POPULATION 1985 AGE	POPULATION 1985 NUMBER
1950	2969	152	66	904	30.5	0	1434
1955	3431	169	71	1088	31.7	5	1213
1960	3964	190	73	1308	33.0	10	1009
1965	4568	208	73	1568	34.3	15	843
1970	5246	234	71	1871	35.7	20	698
1975	6022	267	72	2231	37.1	25	566
1980	6916	295	73	2664	38.5	30	472
1985	7963	325	71	3184	40.0	35	367
1990	*9197*	*356*	*70*	*3861*	*42.0*	40	300
1995	*10621*	*386*	*71*	*4725*	*44.5*	45	260
2000	*12221*	*414*	*73*	*5800*	*47.5*	50	233
2005	*13971*	*436*	*78*	*7103*	*50.8*	55	191
2010	*15827*	*454*	*84*	*8634*	*54.6*	60	143
2015	*17752*	*466*	*93*	*10311*	*58.1*	65	97
2020	*19706*	*477*	*104*	*12104*	*61.4*	70+	137

POPULATION RATIOS

YEAR	AGE DISTRIBUTION UNDER 15	AGE DISTRIBUTION 15-64	AGE DISTRIBUTION 65 & OLDER	AGE DISTRIBUTION 70 & OLDER	DEPENDENCY RATIO	WOMEN 15-49	CHILD-WOMAN RATIO
1950	0.441	0.534	0.025	0.014	0.874	0.230	0.800
1955	0.452	0.522	0.026	0.014	0.915	0.224	0.867
1960	0.460	0.513	0.026	0.015	0.949	0.220	0.860
1965	0.464	0.508	0.027	0.015	0.967	0.219	0.853
1970	0.459	0.513	0.028	0.016	0.951	0.222	0.820
1975	0.457	0.515	0.028	0.017	0.943	0.221	0.820
1980	0.459	0.513	0.028	0.017	0.951	0.219	0.838
1985	0.459	0.512	0.029	0.017	0.955	0.218	0.825
1990	*0.454*	*0.514*	*0.032*	*0.018*	*0.946*	*0.221*	*0.793*
2000	*0.429*	*0.533*	*0.037*	*0.022*	*0.875*	*0.232*	*0.692*
2010	*0.393*	*0.568*	*0.039*	*0.025*	*0.761*	*0.245*	*0.577*
2020	*0.348*	*0.607*	*0.045*	*0.028*	*0.648*	*0.257*	*0.469*

MORTALITY MEASURES (Annual Averages)

PERIOD	CRUDE DEATH RATE	INFANT MORT. RATE	LIFE EXPECTANCY AT BIRTH (years) MALE	LIFE EXPECTANCY AT BIRTH (years) FEMALE	LIFE EXPECTANCY AT BIRTH (years) BOTH SEXES	DIFFERENCE FEMALE-MALE
1950-55	22.38	141.00	41.85	42.35	42.09	0.50
1955-60	20.58	131.00	43.70	44.70	44.19	1.00
1960-65	18.29	119.00	46.20	47.90	47.03	1.70
1965-70	15.94	108.00	49.00	51.30	50.12	2.30
1970-75	13.45	95.00	52.60	55.47	54.00	2.87
1975-80	12.03	82.00	54.50	58.38	56.39	3.88
1980-85	10.52	70.00	56.80	61.26	58.98	4.46
1985-90	*8.95*	*59.00*	*59.70*	*64.40*	*61.99*	*4.70*
1990-95	*7.66*	*48.00*	*62.41*	*67.33*	*64.81*	*4.92*
2000-05	*5.99*	*34.00*	*66.49*	*71.74*	*69.05*	*5.25*
2010-15	*5.32*	*27.00*	*68.67*	*74.09*	*71.31*	*5.42*
2020-25	*5.25*	*24.00*	*69.63*	*75.13*	*72.31*	*5.50*

FERTILITY MEASURES (Annual Averages)

PERIOD	CRUDE BIRTH RATE	FERTILITY RATES GENERAL	FERTILITY RATES TOTAL	REPRODUCTION RATES GROSS	REPRODUCTION RATES NET	RATE OF NATUR. INCR.
1950-55	51.27	226.44	7.090	3.460	2.157	28.89
1955-60	49.38	222.54	6.930	3.380	2.204	28.80
1960-65	47.81	217.68	6.849	3.340	2.301	29.52
1965-70	45.60	206.83	6.599	3.220	2.343	29.66
1970-75	44.55	201.08	6.450	3.150	2.436	31.10
1975-80	44.31	201.15	6.400	3.120	2.517	32.28
1980-85	42.69	195.18	6.120	2.990	2.490	32.16
1985-90	*40.78*	*185.79*	*5.770*	*2.810*	*2.424*	*31.82*
1990-95	*38.67*	*172.99*	*5.360*	*2.610*	*2.314*	*31.01*
2000-05	*33.86*	*144.01*	*4.429*	*2.160*	*1.986*	*27.87*
2010-15	*28.69*	*115.69*	*3.560*	*1.740*	*1.626*	*23.38*
2020-25	*24.23*	*93.24*	*2.920*	*1.420*	*1.345*	*18.98*

AGING MEASURES

YEAR	POPULATION AGE RATIOS 60+/20-59	POPULATION AGE RATIOS 65+/20-64	POPULATION AGE RATIOS 70+/20-69	POPULATION AGE RATIOS 75+/20-74	POPULATION MEAN AGE	POPULATION MEDIAN AGE
1950	0.1046	0.0600	0.0320	0.0148	22.08	17.72
1960	0.1096	0.0637	0.0346	0.0161	21.75	17.03
1970	0.1122	0.0702	0.0385	0.0187	21.82	16.90
1980	0.1149	0.0702	0.0397	0.0211	21.86	16.92
1990	*0.1309*	*0.0780*	*0.0430*	*0.0221*	*22.14*	*17.13*
2000	*0.1353*	*0.0878*	*0.0510*	*0.0259*	*22.93*	*18.22*
2010	*0.1311*	*0.0854*	*0.0531*	*0.0299*	*24.28*	*19.94*
2020	*0.1400*	*0.0895*	*0.0532*	*0.0296*	*26.22*	*22.48*

AGE DISTRIBUTIONS, 1960 - 1985

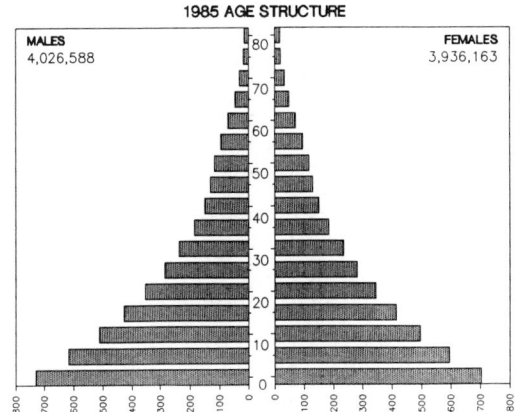

1985 AGE STRUCTURE

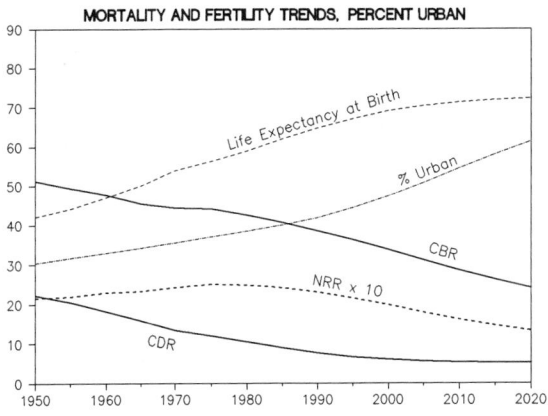

MORTALITY AND FERTILITY TRENDS, PERCENT URBAN

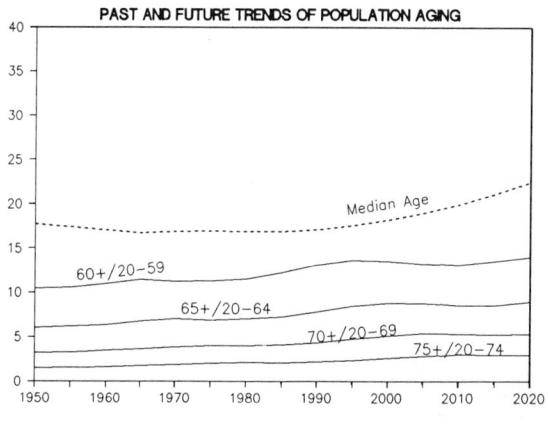

PAST AND FUTURE TRENDS OF POPULATION AGING

OBSERVED AND *PROJECTED* POPULATION DATA

YEAR	MID-YEAR POPULATION	NO. OF BIRTHS	NO. OF DEATHS	URBAN POPULATION NUMBER	URBAN POPULATION PERCENT	POPULATION 1985 AGE	POPULATION 1985 NUMBER
1950	422900	20341	5709	118510	28.0	0	123884
1955	486000	21335	5200	138611	28.5	5	120046
1960	568500	22967	4889	164918	29.0	10	108394
1965	645000	22833	4967	188398	29.2	15	104397
1970	709383	23055	5391	208625	29.4	20	109420
1975	779600	24557	5223	230845	29.6	25	91103
1980	864674	24633	5100	263952	30.5	30	70093
1985	953345	23635	5153	306796	32.2	35	49705
1990	*1039997*	*22513*	*5379*	*359911*	*34.6*	40	35841
1995	*1118950*	*21601*	*5624*	*423275*	*37.8*	45	30497
2000	*1196624*	*21581*	*6030*	*500637*	*41.8*	50	28548
2005	*1271831*	*22164*	*6541*	*582715*	*45.8*	55	24446
2010	*1352427*	*22415*	*7192*	*672292*	*49.7*	60	19853
2015	*1430749*	*22337*	*8087*	*765017*	*53.5*	65	14873
2020	*1503821*	*22192*	*9321*	*858083*	*57.1*	70+	22245

AGE DISTRIBUTIONS, 1960 - 1985

POPULATION RATIOS

YEAR	AGE DISTRIBUTION UNDER 15	AGE DISTRIBUTION 15-64	AGE DISTRIBUTION 65 & OLDER	AGE DISTRIBUTION 70 & OLDER	DEPENDENCY RATIO	WOMEN 15-49	CHILD-WOMAN RATIO
1950	0.411	0.544	0.045	0.027	0.839	0.232	0.783
1955	0.452	0.510	0.038	0.022	0.960	0.218	0.912
1960	0.485	0.482	0.033	0.018	1.074	0.208	0.973
1965	0.471	0.495	0.034	0.020	1.021	0.211	0.862
1970	0.476	0.489	0.035	0.019	1.046	0.211	0.817
1975	0.438	0.528	0.035	0.021	0.894	0.231	0.634
1980	0.394	0.568	0.037	0.021	0.759	0.249	0.570
1985	0.370	0.591	0.039	0.023	0.691	0.258	0.504
1990	*0.346*	*0.613*	*0.042*	*0.025*	*0.632*	*0.267*	*0.429*
2000	*0.282*	*0.669*	*0.049*	*0.030*	*0.494*	*0.287*	*0.318*
2010	*0.243*	*0.702*	*0.055*	*0.034*	*0.425*	*0.276*	*0.302*
2020	*0.225*	*0.693*	*0.082*	*0.045*	*0.444*	*0.252*	*0.299*

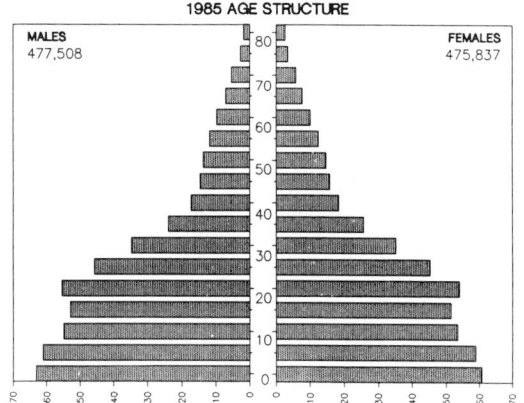

1985 AGE STRUCTURE

MALES 477,508 — FEMALES 475,837

MORTALITY MEASURES (Annual Averages)

PERIOD	CRUDE DEATH RATE	INFANT MORT. RATE	LIFE EXPECTANCY AT BIRTH (years) MALE	LIFE EXPECTANCY AT BIRTH (years) FEMALE	LIFE EXPECTANCY AT BIRTH (years) BOTH SEXES	DIFFERENCE FEMALE-MALE
1950-55	13.50	92.60	53.50	57.00	55.22	3.50
1955-60	10.70	76.00	56.80	60.70	58.71	3.90
1960-65	8.60	60.90	59.10	63.30	61.16	4.20
1965-70	7.70	55.90	60.30	64.70	62.46	4.40
1970-75	7.60	55.70	61.90	66.40	64.11	4.50
1975-80	6.70	48.70	64.10	68.90	66.46	4.80
1980-85	5.90	36.18	65.80	70.80	68.24	5.00
1985-90	*5.41*	*29.69*	*67.30*	*72.30*	*69.74*	*5.00*
1990-95	*5.17*	*25.27*	*68.56*	*73.56*	*71.00*	*5.00*
2000-05	*5.04*	*18.15*	*70.84*	*75.84*	*73.28*	*5.00*
2010-15	*5.32*	*12.76*	*72.80*	*77.80*	*75.24*	*5.00*
2020-25	*6.20*	*9.03*	*74.40*	*79.40*	*76.84*	*5.00*

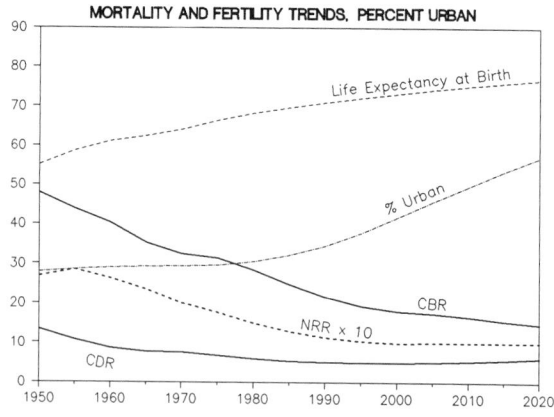

MORTALITY AND FERTILITY TRENDS, PERCENT URBAN

FERTILITY MEASURES (Annual Averages)

PERIOD	CRUDE BIRTH RATE	FERTILITY RATES GENERAL	FERTILITY RATES TOTAL	REPRODUCTION RATES GROSS	REPRODUCTION RATES NET	RATE OF NATUR. INCR.
1950-55	48.10	214.20	6.683	3.260	2.690	34.60
1955-60	43.90	206.29	6.765	3.300	2.850	33.20
1960-65	40.40	192.63	6.047	2.950	2.630	31.80
1965-70	35.40	167.71	5.330	2.600	2.350	27.70
1970-75	32.50	146.78	4.551	2.220	2.010	24.90
1975-80	31.50	131.05	3.936	1.920	1.760	24.80
1980-85	28.49	112.33	3.259	1.590	1.504	22.59
1985-90	*24.79*	*94.35*	*2.747*	*1.340*	*1.282*	*19.39*
1990-95	*21.65*	*79.17*	*2.419*	*1.180*	*1.138*	*16.48*
2000-05	*18.03*	*63.06*	*2.091*	*1.020*	*0.996*	*12.99*
2010-15	*16.57*	*61.75*	*2.091*	*1.020*	*1.005*	*11.26*
2020-25	*14.76*	*59.53*	*2.091*	*1.020*	*1.011*	*8.56*

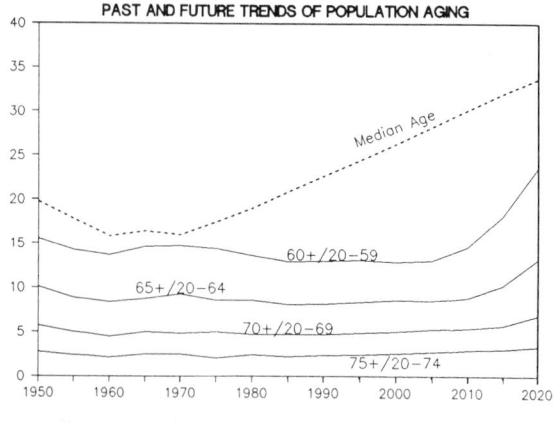

PAST AND FUTURE TRENDS OF POPULATION AGING

AGING MEASURES

YEAR	POPULATION AGE RATIOS 60+/20-59	POPULATION AGE RATIOS 65+/20-64	POPULATION AGE RATIOS 70+/20-69	POPULATION AGE RATIOS 75+/20-74	POPULATION MEAN AGE	POPULATION MEDIAN AGE
1950	0.1554	0.1008	0.0570	0.0274	24.31	19.78
1960	0.1369	0.0837	0.0447	0.0214	21.98	15.87
1970	0.1472	0.0926	0.0482	0.0248	21.96	16.05
1980	0.1363	0.0856	0.0469	0.0242	23.50	19.06
1990	*0.1298*	*0.0817*	*0.0470*	*0.0241*	*25.68*	*22.67*
2000	*0.1290*	*0.0856*	*0.0506*	*0.0259*	*28.68*	*26.31*
2010	*0.1463*	*0.0885*	*0.0536*	*0.0295*	*31.71*	*30.16*
2020	*0.2356*	*0.1318*	*0.0687*	*0.0335*	*34.55*	*33.77*

OBSERVED AND *PROJECTED* POPULATION DATA (000's)

YEAR	MID-YEAR POPULATION	NO. OF BIRTHS	NO. OF DEATHS	URBAN POPULATION NUMBER	URBAN POPULATION PERCENT	POPULATION 1985 AGE	POPULATION 1985 NUMBER
1950	3097	135	82	377	12.2	0	872
1955	3353	146	80	462	13.8	5	779
1960	3675	159	79	573	15.6	10	728
1965	4047	172	78	712	17.6	15	665
1970	4500	178	77	889	19.8	20	547
1975	4957	182	76	1095	22.1	25	440
1980	5413	191	75	1330	24.6	30	357
1985	5922	203	75	1613	27.2	35	314
1990	*6504*	*215*	*75*	*1968*	*30.3*	40	270
1995	*7148*	*224*	*76*	*2403*	*33.6*	45	234
2000	*7837*	*230*	*76*	*2921*	*37.3*	50	200
2005	*8558*	*235*	*77*	*3521*	*41.1*	55	163
2010	*9292*	*239*	*79*	*4194*	*45.1*	60	129
2015	*10036*	*243*	*81*	*4922*	*49.0*	65	97
2020	*10785*	*247*	*85*	*5698*	*52.8*	70+	130

POPULATION RATIOS

YEAR	AGE DISTRIBUTION UNDER 15	AGE DISTRIBUTION 15-64	AGE DISTRIBUTION 65 & OLDER	AGE DISTRIBUTION 70 & OLDER	DEPENDENCY RATIO	WOMEN 15-49	CHILD-WOMAN RATIO
1950	0.395	0.564	0.041	0.023	0.772	0.245	0.633
1955	0.395	0.564	0.041	0.023	0.772	0.246	0.625
1960	0.401	0.560	0.040	0.023	0.787	0.244	0.652
1965	0.409	0.553	0.039	0.022	0.810	0.241	0.676
1970	0.419	0.543	0.038	0.021	0.840	0.236	0.698
1975	0.420	0.542	0.037	0.021	0.843	0.236	0.668
1980	0.414	0.548	0.038	0.022	0.824	0.239	0.629
1985	0.402	0.560	0.038	0.022	0.785	0.245	0.601
1990	*0.392*	*0.569*	*0.039*	*0.022*	*0.756*	*0.249*	*0.582*
2000	*0.378*	*0.582*	*0.040*	*0.023*	*0.717*	*0.255*	*0.536*
2010	*0.351*	*0.606*	*0.042*	*0.025*	*0.649*	*0.263*	*0.465*
2020	*0.320*	*0.633*	*0.046*	*0.028*	*0.579*	*0.267*	*0.414*

MORTALITY MEASURES (Annual Averages)

PERIOD	CRUDE DEATH RATE	INFANT MORT. RATE	LIFE EXPECTANCY AT BIRTH (years) MALE	LIFE EXPECTANCY AT BIRTH (years) FEMALE	LIFE EXPECTANCY AT BIRTH (years) BOTH SEXES	DIFFERENCE FEMALE-MALE
1950-55	26.38	220.00	36.32	38.87	37.56	2.55
1955-60	23.73	205.00	39.39	42.03	40.68	2.64
1960-65	21.40	188.00	42.26	44.94	43.57	2.68
1965-70	19.20	172.00	44.93	47.63	46.25	2.70
1970-75	17.11	155.00	47.07	49.98	48.49	2.91
1975-80	15.31	139.00	49.15	52.23	50.65	3.08
1980-85	13.89	128.00	51.16	54.37	52.73	3.21
1985-90	*12.68*	*117.00*	*53.09*	*56.41*	*54.71*	*3.32*
1990-95	*11.59*	*106.00*	*54.95*	*58.34*	*56.60*	*3.39*
2000-05	*9.64*	*85.00*	*58.52*	*62.20*	*60.31*	*3.68*
2010-15	*8.46*	*67.00*	*61.36*	*65.50*	*63.38*	*4.14*
2020-25	*7.88*	*49.00*	*63.80*	*68.40*	*66.04*	*4.60*

FERTILITY MEASURES (Annual Averages)

PERIOD	CRUDE BIRTH RATE	FERTILITY RATES GENERAL	FERTILITY RATES TOTAL	REPRODUCTION RATES GROSS	REPRODUCTION RATES NET	RATE OF NATUR. INCR.
1950-55	43.67	177.76	6.150	3.000	1.670	17.30
1955-60	43.57	177.85	6.150	3.000	1.810	19.84
1960-65	43.15	177.85	6.150	3.000	1.938	21.75
1965-70	42.48	177.97	6.150	3.000	2.055	23.29
1970-75	39.46	167.13	5.760	2.810	2.022	22.34
1975-80	36.75	154.76	5.350	2.610	1.963	21.44
1980-85	35.37	146.12	5.053	2.460	1.927	21.48
1985-90	*34.33*	*138.88*	*4.739*	*2.310*	*1.869*	*21.65*
1990-95	*33.10*	*132.04*	*4.420*	*2.160*	*1.795*	*21.51*
2000-05	*29.41*	*114.37*	*3.800*	*1.850*	*1.626*	*19.77*
2010-15	*25.72*	*97.10*	*3.270*	*1.600*	*1.452*	*17.26*
2020-25	*22.92*	*85.96*	*2.870*	*1.400*	*1.309*	*15.04*

AGING MEASURES

YEAR	POPULATION AGE RATIOS 60+/20-59	POPULATION AGE RATIOS 65+/20-64	POPULATION AGE RATIOS 70+/20-69	POPULATION AGE RATIOS 75+/20-74	POPULATION MEAN AGE	POPULATION MEDIAN AGE
1950	0.1465	0.0877	0.0470	0.0221	24.81	20.25
1960	0.1420	0.0862	0.0474	0.0223	24.60	20.03
1970	0.1408	0.0848	0.0465	0.0225	24.02	19.17
1980	0.1429	0.0861	0.0471	0.0227	24.05	19.01
1990	*0.1377*	*0.0837*	*0.0467*	*0.0228*	*24.41*	*19.95*
2000	*0.1355*	*0.0832*	*0.0465*	*0.0229*	*25.05*	*21.03*
2010	*0.1358*	*0.0839*	*0.0479*	*0.0240*	*26.21*	*22.45*
2020	*0.1431*	*0.0868*	*0.0501*	*0.0254*	*27.78*	*24.40*

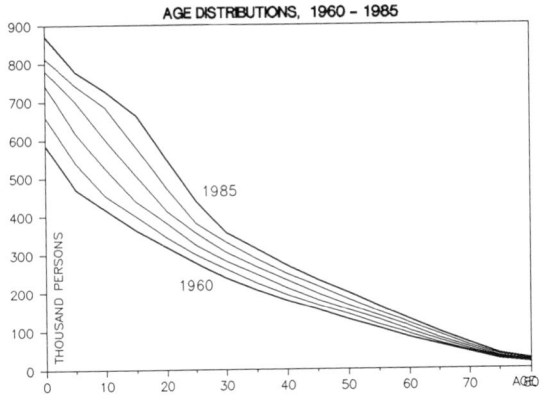

AGE DISTRIBUTIONS, 1960 - 1985

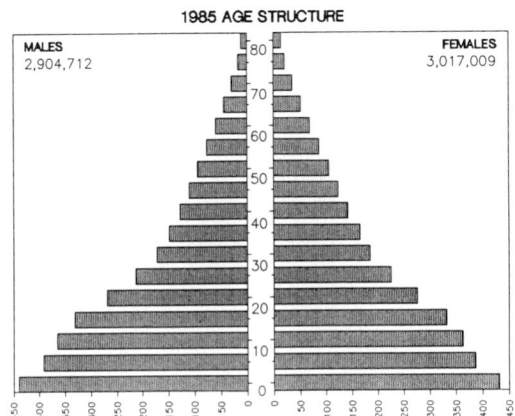

1985 AGE STRUCTURE

MALES 2,904,712   FEMALES 3,017,009

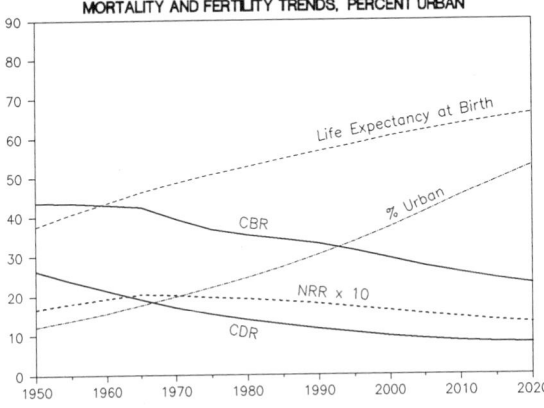

MORTALITY AND FERTILITY TRENDS, PERCENT URBAN

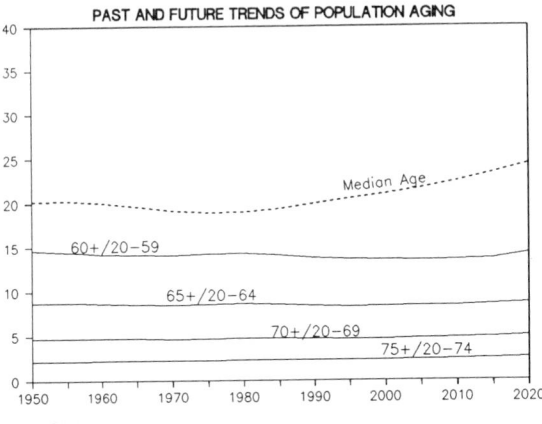

PAST AND FUTURE TRENDS OF POPULATION AGING

OBSERVED AND *PROJECTED* POPULATION DATA (000's)

YEAR	MID-YEAR POPULATION	NO. OF BIRTHS	NO. OF DEATHS	URBAN POPULATION NUMBER	URBAN POPULATION PERCENT	POPULATION 1985 AGE	POPULATION 1985 NUMBER
1950	1401	72	31	246	17.6	0	782
1955	1640	84	33	329	20.0	5	656
1960	1935	99	35	440	22.7	10	595
1965	2293	115	37	590	25.7	15	486
1970	2627	128	36	759	28.9	20	387
1975	3081	135	34	996	32.3	25	307
1980	3662	155	33	1315	35.9	30	246
1985	4383	174	35	1739	39.7	35	199
1990	*5138*	*190*	*37*	*2240*	*43.6*	40	164
1995	*5968*	*202*	*38*	*2838*	*47.5*	45	138
2000	*6846*	*209*	*40*	*3522*	*51.5*	50	115
2005	*7748*	*215*	*42*	*4277*	*55.2*	55	94
2010	*8668*	*222*	*44*	*5088*	*58.7*	60	74
2015	*9606*	*229*	*48*	*5956*	*62.0*	65	59
2020	*10558*	*235*	*53*	*6871*	*65.1*	70+	84

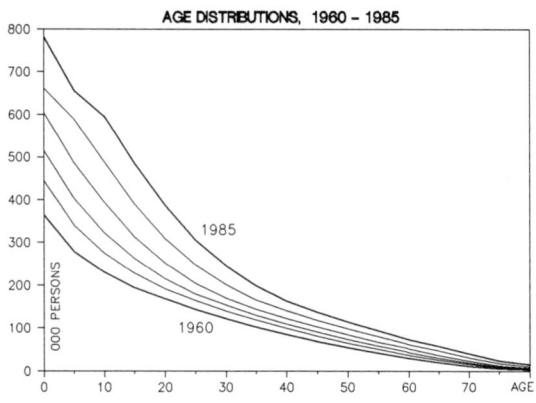

AGE DISTRIBUTIONS, 1960 - 1985

POPULATION RATIOS

YEAR	AGE DISTRIBUTION UNDER 15	AGE DISTRIBUTION 15-64	AGE DISTRIBUTION 65 & OLDER	AGE DISTRIBUTION 70 & OLDER	DEPENDENCY RATIO	WOMEN 15-49	CHILD-WOMAN RATIO
1950	0.447	0.533	0.019	0.011	0.874	0.234	0.775
1955	0.446	0.533	0.021	0.011	0.875	0.232	0.790
1960	0.452	0.526	0.023	0.012	0.903	0.227	0.829
1965	0.462	0.513	0.024	0.013	0.949	0.221	0.876
1970	0.472	0.502	0.026	0.014	0.992	0.216	0.906
1975	0.482	0.491	0.027	0.015	1.035	0.212	0.928
1980	0.475	0.495	0.030	0.017	1.019	0.214	0.845
1985	0.464	0.504	0.032	0.019	0.985	0.218	0.817
1990	*0.446*	*0.521*	*0.033*	*0.020*	*0.918*	*0.227*	*0.749*
2000	*0.412*	*0.554*	*0.035*	*0.021*	*0.805*	*0.243*	*0.614*
2010	*0.361*	*0.600*	*0.039*	*0.024*	*0.667*	*0.260*	*0.484*
2020	*0.317*	*0.636*	*0.047*	*0.029*	*0.572*	*0.266*	*0.413*

MORTALITY MEASURES (Annual Averages)

PERIOD	CRUDE DEATH RATE	INFANT MORT. RATE	LIFE EXPECTANCY AT BIRTH (years) MALE	LIFE EXPECTANCY AT BIRTH (years) FEMALE	LIFE EXPECTANCY AT BIRTH (years) BOTH SEXES	DIFFERENCE FEMALE-MALE
1950-55	22.21	169.00	40.88	43.81	42.31	2.93
1955-60	20.22	152.00	43.43	46.62	44.99	3.19
1960-65	18.10	136.00	46.27	49.70	47.94	3.43
1965-70	16.07	123.00	49.18	52.69	50.89	3.51
1970-75	13.68	110.00	52.20	55.80	53.96	3.60
1975-80	11.06	95.00	55.80	59.60	57.65	3.80
1980-85	8.97	82.00	59.98	63.99	61.94	4.01
1985-90	*8.07*	*69.00*	*61.94*	*66.07*	*63.96*	*4.13*
1990-95	*7.16*	*57.00*	*63.73*	*67.98*	*65.80*	*4.25*
2000-05	*5.79*	*40.00*	*66.83*	*71.23*	*68.98*	*4.40*
2010-15	*5.11*	*32.00*	*69.34*	*73.87*	*71.55*	*4.53*
2020-25	*4.97*	*29.00*	*71.31*	*75.95*	*73.57*	*4.64*

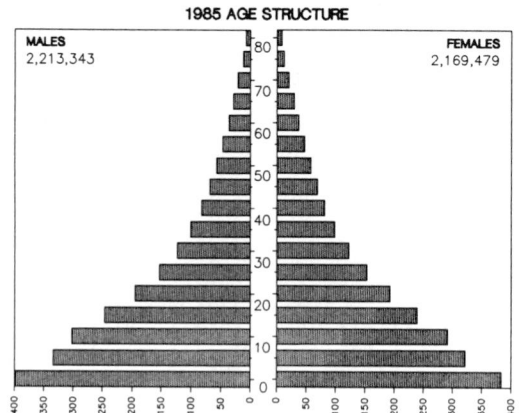

1985 AGE STRUCTURE

MALES 2,213,343 — FEMALES 2,169,479

FERTILITY MEASURES (Annual Averages)

PERIOD	CRUDE BIRTH RATE	FERTILITY RATES GENERAL	FERTILITY RATES TOTAL	REPRODUCTION RATES GROSS	REPRODUCTION RATES NET	RATE OF NATUR. INCR.
1950-55	51.38	220.54	7.052	3.440	2.179	29.17
1955-60	51.31	223.59	7.175	3.500	2.339	31.09
1960-65	51.15	228.47	7.359	3.590	2.535	33.05
1965-70	50.14	229.46	7.421	3.620	2.693	34.07
1970-75	48.67	227.69	7.380	3.600	2.817	34.99
1975-80	43.79	205.71	6.580	3.210	2.637	32.73
1980-85	42.30	195.58	6.156	3.000	2.592	33.34
1985-90	*39.80*	*178.34*	*5.550*	*2.710*	*2.382*	*31.73*
1990-95	*37.06*	*160.62*	*4.936*	*2.410*	*2.155*	*29.90*
2000-05	*30.50*	*123.36*	*3.809*	*1.860*	*1.708*	*24.72*
2010-15	*25.65*	*97.81*	*3.075*	*1.500*	*1.407*	*20.54*
2020-25	*22.24*	*83.80*	*2.685*	*1.310*	*1.247*	*17.26*

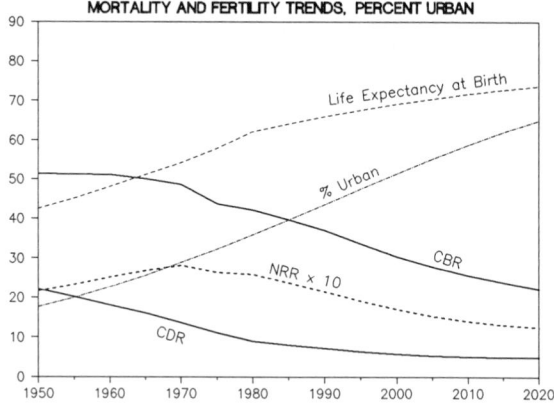

MORTALITY AND FERTILITY TRENDS, PERCENT URBAN

AGING MEASURES

YEAR	POPULATION AGE RATIOS 60+/20-59	POPULATION AGE RATIOS 65+/20-64	POPULATION AGE RATIOS 70+/20-69	POPULATION AGE RATIOS 75+/20-74	POPULATION MEAN AGE	POPULATION MEDIAN AGE
1950	0.0789	0.0450	0.0243	0.0119	21.51	17.46
1960	0.0947	0.0536	0.0275	0.0126	21.83	17.39
1970	0.1093	0.0635	0.0336	0.0153	21.48	16.38
1980	0.1256	0.0767	0.0418	0.0199	21.47	16.17
1990	*0.1273*	*0.0804*	*0.0475*	*0.0242*	*22.06*	*17.36*
2000	*0.1217*	*0.0779*	*0.0465*	*0.0247*	*23.28*	*19.01*
2010	*0.1226*	*0.0786*	*0.0476*	*0.0258*	*25.30*	*21.58*
2020	*0.1382*	*0.0868*	*0.0517*	*0.0281*	*27.66*	*24.51*

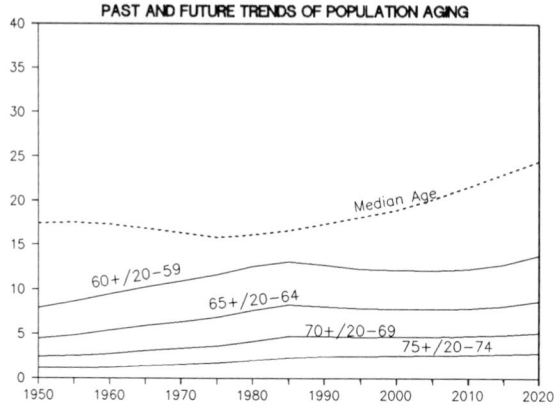

PAST AND FUTURE TRENDS OF POPULATION AGING

OBSERVED AND *PROJECTED* POPULATION DATA

YEAR	MID-YEAR POPULATION	NO. OF BIRTHS	NO. OF DEATHS	URBAN POPULATION NUMBER	URBAN POPULATION PERCENT	POPULATION 1985 AGE	POPULATION 1985 NUMBER
1950	1402900	48821	16133	375352	26.8	0	305650
1955	1541700	60435	15109	464809	30.1	5	272556
1960	1629000	64508	14824	550191	33.8	10	278547
1965	1760441	65664	14084	661956	37.6	15	290095
1970	1869000	60743	13831	776033	41.5	20	279682
1975	2042700	57604	13686	901446	44.1	25	216848
1980	2172900	61106	12229	1016304	46.8	30	125297
1985	2336491	60842	12918	1154967	49.4	35	88510
1990	*2520889*	*57118*	*12821*	*1318841*	*52.3*	40	73807
1995	*2705696*	*54717*	*13047*	*1498017*	*55.4*	45	68372
2000	*2886137*	*53717*	*13314*	*1688605*	*58.5*	50	69600
2005	*3059339*	*53184*	*13782*	*1886643*	*61.7*	55	67279
2010	*3226856*	*53472*	*14592*	*2090221*	*64.8*	60	57687
2015	*3401601*	*53344*	*15879*	*2301761*	*67.7*	65	51375
2020	*3578866*	*53082*	*18055*	*2517518*	*70.3*	70+	91186

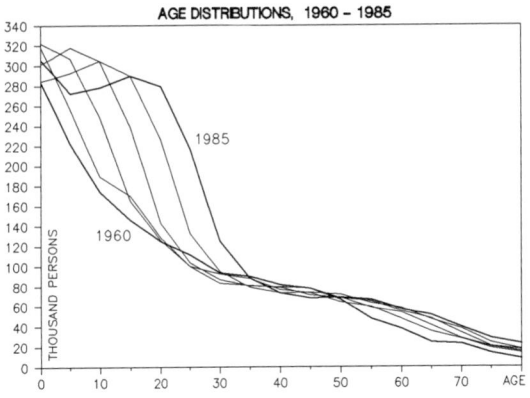

AGE DISTRIBUTIONS, 1960 - 1985

POPULATION RATIOS

YEAR	AGE DISTRIBUTION UNDER 15	AGE DISTRIBUTION 15-64	AGE DISTRIBUTION 65 & OLDER	AGE DISTRIBUTION 70 & OLDER	DEPENDENCY RATIO	WOMEN 15-49	CHILD-WOMAN RATIO
1950	0.360	0.601	0.039	0.021	0.664	0.267	0.505
1955	0.371	0.588	0.041	0.024	0.700	0.256	0.575
1960	0.417	0.540	0.043	0.028	0.851	0.238	0.729
1965	0.434	0.512	0.054	0.034	0.953	0.221	0.821
1970	0.470	0.475	0.056	0.034	1.107	0.197	0.875
1975	0.452	0.490	0.058	0.035	1.042	0.207	0.714
1980	0.406	0.536	0.058	0.036	0.865	0.229	0.573
1985	0.367	0.572	0.061	0.039	0.747	0.247	0.531
1990	*0.344*	*0.596*	*0.060*	*0.039*	*0.678*	*0.259*	*0.471*
2000	*0.298*	*0.643*	*0.059*	*0.040*	*0.556*	*0.282*	*0.341*
2010	*0.250*	*0.694*	*0.056*	*0.039*	*0.441*	*0.283*	*0.296*
2020	*0.225*	*0.707*	*0.068*	*0.041*	*0.414*	*0.251*	*0.302*

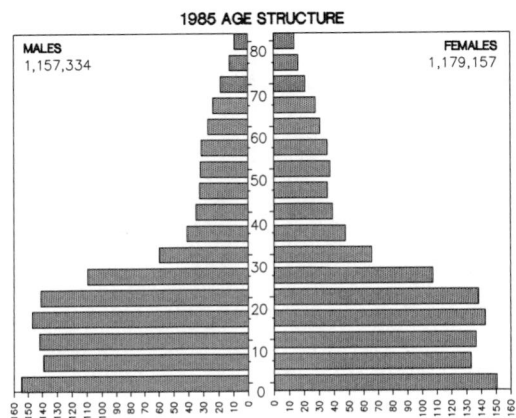

1985 AGE STRUCTURE

MALES 1,157,334   FEMALES 1,179,157

MORTALITY MEASURES (Annual Averages)

PERIOD	CRUDE DEATH RATE	INFANT MORT. RATE	LIFE EXPECTANCY AT BIRTH (years) MALE	LIFE EXPECTANCY AT BIRTH (years) FEMALE	LIFE EXPECTANCY AT BIRTH (years) BOTH SEXES	DIFFERENCE FEMALE-MALE
1950-55	11.50	84.90	55.70	58.70	57.16	3.00
1955-60	9.80	71.30	59.50	63.00	61.21	3.50
1960-65	9.10	54.40	62.40	66.20	64.25	3.80
1965-70	8.00	44.60	64.50	68.10	66.26	3.60
1970-75	7.40	36.20	66.00	69.70	67.81	3.70
1975-80	6.70	24.50	67.00	71.00	68.95	4.00
1980-85	5.63	21.02	70.35	75.67	72.96	5.33
1985-90	*5.53*	*18.00*	*71.34*	*76.67*	*73.95*	*5.33*
1990-95	*5.09*	*16.00*	*72.34*	*77.67*	*74.95*	*5.33*
2000-05	*4.61*	*13.00*	*73.98*	*79.27*	*76.57*	*5.29*
2010-15	*4.52*	*11.00*	*75.40*	*80.57*	*77.93*	*5.17*
2020-25	*5.05*	*9.00*	*76.40*	*81.57*	*78.93*	*5.17*

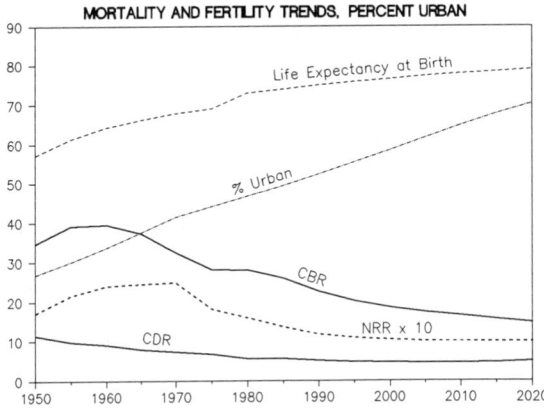

MORTALITY AND FERTILITY TRENDS, PERCENT URBAN

Life Expectancy at Birth

% Urban

CBR

CDR

NRR x 10

FERTILITY MEASURES (Annual Averages)

PERIOD	CRUDE BIRTH RATE	FERTILITY RATES GENERAL	FERTILITY RATES TOTAL	REPRODUCTION RATES GROSS	REPRODUCTION RATES NET	RATE OF NATUR. INCR.
1950-55	34.80	133.43	4.223	2.070	1.720	23.30
1955-60	39.20	158.94	5.018	2.460	2.160	29.40
1960-65	39.60	172.92	5.426	2.660	2.410	30.50
1965-70	37.30	179.03	5.406	2.650	2.450	29.30
1970-75	32.50	160.94	5.406	2.650	2.490	25.10
1975-80	28.20	129.41	3.937	1.930	1.830	21.50
1980-85	28.12	118.21	3.366	1.650	1.601	22.49
1985-90	*26.04*	*102.83*	*2.856*	*1.400*	*1.374*	*20.51*
1990-95	*22.66*	*85.68*	*2.448*	*1.200*	*1.183*	*17.57*
2000-05	*18.61*	*65.09*	*2.142*	*1.050*	*1.040*	*14.00*
2010-15	*16.57*	*60.44*	*2.081*	*1.020*	*1.013*	*12.05*
2020-25	*14.83*	*60.34*	*2.081*	*1.020*	*1.013*	*9.79*

AGING MEASURES

YEAR	POPULATION AGE RATIOS 60+/20-59	POPULATION AGE RATIOS 65+/20-64	POPULATION AGE RATIOS 70+/20-69	POPULATION AGE RATIOS 75+/20-74	POPULATION MEAN AGE	POPULATION MEDIAN AGE
1950	0.1212	0.0773	0.0411	0.0164	25.78	22.19
1960	0.1552	0.0954	0.0600	0.0285	24.78	19.64
1970	0.2365	0.1440	0.0826	0.0442	24.15	16.71
1980	0.2259	0.1442	0.0858	0.0432	24.63	18.53
1990	*0.1817*	*0.1221*	*0.0771*	*0.0420*	*25.90*	*22.21*
2000	*0.1522*	*0.1092*	*0.0708*	*0.0397*	*28.22*	*25.93*
2010	*0.1347*	*0.0926*	*0.0621*	*0.0380*	*31.18*	*29.46*
2020	*0.2048*	*0.1069*	*0.0616*	*0.0353*	*34.26*	*33.39*

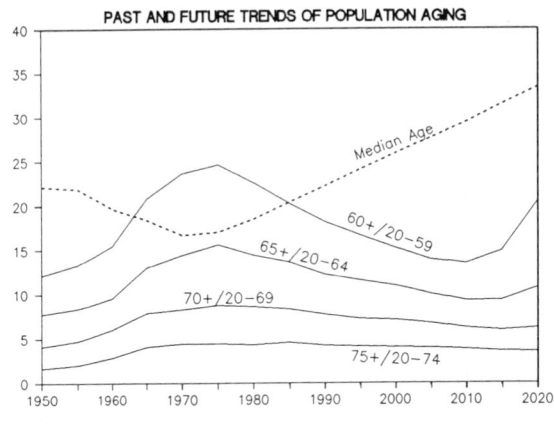

PAST AND FUTURE TRENDS OF POPULATION AGING

Median Age

60+/20-59

65+/20-64

70+/20-69

75+/20-74

OBSERVED AND *PROJECTED* POPULATION DATA

YEAR	MID-YEAR POPULATION	NO. OF BIRTHS	NO. OF DEATHS	URBAN POPULATION NUMBER	URBAN POPULATION PERCENT	POPULATION 1985 AGE	POPULATION 1985 NUMBER
1950	222000	8858	2797	61566	27.7	0	28517
1955	245800	9734	2433	82667	33.6	5	21758
1960	281800	10060	2367	112973	40.1	10	29712
1965	311400	9560	2367	146082	46.9	15	37783
1970	325500	8105	2376	175284	53.9	20	37872
1975	328500	5585	2267	199214	60.6	25	29436
1980	326138	5832	2448	216602	66.4	30	21216
1985	328112	6093	2529	233232	71.1	35	19275
1990	*331046*	*5954*	*2569*	*247303*	*74.7*	40	16811
1995	*338172*	*5421*	*2634*	*261725*	*77.4*	45	14846
2000	*352398*	*5081*	*2751*	*279397*	*79.3*	50	15175
2005	*364240*	*5110*	*2869*	*295088*	*81.0*	55	13502
2010	*375619*	*5390*	*3032*	*310250*	*82.6*	60	12128
2015	*387599*	*5591*	*3181*	*325750*	*84.0*	65	10137
2020	*399841*	*5577*	*3412*	*341324*	*85.4*	70+	19944

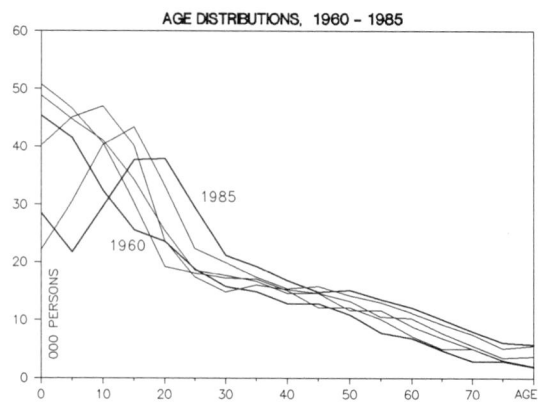

AGE DISTRIBUTIONS, 1960 - 1985

POPULATION RATIOS

YEAR	AGE DISTRIBUTION UNDER 15	AGE DISTRIBUTION 15-64	AGE DISTRIBUTION 65 & OLDER	AGE DISTRIBUTION 70 & OLDER	DEPENDENCY RATIO	WOMEN 15-49	CHILD-WOMAN RATIO
1950	0.374	0.574	0.052	0.030	0.743	0.252	0.607
1955	0.404	0.547	0.049	0.029	0.829	0.240	0.712
1960	0.424	0.532	0.045	0.028	0.881	0.225	0.715
1965	0.443	0.509	0.048	0.032	0.966	0.218	0.747
1970	0.414	0.534	0.052	0.031	0.873	0.227	0.661
1975	0.403	0.535	0.062	0.039	0.870	0.224	0.546
1980	0.285	0.631	0.084	0.056	0.585	0.263	0.259
1985	0.244	0.665	0.092	0.061	0.505	0.275	0.316
1990	*0.239*	*0.661*	*0.100*	*0.066*	*0.512*	*0.272*	*0.332*
2000	*0.245*	*0.644*	*0.111*	*0.075*	*0.554*	*0.256*	*0.303*
2010	*0.209*	*0.674*	*0.117*	*0.081*	*0.484*	*0.254*	*0.270*
2020	*0.203*	*0.664*	*0.134*	*0.091*	*0.507*	*0.223*	*0.316*

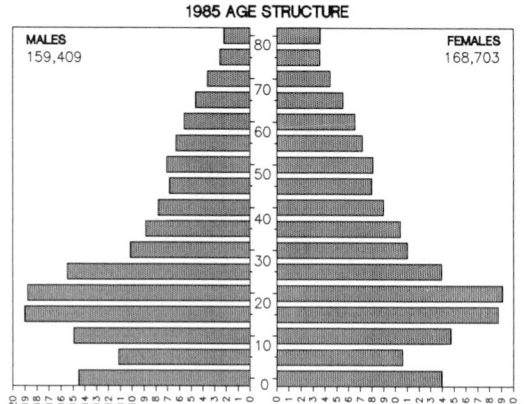

1985 AGE STRUCTURE

MALES 159,409 — FEMALES 168,703

MORTALITY MEASURES (Annual Averages)

PERIOD	CRUDE DEATH RATE	INFANT MORT. RATE	LIFE EXPECTANCY AT BIRTH (years) MALE	LIFE EXPECTANCY AT BIRTH (years) FEMALE	LIFE EXPECTANCY AT BIRTH (years) BOTH SEXES	DIFFERENCE FEMALE-MALE
1950-55	12.60	64.70	55.00	58.10	56.53	3.10
1955-60	9.90	55.70	59.50	63.60	61.53	4.10
1960-65	8.40	47.70	62.80	66.90	64.82	4.10
1965-70	7.60	42.30	64.50	68.60	66.53	4.10
1970-75	7.30	34.70	66.70	71.00	68.82	4.30
1975-80	6.90	21.90	68.90	73.30	71.07	4.40
1980-85	7.51	14.06	71.02	75.50	73.21	4.48
1985-90	*7.71*	*13.00*	*71.98*	*76.51*	*74.20*	*4.53*
1990-95	*7.76*	*11.00*	*72.95*	*77.78*	*75.32*	*4.83*
2000-05	*7.81*	*9.00*	*74.56*	*79.14*	*76.81*	*4.57*
2010-15	*8.07*	*7.00*	*75.76*	*80.47*	*78.07*	*4.71*
2020-25	*8.53*	*7.00*	*77.70*	*81.49*	*79.56*	*3.78*

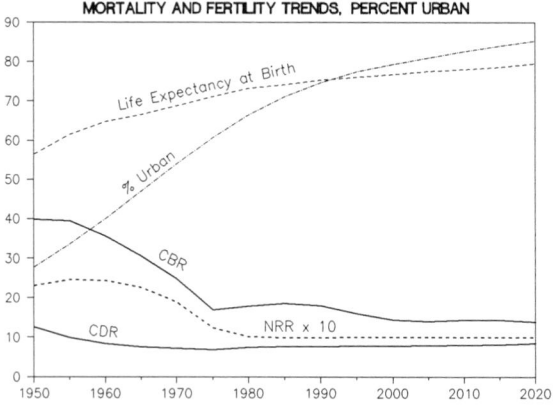

MORTALITY AND FERTILITY TRENDS, PERCENT URBAN

FERTILITY MEASURES (Annual Averages)

PERIOD	CRUDE BIRTH RATE	FERTILITY RATES GENERAL	FERTILITY RATES TOTAL	REPRODUCTION RATES GROSS	REPRODUCTION RATES NET	RATE OF NATUR. INCR.
1950-55	39.90	162.16	5.712	2.800	2.310	27.30
1955-60	39.60	170.42	5.712	2.800	2.470	29.70
1960-65	35.70	161.04	5.447	2.670	2.440	27.30
1965-70	30.70	137.89	4.998	2.450	2.270	23.10
1970-75	24.90	110.48	4.080	2.000	1.890	17.60
1975-80	17.00	69.88	2.652	1.300	1.240	10.10
1980-85	17.88	66.50	2.142	1.050	1.015	10.38
1985-90	*18.57*	*67.89*	*2.081*	*1.020*	*0.992*	*10.86*
1990-95	*17.99*	*68.05*	*2.081*	*1.020*	*0.998*	*10.22*
2000-05	*14.42*	*56.08*	*2.081*	*1.020*	*1.004*	*6.61*
2010-15	*14.35*	*58.51*	*2.081*	*1.020*	*1.007*	*6.28*
2020-25	*13.95*	*63.15*	*2.081*	*1.020*	*1.009*	*5.41*

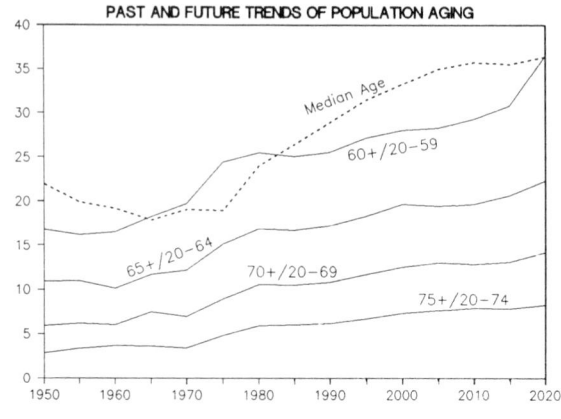

PAST AND FUTURE TRENDS OF POPULATION AGING

AGING MEASURES

YEAR	POPULATION AGE RATIOS 60+/20-59	POPULATION AGE RATIOS 65+/20-64	POPULATION AGE RATIOS 70+/20-69	POPULATION AGE RATIOS 75+/20-74	POPULATION MEAN AGE	POPULATION MEDIAN AGE
1950	0.1683	0.1090	0.0592	0.0288	26.16	21.94
1960	0.1652	0.1014	0.0605	0.0371	24.56	19.20
1970	0.1972	0.1218	0.0697	0.0343	25.28	19.10
1980	0.2550	0.1686	0.1057	0.0596	30.12	24.02
1990	*0.2553*	*0.1724*	*0.1084*	*0.0621*	*32.52*	*28.95*
2000	*0.2804*	*0.1966*	*0.1254*	*0.0734*	*34.27*	*33.29*
2010	*0.2929*	*0.1967*	*0.1284*	*0.0792*	*36.29*	*35.83*
2020	*0.3650*	*0.2229*	*0.1418*	*0.0828*	*37.92*	*36.42*

OBSERVED AND *PROJECTED* POPULATION DATA (000's)

YEAR	MID-YEAR POPULATION	NO. OF BIRTHS	NO. OF DEATHS	URBAN POPULATION NUMBER	URBAN POPULATION PERCENT	POPULATION 1985 AGE	POPULATION 1985 NUMBER
1950	28012	1304	451	11949	42.7	0	11172
1955	32416	1495	427	15132	46.7	5	10440
1960	38019	1730	428	19296	50.8	10	10867
1965	44752	1993	457	24584	54.9	15	9333
1970	52770	2248	471	31146	59.0	20	7743
1975	61918	2132	444	38860	62.8	25	6317
1980	70416	2229	446	46723	66.4	30	5091
1985	79376	2304	462	55276	69.6	35	3864
1990	*88598*	*2361*	*482*	*64304*	*72.6*	40	3377
1995	*97967*	*2378*	*508*	*73632*	*75.2*	45	2751
2000	*107233*	*2391*	*550*	*82985*	*77.4*	50	2273
2005	*116302*	*2413*	*605*	*92202*	*79.3*	55	1836
2010	*125166*	*2446*	*676*	*101396*	*81.0*	60	1454
2015	*133799*	*2484*	*766*	*110507*	*82.6*	65	1025
2020	*142135*	*2523*	*879*	*119448*	*84.0*	70+	1832

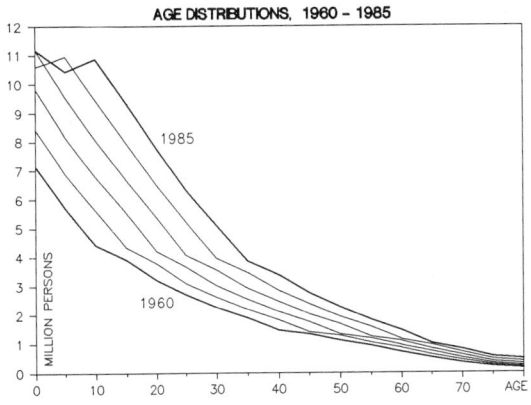

AGE DISTRIBUTIONS, 1960 - 1985

POPULATION RATIOS

YEAR	AGE DISTRIBUTION UNDER 15	AGE DISTRIBUTION 15-64	AGE DISTRIBUTION 65 & OLDER	AGE DISTRIBUTION 70 & OLDER	DEPENDENCY RATIO	WOMEN 15-49	CHILD-WOMAN RATIO
1950	0.437	0.530	0.033	0.019	0.886	0.228	0.751
1955	0.445	0.522	0.033	0.019	0.915	0.224	0.822
1960	0.454	0.513	0.033	0.019	0.948	0.221	0.849
1965	0.467	0.499	0.033	0.020	1.002	0.215	0.875
1970	0.469	0.497	0.034	0.020	1.013	0.216	0.861
1975	0.465	0.501	0.034	0.021	0.996	0.218	0.826
1980	0.441	0.524	0.035	0.022	0.908	0.229	0.657
1985	0.409	0.555	0.036	0.023	0.802	0.243	0.579
1990	*0.372*	*0.590*	*0.038*	*0.024*	*0.696*	*0.259*	*0.506*
2000	*0.328*	*0.627*	*0.046*	*0.028*	*0.596*	*0.272*	*0.411*
2010	*0.287*	*0.657*	*0.056*	*0.035*	*0.523*	*0.275*	*0.354*
2020	*0.259*	*0.670*	*0.071*	*0.044*	*0.492*	*0.264*	*0.334*

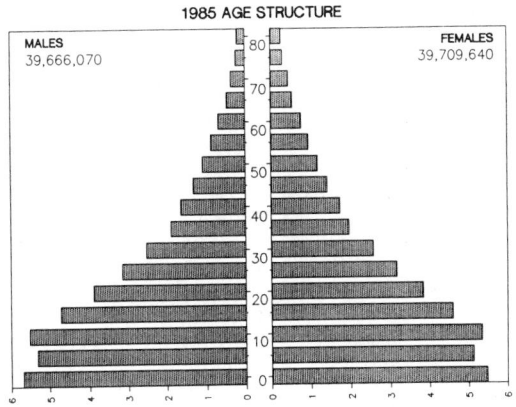

1985 AGE STRUCTURE

MALES 39,666,070   FEMALES 39,709,640

MORTALITY MEASURES (Annual Averages)

PERIOD	CRUDE DEATH RATE	INFANT MORT. RATE	LIFE EXPECTANCY AT BIRTH (years) MALE	LIFE EXPECTANCY AT BIRTH (years) FEMALE	LIFE EXPECTANCY AT BIRTH (years) BOTH SEXES	DIFFERENCE FEMALE-MALE
1950-55	16.08	114.00	49.20	52.37	50.75	3.17
1955-60	13.17	98.00	53.85	57.07	55.42	3.22
1960-65	11.27	86.00	57.01	60.30	58.62	3.29
1965-70	10.22	79.00	58.51	62.21	60.31	3.70
1970-75	8.93	69.00	60.41	64.94	62.62	4.53
1975-80	7.17	60.00	62.62	68.24	65.36	5.62
1980-85	6.33	53.00	64.24	70.64	67.36	6.40
1985-90	*5.82*	*47.00*	*65.70*	*72.28*	*68.91*	*6.58*
1990-95	*5.44*	*41.00*	*67.10*	*73.81*	*70.37*	*6.71*
2000-05	*5.13*	*33.00*	*69.30*	*76.13*	*72.63*	*6.83*
2010-15	*5.40*	*27.00*	*70.81*	*77.70*	*74.17*	*6.89*
2020-25	*6.18*	*22.00*	*71.66*	*78.58*	*75.04*	*6.92*

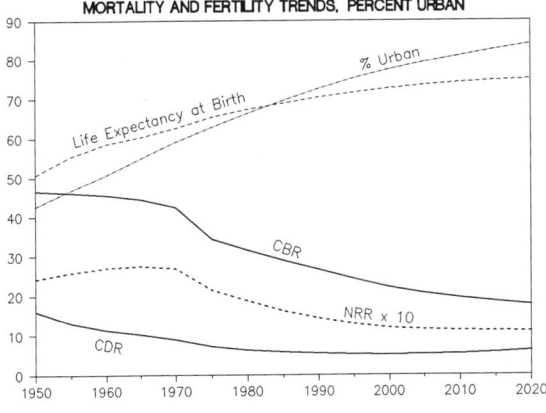

MORTALITY AND FERTILITY TRENDS, PERCENT URBAN

% Urban
Life Expectancy at Birth
CBR
NRR x 10
CDR

FERTILITY MEASURES (Annual Averages)

PERIOD	CRUDE BIRTH RATE	FERTILITY RATES GENERAL	FERTILITY RATES TOTAL	REPRODUCTION RATES GROSS	REPRODUCTION RATES NET	RATE OF NATUR. INCR.
1950-55	46.56	206.11	6.750	3.290	2.426	30.48
1955-60	46.13	207.33	6.750	3.290	2.604	32.96
1960-65	45.49	208.88	6.750	3.290	2.722	34.23
1965-70	44.54	206.52	6.700	3.270	2.767	34.32
1970-75	42.59	195.95	6.366	3.110	2.707	33.67
1975-80	34.44	153.59	4.893	2.390	2.149	27.27
1980-85	31.65	133.83	4.198	2.050	1.886	25.33
1985-90	*29.03*	*115.60*	*3.578*	*1.750*	*1.629*	*23.21*
1990-95	*26.65*	*101.66*	*3.108*	*1.520*	*1.433*	*21.21*
2000-05	*22.30*	*81.48*	*2.578*	*1.260*	*1.209*	*17.17*
2010-15	*19.54*	*71.53*	*2.388*	*1.170*	*1.133*	*14.14*
2020-25	*17.75*	*68.54*	*2.328*	*1.140*	*1.111*	*11.57*

AGING MEASURES

YEAR	POPULATION AGE RATIOS 60+/20-59	POPULATION AGE RATIOS 65+/20-64	POPULATION AGE RATIOS 70+/20-69	POPULATION AGE RATIOS 75+/20-74	POPULATION MEAN AGE	POPULATION MEDIAN AGE
1950	0.1257	0.0770	0.0436	0.0220	22.94	18.06
1960	0.1316	0.0803	0.0453	0.0231	22.31	17.26
1970	0.1381	0.0865	0.0495	0.0255	21.86	16.47
1980	0.1308	0.0861	0.0513	0.0276	22.61	17.64
1990	*0.1287*	*0.0821*	*0.0490*	*0.0279*	*24.47*	*20.33*
2000	*0.1346*	*0.0867*	*0.0523*	*0.0285*	*26.80*	*23.80*
2010	*0.1521*	*0.0993*	*0.0598*	*0.0330*	*29.41*	*26.88*
2020	*0.1955*	*0.1209*	*0.0710*	*0.0398*	*31.95*	*29.84*

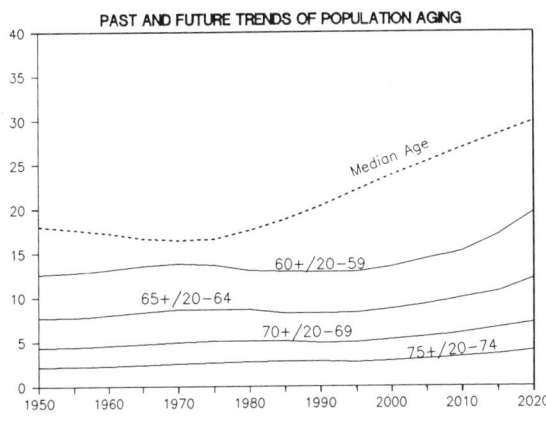

PAST AND FUTURE TRENDS OF POPULATION AGING

Median Age
60+/20-59
65+/20-64
70+/20-69
75+/20-74

OBSERVED AND *PROJECTED* POPULATION DATA

YEAR	MID-YEAR POPULATION	NO. OF BIRTHS	NO. OF DEATHS	URBAN POPULATION NUMBER	URBAN POPULATION PERCENT	POPULATION 1985 AGE	POPULATION 1985 NUMBER
1950	1097916	59433	24881	383600	34.9	0	604131
1955	1277289	66600	25207	475414	37.2	5	499151
1960	1492703	75122	25470	590521	39.6	10	426348
1965	1750397	84682	25738	748074	42.7	15	358282
1970	2052553	96039	26002	964898	47.0	20	297273
1975	2408065	109769	28319	1211366	50.3	25	243771
1980	2771016	122493	26923	1479799	53.4	30	200896
1985	3272068	136763	26134	1851315	56.6	35	148409
1990	*3870822*	*149789*	*25768*	*2313275*	*59.8*	40	115946
1995	*4539500*	*160730*	*26075*	*2854411*	*62.9*	45	97215
2000	*5261316*	*170414*	*27396*	*3465584*	*65.9*	50	80170
2005	*6028546*	*178891*	*29721*	*4140448*	*68.7*	55	66587
2010	*6823589*	*185431*	*33019*	*4863859*	*71.3*	60	51535
2015	*7630687*	*190187*	*37383*	*5621905*	*73.7*	65	35976
2020	*8435001*	*192816*	*42909*	*6400109*	*75.9*	70+	46379

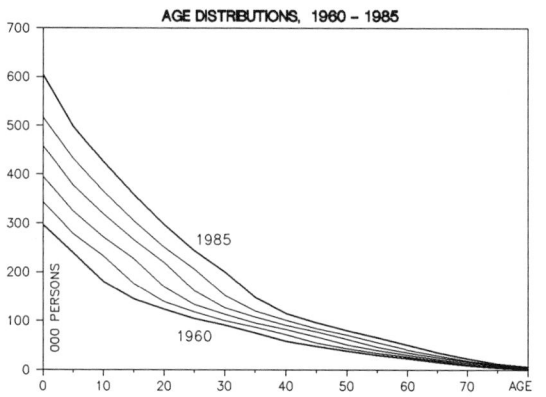

AGE DISTRIBUTIONS, 1960 - 1985

POPULATION RATIOS

YEAR	AGE DISTRIBUTION UNDER 15	15-64	65 & OLDER	70 & OLDER	DEPENDENCY RATIO	WOMEN 15-49	CHILD-WOMAN RATIO
1950	0.446	0.529	0.025	0.013	0.890	0.235	0.784
1955	0.463	0.513	0.024	0.013	0.950	0.227	0.885
1960	0.480	0.497	0.023	0.012	1.013	0.219	0.905
1965	0.488	0.488	0.024	0.013	1.049	0.215	0.910
1970	0.483	0.493	0.024	0.013	1.029	0.218	0.882
1975	0.479	0.497	0.024	0.013	1.014	0.219	0.867
1980	0.474	0.501	0.024	0.013	0.994	0.222	0.840
1985	0.467	0.507	0.025	0.014	0.971	0.225	0.822
1990	*0.458*	*0.515*	*0.027*	*0.015*	*0.943*	*0.228*	*0.782*
2000	*0.427*	*0.542*	*0.031*	*0.019*	*0.845*	*0.239*	*0.655*
2010	*0.380*	*0.585*	*0.035*	*0.022*	*0.708*	*0.251*	*0.534*
2020	*0.333*	*0.622*	*0.045*	*0.026*	*0.607*	*0.261*	*0.440*

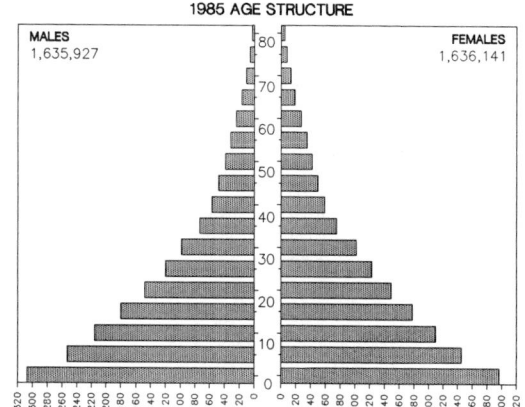

1985 AGE STRUCTURE

MALES 1,635,927   FEMALES 1,636,141

MORTALITY MEASURES (Annual Averages)

PERIOD	CRUDE DEATH RATE	INFANT MORT. RATE	LIFE EXPECTANCY AT BIRTH (years) MALE	FEMALE	BOTH SEXES	DIFFERENCE FEMALE-MALE
1950-55	22.66	167.00	40.89	43.73	42.28	2.84
1955-60	19.74	148.00	44.11	46.76	45.40	2.65
1960-65	17.06	131.00	47.31	49.77	48.51	2.46
1965-70	14.70	115.00	50.51	52.77	51.61	2.26
1970-75	12.67	100.00	53.70	55.76	54.71	2.06
1975-80	11.76	93.00	55.29	57.27	56.26	1.98
1980-85	9.72	76.00	58.68	60.99	59.81	2.31
1985-90	*7.99*	*62.00*	*61.98*	*64.61*	*63.26*	*2.63*
1990-95	*6.66*	*50.00*	*64.80*	*67.71*	*66.22*	*2.91*
2000-05	*5.21*	*35.00*	*68.52*	*71.79*	*70.11*	*3.27*
2010-15	*4.84*	*29.00*	*70.22*	*73.65*	*71.89*	*3.43*
2020-25	*5.09*	*27.00*	*70.88*	*74.38*	*72.59*	*3.50*

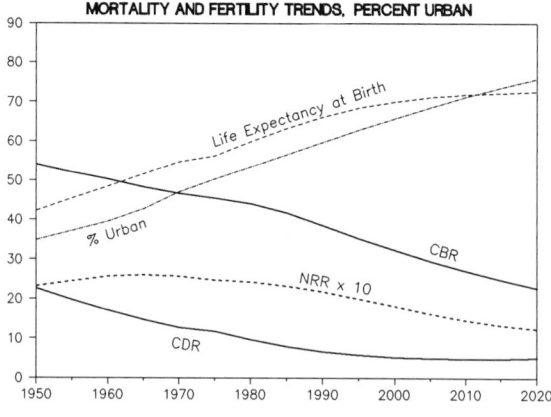

MORTALITY AND FERTILITY TRENDS, PERCENT URBAN

FERTILITY MEASURES (Annual Averages)

PERIOD	CRUDE BIRTH RATE	FERTILITY RATES GENERAL	FERTILITY RATES TOTAL	REPRODUCTION RATES GROSS	REPRODUCTION RATES NET	RATE OF NATUR. INCR.
1950-55	54.13	234.79	7.330	3.580	2.325	31.47
1955-60	52.14	234.05	7.330	3.580	2.454	32.41
1960-65	50.33	231.89	7.330	3.580	2.579	33.26
1965-70	48.38	223.08	7.100	3.460	2.616	33.67
1970-75	46.79	213.84	6.710	3.270	2.581	34.12
1975-80	45.58	206.49	6.311	3.080	2.479	33.83
1980-85	44.21	197.77	5.939	2.900	2.430	34.49
1985-90	*41.80*	*184.55*	*5.500*	*2.680*	*2.333*	*33.81*
1990-95	*38.70*	*167.98*	*5.010*	*2.440*	*2.185*	*32.04*
2000-05	*32.39*	*133.69*	*4.010*	*1.960*	*1.809*	*27.18*
2010-15	*27.17*	*106.89*	*3.200*	*1.560*	*1.464*	*22.33*
2020-25	*22.86*	*87.20*	*2.679*	*1.310*	*1.233*	*17.77*

AGING MEASURES

YEAR	POPULATION AGE RATIOS 60+/20-59	65+/20-64	70+/20-69	75+/20-74	POPULATION MEAN AGE	POPULATION MEDIAN AGE
1950	0.1011	0.0591	0.0309	0.0136	21.94	17.59
1960	0.1020	0.0583	0.0301	0.0134	21.03	16.04
1970	0.1050	0.0619	0.0331	0.0146	20.80	15.75
1980	0.1036	0.0616	0.0331	0.0152	20.90	16.16
1990	*0.1105*	*0.0669*	*0.0366*	*0.0178*	*21.46*	*16.92*
2000	*0.1130*	*0.0719*	*0.0423*	*0.0215*	*22.71*	*18.31*
2010	*0.1166*	*0.0736*	*0.0445*	*0.0240*	*24.57*	*20.58*
2020	*0.1387*	*0.0859*	*0.0487*	*0.0259*	*26.88*	*23.45*

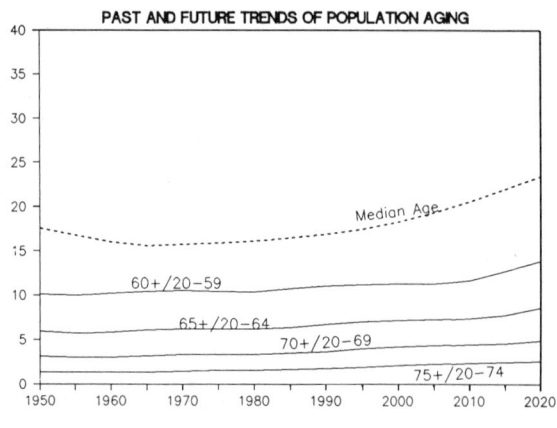

PAST AND FUTURE TRENDS OF POPULATION AGING

OBSERVED AND *PROJECTED* POPULATION DATA

YEAR	MID-YEAR POPULATION	NO. OF BIRTHS	NO. OF DEATHS	URBAN POPULATION NUMBER	URBAN POPULATION PERCENT	POPULATION 1985 AGE	POPULATION 1985 NUMBER
1950	892500	35968	11763	319196	35.8	0	280885
1955	1010700	41449	11057	388820	38.5	5	270153
1960	1147700	46872	10995	473425	41.2	10	267724
1965	1326000	52125	11178	589167	44.4	15	246560
1970	1531000	54703	11207	729394	47.6	20	213763
1975	1747800	54164	10487	858005	49.1	25	180920
1980	1956454	54792	10539	988811	50.5	30	146576
1985	2180488	58175	11258	1143593	52.4	35	122609
1990	*2417954*	*60287*	*12472*	*1324357*	*54.8*	40	99940
1995	*2659055*	*60693*	*13925*	*1527952*	*57.5*	45	80602
2000	*2893281*	*60342*	*15601*	*1748856*	*60.4*	50	68464
2005	*3115686*	*59902*	*17604*	*1982621*	*63.6*	55	57505
2010	*3324361*	*59898*	*19976*	*2214225*	*66.6*	60	47204
2015	*3519945*	*59938*	*22785*	*2441538*	*69.4*	65	38403
2020	*3700586*	*59683*	*26174*	*2661068*	*71.9*	70+	59180

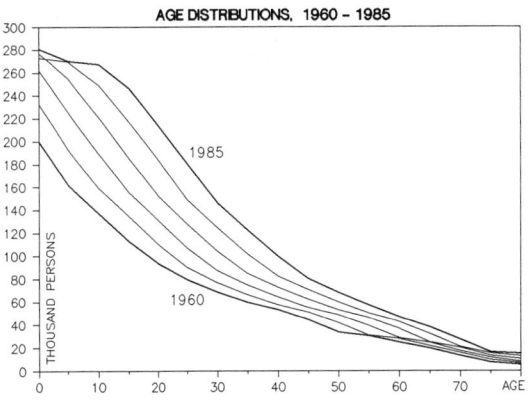

AGE DISTRIBUTIONS, 1960 - 1985

POPULATION RATIOS

YEAR	AGE DISTRIBUTION UNDER 15	AGE DISTRIBUTION 15-64	AGE DISTRIBUTION 65 & OLDER	AGE DISTRIBUTION 70 & OLDER	DEPENDENCY RATIO	WOMEN 15-49	CHILD-WOMAN RATIO
1950	0.410	0.551	0.039	0.023	0.815	0.223	0.743
1955	0.424	0.537	0.039	0.022	0.862	0.219	0.770
1960	0.435	0.525	0.040	0.023	0.905	0.218	0.798
1965	0.441	0.518	0.041	0.024	0.929	0.216	0.811
1970	0.442	0.517	0.041	0.025	0.933	0.216	0.792
1975	0.431	0.530	0.039	0.025	0.888	0.222	0.713
1980	0.405	0.554	0.041	0.025	0.806	0.233	0.600
1985	0.375	0.580	0.045	0.027	0.725	0.245	0.525
1990	*0.350*	*0.603*	*0.048*	*0.030*	*0.659*	*0.256*	*0.482*
2000	*0.315*	*0.631*	*0.054*	*0.035*	*0.585*	*0.264*	*0.406*
2010	*0.275*	*0.661*	*0.065*	*0.041*	*0.513*	*0.267*	*0.341*
2020	*0.243*	*0.674*	*0.083*	*0.052*	*0.484*	*0.258*	*0.316*

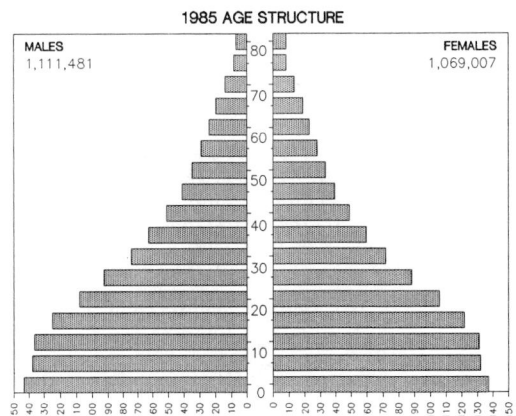

1985 AGE STRUCTURE

MALES 1,111,481   FEMALES 1,069,007

MORTALITY MEASURES (Annual Averages)

PERIOD	CRUDE DEATH RATE	INFANT MORT. RATE	LIFE EXPECTANCY AT BIRTH (years) MALE	LIFE EXPECTANCY AT BIRTH (years) FEMALE	LIFE EXPECTANCY AT BIRTH (years) BOTH SEXES	DIFFERENCE FEMALE-MALE
1950-55	13.18	93.04	54.35	56.22	55.26	1.87
1955-60	10.94	74.91	58.35	60.37	59.33	2.02
1960-65	9.58	62.69	60.91	63.12	61.99	2.21
1965-70	8.43	51.60	63.08	65.52	64.27	2.44
1970-75	7.32	42.82	65.00	67.75	66.34	2.75
1975-80	6.00	31.57	67.60	70.85	69.18	3.25
1980-85	5.39	25.65	69.20	72.85	70.98	3.65
1985-90	*5.16*	*23.00*	*70.15*	*74.10*	*72.08*	*3.95*
1990-95	*5.16*	*21.00*	*70.75*	*74.93*	*72.79*	*4.18*
2000-05	*5.39*	*19.00*	*71.45*	*75.95*	*73.64*	*4.50*
2010-15	*6.01*	*17.00*	*71.81*	*76.46*	*74.08*	*4.65*
2020-25	*7.07*	*17.00*	*72.04*	*76.73*	*74.33*	*4.69*

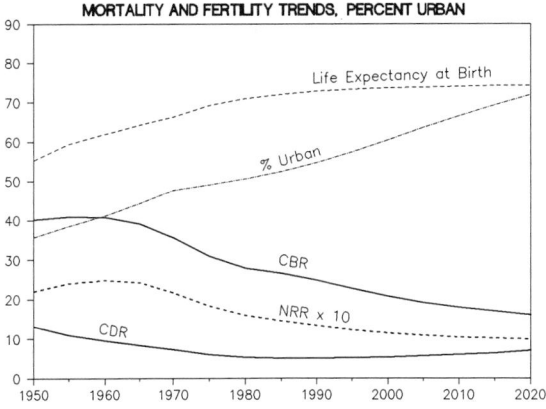

MORTALITY AND FERTILITY TRENDS, PERCENT URBAN

Life Expectancy at Birth

% Urban

CBR

NRR x 10

CDR

FERTILITY MEASURES (Annual Averages)

PERIOD	CRUDE BIRTH RATE	FERTILITY RATES GENERAL	FERTILITY RATES TOTAL	REPRODUCTION RATES GROSS	REPRODUCTION RATES NET	RATE OF NATUR. INCR.
1950-55	40.30	182.57	5.678	2.770	2.217	27.12
1955-60	41.01	187.77	5.883	2.870	2.407	30.07
1960-65	40.84	188.16	5.924	2.890	2.489	31.26
1965-70	39.31	181.79	5.617	2.740	2.426	30.88
1970-75	35.73	162.89	4.940	2.410	2.178	28.41
1975-80	30.99	136.16	4.059	1.980	1.842	24.99
1980-85	28.01	117.02	3.464	1.690	1.596	22.62
1985-90	*26.68*	*106.31*	*3.139*	*1.530*	*1.458*	*21.52*
1990-95	*24.93*	*96.42*	*2.871*	*1.400*	*1.340*	*19.78*
2000-05	*20.86*	*78.65*	*2.480*	*1.210*	*1.164*	*15.46*
2010-15	*18.02*	*67.89*	*2.239*	*1.090*	*1.054*	*12.01*
2020-25	*16.13*	*63.38*	*2.120*	*1.030*	*0.999*	*9.06*

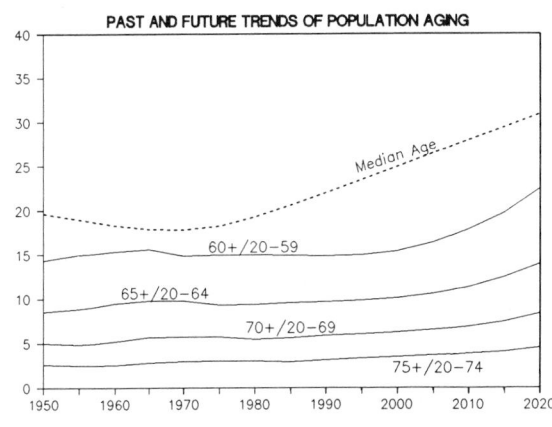

PAST AND FUTURE TRENDS OF POPULATION AGING

Median Age

60+/20-59

65+/20-64

70+/20-69

75+/20-74

AGING MEASURES

YEAR	POPULATION AGE RATIOS 60+/20-59	POPULATION AGE RATIOS 65+/20-64	POPULATION AGE RATIOS 70+/20-69	POPULATION AGE RATIOS 75+/20-74	POPULATION MEAN AGE	POPULATION MEDIAN AGE
1950	0.1437	0.0853	0.0496	0.0261	24.32	19.65
1960	0.1536	0.0946	0.0518	0.0251	23.55	18.31
1970	0.1489	0.0976	0.0571	0.0296	23.15	17.84
1980	0.1497	0.0934	0.0543	0.0303	24.15	19.29
1990	*0.1490*	*0.0969*	*0.0587*	*0.0310*	*25.95*	*22.03*
2000	*0.1539*	*0.1011*	*0.0623*	*0.0346*	*28.05*	*25.00*
2010	*0.1785*	*0.1132*	*0.0684*	*0.0383*	*30.54*	*27.97*
2020	*0.2245*	*0.1399*	*0.0835*	*0.0451*	*33.08*	*30.97*

OBSERVED AND *PROJECTED* POPULATION DATA

YEAR	MID-YEAR POPULATION	NO. OF BIRTHS	NO. OF DEATHS	URBAN POPULATION NUMBER	URBAN POPULATION PERCENT	POPULATION 1985 AGE	POPULATION 1985 NUMBER
1950	1350535	63892	12622	466850	34.6	0	580564
1955	1552008	69060	13864	544240	35.1	5	493061
1960	1773695	75082	14383	630890	35.6	10	439818
1965	2050911	80949	15622	743314	36.2	15	400772
1970	2351486	86043	16879	871591	37.1	20	360800
1975	2681586	94853	18447	1045340	39.0	25	317194
1980	3146759	112572	21206	1311829	41.7	30	277933
1985	3693262	128703	24268	1641484	44.4	35	180157
1990	*4276673*	*141284*	*27285*	*2029894*	*47.5*	40	143120
1995	*4892699*	*151493*	*30477*	*2479969*	*50.7*	45	120997
2000	*5537642*	*161655*	*34034*	*2992627*	*54.0*	50	95115
2005	*6214744*	*172484*	*37494*	*3570165*	*57.4*	55	84172
2010	*6928425*	*183395*	*43240*	*4213901*	*60.8*	60	70496
2015	*7666513*	*193234*	*49004*	*4905352*	*64.0*	65	53355
2020	*8423258*	*201038*	*55754*	*5637846*	*66.9*	70+	75707

POPULATION RATIOS

YEAR	AGE DISTRIBUTION UNDER 15	AGE DISTRIBUTION 15-64	AGE DISTRIBUTION 65 & OLDER	AGE DISTRIBUTION 70 & OLDER	DEPENDENCY RATIO	WOMEN 15-49	CHILD-WOMAN RATIO
1950	0.429	0.539	0.032	0.018	0.856	0.238	0.692
1955	0.454	0.514	0.032	0.019	0.946	0.225	0.895
1960	0.477	0.490	0.033	0.019	1.039	0.213	0.896
1965	0.487	0.480	0.033	0.019	1.085	0.207	0.882
1970	0.464	0.502	0.034	0.020	0.993	0.217	0.792
1975	0.443	0.522	0.035	0.020	0.915	0.223	0.719
1980	0.421	0.545	0.035	0.021	0.836	0.233	0.667
1985	0.410	0.555	0.035	0.020	0.801	0.238	0.659
1990	*0.404*	*0.561*	*0.036*	*0.021*	*0.784*	*0.241*	*0.637*
2000	*0.382*	*0.582*	*0.036*	*0.022*	*0.719*	*0.250*	*0.554*
2010	*0.350*	*0.611*	*0.040*	*0.024*	*0.638*	*0.252*	*0.498*
2020	*0.324*	*0.623*	*0.052*	*0.028*	*0.605*	*0.252*	*0.456*

MORTALITY MEASURES (Annual Averages)

PERIOD	CRUDE DEATH RATE	INFANT MORT. RATE	LIFE EXPECTANCY AT BIRTH (years) MALE	LIFE EXPECTANCY AT BIRTH (years) FEMALE	LIFE EXPECTANCY AT BIRTH (years) BOTH SEXES	DIFFERENCE FEMALE-MALE
1950-55	9.35	106.00	60.68	64.66	62.62	3.98
1955-60	8.93	91.00	61.27	65.24	63.21	3.97
1960-65	8.11	81.00	62.46	66.40	64.38	3.94
1965-70	7.62	67.00	63.07	66.99	64.98	3.92
1970-75	7.18	53.00	63.68	67.58	65.58	3.90
1975-80	6.88	49.00	64.05	68.08	66.02	4.03
1980-85	6.74	45.00	64.42	68.57	66.44	4.15
1985-90	*6.57*	*42.00*	*64.79*	*69.05*	*66.87*	*4.26*
1990-95	*6.38*	*39.00*	*65.15*	*69.53*	*67.29*	*4.38*
2000-05	*6.15*	*33.00*	*65.85*	*70.46*	*68.10*	*4.61*
2010-15	*6.24*	*28.00*	*66.53*	*71.35*	*68.88*	*4.82*
2020-25	*6.62*	*24.00*	*67.18*	*72.21*	*69.63*	*5.03*

FERTILITY MEASURES (Annual Averages)

PERIOD	CRUDE BIRTH RATE	FERTILITY RATES GENERAL	FERTILITY RATES TOTAL	REPRODUCTION RATES GROSS	REPRODUCTION RATES NET	RATE OF NATUR. INCR.
1950-55	47.31	205.15	6.800	3.320	2.885	37.96
1955-60	44.50	203.92	6.800	3.320	2.906	35.56
1960-65	42.33	202.08	6.800	3.320	2.948	34.22
1965-70	39.47	186.16	6.400	3.120	2.795	31.85
1970-75	36.59	166.13	5.650	2.760	2.487	29.41
1975-80	35.37	154.78	5.049	2.460	2.232	28.49
1980-85	35.77	151.66	4.818	2.350	2.138	29.03
1985-90	*34.85*	*145.24*	*4.578*	*2.230*	*2.040*	*28.28*
1990-95	*33.04*	*136.01*	*4.338*	*2.120*	*1.940*	*26.66*
2000-05	*29.19*	*116.68*	*3.868*	*1.890*	*1.742*	*23.05*
2010-15	*26.47*	*105.17*	*3.448*	*1.680*	*1.564*	*20.23*
2020-25	*23.87*	*94.46*	*3.098*	*1.510*	*1.414*	*17.25*

AGING MEASURES

YEAR	POPULATION AGE RATIOS 60+/20-59	POPULATION AGE RATIOS 65+/20-64	POPULATION AGE RATIOS 70+/20-69	POPULATION AGE RATIOS 75+/20-74	POPULATION MEAN AGE	POPULATION MEDIAN AGE
1950	0.1211	0.0739	0.0414	0.0202	22.86	18.26
1960	0.1365	0.0834	0.0470	0.0232	21.91	16.22
1970	0.1463	0.0896	0.0506	0.0251	22.00	16.46
1980	0.1308	0.0804	0.0464	0.0232	22.86	18.43
1990	*0.1227*	*0.0779*	*0.0446*	*0.0224*	*23.62*	*19.69*
2000	*0.1189*	*0.0750*	*0.0454*	*0.0238*	*24.83*	*20.81*
2010	*0.1258*	*0.0777*	*0.0458*	*0.0241*	*26.42*	*22.65*
2020	*0.1679*	*0.0991*	*0.0504*	*0.0256*	*28.05*	*24.57*

AGE DISTRIBUTIONS, 1960 - 1985

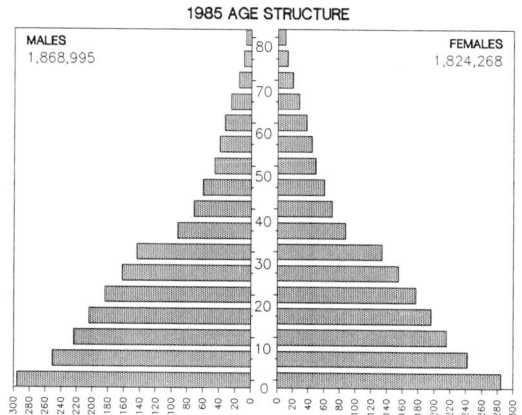

1985 AGE STRUCTURE

MALES 1,868,995 — FEMALES 1,824,268

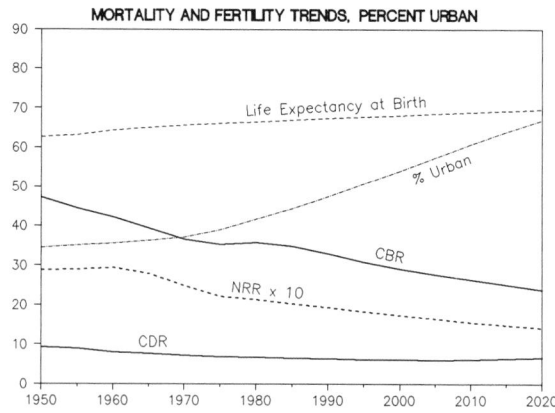

MORTALITY AND FERTILITY TRENDS, PERCENT URBAN

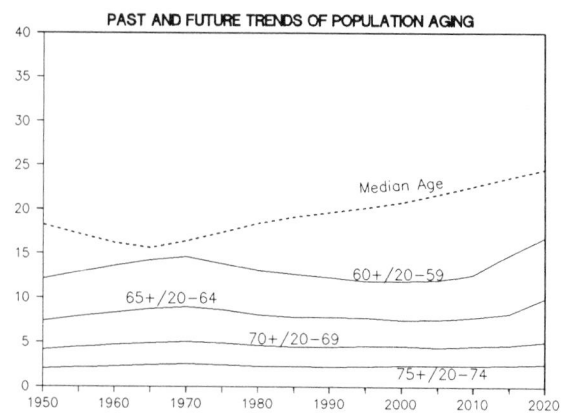

PAST AND FUTURE TRENDS OF POPULATION AGING

OBSERVED AND *PROJECTED* POPULATION DATA (000's)

YEAR	MID-YEAR POPULATION	NO. OF BIRTHS	NO. OF DEATHS	URBAN POPULATION NUMBER	PERCENT	POPULATION 1985 AGE	NUMBER
1950	7632	359	165	2711	35.5	0	3000
1955	8672	406	171	3537	40.8	5	2602
1960	9931	460	174	4597	46.3	10	2369
1965	11467	500	179	5948	51.9	15	2123
1970	13193	535	168	7574	57.4	20	1867
1975	15161	576	177	9313	61.4	25	1555
1980	17295	635	186	11153	64.5	30	1294
1985	19698	676	182	13282	67.4	35	1047
1990	*22332*	*697*	*172*	*15681*	*70.2*	40	865
1995	*25123*	*704*	*168*	*18292*	*72.8*	45	746
2000	*27952*	*704*	*172*	*21014*	*75.2*	50	631
2005	*30746*	*708*	*185*	*23771*	*77.3*	55	503
2010	*33479*	*710*	*201*	*26519*	*79.2*	60	389
2015	*36124*	*710*	*222*	*29242*	*80.9*	65	293
2020	*38647*	*705*	*247*	*31898*	*82.5*	70+	415

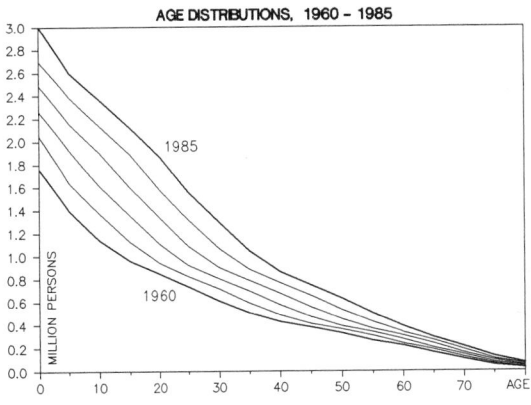

AGE DISTRIBUTIONS, 1960 - 1985

POPULATION RATIOS

YEAR	AGE DISTRIBUTION UNDER 15	15-64	65 & OLDER	70 & OLDER	DEPENDENCY RATIO	WOMEN 15-49	CHILD-WOMAN RATIO
1950	0.416	0.550	0.035	0.020	0.819	0.229	0.734
1955	0.423	0.543	0.034	0.018	0.841	0.227	0.772
1960	0.433	0.532	0.034	0.018	0.878	0.223	0.795
1965	0.441	0.524	0.035	0.019	0.910	0.220	0.812
1970	0.440	0.525	0.035	0.019	0.904	0.222	0.772
1975	0.432	0.532	0.035	0.020	0.879	0.226	0.725
1980	0.418	0.546	0.036	0.021	0.830	0.233	0.669
1985	0.405	0.559	0.036	0.021	0.788	0.238	0.639
1990	*0.392*	*0.572*	*0.037*	*0.021*	*0.749*	*0.243*	*0.597*
2000	*0.356*	*0.601*	*0.043*	*0.025*	*0.664*	*0.254*	*0.485*
2010	*0.307*	*0.641*	*0.052*	*0.032*	*0.561*	*0.265*	*0.392*
2020	*0.268*	*0.666*	*0.066*	*0.039*	*0.502*	*0.265*	*0.340*

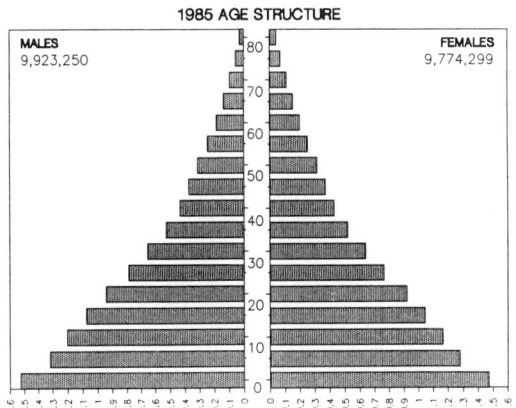

1985 AGE STRUCTURE

MALES 9,923,250   FEMALES 9,774,299

MORTALITY MEASURES (Annual Averages)

PERIOD	CRUDE DEATH RATE	INFANT MORT. RATE	LIFE EXPECTANCY AT BIRTH (years) MALE	FEMALE	BOTH SEXES	DIFFERENCE FEMALE-MALE
1950-55	21.58	159.00	42.86	45.00	43.90	2.14
1955-60	19.71	148.00	45.11	47.50	46.28	2.39
1960-65	17.56	136.00	47.82	50.50	49.13	2.68
1965-70	15.59	126.00	50.07	53.00	51.50	2.93
1970-75	12.75	110.00	53.88	57.25	55.52	3.37
1975-80	11.71	105.00	55.22	58.75	56.94	3.53
1980-85	10.74	99.00	56.78	60.51	58.60	3.72
1985-90	*9.24*	*88.00*	*59.51*	*63.38*	*61.40*	*3.87*
1990-95	*7.69*	*76.00*	*62.74*	*66.55*	*64.60*	*3.81*
2000-05	*6.14*	*60.00*	*66.83*	*70.76*	*68.75*	*3.93*
2010-15	*6.00*	*52.00*	*68.82*	*72.78*	*70.75*	*3.96*
2020-25	*6.40*	*47.00*	*70.05*	*74.04*	*72.00*	*3.99*

FERTILITY MEASURES (Annual Averages)

PERIOD	CRUDE BIRTH RATE	FERTILITY RATES GENERAL	TOTAL	REPRODUCTION RATES GROSS	NET	RATE OF NATUR. INCR.
1950-55	47.08	206.68	6.853	3.350	2.148	25.49
1955-60	46.79	208.32	6.853	3.350	2.250	27.08
1960-65	46.27	209.23	6.853	3.350	2.369	28.72
1965-70	43.58	197.15	6.560	3.200	2.357	27.99
1970-75	40.52	180.58	5.999	2.930	2.297	27.77
1975-80	38.01	165.24	5.378	2.620	2.104	26.30
1980-85	36.71	155.60	5.000	2.440	2.002	25.98
1985-90	*34.31*	*142.44*	*4.490*	*2.190*	*1.863*	*25.07*
1990-95	*31.21*	*127.06*	*3.970*	*1.940*	*1.704*	*23.52*
2000-05	*25.19*	*97.82*	*3.100*	*1.510*	*1.383*	*19.04*
2010-15	*21.20*	*79.94*	*2.550*	*1.240*	*1.156*	*15.20*
2020-25	*18.24*	*69.23*	*2.260*	*1.100*	*1.034*	*11.85*

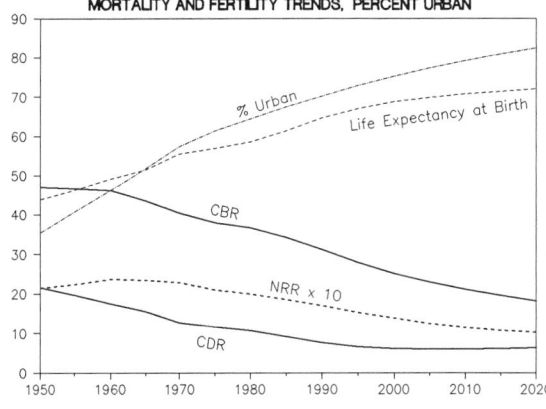

MORTALITY AND FERTILITY TRENDS, PERCENT URBAN

AGING MEASURES

YEAR	POPULATION AGE RATIOS 60+/20-59	65+/20-64	70+/20-69	75+/20-74	POPULATION MEAN AGE	MEDIAN AGE
1950	0.1334	0.0772	0.0425	0.0190	23.93	19.13
1960	0.1364	0.0789	0.0405	0.0172	23.29	18.45
1970	0.1380	0.0820	0.0445	0.0197	22.98	17.91
1980	0.1323	0.0821	0.0454	0.0209	23.47	18.76
1990	*0.1294*	*0.0789*	*0.0445*	*0.0219*	*24.35*	*20.16*
2000	*0.1398*	*0.0867*	*0.0486*	*0.0236*	*26.01*	*22.21*
2010	*0.1528*	*0.0959*	*0.0562*	*0.0284*	*28.31*	*24.97*
2020	*0.1843*	*0.1138*	*0.0651*	*0.0333*	*30.82*	*28.29*

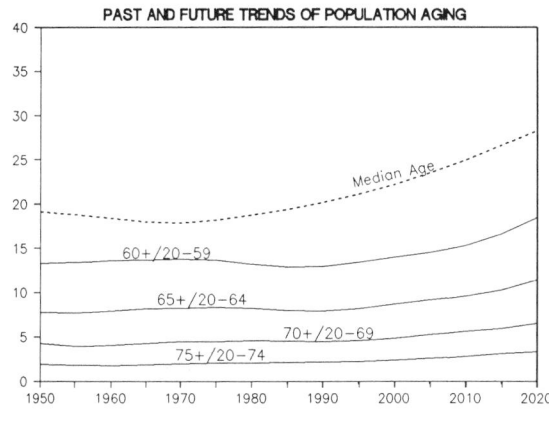

PAST AND FUTURE TRENDS OF POPULATION AGING

OBSERVED AND *PROJECTED* POPULATION DATA

YEAR	MID-YEAR POPULATION	NO. OF BIRTHS	NO. OF DEATHS	URBAN POPULATION NUMBER	URBAN POPULATION PERCENT	POPULATION 1985 AGE	POPULATION 1985 NUMBER
1950	2219000	81215	19971	900730	40.6	0	354070
1955	2250000	75375	15750	954723	42.4	5	340267
1960	2358000	73805	16270	1050411	44.5	10	330128
1965	2594000	69519	17120	1336521	51.5	15	337727
1970	2718000	66455	18075	1585332	58.3	20	335787
1975	2993000	71233	19305	1878701	62.8	25	270949
1980	3199300	69489	21141	2143748	67.0	30	234486
1985	3450532	72375	22549	2440794	70.7	35	227731
1990	3708979	72422	24212	2742288	73.9	40	191976
1995	3958111	70961	25589	3032678	76.6	45	162948
2000	4191670	69422	27149	3303953	78.8	50	141365
2005	4408512	69311	28907	3552882	80.6	55	124766
2010	4615276	70868	31250	3794211	82.2	60	112653
2015	4817726	71529	34273	4031924	83.7	65	96023
2020	5007676	71289	37823	4258608	85.0	70+	189656

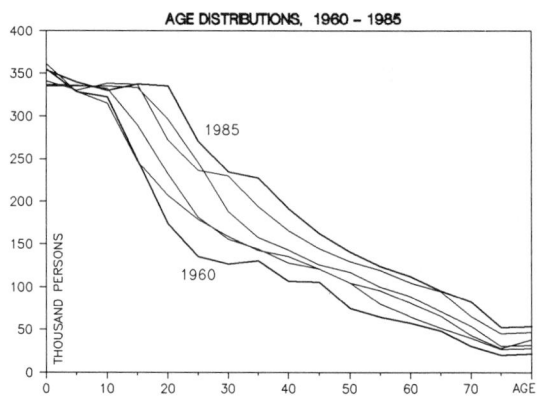

AGE DISTRIBUTIONS, 1960 - 1985

POPULATION RATIOS

YEAR	AGE DISTRIBUTION UNDER 15	AGE DISTRIBUTION 15-64	AGE DISTRIBUTION 65 & OLDER	AGE DISTRIBUTION 70 & OLDER	DEPENDENCY RATIO	WOMEN 15-49	CHILD-WOMAN RATIO
1950	0.433	0.529	0.038	0.024	0.892	0.228	0.729
1955	0.429	0.525	0.046	0.028	0.905	0.228	0.692
1960	0.427	0.521	0.052	0.031	0.920	0.227	0.664
1965	0.387	0.556	0.057	0.037	0.799	0.243	0.573
1970	0.370	0.565	0.065	0.040	0.770	0.242	0.513
1975	0.336	0.601	0.063	0.039	0.664	0.259	0.432
1980	0.316	0.605	0.079	0.049	0.652	0.259	0.412
1985	0.297	0.620	0.083	0.055	0.612	0.265	0.388
1990	0.286	0.628	0.086	0.058	0.593	0.265	0.375
2000	0.262	0.647	0.091	0.062	0.545	0.261	0.330
2010	0.230	0.665	0.105	0.070	0.504	0.257	0.297
2020	0.214	0.660	0.126	0.087	0.515	0.239	0.302

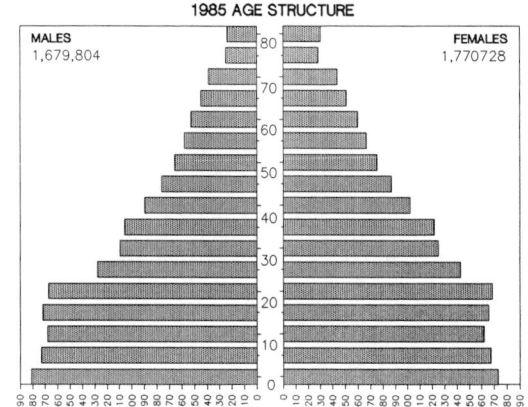

1985 AGE STRUCTURE

MALES 1,679,804   FEMALES 1,770728

MORTALITY MEASURES (Annual Averages)

PERIOD	CRUDE DEATH RATE	INFANT MORT. RATE	LIFE EXPECTANCY AT BIRTH (years) MALE	LIFE EXPECTANCY AT BIRTH (years) FEMALE	LIFE EXPECTANCY AT BIRTH (years) BOTH SEXES	DIFFERENCE FEMALE-MALE
1950-55	9.00	63.23	63.00	66.70	64.81	3.70
1955-60	7.00	51.19	66.60	70.70	68.60	4.10
1960-65	6.90	44.54	67.00	72.50	69.68	5.50
1965-70	6.60	33.26	68.20	73.50	70.79	5.30
1970-75	6.65	25.30	69.00	76.20	72.51	7.20
1975-80	6.45	19.93	70.20	77.00	73.52	6.80
1980-85	6.61	16.60	70.53	77.60	73.98	7.07
1985-90	6.53	15.00	71.51	78.43	74.89	6.91
1990-95	6.53	13.00	72.54	79.18	75.78	6.64
2000-05	6.48	10.00	74.15	80.58	77.28	6.43
2010-15	6.77	9.00	75.54	81.57	78.48	6.04
2020-25	7.55	8.00	76.47	82.55	79.43	6.08

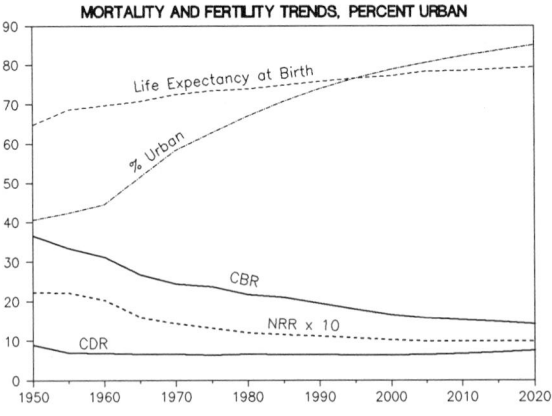

MORTALITY AND FERTILITY TRENDS, PERCENT URBAN

FERTILITY MEASURES (Annual Averages)

PERIOD	CRUDE BIRTH RATE	FERTILITY RATES GENERAL	FERTILITY RATES TOTAL	REPRODUCTION RATES GROSS	REPRODUCTION RATES NET	RATE OF NATUR. INCR.
1950-55	36.60	160.67	5.022	2.450	2.240	27.60
1955-60	33.50	147.30	4.817	2.350	2.230	26.50
1960-65	31.30	133.04	4.366	2.130	2.040	24.40
1965-70	26.80	110.57	3.403	1.660	1.600	20.20
1970-75	24.45	97.38	2.993	1.460	1.430	17.80
1975-80	23.80	91.89	2.747	1.340	1.320	17.35
1980-85	21.72	82.99	2.563	1.250	1.207	15.11
1985-90	20.98	79.15	2.438	1.200	1.162	14.44
1990-95	19.53	73.72	2.336	1.150	1.117	13.00
2000-05	16.56	63.47	2.133	1.050	1.024	10.09
2010-15	15.35	60.93	2.072	1.020	0.996	8.59
2020-25	14.24	60.25	2.072	1.020	0.997	6.68

AGING MEASURES

YEAR	POPULATION AGE RATIOS 60+/20-59	POPULATION AGE RATIOS 65+/20-64	POPULATION AGE RATIOS 70+/20-69	POPULATION AGE RATIOS 75+/20-74	POPULATION MEAN AGE	POPULATION MEDIAN AGE
1950	0.1484	0.0893	0.0539	0.0267	23.34	18.36
1960	0.1965	0.1256	0.0720	0.0406	24.73	18.45
1970	0.2207	0.1413	0.0838	0.0493	27.07	21.35
1980	0.2394	0.1580	0.0934	0.0526	29.26	24.62
1990	0.2320	0.1592	0.1021	0.0596	30.58	26.90
2000	0.2380	0.1612	0.1049	0.0633	32.30	29.74
2010	0.2744	0.1787	0.1127	0.0669	34.46	32.44
2020	0.3226	0.2144	0.1386	0.0794	36.53	34.98

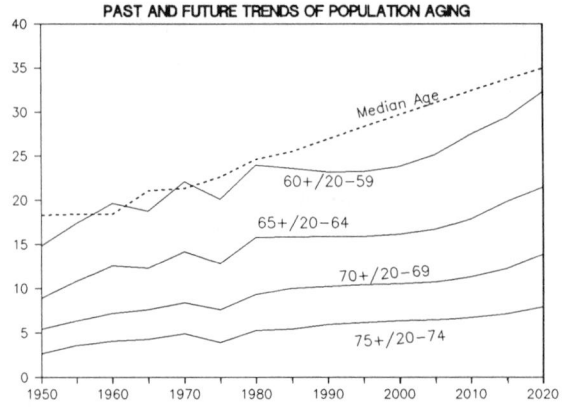

PAST AND FUTURE TRENDS OF POPULATION AGING

OBSERVED AND *PROJECTED* POPULATION DATA

YEAR	MID-YEAR POPULATION	NO. OF BIRTHS	NO. OF DEATHS	URBAN POPULATION NUMBER	URBAN POPULATION PERCENT	POPULATION 1985 AGE	POPULATION 1985 NUMBER
1950	215000	9417	2709	100808	46.9	0	50101
1955	250000	11100	2850	117685	47.1	5	41223
1960	290000	12876	2987	137055	47.3	10	48257
1965	332200	13288	2923	156494	47.1	15	47590
1970	372300	12882	2792	171062	45.9	20	42420
1975	364499	10753	2661	163262	44.8	25	29507
1980	354860	10224	2430	158944	44.8	30	20996
1985	374934	9693	2295	171189	45.7	35	16204
1990	*403380*	*9346*	*2274*	*191718*	*47.5*	40	14990
1995	*435150*	*8824*	*2330*	*219169*	*50.4*	45	14479
2000	*468877*	*8913*	*2503*	*253658*	*54.1*	50	13552
2005	*502061*	*9043*	*2704*	*289477*	*57.7*	55	11043
2010	*534787*	*9219*	*2917*	*326322*	*61.0*	60	8567
2015	*567256*	*9241*	*3170*	*364006*	*64.2*	65	5619
2020	*598444*	*9209*	*3473*	*401581*	*67.1*	70+	10386

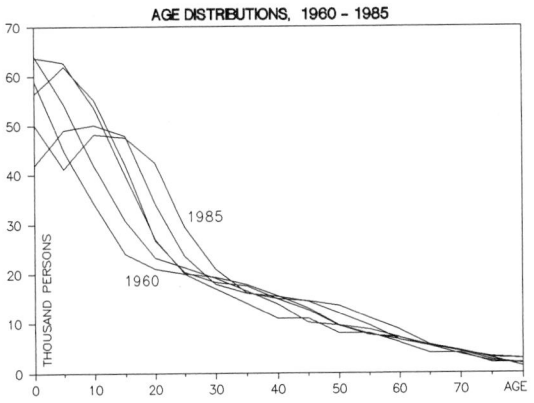

AGE DISTRIBUTIONS, 1960 - 1985

POPULATION RATIOS

YEAR	AGE DISTRIBUTION UNDER 15	AGE DISTRIBUTION 15-64	AGE DISTRIBUTION 65 & OLDER	AGE DISTRIBUTION 70 & OLDER	DEPENDENCY RATIO	WOMEN 15-49	CHILD-WOMAN RATIO
1950	0.400	0.540	0.060	0.042	0.853	0.228	0.755
1955	0.432	0.520	0.048	0.032	0.923	0.216	0.870
1960	0.476	0.483	0.041	0.028	1.071	0.207	0.983
1965	0.482	0.478	0.040	0.024	1.093	0.207	0.932
1970	0.483	0.478	0.039	0.024	1.093	0.208	0.823
1975	0.476	0.485	0.039	0.024	1.063	0.211	0.736
1980	0.398	0.558	0.045	0.029	0.794	0.245	0.483
1985	0.372	0.585	0.043	0.028	0.709	0.254	0.527
1990	*0.344*	*0.611*	*0.045*	*0.027*	*0.637*	*0.264*	*0.455*
2000	*0.298*	*0.647*	*0.055*	*0.033*	*0.546*	*0.281*	*0.339*
2010	*0.254*	*0.685*	*0.061*	*0.040*	*0.460*	*0.287*	*0.299*
2020	*0.233*	*0.697*	*0.069*	*0.043*	*0.434*	*0.261*	*0.301*

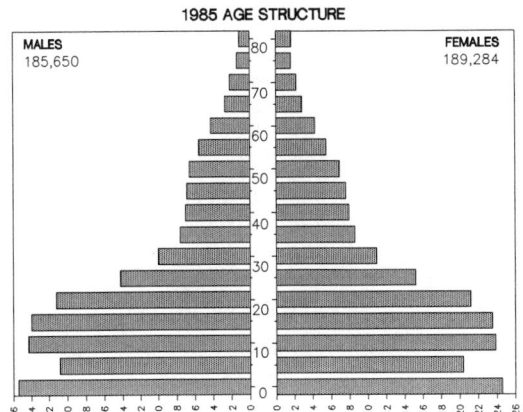

1985 AGE STRUCTURE

MALES 185,650   FEMALES 189,284

MORTALITY MEASURES (Annual Averages)

PERIOD	CRUDE DEATH RATE	INFANT MORT. RATE	LIFE EXPECTANCY AT BIRTH (years) MALE	LIFE EXPECTANCY AT BIRTH (years) FEMALE	LIFE EXPECTANCY AT BIRTH (years) BOTH SEXES	DIFFERENCE FEMALE-MALE
1950-55	12.60	89.23	54.40	57.70	56.01	3.30
1955-60	11.40	76.22	57.00	60.50	58.71	3.50
1960-65	10.30	63.46	59.70	63.40	61.51	3.70
1965-70	8.80	54.62	61.50	65.70	63.55	4.20
1970-75	7.50	48.84	62.70	67.30	64.94	4.60
1975-80	7.30	43.99	63.80	68.60	66.14	4.80
1980-85	6.85	36.18	65.55	70.60	68.01	5.05
1985-90	*6.12*	*30.53*	*67.05*	*72.10*	*69.51*	*5.05*
1990-95	*5.64*	*25.86*	*68.37*	*73.42*	*70.83*	*5.05*
2000-05	*5.34*	*18.66*	*70.65*	*75.70*	*73.11*	*5.05*
2010-15	*5.45*	*13.08*	*72.65*	*77.70*	*75.11*	*5.05*
2020-25	*5.80*	*9.30*	*74.25*	*79.30*	*76.71*	*5.05*

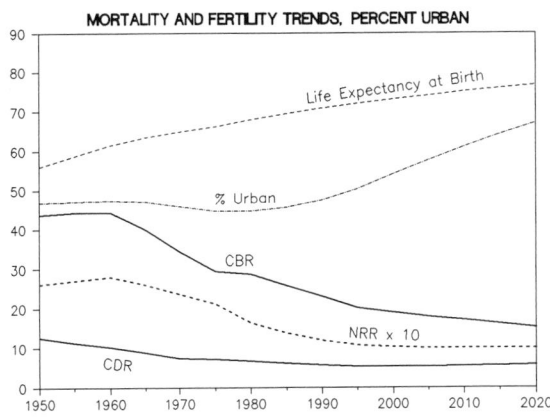

MORTALITY AND FERTILITY TRENDS, PERCENT URBAN

Life Expectancy at Birth

% Urban

CBR

NRR x 10

CDR

FERTILITY MEASURES (Annual Averages)

PERIOD	CRUDE BIRTH RATE	FERTILITY RATES GENERAL	FERTILITY RATES TOTAL	REPRODUCTION RATES GROSS	REPRODUCTION RATES NET	RATE OF NATUR. INCR.
1950-55	43.80	197.74	6.560	3.200	2.620	31.20
1955-60	44.40	210.32	6.560	3.200	2.720	33.00
1960-65	44.40	214.65	6.560	3.200	2.810	34.10
1965-70	40.00	192.88	5.945	2.900	2.610	31.20
1970-75	34.60	165.40	5.289	2.580	2.380	27.10
1975-80	29.50	129.78	4.633	2.260	2.130	22.20
1980-85	28.81	115.58	3.587	1.750	1.652	21.96
1985-90	*25.85*	*99.76*	*2.972*	*1.450*	*1.385*	*19.73*
1990-95	*23.17*	*87.16*	*2.563*	*1.250*	*1.204*	*17.53*
2000-05	*19.01*	*66.67*	*2.152*	*1.050*	*1.025*	*13.67*
2010-15	*17.24*	*61.53*	*2.091*	*1.020*	*1.005*	*11.78*
2020-25	*15.39*	*60.41*	*2.091*	*1.020*	*1.011*	*9.58*

AGING MEASURES

YEAR	POPULATION AGE RATIOS 60+/20-59	POPULATION AGE RATIOS 65+/20-64	POPULATION AGE RATIOS 70+/20-69	POPULATION AGE RATIOS 75+/20-74	POPULATION MEAN AGE	POPULATION MEDIAN AGE
1950	0.2000	0.1368	0.0909	0.0485	25.43	20.14
1960	0.1636	0.1034	0.0667	0.0323	22.60	16.46
1970	0.1635	0.1044	0.0613	0.0304	22.07	15.77
1980	0.1565	0.1057	0.0669	0.0382	24.36	18.78
1990	*0.1495*	*0.0913*	*0.0517*	*0.0287*	*25.67*	*21.78*
2000	*0.1584*	*0.1021*	*0.0579*	*0.0286*	*28.14*	*25.62*
2010	*0.1511*	*0.1026*	*0.0644*	*0.0345*	*30.86*	*28.81*
2020	*0.1891*	*0.1115*	*0.0659*	*0.0372*	*33.51*	*32.49*

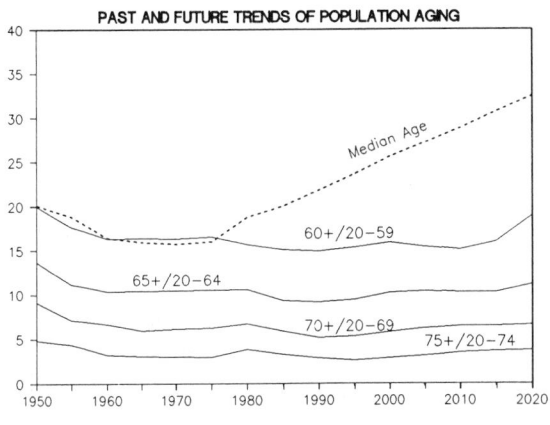

PAST AND FUTURE TRENDS OF POPULATION AGING

Median Age

60+/20-59

65+/20-64

70+/20-69

75+/20-74

OBSERVED AND *PROJECTED* POPULATION DATA

YEAR	MID-YEAR POPULATION	NO. OF BIRTHS	NO. OF DEATHS	URBAN POPULATION NUMBER	URBAN POPULATION PERCENT	POPULATION 1985 AGE	POPULATION 1985 NUMBER
1950	636000	24295	7187	145609	22.9	0	140011
1955	721000	27398	6705	162492	22.5	5	128733
1960	843000	32034	6491	189827	22.5	10	121389
1965	896400	27161	6723	269351	30.0	15	122442
1970	955337	25460	6850	370998	38.8	20	132488
1975	1008769	26541	6759	488360	48.4	25	109898
1980	1094934	27811	7659	623482	56.9	30	87906
1985	1184839	28401	7641	756857	63.9	35	72516
1990	*1282955*	*27518*	*7841*	*886503*	*69.1*	40	56811
1995	*1385265*	*26323*	*7976*	*1007632*	*72.7*	45	47241
2000	*1480141*	*26259*	*8412*	*1110349*	*75.0*	50	37053
2005	*1572151*	*26640*	*8991*	*1212227*	*77.1*	55	34790
2010	*1662940*	*27460*	*9780*	*1314074*	*79.0*	60	29143
2015	*1753757*	*27767*	*11003*	*1416575*	*80.8*	65	23580
2020	*1839633*	*27718*	*12370*	*1515426*	*82.4*	70+	40838

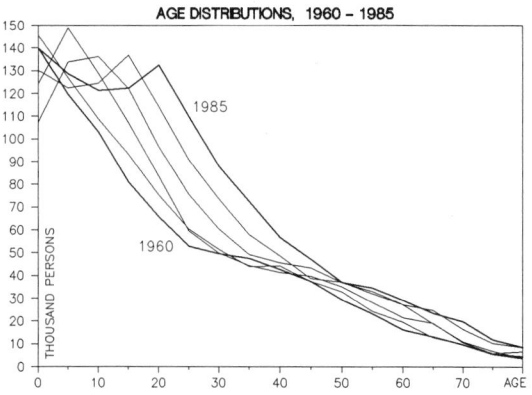

AGE DISTRIBUTIONS, 1960 – 1985

POPULATION RATIOS

YEAR	AGE DISTRIBUTION UNDER 15	AGE DISTRIBUTION 15-64	AGE DISTRIBUTION 65 & OLDER	AGE DISTRIBUTION 70 & OLDER	DEPENDENCY RATIO	WOMEN 15-49	CHILD-WOMAN RATIO
1950	0.404	0.557	0.039	0.024	0.797	0.237	0.702
1955	0.423	0.538	0.039	0.024	0.858	0.226	0.730
1960	0.430	0.530	0.040	0.024	0.887	0.226	0.734
1965	0.426	0.539	0.035	0.021	0.856	0.229	0.708
1970	0.421	0.535	0.044	0.024	0.870	0.229	0.569
1975	0.374	0.585	0.041	0.022	0.709	0.238	0.447
1980	0.344	0.601	0.055	0.032	0.665	0.257	0.462
1985	0.329	0.616	0.054	0.034	0.622	0.267	0.443
1990	*0.320*	*0.626*	*0.054*	*0.034*	*0.599*	*0.269*	*0.418*
2000	*0.282*	*0.663*	*0.055*	*0.035*	*0.508*	*0.277*	*0.327*
2010	*0.242*	*0.692*	*0.065*	*0.039*	*0.444*	*0.272*	*0.300*
2020	*0.226*	*0.683*	*0.091*	*0.054*	*0.464*	*0.250*	*0.307*

MORTALITY MEASURES (Annual Averages)

PERIOD	CRUDE DEATH RATE	INFANT MORT. RATE	LIFE EXPECTANCY AT BIRTH (years) MALE	LIFE EXPECTANCY AT BIRTH (years) FEMALE	LIFE EXPECTANCY AT BIRTH (years) BOTH SEXES	DIFFERENCE FEMALE-MALE
1950-55	11.30	78.60	56.40	59.40	57.86	3.00
1955-60	9.30	64.40	60.60	64.30	62.40	3.70
1960-65	7.70	43.80	62.80	67.00	64.85	4.20
1965-70	7.50	40.80	63.70	67.70	65.65	4.00
1970-75	7.17	30.20	64.40	68.70	66.50	4.30
1975-80	6.70	26.20	65.10	70.00	67.49	4.90
1980-85	6.99	24.03	66.20	71.33	68.71	5.13
1985-90	*6.45*	*20.00*	*67.74*	*72.78*	*70.21*	*5.04*
1990-95	*6.11*	*18.00*	*68.88*	*74.04*	*71.40*	*5.16*
2000-05	*5.68*	*13.00*	*71.12*	*76.19*	*73.61*	*5.06*
2010-15	*5.88*	*11.00*	*73.05*	*78.11*	*75.53*	*5.06*
2020-25	*6.72*	*9.00*	*74.65*	*79.76*	*77.16*	*5.11*

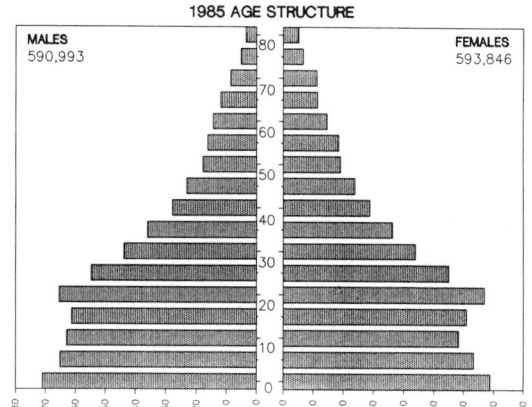

1985 AGE STRUCTURE

MALES 590,993 FEMALES 593,846

FERTILITY MEASURES (Annual Averages)

PERIOD	CRUDE BIRTH RATE	FERTILITY RATES GENERAL	FERTILITY RATES TOTAL	REPRODUCTION RATES GROSS	REPRODUCTION RATES NET	RATE OF NATUR. INCR.
1950-55	38.20	165.09	5.304	2.600	2.180	26.90
1955-60	38.00	167.98	5.304	2.600	2.310	28.70
1960-65	38.00	166.74	4.998	2.450	2.240	30.30
1965-70	30.30	132.34	3.876	1.900	1.750	22.80
1970-75	26.65	114.15	3.468	1.700	1.590	19.48
1975-80	26.31	106.09	3.060	1.500	1.440	19.61
1980-85	25.40	96.92	2.856	1.400	1.366	18.41
1985-90	*23.97*	*89.55*	*2.679*	*1.300*	*1.279*	*17.52*
1990-95	*21.45*	*79.21*	*2.473*	*1.200*	*1.188*	*15.34*
2000-05	*17.74*	*63.98*	*2.164*	*1.050*	*1.048*	*12.06*
2010-15	*16.51*	*62.36*	*2.102*	*1.020*	*1.023*	*10.63*
2020-25	*15.07*	*61.03*	*2.102*	*1.020*	*1.024*	*8.34*

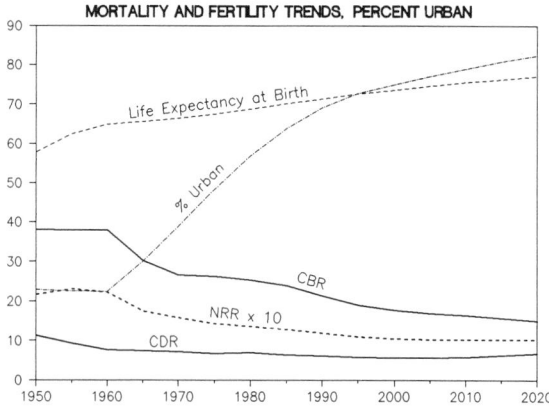

MORTALITY AND FERTILITY TRENDS, PERCENT URBAN

AGING MEASURES

YEAR	POPULATION AGE RATIOS 60+/20-59	POPULATION AGE RATIOS 65+/20-64	POPULATION AGE RATIOS 70+/20-69	POPULATION AGE RATIOS 75+/20-74	POPULATION MEAN AGE	POPULATION MEDIAN AGE
1950	0.1364	0.0833	0.0484	0.0252	24.76	20.70
1960	0.1423	0.0914	0.0531	0.0265	24.00	18.61
1970	0.1674	0.1050	0.0550	0.0291	24.35	18.53
1980	0.1772	0.1155	0.0649	0.0336	26.14	21.47
1990	*0.1555*	*0.1016*	*0.0620*	*0.0341*	*27.46*	*24.62*
2000	*0.1504*	*0.0959*	*0.0599*	*0.0322*	*29.61*	*27.33*
2010	*0.1779*	*0.1071*	*0.0620*	*0.0324*	*32.22*	*30.26*
2020	*0.2524*	*0.1485*	*0.0828*	*0.0412*	*34.65*	*33.37*

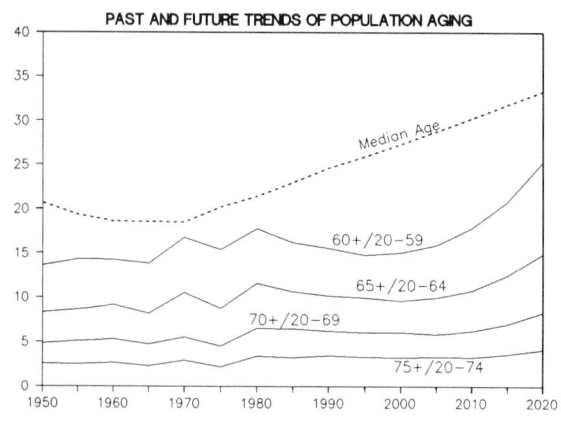

PAST AND FUTURE TRENDS OF POPULATION AGING

OBSERVED AND *PROJECTED* POPULATION DATA

YEAR	MID-YEAR POPULATION	NO. OF BIRTHS	NO. OF DEATHS	URBAN POPULATION NUMBER	URBAN POPULATION PERCENT	POPULATION 1985 AGE	POPULATION 1985 NUMBER
1950	2238505	47523	23536	1746458	78.0	0	275579
1955	2372025	52037	23865	1876221	79.1	5	269649
1960	2537802	55611	24256	2033726	80.1	10	264647
1965	2693381	55152	25967	2185338	81.1	15	241303
1970	2808426	59362	28250	2305671	82.1	20	244819
1975	2828543	57335	28763	2348224	83.0	25	219322
1980	2908416	56714	29750	2438102	83.8	30	188116
1985	3012147	56830	30850	2548519	84.6	35	177032
1990	*3128043*	*57059*	*32200*	*2673297*	*85.5*	40	167756
1995	*3246431*	*57485*	*33230*	*2804002*	*86.4*	45	167948
2000	*3363893*	*57644*	*34594*	*2937233*	*87.3*	50	170629
2005	*3475043*	*57919*	*35831*	*3067660*	*88.3*	55	163110
2010	*3581167*	*58033*	*36703*	*3195665*	*89.2*	60	139180
2015	*3683354*	*58098*	*37467*	*3319146*	*90.1*	65	109266
2020	*3781878*	*58218*	*38602*	*3438272*	*90.9*	70+	213791

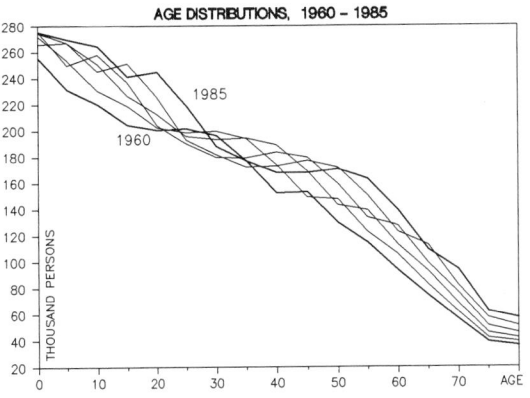

AGE DISTRIBUTIONS, 1960 – 1985

POPULATION RATIOS

YEAR	AGE DISTRIBUTION UNDER 15	AGE DISTRIBUTION 15-64	AGE DISTRIBUTION 65 & OLDER	AGE DISTRIBUTION 70 & OLDER	DEPENDENCY RATIO	WOMEN 15-49	CHILD-WOMAN RATIO
1950	0.279	0.639	0.082	0.053	0.565	0.251	0.392
1955	0.276	0.643	0.081	0.052	0.556	0.253	0.385
1960	0.279	0.640	0.081	0.052	0.562	0.252	0.400
1965	0.281	0.636	0.084	0.053	0.573	0.247	0.408
1970	0.279	0.632	0.089	0.056	0.582	0.245	0.386
1975	0.277	0.627	0.096	0.061	0.595	0.239	0.408
1980	0.271	0.625	0.104	0.065	0.599	0.236	0.400
1985	0.269	0.624	0.107	0.071	0.603	0.233	0.393
1990	*0.262*	*0.626*	*0.112*	*0.073*	*0.599*	*0.236*	*0.378*
2000	*0.250*	*0.629*	*0.122*	*0.081*	*0.590*	*0.244*	*0.346*
2010	*0.238*	*0.644*	*0.118*	*0.082*	*0.552*	*0.248*	*0.322*
2020	*0.227*	*0.657*	*0.117*	*0.080*	*0.523*	*0.245*	*0.309*

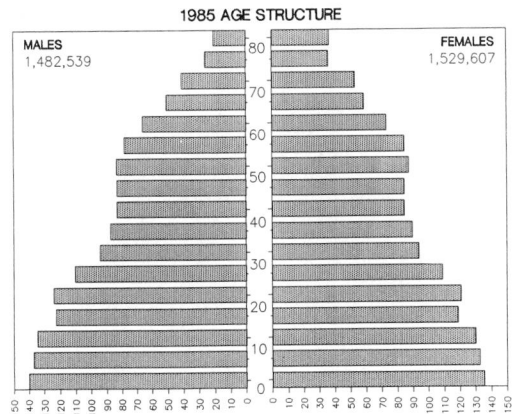

1985 AGE STRUCTURE

MALES 1,482,539   FEMALES 1,529,607

MORTALITY MEASURES (Annual Averages)

PERIOD	CRUDE DEATH RATE	INFANT MORT. RATE	LIFE EXPECTANCY AT BIRTH (years) MALE	LIFE EXPECTANCY AT BIRTH (years) FEMALE	LIFE EXPECTANCY AT BIRTH (years) BOTH SEXES	DIFFERENCE FEMALE-MALE
1950-55	10.51	57.00	63.28	69.40	66.26	6.12
1955-60	10.06	53.00	64.20	70.43	67.24	6.23
1960-65	9.56	48.00	65.38	71.64	68.43	6.26
1965-70	9.64	48.00	65.50	71.92	68.63	6.42
1970-75	10.06	47.00	65.62	72.20	68.83	6.58
1975-80	10.17	44.00	66.39	73.00	69.61	6.61
1980-85	10.23	30.00	67.11	73.74	70.34	6.63
1985-90	*10.24*	*27.00*	*67.76*	*74.44*	*71.02*	*6.68*
1990-95	*10.29*	*25.00*	*68.29*	*75.05*	*71.59*	*6.76*
2000-05	*10.28*	*21.00*	*69.13*	*76.01*	*72.49*	*6.88*
2010-15	*10.25*	*18.00*	*69.68*	*76.66*	*73.08*	*6.98*
2020-25	*10.21*	*16.00*	*70.00*	*77.00*	*73.42*	*7.00*

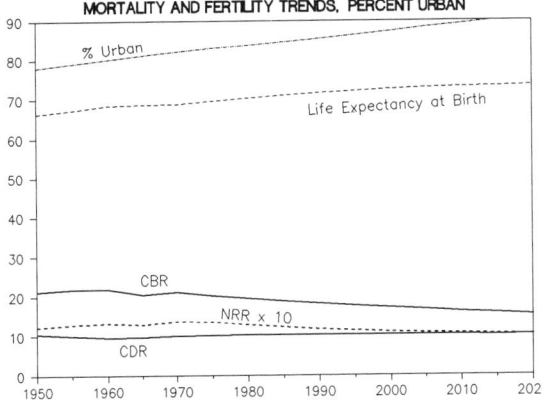

MORTALITY AND FERTILITY TRENDS, PERCENT URBAN

% Urban   Life Expectancy at Birth   CBR   NRR x 10   CDR

FERTILITY MEASURES (Annual Averages)

PERIOD	CRUDE BIRTH RATE	FERTILITY RATES GENERAL	FERTILITY RATES TOTAL	REPRODUCTION RATES GROSS	REPRODUCTION RATES NET	RATE OF NATUR. INCR.
1950-55	21.23	84.37	2.730	1.330	1.230	10.72
1955-60	21.94	86.96	2.831	1.380	1.284	11.88
1960-65	21.91	87.81	2.900	1.410	1.325	12.35
1965-70	20.48	83.12	2.800	1.370	1.281	10.84
1970-75	21.14	87.32	3.000	1.460	1.375	11.08
1975-80	20.27	85.44	2.930	1.430	1.355	10.10
1980-85	19.50	83.24	2.760	1.350	1.286	9.27
1985-90	*18.87*	*80.51*	*2.610*	*1.270*	*1.224*	*8.63*
1990-95	*18.24*	*76.62*	*2.480*	*1.210*	*1.169*	*7.95*
2000-05	*17.14*	*69.66*	*2.300*	*1.120*	*1.093*	*6.85*
2010-15	*16.20*	*65.56*	*2.210*	*1.080*	*1.055*	*5.96*
2020-25	*15.39*	*63.11*	*2.160*	*1.050*	*1.033*	*5.19*

AGING MEASURES

YEAR	POPULATION AGE RATIOS 60+/20-59	POPULATION AGE RATIOS 65+/20-64	POPULATION AGE RATIOS 70+/20-69	POPULATION AGE RATIOS 75+/20-74	POPULATION MEAN AGE	POPULATION MEDIAN AGE
1950	0.2295	0.1498	0.0911	0.0496	31.15	27.85
1960	0.2261	0.1452	0.0880	0.0485	31.50	28.88
1970	0.2519	0.1607	0.0950	0.0514	32.18	29.63
1980	0.2949	0.1934	0.1134	0.0615	33.08	29.94
1990	*0.3262*	*0.2076*	*0.1251*	*0.0711*	*33.57*	*30.07*
2000	*0.3254*	*0.2216*	*0.1379*	*0.0756*	*34.05*	*31.03*
2010	*0.3035*	*0.2085*	*0.1370*	*0.0816*	*34.66*	*32.31*
2020	*0.3081*	*0.2008*	*0.1288*	*0.0765*	*35.49*	*33.69*

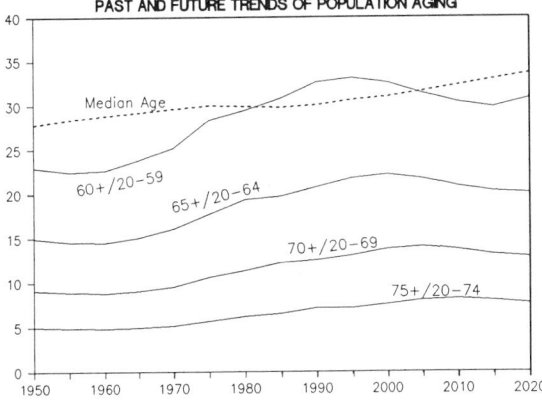

PAST AND FUTURE TRENDS OF POPULATION AGING

Median Age   60+/20-59   65+/20-64   70+/20-69   75+/20-74

OBSERVED AND *PROJECTED* POPULATION DATA (000's)

YEAR	MID-YEAR POPULATION	NO. OF BIRTHS	NO. OF DEATHS	URBAN POPULATION NUMBER	URBAN POPULATION PERCENT	POPULATION 1985 AGE	POPULATION 1985 NUMBER
1950	5009	236	62	2667	53.2	0	2559
1955	6148	279	65	3695	60.1	5	2273
1960	7502	331	69	4996	66.6	10	2007
1965	8970	364	69	6261	69.8	15	1871
1970	10604	382	69	7680	72.4	20	1679
1975	12665	436	75	9857	77.8	25	1436
1980	15024	495	83	12511	83.3	30	1245
1985	17317	532	94	15169	87.6	35	1018
1990	*19736*	*557*	*105*	*17859*	*90.5*	40	760
1995	*22213*	*578*	*118*	*20528*	*92.4*	45	605
2000	*24716*	*615*	*134*	*23151*	*93.7*	50	517
2005	*27322*	*649*	*152*	*25806*	*94.5*	55	431
2010	*30007*	*676*	*172*	*28474*	*94.9*	60	327
2015	*32713*	*696*	*195*	*31174*	*95.3*	65	238
2020	*35395*	*711*	*223*	*33862*	*95.7*	70+	353

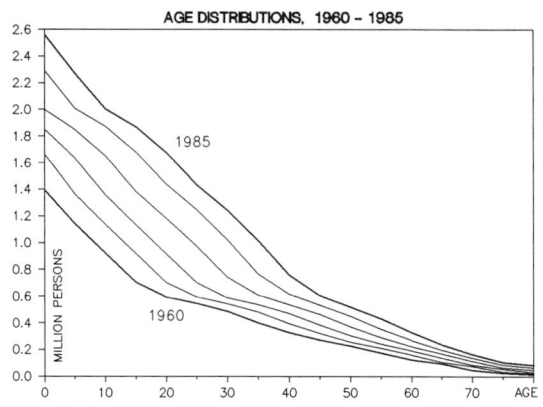

AGE DISTRIBUTIONS, 1960 - 1985

POPULATION RATIOS

YEAR	AGE DISTRIBUTION UNDER 15	15-64	65 & OLDER	70 & OLDER	DEPENDENCY RATIO	WOMEN 15-49	CHILD-WOMAN RATIO
1950	0.436	0.545	0.018	0.009	0.833	0.235	0.792
1955	0.451	0.529	0.021	0.010	0.892	0.224	0.840
1960	0.461	0.515	0.024	0.012	0.944	0.217	0.856
1965	0.464	0.509	0.026	0.015	0.963	0.216	0.859
1970	0.457	0.515	0.029	0.016	0.944	0.220	0.793
1975	0.435	0.535	0.031	0.018	0.871	0.229	0.688
1980	0.411	0.557	0.032	0.019	0.795	0.239	0.636
1985	0.395	0.571	0.034	0.020	0.751	0.246	0.602
1990	*0.383*	*0.581*	*0.037*	*0.022*	*0.722*	*0.250*	*0.556*
2000	*0.345*	*0.612*	*0.044*	*0.027*	*0.635*	*0.259*	*0.461*
2010	*0.312*	*0.636*	*0.051*	*0.031*	*0.571*	*0.260*	*0.424*
2020	*0.290*	*0.642*	*0.068*	*0.041*	*0.558*	*0.255*	*0.392*

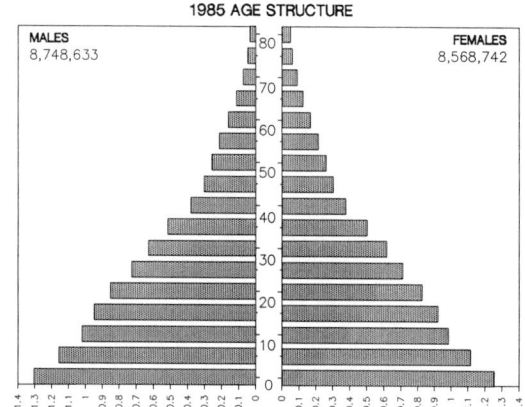

1985 AGE STRUCTURE

MALES 8,748,633   FEMALES 8,568,742

MORTALITY MEASURES (Annual Averages)

PERIOD	CRUDE DEATH RATE	INFANT MORT. RATE	LIFE EXPECTANCY AT BIRTH (years) MALE	FEMALE	BOTH SEXES	DIFFERENCE FEMALE-MALE
1950-55	12.28	106.00	53.83	56.61	55.19	2.78
1955-60	10.61	89.00	56.58	59.62	58.06	3.04
1960-65	9.14	73.00	59.25	62.79	60.98	3.54
1965-70	7.71	60.00	61.48	66.13	63.75	4.65
1970-75	6.47	49.00	63.50	69.10	66.23	5.60
1975-80	5.90	43.00	64.85	70.70	67.70	5.85
1980-85	5.54	39.00	66.02	72.07	68.97	6.05
1985-90	*5.42*	*36.00*	*66.68*	*72.80*	*69.67*	*6.12*
1990-95	*5.34*	*33.00*	*67.31*	*73.50*	*70.33*	*6.19*
2000-05	*5.42*	*28.00*	*68.49*	*74.81*	*71.57*	*6.32*
2010-15	*5.73*	*24.00*	*69.55*	*75.97*	*72.68*	*6.42*
2020-25	*6.30*	*20.00*	*70.50*	*77.00*	*73.67*	*6.50*

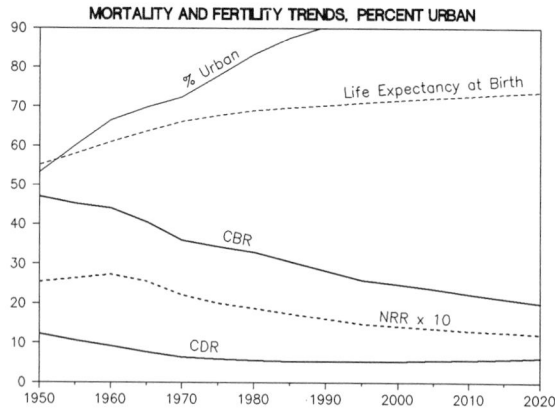

MORTALITY AND FERTILITY TRENDS, PERCENT URBAN

FERTILITY MEASURES (Annual Averages)

PERIOD	CRUDE BIRTH RATE	FERTILITY RATES GENERAL	TOTAL	REPRODUCTION RATES GROSS	NET	RATE OF NATUR. INCR.
1950-55	47.03	205.25	6.460	3.150	2.557	34.75
1955-60	45.30	205.59	6.460	3.150	2.646	34.69
1960-65	44.18	204.09	6.460	3.150	2.733	35.04
1965-70	40.58	186.15	5.887	2.880	2.565	32.88
1970-75	36.06	160.26	4.965	2.420	2.218	29.59
1975-80	34.41	146.53	4.445	2.170	2.016	28.51
1980-85	32.97	135.87	4.100	2.000	1.882	27.43
1985-90	*30.72*	*123.96*	*3.770*	*1.840*	*1.739*	*25.30*
1990-95	*28.25*	*111.84*	*3.469*	*1.690*	*1.607*	*22.91*
2000-05	*24.87*	*95.62*	*3.050*	*1.490*	*1.424*	*19.45*
2010-15	*22.52*	*87.00*	*2.800*	*1.370*	*1.316*	*16.78*
2020-25	*20.09*	*78.89*	*2.600*	*1.270*	*1.229*	*13.79*

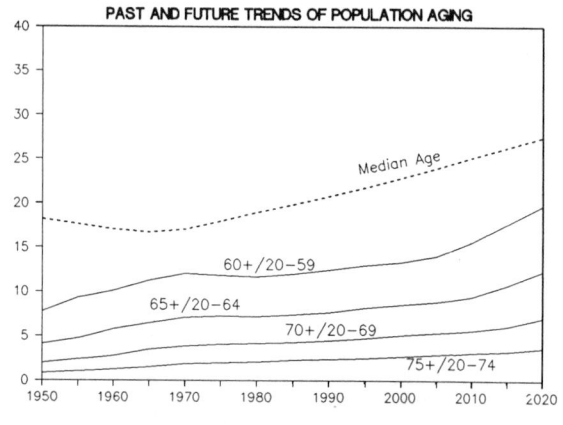

PAST AND FUTURE TRENDS OF POPULATION AGING

AGING MEASURES

YEAR	POPULATION AGE RATIOS 60+/20-59	65+/20-64	70+/20-69	75+/20-74	POPULATION MEAN AGE	POPULATION MEDIAN AGE
1950	0.0775	0.0412	0.0197	0.0082	22.27	18.22
1960	0.1009	0.0579	0.0275	0.0124	21.97	17.07
1970	0.1200	0.0707	0.0381	0.0189	22.11	17.03
1980	0.1165	0.0719	0.0416	0.0210	23.23	18.98
1990	*0.1243*	*0.0767*	*0.0445*	*0.0235*	*24.63*	*20.84*
2000	*0.1330*	*0.0855*	*0.0509*	*0.0269*	*26.51*	*22.89*
2010	*0.1559*	*0.0942*	*0.0559*	*0.0310*	*28.42*	*25.16*
2020	*0.1973*	*0.1227*	*0.0703*	*0.0364*	*30.31*	*27.45*

OBSERVED AND *PROJECTED* POPULATION DATA (000's)

YEAR	MID-YEAR POPULATION	NO. OF BIRTHS	NO. OF DEATHS	URBAN POPULATION		POPULATION 1985	
				NUMBER	PERCENT	AGE	NUMBER
1950	166075	4082	1567	106098	63.9	0	19927
1955	181742	4465	1687	121730	67.0	5	18624
1960	198663	4407	1837	138884	69.9	10	18894
1965	214076	3862	1993	154054	72.0	15	20519
1970	226480	3567	2048	167142	73.8	20	23551
1975	238807	3606	2032	176342	73.8	25	24259
1980	251808	3934	2130	186068	73.9	30	22531
1985	264777	3970	2290	196137	74.1	35	19796
1990	*275880*	*3851*	*2392*	*204940*	*74.3*	40	15694
1995	*285895*	*3742*	*2497*	*213409*	*74.6*	45	12974
2000	*294830*	*3723*	*2596*	*221203*	*75.0*	50	12170
2005	*303160*	*3821*	*2681*	*229012*	*75.5*	55	12536
2010	*311555*	*3900*	*2787*	*236955*	*76.1*	60	12113
2015	*319808*	*3894*	*2960*	*245145*	*76.7*	65	10329
2020	*327153*	*3863*	*3224*	*252687*	*77.2*	70+	20861

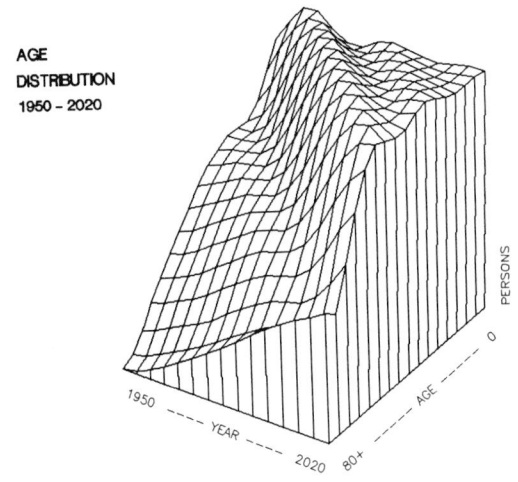

AGE DISTRIBUTION 1950 - 2020

POPULATION RATIOS

YEAR	AGE DISTRIBUTION				DEPENDENCY RATIO	WOMEN 15-49	CHILD-WOMAN RATIO
	UNDER 15	15-64	65 & OLDER	70 & OLDER			
1950	0.272	0.647	0.081	0.048	0.544	0.255	0.426
1955	0.297	0.616	0.087	0.053	0.623	0.240	0.470
1960	0.313	0.597	0.091	0.057	0.676	0.231	0.492
1965	0.307	0.599	0.093	0.060	0.668	0.231	0.446
1970	0.284	0.619	0.096	0.063	0.614	0.239	0.351
1975	0.253	0.644	0.103	0.066	0.553	0.249	0.300
1980	0.225	0.663	0.111	0.073	0.507	0.259	0.279
1985	0.217	0.665	0.118	0.079	0.503	0.263	0.286
1990	*0.214*	*0.661*	*0.125*	*0.084*	*0.513*	*0.264*	*0.278*
2000	*0.202*	*0.670*	*0.128*	*0.093*	*0.492*	*0.255*	*0.253*
2010	*0.186*	*0.678*	*0.136*	*0.093*	*0.475*	*0.234*	*0.266*
2020	*0.182*	*0.643*	*0.175*	*0.116*	*0.555*	*0.216*	*0.280*

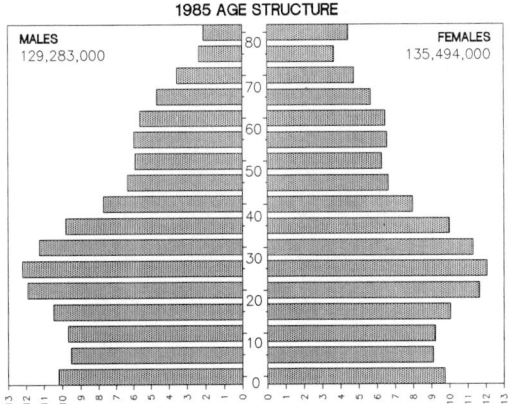

1985 AGE STRUCTURE

MALES 129,283,000   FEMALES 135,494,000

MORTALITY MEASURES (Annual Averages)

PERIOD	CRUDE DEATH RATE	INFANT MORT. RATE	LIFE EXPECTANCY AT BIRTH (years)			DIFFERENCE FEMALE-MALE
			MALE	FEMALE	BOTH SEXES	
1950-55	9.43	28.56	66.25	71.96	69.03	5.70
1955-60	9.28	26.78	66.78	73.08	69.84	6.31
1960-65	9.25	25.32	66.88	73.52	70.11	6.63
1965-70	9.31	22.10	67.10	74.16	70.54	7.07
1970-75	9.04	17.91	67.71	75.44	71.47	7.73
1975-80	8.51	13.83	69.51	77.29	73.29	7.78
1980-85	8.46	11.15	71.04	78.38	74.62	7.33
1985-90	*8.65*	*9.55*	*72.07*	*79.15*	*75.52*	*7.08*
1990-95	*8.67*	*7.69*	*72.92*	*79.95*	*76.35*	*7.03*
2000-05	*8.81*	*6.42*	*74.58*	*80.99*	*77.70*	*6.41*
2010-15	*8.95*	*5.71*	*75.77*	*82.02*	*78.82*	*6.25*
2020-25	*9.85*	*5.18*	*76.73*	*82.91*	*79.74*	*6.18*

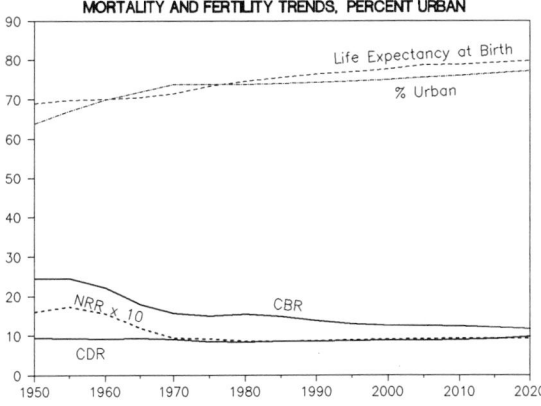

MORTALITY AND FERTILITY TRENDS, PERCENT URBAN

Life Expectancy at Birth / % Urban / NRR x 10 / CBR / CDR

FERTILITY MEASURES (Annual Averages)

PERIOD	CRUDE BIRTH RATE	FERTILITY RATES		REPRODUCTION RATES		RATE OF NATUR. INCR.
		GENERAL	TOTAL	GROSS	NET	
1950-55	24.58	99.35	3.467	1.690	1.611	15.15
1955-60	24.57	104.34	3.723	1.815	1.744	15.28
1960-65	22.18	96.01	3.341	1.629	1.569	12.94
1965-70	18.04	76.65	2.542	1.239	1.197	8.73
1970-75	15.75	64.45	1.969	0.960	0.950	6.70
1975-80	15.10	59.40	1.914	0.933	0.923	6.59
1980-85	15.62	59.85	1.800	0.877	0.862	7.16
1985-90	*14.99*	*56.92*	*1.812*	*0.883*	*0.867*	*6.35*
1990-95	*13.96*	*53.18*	*1.831*	*0.892*	*0.877*	*5.29*
2000-05	*12.63*	*50.37*	*1.885*	*0.919*	*0.905*	*3.82*
2010-15	*12.52*	*54.86*	*1.936*	*0.944*	*0.930*	*3.57*
2020-25	*11.81*	*54.97*	*1.936*	*0.944*	*0.930*	*1.95*

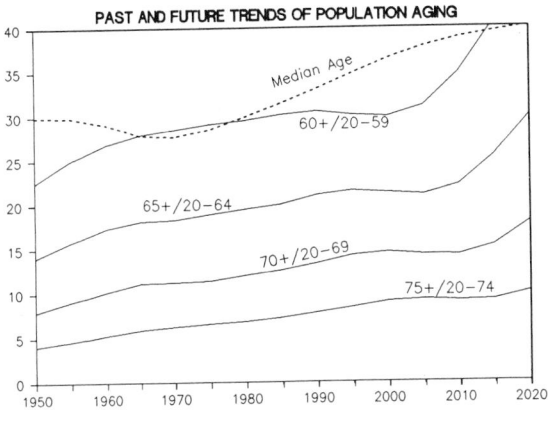

PAST AND FUTURE TRENDS OF POPULATION AGING

Median Age / 60+/20-59 / 65+/20-64 / 70+/20-69 / 75+/20-74

AGING MEASURES

YEAR	POPULATION AGE RATIOS				POPULATION	
	60+/20-59	65+/20-64	70+/20-69	75+/20-74	MEAN AGE	MEDIAN AGE
1950	0.2250	0.1405	0.0789	0.0403	31.95	29.97
1960	0.2684	0.1739	0.1020	0.0528	31.49	29.12
1970	0.2852	0.1833	0.1121	0.0624	32.12	27.74
1980	0.2955	0.1952	0.1200	0.0680	33.90	29.97
1990	*0.3053*	*0.2105*	*0.1336*	*0.0779*	*35.32*	*33.08*
2000	*0.2993*	*0.2128*	*0.1459*	*0.0900*	*37.00*	*36.47*
2010	*0.3488*	*0.2218*	*0.1425*	*0.0904*	*38.73*	*38.83*
2020	*0.4731*	*0.2996*	*0.1801*	*0.1010*	*40.33*	*40.08*

OBSERVED AND *PROJECTED* POPULATION DATA (000's)

YEAR	MID-YEAR POPULATION	NO. OF BIRTHS	NO. OF DEATHS	URBAN POPULATION		POPULATION 1985	
				NUMBER	PERCENT	AGE	NUMBER
1950	13737	381	120	8356	60.8	0	1881
1955	15736	436	127	10224	65.0	5	1795
1960	17909	441	138	12340	68.9	10	1783
1965	19678	362	147	14344	72.9	15	1923
1970	21324	342	157	16133	75.7	20	2333
1975	22727	353	164	17184	75.6	25	2365
1980	23941	363	169	18114	75.7	30	2178
1985	25379	357	189	19253	75.9	35	2025
1990	*26525*	*341*	*205*	*20274*	*76.4*	40	1610
1995	*27567*	*331*	*220*	*21323*	*77.3*	45	1314
2000	*28508*	*333*	*238*	*22400*	*78.6*	50	1222
2005	*29364*	*344*	*254*	*23506*	*80.1*	55	1193
2010	*30197*	*346*	*271*	*24676*	*81.7*	60	1111
2015	*30954*	*343*	*291*	*25765*	*83.2*	65	895
2020	*31587*	*337*	*319*	*26732*	*84.6*	70+	1752

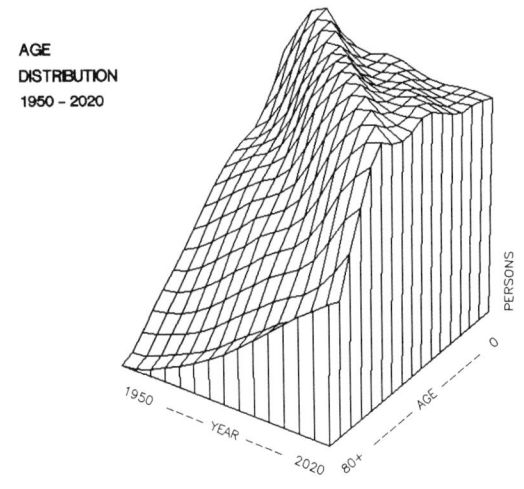

AGE DISTRIBUTION 1950 – 2020

POPULATION RATIOS

YEAR	AGE DISTRIBUTION				DEPENDENCY RATIO	WOMEN 15-49	CHILD-WOMAN RATIO
	UNDER 15	15-64	65 & OLDER	70 & OLDER			
1950	0.297	0.626	0.077	0.046	0.596	0.249	0.479
1955	0.321	0.602	0.077	0.048	0.662	0.239	0.516
1960	0.335	0.590	0.075	0.049	0.696	0.233	0.536
1965	0.334	0.590	0.077	0.050	0.696	0.233	0.494
1970	0.302	0.619	0.079	0.051	0.614	0.244	0.357
1975	0.265	0.650	0.085	0.055	0.538	0.255	0.303
1980	0.225	0.678	0.097	0.062	0.475	0.267	0.274
1985	0.215	0.681	0.104	0.069	0.469	0.269	0.276
1990	*0.209*	*0.676*	*0.114*	*0.075*	*0.478*	*0.268*	*0.258*
2000	*0.189*	*0.684*	*0.127*	*0.090*	*0.462*	*0.256*	*0.234*
2010	*0.174*	*0.682*	*0.144*	*0.097*	*0.467*	*0.231*	*0.253*
2020	*0.170*	*0.643*	*0.186*	*0.126*	*0.555*	*0.212*	*0.261*

MORTALITY MEASURES (Annual Averages)

PERIOD	CRUDE DEATH RATE	INFANT MORT. RATE	LIFE EXPECTANCY AT BIRTH (years)			
			MALE	FEMALE	BOTH SEXES	DIFFERENCE FEMALE-MALE
1950-55	8.72	35.94	66.75	71.55	69.08	4.80
1955-60	8.10	30.12	67.90	73.35	70.55	5.45
1960-65	7.72	26.28	68.50	74.55	71.44	6.05
1965-70	7.46	21.33	68.95	75.25	72.01	6.30
1970-75	7.38	16.38	69.70	76.80	73.15	7.10
1975-80	7.21	12.18	70.50	78.10	74.19	7.60
1980-85	7.07	8.83	72.44	79.60	75.92	7.16
1985-90	*7.43*	*7.34*	*73.32*	*80.25*	*76.69*	*6.93*
1990-95	*7.73*	*6.84*	*74.03*	*80.73*	*77.29*	*6.70*
2000-05	*8.33*	*6.12*	*75.46*	*81.74*	*78.51*	*6.27*
2010-15	*8.96*	*5.55*	*76.40*	*82.74*	*79.48*	*6.33*
2020-25	*10.10*	*5.29*	*77.42*	*83.58*	*80.41*	*6.16*

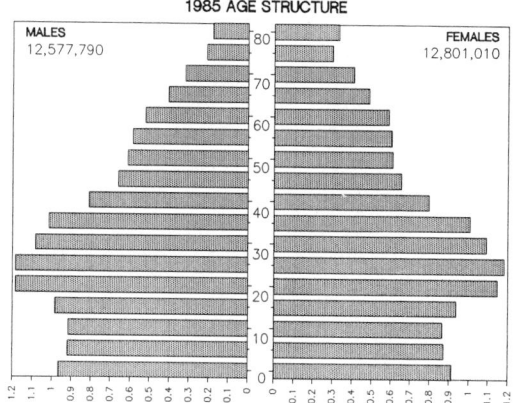

1985 AGE STRUCTURE

MALES 12,577,790

FEMALES 12,801,010

FERTILITY MEASURES (Annual Averages)

PERIOD	CRUDE BIRTH RATE	FERTILITY RATES		REPRODUCTION RATES		RATE OF NATUR. INCR.
		GENERAL	TOTAL	GROSS	NET	
1950-55	27.76	113.84	3.701	1.800	1.703	19.04
1955-60	27.70	117.39	3.896	1.895	1.814	19.60
1960-65	24.61	105.66	3.608	1.755	1.691	16.89
1965-70	18.42	77.14	2.508	1.220	1.178	10.96
1970-75	16.02	64.17	1.974	0.960	1.117	8.64
1975-80	15.52	59.47	1.768	0.860	0.895	8.32
1980-85	15.15	56.57	1.657	0.806	0.792	8.08
1985-90	*14.07*	*52.47*	*1.650*	*0.803*	*0.790*	*6.63*
1990-95	*12.86*	*48.44*	*1.650*	*0.803*	*0.790*	*5.13*
2000-05	*11.67*	*46.62*	*1.750*	*0.851*	*0.839*	*3.34*
2010-15	*11.47*	*51.07*	*1.800*	*0.875*	*0.863*	*2.51*
2020-25	*10.67*	*50.60*	*1.800*	*0.875*	*0.865*	*0.57*

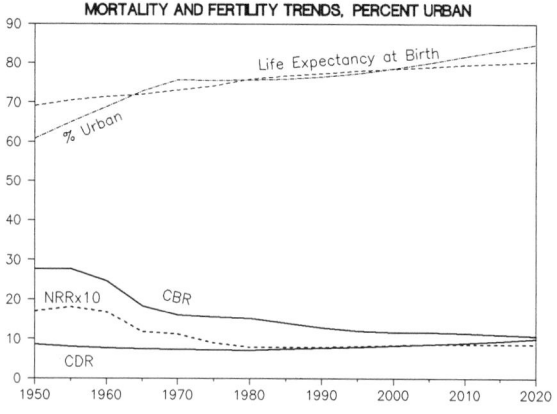

MORTALITY AND FERTILITY TRENDS, PERCENT URBAN

Life Expectancy at Birth

% Urban

NRRx10

CBR

CDR

AGING MEASURES

YEAR	POPULATION AGE RATIOS				POPULATION	
	60+/20-59	65+/20-64	70+/20-69	75+/20-74	MEAN AGE	MEDIAN AGE
1950	0.2215	0.1400	0.0800	0.0404	30.45	27.71
1960	0.2227	0.1464	0.0901	0.0474	29.53	26.39
1970	0.2329	0.1505	0.0930	0.0528	30.49	26.02
1980	0.2529	0.1664	0.1009	0.0564	33.14	29.67
1990	*0.2780*	*0.1878*	*0.1166*	*0.0676*	*35.24*	*33.31*
2000	*0.2962*	*0.2064*	*0.1373*	*0.0824*	*37.54*	*37.25*
2010	*0.3678*	*0.2314*	*0.1460*	*0.0905*	*39.60*	*40.06*
2020	*0.4990*	*0.3181*	*0.1944*	*0.1080*	*41.40*	*41.63*

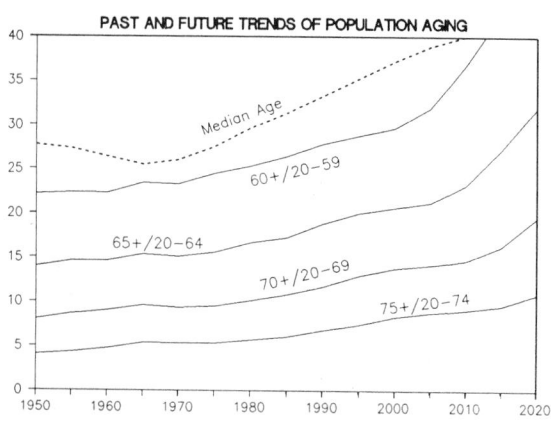

PAST AND FUTURE TRENDS OF POPULATION AGING

Median Age

60+/20-59

65+/20-64

70+/20-69

75+/20-74

OBSERVED AND *PROJECTED* POPULATION DATA (000's)

YEAR	MID-YEAR POPULATION	NO. OF BIRTHS	NO. OF DEATHS	URBAN POPULATION NUMBER	URBAN POPULATION PERCENT	POPULATION 1985 AGE	POPULATION 1985 NUMBER
1950	152271	3698	1447	97682	64.2	0	18037
1955	165932	4026	1560	111440	67.2	5	16821
1960	180671	3964	1698	126470	70.0	10	17103
1965	194303	3497	1846	139626	71.9	15	18587
1970	205051	3223	1890	150918	73.6	20	21208
1975	215972	3251	1867	159063	73.7	25	21884
1980	227757	3569	1960	167857	73.7	30	20343
1985	239283	3611	2100	176782	73.9	35	17762
1990	*249235*	*3508*	*2186*	*184559*	*74.1*	40	14077
1995	*258204*	*3409*	*2277*	*191975*	*74.3*	45	11654
2000	*266194*	*3389*	*2358*	*198687*	*74.6*	50	10943
2005	*273664*	*3475*	*2427*	*205385*	*75.0*	55	11337
2010	*281221*	*3552*	*2516*	*212153*	*75.4*	60	10997
2015	*288713*	*3550*	*2667*	*219248*	*75.9*	65	9430
2020	*295420*	*3524*	*2904*	*225819*	*76.4*	70+	19100

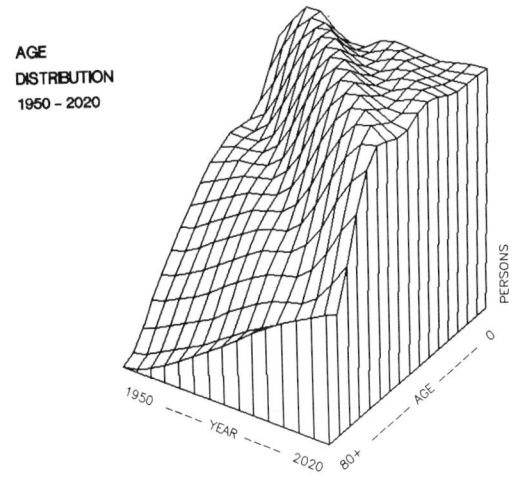

AGE DISTRIBUTION 1950 - 2020

POPULATION RATIOS

YEAR	AGE DISTRIBUTION UNDER 15	AGE DISTRIBUTION 15-64	AGE DISTRIBUTION 65 & OLDER	AGE DISTRIBUTION 70 & OLDER	DEPENDENCY RATIO	WOMEN 15-49	CHILD-WOMAN RATIO
1950	0.269	0.649	0.081	0.048	0.540	0.256	0.422
1955	0.295	0.617	0.088	0.053	0.620	0.241	0.465
1960	0.310	0.597	0.092	0.058	0.674	0.231	0.488
1965	0.305	0.600	0.095	0.061	0.665	0.231	0.441
1970	0.283	0.619	0.098	0.064	0.614	0.239	0.351
1975	0.252	0.643	0.105	0.067	0.555	0.249	0.300
1980	0.225	0.662	0.113	0.074	0.511	0.258	0.280
1985	0.217	0.664	0.119	0.080	0.507	0.262	0.287
1990	*0.215*	*0.659*	*0.126*	*0.085*	*0.517*	*0.263*	*0.280*
2000	*0.203*	*0.669*	*0.128*	*0.093*	*0.495*	*0.255*	*0.255*
2010	*0.187*	*0.678*	*0.135*	*0.093*	*0.476*	*0.234*	*0.268*
2020	*0.183*	*0.643*	*0.173*	*0.115*	*0.555*	*0.216*	*0.282*

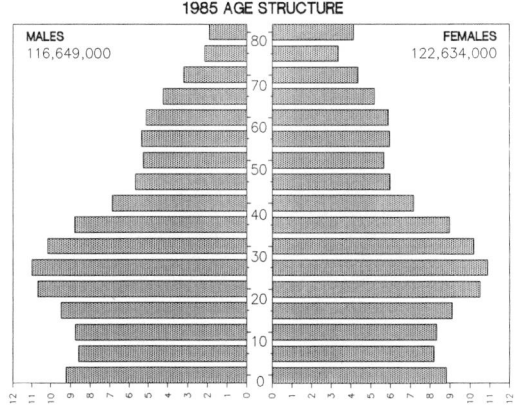

1985 AGE STRUCTURE

MALES 116,649,000   FEMALES 122,634,000

MORTALITY MEASURES (Annual Averages)

PERIOD	CRUDE DEATH RATE	INFANT MORT. RATE	LIFE EXPECTANCY AT BIRTH (years) MALE	FEMALE	BOTH SEXES	DIFFERENCE FEMALE-MALE
1950-55	9.50	27.78	66.20	72.00	69.02	5.80
1955-60	9.40	26.41	66.65	73.05	69.77	6.40
1960-65	9.40	25.21	66.70	73.40	69.96	6.70
1965-70	9.50	22.18	66.90	74.05	70.38	7.15
1970-75	9.22	18.07	67.50	75.30	71.30	7.80
1975-80	8.65	14.01	69.40	77.20	73.20	7.80
1980-85	8.60	11.39	70.90	78.25	74.48	7.35
1985-90	*8.78*	*9.76*	*71.95*	*79.04*	*75.40*	*7.09*
1990-95	*8.77*	*7.78*	*72.81*	*79.87*	*76.25*	*7.06*
2000-05	*8.86*	*6.45*	*74.49*	*80.91*	*77.62*	*6.42*
2010-15	*8.95*	*5.73*	*75.71*	*81.95*	*78.75*	*6.25*
2020-25	*9.83*	*5.16*	*76.67*	*82.85*	*79.68*	*6.18*

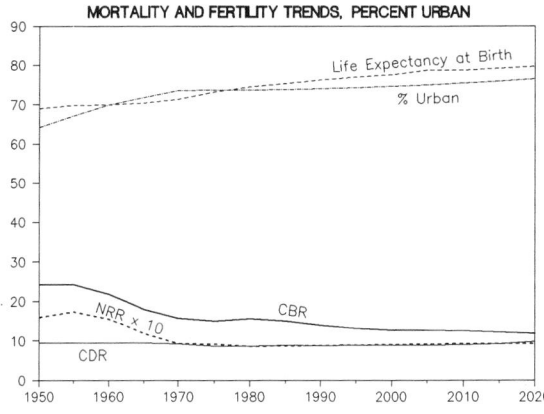

MORTALITY AND FERTILITY TRENDS, PERCENT URBAN

Life Expectancy at Birth — % Urban — NRR x 10 — CBR — CDR

FERTILITY MEASURES (Annual Averages)

PERIOD	CRUDE BIRTH RATE	FERTILITY RATES GENERAL	FERTILITY RATES TOTAL	REPRODUCTION RATES GROSS	REPRODUCTION RATES NET	RATE OF NATUR. INCR.
1950-55	24.28	98.03	3.446	1.680	1.603	14.78
1955-60	24.26	103.07	3.706	1.807	1.737	14.86
1960-65	21.94	95.03	3.314	1.616	1.557	12.54
1965-70	18.00	76.60	2.545	1.241	1.199	8.50
1970-75	15.72	64.48	1.969	0.960	0.932	6.50
1975-80	15.06	59.39	1.930	0.941	0.926	6.41
1980-85	15.67	60.21	1.815	0.885	0.870	7.07
1985-90	*15.09*	*57.40*	*1.830*	*0.892*	*0.875*	*6.32*
1990-95	*14.08*	*53.69*	*1.850*	*0.902*	*0.886*	*5.30*
2000-05	*12.73*	*50.77*	*1.900*	*0.926*	*0.912*	*3.87*
2010-15	*12.63*	*55.26*	*1.950*	*0.951*	*0.937*	*3.68*
2020-25	*11.93*	*55.43*	*1.950*	*0.951*	*0.937*	*2.10*

AGING MEASURES

YEAR	POPULATION AGE RATIOS 60+/20-59	65+/20-64	70+/20-69	75+/20-74	POPULATION MEAN AGE	POPULATION MEDIAN AGE
1950	0.2253	0.1405	0.0788	0.0403	32.09	30.18
1960	0.2729	0.1766	0.1031	0.0533	31.68	29.43
1970	0.2907	0.1867	0.1140	0.0634	32.29	27.93
1980	0.3001	0.1984	0.1220	0.0692	33.98	30.01
1990	*0.3083*	*0.2130*	*0.1354*	*0.0790*	*35.32*	*33.06*
2000	*0.2997*	*0.2135*	*0.1469*	*0.0908*	*36.94*	*36.38*
2010	*0.3467*	*0.2207*	*0.1421*	*0.0904*	*38.64*	*38.69*
2020	*0.4703*	*0.2976*	*0.1786*	*0.1002*	*40.22*	*39.91*

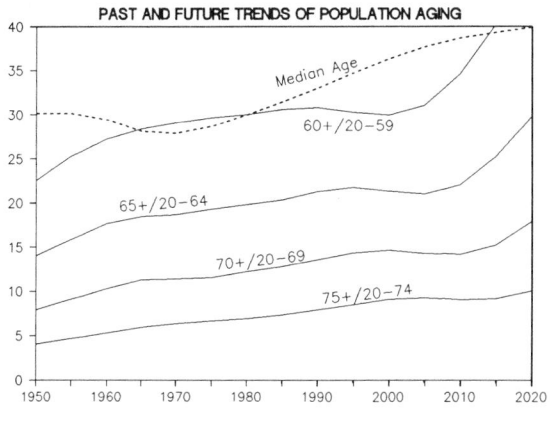

PAST AND FUTURE TRENDS OF POPULATION AGING

Median Age — 60+/20-59 — 65+/20-64 — 70+/20-69 — 75+/20-74

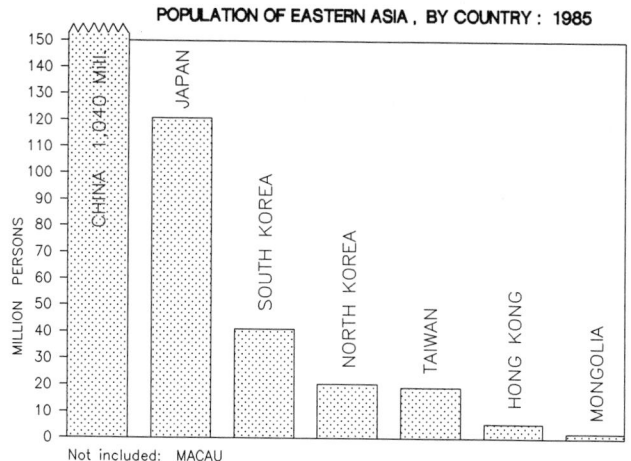

POPULATION OF EASTERN ASIA , BY COUNTRY : 1985

Not included: MACAU

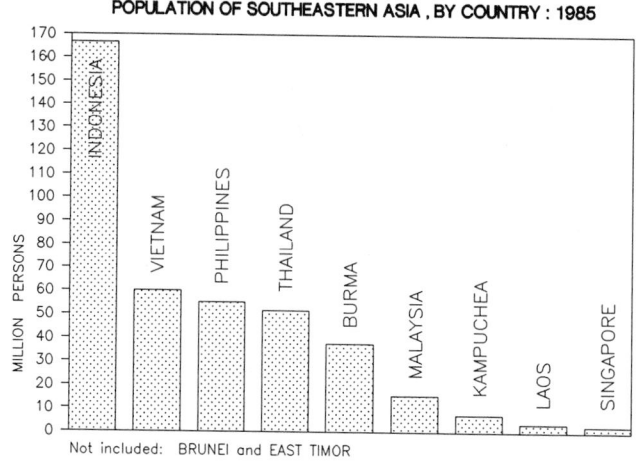

POPULATION OF SOUTHEASTERN ASIA , BY COUNTRY : 1985

Not included: BRUNEI and EAST TIMOR

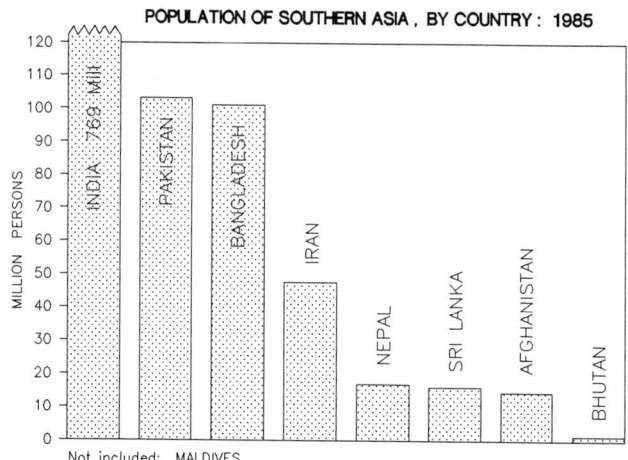

POPULATION OF SOUTHERN ASIA , BY COUNTRY : 1985

Not included: MALDIVES

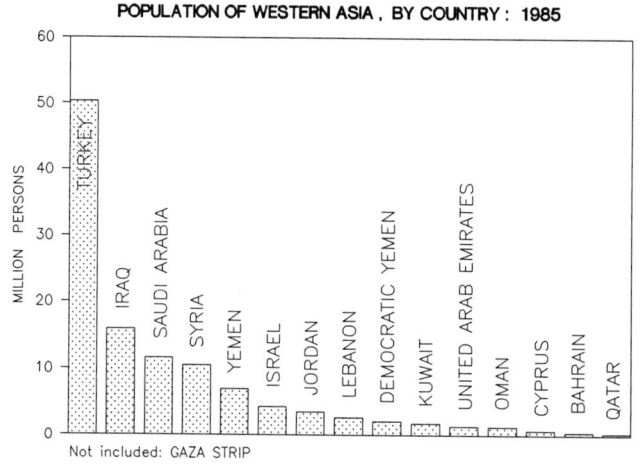

POPULATION OF WESTERN ASIA , BY COUNTRY : 1985

Not included: GAZA STRIP

OBSERVED AND *PROJECTED* POPULATION DATA (000's)

YEAR	MID-YEAR POPULATION	NO. OF BIRTHS	NO. OF DEATHS	URBAN POPULATION NUMBER	URBAN POPULATION PERCENT	POPULATION 1985 AGE	POPULATION 1985 NUMBER
1950	1374552	58959	33116	225750	16.4	0	345192
1955	1511679	59873	30865	275755	18.2	5	313242
1960	1666801	65864	29542	358859	21.5	10	328992
1965	1859966	71369	26319	425228	22.9	15	313604
1970	2101102	73144	26024	502685	23.9	20	269583
1975	2353390	69947	25285	595272	25.3	25	227224
1980	2582836	73435	25356	688176	26.6	30	207022
1985	2834226	78199	25874	796606	28.1	35	163982
1990	*3108476*	*82903*	*26441*	*930694*	*29.9*	40	134779
1995	*3404078*	*83274*	*26936*	*1095979*	*32.2*	45	122636
2000	*3697849*	*80743*	*27579*	*1292455*	*35.0*	50	110429
2005	*3973491*	*77483*	*28518*	*1518521*	*38.2*	55	92081
2010	*4226018*	*75992*	*29857*	*1772152*	*41.9*	60	72957
2015	*4463090*	*74123*	*31679*	*2038036*	*45.7*	65	54694
2020	*4680433*	*75027*	*34130*	*2310155*	*49.4*	70+	77810

POPULATION RATIOS

YEAR	UNDER 15	15-64	65 & OLDER	70 & OLDER	DEPENDENCY RATIO	WOMEN 15-49	CHILD-WOMAN RATIO
1950	0.367	0.593	0.040	0.021	0.687	0.239	0.611
1955	0.383	0.577	0.040	0.022	0.734	0.233	0.685
1960	0.395	0.564	0.041	0.023	0.774	0.228	0.670
1965	0.404	0.556	0.040	0.023	0.798	0.225	0.697
1970	0.403	0.557	0.040	0.022	0.796	0.227	0.696
1975	0.399	0.560	0.041	0.023	0.785	0.228	0.639
1980	0.376	0.580	0.044	0.025	0.725	0.236	0.532
1985	0.348	0.605	0.047	0.027	0.653	0.246	0.495
1990	*0.328*	*0.622*	*0.050*	*0.029*	*0.608*	*0.254*	*0.474*
2000	*0.314*	*0.628*	*0.058*	*0.035*	*0.592*	*0.255*	*0.429*
2010	*0.275*	*0.659*	*0.066*	*0.042*	*0.518*	*0.259*	*0.346*
2020	*0.236*	*0.679*	*0.085*	*0.051*	*0.473*	*0.255*	*0.305*

MORTALITY MEASURES (Annual Averages)

PERIOD	CRUDE DEATH RATE	INFANT MORT. RATE	LIFE EXPECTANCY AT BIRTH (years) MALE	FEMALE	BOTH SEXES	DIFFERENCE FEMALE-MALE
1950-55	24.09	180.63	40.52	41.76	41.13	1.24
1955-60	20.42	163.61	43.98	45.05	44.50	1.07
1960-65	17.72	132.76	47.63	48.36	47.99	0.73
1965-70	14.15	110.26	52.95	53.71	53.32	0.76
1970-75	12.39	98.94	55.46	56.05	55.75	0.59
1975-80	10.74	90.75	57.07	57.85	57.46	0.78
1980-85	9.82	83.43	58.63	60.04	59.30	1.41
1985-90	*9.13*	*72.93*	*60.86*	*62.57*	*61.69*	*1.71*
1990-95	*8.51*	*64.75*	*62.66*	*64.68*	*63.64*	*2.02*
2000-05	*7.46*	*50.42*	*65.90*	*68.36*	*67.10*	*2.46*
2010-15	*7.07*	*37.20*	*68.71*	*71.85*	*70.24*	*3.14*
2020-25	*7.29*	*26.59*	*70.96*	*74.72*	*72.79*	*3.76*

FERTILITY MEASURES (Annual Averages)

PERIOD	CRUDE BIRTH RATE	FERTILITY RATES GENERAL	FERTILITY RATES TOTAL	REPRODUCTION RATES GROSS	REPRODUCTION RATES NET	RATE OF NATUR. INCR.
1950-55	42.89	181.83	5.923	2.882	1.776	18.80
1955-60	39.61	171.60	5.568	2.710	1.782	19.19
1960-65	39.51	174.29	5.708	2.778	1.946	21.79
1965-70	38.37	169.82	5.674	2.762	2.113	24.22
1970-75	34.81	153.08	5.055	2.460	1.936	22.43
1975-80	29.72	127.99	4.061	1.976	1.595	18.98
1980-85	28.43	117.84	3.715	1.808	1.489	18.61
1985-90	*27.59*	*110.36*	*3.447*	*1.678*	*1.425*	*18.46*
1990-95	*26.67*	*105.00*	*3.231*	*1.573*	*1.367*	*18.17*
2000-05	*21.83*	*85.56*	*2.762*	*1.345*	*1.216*	*14.38*
2010-15	*17.98*	*69.46*	*2.306*	*1.123*	*1.048*	*10.92*
2020-25	*16.03*	*63.51*	*2.065*	*1.006*	*0.956*	*8.74*

AGING MEASURES

YEAR	60+/20-59	65+/20-64	70+/20-69	75+/20-74	MEAN AGE	MEDIAN AGE
1950	0.1418	0.0812	0.0411	0.0175	25.83	21.83
1960	0.1429	0.0869	0.0460	0.0203	25.12	20.86
1970	0.1491	0.0880	0.0475	0.0236	24.69	19.69
1980	0.1518	0.0926	0.0507	0.0235	25.62	21.02
1990	*0.1577*	*0.0966*	*0.0546*	*0.0273*	*27.09*	*23.34*
2000	*0.1696*	*0.1080*	*0.0619*	*0.0311*	*28.58*	*25.78*
2010	*0.1850*	*0.1166*	*0.0706*	*0.0375*	*30.77*	*28.07*
2020	*0.2261*	*0.1420*	*0.0801*	*0.0419*	*33.26*	*30.95*

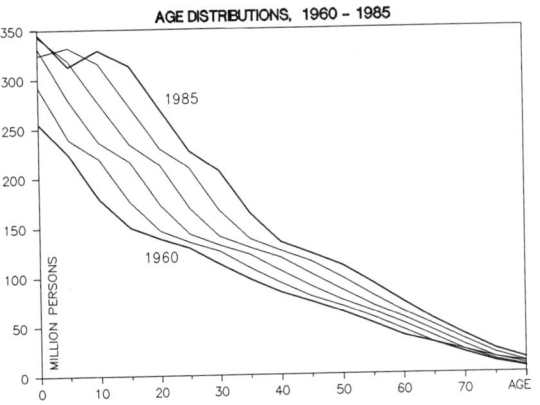

AGE DISTRIBUTIONS, 1960 - 1985

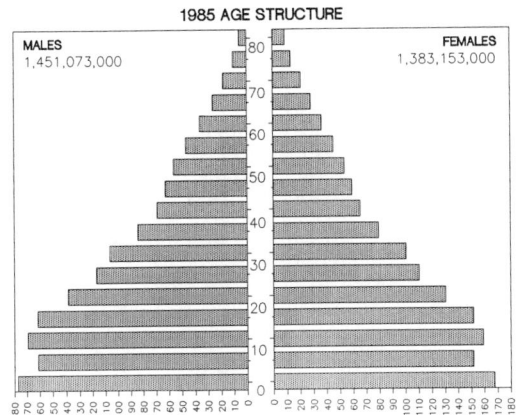

1985 AGE STRUCTURE

MALES 1,451,073,000

FEMALES 1,383,153,000

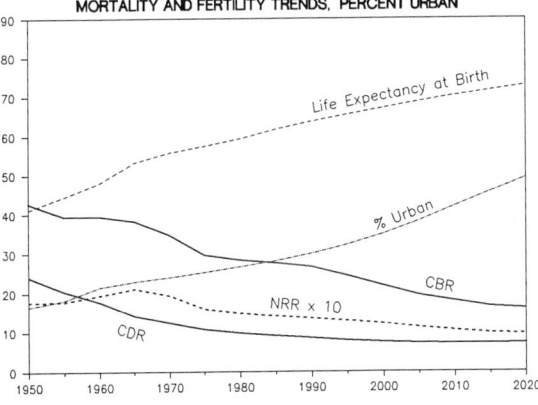

MORTALITY AND FERTILITY TRENDS, PERCENT URBAN

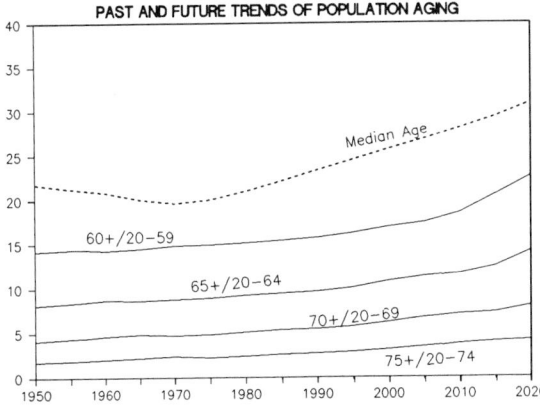

PAST AND FUTURE TRENDS OF POPULATION AGING

OBSERVED AND *PROJECTED* POPULATION DATA (000's)

YEAR	MID-YEAR POPULATION	NO. OF BIRTHS	NO. OF DEATHS	URBAN POPULATION NUMBER	URBAN POPULATION PERCENT	POPULATION 1985 AGE	POPULATION 1985 NUMBER
1950	671392	27412	15653	112475	16.8	0	108031
1955	732836	25026	13727	141619	19.3	5	113013
1960	791292	28074	12422	198094	25.0	10	142337
1965	873686	30249	9107	230307	26.4	15	145575
1970	986255	29000	8366	265547	26.9	20	122947
1975	1096027	23151	7732	302340	27.6	25	100465
1980	1176115	21951	7749	330564	28.1	30	102871
1985	1249474	24667	8313	357406	28.6	35	80161
1990	*1334018*	*25724*	*8841*	*392424*	*29.4*	40	63440
1995	*1421227*	*25018*	*9463*	*436703*	*30.7*	45	59192
2000	*1501277*	*22455*	*10185*	*489957*	*32.6*	50	55272
2005	*1563948*	*20144*	*11024*	*551410*	*35.3*	55	46739
2010	*1610251*	*20397*	*12004*	*621789*	*38.6*	60	37914
2015	*1652777*	*21174*	*13067*	*694936*	*42.0*	65	28798
2020	*1693806*	*21176*	*14291*	*771542*	*45.6*	70+	42719

AGE DISTRIBUTIONS, 1960 - 1985

POPULATION RATIOS

YEAR	AGE DISTRIBUTION UNDER 15	15-64	65 & OLDER	70 & OLDER	DEPENDENCY RATIO	WOMEN 15-49	CHILD-WOMAN RATIO
1950	0.341	0.614	0.045	0.023	0.629	0.243	0.566
1955	0.368	0.586	0.047	0.025	0.708	0.232	0.679
1960	0.380	0.571	0.049	0.027	0.751	0.226	0.607
1965	0.387	0.567	0.045	0.028	0.763	0.224	0.653
1970	0.382	0.572	0.046	0.026	0.747	0.228	0.661
1975	0.379	0.574	0.047	0.027	0.742	0.228	0.575
1980	0.343	0.606	0.051	0.030	0.650	0.241	0.404
1985	0.291	0.652	0.057	0.034	0.534	0.260	0.332
1990	*0.257*	*0.680*	*0.063*	*0.038*	*0.471*	*0.273*	*0.338*
2000	*0.250*	*0.672*	*0.077*	*0.047*	*0.487*	*0.266*	*0.315*
2010	*0.210*	*0.700*	*0.090*	*0.059*	*0.428*	*0.261*	*0.239*
2020	*0.182*	*0.696*	*0.122*	*0.073*	*0.437*	*0.240*	*0.260*

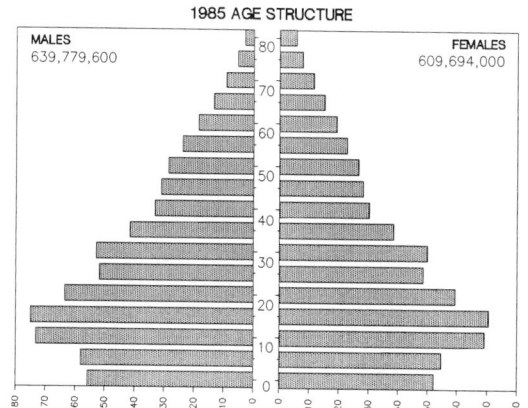

1985 AGE STRUCTURE

MALES 639,779,600   FEMALES 609,694,000

MORTALITY MEASURES (Annual Averages)

PERIOD	CRUDE DEATH RATE	INFANT MORT. RATE	LIFE EXPECTANCY AT BIRTH (years) MALE	FEMALE	BOTH SEXES	DIFFERENCE FEMALE-MALE
1950-55	23.31	181.14	41.25	44.33	42.75	3.08
1955-60	18.73	164.58	45.00	48.21	46.57	3.21
1960-65	15.70	112.34	50.01	52.01	50.99	2.00
1965-70	10.42	75.94	59.23	61.15	60.17	1.92
1970-75	8.48	56.93	62.90	64.77	63.81	1.87
1975-80	7.05	38.68	65.84	67.25	66.53	1.41
1980-85	6.59	36.46	67.06	69.82	68.40	2.76
1985-90	*6.65*	*30.47*	*68.28*	*71.60*	*69.89*	*3.32*
1990-95	*6.63*	*25.19*	*69.53*	*73.24*	*71.33*	*3.71*
2000-05	*6.78*	*17.60*	*71.71*	*75.65*	*73.63*	*3.94*
2010-15	*7.45*	*12.45*	*73.46*	*77.55*	*75.45*	*4.09*
2020-25	*8.44*	*8.59*	*74.98*	*79.28*	*77.07*	*4.30*

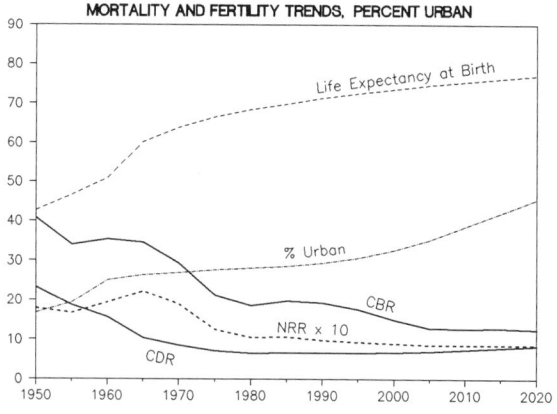

MORTALITY AND FERTILITY TRENDS, PERCENT URBAN

Life Expectancy at Birth

% Urban

CBR

NRR x 10

CDR

FERTILITY MEASURES (Annual Averages)

PERIOD	CRUDE BIRTH RATE	FERTILITY RATES GENERAL	FERTILITY RATES TOTAL	REPRODUCTION RATES GROSS	REPRODUCTION RATES NET	RATE OF NATUR. INCR.
1950-55	40.83	172.15	5.718	2.776	1.792	17.51
1955-60	34.15	149.06	4.958	2.407	1.670	15.42
1960-65	35.48	157.53	5.349	2.597	1.938	19.78
1965-70	34.62	152.99	5.385	2.614	2.229	24.20
1970-75	29.40	128.78	4.397	2.135	1.895	20.92
1975-80	21.12	89.88	2.802	1.360	1.253	14.07
1980-85	18.66	74.37	2.333	1.133	1.048	12.07
1985-90	*19.74*	*74.02*	*2.314*	*1.123*	*1.057*	*13.09*
1990-95	*19.28*	*70.78*	*2.130*	*1.034*	*0.985*	*12.66*
2000-05	*14.96*	*56.88*	*1.909*	*0.927*	*0.897*	*8.17*
2010-15	*12.67*	*49.04*	*1.814*	*0.881*	*0.861*	*5.21*
2020-25	*12.50*	*53.87*	*1.809*	*0.878*	*0.865*	*4.07*

AGING MEASURES

YEAR	POPULATION AGE RATIOS 60+/20-59	65+/20-64	70+/20-69	75+/20-74	POPULATION MEAN AGE	POPULATION MEDIAN AGE
1950	0.1527	0.0867	0.0419	0.0175	27.12	23.49
1960	0.1589	0.1001	0.0531	0.0239	26.22	22.15
1970	0.1632	0.0978	0.0536	0.0287	25.63	20.67
1980	0.1664	0.1021	0.0565	0.0266	27.25	23.00
1990	*0.1773*	*0.1102*	*0.0632*	*0.0324*	*29.96*	*26.53*
2000	*0.1976*	*0.1284*	*0.0750*	*0.0388*	*32.17*	*30.54*
2010	*0.2319*	*0.1454*	*0.0900*	*0.0495*	*35.15*	*35.04*
2020	*0.3024*	*0.1944*	*0.1080*	*0.0566*	*37.86*	*37.60*

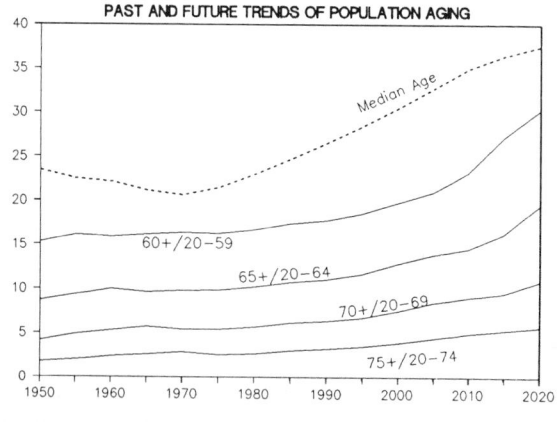

PAST AND FUTURE TRENDS OF POPULATION AGING

Median Age

60+/20-59

65+/20-64

70+/20-69

75+/20-74

OBSERVED AND *PROJECTED* POPULATION DATA (000's)

YEAR	MID-YEAR POPULATION	NO. OF BIRTHS	NO. OF DEATHS	URBAN POPULATION NUMBER	URBAN POPULATION PERCENT	POPULATION 1985 AGE	POPULATION 1985 NUMBER
1950	182033	8019	4438	26937	14.8	0	55963
1955	200415	8959	4378	32437	16.2	5	50848
1960	224605	9552	4230	39487	17.6	10	48777
1965	252829	10359	4083	47674	18.9	15	44608
1970	286709	10712	4141	57894	20.2	20	38446
1975	323532	11375	4157	71215	22.0	25	33235
1980	360063	11830	3961	86479	24.0	30	26635
1985	400558	11581	3878	105413	26.3	35	20422
1990	*440831*	*11852*	*3846*	*127973*	*29.0*	40	17569
1995	*482567*	*11771*	*3822*	*154947*	*32.1*	45	16033
2000	*523814*	*11429*	*3836*	*186122*	*35.5*	50	13777
2005	*563052*	*11142*	*3941*	*221100*	*39.3*	55	11014
2010	*600138*	*11043*	*4127*	*258679*	*43.1*	60	8396
2015	*635678*	*10835*	*4389*	*298281*	*46.9*	65	6110
2020	*668733*	*10938*	*4721*	*338695*	*50.6*	70+	8724

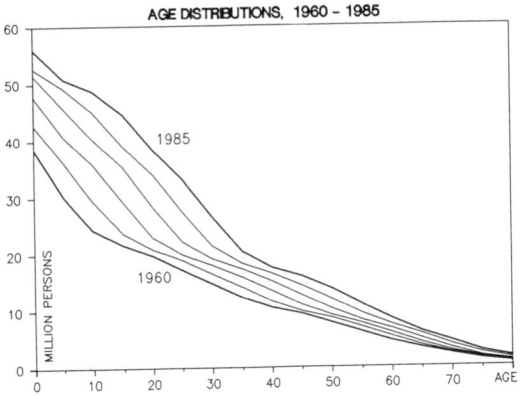

POPULATION RATIOS

YEAR	AGE DISTRIBUTION UNDER 15	AGE DISTRIBUTION 15-64	AGE DISTRIBUTION 65 & OLDER	AGE DISTRIBUTION 70 & OLDER	DEPENDENCY RATIO	WOMEN 15-49	CHILD-WOMAN RATIO
1950	0.393	0.570	0.037	0.021	0.754	0.242	0.622
1955	0.399	0.566	0.035	0.020	0.767	0.241	0.676
1960	0.414	0.553	0.033	0.019	0.809	0.236	0.725
1965	0.429	0.539	0.033	0.018	0.856	0.230	0.733
1970	0.434	0.533	0.033	0.018	0.875	0.230	0.723
1975	0.425	0.542	0.033	0.018	0.846	0.235	0.677
1980	0.408	0.555	0.037	0.021	0.801	0.241	0.607
1985	0.388	0.575	0.037	0.022	0.741	0.248	0.563
1990	*0.363*	*0.598*	*0.039*	*0.023*	*0.673*	*0.257*	*0.490*
2000	*0.320*	*0.634*	*0.046*	*0.027*	*0.577*	*0.272*	*0.403*
2010	*0.277*	*0.668*	*0.054*	*0.034*	*0.497*	*0.275*	*0.333*
2020	*0.242*	*0.689*	*0.069*	*0.040*	*0.451*	*0.267*	*0.300*

MORTALITY MEASURES (Annual Averages)

PERIOD	CRUDE DEATH RATE	INFANT MORT. RATE	LIFE EXPECTANCY AT BIRTH (years) MALE	LIFE EXPECTANCY AT BIRTH (years) FEMALE	LIFE EXPECTANCY AT BIRTH (years) BOTH SEXES	DIFFERENCE FEMALE-MALE
1950-55	24.38	151.86	40.06	42.33	41.17	2.27
1955-60	21.84	135.36	42.66	45.17	43.88	2.50
1960-65	18.83	121.16	45.38	48.13	46.72	2.74
1965-70	16.15	109.61	47.85	50.80	49.29	2.94
1970-75	14.44	100.43	50.02	53.17	51.56	3.16
1975-80	12.85	89.03	52.65	55.87	54.22	3.22
1980-85	11.00	78.29	55.54	58.91	57.18	3.37
1985-90	*9.68*	*67.83*	*57.92*	*61.38*	*59.61*	*3.46*
1990-95	*8.73*	*58.83*	*60.14*	*63.65*	*61.85*	*3.51*
2000-05	*7.32*	*42.15*	*64.32*	*68.06*	*66.14*	*3.74*
2010-15	*6.88*	*30.40*	*67.44*	*71.44*	*69.39*	*4.00*
2020-25	*7.06*	*22.24*	*69.90*	*74.20*	*71.99*	*4.30*

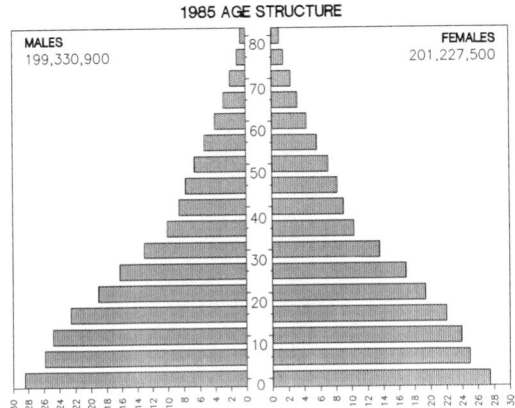

FERTILITY MEASURES (Annual Averages)

PERIOD	CRUDE BIRTH RATE	FERTILITY RATES GENERAL	FERTILITY RATES TOTAL	REPRODUCTION RATES GROSS	REPRODUCTION RATES NET	RATE OF NATUR. INCR.
1950-55	44.05	182.41	5.995	2.922	1.850	19.68
1955-60	44.70	187.40	6.079	2.963	1.984	22.85
1960-65	42.53	182.52	5.894	2.873	2.028	23.69
1965-70	40.97	177.93	5.788	2.821	2.084	24.82
1970-75	37.36	160.46	5.260	2.564	1.959	22.92
1975-80	35.16	147.61	4.787	2.333	1.857	22.31
1980-85	32.86	134.22	4.276	2.084	1.716	21.85
1985-90	*28.91*	*114.36*	*3.578*	*1.744*	*1.481*	*19.23*
1990-95	*26.89*	*103.13*	*3.190*	*1.554*	*1.357*	*18.16*
2000-05	*21.82*	*79.87*	*2.554*	*1.245*	*1.137*	*14.49*
2010-15	*18.40*	*67.25*	*2.210*	*1.077*	*1.012*	*11.52*
2020-25	*16.36*	*62.03*	*2.079*	*1.013*	*0.970*	*9.30*

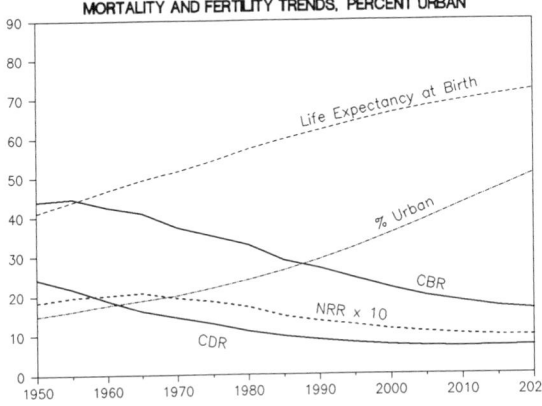

AGING MEASURES

YEAR	POPULATION AGE RATIOS 60+/20-59	POPULATION AGE RATIOS 65+/20-64	POPULATION AGE RATIOS 70+/20-69	POPULATION AGE RATIOS 75+/20-74	POPULATION MEAN AGE	POPULATION MEDIAN AGE
1950	0.1332	0.0798	0.0431	0.0196	24.60	20.21
1960	0.1226	0.0732	0.0398	0.0184	23.80	19.47
1970	0.1290	0.0755	0.0405	0.0193	23.29	18.25
1980	0.1334	0.0817	0.0448	0.0212	23.92	19.24
1990	*0.1320*	*0.0797*	*0.0448*	*0.0226*	*25.26*	*21.35*
2000	*0.1403*	*0.0868*	*0.0485*	*0.0239*	*27.22*	*24.13*
2010	*0.1482*	*0.0945*	*0.0564*	*0.0290*	*29.74*	*27.34*
2020	*0.1905*	*0.1131*	*0.0634*	*0.0337*	*32.43*	*30.63*

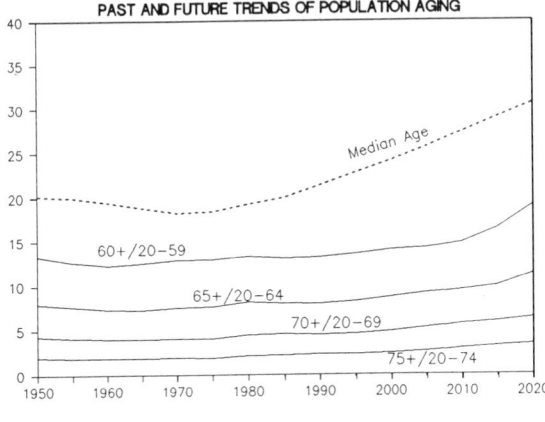

OBSERVED AND *PROJECTED* POPULATION DATA (000's)

YEAR	MID-YEAR POPULATION	NO. OF BIRTHS	NO. OF DEATHS	URBAN POPULATION NUMBER	URBAN POPULATION PERCENT	POPULATION 1985 AGE	POPULATION 1985 NUMBER
1950	478695	21501	12030	76209	15.9	0	163494
1955	529852	23543	11742	87950	16.6	5	134156
1960	595049	25710	11879	102888	17.3	10	124201
1965	669318	28036	12131	122777	18.3	15	111485
1970	754468	30468	12501	147428	19.5	20	97684
1975	848618	31959	12409	180934	21.3	25	84652
1980	948414	35699	12593	220311	23.2	30	70126
1985	1070282	37661	12642	271193	25.3	35	57404
1990	*1202858*	*40608*	*12724*	*334236*	*27.8*	40	48905
1995	*1350597*	*41390*	*12633*	*412779*	*30.6*	45	43116
2000	*1502312*	*41365*	*12514*	*507383*	*33.8*	50	37546
2005	*1653744*	*40401*	*12468*	*617498*	*37.3*	55	31157
2010	*1799526*	*38675*	*12600*	*741790*	*41.2*	60	24419
2015	*1934812*	*36268*	*13031*	*872497*	*45.1*	65	18256
2020	*2054594*	*37005*	*13836*	*1004657*	*48.9*	70+	23682

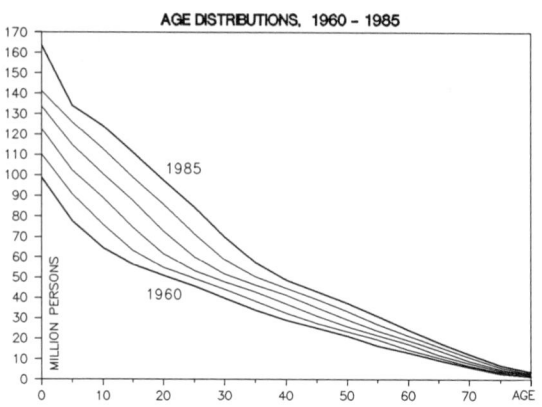

AGE DISTRIBUTIONS, 1960 - 1985

POPULATION RATIOS

YEAR	AGE DISTRIBUTION UNDER 15	15-64	65 & OLDER	70 & OLDER	DEPENDENCY RATIO	WOMEN 15-49	CHILD-WOMAN RATIO
1950	0.390	0.575	0.035	0.019	0.740	0.232	0.667
1955	0.395	0.571	0.035	0.018	0.752	0.233	0.692
1960	0.405	0.560	0.035	0.018	0.785	0.229	0.725
1965	0.414	0.551	0.035	0.019	0.816	0.225	0.731
1970	0.417	0.548	0.035	0.019	0.826	0.224	0.727
1975	0.412	0.551	0.037	0.020	0.814	0.225	0.700
1980	0.401	0.561	0.038	0.021	0.783	0.229	0.650
1985	0.394	0.567	0.039	0.022	0.765	0.231	0.661
1990	*0.386*	*0.573*	*0.041*	*0.023*	*0.744*	*0.234*	*0.622*
2000	*0.366*	*0.589*	*0.045*	*0.026*	*0.699*	*0.241*	*0.544*
2010	*0.322*	*0.627*	*0.051*	*0.031*	*0.596*	*0.253*	*0.427*
2020	*0.268*	*0.669*	*0.063*	*0.038*	*0.495*	*0.264*	*0.323*

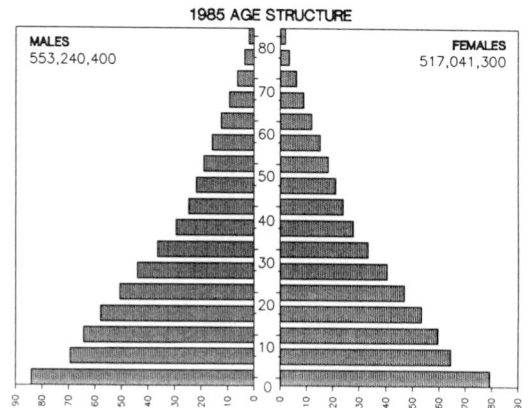

1985 AGE STRUCTURE

MALES 553,240,400   FEMALES 517,041,300

MORTALITY MEASURES (Annual Averages)

PERIOD	CRUDE DEATH RATE	INFANT MORT. RATE	LIFE EXPECTANCY AT BIRTH (years) MALE	FEMALE	BOTH SEXES	DIFFERENCE FEMALE-MALE
1950-55	25.13	188.54	39.61	38.03	38.84	-1.58
1955-60	22.16	171.75	43.22	41.39	42.33	-1.83
1960-65	19.96	156.79	45.74	44.19	44.99	-1.56
1965-70	18.13	145.13	48.13	46.71	47.43	-1.42
1970-75	16.57	136.29	50.39	48.67	49.55	-1.72
1975-80	14.62	127.28	52.36	51.59	51.98	-0.77
1980-85	13.28	113.14	54.52	54.35	54.41	-0.16
1985-90	*11.81*	*101.83*	*56.92*	*56.97*	*56.94*	*0.04*
1990-95	*10.58*	*91.50*	*59.03*	*59.47*	*59.25*	*0.43*
2000-05	*8.33*	*71.22*	*63.14*	*64.31*	*63.71*	*1.17*
2010-15	*7.00*	*53.19*	*66.51*	*68.79*	*67.62*	*2.27*
2020-25	*6.73*	*38.97*	*68.91*	*72.13*	*70.48*	*3.22*

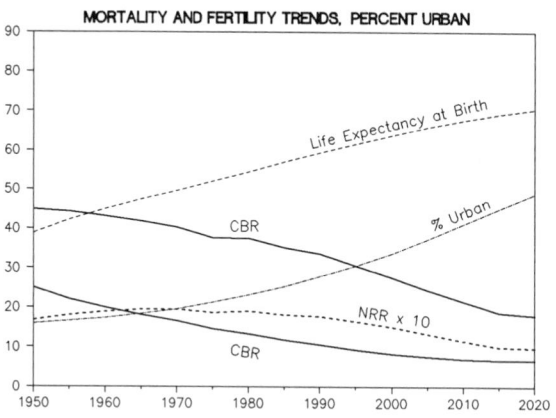

MORTALITY AND FERTILITY TRENDS, PERCENT URBAN

FERTILITY MEASURES (Annual Averages)

PERIOD	CRUDE BIRTH RATE	FERTILITY RATES GENERAL	FERTILITY RATES TOTAL	REPRODUCTION RATES GROSS	REPRODUCTION RATES NET	RATE OF NATUR. INCR.
1950-55	44.92	193.21	6.108	2.979	1.689	19.78
1955-60	44.43	192.47	6.090	2.971	1.814	22.27
1960-65	43.21	190.28	6.033	2.943	1.898	23.24
1965-70	41.89	186.59	5.956	2.905	1.957	23.76
1970-75	40.38	179.79	5.755	2.807	1.954	23.81
1975-80	37.66	165.73	5.267	2.569	1.874	23.04
1980-85	37.64	163.59	5.141	2.508	1.904	24.36
1985-90	*35.19*	*151.36*	*4.716*	*2.300*	*1.811*	*23.38*
1990-95	*33.76*	*144.09*	*4.473*	*2.182*	*1.776*	*23.18*
2000-05	*27.53*	*113.07*	*3.586*	*1.749*	*1.508*	*19.20*
2010-15	*21.49*	*83.92*	*2.645*	*1.290*	*1.160*	*14.49*
2020-25	*18.01*	*67.99*	*2.158*	*1.053*	*0.974*	*11.28*

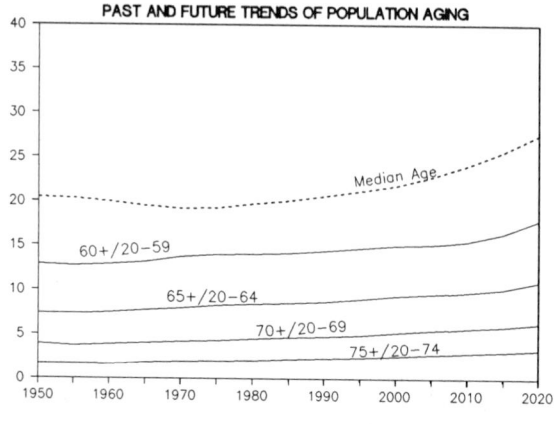

PAST AND FUTURE TRENDS OF POPULATION AGING

AGING MEASURES

YEAR	POPULATION AGE RATIOS 60+/20-59	65+/20-64	70+/20-69	75+/20-74	POPULATION MEAN AGE	POPULATION MEDIAN AGE
1950	0.1285	0.0735	0.0389	0.0167	24.63	20.42
1960	0.1283	0.0744	0.0384	0.0161	24.27	19.98
1970	0.1369	0.0789	0.0417	0.0185	24.08	19.21
1980	0.1401	0.0837	0.0446	0.0198	24.44	19.74
1990	*0.1435*	*0.0863*	*0.0474*	*0.0223*	*24.91*	*20.64*
2000	*0.1498*	*0.0931*	*0.0521*	*0.0250*	*25.88*	*21.78*
2010	*0.1545*	*0.0972*	*0.0569*	*0.0288*	*27.75*	*24.09*
2020	*0.1785*	*0.1094*	*0.0625*	*0.0322*	*30.43*	*27.58*

OBSERVED AND *PROJECTED* POPULATION DATA (000's)

YEAR	MID-YEAR POPULATION	NO. OF BIRTHS	NO. OF DEATHS	URBAN POPULATION NUMBER	URBAN POPULATION PERCENT	POPULATION 1985 AGE	POPULATION 1985 NUMBER
1950	42432	2014	992	10128	23.9	0	17704
1955	48575	2262	994	13749	28.3	5	15224
1960	55856	2494	994	18390	32.9	10	13675
1965	64133	2723	996	24470	38.2	15	11937
1970	73670	2924	990	31817	43.2	20	10506
1975	85212	3254	903	40783	47.9	25	8872
1980	98244	3599	938	50822	51.7	30	7389
1985	113913	4027	960	62594	54.9	35	5996
1990	*130769*	*4443*	*964*	*76061*	*58.2*	40	4865
1995	*149687*	*4822*	*973*	*91549*	*61.2*	45	4296
2000	*170447*	*5183*	*1017*	*108994*	*63.9*	50	3834
2005	*192746*	*5482*	*1082*	*128512*	*66.7*	55	3172
2010	*216102*	*5648*	*1147*	*149894*	*69.4*	60	2227
2015	*239823*	*5703*	*1222*	*172322*	*71.9*	65	1530
2020	*263300*	*5780*	*1325*	*195260*	*74.2*	70+	2686

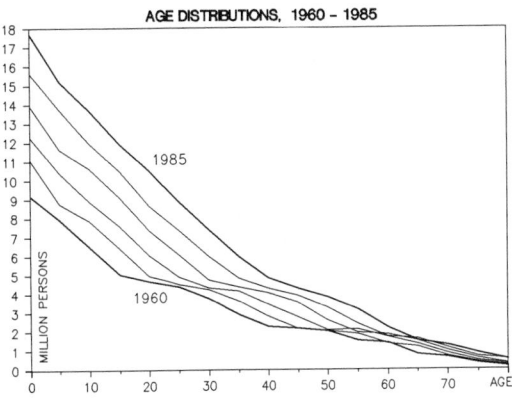

AGE DISTRIBUTIONS, 1960 – 1985

POPULATION RATIOS

YEAR	AGE DISTRIBUTION UNDER 15	AGE DISTRIBUTION 15-64	AGE DISTRIBUTION 65 & OLDER	AGE DISTRIBUTION 70 & OLDER	DEPENDENCY RATIO	WOMEN 15-49	CHILD-WOMAN RATIO
1950	0.401	0.563	0.036	0.021	0.775	0.234	0.681
1955	0.409	0.555	0.036	0.021	0.802	0.228	0.733
1960	0.422	0.542	0.035	0.021	0.844	0.221	0.744
1965	0.432	0.530	0.038	0.020	0.887	0.217	0.794
1970	0.428	0.532	0.040	0.022	0.881	0.221	0.752
1975	0.425	0.536	0.040	0.022	0.867	0.224	0.729
1980	0.421	0.539	0.040	0.024	0.854	0.224	0.711
1985	0.409	0.554	0.037	0.024	0.805	0.225	0.691
1990	*0.401*	*0.562*	*0.037*	*0.022*	*0.779*	*0.229*	*0.668*
2000	*0.388*	*0.570*	*0.042*	*0.024*	*0.753*	*0.236*	*0.608*
2010	*0.363*	*0.593*	*0.044*	*0.027*	*0.686*	*0.244*	*0.531*
2020	*0.325*	*0.622*	*0.053*	*0.031*	*0.608*	*0.253*	*0.438*

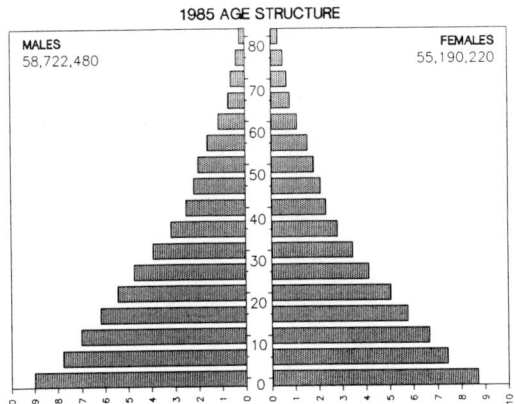

1985 AGE STRUCTURE

MALES 58,722,480   FEMALES 55,190,220

MORTALITY MEASURES (Annual Averages)

PERIOD	CRUDE DEATH RATE	INFANT MORT. RATE	LIFE EXPECTANCY AT BIRTH (years) MALE	LIFE EXPECTANCY AT BIRTH (years) FEMALE	LIFE EXPECTANCY AT BIRTH (years) BOTH SEXES	DIFFERENCE FEMALE-MALE
1950-55	23.39	203.03	42.21	44.74	43.46	2.52
1955-60	20.47	179.95	45.81	48.46	47.10	2.64
1960-65	17.80	156.88	49.06	51.73	50.38	2.67
1965-70	15.53	134.93	51.92	54.66	53.25	2.74
1970-75	13.44	117.97	54.80	58.04	56.38	3.24
1975-80	10.60	100.46	57.50	61.03	59.25	3.53
1980-85	9.55	83.14	59.48	62.60	60.99	3.12
1985-90	*8.43*	*70.43*	*61.62*	*64.75*	*63.15*	*3.13*
1990-95	*7.37*	*58.79*	*63.59*	*66.98*	*65.25*	*3.39*
2000-05	*5.97*	*40.74*	*66.82*	*70.72*	*68.72*	*3.90*
2010-15	*5.31*	*28.35*	*69.36*	*73.53*	*71.39*	*4.17*
2020-25	*5.03*	*20.43*	*71.59*	*76.00*	*73.74*	*4.41*

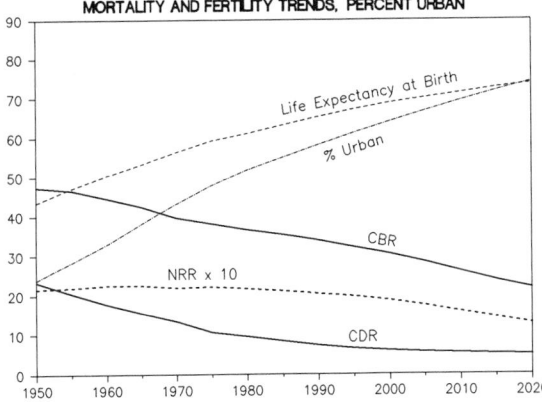

MORTALITY AND FERTILITY TRENDS, PERCENT URBAN

FERTILITY MEASURES (Annual Averages)

PERIOD	CRUDE BIRTH RATE	FERTILITY RATES GENERAL	FERTILITY RATES TOTAL	REPRODUCTION RATES GROSS	REPRODUCTION RATES NET	RATE OF NATUR. INCR.
1950-55	47.46	205.74	6.785	3.309	2.169	24.08
1955-60	46.56	207.81	6.632	3.235	2.202	26.09
1960-65	44.65	204.00	6.483	3.162	2.255	26.85
1965-70	42.45	193.40	6.249	3.048	2.262	26.92
1970-75	39.69	178.13	5.903	2.879	2.206	26.25
1975-80	38.19	170.61	5.480	2.673	2.230	27.59
1980-85	36.63	163.26	5.205	2.539	2.178	27.08
1985-90	*35.35*	*155.76*	*4.919*	*2.399*	*2.113*	*26.92*
1990-95	*33.98*	*147.43*	*4.662*	*2.274*	*2.054*	*26.61*
2000-05	*30.41*	*127.77*	*4.089*	*1.994*	*1.870*	*24.44*
2010-15	*26.14*	*106.09*	*3.398*	*1.657*	*1.589*	*20.83*
2020-25	*21.95*	*86.06*	*2.733*	*1.333*	*1.301*	*16.92*

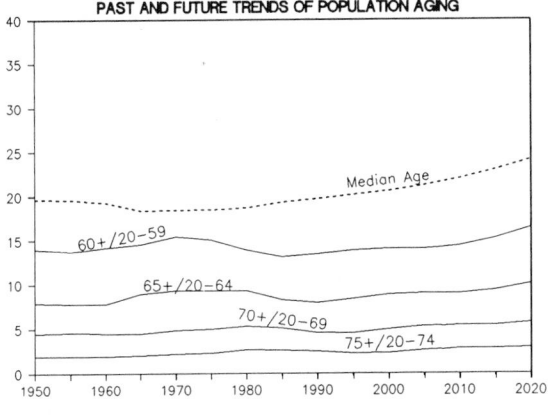

PAST AND FUTURE TRENDS OF POPULATION AGING

AGING MEASURES

YEAR	POPULATION AGE RATIOS 60+/20-59	POPULATION AGE RATIOS 65+/20-64	POPULATION AGE RATIOS 70+/20-69	POPULATION AGE RATIOS 75+/20-74	POPULATION MEAN AGE	POPULATION MEDIAN AGE
1950	0.1400	0.0791	0.0449	0.0190	24.34	19.64
1960	0.1418	0.0779	0.0447	0.0190	23.93	19.28
1970	0.1547	0.0931	0.0484	0.0221	23.72	18.47
1980	0.1394	0.0929	0.0529	0.0264	23.64	18.72
1990	*0.1349*	*0.0797*	*0.0455*	*0.0249*	*24.15*	*19.74*
2000	*0.1407*	*0.0886*	*0.0494*	*0.0231*	*24.90*	*20.63*
2010	*0.1443*	*0.0902*	*0.0536*	*0.0278*	*26.09*	*22.00*
2020	*0.1642*	*0.1007*	*0.0571*	*0.0291*	*27.87*	*24.15*

OBSERVED AND *PROJECTED* POPULATION DATA (000's)

YEAR	MID-YEAR POPULATION	NO. OF BIRTHS	NO. OF DEATHS	URBAN POPULATION		POPULATION 1985	
				NUMBER	PERCENT	AGE	NUMBER
1950	8958	433	284	520	5.8	0	2393
1955	9734	494	296	663	6.8	5	1883
1960	10775	567	322	861	8.0	10	1794
1965	12071	643	338	1129	9.4	15	1573
1970	13623	702	354	1503	11.0	20	1297
1975	15378	781	369	2021	13.1	25	1042
1980	16063	785	369	2512	15.6	30	820
1985	14519	715	335	2686	18.5	35	879
1990	*16557*	*864*	*350*	*3598*	*21.7*	40	726
1995	*23141*	*1104*	*459*	*5850*	*25.3*	45	592
2000	*26608*	*1060*	*455*	*7737*	*29.1*	50	477
2005	*29817*	*1004*	*442*	*9846*	*33.0*	55	374
2010	*32765*	*991*	*438*	*12117*	*37.0*	60	281
2015	*35651*	*974*	*438*	*14613*	*41.0*	65	194
2020	*38440*	*945*	*438*	*17290*	*45.0*	70+	193

AGE DISTRIBUTIONS, 1960 - 1985

POPULATION RATIOS

YEAR	AGE DISTRIBUTION				DEPENDENCY RATIO	WOMEN 15-49	CHILD-WOMAN RATIO
	UNDER 15	15-64	65 & OLDER	70 & OLDER			
1950	0.464	0.517	0.019	0.009	0.935	0.221	0.886
1955	0.440	0.540	0.020	0.010	0.853	0.230	0.696
1960	0.424	0.555	0.021	0.010	0.802	0.235	0.722
1965	0.413	0.565	0.021	0.010	0.769	0.238	0.748
1970	0.430	0.548	0.022	0.011	0.824	0.229	0.796
1975	0.438	0.539	0.024	0.011	0.856	0.224	0.802
1980	0.430	0.545	0.025	0.012	0.836	0.226	0.729
1985	0.418	0.555	0.027	0.013	0.801	0.230	0.717
1990	*0.420*	*0.553*	*0.028*	*0.014*	*0.810*	*0.228*	*0.784*
2000	*0.429*	*0.544*	*0.027*	*0.014*	*0.838*	*0.228*	*0.784*
2010	*0.397*	*0.571*	*0.032*	*0.017*	*0.750*	*0.240*	*0.556*
2020	*0.326*	*0.636*	*0.038*	*0.022*	*0.572*	*0.259*	*0.435*

MORTALITY MEASURES (Annual Averages)

PERIOD	CRUDE DEATH RATE	INFANT MORT. RATE	LIFE EXPECTANCY AT BIRTH (years)			
			MALE	FEMALE	BOTH SEXES	DIFFERENCE FEMALE-MALE
1950-55	31.66	227.13	31.30	31.83	31.56	0.53
1955-60	30.42	219.09	32.50	33.10	32.79	0.60
1960-65	29.93	210.87	34.00	34.00	34.00	0.00
1965-70	28.00	202.85	36.00	36.00	36.00	0.00
1970-75	26.00	193.77	38.00	38.00	38.00	0.00
1975-80	24.00	183.00	40.00	40.00	40.00	0.00
1980-85	23.00	183.00	40.00	41.00	40.50	1.00
1985-90	*23.04*	*172.10*	*41.00*	*42.00*	*41.49*	*1.00*
1990-95	*21.14*	*162.38*	*43.00*	*44.00*	*43.49*	*1.00*
2000-05	*17.09*	*142.20*	*47.00*	*48.00*	*47.49*	*1.00*
2010-15	*13.36*	*121.49*	*51.00*	*52.00*	*51.49*	*1.00*
2020-25	*11.39*	*102.00*	*55.00*	*56.00*	*55.49*	*1.00*

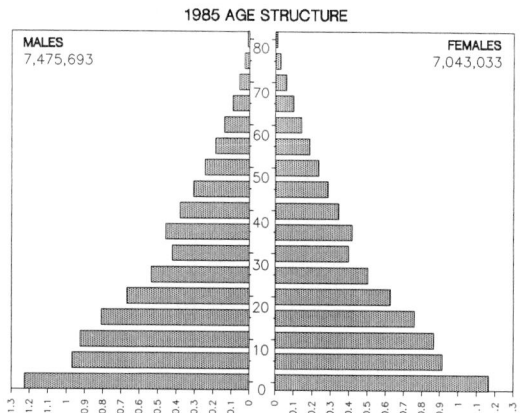

1985 AGE STRUCTURE

MALES 7,475,693   FEMALES 7,043,033

FERTILITY MEASURES (Annual Averages)

PERIOD	CRUDE BIRTH RATE	FERTILITY RATES		REPRODUCTION RATES		RATE OF NATUR. INCR.
		GENERAL	TOTAL	GROSS	NET	
1950-55	48.28	213.72	6.703	3.254	1.554	16.62
1955-60	50.72	218.01	6.860	3.330	1.648	20.30
1960-65	52.62	222.60	7.006	3.401	1.744	22.69
1965-70	53.24	228.53	7.132	3.462	1.850	25.24
1970-75	51.56	227.92	7.138	3.465	1.950	25.56
1975-80	50.80	225.66	7.210	3.500	2.050	26.80
1980-85	48.87	214.43	6.901	3.350	2.000	25.87
1985-90	*49.27*	*215.20*	*6.901*	*3.350*	*2.045*	*26.23*
1990-95	*52.17*	*219.42*	*6.798*	*3.300*	*2.095*	*31.03*
2000-05	*39.84*	*175.18*	*5.562*	*2.700*	*1.840*	*22.75*
2010-15	*30.24*	*122.70*	*4.326*	*2.100*	*1.527*	*16.88*
2020-25	*24.59*	*94.72*	*3.008*	*1.460*	*1.127*	*13.20*

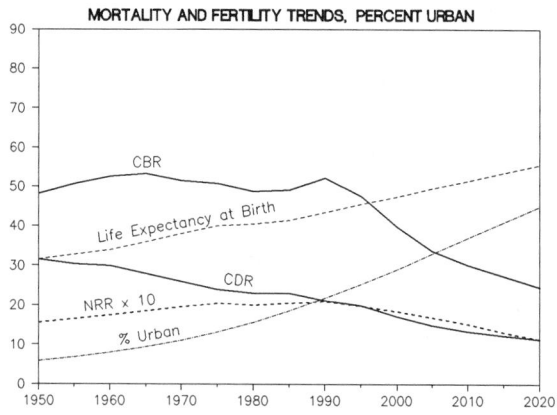

MORTALITY AND FERTILITY TRENDS, PERCENT URBAN

AGING MEASURES

YEAR	POPULATION AGE RATIOS				POPULATION	
	60+/20-59	65+/20-64	70+/20-69	75+/20-74	MEAN AGE	MEDIAN AGE
1950	0.0866	0.0467	0.0220	0.0078	21.11	16.72
1960	0.0862	0.0470	0.0222	0.0083	22.39	18.37
1970	0.0904	0.0482	0.0230	0.0089	22.58	18.87
1980	0.1044	0.0573	0.0273	0.0103	23.02	18.41
1990	*0.1112*	*0.0623*	*0.0307*	*0.0123*	*23.14*	*18.80*
2000	*0.1022*	*0.0579*	*0.0292*	*0.0123*	*23.14*	*19.41*
2010	*0.1248*	*0.0703*	*0.0355*	*0.0151*	*24.55*	*19.46*
2020	*0.1245*	*0.0722*	*0.0405*	*0.0174*	*26.69*	*23.00*

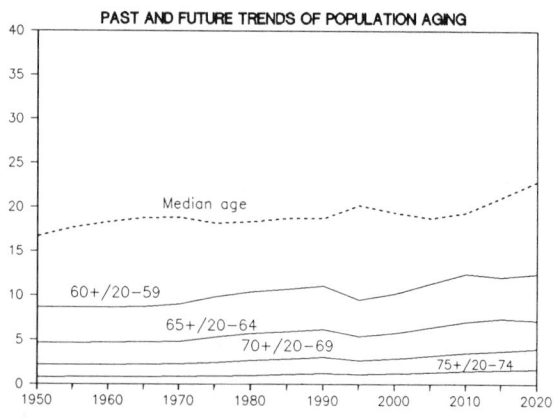

PAST AND FUTURE TRENDS OF POPULATION AGING

OBSERVED AND *PROJECTED* POPULATION DATA

YEAR	MID-YEAR POPULATION	NO. OF BIRTHS	NO. OF DEATHS	URBAN POPULATION NUMBER	URBAN POPULATION PERCENT	POPULATION 1985 AGE	POPULATION 1985 NUMBER
1950	115613	5214	1896	73580	63.6	0	58206
1955	133701	6083	2099	97198	72.7	5	44500
1960	156112	7337	2154	122704	78.6	10	40479
1965	191026	8291	1929	150099	78.6	15	35342
1970	219568	7904	1647	171811	78.2	20	41797
1975	271940	9357	1708	215620	79.3	25	51607
1980	347000	10751	1560	279406	80.5	30	50065
1985	429589	12098	1676	350953	81.7	35	33733
1990	*515462*	*12758*	*1823*	*427295*	*82.9*	40	22705
1995	*600880*	*13012*	*1989*	*505344*	*84.1*	45	16666
2000	*682081*	*13214*	*2250*	*581753*	*85.3*	50	11849
2005	*756956*	*13342*	*2549*	*654389*	*86.5*	55	8681
2010	*822652*	*13475*	*2877*	*720354*	*87.6*	60	5563
2015	*880512*	*13814*	*3199*	*779994*	*88.6*	65	3638
2020	*936507*	*14122*	*3566*	*838326*	*89.5*	70+	4759

POPULATION RATIOS

YEAR	AGE DISTRIBUTION UNDER 15	AGE DISTRIBUTION 15-64	AGE DISTRIBUTION 65 & OLDER	AGE DISTRIBUTION 70 & OLDER	DEPENDENCY RATIO	WOMEN 15-49	CHILD-WOMAN RATIO
1950	0.423	0.548	0.029	0.016	0.824	0.208	0.843
1955	0.427	0.545	0.028	0.016	0.836	0.207	0.856
1960	0.431	0.542	0.027	0.016	0.845	0.205	0.869
1965	0.508	0.470	0.022	0.013	1.126	0.208	1.008
1970	0.460	0.516	0.025	0.015	0.939	0.198	0.867
1975	0.430	0.547	0.023	0.013	0.827	0.205	0.728
1980	0.347	0.633	0.021	0.012	0.581	0.211	0.603
1985	0.333	0.647	0.020	0.011	0.545	0.211	0.644
1990	*0.327*	*0.654*	*0.020*	*0.011*	*0.529*	*0.211*	*0.595*
2000	*0.296*	*0.682*	*0.022*	*0.013*	*0.466*	*0.224*	*0.447*
2010	*0.252*	*0.720*	*0.028*	*0.016*	*0.388*	*0.235*	*0.356*
2020	*0.224*	*0.732*	*0.043*	*0.024*	*0.366*	*0.242*	*0.313*

MORTALITY MEASURES (Annual Averages)

PERIOD	CRUDE DEATH RATE	INFANT MORT. RATE	LIFE EXPECTANCY AT BIRTH (years) MALE	LIFE EXPECTANCY AT BIRTH (years) FEMALE	LIFE EXPECTANCY AT BIRTH (years) BOTH SEXES	DIFFERENCE FEMALE-MALE
1950-55	16.40	175.00	49.60	52.50	51.01	2.90
1955-60	15.70	150.00	52.40	55.60	53.96	3.20
1960-65	13.80	110.00	55.30	58.80	57.01	3.50
1965-70	10.10	78.00	58.10	62.00	60.00	3.90
1970-75	7.50	55.00	61.66	65.43	63.50	3.77
1975-80	6.28	38.00	65.57	69.52	67.50	3.95
1980-85	4.50	31.59	67.07	71.42	69.19	4.35
1985-90	*3.90*	*26.17*	*68.57*	*72.92*	*70.69*	*4.35*
1990-95	*3.54*	*22.33*	*69.77*	*74.12*	*71.89*	*4.35*
2000-05	*3.30*	*15.74*	*71.97*	*76.32*	*74.09*	*4.35*
2010-15	*3.50*	*10.80*	*73.77*	*78.32*	*75.99*	*4.55*
2020-25	*3.81*	*7.41*	*75.37*	*79.92*	*77.59*	*4.55*

FERTILITY MEASURES (Annual Averages)

PERIOD	CRUDE BIRTH RATE	FERTILITY RATES GENERAL	FERTILITY RATES TOTAL	REPRODUCTION RATES GROSS	REPRODUCTION RATES NET	RATE OF NATUR. INCR.
1950-55	45.10	217.68	6.970	3.400	2.490	28.70
1955-60	45.50	220.85	6.970	3.400	2.610	29.80
1960-65	47.00	227.44	7.175	3.500	2.810	33.20
1965-70	43.40	214.21	6.970	3.400	2.840	33.30
1970-75	36.00	178.45	5.945	2.900	2.520	28.50
1975-80	34.41	165.22	5.227	2.550	2.275	28.13
1980-85	30.98	146.98	4.632	2.260	2.139	26.49
1985-90	*28.16*	*133.48*	*4.140*	*2.020*	*1.934*	*24.26*
1990-95	*24.75*	*116.29*	*3.689*	*1.800*	*1.737*	*21.22*
2000-05	*19.37*	*85.27*	*2.910*	*1.420*	*1.388*	*16.08*
2010-15	*16.38*	*69.26*	*2.296*	*1.120*	*1.105*	*12.88*
2020-25	*15.08*	*62.30*	*2.070*	*1.010*	*1.002*	*11.27*

AGING MEASURES

YEAR	POPULATION AGE RATIOS 60+/20-59	POPULATION AGE RATIOS 65+/20-64	POPULATION AGE RATIOS 70+/20-69	POPULATION AGE RATIOS 75+/20-74	POPULATION MEAN AGE	POPULATION MEDIAN AGE
1950	0.1065	0.0639	0.0350	0.0161	22.77	18.89
1960	0.1019	0.0616	0.0343	0.0162	22.40	18.50
1970	0.0990	0.0596	0.0355	0.0192	21.85	16.94
1980	0.0662	0.0392	0.0228	0.0125	24.09	22.33
1990	*0.0575*	*0.0340*	*0.0187*	*0.0094*	*25.72*	*25.65*
2000	*0.0591*	*0.0369*	*0.0219*	*0.0107*	*27.90*	*27.50*
2010	*0.0770*	*0.0438*	*0.0252*	*0.0129*	*30.12*	*29.16*
2020	*0.1158*	*0.0661*	*0.0356*	*0.0172*	*31.94*	*31.45*

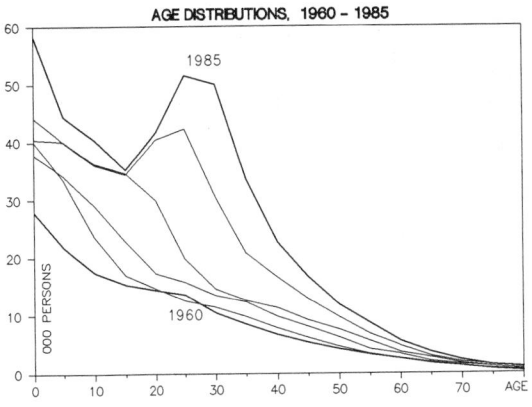

AGE DISTRIBUTIONS, 1960 - 1985

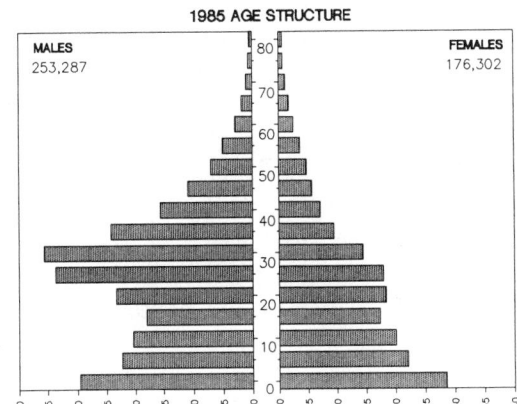

1985 AGE STRUCTURE

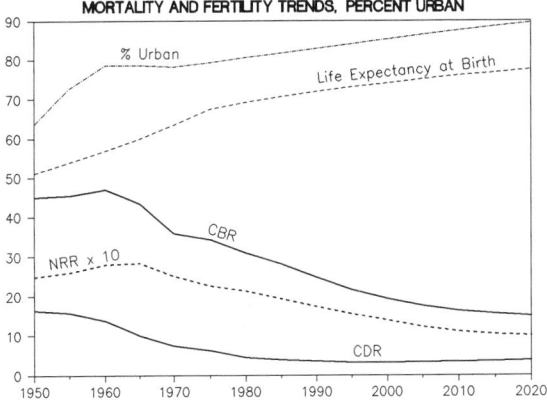

MORTALITY AND FERTILITY TRENDS, PERCENT URBAN

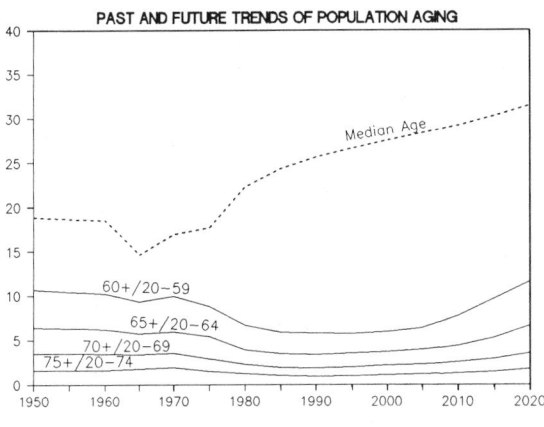

PAST AND FUTURE TRENDS OF POPULATION AGING

OBSERVED AND *PROJECTED* POPULATION DATA (000's)

YEAR	MID-YEAR POPULATION	NO. OF BIRTHS	NO. OF DEATHS	URBAN POPULATION NUMBER	URBAN POPULATION PERCENT	POPULATION 1985 AGE	POPULATION 1985 NUMBER
1950	41783	1964	1013	1818	4.4	0	17855
1955	45486	2127	1044	2153	4.7	5	15283
1960	51419	2401	1131	2647	5.1	10	13119
1965	58312	2772	1225	3629	6.2	15	10921
1970	66671	3233	1388	5073	7.6	20	9068
1975	76582	3614	1451	6985	9.1	25	7658
1980	88219	3950	1541	9189	10.4	30	5530
1985	101147	4264	1567	12008	11.9	35	4584
1990	*115593*	*4695*	*1592*	*15759*	*13.6*	40	3919
1995	*132220*	*5049*	*1613*	*20821*	*15.7*	45	3323
2000	*150589*	*5292*	*1620*	*27491*	*18.3*	50	2793
2005	*170138*	*5005*	*1575*	*36049*	*21.2*	55	2262
2010	*188196*	*4676*	*1527*	*46205*	*24.6*	60	1712
2015	*204631*	*4499*	*1514*	*57625*	*28.2*	65	1262
2020	*220119*	*4413*	*1536*	*70359*	*32.0*	70+	1857

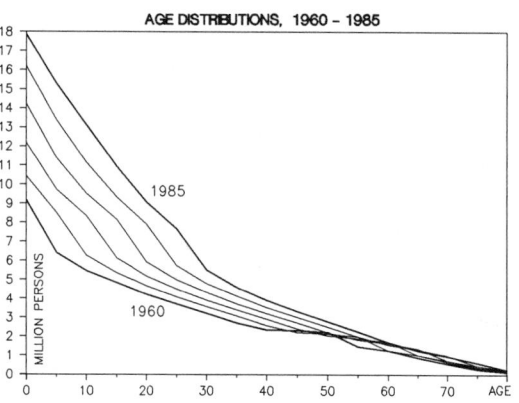

AGE DISTRIBUTIONS, 1960 – 1985

POPULATION RATIOS

YEAR	AGE DISTRIBUTION UNDER 15	15-64	65 & OLDER	70 & OLDER	DEPENDENCY RATIO	WOMEN 15-49	CHILD-WOMAN RATIO
1950	0.376	0.588	0.036	0.019	0.702	0.220	0.665
1955	0.385	0.578	0.037	0.019	0.730	0.222	0.689
1960	0.410	0.553	0.037	0.020	0.808	0.214	0.836
1965	0.433	0.530	0.037	0.020	0.887	0.209	0.857
1970	0.454	0.511	0.035	0.020	0.957	0.206	0.889
1975	0.459	0.505	0.036	0.018	0.980	0.209	0.889
1980	0.462	0.504	0.034	0.019	0.983	0.212	0.866
1985	0.457	0.512	0.031	0.018	0.954	0.217	0.814
1990	*0.439*	*0.532*	*0.029*	*0.017*	*0.879*	*0.227*	*0.725*
2000	*0.406*	*0.565*	*0.029*	*0.016*	*0.769*	*0.242*	*0.638*
2010	*0.367*	*0.602*	*0.031*	*0.018*	*0.661*	*0.253*	*0.490*
2020	*0.296*	*0.666*	*0.038*	*0.022*	*0.501*	*0.272*	*0.355*

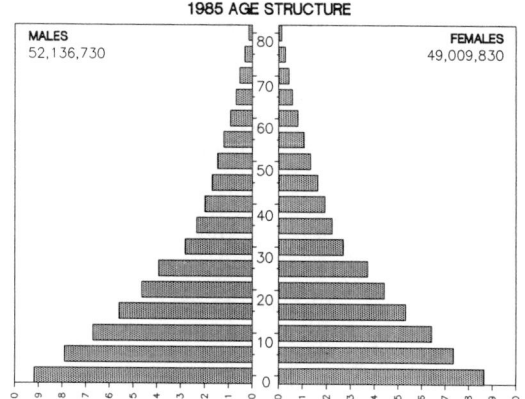

1985 AGE STRUCTURE

MALES 52,136,730 FEMALES 49,009,830

MORTALITY MEASURES (Annual Averages)

PERIOD	CRUDE DEATH RATE	INFANT MORT. RATE	LIFE EXPECTANCY AT BIRTH (years) MALE	FEMALE	BOTH SEXES	DIFFERENCE FEMALE-MALE
1950-55	24.24	179.50	38.30	34.90	36.64	-3.40
1955-60	22.95	161.90	40.00	37.20	38.63	-2.80
1960-65	22.00	150.00	41.70	39.50	40.63	-2.20
1965-70	21.00	140.00	44.10	42.50	43.32	-1.60
1970-75	20.82	140.00	45.59	44.09	44.86	-1.50
1975-80	18.95	136.60	47.11	46.11	46.62	-1.00
1980-85	17.47	128.20	49.10	48.10	48.60	-1.00
1985-90	*15.50*	*119.17*	*51.10*	*50.35*	*50.73*	*-0.75*
1990-95	*13.78*	*107.51*	*53.10*	*52.60*	*52.86*	*-0.50*
2000-05	*10.76*	*85.48*	*57.10*	*57.10*	*57.10*	*0.00*
2010-15	*8.11*	*69.15*	*61.10*	*61.60*	*61.34*	*0.50*
2020-25	*6.98*	*53.40*	*65.10*	*66.10*	*65.59*	*1.00*

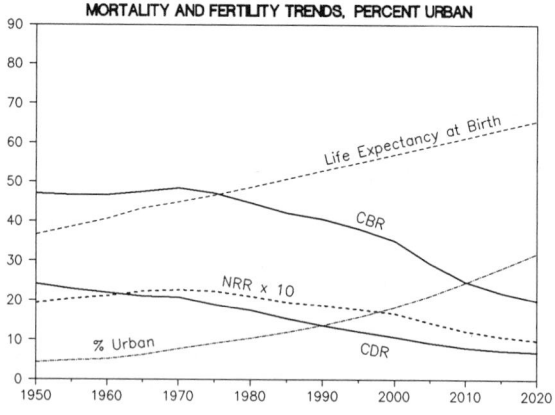

MORTALITY AND FERTILITY TRENDS, PERCENT URBAN

FERTILITY MEASURES (Annual Averages)

PERIOD	CRUDE BIRTH RATE	FERTILITY RATES GENERAL	TOTAL	REPRODUCTION RATES GROSS	NET	RATE OF NATUR. INCR.
1950-55	47.00	212.86	6.662	3.250	1.940	22.76
1955-60	46.76	215.18	6.621	3.230	2.050	23.81
1960-65	46.69	221.26	6.681	3.259	2.115	24.69
1965-70	47.55	229.51	6.906	3.369	2.236	26.54
1970-75	48.49	233.54	7.017	3.423	2.271	27.67
1975-80	47.19	223.81	6.656	3.247	2.234	28.25
1980-85	44.78	208.56	6.150	3.000	2.106	27.31
1985-90	*42.16*	*189.67*	*5.535*	*2.700*	*1.953*	*26.66*
1990-95	*40.61*	*175.50*	*5.125*	*2.500*	*1.873*	*26.84*
2000-05	*35.14*	*143.95*	*4.305*	*2.100*	*1.675*	*24.38*
2010-15	*24.85*	*96.21*	*2.993*	*1.460*	*1.230*	*16.73*
2020-25	*20.05*	*73.32*	*2.296*	*1.120*	*0.989*	*13.07*

AGING MEASURES

YEAR	POPULATION AGE RATIOS 60+/20-59	65+/20-64	70+/20-69	75+/20-74	POPULATION MEAN AGE	POPULATION MEDIAN AGE
1950	0.1321	0.0738	0.0369	0.0156	25.66	21.60
1960	0.1417	0.0809	0.0410	0.0175	24.48	19.80
1970	0.1542	0.0837	0.0462	0.0208	23.08	17.50
1980	0.1359	0.0855	0.0466	0.0189	22.01	16.81
1990	*0.1145*	*0.0691*	*0.0393*	*0.0202*	*22.23*	*17.72*
2000	*0.1037*	*0.0627*	*0.0345*	*0.0168*	*23.16*	*19.34*
2010	*0.1034*	*0.0629*	*0.0351*	*0.0173*	*24.99*	*21.48*
2020	*0.1207*	*0.0682*	*0.0379*	*0.0190*	*27.95*	*24.95*

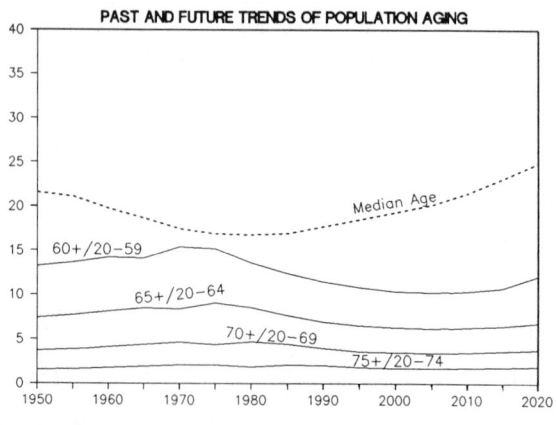

PAST AND FUTURE TRENDS OF POPULATION AGING

OBSERVED AND *PROJECTED* POPULATION DATA

YEAR	MID-YEAR POPULATION	NO. OF BIRTHS	NO. OF DEATHS	URBAN POPULATION NUMBER	URBAN POPULATION PERCENT	POPULATION 1985 AGE	POPULATION 1985 NUMBER
1950	733700	31890	19988	15408	2.1	0	206129
1955	795500	34180	20475	18229	2.3	5	178364
1960	867500	36625	20927	21688	2.5	10	160895
1965	949700	39655	21516	26444	2.8	15	138997
1970	1044600	42829	22271	32384	3.1	20	121085
1975	1143500	45740	22658	39454	3.5	25	105430
1980	1245000	48555	22586	48767	3.9	30	91233
1985	1362000	52128	22924	61742	4.5	35	78525
1990	1516293	57874	23563	81020	5.3	40	66870
1995	1698131	63386	24147	108793	6.4	45	56394
2000	1906351	68177	24590	148701	7.8	50	46638
2005	2137499	72292	24906	201985	9.4	55	37518
2010	2388333	71578	24851	271814	11.4	60	28859
2015	2633986	68175	24609	358626	13.6	65	20689
2020	2861212	64786	24532	462525	16.2	70+	24375

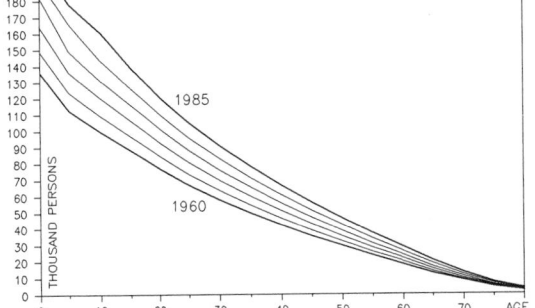

AGE DISTRIBUTIONS, 1960 – 1985

POPULATION RATIOS

YEAR	AGE DISTRIBUTION UNDER 15	AGE DISTRIBUTION 15-64	AGE DISTRIBUTION 65 & OLDER	AGE DISTRIBUTION 70 & OLDER	DEPENDENCY RATIO	WOMEN 15-49	CHILD-WOMAN RATIO
1950	0.398	0.566	0.036	0.019	0.766	0.242	0.644
1955	0.400	0.566	0.034	0.019	0.768	0.241	0.650
1960	0.402	0.566	0.032	0.018	0.767	0.239	0.654
1965	0.402	0.566	0.032	0.017	0.767	0.238	0.657
1970	0.403	0.566	0.032	0.017	0.768	0.236	0.664
1975	0.404	0.564	0.032	0.017	0.774	0.234	0.680
1980	0.404	0.564	0.032	0.017	0.773	0.232	0.666
1985	0.400	0.566	0.033	0.018	0.765	0.232	0.653
1990	0.397	0.569	0.034	0.018	0.756	0.232	0.660
2000	0.400	0.565	0.035	0.020	0.771	0.229	0.673
2010	0.391	0.571	0.038	0.021	0.750	0.231	0.624
2020	0.348	0.609	0.043	0.024	0.641	0.247	0.465

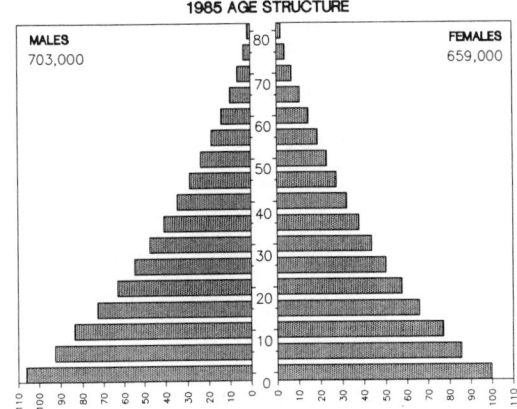

1985 AGE STRUCTURE

MALES 703,000   FEMALES 659,000

MORTALITY MEASURES (Annual Averages)

PERIOD	CRUDE DEATH RATE	INFANT MORT. RATE	LIFE EXPECTANCY AT BIRTH (years) MALE	LIFE EXPECTANCY AT BIRTH (years) FEMALE	LIFE EXPECTANCY AT BIRTH (years) BOTH SEXES	DIFFERENCE FEMALE-MALE
1950-55	27.24	197.10	37.00	35.50	36.27	-1.50
1955-60	25.74	190.60	38.30	36.80	37.57	-1.50
1960-65	24.12	182.10	39.80	38.30	39.07	-1.50
1965-70	22.66	164.30	41.35	39.85	40.62	-1.50
1970-75	21.32	152.90	43.00	41.50	42.27	-1.50
1975-80	19.82	146.50	44.60	43.10	43.87	-1.50
1980-85	18.14	138.70	46.60	45.10	45.87	-1.50
1985-90	16.83	128.20	48.60	47.10	47.87	-1.50
1990-95	15.54	118.20	50.60	49.35	49.99	-1.25
2000-05	12.90	99.28	54.60	53.85	54.23	-0.75
2010-15	10.40	79.47	58.60	58.35	58.48	-0.25
2020-25	8.57	61.44	62.50	62.85	62.67	0.35

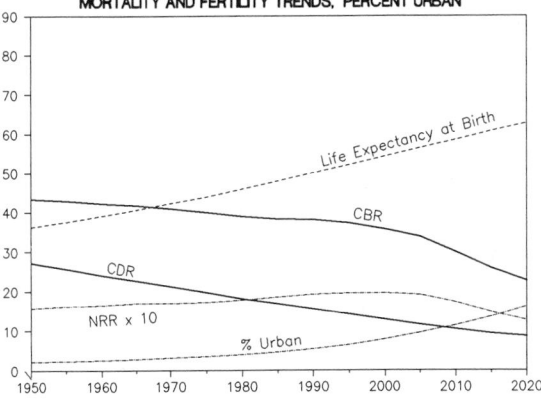

MORTALITY AND FERTILITY TRENDS, PERCENT URBAN

Life Expectancy at Birth

CBR

CDR

NRR x 10

% Urban

FERTILITY MEASURES (Annual Averages)

PERIOD	CRUDE BIRTH RATE	FERTILITY RATES GENERAL	FERTILITY RATES TOTAL	REPRODUCTION RATES GROSS	REPRODUCTION RATES NET	RATE OF NATUR. INCR.
1950-55	43.46	179.93	6.023	2.938	1.565	16.22
1955-60	42.97	178.95	5.988	2.921	1.607	17.23
1960-65	42.22	176.90	5.918	2.887	1.647	18.10
1965-70	41.76	176.09	5.892	2.874	1.699	19.10
1970-75	41.00	174.42	5.740	2.800	1.700	19.68
1975-80	40.00	171.62	5.637	2.750	1.720	20.18
1980-85	39.00	168.09	5.535	2.700	1.780	20.86
1985-90	38.27	165.03	5.535	2.700	1.844	21.44
1990-95	38.17	164.97	5.535	2.700	1.918	22.63
2000-05	35.76	156.52	5.227	2.550	1.951	22.86
2010-15	29.97	127.99	4.305	2.100	1.716	19.57
2020-25	22.64	89.76	2.993	1.460	1.264	14.07

AGING MEASURES

YEAR	POPULATION AGE RATIOS 60+/20-59	POPULATION AGE RATIOS 65+/20-64	POPULATION AGE RATIOS 70+/20-69	POPULATION AGE RATIOS 75+/20-74	POPULATION MEAN AGE	POPULATION MEDIAN AGE
1950	0.1303	0.0770	0.0405	0.0177	24.41	20.07
1960	0.1201	0.0698	0.0368	0.0163	24.11	19.83
1970	0.1184	0.0683	0.0354	0.0155	24.04	19.77
1980	0.1206	0.0699	0.0365	0.0160	24.07	19.75
1990	0.1245	0.0728	0.0383	0.0171	24.32	19.97
2000	0.1290	0.0761	0.0406	0.0184	24.40	20.09
2010	0.1353	0.0806	0.0436	0.0201	24.82	20.37
2020	0.1405	0.0846	0.0464	0.0219	26.34	22.39

PAST AND FUTURE TRENDS OF POPULATION AGING

Median Age

60+/20-59

65+/20-64

70+/20-69

75+/20-74

OBSERVED AND *PROJECTED* POPULATION DATA (000's)

YEAR	MID-YEAR POPULATION	NO. OF BIRTHS	NO. OF DEATHS	URBAN POPULATION NUMBER	URBAN POPULATION PERCENT	POPULATION AGE	1985 NUMBER
1950	17832	753	423	2876	16.1	0	5297
1955	19561	839	426	3451	17.6	5	4782
1960	21746	883	424	4189	19.3	10	4652
1965	24167	945	391	5074	21.0	15	4070
1970	27102	1020	386	6190	22.8	20	3581
1975	30441	1090	378	7276	23.9	25	3017
1980	33821	1160	373	8083	23.9	30	2346
1985	37544	1149	366	8973	23.9	35	1818
1990	*41675*	*1236*	*364*	*10247*	*24.6*	40	1613
1995	*46275*	*1284*	*361*	*12029*	*26.0*	45	1541
2000	*51129*	*1285*	*364*	*14405*	*28.2*	50	1415
2005	*55950*	*1258*	*371*	*17454*	*31.2*	55	1085
2010	*60567*	*1216*	*386*	*21265*	*35.1*	60	904
2015	*64864*	*1159*	*406*	*25364*	*39.1*	65	584
2020	*68743*	*1187*	*433*	*29635*	*43.1*	70+	839

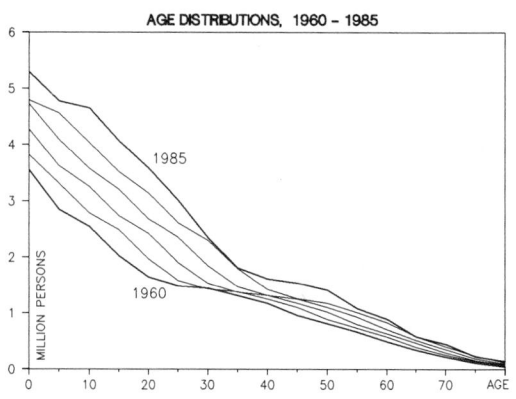

AGE DISTRIBUTIONS, 1960 – 1985

POPULATION RATIOS

YEAR	AGE DISTRIBUTION UNDER 15	15-64	65 & OLDER	70 & OLDER	DEPENDENCY RATIO	WOMEN 15-49	CHILD-WOMAN RATIO
1950	0.378	0.590	0.032	0.017	0.696	0.249	0.642
1955	0.397	0.569	0.033	0.017	0.756	0.238	0.662
1960	0.411	0.554	0.034	0.018	0.803	0.231	0.708
1965	0.411	0.554	0.035	0.019	0.805	0.231	0.686
1970	0.412	0.551	0.037	0.020	0.815	0.229	0.690
1975	0.407	0.554	0.038	0.021	0.804	0.231	0.673
1980	0.396	0.564	0.040	0.022	0.773	0.236	0.602
1985	0.392	0.570	0.038	0.022	0.755	0.243	0.581
1990	*0.372*	*0.587*	*0.041*	*0.022*	*0.703*	*0.251*	*0.534*
2000	*0.349*	*0.605*	*0.047*	*0.026*	*0.654*	*0.261*	*0.479*
2010	*0.314*	*0.637*	*0.050*	*0.031*	*0.571*	*0.267*	*0.391*
2020	*0.264*	*0.678*	*0.058*	*0.034*	*0.475*	*0.270*	*0.313*

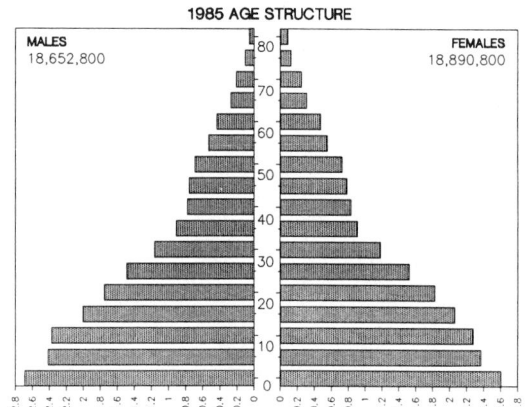

1985 AGE STRUCTURE

MALES 18,652,800   FEMALES 18,890,800

MORTALITY MEASURES (Annual Averages)

PERIOD	CRUDE DEATH RATE	INFANT MORT. RATE	LIFE EXPECTANCY AT BIRTH (years) MALE	FEMALE	BOTH SEXES	DIFFERENCE FEMALE-MALE
1950-55	23.72	183.00	38.66	41.41	40.00	2.75
1955-60	21.76	166.00	41.11	43.96	42.50	2.84
1960-65	19.50	140.00	43.57	46.51	45.00	2.94
1965-70	16.19	110.00	48.08	50.99	49.50	2.91
1970-75	14.24	100.00	50.99	54.08	52.50	3.09
1975-80	12.42	90.00	53.39	56.69	55.00	3.30
1980-85	11.03	80.00	55.80	59.28	57.50	3.48
1985-90	*9.74*	*70.23*	*58.30*	*61.78*	*60.00*	*3.48*
1990-95	*8.73*	*59.13*	*60.76*	*64.28*	*62.48*	*3.52*
2000-05	*7.12*	*40.70*	*65.00*	*68.78*	*66.84*	*3.78*
2010-15	*6.37*	*28.37*	*68.04*	*72.18*	*70.06*	*4.14*
2020-25	*6.29*	*20.38*	*70.40*	*74.70*	*72.50*	*4.30*

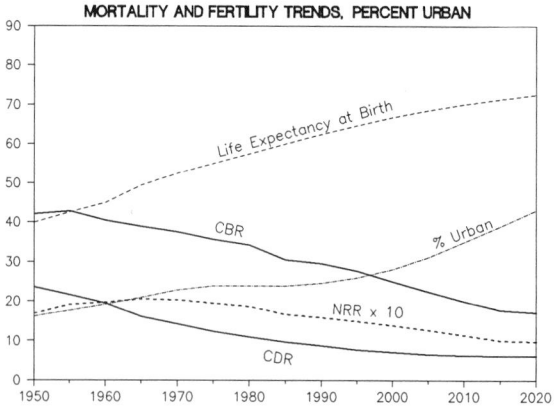

MORTALITY AND FERTILITY TRENDS, PERCENT URBAN

FERTILITY MEASURES (Annual Averages)

PERIOD	CRUDE BIRTH RATE	FERTILITY RATES GENERAL	FERTILITY RATES TOTAL	REPRODUCTION RATES GROSS	REPRODUCTION RATES NET	RATE OF NATUR. INCR.
1950-55	42.22	173.59	5.637	2.750	1.698	18.50
1955-60	42.91	183.29	6.047	2.950	1.921	21.16
1960-65	40.60	176.04	5.945	2.900	1.978	21.09
1965-70	39.09	170.17	5.740	2.800	2.060	22.90
1970-75	37.63	163.70	5.432	2.650	2.045	23.40
1975-80	35.80	153.38	5.022	2.450	1.960	23.38
1980-85	34.30	143.19	4.612	2.250	1.870	23.27
1985-90	*30.60*	*123.94*	*4.024*	*1.963*	*1.681*	*20.86*
1990-95	*29.66*	*117.21*	*3.690*	*1.800*	*1.590*	*20.92*
2000-05	*25.13*	*95.84*	*3.075*	*1.500*	*1.392*	*18.01*
2010-15	*20.07*	*74.97*	*2.460*	*1.200*	*1.147*	*13.70*
2020-25	*17.26*	*64.26*	*2.070*	*1.010*	*0.982*	*10.97*

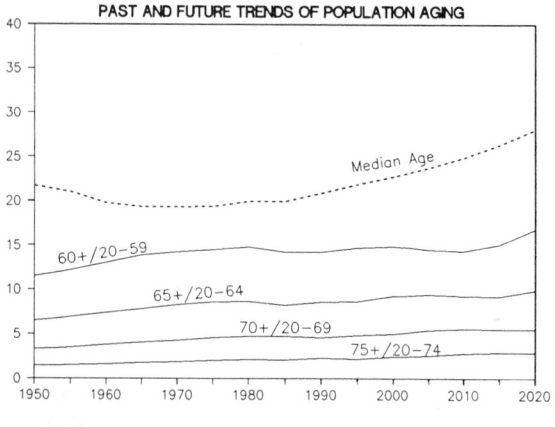

PAST AND FUTURE TRENDS OF POPULATION AGING

AGING MEASURES

YEAR	POPULATION AGE RATIOS 60+/20-59	65+/20-64	70+/20-69	75+/20-74	POPULATION MEAN AGE	POPULATION MEDIAN AGE
1950	0.1149	0.0650	0.0331	0.0143	25.06	21.76
1960	0.1299	0.0739	0.0378	0.0162	24.53	19.75
1970	0.1420	0.0827	0.0426	0.0187	24.30	19.36
1980	0.1478	0.0866	0.0469	0.0216	24.60	19.98
1990	*0.1420*	*0.0859*	*0.0453*	*0.0227*	*25.14*	*20.92*
2000	*0.1482*	*0.0924*	*0.0502*	*0.0244*	*26.28*	*22.81*
2010	*0.1431*	*0.0926*	*0.0558*	*0.0284*	*28.12*	*24.95*
2020	*0.1684*	*0.0989*	*0.0553*	*0.0292*	*30.69*	*28.07*

OBSERVED AND *PROJECTED* POPULATION DATA (000's)

YEAR	MID-YEAR POPULATION	NO. OF BIRTHS	NO. OF DEATHS	URBAN POPULATION NUMBER	PERCENT	POPULATION 1985 AGE	NUMBER
1950	554760	24188	13869	60969	11.0	0	93282
1955	609005	21863	12546	80715	13.3	5	97156
1960	657492	24853	11243	124892	19.0	10	124614
1965	729191	26907	7948	145109	19.9	15	129332
1970	830675	25419	7227	166966	20.1	20	107785
1975	927269	19936	6676	187309	20.2	25	85912
1980	996134	18930	6643	203351	20.4	30	88656
1985	1059522	21728	7060	218576	20.6	35	65196
1990	*1135496*	*22687*	*7470*	*243475*	*21.4*	40	50813
1995	*1214221*	*21883*	*7959*	*277982*	*22.9*	45	47675
2000	*1285894*	*19380*	*8511*	*322125*	*25.1*	50	44608
2005	*1341412*	*17240*	*9154*	*375479*	*28.0*	55	37621
2010	*1382463*	*17624*	*9943*	*439443*	*31.8*	60	30794
2015	*1421408*	*18409*	*10841*	*507696*	*35.7*	65	23372
2020	*1459753*	*18390*	*11904*	*579781*	*39.7*	70+	32707

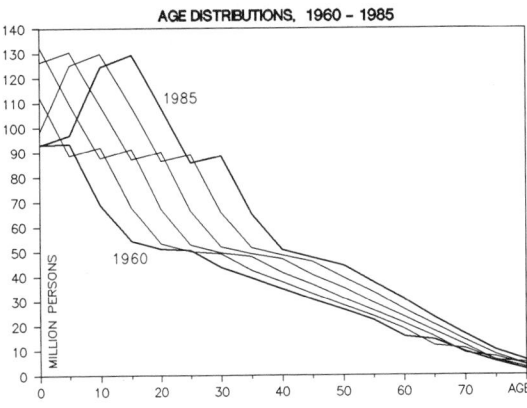

POPULATION RATIOS

YEAR	UNDER 15	15-64	65 & OLDER	70 & OLDER	DEPENDENCY RATIO	WOMEN 15-49	CHILD-WOMAN RATIO
1950	0.335	0.620	0.045	0.022	0.613	0.242	0.567
1955	0.371	0.583	0.046	0.025	0.716	0.227	0.727
1960	0.389	0.563	0.048	0.026	0.777	0.220	0.646
1965	0.402	0.554	0.044	0.027	0.804	0.216	0.713
1970	0.397	0.560	0.043	0.024	0.787	0.221	0.722
1975	0.395	0.561	0.044	0.025	0.781	0.222	0.614
1980	0.355	0.598	0.047	0.027	0.672	0.238	0.416
1985	0.297	0.650	0.053	0.031	0.539	0.260	0.338
1990	*0.262*	*0.680*	*0.058*	*0.034*	*0.472*	*0.275*	*0.347*
2000	*0.257*	*0.673*	*0.070*	*0.043*	*0.486*	*0.269*	*0.317*
2010	*0.211*	*0.708*	*0.081*	*0.052*	*0.413*	*0.266*	*0.234*
2020	*0.182*	*0.704*	*0.114*	*0.066*	*0.421*	*0.243*	*0.260*

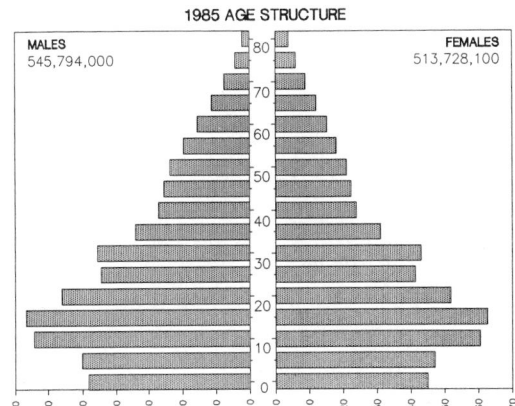

MORTALITY MEASURES (Annual Averages)

PERIOD	CRUDE DEATH RATE	INFANT MORT. RATE	MALE	FEMALE	BOTH SEXES	DIFFERENCE FEMALE-MALE
1950-55	25.00	195.00	39.30	42.30	40.76	3.00
1955-60	20.60	178.70	43.10	46.20	44.61	3.10
1960-65	17.10	120.71	48.70	50.40	49.53	1.70
1965-70	10.90	80.82	58.80	60.40	59.58	1.60
1970-75	8.70	61.10	62.50	63.90	63.18	1.40
1975-80	7.20	41.49	65.50	66.20	65.84	0.70
1980-85	6.67	39.33	66.69	68.95	67.79	2.26
1985-90	*6.66*	*32.45*	*67.98*	*70.94*	*69.42*	*2.96*
1990-95	*6.58*	*26.74*	*69.24*	*72.64*	*70.89*	*3.41*
2000-05	*6.62*	*18.77*	*71.44*	*75.08*	*73.21*	*3.64*
2010-15	*7.19*	*13.08*	*73.30*	*77.10*	*75.14*	*3.81*
2020-25	*8.15*	*8.86*	*74.85*	*78.93*	*76.83*	*4.08*

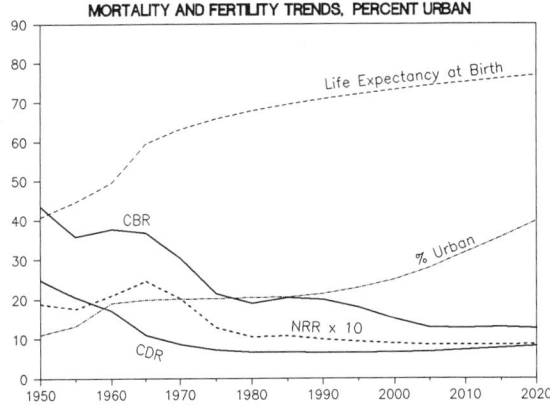

FERTILITY MEASURES (Annual Averages)

PERIOD	CRUDE BIRTH RATE	FERTILITY RATES GENERAL	TOTAL	REPRODUCTION RATES GROSS	NET	RATE OF NATUR. INCR.
1950-55	43.60	186.44	6.242	3.030	1.890	18.60
1955-60	35.90	160.90	5.397	2.620	1.760	15.30
1960-65	37.80	173.65	5.933	2.880	2.100	20.70
1965-70	36.90	168.81	5.995	2.910	2.460	26.00
1970-75	30.60	138.08	4.759	2.310	2.040	21.90
1975-80	21.50	93.38	2.905	1.410	1.290	14.30
1980-85	19.00	76.17	2.365	1.148	1.054	12.33
1985-90	*20.51*	*76.54*	*2.365*	*1.148*	*1.075*	*13.85*
1990-95	*19.98*	*72.70*	*2.151*	*1.044*	*0.991*	*13.40*
2000-05	*15.07*	*56.53*	*1.899*	*0.922*	*0.890*	*8.45*
2010-15	*12.75*	*48.51*	*1.798*	*0.873*	*0.853*	*5.56*
2020-25	*12.60*	*53.88*	*1.798*	*0.873*	*0.859*	*4.44*

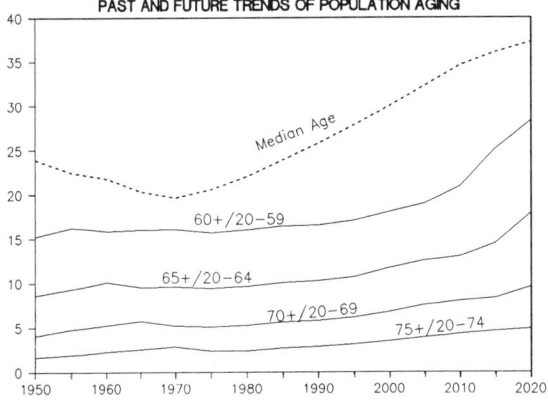

AGING MEASURES

YEAR	60+/20-59	65+/20-64	70+/20-69	75+/20-74	MEAN AGE	MEDIAN AGE
1950	0.1524	0.0858	0.0407	0.0167	27.38	23.93
1960	0.1585	0.1007	0.0524	0.0231	25.99	21.81
1970	0.1610	0.0958	0.0521	0.0285	25.00	19.68
1980	0.1599	0.0965	0.0526	0.0240	26.58	22.09
1990	*0.1652*	*0.1024*	*0.0579*	*0.0288*	*29.28*	*25.81*
2000	*0.1806*	*0.1169*	*0.0677*	*0.0346*	*31.52*	*30.06*
2010	*0.2093*	*0.1301*	*0.0801*	*0.0433*	*34.67*	*34.65*
2020	*0.2830*	*0.1792*	*0.0955*	*0.0488*	*37.53*	*37.24*

OBSERVED AND *PROJECTED* POPULATION DATA

YEAR	MID-YEAR POPULATION	NO. OF BIRTHS	NO. OF DEATHS	URBAN POPULATION NUMBER	URBAN POPULATION PERCENT	POPULATION 1985 AGE	POPULATION 1985 NUMBER
1950	494011	13536	5187	147172	29.8	0	64100
1955	529989	13992	5565	173003	32.6	5	52300
1960	572999	14440	6016	204152	35.6	10	51500
1965	582300	12228	5823	222373	38.2	15	54200
1970	615000	11070	5966	250687	40.8	20	61500
1975	609235	11393	5239	264331	43.4	25	57500
1980	629291	12838	5286	291409	46.3	30	49400
1985	665200	12395	5457	329082	49.5	35	47800
1990	*700819*	*11997*	*5489*	*370101*	*52.8*	40	38200
1995	*734133*	*11521*	*5479*	*412900*	*56.2*	45	35600
2000	*764980*	*11443*	*5507*	*456589*	*59.7*	50	30200
2005	*795248*	*11853*	*5832*	*500395*	*62.9*	55	27600
2010	*825938*	*12051*	*6270*	*544666*	*65.9*	60	24600
2015	*855363*	*12085*	*6825*	*588072*	*68.8*	65	22900
2020	*882075*	*11919*	*7445*	*629317*	*71.3*	70+	47800

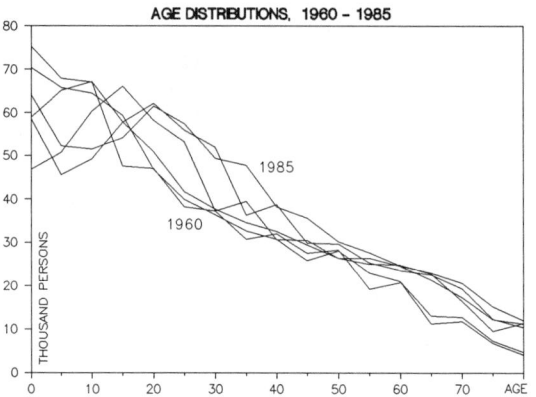

AGE DISTRIBUTIONS, 1960 - 1985

POPULATION RATIOS

YEAR	AGE DISTRIBUTION UNDER 15	AGE DISTRIBUTION 15-64	AGE DISTRIBUTION 65 & OLDER	AGE DISTRIBUTION 70 & OLDER	DEPENDENCY RATIO	WOMEN 15-49	CHILD-WOMAN RATIO
1950	0.345	0.595	0.060	0.036	0.681	0.251	0.537
1955	0.342	0.590	0.067	0.041	0.694	0.249	0.492
1960	0.367	0.574	0.059	0.040	0.743	0.236	0.556
1965	0.344	0.591	0.065	0.042	0.693	0.241	0.502
1970	0.311	0.588	0.101	0.066	0.699	0.236	0.406
1975	0.259	0.642	0.098	0.061	0.557	0.259	0.297
1980	0.244	0.654	0.103	0.067	0.530	0.261	0.356
1985	0.252	0.641	0.106	0.072	0.559	0.257	0.375
1990	*0.256*	*0.642*	*0.103*	*0.071*	*0.559*	*0.254*	*0.354*
2000	*0.238*	*0.659*	*0.103*	*0.069*	*0.517*	*0.248*	*0.307*
2010	*0.213*	*0.669*	*0.118*	*0.078*	*0.495*	*0.239*	*0.304*
2020	*0.206*	*0.648*	*0.146*	*0.097*	*0.544*	*0.224*	*0.309*

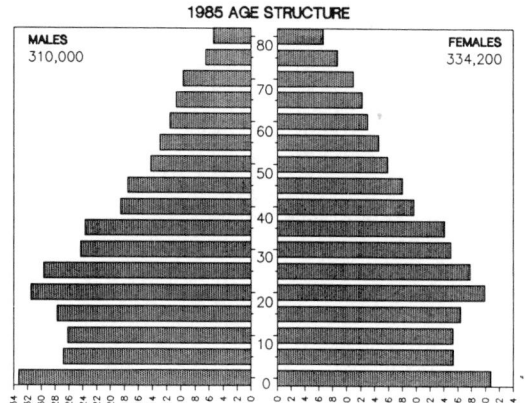

1985 AGE STRUCTURE

MALES 310,000   FEMALES 334,200

MORTALITY MEASURES (Annual Averages)

PERIOD	CRUDE DEATH RATE	INFANT MORT. RATE	LIFE EXPECTANCY AT BIRTH (years) MALE	FEMALE	BOTH SEXES	DIFFERENCE FEMALE-MALE
1950-55	10.50	53.28	65.10	69.00	66.99	3.90
1955-60	10.50	30.64	66.20	70.10	68.09	3.90
1960-65	10.50	29.01	67.50	71.00	69.20	3.50
1965-70	10.00	29.31	68.70	72.00	70.30	3.30
1970-75	9.70	28.50	70.00	72.90	71.41	2.90
1975-80	8.60	20.00	72.00	75.50	73.70	3.50
1980-85	8.40	16.20	72.50	77.50	75.00	5.00
1985-90	*8.20*	*11.91*	*73.29*	*78.21*	*75.68*	*4.92*
1990-95	*7.83*	*9.94*	*74.11*	*79.02*	*76.49*	*4.91*
2000-05	*7.20*	*7.00*	*75.72*	*80.65*	*78.11*	*4.93*
2010-15	*7.59*	*5.80*	*76.65*	*81.64*	*79.07*	*4.99*
2020-25	*8.44*	*5.55*	*77.71*	*82.61*	*80.09*	*4.89*

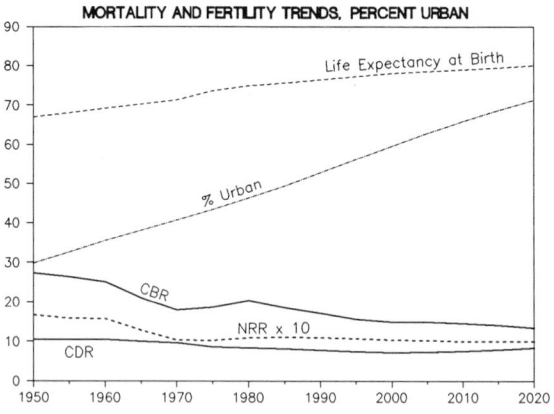

MORTALITY AND FERTILITY TRENDS, PERCENT URBAN

Life Expectancy at Birth — % Urban — CBR — NRR x 10 — CDR

FERTILITY MEASURES (Annual Averages)

PERIOD	CRUDE BIRTH RATE	FERTILITY RATES GENERAL	FERTILITY RATES TOTAL	REPRODUCTION RATES GROSS	REPRODUCTION RATES NET	RATE OF NATUR. INCR.
1950-55	27.40	109.69	3.687	1.790	1.670	16.90
1955-60	26.40	108.97	3.481	1.690	1.590	15.90
1960-65	25.20	105.62	3.420	1.660	1.570	14.70
1965-70	21.00	88.05	2.781	1.350	1.290	11.00
1970-75	18.00	72.69	2.225	1.080	1.040	8.30
1975-80	18.70	71.92	2.184	1.060	1.020	10.10
1980-85	20.40	78.82	2.348	1.140	1.100	12.00
1985-90	*18.63*	*73.02*	*2.307*	*1.120*	*1.109*	*10.43*
1990-95	*17.12*	*68.00*	*2.266*	*1.100*	*1.091*	*9.29*
2000-05	*14.96*	*60.51*	*2.163*	*1.050*	*1.044*	*7.76*
2010-15	*14.59*	*62.37*	*2.081*	*1.010*	*1.004*	*7.00*
2020-25	*13.51*	*60.46*	*2.081*	*1.010*	*1.004*	*5.07*

AGING MEASURES

YEAR	POPULATION AGE RATIOS 60+/20-59	65+/20-64	70+/20-69	75+/20-74	POPULATION MEAN AGE	MEDIAN AGE
1950	0.1929	0.1196	0.0681	0.0309	27.80	23.70
1960	0.2100	0.1205	0.0777	0.0359	27.72	23.04
1970	0.3091	0.2040	0.1250	0.0683	31.01	25.92
1980	0.2669	0.1828	0.1120	0.0577	32.40	28.69
1990	*0.2640*	*0.1809*	*0.1175*	*0.0673*	*32.99*	*30.37*
2000	*0.2733*	*0.1791*	*0.1135*	*0.0650*	*34.36*	*33.05*
2010	*0.3148*	*0.1975*	*0.1228*	*0.0677*	*36.20*	*34.73*
2020	*0.3954*	*0.2509*	*0.1544*	*0.0823*	*37.86*	*36.53*

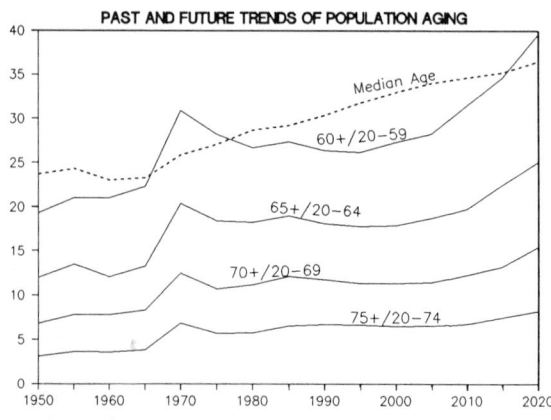

PAST AND FUTURE TRENDS OF POPULATION AGING

Median Age — 60+/20-59 — 65+/20-64 — 70+/20-69 — 75+/20-74

OBSERVED AND *PROJECTED* POPULATION DATA

YEAR	MID-YEAR POPULATION	NO. OF BIRTHS	NO. OF DEATHS	URBAN POPULATION NUMBER	URBAN POPULATION PERCENT	POPULATION 1985 AGE	POPULATION 1985 NUMBER
1950	433400	20557	14952	42871	9.9	0	116140
1955	461900	21716	14386	46148	10.0	5	33160
1960	500500	23403	14139	50505	10.1	10	79196
1965	548600	24509	13893	55912	10.2	15	79050
1970	604500	26782	13916	62224	10.3	20	69903
1975	672400	16810	30258	69903	10.4	25	58120
1980	581384	27883	13368	63208	10.9	30	48391
1985	658786	28879	14132	77495	11.8	35	40599
1990	736893	28135	13806	96876	13.1	40	33417
1995	812197	25297	13110	122931	15.1	45	28377
2000	875508	22158	12395	156539	17.9	50	22956
2005	925727	22361	12157	193792	20.9	55	18792
2010	978192	23870	12196	237464	24.3	60	13341
2015	1038354	23335	12190	289362	27.9	65	9142
2020	1095615	21602	12131	346843	31.7	70+	8203

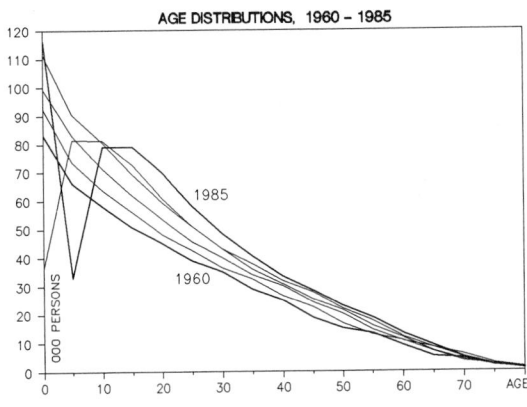

AGE DISTRIBUTIONS, 1960 - 1985

POPULATION RATIOS

YEAR	AGE DISTRIBUTION UNDER 15	AGE DISTRIBUTION 15-64	AGE DISTRIBUTION 65 & OLDER	AGE DISTRIBUTION 70 & OLDER	DEPENDENCY RATIO	WOMEN 15-49	CHILD-WOMAN RATIO
1950	0.405	0.561	0.033	0.018	0.782	0.234	0.696
1955	0.409	0.559	0.031	0.016	0.788	0.233	0.704
1960	0.414	0.559	0.026	0.016	0.788	0.235	0.706
1965	0.419	0.556	0.026	0.013	0.799	0.235	0.716
1970	0.420	0.554	0.027	0.013	0.807	0.234	0.702
1975	0.420	0.553	0.027	0.015	0.809	0.233	0.711
1980	0.342	0.634	0.024	0.012	0.577	0.267	0.233
1985	0.347	0.627	0.026	0.012	0.595	0.263	0.669
1990	0.356	0.615	0.029	0.014	0.626	0.258	0.646
2000	0.385	0.580	0.035	0.019	0.723	0.240	0.525
2010	0.304	0.654	0.042	0.023	0.530	0.268	0.383
2020	0.284	0.664	0.053	0.029	0.507	0.263	0.376

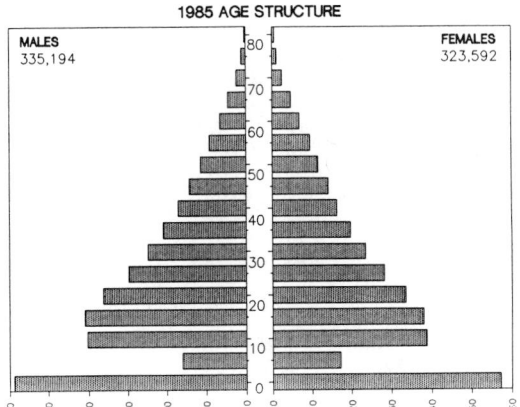

1985 AGE STRUCTURE

MALES 335,194 FEMALES 323,592

MORTALITY MEASURES (Annual Averages)

PERIOD	CRUDE DEATH RATE	INFANT MORT. RATE	LIFE EXPECTANCY AT BIRTH (years) MALE	LIFE EXPECTANCY AT BIRTH (years) FEMALE	LIFE EXPECTANCY AT BIRTH (years) BOTH SEXES	DIFFERENCE FEMALE-MALE
1950-55	34.50	264.30	29.57	30.40	29.98	0.83
1955-60	31.15	241.70	31.94	33.08	32.50	1.14
1960-65	28.25	220.63	34.42	35.60	35.00	1.18
1965-70	25.32	201.05	36.90	38.14	37.51	1.24
1970-75	23.02	183.25	39.24	40.74	39.97	1.50
1975-80	45.00	253.55	30.00	32.50	31.22	2.50
1980-85	22.99	183.25	39.20	40.70	39.93	1.50
1985-90	21.45	165.59	41.65	43.44	42.52	1.79
1990-95	18.74	149.51	44.05	46.06	45.03	2.01
2000-05	14.16	120.83	48.72	51.31	49.98	2.59
2010-15	12.47	94.43	53.59	56.40	54.96	2.81
2020-25	11.07	72.47	58.04	61.02	59.49	2.98

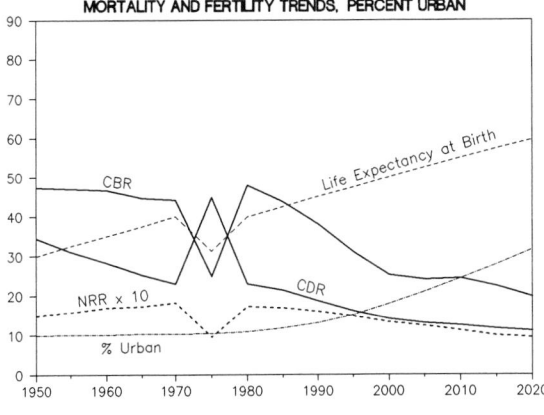

MORTALITY AND FERTILITY TRENDS, PERCENT URBAN

FERTILITY MEASURES (Annual Averages)

PERIOD	CRUDE BIRTH RATE	FERTILITY RATES GENERAL	FERTILITY RATES TOTAL	REPRODUCTION RATES GROSS	REPRODUCTION RATES NET	RATE OF NATUR. INCR.
1950-55	47.43	202.89	6.441	3.142	1.493	12.93
1955-60	47.01	200.65	6.353	3.099	1.585	15.87
1960-65	46.76	198.84	6.371	3.108	1.694	18.51
1965-70	44.67	190.51	6.156	3.003	1.735	19.35
1970-75	44.31	189.78	6.150	3.000	1.829	21.28
1975-80	25.00	100.46	4.305	2.100	0.960	-20.00
1980-85	47.96	180.89	5.842	2.850	1.736	24.97
1985-90	43.84	168.40	5.412	2.640	1.696	22.39
1990-95	38.18	158.42	4.879	2.380	1.604	19.44
2000-05	25.31	101.85	3.690	1.800	1.330	11.15
2010-15	24.40	90.91	2.870	1.400	1.124	11.93
2020-25	19.72	75.28	2.255	1.100	0.942	8.65

AGING MEASURES

YEAR	POPULATION AGE RATIOS 60+/20-59	POPULATION AGE RATIOS 65+/20-64	POPULATION AGE RATIOS 70+/20-69	POPULATION AGE RATIOS 75+/20-74	POPULATION MEAN AGE	POPULATION MEDIAN AGE
1950	0.1278	0.0729	0.0369	0.0152	23.76	19.64
1960	0.1013	0.0576	0.0341	0.0146	23.30	19.23
1970	0.1026	0.0598	0.0285	0.0115	23.21	18.94
1980	0.0898	0.0464	0.0223	0.0092	25.41	21.57
1990	0.1031	0.0564	0.0276	0.0106	24.54	21.89
2000	0.1311	0.0753	0.0390	0.0163	25.52	19.90
2010	0.1348	0.0783	0.0417	0.0187	27.75	23.75
2020	0.1570	0.0908	0.0481	0.0219	29.49	27.15

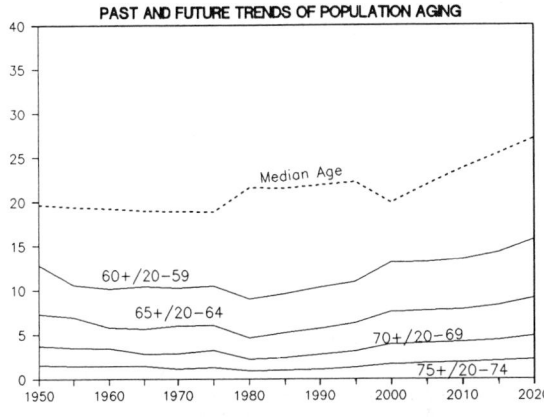

PAST AND FUTURE TRENDS OF POPULATION AGING

OBSERVED AND *PROJECTED* POPULATION DATA

YEAR	MID-YEAR POPULATION	NO. OF BIRTHS	NO. OF DEATHS	URBAN POPULATION NUMBER	URBAN POPULATION PERCENT	POPULATION 1985 AGE	POPULATION 1985 NUMBER
1950	1974000	74420	17569	1746992	88.5	0	397875
1955	2490000	90387	17928	2210732	88.8	5	420626
1960	3075100	101909	19035	2738764	89.1	10	442263
1965	3691900	86723	20121	3299181	89.4	15	456318
1970	3941600	76861	20102	3534031	89.7	20	567744
1975	4395800	81551	19522	3983053	90.6	25	608289
1980	5038500	84143	25193	4614001	91.6	30	501818
1985	5456200	86792	31739	5044177	92.4	35	409806
1990	*5840595*	*79315*	*36603*	*5443545*	*93.2*	40	244691
1995	*6159469*	*78293*	*41139*	*5780630*	*93.8*	45	258846
2000	*6449110*	*78666*	*46550*	*6088265*	*94.4*	50	272193
2005	*6611702*	*76094*	*51287*	*6273165*	*94.9*	55	250353
2010	*6736910*	*75460*	*55532*	*6419275*	*95.3*	60	211930
2015	*6837293*	*74383*	*59368*	*6540388*	*95.7*	65	162385
2020	*6912792*	*72107*	*64151*	*6636264*	*96.0*	70+	251063

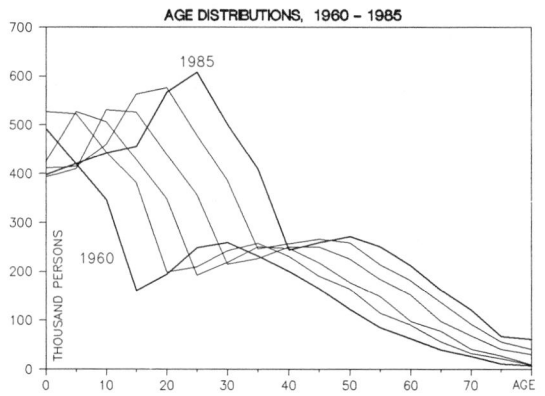

AGE DISTRIBUTIONS, 1960 – 1985

POPULATION RATIOS

YEAR	AGE DISTRIBUTION UNDER 15	AGE DISTRIBUTION 15-64	AGE DISTRIBUTION 65 & OLDER	AGE DISTRIBUTION 70 & OLDER	DEPENDENCY RATIO	WOMEN 15-49	CHILD-WOMAN RATIO
1950	0.304	0.671	0.025	0.015	0.489	0.286	0.560
1955	0.354	0.621	0.025	0.015	0.610	0.255	0.645
1960	0.409	0.563	0.028	0.015	0.776	0.222	0.722
1965	0.405	0.563	0.032	0.017	0.776	0.221	0.646
1970	0.370	0.590	0.040	0.020	0.694	0.229	0.471
1975	0.304	0.642	0.054	0.032	0.557	0.242	0.370
1980	0.255	0.680	0.065	0.038	0.470	0.254	0.322
1985	0.231	0.693	0.076	0.046	0.443	0.267	0.273
1990	*0.220*	*0.692*	*0.088*	*0.054*	*0.445*	*0.268*	*0.288*
2000	*0.199*	*0.692*	*0.108*	*0.072*	*0.444*	*0.263*	*0.238*
2010	*0.175*	*0.711*	*0.114*	*0.083*	*0.407*	*0.232*	*0.244*
2020	*0.163*	*0.669*	*0.167*	*0.103*	*0.495*	*0.208*	*0.258*

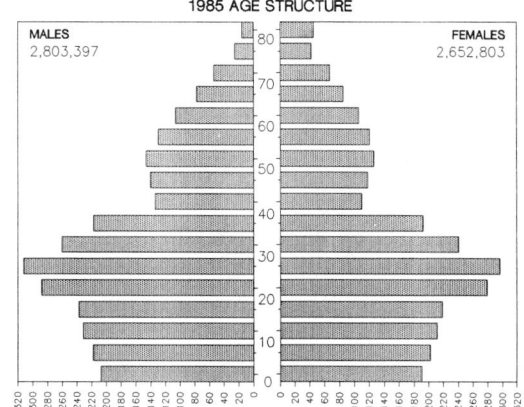

1985 AGE STRUCTURE

MALES 2,803,397 — FEMALES 2,652,803

MORTALITY MEASURES (Annual Averages)

PERIOD	CRUDE DEATH RATE	INFANT MORT. RATE	LIFE EXPECTANCY AT BIRTH (years) MALE	LIFE EXPECTANCY AT BIRTH (years) FEMALE	LIFE EXPECTANCY AT BIRTH (years) BOTH SEXES	DIFFERENCE FEMALE-MALE
1950-55	8.90	78.54	57.20	64.91	60.96	7.71
1955-60	7.20	54.25	61.00	68.50	64.75	7.50
1960-65	6.19	32.51	64.00	71.30	67.65	7.30
1965-70	5.45	22.63	66.50	73.50	70.00	7.00
1970-75	5.10	17.08	68.50	75.60	72.00	7.10
1975-80	4.44	12.87	70.50	76.80	73.60	6.30
1980-85	5.00	9.66	72.60	78.30	75.45	5.70
1985-90	*5.82*	*8.27*	*73.42*	*79.10*	*76.18*	*5.68*
1990-95	*6.27*	*6.66*	*74.17*	*79.91*	*76.96*	*5.74*
2000-05	*7.22*	*5.77*	*75.59*	*80.99*	*78.21*	*5.40*
2010-15	*8.24*	*5.20*	*76.59*	*81.93*	*79.18*	*5.34*
2020-25	*9.28*	*5.03*	*77.52*	*82.90*	*80.13*	*5.38*

FERTILITY MEASURES (Annual Averages)

PERIOD	CRUDE BIRTH RATE	FERTILITY RATES GENERAL	FERTILITY RATES TOTAL	REPRODUCTION RATES GROSS	REPRODUCTION RATES NET	RATE OF NATUR. INCR.
1950-55	37.70	140.26	4.433	2.150	1.900	28.80
1955-60	36.30	153.42	4.703	2.281	2.086	29.10
1960-65	33.14	149.76	5.299	2.570	2.409	26.95
1965-70	23.49	104.28	4.006	1.943	1.844	18.04
1970-75	19.50	82.56	2.887	1.400	1.346	14.40
1975-80	18.55	74.57	2.309	1.120	1.108	14.11
1980-85	16.70	64.00	1.800	0.873	0.857	11.70
1985-90	*15.91*	*59.47*	*1.700*	*0.824*	*0.811*	*10.09*
1990-95	*13.58*	*50.27*	*1.600*	*0.776*	*0.765*	*7.31*
2000-05	*12.20*	*47.34*	*1.800*	*0.873*	*0.862*	*4.98*
2010-15	*11.20*	*50.02*	*1.800*	*0.873*	*0.862*	*2.96*
2020-25	*10.43*	*50.91*	*1.800*	*0.873*	*0.863*	*1.15*

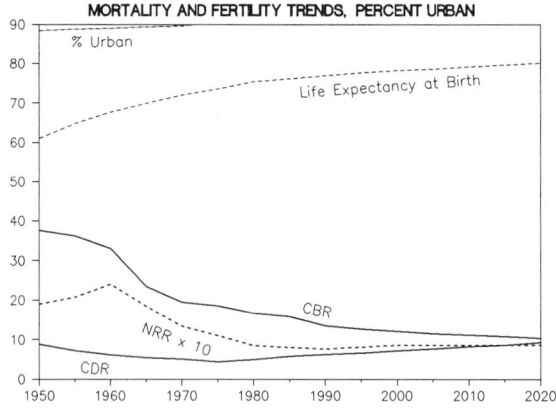

MORTALITY AND FERTILITY TRENDS, PERCENT URBAN

AGING MEASURES

YEAR	POPULATION AGE RATIOS 60+/20-59	POPULATION AGE RATIOS 65+/20-64	POPULATION AGE RATIOS 70+/20-69	POPULATION AGE RATIOS 75+/20-74	POPULATION MEAN AGE	POPULATION MEDIAN AGE
1950	0.0673	0.0444	0.0263	0.0124	25.25	23.71
1960	0.0988	0.0550	0.0286	0.0120	25.26	23.06
1970	0.1413	0.0823	0.0395	0.0184	26.50	21.19
1980	0.1886	0.1136	0.0631	0.0314	30.17	25.98
1990	*0.2234*	*0.1425*	*0.0836*	*0.0444*	*33.08*	*31.10*
2000	*0.2464*	*0.1726*	*0.1084*	*0.0603*	*35.90*	*35.81*
2010	*0.2896*	*0.1763*	*0.1216*	*0.0755*	*38.77*	*39.57*
2020	*0.4738*	*0.2736*	*0.1525*	*0.0783*	*41.39*	*42.57*

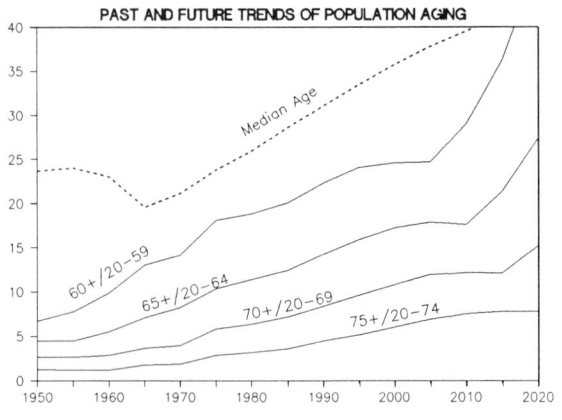

PAST AND FUTURE TRENDS OF POPULATION AGING

OBSERVED AND *PROJECTED* POPULATION DATA (000's)

YEAR	MID-YEAR POPULATION	NO. OF BIRTHS	NO. OF DEATHS	URBAN POPULATION NUMBER	URBAN POPULATION PERCENT	POPULATION 1985 AGE	POPULATION 1985 NUMBER
1950	357561	15762	8929	61695	17.3	0	109504
1955	395097	17206	8587	69540	17.6	5	92383
1960	442346	18560	8593	79414	18.0	10	87739
1965	495157	19922	8651	93084	18.8	15	79279
1970	554911	21191	8769	109616	19.8	20	70207
1975	620701	21546	8625	133267	21.5	25	61245
1980	688856	23901	8721	161402	23.4	30	51357
1985	769183	24650	8686	196228	25.5	35	42649
1990	*853373*	*26500*	*8690*	*238946*	*28.0*	40	36863
1995	*947326*	*26684*	*8554*	*292814*	*30.9*	45	32968
2000	*1042530*	*26358*	*8451*	*356875*	*34.2*	50	29019
2005	*1136085*	*25619*	*8448*	*430932*	*37.9*	55	24135
2010	*1225305*	*24250*	*8576*	*513903*	*41.9*	60	19137
2015	*1306261*	*22220*	*8926*	*599820*	*45.9*	65	14380
2020	*1374470*	*23413*	*9550*	*684609*	*49.8*	70+	18318

POPULATION RATIOS

YEAR	AGE DISTRIBUTION UNDER 15	AGE DISTRIBUTION 15-64	AGE DISTRIBUTION 65 & OLDER	AGE DISTRIBUTION 70 & OLDER	DEPENDENCY RATIO	WOMEN 15-49	CHILD-WOMAN RATIO
1950	0.389	0.577	0.033	0.019	0.732	0.235	0.655
1955	0.390	0.576	0.034	0.017	0.736	0.236	0.670
1960	0.398	0.568	0.034	0.018	0.761	0.233	0.693
1965	0.404	0.561	0.035	0.019	0.784	0.229	0.695
1970	0.404	0.559	0.037	0.020	0.788	0.228	0.686
1975	0.398	0.564	0.038	0.021	0.774	0.229	0.660
1980	0.385	0.574	0.040	0.022	0.742	0.232	0.605
1985	0.377	0.581	0.043	0.024	0.721	0.234	0.609
1990	*0.365*	*0.590*	*0.045*	*0.026*	*0.695*	*0.237*	*0.565*
2000	*0.345*	*0.604*	*0.051*	*0.030*	*0.656*	*0.243*	*0.501*
2010	*0.304*	*0.637*	*0.059*	*0.036*	*0.569*	*0.254*	*0.397*
2020	*0.251*	*0.677*	*0.072*	*0.043*	*0.478*	*0.263*	*0.297*

MORTALITY MEASURES (Annual Averages)

PERIOD	CRUDE DEATH RATE	INFANT MORT. RATE	LIFE EXPECTANCY AT BIRTH (years) MALE	LIFE EXPECTANCY AT BIRTH (years) FEMALE	LIFE EXPECTANCY AT BIRTH (years) BOTH SEXES	DIFFERENCE FEMALE-MALE
1950-55	24.97	190.00	39.37	38.00	38.70	-1.37
1955-60	21.73	173.00	43.50	41.70	42.62	-1.80
1960-65	19.43	157.00	46.20	44.70	45.47	-1.50
1965-70	17.47	145.00	48.70	47.30	48.02	-1.40
1970-75	15.80	135.00	51.20	49.30	50.27	-1.90
1975-80	13.90	126.00	53.30	52.42	52.87	-0.88
1980-85	12.66	110.25	55.56	55.17	55.37	-0.39
1985-90	*11.29*	*98.79*	*57.82*	*57.92*	*57.87*	*0.10*
1990-95	*10.18*	*87.95*	*60.08*	*60.67*	*60.37*	*0.59*
2000-05	*8.11*	*66.67*	*64.44*	*65.92*	*65.16*	*1.48*
2010-15	*7.00*	*47.93*	*67.64*	*70.46*	*69.02*	*2.82*
2020-25	*6.95*	*34.50*	*69.64*	*73.59*	*71.57*	*3.95*

FERTILITY MEASURES (Annual Averages)

PERIOD	CRUDE BIRTH RATE	FERTILITY RATES GENERAL	FERTILITY RATES TOTAL	REPRODUCTION RATES GROSS	REPRODUCTION RATES NET	RATE OF NATUR. INCR.
1950-55	44.08	187.15	5.970	2.912	1.626	19.11
1955-60	43.55	185.66	5.918	2.887	1.748	21.82
1960-65	41.96	181.56	5.810	2.834	1.823	22.53
1965-70	40.23	176.15	5.689	2.775	1.873	22.76
1970-75	38.19	167.39	5.426	2.647	1.851	22.39
1975-80	34.71	150.66	4.826	2.354	1.734	20.82
1980-85	34.70	148.90	4.750	2.317	1.776	22.04
1985-90	*32.05*	*136.01*	*4.305*	*2.100*	*1.672*	*20.75*
1990-95	*31.05*	*130.60*	*4.100*	*2.000*	*1.650*	*20.87*
2000-05	*25.28*	*102.90*	*3.280*	*1.600*	*1.402*	*17.18*
2010-15	*19.79*	*77.20*	*2.460*	*1.200*	*1.096*	*12.79*
2020-25	*17.03*	*64.79*	*2.070*	*1.010*	*0.944*	*10.09*

AGING MEASURES

YEAR	POPULATION AGE RATIOS 60+/20-59	POPULATION AGE RATIOS 65+/20-64	POPULATION AGE RATIOS 70+/20-69	POPULATION AGE RATIOS 75+/20-74	POPULATION MEAN AGE	POPULATION MEDIAN AGE
1950	0.1245	0.0706	0.0379	0.0160	24.57	20.43
1960	0.1260	0.0726	0.0369	0.0151	24.49	20.41
1970	0.1369	0.0793	0.0413	0.0179	24.57	19.86
1980	0.1451	0.0861	0.0456	0.0202	25.17	20.61
1990	*0.1533*	*0.0922*	*0.0502*	*0.0232*	*25.91*	*21.81*
2000	*0.1635*	*0.1019*	*0.0568*	*0.0270*	*26.99*	*23.20*
2010	*0.1713*	*0.1086*	*0.0638*	*0.0322*	*28.90*	*25.48*
2020	*0.1982*	*0.1226*	*0.0707*	*0.0366*	*31.65*	*28.93*

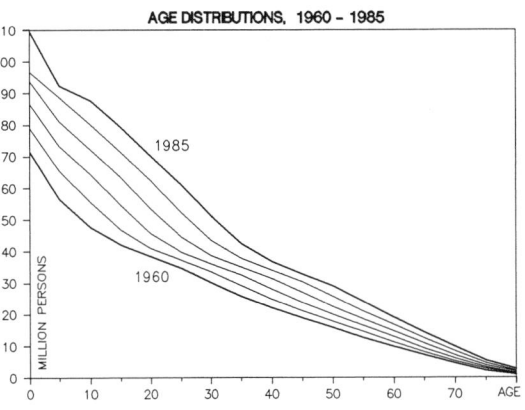

AGE DISTRIBUTIONS, 1960 - 1985

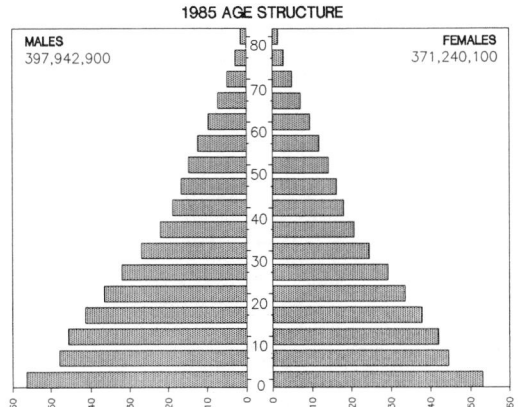

1985 AGE STRUCTURE

MALES 397,942,900   FEMALES 371,240,100

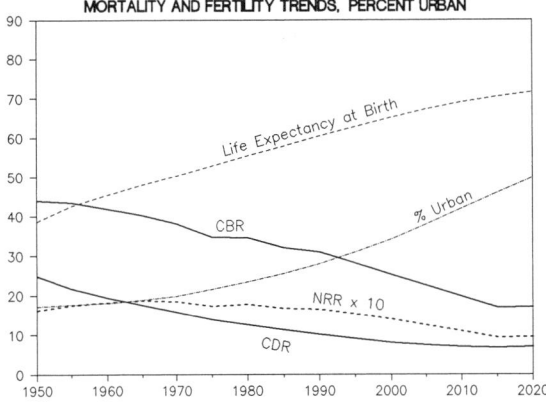

MORTALITY AND FERTILITY TRENDS, PERCENT URBAN

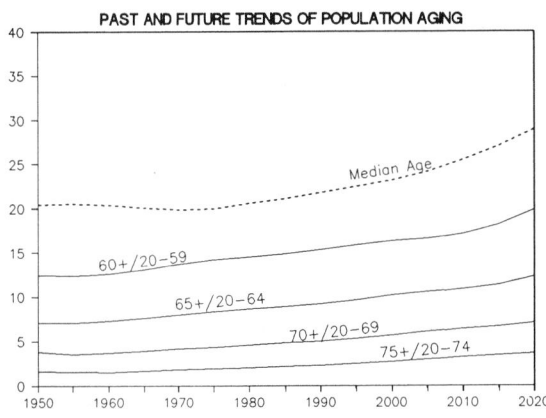

PAST AND FUTURE TRENDS OF POPULATION AGING

OBSERVED AND *PROJECTED* POPULATION DATA (000's)

YEAR	MID-YEAR POPULATION	NO. OF BIRTHS	NO. OF DEATHS	URBAN POPULATION NUMBER	URBAN POPULATION PERCENT	POPULATION 1985 AGE	POPULATION 1985 NUMBER
1950	79538	3422	2078	9871	12.4	0	22233
1955	86552	3929	2102	11651	13.5	5	21259
1960	96194	4122	2069	14032	14.6	10	20810
1965	107041	4561	2067	16902	15.8	15	18206
1970	120280	4595	2084	20534	17.1	20	15431
1975	135666	4803	2046	26259	19.4	25	13686
1980	150958	4859	1910	33514	22.2	30	10885
1985	166464	4553	1857	42170	25.3	35	8578
1990	*180514*	*4578*	*1827*	*51975*	*28.8*	40	7910
1995	*194811*	*4408*	*1795*	*63371*	*32.5*	45	7224
2000	*208329*	*4152*	*1773*	*75960*	*36.5*	50	6048
2005	*220575*	*4007*	*1787*	*89300*	*40.5*	55	4798
2010	*231956*	*4008*	*1843*	*103177*	*44.5*	60	3463
2015	*243040*	*3994*	*1935*	*117654*	*48.4*	65	2501
2020	*253560*	*3954*	*2053*	*132405*	*52.2*	70+	3431

AGE DISTRIBUTIONS, 1960 - 1985

POPULATION RATIOS

YEAR	AGE DISTRIBUTION UNDER 15	15-64	65 & OLDER	70 & OLDER	DEPENDENCY RATIO	WOMEN 15-49	CHILD-WOMAN RATIO
1950	0.392	0.569	0.040	0.022	0.758	0.241	0.593
1955	0.389	0.574	0.036	0.021	0.741	0.247	0.635
1960	0.402	0.565	0.033	0.019	0.770	0.244	0.691
1965	0.416	0.553	0.031	0.018	0.809	0.238	0.686
1970	0.423	0.547	0.031	0.017	0.830	0.236	0.700
1975	0.420	0.548	0.032	0.017	0.824	0.239	0.687
1980	0.410	0.556	0.033	0.018	0.797	0.241	0.614
1985	0.386	0.578	0.036	0.021	0.730	0.248	0.538
1990	*0.350*	*0.611*	*0.039*	*0.022*	*0.637*	*0.260*	*0.446*
2000	*0.295*	*0.655*	*0.050*	*0.029*	*0.527*	*0.278*	*0.358*
2010	*0.252*	*0.685*	*0.063*	*0.039*	*0.461*	*0.281*	*0.294*
2020	*0.225*	*0.697*	*0.078*	*0.047*	*0.434*	*0.268*	*0.284*

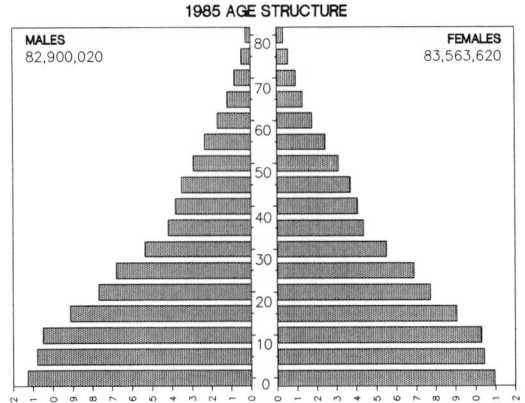

1985 AGE STRUCTURE

MALES 82,900,020   FEMALES 83,563,620

MORTALITY MEASURES (Annual Averages)

PERIOD	CRUDE DEATH RATE	INFANT MORT. RATE	LIFE EXPECTANCY AT BIRTH (years) MALE	FEMALE	BOTH SEXES	DIFFERENCE FEMALE-MALE
1950-55	26.13	160.00	36.90	38.10	37.49	1.20
1955-60	24.28	145.00	39.20	40.70	39.93	1.50
1960-65	21.51	133.00	41.70	43.40	42.53	1.70
1965-70	19.31	124.00	44.10	46.10	45.08	2.00
1970-75	17.33	114.00	46.40	48.70	47.52	2.30
1975-80	15.08	105.00	48.70	51.30	49.97	2.60
1980-85	12.65	95.00	52.20	54.90	53.52	2.70
1985-90	*11.15*	*84.00*	*54.60*	*57.40*	*55.97*	*2.80*
1990-95	*10.12*	*74.00*	*57.10*	*59.90*	*58.47*	*2.80*
2000-05	*8.51*	*55.00*	*61.94*	*64.90*	*63.38*	*2.96*
2010-15	*7.94*	*39.00*	*65.86*	*69.30*	*67.54*	*3.44*
2020-25	*8.10*	*29.00*	*68.62*	*72.50*	*70.51*	*3.88*

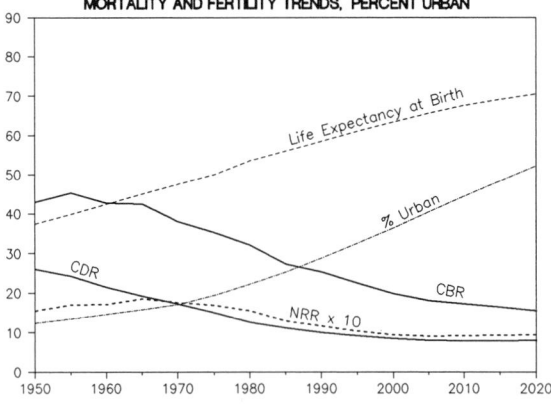

MORTALITY AND FERTILITY TRENDS, PERCENT URBAN

FERTILITY MEASURES (Annual Averages)

PERIOD	CRUDE BIRTH RATE	FERTILITY RATES GENERAL	TOTAL	REPRODUCTION RATES GROSS	NET	RATE OF NATUR. INCR.
1950-55	43.02	176.05	5.486	2.676	1.563	16.89
1955-60	45.39	185.01	5.672	2.767	1.709	21.11
1960-65	42.85	178.05	5.420	2.644	1.722	21.35
1965-70	42.61	179.78	5.568	2.716	1.859	23.30
1970-75	38.20	160.85	5.100	2.488	1.760	20.87
1975-80	35.40	147.52	4.680	2.283	1.700	20.32
1980-85	32.19	131.39	4.100	2.000	1.557	19.54
1985-90	*27.35*	*107.40*	*3.300*	*1.610*	*1.297*	*16.20*
1990-95	*25.36*	*95.62*	*2.900*	*1.415*	*1.175*	*15.24*
2000-05	*19.93*	*71.30*	*2.200*	*1.073*	*0.940*	*11.42*
2010-15	*17.28*	*61.99*	*2.070*	*1.010*	*0.920*	*9.33*
2020-25	*15.60*	*59.62*	*2.070*	*1.010*	*0.942*	*7.50*

AGING MEASURES

YEAR	POPULATION AGE RATIOS 60+/20-59	65+/20-64	70+/20-69	75+/20-74	POPULATION MEAN AGE	MEDIAN AGE
1950	0.1421	0.0859	0.0463	0.0209	24.63	20.02
1960	0.1166	0.0716	0.0393	0.0182	23.89	19.96
1970	0.1209	0.0683	0.0357	0.0168	23.59	18.92
1980	0.1226	0.0739	0.0388	0.0168	23.90	19.32
1990	*0.1323*	*0.0779*	*0.0435*	*0.0219*	*25.80*	*21.78*
2000	*0.1480*	*0.0900*	*0.0498*	*0.0242*	*28.18*	*25.28*
2010	*0.1617*	*0.1055*	*0.0628*	*0.0322*	*31.05*	*29.17*
2020	*0.2065*	*0.1246*	*0.0726*	*0.0405*	*33.77*	*32.67*

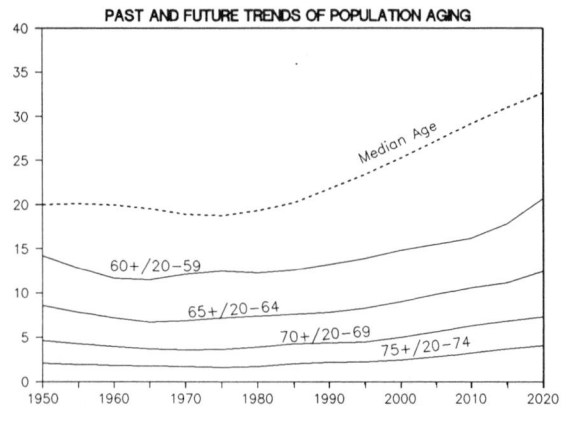

PAST AND FUTURE TRENDS OF POPULATION AGING

OBSERVED AND *PROJECTED* POPULATION DATA (000's)

YEAR	MID-YEAR POPULATION	NO. OF BIRTHS	NO. OF DEATHS	URBAN POPULATION NUMBER	URBAN POPULATION PERCENT	POPULATION 1985 AGE	POPULATION 1985 NUMBER
1950	14206	682	348	3937	27.7	0	8315
1955	17061	802	375	5219	30.6	5	6575
1960	20301	944	398	6828	33.6	10	5670
1965	24078	1091	409	8864	36.8	15	5042
1970	28397	1252	412	11648	41.0	20	4390
1975	33344	1437	397	15240	45.7	25	3825
1980	38900	1630	377	19086	49.1	30	3254
1985	47624	2017	379	24719	51.9	35	2507
1990	*56585*	*2208*	*391*	*31066*	*54.9*	40	1875
1995	*64525*	*2228*	*383*	*37416*	*58.0*	45	1503
2000	*74460*	*2305*	*398*	*45487*	*61.1*	50	1259
2005	*84646*	*2314*	*417*	*54291*	*64.1*	55	1028
2010	*94691*	*2285*	*448*	*63515*	*67.1*	60	819
2015	*104342*	*2252*	*488*	*72828*	*69.8*	65	616
2020	*113550*	*2205*	*544*	*82108*	*72.3*	70+	946

POPULATION RATIOS

YEAR	AGE DISTRIBUTION UNDER 15	AGE DISTRIBUTION 15-64	AGE DISTRIBUTION 65 & OLDER	AGE DISTRIBUTION 70 & OLDER	DEPENDENCY RATIO	WOMEN 15-49	CHILD-WOMAN RATIO
1950	0.438	0.550	0.012	0.005	0.819	0.237	0.816
1955	0.458	0.526	0.016	0.007	0.903	0.220	0.916
1960	0.471	0.508	0.021	0.010	0.967	0.211	0.923
1965	0.471	0.502	0.027	0.013	0.992	0.209	0.908
1970	0.462	0.507	0.031	0.016	0.973	0.214	0.859
1975	0.454	0.513	0.033	0.019	0.949	0.219	0.814
1980	0.444	0.522	0.034	0.020	0.916	0.224	0.770
1985	0.432	0.535	0.033	0.020	0.867	0.234	0.746
1990	*0.439*	*0.529*	*0.032*	*0.020*	*0.891*	*0.230*	*0.779*
2000	*0.430*	*0.536*	*0.034*	*0.021*	*0.866*	*0.228*	*0.667*
2010	*0.366*	*0.597*	*0.038*	*0.023*	*0.676*	*0.248*	*0.502*
2020	*0.305*	*0.644*	*0.051*	*0.030*	*0.553*	*0.265*	*0.380*

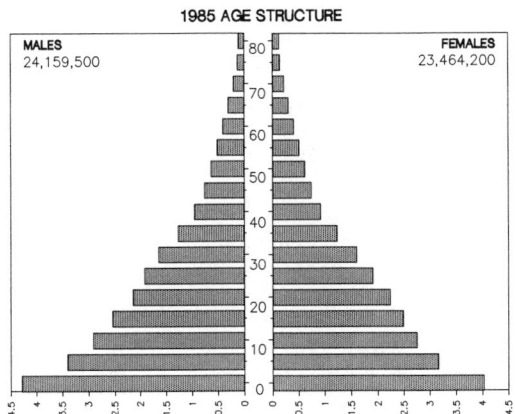

1985 AGE STRUCTURE

MALES 24,159,500　　　FEMALES 23,464,200

MORTALITY MEASURES (Annual Averages)

PERIOD	CRUDE DEATH RATE	INFANT MORT. RATE	LIFE EXPECTANCY AT BIRTH (years) MALE	LIFE EXPECTANCY AT BIRTH (years) FEMALE	LIFE EXPECTANCY AT BIRTH (years) BOTH SEXES	DIFFERENCE FEMALE-MALE
1950-55	24.50	190.00	46.11	46.13	46.12	0.02
1955-60	22.00	175.00	48.31	48.27	48.29	-0.04
1960-65	19.60	163.00	50.92	50.63	50.78	-0.29
1965-70	17.00	145.00	53.46	52.86	53.16	-0.60
1970-75	14.50	122.00	56.24	55.48	55.87	-0.76
1975-80	11.90	100.00	58.20	59.00	58.60	0.80
1980-85	9.70	78.00	59.40	63.00	60.60	3.60
1985-90	*7.96*	*63.00*	*65.00*	*65.50*	*65.24*	*0.50*
1990-95	*6.90*	*53.00*	*66.61*	*67.77*	*67.18*	*1.16*
2000-05	*5.34*	*38.00*	*69.22*	*71.39*	*70.28*	*2.17*
2010-15	*4.74*	*27.24*	*71.41*	*74.04*	*72.69*	*2.64*
2020-25	*4.79*	*18.65*	*73.20*	*76.20*	*74.67*	*3.00*

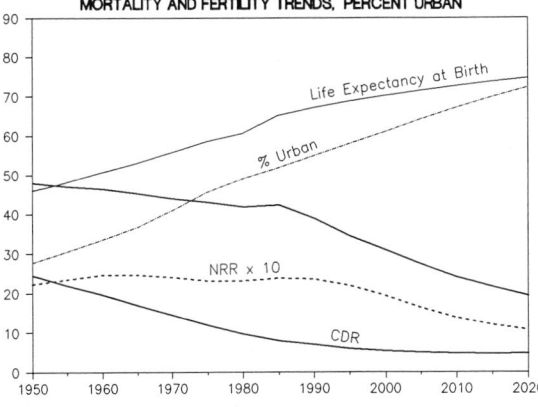

FERTILITY MEASURES (Annual Averages)

PERIOD	CRUDE BIRTH RATE	FERTILITY RATES GENERAL	FERTILITY RATES TOTAL	REPRODUCTION RATES GROSS	REPRODUCTION RATES NET	RATE OF NATUR. INCR.
1950-55	48.00	210.76	7.134	3.480	2.230	23.50
1955-60	47.00	218.58	7.195	3.510	2.350	25.00
1960-65	46.50	221.59	7.257	3.540	2.461	26.90
1965-70	45.30	213.84	6.970	3.400	2.460	28.30
1970-75	44.10	203.64	6.539	3.190	2.412	29.60
1975-80	43.10	194.51	6.047	2.950	2.309	31.20
1980-85	41.90	182.56	5.637	2.750	2.313	32.20
1985-90	*42.36*	*182.51*	*5.637*	*2.750*	*2.384*	*34.40*
1990-95	*39.02*	*172.12*	*5.432*	*2.650*	*2.359*	*32.12*
2000-05	*30.95*	*132.43*	*4.305*	*2.100*	*1.939*	*25.61*
2010-15	*24.13*	*95.50*	*2.993*	*1.460*	*1.377*	*19.40*
2020-25	*19.42*	*72.41*	*2.296*	*1.120*	*1.072*	*14.63*

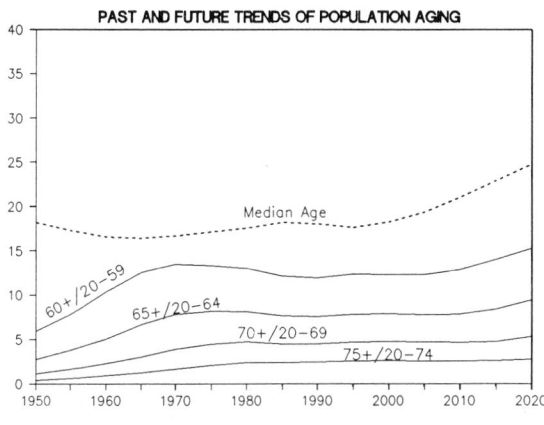

AGING MEASURES

YEAR	POPULATION AGE RATIOS 60+/20-59	POPULATION AGE RATIOS 65+/20-64	POPULATION AGE RATIOS 70+/20-69	POPULATION AGE RATIOS 75+/20-74	POPULATION MEAN AGE	POPULATION MEDIAN AGE
1950	0.0591	0.0275	0.0115	0.0041	22.10	18.20
1960	0.1035	0.0505	0.0229	0.0091	21.94	16.59
1970	0.1345	0.0779	0.0390	0.0163	21.99	16.73
1980	0.1298	0.0810	0.0470	0.0238	22.31	17.57
1990	*0.1191*	*0.0756*	*0.0448*	*0.0243*	*22.51*	*18.07*
2000	*0.1227*	*0.0785*	*0.0470*	*0.0258*	*23.24*	*18.24*
2010	*0.1283*	*0.0777*	*0.0461*	*0.0256*	*25.20*	*21.03*
2020	*0.1525*	*0.0944*	*0.0530*	*0.0275*	*27.93*	*24.77*

OBSERVED AND *PROJECTED* POPULATION DATA (000's)

YEAR	MID-YEAR POPULATION	NO. OF BIRTHS	NO. OF DEATHS	URBAN POPULATION NUMBER	URBAN POPULATION PERCENT	POPULATION 1985 AGE	POPULATION 1985 NUMBER
1950	5158	255	113	1812	35.1	0	2952
1955	5911	292	124	2224	37.6	5	2504
1960	6847	338	129	2937	42.9	10	2006
1965	7976	389	135	4040	50.7	15	1653
1970	9356	443	137	5254	56.2	20	1363
1975	11020	515	103	6764	61.4	25	1128
1980	13291	591	116	8819	66.4	30	935
1985	15898	677	125	11228	70.6	35	773
1990	18920	765	126	14034	74.2	40	635
1995	22411	852	130	17268	77.0	45	519
2000	26339	935	134	20890	79.3	50	419
2005	30677	1006	142	24860	81.0	55	333
2010	35323	1060	152	29184	82.6	60	256
2015	40175	1089	165	33773	84.1	65	187
2020	45080	1113	182	38491	85.4	70+	235

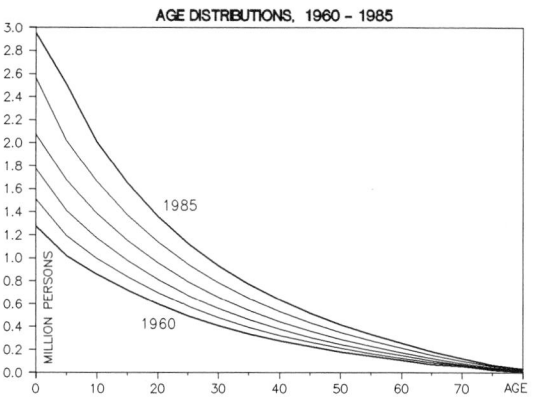

AGE DISTRIBUTIONS, 1960 - 1985

POPULATION RATIOS

YEAR	AGE DISTRIBUTION UNDER 15	AGE DISTRIBUTION 15-64	AGE DISTRIBUTION 65 & OLDER	AGE DISTRIBUTION 70 & OLDER	DEPENDENCY RATIO	WOMEN 15-49	CHILD-WOMAN RATIO
1950	0.457	0.516	0.027	0.015	0.940	0.220	0.842
1955	0.460	0.515	0.025	0.014	0.942	0.220	0.843
1960	0.461	0.514	0.024	0.014	0.945	0.220	0.846
1965	0.464	0.512	0.024	0.013	0.955	0.219	0.864
1970	0.466	0.510	0.024	0.013	0.963	0.219	0.869
1975	0.466	0.509	0.025	0.013	0.964	0.219	0.861
1980	0.470	0.504	0.026	0.014	0.984	0.216	0.894
1985	0.469	0.504	0.027	0.015	0.984	0.216	0.861
1990	0.465	0.508	0.027	0.015	0.969	0.217	0.830
2000	0.441	0.530	0.030	0.017	0.888	0.226	0.736
2010	0.407	0.560	0.033	0.019	0.787	0.239	0.619
2020	0.361	0.599	0.040	0.023	0.669	0.253	0.494

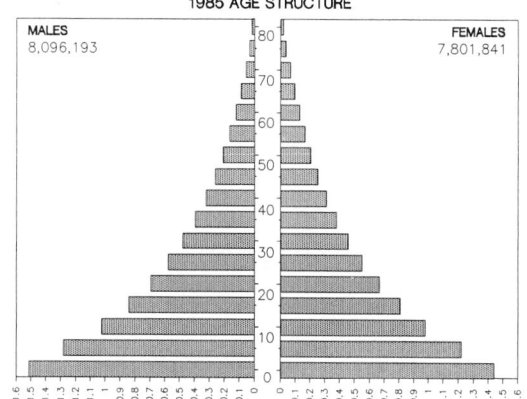

1985 AGE STRUCTURE

MALES 8,096,193 — FEMALES 7,801,841

MORTALITY MEASURES (Annual Averages)

PERIOD	CRUDE DEATH RATE	INFANT MORT. RATE	LIFE EXPECTANCY AT BIRTH (years) MALE	LIFE EXPECTANCY AT BIRTH (years) FEMALE	LIFE EXPECTANCY AT BIRTH (years) BOTH SEXES	DIFFERENCE FEMALE-MALE
1950-55	21.90	165.00	43.10	44.90	43.98	1.80
1955-60	21.00	148.00	46.10	47.90	46.98	1.80
1960-65	18.80	130.00	49.10	50.90	49.98	1.80
1965-70	16.90	111.00	52.10	53.90	52.98	1.80
1970-75	14.60	96.00	56.10	57.90	56.98	1.80
1975-80	9.37	83.08	60.50	62.33	61.39	1.83
1980-85	8.71	77.03	61.53	63.31	62.40	1.78
1985-90	7.85	68.63	62.98	64.82	63.88	1.85
1990-95	6.66	56.11	65.01	67.39	66.17	2.38
2000-05	5.08	37.42	68.01	71.64	69.78	3.63
2010-15	4.30	26.23	70.42	74.39	72.36	3.97
2020-25	4.03	18.15	72.39	76.51	74.40	4.13

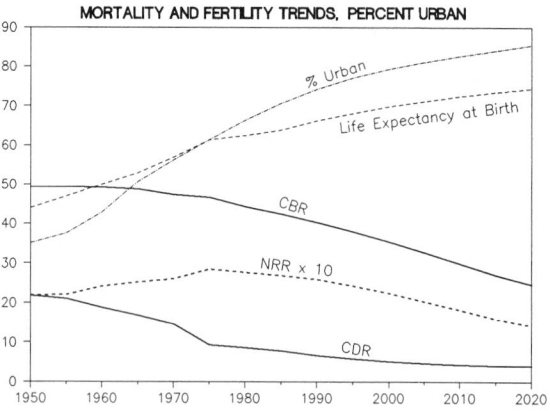

MORTALITY AND FERTILITY TRENDS, PERCENT URBAN

% Urban · Life Expectancy at Birth · CBR · NRR x 10 · CDR

FERTILITY MEASURES (Annual Averages)

PERIOD	CRUDE BIRTH RATE	FERTILITY RATES GENERAL	FERTILITY RATES TOTAL	REPRODUCTION RATES GROSS	REPRODUCTION RATES NET	RATE OF NATUR. INCR.
1950-55	49.40	224.27	7.175	3.500	2.200	27.50
1955-60	49.40	224.35	7.175	3.500	2.210	28.40
1960-65	49.30	224.55	7.175	3.500	2.420	30.50
1965-70	48.80	222.96	7.175	3.500	2.530	31.90
1970-75	47.40	216.79	7.113	3.470	2.610	32.80
1975-80	46.74	215.27	6.970	3.400	2.860	37.37
1980-85	44.44	205.89	6.662	3.250	2.769	35.73
1985-90	42.56	196.57	6.355	3.100	2.692	34.72
1990-95	40.45	184.10	5.945	2.900	2.597	33.79
2000-05	35.52	154.82	4.920	2.400	2.247	30.43
2010-15	30.00	123.73	3.895	1.900	1.820	25.70
2020-25	24.70	96.19	2.993	1.460	1.419	20.67

AGING MEASURES

YEAR	POPULATION AGE RATIOS 60+/20-59	POPULATION AGE RATIOS 65+/20-64	POPULATION AGE RATIOS 70+/20-69	POPULATION AGE RATIOS 75+/20-74	POPULATION MEAN AGE	POPULATION MEDIAN AGE
1950	0.1097	0.0660	0.0358	0.0142	21.77	17.04
1960	0.1028	0.0597	0.0322	0.0124	21.51	16.84
1970	0.1032	0.0602	0.0313	0.0137	21.34	16.62
1980	0.1084	0.0642	0.0343	0.0155	21.31	16.44
1990	0.1133	0.0681	0.0372	0.0174	21.61	16.67
2000	0.1157	0.0705	0.0392	0.0187	22.31	17.73
2010	0.1204	0.0741	0.0418	0.0205	23.58	19.28
2020	0.1292	0.0804	0.0460	0.0230	25.50	21.69

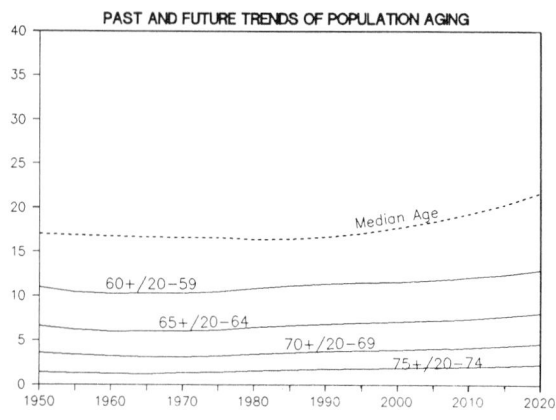

PAST AND FUTURE TRENDS OF POPULATION AGING

Median Age · 60+/20-59 · 65+/20-64 · 70+/20-69 · 75+/20-74

OBSERVED AND *PROJECTED* POPULATION DATA

YEAR	MID-YEAR POPULATION	NO. OF BIRTHS	NO. OF DEATHS	URBAN POPULATION NUMBER	URBAN POPULATION PERCENT	POPULATION 1985 AGE	POPULATION 1985 NUMBER
1950	1257969	40884	8680	812977	64.6	0	479100
1955	1748020	48770	10838	1244342	71.2	5	463700
1960	2114020	53908	12684	1627007	77.0	10	435300
1965	2562660	65348	17170	2074268	80.9	15	374300
1970	2974000	81488	21115	2504011	84.2	20	340200
1975	3455000	89968	23598	2993570	86.6	25	324800
1980	3877700	92444	26174	3434996	88.6	30	323900
1985	4232900	91359	29321	3821134	90.3	35	281700
1990	*4580557*	*92110*	*30461*	*4195961*	*91.6*	40	186700
1995	*4920026*	*97171*	*30671*	*4558235*	*92.6*	45	176000
2000	*5279516*	*101478*	*32369*	*4934096*	*93.5*	50	164800
2005	*5647017*	*102911*	*33651*	*5312764*	*94.1*	55	156200
2010	*6009383*	*101378*	*35894*	*5681977*	*94.6*	60	153600
2015	*6345968*	*98673*	*38704*	*6027653*	*95.0*	65	112400
2020	*6653072*	*97381*	*42713*	*6345759*	*95.4*	70+	259900

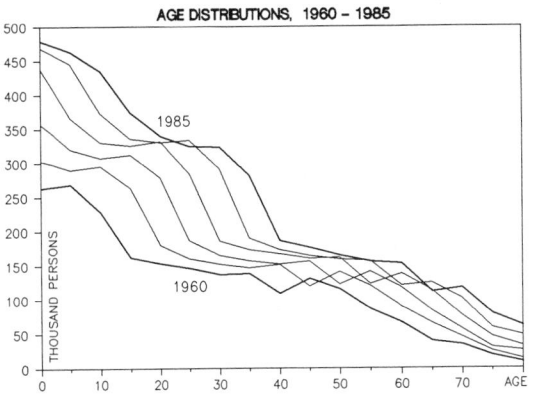

AGE DISTRIBUTIONS, 1960 - 1985

POPULATION RATIOS

YEAR	AGE DISTRIBUTION UNDER 15	AGE DISTRIBUTION 15-64	AGE DISTRIBUTION 65 & OLDER	AGE DISTRIBUTION 70 & OLDER	DEPENDENCY RATIO	WOMEN 15-49	CHILD-WOMAN RATIO
1950	0.317	0.644	0.039	0.022	0.553	0.266	0.525
1955	0.345	0.609	0.047	0.026	0.643	0.247	0.579
1960	0.361	0.591	0.049	0.030	0.693	0.231	0.541
1965	0.347	0.595	0.058	0.033	0.681	0.229	0.516
1970	0.331	0.602	0.067	0.038	0.661	0.237	0.507
1975	0.328	0.594	0.078	0.045	0.684	0.236	0.536
1980	0.332	0.582	0.086	0.054	0.718	0.233	0.518
1985	0.326	0.586	0.088	0.061	0.705	0.236	0.480
1990	*0.309*	*0.602*	*0.089*	*0.058*	*0.662*	*0.245*	*0.420*
2000	*0.275*	*0.639*	*0.086*	*0.059*	*0.565*	*0.256*	*0.371*
2010	*0.258*	*0.656*	*0.086*	*0.059*	*0.524*	*0.248*	*0.355*
2020	*0.233*	*0.654*	*0.114*	*0.071*	*0.530*	*0.246*	*0.307*

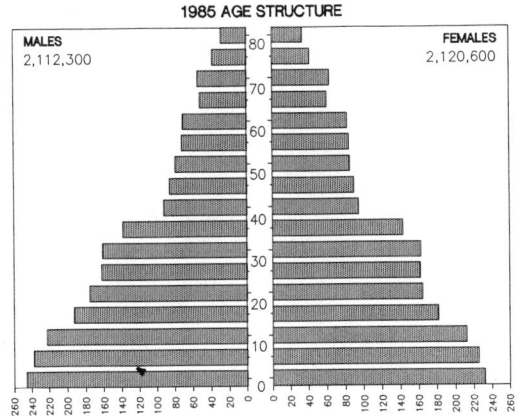

1985 AGE STRUCTURE

MALES 2,112,300   FEMALES 2,120,600

MORTALITY MEASURES (Annual Averages)

PERIOD	CRUDE DEATH RATE	INFANT MORT. RATE	LIFE EXPECTANCY AT BIRTH (years) MALE	LIFE EXPECTANCY AT BIRTH (years) FEMALE	LIFE EXPECTANCY AT BIRTH (years) BOTH SEXES	DIFFERENCE FEMALE-MALE
1950-55	6.90	40.86	64.40	66.44	65.39	2.04
1955-60	6.20	35.55	66.44	69.32	67.84	2.88
1960-65	6.00	29.20	68.12	70.73	69.39	2.61
1965-70	6.70	25.01	69.20	72.40	70.75	3.20
1970-75	7.10	23.39	70.11	73.25	71.63	3.14
1975-80	6.83	17.94	71.38	74.85	73.06	3.47
1980-85	6.75	14.18	72.79	76.21	74.45	3.42
1985-90	*6.93*	*11.95*	*73.63*	*77.21*	*75.37*	*3.58*
1990-95	*6.65*	*9.88*	*74.44*	*78.20*	*76.27*	*3.76*
2000-05	*6.13*	*6.87*	*75.69*	*79.82*	*77.70*	*4.14*
2010-15	*5.97*	*5.64*	*76.67*	*81.05*	*78.80*	*4.38*
2020-25	*6.42*	*5.44*	*77.87*	*82.08*	*79.91*	*4.20*

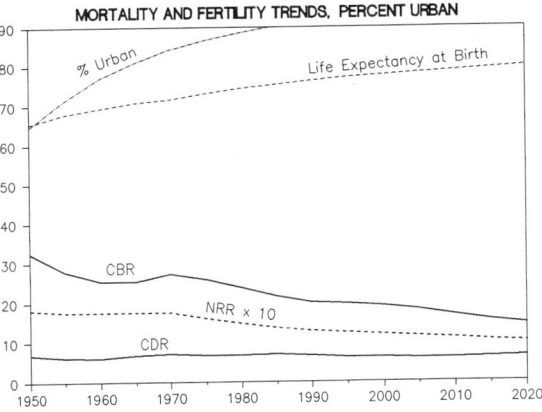

MORTALITY AND FERTILITY TRENDS, PERCENT URBAN

% Urban   Life Expectancy at Birth   CBR   NRR x 10   CDR

FERTILITY MEASURES (Annual Averages)

PERIOD	CRUDE BIRTH RATE	FERTILITY RATES GENERAL	FERTILITY RATES TOTAL	REPRODUCTION RATES GROSS	REPRODUCTION RATES NET	RATE OF NATUR. INCR.
1950-55	32.50	127.55	4.161	2.020	1.830	25.60
1955-60	27.90	117.34	3.893	1.890	1.760	21.70
1960-65	25.50	111.00	3.852	1.870	1.770	19.50
1965-70	25.50	109.35	3.790	1.840	1.760	18.80
1970-75	27.40	115.94	3.770	1.830	1.760	20.30
1975-80	26.04	111.00	3.409	1.655	1.610	19.21
1980-85	23.84	101.60	3.125	1.517	1.483	17.09
1985-90	*21.58*	*89.62*	*2.884*	*1.400*	*1.376*	*14.66*
1990-95	*20.11*	*80.15*	*2.678*	*1.300*	*1.283*	*13.46*
2000-05	*19.22*	*75.75*	*2.472*	*1.200*	*1.191*	*13.09*
2010-15	*16.87*	*68.21*	*2.266*	*1.100*	*1.092*	*10.90*
2020-25	*14.64*	*60.06*	*2.081*	*1.010*	*1.003*	*8.22*

AGING MEASURES

YEAR	POPULATION AGE RATIOS 60+/20-59	POPULATION AGE RATIOS 65+/20-64	POPULATION AGE RATIOS 70+/20-69	POPULATION AGE RATIOS 75+/20-74	POPULATION MEAN AGE	POPULATION MEDIAN AGE
1950	0.1170	0.0706	0.0392	0.0165	27.50	25.51
1960	0.1665	0.0948	0.0557	0.0245	27.98	24.33
1970	0.2324	0.1340	0.0727	0.0350	28.74	23.41
1980	0.2532	0.1742	0.1022	0.0500	29.09	24.77
1990	*0.2566*	*0.1756*	*0.1079*	*0.0657*	*29.99*	*25.87*
2000	*0.2271*	*0.1577*	*0.1029*	*0.0604*	*31.20*	*27.74*
2010	*0.2418*	*0.1485*	*0.0971*	*0.0577*	*32.70*	*30.21*
2020	*0.3001*	*0.1976*	*0.1155*	*0.0590*	*34.79*	*32.98*

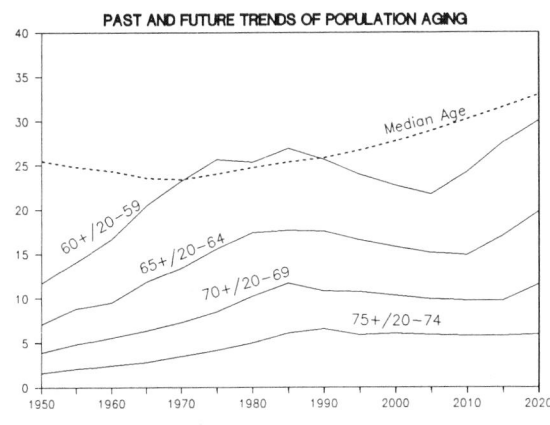

PAST AND FUTURE TRENDS OF POPULATION AGING

Median Age   60+/20-59   65+/20-64   70+/20-69   75+/20-74

OBSERVED AND *PROJECTED* POPULATION DATA (000's)

YEAR	MID-YEAR POPULATION	NO. OF BIRTHS	NO. OF DEATHS	URBAN POPULATION NUMBER	URBAN POPULATION PERCENT	POPULATION 1985 AGE	POPULATION 1985 NUMBER
1950	83625	1979	783	42063	50.3	0	7444
1955	89815	1626	699	49847	55.5	5	8514
1960	94096	1620	685	58810	62.5	10	10021
1965	98881	1756	678	66547	67.3	15	8961
1970	104331	2004	689	74294	71.2	20	8184
1975	111524	1695	681	84413	75.7	25	7807
1980	116807	1485	718	88995	76.2	30	9035
1985	120754	1377	843	92594	76.7	35	10716
1990	*123457*	*1505*	*939*	*95037*	*77.0*	40	9116
1995	*126319*	*1589*	*1038*	*97746*	*77.4*	45	8219
2000	*129105*	*1560*	*1164*	*100276*	*77.7*	50	7917
2005	*131101*	*1420*	*1305*	*102495*	*78.2*	55	6984
2010	*131677*	*1307*	*1431*	*103735*	*78.8*	60	5395
2015	*131056*	*1294*	*1523*	*103822*	*79.2*	65	4184
2020	*129916*	*1343*	*1608*	*103855*	*79.9*	70+	8258

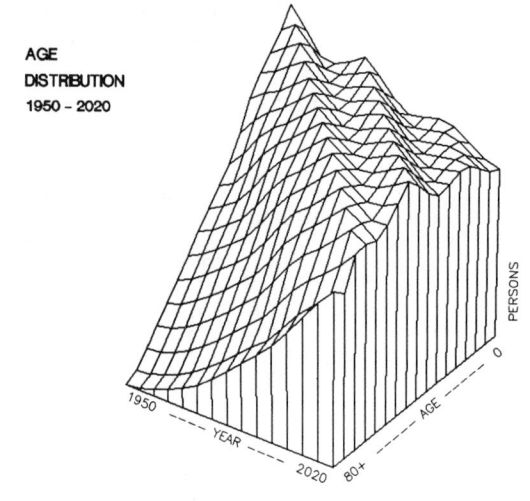

AGE DISTRIBUTION 1950 - 2020

POPULATION RATIOS

YEAR	AGE DISTRIBUTION UNDER 15	AGE DISTRIBUTION 15-64	AGE DISTRIBUTION 65 & OLDER	AGE DISTRIBUTION 70 & OLDER	DEPENDENCY RATIO	WOMEN 15-49	CHILD-WOMAN RATIO
1950	0.354	0.596	0.049	0.028	0.678	0.256	0.522
1955	0.336	0.611	0.053	0.031	0.636	0.260	0.407
1960	0.302	0.641	0.057	0.034	0.561	0.270	0.315
1965	0.259	0.678	0.062	0.037	0.475	0.283	0.293
1970	0.240	0.689	0.071	0.042	0.451	0.285	0.299
1975	0.243	0.678	0.079	0.048	0.475	0.272	0.327
1980	0.236	0.674	0.090	0.057	0.484	0.262	0.281
1985	0.215	0.682	0.103	0.068	0.467	0.255	0.242
1990	*0.185*	*0.698*	*0.117*	*0.076*	*0.433*	*0.255*	*0.220*
2000	*0.174*	*0.668*	*0.158*	*0.104*	*0.497*	*0.227*	*0.273*
2010	*0.174*	*0.631*	*0.195*	*0.134*	*0.584*	*0.212*	*0.253*
2020	*0.153*	*0.611*	*0.235*	*0.174*	*0.636*	*0.209*	*0.236*

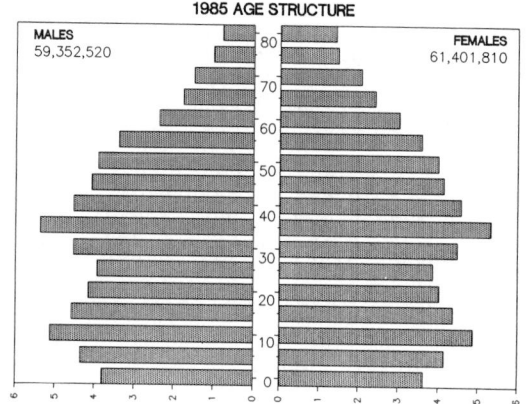

1985 AGE STRUCTURE

MALES 59,352,520   FEMALES 61,401,810

MORTALITY MEASURES (Annual Averages)

PERIOD	CRUDE DEATH RATE	INFANT MORT. RATE	LIFE EXPECTANCY AT BIRTH (years) MALE	LIFE EXPECTANCY AT BIRTH (years) FEMALE	LIFE EXPECTANCY AT BIRTH (years) BOTH SEXES	DIFFERENCE FEMALE-MALE
1950-55	9.36	50.64	62.10	65.90	63.94	3.80
1955-60	7.78	36.83	64.55	69.10	66.75	4.55
1960-65	7.28	24.46	66.50	71.60	68.96	5.10
1965-70	6.86	15.62	68.50	73.90	71.11	5.40
1970-75	6.60	11.54	70.60	76.19	73.30	5.59
1975-80	6.11	8.69	72.76	78.17	75.47	5.41
1980-85	6.15	6.50	74.16	79.67	76.92	5.51
1985-90	*6.98*	*5.00*	*75.38*	*81.06*	*78.14*	*5.68*
1990-95	*7.61*	*5.36*	*75.86*	*81.90*	*78.80*	*6.05*
2000-05	*9.02*	*4.99*	*76.84*	*82.56*	*79.62*	*5.72*
2010-15	*10.87*	*4.89*	*77.75*	*83.41*	*80.50*	*5.66*
2020-25	*12.38*	*4.79*	*78.64*	*84.19*	*81.34*	*5.56*

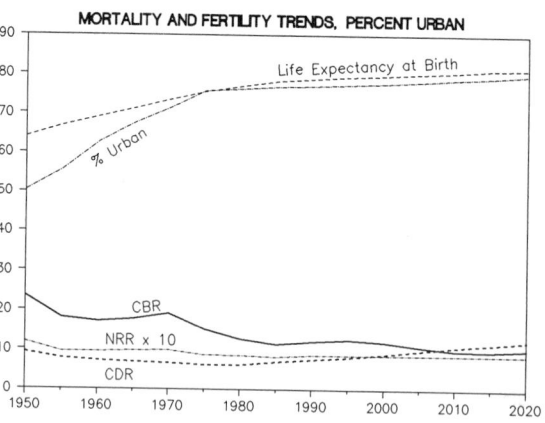

MORTALITY AND FERTILITY TRENDS, PERCENT URBAN

Life Expectancy at Birth
% Urban
CBR
NRR x 10
CDR

FERTILITY MEASURES (Annual Averages)

PERIOD	CRUDE BIRTH RATE	FERTILITY RATES GENERAL	FERTILITY RATES TOTAL	REPRODUCTION RATES GROSS	REPRODUCTION RATES NET	RATE OF NATUR. INCR.
1950-55	23.66	91.65	2.747	1.336	1.194	14.30
1955-60	18.10	68.25	2.077	1.010	0.945	10.32
1960-65	17.22	62.22	2.015	0.980	0.938	9.94
1965-70	17.76	62.53	2.003	0.974	0.965	10.90
1970-75	19.21	68.99	2.068	1.006	0.982	12.60
1975-80	15.20	56.89	1.809	0.880	0.870	9.09
1980-85	12.71	49.17	1.760	0.856	0.850	6.56
1985-90	*11.41*	*44.76*	*1.700*	*0.827*	*0.817*	*4.43*
1990-95	*12.19*	*48.79*	*1.800*	*0.875*	*0.867*	*4.58*
2000-05	*12.09*	*54.82*	*1.800*	*0.875*	*0.866*	*3.07*
2010-15	*9.92*	*46.82*	*1.800*	*0.875*	*0.867*	*-0.94*
2020-25	*10.34*	*50.44*	*1.800*	*0.875*	*0.868*	*-2.04*

AGING MEASURES

YEAR	POPULATION AGE RATIOS 60+/20-59	POPULATION AGE RATIOS 65+/20-64	POPULATION AGE RATIOS 70+/20-69	POPULATION AGE RATIOS 75+/20-74	POPULATION MEAN AGE	POPULATION MEDIAN AGE
1950	0.1654	0.1003	0.0548	0.0241	26.63	22.28
1960	0.1740	0.1061	0.0609	0.0301	29.02	25.53
1970	0.1883	0.1175	0.0665	0.0329	31.52	28.98
1980	0.2276	0.1499	0.0890	0.0467	33.87	32.61
1990	*0.3057*	*0.1902*	*0.1159*	*0.0663*	*37.32*	*37.21*
2000	*0.3936*	*0.2587*	*0.1558*	*0.0834*	*39.72*	*39.52*
2010	*0.5411*	*0.3396*	*0.2118*	*0.1232*	*41.67*	*41.59*
2020	*0.5872*	*0.4267*	*0.2840*	*0.1585*	*43.40*	*44.50*

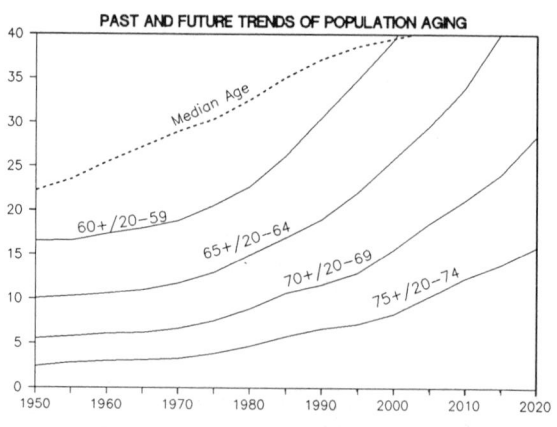

PAST AND FUTURE TRENDS OF POPULATION AGING

Median Age
60+/20-59
65+/20-64
70+/20-69
75+/20-74

OBSERVED AND *PROJECTED* POPULATION DATA (000's)

YEAR	MID-YEAR POPULATION	NO. OF BIRTHS	NO. OF DEATHS	URBAN POPULATION NUMBER	URBAN POPULATION PERCENT	POPULATION 1985 AGE	POPULATION 1985 NUMBER
1950	1237	58	32	429	34.7	0	667
1955	1447	68	33	559	38.6	5	538
1960	1695	89	37	724	42.7	10	481
1965	1962	103	41	908	46.3	15	411
1970	2299	115	33	1162	50.6	20	329
1975	2600	117	25	1440	55.4	25	231
1980	2923	129	23	1756	60.1	30	159
1985	3506	161	23	2257	64.4	35	139
1990	*4270*	*194*	*23*	*2908*	*68.1*	40	127
1995	*5218*	*225*	*24*	*3722*	*71.3*	45	116
2000	*6329*	*254*	*26*	*4684*	*74.0*	50	92
2005	*7585*	*277*	*28*	*5778*	*76.2*	55	70
2010	*8941*	*286*	*30*	*6989*	*78.2*	60	50
2015	*10323*	*296*	*33*	*8258*	*80.0*	65	37
2020	*11728*	*300*	*36*	*9577*	*81.7*	70+	59

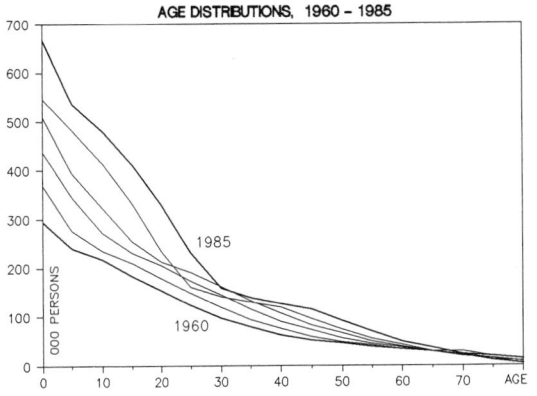

AGE DISTRIBUTIONS, 1960 - 1985

POPULATION RATIOS

YEAR	AGE DISTRIBUTION UNDER 15	AGE DISTRIBUTION 15-64	AGE DISTRIBUTION 65 & OLDER	AGE DISTRIBUTION 70 & OLDER	DEPENDENCY RATIO	WOMEN 15-49	CHILD-WOMAN RATIO
1950	0.457	0.495	0.048	0.028	1.022	0.200	0.930
1955	0.451	0.505	0.044	0.025	0.982	0.209	0.833
1960	0.444	0.515	0.041	0.023	0.942	0.217	0.800
1965	0.448	0.515	0.037	0.022	0.942	0.218	0.859
1970	0.459	0.510	0.031	0.019	0.960	0.216	0.879
1975	0.472	0.500	0.028	0.017	1.002	0.211	0.929
1980	0.494	0.475	0.031	0.021	1.107	0.201	0.929
1985	0.481	0.492	0.027	0.017	1.033	0.208	0.915
1990	*0.479*	*0.496*	*0.025*	*0.015*	*1.014*	*0.209*	*0.952*
2000	*0.486*	*0.489*	*0.025*	*0.014*	*1.046*	*0.210*	*0.906*
2010	*0.450*	*0.523*	*0.027*	*0.016*	*0.913*	*0.229*	*0.719*
2020	*0.386*	*0.586*	*0.027*	*0.017*	*0.706*	*0.252*	*0.526*

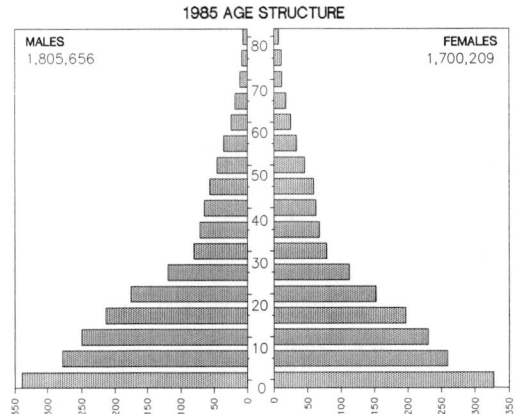

1985 AGE STRUCTURE

MALES 1,805,656   FEMALES 1,700,209

MORTALITY MEASURES (Annual Averages)

PERIOD	CRUDE DEATH RATE	INFANT MORT. RATE	LIFE EXPECTANCY AT BIRTH (years) MALE	LIFE EXPECTANCY AT BIRTH (years) FEMALE	LIFE EXPECTANCY AT BIRTH (years) BOTH SEXES	DIFFERENCE FEMALE-MALE
1950-55	26.00	160.00	42.20	44.30	43.22	2.10
1955-60	23.00	145.00	44.60	46.90	45.72	2.30
1960-65	22.00	125.00	46.90	49.50	48.17	2.60
1965-70	21.00	102.00	50.20	53.20	51.66	3.00
1970-75	14.40	82.00	54.90	58.30	56.56	3.40
1975-80	9.60	65.00	59.36	63.04	61.15	3.68
1980-85	7.91	54.09	61.86	65.54	63.65	3.68
1985-90	*6.62*	*44.42*	*64.16*	*67.84*	*65.96*	*3.68*
1990-95	*5.47*	*36.04*	*66.16*	*69.84*	*67.96*	*3.68*
2000-05	*4.06*	*25.05*	*68.86*	*73.34*	*71.04*	*4.48*
2010-15	*3.35*	*17.88*	*71.06*	*75.74*	*73.34*	*4.68*
2020-25	*3.03*	*12.41*	*73.06*	*77.74*	*75.34*	*4.68*

FERTILITY MEASURES (Annual Averages)

PERIOD	CRUDE BIRTH RATE	FERTILITY RATES GENERAL	FERTILITY RATES TOTAL	REPRODUCTION RATES GROSS	REPRODUCTION RATES NET	RATE OF NATUR. INCR.
1950-55	46.70	227.78	7.380	3.600	2.280	20.70
1955-60	46.70	218.68	7.380	3.600	2.410	23.70
1960-65	52.50	241.14	7.995	3.900	2.790	30.50
1965-70	52.50	241.77	7.995	3.900	2.970	31.50
1970-75	50.00	234.40	7.790	3.800	3.110	35.60
1975-80	45.00	218.87	7.380	3.600	3.150	35.40
1980-85	44.19	215.81	7.277	3.550	3.178	36.28
1985-90	*45.91*	*220.30*	*7.175*	*3.500*	*3.211*	*39.29*
1990-95	*45.45*	*218.62*	*6.867*	*3.350*	*3.135*	*39.97*
2000-05	*40.15*	*186.75*	*5.945*	*2.900*	*2.788*	*36.09*
2010-15	*32.04*	*136.15*	*4.346*	*2.120*	*2.068*	*28.69*
2020-25	*25.59*	*99.46*	*2.993*	*1.460*	*1.439*	*22.56*

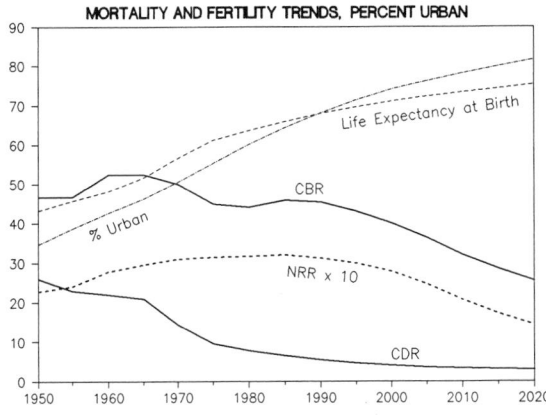

MORTALITY AND FERTILITY TRENDS, PERCENT URBAN

Life Expectancy at Birth / % Urban / CBR / NRR x 10 / CDR

AGING MEASURES

YEAR	POPULATION AGE RATIOS 60+/20-59	POPULATION AGE RATIOS 65+/20-64	POPULATION AGE RATIOS 70+/20-69	POPULATION AGE RATIOS 75+/20-74	POPULATION MEAN AGE	POPULATION MEDIAN AGE
1950	0.2005	0.1221	0.0679	0.0294	23.49	17.19
1960	0.1572	0.1007	0.0554	0.0233	22.67	17.58
1970	0.1208	0.0763	0.0450	0.0224	21.74	17.06
1980	0.1329	0.0867	0.0568	0.0291	20.96	15.26
1990	*0.1079*	*0.0647*	*0.0372*	*0.0191*	*20.57*	*15.95*
2000	*0.1106*	*0.0659*	*0.0357*	*0.0170*	*20.60*	*15.68*
2010	*0.1011*	*0.0661*	*0.0388*	*0.0187*	*21.64*	*17.17*
2020	*0.0966*	*0.0579*	*0.0352*	*0.0190*	*23.81*	*19.93*

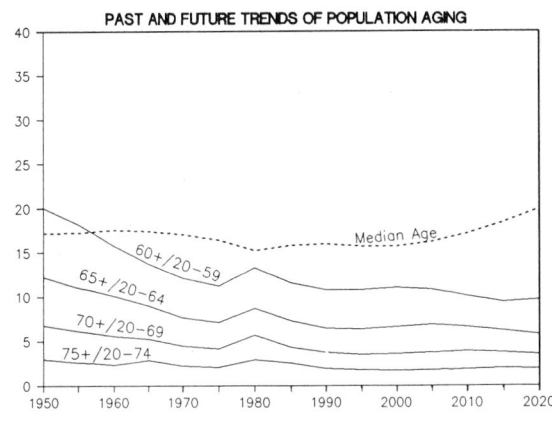

PAST AND FUTURE TRENDS OF POPULATION AGING

Median Age / 60+/20-59 / 65+/20-64 / 70+/20-69 / 75+/20-74

OBSERVED AND *PROJECTED* POPULATION DATA (000's)

YEAR	MID-YEAR POPULATION	NO. OF BIRTHS	NO. OF DEATHS	URBAN POPULATION NUMBER	URBAN POPULATION PERCENT	POPULATION 1985 AGE	POPULATION 1985 NUMBER
1950	4346	197	104	443	10.2	0	1259
1955	4840	219	107	496	10.2	5	333
1960	5433	244	111	559	10.3	10	779
1965	6141	270	119	665	10.8	15	928
1970	6938	277	156	812	11.7	20	798
1975	7098	213	284	731	10.3	25	713
1980	6400	291	126	659	10.3	30	618
1985	7284	302	121	787	10.8	35	476
1990	*8246*	*301*	*120*	*959*	*11.6*	40	335
1995	*9205*	*276*	*115*	*1183*	*12.9*	45	278
2000	*10046*	*254*	*112*	*1460*	*14.5*	50	239
2005	*10784*	*257*	*112*	*1811*	*16.8*	55	194
2010	*11539*	*282*	*115*	*2276*	*19.7*	60	143
2015	*12405*	*285*	*118*	*2849*	*23.0*	65	93
2020	*13266*	*262*	*122*	*3511*	*26.5*	70+	99

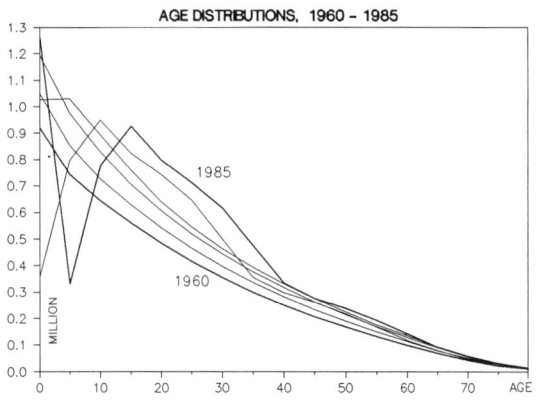

AGE DISTRIBUTIONS, 1960 - 1985

POPULATION RATIOS

YEAR	AGE DISTRIBUTION UNDER 15	AGE DISTRIBUTION 15-64	AGE DISTRIBUTION 65 & OLDER	AGE DISTRIBUTION 70 & OLDER	DEPENDENCY RATIO	WOMEN 15-49	CHILD-WOMAN RATIO
1950	0.422	0.551	0.027	0.015	0.816	0.237	0.704
1955	0.423	0.550	0.027	0.014	0.817	0.237	0.706
1960	0.425	0.548	0.027	0.014	0.825	0.236	0.719
1965	0.428	0.544	0.027	0.015	0.837	0.234	0.732
1970	0.432	0.540	0.028	0.015	0.853	0.232	0.743
1975	0.416	0.556	0.028	0.015	0.798	0.239	0.605
1980	0.329	0.646	0.025	0.012	0.549	0.283	0.198
1985	0.325	0.648	0.026	0.014	0.543	0.283	0.611
1990	*0.349*	*0.622*	*0.029*	*0.015*	*0.607*	*0.270*	*0.610*
2000	*0.385*	*0.580*	*0.035*	*0.019*	*0.724*	*0.245*	*0.517*
2010	*0.310*	*0.650*	*0.040*	*0.023*	*0.540*	*0.263*	*0.399*
2020	*0.292*	*0.650*	*0.058*	*0.030*	*0.539*	*0.254*	*0.407*

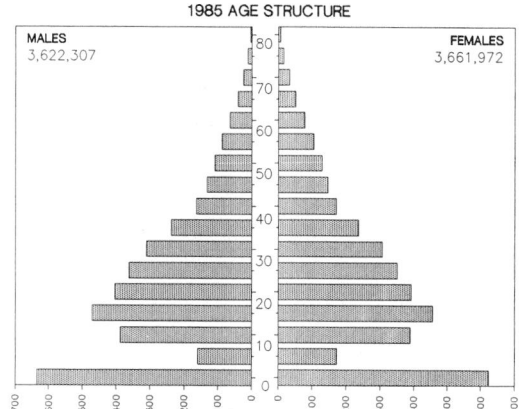

1985 AGE STRUCTURE

MALES 3,622,307 — FEMALES 3,661,972

MORTALITY MEASURES (Annual Averages)

PERIOD	CRUDE DEATH RATE	INFANT MORT. RATE	LIFE EXPECTANCY AT BIRTH (years) MALE	LIFE EXPECTANCY AT BIRTH (years) FEMALE	LIFE EXPECTANCY AT BIRTH (years) BOTH SEXES	DIFFERENCE FEMALE-MALE
1950-55	23.82	165.05	38.10	40.80	39.42	2.70
1955-60	22.09	151.97	40.00	42.80	41.37	2.80
1960-65	20.38	139.53	42.00	44.90	43.42	2.90
1965-70	19.40	129.96	44.00	46.90	45.42	2.90
1970-75	22.54	180.85	39.00	41.70	40.32	2.70
1975-80	40.00	263.19	30.00	32.50	31.22	2.50
1980-85	19.65	159.94	42.00	44.90	43.42	2.90
1985-90	*16.62*	*129.73*	*47.00*	*49.90*	*48.42*	*2.90*
1990-95	*14.55*	*115.67*	*49.50*	*52.40*	*50.92*	*2.90*
2000-05	*11.11*	*89.62*	*54.26*	*57.63*	*55.90*	*3.37*
2010-15	*9.95*	*65.93*	*58.71*	*62.31*	*60.47*	*3.60*
2020-25	*9.16*	*45.37*	*62.63*	*66.47*	*64.50*	*3.84*

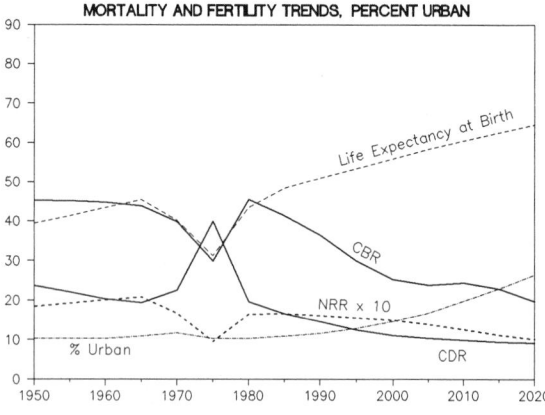

MORTALITY AND FERTILITY TRENDS, PERCENT URBAN

FERTILITY MEASURES (Annual Averages)

PERIOD	CRUDE BIRTH RATE	FERTILITY RATES GENERAL	FERTILITY RATES TOTAL	REPRODUCTION RATES GROSS	REPRODUCTION RATES NET	RATE OF NATUR. INCR.
1950-55	45.35	191.46	6.293	3.070	1.849	21.53
1955-60	45.20	191.43	6.293	3.070	1.927	23.11
1960-65	44.87	191.28	6.291	3.069	2.008	24.49
1965-70	43.90	188.75	6.216	3.032	2.082	24.50
1970-75	39.91	169.65	5.535	2.700	1.676	17.37
1975-80	30.00	115.38	4.100	2.000	0.958	-10.00
1980-85	45.50	160.74	5.125	2.500	1.650	25.85
1985-90	*41.39*	*149.95*	*4.715*	*2.300*	*1.657*	*24.77*
1990-95	*36.53*	*145.16*	*4.407*	*2.150*	*1.614*	*21.98*
2000-05	*25.28*	*101.01*	*3.792*	*1.850*	*1.503*	*14.18*
2010-15	*24.42*	*93.06*	*2.993*	*1.460*	*1.264*	*14.47*
2020-25	*19.76*	*77.43*	*2.296*	*1.120*	*1.018*	*10.60*

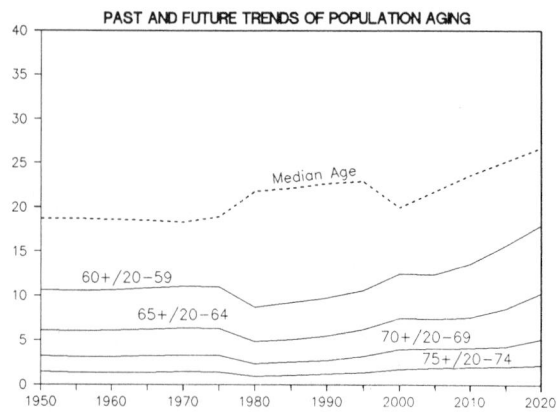

PAST AND FUTURE TRENDS OF POPULATION AGING

AGING MEASURES

YEAR	POPULATION AGE RATIOS 60+/20-59	POPULATION AGE RATIOS 65+/20-64	POPULATION AGE RATIOS 70+/20-69	POPULATION AGE RATIOS 75+/20-74	POPULATION MEAN AGE	POPULATION MEDIAN AGE
1950	0.1060	0.0606	0.0322	0.0144	23.03	18.74
1960	0.1064	0.0608	0.0311	0.0133	22.96	18.64
1970	0.1103	0.0635	0.0329	0.0143	22.82	18.32
1980	0.0869	0.0484	0.0233	0.0092	25.35	21.81
1990	*0.0970*	*0.0546*	*0.0272*	*0.0117*	*24.71*	*22.67*
2000	*0.1242*	*0.0744*	*0.0393*	*0.0171*	*25.72*	*19.99*
2010	*0.1360*	*0.0752*	*0.0411*	*0.0195*	*27.87*	*23.62*
2020	*0.1794*	*0.1026*	*0.0512*	*0.0220*	*29.45*	*26.73*

OBSERVED AND *PROJECTED* POPULATION DATA (000's)

YEAR	MID-YEAR POPULATION	NO. OF BIRTHS	NO. OF DEATHS	URBAN POPULATION NUMBER	URBAN POPULATION PERCENT	POPULATION 1985 AGE	POPULATION 1985 NUMBER
1950	9740	360	312	3024	31.0	0	2836
1955	9100	387	121	3230	35.5	5	2626
1960	10526	416	128	4231	40.2	10	2419
1965	12100	469	136	5456	45.1	15	2193
1970	13892	496	130	6958	50.1	20	1918
1975	15853	517	110	8731	55.1	25	1845
1980	18025	551	108	10759	59.7	30	1360
1985	20385	590	110	13009	63.8	35	1103
1990	*22937*	*608*	*114*	*15457*	*67.4*	40	915
1995	*25548*	*620*	*122*	*17986*	*70.4*	45	803
2000	*28165*	*615*	*134*	*20522*	*72.9*	50	672
2005	*30678*	*617*	*148*	*23049*	*75.1*	55	532
2010	*33115*	*611*	*168*	*25569*	*77.2*	60	431
2015	*35405*	*616*	*190*	*28012*	*79.1*	65	317
2020	*37600*	*607*	*216*	*30405*	*80.9*	70+	418

AGE DISTRIBUTIONS, 1960 - 1985

POPULATION RATIOS

YEAR	AGE DISTRIBUTION UNDER 15	15-64	65 & OLDER	70 & OLDER	DEPENDENCY RATIO	WOMEN 15-49	CHILD-WOMAN RATIO
1950	0.417	0.553	0.031	0.014	0.809	0.228	0.690
1955	0.414	0.551	0.036	0.021	0.816	0.246	0.681
1960	0.437	0.530	0.033	0.019	0.888	0.234	0.807
1965	0.442	0.524	0.034	0.019	0.908	0.229	0.729
1970	0.439	0.526	0.035	0.020	0.900	0.229	0.711
1975	0.416	0.548	0.035	0.020	0.823	0.239	0.647
1980	0.403	0.561	0.035	0.020	0.781	0.245	0.598
1985	0.387	0.577	0.036	0.021	0.732	0.250	0.556
1990	*0.370*	*0.592*	*0.038*	*0.022*	*0.689*	*0.255*	*0.522*
2000	*0.333*	*0.624*	*0.044*	*0.025*	*0.604*	*0.263*	*0.431*
2010	*0.288*	*0.660*	*0.052*	*0.031*	*0.515*	*0.265*	*0.361*
2020	*0.251*	*0.682*	*0.067*	*0.039*	*0.466*	*0.261*	*0.321*

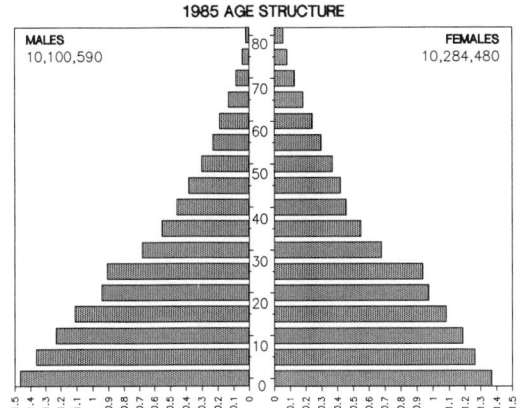

1985 AGE STRUCTURE

MALES 10,100,590 FEMALES 10,284,480

MORTALITY MEASURES (Annual Averages)

PERIOD	CRUDE DEATH RATE	INFANT MORT. RATE	LIFE EXPECTANCY AT BIRTH (years) MALE	FEMALE	BOTH SEXES	DIFFERENCE FEMALE-MALE
1950-55	32.00	115.00	46.03	48.96	47.46	2.93
1955-60	13.34	100.00	51.06	54.15	52.57	3.09
1960-65	12.20	70.00	53.58	56.90	55.20	3.32
1965-70	11.21	57.50	55.97	59.40	57.64	3.43
1970-75	9.36	46.60	59.20	64.00	61.54	4.80
1975-80	6.94	35.00	62.41	68.78	65.52	6.37
1980-85	5.97	29.66	64.57	71.00	67.69	6.43
1985-90	*5.37*	*24.48*	*66.16*	*72.68*	*69.32*	*6.52*
1990-95	*4.97*	*20.72*	*67.67*	*73.93*	*70.71*	*6.26*
2000-05	*4.74*	*15.16*	*69.72*	*76.18*	*72.86*	*6.46*
2010-15	*5.07*	*11.31*	*71.18*	*77.97*	*74.48*	*6.79*
2020-25	*5.74*	*8.67*	*72.57*	*79.43*	*75.90*	*6.86*

FERTILITY MEASURES (Annual Averages)

PERIOD	CRUDE BIRTH RATE	FERTILITY RATES GENERAL	TOTAL	REPRODUCTION RATES GROSS	NET	RATE OF NATUR. INCR.
1950-55	37.00	156.30	5.175	2.512	1.782	5.00
1955-60	42.48	177.16	5.803	2.817	2.179	29.14
1960-65	39.50	170.68	5.601	2.719	2.188	27.30
1965-70	38.79	169.50	5.667	2.751	2.289	27.58
1970-75	35.71	152.49	5.237	2.542	2.196	26.35
1975-80	32.61	134.45	4.553	2.210	2.030	25.67
1980-85	30.54	123.12	4.017	1.950	1.830	24.58
1985-90	*28.93*	*114.53*	*3.605*	*1.750*	*1.666*	*23.56*
1990-95	*26.51*	*103.11*	*3.234*	*1.570*	*1.509*	*21.54*
2000-05	*21.83*	*82.24*	*2.678*	*1.300*	*1.268*	*17.09*
2010-15	*18.44*	*69.73*	*2.266*	*1.100*	*1.083*	*13.37*
2020-25	*16.14*	*62.44*	*2.060*	*1.000*	*0.990*	*10.39*

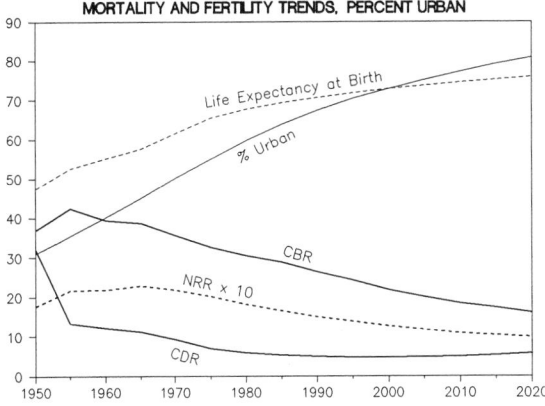

MORTALITY AND FERTILITY TRENDS, PERCENT URBAN

AGING MEASURES

YEAR	POPULATION AGE RATIOS 60+/20-59	65+/20-64	70+/20-69	75+/20-74	POPULATION MEAN AGE	POPULATION MEDIAN AGE
1950	0.1272	0.0676	0.0300	0.0137	23.86	19.15
1960	0.1297	0.0764	0.0434	0.0196	23.08	18.33
1970	0.1362	0.0814	0.0446	0.0239	23.27	18.02
1980	0.1285	0.0774	0.0424	0.0201	23.86	19.52
1990	*0.1269*	*0.0776*	*0.0427*	*0.0206*	*25.07*	*21.28*
2000	*0.1361*	*0.0831*	*0.0461*	*0.0228*	*26.92*	*23.62*
2010	*0.1497*	*0.0922*	*0.0534*	*0.0267*	*29.33*	*26.55*
2020	*0.1962*	*0.1116*	*0.0622*	*0.0315*	*31.93*	*29.83*

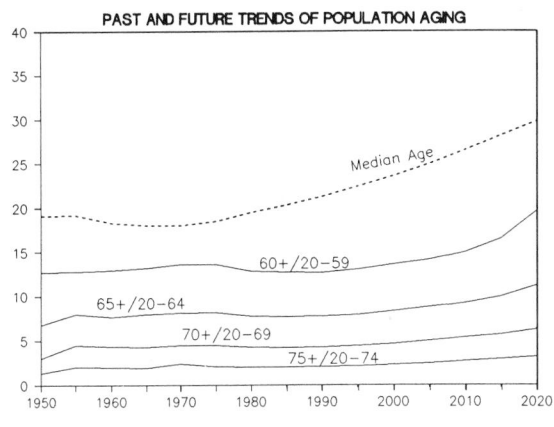

PAST AND FUTURE TRENDS OF POPULATION AGING

OBSERVED AND *PROJECTED* POPULATION DATA (000's)

YEAR	MID-YEAR POPULATION	NO. OF BIRTHS	NO. OF DEATHS	URBAN POPULATION NUMBER	URBAN POPULATION PERCENT	POPULATION 1985 AGE	POPULATION 1985 NUMBER
1950	20357	753	651	4347	21.4	0	3740
1955	21422	983	318	5225	24.4	5	3999
1960	25003	989	313	6929	27.7	10	4563
1965	28530	909	296	9230	32.4	15	4374
1970	31923	921	282	12995	40.7	20	4281
1975	35281	843	229	16947	48.0	25	4120
1980	38124	811	238	21678	56.9	30	3172
1985	41056	773	253	26829	65.3	35	2610
1990	*43582*	*724*	*265*	*31397*	*72.0*	40	2243
1995	*45814*	*729*	*285*	*35282*	*77.0*	45	2145
2000	*48012*	*701*	*313*	*38661*	*80.5*	50	1726
2005	*49989*	*664*	*349*	*41428*	*82.9*	55	1288
2010	*51586*	*645*	*390*	*43485*	*84.3*	60	1033
2015	*52876*	*635*	*435*	*45260*	*85.6*	65	727
2020	*53888*	*626*	*479*	*46766*	*86.8*	70+	1036

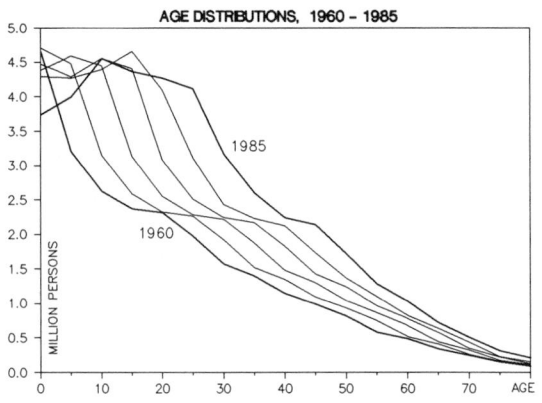

AGE DISTRIBUTIONS, 1960 - 1985

POPULATION RATIOS

YEAR	AGE DISTRIBUTION UNDER 15	AGE DISTRIBUTION 15-64	AGE DISTRIBUTION 65 & OLDER	AGE DISTRIBUTION 70 & OLDER	DEPENDENCY RATIO	WOMEN 15-49	CHILD-WOMAN RATIO
1950	0.417	0.553	0.030	0.014	0.808	0.228	0.690
1955	0.394	0.570	0.037	0.022	0.756	0.251	0.622
1960	0.419	0.547	0.033	0.020	0.827	0.237	0.786
1965	0.432	0.535	0.033	0.018	0.870	0.228	0.722
1970	0.421	0.546	0.033	0.019	0.830	0.232	0.593
1975	0.377	0.586	0.036	0.020	0.705	0.248	0.512
1980	0.340	0.622	0.038	0.021	0.608	0.262	0.430
1985	0.300	0.657	0.043	0.025	0.521	0.274	0.332
1990	*0.265*	*0.688*	*0.047*	*0.027*	*0.454*	*0.282*	*0.314*
2000	*0.231*	*0.706*	*0.063*	*0.035*	*0.416*	*0.281*	*0.271*
2010	*0.203*	*0.712*	*0.084*	*0.051*	*0.404*	*0.261*	*0.248*
2020	*0.181*	*0.707*	*0.112*	*0.067*	*0.414*	*0.238*	*0.248*

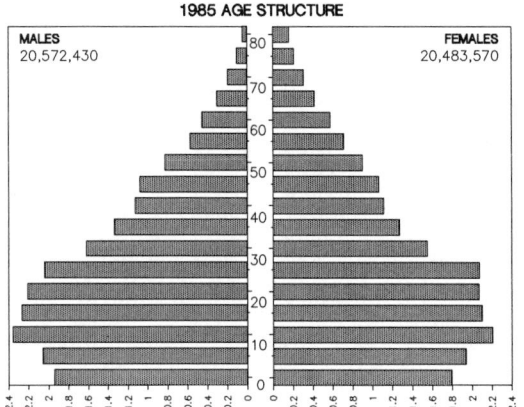

1985 AGE STRUCTURE

MALES 20,572,430   FEMALES 20,483,570

MORTALITY MEASURES (Annual Averages)

PERIOD	CRUDE DEATH RATE	INFANT MORT. RATE	LIFE EXPECTANCY AT BIRTH (years) MALE	LIFE EXPECTANCY AT BIRTH (years) FEMALE	LIFE EXPECTANCY AT BIRTH (years) BOTH SEXES	DIFFERENCE FEMALE-MALE
1950-55	32.00	115.00	46.00	49.00	47.46	3.00
1955-60	14.85	100.00	51.06	54.15	52.57	3.09
1960-65	12.52	70.00	53.58	56.90	55.20	3.32
1965-70	10.39	57.50	55.97	59.40	57.64	3.43
1970-75	8.85	46.60	59.20	64.00	61.54	4.80
1975-80	6.50	35.00	62.40	68.80	65.52	6.40
1980-85	6.25	29.66	64.57	71.00	67.69	6.43
1985-90	*6.17*	*24.78*	*66.20*	*72.48*	*69.25*	*6.28*
1990-95	*6.08*	*21.00*	*67.71*	*73.74*	*70.63*	*6.03*
2000-05	*6.52*	*15.04*	*70.19*	*75.98*	*73.00*	*5.79*
2010-15	*7.57*	*10.64*	*72.12*	*77.90*	*74.92*	*5.78*
2020-25	*8.89*	*7.55*	*73.83*	*79.55*	*76.61*	*5.72*

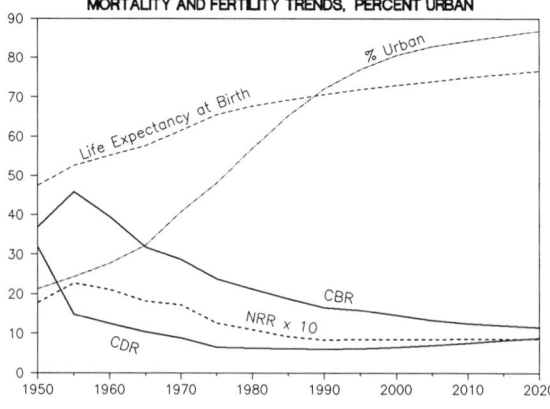

MORTALITY AND FERTILITY TRENDS, PERCENT URBAN

% Urban, Life Expectancy at Birth, CBR, NRR x 10, CDR

FERTILITY MEASURES (Annual Averages)

PERIOD	CRUDE BIRTH RATE	FERTILITY RATES GENERAL	FERTILITY RATES TOTAL	REPRODUCTION RATES GROSS	REPRODUCTION RATES NET	RATE OF NATUR. INCR.
1950-55	37.00	154.50	5.179	2.514	1.791	5.00
1955-60	45.90	188.61	6.073	2.948	2.284	31.05
1960-65	39.56	170.26	5.399	2.621	2.113	27.04
1965-70	31.86	138.47	4.516	2.192	1.827	21.47
1970-75	28.84	120.15	4.106	1.993	1.727	19.99
1975-80	23.90	93.71	2.800	1.359	1.262	17.40
1980-85	21.28	79.33	2.400	1.165	1.096	15.03
1985-90	*18.82*	*67.69*	*2.000*	*0.971*	*0.925*	*12.64*
1990-95	*16.62*	*58.74*	*1.800*	*0.874*	*0.840*	*10.54*
2000-05	*14.59*	*52.51*	*1.800*	*0.874*	*0.852*	*8.07*
2010-15	*12.51*	*49.06*	*1.800*	*0.874*	*0.860*	*4.94*
2020-25	*11.62*	*50.22*	*1.800*	*0.874*	*0.866*	*2.72*

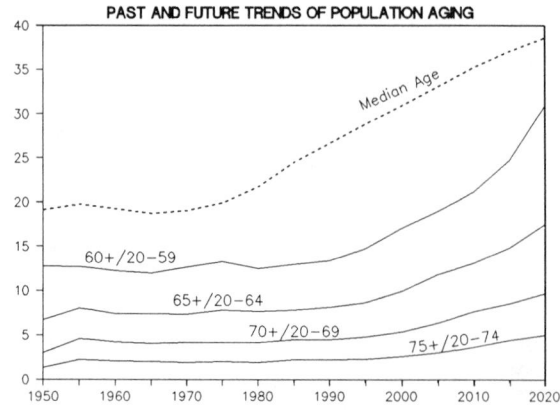

PAST AND FUTURE TRENDS OF POPULATION AGING

Median Age, 60+/20-59, 65+/20-64, 70+/20-69, 75+/20-74

AGING MEASURES

YEAR	POPULATION AGE RATIOS 60+/20-59	POPULATION AGE RATIOS 65+/20-64	POPULATION AGE RATIOS 70+/20-69	POPULATION AGE RATIOS 75+/20-74	POPULATION MEAN AGE	POPULATION MEDIAN AGE
1950	0.1272	0.0673	0.0299	0.0136	23.85	19.15
1960	0.1220	0.0736	0.0423	0.0207	23.35	19.24
1970	0.1266	0.0735	0.0414	0.0194	24.01	19.04
1980	0.1249	0.0763	0.0414	0.0190	25.83	21.76
1990	*0.1338*	*0.0812*	*0.0445*	*0.0223*	*29.14*	*26.61*
2000	*0.1705*	*0.0996*	*0.0534*	*0.0261*	*32.24*	*30.94*
2010	*0.2119*	*0.1311*	*0.0761*	*0.0364*	*35.30*	*35.31*
2020	*0.3087*	*0.1745*	*0.0969*	*0.0496*	*38.12*	*38.61*

OBSERVED AND *PROJECTED* POPULATION DATA

YEAR	MID-YEAR POPULATION	NO. OF BIRTHS	NO. OF DEATHS	URBAN POPULATION NUMBER	URBAN POPULATION PERCENT	POPULATION 1985 AGE	POPULATION 1985 NUMBER
1950	152248	6882	1705	89919	59.1	0	266963
1955	199150	8822	2091	131474	66.0	5	229293
1960	277980	12370	2502	201107	72.3	10	188060
1965	470562	23387	2965	365592	77.7	15	150027
1970	744261	33045	3721	578804	77.8	20	156581
1975	1006552	40363	4228	843572	83.8	25	175503
1980	1374919	48947	4365	1240037	90.2	30	153417
1985	1709859	55300	4757	1601856	93.7	35	122539
1990	*2090231*	*58934*	*5677*	*1998107*	*95.6*	40	98027
1995	*2438452*	*63575*	*6850*	*2356442*	*96.6*	45	64011
2000	*2781910*	*67823*	*8588*	*2703502*	*97.2*	50	43416
2005	*3121054*	*72540*	*10858*	*3039951*	*97.4*	55	23932
2010	*3450731*	*74322*	*13727*	*3368047*	*97.6*	60	16095
2015	*3767627*	*75710*	*17203*	*3684373*	*97.8*	65	8737
2020	*4071976*	*75258*	*21329*	*3988989*	*98.0*	70+	13258

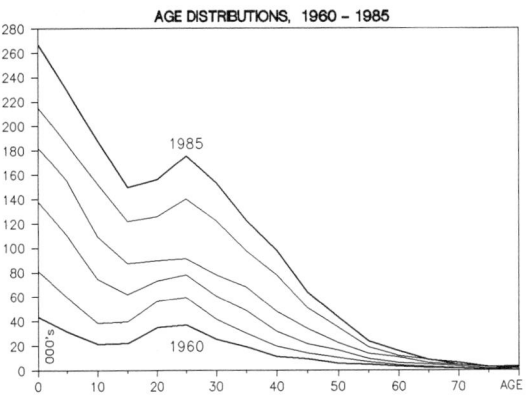

AGE DISTRIBUTIONS, 1960 – 1985

POPULATION RATIOS

YEAR	AGE DISTRIBUTION UNDER 15	AGE DISTRIBUTION 15-64	AGE DISTRIBUTION 65 & OLDER	AGE DISTRIBUTION 70 & OLDER	DEPENDENCY RATIO	WOMEN 15-49	CHILD-WOMAN RATIO
1950	0.361	0.610	0.029	0.015	0.641	0.189	0.802
1955	0.363	0.604	0.033	0.022	0.657	0.183	0.931
1960	0.348	0.629	0.022	0.013	0.589	0.174	0.900
1965	0.382	0.601	0.017	0.010	0.664	0.177	0.973
1970	0.434	0.549	0.017	0.010	0.823	0.194	0.954
1975	0.444	0.540	0.016	0.010	0.850	0.208	0.869
1980	0.402	0.584	0.014	0.008	0.713	0.206	0.760
1985	0.400	0.587	0.013	0.008	0.704	0.208	0.750
1990	*0.387*	*0.598*	*0.015*	*0.007*	*0.673*	*0.210*	*0.700*
2000	*0.347*	*0.627*	*0.025*	*0.012*	*0.594*	*0.224*	*0.543*
2010	*0.311*	*0.641*	*0.048*	*0.024*	*0.561*	*0.233*	*0.470*
2020	*0.283*	*0.639*	*0.078*	*0.044*	*0.566*	*0.245*	*0.392*

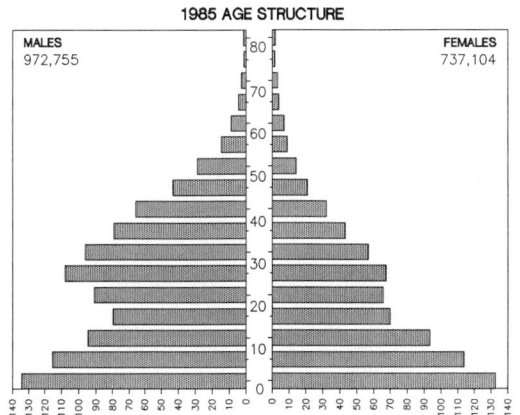

1985 AGE STRUCTURE

MALES 972,755   FEMALES 737,104

MORTALITY MEASURES (Annual Averages)

PERIOD	CRUDE DEATH RATE	INFANT MORT. RATE	LIFE EXPECTANCY AT BIRTH (years) MALE	LIFE EXPECTANCY AT BIRTH (years) FEMALE	LIFE EXPECTANCY AT BIRTH (years) BOTH SEXES	DIFFERENCE FEMALE-MALE
1950-55	11.20	125.00	54.10	57.50	55.76	3.40
1955-60	10.50	101.00	56.60	60.00	58.26	3.40
1960-65	9.00	77.00	59.10	62.50	60.76	3.40
1965-70	6.30	55.00	62.50	66.40	64.40	3.90
1970-75	5.00	43.00	65.30	69.30	67.25	4.00
1975-80	4.20	33.98	67.50	71.70	69.55	4.20
1980-85	3.17	23.03	69.56	73.72	71.58	4.16
1985-90	*2.78*	*19.14*	*70.75*	*74.97*	*72.81*	*4.22*
1990-95	*2.72*	*16.02*	*71.74*	*76.09*	*73.86*	*4.36*
2000-05	*3.09*	*11.03*	*73.53*	*78.13*	*75.78*	*4.60*
2010-15	*3.98*	*7.61*	*75.11*	*79.69*	*77.35*	*4.57*
2020-25	*5.24*	*6.22*	*76.13*	*81.02*	*78.51*	*4.89*

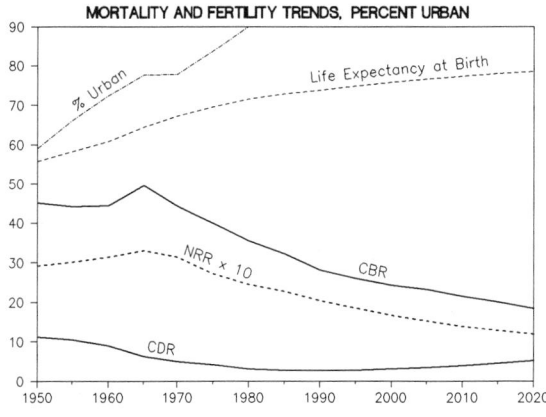

MORTALITY AND FERTILITY TRENDS, PERCENT URBAN

FERTILITY MEASURES (Annual Averages)

PERIOD	CRUDE BIRTH RATE	FERTILITY RATES GENERAL	FERTILITY RATES TOTAL	REPRODUCTION RATES GROSS	REPRODUCTION RATES NET	RATE OF NATUR. INCR.
1950-55	45.20	243.79	7.277	3.550	2.930	34.00
1955-60	44.30	249.11	7.277	3.550	3.020	33.80
1960-65	44.50	252.41	7.380	3.600	3.150	35.50
1965-70	49.70	264.87	7.482	3.650	3.310	43.40
1970-75	44.40	219.59	6.970	3.400	3.150	39.40
1975-80	40.10	193.90	5.945	2.900	2.730	35.90
1980-85	35.60	171.85	5.227	2.550	2.453	32.42
1985-90	*32.34*	*154.62*	*4.817*	*2.350*	*2.280*	*29.56*
1990-95	*28.19*	*132.17*	*4.305*	*2.100*	*2.049*	*25.48*
2000-05	*24.38*	*107.43*	*3.485*	*1.700*	*1.675*	*21.29*
2010-15	*21.54*	*91.25*	*2.870*	*1.400*	*1.386*	*17.56*
2020-25	*18.48*	*74.74*	*2.460*	*1.200*	*1.190*	*13.24*

AGING MEASURES

YEAR	POPULATION AGE RATIOS 60+/20-59	POPULATION AGE RATIOS 65+/20-64	POPULATION AGE RATIOS 70+/20-69	POPULATION AGE RATIOS 75+/20-74	POPULATION MEAN AGE	POPULATION MEDIAN AGE
1950	0.0909	0.0577	0.0283	0.0111	23.87	21.54
1960	0.0665	0.0410	0.0242	0.0094	23.68	22.80
1970	0.0554	0.0367	0.0216	0.0115	21.35	18.93
1980	0.0467	0.0282	0.0151	0.0082	22.61	20.50
1990	*0.0523*	*0.0292*	*0.0146*	*0.0078*	*23.77*	*21.18*
2000	*0.0921*	*0.0476*	*0.0216*	*0.0098*	*26.35*	*23.08*
2010	*0.1590*	*0.0878*	*0.0416*	*0.0179*	*28.76*	*25.37*
2020	*0.2393*	*0.1418*	*0.0754*	*0.0355*	*31.00*	*27.96*

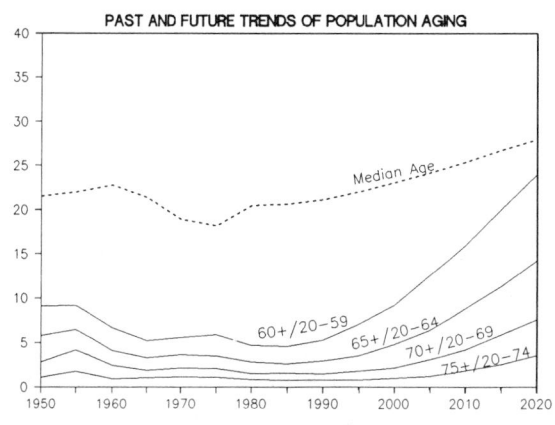

PAST AND FUTURE TRENDS OF POPULATION AGING

OBSERVED AND *PROJECTED* POPULATION DATA

YEAR	MID-YEAR POPULATION	NO. OF BIRTHS	NO. OF DEATHS	URBAN POPULATION NUMBER	URBAN POPULATION PERCENT	POPULATION 1985 AGE	POPULATION 1985 NUMBER
1950	1755000	80261	44337	127055	7.2	0	620827
1955	1944311	88338	44406	147484	7.6	5	490756
1960	2177126	97692	49493	173002	7.9	10	420765
1965	2432240	108101	55083	202433	8.3	15	365097
1970	2712603	120442	61484	261089	9.6	20	319439
1975	3024336	135079	62646	344115	11.4	25	277395
1980	3205428	143334	59852	430966	13.4	30	231211
1985	3594220	148369	59021	569757	15.9	35	191123
1990	*4070568*	*155162*	*58799*	*757612*	*18.6*	40	164344
1995	*4582700*	*162411*	*58480*	*995110*	*21.7*	45	137504
2000	*5133589*	*163299*	*57532*	*1289584*	*25.1*	50	110376
2005	*5691134*	*159813*	*56206*	*1637057*	*28.8*	55	91855
2010	*6233874*	*155199*	*54927*	*2031873*	*32.6*	60	69045
2015	*6756252*	*151279*	*54273*	*2469057*	*36.5*	65	49638
2020	*7259347*	*146813*	*54583*	*2943710*	*40.6*	70+	54843

AGE DISTRIBUTIONS, 1960 - 1985

POPULATION RATIOS

YEAR	AGE DISTRIBUTION UNDER 15	AGE DISTRIBUTION 15-64	AGE DISTRIBUTION 65 & OLDER	AGE DISTRIBUTION 70 & OLDER	DEPENDENCY RATIO	WOMEN 15-49	CHILD-WOMAN RATIO
1950	0.419	0.553	0.028	0.015	0.808	0.237	0.688
1955	0.418	0.555	0.027	0.015	0.803	0.237	0.699
1960	0.421	0.555	0.024	0.014	0.801	0.236	0.716
1965	0.424	0.552	0.024	0.013	0.811	0.234	0.714
1970	0.423	0.551	0.026	0.013	0.815	0.233	0.708
1975	0.421	0.552	0.027	0.014	0.810	0.235	0.704
1980	0.420	0.552	0.028	0.015	0.813	0.234	0.708
1985	0.426	0.545	0.029	0.015	0.836	0.232	0.745
1990	*0.427*	*0.543*	*0.030*	*0.016*	*0.841*	*0.232*	*0.710*
2000	*0.404*	*0.564*	*0.032*	*0.018*	*0.772*	*0.242*	*0.611*
2010	*0.359*	*0.604*	*0.036*	*0.020*	*0.655*	*0.257*	*0.476*
2020	*0.305*	*0.651*	*0.044*	*0.025*	*0.535*	*0.273*	*0.371*

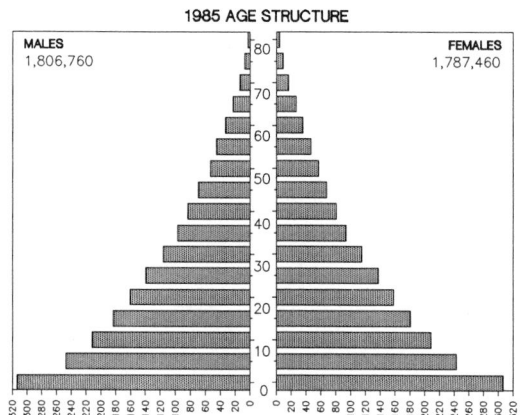

1985 AGE STRUCTURE

MALES 1,806,760   FEMALES 1,787,460

MORTALITY MEASURES (Annual Averages)

PERIOD	CRUDE DEATH RATE	INFANT MORT. RATE	LIFE EXPECTANCY AT BIRTH (years) MALE	LIFE EXPECTANCY AT BIRTH (years) FEMALE	LIFE EXPECTANCY AT BIRTH (years) BOTH SEXES	DIFFERENCE FEMALE-MALE
1950-55	25.26	180.14	36.50	39.20	37.82	2.70
1955-60	22.84	160.00	39.10	41.80	40.42	2.70
1960-65	22.73	149.97	39.10	41.80	40.42	2.70
1965-70	22.65	147.49	39.10	41.80	40.42	2.70
1970-75	22.67	144.98	39.10	41.80	40.42	2.70
1975-80	20.71	135.01	42.10	45.00	43.51	2.90
1980-85	18.67	122.50	44.50	47.50	45.96	3.00
1985-90	*16.42*	*109.99*	*47.00*	*50.00*	*48.46*	*3.00*
1990-95	*14.44*	*97.01*	*49.50*	*52.50*	*50.96*	*3.00*
2000-05	*11.21*	*73.75*	*54.50*	*57.50*	*55.96*	*3.00*
2010-15	*8.81*	*54.89*	*59.50*	*62.50*	*60.96*	*3.00*
2020-25	*7.52*	*39.77*	*63.98*	*67.32*	*65.61*	*3.34*

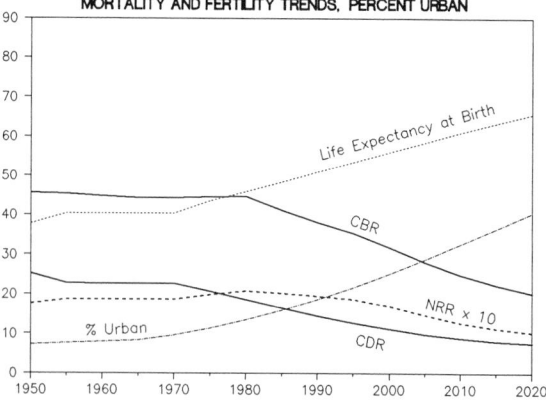

MORTALITY AND FERTILITY TRENDS, PERCENT URBAN

FERTILITY MEASURES (Annual Averages)

PERIOD	CRUDE BIRTH RATE	FERTILITY RATES GENERAL	FERTILITY RATES TOTAL	REPRODUCTION RATES GROSS	REPRODUCTION RATES NET	RATE OF NATUR. INCR.
1950-55	45.73	192.86	6.150	3.000	1.772	20.47
1955-60	45.43	192.21	6.150	3.000	1.873	22.60
1960-65	44.87	191.29	6.150	3.000	1.873	22.14
1965-70	44.44	190.30	6.150	3.000	1.873	21.80
1970-75	44.40	189.70	6.150	3.000	1.873	21.74
1975-80	44.66	190.45	6.150	3.000	1.994	23.95
1980-85	44.72	191.89	6.150	3.000	2.085	26.05
1985-90	*41.28*	*178.16*	*5.740*	*2.800*	*2.026*	*24.86*
1990-95	*38.12*	*163.60*	*5.330*	*2.600*	*1.958*	*23.67*
2000-05	*31.81*	*129.50*	*4.305*	*2.100*	*1.701*	*20.60*
2010-15	*24.90*	*95.18*	*2.993*	*1.460*	*1.267*	*16.08*
2020-25	*20.22*	*73.48*	*2.296*	*1.120*	*1.027*	*12.70*

AGING MEASURES

YEAR	POPULATION AGE RATIOS 60+/20-59	POPULATION AGE RATIOS 65+/20-64	POPULATION AGE RATIOS 70+/20-69	POPULATION AGE RATIOS 75+/20-74	POPULATION MEAN AGE	POPULATION MEDIAN AGE
1950	0.1069	0.0627	0.0333	0.0152	22.98	18.94
1960	0.0937	0.0537	0.0305	0.0135	22.95	18.84
1970	0.1027	0.0572	0.0274	0.0115	23.07	18.72
1980	0.1109	0.0625	0.0316	0.0134	23.17	18.83
1990	*0.1174*	*0.0679*	*0.0355*	*0.0154*	*23.12*	*18.60*
2000	*0.1199*	*0.0707*	*0.0383*	*0.0172*	*23.83*	*19.35*
2010	*0.1212*	*0.0729*	*0.0395*	*0.0183*	*25.42*	*21.69*
2020	*0.1333*	*0.0792*	*0.0431*	*0.0206*	*27.75*	*24.74*

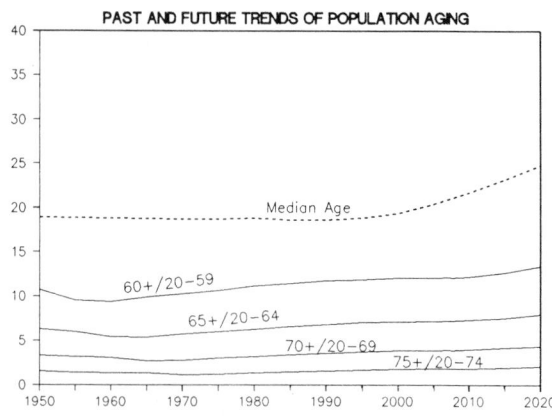

PAST AND FUTURE TRENDS OF POPULATION AGING

OBSERVED AND *PROJECTED* POPULATION DATA

YEAR	MID-YEAR POPULATION	NO. OF BIRTHS	NO. OF DEATHS	URBAN POPULATION NUMBER	URBAN POPULATION PERCENT	POPULATION 1985 AGE	POPULATION 1985 NUMBER
1950	1442712	59151	26979	327250	22.7	0	342139
1955	1613200	70013	24521	491612	30.5	5	319236
1960	1857419	79312	24704	735021	39.6	10	338352
1965	2151356	83473	25386	1063935	49.5	15	326188
1970	2469000	79255	22962	1466066	59.4	20	254811
1975	2767344	83377	24018	1898193	68.6	25	197429
1980	2669248	78190	23487	2016098	75.5	30	159551
1985	2667678	77157	20789	2145722	80.4	35	122866
1990	2965241	81820	20979	2482907	83.7	40	99823
1995	3285898	81572	21020	2820132	85.8	45	100512
2000	3603275	78378	22095	3134625	87.0	50	103385
2005	3896124	76216	23338	3431003	88.1	55	95463
2010	4169816	75278	24443	3712751	89.0	60	71298
2015	4431977	76062	25688	3985774	89.9	65	43589
2020	4691215	78249	27861	4257268	90.7	70+	93036

POPULATION RATIOS

YEAR	AGE DISTRIBUTION UNDER 15	AGE DISTRIBUTION 15-64	AGE DISTRIBUTION 65 & OLDER	AGE DISTRIBUTION 70 & OLDER	DEPENDENCY RATIO	WOMEN 15-49	CHILD-WOMAN RATIO
1950	0.342	0.585	0.073	0.045	0.709	0.235	0.578
1955	0.366	0.567	0.067	0.041	0.764	0.231	0.685
1960	0.408	0.534	0.058	0.037	0.872	0.218	0.809
1965	0.436	0.512	0.052	0.032	0.952	0.208	0.845
1970	0.439	0.512	0.049	0.030	0.953	0.213	0.763
1975	0.412	0.539	0.050	0.030	0.856	0.227	0.608
1980	0.401	0.545	0.054	0.032	0.835	0.237	0.547
1985	0.375	0.574	0.051	0.035	0.742	0.252	0.509
1990	0.353	0.596	0.051	0.030	0.678	0.263	0.499
2000	0.337	0.606	0.057	0.035	0.650	0.271	0.425
2010	0.286	0.659	0.055	0.036	0.516	0.278	0.333
2020	0.245	0.692	0.063	0.037	0.445	0.269	0.305

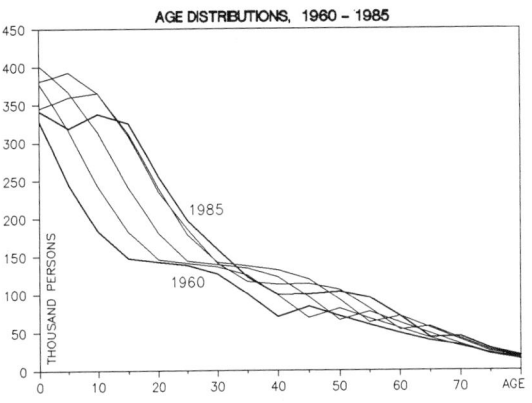

AGE DISTRIBUTIONS, 1960 - 1985

MORTALITY MEASURES (Annual Averages)

PERIOD	CRUDE DEATH RATE	INFANT MORT. RATE	LIFE EXPECTANCY AT BIRTH (years) MALE	LIFE EXPECTANCY AT BIRTH (years) FEMALE	LIFE EXPECTANCY AT BIRTH (years) BOTH SEXES	DIFFERENCE FEMALE-MALE
1950-55	18.70	87.00	54.30	57.70	55.96	3.40
1955-60	15.20	73.00	56.80	60.30	58.51	3.50
1960-65	13.30	62.00	58.90	62.60	60.71	3.70
1965-70	11.80	52.00	61.10	64.80	62.90	3.70
1970-75	9.30	48.00	63.10	67.00	65.00	3.90
1975-80	8.68	48.00	63.10	67.00	65.00	3.90
1980-85	8.80	48.00	63.10	67.00	65.00	3.90
1985-90	7.79	40.06	65.10	69.00	67.00	3.90
1990-95	7.07	34.04	66.60	70.50	68.50	3.90
2000-05	6.13	25.26	69.10	72.90	70.95	3.80
2010-15	5.86	19.21	70.90	74.90	72.85	4.00
2020-25	5.94	14.46	72.50	76.70	74.55	4.20

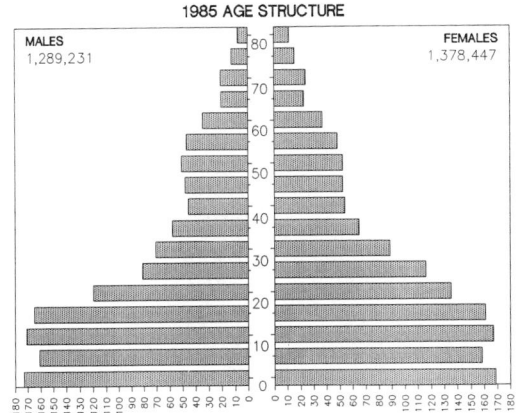

1985 AGE STRUCTURE

MALES 1,289,231   FEMALES 1,378,447

FERTILITY MEASURES (Annual Averages)

PERIOD	CRUDE BIRTH RATE	FERTILITY RATES GENERAL	FERTILITY RATES TOTAL	REPRODUCTION RATES GROSS	REPRODUCTION RATES NET	RATE OF NATUR. INCR.
1950-55	41.00	176.13	5.740	2.800	2.150	22.30
1955-60	43.40	193.54	6.150	3.000	2.390	28.20
1960-65	42.70	200.75	6.355	3.100	2.550	29.40
1965-70	38.80	184.17	6.047	2.950	2.490	27.00
1970-75	32.10	145.75	4.920	2.400	2.080	22.80
1975-80	30.13	130.14	4.305	2.100	1.856	21.45
1980-85	29.29	119.92	3.792	1.850	1.686	20.49
1985-90	28.92	112.19	3.382	1.650	1.536	21.13
1990-95	27.59	104.06	3.075	1.500	1.416	20.52
2000-05	21.75	79.65	2.563	1.250	1.201	15.62
2010-15	18.05	65.15	2.173	1.060	1.031	12.19
2020-25	16.68	63.20	2.070	1.010	0.991	10.74

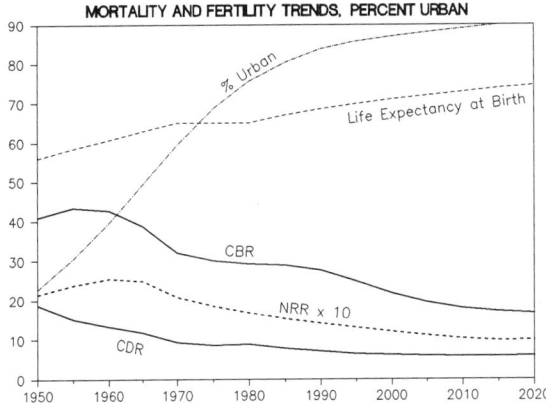

MORTALITY AND FERTILITY TRENDS, PERCENT URBAN

AGING MEASURES

YEAR	POPULATION AGE RATIOS 60+/20-59	POPULATION AGE RATIOS 65+/20-64	POPULATION AGE RATIOS 70+/20-69	POPULATION AGE RATIOS 75+/20-74	POPULATION MEAN AGE	POPULATION MEDIAN AGE
1950	0.2291	0.1500	0.0872	0.0429	28.13	23.18
1960	0.1964	0.1278	0.0782	0.0391	25.63	20.83
1970	0.1915	0.1188	0.0684	0.0352	24.27	18.13
1980	0.1798	0.1252	0.0716	0.0356	25.13	19.26
1990	0.1788	0.1064	0.0601	0.0356	25.95	21.54
2000	0.1655	0.1115	0.0652	0.0311	27.09	24.00
2010	0.1479	0.0974	0.0630	0.0355	29.32	26.48
2020	0.1728	0.1041	0.0588	0.0313	31.98	29.84

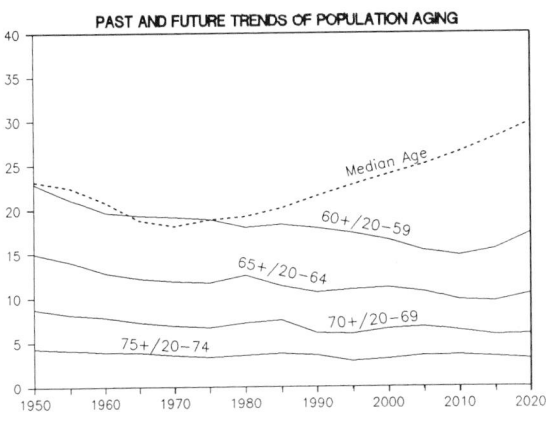

PAST AND FUTURE TRENDS OF POPULATION AGING

OBSERVED AND *PROJECTED* POPULATION DATA (000's)

YEAR	MID-YEAR POPULATION	NO. OF BIRTHS	NO. OF DEATHS	URBAN POPULATION NUMBER	URBAN POPULATION PERCENT	POPULATION 1985 AGE	POPULATION 1985 NUMBER
1950	6110	276	122	1244	20.4	0	2169
1955	7000	318	116	1639	23.4	5	1836
1960	8140	352	108	2053	25.2	10	1829
1965	9502	366	99	2480	26.1	15	1674
1970	10853	377	96	2929	27.0	20	1552
1975	12258	373	88	3736	30.5	25	1330
1980	13763	406	83	4713	34.2	30	1099
1985	15448	442	86	5905	38.2	35	897
1990	*17339*	*441*	*90*	*7336*	*42.3*	40	682
1995	*19186*	*419*	*96*	*8901*	*46.4*	45	628
2000	*20870*	*384*	*103*	*10509*	*50.4*	50	469
2005	*22320*	*381*	*115*	*12072*	*54.1*	55	400
2010	*23692*	*406*	*127*	*13658*	*57.6*	60	298
2015	*25131*	*422*	*144*	*15332*	*61.0*	65	237
2020	*26556*	*422*	*163*	*17038*	*64.2*	70+	348

AGE DISTRIBUTIONS, 1960 - 1985

POPULATION RATIOS

YEAR	AGE DISTRIBUTION UNDER 15	AGE DISTRIBUTION 15-64	AGE DISTRIBUTION 65 & OLDER	AGE DISTRIBUTION 70 & OLDER	DEPENDENCY RATIO	WOMEN 15-49	CHILD-WOMAN RATIO
1950	0.409	0.540	0.051	0.033	0.850	0.222	0.751
1955	0.426	0.532	0.043	0.028	0.880	0.224	0.814
1960	0.453	0.513	0.034	0.022	0.949	0.215	0.867
1965	0.462	0.506	0.032	0.019	0.975	0.214	0.843
1970	0.446	0.520	0.034	0.021	0.923	0.221	0.742
1975	0.421	0.542	0.037	0.022	0.846	0.234	0.653
1980	0.393	0.570	0.037	0.022	0.754	0.248	0.548
1985	0.378	0.584	0.038	0.023	0.711	0.254	0.553
1990	*0.362*	*0.600*	*0.038*	*0.024*	*0.667*	*0.258*	*0.510*
2000	*0.320*	*0.636*	*0.044*	*0.027*	*0.571*	*0.268*	*0.383*
2010	*0.254*	*0.690*	*0.057*	*0.035*	*0.450*	*0.276*	*0.296*
2020	*0.231*	*0.691*	*0.078*	*0.047*	*0.448*	*0.261*	*0.310*

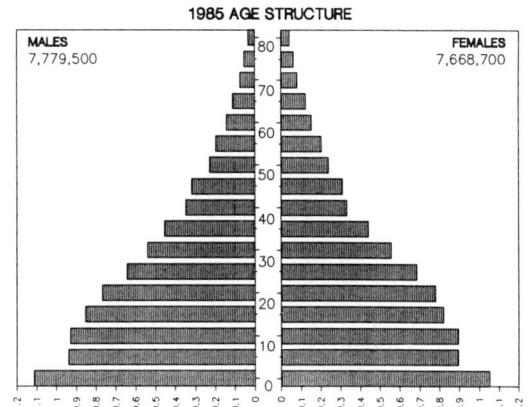

1985 AGE STRUCTURE

MALES 7,779,500 / FEMALES 7,668,700

MORTALITY MEASURES (Annual Averages)

PERIOD	CRUDE DEATH RATE	INFANT MORT. RATE	LIFE EXPECTANCY AT BIRTH (years) MALE	LIFE EXPECTANCY AT BIRTH (years) FEMALE	LIFE EXPECTANCY AT BIRTH (years) BOTH SEXES	DIFFERENCE FEMALE-MALE
1950-55	19.89	98.80	47.00	50.00	48.46	3.00
1955-60	16.54	82.20	50.60	53.68	52.10	3.08
1960-65	13.28	62.70	54.20	57.35	55.74	3.15
1965-70	10.40	49.60	57.80	61.02	59.37	3.22
1970-75	8.80	42.40	61.40	64.70	63.01	3.30
1975-80	7.20	33.80	63.50	67.10	65.26	3.60
1980-85	6.00	28.00	66.00	70.00	68.00	4.00
1985-90	*5.56*	*24.07*	*67.52*	*71.58*	*69.49*	*4.06*
1990-95	*5.19*	*20.44*	*68.74*	*72.97*	*70.79*	*4.24*
2000-05	*4.96*	*14.91*	*70.98*	*75.35*	*73.10*	*4.38*
2010-15	*5.36*	*10.78*	*72.88*	*77.33*	*75.04*	*4.46*
2020-25	*6.12*	*7.93*	*74.50*	*78.97*	*76.67*	*4.47*

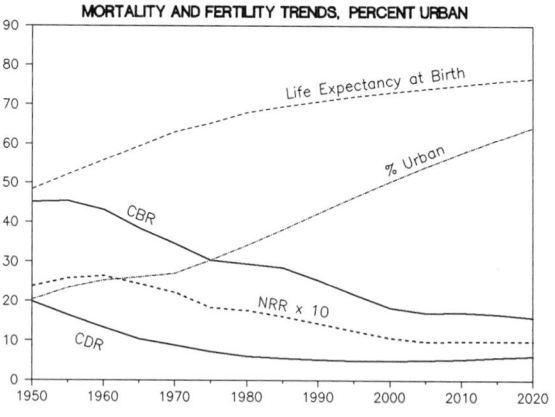

MORTALITY AND FERTILITY TRENDS, PERCENT URBAN

FERTILITY MEASURES (Annual Averages)

PERIOD	CRUDE BIRTH RATE	FERTILITY RATES GENERAL	FERTILITY RATES TOTAL	REPRODUCTION RATES GROSS	REPRODUCTION RATES NET	RATE OF NATUR. INCR.
1950-55	45.19	202.43	6.833	3.317	2.394	25.30
1955-60	45.41	207.33	6.944	3.371	2.582	28.87
1960-65	43.19	201.57	6.724	3.264	2.639	29.91
1965-70	38.48	176.93	5.941	2.884	2.447	28.08
1970-75	34.70	152.36	5.150	2.500	2.220	25.90
1975-80	30.40	126.03	4.161	2.020	1.840	23.20
1980-85	29.50	117.56	3.914	1.900	1.761	23.50
1985-90	*28.63*	*111.69*	*3.502*	*1.700*	*1.614*	*23.07*
1990-95	*25.41*	*97.77*	*3.090*	*1.500*	*1.437*	*20.23*
2000-05	*18.38*	*67.67*	*2.266*	*1.100*	*1.068*	*13.42*
2010-15	*17.15*	*62.75*	*2.081*	*1.010*	*0.989*	*11.79*
2020-25	*15.89*	*62.20*	*2.081*	*1.010*	*0.994*	*9.77*

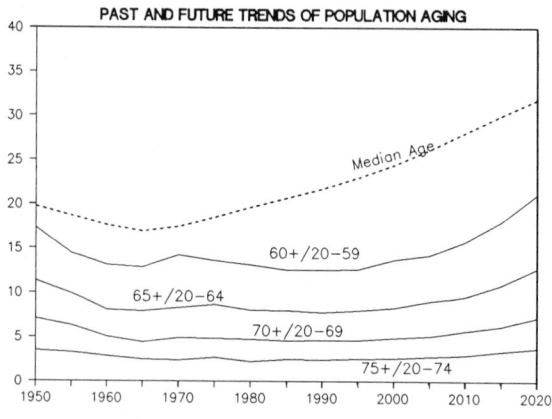

PAST AND FUTURE TRENDS OF POPULATION AGING

AGING MEASURES

YEAR	POPULATION AGE RATIOS 60+/20-59	POPULATION AGE RATIOS 65+/20-64	POPULATION AGE RATIOS 70+/20-69	POPULATION AGE RATIOS 75+/20-74	POPULATION MEAN AGE	POPULATION MEDIAN AGE
1950	0.1732	0.1135	0.0706	0.0348	24.70	19.80
1960	0.1311	0.0805	0.0505	0.0288	22.82	17.65
1970	0.1420	0.0828	0.0487	0.0235	22.81	17.50
1980	0.1313	0.0801	0.0469	0.0224	24.08	19.67
1990	*0.1255*	*0.0776*	*0.0464*	*0.0245*	*25.27*	*21.73*
2000	*0.1367*	*0.0826*	*0.0491*	*0.0261*	*27.54*	*24.46*
2010	*0.1570*	*0.0951*	*0.0569*	*0.0294*	*30.72*	*28.11*
2020	*0.2108*	*0.1268*	*0.0718*	*0.0373*	*33.38*	*31.85*

OBSERVED AND *PROJECTED* POPULATION DATA

YEAR	MID-YEAR POPULATION	NO. OF BIRTHS	NO. OF DEATHS	URBAN POPULATION NUMBER	URBAN POPULATION PERCENT	POPULATION 1985 AGE	POPULATION 1985 NUMBER
1950	747400	29866	15352	141677	19.0	0	298190
1955	824100	33821	13697	218234	26.5	5	261995
1960	930700	38354	12518	332067	35.7	10	233937
1965	1069400	44840	11977	450380	42.1	15	212223
1970	1247800	51160	11664	562174	45.1	20	172652
1975	1444400	57776	12985	702801	48.7	25	141831
1980	1663074	65691	14121	849840	51.1	30	114050
1985	1907770	74203	15291	968498	50.8	35	101912
1990	*2226975*	*84224*	*16279*	*1141182*	*51.2*	40	88468
1995	*2594758*	*91636*	*17136*	*1362904*	*52.5*	45	73257
2000	*2996073*	*98355*	*17680*	*1635260*	*54.6*	50	60620
2005	*3428560*	*105781*	*18627*	*1966175*	*57.3*	55	48863
2010	*3893905*	*112429*	*20019*	*2364637*	*60.7*	60	37850
2015	*4385106*	*121757*	*21658*	*2801925*	*63.9*	65	26601
2020	*4915884*	*118581*	*22706*	*3286287*	*66.9*	70+	35321

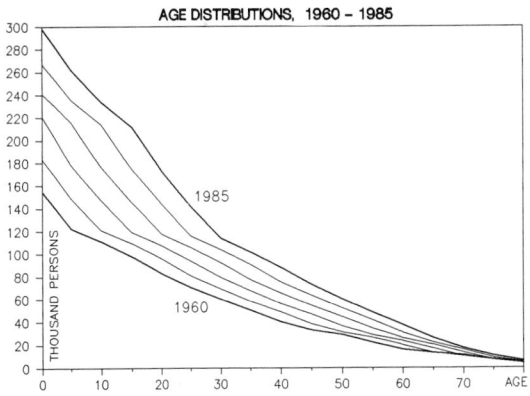

POPULATION RATIOS

YEAR	AGE DISTRIBUTION UNDER 15	AGE DISTRIBUTION 15-64	AGE DISTRIBUTION 65 & OLDER	AGE DISTRIBUTION 70 & OLDER	DEPENDENCY RATIO	WOMEN 15-49	CHILD-WOMAN RATIO
1950	0.415	0.533	0.052	0.031	0.878	0.223	0.723
1955	0.415	0.539	0.046	0.028	0.854	0.230	0.680
1960	0.416	0.543	0.040	0.026	0.840	0.233	0.711
1965	0.423	0.543	0.034	0.022	0.842	0.233	0.732
1970	0.437	0.530	0.032	0.019	0.885	0.228	0.774
1975	0.438	0.530	0.032	0.018	0.887	0.228	0.731
1980	0.431	0.537	0.032	0.019	0.862	0.230	0.697
1985	0.416	0.551	0.032	0.019	0.814	0.237	0.659
1990	*0.418*	*0.549*	*0.033*	*0.019*	*0.823*	*0.235*	*0.720*
2000	*0.423*	*0.541*	*0.036*	*0.020*	*0.849*	*0.231*	*0.681*
2010	*0.390*	*0.571*	*0.039*	*0.023*	*0.751*	*0.244*	*0.575*
2020	*0.356*	*0.601*	*0.043*	*0.026*	*0.665*	*0.251*	*0.510*

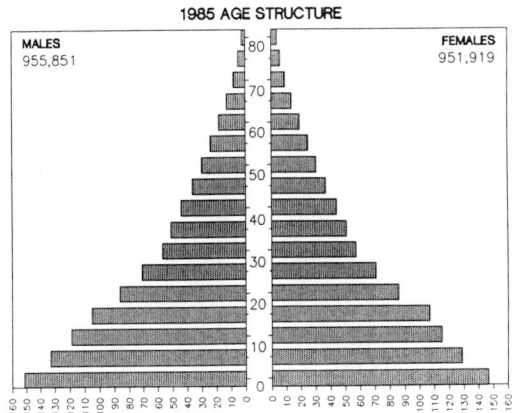

MORTALITY MEASURES (Annual Averages)

PERIOD	CRUDE DEATH RATE	INFANT MORT. RATE	LIFE EXPECTANCY AT BIRTH (years) MALE	LIFE EXPECTANCY AT BIRTH (years) FEMALE	LIFE EXPECTANCY AT BIRTH (years) BOTH SEXES	DIFFERENCE FEMALE-MALE
1950-55	20.54	149.83	43.57	46.51	45.00	2.94
1955-60	16.62	120.73	48.57	51.51	50.00	2.94
1960-65	13.45	96.84	52.91	56.17	54.50	3.26
1965-70	11.20	82.00	56.28	59.80	58.00	3.52
1970-75	9.35	71.00	59.10	62.30	60.66	3.20
1975-80	8.99	62.00	59.29	62.82	61.01	3.53
1980-85	8.49	53.00	60.00	64.10	62.00	4.10
1985-90	*8.02*	*45.00*	*61.50*	*65.60*	*63.50*	*4.10*
1990-95	*7.31*	*39.00*	*63.00*	*67.10*	*65.00*	*4.10*
2000-05	*5.90*	*28.27*	*66.00*	*70.60*	*68.24*	*4.60*
2010-15	*5.14*	*20.83*	*68.60*	*73.20*	*70.84*	*4.60*
2020-25	*4.62*	*15.68*	*71.60*	*75.30*	*73.40*	*3.70*

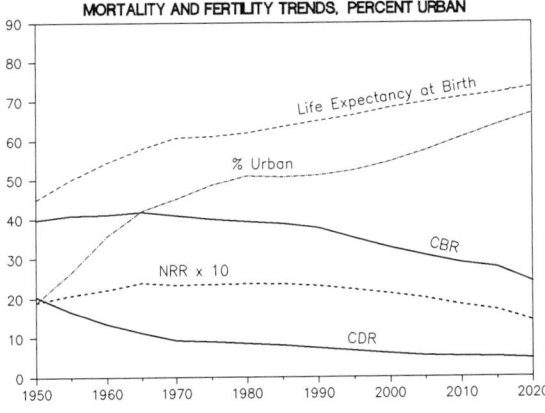

FERTILITY MEASURES (Annual Averages)

PERIOD	CRUDE BIRTH RATE	FERTILITY RATES GENERAL	FERTILITY RATES TOTAL	REPRODUCTION RATES GROSS	REPRODUCTION RATES NET	RATE OF NATUR. INCR.
1950-55	39.96	176.10	5.746	2.803	1.908	19.42
1955-60	41.04	177.16	5.740	2.800	2.077	24.42
1960-65	41.21	176.65	5.715	2.788	2.223	27.76
1965-70	41.93	181.71	5.886	2.871	2.403	30.73
1970-75	41.00	179.77	5.558	2.711	2.338	31.65
1975-80	40.00	174.58	5.500	2.683	2.350	31.01
1980-85	39.50	168.81	5.451	2.659	2.380	31.01
1985-90	*38.90*	*164.67*	*5.400*	*2.634*	*2.360*	*30.88*
1990-95	*37.82*	*161.86*	*5.227*	*2.550*	*2.321*	*30.51*
2000-05	*32.83*	*140.15*	*4.612*	*2.250*	*2.118*	*26.93*
2010-15	*28.87*	*116.94*	*3.895*	*1.900*	*1.825*	*23.73*
2020-25	*24.12*	*95.06*	*2.993*	*1.460*	*1.422*	*19.50*

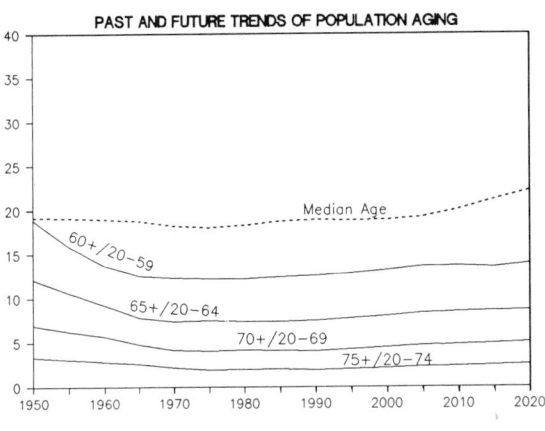

AGING MEASURES

YEAR	POPULATION AGE RATIOS 60+/20-59	POPULATION AGE RATIOS 65+/20-64	POPULATION AGE RATIOS 70+/20-69	POPULATION AGE RATIOS 75+/20-74	POPULATION MEAN AGE	POPULATION MEDIAN AGE
1950	0.1888	0.1213	0.0689	0.0332	24.44	19.19
1960	0.1367	0.0918	0.0565	0.0280	23.62	18.96
1970	0.1232	0.0739	0.0413	0.0221	22.92	18.27
1980	0.1223	0.0739	0.0416	0.0195	23.17	18.29
1990	*0.1256*	*0.0750*	*0.0406*	*0.0194*	*23.36*	*18.92*
2000	*0.1318*	*0.0801*	*0.0444*	*0.0213*	*23.62*	*18.95*
2010	*0.1367*	*0.0848*	*0.0476*	*0.0234*	*24.62*	*20.08*
2020	*0.1394*	*0.0860*	*0.0505*	*0.0256*	*26.03*	*22.20*

OBSERVED AND *PROJECTED* POPULATION DATA (000's)

YEAR	MID-YEAR POPULATION	NO. OF BIRTHS	NO. OF DEATHS	URBAN POPULATION NUMBER	URBAN POPULATION PERCENT	POPULATION 1985 AGE	POPULATION 1985 NUMBER
1950	8182	372	221	187	2.3	0	2882
1955	8675	399	227	231	2.7	5	2287
1960	9404	431	235	292	3.1	10	1981
1965	10344	471	238	362	3.5	15	1653
1970	11488	541	241	450	3.9	20	1416
1975	13000	580	247	629	4.8	25	1253
1980	14858	637	253	909	6.1	30	1128
1985	16915	669	251	1303	7.7	35	970
1990	*19143*	*695*	*247*	*1837*	*9.6*	40	820
1995	*21521*	*729*	*245*	*2539*	*11.8*	45	687
2000	*24084*	*712*	*239*	*3446*	*14.3*	50	560
2005	*26575*	*679*	*234*	*4539*	*17.1*	55	438
2010	*28900*	*646*	*231*	*5794*	*20.0*	60	332
2015	*31055*	*625*	*233*	*7240*	*23.3*	65	235
2020	*33080*	*608*	*240*	*8878*	*26.8*	70+	274

AGE DISTRIBUTIONS, 1960 - 1985

POPULATION RATIOS

YEAR	AGE DISTRIBUTION UNDER 15	15-64	65 & OLDER	70 & OLDER	DEPENDENCY RATIO	WOMEN 15-49	CHILD-WOMAN RATIO
1950	0.392	0.564	0.045	0.025	0.774	0.234	0.627
1955	0.381	0.577	0.042	0.024	0.733	0.248	0.568
1960	0.384	0.577	0.039	0.022	0.733	0.245	0.632
1965	0.395	0.570	0.035	0.020	0.754	0.246	0.661
1970	0.413	0.557	0.030	0.018	0.797	0.240	0.693
1975	0.429	0.538	0.033	0.015	0.858	0.227	0.781
1980	0.412	0.558	0.030	0.017	0.794	0.240	0.680
1985	0.423	0.547	0.030	0.016	0.827	0.232	0.733
1990	*0.422*	*0.547*	*0.031*	*0.017*	*0.828*	*0.230*	*0.700*
2000	*0.396*	*0.569*	*0.034*	*0.019*	*0.756*	*0.235*	*0.613*
2010	*0.346*	*0.614*	*0.041*	*0.023*	*0.629*	*0.250*	*0.454*
2020	*0.284*	*0.666*	*0.050*	*0.029*	*0.502*	*0.271*	*0.342*

MORTALITY MEASURES (Annual Averages)

PERIOD	CRUDE DEATH RATE	INFANT MORT. RATE	LIFE EXPECTANCY AT BIRTH (years) MALE	FEMALE	BOTH SEXES	DIFFERENCE FEMALE-MALE
1950-55	27.01	197.10	36.75	35.75	36.26	-1.00
1955-60	26.20	190.60	38.05	37.05	37.56	-1.00
1960-65	25.03	182.10	39.55	38.55	39.06	-1.00
1965-70	23.00	164.30	41.50	40.50	41.00	-1.00
1970-75	21.00	152.90	44.00	42.50	43.25	-1.50
1975-80	19.00	146.50	46.50	45.00	45.75	-1.50
1980-85	17.00	138.70	49.00	47.50	48.27	-1.50
1985-90	*14.84*	*128.20*	*51.50*	*50.25*	*50.89*	*-1.25*
1990-95	*12.93*	*118.20*	*54.00*	*53.00*	*53.51*	*-1.00*
2000-05	*9.91*	*99.28*	*59.00*	*58.50*	*58.76*	*-0.50*
2010-15	*7.99*	*79.47*	*63.58*	*63.50*	*63.54*	*-0.08*
2020-25	*7.24*	*61.00*	*66.98*	*68.00*	*67.48*	*1.02*

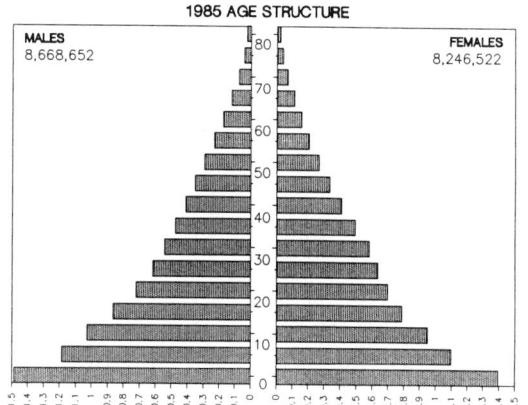

1985 AGE STRUCTURE

MALES 8,668,652   FEMALES 8,246,522

FERTILITY MEASURES (Annual Averages)

PERIOD	CRUDE BIRTH RATE	FERTILITY RATES GENERAL	TOTAL	REPRODUCTION RATES GROSS	NET	RATE OF NATUR. INCR.
1950-55	45.50	188.56	5.637	2.750	1.365	18.49
1955-60	46.00	186.59	5.699	2.780	1.470	19.80
1960-65	45.80	186.47	5.863	2.860	1.575	20.77
1965-70	45.50	187.25	6.170	3.010	1.703	22.50
1970-75	47.10	201.87	6.519	3.180	1.976	26.10
1975-80	44.60	190.70	6.539	3.190	2.048	25.60
1980-85	42.90	181.96	6.252	3.050	2.070	25.91
1985-90	*39.55*	*171.16*	*5.945*	*2.900*	*2.066*	*24.72*
1990-95	*36.32*	*157.98*	*5.535*	*2.700*	*2.015*	*23.39*
2000-05	*29.58*	*124.23*	*4.346*	*2.120*	*1.720*	*19.67*
2010-15	*22.36*	*87.27*	*2.993*	*1.460*	*1.265*	*14.37*
2020-25	*18.37*	*67.38*	*2.296*	*1.120*	*1.022*	*11.13*

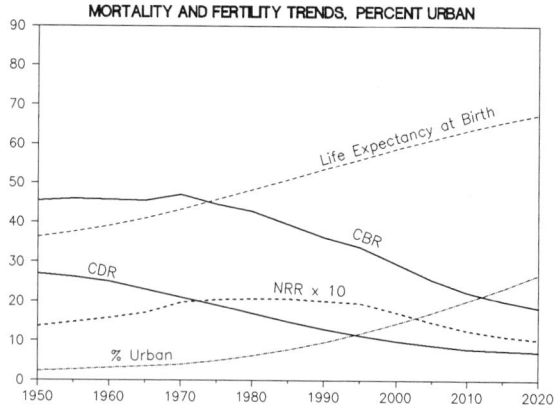

MORTALITY AND FERTILITY TRENDS, PERCENT URBAN

AGING MEASURES

YEAR	POPULATION AGE RATIOS 60+/20-59	65+/20-64	70+/20-69	75+/20-74	POPULATION MEAN AGE	POPULATION MEDIAN AGE
1950	0.1633	0.0976	0.0514	0.0229	25.03	20.22
1960	0.1322	0.0829	0.0447	0.0205	24.62	20.68
1970	0.1257	0.0648	0.0378	0.0183	23.88	19.77
1980	0.1128	0.0656	0.0357	0.0172	23.68	19.48
1990	*0.1199*	*0.0696*	*0.0364*	*0.0161*	*23.54*	*18.84*
2000	*0.1286*	*0.0752*	*0.0397*	*0.0180*	*24.29*	*19.68*
2010	*0.1346*	*0.0804*	*0.0436*	*0.0201*	*26.11*	*22.40*
2020	*0.1431*	*0.0885*	*0.0490*	*0.0234*	*28.69*	*25.89*

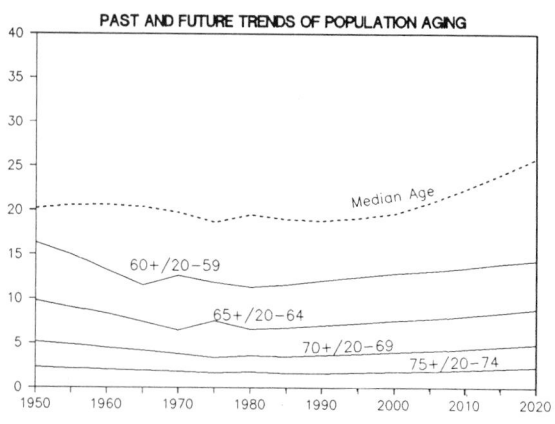

PAST AND FUTURE TRENDS OF POPULATION AGING

OBSERVED AND *PROJECTED* POPULATION DATA

YEAR	MID-YEAR POPULATION	NO. OF BIRTHS	NO. OF DEATHS	URBAN POPULATION NUMBER	URBAN POPULATION PERCENT	POPULATION 1985 AGE	POPULATION 1985 NUMBER
1950	413000	21022	13175	9913	2.4	0	231110
1955	455000	23069	13423	13195	2.9	5	181023
1960	505000	25452	13181	17676	3.5	10	138173
1965	571000	28550	12962	24092	4.2	15	110961
1970	654000	32438	13472	33212	5.1	20	99376
1975	766000	37473	14286	46734	6.1	25	97508
1980	983853	46900	14345	72197	7.3	30	88532
1985	1242314	57150	15770	109646	8.8	35	74353
1990	*1468015*	*64813*	*15856*	*155604*	*10.6*	40	60486
1995	*1735059*	*74743*	*15886*	*220166*	*12.7*	45	46253
2000	*2056613*	*86326*	*16068*	*310814*	*15.1*	50	35981
2005	*2440707*	*97321*	*16448*	*435770*	*17.9*	55	27508
2010	*2881602*	*104573*	*16927*	*602423*	*20.9*	60	20027
2015	*3355916*	*107017*	*17642*	*813651*	*24.2*	65	14313
2020	*3834653*	*108145*	*18836*	*1067369*	*27.8*	70+	16710

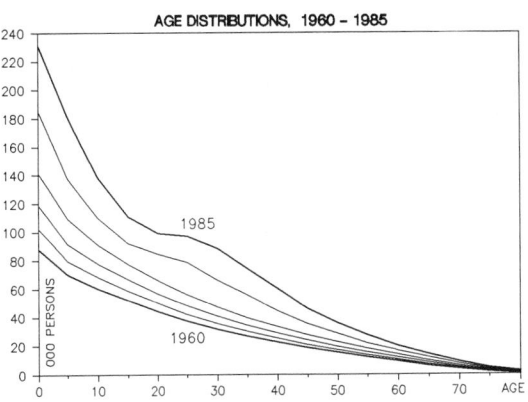

AGE DISTRIBUTIONS, 1960 - 1985

POPULATION RATIOS

YEAR	AGE DISTRIBUTION UNDER 15	AGE DISTRIBUTION 15-64	AGE DISTRIBUTION 65 & OLDER	AGE DISTRIBUTION 70 & OLDER	DEPENDENCY RATIO	WOMEN 15-49	CHILD-WOMAN RATIO
1950	0.423	0.546	0.030	0.016	0.830	0.231	0.739
1955	0.429	0.542	0.029	0.015	0.844	0.230	0.749
1960	0.433	0.540	0.027	0.015	0.853	0.229	0.759
1965	0.439	0.535	0.027	0.014	0.871	0.227	0.790
1970	0.441	0.532	0.027	0.014	0.880	0.226	0.803
1975	0.447	0.526	0.027	0.014	0.901	0.223	0.825
1980	0.440	0.534	0.026	0.014	0.873	0.216	0.870
1985	0.443	0.532	0.025	0.013	0.879	0.210	0.888
1990	*0.458*	*0.517*	*0.025*	*0.014*	*0.936*	*0.206*	*0.900*
2000	*0.458*	*0.514*	*0.028*	*0.015*	*0.947*	*0.210*	*0.864*
2010	*0.451*	*0.517*	*0.032*	*0.017*	*0.935*	*0.216*	*0.804*
2020	*0.413*	*0.549*	*0.038*	*0.022*	*0.821*	*0.237*	*0.607*

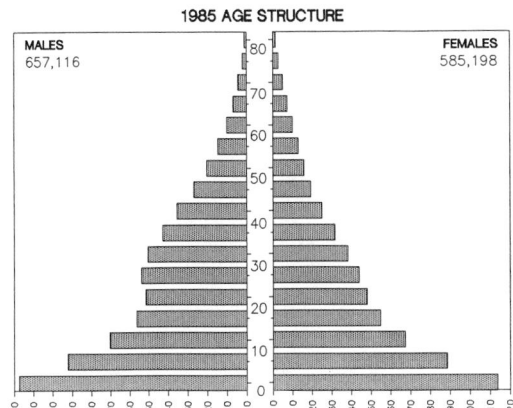

1985 AGE STRUCTURE

MALES 657,116   FEMALES 585,198

MORTALITY MEASURES (Annual Averages)

PERIOD	CRUDE DEATH RATE	INFANT MORT. RATE	LIFE EXPECTANCY AT BIRTH (years) MALE	LIFE EXPECTANCY AT BIRTH (years) FEMALE	LIFE EXPECTANCY AT BIRTH (years) BOTH SEXES	DIFFERENCE FEMALE-MALE
1950-55	31.90	231.00	35.75	36.98	36.35	1.23
1955-60	29.50	220.00	38.13	39.59	38.84	1.46
1960-65	26.10	207.00	40.45	42.29	41.35	1.84
1965-70	22.70	186.00	42.80	44.94	43.84	2.14
1970-75	20.60	160.00	45.18	47.58	46.35	2.40
1975-80	18.65	135.00	48.04	50.75	49.36	2.71
1980-85	14.58	117.20	51.03	53.73	52.35	2.70
1985-90	*12.69*	*100.20*	*54.08*	*56.75*	*55.38*	*2.67*
1990-95	*10.80*	*84.23*	*57.07*	*59.73*	*58.37*	*2.66*
2000-05	*7.81*	*56.50*	*62.56*	*65.67*	*64.07*	*3.12*
2010-15	*5.87*	*37.82*	*66.16*	*70.43*	*68.24*	*4.28*
2020-25	*4.91*	*26.94*	*68.62*	*73.50*	*71.00*	*4.88*

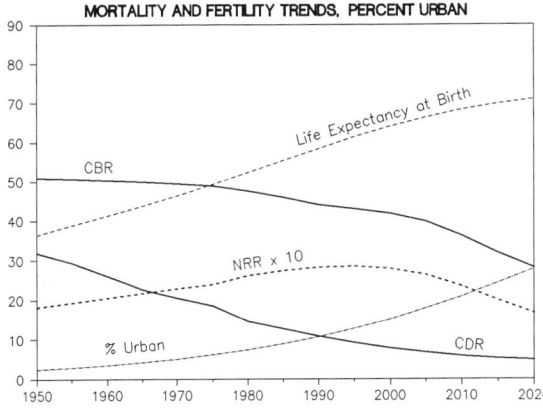

MORTALITY AND FERTILITY TRENDS, PERCENT URBAN

FERTILITY MEASURES (Annual Averages)

PERIOD	CRUDE BIRTH RATE	FERTILITY RATES GENERAL	FERTILITY RATES TOTAL	REPRODUCTION RATES GROSS	REPRODUCTION RATES NET	RATE OF NATUR. INCR.
1950-55	50.90	220.57	7.175	3.500	1.820	19.00
1955-60	50.70	220.74	7.175	3.500	1.940	21.20
1960-65	50.40	221.08	7.175	3.500	2.060	24.30
1965-70	50.00	220.80	7.175	3.500	2.180	27.30
1970-75	49.60	220.79	7.175	3.500	2.290	29.00
1975-80	48.92	223.05	7.175	3.500	2.401	30.27
1980-85	47.67	224.40	7.175	3.500	2.625	33.09
1985-90	*46.00*	*221.45*	*7.175*	*3.500*	*2.750*	*33.31*
1990-95	*44.15*	*213.33*	*7.072*	*3.450*	*2.829*	*33.35*
2000-05	*41.97*	*198.52*	*6.498*	*3.170*	*2.803*	*34.16*
2010-15	*36.29*	*164.51*	*5.186*	*2.530*	*2.357*	*30.42*
2020-25	*28.20*	*115.19*	*3.587*	*1.750*	*1.674*	*23.29*

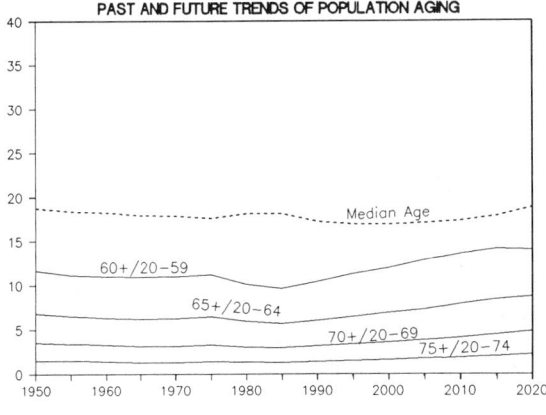

PAST AND FUTURE TRENDS OF POPULATION AGING

AGING MEASURES

YEAR	POPULATION AGE RATIOS 60+/20-59	POPULATION AGE RATIOS 65+/20-64	POPULATION AGE RATIOS 70+/20-69	POPULATION AGE RATIOS 75+/20-74	POPULATION MEAN AGE	POPULATION MEDIAN AGE
1950	0.1167	0.0681	0.0354	0.0150	23.25	18.76
1960	0.1100	0.0626	0.0326	0.0139	22.74	18.25
1970	0.1097	0.0623	0.0311	0.0129	22.42	17.86
1980	0.1012	0.0590	0.0304	0.0133	22.39	18.19
1990	*0.1043*	*0.0601*	*0.0317*	*0.0141*	*22.33*	*17.26*
2000	*0.1195*	*0.0689*	*0.0360*	*0.0160*	*22.25*	*16.98*
2010	*0.1357*	*0.0788*	*0.0410*	*0.0186*	*22.36*	*17.34*
2020	*0.1403*	*0.0874*	*0.0480*	*0.0223*	*23.49*	*18.90*

OBSERVED AND *PROJECTED* POPULATION DATA (000's)

YEAR	MID-YEAR POPULATION	NO. OF BIRTHS	NO. OF DEATHS	URBAN POPULATION NUMBER	URBAN POPULATION PERCENT	POPULATION 1985 AGE	POPULATION 1985 NUMBER
1950	39513	1955	1126	6923	17.5	0	20316
1955	44194	2157	1104	8712	19.7	5	13710
1960	49955	2417	1092	11042	22.1	10	12056
1965	57145	2731	1152	13454	23.5	15	11204
1970	65706	3121	1205	16354	24.9	20	9630
1975	74734	3535	1196	19730	26.4	25	8074
1980	85299	4293	1224	23936	28.1	30	6727
1985	103241	4847	1297	30751	29.8	35	4663
1990	*122666*	*5143*	*1298*	*39229*	*32.0*	40	3825
1995	*141599*	*5125*	*1238*	*49076*	*34.7*	45	3317
2000	*162467*	*5180*	*1204*	*61438*	*37.8*	50	2795
2005	*183641*	*5319*	*1198*	*76062*	*41.4*	55	2358
2010	*205472*	*5364*	*1217*	*93294*	*45.4*	60	1712
2015	*227312*	*5236*	*1258*	*112085*	*49.3*	65	1240
2020	*248112*	*4990*	*1334*	*131709*	*53.1*	70+	1616

POPULATION RATIOS

YEAR	AGE DISTRIBUTION UNDER 15	AGE DISTRIBUTION 15-64	AGE DISTRIBUTION 65 & OLDER	AGE DISTRIBUTION 70 & OLDER	DEPENDENCY RATIO	WOMEN 15-49	CHILD-WOMAN RATIO
1950	0.379	0.567	0.053	0.029	0.763	0.222	0.677
1955	0.409	0.542	0.048	0.027	0.843	0.220	0.831
1960	0.438	0.520	0.042	0.025	0.923	0.214	0.860
1965	0.463	0.501	0.036	0.021	0.995	0.207	0.895
1970	0.463	0.505	0.032	0.019	0.978	0.210	0.877
1975	0.455	0.516	0.030	0.016	0.939	0.216	0.799
1980	0.444	0.527	0.029	0.016	0.896	0.218	0.780
1985	0.446	0.526	0.028	0.016	0.901	0.218	0.901
1990	*0.457*	*0.516*	*0.027*	*0.015*	*0.937*	*0.214*	*0.877*
2000	*0.433*	*0.538*	*0.029*	*0.017*	*0.859*	*0.226*	*0.673*
2010	*0.363*	*0.605*	*0.032*	*0.019*	*0.654*	*0.251*	*0.504*
2020	*0.311*	*0.646*	*0.042*	*0.023*	*0.547*	*0.264*	*0.392*

MORTALITY MEASURES (Annual Averages)

PERIOD	CRUDE DEATH RATE	INFANT MORT. RATE	LIFE EXPECTANCY AT BIRTH (years) MALE	LIFE EXPECTANCY AT BIRTH (years) FEMALE	LIFE EXPECTANCY AT BIRTH (years) BOTH SEXES	DIFFERENCE FEMALE-MALE
1950-55	28.51	190.00	40.15	37.60	38.91	-2.55
1955-60	24.99	170.00	43.05	40.45	41.78	-2.60
1960-65	21.85	155.00	45.65	43.05	44.38	-2.60
1965-70	20.15	145.00	48.00	45.50	46.78	-2.50
1970-75	18.34	140.00	50.00	48.00	49.00	-2.00
1975-80	16.00	130.00	52.00	51.00	51.50	-1.00
1980-85	14.35	120.00	54.00	54.00	54.00	0.00
1985-90	*12.56*	*108.90*	*56.50*	*56.50*	*56.50*	*0.00*
1990-95	*10.58*	*98.40*	*59.00*	*59.00*	*59.00*	*0.00*
2000-05	*7.41*	*78.70*	*63.58*	*64.00*	*63.78*	*0.42*
2010-15	*5.92*	*60.21*	*66.98*	*68.58*	*67.76*	*1.60*
2020-25	*5.38*	*42.90*	*69.50*	*71.98*	*70.71*	*2.48*

FERTILITY MEASURES (Annual Averages)

PERIOD	CRUDE BIRTH RATE	FERTILITY RATES GENERAL	FERTILITY RATES TOTAL	REPRODUCTION RATES GROSS	REPRODUCTION RATES NET	RATE OF NATUR. INCR.
1950-55	49.49	223.85	6.501	3.171	1.827	20.98
1955-60	48.81	225.14	6.800	3.317	2.034	23.82
1960-65	48.38	229.97	7.001	3.415	2.207	26.53
1965-70	47.80	228.77	7.001	3.415	2.309	27.64
1970-75	47.50	222.67	7.001	3.415	2.400	29.16
1975-80	47.30	218.21	7.001	3.415	2.500	31.30
1980-85	50.33	230.86	7.001	3.415	2.604	35.98
1985-90	*46.95*	*217.17*	*6.498*	*3.170*	*2.503*	*34.39*
1990-95	*41.93*	*197.33*	*5.945*	*2.900*	*2.366*	*31.35*
2000-05	*31.88*	*136.49*	*4.346*	*2.120*	*1.832*	*24.47*
2010-15	*26.11*	*102.28*	*2.993*	*1.460*	*1.318*	*20.19*
2020-25	*20.11*	*75.00*	*2.296*	*1.120*	*1.039*	*14.73*

AGING MEASURES

YEAR	POPULATION AGE RATIOS 60+/20-59	POPULATION AGE RATIOS 65+/20-64	POPULATION AGE RATIOS 70+/20-69	POPULATION AGE RATIOS 75+/20-74	POPULATION MEAN AGE	POPULATION MEDIAN AGE
1950	0.1869	0.1140	0.0582	0.0269	25.92	21.25
1960	0.1539	0.0966	0.0561	0.0261	23.48	18.43
1970	0.1326	0.0797	0.0462	0.0228	22.17	16.71
1980	0.1163	0.0694	0.0370	0.0168	22.17	17.52
1990	*0.1101*	*0.0646*	*0.0357*	*0.0175*	*21.67*	*17.22*
2000	*0.1125*	*0.0691*	*0.0389*	*0.0186*	*22.66*	*17.85*
2010	*0.1057*	*0.0654*	*0.0381*	*0.0195*	*24.78*	*21.06*
2020	*0.1308*	*0.0773*	*0.0408*	*0.0211*	*27.45*	*24.68*

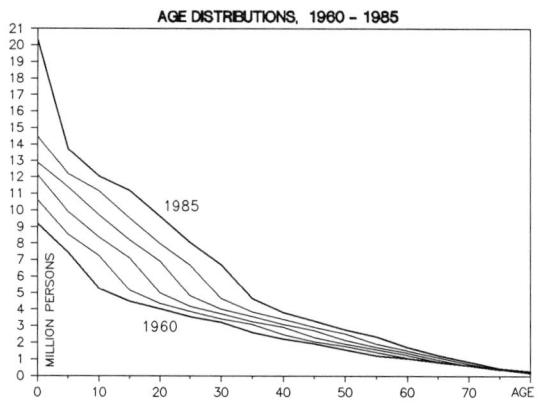

AGE DISTRIBUTIONS, 1960 - 1985

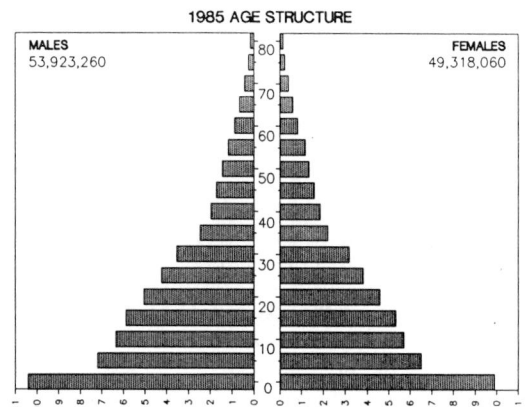

1985 AGE STRUCTURE

MALES 53,923,260   FEMALES 49,318,060

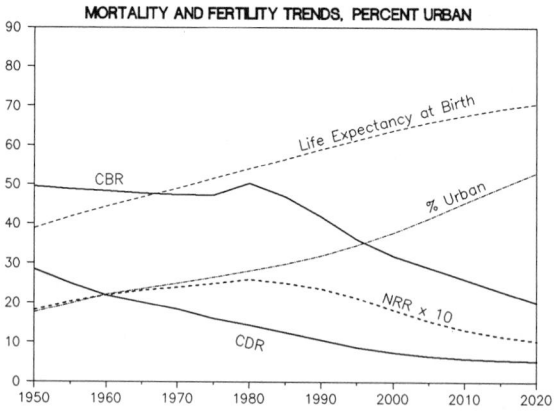

MORTALITY AND FERTILITY TRENDS, PERCENT URBAN

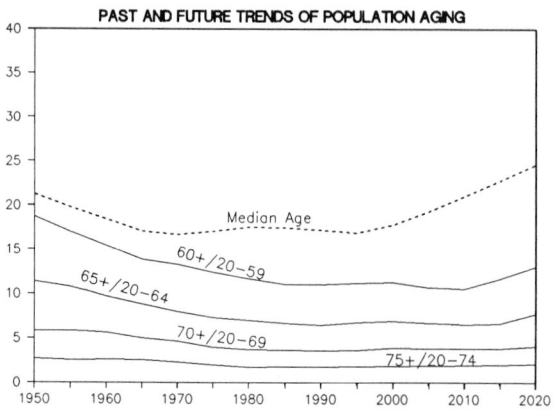

PAST AND FUTURE TRENDS OF POPULATION AGING

OBSERVED AND *PROJECTED* POPULATION DATA (000's)

YEAR	MID-YEAR POPULATION	NO. OF BIRTHS	NO. OF DEATHS	URBAN POPULATION NUMBER	URBAN POPULATION PERCENT	POPULATION 1985 AGE	POPULATION 1985 NUMBER
1950	20988	1034	409	5695	27.1	0	8591
1955	23913	1133	386	6864	28.7	5	7497
1960	27561	1200	360	8350	30.3	10	6570
1965	32030	1286	344	10123	31.6	15	5922
1970	37540	1385	393	12380	33.0	20	5199
1975	42565	1551	389	15136	35.6	25	4519
1980	48317	1721	413	18052	37.4	30	3783
1985	55120	1831	427	21844	39.6	35	2931
1990	*62409*	*1895*	*441*	*26432*	*42.4*	40	2356
1995	*69922*	*1918*	*452*	*31813*	*45.5*	45	2007
2000	*77447*	*1913*	*466*	*37953*	*49.0*	50	1584
2005	*84882*	*1889*	*496*	*44811*	*52.8*	55	1297
2010	*92038*	*1931*	*538*	*51924*	*56.4*	60	990
2015	*99225*	*1762*	*586*	*59385*	*59.8*	65	780
2020	*105289*	*1829*	*642*	*66412*	*63.1*	70+	1095

AGE DISTRIBUTIONS, 1960 - 1985

POPULATION RATIOS

YEAR	AGE DISTRIBUTION UNDER 15	AGE DISTRIBUTION 15-64	AGE DISTRIBUTION 65 & OLDER	AGE DISTRIBUTION 70 & OLDER	DEPENDENCY RATIO	WOMEN 15-49	CHILD-WOMAN RATIO
1950	0.436	0.528	0.036	0.021	0.893	0.228	0.769
1955	0.442	0.525	0.033	0.019	0.904	0.227	0.775
1960	0.446	0.524	0.030	0.018	0.910	0.224	0.796
1965	0.450	0.521	0.029	0.016	0.920	0.221	0.814
1970	0.455	0.518	0.027	0.017	0.929	0.226	0.750
1975	0.428	0.545	0.027	0.015	0.835	0.236	0.638
1980	0.420	0.546	0.034	0.019	0.833	0.240	0.664
1985	0.411	0.555	0.034	0.020	0.802	0.244	0.639
1990	*0.401*	*0.565*	*0.034*	*0.020*	*0.769*	*0.246*	*0.597*
2000	*0.361*	*0.602*	*0.037*	*0.022*	*0.662*	*0.259*	*0.481*
2010	*0.311*	*0.645*	*0.044*	*0.026*	*0.550*	*0.267*	*0.387*
2020	*0.266*	*0.675*	*0.059*	*0.033*	*0.481*	*0.270*	*0.312*

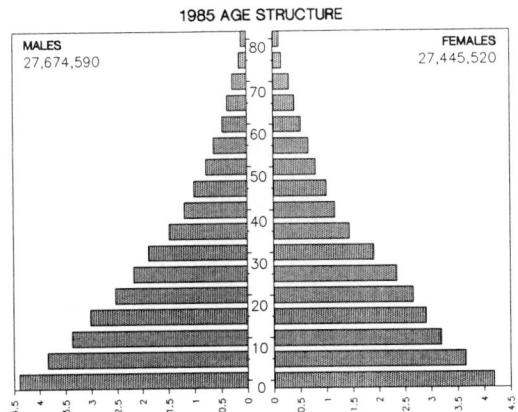

1985 AGE STRUCTURE

MALES 27,674,590 — FEMALES 27,445,520

MORTALITY MEASURES (Annual Averages)

PERIOD	CRUDE DEATH RATE	INFANT MORT. RATE	LIFE EXPECTANCY AT BIRTH (years) MALE	LIFE EXPECTANCY AT BIRTH (years) FEMALE	LIFE EXPECTANCY AT BIRTH (years) BOTH SEXES	DIFFERENCE FEMALE-MALE
1950-55	19.50	99.58	46.00	49.05	47.49	3.05
1955-60	16.13	82.56	49.61	52.62	51.08	3.01
1960-65	13.06	75.89	52.93	56.18	54.51	3.25
1965-70	10.75	69.63	54.60	57.80	56.16	3.20
1970-75	10.48	63.70	56.44	59.44	57.90	3.00
1975-80	9.15	54.00	58.30	61.46	59.84	3.16
1980-85	8.54	50.58	60.17	63.75	61.91	3.57
1985-90	*7.74*	*45.11*	*61.64*	*65.37*	*63.45*	*3.72*
1990-95	*7.07*	*39.84*	*63.10*	*66.98*	*64.98*	*3.87*
2000-05	*6.02*	*29.35*	*66.15*	*70.18*	*68.11*	*4.04*
2010-15	*5.84*	*22.45*	*68.42*	*72.58*	*70.44*	*4.16*
2020-25	*6.10*	*16.52*	*70.43*	*75.07*	*72.68*	*4.64*

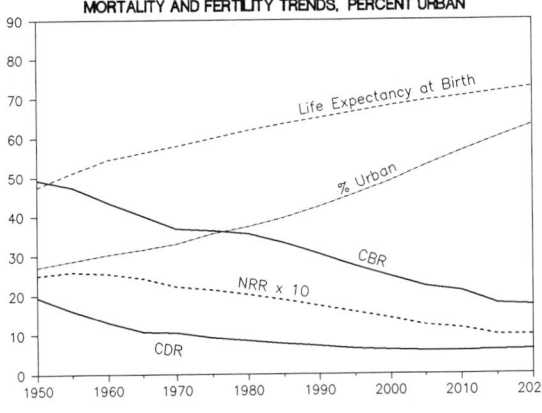

MORTALITY AND FERTILITY TRENDS, PERCENT URBAN

Life Expectancy at Birth — % Urban — CBR — NRR x 10 — CDR

FERTILITY MEASURES (Annual Averages)

PERIOD	CRUDE BIRTH RATE	FERTILITY RATES GENERAL	FERTILITY RATES TOTAL	REPRODUCTION RATES GROSS	REPRODUCTION RATES NET	RATE OF NATUR. INCR.
1950-55	49.29	216.74	7.290	3.539	2.514	29.78
1955-60	47.40	210.11	7.093	3.443	2.595	31.27
1960-65	43.55	195.80	6.606	3.207	2.550	30.49
1965-70	40.15	179.69	6.040	2.932	2.425	29.41
1970-75	36.90	159.55	5.294	2.570	2.230	26.42
1975-80	36.44	152.98	4.965	2.410	2.140	27.29
1980-85	35.62	147.18	4.738	2.300	2.023	27.07
1985-90	*33.22*	*135.51*	*4.326*	*2.100*	*1.880*	*25.48*
1990-95	*30.37*	*121.80*	*3.914*	*1.900*	*1.732*	*23.31*
2000-05	*24.70*	*94.38*	*3.090*	*1.500*	*1.413*	*18.68*
2010-15	*20.98*	*78.31*	*2.472*	*1.200*	*1.152*	*15.14*
2020-25	*17.37*	*64.40*	*2.081*	*1.010*	*0.985*	*11.27*

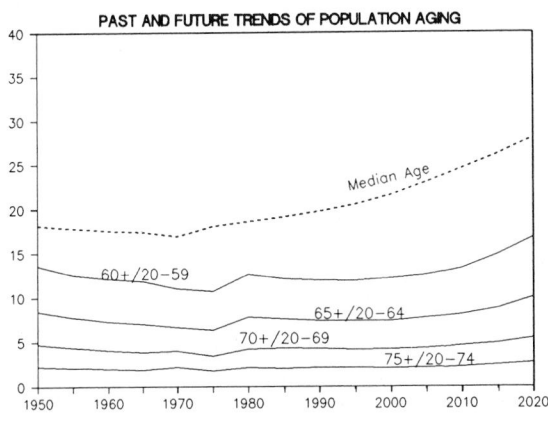

PAST AND FUTURE TRENDS OF POPULATION AGING

Median Age — 60+/20-59 — 65+/20-64 — 70+/20-69 — 75+/20-74

AGING MEASURES

YEAR	POPULATION AGE RATIOS 60+/20-59	POPULATION AGE RATIOS 65+/20-64	POPULATION AGE RATIOS 70+/20-69	POPULATION AGE RATIOS 75+/20-74	POPULATION MEAN AGE	POPULATION MEDIAN AGE
1950	0.1354	0.0840	0.0470	0.0224	23.22	18.17
1960	0.1208	0.0725	0.0406	0.0196	22.53	17.59
1970	0.1104	0.0664	0.0398	0.0218	21.87	17.00
1980	0.1266	0.0780	0.0423	0.0216	23.09	18.64
1990	*0.1193*	*0.0736*	*0.0426*	*0.0212*	*23.86*	*19.75*
2000	*0.1224*	*0.0742*	*0.0422*	*0.0208*	*25.46*	*21.67*
2010	*0.1334*	*0.0809*	*0.0460*	*0.0225*	*27.78*	*24.59*
2020	*0.1682*	*0.1004*	*0.0545*	*0.0268*	*30.48*	*28.09*

OBSERVED AND *PROJECTED* POPULATION DATA

YEAR	MID-YEAR POPULATION	NO. OF BIRTHS	NO. OF DEATHS	URBAN POPULATION NUMBER	URBAN POPULATION PERCENT	POPULATION 1985 AGE	POPULATION 1985 NUMBER
1950	25000	1158	555	15720	62.9	0	46088
1955	35000	1530	679	23747	67.8	5	29069
1960	45000	1836	752	32601	72.4	10	26026
1965	70000	2590	987	53630	76.6	15	25686
1970	111333	3485	1291	89424	80.3	20	25045
1975	171171	5119	1605	143043	83.6	25	29464
1980	229243	7929	1043	197357	86.1	30	32324
1985	298586	9194	1283	262819	88.0	35	27768
1990	*367489*	*10385*	*1525*	*328813*	*89.5*	40	19866
1995	*435751*	*11745*	*1877*	*394567*	*90.5*	45	14503
2000	*498579*	*13496*	*2223*	*455274*	*91.3*	50	8637
2005	*563587*	*15523*	*2709*	*518586*	*92.0*	55	6482
2010	*631521*	*17177*	*3207*	*585151*	*92.7*	60	2861
2015	*705457*	*18492*	*3853*	*657811*	*93.2*	65	2502
2020	*782660*	*19840*	*4495*	*734024*	*93.8*	70+	2265

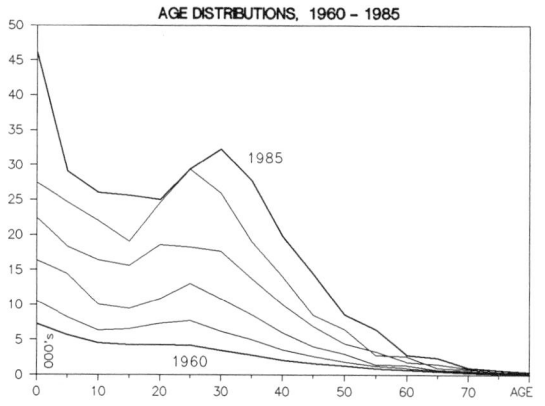

AGE DISTRIBUTIONS, 1960 - 1985

POPULATION RATIOS

YEAR	AGE DISTRIBUTION UNDER 15	15-64	65 & OLDER	70 & OLDER	DEPENDENCY RATIO	WOMEN 15-49	CHILD-WOMAN RATIO
1950	0.423	0.543	0.034	0.018	0.841	0.225	0.768
1955	0.401	0.570	0.030	0.016	0.756	0.206	0.804
1960	0.390	0.583	0.027	0.015	0.714	0.195	0.828
1965	0.359	0.619	0.022	0.012	0.616	0.176	0.859
1970	0.367	0.616	0.017	0.010	0.622	0.151	0.973
1975	0.334	0.646	0.020	0.011	0.548	0.142	0.921
1980	0.323	0.665	0.011	0.007	0.503	0.188	0.635
1985	0.339	0.645	0.016	0.008	0.550	0.180	0.860
1990	*0.351*	*0.631*	*0.018*	*0.010*	*0.584*	*0.175*	*0.799*
2000	*0.346*	*0.624*	*0.030*	*0.016*	*0.602*	*0.184*	*0.680*
2010	*0.339*	*0.609*	*0.052*	*0.027*	*0.642*	*0.203*	*0.631*
2020	*0.341*	*0.579*	*0.080*	*0.045*	*0.726*	*0.219*	*0.563*

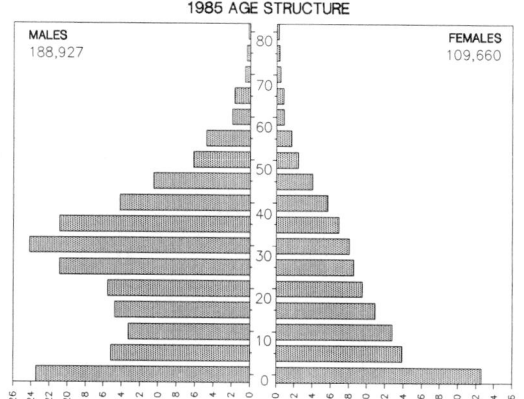

1985 AGE STRUCTURE

MALES 188,927 FEMALES 109,660

MORTALITY MEASURES (Annual Averages)

PERIOD	CRUDE DEATH RATE	INFANT MORT. RATE	LIFE EXPECTANCY AT BIRTH (years) MALE	FEMALE	BOTH SEXES	DIFFERENCE FEMALE-MALE
1950-55	22.20	180.00	46.70	49.30	47.97	2.60
1955-60	19.40	160.00	49.60	52.50	51.01	2.90
1960-65	16.70	130.00	53.50	56.60	55.01	3.10
1965-70	14.10	85.00	57.30	60.80	59.01	3.50
1970-75	11.60	57.00	60.70	64.40	62.51	3.70
1975-80	9.38	46.35	63.53	67.60	65.51	4.07
1980-85	4.55	37.80	65.43	69.80	67.56	4.37
1985-90	*4.30*	*31.26*	*66.93*	*71.80*	*69.31*	*4.87*
1990-95	*4.15*	*25.91*	*68.43*	*73.30*	*70.81*	*4.87*
2000-05	*4.46*	*18.52*	*70.73*	*75.70*	*73.15*	*4.97*
2010-15	*5.08*	*12.95*	*72.73*	*77.70*	*75.15*	*4.97*
2020-25	*5.74*	*9.20*	*74.33*	*79.30*	*76.75*	*4.97*

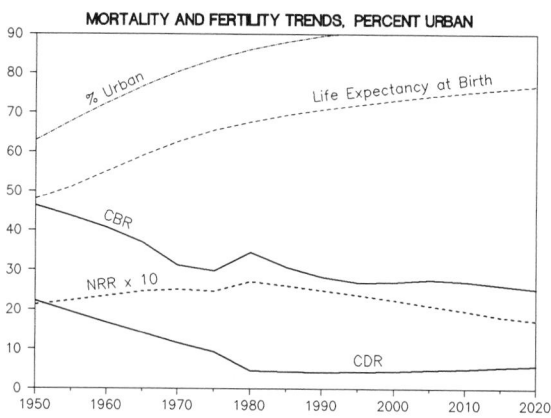

MORTALITY AND FERTILITY TRENDS, PERCENT URBAN

% Urban, Life Expectancy at Birth, CBR, NRR x 10, CDR

FERTILITY MEASURES (Annual Averages)

PERIOD	CRUDE BIRTH RATE	FERTILITY RATES GENERAL	FERTILITY RATES TOTAL	REPRODUCTION RATES GROSS	REPRODUCTION RATES NET	RATE OF NATUR. INCR.
1950-55	46.30	216.42	6.970	3.400	2.130	24.10
1955-60	43.70	218.58	6.970	3.400	2.240	24.30
1960-65	40.80	222.58	6.970	3.400	2.350	24.10
1965-70	37.00	230.50	6.970	3.400	2.470	22.90
1970-75	31.30	214.85	6.765	3.300	2.520	19.70
1975-80	29.90	177.35	6.355	3.100	2.470	20.53
1980-85	34.59	188.64	5.945	2.900	2.713	30.04
1985-90	*30.79*	*173.77*	*5.637*	*2.750*	*2.615*	*26.50*
1990-95	*28.26*	*163.39*	*5.330*	*2.600*	*2.499*	*24.11*
2000-05	*27.07*	*143.01*	*4.715*	*2.300*	*2.243*	*22.61*
2010-15	*27.20*	*131.32*	*4.100*	*2.000*	*1.970*	*22.12*
2020-25	*25.35*	*113.46*	*3.587*	*1.750*	*1.734*	*19.61*

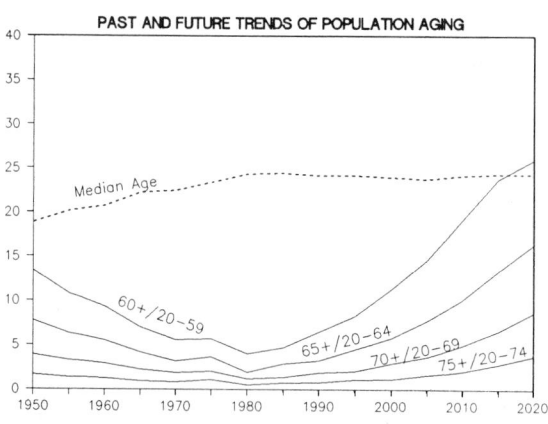

PAST AND FUTURE TRENDS OF POPULATION AGING

Median Age, 60+/20-59, 65+/20-64, 70+/20-69, 75+/20-74

AGING MEASURES

YEAR	POPULATION AGE RATIOS 60+/20-59	65+/20-64	70+/20-69	75+/20-74	POPULATION MEAN AGE	POPULATION MEDIAN AGE
1950	0.1343	0.0773	0.0392	0.0163	23.62	18.88
1960	0.0933	0.0551	0.0291	0.0123	23.65	20.76
1970	0.0555	0.0315	0.0188	0.0085	23.57	22.45
1980	0.0397	0.0194	0.0117	0.0053	24.59	24.36
1990	*0.0647*	*0.0320*	*0.0184*	*0.0076*	*25.63*	*24.18*
2000	*0.1129*	*0.0575*	*0.0290*	*0.0112*	*27.26*	*24.01*
2010	*0.1913*	*0.1007*	*0.0493*	*0.0201*	*28.34*	*24.19*
2020	*0.2591*	*0.1631*	*0.0861*	*0.0375*	*28.87*	*24.36*

OBSERVED AND *PROJECTED* POPULATION DATA (000's)

YEAR	MID-YEAR POPULATION	NO. OF BIRTHS	NO. OF DEATHS	URBAN POPULATION NUMBER	URBAN POPULATION PERCENT	POPULATION 1985 AGE	POPULATION 1985 NUMBER
1950	3201	157	83	508	15.9	0	2127
1955	3593	175	85	791	22.0	5	1746
1960	4075	199	87	1211	29.7	10	1329
1965	4793	231	92	1858	38.8	15	1083
1970	5745	273	97	2796	48.7	20	965
1975	7251	333	78	4255	58.7	25	945
1980	9372	405	84	6265	66.8	30	844
1985	11595	487	88	8463	73.0	35	652
1990	*14131*	*590*	*90*	*10926*	*77.3*	40	493
1995	*17118*	*714*	*95*	*13722*	*80.2*	45	384
2000	*20686*	*845*	*101*	*16924*	*81.8*	50	304
2005	*24856*	*964*	*110*	*20712*	*83.3*	55	235
2010	*29551*	*1045*	*121*	*25033*	*84.7*	60	183
2015	*34567*	*1083*	*133*	*29719*	*86.0*	65	128
2020	*39667*	*1109*	*148*	*34562*	*87.1*	70+	177

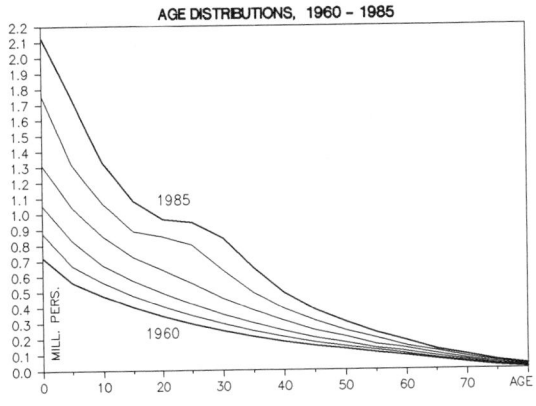

AGE DISTRIBUTIONS, 1960 - 1985

POPULATION RATIOS

YEAR	AGE DISTRIBUTION UNDER 15	AGE DISTRIBUTION 15-64	AGE DISTRIBUTION 65 & OLDER	AGE DISTRIBUTION 70 & OLDER	DEPENDENCY RATIO	WOMEN 15-49	CHILD-WOMAN RATIO
1950	0.420	0.547	0.033	0.017	0.830	0.225	0.765
1955	0.426	0.540	0.033	0.017	0.850	0.224	0.782
1960	0.433	0.534	0.033	0.018	0.874	0.222	0.801
1965	0.440	0.527	0.033	0.018	0.897	0.218	0.840
1970	0.445	0.523	0.032	0.017	0.911	0.214	0.857
1975	0.443	0.527	0.030	0.017	0.897	0.208	0.869
1980	0.442	0.530	0.028	0.016	0.886	0.196	0.955
1985	0.449	0.525	0.026	0.015	0.905	0.192	0.956
1990	*0.455*	*0.520*	*0.026*	*0.015*	*0.924*	*0.191*	*0.947*
2000	*0.457*	*0.517*	*0.026*	*0.015*	*0.933*	*0.199*	*0.921*
2010	*0.453*	*0.518*	*0.028*	*0.016*	*0.929*	*0.210*	*0.826*
2020	*0.412*	*0.552*	*0.036*	*0.020*	*0.811*	*0.234*	*0.614*

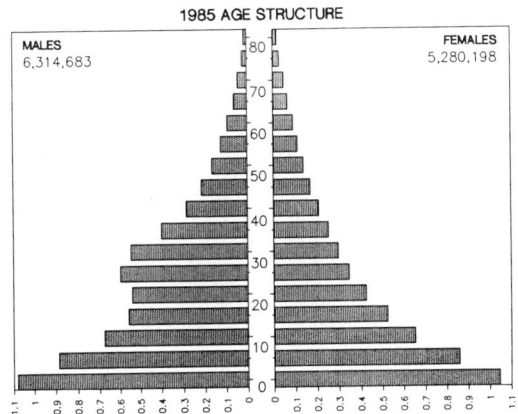

1985 AGE STRUCTURE

MALES 6,314,683   FEMALES 5,280,198

MORTALITY MEASURES (Annual Averages)

PERIOD	CRUDE DEATH RATE	INFANT MORT. RATE	LIFE EXPECTANCY AT BIRTH (years) MALE	LIFE EXPECTANCY AT BIRTH (years) FEMALE	LIFE EXPECTANCY AT BIRTH (years) BOTH SEXES	DIFFERENCE FEMALE-MALE
1950-55	25.90	200.00	39.10	40.70	39.88	1.60
1955-60	23.70	180.00	41.90	43.90	42.88	2.00
1960-65	21.30	160.00	44.80	47.10	45.92	2.30
1965-70	19.20	140.00	48.60	51.30	49.92	2.70
1970-75	16.90	120.00	52.40	55.50	53.91	3.10
1975-80	10.70	100.00	56.20	59.70	57.91	3.50
1980-85	8.92	85.00	59.20	62.70	60.91	3.50
1985-90	*7.57*	*70.88*	*61.70*	*65.20*	*63.41*	*3.50*
1990-95	*6.40*	*58.08*	*64.20*	*67.70*	*65.91*	*3.50*
2000-05	*4.89*	*38.97*	*67.70*	*71.70*	*69.65*	*4.00*
2010-15	*4.08*	*23.83*	*70.10*	*74.40*	*72.20*	*4.30*
2020-25	*3.73*	*21.35*	*72.10*	*76.60*	*74.29*	*4.50*

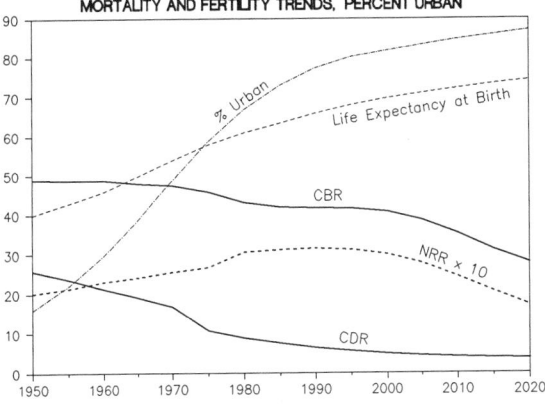

MORTALITY AND FERTILITY TRENDS, PERCENT URBAN

% Urban

Life Expectancy at Birth

CBR

NRR x 10

CDR

FERTILITY MEASURES (Annual Averages)

PERIOD	CRUDE BIRTH RATE	FERTILITY RATES GENERAL	FERTILITY RATES TOTAL	REPRODUCTION RATES GROSS	REPRODUCTION RATES NET	RATE OF NATUR. INCR.
1950-55	49.00	218.49	7.175	3.500	2.020	23.10
1955-60	48.80	219.14	7.175	3.500	2.140	25.10
1960-65	48.90	222.45	7.257	3.540	2.310	27.60
1965-70	48.10	222.84	7.257	3.540	2.420	28.90
1970-75	47.60	225.94	7.298	3.560	2.570	30.70
1975-80	45.89	227.93	7.277	3.550	2.687	35.19
1980-85	43.23	223.13	7.277	3.550	3.076	34.31
1985-90	*42.01*	*219.41*	*7.175*	*3.500*	*3.121*	*34.44*
1990-95	*41.77*	*215.79*	*7.072*	*3.450*	*3.161*	*35.38*
2000-05	*40.87*	*202.74*	*6.498*	*3.170*	*3.011*	*35.98*
2010-15	*35.37*	*163.89*	*5.186*	*2.530*	*2.449*	*31.29*
2020-25	*27.95*	*115.62*	*3.587*	*1.750*	*1.716*	*24.22*

AGING MEASURES

YEAR	POPULATION AGE RATIOS 60+/20-59	POPULATION AGE RATIOS 65+/20-64	POPULATION AGE RATIOS 70+/20-69	POPULATION AGE RATIOS 75+/20-74	POPULATION MEAN AGE	POPULATION MEDIAN AGE
1950	0.1320	0.0746	0.0369	0.0148	23.76	19.03
1960	0.1334	0.0771	0.0394	0.0164	23.22	18.37
1970	0.1264	0.0747	0.0395	0.0173	22.56	17.76
1980	0.1043	0.0643	0.0352	0.0165	22.15	18.07
1990	*0.1003*	*0.0608*	*0.0334*	*0.0165*	*22.05*	*17.40*
2000	*0.1044*	*0.0625*	*0.0343*	*0.0167*	*22.01*	*17.12*
2010	*0.1183*	*0.0685*	*0.0373*	*0.0180*	*22.25*	*17.23*
2020	*0.1358*	*0.0819*	*0.0436*	*0.0204*	*23.54*	*18.91*

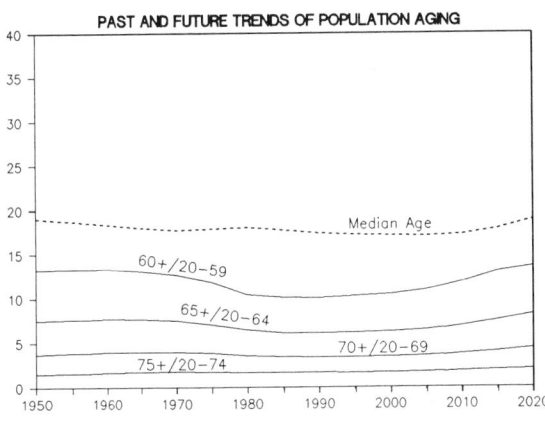

PAST AND FUTURE TRENDS OF POPULATION AGING

Median Age

60+/20-59

65+/20-64

70+/20-69

75+/20-74

OBSERVED AND *PROJECTED* POPULATION DATA

YEAR	MID-YEAR POPULATION	NO. OF BIRTHS	NO. OF DEATHS	URBAN POPULATION NUMBER	URBAN POPULATION PERCENT	1985 POPULATION AGE	1985 POPULATION NUMBER
1950	1022100	45381	10793	1022099	100.0	0	209106
1955	1306100	54268	11193	1306099	100.0	5	193341
1960	1634000	55589	11552	1633998	100.0	10	223660
1965	1880300	46725	10586	1880298	100.0	15	235034
1970	2074600	43984	10684	2074598	100.0	20	286465
1975	2262600	38899	11580	2262598	100.0	25	295007
1980	2414500	41107	13108	2414498	100.0	30	252353
1985	2558670	42205	14339	2558667	100.0	35	209817
1990	2701898	41755	15590	2701895	100.0	40	134491
1995	2835963	39323	16914	2835960	100.0	45	129254
2000	2950276	37129	18743	2950273	100.0	50	103904
2005	3043669	35708	21190	3043667	100.0	55	88279
2010	3117148	35835	23871	3117146	100.0	60	65462
2015	3177549	35983	27518	3177547	100.0	65	52119
2020	3220155	35277	31532	3220153	100.0	70+	80378

POPULATION RATIOS

YEAR	UNDER 15	15-64	65 & OLDER	70 & OLDER	DEPENDENCY RATIO	WOMEN 15-49	CHILD-WOMAN RATIO
1950	0.405	0.571	0.024	0.014	0.750	0.235	0.684
1955	0.414	0.564	0.022	0.013	0.773	0.225	0.801
1960	0.432	0.547	0.021	0.012	0.828	0.215	0.861
1965	0.437	0.537	0.027	0.015	0.864	0.216	0.697
1970	0.388	0.579	0.034	0.017	0.728	0.238	0.477
1975	0.328	0.631	0.041	0.022	0.586	0.264	0.376
1980	0.271	0.682	0.047	0.027	0.466	0.288	0.279
1985	0.245	0.704	0.052	0.031	0.421	0.295	0.277
1990	0.228	0.716	0.056	0.034	0.396	0.294	0.270
2000	0.212	0.717	0.071	0.043	0.395	0.277	0.244
2010	0.182	0.725	0.093	0.059	0.379	0.242	0.238
2020	0.168	0.680	0.153	0.089	0.471	0.214	0.261

MORTALITY MEASURES (Annual Averages)

PERIOD	CRUDE DEATH RATE	INFANT MORT. RATE	LIFE EXPECTANCY AT BIRTH (years) MALE	FEMALE	BOTH SEXES	DIFFERENCE FEMALE-MALE
1950-55	10.56	66.03	58.82	62.05	60.40	3.23
1955-60	8.57	41.08	61.53	64.91	63.18	3.38
1960-65	7.07	30.19	64.11	67.57	65.80	3.46
1965-70	5.63	23.63	66.00	69.99	67.95	3.99
1970-75	5.15	18.86	67.35	71.80	69.52	4.45
1975-80	5.12	12.52	68.60	73.10	70.79	4.50
1980-85	5.43	10.07	69.19	74.60	71.79	5.41
1985-90	5.60	8.97	70.16	75.75	72.85	5.59
1990-95	5.77	7.97	71.15	76.70	73.82	5.54
2000-05	6.35	6.38	73.01	78.48	75.64	5.47
2010-15	7.66	5.39	74.66	80.09	77.28	5.44
2020-25	9.79	4.95	75.82	81.06	78.34	5.24

FERTILITY MEASURES (Annual Averages)

PERIOD	CRUDE BIRTH RATE	FERTILITY RATES GENERAL	FERTILITY RATES TOTAL	REPRODUCTION RATES GROSS	REPRODUCTION RATES NET	RATE OF NATUR. INCR.
1950-55	44.40	193.47	6.408	3.085	2.655	33.84
1955-60	41.55	189.49	6.005	2.891	2.572	32.98
1960-65	34.02	158.02	4.935	2.376	2.178	26.95
1965-70	24.85	109.26	3.462	1.667	1.567	19.22
1970-75	21.20	84.23	2.629	1.266	1.210	16.05
1975-80	17.19	62.19	1.869	0.900	0.867	12.07
1980-85	17.02	58.43	1.695	0.816	0.798	11.60
1985-90	16.50	56.01	1.650	0.794	0.781	10.89
1990-95	15.45	53.01	1.700	0.818	0.807	9.68
2000-05	12.59	46.81	1.800	0.867	0.860	6.23
2010-15	11.50	49.25	1.800	0.867	0.861	3.84
2020-25	10.95	52.07	1.800	0.867	0.861	1.16

AGING MEASURES

YEAR	POPULATION AGE RATIOS 60+/20-59	65+/20-64	70+/20-69	75+/20-74	POPULATION MEAN AGE	POPULATION MEDIAN AGE
1950	0.0809	0.0504	0.0284	0.0171	23.49	19.98
1960	0.0844	0.0450	0.0258	0.0137	22.93	18.80
1970	0.1308	0.0729	0.0365	0.0170	24.69	19.72
1980	0.1336	0.0838	0.0459	0.0208	27.90	24.50
1990	0.1423	0.0879	0.0525	0.0276	31.09	29.84
2000	0.1793	0.1098	0.0638	0.0323	34.28	34.85
2010	0.2542	0.1420	0.0857	0.0436	37.65	38.75
2020	0.4333	0.2453	0.1297	0.0596	40.48	41.34

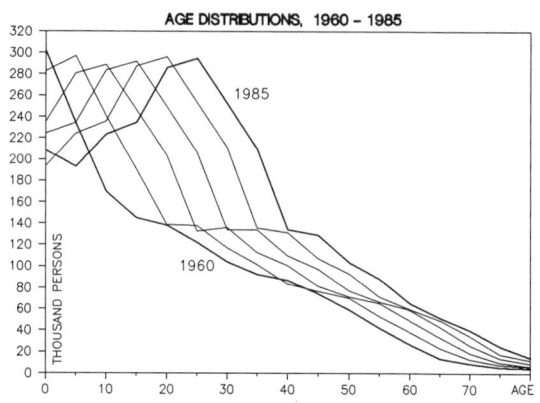

AGE DISTRIBUTIONS, 1960 - 1985

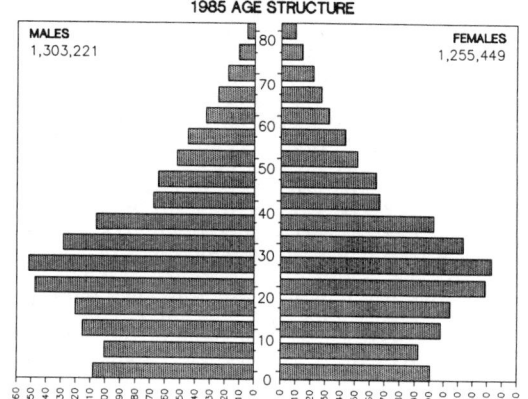

1985 AGE STRUCTURE

MALES 1,303,221

FEMALES 1,255,449

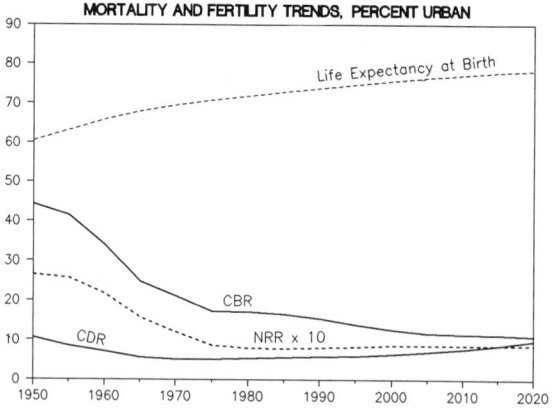

MORTALITY AND FERTILITY TRENDS, PERCENT URBAN

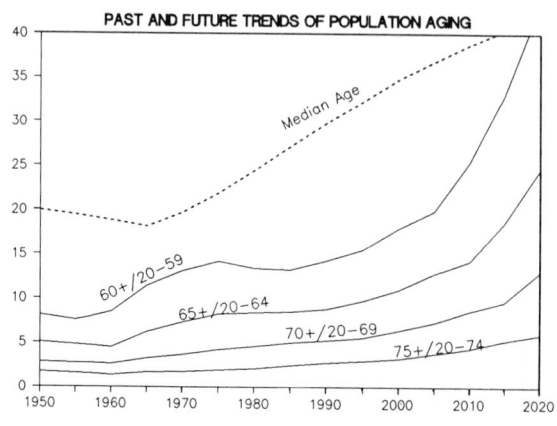

PAST AND FUTURE TRENDS OF POPULATION AGING

OBSERVED AND *PROJECTED* POPULATION DATA (000's)

YEAR	MID-YEAR POPULATION	NO. OF BIRTHS	NO. OF DEATHS	URBAN POPULATION NUMBER	URBAN POPULATION PERCENT	POPULATION 1985 AGE	POPULATION 1985 NUMBER
1950	7678	296	88	1106	14.4	0	1995
1955	8723	319	86	1403	16.1	5	1835
1960	9889	343	84	1772	17.9	10	1660
1965	11164	352	93	2217	19.9	15	1655
1970	12514	362	101	2736	21.9	20	1539
1975	13603	388	97	2998	22.0	25	1435
1980	14819	398	94	3196	21.6	30	1206
1985	16108	362	96	3399	21.1	35	1064
1990	*17209*	*354*	*101*	*3677*	*21.4*	40	802
1995	*18320*	*344*	*108*	*4101*	*22.4*	45	662
2000	*19385*	*332*	*117*	*4694*	*24.2*	50	591
2005	*20388*	*345*	*127*	*5494*	*26.9*	55	517
2010	*21458*	*351*	*139*	*6586*	*30.7*	60	393
2015	*22544*	*350*	*153*	*7799*	*34.6*	65	306
2020	*23554*	*345*	*170*	*9087*	*38.6*	70+	449

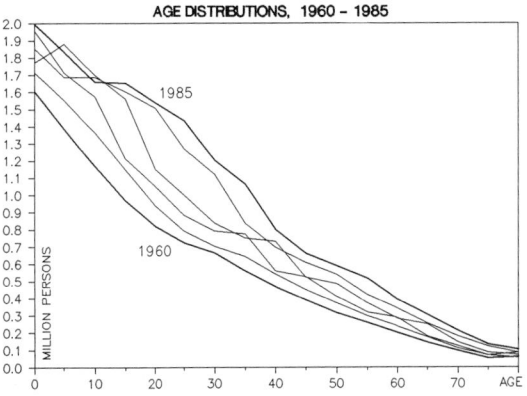

AGE DISTRIBUTIONS, 1960 - 1985

POPULATION RATIOS

YEAR	AGE DISTRIBUTION UNDER 15	AGE DISTRIBUTION 15-64	AGE DISTRIBUTION 65 & OLDER	AGE DISTRIBUTION 70 & OLDER	DEPENDENCY RATIO	WOMEN 15-49	CHILD-WOMAN RATIO
1950	0.407	0.554	0.039	0.023	0.805	0.217	0.746
1955	0.415	0.547	0.038	0.023	0.827	0.219	0.754
1960	0.421	0.543	0.036	0.022	0.841	0.221	0.733
1965	0.415	0.549	0.037	0.021	0.823	0.226	0.680
1970	0.419	0.545	0.036	0.022	0.836	0.222	0.703
1975	0.394	0.566	0.041	0.022	0.768	0.233	0.559
1980	0.353	0.604	0.043	0.026	0.656	0.255	0.490
1985	0.341	0.612	0.047	0.028	0.633	0.260	0.477
1990	*0.325*	*0.623*	*0.052*	*0.031*	*0.605*	*0.265*	*0.397*
2000	*0.272*	*0.662*	*0.065*	*0.040*	*0.510*	*0.276*	*0.323*
2010	*0.238*	*0.683*	*0.079*	*0.050*	*0.465*	*0.268*	*0.303*
2020	*0.224*	*0.671*	*0.105*	*0.066*	*0.490*	*0.251*	*0.299*

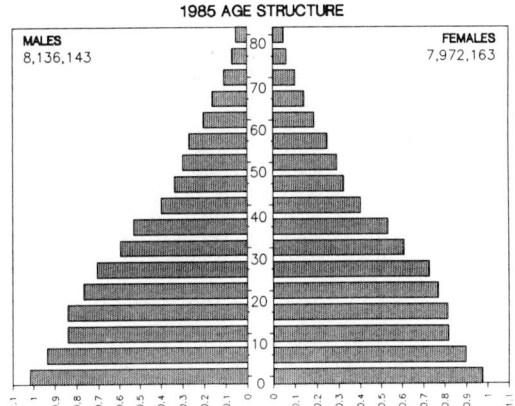

1985 AGE STRUCTURE

MALES 8,136,143   FEMALES 7,972,163

MORTALITY MEASURES (Annual Averages)

PERIOD	CRUDE DEATH RATE	INFANT MORT. RATE	LIFE EXPECTANCY AT BIRTH (years) MALE	LIFE EXPECTANCY AT BIRTH (years) FEMALE	LIFE EXPECTANCY AT BIRTH (years) BOTH SEXES	DIFFERENCE FEMALE-MALE
1950-55	11.50	90.70	57.60	55.50	56.57	-2.10
1955-60	9.90	76.20	61.30	59.70	60.51	-1.60
1960-65	8.50	65.00	63.30	63.70	63.50	0.40
1965-70	8.30	61.00	63.50	65.00	64.24	1.50
1970-75	8.10	56.00	64.00	66.00	64.98	2.00
1975-80	7.10	47.70	65.00	68.50	66.75	3.50
1980-85	6.33	39.38	67.01	70.98	68.94	3.96
1985-90	*5.97*	*33.09*	*68.29*	*72.50*	*70.34*	*4.21*
1990-95	*5.85*	*28.15*	*69.54*	*73.77*	*71.60*	*4.24*
2000-05	*6.01*	*20.72*	*71.61*	*75.96*	*73.73*	*4.35*
2010-15	*6.47*	*15.34*	*73.44*	*77.87*	*75.60*	*4.43*
2020-25	*7.20*	*12.50*	*75.03*	*79.50*	*77.21*	*4.47*

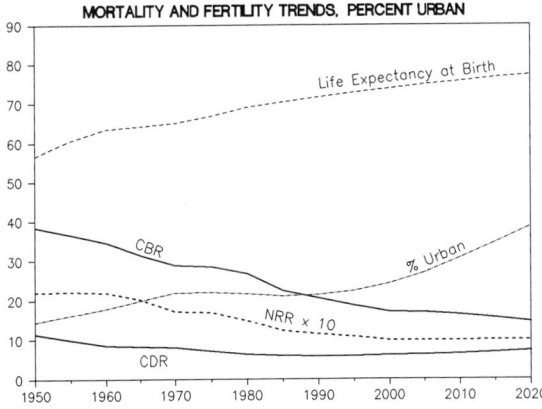

MORTALITY AND FERTILITY TRENDS, PERCENT URBAN

FERTILITY MEASURES (Annual Averages)

PERIOD	CRUDE BIRTH RATE	FERTILITY RATES GENERAL	FERTILITY RATES TOTAL	REPRODUCTION RATES GROSS	REPRODUCTION RATES NET	RATE OF NATUR. INCR.
1950-55	38.50	176.84	5.744	2.802	2.209	27.00
1955-60	36.60	166.41	5.443	2.655	2.222	26.70
1960-65	34.70	155.14	5.156	2.515	2.200	26.20
1965-70	31.50	140.58	4.680	2.283	2.028	23.20
1970-75	28.90	126.73	3.997	1.950	1.720	20.80
1975-80	28.50	116.43	3.829	1.868	1.700	21.40
1980-85	26.87	104.29	3.250	1.585	1.479	20.54
1985-90	*22.47*	*85.68*	*2.667*	*1.302*	*1.231*	*16.51*
1990-95	*20.59*	*76.87*	*2.468*	*1.205*	*1.150*	*14.75*
2000-05	*17.11*	*62.18*	*2.068*	*1.010*	*0.977*	*11.09*
2010-15	*16.35*	*61.94*	*2.068*	*1.010*	*0.987*	*9.88*
2020-25	*14.65*	*59.11*	*2.068*	*1.010*	*0.994*	*7.45*

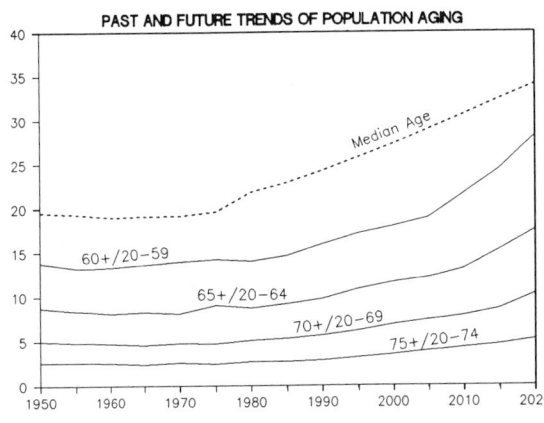

PAST AND FUTURE TRENDS OF POPULATION AGING

AGING MEASURES

YEAR	POPULATION AGE RATIOS 60+/20-59	POPULATION AGE RATIOS 65+/20-64	POPULATION AGE RATIOS 70+/20-69	POPULATION AGE RATIOS 75+/20-74	POPULATION MEAN AGE	POPULATION MEDIAN AGE
1950	0.1380	0.0874	0.0498	0.0258	23.96	19.56
1960	0.1330	0.0812	0.0469	0.0251	23.83	19.06
1970	0.1398	0.0812	0.0477	0.0259	24.08	19.18
1980	0.1404	0.0875	0.0510	0.0267	25.81	21.92
1990	*0.1598*	*0.0980*	*0.0567*	*0.0288*	*27.69*	*24.31*
2000	*0.1797*	*0.1164*	*0.0686*	*0.0345*	*30.28*	*27.33*
2010	*0.2163*	*0.1315*	*0.0785*	*0.0427*	*32.91*	*30.63*
2020	*0.2819*	*0.1753*	*0.1029*	*0.0518*	*35.18*	*34.06*

OBSERVED AND *PROJECTED* POPULATION DATA (000's)

YEAR	MID-YEAR POPULATION	NO. OF BIRTHS	NO. OF DEATHS	URBAN POPULATION NUMBER	URBAN POPULATION PERCENT	POPULATION 1985 AGE	POPULATION 1985 NUMBER
1950	3495	163	75	1071	30.6	0	2025
1955	3967	185	75	1334	33.6	5	1659
1960	4561	216	76	1677	36.8	10	1346
1965	5325	253	81	2130	40.0	15	1094
1970	6258	292	76	2713	43.3	20	1007
1975	7438	342	66	3378	45.4	25	776
1980	8800	400	76	4174	47.4	30	571
1985	10458	462	73	5172	49.5	35	424
1990	12501	521	72	6479	51.8	40	333
1995	14904	575	73	8124	54.5	45	292
2000	17611	625	76	10115	57.4	50	264
2005	20586	651	82	12460	60.5	55	219
2010	23646	652	88	15065	63.7	60	161
2015	26649	641	96	17769	66.7	65	113
2020	29518	634	108	20494	69.4	70+	177

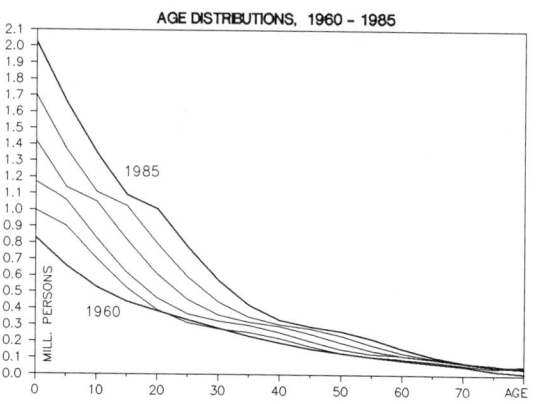

AGE DISTRIBUTIONS, 1960 - 1985

POPULATION RATIOS

YEAR	AGE DISTRIBUTION UNDER 15	AGE DISTRIBUTION 15-64	AGE DISTRIBUTION 65 & OLDER	AGE DISTRIBUTION 70 & OLDER	DEPENDENCY RATIO	WOMEN 15-49	CHILD-WOMAN RATIO
1950	0.414	0.542	0.044	0.025	0.846	0.223	0.748
1955	0.428	0.531	0.041	0.023	0.882	0.222	0.803
1960	0.444	0.518	0.038	0.022	0.930	0.218	0.836
1965	0.489	0.467	0.044	0.029	1.139	0.199	0.938
1970	0.489	0.467	0.044	0.029	1.141	0.199	0.939
1975	0.485	0.478	0.037	0.024	1.092	0.204	0.935
1980	0.475	0.493	0.032	0.020	1.029	0.210	0.922
1985	0.481	0.491	0.028	0.017	1.035	0.210	0.921
1990	0.481	0.493	0.026	0.015	1.028	0.214	0.892
2000	0.458	0.516	0.027	0.015	0.940	0.228	0.752
2010	0.409	0.564	0.027	0.016	0.773	0.247	0.585
2020	0.342	0.626	0.032	0.018	0.598	0.268	0.419

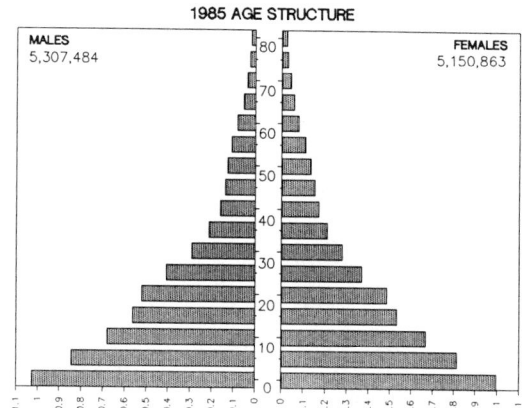

1985 AGE STRUCTURE

MALES 5,307,484

FEMALES 5,150,863

MORTALITY MEASURES (Annual Averages)

PERIOD	CRUDE DEATH RATE	INFANT MORT. RATE	LIFE EXPECTANCY AT BIRTH (years) MALE	LIFE EXPECTANCY AT BIRTH (years) FEMALE	LIFE EXPECTANCY AT BIRTH (years) BOTH SEXES	DIFFERENCE FEMALE-MALE
1950-55	21.40	160.00	44.80	47.20	45.97	2.40
1955-60	18.80	145.00	47.30	49.70	48.47	2.40
1960-65	16.60	125.00	49.70	52.40	51.02	2.70
1965-70	15.30	107.00	52.50	55.50	53.96	3.00
1970-75	12.10	88.00	55.40	58.70	57.01	3.30
1975-80	8.87	70.00	58.28	61.91	60.05	3.63
1980-85	8.62	58.83	60.78	64.41	62.55	3.63
1985-90	7.01	48.45	63.18	66.91	65.00	3.73
1990-95	5.75	39.44	65.18	69.23	67.16	4.05
2000-05	4.32	27.63	67.98	72.74	70.30	4.76
2010-15	3.70	20.45	69.98	75.20	72.53	5.22
2020-25	3.66	15.48	71.44	77.20	74.25	5.76

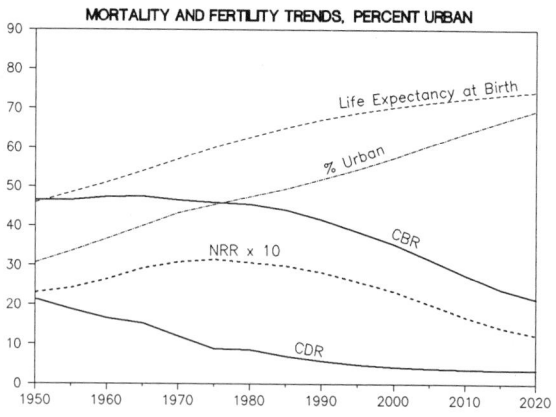

MORTALITY AND FERTILITY TRENDS, PERCENT URBAN

Life Expectancy at Birth

% Urban

NRR x 10

CBR

CDR

FERTILITY MEASURES (Annual Averages)

PERIOD	CRUDE BIRTH RATE	FERTILITY RATES GENERAL	FERTILITY RATES TOTAL	REPRODUCTION RATES GROSS	REPRODUCTION RATES NET	RATE OF NATUR. INCR.
1950-55	46.60	209.78	7.093	3.460	2.320	25.20
1955-60	46.60	212.12	7.093	3.460	2.430	27.80
1960-65	47.40	227.92	7.462	3.640	2.660	30.80
1965-70	47.60	238.89	7.790	3.800	2.940	32.30
1970-75	46.60	230.83	7.688	3.750	3.090	34.50
1975-80	46.00	221.78	7.441	3.630	3.159	37.13
1980-85	45.51	216.48	7.173	3.500	3.085	36.89
1985-90	44.13	208.04	6.763	3.300	2.991	37.13
1990-95	41.68	192.16	6.251	3.050	2.831	35.94
2000-05	35.48	152.33	5.021	2.450	2.343	31.16
2010-15	27.58	109.60	3.586	1.750	1.700	23.88
2020-25	21.48	78.88	2.582	1.260	1.237	17.82

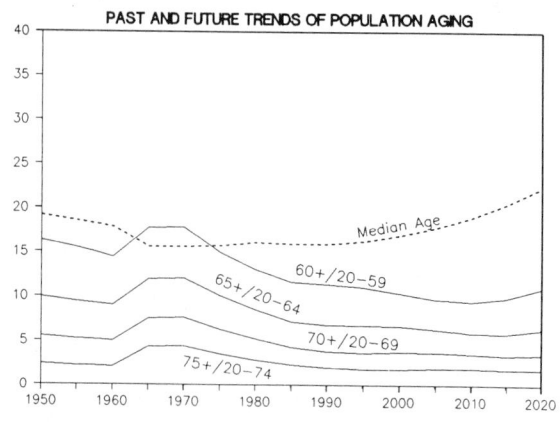

PAST AND FUTURE TRENDS OF POPULATION AGING

Median Age

60+/20-59

65+/20-64

70+/20-69

75+/20-74

AGING MEASURES

YEAR	POPULATION AGE RATIOS 60+/20-59	POPULATION AGE RATIOS 65+/20-64	POPULATION AGE RATIOS 70+/20-69	POPULATION AGE RATIOS 75+/20-74	POPULATION MEAN AGE	POPULATION MEDIAN AGE
1950	0.1637	0.0995	0.0551	0.0236	24.26	19.22
1960	0.1443	0.0901	0.0496	0.0207	22.90	17.89
1970	0.1783	0.1201	0.0758	0.0436	22.02	15.58
1980	0.1299	0.0845	0.0521	0.0283	21.11	16.06
1990	0.1132	0.0676	0.0379	0.0196	20.72	15.90
2000	0.1037	0.0663	0.0373	0.0177	21.37	16.90
2010	0.0941	0.0589	0.0353	0.0184	23.00	18.99
2020	0.1092	0.0630	0.0345	0.0174	25.70	22.36

OBSERVED AND *PROJECTED* POPULATION DATA (000's)

YEAR	MID-YEAR POPULATION	NO. OF BIRTHS	NO. OF DEATHS	URBAN POPULATION NUMBER	URBAN POPULATION PERCENT	POPULATION 1985 AGE	POPULATION 1985 NUMBER
1950	20010	932	384	2097	10.5	0	6400
1955	22762	1008	361	2611	11.5	5	6234
1960	26392	1148	353	3302	12.5	10	6188
1965	30641	1279	350	3941	12.9	15	6066
1970	35745	1255	333	4750	13.3	20	5229
1975	41359	1307	343	6283	15.2	25	4512
1980	46718	1300	372	8088	17.3	30	3694
1985	51604	1150	362	10211	19.8	35	2830
1990	*55702*	*1116*	*362*	*12609*	*22.6*	40	2304
1995	*59605*	*1164*	*378*	*15414*	*25.9*	45	2105
2000	*63670*	*1187*	*401*	*18738*	*29.4*	50	1738
2005	*67724*	*1188*	*436*	*22542*	*33.3*	55	1401
2010	*71594*	*1151*	*474*	*26669*	*37.3*	60	1025
2015	*75065*	*1121*	*523*	*30971*	*41.3*	65	758
2020	*78118*	*1126*	*577*	*35346*	*45.2*	70+	1120

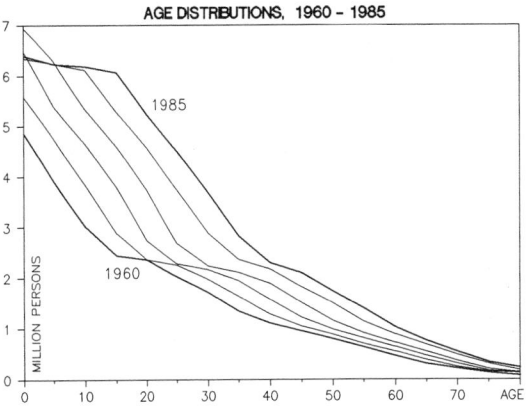

AGE DISTRIBUTIONS, 1960 - 1985

POPULATION RATIOS

YEAR	AGE DISTRIBUTION UNDER 15	AGE DISTRIBUTION 15-64	AGE DISTRIBUTION 65 & OLDER	AGE DISTRIBUTION 70 & OLDER	DEPENDENCY RATIO	WOMEN 15-49	CHILD-WOMAN RATIO
1950	0.425	0.545	0.030	0.017	0.836	0.236	0.709
1955	0.429	0.542	0.029	0.017	0.844	0.235	0.774
1960	0.447	0.526	0.027	0.016	0.903	0.226	0.815
1965	0.463	0.508	0.029	0.017	0.968	0.219	0.830
1970	0.462	0.508	0.030	0.017	0.969	0.222	0.814
1975	0.449	0.521	0.030	0.017	0.919	0.229	0.733
1980	0.400	0.565	0.035	0.021	0.771	0.244	0.556
1985	0.365	0.599	0.036	0.022	0.670	0.257	0.482
1990	*0.326*	*0.635*	*0.039*	*0.023*	*0.576*	*0.270*	*0.376*
2000	*0.265*	*0.685*	*0.050*	*0.029*	*0.460*	*0.289*	*0.315*
2010	*0.246*	*0.692*	*0.062*	*0.038*	*0.445*	*0.274*	*0.303*
2020	*0.221*	*0.695*	*0.084*	*0.049*	*0.439*	*0.255*	*0.282*

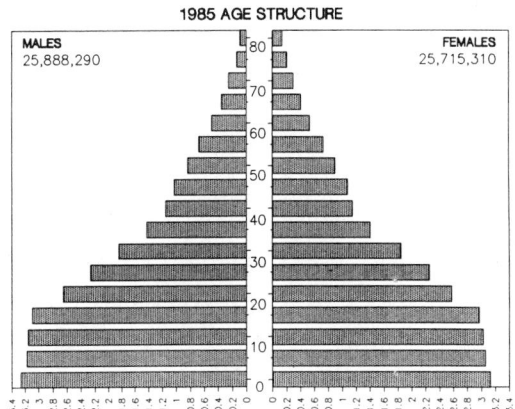

1985 AGE STRUCTURE
MALES 25,888,290   FEMALES 25,715,310

MORTALITY MEASURES (Annual Averages)

PERIOD	CRUDE DEATH RATE	INFANT MORT. RATE	LIFE EXPECTANCY AT BIRTH (years) MALE	FEMALE	BOTH SEXES	DIFFERENCE FEMALE-MALE
1950-55	19.21	132.00	45.00	49.05	46.98	4.05
1955-60	15.88	111.00	48.55	52.85	50.65	4.30
1960-65	13.37	95.00	51.85	56.15	53.95	4.30
1965-70	11.41	84.00	54.65	58.95	56.75	4.30
1970-75	9.30	65.10	57.73	61.57	59.60	3.84
1975-80	8.30	56.00	59.25	63.19	61.17	3.94
1980-85	7.95	47.51	60.73	64.79	62.71	4.06
1985-90	*7.01*	*38.97*	*63.00*	*67.07*	*64.99*	*4.06*
1990-95	*6.50*	*32.26*	*65.06*	*69.18*	*67.07*	*4.12*
2000-05	*6.30*	*23.41*	*68.00*	*72.42*	*70.15*	*4.42*
2010-15	*6.62*	*17.39*	*70.31*	*74.92*	*72.56*	*4.61*
2020-25	*7.38*	*13.12*	*72.26*	*76.98*	*74.56*	*4.71*

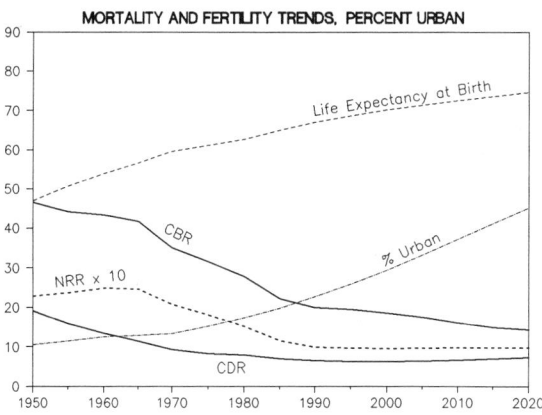

MORTALITY AND FERTILITY TRENDS, PERCENT URBAN

FERTILITY MEASURES (Annual Averages)

PERIOD	CRUDE BIRTH RATE	FERTILITY RATES GENERAL	FERTILITY RATES TOTAL	REPRODUCTION RATES GROSS	REPRODUCTION RATES NET	RATE OF NATUR. INCR.
1950-55	46.58	197.87	6.619	3.229	2.293	27.37
1955-60	44.28	192.59	6.421	3.132	2.369	28.40
1960-65	43.49	195.60	6.421	3.132	2.489	30.11
1965-70	41.75	188.91	6.138	2.994	2.473	30.34
1970-75	35.12	155.52	5.010	2.444	2.087	25.81
1975-80	31.60	133.35	4.274	2.085	1.816	23.30
1980-85	27.83	110.82	3.520	1.717	1.521	19.88
1985-90	*22.29*	*84.38*	*2.600*	*1.268*	*1.152*	*15.28*
1990-95	*20.04*	*72.48*	*2.200*	*1.073*	*0.996*	*13.54*
2000-05	*18.64*	*65.07*	*2.070*	*1.010*	*0.963*	*12.34*
2010-15	*16.08*	*59.61*	*2.070*	*1.010*	*0.978*	*9.47*
2020-25	*14.41*	*57.68*	*2.070*	*1.010*	*0.988*	*7.03*

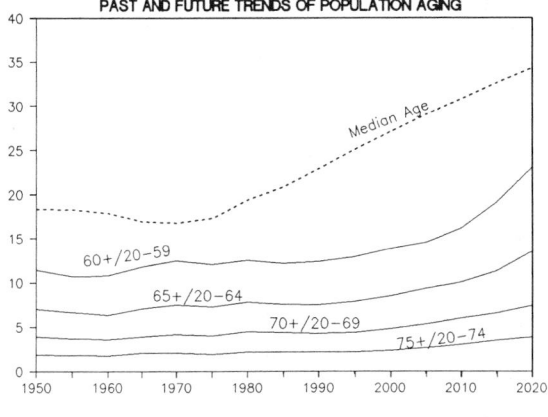

PAST AND FUTURE TRENDS OF POPULATION AGING

AGING MEASURES

YEAR	POPULATION AGE RATIOS 60+/20-59	POPULATION AGE RATIOS 65+/20-64	POPULATION AGE RATIOS 70+/20-69	POPULATION AGE RATIOS 75+/20-74	POPULATION MEAN AGE	POPULATION MEDIAN AGE
1950	0.1144	0.0698	0.0388	0.0188	22.83	18.39
1960	0.1084	0.0635	0.0359	0.0176	22.35	17.86
1970	0.1250	0.0750	0.0416	0.0207	22.10	16.79
1980	0.1251	0.0782	0.0445	0.0218	23.92	19.41
1990	*0.1237*	*0.0745*	*0.0426*	*0.0219*	*26.33*	*22.93*
2000	*0.1384*	*0.0849*	*0.0478*	*0.0234*	*29.27*	*27.12*
2010	*0.1613*	*0.1005*	*0.0598*	*0.0303*	*31.97*	*30.81*
2020	*0.2296*	*0.1351*	*0.0742*	*0.0382*	*34.73*	*34.32*

OBSERVED AND *PROJECTED* POPULATION DATA (000's)

YEAR	MID-YEAR POPULATION	NO. OF BIRTHS	NO. OF DEATHS	URBAN POPULATION NUMBER	PERCENT	POPULATION 1985 AGE	NUMBER
1950	20809	1003	489	4442	21.3	0	6502
1955	23859	1117	472	6134	25.7	5	5851
1960	27509	1180	451	8182	29.7	10	5956
1965	31151	1215	421	10627	34.1	15	5517
1970	35321	1219	410	13571	38.4	20	4911
1975	40025	1281	408	16651	41.6	25	4162
1980	44438	1342	418	19455	43.8	30	3384
1985	50345	1429	421	23118	45.9	35	2725
1990	*55616*	*1473*	*415*	*26928*	*48.4*	40	2276
1995	*61151*	*1457*	*408*	*31332*	*51.2*	45	2122
2000	*66622*	*1426*	*429*	*36188*	*54.3*	50	2017
2005	*71800*	*1399*	*462*	*41346*	*57.6*	55	1703
2010	*76641*	*1373*	*493*	*46713*	*61.0*	60	1083
2015	*81168*	*1356*	*525*	*52033*	*64.1*	65	712
2020	*85432*	*1391*	*568*	*57277*	*67.0*	70+	1424

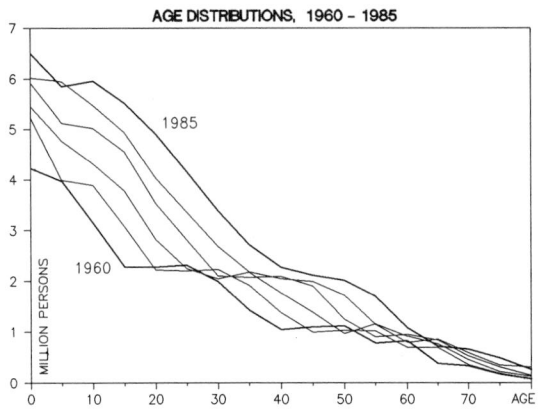

AGE DISTRIBUTIONS, 1960 - 1985

POPULATION RATIOS

YEAR	AGE DISTRIBUTION UNDER 15	15-64	65 & OLDER	70 & OLDER	DEPENDENCY RATIO	WOMEN 15-49	CHILD-WOMAN RATIO
1950	0.383	0.584	0.033	0.020	0.713	0.243	0.609
1955	0.394	0.571	0.034	0.022	0.750	0.232	0.693
1960	0.412	0.552	0.035	0.022	0.811	0.220	0.700
1965	0.420	0.538	0.041	0.019	0.858	0.218	0.770
1970	0.411	0.545	0.044	0.022	0.836	0.225	0.685
1975	0.401	0.554	0.045	0.024	0.806	0.232	0.637
1980	0.392	0.560	0.047	0.028	0.784	0.235	0.576
1985	0.364	0.594	0.042	0.028	0.684	0.240	0.539
1990	*0.344*	*0.614*	*0.043*	*0.025*	*0.629*	*0.248*	*0.501*
2000	*0.317*	*0.627*	*0.056*	*0.032*	*0.595*	*0.257*	*0.421*
2010	*0.276*	*0.662*	*0.063*	*0.040*	*0.512*	*0.265*	*0.343*
2020	*0.240*	*0.683*	*0.077*	*0.046*	*0.464*	*0.261*	*0.304*

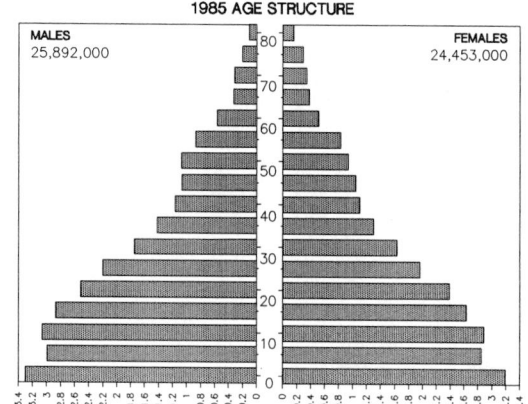

1985 AGE STRUCTURE

MALES 25,892,000   FEMALES 24,453,000

MORTALITY MEASURES (Annual Averages)

PERIOD	CRUDE DEATH RATE	INFANT MORT. RATE	LIFE EXPECTANCY AT BIRTH (years) MALE	FEMALE	BOTH SEXES	DIFFERENCE FEMALE-MALE
1950-55	23.50	233.00	42.00	45.20	43.60	3.20
1955-60	19.80	203.00	46.50	49.78	48.10	3.28
1960-65	16.40	176.00	50.50	53.70	52.10	3.20
1965-70	13.50	153.00	53.40	56.50	54.90	3.10
1970-75	11.60	138.00	55.90	60.00	57.90	4.10
1975-80	10.20	120.00	58.00	62.50	60.28	4.50
1980-85	9.40	92.09	60.00	63.30	61.60	3.30
1985-90	*8.37*	*75.63*	*62.50*	*65.77*	*64.09*	*3.27*
1990-95	*7.46*	*62.20*	*64.46*	*68.13*	*66.25*	*3.67*
2000-05	*6.45*	*40.92*	*67.96*	*71.92*	*69.89*	*3.96*
2010-15	*6.43*	*28.39*	*70.38*	*74.63*	*72.45*	*4.25*
2020-25	*6.65*	*19.38*	*72.41*	*76.81*	*74.56*	*4.40*

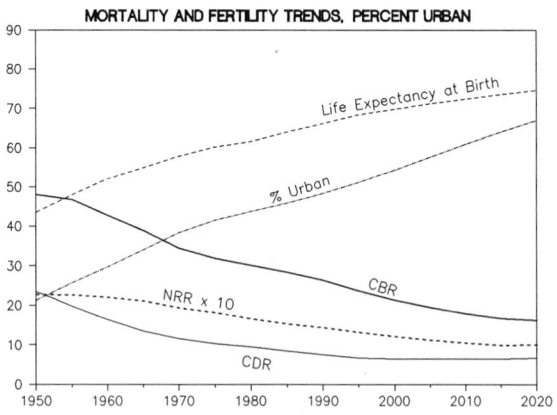

MORTALITY AND FERTILITY TRENDS, PERCENT URBAN

FERTILITY MEASURES (Annual Averages)

PERIOD	CRUDE BIRTH RATE	FERTILITY RATES GENERAL	TOTAL	REPRODUCTION RATES GROSS	NET	RATE OF NATUR. INCR.
1950-55	48.20	203.61	6.847	3.340	2.287	24.70
1955-60	46.80	207.87	6.539	3.190	2.276	27.00
1960-65	42.90	196.23	6.109	2.980	2.212	26.50
1965-70	39.00	175.87	5.617	2.740	2.119	25.50
1970-75	34.50	150.85	5.043	2.460	1.937	22.90
1975-80	32.00	137.10	4.305	2.100	1.830	21.80
1980-85	30.20	127.20	3.895	1.900	1.661	20.80
1985-90	*28.39*	*116.44*	*3.546*	*1.700*	*1.531*	*20.02*
1990-95	*26.48*	*106.01*	*3.233*	*1.550*	*1.432*	*19.03*
2000-05	*21.41*	*82.40*	*2.649*	*1.270*	*1.217*	*14.96*
2010-15	*17.91*	*67.63*	*2.232*	*1.070*	*1.046*	*11.48*
2020-25	*16.28*	*63.12*	*2.107*	*1.010*	*1.001*	*9.63*

AGING MEASURES

YEAR	POPULATION AGE RATIOS 60+/20-59	65+/20-64	70+/20-69	75+/20-74	POPULATION MEAN AGE	MEDIAN AGE
1950	0.1343	0.0701	0.0416	0.0173	24.77	20.13
1960	0.1486	0.0753	0.0448	0.0189	24.57	20.27
1970	0.1689	0.1003	0.0486	0.0203	24.57	19.13
1980	0.1506	0.1052	0.0596	0.0305	24.91	19.84
1990	*0.1476*	*0.0839*	*0.0484*	*0.0279*	*26.34*	*22.54*
2000	*0.1646*	*0.1049*	*0.0575*	*0.0254*	*28.07*	*25.07*
2010	*0.1718*	*0.1100*	*0.0673*	*0.0356*	*30.36*	*27.67*
2020	*0.2108*	*0.1275*	*0.0726*	*0.0380*	*32.87*	*30.79*

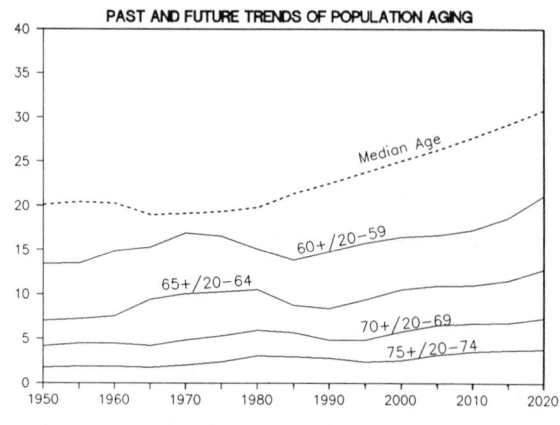

PAST AND FUTURE TRENDS OF POPULATION AGING

OBSERVED AND *PROJECTED* POPULATION DATA

YEAR	MID-YEAR POPULATION	NO. OF BIRTHS	NO. OF DEATHS	URBAN POPULATION NUMBER	URBAN POPULATION PERCENT	POPULATION 1985 AGE	POPULATION 1985 NUMBER
1950	69593	3327	1587	17400	25.0	0	167512
1955	78901	3748	1633	25280	32.0	5	146658
1960	90243	3935	1561	36098	40.0	10	103610
1965	144234	5567	1774	59367	41.2	15	85803
1970	222840	7354	2206	94328	42.3	20	96696
1975	504793	15403	3709	402838	79.8	25	155986
1980	1015200	27014	3646	824268	81.2	30	197572
1985	1349556	30527	4902	1049818	77.8	35	146806
1990	*1588248*	*32097*	*5992*	*1235496*	*77.8*	40	96127
1995	*1776146*	*35688*	*7224*	*1381662*	*77.8*	45	61572
2000	*1950290*	*40418*	*8969*	*1517128*	*77.8*	50	36332
2005	*2114146*	*44120*	*11165*	*1661502*	*78.6*	55	22971
2010	*2285604*	*44302*	*13986*	*1837146*	*80.4*	60	11493
2015	*2442388*	*43826*	*17363*	*2003140*	*82.0*	65	8376
2020	*2578392*	*43219*	*20970*	*2153263*	*83.5*	70+	12041

POPULATION RATIOS

YEAR	AGE DISTRIBUTION UNDER 15	AGE DISTRIBUTION 15-64	AGE DISTRIBUTION 65 & OLDER	AGE DISTRIBUTION 70 & OLDER	DEPENDENCY RATIO	WOMEN 15-49	CHILD-WOMAN RATIO
1950	0.423	0.543	0.034	0.018	0.841	0.225	0.768
1955	0.430	0.536	0.034	0.018	0.865	0.223	0.787
1960	0.437	0.530	0.034	0.018	0.888	0.222	0.803
1965	0.381	0.594	0.026	0.014	0.685	0.192	0.803
1970	0.349	0.627	0.024	0.011	0.595	0.171	0.877
1975	0.282	0.698	0.020	0.013	0.433	0.145	0.834
1980	0.286	0.702	0.012	0.007	0.425	0.154	0.865
1985	0.310	0.675	0.015	0.009	0.481	0.145	0.858
1990	*0.311*	*0.673*	*0.017*	*0.010*	*0.487*	*0.152*	*0.702*
2000	*0.271*	*0.698*	*0.031*	*0.015*	*0.432*	*0.184*	*0.517*
2010	*0.270*	*0.665*	*0.065*	*0.031*	*0.504*	*0.195*	*0.507*
2020	*0.262*	*0.607*	*0.131*	*0.068*	*0.648*	*0.220*	*0.393*

MORTALITY MEASURES (Annual Averages)

PERIOD	CRUDE DEATH RATE	INFANT MORT. RATE	LIFE EXPECTANCY AT BIRTH (years) MALE	LIFE EXPECTANCY AT BIRTH (years) FEMALE	LIFE EXPECTANCY AT BIRTH (years) BOTH SEXES	DIFFERENCE FEMALE-MALE
1950-55	22.80	180.00	46.70	49.30	47.97	2.60
1955-60	20.70	160.00	49.60	52.50	51.01	2.90
1960-65	17.30	130.00	53.50	56.60	55.01	3.10
1965-70	12.30	85.00	57.30	60.80	59.01	3.50
1970-75	9.90	57.00	60.70	64.40	62.51	3.70
1975-80	7.35	38.00	64.70	68.90	66.80	4.20
1980-85	3.59	31.59	67.07	71.42	69.19	4.35
1985-90	*3.63*	*26.17*	*68.57*	*72.92*	*70.69*	*4.35*
1990-95	*3.77*	*22.33*	*69.77*	*74.12*	*71.89*	*4.35*
2000-05	*4.60*	*15.74*	*71.97*	*76.32*	*74.09*	*4.35*
2010-15	*6.12*	*10.80*	*73.77*	*78.32*	*75.99*	*4.55*
2020-25	*8.13*	*7.41*	*75.37*	*79.92*	*77.59*	*4.55*

FERTILITY MEASURES (Annual Averages)

PERIOD	CRUDE BIRTH RATE	FERTILITY RATES GENERAL	FERTILITY RATES TOTAL	REPRODUCTION RATES GROSS	REPRODUCTION RATES NET	RATE OF NATUR. INCR.
1950-55	47.80	213.26	6.970	3.400	2.130	25.00
1955-60	47.50	213.50	6.970	3.400	2.240	26.80
1960-65	43.60	214.13	6.867	3.350	2.330	26.30
1965-70	38.60	215.23	6.765	3.300	2.480	26.30
1970-75	33.00	216.04	6.355	3.100	2.500	23.10
1975-80	30.51	202.40	5.658	2.760	2.347	23.17
1980-85	26.61	179.07	5.227	2.550	2.418	23.02
1985-90	*22.62*	*152.25*	*4.817*	*2.350*	*2.254*	*18.99*
1990-95	*20.21*	*125.95*	*4.305*	*2.100*	*2.030*	*16.44*
2000-05	*20.72*	*110.62*	*3.485*	*1.700*	*1.664*	*16.13*
2010-15	*19.38*	*96.39*	*2.870*	*1.400*	*1.383*	*13.26*
2020-25	*16.76*	*73.92*	*2.460*	*1.200*	*1.192*	*8.63*

AGING MEASURES

YEAR	POPULATION AGE RATIOS 60+/20-59	POPULATION AGE RATIOS 65+/20-64	POPULATION AGE RATIOS 70+/20-69	POPULATION AGE RATIOS 75+/20-74	POPULATION MEAN AGE	POPULATION MEDIAN AGE
1950	0.1343	0.0773	0.0392	0.0163	23.63	18.89
1960	0.1337	0.0787	0.0410	0.0176	23.08	18.18
1970	0.0789	0.0446	0.0191	0.0108	24.26	22.68
1980	0.0313	0.0192	0.0112	0.0053	25.00	26.08
1990	*0.0528*	*0.0281*	*0.0164*	*0.0084*	*27.48*	*28.49*
2000	*0.1017*	*0.0505*	*0.0242*	*0.0100*	*30.54*	*29.12*
2010	*0.2278*	*0.1094*	*0.0495*	*0.0196*	*32.63*	*30.17*
2020	*0.4024*	*0.2488*	*0.1153*	*0.0458*	*34.20*	*31.56*

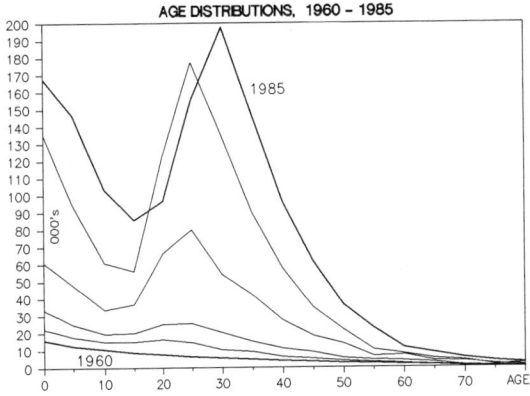

AGE DISTRIBUTIONS, 1960 - 1985

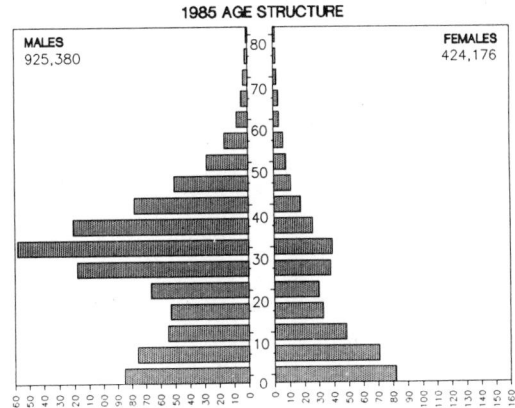

1985 AGE STRUCTURE

MALES 925,380   FEMALES 424,176

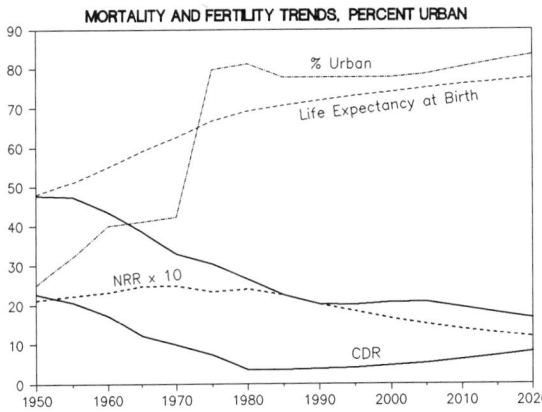

MORTALITY AND FERTILITY TRENDS, PERCENT URBAN

% Urban
Life Expectancy at Birth
NRR x 10
CDR

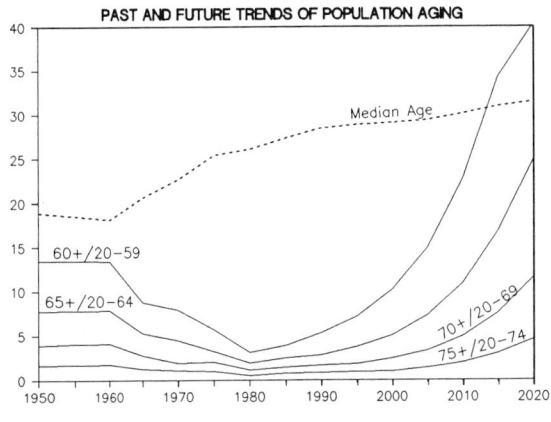

PAST AND FUTURE TRENDS OF POPULATION AGING

Median Age
60+/20-59
65+/20-64
70+/20-69
75+/20-74

OBSERVED AND *PROJECTED* POPULATION DATA (000's)

YEAR	MID-YEAR POPULATION	NO. OF BIRTHS	NO. OF DEATHS	URBAN POPULATION NUMBER	URBAN POPULATION PERCENT	POPULATION 1985 AGE	POPULATION 1985 NUMBER
1950	29954	1252	855	3507	11.7	0	9036
1955	32009	1343	819	4203	13.1	5	8162
1960	34743	1421	737	5107	14.7	10	7200
1965	38341	1468	638	6296	16.4	15	7038
1970	42729	1609	611	7820	18.3	20	5960
1975	48030	1839	547	9021	18.8	25	4808
1980	53700	1869	599	10350	19.3	30	3664
1985	60059	1915	572	12189	20.3	35	2441
1990	*67171*	*2038*	*553*	*14705*	*21.9*	40	2028
1995	*75030*	*2056*	*536*	*18109*	*24.1*	45	1946
2000	*83030*	*2013*	*529*	*22503*	*27.1*	50	2038
2005	*90798*	*1929*	*536*	*28017*	*30.9*	55	1633
2010	*98045*	*1820*	*554*	*34080*	*34.8*	60	1420
2015	*104586*	*1871*	*584*	*40526*	*38.7*	65	1043
2020	*111226*	*1945*	*635*	*47558*	*42.8*	70+	1643

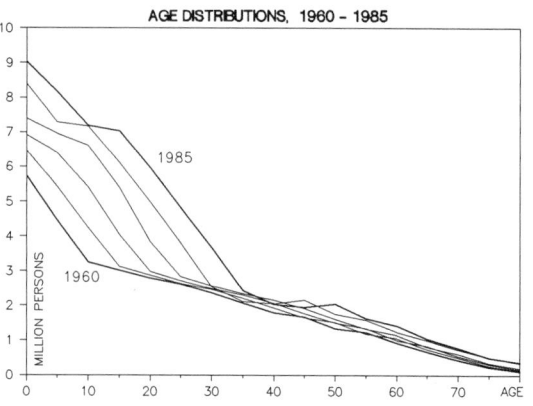

AGE DISTRIBUTIONS, 1960 - 1985

POPULATION RATIOS

YEAR	AGE DISTRIBUTION UNDER 15	AGE DISTRIBUTION 15-64	AGE DISTRIBUTION 65 & OLDER	AGE DISTRIBUTION 70 & OLDER	DEPENDENCY RATIO	WOMEN 15-49	CHILD-WOMAN RATIO
1950	0.343	0.618	0.039	0.021	0.617	0.257	0.496
1955	0.360	0.599	0.040	0.022	0.669	0.249	0.621
1960	0.387	0.571	0.042	0.022	0.751	0.241	0.683
1965	0.421	0.537	0.043	0.023	0.863	0.230	0.735
1970	0.438	0.519	0.043	0.024	0.928	0.226	0.715
1975	0.437	0.523	0.040	0.024	0.912	0.231	0.666
1980	0.426	0.527	0.048	0.029	0.898	0.233	0.672
1985	0.406	0.549	0.045	0.027	0.821	0.241	0.625
1990	*0.392*	*0.563*	*0.044*	*0.026*	*0.775*	*0.248*	*0.564*
2000	*0.356*	*0.600*	*0.045*	*0.026*	*0.668*	*0.268*	*0.463*
2010	*0.305*	*0.652*	*0.042*	*0.027*	*0.533*	*0.276*	*0.358*
2020	*0.253*	*0.694*	*0.052*	*0.029*	*0.440*	*0.276*	*0.308*

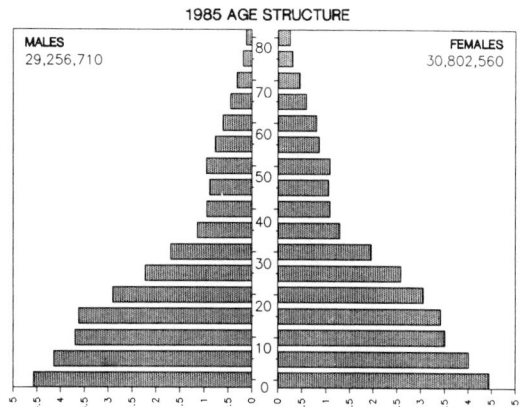

1985 AGE STRUCTURE

MALES 29,256,710   FEMALES 30,802,560

MORTALITY MEASURES (Annual Averages)

PERIOD	CRUDE DEATH RATE	INFANT MORT. RATE	LIFE EXPECTANCY AT BIRTH (years) MALE	LIFE EXPECTANCY AT BIRTH (years) FEMALE	LIFE EXPECTANCY AT BIRTH (years) BOTH SEXES	DIFFERENCE FEMALE-MALE
1950-55	28.53	180.14	39.10	41.80	40.42	2.70
1955-60	25.58	163.41	41.30	44.60	42.91	3.30
1960-65	21.22	147.65	43.50	47.40	45.40	3.90
1965-70	16.65	133.07	45.70	50.20	47.90	4.50
1970-75	14.29	119.61	47.70	53.10	50.33	5.40
1975-80	11.38	90.32	53.70	58.10	55.85	4.40
1980-85	11.15	75.75	56.70	61.10	58.85	4.40
1985-90	*9.52*	*64.29*	*59.20*	*63.60*	*61.35*	*4.40*
1990-95	*8.23*	*53.84*	*61.58*	*66.02*	*63.75*	*4.44*
2000-05	*6.37*	*36.47*	*65.66*	*70.26*	*67.90*	*4.60*
2010-15	*5.65*	*26.03*	*68.48*	*73.14*	*70.75*	*4.66*
2020-25	*5.71*	*18.75*	*70.76*	*75.46*	*73.05*	*4.70*

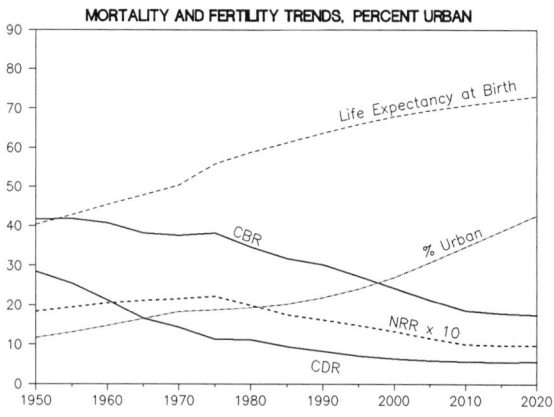

MORTALITY AND FERTILITY TRENDS, PERCENT URBAN

FERTILITY MEASURES (Annual Averages)

PERIOD	CRUDE BIRTH RATE	FERTILITY RATES GENERAL	FERTILITY RATES TOTAL	REPRODUCTION RATES GROSS	REPRODUCTION RATES NET	RATE OF NATUR. INCR.
1950-55	41.80	165.43	6.047	2.950	1.844	13.27
1955-60	41.97	171.45	6.047	2.950	1.950	16.39
1960-65	40.91	174.05	6.047	2.950	2.065	19.69
1965-70	38.30	168.10	5.945	2.900	2.117	21.65
1970-75	37.65	164.49	5.847	2.852	2.164	23.36
1975-80	38.29	165.12	5.588	2.726	2.225	26.91
1980-85	34.80	146.90	4.820	2.351	1.997	23.65
1985-90	*31.88*	*130.29*	*4.100*	*2.000*	*1.750*	*22.36*
1990-95	*30.34*	*119.76*	*3.700*	*1.805*	*1.625*	*22.11*
2000-05	*24.25*	*89.73*	*2.900*	*1.415*	*1.332*	*17.88*
2010-15	*18.57*	*67.06*	*2.150*	*1.049*	*1.010*	*12.91*
2020-25	*17.49*	*64.02*	*2.070*	*1.010*	*0.985*	*11.77*

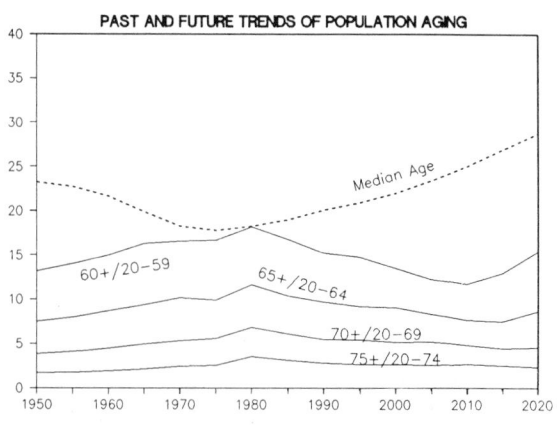

PAST AND FUTURE TRENDS OF POPULATION AGING

AGING MEASURES

YEAR	POPULATION AGE RATIOS 60+/20-59	POPULATION AGE RATIOS 65+/20-64	POPULATION AGE RATIOS 70+/20-69	POPULATION AGE RATIOS 75+/20-74	POPULATION MEAN AGE	POPULATION MEDIAN AGE
1950	0.1316	0.0751	0.0387	0.0168	26.73	23.24
1960	0.1498	0.0868	0.0446	0.0193	25.64	21.63
1970	0.1653	0.1014	0.0533	0.0242	24.19	18.27
1980	0.1813	0.1160	0.0680	0.0353	23.95	18.27
1990	*0.1520*	*0.0966*	*0.0547*	*0.0282*	*24.28*	*20.07*
2000	*0.1346*	*0.0903*	*0.0515*	*0.0266*	*25.53*	*22.02*
2010	*0.1172*	*0.0767*	*0.0484*	*0.0269*	*27.88*	*25.01*
2020	*0.1532*	*0.0866*	*0.0454*	*0.0239*	*30.88*	*28.72*

OBSERVED AND *PROJECTED* POPULATION DATA (000's)

YEAR	MID-YEAR POPULATION	NO. OF BIRTHS	NO. OF DEATHS	URBAN POPULATION NUMBER	URBAN POPULATION PERCENT	POPULATION 1985 AGE	POPULATION 1985 NUMBER
1950	3324	168	106	63	1.9	0	1315
1955	3646	183	108	93	2.5	5	1097
1960	4039	199	113	137	3.4	10	895
1965	4492	219	119	228	5.1	15	727
1970	4835	235	127	364	7.5	20	608
1975	5282	268	107	581	11.0	25	362
1980	5995	291	107	915	15.3	30	299
1985	6888	330	108	1381	20.0	35	296
1990	*8017*	*377*	*111*	*2001*	*25.0*	40	271
1995	*9425*	*432*	*113*	*2786*	*29.6*	45	251
2000	*11145*	*489*	*114*	*3725*	*33.4*	50	223
2005	*13190*	*546*	*114*	*4931*	*37.4*	55	178
2010	*15540*	*584*	*111*	*6433*	*41.4*	60	141
2015	*18100*	*596*	*107*	*8214*	*45.4*	65	102
2020	*20720*	*597*	*104*	*10212*	*49.3*	70+	121

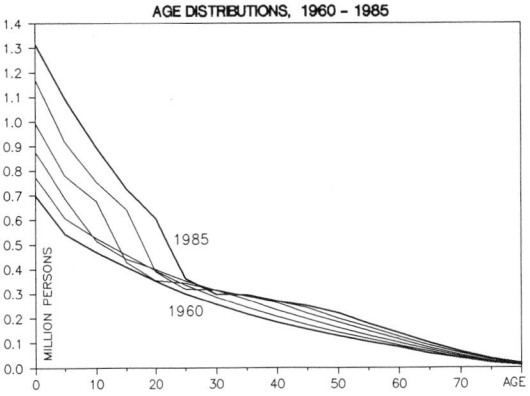

AGE DISTRIBUTIONS, 1960 - 1985

POPULATION RATIOS

YEAR	AGE DISTRIBUTION UNDER 15	AGE DISTRIBUTION 15-64	AGE DISTRIBUTION 65 & OLDER	AGE DISTRIBUTION 70 & OLDER	DEPENDENCY RATIO	WOMEN 15-49	CHILD-WOMAN RATIO
1950	0.418	0.542	0.040	0.022	0.845	0.225	0.766
1955	0.422	0.543	0.035	0.019	0.842	0.227	0.760
1960	0.424	0.544	0.032	0.017	0.838	0.228	0.758
1965	0.425	0.545	0.030	0.016	0.836	0.229	0.752
1970	0.430	0.539	0.031	0.016	0.857	0.238	0.761
1975	0.464	0.504	0.032	0.017	0.985	0.236	0.797
1980	0.474	0.493	0.032	0.017	1.028	0.233	0.836
1985	0.480	0.487	0.032	0.018	1.052	0.229	0.833
1990	*0.481*	*0.487*	*0.032*	*0.018*	*1.054*	*0.227*	*0.844*
2000	*0.476*	*0.494*	*0.030*	*0.017*	*1.025*	*0.226*	*0.838*
2010	*0.461*	*0.512*	*0.027*	*0.016*	*0.955*	*0.232*	*0.763*
2020	*0.418*	*0.558*	*0.024*	*0.015*	*0.793*	*0.245*	*0.598*

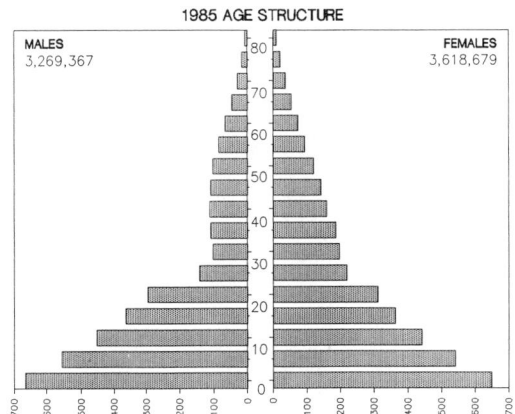

1985 AGE STRUCTURE

MALES 3,269,367   FEMALES 3,618,679

MORTALITY MEASURES (Annual Averages)

PERIOD	CRUDE DEATH RATE	INFANT MORT. RATE	LIFE EXPECTANCY AT BIRTH (years) MALE	LIFE EXPECTANCY AT BIRTH (years) FEMALE	LIFE EXPECTANCY AT BIRTH (years) BOTH SEXES	DIFFERENCE FEMALE-MALE
1950-55	32.00	231.00	32.89	33.89	33.38	1.00
1955-60	29.60	220.00	35.32	36.47	35.88	1.15
1960-65	28.10	207.00	37.70	39.09	38.38	1.39
1965-70	26.60	186.00	40.03	41.77	40.88	1.74
1970-75	26.30	168.00	42.48	44.33	43.38	1.85
1975-80	20.19	144.34	44.73	47.08	45.88	2.35
1980-85	17.83	129.94	46.94	49.89	48.38	2.95
1985-90	*15.73*	*115.67*	*49.50*	*52.40*	*50.92*	*2.90*
1990-95	*13.81*	*102.35*	*52.00*	*54.90*	*53.42*	*2.90*
2000-05	*10.26*	*77.48*	*57.00*	*59.90*	*58.42*	*2.90*
2010-15	*7.17*	*54.97*	*62.00*	*64.90*	*63.42*	*2.90*
2020-25	*5.03*	*36.01*	*66.30*	*69.70*	*67.96*	*3.40*

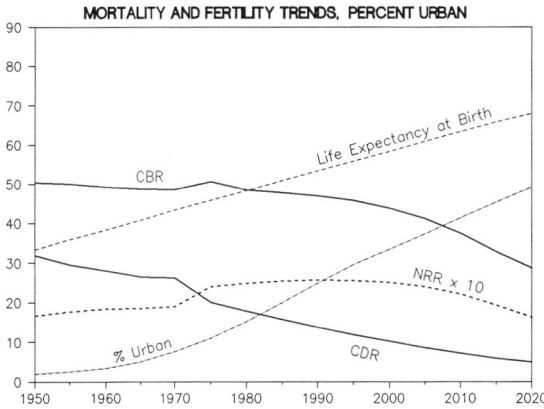

MORTALITY AND FERTILITY TRENDS, PERCENT URBAN

FERTILITY MEASURES (Annual Averages)

PERIOD	CRUDE BIRTH RATE	FERTILITY RATES GENERAL	FERTILITY RATES TOTAL	REPRODUCTION RATES GROSS	REPRODUCTION RATES NET	RATE OF NATUR. INCR.
1950-55	50.50	223.41	6.970	3.400	1.680	18.50
1955-60	50.10	220.23	6.970	3.400	1.780	20.50
1960-65	49.30	215.78	6.970	3.400	1.850	21.20
1965-70	48.80	208.80	6.970	3.400	1.860	22.20
1970-75	48.70	205.51	6.970	3.400	1.910	22.40
1975-80	50.65	215.99	7.175	3.500	2.406	30.46
1980-85	48.60	210.22	7.072	3.450	2.489	30.76
1985-90	*47.87*	*209.96*	*6.970*	*3.400*	*2.556*	*32.13*
1990-95	*47.00*	*207.13*	*6.765*	*3.300*	*2.578*	*33.19*
2000-05	*43.87*	*193.33*	*6.150*	*3.000*	*2.512*	*33.61*
2010-15	*37.61*	*160.48*	*5.125*	*2.500*	*2.224*	*30.44*
2020-25	*28.79*	*114.86*	*3.587*	*1.750*	*1.639*	*23.76*

AGING MEASURES

YEAR	POPULATION AGE RATIOS 60+/20-59	POPULATION AGE RATIOS 65+/20-64	POPULATION AGE RATIOS 70+/20-69	POPULATION AGE RATIOS 75+/20-74	POPULATION MEAN AGE	POPULATION MEDIAN AGE
1950	0.1494	0.0903	0.0482	0.0209	23.95	19.12
1960	0.1244	0.0722	0.0382	0.0167	23.33	18.75
1970	0.1224	0.0699	0.0355	0.0148	23.39	18.84
1980	0.1464	0.0841	0.0433	0.0187	22.32	16.20
1990	*0.1431*	*0.0845*	*0.0448*	*0.0202*	*21.38*	*15.86*
2000	*0.1287*	*0.0788*	*0.0426*	*0.0198*	*20.92*	*16.11*
2010	*0.1055*	*0.0680*	*0.0396*	*0.0193*	*21.20*	*16.77*
2020	*0.0840*	*0.0542*	*0.0334*	*0.0173*	*22.63*	*18.61*

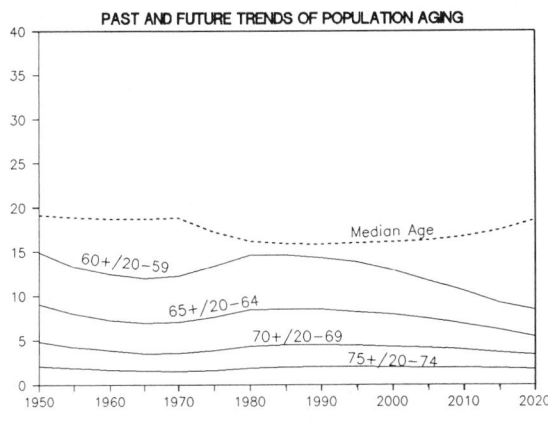

PAST AND FUTURE TRENDS OF POPULATION AGING

OBSERVED AND *PROJECTED* POPULATION DATA

YEAR	MID-YEAR POPULATION	NO. OF BIRTHS	NO. OF DEATHS	URBAN POPULATION NUMBER	PERCENT	POPULATION 1985 AGE	NUMBER
1950	992000	50096	31744	186509	18.8	0	384417
1955	1088000	54944	32205	251135	23.1	5	297543
1960	1208000	60762	33703	338248	28.0	10	281411
1965	1351000	66199	34180	405673	30.0	15	237730
1970	1497000	72155	34581	481074	32.1	20	202656
1975	1654000	78750	34643	567644	34.3	25	139348
1980	1861288	87447	32409	687097	36.9	30	110956
1985	2136842	100976	33773	852764	39.9	35	103222
1990	*2490983*	*115397*	*35031*	*1077597*	*43.3*	40	86958
1995	*2928083*	*128230*	*35854*	*1373546*	*46.9*	45	78421
2000	*3429508*	*138748*	*35917*	*1741148*	*50.8*	50	64088
2005	*3985315*	*146851*	*35557*	*2171414*	*54.5*	55	51185
2010	*4583560*	*148778*	*34588*	*2659564*	*58.0*	60	39299
2015	*5192437*	*148566*	*33533*	*3186257*	*61.4*	65	27875
2020	*5801329*	*147157*	*32754*	*3741349*	*64.5*	70+	31733

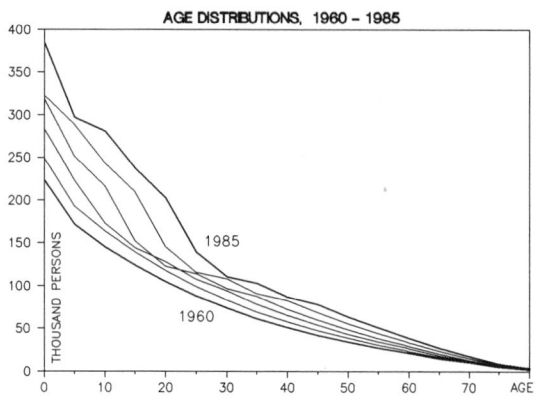

AGE DISTRIBUTIONS, 1960 - 1985

POPULATION RATIOS

YEAR	AGE DISTRIBUTION UNDER 15	15-64	65 & OLDER	70 & OLDER	DEPENDENCY RATIO	WOMEN 15-49	CHILD-WOMAN RATIO
1950	0.439	0.523	0.038	0.021	0.912	0.220	0.836
1955	0.444	0.523	0.033	0.018	0.913	0.222	0.832
1960	0.448	0.524	0.029	0.016	0.910	0.224	0.828
1965	0.448	0.525	0.027	0.014	0.906	0.225	0.820
1970	0.454	0.519	0.026	0.014	0.926	0.226	0.836
1975	0.475	0.498	0.027	0.014	1.007	0.221	0.870
1980	0.459	0.513	0.027	0.014	0.948	0.228	0.759
1985	0.451	0.521	0.028	0.015	0.918	0.232	0.777
1990	*0.447*	*0.525*	*0.028*	*0.015*	*0.905*	*0.232*	*0.796*
2000	*0.456*	*0.514*	*0.029*	*0.016*	*0.944*	*0.225*	*0.796*
2010	*0.428*	*0.541*	*0.030*	*0.018*	*0.848*	*0.237*	*0.664*
2020	*0.374*	*0.594*	*0.032*	*0.019*	*0.683*	*0.254*	*0.504*

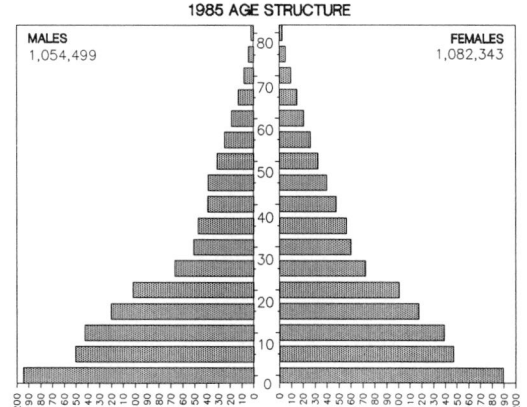

1985 AGE STRUCTURE

MALES 1,054,499   FEMALES 1,082,343

MORTALITY MEASURES (Annual Averages)

PERIOD	CRUDE DEATH RATE	INFANT MORT. RATE	LIFE EXPECTANCY AT BIRTH (years) MALE	FEMALE	BOTH SEXES	DIFFERENCE FEMALE-MALE
1950-55	32.00	231.00	32.89	33.89	33.38	1.00
1955-60	29.60	220.00	35.32	36.47	35.88	1.15
1960-65	27.90	207.00	37.70	39.09	38.38	1.39
1965-70	25.30	186.00	40.03	41.77	40.88	1.74
1970-75	23.10	168.00	42.48	44.33	43.38	1.85
1975-80	20.94	150.00	44.73	47.08	45.88	2.35
1980-85	17.41	134.94	46.94	49.88	48.38	2.94
1985-90	*15.81*	*120.41*	*49.40*	*52.37*	*50.85*	*2.97*
1990-95	*14.06*	*106.53*	*51.90*	*54.90*	*53.36*	*2.99*
2000-05	*10.47*	*80.64*	*56.92*	*59.95*	*58.40*	*3.02*
2010-15	*7.55*	*57.21*	*61.94*	*64.85*	*63.36*	*2.92*
2020-25	*5.65*	*36.83*	*66.55*	*69.74*	*68.10*	*3.19*

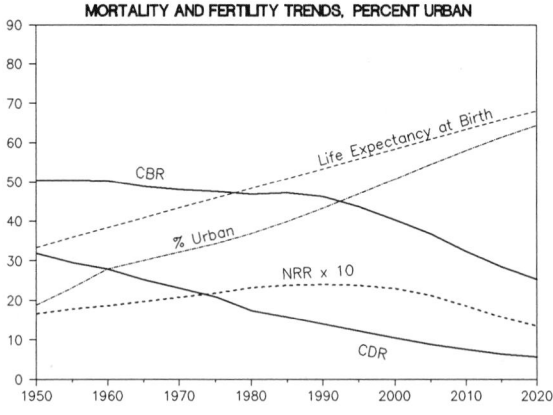

MORTALITY AND FERTILITY TRENDS, PERCENT URBAN

FERTILITY MEASURES (Annual Averages)

PERIOD	CRUDE BIRTH RATE	FERTILITY RATES GENERAL	TOTAL	REPRODUCTION RATES GROSS	NET	RATE OF NATUR. INCR.
1950-55	50.50	228.30	6.970	3.400	1.680	18.50
1955-60	50.50	226.55	6.970	3.400	1.790	20.90
1960-65	50.30	224.48	6.970	3.400	1.870	22.40
1965-70	49.00	217.27	6.970	3.400	1.970	23.70
1970-75	48.20	215.58	6.970	3.400	2.080	25.10
1975-80	47.61	211.65	6.970	3.400	2.195	26.67
1980-85	46.98	204.17	6.765	3.300	2.324	29.57
1985-90	*47.26*	*203.70*	*6.662*	*3.250*	*2.389*	*31.45*
1990-95	*46.33*	*202.20*	*6.478*	*3.160*	*2.419*	*32.26*
2000-05	*40.46*	*178.07*	*5.719*	*2.790*	*2.299*	*29.98*
2010-15	*32.46*	*134.64*	*4.346*	*2.120*	*1.861*	*24.91*
2020-25	*25.37*	*98.20*	*2.993*	*1.460*	*1.356*	*19.72*

AGING MEASURES

YEAR	POPULATION AGE RATIOS 60+/20-59	65+/20-64	70+/20-69	75+/20-74	POPULATION MEAN AGE	MEDIAN AGE
1950	0.1488	0.0893	0.0475	0.0206	23.03	18.01
1960	0.1164	0.0685	0.0367	0.0157	22.25	17.55
1970	0.1090	0.0626	0.0322	0.0139	22.08	17.36
1980	0.1187	0.0681	0.0350	0.0150	22.07	16.81
1990	*0.1181*	*0.0686*	*0.0355*	*0.0155*	*21.98*	*17.41*
2000	*0.1208*	*0.0712*	*0.0377*	*0.0168*	*21.95*	*17.14*
2010	*0.1154*	*0.0707*	*0.0395*	*0.0181*	*22.75*	*18.23*
2020	*0.1077*	*0.0661*	*0.0385*	*0.0185*	*24.62*	*20.74*

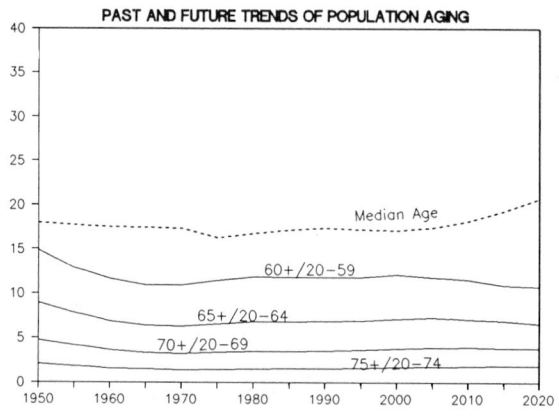

PAST AND FUTURE TRENDS OF POPULATION AGING

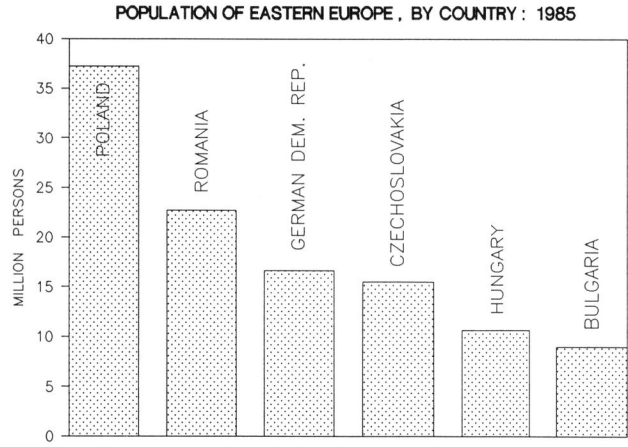

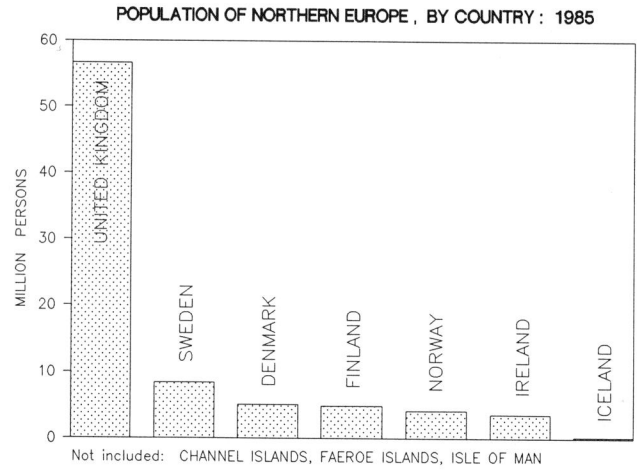

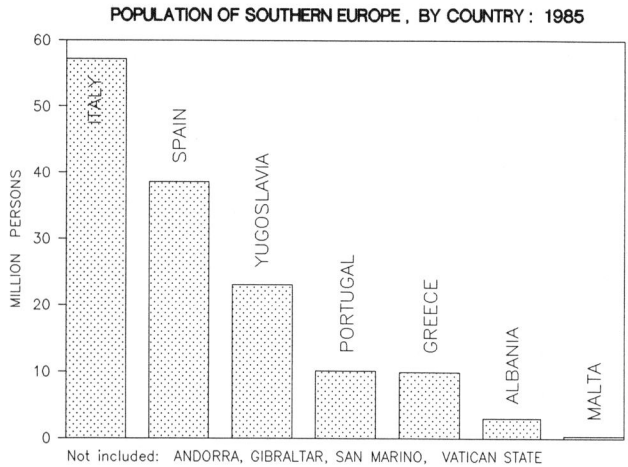

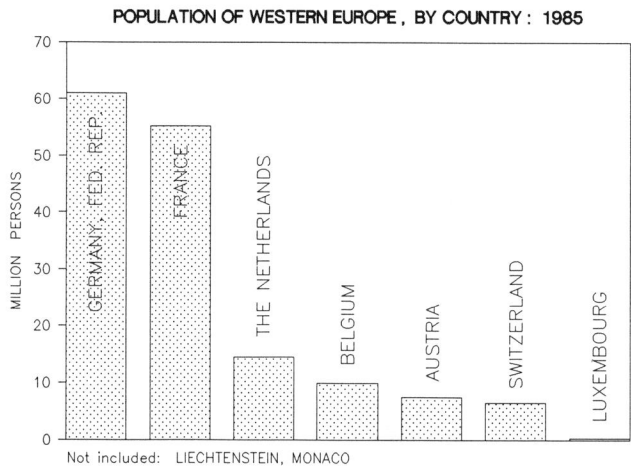

OBSERVED AND *PROJECTED* POPULATION DATA (000's)

YEAR	MID-YEAR POPULATION	NO. OF BIRTHS	NO. OF DEATHS	URBAN POPULATION NUMBER	URBAN POPULATION PERCENT	POPULATION 1985 AGE	POPULATION 1985 NUMBER
1950	392523	7782	4321	221113	56.3	0	32356
1955	408332	7846	4267	238945	58.5	5	33763
1960	425070	7945	4355	258919	60.9	10	36161
1965	444889	7886	4606	284047	63.8	15	39004
1970	460132	7245	4782	306666	66.6	20	39083
1975	473717	6817	4920	325976	68.8	25	37462
1980	484437	6509	5080	340447	70.3	30	36039
1985	492177	6390	5279	352841	71.7	35	34109
1990	*497741*	*6346*	*5268*	*363990*	*73.1*	40	30104
1995	*503156*	*6252*	*5174*	*375371*	*74.6*	45	29886
2000	*508569*	*6074*	*5394*	*386631*	*76.0*	50	28709
2005	*511966*	*5878*	*5542*	*396490*	*77.4*	55	27648
2010	*513637*	*5776*	*5655*	*404793*	*78.8*	60	25448
2015	*514232*	*5699*	*5781*	*411835*	*80.1*	65	16918
2020	*513811*	*5626*	*5927*	*417376*	*81.2*	70+	45486

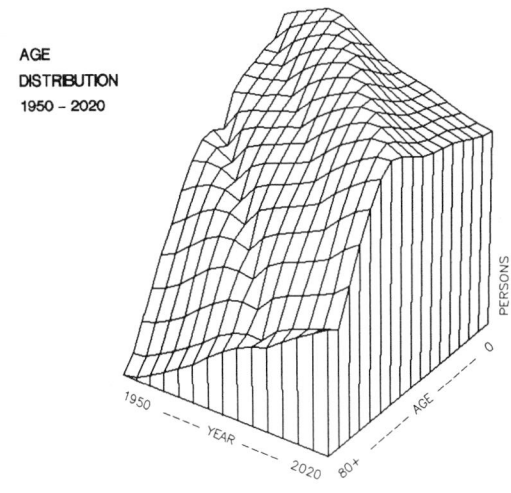

AGE DISTRIBUTION 1950 - 2020

POPULATION RATIOS

YEAR	AGE DISTRIBUTION UNDER 15	AGE DISTRIBUTION 15-64	AGE DISTRIBUTION 65 & OLDER	AGE DISTRIBUTION 70 & OLDER	DEPENDENCY RATIO	WOMEN 15-49	CHILD-WOMAN RATIO
1950	0.254	0.659	0.087	0.053	0.517	0.263	0.349
1955	0.253	0.655	0.092	0.057	0.528	0.255	0.354
1960	0.258	0.645	0.097	0.061	0.550	0.243	0.365
1965	0.254	0.642	0.104	0.064	0.557	0.238	0.367
1970	0.250	0.636	0.114	0.070	0.572	0.241	0.345
1975	0.239	0.638	0.123	0.078	0.568	0.241	0.315
1980	0.224	0.646	0.131	0.088	0.549	0.243	0.290
1985	0.208	0.665	0.127	0.092	0.503	0.247	0.267
1990	*0.196*	*0.670*	*0.134*	*0.087*	*0.493*	*0.248*	*0.257*
2000	*0.185*	*0.665*	*0.149*	*0.102*	*0.503*	*0.243*	*0.252*
2010	*0.176*	*0.662*	*0.161*	*0.113*	*0.509*	*0.229*	*0.248*
2020	*0.168*	*0.646*	*0.186*	*0.128*	*0.548*	*0.213*	*0.258*

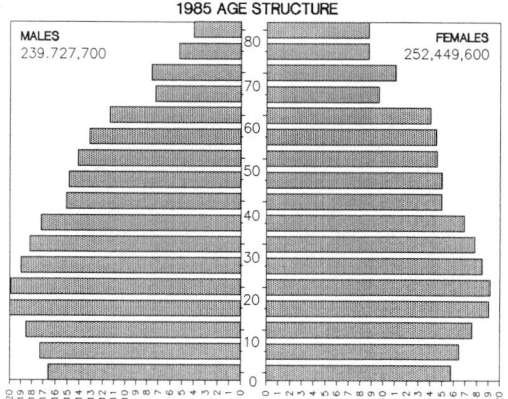

1985 AGE STRUCTURE

MALES 239,727,700   FEMALES 252,449,600

MORTALITY MEASURES (Annual Averages)

PERIOD	CRUDE DEATH RATE	INFANT MORT. RATE	LIFE EXPECTANCY AT BIRTH (years) MALE	LIFE EXPECTANCY AT BIRTH (years) FEMALE	LIFE EXPECTANCY AT BIRTH (years) BOTH SEXES	DIFFERENCE FEMALE-MALE
1950-55	11.01	62.45	63.18	67.56	65.30	4.38
1955-60	10.45	48.60	65.62	70.43	67.96	4.81
1960-65	10.24	36.96	67.12	72.39	69.68	5.27
1965-70	10.35	29.92	67.77	73.54	70.57	5.77
1970-75	10.39	24.22	68.38	74.47	71.34	6.09
1975-80	10.39	18.82	69.17	75.69	72.35	6.52
1980-85	10.49	14.60	69.95	76.68	73.22	6.72
1985-90	*10.73*	*12.72*	*70.95*	*77.57*	*74.16*	*6.62*
1990-95	*10.58*	*10.91*	*71.93*	*78.39*	*75.07*	*6.46*
2000-05	*10.61*	*8.36*	*73.59*	*79.79*	*76.60*	*6.20*
2010-15	*11.01*	*6.72*	*74.98*	*81.04*	*77.93*	*6.06*
2020-25	*11.54*	*5.76*	*76.17*	*82.10*	*79.05*	*5.93*

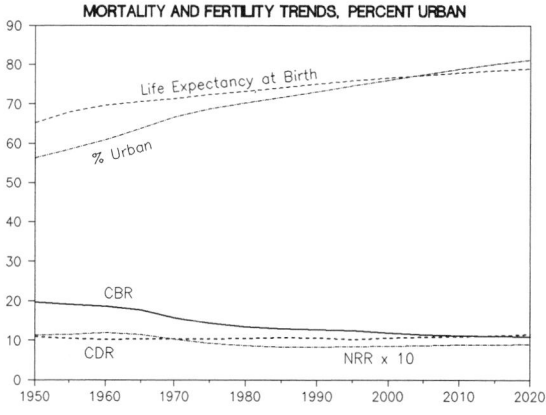

MORTALITY AND FERTILITY TRENDS, PERCENT URBAN

Life Expectancy at Birth

% Urban

CBR

CDR

NRR x 10

FERTILITY MEASURES (Annual Averages)

PERIOD	CRUDE BIRTH RATE	FERTILITY RATES GENERAL	FERTILITY RATES TOTAL	REPRODUCTION RATES GROSS	REPRODUCTION RATES NET	RATE OF NATUR. INCR.
1950-55	19.83	76.59	2.592	1.259	1.134	8.81
1955-60	19.21	77.22	2.591	1.259	1.148	8.76
1960-65	18.69	77.67	2.630	1.278	1.191	8.45
1965-70	17.73	73.90	2.503	1.216	1.148	7.37
1970-75	15.74	65.29	2.195	1.066	1.021	5.35
1975-80	14.39	59.51	1.978	0.961	0.926	4.00
1980-85	13.44	54.91	1.807	0.878	0.859	2.95
1985-90	*12.98*	*52.48*	*1.738*	*0.845*	*0.828*	*2.26*
1990-95	*12.75*	*51.41*	*1.724*	*0.838*	*0.824*	*2.17*
2000-05	*11.94*	*49.88*	*1.780*	*0.865*	*0.855*	*1.34*
2010-15	*11.24*	*49.87*	*1.844*	*0.896*	*0.887*	*0.24*
2020-25	*10.95*	*52.00*	*1.856*	*0.902*	*0.894*	*-0.59*

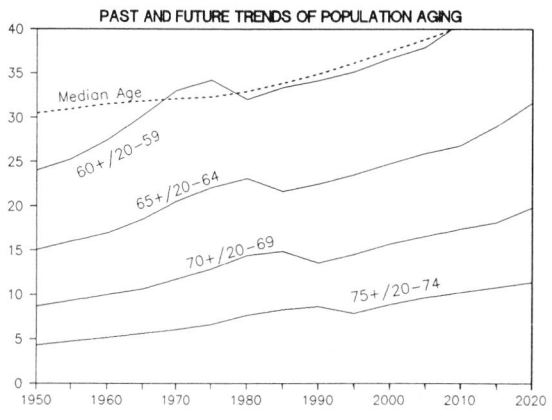

PAST AND FUTURE TRENDS OF POPULATION AGING

Median Age

60+/20-59

65+/20-64

70+/20-69

75+/20-74

AGING MEASURES

YEAR	POPULATION AGE RATIOS 60+/20-59	POPULATION AGE RATIOS 65+/20-64	POPULATION AGE RATIOS 70+/20-69	POPULATION AGE RATIOS 75+/20-74	POPULATION MEAN AGE	POPULATION MEDIAN AGE
1950	0.2404	0.1505	0.0870	0.0429	32.93	30.51
1960	0.2746	0.1696	0.0999	0.0516	33.71	31.59
1970	0.3306	0.2050	0.1170	0.0604	34.39	32.15
1980	0.3206	0.2310	0.1440	0.0766	35.56	32.97
1990	*0.3421*	*0.2245*	*0.1358*	*0.0864*	*36.98*	*35.00*
2000	*0.3669*	*0.2476*	*0.1569*	*0.0885*	*38.47*	*37.55*
2010	*0.4065*	*0.2682*	*0.1738*	*0.1019*	*40.02*	*40.27*
2020	*0.4816*	*0.3167*	*0.1976*	*0.1132*	*41.47*	*42.22*

OBSERVED AND *PROJECTED* POPULATION DATA (000's)

YEAR	MID-YEAR POPULATION	NO. OF BIRTHS	NO. OF DEATHS	URBAN POPULATION NUMBER	URBAN POPULATION PERCENT	POPULATION 1985 AGE	POPULATION 1985 NUMBER
1950	88500	2090	998	37076	41.9	0	8728
1955	93128	1995	930	41688	44.8	5	9172
1960	96713	1695	906	46347	47.9	10	8390
1965	100055	1680	981	50680	50.7	15	8124
1970	103128	1733	1059	55179	53.5	20	7902
1975	106182	1865	1143	60260	56.8	25	8919
1980	109397	1760	1223	64912	59.3	30	9139
1985	111681	1632	1257	68831	61.6	35	7689
1990	*113573*	*1559*	*1232*	*72425*	*63.8*	40	6389
1995	*115219*	*1567*	*1191*	*75806*	*65.8*	45	6786
2000	*117112*	*1595*	*1243*	*79148*	*67.6*	50	6646
2005	*118890*	*1579*	*1275*	*82359*	*69.3*	55	6319
2010	*120417*	*1532*	*1290*	*85180*	*70.7*	60	5527
2015	*121634*	*1490*	*1307*	*87675*	*72.1*	65	3127
2020	*122554*	*1476*	*1329*	*89710*	*73.2*	70+	8827

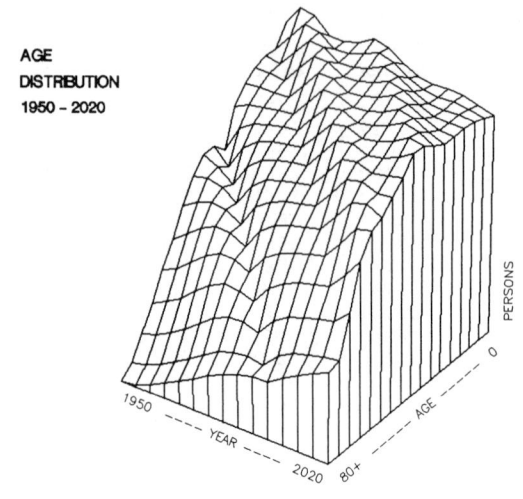

AGE DISTRIBUTION 1950 – 2020

POPULATION RATIOS

YEAR	AGE DISTRIBUTION UNDER 15	AGE DISTRIBUTION 15-64	AGE DISTRIBUTION 65 & OLDER	AGE DISTRIBUTION 70 & OLDER	DEPENDENCY RATIO	WOMEN 15-49	CHILD-WOMAN RATIO
1950	0.267	0.663	0.070	0.042	0.509	0.274	0.351
1955	0.270	0.652	0.078	0.046	0.534	0.261	0.401
1960	0.280	0.638	0.082	0.050	0.567	0.245	0.392
1965	0.268	0.640	0.093	0.054	0.563	0.241	0.336
1970	0.247	0.650	0.104	0.061	0.540	0.254	0.315
1975	0.233	0.653	0.114	0.069	0.531	0.254	0.317
1980	0.236	0.645	0.118	0.079	0.550	0.247	0.342
1985	0.235	0.658	0.107	0.079	0.521	0.244	0.321
1990	*0.228*	*0.659*	*0.113*	*0.069*	*0.517*	*0.244*	*0.291*
2000	*0.201*	*0.669*	*0.129*	*0.084*	*0.494*	*0.250*	*0.266*
2010	*0.196*	*0.669*	*0.135*	*0.093*	*0.495*	*0.233*	*0.280*
2020	*0.187*	*0.652*	*0.161*	*0.102*	*0.534*	*0.228*	*0.265*

MORTALITY MEASURES (Annual Averages)

PERIOD	CRUDE DEATH RATE	INFANT MORT. RATE	LIFE EXPECTANCY AT BIRTH (years) MALE	LIFE EXPECTANCY AT BIRTH (years) FEMALE	LIFE EXPECTANCY AT BIRTH (years) BOTH SEXES	DIFFERENCE FEMALE-MALE
1950-55	11.28	83.13	60.91	65.46	63.12	4.55
1955-60	9.99	62.39	64.28	68.89	66.51	4.61
1960-65	9.36	43.81	66.50	71.28	68.82	4.78
1965-70	9.80	35.76	67.11	72.46	69.71	5.35
1970-75	10.27	28.44	67.21	73.22	70.13	6.01
1975-80	10.76	23.44	67.38	73.94	70.57	6.56
1980-85	11.18	19.29	67.29	74.29	70.69	7.00
1985-90	*11.25*	*17.39*	*67.93*	*74.82*	*71.28*	*6.88*
1990-95	*10.85*	*15.52*	*68.85*	*75.69*	*72.17*	*6.84*
2000-05	*10.61*	*11.31*	*71.05*	*77.64*	*74.25*	*6.59*
2010-15	*10.71*	*8.35*	*72.93*	*79.29*	*76.02*	*6.35*
2020-25	*10.85*	*6.57*	*74.49*	*80.58*	*77.45*	*6.10*

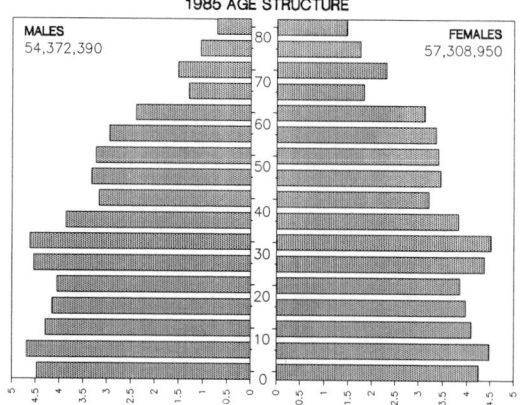

1985 AGE STRUCTURE

MALES 54,372,390

FEMALES 57,308,950

FERTILITY MEASURES (Annual Averages)

PERIOD	CRUDE BIRTH RATE	FERTILITY RATES GENERAL	FERTILITY RATES TOTAL	REPRODUCTION RATES GROSS	REPRODUCTION RATES NET	RATE OF NATUR. INCR.
1950-55	23.62	88.44	2.946	1.432	1.183	12.34
1955-60	21.42	84.77	2.674	1.300	1.110	11.43
1960-65	17.52	72.10	2.328	1.132	0.994	8.15
1965-70	16.79	67.76	2.366	1.150	1.055	6.99
1970-75	16.80	66.20	2.232	1.085	1.034	6.53
1975-80	17.57	70.27	2.248	1.093	1.053	6.80
1980-85	16.09	65.65	2.125	1.033	1.002	4.91
1985-90	*14.61*	*59.94*	*2.022*	*0.983*	*0.958*	*3.36*
1990-95	*13.73*	*55.49*	*1.939*	*0.943*	*0.923*	*2.88*
2000-05	*13.62*	*55.45*	*1.909*	*0.928*	*0.916*	*3.01*
2010-15	*12.73*	*54.81*	*1.932*	*0.939*	*0.932*	*2.01*
2020-25	*12.05*	*53.11*	*1.935*	*0.941*	*0.935*	*1.20*

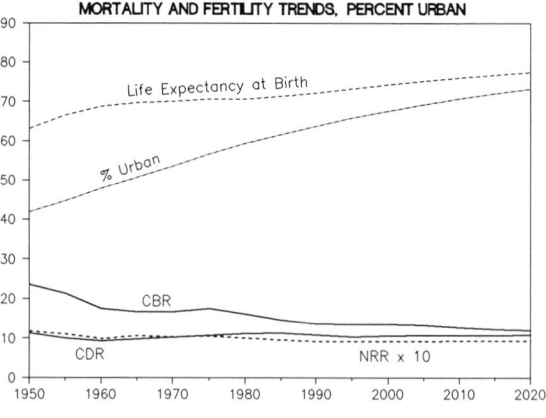

MORTALITY AND FERTILITY TRENDS, PERCENT URBAN

Life Expectancy at Birth

% Urban

CBR

CDR

NRR x 10

AGING MEASURES

YEAR	POPULATION AGE RATIOS 60+/20-59	POPULATION AGE RATIOS 65+/20-64	POPULATION AGE RATIOS 70+/20-69	POPULATION AGE RATIOS 75+/20-74	POPULATION MEAN AGE	POPULATION MEDIAN AGE
1950	0.2033	0.1223	0.0692	0.0328	31.61	28.69
1960	0.2444	0.1455	0.0828	0.0407	32.28	29.82
1970	0.3079	0.1858	0.1023	0.0500	33.72	31.36
1980	0.2791	0.2068	0.1283	0.0650	34.46	31.66
1990	*0.3075*	*0.1923*	*0.1099*	*0.0708*	*35.29*	*33.68*
2000	*0.3294*	*0.2173*	*0.1312*	*0.0679*	*36.70*	*35.55*
2010	*0.3447*	*0.2232*	*0.1445*	*0.0807*	*37.93*	*36.92*
2020	*0.4283*	*0.2743*	*0.1573*	*0.0851*	*39.24*	*39.05*

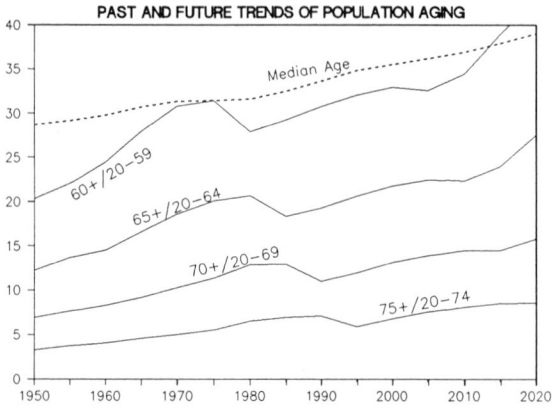

PAST AND FUTURE TRENDS OF POPULATION AGING

Median Age

60+/20-59

65+/20-64

70+/20-69

75+/20-74

OBSERVED AND *PROJECTED* POPULATION DATA (000's)

YEAR	MID-YEAR POPULATION	NO. OF BIRTHS	NO. OF DEATHS	URBAN POPULATION NUMBER	URBAN POPULATION PERCENT	POPULATION 1985 AGE	POPULATION 1985 NUMBER
1950	72477	1213	803	53852	74.3	0	5285
1955	73832	1235	814	55664	75.4	5	5178
1960	75647	1354	848	58016	76.7	10	5820
1965	78396	1357	877	62354	79.5	15	6566
1970	80457	1187	903	66276	82.4	20	6754
1975	81850	1046	930	68703	83.9	25	6030
1980	82494	1066	926	70245	85.2	30	5712
1985	83180	1094	962	71744	86.3	35	6219
1990	*83794*	*1091*	*950*	*73108*	*87.2*	40	5174
1995	*84442*	*1052*	*931*	*74447*	*88.2*	45	4602
2000	*84995*	*1000*	*926*	*75626*	*89.0*	50	4367
2005	*85312*	*971*	*918*	*76563*	*89.7*	55	4437
2010	*85523*	*978*	*918*	*77361*	*90.5*	60	4531
2015	*85769*	*978*	*941*	*78156*	*91.1*	65	3768
2020	*85899*	*963*	*982*	*78792*	*91.7*	70+	8737

POPULATION RATIOS

YEAR	AGE DISTRIBUTION UNDER 15	AGE DISTRIBUTION 15-64	AGE DISTRIBUTION 65 & OLDER	AGE DISTRIBUTION 70 & OLDER	DEPENDENCY RATIO	WOMEN 15-49	CHILD-WOMAN RATIO
1950	0.235	0.662	0.103	0.064	0.510	0.252	0.358
1955	0.241	0.651	0.108	0.068	0.536	0.242	0.327
1960	0.241	0.646	0.113	0.072	0.549	0.234	0.343
1965	0.237	0.646	0.118	0.074	0.548	0.231	0.373
1970	0.242	0.632	0.127	0.080	0.583	0.226	0.358
1975	0.233	0.630	0.137	0.088	0.587	0.225	0.319
1980	0.212	0.640	0.148	0.099	0.562	0.233	0.268
1985	0.196	0.654	0.150	0.105	0.529	0.243	0.261
1990	*0.190*	*0.655*	*0.155*	*0.106*	*0.526*	*0.247*	*0.263*
2000	*0.190*	*0.657*	*0.153*	*0.110*	*0.522*	*0.236*	*0.262*
2010	*0.177*	*0.662*	*0.161*	*0.111*	*0.511*	*0.229*	*0.247*
2020	*0.170*	*0.639*	*0.191*	*0.134*	*0.564*	*0.211*	*0.270*

MORTALITY MEASURES (Annual Averages)

PERIOD	CRUDE DEATH RATE	INFANT MORT. RATE	LIFE EXPECTANCY AT BIRTH (years) MALE	LIFE EXPECTANCY AT BIRTH (years) FEMALE	LIFE EXPECTANCY AT BIRTH (years) BOTH SEXES	DIFFERENCE FEMALE-MALE
1950-55	11.09	28.43	67.13	71.76	69.38	4.64
1955-60	11.02	23.54	68.11	73.28	70.62	5.18
1960-65	11.21	20.87	68.37	73.94	71.08	5.57
1965-70	11.19	17.94	68.78	74.80	71.70	6.01
1970-75	11.22	15.80	69.42	75.54	72.39	6.12
1975-80	11.36	12.43	70.06	76.38	73.13	6.31
1980-85	11.23	9.61	71.26	77.49	74.29	6.23
1985-90	*11.56*	*8.44*	*72.47*	*78.36*	*75.34*	*5.89*
1990-95	*11.34*	*7.41*	*73.35*	*79.14*	*76.17*	*5.80*
2000-05	*10.90*	*5.87*	*74.86*	*80.53*	*77.62*	*5.68*
2010-15	*10.73*	*5.32*	*76.05*	*81.72*	*78.81*	*5.67*
2020-25	*11.44*	*4.97*	*76.99*	*82.48*	*79.66*	*5.49*

FERTILITY MEASURES (Annual Averages)

PERIOD	CRUDE BIRTH RATE	FERTILITY RATES GENERAL	FERTILITY RATES TOTAL	REPRODUCTION RATES GROSS	REPRODUCTION RATES NET	RATE OF NATUR. INCR.
1950-55	16.73	67.76	2.319	1.129	1.083	5.65
1955-60	16.73	70.27	2.550	1.242	1.199	5.71
1960-65	17.89	77.04	2.784	1.356	1.318	6.68
1965-70	17.31	75.86	2.489	1.212	1.178	6.12
1970-75	14.76	65.40	2.070	1.008	0.983	3.54
1975-80	12.77	55.71	1.782	0.868	0.849	1.41
1980-85	12.92	54.23	1.794	0.874	0.864	1.69
1985-90	*13.15*	*53.62*	*1.779*	*0.866*	*0.854*	*1.59*
1990-95	*13.02*	*52.97*	*1.778*	*0.866*	*0.855*	*1.67*
2000-05	*11.77*	*50.11*	*1.825*	*0.888*	*0.879*	*0.87*
2010-15	*11.43*	*50.98*	*1.873*	*0.912*	*0.904*	*0.70*
2020-25	*11.22*	*53.88*	*1.877*	*0.914*	*0.906*	*-0.22*

AGING MEASURES

YEAR	POPULATION AGE RATIOS 60+/20-59	POPULATION AGE RATIOS 65+/20-64	POPULATION AGE RATIOS 70+/20-69	POPULATION AGE RATIOS 75+/20-74	POPULATION MEAN AGE	POPULATION MEDIAN AGE
1950	0.2715	0.1729	0.1012	0.0511	34.68	33.73
1960	0.3135	0.1974	0.1176	0.0623	35.50	34.72
1970	0.3634	0.2267	0.1316	0.0693	35.56	33.30
1980	0.3894	0.2637	0.1617	0.0872	36.90	34.23
1990	*0.3819*	*0.2642*	*0.1663*	*0.0993*	*37.78*	*35.83*
2000	*0.3700*	*0.2576*	*0.1726*	*0.1047*	*38.72*	*37.80*
2010	*0.4261*	*0.2700*	*0.1712*	*0.1040*	*40.10*	*40.60*
2020	*0.4908*	*0.3280*	*0.2109*	*0.1161*	*41.48*	*42.13*

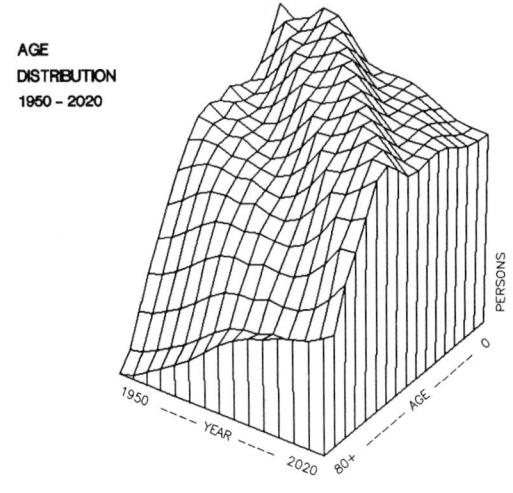

AGE DISTRIBUTION 1950 - 2020

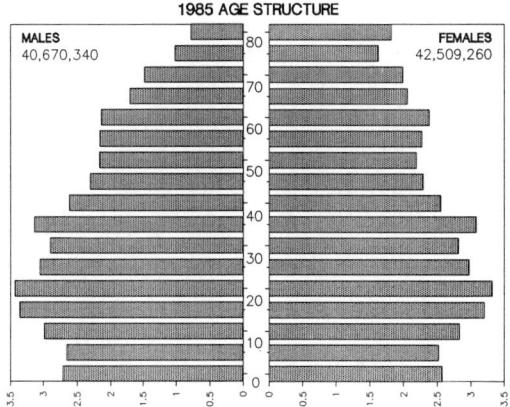

1985 AGE STRUCTURE

MALES 40,670,340　　　FEMALES 42,509,260

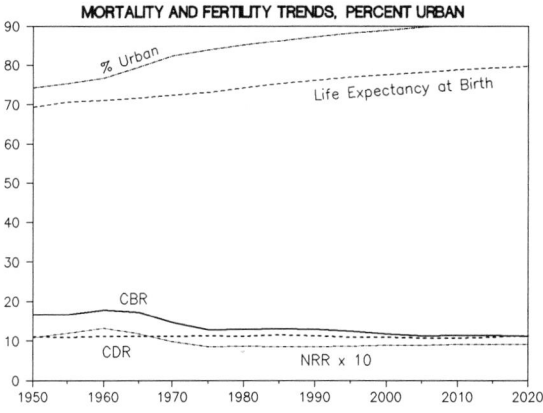

MORTALITY AND FERTILITY TRENDS, PERCENT URBAN

% Urban

Life Expectancy at Birth

CBR

CDR

NRR x 10

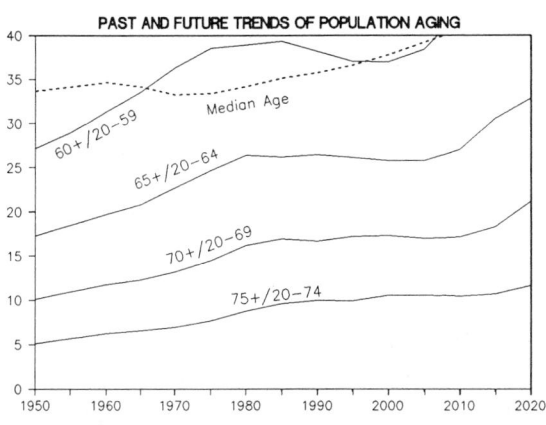

PAST AND FUTURE TRENDS OF POPULATION AGING

Median Age

60+/20-59

65+/20-64

70+/20-69

75+/20-74

OBSERVED AND *PROJECTED* POPULATION DATA (000's)

YEAR	MID-YEAR POPULATION	NO. OF BIRTHS	NO. OF DEATHS	URBAN POPULATION NUMBER	URBAN POPULATION PERCENT	POPULATION 1985 AGE	POPULATION 1985 NUMBER
1950	109014	2312	1128	48604	44.6	0	9262
1955	113675	2365	1098	53397	47.0	5	10512
1960	118197	2444	1113	58473	49.5	10	11454
1965	123427	2415	1138	65029	52.7	15	11856
1970	128339	2285	1175	71965	56.1	20	11690
1975	133358	2109	1207	77952	58.5	25	10664
1980	138806	1827	1232	83945	60.5	30	9754
1985	142342	1797	1354	88897	62.5	35	9256
1990	*144535*	*1824*	*1399*	*93333*	*64.6*	40	8513
1995	*146661*	*1836*	*1414*	*97941*	*66.8*	45	8647
2000	*148768*	*1789*	*1504*	*102691*	*69.0*	50	8772
2005	*150180*	*1710*	*1581*	*107054*	*71.3*	55	8160
2010	*150807*	*1657*	*1636*	*110872*	*73.5*	60	7128
2015	*150899*	*1626*	*1660*	*114079*	*75.6*	65	4866
2020	*150707*	*1608*	*1691*	*116858*	*77.5*	70+	11808

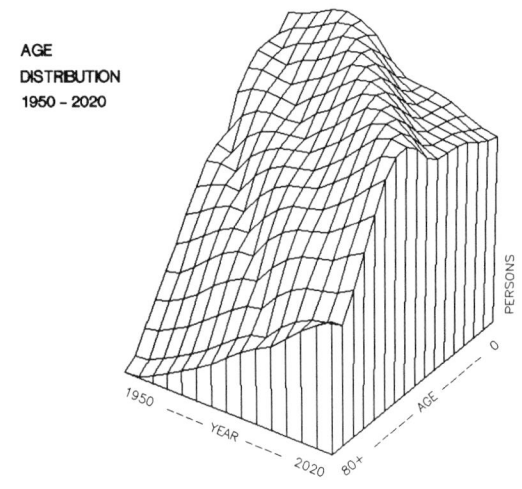

AGE DISTRIBUTION 1950 - 2020

POPULATION RATIOS

YEAR	AGE DISTRIBUTION UNDER 15	AGE DISTRIBUTION 15-64	AGE DISTRIBUTION 65 & OLDER	AGE DISTRIBUTION 70 & OLDER	DEPENDENCY RATIO	WOMEN 15-49	CHILD-WOMAN RATIO
1950	0.278	0.648	0.074	0.045	0.543	0.266	0.369
1955	0.270	0.652	0.078	0.048	0.534	0.263	0.361
1960	0.271	0.646	0.083	0.052	0.548	0.255	0.368
1965	0.267	0.645	0.088	0.054	0.550	0.251	0.376
1970	0.265	0.636	0.099	0.061	0.573	0.248	0.366
1975	0.259	0.634	0.107	0.066	0.576	0.245	0.347
1980	0.244	0.641	0.115	0.073	0.559	0.244	0.320
1985	0.219	0.663	0.117	0.083	0.507	0.246	0.265
1990	*0.198*	*0.675*	*0.127*	*0.082*	*0.482*	*0.249*	*0.247*
2000	*0.182*	*0.667*	*0.151*	*0.101*	*0.499*	*0.246*	*0.250*
2010	*0.176*	*0.661*	*0.163*	*0.116*	*0.513*	*0.233*	*0.242*
2020	*0.164*	*0.654*	*0.182*	*0.127*	*0.529*	*0.215*	*0.249*

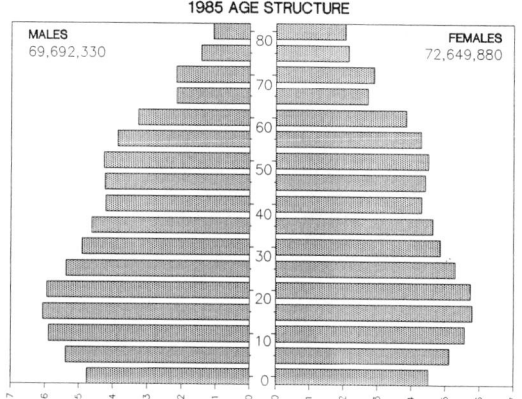

1985 AGE STRUCTURE

MALES 69,692,330   FEMALES 72,649,880

MORTALITY MEASURES (Annual Averages)

PERIOD	CRUDE DEATH RATE	INFANT MORT. RATE	LIFE EXPECTANCY AT BIRTH (years) MALE	LIFE EXPECTANCY AT BIRTH (years) FEMALE	LIFE EXPECTANCY AT BIRTH (years) BOTH SEXES	DIFFERENCE FEMALE-MALE
1950-55	10.35	78.85	61.25	64.90	63.02	3.65
1955-60	9.66	64.91	64.10	68.26	66.12	4.17
1960-65	9.42	52.45	66.21	70.83	68.45	4.62
1965-70	9.22	41.29	67.43	72.59	69.94	5.16
1970-75	9.15	30.73	68.63	74.10	71.28	5.48
1975-80	9.05	22.88	69.87	75.81	72.74	5.94
1980-85	8.87	17.82	70.81	76.93	73.77	6.12
1985-90	*9.51*	*15.29*	*71.83*	*78.00*	*74.81*	*6.17*
1990-95	*9.68*	*12.56*	*72.78*	*78.77*	*75.68*	*5.99*
2000-05	*10.11*	*9.16*	*74.40*	*80.13*	*77.18*	*5.73*
2010-15	*10.85*	*7.13*	*75.59*	*81.22*	*78.31*	*5.64*
2020-25	*11.22*	*6.08*	*76.70*	*82.44*	*79.48*	*5.73*

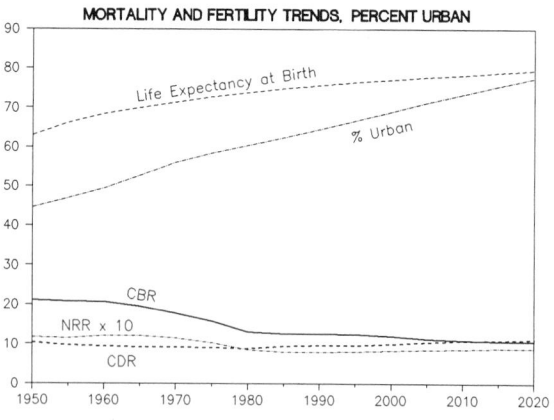

MORTALITY AND FERTILITY TRENDS, PERCENT URBAN

Life Expectancy at Birth

% Urban

CBR

NRR x 10

CDR

FERTILITY MEASURES (Annual Averages)

PERIOD	CRUDE BIRTH RATE	FERTILITY RATES GENERAL	FERTILITY RATES TOTAL	REPRODUCTION RATES GROSS	REPRODUCTION RATES NET	RATE OF NATUR. INCR.
1950-55	21.21	80.09	2.685	1.299	1.172	10.86
1955-60	20.80	80.30	2.616	1.266	1.149	11.14
1960-65	20.67	81.80	2.718	1.315	1.202	11.26
1965-70	19.57	78.51	2.660	1.287	1.202	10.35
1970-75	17.81	72.23	2.517	1.218	1.146	8.65
1975-80	15.81	64.65	2.258	1.092	1.032	6.77
1980-85	13.16	53.72	1.812	0.877	0.854	4.29
1985-90	*12.63*	*51.01*	*1.673*	*0.809*	*0.793*	*3.12*
1990-95	*12.62*	*50.49*	*1.656*	*0.801*	*0.788*	*2.94*
2000-05	*12.03*	*49.54*	*1.728*	*0.836*	*0.826*	*1.91*
2010-15	*10.99*	*48.13*	*1.820*	*0.881*	*0.872*	*0.15*
2020-25	*10.67*	*50.75*	*1.841*	*0.890*	*0.882*	*-0.56*

AGING MEASURES

YEAR	POPULATION AGE RATIOS 60+/20-59	POPULATION AGE RATIOS 65+/20-64	POPULATION AGE RATIOS 70+/20-69	POPULATION AGE RATIOS 75+/20-74	POPULATION MEAN AGE	POPULATION MEDIAN AGE
1950	0.2132	0.1334	0.0774	0.0389	30.83	27.39
1960	0.2336	0.1464	0.0873	0.0448	32.06	29.43
1970	0.2878	0.1778	0.1024	0.0537	33.18	31.01
1980	0.2923	0.2053	0.1226	0.0638	34.32	31.74
1990	*0.3335*	*0.2135*	*0.1278*	*0.0787*	*36.54*	*34.11*
2000	*0.3689*	*0.2497*	*0.1539*	*0.0843*	*38.35*	*36.96*
2010	*0.4014*	*0.2721*	*0.1789*	*0.1059*	*40.03*	*40.06*
2020	*0.4631*	*0.3052*	*0.1950*	*0.1153*	*41.62*	*42.76*

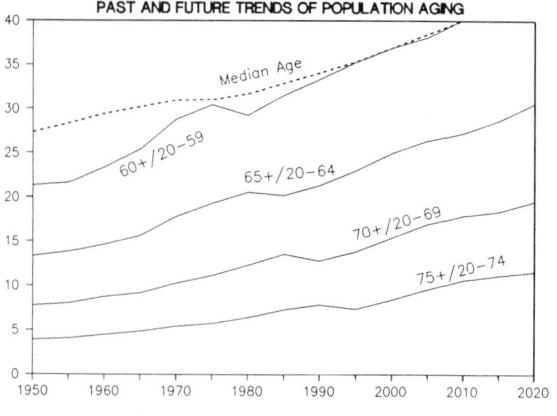

PAST AND FUTURE TRENDS OF POPULATION AGING

Median Age

60+/20-59

65+/20-64

70+/20-69

75+/20-74

OBSERVED AND *PROJECTED* POPULATION DATA (000's)

YEAR	MID-YEAR POPULATION	NO. OF BIRTHS	NO. OF DEATHS	URBAN POPULATION NUMBER	URBAN POPULATION PERCENT	POPULATION 1985 AGE	POPULATION 1985 NUMBER
1950	122532	2162	1391	81582	66.6	0	9082
1955	127697	2251	1425	88196	69.1	5	8901
1960	134513	2454	1487	96083	71.4	10	10496
1965	143012	2434	1611	105984	74.1	15	12457
1970	148209	2037	1647	113246	76.4	20	12736
1975	152327	1791	1644	119060	78.2	25	11849
1980	153740	1855	1701	121345	78.9	30	11434
1985	154974	1866	1707	123368	79.6	35	10945
1990	*155839*	*1872*	*1687*	*125123*	*80.3*	40	10028
1995	*156834*	*1796*	*1638*	*127176*	*81.1*	45	9851
2000	*157694*	*1688*	*1722*	*129166*	*81.9*	50	8925
2005	*157585*	*1616*	*1768*	*130514*	*82.8*	55	8732
2010	*156890*	*1607*	*1812*	*131379*	*83.7*	60	8264
2015	*155929*	*1604*	*1874*	*131925*	*84.6*	65	5158
2020	*154650*	*1577*	*1925*	*132015*	*85.4*	70+	16115

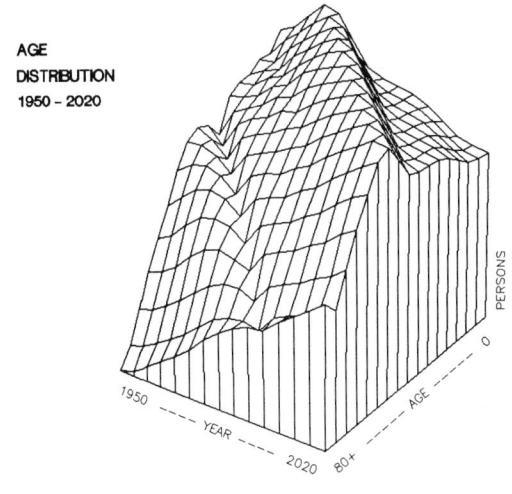

AGE DISTRIBUTION 1950 - 2020

POPULATION RATIOS

YEAR	AGE DISTRIBUTION UNDER 15	AGE DISTRIBUTION 15-64	AGE DISTRIBUTION 65 & OLDER	AGE DISTRIBUTION 70 & OLDER	DEPENDENCY RATIO	WOMEN 15-49	CHILD-WOMAN RATIO
1950	0.234	0.665	0.101	0.062	0.504	0.259	0.323
1955	0.233	0.661	0.106	0.066	0.513	0.250	0.327
1960	0.241	0.649	0.111	0.070	0.542	0.237	0.355
1965	0.243	0.639	0.118	0.073	0.565	0.230	0.378
1970	0.242	0.630	0.128	0.080	0.587	0.235	0.343
1975	0.228	0.635	0.137	0.088	0.576	0.237	0.281
1980	0.203	0.653	0.144	0.101	0.532	0.244	0.238
1985	0.184	0.679	0.137	0.104	0.473	0.251	0.233
1990	*0.175*	*0.680*	*0.145*	*0.096*	*0.470*	*0.251*	*0.238*
2000	*0.175*	*0.666*	*0.160*	*0.112*	*0.502*	*0.238*	*0.239*
2010	*0.162*	*0.659*	*0.179*	*0.126*	*0.517*	*0.223*	*0.229*
2020	*0.155*	*0.638*	*0.208*	*0.145*	*0.568*	*0.202*	*0.255*

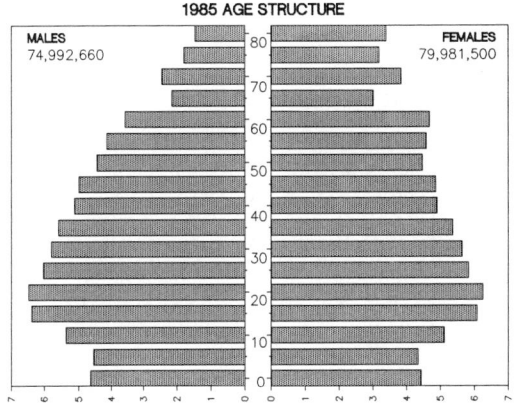

1985 AGE STRUCTURE

MALES 74,992,660   FEMALES 79,981,500

MORTALITY MEASURES (Annual Averages)

PERIOD	CRUDE DEATH RATE	INFANT MORT. RATE	LIFE EXPECTANCY AT BIRTH (years) MALE	LIFE EXPECTANCY AT BIRTH (years) FEMALE	LIFE EXPECTANCY AT BIRTH (years) BOTH SEXES	DIFFERENCE FEMALE-MALE
1950-55	11.35	43.67	65.26	70.09	67.61	4.83
1955-60	11.16	33.00	67.05	72.49	69.69	5.44
1960-65	11.05	25.76	67.77	73.84	70.72	6.07
1965-70	11.26	21.22	67.99	74.51	71.16	6.52
1970-75	11.11	18.16	68.50	75.33	71.82	6.82
1975-80	10.79	12.83	69.70	77.00	73.27	7.31
1980-85	11.06	9.79	70.89	78.24	74.47	7.35
1985-90	*11.01*	*8.62*	*71.86*	*79.11*	*75.39*	*7.25*
1990-95	*10.82*	*7.47*	*72.85*	*79.85*	*76.26*	*7.00*
2000-05	*10.92*	*6.18*	*74.39*	*81.04*	*77.63*	*6.65*
2010-15	*11.55*	*5.61*	*75.67*	*82.13*	*78.82*	*6.45*
2020-25	*12.45*	*5.17*	*76.71*	*82.95*	*79.75*	*6.24*

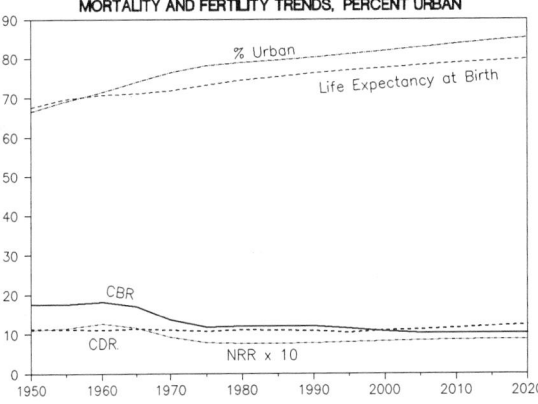

MORTALITY AND FERTILITY TRENDS, PERCENT URBAN

% Urban

Life Expectancy at Birth

CBR

CDR

NRR x 10

FERTILITY MEASURES (Annual Averages)

PERIOD	CRUDE BIRTH RATE	FERTILITY RATES GENERAL	FERTILITY RATES TOTAL	REPRODUCTION RATES GROSS	REPRODUCTION RATES NET	RATE OF NATUR. INCR.
1950-55	17.65	69.33	2.392	1.165	1.090	6.29
1955-60	17.63	72.52	2.529	1.232	1.148	6.47
1960-65	18.24	78.25	2.685	1.307	1.257	7.19
1965-70	17.02	73.14	2.468	1.202	1.153	5.75
1970-75	13.75	58.24	1.939	0.944	0.917	2.64
1975-80	11.76	48.93	1.628	0.793	0.777	0.97
1980-85	12.06	48.73	1.583	0.771	0.759	1.00
1985-90	*12.04*	*47.98*	*1.576*	*0.768*	*0.755*	*1.03*
1990-95	*12.01*	*48.46*	*1.603*	*0.781*	*0.769*	*1.19*
2000-05	*10.70*	*45.71*	*1.707*	*0.831*	*0.821*	*-0.22*
2010-15	*10.24*	*46.94*	*1.779*	*0.867*	*0.857*	*-1.31*
2020-25	*10.20*	*51.19*	*1.789*	*0.871*	*0.862*	*-2.25*

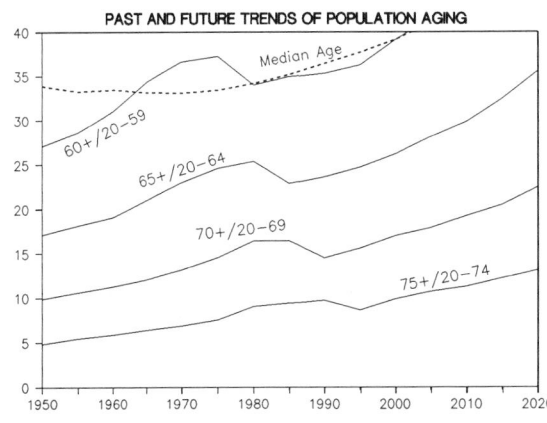

PAST AND FUTURE TRENDS OF POPULATION AGING

Median Age

60+/20-59

65+/20-64

70+/20-69

75+/20-74

AGING MEASURES

YEAR	POPULATION AGE RATIOS 60+/20-59	POPULATION AGE RATIOS 65+/20-64	POPULATION AGE RATIOS 70+/20-69	POPULATION AGE RATIOS 75+/20-74	POPULATION MEAN AGE	POPULATION MEDIAN AGE
1950	0.2713	0.1711	0.0986	0.0481	34.73	33.94
1960	0.3105	0.1909	0.1125	0.0587	35.19	33.48
1970	0.3663	0.2301	0.1317	0.0683	35.28	33.14
1980	0.3401	0.2537	0.1646	0.0904	36.74	34.22
1990	*0.3534*	*0.2364*	*0.1453*	*0.0973*	*38.18*	*36.44*
2000	*0.3909*	*0.2623*	*0.1702*	*0.0987*	*39.77*	*39.19*
2010	*0.4494*	*0.2985*	*0.1925*	*0.1129*	*41.57*	*42.55*
2020	*0.5380*	*0.3557*	*0.2248*	*0.1314*	*43.07*	*44.85*

OBSERVED AND *PROJECTED* POPULATION DATA (000's)

YEAR	MID-YEAR POPULATION	NO. OF BIRTHS	NO. OF DEATHS	URBAN POPULATION NUMBER	PERCENT	POPULATION 1985 AGE	NUMBER
1950	259806	4701	2829	167351	64.4	0	19521
1955	268701	4882	2858	178691	66.5	5	20412
1960	279659	5277	2963	191937	68.6	10	23476
1965	293588	5258	3126	209670	71.4	15	26285
1970	303402	4626	3209	224523	74.0	20	26467
1975	312022	4101	3251	236454	75.8	25	23956
1980	318051	3914	3303	244202	76.8	30	22500
1985	322061	3950	3443	250557	77.8	35	22379
1990	*324523*	*4003*	*3449*	*256049*	*78.9*	40	19913
1995	*327248*	*3920*	*3394*	*262028*	*80.1*	45	19553
2000	*329830*	*3730*	*3535*	*267975*	*81.2*	50	18720
2005	*330743*	*3562*	*3624*	*272784*	*82.5*	55	18232
2010	*330376*	*3513*	*3701*	*276560*	*83.7*	60	17182
2015	*329377*	*3494*	*3789*	*279536*	*84.9*	65	11810
2020	*327848*	*3446*	*3882*	*281662*	*85.9*	70+	31655

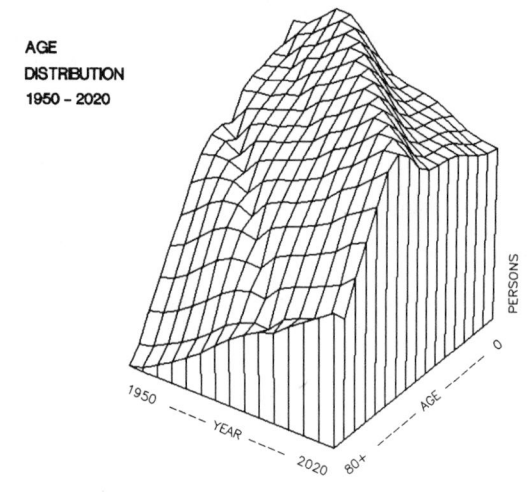

AGE DISTRIBUTION 1950 – 2020

POPULATION RATIOS

YEAR	AGE DISTRIBUTION UNDER 15	15-64	65 & OLDER	70 & OLDER	DEPENDENCY RATIO	WOMEN 15-49	CHILD-WOMAN RATIO
1950	0.246	0.660	0.094	0.058	0.515	0.260	0.342
1955	0.243	0.658	0.099	0.062	0.520	0.253	0.331
1960	0.248	0.648	0.104	0.066	0.542	0.242	0.353
1965	0.247	0.643	0.110	0.068	0.554	0.237	0.376
1970	0.249	0.631	0.120	0.075	0.584	0.236	0.356
1975	0.240	0.632	0.128	0.082	0.583	0.236	0.313
1980	0.219	0.645	0.137	0.092	0.551	0.241	0.271
1985	0.197	0.668	0.135	0.098	0.497	0.247	0.245
1990	*0.183*	*0.673*	*0.143*	*0.095*	*0.485*	*0.249*	*0.243*
2000	*0.179*	*0.663*	*0.158*	*0.109*	*0.508*	*0.240*	*0.247*
2010	*0.169*	*0.660*	*0.171*	*0.121*	*0.516*	*0.228*	*0.235*
2020	*0.160*	*0.644*	*0.196*	*0.138*	*0.553*	*0.208*	*0.255*

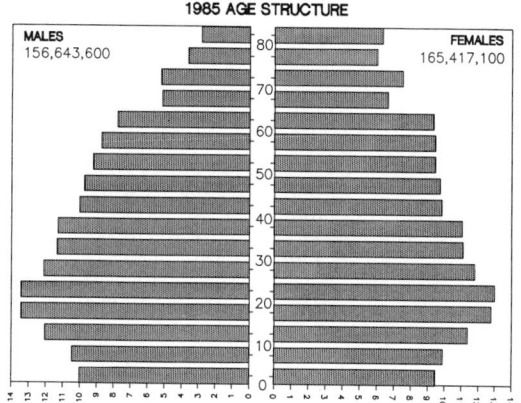

1985 AGE STRUCTURE

MALES 156,643,600

FEMALES 165,417,100

MORTALITY MEASURES (Annual Averages)

PERIOD	CRUDE DEATH RATE	INFANT MORT. RATE	LIFE EXPECTANCY AT BIRTH (years) MALE	FEMALE	BOTH SEXES	DIFFERENCE FEMALE-MALE
1950-55	10.89	47.60	64.73	69.25	66.93	4.52
1955-60	10.64	38.24	66.65	71.75	69.12	5.10
1960-65	10.59	31.51	67.59	73.19	70.31	5.60
1965-70	10.65	25.91	68.13	74.18	71.07	6.05
1970-75	10.58	21.14	68.84	75.06	71.86	6.22
1975-80	10.42	15.17	69.97	76.63	73.21	6.66
1980-85	10.38	11.03	71.21	77.89	74.46	6.68
1985-90	*10.69*	*9.79*	*72.23*	*78.81*	*75.43*	*6.58*
1990-95	*10.63*	*8.31*	*73.15*	*79.54*	*76.26*	*6.39*
2000-05	*10.72*	*6.54*	*74.69*	*80.78*	*77.65*	*6.09*
2010-15	*11.20*	*5.73*	*75.88*	*81.88*	*78.80*	*5.99*
2020-25	*11.84*	*5.27*	*76.89*	*82.82*	*79.77*	*5.93*

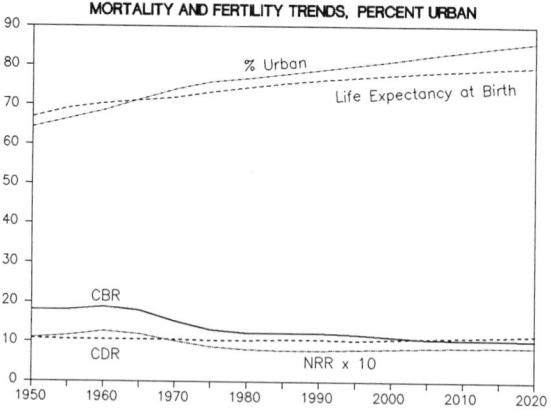

MORTALITY AND FERTILITY TRENDS, PERCENT URBAN

% Urban

Life Expectancy at Birth

CBR

CDR

NRR x 10

FERTILITY MEASURES (Annual Averages)

PERIOD	CRUDE BIRTH RATE	FERTILITY RATES GENERAL	TOTAL	REPRODUCTION RATES GROSS	NET	RATE OF NATUR. INCR.
1950-55	18.09	70.85	2.407	1.170	1.104	7.20
1955-60	18.17	73.62	2.544	1.237	1.160	7.53
1960-65	18.87	78.88	2.721	1.322	1.262	8.28
1965-70	17.91	75.73	2.554	1.241	1.187	7.26
1970-75	15.25	64.60	2.178	1.058	1.018	4.67
1975-80	13.14	55.25	1.876	0.911	0.880	2.73
1980-85	12.31	50.60	1.682	0.817	0.804	1.92
1985-90	*12.27*	*49.49*	*1.629*	*0.792*	*0.779*	*1.57*
1990-95	*12.34*	*49.71*	*1.639*	*0.797*	*0.786*	*1.71*
2000-05	*11.31*	*47.64*	*1.729*	*0.840*	*0.831*	*0.59*
2010-15	*10.63*	*47.62*	*1.806*	*0.877*	*0.869*	*-0.57*
2020-25	*10.51*	*51.44*	*1.819*	*0.883*	*0.875*	*-1.33*

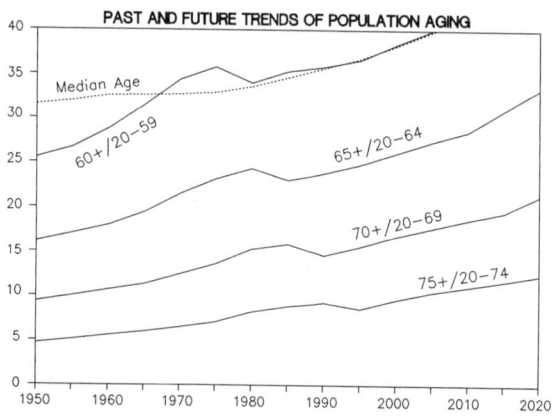

PAST AND FUTURE TRENDS OF POPULATION AGING

Median Age

60+/20-59

65+/20-64

70+/20-69

75+/20-74

AGING MEASURES

YEAR	POPULATION AGE RATIOS 60+/20-59	65+/20-64	70+/20-69	75+/20-74	POPULATION MEAN AGE	MEDIAN AGE
1950	0.2552	0.1613	0.0938	0.0467	33.58	31.57
1960	0.2879	0.1797	0.1067	0.0557	34.41	32.54
1970	0.3435	0.2148	0.1240	0.0650	34.80	32.72
1980	0.3400	0.2433	0.1523	0.0822	36.08	33.59
1990	*0.3583*	*0.2382*	*0.1457*	*0.0925*	*37.70*	*35.66*
2000	*0.3835*	*0.2608*	*0.1677*	*0.0965*	*39.19*	*38.23*
2010	*0.4314*	*0.2858*	*0.1859*	*0.1105*	*40.84*	*41.43*
2020	*0.5025*	*0.3332*	*0.2132*	*0.1235*	*42.35*	*43.76*

OBSERVED AND *PROJECTED* POPULATION DATA

YEAR	MID-YEAR POPULATION	NO. OF BIRTHS	NO. OF DEATHS	URBAN POPULATION NUMBER	PERCENT	POPULATION 1985 AGE	NUMBER
1950	1229630	47005	17477	250180	20.3	0	361593
1955	1389128	57961	15140	349083	25.1	5	343469
1960	1610563	64284	15552	492926	30.6	10	317083
1965	1869942	65040	15513	601455	32.2	15	308443
1970	2138000	68290	14680	716763	33.5	20	300355
1975	2423978	73398	15412	795586	32.8	25	263178
1980	2671300	71404	16242	893056	33.4	30	203719
1985	2962200	71096	17030	1008543	34.0	35	158900
1990	*3245457*	*70942*	*18097*	*1146582*	*35.3*	40	144048
1995	*3520890*	*72027*	*19337*	*1313004*	*37.3*	45	133728
2000	*3794588*	*72184*	*20745*	*1515706*	*39.9*	50	108816
2005	*4060810*	*72745*	*23240*	*1757192*	*43.3*	55	96964
2010	*4316121*	*73456*	*25633*	*2038355*	*47.2*	60	66166
2015	*4562036*	*73262*	*28431*	*2330130*	*51.1*	65	58215
2020	*4791838*	*74288*	*31468*	*2624922*	*54.8*	70+	97523

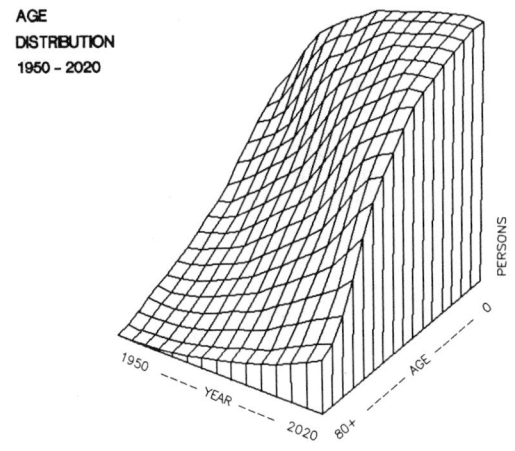

AGE DISTRIBUTION 1950 - 2020

POPULATION RATIOS

YEAR	AGE DISTRIBUTION UNDER 15	15-64	65 & OLDER	70 & OLDER	DEPENDENCY RATIO	WOMEN 15-49	CHILD-WOMAN RATIO
1950	0.389	0.541	0.070	0.043	0.849	0.222	0.643
1955	0.391	0.545	0.064	0.040	0.834	0.229	0.693
1960	0.411	0.537	0.052	0.036	0.863	0.225	0.774
1965	0.429	0.523	0.047	0.030	0.911	0.218	0.775
1970	0.424	0.532	0.044	0.028	0.880	0.223	0.676
1975	0.399	0.556	0.045	0.027	0.799	0.235	0.595
1980	0.359	0.589	0.052	0.031	0.697	0.238	0.542
1985	0.345	0.602	0.053	0.033	0.660	0.244	0.501
1990	*0.326*	*0.621*	*0.053*	*0.035*	*0.611*	*0.248*	*0.443*
2000	*0.282*	*0.653*	*0.065*	*0.040*	*0.532*	*0.262*	*0.366*
2010	*0.253*	*0.668*	*0.079*	*0.051*	*0.496*	*0.257*	*0.331*
2020	*0.231*	*0.673*	*0.096*	*0.060*	*0.485*	*0.245*	*0.316*

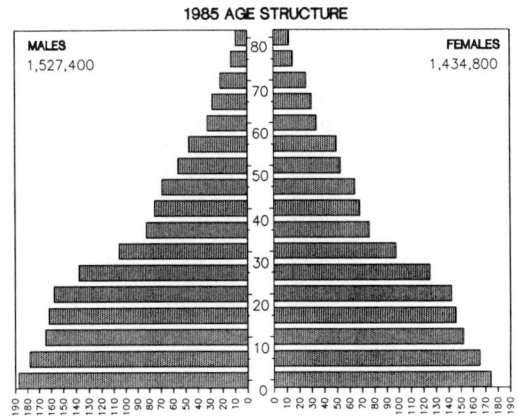

1985 AGE STRUCTURE

MALES 1,527,400 — FEMALES 1,434,800

MORTALITY MEASURES (Annual Averages)

PERIOD	CRUDE DEATH RATE	INFANT MORT. RATE	LIFE EXPECTANCY AT BIRTH (years) MALE	FEMALE	BOTH SEXES	DIFFERENCE FEMALE-MALE
1950-55	14.21	145.00	54.40	56.10	55.22	1.70
1955-60	10.90	125.00	58.50	60.10	59.28	1.60
1960-65	9.66	99.00	63.70	66.00	64.82	2.30
1965-70	8.30	77.00	65.10	67.40	66.22	2.30
1970-75	6.87	58.00	66.00	69.50	67.69	3.50
1975-80	6.36	50.00	66.80	71.20	68.93	4.40
1980-85	6.08	44.76	68.00	73.00	70.42	5.00
1985-90	*5.75*	*38.83*	*69.20*	*74.22*	*71.63*	*5.02*
1990-95	*5.58*	*32.10*	*70.32*	*75.39*	*72.77*	*5.07*
2000-05	*5.47*	*21.53*	*72.37*	*77.40*	*74.80*	*5.03*
2010-15	*5.94*	*14.18*	*74.01*	*78.99*	*76.41*	*4.98*
2020-25	*6.57*	*9.43*	*75.38*	*80.44*	*77.82*	*5.06*

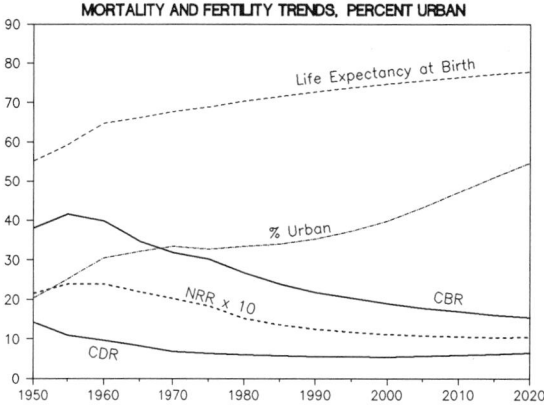

MORTALITY AND FERTILITY TRENDS, PERCENT URBAN

Life Expectancy at Birth — % Urban — NRR x 10 — CBR — CDR

FERTILITY MEASURES (Annual Averages)

PERIOD	CRUDE BIRTH RATE	FERTILITY RATES GENERAL	TOTAL	REPRODUCTION RATES GROSS	NET	RATE OF NATUR. INCR.
1950-55	38.23	169.41	5.597	2.704	2.163	24.01
1955-60	41.72	184.09	5.978	2.888	2.397	30.83
1960-65	39.91	180.48	5.763	2.784	2.401	30.26
1965-70	34.78	157.72	5.113	2.470	2.197	26.49
1970-75	31.94	139.23	4.657	2.250	2.040	25.08
1975-80	30.28	128.00	4.202	2.030	1.853	23.92
1980-85	26.73	111.01	3.403	1.644	1.532	20.65
1985-90	*24.00*	*97.55*	*3.000*	*1.449*	*1.371*	*18.25*
1990-95	*21.86*	*86.76*	*2.700*	*1.304*	*1.246*	*16.28*
2000-05	*19.02*	*72.61*	*2.400*	*1.159*	*1.124*	*13.56*
2010-15	*17.02*	*66.99*	*2.250*	*1.087*	*1.063*	*11.08*
2020-25	*15.50*	*63.98*	*2.200*	*1.063*	*1.046*	*8.94*

AGING MEASURES

YEAR	POPULATION AGE RATIOS 60+/20-59	65+/20-64	70+/20-69	75+/20-74	POPULATION MEAN AGE	MEDIAN AGE
1950	0.2453	0.1584	0.0922	0.0469	26.38	20.64
1960	0.1806	0.1185	0.0784	0.0408	24.61	19.68
1970	0.1617	0.1027	0.0625	0.0324	24.24	18.84
1980	0.1700	0.1098	0.0623	0.0323	25.99	21.35
1990	*0.1652*	*0.1020*	*0.0638*	*0.0343*	*27.56*	*24.05*
2000	*0.1838*	*0.1161*	*0.0692*	*0.0344*	*29.84*	*27.05*
2010	*0.2020*	*0.1342*	*0.0825*	*0.0433*	*32.25*	*30.10*
2020	*0.2643*	*0.1598*	*0.0941*	*0.0528*	*34.57*	*33.10*

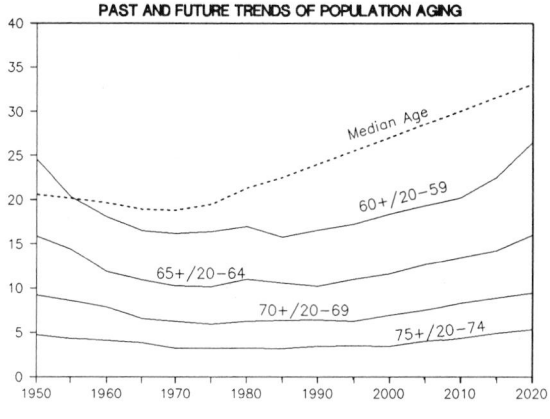

PAST AND FUTURE TRENDS OF POPULATION AGING

Median Age — 60+/20-59 — 65+/20-64 — 70+/20-69 — 75+/20-74

OBSERVED AND *PROJECTED* POPULATION DATA

YEAR	MID-YEAR POPULATION	NO. OF BIRTHS	NO. OF DEATHS	URBAN POPULATION NUMBER	URBAN POPULATION PERCENT	POPULATION 1985 AGE	POPULATION 1985 NUMBER
1950	6935000	104164	85023	3407165	49.1	0	463301
1955	6947000	116849	86560	3440849	49.5	5	432346
1960	7048000	130388	88241	3519771	49.9	10	497828
1965	7255000	123284	94315	3685540	50.8	15	606503
1970	7446800	101708	94969	3852974	51.7	20	643321
1975	7519889	86637	93502	3996069	53.1	25	575335
1980	7549433	91748	91597	4125010	54.6	30	505809
1985	7501785	87043	88949	4210752	56.1	35	505504
1990	*7492286*	*84483*	*87128*	*4323798*	*57.7*	40	516955
1995	*7479059*	*79697*	*83294*	*4433586*	*59.3*	45	452675
2000	*7461085*	*75267*	*86362*	*4545293*	*60.9*	50	396995
2005	*7405787*	*73280*	*86625*	*4630839*	*62.5*	55	420445
2010	*7339380*	*72432*	*86318*	*4712616*	*64.2*	60	425259
2015	*7270250*	*69678*	*89271*	*4787460*	*65.9*	65	255636
2020	*7172913*	*66708*	*93061*	*4843868*	*67.5*	70+	803873

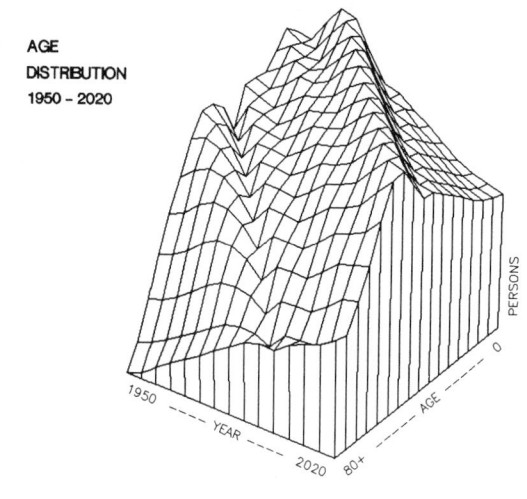

AGE DISTRIBUTION 1950 – 2020

POPULATION RATIOS

YEAR	AGE DISTRIBUTION UNDER 15	AGE DISTRIBUTION 15-64	AGE DISTRIBUTION 65 & OLDER	AGE DISTRIBUTION 70 & OLDER	DEPENDENCY RATIO	WOMEN 15-49	CHILD-WOMAN RATIO
1950	0.228	0.668	0.104	0.062	0.496	0.264	0.280
1955	0.223	0.665	0.113	0.069	0.505	0.252	0.278
1960	0.221	0.658	0.120	0.075	0.519	0.240	0.338
1965	0.232	0.635	0.133	0.081	0.574	0.228	0.384
1970	0.245	0.614	0.141	0.087	0.629	0.230	0.356
1975	0.233	0.617	0.150	0.096	0.620	0.229	0.291
1980	0.204	0.642	0.154	0.104	0.558	0.241	0.236
1985	0.186	0.673	0.141	0.107	0.486	0.251	0.246
1990	*0.177*	*0.673*	*0.150*	*0.098*	*0.486*	*0.252*	*0.227*
2000	*0.166*	*0.676*	*0.158*	*0.113*	*0.480*	*0.243*	*0.218*
2010	*0.154*	*0.668*	*0.178*	*0.120*	*0.496*	*0.230*	*0.215*
2020	*0.148*	*0.650*	*0.202*	*0.143*	*0.538*	*0.203*	*0.237*

MORTALITY MEASURES (Annual Averages)

PERIOD	CRUDE DEATH RATE	INFANT MORT. RATE	LIFE EXPECTANCY AT BIRTH (years) MALE	LIFE EXPECTANCY AT BIRTH (years) FEMALE	LIFE EXPECTANCY AT BIRTH (years) BOTH SEXES	DIFFERENCE FEMALE-MALE
1950-55	12.26	53.45	63.20	68.40	65.73	5.20
1955-60	12.46	41.82	65.00	71.10	67.96	6.10
1960-65	12.52	31.76	66.10	72.60	69.26	6.50
1965-70	13.00	26.54	66.50	73.40	69.85	6.90
1970-75	12.75	24.43	67.00	74.30	70.55	7.30
1975-80	12.43	16.47	68.50	75.65	71.98	7.15
1980-85	12.13	12.22	69.56	76.83	73.11	7.27
1985-90	*11.86*	*10.77*	*70.62*	*77.84*	*74.14*	*7.22*
1990-95	*11.63*	*9.25*	*71.65*	*78.60*	*75.04*	*6.96*
2000-05	*11.57*	*6.63*	*73.47*	*80.11*	*76.70*	*6.64*
2010-15	*11.76*	*5.80*	*75.05*	*81.12*	*78.01*	*6.07*
2020-25	*12.97*	*5.30*	*76.07*	*82.08*	*79.00*	*6.01*

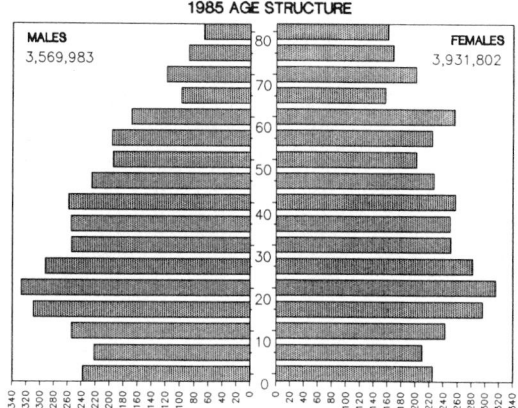

1985 AGE STRUCTURE

MALES 3,569,983   FEMALES 3,931,802

FERTILITY MEASURES (Annual Averages)

PERIOD	CRUDE BIRTH RATE	FERTILITY RATES GENERAL	FERTILITY RATES TOTAL	REPRODUCTION RATES GROSS	REPRODUCTION RATES NET	RATE OF NATUR. INCR.
1950-55	15.02	58.11	2.088	1.018	0.941	2.76
1955-60	16.82	68.27	2.519	1.228	1.135	4.36
1960-65	18.50	78.96	2.777	1.354	1.280	5.98
1965-70	16.99	74.09	2.527	1.232	1.181	3.99
1970-75	13.66	59.52	2.012	0.981	0.948	0.90
1975-80	11.52	49.06	1.641	0.800	0.781	-0.91
1980-85	12.15	49.43	1.614	0.787	0.770	0.02
1985-90	*11.60*	*46.13*	*1.500*	*0.731*	*0.718*	*-0.25*
1990-95	*11.28*	*45.28*	*1.500*	*0.731*	*0.720*	*-0.35*
2000-05	*10.09*	*41.90*	*1.600*	*0.780*	*0.771*	*-1.49*
2010-15	*9.87*	*44.29*	*1.700*	*0.829*	*0.820*	*-1.89*
2020-25	*9.30*	*46.54*	*1.700*	*0.829*	*0.820*	*-3.67*

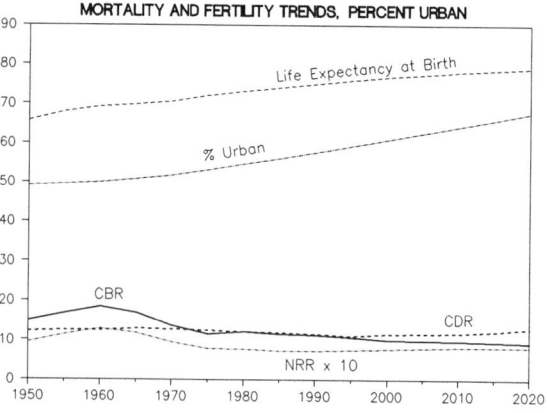

MORTALITY AND FERTILITY TRENDS, PERCENT URBAN

Life Expectancy at Birth

% Urban

CBR   CDR

NRR x 10

AGING MEASURES

YEAR	POPULATION AGE RATIOS 60+/20-59	POPULATION AGE RATIOS 65+/20-64	POPULATION AGE RATIOS 70+/20-69	POPULATION AGE RATIOS 75+/20-74	POPULATION MEAN AGE	POPULATION MEDIAN AGE
1950	0.2796	0.1721	0.0965	0.0455	35.55	35.80
1960	0.3460	0.2079	0.1196	0.0611	36.43	35.40
1970	0.4147	0.2584	0.1454	0.0734	36.02	33.87
1980	0.3698	0.2777	0.1726	0.0920	37.01	34.68
1990	*0.3665*	*0.2475*	*0.1491*	*0.0997*	*38.18*	*36.09*
2000	*0.3786*	*0.2571*	*0.1722*	*0.1011*	*39.85*	*39.00*
2010	*0.4342*	*0.2911*	*0.1794*	*0.1052*	*41.70*	*42.72*
2020	*0.5191*	*0.3371*	*0.2177*	*0.1285*	*43.44*	*45.40*

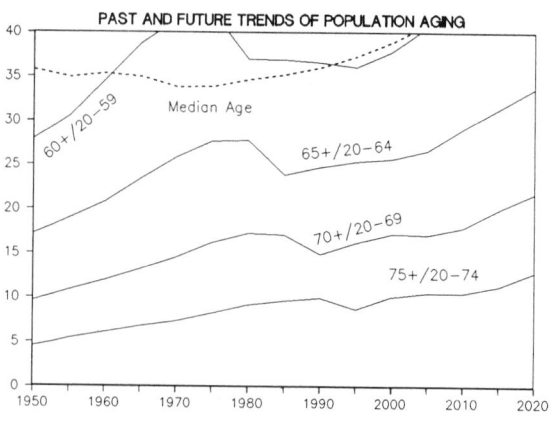

PAST AND FUTURE TRENDS OF POPULATION AGING

60+/20-59   Median Age   65+/20-64   70+/20-69   75+/20-74

OBSERVED AND *PROJECTED* POPULATION DATA

YEAR	MID-YEAR POPULATION	NO. OF BIRTHS	NO. OF DEATHS	URBAN POPULATION		POPULATION 1985	
				NUMBER	PERCENT	AGE	NUMBER
1950	8639000	144530	105741	7901792	91.5	0	608017
1955	8868000	151731	106061	8156567	92.0	5	608097
1960	9153000	156425	111209	8462907	92.5	10	668834
1965	9464000	146787	117164	8835213	93.4	15	738167
1970	9655547	131306	117093	9106336	94.3	20	792512
1975	9796000	121069	114731	9262183	94.6	25	776012
1980	9851860	118882	112114	9395394	95.4	30	733006
1985	9903000	115994	113885	9535022	96.3	35	704420
1990	*9938439*	*116190*	*112771*	*9634374*	*96.9*	40	556804
1995	*9980441*	*115593*	*109964*	*9722014*	*97.4*	45	580258
2000	*10033580*	*111403*	*113971*	*9807394*	*97.7*	50	610326
2005	*10045643*	*109287*	*115384*	*9842737*	*98.0*	55	598631
2010	*10040029*	*106123*	*116555*	*9852972*	*98.1*	60	563514
2015	*10012852*	*104394*	*117120*	*9840761*	*98.3*	65	367219
2020	*9974263*	*103134*	*118983*	*9816109*	*98.4*	70+	997183

POPULATION RATIOS

YEAR	AGE DISTRIBUTION				DEPENDENCY RATIO	WOMEN 15-49	CHILD-WOMAN RATIO
	UNDER 15	15-64	65 & OLDER	70 & OLDER			
1950	0.209	0.681	0.111	0.068	0.469	0.252	0.319
1955	0.218	0.667	0.115	0.073	0.500	0.239	0.330
1960	0.235	0.645	0.120	0.075	0.550	0.226	0.363
1965	0.239	0.635	0.126	0.079	0.575	0.224	0.367
1970	0.236	0.630	0.134	0.084	0.587	0.234	0.319
1975	0.222	0.639	0.139	0.091	0.566	0.236	0.284
1980	0.202	0.655	0.143	0.096	0.527	0.241	0.254
1985	0.190	0.672	0.138	0.101	0.488	0.243	0.253
1990	*0.181*	*0.672*	*0.147*	*0.095*	*0.488*	*0.245*	*0.238*
2000	*0.174*	*0.663*	*0.164*	*0.112*	*0.509*	*0.241*	*0.240*
2010	*0.168*	*0.665*	*0.166*	*0.120*	*0.503*	*0.224*	*0.243*
2020	*0.161*	*0.644*	*0.195*	*0.133*	*0.552*	*0.207*	*0.252*

MORTALITY MEASURES (Annual Averages)

PERIOD	CRUDE DEATH RATE	INFANT MORT. RATE	LIFE EXPECTANCY AT BIRTH (years)			
			MALE	FEMALE	BOTH SEXES	DIFFERENCE FEMALE-MALE
1950-55	12.24	44.99	65.00	70.15	67.50	5.15
1955-60	11.96	34.50	66.90	72.60	69.67	5.70
1960-65	12.15	27.11	67.85	73.85	70.77	6.00
1965-70	12.38	22.65	67.80	74.25	70.94	6.45
1970-75	12.13	18.68	68.24	74.69	71.38	6.45
1975-80	11.71	13.48	69.13	75.70	72.33	6.57
1980-85	11.38	11.17	70.44	77.21	73.73	6.77
1985-90	*11.50*	*9.56*	*71.49*	*78.10*	*74.71*	*6.61*
1990-95	*11.35*	*8.25*	*72.39*	*78.87*	*75.54*	*6.48*
2000-05	*11.36*	*6.29*	*74.08*	*80.30*	*77.11*	*6.22*
2010-15	*11.61*	*5.61*	*75.48*	*81.74*	*78.53*	*6.26*
2020-25	*11.93*	*5.10*	*76.44*	*82.36*	*79.32*	*5.92*

FERTILITY MEASURES (Annual Averages)

PERIOD	CRUDE BIRTH RATE	FERTILITY RATES		REPRODUCTION RATES		RATE OF NATUR. INCR.
		GENERAL	TOTAL	GROSS	NET	
1950-55	16.73	68.19	2.337	1.137	1.055	4.49
1955-60	17.11	73.64	2.507	1.220	1.161	5.15
1960-65	17.09	75.95	2.663	1.296	1.231	4.94
1965-70	15.51	67.71	2.341	1.139	1.102	3.13
1970-75	13.60	57.92	1.938	0.943	0.916	1.47
1975-80	12.36	51.77	1.706	0.830	0.810	0.65
1980-85	12.07	49.86	1.595	0.776	0.761	0.69
1985-90	*11.71*	*48.05*	*1.550*	*0.754*	*0.741*	*0.21*
1990-95	*11.69*	*47.60*	*1.600*	*0.779*	*0.767*	*0.34*
2000-05	*11.10*	*46.87*	*1.750*	*0.852*	*0.842*	*-0.26*
2010-15	*10.57*	*48.12*	*1.800*	*0.876*	*0.867*	*-1.04*
2020-25	*10.34*	*50.43*	*1.800*	*0.876*	*0.868*	*-1.59*

AGING MEASURES

YEAR	POPULATION AGE RATIOS				POPULATION	
	60+/20-59	65+/20-64	70+/20-69	75+/20-74	MEAN AGE	MEDIAN AGE
1950	0.2854	0.1817	0.1048	0.0520	35.93	35.55
1960	0.3326	0.2043	0.1199	0.0633	36.19	35.23
1970	0.3795	0.2411	0.1386	0.0711	35.94	34.49
1980	0.3422	0.2497	0.1548	0.0849	36.85	34.14
1990	*0.3723*	*0.2433*	*0.1455*	*0.0927*	*38.17*	*36.31*
2000	*0.3926*	*0.2721*	*0.1724*	*0.0971*	*39.52*	*38.96*
2010	*0.4218*	*0.2742*	*0.1841*	*0.1120*	*40.89*	*41.61*
2020	*0.5125*	*0.3310*	*0.2042*	*0.1142*	*42.23*	*43.37*

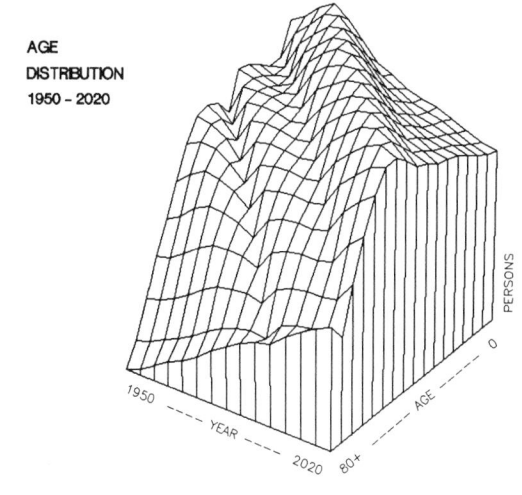

AGE DISTRIBUTION 1950 - 2020

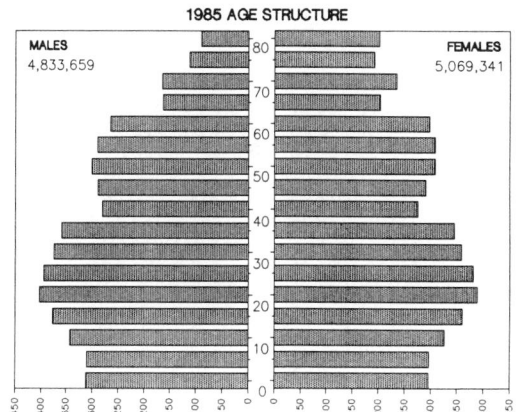

1985 AGE STRUCTURE

MALES 4,833,659

FEMALES 5,069,341

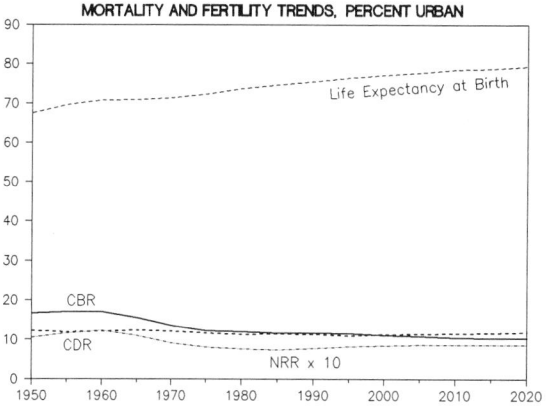

MORTALITY AND FERTILITY TRENDS, PERCENT URBAN

Life Expectancy at Birth

CBR

CDR

NRR x 10

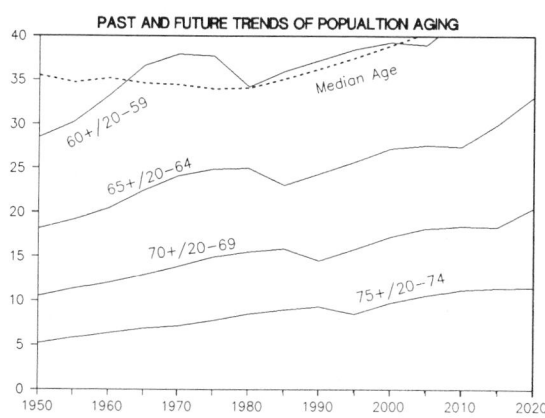

PAST AND FUTURE TRENDS OF POPUALTION AGING

Median Age

60+/20-59

65+/20-64

70+/20-69

75+/20-74

OBSERVED AND *PROJECTED* POPULATION DATA

YEAR	MID-YEAR POPULATION	NO. OF BIRTHS	NO. OF DEATHS	URBAN POPULATION NUMBER	URBAN POPULATION PERCENT	POPULATION 1985 AGE	POPULATION 1985 NUMBER
1950	7251000	152735	73815	1856256	25.6	0	587617
1955	7499000	140231	66591	2379433	31.7	5	661729
1960	7867000	132795	64195	3033515	38.6	10	656166
1965	8200544	129733	71345	3762410	45.9	15	608191
1970	8489574	137370	77654	4440047	52.3	20	603987
1975	8721874	137867	85579	5012461	57.5	25	617811
1980	8861539	122803	99852	5536690	62.5	30	649304
1985	8960416	114084	104156	5957781	66.5	35	673715
1990	*9010202*	*110042*	*104825*	*6331469*	*70.3*	40	561177
1995	*9036318*	*111635*	*104740*	*6613681*	*73.2*	45	553410
2000	*9070855*	*111689*	*110492*	*6886593*	*75.9*	50	622179
2005	*9076881*	*108796*	*112381*	*7076336*	*78.0*	55	598805
2010	*9058983*	*104387*	*112069*	*7235410*	*79.9*	60	552580
2015	*9020671*	*102394*	*109448*	*7329295*	*81.3*	65	297597
2020	*8985446*	*101859*	*110117*	*7417486*	*82.6*	70+	716148

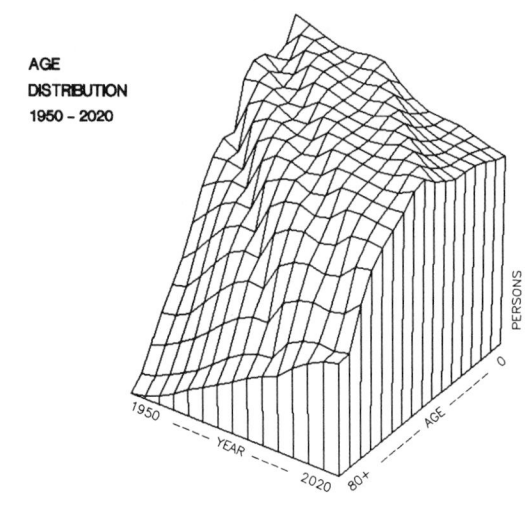

AGE DISTRIBUTION 1950 - 2020

PERSONS

POPULATION RATIOS

YEAR	AGE DISTRIBUTION UNDER 15	AGE DISTRIBUTION 15-64	AGE DISTRIBUTION 65 & OLDER	AGE DISTRIBUTION 70 & OLDER	DEPENDENCY RATIO	WOMEN 15-49	CHILD-WOMAN RATIO
1950	0.268	0.665	0.067	0.039	0.504	0.269	0.376
1955	0.266	0.660	0.074	0.045	0.515	0.263	0.354
1960	0.261	0.664	0.075	0.048	0.505	0.255	0.328
1965	0.242	0.674	0.084	0.051	0.483	0.255	0.308
1970	0.228	0.676	0.096	0.056	0.480	0.260	0.293
1975	0.220	0.671	0.109	0.065	0.491	0.251	0.307
1980	0.221	0.660	0.119	0.074	0.515	0.241	0.316
1985	0.213	0.674	0.113	0.080	0.483	0.236	0.278
1990	*0.201*	*0.670*	*0.130*	*0.075*	*0.493*	*0.238*	*0.262*
2000	*0.182*	*0.659*	*0.158*	*0.103*	*0.517*	*0.235*	*0.259*
2010	*0.181*	*0.657*	*0.162*	*0.112*	*0.523*	*0.225*	*0.264*
2020	*0.174*	*0.642*	*0.184*	*0.125*	*0.558*	*0.221*	*0.255*

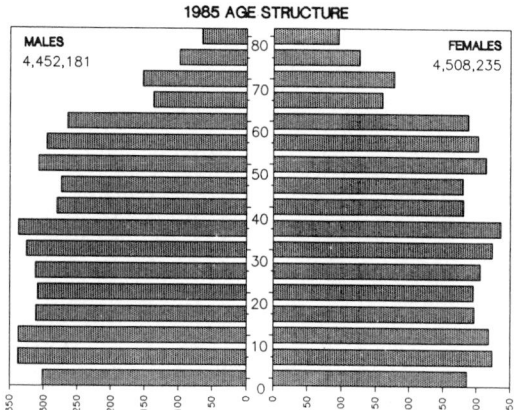

1985 AGE STRUCTURE

MALES 4,452,181   FEMALES 4,508,235

MORTALITY MEASURES (Annual Averages)

PERIOD	CRUDE DEATH RATE	INFANT MORT. RATE	LIFE EXPECTANCY AT BIRTH (years) MALE	LIFE EXPECTANCY AT BIRTH (years) FEMALE	LIFE EXPECTANCY AT BIRTH (years) BOTH SEXES	DIFFERENCE FEMALE-MALE
1950-55	10.18	92.44	62.20	66.10	64.09	3.90
1955-60	8.88	62.30	65.40	68.80	67.05	3.40
1960-65	8.16	36.42	68.10	71.70	69.84	3.60
1965-70	8.70	30.54	68.70	73.10	70.83	4.40
1970-75	9.15	25.56	68.70	73.90	71.22	5.20
1975-80	9.81	22.27	68.70	74.10	71.32	5.40
1980-85	11.27	17.49	68.50	74.40	71.36	5.90
1985-90	*11.62*	*16.30*	*69.20*	*74.96*	*72.00*	*5.76*
1990-95	*11.63*	*14.03*	*70.35*	*76.07*	*73.13*	*5.72*
2000-05	*12.18*	*10.23*	*72.39*	*77.90*	*75.06*	*5.51*
2010-15	*12.37*	*7.53*	*73.99*	*79.54*	*76.68*	*5.56*
2020-25	*12.26*	*6.15*	*75.38*	*80.73*	*77.97*	*5.35*

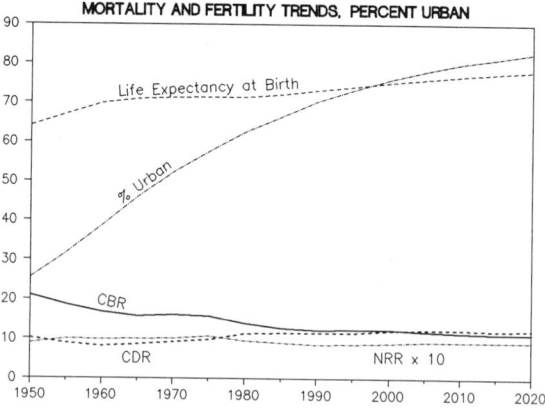

MORTALITY AND FERTILITY TRENDS, PERCENT URBAN

Life Expectancy at Birth

% Urban

CBR

CDR   NRR x 10

FERTILITY MEASURES (Annual Averages)

PERIOD	CRUDE BIRTH RATE	FERTILITY RATES GENERAL	FERTILITY RATES TOTAL	REPRODUCTION RATES GROSS	REPRODUCTION RATES NET	RATE OF NATUR. INCR.
1950-55	21.06	79.24	2.495	1.210	0.890	10.88
1955-60	18.70	72.25	2.283	1.107	0.990	9.82
1960-65	16.88	66.21	2.192	1.063	0.985	8.72
1965-70	15.82	61.45	2.159	1.047	0.996	7.12
1970-75	16.18	63.31	2.165	1.050	1.013	7.03
1975-80	15.81	64.17	2.250	1.091	1.058	5.99
1980-85	13.86	58.02	2.013	0.976	0.939	2.59
1985-90	*12.73*	*53.67*	*1.900*	*0.921*	*0.900*	*1.11*
1990-95	*12.21*	*50.90*	*1.800*	*0.873*	*0.857*	*0.58*
2000-05	*12.31*	*53.05*	*1.850*	*0.897*	*0.888*	*0.13*
2010-15	*11.52*	*51.35*	*1.900*	*0.921*	*0.916*	*-0.85*
2020-25	*11.34*	*51.78*	*1.900*	*0.921*	*0.916*	*-0.92*

AGING MEASURES

YEAR	POPULATION AGE RATIOS 60+/20-59	POPULATION AGE RATIOS 65+/20-64	POPULATION AGE RATIOS 70+/20-69	POPULATION AGE RATIOS 75+/20-74	POPULATION MEAN AGE	POPULATION MEDIAN AGE
1950	0.1895	0.1179	0.0644	0.0298	30.47	27.30
1960	0.2072	0.1275	0.0777	0.0375	32.30	30.42
1970	0.2704	0.1610	0.0884	0.0441	34.39	33.16
1980	0.2838	0.2011	0.1162	0.0572	35.76	34.22
1990	*0.3584*	*0.2172*	*0.1150*	*0.0703*	*37.43*	*36.71*
2000	*0.3926*	*0.2664*	*0.1577*	*0.0804*	*38.85*	*38.24*
2010	*0.4278*	*0.2715*	*0.1735*	*0.1017*	*39.80*	*39.25*
2020	*0.4731*	*0.3177*	*0.1957*	*0.1043*	*40.78*	*41.16*

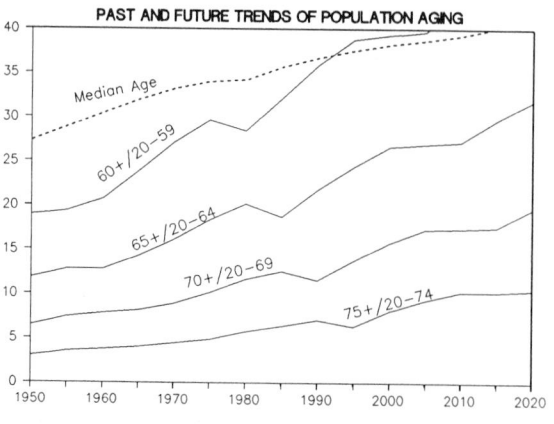

PAST AND FUTURE TRENDS OF POPULATION AGING

Median Age

60+/20-59

65+/20-64

70+/20-69

75+/20-74

OBSERVED AND *PROJECTED* POPULATION DATA (000's)

YEAR	MID-YEAR POPULATION	NO. OF BIRTHS	NO. OF DEATHS	URBAN POPULATION NUMBER	URBAN POPULATION PERCENT	POPULATION 1985 AGE	POPULATION 1985 NUMBER
1950	12389	273	135	4634	37.4	0	1182
1955	13093	242	127	5513	42.1	5	1388
1960	13654	223	130	6411	46.9	10	1218
1965	14159	219	150	7238	51.1	15	1076
1970	14334	259	164	7907	55.2	20	1074
1975	14802	273	172	8694	58.7	25	1186
1980	15311	232	182	9519	62.2	30	1265
1985	15500	218	184	10152	65.5	35	1166
1990	*15667*	*217*	*176*	*10749*	*68.6*	40	942
1995	*15874*	*226*	*165*	*11343*	*71.5*	45	782
2000	*16179*	*229*	*170*	*11977*	*74.0*	50	850
2005	*16478*	*217*	*170*	*12573*	*76.3*	55	851
2010	*16715*	*207*	*170*	*13085*	*78.3*	60	811
2015	*16899*	*204*	*172*	*13535*	*80.1*	65	423
2020	*17061*	*206*	*182*	*13948*	*81.8*	70+	1287

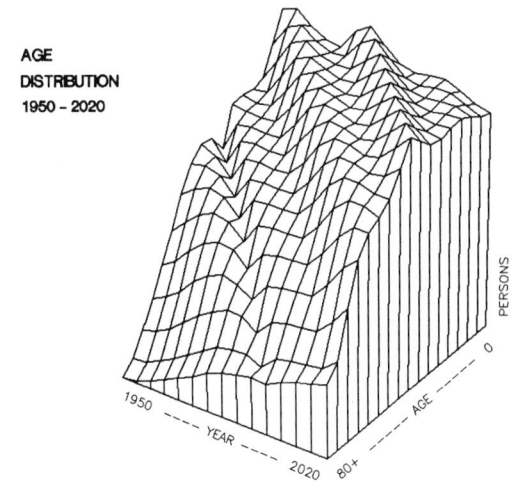

AGE DISTRIBUTION 1950 - 2020

POPULATION RATIOS

YEAR	AGE DISTRIBUTION UNDER 15	AGE DISTRIBUTION 15-64	AGE DISTRIBUTION 65 & OLDER	AGE DISTRIBUTION 70 & OLDER	DEPENDENCY RATIO	WOMEN 15-49	CHILD-WOMAN RATIO
1950	0.259	0.665	0.076	0.046	0.504	0.262	0.397
1955	0.277	0.641	0.082	0.049	0.560	0.242	0.415
1960	0.274	0.640	0.086	0.051	0.564	0.234	0.368
1965	0.253	0.648	0.098	0.057	0.542	0.235	0.334
1970	0.232	0.657	0.112	0.066	0.523	0.251	0.298
1975	0.234	0.645	0.121	0.073	0.550	0.245	0.356
1980	0.243	0.633	0.125	0.083	0.581	0.239	0.371
1985	0.244	0.645	0.110	0.083	0.550	0.239	0.319
1990	*0.232*	*0.652*	*0.116*	*0.070*	*0.534*	*0.248*	*0.277*
2000	*0.203*	*0.675*	*0.123*	*0.081*	*0.482*	*0.252*	*0.276*
2010	*0.201*	*0.675*	*0.124*	*0.081*	*0.482*	*0.235*	*0.276*
2020	*0.184*	*0.657*	*0.159*	*0.100*	*0.522*	*0.234*	*0.256*

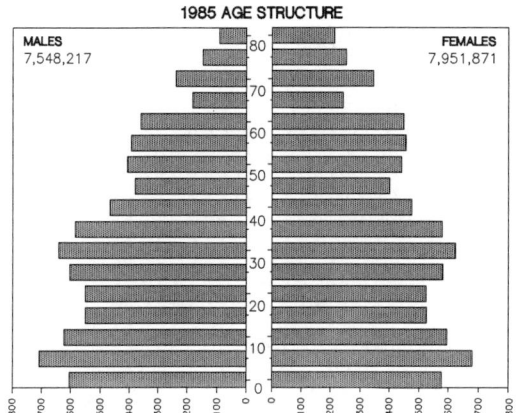

1985 AGE STRUCTURE

MALES 7,548,217   FEMALES 7,951,871

MORTALITY MEASURES (Annual Averages)

PERIOD	CRUDE DEATH RATE	INFANT MORT. RATE	LIFE EXPECTANCY AT BIRTH (years) MALE	LIFE EXPECTANCY AT BIRTH (years) FEMALE	LIFE EXPECTANCY AT BIRTH (years) BOTH SEXES	DIFFERENCE FEMALE-MALE
1950-55	10.90	53.87	63.60	68.40	65.93	4.80
1955-60	9.70	30.03	67.00	72.20	69.53	5.20
1960-65	9.50	22.68	67.50	73.20	70.27	5.70
1965-70	10.59	23.16	66.90	73.40	70.06	6.50
1970-75	11.44	21.25	66.60	73.50	69.96	6.90
1975-80	11.59	19.39	67.00	74.10	70.45	7.10
1980-85	11.90	16.07	67.00	74.40	70.60	7.40
1985-90	*11.89*	*15.28*	*67.52*	*74.96*	*71.14*	*7.44*
1990-95	*11.24*	*13.27*	*68.76*	*76.02*	*72.30*	*7.26*
2000-05	*10.48*	*9.89*	*70.97*	*77.92*	*74.35*	*6.96*
2010-15	*10.19*	*7.49*	*72.93*	*79.53*	*76.14*	*6.60*
2020-25	*10.68*	*6.18*	*74.50*	*80.72*	*77.53*	*6.22*

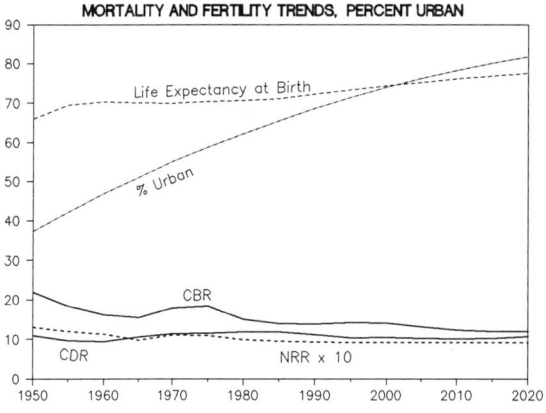

MORTALITY AND FERTILITY TRENDS, PERCENT URBAN

Life Expectancy at Birth — % Urban — CBR — CDR — NRR x 10

FERTILITY MEASURES (Annual Averages)

PERIOD	CRUDE BIRTH RATE	FERTILITY RATES GENERAL	FERTILITY RATES TOTAL	REPRODUCTION RATES GROSS	REPRODUCTION RATES NET	RATE OF NATUR. INCR.
1950-55	22.00	87.35	2.892	1.408	1.307	11.10
1955-60	18.50	77.75	2.578	1.255	1.202	8.80
1960-65	16.30	69.54	2.401	1.169	1.130	6.80
1965-70	15.50	63.75	2.085	1.015	0.983	4.91
1970-75	18.04	72.78	2.342	1.140	1.109	6.60
1975-80	18.45	76.22	2.356	1.147	1.104	6.86
1980-85	15.14	63.26	2.091	1.018	0.995	3.25
1985-90	*14.04*	*57.59*	*2.000*	*0.974*	*0.955*	*2.14*
1990-95	*13.86*	*54.83*	*1.950*	*0.949*	*0.935*	*2.63*
2000-05	*14.15*	*57.31*	*1.900*	*0.925*	*0.917*	*3.67*
2010-15	*12.37*	*52.71*	*1.900*	*0.925*	*0.920*	*2.18*
2020-25	*12.10*	*52.30*	*1.900*	*0.925*	*0.920*	*1.42*

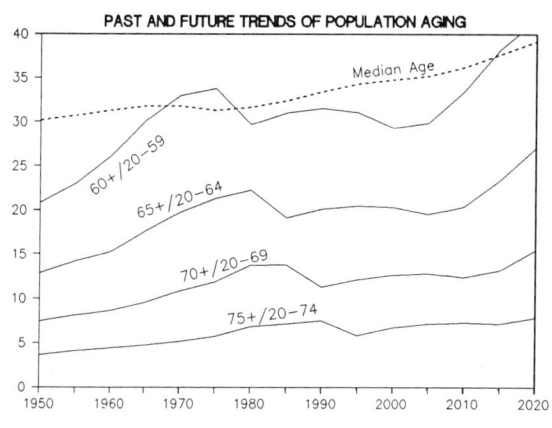

PAST AND FUTURE TRENDS OF POPULATION AGING

Median Age — 60+/20-59 — 65+/20-64 — 70+/20-69 — 75+/20-74

AGING MEASURES

YEAR	POPULATION AGE RATIOS 60+/20-59	POPULATION AGE RATIOS 65+/20-64	POPULATION AGE RATIOS 70+/20-69	POPULATION AGE RATIOS 75+/20-74	POPULATION MEAN AGE	POPULATION MEDIAN AGE
1950	0.2082	0.1285	0.0744	0.0367	32.39	30.15
1960	0.2612	0.1527	0.0860	0.0442	33.15	31.34
1970	0.3297	0.1970	0.1081	0.0515	34.60	31.82
1980	0.2971	0.2227	0.1373	0.0681	34.49	31.70
1990	*0.3158*	*0.2011*	*0.1129*	*0.0748*	*35.11*	*33.53*
2000	*0.2933*	*0.2037*	*0.1264*	*0.0671*	*36.24*	*34.88*
2010	*0.3351*	*0.2040*	*0.1235*	*0.0730*	*37.46*	*36.25*
2020	*0.4158*	*0.2699*	*0.1547*	*0.0779*	*39.09*	*39.17*

OBSERVED AND *PROJECTED* POPULATION DATA

YEAR	MID-YEAR POPULATION	NO. OF BIRTHS	NO. OF DEATHS	URBAN POPULATION NUMBER	PERCENT	POPULATION 1985 AGE	NUMBER
1950	4271000	76451	38524	2903575	68.0	0	276043
1955	4439000	74664	40306	3090405	69.6	5	315431
1960	4581000	78060	44252	3375188	73.7	10	365515
1965	4758000	79078	47390	3665964	77.0	15	392381
1970	4928757	72147	49623	3929191	79.7	20	397396
1975	5059861	62277	52754	4156371	82.1	25	370151
1980	5123027	52783	56635	4290991	83.8	30	372303
1985	5122065	54719	58110	4359824	85.1	35	410356
1990	*5120035*	*56674*	*57892*	*4422469*	*86.4*	40	369189
1995	*5128859*	*56402*	*57274*	*4489194*	*87.5*	45	293824
2000	*5139426*	*53697*	*57238*	*4552318*	*88.6*	50	265323
2005	*5136682*	*50427*	*57366*	*4598563*	*89.5*	55	262182
2010	*5116983*	*48990*	*58421*	*4624536*	*90.4*	60	267928
2015	*5084909*	*48327*	*60831*	*4635213*	*91.2*	65	235370
2020	*5037633*	*48205*	*64441*	*4628099*	*91.9*	70+	528673

POPULATION RATIOS

YEAR	UNDER 15	15-64	65 & OLDER	70 & OLDER	DEPENDENCY RATIO	WOMEN 15-49	CHILD-WOMAN RATIO
1950	0.263	0.646	0.091	0.056	0.549	0.248	0.392
1955	0.265	0.637	0.098	0.061	0.570	0.240	0.352
1960	0.252	0.642	0.106	0.067	0.558	0.237	0.339
1965	0.238	0.649	0.113	0.071	0.541	0.237	0.348
1970	0.233	0.644	0.123	0.078	0.552	0.234	0.336
1975	0.226	0.640	0.134	0.087	0.562	0.232	0.308
1980	0.208	0.647	0.144	0.097	0.545	0.239	0.256
1985	0.187	0.664	0.149	0.103	0.506	0.250	0.216
1990	*0.170*	*0.675*	*0.155*	*0.107*	*0.481*	*0.256*	*0.210*
2000	*0.166*	*0.679*	*0.155*	*0.112*	*0.472*	*0.238*	*0.232*
2010	*0.159*	*0.664*	*0.177*	*0.117*	*0.507*	*0.223*	*0.222*
2020	*0.149*	*0.636*	*0.216*	*0.154*	*0.573*	*0.206*	*0.235*

MORTALITY MEASURES (Annual Averages)

PERIOD	CRUDE DEATH RATE	INFANT MORT. RATE	MALE	FEMALE	BOTH SEXES	DIFFERENCE FEMALE-MALE
1950-55	9.02	27.96	69.60	72.40	70.96	2.80
1955-60	9.08	23.32	70.30	73.70	71.96	3.40
1960-65	9.66	19.92	70.30	74.40	72.29	4.10
1965-70	9.96	16.16	70.60	75.30	72.89	4.70
1970-75	10.07	12.04	70.90	76.40	73.58	5.50
1975-80	10.43	9.20	71.25	77.25	74.17	6.00
1980-85	11.06	7.95	71.55	77.50	74.45	5.95
1985-90	*11.35*	*7.11*	*72.57*	*78.28*	*75.36*	*5.71*
1990-95	*11.31*	*6.41*	*73.33*	*79.14*	*76.17*	*5.81*
2000-05	*11.14*	*5.41*	*74.96*	*80.47*	*77.65*	*5.51*
2010-15	*11.42*	*5.03*	*76.01*	*81.49*	*78.68*	*5.47*
2020-25	*12.79*	*4.77*	*76.96*	*82.49*	*79.66*	*5.53*

FERTILITY MEASURES (Annual Averages)

PERIOD	CRUDE BIRTH RATE	GENERAL	TOTAL	GROSS	NET	RATE OF NATUR. INCR.
1950-55	17.90	73.37	2.528	1.233	1.186	8.88
1955-60	16.82	70.60	2.532	1.235	1.195	7.74
1960-65	17.04	71.94	2.581	1.259	1.223	7.38
1965-70	16.62	70.60	2.237	1.091	1.041	6.66
1970-75	14.64	62.79	1.958	0.955	0.936	4.57
1975-80	12.31	52.19	1.701	0.830	0.814	1.88
1980-85	10.30	42.16	1.423	0.694	0.683	-0.75
1985-90	*10.68*	*42.28*	*1.450*	*0.707*	*0.697*	*-0.66*
1990-95	*11.07*	*43.71*	*1.500*	*0.732*	*0.722*	*-0.24*
2000-05	*10.45*	*44.62*	*1.600*	*0.780*	*0.771*	*-0.69*
2010-15	*9.57*	*43.71*	*1.700*	*0.829*	*0.820*	*-1.84*
2020-25	*9.57*	*47.46*	*1.700*	*0.829*	*0.820*	*-3.22*

AGING MEASURES

YEAR	60+/20-59	65+/20-64	70+/20-69	75+/20-74	MEAN AGE	MEDIAN AGE
1950	0.2505	0.1582	0.0914	0.0454	33.16	31.77
1960	0.3036	0.1895	0.1114	0.0584	34.48	32.99
1970	0.3421	0.2158	0.1279	0.0679	35.33	32.52
1980	0.3749	0.2527	0.1579	0.0874	36.80	34.26
1990	*0.3656*	*0.2566*	*0.1648*	*0.0978*	*38.56*	*37.19*
2000	*0.3601*	*0.2486*	*0.1678*	*0.1043*	*40.02*	*39.49*
2010	*0.4645*	*0.2917*	*0.1761*	*0.1063*	*41.74*	*42.50*
2020	*0.5477*	*0.3713*	*0.2395*	*0.1328*	*43.47*	*45.26*

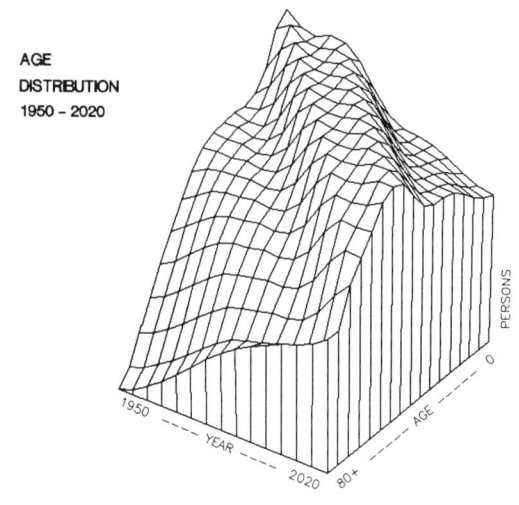

AGE DISTRIBUTION 1950 - 2020

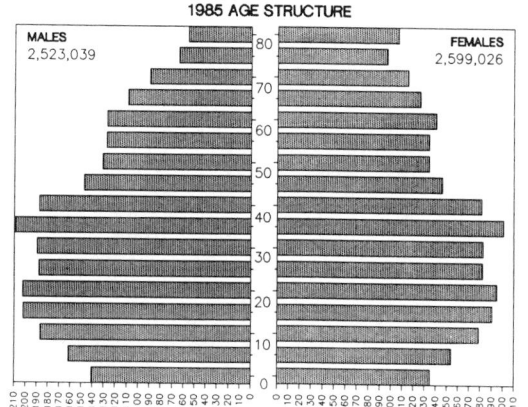

1985 AGE STRUCTURE

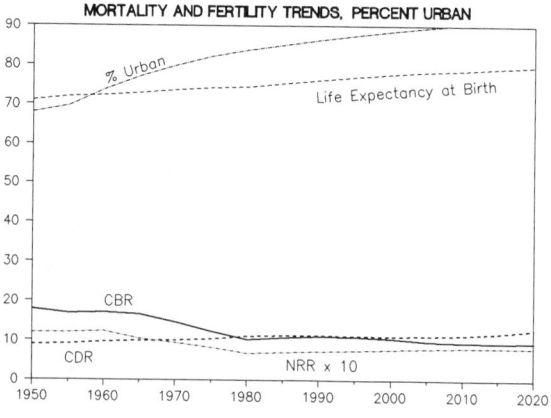

MORTALITY AND FERTILITY TRENDS, PERCENT URBAN

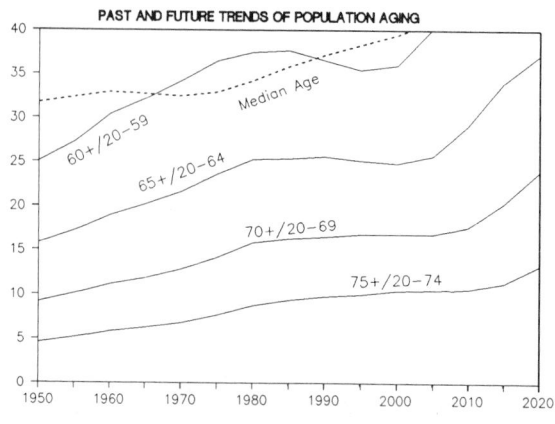

PAST AND FUTURE TRENDS OF POPULATION AGING

OBSERVED AND *PROJECTED* POPULATION DATA

YEAR	MID-YEAR POPULATION	NO. OF BIRTHS	NO. OF DEATHS	URBAN POPULATION NUMBER	URBAN POPULATION PERCENT	POPULATION 1985 AGE	POPULATION 1985 NUMBER
1950	4009000	91485	38807	1283229	32.0	0	325027
1955	4235000	84361	38454	1481648	35.0	5	324057
1960	4430000	80272	41110	1687150	38.1	10	302436
1965	4564000	74302	44088	2005311	43.9	15	350851
1970	4606000	60693	43877	2315215	50.3	20	378409
1975	4711431	64108	43764	2594187	55.1	25	384538
1980	4779536	64299	44349	2848639	59.6	30	408648
1985	4902208	61317	49851	3136499	64.0	35	441265
1990	4974948	58525	50560	3378013	67.9	40	315991
1995	5029983	57226	51140	3586974	71.3	45	283220
2000	5075537	56516	53065	3766545	74.2	50	263214
2005	5107830	56498	54633	3913475	76.6	55	268956
2010	5132159	56454	55987	4032504	78.6	60	242598
2015	5149490	55553	58817	4138332	80.4	65	189969
2020	5148147	54056	62550	4221575	82.0	70+	422031

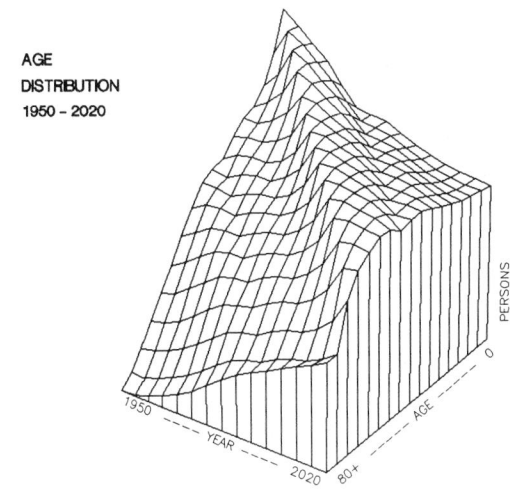

AGE DISTRIBUTION 1950 – 2020

POPULATION RATIOS

YEAR	UNDER 15	15-64	65 & OLDER	70 & OLDER	DEPENDENCY RATIO	WOMEN 15-49	CHILD-WOMAN RATIO
1950	0.300	0.634	0.067	0.039	0.578	0.262	0.476
1955	0.306	0.625	0.069	0.041	0.601	0.252	0.417
1960	0.304	0.624	0.072	0.043	0.603	0.242	0.385
1965	0.271	0.650	0.079	0.046	0.538	0.249	0.345
1970	0.246	0.662	0.092	0.054	0.510	0.252	0.300
1975	0.220	0.674	0.106	0.063	0.484	0.255	0.251
1980	0.203	0.677	0.120	0.078	0.477	0.255	0.263
1985	0.194	0.681	0.125	0.086	0.469	0.256	0.259
1990	0.193	0.675	0.132	0.088	0.480	0.254	0.244
2000	0.175	0.681	0.144	0.100	0.469	0.241	0.235
2010	0.167	0.675	0.159	0.108	0.482	0.223	0.248
2020	0.164	0.628	0.208	0.142	0.593	0.209	0.258

MORTALITY MEASURES (Annual Averages)

PERIOD	CRUDE DEATH RATE	INFANT MORT. RATE	LIFE EXPECTANCY AT BIRTH (years) MALE	LIFE EXPECTANCY AT BIRTH (years) FEMALE	LIFE EXPECTANCY AT BIRTH (years) BOTH SEXES	DIFFERENCE FEMALE-MALE
1950-55	9.68	33.80	63.20	69.60	66.32	6.40
1955-60	9.08	25.47	64.80	71.40	68.02	6.60
1960-65	9.28	19.18	65.40	72.50	68.86	7.10
1965-70	9.66	14.83	65.90	73.50	69.61	7.60
1970-75	9.53	11.55	66.60	75.00	70.70	8.40
1975-80	9.29	8.58	68.00	76.60	72.19	8.60
1980-85	9.28	6.45	70.02	77.94	73.89	7.92
1985-90	10.17	5.87	71.04	78.79	74.82	7.75
1990-95	10.16	5.34	72.07	79.57	75.73	7.51
2000-05	10.45	4.87	73.76	80.67	77.13	6.91
2010-15	10.91	4.70	75.24	81.76	78.42	6.53
2020-25	12.15	4.59	76.19	83.00	79.51	6.81

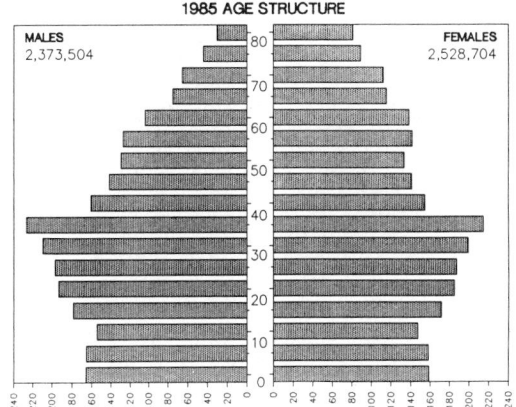

1985 AGE STRUCTURE

MALES 2,373,504   FEMALES 2,528,704

MALE   FEMALE   BOTH SEXES

LIFE EXPECTANCY AT BIRTH (years)

FERTILITY MEASURES (Annual Averages)

PERIOD	CRUDE BIRTH RATE	FERTILITY RATES GENERAL	FERTILITY RATES TOTAL	REPRODUCTION RATES GROSS	REPRODUCTION RATES NET	RATE OF NATUR. INCR.
1950-55	22.82	88.78	2.975	1.452	1.372	13.14
1955-60	19.92	80.62	2.785	1.359	1.300	10.84
1960-65	18.12	73.81	2.580	1.259	1.220	8.84
1965-70	16.28	65.05	2.063	1.007	0.977	6.62
1970-75	13.18	51.95	1.617	0.789	0.769	3.65
1975-80	13.61	53.32	1.639	0.800	0.788	4.32
1980-85	13.45	52.68	1.688	0.824	0.812	4.17
1985-90	12.51	49.08	1.650	0.805	0.795	2.34
1990-95	11.76	46.45	1.650	0.805	0.796	1.60
2000-05	11.14	47.20	1.730	0.844	0.836	0.68
2010-15	11.00	50.33	1.780	0.869	0.861	0.09
2020-25	10.50	50.38	1.800	0.878	0.871	-1.65

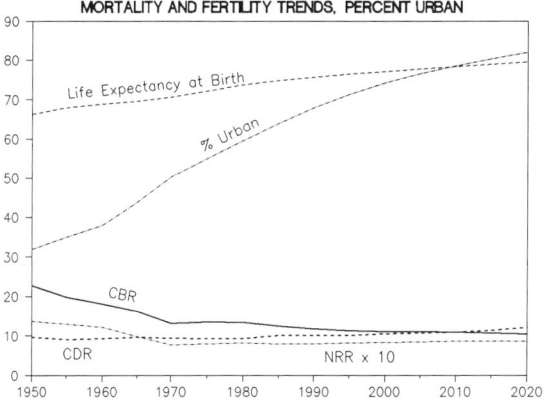

MORTALITY AND FERTILITY TRENDS, PERCENT URBAN

Life Expectancy at Birth
% Urban
CBR
CDR
NRR x 10

AGING MEASURES

YEAR	POPULATION AGE RATIOS 60+/20-59	65+/20-64	70+/20-69	75+/20-74	POPULATION MEAN AGE	POPULATION MEDIAN AGE
1950	0.1947	0.1197	0.0676	0.0331	30.20	27.71
1960	0.2213	0.1325	0.0758	0.0373	31.07	28.24
1970	0.2728	0.1608	0.0882	0.0421	33.10	29.64
1980	0.2955	0.2005	0.1218	0.0617	35.52	32.79
1990	0.3246	0.2149	0.1329	0.0791	37.29	36.32
2000	0.3420	0.2332	0.1523	0.0871	39.11	39.25
2010	0.4355	0.2571	0.1615	0.0959	40.81	41.65
2020	0.5459	0.3641	0.2226	0.1128	42.25	42.79

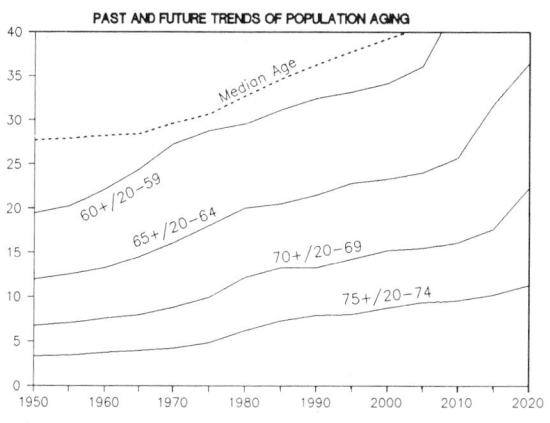

PAST AND FUTURE TRENDS OF POPULATION AGING

Median Age
60+/20-59
65+/20-64
70+/20-69
75+/20-74

OBSERVED AND *PROJECTED* POPULATION DATA (000's)

YEAR	MID-YEAR POPULATION	NO. OF BIRTHS	NO. OF DEATHS	URBAN POPULATION NUMBER	URBAN POPULATION PERCENT	POPULATION 1985 AGE	POPULATION 1985 NUMBER
1950	41829	815	533	23494	56.2	0	3788
1955	43428	798	512	25759	59.3	5	3702
1960	45684	824	513	28501	62.4	10	4208
1965	48758	836	540	32738	67.1	15	4265
1970	50772	826	541	36061	71.0	20	4296
1975	52699	738	541	38479	73.0	25	4207
1980	53880	783	602	39456	73.2	30	4269
1985	55170	771	573	40518	73.4	35	4256
1990	*56173*	*761*	*560*	*41603*	*74.1*	40	2975
1995	*57188*	*743*	*543*	*42929*	*75.1*	45	2969
2000	*58196*	*719*	*581*	*44469*	*76.4*	50	3130
2005	*58889*	*707*	*600*	*45956*	*78.0*	55	3054
2010	*59430*	*701*	*614*	*47469*	*79.9*	60	2904
2015	*59867*	*698*	*626*	*48824*	*81.6*	65	1614
2020	*60229*	*689*	*646*	*50044*	*83.1*	70+	5531

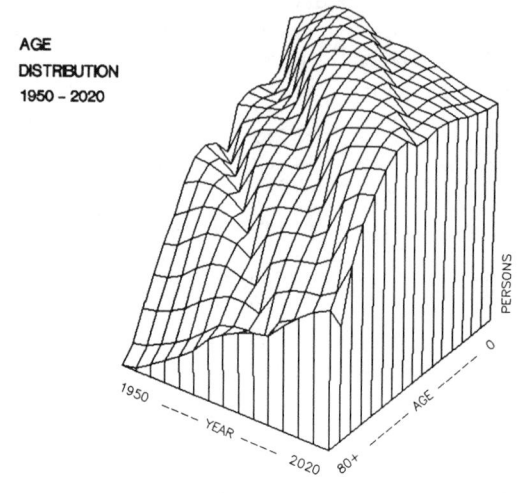

AGE DISTRIBUTION 1950 – 2020

POPULATION RATIOS

YEAR	AGE DISTRIBUTION UNDER 15	15-64	65 & OLDER	70 & OLDER	DEPENDENCY RATIO	WOMEN 15-49	CHILD-WOMAN RATIO
1950	0.227	0.659	0.114	0.072	0.517	0.246	0.386
1955	0.245	0.640	0.116	0.074	0.563	0.232	0.389
1960	0.264	0.620	0.116	0.076	0.613	0.219	0.400
1965	0.256	0.623	0.121	0.077	0.606	0.223	0.388
1970	0.248	0.623	0.129	0.082	0.605	0.236	0.351
1975	0.239	0.626	0.135	0.089	0.597	0.236	0.331
1980	0.223	0.638	0.140	0.101	0.569	0.240	0.286
1985	0.212	0.658	0.130	0.100	0.519	0.244	0.281
1990	*0.202*	*0.661*	*0.138*	*0.090*	*0.514*	*0.249*	*0.276*
2000	*0.195*	*0.651*	*0.153*	*0.108*	*0.536*	*0.241*	*0.265*
2010	*0.182*	*0.662*	*0.156*	*0.114*	*0.511*	*0.228*	*0.261*
2020	*0.174*	*0.634*	*0.191*	*0.132*	*0.577*	*0.214*	*0.270*

1985 AGE STRUCTURE

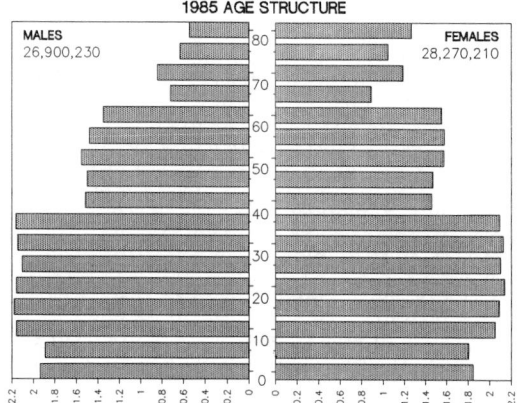

MALES 26,900,230   FEMALES 28,270,210

MORTALITY MEASURES (Annual Averages)

PERIOD	CRUDE DEATH RATE	INFANT MORT. RATE	LIFE EXPECTANCY AT BIRTH (years) MALE	FEMALE	BOTH SEXES	DIFFERENCE FEMALE-MALE
1950-55	12.75	44.97	63.70	69.50	66.52	5.80
1955-60	11.79	32.76	66.50	72.90	69.61	6.40
1960-65	11.24	24.94	67.60	74.50	70.96	6.90
1965-70	11.07	20.53	67.90	75.40	71.55	7.50
1970-75	10.65	15.91	68.60	76.30	72.35	7.70
1975-80	10.26	11.29	69.70	77.80	73.70	8.10
1980-85	11.18	9.20	70.70	78.90	74.70	8.20
1985-90	*10.38*	*7.99*	*71.70*	*79.80*	*75.65*	*8.10*
1990-95	*9.97*	*6.86*	*72.71*	*80.61*	*76.56*	*7.90*
2000-05	*9.99*	*6.19*	*74.29*	*81.59*	*77.85*	*7.30*
2010-15	*10.33*	*5.69*	*75.56*	*82.65*	*79.01*	*7.09*
2020-25	*10.73*	*5.23*	*76.64*	*83.36*	*79.92*	*6.72*

FERTILITY MEASURES (Annual Averages)

PERIOD	CRUDE BIRTH RATE	FERTILITY RATES GENERAL	FERTILITY RATES TOTAL	REPRODUCTION RATES GROSS	REPRODUCTION RATES NET	RATE OF NATUR. INCR.
1950-55	19.48	81.63	2.726	1.328	1.257	6.73
1955-60	18.37	81.47	2.712	1.321	1.267	6.58
1960-65	18.04	81.58	2.850	1.388	1.344	6.80
1965-70	17.15	74.72	2.607	1.270	1.234	6.08
1970-75	16.26	68.93	2.310	1.125	1.099	5.61
1975-80	14.00	58.86	1.862	0.907	0.891	3.74
1980-85	14.53	60.06	1.866	0.909	0.896	3.35
1985-90	*13.98*	*56.69*	*1.850*	*0.901*	*0.887*	*3.60*
1990-95	*13.55*	*54.29*	*1.840*	*0.896*	*0.883*	*3.58*
2000-05	*12.36*	*52.00*	*1.870*	*0.911*	*0.899*	*2.37*
2010-15	*11.80*	*52.63*	*1.900*	*0.925*	*0.914*	*1.47*
2020-25	*11.44*	*54.26*	*1.900*	*0.925*	*0.915*	*0.71*

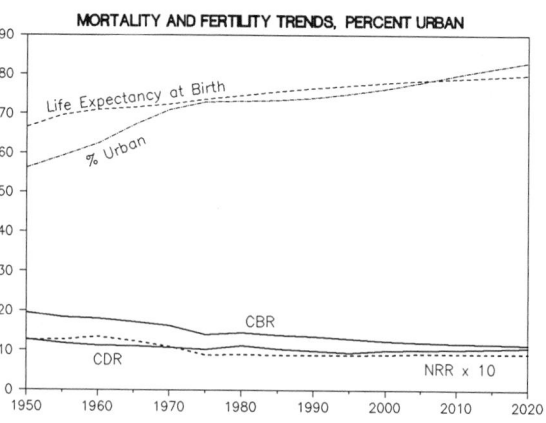

MORTALITY AND FERTILITY TRENDS, PERCENT URBAN

Life Expectancy at Birth
% Urban
CBR
CDR
NRR x 10

AGING MEASURES

YEAR	POPULATION AGE RATIOS 60+/20-59	65+/20-64	70+/20-69	75+/20-74	POPULATION MEAN AGE	POPULATION MEDIAN AGE
1950	0.3031	0.1949	0.1149	0.0593	35.26	34.51
1960	0.3311	0.2082	0.1270	0.0686	34.87	32.96
1970	0.3697	0.2382	0.1406	0.0757	34.79	32.30
1980	0.3277	0.2504	0.1700	0.0972	35.79	32.53
1990	*0.3540*	*0.2351*	*0.1419*	*0.0978*	*36.78*	*34.81*
2000	*0.3685*	*0.2615*	*0.1701*	*0.0985*	*38.18*	*37.23*
2010	*0.4116*	*0.2609*	*0.1784*	*0.1127*	*39.71*	*39.64*
2020	*0.4964*	*0.3332*	*0.2076*	*0.1134*	*41.14*	*41.40*

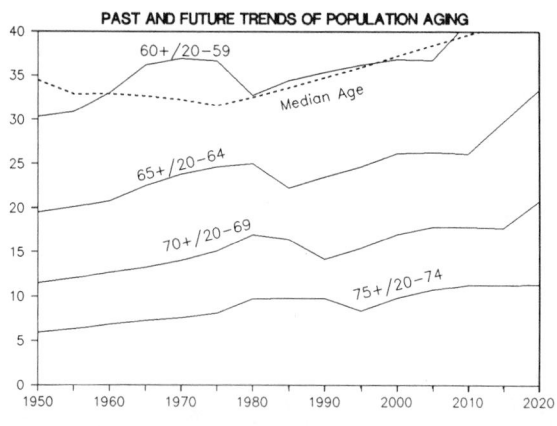

PAST AND FUTURE TRENDS OF POPULATION AGING

60+/20-59
Median Age
65+/20-64
70+/20-69
75+/20-74

OBSERVED AND *PROJECTED* POPULATION DATA (000's)

YEAR	MID-YEAR POPULATION	NO. OF BIRTHS	NO. OF DEATHS	URBAN POPULATION NUMBER	PERCENT	POPULATION 1985 AGE	NUMBER
1950	18387	304	218	13013	70.8	0	1158
1955	17944	288	227	12833	71.5	5	1072
1960	17240	299	229	12456	72.3	10	976
1965	17019	256	233	12420	73.0	15	1226
1970	17066	202	236	12582	73.7	20	1417
1975	16850	221	234	12671	75.2	25	1292
1980	16737	236	228	12747	76.2	30	1269
1985	16644	214	213	12810	77.0	35	887
1990	*16649*	*190*	*196*	*12982*	*78.0*	40	1129
1995	*16618*	*181*	*181*	*13157*	*79.2*	45	1265
2000	*16618*	*186*	*186*	*13380*	*80.5*	50	999
2005	*16621*	*191*	*191*	*13622*	*82.0*	55	904
2010	*16618*	*181*	*196*	*13869*	*83.5*	60	793
2015	*16542*	*170*	*206*	*14033*	*84.8*	65	491
2020	*16363*	*164*	*206*	*14086*	*86.1*	70+	1766

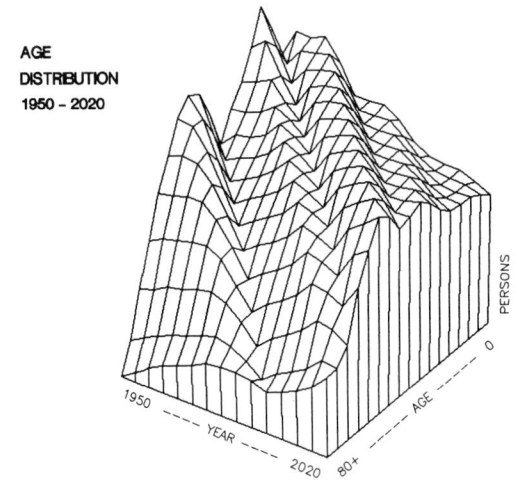

AGE DISTRIBUTION 1950 – 2020

POPULATION RATIOS

YEAR	AGE DISTRIBUTION UNDER 15	15-64	65 & OLDER	70 & OLDER	DEPENDENCY RATIO	WOMEN 15-49	CHILD-WOMAN RATIO
1950	0.228	0.666	0.106	0.062	0.502	0.272	0.216
1955	0.211	0.667	0.123	0.073	0.500	0.260	0.301
1960	0.211	0.652	0.137	0.085	0.533	0.240	0.323
1965	0.238	0.616	0.146	0.090	0.624	0.219	0.385
1970	0.234	0.611	0.155	0.096	0.638	0.231	0.313
1975	0.216	0.621	0.162	0.105	0.610	0.238	0.246
1980	0.197	0.644	0.159	0.113	0.552	0.248	0.261
1985	0.193	0.672	0.136	0.106	0.489	0.251	0.277
1990	*0.197*	*0.672*	*0.131*	*0.088*	*0.488*	*0.241*	*0.264*
2000	*0.174*	*0.682*	*0.143*	*0.094*	*0.465*	*0.245*	*0.221*
2010	*0.167*	*0.661*	*0.173*	*0.117*	*0.514*	*0.229*	*0.249*
2020	*0.164*	*0.651*	*0.184*	*0.120*	*0.535*	*0.208*	*0.247*

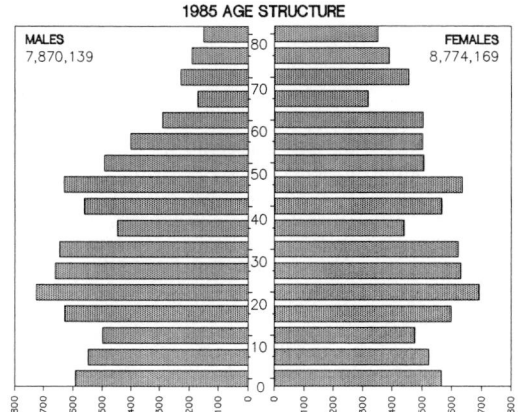

1985 AGE STRUCTURE

MALES 7,870,139   FEMALES 8,774,169

MORTALITY MEASURES (Annual Averages)

PERIOD	CRUDE DEATH RATE	INFANT MORT. RATE	LIFE EXPECTANCY AT BIRTH (years) MALE	FEMALE	BOTH SEXES	DIFFERENCE FEMALE-MALE
1950-55	11.86	57.58	65.10	69.10	67.04	4.00
1955-60	12.65	44.12	66.50	71.20	68.78	4.70
1960-65	13.30	31.40	67.90	72.90	70.33	5.00
1965-70	13.71	21.37	68.80	74.00	71.32	5.20
1970-75	13.81	16.98	68.60	73.90	71.17	5.30
1975-80	13.86	13.33	68.80	74.60	71.62	5.80
1980-85	13.61	11.06	69.27	75.17	72.14	5.90
1985-90	*12.80*	*9.23*	*70.45*	*76.18*	*73.24*	*5.74*
1990-95	*11.79*	*8.16*	*71.45*	*77.20*	*74.25*	*5.75*
2000-05	*11.17*	*6.57*	*73.31*	*78.89*	*76.03*	*5.58*
2010-15	*11.81*	*5.45*	*74.85*	*80.36*	*77.53*	*5.52*
2020-25	*12.59*	*5.07*	*75.92*	*81.33*	*78.55*	*5.41*

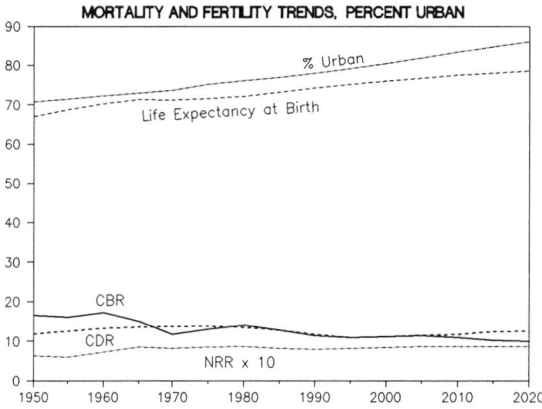

MORTALITY AND FERTILITY TRENDS, PERCENT URBAN

% Urban

Life Expectancy at Birth

CBR

CDR

NRR x 10

FERTILITY MEASURES (Annual Averages)

PERIOD	CRUDE BIRTH RATE	FERTILITY RATES GENERAL	TOTAL	REPRODUCTION RATES GROSS	NET	RATE OF NATUR. INCR.
1950-55	16.56	62.28	2.366	1.150	0.627	4.70
1955-60	16.06	64.20	2.246	1.092	0.599	3.41
1960-65	17.36	75.64	2.448	1.190	0.728	4.06
1965-70	15.06	66.88	2.294	1.115	0.854	1.35
1970-75	11.84	50.42	1.711	0.832	0.813	-1.97
1975-80	13.13	53.96	1.806	0.878	0.851	-0.73
1980-85	14.10	56.43	1.833	0.891	0.872	0.49
1985-90	*12.86*	*52.24*	*1.700*	*0.826*	*0.814*	*0.06*
1990-95	*11.42*	*47.66*	*1.650*	*0.802*	*0.793*	*-0.38*
2000-05	*11.20*	*46.24*	*1.750*	*0.851*	*0.845*	*0.03*
2010-15	*10.90*	*49.10*	*1.800*	*0.875*	*0.870*	*-0.91*
2020-25	*10.04*	*47.95*	*1.800*	*0.875*	*0.870*	*-2.55*

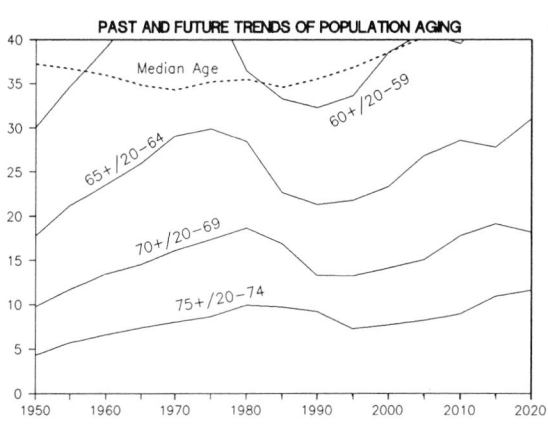

PAST AND FUTURE TRENDS OF POPULATION AGING

Median Age

60+/20-59

65+/20-64

70+/20-69

75+/20-74

AGING MEASURES

YEAR	POPULATION AGE RATIOS 60+/20-59	65+/20-64	70+/20-69	75+/20-74	POPULATION MEAN AGE	MEDIAN AGE
1950	0.3009	0.1782	0.0977	0.0431	36.26	37.27
1960	0.3914	0.2358	0.1346	0.0659	37.39	36.03
1970	0.4706	0.2909	0.1615	0.0803	36.78	34.33
1980	0.3648	0.2844	0.1867	0.0990	37.20	35.52
1990	*0.3230*	*0.2132*	*0.1335*	*0.0921*	*37.38*	*35.57*
2000	*0.3863*	*0.2335*	*0.1414*	*0.0771*	*39.02*	*38.58*
2010	*0.3953*	*0.2859*	*0.1780*	*0.0894*	*40.54*	*41.49*
2020	*0.4874*	*0.3100*	*0.1822*	*0.1159*	*41.90*	*42.51*

OBSERVED AND *PROJECTED* POPULATION DATA (000's)

YEAR	MID-YEAR POPULATION	NO. OF BIRTHS	NO. OF DEATHS	URBAN POPULATION NUMBER	URBAN POPULATION PERCENT	POPULATION 1985 AGE	POPULATION 1985 NUMBER
1950	49989	788	540	36137	72.3	0	2994
1955	52382	863	586	39239	74.9	5	2884
1960	55433	996	630	42883	77.4	10	3638
1965	59012	982	702	46879	79.4	15	5102
1970	60651	683	725	49333	81.3	20	5180
1975	61829	592	722	51374	83.1	25	4553
1980	61566	608	715	51937	84.4	30	4262
1985	61024	638	735	52200	85.5	35	3742
1990	*60539*	*657*	*725*	*52282*	*86.4*	40	4556
1995	*60201*	*617*	*694*	*52459*	*87.1*	45	4613
2000	*59818*	*560*	*722*	*52418*	*87.6*	50	3627
2005	*59011*	*516*	*739*	*51989*	*88.1*	55	3571
2010	*57907*	*518*	*756*	*51155*	*88.3*	60	3342
2015	*56725*	*521*	*792*	*50247*	*88.6*	65	2099
2020	*55389*	*512*	*800*	*49080*	*88.6*	70+	6859

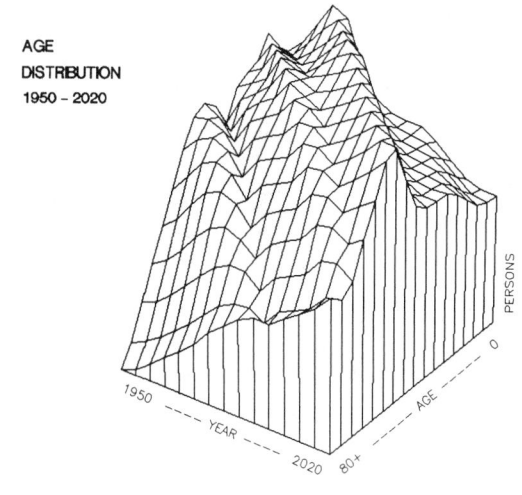

AGE DISTRIBUTION 1950 - 2020

POPULATION RATIOS

YEAR	AGE DISTRIBUTION UNDER 15	AGE DISTRIBUTION 15-64	AGE DISTRIBUTION 65 & OLDER	AGE DISTRIBUTION 70 & OLDER	DEPENDENCY RATIO	WOMEN 15-49	CHILD-WOMAN RATIO
1950	0.233	0.673	0.094	0.056	0.486	0.273	0.253
1955	0.212	0.686	0.101	0.062	0.457	0.268	0.269
1960	0.213	0.678	0.108	0.067	0.475	0.252	0.311
1965	0.226	0.655	0.119	0.072	0.527	0.234	0.365
1970	0.232	0.636	0.132	0.080	0.571	0.235	0.331
1975	0.215	0.641	0.145	0.090	0.561	0.236	0.232
1980	0.182	0.663	0.155	0.107	0.508	0.246	0.194
1985	0.156	0.697	0.147	0.112	0.434	0.256	0.192
1990	*0.149*	*0.697*	*0.154*	*0.103*	*0.434*	*0.249*	*0.209*
2000	*0.158*	*0.674*	*0.168*	*0.118*	*0.484*	*0.231*	*0.221*
2010	*0.144*	*0.649*	*0.207*	*0.142*	*0.541*	*0.218*	*0.201*
2020	*0.138*	*0.639*	*0.223*	*0.158*	*0.565*	*0.190*	*0.244*

MORTALITY MEASURES (Annual Averages)

PERIOD	CRUDE DEATH RATE	INFANT MORT. RATE	LIFE EXPECTANCY AT BIRTH (years) MALE	LIFE EXPECTANCY AT BIRTH (years) FEMALE	LIFE EXPECTANCY AT BIRTH (years) BOTH SEXES	DIFFERENCE FEMALE-MALE
1950-55	10.81	47.89	65.40	69.80	67.54	4.40
1955-60	11.18	36.50	66.60	71.60	69.03	5.00
1960-65	11.36	28.34	67.20	72.90	69.97	5.70
1965-70	11.89	23.28	67.40	73.40	70.31	6.00
1970-75	11.96	22.44	67.60	73.70	70.56	6.10
1975-80	11.69	15.48	69.00	75.80	72.30	6.80
1980-85	11.62	10.64	70.64	77.26	73.86	6.62
1985-90	*12.05*	*9.38*	*71.61*	*78.16*	*74.80*	*6.55*
1990-95	*11.98*	*8.01*	*72.67*	*78.95*	*75.72*	*6.28*
2000-05	*12.07*	*6.08*	*74.22*	*80.32*	*77.18*	*6.10*
2010-15	*13.06*	*5.49*	*75.57*	*81.40*	*78.40*	*5.84*
2020-25	*14.45*	*5.02*	*76.55*	*82.39*	*79.39*	*5.84*

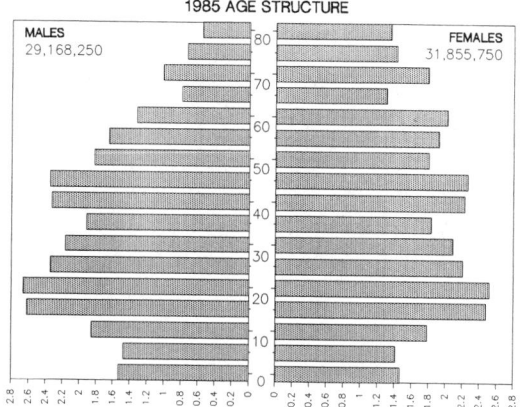

1985 AGE STRUCTURE

MALES 29,168,250   FEMALES 31,855,750

FERTILITY MEASURES (Annual Averages)

PERIOD	CRUDE BIRTH RATE	FERTILITY RATES GENERAL	FERTILITY RATES TOTAL	REPRODUCTION RATES GROSS	REPRODUCTION RATES NET	RATE OF NATUR. INCR.
1950-55	15.77	58.27	2.084	1.014	0.935	4.96
1955-60	16.48	63.38	2.316	1.127	1.068	5.30
1960-65	17.96	73.98	2.484	1.209	1.157	6.60
1965-70	16.64	71.00	2.332	1.135	1.069	4.75
1970-75	11.26	47.81	1.623	0.790	0.760	-0.70
1975-80	9.58	39.76	1.438	0.700	0.685	-2.11
1980-85	9.88	39.38	1.358	0.661	0.648	-1.75
1985-90	*10.45*	*41.42*	*1.380*	*0.672*	*0.660*	*-1.60*
1990-95	*10.86*	*44.76*	*1.430*	*0.696*	*0.686*	*-1.12*
2000-05	*9.35*	*41.01*	*1.600*	*0.779*	*0.769*	*-2.71*
2010-15	*8.94*	*42.22*	*1.700*	*0.827*	*0.819*	*-4.12*
2020-25	*9.24*	*49.35*	*1.700*	*0.827*	*0.819*	*-5.21*

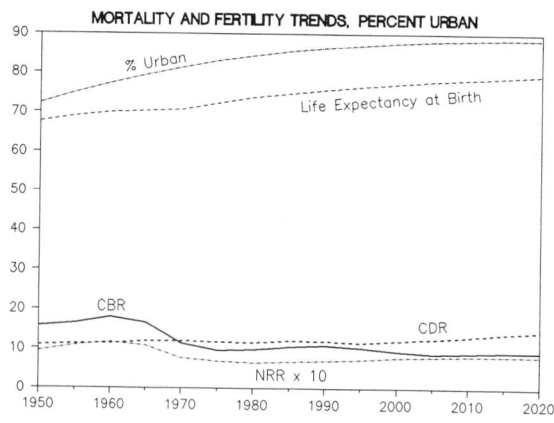

MORTALITY AND FERTILITY TRENDS, PERCENT URBAN

% Urban — Life Expectancy at Birth — CBR — CDR — NRR x 10

AGING MEASURES

YEAR	POPULATION AGE RATIOS 60+/20-59	POPULATION AGE RATIOS 65+/20-64	POPULATION AGE RATIOS 70+/20-69	POPULATION AGE RATIOS 75+/20-74	POPULATION MEAN AGE	POPULATION MEDIAN AGE
1950	0.2528	0.1565	0.0883	0.0405	34.78	34.60
1960	0.2979	0.1793	0.1028	0.0518	35.89	34.41
1970	0.3777	0.2309	0.1278	0.0638	36.15	34.29
1980	0.3573	0.2682	0.1708	0.0902	38.03	36.68
1990	*0.3597*	*0.2410*	*0.1498*	*0.1015*	*39.71*	*38.36*
2000	*0.4287*	*0.2700*	*0.1742*	*0.1003*	*41.35*	*40.93*
2010	*0.4947*	*0.3490*	*0.2152*	*0.1160*	*43.36*	*44.81*
2020	*0.5769*	*0.3785*	*0.2424*	*0.1538*	*44.83*	*47.96*

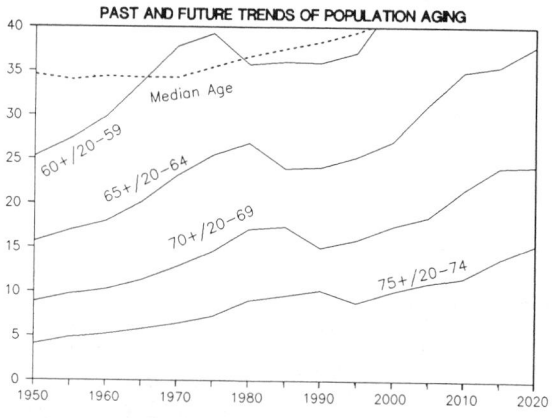

PAST AND FUTURE TRENDS OF POPULATION AGING

Median Age — 60+/20-59 — 65+/20-64 — 70+/20-69 — 75+/20-74

OBSERVED AND *PROJECTED* POPULATION DATA (000's)

YEAR	MID-YEAR POPULATION	NO. OF BIRTHS	NO. OF DEATHS	URBAN POPULATION NUMBER	URBAN POPULATION PERCENT	POPULATION 1985 AGE	POPULATION 1985 NUMBER
1950	7566	147	54	2821	37.3	0	688
1955	7966	154	58	3191	40.1	5	711
1960	8327	150	65	3572	42.9	10	716
1965	8551	154	69	4064	47.5	15	775
1970	8793	139	75	4617	52.5	20	726
1975	9047	142	80	5003	55.3	25	684
1980	9643	132	87	5567	57.7	30	660
1985	9934	118	96	5973	60.1	35	668
1990	*10047*	*116*	*101*	*6293*	*62.6*	40	565
1995	*10124*	*119*	*105*	*6604*	*65.2*	45	678
2000	*10193*	*119*	*108*	*6914*	*67.8*	50	684
2005	*10247*	*116*	*115*	*7212*	*70.4*	55	609
2010	*10249*	*111*	*121*	*7466*	*72.8*	60	449
2015	*10201*	*110*	*122*	*7663*	*75.1*	65	445
2020	*10139*	*108*	*120*	*7827*	*77.2*	70+	876

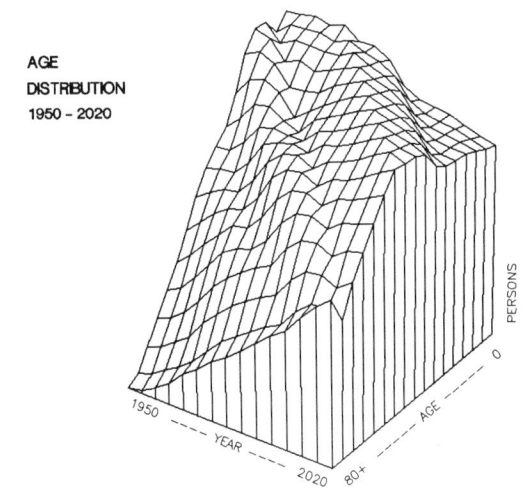

AGE DISTRIBUTION 1950 – 2020

POPULATION RATIOS

YEAR	AGE DISTRIBUTION UNDER 15	AGE DISTRIBUTION 15-64	AGE DISTRIBUTION 65 & OLDER	AGE DISTRIBUTION 70 & OLDER	DEPENDENCY RATIO	WOMEN 15-49	CHILD-WOMAN RATIO
1950	0.287	0.646	0.068	0.042	0.549	0.273	0.360
1955	0.265	0.661	0.074	0.047	0.513	0.274	0.337
1960	0.265	0.653	0.083	0.054	0.532	0.263	0.345
1965	0.255	0.657	0.089	0.055	0.522	0.261	0.323
1970	0.249	0.640	0.111	0.070	0.563	0.245	0.357
1975	0.239	0.639	0.122	0.078	0.565	0.245	0.311
1980	0.228	0.640	0.131	0.087	0.561	0.242	0.308
1985	0.213	0.654	0.133	0.088	0.529	0.239	0.289
1990	*0.197*	*0.665*	*0.137*	*0.096*	*0.503*	*0.235*	*0.247*
2000	*0.171*	*0.659*	*0.169*	*0.111*	*0.517*	*0.236*	*0.245*
2010	*0.171*	*0.645*	*0.184*	*0.137*	*0.550*	*0.223*	*0.251*
2020	*0.164*	*0.637*	*0.199*	*0.143*	*0.570*	*0.210*	*0.255*

MORTALITY MEASURES (Annual Averages)

PERIOD	CRUDE DEATH RATE	INFANT MORT. RATE	LIFE EXPECTANCY AT BIRTH (years) MALE	LIFE EXPECTANCY AT BIRTH (years) FEMALE	LIFE EXPECTANCY AT BIRTH (years) BOTH SEXES	DIFFERENCE FEMALE-MALE
1950-55	7.16	60.00	64.30	67.50	65.86	3.20
1955-60	7.28	56.10	66.30	69.50	67.86	3.20
1960-65	7.76	50.20	67.90	71.20	69.51	3.30
1965-70	8.09	42.40	69.30	72.80	71.00	3.50
1970-75	8.56	34.06	70.60	74.20	72.34	3.60
1975-80	8.84	25.08	71.70	75.80	73.68	4.10
1980-85	9.02	15.27	72.70	76.90	74.72	4.20
1985-90	*9.65*	*16.59*	*73.51*	*77.89*	*75.62*	*4.38*
1990-95	*10.04*	*13.31*	*74.29*	*78.68*	*76.41*	*4.39*
2000-05	*10.58*	*8.18*	*75.61*	*80.20*	*77.82*	*4.60*
2010-15	*11.80*	*6.54*	*76.62*	*81.19*	*78.82*	*4.58*
2020-25	*11.79*	*6.13*	*77.55*	*82.15*	*79.77*	*4.60*

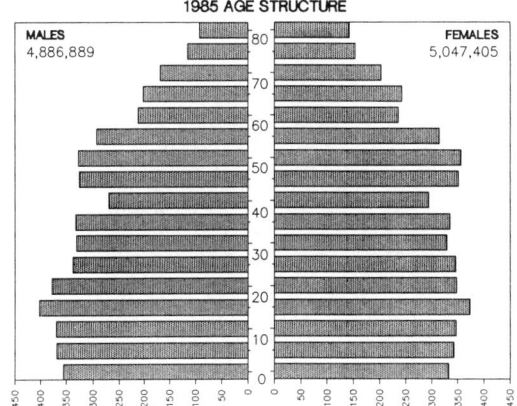

1985 AGE STRUCTURE

MALES 4,886,889

FEMALES 5,047,405

FERTILITY MEASURES (Annual Averages)

PERIOD	CRUDE BIRTH RATE	FERTILITY RATES GENERAL	FERTILITY RATES TOTAL	REPRODUCTION RATES GROSS	REPRODUCTION RATES NET	RATE OF NATUR. INCR.
1950-55	19.44	71.04	2.291	1.104	1.015	12.28
1955-60	19.34	72.12	2.270	1.094	1.006	12.06
1960-65	18.06	68.98	2.202	1.061	0.982	10.30
1965-70	18.00	71.13	2.388	1.151	1.071	9.91
1970-75	15.86	64.62	2.322	1.119	1.062	7.30
1975-80	15.65	64.24	2.324	1.120	1.059	6.80
1980-85	13.67	56.82	1.965	0.947	0.908	4.64
1985-90	*11.91*	*50.19*	*1.700*	*0.819*	*0.800*	*2.26*
1990-95	*11.57*	*48.91*	*1.650*	*0.795*	*0.780*	*1.53*
2000-05	*11.64*	*50.03*	*1.750*	*0.843*	*0.833*	*1.06*
2010-15	*10.87*	*49.39*	*1.850*	*0.892*	*0.882*	*-0.93*
2020-25	*10.63*	*51.23*	*1.900*	*0.916*	*0.906*	*-1.16*

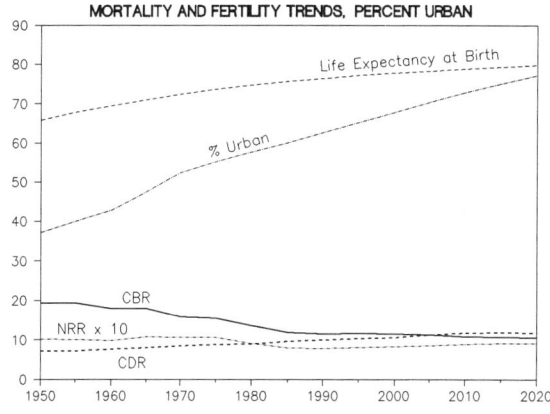

MORTALITY AND FERTILITY TRENDS, PERCENT URBAN

Life Expectancy at Birth

% Urban

CBR

NRR x 10

CDR

AGING MEASURES

YEAR	POPULATION AGE RATIOS 60+/20-59	POPULATION AGE RATIOS 65+/20-64	POPULATION AGE RATIOS 70+/20-69	POPULATION AGE RATIOS 75+/20-74	POPULATION MEAN AGE	POPULATION MEDIAN AGE
1950	0.1953	0.1254	0.0735	0.0380	29.84	25.96
1960	0.2238	0.1429	0.0885	0.0479	32.00	29.10
1970	0.3169	0.1974	0.1150	0.0592	34.63	33.40
1980	0.3343	0.2325	0.1429	0.0776	35.97	34.18
1990	*0.3639*	*0.2313*	*0.1512*	*0.0848*	*37.69*	*36.14*
2000	*0.4342*	*0.2860*	*0.1709*	*0.0920*	*39.54*	*38.35*
2010	*0.4599*	*0.3123*	*0.2145*	*0.1244*	*41.00*	*40.87*
2020	*0.5036*	*0.3432*	*0.2245*	*0.1332*	*42.17*	*42.91*

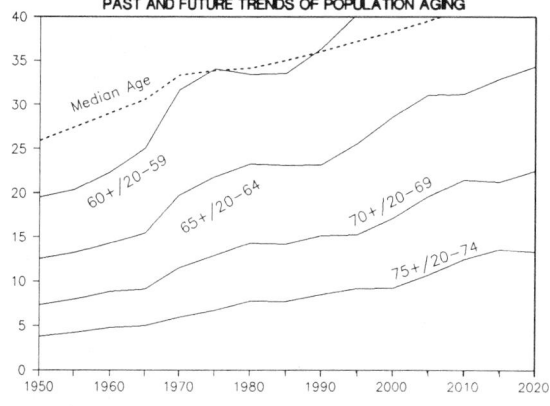

PAST AND FUTURE TRENDS OF POPULATION AGING

Median Age

60+/20-59

65+/20-64

70+/20-69

75+/20-74

OBSERVED AND *PROJECTED* POPULATION DATA (000's)

YEAR	MID-YEAR POPULATION	NO. OF BIRTHS	NO. OF DEATHS	URBAN POPULATION NUMBER	URBAN POPULATION PERCENT	POPULATION 1985 AGE	POPULATION 1985 NUMBER
1950	9338	197	106	3440	36.8	0	654
1955	9825	175	101	3767	38.3	5	842
1960	9984	135	101	3990	40.0	10	792
1965	10148	145	110	4333	42.7	15	710
1970	10353	162	122	4725	45.6	20	643
1975	10541	171	135	5281	50.1	25	782
1980	10711	134	147	5735	53.5	30	895
1985	10649	124	143	6068	57.0	35	764
1990	*10552*	*126*	*134*	*6368*	*60.3*	40	703
1995	*10509*	*134*	*129*	*6680*	*63.6*	45	637
2000	*10531*	*130*	*133*	*7011*	*66.6*	50	648
2005	*10519*	*120*	*132*	*7293*	*69.3*	55	648
2010	*10459*	*113*	*130*	*7518*	*71.9*	60	615
2015	*10375*	*112*	*129*	*7701*	*74.2*	65	351
2020	*10291*	*112*	*131*	*7860*	*76.4*	70+	966

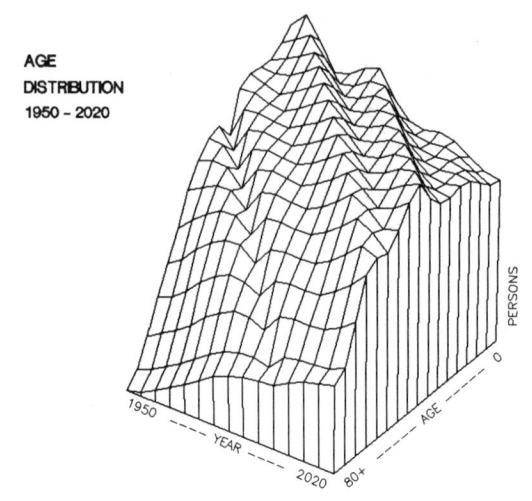

AGE DISTRIBUTION 1950 - 2020

POPULATION RATIOS

YEAR	AGE DISTRIBUTION UNDER 15	15-64	65 & OLDER	70 & OLDER	DEPENDENCY RATIO	WOMEN 15-49	CHILD-WOMAN RATIO
1950	0.251	0.676	0.073	0.041	0.480	0.273	0.327
1955	0.256	0.662	0.082	0.049	0.512	0.259	0.369
1960	0.253	0.656	0.090	0.055	0.524	0.249	0.322
1965	0.232	0.665	0.103	0.060	0.505	0.247	0.257
1970	0.208	0.676	0.115	0.070	0.478	0.259	0.266
1975	0.203	0.670	0.126	0.077	0.492	0.253	0.297
1980	0.219	0.646	0.134	0.088	0.547	0.240	0.328
1985	0.215	0.661	0.124	0.091	0.512	0.240	0.256
1990	*0.199*	*0.667*	*0.134*	*0.081*	*0.498*	*0.245*	*0.233*
2000	*0.178*	*0.673*	*0.148*	*0.100*	*0.485*	*0.244*	*0.257*
2010	*0.181*	*0.664*	*0.155*	*0.104*	*0.507*	*0.224*	*0.253*
2020	*0.166*	*0.648*	*0.187*	*0.119*	*0.544*	*0.226*	*0.238*

MORTALITY MEASURES (Annual Averages)

PERIOD	CRUDE DEATH RATE	INFANT MORT. RATE	LIFE EXPECTANCY AT BIRTH (years) MALE	FEMALE	BOTH SEXES	DIFFERENCE FEMALE-MALE
1950-55	11.36	71.18	62.10	65.90	63.94	3.80
1955-60	10.28	57.55	65.10	69.30	67.13	4.20
1960-65	10.10	43.65	66.80	71.30	69.00	4.50
1965-70	10.80	36.78	67.00	72.30	69.59	5.30
1970-75	11.81	34.14	67.00	72.90	69.88	5.90
1975-80	12.79	26.70	66.80	73.30	70.02	6.50
1980-85	13.69	20.41	65.80	73.50	69.56	7.70
1985-90	*13.44*	*19.63*	*66.46*	*73.99*	*70.13*	*7.53*
1990-95	*12.71*	*16.55*	*67.93*	*75.23*	*71.49*	*7.30*
2000-05	*12.60*	*12.03*	*70.28*	*77.20*	*73.65*	*6.92*
2010-15	*12.42*	*8.85*	*72.27*	*78.89*	*75.50*	*6.62*
2020-25	*12.70*	*6.62*	*73.98*	*80.36*	*77.10*	*6.38*

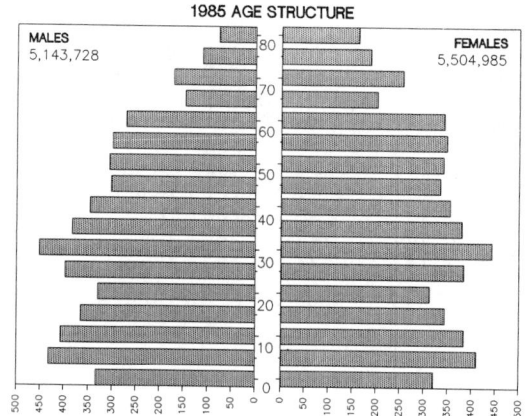

1985 AGE STRUCTURE

MALES 5,143,728   FEMALES 5,504,985

FERTILITY MEASURES (Annual Averages)

PERIOD	CRUDE BIRTH RATE	FERTILITY RATES GENERAL	FERTILITY RATES TOTAL	REPRODUCTION RATES GROSS	REPRODUCTION RATES NET	RATE OF NATUR. INCR.
1950-55	21.06	79.33	2.721	1.328	1.212	9.70
1955-60	17.82	70.19	2.207	1.077	0.979	7.54
1960-65	13.56	54.71	1.817	0.887	0.830	3.46
1965-70	14.28	56.44	1.971	0.962	0.917	3.48
1970-75	15.69	61.27	2.082	1.016	0.974	3.88
1975-80	16.24	65.86	2.110	1.030	0.988	3.45
1980-85	12.52	52.14	1.801	0.879	0.852	-1.17
1985-90	*11.61*	*47.91*	*1.750*	*0.854*	*0.830*	*-1.83*
1990-95	*11.90*	*48.07*	*1.750*	*0.854*	*0.835*	*-0.81*
2000-05	*12.37*	*52.24*	*1.800*	*0.878*	*0.865*	*-0.23*
2010-15	*10.80*	*47.97*	*1.800*	*0.878*	*0.870*	*-1.62*
2020-25	*10.92*	*49.06*	*1.800*	*0.878*	*0.872*	*-1.78*

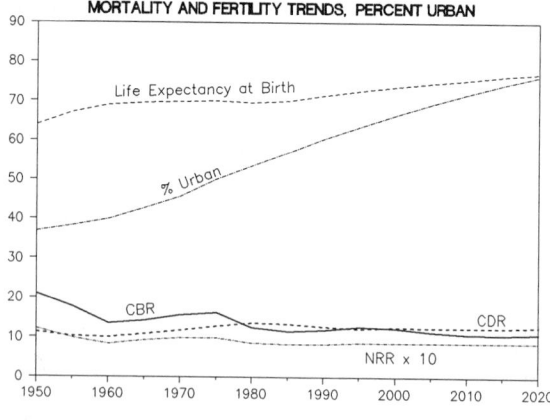

MORTALITY AND FERTILITY TRENDS, PERCENT URBAN

Life Expectancy at Birth
% Urban
CBR
CDR
NRR x 10

AGING MEASURES

YEAR	POPULATION AGE RATIOS 60+/20-59	65+/20-64	70+/20-69	75+/20-74	POPULATION MEAN AGE	POPULATION MEDIAN AGE
1950	0.2044	0.1236	0.0650	0.0308	32.37	29.86
1960	0.2627	0.1556	0.0885	0.0436	33.78	32.10
1970	0.3239	0.1966	0.1101	0.0529	35.73	34.07
1980	0.3130	0.2292	0.1397	0.0701	36.26	34.35
1990	*0.3534*	*0.2260*	*0.1258*	*0.0784*	*37.40*	*36.50*
2000	*0.3546*	*0.2424*	*0.1514*	*0.0795*	*38.60*	*38.27*
2010	*0.3960*	*0.2565*	*0.1585*	*0.0903*	*39.68*	*39.09*
2020	*0.4822*	*0.3192*	*0.1830*	*0.0986*	*41.04*	*41.71*

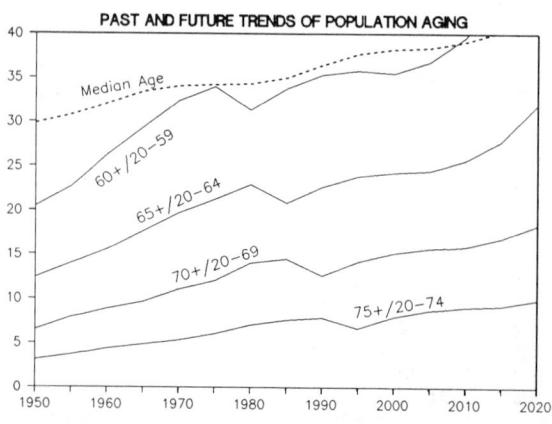

PAST AND FUTURE TRENDS OF POPULATION AGING

Median Age
60+/20-59
65+/20-64
70+/20-69
75+/20-74

OBSERVED AND *PROJECTED* POPULATION DATA

YEAR	MID-YEAR POPULATION	NO. OF BIRTHS	NO. OF DEATHS	URBAN POPULATION NUMBER	URBAN POPULATION PERCENT	POPULATION 1985 AGE	POPULATION 1985 NUMBER
1950	143000	3990	1073	105536	73.8	0	22050
1955	158000	4471	1122	121998	77.2	5	20698
1960	176000	4594	1214	141330	80.3	10	21122
1965	192000	4320	1336	158862	82.7	15	21785
1970	204104	4280	1422	173352	84.9	20	22414
1975	218031	4179	1399	189252	86.8	25	20826
1980	228161	4148	1573	201200	88.2	30	18533
1985	241400	4059	1711	215916	89.4	35	15973
1990	*253434*	*3880*	*1777*	*229432*	*90.5*	40	12297
1995	*264171*	*3785*	*1861*	*241607*	*91.5*	45	10592
2000	*273971*	*3675*	*1977*	*252737*	*92.2*	50	11212
2005	*282597*	*3750*	*2089*	*262591*	*92.9*	55	10324
2010	*291026*	*3720*	*2221*	*272073*	*93.5*	60	9309
2015	*298616*	*3671*	*2357*	*280721*	*94.0*	65	7553
2020	*305261*	*3563*	*2583*	*288423*	*94.5*	70+	16712

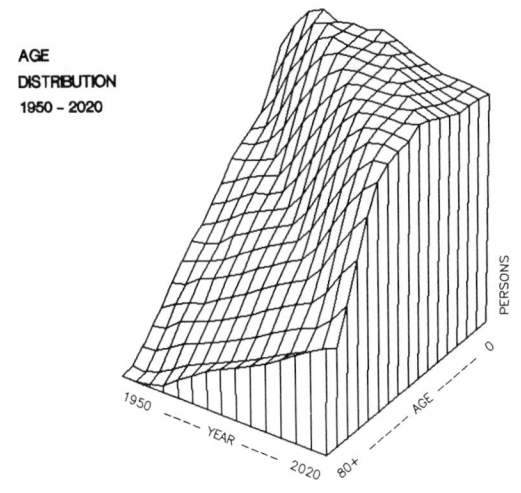

AGE DISTRIBUTION 1950 – 2020

POPULATION RATIOS

YEAR	AGE DISTRIBUTION UNDER 15	AGE DISTRIBUTION 15-64	AGE DISTRIBUTION 65 & OLDER	AGE DISTRIBUTION 70 & OLDER	DEPENDENCY RATIO	WOMEN 15-49	CHILD-WOMAN RATIO
1950	0.308	0.615	0.077	0.049	0.625	0.245	0.514
1955	0.335	0.595	0.070	0.044	0.681	0.228	0.583
1960	0.347	0.574	0.080	0.045	0.743	0.222	0.590
1965	0.344	0.573	0.083	0.052	0.745	0.224	0.535
1970	0.323	0.588	0.089	0.059	0.701	0.228	0.446
1975	0.301	0.608	0.092	0.062	0.645	0.236	0.417
1980	0.275	0.626	0.099	0.067	0.597	0.244	0.375
1985	0.265	0.635	0.101	0.069	0.575	0.248	0.368
1990	*0.250*	*0.646*	*0.104*	*0.070*	*0.549*	*0.255*	*0.320*
2000	*0.217*	*0.669*	*0.114*	*0.079*	*0.495*	*0.261*	*0.268*
2010	*0.194*	*0.685*	*0.121*	*0.084*	*0.460*	*0.247*	*0.263*
2020	*0.184*	*0.662*	*0.155*	*0.102*	*0.511*	*0.224*	*0.269*

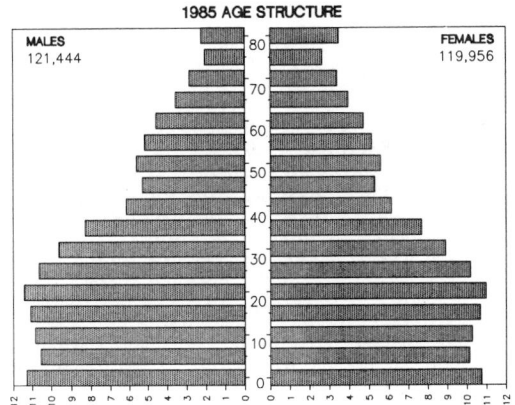

1985 AGE STRUCTURE

MALES 121,444　　　FEMALES 119,956

MORTALITY MEASURES (Annual Averages)

PERIOD	CRUDE DEATH RATE	INFANT MORT. RATE	LIFE EXPECTANCY AT BIRTH (years) MALE	LIFE EXPECTANCY AT BIRTH (years) FEMALE	LIFE EXPECTANCY AT BIRTH (years) BOTH SEXES	DIFFERENCE FEMALE-MALE
1950-55	7.50	21.38	70.00	74.10	71.99	4.10
1955-60	7.10	17.37	70.80	75.40	73.03	4.60
1960-65	6.90	16.98	70.80	76.10	73.37	5.30
1965-70	6.96	13.28	70.70	76.30	73.42	5.60
1970-75	6.97	11.62	71.40	77.40	74.31	6.00
1975-80	6.41	8.75	73.40	79.30	76.26	5.90
1980-85	6.90	6.40	73.94	79.83	76.79	5.89
1985-90	*7.09*	*5.38*	*74.75*	*80.41*	*77.50*	*5.66*
1990-95	*7.01*	*5.20*	*75.33*	*80.98*	*78.08*	*5.65*
2000-05	*7.22*	*4.90*	*76.39*	*81.92*	*79.08*	*5.52*
2010-15	*7.63*	*4.76*	*77.31*	*82.89*	*80.02*	*5.58*
2020-25	*8.46*	*4.70*	*78.15*	*83.62*	*80.81*	*5.47*

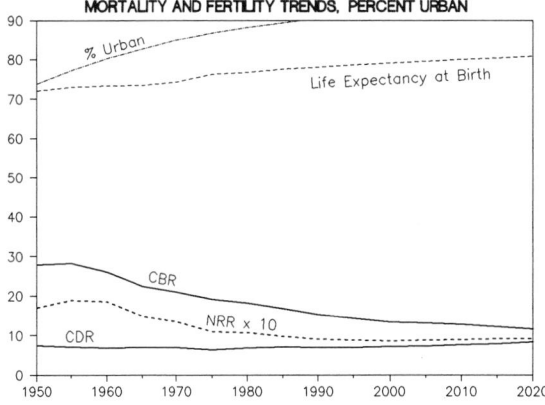

MORTALITY AND FERTILITY TRENDS, PERCENT URBAN

% Urban — Life Expectancy at Birth — CBR — NRR x 10 — CDR

FERTILITY MEASURES (Annual Averages)

PERIOD	CRUDE BIRTH RATE	FERTILITY RATES GENERAL	FERTILITY RATES TOTAL	REPRODUCTION RATES GROSS	REPRODUCTION RATES NET	RATE OF NATUR. INCR.
1950-55	27.90	118.28	3.700	1.796	1.706	20.40
1955-60	28.30	126.03	4.023	1.953	1.898	21.20
1960-65	26.10	117.13	3.943	1.914	1.861	19.20
1965-70	22.50	99.60	3.154	1.531	1.489	15.54
1970-75	20.97	90.33	2.843	1.380	1.353	14.00
1975-80	19.17	79.86	2.287	1.110	1.092	12.75
1980-85	18.18	73.96	2.247	1.091	1.078	11.28
1985-90	*16.81*	*66.83*	*2.050*	*0.995*	*0.984*	*9.73*
1990-95	*15.31*	*59.50*	*1.900*	*0.922*	*0.912*	*8.30*
2000-05	*13.41*	*51.84*	*1.800*	*0.874*	*0.864*	*6.20*
2010-15	*12.78*	*53.04*	*1.870*	*0.908*	*0.898*	*5.15*
2020-25	*11.67*	*52.83*	*1.900*	*0.922*	*0.913*	*3.21*

AGING MEASURES

YEAR	POPULATION AGE RATIOS 60+/20-59	POPULATION AGE RATIOS 65+/20-64	POPULATION AGE RATIOS 70+/20-69	POPULATION AGE RATIOS 75+/20-74	POPULATION MEAN AGE	POPULATION MEDIAN AGE
1950	0.2083	0.1447	0.0875	0.0482	29.81	26.46
1960	0.2469	0.1609	0.0860	0.0412	29.29	25.42
1970	0.2728	0.1815	0.1135	0.0631	30.02	24.60
1980	0.2749	0.1870	0.1204	0.0716	31.50	26.94
1990	*0.2733*	*0.1855*	*0.1181*	*0.0710*	*32.83*	*29.60*
2000	*0.2712*	*0.1942*	*0.1264*	*0.0754*	*34.97*	*33.24*
2010	*0.3015*	*0.1956*	*0.1292*	*0.0826*	*37.28*	*36.53*
2020	*0.4043*	*0.2575*	*0.1566*	*0.0887*	*39.53*	*39.37*

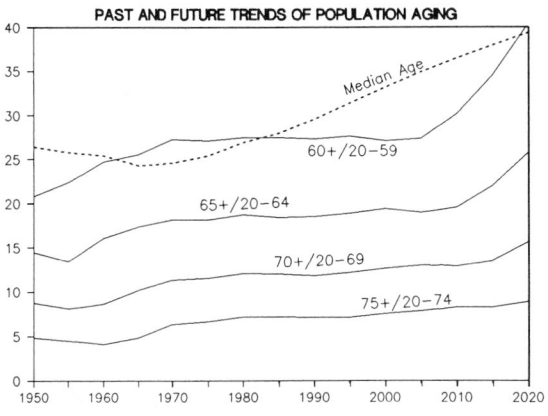

PAST AND FUTURE TRENDS OF POPULATION AGING

Median Age — 60+/20-59 — 65+/20-64 — 70+/20-69 — 75+/20-74

OBSERVED AND *PROJECTED* POPULATION DATA

YEAR	MID-YEAR POPULATION	NO. OF BIRTHS	NO. OF DEATHS	URBAN POPULATION NUMBER	URBAN POPULATION PERCENT	POPULATION 1985 AGE	POPULATION 1985 NUMBER
1950	2969000	63507	37261	1219490	41.1	0	353995
1955	2921000	61516	35169	1281353	43.9	5	349071
1960	2834000	61838	33498	1298590	45.8	10	350979
1965	2876000	61719	33045	1400885	48.7	15	330181
1970	2953700	65129	32381	1527753	51.7	20	290088
1975	3205800	67857	32715	1719556	53.6	25	262155
1980	3401000	67007	31935	1882184	55.3	30	243365
1985	3552000	64210	31403	2025805	57.0	35	218445
1990	*3719899*	*66266*	*31102*	*2196743*	*59.1*	40	183478
1995	*3899971*	*67099*	*30802*	*2392925*	*61.4*	45	159463
2000	*4085765*	*67403*	*30451*	*2610144*	*63.9*	50	149314
2005	*4274790*	*67093*	*30484*	*2845463*	*66.6*	55	146501
2010	*4461855*	*66794*	*31541*	*3093131*	*69.3*	60	139769
2015	*4641665*	*66199*	*33582*	*3336119*	*71.9*	65	130424
2020	*4807672*	*66130*	*36505*	*3568282*	*74.2*	70+	244772

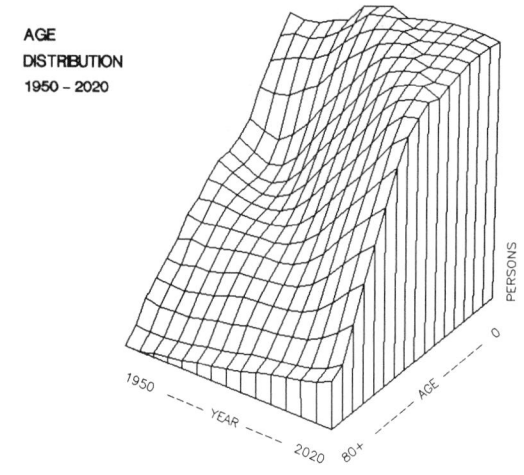

AGE DISTRIBUTION 1950 – 2020

POPULATION RATIOS

YEAR	AGE DISTRIBUTION UNDER 15	15-64	65 & OLDER	70 & OLDER	DEPENDENCY RATIO	WOMEN 15-49	CHILD-WOMAN RATIO
1950	0.289	0.604	0.107	0.070	0.655	0.226	0.468
1955	0.300	0.592	0.109	0.071	0.690	0.222	0.463
1960	0.311	0.577	0.112	0.075	0.732	0.212	0.502
1965	0.312	0.576	0.112	0.072	0.736	0.211	0.520
1970	0.311	0.576	0.112	0.074	0.735	0.210	0.501
1975	0.312	0.578	0.110	0.072	0.731	0.214	0.512
1980	0.306	0.587	0.107	0.068	0.705	0.223	0.458
1985	0.297	0.598	0.106	0.069	0.673	0.233	0.428
1990	*0.276*	*0.620*	*0.103*	*0.070*	*0.612*	*0.247*	*0.355*
2000	*0.245*	*0.658*	*0.096*	*0.066*	*0.519*	*0.260*	*0.322*
2010	*0.230*	*0.672*	*0.098*	*0.064*	*0.487*	*0.254*	*0.301*
2020	*0.211*	*0.670*	*0.119*	*0.076*	*0.492*	*0.242*	*0.289*

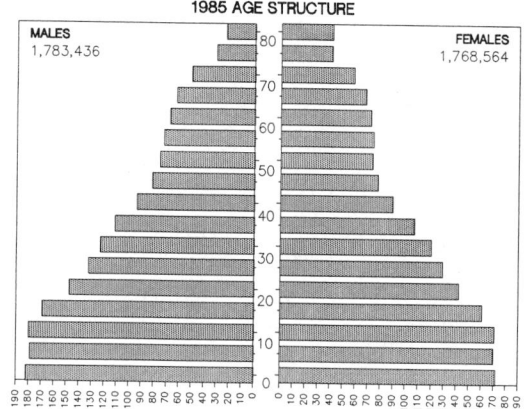

1985 AGE STRUCTURE

MALES 1,783,436   FEMALES 1,768,564

MORTALITY MEASURES (Annual Averages)

PERIOD	CRUDE DEATH RATE	INFANT MORT. RATE	LIFE EXPECTANCY AT BIRTH (years) MALE	FEMALE	BOTH SEXES	DIFFERENCE FEMALE-MALE
1950-55	12.55	41.17	65.70	68.20	66.91	2.50
1955-60	12.04	33.82	67.30	70.60	68.90	3.30
1960-65	11.82	28.01	68.40	72.30	70.29	3.90
1965-70	11.49	22.65	68.90	73.40	71.08	4.50
1970-75	10.96	18.05	68.90	73.80	71.28	4.90
1975-80	10.20	14.57	69.60	74.60	72.03	5.00
1980-85	9.39	9.23	70.44	75.92	73.10	5.48
1985-90	*8.84*	*8.89*	*71.48*	*76.90*	*74.11*	*5.43*
1990-95	*8.36*	*7.81*	*72.46*	*77.86*	*75.08*	*5.40*
2000-05	*7.45*	*6.19*	*74.13*	*79.46*	*76.71*	*5.33*
2010-15	*7.07*	*5.36*	*75.46*	*80.65*	*77.98*	*5.19*
2020-25	*7.59*	*4.95*	*76.44*	*81.65*	*78.97*	*5.21*

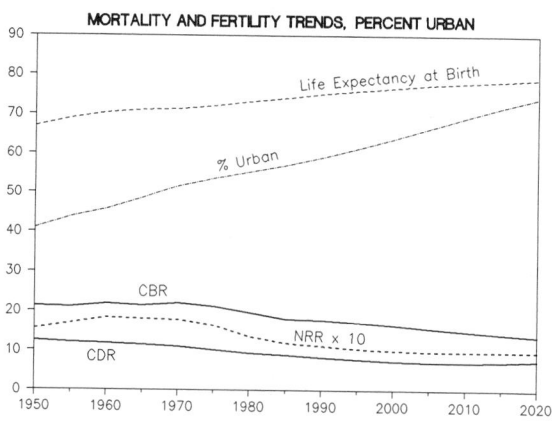

MORTALITY AND FERTILITY TRENDS, PERCENT URBAN

Life Expectancy at Birth

% Urban

CBR

NRR x 10

CDR

FERTILITY MEASURES (Annual Averages)

PERIOD	CRUDE BIRTH RATE	FERTILITY RATES GENERAL	FERTILITY RATES TOTAL	REPRODUCTION RATES GROSS	REPRODUCTION RATES NET	RATE OF NATUR. INCR.
1950-55	21.39	95.52	3.367	1.633	1.562	8.84
1955-60	21.06	96.96	3.666	1.778	1.701	9.02
1960-65	21.82	103.14	3.963	1.922	1.839	10.00
1965-70	21.46	102.03	3.858	1.871	1.804	9.97
1970-75	22.05	103.97	3.800	1.843	1.781	11.09
1975-80	21.17	96.86	3.464	1.680	1.636	10.96
1980-85	19.70	86.46	2.866	1.390	1.359	10.31
1985-90	*18.08*	*75.36*	*2.500*	*1.212*	*1.195*	*9.23*
1990-95	*17.81*	*70.90*	*2.350*	*1.140*	*1.128*	*9.45*
2000-05	*16.50*	*63.86*	*2.100*	*1.018*	*1.011*	*9.04*
2010-15	*14.97*	*59.52*	*2.050*	*0.994*	*0.988*	*7.90*
2020-25	*13.76*	*57.93*	*2.050*	*0.994*	*0.988*	*6.16*

AGING MEASURES

YEAR	POPULATION AGE RATIOS 60+/20-59	65+/20-64	70+/20-69	75+/20-74	POPULATION MEAN AGE	POPULATION MEDIAN AGE
1950	0.3070	0.2043	0.1259	0.0619	32.47	29.56
1960	0.3528	0.2263	0.1415	0.0744	32.78	29.80
1970	0.3537	0.2291	0.1412	0.0740	32.30	27.55
1980	0.3291	0.2184	0.1278	0.0695	31.34	26.44
1990	*0.2865*	*0.1964*	*0.1243*	*0.0682*	*31.74*	*27.63*
2000	*0.2438*	*0.1682*	*0.1060*	*0.0640*	*32.76*	*29.85*
2010	*0.2563*	*0.1641*	*0.1018*	*0.0593*	*34.37*	*32.77*
2020	*0.3062*	*0.1982*	*0.1190*	*0.0640*	*36.38*	*35.64*

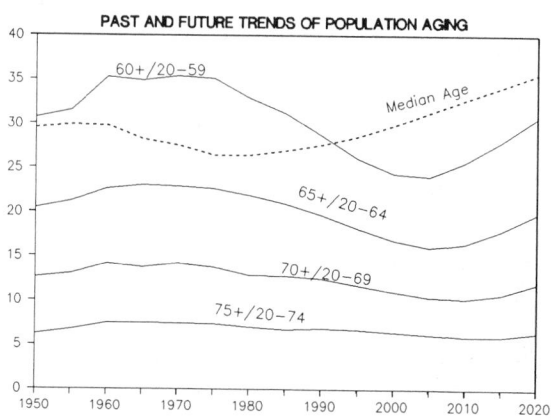

PAST AND FUTURE TRENDS OF POPULATION AGING

60+/20-59

Median Age

65+/20-64

70+/20-69

75+/20-74

OBSERVED AND *PROJECTED* POPULATION DATA (OOO's)

YEAR	MID-YEAR POPULATION	NO. OF BIRTHS	NO. OF DEATHS	URBAN POPULATION NUMBER	URBAN POPULATION PERCENT	POPULATION 1985 AGE	POPULATION 1985 NUMBER
1950	47104	863	464	25584	54.3	0	3054
1955	48633	876	467	27650	56.9	5	3709
1960	50200	945	492	29799	59.4	10	4424
1965	52112	952	505	32228	61.8	15	4740
1970	53822	864	529	34593	64.3	20	4617
1975	55441	721	541	36352	65.6	25	4067
1980	56434	604	537	37509	66.5	30	3808
1985	57128	619	580	38476	67.4	35	3943
1990	*57322*	*656*	*603*	*39320*	*68.6*	40	3555
1995	*57591*	*655*	*598*	*40404*	*70.2*	45	3692
2000	*57881*	*616*	*638*	*41667*	*72.0*	50	3568
2005	*57771*	*567*	*664*	*42763*	*74.0*	55	3438
2010	*57290*	*542*	*682*	*43652*	*76.2*	60	3237
2015	*56598*	*531*	*695*	*44252*	*78.2*	65	1941
2020	*55785*	*526*	*701*	*44633*	*80.0*	70+	5335

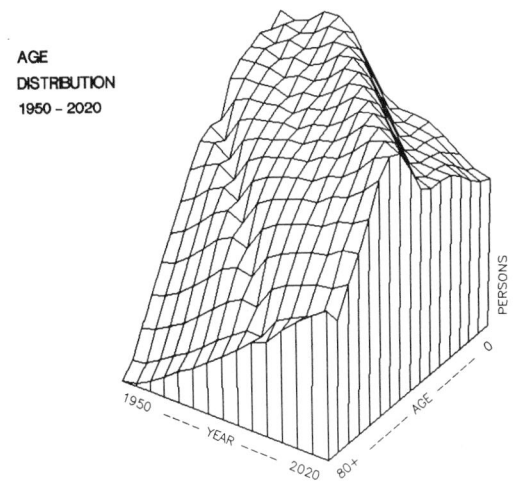

AGE DISTRIBUTION 1950 - 2020

POPULATION RATIOS

YEAR	AGE DISTRIBUTION UNDER 15	AGE DISTRIBUTION 15-64	AGE DISTRIBUTION 65 & OLDER	AGE DISTRIBUTION 70 & OLDER	DEPENDENCY RATIO	WOMEN 15-49	CHILD-WOMAN RATIO
1950	0.263	0.654	0.083	0.050	0.528	0.264	0.348
1955	0.250	0.663	0.087	0.053	0.509	0.263	0.318
1960	0.248	0.659	0.093	0.059	0.517	0.254	0.329
1965	0.243	0.657	0.100	0.063	0.521	0.246	0.360
1970	0.246	0.645	0.109	0.069	0.550	0.246	0.347
1975	0.242	0.637	0.120	0.075	0.569	0.239	0.325
1980	0.223	0.646	0.131	0.085	0.549	0.242	0.265
1985	0.196	0.677	0.127	0.093	0.478	0.248	0.215
1990	*0.171*	*0.686*	*0.142*	*0.090*	*0.457*	*0.251*	*0.212*
2000	*0.165*	*0.668*	*0.166*	*0.114*	*0.497*	*0.240*	*0.235*
2010	*0.159*	*0.657*	*0.184*	*0.131*	*0.521*	*0.227*	*0.215*
2020	*0.145*	*0.649*	*0.206*	*0.148*	*0.540*	*0.206*	*0.228*

MORTALITY MEASURES (Annual Averages)

PERIOD	CRUDE DEATH RATE	INFANT MORT. RATE	LIFE EXPECTANCY AT BIRTH (years) MALE	LIFE EXPECTANCY AT BIRTH (years) FEMALE	LIFE EXPECTANCY AT BIRTH (years) BOTH SEXES	DIFFERENCE FEMALE-MALE
1950-55	9.86	59.72	64.30	67.80	66.00	3.50
1955-60	9.60	47.94	66.30	70.80	68.48	4.50
1960-65	9.80	39.65	67.40	72.60	69.92	5.20
1965-70	9.70	32.90	68.20	73.90	70.97	5.70
1970-75	9.83	26.05	69.20	75.20	72.11	6.00
1975-80	9.76	17.79	70.44	76.93	73.59	6.49
1980-85	9.52	12.59	71.35	78.02	74.59	6.67
1985-90	*10.15*	*11.28*	*72.36*	*79.10*	*75.63*	*6.74*
1990-95	*10.51*	*9.13*	*73.18*	*79.60*	*76.30*	*6.42*
2000-05	*11.03*	*7.03*	*74.83*	*80.78*	*77.72*	*5.94*
2010-15	*11.90*	*6.08*	*75.88*	*81.75*	*78.73*	*5.87*
2020-25	*12.56*	*5.40*	*76.89*	*83.20*	*79.95*	*6.32*

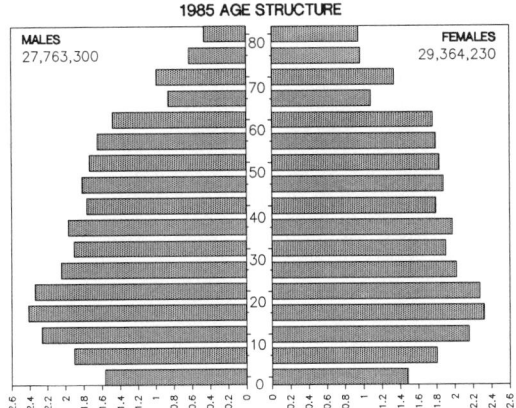

1985 AGE STRUCTURE

MALES 27,763,300   FEMALES 29,364,230

FERTILITY MEASURES (Annual Averages)

PERIOD	CRUDE BIRTH RATE	FERTILITY RATES GENERAL	FERTILITY RATES TOTAL	REPRODUCTION RATES GROSS	REPRODUCTION RATES NET	RATE OF NATUR. INCR.
1950-55	18.32	69.62	2.317	1.125	1.092	8.46
1955-60	18.02	69.81	2.346	1.139	1.071	8.42
1960-65	18.82	75.24	2.548	1.237	1.155	9.02
1965-70	18.27	74.21	2.488	1.208	1.149	8.57
1970-75	16.05	66.14	2.274	1.104	1.050	6.22
1975-80	13.01	54.06	1.916	0.930	0.881	3.24
1980-85	10.70	43.66	1.551	0.753	0.741	1.18
1985-90	*10.83*	*43.35*	*1.450*	*0.704*	*0.692*	*0.68*
1990-95	*11.45*	*45.67*	*1.500*	*0.728*	*0.718*	*0.94*
2000-05	*10.65*	*45.03*	*1.600*	*0.777*	*0.768*	*-0.38*
2010-15	*9.47*	*42.54*	*1.700*	*0.825*	*0.816*	*-2.43*
2020-25	*9.44*	*47.06*	*1.700*	*0.825*	*0.816*	*-3.13*

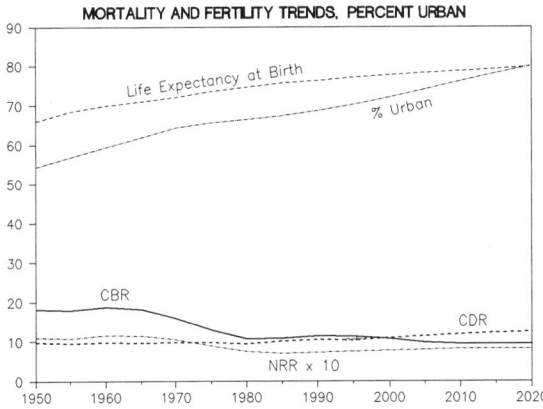

MORTALITY AND FERTILITY TRENDS, PERCENT URBAN

Life Expectancy at Birth
% Urban
CBR
CDR
NRR x 10

AGING MEASURES

YEAR	POPULATION AGE RATIOS 60+/20-59	POPULATION AGE RATIOS 65+/20-64	POPULATION AGE RATIOS 70+/20-69	POPULATION AGE RATIOS 75+/20-74	POPULATION MEAN AGE	POPULATION MEDIAN AGE
1950	0.2311	0.1450	0.0832	0.0421	32.05	29.02
1960	0.2514	0.1594	0.0947	0.0486	33.48	31.31
1970	0.3094	0.1899	0.1120	0.0599	34.55	32.85
1980	0.3228	0.2328	0.1392	0.0729	35.99	34.04
1990	*0.3603*	*0.2335*	*0.1369*	*0.0883*	*38.18*	*36.38*
2000	*0.4021*	*0.2704*	*0.1707*	*0.0958*	*40.00*	*38.87*
2010	*0.4568*	*0.3059*	*0.2014*	*0.1185*	*41.83*	*42.31*
2020	*0.5148*	*0.3459*	*0.2262*	*0.1331*	*43.55*	*45.65*

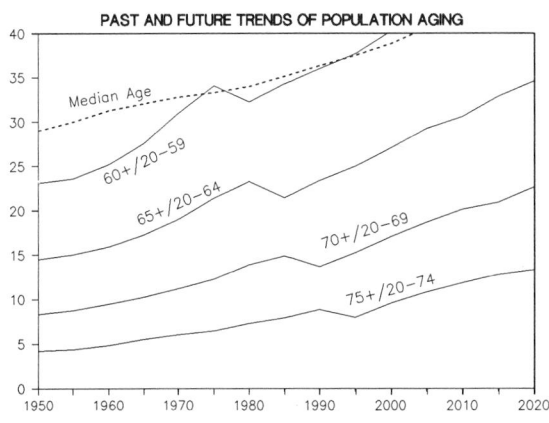

PAST AND FUTURE TRENDS OF POPULATION AGING

Median Age
60+/20-59
65+/20-64
70+/20-69
75+/20-74

OBSERVED AND *PROJECTED* POPULATION DATA

YEAR	MID-YEAR POPULATION	NO. OF BIRTHS	NO. OF DEATHS	URBAN POPULATION NUMBER	URBAN POPULATION PERCENT	POPULATION 1985 AGE	POPULATION 1985 NUMBER
1950	296000	4357	3469	174818	59.1	0	21234
1955	304999	4819	3599	184726	60.6	5	20469
1960	314002	5018	3749	194847	62.1	10	21844
1965	332010	4819	4106	209004	63.0	15	26399
1970	339174	3995	4116	229866	67.8	20	29688
1975	362400	4033	4167	267240	73.7	25	30386
1980	364000	4230	4087	285265	78.4	30	29331
1985	366700	4205	4246	300073	81.8	35	27216
1990	*367492*	*4093*	*4148*	*309943*	*84.3*	40	23939
1995	*368215*	*3798*	*4030*	*317002*	*86.1*	45	23523
2000	*368056*	*3560*	*4175*	*321082*	*87.2*	50	23530
2005	*365988*	*3502*	*4365*	*323111*	*88.3*	55	22626
2010	*362689*	*3547*	*4470*	*323672*	*89.2*	60	18163
2015	*359099*	*3475*	*4575*	*323615*	*90.1*	65	13268
2020	*354629*	*3341*	*4698*	*322430*	*90.9*	70+	35084

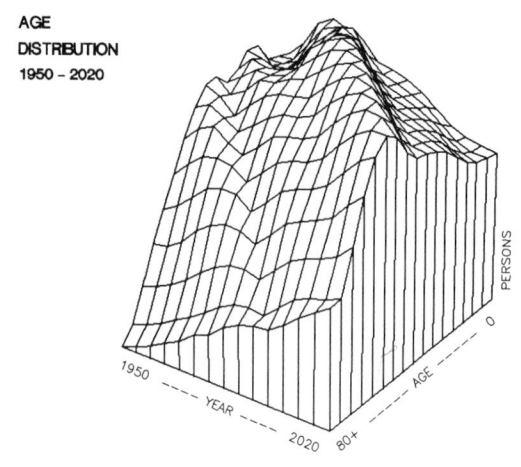

AGE DISTRIBUTION 1950 – 2020

POPULATION RATIOS

YEAR	AGE DISTRIBUTION UNDER 15	15-64	65 & OLDER	70 & OLDER	DEPENDENCY RATIO	WOMEN 15-49	CHILD-WOMAN RATIO
1950	0.199	0.703	0.098	0.057	0.423	0.267	0.241
1955	0.197	0.698	0.105	0.066	0.432	0.252	0.273
1960	0.213	0.678	0.108	0.067	0.474	0.239	0.333
1965	0.225	0.657	0.118	0.070	0.522	0.234	0.330
1970	0.220	0.655	0.125	0.076	0.527	0.238	0.292
1975	0.216	0.654	0.131	0.081	0.529	0.238	0.268
1980	0.190	0.675	0.135	0.088	0.482	0.251	0.225
1985	0.173	0.695	0.132	0.096	0.439	0.256	0.226
1990	*0.170*	*0.696*	*0.134*	*0.089*	*0.438*	*0.253*	*0.225*
2000	*0.164*	*0.679*	*0.157*	*0.104*	*0.472*	*0.242*	*0.212*
2010	*0.149*	*0.676*	*0.175*	*0.120*	*0.479*	*0.220*	*0.217*
2020	*0.147*	*0.642*	*0.210*	*0.141*	*0.557*	*0.198*	*0.245*

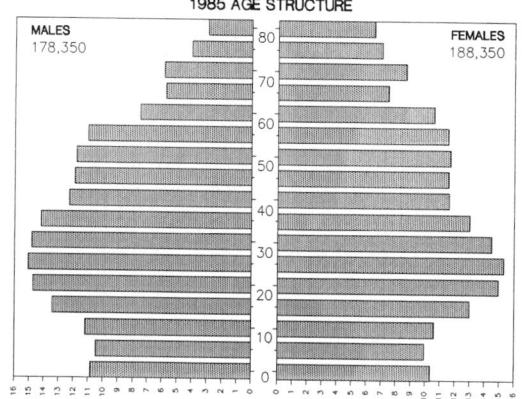

1985 AGE STRUCTURE

MALES 178,350   FEMALES 188,350

MORTALITY MEASURES (Annual Averages)

PERIOD	CRUDE DEATH RATE	INFANT MORT. RATE	LIFE EXPECTANCY AT BIRTH (years) MALE	FEMALE	BOTH SEXES	DIFFERENCE FEMALE-MALE
1950-55	11.72	43.46	63.10	68.90	65.92	5.80
1955-60	11.80	36.67	64.50	70.60	67.47	6.10
1960-65	11.94	28.70	65.70	72.10	68.81	6.40
1965-70	12.37	21.10	66.80	73.20	69.91	6.40
1970-75	12.13	16.17	67.00	74.10	70.45	7.10
1975-80	11.50	12.77	68.20	75.50	71.75	7.30
1980-85	11.23	9.30	70.00	76.70	73.26	6.70
1985-90	*11.58*	*10.13*	*71.00*	*77.72*	*74.27*	*6.73*
1990-95	*11.29*	*8.94*	*72.05*	*78.50*	*75.19*	*6.45*
2000-05	*11.34*	*6.88*	*73.78*	*80.12*	*76.86*	*6.34*
2010-15	*12.32*	*5.94*	*75.22*	*81.13*	*78.10*	*5.91*
2020-25	*13.25*	*5.32*	*76.19*	*82.14*	*79.08*	*5.94*

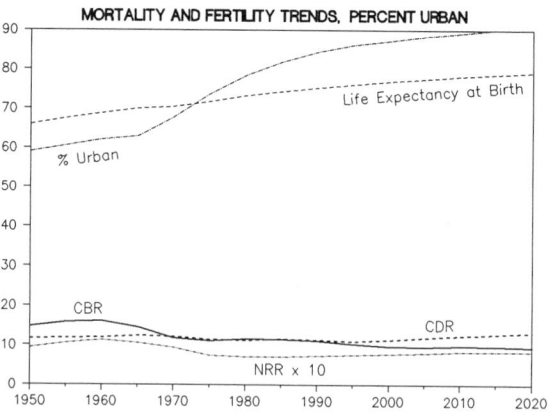

MORTALITY AND FERTILITY TRENDS, PERCENT URBAN

Life Expectancy at Birth

% Urban

CBR

CDR

NRR x 10

FERTILITY MEASURES (Annual Averages)

PERIOD	CRUDE BIRTH RATE	FERTILITY RATES GENERAL	TOTAL	REPRODUCTION RATES GROSS	NET	RATE OF NATUR. INCR.
1950-55	14.72	56.71	1.973	0.960	0.937	3.00
1955-60	15.80	64.34	2.219	1.080	1.054	4.00
1960-65	15.98	67.64	2.359	1.148	1.121	4.04
1965-70	14.51	61.47	2.217	1.079	1.054	2.15
1970-75	11.78	49.44	1.960	0.954	0.932	-0.36
1975-80	11.13	45.54	1.541	0.750	0.732	-0.37
1980-85	11.62	45.89	1.475	0.718	0.694	0.39
1985-90	*11.47*	*45.08*	*1.450*	*0.706*	*0.696*	*-0.11*
1990-95	*11.14*	*44.46*	*1.500*	*0.730*	*0.721*	*-0.15*
2000-05	*9.67*	*40.80*	*1.600*	*0.779*	*0.773*	*-1.67*
2010-15	*9.78*	*45.73*	*1.700*	*0.827*	*0.822*	*-2.54*
2020-25	*9.42*	*47.88*	*1.700*	*0.827*	*0.822*	*-3.83*

AGING MEASURES

YEAR	POPULATION AGE RATIOS 60+/20-59	65+/20-64	70+/20-69	75+/20-74	POPULATION MEAN AGE	POPULATION MEDIAN AGE
1950	0.2529	0.1576	0.0867	0.0435	35.47	35.00
1960	0.2898	0.1762	0.1020	0.0531	36.28	35.23
1970	0.3512	0.2148	0.1194	0.0595	36.36	35.35
1980	0.3154	0.2261	0.1364	0.0698	36.87	34.83
1990	*0.3321*	*0.2109*	*0.1309*	*0.0821*	*38.41*	*37.13*
2000	*0.3797*	*0.2527*	*0.1538*	*0.0810*	*40.22*	*40.46*
2010	*0.4389*	*0.2825*	*0.1788*	*0.1023*	*42.18*	*43.79*
2020	*0.5626*	*0.3555*	*0.2124*	*0.1172*	*43.63*	*45.52*

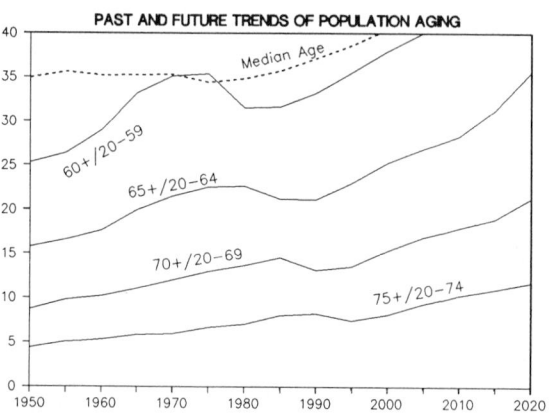

PAST AND FUTURE TRENDS OF POPULATION AGING

Median Age

60+/20-59

65+/20-64

70+/20-69

75+/20-74

OBSERVED AND *PROJECTED* POPULATION DATA

YEAR	MID-YEAR POPULATION	NO. OF BIRTHS	NO. OF DEATHS	URBAN POPULATION NUMBER	URBAN POPULATION PERCENT	POPULATION 1985 AGE	POPULATION 1985 NUMBER
1950	311999	9148	3167	190993	61.2	0	27905
1955	314000	8396	2754	206424	65.7	5	28424
1960	329001	7426	2892	230285	70.0	10	26775
1965	320000	5312	2957	236580	73.9	15	23945
1970	325569	5693	2941	252371	77.5	20	26945
1975	327842	5855	2894	264693	80.7	25	28864
1980	364001	6203	3367	303398	83.4	30	27551
1985	344360	5053	3367	294203	85.4	35	29977
1990	352897	4725	3299	307273	87.1	40	21746
1995	360104	4555	3305	318100	88.3	45	18906
2000	366412	4644	3376	327166	89.3	50	17888
2005	372803	4810	3489	336124	90.2	55	16111
2010	379468	4814	3679	345162	91.0	60	15379
2015	385185	4585	3955	353177	91.7	65	11248
2020	388348	4388	4294	358677	92.4	70+	22696

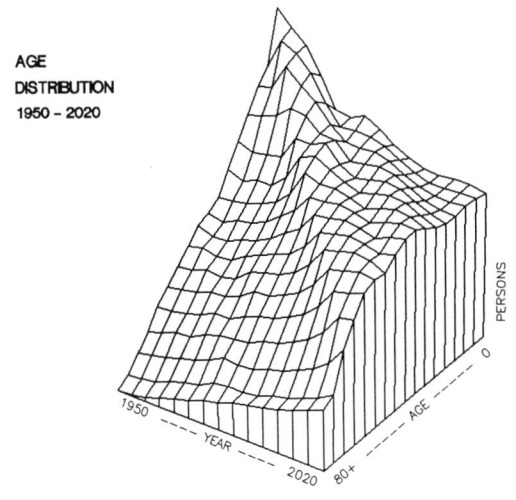

AGE DISTRIBUTION 1950 – 2020

POPULATION RATIOS

YEAR	AGE DISTRIBUTION UNDER 15	15-64	65 & OLDER	70 & OLDER	DEPENDENCY RATIO	WOMEN 15-49	CHILD-WOMAN RATIO
1950	0.349	0.593	0.058	0.035	0.686	0.240	0.627
1955	0.363	0.567	0.070	0.041	0.764	0.236	0.554
1960	0.368	0.559	0.073	0.040	0.788	0.237	0.500
1965	0.331	0.591	0.078	0.050	0.693	0.253	0.407
1970	0.277	0.633	0.090	0.054	0.580	0.268	0.285
1975	0.247	0.657	0.096	0.058	0.521	0.277	0.295
1980	0.231	0.671	0.099	0.067	0.491	0.274	0.309
1985	0.241	0.660	0.099	0.066	0.515	0.258	0.314
1990	0.231	0.667	0.102	0.064	0.499	0.259	0.276
2000	0.196	0.695	0.110	0.071	0.440	0.252	0.247
2010	0.185	0.690	0.125	0.080	0.450	0.232	0.274
2020	0.183	0.649	0.168	0.110	0.542	0.221	0.268

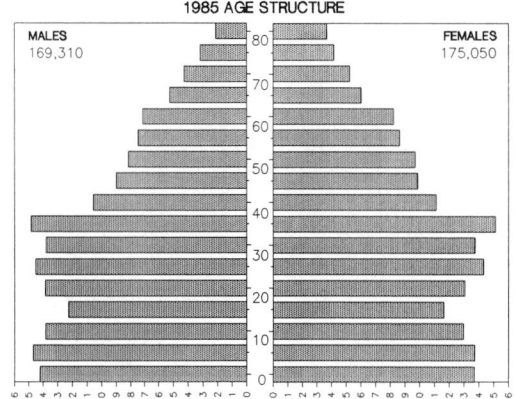

1985 AGE STRUCTURE

MALES 169,310   FEMALES 175,050

MORTALITY MEASURES (Annual Averages)

PERIOD	CRUDE DEATH RATE	INFANT MORT. RATE	LIFE EXPECTANCY AT BIRTH (years) MALE	FEMALE	BOTH SEXES	DIFFERENCE FEMALE-MALE
1950-55	10.15	74.65	64.20	67.70	65.89	3.50
1955-60	8.77	39.99	66.30	70.00	68.09	3.70
1960-65	8.79	34.31	67.04	70.75	68.83	3.71
1965-70	9.24	28.20	67.50	71.40	69.38	3.90
1970-75	9.03	21.80	68.50	72.76	70.56	4.26
1975-80	8.83	15.38	68.80	73.30	70.97	4.50
1980-85	9.25	12.88	69.99	73.38	71.62	3.39
1985-90	9.78	10.27	71.02	74.59	72.74	3.56
1990-95	9.35	9.14	72.01	75.70	73.78	3.69
2000-05	9.21	7.24	73.79	77.65	75.65	3.85
2010-15	9.69	5.99	75.20	79.28	77.16	4.08
2020-25	11.06	5.24	76.24	80.61	78.34	4.37

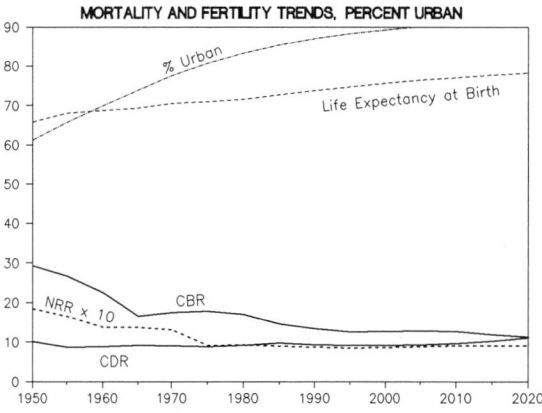

MORTALITY AND FERTILITY TRENDS, PERCENT URBAN

% Urban
Life Expectancy at Birth
NRR x 10
CBR
CDR

FERTILITY MEASURES (Annual Averages)

PERIOD	CRUDE BIRTH RATE	FERTILITY RATES GENERAL	TOTAL	REPRODUCTION RATES GROSS	NET	RATE OF NATUR. INCR.
1950-55	29.32	123.18	4.175	2.008	1.846	19.17
1955-60	26.74	113.12	3.769	1.813	1.666	17.97
1960-65	22.57	92.13	3.127	1.504	1.382	13.78
1965-70	16.60	63.63	2.185	1.051	1.378	7.36
1970-75	17.49	64.13	2.094	1.007	1.320	8.45
1975-80	17.86	64.91	2.037	0.980	0.914	9.03
1980-85	17.04	64.01	1.981	0.953	0.935	7.79
1985-90	14.67	56.69	1.900	0.914	0.897	4.90
1990-95	13.39	51.50	1.850	0.890	0.877	4.04
2000-05	12.67	51.13	1.800	0.866	0.858	3.46
2010-15	12.69	55.73	1.900	0.914	0.908	2.99
2020-25	11.30	51.66	1.900	0.914	0.908	0.24

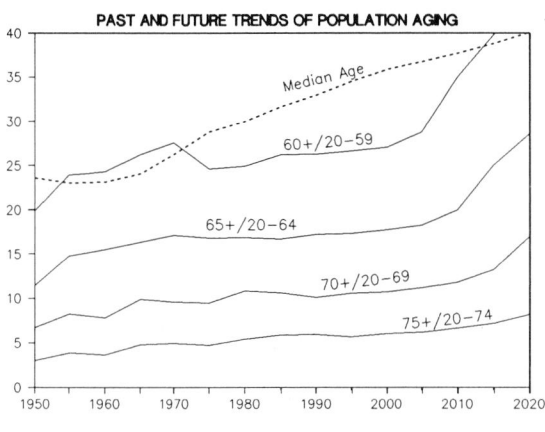

PAST AND FUTURE TRENDS OF POPULATION AGING

Median Age
60+/20-59
65+/20-64
70+/20-69
75+/20-74

AGING MEASURES

YEAR	POPULATION AGE RATIOS 60+/20-59	65+/20-64	70+/20-69	75+/20-74	POPULATION MEAN AGE	POPULATION MEDIAN AGE
1950	0.1986	0.1146	0.0671	0.0304	27.87	23.65
1960	0.2431	0.1548	0.0783	0.0361	28.37	23.15
1970	0.2758	0.1713	0.0956	0.0494	31.35	26.29
1980	0.2495	0.1688	0.1082	0.0536	33.08	30.03
1990	0.2629	0.1722	0.1009	0.0591	34.42	33.02
2000	0.2706	0.1772	0.1072	0.0602	36.43	35.90
2010	0.3502	0.2000	0.1183	0.0665	38.31	37.74
2020	0.4507	0.2857	0.1699	0.0819	39.97	40.08

OBSERVED AND *PROJECTED* POPULATION DATA (000's)

YEAR	MID-YEAR POPULATION	NO. OF BIRTHS	NO. OF DEATHS	URBAN POPULATION NUMBER	URBAN POPULATION PERCENT	POPULATION 1985 AGE	POPULATION 1985 NUMBER
1950	10114	224	76	8362	82.7	0	873
1955	10751	229	82	9018	83.9	5	889
1960	11480	240	89	9759	85.0	10	1056
1965	12292	236	100	10517	85.6	15	1232
1970	13032	201	108	11221	86.1	20	1271
1975	13666	173	111	12081	88.4	25	1209
1980	14150	173	116	12508	88.4	30	1149
1985	14484	172	126	12804	88.4	35	1198
1990	*14752*	*174*	*131*	*13051*	*88.5*	40	916
1995	*15008*	*166*	*135*	*13288*	*88.5*	45	804
2000	*15207*	*155*	*143*	*13484*	*88.7*	50	751
2005	*15301*	*146*	*150*	*13588*	*88.8*	55	709
2010	*15318*	*144*	*157*	*13632*	*89.0*	60	679
2015	*15289*	*147*	*166*	*13633*	*89.2*	65	544
2020	*15225*	*144*	*178*	*13613*	*89.4*	70+	1204

POPULATION RATIOS

YEAR	AGE DISTRIBUTION UNDER 15	AGE DISTRIBUTION 15-64	AGE DISTRIBUTION 65 & OLDER	AGE DISTRIBUTION 70 & OLDER	DEPENDENCY RATIO	WOMEN 15-49	CHILD-WOMAN RATIO
1950	0.293	0.630	0.077	0.047	0.589	0.250	0.478
1955	0.299	0.617	0.084	0.052	0.620	0.240	0.431
1960	0.300	0.610	0.090	0.056	0.639	0.233	0.432
1965	0.283	0.622	0.096	0.061	0.608	0.236	0.420
1970	0.273	0.625	0.102	0.065	0.599	0.237	0.385
1975	0.253	0.639	0.108	0.071	0.566	0.241	0.312
1980	0.223	0.662	0.115	0.077	0.511	0.252	0.248
1985	0.195	0.685	0.121	0.083	0.460	0.262	0.230
1990	*0.178*	*0.693*	*0.129*	*0.087*	*0.444*	*0.266*	*0.220*
2000	*0.170*	*0.688*	*0.142*	*0.099*	*0.452*	*0.248*	*0.222*
2010	*0.153*	*0.684*	*0.162*	*0.111*	*0.461*	*0.227*	*0.210*
2020	*0.144*	*0.645*	*0.211*	*0.146*	*0.551*	*0.200*	*0.239*

MORTALITY MEASURES (Annual Averages)

PERIOD	CRUDE DEATH RATE	INFANT MORT. RATE	LIFE EXPECTANCY AT BIRTH (years) MALE	LIFE EXPECTANCY AT BIRTH (years) FEMALE	LIFE EXPECTANCY AT BIRTH (years) BOTH SEXES	DIFFERENCE FEMALE-MALE
1950-55	7.53	24.24	70.90	73.40	72.11	2.50
1955-60	7.61	18.97	71.40	74.70	73.00	3.30
1960-65	7.78	16.14	71.10	75.80	73.38	4.70
1965-70	8.11	13.70	71.00	76.40	73.62	5.40
1970-75	8.32	11.72	71.10	77.00	73.96	5.90
1975-80	8.13	9.62	72.10	78.60	75.25	6.50
1980-85	8.23	8.31	72.75	79.48	76.04	6.73
1985-90	*8.73*	*7.53*	*73.51*	*80.23*	*76.79*	*6.72*
1990-95	*8.85*	*7.00*	*74.34*	*80.75*	*77.47*	*6.42*
2000-05	*9.40*	*6.20*	*75.65*	*81.76*	*78.63*	*6.10*
2010-15	*10.27*	*5.56*	*76.64*	*82.73*	*79.61*	*6.08*
2020-25	*11.72*	*5.36*	*77.65*	*83.51*	*80.51*	*5.86*

FERTILITY MEASURES (Annual Averages)

PERIOD	CRUDE BIRTH RATE	FERTILITY RATES GENERAL	FERTILITY RATES TOTAL	REPRODUCTION RATES GROSS	REPRODUCTION RATES NET	RATE OF NATUR. INCR.
1950-55	22.10	90.33	3.059	1.493	1.411	14.57
1955-60	21.28	90.11	3.092	1.509	1.150	13.67
1960-65	20.90	89.23	3.123	1.524	1.480	13.12
1965-70	19.18	81.17	2.735	1.335	1.300	11.07
1970-75	15.44	64.55	1.969	0.961	0.939	7.12
1975-80	12.66	51.30	1.578	0.770	0.753	4.53
1980-85	12.22	47.52	1.512	0.738	0.732	4.00
1985-90	*11.85*	*44.86*	*1.450*	*0.708*	*0.698*	*3.12*
1990-95	*11.77*	*44.68*	*1.470*	*0.717*	*0.708*	*2.91*
2000-05	*10.18*	*41.95*	*1.550*	*0.756*	*0.747*	*0.78*
2010-15	*9.43*	*42.82*	*1.650*	*0.805*	*0.796*	*-0.84*
2020-25	*9.43*	*48.07*	*1.700*	*0.830*	*0.821*	*-2.29*

AGING MEASURES

YEAR	POPULATION AGE RATIOS 60+/20-59	POPULATION AGE RATIOS 65+/20-64	POPULATION AGE RATIOS 70+/20-69	POPULATION AGE RATIOS 75+/20-74	POPULATION MEAN AGE	POPULATION MEDIAN AGE
1950	0.2237	0.1409	0.0816	0.0405	30.83	28.03
1960	0.2687	0.1698	0.0999	0.0523	31.77	28.75
1970	0.2925	0.1881	0.1124	0.0607	32.53	28.63
1980	0.2958	0.2009	0.1264	0.0716	34.49	31.28
1990	*0.3041*	*0.2080*	*0.1307*	*0.0781*	*36.87*	*34.86*
2000	*0.3266*	*0.2249*	*0.1476*	*0.0888*	*39.13*	*38.66*
2010	*0.4204*	*0.2588*	*0.1643*	*0.0996*	*41.61*	*42.77*
2020	*0.5475*	*0.3566*	*0.2226*	*0.1196*	*43.80*	*46.01*

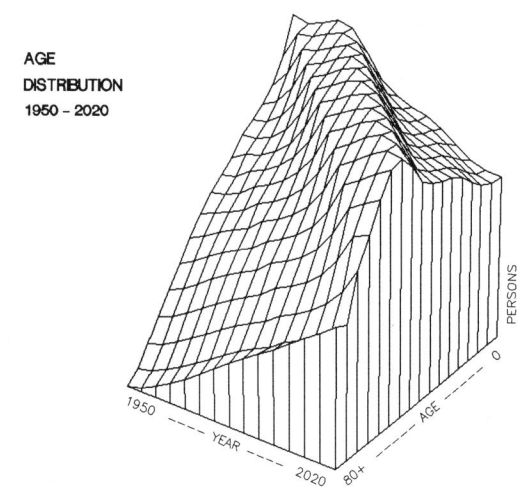

AGE DISTRIBUTION 1950 - 2020

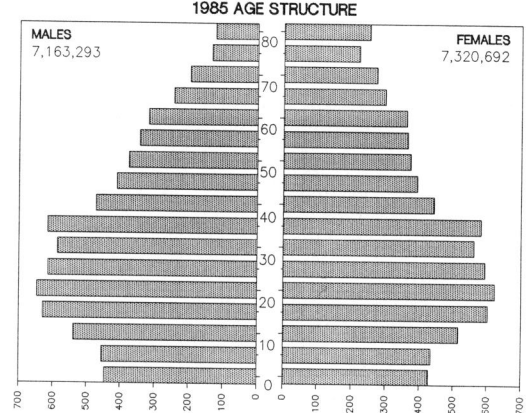

1985 AGE STRUCTURE

MALES 7,163,293

FEMALES 7,320,692

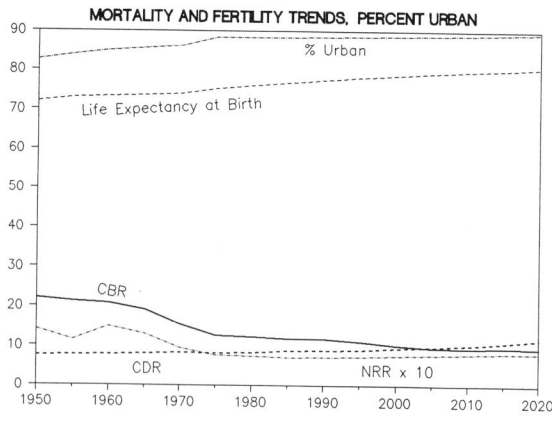

MORTALITY AND FERTILITY TRENDS, PERCENT URBAN

% Urban
Life Expectancy at Birth
CBR
CDR
NRR x 10

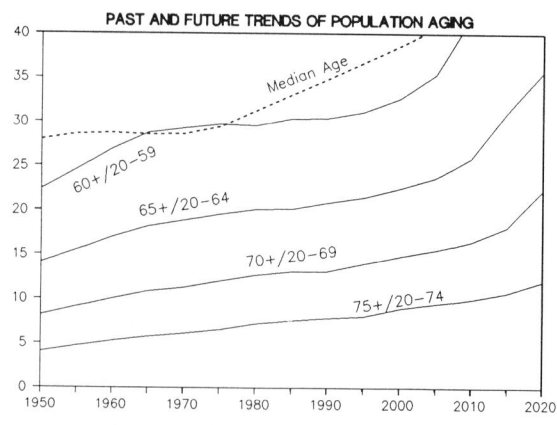

PAST AND FUTURE TRENDS OF POPULATION AGING

Median Age
60+/20-59
65+/20-64
70+/20-69
75+/20-74

OBSERVED AND *PROJECTED* POPULATION DATA

YEAR	MID-YEAR POPULATION	NO. OF BIRTHS	NO. OF DEATHS	URBAN POPULATION NUMBER	URBAN POPULATION PERCENT	POPULATION 1985 AGE	POPULATION 1985 NUMBER
1950	3265000	61121	26675	1051330	32.2	0	255159
1955	3427000	62166	30055	1101780	32.1	5	270652
1960	3581000	62130	33912	1149501	32.1	10	322205
1965	3723000	65934	36262	1769914	47.5	15	334187
1970	3877386	65066	38785	2513322	64.8	20	312781
1975	4007313	51879	40217	2732587	68.2	25	312951
1980	4085619	50237	41788	2882404	70.5	30	304989
1985	4152516	51674	43846	3023032	72.8	35	316252
1990	*4211853*	*52737*	*44903*	*3135303*	*74.4*	40	237094
1995	*4271228*	*53254*	*45305*	*3246560*	*76.0*	45	196298
2000	*4331173*	*50922*	*45638*	*3338901*	*77.1*	50	197725
2005	*4377679*	*48588*	*44876*	*3420281*	*78.1*	55	213618
2010	*4416242*	*47594*	*44366*	*3478232*	*78.8*	60	234105
2015	*4452390*	*47520*	*45063*	*3534307*	*79.4*	65	206963
2020	*4484670*	*47632*	*47659*	*3571591*	*79.6*	70+	437537

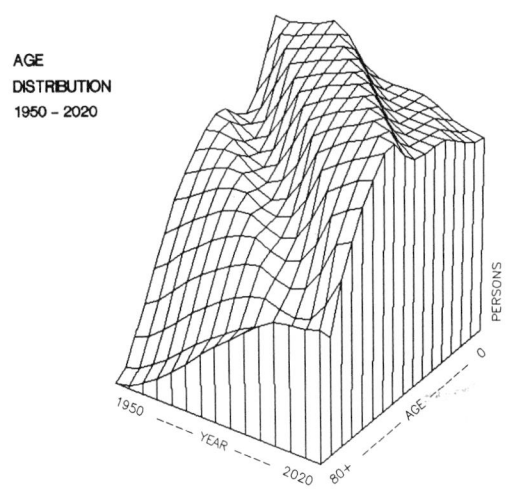

AGE DISTRIBUTION 1950 – 2020

POPULATION RATIOS

YEAR	AGE DISTRIBUTION UNDER 15	AGE DISTRIBUTION 15-64	AGE DISTRIBUTION 65 & OLDER	AGE DISTRIBUTION 70 & OLDER	DEPENDENCY RATIO	WOMEN 15-49	CHILD-WOMAN RATIO
1950	0.244	0.659	0.097	0.063	0.518	0.251	0.389
1955	0.256	0.642	0.102	0.065	0.558	0.237	0.374
1960	0.259	0.630	0.111	0.071	0.587	0.227	0.378
1965	0.248	0.633	0.120	0.075	0.580	0.226	0.371
1970	0.245	0.626	0.129	0.083	0.597	0.221	0.385
1975	0.238	0.625	0.137	0.090	0.600	0.219	0.352
1980	0.222	0.631	0.148	0.099	0.585	0.226	0.282
1985	0.204	0.641	0.155	0.105	0.561	0.237	0.260
1990	*0.188*	*0.648*	*0.164*	*0.113*	*0.542*	*0.248*	*0.250*
2000	*0.185*	*0.657*	*0.158*	*0.118*	*0.522*	*0.240*	*0.259*
2010	*0.176*	*0.668*	*0.156*	*0.110*	*0.497*	*0.228*	*0.244*
2020	*0.163*	*0.644*	*0.193*	*0.134*	*0.554*	*0.212*	*0.252*

MORTALITY MEASURES (Annual Averages)

PERIOD	CRUDE DEATH RATE	INFANT MORT. RATE	LIFE EXPECTANCY AT BIRTH (years) MALE	LIFE EXPECTANCY AT BIRTH (years) FEMALE	LIFE EXPECTANCY AT BIRTH (years) BOTH SEXES	DIFFERENCE FEMALE-MALE
1950-55	8.17	23.41	70.92	74.50	72.66	3.58
1955-60	8.77	20.02	71.30	75.50	73.34	4.20
1960-65	9.47	17.33	71.10	75.90	73.44	4.80
1965-70	9.74	14.31	71.10	76.70	73.82	5.60
1970-75	10.00	11.79	71.38	77.60	74.41	6.22
1975-80	10.04	9.36	72.20	78.60	75.31	6.40
1980-85	10.23	8.00	72.69	79.54	76.02	6.85
1985-90	*10.56*	*6.73*	*73.49*	*80.23*	*76.77*	*6.74*
1990-95	*10.66*	*6.33*	*74.29*	*80.69*	*77.40*	*6.41*
2000-05	*10.54*	*5.74*	*75.59*	*82.04*	*78.72*	*6.45*
2010-15	*10.05*	*5.26*	*76.63*	*82.67*	*79.57*	*6.04*
2020-25	*10.63*	*5.09*	*77.61*	*83.52*	*80.48*	*5.91*

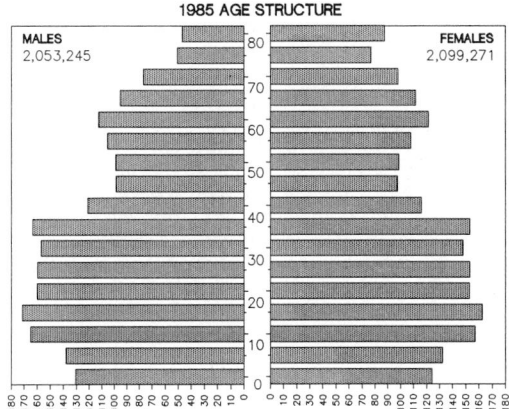

1985 AGE STRUCTURE

MALES 2,053,245 — FEMALES 2,099,271

FERTILITY MEASURES (Annual Averages)

PERIOD	CRUDE BIRTH RATE	FERTILITY RATES GENERAL	FERTILITY RATES TOTAL	REPRODUCTION RATES GROSS	REPRODUCTION RATES NET	RATE OF NATUR. INCR.
1950-55	18.72	76.67	2.602	1.265	1.191	10.55
1955-60	18.14	78.14	2.837	1.379	1.329	9.37
1960-65	17.35	76.57	2.898	1.409	1.365	7.88
1965-70	17.71	79.27	2.719	1.322	1.288	7.97
1970-75	16.78	76.20	2.248	1.093	1.071	6.78
1975-80	12.95	58.06	1.810	0.880	0.862	2.91
1980-85	12.30	53.08	1.687	0.820	0.809	2.07
1985-90	*12.44*	*51.32*	*1.690*	*0.822*	*0.810*	*1.88*
1990-95	*12.52*	*50.34*	*1.690*	*0.822*	*0.810*	*1.86*
2000-05	*11.76*	*49.56*	*1.750*	*0.851*	*0.841*	*1.22*
2010-15	*10.78*	*47.97*	*1.800*	*0.875*	*0.864*	*0.73*
2020-25	*10.62*	*51.06*	*1.800*	*0.875*	*0.866*	*-0.01*

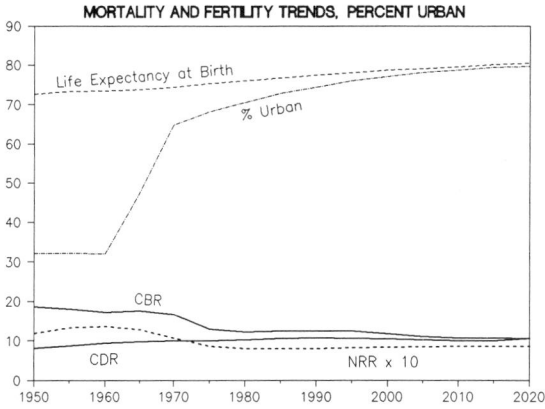

MORTALITY AND FERTILITY TRENDS, PERCENT URBAN

Life Expectancy at Birth — % Urban — CBR — CDR — NRR x 10

AGING MEASURES

YEAR	POPULATION AGE RATIOS 60+/20-59	POPULATION AGE RATIOS 65+/20-64	POPULATION AGE RATIOS 70+/20-69	POPULATION AGE RATIOS 75+/20-74	POPULATION MEAN AGE	POPULATION MEDIAN AGE
1950	0.2503	0.1623	0.1001	0.0545	33.99	32.71
1960	0.3194	0.1996	0.1183	0.0641	34.90	34.36
1970	0.3663	0.2350	0.1405	0.0746	35.47	32.96
1980	0.4061	0.2664	0.1645	0.0920	36.58	33.32
1990	*0.4056*	*0.2868*	*0.1806*	*0.1040*	*37.78*	*35.46*
2000	*0.3590*	*0.2643*	*0.1858*	*0.1177*	*38.78*	*37.57*
2010	*0.4085*	*0.2567*	*0.1682*	*0.1101*	*40.12*	*40.28*
2020	*0.4958*	*0.3301*	*0.2083*	*0.1138*	*41.82*	*42.82*

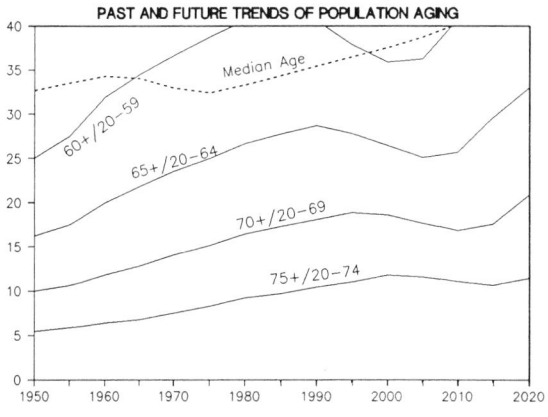

PAST AND FUTURE TRENDS OF POPULATION AGING

Median Age — 60+/20-59 — 65+/20-64 — 70+/20-69 — 75+/20-74

OBSERVED AND *PROJECTED* POPULATION DATA (000's)

YEAR	MID-YEAR POPULATION	NO. OF BIRTHS	NO. OF DEATHS	URBAN POPULATION NUMBER	URBAN POPULATION PERCENT	POPULATION 1985 AGE	POPULATION 1985 NUMBER
1950	24824	748	270	9607	38.7	0	3423
1955	27281	741	241	11796	43.2	5	3224
1960	29561	595	226	14160	47.9	10	2852
1965	31496	522	243	15751	50.0	15	2509
1970	32526	577	271	17008	52.3	20	2750
1975	34022	653	312	18794	55.2	25	3305
1980	35574	682	341	20686	58.1	30	3310
1985	37203	609	369	22698	61.0	35	2731
1990	38423	564	378	24268	63.2	40	1820
1995	39365	570	372	25690	65.3	45	2047
2000	40366	606	390	26944	66.8	50	2091
2005	41462	621	405	28281	68.2	55	1991
2010	42553	604	414	29421	69.1	60	1647
2015	43514	583	421	30486	70.1	65	976
2020	44333	580	434	31259	70.5	70+	2526

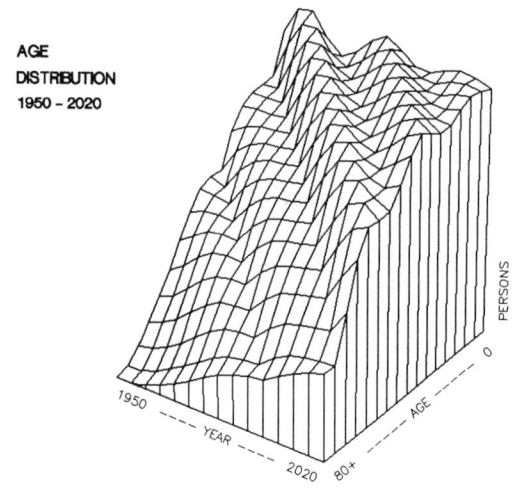

AGE DISTRIBUTION 1950 - 2020

POPULATION RATIOS

YEAR	AGE DISTRIBUTION UNDER 15	15-64	65 & OLDER	70 & OLDER	DEPENDENCY RATIO	WOMEN 15-49	CHILD-WOMAN RATIO
1950	0.294	0.654	0.052	0.031	0.529	0.281	0.422
1955	0.310	0.635	0.055	0.031	0.574	0.264	0.490
1960	0.335	0.608	0.058	0.034	0.646	0.240	0.494
1965	0.310	0.621	0.068	0.038	0.609	0.242	0.372
1970	0.270	0.648	0.082	0.047	0.543	0.261	0.300
1975	0.240	0.664	0.095	0.057	0.505	0.265	0.317
1980	0.243	0.656	0.101	0.067	0.524	0.256	0.356
1985	0.255	0.651	0.094	0.068	0.537	0.246	0.374
1990	0.252	0.649	0.100	0.061	0.542	0.246	0.321
2000	0.215	0.668	0.117	0.076	0.497	0.257	0.274
2010	0.211	0.674	0.115	0.082	0.485	0.234	0.312
2020	0.204	0.646	0.150	0.091	0.547	0.232	0.284

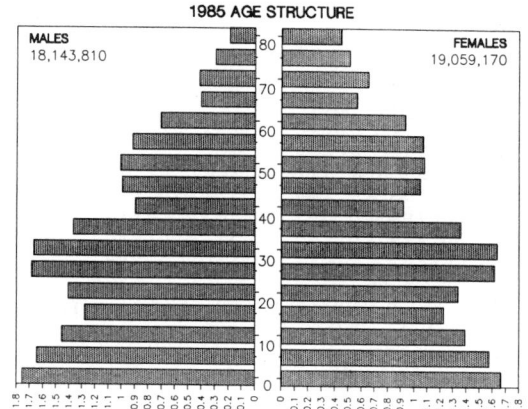

1985 AGE STRUCTURE

MALES 18,143,810

FEMALES 19,059,170

MORTALITY MEASURES (Annual Averages)

PERIOD	CRUDE DEATH RATE	INFANT MORT. RATE	LIFE EXPECTANCY AT BIRTH (years) MALE	FEMALE	BOTH SEXES	DIFFERENCE FEMALE-MALE
1950-55	10.88	95.04	58.60	64.20	61.31	5.60
1955-60	8.84	72.40	63.20	68.50	65.76	5.30
1960-65	7.64	51.16	65.80	71.00	68.32	5.20
1965-70	7.73	36.42	66.90	73.00	69.85	6.10
1970-75	8.32	27.11	67.00	74.10	70.45	7.10
1975-80	9.17	22.98	67.00	75.00	70.89	8.00
1980-85	9.59	19.83	67.00	75.00	70.89	8.00
1985-90	9.91	17.78	67.54	75.50	71.41	7.96
1990-95	9.84	16.57	67.98	76.02	71.89	8.03
2000-05	9.65	11.88	70.38	77.93	74.05	7.55
2010-15	9.72	8.59	72.31	79.48	75.79	7.17
2020-25	9.80	6.82	74.00	80.76	77.29	6.76

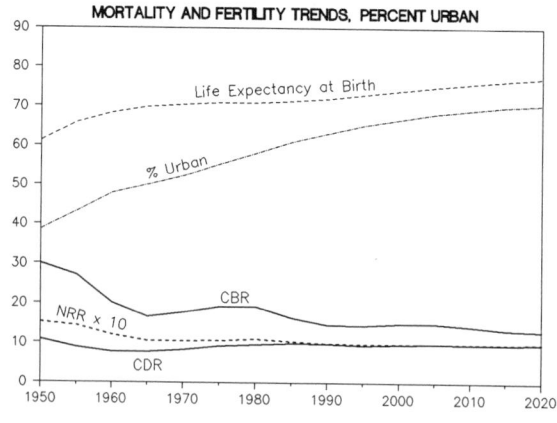

MORTALITY AND FERTILITY TRENDS, PERCENT URBAN

Life Expectancy at Birth

% Urban

NRR x 10

CBR

CDR

FERTILITY MEASURES (Annual Averages)

PERIOD	CRUDE BIRTH RATE	FERTILITY RATES GENERAL	FERTILITY RATES TOTAL	REPRODUCTION RATES GROSS	REPRODUCTION RATES NET	RATE OF NATUR. INCR.
1950-55	30.14	110.76	3.620	1.759	1.519	19.26
1955-60	27.16	108.05	3.287	1.597	1.429	18.33
1960-65	20.12	83.42	2.647	1.286	1.201	12.48
1965-70	16.58	65.91	2.268	1.102	1.053	8.85
1970-75	17.75	67.47	2.245	1.091	1.048	9.42
1975-80	19.20	73.69	2.262	1.099	1.063	10.03
1980-85	19.16	76.41	2.332	1.133	1.103	9.57
1985-90	16.36	66.52	2.200	1.069	1.043	6.45
1990-95	14.68	58.49	2.100	1.020	0.998	4.84
2000-05	15.01	59.72	2.050	0.996	0.982	5.36
2010-15	14.19	61.12	2.050	0.996	0.987	4.47
2020-25	13.07	56.56	2.050	0.996	0.989	3.28

AGING MEASURES

YEAR	POPULATION AGE RATIOS 60+/20-59	65+/20-64	70+/20-69	75+/20-74	POPULATION MEAN AGE	POPULATION MEDIAN AGE
1950	0.1564	0.0939	0.0534	0.0281	29.11	25.80
1960	0.1851	0.1065	0.0594	0.0293	29.25	26.54
1970	0.2576	0.1521	0.0823	0.0398	31.67	28.16
1980	0.2411	0.1750	0.1096	0.0556	33.02	29.55
1990	0.2802	0.1734	0.1001	0.0632	33.78	32.22
2000	0.2967	0.2003	0.1215	0.0627	35.41	34.18
2010	0.3065	0.1897	0.1284	0.0745	36.58	34.84
2020	0.4156	0.2587	0.1429	0.0726	37.93	37.16

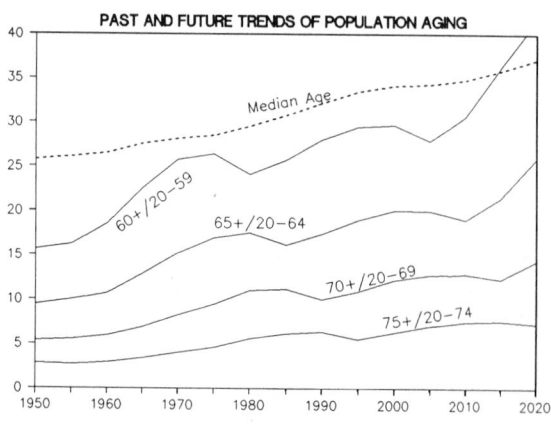

PAST AND FUTURE TRENDS OF POPULATION AGING

Median Age

60+/20-59

65+/20-64

70+/20-69

75+/20-74

OBSERVED AND *PROJECTED* POPULATION DATA (000's)

YEAR	MID-YEAR POPULATION	NO. OF BIRTHS	NO. OF DEATHS	URBAN POPULATION NUMBER	URBAN POPULATION PERCENT	POPULATION 1985 AGE	POPULATION 1985 NUMBER
1950	8405	202	99	1619	19.3	0	712
1955	8610	208	98	1795	20.9	5	810
1960	8826	212	96	1990	22.5	10	867
1965	9129	195	98	2222	24.3	15	860
1970	9044	176	95	2372	26.2	20	855
1975	9093	165	93	2531	27.8	25	757
1980	9766	144	94	2878	29.5	30	677
1985	10157	137	102	3164	31.2	35	627
1990	*10285*	*137*	*105*	*3427*	*33.3*	*40*	*560*
1995	*10429*	*141*	*105*	*3752*	*36.0*	*45*	*577*
2000	*10587*	*138*	*108*	*4141*	*39.1*	*50*	*579*
2005	*10717*	*133*	*111*	*4577*	*42.7*	*55*	*553*
2010	*10809*	*129*	*112*	*5044*	*46.7*	*60*	*505*
2015	*10873*	*125*	*113*	*5494*	*50.5*	*65*	*394*
2020	*10912*	*124*	*116*	*5921*	*54.3*	*70+*	*823*

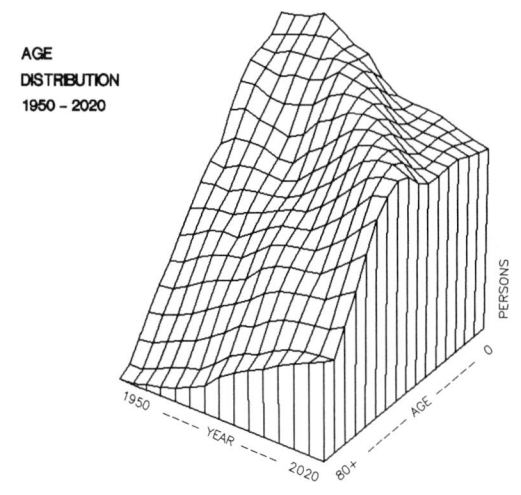

AGE DISTRIBUTION 1950 – 2020

POPULATION RATIOS

YEAR	AGE DISTRIBUTION UNDER 15	AGE DISTRIBUTION 15-64	AGE DISTRIBUTION 65 & OLDER	AGE DISTRIBUTION 70 & OLDER	DEPENDENCY RATIO	WOMEN 15-49	CHILD-WOMAN RATIO
1950	0.295	0.635	0.070	0.043	0.574	0.264	0.398
1955	0.287	0.641	0.073	0.044	0.561	0.264	0.390
1960	0.292	0.629	0.080	0.050	0.591	0.255	0.398
1965	0.290	0.627	0.083	0.052	0.595	0.253	0.419
1970	0.288	0.620	0.092	0.056	0.612	0.252	0.392
1975	0.279	0.622	0.099	0.060	0.608	0.252	0.358
1980	0.259	0.636	0.105	0.066	0.572	0.251	0.342
1985	0.235	0.645	0.120	0.081	0.551	0.245	0.286
1990	*0.212*	*0.659*	*0.129*	*0.084*	*0.518*	*0.252*	*0.260*
2000	*0.193*	*0.664*	*0.144*	*0.097*	*0.507*	*0.254*	*0.260*
2010	*0.188*	*0.663*	*0.148*	*0.106*	*0.508*	*0.241*	*0.253*
2020	*0.175*	*0.661*	*0.164*	*0.112*	*0.513*	*0.223*	*0.256*

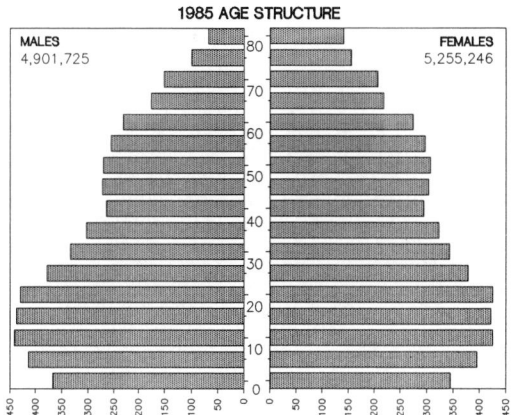

1985 AGE STRUCTURE

MALES 4,901,725   FEMALES 5,255,246

MORTALITY MEASURES (Annual Averages)

PERIOD	CRUDE DEATH RATE	INFANT MORT. RATE	LIFE EXPECTANCY AT BIRTH (years) MALE	LIFE EXPECTANCY AT BIRTH (years) FEMALE	LIFE EXPECTANCY AT BIRTH (years) BOTH SEXES	DIFFERENCE FEMALE-MALE
1950-55	11.75	91.38	56.90	61.90	59.34	5.00
1955-60	11.37	86.43	59.70	65.10	62.33	5.40
1960-65	10.84	76.18	61.40	67.10	64.18	5.70
1965-70	10.69	60.50	63.10	69.30	66.12	6.20
1970-75	10.52	44.55	64.90	71.30	68.02	6.40
1975-80	10.26	30.30	66.70	73.80	70.16	7.10
1980-85	9.60	20.28	68.80	75.82	72.19	7.02
1985-90	*10.09*	*15.47*	*70.00*	*76.83*	*73.31*	*6.83*
1990-95	*10.17*	*12.88*	*71.07*	*77.75*	*74.30*	*6.68*
2000-05	*10.24*	*9.10*	*72.99*	*79.38*	*76.08*	*6.39*
2010-15	*10.38*	*6.95*	*74.54*	*80.61*	*77.48*	*6.08*
2020-25	*10.60*	*6.03*	*75.73*	*82.05*	*78.79*	*6.32*

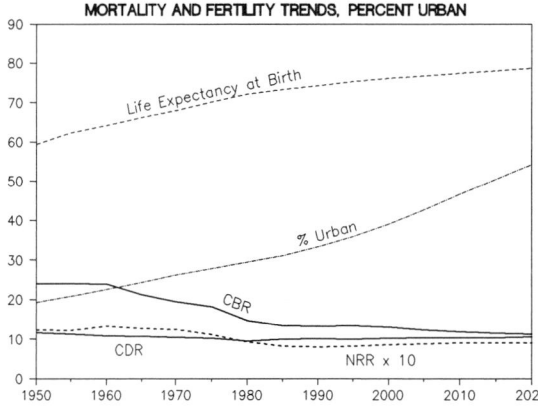

MORTALITY AND FERTILITY TRENDS, PERCENT URBAN

Life Expectancy at Birth — % Urban — CBR — CDR — NRR x 10

FERTILITY MEASURES (Annual Averages)

PERIOD	CRUDE BIRTH RATE	FERTILITY RATES GENERAL	FERTILITY RATES TOTAL	REPRODUCTION RATES GROSS	REPRODUCTION RATES NET	RATE OF NATUR. INCR.
1950-55	24.09	91.21	3.050	1.475	1.235	12.34
1955-60	24.16	93.24	3.042	1.471	1.225	12.79
1960-65	24.01	94.69	3.085	1.492	1.330	13.17
1965-70	21.35	84.68	2.860	1.383	1.268	10.66
1970-75	19.50	77.40	2.759	1.334	1.255	8.98
1975-80	18.19	72.36	2.420	1.170	1.116	7.94
1980-85	14.71	59.34	1.989	0.962	0.929	5.11
1985-90	*13.47*	*54.20*	*1.750*	*0.846*	*0.824*	*3.38*
1990-95	*13.34*	*52.48*	*1.700*	*0.822*	*0.804*	*3.17*
2000-05	*13.07*	*52.08*	*1.800*	*0.870*	*0.858*	*2.83*
2010-15	*11.93*	*50.45*	*1.900*	*0.919*	*0.908*	*1.55*
2020-25	*11.38*	*52.26*	*1.900*	*0.919*	*0.909*	*0.78*

AGING MEASURES

YEAR	POPULATION AGE RATIOS 60+/20-59	POPULATION AGE RATIOS 65+/20-64	POPULATION AGE RATIOS 70+/20-69	POPULATION AGE RATIOS 75+/20-74	POPULATION MEAN AGE	POPULATION MEDIAN AGE
1950	0.2075	0.1295	0.0754	0.0385	29.88	26.18
1960	0.2317	0.1467	0.0872	0.0449	31.10	27.99
1970	0.2788	0.1722	0.0986	0.0513	31.95	28.57
1980	0.2899	0.1924	0.1136	0.0563	32.95	29.14
1990	*0.3426*	*0.2239*	*0.1351*	*0.0776*	*35.77*	*32.73*
2000	*0.3508*	*0.2404*	*0.1514*	*0.0842*	*37.29*	*35.46*
2010	*0.3635*	*0.2470*	*0.1639*	*0.0968*	*38.75*	*38.38*
2020	*0.4190*	*0.2737*	*0.1731*	*0.1010*	*40.37*	*41.21*

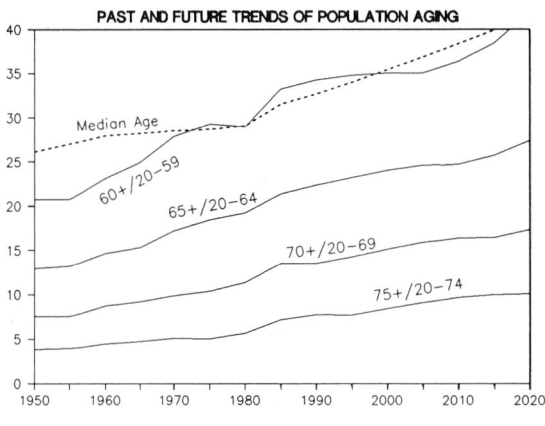

PAST AND FUTURE TRENDS OF POPULATION AGING

Median Age — 60+/20-59 — 65+/20-64 — 70+/20-69 — 75+/20-74

OBSERVED AND *PROJECTED* POPULATION DATA (000's)

YEAR	MID-YEAR POPULATION	NO. OF BIRTHS	NO. OF DEATHS	URBAN POPULATION NUMBER	URBAN POPULATION PERCENT	POPULATION 1985 AGE	POPULATION 1985 NUMBER
1950	16311	407	196	4525	27.7	0	1723
1955	17486	400	170	5400	30.9	5	1984
1960	18407	308	158	6297	34.2	10	1896
1965	19032	405	174	7175	37.7	15	1994
1970	20360	393	191	8517	41.8	20	1414
1975	21245	406	207	9809	46.2	25	1736
1980	22201	351	227	10688	48.1	30	1751
1985	22725	353	245	11147	49.0	35	1466
1990	*23272*	*351*	*244*	*11727*	*50.4*	40	1234
1995	*23816*	*344*	*239*	*12323*	*51.7*	45	1503
2000	*24346*	*332*	*255*	*12950*	*53.2*	50	1436
2005	*24731*	*321*	*265*	*13513*	*54.6*	55	1326
2010	*25013*	*323*	*269*	*14052*	*56.2*	60	1108
2015	*25284*	*318*	*271*	*14591*	*57.7*	65	588
2020	*25521*	*311*	*267*	*15139*	*59.3*	70+	1565

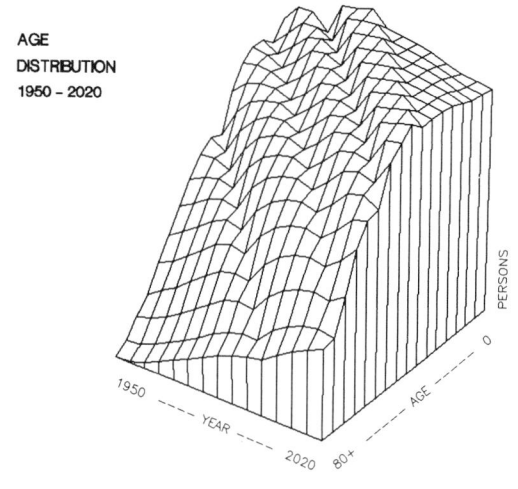

AGE DISTRIBUTION 1950 - 2020

POPULATION RATIOS

YEAR	AGE DISTRIBUTION UNDER 15	15-64	65 & OLDER	70 & OLDER	DEPENDENCY RATIO	WOMEN 15-49	CHILD-WOMAN RATIO
1950	0.284	0.663	0.053	0.034	0.509	0.276	0.361
1955	0.275	0.661	0.064	0.037	0.512	0.271	0.392
1960	0.282	0.651	0.067	0.039	0.536	0.259	0.380
1965	0.264	0.657	0.079	0.046	0.522	0.255	0.297
1970	0.259	0.655	0.086	0.049	0.526	0.260	0.386
1975	0.252	0.652	0.096	0.057	0.535	0.254	0.357
1980	0.267	0.631	0.103	0.065	0.586	0.240	0.377
1985	0.247	0.659	0.095	0.069	0.518	0.242	0.313
1990	*0.233*	*0.664*	*0.103*	*0.060*	*0.506*	*0.242*	*0.309*
2000	*0.213*	*0.661*	*0.126*	*0.079*	*0.512*	*0.249*	*0.282*
2010	*0.197*	*0.670*	*0.132*	*0.094*	*0.492*	*0.241*	*0.264*
2020	*0.187*	*0.664*	*0.149*	*0.094*	*0.506*	*0.236*	*0.263*

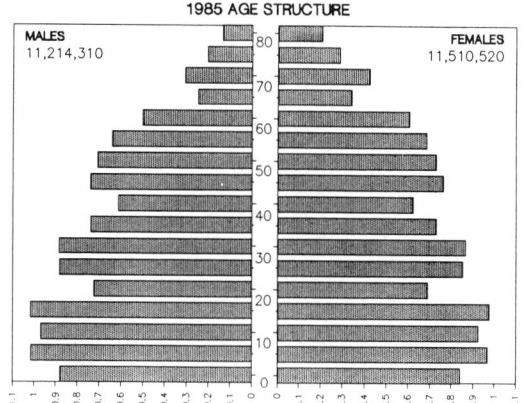

1985 AGE STRUCTURE

MALES 11,214,310

FEMALES 11,510,520

MORTALITY MEASURES (Annual Averages)

PERIOD	CRUDE DEATH RATE	INFANT MORT. RATE	LIFE EXPECTANCY AT BIRTH (years) MALE	FEMALE	BOTH SEXES	DIFFERENCE FEMALE-MALE
1950-55	12.00	100.93	59.40	62.80	61.05	3.40
1955-60	9.74	77.76	62.40	65.90	64.10	3.50
1960-65	8.60	59.76	65.00	68.70	66.80	3.70
1965-70	9.16	51.69	66.00	70.20	68.04	4.20
1970-75	9.37	39.51	66.80	71.30	68.99	4.50
1975-80	9.74	31.29	67.30	72.00	69.58	4.70
1980-85	10.23	26.02	66.90	72.50	69.62	5.60
1985-90	*10.77*	*22.47*	*67.46*	*72.97*	*70.14*	*5.51*
1990-95	*10.47*	*19.24*	*68.76*	*74.18*	*71.39*	*5.42*
2000-05	*10.48*	*14.00*	*70.93*	*76.32*	*73.54*	*5.39*
2010-15	*10.74*	*10.12*	*72.93*	*78.21*	*75.50*	*5.28*
2020-25	*10.45*	*7.28*	*74.53*	*79.81*	*77.09*	*5.28*

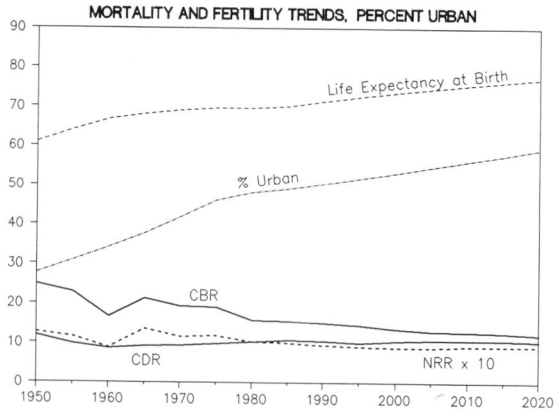

MORTALITY AND FERTILITY TRENDS, PERCENT URBAN

Life Expectancy at Birth

% Urban

CBR

CDR

NRR x 10

FERTILITY MEASURES (Annual Averages)

PERIOD	CRUDE BIRTH RATE	FERTILITY RATES GENERAL	TOTAL	REPRODUCTION RATES GROSS	NET	RATE OF NATUR. INCR.
1950-55	24.94	91.21	2.872	1.395	1.273	12.94
1955-60	22.90	86.46	2.623	1.274	1.162	13.16
1960-65	16.74	65.14	2.014	0.978	0.892	8.14
1965-70	21.26	82.57	3.058	1.485	1.354	12.10
1970-75	19.28	75.10	2.625	1.275	1.162	9.91
1975-80	19.12	77.48	2.553	1.240	1.185	9.39
1980-85	15.82	65.64	2.224	1.080	1.031	5.59
1985-90	*15.53*	*64.16*	*2.150*	*1.044*	*1.007*	*4.76*
1990-95	*15.10*	*61.34*	*2.000*	*0.971*	*0.944*	*4.63*
2000-05	*13.62*	*55.26*	*1.850*	*0.898*	*0.883*	*3.14*
2010-15	*12.89*	*53.10*	*1.900*	*0.923*	*0.914*	*2.15*
2020-25	*12.20*	*52.60*	*1.900*	*0.923*	*0.918*	*1.75*

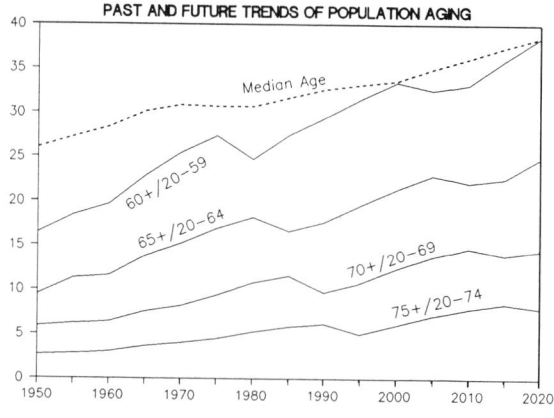

PAST AND FUTURE TRENDS OF POPULATION AGING

Median Age

60+/20-59

65+/20-64

70+/20-69

75+/20-74

AGING MEASURES

YEAR	POPULATION AGE RATIOS 60+/20-59	65+/20-64	70+/20-69	75+/20-74	POPULATION MEAN AGE	MEDIAN AGE
1950	0.1642	0.0948	0.0586	0.0266	29.63	26.07
1960	0.1968	0.1162	0.0641	0.0298	30.91	28.41
1970	0.2545	0.1517	0.0819	0.0398	32.53	30.91
1980	0.2471	0.1815	0.1077	0.0523	33.32	30.74
1990	*0.2939*	*0.1763*	*0.0966*	*0.0611*	*34.60*	*32.67*
2000	*0.3343*	*0.2133*	*0.1236*	*0.0604*	*35.95*	*33.67*
2010	*0.3320*	*0.2204*	*0.1466*	*0.0784*	*37.38*	*36.22*
2020	*0.3848*	*0.2481*	*0.1439*	*0.0791*	*38.65*	*38.54*

OBSERVED AND *PROJECTED* POPULATION DATA (000's)

YEAR	MID-YEAR POPULATION	NO. OF BIRTHS	NO. OF DEATHS	URBAN POPULATION NUMBER	URBAN POPULATION PERCENT	POPULATION 1985 AGE	POPULATION 1985 NUMBER
1950	28009	569	286	14526	51.9	0	2542
1955	29199	622	274	15833	54.2	5	3016
1960	30455	656	268	17228	56.6	10	3272
1965	31954	656	277	19581	61.3	15	3284
1970	33779	658	281	22307	66.0	20	3265
1975	35596	620	290	24765	69.6	25	2936
1980	37542	498	289	27327	72.8	30	2527
1985	38602	496	351	29255	75.8	35	2439
1990	*39333*	*502*	*358*	*30839*	*78.4*	40	2230
1995	*40060*	*519*	*370*	*32310*	*80.7*	45	1992
2000	*40812*	*513*	*392*	*33693*	*82.6*	50	2293
2005	*41420*	*491*	*410*	*34854*	*84.1*	55	2189
2010	*41831*	*474*	*420*	*35749*	*85.5*	60	1929
2015	*42102*	*471*	*419*	*36486*	*86.7*	65	1485
2020	*42366*	*468*	*435*	*37179*	*87.8*	70+	3204

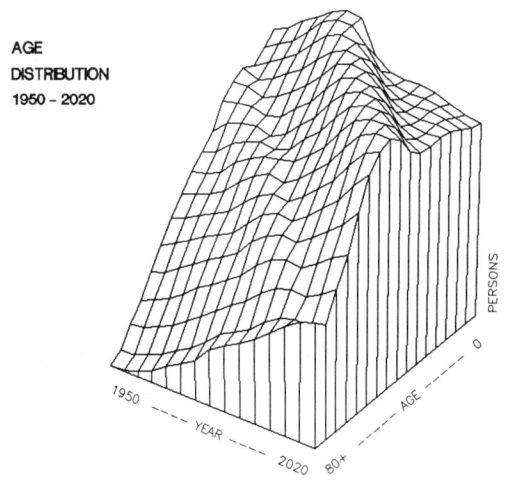

AGE DISTRIBUTION 1950 – 2020

POPULATION RATIOS

YEAR	AGE DISTRIBUTION UNDER 15	AGE DISTRIBUTION 15-64	AGE DISTRIBUTION 65 & OLDER	AGE DISTRIBUTION 70 & OLDER	DEPENDENCY RATIO	WOMEN 15-49	CHILD-WOMAN RATIO
1950	0.271	0.656	0.073	0.046	0.524	0.269	0.363
1955	0.272	0.650	0.078	0.048	0.539	0.262	0.364
1960	0.274	0.644	0.082	0.051	0.554	0.256	0.387
1965	0.273	0.641	0.086	0.051	0.560	0.254	0.377
1970	0.279	0.623	0.098	0.060	0.606	0.241	0.394
1975	0.276	0.624	0.100	0.063	0.604	0.241	0.387
1980	0.266	0.627	0.107	0.068	0.594	0.237	0.377
1985	0.229	0.650	0.121	0.083	0.539	0.240	0.274
1990	*0.204*	*0.666*	*0.130*	*0.085*	*0.503*	*0.249*	*0.253*
2000	*0.186*	*0.663*	*0.151*	*0.102*	*0.508*	*0.249*	*0.256*
2010	*0.182*	*0.663*	*0.155*	*0.109*	*0.509*	*0.236*	*0.249*
2020	*0.169*	*0.658*	*0.173*	*0.121*	*0.520*	*0.216*	*0.257*

1985 AGE STRUCTURE

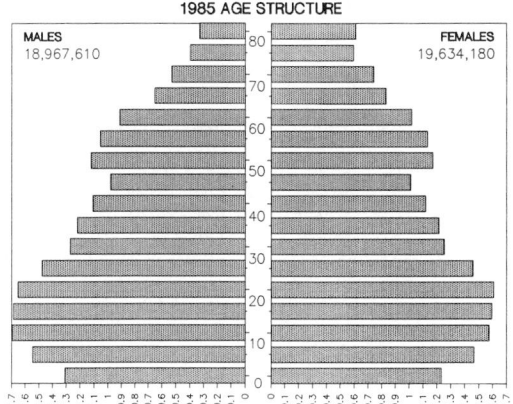

MALES 18,967,610   FEMALES 19,634,180

MORTALITY MEASURES (Annual Averages)

PERIOD	CRUDE DEATH RATE	INFANT MORT. RATE	LIFE EXPECTANCY AT BIRTH (years) MALE	LIFE EXPECTANCY AT BIRTH (years) FEMALE	LIFE EXPECTANCY AT BIRTH (years) BOTH SEXES	DIFFERENCE FEMALE-MALE
1950-55	10.21	61.62	61.60	66.30	63.89	4.70
1955-60	9.37	50.62	65.40	70.20	67.74	4.80
1960-65	8.81	41.99	67.90	72.70	70.24	4.80
1965-70	8.67	32.54	69.10	74.30	71.63	5.20
1970-75	8.32	21.42	70.20	75.70	72.85	5.50
1975-80	8.15	15.67	71.40	77.40	74.30	6.00
1980-85	7.70	10.82	72.80	78.90	75.75	6.10
1985-90	*9.09*	*9.87*	*73.60*	*79.70*	*76.54*	*6.10*
1990-95	*9.11*	*8.52*	*74.40*	*80.32*	*77.26*	*5.92*
2000-05	*9.60*	*7.00*	*75.64*	*81.32*	*78.38*	*5.68*
2010-15	*10.04*	*5.77*	*76.64*	*82.32*	*79.38*	*5.68*
2020-25	*10.27*	*5.53*	*77.62*	*83.16*	*80.29*	*5.54*

MORTALITY AND FERTILITY TRENDS, PERCENT URBAN

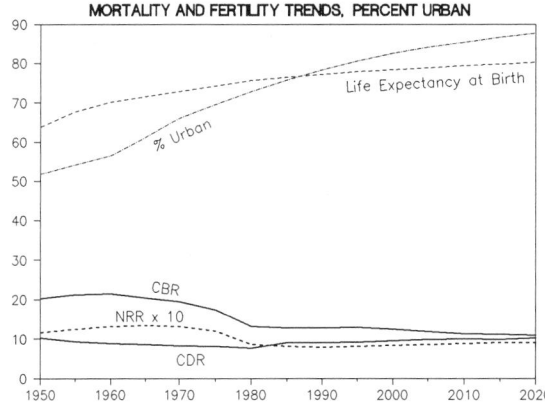

Life Expectancy at Birth
% Urban
CBR
NRR x 10
CDR

FERTILITY MEASURES (Annual Averages)

PERIOD	CRUDE BIRTH RATE	FERTILITY RATES GENERAL	FERTILITY RATES TOTAL	REPRODUCTION RATES GROSS	REPRODUCTION RATES NET	RATE OF NATUR. INCR.
1950-55	20.32	76.54	2.568	1.240	1.172	10.11
1955-60	21.29	82.22	2.750	1.328	1.255	11.92
1960-65	21.53	84.40	2.889	1.395	1.319	12.72
1965-70	20.53	82.96	2.930	1.415	1.338	11.86
1970-75	19.47	80.83	2.891	1.396	1.320	11.15
1975-80	17.41	72.87	2.630	1.270	1.201	9.26
1980-85	13.26	55.55	1.833	0.885	0.870	5.56
1985-90	*12.84*	*52.49*	*1.700*	*0.821*	*0.814*	*3.75*
1990-95	*12.77*	*50.82*	*1.650*	*0.797*	*0.791*	*3.66*
2000-05	*12.56*	*50.99*	*1.750*	*0.845*	*0.839*	*2.96*
2010-15	*11.34*	*49.16*	*1.850*	*0.893*	*0.887*	*1.29*
2020-25	*11.04*	*52.32*	*1.900*	*0.917*	*0.911*	*0.77*

AGING MEASURES

YEAR	POPULATION AGE RATIOS 60+/20-59	POPULATION AGE RATIOS 65+/20-64	POPULATION AGE RATIOS 70+/20-69	POPULATION AGE RATIOS 75+/20-74	POPULATION MEAN AGE	POPULATION MEDIAN AGE
1950	0.2079	0.1298	0.0788	0.0393	30.89	27.68
1960	0.2358	0.1455	0.0857	0.0433	31.92	29.56
1970	0.2844	0.1798	0.1027	0.0537	32.72	30.20
1980	0.2968	0.1968	0.1179	0.0616	33.36	30.33
1990	*0.3467*	*0.2238*	*0.1353*	*0.0786*	*36.14*	*33.13*
2000	*0.3531*	*0.2517*	*0.1575*	*0.0871*	*37.87*	*36.17*
2010	*0.3806*	*0.2578*	*0.1687*	*0.1061*	*39.45*	*39.32*
2020	*0.4444*	*0.2897*	*0.1868*	*0.1100*	*41.14*	*42.32*

PAST AND FUTURE TRENDS OF POPULATION AGING

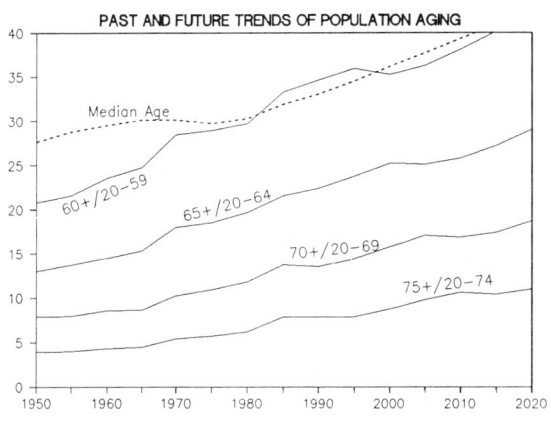

Median Age
60+/20-59
65+/20-64
70+/20-69
75+/20-74

OBSERVED AND *PROJECTED* POPULATION DATA

YEAR	MID-YEAR POPULATION	NO. OF BIRTHS	NO. OF DEATHS	URBAN POPULATION NUMBER	URBAN POPULATION PERCENT	POPULATION 1985 AGE	POPULATION 1985 NUMBER
1950	7014000	108647	68387	4618337	65.8	0	426673
1955	7262000	105154	69860	5033894	69.3	5	484412
1960	7480000	110098	74875	5429420	72.6	10	553420
1965	7734000	114100	79196	5960331	77.1	15	578018
1970	8042845	109616	83766	6524889	81.1	20	586249
1975	8192567	96156	89283	6777686	82.7	25	558752
1980	8310474	93800	91158	6904903	83.1	30	578041
1985	8350366	93466	101724	6967368	83.4	35	654718
1990	8339074	93248	100894	7004261	84.0	40	617277
1995	8325796	94156	99960	7054579	84.7	45	473940
2000	8321768	90566	98854	7125467	85.6	50	426418
2005	8305331	85537	96574	7195599	86.6	55	443293
2010	8275215	84018	95237	7260423	87.7	60	478128
2015	8243985	84971	97732	7315837	88.7	65	446841
2020	8205307	85384	104363	7356903	89.7	70+1	044186

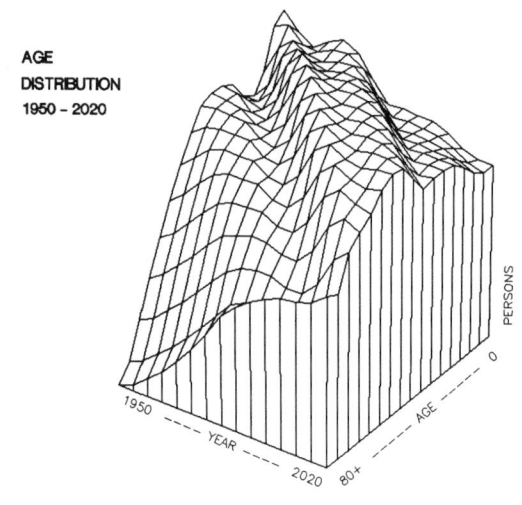

AGE DISTRIBUTION 1950 - 2020

POPULATION RATIOS

YEAR	AGE DISTRIBUTION UNDER 15	15-64	65 & OLDER	70 & OLDER	DEPENDENCY RATIO	WOMEN 15-49	CHILD-WOMAN RATIO
1950	0.234	0.663	0.103	0.064	0.508	0.249	0.348
1955	0.238	0.653	0.109	0.068	0.530	0.239	0.308
1960	0.220	0.660	0.120	0.076	0.514	0.236	0.286
1965	0.209	0.664	0.127	0.080	0.506	0.234	0.307
1970	0.208	0.655	0.137	0.087	0.527	0.230	0.315
1975	0.207	0.642	0.151	0.098	0.558	0.224	0.300
1980	0.196	0.641	0.163	0.111	0.560	0.229	0.256
1985	0.175	0.646	0.179	0.125	0.548	0.237	0.216
1990	0.166	0.651	0.183	0.130	0.535	0.242	0.232
2000	0.169	0.655	0.176	0.132	0.527	0.224	0.253
2010	0.164	0.642	0.194	0.130	0.557	0.215	0.240
2020	0.155	0.617	0.228	0.167	0.621	0.205	0.253

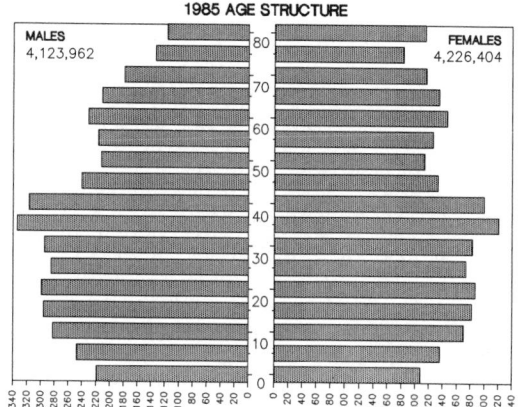

1985 AGE STRUCTURE

MALES 4,123,962   FEMALES 4,226,404

MORTALITY MEASURES (Annual Averages)

PERIOD	CRUDE DEATH RATE	INFANT MORT. RATE	LIFE EXPECTANCY AT BIRTH (years) MALE	FEMALE	BOTH SEXES	DIFFERENCE FEMALE-MALE
1950-55	9.75	19.67	70.40	73.30	71.81	2.90
1955-60	9.62	16.94	70.90	74.50	72.65	3.60
1960-65	10.01	15.09	71.60	75.60	73.54	4.00
1965-70	10.24	12.50	71.90	76.50	74.13	4.60
1970-75	10.41	10.24	72.10	77.50	74.72	5.40
1975-80	10.90	7.89	72.30	78.30	75.21	6.00
1980-85	10.97	6.81	73.37	79.34	76.27	5.97
1985-90	12.18	6.08	74.17	80.12	77.06	5.95
1990-95	12.10	5.78	74.99	80.68	77.75	5.69
2000-05	11.88	5.35	76.02	81.67	78.76	5.66
2010-15	11.51	5.04	77.04	82.64	79.76	5.60
2020-25	12.72	4.93	77.97	83.46	80.64	5.49

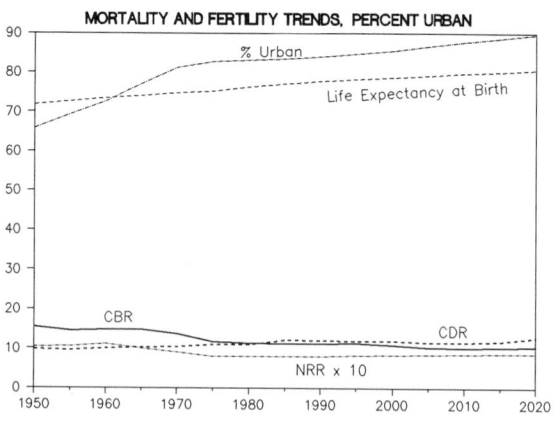

MORTALITY AND FERTILITY TRENDS, PERCENT URBAN

% Urban

Life Expectancy at Birth

CBR

CDR

NRR x 10

FERTILITY MEASURES (Annual Averages)

PERIOD	CRUDE BIRTH RATE	FERTILITY RATES GENERAL	FERTILITY RATES TOTAL	REPRODUCTION RATES GROSS	REPRODUCTION RATES NET	RATE OF NATUR. INCR.
1950-55	15.49	63.51	2.212	1.075	1.040	5.74
1955-60	14.48	60.97	2.233	1.085	1.049	4.86
1960-65	14.72	62.71	2.334	1.134	1.106	4.71
1965-70	14.75	63.67	2.118	1.029	0.991	4.51
1970-75	13.63	60.04	1.887	0.917	0.900	3.21
1975-80	11.74	51.79	1.646	0.800	0.788	0.84
1980-85	11.29	48.47	1.659	0.806	0.796	0.32
1985-90	11.19	46.71	1.650	0.802	0.792	-0.99
1990-95	11.18	46.74	1.650	0.802	0.793	-0.92
2000-05	10.88	49.21	1.730	0.841	0.832	-0***
2010-15	10.15	47.68	1.780	0.865	0.856	-1.36
2020-25	10.41	51.49	1.800	0.875	0.866	-2.31

AGING MEASURES

YEAR	POPULATION AGE RATIOS 60+/20-59	65+/20-64	70+/20-69	75+/20-74	POPULATION MEAN AGE	POPULATION MEDIAN AGE
1950	0.2682	0.1697	0.0999	0.0509	34.95	34.26
1960	0.3269	0.2060	0.1221	0.0637	36.50	36.24
1970	0.3716	0.2332	0.1376	0.0733	37.11	35.39
1980	0.4251	0.2844	0.1768	0.0965	38.40	36.25
1990	0.4386	0.3135	0.2037	0.1202	40.09	39.32
2000	0.4152	0.2923	0.2032	0.1292	40.93	40.69
2010	0.5201	0.3324	0.2010	0.1239	42.05	42.62
2020	0.5814	0.4061	0.2687	0.1528	43.33	44.63

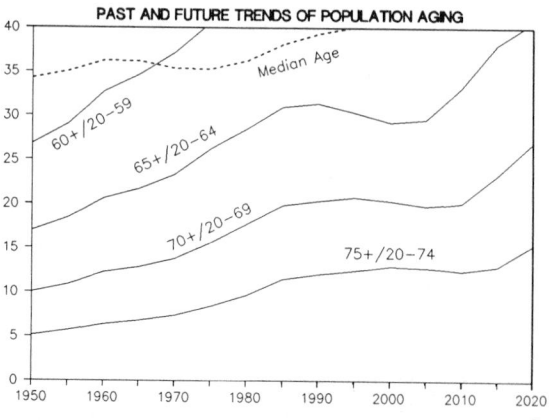

PAST AND FUTURE TRENDS OF POPULATION AGING

Median Age

60+/20-59

65+/20-64

70+/20-69

75+/20-74

OBSERVED AND *PROJECTED* POPULATION DATA

YEAR	MID-YEAR POPULATION	NO. OF BIRTHS	NO. OF DEATHS	URBAN POPULATION NUMBER	URBAN POPULATION PERCENT	POPULATION 1985 AGE	POPULATION 1985 NUMBER
1950	4694000	81394	47597	2080381	44.3	0	331347
1955	4980000	87150	49103	2373468	47.7	5	362706
1960	5362000	101235	51046	2735692	51.0	10	401996
1965	5857000	103552	54353	3093667	52.8	15	482988
1970	6267000	88716	56228	3413008	54.5	20	518467
1975	6405000	74042	57440	3570787	55.7	25	493302
1980	6326716	73409	58864	3606228	57.0	30	481531
1985	6470366	75994	65991	3767694	58.2	35	507011
1990	*6520585*	*73500*	*67195*	*3884312*	*59.6*	40	480001
1995	*6552207*	*68189*	*68018*	*3989639*	*60.9*	45	404778
2000	*6553062*	*62103*	*71173*	*4082558*	*62.3*	50	382696
2005	*6507882*	*59000*	*73858*	*4144870*	*63.7*	55	353667
2010	*6434026*	*59598*	*77047*	*4191768*	*65.2*	60	327527
2015	*6347369*	*59729*	*79888*	*4226078*	*66.6*	65	263021
2020	*6247351*	*58044*	*84214*	*4252572*	*68.1*	70+	678828

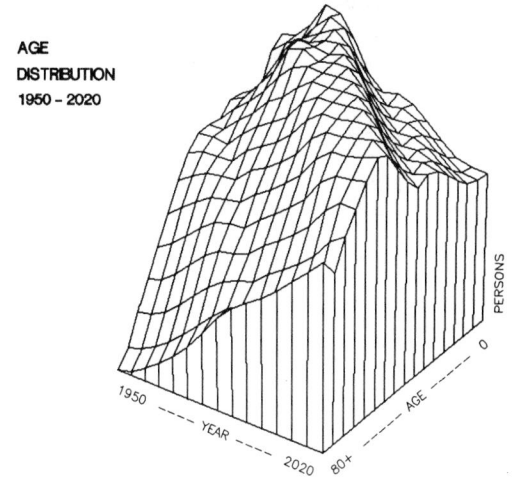

AGE DISTRIBUTION 1950 – 2020

POPULATION RATIOS

YEAR	AGE DISTRIBUTION UNDER 15	AGE DISTRIBUTION 15-64	AGE DISTRIBUTION 65 & OLDER	AGE DISTRIBUTION 70 & OLDER	DEPENDENCY RATIO	WOMEN 15-49	CHILD-WOMAN RATIO
1950	0.235	0.669	0.096	0.059	0.496	0.261	0.335
1955	0.243	0.659	0.099	0.062	0.518	0.251	0.325
1960	0.236	0.663	0.101	0.063	0.508	0.245	0.334
1965	0.241	0.654	0.105	0.065	0.530	0.245	0.359
1970	0.233	0.653	0.114	0.071	0.531	0.242	0.322
1975	0.223	0.650	0.126	0.081	0.537	0.248	0.269
1980	0.197	0.665	0.138	0.096	0.505	0.253	0.223
1985	0.169	0.685	0.146	0.105	0.460	0.258	0.199
1990	*0.164*	*0.683*	*0.153*	*0.106*	*0.465*	*0.254*	*0.229*
2000	*0.165*	*0.664*	*0.171*	*0.121*	*0.506*	*0.229*	*0.226*
2010	*0.145*	*0.651*	*0.203*	*0.140*	*0.536*	*0.213*	*0.212*
2020	*0.141*	*0.617*	*0.243*	*0.177*	*0.622*	*0.192*	*0.246*

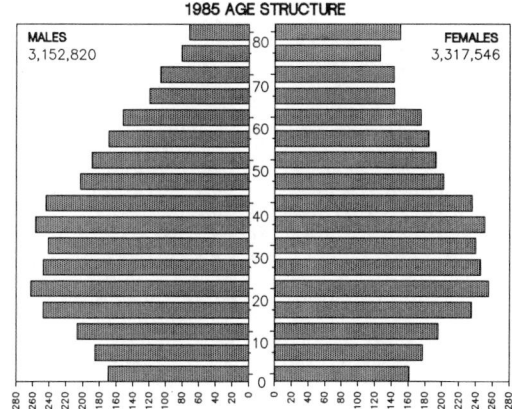

1985 AGE STRUCTURE

MALES 3,152,820

FEMALES 3,317,546

MORTALITY MEASURES (Annual Averages)

PERIOD	CRUDE DEATH RATE	INFANT MORT. RATE	LIFE EXPECTANCY AT BIRTH (years) MALE	LIFE EXPECTANCY AT BIRTH (years) FEMALE	LIFE EXPECTANCY AT BIRTH (years) BOTH SEXES	DIFFERENCE FEMALE-MALE
1950-55	10.14	29.01	67.00	71.60	69.23	4.60
1955-60	9.86	23.34	68.20	73.40	70.72	5.20
1960-65	9.52	20.18	68.90	74.60	71.67	5.70
1965-70	9.28	16.53	69.40	75.10	72.17	5.70
1970-75	8.97	13.32	70.80	77.00	73.81	6.20
1975-80	8.97	9.52	72.00	78.60	75.20	6.60
1980-85	9.30	7.50	72.96	79.73	76.26	6.77
1985-90	*10.20*	*7.21*	*73.75*	*80.35*	*76.97*	*6.60*
1990-95	*10.31*	*6.77*	*74.58*	*80.85*	*77.64*	*6.27*
2000-05	*10.86*	*6.10*	*75.70*	*81.81*	*78.68*	*6.12*
2010-15	*11.98*	*5.55*	*76.71*	*82.75*	*79.65*	*6.03*
2020-25	*13.48*	*5.35*	*77.72*	*83.60*	*80.58*	*5.88*

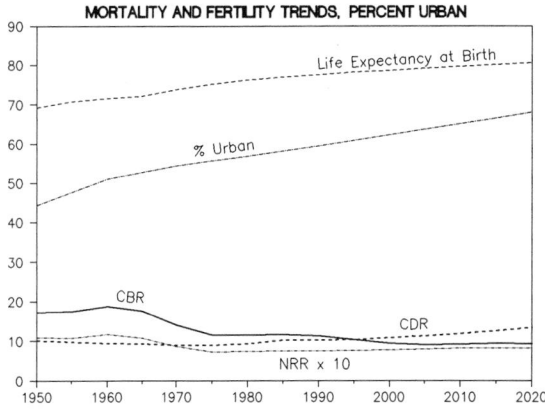

MORTALITY AND FERTILITY TRENDS, PERCENT URBAN

Life Expectancy at Birth

% Urban

CBR

CDR

NRR x 10

FERTILITY MEASURES (Annual Averages)

PERIOD	CRUDE BIRTH RATE	FERTILITY RATES GENERAL	FERTILITY RATES TOTAL	REPRODUCTION RATES GROSS	REPRODUCTION RATES NET	RATE OF NATUR. INCR.
1950-55	17.34	67.83	2.279	1.110	1.080	7.20
1955-60	17.50	70.67	2.336	1.138	1.079	7.64
1960-65	18.88	77.05	2.507	1.221	1.171	9.36
1965-70	17.68	72.56	2.269	1.105	1.068	8.40
1970-75	14.16	57.74	1.817	0.885	0.862	5.18
1975-80	11.56	46.19	1.519	0.740	0.726	2.59
1980-85	11.60	45.49	1.532	0.746	0.736	2.30
1985-90	*11.74*	*45.95*	*1.550*	*0.755*	*0.743*	*1.55*
1990-95	*11.27*	*45.41*	*1.550*	*0.755*	*0.743*	*0.97*
2000-05	*9.48*	*42.08*	*1.600*	*0.779*	*0.768*	*-1.38*
2010-15	*9.26*	*44.56*	*1.700*	*0.828*	*0.816*	*-2.71*
2020-25	*9.29*	*49.01*	*1.700*	*0.828*	*0.818*	*-4.19*

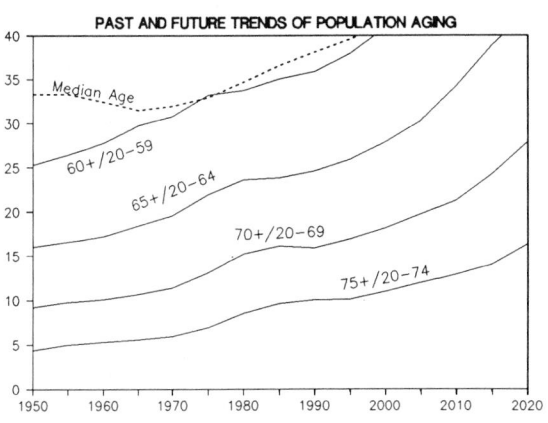

PAST AND FUTURE TRENDS OF POPULATION AGING

Median Age

60+/20-59

65+/20-64

70+/20-69

75+/20-74

AGING MEASURES

YEAR	POPULATION AGE RATIOS 60+/20-59	POPULATION AGE RATIOS 65+/20-64	POPULATION AGE RATIOS 70+/20-69	POPULATION AGE RATIOS 75+/20-74	POPULATION MEAN AGE	POPULATION MEDIAN AGE
1950	0.2531	0.1604	0.0920	0.0438	34.32	33.33
1960	0.2778	0.1719	0.1010	0.0530	34.44	32.47
1970	0.3082	0.1954	0.1140	0.0593	34.61	31.97
1980	0.3376	0.2365	0.1526	0.0851	36.90	34.75
1990	*0.3591*	*0.2461*	*0.1592*	*0.1003*	*39.18*	*38.13*
2000	*0.4087*	*0.2790*	*0.1817*	*0.1100*	*41.14*	*41.22*
2010	*0.5261*	*0.3423*	*0.2126*	*0.1293*	*43.36*	*44.87*
2020	*0.6346*	*0.4277*	*0.2789*	*0.1632*	*45.05*	*47.38*

OBSERVED AND *PROJECTED* POPULATION DATA (000's)

YEAR	MID-YEAR POPULATION	NO. OF BIRTHS	NO. OF DEATHS	URBAN POPULATION NUMBER	URBAN POPULATION PERCENT	POPULATION 1985 AGE	POPULATION 1985 NUMBER
1950	50616	804	591	42609	84.2	0	3610
1955	51199	840	597	43492	84.9	5	3398
1960	52372	953	617	44874	85.7	10	3888
1965	54350	954	634	47330	87.1	15	4540
1970	55632	806	651	49226	88.5	20	4747
1975	56226	695	668	50464	89.8	25	4103
1980	56330	730	656	51166	90.8	30	3770
1985	56618	761	672	51947	91.7	35	4144
1990	*56926*	*756*	*661*	*52671*	*92.5*	40	3424
1995	*57268*	*717*	*642*	*53360*	*93.2*	45	3171
2000	*57509*	*674*	*637*	*53898*	*93.7*	50	3041
2005	*57562*	*656*	*629*	*54236*	*94.2*	55	3079
2010	*57560*	*667*	*627*	*54498*	*94.7*	60	3146
2015	*57622*	*668*	*640*	*54800*	*95.1*	65	2540
2020	*57630*	*655*	*661*	*55031*	*95.5*	70+	6018

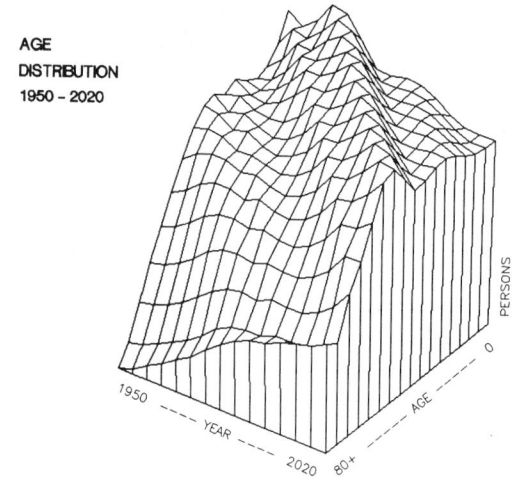

AGE DISTRIBUTION 1950 – 2020

POPULATION RATIOS

YEAR	AGE DISTRIBUTION UNDER 15	AGE DISTRIBUTION 15-64	AGE DISTRIBUTION 65 & OLDER	AGE DISTRIBUTION 70 & OLDER	DEPENDENCY RATIO	WOMEN 15-49	CHILD-WOMAN RATIO
1950	0.223	0.669	0.107	0.067	0.494	0.253	0.339
1955	0.229	0.659	0.113	0.072	0.519	0.244	0.309
1960	0.233	0.651	0.117	0.075	0.537	0.234	0.337
1965	0.232	0.648	0.120	0.076	0.544	0.229	0.380
1970	0.243	0.628	0.129	0.081	0.592	0.224	0.363
1975	0.233	0.627	0.140	0.089	0.595	0.223	0.316
1980	0.209	0.640	0.151	0.101	0.562	0.233	0.259
1985	0.192	0.656	0.151	0.106	0.523	0.244	0.262
1990	*0.189*	*0.655*	*0.155*	*0.105*	*0.526*	*0.246*	*0.269*
2000	*0.193*	*0.653*	*0.154*	*0.110*	*0.532*	*0.236*	*0.263*
2010	*0.177*	*0.662*	*0.161*	*0.112*	*0.510*	*0.230*	*0.246*
2020	*0.172*	*0.641*	*0.187*	*0.132*	*0.561*	*0.209*	*0.276*

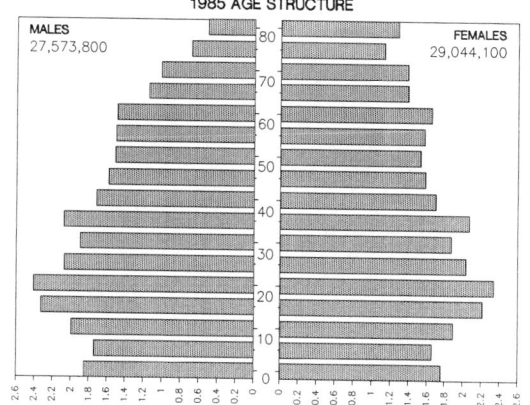

1985 AGE STRUCTURE

MALES 27,573,800   FEMALES 29,044,100

MORTALITY MEASURES (Annual Averages)

PERIOD	CRUDE DEATH RATE	INFANT MORT. RATE	LIFE EXPECTANCY AT BIRTH (years) MALE	LIFE EXPECTANCY AT BIRTH (years) FEMALE	LIFE EXPECTANCY AT BIRTH (years) BOTH SEXES	DIFFERENCE FEMALE-MALE
1950-55	11.68	28.48	66.70	71.80	69.18	5.10
1955-60	11.66	23.76	67.70	73.30	70.42	5.60
1960-65	11.78	21.55	67.90	73.80	70.76	5.90
1965-70	11.66	18.96	68.30	74.60	71.36	6.30
1970-75	11.70	17.38	69.00	75.20	72.01	6.20
1975-80	11.87	13.74	69.70	76.00	72.76	6.30
1980-85	11.65	10.53	71.04	77.20	74.04	6.16
1985-90	*11.88*	*9.12*	*72.37*	*78.11*	*75.16*	*5.74*
1990-95	*11.60*	*7.90*	*73.25*	*78.92*	*76.01*	*5.67*
2000-05	*11.07*	*6.04*	*74.80*	*80.36*	*77.51*	*5.57*
2010-15	*10.90*	*5.43*	*76.01*	*81.66*	*78.76*	*5.65*
2020-25	*11.48*	*5.01*	*76.93*	*82.31*	*79.55*	*5.38*

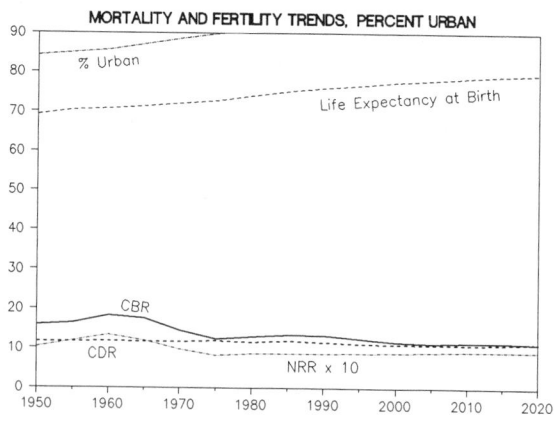

MORTALITY AND FERTILITY TRENDS, PERCENT URBAN

% Urban

Life Expectancy at Birth

CBR

CDR

NRR x 10

FERTILITY MEASURES (Annual Averages)

PERIOD	CRUDE BIRTH RATE	FERTILITY RATES GENERAL	FERTILITY RATES TOTAL	REPRODUCTION RATES GROSS	REPRODUCTION RATES NET	RATE OF NATUR. INCR.
1950-55	15.88	63.95	2.184	1.064	1.022	4.20
1955-60	16.40	68.63	2.496	1.216	1.176	4.74
1960-65	18.20	78.48	2.817	1.372	1.335	6.42
1965-70	17.56	77.52	2.521	1.228	1.197	5.90
1970-75	14.49	64.85	2.045	0.996	0.971	2.80
1975-80	12.37	54.26	1.725	0.840	0.820	0.50
1980-85	12.96	54.43	1.800	0.877	0.869	1.31
1985-90	*13.44*	*54.82*	*1.800*	*0.877*	*0.864*	*1.56*
1990-95	*13.27*	*54.25*	*1.800*	*0.877*	*0.866*	*1.67*
2000-05	*11.72*	*49.91*	*1.850*	*0.901*	*0.892*	*0.65*
2010-15	*11.59*	*51.58*	*1.900*	*0.925*	*0.917*	*0.69*
2020-25	*11.37*	*54.90*	*1.900*	*0.925*	*0.917*	*-0.11*

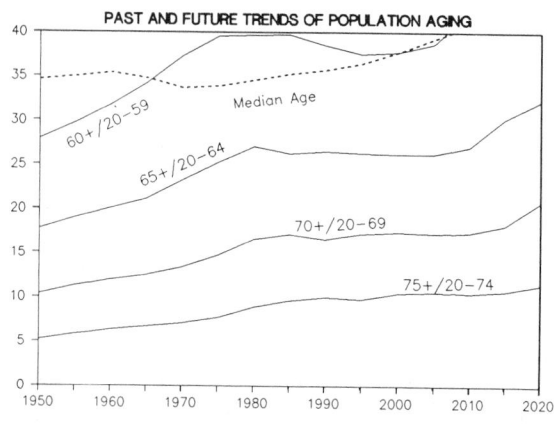

PAST AND FUTURE TRENDS OF POPULATION AGING

Median Age

60+/20-59

65+/20-64

70+/20-69

75+/20-74

AGING MEASURES

YEAR	POPULATION AGE RATIOS 60+/20-59	POPULATION AGE RATIOS 65+/20-64	POPULATION AGE RATIOS 70+/20-69	POPULATION AGE RATIOS 75+/20-74	POPULATION MEAN AGE	POPULATION MEDIAN AGE
1950	0.2791	0.1776	0.1034	0.0520	35.32	34.63
1960	0.3179	0.2006	0.1197	0.0637	36.03	35.44
1970	0.3724	0.2318	0.1337	0.0705	35.75	33.73
1980	0.3966	0.2698	0.1651	0.0887	37.18	34.60
1990	*0.3848*	*0.2649*	*0.1655*	*0.0997*	*37.84*	*35.76*
2000	*0.3771*	*0.2615*	*0.1738*	*0.1046*	*38.68*	*37.76*
2010	*0.4246*	*0.2701*	*0.1731*	*0.1046*	*40.07*	*40.74*
2020	*0.4851*	*0.3217*	*0.2076*	*0.1144*	*41.39*	*42.03*

OBSERVED AND *PROJECTED* POPULATION DATA (000's)

YEAR	MID-YEAR POPULATION	NO. OF BIRTHS	NO. OF DEATHS	URBAN POPULATION NUMBER	URBAN POPULATION PERCENT	POPULATION 1985 AGE	POPULATION 1985 NUMBER
1950	16346	470	203	3589	22.0	0	1870
1955	17519	435	184	4348	24.8	5	1887
1960	18402	406	174	5137	27.9	10	1823
1965	19434	385	170	6070	31.2	15	1857
1970	20371	371	177	7081	34.8	20	1893
1975	21352	377	184	8211	38.5	25	1921
1980	22299	368	205	9438	42.3	30	1845
1985	23118	348	204	10698	46.3	35	1384
1990	*23849*	*333*	*211*	*11970*	*50.2*	40	1432
1995	*24471*	*324*	*214*	*13209*	*54.0*	45	1551
2000	*25026*	*324*	*233*	*14401*	*57.5*	50	1516
2005	*25481*	*323*	*255*	*15521*	*60.9*	55	1252
2010	*25822*	*319*	*271*	*16544*	*64.1*	60	920
2015	*26064*	*308*	*279*	*17466*	*67.0*	65	527
2020	*26211*	*301*	*285*	*18279*	*69.7*	70+	1442

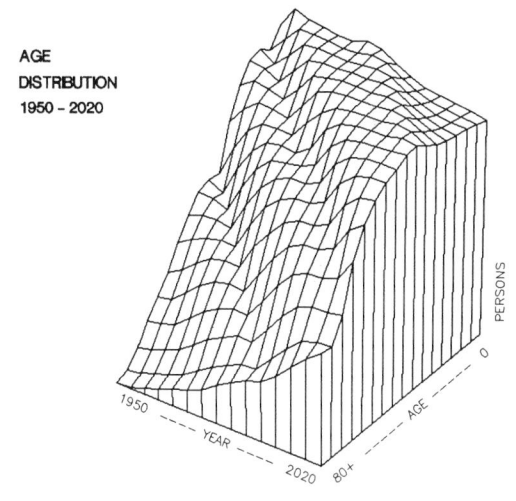

AGE DISTRIBUTION 1950 – 2020

POPULATION RATIOS

YEAR	AGE DISTRIBUTION UNDER 15	AGE DISTRIBUTION 15-64	AGE DISTRIBUTION 65 & OLDER	AGE DISTRIBUTION 70 & OLDER	DEPENDENCY RATIO	WOMEN 15-49	CHILD-WOMAN RATIO
1950	0.311	0.632	0.057	0.032	0.582	0.270	0.406
1955	0.304	0.636	0.060	0.035	0.572	0.266	0.447
1960	0.305	0.632	0.063	0.040	0.583	0.256	0.406
1965	0.297	0.636	0.067	0.039	0.572	0.254	0.382
1970	0.274	0.648	0.078	0.044	0.544	0.266	0.337
1975	0.257	0.657	0.086	0.050	0.522	0.266	0.322
1980	0.248	0.662	0.090	0.055	0.510	0.259	0.332
1985	0.241	0.673	0.085	0.062	0.485	0.253	0.320
1990	*0.229*	*0.680*	*0.091*	*0.056*	*0.471*	*0.249*	*0.291*
2000	*0.199*	*0.677*	*0.125*	*0.075*	*0.478*	*0.253*	*0.255*
2010	*0.187*	*0.669*	*0.145*	*0.100*	*0.495*	*0.237*	*0.262*
2020	*0.180*	*0.659*	*0.161*	*0.104*	*0.519*	*0.223*	*0.262*

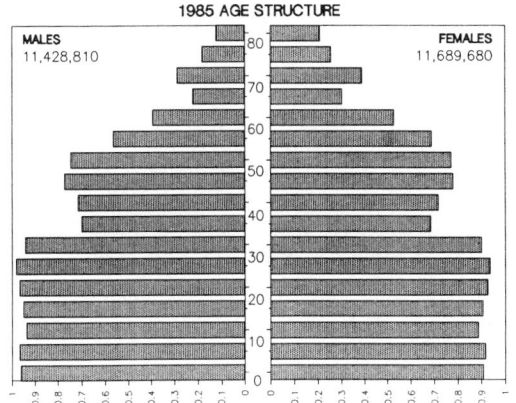

1985 AGE STRUCTURE

MALES 11,428,810   FEMALES 11,689,680

MORTALITY MEASURES (Annual Averages)

PERIOD	CRUDE DEATH RATE	INFANT MORT. RATE	LIFE EXPECTANCY AT BIRTH (years) MALE	LIFE EXPECTANCY AT BIRTH (years) FEMALE	LIFE EXPECTANCY AT BIRTH (years) BOTH SEXES	DIFFERENCE FEMALE-MALE
1950-55	12.44	127.67	56.90	59.30	58.06	2.40
1955-60	10.49	104.11	59.90	62.60	61.20	2.70
1960-65	9.44	79.94	63.00	66.30	64.59	3.30
1965-70	8.75	60.86	64.50	68.90	66.63	4.40
1970-75	8.68	45.29	66.00	70.90	68.37	4.90
1975-80	8.60	34.95	67.60	72.90	70.16	5.30
1980-85	9.17	30.32	67.94	73.80	70.77	5.86
1985-90	*8.83*	*24.62*	*69.10*	*74.96*	*71.93*	*5.87*
1990-95	*8.83*	*20.70*	*70.30*	*76.04*	*73.07*	*5.73*
2000-05	*9.33*	*14.18*	*72.28*	*78.00*	*75.04*	*5.72*
2010-15	*10.51*	*9.52*	*73.98*	*79.51*	*76.65*	*5.54*
2020-25	*10.85*	*7.27*	*75.40*	*80.76*	*77.99*	*5.36*

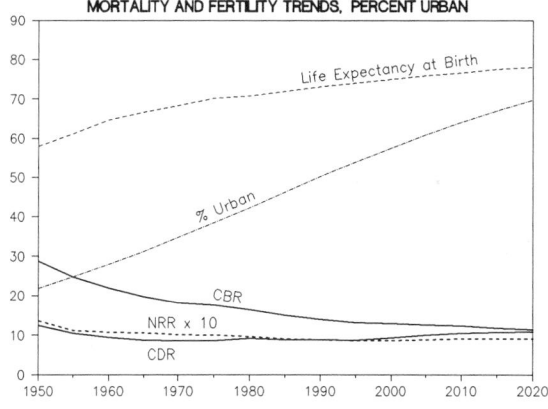

MORTALITY AND FERTILITY TRENDS, PERCENT URBAN

Life Expectancy at Birth
% Urban
CBR
NRR x 10
CDR

FERTILITY MEASURES (Annual Averages)

PERIOD	CRUDE BIRTH RATE	FERTILITY RATES GENERAL	FERTILITY RATES TOTAL	REPRODUCTION RATES GROSS	REPRODUCTION RATES NET	RATE OF NATUR. INCR.
1950-55	28.78	107.26	3.691	1.783	1.363	16.34
1955-60	24.84	95.21	2.819	1.362	1.115	14.35
1960-65	22.06	86.64	2.699	1.304	1.072	12.62
1965-70	19.81	76.21	2.492	1.204	1.061	11.06
1970-75	18.20	68.48	2.318	1.120	1.015	9.52
1975-80	17.66	67.29	2.200	1.063	1.000	9.06
1980-85	16.50	64.44	2.080	1.005	0.964	7.33
1985-90	*15.05*	*60.04*	*1.950*	*0.942*	*0.912*	*6.22*
1990-95	*13.98*	*56.11*	*1.870*	*0.903*	*0.880*	*5.15*
2000-05	*12.93*	*51.94*	*1.820*	*0.879*	*0.865*	*3.61*
2010-15	*12.37*	*53.09*	*1.900*	*0.918*	*0.908*	*1.87*
2020-25	*11.47*	*51.88*	*1.900*	*0.918*	*0.910*	*0.61*

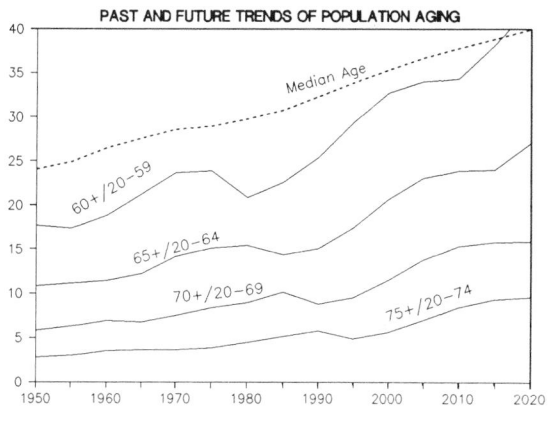

PAST AND FUTURE TRENDS OF POPULATION AGING

Median Age
60+/20-59
65+/20-64
70+/20-69
75+/20-74

AGING MEASURES

YEAR	POPULATION AGE RATIOS 60+/20-59	POPULATION AGE RATIOS 65+/20-64	POPULATION AGE RATIOS 70+/20-69	POPULATION AGE RATIOS 75+/20-74	POPULATION MEAN AGE	POPULATION MEDIAN AGE
1950	0.1771	0.1083	0.0583	0.0278	28.52	24.06
1960	0.1880	0.1141	0.0690	0.0352	29.59	26.54
1970	0.2369	0.1415	0.0746	0.0367	31.20	28.64
1980	0.2085	0.1547	0.0894	0.0445	32.62	29.79
1990	*0.2536*	*0.1508*	*0.0882*	*0.0576*	*34.33*	*32.35*
2000	*0.3274*	*0.2067*	*0.1149*	*0.0561*	*36.55*	*35.42*
2010	*0.3434*	*0.2389*	*0.1537*	*0.0840*	*38.43*	*37.84*
2020	*0.4254*	*0.2700*	*0.1584*	*0.0958*	*39.90*	*39.97*

POPULATION OF AUSTRALIA – NEW ZEALAND, BY COUNTRY : 1985

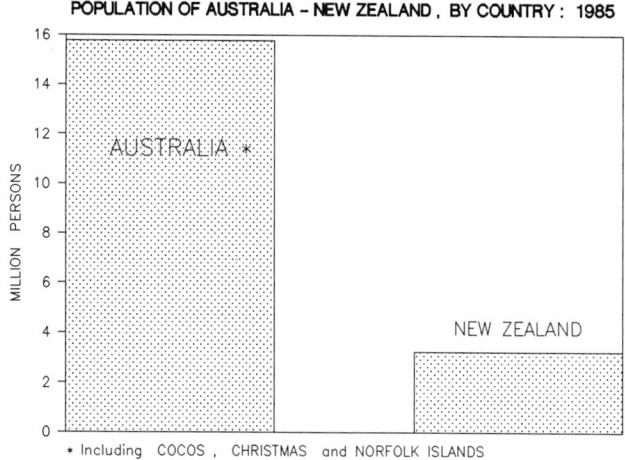

* Including COCOS, CHRISTMAS and NORFOLK ISLANDS

POPULATION OF MELANESIA, BY COUNTRY / TERRITORY : 1980

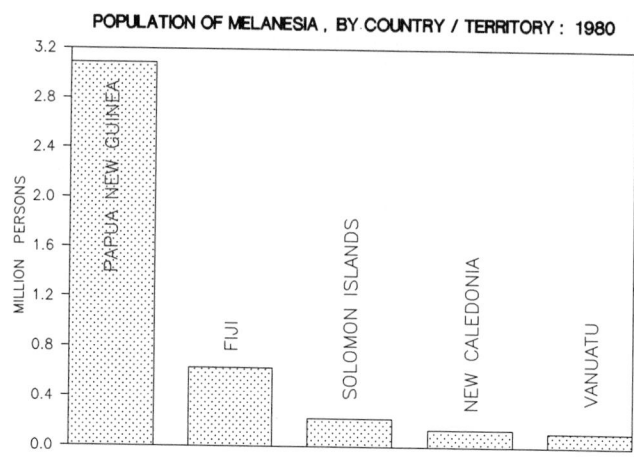

POPULATION OF MICRONESIA, BY COUNTRY / TERRITORY : 1980

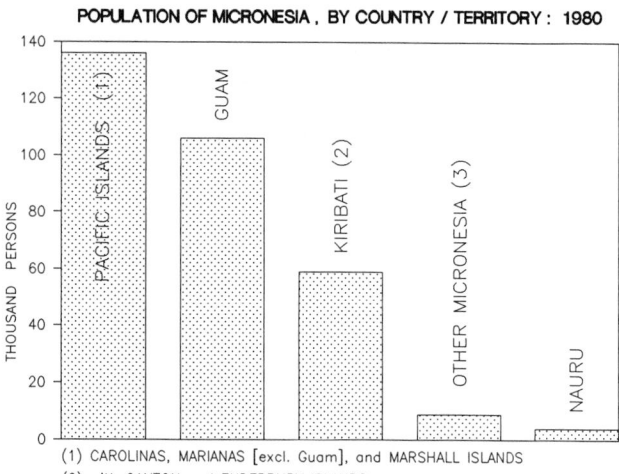

(1) CAROLINAS, MARIANAS [excl. Guam], and MARSHALL ISLANDS
(2) with CANTON and ENDERBURY ISLANDS
(3) including JOHNSTON, MIDWAY, PITCAIRN, TOKELAU and WAKE ISLANDS

POPULATION OF POLYNESIA, BY COUNTRY / TERRITORY : 1980

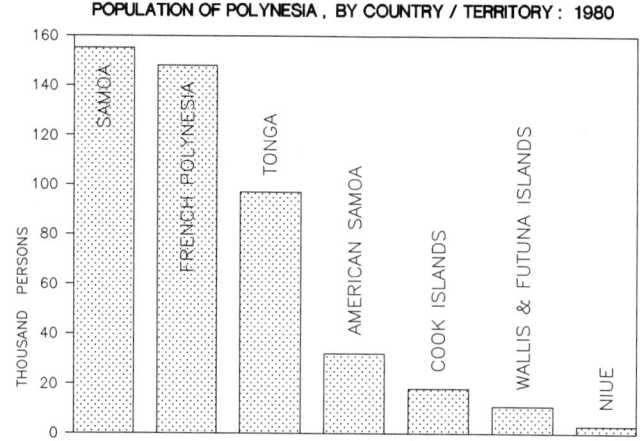

OBSERVED AND *PROJECTED* POPULATION DATA (000's)

YEAR	MID-YEAR POPULATION	NO. OF BIRTHS	NO. OF DEATHS	URBAN POPULATION NUMBER	URBAN POPULATION PERCENT	POPULATION 1985 AGE	POPULATION 1985 NUMBER
1950	12647	349	157	7755	61.3	0	2370
1955	14151	389	160	9036	63.9	5	2183
1960	15782	422	167	10460	66.3	10	2293
1965	17516	429	180	12003	68.5	15	2263
1970	19329	461	187	13680	70.8	20	2126
1975	21132	451	186	15159	71.7	25	2013
1980	22794	469	184	16276	71.4	30	1851
1985	24634	495	198	17492	71.0	35	1747
1990	*26476*	*506*	*211*	*18743*	*70.8*	40	1408
1995	*28304*	*520*	*223*	*20006*	*70.7*	45	1207
2000	*30139*	*531*	*234*	*21377*	*70.9*	50	1065
2005	*31964*	*543*	*246*	*22792*	*71.3*	55	1068
2010	*33787*	*553*	*258*	*24333*	*72.0*	60	946
2015	*35598*	*560*	*275*	*25932*	*72.8*	65	760
2020	*37349*	*558*	*299*	*27617*	*73.9*	70+	1334

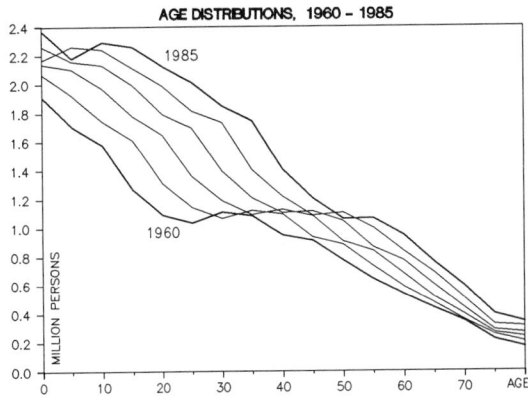

AGE DISTRIBUTIONS, 1960 – 1985

POPULATION RATIOS

YEAR	AGE DISTRIBUTION UNDER 15	AGE DISTRIBUTION 15-64	AGE DISTRIBUTION 65 & OLDER	AGE DISTRIBUTION 70 & OLDER	DEPENDENCY RATIO	WOMEN 15-49	CHILD-WOMAN RATIO
1950	0.297	0.628	0.075	0.044	0.592	0.241	0.499
1955	0.318	0.607	0.075	0.045	0.648	0.233	0.517
1960	0.329	0.596	0.074	0.047	0.677	0.228	0.531
1965	0.328	0.599	0.073	0.046	0.670	0.229	0.515
1970	0.322	0.606	0.073	0.046	0.651	0.232	0.477
1975	0.310	0.615	0.075	0.047	0.627	0.237	0.452
1980	0.293	0.627	0.080	0.050	0.594	0.244	0.390
1985	0.278	0.637	0.085	0.054	0.570	0.251	0.383
1990	*0.268*	*0.641*	*0.091*	*0.058*	*0.560*	*0.255*	*0.373*
2000	*0.259*	*0.647*	*0.095*	*0.065*	*0.547*	*0.251*	*0.351*
2010	*0.242*	*0.656*	*0.101*	*0.067*	*0.524*	*0.244*	*0.335*
2020	*0.228*	*0.649*	*0.123*	*0.081*	*0.541*	*0.237*	*0.323*

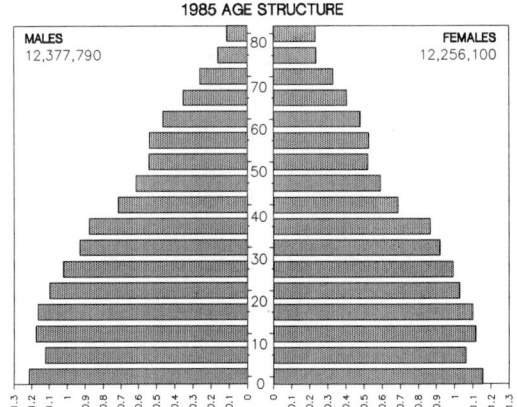

1985 AGE STRUCTURE

MALES 12,377,790   FEMALES 12,256,100

MORTALITY MEASURES (Annual Averages)

PERIOD	CRUDE DEATH RATE	INFANT MORT. RATE	LIFE EXPECTANCY AT BIRTH (years) MALE	LIFE EXPECTANCY AT BIRTH (years) FEMALE	LIFE EXPECTANCY AT BIRTH (years) BOTH SEXES	DIFFERENCE FEMALE-MALE
1950-55	12.41	67.26	58.95	62.72	60.78	3.78
1955-60	11.34	60.66	60.42	64.61	62.46	4.19
1960-65	10.59	54.13	61.61	66.15	63.81	4.54
1965-70	10.28	47.90	61.91	66.62	64.19	4.71
1970-75	9.68	39.74	63.13	67.99	65.49	4.86
1975-80	8.79	35.61	64.08	68.58	66.26	4.50
1980-85	8.09	30.53	65.56	70.51	67.97	4.95
1985-90	*8.04*	*25.79*	*66.43*	*71.33*	*68.81*	*4.90*
1990-95	*7.97*	*23.12*	*67.45*	*72.30*	*69.81*	*4.85*
2000-05	*7.77*	*18.92*	*69.44*	*74.10*	*71.71*	*4.65*
2010-15	*7.64*	*15.09*	*71.33*	*76.01*	*73.61*	*4.68*
2020-25	*8.00*	*11.48*	*73.20*	*78.11*	*75.58*	*4.92*

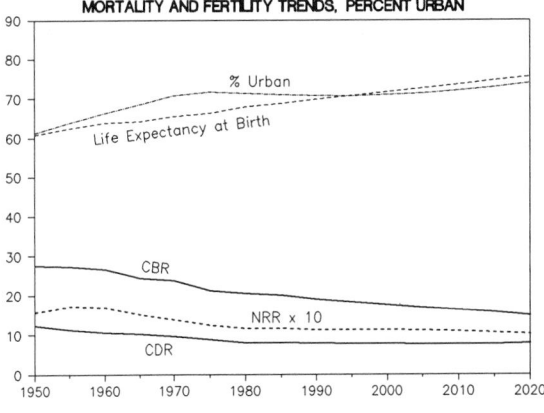

MORTALITY AND FERTILITY TRENDS, PERCENT URBAN

% Urban

Life Expectancy at Birth

CBR

NRR x 10

CDR

FERTILITY MEASURES (Annual Averages)

PERIOD	CRUDE BIRTH RATE	FERTILITY RATES GENERAL	FERTILITY RATES TOTAL	REPRODUCTION RATES GROSS	REPRODUCTION RATES NET	RATE OF NATUR. INCR.
1950-55	27.63	116.71	3.832	1.863	1.583	15.22
1955-60	27.47	119.27	4.063	1.976	1.720	16.14
1960-65	26.71	116.80	3.942	1.917	1.698	16.12
1965-70	24.47	106.00	3.539	1.721	1.529	14.18
1970-75	23.85	101.60	3.194	1.553	1.390	14.17
1975-80	21.33	88.68	2.850	1.386	1.248	12.53
1980-85	20.56	83.04	2.635	1.281	1.174	12.47
1985-90	*20.09*	*79.32*	*2.568*	*1.248*	*1.171*	*12.05*
1990-95	*19.12*	*75.10*	*2.472*	*1.201*	*1.137*	*11.15*
2000-05	*17.62*	*70.69*	*2.408*	*1.170*	*1.126*	*9.85*
2010-15	*16.38*	*67.54*	*2.301*	*1.118*	*1.091*	*8.74*
2020-25	*14.93*	*63.51*	*2.130*	*1.035*	*1.021*	*6.93*

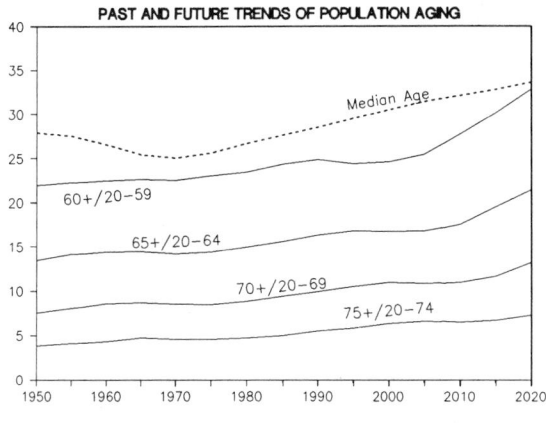

PAST AND FUTURE TRENDS OF POPULATION AGING

Median Age

60+/20-59

65+/20-64

70+/20-69

75+/20-74

AGING MEASURES

YEAR	POPULATION AGE RATIOS 60+/20-59	POPULATION AGE RATIOS 65+/20-64	POPULATION AGE RATIOS 70+/20-69	POPULATION AGE RATIOS 75+/20-74	POPULATION MEAN AGE	POPULATION MEDIAN AGE
1950	0.2194	0.1349	0.0755	0.0381	30.55	27.94
1960	0.2245	0.1441	0.0857	0.0432	29.77	26.59
1970	0.2253	0.1417	0.0851	0.0459	29.58	25.07
1980	0.2345	0.1498	0.0884	0.0474	30.51	26.71
1990	*0.2488*	*0.1636*	*0.0993*	*0.0551*	*31.65*	*28.58*
2000	*0.2459*	*0.1674*	*0.1099*	*0.0632*	*32.85*	*30.53*
2010	*0.2775*	*0.1755*	*0.1097*	*0.0652*	*34.19*	*32.17*
2020	*0.3285*	*0.2141*	*0.1321*	*0.0726*	*35.64*	*33.66*

OBSERVED AND *PROJECTED* POPULATION DATA (000's)

YEAR	MID-YEAR POPULATION	NO. OF BIRTHS	NO. OF DEATHS	URBAN POPULATION NUMBER	URBAN POPULATION PERCENT	POPULATION 1985 AGE	POPULATION 1985 NUMBER
1950	10127	238	95	7565	74.7	0	1482
1955	11376	265	101	8783	77.2	5	1428
1960	12687	287	111	10118	79.7	10	1599
1965	14015	284	124	11520	82.2	15	1648
1970	15371	304	131	12979	84.4	20	1623
1975	16714	271	130	14264	85.3	25	1588
1980	17808	279	133	15197	85.3	30	1497
1985	19005	287	144	16186	85.2	35	1426
1990	*20124*	*289*	*156*	*17162*	*85.3*	40	1167
1995	*21197*	*295*	*166*	*18100*	*85.4*	45	986
2000	*22242*	*296*	*177*	*19082*	*85.8*	50	888
2005	*23237*	*299*	*189*	*20028*	*86.2*	55	909
2010	*24186*	*304*	*199*	*21008*	*86.9*	60	827
2015	*25108*	*308*	*215*	*21972*	*87.5*	65	675
2020	*25972*	*312*	*235*	*22955*	*88.4*	70+	1262

POPULATION RATIOS

YEAR	UNDER 15	15-64	65 & OLDER	70 & OLDER	DEPENDENCY RATIO	WOMEN 15-49	CHILD-WOMAN RATIO
1950	0.270	0.647	0.083	0.049	0.545	0.246	0.449
1955	0.294	0.621	0.085	0.051	0.610	0.235	0.464
1960	0.306	0.609	0.085	0.053	0.643	0.230	0.475
1965	0.302	0.614	0.084	0.054	0.629	0.232	0.454
1970	0.294	0.623	0.084	0.054	0.606	0.235	0.412
1975	0.280	0.633	0.087	0.054	0.580	0.241	0.387
1980	0.255	0.648	0.097	0.061	0.543	0.249	0.313
1985	0.237	0.661	0.102	0.066	0.513	0.258	0.302
1990	*0.222*	*0.668*	*0.110*	*0.072*	*0.497*	*0.263*	*0.282*
2000	*0.209*	*0.674*	*0.117*	*0.082*	*0.483*	*0.255*	*0.270*
2010	*0.196*	*0.677*	*0.128*	*0.086*	*0.478*	*0.241*	*0.267*
2020	*0.186*	*0.656*	*0.158*	*0.106*	*0.524*	*0.225*	*0.273*

MORTALITY MEASURES (Annual Averages)

PERIOD	CRUDE DEATH RATE	INFANT MORT. RATE	LIFE EXPECTANCY AT BIRTH (years) MALE	FEMALE	BOTH SEXES	DIFFERENCE FEMALE-MALE
1950-55	9.37	24.15	67.02	72.28	69.57	5.25
1955-60	8.88	21.75	67.67	73.44	70.47	5.77
1960-65	8.72	19.80	67.91	74.14	70.93	6.23
1965-70	8.83	18.01	67.74	74.32	70.94	6.58
1970-75	8.51	16.49	68.46	75.12	71.69	6.66
1975-80	7.79	12.73	69.95	76.75	73.25	6.80
1980-85	7.47	10.32	71.73	78.35	74.95	6.62
1985-90	*7.58*	*8.77*	*72.66*	*79.19*	*75.84*	*6.53*
1990-95	*7.73*	*7.25*	*73.50*	*79.96*	*76.64*	*6.46*
2000-05	*7.97*	*6.08*	*75.04*	*81.06*	*77.97*	*6.01*
2010-15	*8.24*	*5.47*	*76.13*	*82.04*	*79.00*	*5.91*
2020-25	*9.03*	*5.10*	*77.10*	*82.97*	*79.96*	*5.86*

FERTILITY MEASURES (Annual Averages)

PERIOD	CRUDE BIRTH RATE	FERTILITY RATES GENERAL	FERTILITY RATES TOTAL	REPRODUCTION RATES GROSS	REPRODUCTION RATES NET	RATE OF NATUR. INCR.
1950-55	23.52	97.95	3.247	1.580	1.511	14.15
1955-60	23.30	100.28	3.503	1.705	1.641	14.42
1960-65	22.60	97.93	3.369	1.640	1.586	13.88
1965-70	20.27	86.81	2.935	1.428	1.383	11.44
1970-75	19.78	83.10	2.581	1.256	1.219	11.27
1975-80	16.19	66.14	2.112	1.028	1.008	8.39
1980-85	15.67	61.86	1.936	0.942	0.927	8.20
1985-90	*15.08*	*57.86*	*1.858*	*0.904*	*0.889*	*7.50*
1990-95	*14.38*	*54.86*	*1.809*	*0.880*	*0.867*	*6.65*
2000-05	*13.33*	*52.94*	*1.858*	*0.904*	*0.893*	*5.36*
2010-15	*12.59*	*53.19*	*1.901*	*0.925*	*0.913*	*4.35*
2020-25	*12.03*	*54.26*	*1.901*	*0.925*	*0.914*	*2.99*

AGING MEASURES

YEAR	60+/20-59	65+/20-64	70+/20-69	75+/20-74	MEAN AGE	MEDIAN AGE
1950	0.2347	0.1431	0.0801	0.0408	32.18	30.20
1960	0.2468	0.1593	0.0943	0.0474	31.36	29.21
1970	0.2488	0.1570	0.0950	0.0517	31.24	27.27
1980	0.2662	0.1728	0.1026	0.0553	32.63	29.22
1990	*0.2807*	*0.1868*	*0.1149*	*0.0647*	*34.26*	*31.82*
2000	*0.2808*	*0.1937*	*0.1289*	*0.0751*	*35.95*	*34.55*
2010	*0.3298*	*0.2094*	*0.1316*	*0.0794*	*37.65*	*37.18*
2020	*0.4091*	*0.2669*	*0.1652*	*0.0915*	*39.30*	*38.93*

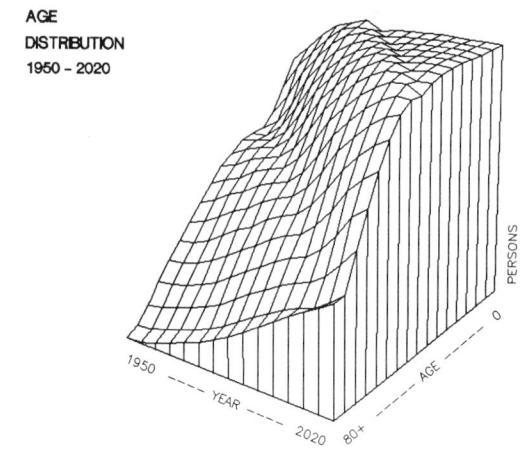

AGE DISTRIBUTION 1950 - 2020

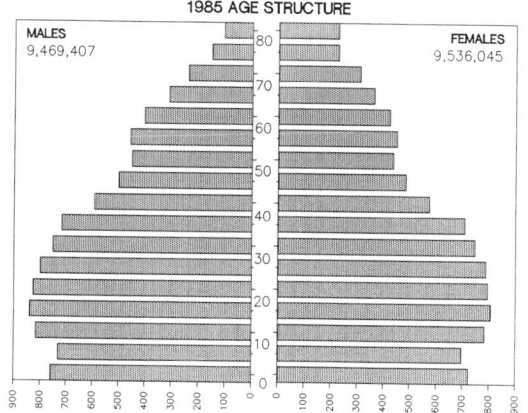

1985 AGE STRUCTURE

MALES 9,469,407   FEMALES 9,536,045

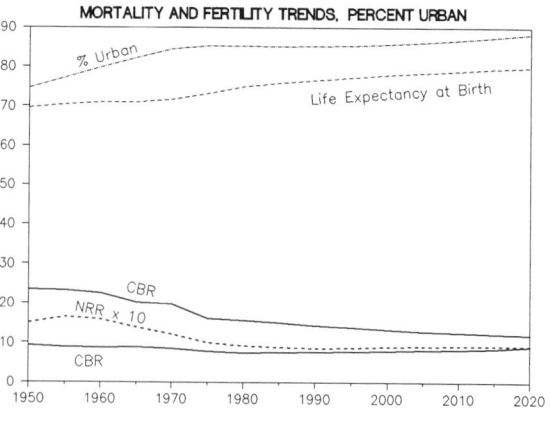

MORTALITY AND FERTILITY TRENDS, PERCENT URBAN

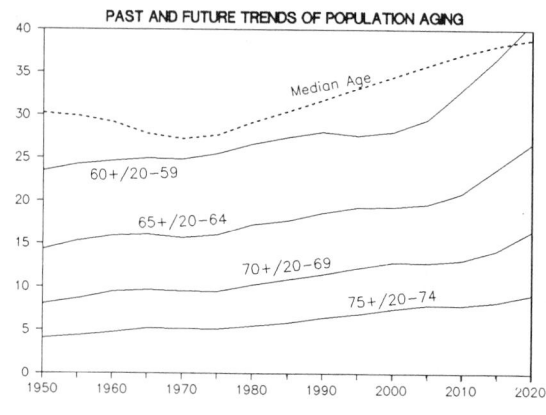

PAST AND FUTURE TRENDS OF POPULATION AGING

OBSERVED AND *PROJECTED* POPULATION DATA (000's)

YEAR	MID-YEAR POPULATION	NO. OF BIRTHS	NO. OF DEATHS	URBAN POPULATION NUMBER	URBAN POPULATION PERCENT	POPULATION 1985 AGE	POPULATION 1985 NUMBER
1950	2119	93	55	117	5.5	0	754
1955	2319	103	52	155	6.7	5	631
1960	2583	112	49	217	8.4	10	583
1965	2921	120	49	322	11.0	15	520
1970	3300	130	49	498	15.1	20	425
1975	3695	150	50	646	17.5	25	361
1980	4196	159	47	787	18.8	30	302
1985	4767	176	49	963	20.2	35	279
1990	*5417*	*185*	*50*	*1180*	*21.8*	40	205
1995	*6104*	*194*	*51*	*1446*	*23.7*	45	193
2000	*6832*	*204*	*52*	*1772*	*25.9*	50	150
2005	*7603*	*213*	*52*	*2177*	*28.6*	55	136
2010	*8421*	*220*	*53*	*2673*	*31.7*	60	101
2015	*9261*	*223*	*55*	*3244*	*35.0*	65	71
2020	*10109*	*219*	*57*	*3886*	*38.4*	70+	55

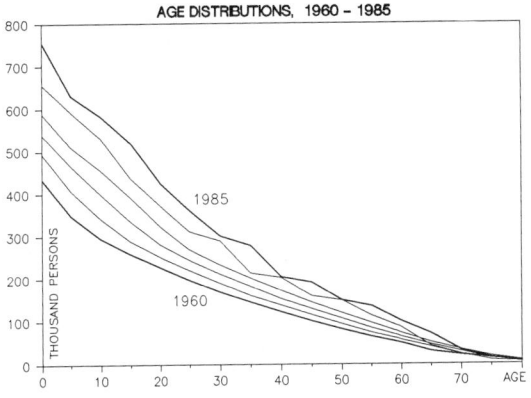

AGE DISTRIBUTIONS, 1960 - 1985

POPULATION RATIOS

YEAR	AGE DISTRIBUTION UNDER 15	AGE DISTRIBUTION 15-64	AGE DISTRIBUTION 65 & OLDER	AGE DISTRIBUTION 70 & OLDER	DEPENDENCY RATIO	WOMEN 15-49	CHILD-WOMAN RATIO
1950	0.405	0.554	0.041	0.023	0.804	0.224	0.707
1955	0.410	0.555	0.035	0.022	0.803	0.226	0.724
1960	0.418	0.552	0.030	0.018	0.811	0.224	0.750
1965	0.425	0.545	0.029	0.016	0.834	0.222	0.762
1970	0.426	0.545	0.030	0.016	0.837	0.222	0.736
1975	0.421	0.549	0.030	0.017	0.821	0.225	0.708
1980	0.424	0.557	0.019	0.009	0.796	0.228	0.685
1985	0.413	0.561	0.026	0.011	0.783	0.230	0.688
1990	*0.414*	*0.557*	*0.028*	*0.014*	*0.795*	*0.230*	*0.714*
2000	*0.404*	*0.566*	*0.030*	*0.016*	*0.766*	*0.235*	*0.612*
2010	*0.365*	*0.603*	*0.032*	*0.018*	*0.658*	*0.252*	*0.513*
2020	*0.329*	*0.632*	*0.039*	*0.022*	*0.583*	*0.262*	*0.431*

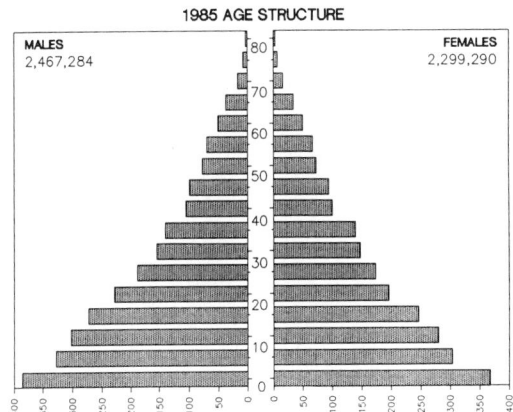

1985 AGE STRUCTURE

MALES 2,467,284   FEMALES 2,299,290

MORTALITY MEASURES (Annual Averages)

PERIOD	CRUDE DEATH RATE	INFANT MORT. RATE	LIFE EXPECTANCY AT BIRTH (years) MALE	FEMALE	BOTH SEXES	DIFFERENCE FEMALE-MALE
1950-55	26.02	170.75	39.60	39.51	39.55	-0.09
1955-60	22.44	155.94	42.98	43.15	43.06	0.17
1960-65	19.03	137.94	46.58	46.96	46.77	0.37
1965-70	16.89	116.05	48.77	49.23	48.99	0.46
1970-75	14.99	91.59	51.23	52.01	51.61	0.78
1975-80	13.65	74.89	53.67	54.14	53.90	0.47
1980-85	11.09	64.66	54.86	57.00	55.90	2.14
1985-90	*10.30*	*52.19*	*56.44*	*58.74*	*57.56*	*2.31*
1990-95	*9.30*	*47.03*	*58.09*	*60.43*	*59.22*	*2.34*
2000-05	*7.55*	*37.20*	*61.38*	*63.97*	*62.64*	*2.58*
2010-15	*6.29*	*28.23*	*64.79*	*67.63*	*66.17*	*2.83*
2020-25	*5.66*	*20.41*	*67.79*	*71.18*	*69.44*	*3.39*

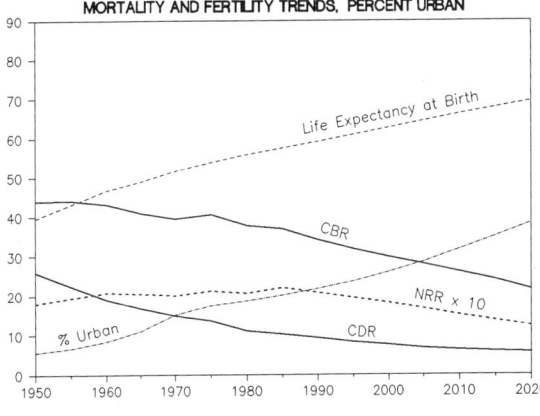

MORTALITY AND FERTILITY TRENDS, PERCENT URBAN

Life Expectancy at Birth · CBR · NRR x 10 · % Urban · CDR

FERTILITY MEASURES (Annual Averages)

PERIOD	CRUDE BIRTH RATE	FERTILITY RATES GENERAL	FERTILITY RATES TOTAL	REPRODUCTION RATES GROSS	REPRODUCTION RATES NET	RATE OF NATUR. INCR.
1950-55	44.10	195.95	6.313	3.064	1.804	18.08
1955-60	44.21	196.62	6.351	3.082	1.958	21.77
1960-65	43.22	193.94	6.274	3.045	2.080	24.18
1965-70	40.97	184.62	5.990	2.907	2.057	24.08
1970-75	39.53	176.83	5.639	2.737	2.010	24.55
1975-80	40.60	179.21	5.810	2.820	2.136	26.94
1980-85	37.80	165.00	5.339	2.591	2.071	26.71
1985-90	*37.00*	*160.84*	*5.263*	*2.554*	*2.210*	*26.70*
1990-95	*34.19*	*148.08*	*4.859*	*2.358*	*2.084*	*24.89*
2000-05	*29.81*	*124.13*	*4.076*	*1.978*	*1.821*	*22.27*
2010-15	*26.07*	*102.19*	*3.281*	*1.592*	*1.522*	*19.78*
2020-25	*21.66*	*82.02*	*2.581*	*1.253*	*1.232*	*15.99*

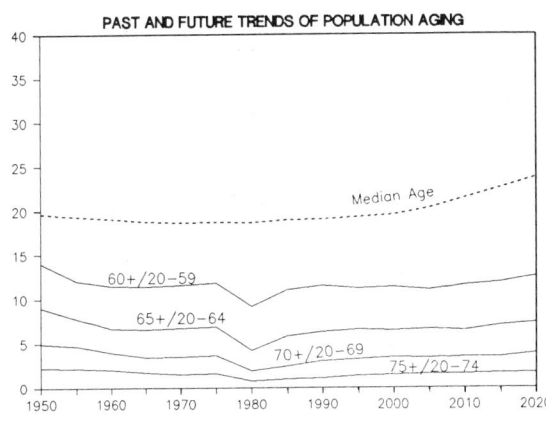

PAST AND FUTURE TRENDS OF POPULATION AGING

Median Age · 60+/20-59 · 65+/20-64 · 70+/20-69 · 75+/20-74

AGING MEASURES

YEAR	POPULATION AGE RATIOS 60+/20-59	POPULATION AGE RATIOS 65+/20-64	POPULATION AGE RATIOS 70+/20-69	POPULATION AGE RATIOS 75+/20-74	POPULATION MEAN AGE	POPULATION MEDIAN AGE
1950	0.1397	0.0901	0.0494	0.0225	24.11	19.63
1960	0.1142	0.0666	0.0393	0.0202	23.42	19.09
1970	0.1158	0.0670	0.0348	0.0151	23.27	18.65
1980	0.0913	0.0423	0.0194	0.0076	22.98	18.65
1990	*0.1150*	*0.0628*	*0.0300*	*0.0107*	*23.31*	*19.06*
2000	*0.1135*	*0.0645*	*0.0342*	*0.0145*	*23.89*	*19.58*
2010	*0.1157*	*0.0645*	*0.0350*	*0.0154*	*25.15*	*21.41*
2020	*0.1259*	*0.0733*	*0.0392*	*0.0171*	*26.92*	*23.78*

OBSERVED AND *PROJECTED* POPULATION DATA

YEAR	MID-YEAR POPULATION	NO. OF BIRTHS	NO. OF DEATHS	URBAN POPULATION NUMBER	URBAN POPULATION PERCENT	POPULATION 1985 AGE	POPULATION 1985 NUMBER
1950	155692	6042	2592	26243	16.9	0	52970
1955	176818	7136	2571	34884	19.7	5	47027
1960	194411	7578	2409	44799	23.0	10	41877
1965	218443	8170	2296	58036	26.6	15	35497
1970	251514	9039	2252	76850	30.6	20	31478
1975	284607	10280	2015	102854	36.1	25	27528
1980	316333	10970	1957	130246	41.2	30	22392
1985	348204	11171	1946	160713	46.2	35	19856
1990	*379318*	*11212*	*2051*	*192495*	*50.7*	40	15960
1995	*408372*	*11343*	*2194*	*223445*	*54.7*	45	12364
2000	*435804*	*11425*	*2361*	*253343*	*58.1*	50	11611
2005	*461353*	*11490*	*2549*	*282243*	*61.2*	55	9415
2010	*484934*	*11339*	*2754*	*310281*	*64.0*	60	7585
2015	*505451*	*10901*	*2976*	*336609*	*66.6*	65	5583
2020	*521514*	*10608*	*3299*	*359569*	*68.9*	70+	7061

POPULATION RATIOS

YEAR	AGE DISTRIBUTION UNDER 15	15-64	65 & OLDER	70 & OLDER	DEPENDENCY RATIO	WOMEN 15-49	CHILD-WOMAN RATIO
1950	0.401	0.557	0.042	0.024	0.796	0.216	0.775
1955	0.425	0.533	0.042	0.026	0.875	0.205	0.845
1960	0.443	0.528	0.029	0.019	0.893	0.205	0.867
1965	0.427	0.534	0.039	0.026	0.871	0.211	0.777
1970	0.423	0.539	0.037	0.022	0.854	0.221	0.730
1975	0.416	0.549	0.035	0.023	0.823	0.216	0.755
1980	0.413	0.553	0.034	0.019	0.808	0.223	0.702
1985	0.407	0.556	0.036	0.020	0.798	0.226	0.674
1990	*0.401*	*0.558*	*0.041*	*0.023*	*0.791*	*0.235*	*0.597*
2000	*0.361*	*0.587*	*0.052*	*0.031*	*0.704*	*0.258*	*0.474*
2010	*0.326*	*0.611*	*0.062*	*0.038*	*0.636*	*0.274*	*0.403*
2020	*0.295*	*0.625*	*0.080*	*0.050*	*0.600*	*0.285*	*0.335*

MORTALITY MEASURES (Annual Averages)

PERIOD	CRUDE DEATH RATE	INFANT MORT. RATE	LIFE EXPECTANCY AT BIRTH (years) MALE	FEMALE	BOTH SEXES	DIFFERENCE FEMALE-MALE
1950-55	16.65	102.00	45.92	49.51	47.67	3.59
1955-60	14.54	84.00	48.42	52.01	50.17	3.59
1960-65	12.39	77.00	50.92	54.51	52.67	3.59
1965-70	10.51	65.00	53.42	57.01	55.17	3.59
1970-75	8.95	54.00	55.92	59.51	57.67	3.59
1975-80	7.08	44.32	64.03	68.06	66.00	4.03
1980-85	6.19	35.83	65.93	70.26	68.04	4.33
1985-90	*5.59*	*29.97*	*67.43*	*71.96*	*69.64*	*4.53*
1990-95	*5.41*	*25.57*	*68.53*	*73.39*	*70.90*	*4.86*
2000-05	*5.42*	*19.03*	*70.41*	*75.74*	*73.01*	*5.33*
2010-15	*5.68*	*14.39*	*71.81*	*77.68*	*74.67*	*5.87*
2020-25	*6.33*	*11.59*	*72.81*	*79.08*	*75.87*	*6.27*

FERTILITY MEASURES (Annual Averages)

PERIOD	CRUDE BIRTH RATE	FERTILITY RATES GENERAL	TOTAL	REPRODUCTION RATES GROSS	NET	RATE OF NATUR. INCR.
1950-55	38.81	184.61	5.935	2.895	2.225	22.16
1955-60	40.36	196.74	6.339	3.092	2.467	25.82
1960-65	38.98	187.13	6.209	3.029	2.505	26.59
1965-70	37.40	173.04	5.924	2.890	2.456	26.89
1970-75	35.94	164.67	5.601	2.732	2.389	26.99
1975-80	36.12	164.37	5.330	2.600	2.391	29.04
1980-85	34.68	154.50	4.981	2.430	2.282	28.49
1985-90	*32.08*	*139.27*	*4.530*	*2.210*	*2.103*	*26.49*
1990-95	*29.56*	*122.93*	*4.100*	*2.000*	*1.923*	*24.15*
2000-05	*26.22*	*99.70*	*3.280*	*1.600*	*1.562*	*20.80*
2010-15	*23.38*	*84.59*	*2.665*	*1.300*	*1.281*	*17.70*
2020-25	*20.34*	*70.95*	*2.357*	*1.150*	*1.139*	*14.02*

AGING MEASURES

YEAR	POPULATION AGE RATIOS 60+/20-59	65+/20-64	70+/20-69	75+/20-74	POPULATION MEAN AGE	MEDIAN AGE
1950	0.1527	0.0920	0.0507	0.0247	23.84	19.85
1960	0.1180	0.0676	0.0441	0.0216	22.56	17.83
1970	0.1340	0.0855	0.0496	0.0325	23.66	18.80
1980	0.1286	0.0759	0.0418	0.0218	23.73	19.16
1990	*0.1478*	*0.0900*	*0.0494*	*0.0232*	*24.70*	*19.88*
2000	*0.1680*	*0.1086*	*0.0614*	*0.0306*	*26.43*	*21.58*
2010	*0.1975*	*0.1214*	*0.0698*	*0.0375*	*28.36*	*24.19*
2020	*0.2399*	*0.1505*	*0.0895*	*0.0453*	*30.60*	*27.06*

AGE DISTRIBUTIONS, 1960 - 1985

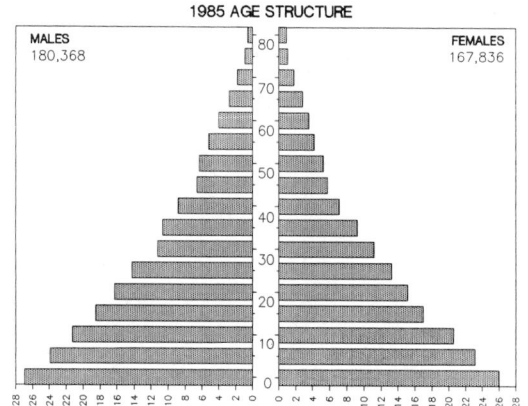

1985 AGE STRUCTURE

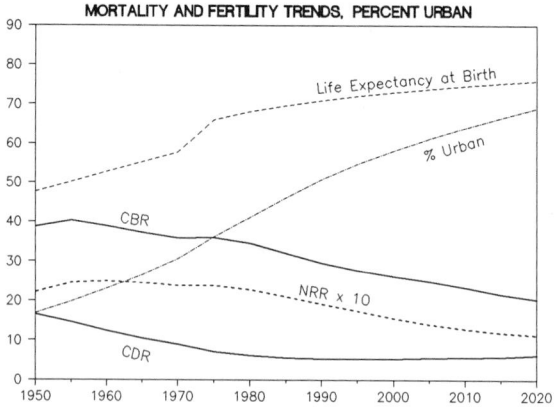

MORTALITY AND FERTILITY TRENDS, PERCENT URBAN

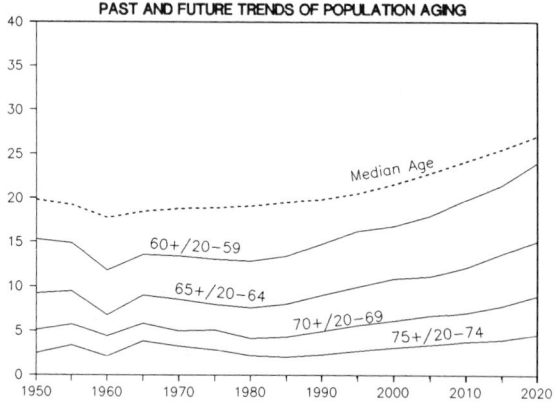

PAST AND FUTURE TRENDS OF POPULATION AGING

OBSERVED AND *PROJECTED* POPULATION DATA

YEAR	MID-YEAR POPULATION	NO. OF BIRTHS	NO. OF DEATHS	URBAN POPULATION NUMBER	URBAN POPULATION PERCENT	POPULATION 1985 AGE	POPULATION 1985 NUMBER
1950	245300	12103	4715	46713	19.0	0	80610
1955	278973	13996	4754	63644	22.8	5	76985
1960	317381	15015	4618	81344	25.6	10	69635
1965	361557	15695	4465	102576	28.4	15	59867
1970	406528	16623	4236	126549	31.1	20	46479
1975	437599	17268	2494	146320	33.4	25	35810
1980	473329	17476	2481	162098	34.2	30	29229
1985	513664	17587	2559	182061	35.4	35	22073
1990	*555023*	*17349*	*2697*	*207755*	*37.4*	40	19262
1995	*594018*	*16938*	*2889*	*236504*	*39.8*	45	15916
2000	*629503*	*16692*	*3081*	*268982*	*42.7*	50	15430
2005	*662466*	*16330*	*3264*	*304586*	*46.0*	55	13041
2010	*694476*	*15553*	*3486*	*342607*	*49.3*	60	11013
2015	*723144*	*14735*	*3750*	*380101*	*52.6*	65	8201
2020	*746017*	*14105*	*4102*	*415748*	*55.7*	70+	10113

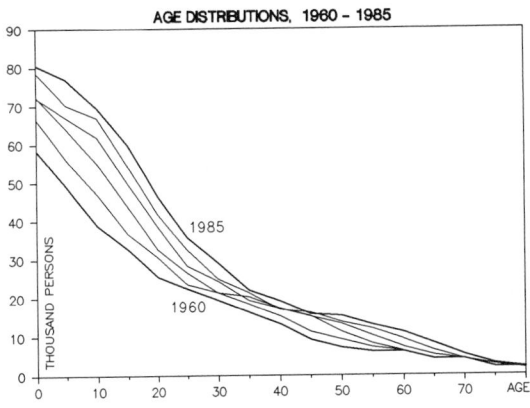

AGE DISTRIBUTIONS, 1960 - 1985

POPULATION RATIOS

YEAR	AGE DISTRIBUTION UNDER 15	AGE DISTRIBUTION 15-64	AGE DISTRIBUTION 65 & OLDER	AGE DISTRIBUTION 70 & OLDER	DEPENDENCY RATIO	WOMEN 15-49	CHILD-WOMAN RATIO
1950	0.439	0.515	0.046	0.029	0.943	0.213	0.804
1955	0.456	0.507	0.037	0.022	0.971	0.210	0.877
1960	0.461	0.500	0.039	0.026	1.000	0.210	0.877
1965	0.469	0.497	0.034	0.023	1.011	0.206	0.890
1970	0.471	0.499	0.030	0.020	1.005	0.211	0.845
1975	0.459	0.510	0.030	0.019	0.959	0.216	0.763
1980	0.456	0.514	0.031	0.017	0.947	0.215	0.772
1985	0.442	0.522	0.036	0.020	0.916	0.218	0.719
1990	*0.427*	*0.531*	*0.041*	*0.023*	*0.882*	*0.225*	*0.653*
2000	*0.376*	*0.573*	*0.051*	*0.031*	*0.746*	*0.248*	*0.501*
2010	*0.327*	*0.616*	*0.057*	*0.036*	*0.625*	*0.262*	*0.414*
2020	*0.284*	*0.649*	*0.067*	*0.042*	*0.542*	*0.266*	*0.340*

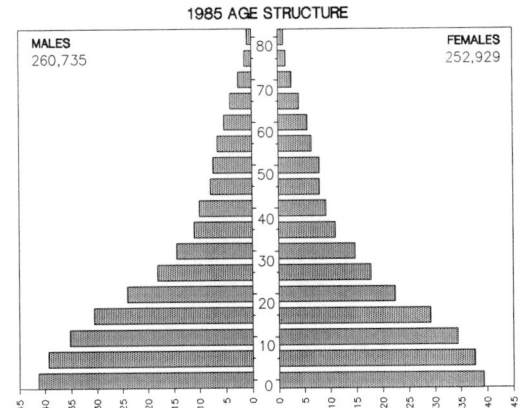

1985 AGE STRUCTURE

MALES 260,735   FEMALES 252,929

MORTALITY MEASURES (Annual Averages)

PERIOD	CRUDE DEATH RATE	INFANT MORT. RATE	LIFE EXPECTANCY AT BIRTH (years) MALE	LIFE EXPECTANCY AT BIRTH (years) FEMALE	LIFE EXPECTANCY AT BIRTH (years) BOTH SEXES	DIFFERENCE FEMALE-MALE
1950-55	19.22	110.00	54.30	57.60	55.89	3.30
1955-60	17.04	88.00	57.30	60.60	58.89	3.30
1960-65	14.55	67.00	60.30	63.60	61.89	3.30
1965-70	12.35	52.00	62.80	66.60	64.63	3.80
1970-75	10.42	44.00	64.80	69.20	66.92	4.40
1975-80	5.70	35.79	65.97	70.26	68.04	4.29
1980-85	5.24	29.95	67.47	71.96	69.64	4.49
1985-90	*4.98*	*25.55*	*68.57*	*73.39*	*70.89*	*4.82*
1990-95	*4.86*	*22.00*	*69.57*	*74.64*	*72.02*	*5.07*
2000-05	*4.89*	*16.56*	*71.15*	*76.74*	*73.85*	*5.59*
2010-15	*5.02*	*12.68*	*72.55*	*78.38*	*75.36*	*5.83*
2020-25	*5.50*	*10.50*	*73.15*	*79.78*	*76.35*	*6.63*

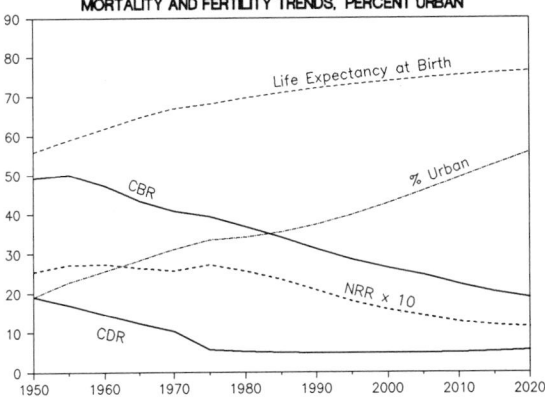

MORTALITY AND FERTILITY TRENDS, PERCENT URBAN

Life Expectancy at Birth

CBR

% Urban

NRR x 10

CDR

FERTILITY MEASURES (Annual Averages)

PERIOD	CRUDE BIRTH RATE	FERTILITY RATES GENERAL	FERTILITY RATES TOTAL	REPRODUCTION RATES GROSS	REPRODUCTION RATES NET	RATE OF NATUR. INCR.
1950-55	49.34	233.45	7.378	3.559	2.560	30.12
1955-60	50.17	239.33	7.537	3.636	2.726	33.13
1960-65	47.31	227.63	7.285	3.514	2.736	32.76
1965-70	43.41	208.21	6.816	3.288	2.644	31.06
1970-75	40.89	191.75	6.418	3.096	2.581	30.47
1975-80	39.46	183.16	6.012	2.900	2.725	33.76
1980-85	36.92	170.33	5.597	2.700	2.571	31.68
1985-90	*34.24*	*154.24*	*5.079*	*2.450*	*2.356*	*29.26*
1990-95	*31.26*	*135.24*	*4.457*	*2.150*	*2.084*	*26.40*
2000-05	*26.52*	*105.12*	*3.358*	*1.620*	*1.589*	*21.62*
2010-15	*22.40*	*84.79*	*2.695*	*1.300*	*1.284*	*17.38*
2020-25	*18.91*	*71.37*	*2.384*	*1.150*	*1.141*	*13.41*

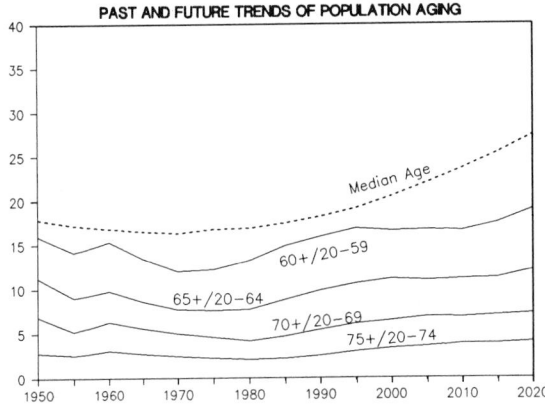

PAST AND FUTURE TRENDS OF POPULATION AGING

Median Age

60+/20-59

65+/20-64

70+/20-69

75+/20-74

AGING MEASURES

YEAR	POPULATION AGE RATIOS 60+/20-59	POPULATION AGE RATIOS 65+/20-64	POPULATION AGE RATIOS 70+/20-69	POPULATION AGE RATIOS 75+/20-74	POPULATION MEAN AGE	POPULATION MEDIAN AGE
1950	0.1596	0.1122	0.0686	0.0283	23.02	17.90
1960	0.1538	0.0975	0.0630	0.0305	22.16	16.88
1970	0.1200	0.0769	0.0500	0.0244	21.74	16.34
1980	0.1323	0.0768	0.0418	0.0207	22.15	16.93
1990	*0.1592*	*0.0985*	*0.0538*	*0.0250*	*23.36*	*18.21*
2000	*0.1661*	*0.1110*	*0.0648*	*0.0332*	*25.23*	*20.49*
2010	*0.1659*	*0.1114*	*0.0681*	*0.0382*	*27.51*	*23.63*
2020	*0.1897*	*0.1213*	*0.0721*	*0.0404*	*30.30*	*27.35*

OBSERVED AND *PROJECTED* POPULATION DATA (000's)

YEAR	MID-YEAR POPULATION	NO. OF BIRTHS	NO. OF DEATHS	URBAN POPULATION NUMBER	URBAN POPULATION PERCENT	POPULATION 1985 AGE	POPULATION 1985 NUMBER
1950	8219	189	77	6182	75.2	0	1234
1955	9240	209	82	7210	78.0	5	1175
1960	10315	225	90	8315	80.6	10	1309
1965	11387	225	101	9447	83.0	15	1349
1970	12552	245	107	10692	85.2	20	1342
1975	13627	218	105	11708	85.9	25	1323
1980	14695	229	108	12603	85.8	30	1253
1985	15758	236	117	13467	85.5	35	1187
1990	*16746*	*238*	*127*	*14318*	*85.5*	40	977
1995	*17690*	*244*	*137*	*15132*	*85.5*	45	821
2000	*18610*	*247*	*147*	*15990*	*85.9*	50	744
2005	*19492*	*251*	*157*	*16822*	*86.3*	55	760
2010	*20344*	*257*	*167*	*17697*	*87.0*	60	689
2015	*21179*	*261*	*180*	*18566*	*87.7*	65	561
2020	*21966*	*265*	*196*	*19460*	*88.6*	70+	1035

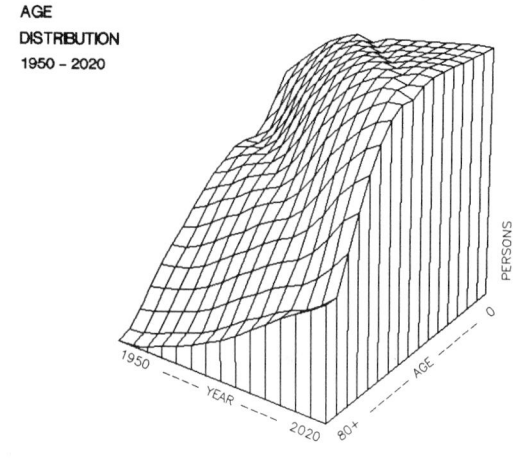

AGE DISTRIBUTION 1950 - 2020

POPULATION RATIOS

YEAR	AGE DISTRIBUTION UNDER 15	15-64	65 & OLDER	70 & OLDER	DEPENDENCY RATIO	WOMEN 15-49	CHILD-WOMAN RATIO
1950	0.265	0.654	0.081	0.048	0.530	0.247	0.435
1955	0.290	0.627	0.084	0.049	0.596	0.236	0.453
1960	0.301	0.614	0.085	0.052	0.628	0.232	0.459
1965	0.296	0.619	0.085	0.054	0.616	0.233	0.441
1970	0.288	0.628	0.083	0.054	0.592	0.237	0.400
1975	0.276	0.637	0.087	0.054	0.569	0.242	0.381
1980	0.253	0.651	0.096	0.060	0.536	0.249	0.310
1985	0.236	0.663	0.101	0.066	0.509	0.258	0.304
1990	*0.222*	*0.669*	*0.110*	*0.072*	*0.496*	*0.263*	*0.282*
2000	*0.208*	*0.675*	*0.118*	*0.083*	*0.482*	*0.255*	*0.269*
2010	*0.195*	*0.676*	*0.128*	*0.086*	*0.479*	*0.240*	*0.268*
2020	*0.187*	*0.655*	*0.158*	*0.107*	*0.527*	*0.225*	*0.274*

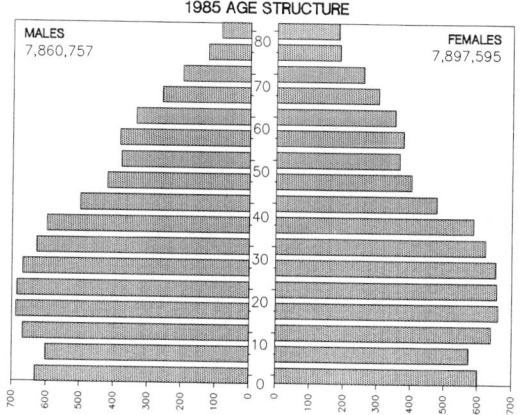

1985 AGE STRUCTURE

MALES 7,860,757   FEMALES 7,897,595

MORTALITY MEASURES (Annual Averages)

PERIOD	CRUDE DEATH RATE	INFANT MORT. RATE	LIFE EXPECTANCY AT BIRTH (years) MALE	FEMALE	BOTH SEXES	DIFFERENCE FEMALE-MALE
1950-55	9.38	23.59	66.90	72.40	69.57	5.50
1955-60	8.84	21.24	67.50	73.50	70.41	6.00
1960-65	8.69	19.58	67.80	74.20	70.91	6.40
1965-70	8.85	18.05	67.60	74.30	70.85	6.70
1970-75	8.53	16.59	68.40	75.20	71.70	6.80
1975-80	7.70	12.48	70.10	77.00	73.45	6.90
1980-85	7.34	9.99	71.94	78.66	75.21	6.72
1985-90	*7.41*	*8.31*	*72.85*	*79.47*	*76.07*	*6.62*
1990-95	*7.61*	*6.80*	*73.66*	*80.25*	*76.87*	*6.59*
2000-05	*7.91*	*5.95*	*75.20*	*81.24*	*78.14*	*6.04*
2010-15	*8.19*	*5.40*	*76.23*	*82.20*	*79.14*	*5.97*
2020-25	*8.94*	*5.08*	*77.20*	*83.11*	*80.07*	*5.90*

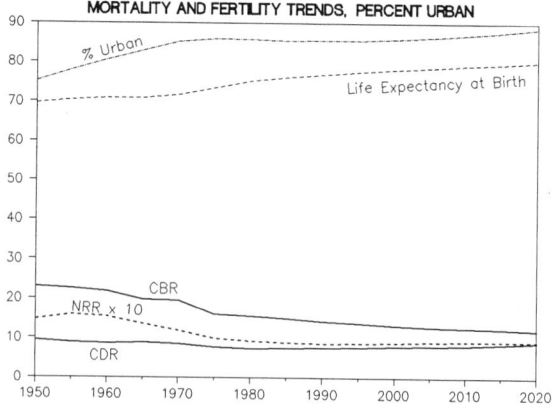

MORTALITY AND FERTILITY TRENDS, PERCENT URBAN

% Urban
Life Expectancy at Birth
CBR
NRR x 10
CDR

FERTILITY MEASURES (Annual Averages)

PERIOD	CRUDE BIRTH RATE	FERTILITY RATES GENERAL	FERTILITY RATES TOTAL	REPRODUCTION RATES GROSS	REPRODUCTION RATES NET	RATE OF NATUR. INCR.
1950-55	23.01	95.29	3.181	1.548	1.477	13.63
1955-60	22.62	96.75	3.407	1.658	1.595	13.78
1960-65	21.85	94.03	3.276	1.594	1.542	13.16
1965-70	19.75	83.96	2.873	1.398	1.353	10.90
1970-75	19.55	81.60	2.536	1.234	1.197	11.02
1975-80	15.97	64.99	2.092	1.018	0.998	8.27
1980-85	15.61	61.54	1.932	0.940	0.926	8.27
1985-90	*14.97*	*57.53*	*1.850*	*0.900*	*0.886*	*7.56*
1990-95	*14.24*	*54.46*	*1.800*	*0.876*	*0.864*	*6.63*
2000-05	*13.25*	*52.71*	*1.850*	*0.900*	*0.889*	*5.34*
2010-15	*12.63*	*53.46*	*1.900*	*0.925*	*0.913*	*4.45*
2020-25	*12.04*	*54.26*	*1.900*	*0.925*	*0.914*	*3.10*

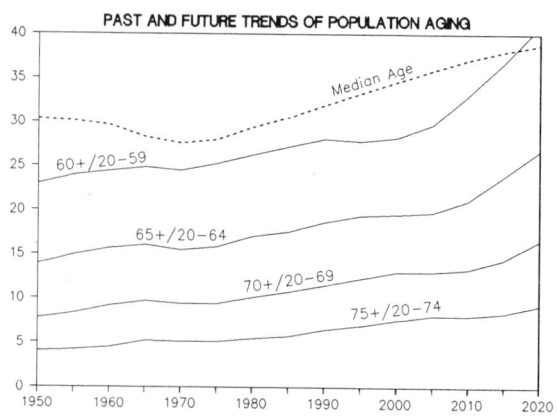

PAST AND FUTURE TRENDS OF POPULATION AGING

Median Age
60+/20-59
65+/20-64
70+/20-69
75+/20-74

AGING MEASURES

YEAR	POPULATION AGE RATIOS 60+/20-59	65+/20-64	70+/20-69	75+/20-74	POPULATION MEAN AGE	POPULATION MEDIAN AGE
1950	0.2297	0.1388	0.0776	0.0404	32.31	30.38
1960	0.2442	0.1569	0.0916	0.0450	31.53	29.61
1970	0.2448	0.1547	0.0940	0.0511	31.40	27.61
1980	0.2627	0.1702	0.1010	0.0545	32.72	29.41
1990	*0.2806*	*0.1863*	*0.1143*	*0.0642*	*34.32*	*31.96*
2000	*0.2823*	*0.1951*	*0.1297*	*0.0755*	*36.01*	*34.64*
2010	*0.3305*	*0.2105*	*0.1325*	*0.0803*	*37.67*	*37.15*
2020	*0.4094*	*0.2675*	*0.1657*	*0.0922*	*39.24*	*38.80*

OBSERVED AND *PROJECTED* POPULATION DATA

YEAR	MID-YEAR POPULATION	NO. OF BIRTHS	NO. OF DEATHS	URBAN POPULATION		POPULATION 1985	
				NUMBER	PERCENT	AGE	NUMBER
1950	288994	12802	4075	70381	24.4	0	97590
1955	335995	15019	3730	90498	26.9	5	86780
1960	393995	15523	3625	116942	29.7	10	72824
1965	463966	14856	3526	151175	32.6	15	68575
1970	520307	16390	3382	180853	34.8	20	69457
1975	576000	18012	3335	211517	36.7	25	64736
1980	629267	19551	3383	243712	38.7	30	51189
1985	691080	18899	3478	284493	41.2	35	40545
1990	*748512*	*16916*	*3706*	*329425*	*44.0*	40	33585
1995	*793660*	*16349*	*3969*	*374762*	*47.2*	45	28216
2000	*834237*	*16205*	*4341*	*423179*	*50.7*	50	22102
2005	*871985*	*15704*	*4780*	*474745*	*54.4*	55	17416
2010	*904699*	*15067*	*5341*	*524589*	*58.0*	60	13806
2015	*931098*	*13894*	*6074*	*571011*	*61.3*	65	10905
2020	*947603*	*12676*	*6908*	*610796*	*64.5*	70+	13354

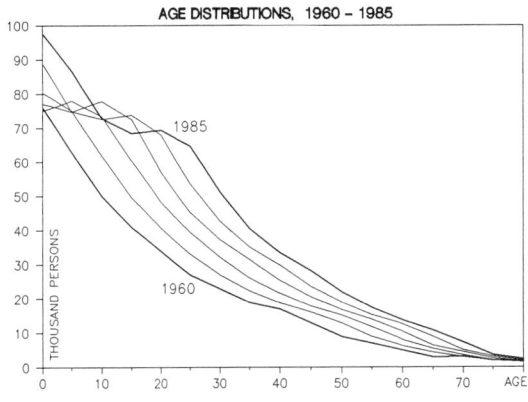

AGE DISTRIBUTIONS, 1960 – 1985

POPULATION RATIOS

YEAR	AGE DISTRIBUTION				DEPENDENCY RATIO	WOMEN 15-49	CHILD-WOMAN RATIO
	UNDER 15	15-64	65 & OLDER	70 & OLDER			
1950	0.467	0.505	0.028	0.017	0.979	0.215	0.887
1955	0.476	0.494	0.030	0.021	1.024	0.220	0.878
1960	0.480	0.495	0.025	0.018	1.020	0.216	0.894
1965	0.468	0.508	0.023	0.014	0.968	0.221	0.781
1970	0.435	0.540	0.024	0.014	0.850	0.234	0.615
1975	0.399	0.575	0.027	0.015	0.740	0.251	0.532
1980	0.375	0.594	0.031	0.016	0.684	0.261	0.541
1985	0.372	0.593	0.035	0.019	0.687	0.259	0.545
1990	*0.367*	*0.594*	*0.039*	*0.023*	*0.683*	*0.256*	*0.492*
2000	*0.303*	*0.647*	*0.050*	*0.029*	*0.545*	*0.270*	*0.359*
2010	*0.257*	*0.676*	*0.067*	*0.040*	*0.480*	*0.263*	*0.325*
2020	*0.226*	*0.680*	*0.094*	*0.056*	*0.471*	*0.253*	*0.283*

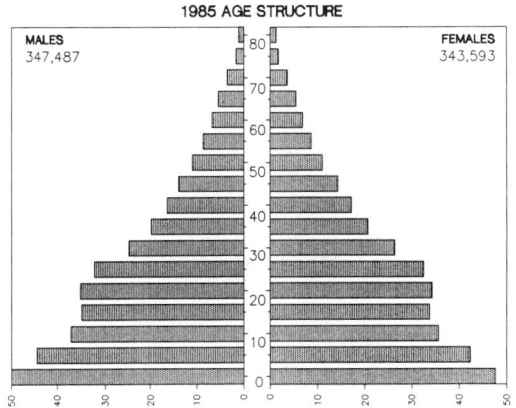

1985 AGE STRUCTURE

MALES 347,487   FEMALES 343,593

MORTALITY MEASURES (Annual Averages)

PERIOD	CRUDE DEATH RATE	INFANT MORT. RATE	LIFE EXPECTANCY AT BIRTH (years)			
			MALE	FEMALE	BOTH SEXES	DIFFERENCE FEMALE-MALE
1950-55	14.10	88.00	53.80	56.68	55.21	2.88
1955-60	11.10	75.00	56.30	59.18	57.71	2.88
1960-65	9.20	66.00	58.80	61.68	60.21	2.88
1965-70	7.60	55.00	61.30	64.18	62.71	2.88
1970-75	6.50	45.00	63.60	66.68	65.10	3.08
1975-80	5.79	36.74	65.50	69.00	67.21	3.50
1980-85	5.38	30.81	67.00	71.00	68.94	4.00
1985-90	*5.03*	*27.26*	*68.20*	*72.70*	*70.38*	*4.50*
1990-95	*4.95*	*23.60*	*69.20*	*73.95*	*71.51*	*4.75*
2000-05	*5.20*	*17.63*	*70.90*	*76.20*	*73.47*	*5.30*
2010-15	*5.90*	*13.35*	*72.30*	*78.02*	*75.08*	*5.72*
2020-25	*7.29*	*10.93*	*73.06*	*79.42*	*76.15*	*6.36*

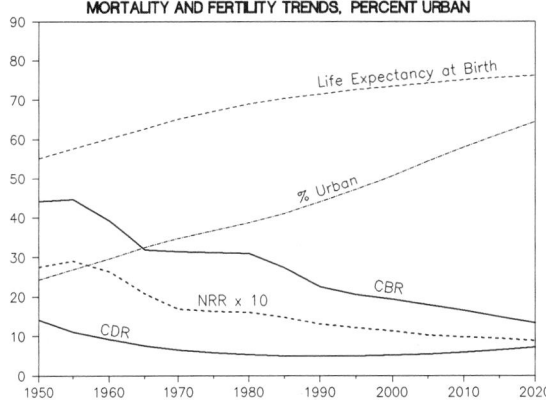

MORTALITY AND FERTILITY TRENDS, PERCENT URBAN

Life Expectancy at Birth

% Urban

NRR x 10   CBR

CDR

FERTILITY MEASURES (Annual Averages)

PERIOD	CRUDE BIRTH RATE	FERTILITY RATES		REPRODUCTION RATES		RATE OF NATUR. INCR.
		GENERAL	TOTAL	GROSS	NET	
1950-55	44.30	203.58	6.625	3.216	2.767	30.20
1955-60	44.70	205.22	6.792	3.297	2.913	33.60
1960-65	39.40	180.07	5.953	2.890	2.639	30.20
1965-70	32.02	140.25	4.596	2.231	2.087	24.42
1970-75	31.50	129.49	3.708	1.800	1.700	25.00
1975-80	31.27	122.03	3.605	1.750	1.632	25.48
1980-85	31.07	119.53	3.502	1.700	1.612	25.69
1985-90	*27.35*	*106.28*	*3.193*	*1.550*	*1.488*	*22.31*
1990-95	*22.60*	*87.41*	*2.781*	*1.350*	*1.306*	*17.65*
2000-05	*19.42*	*71.81*	*2.369*	*1.150*	*1.126*	*14.22*
2010-15	*16.65*	*64.21*	*2.060*	*1.000*	*0.987*	*10.75*
2020-25	*13.38*	*52.94*	*1.854*	*0.900*	*0.892*	*6.09*

AGING MEASURES

YEAR	POPULATION AGE RATIOS				POPULATION	
	60+/20-59	65+/20-64	70+/20-69	75+/20-74	MEAN AGE	MEDIAN AGE
1950	0.1171	0.0689	0.0420	0.0222	21.32	16.58
1960	0.1006	0.0649	0.0446	0.0243	20.91	15.98
1970	0.0972	0.0573	0.0321	0.0163	22.32	17.79
1980	0.1108	0.0643	0.0333	0.0166	24.06	20.34
1990	*0.1254*	*0.0778*	*0.0441*	*0.0207*	*25.66*	*22.39*
2000	*0.1507*	*0.0918*	*0.0524*	*0.0266*	*28.49*	*24.85*
2010	*0.1826*	*0.1128*	*0.0649*	*0.0323*	*31.43*	*28.69*
2020	*0.2660*	*0.1563*	*0.0875*	*0.0448*	*34.51*	*33.15*

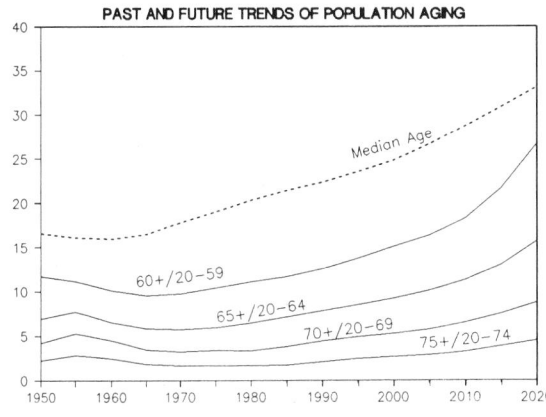

PAST AND FUTURE TRENDS OF POPULATION AGING

Median Age

60+/20-59

65+/20-64

70+/20-69

75+/20-74

NEW ZEALAND

290

OBSERVED AND *PROJECTED* POPULATION DATA

YEAR	MID-YEAR POPULATION	NO. OF BIRTHS	NO. OF DEATHS	URBAN POPULATION NUMBER	URBAN POPULATION PERCENT	POPULATION 1985 AGE	POPULATION 1985 NUMBER
1950	1908000	49112	17783	1383682	72.5	0	247843
1955	2136000	56070	19352	1572737	73.6	5	252763
1960	2372000	61316	21040	1802720	76.0	10	290441
1965	2628000	59288	22916	2073229	78.9	15	298605
1970	2819602	58653	23803	2286979	81.1	20	281491
1975	3086900	53002	25343	2555336	82.8	25	265736
1980	3112900	49744	25277	2594291	83.3	30	244791
1985	3247100	50665	27321	2719122	83.7	35	238926
1990	3378582	51003	28221	2844428	84.2	40	190388
1995	3507078	51151	29060	2968391	84.6	45	165292
2000	3631928	49808	30065	3092587	85.2	50	143853
2005	3744613	47886	31129	3206887	85.6	55	148435
2010	3841920	47398	32606	3310582	86.2	60	138118
2015	3929162	47700	35025	3406191	86.7	65	113892
2020	4005593	47807	38149	3494880	87.3	70+	226526

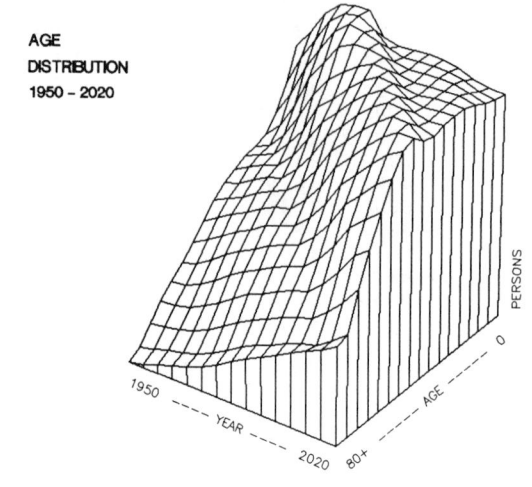

AGE DISTRIBUTION 1950 – 2020

POPULATION RATIOS

YEAR	AGE DISTRIBUTION UNDER 15	15-64	65 & OLDER	70 & OLDER	DEPENDENCY RATIO	WOMEN 15-49	CHILD-WOMAN RATIO
1950	0.291	0.619	0.090	0.053	0.614	0.240	0.508
1955	0.312	0.598	0.090	0.057	0.673	0.230	0.515
1960	0.329	0.585	0.086	0.057	0.710	0.223	0.547
1965	0.326	0.592	0.081	0.052	0.688	0.225	0.513
1970	0.318	0.598	0.085	0.054	0.673	0.227	0.464
1975	0.300	0.613	0.087	0.054	0.631	0.235	0.418
1980	0.267	0.633	0.100	0.063	0.579	0.245	0.324
1985	0.244	0.652	0.105	0.070	0.535	0.258	0.295
1990	0.225	0.666	0.110	0.073	0.502	0.266	0.285
2000	0.214	0.673	0.113	0.079	0.485	0.257	0.278
2010	0.197	0.679	0.124	0.083	0.474	0.243	0.260
2020	0.181	0.661	0.158	0.106	0.512	0.224	0.268

MORTALITY MEASURES (Annual Averages)

PERIOD	CRUDE DEATH RATE	INFANT MORT. RATE	LIFE EXPECTANCY AT BIRTH (years) MALE	FEMALE	BOTH SEXES	DIFFERENCE FEMALE-MALE
1950-55	9.32	26.30	67.50	71.80	69.59	4.30
1955-60	9.06	23.64	68.30	73.20	70.68	4.90
1960-65	8.87	20.61	68.30	73.90	71.03	5.60
1965-70	8.72	17.87	68.30	74.40	71.27	6.10
1970-75	8.44	16.05	68.70	74.80	71.67	6.10
1975-80	8.21	13.81	69.30	75.70	72.41	6.40
1980-85	8.12	11.87	70.74	76.89	73.74	6.15
1985-90	8.41	10.99	71.75	77.89	74.75	6.14
1990-95	8.35	9.36	72.73	78.62	75.60	5.88
2000-05	8.28	6.69	74.28	80.18	77.15	5.89
2010-15	8.49	5.86	75.55	81.14	78.28	5.59
2020-25	9.52	5.21	76.56	82.19	79.30	5.62

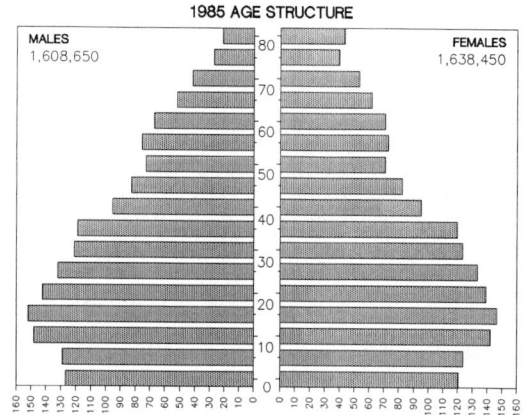

1985 AGE STRUCTURE

MALES 1,608,650

FEMALES 1,638,450

FERTILITY MEASURES (Annual Averages)

PERIOD	CRUDE BIRTH RATE	FERTILITY RATES GENERAL	TOTAL	REPRODUCTION RATES GROSS	NET	RATE OF NATUR. INCR.
1950-55	25.74	109.80	3.541	1.725	1.660	16.42
1955-60	26.25	116.13	3.934	1.916	1.847	17.19
1960-65	25.85	115.50	3.790	1.846	1.787	16.98
1965-70	22.56	99.85	3.217	1.567	1.522	13.84
1970-75	20.80	90.02	2.790	1.359	1.321	12.36
1975-80	17.17	71.52	2.205	1.074	1.052	8.96
1980-85	15.98	63.41	1.957	0.953	0.933	7.86
1985-90	15.60	59.46	1.898	0.925	0.906	7.19
1990-95	15.10	56.85	1.848	0.901	0.884	6.74
2000-05	13.71	54.10	1.898	0.925	0.912	5.44
2010-15	12.34	51.74	1.898	0.925	0.913	3.85
2020-25	11.94	54.27	1.898	0.925	0.914	2.41

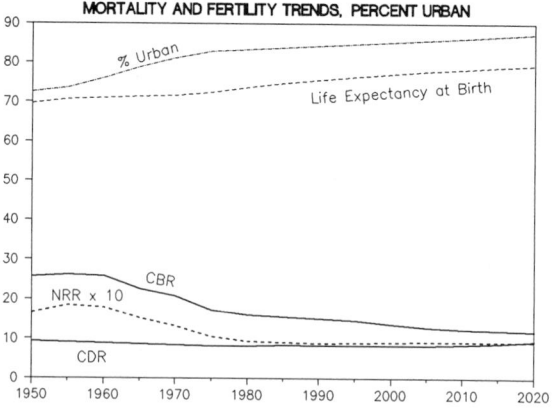

MORTALITY AND FERTILITY TRENDS, PERCENT URBAN

% Urban

Life Expectancy at Birth

CBR

NRR x 10

CDR

AGING MEASURES

YEAR	POPULATION AGE RATIOS 60+/20-59	65+/20-64	70+/20-69	75+/20-74	POPULATION MEAN AGE	MEDIAN AGE
1950	0.2577	0.1630	0.0912	0.0427	31.65	29.41
1960	0.2592	0.1703	0.1068	0.0586	30.63	27.43
1970	0.2682	0.1680	0.1000	0.0543	30.49	25.61
1980	0.2833	0.1856	0.1105	0.0588	32.20	28.27
1990	0.2809	0.1894	0.1177	0.0676	33.96	31.12
2000	0.2733	0.1866	0.1245	0.0730	35.60	34.08
2010	0.3259	0.2037	0.1271	0.0748	37.56	37.36
2020	0.4075	0.2639	0.1626	0.0876	39.59	39.69

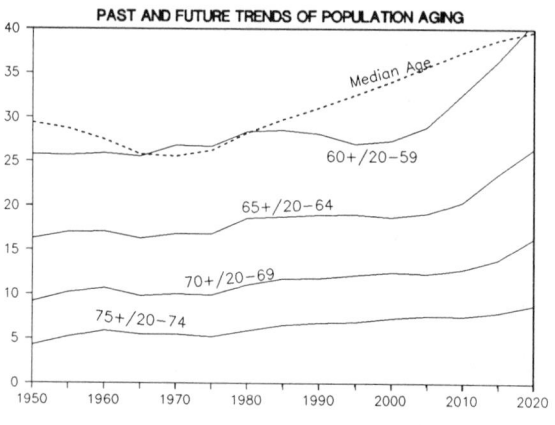

PAST AND FUTURE TRENDS OF POPULATION AGING

Median Age

60+/20-59

65+/20-64

70+/20-69

75+/20-74

OBSERVED AND *PROJECTED* POPULATION DATA

YEAR	MID-YEAR POPULATION	NO. OF BIRTHS	NO. OF DEATHS	URBAN POPULATION NUMBER	URBAN POPULATION PERCENT	POPULATION 1985 AGE	POPULATION 1985 NUMBER
1950	1613198	71674	46492	11183	.7	0	557954
1955	1744257	77305	43798	23852	1.4	5	463157
1960	1920275	83935	40921	51460	2.7	10	438078
1965	2148094	90972	41050	111391	5.2	15	390274
1970	2422002	98384	41334	237317	9.8	20	304314
1975	2696000	114610	42198	321642	11.9	25	257074
1980	3086046	119853	40322	402654	13.0	30	218194
1985	3511072	135942	42600	500415	14.3	35	210976
1990	*4011003*	*145006*	*43483*	*634102*	*15.8*	40	147848
1995	*4552912*	*154098*	*43580*	*809245*	*17.8*	45	143944
2000	*5141211*	*162617*	*43428*	*1038930*	*20.2*	50	110213
2005	*5773816*	*171904*	*43055*	*1337480*	*23.2*	55	106967
2010	*6456101*	*177665*	*43030*	*1722506*	*26.7*	60	76194
2015	*7166323*	*182490*	*43478*	*2179449*	*30.4*	65	53604
2020	*7896830*	*179511*	*44704*	*2708803*	*34.3*	70+	32281

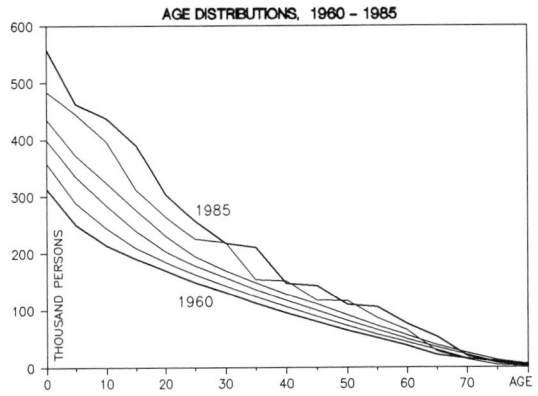

AGE DISTRIBUTIONS, 1960 - 1985

POPULATION RATIOS

YEAR	AGE DISTRIBUTION UNDER 15	AGE DISTRIBUTION 15-64	AGE DISTRIBUTION 65 & OLDER	AGE DISTRIBUTION 70 & OLDER	DEPENDENCY RATIO	WOMEN 15-49	CHILD-WOMAN RATIO
1950	0.393	0.565	0.041	0.023	0.769	0.230	0.667
1955	0.397	0.568	0.034	0.021	0.759	0.230	0.687
1960	0.405	0.566	0.029	0.017	0.766	0.227	0.716
1965	0.415	0.556	0.029	0.015	0.797	0.223	0.745
1970	0.420	0.550	0.030	0.016	0.819	0.221	0.746
1975	0.420	0.549	0.031	0.016	0.821	0.221	0.729
1980	0.430	0.555	0.016	0.006	0.802	0.223	0.705
1985	0.416	0.560	0.024	0.009	0.786	0.226	0.702
1990	*0.419*	*0.555*	*0.026*	*0.012*	*0.802*	*0.226*	*0.754*
2000	*0.420*	*0.554*	*0.025*	*0.013*	*0.804*	*0.229*	*0.665*
2010	*0.382*	*0.593*	*0.025*	*0.013*	*0.687*	*0.249*	*0.548*
2020	*0.344*	*0.625*	*0.030*	*0.016*	*0.599*	*0.262*	*0.454*

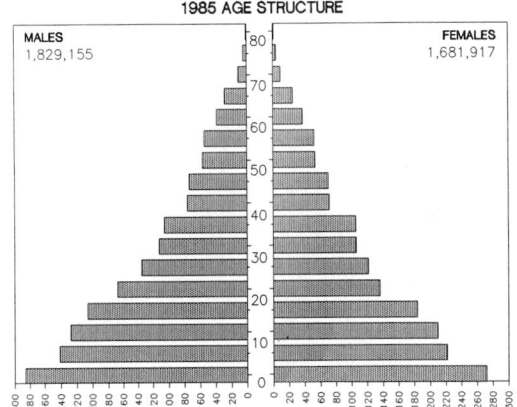

1985 AGE STRUCTURE

MALES 1,829,155   FEMALES 1,681,917

MORTALITY MEASURES (Annual Averages)

PERIOD	CRUDE DEATH RATE	INFANT MORT. RATE	LIFE EXPECTANCY AT BIRTH (years) MALE	LIFE EXPECTANCY AT BIRTH (years) FEMALE	LIFE EXPECTANCY AT BIRTH (years) BOTH SEXES	DIFFERENCE FEMALE-MALE
1950-55	28.82	190.00	35.62	34.48	35.06	-1.14
1955-60	25.11	175.00	39.00	38.14	38.58	-0.86
1960-65	21.31	155.00	42.99	42.38	42.69	-0.61
1965-70	19.11	130.00	45.35	44.90	45.13	-0.45
1970-75	17.07	105.00	47.70	47.60	47.65	-0.10
1975-80	15.65	85.00	50.50	50.00	50.26	-0.50
1980-85	13.07	74.40	51.20	52.70	51.93	1.50
1985-90	*12.13*	*58.80*	*53.18*	*54.84*	*53.98*	*1.66*
1990-95	*10.84*	*52.87*	*55.23*	*56.89*	*56.04*	*1.66*
2000-05	*8.45*	*41.68*	*59.15*	*61.07*	*60.08*	*1.92*
2010-15	*6.66*	*31.38*	*63.19*	*65.33*	*64.23*	*2.15*
2020-25	*5.66*	*22.29*	*66.71*	*69.50*	*68.07*	*2.79*

FERTILITY MEASURES (Annual Averages)

PERIOD	CRUDE BIRTH RATE	FERTILITY RATES GENERAL	FERTILITY RATES TOTAL	REPRODUCTION RATES GROSS	REPRODUCTION RATES NET	RATE OF NATUR. INCR.
1950-55	44.43	193.34	6.240	3.029	1.600	15.61
1955-60	44.32	193.89	6.264	3.041	1.753	19.21
1960-65	43.71	194.09	6.285	3.051	1.929	22.40
1965-70	42.35	190.77	6.207	3.013	1.997	23.24
1970-75	40.62	183.65	5.953	2.890	2.010	23.56
1975-80	42.51	191.36	6.283	3.050	2.212	26.86
1980-85	38.84	172.92	5.665	2.750	2.079	25.77
1985-90	*38.72*	*171.06*	*5.665*	*2.750*	*2.311*	*26.58*
1990-95	*36.15*	*159.33*	*5.253*	*2.550*	*2.200*	*25.31*
2000-05	*31.63*	*134.82*	*4.429*	*2.150*	*1.950*	*23.18*
2010-15	*27.52*	*108.70*	*3.502*	*1.700*	*1.614*	*20.85*
2020-25	*22.73*	*85.92*	*2.678*	*1.300*	*1.277*	*17.07*

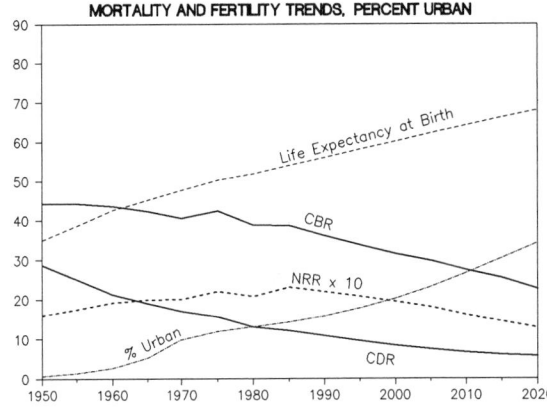

MORTALITY AND FERTILITY TRENDS, PERCENT URBAN

AGING MEASURES

YEAR	POPULATION AGE RATIOS 60+/20-59	POPULATION AGE RATIOS 65+/20-64	POPULATION AGE RATIOS 70+/20-69	POPULATION AGE RATIOS 75+/20-74	POPULATION MEAN AGE	POPULATION MEDIAN AGE
1950	0.1358	0.0893	0.0481	0.0213	24.47	20.26
1960	0.1097	0.0620	0.0361	0.0186	23.89	19.78
1970	0.1177	0.0667	0.0333	0.0135	23.60	19.03
1980	0.0845	0.0342	0.0140	0.0044	22.88	18.49
1990	*0.1123*	*0.0579*	*0.0257*	*0.0074*	*22.98*	*18.75*
2000	*0.1027*	*0.0562*	*0.0291*	*0.0108*	*23.15*	*18.87*
2010	*0.1005*	*0.0521*	*0.0269*	*0.0105*	*24.16*	*20.40*
2020	*0.1034*	*0.0582*	*0.0295*	*0.0109*	*25.83*	*22.72*

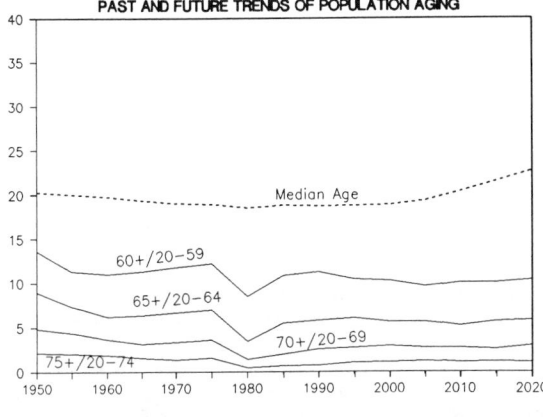

PAST AND FUTURE TRENDS OF POPULATION AGING

OBSERVED AND *PROJECTED* POPULATION DATA (000's)

YEAR	MID-YEAR POPULATION	NO. OF BIRTHS	NO. OF DEATHS	URBAN POPULATION NUMBER	URBAN POPULATION PERCENT	POPULATION 1985 AGE	POPULATION 1985 NUMBER
1950	180075	4736	1657	70769	39.3	0	25199
1955	196159	4967	1491	86114	43.9	5	23105
1960	214335	4737	1539	104595	48.8	10	21488
1965	230940	4138	1795	121013	52.4	15	20687
1970	242959	4405	2083	137758	56.7	20	23555
1975	254851	4651	2556	152936	60.0	25	24310
1980	265546	5077	2844	167453	63.1	30	21718
1985	276946	5097	2931	181760	65.6	35	15643
1990	*287991*	*4823*	*2855*	*194509*	*67.5*	40	13074
1995	*298000*	*4749*	*2833*	*206752*	*69.4*	45	19038
2000	*307737*	*4833*	*2957*	*217447*	*70.7*	50	15622
2005	*317266*	*4931*	*3127*	*228146*	*71.9*	55	16136
2010	*326415*	*4896*	*3185*	*237205*	*72.7*	60	10771
2015	*335083*	*4872*	*3266*	*246018*	*73.4*	65	7198
2020	*343212*	*4849*	*3221*	*253119*	*73.8*	70+	19402

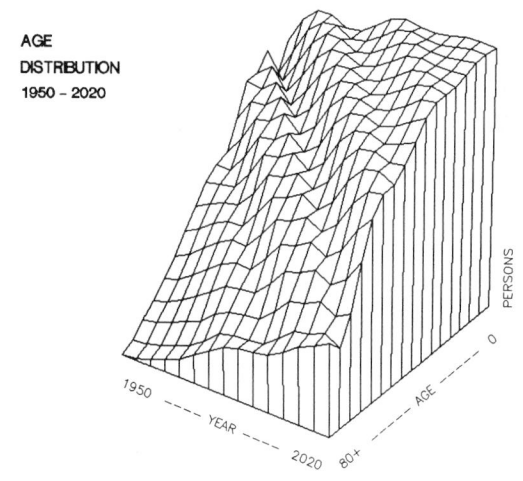

AGE DISTRIBUTION 1950 - 2020

POPULATION RATIOS

YEAR	AGE DISTRIBUTION UNDER 15	AGE DISTRIBUTION 15-64	AGE DISTRIBUTION 65 & OLDER	AGE DISTRIBUTION 70 & OLDER	DEPENDENCY RATIO	WOMEN 15-49	CHILD-WOMAN RATIO
1950	0.301	0.638	0.061	0.039	0.567	0.302	0.347
1955	0.278	0.657	0.065	0.041	0.523	0.299	0.391
1960	0.307	0.626	0.068	0.043	0.598	0.271	0.423
1965	0.306	0.621	0.074	0.046	0.611	0.258	0.394
1970	0.289	0.637	0.074	0.043	0.570	0.267	0.325
1975	0.260	0.644	0.095	0.059	0.552	0.265	0.320
1980	0.248	0.650	0.103	0.070	0.539	0.257	0.343
1985	0.252	0.652	0.096	0.070	0.534	0.249	0.365
1990	*0.255*	*0.649*	*0.096*	*0.063*	*0.540*	*0.240*	*0.366*
2000	*0.236*	*0.647*	*0.117*	*0.077*	*0.545*	*0.252*	*0.306*
2010	*0.222*	*0.658*	*0.121*	*0.090*	*0.520*	*0.240*	*0.315*
2020	*0.214*	*0.655*	*0.131*	*0.082*	*0.527*	*0.234*	*0.304*

MORTALITY MEASURES (Annual Averages)

PERIOD	CRUDE DEATH RATE	INFANT MORT. RATE	LIFE EXPECTANCY AT BIRTH (years) MALE	LIFE EXPECTANCY AT BIRTH (years) FEMALE	LIFE EXPECTANCY AT BIRTH (years) BOTH SEXES	DIFFERENCE FEMALE-MALE
1950-55	9.20	73.00	60.00	68.50	64.15	8.50
1955-60	7.60	44.00	64.00	71.00	67.42	7.00
1960-65	7.18	31.56	65.50	73.00	69.16	7.50
1965-70	7.77	26.15	65.30	73.50	69.30	8.20
1970-75	8.57	25.55	64.00	73.50	68.64	9.50
1975-80	10.03	28.00	63.00	73.00	67.88	10.00
1980-85	10.71	26.00	63.00	73.00	67.88	10.00
1985-90	*10.58*	*24.32*	*65.04*	*74.17*	*69.50*	*9.14*
1990-95	*9.91*	*20.33*	*66.59*	*75.33*	*70.86*	*8.74*
2000-05	*9.61*	*14.35*	*69.25*	*77.33*	*73.19*	*8.08*
2010-15	*9.76*	*10.35*	*71.43*	*79.02*	*75.13*	*7.59*
2020-25	*9.39*	*7.64*	*73.22*	*80.39*	*76.72*	*7.17*

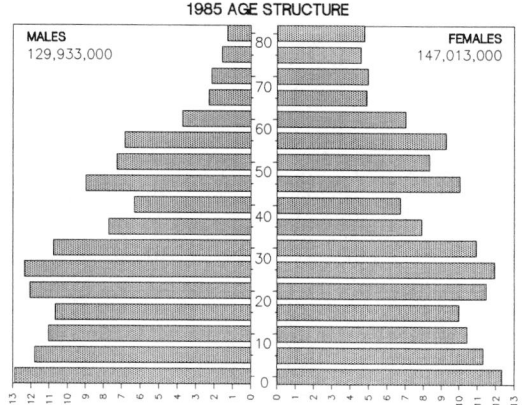

1985 AGE STRUCTURE

MALES 129,933,000

FEMALES 147,013,000

FERTILITY MEASURES (Annual Averages)

PERIOD	CRUDE BIRTH RATE	FERTILITY RATES GENERAL	FERTILITY RATES TOTAL	REPRODUCTION RATES GROSS	REPRODUCTION RATES NET	RATE OF NATUR. INCR.
1950-55	26.30	87.64	2.819	1.376	1.281	17.10
1955-60	25.32	89.14	2.807	1.370	1.276	17.72
1960-65	22.10	83.68	2.537	1.238	1.153	14.92
1965-70	17.92	68.28	2.418	1.180	1.122	10.15
1970-75	18.13	68.16	2.438	1.190	1.123	9.56
1975-80	18.25	69.86	2.336	1.140	1.105	8.22
1980-85	19.12	75.50	2.350	1.147	1.120	8.41
1985-90	*18.40*	*75.28*	*2.380*	*1.162*	*1.113*	*7.82*
1990-95	*16.75*	*68.93*	*2.300*	*1.122*	*1.084*	*6.83*
2000-05	*15.71*	*62.89*	*2.200*	*1.074*	*1.048*	*6.10*
2010-15	*15.00*	*63.20*	*2.100*	*1.025*	*1.007*	*5.24*
2020-25	*14.13*	*60.46*	*2.100*	*1.025*	*1.011*	*4.74*

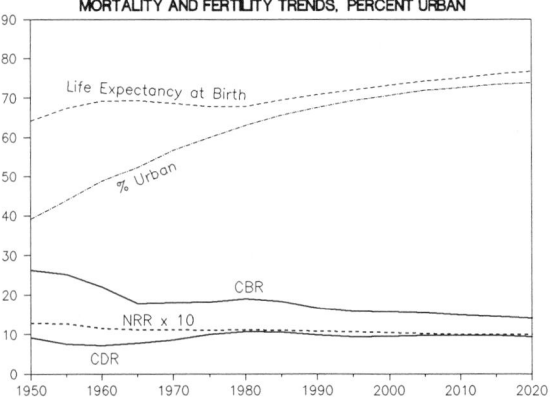

MORTALITY AND FERTILITY TRENDS, PERCENT URBAN

Life Expectancy at Birth

% Urban

CBR

NRR x 10

CDR

AGING MEASURES

YEAR	POPULATION AGE RATIOS 60+/20-59	POPULATION AGE RATIOS 65+/20-64	POPULATION AGE RATIOS 70+/20-69	POPULATION AGE RATIOS 75+/20-74	POPULATION MEAN AGE	POPULATION MEDIAN AGE
1950	0.1761	0.1127	0.0685	0.0328	29.04	24.67
1960	0.1894	0.1197	0.0722	0.0362	29.78	26.90
1970	0.2281	0.1364	0.0756	0.0402	31.03	28.88
1980	0.2481	0.1830	0.1174	0.0662	33.01	29.27
1990	*0.2818*	*0.1667*	*0.1028*	*0.0660*	*33.52*	*31.09*
2000	*0.3296*	*0.2060*	*0.1268*	*0.0627*	*34.71*	*32.99*
2010	*0.2950*	*0.2061*	*0.1463*	*0.0789*	*35.80*	*33.80*
2020	*0.3633*	*0.2234*	*0.1293*	*0.0777*	*36.85*	*35.40*

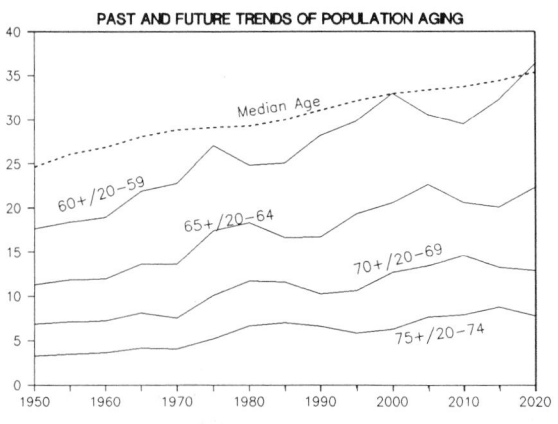

PAST AND FUTURE TRENDS OF POPULATION AGING

Median Age

60+/20-59

65+/20-64

70+/20-69

75+/20-74

Detailed Country
Tabulations

TABLE 1 — DATA

AGE AT LAST BIRTHDAY	ESTIMATED MID-YEAR POPULATION BOTH SEXES	MALES Number	MALES Percent	FEMALES Number	FEMALES Percent	BIRTHS BY AGE OF MOTHER AND SEX	DEATHS BOTH SEXES	DEATHS MALES	DEATHS FEMALES	AGE AT LAST BIRTHDAY
0	21700	11100	2.7	10600	2.6		1232	706	526	0
1-4	88200	44450	10.9	43750	10.8		502	240	262	1-4
5-9	118500	59900	14.7	58600	14.5		113	57	56	5-9
10-14	106300	53750	13.2	52550	13.0	19	77	41	36	10-14
15-19	97950	49100	12.1	48850	12.1	2790	80	46	34	15-19
20-24	74400	37350	9.2	37050	9.2	6952	110	57	53	20-24
25-29	50400	25300	6.2	25100	6.2	5166	95	39	56	25-29
30-34	44500	22050	5.4	22450	5.6	3244	108	43	65	30-34
35-39	37600	18900	4.6	18700	4.6	2076	131	60	71	35-39
40-44	40100	20400	5.0	19700	4.9	733	208	121	87	40-44
45-49	35350	18350	4.5	17000	4.2	78	271	169	102	45-49
50-54	26150	13600	3.3	12550	3.1	13	289	185	104	50-54
55-59	23800	12450	3.1	11350	2.8		414	280	134	55-59
60-64	16150	7950	2.0	8200	2.0		500	321	179	60-64
65-69	13300	6200	1.5	7100	1.8		571	341	230	65-69
70-74	8500	3450	0.8	5050	1.2		604	344	260	70-74
75-79	5350	1800	0.4	3550	0.9		446	213	233	75-79
80-84	2400	700	0.2	1700	0.4	10812 M	326	125	201	80-84
85+	650	200	0.0	450	0.1	10259 F	232	56	176	85+
TOTAL	811300	407000		404300		21071	6309	3444	2865	TOTAL

TABLE 2 — MALE LIFE TABLE

x	nM_x	nq_x	l_x	nd_x	nL_x	nm_x	na_x	T_x	$\overset{\circ}{e}_x$	x
0	0.063604	0.060444	100000	6044	95032	0.063604	0.178	6086506	60.865	0
1	0.005399	0.021310	93956	2002	370817	0.005399	1.500	5991474	63.769	1
5	0.000952	0.004747	91953	436	458676	0.000952	2.500	5620657	61.125	5
10	0.000763	0.003806	91517	348	456712	0.000763	2.495	5161981	56.405	10
15	0.000937	0.004693	91169	428	454845	0.000941	2.668	4705269	51.611	15
20	0.001526	0.007631	90741	692	452028	0.001532	2.579	4250424	46.841	20
25	0.001542	0.007686	90048	692	448549	0.001543	2.554	3798396	42.182	25
30	0.001950	0.009755	89356	872	444750	0.001960	2.669	3349847	37.489	30
35	0.003175	0.015810	88485	1399	439275	0.003185	2.750	2905097	32.832	35
40	0.005931	0.029257	87086	2548	429565	0.005931	2.698	2465822	28.315	40
45	0.009210	0.045263	84538	3826	413705	0.009249	2.652	2036258	24.087	45
50	0.013603	0.066192	80711	5342	391091	0.013660	2.667	1622552	20.103	50
55	0.022490	0.107476	75369	8100	358074	0.022622	2.683	1231461	16.339	55
60	0.040377	0.185040	67269	12447	306316	0.040636	2.588	873387	12.984	60
65	0.055000	0.243294	54821	13338	241630	0.055199	2.565	567072	10.344	65
70	0.099710	0.400568	41484	16617	165430	0.100448	2.473	325441	7.845	70
75	0.118333	0.450345	24867	11199	94602	0.118375	2.345	160012	6.435	75
80	0.178571	0.606619	13668	8291	46207	0.179437	2.331	65410	4.786	80
85	0.280000	1.000000	5377	5377	19203	0.232063	3.571	19203	3.571	85

TABLE 3 — FEMALE LIFE TABLE

x	nM_x	nq_x	l_x	nd_x	nL_x	nm_x	na_x	T_x	$\overset{\circ}{e}_x$	x
0	0.049623	0.047624	100000	4762	95973	0.049623	0.154	6575811	65.758	0
1	0.005989	0.023601	95238	2248	375331	0.005989	1.500	6479839	68.039	1
5	0.000956	0.004767	92990	443	463841	0.000956	2.500	6104508	65.647	5
10	0.000685	0.003416	92547	316	461918	0.000684	2.420	5640666	60.949	10
15	0.000696	0.003491	92230	322	460419	0.000699	2.723	5178749	56.150	15
20	0.001430	0.007190	91909	661	458036	0.001443	2.719	4718329	51.337	20
25	0.002231	0.011156	91248	1018	453842	0.002243	2.631	4260294	46.689	25
30	0.002895	0.014425	90230	1302	448032	0.002905	2.605	3806466	42.186	30
35	0.003797	0.018838	88928	1675	440579	0.003802	2.575	3358434	37.766	35
40	0.004416	0.021853	87253	1907	431677	0.004417	2.594	2917855	33.441	40
45	0.006000	0.029698	85346	2535	420702	0.006025	2.621	2486178	29.130	45
50	0.008287	0.040815	82812	3380	406037	0.008324	2.627	2065477	24.942	50
55	0.011806	0.057815	79432	4592	386601	0.011879	2.701	1659440	20.891	55
60	0.021829	0.104392	74839	7813	355813	0.021957	2.647	1272839	17.008	60
65	0.032394	0.150742	67027	10104	310962	0.032492	2.608	917026	13.682	65
70	0.051485	0.229039	56923	13038	252506	0.051633	2.537	606063	10.647	70
75	0.065634	0.283277	43885	12432	188667	0.065892	2.526	353558	8.056	75
80	0.118235	0.463270	31454	14572	121726	0.119707	2.561	164891	5.242	80
85	0.391111	1.000000	16882	16882	43165	0.386631	2.557	43165	2.557	85

TABLE 4 — OBSERVED VITAL RATES AND RATIOS

CRUDE RATES

Per Thousand	BOTH SEXES	MALES	FEMALES
BIRTH RATE	25.97	26.57	25.37
DEATH RATE	7.78	8.46	7.09
RATE OF INCREASE	18.20	18.10	18.29

PERCENT OF POPULATION IN AGE GROUP

	BOTH SEXES	MALES	FEMALES
UNDER 15	41.25	41.57	40.93
15 - 64	55.02	55.39	54.65
65 AND OLDER	3.72	3.03	4.42

RATES STANDARDIZED ON USA 1980

Per Thousand	BOTH SEXES	MALES	FEMALES
BIRTH RATE	30.65		29.02
DEATH RATE	16.48	16.43	16.54
RATE OF INCREASE	14.17		12.49

RATES STANDARDIZED ON MEXICO 1980

	BOTH SEXES	MALES	FEMALES
BIRTH RATE	26.93		26.43
DEATH RATE	7.80	8.58	7.01
RATE OF INCREASE	19.13		19.42

VITAL STATISTICS

GFR x 1000	111.575
TFR	3.746
GRR	1.824
NRR	1.645
μ	28.707
σ^2	45.823
GENERATION	28.304
POP. SEX RATIO	0.993
SEX RATIO AT BIRTH	1.054
DEP. RATIO x 100	81.743

PROJECTED POPULATION

STABLE EQUIVALENT TO ORIGINAL POPULATION

AGE GROUP	1975			1980			MALES		FEMALES		AGE GROUP	
	BOTH SEXES	MALES	FEMALES	BOTH SEXES	MALES	FEMALES	Number	Percent	Number	Percent		
0-4	112	57	55	137	70	67	60	12.6	58	12.2	0-4	
5-9	108	55	53	110	56	54	54	11.4	52	11.0	5-9	TABLE 5
10-14	118	60	58	107	54	53	49	10.4	47	10.0	10-14	
15-19	106	54	52	117	59	58	45	9.5	43	9.2	15-19	POPULATION
20-24	98	49	49	105	53	52	41	8.6	39	8.3	20-24	PROJECTED
25-29	74	37	37	96	48	48	37	7.8	36	7.6	25-29	WITH
30-34	50	25	25	73	37	36	34	7.1	32	6.8	30-34	FIXED
35-39	44	22	22	49	25	24	31	6.4	29	6.2	35-39	AGE-
40-44	36	18	18	43	21	22	27	5.7	26	5.5	40-44	SPECIFIC
45-49	39	20	19	36	18	18	24	5.1	23	4.9	45-49	BIRTH
50-54	33	17	16	38	19	19	21	4.4	21	4.4	50-54	AND
55-59	24	12	12	32	16	16	18	3.7	18	3.8	55-59	DEATH
60-64	21	11	10	22	11	11	14	2.9	15	3.2	60-64	RATES
65-69	13	6	7	17	8	9	10	2.1	12	2.6	65-69	(female
70-74	10	4	6	10	4	6	6	1.3	9	1.9	70-74	dominant,
75-79	6	2	4	6	2	4	3	0.7	6	1.3	75-79	in 000s)
80-84	3	1	2	3	1	2	1	0.3	4	0.8	80-84	
85+	1	0	1	1	0	1	1	0.1	1	0.3	85+	
TOTAL	896	450	446	1002	502	500	476		471		TOTAL	

VITAL RATES OF PROJECTED POPULATION

VITAL RATES OF STABLE POPULATION

Per Thousand	1975			1980				MALES	FEMALES	
	BOTH SEXES	MALES	FEMALES	BOTH SEXES	MALES	FEMALES	Per Thousand			TABLE 6
BIRTH RATE	29.56	30.24	28.88	31.76	32.49	31.03	BIRTH RATE	28.27	27.06	
DEATH RATE	7.87	8.54	7.18	8.14	8.79	7.48	DEATH RATE	10.54	9.45	PROJECTED
RATE OF INCREASE	21.70	21.70	21.69	23.62	23.70	23.55	RATE OF INCREASE		17.62	VITAL RATES

AGE STRUCTURE OF PROJECTED POPULATION

STABLE AGE STRUCTURE

										AND RATIOS
% UNDER 15	37.66	38.07	37.24	35.29	35.80	34.78	% UNDER 15	34.35	33.27	(female
% 15-64	58.63	58.89	58.37	60.82	60.93	60.72	% 15-64	61.16	59.93	dominant)
% 65 AND OLDER	3.71	3.04	4.39	3.88	3.27	4.50	% 65 AND OLDER	4.49	6.80	
DEPEND. RATIO x 100	70.55	69.80	71.31	64.41	64.12	64.70	DEPEND. RATIO x 100	63.51	66.85	

AGE GROUP	FEMALE BIRTH RATES	NET MATERNITY FUNCTION	COEFF. OF MATRIX EQUATION	ORIGINAL MATRIX		STABLE MATRIX		MATRIX PARAMETERS		
				SUB-DIAGONAL	FIRST ROW	FISHER VALUES	REPRODUCTIVE VALUES			
0-4	0.0000	0.0000	0.0000	0.98417	0.00000	1.108	60236	λ_1	1.09208	
5-9	0.0000	0.0000	0.0004	0.99585	0.00041	1.230	72068	λ_2	0.41403+0.74788i	TABLE 7
10-14	0.0002	0.0008	0.0644	0.99676	0.06573	1.348	70849	λ_4	-0.00695+0.64974i	
15-19	0.0278	0.1280	0.2732	0.99482	0.27970	1.404	68589	λ_6	-0.46141+0.43616i	LESLIE
20-24	0.0914	0.4184	0.4366	0.99081	0.44926	1.230	45562	r_1	0.01762	MATRIX
25-29	0.1002	0.4548	0.3850	0.98723	0.39981	0.853	21408	r_2	-0.03137+0.21304i	AND ITS
30-34	0.0704	0.3152	0.2767	0.98336	0.29104	0.495	11105	r_4	-0.08622+0.31630i	ANALYSIS
35-39	0.0541	0.2381	0.1582	0.97979	0.16920	0.221	4139	r_6	-0.09085+0.47686i	(females)
40-44	0.0181	0.0782	0.0438	0.97457	0.04782	0.055	1089	c_1	4716	
45-49	0.0022	0.0094	0.0057	0.96514	0.00641	0.008	129	$2\pi/y$	29.4932	
50-54	0.0005	0.0020	0.0010	0.95213	0.00119	0.001	15	Δ	11.4014	

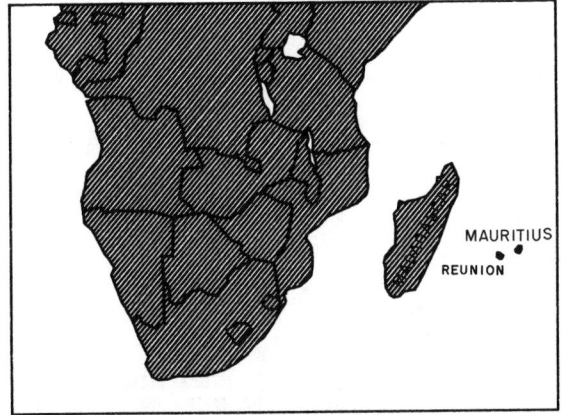

EDUCATION [1984]

% of primary school-age children enrolled:	106
secondary school-age children enrolled:	51
ca. 20-24 year olds in higher education:	1

LABOR FORCE

Average annual labor force growth (%) 1980-85:	3.3	
% of the 1980 labor force in agriculture:	28	TABLE 8
in industry:	24	
in services:	48	SOCIO-ECONOMIC

GNP & INCOME DISTRIBUTION

GNP per capita (in US Dollars) 1985:	1090	INDICATORS
GNP average annual growth rate (%) 1965-85:	2.7	
% share of total household income 1980-81		
Lowest 20% of households:	4.0	
Highest 10% of households:	46.7	

HEALTH & NUTRITION

Population per physician 1981:	1800
Daily calorie supply per capita 1985:	2740

TABLE 1 DATA

AGE AT LAST BIRTHDAY	ESTIMATED MID-YEAR POPULATION BOTH SEXES	MALES Number	Percent	FEMALES Number	Percent	BIRTHS BY AGE OF MOTHER AND SEX	DEATHS BOTH SEXES	MALES	FEMALES	AGE AT LAST BIRTHDAY
0	24652	12550	2.8	12102	2.6		808	438	370	0
1-4	87385	44406	9.8	42979	9.1		207	112	95	1-4
5-9	95630	48008	10.6	47622	10.1		60	35	25	5-9
10-14	106311	53026	11.7	53285	11.3	38	67	40	27	10-14
15-19	115041	57659	12.7	57382	12.2	3439	111	55	56	15-19
20-24	99261	48790	10.7	50471	10.7	8696	129	68	61	20-24
25-29	86032	41808	9.2	44224	9.4	7050	120	66	54	25-29
30-34	63325	30658	6.7	32667	6.9	3427	134	82	52	30-34
35-39	44327	21125	4.6	23202	4.9	1352	160	105	55	35-39
40-44	41321	20196	4.4	21125	4.5	411	206	139	67	40-44
45-49	34810	16643	3.7	18167	3.9	39	254	185	69	45-49
50-54	36358	18107	4.0	18251	3.9	6	380	271	109	50-54
55-59	31221	16223	3.6	14998	3.2		553	371	182	55-59
60-64	21431	10263	2.3	11168	2.4		650	455	195	60-64
65-69	18173	7893	1.7	10280	2.2		735	460	275	65-69
70-74	10246	4030	0.9	6216	1.3		688	408	280	70-74
75-79	6648	2536	0.6	4112	0.9		580	261	319	75-79
80-84	3369	925	0.2	2444	0.5	12435 M	432	155	277	80-84
85+	1037	185	0.0	852	0.2	12023 F	411	112	299	85+
TOTAL	926578	455031		471547		24458	6685	3818	2867	TOTAL

TABLE 2 MALE LIFE TABLE

x	nM_x	nq_x	l_x	nd_x	nL_x	nm_x	na_x	T_x	$\overset{\circ}{e}_x$	x
0	0.034900	0.033871	100000	3387	97051	0.034900	0.129	6234527	62.345	0
1	0.002522	0.010026	96613	969	384030	0.002522	1.500	6137476	63.526	1
5	0.000729	0.003639	95644	348	477351	0.000729	2.500	5753446	60.155	5
10	0.000754	0.003765	95296	359	475606	0.000754	2.560	5276095	55.365	10
15	0.000954	0.004760	94938	452	473620	0.000954	2.638	4800489	50.565	15
20	0.001394	0.006960	94486	658	470844	0.001397	2.592	4326869	45.794	20
25	0.001579	0.007902	93828	741	467409	0.001586	2.666	3856024	41.097	25
30	0.002675	0.013418	93087	1249	462629	0.002700	2.755	3388615	36.403	30
35	0.004970	0.024746	91838	2273	453880	0.005007	2.665	2925986	31.860	35
40	0.006883	0.034007	89565	3046	440713	0.006911	2.665	2472106	27.601	40
45	0.011116	0.054200	86519	4689	421469	0.011126	2.627	2031392	23.479	45
50	0.014967	0.072266	81830	5914	395114	0.014967	2.627	1609923	19.674	50
55	0.022869	0.109168	75916	8288	360467	0.022991	2.694	1214809	16.002	55
60	0.044334	0.201380	67629	13619	305247	0.044617	2.585	854341	12.633	60
65	0.058279	0.255793	54010	13815	236056	0.058525	2.540	549094	10.167	65
70	0.101241	0.404077	40194	16242	159500	0.101828	2.447	313038	7.788	70
75	0.102918	0.402960	23953	9652	94009	0.102671	2.332	153538	6.410	75
80	0.167568	0.590389	14301	8443	49854	0.169355	2.436	59530	4.163	80
85	0.605405	1.000000	5858	5858	9676	0.728542	1.652	9676	1.652	85

TABLE 3 FEMALE LIFE TABLE

x	nM_x	nq_x	l_x	nd_x	nL_x	nm_x	na_x	T_x	$\overset{\circ}{e}_x$	x
0	0.030573	0.029774	100000	2977	97386	0.030573	0.122	7006479	70.065	0
1	0.002210	0.008793	97023	853	385958	0.002210	1.500	6909094	71.211	1
5	0.000525	0.002621	96169	252	480217	0.000525	2.500	6523136	67.830	5
10	0.000507	0.002531	95917	243	479025	0.000507	2.683	6042919	63.001	10
15	0.000976	0.004869	95675	466	477278	0.000976	2.648	5563895	58.154	15
20	0.001209	0.006030	95209	574	474632	0.001209	2.540	5086617	53.426	20
25	0.001221	0.006095	94635	577	471768	0.001223	2.563	4611985	48.735	25
30	0.001592	0.007968	94058	749	468526	0.001600	2.647	4140217	44.018	30
35	0.002370	0.011848	93308	1106	463926	0.002383	2.633	3671691	39.350	35
40	0.003172	0.015779	92203	1455	457504	0.003180	2.587	3207765	34.790	40
45	0.003798	0.018862	90748	1712	449706	0.003806	2.643	2750261	30.307	45
50	0.005972	0.029524	89036	2629	439323	0.005984	2.771	2300555	25.838	50
55	0.012135	0.059414	86408	5134	420080	0.012221	2.671	1861232	21.540	55
60	0.017461	0.084102	81274	6835	390172	0.017519	2.630	1441152	17.732	60
65	0.026751	0.126404	74439	9409	350023	0.026882	2.644	1050980	14.119	65
70	0.045045	0.205014	65029	13332	293376	0.045443	2.617	700957	10.779	70
75	0.077578	0.326817	51697	16896	216684	0.077973	2.526	407581	7.884	75
80	0.113339	0.443297	34802	15428	135690	0.113697	2.516	190897	5.485	80
85	0.350939	1.000000	19374	19374	55207	0.327740	2.849	55207	2.849	85

TABLE 4 OBSERVED VITAL RATES AND RATIOS

CRUDE RATES

Per Thousand	BOTH SEXES	MALES	FEMALES
BIRTH RATE	26.40	27.33	25.50
DEATH RATE	7.21	8.39	6.08
RATE OF INCREASE	19.18	18.94	19.42

PERCENT OF POPULATION IN AGE GROUP

UNDER 15	33.89	34.72	33.08
15 - 64	61.85	61.86	61.85
65 AND OLDER	4.26	3.42	5.07

RATES STANDARDIZED ON USA 1980

Per Thousand	BOTH SEXES	MALES	FEMALES
BIRTH RATE	24.31		23.24
DEATH RATE	16.26	18.14	14.49
RATE OF INCREASE	8.05		8.75

RATES STANDARDIZED ON MEXICO 1980

	BOTH SEXES	MALES	FEMALES
BIRTH RATE	21.88		21.68
DEATH RATE	6.71	8.09	5.30
RATE OF INCREASE	15.18		16.38

VITAL STATISTICS

GFR x 1000	98.925
TFR	2.887
GRR	1.419
NRR	1.338
μ	27.399
σ^2	41.856
GENERATION	27.175
POP. SEX RATIO	1.036
SEX RATIO AT BIRTH	1.034
DEP. RATIO x 100	61.671

PROJECTED POPULATION

AGE GROUP	1985 BOTH SEXES	1985 MALES	1985 FEMALES	1990 BOTH SEXES	1990 MALES	1990 FEMALES
0-4	126	64	62	138	70	68
5-9	112	57	55	126	64	62
10-14	96	48	48	111	56	55
15-19	106	53	53	95	48	47
20-24	114	57	57	105	52	53
25-29	98	48	50	114	57	57
30-34	85	41	44	98	48	50
35-39	62	30	32	84	41	43
40-44	44	21	23	61	29	32
45-49	40	19	21	42	20	22
50-54	34	16	18	38	18	20
55-59	34	17	17	31	14	17
60-64	28	14	14	30	14	16
65-69	18	8	10	23	11	12
70-74	14	5	9	13	5	8
75-79	7	2	5	9	3	6
80-84	4	1	3	4	1	3
85+	1	0	1	1	0	1
TOTAL	1023	501	522	1123	551	572

STABLE EQUIVALENT TO ORIGINAL POPULATION

MALES Number	MALES Percent	FEMALES Number	FEMALES Percent	AGE GROUP	
60	10.6	58	9.8	0-4	
56	9.9	55	9.2	5-9	TABLE 5
53	9.4	52	8.7	10-14	
50	8.9	49	8.2	15-19	POPULATION
47	8.4	46	7.8	20-24	PROJECTED
45	7.9	43	7.3	25-29	WITH
42	7.4	41	6.9	30-34	FIXED
39	6.9	38	6.5	35-39	AGE-
36	6.3	36	6.0	40-44	SPECIFIC
32	5.7	33	5.6	45-49	BIRTH
29	5.1	31	5.2	50-54	AND
25	4.4	28	4.7	55-59	DEATH
20	3.5	25	4.2	60-64	RATES
15	2.6	21	3.5	65-69	(female
9	1.7	17	2.8	70-74	dominant,
5	0.9	12	2.0	75-79	in 000s)
3	0.5	7	1.2	80-84	
0	0.1	3	0.4	85+	
566		595		TOTAL	

VITAL RATES OF PROJECTED POPULATION

Per Thousand	1985 BOTH SEXES	1985 MALES	1985 FEMALES	1990 BOTH SEXES	1990 MALES	1990 FEMALES
BIRTH RATE	27.43	28.42	26.46	26.16	27.14	25.22
DEATH RATE	7.43	8.62	6.29	7.54	8.69	6.44
RATE OF INCREASE	20.00	19.81	20.18	18.62	18.45	18.78

VITAL RATES OF STABLE POPULATION

Per Thousand	MALES	FEMALES	
BIRTH RATE	22.58	20.79	TABLE 6
DEATH RATE	11.86	10.07	PROJECTED
RATE OF INCREASE		10.72	VITAL RATES AND RATIOS (female dominant)

AGE STRUCTURE OF PROJECTED POPULATION

	1985 BOTH SEXES	1985 MALES	1985 FEMALES	1990 BOTH SEXES	1990 MALES	1990 FEMALES
% UNDER 15	32.59	33.61	31.61	33.33	34.50	32.20
% 15-64	63.11	62.96	63.25	62.07	61.76	62.37
% 65 AND OLDER	4.30	3.42	5.15	4.60	3.74	5.43
DEPEND. RATIO x 100	58.46	58.82	58.11	61.11	61.91	60.34

STABLE AGE STRUCTURE

	MALES	FEMALES
% UNDER 15	29.92	27.72
% 15-64	64.36	62.36
% 65 AND OLDER	5.72	9.92
DEPEND. RATIO x 100	55.38	60.35

MATRIX PARAMETERS

AGE GROUP	FEMALE BIRTH RATES	NET MATERNITY FUNCTION	COEFF. OF MATRIX EQUATION	ORIGINAL MATRIX SUB-DIAGONAL	ORIGINAL MATRIX FIRST ROW	STABLE MATRIX FISHER VALUES	STABLE MATRIX REPRODUCTIVE VALUES		
0-4	0.0000	0.0000	0.0000	0.99353	0.00000	1.062	58521	λ_1	1.05506
5-9	0.0000	0.0000	0.0008	0.99752	0.00085	1.128	53729	λ_2	0.35668+0.73347i
10-14	0.0004	0.0017	0.0711	0.99635	0.07179	1.192	63539	λ_4	0.00169+0.56239i
15-19	0.0295	0.1406	0.2713	0.99446	0.27475	1.186	68063	λ_6	-0.39172-0.39339i
20-24	0.0847	0.4020	0.3859	0.99397	0.39293	0.965	48699	r_1	0.01072
25-29	0.0784	0.3697	0.3057	0.99313	0.31316	0.604	26719	r_2	-0.04077+0.22364i
30-34	0.0516	0.2416	0.1873	0.99018	0.19318	0.307	10024	r_4	-0.11511+0.31356i
35-39	0.0286	0.1329	0.0883	0.98616	0.09202	0.120	2777	r_6	-0.11770-0.47081i
40-44	0.0096	0.0438	0.0243	0.98296	0.02562	0.029	610	c_1	5949
45-49	0.0011	0.0047	0.0027	0.97691	0.00293	0.003	60	$2\pi/y$	28.0957
50-54	0.0002	0.0007	0.0004	0.95620	0.00039	0.000	7	Δ	14.3635

TABLE 7

LESLIE MATRIX AND ITS ANALYSIS (females)

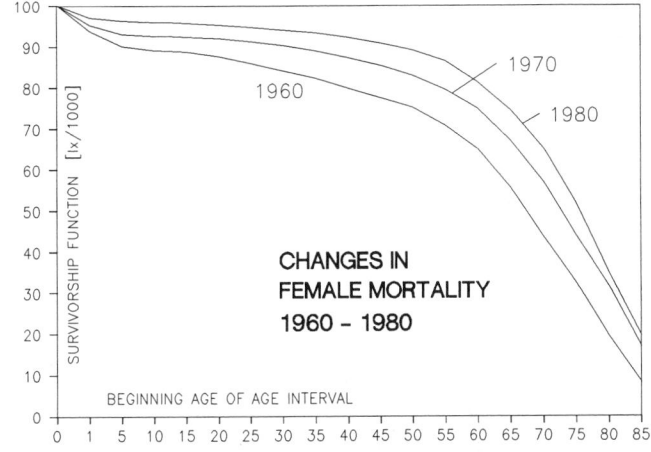

CHANGES IN FEMALE MORTALITY 1960 - 1980

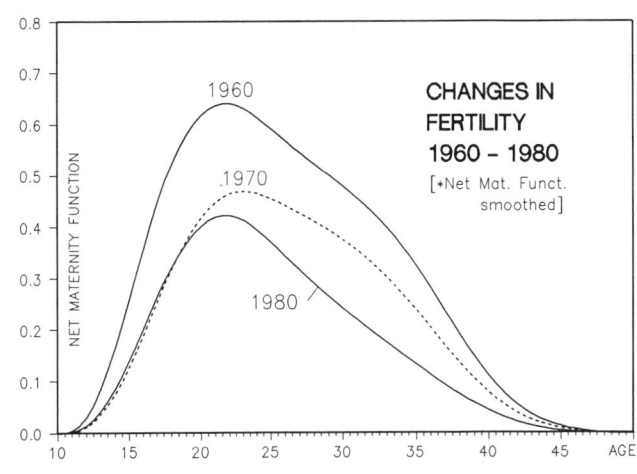

CHANGES IN FERTILITY 1960 - 1980

[+Net Mat. Funct. smoothed]

TABLE 1 — DATA

AGE AT LAST BIRTHDAY	ESTIMATED MID-YEAR POPULATION BOTH SEXES	MALES Number	MALES Percent	FEMALES Number	FEMALES Percent	BIRTHS BY AGE OF MOTHER AND SEX	DEATHS BOTH SEXES	DEATHS MALES	DEATHS FEMALES	AGE AT LAST BIRTHDAY
0	175311	88250	2.8	87061	2.7		12559	6806	5753	0
1-4	673396	338514	10.6	334882	10.3		4617	2333	2284	1-4
5-9	804973	405969	12.7	399004	12.3		734	428	306	5-9
10-14	736428	372610	11.6	363818	11.2	121	502	292	210	10-14
15-19	633793	316889	9.9	316904	9.7	17913	910	610	300	15-19
20-24	560727	275157	8.6	285570	8.8	60990	1313	948	365	20-24
25-29	476929	238164	7.4	238765	7.3	53070	1203	777	426	25-29
30-34	414076	207349	6.5	206727	6.4	31292	1344	853	491	30-34
35-39	367985	184580	5.8	183405	5.6	14738	1577	971	606	35-39
40-44	326189	162712	5.1	163477	5.0	5180	2232	1409	823	40-44
45-49	291785	146425	4.6	145360	4.5	893	2768	1786	982	45-49
50-54	250946	124487	3.9	126459	3.9	200	3606	2289	1317	50-54
55-59	227738	112615	3.5	115123	3.5		4499	2883	1616	55-59
60-64	190495	90567	2.8	99928	3.1		5572	3510	2062	60-64
65-69	130006	60788	1.9	69218	2.1		5542	3310	2232	65-69
70-74	84573	36107	1.1	48466	1.5		5332	2983	2349	70-74
75-79	55735	22397	0.7	33338	1.0		4937	2467	2470	75-79
80-84	31403	11707	0.4	19696	0.6	93619 M	4127	1819	2308	80-84
85+	21865	8225	0.3	13640	0.4	90778 F	4392	1815	2577	85+
TOTAL	6454353	3203512		3250841		184397	67766	38289	29477	TOTAL

TABLE 2 — MALE LIFE TABLE

x	$_nM_x$	$_nq_x$	l_x	$_nd_x$	$_nL_x$	$_nm_x$	$_na_x$	T_x	$\overset{\circ}{e}_x$	x
0	0.077122	0.072646	100000	7265	94196	0.077122	0.201	5765165	57.652	0
1	0.006892	0.027101	92735	2513	364659	0.006892	1.500	5670969	61.152	1
5	0.001054	0.005258	90222	474	449925	0.001054	2.500	5306310	58.814	5
10	0.000784	0.003924	89748	352	447940	0.000786	2.730	4856385	54.111	10
15	0.001925	0.009655	89396	863	445064	0.001939	2.781	4408445	49.314	15
20	0.003445	0.017130	88533	1517	438986	0.003455	2.575	3963381	44.767	20
25	0.003262	0.016192	87016	1409	431606	0.003265	2.534	3524396	40.503	25
30	0.004114	0.020413	85607	1747	423829	0.004123	2.593	3092789	36.128	30
35	0.005261	0.026068	83860	2186	414193	0.005278	2.665	2668961	31.827	35
40	0.008659	0.042544	81674	3475	400194	0.008683	2.647	2254768	27.607	40
45	0.012197	0.059414	78199	4646	380007	0.012226	2.635	1854574	23.716	45
50	0.018387	0.088202	73553	6487	352263	0.018417	2.611	1474567	20.048	50
55	0.025600	0.120667	67065	8093	315925	0.025615	2.603	1122304	16.734	55
60	0.038756	0.177534	58973	10470	269441	0.038857	2.572	806379	13.674	60
65	0.054452	0.241169	48503	11697	213722	0.054732	2.538	536939	11.070	65
70	0.082616	0.343154	36806	12630	152173	0.082997	2.478	323217	8.782	70
75	0.110149	0.428291	24176	10354	93944	0.110217	2.399	171044	7.075	75
80	0.155377	0.549607	13821	7596	48890	0.155377	2.339	77100	5.578	80
85	0.220669	1.000000	6225	6225	28210	0.158344	4.532	28210	4.532	85

TABLE 3 — FEMALE LIFE TABLE

x	$_nM_x$	$_nq_x$	l_x	$_nd_x$	$_nL_x$	$_nm_x$	$_na_x$	T_x	$\overset{\circ}{e}_x$	x
0	0.066080	0.062693	100000	6269	94874	0.066080	0.182	6479558	64.796	0
1	0.006820	0.026824	93731	2514	368637	0.006820	1.500	6384684	68.117	1
5	0.000767	0.003827	91217	349	455210	0.000767	2.500	6016046	65.953	5
10	0.000577	0.002884	90867	262	453699	0.000578	2.564	5560836	61.197	10
15	0.000947	0.004739	90605	429	452019	0.000950	2.653	5107138	56.367	15
20	0.001278	0.006392	90176	576	449516	0.001282	2.634	4655119	51.623	20
25	0.001784	0.008916	89600	799	446100	0.001791	2.624	4205603	46.938	25
30	0.002375	0.011848	88801	1052	441508	0.002383	2.628	3759503	42.336	30
35	0.003304	0.016450	87749	1443	435364	0.003316	2.659	3317995	37.813	35
40	0.005034	0.024942	86305	2153	426428	0.005048	2.632	2882632	33.400	40
45	0.006756	0.033346	84152	2806	414162	0.006776	2.648	2456204	29.188	45
50	0.010414	0.050930	81346	4143	396883	0.010439	2.623	2042042	25.103	50
55	0.014037	0.067985	77203	5249	373512	0.014052	2.618	1645160	21.309	55
60	0.020635	0.098724	71955	7104	342956	0.020713	2.633	1271648	17.673	60
65	0.032246	0.150624	64851	9768	300853	0.032468	2.604	928692	14.320	65
70	0.048467	0.217689	55083	11991	246221	0.048700	2.565	627839	11.398	70
75	0.074090	0.313953	43092	13529	181918	0.074368	2.521	381619	8.856	75
80	0.117181	0.451149	29563	13337	113818	0.117181	2.451	199701	6.755	80
85	0.188930	1.000000	16226	16226	85882	0.120982	5.293	85882	5.293	85

TABLE 4 — OBSERVED VITAL RATES AND RATIOS

CRUDE RATES

Per Thousand	BOTH SEXES	MALES	FEMALES
BIRTH RATE	28.57	29.22	27.92
DEATH RATE	10.50	11.95	9.07
RATE OF INCREASE	18.07	17.27	18.86

RATES STANDARDIZED ON USA 1980

Per Thousand	BOTH SEXES	MALES	FEMALES
BIRTH RATE	31.77		30.42
DEATH RATE	15.59	16.92	14.33
RATE OF INCREASE	16.19		16.09

VITAL STATISTICS

GFR x 1000	119.722
TFR	3.819
GRR	1.880
NRR	1.671
μ	28.135
σ^2	42.644
GENERATION	27.740
POP. SEX RATIO	1.015
SEX RATIO AT BIRTH	1.031
DEP. RATIO x 100	72.546

PERCENT OF POPULATION IN AGE GROUP

	BOTH SEXES	MALES	FEMALES
UNDER 15	37.03	37.63	36.44
15 - 64	57.96	58.03	57.88
65 AND OLDER	5.01	4.35	5.67

RATES STANDARDIZED ON MEXICO 1980

	BOTH SEXES	MALES	FEMALES
BIRTH RATE	28.05		27.83
DEATH RATE	8.54	9.84	7.21
RATE OF INCREASE	19.51		20.62

PROJECTED POPULATION

AGE GROUP	1975 BOTH SEXES	1975 MALES	1975 FEMALES	1980 BOTH SEXES	1980 MALES	1980 FEMALES
0-4	909	459	450	1033	522	511
5-9	832	418	414	892	450	442
10-14	802	404	398	830	417	413
15-19	732	370	362	798	402	396
20-24	628	313	315	725	365	360
25-29	554	271	283	620	307	313
30-34	470	234	236	546	266	280
35-39	407	203	204	462	229	233
40-44	358	178	180	396	196	200
45-49	314	155	159	343	169	174
50-54	275	136	139	295	143	152
55-59	231	112	119	253	122	131
60-64	202	96	106	204	95	109
65-69	160	72	88	169	76	93
70-74	100	43	57	123	51	72
75-79	58	22	36	69	27	42
80-84	33	12	21	34	12	22
85+	22	7	15	23	7	16
TOTAL	7087	3505	3582	7815	3856	3959

STABLE EQUIVALENT TO ORIGINAL POPULATION

MALES Number	MALES Percent	FEMALES Number	FEMALES Percent	AGE GROUP
437	13.3	428	12.5	0-4
391	11.9	383	11.2	5-9
354	10.8	348	10.2	10-14
321	9.8	316	9.2	15-19
289	8.8	287	8.4	20-24
259	7.9	259	7.6	25-29
231	7.0	234	6.8	30-34
206	6.3	210	6.1	35-39
182	5.5	188	5.5	40-44
157	4.8	166	4.9	45-49
133	4.0	145	4.2	50-54
109	3.3	124	3.6	55-59
84	2.6	104	3.0	60-64
61	1.9	83	2.4	65-69
40	1.2	62	1.8	70-74
22	0.7	42	1.2	75-79
11	0.3	24	0.7	80-84
6	0.2	16	0.5	85+
3293		3419		TOTAL

TABLE 5

POPULATION PROJECTED WITH FIXED AGE-SPECIFIC BIRTH AND DEATH RATES (female dominant, in 000s)

VITAL RATES OF PROJECTED POPULATION

Per Thousand	1975 BOTH SEXES	1975 MALES	1975 FEMALES	1980 BOTH SEXES	1980 MALES	1980 FEMALES
BIRTH RATE	29.63	30.42	28.86	30.44	31.33	29.57
DEATH RATE	10.36	11.71	9.04	10.40	11.70	9.13
RATE OF INCREASE	19.27	18.71	19.82	20.04	19.63	20.44

VITAL RATES OF STABLE POPULATION

Per Thousand	MALES	FEMALES
BIRTH RATE	30.27	28.25
DEATH RATE	11.68	9.72
RATE OF INCREASE		18.53

TABLE 6

PROJECTED VITAL RATES AND RATIOS (female dominant)

AGE STRUCTURE OF PROJECTED POPULATION

	1975 BOTH SEXES	1975 MALES	1975 FEMALES	1980 BOTH SEXES	1980 MALES	1980 FEMALES
% UNDER 15	35.90	36.59	35.24	35.25	36.03	34.49
% 15-64	58.85	58.97	58.74	59.42	59.50	59.34
% 65 AND OLDER	5.25	4.45	6.03	5.33	4.47	6.17
DEPEND. RATIO x 100	69.92	69.59	70.25	68.30	68.06	68.53

STABLE AGE STRUCTURE

	MALES	FEMALES
% UNDER 15	35.91	33.90
% 15-64	59.86	59.45
% 65 AND OLDER	4.22	6.65
DEPEND. RATIO x 100	67.04	68.21

AGE GROUP	FEMALE BIRTH RATES	NET MATERNITY FUNCTION	COEFF. OF MATRIX EQUATION	ORIGINAL MATRIX SUB-DIAGONAL	ORIGINAL MATRIX FIRST ROW	STABLE MATRIX FISHER VALUES	STABLE MATRIX REPRODUCTIVE VALUES
0-4	0.0000	0.0000	0.0000	0.98209	0.00000	1.129	476558
5-9	0.0000	0.0000	0.0004	0.99668	0.00038	1.262	503423
10-14	0.0002	0.0007	0.0633	0.99630	0.06463	1.388	505121
15-19	0.0278	0.1258	0.2992	0.99446	0.30681	1.456	461283
20-24	0.1051	0.4726	0.4804	0.99240	0.49534	1.257	359066
25-29	0.1094	0.4881	0.4086	0.98971	0.42451	0.826	197287
30-34	0.0745	0.3290	0.2506	0.98608	0.26311	0.431	89201
35-39	0.0396	0.1722	0.1194	0.97948	0.12709	0.179	32777
40-44	0.0156	0.0665	0.0395	0.97123	0.04296	0.054	8767
45-49	0.0030	0.0125	0.0078	0.95828	0.00874	0.011	1543
50-54	0.0008	0.0031	0.0015	0.94111	0.00180	0.002	235

MATRIX PARAMETERS

λ_1	1.09710
λ_2	$0.37436 - 0.77893i$
λ_4	$-0.38653 - 0.41373i$
λ_6	$-0.49711 + 0.15211i$
r_1	0.01853
r_2	$-0.02919 - 0.22456i$
r_4	$-0.11376 - 0.46444i$
r_6	$-0.13084 + 0.56893i$
c_1	34200
$2\pi/y$	27.9805
Δ	3.4887

TABLE 7

LESLIE MATRIX AND ITS ANALYSIS (females)

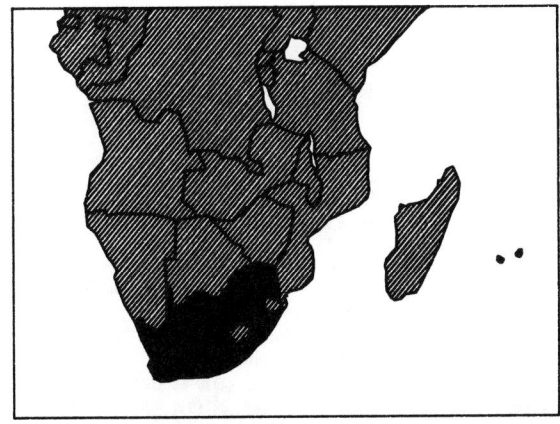

EDUCATION [1984]

% of primary school-age children enrolled:	na
secondary school-age children enrolled:	na
ca. 20-24 year olds in higher education:	na

LABOR FORCE [incl. Black Pop.]

Average annual labor force growth (%) 1980-85:	2.8
% of the 1980 labor force in agriculture:	17
in industry:	35
in services:	49

TABLE 8

SOCIO-ECONOMIC INDICATORS

GNP & INCOME DISTRIBUTION [incl. Black Pop.]

GNP per capita (in US Dollars) 1985:	2010
GNP average annual growth rate (%) 1965-85:	1.1
% share of total household income	
Lowest 20% of households:	na
Highest 10% of households:	na

HEALTH & NUTRITION [incl. Black Pop.]

Population per physician 1981:	na
Daily calorie supply per capita 1985:	2979

TABLE 1 — DATA

AGE AT LAST BIRTHDAY	ESTIMATED MID-YEAR POPULATION BOTH SEXES	MALES Number	Percent	FEMALES Number	Percent	BIRTHS BY AGE OF MOTHER AND SEX	DEATHS BOTH SEXES	MALES	FEMALES	AGE AT LAST BIRTHDAY
0	159827	81324	2.0	78503	1.9		4476	2468	2008	0
1-4	658712	333712	8.3	325000	7.8		1316	676	640	1-4
5-9	785923	398943	9.9	386980	9.2		333	193	140	5-9
10-14	899894	456305	11.3	443589	10.6	135	356	231	125	10-14
15-19	841559	423086	10.5	418473	10.0	20260	793	536	257	15-19
20-24	774318	378156	9.4	396162	9.5	59853	1364	1008	356	20-24
25-29	697038	340656	8.4	356382	8.5	57698	1373	963	410	25-29
30-34	620316	303060	7.5	317256	7.6	31178	1418	927	491	30-34
35-39	561071	276559	6.9	284512	6.8	11729	1792	1159	633	35-39
40-44	470767	233604	5.8	237163	5.7	2654	2221	1395	826	40-44
45-49	397959	197537	4.9	200422	4.8	352	3005	1851	1154	45-49
50-54	332970	162540	4.0	170430	4.1	105	3623	2249	1374	50-54
55-59	277398	133063	3.3	144335	3.4		4721	2931	1790	55-59
60-64	239187	110212	2.7	128975	3.1		5903	3603	2300	60-64
65-69	184845	83428	2.1	101417	2.4		6776	4045	2731	65-69
70-74	148326	62494	1.5	85832	2.1		7523	4216	3307	70-74
75-79	95024	36879	0.9	58145	1.4		7201	3653	3548	75-79
80-84	48720	16694	0.4	32026	0.8	93737 M	5171	2173	2998	80-84
85+	28951	8278	0.2	20673	0.5	90227 F	5577	1744	3833	85+
TOTAL	8222805	4036530		4186275		183964	64942	36021	28921	TOTAL

TABLE 2 — MALE LIFE TABLE

x	nM_x	nq_x	l_x	nd_x	nL_x	nm_x	na_x	T_x	$\overset{\circ}{e}_x$	x
0	0.030348	0.029560	100000	2956	97403	0.030348	0.122	6430880	64.309	0
1	0.002026	0.008062	97044	782	386220	0.002026	1.500	6333477	65.264	1
5	0.000484	0.002416	96262	233	480727	0.000484	2.500	5947257	61.782	5
10	0.000506	0.002528	96029	243	479617	0.000506	2.822	5466530	56.926	10
15	0.001267	0.006345	95786	608	477625	0.001272	2.850	4986913	52.063	15
20	0.002666	0.013275	95179	1263	472882	0.002672	2.617	4509288	47.377	20
25	0.002827	0.014043	93915	1319	466308	0.002828	2.523	4036406	42.979	25
30	0.003059	0.015203	92596	1408	459582	0.003063	2.586	3570098	38.556	30
35	0.004191	0.020803	91188	1897	451456	0.004202	2.635	3110516	34.111	35
40	0.005972	0.029569	89291	2640	440292	0.005997	2.665	2659059	29.780	40
45	0.009370	0.046041	86651	3990	423891	0.009412	2.653	2218767	25.606	45
50	0.013837	0.067305	82662	5564	400255	0.013900	2.654	1794876	21.714	50
55	0.022027	0.104994	77098	8095	366278	0.022100	2.627	1394621	18.089	55
60	0.032692	0.151880	69003	10480	319775	0.032774	2.591	1028343	14.903	60
65	0.048485	0.216947	58523	12696	261449	0.048562	2.545	708569	12.108	65
70	0.067462	0.288600	45827	13239	196086	0.067518	2.504	447120	9.757	70
75	0.099054	0.397104	32587	12941	129812	0.099687	2.440	251034	7.703	75
80	0.130167	0.484862	19647	9526	73183	0.130167	2.370	121222	6.170	80
85	0.210679	1.000000	10121	10121	48039	0.145877	4.747	48039	4.747	85

TABLE 3 — FEMALE LIFE TABLE

x	nM_x	nq_x	l_x	nd_x	nL_x	nm_x	na_x	T_x	$\overset{\circ}{e}_x$	x
0	0.025579	0.025011	100000	2501	97783	0.025579	0.113	7143028	71.430	0
1	0.001969	0.007838	97499	764	388085	0.001969	1.500	7045246	72.260	1
5	0.000362	0.001807	96735	175	483236	0.000362	2.500	6657161	68.819	5
10	0.000282	0.001408	96560	136	482484	0.000282	2.686	6173925	63.939	10
15	0.000614	0.003071	96424	296	481440	0.000615	2.708	5691440	59.025	15
20	0.000899	0.004490	96128	432	479612	0.000900	2.623	5210000	54.199	20
25	0.001150	0.005749	95696	550	477168	0.001153	2.615	4730387	49.431	25
30	0.001548	0.007730	95146	736	473995	0.001552	2.641	4253219	44.702	30
35	0.002225	0.011111	94410	1049	469614	0.002234	2.676	3779224	40.030	35
40	0.003483	0.017376	93361	1622	463078	0.003503	2.701	3309609	35.449	40
45	0.005758	0.028534	91739	2618	452551	0.005784	2.653	2846531	31.029	45
50	0.008062	0.039724	89122	3540	437289	0.008096	2.650	2393979	26.862	50
55	0.012402	0.060405	85581	5170	415682	0.012436	2.635	1956691	22.864	55
60	0.017833	0.085768	80412	6897	385681	0.017882	2.625	1541009	19.164	60
65	0.026928	0.126750	73515	9318	345203	0.026993	2.599	1155328	15.716	65
70	0.038529	0.176502	64197	11331	293659	0.038585	2.588	810125	12.619	70
75	0.061020	0.267197	52866	14126	229720	0.061491	2.550	516466	9.769	75
80	0.093611	0.379714	38740	14710	157142	0.093611	2.515	286746	7.402	80
85	0.185411	1.000000	24030	24030	129605	0.116968	5.393	129605	5.393	85

TABLE 4 — OBSERVED VITAL RATES AND RATIOS

CRUDE RATES

Per Thousand	BOTH SEXES	MALES	FEMALES
BIRTH RATE	22.37	23.22	21.55
DEATH RATE	7.90	8.92	6.91
RATE OF INCREASE	14.47	14.30	14.64

RATES STANDARDIZED ON USA 1980

Per Thousand	BOTH SEXES	MALES	FEMALES
BIRTH RATE	21.86		20.85
DEATH RATE	12.38	13.43	11.38
RATE OF INCREASE	9.48		9.47

VITAL STATISTICS

GFR x 1000	83.228
TFR	2.574
GRR	1.262
NRR	1.203
μ	27.212
σ^2	36.306
GENERATION	27.088
POP. SEX RATIO	1.037
SEX RATIO AT BIRTH	1.039
DEP. RATIO x 100	57.749

PERCENT OF POPULATION IN AGE GROUP

	BOTH SEXES	MALES	FEMALES
UNDER 15	30.46	31.47	29.48
15 - 64	63.39	63.38	63.40
65 AND OLDER	6.15	5.15	7.12

RATES STANDARDIZED ON MEXICO 1980

	BOTH SEXES	MALES	FEMALES
BIRTH RATE	19.57		19.34
DEATH RATE	5.58	6.60	4.55
RATE OF INCREASE	13.99		14.80

PROJECTED POPULATION

AGE GROUP	1990 BOTH SEXES	1990 MALES	1990 FEMALES	1995 BOTH SEXES	1995 MALES	1995 FEMALES
0-4	930	473	457	992	504	488
5-9	814	413	401	925	470	455
10-14	784	398	386	813	412	401
15-19	897	454	443	782	396	386
20-24	836	419	417	891	450	441
25-29	767	373	394	828	413	415
30-34	690	336	354	760	368	392
35-39	612	298	314	681	330	351
40-44	551	270	281	600	290	310
45-49	457	225	232	534	260	274
50-54	381	187	194	436	212	224
55-59	311	149	162	355	171	184
60-64	250	116	134	280	130	150
65-69	205	90	115	215	95	120
70-74	149	63	86	166	68	98
75-79	108	41	67	108	41	67
80-84	61	21	40	69	23	46
85+	37	11	26	47	14	33
TOTAL	8840	4337	4503	9482	4647	4835

STABLE EQUIVALENT TO ORIGINAL POPULATION

MALES Number	MALES Percent	FEMALES Number	FEMALES Percent	AGE GROUP	
453	9.3	438	8.6	0-4	
435	8.9	421	8.3	5-9	TABLE 5
419	8.6	406	8.0	10-14	
404	8.3	392	7.7	15-19	POPULATION
386	7.9	377	7.4	20-24	PROJECTED
368	7.6	362	7.1	25-29	WITH
350	7.2	348	6.8	30-34	FIXED
333	6.8	333	6.5	35-39	AGE-
314	6.4	317	6.2	40-44	SPECIFIC
292	6.0	300	5.9	45-49	BIRTH
266	5.5	280	5.5	50-54	AND
235	4.8	257	5.0	55-59	DEATH
199	4.1	231	4.5	60-64	RATES
157	3.2	199	3.9	65-69	(female
114	2.3	164	3.2	70-74	dominant,
73	1.5	124	2.4	75-79	in 000s)
40	0.8	82	1.6	80-84	
25	0.5	65	1.3	85+	
4863		5096		TOTAL	

VITAL RATES OF PROJECTED POPULATION

Per Thousand	1990 BOTH SEXES	1990 MALES	1990 FEMALES	1995 BOTH SEXES	1995 MALES	1995 FEMALES
BIRTH RATE	22.60	23.48	21.75	22.11	22.98	21.27
DEATH RATE	8.27	9.25	7.33	8.53	9.45	7.64
RATE OF INCREASE	14.33	14.23	14.42	13.58	13.53	13.63

VITAL RATES OF STABLE POPULATION

Per Thousand	MALES	FEMALES	
BIRTH RATE	19.59	17.99	TABLE 6
DEATH RATE	12.71	11.15	PROJECTED
RATE OF INCREASE		6.84	VITAL RATES

AGE STRUCTURE OF PROJECTED POPULATION

	1990 BOTH SEXES	1990 MALES	1990 FEMALES	1995 BOTH SEXES	1995 MALES	1995 FEMALES
% UNDER 15	28.60	29.61	27.64	28.79	29.83	27.79
% 15-64	65.05	65.19	64.92	64.83	64.99	64.67
% 65 AND OLDER	6.35	5.21	7.44	6.38	5.19	7.54
DEPEND. RATIO x 100	53.73	53.41	54.04	54.26	53.88	54.62

STABLE AGE STRUCTURE

	MALES	FEMALES	
% UNDER 15	26.89	24.82	AND RATIOS
% 15-64	64.72	62.73	(female
% 65 AND OLDER	8.40	12.45	dominant)
DEPEND. RATIO x 100	54.52	59.41	

AGE GROUP	FEMALE BIRTH RATES	NET MATERNITY FUNCTION	COEFF. OF MATRIX EQUATION	ORIGINAL MATRIX SUB-DIAGONAL	ORIGINAL MATRIX FIRST ROW	STABLE MATRIX FISHER VALUES	STABLE MATRIX REPRODUCTIVE VALUES	MATRIX PARAMETERS		
0-4	0.0000	0.0000	0.0000	0.99458	0.00000	1.047	422382	λ_1	1.03479	
5-9	0.0000	0.0000	0.0004	0.99844	0.00036	1.089	421462	λ_2	0.35545+0.75752i	TABLE 7
10-14	0.0001	0.0007	0.0575	0.99784	0.05792	1.128	500533	λ_4	-0.35661+0.37861i	
15-19	0.0237	0.1143	0.2349	0.99620	0.23701	1.109	464252	λ_6	-0.11844+0.47079i	LESLIE
20-24	0.0741	0.3554	0.3671	0.99490	0.37193	0.903	357860	r_1	0.00684	MATRIX
25-29	0.0794	0.3789	0.3037	0.99335	0.30922	0.548	195370	r_2	-0.03564+0.22641i	AND ITS
30-34	0.0482	0.2285	0.1617	0.99076	0.16576	0.245	77798	r_4	-0.13074+0.46526i	ANALYSIS
35-39	0.0202	0.0950	0.0602	0.98608	0.06227	0.081	23042	r_6	-0.14453+0.36345i	(females)
40-44	0.0055	0.0254	0.0147	0.97727	0.01538	0.019	4480	c_1	50963	
45-49	0.0009	0.0039	0.0026	0.96627	0.00280	0.004	707	$2\pi/\gamma$	27.7509	
50-54	0.0003	0.0013	0.0007	0.95059	0.00073	0.001	127	Δ	11.4534	

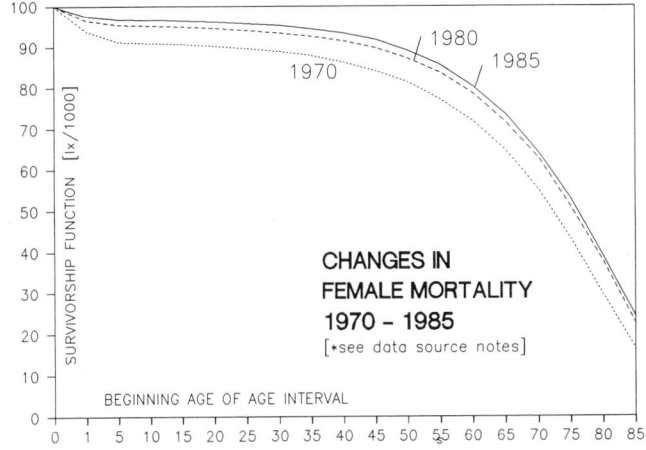

CHANGES IN FEMALE MORTALITY 1970 – 1985

[*see data source notes]

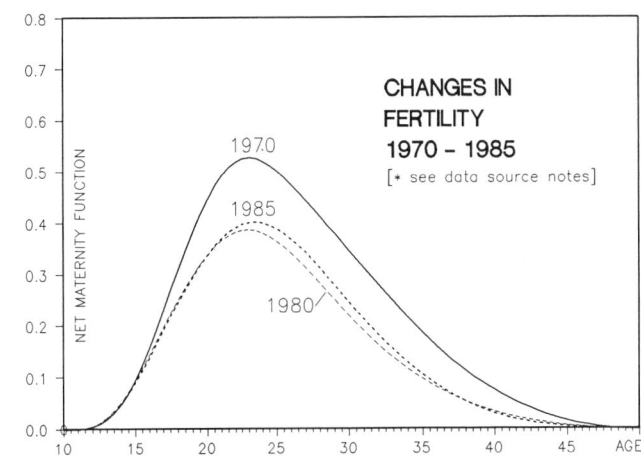

CHANGES IN FERTILITY 1970 – 1985

[* see data source notes]

AGE AT LAST BIRTHDAY	ESTIMATED MID-YEAR POPULATION					BIRTHS BY AGE OF MOTHER AND SEX	DEATHS			AGE AT LAST BIRTHDAY
	BOTH SEXES	MALES Number	MALES Percent	FEMALES Number	FEMALES Percent		BOTH SEXES	MALES	FEMALES	
0	522369	271019	2.3	251350	2.1		32355	17829	14526	0
1-4	1890525	955200	8.0	935325	7.8		6285	3228	3057	1-4
5-9	2353168	1191490	10.0	1161678	9.6		1698	971	727	5-9
10-14	2254974	1141547	9.6	1113427	9.2	1993	1454	873	581	10-14
15-19	2150018	1084741	9.1	1065277	8.8	67981	2561	1546	1015	15-19
20-24	1998195	993668	8.3	1004527	8.3	154447	3188	1997	1191	20-24
25-29	1744336	863153	7.3	881183	7.3	146058	3262	2014	1248	25-29
30-34	1618994	803888	6.8	815106	6.8	94232	3753	2272	1481	30-34
35-39	1584214	798049	6.7	786165	6.5	54092	5038	3170	1868	35-39
40-44	1576735	788316	6.6	788419	6.5	20460	6937	4614	2323	40-44
45-49	1416305	700264	5.9	716041	5.9	3914	9026	5992	3034	45-49
50-54	1175149	576049	4.8	599100	5.0	1344	11439	7750	3689	50-54
55-59	1093142	530462	4.5	562680	4.7		15420	10349	5071	55-59
60-64	912582	446712	3.8	465870	3.9		19421	12940	6481	60-64
65-69	688995	329976	2.8	359019	3.0		22727	14656	8071	65-69
70-74	457367	207196	1.7	250171	2.1		23221	13785	9436	70-74
75-79	286541	126162	1.1	160379	1.3		21476	11767	9709	75-79
80-84	155563	63977	0.5	91586	0.8	276206 M	17580	8654	8926	80-84
85+	82828	29197	0.2	53631	0.4	268315 F	15272	6324	8948	85+
TOTAL	23962000	11901066		12060934		544521	222113	130731	91382	TOTAL

TABLE 1 — DATA

TABLE 2 — MALE LIFE TABLE

x	nM_x	nq_x	l_x	nd_x	nL_x	nm_x	na_x	T_x	$\overset{\circ}{e}_x$	x
0	0.065785	0.062425	100000	6243	94893	0.065785	0.182	6250840	62.508	0
1	0.003379	0.013404	93757	1257	371888	0.003379	1.500	6155947	65.658	1
5	0.000815	0.004066	92501	376	461563	0.000815	2.500	5784059	62.530	5
10	0.000765	0.003821	92125	352	459801	0.000765	2.664	5322496	57.775	10
15	0.001425	0.007114	91773	653	457348	0.001428	2.679	4862696	52.986	15
20	0.002010	0.010017	91120	913	453399	0.002013	2.590	4405348	48.347	20
25	0.002333	0.011617	90207	1048	448486	0.002337	2.568	3951949	43.810	25
30	0.002826	0.014053	89159	1253	442805	0.002830	2.613	3503463	39.295	30
35	0.003972	0.019677	87906	1730	435643	0.003972	2.649	3060658	34.817	35
40	0.005853	0.028877	86176	2489	425034	0.005855	2.650	2625195	30.463	40
45	0.008557	0.042075	83688	3521	410210	0.008584	2.663	2200161	26.290	45
50	0.013454	0.065378	80167	5241	388454	0.013492	2.638	1789951	22.328	50
55	0.019509	0.093307	74926	6991	357979	0.019529	2.619	1401498	18.705	55
60	0.028967	0.135706	67934	9219	317631	0.029025	2.609	1043519	15.361	60
65	0.044415	0.201322	58715	11821	264905	0.044622	2.574	725888	12.363	65
70	0.066531	0.286633	46895	13442	201042	0.066860	2.513	460983	9.830	70
75	0.093269	0.378093	33453	12648	135011	0.093684	2.450	259942	7.770	75
80	0.135267	0.500031	20805	10403	76907	0.135267	2.393	124930	6.005	80
85	0.216598	1.000000	10402	10402	48023	0.152523	4.617	48023	4.617	85

TABLE 3 — FEMALE LIFE TABLE

x	nM_x	nq_x	l_x	nd_x	nL_x	nm_x	na_x	T_x	$\overset{\circ}{e}_x$	x
0	0.057792	0.055141	100000	5514	95414	0.057792	0.168	6982804	69.828	0
1	0.003268	0.012968	94486	1225	374880	0.003268	1.500	6887391	72.893	1
5	0.000626	0.003124	93261	291	465575	0.000626	2.500	6512510	69.831	5
10	0.000522	0.002608	92969	242	464271	0.000522	2.629	6046936	65.042	10
15	0.000953	0.004758	92727	441	462594	0.000954	2.643	5582664	60.205	15
20	0.001186	0.005918	92286	546	460106	0.001187	2.579	5120070	55.481	20
25	0.001416	0.007069	91739	649	457134	0.001419	2.590	4659964	50.796	25
30	0.001817	0.009059	91091	825	453479	0.001820	2.606	4202830	46.139	30
35	0.002376	0.011818	90266	1067	448762	0.002377	2.594	3749351	41.537	35
40	0.002946	0.014633	89199	1305	442895	0.002947	2.625	3300589	37.003	40
45	0.004237	0.021036	87894	1849	435120	0.004249	2.648	2857694	32.513	45
50	0.006158	0.030435	86045	2619	424061	0.006176	2.646	2422573	28.155	50
55	0.009012	0.044231	83426	3690	408484	0.009033	2.657	1998512	23.955	55
60	0.013912	0.067671	79736	5396	386087	0.013976	2.666	1590029	19.941	60
65	0.022481	0.107504	74340	7992	353008	0.022639	2.661	1203942	16.195	65
70	0.037718	0.174369	66348	11569	304186	0.038033	2.618	850934	12.825	70
75	0.060538	0.265629	54779	14551	238392	0.061038	2.560	546749	9.981	75
80	0.097460	0.391739	40228	15759	161697	0.097460	2.497	308357	7.665	80
85	0.166844	1.000000	24469	24469	146660	0.097657	5.994	146660	5.994	85

TABLE 4 — OBSERVED VITAL RATES AND RATIOS

CRUDE RATES

Per Thousand	BOTH SEXES	MALES	FEMALES
BIRTH RATE	22.72	23.21	22.25
DEATH RATE	9.27	10.98	7.58
RATE OF INCREASE	13.45	12.22	14.67

PERCENT OF POPULATION IN AGE GROUP

	BOTH SEXES	MALES	FEMALES
UNDER 15	29.30	29.91	28.70
15 - 64	63.72	63.74	63.71
65 AND OLDER	6.97	6.36	7.58

RATES STANDARDIZED ON USA 1980

Per Thousand	BOTH SEXES	MALES	FEMALES
BIRTH RATE	24.99		23.95
DEATH RATE	12.26	13.49	11.10
RATE OF INCREASE	12.73		12.85

RATES STANDARDIZED ON MEXICO 1980

	BOTH SEXES	MALES	FEMALES
BIRTH RATE	22.34		22.19
DEATH RATE	6.51	7.56	5.43
RATE OF INCREASE	15.83		16.75

VITAL STATISTICS

GFR x 1000	89.904
TFR	3.016
GRR	1.486
NRR	1.355
μ	28.057
σ^2	48.556
GENERATION	27.792
POP. SEX RATIO	1.013
SEX RATIO AT BIRTH	1.029
DEP. RATIO x 100	56.925

PROJECTED POPULATION

STABLE EQUIVALENT TO ORIGINAL POPULATION

AGE GROUP	1975 BOTH SEXES	1975 MALES	1975 FEMALES	1980 BOTH SEXES	1980 MALES	1980 FEMALES	MALES Number	MALES Percent	FEMALES Number	FEMALES Percent	AGE GROUP	
0-4	2643	1336	1307	2820	1425	1395	1265	*10.4*	1238	*9.7*	0-4	
5-9	2388	1213	1175	2615	1321	1294	1184	*9.8*	1160	*9.1*	5-9	TABLE 5
10-14	2345	1187	1158	2379	1208	1171	1117	*9.2*	1095	*8.6*	10-14	
15-19	2244	1135	1109	2335	1181	1154	1051	*8.7*	1033	*8.1*	15-19	POPULATION
20-24	2135	1075	1060	2229	1126	1103	987	*8.1*	973	*7.6*	20-24	PROJECTED
25-29	1981	983	998	2117	1064	1053	924	*7.6*	915	*7.2*	25-29	WITH
30-34	1726	852	874	1960	970	990	864	*7.1*	859	*6.8*	30-34	FIXED
35-39	1598	791	807	1703	838	865	804	*6.6*	805	*6.3*	35-39	AGE-
40-44	1555	779	776	1568	772	796	743	*6.1*	752	*5.9*	40-44	SPECIFIC
45-49	1536	761	775	1514	752	762	679	*5.6*	700	*5.5*	45-49	BIRTH
50-54	1361	663	698	1475	720	755	609	*5.0*	646	*5.1*	50-54	AND
55-59	1108	531	577	1283	611	672	531	*4.4*	589	*4.6*	55-59	DEATH
60-64	1003	471	532	1016	471	545	446	*3.7*	527	*4.1*	60-64	RATES
65-69	799	373	426	879	393	486	352	*2.9*	456	*3.6*	65-69	(female
70-74	559	250	309	650	283	367	253	*2.1*	372	*2.9*	70-74	dominant,
75-79	335	139	196	410	168	242	161	*1.3*	276	*2.2*	75-79	in 000s)
80-84	181	72	109	212	79	133	87	*0.7*	177	*1.4*	80-84	
85+	123	40	83	144	45	99	51	*0.4*	152	*1.2*	85+	
TOTAL	25620	12651	12969	27309	13427	13882	12108		12725		TOTAL	

VITAL RATES OF PROJECTED POPULATION

VITAL RATES OF STABLE POPULATION

Per Thousand	1975 BOTH SEXES	1975 MALES	1975 FEMALES	1980 BOTH SEXES	1980 MALES	1980 FEMALES	Per Thousand	MALES	FEMALES	
BIRTH RATE	22.78	23.41	22.18	22.72	23.44	22.02	BIRTH RATE	22.99	21.25	TABLE 6
DEATH RATE	9.87	11.46	8.33	10.26	11.74	8.83	DEATH RATE	12.12	10.30	PROJECTED
RATE OF INCREASE	12.91	11.94	13.85	12.46	11.70	13.19	RATE OF INCREASE		10.94	VITAL RATES

AGE STRUCTURE OF PROJECTED POPULATION

STABLE AGE STRUCTURE

								MALES	FEMALES	AND RATIOS
% UNDER 15	28.79	29.53	28.07	28.61	29.45	27.81	% UNDER 15	29.44	27.45	(female
% 15-64	63.41	63.56	63.27	62.98	63.34	62.63	% 15-64	63.09	61.29	dominant)
% 65 AND OLDER	7.80	6.91	8.66	8.40	7.21	9.56	% 65 AND OLDER	7.47	11.27	
DEPEND. RATIO x 100	57.69	57.32	58.06	58.78	57.87	59.66	DEPEND. RATIO x 100	58.51	63.17	

AGE GROUP	FEMALE BIRTH RATES	NET MATERNITY FUNCTION	COEFF. OF MATRIX EQUATION	ORIGINAL MATRIX SUB-DIAGONAL	ORIGINAL MATRIX FIRST ROW	STABLE MATRIX FISHER VALUES	STABLE MATRIX REPRODUCTIVE VALUES	MATRIX PARAMETERS		
0-4	0.0000	0.0000	0.0000	0.98997	0.00000	1.093	1296445	λ_1	1.05625	
5-9	0.0000	0.0000	0.0020	0.99720	0.00207	1.166	1354108	λ_2	0.37978-0.72002i	TABLE 7
10-14	0.0009	0.0041	0.0748	0.99639	0.07575	1.232	1372189	λ_4	-0.40454+0.41498i	
15-19	0.0314	0.1455	0.2470	0.99462	0.25113	1.223	1303240	λ_6	-0.04569+0.55059i	LESLIE
20-24	0.0758	0.3486	0.3610	0.99354	0.36897	1.023	1027963	r_1	0.01094	MATRIX
25-29	0.0817	0.3734	0.3158	0.99200	0.32494	0.682	601141	r_2	-0.04115-0.21708i	AND ITS
30-34	0.0570	0.2583	0.2052	0.98960	0.21285	0.369	300381	r_4	-0.10911+0.46869i	ANALYSIS
35-39	0.0339	0.1521	0.1044	0.98693	0.10940	0.158	124493	r_6	-0.11867+0.33072i	(females)
40-44	0.0128	0.0566	0.0342	0.98245	0.03629	0.048	38140	c_1	127258	
45-49	0.0027	0.0117	0.0082	0.97458	0.00887	0.012	8343	$2\pi/y$	28.9436	
50-54	0.0011	0.0047	0.0023	0.96327	0.00260	0.003	1611	Δ	4.0669	

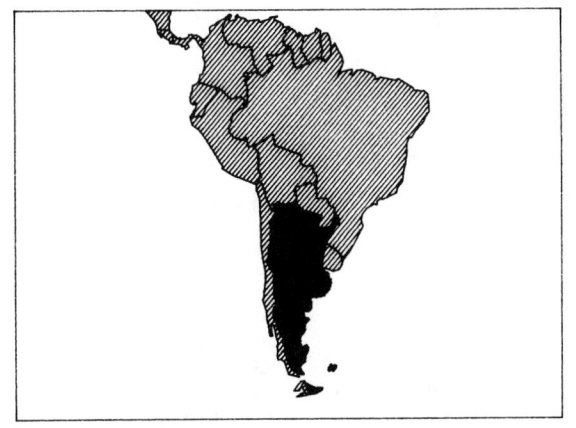

EDUCATION [1984]

% of primary school-age children enrolled:	107
secondary school-age children enrolled:	65
ca. 20-24 year olds in higher education:	29

LABOR FORCE

Average annual labor force growth (%) 1980-85:	1.1	
% of the 1980 labor force in agriculture:	13	TABLE 8
in industry:	34	
in services:	53	SOCIO-ECONOMIC

GNP & INCOME DISTRIBUTION

GNP per capita (in US Dollars) 1985:	2130	INDICATORS
GNP average annual growth rate (%) 1965-85:	0.2	
% share of total household income 1970		
Lowest 20% of households:	4.4	
Highest 10% of households:	35.2	

HEALTH & NUTRITION

Population per physician 1981:	*na*
Daily calorie supply per capita 1985:	3221

TABLE 1 — DATA

AGE AT LAST BIRTHDAY	ESTIMATED MID-YEAR POPULATION BOTH SEXES	MALES Number	MALES Percent	FEMALES Number	FEMALES Percent	BIRTHS BY AGE OF MOTHER AND SEX	DEATHS BOTH SEXES	DEATHS MALES	DEATHS FEMALES	AGE AT LAST BIRTHDAY
0	4367	2206	2.0	2161	1.7		228	129	99	0
1-4	21445	10859	9.8	10586	8.5		46	26	20	1-4
5-9	31305	15796	14.3	15509	12.4		19	12	7	5-9
10-14	30318	15042	13.6	15276	12.2	27	13	8	5	10-14
15-19	25781	12869	11.6	12912	10.3	1188	18	10	8	15-19
20-24	19496	9905	8.9	9591	7.7	1567	28	20	8	20-24
25-29	12026	5742	5.2	6284	5.0	979	23	15	8	25-29
30-34	10691	4823	4.4	5868	4.7	596	20	12	8	30-34
35-39	10141	4308	3.9	5833	4.7	351	26	18	8	35-39
40-44	10786	4554	4.1	6232	5.0	154	47	28	19	40-44
45-49	9896	4313	3.9	5583	4.5	19	54	30	24	45-49
50-54	10873	4801	4.3	6072	4.9	2	84	43	41	50-54
55-59	10026	4481	4.0	5545	4.4		105	45	60	55-59
60-64	9194	4210	3.8	4984	4.0		171	104	67	60-64
65-69	8134	3412	3.1	4722	3.8		254	142	112	65-69
70-74	5300	1938	1.7	3362	2.7		263	125	138	70-74
75-79	3102	929	0.8	2173	1.7		205	71	134	75-79
80-84	1668	364	0.3	1304	1.0	2421 M	200	61	139	80-84
85+	1337	259	0.2	1078	0.9	2462 F	260	58	202	85+
TOTAL	235886	110811		125075		4883	2064	957	1107	TOTAL

TABLE 2 — MALE LIFE TABLE

x	nM_x	nq_x	l_x	nd_x	nL_x	nm_x	na_x	T_x	$\overset{\circ}{e}_x$	x
0	0.058477	0.055768	100000	5577	95368	0.058477	0.169	6486348	64.863	0
1	0.002394	0.009520	94423	899	375445	0.002394	1.500	6390980	67.684	1
5	0.000760	0.003791	93524	355	466735	0.000760	2.500	6015535	64.321	5
10	0.000532	0.002655	93170	247	465232	0.000532	2.508	5548800	59.556	10
15	0.000777	0.003921	92922	364	463844	0.000786	2.895	5083568	54.708	15
20	0.002019	0.010131	92558	938	460617	0.002036	2.684	4619724	49.912	20
25	0.002612	0.013001	91620	1191	455161	0.002617	2.532	4159106	45.395	25
30	0.002488	0.012402	90429	1122	449479	0.002495	2.623	3703945	40.960	30
35	0.004178	0.020726	89308	1851	442228	0.004186	2.672	3254466	36.441	35
40	0.006148	0.030292	87456	2649	430878	0.006148	2.583	2812238	32.156	40
45	0.006956	0.034200	84807	2900	416981	0.006956	2.568	2381360	28.080	45
50	0.008956	0.043823	81907	3589	400758	0.008956	2.555	1964379	23.983	50
55	0.010042	0.049119	78317	3847	383036	0.010043	2.777	1563621	19.965	55
60	0.024703	0.116895	74471	8705	352393	0.024703	2.707	1180585	15.853	60
65	0.041618	0.190107	65765	12502	298858	0.041834	2.603	828192	12.593	65
70	0.064499	0.279407	53263	14882	229078	0.064965	2.498	529334	9.938	70
75	0.076426	0.321795	38381	12351	161106	0.076662	2.506	300256	7.823	75
80	0.167582	0.586159	26030	15258	91046	0.167583	2.437	139150	5.346	80
85	0.223938	1.000000	10772	10772	48104	0.160983	4.466	48104	4.466	85

TABLE 3 — FEMALE LIFE TABLE

x	nM_x	nq_x	l_x	nd_x	nL_x	nm_x	na_x	T_x	$\overset{\circ}{e}_x$	x
0	0.045812	0.044091	100000	4409	96243	0.045812	0.148	7095717	70.957	0
1	0.001889	0.007522	95591	719	380566	0.001889	1.500	6999474	73.223	1
5	0.000451	0.002254	94872	214	473825	0.000451	2.500	6618908	69.767	5
10	0.000327	0.001637	94658	155	472920	0.000328	2.608	6145083	64.919	10
15	0.000620	0.003111	94503	294	471830	0.000623	2.669	5672164	60.021	15
20	0.000834	0.004182	94209	394	470124	0.000838	2.660	5200333	55.200	20
25	0.001273	0.006368	93815	597	467632	0.001277	2.583	4730210	50.421	25
30	0.001363	0.006795	93218	633	464512	0.001364	2.512	4262578	45.727	30
35	0.001372	0.006836	92584	633	461497	0.001372	2.750	3798065	41.023	35
40	0.003049	0.015142	91951	1392	456545	0.003050	2.694	3336568	36.286	40
45	0.004299	0.021280	90559	1927	448301	0.004299	2.668	2880023	31.803	45
50	0.006752	0.033242	88632	2946	436335	0.006752	2.684	2431722	27.436	50
55	0.010821	0.052800	85686	4524	417606	0.010834	2.608	1995387	23.287	55
60	0.013443	0.065179	81161	5290	393419	0.013446	2.658	1577782	19.440	60
65	0.023719	0.112596	75871	8543	359533	0.023761	2.680	1184362	15.610	65
70	0.041047	0.187911	67329	12652	306304	0.041305	2.602	824829	12.251	70
75	0.061666	0.269540	54677	14738	237406	0.062078	2.559	518525	9.483	75
80	0.106595	0.420815	39939	16807	157671	0.106595	2.500	281119	7.039	80
85	0.187384	1.000000	23132	23132	123448	0.119109	5.337	123448	5.337	85

TABLE 4 — OBSERVED VITAL RATES AND RATIOS

CRUDE RATES

Per Thousand	BOTH SEXES	MALES	FEMALES
BIRTH RATE	20.70	21.85	19.68
DEATH RATE	8.75	8.64	8.85
RATE OF INCREASE	11.95	13.21	10.83

PERCENT OF POPULATION IN AGE GROUP

	BOTH SEXES	MALES	FEMALES
UNDER 15	37.07	39.62	34.80
15 - 64	54.65	54.15	55.09
65 AND OLDER	8.28	6.23	10.11

RATES STANDARDIZED ON USA 1980

Per Thousand	BOTH SEXES	MALES	FEMALES
BIRTH RATE	25.35		24.85
DEATH RATE	11.78	12.20	11.38
RATE OF INCREASE	13.57		13.47

RATES STANDARDIZED ON MEXICO 1980

	BOTH SEXES	MALES	FEMALES
BIRTH RATE	23.26		23.64
DEATH RATE	5.79	6.66	4.91
RATE OF INCREASE	17.47		18.73

VITAL STATISTICS

GFR x 1000	93.360
TFR	3.016
GRR	1.521
NRR	1.421
μ	27.096
σ^2	48.254
GENERATION	26.780
POP. SEX RATIO	1.129
SEX RATIO AT BIRTH	0.983
DEP. RATIO x 100	82.985

PROJECTED POPULATION

STABLE EQUIVALENT TO ORIGINAL POPULATION

AGE GROUP	1975			1980			MALES		FEMALES		AGE GROUP	
	BOTH SEXES	MALES	FEMALES	BOTH SEXES	MALES	FEMALES	Number	Percent	Number	Percent		
0-4	26	13	13	32	16	16	14	10.9	14	10.3	0-4	
5-9	26	13	13	26	13	13	13	10.1	13	9.6	5-9	TABLE 5
10-14	31	16	15	26	13	13	12	9.4	13	9.0	10-14	
15-19	30	15	15	31	16	15	11	8.8	12	8.4	15-19	POPULATION
20-24	26	13	13	30	15	15	11	8.2	11	7.8	20-24	PROJECTED
25-29	20	10	10	26	13	13	10	7.6	10	7.3	25-29	WITH
30-34	12	6	6	19	10	9	9	7.0	9	6.8	30-34	FIXED
35-39	11	5	6	12	6	6	8	6.5	9	6.3	35-39	AGE-
40-44	10	4	6	11	5	6	8	5.9	8	5.9	40-44	SPECIFIC
45-49	10	4	6	10	4	6	7	5.3	8	5.4	45-49	BIRTH
50-54	9	4	5	10	4	6	6	4.8	7	4.9	50-54	AND
55-59	11	5	6	9	4	5	6	4.3	6	4.4	55-59	DEATH
60-64	9	4	5	9	4	5	5	3.7	5	3.9	60-64	RATES
65-69	9	4	5	8	3	5	4	2.9	5	3.3	65-69	(female
70-74	7	3	4	7	3	4	3	2.1	4	2.6	70-74	dominant,
75-79	4	1	3	5	2	3	2	1.4	3	1.9	75-79	in 000s)
80-84	2	1	1	3	1	2	1	0.7	2	1.2	80-84	
85+	1	0	1	1	0	1	0	0.4	1	0.9	85+	
TOTAL	254	121	133	275	132	143	130		140		TOTAL	

VITAL RATES OF PROJECTED POPULATION

VITAL RATES OF STABLE POPULATION

Per Thousand	1975			1980				MALES	FEMALES	TABLE 6
	BOTH SEXES	MALES	FEMALES	BOTH SEXES	MALES	FEMALES	Per Thousand			
BIRTH RATE	24.43	25.63	23.36	27.05	28.24	25.98	BIRTH RATE	23.87	22.40	
DEATH RATE	8.87	8.90	8.83	9.17	9.37	9.00	DEATH RATE	10.50	9.26	PROJECTED
RATE OF INCREASE	15.56	16.73	14.52	17.88	18.87	16.98	RATE OF INCREASE		13.14	VITAL RATES AND RATIOS (female dominant)

AGE STRUCTURE OF PROJECTED POPULATION

STABLE AGE STRUCTURE

	1975 BOTH SEXES	MALES	FEMALES	1980 BOTH SEXES	MALES	FEMALES		MALES	FEMALES	
% UNDER 15	32.89	34.87	31.11	30.53	31.90	29.29	% UNDER 15	30.41	28.96	
% 15-64	58.43	58.21	58.64	60.81	61.09	60.54	% 15-64	62.05	61.08	
% 65 AND OLDER	8.68	6.93	10.25	8.66	7.00	10.16	% 65 AND OLDER	7.54	9.96	
DEPEND. RATIO x 100	71.14	71.80	70.54	64.46	63.68	65.17	DEPEND. RATIO x 100	61.16	63.72	

AGE GROUP	FEMALE BIRTH RATES	NET MATERNITY FUNCTION	COEFF. OF MATRIX EQUATION	ORIGINAL MATRIX SUB-DIAGONAL	FIRST ROW	STABLE MATRIX FISHER VALUES	REPRODUCTIVE VALUES	MATRIX PARAMETERS		
0-4	0.0000	0.0000	0.0000	0.99374	0.00000	1.083	13811	λ_1	1.06788	
5-9	0.0000	0.0000	0.0021	0.99809	0.00212	1.164	18057	λ_2	0.34956+0.69909i	TABLE 7
10-14	0.0009	0.0042	0.1115	0.99770	0.11247	1.243	18995	λ_4	0.03827+0.59756i	
15-19	0.0464	0.2189	0.3031	0.99638	0.30628	1.209	15608	λ_6	-0.36289+0.43203i	LESLIE
20-24	0.0824	0.3873	0.3773	0.99470	0.38267	0.962	9231	r_1	0.01314	MATRIX
25-29	0.0786	0.3673	0.3026	0.99333	0.30854	0.616	3874	r_2	-0.04928+0.22143i	AND ITS
30-34	0.0512	0.2379	0.1889	0.99351	0.19395	0.326	1914	r_4	-0.10257+0.30137i	ANALYSIS
35-39	0.0303	0.1400	0.0985	0.98927	0.10172	0.139	811	r_6	-0.11446+0.45389i	(females)
40-44	0.0125	0.0569	0.0323	0.98194	0.03372	0.039	241	c_1	1396	
45-49	0.0017	0.0077	0.0042	0.97331	0.00448	0.005	27	$2x/y$	28.3760	
50-54	0.0002	0.0007	0.0004	0.95708	0.00040	0.000	2	Δ	8.5534	

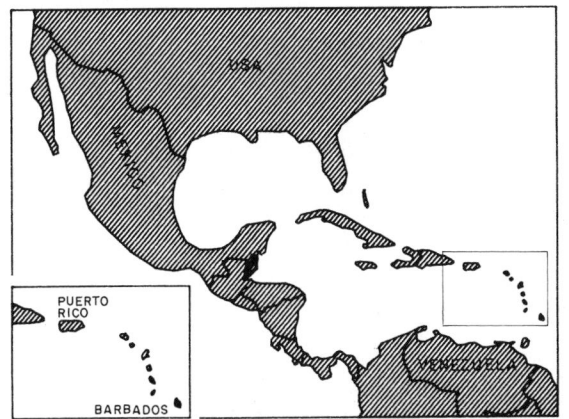

EDUCATION [1984]

% of primary school-age children enrolled:	na
secondary school-age children enrolled:	na
ca. 20-24 year olds in higher education:	na

LABOR FORCE

Average annual labor force growth (%) 1980-85:	1.5	
% of the 1980 labor force in agriculture:	10	TABLE 8
in industry and services:	90	SOCIO-ECONOMIC INDICATORS

GNP & INCOME DISTRIBUTION

GNP per capita (in US Dollars) 1985:	4630
GNP average annual growth rate (%) 1965-85:	2.3
% share of total household income	
Lowest 20% of households:	na
Highest 10% of households:	na

HEALTH & NUTRITION

Population per physician 1981:	na
Daily calorie supply per capita 1985:	na

AGE AT LAST BIRTHDAY	ESTIMATED MID-YEAR POPULATION					BIRTHS BY AGE OF MOTHER AND SEX	DEATHS			AGE AT LAST BIRTHDAY
	BOTH SEXES	MALES Number	Percent	FEMALES Number	Percent		BOTH SEXES	MALES	FEMALES	
0	211567	107449	2.3	104118	2.2		20687	11435	9252	0
1-4	983458	496253	10.7	487205	10.1		3686	1932	1754	1-4
5-9	1323905	664261	14.4	659644	13.6		1188	688	500	5-9
10-14	1186025	595535	12.9	590490	12.2	684	865	506	359	10-14
15-19	972194	475450	10.3	496744	10.3	33682	1244	757	487	15-19
20-24	818480	394484	8.5	423996	8.8	73176	1525	942	583	20-24
25-29	666239	321270	6.9	344969	7.1	60408	1620	1017	603	25-29
30-34	549942	265444	5.7	284498	5.9	36791	1762	1070	692	30-34
35-39	547634	263384	5.7	284250	5.9	22327	2176	1347	829	35-39
40-44	485097	237353	5.1	247744	5.1	10087	2712	1698	1014	40-44
45-49	379796	183335	4.0	196461	4.1	1325	3046	1875	1171	45-49
50-54	332715	158940	3.4	173775	3.6	189	3607	2197	1410	50-54
55-59	285965	135422	2.9	150543	3.1		4609	2759	1850	55-59
60-64	237549	112512	2.4	125037	2.6		5618	3201	2417	60-64
65-69	182921	84733	1.8	98188	2.0		6346	3513	2833	65-69
70-74	125344	57110	1.2	68234	1.4		6597	3482	3115	70-74
75-79	74187	33016	0.7	41171	0.9		6010	2981	3029	75-79
80-84	44595	17886	0.4	26709	0.6	121558 N	4841	2117	2724	80-84
85+	48387	18935	0.4	29452	0.6	117111 F	4875	1761	3114	85+
TOTAL	9456000	4622772		4833228		238669	83014	45278	37736	TOTAL

TABLE 1 DATA

TABLE 2 MALE LIFE TABLE

x	$_nM_x$	$_nq_x$	l_x	$_nd_x$	$_nL_x$	$_nm_x$	$_na_x$	T_x	$\overset{o}{e}_x$	x
0	0.106423	0.098565	100000	9857	92617	0.106423	0.251	5990209	59.902	0
1	0.003893	0.015423	90143	1390	357098	0.003893	1.500	5897592	65.424	1
5	0.001036	0.005165	88753	458	442620	0.001036	2.500	5540494	62.426	5
10	0.000850	0.004249	88295	375	440587	0.000852	2.635	5097874	57.737	10
15	0.001592	0.007987	87920	702	437981	0.001603	2.697	4657287	52.972	15
20	0.002388	0.011929	87217	1040	433623	0.002399	2.632	4219306	48.377	20
25	0.003166	0.015771	86177	1359	427624	0.003178	2.601	3785683	43.929	25
30	0.004031	0.020008	84818	1697	420002	0.004041	2.591	3358059	39.591	30
35	0.005114	0.025280	83121	2101	410593	0.005118	2.615	2938058	35.347	35
40	0.007154	0.035282	81020	2859	398330	0.007176	2.632	2527465	31.196	40
45	0.010227	0.050114	78161	3917	381455	0.010268	2.613	2129135	27.240	45
50	0.013823	0.067089	74244	4981	359356	0.013861	2.618	1747680	23.540	50
55	0.020373	0.097331	69263	6741	330162	0.020419	2.604	1388324	20.044	55
60	0.028450	0.133394	62522	8340	292486	0.028514	2.587	1058163	16.925	60
65	0.041460	0.188200	54182	10234	246021	0.041599	2.568	765677	14.132	65
70	0.060970	0.266057	43947	11692	190852	0.061265	2.530	519656	11.825	70
75	0.090290	0.368875	32255	11898	131000	0.090824	2.456	328804	10.194	75
80	0.118361	0.449547	20357	9151	77318	0.118361	2.326	197804	9.717	80
85	0.093002	1.000000	11206	11206	120486	0.035472	10.752	120486	10.752	85

TABLE 3 FEMALE LIFE TABLE

x	$_nM_x$	$_nq_x$	l_x	$_nd_x$	$_nL_x$	$_nm_x$	$_na_x$	T_x	$\overset{o}{e}_x$	x
0	0.088861	0.083108	100000	8311	93526	0.088861	0.221	6593688	65.937	0
1	0.003600	0.014272	91689	1309	363485	0.003600	1.500	6500161	70.893	1
5	0.000758	0.003783	90381	342	451048	0.000758	2.500	6136676	67.898	5
10	0.000608	0.003038	90039	274	449530	0.000609	2.575	5685628	63.146	10
15	0.000980	0.004912	89765	441	447794	0.000985	2.661	5236098	58.331	15
20	0.001375	0.006877	89324	614	445155	0.001380	2.613	4788304	53.606	20
25	0.001748	0.008739	88710	775	441705	0.001755	2.621	4343149	48.959	25
30	0.002432	0.012121	87935	1066	437109	0.002438	2.595	3901444	44.368	30
35	0.002916	0.014497	86869	1259	431336	0.002920	2.612	3464334	39.880	35
40	0.004093	0.020348	85609	1742	423945	0.004109	2.645	3032998	35.428	40
45	0.005960	0.029509	83867	2475	413464	0.005986	2.627	2609053	31.109	45
50	0.008114	0.039929	81393	3250	399298	0.008139	2.642	2195588	26.975	50
55	0.012289	0.059931	78143	4683	379748	0.012332	2.659	1796290	22.987	55
60	0.019330	0.092745	73459	6813	351171	0.019401	2.633	1416543	19.283	60
65	0.028853	0.135551	66646	9034	311713	0.028982	2.618	1065372	15.985	65
70	0.045652	0.207044	57612	11928	259333	0.045996	2.592	753659	13.082	70
75	0.073571	0.312501	45684	14276	192881	0.074016	2.511	494325	10.821	75
80	0.101988	0.402856	31408	12653	124062	0.101988	2.394	301445	9.598	80
85	0.105731	1.000000	18755	18755	177383	0.044078	9.458	177383	9.458	85

CRUDE RATES

TABLE 4 OBSERVED VITAL RATES AND RATIOS

Per Thousand	BOTH SEXES	MALES	FEMALES
BIRTH RATE	25.24	26.30	24.23
DEATH RATE	8.78	9.79	7.81
RATE OF INCREASE	16.46	16.50	16.42

PERCENT OF POPULATION IN AGE GROUP

UNDER 15	39.18	40.31	38.10
15 - 64	55.79	55.11	56.44
65 AND OLDER	5.03	4.58	5.46

RATES STANDARDIZED ON USA 1980

Per Thousand	BOTH SEXES	MALES	FEMALES
BIRTH RATE	27.67		26.41
DEATH RATE	12.98	13.47	12.51
RATE OF INCREASE	14.69		13.89

RATES STANDARDIZED ON MEXICO 1980

	BOTH SEXES	MALES	FEMALES
BIRTH RATE	24.65		24.38
DEATH RATE	7.93	8.88	6.97
RATE OF INCREASE	16.72		17.42

VITAL STATISTICS

GFR x 1000	104.741
TFR	3.365
GRR	1.651
NRR	1.452
μ	28.349
σ^2	50.456
GENERATION	28.013
POP. SEX RATIO	1.046
SEX RATIO AT BIRTH	1.038
DEP. RATIO x 100	79.240

PROJECTED POPULATION

AGE GROUP	1975 BOTH SEXES	1975 MALES	1975 FEMALES	1980 BOTH SEXES	1980 MALES	1980 FEMALES
0-4	1173	593	580	1370	692	678
5-9	1178	594	584	1156	583	573
10-14	1318	661	657	1173	591	582
15-19	1180	592	588	1312	657	655
20-24	965	471	494	1171	586	585
25-29	810	389	421	954	464	490
30-34	657	316	341	798	382	416
35-39	540	259	281	645	308	337
40-44	535	256	279	528	252	276
45-49	469	227	242	517	245	272
50-54	363	173	190	447	214	233
55-59	311	146	165	339	159	180
60-64	259	120	139	282	129	153
65-69	206	95	111	225	101	124
70-74	148	66	82	165	73	92
75-79	90	39	51	106	45	61
80-84	45	19	26	56	23	33
85+	66	28	38	68	30	38
TOTAL	10313	5044	5269	11312	5534	5778

STABLE EQUIVALENT TO ORIGINAL POPULATION

	MALES Number	MALES Percent	FEMALES Number	FEMALES Percent	AGE GROUP	
	628	11.3	615	10.7	0-4	
	578	10.4	568	9.8	5-9	TABLE 5
	539	9.7	529	9.2	10-14	
	501	9.0	493	8.6	15-19	POPULATION
	464	8.3	459	8.0	20-24	PROJECTED
	428	7.7	426	7.4	25-29	WITH
	393	7.0	394	6.8	30-34	FIXED
	360	6.4	364	6.3	35-39	AGE-
	326	5.8	335	5.8	40-44	SPECIFIC
	292	5.2	305	5.3	45-49	BIRTH
	258	4.6	276	4.8	50-54	AND
	221	4.0	245	4.3	55-59	DEATH
	184	3.3	212	3.7	60-64	RATES
	144	2.6	176	3.1	65-69	(female
	105	1.9	137	2.4	70-74	dominant,
	67	1.2	95	1.7	75-79	in 000s)
	37	0.7	57	1.0	80-84	
	54	1.0	77	1.3	85+	
	5579		5763		TOTAL	

VITAL RATES OF PROJECTED POPULATION

Per Thousand	1975 BOTH SEXES	1975 MALES	1975 FEMALES	1980 BOTH SEXES	1980 MALES	1980 FEMALES
BIRTH RATE	27.05	28.17	25.98	28.76	29.94	27.64
DEATH RATE	8.83	9.81	7.88	9.11	10.10	8.15
RATE OF INCREASE	18.22	18.36	18.09	19.66	19.83	19.49

VITAL RATES OF STABLE POPULATION

Per Thousand	MALES	FEMALES	
BIRTH RATE	25.87	24.12	TABLE 6
DEATH RATE	12.22	10.78	PROJECTED
RATE OF INCREASE		13.33	VITAL RATES AND RATIOS (female dominant)

AGE STRUCTURE OF PROJECTED POPULATION

	1975 BOTH SEXES	1975 MALES	1975 FEMALES	1980 BOTH SEXES	1980 MALES	1980 FEMALES
% UNDER 15	35.58	36.65	34.56	32.70	33.72	31.71
% 15-64	59.04	58.46	59.59	61.82	61.35	62.28
% 65 AND OLDER	5.38	4.90	5.85	5.48	4.93	6.01
DEPEND. RATIO x 100	69.39	71.06	67.82	61.75	63.00	60.57

STABLE AGE STRUCTURE

	MALES	FEMALES
% UNDER 15	31.27	29.70
% 15-64	61.42	60.88
% 65 AND OLDER	7.31	9.42
DEPEND. RATIO x 100	62.82	64.26

AGE GROUP	FEMALE BIRTH RATES	NET MATERNITY FUNCTION	COEFF. OF MATRIX EQUATION	ORIGINAL MATRIX SUB-DIAGONAL	ORIGINAL MATRIX FIRST ROW	STABLE MATRIX FISHER VALUES	STABLE MATRIX REPRODUCTIVE VALUES
0-4	0.0000	0.0000	0.0000	0.98695	0.00000	1.131	668712
5-9	0.0000	0.0000	0.0013	0.99663	0.00129	1.225	807950
10-14	0.0006	0.0026	0.0758	0.99614	0.07703	1.312	774859
15-19	0.0333	0.1490	0.2630	0.99411	0.26840	1.321	656046
20-24	0.0847	0.3770	0.3783	0.99225	0.38833	1.115	472671
25-29	0.0859	0.3795	0.3284	0.98959	0.33983	0.758	261619
30-34	0.0635	0.2774	0.2218	0.98679	0.23190	0.431	122576
35-39	0.0385	0.1662	0.1255	0.98287	0.13294	0.201	57122
40-44	0.0200	0.0847	0.0492	0.97528	0.05303	0.066	16252
45-49	0.0033	0.0137	0.0079	0.96574	0.00874	0.010	2045
50-54	0.0005	0.0021	0.0011	0.95104	0.00122	0.001	224

MATRIX PARAMETERS

λ_1	1.06895	
λ_2	$0.39063+0.70691i$	TABLE 7
λ_4	$0.05379+0.61239i$	
λ_6	$-0.36638+0.46457i$	LESLIE
r_1	0.01333	MATRIX
r_2	$-0.04272+0.21319i$	AND ITS
r_4	$-0.09731+0.29664i$	ANALYSIS
r_6	$-0.10496+0.44772i$	(females)
c_1	57652	
$2\pi/\gamma$	29.4716	
Δ	10.9367	

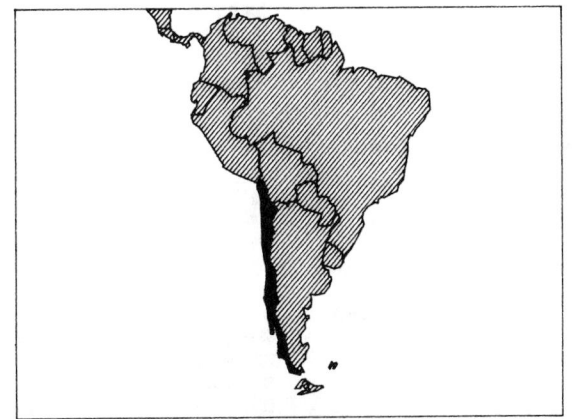

EDUCATION [1984]

% of primary school-age children enrolled:	107
secondary school-age children enrolled:	66
ca. 20-24 year olds in higher education:	15

LABOR FORCE

Average annual labor force growth (%) 1980-85:	2.6	
% of the 1980 labor force in agriculture:	17	TABLE 8
in industry:	25	
in services:	58	SOCIO-

GNP & INCOME DISTRIBUTION

ECONOMIC INDICATORS

GNP per capita (in US Dollars) 1985:	1430
GNP average annual growth rate (%) 1965-85:	-0.2
% share of total household income	
Lowest 20% of households:	na
Highest 10% of households:	na

HEALTH & NUTRITION

Population per physician 1981:	na
Daily calorie supply per capita 1985:	2602

TABLE 1 — DATA

AGE AT LAST BIRTHDAY	ESTIMATED MID-YEAR POPULATION — BOTH SEXES	MALES Number	MALES Percent	FEMALES Number	FEMALES Percent	BIRTHS BY AGE OF MOTHER AND SEX	DEATHS BOTH SEXES	DEATHS MALES	DEATHS FEMALES	AGE AT LAST BIRTHDAY
0	270782	137454	2.5	133328	2.4		8158	4562	3596	0
1-4	995126	505586	9.2	489540	8.7		1235	651	584	1-4
5-9	1163667	591091	10.7	572576	10.2		672	389	283	5-9
10-14	1183822	599982	10.9	583840	10.4	596	633	364	269	10-14
15-19	1220838	617045	11.2	603793	10.8	38562	1143	751	392	15-19
20-24	1105957	557214	10.1	548743	9.8	79724	1496	1069	427	20-24
25-29	895257	450052	8.2	445205	7.9	59771	1460	1014	446	25-29
30-34	810274	401950	7.3	408324	7.3	33769	1497	1013	484	30-34
35-39	701238	346739	6.3	354499	6.3	16428	1906	1255	651	35-39
40-44	571020	280987	5.1	290033	5.2	5109	2162	1428	734	40-44
45-49	485559	236978	4.3	248581	4.4	620	2879	1822	1057	45-49
50-54	451216	217674	4.0	233542	4.2	83	4009	2448	1561	50-54
55-59	350085	166365	3.0	183720	3.3		4454	2741	1713	55-59
60-64	292573	135245	2.5	157328	2.8		5385	3188	2197	60-64
65-69	235158	104798	1.9	130360	2.3		6992	3972	3020	65-69
70-74	172593	74505	1.4	98088	1.8		7923	4405	3518	70-74
75-79	106768	42802	0.8	63966	1.1		8368	4146	4222	75-79
80-84	44258	15937	0.3	28321	0.5	119821 M	6693	3018	3675	80-84
85+	48102	16873	0.3	31229	0.6	114841 F	7044	2595	4449	85+
TOTAL	11104293	5499277		5605016		234662	74109	40831	33278	TOTAL

TABLE 2 — MALE LIFE TABLE

x	nM_x	nq_x	l_x	nd_x	nL_x	nm_x	na_x	T_x	$\overset{\circ}{e}_x$	x
0	0.033189	0.032254	100000	3225	97182	0.033189	0.126	6640087	66.401	0
1	0.001288	0.005134	96775	497	385856	0.001288	1.500	6542904	67.610	1
5	0.000658	0.003285	96278	316	480598	0.000658	2.500	6157048	63.951	5
10	0.000607	0.003029	95961	291	479136	0.000607	2.689	5676450	59.153	10
15	0.001217	0.006069	95671	581	477031	0.001217	2.722	5197315	54.325	15
20	0.001918	0.009573	95090	910	473274	0.001924	2.609	4720283	49.640	20
25	0.002253	0.011221	94180	1057	468311	0.002257	2.551	4247009	45.095	25
30	0.002520	0.012554	93123	1169	462817	0.002526	2.607	3778698	40.577	30
35	0.003619	0.018016	91954	1657	455859	0.003634	2.640	3315881	36.060	35
40	0.005082	0.025242	90297	2279	446138	0.005109	2.653	2860022	31.673	40
45	0.007688	0.037884	88018	3334	432248	0.007714	2.648	2413884	27.425	45
50	0.011246	0.054949	84684	4653	412417	0.011283	2.636	1981636	23.400	50
55	0.016476	0.079613	80030	6371	384973	0.016550	2.618	1569219	19.608	55
60	0.023572	0.112029	73659	8252	348713	0.023664	2.627	1184246	16.077	60
65	0.037901	0.174355	65407	11404	299724	0.038048	2.605	835533	12.774	65
70	0.059124	0.259640	54003	14010	235892	0.059391	2.564	535809	9.922	70
75	0.096865	0.393492	39993	15737	160892	0.097811	2.517	299917	7.499	75
80	0.189371	0.630827	24256	15301	80801	0.189371	2.355	139025	5.732	80
85	0.153796	1.000000	8955	8955	58224	0.086803	6.502	58224	6.502	85

TABLE 3 — FEMALE LIFE TABLE

x	nM_x	nq_x	l_x	nd_x	nL_x	nm_x	na_x	T_x	$\overset{\circ}{e}_x$	x
0	0.026971	0.026343	100000	2634	97671	0.026971	0.116	7285947	72.859	0
1	0.001193	0.004758	97366	463	388305	0.001193	1.500	7188276	73.828	1
5	0.000494	0.002468	96902	239	483914	0.000494	2.500	6799972	70.173	5
10	0.000461	0.002301	96663	222	482776	0.000461	2.569	6316057	65.341	10
15	0.000649	0.003241	96441	313	481454	0.000649	2.601	5833282	60.486	15
20	0.000778	0.003891	96128	374	479741	0.000780	2.593	5351827	55.674	20
25	0.001002	0.005009	95754	480	477612	0.001004	2.583	4872086	50.881	25
30	0.001185	0.005927	95275	565	475043	0.001189	2.644	4394474	46.124	30
35	0.001836	0.009183	94710	870	471505	0.001845	2.649	3919432	41.384	35
40	0.002531	0.012656	93840	1188	466459	0.002546	2.691	3447926	36.743	40
45	0.004252	0.021140	92653	1959	458742	0.004270	2.692	2981468	32.179	45
50	0.006684	0.033013	90694	2994	446413	0.006707	2.643	2522725	27.816	50
55	0.009324	0.045818	87700	4018	429013	0.009366	2.639	2076312	23.675	55
60	0.013964	0.067886	83682	5681	405161	0.014021	2.668	1647299	19.685	60
65	0.023167	0.110283	78001	8602	369718	0.023267	2.642	1242138	15.925	65
70	0.035866	0.166245	69399	11537	319825	0.036073	2.645	872419	12.571	70
75	0.066004	0.287646	57861	16644	249477	0.066714	2.607	552594	9.550	75
80	0.129762	0.487122	41218	20078	154730	0.129762	2.442	303116	7.354	80
85	0.142464	1.000000	21140	21140	148387	0.074507	7.019	148387	7.019	85

TABLE 4 — OBSERVED VITAL RATES AND RATIOS

CRUDE RATES

Per Thousand	BOTH SEXES	MALES	FEMALES
BIRTH RATE	21.13	21.79	20.49
DEATH RATE	6.67	7.42	5.94
RATE OF INCREASE	14.46	14.36	14.55

RATES STANDARDIZED ON USA 1980

Per Thousand	BOTH SEXES	MALES	FEMALES
BIRTH RATE	20.86		19.85
DEATH RATE	11.27	11.90	10.67
RATE OF INCREASE	9.59		9.18

VITAL STATISTICS

GFR x 1000	80.941
TFR	2.470
GRR	1.209
NRR	1.154
μ	27.083
σ^2	44.375
GENERATION	26.965
POP. SEX RATIO	1.019
SEX RATIO AT BIRTH	1.043
DEP. RATIO x 100	61.305

PERCENT OF POPULATION IN AGE GROUP

	BOTH SEXES	MALES	FEMALES
UNDER 15	32.54	33.35	31.74
15 - 64	61.99	62.01	61.98
65 AND OLDER	5.47	4.64	6.28

RATES STANDARDIZED ON MEXICO 1980

	BOTH SEXES	MALES	FEMALES
BIRTH RATE	19.01		18.75
DEATH RATE	5.09	5.93	4.23
RATE OF INCREASE	13.92		14.52

PROJECTED POPULATION

AGE GROUP	1985 BOTH SEXES	1985 MALES	1985 FEMALES	1990 BOTH SEXES	1990 MALES	1990 FEMALES
0-4	1200	611	589	1298	661	637
5-9	1260	640	620	1195	608	587
10-14	1160	589	571	1257	638	619
15-19	1179	597	582	1157	587	570
20-24	1214	612	602	1173	593	580
25-29	1097	551	546	1205	606	599
30-34	888	445	443	1088	545	543
35-39	801	396	405	878	438	440
40-44	690	339	351	788	387	401
45-49	557	272	285	674	329	345
50-54	468	226	242	538	260	278
55-59	427	203	224	443	211	232
60-64	325	151	174	396	184	212
65-69	260	116	144	288	130	158
70-74	195	82	113	215	91	124
75-79	128	51	77	144	56	88
80-84	61	21	40	73	26	47
85+	38	11	27	53	15	38
TOTAL	11948	5913	6035	12863	6365	6498

STABLE EQUIVALENT TO ORIGINAL POPULATION

	MALES Number	MALES Percent	FEMALES Number	FEMALES Percent	AGE GROUP	
	627	8.6	605	8.0	0-4	
	608	8.4	586	7.8	5-9	TABLE 5
	590	8.1	570	7.6	10-14	
	572	7.9	553	7.4	15-19	POPULATION
	553	7.6	537	7.1	20-24	PROJECTED
	533	7.3	521	6.9	25-29	WITH
	513	7.1	504	6.7	30-34	FIXED
	492	6.8	487	6.5	35-39	AGE-
	469	6.5	470	6.2	40-44	SPECIFIC
	442	6.1	450	6.0	45-49	BIRTH
	411	5.7	426	5.7	50-54	AND
	373	5.1	399	5.3	55-59	DEATH
	329	4.5	367	4.9	60-64	RATES
	276	3.8	326	4.3	65-69	(female
	211	2.9	275	3.6	70-74	dominant,
	140	1.9	209	2.8	75-79	in 000s)
	69	0.9	126	1.7	80-84	
	48	0.7	118	1.6	85+	
	7256		7529		TOTAL	

VITAL RATES OF PROJECTED POPULATION

Per Thousand	1985 BOTH SEXES	1985 MALES	1985 FEMALES	1990 BOTH SEXES	1990 MALES	1990 FEMALES
BIRTH RATE	21.83	22.52	21.16	21.38	22.07	20.71
DEATH RATE	6.83	7.56	6.11	7.25	7.94	6.57
RATE OF INCREASE	15.00	14.96	15.05	14.13	14.13	14.14

AGE STRUCTURE OF PROJECTED POPULATION

	BOTH SEXES	MALES	FEMALES	BOTH SEXES	MALES	FEMALES
% UNDER 15	30.30	31.11	29.51	29.15	29.96	28.36
% 15-64	63.99	64.12	63.87	64.83	65.04	64.62
% 65 AND OLDER	5.71	4.78	6.62	6.02	5.00	7.02
DEPEND. RATIO x 100	56.27	55.96	56.57	54.25	53.76	54.74

VITAL RATES OF STABLE POPULATION

Per Thousand	MALES	FEMALES	
BIRTH RATE	18.13	16.75	TABLE 6
DEATH RATE	12.84	11.45	PROJECTED
RATE OF INCREASE		5.30	VITAL RATES

STABLE AGE STRUCTURE

	MALES	FEMALES	AND RATIOS
% UNDER 15	25.15	23.39	(female
% 15-64	64.59	62.62	dominant)
% 65 AND OLDER	10.26	13.99	
DEPEND. RATIO x 100	54.83	59.70	

AGE GROUP	FEMALE BIRTH RATES	NET MATERNITY FUNCTION	COEFF. OF MATRIX EQUATION	ORIGINAL MATRIX SUB-DIAGONAL	ORIGINAL MATRIX FIRST ROW	STABLE MATRIX FISHER VALUES	STABLE MATRIX REPRODUCTIVE VALUES	MATRIX PARAMETERS		
0-4	0.0000	0.0000	0.0000	0.99576	0.00000	1.043	649375	λ_1	1.02686	
5-9	0.0000	0.0000	0.0012	0.99765	0.00121	1.075	615589	λ_2	0.34101+0.69658i	TABLE 7
10-14	0.0005	0.0024	0.0764	0.99726	0.07695	1.105	645342	λ_4	0.03580+0.54854i	
15-19	0.0313	0.1505	0.2458	0.99644	0.24810	1.058	638631	λ_6	-0.36646+0.40869i	LESLIE
20-24	0.0711	0.3411	0.3275	0.99556	0.33171	0.830	455681	r_1	0.00530	MATRIX
25-29	0.0657	0.3138	0.2530	0.99462	0.25747	0.509	226677	r_2	-0.05083+0.22311i	AND ITS
30-34	0.0405	0.1923	0.1496	0.99255	0.15304	0.256	104442	r_4	-0.11967+0.30112i	ANALYSIS
35-39	0.0227	0.1069	0.0736	0.98930	0.07583	0.104	36822	r_6	-0.11996+0.46035i	(females)
40-44	0.0086	0.0402	0.0229	0.98346	0.02386	0.028	8093	c_1	75276	
45-49	0.0012	0.0056	0.0032	0.97312	0.00338	0.004	953	$2\pi/y$	28.1620	
50-54	0.0002	0.0008	0.0004	0.96102	0.00042	0.000	100	Δ	16.0424	

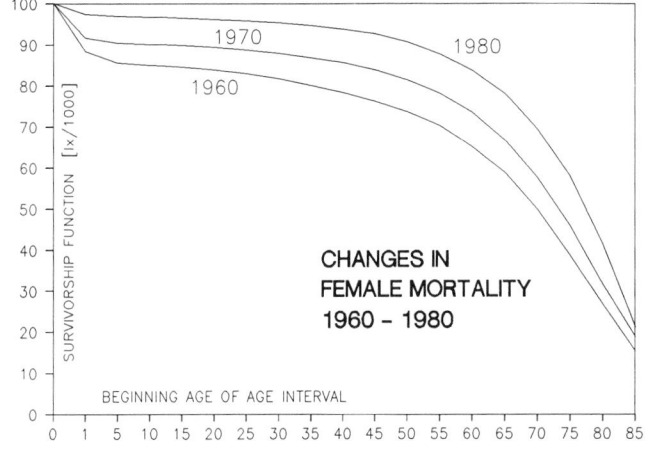

CHANGES IN FEMALE MORTALITY 1960 - 1980

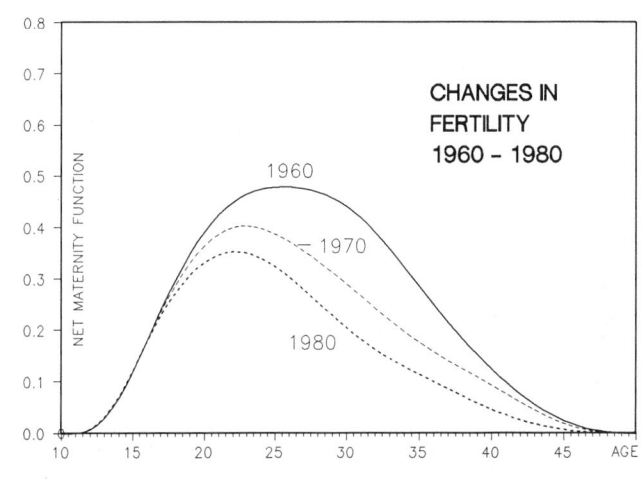

CHANGES IN FERTILITY 1960 - 1980

TABLE 1 — DATA

AGE AT LAST BIRTHDAY	ESTIMATED MID-YEAR POPULATION BOTH SEXES	MALES Number	MALES Percent	FEMALES Number	FEMALES Percent	BIRTHS BY AGE OF MOTHER AND SEX	DEATHS BOTH SEXES	DEATHS MALES	DEATHS FEMALES	AGE AT LAST BIRTHDAY
0	354667	180924	4.5	173743	4.4		18292	10157	8135	0
1-4	1078878	549493	13.6	529385	13.4		12066	6087	5979	1-4
5-9	1213314	617762	15.3	595552	15.1		2454	1265	1189	5-9
10-14	1008947	512671	12.7	496276	12.6	1208	1215	675	540	10-14
15-19	842567	427756	10.6	414811	10.5	51232	1399	801	598	15-19
20-24	698447	353237	8.8	345210	8.8	95150	1928	1152	776	20-24
25-29	566270	285362	7.1	280908	7.1	76714	1860	1136	724	25-29
30-34	471868	236625	5.9	235243	6.0	53472	1867	1140	727	30-34
35-39	366969	184164	4.6	182805	4.6	33708	2017	1180	837	35-39
40-44	299985	150434	3.7	149551	3.8	12290	1695	987	708	40-44
45-49	259788	130842	3.2	128946	3.3	2410	1824	1075	749	45-49
50-54	233166	116740	2.9	116426	3.0	665	2228	1334	894	50-54
55-59	191326	95585	2.4	95741	2.4		2486	1416	1070	55-59
60-64	143085	71229	1.8	71856	1.8		2913	1627	1286	60-64
65-69	96917	47757	1.2	49160	1.2		2938	1709	1229	65-69
70-74	65552	32174	0.8	33378	0.8		3519	1880	1639	70-74
75-79	37544	18241	0.5	19303	0.5		3065	1607	1458	75-79
80-84	19471	8963	0.2	10508	0.3	167444 M	2604	1224	1380	80-84
85+	14595	6654	0.2	7941	0.2	159405 F	3085	1443	1642	85+
TOTAL	7963356	4026613		3936743		326849	69455	37895	31560	TOTAL

TABLE 2 — MALE LIFE TABLE

x	nM_x	nq_x	l_x	nd_x	nL_x	nm_x	na_x	T_x	$\overset{o}{e}_x$	x
0	0.056140	0.053627	100000	5363	95524	0.056140	0.165	6058158	60.582	0
1	0.011077	0.043116	94637	4080	368348	0.011077	1.500	5962633	63.005	1
5	0.002048	0.010186	90557	922	450478	0.002048	2.500	5594285	61.776	5
10	0.001317	0.006548	89634	587	446687	0.001314	2.469	5143807	57.386	10
15	0.001873	0.009380	89048	835	443326	0.001884	2.711	4697120	52.748	15
20	0.003261	0.016267	88212	1435	437657	0.003279	2.628	4253794	48.222	20
25	0.003981	0.019767	86777	1715	429723	0.003992	2.573	3816136	43.976	25
30	0.004818	0.023894	85062	2032	420419	0.004834	2.593	3386413	39.811	30
35	0.006407	0.031629	83030	2626	408700	0.006425	2.545	2965995	35.722	35
40	0.006561	0.032325	80403	2599	395627	0.006569	2.541	2557294	31.806	40
45	0.008216	0.040378	77804	3142	381493	0.008235	2.604	2161667	27.783	45
50	0.011427	0.055723	74663	4160	363313	0.011451	2.596	1780174	23.843	50
55	0.014814	0.071821	70502	5064	340474	0.014872	2.623	1416860	20.097	55
60	0.022842	0.109098	65439	7139	310308	0.023007	2.635	1076387	16.449	60
65	0.035785	0.166024	58300	9679	268420	0.036060	2.616	766079	13.140	65
70	0.058432	0.257372	48620	12514	212532	0.058879	2.557	497659	10.236	70
75	0.088098	0.362872	36107	13102	147589	0.088775	2.486	285128	7.897	75
80	0.136561	0.504333	23005	11602	84958	0.136561	2.409	137539	5.979	80
85	0.216862	1.000000	11403	11403	52580	0.152398	4.611	52580	4.611	85

TABLE 3 — FEMALE LIFE TABLE

x	nM_x	nq_x	l_x	nd_x	nL_x	nm_x	na_x	T_x	$\overset{o}{e}_x$	x
0	0.046822	0.045029	100000	4503	96171	0.046822	0.150	6441543	64.415	0
1	0.011294	0.043936	95497	4196	371499	0.011294	1.500	6345372	66.446	1
5	0.001996	0.009933	91301	907	454239	0.001996	2.500	5973873	65.430	5
10	0.001088	0.005402	90394	488	450698	0.001083	2.390	5519634	61.062	10
15	0.001442	0.007218	89906	649	448015	0.001448	2.665	5068936	56.380	15
20	0.002248	0.011224	89257	1002	443882	0.002257	2.601	4620921	51.771	20
25	0.002577	0.012832	88255	1133	438516	0.002583	2.563	4177039	47.329	25
30	0.003090	0.015404	87123	1342	432429	0.003104	2.627	3738522	42.911	30
35	0.004579	0.022724	85781	1949	424160	0.004596	2.566	3306093	38.541	35
40	0.004734	0.023428	83832	1964	414331	0.004740	2.543	2881932	34.378	40
45	0.005809	0.028706	81868	2350	403679	0.005822	2.592	2467601	30.141	45
50	0.007679	0.037803	79517	3006	390455	0.007699	2.627	2063922	25.956	50
55	0.011176	0.054745	76511	4189	372761	0.011237	2.661	1673466	21.872	55
60	0.017897	0.086391	72323	6248	346760	0.018018	2.623	1300705	17.985	60
65	0.025000	0.118994	66075	7863	312105	0.025192	2.676	953946	14.437	65
70	0.049104	0.221701	58212	12906	260184	0.049602	2.607	641841	11.026	70
75	0.075532	0.320461	45307	14519	190701	0.076135	2.532	381657	8.424	75
80	0.131329	0.491742	30788	15140	115280	0.131329	2.447	190957	6.202	80
85	0.206775	1.000000	15648	15648	75677	0.140526	4.836	75677	4.836	85

TABLE 4 — OBSERVED VITAL RATES AND RATIOS

CRUDE RATES

Per Thousand	BOTH SEXES	MALES	FEMALES
BIRTH RATE	41.04	41.58	40.49
DEATH RATE	8.72	9.41	8.02
RATE OF INCREASE	32.32	32.17	32.47

PERCENT OF POPULATION IN AGE GROUP

	BOTH SEXES	MALES	FEMALES
UNDER 15	45.91	46.21	45.59
15 - 64	51.15	50.96	51.35
65 AND OLDER	2.94	2.83	3.06

RATES STANDARDIZED ON USA 1980

Per Thousand	BOTH SEXES	MALES	FEMALES
BIRTH RATE	48.05		45.57
DEATH RATE	13.95	13.39	14.49
RATE OF INCREASE	34.10		31.09

RATES STANDARDIZED ON MEXICO 1980

	BOTH SEXES	MALES	FEMALES
BIRTH RATE	42.59		41.87
DEATH RATE	8.09	8.61	7.56
RATE OF INCREASE	34.50		34.30

VITAL STATISTICS

GFR x 1000	188.117
TFR	5.965
GRR	2.909
NRR	2.531
μ	29.060
σ^2	57.679
GENERATION	28.107
POP. SEX RATIO	0.978
SEX RATIO AT BIRTH	1.050
DEP. RATIO x 100	95.493

PROJECTED POPULATION

AGE GROUP	1990 BOTH SEXES	1990 MALES	1990 FEMALES	1995 BOTH SEXES	1995 MALES	1995 FEMALES
0-4	1675	855	820	2005	1023	982
5-9	1392	709	683	1627	830	797
10-14	1204	613	591	1381	703	678
15-19	1002	509	493	1195	608	587
20-24	833	422	411	991	502	489
25-29	688	347	341	821	415	406
30-34	556	279	277	675	339	336
35-39	461	230	231	543	271	272
40-44	357	178	179	448	223	225
45-49	291	145	146	346	172	174
50-54	250	125	125	279	138	141
55-59	220	109	111	236	117	119
60-64	176	87	89	203	100	103
65-69	127	62	65	155	75	80
70-74	79	38	41	103	49	54
75-79	46	22	24	56	26	30
80-84	23	11	12	28	13	15
85+	13	6	7	14	6	8
TOTAL	9393	4747	4646	11106	5610	5496

STABLE EQUIVALENT TO ORIGINAL POPULATION

MALES Number	MALES Percent	FEMALES Number	FEMALES Percent	AGE GROUP
737	*18.1*	708	*17.7*	0-4
607	*14.9*	582	*14.6*	5-9
510	*12.5*	490	*12.3*	10-14
429	*10.5*	412	*10.3*	15-19
359	*8.8*	346	*8.7*	20-24
298	*7.3*	290	*7.3*	25-29
247	*6.1*	242	*6.1*	30-34
204	*5.0*	201	*5.0*	35-39
167	*4.1*	167	*4.2*	40-44
137	*3.4*	138	*3.4*	45-49
110	*2.7*	113	*2.8*	50-54
88	*2.1*	91	*2.3*	55-59
68	*1.7*	72	*1.8*	60-64
50	*1.2*	55	*1.4*	65-69
33	*0.8*	39	*1.0*	70-74
20	*0.5*	24	*0.6*	75-79
10	*0.2*	12	*0.3*	80-84
5	*0.1*	7	*0.2*	85+
4079		3989		TOTAL

TABLE 5

POPULATION PROJECTED WITH FIXED AGE-SPECIFIC BIRTH AND DEATH RATES (female dominant, in 000s)

VITAL RATES OF PROJECTED POPULATION

Per Thousand

	1990 BOTH SEXES	1990 MALES	1990 FEMALES	1995 BOTH SEXES	1995 MALES	1995 FEMALES
BIRTH RATE	41.79	42.36	41.20	42.22	42.81	41.61
DEATH RATE	8.63	9.32	7.93	8.71	9.39	8.03
RATE OF INCREASE	33.16	33.04	33.27	33.50	33.42	33.58

AGE STRUCTURE OF PROJECTED POPULATION

	1990 BOTH SEXES	1990 MALES	1990 FEMALES	1995 BOTH SEXES	1995 MALES	1995 FEMALES
% UNDER 15	45.48	45.86	45.08	45.13	45.56	44.70
% 15-64	51.47	51.24	51.72	51.66	51.41	51.91
% 65 AND OLDER	3.05	2.90	3.20	3.21	3.03	3.39
DEPEND. RATIO x 100	94.27	95.18	93.36	93.58	94.51	92.65

VITAL RATES OF STABLE POPULATION

Per Thousand

	MALES	FEMALES
BIRTH RATE	42.20	41.06
DEATH RATE	9.35	7.94
RATE OF INCREASE		33.12

STABLE AGE STRUCTURE

	MALES	FEMALES
% UNDER 15	45.47	44.61
% 15-64	51.66	51.96
% 65 AND OLDER	2.87	3.43
DEPEND. RATIO x 100	93.56	92.47

TABLE 6

PROJECTED VITAL RATES AND RATIOS (female dominant)

MATRIX

AGE GROUP	FEMALE BIRTH RATES	NET MATERNITY FUNCTION	COEFF. OF MATRIX EQUATION	ORIGINAL MATRIX SUB-DIAGONAL	ORIGINAL MATRIX FIRST ROW	STABLE MATRIX FISHER VALUES	STABLE MATRIX REPRODUCTIVE VALUES
0-4	0.0000	0.0000	0.0000	0.97128	0.00000	1.160	815780
5-9	0.0000	0.0000	0.0027	0.99220	0.00275	1.410	839515
10-14	0.0012	0.0054	0.1376	0.99405	0.14279	1.673	830447
15-19	0.0602	0.2699	0.4333	0.99077	0.45228	1.820	754907
20-24	0.1344	0.5967	0.5904	0.98791	0.62201	1.638	565451
25-29	0.1332	0.5841	0.5317	0.98612	0.56706	1.226	344433
30-34	0.1109	0.4794	0.4304	0.98088	0.46549	0.800	188229
35-39	0.0899	0.3814	0.2738	0.97683	0.30183	0.412	75327
40-44	0.0401	0.1661	0.1014	0.97429	0.11449	0.139	20833
45-49	0.0091	0.0368	0.0238	0.96724	0.02761	0.032	4178
50-54	0.0028	0.0109	0.0054	0.95468	0.00651	0.006	746

MATRIX PARAMETERS

λ_1	1.18009
λ_2	$0.42583+0.75100i$
λ_4	$0.01184+0.71299i$
λ_6	$-0.46402+0.43788i$
r_1	0.03312
r_2	$-0.02939+0.21100i$
r_4	$-0.06763+0.31084i$
r_6	$-0.08988+0.47704i$
c_1	39890
$2\pi/y$	29.7787
Δ	1.5925

TABLE 7

LESLIE MATRIX AND ITS ANALYSIS (females)

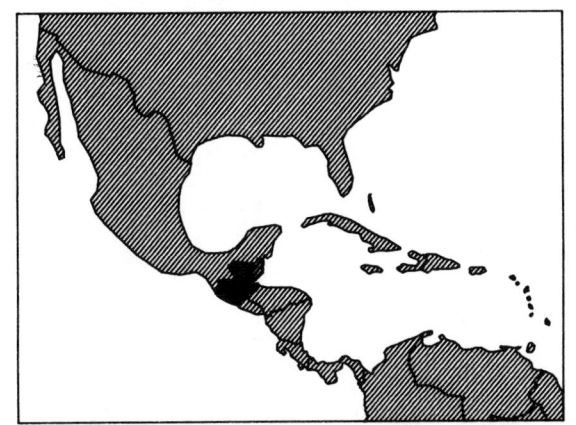

EDUCATION [1984]

% of primary school-age children enrolled:	76
secondary school-age children enrolled:	17
ca. 20-24 year olds in higher education:	7

LABOR FORCE

Average annual labor force growth (%) 1980-85:	2.8
% of the 1980 labor force in agriculture:	57
in industry:	17
in services:	26

GNP & INCOME DISTRIBUTION

GNP per capita (in US Dollars) 1985:	1250
GNP average annual growth rate (%) 1965-85:	1.7
% share of total household income	
Lowest 20% of households:	na
Highest 10% of households:	na

HEALTH & NUTRITION

Population per physician 1981:	na
Daily calorie supply per capita 1985:	2294

TABLE 8

SOCIO-ECONOMIC INDICATORS

AGE AT LAST BIRTHDAY	ESTIMATED MID-YEAR POPULATION					BIRTHS BY AGE OF MOTHER AND SEX	DEATHS			AGE AT LAST BIRTHDAY
	BOTH SEXES	MALES		FEMALES			BOTH SEXES	MALES	FEMALES	
		Number	Percent	Number	Percent					
0	1961258	995882	3.9	965376	3.8		146022	80811	65211	0
1-4	7497765	3820818	14.9	3676947	14.4		70570	35348	35222	1-4
5-9	7844776	3995682	15.6	3849094	15.1		15839	8326	7513	5-9
10-14	6574060	3347347	13.1	3226713	12.6	11561	7452	4183	3269	10-14
15-19	5406849	2743556	10.7	2663293	10.4	227386	8698	5147	3551	15-19
20-24	4201558	2112212	8.2	2089346	8.2	594957	11103	6572	4531	20-24
25-29	3389830	1687848	6.6	1701982	6.7	537727	10926	6285	4641	25-29
30-34	2880535	1422916	5.6	1457619	5.7	357999	10922	6351	4571	30-34
35-39	2467904	1215314	4.7	1252590	4.9	258863	13910	8128	5782	35-39
40-44	1978512	971774	3.8	1006738	3.9	99902	12835	7639	5196	40-44
45-49	1742569	849194	3.3	893375	3.5	37994	14167	8466	5701	45-49
50-54	1322830	637666	2.5	685164	2.7	6241	13405	7915	5490	50-54
55-59	1179655	561426	2.2	618229	2.4		16150	9366	6784	55-59
60-64	938124	442127	1.7	495997	1.9		20602	11317	9285	60-64
65-69	728414	339456	1.3	388958	1.5		23416	12598	10818	65-69
70-74	501265	230590	0.9	270675	1.1		24580	13036	11544	70-74
75-79	319390	144811	0.6	174579	0.7		18090	9050	9040	75-79
80-84	125246	56151	0.2	69095	0.3	1071017 M	17434	8006	9428	80-84
85+	115573	49705	0.2	65868	0.3	1061613 F	29535	12282	17253	85+
TOTAL	51176113	25624475		25551638		2132630	485656	260826	224830	TOTAL

TABLE 1 DATA

TABLE 2 — MALE LIFE TABLE

x	$_nM_x$	$_nq_x$	l_x	$_nd_x$	$_nL_x$	$_nm_x$	$_na_x$	T_x	$\overset{\circ}{e}_x$	x
0	0.081145	0.076245	100000	7624	93961	0.081145	0.208	5920049	59.200	0
1	0.009251	0.036169	92376	3341	361149	0.009251	1.500	5826088	63.070	1
5	0.002084	0.010365	89034	923	442865	0.002084	2.500	5464939	61.380	5
10	0.001250	0.006214	88112	547	439168	0.001247	2.462	5022074	56.997	10
15	0.001876	0.009407	87564	824	435928	0.001890	2.702	4582906	52.338	15
20	0.003111	0.015524	86740	1347	430493	0.003128	2.617	4146978	47.809	20
25	0.003724	0.018499	85394	1580	423126	0.003733	2.567	3716485	43.522	25
30	0.004463	0.022161	83814	1857	414662	0.004479	2.626	3293359	39.294	30
35	0.006688	0.033034	81957	2707	403266	0.006714	2.593	2878698	35.125	35
40	0.007861	0.038652	79249	3063	388799	0.007879	2.569	2475432	31.236	40
45	0.009969	0.048812	76186	3719	371908	0.009999	2.574	2086632	27.389	45
50	0.012412	0.060444	72467	4380	351753	0.012453	2.584	1714724	23.662	50
55	0.016683	0.080469	68087	5479	327405	0.016734	2.622	1362971	20.018	55
60	0.025597	0.121048	62608	7579	294913	0.025698	2.608	1035567	16.540	60
65	0.037112	0.170931	55030	9406	252417	0.037265	2.583	740654	13.459	65
70	0.056533	0.248634	45623	11344	199737	0.056792	2.498	488237	10.701	70
75	0.062495	0.271446	34280	9305	148506	0.062658	2.540	288500	8.416	75
80	0.142580	0.525327	24975	13120	92018	0.142580	2.496	139994	5.605	80
85	0.247098	1.000000	11855	11855	47976	0.188355	4.047	47976	4.047	85

TABLE 3 — FEMALE LIFE TABLE

x	$_nM_x$	$_nq_x$	l_x	$_nd_x$	$_nL_x$	$_nm_x$	$_na_x$	T_x	$\overset{\circ}{e}_x$	x
0	0.067550	0.064024	100000	6402	94781	0.067550	0.185	6361248	63.612	0
1	0.009579	0.037420	93598	3502	365634	0.009579	1.500	6266467	66.951	1
5	0.001952	0.009712	90095	875	448288	0.001952	2.500	5900833	65.496	5
10	0.001013	0.005028	89220	449	444920	0.001008	2.369	5452545	61.113	10
15	0.001333	0.006684	88772	593	442480	0.001341	2.678	5007625	56.410	15
20	0.002169	0.010845	88178	956	438623	0.002180	2.629	4565145	51.772	20
25	0.002727	0.013579	87222	1184	433229	0.002734	2.568	4126521	47.311	25
30	0.003136	0.015609	86037	1343	426987	0.003145	2.617	3693292	42.927	30
35	0.004616	0.022900	84695	1939	418784	0.004631	2.583	3266305	38.566	35
40	0.005161	0.025529	82755	2113	408619	0.005170	2.559	2847521	34.409	40
45	0.006381	0.031507	80642	2541	397061	0.006399	2.579	2438902	30.243	45
50	0.008013	0.039437	78102	3080	383118	0.008040	2.601	2041841	26.143	50
55	0.010973	0.053698	75021	4029	365726	0.011015	2.671	1658723	22.110	55
60	0.018720	0.090058	70993	6394	339904	0.018810	2.644	1292997	18.213	60
65	0.027813	0.130974	64599	8461	302782	0.027944	2.611	953092	14.754	65
70	0.042649	0.194004	56139	10891	253888	0.042897	2.539	650310	11.584	70
75	0.051782	0.231869	45248	10491	201436	0.052083	2.636	396422	8.761	75
80	0.136450	0.510503	34756	17743	130033	0.136450	2.534	194985	5.610	80
85	0.261933	1.000000	17013	17013	64952	0.206673	3.818	64952	3.818	85

TABLE 4 — OBSERVED VITAL RATES AND RATIOS

CRUDE RATES

Per Thousand	BOTH SEXES	MALES	FEMALES
BIRTH RATE	41.67	41.80	41.55
DEATH RATE	9.49	10.18	8.80
RATE OF INCREASE	32.18	31.62	32.75

RATES STANDARDIZED ON USA 1980

Per Thousand	BOTH SEXES	MALES	FEMALES
BIRTH RATE	51.19		49.55
DEATH RATE	14.40	13.86	14.91
RATE OF INCREASE	36.79		34.64

VITAL STATISTICS

GFR x 1000	192.738
TFR	6.464
GRR	3.218
NRR	2.755
μ	30.024
σ^2	59.747
GENERATION	28.979
POP. SEX RATIO	0.997
SEX RATIO AT BIRTH	1.009
DEP. RATIO x 100	100.625

PERCENT OF POPULATION IN AGE GROUP

	BOTH SEXES	MALES	FEMALES
UNDER 15	46.66	47.45	45.86
15 - 64	49.84	49.34	50.35
65 AND OLDER	3.50	3.20	3.79

RATES STANDARDIZED ON MEXICO 1980

	BOTH SEXES	MALES	FEMALES
BIRTH RATE	44.38		44.53
DEATH RATE	8.56	9.20	7.92
RATE OF INCREASE	35.82		36.61

PROJECTED POPULATION

STABLE EQUIVALENT TO ORIGINAL POPULATION

AGE GROUP	1975 BOTH SEXES	1975 MALES	1975 FEMALES	1980 BOTH SEXES	1980 MALES	1980 FEMALES	MALES Number	MALES Percent	FEMALES Number	FEMALES Percent	AGE GROUP	
0-4	10763	5374	5389	12992	6487	6505	4608	18.8	4621	18.4	0-4	
5-9	9207	4687	4520	10476	5229	5247	3763	15.3	3776	15.0	5-9	TABLE 5
10-14	7782	3962	3820	9134	4648	4486	3132	12.8	3145	12.5	10-14	
15-19	6532	3323	3209	7732	3933	3799	2609	10.6	2625	10.4	15-19	POPULATION
20-24	5349	2709	2640	6462	3281	3181	2162	8.8	2184	8.7	20-24	PROJECTED
25-29	4140	2076	2064	5271	2663	2608	1783	7.3	1810	7.2	25-29	WITH
30-34	3331	1654	1677	4069	2035	2034	1467	6.0	1497	6.0	30-34	FIXED
35-39	2814	1384	1430	3254	1609	1645	1197	4.9	1232	4.9	35-39	AGE-
40-44	2394	1172	1222	2729	1334	1395	969	3.9	1009	4.0	40-44	SPECIFIC
45-49	1908	930	978	2309	1121	1188	777	3.2	823	3.3	45-49	BIRTH
50-54	1665	803	862	1823	879	944	617	2.5	666	2.7	50-54	AND
55-59	1248	594	654	1571	748	823	482	2.0	534	2.1	55-59	DEATH
60-64	1081	506	575	1143	535	608	364	1.5	416	1.7	60-64	RATES
65-69	820	378	442	945	433	512	262	1.1	311	1.2	65-69	(female
70-74	595	269	326	669	299	370	174	0.7	219	0.9	70-74	dominant,
75-79	386	171	215	459	200	259	108	0.4	146	0.6	75-79	in 000s)
80-84	203	90	113	245	106	139	56	0.2	79	0.3	80-84	
85+	64	29	35	103	47	56	25	0.1	33	0.1	85+	
TOTAL	60282	30111	30171	71386	35587	35799	24555		25126		TOTAL	

VITAL RATES OF PROJECTED POPULATION

VITAL RATES OF STABLE POPULATION

Per Thousand	1975 BOTH SEXES	1975 MALES	1975 FEMALES	1980 BOTH SEXES	1980 MALES	1980 FEMALES		MALES	FEMALES	
BIRTH RATE	42.63	42.86	42.40	43.53	43.85	43.21	BIRTH RATE	44.84	43.44	TABLE 6
DEATH RATE	9.13	9.78	8.48	9.24	9.87	8.62	DEATH RATE	9.63	8.38	PROJECTED
RATE OF INCREASE	33.50	33.07	33.92	34.28	33.97	34.59	RATE OF INCREASE		35.06	VITAL

AGE STRUCTURE OF PROJECTED POPULATION

STABLE AGE STRUCTURE

								MALES	FEMALES	RATES AND RATIOS
% UNDER 15	46.04	46.57	45.51	45.67	45.99	45.36	% UNDER 15	46.85	45.94	(female
% 15-64	50.53	50.31	50.75	50.94	50.97	50.91	% 15-64	50.61	50.93	dominant)
% 65 AND OLDER	3.43	3.11	3.75	3.39	3.05	3.73	% 65 AND OLDER	2.55	3.14	
DEPEND. RATIO x 100	97.90	98.75	97.05	96.32	96.21	96.43	DEPEND. RATIO x 100	97.59	96.36	

AGE GROUP	FEMALE BIRTH RATES	NET MATERNITY FUNCTION	COEFF. OF MATRIX EQUATION	ORIGINAL MATRIX SUB-DIAGONAL	ORIGINAL MATRIX FIRST ROW	STABLE MATRIX FISHER VALUES	STABLE MATRIX REPRODUCTIVE VALUES	MATRIX PARAMETERS		
0-4	0.0000	0.0000	0.0000	0.97366	0.00000	1.184	5496928	λ_1	1.19160	
5-9	0.0000	0.0000	0.0040	0.99249	0.00408	1.449	5577822	λ_2	$0.42900-0.76750i$	TABLE 7
10-14	0.0018	0.0079	0.0980	0.99452	0.10141	1.735	5598290	λ_4	$0.10344-0.65238i$	
15-19	0.0425	0.1881	0.4049	0.99128	0.42132	1.958	5214889	λ_6	$-0.50778-0.41269i$	LESLIE
20-24	0.1418	0.6218	0.6516	0.98770	0.68393	1.850	3866273	r_1	0.03506	MATRIX
25-29	0.1573	0.6814	0.6017	0.98559	0.63946	1.413	2404146	r_2	$-0.02574-0.21222i$	AND ITS
30-34	0.1223	0.5220	0.4764	0.98079	0.51373	0.940	1369521	r_4	$-0.08294-0.28271i$	ANALYSIS
35-39	0.1029	0.4308	0.3163	0.97573	0.34778	0.521	652959	r_6	$-0.08483-0.49183i$	(females)
40-44	0.0494	0.2018	0.1430	0.97172	0.16108	0.215	216010	c_1	251252	
45-49	0.0212	0.0841	0.0507	0.96488	0.05881	0.067	59710	$2\pi/\gamma$	29.6070	
50-54	0.0045	0.0174	0.0087	0.95461	0.01044	0.010	7107	Δ	1.6785	

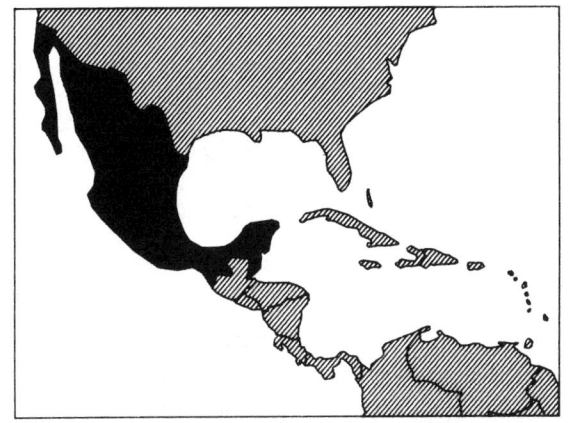

EDUCATION [1984]

% of primary school-age children enrolled:	116
secondary school-age children enrolled:	55
ca. 20-24 year olds in higher education:	15

LABOR FORCE

Average annual labor force growth (%) 1980-85:	3.2	
% of the 1980 labor force in agriculture:	37	TABLE 8
in industry:	29	
in services:	35	SOCIO-ECONOMIC INDICATORS

GNP & INCOME DISTRIBUTION

GNP per capita (in US Dollars) 1985:	2080
GNP average annual growth rate (%) 1965-85:	2.7
% share of total household income 1977	
Lowest 20% of households:	2.9
Highest 10% of households:	40.6

HEALTH & NUTRITION

Population per physician 1981:	1200
Daily calorie supply per capita 1985:	3177

TABLE 1 DATA

AGE AT LAST BIRTHDAY	ESTIMATED MID-YEAR POPULATION BOTH SEXES	MALES Number	MALES Percent	FEMALES Number	FEMALES Percent	BIRTHS BY AGE OF MOTHER AND SEX	DEATHS BOTH SEXES	DEATHS MALES	DEATHS FEMALES	AGE AT LAST BIRTHDAY
0	2093367	1063110	2.8	1030257	2.8		79878	44893	34985	0
1-4	8382014	4255950	11.3	4126064	11.1		22446	11659	10787	1-4
5-9	10532933	5349547	14.3	5183386	14.0		7032	4071	2961	5-9
10-14	10174699	5168710	13.8	5005989	13.5	7393	5772	3573	2199	10-14
15-19	8720535	4422967	11.8	4297568	11.6	407852	9461	6525	2936	15-19
20-24	7147209	3607927	9.6	3539282	9.5	827602	13164	9545	3619	20-24
25-29	5774486	2904145	7.7	2870341	7.7	631662	12917	9291	3626	25-29
30-34	4656514	2341445	6.2	2315069	6.2	380631	12285	8637	3648	30-34
35-39	3826568	1924093	5.1	1902475	5.1	224258	13594	9337	4257	35-39
40-44	3100434	1551538	4.1	1548901	4.2	84779	13796	9086	4710	40-44
45-49	2543016	1265930	3.4	1277086	3.4	37725	15781	10157	5624	45-49
50-54	2105021	1040022	2.8	1064999	2.9	7186	17583	10966	6617	50-54
55-59	1708777	832837	2.2	875940	2.4		19993	11880	8113	55-59
60-64	1318842	632450	1.7	686392	1.9		22472	12913	9559	60-64
65-69	957176	452465	1.2	504711	1.4		22731	12615	10116	65-69
70-74	690168	320401	0.9	369767	1.0		29335	15764	13571	70-74
75-79	471389	213363	0.6	258026	0.7		28324	14638	13686	75-79
80-84	272919	120111	0.3	152808	0.4	1317916 M	30039	14544	15495	80-84
85+	148943	63112	0.2	85831	0.2	1291172 F	36800	14845	21955	85+
TOTAL	74625010	37530118		37094892		2609088	413403	234939	178464	TOTAL

TABLE 2 MALE LIFE TABLE

x	$_nM_x$	$_nq_x$	l_x	$_nd_x$	$_nL_x$	$_nm_x$	$_na_x$	T_x	$\overset{\circ}{e}_x$	x
0	0.042228	0.040751	100000	4075	96503	0.042228	0.142	6585448	65.854	0
1	0.002739	0.010883	95925	1044	381090	0.002739	1.500	6488946	67.646	1
5	0.000761	0.003798	94881	360	473504	0.000761	2.500	6107856	64.374	5
10	0.000691	0.003459	94521	327	471856	0.000693	2.715	5634353	59.610	10
15	0.001475	0.007407	94194	698	469413	0.001486	2.771	5162497	54.807	15
20	0.002646	0.013216	93496	1236	464551	0.002660	2.630	4693083	50.196	20
25	0.003199	0.015911	92260	1468	457721	0.003207	2.561	4228532	45.833	25
30	0.003689	0.018334	90792	1665	449941	0.003700	2.585	3770811	41.532	30
35	0.004853	0.024064	89128	2145	440455	0.004869	2.583	3320870	37.260	35
40	0.005856	0.028977	86983	2521	428862	0.005877	2.599	2880415	33.115	40
45	0.008023	0.039517	84462	3338	414315	0.008056	2.604	2451553	29.025	45
50	0.010544	0.051603	81125	4186	395573	0.010583	2.599	2037238	25.112	50
55	0.014264	0.069269	76938	5329	371956	0.014328	2.610	1641665	21.337	55
60	0.020417	0.097817	71609	7005	341194	0.020530	2.594	1269709	17.731	60
65	0.027881	0.131577	64604	8500	302895	0.028064	2.632	928515	14.372	65
70	0.049201	0.220994	56104	12399	250434	0.049509	2.573	625620	11.151	70
75	0.068606	0.294555	43705	12874	186742	0.068938	2.531	375185	8.584	75
80	0.121088	0.464327	30832	14316	118228	0.121088	2.490	188443	6.112	80
85	0.235217	1.000000	16516	16516	70215	0.173726	4.251	70215	4.251	85

TABLE 3 FEMALE LIFE TABLE

x	$_nM_x$	$_nq_x$	l_x	$_nd_x$	$_nL_x$	$_nm_x$	$_na_x$	T_x	$\overset{\circ}{e}_x$	x
0	0.033958	0.032981	100000	3298	97123	0.033958	0.128	7158166	71.582	0
1	0.002614	0.010390	96702	1005	384296	0.002614	1.500	7061043	73.019	1
5	0.000571	0.002852	95697	273	477804	0.000571	2.500	6676747	69.769	5
10	0.000439	0.002195	95424	209	476609	0.000439	2.553	6198943	64.962	10
15	0.000683	0.003426	95215	326	475316	0.000686	2.676	5722334	60.099	15
20	0.001023	0.005121	94889	486	473285	0.001027	2.616	5247018	55.297	20
25	0.001263	0.006315	94403	596	470576	0.001267	2.589	4773733	50.568	25
30	0.001576	0.007881	93807	739	467277	0.001582	2.625	4303157	45.873	30
35	0.002238	0.011183	93067	1041	462871	0.002249	2.631	3835880	41.216	35
40	0.003041	0.015172	92027	1396	456839	0.003056	2.641	3373009	36.653	40
45	0.004404	0.021901	90630	1985	448467	0.004426	2.640	2916170	32.177	45
50	0.006213	0.030765	88645	2727	436811	0.006243	2.647	2467704	27.838	50
55	0.009262	0.045563	85918	3915	420395	0.009312	2.651	2030892	23.638	55
60	0.013926	0.067814	82004	5561	396836	0.014013	2.630	1610498	19.639	60
65	0.020043	0.096449	76443	7373	365065	0.020196	2.674	1213662	15.877	65
70	0.036701	0.169768	69070	11726	317325	0.036952	2.610	848597	12.286	70
75	0.053041	0.236590	57344	13567	254071	0.053398	2.594	531273	9.265	75
80	0.101402	0.407020	43777	17818	175718	0.101402	2.577	277201	6.332	80
85	0.255793	1.000000	25959	25959	101484	0.198865	3.909	101484	3.909	85

TABLE 4 OBSERVED VITAL RATES AND RATIOS

CRUDE RATES

Per Thousand	BOTH SEXES	MALES	FEMALES
BIRTH RATE	34.96	35.12	34.81
DEATH RATE	5.54	6.26	4.81
RATE OF INCREASE	29.42	28.86	30.00

PERCENT OF POPULATION IN AGE GROUP

UNDER 15	41.79	42.20	41.37
15 - 64	54.81	54.69	54.93
65 AND OLDER	3.40	3.12	3.70

RATES STANDARDIZED ON USA 1980

Per Thousand	BOTH SEXES	MALES	FEMALES
BIRTH RATE	37.46		36.05
DEATH RATE	11.33	11.06	11.58
RATE OF INCREASE	26.14		24.47

RATES STANDARDIZED ON MEXICO 1980

	BOTH SEXES	MALES	FEMALES
BIRTH RATE	33.30		33.22
DEATH RATE	5.44	6.16	4.70
RATE OF INCREASE	27.87		28.52

VITAL STATISTICS

GFR x 1000	146.985
TFR	4.618
GRR	2.285
NRR	2.141
μ	28.953
σ^2	61.640
GENERATION	28.118
POP. SEX RATIO	0.988
SEX RATIO AT BIRTH	1.021
DEP. RATIO x 100	82.451

PROJECTED POPULATION

AGE GROUP	1988			1993		
	BOTH SEXES	MALES	FEMALES	BOTH SEXES	MALES	FEMALES
0-4	13811	6949	6862	16405	8254	8151
5-9	10392	5274	5118	13700	6889	6811
10-14	10501	5331	5170	10360	5255	5105
15-19	10134	5142	4992	10459	5303	5156
20-24	8656	4377	4279	10060	5089	4971
25-29	7074	3555	3519	8568	4313	4255
30-34	5705	2855	2850	6988	3494	3494
35-39	4585	2292	2293	5618	2795	2823
40-44	3751	1873	1878	4495	2232	2263
45-49	3020	1499	1521	3653	1810	1843
50-54	2453	1209	1244	2912	1431	1481
55-59	2003	978	1025	2334	1137	1197
60-64	1591	764	827	1865	897	968
65-69	1192	561	631	1439	678	761
70-74	813	374	439	1013	464	549
75-79	535	239	296	630	279	351
80-84	313	135	178	356	151	205
85+	159	71	88	183	80	103
TOTAL	86688	43478	43210	101038	50551	50487

STABLE EQUIVALENT TO ORIGINAL POPULATION

	MALES		FEMALES		AGE GROUP	
	Number	Percent	Number	Percent		
	6076	15.5	6001	14.9	0-4	
	5260	13.4	5200	12.9	5-9	TABLE 5
	4577	11.6	4530	11.3	10-14	
	3976	10.1	3944	9.8	15-19	POPULATION
	3436	8.7	3429	8.5	20-24	PROJECTED
	2956	7.5	2977	7.4	25-29	WITH
	2537	6.5	2582	6.4	30-34	FIXED
	2169	5.5	2233	5.6	35-39	AGE-
	1844	4.7	1924	4.8	40-44	SPECIFIC
	1555	4.0	1649	4.1	45-49	BIRTH
	1297	3.3	1403	3.5	50-54	AND
	1065	2.7	1179	2.9	55-59	DEATH
	853	2.2	972	2.4	60-64	RATES
	661	1.7	781	1.9	65-69	(female
	477	1.2	592	1.5	70-74	dominant,
	311	0.8	414	1.0	75-79	in 000s)
	172	0.4	250	0.6	80-84	
	89	0.2	126	0.3	85+	
	39311		40186		TOTAL	

VITAL RATES OF PROJECTED POPULATION

Per Thousand	1988			1993		
	BOTH SEXES	MALES	FEMALES	BOTH SEXES	MALES	FEMALES
BIRTH RATE	36.35	36.61	36.09	36.53	36.88	36.18
DEATH RATE	5.73	6.50	4.96	5.82	6.60	5.04
RATE OF INCREASE	30.62	30.11	31.13	30.72	30.29	31.15

VITAL RATES OF STABLE POPULATION

Per Thousand	MALES	FEMALES	
BIRTH RATE	34.56	33.12	TABLE 6
DEATH RATE	7.39	5.99	PROJECTED
RATE OF INCREASE		27.12	VITAL RATES

AGE STRUCTURE OF PROJECTED POPULATION

	BOTH SEXES	MALES	FEMALES	BOTH SEXES	MALES	FEMALES
% UNDER 15	40.03	40.37	39.69	40.05	40.35	39.75
% 15-64	56.49	56.45	56.53	56.37	56.38	56.36
% 65 AND OLDER	3.48	3.18	3.78	3.58	3.27	3.90
DEPEND. RATIO x 100	77.02	77.14	76.89	77.41	77.37	77.45

STABLE AGE STRUCTURE

	MALES	FEMALES	
% UNDER 15	40.48	39.14	AND RATIOS
% 15-64	55.17	55.47	(female
% 65 AND OLDER	4.35	5.38	dominant)
DEPEND. RATIO x 100	81.26	80.27	

AGE GROUP	FEMALE BIRTH RATES	NET MATERNITY FUNCTION	COEFF. OF MATRIX EQUATION	ORIGINAL MATRIX SUB-DIAGONAL	ORIGINAL MATRIX FIRST ROW	STABLE MATRIX FISHER VALUES	STABLE MATRIX REPRODUCTIVE VALUES	MATRIX PARAMETERS		
0-4	0.0000	0.0000	0.0000	0.99249	0.00000	1.111	5728234	λ_1	1.14524	
5-9	0.0000	0.0000	0.0017	0.99750	0.00175	1.282	6644541	λ_2	0.35359-0.70745i	TABLE 7
10-14	0.0007	0.0035	0.1134	0.99729	0.11450	1.470	7357813	λ_4	0.20187-0.61457i	
15-19	0.0470	0.2232	0.3855	0.99573	0.39040	1.560	6705528	λ_6	-0.50593-0.36960i	LESLIE
20-24	0.1157	0.5477	0.5301	0.99428	0.53919	1.359	4809999	r_1	0.02712	MATRIX
25-29	0.1089	0.5125	0.4463	0.99299	0.45662	0.963	2763959	r_2	-0.04692-0.22146i	AND ITS
30-34	0.0814	0.3802	0.3251	0.99057	0.33494	0.600	1388416	r_4	-0.08712-0.25068i	ANALYSIS
35-39	0.0583	0.2700	0.1969	0.98697	0.20477	0.318	604485	r_6	-0.09350-0.50213i	(females)
40-44	0.0271	0.1237	0.0947	0.98167	0.09974	0.138	214068	c_1	401869	
45-49	0.0146	0.0656	0.0401	0.97401	0.04302	0.048	61758	$2\pi/y$	28.3717	
50-54	0.0033	0.0146	0.0073	0.96242	0.00804	0.008	8303	Δ	6.3635	

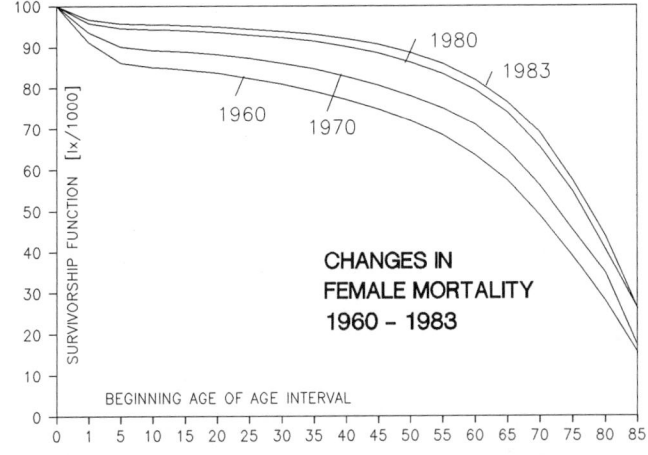

CHANGES IN FEMALE MORTALITY 1960 – 1983

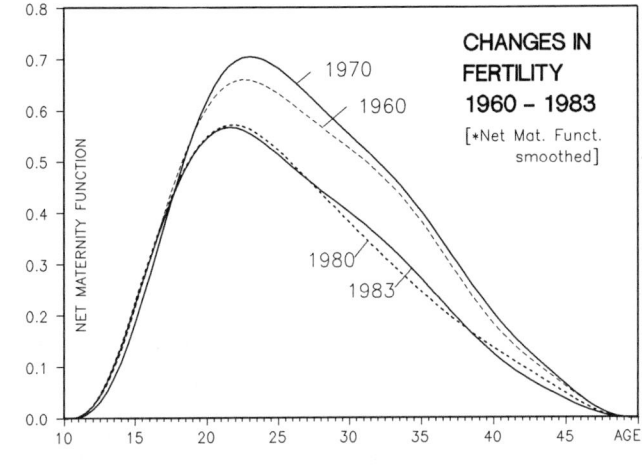

CHANGES IN FERTILITY 1960 – 1983

[*Net Mat. Funct. smoothed]

TABLE 1 — DATA

AGE AT LAST BIRTHDAY	ESTIMATED MID-YEAR POPULATION BOTH SEXES	MALES Number	MALES Percent	FEMALES Number	FEMALES Percent	BIRTHS BY AGE OF MOTHER AND SEX	DEATHS BOTH SEXES	DEATHS MALES	DEATHS FEMALES	AGE AT LAST BIRTHDAY
0	46710	23837	3.3	22873	3.2		2180	1230	950	0
1-4	185695	94065	12.9	91630	13.0		1416	737	679	1-4
5-9	216369	108969	15.0	107400	15.2		377	208	169	5-9
10-14	174294	88678	12.2	85616	12.1	206	173	101	72	10-14
15-19	145839	72145	9.9	73694	10.4	9675	223	127	96	15-19
20-24	125868	62589	8.6	63279	8.9	17323	232	132	100	20-24
25-29	102127	50986	7.0	51141	7.2	12566	218	113	105	25-29
30-34	82875	41816	5.8	41059	5.8	7532	216	121	95	30-34
35-39	73704	37435	5.2	36269	5.1	4449	220	102	118	35-39
40-44	61201	31667	4.4	29534	4.2	1308	236	125	111	40-44
45-49	53554	28086	3.9	25468	3.6	226	303	164	139	45-49
50-54	46757	24889	3.4	21868	3.1	2	370	207	163	50-54
55-59	37975	20268	2.8	17707	2.5		446	258	188	55-59
60-64	28006	14947	2.1	13059	1.8		525	289	236	60-64
65-69	20483	10379	1.4	10104	1.4		618	346	272	65-69
70-74	13583	6864	0.9	6719	0.9		617	343	274	70-74
75-79	9403	4781	0.7	4622	0.7		590	333	257	75-79
80-84	5261	2484	0.3	2777	0.4	27105 M	570	291	279	80-84
85+	4393	1876	0.3	2517	0.4	26182 F	695	306	389	85+
TOTAL	1434097	726761		707336		53287	10225	5533	4692	TOTAL

TABLE 2 — MALE LIFE TABLE

x	nM_x	nq_x	l_x	nd_x	nL_x	nm_x	na_x	T_x	$\overset{o}{e}_x$	x
0	0.051600	0.049451	100000	4945	95835	0.051600	0.158	6522430	65.224	0
1	0.007835	0.030738	95055	2922	372915	0.007835	1.500	6426595	67.609	1
5	0.001909	0.009499	92133	875	458478	0.001909	2.500	6053680	65.706	5
10	0.001139	0.005660	91258	517	454982	0.001135	2.469	5595202	61.312	10
15	0.001760	0.008799	90741	798	451800	0.001767	2.612	5140220	56.647	15
20	0.002109	0.010505	89943	945	447391	0.002112	2.541	4688420	52.127	20
25	0.002216	0.011042	88998	983	442600	0.002220	2.568	4241029	47.653	25
30	0.002894	0.014387	88015	1266	436951	0.002898	2.532	3798428	43.156	30
35	0.002725	0.013553	86749	1176	430892	0.002729	2.573	3361477	38.749	35
40	0.003947	0.019635	85573	1680	423926	0.003964	2.655	2930585	34.246	40
45	0.005839	0.028884	83893	2423	413752	0.005857	2.642	2506659	29.879	45
50	0.008317	0.040918	81470	3334	399523	0.008344	2.652	2092907	25.689	50
55	0.012729	0.062141	78136	4856	379271	0.012802	2.650	1693384	21.672	55
60	0.019335	0.093186	73281	6829	350475	0.019484	2.667	1314113	17.933	60
65	0.033337	0.155574	66452	10338	307605	0.033609	2.615	963638	14.501	65
70	0.049971	0.223475	56114	12540	249773	0.050206	2.544	656033	11.691	70
75	0.069651	0.298292	43574	12998	185635	0.070017	2.520	406260	9.323	75
80	0.117150	0.451019	30576	13790	117716	0.117150	2.450	220624	7.216	80
85	0.163113	1.000000	16786	16786	102908	0.094185	6.131	102908	6.131	85

TABLE 3 — FEMALE LIFE TABLE

x	nM_x	nq_x	l_x	nd_x	nL_x	nm_x	na_x	T_x	$\overset{o}{e}_x$	x
0	0.041534	0.040102	100000	4010	96554	0.041534	0.141	6787143	67.871	0
1	0.007410	0.029102	95990	2793	376975	0.007410	1.500	6690590	69.701	1
5	0.001574	0.007837	93196	730	464156	0.001574	2.500	6313614	67.745	5
10	0.000841	0.004177	92466	386	461337	0.000837	2.430	5849459	63.261	10
15	0.001303	0.006516	92080	600	458969	0.001307	2.617	5388122	58.516	15
20	0.001580	0.007893	91480	722	455662	0.001585	2.595	4929153	53.882	20
25	0.002053	0.010243	90758	930	451530	0.002059	2.570	4473491	49.291	25
30	0.002314	0.011539	89828	1037	446654	0.002321	2.602	4021961	44.774	30
35	0.003253	0.016189	88791	1437	440488	0.003263	2.586	3575307	40.266	35
40	0.003758	0.018686	87354	1632	432873	0.003771	2.612	3134819	35.886	40
45	0.005458	0.027038	85722	2318	423113	0.005478	2.629	2701947	31.520	45
50	0.007454	0.036750	83404	3065	409747	0.007481	2.627	2278834	27.323	50
55	0.010617	0.052148	80339	4190	391966	0.010689	2.678	1869087	23.265	55
60	0.018072	0.087273	76149	6646	365101	0.018202	2.646	1477121	19.398	60
65	0.026920	0.127221	69504	8842	326385	0.027092	2.610	1112019	15.999	65
70	0.040780	0.186507	60661	11314	275709	0.041035	2.561	785635	12.951	70
75	0.055604	0.246028	49348	12141	217141	0.055912	2.562	509926	10.333	75
80	0.100468	0.401584	37207	14942	148720	0.100468	2.503	292784	7.869	80
85	0.154549	1.000000	22265	22265	144065	0.085618	6.470	144065	6.470	85

TABLE 4 — OBSERVED VITAL RATES AND RATIOS

CRUDE RATES

Per Thousand	BOTH SEXES	MALES	FEMALES
BIRTH RATE	37.16	37.30	37.01
DEATH RATE	7.13	7.61	6.63
RATE OF INCREASE	30.03	29.68	30.38

PERCENT OF POPULATION IN AGE GROUP

	BOTH SEXES	MALES	FEMALES
UNDER 15	43.45	43.42	43.48
15 - 64	52.85	52.95	52.74
65 AND OLDER	3.70	3.63	3.78

RATES STANDARDIZED ON USA 1980

Per Thousand	BOTH SEXES	MALES	FEMALES
BIRTH RATE	42.08		40.21
DEATH RATE	11.28	10.64	11.88
RATE OF INCREASE	30.81		28.33

RATES STANDARDIZED ON MEXICO 1980

	BOTH SEXES	MALES	FEMALES
BIRTH RATE	38.15		37.78
DEATH RATE	6.45	6.77	6.12
RATE OF INCREASE	31.70		31.66

VITAL STATISTICS

GFR x 1000	166.291
TFR	5.063
GRR	2.487
NRR	2.240
μ	27.655
σ^2	49.724
GENERATION	26.910
POP. SEX RATIO	0.973
SEX RATIO AT BIRTH	1.035
DEP. RATIO x 100	89.218

PROJECTED POPULATION

TABLE 5

POPULATION PROJECTED WITH FIXED AGE-SPECIFIC BIRTH AND DEATH RATES (female dominant, in 000s)

AGE GROUP	1975 BOTH SEXES	1975 MALES	1975 FEMALES	1980 BOTH SEXES	1980 MALES	1980 FEMALES	STABLE EQUIVALENT TO ORIGINAL POPULATION: MALES Number	MALES Percent	FEMALES Number	FEMALES Percent	AGE GROUP
0-4	274	139	135	324	164	160	122	*16.5*	119	*16.3*	0-4
5-9	227	115	112	269	136	133	103	*13.9*	100	*13.8*	5-9
10-14	215	108	107	226	114	112	88	*11.9*	86	*11.8*	10-14
15-19	173	88	85	213	107	106	75	*10.2*	73	*10.1*	15-19
20-24	144	71	73	172	87	85	64	*8.6*	63	*8.6*	20-24
25-29	125	62	63	144	71	73	54	*7.4*	53	*7.3*	25-29
30-34	101	50	51	123	61	62	46	*6.3*	46	*6.3*	30-34
35-39	81	41	40	100	50	50	39	*5.3*	39	*5.3*	35-39
40-44	73	37	36	81	41	40	33	*4.5*	33	*4.5*	40-44
45-49	60	31	29	71	36	35	28	*3.8*	27	*3.8*	45-49
50-54	52	27	25	58	30	28	23	*3.1*	23	*3.1*	50-54
55-59	45	24	21	50	26	24	19	*2.6*	19	*2.6*	55-59
60-64	35	19	16	41	22	19	15	*2.0*	15	*2.1*	60-64
65-69	25	13	12	31	16	15	11	*1.5*	12	*1.6*	65-69
70-74	17	8	9	21	11	10	8	*1.1*	8	*1.2*	70-74
75-79	10	5	5	13	6	7	5	*0.7*	6	*0.8*	75-79
80-84	6	3	3	7	3	4	3	*0.4*	3	*0.5*	80-84
85+	5	2	3	6	3	3	2	*0.3*	3	*0.4*	85+
TOTAL	1668	843	825	1950	984	966	738		728		TOTAL

VITAL RATES OF PROJECTED POPULATION / VITAL RATES OF STABLE POPULATION

TABLE 6

PROJECTED VITAL RATES AND RATIOS (female dominant)

Per Thousand	1975 BOTH SEXES	1975 MALES	1975 FEMALES	1980 BOTH SEXES	1980 MALES	1980 FEMALES	STABLE MALES	STABLE FEMALES
BIRTH RATE	37.74	37.94	37.53	38.40	38.66	38.13	37.91	37.10
DEATH RATE	7.18	7.69	6.65	7.26	7.80	6.72	7.81	7.04
RATE OF INCREASE	30.56	30.25	30.88	31.14	30.87	31.41		30.06

AGE STRUCTURE OF PROJECTED POPULATION / STABLE AGE STRUCTURE

	1975 BOTH SEXES	1975 MALES	1975 FEMALES	1980 BOTH SEXES	1980 MALES	1980 FEMALES	STABLE MALES	STABLE FEMALES
% UNDER 15	42.93	42.89	42.97	42.05	42.12	41.98	42.32	41.91
% 15-64	53.28	53.34	53.22	53.98	53.89	54.08	53.72	53.70
% 65 AND OLDER	3.79	3.77	3.80	3.97	3.99	3.95	3.96	4.39
DEPEND. RATIO x 100	87.69	87.49	87.89	85.24	85.55	84.92	86.15	86.23

TABLE 7

LESLIE MATRIX AND ITS ANALYSIS (females)

AGE GROUP	FEMALE BIRTH RATES	NET MATERNITY FUNCTION	COEFF. OF MATRIX EQUATION	ORIGINAL MATRIX SUB-DIAGONAL	ORIGINAL MATRIX FIRST ROW	STABLE MATRIX FISHER VALUES	STABLE MATRIX REPRODUCTIVE VALUES
0-4	0.0000	0.0000	0.0000	0.98021	0.00000	1.137	130240
5-9	0.0000	0.0000	0.0027	0.99393	0.00278	1.349	144838
10-14	0.0012	0.0055	0.1508	0.99487	0.15474	1.574	134732
15-19	0.0645	0.2961	0.4545	0.99280	0.46890	1.661	122434
20-24	0.1345	0.6129	0.5790	0.99093	0.60171	1.408	89072
25-29	0.1207	0.5451	0.4739	0.98920	0.49694	0.960	49104
30-34	0.0901	0.4026	0.3340	0.98619	0.35413	0.557	22855
35-39	0.0603	0.2655	0.1798	0.98271	0.19333	0.248	8977
40-44	0.0218	0.0942	0.0563	0.97745	0.06161	0.069	2037
45-49	0.0044	0.0184	0.0093	0.96841	0.01043	0.010	262
50-54	0.0000	0.0002	0.0001	0.95661	0.00011	0.000	2

MATRIX PARAMETERS

λ_1	1.16217
λ_2	0.36547-0.75582i
λ_4	0.02434-0.65879i
λ_6	-0.44260-0.35400i
r_1	0.03006
r_2	-0.03498-0.22408i
r_4	-0.08333-0.30677i
r_6	-0.11357-0.49339i
c_1	7277
$2\pi/y$	28.0400
Δ	2.3742

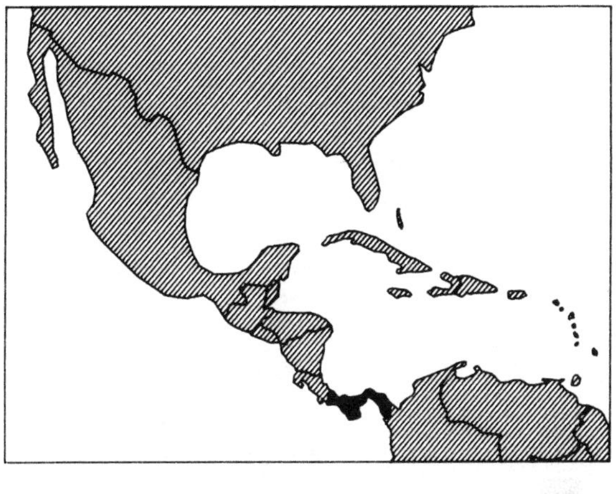

TABLE 8

SOCIO-ECONOMIC INDICATORS

EDUCATION [1984]

% of primary school-age children enrolled:	105
secondary school-age children enrolled:	59
ca. 20-24 year olds in higher education:	25

LABOR FORCE

Average annual labor force growth (%) 1980-85:	3.0
% of the 1980 labor force in agriculture:	32
in industry:	18
in services:	50

GNP & INCOME DISTRIBUTION

GNP per capita (in US Dollars) 1985:	2100
GNP average annual growth rate (%) 1965-85:	2.5
% share of total household income 1973	
Lowest 20% of households:	2.0
Highest 10% of households:	44.2

HEALTH & NUTRITION

Population per physician 1981:	1010
Daily calorie supply per capita 1985:	2419

AGE AT LAST BIRTHDAY	ESTIMATED MID-YEAR POPULATION					BIRTHS BY AGE OF MOTHER AND SEX	DEATHS			AGE AT LAST BIRTHDAY
	BOTH SEXES	MALES Number	Percent	FEMALES Number	Percent		BOTH SEXES	MALES	FEMALES	
0	45514	23104	2.5	22410	2.5		1162	636	526	0
1-4	213146	108216	11.6	104930	11.7		515	250	265	1-4
5-9	246670	125210	13.4	121460	13.5		158	89	69	5-9
10-14	225690	115230	12.3	110460	12.3	295	107	60	47	10-14
15-19	198850	101890	10.9	96960	10.8	10598	195	133	62	15-19
20-24	172250	88310	9.4	83940	9.3	17352	223	155	68	20-24
25-29	146830	75180	8.0	71650	8.0	12397	184	121	63	25-29
30-34	117640	60520	6.5	57120	6.3	7128	197	128	69	30-34
35-39	97840	50510	5.4	47330	5.3	3502	210	121	89	35-39
40-44	79410	40640	4.3	38770	4.3	1135	205	119	86	40-44
45-49	69060	35050	3.7	34010	3.8	199	244	152	92	45-49
50-54	56820	29040	3.1	27780	3.1	20	324	188	136	50-54
55-59	49010	25120	2.7	23890	2.7		401	256	145	55-59
60-64	41150	21090	2.3	20060	2.2		539	332	207	60-64
65-69	32250	16230	1.7	16020	1.8		633	414	219	65-69
70-74	21390	10450	1.1	10940	1.2		594	358	236	70-74
75-79	12680	6030	0.6	6650	0.7		683	390	293	75-79
80-84	5881	2707	0.3	3174	0.4	26853 M	575	316	259	80-84
85+	4479	1803	0.2	2676	0.3	25773 F	810	355	455	85+
TOTAL	1836560	936330		900230		52626	7959	4573	3386	TOTAL

TABLE 1 — DATA

TABLE 2 — MALE LIFE TABLE

x	$_nM_x$	$_nq_x$	l_x	$_nd_x$	$_nL_x$	$_nm_x$	$_na_x$	T_x	$\mathring{e}_x$	x
0	0.027528	0.026874	100000	2687	97626	0.027528	0.117	7098321	70.983	0
1	0.002310	0.009188	97313	894	387015	0.002310	1.500	7000694	71.940	1
5	0.000711	0.003548	96418	342	481237	0.000711	2.500	6613679	68.593	5
10	0.000521	0.002608	96076	251	479815	0.000522	2.736	6132442	63.829	10
15	0.001305	0.006536	95826	626	477685	0.001311	2.694	5652627	58.989	15
20	0.001755	0.008749	95200	833	473943	0.001757	2.533	5174942	54.359	20
25	0.001609	0.008020	94367	757	469974	0.001610	2.543	4700999	49.816	25
30	0.002115	0.010551	93610	988	465653	0.002121	2.573	4231025	45.198	30
35	0.002396	0.011933	92622	1105	460421	0.002401	2.566	3765372	40.653	35
40	0.002928	0.014599	91517	1336	454420	0.002940	2.631	3304952	36.113	40
45	0.004337	0.021569	90181	1945	446352	0.004358	2.660	2850532	31.609	45
50	0.006474	0.032045	88236	2828	434594	0.006506	2.671	2404180	27.247	50
55	0.010191	0.049968	85408	4268	417071	0.010233	2.664	1969586	23.061	55
60	0.015742	0.076228	81141	6185	391239	0.015809	2.662	1552515	19.134	60
65	0.025508	0.120958	74955	9066	353010	0.025683	2.599	1161275	15.493	65
70	0.034258	0.159405	65889	10503	304558	0.034486	2.631	808265	12.267	70
75	0.064677	0.282532	55386	15648	239356	0.065377	2.599	503707	9.094	75
80	0.116734	0.451187	39738	17929	153588	0.116734	2.485	264351	6.652	80
85	0.196894	1.000000	21809	21809	110763	0.129284	5.079	110763	5.079	85

TABLE 3 — FEMALE LIFE TABLE

x	$_nM_x$	$_nq_x$	l_x	$_nd_x$	$_nL_x$	$_nm_x$	$_na_x$	T_x	$\mathring{e}_x$	x
0	0.023472	0.022991	100000	2299	97954	0.023472	0.110	7586049	75.860	0
1	0.002525	0.010039	97701	981	388352	0.002525	1.500	7488095	76.643	1
5	0.000568	0.002836	96720	274	482915	0.000568	2.500	7099744	73.405	5
10	0.000425	0.002126	96446	205	481723	0.000426	2.534	6616829	68.607	10
15	0.000639	0.003202	96241	308	480472	0.000641	2.624	6135106	63.747	15
20	0.000810	0.004049	95933	388	478715	0.000811	2.560	5654634	58.944	20
25	0.000879	0.004397	95544	420	476710	0.000881	2.593	5175919	54.173	25
30	0.001208	0.006056	95124	576	474278	0.001215	2.669	4699210	49.401	30
35	0.001880	0.009401	94548	889	470614	0.001889	2.608	4224932	44.686	35
40	0.002218	0.011056	93659	1036	465783	0.002223	2.573	3754318	40.085	40
45	0.002705	0.013511	92624	1251	460237	0.002719	2.697	3288536	35.504	45
50	0.004896	0.024315	91372	2222	451604	0.004920	2.634	2828299	30.954	50
55	0.006069	0.030047	89150	2679	439504	0.006095	2.667	2376695	26.659	55
60	0.010319	0.050579	86472	4374	422006	0.010364	2.633	1937191	22.403	60
65	0.013670	0.066588	82098	5467	397569	0.013750	2.636	1515185	18.456	65
70	0.021572	0.103722	76631	7948	365034	0.021774	2.720	1117617	14.584	70
75	0.044060	0.201712	68683	13854	311017	0.044545	2.661	752583	10.957	75
80	0.081601	0.340820	54829	18687	229003	0.081601	2.584	441566	8.054	80
85	0.170030	1.000000	36142	36142	212563	0.100751	5.881	212563	5.881	85

TABLE 4 — OBSERVED VITAL RATES AND RATIOS

CRUDE RATES

Per Thousand	BOTH SEXES	MALES	FEMALES
BIRTH RATE	28.65	28.68	28.63
DEATH RATE	4.33	4.88	3.76
RATE OF INCREASE	24.32	23.80	24.87

PERCENT OF POPULATION IN AGE GROUP

	BOTH SEXES	MALES	FEMALES
UNDER 15	39.80	39.70	39.91
15 - 64	56.02	56.32	55.71
65 AND OLDER	4.18	3.98	4.38

RATES STANDARDIZED ON USA 1980

Per Thousand	BOTH SEXES	MALES	FEMALES
BIRTH RATE	30.50		29.05
DEATH RATE	8.40	8.49	8.30
RATE OF INCREASE	22.10		20.74

RATES STANDARDIZED ON MEXICO 1980

	BOTH SEXES	MALES	FEMALES
BIRTH RATE	28.03		27.67
DEATH RATE	3.98	4.46	3.49
RATE OF INCREASE	24.05		24.18

VITAL STATISTICS

GFR x 1000	122.449
TFR	3.632
GRR	1.779
NRR	1.694
μ	27.128
σ^2	49.949
GENERATION	26.634
POP. SEX RATIO	0.961
SEX RATIO AT BIRTH	1.042
DEP. RATIO x 100	78.504

PROJECTED POPULATION

AGE GROUP	1985			1990			STABLE EQUIVALENT TO ORIGINAL POPULATION				AGE GROUP	
							MALES		FEMALES			
	BOTH SEXES	MALES	FEMALES	BOTH SEXES	MALES	FEMALES	Number	Percent	Number	Percent		
0-4	277	141	136	320	163	157	134	12.6	129	12.2	0-4	
5-9	256	130	126	275	140	135	121	11.3	116	11.0	5-9	TABLE 5
10-14	246	125	121	256	130	126	109	10.2	105	9.9	10-14	
15-19	225	115	110	245	124	121	98	9.2	95	9.0	15-19	POPULATION
20-24	198	101	97	224	114	110	88	8.3	86	8.1	20-24	PROJECTED
25-29	172	88	84	196	100	96	79	7.4	77	7.3	25-29	WITH
30-34	145	74	71	170	87	83	71	6.7	70	6.6	30-34	FIXED
35-39	117	60	57	145	74	71	64	6.0	63	5.9	35-39	AGE-
40-44	97	50	47	115	59	56	57	5.3	56	5.3	40-44	SPECIFIC
45-49	78	40	38	95	49	46	51	4.8	50	4.7	45-49	BIRTH
50-54	67	34	33	77	39	38	45	4.2	45	4.2	50-54	AND
55-59	55	28	27	65	33	32	39	3.6	39	3.7	55-59	DEATH
60-64	47	24	23	52	26	26	33	3.1	34	3.2	60-64	RATES
65-69	38	19	19	43	21	22	27	2.5	29	2.7	65-69	(female
70-74	29	14	15	33	16	17	21	2.0	24	2.3	70-74	dominant,
75-79	17	8	9	24	11	13	15	1.4	19	1.8	75-79	in 000s)
80-84	9	4	5	12	5	7	9	0.8	12	1.2	80-84	
85+	5	2	3	8	3	5	6	0.5	10	1.0	85+	
TOTAL	2078	1057	1021	2355	1194	1161	1067		1059		TOTAL	

VITAL RATES OF PROJECTED POPULATION

Per Thousand	1985			1990			VITAL RATES OF STABLE POPULATION		
	BOTH SEXES	MALES	FEMALES	BOTH SEXES	MALES	FEMALES		MALES	FEMALES
BIRTH RATE	29.61	29.71	29.50	29.91	30.09	29.73	BIRTH RATE	27.27	26.34
DEATH RATE	4.55	5.12	3.96	4.91	5.45	4.35	DEATH RATE	7.38	6.51
RATE OF INCREASE	25.06	24.59	25.54	25.00	24.63	25.38	RATE OF INCREASE		19.83

TABLE 6

PROJECTED VITAL RATES AND RATIOS (female dominant)

AGE STRUCTURE OF PROJECTED POPULATION

	BOTH SEXES	MALES	FEMALES	BOTH SEXES	MALES	FEMALES	STABLE AGE STRUCTURE	MALES	FEMALES
% UNDER 15	37.54	37.52	37.56	36.16	36.27	36.05	% UNDER 15	34.14	33.09
% 15-64	57.75	58.03	57.47	58.76	58.98	58.53	% 15-64	58.60	57.94
% 65 AND OLDER	4.71	4.46	4.97	5.08	4.75	5.42	% 65 AND OLDER	7.26	8.96
DEPEND. RATIO x 100	73.15	72.33	74.01	70.19	69.55	70.84	DEPEND. RATIO x 100	70.64	72.59

AGE GROUP	FEMALE BIRTH RATES	NET MATERNITY FUNCTION	COEFF. OF MATRIX EQUATION	ORIGINAL MATRIX		STABLE MATRIX		MATRIX PARAMETERS		
				SUB-DIAGONAL	FIRST ROW	FISHER VALUES	REPRODUCTIVE VALUES			
0-4	0.0000	0.0000	0.0000	0.99303	0.00000	1.080	137543	λ_1	1.10422	
5-9	0.0000	0.0000	0.0032	0.99753	0.00317	1.201	145882	λ_2	$0.34088+0.71134i$	TABLE 7
10-14	0.0013	0.0063	0.1317	0.99740	0.13300	1.326	146480	λ_4	$0.03862+0.61042i$	
15-19	0.0535	0.2572	0.3709	0.99634	0.37542	1.324	128383	λ_6	$-0.35677+0.35948i$	LESLIE
20-24	0.1012	0.4846	0.4443	0.99581	0.45134	1.060	89015	r_1	0.01983	MATRIX
25-29	0.0847	0.4039	0.3469	0.99490	0.35388	0.686	49178	r_2	$-0.04745+0.22478i$	AND ITS
30-34	0.0611	0.2899	0.2302	0.99227	0.23603	0.378	21568	r_4	$-0.09832+0.30152i$	ANALYSIS
35-39	0.0362	0.1705	0.1187	0.98973	0.12261	0.163	7727	r_6	$-0.13606+0.47048i$	(females)
40-44	0.0143	0.0668	0.0400	0.98809	0.04175	0.048	1874	c_1	10599	
45-49	0.0029	0.0132	0.0074	0.98124	0.00781	0.008	285	$2\pi/y$	27.9521	
50-54	0.0004	0.0016	0.0008	0.97321	0.00086	0.001	23	Δ	10.5461	

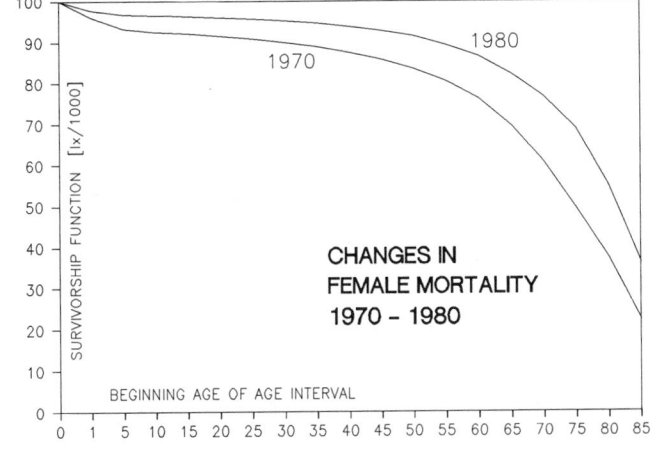

CHANGES IN FEMALE MORTALITY 1970 - 1980

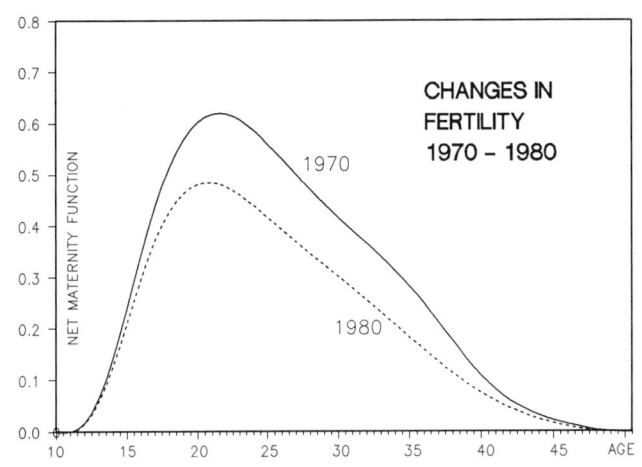

CHANGES IN FERTILITY 1970 - 1980

TABLE 1 — DATA

AGE AT LAST BIRTHDAY	ESTIMATED MID-YEAR POPULATION BOTH SEXES	MALES Number	MALES Percent	FEMALES Number	FEMALES Percent	BIRTHS BY AGE OF MOTHER AND SEX	DEATHS BOTH SEXES	DEATHS MALES	DEATHS FEMALES	AGE AT LAST BIRTHDAY
0	62700	31700	2.4	31000	2.2		1937	1143	794	0
1-4	255900	129800	9.7	126100	9.1		264	144	120	1-4
5-9	338800	171300	12.9	167500	12.1		143	76	67	5-9
10-14	335100	170100	12.8	165000	11.9	184	158	96	62	10-14
15-19	291800	144000	10.8	147800	10.7	10582	236	164	72	15-19
20-24	234200	108200	8.1	126000	9.1	24375	327	232	95	20-24
25-29	182900	84900	6.4	98000	7.1	17793	290	190	100	25-29
30-34	156900	73600	5.5	83300	6.0	8577	281	195	86	30-34
35-39	145400	68300	5.1	77100	5.6	4322	366	230	136	35-39
40-44	129000	61600	4.6	67400	4.9	1403	458	312	146	40-44
45-49	122200	59600	4.5	62600	4.5	198	624	419	205	45-49
50-54	105700	53100	4.0	52600	3.8	4	827	536	291	50-54
55-59	96600	49200	3.7	47400	3.4		1074	679	395	55-59
60-64	81700	40700	3.1	41000	3.0		1368	834	534	60-64
65-69	66500	33000	2.5	33500	2.4		1632	966	666	65-69
70-74	43500	21900	1.6	21600	1.6		1721	977	744	70-74
75-79	28400	13900	1.0	14500	1.0		1513	863	650	75-79
80-84	20000	9300	0.7	10700	0.8	34520 M	1648	855	793	80-84
85+	19000	7800	0.6	11200	0.8	32918 F	3213	1402	1811	85+
TOTAL	2716300	1332000		1384300		67438	18080	10313	7767	TOTAL

TABLE 2 — MALE LIFE TABLE

x	$_nM_x$	$_nq_x$	l_x	$_nd_x$	$_nL_x$	$_nm_x$	$_na_x$	T_x	$\overset{\circ}{e}_x$	x
0	0.036057	0.034962	100000	3496	96963	0.036057	0.131	6858819	68.588	0
1	0.001109	0.004425	96504	427	384948	0.001109	1.500	6761856	70.068	1
5	0.000444	0.002216	96077	213	479852	0.000444	2.500	6376908	66.373	5
10	0.000564	0.002824	95864	271	478712	0.000565	2.758	5897057	61.515	10
15	0.001139	0.005734	95593	548	476751	0.001150	2.784	5418344	56.681	15
20	0.002144	0.010720	95045	1019	472782	0.002155	2.602	4941593	51.992	20
25	0.002238	0.011139	94026	1047	467556	0.002240	2.541	4468811	47.527	25
30	0.002649	0.013190	92979	1226	461930	0.002655	2.583	4001255	43.034	30
35	0.003367	0.016746	91752	1536	455137	0.003376	2.640	3539325	38.575	35
40	0.005065	0.025065	90216	2261	445741	0.005073	2.639	3084188	34.187	40
45	0.007030	0.034616	87955	3045	432564	0.007039	2.632	2638447	29.998	45
50	0.010094	0.049342	84910	4190	414567	0.010106	2.617	2205883	25.979	50
55	0.013801	0.066915	80720	5401	390762	0.013823	2.623	1791316	22.192	55
60	0.020491	0.097904	75319	7374	358978	0.020542	2.611	1400554	18.595	60
65	0.029273	0.137277	67945	9327	317342	0.029392	2.600	1041576	15.330	65
70	0.044612	0.202385	58618	11863	264117	0.044917	2.558	724234	12.355	70
75	0.062086	0.270008	46754	12624	202400	0.062372	2.515	460117	9.841	75
80	0.091935	0.374031	34130	12766	138856	0.091936	2.509	257717	7.551	80
85	0.179744	1.000000	21365	21365	118861	0.111008	5.563	118861	5.563	85

TABLE 3 — FEMALE LIFE TABLE

x	$_nM_x$	$_nq_x$	l_x	$_nd_x$	$_nL_x$	$_nm_x$	$_na_x$	T_x	$\overset{\circ}{e}_x$	x
0	0.025613	0.025044	100000	2504	97780	0.025613	0.114	7493805	74.938	0
1	0.000952	0.003797	97496	370	389057	0.000952	1.500	7396025	75.860	1
5	0.000400	0.001998	97125	194	485142	0.000400	2.500	7006968	72.144	5
10	0.000376	0.001878	96931	182	484210	0.000376	2.548	6521827	67.283	10
15	0.000487	0.002440	96749	236	483194	0.000489	2.661	6037617	62.405	15
20	0.000754	0.003780	96513	365	481707	0.000757	2.645	5554422	57.551	20
25	0.001020	0.005099	96148	490	479543	0.001022	2.555	5072715	52.759	25
30	0.001032	0.005166	95658	494	477128	0.001036	2.647	4593172	48.017	30
35	0.001771	0.008809	95164	838	473833	0.001769	2.630	4116045	43.252	35
40	0.002166	0.010802	94326	1019	469223	0.002172	2.640	3642211	38.613	40
45	0.003275	0.016316	93307	1522	463040	0.003288	2.705	3172988	34.006	45
50	0.005532	0.027425	91784	2517	453074	0.005556	2.677	2709948	29.525	50
55	0.008333	0.040996	89267	3660	437792	0.008359	2.665	2256874	25.282	55
60	0.013024	0.063364	85607	5424	415312	0.013061	2.654	1819082	21.249	60
65	0.019881	0.095656	80183	7670	383029	0.020025	2.668	1403770	17.507	65
70	0.034444	0.160110	72513	11610	334516	0.034707	2.584	1020742	14.077	70
75	0.044828	0.202821	60903	12352	274396	0.045017	2.562	686226	11.268	75
80	0.074112	0.314433	48551	15266	205984	0.074112	2.591	411830	8.483	80
85	0.161696	1.000000	33285	33285	205847	0.092549	6.184	205847	6.184	85

TABLE 4 — OBSERVED VITAL RATES AND RATIOS

CRUDE RATES

Per Thousand	BOTH SEXES	MALES	FEMALES
BIRTH RATE	24.83	25.92	23.78
DEATH RATE	6.66	7.74	5.61
RATE OF INCREASE	18.17	18.17	18.17

PERCENT OF POPULATION IN AGE GROUP

	BOTH SEXES	MALES	FEMALES
UNDER 15	36.54	37.76	35.37
15 - 64	56.93	55.80	58.02
65 AND OLDER	6.53	6.45	6.61

RATES STANDARDIZED ON USA 1980

Per Thousand	BOTH SEXES	MALES	FEMALES
BIRTH RATE	26.73		25.37
DEATH RATE	9.27	9.56	8.99
RATE OF INCREASE	17.46		16.38

RATES STANDARDIZED ON MEXICO 1980

	BOTH SEXES	MALES	FEMALES
BIRTH RATE	24.24		23.85
DEATH RATE	4.36	5.10	3.60
RATE OF INCREASE	19.88		20.25

VITAL STATISTICS

GFR x 1000	101.839
TFR	3.154
GRR	1.540
NRR	1.476
μ	27.063
σ^2	41.484
GENERATION	26.761
POP. SEX RATIO	1.039
SEX RATIO AT BIRTH	1.049
DEP. RATIO x 100	75.653

PROJECTED POPULATION

STABLE EQUIVALENT TO ORIGINAL POPULATION

AGE GROUP	1975 BOTH SEXES	1975 MALES	1975 FEMALES	1980 BOTH SEXES	1980 MALES	1980 FEMALES	MALES Number	MALES Percent	FEMALES Number	FEMALES Percent	AGE GROUP	
0-4	357	182	175	413	210	203	179	11.1	173	10.6	0-4	
5-9	318	161	157	355	181	174	166	10.3	160	9.8	5-9	TABLE 5
10-14	338	171	167	316	160	156	154	9.5	148	9.1	10-14	
15-19	334	169	165	337	170	167	142	8.8	138	8.4	15-19	POPULATION
20-24	290	143	147	332	168	164	131	8.1	128	7.8	20-24	PROJECTED
25-29	232	107	125	288	141	147	121	7.5	118	7.2	25-29	WITH
30-34	182	84	98	231	106	125	111	6.9	109	6.7	30-34	FIXED
35-39	156	73	83	180	83	97	102	6.3	101	6.2	35-39	AGE-
40-44	143	67	76	153	71	82	93	5.7	93	5.7	40-44	SPECIFIC
45-49	127	60	67	140	65	75	83	5.2	85	5.2	45-49	BIRTH
50-54	118	57	61	122	57	65	74	4.6	78	4.7	50-54	AND
55-59	101	50	51	113	54	59	65	4.0	70	4.3	55-59	DEATH
60-64	90	45	45	94	46	48	56	3.5	61	3.8	60-64	RATES
65-69	74	36	38	81	40	41	46	2.8	53	3.2	65-69	(female
70-74	56	27	29	63	30	33	35	2.2	43	2.6	70-74	dominant,
75-79	35	17	18	45	21	24	25	1.6	33	2.0	75-79	in 000s)
80-84	21	10	11	25	12	13	16	1.0	23	1.4	80-84	
85+	19	8	11	19	8	11	13	0.8	21	1.3	85+	
TOTAL	2991	1467	1524	3307	1623	1684	1612		1635		TOTAL	

VITAL RATES OF PROJECTED POPULATION

VITAL RATES OF STABLE POPULATION

Per Thousand	1975 BOTH SEXES	1975 MALES	1975 FEMALES	1980 BOTH SEXES	1980 MALES	1980 FEMALES		STABLE MALES	STABLE FEMALES	
BIRTH RATE	26.68	27.85	25.56	27.43	28.62	26.29	BIRTH RATE	23.89	22.50	TABLE 6
DEATH RATE	6.67	7.78	5.60	6.75	7.82	5.73	DEATH RATE	9.34	7.93	PROJECTED
RATE OF INCREASE	20.01	20.07	19.96	20.68	20.80	20.56	RATE OF INCREASE		14.57	VITAL RATES AND RATIOS (female dominant)

AGE STRUCTURE OF PROJECTED POPULATION

STABLE AGE STRUCTURE

	BOTH SEXES	MALES	FEMALES	BOTH SEXES	MALES	FEMALES		MALES	FEMALES
% UNDER 15	33.86	35.02	32.75	32.79	33.98	31.64	% UNDER 15	30.93	29.44
% 15-64	59.31	58.31	60.27	60.16	59.20	61.08	% 15-64	60.67	60.02
% 65 AND OLDER	6.83	6.67	6.99	7.05	6.82	7.28	% 65 AND OLDER	8.39	10.53
DEPEND. RATIO x 100	68.61	71.49	65.93	66.22	68.91	63.72	DEPEND. RATIO x 100	64.82	66.60

AGE GROUP	FEMALE BIRTH RATES	NET MATERNITY FUNCTION	COEFF. OF MATRIX EQUATION	ORIGINAL MATRIX SUB-DIAGONAL	ORIGINAL MATRIX FIRST ROW	STABLE MATRIX FISHER VALUES	STABLE MATRIX REPRODUCTIVE VALUES	MATRIX PARAMETERS		
0-4	0.0000	0.0000	0.0000	0.99652	0.00000	1.065	167308	λ_1	1.07555	
5-9	0.0000	0.0000	0.0013	0.99808	0.00132	1.149	192531	λ_2	0.32928+0.75377i	TABLE 7
10-14	0.0005	0.0026	0.0858	0.99790	0.08622	1.237	204144	λ_4	-0.38204+0.41760i	
15-19	0.0349	0.1689	0.3119	0.99692	0.31422	1.241	183493	λ_6	0.06029+0.52686i	LESLIE
20-24	0.0944	0.4549	0.4399	0.99551	0.44461	1.004	126471	r_1	0.01457	MATRIX
25-29	0.0886	0.4250	0.3324	0.99496	0.33745	0.609	59662	r_2	-0.03907+0.23179i	AND ITS
30-34	0.0503	0.2398	0.1847	0.99310	0.18849	0.297	24732	r_4	-0.11384+0.46235i	ANALYSIS
35-39	0.0274	0.1297	0.0887	0.99027	0.09110	0.119	9207	r_6	-0.12686+0.29137i	(females)
40-44	0.0102	0.0477	0.0274	0.98682	0.02844	0.032	2139	c_1	16333	
45-49	0.0015	0.0071	0.0037	0.97848	0.00385	0.004	244	$2\pi/\gamma$	27.1075	
50-54	0.0000	0.0002	0.0001	0.96627	0.00009	0.000	5	Δ	9.4598	

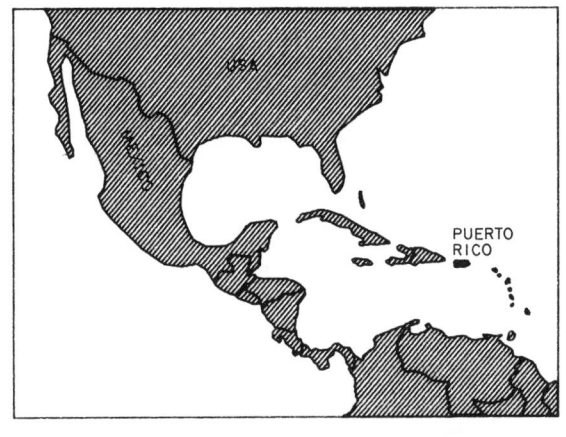

EDUCATION [1984]
% of primary school-age children enrolled: na
    secondary school-age children enrolled: na
    ca. 20-24 year olds in higher education: na

LABOR FORCE
Average annual labor force growth (%) 1980-85:   na
% of the 1980 labor force in agriculture: 4   TABLE 8
            in industry
            and services: 96   SOCIO-ECONOMIC INDICATORS

GNP & INCOME DISTRIBUTION
GNP per capita (in US Dollars) 1985:   na
GNP average annual growth rate (%) 1965-85:   na
% share of total household income
        Lowest 20% of households: na
        Highest 10% of households: na

HEALTH & NUTRITION
Population per physician 1981:   na
Daily calorie supply per capita 1985:   na

PUERTO RICO 1985   322

TABLE 1 — DATA

AGE AT LAST BIRTHDAY	ESTIMATED MID-YEAR POPULATION BOTH SEXES	MALES Number	MALES Percent	FEMALES Number	FEMALES Percent	BIRTHS BY AGE OF MOTHER AND SEX	DEATHS BOTH SEXES	DEATHS MALES	DEATHS FEMALES	AGE AT LAST BIRTHDAY
0	54241	28054	1.8	26187	1.5		948	519	429	0
1-4	221538	114932	7.2	106606	6.3		122	76	46	1-4
5-9	311525	159495	10.0	152030	9.0		71	46	25	5-9
10-14	327604	170693	10.7	156911	9.3	254	107	68	39	10-14
15-19	341673	175718	11.0	165955	9.8	10729	236	181	55	15-19
20-24	282096	135665	8.5	146431	8.7	21656	324	256	68	20-24
25-29	222374	105229	6.6	117145	6.9	17559	359	269	90	25-29
30-34	200841	90443	5.7	110398	6.5	9036	458	347	111	30-34
35-39	213331	97047	6.1	116284	6.9	3593	539	394	145	35-39
40-44	192802	90156	5.7	102646	6.1	753	578	426	152	40-44
45-49	165955	76373	4.8	89582	5.3	47	682	484	198	45-49
50-54	152891	70919	4.5	81972	4.8	2	916	629	287	50-54
55-59	136094	63166	4.0	72928	4.3		1259	813	446	55-59
60-64	130497	58573	3.7	71924	4.3		1637	1044	593	60-64
65-69	112694	52830	3.3	59864	3.5		2156	1262	894	65-69
70-74	88864	42781	2.7	46083	2.7		2784	1662	1122	70-74
75-79	62571	30625	1.9	31946	1.9		2857	1598	1259	75-79
80-84	33401	15742	1.0	17659	1.0	32608 M	2761	1421	1340	80-84
85+	31508	13497	0.8	18011	1.1	31021 F	4399	1951	2448	85+
TOTAL	3282500	1591938		1690562		63629	23193	13446	9747	TOTAL

TABLE 2 — MALE LIFE TABLE

x	nM_x	nq_x	l_x	nd_x	nL_x	nm_x	na_x	T_x	$\overset{\circ}{e}_x$	x
0	0.018500	0.018197	100000	1820	98365	0.018500	0.101	7117664	71.177	0
1	0.000661	0.002641	98180	259	392073	0.000661	1.500	7019299	71.494	1
5	0.000288	0.001441	97921	141	489252	0.000288	2.500	6627226	67.679	5
10	0.000398	0.001990	97780	195	488488	0.000398	2.888	6137974	62.773	10
15	0.001030	0.005157	97585	503	486819	0.001034	2.799	5649485	57.893	15
20	0.001887	0.009457	97082	918	483266	0.001900	2.665	5162666	53.178	20
25	0.002556	0.012774	96164	1228	477934	0.002570	2.651	4679400	48.661	25
30	0.003837	0.019031	94936	1807	470295	0.003842	2.574	4201466	44.256	30
35	0.004060	0.020098	93129	1872	461033	0.004060	2.537	3731171	40.065	35
40	0.004725	0.023392	91257	2135	451140	0.004732	2.589	3270138	35.834	40
45	0.006337	0.031290	89122	2789	438978	0.006352	2.621	2818999	31.631	45
50	0.008869	0.043509	86334	3756	422773	0.008885	2.632	2380020	27.568	50
55	0.012871	0.062512	82577	5162	400578	0.012887	2.615	1957247	23.702	55
60	0.017824	0.085461	77415	6616	371129	0.017827	2.590	1556669	20.108	60
65	0.023888	0.113084	70799	8006	334928	0.023904	2.618	1185540	16.745	65
70	0.038849	0.177744	62793	11161	286897	0.038903	2.575	850612	13.546	70
75	0.052180	0.232639	51632	12012	228849	0.052487	2.560	563715	10.918	75
80	0.090268	0.368707	39620	14608	161832	0.090268	2.517	334866	8.452	80
85	0.144551	1.000000	25012	25012	173033	0.076387	6.918	173033	6.918	85

TABLE 3 — FEMALE LIFE TABLE

x	nM_x	nq_x	l_x	nd_x	nL_x	nm_x	na_x	T_x	$\overset{\circ}{e}_x$	x
0	0.016382	0.016144	100000	1614	98544	0.016382	0.098	7879640	78.796	0
1	0.000431	0.001724	98386	170	393119	0.000431	1.500	7781096	79.088	1
5	0.000164	0.000822	98216	81	490878	0.000164	2.500	7387978	75.222	5
10	0.000249	0.001242	98135	122	490389	0.000249	2.639	6897099	70.282	10
15	0.000331	0.001656	98013	162	489683	0.000331	2.636	6406711	65.366	15
20	0.000464	0.002330	97851	228	488730	0.000467	2.695	5917027	60.470	20
25	0.000768	0.003852	97623	376	487230	0.000772	2.644	5428297	55.605	25
30	0.001005	0.005019	97247	488	485062	0.001006	2.596	4941068	50.809	30
35	0.001247	0.006217	96759	602	482338	0.001247	2.577	4456005	46.053	35
40	0.001481	0.007397	96157	711	479103	0.001485	2.632	3973667	41.325	40
45	0.002210	0.011036	95446	1053	474792	0.002219	2.685	3494564	36.613	45
50	0.003501	0.017440	94393	1646	468213	0.003516	2.721	3019772	31.992	50
55	0.006116	0.030194	92747	2800	457148	0.006126	2.649	2551559	27.511	55
60	0.008245	0.040520	89946	3645	441340	0.008258	2.698	2094411	23.285	60
65	0.014934	0.072530	86302	6259	417032	0.015010	2.687	1653070	19.155	65
70	0.024347	0.115871	80042	9275	378401	0.024510	2.648	1236038	15.442	70
75	0.039410	0.181807	70768	12866	323607	0.039758	2.650	857637	12.119	75
80	0.075882	0.320504	57902	18558	244560	0.075882	2.578	534030	9.223	80
85	0.135917	1.000000	39344	39344	289470	0.068433	7.357	289470	7.357	85

TABLE 4 — OBSERVED VITAL RATES AND RATIOS

CRUDE RATES

Per Thousand	BOTH SEXES	MALES	FEMALES
BIRTH RATE	19.38	20.48	18.35
DEATH RATE	7.07	8.45	5.77
RATE OF INCREASE	12.32	12.04	12.58

PERCENT OF POPULATION IN AGE GROUP

	BOTH SEXES	MALES	FEMALES
UNDER 15	27.87	29.72	26.13
15 - 64	62.10	60.51	63.60
65 AND OLDER	10.02	9.77	10.27

RATES STANDARDIZED ON USA 1980

Per Thousand	BOTH SEXES	MALES	FEMALES
BIRTH RATE	20.87		19.79
DEATH RATE	7.73	8.33	7.17
RATE OF INCREASE	13.14		12.62

RATES STANDARDIZED ON MEXICO 1980

	BOTH SEXES	MALES	FEMALES
BIRTH RATE	19.13		18.80
DEATH RATE	3.43	4.23	2.63
RATE OF INCREASE	15.70		16.17

VITAL STATISTICS

GFR x 1000	74.995
TFR	2.423
GRR	1.181
NRR	1.151
μ	26.296
σ^2	34.680
GENERATION	26.203
POP. SEX RATIO	1.062
SEX RATIO AT BIRTH	1.051
DEP. RATIO x 100	61.021

PROJECTED POPULATION

STABLE EQUIVALENT TO ORIGINAL POPULATION

AGE GROUP	1990 BOTH SEXES	1990 MALES	1990 FEMALES	1995 BOTH SEXES	1995 MALES	1995 FEMALES	MALES Number	MALES Percent	FEMALES Number	FEMALES Percent	AGE GROUP	
0-4	330	169	161	356	182	174	164	8.3	157	7.6	0-4	
5-9	276	143	133	329	168	161	159	8.1	152	7.4	5-9	TABLE 5
10-14	311	159	152	274	142	132	155	7.8	148	7.2	10-14	
15-19	327	170	157	311	159	152	150	7.6	144	7.0	15-19	POPULATION
20-24	340	174	166	325	169	156	145	7.3	140	6.8	20-24	PROJECTED
25-29	280	134	146	338	173	165	140	7.1	136	6.6	25-29	WITH
30-34	221	104	117	277	132	145	134	6.8	131	6.4	30-34	FIXED
35-39	199	89	110	218	102	116	128	6.5	127	6.2	35-39	AGE-
40-44	211	95	116	196	87	109	122	6.2	123	6.0	40-44	SPECIFIC
45-49	190	88	102	206	92	114	115	5.8	119	5.8	45-49	BIRTH
50-54	162	74	88	184	84	100	108	5.5	114	5.5	50-54	AND
55-59	147	67	80	156	70	86	100	5.0	108	5.3	55-59	DEATH
60-64	129	59	70	139	62	77	90	4.5	102	5.0	60-64	RATES
65-69	121	53	68	120	53	67	79	4.0	94	4.6	65-69	(female
70-74	99	45	54	107	45	62	66	3.3	83	4.0	70-74	dominant,
75-79	73	34	39	82	36	46	51	2.6	69	3.4	75-79	in 000s)
80-84	46	22	24	54	24	30	35	1.8	51	2.5	80-84	
85+	38	17	21	52	23	29	37	1.9	58	2.8	85+	
TOTAL	3500	1696	1804	3724	1803	1921	1978		2056		TOTAL	

VITAL RATES OF PROJECTED POPULATION

VITAL RATES OF STABLE POPULATION

Per Thousand	1990 BOTH SEXES	1990 MALES	1990 FEMALES	1995 BOTH SEXES	1995 MALES	1995 FEMALES	Per Thousand	MALES	FEMALES	
BIRTH RATE	20.19	21.35	19.09	19.93	21.10	18.84	BIRTH RATE	17.14	15.71	TABLE 6
DEATH RATE	7.62	8.95	6.36	8.19	9.36	7.09	DEATH RATE	11.81	10.33	
RATE OF INCREASE	12.57	12.40	12.73	11.74	11.73	11.75	RATE OF INCREASE		5.38	PROJECTED

AGE STRUCTURE OF PROJECTED POPULATION

STABLE AGE STRUCTURE

	1990 BOTH SEXES	1990 MALES	1990 FEMALES	1995 BOTH SEXES	1995 MALES	1995 FEMALES		MALES	FEMALES	
% UNDER 15	26.19	27.78	24.70	25.75	27.32	24.29	% UNDER 15	24.18	22.23	VITAL RATES AND RATIOS
% 15-64	63.01	62.15	63.83	63.12	62.62	63.59	% 15-64	62.27	60.53	(female
% 65 AND OLDER	10.79	10.08	11.47	11.13	10.06	12.13	% 65 AND OLDER	13.54	17.24	dominant)
DEPEND. RATIO x 100	58.69	60.91	56.67	58.43	59.70	57.26	DEPEND. RATIO x 100	60.58	65.20	

AGE GROUP	FEMALE BIRTH RATES	NET MATERNITY FUNCTION	COEFF. OF MATRIX EQUATION	ORIGINAL MATRIX SUB-DIAGONAL	ORIGINAL MATRIX FIRST ROW	STABLE MATRIX FISHER VALUES	STABLE MATRIX REPRODUCTIVE VALUES	MATRIX PARAMETERS		
0-4	0.0000	0.0000	0.0000	0.99841	0.00000	1.031	136871	λ_1	1.02726	
5-9	0.0000	0.0000	0.0019	0.99900	0.00194	1.060	161227	λ_2	0.32963+0.75015i	TABLE 7
10-14	0.0008	0.0039	0.0791	0.99856	0.07931	1.088	170797	λ_4	-0.31331+0.39341i	
15-19	0.0315	0.1543	0.2534	0.99805	0.25439	1.038	172247	λ_6	-0.07683+0.42503i	LESLIE
20-24	0.0721	0.3524	0.3542	0.99693	0.35634	0.806	117962	r_1	0.00538	MATRIX
25-29	0.0731	0.3560	0.2748	0.99555	0.27730	0.462	54083	r_2	-0.03984+0.23135i	AND ITS
30-34	0.0399	0.1936	0.1331	0.99438	0.13492	0.189	20897	r_4	-0.13746+0.44867i	ANALYSIS
35-39	0.0151	0.0727	0.0449	0.99329	0.04576	0.056	6476	r_6	-0.16790+0.34992i	(females)
40-44	0.0036	0.0171	0.0092	0.99100	0.00942	0.010	1038	c_1	20546	
45-49	0.0003	0.0012	0.0006	0.98614	0.00066	0.001	62	$2\pi/y$	27.1583	
50-54	0.0000	0.0001	0.0000	0.97637	0.00003	0.000	2	Δ	9.8020	

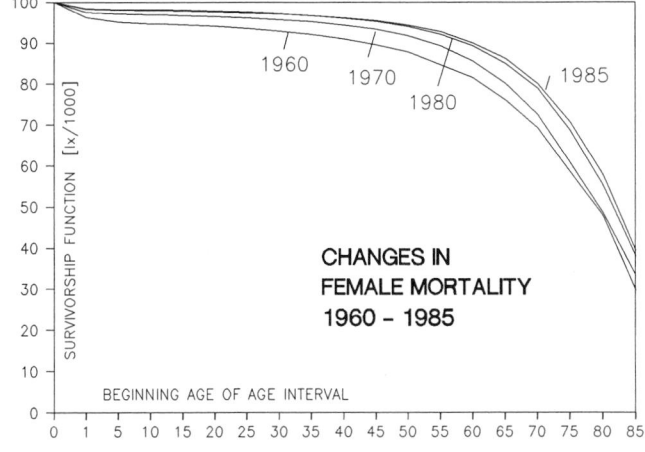

CHANGES IN FEMALE MORTALITY 1960 - 1985

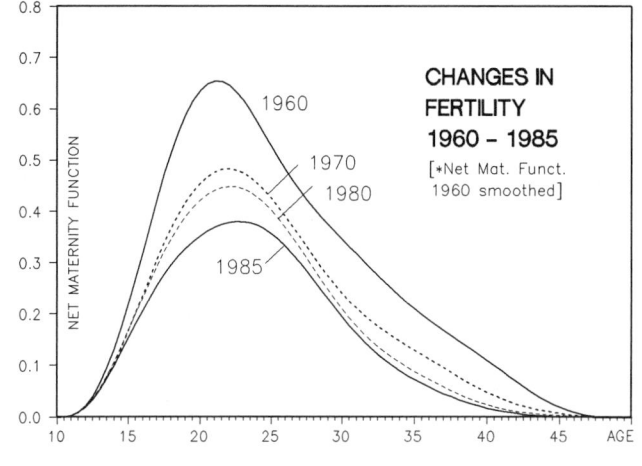

CHANGES IN FERTILITY 1960 - 1985
[*Net Mat. Funct. 1960 smoothed]

TABLE 1 — DATA

AGE AT LAST BIRTHDAY	ESTIMATED MID-YEAR POPULATION BOTH SEXES	MALES Number	MALES Percent	FEMALES Number	FEMALES Percent	BIRTHS BY AGE OF MOTHER AND SEX	DEATHS BOTH SEXES	DEATHS MALES	DEATHS FEMALES	AGE AT LAST BIRTHDAY
0	955	477	2.3	478	2.0		59	39	20	0
1-4	5674	2807	13.3	2867	12.0		25	11	14	1-4
5-9	7900	4016	19.0	3884	16.2		9	4	5	5-9
10-14	7405	3612	17.1	3793	15.9	13	11	8	3	10-14
15-19	4815	2404	11.4	2411	10.1	353	10	4	6	15-19
20-24	2266	1075	5.1	1191	5.0	303	9	3	6	20-24
25-29	1402	591	2.8	811	3.4	208	8	3	5	25-29
30-34	1187	502	2.4	685	2.9	125	6	2	4	30-34
35-39	1461	623	2.9	838	3.5	115	16	5	11	35-39
40-44	1603	649	3.1	954	4.0	36	12	4	8	40-44
45-49	1740	791	3.7	949	4.0	3	15	9	6	45-49
50-54	1802	813	3.8	989	4.1		24	8	16	50-54
55-59	1869	862	4.1	1007	4.2		27	12	15	55-59
60-64	1792	790	3.7	1002	4.2		40	21	19	60-64
65-69	1283	527	2.5	756	3.2		51	20	31	65-69
70-74	828	301	1.4	527	2.2		41	16	25	70-74
75-79	496	166	0.8	330	1.4		46	21	25	75-79
80-84	313	74	0.4	239	1.0	608 M	31	13	18	80-84
85+	258	60	0.3	198	0.8	548 F	48	18	30	85+
TOTAL	45049	21140		23909		1156	488	221	267	TOTAL

TABLE 2 — MALE LIFE TABLE

x	nM_x	nq_x	l_x	nd_x	nL_x	nm_x	na_x	T_x	$\overset{\circ}{e}_x$	x
0	0.081761	0.076794	100000	7679	93926	0.081761	0.209	5986015	59.860	0
1	0.003919	0.015523	92321	1433	365700	0.003919	1.500	5892089	63.822	1
5	0.000996	0.004968	90887	452	453309	0.000996	2.500	5526390	60.805	5
10	0.002215	0.011062	90436	1000	449739	0.002224	2.560	5073081	56.096	10
15	0.001664	0.008282	89436	741	445376	0.001663	2.568	4623342	51.695	15
20	0.002791	0.013992	88695	1241	440676	0.002816	2.745	4177966	47.105	20
25	0.005076	0.025161	87454	2200	431860	0.005095	2.542	3737290	42.734	25
30	0.003984	0.019734	85253	1682	422288	0.003984	2.635	3305430	38.772	30
35	0.008026	0.039453	83571	3289	409790	0.008026	2.548	2883142	34.499	35
40	0.006163	0.030365	80282	2438	395529	0.006163	2.587	2473352	30.808	40
45	0.011378	0.055349	77844	4309	378678	0.011378	2.553	2077823	26.692	45
50	0.009840	0.048030	73536	3532	358935	0.009840	2.524	1699144	23.106	50
55	0.013921	0.067451	70004	4722	339184	0.013921	2.705	1340209	19.145	55
60	0.026582	0.125371	65282	8184	307043	0.026656	2.634	1001025	15.334	60
65	0.037951	0.174638	57098	9971	261188	0.038177	2.563	693983	12.154	65
70	0.053156	0.237754	47126	11204	209173	0.053565	2.639	432794	9.184	70
75	0.126506	0.485125	35922	17427	136001	0.128135	2.498	223621	6.225	75
80	0.175676	0.595223	18495	11009	62665	0.175676	2.292	87620	4.737	80
85	0.300000	1.000000	7486	7486	24955	0.258077	3.333	24955	3.333	85

TABLE 3 — FEMALE LIFE TABLE

x	nM_x	nq_x	l_x	nd_x	nL_x	nm_x	na_x	T_x	$\overset{\circ}{e}_x$	x
0	0.041841	0.040390	100000	4039	96531	0.041841	0.141	6188127	61.881	0
1	0.004883	0.019297	95961	1852	379215	0.004883	1.500	6091596	63.480	1
5	0.001287	0.006416	94109	604	469037	0.001287	2.500	5712381	60.699	5
10	0.000791	0.003968	93505	371	466717	0.000795	2.817	5243344	56.075	10
15	0.002489	0.012543	93134	1168	463154	0.002522	2.845	4776627	51.287	15
20	0.005038	0.025064	91966	2305	454393	0.005073	2.641	4313472	46.903	20
25	0.006165	0.030407	89661	2726	441532	0.006175	2.515	3859079	43.041	25
30	0.005839	0.028813	86935	2505	428962	0.005839	2.720	3417547	39.312	30
35	0.013126	0.063570	84430	5367	408885	0.013126	2.529	2988585	35.397	35
40	0.008386	0.041003	79063	3242	386583	0.008386	2.307	2579700	32.629	40
45	0.006322	0.031163	75821	2363	373714	0.006322	2.718	2193116	28.925	45
50	0.016178	0.077856	73458	5719	353514	0.016178	2.591	1819402	24.768	50
55	0.014896	0.071804	67739	4864	326534	0.014896	2.500	1465888	21.640	55
60	0.018962	0.090885	62875	5714	301306	0.018966	2.713	1139354	18.121	60
65	0.041005	0.187227	57161	10702	259916	0.041175	2.581	838049	14.661	65
70	0.047438	0.212711	46459	9882	207786	0.047560	2.520	578132	12.444	70
75	0.075758	0.318635	36576	11655	153326	0.076012	2.464	370347	10.125	75
80	0.075314	0.315684	24922	7867	104462	0.075314	2.439	217021	8.708	80
85	0.151515	1.000000	17054	17054	112559	0.083123	6.600	112559	6.600	85

TABLE 4 — OBSERVED VITAL RATES AND RATIOS

CRUDE RATES

Per Thousand	BOTH SEXES	MALES	FEMALES
BIRTH RATE	25.66	28.76	22.92
DEATH RATE	10.83	10.45	11.17
RATE OF INCREASE	14.83	18.31	11.75

PERCENT OF POPULATION IN AGE GROUP

	BOTH SEXES	MALES	FEMALES
UNDER 15	48.69	51.62	46.10
15 - 64	44.26	43.05	45.33
65 AND OLDER	7.05	5.34	8.57

RATES STANDARDIZED ON USA 1980

Per Thousand	BOTH SEXES	MALES	FEMALES
BIRTH RATE	42.48		39.16
DEATH RATE	15.16	15.07	15.24
RATE OF INCREASE	27.32		23.92

RATES STANDARDIZED ON MEXICO 1980

	BOTH SEXES	MALES	FEMALES
BIRTH RATE	38.66		36.94
DEATH RATE	8.53	8.99	8.06
RATE OF INCREASE	30.14		28.88

VITAL STATISTICS

GFR x 1000	147.468
TFR	5.107
GRR	2.421
NRR	2.126
μ	27.310
σ^2	47.586
GENERATION	26.636
POP. SEX RATIO	1.131
SEX RATIO AT BIRTH	1.109
DEP. RATIO x 100	125.957

PROJECTED POPULATION

STABLE EQUIVALENT TO ORIGINAL POPULATION

AGE GROUP	1975 BOTH SEXES	1975 MALES	1975 FEMALES	1980 BOTH SEXES	1980 MALES	1980 FEMALES	MALES Number	MALES Percent	FEMALES Number	FEMALES Percent	AGE GROUP	
0-4	6	3	3	10	5	5	4	16.3	4	16.5	0-4	
5-9	6	3	3	6	3	3	3	14.0	3	14.1	5-9	TABLE 5
10-14	8	4	4	6	3	3	3	12.0	3	12.2	10-14	
15-19	8	4	4	8	4	4	2	10.3	2	10.5	15-19	POPULATION
20-24	4	2	2	8	4	4	2	8.9	2	8.9	20-24	PROJECTED
25-29	2	1	1	4	2	2	2	7.5	2	7.5	25-29	WITH
30-34	2	1	1	2	1	1	2	6.4	1	6.3	30-34	FIXED
35-39	1	0	1	2	1	1	1	5.4	1	5.2	35-39	AGE-
40-44	2	1	1	1	0	1	1	4.5	1	4.3	40-44	SPECIFIC
45-49	2	1	1	2	1	1	1	3.7	1	3.6	45-49	BIRTH
50-54	2	1	1	2	1	1	1	3.1	1	3.0	50-54	AND
55-59	2	1	1	2	1	1	1	2.5	1	2.4	55-59	DEATH
60-64	2	1	1	2	1	1	0	2.0	0	1.9	60-64	RATES
65-69	2	1	1	2	1	1	0	1.5	0	1.4	65-69	(female
70-74	1	0	1	2	1	1	0	1.0	0	1.0	70-74	dominant,
75-79	0	0	0	0	0	0	0	0.6	0	0.6	75-79	in 000s)
80-84	0	0	0	0	0	0	0	0.2	0	0.4	80-84	
85+	0	0	0	0	0	0	0	0.1	0	0.3	85+	
TOTAL	50	24	26	59	29	30	23		22		TOTAL	

VITAL RATES OF PROJECTED POPULATION

VITAL RATES OF STABLE POPULATION

Per Thousand	1975 BOTH SEXES	1975 MALES	1975 FEMALES	1980 BOTH SEXES	1980 MALES	1980 FEMALES	MALES	FEMALES	
BIRTH RATE	34.83	38.37	31.60	42.74	46.20	39.46	38.00	37.03	TABLE 6
DEATH RATE	10.55	9.87	11.17	10.58	10.14	11.00	8.73	8.64	
RATE OF INCREASE	24.29	28.50	20.43	32.16	36.06	28.46		28.39	PROJECTED

AGE STRUCTURE OF PROJECTED POPULATION

STABLE AGE STRUCTURE

	BOTH SEXES	MALES	FEMALES	BOTH SEXES	MALES	FEMALES	MALES	FEMALES	
% UNDER 15	42.56	45.19	40.16	40.13	42.15	38.23	42.29	42.68	VITAL RATES AND RATIOS (female dominant)
% 15-64	49.91	48.92	50.82	52.77	52.10	53.42	54.35	53.56	
% 65 AND OLDER	7.53	5.89	9.02	7.09	5.76	8.36	3.36	3.76	
DEPEND. RATIO x 100	00.34	104.41	96.76	89.49	91.96	87.21	84.00	86.69	

AGE GROUP	FEMALE BIRTH RATES	NET MATERNITY FUNCTION	COEFF. OF MATRIX EQUATION	ORIGINAL MATRIX SUB-DIAGONAL	ORIGINAL MATRIX FIRST ROW	STABLE MATRIX FISHER VALUES	STABLE MATRIX REPRODUCTIVE VALUES	MATRIX PARAMETERS		
0-4	0.0000	0.0000	0.0000	0.98590	0.00000	1.128	3772	λ_1	1.15252	
5-9	0.0000	0.0000	0.0038	0.99505	0.00385	1.318	5120	λ_2	$0.37714-0.75554i$	TABLE 7
10-14	0.0016	0.0076	0.1645	0.99237	0.16770	1.522	5774	λ_4	$-0.02299-0.68646i$	
15-19	0.0694	0.3215	0.4347	0.98108	0.44655	1.578	3803	λ_6	$-0.46441+0.41697i$	LESLIE
20-24	0.1206	0.5480	0.5424	0.97170	0.56790	1.340	1596	r_1	0.02839	MATRIX
25-29	0.1216	0.5368	0.4539	0.97153	0.48912	0.930	754	r_2	$-0.03382-0.22156i$	AND ITS
30-34	0.0865	0.3711	0.3185	0.95320	0.35328	0.536	367	r_4	$-0.07513-0.32086i$	ANALYSIS
35-39	0.0651	0.2660	0.1676	0.94546	0.19498	0.230	193	r_6	$-0.09428+0.48199i$	(females)
40-44	0.0179	0.0692	0.0374	0.96671	0.04600	0.048	46	c_1	224	
45-49	0.0015	0.0056	0.0028	0.94595	0.00356	0.003	3	$2\pi/\gamma$	28.3584	
50-54	0.0000	0.0000	0.0000	0.00000	0.00000	0.000	0	Δ	16.3835	

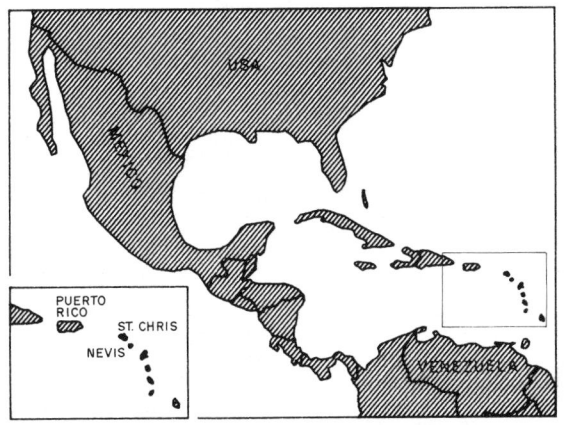

EDUCATION [1984]

% of primary school-age children enrolled:	na
secondary school-age children enrolled:	na
ca. 20-24 year olds in higher education:	na

LABOR FORCE

Average annual labor force growth (%) 1980-85:	na	
% of the 1980 labor force in agriculture:	na	TABLE 8
in industry:	na	
in services:	na	SOCIO-ECONOMIC

GNP & INCOME DISTRIBUTION

GNP per capita (in US Dollars) 1985:	1550	INDICATORS
GNP average annual growth rate (%) 1965-85:	2.4	
% share of total household income		
Lowest 20% of households:	na	
Highest 10% of households:	na	

HEALTH & NUTRITION

Population per physician 1981:	na
Daily calorie supply per capita 1985:	na

AGE AT LAST BIRTHDAY	ESTIMATED MID-YEAR POPULATION					BIRTHS BY AGE OF MOTHER AND SEX	DEATHS			AGE AT LAST BIRTHDAY
	BOTH SEXES	MALES Number	Percent	FEMALES Number	Percent		BOTH SEXES	MALES	FEMALES	
0	1047	541	2.6	506	2.2		62	31	31	0
1-4	4239	2140	10.2	2099	9.3		14	12	2	1-4
5-9	5374	2671	12.8	2703	12.0		3	1	2	5-9
10-14	5534	2823	13.5	2711	12.0	9	3	1	2	10-14
15-19	5649	2899	13.9	2750	12.2	346	3	2	1	15-19
20-24	4676	2250	10.8	2426	10.8	427	3	1	2	20-24
25-29	2887	1441	6.9	1446	6.4	227	3	2	1	25-29
30-34	1668	792	3.8	876	3.9	90	6	4	2	30-34
35-39	1265	572	2.7	693	3.1	53	9	6	3	35-39
40-44	1181	515	2.5	666	3.0	18	7	5	2	40-44
45-49	1287	570	2.7	717	3.2		15	11	4	45-49
50-54	1417	601	2.9	816	3.6		17	14	3	50-54
55-59	1368	625	3.0	743	3.3		21	13	8	55-59
60-64	1662	765	3.7	897	4.0		39	19	20	60-64
65-69	1542	693	3.3	849	3.8		51	25	26	65-69
70-74	1143	487	2.3	656	2.9		74	41	33	70-74
75-79	786	295	1.4	491	2.2		54	22	32	75-79
80-84	400	138	0.7	262	1.2	583 M	48	16	32	80-84
85+	272	67	0.3	205	0.9	587 F	61	18	43	85+
TOTAL	43397	20885		22512		1170	493	244	249	TOTAL

TABLE 1
DATA

TABLE 2 — MALE LIFE TABLE

x	$_nM_x$	$_nq_x$	l_x	$_nd_x$	$_nL_x$	$_nm_x$	$_na_x$	T_x	$\overset{\circ}{e}_x$	x
0	0.057301	0.054692	100000	5469	95446	0.057301	0.167	6012517	60.125	0
1	0.005607	0.022120	94531	2091	372896	0.005607	1.500	5917071	62.594	1
5	0.000374	0.001870	92440	173	461767	0.000374	2.500	5544175	59.976	5
10	0.000354	0.001770	92267	163	460956	0.000354	2.684	5082408	55.084	10
15	0.000690	0.003448	92104	318	459733	0.000691	2.527	4621452	50.177	15
20	0.000444	0.002231	91786	205	458487	0.000447	2.837	4161719	45.342	20
25	0.001388	0.007082	91581	649	456723	0.001420	3.174	3703231	40.437	25
30	0.005051	0.025337	90933	2304	449719	0.005123	2.854	3246509	35.702	30
35	0.010490	0.051441	88629	4559	432097	0.010551	2.577	2796790	31.556	35
40	0.009709	0.047460	84070	3990	410962	0.009709	2.648	2364693	28.128	40
45	0.019298	0.092242	80080	7387	382766	0.019298	2.613	1953730	24.397	45
50	0.023295	0.110000	72693	7996	343267	0.023294	2.474	1570964	21.611	50
55	0.020800	0.098785	64697	6391	307263	0.020800	2.462	1227697	18.976	55
60	0.024837	0.117105	58306	6828	274914	0.024837	2.567	920434	15.786	60
65	0.036075	0.166596	51478	8576	237647	0.036087	2.698	645520	12.540	65
70	0.084189	0.349077	42902	14976	177084	0.084570	2.501	407873	9.507	70
75	0.074576	0.309690	27926	8648	116697	0.074109	2.348	230789	8.264	75
80	0.115942	0.450380	19277	8682	74654	0.116299	2.497	114092	5.918	80
85	0.268657	1.000000	10595	10595	39438	0.215900	3.722	39438	3.722	85

TABLE 3 — FEMALE LIFE TABLE

x	$_nM_x$	$_nq_x$	l_x	$_nd_x$	$_nL_x$	$_nm_x$	$_na_x$	T_x	$\overset{\circ}{e}_x$	x
0	0.061265	0.058314	100000	5831	95184	0.061265	0.174	6817046	68.170	0
1	0.000953	0.003802	94169	358	375779	0.000953	1.500	6721862	71.381	1
5	0.000740	0.003693	93811	346	468187	0.000740	2.500	6346083	67.648	5
10	0.000738	0.003682	93464	344	466423	0.000738	2.393	5877896	62.889	10
15	0.000364	0.001817	93120	169	465185	0.000364	2.549	5411473	58.113	15
20	0.000824	0.004131	92951	384	463826	0.000828	2.583	4946287	53.214	20
25	0.000692	0.003489	92567	323	462168	0.000699	2.937	4482461	48.424	25
30	0.002283	0.011504	92244	1061	458907	0.002312	2.821	4020293	43.583	30
35	0.004329	0.021473	91183	1958	451075	0.004341	2.529	3561385	39.058	35
40	0.003003	0.014907	89225	1330	442894	0.003003	2.572	3110311	34.859	40
45	0.005579	0.027513	87895	2418	433475	0.005579	2.520	2667417	30.348	45
50	0.003676	0.018233	85476	1558	423901	0.003676	2.767	2233942	26.135	50
55	0.010767	0.052603	83918	4414	409983	0.010767	2.824	1810040	21.569	55
60	0.022297	0.105914	79504	8421	377660	0.022297	2.642	1400057	17.610	60
65	0.030624	0.142668	71083	10141	331151	0.030624	2.607	1022398	14.383	65
70	0.050305	0.223960	60942	13649	271247	0.050318	2.548	691246	11.343	70
75	0.065173	0.281404	47293	13309	203660	0.065347	2.535	419999	8.881	75
80	0.122137	0.467338	33985	15882	130037	0.122137	2.489	216339	6.366	80
85	0.209756	1.000000	18102	18102	86302	0.144131	4.767	86302	4.767	85

TABLE 4 — OBSERVED VITAL RATES AND RATIOS

CRUDE RATES

Per Thousand	BOTH SEXES	MALES	FEMALES
BIRTH RATE	26.96	27.91	26.07
DEATH RATE	11.36	11.68	11.06
RATE OF INCREASE	15.60	16.23	15.01

PERCENT OF POPULATION IN AGE GROUP

UNDER 15	37.32	39.14	35.62
15 - 64	53.14	52.81	53.44
65 AND OLDER	9.55	8.04	10.94

RATES STANDARDIZED ON USA 1980

Per Thousand	BOTH SEXES	MALES	FEMALES
BIRTH RATE	28.13		27.45
DEATH RATE	14.05	14.80	13.34
RATE OF INCREASE	14.08		14.10

RATES STANDARDIZED ON MEXICO 1980

	BOTH SEXES	MALES	FEMALES
BIRTH RATE	26.27		26.56
DEATH RATE	7.11	8.32	5.88
RATE OF INCREASE	19.16		20.68

VITAL STATISTICS

GFR x 1000	122.206
TFR	3.342
GRR	1.677
NRR	1.545
μ	26.667
σ^2	49.858
GENERATION	26.254
POP. SEX RATIO	1.078
SEX RATIO AT BIRTH	0.993
DEP. RATIO x 100	88.192

PROJECTED POPULATION

AGE GROUP	1985			1990			STABLE EQUIVALENT TO ORIGINAL POPULATION				AGE GROUP	
							MALES		FEMALES			
	BOTH SEXES	MALES	FEMALES	BOTH SEXES	MALES	FEMALES	Number	Percent	Number	Percent		
0-4	6	3	3	8	4	4	3	12.5	3	11.6	0-4	
5-9	6	3	3	6	3	3	3	11.3	3	10.6	5-9	TABLE 5
10-14	6	3	3	6	3	3	2	10.4	2	9.7	10-14	
15-19	6	3	3	6	3	3	2	9.5	2	8.9	15-19	POPULATION
20-24	6	3	3	6	3	3	2	8.8	2	8.2	20-24	PROJECTED
25-29	4	2	2	6	3	3	2	8.0	2	7.5	25-29	WITH
30-34	2	1	1	4	2	2	2	7.3	2	6.9	30-34	FIXED
35-39	2	1	1	2	1	1	2	6.4	2	6.2	35-39	AGE-
40-44	2	1	1	2	1	1	1	5.6	1	5.6	40-44	SPECIFIC
45-49	1	0	1	2	1	1	1	4.8	1	5.1	45-49	BIRTH
50-54	2	1	1	1	0	1	1	4.0	1	4.6	50-54	AND
55-59	2	1	1	1	0	1	1	3.3	1	4.1	55-59	DEATH
60-64	2	1	1	1	0	1	1	2.7	1	3.4	60-64	RATES
65-69	2	1	1	1	0	1	1	2.2	1	2.8	65-69	(female
70-74	2	1	1	1	0	1	0	1.5	1	2.1	70-74	dominant,
75-79	0	0	0	1	0	1	0	0.9	0	1.4	75-79	in 000s)
80-84	0	0	0	0	0	0	0	0.5	0	0.8	80-84	
85+	0	0	0	0	0	0	0	0.3	0	0.5	85+	
TOTAL	51	25	26	54	24	30	24		25		TOTAL	

VITAL RATES OF PROJECTED POPULATION / VITAL RATES OF STABLE POPULATION

Per Thousand	1985			1990			STABLE		
	BOTH SEXES	MALES	FEMALES	BOTH SEXES	MALES	FEMALES	MALES	FEMALES	TABLE 6
BIRTH RATE	30.46	31.43	29.55	31.05	31.97	30.19	27.73	25.63	
DEATH RATE	10.75	11.21	10.32	10.32	10.85	9.83	11.09	9.04	PROJECTED
RATE OF INCREASE	19.70	20.21	19.23	20.73	21.12	20.36		16.59	VITAL RATES

AGE STRUCTURE OF PROJECTED POPULATION / STABLE AGE STRUCTURE

	BOTH SEXES	MALES	FEMALES	BOTH SEXES	MALES	FEMALES	MALES	FEMALES	AND RATIOS
% UNDER 15	35.31	36.53	34.16	35.31	36.38	34.30	34.19	31.92	(female
% 15-64	55.78	55.77	55.79	57.23	57.23	57.24	60.50	60.41	dominant)
% 65 AND OLDER	8.91	7.69	10.05	7.46	6.39	8.46	5.31	7.67	
DEPEND. RATIO x 100	79.28	79.30	79.25	74.72	74.73	74.71	65.28	65.54	

AGE GROUP	FEMALE BIRTH RATES	NET MATERNITY FUNCTION	COEFF. OF MATRIX EQUATION	ORIGINAL MATRIX		STABLE MATRIX		MATRIX PARAMETERS		
				SUB-DIAGONAL	FIRST ROW	FISHER VALUES	REPRODUCTIVE VALUES			
0-4	0.0000	0.0000	0.0000	0.99410	0.00000	1.106	2882	λ_1	1.08649	
5-9	0.0000	0.0000	0.0039	0.99623	0.00391	1.209	3268	λ_2	0.36497+0.68042i	TABLE 7
10-14	0.0017	0.0078	0.1507	0.99735	0.15217	1.314	3563	λ_4	0.01038-0.69103i	
15-19	0.0631	0.2936	0.3516	0.99708	0.35598	1.263	3473	λ_6	-0.41371+0.44187i	LESLIE
20-24	0.0883	0.4096	0.3868	0.99642	0.39275	0.981	2381	r_1	0.01659	MATRIX
25-29	0.0788	0.3640	0.3003	0.99294	0.30599	0.634	917	r_2	-0.05172+0.21569i	AND ITS
30-34	0.0515	0.2365	0.2048	0.98293	0.21019	0.353	309	r_4	-0.07389-0.31116i	ANALYSIS
35-39	0.0384	0.1731	0.1166	0.98186	0.12171	0.153	106	r_6	-0.10040+0.46466i	(females)
40-44	0.0136	0.0601	0.0300	0.97873	0.03193	0.033	22	c_1	256	
45-49	0.0000	0.0000	0.0000	0.00000	0.00000	0.000	0	$2\pi/y$	29.1303	
50-54	0.0000	0.0000	0.0000	0.00000	0.00000	0.000	0	Δ	13.4155	

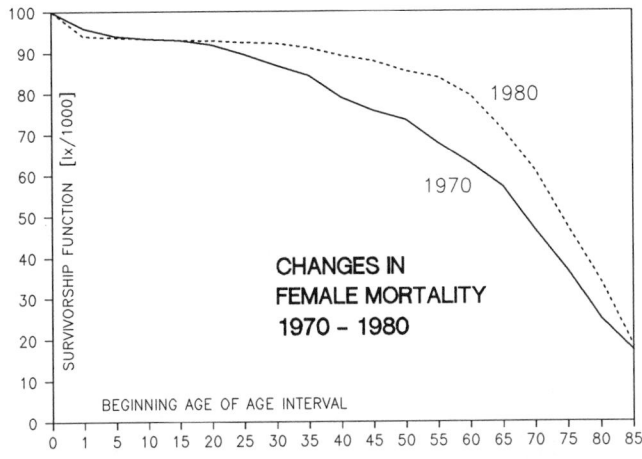

CHANGES IN FEMALE MORTALITY 1970 – 1980

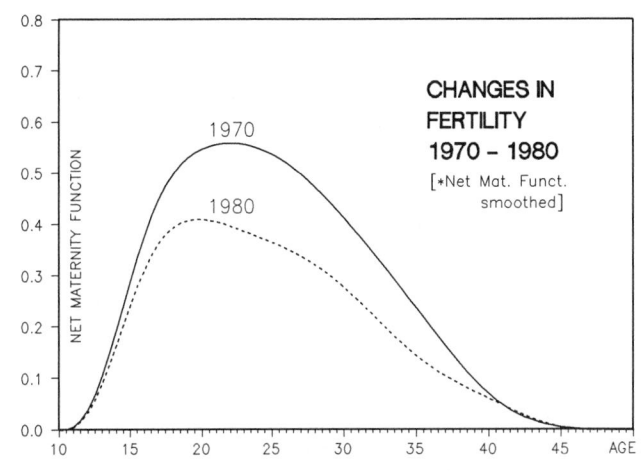

CHANGES IN FERTILITY 1970 – 1980
[*Net Mat. Funct. smoothed]

TABLE 1 — DATA

AGE AT LAST BIRTHDAY	ESTIMATED MID-YEAR POPULATION BOTH SEXES	MALES Number	MALES Percent	FEMALES Number	FEMALES Percent	BIRTHS BY AGE OF MOTHER AND SEX	DEATHS BOTH SEXES	DEATHS MALES	DEATHS FEMALES	AGE AT LAST BIRTHDAY
0	18585	9419	2.0	9166	1.9		866	480	386	0
1-4	105696	52987	11.2	52709	10.9		197	108	89	1-4
5-9	148739	74810	15.9	73929	15.3		104	62	42	5-9
10-14	128761	64464	13.7	64297	13.3	51	80	50	30	10-14
15-19	107232	52512	11.1	54720	11.3	4552	97	51	46	15-19
20-24	83634	40881	8.7	42753	8.8	8525	121	72	49	20-24
25-29	59731	29024	6.2	30707	6.3	5911	117	68	49	25-29
30-34	49949	24109	5.1	25840	5.3	3411	136	76	60	30-34
35-39	44412	21207	4.5	23205	4.8	1998	136	77	59	35-39
40-44	41300	20056	4.3	21244	4.4	614	198	105	93	40-44
45-49	39834	20015	4.2	19819	4.1	79	294	174	120	45-49
50-54	35051	18024	3.8	17027	3.5	10	444	263	181	50-54
55-59	28105	14522	3.1	13583	2.8		505	295	210	55-59
60-64	21568	10840	2.3	10728	2.2		618	355	263	60-64
65-69	19142	8639	1.8	10503	2.2		773	418	355	65-69
70-74	10655	4842	1.0	5813	1.2		670	359	311	70-74
75-79	5986	2521	0.5	3465	0.7		527	264	263	75-79
80-84	3617	1405	0.3	2212	0.5	12755 M	486	220	266	80-84
85+	3003	1057	0.2	1946	0.4	12396 F	587	230	357	85+
TOTAL	955000	471334		483666		25151	6956	3727	3229	TOTAL

TABLE 2 — MALE LIFE TABLE

x	nM_x	nq_x	l_x	nd_x	nL_x	nm_x	na_x	T_x	$\overset{\circ}{e}_x$	x
0	0.050961	0.048861	100000	4886	95879	0.050961	0.157	6320375	63.204	0
1	0.002038	0.008112	95114	772	378527	0.002038	1.500	6224496	65.443	1
5	0.000829	0.004135	94342	390	470737	0.000829	2.500	5845969	61.965	5
10	0.000776	0.003873	93952	364	468865	0.000776	2.538	5375233	57.212	10
15	0.000971	0.004875	93588	456	466897	0.000977	2.709	4906367	52.425	15
20	0.001761	0.008826	93132	822	463736	0.001773	2.658	4439470	47.669	20
25	0.002343	0.011700	92310	1080	458978	0.002353	2.617	3975735	43.069	25
30	0.003152	0.015687	91230	1431	452685	0.003161	2.579	3516757	38.548	30
35	0.003631	0.018039	89799	1620	445123	0.003639	2.610	3064072	34.121	35
40	0.005235	0.025891	88179	2283	435613	0.005241	2.686	2618949	29.700	40
45	0.008693	0.042618	85896	3661	421063	0.008694	2.701	2183336	25.418	45
50	0.014592	0.070648	82235	5810	397439	0.014618	2.635	1762273	21.430	50
55	0.020314	0.097309	76426	7437	364515	0.020402	2.632	1364833	17.858	55
60	0.032749	0.152305	68989	10507	319773	0.032859	2.604	1000319	14.500	60
65	0.048385	0.217249	58481	12705	261458	0.048593	2.564	680546	11.637	65
70	0.074143	0.314845	45776	14412	192908	0.074712	2.504	419088	9.155	70
75	0.104720	0.413910	31364	12982	123482	0.105131	2.432	226180	7.211	75
80	0.156584	0.553525	18382	10175	64981	0.156584	2.353	102698	5.587	80
85	0.217597	1.000000	8207	8207	37717	0.154294	4.596	37717	4.596	85

TABLE 3 — FEMALE LIFE TABLE

x	nM_x	nq_x	l_x	nd_x	nL_x	nm_x	na_x	T_x	$\overset{\circ}{e}_x$	x
0	0.042112	0.040643	100000	4064	96511	0.042112	0.142	6756587	67.566	0
1	0.001689	0.006726	95936	645	382130	0.001689	1.500	6660076	69.422	1
5	0.000568	0.002837	95290	270	475777	0.000568	2.500	6277946	65.882	5
10	0.000467	0.002335	95020	222	474573	0.000467	2.622	5802170	61.063	10
15	0.000841	0.004219	94798	400	473059	0.000845	2.667	5327596	56.199	15
20	0.001146	0.005740	94398	542	470710	0.001151	2.635	4854538	51.426	20
25	0.001596	0.007990	93857	750	467520	0.001604	2.649	4383827	46.708	25
30	0.002322	0.011578	93107	1078	462925	0.002329	2.581	3916307	42.063	30
35	0.002543	0.012675	92029	1167	457413	0.002550	2.660	3453383	37.525	35
40	0.004378	0.021716	90862	1973	449689	0.004388	2.658	2995969	32.973	40
45	0.006055	0.029938	88889	2661	438316	0.006071	2.697	2546280	28.646	45
50	0.010630	0.052073	86228	4490	420636	0.010675	2.661	2107964	24.446	50
55	0.015461	0.075000	81738	6130	394252	0.015549	2.645	1687328	20.643	55
60	0.024515	0.115871	75607	8761	357040	0.024537	2.603	1293076	17.103	60
65	0.033800	0.156672	66847	10473	309022	0.033891	2.593	936036	14.003	65
70	0.053501	0.238109	56374	13423	248993	0.053910	2.551	627014	11.122	70
75	0.075902	0.320110	42951	13749	180381	0.076221	2.500	378021	8.801	75
80	0.120253	0.459752	29202	13426	111644	0.120253	2.440	197639	6.768	80
85	0.183453	1.000000	15776	15776	85995	0.115194	5.451	85995	5.451	85

TABLE 4 — OBSERVED VITAL RATES AND RATIOS

CRUDE RATES

Per Thousand	BOTH SEXES	MALES	FEMALES
BIRTH RATE	26.34	27.06	25.63
DEATH RATE	7.28	7.91	6.68
RATE OF INCREASE	19.05	19.15	18.95

PERCENT OF POPULATION IN AGE GROUP

	BOTH SEXES	MALES	FEMALES
UNDER 15	42.07	42.79	41.37
15 - 64	53.49	53.29	53.68
65 AND OLDER	4.44	3.92	4.95

RATES STANDARDIZED ON USA 1980

Per Thousand	BOTH SEXES	MALES	FEMALES
BIRTH RATE	30.33		29.07
DEATH RATE	14.06	14.07	14.05
RATE OF INCREASE	16.27		15.02

RATES STANDARDIZED ON MEXICO 1980

Per Thousand	BOTH SEXES	MALES	FEMALES
BIRTH RATE	27.30		27.12
DEATH RATE	6.58	7.23	5.93
RATE OF INCREASE	20.71		21.19

VITAL STATISTICS

GFR x 1000	115.219
TFR	3.637
GRR	1.793
NRR	1.671
μ	27.698
σ^2	45.999
GENERATION	27.264
POP. SEX RATIO	1.026
SEX RATIO AT BIRTH	1.029
DEP. RATIO x 100	86.956

PROJECTED POPULATION

AGE GROUP	1975			1980		
	BOTH SEXES	MALES	FEMALES	BOTH SEXES	MALES	FEMALES
0-4	135	68	67	166	84	82
5-9	124	62	62	133	67	66
10-14	149	75	74	123	62	61
15-19	128	64	64	148	74	74
20-24	106	52	54	128	64	64
25-29	82	40	42	106	52	54
30-34	59	29	30	82	40	42
35-39	50	24	26	58	28	30
40-44	44	21	23	48	23	25
45-49	40	19	21	42	20	22
50-54	38	19	19	38	18	20
55-59	33	17	16	35	17	18
60-64	25	13	12	29	15	14
65-69	18	9	9	21	10	11
70-74	14	6	8	14	7	7
75-79	7	3	4	10	4	6
80-84	3	1	2	5	2	3
85+	3	1	2	3	1	2
TOTAL	1058	523	535	1189	588	601

STABLE EQUIVALENT TO ORIGINAL POPULATION

	MALES		FEMALES		AGE GROUP	
	Number	Percent	Number	Percent		
0-4	71	12.9	69	12.5	0-4	
5-9	64	11.6	63	11.3	5-9	TABLE 5
10-14	58	10.5	57	10.2	10-14	
15-19	52	9.5	51	9.3	15-19	POPULATION
20-24	47	8.6	47	8.4	20-24	PROJECTED
25-29	43	7.8	42	7.6	25-29	WITH
30-34	38	7.0	38	6.9	30-34	FIXED
35-39	34	6.2	34	6.2	35-39	AGE-
40-44	30	5.6	31	5.5	40-44	SPECIFIC
45-49	27	4.9	27	4.9	45-49	BIRTH
50-54	23	4.2	24	4.3	50-54	AND
55-59	19	3.5	20	3.6	55-59	DEATH
60-64	15	2.8	17	3.0	60-64	RATES
65-69	11	2.1	13	2.4	65-69	(female
70-74	8	1.4	10	1.7	70-74	dominant,
75-79	4	0.8	6	1.1	75-79	in 000s)
80-84	2	0.4	4	0.6	80-84	
85+	1	0.2	2	0.5	85+	
TOTAL	547		555		TOTAL	

VITAL RATES OF PROJECTED POPULATION

Per Thousand	1975			1980		
	BOTH SEXES	MALES	FEMALES	BOTH SEXES	MALES	FEMALES
BIRTH RATE	29.67	30.47	28.89	32.18	33.03	31.36
DEATH RATE	7.21	7.83	6.60	7.30	7.93	6.69
RATE OF INCREASE	22.46	22.64	22.29	24.88	25.10	24.67

VITAL RATES OF STABLE POPULATION

Per Thousand	MALES	FEMALES	
BIRTH RATE	28.41	27.31	TABLE 6
DEATH RATE	9.17	8.44	PROJECTED
RATE OF INCREASE		18.87	VITAL RATES

AGE STRUCTURE OF PROJECTED POPULATION

	BOTH SEXES	MALES	FEMALES	BOTH SEXES	MALES	FEMALES
% UNDER 15	38.42	39.14	37.71	35.56	36.25	34.89
% 15-64	57.21	56.94	57.47	60.07	59.76	60.37
% 65 AND OLDER	4.38	3.92	4.82	4.37	3.99	4.74
DEPEND. RATIO x 100	74.80	75.62	74.00	66.48	67.34	65.66

STABLE AGE STRUCTURE

	MALES	FEMALES	
% UNDER 15	35.02	34.02	AND RATIOS
% 15-64	60.09	59.65	(female
% 65 AND OLDER	4.89	6.33	dominant)
DEPEND. RATIO x 100	66.42	67.65	

AGE GROUP	FEMALE BIRTH RATES	NET MATERNITY FUNCTION	COEFF. OF MATRIX EQUATION	ORIGINAL MATRIX SUB-DIAGONAL	FIRST ROW	STABLE MATRIX FISHER VALUES	REPRODUCTIVE VALUES	MATRIX PARAMETERS		
0-4	0.0000	0.0000	0.0000	0.99402	0.00000	1.095	67741	λ_1	1.09894	
5-9	0.0000	0.0000	0.0009	0.99747	0.00093	1.210	89481	λ_2	$0.37236+0.74228i$	TABLE 7
10-14	0.0004	0.0019	0.0979	0.99681	0.09874	1.332	85674	λ_4	$0.00344+0.61843i$	
15-19	0.0410	0.1940	0.3283	0.99504	0.33215	1.361	74450	λ_6	$-0.42744+0.40628i$	LESLIE
20-24	0.0983	0.4626	0.4531	0.99322	0.46071	1.137	48618	r_1	0.01887	MATRIX
25-29	0.0949	0.4436	0.3724	0.99017	0.38123	0.750	23042	r_2	$-0.03716+0.22117i$	AND ITS
30-34	0.0651	0.3012	0.2476	0.98809	0.25605	0.411	10628	r_4	$-0.09611+0.31305i$	ANALYSIS
35-39	0.0424	0.1941	0.1291	0.98311	0.13507	0.174	4032	r_6	$-0.10562+0.47631i$	(females)
40-44	0.0142	0.0641	0.0363	0.97471	0.03867	0.044	931	c_1	5539	
45-49	0.0020	0.0086	0.0049	0.95966	0.00537	0.006	118	$2\pi/y$	28.4093	
50-54	0.0003	0.0012	0.0006	0.93728	0.00069	0.001	12	Δ	9.7950	

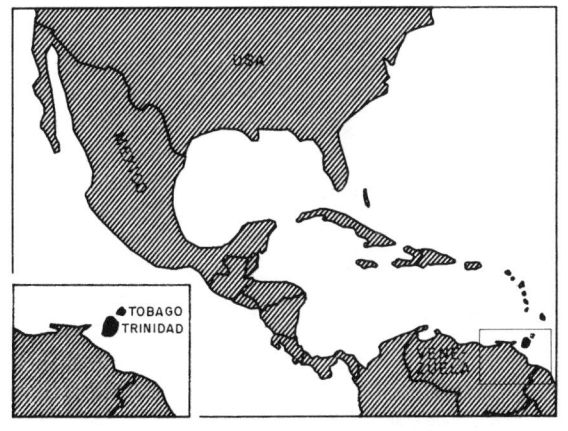

EDUCATION [1984]

% of primary school-age children enrolled:	96
secondary school-age children enrolled:	76
ca. 20-24 year olds in higher education:	4

LABOR FORCE

Average annual labor force growth (%) 1980-85:	2.5	
% of the 1980 labor force in agriculture:	10	TABLE 8
in industry:	39	
in services:	51	SOCIO-ECONOMIC

GNP & INCOME DISTRIBUTION

GNP per capita (in US Dollars) 1985:	6020	INDICATORS
GNP average annual growth rate (%) 1965-85:	2.3	
% share of total household income 1975-76		
Lowest 20% of households:	4.2	
Highest 10% of households:	31.8	

HEALTH & NUTRITION

Population per physician 1981:	1500
Daily calorie supply per capita 1985:	3006

TABLE 1 — DATA

AGE AT LAST BIRTHDAY	ESTIMATED MID-YEAR POPULATION BOTH SEXES	MALES Number	MALES Percent	FEMALES Number	FEMALES Percent	BIRTHS BY AGE OF MOTHER AND SEX	DEATHS BOTH SEXES	DEATHS MALES	DEATHS FEMALES	AGE AT LAST BIRTHDAY
0	399737	202797	3.8	196940	3.8		19356	10832	8524	0
1-4	1448948	739835	13.8	709113	13.5		7515	3647	3868	1-4
5-9	1635302	833395	15.5	801907	15.3		1632	888	744	5-9
10-14	1358563	691411	12.9	667152	12.7	1056	960	565	395	10-14
15-19	1132433	575437	10.7	556996	10.6	60918	1387	847	540	15-19
20-24	915989	463738	8.6	452251	8.6	119693	1530	1052	478	20-24
25-29	676632	334424	6.2	342208	6.5	92354	1339	844	495	25-29
30-34	630555	318335	5.9	312220	6.0	61504	1355	808	547	30-34
35-39	535523	273579	5.1	261944	5.0	40916	1622	922	700	35-39
40-44	492945	253360	4.7	239585	4.6	13788	1976	1121	855	40-44
45-49	372184	189315	3.5	182869	3.5	2219	2215	1323	892	45-49
50-54	312620	156752	2.9	155868	3.0	135	2726	1669	1057	50-54
55-59	242349	121026	2.3	121323	2.3		3452	2042	1410	55-59
60-64	186149	91982	1.7	94167	1.8		4110	2280	1830	60-64
65-69	100469	48838	0.9	51631	1.0		4005	2235	1770	65-69
70-74	74058	34716	0.6	39342	0.8		3702	1997	1705	70-74
75-79	38346	16968	0.3	21378	0.4		3060	1511	1549	75-79
80-84	26604	10628	0.2	15976	0.3	200079 M	2629	1152	1477	80-84
85+	24665	8934	0.2	15731	0.3	192504 F	3922	1346	2576	85+
TOTAL	10604071	5365470		5238601		392583	68493	37081	31412	TOTAL

TABLE 2 — MALE LIFE TABLE

x	$_nM_x$	$_nq_x$	l_x	$_nd_x$	$_nL_x$	$_nm_x$	$_na_x$	T_x	$\overset{\circ}{e}_x$	x
0	0.053413	0.051122	100000	5112	95710	0.053413	0.161	6430976	64.310	0
1	0.004929	0.019478	94888	1848	374931	0.004929	1.500	6335266	66.766	1
5	0.001066	0.005313	93040	494	463962	0.001066	2.500	5960335	64.062	5
10	0.000817	0.004083	92545	378	461820	0.000818	2.603	5496373	59.391	10
15	0.001472	0.007385	92167	681	459272	0.001482	2.701	5034552	54.624	15
20	0.002269	0.011327	91487	1036	454937	0.002278	2.591	4575280	50.010	20
25	0.002524	0.012548	90450	1135	449434	0.002525	2.517	4120342	45.554	25
30	0.002538	0.012629	89315	1128	443828	0.002541	2.563	3670909	41.101	30
35	0.003370	0.016750	88187	1477	437407	0.003377	2.610	3227081	36.593	35
40	0.004425	0.021984	86710	1906	429090	0.004443	2.659	2789674	32.172	40
45	0.006988	0.034616	84804	2936	417175	0.007037	2.668	2360584	27.836	45
50	0.010647	0.052256	81868	4278	399354	0.010713	2.665	1943409	23.738	50
55	0.016872	0.081600	77590	6331	372984	0.016975	2.636	1544055	19.900	55
60	0.024787	0.118020	71259	8410	336667	0.024980	2.666	1171071	16.434	60
65	0.045764	0.207493	62849	13041	282511	0.046160	2.567	834404	13.276	65
70	0.057524	0.252502	49808	12577	217718	0.057766	2.509	551893	11.080	70
75	0.089050	0.365517	37232	13609	151591	0.089772	2.460	334175	8.976	75
80	0.108393	0.421793	23623	9964	91924	0.108393	2.372	182584	7.729	80
85	0.150660	1.000000	13659	13659	90660	0.082345	6.637	90660	6.637	85

TABLE 3 — FEMALE LIFE TABLE

x	$_nM_x$	$_nq_x$	l_x	$_nd_x$	$_nL_x$	$_nm_x$	$_na_x$	T_x	$\overset{\circ}{e}_x$	x
0	0.043282	0.041735	100000	4174	96426	0.043282	0.144	6833514	68.335	0
1	0.005455	0.021525	95826	2063	378149	0.005455	1.500	6737088	70.305	1
5	0.000928	0.004628	93764	434	467734	0.000928	2.500	6358939	67.819	5
10	0.000592	0.002952	93330	276	465964	0.000591	2.513	5891205	63.122	10
15	0.000969	0.004854	93054	452	464187	0.000973	2.599	5425241	58.302	15
20	0.001057	0.005282	92603	489	461835	0.001059	2.591	4961054	53.574	20
25	0.001446	0.007233	92113	666	458967	0.001452	2.597	4499219	48.844	25
30	0.001752	0.008755	91447	801	455347	0.001758	2.641	4040252	44.181	30
35	0.002672	0.013321	90647	1208	450378	0.002681	2.636	3584905	39.548	35
40	0.003569	0.017754	89439	1588	443418	0.003581	2.621	3134527	35.046	40
45	0.004878	0.024223	87851	2128	434205	0.004901	2.626	2691109	30.633	45
50	0.006781	0.033581	85723	2879	421960	0.006822	2.688	2256904	26.328	50
55	0.011622	0.057029	82844	4725	403337	0.011714	2.696	1834944	22.149	55
60	0.019434	0.093763	78120	7325	373654	0.019603	2.687	1431607	18.326	60
65	0.034282	0.159401	70795	11285	326678	0.034544	2.581	1057952	14.944	65
70	0.043338	0.196847	59510	11714	268987	0.043550	2.562	731274	12.288	70
75	0.072458	0.308582	47796	14749	202243	0.072927	2.509	462287	9.672	75
80	0.092451	0.374153	33047	12365	133742	0.092451	2.453	260044	7.869	80
85	0.163753	1.000000	20682	20682	126302	0.094688	6.107	126302	6.107	85

TABLE 4 — OBSERVED VITAL RATES AND RATIOS

CRUDE RATES

Per Thousand	BOTH SEXES	MALES	FEMALES
BIRTH RATE	37.02	37.29	36.75
DEATH RATE	6.46	6.91	6.00
RATE OF INCREASE	30.56	30.38	30.75

PERCENT OF POPULATION IN AGE GROUP

	BOTH SEXES	MALES	FEMALES
UNDER 15	45.67	45.99	45.34
15 - 64	51.84	51.77	51.91
65 AND OLDER	2.49	2.24	2.75

RATES STANDARDIZED ON USA 1980

Per Thousand	BOTH SEXES	MALES	FEMALES
BIRTH RATE	43.70		41.67
DEATH RATE	12.14	11.87	12.39
RATE OF INCREASE	31.56		29.28

RATES STANDARDIZED ON MEXICO 1980

	BOTH SEXES	MALES	FEMALES
BIRTH RATE	38.89		38.43
DEATH RATE	6.35	6.86	5.83
RATE OF INCREASE	32.54		32.60

VITAL STATISTICS

GFR x 1000	167.194
TFR	5.346
GRR	2.621
NRR	2.397
μ	28.563
σ^2	51.354
GENERATION	27.754
POP. SEX RATIO	0.976
SEX RATIO AT BIRTH	1.039
DEP. RATIO x 100	92.893

PROJECTED POPULATION

AGE GROUP	1975 BOTH SEXES	1975 MALES	1975 FEMALES	1980 BOTH SEXES	1980 MALES	1980 FEMALES
0-4	2049	1040	1009	2476	1257	1219
5-9	1822	929	893	2021	1026	995
10-14	1629	830	799	1815	925	890
15-19	1353	688	665	1621	825	796
20-24	1124	570	554	1342	681	661
25-29	907	458	449	1114	563	551
30-34	670	330	340	898	452	446
35-39	623	314	309	661	325	336
40-44	526	268	258	612	308	304
45-49	481	246	235	514	261	253
50-54	359	181	178	464	236	228
55-59	295	146	149	339	169	170
60-64	221	109	112	270	132	138
65-69	159	77	82	190	92	98
70-74	81	38	43	127	59	68
75-79	54	24	30	58	26	32
80-84	24	10	14	35	15	20
85+	25	10	15	23	10	13
TOTAL	12402	6268	6134	14580	7362	7218

STABLE EQUIVALENT TO ORIGINAL POPULATION

MALES Number	MALES Percent	FEMALES Number	FEMALES Percent	AGE GROUP	
931	17.0	903	16.7	0-4	
784	14.4	760	14.1	5-9	TABLE 5
666	12.2	647	12.0	10-14	
566	10.4	550	10.2	15-19	POPULATION
478	8.8	467	8.7	20-24	PROJECTED
404	7.4	397	7.3	25-29	WITH
340	6.2	336	6.2	30-34	FIXED
286	5.2	284	5.3	35-39	AGE-
240	4.4	239	4.4	40-44	SPECIFIC
199	3.6	199	3.7	45-49	BIRTH
163	3.0	166	3.1	50-54	AND
130	2.4	135	2.5	55-59	DEATH
100	1.8	107	2.0	60-64	RATES
72	1.3	80	1.5	65-69	(female
47	0.9	56	1.0	70-74	dominant,
28	0.5	36	0.7	75-79	in 000s)
15	0.3	20	0.4	80-84	
12	0.2	16	0.3	85+	
5461		5398		TOTAL	

VITAL RATES OF PROJECTED POPULATION

Per Thousand	1975 BOTH SEXES	1975 MALES	1975 FEMALES	1980 BOTH SEXES	1980 MALES	1980 FEMALES
BIRTH RATE	38.29	38.60	37.97	39.31	39.67	38.94
DEATH RATE	6.43	6.95	5.90	6.56	7.13	5.99
RATE OF INCREASE	31.86	31.65	32.07	32.75	32.55	32.96

VITAL RATES OF STABLE POPULATION

Per Thousand	MALES	FEMALES	
BIRTH RATE	39.08	38.03	TABLE 6
DEATH RATE	7.55	6.45	PROJECTED
RATE OF INCREASE		31.58	VITAL RATES

AGE STRUCTURE OF PROJECTED POPULATION

	BOTH SEXES	MALES	FEMALES	BOTH SEXES	MALES	FEMALES
% UNDER 15	44.35	44.64	44.04	43.29	43.56	43.01
% 15-64	52.89	52.81	52.96	53.74	53.69	53.79
% 65 AND OLDER	2.77	2.55	2.99	2.97	2.75	3.20
DEPEND. RATIO x 100	89.09	89.36	88.81	86.08	86.25	85.90

STABLE AGE STRUCTURE

	MALES	FEMALES	
% UNDER 15	43.59	42.79	AND RATIOS
% 15-64	53.22	53.34	(female
% 65 AND OLDER	3.18	3.87	dominant)
DEPEND. RATIO x 100	87.89	87.47	

AGE GROUP	FEMALE BIRTH RATES	NET MATERNITY FUNCTION	COEFF. OF MATRIX EQUATION	ORIGINAL MATRIX SUB-DIAGONAL	ORIGINAL MATRIX FIRST ROW	STABLE MATRIX FISHER VALUES	STABLE MATRIX REPRODUCTIVE VALUES	MATRIX PARAMETERS		
0-4	0.0000	0.0000	0.0000	0.98559	0.00000	1.139	1032236	λ_1	1.17107	
5-9	0.0000	0.0000	0.0018	0.99622	0.00183	1.354	1085521	λ_2	$0.40521-0.76809i$	TABLE 7
10-14	0.0008	0.0036	0.1263	0.99619	0.12861	1.589	1060221	λ_4	$0.02043+0.68815i$	
15-19	0.0536	0.2489	0.4241	0.99493	0.43364	1.721	958634	λ_6	$-0.47626+0.42052i$	LESLIE
20-24	0.1298	0.5994	0.6034	0.99379	0.62001	1.529	691592	r_1	0.03158	MATRIX
25-29	0.1323	0.6074	0.5236	0.99211	0.54141	1.091	373435	r_2	$-0.02822-0.21707i$	AND ITS
30-34	0.0966	0.4398	0.3924	0.98909	0.40897	0.666	208056	r_4	$-0.07466+0.30822i$	ANALYSIS
35-39	0.0766	0.3450	0.2350	0.98454	0.24767	0.318	83277	r_6	$-0.09072+0.48365i$	(females)
40-44	0.0282	0.1251	0.0755	0.97922	0.08079	0.092	21935	c_1	53970	
45-49	0.0060	0.0258	0.0138	0.97180	0.01510	0.016	2835	$2\pi/\gamma$	28.9455	
50-54	0.0004	0.0018	0.0009	0.95587	0.00101	0.001	153	Δ	3.1419	

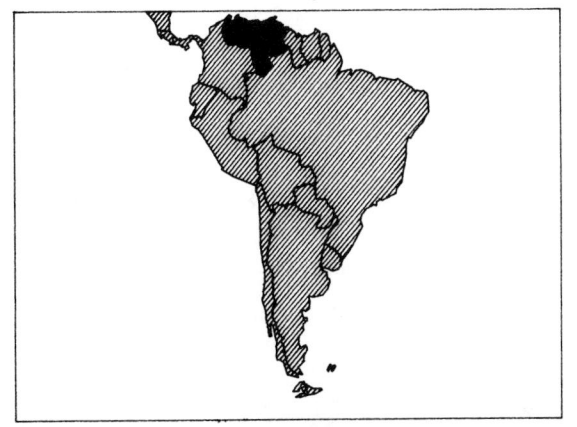

EDUCATION [1984]

% of primary school-age children enrolled:	109
secondary school-age children enrolled:	45
ca. 20-24 year olds in higher education:	23

LABOR FORCE

Average annual labor force growth (%) 1980-85:	3.5	
% of the 1980 labor force in agriculture:	16	TABLE 8
in industry:	28	
in services:	56	SOCIO-

GNP & INCOME DISTRIBUTION

GNP per capita (in US Dollars) 1985:	3080	ECONOMIC
GNP average annual growth rate (%) 1965-85:	0.5	INDICATORS
% share of total household income 1970		
Lowest 20% of households:	3.0	
Highest 10% of households:	35.7	

HEALTH & NUTRITION

Population per physician 1981:	1000
Daily calorie supply per capita 1985:	2583

AGE AT LAST BIRTHDAY	ESTIMATED MID-YEAR POPULATION BOTH SEXES	MALES Number	MALES Percent	FEMALES Number	FEMALES Percent	BIRTHS BY AGE OF MOTHER AND SEX	DEATHS BOTH SEXES	DEATHS MALES	DEATHS FEMALES	AGE AT LAST BIRTHDAY
0	536364	275212	3.1	261152	3.0		13105	7483	5622	0
1-4	2022147	1029581	11.8	992566	11.6		3079	1553	1526	1-4
5-9	2273390	1158483	13.2	1114907	13.0		1031	597	434	5-9
10-14	2006568	1021657	11.7	984911	11.5	4158	992	594	398	10-14
15-19	1870760	950940	10.9	919820	10.7	75411	1696	1187	509	15-19
20-24	1678987	851927	9.7	827060	9.7	152301	2372	1756	616	20-24
25-29	1436379	727415	8.3	708964	8.3	128193	2281	1648	633	25-29
30-34	1245110	630454	7.2	614656	7.2	85161	2188	1490	698	30-34
35-39	1017986	515837	5.9	502149	5.9	41462	2116	1330	786	35-39
40-44	759828	382875	4.4	376953	4.4	13007	2289	1406	883	40-44
45-49	604770	302333	3.5	302437	3.5	2247	2842	1717	1125	45-49
50-54	516839	258140	3.0	258699	3.0	389	3661	2253	1408	50-54
55-59	430573	214413	2.5	216160	2.5		4602	2765	1837	55-59
60-64	327294	160423	1.8	166871	1.9		5250	3086	2164	60-64
65-69	237641	113182	1.3	124459	1.5		5902	3364	2538	65-69
70-74	162869	74880	0.9	87989	1.0		7054	3875	3179	70-74
75-79	81191	37464	0.4	43727	0.5		6251	3214	3037	75-79
80-84	56143	23465	0.3	32678	0.4	256707 M	5600	2670	2930	80-84
85+	51902	19725	0.2	32177	0.4	245622 F	6627	2523	4104	85+
TOTAL	17316741	8748406		8568335		502329	78938	44511	34427	TOTAL

TABLE 1 DATA

TABLE 2 — MALE LIFE TABLE

x	nM_x	nq_x	l_x	nd_x	nL_x	nm_x	na_x	T_x	$\overset{\circ}{e}_x$	x
0	0.027190	0.026552	100000	2655	97653	0.027190	0.116	6943588	69.436	0
1	0.001508	0.006011	97345	585	387916	0.001508	1.500	6845934	70.327	1
5	0.000515	0.002573	96760	249	483176	0.000515	2.500	6458018	66.743	5
10	0.000581	0.002914	96511	281	481924	0.000584	2.761	5974842	61.909	10
15	0.001248	0.006246	96229	601	479791	0.001253	2.743	5492918	57.081	15
20	0.002061	0.010280	95628	983	475782	0.002066	2.599	5013127	52.423	20
25	0.002266	0.011272	94645	1067	470584	0.002267	2.523	4537345	47.940	25
30	0.002363	0.011755	93578	1100	465168	0.002365	2.523	4066761	43.458	30
35	0.002578	0.012851	92478	1188	459540	0.002586	2.600	3601594	38.945	35
40	0.003672	0.018319	91290	1672	452548	0.003695	2.667	3142054	34.418	40
45	0.005679	0.028203	89618	2528	442200	0.005716	2.670	2689506	30.011	45
50	0.008728	0.042945	87090	3740	426666	0.008766	2.651	2247305	25.804	50
55	0.012896	0.062876	83350	5241	404376	0.012960	2.639	1820640	21.843	55
60	0.019237	0.092596	78109	7233	373439	0.019368	2.635	1416264	18.132	60
65	0.029722	0.139911	70877	9916	331033	0.029956	2.645	1042824	14.713	65
70	0.051749	0.232033	60960	14145	270842	0.052225	2.599	711791	11.676	70
75	0.085789	0.355567	46816	16646	192267	0.086578	2.488	440950	9.419	75
80	0.113786	0.437767	30169	13207	116070	0.113787	2.367	248682	8.243	80
85	0.127909	1.000000	16962	16962	132612	0.061842	7.818	132612	7.818	85

TABLE 3 — FEMALE LIFE TABLE

x	nM_x	nq_x	l_x	nd_x	nL_x	nm_x	na_x	T_x	$\overset{\circ}{e}_x$	x
0	0.021528	0.021121	100000	2112	98113	0.021528	0.107	7448777	74.488	0
1	0.001537	0.006126	97888	600	390052	0.001537	1.500	7350664	75.093	1
5	0.000389	0.001944	97288	189	485968	0.000389	2.500	6960612	71.546	5
10	0.000404	0.002021	97099	196	485021	0.000405	2.584	6474644	66.681	10
15	0.000553	0.002768	96903	268	483877	0.000554	2.627	5989623	61.811	15
20	0.000745	0.003725	96635	360	482306	0.000746	2.593	5505746	56.975	20
25	0.000893	0.004464	96275	430	480337	0.000895	2.589	5023439	52.178	25
30	0.001136	0.005681	95845	545	477929	0.001139	2.621	4543102	47.401	30
35	0.001565	0.007840	95300	747	474751	0.001574	2.657	4065174	42.656	35
40	0.002342	0.011728	94553	1109	470199	0.002358	2.685	3590423	37.973	40
45	0.003720	0.018551	93444	1733	463172	0.003743	2.664	3120224	33.391	45
50	0.005443	0.027000	91711	2476	452781	0.005469	2.669	2657052	28.972	50
55	0.008498	0.041898	89235	3739	437439	0.008547	2.664	2204271	24.702	55
60	0.012968	0.063365	85496	5417	414794	0.013060	2.658	1766833	20.666	60
65	0.020392	0.098119	80078	7857	382150	0.020560	2.678	1352039	16.884	65
70	0.036130	0.168142	72221	12143	332855	0.036483	2.674	969889	13.429	70
75	0.069454	0.299199	60078	17975	256117	0.070184	2.537	637033	10.603	75
80	0.089663	0.364361	42103	15341	171091	0.089663	2.430	380916	9.047	80
85	0.127545	1.000000	26762	26762	209825	0.061190	7.840	209825	7.840	85

TABLE 4 — OBSERVED VITAL RATES AND RATIOS

CRUDE RATES

Per Thousand	BOTH SEXES	MALES	FEMALES
BIRTH RATE	29.01	29.34	28.67
DEATH RATE	4.56	5.09	4.02
RATE OF INCREASE	24.45	24.26	24.65

PERCENT OF POPULATION IN AGE GROUP

	BOTH SEXES	MALES	FEMALES
UNDER 15	39.49	39.84	39.14
15 - 64	57.10	57.09	57.11
65 AND OLDER	3.41	3.07	3.75

RATES STANDARDIZED ON USA 1980

Per Thousand	BOTH SEXES	MALES	FEMALES
BIRTH RATE	29.59		28.14
DEATH RATE	9.52	9.55	9.49
RATE OF INCREASE	20.07		18.65

RATES STANDARDIZED ON MEXICO 1980

	BOTH SEXES	MALES	FEMALES
BIRTH RATE	26.64		26.25
DEATH RATE	4.32	4.88	3.76
RATE OF INCREASE	22.32		22.50

VITAL STATISTICS

GFR x 1000	118.138
TFR	3.579
GRR	1.750
NRR	1.678
μ	28.027
σ^2	51.234
GENERATION	27.546
POP. SEX RATIO	0.979
SEX RATIO AT BIRTH	1.045
DEP. RATIO x 100	75.120

PROJECTED POPULATION

AGE GROUP	1990 BOTH SEXES	1990 MALES	1990 FEMALES	1995 BOTH SEXES	1995 MALES	1995 FEMALES
0-4	2614	1332	1282	2945	1501	1444
5-9	2546	1298	1248	2602	1326	1276
10-14	2268	1155	1113	2541	1295	1246
15-19	2000	1017	983	2260	1150	1110
20-24	1860	943	917	1988	1009	979
25-29	1667	843	824	1846	933	913
30-34	1424	719	705	1653	833	820
35-39	1234	623	611	1411	710	701
40-44	1005	508	497	1218	613	605
45-49	745	374	371	986	496	490
50-54	588	292	296	724	361	363
55-59	495	245	250	562	276	286
60-64	403	198	205	463	226	237
65-69	296	142	154	365	176	189
70-74	201	93	108	250	116	134
75-79	121	53	68	149	66	83
80-84	52	23	29	77	32	45
85+	67	27	40	62	26	36
TOTAL	19586	9885	9701	22102	11145	10957

STABLE EQUIVALENT TO ORIGINAL POPULATION

MALES Number	MALES Percent	FEMALES Number	FEMALES Percent	AGE GROUP	
1257	12.4	1210	12.0	0-4	
1139	11.2	1096	10.9	5-9	TABLE 5
1034	10.2	996	9.9	10-14	
937	9.2	904	9.0	15-19	POPULATION
846	8.3	820	8.1	20-24	PROJECTED
761	7.5	743	7.4	25-29	WITH
685	6.8	673	6.7	30-34	FIXED
616	6.1	609	6.0	35-39	AGE-
552	5.4	549	5.4	40-44	SPECIFIC
491	4.8	492	4.9	45-49	BIRTH
431	4.3	438	4.3	50-54	AND
372	3.7	385	3.8	55-59	DEATH
313	3.1	332	3.3	60-64	RATES
252	2.5	279	2.8	65-69	(female
188	1.9	221	2.2	70-74	dominant,
121	1.2	155	1.5	75-79	in 000s)
67	0.7	94	0.9	80-84	
69	0.7	105	1.0	85+	
10131		10101		TOTAL	

VITAL RATES OF PROJECTED POPULATION

Per Thousand	1990 BOTH SEXES	1990 MALES	1990 FEMALES	1995 BOTH SEXES	1995 MALES	1995 FEMALES
BIRTH RATE	29.18	29.55	28.81	28.88	29.26	28.48
DEATH RATE	4.72	5.27	4.16	4.91	5.49	4.31
RATE OF INCREASE	24.46	24.28	24.65	23.97	23.77	24.17

AGE STRUCTURE OF PROJECTED POPULATION

	1990 BOTH SEXES	1990 MALES	1990 FEMALES	1995 BOTH SEXES	1995 MALES	1995 FEMALES
% UNDER 15	37.93	38.30	37.55	36.59	36.98	36.19
% 15-64	58.31	58.28	58.33	59.32	59.29	59.36
% 65 AND OLDER	3.76	3.41	4.11	4.08	3.73	4.45
DEPEND. RATIO x 100	71.50	71.58	71.43	68.57	68.66	68.47

VITAL RATES OF STABLE POPULATION

Per Thousand	MALES	FEMALES	
BIRTH RATE	26.76	25.69	TABLE 6
DEATH RATE	8.02	6.86	
RATE OF INCREASE		18.82	PROJECTED VITAL RATES AND

STABLE AGE STRUCTURE

	MALES	FEMALES	
% UNDER 15	33.86	32.69	RATIOS
% 15-64	59.26	58.87	(female
% 65 AND OLDER	6.88	8.45	dominant)
DEPEND. RATIO x 100	68.76	69.88	

MATRIX PARAMETERS

AGE GROUP	FEMALE BIRTH RATES	NET MATERNITY FUNCTION	COEFF. OF MATRIX EQUATION	ORIGINAL MATRIX SUB-DIAGONAL	ORIGINAL MATRIX FIRST ROW	STABLE MATRIX FISHER VALUES	STABLE MATRIX REPRODUCTIVE VALUES		MATRIX PARAMETERS	
0-4	0.0000	0.0000	0.0000	0.99550	0.00000	1.073	1345679	λ_1	1.09868	
5-9	0.0000	0.0000	0.0050	0.99805	0.00503	1.185	1320724	λ_2	$0.38380+0.72861i$	TABLE 7
10-14	0.0021	0.0100	0.1020	0.99764	0.10265	1.299	1279044	λ_4	$0.00758+0.58753i$	
15-19	0.0401	0.1940	0.3141	0.99675	0.31691	1.320	1213906	λ_6	$-0.36805+0.39343i$	LESLIE
20-24	0.0900	0.4343	0.4295	0.99592	0.43470	1.113	920862	r_1	0.01882	MATRIX
25-29	0.0884	0.4247	0.3742	0.99499	0.38033	0.760	538679	r_2	$-0.03883+0.21720i$	AND ITS
30-34	0.0677	0.3238	0.2577	0.99335	0.26325	0.429	263512	r_4	$-0.10635+0.31158i$	ANALYSIS
35-39	0.0404	0.1917	0.1355	0.99041	0.13933	0.190	95271	r_6	$-0.12370+0.46457i$	(females)
40-44	0.0169	0.0793	0.0481	0.98506	0.04992	0.059	22416	c_1	100995	
45-49	0.0036	0.0168	0.0101	0.97757	0.01062	0.012	3610	$2x/y$	28.9287	
50-54	0.0007	0.0033	0.0017	0.96612	0.00179	0.002	454	Δ	11.1885	

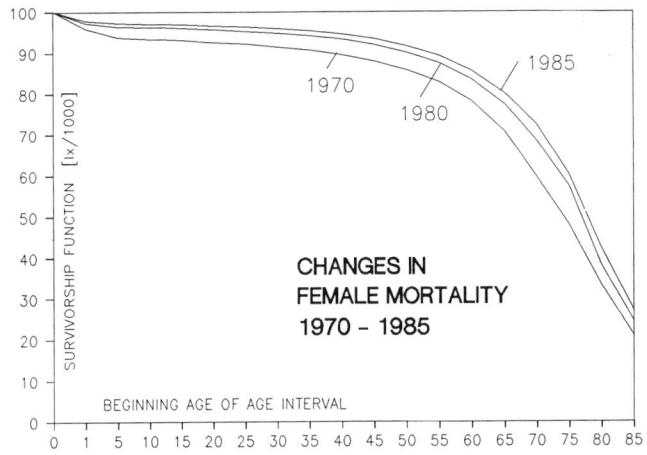

CHANGES IN FEMALE MORTALITY 1970 - 1985

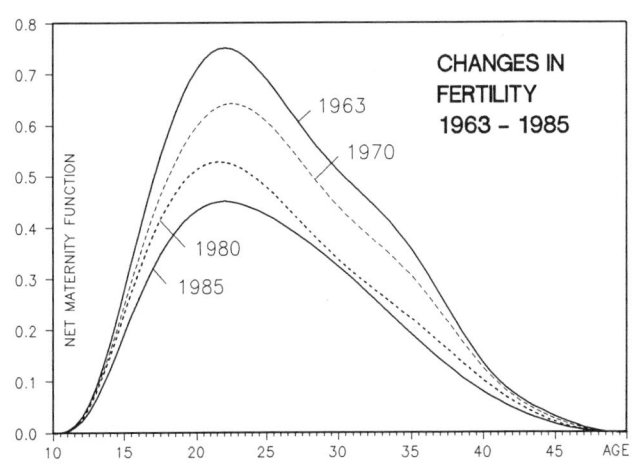

CHANGES IN FERTILITY 1963 - 1985

TABLE 1 — DATA

AGE AT LAST BIRTHDAY	ESTIMATED MID-YEAR POPULATION BOTH SEXES	MALES Number	MALES Percent	FEMALES Number	FEMALES Percent	BIRTHS BY AGE OF MOTHER AND SEX	DEATHS BOTH SEXES	DEATHS MALES	DEATHS FEMALES	AGE AT LAST BIRTHDAY
0	360800	184400	1.7	176400	1.7		7002	4057	2945	0
1-4	1518800	777200	7.3	741600	7.0		1263	714	549	1-4
5-9	2288600	1171400	11.0	1117200	10.5		1102	676	426	5-9
10-14	2285600	1167500	10.9	1118100	10.5	308	988	615	373	10-14
15-19	2064800	1049000	9.8	1015800	9.6	43823	1948	1410	538	15-19
20-24	1822400	911900	8.5	910500	8.6	131907	2105	1585	520	20-24
25-29	1503800	758400	7.1	745400	7.0	111226	1564	1088	476	25-29
30-34	1276700	645900	6.1	630800	5.9	52395	1636	1045	591	30-34
35-39	1265900	646200	6.1	619500	5.8	24547	2217	1402	815	35-39
40-44	1270600	641900	6.0	628700	5.9	7219	3566	2260	1306	40-44
45-49	1218900	603100	5.7	615800	5.8	563	5327	3372	1955	45-49
50-54	1037800	513600	4.8	524200	4.9		7363	4785	2578	50-54
55-59	934400	464300	4.4	470100	4.4		10420	6889	3531	55-59
60-64	752700	370600	3.5	382100	3.6		13061	8774	4287	60-64
65-69	597400	284500	2.7	312900	2.9		16056	10336	5720	65-69
70-74	447500	202200	1.9	245300	2.3		17992	10781	7211	70-74
75-79	323400	140800	1.3	182600	1.7		19919	11024	8895	75-79
80-84	199600	85100	0.8	114500	1.1	191435 M	19776	10166	9610	80-84
85+	128100	51500	0.5	76600	0.7	180553 F	22656	10130	12526	85+
TOTAL	21297600	10669500		10628100		371988	155961	91109	64852	TOTAL

TABLE 2 — MALE LIFE TABLE

x	nM_x	nq_x	l_x	nd_x	nL_x	nm_x	na_x	T_x	$\mathring{e}_x$	x
0	0.022001	0.021577	100000	2158	98074	0.022001	0.107	6927758	69.278	0
1	0.000919	0.003666	97842	359	390472	0.000919	1.500	6829684	69.803	1
5	0.000577	0.002881	97484	281	486716	0.000577	2.500	6439212	66.054	5
10	0.000527	0.002635	97203	256	485450	0.000528	2.802	5952497	61.238	10
15	0.001344	0.006724	96947	652	483223	0.001349	2.685	5467046	56.392	15
20	0.001738	0.008659	96295	834	479395	0.001739	2.507	4983823	51.756	20
25	0.001435	0.007135	95461	681	475587	0.001432	2.479	4504428	47.186	25
30	0.001618	0.008073	94780	765	472055	0.001621	2.591	4028841	42.507	30
35	0.002170	0.010800	94015	1015	467713	0.002171	2.676	3556786	37.832	35
40	0.003521	0.017465	92999	1624	461251	0.003521	2.694	3089073	33.216	40
45	0.005591	0.027673	91375	2529	451061	0.005606	2.701	2627822	28.759	45
50	0.009317	0.045740	88846	4064	434815	0.009346	2.683	2176761	24.500	50
55	0.014837	0.071909	84782	6097	409669	0.014882	2.664	1741946	20.546	55
60	0.023675	0.112535	78686	8855	372461	0.023774	2.632	1332277	16.932	60
65	0.036330	0.167658	69831	11708	320903	0.036484	2.587	959816	13.745	65
70	0.053318	0.236372	58123	13739	256862	0.053487	2.543	638913	10.992	70
75	0.078295	0.327852	44385	14552	185525	0.078435	2.499	382052	8.608	75
80	0.119459	0.457443	29833	13647	114238	0.119459	2.441	196527	6.588	80
85	0.196699	1.000000	16186	16186	82289	0.129642	5.084	82289	5.084	85

TABLE 3 — FEMALE LIFE TABLE

x	nM_x	nq_x	l_x	nd_x	nL_x	nm_x	na_x	T_x	$\mathring{e}_x$	x
0	0.016695	0.016447	100000	1645	98517	0.016695	0.098	7630985	76.310	0
1	0.000740	0.002956	98355	291	392694	0.000740	1.500	7532468	76.584	1
5	0.000381	0.001905	98065	187	489856	0.000381	2.500	7139774	72.807	5
10	0.000334	0.001667	97878	163	488996	0.000334	2.592	6649919	67.941	10
15	0.000530	0.002649	97715	259	487950	0.000530	2.592	6160923	63.050	15
20	0.000571	0.002854	97456	278	486594	0.000572	2.539	5672973	58.211	20
25	0.000639	0.003197	97178	311	485149	0.000640	2.618	5186379	53.370	25
30	0.000937	0.004691	96867	454	483266	0.000940	2.648	4701231	48.533	30
35	0.001316	0.006564	96413	633	480592	0.001317	2.676	4217966	43.749	35
40	0.002077	0.010337	95780	990	476603	0.002077	2.682	3737373	39.021	40
45	0.003175	0.015786	94790	1496	470475	0.003181	2.679	3260770	34.400	45
50	0.004918	0.024394	93293	2276	461168	0.004935	2.672	2790295	29.909	50
55	0.007511	0.037042	91018	3371	447188	0.007539	2.657	2329128	25.590	55
60	0.011220	0.054942	87646	4815	427010	0.011277	2.670	1881940	21.472	60
65	0.018281	0.088097	82831	7297	397079	0.018377	2.660	1454930	17.565	65
70	0.029397	0.138020	75533	10425	353060	0.029528	2.640	1057851	14.005	70
75	0.048713	0.219397	65108	14285	291346	0.049030	2.606	704791	10.825	75
80	0.083930	0.348243	50824	17699	210878	0.083930	2.557	413445	8.135	80
85	0.163525	1.000000	33125	33125	202567	0.094366	6.115	202567	6.115	85

TABLE 4 — OBSERVED VITAL RATES AND RATIOS

CRUDE RATES

Per Thousand	BOTH SEXES	MALES	FEMALES
BIRTH RATE	17.47	17.94	16.99
DEATH RATE	7.32	8.54	6.10
RATE OF INCREASE	10.14	9.40	10.89

PERCENT OF POPULATION IN AGE GROUP

	BOTH SEXES	MALES	FEMALES
UNDER 15	30.30	30.93	29.67
15 - 64	61.73	61.90	61.56
65 AND OLDER	7.96	7.16	8.77

RATES STANDARDIZED ON USA 1980

Per Thousand	BOTH SEXES	MALES	FEMALES
BIRTH RATE	20.10		18.97
DEATH RATE	9.39	10.18	8.64
RATE OF INCREASE	10.71		10.33

RATES STANDARDIZED ON MEXICO 1980

	BOTH SEXES	MALES	FEMALES
BIRTH RATE	18.03		17.64
DEATH RATE	3.99	4.80	3.17
RATE OF INCREASE	14.04		14.47

VITAL STATISTICS

GFR x 1000	72.000
TFR	2.363
GRR	1.147
NRR	1.112
μ	27.137
σ^2	35.690
GENERATION	27.067
POP. SEX RATIO	0.996
SEX RATIO AT BIRTH	1.060
DEP. RATIO x 100	61.986

PROJECTED POPULATION

AGE GROUP	1975 BOTH SEXES	1975 MALES	1975 FEMALES	1980 BOTH SEXES	1980 MALES	1980 FEMALES
0-4	1952	1002	950	2197	1128	1069
5-9	1873	958	915	1945	998	947
10-14	2283	1168	1115	1870	956	914
15-19	2278	1162	1116	2276	1163	1113
20-24	2054	1041	1013	2266	1153	1113
25-29	1813	905	908	2042	1032	1010
30-34	1496	753	743	1802	898	904
35-39	1267	640	627	1484	746	738
40-44	1251	637	614	1253	631	622
45-49	1249	628	621	1229	623	606
50-54	1185	581	604	1213	605	608
55-59	992	484	508	1133	548	585
60-64	871	422	449	925	440	485
65-69	674	319	355	781	364	417
70-74	506	228	278	572	256	316
75-79	348	146	202	394	164	230
80-84	219	87	132	237	90	147
85+	171	61	110	189	62	127
TOTAL	22482	11222	11260	23808	11857	11951

STABLE EQUIVALENT TO ORIGINAL POPULATION

MALES Number	MALES Percent	FEMALES Number	FEMALES Percent	AGE GROUP	
1086	*8.1*	1030	*7.4*	0-4	
1061	*7.9*	1007	*7.3*	5-9	TABLE 5
1037	*7.7*	985	*7.1*	10-14	
1012	*7.5*	964	*7.0*	15-19	POPULATION
985	*7.3*	943	*6.8*	20-24	PROJECTED
958	*7.1*	922	*6.7*	25-29	WITH
932	*6.9*	900	*6.5*	30-34	FIXED
906	*6.7*	878	*6.3*	35-39	AGE-
876	*6.5*	854	*6.2*	40-44	SPECIFIC
840	*6.2*	826	*6.0*	45-49	BIRTH
794	*5.9*	794	*5.7*	50-54	AND
733	*5.4*	755	*5.5*	55-59	DEATH
654	*4.8*	707	*5.1*	60-64	RATES
552	*4.1*	645	*4.7*	65-69	(female
433	*3.2*	562	*4.1*	70-74	dominant,
307	*2.3*	455	*3.3*	75-79	in 000s)
185	*1.4*	323	*2.3*	80-84	
131	*1.0*	304	*2.2*	85+	
13482		13854		TOTAL	

VITAL RATES OF PROJECTED POPULATION

Per Thousand	1975 BOTH SEXES	1975 MALES	1975 FEMALES	1980 BOTH SEXES	1980 MALES	1980 FEMALES
BIRTH RATE	18.89	19.48	18.31	19.83	20.50	19.18
DEATH RATE	7.81	8.85	6.77	8.11	9.06	7.16
RATE OF INCREASE	11.08	10.63	11.54	11.72	11.44	12.01

VITAL RATES OF STABLE POPULATION

Per Thousand	MALES	FEMALES	
BIRTH RATE	16.65	15.28	TABLE 6
DEATH RATE	12.69	11.35	PROJECTED
RATE OF INCREASE		3.93	VITAL RATES AND RATIOS (female dominant)

AGE STRUCTURE OF PROJECTED POPULATION

	1975 BOTH SEXES	1975 MALES	1975 FEMALES	1980 BOTH SEXES	1980 MALES	1980 FEMALES
% UNDER 15	27.17	27.87	26.47	25.25	25.99	24.52
% 15-64	64.29	64.63	63.96	65.63	66.12	65.14
% 65 AND OLDER	8.54	7.50	9.57	9.12	7.90	10.34
DEPEND. RATIO x 100	55.54	54.73	56.35	52.38	51.24	53.52

STABLE AGE STRUCTURE

	MALES	FEMALES
% UNDER 15	23.61	21.82
% 15-64	64.45	61.67
% 65 AND OLDER	11.93	16.52
DEPEND. RATIO x 100	55.15	62.16

MATRIX

AGE GROUP	FEMALE BIRTH RATES	NET MATERNITY FUNCTION	COEFF. OF MATRIX EQUATION	ORIGINAL MATRIX SUB-DIAGONAL	ORIGINAL MATRIX FIRST ROW	STABLE MATRIX FISHER VALUES	STABLE MATRIX REPRODUCTIVE VALUES	MATRIX PARAMETERS		
0-4	0.0000	0.0000	0.0000	0.99724	0.00000	1.028	943645	λ_1	1.01986	
5-9	0.0000	0.0000	0.0003	0.99824	0.00033	1.051	1174458	λ_2	0.34819+0.74114i	TABLE 7
10-14	0.0001	0.0007	0.0514	0.99786	0.05165	1.074	1200477	λ_4	-0.37349-0.41005i	
15-19	0.0209	0.1022	0.2222	0.99722	0.22365	1.044	1060640	λ_6	-0.00990+0.48683i	LESLIE
20-24	0.0703	0.3422	0.3468	0.99703	0.35006	0.837	762365	r_1	0.00393	MATRIX
25-29	0.0724	0.3514	0.2731	0.99612	0.27652	0.496	369397	r_2	-0.03997+0.22632i	AND ITS
30-34	0.0403	0.1948	0.1436	0.99447	0.14599	0.222	140058	r_4	-0.11788-0.46191i	ANALYSIS
35-39	0.0192	0.0924	0.0595	0.99170	0.06081	0.077	47575	r_6	-0.14393+0.31822i	(females)
40-44	0.0056	0.0266	0.0143	0.98714	0.01476	0.016	10024	c_1	138515	
45-49	0.0004	0.0021	0.0010	0.98022	0.00109	0.001	676	$2\pi/\gamma$	27.7626	
50-54	0.0000	0.0000	0.0000	0.00000	0.00000	0.000	0	Δ	12.5722	

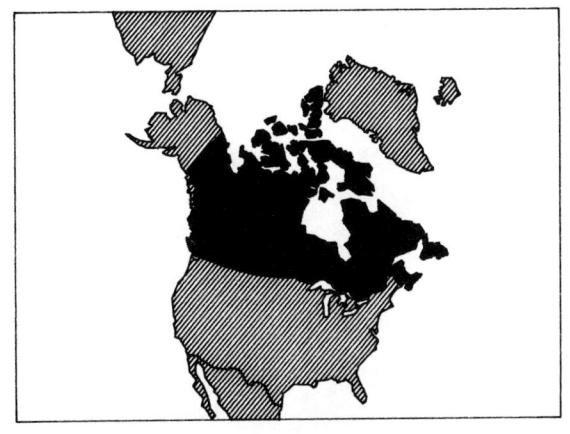

EDUCATION [1984]

% of primary school-age children enrolled:	106
secondary school-age children enrolled:	102
ca. 20-24 year olds in higher education:	44

LABOR FORCE

Average annual labor force growth (%) 1980-85:	1.4	
% of the 1980 labor force in agriculture:	5	TABLE 8
in industry:	29	
in services:	65	SOCIO-ECONOMIC INDICATORS

GNP & INCOME DISTRIBUTION

GNP per capita (in US Dollars) 1985:	13680
GNP average annual growth rate (%) 1965-85:	2.4
% share of total household income 1981	
Lowest 20% of households:	5.3
Highest 10% of households:	23.8

HEALTH & NUTRITION

Population per physician 1981:	550
Daily calorie supply per capita 1985:	3432

TABLE 1 — DATA

AGE AT LAST BIRTHDAY	ESTIMATED MID-YEAR POPULATION BOTH SEXES	MALES Number	MALES Percent	FEMALES Number	FEMALES Percent	BIRTHS BY AGE OF MOTHER AND SEX	DEATHS BOTH SEXES	DEATHS MALES	DEATHS FEMALES	AGE AT LAST BIRTHDAY
0	347600	178400	1.6	169200	1.5		4908	2802	2106	0
1-4	1404400	720300	6.4	684100	6.0		1082	621	461	1-4
5-9	1914900	979800	8.7	935100	8.2		827	500	327	5-9
10-14	2337300	1196100	10.6	1141200	10.0	383	898	551	347	10-14
15-19	2296600	1169200	10.3	1127400	9.9	40350	2553	1933	620	15-19
20-24	2078900	1039900	9.2	1039000	9.1	120176	2652	2041	611	20-24
25-29	1924700	966500	8.5	958200	8.4	129341	2072	1488	584	25-29
30-34	1560800	789400	7.0	771400	6.8	51685	1891	1276	615	30-34
35-39	1296000	655500	5.8	640500	5.6	14094	2274	1487	787	35-39
40-44	1269300	645300	5.7	624000	5.5	3065	3437	2214	1223	40-44
45-49	1249300	626200	5.5	623100	5.5	230	5485	3481	2004	45-49
50-54	1203600	587800	5.2	615800	5.4		8143	5382	2761	50-54
55-59	985600	478500	4.2	507100	4.5		10516	6917	3599	55-59
60-64	890600	429900	3.8	460700	4.0		14577	9626	4951	60-64
65-69	693600	326700	2.9	366800	3.2		17533	11244	6289	65-69
70-74	519400	235200	2.1	284200	2.5		19984	12125	7859	70-74
75-79	350400	145400	1.3	205000	1.8		20740	11317	9423	75-79
80-84	215900	84900	0.8	131000	1.2	184535 M	20337	10106	10231	80-84
85+	158900	59200	0.5	99700	0.9	174789 F	27267	11816	15451	85+
TOTAL	22697700	11314200		11383500		359324	167176	96927	70249	TOTAL

TABLE 2 — MALE LIFE TABLE

x	$_nM_x$	$_nq_x$	l_x	$_nd_x$	$_nL_x$	$_nm_x$	$_na_x$	T_x	$\overset{\circ}{e}_x$	x
0	0.015706	0.015487	100000	1549	98601	0.015706	0.097	6984567	69.846	0
1	0.000862	0.003441	98451	339	392958	0.000862	1.500	6885966	69.943	1
5	0.000510	0.002548	98113	250	489938	0.000510	2.500	6493007	66.179	5
10	0.000461	0.002301	97863	225	488865	0.000461	3.014	6003069	61.342	10
15	0.001653	0.008250	97637	805	486323	0.001656	2.686	5514204	56.476	15
20	0.001963	0.009765	96832	946	481781	0.001963	2.484	5027881	51.924	20
25	0.001540	0.007659	95886	734	477558	0.001538	2.450	4546100	47.411	25
30	0.001616	0.008069	95152	768	473910	0.001620	2.591	4068542	42.758	30
35	0.002268	0.011327	94384	1069	469419	0.002277	2.660	3594632	38.085	35
40	0.003431	0.017044	93315	1590	462901	0.003436	2.690	3125213	33.491	40
45	0.005559	0.027453	91725	2518	452832	0.005561	2.700	2662312	29.025	45
50	0.009156	0.044943	89206	4009	436729	0.009180	2.680	2209480	24.768	50
55	0.014456	0.070105	85197	5973	411978	0.014498	2.655	1772751	20.808	55
60	0.022391	0.106552	79224	8442	376126	0.022443	2.631	1360774	17.176	60
65	0.034417	0.159473	70783	11288	326785	0.034543	2.597	984648	13.911	65
70	0.051552	0.229835	59495	13674	264063	0.051783	2.557	657863	11.057	70
75	0.077834	0.327331	45821	14999	191689	0.078244	2.505	393801	8.594	75
80	0.119034	0.456286	30822	14064	118149	0.119034	2.443	202112	6.557	80
85	0.199595	1.000000	16759	16759	83963	0.132724	5.010	83963	5.010	85

TABLE 3 — FEMALE LIFE TABLE

x	$_nM_x$	$_nq_x$	l_x	$_nd_x$	$_nL_x$	$_nm_x$	$_na_x$	T_x	$\overset{\circ}{e}_x$	x
0	0.012447	0.012308	100000	1231	98881	0.012447	0.091	7731198	77.312	0
1	0.000674	0.002691	98769	266	394413	0.000674	1.500	7632317	77.274	1
5	0.000350	0.001747	98503	172	492087	0.000350	2.500	7237904	73.479	5
10	0.000304	0.001519	98331	149	491304	0.000304	2.636	6745817	68.603	10
15	0.000550	0.002748	98182	270	490264	0.000550	2.607	6254513	63.703	15
20	0.000588	0.002937	97912	288	488848	0.000588	2.520	5764249	58.872	20
25	0.000609	0.003047	97625	297	487401	0.000610	2.571	5275401	54.038	25
30	0.000797	0.003997	97327	389	485726	0.000801	2.660	4788001	49.195	30
35	0.001229	0.006157	96938	597	483314	0.001235	2.693	4302275	44.382	35
40	0.001960	0.009771	96341	941	479546	0.001963	2.705	3818962	39.640	40
45	0.003216	0.015961	95400	1523	473432	0.003216	2.657	3339416	35.004	45
50	0.004484	0.022227	93877	2087	464523	0.004492	2.669	2865984	30.529	50
55	0.007097	0.035026	91791	3215	451451	0.007122	2.667	2401462	26.162	55
60	0.010747	0.052590	88576	4658	432011	0.010783	2.667	1950010	22.015	60
65	0.017146	0.082840	83917	6952	403329	0.017236	2.661	1517999	18.089	65
70	0.027653	0.130460	76966	10041	361185	0.027800	2.645	1114670	14.483	70
75	0.045966	0.208510	66925	13954	301267	0.046319	2.610	753485	11.259	75
80	0.078099	0.328197	52970	17385	222597	0.078099	2.569	452218	8.537	80
85	0.154975	1.000000	35586	35586	229621	0.086017	6.453	229621	6.453	85

TABLE 4 — OBSERVED VITAL RATES AND RATIOS

CRUDE RATES

Per Thousand	BOTH SEXES	MALES	FEMALES
BIRTH RATE	15.83	16.31	15.35
DEATH RATE	7.37	8.57	6.17
RATE OF INCREASE	8.47	7.74	9.18

PERCENT OF POPULATION IN AGE GROUP

UNDER 15	26.45	27.17	25.74
15 - 64	65.01	65.30	64.72
65 AND OLDER	8.54	7.53	9.55

RATES STANDARDIZED ON USA 1980

Per Thousand	BOTH SEXES	MALES	FEMALES
BIRTH RATE	16.40		15.52
DEATH RATE	8.99	9.93	8.10
RATE OF INCREASE	7.41		7.42

RATES STANDARDIZED ON MEXICO 1980

	BOTH SEXES	MALES	FEMALES
BIRTH RATE	14.74		14.45
DEATH RATE	3.75	4.58	2.90
RATE OF INCREASE	11.00		11.56

VITAL STATISTICS

GFR x 1000	62.128
TFR	1.905
GRR	0.927
NRR	0.904
μ	26.678
σ^2	29.914
GENERATION	26.734
POP. SEX RATIO	1.006
SEX RATIO AT BIRTH	1.056
DEP. RATIO x 100	53.826

Table 1 Data

AGE AT LAST BIRTHDAY	ESTIMATED MID-YEAR POPULATION BOTH SEXES	MALES Number	MALES Percent	FEMALES Number	FEMALES Percent	BIRTHS BY AGE OF MOTHER AND SEX	DEATHS BOTH SEXES	DEATHS MALES	DEATHS FEMALES	AGE AT LAST BIRTHDAY
0	363500	186800	1.6	176700	1.5		3870	2218	1652	0
1-4	1412300	724100	6.1	688200	5.7		829	489	340	1-4
5-9	1795200	921300	7.7	873900	7.2		590	372	218	5-9
10-14	1953300	1001200	8.4	952100	7.9		628	394	234	10-14
15-19	2359100	1202000	10.1	1157100	9.6	31958	2187	1619	568	15-19
20-24	2305600	1156600	9.7	1149000	9.5	116019	2574	1955	619	20-24
25-29	2131400	1061600	8.9	1069800	8.8	137944	2076	1498	578	25-29
30-34	1968700	988400	8.3	980300	8.1	67321	2078	1416	662	30-34
35-39	1564000	789200	6.6	774800	6.4	15069	2324	1506	818	35-39
40-44	1301400	656800	5.5	644600	5.3	2006	2859	1819	1040	40-44
45-49	1258300	636900	5.3	621400	5.1	111	4772	3107	1665	45-49
50-54	1232400	613200	5.1	619200	5.1		7538	4963	2575	50-54
55-59	1165800	560400	4.7	605400	5.0		11097	7217	3880	55-59
60-64	944500	446900	3.7	497600	4.1		13851	8995	4856	60-64
65-69	825300	382900	3.2	442400	3.7		18853	12046	6807	65-69
70-74	610400	271500	2.3	338900	2.8		21424	12998	8426	70-74
75-79	417600	175000	1.5	242600	2.0		22864	12830	10034	75-79
80-84	247700	91800	0.8	155900	1.3	190395 M	20952	10122	10830	80-84
85+	186200	62500	0.5	123700	1.0	180314 F	30107	12012	18095	85+
TOTAL	24042700	11929100		12113600		370709	171473	97576	73897	TOTAL

Table 2 Male Life Table

x	$_nM_x$	$_nq_x$	l_x	$_nd_x$	$_nL_x$	$_nm_x$	$_na_x$	T_x	$\overset{\circ}{e}_x$	x
0	0.011874	0.011747	100000	1175	98931	0.011874	0.090	7144474	71.445	0
1	0.000675	0.002697	98825	267	394635	0.000675	1.500	7045543	71.293	1
5	0.000404	0.002017	98559	199	492297	0.000404	2.500	6650908	67.482	5
10	0.000394	0.001966	98360	193	491413	0.000394	2.996	6158611	62.613	10
15	0.001347	0.006714	98167	659	489316	0.001347	2.698	5667198	57.730	15
20	0.001690	0.008417	97508	821	485490	0.001690	2.505	5177882	53.102	20
25	0.001411	0.007027	96687	679	481708	0.001410	2.459	4692391	48.532	25
30	0.001433	0.007148	96007	686	478370	0.001435	2.570	4210683	43.858	30
35	0.001908	0.009544	95321	910	474461	0.001917	2.642	3732313	39.155	35
40	0.002769	0.013832	94411	1306	469072	0.002784	2.714	3257853	34.507	40
45	0.004878	0.024161	93106	2250	460384	0.004886	2.713	2788781	29.953	45
50	0.008094	0.039744	90856	3611	445923	0.008098	2.686	2328397	25.627	50
55	0.012878	0.062678	87245	5468	423444	0.012914	2.663	1882474	21.577	55
60	0.020128	0.096363	81777	7880	390302	0.020190	2.642	1459030	17.842	60
65	0.031460	0.146690	73896	10840	343569	0.031551	2.609	1068729	14.463	65
70	0.047875	0.215253	63057	13573	282309	0.048079	2.571	725160	11.500	70
75	0.073314	0.312038	49483	15441	209042	0.073864	2.515	442851	8.949	75
80	0.110261	0.430647	34043	14660	132960	0.110261	2.459	233809	6.868	80
85	0.192192	1.000000	19382	19382	100849	0.124435	5.203	100849	5.203	85

Table 3 Female Life Table

x	$_nM_x$	$_nq_x$	l_x	$_nd_x$	$_nL_x$	$_nm_x$	$_na_x$	T_x	$\overset{\circ}{e}_x$	x
0	0.009349	0.009270	100000	927	99153	0.009349	0.086	7883332	78.833	0
1	0.000494	0.001974	99073	196	395803	0.000494	1.500	7784179	78.570	1
5	0.000249	0.001246	98877	123	494079	0.000249	2.500	7388376	74.723	5
10	0.000246	0.001228	98754	121	493493	0.000246	2.704	6894297	69.813	10
15	0.000491	0.002452	98633	242	492590	0.000491	2.624	6400805	64.895	15
20	0.000539	0.002690	98391	265	491299	0.000539	2.518	5908215	60.048	20
25	0.000540	0.002699	98126	265	489984	0.000541	2.552	5416916	55.203	25
30	0.000675	0.003383	97862	331	488533	0.000678	2.658	4926933	50.346	30
35	0.001056	0.005299	97531	517	486455	0.001062	2.683	4438400	45.508	35
40	0.001613	0.008081	97014	784	483268	0.001622	2.704	3951945	40.736	40
45	0.002679	0.013336	96230	1283	478185	0.002684	2.690	3468677	36.046	45
50	0.004159	0.020594	94946	1955	470189	0.004159	2.677	2990492	31.497	50
55	0.006409	0.031631	92991	2941	458093	0.006421	2.667	2520303	27.103	55
60	0.009759	0.047865	90050	4310	440192	0.009792	2.667	2062210	22.901	60
65	0.015387	0.074521	85740	6389	413779	0.015442	2.665	1622019	18.918	65
70	0.024863	0.118102	79350	9371	374757	0.025007	2.653	1208240	15.227	70
75	0.041360	0.189711	69979	13276	318268	0.041712	2.618	833483	11.911	75
80	0.069468	0.297663	56703	16878	242968	0.069468	2.598	515215	9.086	80
85	0.146281	1.000000	39825	39825	272247	0.077835	6.836	272247	6.836	85

CRUDE RATES

Per Thousand	BOTH SEXES	MALES	FEMALES
BIRTH RATE	15.42	15.96	14.89
DEATH RATE	7.13	8.18	6.10
RATE OF INCREASE	8.29	7.78	8.78

PERCENT OF POPULATION IN AGE GROUP

UNDER 15	22.98	23.75	22.21
15 - 64	67.51	68.00	67.03
65 AND OLDER	9.51	8.25	10.76

RATES STANDARDIZED ON USA 1980

Per Thousand	BOTH SEXES	MALES	FEMALES
BIRTH RATE	15.01		14.19
DEATH RATE	8.15	9.04	7.31
RATE OF INCREASE	6.86		6.88

RATES STANDARDIZED ON MEXICO 1980

	BOTH SEXES	MALES	FEMALES
BIRTH RATE	13.35		13.09
DEATH RATE	3.29	4.05	2.52
RATE OF INCREASE	10.06		10.57

VITAL STATISTICS

Table 4 — Observed Vital Rates and Ratios

GFR x 1000	57.950
TFR	1.746
GRR	0.849
NRR	0.832
μ	26.918
σ^2	27.655
GENERATION	27.012
POP. SEX RATIO	1.015
SEX RATIO AT BIRTH	1.056
DEP. RATIO x 100	48.126

AGE AT LAST BIRTHDAY	ESTIMATED MID-YEAR POPULATION BOTH SEXES	MALES Number	MALES Percent	FEMALES Number	FEMALES Percent	BIRTHS BY AGE OF MOTHER AND SEX	DEATHS BOTH SEXES	DEATHS MALES	DEATHS FEMALES	AGE AT LAST BIRTHDAY
0	373700	192300	1.5	181400	1.4		2982	1680	1302	0
1-4	1478300	757600	6.0	720700	5.6		633	363	270	1-4
5-9	1784100	914900	7.3	869200	6.8		403	241	162	5-9
10-14	1813700	930700	7.4	883000	6.9	231	469	290	179	10-14
15-19	1975600	1012100	8.1	963400	7.5	22617	1433	1028	405	15-19
20-24	2396300	1215000	9.7	1181300	9.2	100612	2151	1674	477	20-24
25-29	2341200	1167600	9.3	1173600	9.2	147258	1987	1467	520	25-29
30-34	2159300	1074200	8.6	1085100	8.5	81005	2137	1470	667	30-34
35-39	1978800	990900	7.9	987900	7.7	21549	2348	1541	807	35-39
40-44	1558300	783800	6.2	774500	6.0	2372	3015	1918	1097	40-44
45-49	1293100	649300	5.2	643800	5.0	83	4089	2549	1540	45-49
50-54	1241700	622700	5.0	619000	4.8		6608	4273	2335	50-54
55-59	1207300	591900	4.7	615400	4.8		10362	6710	3652	55-59
60-64	1120600	527100	4.2	593500	4.6		14935	9520	5415	60-64
65-69	880200	403200	3.2	477000	3.7		18659	11703	6956	65-69
70-74	729700	321600	2.6	408100	3.2		23897	14543	9354	70-74
75-79	500800	206300	1.6	294500	2.3		25491	14099	11392	75-79
80-84	303600	113900	0.9	189700	1.5	193247 M	24141	12030	12111	80-84
85+	221900	68000	0.5	153900	1.2	182480 F	35583	13361	22222	85+
TOTAL	25358200	12543200		12815000		375727	181323	100460	80863	TOTAL

TABLE 1 DATA

TABLE 2 — MALE LIFE TABLE

x	nM_x	nq_x	l_x	nd_x	nL_x	nm_x	na_x	T_x	$\overset{\circ}{e}_x$	x
0	0.008736	0.008667	100000	867	99207	0.008736	0.085	7294618	72.946	0
1	0.000479	0.001914	99133	190	396059	0.000479	1.500	7195411	72.583	1
5	0.000263	0.001316	98944	130	494392	0.000263	2.500	6799352	68.720	5
10	0.000312	0.001557	98813	154	493759	0.000312	3.000	6304960	63.807	10
15	0.001016	0.005066	98659	500	492156	0.001016	2.717	5811201	58.902	15
20	0.001378	0.006866	98160	674	489136	0.001378	2.534	5319045	54.188	20
25	0.001256	0.006262	97486	610	485900	0.001256	2.496	4829908	49.545	25
30	0.001368	0.006823	96875	661	482752	0.001369	2.543	4344009	44.841	30
35	0.001555	0.007770	96214	748	479308	0.001560	2.642	3861256	40.132	35
40	0.002447	0.012254	95467	1170	474637	0.002465	2.695	3381948	35.425	40
45	0.003926	0.019565	94297	1845	467280	0.003948	2.721	2907311	30.831	45
50	0.006862	0.033834	92452	3128	455083	0.006874	2.706	2440031	26.392	50
55	0.011336	0.055260	89324	4936	435155	0.011343	2.677	1984948	22.222	55
60	0.018061	0.086892	84388	7333	404766	0.018116	2.658	1549793	18.365	60
65	0.029025	0.136230	77055	10497	360339	0.029132	2.624	1145026	14.860	65
70	0.045221	0.204342	66558	13601	299846	0.045359	2.578	784688	11.790	70
75	0.068342	0.294035	52957	15571	226275	0.068816	2.527	484842	9.155	75
80	0.105619	0.417195	37386	15597	147675	0.105619	2.483	258568	6.916	80
85	0.196485	1.000000	21789	21789	110893	0.129063	5.089	110893	5.089	85

TABLE 3 — FEMALE LIFE TABLE

x	nM_x	nq_x	l_x	nd_x	nL_x	nm_x	na_x	T_x	$\overset{\circ}{e}_x$	x
0	0.007178	0.007131	100000	713	99346	0.007178	0.082	7988702	79.887	0
1	0.000375	0.001497	99287	149	396776	0.000375	1.500	7889357	79.460	1
5	0.000186	0.000931	99138	92	495461	0.000186	2.500	7492581	75.577	5
10	0.000203	0.001013	99046	100	495003	0.000203	2.739	6997120	70.645	10
15	0.000420	0.002100	98946	208	494229	0.000420	2.599	6502117	65.714	15
20	0.000404	0.002017	98738	199	493194	0.000404	2.511	6007888	60.847	20
25	0.000443	0.002214	98539	218	492169	0.000443	2.598	5514695	55.965	25
30	0.000615	0.003074	98321	302	490885	0.000616	2.626	5022525	51.083	30
35	0.000817	0.004096	98018	401	489170	0.000821	2.704	4531640	46.233	35
40	0.001416	0.007117	97617	695	486505	0.001428	2.727	4042470	41.412	40
45	0.002392	0.011960	96922	1159	481941	0.002405	2.697	3555965	36.689	45
50	0.003772	0.018724	95763	1793	474663	0.003778	2.685	3074024	32.100	50
55	0.005934	0.029268	93970	2750	463451	0.005934	2.673	2599361	27.662	55
60	0.009124	0.044764	91220	4083	446601	0.009143	2.674	2135910	23.415	60
65	0.014583	0.070775	87136	6167	421254	0.014640	2.661	1689309	19.387	65
70	0.022921	0.109163	80969	8839	384146	0.023009	2.658	1268055	15.661	70
75	0.038683	0.178514	72130	12876	330041	0.039014	2.623	883908	12.254	75
80	0.063843	0.277157	59254	16423	257235	0.063843	2.623	553867	9.347	80
85	0.144392	1.000000	42831	42831	296632	0.076124	6.926	296632	6.926	85

TABLE 4 — OBSERVED VITAL RATES AND RATIOS

CRUDE RATES Per Thousand	BOTH SEXES	MALES	FEMALES
BIRTH RATE	14.82	15.41	14.24
DEATH RATE	7.15	8.01	6.31
RATE OF INCREASE	7.67	7.40	7.93

PERCENT OF POPULATION IN AGE GROUP

	BOTH SEXES	MALES	FEMALES
UNDER 15	21.49	22.29	20.71
15 - 64	68.11	68.84	67.40
65 AND OLDER	10.40	8.87	11.89

RATES STANDARDIZED ON USA 1980

Per Thousand	BOTH SEXES	MALES	FEMALES
BIRTH RATE	14.23		13.44
DEATH RATE	7.55	8.31	6.83
RATE OF INCREASE	6.68		6.60

RATES STANDARDIZED ON MEXICO 1980

	BOTH SEXES	MALES	FEMALES
BIRTH RATE	12.51		12.25
DEATH RATE	2.92	3.57	2.26
RATE OF INCREASE	9.59		9.99

VITAL STATISTICS

GFR x 1000	55.176
TFR	1.670
GRR	0.811
NRR	0.798
μ	27.412
σ^2	27.875
GENERATION	27.526
POP. SEX RATIO	1.022
SEX RATIO AT BIRTH	1.059
DEP. RATIO x 100	46.815

PROJECTED POPULATION

AGE GROUP	1990 BOTH SEXES	1990 MALES	1990 FEMALES	1995 BOTH SEXES	1995 MALES	1995 FEMALES
0-4	1835	943	892	1728	888	840
5-9	1849	948	901	1833	942	891
10-14	1782	914	868	1847	947	900
15-19	1810	928	882	1778	911	867
20-24	1967	1006	961	1802	922	880
25-29	2386	1207	1179	1958	999	959
30-34	2331	1160	1171	2375	1199	1176
35-39	2148	1067	1081	2318	1152	1166
40-44	1964	981	983	2131	1056	1075
45-49	1539	772	767	1939	966	973
50-54	1266	632	634	1508	752	756
55-59	1199	595	604	1224	605	619
60-64	1144	551	593	1136	554	582
65-69	1029	469	560	1049	490	559
70-74	771	336	435	901	390	511
75-79	594	243	351	627	253	374
80-84	365	135	230	431	158	273
85+	305	86	219	366	101	265
TOTAL	26284	12973	13311	26951	13285	13666

STABLE EQUIVALENT TO ORIGINAL POPULATION

	MALES Number	MALES Percent	FEMALES Number	FEMALES Percent	AGE GROUP	
	935	5.0	884	4.4	0-4	
	972	5.2	920	4.6	5-9	TABLE 5
	1012	5.4	958	4.8	10-14	
	1050	5.6	996	5.0	15-19	POPULATION
	1088	5.8	1035	5.2	20-24	PROJECTED
	1125	6.0	1076	5.4	25-29	WITH
	1165	6.2	1118	5.6	30-34	FIXED
	1205	6.4	1161	5.8	35-39	AGE-
	1243	6.6	1203	6.0	40-44	SPECIFIC
	1275	6.8	1241	6.2	45-49	BIRTH
	1293	6.9	1274	6.4	50-54	AND
	1288	6.9	1296	6.5	55-59	DEATH
	1248	6.6	1301	6.5	60-64	RATES
	1158	6.2	1278	6.4	65-69	(female
	1004	5.3	1214	6.1	70-74	dominant,
	789	4.2	1087	5.4	75-79	in 000s)
	536	2.9	882	4.4	80-84	
	420	2.2	1060	5.3	85+	
	18806		19984		TOTAL	

VITAL RATES OF PROJECTED POPULATION

Per Thousand	1990 BOTH SEXES	1990 MALES	1990 FEMALES	1995 BOTH SEXES	1995 MALES	1995 FEMALES
BIRTH RATE	13.88	14.46	13.31	12.34	12.87	11.82
DEATH RATE	7.99	8.67	7.31	8.68	9.30	8.07
RATE OF INCREASE	5.90	5.79	6.00	3.66	3.58	3.75

VITAL RATES OF STABLE POPULATION

Per Thousand	MALES	FEMALES	
BIRTH RATE	9.83	8.74	TABLE 6
DEATH RATE	17.87	16.92	PROJECTED
RATE OF INCREASE		-8.18	VITAL RATES AND RATIOS (female dominant)

AGE STRUCTURE OF PROJECTED POPULATION

	1990 BOTH SEXES	1990 MALES	1990 FEMALES	1995 BOTH SEXES	1995 MALES	1995 FEMALES
% UNDER 15	20.80	21.63	20.00	20.06	20.90	19.25
% 15-64	67.55	68.60	66.53	67.41	68.61	66.25
% 65 AND OLDER	11.65	9.77	13.48	12.52	10.49	14.50
DEPEND. RATIO x 100	48.04	45.77	50.31	48.34	45.75	50.95

STABLE AGE STRUCTURE

	MALES	FEMALES
% UNDER 15	15.52	13.82
% 15-64	63.71	58.55
% 65 AND OLDER	20.77	27.62
DEPEND. RATIO x 100	56.97	70.78

AGE GROUP	FEMALE BIRTH RATES	NET MATERNITY FUNCTION	COEFF. OF MATRIX EQUATION	ORIGINAL MATRIX SUB-DIAGONAL	ORIGINAL MATRIX FIRST ROW	STABLE MATRIX FISHER VALUES	STABLE MATRIX REPRODUCTIVE VALUES
0-4	0.0000	0.0000	0.0000	0.99867	0.00000	0.987	890727
5-9	0.0000	0.0000	0.0003	0.99908	0.00031	0.949	824954
10-14	0.0001	0.0006	0.0285	0.99844	0.02855	0.912	804942
15-19	0.0114	0.0564	0.1302	0.99790	0.13068	0.848	817162
20-24	0.0414	0.2040	0.2520	0.99792	0.25346	0.687	811115
25-29	0.0609	0.2999	0.2390	0.99739	0.24087	0.410	480823
30-34	0.0363	0.1780	0.1149	0.99651	0.11613	0.156	169120
35-39	0.0106	0.0518	0.0295	0.99455	0.02995	0.035	34648
40-44	0.0015	0.0072	0.0038	0.99062	0.00384	0.004	3190
45-49	0.0001	0.0003	0.0002	0.98490	0.00016	0.000	103
50-54	0.0000	0.0000	0.0000	0.00000	0.00000	0.000	0

MATRIX PARAMETERS

λ_1	0.95993	
λ_2	$0.37418+0.73350i$	TABLE 7
λ_4	$-0.24855-0.50687i$	
λ_6	$-0.34451+0.06304i$	LESLIE
r_1	-0.00818	MATRIX
r_2	$-0.03886+0.21982i$	AND ITS
r_4	$-0.11435-0.40534i$	ANALYSIS
r_6	$-0.20983+0.59212i$	(females)
c_1	199846	
$2\pi/\gamma$	28.5838	
Δ	22.0257	

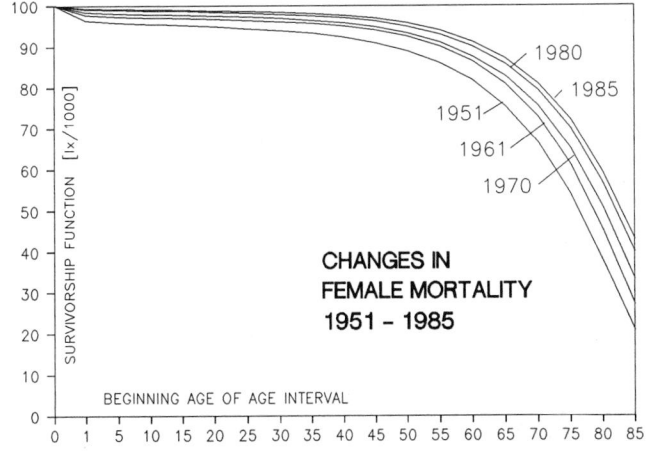

CHANGES IN FEMALE MORTALITY 1951 – 1985

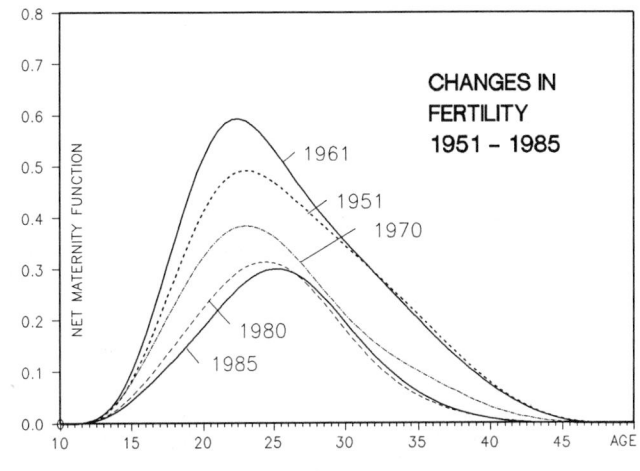

CHANGES IN FERTILITY 1951 - 1985

TABLE 1 — DATA

AGE AT LAST BIRTHDAY	ESTIMATED MID-YEAR POPULATION BOTH SEXES	MALES Number	MALES Percent	FEMALES Number	FEMALES Percent	BIRTHS BY AGE OF MOTHER AND SEX	DEATHS BOTH SEXES	DEATHS MALES	DEATHS FEMALES	AGE AT LAST BIRTHDAY
0	1179	608	2.5	571	2.6		54	35	19	0
1-4	6136	3121	13.0	3015	13.8		15	8	7	1-4
5-9	7411	3745	15.6	3666	16.7		6	5	1	5-9
10-14	5415	2800	11.6	2615	11.9	1	7	6	1	10-14
15-19	3656	1798	7.5	1858	8.5	207	4	1	3	15-19
20-24	3456	1844	7.7	1612	7.4	343	16	14	2	20-24
25-29	4340	2462	10.2	1878	8.6	315	8	5	3	25-29
30-34	3463	2030	8.4	1433	6.5	155	9	6	3	30-34
35-39	2770	1568	6.5	1202	5.5	82	9	8	1	35-39
40-44	2268	1211	5.0	1057	4.8	39	9	5	4	40-44
45-49	1534	809	3.4	725	3.3	2	11	6	5	45-49
50-54	1287	676	2.8	611	2.8		21	12	9	50-54
55-59	1042	511	2.1	531	2.4		24	17	7	55-59
60-64	811	372	1.5	439	2.0		19	11	8	60-64
65-69	590	261	1.1	329	1.5		23	12	11	65-69
70-74	386	170	0.7	216	1.0		14	9	5	70-74
75-79	183	75	0.3	108	0.5		24	9	15	75-79
80-84	53	16	0.1	37	0.2	622 M	4	1	3	80-84
85+	16	2	0.0	14	0.1	522 F	6	1	5	85+
TOTAL	45996	24079		21917		1144	283	171	112	TOTAL

TABLE 2 — MALE LIFE TABLE

x	$_nM_x$	$_nq_x$	l_x	$_nd_x$	$_nL_x$	$_nm_x$	$_na_x$	T_x	$\overset{\circ}{e}_x$	x
0	0.057566	0.054934	100000	5493	95429	0.057566	0.168	6067707	60.677	0
1	0.002563	0.010188	94507	963	375619	0.002563	1.500	5972279	63.194	1
5	0.001335	0.006653	93544	622	466163	0.001335	2.500	5596660	59.829	5
10	0.002143	0.010649	92921	990	462059	0.002142	2.425	5130497	55.213	10
15	0.000556	0.002896	91932	266	459499	0.000579	4.398	4668438	50.782	15
20	0.007592	0.037264	91666	3416	449918	0.007592	2.538	4208939	45.916	20
25	0.002031	0.010093	88250	891	438579	0.002031	2.003	3759020	42.595	25
30	0.002956	0.014770	87359	1290	433837	0.002974	2.708	3320441	38.009	30
35	0.005102	0.025283	86069	2176	424992	0.005120	2.541	2886604	33.538	35
40	0.004129	0.020471	83893	1717	415349	0.004135	2.604	2461612	29.342	40
45	0.007417	0.036960	82175	3037	404344	0.007511	2.849	2046264	24.901	45
50	0.017751	0.086051	79138	6810	380359	0.017904	2.749	1641920	20.748	50
55	0.033268	0.154415	72328	11169	334054	0.033433	2.530	1261561	17.442	55
60	0.029570	0.137616	61160	8417	284709	0.029562	2.494	927507	15.165	60
65	0.045977	0.207429	52743	10940	236662	0.046228	2.527	642798	12.187	65
70	0.052941	0.235533	41803	9846	185210	0.053161	2.582	406136	9.716	70
75	0.120000	0.464229	31957	14835	121586	0.122014	2.425	220926	6.913	75
80	0.062500	0.263965	17121	4519	74136	0.060962	2.462	99340	5.802	80
85	0.500000	1.000000	12602	12602	25204	0.555739	2.000	25204	2.000	85

TABLE 3 — FEMALE LIFE TABLE

x	$_nM_x$	$_nq_x$	l_x	$_nd_x$	$_nL_x$	$_nm_x$	$_na_x$	T_x	$\overset{\circ}{e}_x$	x
0	0.033275	0.032335	100000	3234	97176	0.033275	0.127	6798975	67.990	0
1	0.002322	0.009233	96766	893	384832	0.002322	1.500	6701799	69.257	1
5	0.000273	0.001363	95873	131	479038	0.000273	2.500	6316967	65.889	5
10	0.000382	0.001950	95742	187	478379	0.000390	3.217	5837929	60.975	10
15	0.001615	0.008095	95556	774	475928	0.001625	2.608	5359550	56.088	15
20	0.001241	0.006184	94782	586	472440	0.001241	2.492	4883622	51.525	20
25	0.001597	0.007958	94196	750	469186	0.001598	2.607	4411182	46.830	25
30	0.002094	0.010398	93446	972	464727	0.002091	2.422	3941995	42.185	30
35	0.000832	0.004175	92475	386	461571	0.000837	2.921	3477268	37.602	35
40	0.003784	0.019021	92089	1752	456630	0.003836	2.823	3015697	32.748	40
45	0.006897	0.034347	90337	3103	444859	0.006975	2.800	2559067	28.328	45
50	0.014730	0.071334	87234	6223	421045	0.014779	2.569	2114208	24.236	50
55	0.013183	0.063848	81011	5172	392216	0.013188	2.517	1693163	20.900	55
60	0.018223	0.087762	75839	6656	363714	0.018300	2.674	1300947	17.154	60
65	0.033435	0.155126	69183	10732	319059	0.033637	2.497	937233	13.547	65
70	0.023148	0.111663	58451	6527	279404	0.023360	3.031	618174	10.576	70
75	0.138889	0.527094	51924	27369	191483	0.142932	2.510	338769	6.524	75
80	0.081081	0.321315	24555	7890	100624	0.078411	2.192	147287	5.998	80
85	0.357143	1.000000	16665	16665	46663	0.336801	2.800	46663	2.800	85

TABLE 4 — OBSERVED VITAL RATES AND RATIOS

CRUDE RATES

Per Thousand	BOTH SEXES	MALES	FEMALES
BIRTH RATE	24.87	25.83	23.82
DEATH RATE	6.15	7.10	5.11
RATE OF INCREASE	18.72	18.73	18.71

PERCENT OF POPULATION IN AGE GROUP

	BOTH SEXES	MALES	FEMALES
UNDER 15	43.79	42.67	45.02
15 - 64	53.54	55.16	51.77
65 AND OLDER	2.67	2.18	3.21

RATES STANDARDIZED ON USA 1980

Per Thousand	BOTH SEXES	MALES	FEMALES
BIRTH RATE	29.83		26.47
DEATH RATE	15.95	15.99	15.92
RATE OF INCREASE	13.88		10.55

RATES STANDARDIZED ON MEXICO 1980

	BOTH SEXES	MALES	FEMALES
BIRTH RATE	27.53		25.32
DEATH RATE	7.24	8.49	5.96
RATE OF INCREASE	20.30		19.36

VITAL STATISTICS

GFR x 1000	117.153
TFR	3.542
GRR	1.616
NRR	1.516
μ	26.922
σ^2	49.457
GENERATION	26.534
POP. SEX RATIO	0.910
SEX RATIO AT BIRTH	1.192
DEP. RATIO x 100	86.771

PROJECTED POPULATION

STABLE EQUIVALENT TO ORIGINAL POPULATION

AGE GROUP	1975 BOTH SEXES	1975 MALES	1975 FEMALES	1980 BOTH SEXES	1980 MALES	1980 FEMALES	MALES Number	MALES Percent	FEMALES Number	FEMALES Percent	AGE GROUP	
0-4	6	3	3	7	4	3	4	12.2	3	11.5	0-4	
5-9	8	4	4	6	3	3	3	11.2	3	10.5	5-9	TABLE 5
10-14	8	4	4	8	4	4	3	10.2	3	9.7	10-14	
15-19	6	3	3	8	4	4	3	9.4	2	9.0	15-19	POPULATION
20-24	4	2	2	6	3	3	2	8.5	2	8.2	20-24	PROJECTED
25-29	4	2	2	4	2	2	2	7.7	2	7.5	25-29	WITH
30-34	4	2	2	4	2	2	2	7.0	2	6.9	30-34	FIXED
35-39	3	2	1	4	2	2	2	6.4	2	6.3	35-39	AGE-
40-44	3	2	1	3	2	1	2	5.7	2	5.8	40-44	SPECIFIC
45-49	2	1	1	2	1	1	2	5.2	1	5.2	45-49	BIRTH
50-54	2	1	1	2	1	1	1	4.5	1	4.6	50-54	AND
55-59	2	1	1	2	1	1	1	3.6	1	3.9	55-59	DEATH
60-64	0	0	0	2	1	1	1	2.9	1	3.4	60-64	RATES
65-69	0	0	0	0	0	0	1	2.2	1	2.7	65-69	(female
70-74	0	0	0	0	0	0	0	1.6	1	2.2	70-74	dominant,
75-79	0	0	0	0	0	0	0	1.0	0	1.4	75-79	in 000s)
80-84	0	0	0	0	0	0	0	0.5	0	0.7	80-84	
85+	0	0	0	0	0	0	0	0.2	0	0.3	85+	
TOTAL	52	27	25	58	30	28	29		27		TOTAL	

VITAL RATES OF PROJECTED POPULATION

VITAL RATES OF STABLE POPULATION

Per Thousand	1975 BOTH SEXES	1975 MALES	1975 FEMALES	1980 BOTH SEXES	1980 MALES	1980 FEMALES	Per Thousand	MALES	FEMALES	
BIRTH RATE	25.65	26.64	24.56	28.86	29.98	27.63	BIRTH RATE	26.93	24.76	TABLE 6
DEATH RATE	6.23	7.18	5.19	6.88	7.92	5.74	DEATH RATE	10.87	9.05	PROJECTED
RATE OF INCREASE	19.42	19.46	19.37	21.98	22.06	21.89	RATE OF INCREASE		15.71	VITAL RATES

AGE STRUCTURE OF PROJECTED POPULATION

STABLE AGE STRUCTURE

	1975 BOTH SEXES	1975 MALES	1975 FEMALES	1980 BOTH SEXES	1980 MALES	1980 FEMALES		MALES	FEMALES	AND RATIOS
% UNDER 15	40.41	39.77	41.12	35.55	35.75	35.32	% UNDER 15	33.61	31.77	(female
% 15-64	56.48	57.67	55.17	61.07	61.45	60.67	% 15-64	60.90	60.90	dominant)
% 65 AND OLDER	3.11	2.55	3.71	3.38	2.80	4.01	% 65 AND OLDER	5.50	7.33	
DEPEND. RATIO x 100	77.05	73.39	81.26	63.74	62.75	64.84	DEPEND. RATIO x 100	64.21	64.21	

AGE GROUP	FEMALE BIRTH RATES	NET MATERNITY FUNCTION	COEFF. OF MATRIX EQUATION	ORIGINAL MATRIX SUB-DIAGONAL	ORIGINAL MATRIX FIRST ROW	STABLE MATRIX FISHER VALUES	STABLE MATRIX REPRODUCTIVE VALUES	MATRIX PARAMETERS		
0-4	0.0000	0.0000	0.0000	0.99384	0.00000	1.079	3868	λ_1	1.08170	
5-9	0.0000	0.0000	0.0004	0.99862	0.00042	1.174	4304	λ_2	0.33209+0.66334i	TABLE 7
10-14	0.0002	0.0008	0.1214	0.99488	0.12231	1.271	3324	λ_4	0.09491+0.67922i	
15-19	0.0508	0.2419	0.3503	0.99267	0.35479	1.250	2322	λ_6	-0.38237+0.46681i	LESLIE
20-24	0.0971	0.4587	0.4089	0.99311	0.41717	0.976	1574	r_1	0.01571	MATRIX
25-29	0.0765	0.3591	0.2942	0.99050	0.30227	0.610	1146	r_2	-0.05973+0.22133i	AND ITS
30-34	0.0494	0.2294	0.1865	0.99321	0.19346	0.337	483	r_4	-0.07543+0.28639i	ANALYSIS
35-39	0.0311	0.1437	0.1103	0.98930	0.11516	0.157	189	r_6	-0.10103+0.45141i	(females)
40-44	0.0168	0.0769	0.0412	0.97422	0.04353	0.046	49	c_1	267	
45-49	0.0013	0.0056	0.0028	0.94647	0.00303	0.003	2	$2\pi/y$	28.3886	
50-54	0.0000	0.0000	0.0000	0.00000	0.00000	0.000	0	Δ	14.2718	

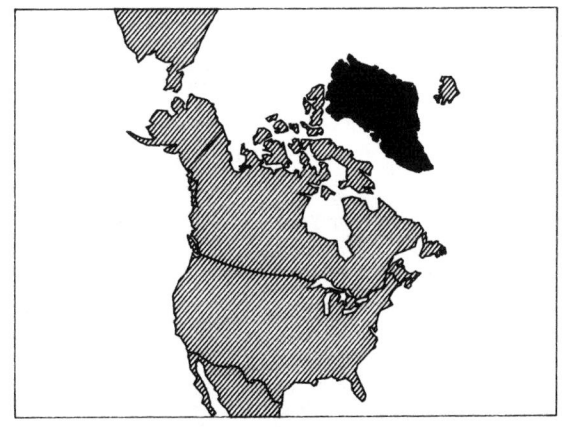

AGE AT LAST BIRTHDAY	ESTIMATED MID-YEAR POPULATION BOTH SEXES	MALES Number	MALES Percent	FEMALES Number	FEMALES Percent	BIRTHS BY AGE OF MOTHER AND SEX	DEATHS BOTH SEXES	DEATHS MALES	DEATHS FEMALES	AGE AT LAST BIRTHDAY
0	1025	541	1.9	484	2.0		28	15	13	0
1-4	3996	2051	7.1	1945	8.0		6	2	4	1-4
5-9	4213	2161	7.5	2052	8.4		6	3	3	5-9
10-14	3910	2041	7.1	1869	7.7		3	2	1	10-14
15-19	5912	3070	10.6	2842	11.7	213	17	12	5	15-19
20-24	6494	3388	11.7	3106	12.8	404	37	29	8	20-24
25-29	5708	3172	11.0	2536	10.4	288	29	24	5	25-29
30-34	4647	2630	9.1	2017	8.3	170	16	11	5	30-34
35-39	3933	2413	8.4	1520	6.3	50	20	16	4	35-39
40-44	3683	2268	7.9	1415	5.8	13	14	9	5	40-44
45-49	2655	1590	5.5	1065	4.4	2	23	17	6	45-49
50-54	2218	1250	4.3	968	4.0		30	19	11	50-54
55-59	1771	945	3.3	826	3.4		34	18	16	55-59
60-64	1071	544	1.9	527	2.2		36	18	18	60-64
65-69	784	382	1.3	402	1.7		33	22	11	65-69
70-74	545	236	0.8	309	1.3		33	14	19	70-74
75-79	362	131	0.5	231	1.0		29	14	15	75-79
80-84	190	60	0.2	130	0.5	603 M	26	8	18	80-84
85+	56	14	0.0	42	0.2	537 F	16	2	14	85+
TOTAL	53173	28887		24286		1140	436	255	181	TOTAL

TABLE 1 — DATA

TABLE 2 — MALE LIFE TABLE

x	$_nM_x$	$_nq_x$	l_x	$_nd_x$	$_nL_x$	$_nm_x$	$_na_x$	T_x	$\overset{\circ}{e}_x$	x
0	0.027726	0.027064	100000	2706	97611	0.027726	0.117	6129543	61.295	0
1	0.000975	0.003891	97294	379	388228	0.000975	1.500	6031932	61.997	1
5	0.001388	0.006917	96915	670	482899	0.001388	2.500	5643704	58.234	5
10	0.000980	0.004890	96245	471	480294	0.000980	3.025	5160805	53.622	10
15	0.003909	0.019384	95774	1856	474951	0.003909	2.889	4680512	48.870	15
20	0.008560	0.041929	93918	3938	460051	0.008560	2.578	4205561	44.779	20
25	0.007566	0.037044	89980	3333	441117	0.007556	2.366	3745510	41.626	25
30	0.004183	0.020640	86646	1788	428643	0.004172	2.434	3304392	38.137	30
35	0.006631	0.032614	84858	2768	417336	0.006631	2.487	2875749	33.889	35
40	0.003968	0.019706	82091	1618	406715	0.003977	2.690	2458413	29.948	40
45	0.010692	0.052682	80473	4239	392598	0.010799	2.696	2051698	25.496	45
50	0.015200	0.073627	76233	5613	367600	0.015269	2.583	1659101	21.763	50
55	0.019048	0.091646	70620	6472	337822	0.019158	2.639	1291501	18.288	55
60	0.033088	0.154799	64148	9930	297428	0.033387	2.652	953679	14.867	60
65	0.057592	0.253170	54218	13726	236884	0.057946	2.508	656251	12.104	65
70	0.059322	0.258174	40492	10454	176118	0.059358	2.480	419367	10.357	70
75	0.106870	0.424014	30038	12736	117938	0.107993	2.468	243249	8.098	75
80	0.133333	0.490539	17301	8487	63610	0.133423	2.302	125311	7.243	80
85	0.142857	1.000000	8814	8814	61701	0.075774	7.000	61701	7.000	85

TABLE 3 — FEMALE LIFE TABLE

x	$_nM_x$	$_nq_x$	l_x	$_nd_x$	$_nL_x$	$_nm_x$	$_na_x$	T_x	$\overset{\circ}{e}_x$	x
0	0.026860	0.026236	100000	2624	97680	0.026860	0.116	6653738	66.537	0
1	0.002057	0.008184	97376	797	387513	0.002057	1.500	6556058	67.327	1
5	0.001462	0.007283	96579	703	481139	0.001462	2.500	6168545	63.870	5
10	0.000535	0.002672	95876	256	478768	0.000535	2.609	5687407	59.320	10
15	0.001759	0.008762	95620	838	476204	0.001759	2.738	5208639	54.472	15
20	0.002576	0.012797	94782	1213	470894	0.002576	2.514	4732435	49.930	20
25	0.001972	0.009795	93569	917	465540	0.001969	2.484	4261541	45.544	25
30	0.002479	0.012347	92653	1144	460462	0.002484	2.551	3796000	40.970	30
35	0.002632	0.013102	91509	1199	454639	0.002637	2.578	3335538	36.451	35
40	0.003534	0.017609	90310	1590	447842	0.003551	2.669	2880900	31.900	40
45	0.005634	0.028065	88719	2490	438039	0.005684	2.768	2433058	27.424	45
50	0.011364	0.055564	86229	4791	420235	0.011401	2.722	1995019	23.136	50
55	0.019370	0.093364	81438	7603	389619	0.019515	2.689	1574784	19.337	55
60	0.034156	0.158255	73835	11685	340040	0.034363	2.507	1185166	16.052	60
65	0.027363	0.128377	62150	7979	291388	0.027381	2.573	845125	13.598	65
70	0.061489	0.267482	54171	14490	235281	0.061585	2.545	553737	10.222	70
75	0.064935	0.279519	39682	11092	170740	0.064963	2.505	318456	8.025	75
80	0.138462	0.517057	28590	14783	106294	0.139072	2.520	147716	5.167	80
85	0.333333	1.000000	13807	13807	41422	0.302705	3.000	41422	3.000	85

TABLE 4 — OBSERVED VITAL RATES AND RATIOS

CRUDE RATES

Per Thousand	BOTH SEXES	MALES	FEMALES
BIRTH RATE	21.44	20.87	22.11
DEATH RATE	8.20	8.83	7.45
RATE OF INCREASE	13.24	12.05	14.66

PERCENT OF POPULATION IN AGE GROUP

	BOTH SEXES	MALES	FEMALES
UNDER 15	24.72	23.52	26.15
15 - 64	71.64	73.63	69.27
65 AND OLDER	3.64	2.85	4.59

RATES STANDARDIZED ON USA 1980

Per Thousand	BOTH SEXES	MALES	FEMALES
BIRTH RATE	19.11		17.51
DEATH RATE	15.78	14.68	16.83
RATE OF INCREASE	3.33		0.68

RATES STANDARDIZED ON MEXICO 1980

	BOTH SEXES	MALES	FEMALES
BIRTH RATE	17.66		16.76
DEATH RATE	7.20	7.90	6.49
RATE OF INCREASE	10.46		10.28

VITAL STATISTICS

GFR x 1000	78.615
TFR	2.234
GRR	1.052
NRR	0.982
μ	26.342
σ^2	40.964
GENERATION	26.357
POP. SEX RATIO	0.841
SEX RATIO AT BIRTH	1.123
DEP. RATIO x 100	39.591

PROJECTED POPULATION

AGE GROUP	1990 BOTH SEXES	1990 MALES	1990 FEMALES	1995 BOTH SEXES	1995 MALES	1995 FEMALES
0-4	6	3	3	6	3	3
5-9	5	3	2	6	3	3
10-14	4	2	2	5	3	2
15-19	4	2	2	4	2	2
20-24	6	3	3	4	2	2
25-29	6	3	3	6	3	3
30-34	6	3	3	6	3	3
35-39	5	3	2	5	3	2
40-44	3	2	1	4	2	2
45-49	3	2	1	3	2	1
50-54	2	1	1	3	2	1
55-59	2	1	1	2	1	1
60-64	2	1	1	2	1	1
65-69	0	0	0	2	1	1
70-74	0	0	0	0	0	0
75-79	0	0	0	0	0	0
80-84	0	0	0	0	0	0
85+	0	0	0	0	0	0
TOTAL	54	29	25	58	31	27

STABLE EQUIVALENT TO ORIGINAL POPULATION

MALES Number	MALES Percent	FEMALES Number	FEMALES Percent	AGE GROUP	
3	7.8	2	7.1	0-4	
3	7.7	2	7.1	5-9	TABLE 5
3	7.7	2	7.1	10-14	
3	7.7	2	7.1	15-19	POPULATION
3	7.4	2	7.0	20-24	PROJECTED
3	7.2	2	7.0	25-29	WITH
2	7.0	2	6.9	30-34	FIXED
2	6.8	2	6.8	35-39	AGE-
2	6.7	2	6.8	40-44	SPECIFIC
2	6.5	2	6.6	45-49	BIRTH
2	6.1	2	6.4	50-54	AND
2	5.6	2	5.9	55-59	DEATH
2	4.9	2	5.2	60-64	RATES
1	4.0	2	4.5	65-69	(female
1	2.9	1	3.6	70-74	dominant,
1	2.0	1	2.6	75-79	in 000s)
0	1.1	1	1.6	80-84	
0	1.0	0	0.6	85+	
35		31		TOTAL	

VITAL RATES OF PROJECTED POPULATION

Per Thousand	1990 BOTH SEXES	1990 MALES	1990 FEMALES	1995 BOTH SEXES	1995 MALES	1995 FEMALES
BIRTH RATE	20.27	19.85	20.76	17.90	17.64	18.19
DEATH RATE	8.75	9.62	7.74	9.19	10.29	7.93
RATE OF INCREASE	11.52	10.23	13.03	8.70	7.35	10.27

VITAL RATES OF STABLE POPULATION

Per Thousand	MALES	FEMALES	
BIRTH RATE	15.93	14.66	TABLE 6
DEATH RATE	16.55	15.34	PROJECTED
RATE OF INCREASE		-.68	VITAL RATES

AGE STRUCTURE OF PROJECTED POPULATION

	BOTH SEXES	MALES	FEMALES	BOTH SEXES	MALES	FEMALES
% UNDER 15	26.03	25.08	27.15	26.62	26.07	27.26
% 15-64	70.08	71.64	68.26	68.77	69.77	67.62
% 65 AND OLDER	3.89	3.29	4.59	4.61	4.16	5.13
DEPEND. RATIO x 100	42.69	39.59	46.50	45.40	43.32	47.89

STABLE AGE STRUCTURE

	MALES	FEMALES	
% UNDER 15	23.20	21.29	AND RATIOS
% 15-64	65.80	65.68	(female
% 65 AND OLDER	11.00	13.03	dominant)
DEPEND. RATIO x 100	51.97	52.25	

AGE GROUP	FEMALE BIRTH RATES	NET MATERNITY FUNCTION	COEFF. OF MATRIX EQUATION	ORIGINAL MATRIX SUB-DIAGONAL	ORIGINAL MATRIX FIRST ROW	STABLE MATRIX FISHER VALUES	STABLE MATRIX REPRODUCTIVE VALUES	MATRIX PARAMETERS		
0-4	0.0000	0.0000	0.0000	0.99164	0.00000	1.029	2499	λ_1	0.99660	
5-9	0.0000	0.0000	0.0000	0.99507	0.00000	1.034	2122	λ_2	0.33448+0.68959i	TABLE 7
10-14	0.0000	0.0000	0.0841	0.99465	0.08519	1.035	1935	λ_4	-0.13403+0.50628i	
15-19	0.0353	0.1681	0.2283	0.98885	0.23263	0.949	2698	λ_6	-0.45376+0.22320i	LESLIE
20-24	0.0613	0.2885	0.2688	0.98863	0.27694	0.715	2220	r_1	-0.00068	MATRIX
25-29	0.0535	0.2490	0.2159	0.98909	0.22504	0.432	1097	r_2	-0.05320+0.22384i	AND ITS
30-34	0.0397	0.1828	0.1266	0.98735	0.13343	0.202	407	r_4	-0.12936+0.36592i	ANALYSIS
35-39	0.0155	0.0704	0.0449	0.98505	0.04793	0.064	98	r_6	-0.13637+0.53689i	(females)
40-44	0.0043	0.0194	0.0116	0.97811	0.01260	0.015	21	c_1	339	
45-49	0.0009	0.0039	0.0019	0.95935	0.00215	0.002	2	$2x/y$	28.0703	
50-54	0.0000	0.0000	0.0000	0.00000	0.00000	0.000	0	Δ	20.1660	

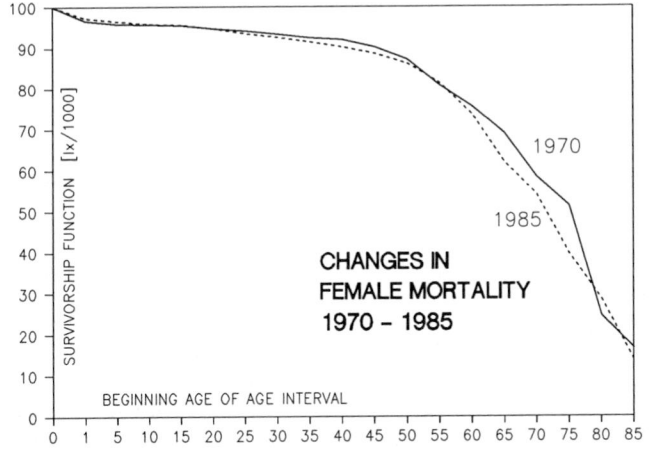

CHANGES IN FEMALE MORTALITY 1970 – 1985

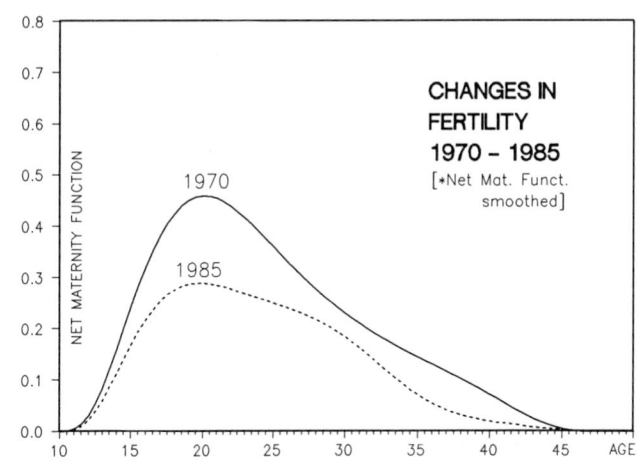

CHANGES IN FERTILITY 1970 – 1985
[*Net Mat. Funct. smoothed]

TABLE 1 — DATA

AGE AT LAST BIRTHDAY	ESTIMATED MID-YEAR POPULATION BOTH SEXES	MALES Number	Percent	FEMALES Number	Percent	BIRTHS BY AGE OF MOTHER AND SEX	DEATHS BOTH SEXES	MALES	FEMALES	AGE AT LAST BIRTHDAY
0	3493022	1781676	1.8	1711346	1.6		74695	42866	31829	0
1-4	13699435	6982322	7.0	6717113	6.4		11552	6497	5055	1-4
5-9	20000594	10190005	10.3	9810589	9.4		8404	5056	3348	5-9
10-14	20835667	10613139	10.7	10222528	9.8	11752	8449	5439	3010	10-14
15-19	19112744	9654225	9.7	9458519	9.0	644708	21038	15214	5824	15-19
20-24	16407493	7934016	8.0	8473477	8.1	1418874	24242	17877	6365	20-24
25-29	13506995	6635573	6.7	6871422	6.6	994904	19443	13427	6016	25-29
30-34	11455887	5607627	5.7	5848260	5.6	427806	19766	12884	6882	30-34
35-39	11131587	5423872	5.5	5707715	5.5	180244	27460	17011	10449	35-39
40-44	12007640	5831121	5.9	6176519	5.9	49952	45184	28226	16958	40-44
45-49	12142933	5863711	5.9	6279222	6.0	3146	70792	44294	26498	45-49
50-54	11128761	5359228	5.4	5769533	5.5		98790	63094	35696	50-54
55-59	9995259	4775902	4.8	5219357	5.0		135790	88548	47242	55-59
60-64	8636011	4035490	4.1	4600521	4.4		172703	112252	60451	60-64
65-69	7007258	3128688	3.2	3878570	3.7		207673	128619	79054	65-69
70-74	5456029	2319897	2.3	3136132	3.0		238027	136492	101535	70-74
75-79	3843441	1563962	1.6	2279479	2.2		257863	135475	122388	75-79
80-84	2289450	877436	0.9	1412014	1.4	1915378 M	232119	108505	123614	80-84
85+	1514308	543526	0.5	970782	0.9	1816008 F	247041	96702	150339	85+
TOTAL	203664514	99121416		104543098		3731386	1921031	1078478	842553	TOTAL

TABLE 2 — MALE LIFE TABLE

x	$_nM_x$	$_nq_x$	l_x	$_nd_x$	$_nL_x$	$_nm_x$	$_na_x$	T_x	$\overset{\circ}{e}_x$	x
0	0.024059	0.023555	100000	2356	97906	0.024059	0.111	6709689	67.097	0
1	0.000930	0.003713	97644	363	389671	0.000930	1.500	6611784	67.713	1
5	0.000496	0.002478	97282	241	485807	0.000496	2.500	6222112	63.960	5
10	0.000512	0.002560	97041	248	484692	0.000512	2.938	5736306	59.112	10
15	0.001576	0.007887	96792	763	482226	0.001583	2.726	5251614	54.256	15
20	0.002253	0.011224	96029	1078	477490	0.002257	2.537	4769387	49.666	20
25	0.002023	0.010060	94951	955	472368	0.002022	2.500	4291897	45.201	25
30	0.002298	0.011451	93996	1076	467391	0.002303	2.595	3819529	40.635	30
35	0.003136	0.015567	92920	1447	461213	0.003136	2.660	3352138	36.076	35
40	0.004841	0.023934	91473	2189	452281	0.004841	2.678	2890925	31.604	40
45	0.007554	0.037117	89284	3314	438705	0.007554	2.672	2438644	27.313	45
50	0.011773	0.057354	85970	4931	418333	0.011787	2.664	1999939	23.263	50
55	0.018541	0.088922	81039	7206	388162	0.018565	2.636	1581606	19.517	55
60	0.027816	0.130626	73833	9644	346056	0.027870	2.604	1193444	16.164	60
65	0.041110	0.187221	64188	12017	291684	0.041200	2.565	847388	13.202	65
70	0.058835	0.257144	52171	13415	227687	0.058921	2.528	555704	10.652	70
75	0.086623	0.355960	38756	13795	158927	0.086803	2.474	328018	8.464	75
80	0.123661	0.467887	24960	11679	94439	0.123661	2.400	169090	6.774	80
85	0.177916	1.000000	13282	13282	74651	0.109892	5.621	74651	5.621	85

TABLE 3 — FEMALE LIFE TABLE

x	$_nM_x$	$_nq_x$	l_x	$_nd_x$	$_nL_x$	$_nm_x$	$_na_x$	T_x	$\overset{\circ}{e}_x$	x
0	0.018599	0.018293	100000	1829	98357	0.018599	0.102	7484240	74.842	0
1	0.000753	0.003005	98171	295	391945	0.000753	1.500	7385884	75.235	1
5	0.000341	0.001705	97876	167	488961	0.000341	2.500	6993938	71.457	5
10	0.000294	0.001471	97709	144	488213	0.000294	2.693	6504977	66.575	10
15	0.000616	0.003080	97565	300	487120	0.000617	2.654	6016764	61.669	15
20	0.000751	0.003755	97265	365	485436	0.000752	2.571	5529644	56.852	20
25	0.000876	0.004380	96899	424	483478	0.000878	2.600	5044208	52.056	25
30	0.001177	0.005891	96475	568	481048	0.001182	2.665	4560730	47.274	30
35	0.001831	0.009115	95907	874	477499	0.001831	2.673	4079683	42.538	35
40	0.002746	0.013641	95032	1296	472147	0.002746	2.674	3602183	37.905	40
45	0.004220	0.020894	93736	1959	464098	0.004220	2.660	3130036	33.392	45
50	0.006187	0.030534	91778	2802	452297	0.006196	2.648	2665938	29.048	50
55	0.009051	0.044387	88975	3949	435551	0.009067	2.639	2213641	24.879	55
60	0.013140	0.063879	85026	5431	412345	0.013172	2.646	1778090	20.912	60
65	0.020382	0.097518	79595	7762	379693	0.020442	2.645	1365745	17.159	65
70	0.032376	0.150780	71833	10831	333505	0.032476	2.631	986052	13.727	70
75	0.053691	0.238883	61002	14572	269801	0.054011	2.584	652548	10.697	75
80	0.087544	0.359749	46429	16703	190794	0.087544	2.524	382746	8.244	80
85	0.154864	1.000000	29726	29726	191952	0.086018	6.457	191952	6.457	85

TABLE 4 — OBSERVED VITAL RATES AND RATIOS

CRUDE RATES

Per Thousand	BOTH SEXES	MALES	FEMALES
BIRTH RATE	18.32	19.32	17.37
DEATH RATE	9.43	10.88	8.06
RATE OF INCREASE	8.89	8.44	9.31

PERCENT OF POPULATION IN AGE GROUP

	BOTH SEXES	MALES	FEMALES
UNDER 15	28.49	29.83	27.22
15 - 64	61.63	61.66	61.61
65 AND OLDER	9.87	8.51	11.17

RATES STANDARDIZED ON USA 1980

Per Thousand	BOTH SEXES	MALES	FEMALES
BIRTH RATE	21.41		20.27
DEATH RATE	10.37	11.47	9.34
RATE OF INCREASE	11.04		10.93

RATES STANDARDIZED ON MEXICO 1980

	BOTH SEXES	MALES	FEMALES
BIRTH RATE	19.77		19.39
DEATH RATE	4.54	5.51	3.55
RATE OF INCREASE	15.23		15.84

VITAL STATISTICS

GFR x 1000	76.439
TFR	2.474
GRR	1.204
NRR	1.165
μ	26.004
σ^2	34.601
GENERATION	25.901
POP. SEX RATIO	1.055
SEX RATIO AT BIRTH	1.055
DEP. RATIO x 100	62.250

PROJECTED POPULATION

AGE GROUP	1975 BOTH SEXES	MALES	FEMALES	1980 BOTH SEXES	MALES	FEMALES
0-4	19483	9974	9509	21643	11080	10563
5-9	17137	8732	8405	19421	9938	9483
10-14	19963	10167	9796	17105	8712	8393
15-19	20759	10559	10200	19889	10115	9774
20-24	18985	9559	9426	20619	10455	10164
25-29	16288	7849	8439	18845	9457	9388
30-34	13403	6566	6837	16163	7766	8397
35-39	11339	5534	5805	13265	6479	6786
40-44	10963	5319	5644	11166	5426	5740
45-49	11727	5656	6071	10707	5159	5548
50-54	11711	5591	6120	11310	5393	5917
55-59	10529	4973	5556	11081	5188	5893
60-64	9199	4258	4941	9693	4433	5260
65-69	7637	3401	4236	8139	3589	4550
70-74	5849	2442	3407	6376	2655	3721
75-79	4156	1619	2537	4461	1705	2756
80-84	2541	929	1612	2756	962	1794
85+	2115	694	1421	2357	735	1622
TOTAL	213784	103822	109962	224996	109247	115749

STABLE EQUIVALENT TO ORIGINAL POPULATION

	MALES Number	Percent	FEMALES Number	Percent	AGE GROUP	
0-4	10148	8.8	9675	8.1	0-4	
5-9	9817	8.5	9368	7.8	5-9	TABLE 5
10-14	9510	8.2	9082	7.6	10-14	
15-19	9187	8.0	8798	7.3	15-19	POPULATION
20-24	8832	7.7	8513	7.1	20-24	PROJECTED
25-29	8483	7.4	8232	6.9	25-29	WITH
30-34	8150	7.1	7953	6.6	30-34	FIXED
35-39	7808	6.8	7665	6.4	35-39	AGE-
40-44	7435	6.4	7359	6.1	40-44	SPECIFIC
45-49	7002	6.1	7023	5.9	45-49	BIRTH
50-54	6483	5.6	6645	5.5	50-54	AND
55-59	5840	5.1	6213	5.2	55-59	DEATH
60-64	5055	4.4	5711	4.8	60-64	RATES
65-69	4137	3.6	5106	4.3	65-69	(female
70-74	3136	2.7	4355	3.6	70-74	dominant,
75-79	2125	1.8	3420	2.9	75-79	in 000s)
80-84	1226	1.1	2349	2.0	80-84	
85+	941	0.8	2294	1.9	85+	
TOTAL	115315	·	119761		TOTAL	

VITAL RATES OF PROJECTED POPULATION

Per Thousand	1975 BOTH SEXES	MALES	FEMALES	1980 BOTH SEXES	MALES	FEMALES
BIRTH RATE	19.83	20.96	18.76	20.51	21.68	19.40
DEATH RATE	9.98	11.17	8.87	10.14	11.15	9.19
RATE OF INCREASE	9.84	9.79	9.89	10.37	10.53	10.21

VITAL RATES OF STABLE POPULATION

Per Thousand	MALES	FEMALES	
BIRTH RATE	18.32	16.72	TABLE 6
DEATH RATE	12.43	10.82	PROJECTED
RATE OF INCREASE		5.90	VITAL RATES AND RATIOS

AGE STRUCTURE OF PROJECTED POPULATION

	BOTH SEXES	MALES	FEMALES	BOTH SEXES	MALES	FEMALES
% UNDER 15	26.47	27.81	25.20	25.85	27.21	24.57
% 15-64	63.10	63.44	62.78	63.44	63.96	62.95
% 65 AND OLDER	10.43	8.75	12.02	10.71	8.83	12.48
DEPEND. RATIO x 100	58.47	57.63	59.28	57.63	56.35	58.85

STABLE AGE STRUCTURE

	MALES	FEMALES	
% UNDER 15	25.56	23.48	(female
% 15-64	64.41	61.88	dominant)
% 65 AND OLDER	10.03	14.63	
DEPEND. RATIO x 100	55.25	61.59	

AGE GROUP	FEMALE BIRTH RATES	NET MATERNITY FUNCTION	COEFF. OF MATRIX EQUATION	ORIGINAL MATRIX SUB-DIAGONAL	FIRST ROW	STABLE MATRIX FISHER VALUES	REPRODUCTIVE VALUES	MATRIX PARAMETERS		
0-4	0.0000	0.0000	0.0000	0.99727	0.00000	1.035	8722654	λ_1	1.02994	
5-9	0.0000	0.0000	0.0014	0.99847	0.00137	1.069	10485656	λ_2	0.30392+0.74778i	TABLE 7
10-14	0.0006	0.0027	0.0822	0.99776	0.08251	1.101	11255784	λ_4	-0.37092+0.38351i	
15-19	0.0332	0.1616	0.2786	0.99654	0.28042	1.051	9940880	λ_6	-0.00507+0.45892i	LESLIE
20-24	0.0815	0.3956	0.3681	0.99597	0.37184	0.795	6736454	r_1	0.00590	MATRIX
25-29	0.0705	0.3407	0.2560	0.99497	0.25959	0.436	2994194	r_2	-0.04284+0.23695i	AND ITS
30-34	0.0356	0.1713	0.1223	0.99262	0.12468	0.181	1058845	r_4	-0.12565+0.46790i	ANALYSIS
35-39	0.0154	0.0734	0.0460	0.98879	0.04722	0.058	330315	r_6	-0.15576+0.31637i	(females)
40-44	0.0039	0.0186	0.0099	0.98295	0.01024	0.011	67073	c_1	1197626	
45-49	0.0002	0.0011	0.0006	0.97457	0.00060	0.001	3772	$2\pi/y$	26.5167	
50-54	0.0000	0.0000	0.0000	0.00000	0.00000	0.000	0	Δ	6.5967	

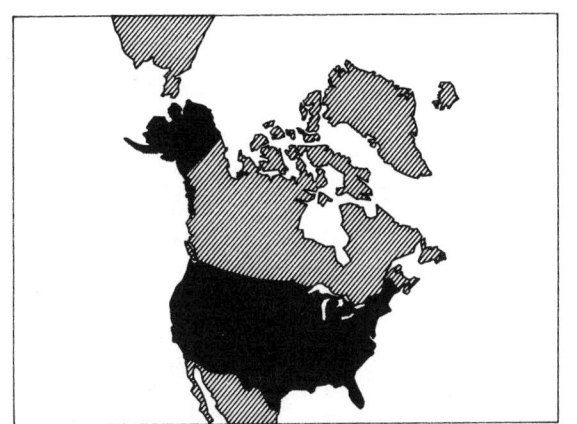

EDUCATION [1984]

% of primary school-age children enrolled:	101
secondary school-age children enrolled:	95
ca. 20-24 year olds in higher education:	57

LABOR FORCE

Average annual labor force growth (%) 1980-85:	1.2
% of the 1980 labor force in agriculture:	4
in industry:	31
in services:	66

TABLE 8

SOCIO-ECONOMIC INDICATORS

GNP & INCOME DISTRIBUTION

GNP per capita (in US Dollars) 1985:	16690
GNP average annual growth rate (%) 1965-85:	1.7
% share of total household income 1980	
Lowest 20% of households:	5.3
Highest 10% of households:	23.3

HEALTH & NUTRITION

Population per physician 1981:	500
Daily calorie supply per capita 1985:	3663

TABLE 1 — DATA

AGE AT LAST BIRTHDAY	ESTIMATED MID-YEAR POPULATION BOTH SEXES	MALES Number	MALES Percent	FEMALES Number	FEMALES Percent	BIRTHS BY AGE OF MOTHER AND SEX	DEATHS BOTH SEXES	DEATHS MALES	DEATHS FEMALES	AGE AT LAST BIRTHDAY
0	3079000	1575000	1.5	1504000	1.4		50536	28819	21717	0
1-4	12803000	6540000	6.3	6263000	5.7		9062	5087	3975	1-4
5-9	17325000	8831000	8.5	8494000	7.8		6187	3718	2469	5-9
10-14	20408000	10405000	10.0	10003000	9.2	12642	7296	4735	2561	10-14
15-19	20953000	10607000	10.2	10346000	9.5	582238	21272	15641	5631	15-19
20-24	19019000	9480000	9.1	9539000	8.7	1093676	26284	19876	6408	20-24
25-29	16835000	8339000	8.0	8496000	7.8	936786	23015	16682	6333	25-29
30-34	13927000	6856000	6.6	7071000	6.5	375500	21035	14122	6913	30-34
35-39	11576000	5626000	5.4	5950000	5.4	115409	24271	15571	8700	35-39
40-44	11169000	5453000	5.3	5716000	5.2	26319	36436	22875	13561	40-44
45-49	11782000	5720000	5.5	6062000	5.5	1628	60376	38176	22200	45-49
50-54	11978000	5761000	5.6	6217000	5.7		94003	60166	33837	50-54
55-59	10535000	5024000	4.8	5511000	5.0		126434	81163	45271	55-59
60-64	9239000	4319000	4.2	4920000	4.5		169360	108988	60372	60-64
65-69	8098000	3585000	3.5	4513000	4.1		208550	130394	78156	65-69
70-74	5778000	2445000	2.4	3333000	3.0		234050	135870	98180	70-74
75-79	4002000	1573000	1.5	2429000	2.2		248387	129863	118524	75-79
80-84	2649000	960000	0.9	1689000	1.5	1613135 M	241184	111325	129859	80-84
85+	1877000	613000	0.6	1264000	1.2	1531063 F	285141	107748	177393	85+
TOTAL	213032000	103712000		109320000		3144198	1892879	1050819	842060	TOTAL

TABLE 2 — MALE LIFE TABLE

x	$_nM_x$	$_nq_x$	l_x	$_nd_x$	$_nL_x$	$_nm_x$	$_na_x$	T_x	$\overset{\circ}{e}_x$	x
0	0.018298	0.018002	100000	1800	98382	0.018298	0.101	6870530	68.705	0
1	0.000778	0.003105	98200	305	392037	0.000778	1.500	6772148	68.963	1
5	0.000421	0.002103	97895	206	488960	0.000421	2.500	6380111	65.173	5
10	0.000455	0.002273	97689	222	487996	0.000455	2.979	5891151	60.305	10
15	0.001475	0.007355	97467	717	485707	0.001476	2.729	5403154	55.436	15
20	0.002097	0.010440	96750	1010	481274	0.002099	2.549	4917447	50.826	20
25	0.002000	0.009950	95740	953	476311	0.002000	2.492	4436173	46.336	25
30	0.002060	0.010267	94787	973	471576	0.002064	2.573	3959862	41.776	30
35	0.002768	0.013807	93814	1295	466031	0.002779	2.653	3488286	37.183	35
40	0.004195	0.020778	92519	1922	458139	0.004196	2.682	3022256	32.666	40
45	0.006674	0.032861	90597	2977	446070	0.006674	2.678	2564116	28.303	45
50	0.010444	0.050974	87619	4466	427662	0.010444	2.664	2118046	24.173	50
55	0.016155	0.077961	83153	6483	400531	0.016185	2.650	1690384	20.329	55
60	0.025235	0.119122	76670	9133	361526	0.025263	2.610	1289853	16.823	60
65	0.036372	0.167521	67537	11314	310375	0.036453	2.586	928327	13.745	65
70	0.055571	0.245502	56223	13803	247279	0.055819	2.549	617952	10.991	70
75	0.082558	0.342525	42420	14530	175493	0.082795	2.480	370673	8.738	75
80	0.115964	0.446086	27890	12441	107288	0.115964	2.415	195180	6.998	80
85	0.175772	1.000000	15449	15449	87892	0.107423	5.689	87892	5.689	85

TABLE 3 — FEMALE LIFE TABLE

x	$_nM_x$	$_nq_x$	l_x	$_nd_x$	$_nL_x$	$_nm_x$	$_na_x$	T_x	$\overset{\circ}{e}_x$	x
0	0.014439	0.014253	100000	1425	98709	0.014439	0.095	7663117	76.631	0
1	0.000635	0.002535	98575	250	393674	0.000635	1.500	7564407	76.738	1
5	0.000291	0.001452	98325	143	491267	0.000291	2.500	7170733	72.929	5
10	0.000256	0.001279	98182	126	490622	0.000256	2.705	6679466	68.031	10
15	0.000544	0.002718	98056	267	489658	0.000544	2.658	6188844	63.115	15
20	0.000672	0.003356	97790	328	488149	0.000672	2.561	5699186	58.280	20
25	0.000745	0.003727	97462	363	486431	0.000747	2.585	5211037	53.468	25
30	0.000978	0.004898	97098	476	484375	0.000982	2.651	4724606	48.658	30
35	0.001462	0.007323	96623	708	481482	0.001470	2.693	4240231	43.884	35
40	0.002372	0.011804	95915	1132	476957	0.002374	2.686	3758749	39.188	40
45	0.003662	0.018156	94783	1721	469899	0.003662	2.666	3281792	34.624	45
50	0.005443	0.026873	93062	2501	459463	0.005443	2.661	2811893	30.215	50
55	0.008215	0.040385	90561	3657	444223	0.008233	2.653	2352431	25.976	55
60	0.012271	0.059678	86904	5186	422213	0.012283	2.627	1908208	21.958	60
65	0.017318	0.083417	81718	6817	392628	0.017362	2.659	1485995	18.184	65
70	0.029457	0.138506	74901	10374	350098	0.029632	2.647	1093366	14.597	70
75	0.048795	0.219268	64527	14149	288496	0.049043	2.587	743268	11.519	75
80	0.076885	0.323369	50378	16291	211885	0.076885	2.544	454773	9.027	80
85	0.140343	1.000000	34087	34087	242888	0.072489	7.125	242888	7.125	85

TABLE 4 — OBSERVED VITAL RATES AND RATIOS

CRUDE RATES

Per Thousand	BOTH SEXES	MALES	FEMALES
BIRTH RATE	14.76	15.55	14.01
DEATH RATE	8.89	10.13	7.70
RATE OF INCREASE	5.87	5.42	6.30

PERCENT OF POPULATION IN AGE GROUP

	BOTH SEXES	MALES	FEMALES
UNDER 15	25.17	26.37	24.02
15 - 64	64.32	64.78	63.87
65 AND OLDER	10.52	8.85	12.10

RATES STANDARDIZED ON USA 1980

Per Thousand	BOTH SEXES	MALES	FEMALES
BIRTH RATE	15.63		14.80
DEATH RATE	9.38	10.51	8.31
RATE OF INCREASE	6.25		6.48

RATES STANDARDIZED ON MEXICO 1980

	BOTH SEXES	MALES	FEMALES
BIRTH RATE	14.52		14.25
DEATH RATE	4.02	4.93	3.09
RATE OF INCREASE	10.50		11.16

VITAL STATISTICS

GFR x 1000	59.124
TFR	1.799
GRR	0.876
NRR	0.853
μ	25.746
σ^2	33.552
GENERATION	25.849
POP. SEX RATIO	1.054
SEX RATIO AT BIRTH	1.054
DEP. RATIO x 100	55.483

AGE AT LAST BIRTHDAY	ESTIMATED MID-YEAR POPULATION BOTH SEXES	MALES Number	MALES Percent	FEMALES Number	FEMALES Percent	BIRTHS BY AGE OF MOTHER AND SEX	DEATHS BOTH SEXES	MALES	FEMALES	AGE AT LAST BIRTHDAY	
0	3540014	1809528	1.6	1730486	1.5		45539	25813	19726	0	
1-4	12837489	6567250	6.0	6270239	5.4		8190	4763	3427	1-4	
5-9	16729835	8554162	7.8	8175673	7.0		5076	2990	2086	5-9	
10-14	18274768	9332676	8.5	8942092	7.7	10169	5615	3572	2043	10-14	
15-19	21206001	10774406	9.8	10431595	8.9	552161	20740	15213	5527	15-19	
20-24	21356858	10682065	9.7	10674793	9.1	1226200	28303	21704	6599	20-24	
25-29	19555859	9722249	8.8	9833610	8.4	1108291	25740	19044	6696	25-29	
30-34	17592354	8692122	7.9	8900232	7.6	550354	24515	17009	7506	30-34	
35-39	13990301	6873628	6.2	7116673	6.1	140793	25664	16828	8836	35-39	TABLE 1
40-44	11690299	5718292	5.2	5972007	5.1	23090	32772	20798	11974	40-44	
45-49	11109610	5397766	4.9	5711844	4.9	1200	49802	31481	18321	45-49	DATA
50-54	11731001	5630598	5.1	6100403	5.2		83395	53022	30373	50-54	
55-59	11636057	5491545	5.0	6144512	5.3		126054	80104	45950	55-59	
60-64	10105692	4678140	4.2	5427552	4.7		166216	104225	61990	60-64	
65-69	8798222	3909849	3.5	4888373	4.2		216342	132508	83834	65-69	
70-74	6810316	2858587	2.6	3951729	3.4		250417	144965	105452	70-74	
75-79	4802327	1850924	1.7	2951403	2.5		263686	138259	125427	75-79	
80-84	2940307	1021027	0.9	1919280	1.6	1852616 M	253714	114599	139115	80-84	
85+	2244097	682729	0.6	1561368	1.3	1759642 F	358061	128181	229880	85+	
TOTAL	226951407	110247543		116703864		3612258	1989841	1075078	914763	TOTAL	

x	$_nM_x$	$_nq_x$	l_x	$_nd_x$	$_nL_x$	$_nm_x$	$_na_x$	T_x	$\overset{\circ}{e}_x$	x	
0	0.014265	0.014083	100000	1408	98724	0.014265	0.094	7002536	70.025	0	
1	0.000725	0.002896	98592	286	393653	0.000725	1.500	6903811	70.024	1	
5	0.000350	0.001746	98306	172	491102	0.000350	2.500	6510158	66.223	5	
10	0.000383	0.001912	98135	188	490311	0.000383	3.074	6019056	61.335	10	
15	0.001412	0.007037	97947	689	488177	0.001412	2.740	5528745	56.446	15	
20	0.002032	0.010112	97258	983	483881	0.002032	2.553	5040568	51.827	20	
25	0.001959	0.009745	96274	938	479014	0.001959	2.488	4556687	47.330	25	TABLE 2
30	0.001957	0.009747	95336	929	474402	0.001959	2.548	4077673	42.772	30	
35	0.002448	0.012227	94407	1154	469306	0.002460	2.637	3603271	38.168	35	MALE
40	0.003637	0.018127	93252	1690	462345	0.003656	2.683	3133965	33.607	40	LIFE
45	0.005832	0.028788	91562	2636	451722	0.005835	2.690	2671620	29.178	45	TABLE
50	0.009417	0.046073	88926	4097	435085	0.009417	2.670	2219899	24.963	50	
55	0.014587	0.070533	84829	5983	410074	0.014591	2.648	1784814	21.040	55	
60	0.022279	0.105953	78846	8354	374440	0.022313	2.627	1374740	17.436	60	
65	0.033891	0.156993	70492	11067	325853	0.033962	2.596	1000337	14.191	65	
70	0.050712	0.226221	59425	13443	264242	0.050875	2.554	674484	11.350	70	
75	0.074697	0.316224	45982	14541	193616	0.075100	2.504	410242	8.922	75	
80	0.112239	0.436351	31441	13719	122235	0.112239	2.451	216627	6.890	80	
85	0.187748	1.000000	17722	17722	94392	0.119791	5.326	94392	5.326	85	

x	$_nM_x$	$_nq_x$	l_x	$_nd_x$	$_nL_x$	$_nm_x$	$_na_x$	T_x	$\overset{\circ}{e}_x$	x	
0	0.011399	0.011282	100000	1128	98973	0.011399	0.089	7766667	77.667	0	
1	0.000547	0.002183	98872	216	394948	0.000547	1.500	7667695	77.552	1	
5	0.000255	0.001275	98656	126	492965	0.000255	2.500	7272747	73.718	5	
10	0.000228	0.001142	98530	113	492398	0.000228	2.749	6779782	68.809	10	
15	0.000530	0.002646	98418	260	491477	0.000530	2.652	6287384	63.885	15	
20	0.000618	0.003087	98157	303	490044	0.000618	2.550	5795907	59.047	20	
25	0.000681	0.003402	97854	333	488462	0.000681	2.568	5305863	54.222	25	TABLE 3
30	0.000843	0.004221	97521	412	486635	0.000846	2.638	4817401	49.398	30	
35	0.001242	0.006229	97110	605	484153	0.001249	2.692	4330767	44.597	35	FEMALE
40	0.002005	0.010034	96505	968	480295	0.002016	2.697	3846614	39.859	40	LIFE
45	0.003208	0.015925	95537	1521	474159	0.003209	2.684	3366319	35.236	45	TABLE
50	0.004979	0.024608	94015	2314	464677	0.004979	2.667	2892160	30.763	50	
55	0.007478	0.036759	91702	3371	450623	0.007481	2.661	2427483	26.472	55	
60	0.011422	0.055694	88331	4919	430087	0.011438	2.649	1976860	22.380	60	
65	0.017150	0.082565	83411	6887	400821	0.017182	2.643	1546773	18.544	65	
70	0.026685	0.125867	76524	9632	359811	0.026769	2.632	1145952	14.975	70	
75	0.042497	0.194032	66892	12979	303472	0.042769	2.612	786141	11.752	75	
80	0.072483	0.308470	53913	16631	229442	0.072483	2.587	482669	8.953	80	
85	0.147230	1.000000	37283	37283	253227	0.078782	6.792	253227	6.792	85	

CRUDE RATES

Per Thousand	BOTH SEXES	MALES	FEMALES
BIRTH RATE	15.92	16.80	15.08
DEATH RATE	8.77	9.75	7.84
RATE OF INCREASE	7.15	7.05	7.24

PERCENT OF POPULATION IN AGE GROUP

UNDER 15	22.64	23.82	21.52
15 - 64	66.08	66.81	65.39
65 AND OLDER	11.28	9.36	13.09

RATES STANDARDIZED ON USA 1980

Per Thousand	BOTH SEXES	MALES	FEMALES
BIRTH RATE	15.92		15.08
DEATH RATE	8.77	9.75	7.84
RATE OF INCREASE	7.15		7.24

RATES STANDARDIZED ON MEXICO 1980

	BOTH SEXES	MALES	FEMALES
BIRTH RATE	14.67		14.41
DEATH RATE	3.65	4.48	2.80
RATE OF INCREASE	11.03		11.61

VITAL STATISTICS

GFR x 1000	61.600	TABLE 4
TFR	1.837	
GRR	0.895	OBSERVED
NRR	0.875	VITAL
μ	25.974	RATES
σ^2	32.776	AND
GENERATION	26.059	RATIOS
POP. SEX RATIO	1.059	
SEX RATIO AT BIRTH	1.053	
DEP. RATIO x 100	51.327	

TABLE 1 — DATA

AGE AT LAST BIRTHDAY	ESTIMATED MID-YEAR POPULATION BOTH SEXES	MALES Number	MALES Percent	FEMALES Number	FEMALES Percent	BIRTHS BY AGE OF MOTHER AND SEX	DEATHS BOTH SEXES	DEATHS MALES	DEATHS FEMALES	AGE AT LAST BIRTHDAY
0	3749000	1918000	1.7	1831000	1.5		40047	22968	17079	0
1-4	14269000	7301000	6.3	6968000	5.7		7342	4243	3099	1-4
5-9	16822000	8608000	7.4	8214000	6.7		4170	2431	1739	5-9
10-14	17101000	8762000	7.5	8339000	6.8	10220	4767	3056	1711	10-14
15-19	18551000	9445000	8.1	9106000	7.4	467485	15075	10836	4239	15-19
20-24	21000000	10517000	9.1	10483000	8.6	1141320	22877	17339	5538	20-24
25-29	21758000	10889000	9.4	10869000	8.9	1201350	24740	18221	6519	25-29
30-34	20269000	10097000	8.7	10172000	8.3	696354	27135	19150	7985	30-34
35-39	17708000	8741000	7.5	8967000	7.3	214336	30452	20570	9882	35-39
40-44	14055000	6888000	5.9	7167000	5.8	28334	35391	22943	12448	40-44
45-49	11646000	5678000	4.9	5968000	4.9	1162	46274	29194	17080	45-49
50-54	10943000	5282000	4.5	5661000	4.6		70410	44159	26251	50-54
55-59	11341000	5382000	4.6	5959000	4.9		115241	72255	42986	55-59
60-64	10994000	5117000	4.4	5877000	4.8		171361	105536	65825	60-64
65-69	9431000	4255000	3.7	5176000	4.2		216841	130324	86517	65-69
70-74	7571000	3217000	2.8	4354000	3.6		266009	152820	113189	70-74
75-79	5496000	2137000	1.8	3359000	2.7		290271	152717	137554	75-79
80-84	3331000	1154000	1.0	2177000	1.8	1927983 M	278815	127280	151535	80-84
85+	2707000	773000	0.7	1934000	1.6	1832578 F	419222	141716	277506	85+
TOTAL	238742000	116161000		122581000		3760561	2086440	1097758	988682	TOTAL

TABLE 2 — MALE LIFE TABLE

x	nM_x	nq_x	l_x	nd_x	nL_x	nm_x	na_x	T_x	$\overset{\circ}{e}_x$	x
0	0.011975	0.011846	100000	1185	98922	0.011975	0.090	7126580	71.266	0
1	0.000581	0.002321	98815	229	394688	0.000581	1.500	7027658	71.119	1
5	0.000282	0.001411	98586	139	492582	0.000282	2.500	6632970	67.281	5
10	0.000349	0.001743	98447	172	491894	0.000349	3.014	6140387	62.373	10
15	0.001147	0.005721	98275	562	490102	0.001147	2.734	5648493	57.476	15
20	0.001649	0.008210	97713	802	486611	0.001649	2.564	5158391	52.791	20
25	0.001673	0.008332	96911	807	482557	0.001673	2.527	4671780	48.207	25
30	0.001897	0.009448	96103	908	478311	0.001898	2.571	4189222	43.591	30
35	0.002353	0.011740	95195	1118	473320	0.002361	2.622	3710911	38.982	35
40	0.003331	0.016626	94078	1564	466738	0.003351	2.666	3237592	34.414	40
45	0.005142	0.025548	92514	2364	457104	0.005171	2.688	2770853	29.951	45
50	0.008360	0.041041	90150	3700	442181	0.008367	2.684	2313749	25.666	50
55	0.013425	0.065080	86450	5626	419071	0.013425	2.657	1871569	21.649	55
60	0.020625	0.098308	80824	7946	385254	0.020625	2.626	1452498	17.971	60
65	0.030628	0.142922	72878	10416	339475	0.030682	2.608	1067244	14.644	65
70	0.047504	0.213448	62463	13332	279934	0.047627	2.571	727769	11.651	70
75	0.071463	0.305045	49130	14987	208470	0.071890	2.519	447836	9.115	75
80	0.110295	0.430804	34143	14709	133361	0.110295	2.460	239366	7.011	80
85	0.183332	1.000000	19434	19434	106005	0.115019	5.455	106005	5.455	85

TABLE 3 — FEMALE LIFE TABLE

x	nM_x	nq_x	l_x	nd_x	nL_x	nm_x	na_x	T_x	$\overset{\circ}{e}_x$	x
0	0.009328	0.009249	100000	925	99155	0.009328	0.086	7842248	78.422	0
1	0.000445	0.001777	99075	176	395860	0.000445	1.500	7743094	78.154	1
5	0.000212	0.001058	98899	105	494234	0.000212	2.500	7347233	74.290	5
10	0.000205	0.001025	98794	101	493745	0.000205	2.757	6853000	69.366	10
15	0.000466	0.002325	98693	229	492925	0.000466	2.644	6359255	64.435	15
20	0.000528	0.002638	98464	260	491682	0.000528	2.552	5866330	59.579	20
25	0.000600	0.002995	98204	294	490310	0.000600	2.588	5374647	54.729	25
30	0.000785	0.003923	97910	384	488640	0.000786	2.632	4884337	49.886	30
35	0.001102	0.005520	97526	538	486379	0.001107	2.678	4395697	45.072	35
40	0.001737	0.008712	96987	845	482999	0.001749	2.706	3909319	40.308	40
45	0.002862	0.014299	96142	1375	477552	0.002879	2.702	3426320	35.638	45
50	0.004637	0.022952	94768	2175	468798	0.004640	2.683	2948768	31.116	50
55	0.007214	0.035472	92593	3284	455314	0.007214	2.671	2479970	26.784	55
60	0.011200	0.054569	89308	4873	435089	0.011201	2.650	2024656	22.670	60
65	0.016715	0.080532	84435	6800	406143	0.016742	2.642	1589567	18.826	65
70	0.025997	0.122670	77635	9523	365610	0.026048	2.631	1183424	15.243	70
75	0.040951	0.187502	68111	12771	310083	0.041186	2.614	817814	12.007	75
80	0.069607	0.298151	55340	16500	237042	0.069607	2.596	507731	9.175	80
85	0.143488	1.000000	38841	38841	270689	0.075358	6.969	270689	6.969	85

TABLE 4 — OBSERVED VITAL RATES AND RATIOS

CRUDE RATES

Per Thousand	BOTH SEXES	MALES	FEMALES
BIRTH RATE	15.75	16.60	14.95
DEATH RATE	8.74	9.45	8.07
RATE OF INCREASE	7.01	7.15	6.88

PERCENT OF POPULATION IN AGE GROUP

	BOTH SEXES	MALES	FEMALES
UNDER 15	21.76	22.89	20.68
15 - 64	66.29	67.18	65.45
65 AND OLDER	11.95	9.93	13.87

RATES STANDARDIZED ON USA 1980

Per Thousand	BOTH SEXES	MALES	FEMALES
BIRTH RATE	15.86		15.03
DEATH RATE	8.27	9.07	7.51
RATE OF INCREASE	7.59		7.52

RATES STANDARDIZED ON MEXICO 1980

	BOTH SEXES	MALES	FEMALES
BIRTH RATE	14.54		14.28
DEATH RATE	3.35	4.08	2.60
RATE OF INCREASE	11.19		11.68

VITAL STATISTICS

GFR x 1000	59.946
TFR	1.842
GRR	0.898
NRR	0.881
μ	26.306
σ^2	34.380
GENERATION	26.389
POP. SEX RATIO	1.055
SEX RATIO AT BIRTH	1.052
DEP. RATIO x 100	50.850

PROJECTED POPULATION

AGE GROUP	1990 BOTH SEXES	1990 MALES	1990 FEMALES	1995 BOTH SEXES	1995 MALES	1995 FEMALES
0-4	18196	9316	8880	17179	8795	8384
5-9	17985	9200	8785	18163	9297	8866
10-14	16802	8596	8206	17963	9187	8776
15-19	17055	8730	8325	16757	8565	8192
20-24	18461	9378	9083	16972	8668	8304
25-29	20883	10429	10454	18358	9300	9058
30-34	21625	10793	10832	20756	10338	10418
35-39	20117	9992	10125	21463	10681	10782
40-44	17524	8619	8905	19908	9853	10055
45-49	13832	6746	7086	17246	8442	8804
50-54	11352	5493	5859	13482	6526	6956
55-59	10504	5006	5498	10896	5206	5690
60-64	10642	4948	5694	9856	4602	5254
65-69	9995	4509	5486	9675	4360	5315
70-74	8168	3509	4659	8657	3718	4939
75-79	6089	2396	3693	6565	2613	3952
80-84	3935	1367	2568	4356	1533	2823
85+	3403	917	2486	4019	1087	2932
TOTAL	246568	119944	126624	252271	122771	129500

STABLE EQUIVALENT TO ORIGINAL POPULATION

MALES Number	MALES Percent	FEMALES Number	FEMALES Percent	AGE GROUP	
9041	5.8	8618	5.2	0-4	
9242	5.9	8814	5.3	5-9	TABLE 5
9454	6.1	9020	5.5	10-14	
9649	6.2	9224	5.6	15-19	POPULATION
9814	6.3	9425	5.7	20-24	PROJECTED
9969	6.4	9628	5.8	25-29	WITH
10122	6.5	9829	5.9	30-34	FIXED
10260	6.6	10022	6.1	35-39	AGE-
10364	6.7	10194	6.2	40-44	SPECIFIC
10397	6.7	10325	6.2	45-49	BIRTH
10303	6.6	10383	6.3	50-54	AND
10002	6.4	10330	6.2	55-59	DEATH
9419	6.0	10111	6.1	60-64	RATES
8502	5.5	9668	5.8	65-69	(female
7182	4.6	8916	5.4	70-74	dominant,
5479	3.5	7746	4.7	75-79	in 000s)
3590	2.3	6065	3.7	80-84	
2923	1.9	7095	4.3	85+	
155712		165413		TOTAL	

VITAL RATES OF PROJECTED POPULATION

Per Thousand	1990 BOTH SEXES	1990 MALES	1990 FEMALES	1995 BOTH SEXES	1995 MALES	1995 FEMALES
BIRTH RATE	14.61	15.40	13.86	13.28	13.99	12.60
DEATH RATE	9.40	9.95	8.88	9.93	10.40	9.48
RATE OF INCREASE	5.21	5.45	4.98	3.35	3.58	3.12

AGE STRUCTURE OF PROJECTED POPULATION

	1990 BOTH SEXES	1990 MALES	1990 FEMALES	1995 BOTH SEXES	1995 MALES	1995 FEMALES
% UNDER 15	21.49	22.60	20.43	21.13	22.22	20.10
% 15-64	65.70	66.81	64.65	65.68	66.94	64.49
% 65 AND OLDER	12.81	10.59	14.92	13.19	10.84	15.41
DEPEND. RATIO x 100	52.21	49.68	54.68	52.25	49.39	55.07

VITAL RATES OF STABLE POPULATION

Per Thousand	MALES	FEMALES	
BIRTH RATE	11.62	10.40	TABLE 6
DEATH RATE	16.36	15.21	PROJECTED
RATE OF INCREASE		-4.81	VITAL RATES AND RATIOS

STABLE AGE STRUCTURE

	MALES	FEMALES	(female dominant)
% UNDER 15	17.81	15.99	
% 15-64	64.41	60.13	
% 65 AND OLDER	17.77	23.87	
DEPEND. RATIO x 100	55.25	66.29	

AGE GROUP	FEMALE BIRTH RATES	NET MATERNITY FUNCTION	COEFF. OF MATRIX EQUATION	ORIGINAL MATRIX SUB-DIAGONAL	ORIGINAL MATRIX FIRST ROW	STABLE MATRIX FISHER VALUES	STABLE MATRIX REPRODUCTIVE VALUES
0-4	0.0000	0.0000	0.0000	0.99842	0.00000	0.998	8781238
5-9	0.0000	0.0000	0.0015	0.99901	0.00148	0.976	8015140
10-14	0.0006	0.0029	0.0631	0.99834	0.06330	0.952	7939182
15-19	0.0250	0.1233	0.1921	0.99748	0.19291	0.868	7901164
20-24	0.0531	0.2609	0.2625	0.99721	0.26426	0.656	6878856
25-29	0.0539	0.2641	0.2136	0.99659	0.21560	0.378	4107577
30-34	0.0334	0.1630	0.1098	0.99537	0.11127	0.154	1569416
35-39	0.0116	0.0567	0.0330	0.99305	0.03357	0.040	356537
40-44	0.0019	0.0093	0.0049	0.98872	0.00500	0.005	38380
45-49	0.0001	0.0005	0.0002	0.98167	0.00023	0.000	1433
50-54	0.0000	0.0000	0.0000	0.00000	0.00000	0.000	0

MATRIX PARAMETERS

λ_1	0.97622	
λ_2	$0.34008+0.71129i$	TABLE 7
λ_4	$-0.14827+0.49804i$	
λ_6	$-0.32589-0.24911i$	LESLIE
r_1	-0.00481	MATRIX
r_2	$-0.04755+0.22496i$	AND ITS
r_4	$-0.13092+0.37203i$	ANALYSIS
r_6	$-0.17822-0.49779i$	(females)
c_1	1654143	
$2\pi/y$	27.9302	
Δ	16.0550	

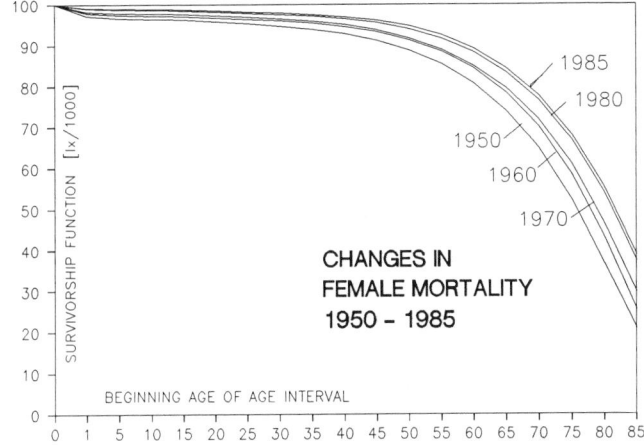

CHANGES IN FEMALE MORTALITY 1950 – 1985

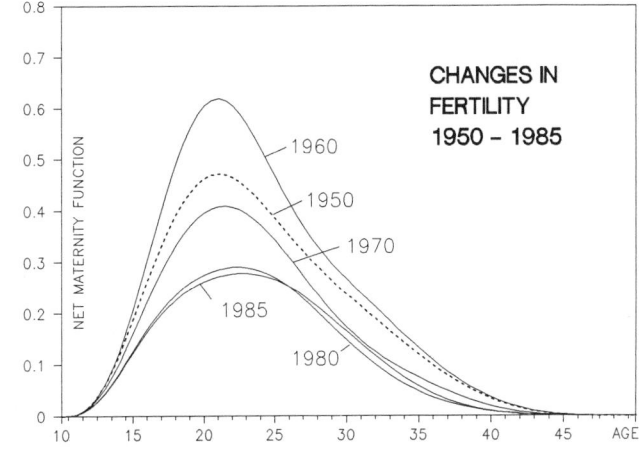

CHANGES IN FERTILITY 1950 – 1985

AGE AT LAST BIRTHDAY	ESTIMATED MID-YEAR POPULATION BOTH SEXES	MALES Number	MALES Percent	FEMALES Number	FEMALES Percent	BIRTHS BY AGE OF MOTHER AND SEX	DEATHS BOTH SEXES	DEATHS MALES	DEATHS FEMALES	AGE AT LAST BIRTHDAY
0	17577613	9121465	1.8	8456148	1.8		682052	363504	318548	0
1-4	76033388	39230804	7.7	36802584	7.7		321088	157287	163801	1-4
5-9	116437660	59968708	11.8	56468952	11.8		136044	76721	59323	5-9
10-14	129211104	66499112	13.1	62711992	13.1		93328	52285	41043	10-14
15-19	118165180	59756396	11.8	58408784	12.2	381083	117072	63478	53594	15-19
20-24	77577932	39943232	7.9	37634700	7.8	5335838	107288	56690	50598	20-24
25-29	91040912	46884120	9.3	44156792	9.2	10683875	133967	68520	65447	25-29
30-34	68014868	35535732	7.0	32479136	6.8	3035240	117154	62470	54684	30-34
35-39	51897356	27403840	5.4	24493516	5.1	852963	119794	66728	53066	35-39
40-44	48044328	25649620	5.1	22394708	4.7	327021	155418	90181	65237	40-44
45-49	46531164	24594232	4.9	21936932	4.6	73684	224404	131782	92622	45-49
50-54	39564024	20856760	4.1	18707264	3.9		306032	182430	123602	50-54
55-59	33345449	17150112	3.4	16195337	3.4		411604	246363	165241	55-59
60-64	26526511	13219004	2.6	13307507	2.8		551864	323519	228345	60-64
65-69	20354171	9723855	1.9	10630316	2.2		659026	373044	285982	65-69
70-74	13951343	6206760	1.2	7744583	1.6		750633	395112	355521	70-74
75-79	8282540	3345785	0.7	4936755	1.0		672147	322944	349203	75-79
80-84	3374313	1228356	0.2	2145957	0.4	10765292 M	452591	192310	260281	80-84
85+	1235921	379804	0.1	856117	0.2	9924412 F	262434	90545	171889	85+
TOTAL	987165777	506697697		480468080		20689704	6273940	3315913	2958027	TOTAL

TABLE 1 DATA

TABLE 2 — MALE LIFE TABLE

x	nM_x	nq_x	l_x	nd_x	nL_x	nm_x	na_x	T_x	$\overset{\circ}{e}_x$	x
0	0.039851	0.038528	100000	3853	96678	0.039851	0.138	6626780	66.268	0
1	0.004009	0.015878	96147	1527	380772	0.004009	1.500	6530102	67.918	1
5	0.001279	0.006376	94621	603	471595	0.001279	2.500	6149329	64.989	5
10	0.000786	0.003923	94017	369	469142	0.000786	2.441	5677734	60.390	10
15	0.001062	0.005319	93648	498	467058	0.001067	2.622	5208592	55.619	15
20	0.001419	0.007086	93150	660	464138	0.001422	2.555	4741534	50.902	20
25	0.001461	0.007284	92490	674	460798	0.001462	2.545	4277396	46.247	25
30	0.001758	0.008784	91817	807	457157	0.001764	2.612	3816598	41.568	30
35	0.002435	0.012166	91010	1107	452442	0.002447	2.644	3359441	36.913	35
40	0.003516	0.017474	89903	1571	445844	0.003524	2.664	2907000	32.335	40
45	0.005358	0.026526	88332	2343	436246	0.005371	2.690	2461155	27.863	45
50	0.008747	0.043059	85989	3703	421398	0.008786	2.692	2024910	23.549	50
55	0.014365	0.069909	82286	5753	398133	0.014449	2.688	1603512	19.487	55
60	0.024474	0.116357	76534	8905	361697	0.024621	2.645	1205378	15.750	60
65	0.038364	0.176756	67628	11954	309620	0.038608	2.614	843681	12.475	65
70	0.063658	0.277431	55675	15446	240542	0.064213	2.551	534061	9.593	70
75	0.096523	0.390570	40229	15712	161503	0.097287	2.477	293519	7.296	75
80	0.156559	0.559376	24517	13714	86703	0.158172	2.384	132016	5.385	80
85	0.238399	1.000000	10803	10803	45313	0.177814	4.195	45313	4.195	85

TABLE 3 — FEMALE LIFE TABLE

x	nM_x	nq_x	l_x	nd_x	nL_x	nm_x	na_x	T_x	$\overset{\circ}{e}_x$	x
0	0.037671	0.036481	100000	3648	96841	0.037671	0.134	6923793	69.238	0
1	0.004451	0.017607	96352	1697	381167	0.004451	1.500	6826952	70.854	1
5	0.001051	0.005239	94655	496	472037	0.001051	2.500	6445786	68.097	5
10	0.000654	0.003267	94160	308	470015	0.000654	2.457	5973748	63.443	10
15	0.000918	0.004600	93852	432	468247	0.000922	2.654	5503733	58.643	15
20	0.001344	0.006721	93420	628	465584	0.001349	2.584	5035486	53.901	20
25	0.001482	0.007388	92792	686	462278	0.001483	2.544	4569902	49.249	25
30	0.001684	0.008404	92107	774	458662	0.001688	2.581	4107623	44.596	30
35	0.002167	0.010820	91333	988	454304	0.002175	2.613	3648962	39.952	35
40	0.002913	0.014496	90344	1310	448631	0.002919	2.639	3194657	35.361	40
45	0.004222	0.020948	89035	1865	440831	0.004231	2.672	2746027	30.842	45
50	0.006607	0.032640	87170	2846	429223	0.006632	2.672	2305195	26.445	50
55	0.010203	0.050050	84323	4220	411855	0.010247	2.687	1875972	22.247	55
60	0.017159	0.082852	80103	6637	384989	0.017239	2.661	1464117	18.278	60
65	0.026902	0.127081	73466	9336	345384	0.027031	2.649	1079128	14.689	65
70	0.045906	0.207732	64130	13322	288612	0.046158	2.595	733745	11.442	70
75	0.070735	0.303378	50808	15414	216175	0.071304	2.543	445133	8.761	75
80	0.121289	0.467184	35394	16536	135030	0.122458	2.464	228958	6.469	80
85	0.200777	1.000000	18859	18859	93928	0.133370	4.981	93928	4.981	85

TABLE 4 — OBSERVED VITAL RATES AND RATIOS

CRUDE RATES

Per Thousand	BOTH SEXES	MALES	FEMALES
BIRTH RATE	20.96	21.25	20.66
DEATH RATE	6.36	6.54	6.16
RATE OF INCREASE	14.60	14.70	14.50

PERCENT OF POPULATION IN AGE GROUP

UNDER 15	34.37	34.50	34.22
15 - 64	60.85	61.38	60.30
65 AND OLDER	4.78	4.12	5.48

RATES STANDARDIZED ON USA 1980

Per Thousand	BOTH SEXES	MALES	FEMALES
BIRTH RATE	22.68		21.15
DEATH RATE	12.32	11.92	12.70
RATE OF INCREASE	10.36		8.46

RATES STANDARDIZED ON MEXICO 1980

	BOTH SEXES	MALES	FEMALES
BIRTH RATE	19.48		18.84
DEATH RATE	5.87	6.19	5.56
RATE OF INCREASE	13.61		13.28

VITAL STATISTICS

GFR x 1000	85.670
TFR	2.682
GRR	1.287
NRR	1.188
μ	28.065
σ^2	26.640
GENERATION	27.983
POP. SEX RATIO	0.948
SEX RATIO AT BIRTH	1.085
DEP. RATIO x 100	64.334

PROJECTED POPULATION

AGE GROUP	1986 BOTH SEXES	MALES	FEMALES	1991 BOTH SEXES	MALES	FEMALES
0-4	105132	54672	50460	124133	64553	59580
5-9	92452	47759	44693	103831	54001	49830
10-14	115884	59657	56227	92013	47511	44502
15-19	128680	66204	62476	115408	59392	56016
20-24	117460	59383	58077	127911	65790	62121
25-29	77023	39656	37367	116620	58956	57664
30-34	90325	46514	43811	76417	39342	37075
35-39	67340	35169	32171	89429	46034	43395
40-44	51192	27004	24188	66425	34656	31769
45-49	47102	25097	22005	50190	26423	23767
50-54	45116	23757	21359	45669	24243	21426
55-59	37655	19705	17950	42941	22446	20495
60-64	30720	15581	15139	34681	17902	16779
65-69	23255	11316	11939	26918	13337	13581
70-74	16437	7554	8883	18767	8791	9976
75-79	9968	4167	5801	11726	5072	6654
80-84	4880	1796	3084	5860	2237	3623
85+	2135	642	1493	3084	939	2145
TOTAL	1062756	545633	517123	1152023	591625	560398

STABLE EQUIVALENT TO ORIGINAL POPULATION

MALES Number	Percent	FEMALES Number	Percent	AGE GROUP	
60108	8.8	55478	8.5	0-4	
57571	8.4	53124	8.2	5-9	TABLE 5
55536	8.1	51294	7.9	10-14	
53614	7.9	49552	7.6	15-19	POPULATION
51664	7.6	47777	7.3	20-24	PROJECTED
49737	7.3	46000	7.1	25-29	WITH
47849	7.0	44257	6.8	30-34	FIXED
45920	6.7	42508	6.5	35-39	AGE-
43879	6.4	40705	6.2	40-44	SPECIFIC
41633	6.1	38785	6.0	45-49	BIRTH
38997	5.7	36619	5.6	50-54	AND
35728	5.2	34072	5.2	55-59	DEATH
31474	4.6	30884	4.7	60-64	RATES
26126	3.8	26867	4.1	65-69	(female
19682	2.9	21771	3.3	70-74	dominant,
12814	1.9	15812	2.4	75-79	in 000s)
6671	1.0	9578	1.5	80-84	
3381	0.5	6460	1.0	85+	
682384		651543		TOTAL	

VITAL RATES OF PROJECTED POPULATION

Per Thousand	1986 BOTH SEXES	MALES	FEMALES	1991 BOTH SEXES	MALES	FEMALES
BIRTH RATE	21.95	22.24	21.64	24.86	25.19	24.52
DEATH RATE	7.01	7.20	6.80	7.54	7.77	7.30
RATE OF INCREASE	14.94	15.04	14.84	17.33	17.42	17.22

AGE STRUCTURE OF PROJECTED POPULATION

	BOTH SEXES	MALES	FEMALES	BOTH SEXES	MALES	FEMALES
% UNDER 15	29.50	29.71	29.27	27.78	28.07	27.46
% 15-64	65.17	65.62	64.69	66.46	66.80	66.11
% 65 AND OLDER	5.33	4.67	6.03	5.76	5.13	6.42
DEPEND. RATIO x 100	53.44	52.38	54.58	50.46	49.71	51.25

VITAL RATES OF STABLE POPULATION

Per Thousand	MALES	FEMALES	
BIRTH RATE	18.73	18.09	TABLE 6
DEATH RATE	12.47	11.93	PROJECTED
RATE OF INCREASE		6.16	VITAL RATES AND RATIOS (female dominant)

STABLE AGE STRUCTURE

	MALES	FEMALES
% UNDER 15	25.38	24.54
% 15-64	64.55	63.11
% 65 AND OLDER	10.06	12.35
DEPEND. RATIO x 100	54.91	58.47

AGE GROUP	FEMALE BIRTH RATES	NET MATERNITY FUNCTION	COEFF. OF MATRIX EQUATION	ORIGINAL MATRIX SUB-DIAGONAL	FIRST ROW	STABLE MATRIX FISHER VALUES	REPRODUCTIVE VALUES	MATRIX PARAMETERS	
0-4	0.0000	0.0000	0.0000	0.98751	0.00000	1.062	48072328	λ_1 1.03126	
5-9	0.0000	0.0000	0.0000	0.99572	0.00000	1.109	62636392	λ_2 0.37484+0.81131i	TABLE 7
10-14	0.0000	0.0000	0.0073	0.99624	0.00745	1.149	72044096	λ_4 −0.41634+0.53128i	
15-19	0.0031	0.0147	0.1656	0.99431	0.16910	1.181	68995032	λ_6 −0.55551−0.00000i	LESLIE
20-24	0.0680	0.3166	0.4266	0.99290	0.43796	1.044	39309184	r_1 0.00616	MATRIX
25-29	0.1161	0.5365	0.3711	0.99218	0.38369	0.616	27215040	r_2 −0.02247+0.22760i	AND ITS
30-34	0.0448	0.2056	0.1407	0.99050	0.14668	0.230	7465304	r_4 −0.07861+0.44710i	ANALYSIS
35-39	0.0167	0.0759	0.0537	0.98751	0.05646	0.082	2008732	r_6 −0.11758−0.62832i	(females)
40-44	0.0070	0.0314	0.0193	0.98262	0.02053	0.025	558063	c_1 6515411	
45-49	0.0016	0.0071	0.0036	0.97367	0.00385	0.004	87007	$2\pi/y$ 27.6064	
50-54	0.0000	0.0000	0.0000	0.00000	0.00000	0.000	0	Δ 16.8653	

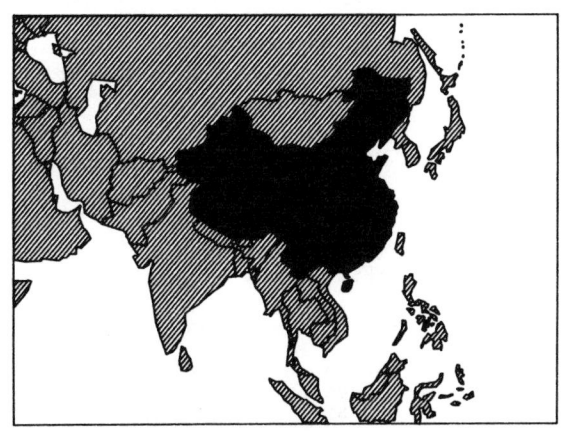

EDUCATION [1984]

% of primary school-age children enrolled:	118
secondary school-age children enrolled:	37
ca. 20-24 year olds in higher education:	1

LABOR FORCE

Average annual labor force growth (%) 1980-85:	2.5	
% of the 1980 labor force in agriculture:	74	TABLE 8
in industry:	14	
in services:	12	SOCIO-ECONOMIC INDICATORS

GNP & INCOME DISTRIBUTION

GNP per capita (in US Dollars) 1985:	310
GNP average annual growth rate (%) 1965-85:	4.8
% share of total household income	
Lowest 20% of households:	na
Highest 10% of households:	na

HEALTH & NUTRITION

Population per physician 1981:	1730
Daily calorie supply per capita 1985:	2602

AGE AT LAST BIRTHDAY	ESTIMATED MID-YEAR POPULATION BOTH SEXES	MALES Number	MALES Percent	FEMALES Number	FEMALES Percent	BIRTHS BY AGE OF MOTHER AND SEX	DEATHS BOTH SEXES	DEATHS MALES	DEATHS FEMALES	AGE AT LAST BIRTHDAY
0	354092	183233	2.4	170859	2.5		6166	3396	2770	0
1-4	1534298	790578	10.3	743720	10.8		4377	2387	1990	1-4
5-9	2010688	1034644	13.5	976044	14.2		1250	733	517	5-9
10-14	1914591	982310	12.9	932281	13.6		1035	607	428	10-14
15-19	1715897	878808	11.5	837089	12.2	33652	1721	1107	614	15-19
20-24	1131529	579192	7.6	552337	8.0	131472	1572	1052	520	20-24
25-29	943043	484755	6.3	458288	6.7	134219	1506	980	526	25-29
30-34	897345	459165	6.0	438180	6.4	64452	1872	1165	707	30-34
35-39	848090	464948	6.1	383142	5.6	22686	2253	1487	766	35-39
40-44	839807	506260	6.6	333547	4.9	6591	3008	2093	915	40-44
45-49	679694	406801	5.3	272893	4.0	940	3784	2653	1131	45-49
50-54	501576	292149	3.8	209427	3.1	3	4408	3027	1381	50-54
55-59	424817	239950	3.1	184867	2.7		5309	3605	1704	55-59
60-64	293781	153629	2.0	140152	2.0		6730	4319	2411	60-64
65-69	194468	95893	1.3	98575	1.4		6989	4231	2758	65-69
70-74	118368	53190	0.7	65178	0.9		6741	3680	3061	70-74
75-79	61203	24523	0.3	36680	0.5		5393	2585	2808	75-79
80-84	28527	9792	0.1	18735	0.3	203168 M	3725	1496	2229	80-84
85+	13600	3680	0.0	9920	0.1	190847 F	3296	1047	2249	85+
TOTAL	14505414	7643500		6861914		394015	71135	41650	29485	TOTAL

TABLE 1 — DATA

TABLE 2 — MALE LIFE TABLE

x	$_nM_x$	$_nq_x$	l_x	$_nd_x$	$_nL_x$	$_nm_x$	$_na_x$	T_x	$\overset{\circ}{e}_x$	x
0	0.018534	0.018230	100000	1823	98362	0.018534	0.102	6658462	66.585	0
1	0.003019	0.011987	98177	1177	389766	0.003019	1.500	6560100	66.819	1
5	0.000708	0.003536	97000	343	484143	0.000708	2.500	6170334	63.612	5
10	0.000618	0.003088	96657	299	482595	0.000619	2.686	5686191	58.828	10
15	0.001260	0.006328	96359	610	480388	0.001269	2.695	5203596	54.002	15
20	0.001816	0.009073	95749	869	476645	0.001823	2.583	4723208	49.329	20
25	0.002022	0.010078	94880	956	472076	0.002025	2.569	4246563	44.757	25
30	0.002537	0.012620	93924	1185	466764	0.002539	2.591	3774487	40.187	30
35	0.003198	0.015869	92739	1472	460156	0.003198	2.597	3307723	35.667	35
40	0.004134	0.020473	91267	1869	451960	0.004134	2.658	2847566	31.200	40
45	0.006522	0.032360	89398	2893	440288	0.006570	2.683	2395606	26.797	45
50	0.010361	0.050910	86506	4404	422167	0.010432	2.647	1955318	22.603	50
55	0.015024	0.073173	82102	6008	396679	0.015145	2.698	1533151	18.674	55
60	0.028113	0.132966	76094	10118	356683	0.028367	2.649	1136472	14.935	60
65	0.044122	0.200752	65976	13245	297928	0.044457	2.588	779789	11.819	65
70	0.069186	0.297457	52731	15685	224909	0.069740	2.530	481861	9.138	70
75	0.105411	0.417955	37046	15484	145706	0.106265	2.447	256952	6.936	75
80	0.152778	0.546088	21562	11775	76845	0.153230	2.370	111246	5.159	80
85	0.284511	1.000000	9787	9787	34401	0.236684	3.515	34401	3.515	85

TABLE 3 — FEMALE LIFE TABLE

x	$_nM_x$	$_nq_x$	l_x	$_nd_x$	$_nL_x$	$_nm_x$	$_na_x$	T_x	$\overset{\circ}{e}_x$	x
0	0.016212	0.015978	100000	1598	98558	0.016212	0.098	7152423	71.524	0
1	0.002676	0.010632	98402	1046	390993	0.002676	1.500	7053865	71.684	1
5	0.000530	0.002645	97356	258	486136	0.000530	2.500	6662872	68.438	5
10	0.000459	0.002294	97098	223	484956	0.000459	2.592	6176736	63.613	10
15	0.000733	0.003678	96876	356	483536	0.000737	2.636	5691780	58.753	15
20	0.000941	0.004709	96519	455	481502	0.000944	2.589	5208244	53.961	20
25	0.001148	0.005740	96065	551	479012	0.001151	2.619	4726742	49.204	25
30	0.001613	0.008052	95514	769	475727	0.001617	2.607	4247731	44.473	30
35	0.001999	0.009973	94744	945	471467	0.002004	2.613	3772004	39.812	35
40	0.002743	0.013683	93800	1283	465991	0.002754	2.657	3300537	35.187	40
45	0.004144	0.020669	92516	1912	458149	0.004174	2.682	2834546	30.638	45
50	0.006594	0.032646	90604	2958	446055	0.006631	2.646	2376398	26.228	50
55	0.009217	0.045391	87646	3978	429122	0.009271	2.711	1930343	22.024	55
60	0.017203	0.083436	83668	6981	402170	0.017358	2.684	1501221	17.943	60
65	0.027979	0.132255	76687	10142	359572	0.028206	2.647	1099051	14.332	65
70	0.046964	0.212668	66545	14152	298768	0.047367	2.601	739478	11.113	70
75	0.076554	0.324180	52393	16985	219923	0.077230	2.525	440710	8.412	75
80	0.118975	0.456821	35408	16175	135954	0.118975	2.460	220787	6.236	80
85	0.226714	1.000000	19233	19233	84833	0.163520	4.411	84833	4.411	85

TABLE 4 — OBSERVED VITAL RATES AND RATIOS

CRUDE RATES

Per Thousand	BOTH SEXES	MALES	FEMALES
BIRTH RATE	27.16	26.58	27.81
DEATH RATE	4.90	5.45	4.30
RATE OF INCREASE	22.26	21.13	23.52

PERCENT OF POPULATION IN AGE GROUP

	BOTH SEXES	MALES	FEMALES
UNDER 15	40.08	39.13	41.14
15 - 64	57.05	58.42	55.52
65 AND OLDER	2.87	2.45	3.34

RATES STANDARDIZED ON USA 1980

Per Thousand	BOTH SEXES	MALES	FEMALES
BIRTH RATE	33.97		31.99
DEATH RATE	12.69	12.78	12.61
RATE OF INCREASE	21.27		19.38

RATES STANDARDIZED ON MEXICO 1980

Per Thousand	BOTH SEXES	MALES	FEMALES
BIRTH RATE	29.83		29.13
DEATH RATE	5.27	5.91	4.61
RATE OF INCREASE	24.57		24.52

VITAL STATISTICS

GFR x 1000	120.292
TFR	4.003
GRR	1.939
NRR	1.855
μ	27.582
σ^2	31.473
GENERATION	27.225
POP. SEX RATIO	0.898
SEX RATIO AT BIRTH	1.065
DEP. RATIO x 100	75.280

PROJECTED POPULATION

STABLE EQUIVALENT TO ORIGINAL POPULATION

AGE GROUP	1975 BOTH SEXES	1975 MALES	1975 FEMALES	1980 BOTH SEXES	1980 MALES	1980 FEMALES	MALES Number	MALES Percent	FEMALES Number	FEMALES Percent	AGE GROUP	
0-4	2181	1123	1058	2730	1406	1324	1101	14.0	1038	13.5	0-4	
5-9	1874	966	908	2163	1113	1050	975	12.4	920	12.0	5-9	TABLE 5
10-14	2005	1031	974	1869	963	906	867	11.0	819	10.7	10-14	
15-19	1908	978	930	1998	1027	971	771	9.8	729	9.5	15-19	POPULATION
20-24	1706	872	834	1896	970	926	682	8.6	647	8.4	20-24	PROJECTED
25-29	1123	574	549	1693	864	829	603	7.6	575	7.5	25-29	WITH
30-34	934	479	455	1113	567	546	532	6.7	510	6.6	30-34	FIXED
35-39	887	453	434	924	473	451	468	5.9	451	5.9	35-39	AGE-
40-44	836	457	379	874	445	429	410	5.2	398	5.2	40-44	SPECIFIC
45-49	821	493	328	817	445	372	357	4.5	349	4.5	45-49	BIRTH
50-54	656	390	266	792	473	319	305	3.9	303	3.9	50-54	AND
55-59	476	275	201	623	367	256	256	3.2	260	3.4	55-59	DEATH
60-64	389	216	173	436	247	189	206	2.6	218	2.8	60-64	RATES
65-69	253	128	125	335	180	155	153	1.9	174	2.3	65-69	(female
70-74	154	72	82	201	97	104	103	1.3	129	1.7	70-74	dominant,
75-79	82	34	48	107	47	60	60	0.8	85	1.1	75-79	in 000s)
80-84	36	13	23	48	18	30	28	0.4	47	0.6	80-84	
85+	16	4	12	20	6	14	11	0.1	26	0.3	85+	
TOTAL	16337	8558	7779	18639	9708	8931	7888		7678		TOTAL	

VITAL RATES OF PROJECTED POPULATION

VITAL RATES OF STABLE POPULATION

Per Thousand	1975 BOTH SEXES	1975 MALES	1975 FEMALES	1980 BOTH SEXES	1980 MALES	1980 FEMALES	MALES	FEMALES	
BIRTH RATE	30.48	30.01	31.01	33.21	32.88	33.57	30.22	29.19	TABLE 6
DEATH RATE	5.32	6.02	4.56	5.73	6.55	4.84	7.42	6.44	
RATE OF INCREASE	25.16	23.99	26.45	27.48	26.33	28.73		22.75	PROJECTED

AGE STRUCTURE OF PROJECTED POPULATION

STABLE AGE STRUCTURE

	BOTH SEXES	MALES	FEMALES	BOTH SEXES	MALES	FEMALES	MALES	FEMALES	
% UNDER 15	37.09	36.46	37.79	36.28	35.87	36.73	37.31	36.17	VITAL RATES AND RATIOS
% 15-64	59.59	60.59	58.49	59.90	60.54	59.20	58.19	57.84	(female dominant)
% 65 AND OLDER	3.32	2.95	3.72	3.82	3.59	4.07	4.50	5.99	
DEPEND. RATIO x 100	67.81	65.03	70.98	66.94	65.18	68.91	71.86	72.90	

AGE GROUP	FEMALE BIRTH RATES	NET MATERNITY FUNCTION	COEFF. OF MATRIX EQUATION	ORIGINAL MATRIX SUB-DIAGONAL	ORIGINAL MATRIX FIRST ROW	STABLE MATRIX FISHER VALUES	STABLE MATRIX REPRODUCTIVE VALUES	MATRIX PARAMETERS		
0-4	0.0000	0.0000	0.0000	0.99302	0.00000	1.081	988437	λ_1	1.12048	
5-9	0.0000	0.0000	0.0000	0.99757	0.00000	1.219	1190262	λ_2	0.36889+0.85794i	TABLE 7
10-14	0.0000	0.0000	0.0471	0.99707	0.04752	1.370	1276971	λ_4	-0.40070-0.48650i	
15-19	0.0195	0.0942	0.3246	0.99579	0.32868	1.488	1245380	λ_6	-0.48962-0.00000i	LESLIE
20-24	0.1153	0.5551	0.6173	0.99483	0.62764	1.317	727602	r_1	0.02275	MATRIX
25-29	0.1419	0.6795	0.5092	0.99314	0.52042	0.802	367478	r_2	-0.01368+0.23294i	AND ITS
30-34	0.0712	0.3389	0.2371	0.99105	0.24396	0.338	148248	r_4	-0.09232-0.45196i	ANALYSIS
35-39	0.0287	0.1352	0.0899	0.98838	0.09336	0.116	44624	r_6	-0.14282-0.62832i	(females)
40-44	0.0096	0.0446	0.0261	0.98317	0.02744	0.030	9991	c_1	76740	
45-49	0.0017	0.0076	0.0038	0.97360	0.00410	0.004	1083	$2\pi/y$	26.9729	
50-54	0.0000	0.0000	0.0000	0.96204	0.00002	0.000	3	Δ	7.8644	

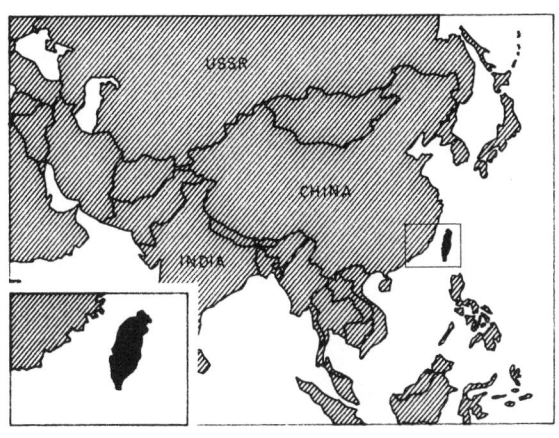

EDUCATION [1984]

% of primary school-age children enrolled:	na
secondary school-age children enrolled:	na
ca. 20-24 year olds in higher education:	na

LABOR FORCE

Average annual labor force growth (%) 1980-85:	na	
% of the 1979 labor force in agriculture:	21	TABLE 8
in industry:	42	
in services:	37	SOCIO-ECONOMIC

GNP & INCOME DISTRIBUTION

GNP per capita (in US Dollars) 1979:	1830	INDICATORS
GNP growth rate (%) 1979:	8.0	
% share of total household income		
Lowest 20% of households:	na	
Highest 10% of households:	na	

HEALTH & NUTRITION

Population per physician 1981:	na
Daily calorie supply per capita 1985:	na

AGE AT LAST BIRTHDAY	ESTIMATED MID-YEAR POPULATION BOTH SEXES	MALES Number	Percent	FEMALES Number	Percent	BIRTHS BY AGE OF MOTHER AND SEX	DEATHS BOTH SEXES	MALES	FEMALES	AGE AT LAST BIRTHDAY
0	331760	171372	2.0	160388	2.1		4598	2572	2026	0
1-4	1455817	749284	8.9	706533	9.3		2550	1430	1120	1-4
5-9	1923005	989135	11.8	933870	12.3		980	610	370	5-9
10-14	2008391	1031734	12.3	976657	12.8		1010	630	380	10-14
15-19	1908412	976658	11.6	931754	12.2	34284	1911	1300	611	15-19
20-24	1712277	875607	10.4	836670	11.0	162642	2224	1539	685	20-24
25-29	1122860	576542	6.9	546318	7.2	117349	1652	1140	512	25-29
30-34	930593	477450	5.7	453143	6.0	37638	1688	1119	569	30-34
35-39	882336	450459	5.4	431877	5.7	11847	2304	1490	814	35-39
40-44	834143	455822	5.4	378321	5.0	3161	3049	2044	1005	40-44
45-49	821771	494258	5.9	327513	4.3	676	4284	3053	1231	45-49
50-54	660109	394891	4.7	265218	3.5		5137	3552	1585	50-54
55-59	473822	273549	3.3	200273	2.6		6037	4185	1852	55-59
60-64	386713	214790	2.6	171923	2.3		6009	4017	1992	60-64
65-69	256245	130317	1.6	125928	1.7		7783	4924	2859	65-69
70-74	156218	73970	0.9	82248	1.1		7901	4422	3479	70-74
75-79	83645	35173	0.4	48472	0.6		6822	3448	3374	75-79
80-84	35786	13200	0.2	22586	0.3	189266 M	4840	2045	2795	80-84
85+	17060	5010	0.1	12050	0.2	178381 F	4282	1443	2839	85+
TOTAL	16000963	8389221		7611742		367647	75061	44963	30098	TOTAL

TABLE 1 DATA

TABLE 2 — MALE LIFE TABLE

x	$_nM_x$	$_nq_x$	l_x	$_nd_x$	$_nL_x$	$_nm_x$	$_na_x$	T_x	$\overset{\circ}{e}_x$	x
0	0.015008	0.014807	100000	1481	98661	0.015008	0.096	6819474	68.195	0
1	0.001908	0.007598	98519	749	392206	0.001908	1.500	6720814	68.218	1
5	0.000617	0.003079	97771	301	488101	0.000617	2.500	6328608	64.729	5
10	0.000611	0.003049	97470	297	486677	0.000611	2.741	5840507	59.921	10
15	0.001331	0.006641	97173	645	484364	0.001332	2.677	5353829	55.096	15
20	0.001758	0.008776	96527	847	480580	0.001763	2.573	4869465	50.447	20
25	0.001977	0.009856	95680	943	476097	0.001981	2.557	4388885	45.870	25
30	0.002344	0.011690	94737	1107	471041	0.002351	2.612	3912787	41.302	30
35	0.003308	0.016430	93630	1538	464497	0.003312	2.627	3441747	36.759	35
40	0.004484	0.022184	92091	2043	455600	0.004484	2.623	2977249	32.329	40
45	0.006177	0.030441	90048	2741	443770	0.006177	2.639	2521650	28.003	45
50	0.008995	0.044375	87307	3874	427570	0.009061	2.686	2077879	23.800	50
55	0.015299	0.074244	83433	6194	402323	0.015396	2.604	1650310	19.780	55
60	0.018702	0.090203	77239	6967	370047	0.018828	2.683	1247987	16.158	60
65	0.037785	0.175054	70271	12301	322326	0.038164	2.640	877939	12.494	65
70	0.059781	0.262740	57970	15231	252739	0.060264	2.563	555614	9.584	70
75	0.098030	0.396335	42739	16939	171152	0.098971	2.488	302875	7.087	75
80	0.154924	0.553825	25800	14289	91756	0.155725	2.393	131723	5.106	80
85	0.288024	1.000000	11511	11511	39967	0.241011	3.472	39967	3.472	85

TABLE 3 — FEMALE LIFE TABLE

x	$_nM_x$	$_nq_x$	l_x	$_nd_x$	$_nL_x$	$_nm_x$	$_na_x$	T_x	$\overset{\circ}{e}_x$	x
0	0.012632	0.012489	100000	1249	98865	0.012632	0.091	7330827	73.308	0
1	0.001585	0.006316	98751	624	393445	0.001585	1.500	7231961	73.234	1
5	0.000396	0.001979	98127	194	490152	0.000396	2.500	6838516	69.690	5
10	0.000389	0.001944	97933	190	489217	0.000389	2.638	6348364	64.823	10
15	0.000656	0.003276	97743	320	487957	0.000657	2.636	5859147	59.944	15
20	0.000819	0.004093	97423	399	486145	0.000820	2.570	5371190	55.133	20
25	0.000937	0.004686	97024	455	484026	0.000939	2.595	4885045	50.349	25
30	0.001256	0.006285	96569	607	481422	0.001261	2.654	4401019	45.574	30
35	0.001885	0.009407	95962	903	477691	0.001890	2.650	3919596	40.845	35
40	0.002656	0.013241	95060	1259	472329	0.002665	2.641	3441906	36.208	40
45	0.003759	0.018715	93801	1756	464923	0.003776	2.675	2969576	31.658	45
50	0.005976	0.029683	92045	2732	453877	0.006020	2.676	2504653	27.211	50
55	0.009247	0.045457	89313	4060	436856	0.009293	2.608	2050776	22.962	55
60	0.011587	0.056759	85253	4839	415150	0.011656	2.703	1613920	18.931	60
65	0.022703	0.108989	80415	8764	382048	0.022940	2.715	1198770	14.907	65
70	0.042299	0.193886	71650	13892	325304	0.042705	2.628	816722	11.399	70
75	0.069607	0.299844	57758	17318	246576	0.070226	2.562	491418	8.508	75
80	0.123749	0.471803	40440	19080	154180	0.123749	2.483	244842	6.054	80
85	0.235602	1.000000	21360	21360	90662	0.174072	4.244	90662	4.244	85

TABLE 4 — OBSERVED VITAL RATES AND RATIOS

CRUDE RATES Per Thousand	BOTH SEXES	MALES	FEMALES	RATES STANDARDIZED ON USA 1980 Per Thousand	BOTH SEXES	MALES	FEMALES	VITAL STATISTICS	
BIRTH RATE	22.98	22.56	23.43	BIRTH RATE	24.54		23.15	GFR x 1000	94.133
DEATH RATE	4.69	5.36	3.95	DEATH RATE	11.69	11.63	11.74	TFR	2.835
RATE OF INCREASE	18.29	17.20	19.48	RATE OF INCREASE	12.85		11.41	GRR	1.376
								NRR	1.332
PERCENT OF POPULATION IN AGE GROUP				RATES STANDARDIZED ON MEXICO 1980				μ	26.617
								σ^2	27.423
								GENERATION	26.468
UNDER 15	35.74	35.06	36.49	BIRTH RATE	21.93		21.45	POP. SEX RATIO	0.907
15 - 64	60.83	61.87	59.68	DEATH RATE	4.66	5.29	4.03	SEX RATIO AT BIRTH	1.061
65 AND OLDER	3.43	3.07	3.83	RATE OF INCREASE	17.27		17.42	DEP. RATIO x 100	64.398

AGE AT LAST BIRTHDAY	ESTIMATED MID-YEAR POPULATION BOTH SEXES	MALES Number	MALES Percent	FEMALES Number	FEMALES Percent	BIRTHS BY AGE OF MOTHER AND SEX	DEATHS BOTH SEXES	DEATHS MALES	DEATHS FEMALES	AGE AT LAST BIRTHDAY	
0	376971	195047	2.1	181924	2.2		4154	2350	1804	0	
1-4	1597348	824619	9.0	772729	9.2		2135	1188	947	1-4	
5-9	1819709	936375	10.2	883334	10.5		843	538	305	5-9	
10-14	1920151	987773	10.7	932378	11.1		771	473	298	10-14	
15-19	2004250	1027423	11.2	976827	11.6	32601	2040	1476	564	15-19	
20-24	1906129	974743	10.6	931386	11.0	168063	2417	1669	748	20-24	
25-29	1692411	865504	9.4	826907	9.8	164968	2137	1464	673	25-29	
30-34	1108065	569624	6.2	538441	6.4	37639	1726	1176	550	30-34	
35-39	920351	472465	5.1	447886	5.3	7168	2094	1436	658	35-39	TABLE 1
40-44	870598	443454	4.8	427144	5.1	1668	2816	1879	937	40-44	
45-49	817426	444672	4.8	372754	4.4	236	4112	2767	1345	45-49	DATA
50-54	798569	477756	5.2	320813	3.8		5993	4147	1846	50-54	
55-59	626746	370065	4.0	256681	3.0		7144	4840	2304	55-59	
60-64	440466	250261	2.7	190205	2.3		7997	5389	2608	60-64	
65-69	343582	185999	2.0	157583	1.9		9931	6331	3600	65-69	
70-74	211631	103359	1.1	108272	1.3		9432	5458	3974	70-74	
75-79	114055	51083	0.6	62972	0.7		8282	4265	4017	75-79	
80-84	51371	20133	0.2	31238	0.4	212399 M	5710	2570	3140	80-84	
85+	22363	7208	0.1	15155	0.2	199494 F	4280	1525	2755	85+	
TOTAL	17642192	9207563		8434629		411893	84014	50941	33073	TOTAL	

x	$_nM_x$	$_nq_x$	l_x	$_nd_x$	$_nL_x$	$_nm_x$	$_na_x$	T_x	$\overset{\circ}{e}_x$	x	
0	0.012048	0.011918	100000	1192	98916	0.012048	0.090	6956616	69.566	0	
1	0.001441	0.005742	98808	567	393815	0.001441	1.500	6857700	69.404	1	
5	0.000575	0.002869	98241	282	490500	0.000575	2.500	6463885	65.796	5	
10	0.000479	0.002392	97959	234	489297	0.000479	2.871	5973385	60.978	10	
15	0.001437	0.007159	97725	700	486998	0.001437	2.677	5484089	56.118	15	
20	0.001712	0.008527	97025	827	483080	0.001713	2.528	4997091	51.503	20	
25	0.001691	0.008427	96198	811	478995	0.001692	2.540	4514010	46.924	25	TABLE 2
30	0.002065	0.010317	95387	984	474605	0.002073	2.631	4035015	42.301	30	
35	0.003039	0.015154	94403	1431	468641	0.003053	2.641	3560410	37.715	35	MALE
40	0.004237	0.021006	92973	1953	460263	0.004243	2.645	3091770	33.255	40	LIFE
45	0.006223	0.030661	91020	2791	448496	0.006223	2.634	2631506	28.911	45	TABLE
50	0.008680	0.042531	88229	3752	432306	0.008680	2.645	2183011	24.743	50	
55	0.013079	0.063917	84476	5399	409802	0.013176	2.670	1750705	20.724	55	
60	0.021534	0.103244	79077	8164	376189	0.021702	2.649	1340903	16.957	60	
65	0.034038	0.158471	70913	11238	327696	0.034293	2.609	964714	13.604	65	
70	0.052806	0.235570	59675	14058	264196	0.053209	2.569	637017	10.675	70	
75	0.083492	0.347897	45617	15870	188478	0.084202	2.504	372821	8.173	75	
80	0.127651	0.483293	29747	14377	111694	0.128714	2.423	184344	6.197	80	
85	0.211570	1.000000	15371	15371	72650	0.145738	4.727	72650	4.727	85	

x	$_nM_x$	$_nq_x$	l_x	$_nd_x$	$_nL_x$	$_nm_x$	$_na_x$	T_x	$\overset{\circ}{e}_x$	x	
0	0.009916	0.009827	100000	983	99103	0.009916	0.087	7463945	74.639	0	
1	0.001226	0.004887	99017	484	394859	0.001226	1.500	7364842	74.379	1	
5	0.000345	0.001725	98533	170	492242	0.000345	2.500	6969983	70.737	5	
10	0.000320	0.001597	98363	157	491448	0.000320	2.650	6477741	65.855	10	
15	0.000577	0.002883	98206	283	490373	0.000577	2.673	5986293	60.956	15	
20	0.000803	0.004009	97923	393	488658	0.000803	2.560	5495920	56.125	20	
25	0.000814	0.004063	97531	396	486684	0.000814	2.555	5007262	51.340	25	TABLE 3
30	0.001021	0.005115	97134	497	484495	0.001025	2.632	4520578	46.539	30	
35	0.001469	0.007351	96638	710	481527	0.001475	2.662	4036082	41.765	35	FEMALE
40	0.002194	0.010949	95927	1050	477217	0.002201	2.697	3554556	37.055	40	LIFE
45	0.003608	0.017970	94877	1705	470457	0.003624	2.696	3077339	32.435	45	TABLE
50	0.005754	0.028531	93172	2658	459693	0.005783	2.680	2606882	27.979	50	
55	0.008976	0.044262	90514	4006	443203	0.009039	2.663	2147189	23.722	55	
60	0.013712	0.066878	86507	5785	419072	0.013805	2.673	1703986	19.698	60	
65	0.022845	0.109065	80722	8804	382943	0.022990	2.653	1284913	15.918	65	
70	0.036704	0.170134	71918	12236	330627	0.037007	2.633	901970	12.542	70	
75	0.063790	0.278299	59682	16609	257952	0.064390	2.564	571343	9.573	75	
80	0.100519	0.402700	43073	17345	171867	0.100923	2.492	313391	7.276	80	
85	0.181788	1.000000	25727	25727	141524	0.112840	5.501	141524	5.501	85	

CRUDE RATES

Per Thousand	BOTH SEXES	MALES	FEMALES
BIRTH RATE	23.35	23.07	23.65
DEATH RATE	4.76	5.53	3.92
RATE OF INCREASE	18.58	17.54	19.73

PERCENT OF POPULATION IN AGE GROUP

UNDER 15	32.39	31.97	32.85
15 - 64	63.40	64.03	62.71
65 AND OLDER	4.21	3.99	4.45

RATES STANDARDIZED ON USA 1980

Per Thousand	BOTH SEXES	MALES	FEMALES
BIRTH RATE	21.99		20.72
DEATH RATE	10.20	10.18	10.22
RATE OF INCREASE	11.79		10.50

RATES STANDARDIZED ON MEXICO 1980

BIRTH RATE	19.75		19.28
DEATH RATE	4.11	4.67	3.54
RATE OF INCREASE	15.64		15.74

VITAL STATISTICS

GFR x 1000	91.100	TABLE 4
TFR	2.515	
GRR	1.218	OBSERVED
NRR	1.186	VITAL
μ	26.168	RATES
σ^2	22.665	AND
GENERATION	26.094	RATIOS
POP. SEX RATIO	0.916	
SEX RATIO AT BIRTH	1.065	
DEP. RATIO x 100	57.731	

AGE AT LAST BIRTHDAY	ESTIMATED MID-YEAR POPULATION BOTH SEXES	MALES Number	MALES Percent	FEMALES Number	FEMALES Percent	BIRTHS BY AGE OF MOTHER AND SEX	DEATHS BOTH SEXES	DEATHS MALES	DEATHS FEMALES	AGE AT LAST BIRTHDAY
0	325083	168196	1.7	156887	1.7		2397	1318	1079	0
1-4	1566914	807667	8.1	759247	8.3		1527	861	666	1-4
5-9	2009575	1034818	10.4	974757	10.6		807	514	293	5-9
10-14	1815035	932719	9.4	882316	9.6		699	447	252	10-14
15-19	1912802	980840	9.9	931962	10.1	18199	1542	1121	421	15-19
20-24	1998967	1023940	10.3	975027	10.6	125768	2187	1552	635	20-24
25-29	1884245	962374	9.7	921871	10.0	145446	2225	1563	662	25-29
30-34	1673025	854427	8.6	818598	8.9	46040	2375	1621	754	30-34
35-39	1095542	561769	5.7	533773	5.8	6507	2174	1492	682	35-39
40-44	908134	464215	4.7	443919	4.8	896	2647	1835	812	40-44
45-49	853665	432019	4.3	421646	4.6	103	3712	2475	1237	45-49
50-54	795078	428865	4.3	366213	4.0		5264	3555	1709	50-54
55-59	764266	453213	4.6	311053	3.4		7611	5301	2310	55-59
60-64	585572	341120	3.4	244452	2.7		9357	6400	2957	60-64
65-69	395149	220087	2.2	175062	1.9		10306	6719	3587	65-69
70-74	288336	151934	1.5	136402	1.5		12377	7498	4879	70-74
75-79	158285	73905	0.7	84380	0.9		10887	5769	5118	75-79
80-84	72759	31069	0.3	41690	0.5	177006 M	7798	3648	4150	80-84
85+	32851	11666	0.1	21185	0.2	165953 F	6025	2283	3742	85+
TOTAL	19135283	9934843		9200440		342959	91917	55972	35945	TOTAL

TABLE 1 DATA

TABLE 2 — MALE LIFE TABLE

x	nM_x	nq_x	l_x	nd_x	nL_x	nm_x	na_x	T_x	$\overset{\circ}{e}_x$	x
0	0.007836	0.007780	100000	778	99287	0.007836	0.083	7109782	71.098	0
1	0.001066	0.004253	99222	422	395833	0.001066	1.500	7010495	70.655	1
5	0.000497	0.002480	98800	245	493387	0.000497	2.500	6614662	66.950	5
10	0.000479	0.002397	98555	236	492250	0.000480	2.778	6121274	62.110	10
15	0.001143	0.005699	98319	560	490297	0.001143	2.687	5629024	57.253	15
20	0.001516	0.007551	97758	738	486993	0.001516	2.563	5138727	52.566	20
25	0.001624	0.008091	97020	785	483175	0.001625	2.546	4651733	47.946	25
30	0.001897	0.009476	96235	912	478997	0.001904	2.610	4168558	43.316	30
35	0.002656	0.013273	95323	1265	473649	0.002671	2.655	3689562	38.706	35
40	0.003953	0.019674	94058	1851	465945	0.003972	2.651	3215912	34.191	40
45	0.005729	0.028305	92208	2610	454887	0.005738	2.643	2749967	29.824	45
50	0.008289	0.040648	89598	3642	439359	0.008289	2.631	2295081	25.615	50
55	0.011696	0.056931	85956	4894	418315	0.011698	2.657	1855721	21.589	55
60	0.018762	0.090542	81062	7340	388145	0.018909	2.661	1437406	17.732	60
65	0.030529	0.143408	73723	10572	343575	0.030772	2.632	1049260	14.233	65
70	0.049350	0.222049	63150	14022	281861	0.049750	2.583	705686	11.175	70
75	0.078060	0.329108	49128	16168	205415	0.078711	2.512	423825	8.627	75
80	0.117416	0.454069	32959	14966	126464	0.118341	2.439	218410	6.627	80
85	0.195697	1.000000	17994	17994	91946	0.127866	5.110	91946	5.110	85

TABLE 3 — FEMALE LIFE TABLE

x	nM_x	nq_x	l_x	nd_x	nL_x	nm_x	na_x	T_x	$\overset{\circ}{e}_x$	x
0	0.006878	0.006834	100000	683	99372	0.006878	0.082	7601695	76.017	0
1	0.000877	0.003501	99317	348	396397	0.000877	1.500	7502323	75.539	1
5	0.000301	0.001502	98969	149	494473	0.000301	2.500	7105926	71.800	5
10	0.000286	0.001428	98820	141	493764	0.000286	2.609	6611453	66.904	10
15	0.000452	0.002256	98679	223	492876	0.000452	2.667	6117689	61.996	15
20	0.000651	0.003251	98456	320	491509	0.000651	2.584	5624813	57.130	20
25	0.000718	0.003586	98136	352	489829	0.000718	2.577	5133304	52.308	25
30	0.000921	0.004612	97784	451	487851	0.000925	2.625	4643474	47.487	30
35	0.001278	0.006401	97333	623	485200	0.001284	2.645	4155623	42.695	35
40	0.001829	0.009150	96710	885	481502	0.001838	2.683	3670423	37.953	40
45	0.002934	0.014618	95826	1401	475897	0.002944	2.694	3188921	33.278	45
50	0.004667	0.023182	94425	2189	467065	0.004687	2.689	2713024	28.732	50
55	0.007426	0.036704	92236	3385	453357	0.007467	2.690	2245959	24.350	55
60	0.012096	0.059313	88850	5270	432088	0.012196	2.692	1792602	20.176	60
65	0.020490	0.098577	83580	8239	398814	0.020659	2.683	1360514	16.278	65
70	0.035769	0.166117	75341	12515	347189	0.036048	2.642	961700	12.765	70
75	0.060654	0.266452	62826	16740	273510	0.061205	2.574	614511	9.781	75
80	0.099544	0.399751	46086	18423	184390	0.099912	2.501	341001	7.399	80
85	0.176634	1.000000	27663	27663	156611	0.107456	5.661	156611	5.661	85

TABLE 4 — OBSERVED VITAL RATES AND RATIOS

CRUDE RATES

Per Thousand	BOTH SEXES	MALES	FEMALES
BIRTH RATE	17.92	17.82	18.04
DEATH RATE	4.80	5.63	3.91
RATE OF INCREASE	13.12	12.18	14.13

PERCENT OF POPULATION IN AGE GROUP

	BOTH SEXES	MALES	FEMALES
UNDER 15	29.87	29.63	30.14
15 - 64	65.17	65.45	64.87
65 AND OLDER	4.95	4.92	4.99

RATES STANDARDIZED ON USA 1980

Per Thousand	BOTH SEXES	MALES	FEMALES
BIRTH RATE	16.45		15.48
DEATH RATE	9.40	9.25	9.54
RATE OF INCREASE	7.05		5.94

RATES STANDARDIZED ON MEXICO 1980

	BOTH SEXES	MALES	FEMALES
BIRTH RATE	14.63		14.27
DEATH RATE	3.64	4.14	3.14
RATE OF INCREASE	10.98		11.12

VITAL STATISTICS

GFR x 1000	67.956
TFR	1.885
GRR	0.912
NRR	0.894
μ	26.417
σ^2	20.967
GENERATION	26.462
POP. SEX RATIO	0.926
SEX RATIO AT BIRTH	1.067
DEP. RATIO x 100	53.435

PROJECTED POPULATION

AGE GROUP	1990 BOTH SEXES	1990 MALES	1990 FEMALES	1995 BOTH SEXES	1995 MALES	1995 FEMALES
0-4	1724	889	835	1731	893	838
5-9	1886	972	914	1719	886	833
10-14	2005	1032	973	1882	970	912
15-19	1810	929	881	2000	1028	972
20-24	1903	974	929	1801	923	878
25-29	1988	1016	972	1893	967	926
30-34	1872	954	918	1975	1007	968
35-39	1659	845	814	1856	943	913
40-44	1083	553	530	1639	831	808
45-49	892	453	439	1064	540	524
50-54	831	417	414	869	438	431
55-59	763	408	355	799	397	402
60-64	717	421	296	718	379	339
65-69	528	302	226	646	372	274
70-74	333	181	152	444	248	196
75-79	218	111	107	252	132	120
80-84	103	46	57	140	68	72
85+	58	23	35	81	33	48
TOTAL	20373	10526	9847	21509	11055	10454

STABLE EQUIVALENT TO ORIGINAL POPULATION

	MALES Number	MALES Percent	FEMALES Number	FEMALES Percent	AGE GROUP	
	948	6.0	890	5.5	0-4	
	965	6.1	907	5.6	5-9	TABLE 5
	984	6.2	925	5.8	10-14	
	1001	6.3	943	5.9	15-19	POPULATION
	1015	6.4	961	6.0	20-24	PROJECTED
	1029	6.5	978	6.1	25-29	WITH
	1042	6.6	995	6.2	30-34	FIXED
	1052	6.6	1011	6.3	35-39	AGE-
	1057	6.7	1024	6.4	40-44	SPECIFIC
	1054	6.6	1034	6.4	45-49	BIRTH
	1040	6.5	1037	6.5	50-54	AND
	1011	6.4	1028	6.4	55-59	DEATH
	959	6.0	1000	6.2	60-64	RATES
	867	5.5	943	5.9	65-69	(female
	726	4.6	839	5.2	70-74	dominant,
	541	3.4	675	4.2	75-79	in 000s)
	340	2.1	465	2.9	80-84	
	252	1.6	403	2.5	85+	
	15883		16058		TOTAL	

VITAL RATES OF PROJECTED POPULATION

Per Thousand	1990 BOTH SEXES	1990 MALES	1990 FEMALES	1995 BOTH SEXES	1995 MALES	1995 FEMALES
BIRTH RATE	17.33	17.32	17.35	16.07	16.14	16.00
DEATH RATE	5.56	6.52	4.53	6.28	7.38	5.13
RATE OF INCREASE	11.77	10.79	12.82	9.79	8.76	10.87

VITAL RATES OF STABLE POPULATION

Per Thousand	MALES	FEMALES	
BIRTH RATE	11.93	11.07	TABLE 6
DEATH RATE	16.03	15.30	PROJECTED
RATE OF INCREASE		-4.23	VITAL RATES

AGE STRUCTURE OF PROJECTED POPULATION

	1990 BOTH SEXES	1990 MALES	1990 FEMALES	1995 BOTH SEXES	1995 MALES	1995 FEMALES
% UNDER 15	27.57	27.50	27.64	24.79	24.87	24.71
% 15-64	66.35	66.22	66.49	67.94	67.42	68.49
% 65 AND OLDER	6.08	6.28	5.87	7.27	7.71	6.80
DEPEND. RATIO x 100	50.71	51.01	50.39	47.20	48.33	46.01

STABLE AGE STRUCTURE

	MALES	FEMALES	
% UNDER 15	18.24	16.96	AND RATIOS
% 15-64	64.60	62.34	(female
% 65 AND OLDER	17.16	20.70	dominant)
DEPEND. RATIO x 100	54.80	60.41	

AGE GROUP	FEMALE BIRTH RATES	NET MATERNITY FUNCTION	COEFF. OF MATRIX EQUATION	ORIGINAL MATRIX SUB-DIAGONAL	ORIGINAL MATRIX FIRST ROW	STABLE MATRIX FISHER VALUES	STABLE MATRIX REPRODUCTIVE VALUES	MATRIX PARAMETERS		
0-4	0.0000	0.0000	0.0000	0.99738	0.00000	0.998	914220	λ_1	0.97905	
5-9	0.0000	0.0000	0.0000	0.99857	0.00000	0.980	954843	λ_2	0.33283+0.78232i	TABLE 7
10-14	0.0000	0.0000	0.0233	0.99820	0.02338	0.960	847402	λ_4	-0.36878-0.47473i	
15-19	0.0094	0.0466	0.1767	0.99723	0.17771	0.919	856128	λ_6	-0.48819+0.00000i	LESLIE
20-24	0.0624	0.3068	0.3404	0.99658	0.34332	0.724	705972	r_1	-0.00423	MATRIX
25-29	0.0763	0.3740	0.2534	0.99596	0.25643	0.368	338827	r_2	-0.03246+0.23371i	AND ITS
30-34	0.0272	0.1328	0.0807	0.99457	0.08200	0.104	85435	r_4	-0.10179-0.44625i	ANALYSIS
35-39	0.0059	0.0286	0.0167	0.99238	0.01702	0.020	10920	r_6	-0.14341+0.62832i	(females)
40-44	0.0010	0.0047	0.0026	0.98836	0.00271	0.003	1360	c_1	160580	
45-49	0.0001	0.0006	0.0003	0.98144	0.00029	0.000	126	$2\pi/y$	26.8844	
50-54	0.0000	0.0000	0.0000	0.00000	0.00000	0.000	0	Δ	28.6883	

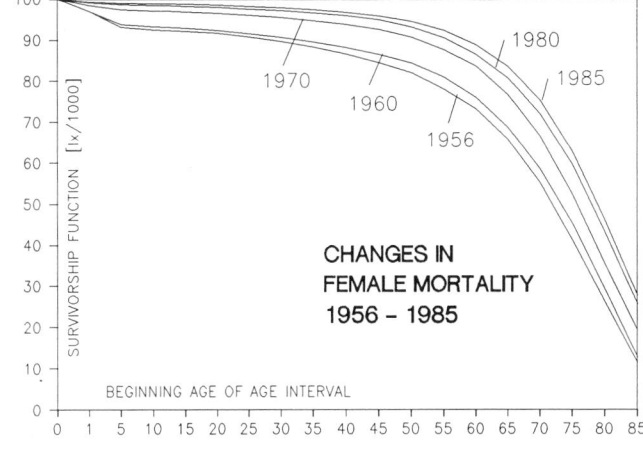

CHANGES IN FEMALE MORTALITY 1956 – 1985

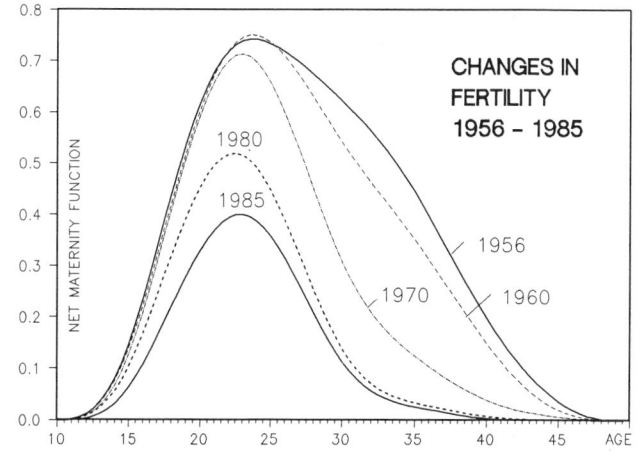

CHANGES IN FERTILITY 1956 – 1985

TABLE 1 — DATA

AGE AT LAST BIRTHDAY	ESTIMATED MID-YEAR POPULATION BOTH SEXES	MALES Number	MALES Percent	FEMALES Number	FEMALES Percent	BIRTHS BY AGE OF MOTHER AND SEX	DEATHS BOTH SEXES	DEATHS MALES	DEATHS FEMALES	AGE AT LAST BIRTHDAY
0	11169	5721	1.8	5448	1.7		245	145	100	0
1-4	45873	23513	7.6	22360	7.1		9	6	3	1-4
5-9	47331	23947	7.7	23384	7.4		10	9	1	5-9
10-14	49839	25191	8.1	24648	7.8		11	3	8	10-14
15-19	59234	30478	9.8	28756	9.1	1011	24	18	6	15-19
20-24	64255	32655	10.5	31600	10.0	4887	34	20	14	20-24
25-29	56099	28923	9.3	27176	8.6	4191	7	1	6	25-29
30-34	51098	25502	8.2	25596	8.1	2090	23	6	17	30-34
35-39	34801	17105	5.5	17696	5.6	531	53	44	9	35-39
40-44	39190	19282	6.2	19908	6.3	76	73	39	34	40-44
45-49	28847	13995	4.5	14852	4.7	2	123	83	40	45-49
50-54	29484	13684	4.4	15800	5.0	4	142	71	71	50-54
55-59	24142	11818	3.8	12324	3.9		272	172	100	55-59
60-64	23841	10885	3.5	12956	4.1		354	178	176	60-64
65-69	21955	10263	3.3	11692	3.7		589	353	236	65-69
70-74	17654	8348	2.7	9306	2.9		823	456	367	70-74
75-79	11857	5449	1.8	6408	2.0		992	498	494	75-79
80-84	6491	2754	0.9	3737	1.2	6710 M	923	416	507	80-84
85+	3840	1487	0.5	2353	0.7	6082 F	1107	445	662	85+
TOTAL	627000	311000		316000		12792	5814	2963	2851	TOTAL

TABLE 2 — MALE LIFE TABLE

x	$_nM_x$	$_nq_x$	l_x	$_nd_x$	$_nL_x$	$_nm_x$	$_na_x$	T_x	$\mathring{e}_x$	x
0	0.025345	0.024788	100000	2479	97802	0.025345	0.113	7086300	70.863	0
1	0.000255	0.001020	97521	99	389836	0.000255	1.500	6988498	71.661	1
5	0.000376	0.001877	97422	183	486651	0.000376	2.500	6598662	67.733	5
10	0.000119	0.000595	97239	58	486071	0.000119	2.873	6112011	62.856	10
15	0.000591	0.002949	97181	287	485238	0.000591	2.673	5625940	57.891	15
20	0.000612	0.003057	96894	296	483675	0.000612	2.310	5140702	53.055	20
25	0.000035	0.000166	96598	16	482914	0.000033	0.223	4657027	48.210	25
30	0.000235	0.001255	96582	121	482863	0.000251	4.606	4174112	43.218	30
35	0.002572	0.012867	96461	1241	479377	0.002589	2.641	3691249	38.267	35
40	0.002023	0.010114	95220	963	474010	0.002032	2.831	3211872	33.731	40
45	0.005931	0.029379	94257	2769	464651	0.005960	2.605	2737862	29.047	45
50	0.005189	0.025742	91488	2355	452283	0.005207	2.811	2273211	24.847	50
55	0.014554	0.070539	89133	6287	430814	0.014594	2.638	1820928	20.429	55
60	0.016353	0.078784	82845	6527	399129	0.016353	2.687	1390114	16.780	60
65	0.034395	0.159135	76318	12145	353096	0.034395	2.654	990985	12.985	65
70	0.054624	0.241314	64173	15486	283411	0.054641	2.581	637889	9.940	70
75	0.091393	0.373531	48688	18186	198200	0.091757	2.513	354477	7.281	75
80	0.151053	0.543545	30501	16579	109755	0.151053	2.421	156278	5.124	80
85	0.299260	1.000000	13922	13922	46523	0.256340	3.342	46523	3.342	85

TABLE 3 — FEMALE LIFE TABLE

x	$_nM_x$	$_nq_x$	l_x	$_nd_x$	$_nL_x$	$_nm_x$	$_na_x$	T_x	$\mathring{e}_x$	x
0	0.018355	0.018057	100000	1806	98377	0.018355	0.101	7454751	74.548	0
1	0.000134	0.000536	98194	53	392645	0.000134	1.500	7356374	74.917	1
5	0.000043	0.000214	98142	21	490655	0.000043	2.500	6963728	70.956	5
10	0.000325	0.001622	98121	159	490222	0.000325	2.606	6473073	65.971	10
15	0.000209	0.001043	97961	102	489564	0.000209	2.617	5982851	61.073	15
20	0.000443	0.002213	97859	217	488757	0.000443	2.506	5493287	56.135	20
25	0.000221	0.001105	97643	108	487967	0.000221	2.709	5004530	51.253	25
30	0.000664	0.003330	97535	325	486892	0.000667	2.590	4516563	46.307	30
35	0.000509	0.002562	97210	249	485533	0.000513	2.921	4029671	41.453	35
40	0.001708	0.008547	96961	829	482950	0.001716	2.762	3544139	36.552	40
45	0.002693	0.013439	96132	1292	477700	0.002705	2.708	3061188	31.844	45
50	0.004494	0.022320	94840	2117	469412	0.004510	2.738	2583488	27.240	50
55	0.008114	0.039965	92723	3706	455133	0.008142	2.710	2114076	22.800	55
60	0.013584	0.065824	89018	5860	431341	0.013584	2.654	1658944	18.636	60
65	0.020185	0.096581	83158	8032	397330	0.020214	2.701	1227603	14.762	65
70	0.039437	0.181340	75127	13623	344077	0.039594	2.684	830273	11.052	70
75	0.077091	0.325891	61503	20043	258931	0.077408	2.576	486195	7.905	75
80	0.135670	0.504962	41460	20936	154313	0.135670	2.469	227264	5.482	80
85	0.281343	1.000000	20524	20524	72951	0.232138	3.554	72951	3.554	85

TABLE 4 — OBSERVED VITAL RATES AND RATIOS

CRUDE RATES

Per Thousand	BOTH SEXES	MALES	FEMALES
BIRTH RATE	20.40	21.58	19.25
DEATH RATE	9.27	9.53	9.02
RATE OF INCREASE	11.13	12.05	10.22

RATES STANDARDIZED ON USA 1980

Per Thousand	BOTH SEXES	MALES	FEMALES
BIRTH RATE	19.83		18.33
DEATH RATE	11.21	10.27	12.11
RATE OF INCREASE	8.61		6.23

VITAL STATISTICS

GFR x 1000	77.254
TFR	2.299
GRR	1.093
NRR	1.067
μ	26.726
σ^2	28.708
GENERATION	26.691
POP. SEX RATIO	1.016
SEX RATIO AT BIRTH	1.103
DEP. RATIO x 100	52.558

PERCENT OF POPULATION IN AGE GROUP

	BOTH SEXES	MALES	FEMALES
UNDER 15	24.60	25.20	24.00
15 - 64	65.55	65.70	65.40
65 AND OLDER	9.86	9.10	10.60

RATES STANDARDIZED ON MEXICO 1980

	BOTH SEXES	MALES	FEMALES
BIRTH RATE	17.75		17.01
DEATH RATE	4.07	4.41	3.73
RATE OF INCREASE	13.68		13.28

PROJECTED POPULATION

AGE GROUP	1985			1990			STABLE EQUIVALENT TO ORIGINAL POPULATION				AGE GROUP	
							MALES		FEMALES			
	BOTH SEXES	MALES	FEMALES	BOTH SEXES	MALES	FEMALES	Number	Percent	Number	Percent		
0-4	63	33	30	63	33	30	30	7.5	28	7.2	0-4	
5-9	57	29	28	63	33	30	30	7.4	27	7.1	5-9	TABLE 5
10-14	47	24	23	57	29	28	30	7.3	27	7.0	10-14	
15-19	50	25	25	47	24	23	29	7.2	27	6.9	15-19	POPULATION
20-24	59	30	29	50	25	25	29	7.1	26	6.8	20-24	PROJECTED
25-29	65	33	32	59	30	29	28	7.0	26	6.7	25-29	WITH
30-34	56	29	27	64	33	31	28	6.9	26	6.6	30-34	FIXED
35-39	51	25	26	56	29	27	27	6.8	25	6.5	35-39	AGE-
40-44	35	17	18	50	25	25	27	6.6	25	6.4	40-44	SPECIFIC
45-49	39	19	20	34	17	17	26	6.4	24	6.3	45-49	BIRTH
50-54	29	14	15	37	18	19	25	6.1	23	6.1	50-54	AND
55-59	28	13	15	27	13	14	24	5.8	23	5.8	55-59	DEATH
60-64	23	11	12	27	12	15	22	5.3	21	5.5	60-64	RATES
65-69	22	10	12	21	10	11	19	4.6	19	5.0	65-69	(female
70-74	18	8	10	18	8	10	15	3.7	16	4.2	70-74	dominant,
75-79	13	6	7	14	6	8	10	2.5	12	3.2	75-79	in 000s)
80-84	7	3	4	7	3	4	6	1.4	7	1.9	80-84	
85+	3	1	2	3	1	2	2	0.6	3	0.9	85+	
TOTAL	665	330	335	697	349	348	407		385		TOTAL	

VITAL RATES OF PROJECTED POPULATION / VITAL RATES OF STABLE POPULATION

Per Thousand	1985			1990			STABLE	MALES	FEMALES	TABLE 6
	BOTH SEXES	MALES	FEMALES	BOTH SEXES	MALES	FEMALES	Per Thousand			
BIRTH RATE	19.96	21.02	18.91	17.96	18.85	17.08	BIRTH RATE	15.43	14.72	PROJECTED
DEATH RATE	8.76	9.08	8.43	8.65	8.84	8.47	DEATH RATE	12.98	12.29	VITAL
RATE OF INCREASE	11.20	11.93	10.47	9.31	10.01	8.61	RATE OF INCREASE		2.43	RATES AND RATIOS

AGE STRUCTURE OF PROJECTED POPULATION / STABLE AGE STRUCTURE

	BOTH SEXES	MALES	FEMALES	BOTH SEXES	MALES	FEMALES		MALES	FEMALES	(female dominant)
% UNDER 15	25.34	26.17	24.51	26.31	27.33	25.28	% UNDER 15	22.13	21.28	
% 15-64	65.23	65.38	65.07	64.75	64.73	64.77	% 15-64	65.07	63.63	
% 65 AND OLDER	9.44	8.45	10.42	8.94	7.94	9.95	% 65 AND OLDER	12.80	15.10	
DEPEND. RATIO x 100	53.32	52.95	53.68	54.44	54.49	54.39	DEPEND. RATIO x 100	53.68	57.17	

MATRIX

AGE GROUP	FEMALE BIRTH RATES	NET MATERNITY FUNCTION	COEFF. OF MATRIX EQUATION	ORIGINAL MATRIX SUB-DIAGONAL	FIRST ROW	STABLE MATRIX FISHER VALUES	REPRODUCTIVE VALUES	MATRIX PARAMETERS		
0-4	0.0000	0.0000	0.0000	0.99925	0.00000	1.024	28489	λ_1	1.01221	
5-9	0.0000	0.0000	0.0000	0.99912	0.00000	1.038	24267	λ_2	0.34295+0.76814i	TABLE 7
10-14	0.0000	0.0000	0.0409	0.99866	0.04098	1.051	25914	λ_4	-0.40090-0.36609i	
15-19	0.0167	0.0818	0.2206	0.99835	0.22127	1.024	29435	λ_6	-0.12653-0.47760i	LESLIE
20-24	0.0735	0.3594	0.3586	0.99838	0.36025	0.811	25620	r_1	0.00243	MATRIX
25-29	0.0733	0.3578	0.2734	0.99780	0.27512	0.452	12292	r_2	-0.03458+0.23018i	AND ITS
30-34	0.0388	0.1890	0.1291	0.99721	0.13024	0.176	4515	r_4	-0.12216-0.48031i	ANALYSIS
35-39	0.0143	0.0693	0.0390	0.99468	0.03946	0.045	801	r_6	-0.14101-0.36595i	(females)
40-44	0.0018	0.0088	0.0045	0.98913	0.00461	0.005	107	c_1	3862	
45-49	0.0001	0.0003	0.0004	0.98265	0.00045	0.001	11	$2\pi/\gamma$	27.2972	
50-54	0.0001	0.0006	0.0003	0.96958	0.00030	0.000	5	Δ	11.4634	

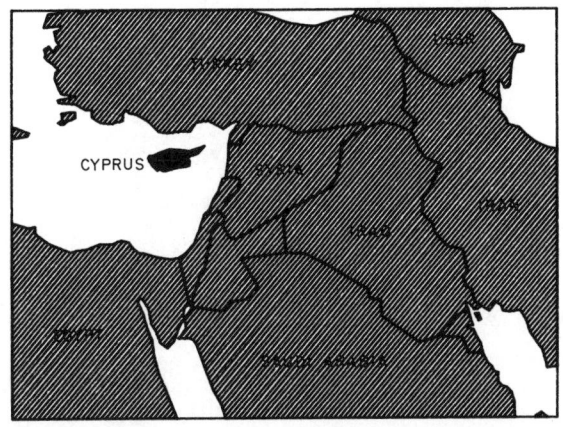

EDUCATION [1984]

% of primary school-age children enrolled:	na
secondary school-age children enrolled:	na
ca. 20-24 year olds in higher education:	na

LABOR FORCE

Average annual labor force growth (%) 1980-85:	1.3	
% of the 1980 labor force in agriculture:	26	TABLE 8
in industry and services:	74	SOCIO-ECONOMIC INDICATORS

GNP & INCOME DISTRIBUTION

GNP per capita (in US Dollars) 1985:	3790
GNP average annual growth rate (%) 1965-85:	na
% share of total household income	
Lowest 20% of households:	na
Highest 10% of households:	na

HEALTH & NUTRITION

Population per physician 1981:	na
Daily calorie supply per capita 1985:	na

TABLE 1 — DATA

AGE AT LAST BIRTHDAY	ESTIMATED MID-YEAR POPULATION BOTH SEXES	MALES Number	MALES Percent	FEMALES Number	FEMALES Percent	BIRTHS BY AGE OF MOTHER AND SEX	DEATHS BOTH SEXES	DEATHS MALES	DEATHS FEMALES	AGE AT LAST BIRTHDAY
0	12800	6600	2.0	6200	1.9		156	82	74	0
1-4	51300	26700	8.1	24600	7.4		21	12	9	1-4
5-9	54400	28100	8.5	26300	7.9		19	12	7	5-9
10-14	49900	25400	7.7	24500	7.3		12	8	4	10-14
15-19	53200	27300	8.2	25900	7.8	887	30	20	10	15-19
20-24	58300	29900	9.0	28400	8.5	4523	36	25	11	20-24
25-29	59500	30700	9.3	28800	8.6	4423	34	20	14	25-29
30-34	49700	25000	7.5	24700	7.4	2251	48	33	15	30-34
35-39	48500	23900	7.2	24600	7.4	809	56	41	15	35-39
40-44	37800	18400	5.6	19400	5.8	95	67	45	22	40-44
45-49	37400	18500	5.6	18900	5.7	4	116	72	44	45-49
50-54	29700	14200	4.3	15500	4.6		143	84	59	50-54
55-59	28200	13300	4.0	14900	4.5		213	135	78	55-59
60-64	23900	11200	3.4	12700	3.8		323	196	127	60-64
65-69	22900	10600	3.2	12300	3.7		456	244	212	65-69
70-74	21300	9700	2.9	11600	3.5		780	374	406	70-74
75-79	13713	6476	2.0	7237	2.2		997	527	470	75-79
80-84	8288	3600	1.1	4688	1.4	6822 M	997	474	523	80-84
85+	4399	1724	0.5	2675	0.8	6170 F	1149	464	685	85+
TOTAL	665200	331300		333900		12992	5653	2868	2785	TOTAL

TABLE 2 — MALE LIFE TABLE

x	nM_x	nq_x	l_x	nd_x	nL_x	nm_x	na_x	T_x	$\overset{\circ}{e}_x$	x
0	0.012424	0.012286	100000	1229	98883	0.012424	0.091	7301849	73.018	0
1	0.000449	0.001796	98771	177	394642	0.000449	1.500	7202966	72.926	1
5	0.000427	0.002133	98594	210	492445	0.000427	2.500	6808323	69.054	5
10	0.000315	0.001574	98384	155	491563	0.000315	2.700	6315879	64.196	10
15	0.000733	0.003657	98229	359	490299	0.000733	2.647	5824316	59.293	15
20	0.000836	0.004172	97870	408	488319	0.000836	2.479	5334017	54.501	20
25	0.000651	0.003258	97461	317	486562	0.000653	2.653	4845698	49.719	25
30	0.001320	0.006603	97144	641	484222	0.001325	2.666	4359136	44.873	30
35	0.001715	0.008573	96502	827	480554	0.001722	2.633	3874914	40.154	35
40	0.002446	0.012211	95675	1168	475664	0.002456	2.679	3394360	35.478	40
45	0.003892	0.019358	94507	1830	468284	0.003907	2.677	2918696	30.883	45
50	0.005915	0.029340	92677	2719	457141	0.005948	2.703	2450413	26.440	50
55	0.010150	0.049781	89958	4478	439527	0.010189	2.708	1993271	22.158	55
60	0.017500	0.084130	85480	7191	410269	0.017529	2.618	1553744	18.177	60
65	0.023019	0.109130	78289	8544	371158	0.023019	2.626	1143475	14.606	65
70	0.038557	0.177049	69745	12348	320154	0.038570	2.686	772317	11.073	70
75	0.081377	0.341177	57397	19582	239339	0.081819	2.567	452163	7.878	75
80	0.131667	0.493021	37814	18643	141594	0.131667	2.453	212824	5.628	80
85	0.269142	1.000000	19171	19171	71230	0.216350	3.716	71230	3.716	85

TABLE 3 — FEMALE LIFE TABLE

x	nM_x	nq_x	l_x	nd_x	nL_x	nm_x	na_x	T_x	$\overset{\circ}{e}_x$	x
0	0.011935	0.011807	100000	1181	98926	0.011935	0.090	7644220	76.442	0
1	0.000366	0.001462	98819	144	394916	0.000366	1.500	7545294	76.354	1
5	0.000266	0.001330	98675	131	493046	0.000266	2.500	7150378	72.464	5
10	0.000163	0.000816	98544	80	492529	0.000163	2.652	6657332	67.557	10
15	0.000386	0.001929	98463	190	491864	0.000386	2.620	6164803	62.610	15
20	0.000387	0.001935	98273	190	490901	0.000387	2.553	5672939	57.726	20
25	0.000486	0.002430	98083	238	489842	0.000487	2.593	5182038	52.833	25
30	0.000607	0.003034	97845	297	488494	0.000608	2.542	4692197	47.956	30
35	0.000610	0.003054	97548	298	487048	0.000612	2.680	4203703	43.094	35
40	0.001134	0.005696	97250	554	485038	0.001142	2.811	3716654	38.218	40
45	0.002328	0.011634	96696	1125	480929	0.002339	2.732	3231617	33.420	45
50	0.003806	0.018926	95571	1809	473606	0.003819	2.651	2750687	28.782	50
55	0.005235	0.025957	93762	2434	463283	0.005253	2.729	2277081	24.286	55
60	0.010000	0.049035	91329	4478	446441	0.010031	2.722	1813798	19.860	60
65	0.017236	0.082954	86850	7205	417999	0.017236	2.744	1367357	15.744	65
70	0.035000	0.162272	79646	12924	368341	0.035088	2.688	949358	11.920	70
75	0.064944	0.282334	66721	18838	288179	0.065368	2.588	581017	8.708	75
80	0.111561	0.436980	47884	20924	187558	0.111561	2.521	292837	6.116	80
85	0.256075	1.000000	26959	26959	105280	0.199439	3.905	105280	3.905	85

TABLE 4 — OBSERVED VITAL RATES AND RATIOS

CRUDE RATES

Per Thousand	BOTH SEXES	MALES	FEMALES
BIRTH RATE	19.53	20.59	18.48
DEATH RATE	8.50	8.66	8.34
RATE OF INCREASE	11.03	11.93	10.14

PERCENT OF POPULATION IN AGE GROUP

	BOTH SEXES	MALES	FEMALES
UNDER 15	25.32	26.20	24.44
15 - 64	64.07	64.11	64.03
65 AND OLDER	10.61	9.69	11.53

RATES STANDARDIZED ON USA 1980

Per Thousand	BOTH SEXES	MALES	FEMALES
BIRTH RATE	20.46		18.89
DEATH RATE	9.52	8.65	10.34
RATE OF INCREASE	10.94		8.55

RATES STANDARDIZED ON MEXICO 1980

	BOTH SEXES	MALES	FEMALES
BIRTH RATE	18.26		17.48
DEATH RATE	3.40	3.66	3.13
RATE OF INCREASE	14.86		14.35

VITAL STATISTICS

GFR x 1000	76.110
TFR	2.381
GRR	1.131
NRR	1.108
μ	26.904
σ^2	29.349
GENERATION	26.849
POP. SEX RATIO	1.008
SEX RATIO AT BIRTH	1.106
DEP. RATIO x 100	56.077

PROJECTED POPULATION

AGE GROUP	1990 BOTH SEXES	1990 MALES	1990 FEMALES	1995 BOTH SEXES	1995 MALES	1995 FEMALES
0-4	63	33	30	63	33	30
5-9	64	33	31	63	33	30
10-14	54	28	26	64	33	31
15-19	49	25	24	54	28	26
20-24	53	27	26	49	25	24
25-29	58	30	28	53	27	26
30-34	60	31	29	58	30	28
35-39	50	25	25	59	30	29
40-44	48	24	24	50	25	25
45-49	37	18	19	47	23	24
50-54	37	18	19	37	18	19
55-59	29	14	15	35	17	18
60-64	26	12	14	28	13	15
65-69	22	10	12	24	11	13
70-74	20	9	11	19	9	10
75-79	16	7	9	15	7	8
80-84	9	4	5	10	4	6
85+	5	2	3	5	2	3
TOTAL	700	350	350	733	368	365

STABLE EQUIVALENT TO ORIGINAL POPULATION

MALES Number	MALES Percent	FEMALES Number	FEMALES Percent	AGE GROUP	
31	7.7	28	7.4	0-4	
31	7.6	28	7.3	5-9	TABLE 5
30	7.4	27	7.1	10-14	
30	7.2	27	7.0	15-19	POPULATION
29	7.1	26	6.8	20-24	PROJECTED
28	6.9	26	6.7	25-29	WITH
28	6.8	25	6.5	30-34	FIXED
27	6.6	25	6.4	35-39	AGE-
26	6.4	24	6.3	40-44	SPECIFIC
25	6.2	23	6.1	45-49	BIRTH
24	5.9	23	5.9	50-54	AND
23	5.6	22	5.6	55-59	DEATH
21	5.1	20	5.3	60-64	RATES
18	4.5	19	4.9	65-69	(female
16	3.8	16	4.2	70-74	dominant,
11	2.8	12	3.3	75-79	in 000s)
7	1.6	8	2.1	80-84	
3	0.8	4	1.1	85+	
408		383		TOTAL	

VITAL RATES OF PROJECTED POPULATION

Per Thousand	1990 BOTH SEXES	1990 MALES	1990 FEMALES	1995 BOTH SEXES	1995 MALES	1995 FEMALES
BIRTH RATE	18.35	19.26	17.43	16.89	17.67	16.10
DEATH RATE	8.45	8.62	8.28	8.45	8.57	8.33
RATE OF INCREASE	9.90	10.65	9.15	8.44	9.10	7.78

VITAL RATES OF STABLE POPULATION

Per Thousand	MALES	FEMALES	
BIRTH RATE	15.79	15.16	TABLE 6
DEATH RATE	11.96	11.34	PROJECTED
RATE OF INCREASE		3.81	VITAL RATES

AGE STRUCTURE OF PROJECTED POPULATION

	BOTH SEXES	MALES	FEMALES	BOTH SEXES	MALES	FEMALES
% UNDER 15	25.98	27.04	24.93	25.88	26.97	24.79
% 15-64	63.84	63.78	63.90	64.04	64.06	64.01
% 65 AND OLDER	10.18	9.18	11.17	10.08	8.97	11.21
DEPEND. RATIO x 100	56.64	56.78	56.50	56.16	56.09	56.23

STABLE AGE STRUCTURE

	MALES	FEMALES	
% UNDER 15	22.68	21.79	AND RATIOS
% 15-64	63.71	62.61	(female
% 65 AND OLDER	13.61	15.60	dominant)
DEPEND. RATIO x 100	56.96	59.73	

MATRIX PARAMETERS (TABLE 7)

AGE GROUP	FEMALE BIRTH RATES	NET MATERNITY FUNCTION	COEFF. OF MATRIX EQUATION	ORIGINAL MATRIX SUB-DIAGONAL	ORIGINAL MATRIX FIRST ROW	STABLE MATRIX FISHER VALUES	STABLE MATRIX REPRODUCTIVE VALUES
0-4	0.0000	0.0000	0.0000	0.99839	0.00000	1.022	31483
5-9	0.0000	0.0000	0.0000	0.99895	0.00000	1.044	27445
10-14	0.0000	0.0000	0.0400	0.99865	0.04011	1.065	26086
15-19	0.0163	0.0800	0.2256	0.99804	0.22655	1.046	27083
20-24	0.0756	0.3713	0.3643	0.99784	0.36646	0.836	23738
25-29	0.0729	0.3573	0.2843	0.99725	0.28666	0.478	13778
30-34	0.0433	0.2114	0.1437	0.99704	0.14532	0.195	4820
35-39	0.0156	0.0761	0.0437	0.99587	0.04428	0.051	1243
40-44	0.0023	0.0113	0.0059	0.99153	0.00599	0.006	121
45-49	0.0001	0.0005	0.0002	0.98477	0.00025	0.000	5
50-54	0.0000	0.0000	0.0000	0.00000	0.00000	0.000	0

	MATRIX PARAMETERS	
λ_1	1.01926	
λ_2	0.35051+0.76824i	TABLE 7
λ_4	-0.40366+0.31222i	
λ_6	-0.13215+0.48179i	LESLIE
r_1	0.00381	MATRIX
r_2	-0.03382+0.22855i	AND ITS
r_4	-0.13455+0.49665i	ANALYSIS
r_6	-0.13879+0.36770i	(females)
c_1	3840	
$2\pi/y$	27.4913	
Δ	8.8697	

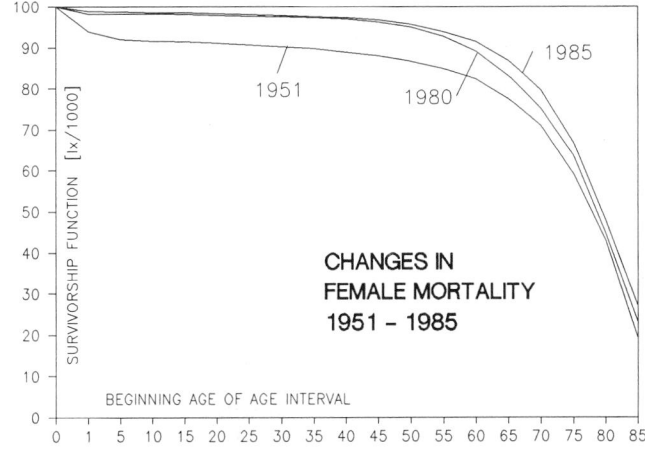

CHANGES IN FEMALE MORTALITY 1951 – 1985

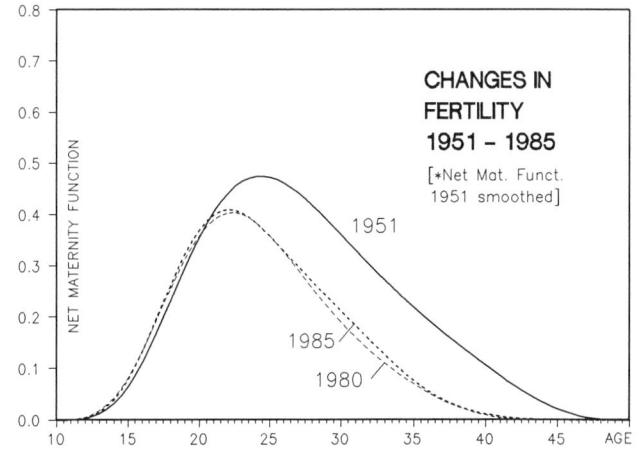

CHANGES IN FERTILITY 1951 – 1985

[*Net Mat. Funct. 1951 smoothed]

Table 1 — DATA

AGE AT LAST BIRTHDAY	ESTIMATED MID-YEAR POPULATION BOTH SEXES	MALES Number	MALES Percent	FEMALES Number	FEMALES Percent	BIRTHS BY AGE OF MOTHER AND SEX	DEATHS BOTH SEXES	DEATHS MALES	DEATHS FEMALES	AGE AT LAST BIRTHDAY
0	76500	39500	2.0	37000	1.9		1519	890	629	0
1-4	344900	177500	8.8	167400	8.6		407	200	207	1-4
5-9	531400	271000	13.5	260400	13.3		237	142	95	5-9
10-14	516600	264500	13.2	252100	12.9		216	134	82	10-14
15-19	421400	215500	10.7	205900	10.5	3744	301	194	107	15-19
20-24	305800	158100	7.9	147700	7.6	22937	324	205	119	20-24
25-29	199800	109900	5.5	89900	4.6	20982	253	181	72	25-29
30-34	215400	116800	5.8	98600	5.0	16643	376	254	122	30-34
35-39	255300	133900	6.7	121400	6.2	10570	559	362	197	35-39
40-44	252100	130700	6.5	121400	6.2	3759	887	600	287	40-44
45-49	218800	113100	5.6	105700	5.4	497	1172	830	342	45-49
50-54	188400	96800	4.8	91600	4.7		1534	1045	489	50-54
55-59	150000	73300	3.7	76700	3.9		2157	1434	723	55-59
60-64	110900	49700	2.5	61200	3.1		2270	1464	806	60-64
65-69	72400	26700	1.3	45700	2.3		2211	1260	951	65-69
70-74	51000	16900	0.8	34100	1.7		2187	1045	1142	70-74
75-79	27200	7100	0.4	20100	1.0		1822	714	1108	75-79
80-84	14100	3600	0.2	10500	0.5	40922 M	1353	458	895	80-84
85+	7000	1700	0.1	5300	0.3	38210 F	978	257	721	85+
TOTAL	3959000	2006300		1952700		79132	20763	11669	9094	TOTAL

Table 2 — MALE LIFE TABLE

x	$_nM_x$	$_nq_x$	l_x	$_nd_x$	$_nL_x$	$_nm_x$	$_na_x$	T_x	$\mathring{e}_x$	x
0	0.022532	0.022088	100000	2209	98030	0.022532	0.108	6730510	67.305	0
1	0.001127	0.004494	97791	440	390066	0.001127	1.500	6632480	67.823	1
5	0.000524	0.002616	97352	255	486122	0.000524	2.500	6242414	64.122	5
10	0.000507	0.002535	97097	246	484908	0.000508	2.655	5756292	59.284	10
15	0.000900	0.004521	96851	438	483239	0.000906	2.681	5271384	54.428	15
20	0.001297	0.006491	96413	626	480574	0.001302	2.617	4788145	49.663	20
25	0.001647	0.008232	95787	788	477049	0.001653	2.606	4307571	44.970	25
30	0.002175	0.010817	94999	1028	472524	0.002175	2.596	3830522	40.322	30
35	0.002704	0.013433	93971	1262	466926	0.002704	2.678	3357999	35.734	35
40	0.004591	0.022749	92709	2109	458692	0.004598	2.699	2891073	31.184	40
45	0.007339	0.036180	90600	3278	445328	0.007361	2.660	2432381	26.848	45
50	0.010795	0.052945	87322	4623	425993	0.010853	2.704	1987053	22.755	50
55	0.019563	0.094267	82699	7796	395203	0.019726	2.654	1561060	18.876	55
60	0.029457	0.138541	74903	10377	349809	0.029665	2.619	1165858	15.565	60
65	0.047191	0.212883	64526	13736	288975	0.047535	2.550	816048	12.647	65
70	0.061834	0.269227	50789	13674	220020	0.062148	2.519	527074	10.378	70
75	0.100563	0.403403	37115	14972	147488	0.101517	2.456	307054	8.273	75
80	0.127222	0.474831	22143	10514	82644	0.127222	2.330	159566	7.206	80
85	0.151176	1.000000	11629	11629	76922	0.083238	6.615	76922	6.615	85

Table 3 — FEMALE LIFE TABLE

x	$_nM_x$	$_nq_x$	l_x	$_nd_x$	$_nL_x$	$_nm_x$	$_na_x$	T_x	$\mathring{e}_x$	x
0	0.017000	0.016744	100000	1674	98491	0.017000	0.099	7529161	75.292	0
1	0.001237	0.004931	98326	485	392091	0.001237	1.500	7430670	75.572	1
5	0.000365	0.001822	97841	178	488758	0.000365	2.500	7038579	71.939	5
10	0.000325	0.001627	97662	159	487931	0.000326	2.600	6549821	67.066	10
15	0.000520	0.002610	97504	254	486930	0.000523	2.691	6061890	62.171	15
20	0.000806	0.004031	97249	392	485293	0.000808	2.571	5574960	57.327	20
25	0.000801	0.004004	96857	388	483358	0.000802	2.609	5089666	52.548	25
30	0.001237	0.006169	96469	595	480939	0.001237	2.636	4606308	47.749	30
35	0.001623	0.008083	95874	775	477543	0.001623	2.641	4125369	43.029	35
40	0.002364	0.011765	95099	1119	472853	0.002366	2.638	3647826	38.358	40
45	0.003236	0.016113	93980	1514	466394	0.003247	2.683	3174973	33.783	45
50	0.005338	0.026510	92466	2451	456756	0.005367	2.726	2708579	29.293	50
55	0.009426	0.046334	90015	4171	440285	0.009473	2.653	2251824	25.016	55
60	0.013170	0.064223	85844	5513	416239	0.013245	2.645	1811539	21.103	60
65	0.020810	0.099843	80331	8020	382809	0.020952	2.650	1395299	17.369	65
70	0.033490	0.156270	72310	11300	334743	0.033757	2.628	1012490	14.002	70
75	0.055124	0.244843	61010	14938	268738	0.055586	2.569	677747	11.109	75
80	0.085238	0.352623	46072	16246	189759	0.085615	2.501	409009	8.878	80
85	0.136038	1.000000	29826	29826	219250	0.068397	7.351	219250	7.351	85

Table 4 — OBSERVED VITAL RATES AND RATIOS

CRUDE RATES

Per Thousand	BOTH SEXES	MALES	FEMALES
BIRTH RATE	19.99	20.40	19.57
DEATH RATE	5.24	5.82	4.66
RATE OF INCREASE	14.74	14.58	14.91

PERCENT OF POPULATION IN AGE GROUP

	BOTH SEXES	MALES	FEMALES
UNDER 15	37.12	37.51	36.71
15 - 64	58.55	59.70	57.36
65 AND OLDER	4.34	2.79	5.93

RATES STANDARDIZED ON USA 1980

Per Thousand	BOTH SEXES	MALES	FEMALES
BIRTH RATE	28.54		26.80
DEATH RATE	10.32	11.67	9.04
RATE OF INCREASE	18.22		17.76

RATES STANDARDIZED ON MEXICO 1980

	BOTH SEXES	MALES	FEMALES
BIRTH RATE	24.29		23.64
DEATH RATE	4.46	5.43	3.47
RATE OF INCREASE	19.83		20.17

VITAL STATISTICS

GFR x 1000	88.852
TFR	3.492
GRR	1.686
NRR	1.625
μ	29.341
σ^2	35.610
GENERATION	29.043
POP. SEX RATIO	0.973
SEX RATIO AT BIRTH	1.071
DEP. RATIO x 100	70.801

PROJECTED POPULATION

AGE GROUP	1975 BOTH SEXES	MALES	FEMALES	1980 BOTH SEXES	MALES	FEMALES
0-4	435	224	211	553	285	268
5-9	420	216	204	434	224	210
10-14	530	270	260	419	216	203
15-19	516	264	252	528	269	259
20-24	419	214	205	513	262	251
25-29	304	157	147	417	213	204
30-34	198	109	89	301	155	146
35-39	213	115	98	197	108	89
40-44	252	132	120	210	113	97
45-49	247	127	120	247	128	119
50-54	212	108	104	238	121	117
55-59	178	90	88	200	100	100
60-64	138	65	73	162	79	83
65-69	97	41	56	121	54	67
70-74	60	20	40	80	31	49
75-79	38	11	27	46	14	32
80-84	18	4	14	25	6	19
85+	15	3	12	20	4	16
TOTAL	4290	2170	2120	4711	2382	2329

STABLE EQUIVALENT TO ORIGINAL POPULATION

MALES Number	Percent	FEMALES Number	Percent	AGE GROUP	
255	*11.9*	239	*11.3*	0-4	
233	*10.9*	219	*10.3*	5-9	TABLE 5
214	*10.0*	201	*9.5*	10-14	
196	*9.2*	184	*8.7*	15-19	POPULATION
179	*8.4*	169	*8.0*	20-24	PROJECTED
164	*7.7*	155	*7.3*	25-29	WITH
149	*7.0*	142	*6.7*	30-34	FIXED
135	*6.4*	129	*6.1*	35-39	AGE-
122	*5.7*	118	*5.6*	40-44	SPECIFIC
109	*5.1*	107	*5.0*	45-49	BIRTH
96	*4.5*	96	*4.5*	50-54	AND
82	*3.8*	85	*4.0*	55-59	DEATH
67	*3.1*	74	*3.5*	60-64	RATES
51	*2.4*	63	*3.0*	65-69	(female
36	*1.7*	50	*2.4*	70-74	dominant,
22	*1.0*	37	*1.8*	75-79	in 000s)
11	*0.5*	24	*1.1*	80-84	
10	*0.5*	26	*1.2*	85+	
2131		2118		TOTAL	

VITAL RATES OF PROJECTED POPULATION

Per Thousand	1975 BOTH SEXES	MALES	FEMALES	1980 BOTH SEXES	MALES	FEMALES
BIRTH RATE	23.00	23.50	22.48	27.02	27.64	26.39
DEATH RATE	6.06	6.64	5.47	6.69	7.34	6.02
RATE OF INCREASE	16.94	16.86	17.01	20.34	20.30	20.37

AGE STRUCTURE OF PROJECTED POPULATION

% UNDER 15	32.28	32.74	31.81	29.82	30.40	29.22
% 15-64	62.36	63.58	61.12	63.98	65.04	62.90
% 65 AND OLDER	5.36	3.69	7.07	6.20	4.56	7.88
DEPEND. RATIO x 100	60.35	57.29	63.62	56.29	53.75	58.98

VITAL RATES OF STABLE POPULATION

Per Thousand	MALES	FEMALES	
BIRTH RATE	25.50	23.94	TABLE 6
DEATH RATE	8.70	7.19	PROJECTED
RATE OF INCREASE		16.75	VITAL RATES

STABLE AGE STRUCTURE

	MALES	FEMALES	
% UNDER 15	32.93	31.09	AND RATIOS
% 15-64	61.02	59.46	(female
% 65 AND OLDER	6.06	9.45	dominant)
DEPEND. RATIO x 100	63.89	68.19	

AGE GROUP	FEMALE BIRTH RATES	NET MATERNITY FUNCTION	COEFF. OF MATRIX EQUATION	ORIGINAL MATRIX SUB-DIAGONAL	FIRST ROW	STABLE MATRIX FISHER VALUES	REPRODUCTIVE VALUES	MATRIX PARAMETERS		
0-4	0.0000	0.0000	0.0000	0.99628	0.00000	1.063	217197	λ_1	1.08738	
5-9	0.0000	0.0000	0.0000	0.99831	0.00000	1.160	302003	λ_2	0.43420+0.80154i	TABLE 7
10-14	0.0000	0.0000	0.0214	0.99795	0.02149	1.263	318463	λ_4	-0.35227+0.46802i	
15-19	0.0088	0.0428	0.2033	0.99664	0.20485	1.354	278697	λ_6	-0.03675+0.51017i	LESLIE
20-24	0.0750	0.3639	0.4543	0.99601	0.45927	1.258	185862	r_1	0.01675	MATRIX
25-29	0.1127	0.5447	0.4684	0.99500	0.47536	0.884	79456	r_2	-0.01851+0.21487i	AND ITS
30-34	0.0815	0.3920	0.2964	0.99294	0.30232	0.458	45181	r_4	-0.10696+0.44320i	ANALYSIS
35-39	0.0420	0.2008	0.1357	0.99018	0.13944	0.178	21643	r_6	-0.13408+0.32854i	(females)
40-44	0.0150	0.0707	0.0406	0.98634	0.04217	0.046	5602	c_1	21188	
45-49	0.0023	0.0106	0.0053	0.97933	0.00557	0.005	575	$2\pi/y$	29.2419	
50-54	0.0000	0.0000	0.0000	0.00000	0.00000	0.000	0	Δ	9.5576	

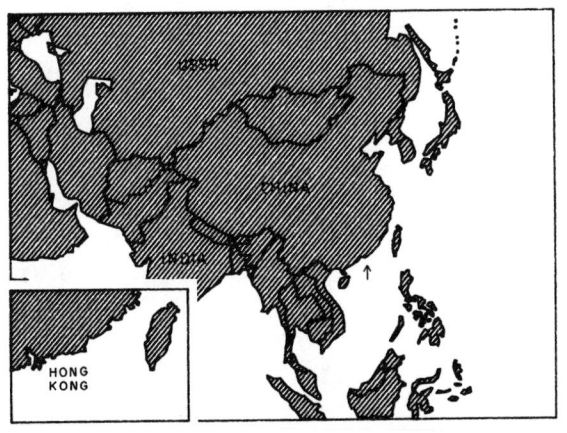

EDUCATION [1984]

% of primary school-age children enrolled:	105
secondary school-age children enrolled:	69
ca. 20-24 year olds in higher education:	13

LABOR FORCE

Average annual labor force growth (%) 1980-85:	2.5
% of the 1980 labor force in agriculture:	2
in industry:	51
in services:	47

TABLE 8

SOCIO-ECONOMIC INDICATORS

GNP & INCOME DISTRIBUTION

GNP per capita (in US Dollars) 1985:	6230
GNP average annual growth rate (%) 1965-85:	6.1
% share of total household income 1980	
Lowest 20% of households:	5.4
Highest 10% of households:	31.3

HEALTH & NUTRITION

Population per physician 1981:	1300
Daily calorie supply per capita 1985:	2698

TABLE 1 — DATA

AGE AT LAST BIRTHDAY	ESTIMATED MID-YEAR POPULATION — BOTH SEXES	MALES Number	MALES Percent	FEMALES Number	FEMALES Percent	BIRTHS BY AGE OF MOTHER AND SEX	DEATHS BOTH SEXES	DEATHS MALES	DEATHS FEMALES	AGE AT LAST BIRTHDAY
0	82600	42800	1.6	39800	1.6		956	542	414	0
1-4	320500	165800	6.4	154700	6.4		200	107	93	1-4
5-9	417400	215400	8.3	202000	8.4		100	68	32	5-9
10-14	459300	236300	9.1	223000	9.2		117	71	46	10-14
15-19	580500	299100	11.5	281400	11.6	3477	238	154	84	15-19
20-24	574900	301800	11.6	273100	11.3	24060	333	227	106	20-24
25-29	473000	252600	9.7	220400	9.1	35209	344	244	100	25-29
30-34	379000	208800	8.0	170200	7.0	17632	377	260	117	30-34
35-39	229400	131000	5.0	98400	4.1	3849	335	227	108	35-39
40-44	259700	144800	5.6	114900	4.8	960	592	392	200	40-44
45-49	268800	144800	5.6	124000	5.1	103	1059	741	318	45-49
50-54	259100	136700	5.2	122400	5.1		1584	1075	509	50-54
55-59	216000	110600	4.2	105400	4.4		2255	1519	736	55-59
60-64	180300	89900	3.4	90400	3.7		2717	1774	943	60-64
65-69	136900	63900	2.4	73000	3.0		3452	2163	1289	65-69
70-74	89700	36000	1.4	53700	2.2		3170	1691	1479	70-74
75-79	54400	17700	0.7	36700	1.5		2881	1337	1544	75-79
80-84	27300	7400	0.3	19900	0.8	44101 M	2178	764	1414	80-84
85+	15600	3100	0.1	12500	0.5	41189 F	2120	501	1619	85+
TOTAL	5024400	2608500		2415900		85290	25008	13857	11151	TOTAL

TABLE 2 — MALE LIFE TABLE

x	$_nM_x$	$_nq_x$	l_x	$_nd_x$	$_nL_x$	$_nm_x$	$_na_x$	T_x	$\overset{\circ}{e}_x$	x
0	0.012664	0.012520	100000	1252	98863	0.012664	0.092	7214871	72.149	0
1	0.000645	0.002577	98748	255	394356	0.000645	1.500	7116008	72.062	1
5	0.000316	0.001577	98494	155	492079	0.000316	2.500	6721652	68.245	5
10	0.000300	0.001501	98338	148	491342	0.000300	2.637	6229573	63.348	10
15	0.000515	0.002571	98191	252	490368	0.000515	2.682	5738231	58.440	15
20	0.000752	0.003759	97938	368	488816	0.000753	2.624	5247863	53.583	20
25	0.000966	0.004832	97570	471	486721	0.000969	2.605	4759047	48.776	25
30	0.001245	0.006233	97099	605	484056	0.001250	2.626	4272327	44.000	30
35	0.001733	0.008680	96493	838	480515	0.001743	2.670	3788271	39.259	35
40	0.002707	0.013454	95656	1287	475384	0.002707	2.751	3307756	34.580	40
45	0.005117	0.025289	94369	2387	466352	0.005117	2.699	2832372	30.014	45
50	0.007864	0.038726	91982	3562	451740	0.007885	2.706	2366020	25.723	50
55	0.013734	0.066818	88420	5908	428218	0.013797	2.650	1914280	21.650	55
60	0.019733	0.094791	82512	7821	394229	0.019840	2.656	1486062	18.010	60
65	0.033850	0.157650	74691	11775	345164	0.034114	2.597	1091833	14.618	65
70	0.046972	0.211897	62916	13332	282103	0.047258	2.564	746669	11.868	70
75	0.075537	0.320074	49584	15871	208345	0.076175	2.506	464566	9.369	75
80	0.103243	0.409771	33714	13815	133095	0.103796	2.432	256221	7.600	80
85	0.161613	1.000000	19899	19899	123126	0.092443	6.188	123126	6.188	85

TABLE 3 — FEMALE LIFE TABLE

x	$_nM_x$	$_nq_x$	l_x	$_nd_x$	$_nL_x$	$_nm_x$	$_na_x$	T_x	$\overset{\circ}{e}_x$	x
0	0.010402	0.010304	100000	1030	99060	0.010402	0.088	7872723	78.727	0
1	0.000601	0.002401	98970	238	395284	0.000601	1.500	7773663	78.546	1
5	0.000158	0.000792	98732	78	493464	0.000158	2.500	7378379	74.731	5
10	0.000206	0.001031	98654	102	493029	0.000206	2.641	6884915	69.789	10
15	0.000299	0.001491	98552	147	492411	0.000298	2.626	6391886	64.858	15
20	0.000388	0.001941	98405	191	491564	0.000389	2.583	5899474	59.951	20
25	0.000454	0.002272	98214	223	490543	0.000455	2.637	5407911	55.062	25
30	0.000687	0.003452	97991	338	489175	0.000692	2.694	4917368	50.182	30
35	0.001098	0.005511	97653	538	487023	0.001105	2.695	4428193	45.346	35
40	0.001741	0.008668	97114	842	483611	0.001741	2.671	3941171	40.583	40
45	0.002565	0.012747	96273	1227	478528	0.002565	2.690	3457559	35.914	45
50	0.004158	0.020627	95045	1960	470739	0.004165	2.711	2979031	31.343	50
55	0.006983	0.034474	93085	3209	457952	0.007007	2.671	2508292	26.946	55
60	0.010431	0.051139	89876	4596	438736	0.010476	2.684	2050340	22.813	60
65	0.017658	0.085259	85280	7271	409378	0.017761	2.659	1611604	18.898	65
70	0.027542	0.130067	78009	10146	365884	0.027731	2.619	1202226	15.411	70
75	0.042071	0.192399	67863	13057	308022	0.042389	2.603	836342	12.324	75
80	0.071055	0.303473	54806	16632	233587	0.071203	2.568	528320	9.640	80
85	0.129520	1.000000	38174	38174	294733	0.062836	7.721	294733	7.721	85

TABLE 4 — OBSERVED VITAL RATES AND RATIOS

CRUDE RATES

Per Thousand	BOTH SEXES	MALES	FEMALES
BIRTH RATE	16.98	16.91	17.05
DEATH RATE	4.98	5.31	4.62
RATE OF INCREASE	12.00	11.59	12.43

PERCENT OF POPULATION IN AGE GROUP

UNDER 15	25.47	25.31	25.64
15 - 64	68.08	69.78	66.25
65 AND OLDER	6.45	4.91	8.10

RATES STANDARDIZED ON USA 1980

Per Thousand	BOTH SEXES	MALES	FEMALES
BIRTH RATE	17.16		16.12
DEATH RATE	7.99	8.67	7.36
RATE OF INCREASE	9.17		8.76

RATES STANDARDIZED ON MEXICO 1980

	BOTH SEXES	MALES	FEMALES
BIRTH RATE	14.65		14.26
DEATH RATE	3.18	3.78	2.57
RATE OF INCREASE	11.47		11.69

VITAL STATISTICS

GFR x 1000	66.508
TFR	2.061
GRR	0.995
NRR	0.975
μ	28.664
σ^2	28.019
GENERATION	28.676
POP. SEX RATIO	0.926
SEX RATIO AT BIRTH	1.071
DEP. RATIO x 100	46.882

PROJECTED POPULATION

STABLE EQUIVALENT TO ORIGINAL POPULATION

AGE GROUP	1985 BOTH SEXES	1985 MALES	1985 FEMALES	1990 BOTH SEXES	1990 MALES	1990 FEMALES	MALES Number	MALES Percent	FEMALES Number	FEMALES Percent	AGE GROUP	
0-4	461	238	223	509	263	246	241	6.6	226	6.1	0-4	
5-9	402	208	194	459	237	222	242	6.6	227	6.1	5-9	TABLE 5
10-14	417	215	202	402	208	194	243	6.7	227	6.1	10-14	
15-19	459	236	223	417	215	202	243	6.7	228	6.1	15-19	POPULATION
20-24	579	298	281	457	235	222	243	6.7	229	6.1	20-24	PROJECTED
25-29	574	301	273	577	297	280	244	6.7	229	6.2	25-29	WITH
30-34	471	251	220	571	299	272	243	6.7	230	6.2	30-34	FIXED
35-39	376	207	169	468	249	219	243	6.7	230	6.2	35-39	AGE-
40-44	228	130	98	373	205	168	241	6.6	229	6.1	40-44	SPECIFIC
45-49	256	142	114	224	127	97	237	6.5	228	6.1	45-49	BIRTH
50-54	262	140	122	250	138	112	231	6.3	225	6.0	50-54	AND
55-59	249	130	119	252	133	119	220	6.0	220	5.9	55-59	DEATH
60-64	203	102	101	233	119	114	203	5.6	211	5.7	60-64	RATES
65-69	163	79	84	183	89	94	179	4.9	198	5.3	65-69	(female
70-74	117	52	65	139	64	75	147	4.0	178	4.8	70-74	dominant,
75-79	72	27	45	94	39	55	109	3.0	150	4.0	75-79	in 000s)
80-84	39	11	28	51	17	34	70	1.9	115	3.1	80-84	
85+	32	7	25	45	10	35	65	1.8	145	3.9	85+	
TOTAL	5360	2774	2586	5704	2944	2760	3644		3725		TOTAL	

VITAL RATES OF PROJECTED POPULATION

VITAL RATES OF STABLE POPULATION

Per Thousand	1985 BOTH SEXES	1985 MALES	1985 FEMALES	1990 BOTH SEXES	1990 MALES	1990 FEMALES	STABLE MALES	STABLE FEMALES	
BIRTH RATE	18.91	18.90	18.93	18.41	18.45	18.38	13.40	12.25	TABLE 6
DEATH RATE	5.99	6.33	5.63	6.78	7.20	6.33	14.21	13.13	PROJECTED
RATE OF INCREASE	12.92	12.57	13.30	11.63	11.25	12.05		-.88	VITAL RATES

AGE STRUCTURE OF PROJECTED POPULATION

STABLE AGE STRUCTURE

	1985 BOTH SEXES	1985 MALES	1985 FEMALES	1990 BOTH SEXES	1990 MALES	1990 FEMALES	STABLE MALES	STABLE FEMALES	AND RATIOS
% UNDER 15	23.89	23.84	23.93	24.03	24.06	24.00	19.92	18.26	(female
% 15-64	68.21	69.82	66.48	66.97	68.49	65.35	64.45	60.63	dominant)
% 65 AND OLDER	7.90	6.33	9.58	9.00	7.45	10.65	15.63	21.11	
DEPEND. RATIO x 100	46.60	43.22	50.41	49.32	46.01	53.02	55.15	64.94	

AGE GROUP	FEMALE BIRTH RATES	NET MATERNITY FUNCTION	COEFF. OF MATRIX EQUATION	ORIGINAL MATRIX SUB-DIAGONAL	ORIGINAL MATRIX FIRST ROW	STABLE MATRIX FISHER VALUES	STABLE MATRIX REPRODUCTIVE VALUES	MATRIX PARAMETERS		
0-4	0.0000	0.0000	0.0000	0.99822	0.00000	1.009	196294	λ_1	0.99562	
5-9	0.0000	0.0000	0.0000	0.99912	0.00000	1.007	203332	λ_2	0.41183+0.75907i	TABLE 7
10-14	0.0000	0.0000	0.0147	0.99875	0.01473	1.003	223684	λ_4	-0.26963+0.49840i	
15-19	0.0060	0.0294	0.1193	0.99828	0.11973	0.985	277191	λ_6	-0.45701-0.00000i	LESLIE
20-24	0.0425	0.2091	0.2938	0.99792	0.29545	0.861	235242	r_1	-0.00088	MATRIX
25-29	0.0771	0.3784	0.3116	0.99721	0.31400	0.561	123553	r_2	-0.02933+0.21474i	AND ITS
30-34	0.0500	0.2447	0.1684	0.99560	0.17014	0.242	41173	r_4	-0.11360+0.41334i	ANALYSIS
35-39	0.0189	0.0920	0.0558	0.99300	0.05659	0.069	6833	r_6	-0.15661-0.62832i	(females)
40-44	0.0040	0.0195	0.0107	0.98949	0.01095	0.012	1391	c_1	37237	
45-49	0.0004	0.0019	0.0010	0.98372	0.00099	0.001	125	$2\pi/\gamma$	29.2595	
50-54	0.0000	0.0000	0.0000	0.00000	0.00000	0.000	0	Δ	21.9155	

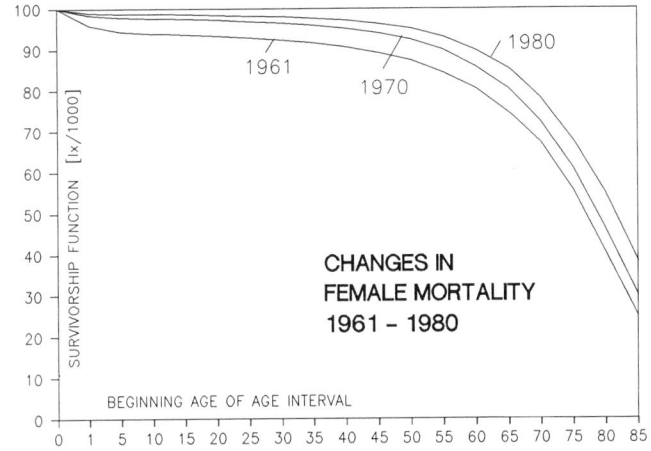

CHANGES IN FEMALE MORTALITY 1961 – 1980

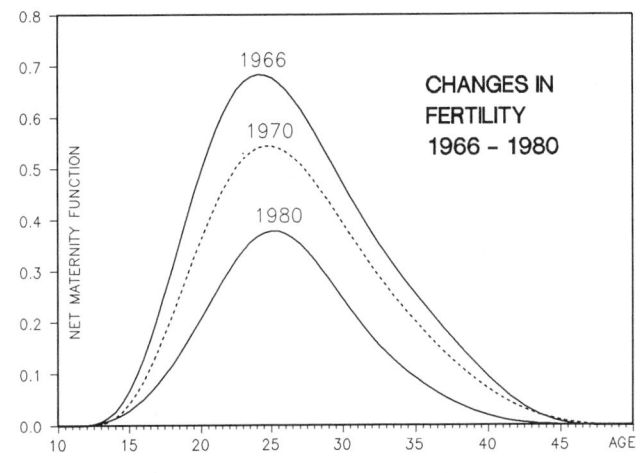

CHANGES IN FERTILITY 1966 – 1980

TABLE 1 DATA

AGE AT LAST BIRTHDAY	ESTIMATED MID-YEAR POPULATION BOTH SEXES	MALES Number	MALES Percent	FEMALES Number	FEMALES Percent	BIRTHS BY AGE OF MOTHER AND SEX	DEATHS BOTH SEXES	DEATHS MALES	DEATHS FEMALES	AGE AT LAST BIRTHDAY
0	77400	39800	2.7	37600	2.5		1765	977	788	0
1-4	278400	143100	9.5	135300	9.2		269	145	124	1-4
5-9	319300	164100	11.0	155200	10.5		161	105	56	5-9
10-14	307000	158200	10.6	148800	10.1		134	79	55	10-14
15-19	313000	160800	10.7	152200	10.3	5678	343	260	83	15-19
20-24	281000	143900	9.6	137100	9.3	27750	372	310	62	20-24
25-29	187700	95200	6.4	92500	6.3	22059	175	125	50	25-29
30-34	165400	82200	5.5	83200	5.6	15107	172	108	64	30-34
35-39	157000	76000	5.1	81000	5.5	7782	240	143	97	35-39
40-44	152200	71500	4.8	80700	5.5	2100	349	200	149	40-44
45-49	156000	76000	5.1	80000	5.4	367	590	356	234	45-49
50-54	122600	59700	4.0	62900	4.3		823	436	387	50-54
55-59	141100	69500	4.6	71600	4.9		1441	798	643	55-59
60-64	118000	60900	4.1	57100	3.9		2138	1274	864	60-64
65-69	84400	43100	2.9	41300	2.8		2571	1450	1121	65-69
70-74	57000	27800	1.9	29200	2.0		2765	1496	1269	70-74
75-79	30400	14700	1.0	15700	1.1		2327	1227	1100	75-79
80-84	17000	8000	0.5	9000	0.6	41717 M	2028	958	1070	80-84
85+	9200	4100	0.3	5100	0.3	39126 F	1707	721	986	85+
TOTAL	2974100	1498600		1475500		80843	20370	11168	9202	TOTAL

TABLE 2 MALE LIFE TABLE

x	nM_x	nq_x	l_x	nd_x	nL_x	nm_x	na_x	T_x	$\overset{\circ}{e}_x$	x
0	0.024548	0.024024	100000	2402	97866	0.024548	0.112	6998084	69.981	0
1	0.001013	0.004043	97598	395	389404	0.001013	1.500	6900218	70.701	1
5	0.000640	0.003194	97203	310	485239	0.000640	2.500	6510814	66.982	5
10	0.000499	0.002495	96893	242	483956	0.000500	2.903	6025575	62.188	10
15	0.001617	0.008055	96651	779	481471	0.001617	2.710	5541619	57.337	15
20	0.002154	0.010712	95872	1027	476760	0.002154	2.467	5060148	52.780	20
25	0.001313	0.006489	94845	615	472603	0.001302	2.362	4583388	48.325	25
30	0.001314	0.006561	94230	618	469659	0.001316	2.589	4110786	43.625	30
35	0.001882	0.009394	93612	879	465999	0.001887	2.659	3641127	38.896	35
40	0.002797	0.013897	92732	1289	460699	0.002797	2.701	3175128	34.240	40
45	0.004684	0.023225	91444	2124	452309	0.004695	2.688	2714429	29.684	45
50	0.007303	0.035935	89320	3210	439136	0.007309	2.675	2262120	25.326	50
55	0.011482	0.055941	86110	4817	419534	0.011482	2.713	1822984	21.170	55
60	0.020920	0.100083	81293	8136	387511	0.020996	2.670	1403450	17.264	60
65	0.033643	0.156819	73157	11472	338488	0.033893	2.621	1015939	13.887	65
70	0.053813	0.239605	61685	14780	272477	0.054243	2.568	677451	10.983	70
75	0.083469	0.347345	46905	16292	193628	0.084141	2.490	404974	8.634	75
80	0.119750	0.456939	30613	13988	116811	0.119750	2.408	211346	6.904	80
85	0.175854	1.000000	16624	16624	94536	0.107251	5.687	94536	5.687	85

TABLE 3 FEMALE LIFE TABLE

x	nM_x	nq_x	l_x	nd_x	nL_x	nm_x	na_x	T_x	$\overset{\circ}{e}_x$	x
0	0.020957	0.020572	100000	2057	98160	0.020957	0.106	7334085	73.341	0
1	0.000916	0.003658	97943	358	390876	0.000916	1.500	7235925	73.879	1
5	0.000361	0.001803	97585	176	487483	0.000361	2.500	6845049	70.145	5
10	0.000370	0.001847	97409	180	486612	0.000370	2.603	6357566	65.267	10
15	0.000545	0.002723	97229	265	485490	0.000545	2.530	5870954	60.383	15
20	0.000452	0.002251	96964	218	484274	0.000451	2.497	5385464	55.541	20
25	0.000541	0.002706	96746	262	483106	0.000542	2.622	4901190	50.661	25
30	0.000769	0.003852	96484	372	481556	0.000772	2.675	4418084	45.791	30
35	0.001198	0.005979	96112	575	479230	0.001199	2.684	3936528	40.958	35
40	0.001846	0.009193	95538	878	475661	0.001846	2.692	3457298	36.188	40
45	0.002925	0.014608	94659	1383	470247	0.002941	2.795	2981638	31.499	45
50	0.006153	0.030393	93277	2835	459836	0.006165	2.691	2511390	26.924	50
55	0.008980	0.043988	90442	3978	442997	0.008980	2.685	2051554	22.684	55
60	0.015131	0.073591	86463	6363	417725	0.015232	2.707	1608557	18.604	60
65	0.027143	0.128543	80100	10296	376317	0.027361	2.651	1190832	14.867	65
70	0.043459	0.198175	69804	13833	315804	0.043804	2.599	814514	11.669	70
75	0.070064	0.301200	55971	16858	238547	0.070671	2.550	498711	8.910	75
80	0.118889	0.456748	39112	17864	150262	0.118889	2.464	260164	6.652	80
85	0.193333	1.000000	21248	21248	109902	0.125514	5.172	109902	5.172	85

TABLE 4 OBSERVED VITAL RATES AND RATIOS

CRUDE RATES

Per Thousand	BOTH SEXES	MALES	FEMALES
BIRTH RATE	27.18	27.84	26.52
DEATH RATE	6.85	7.45	6.24
RATE OF INCREASE	20.33	20.39	20.28

PERCENT OF POPULATION IN AGE GROUP

	BOTH SEXES	MALES	FEMALES
UNDER 15	33.02	33.71	32.32
15 - 64	60.32	59.77	60.88
65 AND OLDER	6.66	6.52	6.80

RATES STANDARDIZED ON USA 1980

Per Thousand	BOTH SEXES	MALES	FEMALES
BIRTH RATE	32.50		30.59
DEATH RATE	10.52	9.65	11.34
RATE OF INCREASE	21.98		19.25

RATES STANDARDIZED ON MEXICO 1980

	BOTH SEXES	MALES	FEMALES
BIRTH RATE	28.16		27.47
DEATH RATE	4.33	4.66	4.00
RATE OF INCREASE	23.83		23.47

VITAL STATISTICS

GFR x 1000	114.395
TFR	3.932
GRR	1.903
NRR	1.836
μ	28.700
σ^2	37.309
GENERATION	28.299
POP. SEX RATIO	0.985
SEX RATIO AT BIRTH	1.066
DEP. RATIO x 100	65.780

PROJECTED POPULATION

AGE GROUP	1975			1980		
	BOTH SEXES	MALES	FEMALES	BOTH SEXES	MALES	FEMALES
0-4	431	222	209	497	256	241
5-9	354	182	172	430	221	209
10-14	319	164	155	354	182	172
15-19	305	157	148	318	163	155
20-24	311	159	152	304	156	148
25-29	280	143	137	309	158	151
30-34	187	95	92	278	142	136
35-39	165	82	83	186	94	92
40-44	155	75	80	163	81	82
45-49	150	70	80	153	74	79
50-54	152	74	78	146	68	78
55-59	118	57	61	145	70	75
60-64	132	64	68	110	53	57
65-69	104	53	51	117	56	61
70-74	70	35	35	86	43	43
75-79	42	20	22	51	25	26
80-84	19	9	10	26	12	14
85+	13	6	7	14	7	7
TOTAL	3307	1667	1640	3687	1861	1826

STABLE EQUIVALENT TO ORIGINAL POPULATION

	MALES		FEMALES		AGE GROUP	
	Number	Percent	Number	Percent		
	198	13.2	186	12.9	0-4	
	177	11.8	167	11.6	5-9	TABLE 5
	158	10.6	149	10.4	10-14	
	142	9.5	134	9.3	15-19	POPULATION
	126	8.4	120	8.3	20-24	PROJECTED
	112	7.5	107	7.4	25-29	WITH
	100	6.7	96	6.7	30-34	FIXED
	89	6.0	86	6.0	35-39	AGE-
	79	5.3	77	5.3	40-44	SPECIFIC
	70	4.7	68	4.7	45-49	BIRTH
	61	4.1	60	4.1	50-54	AND
	52	3.5	52	3.6	55-59	DEATH
	43	2.9	44	3.0	60-64	RATES
	34	2.3	35	2.5	65-69	(female
	25	1.6	27	1.8	70-74	dominant,
	16	1.0	18	1.3	75-79	in 000s)
	8	0.6	10	0.7	80-84	
	6	0.4	7	0.5	85+	
	1496		1443		TOTAL	

VITAL RATES OF PROJECTED POPULATION

Per Thousand	1975			1980		
	BOTH SEXES	MALES	FEMALES	BOTH SEXES	MALES	FEMALES
BIRTH RATE	29.04	29.73	28.35	29.27	29.94	28.58
DEATH RATE	7.30	7.92	6.67	7.48	8.01	6.94
RATE OF INCREASE	21.74	21.81	21.67	21.79	21.94	21.64

VITAL RATES OF STABLE POPULATION

Per Thousand	MALES	FEMALES	
			TABLE 6
BIRTH RATE	28.61	27.82	
DEATH RATE	7.17	6.30	PROJECTED
RATE OF INCREASE		21.52	VITAL RATES

AGE STRUCTURE OF PROJECTED POPULATION

	1975			1980		
% UNDER 15	33.41	34.09	32.72	34.75	35.46	34.04
% 15-64	59.10	58.54	59.68	57.28	56.87	57.69
% 65 AND OLDER	7.49	7.38	7.60	7.97	7.67	8.28
DEPEND. RATIO x 100	69.20	70.83	67.57	74.59	75.83	73.35

STABLE AGE STRUCTURE

	MALES	FEMALES	
			AND RATIOS
% UNDER 15	35.65	34.82	(female
% 15-64	58.41	58.44	dominant)
% 65 AND OLDER	5.94	6.73	
DEPEND. RATIO x 100	71.19	71.11	

AGE GROUP	FEMALE BIRTH RATES	NET MATERNITY FUNCTION	COEFF. OF MATRIX EQUATION	ORIGINAL MATRIX		STABLE MATRIX		MATRIX PARAMETERS		
				SUB-DIAGONAL	FIRST ROW	FISHER VALUES	REPRODUCTIVE VALUES			
0-4	0.0000	0.0000	0.0000	0.99683	0.00000	1.079	186495	λ_1	1.11358	
5-9	0.0000	0.0000	0.0000	0.99821	0.00000	1.205	187011	λ_2	0.41738-0.81105i	TABLE 7
10-14	0.0000	0.0000	0.0438	0.99769	0.04405	1.344	200021	λ_4	-0.09417-0.55863i	
15-19	0.0181	0.0877	0.2810	0.99749	0.28308	1.453	221108	λ_6	-0.44922-0.34446i	LESLIE
20-24	0.0980	0.4744	0.5160	0.99759	0.52106	1.316	180384	r_1	0.02152	MATRIX
25-29	0.1154	0.5576	0.4904	0.99679	0.49640	0.905	83740	r_2	-0.01839-0.21910i	AND ITS
30-34	0.0879	0.4232	0.3230	0.99517	0.32802	0.474	39455	r_4	-0.11365-0.34756i	ANALYSIS
35-39	0.0465	0.2228	0.1414	0.99255	0.14426	0.175	14184	r_6	-0.11380-0.49749i	(females)
40-44	0.0126	0.0599	0.0352	0.98862	0.03616	0.040	3203	c_1	14423	
45-49	0.0022	0.0104	0.0052	0.97786	0.00543	0.005	421	$2\pi/\gamma$	28.6768	
50-54	0.0000	0.0000	0.0000	0.00000	0.00000	0.000	0	Δ	5.5874	

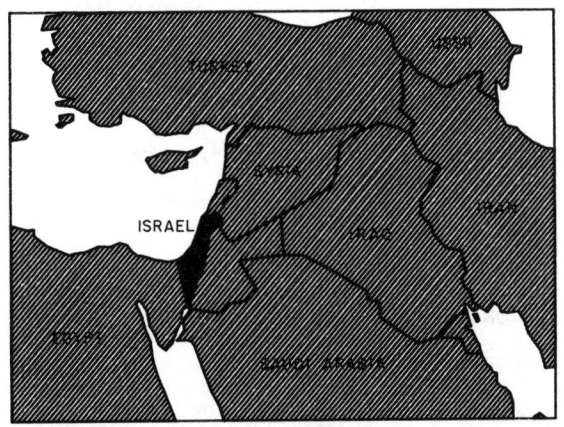

EDUCATION [1984]

% of primary school-age children enrolled:	98
secondary school-age children enrolled:	74
ca. 20-24 year olds in higher education:	34

LABOR FORCE

Average annual labor force growth (%) 1980-85:	2.2	
% of the 1980 labor force in agriculture:	6	TABLE 8
in industry:	32	
in services:	62	SOCIO-ECONOMIC INDICATORS

GNP & INCOME DISTRIBUTION

GNP per capita (in US Dollars) 1985:	4990
GNP average annual growth rate (%) 1965-85:	2.5
% share of total household income 1979-80	
Lowest 20% of households:	6.0
Highest 10% of households:	22.6

HEALTH & NUTRITION

Population per physician 1981:	400
Daily calorie supply per capita 1985:	3060

ISRAEL 1975 (incl. Jewish pop. in occupied territories)

368

TABLE 1 — DATA

AGE AT LAST BIRTHDAY	ESTIMATED MID-YEAR POPULATION BOTH SEXES	MALES Number	MALES Percent	FEMALES Number	FEMALES Percent	BIRTHS BY AGE OF MOTHER AND SEX	DEATHS BOTH SEXES	MALES	FEMALES	AGE AT LAST BIRTHDAY
0	92900	47700	2.8	45200	2.6		2194	1238	956	0
1-4	344400	176600	10.2	167800	9.7		349	188	161	1-4
5-9	366600	188500	10.9	178100	10.3		151	84	67	5-9
10-14	330800	170400	9.8	160400	9.3		139	91	48	10-14
15-19	325500	167700	9.7	157800	9.2	6912	307	232	75	15-19
20-24	331900	168400	9.7	163500	9.5	33337	379	293	86	20-24
25-29	284300	142600	8.2	141700	8.2	30530	271	188	83	25-29
30-34	185900	92700	5.4	93200	5.4	15399	202	123	79	30-34
35-39	173200	85400	4.9	87800	5.1	7430	277	173	104	35-39
40-44	167000	81200	4.7	85800	5.0	1780	346	204	142	40-44
45-49	160600	75300	4.4	85300	4.9	240	592	335	257	45-49
50-54	161400	78000	4.5	83400	4.8		975	541	434	50-54
55-59	123000	59300	3.4	63700	3.7		1245	690	555	55-59
60-64	138600	66400	3.8	72200	4.2		2321	1317	1004	60-64
65-69	113400	56400	3.3	57000	3.3		3158	1784	1374	65-69
70-74	76300	37600	2.2	38700	2.2		3591	1990	1601	70-74
75-79	42525	20185	1.2	22340	1.3		3354	1734	1620	75-79
80-84	23785	10985	0.6	12800	0.7	48976 M	2411	1204	1207	80-84
85+	12890	5630	0.3	7260	0.4	46652 F	2338	1036	1302	85+
TOTAL	3455000	1731000		1724000		95628	24600	13445	11155	TOTAL

TABLE 2 — MALE LIFE TABLE

x	nM_x	nq_x	l_x	nd_x	nL_x	nm_x	na_x	T_x	$\mathring{e}_x$	x
0	0.025954	0.025371	100000	2537	97752	0.025954	0.114	7032797	70.328	0
1	0.001065	0.004247	97463	414	388817	0.001065	1.500	6935044	71.156	1
5	0.000446	0.002226	97049	216	484705	0.000446	2.500	6546227	67.453	5
10	0.000534	0.002677	96833	259	483611	0.000536	2.862	6061522	62.598	10
15	0.001383	0.006896	96574	666	481323	0.001384	2.679	5577911	57.758	15
20	0.001740	0.008662	95908	831	477453	0.001740	2.489	5096588	53.140	20
25	0.001318	0.006540	95077	622	473788	0.001312	2.431	4619135	48.583	25
30	0.001327	0.006630	94455	626	470779	0.001330	2.608	4145347	43.887	30
35	0.002026	0.010102	93829	948	466888	0.002030	2.618	3674568	39.162	35
40	0.002512	0.012522	92881	1163	461722	0.002519	2.692	3207680	34.535	40
45	0.004449	0.022019	91718	2020	453939	0.004449	2.697	2745959	29.939	45
50	0.006936	0.034234	89699	3071	441420	0.006957	2.697	2292019	25.552	50
55	0.011636	0.056750	86628	4916	421823	0.011655	2.698	1850599	21.363	55
60	0.019834	0.094775	81712	7744	390447	0.019834	2.661	1428777	17.486	60
65	0.031631	0.147539	73967	10913	344048	0.031720	2.637	1038329	14.038	65
70	0.052926	0.236473	63054	14911	279288	0.053388	2.587	694282	11.011	70
75	0.085905	0.355630	48144	17121	197567	0.086661	2.480	414993	8.620	75
80	0.109604	0.426726	31022	13238	120781	0.109604	2.407	217427	7.009	80
85	0.184014	1.000000	17784	17784	96646	0.115776	5.434	96646	5.434	85

TABLE 3 — FEMALE LIFE TABLE

x	nM_x	nq_x	l_x	nd_x	nL_x	nm_x	na_x	T_x	$\mathring{e}_x$	x
0	0.021150	0.020758	100000	2076	98144	0.021150	0.106	7406359	74.064	0
1	0.000959	0.003829	97924	375	390760	0.000959	1.500	7308215	74.631	1
5	0.000376	0.001879	97549	183	487288	0.000376	2.500	6917455	70.912	5
10	0.000299	0.001496	97366	146	486476	0.000299	2.568	6430167	66.041	10
15	0.000475	0.002374	97220	231	485547	0.000475	2.598	5943692	61.136	15
20	0.000526	0.002627	96990	255	484322	0.000526	2.543	5458144	56.276	20
25	0.000586	0.002931	96735	284	482997	0.000587	2.614	4973823	51.417	25
30	0.000848	0.004249	96451	410	481291	0.000852	2.645	4490825	46.561	30
35	0.001185	0.005919	96041	568	478865	0.001187	2.639	4009534	41.748	35
40	0.001655	0.008253	95473	788	475572	0.001657	2.724	3530670	36.981	40
45	0.003013	0.014963	94685	1417	470221	0.003013	2.738	3055098	32.266	45
50	0.005204	0.025830	93268	2409	460833	0.005228	2.714	2584877	27.714	50
55	0.008713	0.042792	90859	3888	445294	0.008731	2.685	2124044	23.377	55
60	0.013906	0.067368	86971	5859	421338	0.013906	2.693	1678750	19.302	60
65	0.024105	0.114788	81112	9311	383904	0.024253	2.674	1257412	15.502	65
70	0.041370	0.189951	71801	13639	326724	0.041744	2.633	873508	12.166	70
75	0.072516	0.309757	58163	18016	246113	0.073203	2.519	546784	9.401	75
80	0.094297	0.380476	40146	15275	161985	0.094297	2.463	300671	7.489	80
85	0.179339	1.000000	24872	24872	138685	0.110534	5.576	138685	5.576	85

TABLE 4 — OBSERVED VITAL RATES AND RATIOS

CRUDE RATES

Per Thousand	BOTH SEXES	MALES	FEMALES
BIRTH RATE	27.68	28.29	27.06
DEATH RATE	7.12	7.77	6.47
RATE OF INCREASE	20.56	20.53	20.59

RATES STANDARDIZED ON USA 1980

Per Thousand	BOTH SEXES	MALES	FEMALES
BIRTH RATE	30.69		29.11
DEATH RATE	9.98	9.43	10.50
RATE OF INCREASE	20.71		18.62

VITAL STATISTICS

GFR x 1000	117.321
TFR	3.683
GRR	1.797
NRR	1.733
μ	28.262
σ^2	37.090
GENERATION	27.897
POP. SEX RATIO	0.996
SEX RATIO AT BIRTH	1.050
DEP. RATIO x 100	68.422

PERCENT OF POPULATION IN AGE GROUP

	BOTH SEXES	MALES	FEMALES
UNDER 15	32.84	33.69	31.99
15 - 64	59.37	58.75	60.00
65 AND OLDER	7.78	7.56	8.01

RATES STANDARDIZED ON MEXICO 1980

	BOTH SEXES	MALES	FEMALES
BIRTH RATE	26.86		26.41
DEATH RATE	4.17	4.55	3.78
RATE OF INCREASE	22.69		22.63

ISRAEL 1980 (incl. Jewish pop. in occupied territories)

AGE AT LAST BIRTHDAY	ESTIMATED MID-YEAR POPULATION BOTH SEXES	MALES Number	MALES Percent	FEMALES Number	FEMALES Percent	BIRTHS BY AGE OF MOTHER AND SEX	DEATHS BOTH SEXES	DEATHS MALES	DEATHS FEMALES	AGE AT LAST BIRTHDAY	
0	93600	48000	2.4	45600	2.3		1426	831	595	0	
1-4	380100	195200	10.0	184900	9.4		255	134	121	1-4	
5-9	450900	231000	11.8	219900	11.2		139	79	60	5-9	
10-14	377700	194200	9.9	183500	9.4		97	61	36	10-14	
15-19	338500	174000	8.9	164500	8.4	5815	185	144	41	15-19	
20-24	334400	170100	8.7	164300	8.4	29289	247	183	64	20-24	
25-29	337500	170100	8.7	167400	8.5	32140	218	140	78	25-29	
30-34	295100	147300	7.5	147800	7.5	18647	258	173	85	30-34	
35-39	192400	95600	4.9	96800	4.9	6877	202	127	75	35-39	TABLE 1
40-44	174700	85800	4.4	88900	4.5	1433	317	193	124	40-44	
45-49	166600	80900	4.1	85700	4.4	120	547	328	219	45-49	DATA
50-54	160900	75000	3.8	85900	4.4		867	527	340	50-54	
55-59	158500	74700	3.8	83800	4.3		1425	822	603	55-59	
60-64	122600	58200	3.0	64400	3.3		1813	1021	792	60-64	
65-69	126800	59300	3.0	67500	3.4		3193	1736	1457	65-69	
70-74	103000	49400	2.5	53600	2.7		4292	2394	1898	70-74	
75-79	59700	28700	1.5	31000	1.6		4046	2127	1919	75-79	
80-84	32125	14625	0.7	17500	0.9	48488 M	3610	1715	1895	80-84	
85+	16675	7275	0.4	9400	0.5	45833 F	3141	1420	1721	85+	
TOTAL	3921800	1959400		1962400		94321	26278	14155	12123	TOTAL	

x	$_nM_x$	$_nq_x$	l_x	$_nd_x$	$_nL_x$	$_nm_x$	$_na_x$	T_x	$\mathring{e}_x$	x	
0	0.017313	0.017047	100000	1705	98465	0.017312	0.099	7231330	72.313	0	
1	0.000686	0.002741	98295	269	392508	0.000686	1.500	7132865	72.566	1	
5	0.000342	0.001708	98026	167	489711	0.000342	2.500	6740358	68.761	5	
10	0.000314	0.001579	97858	155	488955	0.000316	2.820	6250647	63.874	10	
15	0.000828	0.004145	97704	405	487584	0.000830	2.689	5761692	58.971	15	
20	0.001076	0.005365	97299	522	485188	0.001076	2.497	5274109	54.205	20	
25	0.000823	0.004107	96777	397	482900	0.000823	2.523	4788920	49.484	25	TABLE 2
30	0.001174	0.005875	96379	566	480532	0.001178	2.588	4306020	44.678	30	
35	0.001328	0.006653	95813	637	477578	0.001335	2.665	3825488	39.926	35	MALE
40	0.002249	0.011245	95176	1070	473466	0.002260	2.745	3347910	35.176	40	LIFE
45	0.004054	0.020154	94106	1897	466228	0.004068	2.733	2874444	30.545	45	TABLE
50	0.007027	0.034578	92209	3188	453676	0.007028	2.689	2408216	26.117	50	
55	0.011004	0.053766	89021	4786	433954	0.011029	2.671	1954540	21.956	55	
60	0.017543	0.084393	84234	7109	404603	0.017570	2.669	1520586	18.052	60	
65	0.029275	0.136935	77126	10561	360760	0.029275	2.645	1115983	14.470	65	
70	0.048462	0.217451	66564	14475	297855	0.048596	2.584	755223	11.346	70	
75	0.074111	0.315109	52090	16414	219755	0.074692	2.521	457368	8.780	75	
80	0.117265	0.451497	35676	16108	137360	0.117265	2.453	237614	6.660	80	
85	0.195189	1.000000	19568	19568	100253	0.127797	5.123	100253	5.123	85	

x	$_nM_x$	$_nq_x$	l_x	$_nd_x$	$_nL_x$	$_nm_x$	$_na_x$	T_x	$\mathring{e}_x$	x	
0	0.013048	0.012895	100000	1290	98829	0.013048	0.092	7604000	76.040	0	
1	0.000654	0.002613	98710	258	394197	0.000654	1.500	7505171	76.032	1	
5	0.000273	0.001363	98452	134	491927	0.000273	2.500	7110974	72.227	5	
10	0.000196	0.000979	98318	96	491348	0.000196	2.475	6619047	67.323	10	
15	0.000249	0.001249	98222	123	490823	0.000250	2.661	6127698	62.386	15	
20	0.000390	0.001946	98099	191	490042	0.000390	2.615	5636875	57.461	20	
25	0.000466	0.002327	97908	228	488991	0.000466	2.583	5146834	52.568	25	TABLE 3
30	0.000575	0.002879	97681	281	487732	0.000577	2.612	4657842	47.684	30	
35	0.000775	0.003892	97399	379	486132	0.000780	2.718	4170110	42.815	35	FEMALE
40	0.001395	0.006986	97020	678	483583	0.001402	2.760	3683978	37.971	40	LIFE
45	0.002555	0.012718	96343	1225	478897	0.002558	2.702	3200395	33.219	45	TABLE
50	0.003958	0.019615	95117	1866	471358	0.003958	2.733	2721498	28.612	50	
55	0.007196	0.035543	93252	3314	458707	0.007226	2.722	2250140	24.130	55	
60	0.012298	0.059976	89937	5394	437320	0.012334	2.708	1791433	19.919	60	
65	0.021585	0.102757	84543	8687	402471	0.021585	2.670	1354113	16.017	65	
70	0.035410	0.164400	75856	12471	349878	0.035643	2.642	951642	12.545	70	
75	0.061903	0.271559	63385	17213	275391	0.062503	2.587	601764	9.494	75	
80	0.108286	0.425836	46172	19662	181574	0.108286	2.493	326372	7.069	80	
85	0.183085	1.000000	26510	26510	144799	0.114460	5.462	144799	5.462	85	

CRUDE RATES

Per Thousand	BOTH SEXES	MALES	FEMALES
BIRTH RATE	24.05	24.75	23.36
DEATH RATE	6.70	7.22	6.18
RATE OF INCREASE	17.35	17.52	17.18

PERCENT OF POPULATION IN AGE GROUP

	BOTH SEXES	MALES	FEMALES
UNDER 15	33.21	34.11	32.30
15 - 64	58.17	57.76	58.58
65 AND OLDER	8.63	8.13	9.12

RATES STANDARDIZED ON USA 1980

Per Thousand	BOTH SEXES	MALES	FEMALES
BIRTH RATE	25.96		24.53
DEATH RATE	9.17	8.61	9.70
RATE OF INCREASE	16.79		14.83

RATES STANDARDIZED ON MEXICO 1980

	BOTH SEXES	MALES	FEMALES
BIRTH RATE	22.78		22.31
DEATH RATE	3.51	3.84	3.18
RATE OF INCREASE	19.27		19.13

VITAL STATISTICS

GFR x 1000	103.038	TABLE 4
TFR	3.102	
GRR	1.507	OBSERVED
NRR	1.473	VITAL
μ	28.071	RATES
σ^2	35.741	AND
GENERATION	27.822	RATIOS
POP. SEX RATIO	1.002	
SEX RATIO AT BIRTH	1.058	
DEP. RATIO x 100	71.918	

TABLE 1 — DATA

AGE AT LAST BIRTHDAY	ESTIMATED MID-YEAR POPULATION BOTH SEXES	MALES Number	MALES Percent	FEMALES Number	FEMALES Percent	BIRTHS BY AGE OF MOTHER AND SEX	DEATHS BOTH SEXES	DEATHS MALES	DEATHS FEMALES	AGE AT LAST BIRTHDAY
0	98500	50700	2.4	47800	2.3		1184	652	532	0
1-4	380600	195900	9.3	184700	8.7		215	106	109	1-4
5-9	463700	238100	11.3	225600	10.6		119	74	45	5-9
10-14	435300	223100	10.6	212200	10.0		96	56	40	10-14
15-19	374400	192800	9.1	181600	8.6	4614	201	148	53	15-19
20-24	340200	175600	8.3	164600	7.8	26863	234	173	61	20-24
25-29	324800	162600	7.7	162200	7.6	32587	210	142	68	25-29
30-34	323900	161400	7.6	162500	7.7	23409	239	158	81	30-34
35-39	281700	139000	6.6	142700	6.7	10186	279	158	121	35-39
40-44	186800	92200	4.4	94600	4.5	1593	317	188	129	40-44
45-49	176100	86000	4.1	90100	4.2	124	487	312	175	45-49
50-54	164800	79200	3.7	85600	4.0		793	483	310	50-54
55-59	156200	71800	3.4	84400	4.0		1370	800	570	55-59
60-64	153600	71100	3.4	82500	3.9		2082	1211	871	60-64
65-69	112400	52000	2.5	60400	2.8		2520	1299	1221	65-69
70-74	117800	54200	2.6	63600	3.0		4271	2297	1974	70-74
75-79	80000	38300	1.8	41700	2.0		5132	2653	2479	75-79
80-84	40900	18900	0.9	22000	1.0	50911 M	4028	2042	1986	80-84
85+	21200	9400	0.4	11800	0.6	48465 F	4316	1962	2354	85+
TOTAL	4232900	2112300		2120600		99376	28093	14914	13179	TOTAL

TABLE 2 — MALE LIFE TABLE

x	nM_x	nq_x	l_x	nd_x	nL_x	nm_x	na_x	T_x	$\overset{\circ}{e}_x$	x
0	0.012860	0.012711	100000	1271	98846	0.012860	0.092	7351535	73.515	0
1	0.000541	0.002161	98729	213	394382	0.000541	1.500	7252690	73.461	1
5	0.000311	0.001553	98515	153	492195	0.000311	2.500	6858308	69.617	5
10	0.000251	0.001260	98362	124	491549	0.000252	2.879	6366113	64.721	10
15	0.000768	0.003851	98239	378	490321	0.000772	2.697	5874563	59.799	15
20	0.000985	0.004917	97860	481	488107	0.000986	2.520	5384242	55.020	20
25	0.000873	0.004357	97379	424	485833	0.000873	2.496	4896135	50.279	25
30	0.000979	0.004885	96955	474	483616	0.000979	2.555	4410302	45.488	30
35	0.001137	0.005700	96481	550	481137	0.001143	2.693	3926687	40.699	35
40	0.002039	0.010241	95931	982	477442	0.002058	2.747	3445550	35.917	40
45	0.003628	0.018065	94949	1715	470837	0.003643	2.723	2968108	31.260	45
50	0.006098	0.030196	93233	2815	459794	0.006123	2.736	2497271	26.785	50
55	0.011142	0.054306	90418	4910	440690	0.011142	2.678	2037476	22.534	55
60	0.017032	0.082059	85508	7017	410905	0.017076	2.629	1596786	18.674	60
65	0.024981	0.118039	78491	9265	370607	0.025000	2.642	1185881	15.108	65
70	0.042380	0.192452	69226	13323	314363	0.042380	2.615	815274	11.777	70
75	0.069269	0.297850	55903	16651	238593	0.069788	2.542	500911	8.960	75
80	0.108042	0.425413	39253	16699	154260	0.108249	2.485	262318	6.683	80
85	0.208723	1.000000	22554	22554	108057	0.142715	4.791	108057	4.791	85

TABLE 3 — FEMALE LIFE TABLE

x	nM_x	nq_x	l_x	nd_x	nL_x	nm_x	na_x	T_x	$\overset{\circ}{e}_x$	x
0	0.011130	0.011018	100000	1102	98996	0.011130	0.089	7696509	76.965	0
1	0.000590	0.002357	98898	233	395010	0.000590	1.500	7597513	76.822	1
5	0.000199	0.000997	98665	98	493080	0.000199	2.500	7202503	73.000	5
10	0.000189	0.000943	98567	93	492611	0.000189	2.602	6709423	68.070	10
15	0.000292	0.001463	98474	144	492027	0.000293	2.629	6216813	63.132	15
20	0.000371	0.001853	98330	182	491206	0.000371	2.570	5724785	58.220	20
25	0.000419	0.002095	98147	206	490236	0.000419	2.562	5233579	53.324	25
30	0.000498	0.002491	97942	244	489144	0.000499	2.680	4743343	48.430	30
35	0.000848	0.004262	97698	416	487537	0.000854	2.711	4254199	43.544	35
40	0.001364	0.006837	97282	665	484854	0.001372	2.663	3766662	38.719	40
45	0.001942	0.009703	96616	938	480959	0.001949	2.735	3281809	33.967	45
50	0.003621	0.017994	95679	1722	474546	0.003628	2.765	2800850	29.273	50
55	0.006754	0.033251	93957	3124	462597	0.006754	2.699	2326304	24.759	55
60	0.010558	0.051779	90833	4703	443492	0.010605	2.731	1863707	20.518	60
65	0.020215	0.096725	86130	8331	411188	0.020261	2.664	1420215	16.489	65
70	0.031038	0.144717	77799	11259	362747	0.031038	2.669	1009027	12.970	70
75	0.059448	0.262250	66540	17450	290512	0.060067	2.582	646280	9.713	75
80	0.090273	0.369823	49090	18155	200697	0.090458	2.535	355768	7.247	80
85	0.199492	1.000000	30935	30935	155071	0.132155	5.013	155071	5.013	85

TABLE 4 — OBSERVED VITAL RATES AND RATIOS

CRUDE RATES

Per Thousand	BOTH SEXES	MALES	FEMALES
BIRTH RATE	23.48	24.10	22.85
DEATH RATE	6.64	7.06	6.21
RATE OF INCREASE	16.84	17.04	16.64

PERCENT OF POPULATION IN AGE GROUP

	BOTH SEXES	MALES	FEMALES
UNDER 15	32.56	33.51	31.61
15 - 64	58.65	58.31	58.98
65 AND OLDER	8.80	8.18	9.41

RATES STANDARDIZED ON USA 1980

Per Thousand	BOTH SEXES	MALES	FEMALES
BIRTH RATE	25.91		24.58
DEATH RATE	8.60	8.00	9.17
RATE OF INCREASE	17.32		15.41

RATES STANDARDIZED ON MEXICO 1980

	BOTH SEXES	MALES	FEMALES
BIRTH RATE	22.42		22.04
DEATH RATE	3.19	3.45	2.91
RATE OF INCREASE	19.24		19.13

VITAL STATISTICS

GFR x 1000	99.545
TFR	3.116
GRR	1.520
NRR	1.489
μ	28.516
σ^2	33.686
GENERATION	28.279
POP. SEX RATIO	1.004
SEX RATIO AT BIRTH	1.050
DEP. RATIO x 100	70.510

PROJECTED POPULATION

AGE GROUP	1990 BOTH SEXES	1990 MALES	1990 FEMALES	1995 BOTH SEXES	1995 MALES	1995 FEMALES		
0-4	506	259	247	543	278	265		
5-9	478	246	232	504	258	246		
10-14	463	238	225	478	246	232		
15-19	435	223	212	462	237	225		
20-24	373	192	181	434	222	212		
25-29	339	175	164	372	191	181		
30-34	324	162	162	338	174	164		
35-39	323	161	162	322	161	161		
40-44	280	138	142	320	159	161		
45-49	185	91	94	277	136	141		
50-54	173	84	89	182	89	93		
55-59	159	76	83	167	80	87		
60-64	148	67	81	151	71	80		
65-69	140	64	76	135	60	75		
70-74	97	44	53	121	54	67		
75-79	92	41	51	76	33	43		
80-84	54	25	29	62	27	35		
85+	30	13	17	39	17	22		
TOTAL	4599	2299	2300	4983	2493	2490		

STABLE EQUIVALENT TO ORIGINAL POPULATION

MALES Number	MALES Percent	FEMALES Number	FEMALES Percent	AGE GROUP	
245	10.6	234	10.3	0-4	
228	9.9	218	9.6	5-9	TABLE 5
212	9.2	203	8.9	10-14	
198	8.5	189	8.3	15-19	POPULATION
183	7.9	176	7.7	20-24	PROJECTED
170	7.3	163	7.2	25-29	WITH
158	6.8	152	6.7	30-34	FIXED
146	6.3	141	6.2	35-39	AGE-
135	5.8	131	5.8	40-44	SPECIFIC
124	5.4	121	5.3	45-49	BIRTH
113	4.9	111	4.9	50-54	AND
101	4.4	101	4.4	55-59	DEATH
88	3.8	90	4.0	60-64	RATES
74	3.2	78	3.4	65-69	(female
58	2.5	64	2.8	70-74	dominant,
41	1.8	48	2.1	75-79	in 000s)
25	1.1	31	1.4	80-84	
16	0.7	22	1.0	85+	
2315		2273		TOTAL	

VITAL RATES OF PROJECTED POPULATION

Per Thousand	1990 BOTH SEXES	1990 MALES	1990 FEMALES	1995 BOTH SEXES	1995 MALES	1995 FEMALES
BIRTH RATE	22.92	23.50	22.33	23.00	23.55	22.46
DEATH RATE	7.00	7.25	6.75	7.08	7.22	6.94
RATE OF INCREASE	15.92	16.25	15.59	15.92	16.33	15.51

VITAL RATES OF STABLE POPULATION

Per Thousand	MALES	FEMALES	
BIRTH RATE	22.24	21.59	TABLE 6
DEATH RATE	8.19	7.50	PROJECTED
RATE OF INCREASE		14.09	VITAL RATES AND RATIOS

AGE STRUCTURE OF PROJECTED POPULATION

	BOTH SEXES	MALES	FEMALES	BOTH SEXES	MALES	FEMALES
% UNDER 15	31.46	32.32	30.60	30.60	31.35	29.85
% 15-64	59.54	59.52	59.56	60.68	60.95	60.41
% 65 AND OLDER	9.00	8.16	9.84	8.72	7.71	9.75
DEPEND. RATIO x 100	67.96	68.01	67.91	64.80	64.07	65.54

STABLE AGE STRUCTURE

	MALES	FEMALES	
% UNDER 15	29.62	28.81	(female dominant)
% 15-64	61.12	60.50	
% 65 AND OLDER	9.26	10.69	
DEPEND. RATIO x 100	63.60	65.29	

MATRIX

AGE GROUP	FEMALE BIRTH RATES	NET MATERNITY FUNCTION	COEFF. OF MATRIX EQUATION	ORIGINAL MATRIX SUB-DIAGONAL	ORIGINAL MATRIX FIRST ROW	STABLE MATRIX FISHER VALUES	STABLE MATRIX REPRODUCTIVE VALUES
0-4	0.0000	0.0000	0.0000	0.99812	0.00000	1.048	243731
5-9	0.0000	0.0000	0.0000	0.99905	0.00000	1.127	254238
10-14	0.0000	0.0000	0.0305	0.99882	0.03057	1.210	256837
15-19	0.0124	0.0610	0.2260	0.99833	0.22687	1.268	230298
20-24	0.0796	0.3910	0.4356	0.99803	0.43813	1.125	185138
25-29	0.0980	0.4803	0.4120	0.99777	0.41516	0.749	121498
30-34	0.0703	0.3436	0.2567	0.99671	0.25924	0.369	60019
35-39	0.0348	0.1697	0.1048	0.99450	0.10616	0.125	17832
40-44	0.0082	0.0398	0.0215	0.99197	0.02193	0.023	2168
45-49	0.0007	0.0032	0.0016	0.98667	0.00166	0.002	146
50-54	0.0000	0.0000	0.0000	0.00000	0.00000	0.000	0

MATRIX PARAMETERS

λ_1	1.07300	
λ_2	$0.41207+0.79334i$	TABLE 7
λ_4	$-0.10158-0.55172i$	
λ_6	$-0.40972+0.37202i$	LESLIE
r_1	0.01409	MATRIX
r_2	$-0.02242+0.21835i$	AND ITS
r_4	$-0.11561-0.35057i$	ANALYSIS
r_6	$-0.11833+0.48088i$	(females)
c_1	22715	
$2\pi/y$	28.7761	
Δ	5.2273	

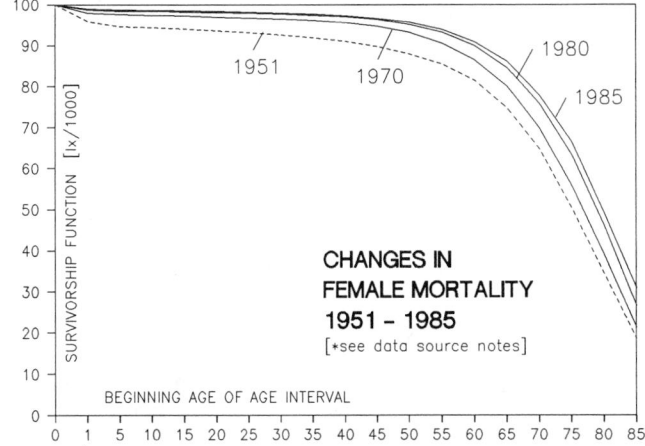

CHANGES IN FEMALE MORTALITY 1951 - 1985
[*see data source notes]

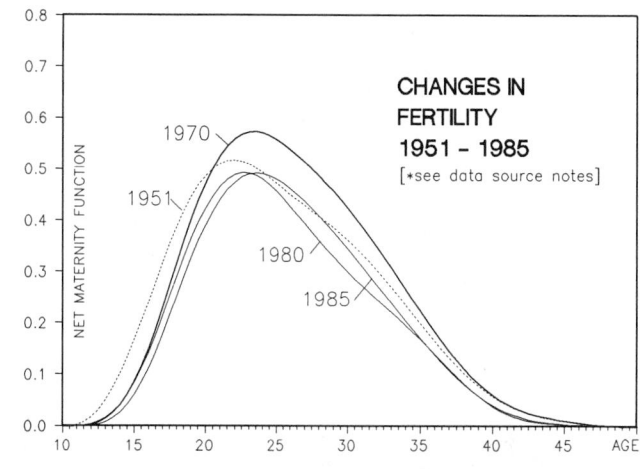

CHANGES IN FERTILITY 1951 - 1985
[*see data source notes]

AGE AT LAST BIRTHDAY	ESTIMATED MID-YEAR POPULATION BOTH SEXES	MALES Number	MALES Percent	FEMALES Number	FEMALES Percent	BIRTHS BY AGE OF MOTHER AND SEX	DEATHS BOTH SEXES	DEATHS MALES	DEATHS FEMALES	AGE AT LAST BIRTHDAY
0	1892710	971596	1.9	921114	1.7		25428	14760	10668	0
1-4	6988897	3579739	7.0	3409158	6.4		7472	4342	3130	1-4
5-9	8243246	4213331	8.2	4029915	7.6		3811	2386	1425	5-9
10-14	7954634	4054473	7.9	3900161	7.3	12	2626	1653	973	10-14
15-19	9140340	4609120	9.0	4531220	8.5	20168	6930	4967	1963	15-19
20-24	10696394	5328984	10.4	5367410	10.1	513246	10387	6819	3568	20-24
25-29	9121557	4532256	8.8	4589301	8.6	951384	10378	6509	3869	25-29
30-34	8416748	4203234	8.2	4213514	7.9	358427	11470	7176	4294	30-34
35-39	8248745	4142318	8.1	4106427	7.7	80593	16131	10358	5773	35-39
40-44	7372095	3679895	7.2	3692200	6.9	9861	20471	12847	7624	40-44
45-49	5902489	2688796	5.2	3213693	6.0	523	23161	13272	9889	45-49
50-54	4827320	2165920	4.2	2661400	5.0	25	29598	17028	12570	50-54
55-59	4442259	2049021	4.0	2393238	4.5		44491	26735	17756	55-59
60-64	3741205	1761138	3.4	1980067	3.7		61998	38113	23885	60-64
65-69	2996845	1403682	2.7	1593163	3.0		85292	52180	33112	65-69
70-74	2144156	965196	1.9	1178960	2.2		102193	58328	43865	70-74
75-79	1276714	534773	1.0	741941	1.4		101574	52131	49443	75-79
80-84	654676	242807	0.5	411869	0.8	1000403 M	83523	36454	47069	80-84
85+	299424	90075	0.2	209349	0.4	933836 F	66028	21824	44204	85+
TOTAL	104360454	51216354		53144100		1934239	712962	387882	325080	TOTAL

TABLE 1
DATA

x	$_nM_x$	$_nq_x$	l_x	$_nd_x$	$_nL_x$	$_nm_x$	$_na_x$	T_x	$\overset{\circ}{e}_x$	x
0	0.015191	0.014986	100000	1499	98645	0.015191	0.096	6951510	69.515	0
1	0.001213	0.004837	98501	476	392815	0.001213	1.500	6852865	69.571	1
5	0.000566	0.002827	98025	277	489432	0.000566	2.500	6460051	65.902	5
10	0.000408	0.002037	97748	199	488293	0.000408	2.759	5970619	61.082	10
15	0.001078	0.005375	97549	524	486520	0.001078	2.667	5482326	56.201	15
20	0.001280	0.006378	97024	619	483610	0.001280	2.556	4995805	51.490	20
25	0.001436	0.007164	96406	691	480342	0.001438	2.559	4512195	46.804	25
30	0.001707	0.008513	95715	815	476640	0.001710	2.625	4031853	42.124	30
35	0.002501	0.012440	94900	1181	471719	0.002503	2.644	3555213	37.463	35
40	0.003491	0.017388	93720	1630	464749	0.003506	2.638	3083494	32.901	40
45	0.004936	0.024558	92090	2262	455183	0.004968	2.671	2618745	28.437	45
50	0.007862	0.038808	89828	3486	441097	0.007903	2.692	2163563	24.086	50
55	0.013048	0.063458	86342	5479	419028	0.013076	2.685	1722466	19.949	55
60	0.021641	0.103298	80863	8353	384881	0.021703	2.673	1303438	16.119	60
65	0.037174	0.171409	72510	12429	333053	0.037318	2.627	918556	12.668	65
70	0.060431	0.264795	60081	15909	261672	0.060798	2.565	585503	9.745	70
75	0.097482	0.394270	44172	17416	177015	0.098386	2.482	323831	7.331	75
80	0.150136	0.539737	26756	14441	95988	0.150451	2.383	146815	5.487	80
85	0.242287	1.000000	12315	12315	50828	0.182975	4.127	50828	4.127	85

TABLE 2
MALE LIFE TABLE

x	$_nM_x$	$_nq_x$	l_x	$_nd_x$	$_nL_x$	$_nm_x$	$_na_x$	T_x	$\overset{\circ}{e}_x$	x
0	0.011582	0.011461	100000	1146	98957	0.011582	0.090	7491578	74.916	0
1	0.000918	0.003664	98854	362	394510	0.000918	1.500	7392622	74.783	1
5	0.000354	0.001766	98492	174	492024	0.000354	2.500	6998112	71.053	5
10	0.000249	0.001247	98318	123	491290	0.000249	2.565	6506088	66.174	10
15	0.000433	0.002164	98195	212	490487	0.000433	2.699	6014798	61.253	15
20	0.000665	0.003319	97983	325	489142	0.000665	2.627	5524311	56.380	20
25	0.000843	0.004214	97658	412	487294	0.000845	2.586	5035169	51.559	25
30	0.001019	0.005090	97246	495	485048	0.001021	2.613	4547875	46.767	30
35	0.001406	0.007017	96751	679	482161	0.001408	2.652	4062827	41.993	35
40	0.002065	0.010304	96072	990	478048	0.002071	2.664	3580666	37.271	40
45	0.003077	0.015346	95082	1459	472015	0.003091	2.672	3102617	32.631	45
50	0.004723	0.023467	93623	2197	463016	0.004745	2.679	2630603	28.098	50
55	0.007419	0.036619	91426	3348	449385	0.007450	2.687	2167586	23.709	55
60	0.012063	0.058998	88078	5196	428424	0.012129	2.697	1718201	19.508	60
65	0.020784	0.099743	82882	8267	395338	0.020911	2.693	1289776	15.562	65
70	0.037207	0.172374	74615	12862	342921	0.037506	2.656	894438	11.987	70
75	0.066640	0.289368	61753	17869	265472	0.067312	2.577	551518	8.931	75
80	0.114281	0.443977	43884	19483	170486	0.114282	2.488	286046	6.518	80
85	0.211150	1.000000	24400	24400	115560	0.145307	4.736	115560	4.736	85

TABLE 3
FEMALE LIFE TABLE

CRUDE RATES

Per Thousand	BOTH SEXES	MALES	FEMALES
BIRTH RATE	18.53	19.53	17.57
DEATH RATE	6.83	7.57	6.12
RATE OF INCREASE	11.70	11.96	11.45

PERCENT OF POPULATION IN AGE GROUP

	BOTH SEXES	MALES	FEMALES
UNDER 15	24.03	25.03	23.07
15 - 64	68.90	68.65	69.15
65 AND OLDER	7.06	6.32	7.78

RATES STANDARDIZED ON USA 1980

Per Thousand	BOTH SEXES	MALES	FEMALES
BIRTH RATE	17.71		16.63
DEATH RATE	10.71	10.85	10.57
RATE OF INCREASE	7.00		6.05

RATES STANDARDIZED ON MEXICO 1980

	BOTH SEXES	MALES	FEMALES
BIRTH RATE	15.12		14.71
DEATH RATE	4.15	4.78	3.51
RATE OF INCREASE	10.97		11.20

VITAL STATISTICS

GFR x 1000	65.096
TFR	2.075
GRR	1.002
NRR	0.976
μ	27.827
σ^2	18.138
GENERATION	27.836
POP. SEX RATIO	1.038
SEX RATIO AT BIRTH	1.071
DEP. RATIO x 100	45.128

TABLE 4

OBSERVED VITAL RATES AND RATIOS

PROJECTED POPULATION

AGE GROUP	1975 BOTH SEXES	1975 MALES	1975 FEMALES	1980 BOTH SEXES	1980 MALES	1980 FEMALES
0-4	9785	5051	4734	9642	4977	4665
5-9	8851	4533	4318	9751	5030	4721
10-14	8228	4204	4024	8833	4522	4311
15-19	7934	4040	3894	8205	4188	4017
20-24	9101	4582	4519	7899	4016	3883
25-29	10640	5293	5347	9053	4551	4502
30-34	9065	4497	4568	10574	5252	5322
35-39	8348	4160	4188	8992	4451	4541
40-44	8152	4081	4071	8251	4098	4153
45-49	7250	3604	3646	8017	3997	4020
50-54	5758	2606	3152	7069	3493	3576
55-59	4641	2058	2583	5535	2475	3060
60-64	4164	1882	2282	4353	1890	2463
65-69	3351	1524	1827	3734	1629	2105
70-74	2485	1103	1382	2782	1197	1585
75-79	1566	653	913	1816	746	1070
80-84	766	290	476	940	354	586
85+	408	129	279	477	154	323
TOTAL	110493	54290	56203	115923	57020	58903

STABLE EQUIVALENT TO ORIGINAL POPULATION

AGE GROUP	MALES Number	MALES Percent	FEMALES Number	FEMALES Percent
0-4	4687	6.9	4393	6.4
5-9	4689	6.9	4400	6.4
10-14	4699	6.9	4413	6.4
15-19	4703	6.9	4426	6.4
20-24	4696	6.9	4433	6.4
25-29	4685	6.9	4436	6.4
30-34	4669	6.8	4435	6.4
35-39	4642	6.8	4429	6.4
40-44	4593	6.7	4411	6.4
45-49	4519	6.6	4374	6.3
50-54	4399	6.4	4310	6.3
55-59	4197	6.1	4202	6.1
60-64	3872	5.7	4024	5.8
65-69	3366	4.9	3730	5.4
70-74	2656	3.9	3249	4.7
75-79	1805	2.6	2527	3.7
80-84	983	1.4	1630	2.4
85+	523	0.8	1110	1.6
TOTAL	68383		68932	

TABLE 5

POPULATION PROJECTED WITH FIXED AGE-SPECIFIC BIRTH AND DEATH RATES (female dominant, in 000s)

VITAL RATES OF PROJECTED POPULATION

Per Thousand	1975 BOTH SEXES	1975 MALES	1975 FEMALES	1980 BOTH SEXES	1980 MALES	1980 FEMALES
BIRTH RATE	18.47	19.44	17.53	16.18	17.02	15.38
DEATH RATE	7.47	8.16	6.80	8.02	8.64	7.42
RATE OF INCREASE	11.00	11.28	10.73	8.17	8.38	7.96

VITAL RATES OF STABLE POPULATION

Per Thousand	MALES	FEMALES
BIRTH RATE	13.92	12.89
DEATH RATE	14.76	13.78
RATE OF INCREASE		-.89

TABLE 6

PROJECTED VITAL RATES AND RATIOS (female dominant)

AGE STRUCTURE OF PROJECTED POPULATION

	1975 BOTH SEXES	1975 MALES	1975 FEMALES	1980 BOTH SEXES	1980 MALES	1980 FEMALES
% UNDER 15	24.31	25.40	23.27	24.35	25.48	23.25
% 15-64	67.93	67.79	68.06	67.24	67.36	67.12
% 65 AND OLDER	7.76	6.81	8.68	8.41	7.15	9.62
DEPEND. RATIO x 100	47.22	47.51	46.94	48.72	48.45	48.98

STABLE AGE STRUCTURE

	MALES	FEMALES
% UNDER 15	20.58	19.16
% 15-64	65.77	63.08
% 65 AND OLDER	13.65	17.76
DEPEND. RATIO x 100	52.05	58.54

MATRIX

AGE GROUP	FEMALE BIRTH RATES	NET MATERNITY FUNCTION	COEFF. OF MATRIX EQUATION	ORIGINAL MATRIX SUB-DIAGONAL	ORIGINAL MATRIX FIRST ROW	STABLE MATRIX FISHER VALUES	STABLE MATRIX REPRODUCTIVE VALUES
0-4	0.0000	0.0000	0.0000	0.99708	0.00000	1.011	4377854
5-9	0.0000	0.0000	0.0000	0.99851	0.00000	1.009	4068000
10-14	0.0000	0.0000	0.0053	0.99836	0.00530	1.006	3925366
15-19	0.0021	0.0105	0.1182	0.99726	0.11890	0.998	4523376
20-24	0.0462	0.2258	0.3568	0.99622	0.35992	0.876	4702033
25-29	0.1001	0.4877	0.3435	0.99539	0.34781	0.510	2341455
30-34	0.0411	0.1992	0.1224	0.99405	0.12457	0.157	661636
35-39	0.0095	0.0457	0.0259	0.99147	0.02653	0.031	125541
40-44	0.0013	0.0062	0.0033	0.98738	0.00337	0.004	13449
45-49	0.0001	0.0004	0.0002	0.98094	0.00020	0.000	704
50-54	0.0000	0.0000	0.0000	0.97056	0.00001	0.000	30

MATRIX PARAMETERS

λ_1	0.99556
λ_2	$0.38875 + 0.80227i$
λ_4	$-0.38549 + 0.54369i$
λ_6	$-0.54941 - 0.00000i$
r_1	-0.00089
r_2	$-0.02297 + 0.22392i$
r_4	$-0.08115 + 0.43751i$
r_6	$-0.11978 - 0.62832i$
c_1	689316
$2\pi/y$	28.0605
Δ	15.2303

TABLE 7

LESLIE MATRIX AND ITS ANALYSIS (females)

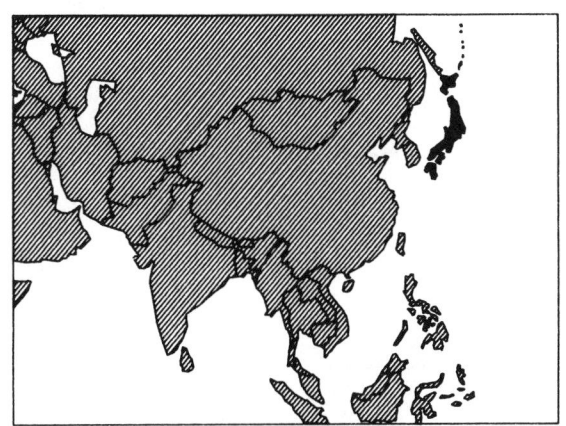

EDUCATION [1984]

% of primary school-age children enrolled:	100
secondary school-age children enrolled:	95
ca. 20-24 year olds in higher education:	30

LABOR FORCE

Average annual labor force growth (%) 1980-85:	0.9
% of the 1980 labor force in agriculture:	11
in industry:	34
in services:	55

GNP & INCOME DISTRIBUTION

GNP per capita (in US Dollars) 1985:	11300
GNP average annual growth rate (%) 1965-85:	4.7
% share of total household income 1979	
Lowest 20% of households:	8.7
Highest 10% of households:	22.4

HEALTH & NUTRITION

Population per physician 1981:	740
Daily calorie supply per capita 1985:	2856

TABLE 8

SOCIO-ECONOMIC INDICATORS

TABLE 1 — DATA

AGE AT LAST BIRTHDAY	ESTIMATED MID-YEAR POPULATION BOTH SEXES	MALES Number	MALES Percent	FEMALES Number	FEMALES Percent	BIRTHS BY AGE OF MOTHER AND SEX	DEATHS BOTH SEXES	MALES	FEMALES	AGE AT LAST BIRTHDAY
0	1573852	798944	1.4	774908	1.3		11847	6759	5088	0
1-4	6974793	3570830	6.2	3403963	5.7		4459	2600	1859	1-4
5-9	10016448	5126570	8.9	4889878	8.2		2774	1749	1025	5-9
10-14	8930828	4575029	8.0	4355799	7.3	14	1628	1031	597	10-14
15-19	8216406	4218056	7.4	3998350	6.7	14577	4045	2969	1076	15-19
20-24	7797249	3922609	6.8	3874640	6.5	296856	4852	3422	1430	20-24
25-29	9056230	4557251	7.9	4498979	7.6	810209	6276	4098	2178	25-29
30-34	10766193	5414426	9.4	5351767	9.0	388937	8777	5550	3227	30-34
35-39	9198323	4593807	8.0	4604516	7.8	59127	11468	7307	4161	35-39
40-44	8306240	4136654	7.2	4169586	7.0	6911	16132	10519	5613	40-44
45-49	8078159	4045962	7.1	4032197	6.8	257	26139	17613	8526	45-49
50-54	7144910	3504310	6.1	3640600	6.1	1	34191	22357	11834	50-54
55-59	5622213	2512796	4.4	3109417	5.2		38018	22996	15022	55-59
60-64	4461105	1949269	3.4	2511836	4.2		48909	29233	19676	60-64
65-69	3931443	1725137	3.0	2206306	3.7		73690	43932	29758	65-69
70-74	2989448	1303342	2.3	1686106	2.8		99383	57206	42177	70-74
75-79	2019982	844191	1.5	1175791	2.0		120098	63938	56160	75-79
80-84	1086171	413406	0.7	672765	1.1	811418 M	110324	51133	59191	80-84
85+	532539	172693	0.3	359846	0.6	765471 F	99791	36232	63559	85+
TOTAL	116702532	57385282		59317250		1576889	722801	390644	332157	TOTAL

TABLE 2 — MALE LIFE TABLE

x	$_nM_x$	$_nq_x$	l_x	$_nd_x$	$_nL_x$	$_nm_x$	$_na_x$	T_x	$\overset{\circ}{e}_x$	x
0	0.008460	0.008395	100000	839	99231	0.008460	0.084	7349079	73.491	0
1	0.000728	0.002907	99161	288	395921	0.000728	1.500	7249847	73.112	1
5	0.000341	0.001704	98872	169	493940	0.000341	2.500	6853926	69.321	5
10	0.000225	0.001131	98704	112	493277	0.000226	2.834	6359986	64.435	10
15	0.000704	0.003527	98592	348	492157	0.000707	2.689	5866709	59.505	15
20	0.000872	0.004353	98244	428	490172	0.000872	2.544	5374552	54.706	20
25	0.000899	0.004486	97817	439	488001	0.000899	2.533	4884380	49.934	25
30	0.001025	0.005113	97378	498	485714	0.001025	2.639	4396378	45.148	30
35	0.001591	0.007957	96880	771	482623	0.001597	2.695	3910664	40.366	35
40	0.002543	0.012679	96109	1219	477765	0.002551	2.718	3428041	35.668	40
45	0.004353	0.021578	94891	2048	469691	0.004359	2.674	2950275	31.091	45
50	0.006380	0.031584	92843	2932	457303	0.006412	2.643	2480584	26.718	50
55	0.009152	0.045107	89911	4056	440107	0.009215	2.671	2023281	22.503	55
60	0.014997	0.072876	85855	6257	414788	0.015084	2.685	1583174	18.440	60
65	0.025466	0.120575	79598	9598	375605	0.025552	2.667	1168385	14.679	65
70	0.043892	0.199560	70001	13969	316838	0.044090	2.626	792781	11.325	70
75	0.075739	0.321827	56031	18032	235898	0.076442	2.546	475943	8.494	75
80	0.123687	0.471464	37999	17915	144319	0.124136	2.450	240045	6.317	80
85	0.209806	1.000000	20084	20084	95726	0.143848	4.766	95726	4.766	85

TABLE 3 — FEMALE LIFE TABLE

x	$_nM_x$	$_nq_x$	l_x	$_nd_x$	$_nL_x$	$_nm_x$	$_na_x$	T_x	$\overset{\circ}{e}_x$	x
0	0.006566	0.006527	100000	653	99400	0.006566	0.081	7902958	79.030	0
1	0.000546	0.002182	99347	217	396848	0.000546	1.500	7803558	78.548	1
5	0.000210	0.001048	99131	104	495393	0.000210	2.500	7406710	74.717	5
10	0.000137	0.000686	99027	68	494970	0.000137	2.590	6911317	69.792	10
15	0.000269	0.001348	98959	133	494485	0.000270	2.678	6416346	64.839	15
20	0.000369	0.001844	98825	182	493694	0.000369	2.620	5921862	59.922	20
25	0.000484	0.002418	98643	238	492644	0.000484	2.600	5428168	55.028	25
30	0.000603	0.003011	98405	296	491326	0.000603	2.644	4935525	50.155	30
35	0.000904	0.004524	98108	444	489508	0.000907	2.669	4444199	45.299	35
40	0.001346	0.006727	97665	657	486801	0.001350	2.683	3954691	40.493	40
45	0.002114	0.010540	97008	1023	482668	0.002118	2.683	3467890	35.749	45
50	0.003251	0.016177	95985	1553	476303	0.003260	2.667	2985221	31.101	50
55	0.004831	0.024014	94432	2268	466912	0.004857	2.685	2508918	26.568	55
60	0.007833	0.038693	92165	3566	452650	0.007878	2.708	2042006	22.156	60
65	0.013488	0.065789	88599	5829	429733	0.013564	2.725	1589356	17.939	65
70	0.025014	0.119206	82770	9867	391258	0.025218	2.710	1159623	14.010	70
75	0.047764	0.216668	72903	15796	327287	0.048263	2.643	768365	10.540	75
80	0.087982	0.362807	57107	20719	235061	0.088143	2.564	441078	7.724	80
85	0.176628	1.000000	36388	36388	206016	0.107481	5.662	206016	5.662	85

TABLE 4 — OBSERVED VITAL RATES AND RATIOS

CRUDE RATES

Per Thousand	BOTH SEXES	MALES	FEMALES
BIRTH RATE	13.51	14.14	12.90
DEATH RATE	6.19	6.81	5.60
RATE OF INCREASE	7.32	7.33	7.31

RATES STANDARDIZED ON USA 1980

Per Thousand	BOTH SEXES	MALES	FEMALES
BIRTH RATE	14.87		14.04
DEATH RATE	7.95	8.16	7.74
RATE OF INCREASE	6.93		6.30

VITAL STATISTICS

GFR x 1000	51.650
TFR	1.738
GRR	0.844
NRR	0.831
μ	27.774
σ^2	16.524
GENERATION	27.829
POP. SEX RATIO	1.034
SEX RATIO AT BIRTH	1.060
DEP. RATIO x 100	48.388

PERCENT OF POPULATION IN AGE GROUP

	BOTH SEXES	MALES	FEMALES
UNDER 15	23.56	24.52	22.63
15 - 64	67.39	67.71	67.08
65 AND OLDER	9.05	7.77	10.29

RATES STANDARDIZED ON MEXICO 1980

	BOTH SEXES	MALES	FEMALES
BIRTH RATE	12.68		12.40
DEATH RATE	2.93	3.44	2.41
RATE OF INCREASE	9.75		10.00

PROJECTED POPULATION

AGE GROUP	1985 BOTH SEXES	1985 MALES	1985 FEMALES	1990 BOTH SEXES	1990 MALES	1990 FEMALES
0-4	7428	3818	3610	7027	3612	3415
5-9	8531	4359	4172	7413	3809	3604
10-14	10006	5120	4886	8521	4353	4168
15-19	8917	4565	4352	9989	5108	4881
20-24	8193	4201	3992	8891	4546	4345
25-29	7771	3905	3866	8165	4182	3983
30-34	9023	4536	4487	7743	3887	3856
35-39	10712	5380	5332	8977	4507	4470
40-44	9127	4548	4579	10628	5326	5302
45-49	8201	4067	4134	9011	4471	4540
50-54	7918	3939	3979	8039	3959	4080
55-59	6942	3373	3569	7692	3791	3901
60-64	5382	2368	3014	6639	3179	3460
65-69	4150	1765	2385	5007	2145	2862
70-74	3464	1455	2009	3660	1489	2171
75-79	2380	970	1410	2763	1083	1680
80-84	1360	516	844	1607	594	1013
85+	864	274	590	1083	343	740
TOTAL	120369	59159	61210	122855	60384	62471

STABLE EQUIVALENT TO ORIGINAL POPULATION

MALES Number	MALES Percent	FEMALES Number	FEMALES Percent	AGE GROUP	
4247	5.2	4015	4.8	0-4	
4380	5.4	4144	5.0	5-9	TABLE 5
4522	5.6	4280	5.1	10-14	
4664	5.8	4421	5.3	15-19	POPULATION
4802	5.9	4563	5.5	20-24	PROJECTED
4942	6.1	4707	5.6	25-29	WITH
5086	6.3	4853	5.8	30-34	FIXED
5224	6.4	4999	6.0	35-39	AGE-
5346	6.6	5139	6.1	40-44	SPECIFIC
5434	6.7	5268	6.3	45-49	BIRTH
5469	6.7	5374	6.4	50-54	AND
5441	6.7	5446	6.5	55-59	DEATH
5302	6.5	5458	6.5	60-64	RATES
4963	6.1	5357	6.4	65-69	(female
4328	5.3	5042	6.0	70-74	dominant,
3331	4.1	4360	5.2	75-79	in 000s)
2107	2.6	3238	3.9	80-84	
1445	1.8	2933	3.5	85+	
81033		83597		TOTAL	

VITAL RATES OF PROJECTED POPULATION

Per Thousand	1985 BOTH SEXES	1985 MALES	1985 FEMALES	1990 BOTH SEXES	1990 MALES	1990 FEMALES
BIRTH RATE	11.80	12.35	11.26	11.52	12.06	10.99
DEATH RATE	7.27	7.76	6.80	8.20	8.62	7.80
RATE OF INCREASE	4.53	4.60	4.46	3.31	3.44	3.19

AGE STRUCTURE OF PROJECTED POPULATION

	1985 BOTH SEXES	1985 MALES	1985 FEMALES	1990 BOTH SEXES	1990 MALES	1990 FEMALES
% UNDER 15	21.57	22.48	20.70	18.69	19.50	17.91
% 15-64	68.28	69.10	67.48	69.82	71.14	68.54
% 65 AND OLDER	10.15	8.42	11.82	11.49	9.36	13.55
DEPEND. RATIO x 100	46.46	44.71	48.19	43.23	40.57	45.90

VITAL RATES OF STABLE POPULATION

Per Thousand	MALES	FEMALES	
BIRTH RATE	10.41	9.52	TABLE 6
DEATH RATE	16.92	16.17	PROJECTED
RATE OF INCREASE		-6.65	VITAL RATES

STABLE AGE STRUCTURE

	MALES	FEMALES	AND RATIOS
% UNDER 15	16.23	14.88	(female
% 15-64	63.81	60.08	dominant)
% 65 AND OLDER	19.96	25.04	
DEPEND. RATIO x 100	56.71	66.44	

AGE GROUP	FEMALE BIRTH RATES	NET MATERNITY FUNCTION	COEFF. OF MATRIX EQUATION	ORIGINAL MATRIX SUB-DIAGONAL	ORIGINAL MATRIX FIRST ROW	STABLE MATRIX FISHER VALUES	STABLE MATRIX REPRODUCTIVE VALUES	MATRIX PARAMETERS		
0-4	0.0000	0.0000	0.0000	0.99828	0.00000	0.991	4140992	λ_1	0.96730	
5-9	0.0000	0.0000	0.0000	0.99915	0.00000	0.960	4695205	λ_2	0.38406+0.78417i	TABLE 7
10-14	0.0000	0.0000	0.0044	0.99902	0.00439	0.930	4049064	λ_4	-0.37466+0.55033i	
15-19	0.0018	0.0088	0.0962	0.99840	0.09652	0.896	3581355	λ_6	-0.52876-0.00000i	LESLIE
20-24	0.0372	0.1836	0.3071	0.99787	0.30873	0.772	2991232	r_1	-0.00665	MATRIX
25-29	0.0874	0.4307	0.3020	0.99732	0.30421	0.442	1987501	r_2	-0.02713+0.22307i	AND ITS
30-34	0.0353	0.1733	0.1019	0.99630	0.10294	0.126	675433	r_4	-0.08137+0.43370i	ANALYSIS
35-39	0.0062	0.0305	0.0172	0.99447	0.01745	0.020	92757	r_6	-0.12744-0.62832i	(females)
40-44	0.0008	0.0039	0.0020	0.99151	0.00207	0.002	9192	c_1	835959	
45-49	0.0000	0.0001	0.0001	0.98681	0.00008	0.000	320	$2\pi/y$	28.1664	
50-54	0.0000	0.0000	0.0000	0.98028	0.00000	0.000	1	Δ	18.6106	

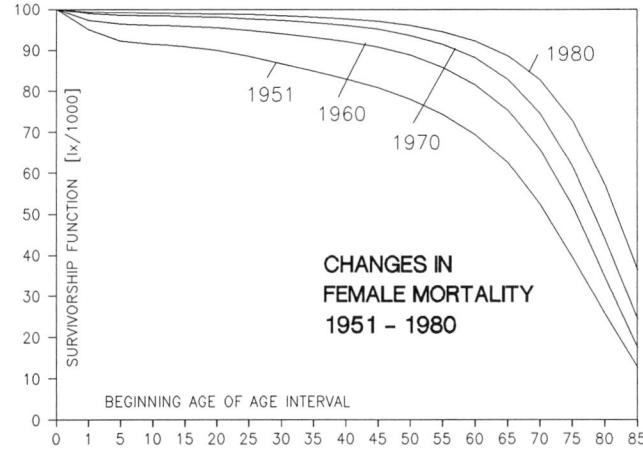

CHANGES IN FEMALE MORTALITY 1951 – 1980

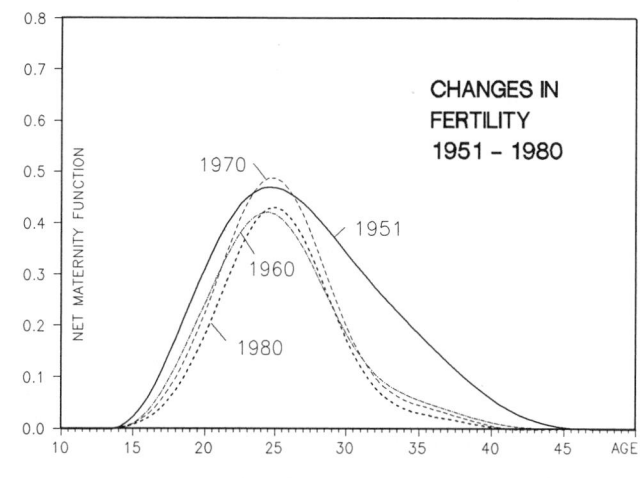

CHANGES IN FERTILITY 1951 – 1980

AGE AT LAST BIRTHDAY	ESTIMATED MID-YEAR POPULATION BOTH SEXES	MALES Number	MALES Percent	FEMALES Number	FEMALES Percent	BIRTHS BY AGE OF MOTHER AND SEX	DEATHS BOTH SEXES	DEATHS MALES	DEATHS FEMALES	AGE AT LAST BIRTHDAY
0	26955	13654	3.2	13301	4.1		1396	721	675	0
1-4	110628	56002	13.2	54626	17.0		418	202	216	1-4
5-9	110261	56065	13.3	54196	16.8		149	82	67	5-9
10-14	74069	38605	9.1	35464	11.0		51	34	17	10-14
15-19	62260	33078	7.8	29182	9.1	3818	45	26	19	15-19
20-24	73651	42163	10.0	31488	9.8	9938	66	46	20	20-24
25-29	78560	47686	11.3	30874	9.6	10464	96	61	35	25-29
30-34	60978	40486	9.6	20492	6.4	5667	109	82	27	30-34
35-39	48770	32967	7.8	15803	4.9	3311	108	76	32	35-39
40-44	31819	22212	5.3	9607	3.0	548	102	78	24	40-44
45-49	21511	14697	3.5	6814	2.1	96	108	83	25	45-49
50-54	16191	9916	2.3	6275	2.0		144	107	37	50-54
55-59	7958	4910	1.2	3048	0.9		77	56	21	55-59
60-64	8055	4123	1.0	3932	1.2		161	93	68	60-64
65-69	3878	1995	0.5	1883	0.6		138	89	49	65-69
70-74	4724	2156	0.5	2568	0.8		180	114	66	70-74
75-79	1679	856	0.2	823	0.3		113	64	49	75-79
80-84	1503	726	0.2	777	0.2	17165 M	135	74	61	80-84
85+	981	456	0.1	525	0.2	16677 F	139	75	64	85+
TOTAL	744431	422753		321678		33842	3735	2163	1572	TOTAL

TABLE 1 DATA

TABLE 2 — MALE LIFE TABLE

x	nM_x	nq_x	l_x	nd_x	nL_x	nm_x	na_x	T_x	$\overset{\circ}{e}_x$	x
0	0.052805	0.050562	100000	5056	95752	0.052805	0.160	6657255	66.573	0
1	0.003607	0.014299	94944	1358	376381	0.003607	1.500	6561504	69.109	1
5	0.001463	0.007286	93586	682	466226	0.001463	2.500	6185122	66.090	5
10	0.000881	0.004352	92904	404	463444	0.000872	2.336	5718896	61.557	10
15	0.000786	0.003923	92500	363	461613	0.000786	2.556	5255451	56.816	15
20	0.001091	0.005441	92137	501	459479	0.001091	2.592	4793838	52.029	20
25	0.001279	0.006377	91636	584	456806	0.001279	2.649	4334359	47.300	25
30	0.002025	0.010107	91052	920	453051	0.002031	2.603	3877553	42.586	30
35	0.002305	0.011510	90131	1037	448197	0.002315	2.629	3424502	37.995	35
40	0.003512	0.017542	89094	1563	441859	0.003537	2.690	2976305	33.406	40
45	0.005647	0.028140	87531	2463	432109	0.005700	2.748	2534446	28.955	45
50	0.010791	0.052902	85068	4500	414513	0.010857	2.594	2102336	24.714	50
55	0.011405	0.055842	80568	4499	392371	0.011466	2.673	1687823	20.949	55
60	0.022556	0.108407	76069	8246	361648	0.022802	2.733	1295453	17.030	60
65	0.044612	0.202276	67822	13719	305732	0.044872	2.567	933805	13.768	65
70	0.052876	0.233838	54103	12651	238761	0.052988	2.490	628074	11.609	70
75	0.074766	0.316222	41452	13108	174241	0.075229	2.481	389312	9.392	75
80	0.101928	0.404180	28344	11456	112393	0.101928	2.440	215072	7.588	80
85	0.164474	1.000000	16888	16888	102678	0.095565	6.080	102678	6.080	85

TABLE 3 — FEMALE LIFE TABLE

x	nM_x	nq_x	l_x	nd_x	nL_x	nm_x	na_x	T_x	$\overset{\circ}{e}_x$	x
0	0.050748	0.048664	100000	4866	95894	0.050748	0.156	7163023	71.630	0
1	0.003954	0.015662	95134	1490	376809	0.003954	1.500	7067129	74.286	1
5	0.001236	0.006162	93644	577	466775	0.001236	2.500	6690320	71.444	5
10	0.000479	0.002351	93067	219	464729	0.000471	2.238	6223544	66.872	10
15	0.000651	0.003254	92848	302	463499	0.000652	2.551	5758816	62.024	15
20	0.000635	0.003171	92546	293	462041	0.000635	2.657	5295317	57.218	20
25	0.001134	0.005677	92252	524	460016	0.001139	2.624	4833276	52.392	25
30	0.001318	0.006594	91728	605	457213	0.001323	2.637	4373260	47.676	30
35	0.002025	0.010124	91124	923	453420	0.002035	2.617	3916047	42.975	35
40	0.002498	0.012473	90201	1125	448340	0.002509	2.631	3462628	38.388	40
45	0.003669	0.018311	89076	1631	441600	0.003694	2.683	3014288	33.840	45
50	0.005896	0.029222	87445	2555	431102	0.005927	2.604	2572688	29.421	50
55	0.006890	0.034255	84890	2908	418079	0.006955	2.810	2141585	25.228	55
60	0.017294	0.083896	81982	6878	394024	0.017456	2.691	1723506	21.023	60
65	0.026022	0.122460	75104	9197	352764	0.026072	2.526	1329482	17.702	65
70	0.025701	0.121695	65907	8021	310737	0.025811	2.656	976718	14.820	70
75	0.059538	0.262930	57886	15220	252621	0.060248	2.581	665982	11.505	75
80	0.078507	0.327514	42666	13974	177994	0.078507	2.471	413361	9.688	80
85	0.121905	1.000000	28692	28692	235367	0.056454	8.203	235367	8.203	85

TABLE 4 — OBSERVED VITAL RATES AND RATIOS

CRUDE RATES

Per Thousand	BOTH SEXES	MALES	FEMALES
BIRTH RATE	45.46	40.60	51.84
DEATH RATE	5.02	5.12	4.89
RATE OF INCREASE	40.44	35.49	46.96

PERCENT OF POPULATION IN AGE GROUP

	BOTH SEXES	MALES	FEMALES
UNDER 15	43.24	38.87	48.99
15 - 64	55.04	59.67	48.97
65 AND OLDER	1.71	1.46	2.04

RATES STANDARDIZED ON USA 1980

Per Thousand	BOTH SEXES	MALES	FEMALES
BIRTH RATE	54.81		52.53
DEATH RATE	10.12	10.57	9.69
RATE OF INCREASE	44.69		42.84

RATES STANDARDIZED ON MEXICO 1980

	BOTH SEXES	MALES	FEMALES
BIRTH RATE	48.44		48.11
DEATH RATE	5.50	6.03	4.97
RATE OF INCREASE	42.94		43.14

VITAL STATISTICS

GFR x 1000	234.590
TFR	6.713
GRR	3.308
NRR	3.034
μ	28.726
σ^2	48.226
GENERATION	27.762
POP. SEX RATIO	0.761
SEX RATIO AT BIRTH	1.029
DEP. RATIO x 100	81.678

PROJECTED POPULATION

AGE GROUP	1975 BOTH SEXES	1975 MALES	1975 FEMALES	1980 BOTH SEXES	1980 MALES	1980 FEMALES
0-4	170	86	84	195	99	96
5-9	136	69	67	168	85	83
10-14	110	56	54	135	68	67
15-19	73	38	35	110	56	54
20-24	62	33	29	73	38	35
25-29	73	42	31	62	33	29
30-34	78	47	31	73	42	31
35-39	60	40	20	77	47	30
40-44	49	33	16	59	39	20
45-49	31	22	9	47	32	15
50-54	21	14	7	30	21	9
55-59	15	9	6	19	13	6
60-64	8	5	3	15	9	6
65-69	7	3	4	7	4	3
70-74	4	2	2	6	3	3
75-79	4	2	2	2	1	1
80-84	2	1	1	2	1	1
85+	2	1	1	2	1	1
TOTAL	905	503	402	1082	592	490

STABLE EQUIVALENT TO ORIGINAL POPULATION

MALES Number	MALES Percent	FEMALES Number	FEMALES Percent	AGE GROUP	
67	*19.8*	65	*19.5*	0-4	
54	*16.0*	52	*15.8*	5-9	TABLE 5
44	*13.0*	43	*12.9*	10-14	
36	*10.6*	35	*10.5*	15-19	POPULATION
29	*8.6*	28	*8.6*	20-24	PROJECTED
24	*7.0*	23	*7.0*	25-29	WITH
19	*5.7*	19	*5.7*	30-34	FIXED
16	*4.6*	15	*4.6*	35-39	AGE-
13	*3.7*	12	*3.7*	40-44	SPECIFIC
10	*3.0*	10	*3.0*	45-49	BIRTH
8	*2.3*	8	*2.4*	50-54	AND
6	*1.8*	6	*1.9*	55-59	DEATH
5	*1.4*	5	*1.5*	60-64	RATES
3	*0.9*	4	*1.1*	65-69	(female
2	*0.6*	3	*0.8*	70-74	dominant,
1	*0.4*	2	*0.5*	75-79	in 000s)
1	*0.2*	1	*0.3*	80-84	
0	*0.1*	1	*0.3*	85+	
338		332		TOTAL	

VITAL RATES OF PROJECTED POPULATION

Per Thousand	1975 BOTH SEXES	1975 MALES	1975 FEMALES	1980 BOTH SEXES	1980 MALES	1980 FEMALES
BIRTH RATE	42.31	38.64	46.91	40.97	38.08	44.45
DEATH RATE	5.23	5.42	4.99	5.19	5.57	4.74
RATE OF INCREASE	37.09	33.22	41.92	35.78	32.51	39.71

VITAL RATES OF STABLE POPULATION

Per Thousand	MALES	FEMALES	
BIRTH RATE	46.19	45.48	TABLE 6
DEATH RATE	5.97	5.36	PROJECTED
RATE OF INCREASE		40.12	VITAL RATES AND RATIOS

AGE STRUCTURE OF PROJECTED POPULATION

	BOTH SEXES	MALES	FEMALES	BOTH SEXES	MALES	FEMALES
% UNDER 15	46.05	42.03	51.07	46.04	42.74	50.00
% 15-64	52.10	56.41	46.72	52.26	55.71	48.12
% 65 AND OLDER	1.85	1.56	2.21	1.71	1.56	1.88
DEPEND. RATIO x 100	91.93	77.28	114.03	91.36	79.52	107.82

STABLE AGE STRUCTURE

	MALES	FEMALES	
% UNDER 15	48.88	48.20	(female
% 15-64	48.88	48.81	dominant)
% 65 AND OLDER	2.25	2.98	
DEPEND. RATIO x 100	04.60	104.86	

AGE GROUP	FEMALE BIRTH RATES	NET MATERNITY FUNCTION	COEFF. OF MATRIX EQUATION	ORIGINAL MATRIX SUB-DIAGONAL	ORIGINAL MATRIX FIRST ROW	STABLE MATRIX FISHER VALUES	STABLE MATRIX REPRODUCTIVE VALUES	MATRIX PARAMETERS		
0-4	0.0000	0.0000	0.0000	0.98746	0.00000	1.168	79341	λ_1	1.22213	
5-9	0.0000	0.0000	0.0000	0.99561	0.00000	1.446	78347	λ_2	0.42420+0.82316i	TABLE 7
10-14	0.0000	0.0000	0.1494	0.99735	0.15198	1.775	62932	λ_4	-0.04751+0.70765i	
15-19	0.0645	0.2988	0.5087	0.99685	0.51883	1.996	58261	λ_6	-0.53202-0.40876i	LESLIE
20-24	0.1555	0.7186	0.7435	0.99562	0.76062	1.840	57929	r_1	0.04012	MATRIX
25-29	0.1670	0.7683	0.6957	0.99391	0.71489	1.366	42172	r_2	-0.01537+0.21899i	AND ITS
30-34	0.1363	0.6231	0.5456	0.99170	0.56410	0.839	17202	r_4	-0.06871+0.32757i	ANALYSIS
35-39	0.1032	0.4681	0.2971	0.98880	0.30972	0.370	5849	r_6	-0.07982-0.49729i	(females)
40-44	0.0281	0.1260	0.0783	0.98497	0.08260	0.092	880	c_1	3315	
45-49	0.0069	0.0307	0.0153	0.97623	0.01641	0.016	107	$2\pi/y$	28.6915	
50-54	0.0000	0.0000	0.0000	0.00000	0.00000	0.000	0	Δ	7.5012	

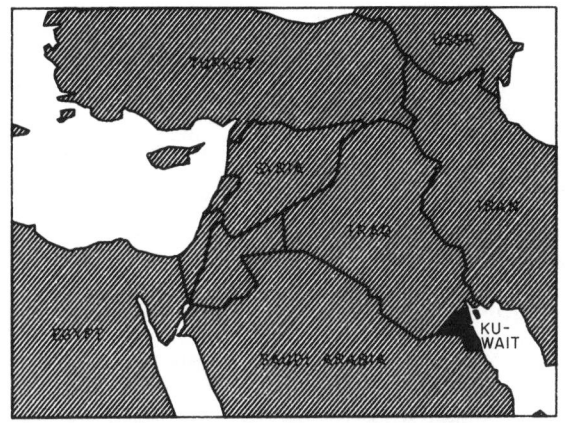

EDUCATION [1984]

% of primary school-age children enrolled:	103
secondary school-age children enrolled:	82
ca. 20-24 year olds in higher education:	16

LABOR FORCE

Average annual labor force growth (%) 1980-85:	6.2	
% of the 1980 labor force in agriculture:	2	TABLE 8
in industry:	32	
in services:	67	SOCIO-ECONOMIC INDICATORS

GNP & INCOME DISTRIBUTION

GNP per capita (in US Dollars) 1985:	14480
GNP average annual growth rate (%) 1965-85:	-0.3
% share of total household income	
Lowest 20% of households:	na
Highest 10% of households:	na

HEALTH & NUTRITION

Population per physician 1981:	700
Daily calorie supply per capita 1985:	3138

TABLE 1 — DATA

AGE AT LAST BIRTHDAY	ESTIMATED MID-YEAR POPULATION BOTH SEXES	MALES Number	MALES Percent	FEMALES Number	FEMALES Percent	BIRTHS BY AGE OF MOTHER AND SEX	DEATHS BOTH SEXES	DEATHS MALES	DEATHS FEMALES	AGE AT LAST BIRTHDAY
0	43220	22056	2.8	21164	3.6		1426	773	653	0
1-4	170896	86798	11.1	84098	14.4		263	131	132	1-4
5-9	183814	93432	12.0	90382	15.5		111	66	45	5-9
10-14	150880	76656	9.8	74224	12.7		77	51	26	10-14
15-19	120481	64622	8.3	55859	9.6	4452	96	73	23	15-19
20-24	125043	72905	9.3	52138	8.9	14022	85	62	23	20-24
25-29	139270	86181	11.0	53089	9.1	15954	137	108	29	25-29
30-34	121379	76627	9.8	44752	7.7	9606	132	104	28	30-34
35-39	97106	63198	8.1	33908	5.8	5613	137	97	40	35-39
40-44	77801	52553	6.7	25248	4.3	1146	173	128	45	40-44
45-49	50935	34476	4.4	16459	2.8	297	217	160	57	45-49
50-54	34670	23196	3.0	11474	2.0		259	189	70	50-54
55-59	19209	12030	1.5	7179	1.2		195	153	42	55-59
60-64	13031	7296	0.9	5735	1.0		291	193	98	60-64
65-69	7099	3809	0.5	3290	0.6		265	156	109	65-69
70-74	5231	2538	0.3	2693	0.5		288	180	108	70-74
75-79	2584	1233	0.2	1351	0.2		221	125	96	75-79
80-84	1848	882	0.1	966	0.2	25971 M	205	106	99	80-84
85+	1138	545	0.1	593	0.1	25119 F	354	172	182	85+
TOTAL	1365635	781033		584602		51090	4932	3027	1905	TOTAL

TABLE 2 — MALE LIFE TABLE

x	$_nM_x$	$_nq_x$	l_x	$_nd_x$	$_nL_x$	$_nm_x$	$_na_x$	T_x	$\overset{\circ}{e}_x$	x
0	0.035047	0.034010	100000	3401	97040	0.035047	0.130	6783677	67.837	0
1	0.001509	0.006014	96599	581	384944	0.001509	1.500	6686638	69.221	1
5	0.000706	0.003526	96018	339	479244	0.000706	2.500	6301694	65.630	5
10	0.000665	0.003329	95680	319	477643	0.000667	2.630	5822450	60.854	10
15	0.001130	0.005636	95361	537	475479	0.001130	2.532	5344808	56.048	15
20	0.000850	0.004243	94823	402	473122	0.000850	2.527	4869329	51.352	20
25	0.001253	0.006247	94421	590	470680	0.001253	2.582	4396207	46.560	25
30	0.001357	0.006769	93831	635	467595	0.001358	2.541	3925527	41.836	30
35	0.001535	0.007677	93196	715	464295	0.001541	2.644	3457932	37.104	35
40	0.002436	0.012223	92481	1130	459870	0.002458	2.758	2993637	32.370	40
45	0.004641	0.023183	91350	2118	451971	0.004686	2.743	2533767	27.737	45
50	0.008148	0.040305	89232	3597	437843	0.008214	2.687	2081797	23.330	50
55	0.012718	0.062411	85636	5345	416172	0.012842	2.753	1643953	19.197	55
60	0.026453	0.125698	80291	10092	377860	0.026710	2.662	1227782	15.292	60
65	0.040956	0.187877	70199	13189	319533	0.041275	2.615	849922	12.107	65
70	0.070922	0.304228	57010	17344	242269	0.071590	2.533	530389	9.303	70
75	0.101379	0.402520	39666	15966	157064	0.101655	2.415	288119	7.264	75
80	0.120181	0.458303	23700	10862	90377	0.120181	2.411	131056	5.530	80
85	0.315596	1.000000	12838	12838	40679	0.278360	3.169	40679	3.169	85

TABLE 3 — FEMALE LIFE TABLE

x	$_nM_x$	$_nq_x$	l_x	$_nd_x$	$_nL_x$	$_nm_x$	$_na_x$	T_x	$\overset{\circ}{e}_x$	x
0	0.030854	0.030041	100000	3004	97364	0.030854	0.122	7206805	72.068	0
1	0.001570	0.006254	96996	607	386467	0.001570	1.500	7109441	73.296	1
5	0.000498	0.002486	96389	240	481347	0.000498	2.500	6722974	69.748	5
10	0.000350	0.001739	96150	167	480321	0.000348	2.447	6241627	64.916	10
15	0.000412	0.002056	95982	197	479428	0.000412	2.546	5761305	60.025	15
20	0.000441	0.002205	95785	211	478411	0.000441	2.563	5281877	55.143	20
25	0.000546	0.002729	95574	261	477236	0.000547	2.570	4803466	50.259	25
30	0.000626	0.003140	95313	299	475880	0.000629	2.710	4326230	45.390	30
35	0.001180	0.005927	95014	563	473775	0.001189	2.702	3850350	40.524	35
40	0.001782	0.008955	94451	846	470360	0.001798	2.761	3376576	35.750	40
45	0.003463	0.017347	93605	1624	464367	0.003497	2.748	2906216	31.048	45
50	0.006101	0.030198	91981	2778	453165	0.006129	2.573	2441849	26.547	50
55	0.005850	0.029171	89203	2602	440436	0.005908	2.855	1988685	22.294	55
60	0.017088	0.083347	86601	7218	416975	0.017310	2.779	1548248	17.878	60
65	0.033131	0.154556	79383	12269	367305	0.033403	2.587	1131273	14.251	65
70	0.040104	0.183513	67114	12316	305705	0.040288	2.575	763968	11.383	70
75	0.071058	0.304974	54798	16712	232890	0.071759	2.541	458263	8.363	75
80	0.102484	0.409156	38086	15583	152053	0.102484	2.537	225373	5.917	80
85	0.306914	1.000000	22503	22503	73320	0.265988	3.258	73320	3.258	85

TABLE 4 — OBSERVED VITAL RATES AND RATIOS

CRUDE RATES

Per Thousand	BOTH SEXES	MALES	FEMALES
BIRTH RATE	37.41	33.25	42.97
DEATH RATE	3.61	3.88	3.26
RATE OF INCREASE	33.80	29.38	39.71

PERCENT OF POPULATION IN AGE GROUP

	BOTH SEXES	MALES	FEMALES
UNDER 15	40.19	35.71	46.16
15 - 64	58.50	63.13	52.32
65 AND OLDER	1.31	1.15	1.52

RATES STANDARDIZED ON USA 1980

Per Thousand	BOTH SEXES	MALES	FEMALES
BIRTH RATE	44.59		42.63
DEATH RATE	12.38	11.87	12.86
RATE OF INCREASE	32.21		29.77

RATES STANDARDIZED ON MEXICO 1980

	BOTH SEXES	MALES	FEMALES
BIRTH RATE	39.04		38.68
DEATH RATE	5.04	5.53	4.54
RATE OF INCREASE	33.99		34.14

VITAL STATISTICS

GFR x 1000	181.522
TFR	5.464
GRR	2.686
NRR	2.560
μ	28.955
σ^2	47.037
GENERATION	28.170
POP. SEX RATIO	0.748
SEX RATIO AT BIRTH	1.034
DEP. RATIO x 100	70.934

PROJECTED POPULATION

AGE GROUP	1985 BOTH SEXES	1985 MALES	1985 FEMALES	1990 BOTH SEXES	1990 MALES	1990 FEMALES
0-4	262	133	129	298	151	147
5-9	213	108	105	260	132	128
10-14	183	93	90	212	108	104
15-19	150	76	74	183	93	90
20-24	120	64	56	150	76	74
25-29	125	73	52	120	64	56
30-34	139	86	53	124	72	52
35-39	121	76	45	138	85	53
40-44	97	63	34	119	75	44
45-49	77	52	25	95	62	33
50-54	49	33	16	74	50	24
55-59	33	22	11	48	32	16
60-64	18	11	7	31	20	11
65-69	11	6	5	15	9	6
70-74	6	3	3	9	5	4
75-79	4	2	2	4	2	2
80-84	2	1	1	2	1	1
85+	0	0	0	0	0	0
TOTAL	1610	902	708	1882	1037	845

STABLE EQUIVALENT TO ORIGINAL POPULATION

MALES Number	MALES Percent	FEMALES Number	FEMALES Percent	AGE GROUP	
109	17.3	105	17.0	0-4	
91	14.6	89	14.3	5-9	TABLE 5
77	12.3	75	12.1	10-14	
65	10.4	63	10.2	15-19	POPULATION
55	8.7	53	8.6	20-24	PROJECTED
46	7.3	45	7.3	25-29	WITH
39	6.2	38	6.1	30-34	FIXED
32	5.2	32	5.2	35-39	AGE-
27	4.3	27	4.3	40-44	SPECIFIC
23	3.6	22	3.6	45-49	BIRTH
19	3.0	19	3.0	50-54	AND
15	2.4	15	2.5	55-59	DEATH
11	1.8	12	2.0	60-64	RATES
8	1.3	9	1.5	65-69	(female
5	0.8	6	1.0	70-74	dominant,
3	0.5	4	0.7	75-79	in 000s)
1	0.2	2	0.4	80-84	
1	0.1	1	0.2	85+	
627		617		TOTAL	

VITAL RATES OF PROJECTED POPULATION

Per Thousand	1985 BOTH SEXES	1985 MALES	1985 FEMALES	1990 BOTH SEXES	1990 MALES	1990 FEMALES
BIRTH RATE	35.59	32.28	39.81	35.19	32.48	38.51
DEATH RATE	3.77	4.19	3.25	4.04	4.65	3.30
RATE OF INCREASE	31.82	28.10	36.57	31.15	27.83	35.21

VITAL RATES OF STABLE POPULATION

Per Thousand	MALES	FEMALES	
BIRTH RATE	38.98	38.15	TABLE 6
DEATH RATE	5.50	4.69	PROJECTED
RATE OF INCREASE		33.46	VITAL RATES

AGE STRUCTURE OF PROJECTED POPULATION

	1985 BOTH SEXES	1985 MALES	1985 FEMALES	1990 BOTH SEXES	1990 MALES	1990 FEMALES
% UNDER 15	40.90	37.06	45.80	40.94	37.73	44.88
% 15-64	57.67	61.63	52.62	57.40	60.62	53.46
% 65 AND OLDER	1.43	1.31	1.58	1.65	1.65	1.66
DEPEND. RATIO x 100	73.41	62.27	90.06	74.21	64.96	87.06

STABLE AGE STRUCTURE

	MALES	FEMALES	
% UNDER 15	44.23	43.47	AND RATIOS
% 15-64	52.86	52.84	(female
% 65 AND OLDER	2.91	3.69	dominant)
DEPEND. RATIO x 100	89.17	89.26	

AGE GROUP	FEMALE BIRTH RATES	NET MATERNITY FUNCTION	COEFF. OF MATRIX EQUATION	ORIGINAL MATRIX SUB-DIAGONAL	ORIGINAL MATRIX FIRST ROW	STABLE MATRIX FISHER VALUES	STABLE MATRIX REPRODUCTIVE VALUES	MATRIX PARAMETERS	
0-4	0.0000	0.0000	0.0000	0.99487	0.00000	1.123	118191	λ_1	1.18211
5-9	0.0000	0.0000	0.0000	0.99787	0.00000	1.334	120583	λ_2	0.41396-0.81426i
10-14	0.0000	0.0000	0.0939	0.99814	0.09462	1.580	117309	λ_4	-0.54103+0.41311i
15-19	0.0392	0.1879	0.4102	0.99788	0.41400	1.765	98609	λ_6	-0.63957-0.00000i
20-24	0.1322	0.6326	0.6689	0.99754	0.67643	1.625	84745	r_1	0.03346
25-29	0.1478	0.7051	0.6037	0.99716	0.61201	1.165	61835	r_2	-0.01811-0.22009i
30-34	0.1055	0.5022	0.4439	0.99558	0.45132	0.692	30952	r_4	-0.07692+0.49789i
35-39	0.0814	0.3856	0.2453	0.99279	0.25049	0.312	10586	r_6	-0.08939-0.62832i
40-44	0.0223	0.1050	0.0731	0.98726	0.07518	0.088	2233	c_1	6191
45-49	0.0089	0.0412	0.0206	0.97588	0.02146	0.020	336	$2\pi/y$	28.5479
50-54	0.0000	0.0000	0.0000	0.00000	0.00000	0.000	0	Δ	6.9255

TABLE 7

LESLIE MATRIX AND ITS ANALYSIS (females)

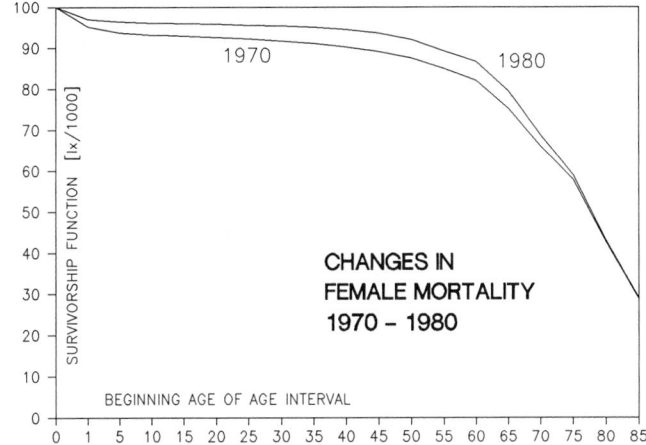

CHANGES IN FEMALE MORTALITY 1970 – 1980

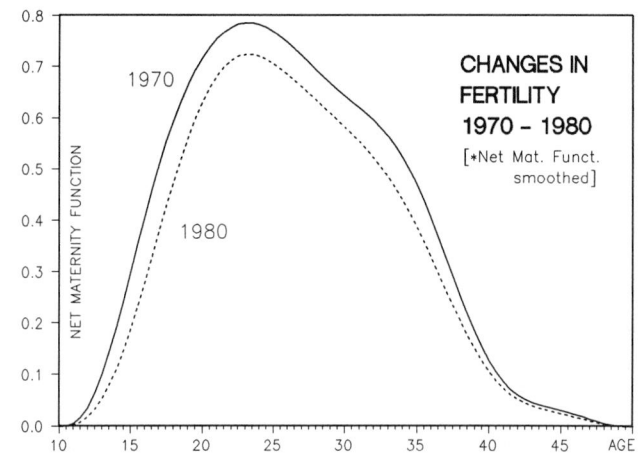

CHANGES IN FERTILITY 1970 – 1980
[*Net Mat. Funct. smoothed]

AGE AT LAST BIRTHDAY	ESTIMATED MID-YEAR POPULATION BOTH SEXES	MALES Number	MALES Percent	FEMALES Number	FEMALES Percent	BIRTHS BY AGE OF MOTHER AND SEX	DEATHS BOTH SEXES	DEATHS MALES	DEATHS FEMALES	AGE AT LAST BIRTHDAY
0	264547	134632	2.9	129915	2.9		12146	7024	5122	0
1-4	1125234	573627	12.4	551607	12.2		4840	2452	2388	1-4
5-9	1402596	715406	15.5	687190	15.2		1999	1056	943	5-9
10-14	1241368	630204	13.6	611164	13.5	270	1143	630	513	10-14
15-19	1026032	512628	11.1	513404	11.4	27778	1280	709	571	15-19
20-24	784871	391967	8.5	392904	8.7	88673	1265	679	586	20-24
25-29	574711	287989	6.2	286722	6.3	76088	1129	557	572	25-29
30-34	555435	279824	6.1	275611	6.1	60386	1408	751	657	30-34
35-39	432325	212247	4.6	219704	4.9	30679	1374	725	649	35-39
40-44	382900	192287	4.2	190613	4.2	10746	1814	996	818	40-44
45-49	319622	157951	3.4	161671	3.6	2075	2264	1279	985	45-49
50-54	285964	144460	3.1	141504	3.1	470	3408	2028	1380	50-54
55-59	234137	122907	2.7	111230	2.5		4102	2523	1579	55-59
60-64	205501	107199	2.3	98302	2.2		6081	3691	2390	60-64
65-69	126375	69336	1.5	57039	1.3		5408	3461	1947	65-69
70-74	88345	44749	1.0	43596	1.0		5543	3325	2218	70-74
75-79	43745	22599	0.5	21146	0.5		3224	1919	1305	75-79
80-84	32738	14988	0.3	17750	0.4	152443 M	3160	1642	1518	80-84
85+	20235	8959	0.2	11276	0.2	144722 F	2386	1050	1336	85+
TOTAL	9146681	4624333		4522348		297165	63974	36497	27477	TOTAL

TABLE 1 DATA

TABLE 2 — MALE LIFE TABLE

x	$_nM_x$	$_nq_x$	l_x	$_nd_x$	$_nL_x$	$_nm_x$	$_na_x$	T_x	$\overset{\circ}{e}_x$	x
0	0.052172	0.049978	100000	4998	95795	0.052172	0.159	6322693	63.227	0
1	0.004275	0.016917	95002	1607	375991	0.004275	1.500	6226898	65.545	1
5	0.001476	0.007353	93395	687	465258	0.001476	2.500	5850907	62.647	5
10	0.001000	0.004980	92708	462	462377	0.000998	2.478	5385649	58.092	10
15	0.001383	0.006919	92247	638	459706	0.001388	2.608	4923272	53.371	15
20	0.001732	0.008645	91608	792	456111	0.001736	2.563	4463566	48.724	20
25	0.001934	0.009652	90816	877	451976	0.001939	2.598	4007455	44.127	25
30	0.002684	0.013377	89940	1203	446822	0.002693	2.609	3555479	39.532	30
35	0.003410	0.016990	88737	1508	440131	0.003425	2.644	3108657	35.032	35
40	0.005180	0.025714	87229	2243	430931	0.005205	2.675	2668526	30.592	40
45	0.008097	0.039934	84986	3394	417136	0.008136	2.704	2237596	26.329	45
50	0.014038	0.068135	81592	5559	394909	0.014077	2.652	1820459	22.312	50
55	0.020528	0.098046	76033	7455	362649	0.020556	2.650	1425550	18.749	55
60	0.034431	0.159521	68578	10940	316671	0.034546	2.603	1062902	15.499	60
65	0.049916	0.223373	57638	12875	256659	0.050163	2.551	746231	12.947	65
70	0.074303	0.314470	44764	14077	188168	0.074810	2.467	489572	10.937	70
75	0.084915	0.347861	30687	10675	125587	0.084999	2.391	301404	9.822	75
80	0.109554	0.425145	20012	8508	77660	0.109554	2.367	175817	8.786	80
85	0.117201	1.000000	11504	11504	98157	0.053494	8.532	98157	8.532	85

TABLE 3 — FEMALE LIFE TABLE

x	$_nM_x$	$_nq_x$	l_x	$_nd_x$	$_nL_x$	$_nm_x$	$_na_x$	T_x	$\overset{\circ}{e}_x$	x
0	0.039426	0.038129	100000	3813	96710	0.039426	0.137	6773655	67.737	0
1	0.004329	0.017131	96187	1648	380629	0.004329	1.500	6676946	69.416	1
5	0.001372	0.006838	94539	646	471081	0.001372	2.500	6296317	66.600	5
10	0.000839	0.004181	93893	393	468457	0.000838	2.433	5825236	62.041	10
15	0.001112	0.005568	93500	521	466263	0.001117	2.621	5356779	57.292	15
20	0.001491	0.007462	92980	694	463248	0.001498	2.620	4890516	52.598	20
25	0.001995	0.009960	92286	919	459214	0.002002	2.589	4427269	47.973	25
30	0.002384	0.011873	91367	1085	454208	0.002388	2.579	3968055	43.430	30
35	0.002954	0.014723	90282	1329	448256	0.002965	2.627	3513847	38.921	35
40	0.004291	0.021329	88953	1897	440291	0.004309	2.642	3065591	34.463	40
45	0.006093	0.030154	87056	2625	429162	0.006117	2.670	2625300	30.157	45
50	0.009752	0.047897	84430	4044	412650	0.009800	2.650	2196138	26.011	50
55	0.014196	0.068938	80386	5542	389039	0.014245	2.673	1783488	22.186	55
60	0.024313	0.115683	74845	8658	353609	0.024485	2.619	1394449	18.631	60
65	0.034135	0.158508	66186	10491	305536	0.034337	2.579	1040840	15.726	65
70	0.050876	0.227102	55695	12649	247070	0.051194	2.517	735304	13.202	70
75	0.061714	0.267586	43047	11519	186109	0.061892	2.472	488234	11.342	75
80	0.085521	0.351252	31528	11074	129492	0.085521	2.458	302125	9.583	80
85	0.118482	1.000000	20454	20454	172633	0.053862	8.440	172633	8.440	85

TABLE 4 — OBSERVED VITAL RATES AND RATIOS

CRUDE RATES

Per Thousand	BOTH SEXES	MALES	FEMALES
BIRTH RATE	32.49	32.97	32.00
DEATH RATE	6.99	7.89	6.08
RATE OF INCREASE	25.49	25.07	25.93

RATES STANDARDIZED ON USA 1980

Per Thousand	BOTH SEXES	MALES	FEMALES
BIRTH RATE	39.48		37.40
DEATH RATE	12.64	12.94	12.35
RATE OF INCREASE	26.85		25.04

VITAL STATISTICS

GFR x 1000	145.624
TFR	4.884
GRR	2.379
NRR	2.170
μ	29.435
σ^2	46.914
GENERATION	28.804
POP. SEX RATIO	0.978
SEX RATIO AT BIRTH	1.053
DEP. RATIO x 100	90.496

PERCENT OF POPULATION IN AGE GROUP

	BOTH SEXES	MALES	FEMALES
UNDER 15	44.10	44.41	43.78
15 - 64	52.49	52.11	52.89
65 AND OLDER	3.40	3.47	3.33

RATES STANDARDIZED ON MEXICO 1980

Per Thousand	BOTH SEXES	MALES	FEMALES
BIRTH RATE	34.11		33.48
DEATH RATE	6.64	7.26	6.01
RATE OF INCREASE	27.47		27.47

PROJECTED POPULATION

AGE GROUP	1975			1980		
	BOTH SEXES	MALES	FEMALES	BOTH SEXES	MALES	FEMALES
0-4	1576	804	772	1937	988	949
5-9	1371	698	673	1554	792	762
10-14	1394	711	683	1363	694	669
15-19	1235	627	608	1387	707	680
20-24	1019	509	510	1226	622	604
25-29	777	388	389	1010	504	506
30-34	569	285	284	769	384	385
35-39	548	276	272	560	280	280
40-44	424	208	216	537	270	267
45-49	372	186	186	412	202	210
50-54	305	150	155	355	176	179
55-59	266	133	133	284	137	147
60-64	208	107	101	237	116	121
65-69	172	87	85	174	87	87
70-74	97	51	46	133	64	69
75-79	63	30	33	69	34	35
80-84	29	14	15	41	18	23
85+	43	19	24	38	18	20
TOTAL	10468	5283	5185	12086	6093	5993

STABLE EQUIVALENT TO ORIGINAL POPULATION

MALES		FEMALES		AGE GROUP	
Number	Percent	Number	Percent		
764	15.6	734	15.3	0-4	
659	13.4	633	13.2	5-9	TABLE 5
572	11.6	550	11.4	10-14	
497	10.1	478	9.9	15-19	POPULATION
431	8.8	415	8.6	20-24	PROJECTED
373	7.6	360	7.5	25-29	WITH
322	6.6	311	6.5	30-34	FIXED
277	5.6	268	5.6	35-39	AGE-
237	4.8	230	4.8	40-44	SPECIFIC
201	4.1	196	4.1	45-49	BIRTH
166	3.4	165	3.4	50-54	AND
133	2.7	136	2.8	55-59	DEATH
102	2.1	108	2.2	60-64	RATES
72	1.5	81	1.7	65-69	(female
46	0.9	58	1.2	70-74	dominant,
27	0.5	38	0.8	75-79	in 000s)
15	0.3	23	0.5	80-84	
16	0.3	27	0.6	85+	
4910		4811		TOTAL	

VITAL RATES OF PROJECTED POPULATION

Per Thousand	1975			1980		
	BOTH SEXES	MALES	FEMALES	BOTH SEXES	MALES	FEMALES
BIRTH RATE	35.05	35.64	34.46	37.20	37.85	36.54
DEATH RATE	7.18	7.99	6.36	7.20	7.95	6.44
RATE OF INCREASE	27.87	27.65	28.10	29.99	29.89	30.10

VITAL RATES OF STABLE POPULATION

Per Thousand	MALES	FEMALES	
BIRTH RATE	35.21	34.11	TABLE 6
DEATH RATE	8.14	7.14	PROJECTED
RATE OF INCREASE		26.97	VITAL RATES AND RATIOS (female dominant)

AGE STRUCTURE OF PROJECTED POPULATION

	BOTH SEXES	MALES	FEMALES	BOTH SEXES	MALES	FEMALES
% UNDER 15	41.47	41.90	41.04	40.17	40.61	39.71
% 15-64	54.68	54.30	55.06	56.08	55.76	56.40
% 65 AND OLDER	3.85	3.80	3.90	3.76	3.62	3.89
DEPEND. RATIO x 100	82.89	84.16	81.61	78.32	79.33	77.32

STABLE AGE STRUCTURE

	MALES	FEMALES
% UNDER 15	40.62	39.85
% 15-64	55.80	55.44
% 65 AND OLDER	3.58	4.71
DEPEND. RATIO x 100	79.22	80.36

AGE GROUP	FEMALE BIRTH RATES	NET MATERNITY FUNCTION	COEFF. OF MATRIX EQUATION	ORIGINAL MATRIX SUB-DIAGONAL	ORIGINAL MATRIX FIRST ROW	STABLE MATRIX FISHER VALUES	STABLE MATRIX REPRODUCTIVE VALUES
0-4	0.0000	0.0000	0.0000	0.98689	0.00000	1.120	763247
5-9	0.0000	0.0000	0.0005	0.99443	0.00051	1.299	892386
10-14	0.0002	0.0010	0.0619	0.99532	0.06311	1.494	912960
15-19	0.0263	0.1229	0.3160	0.99353	0.32352	1.646	845306
20-24	0.1099	0.5092	0.5513	0.99129	0.56809	1.532	601826
25-29	0.1292	0.5935	0.5391	0.98910	0.56034	1.126	322976
30-34	0.1067	0.4847	0.3947	0.98690	0.41485	0.669	184328
35-39	0.0680	0.3048	0.2129	0.98223	0.22667	0.305	66952
40-44	0.0275	0.1209	0.0739	0.97472	0.08007	0.097	18412
45-49	0.0063	0.0268	0.0168	0.96152	0.01863	0.021	3461
50-54	0.0016	0.0067	0.0033	0.94278	0.00386	0.004	535

MATRIX PARAMETERS

λ_1	1.14435	
λ_2	$0.43239-0.79753i$	TABLE 7
λ_4	$-0.03724-0.59924i$	
λ_6	$-0.42724-0.41216i$	LESLIE
r_1	0.02697	MATRIX
r_2	$-0.01948-0.21480i$	AND ITS
r_4	$-0.10203-0.32657i$	ANALYSIS
r_6	$-0.10430-0.47483i$	(females)
c_1	48118	
$2\pi/y$	29.2517	
Δ	5.5825	

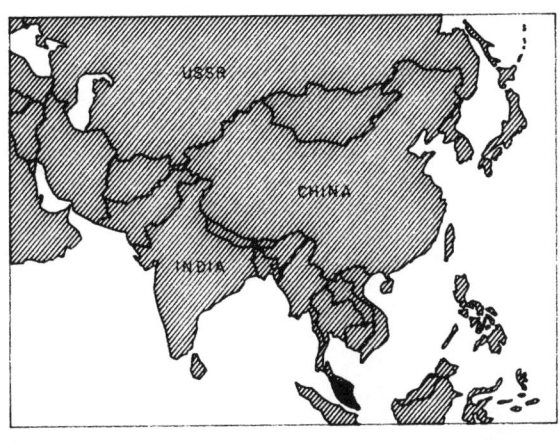

EDUCATION [1984]

% of primary school-age children enrolled:	97
secondary school-age children enrolled:	53
ca. 20-24 year olds in higher education:	6

LABOR FORCE

Average annual labor force growth (%) 1980-85:	2.9	
% of the 1980 labor force in agriculture:	42	TABLE 8
in industry:	19	
in services:	39	SOCIO-

GNP & INCOME DISTRIBUTION

GNP per capita (in US Dollars) 1985:	2000	ECONOMIC
GNP average annual growth rate (%) 1965-85:	4.4	INDICATORS
% share of total household income 1973		
Lowest 20% of households:	3.5	
Highest 10% of households:	39.8	

HEALTH & NUTRITION

Population per physician 1981:	3920
Daily calorie supply per capita 1985:	2684

TABLE 1 DATA

AGE AT LAST BIRTHDAY	ESTIMATED MID-YEAR POPULATION BOTH SEXES	MALES Number	MALES Percent	FEMALES Number	FEMALES Percent	BIRTHS BY AGE OF MOTHER AND SEX	DEATHS BOTH SEXES	DEATHS MALES	DEATHS FEMALES	AGE AT LAST BIRTHDAY
0	314204	160519	3.1	153685	3.0		10372	5965	4407	0
1-4	1180484	602136	11.7	578348	11.4		3626	1854	1772	1-4
5-9	1390071	708420	13.7	681651	13.4		1501	787	714	5-9
10-14	1357131	684147	13.3	672984	13.2	214	1000	546	454	10-14
15-19	1179725	585693	11.4	594032	11.7	28255	1278	773	505	15-19
20-24	976279	482832	9.4	493447	9.7	95049	1470	904	566	20-24
25-29	777701	390967	7.6	386734	7.6	92663	1284	784	500	25-29
30-34	576131	291441	5.7	284690	5.6	51978	1203	680	523	30-34
35-39	552368	280134	5.4	272234	5.3	33588	1573	883	690	35-39
40-44	420443	207534	4.0	212909	4.2	9911	1718	1029	689	40-44
45-49	374728	187835	3.6	186893	3.7	1387	2361	1427	934	45-49
50-54	300683	147943	2.9	152740	3.0	245	3138	1874	1264	50-54
55-59	264443	131432	2.5	133011	2.6		4120	2435	1685	55-59
60-64	203984	104757	2.0	99227	1.9		5597	3405	2192	60-64
65-69	171306	87198	1.7	84108	1.7		6872	4049	2823	65-69
70-74	93733	49889	1.0	43844	0.9		5874	3624	2250	70-74
75-79	53130	26763	0.5	26367	0.5		5049	2852	2197	75-79
80-84	39879	17747	0.3	22132	0.4	160621 M	2779	1526	1253	80-84
85+	24669	10609	0.2	14060	0.3	152669 F	3256	1439	1817	85+
TOTAL	10251092	5157996		5093096		313290	64071	36836	27235	TOTAL

TABLE 2 MALE LIFE TABLE

x	nM_x	nq_x	l_x	nd_x	nL_x	nm_x	na_x	T_x	$\overset{\circ}{e}_x$	x
0	0.037161	0.036001	100000	3600	96879	0.037161	0.133	6498819	64.988	0
1	0.003079	0.012222	96400	1178	382654	0.003079	1.500	6401939	66.410	1
5	0.001111	0.005539	95222	527	474790	0.001111	2.500	6019285	63.213	5
10	0.000798	0.003984	94694	377	472548	0.000798	2.553	5544495	58.552	10
15	0.001320	0.006609	94317	623	470130	0.001326	2.667	5071947	53.776	15
20	0.001872	0.009346	93694	876	466342	0.001878	2.572	4601817	49.116	20
25	0.002005	0.009988	92818	927	461812	0.002008	2.543	4135475	44.555	25
30	0.002333	0.011635	91891	1069	456886	0.002340	2.598	3673662	39.979	30
35	0.003152	0.015720	90822	1428	450776	0.003167	2.666	3216777	35.419	35
40	0.004958	0.024663	89394	2205	441843	0.004990	2.674	2766001	30.942	40
45	0.007597	0.037532	87189	3272	428386	0.007639	2.690	2324159	26.656	45
50	0.012667	0.061779	83917	5184	407403	0.012725	2.650	1895772	22.591	50
55	0.018527	0.089098	78733	7015	377302	0.018592	2.668	1488369	18.904	55
60	0.032504	0.151049	71718	10833	332698	0.032561	2.610	1111066	15.492	60
65	0.046435	0.209159	60885	12735	273438	0.046572	2.567	778369	12.784	65
70	0.072641	0.309782	48150	14916	203698	0.073226	2.516	504931	10.487	70
75	0.106565	0.417410	33234	13872	129787	0.106885	2.377	301233	9.064	75
80	0.085986	0.348200	19362	6742	78405	0.085986	2.270	171446	8.855	80
85	0.135640	1.000000	12620	12620	93041	0.069163	7.372	93041	7.372	85

TABLE 3 FEMALE LIFE TABLE

x	nM_x	nq_x	l_x	nd_x	nL_x	nm_x	na_x	T_x	$\overset{\circ}{e}_x$	x
0	0.028676	0.027969	100000	2797	97535	0.028676	0.119	6989271	69.893	0
1	0.003064	0.012162	97203	1182	385857	0.003064	1.500	6891736	70.900	1
5	0.001047	0.005224	96021	502	478851	0.001047	2.500	6505879	67.755	5
10	0.000675	0.003365	95519	321	476773	0.000674	2.437	6027028	63.097	10
15	0.000850	0.004252	95198	405	475024	0.000852	2.614	5550255	58.302	15
20	0.001147	0.005735	94793	544	472649	0.001150	2.578	5075232	53.540	20
25	0.001293	0.006463	94249	609	469790	0.001297	2.608	4602583	48.834	25
30	0.001837	0.009189	93640	860	466168	0.001846	2.636	4132792	44.135	30
35	0.002535	0.012634	92780	1172	461097	0.002542	2.610	3666625	39.520	35
40	0.003236	0.016132	91608	1478	454566	0.003251	2.650	3205528	34.992	40
45	0.004998	0.024842	90130	2239	445490	0.005026	2.696	2750962	30.522	45
50	0.008276	0.040784	87891	3585	431113	0.008315	2.673	2305471	26.231	50
55	0.012668	0.061902	84306	5219	409475	0.012745	2.690	1874358	22.233	55
60	0.022091	0.105407	79088	8336	375814	0.022182	2.646	1464883	18.522	60
65	0.033564	0.156323	70751	11060	327225	0.033799	2.601	1089069	15.393	65
70	0.051318	0.229672	59691	13709	265166	0.051701	2.572	761844	12.763	70
75	0.083324	0.343228	45982	15782	189147	0.083439	2.417	496678	10.802	75
80	0.056615	0.246371	30200	7440	131419	0.056615	2.369	307531	10.183	80
85	0.129232	1.000000	22759	22759	176112	0.062970	7.738	176112	7.738	85

TABLE 4 OBSERVED VITAL RATES AND RATIOS

CRUDE RATES

Per Thousand	BOTH SEXES	MALES	FEMALES
BIRTH RATE	30.56	31.14	29.98
DEATH RATE	6.25	7.14	5.35
RATE OF INCREASE	24.31	24.00	24.63

PERCENT OF POPULATION IN AGE GROUP

	BOTH SEXES	MALES	FEMALES
UNDER 15	41.38	41.78	40.97
15 - 64	54.89	54.49	55.29
65 AND OLDER	3.73	3.73	3.74

RATES STANDARDIZED ON USA 1980

Per Thousand	BOTH SEXES	MALES	FEMALES
BIRTH RATE	34.12		32.34
DEATH RATE	12.04	12.35	11.75
RATE OF INCREASE	22.09		20.59

RATES STANDARDIZED ON MEXICO 1980

	BOTH SEXES	MALES	FEMALES
BIRTH RATE	29.52		28.99
DEATH RATE	5.81	6.45	5.17
RATE OF INCREASE	23.71		23.82

VITAL STATISTICS

GFR x 1000	128.876
TFR	4.208
GRR	2.051
NRR	1.918
μ	29.309
σ^2	44.762
GENERATION	28.803
POP. SEX RATIO	0.987
SEX RATIO AT BIRTH	1.052
DEP. RATIO x 100	82.194

AGE AT LAST BIRTHDAY	ESTIMATED MID-YEAR POPULATION BOTH SEXES	MALES Number	Percent	FEMALES Number	Percent	BIRTHS BY AGE OF MOTHER AND SEX	DEATHS BOTH SEXES	MALES	FEMALES	AGE AT LAST BIRTHDAY	
0	295952	152022	2.6	143930	2.5		8333	4775	3558	0	
1-4	1248907	639738	11.1	609169	10.7		2558	1313	1245	1-4	
5-9	1502809	766132	13.4	736677	12.9		1173	654	519	5-9	
10-14	1405417	716436	12.5	688981	12.1	162	847	511	336	10-14	
15-19	1316692	655309	11.4	661383	11.6	22939	1231	788	443	15-19	
20-24	1120254	541938	9.4	578316	10.1	101631	1425	967	458	20-24	
25-29	928963	454020	7.9	474943	8.3	111568	1375	887	488	25-29	
30-34	772851	391091	6.8	381760	6.7	68350	1368	753	615	30-34	
35-39	578832	295453	5.1	283379	5.0	29766	1291	736	555	35-39	TABLE 1
40-44	549805	280346	4.9	269459	4.7	11040	1851	1122	729	40-44	
45-49	407744	201456	3.5	206288	3.6	997	2210	1338	872	45-49	DATA
50-54	364130	181537	3.2	182593	3.2	115	3196	1955	1241	50-54	
55-59	278149	135591	2.4	142558	2.5		3991	2430	1561	55-59	
60-64	238075	115558	2.0	122517	2.1		5563	3228	2335	60-64	
65-69	169247	84209	1.5	85038	1.5		6232	3664	2568	65-69	
70-74	134642	66411	1.2	68231	1.2		7574	4214	3360	70-74	
75-79	70264	35664	0.6	34600	0.6		5679	3289	2390	75-79	
80-84	36445	16524	0.3	19921	0.3	178483 N	4084	2099	1985	80-84	
85+	22908	9362	0.2	13546	0.2	168085 F	3501	1516	1985	85+	
TOTAL	11442086	5738797		5703289		346568	63482	36239	27243	TOTAL	

x	$_nM_x$	$_nq_x$	l_x	$_nd_x$	$_nL_x$	$_nm_x$	$_na_x$	T_x	$\overset{\circ}{e}_x$	x	
0	0.031410	0.030568	100000	3057	97320	0.031410	0.123	6665640	66.656	0	
1	0.002052	0.008168	96943	792	385793	0.002052	1.500	6568320	67.754	1	
5	0.000854	0.004259	96151	410	479733	0.000854	2.500	6182527	64.300	5	
10	0.000713	0.003563	95742	341	477891	0.000714	2.601	5702794	59.564	10	
15	0.001202	0.006019	95401	574	475673	0.001207	2.683	5224903	54.768	15	
20	0.001784	0.008911	94826	845	472090	0.001790	2.584	4749230	50.083	20	
25	0.001954	0.009725	93981	914	467632	0.001955	2.511	4277140	45.510	25	TABLE 2
30	0.001925	0.009591	93067	893	463154	0.001927	2.554	3809508	40.933	30	
35	0.002491	0.012445	92175	1147	458199	0.002504	2.668	3346354	36.304	35	MALE
40	0.004002	0.019961	91028	1817	450969	0.004029	2.706	2888155	31.728	40	LIFE
45	0.006642	0.032950	89211	2939	439276	0.006692	2.694	2437185	27.319	45	TABLE
50	0.010769	0.052856	86271	4560	420816	0.010836	2.688	1997909	23.158	50	
55	0.017922	0.086454	81711	7064	391991	0.018022	2.655	1577093	19.301	55	
60	0.027934	0.131467	74647	9814	349893	0.028048	2.621	1185103	15.876	60	
65	0.043511	0.197189	64833	12784	293140	0.043612	2.573	835210	12.882	65	
70	0.063453	0.274719	52049	14299	224788	0.063610	2.520	542069	10.415	70	
75	0.092222	0.375558	37750	14177	152666	0.092865	2.455	317281	8.405	75	
80	0.127027	0.476059	23573	11222	88344	0.127027	2.369	164615	6.983	80	
85	0.161931	1.000000	12351	12351	76272	0.093661	6.175	76272	6.175	85	

x	$_nM_x$	$_nq_x$	l_x	$_nd_x$	$_nL_x$	$_nm_x$	$_na_x$	T_x	$\overset{\circ}{e}_x$	x	
0	0.024720	0.024189	100000	2419	97852	0.024720	0.112	7145142	71.451	0	
1	0.002044	0.008134	97581	794	388340	0.002044	1.500	7047290	72.220	1	
5	0.000705	0.003516	96787	340	483086	0.000705	2.500	6658950	68.800	5	
10	0.000488	0.002435	96447	235	481644	0.000488	2.484	6175864	64.034	10	
15	0.000670	0.003347	96212	322	480286	0.000671	2.594	5694220	59.184	15	
20	0.000792	0.003961	95890	380	478537	0.000794	2.593	5213934	54.374	20	
25	0.001027	0.005150	95510	492	476402	0.001033	2.664	4735398	49.580	25	TABLE 3
30	0.001611	0.008062	95018	766	473267	0.001619	2.617	4258995	44.823	30	
35	0.001959	0.009781	94252	922	469061	0.001965	2.612	3785728	40.166	35	FEMALE
40	0.002705	0.013503	93331	1260	463714	0.002718	2.668	3316668	35.537	40	LIFE
45	0.004227	0.021062	92070	1939	455873	0.004254	2.690	2852953	30.987	45	TABLE
50	0.006797	0.033654	90131	3033	443643	0.006837	2.688	2397080	26.595	50	
55	0.010950	0.053708	87098	4678	424739	0.011014	2.702	1953437	22.428	55	
60	0.019059	0.091810	82420	7567	394415	0.019185	2.663	1528698	18.548	60	
65	0.030198	0.141539	74853	10595	349164	0.030343	2.631	1134283	15.153	65	
70	0.049244	0.221259	64258	14218	286626	0.049604	2.562	785119	12.218	70	
75	0.069075	0.295967	50041	14810	213131	0.069490	2.497	498492	9.962	75	
80	0.099644	0.397220	35230	13994	140442	0.099644	2.448	285362	8.100	80	
85	0.146538	1.000000	21236	21236	144919	0.078223	6.824	144919	6.824	85	

CRUDE RATES

Per Thousand	BOTH SEXES	MALES	FEMALES
BIRTH RATE	30.29	31.10	29.47
DEATH RATE	5.55	6.31	4.78
RATE OF INCREASE	24.74	24.79	24.69

RATES STANDARDIZED ON USA 1980

Per Thousand	BOTH SEXES	MALES	FEMALES
BIRTH RATE	31.58		29.78
DEATH RATE	11.54	11.61	11.47
RATE OF INCREASE	20.04		18.32

VITAL STATISTICS

GFR x 1000	121.367	TABLE 4
TFR	3.880	
GRR	1.882	OBSERVED
NRR	1.786	VITAL
μ	29.302	RATES
σ^2	40.661	AND
GENERATION	28.894	RATIOS
POP. SEX RATIO	0.994	
SEX RATIO AT BIRTH	1.062	
DEP. RATIO x 100	74.542	

PERCENT OF POPULATION IN AGE GROUP

UNDER 15	38.92	39.63	38.20
15 - 64	57.29	56.67	57.92
65 AND OLDER	3.79	3.70	3.88

RATES STANDARDIZED ON MEXICO 1980

	BOTH SEXES	MALES	FEMALES
BIRTH RATE	27.15		26.54
DEATH RATE	5.20	5.79	4.61
RATE OF INCREASE	21.94		21.93

TABLE 1 — DATA

AGE AT LAST BIRTHDAY	ESTIMATED MID-YEAR POPULATION — BOTH SEXES	MALES Number	MALES Percent	FEMALES Number	FEMALES Percent	BIRTHS BY AGE OF MOTHER AND SEX	DEATHS BOTH SEXES	DEATHS MALES	DEATHS FEMALES	AGE AT LAST BIRTHDAY
0	393316	201381	3.1	191935	3.0		6920	3983	2937	0
1-4	1429108	734437	11.3	694671	10.7		2002	1077	925	1-4
5-9	1535125	786519	12.1	748606	11.6		962	543	419	5-9
10-14	1498910	763863	11.7	735047	11.4	130	831	476	355	10-14
15-19	1400030	712941	10.9	687089	10.6	17669	1388	951	437	15-19
20-24	1309358	650324	10.0	659034	10.2	103486	1704	1197	507	20-24
25-29	1112970	537137	8.2	575833	8.9	137470	1619	1065	554	25-29
30-34	922304	449926	6.9	472378	7.3	91283	1462	884	578	30-34
35-39	766066	386998	5.9	379068	5.9	44009	1629	1013	616	35-39
40-44	571274	290903	4.5	280371	4.3	11465	1892	1157	735	40-44
45-49	539160	273798	4.2	265362	4.1	1219	2633	1651	982	45-49
50-54	393335	192717	3.0	200618	3.1	75	3378	2042	1336	50-54
55-59	345133	170012	2.6	175121	2.7		4670	2885	1785	55-59
60-64	253242	121132	1.9	132110	2.0		5816	3358	2458	60-64
65-69	208042	98437	1.5	109605	1.7		6773	3839	2934	65-69
70-74	133343	63886	1.0	69457	1.1		7811	4318	3493	70-74
75-79	97466	45873	0.7	51593	0.8		7512	3964	3548	75-79
80-84	43833	21094	0.3	22739	0.4	208422 M	4836	2557	2279	80-84
85+	28953	11496	0.2	17457	0.3	198384 F	4529	1963	2566	85+
TOTAL	12980968	6512874		6468094		406806	68367	38923	29444	TOTAL

TABLE 2 — MALE LIFE TABLE

x	nM_x	nq_x	l_x	nd_x	nL_x	nm_x	na_x	T_x	$\overset{\circ}{e}_x$	x
0	0.019778	0.019434	100000	1943	98258	0.019778	0.104	6786738	67.867	0
1	0.001466	0.005844	98057	573	390794	0.001466	1.500	6688480	68.210	1
5	0.000690	0.003446	97484	336	486578	0.000690	2.500	6297687	64.603	5
10	0.000623	0.003115	97148	303	485046	0.000624	2.713	5811109	59.817	10
15	0.001334	0.006663	96845	645	482733	0.001337	2.687	5326063	54.996	15
20	0.001841	0.009178	96200	883	478853	0.001844	2.570	4843330	50.347	20
25	0.001983	0.009868	95317	941	474241	0.001983	2.509	4364478	45.789	25
30	0.001965	0.009791	94376	924	469630	0.001968	2.564	3890237	41.221	30
35	0.002618	0.013079	93452	1222	464393	0.002632	2.654	3420607	36.603	35
40	0.003977	0.019811	92230	1827	456891	0.003999	2.669	2956214	32.053	40
45	0.006030	0.029942	90403	2707	445818	0.006072	2.711	2499323	27.647	45
50	0.010596	0.052108	87696	4570	427913	0.010679	2.688	2053505	23.416	50
55	0.016969	0.082087	83126	6824	399696	0.017072	2.665	1625592	19.556	55
60	0.027722	0.130599	76303	9965	357654	0.027862	2.606	1225896	16.066	60
65	0.039000	0.179026	66338	11876	303214	0.039168	2.602	868242	13.088	65
70	0.067589	0.290131	54461	15801	233185	0.067761	2.524	565029	10.375	70
75	0.086412	0.354407	38661	13702	158153	0.086635	2.435	331843	8.584	75
80	0.121219	0.460766	24959	11500	94871	0.121219	2.398	173690	6.959	80
85	0.170755	1.000000	13459	13459	78819	0.102413	5.856	78819	5.856	85

TABLE 3 — FEMALE LIFE TABLE

x	nM_x	nq_x	l_x	nd_x	nL_x	nm_x	na_x	T_x	$\overset{\circ}{e}_x$	x
0	0.015302	0.015093	100000	1509	98636	0.015302	0.096	7286320	72.863	0
1	0.001332	0.005309	98491	523	392656	0.001332	1.500	7187684	72.978	1
5	0.000560	0.002795	97968	274	489155	0.000560	2.500	6795029	69.360	5
10	0.000483	0.002412	97694	236	487889	0.000483	2.532	6305874	64.547	10
15	0.000636	0.003178	97458	310	486546	0.000637	2.593	5817986	59.697	15
20	0.000769	0.003843	97149	373	484842	0.000770	2.587	5331439	54.879	20
25	0.000962	0.004811	96775	466	482758	0.000964	2.597	4846597	50.081	25
30	0.001224	0.006121	96310	590	480140	0.001228	2.611	4363839	45.310	30
35	0.001625	0.008142	95720	779	476789	0.001635	2.675	3883699	40.573	35
40	0.002622	0.013012	94941	1244	471793	0.002637	2.659	3406910	35.885	40
45	0.003701	0.018454	93697	1729	464536	0.003722	2.716	2935118	31.326	45
50	0.006659	0.033013	91968	3036	452818	0.006705	2.687	2470582	26.864	50
55	0.010193	0.050129	88932	4458	434458	0.010261	2.712	2017764	22.689	55
60	0.018606	0.089582	84474	7567	404552	0.018705	2.646	1583306	18.743	60
65	0.026769	0.126742	76906	9747	361739	0.026946	2.662	1178754	15.327	65
70	0.050290	0.225268	67159	15129	299137	0.050575	2.577	817015	12.165	70
75	0.068769	0.294679	52030	15332	221720	0.069151	2.493	517879	9.953	75
80	0.100224	0.399111	36698	14647	146138	0.100224	2.450	296158	8.070	80
85	0.146990	1.000000	22051	22051	150020	0.078670	6.803	150020	6.803	85

TABLE 4 — OBSERVED VITAL RATES AND RATIOS

CRUDE RATES

Per Thousand	BOTH SEXES	MALES	FEMALES
BIRTH RATE	31.34	32.00	30.67
DEATH RATE	5.27	5.98	4.55
RATE OF INCREASE	26.07	26.03	26.12

PERCENT OF POPULATION IN AGE GROUP

	BOTH SEXES	MALES	FEMALES
UNDER 15	37.41	38.17	36.65
15 - 64	58.65	58.13	59.17
65 AND OLDER	3.94	3.70	4.19

RATES STANDARDIZED ON USA 1980

Per Thousand	BOTH SEXES	MALES	FEMALES
BIRTH RATE	31.34		29.72
DEATH RATE	11.08	11.15	11.02
RATE OF INCREASE	20.26		18.70

RATES STANDARDIZED ON MEXICO 1980

	BOTH SEXES	MALES	FEMALES
BIRTH RATE	26.62		26.16
DEATH RATE	4.69	5.27	4.10
RATE OF INCREASE	21.93		22.06

VITAL STATISTICS

GFR x 1000	122.564
TFR	3.884
GRR	1.894
NRR	1.822
μ	29.766
σ^2	38.562
GENERATION	29.372
POP. SEX RATIO	0.993
SEX RATIO AT BIRTH	1.051
DEP. RATIO x 100	70.513

PROJECTED POPULATION

AGE GROUP	1990 BOTH SEXES	1990 MALES	1990 FEMALES	1995 BOTH SEXES	1995 MALES	1995 FEMALES
0-4	2136	1092	1044	2389	1221	1168
5-9	1814	931	883	2127	1087	1040
10-14	1531	784	747	1808	928	880
15-19	1493	760	733	1525	780	745
20-24	1392	707	685	1484	754	730
25-29	1300	644	656	1382	700	682
30-34	1105	532	573	1291	638	653
35-39	914	445	469	1095	526	569
40-44	756	381	375	902	438	464
45-49	560	284	276	741	372	369
50-54	522	263	259	541	272	269
55-59	372	180	192	493	245	248
60-64	315	152	163	340	161	179
65-69	221	103	118	275	129	146
70-74	167	76	91	177	79	98
75-79	94	43	51	118	51	67
80-84	62	28	34	60	26	34
85+	41	18	23	58	23	35
TOTAL	14795	7423	7372	16806	8430	8376

STABLE EQUIVALENT TO ORIGINAL POPULATION

AGE GROUP	MALES Number	MALES Percent	FEMALES Number	FEMALES Percent	
0-4	956	13.1	914	12.7	
5-9	859	11.8	822	11.4	TABLE 5
10-14	773	10.6	740	10.3	
15-19	694	9.5	666	9.2	POPULATION
20-24	622	8.5	599	8.3	PROJECTED
25-29	556	7.6	539	7.5	WITH
30-34	497	6.8	484	6.7	FIXED
35-39	444	6.1	433	6.0	AGE-
40-44	394	5.4	387	5.4	SPECIFIC
45-49	347	4.8	344	4.8	BIRTH
50-54	301	4.1	303	4.2	AND
55-59	253	3.5	262	3.6	DEATH
60-64	205	2.8	220	3.1	RATES
65-69	157	2.1	178	2.5	(female
70-74	109	1.5	133	1.8	dominant,
75-79	67	0.9	89	1.2	in 000s)
80-84	36	0.5	53	0.7	
85+	27	0.4	49	0.7	
TOTAL	7297		7215		

VITAL RATES OF PROJECTED POPULATION

Per Thousand	1990 BOTH SEXES	1990 MALES	1990 FEMALES	1995 BOTH SEXES	1995 MALES	1995 FEMALES
BIRTH RATE	31.43	32.10	30.76	30.33	30.97	29.68
DEATH RATE	5.45	6.11	4.79	5.56	6.14	4.98
RATE OF INCREASE	25.98	25.99	25.97	24.77	24.84	24.70

VITAL RATES OF STABLE POPULATION

Per Thousand	MALES	FEMALES	
BIRTH RATE	28.18	27.12	TABLE 6
DEATH RATE	7.76	6.64	PROJECTED
RATE OF INCREASE		20.48	VITAL RATES

AGE STRUCTURE OF PROJECTED POPULATION

	BOTH SEXES	MALES	FEMALES	BOTH SEXES	MALES	FEMALES
% UNDER 15	37.05	37.82	36.27	37.63	38.38	36.87
% 15-64	59.00	58.58	59.43	58.28	57.96	58.60
% 65 AND OLDER	3.95	3.59	4.31	4.09	3.65	4.53
DEPEND. RATIO x 100	69.49	70.70	68.28	71.58	72.52	70.64

STABLE AGE STRUCTURE

	MALES	FEMALES	
% UNDER 15	35.48	34.32	AND RATIOS
% 15-64	59.11	58.73	(female
% 65 AND OLDER	5.42	6.95	dominant)
DEPEND. RATIO x 100	69.19	70.27	

AGE GROUP	FEMALE BIRTH RATES	NET MATERNITY FUNCTION	COEFF. OF MATRIX EQUATION	ORIGINAL MATRIX SUB-DIAGONAL	ORIGINAL MATRIX FIRST ROW	STABLE MATRIX FISHER VALUES	STABLE MATRIX REPRODUCTIVE VALUES	MATRIX PARAMETERS		
0-4	0.0000	0.0000	0.0000	0.99565	0.00000	1.071	949476	λ_1	1.10780	
5-9	0.0000	0.0000	0.0002	0.99741	0.00021	1.192	891994	λ_2	0.45798-0.80162i	TABLE 7
10-14	0.0001	0.0004	0.0307	0.99725	0.03093	1.323	972608	λ_4	-0.06409-0.60022i	
15-19	0.0125	0.0610	0.2161	0.99650	0.21825	1.437	987115	λ_6	-0.39878-0.45000i	LESLIE
20-24	0.0766	0.3713	0.4667	0.99570	0.47286	1.363	897988	r_1	0.02048	MATRIX
25-29	0.1164	0.5620	0.5072	0.99458	0.51622	1.007	580103	r_2	-0.01598-0.21035i	AND ITS
30-34	0.0942	0.4525	0.3612	0.99302	0.36959	0.566	267493	r_4	-0.10096-0.33544i	ANALYSIS
35-39	0.0566	0.2699	0.1820	0.98952	0.18755	0.233	88376	r_6	-0.10174-0.45918i	(females)
40-44	0.0199	0.0941	0.0522	0.98462	0.05440	0.058	16271	c_1	72150	
45-49	0.0022	0.0104	0.0056	0.97478	0.00594	0.006	1625	$2\pi/y$	29.8706	
50-54	0.0002	0.0008	0.0004	0.95945	0.00045	0.000	87	Δ	7.6398	

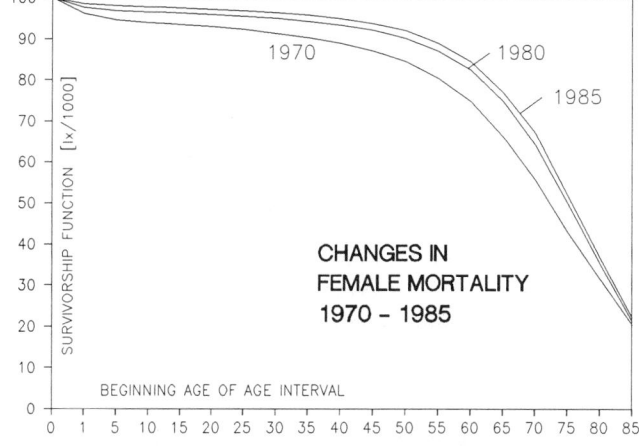

CHANGES IN FEMALE MORTALITY 1970 - 1985

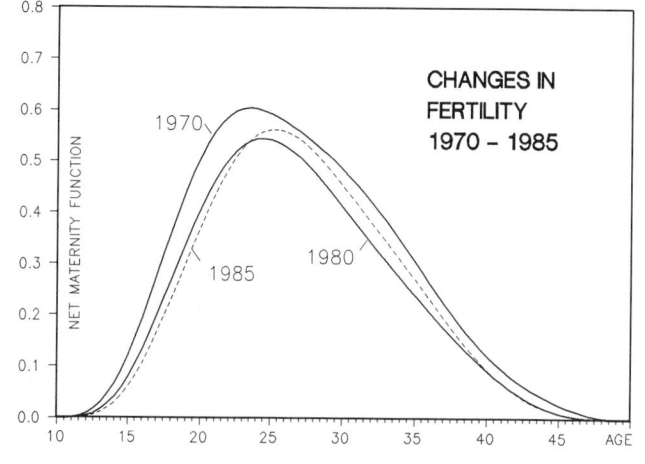

CHANGES IN FERTILITY 1970 - 1985

TABLE 1 — DATA

AGE AT LAST BIRTHDAY	ESTIMATED MID-YEAR POPULATION BOTH SEXES	MALES Number	MALES Percent	FEMALES Number	FEMALES Percent	BIRTHS BY AGE OF MOTHER AND SEX	DEATHS BOTH SEXES	DEATHS MALES	DEATHS FEMALES	AGE AT LAST BIRTHDAY
0	41141	21500	2.0	19641	1.9		947	528	419	0
1-4	194315	99539	9.4	94776	9.4		280	155	125	1-4
5-9	280533	143926	13.6	136607	13.5		130	74	56	5-9
10-14	288847	148506	14.0	140341	13.9	24	104	68	36	10-14
15-19	246417	126358	11.9	120059	11.9	3126	206	152	54	15-19
20-24	203735	103181	9.7	100554	9.9	14021	196	136	60	20-24
25-29	132745	66650	6.3	66095	6.5	13851	159	88	71	25-29
30-34	136381	68462	6.4	67919	6.7	9405	185	100	85	30-34
35-39	112895	58441	5.5	54454	5.4	4073	247	162	85	35-39
40-44	100877	54015	5.1	46862	4.6	1256	342	222	120	40-44
45-49	81746	44148	4.2	37598	3.7	163	488	322	166	45-49
50-54	71223	37770	3.6	33453	3.3	13	695	472	223	50-54
55-59	65365	34044	3.2	31321	3.1		1042	698	344	55-59
60-64	48923	24998	2.4	23925	2.4		1271	855	416	60-64
65-69	33499	16488	1.6	17011	1.7		1336	853	483	65-69
70-74	18838	8261	0.8	10577	1.0		1203	688	515	70-74
75-79	10162	3855	0.4	6307	0.6		897	447	450	75-79
80-84	4642	1430	0.1	3212	0.3	23609 M	576	216	360	80-84
85+	2223	555	0.1	1668	0.2	22323 F	410	114	296	85+
TOTAL	2074507	1062127		1012380		45932	10714	6350	4364	TOTAL

TABLE 2 — MALE LIFE TABLE

x	$_nM_x$	$_nq_x$	l_x	$_nd_x$	$_nL_x$	$_nm_x$	$_na_x$	T_x	$\overset{\circ}{e}_x$	x
0	0.024558	0.024034	100000	2403	97865	0.024558	0.112	6587837	65.878	0
1	0.001557	0.006205	97597	606	388873	0.001557	1.500	6489972	66.498	1
5	0.000514	0.002567	96991	249	484333	0.000514	2.500	6101099	62.904	5
10	0.000458	0.002291	96742	222	483225	0.000459	2.812	5616766	58.059	10
15	0.001203	0.006025	96520	581	481234	0.001208	2.646	5133541	53.186	15
20	0.001318	0.006569	95939	630	478129	0.001318	2.515	4652307	48.492	20
25	0.001320	0.006579	95309	627	474989	0.001320	2.520	4174179	43.796	25
30	0.001461	0.007301	94682	691	471820	0.001465	2.703	3699190	39.070	30
35	0.002772	0.013825	93990	1299	466954	0.002783	2.693	3227370	34.337	35
40	0.004110	0.020445	92691	1895	459130	0.004128	2.718	2760416	29.781	40
45	0.007294	0.036104	90796	3278	446500	0.007342	2.718	2301286	25.346	45
50	0.012497	0.060929	87518	5332	425255	0.012539	2.687	1854786	21.193	50
55	0.020503	0.098126	82185	8065	392110	0.020567	2.667	1429530	17.394	55
60	0.034203	0.159016	74121	11786	342462	0.034417	2.612	1037420	13.996	60
65	0.051735	0.231282	62334	14417	276639	0.052114	2.570	694958	11.149	65
70	0.083283	0.347005	47918	16628	197929	0.084008	2.495	418319	8.730	70
75	0.115953	0.447021	31290	13987	119956	0.116604	2.391	220390	7.043	75
80	0.151049	0.537615	17303	9302	61485	0.151293	2.309	100434	5.805	80
85	0.205405	1.000000	8001	8001	38950	0.140550	4.868	38950	4.868	85

TABLE 3 — FEMALE LIFE TABLE

x	$_nM_x$	$_nq_x$	l_x	$_nd_x$	$_nL_x$	$_nm_x$	$_na_x$	T_x	$\overset{\circ}{e}_x$	x
0	0.021333	0.020934	100000	2093	98129	0.021333	0.106	7210859	72.109	0
1	0.001319	0.005258	97907	515	390339	0.001319	1.500	7112730	72.648	1
5	0.000410	0.002048	97392	199	486460	0.000410	2.500	6722390	69.024	5
10	0.000257	0.001282	97192	125	485654	0.000257	2.532	6235930	64.161	10
15	0.000450	0.002255	97068	219	484826	0.000451	2.658	5750275	59.240	15
20	0.000597	0.002997	96849	290	483581	0.000600	2.716	5265449	54.368	20
25	0.001074	0.005384	96559	520	481558	0.001080	2.624	4781868	49.523	25
30	0.001251	0.006248	96039	600	478741	0.001253	2.578	4300310	44.777	30
35	0.001561	0.007813	95439	746	475457	0.001568	2.671	3821569	40.042	35
40	0.002561	0.012819	94693	1214	470704	0.002579	2.725	3346112	35.336	40
45	0.004415	0.021991	93479	2056	462631	0.004444	2.682	2875408	30.760	45
50	0.006666	0.032920	91423	3010	450155	0.006686	2.686	2412778	26.391	50
55	0.010983	0.053714	88414	4749	431036	0.011018	2.677	1962623	22.198	55
60	0.017388	0.084123	83665	7038	401880	0.017513	2.664	1531587	18.306	60
65	0.028393	0.134133	76627	10278	359005	0.028630	2.652	1129707	14.743	65
70	0.048691	0.219434	66348	14559	296492	0.049104	2.579	770702	11.616	70
75	0.071349	0.304805	51789	15786	219720	0.071844	2.515	474210	9.157	75
80	0.112080	0.436043	36004	15699	140071	0.112080	2.455	254490	7.068	80
85	0.177458	1.000000	20305	20305	114419	0.108624	5.635	114419	5.635	85

TABLE 4 — OBSERVED VITAL RATES AND RATIOS

CRUDE RATES

Per Thousand	BOTH SEXES	MALES	FEMALES
BIRTH RATE	22.14	22.23	22.05
DEATH RATE	5.16	5.98	4.31
RATE OF INCREASE	16.98	16.25	17.74

PERCENT OF POPULATION IN AGE GROUP

UNDER 15	38.80	38.93	38.66
15 - 64	57.86	58.19	57.51
65 AND OLDER	3.34	2.88	3.83

RATES STANDARDIZED ON USA 1980

Per Thousand	BOTH SEXES	MALES	FEMALES
BIRTH RATE	25.44		24.05
DEATH RATE	12.61	13.52	11.75
RATE OF INCREASE	12.83		12.29

RATES STANDARDIZED ON MEXICO 1980

	BOTH SEXES	MALES	FEMALES
BIRTH RATE	21.87		21.43
DEATH RATE	5.23	6.11	4.34
RATE OF INCREASE	16.64		17.09

VITAL STATISTICS

GFR x 1000	93.066
TFR	3.100
GRR	1.507
NRR	1.447
μ	29.032
σ^2	37.727
GENERATION	28.790
POP. SEX RATIO	0.953
SEX RATIO AT BIRTH	1.058
DEP. RATIO x 100	72.831

PROJECTED POPULATION

AGE GROUP	1975			1980			STABLE EQUIVALENT TO ORIGINAL POPULATION				AGE GROUP	
							MALES		FEMALES			
	BOTH SEXES	MALES	FEMALES	BOTH SEXES	MALES	FEMALES	Number	Percent	Number	Percent		
0-4	251	129	122	306	157	149	140	10.9	133	10.3	0-4	
5-9	234	120	114	250	128	122	131	10.1	124	9.6	5-9	TABLE 5
10-14	280	144	136	234	120	114	122	9.5	116	9.0	10-14	
15-19	288	148	140	279	143	136	114	8.9	109	8.4	15-19	POPULATION
20-24	246	126	120	287	147	140	106	8.3	102	7.9	20-24	PROJECTED
25-29	203	103	100	244	125	119	99	7.7	95	7.4	25-29	WITH
30-34	132	66	66	202	102	100	92	7.2	89	6.9	30-34	FIXED
35-39	135	68	67	131	66	65	86	6.7	83	6.4	35-39	AGE-
40-44	111	57	54	134	67	67	79	6.1	77	5.9	40-44	SPECIFIC
45-49	99	53	46	109	56	53	72	5.6	71	5.5	45-49	BIRTH
50-54	79	42	37	95	50	45	64	5.0	64	5.0	50-54	AND
55-59	67	35	32	74	39	35	56	4.3	58	4.5	55-59	DEATH
60-64	59	30	29	60	30	30	46	3.5	51	3.9	60-64	RATES
65-69	41	20	21	50	24	26	35	2.7	42	3.3	65-69	(female
70-74	26	12	14	32	14	18	23	1.8	33	2.5	70-74	dominant,
75-79	13	5	8	17	7	10	13	1.0	23	1.8	75-79	in 000s)
80-84	6	2	4	8	3	5	6	0.5	14	1.1	80-84	
85+	4	1	3	4	1	3	4	0.3	10	0.8	85+	
TOTAL	2274	1161	1113	2516	1279	1237	1288		1294		TOTAL	

VITAL RATES OF PROJECTED POPULATION

Per Thousand	1975			1980			VITAL RATES OF STABLE POPULATION		
	BOTH SEXES	MALES	FEMALES	BOTH SEXES	MALES	FEMALES	MALES	FEMALES	
BIRTH RATE	25.15	25.34	24.95	27.32	27.62	27.01	23.05	21.73	TABLE 6
DEATH RATE	5.67	6.54	4.76	6.09	6.98	5.16	10.11	8.89	PROJECTED
RATE OF INCREASE	19.48	18.80	20.18	21.24	20.64	21.85	12.85		VITAL RATES AND RATIOS

AGE STRUCTURE OF PROJECTED POPULATION

							STABLE AGE STRUCTURE		
% UNDER 15	33.69	33.90	33.47	31.44	31.74	31.13	30.50	28.89	(female dominant)
% 15-64	62.36	62.66	62.05	64.11	64.40	63.82	63.21	61.67	
% 65 AND OLDER	3.95	3.44	4.48	4.45	3.86	5.05	6.28	9.45	
DEPEND. RATIO x 100	60.35	59.58	61.16	55.97	55.29	56.69	58.20	62.17	

AGE GROUP	FEMALE BIRTH RATES	NET MATERNITY FUNCTION	COEFF. OF MATRIX EQUATION	ORIGINAL MATRIX		STABLE MATRIX		MATRIX PARAMETERS		
				SUB-DIAGONAL	FIRST ROW	FISHER VALUES	REPRODUCTIVE VALUES			
0-4	0.0000	0.0000	0.0000	0.99589	0.00000	1.057	120927	λ_1	1.06634	
5-9	0.0000	0.0000	0.0002	0.99834	0.00020	1.132	154594	λ_2	$0.41891+0.77814i$	TABLE 7
10-14	0.0001	0.0004	0.0309	0.99829	0.03106	1.209	169607	λ_4	$-0.37584+0.46464i$	
15-19	0.0127	0.0614	0.1945	0.99743	0.19599	1.258	151038	λ_6	$-0.02265+0.50521i$	LESLIE
20-24	0.0678	0.3277	0.4091	0.99582	0.41321	1.137	114358	r_1	0.01285	MATRIX
25-29	0.1018	0.4905	0.4063	0.99415	0.41215	0.779	51505	r_2	$-0.02472+0.21539i$	AND ITS
30-34	0.0673	0.3222	0.2475	0.99314	0.25254	0.398	27010	r_4	$-0.10296+0.45019i$	ANALYSIS
35-39	0.0364	0.1728	0.1171	0.99000	0.12028	0.158	8617	r_6	$-0.13635+0.32312i$	(females)
40-44	0.0130	0.0613	0.0355	0.98285	0.03687	0.042	1970	c_1	12919	
45-49	0.0021	0.0097	0.0053	0.97303	0.00559	0.006	224	$2\pi/y$	29.1713	
50-54	0.0002	0.0009	0.0004	0.95753	0.00046	0.000	15	Δ	15.2686	

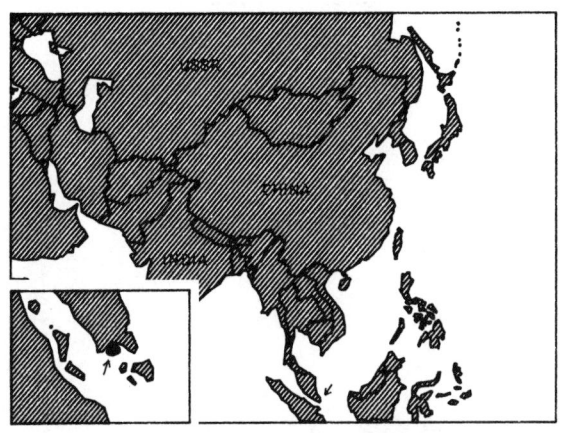

EDUCATION [1984]

% of primary school-age children enrolled:	115
secondary school-age children enrolled:	71
ca. 20-24 year olds in higher education:	12

LABOR FORCE

Average annual labor force growth (%) 1980-85:	1.9
% of the 1980 labor force in agriculture:	2
in industry:	38
in services:	61

TABLE 8

SOCIO-ECONOMIC INDICATORS

GNP & INCOME DISTRIBUTION

GNP per capita (in US Dollars) 1985:	7420
GNP average annual growth rate (%) 1965-85:	7.6
% share of total household income	
Lowest 20% of households:	na
Highest 10% of households:	na

HEALTH & NUTRITION

Population per physician 1981:	1100
Daily calorie supply per capita 1985:	2771

TABLE 1 — DATA

AGE AT LAST BIRTHDAY	ESTIMATED MID-YEAR POPULATION BOTH SEXES	MALES Number	MALES Percent	FEMALES Number	FEMALES Percent	BIRTHS BY AGE OF MOTHER AND SEX	DEATHS BOTH SEXES	DEATHS MALES	DEATHS FEMALES	AGE AT LAST BIRTHDAY
0	42200	21900	1.9	20300	1.8		558	333	225	0
1-4	185800	96000	8.3	89800	8.1		162	78	84	1-4
5-9	234300	120300	10.4	114000	10.3		82	46	36	5-9
10-14	283600	145900	12.6	137700	12.4	14	104	68	36	10-14
15-19	292800	150900	13.1	141900	12.8	2389	159	114	45	15-19
20-24	249600	127500	11.0	122100	11.0	12478	259	179	80	20-24
25-29	207100	105200	9.1	101900	9.2	15765	228	148	80	25-29
30-34	134100	67900	5.9	66200	6.0	6288	198	124	74	30-34
35-39	134000	67400	5.8	66600	6.0	2419	256	159	97	35-39
40-44	110200	56500	4.9	53700	4.9	540	376	232	144	40-44
45-49	97000	51300	4.4	45700	4.1	52	558	384	174	45-49
50-54	76900	40900	3.5	36000	3.3	2	715	482	233	50-54
55-59	66000	34100	2.9	31900	2.9		983	665	318	55-59
60-64	57500	29100	2.5	28400	2.6		1264	843	421	60-64
65-69	41400	20400	1.8	21000	1.9		1579	1019	560	65-69
70-74	27900	13000	1.1	14900	1.3		1550	944	606	70-74
75-79	13300	5200	0.4	8100	0.7		1137	577	560	75-79
80-84	6300	2000	0.2	4300	0.4	20627 M	689	305	384	80-84
85+	2600	600	0.1	2000	0.2	19320 F	586	177	409	85+
TOTAL	2262600	1156100		1106500		39947	11443	6877	4566	TOTAL

TABLE 2 — MALE LIFE TABLE

x	$_nM_x$	$_nq_x$	l_x	$_nd_x$	$_nL_x$	$_nm_x$	$_na_x$	T_x	$\overset{\circ}{e}_x$	x
0	0.015205	0.014999	100000	1500	98644	0.015206	0.096	6726938	67.269	0
1	0.000813	0.003243	98500	319	393202	0.000813	1.500	6628294	67.292	1
5	0.000382	0.001910	98181	188	490434	0.000382	2.500	6235093	63.506	5
10	0.000466	0.002328	97993	228	489433	0.000466	2.666	5744659	58.623	10
15	0.000755	0.003776	97765	369	487997	0.000757	2.757	5255226	53.754	15
20	0.001404	0.007017	97396	683	485335	0.001408	2.594	4767229	48.947	20
25	0.001407	0.007017	96712	679	481905	0.001408	2.559	4281895	44.275	25
30	0.001826	0.009125	96034	876	478070	0.001833	2.605	3799989	39.569	30
35	0.002359	0.011774	95157	1120	473204	0.002368	2.695	3321919	34.910	35
40	0.004106	0.020450	94037	1923	465853	0.004128	2.747	2848715	30.294	40
45	0.007485	0.036959	92114	3404	452724	0.007520	2.695	2382862	25.869	45
50	0.011785	0.057677	88710	5117	431675	0.011853	2.680	1930138	21.758	50
55	0.019501	0.093492	83593	7815	399508	0.019562	2.638	1498463	17.926	55
60	0.028969	0.135990	75778	10305	354551	0.029065	2.638	1098955	14.502	60
65	0.049951	0.223841	65473	14655	291852	0.050215	2.577	744404	11.370	65
70	0.072615	0.309217	50817	15714	214927	0.073111	2.508	452552	8.905	70
75	0.110962	0.434593	35104	15256	136358	0.111881	2.433	237625	6.769	75
80	0.152500	0.544699	19848	10811	70634	0.153059	2.354	101267	5.102	80
85	0.295000	1.000000	9037	9037	30633	0.250790	3.390	30633	3.390	85

TABLE 3 — FEMALE LIFE TABLE

x	$_nM_x$	$_nq_x$	l_x	$_nd_x$	$_nL_x$	$_nm_x$	$_na_x$	T_x	$\overset{\circ}{e}_x$	x
0	0.011084	0.010973	100000	1097	99000	0.011084	0.089	7390734	73.907	0
1	0.000935	0.003733	98903	369	394688	0.000935	1.500	7291734	73.726	1
5	0.000316	0.001578	98534	155	492279	0.000316	2.500	6897046	69.997	5
10	0.000261	0.001306	98378	129	491569	0.000261	2.501	6404767	65.104	10
15	0.000317	0.001587	98250	156	490898	0.000318	2.759	5913198	60.185	15
20	0.000655	0.003283	98094	322	489711	0.000658	2.648	5422299	55.277	20
25	0.000785	0.003930	97772	384	487944	0.000788	2.621	4932589	50.450	25
30	0.001118	0.005598	97387	545	485641	0.001123	2.623	4444645	45.639	30
35	0.001456	0.007289	96842	706	482601	0.001463	2.719	3959004	40.881	35
40	0.002682	0.013400	96136	1288	477689	0.002697	2.677	3476403	36.161	40
45	0.003807	0.018991	94848	1801	470091	0.003832	2.696	2998714	31.616	45
50	0.006472	0.032088	93047	2986	458311	0.006515	2.681	2528623	27.176	50
55	0.009969	0.048836	90061	4398	439973	0.009997	2.651	2070312	22.988	55
60	0.014824	0.071963	85663	6165	414078	0.014887	2.691	1630339	19.032	60
65	0.026667	0.126264	79498	10038	373814	0.026852	2.641	1216261	15.299	65
70	0.040671	0.186608	69461	12962	316307	0.040979	2.609	842447	12.128	70
75	0.069136	0.297316	56499	16798	240825	0.069752	2.519	526140	9.312	75
80	0.089302	0.365916	39701	14527	162217	0.089554	2.502	285315	7.187	80
85	0.204500	1.000000	25174	25174	123098	0.137678	4.890	123098	4.890	85

TABLE 4 — OBSERVED VITAL RATES AND RATIOS

CRUDE RATES

Per Thousand	BOTH SEXES	MALES	FEMALES
BIRTH RATE	17.66	17.84	17.46
DEATH RATE	5.06	5.95	4.13
RATE OF INCREASE	12.60	11.89	13.33

PERCENT OF POPULATION IN AGE GROUP

	BOTH SEXES	MALES	FEMALES
UNDER 15	32.97	33.22	32.70
15 - 64	62.99	63.21	62.76
65 AND OLDER	4.04	3.56	4.55

RATES STANDARDIZED ON USA 1980

Per Thousand	BOTH SEXES	MALES	FEMALES
BIRTH RATE	17.45		16.41
DEATH RATE	11.99	13.13	10.91
RATE OF INCREASE	5.46		5.50

RATES STANDARDIZED ON MEXICO 1980

	BOTH SEXES	MALES	FEMALES
BIRTH RATE	15.08		14.70
DEATH RATE	4.64	5.57	3.70
RATE OF INCREASE	10.43		11.00

VITAL STATISTICS

GFR x 1000	66.790
TFR	2.082
GRR	1.007
NRR	0.981
μ	28.267
σ^2	30.493
GENERATION	28.279
POP. SEX RATIO	0.957
SEX RATIO AT BIRTH	1.068
DEP. RATIO x 100	58.757

AGE AT LAST BIRTHDAY	ESTIMATED MID-YEAR POPULATION					BIRTHS BY AGE OF MOTHER AND SEX	DEATHS			AGE AT LAST BIRTHDAY
	BOTH SEXES	MALES		FEMALES			BOTH SEXES	MALES	FEMALES	
		Number	Percent	Number	Percent					
0	36620	19239	1.6	17381	1.5		484	253	231	0
1-4	157064	81608	6.6	75456	6.4		110	63	47	1-4
5-9	223883	115770	9.4	108113	9.1		51	20	31	5-9
10-14	235556	120857	9.8	114699	9.7	14	79	41	38	10-14
15-19	287420	148236	12.0	139184	11.8	1705	176	119	57	15-19
20-24	296192	152832	12.4	143360	12.1	11463	302	211	91	20-24
25-29	253531	129407	10.5	124124	10.5	17049	236	164	72	25-29
30-34	211040	107368	8.7	103672	8.8	8767	240	152	88	30-34
35-39	135767	68882	5.6	66885	5.7	1820	211	135	76	35-39
40-44	131475	66497	5.4	64978	5.5	371	334	211	123	40-44
45-49	107245	54756	4.4	52489	4.4	25	526	346	180	45-49
50-54	93136	48322	3.9	44814	3.8	2	740	511	229	50-54
55-59	71384	36989	3.0	34395	2.9		978	610	368	55-59
60-64	59708	29795	2.4	29913	2.5		1329	862	467	60-64
65-69	49310	23737	1.9	25573	2.2		1723	1069	654	65-69
70-74	33344	15429	1.3	17915	1.5		1704	970	734	70-74
75-79	18616	7857	0.6	10759	0.9		1440	752	688	75-79
80-84	8035	2891	0.2	5144	0.4	21308 M	969	424	545	80-84
85+	4619	1288	0.1	3331	0.3	19908 F	870	252	618	85+
TOTAL	2413945	1231760		1182185		41216	12502	7165	5337	TOTAL

TABLE 1 — DATA

x	nM_x	nq_x	l_x	nd_x	nL_x	nm_x	na_x	T_x	$\overset{\circ}{e}_x$	x
0	0.013150	0.012995	100000	1300	98820	0.013150	0.092	6893292	68.933	0
1	0.000772	0.003082	98700	304	394041	0.000772	1.500	6794472	68.839	1
5	0.000173	0.000863	98396	85	491769	0.000173	2.500	6400430	65.047	5
10	0.000339	0.001695	98311	167	491204	0.000339	2.885	5908661	60.102	10
15	0.000803	0.004007	98145	393	489846	0.000803	2.768	5417457	55.199	15
20	0.001381	0.006883	97751	673	487121	0.001381	2.568	4927611	50.410	20
25	0.001267	0.006316	97079	613	483862	0.001267	2.503	4440490	45.741	25
30	0.001416	0.007074	96466	682	480690	0.001420	2.600	3956627	41.016	30
35	0.001960	0.009816	95783	940	476736	0.001972	2.682	3475938	36.290	35
40	0.003173	0.015848	94843	1503	470870	0.003192	2.775	2999202	31.623	40
45	0.006319	0.031322	93340	2924	460054	0.006355	2.727	2528332	27.087	45
50	0.010575	0.051855	90416	4689	441178	0.010627	2.675	2068278	22.875	50
55	0.016491	0.079926	85728	6852	412765	0.016600	2.683	1627100	18.980	55
60	0.028931	0.135877	78876	10717	369046	0.029041	2.636	1214335	15.396	60
65	0.045035	0.203384	68158	13862	306995	0.045155	2.562	845289	12.402	65
70	0.062869	0.273358	54296	14842	234674	0.063246	2.520	538293	9.914	70
75	0.095711	0.387830	39454	15301	158593	0.096482	2.472	303619	7.696	75
80	0.146662	0.530655	24152	12817	87087	0.147170	2.373	145026	6.005	80
85	0.195652	1.000000	11336	11336	57939	0.128775	5.111	57939	5.111	85

TABLE 2 — MALE LIFE TABLE

x	nM_x	nq_x	l_x	nd_x	nL_x	nm_x	na_x	T_x	$\overset{\circ}{e}_x$	x
0	0.013290	0.013132	100000	1313	98808	0.013290	0.093	7429682	74.297	0
1	0.000623	0.002488	98687	246	394133	0.000623	1.500	7330873	74.284	1
5	0.000287	0.001433	98441	141	491854	0.000287	2.500	6936740	70.466	5
10	0.000331	0.001655	98300	163	491107	0.000331	2.576	6444886	65.563	10
15	0.000410	0.002046	98138	201	490217	0.000410	2.653	5953779	60.668	15
20	0.000635	0.003170	97937	310	488925	0.000635	2.555	5463562	55.787	20
25	0.000580	0.002900	97626	283	487446	0.000581	2.576	4974637	50.956	25
30	0.000849	0.004254	97343	414	485737	0.000853	2.635	4487192	46.097	30
35	0.001136	0.005700	96929	553	483368	0.001143	2.688	4001455	41.282	35
40	0.001893	0.009478	96377	913	479825	0.001904	2.747	3518086	36.504	40
45	0.003429	0.017111	95463	1633	473540	0.003449	2.688	3038261	31.827	45
50	0.005110	0.025481	93830	2391	463833	0.005155	2.777	2564721	27.334	50
55	0.010699	0.052583	91439	4808	446039	0.010780	2.680	2100888	22.976	55
60	0.015612	0.075518	86631	6542	417816	0.015658	2.656	1654849	19.102	60
65	0.025574	0.121026	80089	9693	377603	0.025669	2.644	1237033	15.446	65
70	0.040971	0.187812	70396	13221	320223	0.041287	2.598	859430	12.209	70
75	0.063946	0.278383	57175	15916	246925	0.064459	2.553	539207	9.431	75
80	0.105949	0.418481	41258	17266	162964	0.105949	2.491	292282	7.084	80
85	0.185530	1.000000	23992	23992	129319	0.117027	5.390	129319	5.390	85

TABLE 3 — FEMALE LIFE TABLE

CRUDE RATES

Per Thousand	BOTH SEXES	MALES	FEMALES
BIRTH RATE	17.07	17.30	16.84
DEATH RATE	5.18	5.82	4.51
RATE OF INCREASE	11.90	11.48	12.33

PERCENT OF POPULATION IN AGE GROUP

UNDER 15	27.06	27.40	26.70
15 - 64	68.22	68.45	67.99
65 AND OLDER	4.72	4.16	5.31

RATES STANDARDIZED ON USA 1980

Per Thousand	BOTH SEXES	MALES	FEMALES
BIRTH RATE	14.61		13.73
DEATH RATE	10.99	11.33	10.68
RATE OF INCREASE	3.62		3.05

RATES STANDARDIZED ON MEXICO 1980

	BOTH SEXES	MALES	FEMALES
BIRTH RATE	12.56		12.23
DEATH RATE	4.23	4.84	3.62
RATE OF INCREASE	8.33		8.61

VITAL STATISTICS

GFR x 1000	59.330	TABLE 4
TFR	1.738	
GRR	0.840	OBSERVED
NRR	0.818	VITAL
μ	28.248	RATES
σ^2	26.921	AND
GENERATION	28.343	RATIOS
POP. SEX RATIO	0.960	
SEX RATIO AT BIRTH	1.070	
DEP. RATIO x 100	46.575	

TABLE 1 — DATA

AGE AT LAST BIRTHDAY	ESTIMATED MID-YEAR POPULATION BOTH SEXES	MALES Number	MALES Percent	FEMALES Number	FEMALES Percent	BIRTHS BY AGE OF MOTHER AND SEX	DEATHS BOTH SEXES	DEATHS MALES	DEATHS FEMALES	AGE AT LAST BIRTHDAY
0	42300	21900	1.7	20400	1.6		394	225	169	0
1-4	165200	85800	6.6	79400	6.3		65	31	34	1-4
5-9	192700	100300	7.7	92400	7.4		44	24	20	5-9
10-14	223600	115600	8.9	108000	8.6	8	56	36	20	10-14
15-19	235100	120600	9.3	114500	9.1	1106	164	112	52	15-19
20-24	286300	147400	11.3	138900	11.1	9293	210	149	61	20-24
25-29	294900	151900	11.7	143000	11.4	17834	279	186	93	25-29
30-34	252300	128600	9.9	123700	9.9	10715	283	179	104	30-34
35-39	209700	106500	8.2	103200	8.2	3214	329	205	124	35-39
40-44	134400	68000	5.2	66400	5.3	299	305	205	100	40-44
45-49	129400	65200	5.0	64200	5.1	12	513	335	178	45-49
50-54	104200	52800	4.1	51400	4.1		726	469	257	50-54
55-59	88600	45300	3.5	43300	3.4		1125	771	354	55-59
60-64	65700	33300	2.6	32400	2.6		1307	825	482	60-64
65-69	52600	25300	1.9	27300	2.2		1577	942	635	65-69
70-74	40600	18500	1.4	22100	1.8		1989	1111	878	70-74
75-79	24200	10300	0.8	13900	1.1		1750	926	824	75-79
80-84	11500	4300	0.3	7200	0.6	22028 M	1209	547	662	80-84
85+	4700	1300	0.1	3400	0.3	20452 F	1022	337	685	85+
TOTAL	2558000	1302900		1255100		42481	13347	7615	5732	TOTAL

TABLE 2 — MALE LIFE TABLE

x	nM_x	nq_x	l_x	nd_x	nL_x	nm_x	na_x	T_x	$\overset{\circ}{e}_x$	x
0	0.010274	0.010179	100000	1018	99071	0.010274	0.087	7015026	70.150	0
1	0.000361	0.001444	98982	143	395571	0.000361	1.500	6915955	69.871	1
5	0.000239	0.001196	98839	118	493901	0.000239	2.500	6520383	65.970	5
10	0.000311	0.001556	98721	154	493292	0.000311	2.959	6026483	61.046	10
15	0.000929	0.004633	98567	457	491766	0.000929	2.656	5533191	56.136	15
20	0.001011	0.005042	98111	495	489346	0.001011	2.559	5041425	51.385	20
25	0.001224	0.006107	97616	596	486628	0.001225	2.563	4552079	46.632	25
30	0.001392	0.006953	97020	675	483483	0.001395	2.603	4065451	41.903	30
35	0.001925	0.009639	96345	929	479565	0.001936	2.672	3581968	37.178	35
40	0.003015	0.015088	95417	1440	473791	0.003039	2.713	3102403	32.514	40
45	0.005138	0.025524	93977	2399	464425	0.005165	2.723	2628612	27.971	45
50	0.008883	0.043811	91578	4012	448863	0.008939	2.749	2164187	23.632	50
55	0.017020	0.082260	87566	7203	420955	0.017112	2.657	1715324	19.589	55
60	0.024775	0.117537	80363	9446	379234	0.024907	2.609	1294369	16.107	60
65	0.037233	0.171507	70917	12163	325430	0.037375	2.603	915134	12.904	65
70	0.060054	0.262394	58755	15446	255948	0.060349	2.551	589704	10.037	70
75	0.089903	0.368466	43308	15958	176172	0.090580	2.470	333756	7.707	75
80	0.127209	0.481197	27351	13161	102847	0.127967	2.424	157585	5.762	80
85	0.259231	1.000000	14190	14190	54737	0.203544	3.858	54737	3.858	85

TABLE 3 — FEMALE LIFE TABLE

x	nM_x	nq_x	l_x	nd_x	nL_x	nm_x	na_x	T_x	$\overset{\circ}{e}_x$	x
0	0.008284	0.008222	100000	822	99247	0.008284	0.084	7558091	75.581	0
1	0.000428	0.001711	99178	170	396287	0.000428	1.500	7458844	75.207	1
5	0.000216	0.001082	99008	107	494773	0.000216	2.500	7062557	71.333	5
10	0.000185	0.000926	98901	92	494301	0.000185	2.766	6567784	66.408	10
15	0.000454	0.002268	98809	224	493513	0.000454	2.616	6073483	61.467	15
20	0.000439	0.002194	98585	216	492406	0.000439	2.592	5579970	56.600	20
25	0.000650	0.003249	98369	320	491087	0.000651	2.628	5087564	51.719	25
30	0.000841	0.004207	98050	413	489272	0.000843	2.635	4596477	46.879	30
35	0.001202	0.006015	97637	587	486784	0.001206	2.614	4107205	42.066	35
40	0.001506	0.007554	97050	733	483572	0.001516	2.712	3620421	37.305	40
45	0.002773	0.013861	96317	1335	478585	0.002789	2.754	3136850	32.568	45
50	0.005000	0.024879	94982	2363	469503	0.005033	2.713	2658265	27.987	50
55	0.008176	0.040449	92619	3746	454576	0.008241	2.726	2188762	23.632	55
60	0.014877	0.072418	88872	6436	429391	0.014989	2.674	1734186	19.513	60
65	0.023260	0.110632	82436	9120	390822	0.023336	2.658	1304795	15.828	65
70	0.039729	0.182082	73316	13350	334560	0.039902	2.601	913974	12.466	70
75	0.059281	0.260356	59967	15613	261498	0.059705	2.545	579414	9.662	75
80	0.091944	0.376368	44354	16693	180623	0.092421	2.535	317916	7.168	80
85	0.201471	1.000000	27661	27661	137293	0.134225	4.964	137293	4.964	85

TABLE 4 — OBSERVED VITAL RATES AND RATIOS

CRUDE RATES

Per Thousand	BOTH SEXES	MALES	FEMALES
BIRTH RATE	16.61	16.91	16.30
DEATH RATE	5.22	5.84	4.57
RATE OF INCREASE	11.39	11.06	11.73

RATES STANDARDIZED ON USA 1980

Per Thousand	BOTH SEXES	MALES	FEMALES
BIRTH RATE	13.49		12.63
DEATH RATE	10.37	10.69	10.07
RATE OF INCREASE	3.12		2.56

VITAL STATISTICS

GFR x 1000	56.347
TFR	1.619
GRR	0.779
NRR	0.765
μ	28.665
σ^2	26.412
GENERATION	28.788
POP. SEX RATIO	0.963
SEX RATIO AT BIRTH	1.077
DEP. RATIO x 100	42.064

PERCENT OF POPULATION IN AGE GROUP

	BOTH SEXES	MALES	FEMALES
UNDER 15	24.39	24.84	23.92
15 - 64	70.39	70.58	70.19
65 AND OLDER	5.22	4.58	5.89

RATES STANDARDIZED ON MEXICO 1980

	BOTH SEXES	MALES	FEMALES
BIRTH RATE	11.49		11.15
DEATH RATE	3.82	4.42	3.21
RATE OF INCREASE	7.67		7.94

PROJECTED POPULATION

AGE GROUP	1990			1995			STABLE EQUIVALENT TO ORIGINAL POPULATION				AGE GROUP
							MALES		FEMALES		
	BOTH SEXES	MALES	FEMALES	BOTH SEXES	MALES	FEMALES	Number	Percent	Number	Percent	
0-4	211	109	102	203	105	98	109	5.0	101	4.5	0-4
5-9	208	108	100	210	109	101	114	5.2	106	4.7	5-9
10-14	192	100	92	207	107	100	119	5.5	111	5.0	10-14
15-19	223	115	108	192	100	92	124	5.7	116	5.2	15-19
20-24	234	120	114	223	115	108	129	6.0	121	5.4	20-24
25-29	286	147	139	233	119	114	135	6.2	126	5.7	25-29
30-34	293	151	142	284	146	138	140	6.5	132	5.9	30-34
35-39	251	128	123	292	150	142	146	6.7	137	6.2	35-39
40-44	208	105	103	248	126	122	151	7.0	143	6.4	40-44
45-49	133	67	66	204	103	101	155	7.1	148	6.7	45-49
50-54	126	63	63	128	64	64	157	7.2	152	6.9	50-54
55-59	100	50	50	120	59	61	154	7.1	155	7.0	55-59
60-64	82	41	41	92	45	47	146	6.7	153	6.9	60-64
65-69	58	29	29	72	35	37	131	6.0	146	6.6	65-69
70-74	43	20	23	47	22	25	108	5.0	131	5.9	70-74
75-79	30	13	17	32	14	18	78	3.6	107	4.8	75-79
80-84	16	6	10	19	7	12	48	2.2	78	3.5	80-84
85+	7	2	5	10	3	7	27	1.2	62	2.8	85+
TOTAL	2701	1374	1327	2816	1429	1387	2171		2225		TOTAL

TABLE 5 POPULATION PROJECTED WITH FIXED AGE-SPECIFIC BIRTH AND DEATH RATES (female dominant, in 000s)

VITAL RATES OF PROJECTED POPULATION

Per Thousand	1990			1995			VITAL RATES OF STABLE POPULATION	
	BOTH SEXES	MALES	FEMALES	BOTH SEXES	MALES	FEMALES	MALES	FEMALES
BIRTH RATE	15.79	16.11	15.46	13.93	14.23	13.61	9.88	8.95
DEATH RATE	5.93	6.57	5.27	6.60	7.28	5.90	19.07	18.27
RATE OF INCREASE	9.86	9.54	10.19	7.33	6.95	7.71		-9.32

AGE STRUCTURE OF PROJECTED POPULATION

							STABLE AGE STRUCTURE	
% UNDER 15	22.62	23.10	22.12	22.00	22.48	21.51	15.72	14.26
% 15-64	71.65	71.84	71.46	71.55	71.80	71.29	66.27	62.21
% 65 AND OLDER	5.73	5.07	6.42	6.45	5.72	7.20	18.01	23.53
DEPEND. RATIO x 100	39.57	39.20	39.94	39.76	39.28	40.27	50.90	60.74

TABLE 6 PROJECTED VITAL RATES AND RATIOS (female dominant)

AGE GROUP	FEMALE BIRTH RATES	NET MATERNITY FUNCTION	COEFF. OF MATRIX EQUATION	ORIGINAL MATRIX		STABLE MATRIX		MATRIX PARAMETERS	
				SUB-DIAGONAL	FIRST ROW	FISHER VALUES	REPRODUCTIVE VALUES		
0-4	0.0000	0.0000	0.0000	0.99846	0.00000	0.986	98378	λ_1	0.95449
5-9	0.0000	0.0000	0.0001	0.99905	0.00009	0.942	87071	λ_2	0.40965+0.72988i
10-14	0.0000	0.0002	0.0116	0.99841	0.01159	0.900	97223	λ_4	-0.21994-0.53202i
15-19	0.0047	0.0230	0.0908	0.99776	0.09115	0.849	97230	λ_6	-0.45075-0.00000i
20-24	0.0322	0.1586	0.2267	0.99732	0.22818	0.722	100326	r_1	-0.00932
25-29	0.0600	0.2949	0.2495	0.99630	0.25171	0.466	66601	r_2	-0.03559+0.21187i
30-34	0.0417	0.2040	0.1385	0.99491	0.14029	0.197	24387	r_4	-0.11044-0.39256i
35-39	0.0150	0.0730	0.0417	0.99340	0.04249	0.050	5174	r_6	-0.15937-0.62832i
40-44	0.0022	0.0105	0.0055	0.98969	0.00559	0.006	399	c_1	22243
45-49	0.0001	0.0004	0.0002	0.98102	0.00022	0.000	15	$2\pi/y$	29.6558
50-54	0.0000	0.0000	0.0000	0.00000	0.00000	0.000	0	Δ	30.8955

TABLE 7 LESLIE MATRIX AND ITS ANALYSIS (females)

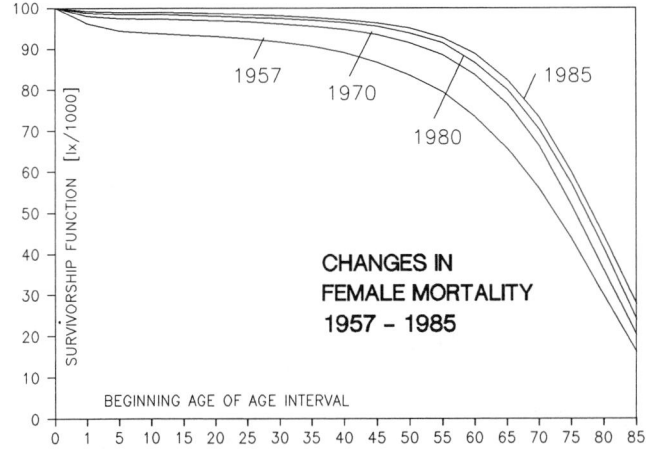

CHANGES IN FEMALE MORTALITY 1957 - 1985

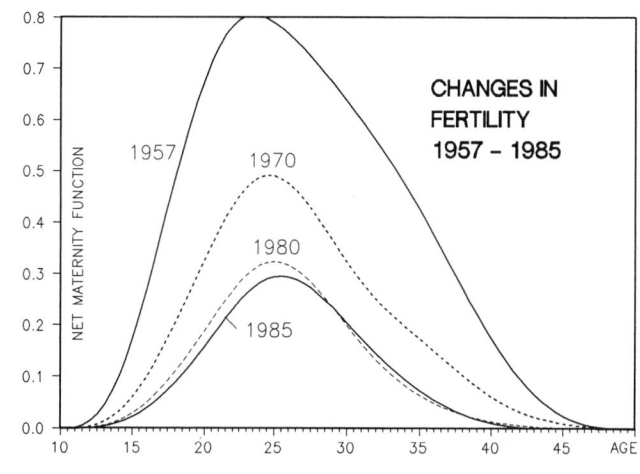

CHANGES IN FERTILITY 1957 - 1985

AGE AT LAST BIRTHDAY	ESTIMATED MID-YEAR POPULATION BOTH SEXES	MALES Number	Percent	FEMALES Number	Percent	BIRTHS BY AGE OF MOTHER AND SEX	DEATHS BOTH SEXES	MALES	FEMALES	AGE AT LAST BIRTHDAY
0	1683621	863975	1.7	819646	1.5		57911	33195	24716	0
1-4	6563994	3362002	6.7	3201992	6.0		8879	4878	4001	1-4
5-9	8010920	4102015	8.2	3908905	7.4		3896	2376	1520	5-9
10-14	9158837	4679484	9.4	4479353	8.4	1108	3912	2500	1412	10-14
15-19	9457061	4827493	9.7	4629568	8.7	220315	7514	5220	2294	15-19
20-24	7984166	4051759	8.1	3932407	7.4	700650	8816	6352	2464	20-24
25-29	6689861	3362386	6.7	3327475	6.3	420646	8221	5787	2434	25-29
30-34	7148372	3569046	7.2	3579326	6.7	241760	10853	7337	3516	30-34
35-39	7139114	3568498	7.2	3570616	6.7	112164	14972	9785	5187	35-39
40-44	7040167	3422653	6.9	3617514	6.8	30309	21479	13770	7709	40-44
45-49	6506618	2996269	6.0	3510349	6.6	2028	29856	17799	12057	45-49
50-54	3996788	1801635	3.6	2195153	4.1	51	28214	16711	11503	50-54
55-59	5576026	2502605	5.0	3073421	5.8		63524	38361	25163	55-59
60-64	5361467	2411270	4.8	2950197	5.5		101862	61465	40397	60-64
65-69	4375088	1919127	3.9	2455961	4.6		139246	80538	58708	65-69
70-74	3088576	1235665	2.5	1852911	3.5		163483	81948	81535	70-74
75-79	1860017	679839	1.4	1180178	2.2		157099	68047	89052	75-79
80-84	927368	329489	0.7	597879	1.1	890225 M	131557	51299	80258	80-84
85+	429608	145267	0.3	284341	0.5	838806 F	102440	37024	65416	85+
TOTAL	102997669	49830477		53167192		1729031	1063734	544392	519342	TOTAL

TABLE 1 DATA

x	nM_x	nq_x	l_x	nd_x	nL_x	nm_x	na_x	T_x	$\overset{\circ}{e}_x$	x
0	0.038421	0.037186	100000	3719	96785	0.038421	0.135	6659420	66.594	0
1	0.001451	0.005783	96281	557	383734	0.001451	1.500	6562635	68.161	1
5	0.000579	0.002892	95725	277	477931	0.000579	2.500	6178902	64.549	5
10	0.000534	0.002668	95448	255	476652	0.000534	2.694	5700971	59.729	10
15	0.001081	0.005398	95193	514	474783	0.001082	2.697	5224319	54.881	15
20	0.001568	0.007831	94679	741	471604	0.001572	2.582	4749536	50.164	20
25	0.001721	0.008578	93938	806	467719	0.001723	2.555	4277933	45.540	25
30	0.002056	0.010228	93132	953	463373	0.002056	2.598	3810214	40.912	30
35	0.002742	0.013623	92180	1256	457937	0.002742	2.643	3346841	36.308	35
40	0.004023	0.019940	90924	1813	450372	0.004026	2.658	2888904	31.773	40
45	0.005940	0.029492	89111	2628	439427	0.005981	2.669	2438532	27.365	45
50	0.009275	0.045560	86483	3940	423288	0.009308	2.684	1999105	23.116	50
55	0.015328	0.074009	82543	6109	398535	0.015328	2.679	1575817	19.091	55
60	0.025491	0.120258	76434	9192	360595	0.025491	2.653	1177282	15.403	60
65	0.041966	0.191187	67242	12856	305402	0.042095	2.604	816687	12.146	65
70	0.066319	0.286533	54386	15583	233538	0.066728	2.536	511286	9.401	70
75	0.100093	0.401350	38803	15573	154509	0.100793	2.463	277748	7.158	75
80	0.155693	0.552850	23229	12842	82485	0.155693	2.379	123239	5.305	80
85	0.254869	1.000000	10387	10387	40754	0.198913	3.924	40754	3.924	85

TABLE 2 MALE LIFE TABLE

x	nM_x	nq_x	l_x	nd_x	nL_x	nm_x	na_x	T_x	$\overset{\circ}{e}_x$	x
0	0.030154	0.029376	100000	2938	97419	0.030154	0.121	7236168	72.362	0
1	0.001250	0.004983	97062	484	387041	0.001250	1.500	7138749	73.548	1
5	0.000389	0.001942	96579	188	482425	0.000389	2.500	6751709	69.909	5
10	0.000315	0.001575	96391	152	481587	0.000315	2.570	6269284	65.040	10
15	0.000496	0.002476	96239	238	480632	0.000496	2.630	5787697	60.139	15
20	0.000627	0.003135	96001	301	479276	0.000628	2.577	5307065	55.281	20
25	0.000731	0.003657	95700	350	477660	0.000733	2.599	4827789	50.447	25
30	0.000982	0.004900	95350	467	475653	0.000982	2.650	4350128	45.623	30
35	0.001453	0.007239	94883	687	472808	0.001453	2.661	3874475	40.834	35
40	0.002131	0.010603	94196	999	468674	0.002131	2.690	3401666	36.113	40
45	0.003435	0.017158	93197	1599	462276	0.003459	2.680	2932993	31.471	45
50	0.005240	0.025967	91598	2379	452459	0.005257	2.674	2470716	26.973	50
55	0.008187	0.040177	89220	3585	437827	0.008187	2.692	2018257	22.621	55
60	0.013693	0.066433	85635	5689	415100	0.013705	2.702	1580431	18.455	60
65	0.023904	0.113699	79946	9090	378777	0.023998	2.695	1165331	14.576	65
70	0.044004	0.200247	70856	14189	320707	0.044242	2.634	786554	11.101	70
75	0.075456	0.321089	56668	18195	238903	0.076162	2.558	465847	8.221	75
80	0.134238	0.500264	38472	19246	143375	0.134238	2.455	226943	5.899	80
85	0.230062	1.000000	19226	19226	83569	0.167699	4.347	83569	4.347	85

TABLE 3 FEMALE LIFE TABLE

CRUDE RATES

TABLE 4 OBSERVED VITAL RATES AND RATIOS

Per Thousand	BOTH SEXES	MALES	FEMALES
BIRTH RATE	16.79	17.87	15.78
DEATH RATE	10.33	10.92	9.77
RATE OF INCREASE	6.46	6.94	6.01

PERCENT OF POPULATION IN AGE GROUP

UNDER 15	24.68	26.10	23.34
15 - 64	64.95	65.25	64.68
65 AND OLDER	10.37	8.65	11.98

RATES STANDARDIZED ON USA 1980

Per Thousand	BOTH SEXES	MALES	FEMALES
BIRTH RATE	19.92		18.80
DEATH RATE	12.24	12.28	12.20
RATE OF INCREASE	7.69		6.60

RATES STANDARDIZED ON MEXICO 1980

	BOTH SEXES	MALES	FEMALES
BIRTH RATE	18.23		17.83
DEATH RATE	5.20	5.95	4.45
RATE OF INCREASE	13.03		13.38

VITAL STATISTICS

GFR x 1000	66.076
TFR	2.302
GRR	1.117
NRR	1.067
μ	26.210
σ^2	33.498
GENERATION	26.168
POP. SEX RATIO	1.067
SEX RATIO AT BIRTH	1.061
DEP. RATIO x 100	53.958

PROJECTED POPULATION

AGE GROUP	1975 BOTH SEXES	1975 MALES	1975 FEMALES	1980 BOTH SEXES	1980 MALES	1980 FEMALES	STABLE EQUIVALENT TO ORIGINAL POPULATION MALES Number	MALES Percent	FEMALES Number	FEMALES Percent	AGE GROUP	
0-4	8751	4488	4263	9311	4775	4536	4488	7.8	4264	7.3	0-4	
5-9	8208	4203	4005	8710	4464	4246	4409	7.7	4193	7.2	5-9	TABLE 5
10-14	7993	4091	3902	8190	4192	3998	4343	7.6	4134	7.1	10-14	
15-19	9131	4661	4470	7969	4075	3894	4273	7.5	4075	7.0	15-19	POPULATION
20-24	9412	4795	4617	9088	4630	4458	4192	7.3	4014	6.9	20-24	PROJECTED
25-29	7937	4018	3919	9357	4756	4601	4106	7.2	3951	6.8	25-29	WITH
30-34	6644	3331	3313	7884	3981	3903	4018	7.0	3886	6.7	30-34	FIXED
35-39	7085	3527	3558	6586	3292	3294	3921	6.8	3815	6.5	35-39	AGE-
40-44	7049	3510	3539	6996	3469	3527	3809	6.7	3735	6.4	40-44	SPECIFIC
45-49	6907	3339	3568	6915	3424	3491	3671	6.4	3639	6.2	45-49	BIRTH
50-54	6322	2886	3436	6709	3217	3492	3492	6.1	3517	6.0	50-54	AND
55-59	3820	1696	2124	6042	2717	3325	3248	5.7	3362	5.8	55-59	DEATH
60-64	5178	2264	2914	3549	1535	2014	2902	5.1	3148	5.4	60-64	RATES
65-69	4734	2042	2692	4577	1918	2659	2428	4.2	2837	4.9	65-69	(female
70-74	3547	1468	2079	3841	1562	2279	1834	3.2	2372	4.1	70-74	dominant,
75-79	2198	818	1380	2520	971	1549	1198	2.1	1746	3.0	75-79	in 000s)
80-84	1071	363	708	1264	436	828	632	1.1	1035	1.8	80-84	
85+	511	163	348	592	179	413	308	0.5	596	1.0	85+	
TOTAL	106498	51663	54835	110100	53593	56507	57272		58319		TOTAL	

VITAL RATES OF PROJECTED POPULATION

Per Thousand	1975 BOTH SEXES	1975 MALES	1975 FEMALES	1980 BOTH SEXES	1980 MALES	1980 FEMALES	VITAL RATES OF STABLE POPULATION MALES	FEMALES	
BIRTH RATE	17.83	18.93	16.80	17.81	18.84	16.84	16.41	15.18	TABLE 6
DEATH RATE	10.97	11.39	10.58	11.41	11.66	11.18	13.90	12.70	PROJECTED
RATE OF INCREASE	6.86	7.54	6.22	6.40	7.18	5.66		2.48	VITAL RATES

AGE STRUCTURE OF PROJECTED POPULATION

							STABLE AGE STRUCTURE		AND RATIOS
% UNDER 15	23.43	24.74	22.19	23.81	25.06	22.62	23.12	21.59	(female
% 15-64	65.25	65.87	64.66	64.57	65.49	63.71	65.71	63.69	dominant)
% 65 AND OLDER	11.33	9.39	13.15	11.62	9.45	13.68	11.17	14.72	
DEPEND. RATIO x 100	53.27	51.82	54.65	54.86	52.70	56.97	52.19	57.02	

AGE GROUP	FEMALE BIRTH RATES	NET MATERNITY FUNCTION	COEFF. OF MATRIX EQUATION	ORIGINAL MATRIX SUB-DIAGONAL	ORIGINAL MATRIX FIRST ROW	STABLE MATRIX FISHER VALUES	STABLE MATRIX REPRODUCTIVE VALUES	MATRIX PARAMETERS		
0-4	0.0000	0.0000	0.0000	0.99580	0.00000	1.038	4176433	λ_1	1.01248	
5-9	0.0000	0.0000	0.0003	0.99826	0.00029	1.056	4127366	λ_2	$0.29572+0.73855i$	TABLE 7
10-14	0.0001	0.0006	0.0558	0.99802	0.05610	1.071	4795719	λ_4	$-0.41217+0.34093i$	
15-19	0.0231	0.1110	0.2626	0.99718	0.26471	1.028	4758124	λ_6	$0.02727+0.48146i$	LESLIE
20-24	0.0864	0.4143	0.3536	0.99663	0.35743	0.768	3019566	r_1	0.00248	MATRIX
25-29	0.0613	0.2929	0.2244	0.99580	0.22759	0.408	1356406	r_2	$-0.04574+0.23799i$	AND ITS
30-34	0.0328	0.1559	0.1140	0.99402	0.11607	0.177	633960	r_4	$-0.12514+0.49010i$	ANALYSIS
35-39	0.0152	0.0721	0.0456	0.99126	0.04667	0.059	211196	r_6	$-0.14586+0.30284i$	(females)
40-44	0.0041	0.0190	0.0102	0.98635	0.01052	0.012	41662	c_1	583181	
45-49	0.0003	0.0013	0.0007	0.97876	0.00071	0.001	2636	$2\pi/y$	26.4013	
50-54	0.0000	0.0001	0.0000	0.96766	0.00003	0.000	61	Δ	5.1568	

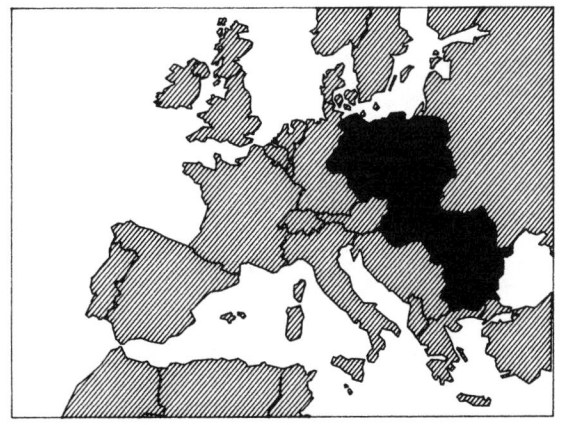

TABLE 1 — DATA

AGE AT LAST BIRTHDAY	ESTIMATED MID-YEAR POPULATION — BOTH SEXES	MALES Number	MALES Percent	FEMALES Number	FEMALES Percent	BIRTHS BY AGE OF MOTHER AND SEX	DEATHS BOTH SEXES	DEATHS MALES	DEATHS FEMALES	AGE AT LAST BIRTHDAY
0	1876443	962416	1.8	914027	1.6		40093	23272	16821	0
1-4	7350340	3764168	7.1	3586172	6.4		6914	3927	2987	1-4
5-9	8488539	4347354	8.2	4141185	7.4		3825	2380	1445	5-9
10-14	8162033	4178298	7.9	3983735	7.1	968	2947	1896	1051	10-14
15-19	7991509	4099260	7.7	3892249	6.9	205165	5839	4172	1667	15-19
20-24	8989706	4596592	8.6	4393114	7.8	817218	9555	7195	2360	20-24
25-29	9259751	4704299	8.8	4555452	8.1	549548	11154	8168	2986	25-29
30-34	7823716	3951054	7.4	3872662	6.9	208460	11930	8542	3388	30-34
35-39	6532684	3263270	6.1	3269414	5.8	62871	14980	10480	4500	35-39
40-44	6961454	3446127	6.5	3515327	6.3	17059	24890	17334	7556	40-44
45-49	6852085	3384246	6.4	3467839	6.4	1266	38158	26278	11880	45-49
50-54	6644982	3173248	6.0	3471734	6.2	43	55921	37373	18548	50-54
55-59	5983889	2680393	5.0	3303496	5.9		75137	47472	27665	55-59
60-64	3540005	1530721	2.9	2009284	3.6		66804	39980	26824	60-64
65-69	4615479	1947151	3.7	2668328	4.7		142172	81102	61070	65-69
70-74	3883070	1586485	3.0	2296585	4.1		199110	105728	93382	70-74
75-79	2579153	983518	1.8	1595635	2.8		219070	103084	115986	75-79
80-84	1276517	429299	0.8	847218	1.5	956778 M	179909	70380	109529	80-84
85+	588972	174359	0.3	414613	0.7	905820 F	141346	45772	95574	85+
TOTAL	109400327	53202258		56198069		1862598	1249754	644535	605219	TOTAL

TABLE 2 — MALE LIFE TABLE

x	$_nM_x$	$_nq_x$	l_x	$_nd_x$	$_nL_x$	$_nm_x$	$_na_x$	T_x	$\overset{\circ}{e}_x$	x
0	0.024181	0.023672	100000	2367	97896	0.024181	0.111	6676085	66.761	0
1	0.001043	0.004162	97633	406	389515	0.001043	1.500	6578189	67.377	1
5	0.000547	0.002734	97226	266	485468	0.000547	2.500	6188674	63.652	5
10	0.000454	0.002269	96961	220	484300	0.000454	2.713	5703206	58.820	10
15	0.001018	0.005077	96741	491	482586	0.001018	2.725	5218906	53.947	15
20	0.001565	0.007797	96250	750	479441	0.001565	2.593	4736320	49.209	20
25	0.001736	0.008647	95499	826	475487	0.001737	2.569	4256879	44.575	25
30	0.002162	0.010797	94673	1022	470951	0.002170	2.637	3781392	39.942	30
35	0.003212	0.015992	93651	1498	464776	0.003222	2.676	3310441	35.349	35
40	0.005030	0.024859	92153	2291	455442	0.005030	2.675	2845666	30.880	40
45	0.007765	0.038132	89863	3427	441301	0.007765	2.662	2390224	26.599	45
50	0.011778	0.057315	86436	4954	420532	0.011781	2.649	1948923	22.548	50
55	0.017711	0.085517	81482	6968	390870	0.017827	2.626	1528390	18.757	55
60	0.026118	0.123240	74514	9183	350736	0.026182	2.623	1137520	15.266	60
65	0.041652	0.189337	65331	12370	296976	0.041652	2.601	786784	12.043	65
70	0.066643	0.286379	52961	15167	227585	0.066643	2.546	489808	9.248	70
75	0.104812	0.415763	37794	15713	149161	0.105346	2.466	262223	6.938	75
80	0.163942	0.572418	22081	12639	77097	0.163942	2.365	113062	5.120	80
85	0.262516	1.000000	9441	9441	35965	0.208936	3.809	35965	3.809	85

TABLE 3 — FEMALE LIFE TABLE

x	$_nM_x$	$_nq_x$	l_x	$_nd_x$	$_nL_x$	$_nm_x$	$_na_x$	T_x	$\overset{\circ}{e}_x$	x
0	0.018403	0.018104	100000	1810	98373	0.018403	0.101	7369202	73.692	0
1	0.000833	0.003325	98190	326	391942	0.000833	1.500	7270829	74.049	1
5	0.000349	0.001743	97863	171	488889	0.000349	2.500	6878887	70.291	5
10	0.000264	0.001319	97693	129	488149	0.000264	2.562	6389997	65.409	10
15	0.000428	0.002139	97564	209	487325	0.000428	2.632	5901849	60.492	15
20	0.000537	0.002683	97355	261	486145	0.000537	2.587	5414524	55.616	20
25	0.000655	0.003274	97094	318	484709	0.000656	2.607	4928379	50.759	25
30	0.000875	0.004384	96776	424	482891	0.000879	2.669	4443670	45.917	30
35	0.001376	0.006880	96352	663	480226	0.001380	2.688	3960779	41.108	35
40	0.002149	0.010694	95689	1023	476083	0.002149	2.693	3480553	36.374	40
45	0.003426	0.016994	94666	1609	469604	0.003426	2.685	3004470	31.738	45
50	0.005343	0.026386	93057	2455	459591	0.005343	2.682	2534866	27.240	50
55	0.008374	0.041374	90601	3749	444300	0.008437	2.677	2075275	22.906	55
60	0.013350	0.064972	86853	5643	421214	0.013397	2.687	1630976	18.779	60
65	0.022887	0.108675	81210	8825	385610	0.022887	2.684	1209761	14.897	65
70	0.040661	0.185648	72384	13438	330301	0.040684	2.647	824152	11.386	70
75	0.072690	0.310498	58946	18303	250299	0.073123	2.572	493850	8.378	75
80	0.129281	0.486973	40644	19792	153096	0.129281	2.468	243552	5.992	80
85	0.230514	1.000000	20851	20851	90456	0.168305	4.338	90456	4.338	85

TABLE 4 — OBSERVED VITAL RATES AND RATIOS

CRUDE RATES

Per Thousand	BOTH SEXES	MALES	FEMALES
BIRTH RATE	17.03	17.98	16.12
DEATH RATE	11.42	12.11	10.77
RATE OF INCREASE	5.60	5.87	5.35

PERCENT OF POPULATION IN AGE GROUP

	BOTH SEXES	MALES	FEMALES
UNDER 15	23.65	24.91	22.47
15 - 64	64.52	65.47	63.62
65 AND OLDER	11.83	9.63	13.92

RATES STANDARDIZED ON USA 1980

Per Thousand	BOTH SEXES	MALES	FEMALES
BIRTH RATE	19.26		18.22
DEATH RATE	12.14	12.66	11.66
RATE OF INCREASE	7.12		6.56

RATES STANDARDIZED ON MEXICO 1980

	BOTH SEXES	MALES	FEMALES
BIRTH RATE	17.88		17.53
DEATH RATE	4.86	5.78	3.93
RATE OF INCREASE	13.02		13.60

VITAL STATISTICS

GFR x 1000	69.072
TFR	2.190
GRR	1.065
NRR	1.033
μ	25.380
σ^2	28.560
GENERATION	25.362
POP. SEX RATIO	1.056
SEX RATIO AT BIRTH	1.056
DEP. RATIO x 100	55.002

PROJECTED POPULATION

AGE GROUP	1985 BOTH SEXES	1985 MALES	1985 FEMALES	1990 BOTH SEXES	1990 MALES	1990 FEMALES
0-4	8944	4581	4363	8706	4459	4247
5-9	9195	4708	4487	8913	4563	4350
10-14	8472	4337	4135	9176	4696	4480
15-19	8141	4164	3977	8450	4322	4128
20-24	7956	4073	3883	8103	4136	3967
25-29	8939	4559	4380	7910	4039	3871
30-34	9197	4659	4538	8879	4515	4364
35-39	7750	3899	3851	9111	4598	4513
40-44	6439	3198	3241	7639	3821	3818
45-49	6806	3339	3467	6295	3098	3197
50-54	6619	3225	3394	6576	3182	3394
55-59	6305	2949	3356	6279	2998	3281
60-64	5537	2405	3132	5829	2647	3182
65-69	3135	1296	1839	4904	2037	2867
70-74	3778	1492	2286	2569	993	1576
75-79	2780	1040	1740	2710	978	1732
80-84	1484	508	976	1601	537	1064
85+	701	200	501	814	237	577
TOTAL	112178	54632	57546	114464	55856	58608

STABLE EQUIVALENT TO ORIGINAL POPULATION

MALES Number	MALES Percent	FEMALES Number	FEMALES Percent	AGE GROUP	
4473	7.6	4260	7.0	0-4	
4427	7.5	4220	6.9	5-9	TABLE 5
4388	7.5	4187	6.8	10-14	
4344	7.4	4153	6.8	15-19	POPULATION
4288	7.3	4117	6.7	20-24	PROJECTED
4226	7.2	4078	6.7	25-29	WITH
4159	7.1	4037	6.6	30-34	FIXED
4078	6.9	3989	6.5	35-39	AGE-
3970	6.8	3929	6.4	40-44	SPECIFIC
3822	6.5	3851	6.3	45-49	BIRTH
3619	6.2	3745	6.1	50-54	AND
3342	5.7	3597	5.9	55-59	DEATH
2980	5.1	3388	5.5	60-64	RATES
2507	4.3	3082	5.0	65-69	(female
1909	3.3	2623	4.3	70-74	dominant,
1243	2.1	1975	3.2	75-79	in 000s)
638	1.1	1200	2.0	80-84	
296	0.5	705	1.2	85+	
58709		61136		TOTAL	

VITAL RATES OF PROJECTED POPULATION

Per Thousand	1985 BOTH SEXES	1985 MALES	1985 FEMALES	1990 BOTH SEXES	1990 MALES	1990 FEMALES
BIRTH RATE	16.02	16.89	15.18	15.42	16.23	14.65
DEATH RATE	11.71	12.18	11.26	11.80	12.17	11.45
RATE OF INCREASE	4.31	4.71	3.93	3.62	4.07	3.19

AGE STRUCTURE OF PROJECTED POPULATION

% UNDER 15	23.72	24.94	22.56	23.41	24.56	22.31
% 15-64	65.69	66.76	64.68	65.58	66.88	64.35
% 65 AND OLDER	10.59	8.30	12.76	11.01	8.56	13.34
DEPEND. RATIO x 100	52.23	49.80	54.61	52.47	49.52	55.40

VITAL RATES OF STABLE POPULATION

Per Thousand	MALES	FEMALES	
BIRTH RATE	15.68	14.26	TABLE 6
DEATH RATE	14.38	12.97	PROJECTED
RATE OF INCREASE		1.28	VITAL RATES

STABLE AGE STRUCTURE

	MALES	FEMALES	
% UNDER 15	22.63	20.72	AND RATIOS (female dominant)
% 15-64	66.14	63.60	
% 65 AND OLDER	11.23	15.68	
DEPEND. RATIO x 100	51.20	57.23	

AGE GROUP	FEMALE BIRTH RATES	NET MATERNITY FUNCTION	COEFF. OF MATRIX EQUATION	ORIGINAL MATRIX SUB-DIAGONAL	ORIGINAL MATRIX FIRST ROW	STABLE MATRIX FISHER VALUES	STABLE MATRIX REPRODUCTIVE VALUES
0-4	0.0000	0.0000	0.0000	0.99709	0.00000	1.023	4603823
5-9	0.0000	0.0000	0.0003	0.99849	0.00029	1.033	4276255
10-14	0.0001	0.0006	0.0628	0.99831	0.06303	1.041	4145255
15-19	0.0256	0.1249	0.2824	0.99758	0.28409	0.984	3831634
20-24	0.0905	0.4398	0.3621	0.99705	0.36519	0.702	3083210
25-29	0.0587	0.2844	0.2054	0.99625	0.20776	0.334	1520313
30-34	0.0262	0.1264	0.0857	0.99448	0.08698	0.124	479433
35-39	0.0094	0.0449	0.0281	0.99137	0.02866	0.036	117089
40-44	0.0024	0.0112	0.0060	0.98639	0.00622	0.007	23833
45-49	0.0002	0.0008	0.0004	0.97868	0.00045	0.000	1636
50-54	0.0000	0.0000	0.0000	0.96673	0.00001	0.000	52

MATRIX PARAMETERS

λ_1	1.00644	
λ_2	0.26672+0.76452i	TABLE 7
λ_4	-0.40182-0.31204i	
λ_6	-0.34706-0.17902i	LESLIE MATRIX
r_1	0.00128	AND ITS
r_2	-0.04222+0.24702i	ANALYSIS
r_4	-0.13516-0.49626i	(females)
r_6	-0.18806-0.53307i	
c_1	611366	
$2\pi/y$	25.4355	
Δ	4.7380	

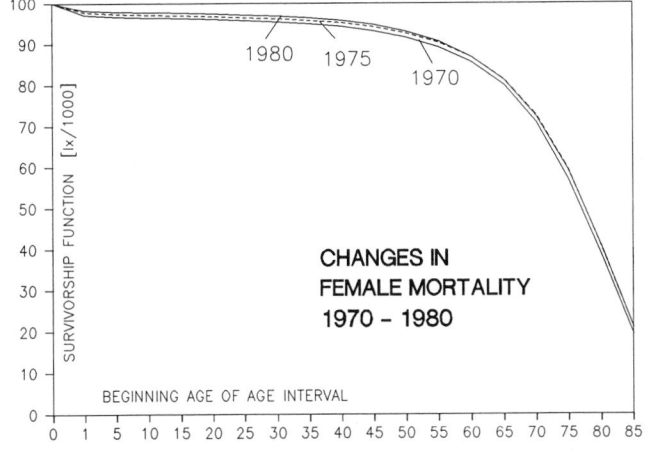

CHANGES IN FEMALE MORTALITY 1970 - 1980

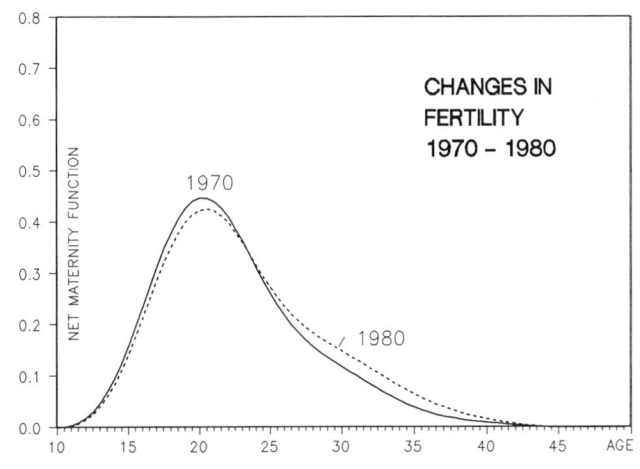

CHANGES IN FERTILITY 1970 - 1980

TABLE 1 — DATA

AGE AT LAST BIRTHDAY	ESTIMATED MID-YEAR POPULATION BOTH SEXES	MALES Number	MALES Percent	FEMALES Number	FEMALES Percent	BIRTHS BY AGE OF MOTHER AND SEX	DEATHS BOTH SEXES	MALES	FEMALES	AGE AT LAST BIRTHDAY
0	4864339	2478570	1.7	2385769	1.5		117877	67717	50160	0
1-4	20555807	10506321	7.1	10049486	6.5		19915	11122	8793	1-4
5-9	25969475	13281668	9.0	12687807	8.1		11572	7090	4482	5-9
10-14	23866175	12219754	8.3	11646421	7.5	1051	9019	5654	3365	10-14
15-19	22426141	11410032	7.8	11016109	7.1	361898	17996	12882	5114	15-19
20-24	22612511	11478946	7.8	11133565	7.1	1589032	21408	15376	6032	20-24
25-29	19646554	9982365	6.8	9664189	6.2	1457596	19536	13328	6208	25-29
30-34	20273996	10288603	7.0	9985393	6.4	931172	24741	16292	8449	30-34
35-39	19623498	9910192	6.7	9713306	6.2	471858	34676	22018	12658	35-39
40-44	19731895	9801925	6.7	9929970	6.4	141709	54269	34180	20089	40-44
45-49	19381060	9243227	6.3	10137833	6.5	11276	85018	51929	33089	45-49
50-54	14230271	6682961	4.5	7547310	4.8	535	96805	59621	37184	50-54
55-59	17240036	8008017	5.4	9232019	5.9		186668	118704	67964	55-59
60-64	16232826	7420282	5.0	8812544	5.7		285966	181454	104512	60-64
65-69	13712078	6044870	4.1	7667208	4.9		392002	238136	153866	65-69
70-74	10060568	4012984	2.7	6047584	3.9		462061	245949	216112	70-74
75-79	6600936	2404840	1.6	4196096	2.7		488550	222974	265576	75-79
80-84	3830474	1326276	0.9	2504198	1.6	2553042 M	451620	183746	267874	80-84
85+	2105778	674286	0.5	1431492	0.9	2413085 F	440900	155669	285231	85+
TOTAL	302964418	147176119		155788299		4966127	3220599	1663841	1556758	TOTAL

TABLE 2 — MALE LIFE TABLE

x	nM_x	nq_x	l_x	nd_x	nL_x	nm_x	na_x	T_x	$\overset{\circ}{e}_x$	x
0	0.027321	0.026677	100000	2668	97643	0.027321	0.116	6837937	68.379	0
1	0.001059	0.004223	97332	411	388302	0.001059	1.500	6740294	69.250	1
5	0.000534	0.002666	96921	258	483960	0.000534	2.500	6351993	65.538	5
10	0.000463	0.002318	96663	224	482814	0.000464	2.765	5868032	60.706	10
15	0.001129	0.005635	96439	543	480922	0.001130	2.660	5385219	55.841	15
20	0.001339	0.006678	95895	640	477895	0.001340	2.529	4904297	51.142	20
25	0.001335	0.006656	95255	634	474712	0.001336	2.535	4426402	46.469	25
30	0.001583	0.007889	94621	746	471323	0.001584	2.613	3951690	41.763	30
35	0.002222	0.011057	93874	1038	466956	0.002223	2.672	3480367	37.075	35
40	0.003487	0.017296	92836	1606	460482	0.003487	2.695	3013411	32.459	40
45	0.005618	0.027885	91231	2544	450269	0.005650	2.687	2552929	27.983	45
50	0.008921	0.043811	88687	3885	434456	0.008943	2.689	2102660	23.709	50
55	0.014823	0.071651	84801	6076	409903	0.014823	2.679	1668204	19.672	55
60	0.024454	0.115620	78725	9102	372222	0.024454	2.648	1258301	15.983	60
65	0.039395	0.180403	69623	12560	317999	0.039498	2.602	886079	12.727	65
70	0.061288	0.267533	57063	15266	247814	0.061603	2.544	568080	9.955	70
75	0.092719	0.376924	41797	15754	169181	0.093121	2.474	320265	7.662	75
80	0.138543	0.509255	26043	13262	95727	0.138543	2.400	151085	5.801	80
85	0.230865	1.000000	12780	12780	55358	0.169279	4.332	55358	4.332	85

TABLE 3 — FEMALE LIFE TABLE

x	nM_x	nq_x	l_x	nd_x	nL_x	nm_x	na_x	T_x	$\overset{\circ}{e}_x$	x
0	0.021025	0.020637	100000	2064	98155	0.021025	0.106	7465861	74.659	0
1	0.000875	0.003492	97936	342	390890	0.000875	1.500	7367706	75.230	1
5	0.000353	0.001765	97594	172	487541	0.000353	2.500	6976816	71.488	5
10	0.000289	0.001445	97422	141	486770	0.000289	2.579	6489275	66.610	10
15	0.000464	0.002320	97281	226	485868	0.000464	2.613	6002505	61.703	15
20	0.000542	0.002707	97056	263	484639	0.000542	2.567	5516637	56.840	20
25	0.000642	0.003211	96793	311	483218	0.000643	2.597	5031998	51.987	25
30	0.000846	0.004223	96482	407	481457	0.000846	2.660	4548780	47.146	30
35	0.001303	0.006496	96075	624	478928	0.001303	2.685	4067322	42.335	35
40	0.002023	0.010068	95451	961	475040	0.002023	2.698	3588394	37.594	40
45	0.003264	0.016260	94490	1536	468879	0.003277	2.677	3113353	32.949	45
50	0.004927	0.024392	92953	2267	459461	0.004935	2.660	2644475	28.450	50
55	0.007362	0.036190	90686	3282	445803	0.007362	2.676	2185014	24.094	55
60	0.011859	0.057753	87404	5048	425366	0.011867	2.691	1739210	19.899	60
65	0.020068	0.096135	82356	7917	393502	0.020120	2.691	1313845	15.953	65
70	0.035735	0.165507	74439	12320	343315	0.035886	2.656	920343	12.364	70
75	0.063291	0.275970	62119	17143	269124	0.063699	2.581	577027	9.289	75
80	0.106970	0.422031	44976	18981	177444	0.106970	2.501	307903	6.846	80
85	0.199254	1.000000	25995	25995	130459	0.132061	5.019	130459	5.019	85

TABLE 4 — OBSERVED VITAL RATES AND RATIOS

CRUDE RATES

Per Thousand	BOTH SEXES	MALES	FEMALES
BIRTH RATE	16.39	17.35	15.49
DEATH RATE	10.63	11.31	9.99
RATE OF INCREASE	5.76	6.04	5.50

PERCENT OF POPULATION IN AGE GROUP

UNDER 15	24.84	26.15	23.60
15 - 64	63.18	64.02	62.37
65 AND OLDER	11.98	9.83	14.02

RATES STANDARDIZED ON USA 1980

Per Thousand	BOTH SEXES	MALES	FEMALES
BIRTH RATE	20.35		19.23
DEATH RATE	10.68	11.16	10.23
RATE OF INCREASE	9.67		9.00

RATES STANDARDIZED ON MEXICO 1980

	BOTH SEXES	MALES	FEMALES
BIRTH RATE	17.99		17.62
DEATH RATE	4.42	5.19	3.64
RATE OF INCREASE	13.57		13.97

VITAL STATISTICS

GFR x 1000	69.378
TFR	2.419
GRR	1.175
NRR	1.135
μ	27.774
σ^2	36.485
GENERATION	27.690
POP. SEX RATIO	1.059
SEX RATIO AT BIRTH	1.058
DEP. RATIO x 100	58.290

PROJECTED POPULATION   STABLE EQUIVALENT TO ORIGINAL POPULATION

AGE GROUP	1975 BOTH SEXES	1975 MALES	1975 FEMALES	1980 BOTH SEXES	1980 MALES	1980 FEMALES	MALES Number	MALES Percent	FEMALES Number	FEMALES Percent	AGE GROUP	
0-4	24669	12643	12026	25659	13150	12509	12852	8.3	12225	7.7	0-4	
5-9	25329	12932	12397	24580	12591	11989	12510	8.1	11912	7.5	5-9	TABLE 5
10-14	25918	13250	12668	25278	12901	12377	12198	7.9	11624	7.3	10-14	
15-19	23797	12172	11625	25842	13198	12644	11876	7.6	11340	7.2	15-19	POPULATION
20-24	22326	11338	10988	23690	12095	11595	11535	7.4	11056	7.0	20-24	PROJECTED
25-29	22503	11402	11101	22219	11263	10956	11199	7.2	10775	6.8	25-29	WITH
30-34	19540	9911	9629	22381	11321	11060	10868	7.0	10493	6.6	30-34	FIXED
35-39	20126	10193	9933	19397	9819	9578	10524	6.8	10202	6.4	35-39	AGE-
40-44	19407	9773	9634	19904	10052	9852	10143	6.5	9890	6.2	40-44	SPECIFIC
45-49	19386	9585	9801	19065	9556	9509	9694	6.2	9542	6.0	45-49	BIRTH
50-54	18853	8919	9934	18852	9248	9604	9143	5.9	9139	5.8	50-54	AND
55-59	13628	6305	7323	18054	8415	9639	8431	5.4	8667	5.5	55-59	DEATH
60-64	16081	7272	8809	12713	5726	6987	7483	4.8	8083	5.1	60-64	RATES
65-69	14491	6339	8152	14362	6213	8149	6248	4.0	7308	4.6	65-69	(female
70-74	11400	4711	6689	12053	4940	7113	4759	3.1	6232	3.9	70-74	dominant,
75-79	7481	2740	4741	8460	3216	5244	3176	2.0	4775	3.0	75-79	in 000s)
80-84	4128	1361	2767	4676	1550	3126	1756	1.1	3077	1.9	80-84	
85+	2608	767	1841	2821	787	2034	993	0.6	2211	1.4	85+	
TOTAL	311671	151613	160058	320006	156041	163965	155388		158551		TOTAL	

VITAL RATES OF PROJECTED POPULATION   VITAL RATES OF STABLE POPULATION

Per Thousand	1975 BOTH SEXES	1975 MALES	1975 FEMALES	1980 BOTH SEXES	1980 MALES	1980 FEMALES	STABLE MALES	STABLE FEMALES	
BIRTH RATE	16.54	17.48	15.65	16.79	17.70	15.92	17.21	15.95	TABLE 6
DEATH RATE	11.22	11.67	10.80	11.58	11.90	11.28	12.61	11.38	
RATE OF INCREASE	5.32	5.81	4.85	5.21	5.80	4.64		4.57	PROJECTED

AGE STRUCTURE OF PROJECTED POPULATION   STABLE AGE STRUCTURE

	1975 BOTH SEXES	1975 MALES	1975 FEMALES	1980 BOTH SEXES	1980 MALES	1980 FEMALES	STABLE MALES	STABLE FEMALES	
% UNDER 15	24.36	25.61	23.17	23.60	24.76	22.49	24.17	22.55	VITAL RATES AND RATIOS (female dominant)
% 15-64	62.77	63.89	61.71	63.16	64.53	61.86	64.93	62.56	
% 65 AND OLDER	12.87	10.50	15.11	13.24	10.71	15.65	10.90	14.89	
DEPEND. RATIO x 100	59.30	56.51	62.04	58.33	54.97	61.66	54.01	59.85	

AGE GROUP	FEMALE BIRTH RATES	NET MATERNITY FUNCTION	COEFF. OF MATRIX EQUATION	ORIGINAL MATRIX SUB-DIAGONAL	ORIGINAL MATRIX FIRST ROW	STABLE MATRIX FISHER VALUES	STABLE MATRIX REPRODUCTIVE VALUES	MATRIX PARAMETERS		
0-4	0.0000	0.0000	0.0000	0.99692	0.00000	1.034	12859696	λ_1	1.02312	
5-9	0.0000	0.0000	0.0001	0.99842	0.00011	1.061	13465590	λ_2	0.37194+0.73974i	TABLE 7
10-14	0.0000	0.0002	0.0389	0.99815	0.03907	1.087	12664850	λ_4	-0.39003+0.40388i	
15-19	0.0160	0.0776	0.2068	0.99747	0.20818	1.074	11833206	λ_6	-0.02194+0.52689i	LESLIE
20-24	0.0694	0.3361	0.3451	0.99707	0.34826	0.886	9863856	r_1	0.00457	MATRIX
25-29	0.0733	0.3541	0.2861	0.99636	0.28960	0.548	5295024	r_2	-0.03775+0.22098i	AND ITS
30-34	0.0453	0.2182	0.1656	0.99475	0.16822	0.262	2616560	r_4	-0.11544+0.46775i	ANALYSIS
35-39	0.0236	0.1130	0.0730	0.99188	0.07454	0.095	919235	r_6	-0.12798+0.32248i	(females)
40-44	0.0069	0.0329	0.0177	0.98703	0.01826	0.020	197654	c_1	1585499	
45-49	0.0005	0.0025	0.0013	0.97991	0.00140	0.002	15214	$2\pi/\gamma$	28.4328	
50-54	0.0000	0.0002	0.0001	0.97027	0.00008	0.000	643	Δ	3.1770	

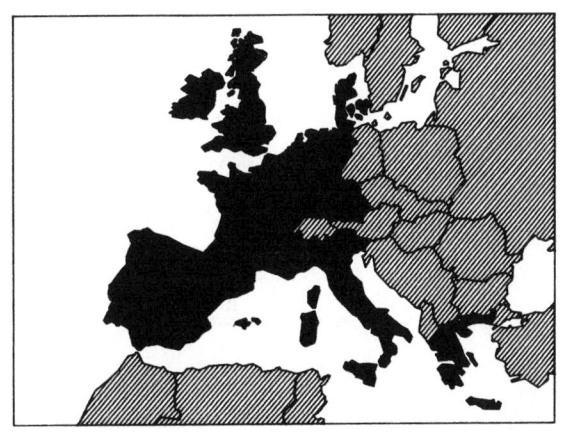

TABLE 1 — DATA

AGE AT LAST BIRTHDAY	ESTIMATED MID-YEAR POPULATION BOTH SEXES	MALES Number	MALES Percent	FEMALES Number	FEMALES Percent	BIRTHS BY AGE OF MOTHER AND SEX	DEATHS BOTH SEXES	DEATHS MALES	DEATHS FEMALES	AGE AT LAST BIRTHDAY
0	4090854	2096513	1.4	1994341	1.2		52662	30416	22246	0
1-4	16398554	8406769	5.4	7991785	4.9		9924	5553	4371	1-4
5-9	23063809	11813481	7.6	11250328	6.9		7401	4477	2924	5-9
10-14	25846470	13244418	8.6	12602052	7.7	1225	7503	4621	2882	10-14
15-19	26439798	13516882	8.7	12922916	7.9	303200	19103	13939	5164	15-19
20-24	24268747	12338109	8.0	11930638	7.3	1289286	21551	16126	5425	20-24
25-29	22708718	11497101	7.4	11211617	6.9	1427461	19429	13721	5708	25-29
30-34	22815524	11548105	7.5	11267419	6.9	793210	22821	15107	7714	30-34
35-39	19663523	9927946	6.4	9735577	6.0	250866	28677	18584	10093	35-39
40-44	20045213	10073442	6.5	9971771	6.1	62754	47019	30929	16090	40-44
45-49	19225534	9578108	6.2	9647426	5.9	5504	74381	49457	24924	45-49
50-54	18934399	9243576	6.0	9690823	5.9	310	118460	79315	39145	50-54
55-59	18186178	8448430	5.5	9737748	6.0		176504	115154	61350	55-59
60-64	12874803	5813244	3.8	7061559	4.3		193008	123062	69946	60-64
65-69	14633759	6342696	4.1	8291063	5.1		349518	214900	134618	65-69
70-74	12396613	5086078	3.3	7310535	4.5		486191	276974	209217	70-74
75-79	8778887	3308637	2.1	5470250	3.3		568166	285180	282986	75-79
80-84	4846487	1572592	1.0	3273895	2.0	2127084 M	518862	211097	307765	80-84
85+	2800569	776629	0.5	2023940	1.2	2006732 F	555141	175001	380140	85+
TOTAL	318018439	154632756		163385683		4133816	3276321	1683613	1592708	TOTAL

TABLE 2 — MALE LIFE TABLE

x	$_nM_x$	$_nq_x$	l_x	$_nd_x$	$_nL_x$	$_nm_x$	$_na_x$	T_x	$\overset{\circ}{e}_x$	x
0	0.014508	0.014320	100000	1432	98704	0.014508	0.095	7053114	70.531	0
1	0.000661	0.002638	98568	260	393622	0.000661	1.500	6954410	70.554	1
5	0.000379	0.001893	98308	186	491075	0.000379	2.500	6560788	66.737	5
10	0.000349	0.001743	98122	171	490248	0.000349	2.887	6069713	61.859	10
15	0.001031	0.005146	97951	504	488591	0.001032	2.692	5579465	56.962	15
20	0.001307	0.006517	97447	635	485661	0.001308	2.524	5090874	52.243	20
25	0.001193	0.005949	96812	576	482617	0.001193	2.497	4605213	47.569	25
30	0.001308	0.006528	96236	628	479674	0.001310	2.605	4122596	42.838	30
35	0.001872	0.009343	95608	893	475975	0.001877	2.690	3642921	38.103	35
40	0.003070	0.015255	94714	1445	470270	0.003072	2.715	3166947	33.437	40
45	0.005164	0.025538	93269	2382	460888	0.005168	2.708	2696677	28.913	45
50	0.008581	0.042067	90888	3823	445587	0.008581	2.685	2235789	24.600	50
55	0.013630	0.066384	87064	5780	421787	0.013703	2.658	1790202	20.562	55
60	0.021169	0.101058	81285	8214	387069	0.021222	2.644	1368415	16.835	60
65	0.033881	0.156767	73070	11455	338090	0.033882	2.620	981346	13.430	65
70	0.054457	0.240575	61615	14823	272106	0.054475	2.573	643257	10.440	70
75	0.086193	0.356449	46792	16679	192302	0.086733	2.502	371151	7.932	75
80	0.134235	0.498508	30113	15012	111831	0.134235	2.420	178849	5.939	80
85	0.225334	1.000000	15101	15101	67018	0.162517	4.438	67018	4.438	85

TABLE 3 — FEMALE LIFE TABLE

x	$_nM_x$	$_nq_x$	l_x	$_nd_x$	$_nL_x$	$_nm_x$	$_na_x$	T_x	$\overset{\circ}{e}_x$	x
0	0.011155	0.011042	100000	1104	98994	0.011155	0.089	7730114	77.301	0
1	0.000547	0.002185	98896	216	395043	0.000547	1.500	7631120	77.163	1
5	0.000260	0.001299	98680	128	493078	0.000260	2.500	7236077	73.329	5
10	0.000229	0.001143	98552	113	492490	0.000229	2.626	6742999	68.421	10
15	0.000400	0.001997	98439	197	491726	0.000400	2.617	6250508	63.496	15
20	0.000455	0.002272	98242	223	490665	0.000455	2.549	5758782	58.618	20
25	0.000509	0.002544	98019	249	489496	0.000509	2.593	5268117	53.746	25
30	0.000685	0.003424	97770	335	488066	0.000686	2.659	4778621	48.876	30
35	0.001037	0.005184	97435	505	486005	0.001039	2.683	4290556	44.035	35
40	0.001614	0.008042	96930	780	482853	0.001614	2.695	3804550	39.250	40
45	0.002583	0.012843	96151	1235	477899	0.002584	2.689	3321697	34.547	45
50	0.004039	0.020010	94916	1899	470177	0.004039	2.683	2843798	29.961	50
55	0.006300	0.031173	93016	2900	458348	0.006326	2.678	2373621	25.518	55
60	0.009905	0.048519	90117	4372	440447	0.009927	2.682	1915272	21.253	60
65	0.016237	0.078252	85744	6710	413249	0.016237	2.694	1474825	17.200	65
70	0.028619	0.134311	79035	10615	370540	0.028648	2.679	1061577	13.432	70
75	0.051732	0.231678	68420	15851	304442	0.052067	2.624	691036	10.100	75
80	0.094006	0.382040	52568	20083	213638	0.094006	2.550	386594	7.354	80
85	0.187822	1.000000	32485	32485	172957	0.119526	5.324	172957	5.324	85

TABLE 4 — OBSERVED VITAL RATES AND RATIOS

CRUDE RATES

Per Thousand	BOTH SEXES	MALES	FEMALES
BIRTH RATE	13.00	13.76	12.28
DEATH RATE	10.30	10.89	9.75
RATE OF INCREASE	2.70	2.87	2.53

PERCENT OF POPULATION IN AGE GROUP

UNDER 15	21.82	23.00	20.71
15 - 64	64.51	65.95	63.15
65 AND OLDER	13.66	11.05	16.14

RATES STANDARDIZED ON USA 1980

Per Thousand	BOTH SEXES	MALES	FEMALES
BIRTH RATE	15.43		14.57
DEATH RATE	9.34	10.02	8.69
RATE OF INCREASE	6.09		5.87

RATES STANDARDIZED ON MEXICO 1980

	BOTH SEXES	MALES	FEMALES
BIRTH RATE	13.65		13.35
DEATH RATE	3.62	4.37	2.86
RATE OF INCREASE	10.03		10.50

VITAL STATISTICS

GFR x 1000	53.905
TFR	1.810
GRR	0.879
NRR	0.860
μ	27.315
σ^2	30.470
GENERATION	27.399
POP. SEX RATIO	1.057
SEX RATIO AT BIRTH	1.060
DEP. RATIO x 100	55.008

PROJECTED POPULATION / STABLE EQUIVALENT TO ORIGINAL POPULATION

AGE GROUP	1985 BOTH SEXES	1985 MALES	1985 FEMALES	1990 BOTH SEXES	1990 MALES	1990 FEMALES	MALES Number	MALES Percent	FEMALES Number	FEMALES Percent	AGE GROUP	
0-4	20915	10744	10171	21712	11153	10559	11552	5.7	10937	5.1	0-4	
5-9	20444	10477	9967	20867	10716	10151	11845	5.9	11220	5.3	5-9	TABLE 5
10-14	23031	11794	11237	20414	10459	9955	12155	6.0	11519	5.4	10-14	
15-19	25782	13200	12582	22973	11754	11219	12452	6.2	11822	5.6	15-19	POPULATION
20-24	26331	13436	12895	25675	13120	12555	12722	6.3	12126	5.7	20-24	PROJECTED
25-29	24163	12261	11902	26216	13352	12864	12995	6.4	12435	5.9	25-29	WITH
30-34	22606	11427	11179	24053	12186	11867	13277	6.6	12744	6.0	30-34	FIXED
35-39	22679	11459	11220	22471	11339	11132	13542	6.7	13045	6.1	35-39	AGE-
40-44	19481	9809	9672	22469	11322	11147	13753	6.8	13322	6.3	40-44	SPECIFIC
45-49	19741	9872	9869	19186	9613	9573	13855	6.9	13553	6.4	45-49	BIRTH
50-54	18752	9260	9492	19255	9545	9710	13768	6.8	13706	6.4	50-54	AND
55-59	18197	8750	9447	18019	8766	9253	13397	6.6	13734	6.5	55-59	DEATH
60-64	17110	7753	9357	17108	8030	9078	12637	6.3	13566	6.4	60-64	RATES
65-69	11703	5078	6625	15552	6772	8780	11346	5.6	13084	6.2	65-69	(female
70-74	12539	5105	7434	10028	4087	5941	9387	4.6	12059	5.7	70-74	dominant,
75-79	9600	3594	6006	9716	3608	6108	6819	3.4	10184	4.8	75-79	in 000s)
80-84	5763	1924	3839	6305	2090	4215	4076	2.0	7346	3.5	80-84	
85+	3592	942	2650	4261	1153	3108	2511	1.2	6113	2.9	85+	
TOTAL	322429	156885	165544	326280	159065	167215	202089		212515		TOTAL	

VITAL RATES OF PROJECTED POPULATION / VITAL RATES OF STABLE POPULATION

Per Thousand	1985 BOTH SEXES	1985 MALES	1985 FEMALES	1990 BOTH SEXES	1990 MALES	1990 FEMALES	STABLE MALES	STABLE FEMALES	
BIRTH RATE	13.49	14.26	12.75	13.66	14.42	12.94	11.45	10.27	TABLE 6
DEATH RATE	11.14	11.48	10.81	11.63	11.87	11.41	16.89	15.78	PROJECTED
RATE OF INCREASE	2.35	2.78	1.94	2.03	2.55	1.53		-5.50	VITAL RATES AND RATIOS

AGE STRUCTURE OF PROJECTED POPULATION / STABLE AGE STRUCTURE

	1985 BOTH SEXES	1985 MALES	1985 FEMALES	1990 BOTH SEXES	1990 MALES	1990 FEMALES	STABLE MALES	STABLE FEMALES	
% UNDER 15	19.97	21.04	18.95	19.31	20.32	18.34	17.59	15.85	(female
% 15-64	66.63	68.35	65.01	66.64	68.54	64.83	65.52	61.20	dominant)
% 65 AND OLDER	13.40	10.61	16.04	14.06	11.13	16.84	16.89	22.96	
DEPEND. RATIO x 100	50.08	46.31	53.83	50.06	45.90	54.26	52.64	63.41	

MATRIX PARAMETERS

AGE GROUP	FEMALE BIRTH RATES	NET MATERNITY FUNCTION	COEFF. OF MATRIX EQUATION	ORIGINAL MATRIX SUB-DIAGONAL	ORIGINAL MATRIX FIRST ROW	STABLE MATRIX FISHER VALUES	STABLE MATRIX REPRODUCTIVE VALUES			
0-4	0.0000	0.0000	0.0000	0.99806	0.00000	0.998	9968426	λ_1	0.97285	
5-9	0.0000	0.0000	0.0001	0.99881	0.00012	0.973	10946736	λ_2	$0.35750+0.73200i$	TABLE 7
10-14	0.0000	0.0000	0.0002	0.0281	0.99845	0.02821	0.948	11941854	λ_4	$-0.30680+0.41424i$
15-19	0.0114	0.0560	0.1567	0.99784	0.15744	0.895	11567520	λ_6	$-0.40279+0.10105i$	LESLIE
20-24	0.0525	0.2574	0.2800	0.99762	0.28189	0.715	8532784	r_1	-0.00550	MATRIX
25-29	0.0618	0.3025	0.2347	0.99708	0.23684	0.415	4657055	r_2	$-0.04100+0.22330i$	AND ITS
30-34	0.0342	0.1668	0.1138	0.99578	0.11519	0.168	1894816	r_4	$-0.13253+0.44166i$	ANALYSIS
35-39	0.0125	0.0608	0.0378	0.99351	0.03840	0.049	475352	r_6	$-0.17577+0.57916i$	(females)
40-44	0.0031	0.0148	0.0080	0.98974	0.00822	0.009	92059	c_1	2125167	
45-49	0.0003	0.0013	0.0007	0.98384	0.00072	0.001	7530	$2\pi/\gamma$	28.1383	
50-54	0.0000	0.0001	0.0000	0.97484	0.00004	0.000	381	Δ	10.7173	

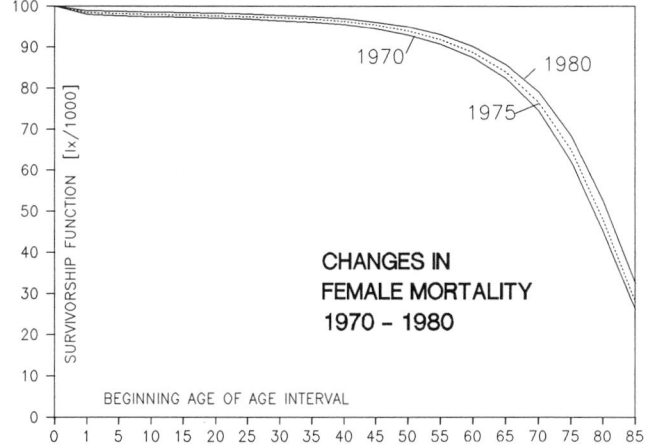

CHANGES IN FEMALE MORTALITY 1970 – 1980

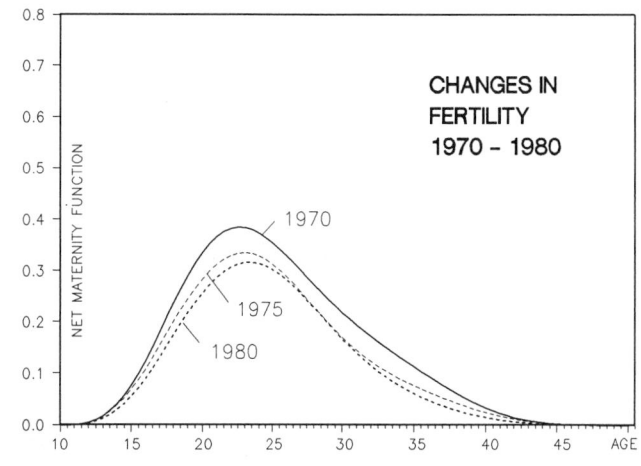

CHANGES IN FERTILITY 1970 – 1980

TABLE 1 — DATA

AGE AT LAST BIRTHDAY	ESTIMATED MID-YEAR POPULATION BOTH SEXES	MALES Number	MALES Percent	FEMALES Number	FEMALES Percent	BIRTHS BY AGE OF MOTHER AND SEX	DEATHS BOTH SEXES	DEATHS MALES	DEATHS FEMALES	AGE AT LAST BIRTHDAY
0	114564	58695	1.7	55869	1.4		2908	1694	1214	0
1-4	493732	252519	7.2	241213	6.1		500	271	229	1-4
5-9	641491	327946	9.3	313545	7.9		317	214	103	5-9
10-14	569472	291240	8.3	278232	7.0	37	236	162	74	10-14
15-19	501723	254504	7.2	247219	6.3	14361	535	389	146	15-19
20-24	508659	259692	7.4	248967	6.3	38563	642	504	138	20-24
25-29	532485	271609	7.7	260876	6.6	30045	612	448	164	25-29
30-34	472990	242138	6.9	230852	5.8	18077	647	444	203	30-34
35-39	426088	217722	6.2	208366	5.3	8335	956	667	289	35-39
40-44	463987	227169	6.5	236818	6.0	2677	1496	987	509	40-44
45-49	485402	205150	5.8	280252	7.1	203	2257	1267	990	45-49
50-54	312471	131499	3.7	180972	4.6	3	2192	1277	915	50-54
55-59	443863	189171	5.4	254692	6.4		5030	2994	2036	55-59
60-64	449099	191269	5.4	257830	6.5		8842	5411	3431	60-64
65-69	401048	168570	4.8	232332	5.9		13081	7749	5332	65-69
70-74	299783	114150	3.2	185633	4.7		15960	8122	7838	70-74
75-79	191909	65055	1.8	126854	3.2		16106	6969	9137	75-79
80-84	105277	33506	1.0	71771	1.8	57878 M	14058	5293	8765	80-84
85+	53043	16280	0.5	36763	0.9	54423 F	12444	4220	8224	85+
TOTAL	7467086	3518030		3949056		112301	98819	49082	49737	TOTAL

TABLE 2 — MALE LIFE TABLE

x	nM_x	nq_x	l_x	nd_x	nL_x	nm_x	na_x	T_x	$\overset{\circ}{e}_x$	x
0	0.028861	0.028145	100000	2815	97521	0.028861	0.119	6652973	66.530	0
1	0.001073	0.004281	97185	416	387702	0.001073	1.500	6555453	67.453	1
5	0.000653	0.003257	96769	315	483059	0.000653	2.500	6167751	63.737	5
10	0.000556	0.002793	96454	269	481685	0.000559	2.824	5684692	58.937	10
15	0.001528	0.007638	96185	735	479223	0.001533	2.685	5203008	54.094	15
20	0.001941	0.009657	95450	922	474955	0.001941	2.509	4723785	49.490	20
25	0.001649	0.008213	94528	776	470687	0.001649	2.483	4248830	44.948	25
30	0.001834	0.009152	93752	858	466748	0.001838	2.655	3778143	40.299	30
35	0.003064	0.015229	92894	1415	461164	0.003068	2.663	3311395	35.647	35
40	0.004345	0.021503	91479	1967	452755	0.004345	2.641	2850232	31.157	40
45	0.006176	0.030636	89512	2742	441155	0.006216	2.664	2397477	26.784	45
50	0.009711	0.047557	86770	4126	424276	0.009726	2.680	1956322	22.546	50
55	0.015827	0.076353	82643	6310	398691	0.015827	2.698	1532046	18.538	55
60	0.028290	0.132639	76333	10125	357892	0.028290	2.652	1133355	14.847	60
65	0.045929	0.206746	66209	13688	298032	0.045929	2.588	775463	11.712	65
70	0.071152	0.303356	52520	15932	223132	0.071403	2.523	477432	9.090	70
75	0.107125	0.421646	36588	15427	143509	0.107499	2.444	254300	6.950	75
80	0.157972	0.557288	21161	11793	74650	0.157972	2.358	110791	5.236	80
85	0.259214	1.000000	9368	9368	36140	0.204823	3.858	36140	3.858	85

TABLE 3 — FEMALE LIFE TABLE

x	nM_x	nq_x	l_x	nd_x	nL_x	nm_x	na_x	T_x	$\overset{\circ}{e}_x$	x
0	0.021729	0.021316	100000	2132	98096	0.021729	0.107	7348030	73.480	0
1	0.000949	0.003788	97868	371	390547	0.000949	1.500	7249933	74.078	1
5	0.000329	0.001641	97498	160	487088	0.000328	2.500	6859387	70.354	5
10	0.000266	0.001333	97338	130	486390	0.000267	2.704	6372299	65.466	10
15	0.000591	0.002954	97208	287	485350	0.000592	2.600	5885908	60.550	15
20	0.000554	0.002768	96921	268	483936	0.000554	2.513	5400558	55.721	20
25	0.000629	0.003139	96652	303	482537	0.000629	2.607	4916621	50.869	25
30	0.000879	0.004404	96349	424	480760	0.000883	2.677	4434085	46.021	30
35	0.001387	0.006915	95925	663	478090	0.001387	2.687	3953325	41.213	35
40	0.002149	0.010694	95262	1019	473968	0.002149	2.703	3475235	36.481	40
45	0.003533	0.017580	94243	1657	467343	0.003545	2.663	3001267	31.846	45
50	0.005056	0.025027	92586	2317	457530	0.005064	2.670	2533925	27.368	50
55	0.007994	0.039246	90269	3543	443171	0.007994	2.693	2076394	23.002	55
60	0.013307	0.064558	86726	5599	420740	0.013307	2.698	1633223	18.832	60
65	0.022950	0.109102	81127	8851	385240	0.022976	2.696	1212483	14.945	65
70	0.042223	0.192437	72276	13909	328506	0.042339	2.636	827243	11.446	70
75	0.072028	0.307630	58368	17956	247979	0.072408	2.557	498737	8.545	75
80	0.122125	0.466584	40412	18856	154396	0.122125	2.472	250758	6.205	80
85	0.223703	1.000000	21556	21556	96361	0.160209	4.470	96361	4.470	85

TABLE 4 — OBSERVED VITAL RATES AND RATIOS

CRUDE RATES

Per Thousand	BOTH SEXES	MALES	FEMALES
BIRTH RATE	15.04	16.45	13.78
DEATH RATE	13.23	13.95	12.59
RATE OF INCREASE	1.81	2.50	1.19

PERCENT OF POPULATION IN AGE GROUP

	BOTH SEXES	MALES	FEMALES
UNDER 15	24.36	26.45	22.51
15 - 64	61.56	62.25	60.95
65 AND OLDER	14.08	11.30	16.54

RATES STANDARDIZED ON USA 1980

Per Thousand	BOTH SEXES	MALES	FEMALES
BIRTH RATE	19.59		18.46
DEATH RATE	12.15	12.81	11.53
RATE OF INCREASE	7.44		6.94

RATES STANDARDIZED ON MEXICO 1980

	BOTH SEXES	MALES	FEMALES
BIRTH RATE	17.93		17.52
DEATH RATE	4.99	5.95	4.01
RATE OF INCREASE	12.94		13.50

VITAL STATISTICS

GFR x 1000	65.545
TFR	2.293
GRR	1.111
NRR	1.072
μ	26.637
σ^2	39.511
GENERATION	26.585
POP. SEX RATIO	1.123
SEX RATIO AT BIRTH	1.063
DEP. RATIO x 100	62.442

PROJECTED POPULATION

AGE GROUP	1975 BOTH SEXES	MALES	FEMALES	1980 BOTH SEXES	MALES	FEMALES
0-4	553	284	269	576	296	280
5-9	606	310	296	551	283	268
10-14	640	327	313	605	309	296
15-19	568	290	278	637	325	312
20-24	498	252	246	564	287	277
25-29	505	257	248	496	250	246
30-34	529	269	260	502	255	247
35-39	469	239	230	524	266	258
40-44	421	214	207	463	235	228
45-49	455	221	234	412	208	204
50-54	471	197	274	442	213	229
55-59	299	124	175	451	185	266
60-64	412	170	242	277	111	166
65-69	395	159	236	362	141	221
70-74	324	126	198	320	119	201
75-79	213	73	140	231	81	150
80-84	113	34	79	125	38	87
85+	61	16	45	65	16	49
TOTAL	7532	3562	3970	7603	3618	3985

STABLE EQUIVALENT TO ORIGINAL POPULATION

AGE GROUP	MALES Number	Percent	FEMALES Number	Percent
0-4	301	8.0	285	7.3
5-9	295	7.8	280	7.2
10-14	291	7.7	276	7.1
15-19	286	7.6	272	7.0
20-24	279	7.4	268	6.9
25-29	273	7.2	263	6.8
30-34	267	7.1	259	6.6
35-39	261	6.9	254	6.5
40-44	253	6.7	249	6.4
45-49	243	6.4	242	6.2
50-54	231	6.1	234	6.0
55-59	214	5.7	224	5.7
60-64	189	5.0	209	5.4
65-69	156	4.1	189	4.9
70-74	115	3.0	159	4.1
75-79	73	1.9	119	3.0
80-84	37	1.0	73	1.9
85+	18	0.5	45	1.2
TOTAL	3782		3900	

TABLE 5 — POPULATION PROJECTED WITH FIXED AGE-SPECIFIC BIRTH AND DEATH RATES (female dominant, in 000s)

VITAL RATES OF PROJECTED POPULATION

Per Thousand	1975 BOTH SEXES	MALES	FEMALES	1980 BOTH SEXES	MALES	FEMALES
BIRTH RATE	15.26	16.63	14.04	16.01	17.34	14.81
DEATH RATE	13.64	13.88	13.43	13.77	13.64	13.88
RATE OF INCREASE	1.62	2.75	0.61	2.25	3.70	0.93

AGE STRUCTURE OF PROJECTED POPULATION

% UNDER 15	23.88	25.84	22.13	22.77	24.53	21.18
% 15-64	61.42	62.68	60.29	62.70	64.52	61.04
% 65 AND OLDER	14.70	11.48	17.58	14.53	10.95	17.78
DEPEND. RATIO x 100	62.82	59.55	65.87	59.50	54.98	63.84

VITAL RATES OF STABLE POPULATION

Per Thousand	MALES	FEMALES
BIRTH RATE	16.50	15.04
DEATH RATE	13.83	12.42
RATE OF INCREASE		2.63

STABLE AGE STRUCTURE

	MALES	FEMALES
% UNDER 15	23.45	21.57
% 15-64	65.99	63.43
% 65 AND OLDER	10.56	15.00
DEPEND. RATIO x 100	51.54	57.66

TABLE 6 — PROJECTED VITAL RATES AND RATIOS (female dominant)

AGE GROUP	FEMALE BIRTH RATES	NET MATERNITY FUNCTION	COEFF. OF MATRIX EQUATION	ORIGINAL MATRIX SUB-DIAGONAL	FIRST ROW	STABLE MATRIX FISHER VALUES	REPRODUCTIVE VALUES
0-4	0.0000	0.0000	0.0000	0.99682	0.00000	1.030	305986
5-9	0.0000	0.0000	0.0002	0.99857	0.00016	1.047	328256
10-14	0.0001	0.0003	0.0685	0.99786	0.06879	1.062	295514
15-19	0.0282	0.1366	0.2499	0.99709	0.25164	1.007	249062
20-24	0.0751	0.3633	0.3163	0.99711	0.31937	0.764	190163
25-29	0.0558	0.2693	0.2259	0.99632	0.22874	0.446	116418
30-34	0.0379	0.1824	0.1376	0.99445	0.13982	0.217	50179
35-39	0.0194	0.0927	0.0593	0.99138	0.06063	0.077	15972
40-44	0.0055	0.0260	0.0138	0.98602	0.01423	0.015	3635
45-49	0.0004	0.0016	0.0008	0.97900	0.00088	0.001	255
50-54	0.0000	0.0000	0.0000	0.96862	0.00002	0.000	4

MATRIX PARAMETERS

λ_1 1.01322
λ_2 0.33053+0.69915i
λ_4 -0.00172+0.56416i
λ_6 -0.38072+0.32661i
r_1 0.00263
r_2 -0.05141+0.22584i
r_4 -0.11448+0.31477i
r_6 -0.13798+0.48651i
c_1 38994
$2\pi/y$ 27.8220
Δ 5.5556

TABLE 7 — LESLIE MATRIX AND ITS ANALYSIS (females)

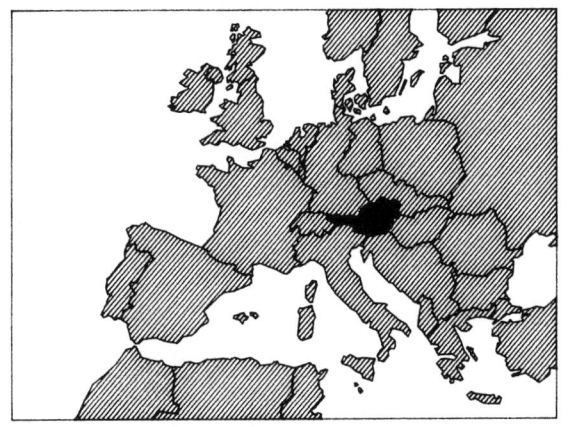

EDUCATION [1984]
% of primary school-age children enrolled: 97
secondary school-age children enrolled: 76
ca. 20-24 year olds in higher education: 26

LABOR FORCE
Average annual labor force growth (%) 1980-85: 0.8
% of the 1980 labor force in agriculture: 9
in industry: 41
in services: 50

GNP & INCOME DISTRIBUTION
GNP per capita (in US Dollars) 1985: 9120
GNP average annual growth rate (%) 1965-85: 3.5
% share of total household income
Lowest 20% of households: na
Highest 10% of households: na

HEALTH & NUTRITION
Population per physician 1981: 440
Daily calorie supply per capita 1985: 3514

TABLE 8 — SOCIO-ECONOMIC INDICATORS

TABLE 1 — DATA

AGE AT LAST BIRTHDAY	ESTIMATED MID-YEAR POPULATION BOTH SEXES	MALES Number	MALES Percent	FEMALES Number	FEMALES Percent	BIRTHS BY AGE OF MOTHER AND SEX	DEATHS BOTH SEXES	DEATHS MALES	DEATHS FEMALES	AGE AT LAST BIRTHDAY
0	94503	48381	1.4	46122	1.2		1926	1124	802	0
1-4	406050	207890	5.9	198160	5.0		340	189	151	1-4
5-9	608839	311608	8.8	297231	7.5		246	152	94	5-9
10-14	642781	328590	9.3	314191	7.9	40	238	154	84	10-14
15-19	574020	293030	8.3	280990	7.1	13466	633	484	149	15-19
20-24	511784	258603	7.3	253181	6.4	33081	626	487	139	20-24
25-29	511415	259782	7.3	251633	6.3	25207	558	394	164	25-29
30-34	526509	265734	7.5	260775	6.6	13526	784	558	226	30-34
35-39	465724	234859	6.6	230865	5.8	6586	898	608	290	35-39
40-44	416656	208924	5.9	207732	5.2	1730	1335	922	413	40-44
45-49	451806	217275	6.1	234531	5.9	121	2117	1403	714	45-49
50-54	470030	195334	5.5	274696	6.9		3159	1877	1282	50-54
55-59	299312	123482	3.5	175830	4.4		3140	1844	1296	55-59
60-64	414810	171641	4.8	243169	6.1		7048	4129	2919	60-64
65-69	400441	162203	4.6	238238	6.0		11311	6505	4806	65-69
70-74	330960	129097	3.6	201863	5.1		15678	8418	7260	70-74
75-79	218633	75100	2.1	143533	3.6		17248	7804	9444	75-79
80-84	115251	34712	1.0	80539	2.0	48165 M	14825	5474	9351	80-84
85+	60367	16925	0.5	43442	1.1	45592 F	13931	4295	9636	85+
TOTAL	7519891	3543170		3976721		93757	96041	46821	49220	TOTAL

TABLE 2 — MALE LIFE TABLE

x	nM_x	nq_x	l_x	nd_x	nL_x	nm_x	na_x	T_x	$\overset{\circ}{e}_x$	x
0	0.023232	0.022761	100000	2276	97973	0.023232	0.109	6762842	67.628	0
1	0.000909	0.003628	97724	355	390009	0.000909	1.500	6664869	68.201	1
5	0.000488	0.002436	97369	237	486254	0.000488	2.500	6274860	64.444	5
10	0.000469	0.002341	97132	227	485209	0.000469	3.016	5788606	59.595	10
15	0.001652	0.008257	96905	800	482663	0.001658	2.675	5303397	54.728	15
20	0.001883	0.009371	96105	901	478254	0.001883	2.481	4820734	50.161	20
25	0.001517	0.007555	95204	719	474240	0.001517	2.525	4342479	45.612	25
30	0.002100	0.010449	94485	987	470057	0.002100	2.603	3868239	40.940	30
35	0.002589	0.012908	93497	1207	464685	0.002597	2.678	3398182	36.345	35
40	0.004413	0.021873	92291	2019	456752	0.004420	2.672	2933498	31.785	40
45	0.006457	0.031804	90272	2871	444622	0.006457	2.653	2476745	27.437	45
50	0.009609	0.047302	87401	4134	427323	0.009675	2.658	2032123	23.251	50
55	0.014933	0.072240	83267	6015	402266	0.014953	2.661	1604799	19.273	55
60	0.024056	0.113855	77251	8795	365625	0.024056	2.654	1202534	15.567	60
65	0.040104	0.183018	68456	12529	312404	0.040104	2.615	836909	12.226	65
70	0.065207	0.281351	55927	15735	241148	0.065251	2.554	524505	9.378	70
75	0.103915	0.413271	40192	16610	158893	0.104537	2.467	283357	7.050	75
80	0.157698	0.557069	23582	13137	83303	0.157698	2.366	124463	5.278	80
85	0.253767	1.000000	10445	10445	41160	0.197805	3.941	41160	3.941	85

TABLE 3 — FEMALE LIFE TABLE

x	nM_x	nq_x	l_x	nd_x	nL_x	nm_x	na_x	T_x	$\overset{\circ}{e}_x$	x
0	0.017389	0.017121	100000	1712	98458	0.017389	0.100	7473580	74.736	0
1	0.000762	0.003042	98288	299	392404	0.000762	1.500	7375121	75.036	1
5	0.000316	0.001580	97989	155	489558	0.000316	2.500	6982717	71.260	5
10	0.000267	0.001336	97834	131	488865	0.000267	2.666	6493160	66.369	10
15	0.000530	0.002654	97703	259	487897	0.000531	2.610	6004294	61.454	15
20	0.000549	0.002743	97444	267	486564	0.000549	2.544	5516397	56.611	20
25	0.000652	0.003254	97177	316	485125	0.000652	2.600	5029833	51.760	25
30	0.000867	0.004326	96861	419	483316	0.000867	2.644	4544707	46.920	30
35	0.001256	0.006286	96442	606	480803	0.001261	2.682	4061391	42.112	35
40	0.001988	0.009898	95835	949	476978	0.001989	2.682	3580587	37.362	40
45	0.003044	0.015115	94887	1434	471102	0.003044	2.677	3103609	32.709	45
50	0.004667	0.023175	93453	2166	462240	0.004685	2.681	2632507	28.169	50
55	0.007371	0.036305	91287	3314	448768	0.007385	2.687	2170267	23.774	55
60	0.012004	0.058400	87973	5138	427992	0.012004	2.689	1721499	19.569	60
65	0.020173	0.096375	82835	7983	395737	0.020173	2.690	1293507	15.615	65
70	0.035965	0.166114	74852	12434	345223	0.036017	2.665	897770	11.994	70
75	0.065797	0.285453	62418	17817	269135	0.066203	2.589	552547	8.852	75
80	0.116105	0.449781	44600	20060	172778	0.116105	2.496	283412	6.354	80
85	0.221813	1.000000	24540	24540	110634	0.157868	4.508	110634	4.508	85

TABLE 4 — OBSERVED VITAL RATES AND RATIOS

CRUDE RATES

Per Thousand	BOTH SEXES	MALES	FEMALES
BIRTH RATE	12.47	13.59	11.46
DEATH RATE	12.77	13.21	12.38
RATE OF INCREASE	-0.30	0.38	-0.91

RATES STANDARDIZED ON USA 1980

Per Thousand	BOTH SEXES	MALES	FEMALES
BIRTH RATE	15.85		14.99
DEATH RATE	11.33	12.01	10.68
RATE OF INCREASE	4.53		4.31

VITAL STATISTICS

GFR x 1000	54.519
TFR	1.841
GRR	0.895
NRR	0.869
μ	26.237
σ^2	37.207
GENERATION	26.336
POP. SEX RATIO	1.122
SEX RATIO AT BIRTH	1.056
DEP. RATIO x 100	61.994

PERCENT OF POPULATION IN AGE GROUP

	BOTH SEXES	MALES	FEMALES
UNDER 15	23.30	25.30	21.52
15 - 64	61.73	62.90	60.69
65 AND OLDER	14.97	11.80	17.79

RATES STANDARDIZED ON MEXICO 1980

Per Thousand	BOTH SEXES	MALES	FEMALES
BIRTH RATE	14.60		14.31
DEATH RATE	4.56	5.49	3.61
RATE OF INCREASE	10.04		10.70

AGE AT LAST BIRTHDAY	ESTIMATED MID-YEAR POPULATION					BIRTHS BY AGE OF MOTHER AND SEX	DEATHS			AGE AT LAST BIRTHDAY	
	BOTH SEXES	MALES		FEMALES			BOTH SEXES	MALES	FEMALES		
		Number	Percent	Number	Percent						
0	88615	45580	1.3	43035	1.1		1303	765	538	0	
1-4	344646	176833	5.0	167813	4.2		232	120	112	1-4	
5-9	498431	255061	7.2	243370	6.2		168	105	63	5-9	
10-14	608145	311098	8.8	297047	7.5	35	176	119	57	10-14	
15-19	646852	329799	9.3	317053	8.0	11173	665	505	160	15-19	
20-24	578371	294630	8.3	283741	7.2	34615	674	535	139	20-24	
25-29	508362	256732	7.2	251630	6.4	25908	558	417	141	25-29	
30-34	509078	258065	7.3	251013	6.3	12896	622	426	196	30-34	
35-39	522649	262941	7.4	259708	6.6	4941	940	642	298	35-39	TABLE 1
40-44	460599	231301	6.5	229296	5.8	1227	1238	840	398	40-44	
45-49	408159	202944	5.7	205215	5.2	75	1965	1370	595	45-49	DATA
50-54	438204	208353	5.9	229851	5.8	2	3028	2029	999	50-54	
55-59	450971	183994	5.2	266977	6.8		4574	2750	1824	55-59	
60-64	280847	112610	3.2	168237	4.3		4223	2443	1780	60-64	
65-69	374716	148379	4.2	226337	5.7		9335	5354	3981	65-69	
70-74	336686	126859	3.6	209827	5.3		14132	7392	6740	70-74	
75-79	246683	86887	2.4	159796	4.0		17809	8228	9581	75-79	
80-84	133918	40509	1.1	93409	2.4	46874 M	16136	5948	10188	80-84	
85+	69219	18443	0.5	50776	1.3	43998 F	14664	4151	10513	85+	
TOTAL	7505151	3551020		3954131		90872	92442	44139	48303	TOTAL	

x	$_nM_x$	$_nq_x$	l_x	$_nd_x$	$_nL_x$	$_nm_x$	$_na_x$	T_x	$\overset{\circ}{e}_x$	x	
0	0.016784	0.016534	100000	1653	98510	0.016784	0.099	6898005	68.980	0	
1	0.000679	0.002710	98347	267	392720	0.000679	1.500	6799495	69.138	1	
5	0.000412	0.002056	98080	202	489897	0.000412	2.500	6406775	65.322	5	
10	0.000383	0.001911	97878	187	489038	0.000383	3.105	5916878	60.451	10	
15	0.001531	0.007629	97691	745	486737	0.001531	2.693	5427840	55.561	15	
20	0.001816	0.009042	96946	877	482546	0.001817	2.507	4941103	50.968	20	
25	0.001624	0.008084	96070	777	478386	0.001624	2.475	4458557	46.410	25	TABLE 2
30	0.001651	0.008221	95293	783	474583	0.001651	2.599	3980171	41.768	30	
35	0.002442	0.012145	94509	1148	469866	0.002443	2.665	3505588	37.092	35	MALE
40	0.003632	0.018103	93362	1690	462979	0.003651	2.735	3035721	32.516	40	LIFE
45	0.006751	0.033291	91671	3052	451255	0.006763	2.673	2572742	28.065	45	TABLE
50	0.009738	0.047603	88620	4219	433193	0.009738	2.652	2121487	23.939	50	
55	0.014946	0.072637	84401	6131	407485	0.015045	2.631	1688294	20.003	55	
60	0.021694	0.103337	78270	8088	372284	0.021726	2.642	1280809	16.364	60	
65	0.036083	0.166161	70182	11662	323184	0.036083	2.622	908525	12.945	65	
70	0.058269	0.255220	58521	14936	256320	0.058269	2.571	585341	10.002	70	
75	0.094698	0.383833	43585	16729	175959	0.095075	2.491	329021	7.549	75	
80	0.146832	0.530676	26856	14252	97061	0.146832	2.389	153061	5.699	80	
85	0.225072	1.000000	12604	12604	56000	0.162621	4.443	56000	4.443	85	

x	$_nM_x$	$_nq_x$	l_x	$_nd_x$	$_nL_x$	$_nm_x$	$_na_x$	T_x	$\overset{\circ}{e}_x$	x	
0	0.012501	0.012361	100000	1236	98877	0.012501	0.091	7609938	76.099	0	
1	0.000667	0.002665	98764	263	394398	0.000667	1.500	7511061	76.051	1	
5	0.000259	0.001293	98501	127	492185	0.000259	2.500	7116664	72.250	5	
10	0.000192	0.000959	98373	94	491656	0.000192	2.765	6624479	67.340	10	
15	0.000505	0.002520	98279	248	490806	0.000505	2.622	6132823	62.402	15	
20	0.000490	0.002447	98031	240	489562	0.000490	2.523	5642018	57.553	20	
25	0.000560	0.002803	97791	274	488301	0.000561	2.606	5152456	52.688	25	TABLE 3
30	0.000781	0.003897	97517	380	486695	0.000781	2.654	4664155	47.829	30	
35	0.001147	0.005724	97137	556	484392	0.001148	2.672	4177460	43.006	35	FEMALE
40	0.001736	0.008681	96581	838	480982	0.001743	2.705	3693068	38.238	40	LIFE
45	0.002899	0.014406	95743	1379	475514	0.002901	2.680	3212087	33.549	45	TABLE
50	0.004346	0.021514	94364	2030	467104	0.004346	2.678	2736573	29.000	50	
55	0.006832	0.033756	92333	3117	454414	0.006859	2.673	2269469	24.579	55	
60	0.010580	0.051742	89217	4616	435383	0.010603	2.682	1815055	20.344	60	
65	0.017589	0.084529	84600	7151	406574	0.017589	2.703	1379672	16.308	65	
70	0.032122	0.149485	77449	11577	360425	0.032122	2.683	973098	12.564	70	
75	0.059958	0.263249	65872	17341	287933	0.060225	2.611	612673	9.301	75	
80	0.109069	0.429057	48531	20823	190913	0.109069	2.515	324740	6.691	80	
85	0.207047	1.000000	27708	27708	133827	0.140829	4.830	133827	4.830	85	

CRUDE RATES

Per Thousand	BOTH SEXES	MALES	FEMALES
BIRTH RATE	12.11	13.20	11.13
DEATH RATE	12.32	12.43	12.22
RATE OF INCREASE	-0.21	0.77	-1.09

PERCENT OF POPULATION IN AGE GROUP

UNDER 15	20.52	22.21	19.00
15 - 64	64.01	65.94	62.28
65 AND OLDER	15.47	11.86	18.72

RATES STANDARDIZED ON USA 1980

Per Thousand	BOTH SEXES	MALES	FEMALES
BIRTH RATE	14.59		13.73
DEATH RATE	10.32	10.95	9.73
RATE OF INCREASE	4.26		4.00

RATES STANDARDIZED ON MEXICO 1980

	BOTH SEXES	MALES	FEMALES
BIRTH RATE	13.30		12.98
DEATH RATE	4.06	4.92	3.19
RATE OF INCREASE	9.24		9.79

VITAL STATISTICS

GFR x 1000	50.550	TABLE 4
TFR	1.682	
GRR	0.814	OBSERVED
NRR	0.796	VITAL
μ	26.203	RATES
σ^2	31.384	AND
GENERATION	26.340	RATIOS
POP. SEX RATIO	1.114	
SEX RATIO AT BIRTH	1.065	
DEP. RATIO x 100	56.224	

AGE AT LAST BIRTHDAY	ESTIMATED MID-YEAR POPULATION BOTH SEXES	MALES Number	Percent	FEMALES Number	Percent	BIRTHS BY AGE OF MOTHER AND SEX	DEATHS BOTH SEXES	MALES	FEMALES	AGE AT LAST BIRTHDAY
0	96988	49427	1.4	47561	1.2		977	591	386	0
1-4	355687	181341	5.1	174346	4.4		195	113	82	1-4
5-9	427026	218507	6.1	208519	5.2		81	46	35	5-9
10-14	498419	254542	7.1	243877	6.1		128	83	45	10-14
15-19	619233	316536	8.8	302697	7.6	7507	500	387	113	15-19
20-24	658900	332423	9.3	326477	8.2	32632	695	550	145	20-24
25-29	588151	293771	8.2	294380	7.4	28771	544	411	133	25-29
30-34	503952	251627	7.0	252325	6.3	12984	553	389	164	30-34
35-39	502811	253689	7.1	249122	6.3	4559	819	552	267	35-39
40-44	518740	259794	7.3	258946	6.5	927	1428	965	463	40-44
45-49	456250	228529	6.4	227721	5.7	60	1760	1192	568	45-49
50-54	400378	197908	5.5	202470	5.1		2592	1797	795	50-54
55-59	423066	198345	5.5	224721	5.7		4109	2751	1358	55-59
60-64	427295	169025	4.7	258270	6.5		6071	3532	2539	60-64
65-69	257330	98880	2.8	158450	4.0		5530	3104	2426	65-69
70-74	321964	119475	3.3	202489	5.1		11921	6130	5791	70-74
75-79	260350	89423	2.5	170927	4.3		16910	7698	9212	75-79
80-84	157659	48982	1.4	108677	2.7	45054 M	17515	6698	10817	80-84
85+	83468	21098	0.6	62370	1.6	42386 F	17250	4884	12366	85+
TOTAL	7557667	3583322		3974345		87440	89578	41873	47705	TOTAL

TABLE 1 DATA

x	$_nM_x$	$_nq_x$	l_x	$_nd_x$	$_nL_x$	$_nm_x$	$_na_x$	T_x	$\overset{\circ}{e}_x$	x
0	0.011957	0.011828	100000	1183	98924	0.011957	0.090	7050021	70.500	0
1	0.000623	0.002489	98817	246	394654	0.000623	1.500	6951097	70.343	1
5	0.000211	0.001052	98571	104	492597	0.000211	2.500	6556443	66.515	5
10	0.000326	0.001629	98468	160	492040	0.000326	3.143	6063846	61.582	10
15	0.001223	0.006096	98307	599	490172	0.001223	2.724	5571806	56.678	15
20	0.001655	0.008239	97708	805	486542	0.001655	2.520	5081635	52.008	20
25	0.001399	0.006966	96903	675	482813	0.001398	2.481	4595092	47.420	25
30	0.001546	0.007714	96228	742	479358	0.001549	2.601	4112279	42.735	30
35	0.002176	0.010825	95485	1034	475051	0.002176	2.701	3632921	38.047	35
40	0.003714	0.018417	94452	1740	468194	0.003715	2.663	3157870	33.434	40
45	0.005216	0.025866	92712	2398	458042	0.005236	2.698	2689676	29.011	45
50	0.009080	0.044544	90314	4023	442221	0.009097	2.676	2231635	24.710	50
55	0.013870	0.067156	86291	5795	417810	0.013870	2.645	1789414	20.737	55
60	0.020896	0.100178	80496	8064	383322	0.021037	2.624	1371604	17.039	60
65	0.031392	0.146316	72432	10598	336928	0.031455	2.619	988282	13.644	65
70	0.051308	0.228343	61834	14119	275191	0.051308	2.593	651354	10.534	70
75	0.086085	0.354706	47715	16925	196564	0.086103	2.518	376164	7.884	75
80	0.136744	0.505568	30790	15566	113837	0.136744	2.423	179600	5.833	80
85	0.231491	1.000000	15224	15224	65763	0.169945	4.320	65763	4.320	85

TABLE 2 MALE LIFE TABLE

x	$_nM_x$	$_nq_x$	l_x	$_nd_x$	$_nL_x$	$_nm_x$	$_na_x$	T_x	$\overset{\circ}{e}_x$	x
0	0.008116	0.008056	100000	806	99262	0.008116	0.084	7750768	77.508	0
1	0.000470	0.001879	99194	186	396312	0.000470	1.500	7651506	77.136	1
5	0.000168	0.000839	99008	83	494832	0.000168	2.500	7255195	73.279	5
10	0.000185	0.000922	98925	91	494418	0.000185	2.731	6760362	68.338	10
15	0.000373	0.001865	98834	184	493734	0.000373	2.644	6265944	63.399	15
20	0.000444	0.002218	98649	219	492708	0.000444	2.536	5772210	58.512	20
25	0.000452	0.002260	98431	222	491618	0.000453	2.595	5279502	53.637	25
30	0.000650	0.003258	98208	320	490303	0.000652	2.696	4787884	48.752	30
35	0.001072	0.005347	97888	523	488246	0.001072	2.718	4297580	43.903	35
40	0.001788	0.008905	97365	867	484798	0.001788	2.663	3809334	39.124	40
45	0.002494	0.012444	96498	1201	479693	0.002503	2.671	3324536	34.452	45
50	0.003927	0.019465	95297	1855	472177	0.003928	2.678	2844843	29.852	50
55	0.006043	0.029799	93442	2784	460774	0.006043	2.688	2372666	25.392	55
60	0.009831	0.048247	90658	4374	443106	0.009871	2.672	1911892	21.089	60
65	0.015311	0.074164	86284	6399	416742	0.015355	2.707	1468786	17.023	65
70	0.028599	0.134160	79884	10717	374743	0.028599	2.697	1052045	13.170	70
75	0.053894	0.239215	69167	16546	306622	0.053962	2.630	677302	9.792	75
80	0.099533	0.399869	52621	21042	211402	0.099534	2.543	370680	7.044	80
85	0.198268	1.000000	31580	31580	159277	0.130994	5.044	159277	5.044	85

TABLE 3 FEMALE LIFE TABLE

CRUDE RATES

Per Thousand	BOTH SEXES	MALES	FEMALES
BIRTH RATE	11.57	12.57	10.66
DEATH RATE	11.85	11.69	12.00
RATE OF INCREASE	-0.28	0.89	-1.34

PERCENT OF POPULATION IN AGE GROUP

UNDER 15	18.23	19.64	16.97
15 - 64	67.46	69.81	65.35
65 AND OLDER	14.30	10.54	17.69

RATES STANDARDIZED ON USA 1980

Per Thousand	BOTH SEXES	MALES	FEMALES
BIRTH RATE	12.77		12.04
DEATH RATE	9.42	10.02	8.85
RATE OF INCREASE	3.35		3.18

RATES STANDARDIZED ON MEXICO 1980

	BOTH SEXES	MALES	FEMALES
BIRTH RATE	11.48		11.21
DEATH RATE	3.57	4.36	2.77
RATE OF INCREASE	7.90		8.44

VITAL STATISTICS

GFR x 1000	45.740
TFR	1.480
GRR	0.718
NRR	0.706
μ	26.644
σ^2	29.638
GENERATION	26.836
POP. SEX RATIO	1.109
SEX RATIO AT BIRTH	1.063
DEP. RATIO x 100	48.225

TABLE 4 OBSERVED VITAL RATES AND RATIOS

PROJECTED POPULATION

AGE GROUP	1990 BOTH SEXES	1990 MALES	1990 FEMALES	1995 BOTH SEXES	1995 MALES	1995 FEMALES
0-4	436	224	212	422	217	205
5-9	452	230	222	435	224	211
10-14	426	218	208	451	230	221
15-19	498	254	244	425	217	208
20-24	616	314	302	495	252	243
25-29	656	330	326	613	312	301
30-34	586	292	294	653	328	325
35-39	500	249	251	581	289	292
40-44	497	250	247	495	246	249
45-49	510	254	256	490	245	245
50-54	445	221	224	497	245	252
55-59	385	187	198	427	208	219
60-64	398	182	216	362	172	190
65-69	392	149	243	363	160	203
70-74	223	81	142	339	121	218
75-79	251	85	166	175	58	117
80-84	170	52	118	163	49	114
85+	110	28	82	119	30	89
TOTAL	7551	3600	3951	7505	3603	3902

STABLE EQUIVALENT TO ORIGINAL POPULATION

MALES Number	MALES Percent	FEMALES Number	FEMALES Percent	AGE GROUP	
235	4.3	222	3.7	0-4	
251	4.5	237	4.0	5-9	TABLE 5
267	4.8	252	4.2	10-14	
284	5.1	269	4.5	15-19	POPULATION
301	5.4	286	4.8	20-24	PROJECTED
318	5.8	305	5.1	25-29	WITH
337	6.1	325	5.5	30-34	FIXED
357	6.5	345	5.8	35-39	AGE-
375	6.8	365	6.1	40-44	SPECIFIC
391	7.1	386	6.5	45-49	BIRTH
403	7.3	405	6.8	50-54	AND
407	7.4	422	7.1	55-59	DEATH
398	7.2	433	7.3	60-64	RATES
373	6.8	434	7.3	65-69	(female
325	5.9	417	7.0	70-74	dominant,
248	4.5	364	6.1	75-79	in 000s)
153	2.8	268	4.5	80-84	
94	1.7	215	3.6	85+	
5517		5950		TOTAL	

VITAL RATES OF PROJECTED POPULATION

Per Thousand	1990 BOTH SEXES	1990 MALES	1990 FEMALES	1995 BOTH SEXES	1995 MALES	1995 FEMALES
BIRTH RATE	11.75	12.70	10.89	10.92	11.72	10.17
DEATH RATE	12.56	12.09	12.99	12.66	12.17	13.12
RATE OF INCREASE	-0.81	0.61	-2.10	-1.75	-0.45	-2.94

VITAL RATES OF STABLE POPULATION

Per Thousand	MALES	FEMALES	
BIRTH RATE	8.36	7.29	TABLE 6
DEATH RATE	21.21	20.27	PROJECTED
RATE OF INCREASE		-12.97	VITAL RATES

AGE STRUCTURE OF PROJECTED POPULATION

	BOTH SEXES	MALES	FEMALES	BOTH SEXES	MALES	FEMALES
% UNDER 15	17.41	18.68	16.24	17.43	18.62	16.33
% 15-64	67.42	70.35	64.75	67.12	69.77	64.68
% 65 AND OLDER	15.17	10.97	19.01	15.45	11.61	18.99
DEPEND. RATIO x 100	48.32	42.15	54.44	48.98	43.33	54.61

STABLE AGE STRUCTURE

	MALES	FEMALES	
% UNDER 15	13.65	11.96	AND RATIOS
% 15-64	64.72	59.51	(female
% 65 AND OLDER	21.64	28.53	dominant)
DEPEND. RATIO x 100	54.52	68.05	

AGE GROUP	FEMALE BIRTH RATES	NET MATERNITY FUNCTION	COEFF. OF MATRIX EQUATION	ORIGINAL MATRIX SUB-DIAGONAL	ORIGINAL MATRIX FIRST ROW	STABLE MATRIX FISHER VALUES	STABLE MATRIX REPRODUCTIVE VALUES	MATRIX PARAMETERS		
0-4	0.0000	0.0000	0.0000	0.99850	0.00000	0.977	216729	λ_1	0.93720	
5-9	0.0000	0.0000	0.0000	0.99916	0.00000	0.917	191149	λ_2	0.33133+0.70313i	TABLE 7
10-14	0.0000	0.0000	0.0297	0.99862	0.02975	0.860	209698	λ_4	-0.31872+0.33581i	
15-19	0.0120	0.0594	0.1490	0.99792	0.14959	0.778	235460	λ_6	-0.09462+0.40051i	LESLIE
20-24	0.0485	0.2387	0.2358	0.99779	0.23719	0.584	190706	r_1	-0.01297	MATRIX
25-29	0.0474	0.2329	0.1776	0.99733	0.17903	0.316	93170	r_2	-0.05039+0.22609i	AND ITS
30-34	0.0249	0.1223	0.0828	0.99580	0.08370	0.122	30807	r_4	-0.15401+0.46602i	ANALYSIS
35-39	0.0089	0.0433	0.0259	0.99294	0.02625	0.033	8176	r_6	-0.17757+0.36056i	(females)
40-44	0.0017	0.0084	0.0045	0.98947	0.00461	0.005	1335	c_1	59497	
45-49	0.0001	0.0006	0.0003	0.98433	0.00032	0.000	75	$2\pi/y$	27.7909	
50-54	0.0000	0.0000	0.0000	0.00000	0.00000	0.000	0	Δ	15.5263	

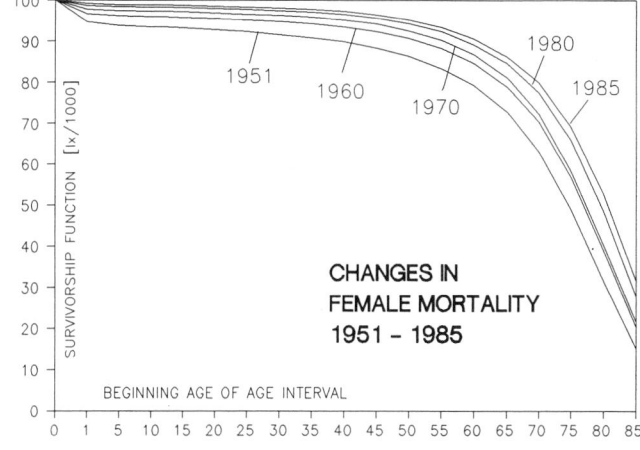

CHANGES IN FEMALE MORTALITY 1951 - 1985

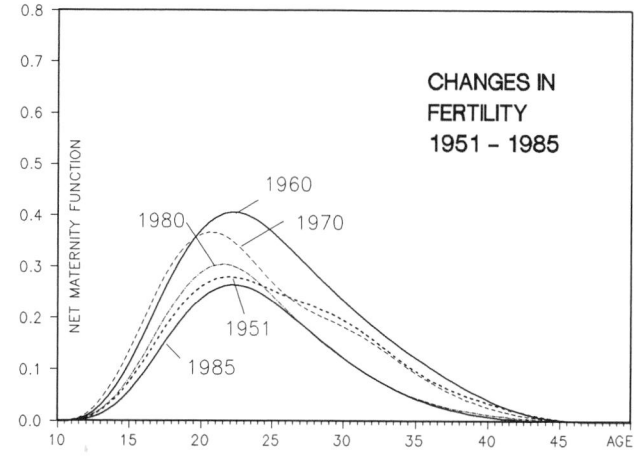

CHANGES IN FERTILITY 1951 - 1985

TABLE 1 — DATA

AGE AT LAST BIRTHDAY	ESTIMATED MID-YEAR POPULATION BOTH SEXES	MALES Number	MALES Percent	FEMALES Number	FEMALES Percent	BIRTHS BY AGE OF MOTHER AND SEX	DEATHS BOTH SEXES	DEATHS MALES	DEATHS FEMALES	AGE AT LAST BIRTHDAY
0	136642	69991	1.5	66651	1.4		2999	1762	1237	0
1-4	583874	298925	6.3	284949	5.8		505	289	216	1-4
5-9	788198	403301	8.5	384897	7.8		352	222	130	5-9
10-14	768332	392360	8.3	375972	7.6	31	304	191	113	10-14
15-19	724717	369600	7.8	355117	7.2	11066	554	405	149	15-19
20-24	716550	365922	7.7	350628	7.1	52869	692	514	178	20-24
25-29	571824	291881	6.2	279943	5.7	40431	575	393	182	25-29
30-34	596019	301118	6.4	294901	6.0	22894	731	455	276	30-34
35-39	637119	320010	6.8	317109	6.4	11423	1146	722	424	35-39
40-44	649823	324248	6.9	325575	6.6	3234	1793	1106	687	40-44
45-49	652177	322860	6.8	329287	6.7	209	2940	1826	1114	45-49
50-54	444211	217661	4.6	226550	4.6	11	3113	2032	1081	50-54
55-59	551401	265036	5.6	286365	5.8		6783	4476	2307	55-59
60-64	537772	249969	5.3	287803	5.8		10685	6920	3765	60-64
65-69	481342	213239	4.5	268103	5.4		15424	9410	6014	65-69
70-74	367026	151200	3.2	215826	4.4		18302	9943	8359	70-74
75-79	238387	91184	1.9	147203	3.0		19013	8934	10079	75-79
80-84	131937	48823	1.0	83114	1.7	73171 M	16758	7085	9673	80-84
85+	71954	25125	0.5	46829	1.0	68997 F	15991	6193	9798	85+
TOTAL	9649305	4722483		4926822		142168	118660	62878	55782	TOTAL

TABLE 2 — MALE LIFE TABLE

x	nM_x	nq_x	l_x	nd_x	nL_x	nm_x	na_x	T_x	$\overset{\circ}{e}_x$	x
0	0.025175	0.024625	100000	2462	97815	0.025175	0.113	6781704	67.817	0
1	0.000967	0.003858	97538	376	389209	0.000967	1.500	6683888	68.526	1
5	0.000550	0.002748	97161	267	485139	0.000550	2.500	6294679	64.786	5
10	0.000487	0.002435	96894	236	483936	0.000488	2.731	5809540	59.958	10
15	0.001096	0.005467	96658	528	482061	0.001096	2.672	5325605	55.097	15
20	0.001405	0.007004	96130	673	478989	0.001406	2.535	4843544	50.385	20
25	0.001346	0.006711	95456	641	475689	0.001347	2.513	4364555	45.723	25
30	0.001511	0.007528	94816	714	472381	0.001511	2.621	3888865	41.015	30
35	0.002256	0.011222	94102	1056	468050	0.002256	2.670	3416484	36.306	35
40	0.003411	0.016922	93046	1575	461609	0.003411	2.700	2948435	31.688	40
45	0.005655	0.028083	91472	2569	451457	0.005690	2.703	2486826	27.187	45
50	0.009336	0.045880	88903	4079	435218	0.009372	2.721	2035368	22.894	50
55	0.016888	0.081261	84824	6893	408147	0.016888	2.683	1600151	18.864	55
60	0.027683	0.129916	77931	10125	365725	0.027683	2.636	1192004	15.296	60
65	0.044129	0.199418	67807	13522	306323	0.044142	2.581	826279	12.186	65
70	0.065761	0.283348	54285	15381	233340	0.065919	2.524	519956	9.578	70
75	0.097978	0.393225	38903	15298	155654	0.098280	2.460	286617	7.367	75
80	0.145116	0.526089	23605	12419	85577	0.145116	2.387	130962	5.548	80
85	0.246488	1.000000	11187	11187	45385	0.188562	4.057	45385	4.057	85

TABLE 3 — FEMALE LIFE TABLE

x	nM_x	nq_x	l_x	nd_x	nL_x	nm_x	na_x	T_x	$\overset{\circ}{e}_x$	x
0	0.018559	0.018255	100000	1826	98360	0.018559	0.102	7420495	74.205	0
1	0.000758	0.003026	98175	297	391955	0.000758	1.500	7322135	74.583	1
5	0.000338	0.001687	97877	165	488974	0.000338	2.500	6930180	70.805	5
10	0.000301	0.001502	97712	147	488202	0.000301	2.556	6441206	65.920	10
15	0.000420	0.002097	97565	205	487337	0.000420	2.602	5953004	61.015	15
20	0.000508	0.002540	97361	247	486210	0.000509	2.594	5465667	56.138	20
25	0.000650	0.003254	97114	316	484821	0.000652	2.635	4979457	51.275	25
30	0.000936	0.004669	96798	452	482926	0.000936	2.650	4494637	46.433	30
35	0.001337	0.006665	96346	642	480238	0.001337	2.679	4011711	41.639	35
40	0.002110	0.010500	95704	1005	476204	0.002110	2.698	3531473	36.900	40
45	0.003383	0.016862	94699	1597	469751	0.003399	2.656	3055268	32.263	45
50	0.004772	0.023668	93102	2204	460417	0.004786	2.689	2585517	27.771	50
55	0.008056	0.039546	90898	3595	446201	0.008056	2.694	2125101	23.379	55
60	0.013082	0.063493	87304	5543	423728	0.013082	2.693	1678900	19.231	60
65	0.022432	0.106656	81761	8720	388555	0.022443	2.678	1255171	15.352	65
70	0.038730	0.177938	73040	12997	334586	0.038844	2.644	866616	11.865	70
75	0.068470	0.295202	60044	17725	257165	0.068925	2.571	532031	8.861	75
80	0.116382	0.449972	42319	19042	163618	0.116382	2.481	274866	6.495	80
85	0.209229	1.000000	23276	23276	111248	0.143366	4.779	111248	4.779	85

TABLE 4 — OBSERVED VITAL RATES AND RATIOS

CRUDE RATES

Per Thousand	BOTH SEXES	MALES	FEMALES
BIRTH RATE	14.73	15.49	14.00
DEATH RATE	12.30	13.31	11.32
RATE OF INCREASE	2.44	2.18	2.68

PERCENT OF POPULATION IN AGE GROUP

	BOTH SEXES	MALES	FEMALES
UNDER 15	23.60	24.66	22.58
15 - 64	63.03	64.13	61.97
65 AND OLDER	13.38	11.21	15.45

RATES STANDARDIZED ON USA 1980

Per Thousand	BOTH SEXES	MALES	FEMALES
BIRTH RATE	19.24		18.16
DEATH RATE	11.39	11.91	10.91
RATE OF INCREASE	7.85		7.25

RATES STANDARDIZED ON MEXICO 1980

	BOTH SEXES	MALES	FEMALES
BIRTH RATE	17.16		16.79
DEATH RATE	4.58	5.39	3.75
RATE OF INCREASE	12.59		13.04

VITAL STATISTICS

GFR x 1000	63.114
TFR	2.254
GRR	1.094
NRR	1.060
μ	27.129
σ^2	32.944
GENERATION	27.094
POP. SEX RATIO	1.043
SEX RATIO AT BIRTH	1.060
DEP. RATIO x 100	58.664

PROJECTED POPULATION

AGE GROUP	1975 BOTH SEXES	1975 MALES	1975 FEMALES	1980 BOTH SEXES	1980 MALES	1980 FEMALES
0-4	717	368	349	760	390	370
5-9	718	367	351	714	366	348
10-14	786	402	384	717	367	350
15-19	766	391	375	785	401	384
20-24	721	367	354	762	388	374
25-29	713	363	350	718	365	353
30-34	569	290	279	709	361	348
35-39	591	298	293	564	287	277
40-44	630	316	314	585	294	291
45-49	638	317	321	619	309	310
50-54	634	311	323	621	306	315
55-59	424	204	220	605	292	313
60-64	509	237	272	391	183	208
65-69	473	209	264	448	199	249
70-74	393	162	231	386	159	227
75-79	267	101	166	285	108	177
80-84	144	50	94	161	55	106
85+	83	26	57	91	27	64
TOTAL	9776	4779	4997	9921	4857	5064

STABLE EQUIVALENT TO ORIGINAL POPULATION

MALES Number	MALES Percent	FEMALES Number	FEMALES Percent	AGE GROUP	
385	7.7	365	7.1	0-4	
379	7.6	360	7.0	5-9	TABLE 5
374	7.5	356	7.0	10-14	
369	7.4	352	6.9	15-19	POPULATION
363	7.3	347	6.8	20-24	PROJECTED
356	7.1	342	6.7	25-29	WITH
350	7.0	337	6.6	30-34	FIXED
343	6.9	332	6.5	35-39	AGE-
335	6.7	326	6.4	40-44	SPECIFIC
324	6.5	318	6.2	45-49	BIRTH
309	6.2	308	6.0	50-54	AND
287	5.7	295	5.8	55-59	DEATH
254	5.1	278	5.4	60-64	RATES
210	4.2	252	4.9	65-69	(female
159	3.2	214	4.2	70-74	dominant,
105	2.1	163	3.2	75-79	in 000s)
57	1.1	103	2.0	80-84	
30	0.6	69	1.3	85+	
4989		5117		TOTAL	

VITAL RATES OF PROJECTED POPULATION

Per Thousand	1975 BOTH SEXES	1975 MALES	1975 FEMALES	1980 BOTH SEXES	1980 MALES	1980 FEMALES
BIRTH RATE	15.46	16.28	14.69	16.09	16.91	15.29
DEATH RATE	12.75	13.44	12.10	12.99	13.44	12.55
RATE OF INCREASE	2.71	2.84	2.59	3.09	3.47	2.74

VITAL RATES OF STABLE POPULATION

Per Thousand	MALES	FEMALES	
BIRTH RATE	15.93	14.64	TABLE 6
DEATH RATE	13.75	12.49	PROJECTED
RATE OF INCREASE		2.15	VITAL RATES

AGE STRUCTURE OF PROJECTED POPULATION

	BOTH SEXES	MALES	FEMALES	BOTH SEXES	MALES	FEMALES
% UNDER 15	22.72	23.79	21.70	22.08	23.11	21.08
% 15-64	63.38	64.74	62.07	64.09	65.59	62.66
% 65 AND OLDER	13.90	11.48	16.23	13.83	11.30	16.25
DEPEND. RATIO x 100	57.79	54.47	61.10	56.02	52.46	59.59

STABLE AGE STRUCTURE

	MALES	FEMALES	
% UNDER 15	22.82	21.14	AND RATIOS
% 15-64	65.94	63.21	(female
% 65 AND OLDER	11.24	15.65	dominant)
DEPEND. RATIO x 100	51.66	58.21	

AGE GROUP	FEMALE BIRTH RATES	NET MATERNITY FUNCTION	COEFF. OF MATRIX EQUATION	ORIGINAL MATRIX SUB-DIAGONAL	ORIGINAL MATRIX FIRST ROW	STABLE MATRIX FISHER VALUES	STABLE MATRIX REPRODUCTIVE VALUES
0-4	0.0000	0.0000	0.0000	0.99726	0.00000	1.025	360475
5-9	0.0000	0.0000	0.0001	0.99842	0.00010	1.039	399969
10-14	0.0000	0.0002	0.0369	0.99823	0.03711	1.052	395502
15-19	0.0151	0.0737	0.2148	0.99769	0.21606	1.027	364736
20-24	0.0732	0.3558	0.3478	0.99714	0.35075	0.819	287010
25-29	0.0701	0.3398	0.2609	0.99609	0.26384	0.469	131333
30-34	0.0377	0.1820	0.1330	0.99443	0.13499	0.205	60309
35-39	0.0175	0.0840	0.0535	0.99160	0.05458	0.069	21786
40-44	0.0048	0.0230	0.0122	0.98645	0.01256	0.014	4428
45-49	0.0003	0.0014	0.0008	0.98013	0.00081	0.001	290
50-54	0.0000	0.0001	0.0001	0.96912	0.00006	0.000	13

MATRIX PARAMETERS

λ_1	1.01080	
λ_2	$0.34212+0.74702i$	TABLE 7
λ_4	$-0.38997+0.39856i$	
λ_6	$-0.00900+0.47439i$	LESLIE
r_1	0.00215	MATRIX
r_2	$-0.03929+0.22826i$	AND ITS
r_4	$-0.11682+0.46906i$	ANALYSIS
r_6	$-0.14911+0.31795i$	(females)
c_1	51172	
$2\pi/y$	27.5260	
Δ	4.0056	

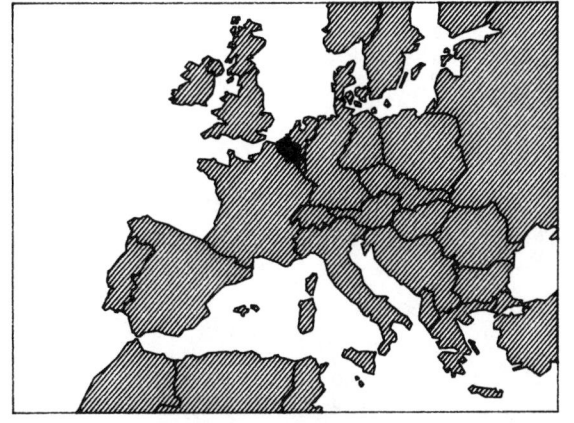

EDUCATION [1984]

% of primary school-age children enrolled:	98
secondary school-age children enrolled:	91
ca. 20-24 year olds in higher education:	31

LABOR FORCE

Average annual labor force growth (%) 1980-85:	0.7
% of the 1980 labor force in agriculture:	3
in industry:	36
in services:	61

TABLE 8

SOCIO-ECONOMIC INDICATORS

GNP & INCOME DISTRIBUTION

GNP per capita (in US Dollars) 1985:	8280
GNP average annual growth rate (%) 1965-85:	2.8
% share of total household income 1978-79	
Lowest 20% of households:	7.9
Highest 10% of households:	21.5

HEALTH & NUTRITION

Population per physician 1981:	370
Daily calorie supply per capita 1985:	3679

TABLE 1 — DATA

AGE AT LAST BIRTHDAY	ESTIMATED MID-YEAR POPULATION BOTH SEXES	MALES Number	MALES Percent	FEMALES Number	FEMALES Percent	BIRTHS BY AGE OF MOTHER AND SEX	DEATHS BOTH SEXES	DEATHS MALES	DEATHS FEMALES	AGE AT LAST BIRTHDAY
0	122078	62648	1.3	59430	1.2		1932	1120	812	0
1-4	533555	273786	5.7	259769	5.2		381	230	151	1-4
5-9	727012	371648	7.7	355364	7.1		244	163	81	5-9
10-14	794748	406060	8.5	388688	7.8	29	250	161	89	10-14
15-19	777918	397216	8.3	380702	7.6	10647	613	439	174	15-19
20-24	748507	384264	8.0	364243	7.3	43569	758	573	185	20-24
25-29	728427	374661	7.8	353766	7.1	42185	660	447	213	25-29
30-34	571690	291496	6.1	280194	5.6	15388	655	429	226	30-34
35-39	595285	300028	6.3	295257	5.9	6107	928	579	349	35-39
40-44	633578	316983	6.6	316595	6.3	1655	1616	996	620	40-44
45-49	637439	316274	6.6	321165	6.4	103	2661	1662	999	45-49
50-54	637682	313127	6.5	324555	6.5	10	4400	2824	1576	50-54
55-59	415517	200410	4.2	215107	4.3		4708	3077	1631	55-59
60-64	512541	239192	5.0	273349	5.5		9177	6024	3153	60-64
65-69	474356	209664	4.4	264692	5.3		14058	8765	5293	65-69
70-74	395802	163137	3.4	232665	4.7		19102	10793	8309	70-74
75-79	269000	101524	2.1	167476	3.3		20982	10100	10882	75-79
80-84	144951	50082	1.0	94869	1.9	61574 M	18452	7621	10831	80-84
85+	80614	26488	0.6	54126	1.1	58119 F	17848	6606	11242	85+
TOTAL	9800700	4798688		5002012		119693	119425	62609	56816	TOTAL

TABLE 2 — MALE LIFE TABLE

x	$_nM_x$	$_nq_x$	l_x	$_nd_x$	$_nL_x$	$_nm_x$	$_na_x$	T_x	$\overset{\circ}{e}_x$	x
0	0.017878	0.017595	100000	1759	98417	0.017878	0.100	6883944	68.839	0
1	0.000840	0.003353	98241	329	392139	0.000840	1.500	6785527	69.071	1
5	0.000439	0.002191	97911	214	489019	0.000439	2.500	6393389	65.298	5
10	0.000396	0.001981	97697	194	488067	0.000396	2.848	5904369	60.436	10
15	0.001105	0.005517	97503	538	486280	0.001106	2.704	5416303	55.550	15
20	0.001491	0.007428	96965	720	483032	0.001491	2.510	4930022	50.843	20
25	0.001193	0.005945	96245	572	479790	0.001193	2.494	4446990	46.205	25
30	0.001472	0.007351	95673	703	476676	0.001475	2.601	3967199	41.466	30
35	0.001930	0.009606	94969	912	472726	0.001930	2.674	3490523	36.754	35
40	0.003142	0.015598	94057	1467	466929	0.003142	2.712	3017797	32.085	40
45	0.005255	0.025964	92590	2404	457470	0.005255	2.720	2550869	27.550	45
50	0.009019	0.044478	90186	4011	441737	0.009081	2.708	2093399	23.212	50
55	0.015354	0.074401	86175	6412	415985	0.015413	2.678	1651662	19.166	55
60	0.025185	0.118895	79763	9483	376554	0.025185	2.652	1235677	15.492	60
65	0.041805	0.190000	70280	13353	319414	0.041805	2.605	859124	12.224	65
70	0.066159	0.284499	56927	16196	244741	0.066174	2.537	539710	9.481	70
75	0.099484	0.398180	40731	16218	162514	0.099796	2.463	294968	7.242	75
80	0.152170	0.544051	24513	13336	87640	0.152170	2.381	132454	5.403	80
85	0.249396	1.000000	11177	11177	44815	0.192288	4.010	44815	4.010	85

TABLE 3 — FEMALE LIFE TABLE

x	$_nM_x$	$_nq_x$	l_x	$_nd_x$	$_nL_x$	$_nm_x$	$_na_x$	T_x	$\overset{\circ}{e}_x$	x
0	0.013663	0.013496	100000	1350	98776	0.013663	0.093	7529579	75.296	0
1	0.000581	0.002322	98650	229	394029	0.000581	1.500	7430803	75.325	1
5	0.000228	0.001139	98421	112	491827	0.000228	2.500	7036774	71.496	5
10	0.000229	0.001144	98309	112	491288	0.000229	2.708	6544947	66.575	10
15	0.000457	0.002284	98197	224	490451	0.000457	2.626	6053659	61.648	15
20	0.000508	0.002537	97972	249	489255	0.000508	2.559	5563207	56.783	20
25	0.000602	0.003012	97724	294	487914	0.000603	2.603	5073952	51.921	25
30	0.000807	0.004038	97430	393	486222	0.000809	2.647	4586038	47.070	30
35	0.001182	0.005894	97036	572	483865	0.001182	2.699	4099815	42.250	35
40	0.001958	0.009748	96464	940	480159	0.001958	2.700	3615950	37.485	40
45	0.003111	0.015442	95524	1475	474209	0.003111	2.688	3135792	32.827	45
50	0.004856	0.024142	94049	2271	464975	0.004883	2.679	2661583	28.300	50
55	0.007582	0.037361	91778	3429	450880	0.007605	2.664	2196608	23.934	55
60	0.011535	0.056177	88349	4963	430285	0.011535	2.691	1745728	19.759	60
65	0.019997	0.095579	83386	7970	398563	0.019997	2.695	1315443	15.775	65
70	0.035712	0.164891	75416	12435	348035	0.035730	2.664	916880	12.158	70
75	0.064976	0.282226	62981	17775	272056	0.065335	2.589	568845	9.032	75
80	0.114168	0.443830	45206	20064	175739	0.114168	2.493	296789	6.565	80
85	0.207701	1.000000	25142	25142	121050	0.141622	4.815	121050	4.815	85

TABLE 4 — OBSERVED VITAL RATES AND RATIOS

CRUDE RATES

Per Thousand	BOTH SEXES	MALES	FEMALES
BIRTH RATE	12.21	12.83	11.62
DEATH RATE	12.19	13.05	11.36
RATE OF INCREASE	0.03	-0.22	0.26

PERCENT OF POPULATION IN AGE GROUP

	BOTH SEXES	MALES	FEMALES
UNDER 15	22.22	23.22	21.26
15 - 64	63.86	65.30	62.47
65 AND OLDER	13.92	11.48	16.27

RATES STANDARDIZED ON USA 1980

Per Thousand	BOTH SEXES	MALES	FEMALES
BIRTH RATE	15.03		14.19
DEATH RATE	10.92	11.54	10.33
RATE OF INCREASE	4.11		3.87

RATES STANDARDIZED ON MEXICO 1980

	BOTH SEXES	MALES	FEMALES
BIRTH RATE	13.52		13.23
DEATH RATE	4.22	5.02	3.40
RATE OF INCREASE	9.30		9.83

VITAL STATISTICS

GFR x 1000	51.772
TFR	1.740
GRR	0.845
NRR	0.825
μ	26.583
σ^2	29.457
GENERATION	26.690
POP. SEX RATIO	1.042
SEX RATIO AT BIRTH	1.059
DEP. RATIO x 100	56.596

TABLE 1 — DATA

AGE AT LAST BIRTHDAY	ESTIMATED MID-YEAR POPULATION BOTH SEXES	MALES Number	MALES Percent	FEMALES Number	FEMALES Percent	BIRTHS BY AGE OF MOTHER AND SEX	DEATHS BOTH SEXES	DEATHS MALES	DEATHS FEMALES	AGE AT LAST BIRTHDAY
0	122786	63049	1.3	59737	1.2		1510	871	639	0
1-4	481874	246424	5.1	235450	4.7		312	159	153	1-4
5-9	657458	336434	7.0	321024	6.4		206	128	78	5-9
10-14	726843	371222	7.7	355621	7.1	23	199	108	91	10-14
15-19	797224	406718	8.4	390506	7.8	7880	614	457	157	15-19
20-24	791303	404109	8.4	387194	7.7	44329	808	604	204	20-24
25-29	751782	385908	8.0	365874	7.3	47235	744	528	216	25-29
30-34	724159	371008	7.7	353151	7.0	19101	835	547	288	30-34
35-39	565231	287100	6.0	278131	5.5	4730	911	567	344	35-39
40-44	586413	293969	6.1	292444	5.8	991	1465	922	543	40-44
45-49	620500	308703	6.4	311797	6.2	109	2365	1518	847	45-49
50-54	617777	303739	6.3	314038	6.2		3997	2649	1348	50-54
55-59	609117	294305	6.1	314812	6.2		6188	4123	2065	55-59
60-64	386757	181150	3.8	205607	4.1		6326	4261	2065	60-64
65-69	458694	203644	4.2	255050	5.1		12176	7683	4493	65-69
70-74	396834	162407	3.4	234427	4.7		16828	9752	7076	70-74
75-79	296570	110826	2.3	185744	3.7		20562	10340	10222	75-79
80-84	169098	56787	1.2	112311	2.2	63778 M	18966	7867	11099	80-84
85+	93035	28225	0.6	64810	1.3	60620 F	18686	6409	12277	85+
TOTAL	9853455	4815727		5037728		124398	113698	59493	54205	TOTAL

TABLE 2 — MALE LIFE TABLE

x	nM_x	nq_x	l_x	nd_x	nL_x	nm_x	na_x	T_x	$\overset{\circ}{e}_x$	x
0	0.013815	0.013644	100000	1364	98763	0.013815	0.093	6988418	69.884	0
1	0.000645	0.002577	98636	254	393907	0.000645	1.500	6889655	69.850	1
5	0.000380	0.001901	98381	187	491440	0.000380	2.500	6495748	66.026	5
10	0.000291	0.001454	98194	143	490691	0.000291	3.029	6004308	61.147	10
15	0.001124	0.005604	98052	549	489007	0.001124	2.721	5513617	56.232	15
20	0.001495	0.007447	97502	726	485719	0.001495	2.532	5024610	51.533	20
25	0.001368	0.006818	96776	660	482228	0.001368	2.494	4538891	46.901	25
30	0.001474	0.007357	96116	707	478873	0.001477	2.583	4056663	42.206	30
35	0.001975	0.009871	95409	942	474851	0.001983	2.669	3577791	37.499	35
40	0.003136	0.015569	94467	1471	468935	0.003136	2.687	3102940	32.847	40
45	0.004917	0.024314	92997	2261	459832	0.004917	2.722	2634004	28.324	45
50	0.008721	0.042748	90736	3879	444745	0.008721	2.697	2174172	23.962	50
55	0.014009	0.068266	86857	5929	420539	0.014099	2.682	1729427	19.911	55
60	0.023522	0.111875	80927	9054	383358	0.023617	2.650	1308888	16.174	60
65	0.037728	0.173030	71874	12436	329633	0.037728	2.609	925530	12.877	65
70	0.060047	0.261808	59437	15561	259151	0.060047	2.556	595897	10.026	70
75	0.093299	0.378312	43876	16599	177535	0.093496	2.479	336746	7.675	75
80	0.138535	0.509087	27277	13887	100238	0.138535	2.397	159211	5.837	80
85	0.227068	1.000000	13391	13391	58973	0.164914	4.404	58973	4.404	85

TABLE 3 — FEMALE LIFE TABLE

x	nM_x	nq_x	l_x	nd_x	nL_x	nm_x	na_x	T_x	$\overset{\circ}{e}_x$	x
0	0.010697	0.010594	100000	1059	99034	0.010697	0.088	7674291	76.743	0
1	0.000650	0.002595	98941	257	395121	0.000650	1.500	7575257	76.564	1
5	0.000243	0.001214	98684	120	493120	0.000243	2.500	7180136	72.759	5
10	0.000256	0.001279	98564	126	492521	0.000256	2.629	6687016	67.844	10
15	0.000402	0.002008	98438	198	491724	0.000402	2.640	6194495	62.928	15
20	0.000527	0.002632	98240	259	490574	0.000527	2.573	5702771	58.049	20
25	0.000590	0.002949	97982	289	489216	0.000591	2.601	5212197	53.196	25
30	0.000816	0.004085	97693	399	487532	0.000819	2.664	4722981	48.345	30
35	0.001237	0.006192	97294	602	485066	0.001242	2.671	4235449	43.533	35
40	0.001857	0.009244	96691	894	481366	0.001857	2.661	3750383	38.787	40
45	0.002717	0.013497	95798	1293	475987	0.002717	2.680	3269017	34.124	45
50	0.004292	0.021251	94505	2008	467859	0.004292	2.678	2793029	29.554	50
55	0.006559	0.032487	92496	3005	455469	0.006598	2.666	2325170	25.138	55
60	0.010043	0.049272	89491	4409	437307	0.010083	2.698	1869701	20.893	60
65	0.017616	0.084637	85082	7201	408776	0.017616	2.690	1432394	16.835	65
70	0.030184	0.141017	77881	10983	363849	0.030184	2.673	1023618	13.143	70
75	0.055033	0.244066	66898	16328	295570	0.055241	2.616	659769	9.862	75
80	0.098824	0.397270	50571	20090	203293	0.098824	2.533	364199	7.202	80
85	0.189431	1.000000	30480	30480	160906	0.121330	5.279	160906	5.279	85

TABLE 4 — OBSERVED VITAL RATES AND RATIOS

CRUDE RATES

Per Thousand	BOTH SEXES	MALES	FEMALES
BIRTH RATE	12.62	13.24	12.03
DEATH RATE	11.54	12.35	10.76
RATE OF INCREASE	1.09	0.89	1.27

RATES STANDARDIZED ON USA 1980

Per Thousand	BOTH SEXES	MALES	FEMALES
BIRTH RATE	14.66		13.89
DEATH RATE	9.83	10.63	9.08
RATE OF INCREASE	4.83		4.82

VITAL STATISTICS

GFR x 1000	52.288
TFR	1.693
GRR	0.825
NRR	0.807
μ	26.665
σ^2	25.382
GENERATION	26.766
POP. SEX RATIO	1.046
SEX RATIO AT BIRTH	1.052
DEP. RATIO x 100	52.761

PERCENT OF POPULATION IN AGE GROUP

	BOTH SEXES	MALES	FEMALES
UNDER 15	20.19	21.12	19.29
15 - 64	65.46	67.21	63.79
65 AND OLDER	14.35	11.67	16.92

RATES STANDARDIZED ON MEXICO 1980

	BOTH SEXES	MALES	FEMALES
BIRTH RATE	13.06		12.83
DEATH RATE	3.80	4.59	2.99
RATE OF INCREASE	9.26		9.83

AGE AT LAST BIRTHDAY	ESTIMATED MID-YEAR POPULATION					BIRTHS BY AGE OF MOTHER AND SEX	DEATHS			AGE AT LAST BIRTHDAY
	BOTH SEXES	MALES		FEMALES			BOTH SEXES	MALES	FEMALES	
		Number	Percent	Number	Percent					
0	115134	58919	1.2	56215	1.1		1156	689	467	0
1-4	482986	247437	5.1	235549	4.7		248	153	95	1-4
5-9	600690	307081	6.4	293609	5.8		146	87	59	5-9
10-14	678194	347093	7.2	331101	6.6	18	166	94	72	10-14
15-19	738750	377646	7.8	361104	7.2	5115	445	308	137	15-19
20-24	798750	406964	8.5	391786	7.8	37645	704	541	163	20-24
25-29	779210	396926	8.2	382284	7.6	47646	675	484	191	25-29
30-34	727229	371833	7.7	355396	7.0	19196	835	580	255	30-34
35-39	691225	352662	7.3	338563	6.7	5135	1030	678	352	35-39
40-44	540770	273499	5.7	267271	5.3	822	1226	753	473	40-44
45-49	583869	290361	6.0	293508	5.8	74	2128	1350	778	45-49
50-54	618854	305123	6.3	313731	6.2		3464	2292	1172	50-54
55-59	590152	285717	5.9	304435	6.0		5618	3712	1906	55-59
60-64	574094	270078	5.6	304016	6.0		8494	5635	2859	60-64
65-69	320763	143679	3.0	177084	3.5		8182	5264	2918	65-69
70-74	406364	168605	3.5	237759	4.7		15602	9277	6325	70-74
75-79	305786	113055	2.3	192731	3.8		19612	10015	9597	75-79
80-84	191905	62882	1.3	129023	2.6	59328 M	20021	8348	11673	80-84
85+	112411	31684	0.7	80727	1.6	56323 F	20836	6766	14070	85+
TOTAL	9857136	4811244		5045892		115651	110588	57026	53562	TOTAL

TABLE 1 DATA

TABLE 2 — MALE LIFE TABLE

x	nM_x	nq_x	l_x	nd_x	nL_x	nm_x	na_x	T_x	$\mathring{e}_x$	x
0	0.011694	0.011571	100000	1157	98947	0.011694	0.090	7095316	70.953	0
1	0.000618	0.002470	98843	244	394761	0.000618	1.500	6996369	70.783	1
5	0.000283	0.001416	98599	140	492645	0.000283	2.500	6601607	66.954	5
10	0.000271	0.001353	98459	133	492017	0.000271	2.907	6108962	62.046	10
15	0.000816	0.004070	98326	400	490737	0.000816	2.768	5616945	57.126	15
20	0.001329	0.006625	97926	649	488047	0.001329	2.561	5126208	52.348	20
25	0.001219	0.006080	97277	591	484928	0.001220	2.536	4638161	47.680	25
30	0.001560	0.007774	96686	752	481617	0.001561	2.591	4153234	42.956	30
35	0.001923	0.009600	95934	921	477483	0.001929	2.625	3671616	38.272	35
40	0.002753	0.013742	95013	1306	472058	0.002766	2.697	3194133	33.618	40
45	0.004649	0.023001	93707	2155	463581	0.004649	2.701	2722075	29.049	45
50	0.007512	0.036923	91552	3380	450018	0.007512	2.710	2258495	24.669	50
55	0.012992	0.063062	88172	5560	427979	0.012992	2.684	1808477	20.511	55
60	0.020864	0.100292	82611	8285	393803	0.021039	2.676	1380498	16.711	60
65	0.036637	0.169073	74326	12567	341609	0.036786	2.611	986695	13.275	65
70	0.055022	0.242565	61759	14981	272266	0.055022	2.561	645086	10.445	70
75	0.088585	0.363110	46779	16986	191374	0.088757	2.497	372820	7.970	75
80	0.132757	0.493866	29793	14714	110832	0.132757	2.408	181446	6.090	80
85	0.213546	1.000000	15079	15079	70613	0.148916	4.683	70613	4.683	85

TABLE 3 — FEMALE LIFE TABLE

x	nM_x	nq_x	l_x	nd_x	nL_x	nm_x	na_x	T_x	$\mathring{e}_x$	x
0	0.008307	0.008245	100000	824	99245	0.008307	0.084	7796172	77.962	0
1	0.000403	0.001612	99176	160	396303	0.000403	1.500	7696927	77.609	1
5	0.000201	0.001004	99016	99	494830	0.000201	2.500	7300624	73.732	5
10	0.000217	0.001087	98916	107	494331	0.000217	2.670	6805794	68.804	10
15	0.000379	0.001895	98809	187	493596	0.000379	2.608	6311463	63.876	15
20	0.000416	0.002078	98622	205	492607	0.000416	2.559	5817867	58.992	20
25	0.000500	0.002497	98417	246	491499	0.000500	2.625	5325260	54.109	25
30	0.000718	0.003586	98171	352	490029	0.000718	2.656	4833761	49.238	30
35	0.001040	0.005214	97819	510	487925	0.001045	2.708	4343732	44.406	35
40	0.001770	0.008845	97309	861	484551	0.001776	2.684	3855807	39.624	40
45	0.002651	0.013171	96448	1270	479252	0.002651	2.648	3371256	34.954	45
50	0.003736	0.018519	95178	1763	471818	0.003736	2.691	2892003	30.385	50
55	0.006261	0.030855	93415	2882	460378	0.006261	2.676	2420185	25.908	55
60	0.009404	0.046382	90533	4199	442998	0.009479	2.698	1959808	21.647	60
65	0.016478	0.079629	86334	6875	415681	0.016538	2.674	1516809	17.569	65
70	0.026603	0.125283	79459	9955	374208	0.026603	2.681	1101128	13.858	70
75	0.049795	0.223162	69504	15511	310837	0.049900	2.635	726920	10.459	75
80	0.090472	0.370354	53994	19997	221026	0.090472	2.553	416084	7.706	80
85	0.174291	1.000000	33997	33997	195058	0.105358	5.738	195058	5.738	85

TABLE 4 — OBSERVED VITAL RATES AND RATIOS

CRUDE RATES

Per Thousand	BOTH SEXES	MALES	FEMALES
BIRTH RATE	11.73	12.33	11.16
DEATH RATE	11.22	11.85	10.61
RATE OF INCREASE	0.51	0.48	0.55

PERCENT OF POPULATION IN AGE GROUP

UNDER 15	19.04	19.96	18.16
15 - 64	67.39	69.23	65.64
65 AND OLDER	13.57	10.81	16.20

RATES STANDARDIZED ON USA 1980

Per Thousand	BOTH SEXES	MALES	FEMALES
BIRTH RATE	13.25		12.55
DEATH RATE	9.05	9.88	8.26
RATE OF INCREASE	4.20		4.29

RATES STANDARDIZED ON MEXICO 1980

	BOTH SEXES	MALES	FEMALES
BIRTH RATE	11.68		11.46
DEATH RATE	3.44	4.20	2.66
RATE OF INCREASE	8.24		8.80

VITAL STATISTICS

GFR x 1000	48.391
TFR	1.537
GRR	0.749
NRR	0.736
μ	26.998
σ^2	24.064
GENERATION	27.134
POP. SEX RATIO	1.049
SEX RATIO AT BIRTH	1.053
DEP. RATIO x 100	48.386

PROJECTED POPULATION

AGE GROUP	1989 BOTH SEXES	1989 MALES	1989 FEMALES	1994 BOTH SEXES	1994 MALES	1994 FEMALES
0-4	570	292	278	553	283	270
5-9	597	306	291	570	292	278
10-14	600	307	293	596	305	291
15-19	677	346	331	599	306	293
20-24	736	376	360	674	344	330
25-29	795	404	391	733	373	360
30-34	775	394	381	792	402	390
35-39	723	369	354	771	391	380
40-44	685	349	336	715	364	351
45-49	533	269	264	675	342	333
50-54	571	282	289	521	261	260
55-59	596	290	306	550	268	282
60-64	556	263	293	562	267	295
65-69	519	234	285	503	228	275
70-74	274	115	159	444	187	257
75-79	316	119	197	212	80	132
80-84	202	65	137	209	69	140
85+	154	40	114	163	42	121
TOTAL	9879	4820	5059	9842	4804	5038

STABLE EQUIVALENT TO ORIGINAL POPULATION

	MALES Number	MALES Percent	FEMALES Number	FEMALES Percent	AGE GROUP	
0-4	309	4.5	294	4.0	0-4	
5-9	326	4.8	311	4.2	5-9	TABLE 5
10-14	345	5.1	329	4.5	10-14	
15-19	364	5.3	347	4.7	15-19	POPULATION
20-24	383	5.6	367	5.0	20-24	PROJECTED
25-29	402	5.9	387	5.2	25-29	WITH
30-34	423	6.2	408	5.5	30-34	FIXED
35-39	443	6.5	430	5.8	35-39	AGE-
40-44	464	6.8	452	6.1	40-44	SPECIFIC
45-49	482	7.1	473	6.4	45-49	BIRTH
50-54	495	7.3	493	6.7	50-54	AND
55-59	498	7.3	509	6.9	55-59	DEATH
60-64	485	7.1	518	7.0	60-64	RATES
65-69	445	6.5	514	7.0	65-69	(female
70-74	375	5.5	490	6.6	70-74	dominant,
75-79	279	4.1	430	5.8	75-79	in 000s)
80-84	171	2.5	324	4.4	80-84	
85+	115	1.7	302	4.1	85+	
TOTAL	6804		7378		TOTAL	

VITAL RATES OF PROJECTED POPULATION

Per Thousand	1989 BOTH SEXES	1989 MALES	1989 FEMALES	1994 BOTH SEXES	1994 MALES	1994 FEMALES
BIRTH RATE	11.65	12.25	11.07	11.04	11.60	10.51
DEATH RATE	12.11	12.41	11.82	12.33	12.67	12.01
RATE OF INCREASE	-0.46	-0.15	-0.75	-1.29	-1.07	-1.50

VITAL RATES OF STABLE POPULATION

Per Thousand	MALES	FEMALES	
BIRTH RATE	8.93	7.82	TABLE 6
DEATH RATE	20.09	19.11	PROJECTED
RATE OF INCREASE		-11.29	VITAL RATES

AGE STRUCTURE OF PROJECTED POPULATION

	1989 BOTH SEXES	1989 MALES	1989 FEMALES	1994 BOTH SEXES	1994 MALES	1994 FEMALES
% UNDER 15	17.89	18.77	17.05	17.47	18.32	16.66
% 15-64	67.27	69.34	65.30	66.97	69.07	64.97
% 65 AND OLDER	14.84	11.89	17.64	15.56	12.61	18.37
DEPEND. RATIO x 100	48.65	44.22	53.13	49.32	44.78	53.92

STABLE AGE STRUCTURE

	MALES	FEMALES	
% UNDER 15	14.39	12.66	AND RATIOS
% 15-64	65.23	59.41	(female
% 65 AND OLDER	20.37	27.93	dominant)
DEPEND. RATIO x 100	53.29	68.31	

AGE GROUP	FEMALE BIRTH RATES	NET MATERNITY FUNCTION	COEFF. OF MATRIX EQUATION	ORIGINAL MATRIX SUB-DIAGONAL	ORIGINAL MATRIX FIRST ROW	STABLE MATRIX FISHER VALUES	STABLE MATRIX REPRODUCTIVE VALUES	MATRIX PARAMETERS		
0-4	0.0000	0.0000	0.0000	0.99855	0.00000	0.981	286176	λ_1	0.94511	
5-9	0.0000	0.0000	0.0001	0.99899	0.00007	0.928	272573	λ_2	0.34468+0.73856i	TABLE 7
10-14	0.0000	0.0001	0.0171	0.99851	0.01713	0.878	290778	λ_4	-0.33442+0.45917i	
15-19	0.0069	0.0341	0.1323	0.99800	0.13280	0.814	294089	λ_6	-0.44361-0.00000i	LESLIE
20-24	0.0468	0.2305	0.2644	0.99775	0.26600	0.641	251031	r_1	-0.01129	MATRIX
25-29	0.0607	0.2983	0.2136	0.99701	0.21538	0.345	132054	r_2	-0.04091+0.22683i	AND ITS
30-34	0.0263	0.1289	0.0825	0.99571	0.08340	0.116	41073	r_4	-0.11311+0.44005i	ANALYSIS
35-39	0.0074	0.0360	0.0216	0.99308	0.02199	0.028	9324	r_6	-0.16256-0.62832i	(females)
40-44	0.0015	0.0073	0.0039	0.98907	0.00401	0.004	1201	c_1	73781	
45-49	0.0001	0.0006	0.0003	0.98449	0.00030	0.000	93	$2\pi/\gamma$	27.7000	
50-54	0.0000	0.0000	0.0000	0.00000	0.00000	0.000	0	Δ	15.4725	

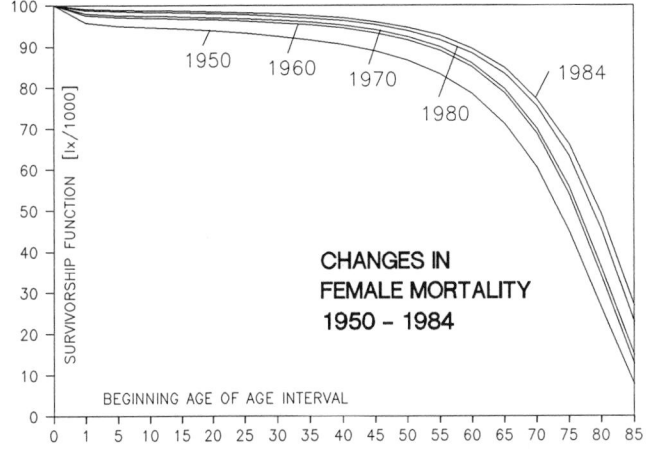

CHANGES IN FEMALE MORTALITY 1950 - 1984

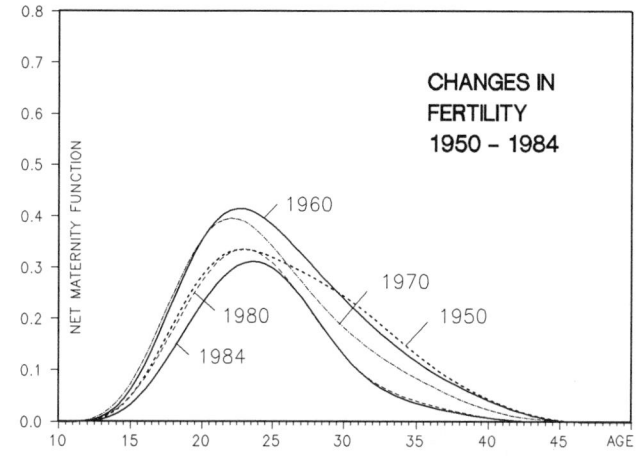

CHANGES IN FERTILITY 1950 - 1984

TABLE 1 DATA

AGE AT LAST BIRTHDAY	ESTIMATED MID-YEAR POPULATION BOTH SEXES	MALES Number	MALES Percent	FEMALES Number	FEMALES Percent	BIRTHS BY AGE OF MOTHER AND SEX	DEATHS BOTH SEXES	DEATHS MALES	DEATHS FEMALES	AGE AT LAST BIRTHDAY
0	137742	70777	1.7	66965	1.6		3788	2241	1547	0
1-4	508521	260769	6.1	247752	5.8		620	342	278	1-4
5-9	632438	324258	7.6	308180	7.3		309	195	114	5-9
10-14	659178	336606	7.9	322572	7.6	213	296	201	95	10-14
15-19	680520	347443	8.2	333077	7.8	23601	501	343	158	15-19
20-24	688288	349020	8.2	339268	8.0	64203	641	442	199	20-24
25-29	575257	288994	6.8	286263	6.7	31959	642	423	219	25-29
30-34	573881	287930	6.8	285951	6.7	12854	707	466	241	30-34
35-39	648563	326656	7.7	321907	7.6	4765	1115	700	415	35-39
40-44	650274	327180	7.7	323094	7.6	1029	1601	1008	593	40-44
45-49	633694	315202	7.4	318492	7.5	112	2459	1464	995	45-49
50-54	377256	187701	4.4	189555	4.5	9	2304	1392	912	50-54
55-59	474410	237969	5.6	236441	5.6		4620	2901	1719	55-59
60-64	435389	213001	5.0	222388	5.2		7405	4515	2890	60-64
65-69	337076	161883	3.8	175193	4.1		9923	5755	4168	65-69
70-74	228756	105156	2.5	123600	2.9		11389	5922	5467	70-74
75-79	129338	55063	1.3	74275	1.7		10148	4717	5431	75-79
80-84	76517	30946	0.7	45571	1.1	71824 M	9759	4135	5624	80-84
85+	42476	17443	0.4	25033	0.6	66921 F	8868	3888	4980	85+
TOTAL	8489574	4243997		4245577		138745	77095	41050	36045	TOTAL

TABLE 2 MALE LIFE TABLE

x	$_nM_x$	$_nq_x$	l_x	$_nd_x$	$_nL_x$	$_nm_x$	$_na_x$	T_x	$\mathring{e}_x$	x
0	0.031663	0.030808	100000	3081	97301	0.031663	0.124	6907041	69.070	0
1	0.001312	0.005229	96919	507	386410	0.001312	1.500	6809740	70.262	1
5	0.000601	0.003002	96412	289	481338	0.000601	2.500	6423330	66.623	5
10	0.000597	0.002981	96123	287	479936	0.000597	2.633	5941992	61.817	10
15	0.000987	0.004925	95836	472	478068	0.000987	2.639	5462055	56.994	15
20	0.001266	0.006319	95364	603	475361	0.001268	2.576	4983988	52.263	20
25	0.001464	0.007300	94762	692	472112	0.001465	2.547	4508626	47.579	25
30	0.001618	0.008061	94070	758	468518	0.001618	2.583	4036514	42.910	30
35	0.002143	0.010661	93312	995	464208	0.002143	2.637	3567996	38.237	35
40	0.003081	0.015294	92317	1412	458286	0.003081	2.664	3103788	33.621	40
45	0.004645	0.023138	90905	2103	449651	0.004678	2.683	2645502	29.102	45
50	0.007416	0.036669	88802	3256	436486	0.007460	2.690	2195850	24.728	50
55	0.012191	0.059291	85545	5072	416065	0.012191	2.701	1759364	20.566	55
60	0.021197	0.101218	80473	8145	383429	0.021243	2.675	1343298	16.692	60
65	0.035550	0.164722	72328	11914	333295	0.035746	2.621	959870	13.271	65
70	0.056316	0.249251	60414	15058	265296	0.056760	2.558	626574	10.371	70
75	0.085666	0.354877	45356	16096	186431	0.086336	2.493	361279	7.965	75
80	0.133620	0.496836	29260	14537	108797	0.133620	2.420	174848	5.976	80
85	0.222897	1.000000	14723	14723	66051	0.159422	4.486	66051	4.486	85

TABLE 3 FEMALE LIFE TABLE

x	$_nM_x$	$_nq_x$	l_x	$_nd_x$	$_nL_x$	$_nm_x$	$_na_x$	T_x	$\mathring{e}_x$	x
0	0.023102	0.022636	100000	2264	97984	0.023102	0.109	7350755	73.508	0
1	0.001122	0.004476	97736	437	389852	0.001122	1.500	7252771	74.207	1
5	0.000370	0.001848	97299	180	486045	0.000370	2.500	6862919	70.534	5
10	0.000295	0.001471	97119	143	485249	0.000295	2.573	6376873	65.660	10
15	0.000474	0.002369	96976	230	484336	0.000474	2.628	5891624	60.753	15
20	0.000587	0.002932	96747	284	483053	0.000587	2.602	5407288	55.891	20
25	0.000765	0.003823	96463	369	481418	0.000766	2.568	4924236	51.048	25
30	0.000843	0.004206	96094	404	479511	0.000843	2.627	4442818	46.234	30
35	0.001289	0.006427	95690	615	477009	0.001289	2.657	3963307	41.418	35
40	0.001835	0.009138	95075	869	473382	0.001835	2.706	3486298	36.669	40
45	0.003124	0.015626	94206	1472	467632	0.003148	2.691	3012916	31.982	45
50	0.004811	0.023928	92734	2219	458491	0.004840	2.666	2545284	27.447	50
55	0.007270	0.035757	90515	3237	445172	0.007270	2.713	2086793	23.055	55
60	0.012995	0.063255	87279	5521	423850	0.013025	2.728	1641621	18.809	60
65	0.023791	0.113465	81758	9277	387495	0.023940	2.705	1217771	14.895	65
70	0.044231	0.201826	72481	14629	327661	0.044645	2.625	830276	11.455	70
75	0.073120	0.311885	57853	18043	245001	0.073646	2.547	502615	8.688	75
80	0.123412	0.469565	39809	18693	151469	0.123412	2.455	257614	6.471	80
85	0.198937	1.000000	21116	21116	106145	0.131775	5.027	106145	5.027	85

TABLE 4 OBSERVED VITAL RATES AND RATIOS

CRUDE RATES

Per Thousand	BOTH SEXES	MALES	FEMALES
BIRTH RATE	16.34	16.92	15.76
DEATH RATE	9.08	9.67	8.49
RATE OF INCREASE	7.26	7.25	7.27

PERCENT OF POPULATION IN AGE GROUP

UNDER 15	22.83	23.38	22.27
15 - 64	67.58	67.89	67.28
65 AND OLDER	9.59	8.73	10.45

RATES STANDARDIZED ON USA 1980

Per Thousand	BOTH SEXES	MALES	FEMALES
BIRTH RATE	19.34		18.14
DEATH RATE	10.83	10.35	11.27
RATE OF INCREASE	8.51		6.87

RATES STANDARDIZED ON MEXICO 1980

	BOTH SEXES	MALES	FEMALES
BIRTH RATE	18.33		17.82
DEATH RATE	4.51	5.01	4.02
RATE OF INCREASE	13.82		13.81

VITAL STATISTICS

GFR x 1000	62.836
TFR	2.179
GRR	1.051
NRR	1.013
μ	24.643
σ^2	27.311
GENERATION	24.637
POP. SEX RATIO	1.000
SEX RATIO AT BIRTH	1.073
DEP. RATIO x 100	47.966

PROJECTED POPULATION

AGE GROUP	1975 BOTH SEXES	1975 MALES	1975 FEMALES	1980 BOTH SEXES	1980 MALES	1980 FEMALES
0-4	681	351	330	685	353	332
5-9	644	330	314	679	350	329
10-14	631	323	308	642	329	313
15-19	657	335	322	629	322	307
20-24	677	345	332	654	333	321
25-29	685	347	338	674	343	331
30-34	572	287	285	681	344	337
35-39	569	285	284	568	284	284
40-44	641	322	319	564	282	282
45-49	640	321	319	632	316	316
50-54	618	306	312	625	312	313
55-59	363	179	184	595	292	303
60-64	444	219	225	340	165	175
65-69	388	185	203	397	191	206
70-74	277	129	148	319	147	172
75-79	166	74	92	202	91	111
80-84	78	32	46	100	43	57
85+	51	19	32	52	20	32
TOTAL	8782	4389	4393	9038	4517	4521

STABLE EQUIVALENT TO ORIGINAL POPULATION

AGE GROUP	MALES Number	MALES Percent	FEMALES Number	FEMALES Percent	
0-4	344	7.1	323	6.8	TABLE 5
5-9	341	7.1	321	6.7	
10-14	339	7.0	320	6.7	POPULATION
15-19	337	7.0	318	6.7	PROJECTED
20-24	334	6.9	316	6.6	WITH
25-29	331	6.9	315	6.6	FIXED
30-34	328	6.8	312	6.5	AGE-
35-39	324	6.7	310	6.5	SPECIFIC
40-44	319	6.6	307	6.4	BIRTH
45-49	312	6.5	302	6.3	AND
50-54	302	6.3	296	6.2	DEATH
55-59	287	6.0	286	6.0	RATES
60-64	264	5.5	272	5.7	(female
65-69	229	4.7	248	5.2	dominant,
70-74	182	3.8	209	4.4	in 000s)
75-79	127	2.6	156	3.3	
80-84	74	1.5	96	2.0	
85+	45	0.9	67	1.4	
TOTAL	4819		4774		TOTAL

VITAL RATES OF PROJECTED POPULATION

Per Thousand	1975 BOTH SEXES	1975 MALES	1975 FEMALES	1980 BOTH SEXES	1980 MALES	1980 FEMALES
BIRTH RATE	16.14	16.72	15.56	15.50	16.06	14.94
DEATH RATE	9.85	10.41	9.29	10.53	11.12	9.94
RATE OF INCREASE	6.29	6.31	6.27	4.97	4.94	5.01

VITAL RATES OF STABLE POPULATION

Per Thousand	MALES	FEMALES	
BIRTH RATE	14.77	13.89	TABLE 6
DEATH RATE	14.21	13.35	PROJECTED
RATE OF INCREASE		.54	VITAL RATES AND RATIOS (female dominant)

AGE STRUCTURE OF PROJECTED POPULATION

	1975 BOTH SEXES	1975 MALES	1975 FEMALES	1980 BOTH SEXES	1980 MALES	1980 FEMALES
% UNDER 15	22.26	22.88	21.65	22.19	22.84	21.54
% 15-64	66.80	67.13	66.48	65.98	66.28	65.68
% 65 AND OLDER	10.93	9.99	11.87	11.83	10.88	12.78
DEPEND. RATIO x 100	49.69	48.97	50.41	51.56	50.87	52.25

STABLE AGE STRUCTURE

	MALES	FEMALES
% UNDER 15	21.26	20.19
% 15-64	65.12	63.56
% 65 AND OLDER	13.62	16.25
DEPEND. RATIO x 100	53.57	57.33

AGE GROUP	FEMALE BIRTH RATES	NET MATERNITY FUNCTION	COEFF. OF MATRIX EQUATION	ORIGINAL MATRIX SUB-DIAGONAL	ORIGINAL MATRIX FIRST ROW	STABLE MATRIX FISHER VALUES	STABLE MATRIX REPRODUCTIVE VALUES
0-4	0.0000	0.0000	0.0000	0.99633	0.00000	1.026	323001
5-9	0.0000	0.0000	0.0008	0.99836	0.00078	1.033	318317
10-14	0.0003	0.0015	0.0835	0.99812	0.08398	1.037	334376
15-19	0.0342	0.1655	0.3032	0.99735	0.30541	0.955	318089
20-24	0.0913	0.4409	0.3501	0.99662	0.35354	0.646	219116
25-29	0.0538	0.2592	0.1816	0.99604	0.18402	0.286	81791
30-34	0.0217	0.1040	0.0690	0.99478	0.07021	0.098	28028
35-39	0.0071	0.0341	0.0207	0.99239	0.02113	0.026	8486
40-44	0.0015	0.0073	0.0040	0.98785	0.00416	0.005	1545
45-49	0.0002	0.0008	0.0004	0.98045	0.00047	0.001	171
50-54	0.0000	0.0001	0.0001	0.97095	0.00006	0.000	11

MATRIX PARAMETERS

λ_1	1.00271	
λ_2	$0.23919+0.76520i$	TABLE 7
λ_4	$-0.41613+0.30493i$	
λ_6	$0.00492-0.33239i$	LESLIE
r_1	0.00054	MATRIX
r_2	$-0.04420+0.25357i$	AND ITS
r_4	$-0.13237+0.50184i$	ANALYSIS
r_6	$-0.22027-0.31120i$	(females)
c_1	47732	
$2\pi/y$	24.7793	
Δ	8.4066	

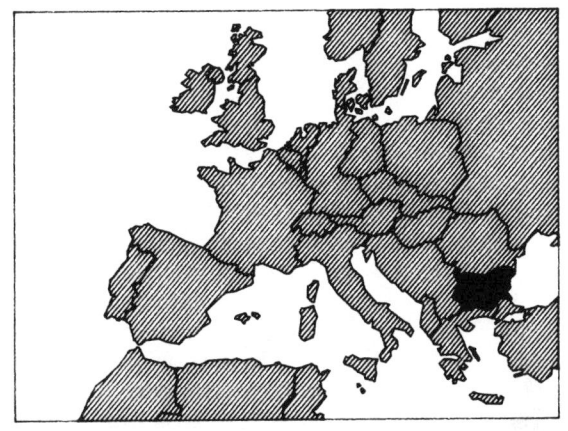

EDUCATION [1984]

% of primary school-age children enrolled:	102
secondary school-age children enrolled:	90
ca. 20-24 year olds in higher education:	17

LABOR FORCE

Average annual labor force growth (%) 1980-85:	0.0	
% of the 1980 labor force in agriculture:	18	TABLE 8
in industry:	45	
in services:	37	SOCIO-

GNP & INCOME DISTRIBUTION

GNP per capita (in US Dollars) 1979:	3020	ECONOMIC
GNP growth rate (%) 1979:	2.6	INDICATORS
% share of total household income		
Lowest 20% of households:	na	
Highest 10% of households:	na	

HEALTH & NUTRITION

Population per physician 1981:	400
Daily calorie supply per capita 1985:	3663

TABLE 1 — DATA

AGE AT LAST BIRTHDAY	ESTIMATED MID-YEAR POPULATION BOTH SEXES	MALES Number	MALES Percent	FEMALES Number	FEMALES Percent	BIRTHS BY AGE OF MOTHER AND SEX	DEATHS BOTH SEXES	DEATHS MALES	DEATHS FEMALES	AGE AT LAST BIRTHDAY
0	144313	74250	1.7	70063	1.6		3335	1923	1412	0
1-4	532781	273565	6.3	259216	5.9		609	322	287	1-4
5-9	636848	327139	7.5	309709	7.1		320	200	120	5-9
10-14	627563	322061	7.4	305502	7.0	238	274	175	99	10-14
15-19	648109	331158	7.6	316951	7.3	23656	455	319	136	15-19
20-24	667459	338169	7.8	329290	7.5	65299	623	457	166	20-24
25-29	680716	344108	7.9	336608	7.7	38771	712	492	220	25-29
30-34	570605	286057	6.6	284548	6.5	12066	742	491	251	30-34
35-39	568304	284479	6.5	283825	6.5	3647	1025	699	326	35-39
40-44	639239	321349	7.4	317890	7.3	914	1658	1108	550	40-44
45-49	636171	319171	7.3	317000	7.3	69	2708	1780	928	45-49
50-54	613206	304164	7.0	309042	7.1	8	4064	2620	1444	50-54
55-59	362404	176845	4.1	185559	4.3		3727	2374	1353	55-59
60-64	446578	219626	5.0	226952	5.2		7840	4823	3017	60-64
65-69	386704	185352	4.3	201352	4.6		11573	6749	4824	65-69
70-74	278018	128280	2.9	149738	3.4		14511	7901	6610	70-74
75-79	162420	71617	1.6	90803	2.1		14618	7173	7445	75-79
80-84	74502	30207	0.7	44295	1.0	74352 M	10654	4571	6083	80-84
85+	44802	17155	0.4	27647	0.6	70316 F	10526	4317	6209	85+
TOTAL	8720742	4354752		4365990		144668	89974	48494	41480	TOTAL

TABLE 2 — MALE LIFE TABLE

x	nM_x	nq_x	l_x	nd_x	nL_x	nm_x	na_x	T_x	$\overset{\circ}{e}_x$	x
0	0.025899	0.025318	100000	2532	97757	0.025899	0.114	6853517	68.535	0
1	0.001177	0.004694	97468	458	388729	0.001177	1.500	6755760	69.312	1
5	0.000611	0.003052	97011	296	484313	0.000611	2.500	6367031	65.632	5
10	0.000543	0.002713	96715	262	482952	0.000543	2.633	5882718	60.826	10
15	0.000963	0.004806	96452	464	481182	0.000963	2.673	5399767	55.984	15
20	0.001351	0.006735	95989	646	478372	0.001351	2.570	4918585	51.241	20
25	0.001430	0.007128	95342	680	475046	0.001431	2.550	4440213	46.571	25
30	0.001716	0.008567	94663	811	471383	0.001720	2.620	3965166	41.887	30
35	0.002457	0.012215	93852	1146	466554	0.002457	2.641	3493784	37.227	35
40	0.003448	0.017103	92705	1586	459846	0.003448	2.679	3027230	32.654	40
45	0.005577	0.027529	91120	2508	449782	0.005577	2.681	2567384	28.176	45
50	0.008614	0.042518	88611	3768	434271	0.008676	2.668	2117602	23.898	50
55	0.013424	0.065424	84844	5551	411282	0.013496	2.669	1683331	19.840	55
60	0.021960	0.104435	79293	8281	377090	0.021960	2.660	1272049	16.042	60
65	0.036412	0.167931	71012	11925	326835	0.036487	2.633	894958	12.603	65
70	0.061592	0.269167	59087	15904	256813	0.061929	2.572	568123	9.615	70
75	0.100158	0.402785	43183	17393	172027	0.101108	2.477	311310	7.209	75
80	0.151323	0.541630	25789	13968	92308	0.151323	2.377	139283	5.401	80
85	0.251647	1.000000	11821	11821	46975	0.194729	3.974	46975	3.974	85

TABLE 3 — FEMALE LIFE TABLE

x	nM_x	nq_x	l_x	nd_x	nL_x	nm_x	na_x	T_x	$\overset{\circ}{e}_x$	x
0	0.020153	0.019796	100000	1980	98227	0.020153	0.104	7343982	73.440	0
1	0.001107	0.004416	98020	433	390999	0.001107	1.500	7245755	73.921	1
5	0.000387	0.001935	97588	189	487465	0.000387	2.500	6854755	70.242	5
10	0.000324	0.001619	97399	158	486603	0.000324	2.526	6367290	65.374	10
15	0.000429	0.002143	97241	208	485702	0.000429	2.586	5880687	60.475	15
20	0.000504	0.002518	97033	244	484574	0.000504	2.592	5394985	55.600	20
25	0.000654	0.003266	96788	316	483199	0.000654	2.619	4910411	50.734	25
30	0.000882	0.004411	96472	425	481345	0.000884	2.615	4427222	45.891	30
35	0.001149	0.005728	96047	550	478941	0.001149	2.650	3945877	41.083	35
40	0.001730	0.008617	95496	823	475597	0.001730	2.709	3466936	36.304	40
45	0.002927	0.014540	94674	1377	470208	0.002927	2.704	2991339	31.596	45
50	0.004673	0.023281	93297	2172	461454	0.004707	2.684	2521131	27.023	50
55	0.007291	0.036114	91125	3291	448126	0.007344	2.721	2059676	22.603	55
60	0.013294	0.064515	87834	5667	426267	0.013294	2.723	1611550	18.348	60
65	0.023958	0.113796	82168	9350	389333	0.024016	2.700	1185283	14.425	65
70	0.044144	0.201142	72817	14647	329697	0.044425	2.652	795950	10.931	70
75	0.081991	0.344524	58171	20041	241730	0.082907	2.549	466253	8.015	75
80	0.137329	0.507493	38129	19350	140905	0.137329	2.429	224523	5.888	80
85	0.224581	1.000000	18779	18779	83618	0.161275	4.453	83618	4.453	85

TABLE 4 — OBSERVED VITAL RATES AND RATIOS

CRUDE RATES

Per Thousand	BOTH SEXES	MALES	FEMALES
BIRTH RATE	16.59	17.07	16.11
DEATH RATE	10.32	11.14	9.50
RATE OF INCREASE	6.27	5.94	6.60

PERCENT OF POPULATION IN AGE GROUP

	BOTH SEXES	MALES	FEMALES
UNDER 15	22.26	22.89	21.63
15 - 64	66.88	67.17	66.60
65 AND OLDER	10.85	9.93	11.77

RATES STANDARDIZED ON USA 1980

Per Thousand	BOTH SEXES	MALES	FEMALES
BIRTH RATE	19.93		18.84
DEATH RATE	11.64	11.25	12.00
RATE OF INCREASE	8.29		6.83

RATES STANDARDIZED ON MEXICO 1980

	BOTH SEXES	MALES	FEMALES
BIRTH RATE	18.96		18.57
DEATH RATE	4.64	5.19	4.07
RATE OF INCREASE	14.32		14.50

VITAL STATISTICS

GFR x 1000	66.176
TFR	2.236
GRR	1.087
NRR	1.052
μ	24.440
σ^2	25.729
GENERATION	24.413
POP. SEX RATIO	1.003
SEX RATIO AT BIRTH	1.057
DEP. RATIO x 100	49.512

AGE AT LAST BIRTHDAY	ESTIMATED MID-YEAR POPULATION						BIRTHS BY AGE OF MOTHER AND SEX	DEATHS			AGE AT LAST BIRTHDAY	
	BOTH SEXES	MALES			FEMALES			BOTH SEXES	MALES	FEMALES		
		Number	Percent		Number	Percent						
0	144330	74169	1.7		70161	1.6		2594	1523	1071	0	
1-4	532840	273264	6.2		259576	5.8		605	328	277	1-4	
5-9	659941	339028	7.7		320913	7.2		292	177	115	5-9	
10-14	624599	321247	7.3		303352	6.8	262	253	158	95	10-14	
15-19	621965	319383	7.2		302582	6.8	24311	442	294	148	15-19	
20-24	630929	322668	7.3		308261	6.9	59463	599	434	165	20-24	
25-29	651595	327830	7.4		323765	7.3	30042	667	452	215	25-29	
30-34	669615	336587	7.6		333028	7.5	10732	856	584	272	30-34	
35-39	562273	281627	6.4		280646	6.3	2734	1062	730	332	35-39	TABLE 1
40-44	557525	277861	6.3		279664	6.3	595	1505	1029	476	40-44	
45-49	624001	312126	7.1		311875	7.0	43	2798	1869	929	45-49	DATA
50-54	612251	304610	6.9		307641	6.9	8	4328	2873	1455	50-54	
55-59	581928	284692	6.4		297236	6.7		6519	4250	2269	55-59	
60-64	336434	160131	3.6		176303	4.0		5878	3708	2170	60-64	
65-69	397592	189514	4.3		208078	4.7		11958	7181	4777	65-69	
70-74	314114	145472	3.3		168642	3.8		16278	8884	7394	70-74	
75-79	200026	87686	2.0		112340	2.5		17012	8504	8508	75-79	
80-84	92289	39351	0.9		52938	1.2	66072 M	13385	6125	7260	80-84	
85+	47288	18186	0.4		29102	0.7	62118 F	10919	4401	6518	85+	
TOTAL	8861535	4415432			4446103		128190	97950	53504	44446	TOTAL	

x	nM_x	nq_x	l_x	nd_x	nL_x	nm_x	na_x	T_x	$\overset{o}{e}_x$	x	
0	0.020534	0.020164	100000	2016	98195	0.020534	0.105	6859400	68.594	0	
1	0.001200	0.004787	97984	469	390762	0.001200	1.500	6761205	69.003	1	
5	0.000522	0.002607	97515	254	486938	0.000522	2.500	6370443	65.328	5	
10	0.000492	0.002459	97260	239	485744	0.000492	2.667	5883505	60.492	10	
15	0.000921	0.004593	97021	446	484077	0.000921	2.691	5397761	55.635	15	
20	0.001345	0.006703	96576	647	481304	0.001345	2.569	4913684	50.879	20	
25	0.001379	0.006871	95928	659	478031	0.001379	2.556	4432379	46.205	25	TABLE 2
30	0.001735	0.008650	95269	824	474403	0.001737	2.642	3954348	41.507	30	
35	0.002592	0.012919	94445	1220	469360	0.002600	2.652	3479946	36.846	35	MALE
40	0.003703	0.018359	93225	1711	462155	0.003703	2.680	3010586	32.294	40	LIFE
45	0.005988	0.029530	91513	2702	451309	0.005988	2.684	2548431	27.848	45	TABLE
50	0.009432	0.046147	88811	4098	434528	0.009432	2.675	2097122	23.613	50	
55	0.014928	0.072630	84713	6153	409133	0.015038	2.655	1662594	19.626	55	
60	0.023156	0.110299	78560	8665	372546	0.023269	2.644	1253461	15.955	60	
65	0.037892	0.173755	69895	12145	320509	0.037892	2.615	881075	12.606	65	
70	0.061070	0.266054	57750	15365	251272	0.061148	2.561	560567	9.707	70	
75	0.096982	0.392079	42386	16618	170150	0.097670	2.486	309295	7.297	75	
80	0.155650	0.553079	25767	14251	91559	0.155650	2.384	139146	5.400	80	
85	0.241999	1.000000	11516	11516	47586	0.182972	4.132	47586	4.132	85	

x	nM_x	nq_x	l_x	nd_x	nL_x	nm_x	na_x	T_x	$\overset{o}{e}_x$	x	
0	0.015265	0.015057	100000	1506	98639	0.015265	0.096	7400870	74.009	0	
1	0.001067	0.004257	98494	419	392929	0.001067	1.500	7302231	74.139	1	
5	0.000358	0.001790	98075	176	489936	0.000358	2.500	6909302	70.449	5	
10	0.000313	0.001565	97899	153	489127	0.000313	2.586	6419366	65.571	10	
15	0.000489	0.002443	97746	239	488156	0.000489	2.594	5930239	60.670	15	
20	0.000535	0.002673	97507	261	486903	0.000535	2.567	5442083	55.812	20	
25	0.000664	0.003315	97247	322	485456	0.000664	2.587	4955180	50.955	25	TABLE 3
30	0.000817	0.004080	96924	395	483685	0.000818	2.631	4469724	46.116	30	
35	0.001183	0.005915	96529	571	481304	0.001186	2.652	3986039	41.294	35	FEMALE
40	0.001702	0.008477	95958	813	477930	0.001702	2.714	3504734	36.524	40	LIFE
45	0.002979	0.014793	95144	1407	472491	0.002979	2.704	3026804	31.813	45	TABLE
50	0.004730	0.023393	93737	2193	463631	0.004730	2.695	2554313	27.250	50	
55	0.007634	0.037794	91544	3460	449721	0.007693	2.688	2090682	22.838	55	
60	0.012308	0.060283	88084	5310	428308	0.012398	2.718	1640961	18.629	60	
65	0.022958	0.109070	82774	9028	393253	0.022958	2.716	1212653	14.650	65	
70	0.043844	0.198988	73746	14675	334128	0.043919	2.642	819400	11.111	70	
75	0.075734	0.322106	59072	19027	248971	0.076424	2.562	485272	8.215	75	
80	0.137142	0.508029	40044	20344	148341	0.137142	2.450	236301	5.901	80	
85	0.223971	1.000000	19701	19701	87961	0.160563	4.465	87961	4.465	85	

CRUDE RATES

Per Thousand	BOTH SEXES	MALES	FEMALES
BIRTH RATE	14.47	14.96	13.97
DEATH RATE	11.05	12.12	10.00
RATE OF INCREASE	3.41	2.85	3.97

RATES STANDARDIZED ON USA 1980

Per Thousand	BOTH SEXES	MALES	FEMALES
BIRTH RATE	18.45		17.39
DEATH RATE	11.51	11.32	11.68
RATE OF INCREASE	6.94		5.70

VITAL STATISTICS

GFR x 1000	59.907	TABLE 4
TFR	2.056	
GRR	0.996	OBSERVED
NRR	0.969	VITAL
μ	23.867	RATES
σ^2	24.237	AND
GENERATION	23.883	RATIOS
POP. SEX RATIO	1.007	
SEX RATIO AT BIRTH	1.064	
DEP. RATIO x 100	51.518	

PERCENT OF POPULATION IN AGE GROUP

	BOTH SEXES	MALES	FEMALES
UNDER 15	22.14	22.82	21.46
15 - 64	66.00	66.30	65.70
65 AND OLDER	11.86	10.88	12.84

RATES STANDARDIZED ON MEXICO 1980

	BOTH SEXES	MALES	FEMALES
BIRTH RATE	17.83		17.41
DEATH RATE	4.49	5.11	3.86
RATE OF INCREASE	13.34		13.55

TABLE 1 — DATA

AGE AT LAST BIRTHDAY	ESTIMATED MID-YEAR POPULATION BOTH SEXES	MALES Number	MALES Percent	FEMALES Number	FEMALES Percent	BIRTHS BY AGE OF MOTHER AND SEX	DEATHS BOTH SEXES	DEATHS MALES	DEATHS FEMALES	AGE AT LAST BIRTHDAY
0	125243	64443	1.4	60800	1.3		1831	1022	809	0
1-4	462374	237429	5.3	224945	5.0		470	258	212	1-4
5-9	661729	338406	7.6	323323	7.2		293	178	115	5-9
10-14	656166	337847	7.6	318319	7.1	407	269	175	94	10-14
15-19	608191	312076	7.0	296115	6.6	22805	442	287	155	15-19
20-24	603987	308888	6.9	295099	6.5	52979	583	424	159	20-24
25-29	617811	312476	7.0	305335	6.8	28283	650	452	198	25-29
30-34	649305	325825	7.3	323480	7.2	10753	900	643	257	30-34
35-39	673715	337381	7.6	336334	7.5	3180	1379	986	393	35-39
40-44	561177	280330	6.3	280847	6.2	521	1709	1216	493	40-44
45-49	553410	273642	6.1	279768	6.2	24	2702	1925	777	45-49
50-54	622179	307888	6.9	314291	7.0	3	4603	3161	1442	50-54
55-59	598805	296152	6.7	302653	6.7		7068	4752	2316	55-59
60-64	552580	264777	5.9	287803	6.4		10453	6735	3718	60-64
65-69	297597	137192	3.1	160405	3.6		8830	5327	3503	65-69
70-74	330153	153071	3.4	177082	3.9		16459	9171	7288	70-74
75-79	225467	98956	2.2	126511	2.8		19768	9948	9820	75-79
80-84	113919	46973	1.1	66946	1.5	60939 M	16294	7480	8814	80-84
85+	46608	18429	0.4	28179	0.6	58016 F	12782	5205	7577	85+
TOTAL	8960416	4452181		4508235		118955	107485	59345	48140	TOTAL

TABLE 2 — MALE LIFE TABLE

x	$_nM_x$	$_nq_x$	l_x	$_nd_x$	$_nL_x$	$_nm_x$	$_na_x$	T_x	$\overset{\circ}{e}_x$	x
0	0.015859	0.015635	100000	1564	98588	0.015859	0.097	6820481	68.205	0
1	0.001087	0.004335	98436	427	392679	0.001087	1.500	6721893	68.287	1
5	0.000526	0.002626	98010	257	489405	0.000526	2.500	6329214	64.577	5
10	0.000518	0.002589	97752	253	488169	0.000518	2.657	5839808	59.741	10
15	0.000920	0.004597	97499	448	486461	0.000921	2.691	5351639	54.889	15
20	0.001373	0.006841	97051	664	483647	0.001373	2.577	4865178	50.130	20
25	0.001447	0.007207	96387	695	480256	0.001447	2.583	4381531	45.458	25
30	0.001973	0.009822	95692	940	476255	0.001973	2.651	3901274	40.769	30
35	0.002923	0.014533	94753	1377	470544	0.002926	2.662	3425020	36.147	35
40	0.004338	0.021550	93376	2012	462219	0.004353	2.685	2954476	31.641	40
45	0.007035	0.034604	91363	3162	449415	0.007035	2.659	2492257	27.279	45
50	0.010267	0.050127	88202	4421	430647	0.010267	2.656	2042842	23.161	50
55	0.016046	0.077323	83780	6478	403731	0.016046	2.658	1612196	19.243	55
60	0.025437	0.120773	77302	9336	364345	0.025624	2.626	1208465	15.633	60
65	0.038829	0.178231	67966	12114	310644	0.038995	2.591	844119	12.420	65
70	0.059913	0.261416	55853	14601	243697	0.059913	2.564	533475	9.551	70
75	0.100530	0.402617	41252	16609	164582	0.100915	2.491	289778	7.025	75
80	0.159240	0.562116	24643	13852	86990	0.159240	2.385	125196	5.080	80
85	0.282435	1.000000	10791	10791	38206	0.234306	3.541	38206	3.541	85

TABLE 3 — FEMALE LIFE TABLE

x	$_nM_x$	$_nq_x$	l_x	$_nd_x$	$_nL_x$	$_nm_x$	$_na_x$	T_x	$\overset{\circ}{e}_x$	x
0	0.013306	0.013147	100000	1315	98807	0.013306	0.093	7418978	74.190	0
1	0.000942	0.003761	98685	371	393813	0.000942	1.500	7320171	74.177	1
5	0.000356	0.001777	98314	175	491134	0.000356	2.500	6926358	70.451	5
10	0.000295	0.001476	98139	145	490352	0.000295	2.617	6435224	65.572	10
15	0.000523	0.002616	97995	256	489356	0.000524	2.596	5944872	60.665	15
20	0.000539	0.002690	97738	263	488046	0.000539	2.547	5455515	55.818	20
25	0.000648	0.003237	97475	316	486613	0.000648	2.581	4967470	50.961	25
30	0.000794	0.003965	97160	385	484887	0.000794	2.635	4480857	46.118	30
35	0.001168	0.005835	96774	565	482556	0.001170	2.669	3995970	41.292	35
40	0.001755	0.008773	96210	844	479095	0.001762	2.685	3513414	36.518	40
45	0.002777	0.013799	95366	1316	473807	0.002777	2.704	3034319	31.818	45
50	0.004588	0.022702	94050	2135	465357	0.004588	2.709	2560512	27.225	50
55	0.007652	0.037602	91915	3456	451653	0.007652	2.709	2095155	22.795	55
60	0.012919	0.063247	88458	5595	429394	0.013029	2.695	1643502	18.579	60
65	0.021838	0.104764	82864	8681	394351	0.022014	2.700	1214108	14.652	65
70	0.041156	0.187742	74183	13927	338399	0.041156	2.665	819757	11.051	70
75	0.077622	0.327676	60255	19744	253181	0.077985	2.564	481357	7.989	75
80	0.131658	0.493610	40511	19997	151883	0.131658	2.466	228177	5.632	80
85	0.268888	1.000000	20514	20514	76294	0.215956	3.719	76294	3.719	85

TABLE 4 — OBSERVED VITAL RATES AND RATIOS

CRUDE RATES

Per Thousand	BOTH SEXES	MALES	FEMALES
BIRTH RATE	13.28	13.69	12.87
DEATH RATE	12.00	13.33	10.68
RATE OF INCREASE	1.28	0.36	2.19

RATES STANDARDIZED ON USA 1980

Per Thousand	BOTH SEXES	MALES	FEMALES
BIRTH RATE	17.70		16.79
DEATH RATE	12.00	11.91	12.08
RATE OF INCREASE	5.70		4.71

VITAL STATISTICS

GFR x 1000	56.191
TFR	1.975
GRR	0.963
NRR	0.939
μ	23.950
σ^2	24.661
GENERATION	23.982
POP. SEX RATIO	1.013
SEX RATIO AT BIRTH	1.050
DEP. RATIO x 100	48.323

PERCENT OF POPULATION IN AGE GROUP

	BOTH SEXES	MALES	FEMALES
UNDER 15	21.27	21.97	20.57
15 - 64	67.42	67.82	67.03
65 AND OLDER	11.31	10.21	12.40

RATES STANDARDIZED ON MEXICO 1980

Per Thousand	BOTH SEXES	MALES	FEMALES
BIRTH RATE	17.08		16.79
DEATH RATE	4.54	5.24	3.83
RATE OF INCREASE	12.54		12.96

PROJECTED POPULATION

AGE GROUP	1990 BOTH SEXES	1990 MALES	1990 FEMALES	1995 BOTH SEXES	1995 MALES	1995 FEMALES
0-4	585	299	286	594	304	290
5-9	586	301	285	583	298	285
10-14	661	338	323	584	300	284
15-19	655	337	318	658	336	322
20-24	605	310	295	652	335	317
25-29	601	307	294	602	308	294
30-34	614	310	304	597	304	293
35-39	644	322	322	609	306	303
40-44	665	331	334	636	316	320
45-49	551	273	278	652	322	330
50-54	537	262	275	534	261	273
55-59	594	289	305	513	246	267
60-64	555	267	288	550	260	290
65-69	490	226	264	492	228	264
70-74	246	108	138	404	177	227
75-79	235	103	132	176	73	103
80-84	128	52	76	134	55	79
85+	55	21	34	61	23	38
TOTAL	9007	4456	4551	9031	4452	4579

STABLE EQUIVALENT TO ORIGINAL POPULATION

AGE GROUP	MALES Number	MALES Percent	FEMALES Number	FEMALES Percent	AGE GROUP	
0-4	313	6.6	299	6.0	0-4	
5-9	316	6.6	302	6.1	5-9	TABLE 5
10-14	319	6.7	305	6.2	10-14	
15-19	322	6.8	308	6.2	15-19	POPULATION
20-24	324	6.8	312	6.3	20-24	PROJECTED
25-29	326	6.9	315	6.4	25-29	WITH
30-34	328	6.9	318	6.4	30-34	FIXED
35-39	328	6.9	320	6.5	35-39	AGE-
40-44	327	6.9	322	6.5	40-44	SPECIFIC
45-49	322	6.8	323	6.5	45-49	BIRTH
50-54	312	6.6	321	6.5	50-54	AND
55-59	297	6.2	316	6.4	55-59	DEATH
60-64	271	5.7	304	6.1	60-64	RATES
65-69	234	4.9	283	5.7	65-69	(female
70-74	186	3.9	246	5.0	70-74	dominant,
75-79	127	2.7	187	3.8	75-79	in 000s)
80-84	68	1.4	113	2.3	80-84	
85+	30	0.6	58	1.2	85+	
TOTAL	4750		4952		TOTAL	

VITAL RATES OF PROJECTED POPULATION

Per Thousand	1990 BOTH SEXES	1990 MALES	1990 FEMALES	1995 BOTH SEXES	1995 MALES	1995 FEMALES
BIRTH RATE	13.21	13.68	12.75	13.57	14.10	13.05
DEATH RATE	12.59	13.82	11.38	13.04	14.18	11.94
RATE OF INCREASE	0.62	-0.14	1.37	0.52	-0.08	1.11

VITAL RATES OF STABLE POPULATION

Per Thousand	MALES	FEMALES	
BIRTH RATE	13.31	12.16	TABLE 6
DEATH RATE	15.89	14.76	PROJECTED
RATE OF INCREASE		-2.60	VITAL RATES AND RATIOS (female dominant)

AGE STRUCTURE OF PROJECTED POPULATION

	1990 BOTH SEXES	1990 MALES	1990 FEMALES	1995 BOTH SEXES	1995 MALES	1995 FEMALES
% UNDER 15	20.33	21.05	19.64	19.50	20.26	18.77
% 15-64	66.85	67.51	66.21	66.47	67.27	65.69
% 65 AND OLDER	12.81	11.44	14.15	14.03	12.47	15.54
DEPEND. RATIO x 100	49.58	48.12	51.03	50.44	48.65	52.22

STABLE AGE STRUCTURE

	MALES	FEMALES
% UNDER 15	19.94	18.28
% 15-64	66.45	63.81
% 65 AND OLDER	13.60	17.91
DEPEND. RATIO x 100	50.48	56.72

AGE GROUP	FEMALE BIRTH RATES	NET MATERNITY FUNCTION	COEFF. OF MATRIX EQUATION	ORIGINAL MATRIX SUB-DIAGONAL	ORIGINAL MATRIX FIRST ROW	STABLE MATRIX FISHER VALUES	STABLE MATRIX REPRODUCTIVE VALUES
0-4	0.0000	0.0000	0.0000	0.99698	0.00000	1.008	288144
5-9	0.0000	0.0000	0.0015	0.99841	0.00153	0.998	322794
10-14	0.0006	0.0031	0.0934	0.99797	0.09386	0.985	313695
15-19	0.0376	0.1838	0.3056	0.99732	0.30761	0.880	260540
20-24	0.0876	0.4273	0.3236	0.99706	0.32661	0.560	165194
25-29	0.0452	0.2198	0.1492	0.99645	0.15107	0.224	68350
30-34	0.0162	0.0786	0.0504	0.99519	0.05124	0.069	22277
35-39	0.0046	0.0223	0.0133	0.99283	0.01357	0.016	5512
40-44	0.0009	0.0043	0.0023	0.98896	0.00233	0.003	705
45-49	0.0002	0.0008	0.0001	0.98216	0.00011	0.000	36
50-54	0.0000	0.0000	0.0000	0.97055	0.00001	0.000	4

MATRIX PARAMETERS

λ_1	0.98707	
λ_2	$0.21377+0.76190i$	TABLE 7
λ_4	$-0.41896+0.28539i$	
λ_6	$-0.29122+0.15738i$	LESLIE
r_1	-0.00260	MATRIX
r_2	$-0.04681+0.25945i$	AND ITS
r_4	$-0.13588+0.50872i$	ANALYSIS
r_6	$-0.22111+0.52923i$	(females)
c_1	49523	
$2\pi/y$	24.2173	
Δ	6.1013	

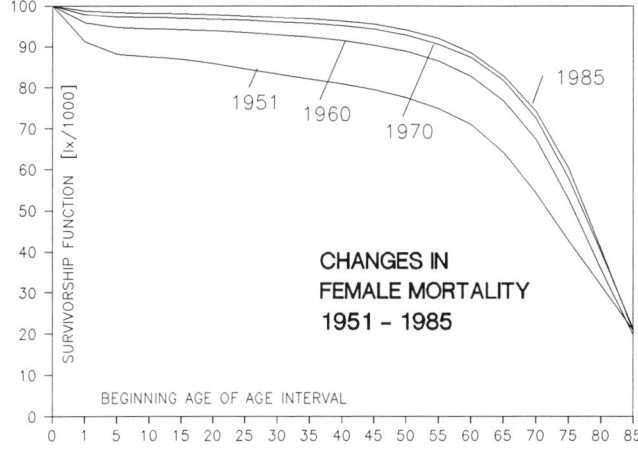

CHANGES IN FEMALE MORTALITY 1951 – 1985

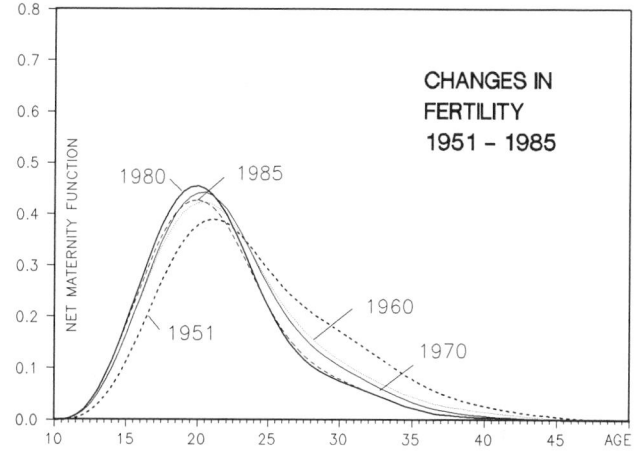

CHANGES IN FERTILITY 1951 – 1985

AGE AT LAST BIRTHDAY	ESTIMATED MID-YEAR POPULATION BOTH SEXES	MALES Number	MALES Percent	FEMALES Number	FEMALES Percent	BIRTHS BY AGE OF MOTHER AND SEX	DEATHS BOTH SEXES	DEATHS MALES	DEATHS FEMALES	AGE AT LAST BIRTHDAY
0	219755	112440	1.6	107315	1.5		5059	2915	2144	0
1-4	854404	437379	6.3	417025	5.7		813	457	356	1-4
5-9	1093881	559097	8.0	534784	7.3		454	276	178	5-9
10-14	1152593	587618	8.4	564975	7.7	62	476	306	170	10-14
15-19	1285298	655259	9.4	630039	8.6	28675	1132	802	330	15-19
20-24	1239061	628404	9.0	610657	8.3	110240	1449	1125	324	20-24
25-29	1017472	512989	7.3	504483	6.9	57447	1200	894	306	25-29
30-34	836079	418880	6.0	417199	5.7	21480	1359	982	377	30-34
35-39	890407	443484	6.4	446923	6.1	8320	1957	1336	621	35-39
40-44	945970	465214	6.7	480756	6.5	2174	2981	2019	962	40-44
45-49	981811	473259	6.8	508552	6.9	130	5112	3348	1764	45-49
50-54	561283	269290	3.9	291993	4.0	3	4524	2927	1597	50-54
55-59	843874	400708	5.7	443166	6.0		11089	7221	3868	55-59
60-64	810477	377270	5.4	433207	5.9		17492	11178	6314	60-64
65-69	658959	289917	4.2	369042	5.0		23460	14179	9281	65-69
70-74	466869	185376	2.7	281493	3.8		26838	13860	12978	70-74
75-79	271703	98697	1.4	173006	2.4		25069	11159	13910	75-79
80-84	137241	46940	0.7	90301	1.2	117137 M	19525	7653	11872	80-84
85+	66479	21237	0.3	45242	0.6	111394 F	15578	5406	10172	85+
TOTAL	14333616	6983458		7350158		228531	165567	88043	77524	TOTAL

TABLE 1 DATA

TABLE 2 — MALE LIFE TABLE

x	nM_x	nq_x	l_x	nd_x	nL_x	nm_x	na_x	T_x	$\overset{\circ}{e}_x$	x
0	0.025925	0.025343	100000	2534	97755	0.025925	0.114	6616991	66.170	0
1	0.001045	0.004169	97466	406	388847	0.001045	1.500	6519236	66.887	1
5	0.000494	0.002465	97059	239	484699	0.000494	2.500	6130389	63.161	5
10	0.000521	0.002601	96820	252	483544	0.000521	2.790	5645690	58.311	10
15	0.001224	0.006103	96568	589	481494	0.001224	2.714	5162146	53.456	15
20	0.001790	0.008920	95979	856	477804	0.001792	2.558	4680651	48.767	20
25	0.001743	0.008687	95123	826	473600	0.001745	2.562	4202847	44.183	25
30	0.002344	0.011684	94296	1102	468846	0.002350	2.607	3729248	39.548	30
35	0.003013	0.014956	93195	1394	462671	0.003013	2.630	3260401	34.985	35
40	0.004340	0.021484	91801	1972	454440	0.004340	2.685	2797731	30.476	40
45	0.007074	0.035054	89829	3149	441821	0.007127	2.674	2343291	26.086	45
50	0.010869	0.053159	86680	4608	422702	0.010901	2.679	1901470	21.937	50
55	0.018021	0.086471	82072	7097	393821	0.018021	2.669	1478768	18.018	55
60	0.029629	0.138468	74975	10382	350393	0.029629	2.642	1084947	14.471	60
65	0.048907	0.219224	64594	14160	288730	0.049044	2.582	734554	11.372	65
70	0.074767	0.316598	50433	15967	212458	0.075154	2.513	445824	8.840	70
75	0.113063	0.440079	34466	15168	133369	0.113728	2.431	233366	6.771	75
80	0.163038	0.568321	19298	10968	67270	0.163038	2.336	99997	5.182	80
85	0.254556	1.000000	8331	8331	32726	0.199163	3.928	32726	3.928	85

TABLE 3 — FEMALE LIFE TABLE

x	nM_x	nq_x	l_x	nd_x	nL_x	nm_x	na_x	T_x	$\overset{\circ}{e}_x$	x
0	0.019979	0.019627	100000	1963	98241	0.019979	0.104	7300803	73.008	0
1	0.000854	0.003407	98037	334	391314	0.000854	1.500	7202561	73.468	1
5	0.000333	0.001663	97703	162	488110	0.000333	2.500	6811247	69.714	5
10	0.000301	0.001503	97541	147	487356	0.000301	2.631	6323137	64.826	10
15	0.000524	0.002616	97394	255	486357	0.000524	2.591	5835781	59.919	15
20	0.000531	0.002650	97139	257	485062	0.000531	2.532	5349424	55.070	20
25	0.000607	0.003038	96882	294	483711	0.000608	2.627	4864362	50.209	25
30	0.000904	0.004524	96588	437	481923	0.000907	2.677	4380651	45.354	30
35	0.001390	0.006925	96151	666	479196	0.001390	2.661	3898727	40.548	35
40	0.002001	0.009960	95485	951	475249	0.002001	2.713	3419532	35.812	40
45	0.003469	0.017342	94534	1639	468897	0.003496	2.699	2944282	31.145	45
50	0.005469	0.027096	92894	2517	458643	0.005488	2.684	2475386	26.647	50
55	0.008728	0.042779	90377	3866	442968	0.008728	2.693	2016742	22.315	55
60	0.014575	0.070513	86511	6100	418495	0.014576	2.695	1573774	18.192	60
65	0.025149	0.119106	80411	9577	379921	0.025209	2.689	1155279	14.367	65
70	0.046104	0.208757	70834	14787	319153	0.046332	2.632	775358	10.946	70
75	0.080402	0.338080	56047	18948	233582	0.081120	2.538	456205	8.140	75
80	0.131471	0.491747	37098	18243	138760	0.131471	2.438	222623	6.001	80
85	0.224835	1.000000	18855	18855	83863	0.161601	4.448	83863	4.448	85

TABLE 4 — OBSERVED VITAL RATES AND RATIOS

CRUDE RATES

Per Thousand	BOTH SEXES	MALES	FEMALES
BIRTH RATE	15.94	16.77	15.16
DEATH RATE	11.55	12.61	10.55
RATE OF INCREASE	4.39	4.17	4.61

PERCENT OF POPULATION IN AGE GROUP

	BOTH SEXES	MALES	FEMALES
UNDER 15	23.17	24.29	22.10
15 - 64	65.66	66.51	64.86
65 AND OLDER	11.17	9.20	13.05

RATES STANDARDIZED ON USA 1980

Per Thousand	BOTH SEXES	MALES	FEMALES
BIRTH RATE	18.25		17.30
DEATH RATE	12.75	13.33	12.20
RATE OF INCREASE	5.50		5.10

RATES STANDARDIZED ON MEXICO 1980

	BOTH SEXES	MALES	FEMALES
BIRTH RATE	16.89		16.59
DEATH RATE	5.11	6.05	4.15
RATE OF INCREASE	11.78		12.44

VITAL STATISTICS

GFR x 1000	63.505
TFR	2.075
GRR	1.011
NRR	0.979
μ	25.449
σ^2	27.965
GENERATION	25.460
POP. SEX RATIO	1.053
SEX RATIO AT BIRTH	1.052
DEP. RATIO x 100	52.295

PROJECTED POPULATION

AGE GROUP	1975			1980			STABLE EQUIVALENT TO ORIGINAL POPULATION				AGE GROUP
							MALES		FEMALES		
	BOTH SEXES	MALES	FEMALES	BOTH SEXES	MALES	FEMALES	Number	Percent	Number	Percent	
0-4	1154	590	564	1180	603	577	584	7.2	559	6.5	0-4
5-9	1071	548	523	1149	587	562	584	7.2	560	6.5	5-9
10-14	1092	558	534	1068	546	522	585	7.2	561	6.5	10-14
15-19	1149	585	564	1088	555	533	585	7.2	562	6.5	15-19
20-24	1278	650	628	1143	581	562	583	7.1	563	6.6	20-24
25-29	1232	623	609	1272	645	627	580	7.1	564	6.6	25-29
30-34	1011	508	503	1224	617	607	577	7.1	564	6.6	30-34
35-39	828	413	415	1001	501	500	572	7.0	563	6.6	35-39
40-44	879	436	443	817	406	411	564	6.9	561	6.5	40-44
45-49	926	452	474	860	423	437	551	6.7	556	6.5	45-49
50-54	950	453	497	897	433	464	529	6.5	546	6.4	50-54
55-59	533	251	282	902	422	480	495	6.1	529	6.2	55-59
60-64	776	357	419	489	223	266	442	5.4	502	5.8	60-64
65-69	704	311	393	674	294	380	366	4.5	458	5.3	65-69
70-74	523	213	310	559	229	330	270	3.3	386	4.5	70-74
75-79	322	116	206	361	134	227	170	2.1	284	3.3	75-79
80-84	153	50	103	181	59	122	86	1.1	169	2.0	80-84
85+	78	23	55	86	24	62	42	0.5	103	1.2	85+
TOTAL	14659	7137	7522	14951	7282	7669	8165		8590		TOTAL

TABLE 5

POPULATION PROJECTED WITH FIXED AGE-SPECIFIC BIRTH AND DEATH RATES (female dominant, in 000s)

VITAL RATES OF PROJECTED POPULATION

Per Thousand	1975			1980			VITAL RATES OF STABLE POPULATION		
	BOTH SEXES	MALES	FEMALES	BOTH SEXES	MALES	FEMALES		MALES	FEMALES
							Per Thousand		
BIRTH RATE	16.66	17.54	15.83	16.03	16.87	15.23	BIRTH RATE	14.67	13.26
DEATH RATE	12.17	13.02	11.35	12.53	13.20	11.91	DEATH RATE	15.47	14.10
RATE OF INCREASE	4.50	4.52	4.47	3.49	3.67	3.32	RATE OF INCREASE		-.83

AGE STRUCTURE OF PROJECTED POPULATION

	BOTH SEXES	MALES	FEMALES	BOTH SEXES	MALES	FEMALES	STABLE AGE STRUCTURE	MALES	FEMALES
% UNDER 15	22.62	23.75	21.55	22.73	23.85	21.66	% UNDER 15	21.47	19.55
% 15-64	65.24	66.25	64.27	64.82	65.99	63.71	% 15-64	67.08	64.15
% 65 AND OLDER	12.14	9.99	14.18	12.45	10.15	14.62	% 65 AND OLDER	11.45	16.30
DEPEND. RATIO x 100	53.29	50.94	55.59	54.26	51.53	56.95	DEPEND. RATIO x 100	49.08	55.88

TABLE 6

PROJECTED VITAL RATES AND RATIOS (female dominant)

AGE GROUP	FEMALE BIRTH RATES	NET MATERNITY FUNCTION	COEFF. OF MATRIX EQUATION	ORIGINAL MATRIX		STABLE MATRIX		MATRIX PARAMETERS		
				SUB-DIAGONAL	FIRST ROW	FISHER VALUES	REPRODUCTIVE VALUES			
0-4	0.0000	0.0000	0.0000	0.99705	0.00000	1.019	534412	λ_1	0.99584	
5-9	0.0000	0.0000	0.0001	0.99846	0.00013	1.018	544395	λ_2	$0.26822+0.75813i$	
10-14	0.0001	0.0003	0.0541	0.99795	0.05432	1.015	573545	λ_4	$-0.41471+0.30943i$	
15-19	0.0222	0.1079	0.2674	0.99734	0.26912	0.958	603289	λ_6	$0.02163+0.39269i$	
20-24	0.0880	0.4268	0.3477	0.99722	0.35088	0.681	415906	r_1	-0.00083	
25-29	0.0555	0.2685	0.1947	0.99630	0.19707	0.322	162202	r_2	$-0.04359+0.24615i$	
30-34	0.0251	0.1209	0.0822	0.99434	0.08352	0.120	49969	r_4	$-0.13178+0.50011i$	
35-39	0.0091	0.0435	0.0270	0.99176	0.02756	0.034	15351	r_6	$-0.18664+0.30315i$	
40-44	0.0022	0.0105	0.0055	0.98663	0.00570	0.006	2963	c_1	85897	
45-49	0.0001	0.0006	0.0003	0.97813	0.00032	0.000	171	$2\pi/y$	25.5258	
50-54	0.0000	0.0000	0.0000	0.96582	0.00001	0.000	4	Δ	7.1330	

TABLE 7

LESLIE MATRIX AND ITS ANALYSIS (females)

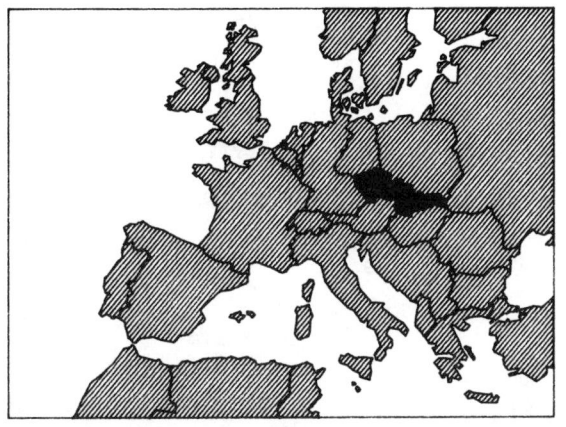

EDUCATION [1984]

% of primary school-age children enrolled:	87
secondary school-age children enrolled:	42
ca. 20-24 year olds in higher education:	16

LABOR FORCE

Average annual labor force growth (%) 1980-85:	0.4
% of the 1980 labor force in agriculture:	13
in industry:	49
in services:	37

GNP & INCOME DISTRIBUTION

GNP per capita (in US Dollars) 1979:	5020
GNP growth rate (%) 1979:	0.7
% share of total household income	
Lowest 20% of households:	na
Highest 10% of households:	na

HEALTH & NUTRITION

Population per physician 1981:	350
Daily calorie supply per capita 1985:	3465

TABLE 8

SOCIO-ECONOMIC INDICATORS

TABLE 1 — DATA

AGE AT LAST BIRTHDAY	ESTIMATED MID-YEAR POPULATION BOTH SEXES	MALES Number	MALES Percent	FEMALES Number	FEMALES Percent	BIRTHS BY AGE OF MOTHER AND SEX	DEATHS BOTH SEXES	DEATHS MALES	DEATHS FEMALES	AGE AT LAST BIRTHDAY
0	285180	145688	2.0	139492	1.8		6027	3482	2545	0
1-4	1002009	512909	7.1	489100	6.4		732	429	303	1-4
5-9	1071877	548973	7.6	522904	6.9		473	289	184	5-9
10-14	1097937	562617	7.8	535320	7.1	42	374	244	130	10-14
15-19	1156954	592009	8.2	564945	7.4	31354	834	614	220	15-19
20-24	1286277	656425	9.1	629852	8.3	133219	1196	930	266	20-24
25-29	1225841	622438	8.6	603403	7.9	84547	1290	974	316	25-29
30-34	996954	500734	6.9	496220	6.5	30079	1310	916	394	30-34
35-39	820554	407655	5.7	412899	5.4	8410	1671	1187	484	35-39
40-44	874038	431978	6.0	442060	5.8	1685	2761	1947	814	40-44
45-49	920423	446695	6.2	473728	6.2	86	4519	3060	1459	45-49
50-54	951839	452397	6.3	499442	6.6	3	7743	5152	2591	50-54
55-59	535250	250854	3.5	284396	3.7		6599	4322	2277	55-59
60-64	783315	362053	5.0	421262	5.5		15617	10021	5596	60-64
65-69	711624	315306	4.4	396318	5.2		23216	14124	9092	65-69
70-74	529498	215479	3.0	314019	4.1		28363	15333	13030	70-74
75-79	328396	117520	1.6	210876	2.8		28555	12846	15709	75-79
80-84	153719	48983	0.7	104736	1.4	147828 M	21542	8255	13287	80-84
85+	69982	20570	0.3	49412	0.7	141597 F	16740	5517	11223	85+
TOTAL	14801667	7211283		7590384		289425	169562	89642	79920	TOTAL

TABLE 2 — MALE LIFE TABLE

x	nM_x	nq_x	l_x	nd_x	nL_x	nm_x	na_x	T_x	$\overset{\circ}{e}_x$	x
0	0.023900	0.023403	100000	2340	97919	0.023900	0.111	6692294	66.923	0
1	0.000836	0.003339	97660	326	389824	0.000836	1.500	6594375	67.524	1
5	0.000526	0.002629	97334	256	486029	0.000526	2.500	6204552	63.745	5
10	0.000434	0.002166	97078	210	484914	0.000434	2.743	5718523	58.907	10
15	0.001037	0.005173	96867	501	483183	0.001037	2.695	5233609	54.029	15
20	0.001417	0.007060	96366	680	480182	0.001417	2.575	4750426	49.295	20
25	0.001565	0.007801	95686	746	476603	0.001566	2.553	4270244	44.628	25
30	0.001829	0.009149	94940	869	472656	0.001838	2.649	3793641	39.958	30
35	0.002912	0.014518	94071	1366	467191	0.002923	2.683	3320985	35.303	35
40	0.004507	0.022302	92705	2067	458710	0.004507	2.670	2853794	30.783	40
45	0.006850	0.033719	90638	3056	446138	0.006850	2.693	2395084	26.425	45
50	0.011388	0.055871	87582	4893	426468	0.011474	2.662	1948947	22.253	50
55	0.017229	0.082995	82688	6863	397318	0.017273	2.650	1522478	18.412	55
60	0.027678	0.129896	75826	9849	355855	0.027678	2.637	1125161	14.839	60
65	0.044795	0.202255	65976	13344	297798	0.044809	2.596	769305	11.660	65
70	0.071158	0.303543	52632	15976	223726	0.071410	2.532	471508	8.959	70
75	0.109309	0.430157	36656	15768	143067	0.110213	2.450	247782	6.760	75
80	0.168528	0.582526	20888	12168	72201	0.168528	2.350	104715	5.013	80
85	0.268206	1.000000	8720	8720	32513	0.216280	3.728	32513	3.728	85

TABLE 3 — FEMALE LIFE TABLE

x	nM_x	nq_x	l_x	nd_x	nL_x	nm_x	na_x	T_x	$\overset{\circ}{e}_x$	x
0	0.018245	0.017950	100000	1795	98386	0.018245	0.101	7401557	74.016	0
1	0.000620	0.002474	98205	243	392212	0.000620	1.500	7303171	74.367	1
5	0.000352	0.001758	97962	172	489379	0.000352	2.500	6910958	70.547	5
10	0.000243	0.001213	97790	119	488656	0.000243	2.531	6421579	65.667	10
15	0.000389	0.001945	97671	190	487899	0.000389	2.595	5932923	60.744	15
20	0.000422	0.002109	97481	206	486905	0.000422	2.566	5445024	55.857	20
25	0.000524	0.002621	97275	255	485778	0.000525	2.648	4958119	50.970	25
30	0.000794	0.003984	97021	386	484202	0.000798	2.668	4472341	46.097	30
35	0.001172	0.005865	96634	567	481856	0.001176	2.682	3988140	41.271	35
40	0.001841	0.009168	96067	881	478320	0.001841	2.710	3506283	36.498	40
45	0.003080	0.015292	95187	1456	472615	0.003080	2.720	3027963	31.811	45
50	0.005188	0.025825	93731	2421	463051	0.005228	2.685	2555349	27.263	50
55	0.008006	0.039443	91310	3602	448221	0.008035	2.687	2092298	22.914	55
60	0.013284	0.064448	87709	5653	425525	0.013284	2.697	1644077	18.745	60
65	0.022941	0.108992	82056	8943	389631	0.022954	2.691	1218552	14.850	65
70	0.041494	0.189502	73113	13855	332984	0.041609	2.649	828921	11.338	70
75	0.074494	0.317610	59258	18821	250392	0.075166	2.561	495937	8.369	75
80	0.126862	0.479783	40437	19401	152929	0.126862	2.461	245545	6.072	80
85	0.227131	1.000000	21036	21036	92616	0.164211	4.403	92616	4.403	85

TABLE 4 — OBSERVED VITAL RATES AND RATIOS

CRUDE RATES

Per Thousand	BOTH SEXES	MALES	FEMALES
BIRTH RATE	19.55	20.50	18.65
DEATH RATE	11.46	12.43	10.53
RATE OF INCREASE	8.10	8.07	8.13

PERCENT OF POPULATION IN AGE GROUP

	BOTH SEXES	MALES	FEMALES
UNDER 15	23.36	24.55	22.22
15 - 64	64.53	65.50	63.61
65 AND OLDER	12.11	9.95	14.17

RATES STANDARDIZED ON USA 1980

Per Thousand	BOTH SEXES	MALES	FEMALES
BIRTH RATE	21.69		20.64
DEATH RATE	12.19	12.90	11.53
RATE OF INCREASE	9.50		9.11

RATES STANDARDIZED ON MEXICO 1980

	BOTH SEXES	MALES	FEMALES
BIRTH RATE	20.09		19.81
DEATH RATE	4.80	5.76	3.83
RATE OF INCREASE	15.29		15.98

VITAL STATISTICS

GFR x 1000	79.883
TFR	2.461
GRR	1.204
NRR	1.170
μ	25.359
σ^2	26.566
GENERATION	25.276
POP. SEX RATIO	1.053
SEX RATIO AT BIRTH	1.044
DEP. RATIO x 100	54.968

TABLE 1 DATA

AGE AT LAST BIRTHDAY	ESTIMATED MID-YEAR POPULATION BOTH SEXES	MALES Number	MALES Percent	FEMALES Number	FEMALES Percent	BIRTHS BY AGE OF MOTHER AND SEX	DEATHS BOTH SEXES	DEATHS MALES	DEATHS FEMALES	AGE AT LAST BIRTHDAY
0	256483	131450	1.8	125033	1.6		4580	2703	1877	0
1-4	1104284	564557	7.6	539727	6.9		708	397	311	1-4
5-9	1282971	656094	8.8	626877	8.0		503	322	181	5-9
10-14	1069746	547685	7.3	522061	6.7	42	335	204	131	10-14
15-19	1095666	561094	7.5	534572	6.8	27393	666	485	181	15-19
20-24	1152942	589158	7.9	563784	7.2	112457	1013	804	209	20-24
25-29	1280228	652110	8.7	628118	8.0	72835	1192	877	315	25-29
30-34	1217383	616855	8.3	600528	7.7	27629	1493	1080	413	30-34
35-39	987770	494480	6.6	493290	6.3	7302	1928	1383	545	35-39
40-44	809618	400112	5.4	409506	5.2	1185	2635	1813	822	40-44
45-49	855790	419350	5.6	436440	5.6	55	4546	3200	1346	45-49
50-54	890003	425988	5.7	464015	5.9	3	7713	5367	2346	50-54
55-59	902493	419356	5.6	483137	6.2		12425	8250	4175	55-59
60-64	493288	223834	3.0	269454	3.4		10220	6473	3747	60-64
65-69	688581	303200	4.1	385381	4.9		23147	13927	9220	65-69
70-74	576483	237313	3.2	339170	4.3		32065	17496	14569	70-74
75-79	375924	137868	1.8	238056	3.0		33595	15485	18110	75-79
80-84	189365	59846	0.8	129519	1.7	128251 M	27332	10430	16902	80-84
85+	82105	22350	0.3	59755	0.8	120650 F	20020	6047	13973	85+
TOTAL	15311123	7462700		7848423		248901	186116	96743	89373	TOTAL

TABLE 2 MALE LIFE TABLE

x	nM_x	nq_x	l_x	nd_x	nL_x	nm_x	na_x	T_x	$\mathring{e}_x$	x
0	0.020563	0.020191	100000	2019	98193	0.020563	0.105	6680651	66.807	0
1	0.000703	0.002808	97981	275	391236	0.000703	1.500	6582458	67.181	1
5	0.000491	0.002451	97706	239	487930	0.000491	2.500	6191222	63.366	5
10	0.000372	0.001865	97466	182	486914	0.000373	2.706	5703292	58.516	10
15	0.000864	0.004313	97284	420	485473	0.000864	2.737	5216378	53.620	15
20	0.001365	0.006801	96865	659	482724	0.001365	2.571	4730905	48.840	20
25	0.001345	0.006702	96206	645	479455	0.001345	2.557	4248181	44.157	25
30	0.001751	0.008741	95561	835	475860	0.001755	2.670	3768726	39.438	30
35	0.002797	0.013997	94726	1326	470579	0.002818	2.699	3292866	34.762	35
40	0.004531	0.022523	93400	2104	462178	0.004552	2.708	2822287	30.217	40
45	0.007631	0.037496	91296	3423	448606	0.007631	2.699	2360109	25.851	45
50	0.012599	0.061198	87873	5378	426834	0.012599	2.670	1911504	21.753	50
55	0.019673	0.094598	82495	7804	393956	0.019809	2.627	1484670	17.997	55
60	0.028919	0.135514	74692	10122	349309	0.028976	2.614	1090714	14.603	60
65	0.045933	0.206787	64570	13352	290687	0.045933	2.591	741404	11.482	65
70	0.073725	0.311786	51218	15969	216599	0.073726	2.527	450718	8.800	70
75	0.112318	0.437871	35249	15434	136789	0.112834	2.444	234118	6.642	75
80	0.174281	0.595558	19814	11801	67710	0.174281	2.342	97329	4.912	80
85	0.270559	1.000000	8014	8014	29619	0.219659	3.696	29619	3.696	85

TABLE 3 FEMALE LIFE TABLE

x	nM_x	nq_x	l_x	nd_x	nL_x	nm_x	na_x	T_x	$\mathring{e}_x$	x
0	0.015012	0.014811	100000	1481	98660	0.015012	0.096	7406214	74.062	0
1	0.000576	0.002302	98519	227	393509	0.000576	1.500	7307553	74.174	1
5	0.000289	0.001443	98292	142	491106	0.000289	2.500	6914045	70.342	5
10	0.000251	0.001254	98150	123	490449	0.000251	2.541	6422938	65.440	10
15	0.000339	0.001692	98027	166	489734	0.000339	2.573	5932489	60.519	15
20	0.000371	0.001852	97861	181	488870	0.000371	2.590	5442755	55.617	20
25	0.000501	0.002505	97680	245	487821	0.000501	2.631	4953885	50.715	25
30	0.000688	0.003441	97436	335	486401	0.000689	2.683	4466063	45.836	30
35	0.001105	0.005553	97100	539	484285	0.001113	2.745	3979662	40.985	35
40	0.002007	0.010031	96561	969	480576	0.002015	2.699	3495377	36.199	40
45	0.003084	0.015312	95592	1464	474591	0.003084	2.697	3014801	31.538	45
50	0.005056	0.024991	94129	2352	465275	0.005056	2.717	2540210	26.987	50
55	0.008641	0.042703	91776	3919	449832	0.008712	2.691	2074935	22.609	55
60	0.013906	0.067605	87857	5940	425556	0.013957	2.688	1625104	18.497	60
65	0.023924	0.113343	81918	9285	388090	0.023924	2.685	1199548	14.643	65
70	0.042955	0.195008	72633	14164	329742	0.042955	2.640	811458	11.172	70
75	0.076075	0.321918	58469	18822	246385	0.076393	2.558	481716	8.239	75
80	0.130498	0.489960	39647	19425	148855	0.130498	2.458	235331	5.936	80
85	0.233838	1.000000	20221	20221	86476	0.172396	4.276	86476	4.276	85

CRUDE RATES

Per Thousand	BOTH SEXES	MALES	FEMALES
BIRTH RATE	16.26	17.19	15.37
DEATH RATE	12.16	12.96	11.39
RATE OF INCREASE	4.10	4.22	3.99

PERCENT OF POPULATION IN AGE GROUP

UNDER 15	24.25	25.46	23.11
15 - 64	63.26	64.35	62.21
65 AND OLDER	12.49	10.19	14.68

RATES STANDARDIZED ON USA 1980

Per Thousand	BOTH SEXES	MALES	FEMALES
BIRTH RATE	19.11		18.02
DEATH RATE	12.51	13.27	11.79
RATE OF INCREASE	6.60		6.22

RATES STANDARDIZED ON MEXICO 1980

BIRTH RATE	17.85		17.44
DEATH RATE	4.80	5.79	3.80
RATE OF INCREASE	13.05		13.64

VITAL STATISTICS

TABLE 4 OBSERVED VITAL RATES AND RATIOS

GFR x 1000	67.890
TFR	2.153
GRR	1.044
NRR	1.019
μ	24.963
σ^2	24.821
GENERATION	24.953
POP. SEX RATIO	1.052
SEX RATIO AT BIRTH	1.063
DEP. RATIO x 100	58.088

AGE AT LAST BIRTHDAY	ESTIMATED MID-YEAR POPULATION BOTH SEXES	MALES Number	Percent	FEMALES Number	Percent	BIRTHS BY AGE OF MOTHER AND SEX	DEATHS BOTH SEXES	MALES	FEMALES	AGE AT LAST BIRTHDAY
0	223995	114584	1.5	109411	1.4		3165	1826	1339	0
1-4	922900	472254	6.3	450646	5.7		462	259	203	1-4
5-9	1355647	692848	9.2	662799	8.3		426	250	176	5-9
10-14	1278081	653272	8.7	624809	7.9	23	341	232	109	10-14
15-19	1065057	544479	7.2	520578	6.5	27467	626	457	169	15-19
20-24	1088995	557154	7.4	531841	6.7	102565	860	664	196	20-24
25-29	1139994	581711	7.7	558283	7.0	60956	1050	778	272	25-29
30-34	1261890	639334	8.5	622556	7.8	26290	1529	1156	373	30-34
35-39	1200719	604957	8.0	595762	7.5	7725	2284	1618	666	35-39
40-44	969858	481861	6.4	487997	6.1	974	3115	2248	867	40-44
45-49	790506	386759	5.1	403747	5.1	36	4238	3013	1225	45-49
50-54	823647	397248	5.3	426399	5.4		7219	5053	2166	50-54
55-59	841503	392992	5.2	448511	5.6		11303	7613	3690	55-59
60-64	826185	369056	4.9	457129	5.7		17797	11616	6181	60-64
65-69	432110	186396	2.5	245714	3.1		13803	8289	5514	65-69
70-74	558025	227620	3.0	330405	4.2		29393	15992	13401	70-74
75-79	408228	151366	2.0	256862	3.2		34756	16351	18405	75-79
80-84	213194	68045	0.9	145149	1.8	115851 M	29012	11198	17814	80-84
85+	97997	25871	0.3	72126	0.9	110185 F	22726	6589	16137	85+
TOTAL	15498531	7547807		7950724		226036	184105	95202	88903	TOTAL

TABLE 1 DATA

TABLE 2 — MALE LIFE TABLE

x	$_nM_x$	$_nq_x$	l_x	$_nd_x$	$_nL_x$	$_nm_x$	$_na_x$	T_x	$\overset{\circ}{e}_x$	x
0	0.015936	0.015710	100000	1571	98582	0.015936	0.097	6729204	67.292	0
1	0.000548	0.002191	98429	216	393177	0.000548	1.500	6630623	67.365	1
5	0.000361	0.001803	98213	177	490624	0.000361	2.500	6237446	63.509	5
10	0.000355	0.001783	98036	175	489794	0.000357	2.780	5746821	58.619	10
15	0.000839	0.004207	97862	412	488363	0.000843	2.705	5257027	53.719	15
20	0.001192	0.005942	97450	579	485851	0.001192	2.584	4768664	48.935	20
25	0.001337	0.006666	96871	646	482800	0.001337	2.593	4282814	44.212	25
30	0.001808	0.009002	96225	866	479090	0.001808	2.651	3800014	39.491	30
35	0.002675	0.013336	95359	1272	473891	0.002684	2.717	3320923	34.826	35
40	0.004665	0.023276	94087	2190	465432	0.004705	2.715	2847032	30.260	40
45	0.007790	0.038426	91897	3531	451339	0.007824	2.693	2381601	25.916	45
50	0.012720	0.061761	88366	5458	429050	0.012720	2.658	1930262	21.844	50
55	0.019372	0.092646	82908	7681	396511	0.019372	2.653	1501212	18.107	55
60	0.031475	0.147308	75227	11082	349518	0.031705	2.598	1104701	14.685	60
65	0.044470	0.200970	64146	12891	289388	0.044547	2.569	755183	11.773	65
70	0.070257	0.299373	51254	15344	218400	0.070257	2.532	465795	9.088	70
75	0.108023	0.424255	35910	15235	140735	0.108253	2.452	247395	6.889	75
80	0.164568	0.573200	20675	11851	72013	0.164568	2.354	106660	5.159	80
85	0.254687	1.000000	8824	8824	34647	0.199301	3.926	34647	3.926	85

TABLE 3 — FEMALE LIFE TABLE

x	$_nM_x$	$_nq_x$	l_x	$_nd_x$	$_nL_x$	$_nm_x$	$_na_x$	T_x	$\overset{\circ}{e}_x$	x
0	0.012238	0.012104	100000	1210	98900	0.012238	0.091	7480421	74.804	0
1	0.000450	0.001800	98790	178	394714	0.000450	1.500	7381521	74.720	1
5	0.000266	0.001327	98612	131	492732	0.000266	2.500	6986807	70.852	5
10	0.000174	0.000872	98481	86	492196	0.000175	2.570	6494075	65.942	10
15	0.000325	0.001627	98395	160	491595	0.000326	2.623	6001879	60.998	15
20	0.000369	0.001841	98235	181	490739	0.000369	2.590	5510284	56.093	20
25	0.000487	0.002433	98054	239	489698	0.000487	2.598	5019544	51.192	25
30	0.000599	0.002992	97816	293	488410	0.000599	2.718	4529847	46.310	30
35	0.001118	0.005593	97523	545	486371	0.001121	2.719	4041436	41.441	35
40	0.001777	0.008917	96978	865	482915	0.001791	2.719	3555066	36.659	40
45	0.003034	0.015132	96113	1454	477243	0.003047	2.717	3072150	31.964	45
50	0.005080	0.025105	94659	2376	467825	0.005080	2.699	2594907	27.413	50
55	0.008227	0.040370	92282	3725	452821	0.008227	2.694	2127082	23.050	55
60	0.013521	0.066073	88557	5851	429224	0.013632	2.683	1674261	18.906	60
65	0.022441	0.107067	82705	8855	393019	0.022531	2.684	1245038	15.054	65
70	0.040559	0.185117	73850	13671	337061	0.040559	2.645	852019	11.537	70
75	0.071653	0.305550	60179	18388	256158	0.071783	2.567	514958	8.557	75
80	0.122729	0.468413	41792	19576	159504	0.122729	2.474	258800	6.193	80
85	0.223733	1.000000	22216	22216	99296	0.160291	4.470	99296	4.470	85

TABLE 4 — OBSERVED VITAL RATES AND RATIOS

CRUDE RATES

Per Thousand	BOTH SEXES	MALES	FEMALES
BIRTH RATE	14.58	15.35	13.86
DEATH RATE	11.88	12.61	11.18
RATE OF INCREASE	2.71	2.74	2.68

PERCENT OF POPULATION IN AGE GROUP

UNDER 15	24.39	25.61	23.24
15 - 64	64.58	65.66	63.55
65 AND OLDER	11.03	8.73	13.21

RATES STANDARDIZED ON USA 1980

Per Thousand	BOTH SEXES	MALES	FEMALES
BIRTH RATE	18.35		17.39
DEATH RATE	11.99	12.86	11.16
RATE OF INCREASE	6.36		6.23

RATES STANDARDIZED ON MEXICO 1980

	BOTH SEXES	MALES	FEMALES
BIRTH RATE	17.21		16.91
DEATH RATE	4.53	5.51	3.53
RATE OF INCREASE	12.68		13.38

VITAL STATISTICS

GFR x 1000	60.750
TFR	2.061
GRR	1.004
NRR	0.985
μ	24.771
σ^2	23.956
GENERATION	24.779
POP. SEX RATIO	1.053
SEX RATIO AT BIRTH	1.051
DEP. RATIO x 100	54.856

PROJECTED POPULATION

AGE GROUP	1990 BOTH SEXES	MALES	FEMALES	1995 BOTH SEXES	MALES	FEMALES
0-4	1108	567	541	1149	588	561
5-9	1144	585	559	1106	566	540
10-14	1354	692	662	1142	584	558
15-19	1275	651	624	1351	690	661
20-24	1062	542	520	1271	648	623
25-29	1085	554	531	1057	538	519
30-34	1134	577	557	1078	549	529
35-39	1252	632	620	1125	571	554
40-44	1186	594	592	1237	621	616
45-49	949	467	482	1161	576	585
50-54	764	368	396	917	444	473
55-59	780	367	413	723	340	383
60-64	771	346	425	715	324	391
65-69	725	306	419	676	287	389
70-74	352	141	211	590	231	359
75-79	398	147	251	251	91	160
80-84	237	77	160	231	75	156
85+	123	33	90	137	37	100
TOTAL	15699	7646	8053	15917	7760	8157

STABLE EQUIVALENT TO ORIGINAL POPULATION

AGE GROUP	MALES Number	Percent	FEMALES Number	Percent	AGE GROUP
0-4	610	7.2	582	6.4	0-4
5-9	610	7.2	583	6.5	5-9
10-14	611	7.2	584	6.5	10-14
15-19	611	7.2	585	6.5	15-19
20-24	610	7.2	586	6.5	20-24
25-29	608	7.1	586	6.5	25-29
30-34	605	7.1	587	6.5	30-34
35-39	600	7.0	586	6.5	35-39
40-44	592	6.9	584	6.5	40-44
45-49	575	6.8	579	6.4	45-49
50-54	549	6.4	569	6.3	50-54
55-59	509	6.0	552	6.1	55-59
60-64	450	5.3	525	5.8	60-64
65-69	374	4.4	483	5.3	65-69
70-74	283	3.3	415	4.6	70-74
75-79	183	2.1	316	3.5	75-79
80-84	94	1.1	198	2.2	80-84
85+	45	0.5	123	1.4	85+
TOTAL	8519		9023		TOTAL

TABLE 5

POPULATION PROJECTED WITH FIXED AGE-SPECIFIC BIRTH AND DEATH RATES (female dominant, in 000s)

VITAL RATES OF PROJECTED POPULATION

Per Thousand	1990 BOTH SEXES	MALES	FEMALES	1995 BOTH SEXES	MALES	FEMALES
BIRTH RATE	14.26	15.01	13.55	15.23	16.02	14.49
DEATH RATE	12.07	12.64	11.54	11.99	12.56	11.44
RATE OF INCREASE	2.19	2.37	2.02	3.24	3.45	3.04

VITAL RATES OF STABLE POPULATION

Per Thousand	MALES	FEMALES
BIRTH RATE	14.53	13.05
DEATH RATE	15.12	13.67
RATE OF INCREASE		-.62

TABLE 6

PROJECTED VITAL RATES AND RATIOS (female dominant)

AGE STRUCTURE OF PROJECTED POPULATION

	BOTH SEXES	MALES	FEMALES	BOTH SEXES	MALES	FEMALES
% UNDER 15	22.97	24.12	21.89	21.35	22.40	20.35
% 15-64	65.34	66.69	64.07	66.81	68.32	65.38
% 65 AND OLDER	11.68	9.20	14.04	11.84	9.28	14.27
DEPEND. RATIO x 100	53.04	49.96	56.08	49.67	46.37	52.95

STABLE AGE STRUCTURE

	MALES	FEMALES
% UNDER 15	21.49	19.38
% 15-64	67.02	63.61
% 65 AND OLDER	11.49	17.01
DEPEND. RATIO x 100	49.21	57.22

AGE GROUP	FEMALE BIRTH RATES	NET MATERNITY FUNCTION	COEFF. OF MATRIX EQUATION	ORIGINAL MATRIX SUB-DIAGONAL	FIRST ROW	STABLE MATRIX FISHER VALUES	REPRODUCTIVE VALUES
0-4	0.0000	0.0000	0.0000	0.99821	0.00000	1.011	566421
5-9	0.0000	0.0000	0.0000	0.99891	0.00004	1.010	669441
10-14	0.0000	0.0001	0.0633	0.99878	0.06345	1.008	629765
15-19	0.0257	0.1264	0.2939	0.99826	0.29509	0.942	490271
20-24	0.0940	0.4613	0.3610	0.99788	0.36310	0.642	341189
25-29	0.0532	0.2606	0.1806	0.99737	0.18203	0.273	152347
30-34	0.0206	0.1005	0.0656	0.99582	0.06634	0.088	54889
35-39	0.0063	0.0307	0.0177	0.99290	0.01798	0.021	12443
40-44	0.0010	0.0047	0.0025	0.98825	0.00251	0.003	1294
45-49	0.0000	0.0002	0.0001	0.98026	0.00011	0.000	44
50-54	0.0000	0.0000	0.0000	0.00000	0.00000	0.000	0

MATRIX PARAMETERS

λ_1 0.99689
λ_2 0.24799+0.77777i
λ_4 -0.44933+0.31474i
λ_6 -0.01541+0.34365i
r_1 -0.00062
r_2 -0.04058+0.25243i
r_4 -0.12008+0.50611i
r_6 -0.21342+0.32312i
c_1 90230
$2\pi/\gamma$ 24.8910
Δ 6.9684

TABLE 7

LESLIE MATRIX AND ITS ANALYSIS (females)

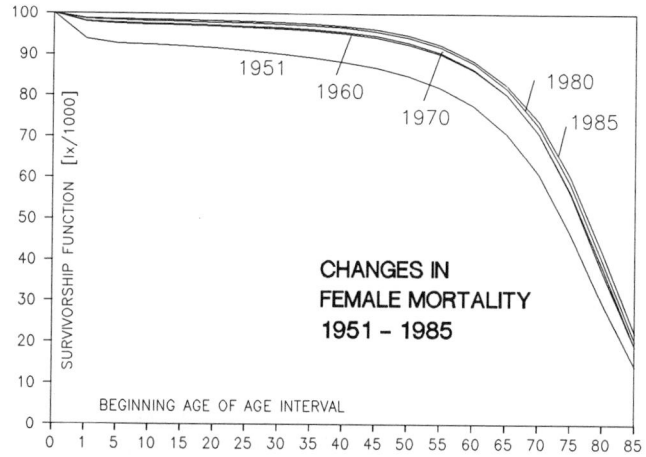

CHANGES IN FEMALE MORTALITY 1951 – 1985

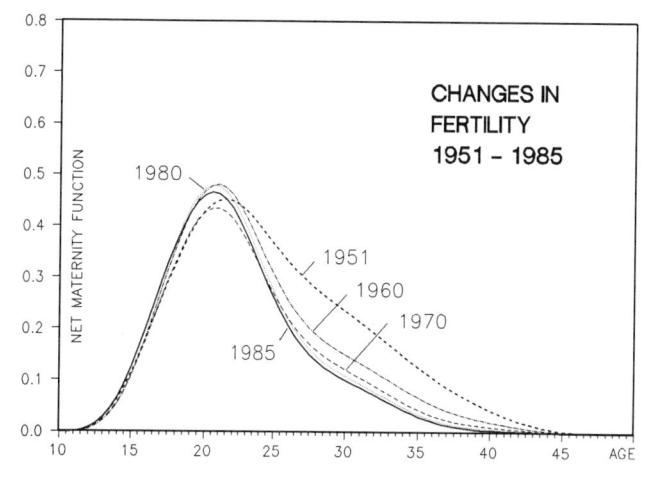

CHANGES IN FERTILITY 1951 – 1985

AGE AT LAST BIRTHDAY	ESTIMATED MID-YEAR POPULATION					BIRTHS BY AGE OF MOTHER AND SEX	DEATHS			AGE AT LAST BIRTHDAY
	BOTH SEXES	MALES		FEMALES			BOTH SEXES	MALES	FEMALES	
		Number	Percent	Number	Percent					
0	70157	36061	1.5	34096	1.4		1005	625	380	0
1-4	317428	162901	6.7	154527	6.2		221	139	82	1-4
5-9	392205	200489	8.2	191716	7.7		173	100	73	5-9
10-14	368246	188618	7.7	179628	7.2	11	113	72	41	10-14
15-19	372722	191364	7.8	181358	7.3	5873	258	175	83	15-19
20-24	415809	213985	8.7	201824	8.1	26588	322	219	103	20-24
25-29	375462	192886	7.9	182576	7.4	24193	298	205	93	25-29
30-34	302053	153251	6.3	148802	6.0	9864	310	183	127	30-34
35-39	279169	139747	5.7	139422	5.6	3453	443	258	185	35-39
40-44	285037	141572	5.8	143465	5.8	774	708	403	305	40-44
45-49	305968	150878	6.2	155090	6.2	46	1268	761	507	45-49
50-54	288645	142429	5.8	146216	5.9		1921	1105	816	50-54
55-59	287095	140249	5.7	146846	5.9		2881	1792	1089	55-59
60-64	263814	125980	5.2	137834	5.6		4274	2600	1674	60-64
65-69	218530	100365	4.1	118165	4.8		5572	3359	2213	65-69
70-74	169773	74520	3.0	95253	3.8		7106	4037	3069	70-74
75-79	115432	49194	2.0	66238	2.7		7472	3805	3667	75-79
80-84	65484	27276	1.1	38208	1.5	36382 M	6944	3257	3687	80-84
85+	35728	14387	0.6	21341	0.9	34420 F	6944	3032	3912	85+
TOTAL	4928757	2446152		2482605		70802	48233	26127	22106	TOTAL

TABLE 1
DATA

TABLE 2 — MALE LIFE TABLE

x	nM_x	nq_x	l_x	nd_x	nL_x	nm_x	na_x	T_x	$\overset{\circ}{e}_x$	x
0	0.017332	0.017065	100000	1707	98463	0.017332	0.099	7091655	70.917	0
1	0.000853	0.003406	98293	335	392337	0.000853	1.500	6993192	71.146	1
5	0.000499	0.002491	97959	244	489183	0.000499	2.500	6600855	67.384	5
10	0.000382	0.001909	97715	187	488149	0.000382	2.724	6111671	62.546	10
15	0.000914	0.004563	97528	445	486593	0.000914	2.645	5623522	57.660	15
20	0.001023	0.005104	97083	496	484191	0.001023	2.528	5136929	52.913	20
25	0.001063	0.005304	96588	512	481674	0.001063	2.532	4652738	48.171	25
30	0.001194	0.005975	96075	574	479019	0.001198	2.633	4171064	43.414	30
35	0.001846	0.009215	95501	880	475466	0.001851	2.681	3692045	38.660	35
40	0.002847	0.014141	94621	1338	470063	0.002847	2.725	3216579	33.994	40
45	0.005044	0.024929	93283	2325	461046	0.005044	2.691	2746517	29.443	45
50	0.007758	0.038107	90958	3466	446770	0.007758	2.686	2285471	25.127	50
55	0.012777	0.062045	87492	5428	424850	0.012777	2.677	1838701	21.016	55
60	0.020638	0.098577	82063	8090	391357	0.020670	2.656	1413850	17.229	60
65	0.033468	0.155444	73974	11499	342557	0.033567	2.625	1022493	13.822	65
70	0.054173	0.239772	62475	14980	275746	0.054324	2.555	679936	10.883	70
75	0.077347	0.325040	47495	15438	198818	0.077648	2.496	404190	8.510	75
80	0.119409	0.457728	32057	14674	122885	0.119409	2.451	205372	6.406	80
85	0.210746	1.000000	17384	17384	82487	0.145361	4.745	82487	4.745	85

TABLE 3 — FEMALE LIFE TABLE

x	nM_x	nq_x	l_x	nd_x	nL_x	nm_x	na_x	T_x	$\overset{\circ}{e}_x$	x
0	0.011145	0.011033	100000	1103	98995	0.011145	0.089	7604965	76.050	0
1	0.000531	0.002120	98897	210	395063	0.000531	1.500	7505970	75.897	1
5	0.000381	0.001902	98687	188	492966	0.000381	2.500	7110907	72.055	5
10	0.000228	0.001141	98499	112	492224	0.000228	2.569	6617941	67.188	10
15	0.000458	0.002286	98387	225	491401	0.000458	2.628	6125718	62.261	15
20	0.000510	0.002548	98162	250	490190	0.000510	2.521	5634316	57.398	20
25	0.000509	0.002550	97912	250	488970	0.000511	2.640	5144126	52.538	25
30	0.000853	0.004282	97662	418	487348	0.000858	2.697	4655156	47.666	30
35	0.001327	0.006627	97244	644	484735	0.001329	2.695	4167808	42.859	35
40	0.002126	0.010578	96600	1022	480632	0.002126	2.685	3683073	38.127	40
45	0.003269	0.016224	95578	1551	474339	0.003269	2.711	3202441	33.506	45
50	0.005581	0.027542	94027	2590	464033	0.005581	2.643	2728102	29.014	50
55	0.007416	0.036448	91437	3333	449401	0.007416	2.664	2264069	24.761	55
60	0.012145	0.059116	88105	5208	428362	0.012159	2.665	1814668	20.597	60
65	0.018728	0.089952	82896	7457	397117	0.018777	2.671	1386306	16.723	65
70	0.032219	0.150304	75440	11339	350585	0.032343	2.653	989189	13.112	70
75	0.055361	0.246183	64101	15781	282612	0.055838	2.599	638604	9.962	75
80	0.096498	0.389610	48320	18826	195093	0.096498	2.530	355991	7.367	80
85	0.183309	1.000000	29494	29494	160899	0.114681	5.455	160899	5.455	85

TABLE 4 — OBSERVED VITAL RATES AND RATIOS

CRUDE RATES

Per Thousand	BOTH SEXES	MALES	FEMALES
BIRTH RATE	14.37	14.87	13.86
DEATH RATE	9.79	10.68	8.90
RATE OF INCREASE	4.58	4.19	4.96

PERCENT OF POPULATION IN AGE GROUP

UNDER 15	23.29	24.04	22.56
15 - 64	64.43	65.10	63.78
65 AND OLDER	12.27	10.86	13.66

RATES STANDARDIZED ON USA 1980

Per Thousand	BOTH SEXES	MALES	FEMALES
BIRTH RATE	16.95		16.03
DEATH RATE	9.42	9.50	9.35
RATE OF INCREASE	7.53		6.68

RATES STANDARDIZED ON MEXICO 1980

	BOTH SEXES	MALES	FEMALES
BIRTH RATE	15.23		14.92
DEATH RATE	3.71	4.25	3.15
RATE OF INCREASE	11.52		11.77

VITAL STATISTICS

GFR x 1000	61.431
TFR	1.967
GRR	0.956
NRR	0.935
μ	26.672
σ^2	29.781
GENERATION	26.710
POP. SEX RATIO	1.015
SEX RATIO AT BIRTH	1.057
DEP. RATIO x 100	55.199

PROJECTED POPULATION

AGE GROUP	1975			1980			STABLE EQUIVALENT TO ORIGINAL POPULATION				AGE GROUP
							MALES		FEMALES		
	BOTH SEXES	MALES	FEMALES	BOTH SEXES	MALES	FEMALES	Number	Percent	Number	Percent	
0-4	354	181	173	357	183	174	191	6.3	181	5.9	0-4
5-9	386	198	188	353	181	172	192	6.4	183	6.0	5-9
10-14	391	200	191	386	198	188	194	6.5	185	6.0	10-14
15-19	367	188	179	390	199	191	196	6.5	187	6.1	15-19
20-24	371	190	181	366	187	179	198	6.6	189	6.2	20-24
25-29	414	213	201	369	189	180	199	6.6	191	6.2	25-29
30-34	374	192	182	413	212	201	201	6.7	193	6.3	30-34
35-39	300	152	148	371	190	181	202	6.7	194	6.3	35-39
40-44	276	138	138	297	150	147	202	6.7	195	6.4	40-44
45-49	281	139	142	272	136	136	200	6.7	195	6.3	45-49
50-54	298	146	152	274	135	139	197	6.5	193	6.3	50-54
55-59	277	135	142	286	139	147	189	6.3	190	6.2	55-59
60-64	269	129	140	260	125	135	177	5.9	183	6.0	60-64
65-69	238	110	128	243	113	130	157	5.2	172	5.6	65-69
70-74	185	81	104	202	89	113	128	4.2	154	5.0	70-74
75-79	131	54	77	142	58	84	93	3.1	125	4.1	75-79
80-84	76	30	46	86	33	53	58	1.9	88	2.9	80-84
85+	50	18	32	58	20	38	40	1.3	73	2.4	85+
TOTAL	5038	2494	2544	5125	2537	2588	3014		3071		TOTAL

TABLE 5

POPULATION PROJECTED WITH FIXED AGE-SPECIFIC BIRTH AND DEATH RATES (female dominant, in 000s)

VITAL RATES OF PROJECTED POPULATION

Per Thousand	1975			1980			VITAL RATES OF STABLE POPULATION	
	BOTH SEXES	MALES	FEMALES	BOTH SEXES	MALES	FEMALES	MALES	FEMALES
BIRTH RATE	14.46	15.00	13.93	14.11	14.64	13.58	12.81	11.88
DEATH RATE	10.72	11.34	10.11	11.35	11.79	10.91	15.26	14.39
RATE OF INCREASE	3.73	3.65	3.81	2.76	2.85	2.67		-2.51

AGE STRUCTURE OF PROJECTED POPULATION / STABLE AGE STRUCTURE

	1975 BOTH SEXES	MALES	FEMALES	1980 BOTH SEXES	MALES	FEMALES	STABLE MALES	FEMALES
% UNDER 15	22.46	23.22	21.71	21.38	22.13	20.65	19.16	17.91
% 15-64	64.06	65.03	63.10	64.35	65.51	63.22	65.06	62.20
% 65 AND OLDER	13.49	11.76	15.18	14.27	12.36	16.13	15.78	19.89
DEPEND. RATIO x 100	56.12	53.79	58.47	55.39	52.65	58.18	53.71	60.77

TABLE 6

PROJECTED VITAL RATES AND RATIOS (female dominant)

AGE GROUP	FEMALE BIRTH RATES	NET MATERNITY FUNCTION	COEFF. OF MATRIX EQUATION	ORIGINAL MATRIX SUB-DIAGONAL	FIRST ROW	STABLE MATRIX FISHER VALUES	REPRODUCTIVE VALUES	MATRIX PARAMETERS	
0-4	0.0000	0.0000	0.0000	0.99779	0.00000	1.006	189698	λ_1	0.98753
5-9	0.0000	0.0000	0.0001	0.99849	0.00007	0.995	190825	λ_2	$0.33389+0.74423i$
10-14	0.0000	0.0001	0.0388	0.99833	0.03890	0.984	176817	λ_4	$-0.35163+0.39019i$
15-19	0.0157	0.0774	0.1956	0.99754	0.19671	0.935	169482	λ_6	$-0.05811+0.40466i$
20-24	0.0640	0.3139	0.3145	0.99751	0.31694	0.727	146690	r_1	-0.00251
25-29	0.0644	0.3150	0.2360	0.99668	0.23848	0.400	73031	r_2	$-0.04074+0.22981i$
30-34	0.0322	0.1571	0.1077	0.99464	0.10919	0.156	23168	r_4	$-0.12878+0.46085i$
35-39	0.0120	0.0584	0.0355	0.99154	0.03617	0.044	6160	r_6	$-0.17890+0.34269i$
40-44	0.0026	0.0126	0.0066	0.98691	0.00683	0.007	1050	c_1	30731
45-49	0.0001	0.0007	0.0003	0.97827	0.00036	0.000	56	$2\pi/y$	27.3402
50-54	0.0000	0.0000	0.0000	0.00000	0.00000	0.000	0	Δ	8.9540

TABLE 7

LESLIE MATRIX AND ITS ANALYSIS (females)

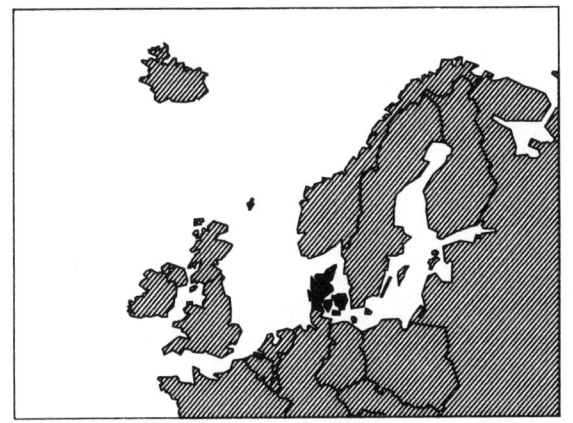

EDUCATION [1984]

% of primary school-age children enrolled:	101
secondary school-age children enrolled:	104
ca. 20-24 year olds in higher education:	29

LABOR FORCE

Average annual labor force growth (%) 1980-85:	0.6
% of the 1980 labor force in agriculture:	7
in industry:	32
in services:	61

GNP & INCOME DISTRIBUTION

GNP per capita (in US Dollars) 1985:	11200
GNP average annual growth rate (%) 1965-85:	1.8
% share of total household income 1981	
Lowest 20% of households:	5.4
Highest 10% of households:	22.3

HEALTH & NUTRITION

Population per physician 1981:	420
Daily calorie supply per capita 1985:	3547

TABLE 8

SOCIO-ECONOMIC INDICATORS

TABLE 1 — DATA

AGE AT LAST BIRTHDAY	ESTIMATED MID-YEAR POPULATION BOTH SEXES	MALES Number	MALES Percent	FEMALES Number	FEMALES Percent	BIRTHS BY AGE OF MOTHER AND SEX	DEATHS BOTH SEXES	DEATHS MALES	DEATHS FEMALES	AGE AT LAST BIRTHDAY
0	70601	36030	1.4	34571	1.4		746	435	311	0
1-4	291204	148948	5.9	142256	5.6		164	101	63	1-4
5-9	388551	199224	8.0	189327	7.4		170	95	75	5-9
10-14	393077	200980	8.0	192097	7.5	13	128	83	45	10-14
15-19	369725	189875	7.6	179850	7.0	4826	225	169	56	15-19
20-24	374969	192245	7.7	182724	7.2	24980	302	234	68	20-24
25-29	415701	213842	8.5	201859	7.9	27447	339	244	95	25-29
30-34	374537	191920	7.7	182617	7.1	11614	338	216	122	30-34
35-39	301229	152539	6.1	148690	5.8	2705	465	281	184	35-39
40-44	276919	138339	5.5	138580	5.4	465	699	413	286	40-44
45-49	280706	139101	5.6	141605	5.5	20	1140	638	502	45-49
50-54	298267	146359	5.8	151908	5.9	1	2010	1225	785	50-54
55-59	277184	135499	5.4	141685	5.5		2773	1710	1063	55-59
60-64	269634	129261	5.2	140373	5.5		4197	2665	1532	60-64
65-69	238647	110102	4.4	128545	5.0		5846	3642	2204	65-69
70-74	186145	80977	3.2	105168	4.1		7233	4249	2984	70-74
75-79	131244	53490	2.1	77754	3.0		8212	4270	3942	75-79
80-84	76680	30042	1.2	46638	1.8	36811 M	7503	3542	3961	80-84
85+	44841	16757	0.7	28084	1.1	35260 F	8405	3556	4849	85+
TOTAL	5059861	2505530		2554331		72071	50895	27768	23127	TOTAL

TABLE 2 — MALE LIFE TABLE

x	$_nM_x$	$_nq_x$	l_x	$_nd_x$	$_nL_x$	$_nm_x$	$_na_x$	T_x	$\overset{\circ}{e}_x$	x
0	0.012073	0.011942	100000	1194	98914	0.012073	0.091	7130658	71.307	0
1	0.000678	0.002708	98806	268	394554	0.000678	1.500	7031744	71.167	1
5	0.000477	0.002381	98538	235	492105	0.000477	2.500	6637189	67.356	5
10	0.000413	0.002064	98304	203	491053	0.000413	2.707	6145085	62.511	10
15	0.000890	0.004445	98101	436	489494	0.000891	2.686	5654032	57.635	15
20	0.001217	0.006068	97665	593	486866	0.001217	2.541	5164538	52.880	20
25	0.001141	0.005689	97072	552	483969	0.001141	2.481	4677672	48.188	25
30	0.001125	0.005626	96520	543	481311	0.001128	2.628	4193702	43.449	30
35	0.001842	0.009231	95977	886	477850	0.001854	2.705	3712391	38.680	35
40	0.002985	0.014864	95091	1413	472179	0.002993	2.683	3234541	34.015	40
45	0.004587	0.022697	93677	2126	463560	0.004587	2.730	2762362	29.488	45
50	0.008370	0.041052	91551	3758	449038	0.008370	2.680	2298802	25.109	50
55	0.012620	0.061296	87793	5381	426416	0.012620	2.668	1849764	21.070	55
60	0.020617	0.098332	82411	8104	393054	0.020617	2.655	1423348	17.271	60
65	0.033078	0.153547	74308	11410	344383	0.033131	2.620	1030294	13.865	65
70	0.052472	0.233235	62898	14670	278793	0.052620	2.567	685911	10.905	70
75	0.079828	0.333837	48228	16100	200865	0.080155	2.498	407118	8.442	75
80	0.117902	0.452990	32128	14554	123438	0.117902	2.444	206253	6.420	80
85	0.212210	1.000000	17574	17574	82815	0.147069	4.712	82815	4.712	85

TABLE 3 — FEMALE LIFE TABLE

x	$_nM_x$	$_nq_x$	l_x	$_nd_x$	$_nL_x$	$_nm_x$	$_na_x$	T_x	$\overset{\circ}{e}_x$	x
0	0.008996	0.008923	100000	892	99184	0.008996	0.085	7714087	77.141	0
1	0.000443	0.001769	99108	175	395993	0.000443	1.500	7614903	76.835	1
5	0.000396	0.001979	98932	196	494172	0.000396	2.500	7218911	72.968	5
10	0.000234	0.001170	98737	116	493385	0.000234	2.424	6724738	68.108	10
15	0.000311	0.001557	98621	154	492736	0.000312	2.591	6231353	63.185	15
20	0.000372	0.001859	98468	183	491896	0.000372	2.588	5738617	58.279	20
25	0.000471	0.002350	98285	231	490875	0.000471	2.631	5246721	53.383	25
30	0.000668	0.003351	98053	329	489524	0.000671	2.738	4755845	48.503	30
35	0.001237	0.006210	97725	607	487247	0.001246	2.730	4266321	43.656	35
40	0.002064	0.010294	97118	1000	483316	0.002068	2.726	3779074	38.912	40
45	0.003545	0.017580	96118	1690	476661	0.003545	2.674	3295757	34.289	45
50	0.005168	0.025528	94429	2411	466471	0.005168	2.647	2819096	29.854	50
55	0.007503	0.036862	92018	3392	452090	0.007503	2.642	2352625	25.567	55
60	0.010914	0.053208	88626	4716	432077	0.010914	2.656	1900535	21.444	60
65	0.017146	0.082542	83910	6926	403394	0.017170	2.667	1468458	17.500	65
70	0.028374	0.133418	76984	10271	360964	0.028455	2.667	1065064	13.835	70
75	0.050698	0.227591	66713	15183	297243	0.051080	2.608	704100	10.554	75
80	0.084931	0.351658	51530	18121	213361	0.084931	2.556	406856	7.896	80
85	0.172661	1.000000	33409	33409	193495	0.103620	5.792	193495	5.792	85

TABLE 4 — OBSERVED VITAL RATES AND RATIOS

CRUDE RATES

Per Thousand	BOTH SEXES	MALES	FEMALES
BIRTH RATE	14.24	14.69	13.80
DEATH RATE	10.06	11.08	9.05
RATE OF INCREASE	4.19	3.61	4.75

PERCENT OF POPULATION IN AGE GROUP

	BOTH SEXES	MALES	FEMALES
UNDER 15	22.60	23.36	21.86
15 - 64	64.01	65.02	63.03
65 AND OLDER	13.39	11.63	15.12

RATES STANDARDIZED ON USA 1980

Per Thousand	BOTH SEXES	MALES	FEMALES
BIRTH RATE	16.71		15.90
DEATH RATE	8.97	9.41	8.55
RATE OF INCREASE	7.75		7.35

RATES STANDARDIZED ON MEXICO 1980

	BOTH SEXES	MALES	FEMALES
BIRTH RATE	14.99		14.78
DEATH RATE	3.48	4.09	2.85
RATE OF INCREASE	11.51		11.93

VITAL STATISTICS

GFR x 1000	61.289
TFR	1.924
GRR	0.941
NRR	0.924
μ	26.447
σ^2	25.723
GENERATION	26.485
POP. SEX RATIO	1.019
SEX RATIO AT BIRTH	1.044
DEP. RATIO x 100	56.223

AGE AT LAST BIRTHDAY	ESTIMATED MID-YEAR POPULATION					BIRTHS BY AGE OF MOTHER AND SEX	DEATHS			AGE AT LAST BIRTHDAY
	BOTH SEXES	MALES		FEMALES			BOTH SEXES	MALES	FEMALES	
		Number	Percent	Number	Percent					
0	58200	29777	1.2	28423	1.1		484	274	210	0
1-4	255762	130863	5.2	124899	4.8		124	73	51	1-4
5-9	364091	185962	7.4	178129	6.9		80	51	29	5-9
10-14	390097	199958	7.9	190139	7.3	5	84	50	34	10-14
15-19	395539	202291	8.0	193248	7.4	3142	264	179	85	15-19
20-24	371658	190163	7.5	181495	7.0	18467	314	236	78	20-24
25-29	373793	191442	7.6	182351	7.0	21498	367	267	100	25-29
30-34	413322	211792	8.4	201530	7.8	10830	453	295	158	30-34
35-39	372721	190543	7.5	182178	7.0	2967	626	385	241	35-39
40-44	298587	150770	6.0	147817	5.7	367	778	451	327	40-44
45-49	272434	135634	5.4	136800	5.3	17	1150	651	499	45-49
50-54	273268	134603	5.3	138665	5.3		1824	1090	734	50-54
55-59	285799	138653	5.5	147146	5.7		3016	1886	1130	55-59
60-64	259662	124456	4.9	135206	5.2		4281	2736	1545	60-64
65-69	244339	113244	4.5	131095	5.1		6031	3806	2225	65-69
70-74	203946	88931	3.5	115015	4.4		8022	4816	3206	70-74
75-79	145520	58112	2.3	87408	3.4		8974	4884	4090	75-79
80-84	88782	32529	1.3	56253	2.2	29352 M	8671	3964	4707	80-84
85+	55507	18916	0.7	36591	1.4	27941 F	10396	4099	6297	85+
TOTAL	5123027	2528639		2594388		57293	55939	30193	25746	TOTAL

TABLE 1 DATA

x	$_nM_x$	$_nq_x$	l_x	$_nd_x$	$_nL_x$	$_nm_x$	$_na_x$	T_x	$\overset{\circ}{e}_x$	x
0	0.009202	0.009125	100000	912	99166	0.009202	0.086	7118105	71.181	0
1	0.000558	0.002228	99088	221	395798	0.000558	1.500	7018939	70.836	1
5	0.000274	0.001370	98867	135	493995	0.000274	2.500	6623141	66.991	5
10	0.000250	0.001250	98731	123	493410	0.000250	3.007	6129146	62.079	10
15	0.000885	0.004418	98608	436	492051	0.000885	2.732	5635736	57.153	15
20	0.001241	0.006189	98172	608	489392	0.001242	2.583	5143685	52.395	20
25	0.001395	0.006949	97565	678	486141	0.001395	2.520	4654292	47.705	25
30	0.001393	0.006941	96887	673	482813	0.001393	2.591	4168151	43.021	30
35	0.002021	0.010092	96214	971	478799	0.002028	2.661	3685338	38.304	35
40	0.002991	0.014939	95243	1423	472921	0.003009	2.685	3206539	33.667	40
45	0.004800	0.023809	93820	2234	463979	0.004814	2.707	2733618	29.137	45
50	0.008098	0.039750	91586	3641	449573	0.008098	2.704	2269639	24.781	50
55	0.013602	0.065929	87946	5798	426264	0.013602	2.678	1820065	20.695	55
60	0.021984	0.104490	82148	8584	390456	0.021984	2.637	1393802	16.967	60
65	0.033609	0.155572	73564	11445	340521	0.033609	2.615	1003346	13.639	65
70	0.054154	0.239563	62120	14882	274435	0.054226	2.570	662825	10.670	70
75	0.084045	0.348072	47238	16442	194961	0.084336	2.492	388390	8.222	75
80	0.121860	0.463969	30796	14288	117251	0.121861	2.430	193430	6.281	80
85	0.216695	1.000000	16507	16507	76178	0.152387	4.615	76178	4.615	85

TABLE 2 MALE LIFE TABLE

x	$_nM_x$	$_nq_x$	l_x	$_nd_x$	$_nL_x$	$_nm_x$	$_na_x$	T_x	$\overset{\circ}{e}_x$	x
0	0.007388	0.007339	100000	734	99327	0.007388	0.083	7730920	77.309	0
1	0.000408	0.001632	99266	162	396660	0.000408	1.500	7631593	76.880	1
5	0.000163	0.000814	99104	81	495319	0.000163	2.500	7234934	73.003	5
10	0.000179	0.000894	99024	89	494925	0.000179	2.822	6739615	68.061	10
15	0.000440	0.002198	98935	217	494157	0.000440	2.618	6244690	63.119	15
20	0.000430	0.002147	98718	212	493069	0.000430	2.551	5750532	58.252	20
25	0.000548	0.002738	98506	270	491890	0.000548	2.633	5257463	53.372	25
30	0.000784	0.003913	98236	384	490297	0.000784	2.705	4765573	48.512	30
35	0.001323	0.006625	97852	648	487781	0.001329	2.722	4275276	43.691	35
40	0.002212	0.011071	97203	1076	483553	0.002225	2.712	3787495	38.965	40
45	0.003648	0.018116	96127	1741	476572	0.003654	2.666	3303941	34.371	45
50	0.005293	0.026141	94386	2467	466119	0.005293	2.646	2827370	29.955	50
55	0.007679	0.037716	91918	3467	451436	0.007679	2.647	2361250	25.689	55
60	0.011427	0.055506	88452	4921	430653	0.011427	2.642	1909814	21.592	60
65	0.016972	0.081616	83530	6817	401676	0.016972	2.657	1479161	17.708	65
70	0.027875	0.130946	76713	10045	359969	0.027906	2.651	1077485	14.046	70
75	0.046792	0.211498	66668	14100	299804	0.047031	2.622	717515	10.763	75
80	0.083676	0.347764	52568	18281	218477	0.083676	2.573	417711	7.946	80
85	0.172091	1.000000	34287	34287	199234	0.103082	5.811	199234	5.811	85

TABLE 3 FEMALE LIFE TABLE

CRUDE RATES

Per Thousand	BOTH SEXES	MALES	FEMALES
BIRTH RATE	11.18	11.61	10.77
DEATH RATE	10.92	11.94	9.92
RATE OF INCREASE	0.26	-0.33	0.85

PERCENT OF POPULATION IN AGE GROUP

UNDER 15	20.85	21.61	20.10
15 - 64	64.74	66.06	63.46
65 AND OLDER	14.41	12.33	16.43

RATES STANDARDIZED ON USA 1980

Per Thousand	BOTH SEXES	MALES	FEMALES
BIRTH RATE	13.33		12.64
DEATH RATE	9.05	9.68	8.44
RATE OF INCREASE	4.28		4.20

RATES STANDARDIZED ON MEXICO 1980

	BOTH SEXES	MALES	FEMALES
BIRTH RATE	11.81		11.61
DEATH RATE	3.44	4.09	2.78
RATE OF INCREASE	8.37		8.82

VITAL STATISTICS

GFR x 1000	46.754	TABLE 4
TFR	1.543	
GRR	0.752	OBSERVED
NRR	0.740	VITAL
μ	26.834	RATES
σ^2	24.646	AND
GENERATION	26.972	RATIOS
POP. SEX RATIO	1.026	
SEX RATIO AT BIRTH	1.050	
DEP. RATIO x 100	54.458	

TABLE 1 — DATA

AGE AT LAST BIRTHDAY	ESTIMATED MID-YEAR POPULATION BOTH SEXES	MALES Number	MALES Percent	FEMALES Number	FEMALES Percent	BIRTHS BY AGE OF MOTHER AND SEX	DEATHS BOTH SEXES	DEATHS MALES	DEATHS FEMALES	AGE AT LAST BIRTHDAY
0	52816	26972	1.1	25844	1.0		427	245	182	0
1-4	211948	108129	4.3	103819	4.0		84	47	37	1-4
5-9	314033	160542	6.4	153491	5.9		90	58	32	5-9
10-14	364126	185930	7.4	178196	6.9	5	103	66	37	10-14
15-19	391805	201005	8.0	190800	7.4	1861	229	167	62	15-19
20-24	397633	203726	8.1	193907	7.5	14713	296	220	76	20-24
25-29	371241	190245	7.6	180996	7.0	21369	344	264	80	25-29
30-34	371318	189759	7.5	181559	7.0	11630	411	277	134	30-34
35-39	410211	209659	8.3	200552	7.7	3611	632	387	245	35-39
40-44	368843	188020	7.5	180823	7.0	542	836	501	335	40-44
45-49	293676	147745	5.9	145931	5.6	18	1183	703	480	45-49
50-54	265132	131281	5.2	133851	5.2		1810	1066	744	50-54
55-59	261926	127736	5.1	134190	5.2		2792	1689	1103	55-59
60-64	267488	127189	5.0	140299	5.4		4371	2718	1653	60-64
65-69	234775	108762	4.3	126013	4.9		5727	3649	2078	65-69
70-74	209882	92185	3.7	117697	4.5		7998	4676	3322	70-74
75-79	160478	63965	2.5	96513	3.7		9404	5118	4286	75-79
80-84	99485	35128	1.4	64357	2.5	27498 M	9292	4247	5045	80-84
85+	66875	20840	0.8	46035	1.8	26251 F	12349	4435	7914	85+
TOTAL	5113691	2518818		2594873		53749	58378	30533	27845	TOTAL

TABLE 2 — MALE LIFE TABLE

x	$_nM_x$	$_nq_x$	l_x	$_nd_x$	$_nL_x$	$_nm_x$	$_na_x$	T_x	$\overset{\circ}{e}_x$	x
0	0.009083	0.009009	100000	901	99176	0.009084	0.085	7152877	71.529	0
1	0.000435	0.001737	99099	172	395966	0.000435	1.500	7053701	71.178	1
5	0.000361	0.001805	98927	179	494189	0.000361	2.500	6657735	67.299	5
10	0.000355	0.001773	98748	175	493353	0.000355	2.774	6163546	62.417	10
15	0.000831	0.004146	98573	409	491919	0.000831	2.680	5670193	57.523	15
20	0.001080	0.005387	98165	529	489557	0.001080	2.605	5178275	52.751	20
25	0.001388	0.006918	97636	675	486527	0.001388	2.554	4688718	48.022	25
30	0.001460	0.007273	96960	705	483083	0.001460	2.562	4202190	43.339	30
35	0.001846	0.009189	96255	885	479183	0.001846	2.633	3719107	38.638	35
40	0.002665	0.013306	95371	1269	473962	0.002678	2.721	3239925	33.972	40
45	0.004758	0.023708	94102	2231	465432	0.004793	2.724	2765963	29.393	45
50	0.008120	0.039971	91871	3672	450887	0.008144	2.694	2300531	25.041	50
55	0.013223	0.064140	88199	5657	427834	0.013223	2.674	1849644	20.971	55
60	0.021370	0.101730	82541	8397	392935	0.021370	2.645	1421810	17.225	60
65	0.033550	0.155270	74145	11512	343138	0.033550	2.604	1028875	13.877	65
70	0.050724	0.225783	62632	14141	278788	0.050724	2.569	685736	10.949	70
75	0.080013	0.334451	48491	16218	202068	0.080259	2.510	406948	8.392	75
80	0.120901	0.461712	32273	14901	123249	0.120901	2.442	204880	6.348	80
85	0.212812	1.000000	17372	17372	81632	0.147843	4.699	81632	4.699	85

TABLE 3 — FEMALE LIFE TABLE

x	$_nM_x$	$_nq_x$	l_x	$_nd_x$	$_nL_x$	$_nm_x$	$_na_x$	T_x	$\overset{\circ}{e}_x$	x
0	0.007042	0.006997	100000	700	99358	0.007042	0.082	7759288	77.593	0
1	0.000356	0.001424	99300	141	396848	0.000356	1.500	7659930	77.139	1
5	0.000208	0.001042	99159	103	495536	0.000208	2.500	7263083	73.247	5
10	0.000208	0.001038	99056	103	495033	0.000208	2.616	6767547	68.321	10
15	0.000325	0.001623	98953	161	494381	0.000325	2.618	6272514	63.389	15
20	0.000392	0.001958	98792	193	493489	0.000392	2.562	5778133	58.488	20
25	0.000442	0.002210	98599	218	492484	0.000442	2.661	5284644	53.598	25
30	0.000738	0.003684	98381	362	491077	0.000738	2.718	4792161	48.710	30
35	0.001222	0.006091	98018	597	488712	0.001222	2.689	4301084	43.880	35
40	0.001853	0.009271	97421	903	485055	0.001862	2.728	3812373	39.133	40
45	0.003289	0.016444	96518	1587	478978	0.003314	2.724	3327318	34.474	45
50	0.005558	0.027492	94931	2610	468575	0.005570	2.670	2848340	30.004	50
55	0.008220	0.040316	92321	3722	452815	0.008220	2.638	2379765	25.777	55
60	0.011782	0.057303	88599	5077	430909	0.011782	2.619	1926951	21.749	60
65	0.016490	0.079389	83522	6631	402096	0.016490	2.660	1496041	17.912	65
70	0.028225	0.132309	76891	10173	360440	0.028225	2.639	1093946	14.227	70
75	0.044409	0.201254	66718	13427	301564	0.044525	2.615	733506	10.994	75
80	0.078391	0.329767	53291	17574	224178	0.078391	2.594	431942	8.105	80
85	0.171913	1.000000	35717	35717	207764	0.102941	5.817	207764	5.817	85

TABLE 4 — OBSERVED VITAL RATES AND RATIOS

CRUDE RATES

Per Thousand	BOTH SEXES	MALES	FEMALES
BIRTH RATE	10.51	10.92	10.12
DEATH RATE	11.42	12.12	10.73
RATE OF INCREASE	-0.91	-1.20	-0.61

PERCENT OF POPULATION IN AGE GROUP

	BOTH SEXES	MALES	FEMALES
UNDER 15	18.44	19.12	17.78
15 - 64	66.47	68.14	64.86
65 AND OLDER	15.09	12.74	17.37

RATES STANDARDIZED ON USA 1980

Per Thousand	BOTH SEXES	MALES	FEMALES
BIRTH RATE	12.29		11.68
DEATH RATE	8.82	9.41	8.27
RATE OF INCREASE	3.47		3.40

RATES STANDARDIZED ON MEXICO 1980

	BOTH SEXES	MALES	FEMALES
BIRTH RATE	10.64		10.48
DEATH RATE	3.35	3.98	2.70
RATE OF INCREASE	7.29		7.77

VITAL STATISTICS

GFR x 1000	42.170
TFR	1.445
GRR	0.706
NRR	0.694
μ	27.729
σ^2	24.130
GENERATION	27.887
POP. SEX RATIO	1.030
SEX RATIO AT BIRTH	1.048
DEP. RATIO x 100	50.435

PROJECTED POPULATION

AGE GROUP	1990 BOTH SEXES	1990 MALES	1990 FEMALES	1995 BOTH SEXES	1995 MALES	1995 FEMALES
0-4	268	137	131	268	137	131
5-9	264	135	129	268	137	131
10-14	313	160	153	264	135	129
15-19	363	185	178	313	160	153
20-24	390	200	190	363	185	178
25-29	396	202	194	389	199	190
30-34	369	189	180	394	201	193
35-39	369	188	181	367	187	180
40-44	406	207	199	365	186	179
45-49	364	185	179	401	204	197
50-54	286	143	143	354	179	175
55-59	254	125	129	274	136	138
60-64	245	117	128	237	114	123
65-69	242	111	131	221	102	119
70-74	201	88	113	207	90	117
75-79	165	67	98	159	64	95
80-84	111	39	72	114	41	73
85+	83	23	60	92	26	66
TOTAL	5089	2501	2588	5050	2483	2567

STABLE EQUIVALENT TO ORIGINAL POPULATION

MALES Number	MALES Percent	FEMALES Number	FEMALES Percent	AGE GROUP	
151	4.2	145	3.7	0-4	
161	4.5	155	4.0	5-9	TABLE 5
172	4.7	165	4.2	10-14	
183	5.1	176	4.5	15-19	POPULATION
194	5.4	187	4.8	20-24	PROJECTED
206	5.7	199	5.1	25-29	WITH
219	6.0	212	5.4	30-34	FIXED
232	6.4	225	5.8	35-39	AGE-
244	6.7	239	6.1	40-44	SPECIFIC
256	7.1	252	6.4	45-49	BIRTH
265	7.3	263	6.7	50-54	AND
268	7.4	271	6.9	55-59	DEATH
263	7.3	275	7.1	60-64	RATES
245	6.8	274	7.0	65-69	(female
213	5.9	263	6.7	70-74	dominant,
165	4.5	234	6.0	75-79	in 000s)
107	3.0	186	4.8	80-84	
76	2.1	184	4.7	85+	
3620		3905		TOTAL	

VITAL RATES OF PROJECTED POPULATION

Per Thousand	1990 BOTH SEXES	1990 MALES	1990 FEMALES	1995 BOTH SEXES	1995 MALES	1995 FEMALES
BIRTH RATE	10.70	11.13	10.28	10.61	11.04	10.19
DEATH RATE	12.26	12.64	11.89	12.75	13.04	12.47
RATE OF INCREASE	-1.56	-1.51	-1.61	-2.14	-2.00	-2.28

AGE STRUCTURE OF PROJECTED POPULATION

	1990 BOTH SEXES	1990 MALES	1990 FEMALES	1995 BOTH SEXES	1995 MALES	1995 FEMALES
% UNDER 15	16.62	17.27	15.99	15.83	16.45	15.24
% 15-64	67.62	69.61	65.70	68.44	70.52	66.42
% 65 AND OLDER	15.76	13.13	18.30	15.73	13.03	18.34
DEPEND. RATIO x 100	47.88	43.67	52.20	46.12	41.80	50.55

VITAL RATES OF STABLE POPULATION

Per Thousand	MALES	FEMALES	
BIRTH RATE	8.17	7.23	TABLE 6
DEATH RATE	21.07	20.29	PROJECTED
RATE OF INCREASE		-13.05	VITAL RATES AND RATIOS (female dominant)

STABLE AGE STRUCTURE

	MALES	FEMALES
% UNDER 15	13.39	11.89
% 15-64	64.37	58.89
% 65 AND OLDER	22.24	29.23
DEPEND. RATIO x 100	55.35	69.82

AGE GROUP	FEMALE BIRTH RATES	NET MATERNITY FUNCTION	COEFF. OF MATRIX EQUATION	ORIGINAL MATRIX SUB-DIAGONAL	ORIGINAL MATRIX FIRST ROW	STABLE MATRIX FISHER VALUES	STABLE MATRIX REPRODUCTIVE VALUES
0-4	0.0000	0.0000	0.0000	0.99865	0.00000	0.975	126450
5-9	0.0000	0.0000	0.0000	0.99898	0.00003	0.915	140418
10-14	0.0000	0.0001	0.0118	0.99868	0.01184	0.858	152867
15-19	0.0048	0.0236	0.1032	0.99820	0.10360	0.793	151334
20-24	0.0371	0.1829	0.2334	0.99796	0.23471	0.643	124715
25-29	0.0577	0.2840	0.2188	0.99714	0.22046	0.374	67764
30-34	0.0313	0.1536	0.0983	0.99518	0.09933	0.136	24716
35-39	0.0088	0.0430	0.0250	0.99252	0.02542	0.031	6178
40-44	0.0015	0.0071	0.0037	0.98747	0.00378	0.004	741
45-49	0.0001	0.0003	0.0001	0.97828	0.00015	0.000	23
50-54	0.0000	0.0000	0.0000	0.00000	0.00000	0.000	0

MATRIX PARAMETERS

λ_1	0.93681	
λ_2	$0.37269+0.72772i$	TABLE 7
λ_4	$-0.28453-0.48452i$	
λ_6	$-0.39280+0.07995i$	LESLIE
r_1	-0.01305	MATRIX
r_2	$-0.04027+0.21950i$	AND ITS
r_4	$-0.11529-0.42036i$	ANALYSIS
r_6	$-0.18283+0.58816i$	(females)
c_1	39057	
$2\pi/\gamma$	28.6252	
Δ	17.6758	

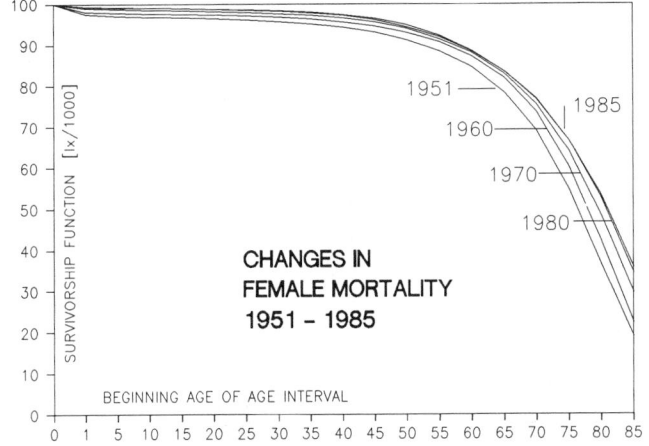

CHANGES IN FEMALE MORTALITY 1951 - 1985

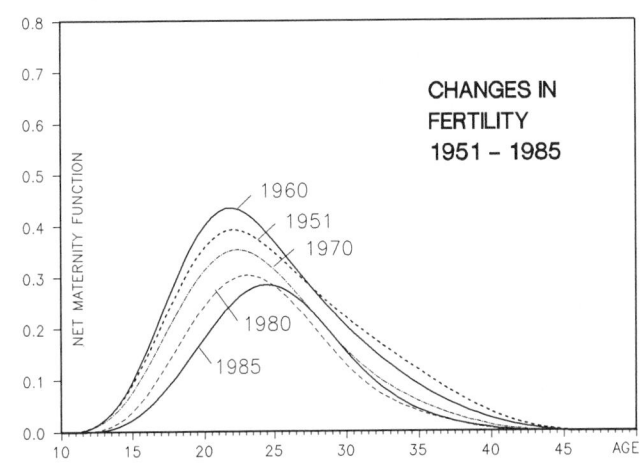

CHANGES IN FERTILITY 1951 - 1985

TABLE 1 — DATA

AGE AT LAST BIRTHDAY	ESTIMATED MID-YEAR POPULATION — BOTH SEXES	MALES Number	MALES Percent	FEMALES Number	FEMALES Percent	BIRTHS BY AGE OF MOTHER AND SEX	DEATHS BOTH SEXES	DEATHS MALES	DEATHS FEMALES	AGE AT LAST BIRTHDAY
0	62905	32164	1.4	30741	1.3		854	483	371	0
1-4	284842	145229	6.5	139613	5.9		211	133	78	1-4
5-9	384263	196029	8.8	188234	7.9		192	126	66	5-9
10-14	402007	205098	9.2	196909	8.3	2	142	97	45	10-14
15-19	426135	218178	9.8	207957	8.7	6686	357	270	87	15-19
20-24	447159	229782	10.3	217377	9.1	25965	467	356	111	20-24
25-29	319071	162946	7.3	156125	6.6	16948	348	269	79	25-29
30-34	290831	147146	6.6	143685	6.0	9286	460	344	116	30-34
35-39	277438	140224	6.3	137214	5.8	4183	693	528	165	35-39
40-44	294371	146191	6.6	148180	6.2	1372	1052	776	276	40-44
45-49	278927	129441	5.8	149486	6.3	116	1585	1124	461	45-49
50-54	235844	105235	4.7	130609	5.5	1	2066	1391	675	50-54
55-59	250179	111078	5.0	139101	5.8		3350	2316	1034	55-59
60-64	230851	99459	4.5	131392	5.5		4898	3174	1724	60-64
65-69	175431	71304	3.2	104127	4.4		5738	3363	2375	65-69
70-74	122925	45394	2.0	77531	3.3		6575	3361	3214	70-74
75-79	71775	24605	1.1	47170	2.0		6265	2642	3623	75-79
80-84	35878	11229	0.5	24649	1.0	33014 M	5094	1881	3213	80-84
85+	15488	4377	0.2	11111	0.5	31545 F	3772	1163	2609	85+
TOTAL	4606320	2225109		2381211		64559	44119	23797	20322	TOTAL

TABLE 2 — MALE LIFE TABLE

x	nM_x	nq_x	l_x	nd_x	nL_x	nm_x	na_x	T_x	$\overset{\circ}{e}_x$	x
0	0.015017	0.014816	100000	1482	98660	0.015017	0.096	6614864	66.149	0
1	0.000916	0.003655	98518	360	393174	0.000916	1.500	6516204	66.142	1
5	0.000643	0.003209	98158	315	490005	0.000643	2.500	6123030	62.379	5
10	0.000473	0.002362	97843	231	488699	0.000473	2.759	5633026	57.572	10
15	0.001238	0.006170	97612	602	486664	0.001238	2.679	5144327	52.702	15
20	0.001549	0.007725	97010	749	483216	0.001551	2.553	4657663	48.012	20
25	0.001651	0.008242	96261	793	479395	0.001655	2.596	4174446	43.366	25
30	0.002338	0.011671	95467	1114	474752	0.002347	2.681	3695051	38.705	30
35	0.003765	0.018670	94353	1762	467635	0.003767	2.655	3220298	34.130	35
40	0.005308	0.026218	92591	2428	457324	0.005308	2.679	2752663	29.729	40
45	0.008683	0.042728	90164	3853	441837	0.008719	2.668	2295339	25.457	45
50	0.013218	0.064183	86311	5540	418577	0.013235	2.657	1853502	21.475	50
55	0.020850	0.099354	80772	8025	384890	0.020850	2.636	1434925	17.765	55
60	0.031913	0.148344	72747	10792	337823	0.031944	2.599	1050035	14.434	60
65	0.047164	0.212329	61955	13155	277540	0.047348	2.572	712211	11.496	65
70	0.074041	0.314146	48800	15330	205885	0.074461	2.514	434377	8.901	70
75	0.107377	0.423088	33470	14161	131089	0.108024	2.439	228492	6.827	75
80	0.167513	0.580574	19309	11210	66923	0.167513	2.358	97403	5.044	80
85	0.265707	1.000000	8099	8099	30480	0.213061	3.764	30480	3.764	85

TABLE 3 — FEMALE LIFE TABLE

x	nM_x	nq_x	l_x	nd_x	nL_x	nm_x	na_x	T_x	$\overset{\circ}{e}_x$	x
0	0.012069	0.011938	100000	1194	98914	0.012069	0.091	7441785	74.418	0
1	0.000559	0.002232	98806	221	394674	0.000559	1.500	7342871	74.316	1
5	0.000351	0.001752	98586	173	492497	0.000351	2.500	6948197	70.479	5
10	0.000229	0.001142	98413	112	491791	0.000229	2.561	6455700	65.598	10
15	0.000418	0.002090	98301	205	491019	0.000418	2.640	5963909	60.670	15
20	0.000511	0.002552	98095	250	489859	0.000511	2.535	5472891	55.792	20
25	0.000506	0.002531	97845	248	488636	0.000507	2.621	4983032	50.928	25
30	0.000807	0.004044	97597	395	487070	0.000810	2.677	4494396	46.050	30
35	0.001203	0.005997	97203	583	484660	0.001203	2.679	4007326	41.227	35
40	0.001863	0.009273	96620	896	481043	0.001863	2.706	3522666	36.459	40
45	0.003084	0.015339	95724	1468	475263	0.003089	2.715	3041624	31.775	45
50	0.005168	0.025550	94255	2408	465650	0.005172	2.663	2566361	27.228	50
55	0.007433	0.036543	91847	3356	451520	0.007433	2.701	2100711	22.872	55
60	0.013121	0.063824	88491	5648	429514	0.013149	2.709	1649192	18.637	60
65	0.022809	0.108872	82843	9019	393415	0.022926	2.694	1219678	14.723	65
70	0.041454	0.190199	73824	14041	336202	0.041764	2.656	826262	11.192	70
75	0.076807	0.326403	59782	19513	251310	0.077646	2.560	490061	8.197	75
80	0.130350	0.489357	40269	19706	151178	0.130350	2.454	238751	5.929	80
85	0.234812	1.000000	20563	20563	87573	0.173314	4.259	87573	4.259	85

TABLE 4 — OBSERVED VITAL RATES AND RATIOS

CRUDE RATES

Per Thousand	BOTH SEXES	MALES	FEMALES
BIRTH RATE	14.02	14.84	13.25
DEATH RATE	9.58	10.69	8.53
RATE OF INCREASE	4.44	4.14	4.71

PERCENT OF POPULATION IN AGE GROUP

UNDER 15	24.62	26.00	23.33
15 - 64	66.23	66.95	65.56
65 AND OLDER	9.15	7.05	11.11

RATES STANDARDIZED ON USA 1980

Per Thousand	BOTH SEXES	MALES	FEMALES
BIRTH RATE	15.55		14.78
DEATH RATE	12.57	13.59	11.62
RATE OF INCREASE	2.98		3.16

RATES STANDARDIZED ON MEXICO 1980

	BOTH SEXES	MALES	FEMALES
BIRTH RATE	13.97		13.75
DEATH RATE	4.84	5.97	3.68
RATE OF INCREASE	9.13		10.07

VITAL STATISTICS

GFR x 1000	55.653
TFR	1.827
GRR	0.893
NRR	0.872
μ	27.102
σ^2	36.041
GENERATION	27.192
POP. SEX RATIO	1.070
SEX RATIO AT BIRTH	1.047
DEP. RATIO x 100	50.987

PROJECTED POPULATION

AGE GROUP	1975			1980			STABLE EQUIVALENT TO ORIGINAL POPULATION				AGE GROUP	
							MALES		FEMALES			
	BOTH SEXES	MALES	FEMALES	BOTH SEXES	MALES	FEMALES	Number	Percent	Number	Percent		
0-4	333	170	163	351	179	172	187	6.3	179	5.5	0-4	
5-9	347	177	170	331	169	162	191	6.4	183	5.6	5-9	TABLE 5
10-14	384	196	188	346	176	170	195	6.5	187	5.7	10-14	
15-19	401	204	197	383	195	188	199	6.7	192	5.9	15-19	POPULATION
20-24	424	217	207	399	203	196	203	6.8	196	6.0	20-24	PROJECTED
25-29	445	228	217	422	215	207	206	6.9	201	6.2	25-29	WITH
30-34	317	161	156	442	226	216	209	7.0	205	6.3	30-34	FIXED
35-39	288	145	143	314	159	155	212	7.1	210	6.4	35-39	AGE-
40-44	273	137	136	284	142	142	212	7.1	213	6.5	40-44	SPECIFIC
45-49	287	141	146	267	132	135	210	7.1	216	6.6	45-49	BIRTH
50-54	269	123	146	277	134	143	204	6.9	217	6.7	50-54	AND
55-59	224	97	127	255	113	142	193	6.5	216	6.6	55-59	DEATH
60-64	229	97	132	205	85	120	173	5.8	211	6.5	60-64	RATES
65-69	202	82	120	201	80	121	146	4.9	198	6.1	65-69	(female
70-74	142	53	89	164	61	103	111	3.7	173	5.3	70-74	dominant,
75-79	87	29	58	101	34	67	73	2.4	133	4.1	75-79	in 000s)
80-84	41	13	28	50	15	35	38	1.3	82	2.5	80-84	
85+	19	5	14	22	6	16	18	0.6	49	1.5	85+	
TOTAL	4712	2275	2437	4814	2324	2490	2980		3261		TOTAL	

VITAL RATES OF PROJECTED POPULATION

Per Thousand	1975			1980			VITAL RATES OF STABLE POPULATION		
	BOTH SEXES	MALES	FEMALES	BOTH SEXES	MALES	FEMALES	MALES	FEMALES	TABLE 6
BIRTH RATE	14.95	15.84	14.12	14.97	15.86	14.14	12.57	10.97	
DEATH RATE	10.38	11.31	9.52	11.06	11.82	10.36	17.54	16.01	PROJECTED
RATE OF INCREASE	4.56	4.53	4.60	3.90	4.04	3.78		-5.04	VITAL RATES AND RATIOS

AGE STRUCTURE OF PROJECTED POPULATION / STABLE AGE STRUCTURE

	BOTH SEXES	MALES	FEMALES	BOTH SEXES	MALES	FEMALES	MALES	FEMALES	(female dominant)
% UNDER 15	22.55	23.84	21.36	21.37	22.59	20.24	19.20	16.84	
% 15-64	67.02	68.19	65.93	67.47	69.02	66.03	67.86	63.69	
% 65 AND OLDER	10.42	7.97	12.71	11.15	8.39	13.73	12.94	19.47	
DEPEND. RATIO x 100	49.21	46.65	51.67	48.21	44.89	51.45	47.37	57.02	

AGE GROUP	FEMALE BIRTH RATES	NET MATERNITY FUNCTION	COEFF. OF MATRIX EQUATION	ORIGINAL MATRIX SUB-DIAGONAL	FIRST ROW	STABLE MATRIX FISHER VALUES	REPRODUCTIVE VALUES	MATRIX PARAMETERS		
0-4	0.0000	0.0000	0.0000	0.99779	0.00000	1.000	170405	λ_1	0.97511	
5-9	0.0000	0.0000	0.0000	0.99857	0.00001	0.978	184010	λ_2	0.34218+0.70036i	TABLE 7
10-14	0.0000	0.0000	0.0386	0.99843	0.03872	0.955	187966	λ_4	-0.35132+0.37665i	
15-19	0.0157	0.0771	0.1815	0.99764	0.18247	0.893	185809	λ_6	-0.00184+0.49510i	LESLIE
20-24	0.0584	0.2859	0.2725	0.99750	0.27462	0.690	150069	r_1	-0.00504	MATRIX
25-29	0.0530	0.2592	0.2065	0.99679	0.20859	0.399	62369	r_2	-0.04982+0.22327i	AND ITS
30-34	0.0316	0.1538	0.1130	0.99505	0.11451	0.181	26074	r_4	-0.13269+0.46428i	ANALYSIS
35-39	0.0149	0.0722	0.0470	0.99254	0.04784	0.063	8605	r_6	-0.14060+0.31490i	(females)
40-44	0.0045	0.0218	0.0118	0.98798	0.01209	0.013	1985	c_1	32610	
45-49	0.0004	0.0018	0.0009	0.97977	0.00094	0.001	146	$2\pi/y$	28.1421	
50-54	0.0000	0.0000	0.0000	0.96966	0.00001	0.000	1	Δ	12.8374	

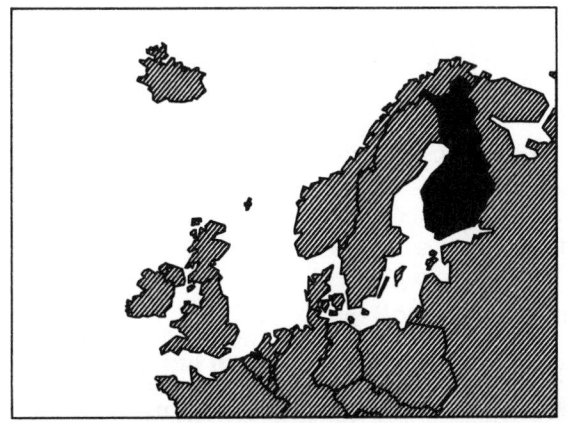

EDUCATION [1984]

% of primary school-age children enrolled:	103
secondary school-age children enrolled:	101
ca. 20-24 year olds in higher education:	31

LABOR FORCE

Average annual labor force growth (%) 1980-85:	0.9
% of the 1980 labor force in agriculture:	12
in industry:	35
in services:	53

TABLE 8

SOCIO-ECONOMIC INDICATORS

GNP & INCOME DISTRIBUTION

GNP per capita (in US Dollars) 1985:	10890
GNP average annual growth rate (%) 1965-85:	3.3
% share of total household income 1981	
Lowest 20% of households:	6.3
Highest 10% of households:	21.7

HEALTH & NUTRITION

Population per physician 1981:	460
Daily calorie supply per capita 1985:	3026

TABLE 1 DATA

AGE AT LAST BIRTHDAY	ESTIMATED MID-YEAR POPULATION BOTH SEXES	MALES Number	MALES Percent	FEMALES Number	FEMALES Percent	BIRTHS BY AGE OF MOTHER AND SEX	DEATHS BOTH SEXES	DEATHS MALES	DEATHS FEMALES	AGE AT LAST BIRTHDAY
0	64001	32764	1.4	31237	1.3		630	373	257	0
1-4	238176	121871	5.4	116305	4.8		159	93	66	1-4
5-9	350297	178716	7.8	171581	7.1		137	85	52	5-9
10-14	384608	196101	8.6	188507	7.7	10	124	80	44	10-14
15-19	398789	203510	8.9	195279	8.0	5366	347	267	80	15-19
20-24	420509	215469	9.5	205040	8.4	21625	491	390	101	20-24
25-29	451071	232311	10.2	218760	9.0	24919	531	426	105	25-29
30-34	322688	165335	7.3	157353	6.5	9380	439	326	113	30-34
35-39	291383	147565	6.5	143818	5.9	3547	621	461	160	35-39
40-44	274954	138493	6.1	136461	5.6	811	933	694	239	40-44
45-49	288804	142134	6.2	146670	6.0	61	1508	1111	397	45-49
50-54	270158	123267	5.4	146891	6.0		2174	1534	640	50-54
55-59	224414	97341	4.3	127073	5.2		2646	1762	884	55-59
60-64	231418	98398	4.3	133020	5.5		4376	2930	1446	60-64
65-69	204015	82477	3.6	121538	5.0		6041	3710	2331	65-69
70-74	144210	53784	2.4	90426	3.7		6610	3499	3111	70-74
75-79	89716	30022	1.3	59694	2.5		6734	2953	3781	75-79
80-84	42606	13090	0.6	29516	1.2	33817 M	5177	1910	3267	80-84
85+	19612	5313	0.2	14299	0.6	31902 F	4150	1297	2853	85+
TOTAL	4711429	2277961		2433468		65719	43828	23901	19927	TOTAL

TABLE 2 MALE LIFE TABLE

x	$_nM_x$	$_nq_x$	l_x	$_nd_x$	$_nL_x$	$_nm_x$	$_na_x$	T_x	$\overset{\circ}{e}_x$	x
0	0.011384	0.011268	100000	1127	98974	0.011384	0.089	6742171	67.422	0
1	0.000763	0.003047	98873	301	394740	0.000763	1.500	6643197	67.189	1
5	0.000476	0.002375	98572	234	492275	0.000476	2.500	6248457	63.390	5
10	0.000408	0.002038	98338	200	491273	0.000408	2.924	5756182	58.535	10
15	0.001312	0.006540	98137	642	489224	0.001312	2.720	5264909	53.648	15
20	0.001810	0.009010	97496	878	485332	0.001810	2.557	4775685	48.984	20
25	0.001834	0.009129	96617	882	480894	0.001834	2.515	4290353	44.406	25
30	0.001972	0.009849	95735	943	476442	0.001979	2.631	3809459	39.792	30
35	0.003124	0.015578	94792	1477	470555	0.003138	2.693	3333017	35.161	35
40	0.005011	0.024788	93316	2313	461215	0.005015	2.682	2862462	30.675	40
45	0.007817	0.038386	91002	3493	446903	0.007817	2.679	2401247	26.387	45
50	0.012445	0.060683	87509	5310	425031	0.012494	2.643	1954343	22.333	50
55	0.018101	0.086945	82199	7147	394195	0.018130	2.649	1529312	18.605	55
60	0.029777	0.139029	75052	10434	350418	0.029777	2.619	1135118	15.124	60
65	0.044982	0.202965	64618	13115	291144	0.045047	2.564	784700	12.144	65
70	0.065057	0.281206	51503	14483	221628	0.065347	2.522	493556	9.583	70
75	0.098361	0.396059	37020	14662	147888	0.099143	2.462	271928	7.346	75
80	0.145913	0.528527	22358	11817	80860	0.146137	2.383	124040	5.548	80
85	0.244118	1.000000	10541	10541	43180	0.185406	4.096	43180	4.096	85

TABLE 3 FEMALE LIFE TABLE

x	$_nM_x$	$_nq_x$	l_x	$_nd_x$	$_nL_x$	$_nm_x$	$_na_x$	T_x	$\overset{\circ}{e}_x$	x
0	0.008227	0.008166	100000	817	99252	0.008227	0.084	7623046	76.230	0
1	0.000567	0.002267	99183	225	396172	0.000567	1.500	7523794	75.857	1
5	0.000303	0.001514	98959	150	494418	0.000303	2.500	7127622	72.026	5
10	0.000233	0.001166	98809	115	493766	0.000233	2.594	6633204	67.132	10
15	0.000410	0.002046	98694	202	492989	0.000410	2.631	6139437	62.207	15
20	0.000493	0.002460	98492	242	491859	0.000493	2.529	5646448	57.329	20
25	0.000480	0.002400	98249	236	490680	0.000481	2.598	5154589	52.464	25
30	0.000718	0.003605	98013	353	489248	0.000722	2.682	4663909	47.584	30
35	0.001113	0.005571	97660	544	487043	0.001117	2.689	4174661	42.747	35
40	0.001751	0.008725	97116	847	483618	0.001752	2.685	3687618	37.971	40
45	0.002707	0.013450	96269	1295	478358	0.002707	2.694	3204000	33.282	45
50	0.004357	0.021604	94974	2052	470133	0.004364	2.692	2725642	28.699	50
55	0.006957	0.034261	92922	3184	457215	0.006963	2.677	2255509	24.273	55
60	0.010871	0.053029	89738	4759	437763	0.010871	2.703	1798293	20.039	60
65	0.019179	0.092092	84980	7826	406918	0.019232	2.702	1360531	16.010	65
70	0.034404	0.160240	77154	12363	356973	0.034633	2.671	953613	12.360	70
75	0.063340	0.277267	64791	17964	280704	0.063997	2.593	596640	9.209	75
80	0.110686	0.434386	46826	20341	183191	0.111035	2.496	315935	6.747	80
85	0.199524	1.000000	26486	26486	132744	0.132129	5.012	132744	5.012	85

TABLE 4 OBSERVED VITAL RATES AND RATIOS

CRUDE RATES

Per Thousand	BOTH SEXES	MALES	FEMALES
BIRTH RATE	13.95	14.85	13.11
DEATH RATE	9.30	10.49	8.19
RATE OF INCREASE	4.65	4.35	4.92

PERCENT OF POPULATION IN AGE GROUP

	BOTH SEXES	MALES	FEMALES
UNDER 15	22.01	23.24	20.86
15 - 64	67.37	68.65	66.18
65 AND OLDER	10.62	8.11	12.96

RATES STANDARDIZED ON USA 1980

Per Thousand	BOTH SEXES	MALES	FEMALES
BIRTH RATE	14.44		13.63
DEATH RATE	11.05	12.36	9.82
RATE OF INCREASE	3.39		3.81

RATES STANDARDIZED ON MEXICO 1980

	BOTH SEXES	MALES	FEMALES
BIRTH RATE	12.91		12.63
DEATH RATE	4.26	5.39	3.11
RATE OF INCREASE	8.65		9.52

VITAL STATISTICS

GFR x 1000	54.612
TFR	1.688
GRR	0.819
NRR	0.804
μ	27.004
σ^2	31.845
GENERATION	27.132
POP. SEX RATIO	1.068
SEX RATIO AT BIRTH	1.060
DEP. RATIO x 100	48.429

AGE AT LAST BIRTHDAY	ESTIMATED MID-YEAR POPULATION					BIRTHS BY AGE OF MOTHER AND SEX	DEATHS			AGE AT LAST BIRTHDAY	
	BOTH SEXES	MALES		FEMALES			BOTH SEXES	MALES	FEMALES		
		Number	Percent	Number	Percent						
0	62821	32056	1.4	30765	1.2		481	271	210	0	
1-4	257428	131727	5.7	125701	5.1		96	60	36	1-4	
5-9	299677	153330	6.6	146347	5.9		70	48	22	5-9	
10-14	350690	178883	7.7	171807	7.0	1	77	47	30	10-14	
15-19	381773	194891	8.4	186882	7.6	3527	229	171	58	15-19	
20-24	384127	196846	8.5	187281	7.6	17135	338	273	65	20-24	
25-29	406636	208748	9.0	197888	8.0	22672	424	329	95	25-29	
30-34	441805	227768	9.9	214037	8.7	14563	589	447	142	30-34	
35-39	317874	162545	7.0	155329	6.3	4216	555	418	137	35-39	TABLE 1
40-44	287189	144868	6.3	142321	5.8	904	771	563	208	40-44	
45-49	269553	134691	5.8	134862	5.5	46	1062	788	274	45-49	DATA
50-54	280084	135837	5.9	144247	5.8		1968	1462	506	50-54	
55-59	258129	114899	5.0	143230	5.8		2720	1910	810	55-59	
60-64	209300	87201	3.8	122099	4.9		3464	2302	1162	60-64	
65-69	207685	83057	3.6	124628	5.0		5455	3408	2047	65-69	
70-74	171425	63539	2.7	107886	4.4		7200	3918	3282	70-74	
75-79	109130	36312	1.6	72818	2.9		7218	3348	3870	75-79	
80-84	57426	16739	0.7	40687	1.6	32349 M	6348	2389	3959	80-84	
85+	26826	6901	0.3	19925	0.8	30715 F	5333	1592	3741	85+	
TOTAL	4779578	2310838		2468740		63064	44398	23744	20654	TOTAL	

x	$_nM_x$	$_nq_x$	l_x	$_nd_x$	$_nL_x$	$_nm_x$	$_na_x$	T_x	$\overset{\circ}{e}_x$	x	
0	0.008454	0.008389	100000	839	99232	0.008454	0.084	6924696	69.247	0	
1	0.000455	0.001820	99161	180	396193	0.000455	1.500	6825464	68.832	1	
5	0.000313	0.001564	98981	155	494516	0.000313	2.500	6429271	64.955	5	
10	0.000263	0.001313	98826	130	493863	0.000263	2.945	5934755	60.053	10	
15	0.000877	0.004378	98696	432	492514	0.000877	2.765	5440893	55.128	15	
20	0.001387	0.006911	98264	679	489691	0.001387	2.602	4948378	50.358	20	
25	0.001576	0.007850	97585	766	486065	0.001576	2.573	4458687	45.690	25	TABLE 2
30	0.001963	0.009780	96819	947	481823	0.001965	2.602	3972622	41.032	30	
35	0.002572	0.012848	95872	1232	476464	0.002585	2.649	3490798	36.411	35	MALE
40	0.003886	0.019342	94640	1830	468929	0.003902	2.665	3014335	31.851	40	LIFE
45	0.005850	0.028906	92810	2683	457950	0.005858	2.725	2545406	27.426	45	TABLE
50	0.010763	0.052506	90128	4732	439678	0.010763	2.684	2087456	23.161	50	
55	0.016623	0.080335	85395	6860	410877	0.016697	2.653	1647778	19.296	55	
60	0.026399	0.124450	78535	9774	369486	0.026452	2.627	1236901	15.750	60	
65	0.041032	0.186661	68761	12835	312807	0.041032	2.585	867414	12.615	65	
70	0.061663	0.268067	55926	14992	242687	0.061775	2.536	554607	9.917	70	
75	0.092201	0.376278	40934	15403	165812	0.092892	2.477	311921	7.620	75	
80	0.142721	0.520806	25532	13297	93074	0.142865	2.399	146109	5.723	80	
85	0.230691	1.000000	12235	12235	53035	0.169041	4.335	53035	4.335	85	

x	$_nM_x$	$_nq_x$	l_x	$_nd_x$	$_nL_x$	$_nm_x$	$_na_x$	T_x	$\overset{\circ}{e}_x$	x	
0	0.006826	0.006783	100000	678	99377	0.006826	0.082	7797306	77.973	0	
1	0.000286	0.001145	99322	114	397002	0.000286	1.500	7697929	77.505	1	
5	0.000150	0.000751	99208	75	495853	0.000150	2.500	7300926	73.592	5	
10	0.000175	0.000873	99133	87	495467	0.000175	2.690	6805073	68.646	10	
15	0.000310	0.001551	99047	154	494868	0.000310	2.615	6309605	63.703	15	
20	0.000347	0.001734	98893	171	494055	0.000347	2.601	5814737	58.798	20	
25	0.000480	0.002398	98722	237	493050	0.000480	2.637	5320682	53.896	25	TABLE 3
30	0.000663	0.003318	98485	327	491650	0.000665	2.626	4827632	49.019	30	
35	0.000882	0.004425	98158	434	489787	0.000887	2.686	4335982	44.173	35	FEMALE
40	0.001461	0.007308	97724	714	486949	0.001467	2.660	3846195	39.358	40	LIFE
45	0.002032	0.010116	97010	981	482795	0.002033	2.703	3359247	34.628	45	TABLE
50	0.003508	0.017399	96029	1671	476311	0.003508	2.707	2876452	29.954	50	
55	0.005655	0.027967	94358	2639	465734	0.005666	2.706	2400141	25.437	55	
60	0.009517	0.046632	91719	4277	448794	0.009530	2.709	1934407	21.091	60	
65	0.016425	0.079156	87442	6922	421403	0.016425	2.716	1485613	16.990	65	
70	0.030421	0.142437	80520	11469	375909	0.030510	2.673	1064209	13.217	70	
75	0.053146	0.237880	69051	16426	306115	0.053659	2.617	688301	9.968	75	
80	0.097304	0.393426	52625	20704	212170	0.097583	2.539	382185	7.262	80	
85	0.187754	1.000000	31921	31921	170016	0.119294	5.326	170016	5.326	85	

CRUDE RATES

Per Thousand	BOTH SEXES	MALES	FEMALES
BIRTH RATE	13.19	14.00	12.44
DEATH RATE	9.29	10.28	8.37
RATE OF INCREASE	3.91	3.72	4.08

PERCENT OF POPULATION IN AGE GROUP

UNDER 15	20.31	21.46	19.23
15 - 64	67.71	69.60	65.95
65 AND OLDER	11.98	8.94	14.82

RATES STANDARDIZED ON USA 1980

Per Thousand	BOTH SEXES	MALES	FEMALES
BIRTH RATE	13.83		13.10
DEATH RATE	9.88	11.22	8.62
RATE OF INCREASE	3.95		4.48

RATES STANDARDIZED ON MEXICO 1980

	BOTH SEXES	MALES	FEMALES
BIRTH RATE	12.14		11.91
DEATH RATE	3.68	4.71	2.63
RATE OF INCREASE	8.46		9.29

VITAL STATISTICS

GFR x 1000	51.751	TABLE 4
TFR	1.634	
GRR	0.796	OBSERVED
NRR	0.784	VITAL
μ	27.689	RATES
σ^2	30.964	AND
GENERATION	27.824	RATIOS
POP. SEX RATIO	1.068	
SEX RATIO AT BIRTH	1.053	
DEP. RATIO x 100	47.679	

TABLE 1 — DATA

AGE AT LAST BIRTHDAY	ESTIMATED MID-YEAR POPULATION BOTH SEXES	MALES Number	MALES Percent	FEMALES Number	FEMALES Percent	BIRTHS BY AGE OF MOTHER AND SEX	DEATHS BOTH SEXES	DEATHS MALES	DEATHS FEMALES	AGE AT LAST BIRTHDAY
0	63749	32501	1.4	31248	1.2		384	207	177	0
1-4	261278	133728	5.6	127550	5.0		83	51	32	1-4
5-9	324057	165608	7.0	158449	6.3		76	46	30	5-9
10-14	302436	154732	6.5	147704	5.8	4	71	49	22	10-14
15-19	350851	178889	7.5	171962	6.8	2370	205	157	48	15-19
20-24	378409	193441	8.2	184968	7.3	14122	282	224	58	20-24
25-29	384538	197053	8.3	187485	7.4	22788	335	262	73	25-29
30-34	408648	209666	8.8	198982	7.9	15383	480	369	111	30-34
35-39	442265	227745	9.6	214520	8.5	7032	743	559	184	35-39
40-44	315991	161111	6.8	154880	6.1	1049	789	587	202	40-44
45-49	283220	141983	6.0	141237	5.6	48	1122	837	285	45-49
50-54	263214	130039	5.5	133175	5.3		1660	1242	418	50-54
55-59	268956	127585	5.4	141371	5.6		2684	1937	747	55-59
60-64	242599	104160	4.4	138439	5.5		3809	2606	1203	60-64
65-69	189970	74868	3.2	115102	4.6		4566	2759	1807	65-69
70-74	177700	65626	2.8	112074	4.4		7011	3862	3149	70-74
75-79	133165	44371	1.9	88794	3.5		8572	4003	4569	75-79
80-84	72392	21001	0.9	51391	2.0	32012 M	7731	2872	4859	80-84
85+	38777	9401	0.4	29376	1.2	30784 F	7595	2262	5333	85+
TOTAL	4902215	2373508		2528707		62796	48198	24891	23307	TOTAL

TABLE 2 — MALE LIFE TABLE

x	nM_x	nq_x	l_x	nd_x	nL_x	nm_x	na_x	T_x	$\dot{e}_x$	x
0	0.006369	0.006332	100000	633	99418	0.006369	0.081	7014038	70.140	0
1	0.000381	0.001524	99367	151	397089	0.000381	1.500	6914620	69.587	1
5	0.000278	0.001388	99215	138	495733	0.000278	2.500	6517532	65.691	5
10	0.000317	0.001582	99078	157	495058	0.000317	2.893	6021799	60.779	10
15	0.000878	0.004379	98921	433	493607	0.000878	2.698	5526741	55.870	15
20	0.001158	0.005774	98488	569	491062	0.001158	2.579	5033134	51.104	20
25	0.001330	0.006627	97919	649	488032	0.001330	2.591	4542073	46.386	25
30	0.001760	0.008763	97270	852	484330	0.001760	2.630	4054041	41.678	30
35	0.002454	0.012229	96418	1179	479325	0.002460	2.655	3569710	37.023	35
40	0.003643	0.018192	95239	1733	472186	0.003669	2.687	3090386	32.449	40
45	0.005895	0.029215	93506	2732	461225	0.005923	2.692	2618200	28.000	45
50	0.009551	0.046777	90774	4246	444009	0.009563	2.677	2156975	23.762	50
55	0.015182	0.073330	86528	6345	417875	0.015184	2.673	1712966	19.797	55
60	0.025019	0.118583	80183	9508	378320	0.025133	2.624	1295091	16.152	60
65	0.036852	0.169624	70675	11988	324568	0.036936	2.597	916771	12.972	65
70	0.058849	0.257251	58687	15097	256543	0.058849	2.556	592203	10.091	70
75	0.090217	0.368951	43589	16082	177490	0.090610	2.484	335660	7.700	75
80	0.136755	0.505054	27507	13893	101587	0.136755	2.412	158170	5.750	80
85	0.240613	1.000000	13615	13615	56583	0.180985	4.156	56583	4.156	85

TABLE 3 — FEMALE LIFE TABLE

x	nM_x	nq_x	l_x	nd_x	nL_x	nm_x	na_x	T_x	$\dot{e}_x$	x
0	0.005664	0.005635	100000	564	99481	0.005664	0.080	7863731	78.637	0
1	0.000251	0.001003	99437	100	397497	0.000251	1.500	7764250	78.082	1
5	0.000189	0.000946	99337	94	496449	0.000189	2.500	7366753	74.159	5
10	0.000149	0.000744	99243	74	496038	0.000149	2.625	6870304	69.227	10
15	0.000279	0.001395	99169	138	495516	0.000279	2.622	6374266	64.277	15
20	0.000314	0.001567	99031	155	494776	0.000314	2.572	5878750	59.363	20
25	0.000389	0.001945	98875	192	493921	0.000389	2.630	5383974	54.452	25
30	0.000558	0.002786	98683	275	492776	0.000558	2.674	4890052	49.553	30
35	0.000858	0.004291	98408	422	491062	0.000860	2.681	4397276	44.684	35
40	0.001304	0.006543	97986	641	488443	0.001313	2.682	3906214	39.865	40
45	0.002018	0.010084	97345	982	484450	0.002026	2.683	3417770	35.110	45
50	0.003139	0.015589	96363	1502	478372	0.003140	2.707	2933321	30.440	50
55	0.005284	0.026103	94861	2476	468624	0.005284	2.706	2454949	25.879	55
60	0.008690	0.042706	92385	3945	452943	0.008711	2.724	1986325	21.501	60
65	0.015699	0.075902	88439	6713	426839	0.015727	2.712	1533382	17.338	65
70	0.028098	0.131912	81727	10781	383690	0.028098	2.686	1106542	13.540	70
75	0.051456	0.230489	70946	16352	315967	0.051753	2.630	722852	10.189	75
80	0.094550	0.383699	54594	20948	221551	0.094550	2.545	406885	7.453	80
85	0.181543	1.000000	33646	33646	185334	0.112872	5.508	185334	5.508	85

TABLE 4 — OBSERVED VITAL RATES AND RATIOS

CRUDE RATES

Per Thousand	BOTH SEXES	MALES	FEMALES
BIRTH RATE	12.81	13.49	12.17
DEATH RATE	9.83	10.49	9.22
RATE OF INCREASE	2.98	3.00	2.96

PERCENT OF POPULATION IN AGE GROUP

	BOTH SEXES	MALES	FEMALES
UNDER 15	19.41	20.50	18.39
15 - 64	68.11	70.43	65.92
65 AND OLDER	12.48	9.07	15.69

RATES STANDARDIZED ON USA 1980

Per Thousand	BOTH SEXES	MALES	FEMALES
BIRTH RATE	13.74		13.10
DEATH RATE	9.40	10.67	8.21
RATE OF INCREASE	4.33		4.89

RATES STANDARDIZED ON MEXICO 1980

	BOTH SEXES	MALES	FEMALES
BIRTH RATE	11.84		11.70
DEATH RATE	3.44	4.40	2.47
RATE OF INCREASE	8.40		9.24

VITAL STATISTICS

GFR x 1000	50.075
TFR	1.645
GRR	0.806
NRR	0.796
μ	28.406
σ^2	30.000
GENERATION	28.526
POP. SEX RATIO	1.065
SEX RATIO AT BIRTH	1.040
DEP. RATIO x 100	46.830

PROJECTED POPULATION

AGE GROUP	1990 BOTH SEXES	1990 MALES	1990 FEMALES	1995 BOTH SEXES	1995 MALES	1995 FEMALES
0-4	305	155	150	288	147	141
5-9	325	166	159	304	155	149
10-14	323	165	158	324	166	158
15-19	302	154	148	323	165	158
20-24	350	178	172	300	153	147
25-29	377	192	185	348	177	171
30-34	383	196	187	375	191	184
35-39	405	207	198	380	194	186
40-44	437	224	213	401	204	197
45-49	311	157	154	431	219	212
50-54	276	137	139	303	151	152
55-59	252	122	130	266	129	137
60-64	253	116	137	237	111	126
65-69	219	89	130	228	99	129
70-74	162	59	103	188	71	117
75-79	137	45	92	126	41	85
80-84	87	25	62	91	26	65
85+	55	12	43	66	14	52
TOTAL	4959	2399	2560	4979	2413	2566

STABLE EQUIVALENT TO ORIGINAL POPULATION

	MALES Number	MALES Percent	FEMALES Number	FEMALES Percent	AGE GROUP
	158	5.3	152	4.6	0-4
	164	5.5	158	4.8	5-9
	171	5.7	165	4.9	10-14
	177	5.9	171	5.1	15-19
	184	6.1	178	5.3	20-24
	190	6.4	185	5.6	25-29
	196	6.6	192	5.8	30-34
	202	6.8	199	6.0	35-39
	207	6.9	206	6.2	40-44
	211	7.0	213	6.4	45-49
	211	7.1	219	6.6	50-54
	207	6.9	223	6.7	55-59
	195	6.5	224	6.7	60-64
	174	5.8	220	6.6	65-69
	143	4.8	206	6.2	70-74
	103	3.4	176	5.3	75-79
	61	2.1	129	3.9	80-84
	36	1.2	112	3.4	85+
TOTAL	2990		3328		TOTAL

TABLE 5 — POPULATION PROJECTED WITH FIXED AGE-SPECIFIC BIRTH AND DEATH RATES (female dominant, in 000s)

VITAL RATES OF PROJECTED POPULATION

Per Thousand	1990 BOTH SEXES	1990 MALES	1990 FEMALES	1995 BOTH SEXES	1995 MALES	1995 FEMALES
BIRTH RATE	12.10	12.75	11.49	11.25	11.84	10.69
DEATH RATE	10.83	11.14	10.54	11.50	11.75	11.26
RATE OF INCREASE	1.27	1.61	0.96	-0.25	0.08	-0.56

AGE STRUCTURE OF PROJECTED POPULATION

	BOTH SEXES	MALES	FEMALES	BOTH SEXES	MALES	FEMALES
% UNDER 15	19.21	20.27	18.22	18.42	19.39	17.50
% 15-64	67.44	70.11	64.93	67.55	70.21	65.06
% 65 AND OLDER	13.35	9.62	16.85	14.03	10.39	17.45
DEPEND. RATIO x 100	48.28	42.63	54.01	48.03	42.42	53.71

VITAL RATES OF STABLE POPULATION

Per Thousand	MALES	FEMALES
BIRTH RATE	10.44	9.02
DEATH RATE	18.37	17.02
RATE OF INCREASE		-8.00

STABLE AGE STRUCTURE

	MALES	FEMALES
% UNDER 15	16.50	14.28
% 15-64	66.20	60.39
% 65 AND OLDER	17.29	25.33
DEPEND. RATIO x 100	51.05	65.60

TABLE 6 — PROJECTED VITAL RATES AND RATIOS (female dominant)

AGE GROUP	FEMALE BIRTH RATES	NET MATERNITY FUNCTION	COEFF. OF MATRIX EQUATION	ORIGINAL MATRIX SUB-DIAGONAL	ORIGINAL MATRIX FIRST ROW	STABLE MATRIX FISHER VALUES	STABLE MATRIX REPRODUCTIVE VALUES
0-4	0.0000	0.0000	0.0000	0.99894	0.00000	0.986	156594
5-9	0.0000	0.0000	0.0000	0.99917	0.00003	0.948	150281
10-14	0.0000	0.0001	0.0168	0.99895	0.01680	0.912	134701
15-19	0.0068	0.0335	0.1093	0.99851	0.10965	0.861	147978
20-24	0.0374	0.1852	0.2397	0.99827	0.24081	0.720	133124
25-29	0.0596	0.2943	0.2405	0.99768	0.24202	0.455	85268
30-34	0.0379	0.1868	0.1328	0.99652	0.13397	0.199	39550
35-39	0.0161	0.0789	0.0476	0.99467	0.04814	0.059	12671
40-44	0.0033	0.0162	0.0085	0.99182	0.00866	0.009	1445
45-49	0.0002	0.0008	0.0004	0.98745	0.00041	0.000	60
50-54	0.0000	0.0000	0.0000	0.00000	0.00000	0.000	0

MATRIX PARAMETERS

λ_1	0.96077
λ_2	$0.39818+0.72193i$
λ_4	$-0.31793+0.39065i$
λ_6	$-0.14046+0.47253i$
r_1	-0.00800
r_2	$-0.03861+0.21335i$
r_4	$-0.13717+0.45079i$
r_6	$-0.14146+0.37194i$
c_1	33278
$2\pi/y$	29.4498
Δ	14.1987

TABLE 7 — LESLIE MATRIX AND ITS ANALYSIS (females)

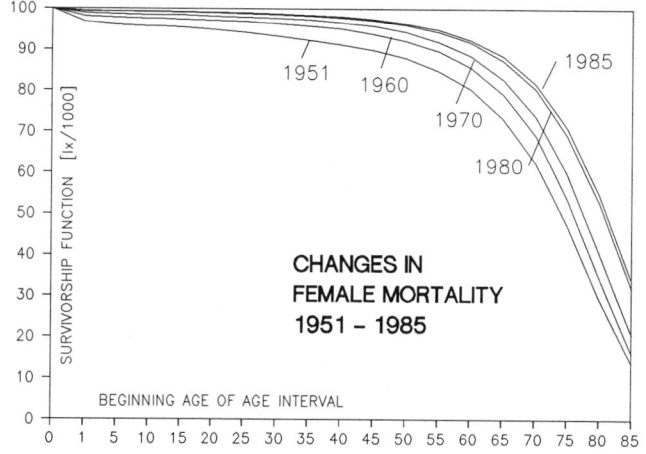

CHANGES IN FEMALE MORTALITY 1951 – 1985

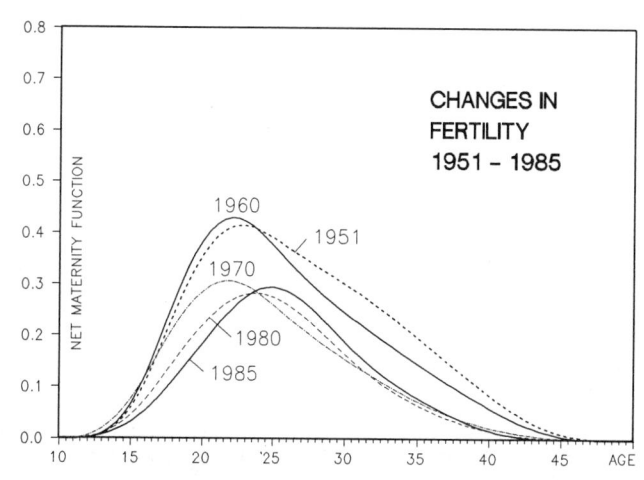

CHANGES IN FERTILITY 1951 – 1985

| AGE AT LAST BIRTHDAY | ESTIMATED MID-YEAR POPULATION | | | | | BIRTHS BY AGE OF MOTHER AND SEX | DEATHS | | | AGE AT LAST BIRTHDAY |
| | BOTH SEXES | MALES | | FEMALES | | | BOTH SEXES | MALES | FEMALES | |
		Number	Percent	Number	Percent					
0	832673	426023	1.7	406650	1.6		12839	7418	5421	0
1-4	3337715	1705276	6.9	1632439	6.3		2662	1537	1125	1-4
5-9	4261923	2174804	8.8	2087119	8.0		1712	1037	675	5-9
10-14	4172471	2125675	8.6	2046796	7.9	206	1474	933	541	10-14
15-19	4155324	2105871	8.5	2049453	7.9	76749	3812	2684	1128	15-19
20-24	4191032	2144631	8.7	2046401	7.9	340695	4747	3459	1288	20-24
25-29	2968061	1539441	6.2	1428620	5.5	217102	3453	2459	994	25-29
30-34	3061349	1580584	6.4	1480765	5.7	128299	4423	3042	1381	30-34
35-39	3328999	1702561	6.9	1626438	6.3	67198	7139	4875	2264	35-39
40-44	3354531	1697889	6.8	1656642	6.4	18841	10915	7370	3545	40-44
45-49	3296959	1634036	6.6	1662923	6.4	1274	16073	10695	5378	45-49
50-54	1942927	948821	3.8	994106	3.8	17	14027	9238	4789	50-54
55-59	2692458	1285207	5.2	1407251	5.4		29837	20198	9639	55-59
60-64	2640195	1225739	4.9	1414456	5.4		45331	30463	14868	60-64
65-69	2355655	1042456	4.2	1313199	5.1		62105	39301	22804	65-69
70-74	1804506	711946	2.9	1092560	4.2		73822	40500	33322	70-74
75-79	1207206	402484	1.6	804722	3.1		79190	35128	44062	75-79
80-84	736966	225239	0.9	511727	2.0	436599 M	79831	31007	48824	80-84
85+	431283	113764	0.5	317519	1.2	413782 F	86287	26373	59914	85+
TOTAL	50772233	24792447		25979786		850381	539679	277717	261962	TOTAL

TABLE 1 DATA

TABLE 2 — MALE LIFE TABLE

x	nM_x	nq_x	l_x	nd_x	nL_x	nm_x	na_x	T_x	$\overset{\circ}{e}_x$	x
0	0.017412	0.017143	100000	1714	98456	0.017412	0.100	6862085	68.621	0
1	0.000901	0.003597	98286	354	392259	0.000901	1.500	6763628	68.816	1
5	0.000477	0.002381	97932	233	489078	0.000477	2.500	6371369	65.059	5
10	0.000439	0.002195	97699	214	488039	0.000439	2.875	5882292	60.208	10
15	0.001275	0.006354	97484	619	485991	0.001275	2.690	5394253	55.334	15
20	0.001613	0.008041	96865	779	482409	0.001615	2.539	4908261	50.671	20
25	0.001597	0.007960	96086	765	478547	0.001598	2.537	4425853	46.061	25
30	0.001925	0.009579	95321	913	474444	0.001925	2.632	3947306	41.411	30
35	0.002863	0.014222	94408	1343	468911	0.002863	2.669	3472861	36.786	35
40	0.004341	0.021486	93066	2000	460664	0.004341	2.668	3003951	32.278	40
45	0.006545	0.032439	91066	2954	448405	0.006588	2.656	2543286	27.928	45
50	0.009736	0.047799	88112	4212	430739	0.009778	2.668	2094881	23.775	50
55	0.015716	0.075792	83900	6359	404622	0.015716	2.660	1664141	19.835	55
60	0.024853	0.117339	77541	9099	366102	0.024853	2.626	1259520	16.243	60
65	0.037700	0.173002	68443	11841	313674	0.037748	2.590	893418	13.054	65
70	0.056886	0.250835	56602	14198	248228	0.057196	2.550	579744	10.242	70
75	0.087278	0.359948	42404	15263	173776	0.087833	2.494	331516	7.818	75
80	0.137663	0.507790	27141	13782	100113	0.137663	2.418	157740	5.812	80
85	0.231822	1.000000	13359	13359	57626	0.170213	4.314	57626	4.314	85

TABLE 3 — FEMALE LIFE TABLE

x	nM_x	nq_x	l_x	nd_x	nL_x	nm_x	na_x	T_x	$\overset{\circ}{e}_x$	x
0	0.013331	0.013172	100000	1317	98805	0.013331	0.093	7613996	76.140	0
1	0.000689	0.002752	98683	272	394052	0.000689	1.500	7515191	76.155	1
5	0.000323	0.001616	98411	159	491659	0.000323	2.500	7121138	72.361	5
10	0.000264	0.001321	98252	130	490960	0.000264	2.678	6629479	67.474	10
15	0.000550	0.002748	98122	270	489975	0.000550	2.637	6138519	62.560	15
20	0.000629	0.003146	97853	308	488509	0.000630	2.547	5648544	57.725	20
25	0.000696	0.003479	97545	339	486907	0.000697	2.589	5160035	52.899	25
30	0.000933	0.004653	97206	452	484966	0.000933	2.653	4673129	48.075	30
35	0.001392	0.006938	96753	671	482207	0.001392	2.677	4188162	43.287	35
40	0.002140	0.010646	96082	1023	478033	0.002140	2.676	3705955	38.571	40
45	0.003234	0.016152	95059	1535	471710	0.003255	2.664	3227922	33.957	45
50	0.004817	0.023894	93524	2235	462353	0.004833	2.644	2756212	29.471	50
55	0.006850	0.033706	91289	3077	449230	0.006850	2.655	2293859	25.127	55
60	0.010511	0.051306	88212	4526	430561	0.010511	2.680	1844629	20.911	60
65	0.017365	0.083550	83686	6992	402289	0.017380	2.691	1414067	16.897	65
70	0.030499	0.142742	76694	10947	357977	0.030582	2.671	1011778	13.192	70
75	0.054754	0.243155	65747	15987	290491	0.055033	2.608	653802	9.944	75
80	0.095410	0.386310	49760	19223	201476	0.095410	2.538	363310	7.301	80
85	0.188694	1.000000	30537	30537	161835	0.120496	5.300	161835	5.300	85

TABLE 4 — OBSERVED VITAL RATES AND RATIOS

CRUDE RATES

Per Thousand	BOTH SEXES	MALES	FEMALES
BIRTH RATE	16.75	17.61	15.93
DEATH RATE	10.63	11.20	10.08
RATE OF INCREASE	6.12	6.41	5.84

PERCENT OF POPULATION IN AGE GROUP

UNDER 15	24.83	25.94	23.76
15 - 64	62.30	63.99	60.69
65 AND OLDER	12.87	10.07	15.55

RATES STANDARDIZED ON USA 1980

Per Thousand	BOTH SEXES	MALES	FEMALES
BIRTH RATE	21.15		20.02
DEATH RATE	10.09	11.03	9.21
RATE OF INCREASE	11.06		10.81

RATES STANDARDIZED ON MEXICO 1980

	BOTH SEXES	MALES	FEMALES
BIRTH RATE	18.92		18.56
DEATH RATE	4.10	5.00	3.18
RATE OF INCREASE	14.83		15.38

VITAL STATISTICS

GFR x 1000	71.154
TFR	2.481
GRR	1.207
NRR	1.175
μ	27.117
σ^2	34.204
GENERATION	27.015
POP. SEX RATIO	1.048
SEX RATIO AT BIRTH	1.055
DEP. RATIO x 100	60.510

PROJECTED POPULATION

AGE GROUP	1975 BOTH SEXES	1975 MALES	1975 FEMALES	1980 BOTH SEXES	1980 MALES	1980 FEMALES
0-4	4379	2243	2136	4695	2405	2290
5-9	4158	2124	2034	4366	2236	2130
10-14	4254	2170	2084	4151	2120	2031
15-19	4160	2117	2043	4241	2161	2080
20-24	4133	2090	2043	4138	2101	2037
25-29	4167	2127	2040	4111	2074	2037
30-34	2949	1526	1423	4141	2109	2032
35-39	3034	1562	1472	2923	1508	1415
40-44	3285	1673	1612	2995	1535	1460
45-49	3288	1653	1635	3219	1628	1591
50-54	3200	1570	1630	3190	1588	1602
55-59	1857	891	966	3058	1474	1584
60-64	2512	1163	1349	1732	806	926
65-69	2372	1050	1322	2256	996	1260
70-74	1994	825	1169	2007	831	1176
75-79	1385	498	887	1526	578	948
80-84	790	232	558	902	287	615
85+	541	130	411	581	133	448
TOTAL	52458	25644	26814	54232	26570	27662

STABLE EQUIVALENT TO ORIGINAL POPULATION

MALES Number	MALES Percent	FEMALES Number	FEMALES Percent	AGE GROUP
2237	8.7	2130	8.0	0-4
2164	8.4	2062	7.8	5-9
2096	8.1	1999	7.5	10-14
2026	7.9	1936	7.3	15-19
1952	7.6	1873	7.0	20-24
1879	7.3	1812	6.8	25-29
1808	7.0	1752	6.6	30-34
1735	6.7	1691	6.4	35-39
1654	6.4	1627	6.1	40-44
1563	6.1	1558	5.9	45-49
1457	5.7	1482	5.6	50-54
1328	5.2	1398	5.3	55-59
1167	4.5	1300	4.9	60-64
970	3.8	1179	4.4	65-69
745	2.9	1018	3.8	70-74
506	2.0	802	3.0	75-79
283	1.1	540	2.0	80-84
158	0.6	421	1.6	85+
25728		26580		TOTAL

TABLE 5

POPULATION PROJECTED WITH FIXED AGE-SPECIFIC BIRTH AND DEATH RATES (female dominant, in 000s)

VITAL RATES OF PROJECTED POPULATION

Per Thousand	1975 BOTH SEXES	1975 MALES	1975 FEMALES	1980 BOTH SEXES	1980 MALES	1980 FEMALES
BIRTH RATE	17.74	18.63	16.89	18.05	18.92	17.22
DEATH RATE	11.19	11.56	10.84	11.38	11.73	11.05
RATE OF INCREASE	6.55	7.07	6.05	6.67	7.19	6.17

AGE STRUCTURE OF PROJECTED POPULATION

	BOTH SEXES	MALES	FEMALES	BOTH SEXES	MALES	FEMALES
% UNDER 15	24.38	25.49	23.32	24.36	25.45	23.32
% 15-64	62.12	63.84	60.47	62.23	63.92	60.60
% 65 AND OLDER	13.50	10.67	16.21	13.41	10.63	16.08
DEPEND. RATIO x 100	60.99	56.64	65.38	60.70	56.44	65.02

VITAL RATES OF STABLE POPULATION

Per Thousand	MALES	FEMALES
BIRTH RATE	17.99	16.50
DEATH RATE	12.00	10.53
RATE OF INCREASE		5.97

STABLE AGE STRUCTURE

	MALES	FEMALES
% UNDER 15	25.25	23.29
% 15-64	64.40	61.81
% 65 AND OLDER	10.35	14.90
DEPEND. RATIO x 100	55.29	61.79

TABLE 6

PROJECTED VITAL RATES AND RATIOS (female dominant)

MATRIX PARAMETERS

AGE GROUP	FEMALE BIRTH RATES	NET MATERNITY FUNCTION	COEFF. OF MATRIX EQUATION	ORIGINAL MATRIX SUB-DIAGONAL	ORIGINAL MATRIX FIRST ROW	STABLE MATRIX FISHER VALUES	STABLE MATRIX REPRODUCTIVE VALUES
0-4	0.0000	0.0000	0.0000	0.99757	0.00000	1.030	2099705
5-9	0.0000	0.0000	0.0001	0.99858	0.00012	1.064	2219704
10-14	0.0000	0.0002	0.0448	0.99799	0.04493	1.097	2245739
15-19	0.0182	0.0893	0.2425	0.99701	0.24394	1.086	2226449
20-24	0.0810	0.3957	0.3779	0.99672	0.38125	0.871	1781822
25-29	0.0739	0.3600	0.2822	0.99602	0.28570	0.506	723135
30-34	0.0422	0.2045	0.1507	0.99431	0.15315	0.228	337966
35-39	0.0201	0.0969	0.0617	0.99134	0.06306	0.078	126688
40-44	0.0055	0.0265	0.0141	0.98677	0.01454	0.015	25600
45-49	0.0004	0.0018	0.0009	0.98016	0.00094	0.001	1593
50-54	0.0000	0.0000	0.0000	0.97162	0.00002	0.000	20

λ_1	1.03031
λ_2	0.34239+0.75451i
λ_4	-0.39637-0.38372i
λ_6	-0.00824+0.49665i
r_1	0.00597
r_2	-0.03761+0.22896i
r_4	-0.11896-0.47448i
r_6	-0.13995+0.31748i
c_1	265794
$2\pi/y$	27.4424
Δ	4.6480

TABLE 7

LESLIE MATRIX AND ITS ANALYSIS (females)

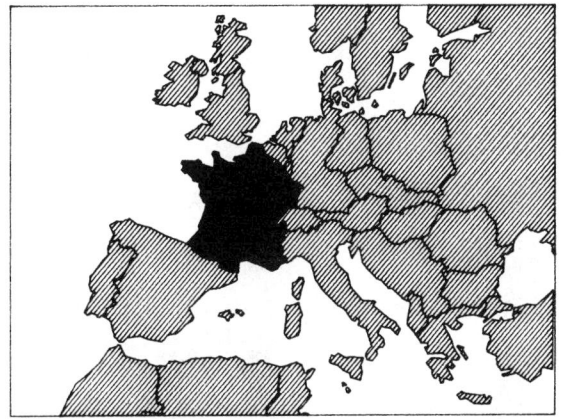

EDUCATION [1984]

% of primary school-age children enrolled:	108
secondary school-age children enrolled:	90
ca. 20-24 year olds in higher education:	27

LABOR FORCE

Average annual labor force growth (%) 1980-85:	0.9
% of the 1980 labor force in agriculture:	9
in industry:	35
in services:	56

GNP & INCOME DISTRIBUTION

GNP per capita (in US Dollars) 1985:	9540
GNP average annual growth rate (%) 1965-85:	2.8
% share of total household income 1975	
Lowest 20% of households:	5.5
Highest 10% of households:	26.4

HEALTH & NUTRITION

Population per physician 1981:	460
Daily calorie supply per capita 1985:	3359

TABLE 8

SOCIO-ECONOMIC INDICATORS

AGE AT LAST BIRTHDAY	ESTIMATED MID-YEAR POPULATION BOTH SEXES	MALES Number	MALES Percent	FEMALES Number	FEMALES Percent	BIRTHS BY AGE OF MOTHER AND SEX	DEATHS BOTH SEXES	DEATHS MALES	DEATHS FEMALES	AGE AT LAST BIRTHDAY
0	751186	384559	1.5	366627	1.4		10277	5906	4371	0
1-4	3358766	1718920	6.7	1639846	6.1		2264	1287	977	1-4
5-9	4195476	2144764	8.3	2050712	7.6		1487	922	565	5-9
10-14	4306324	2199814	8.5	2106510	7.8	181	1413	906	507	10-14
15-19	4236890	2157332	8.4	2079558	7.7	70692	3914	2806	1108	15-19
20-24	4238904	2153789	8.3	2085115	7.8	279310	4778	3549	1229	20-24
25-29	4270863	2205084	8.5	2065779	7.7	253164	4536	3190	1346	25-29
30-34	3017732	1571339	6.1	1446393	5.4	90277	3853	2633	1220	30-34
35-39	3055134	1567918	6.1	1487216	5.5	39583	5915	4098	1817	35-39
40-44	3298820	1672707	6.5	1626113	6.0	11079	10678	7461	3217	40-44
45-49	3285391	1644550	6.4	1640841	6.1	747	16563	11541	5022	45-49
50-54	3200648	1563096	6.1	1637552	6.1	32	23767	16449	7318	50-54
55-59	1854832	890837	3.5	963995	3.6		19268	13126	6142	55-59
60-64	2527950	1169792	4.5	1358158	5.1		40491	27503	12988	60-64
65-69	2393114	1061915	4.1	1331199	5.0		59531	38436	21095	65-69
70-74	2017672	836906	3.2	1180766	4.4		79369	46710	32659	70-74
75-79	1395086	504015	2.0	891071	3.3		89290	43674	45616	75-79
80-84	795598	232559	0.9	563039	2.1	381804 M	83448	31297	52151	80-84
85+	498795	127194	0.5	371601	1.4	363261 F	99511	29614	69897	85+
TOTAL	52699181	25807090		26892091		745065	560353	291108	269245	TOTAL

TABLE 1 — DATA

TABLE 2 — MALE LIFE TABLE

x	nM_x	nq_x	l_x	nd_x	nL_x	nm_x	na_x	T_x	$\overset{\circ}{e}_x$	x
0	0.015358	0.015148	100000	1515	98631	0.015358	0.096	6902952	69.030	0
1	0.000749	0.002989	98485	294	393205	0.000749	1.500	6804321	69.090	1
5	0.000430	0.002147	98191	211	490427	0.000430	2.500	6411116	65.292	5
10	0.000412	0.002057	97980	202	489484	0.000412	2.937	5920689	60.428	10
15	0.001301	0.006485	97778	634	487431	0.001301	2.696	5431205	55.546	15
20	0.001648	0.008205	97144	797	483741	0.001648	2.516	4943774	50.891	20
25	0.001447	0.007206	96347	694	480001	0.001446	2.501	4460032	46.291	25
30	0.001676	0.008380	95653	802	476373	0.001683	2.640	3980031	41.609	30
35	0.002614	0.012993	94851	1232	471439	0.002614	2.714	3503658	36.938	35
40	0.004460	0.022075	93619	2067	463330	0.004460	2.694	3032219	32.389	40
45	0.007018	0.034523	91552	3161	450380	0.007018	2.665	2568889	28.059	45
50	0.010523	0.051642	88392	4565	431136	0.010588	2.629	2118508	23.967	50
55	0.014734	0.071460	83827	5990	405014	0.014790	2.643	1687372	20.129	55
60	0.023511	0.111358	77837	8668	368666	0.023511	2.633	1282358	16.475	60
65	0.036195	0.166509	69169	11517	318200	0.036195	2.600	913692	13.210	65
70	0.055813	0.245916	57652	14177	253663	0.055891	2.560	595492	10.329	70
75	0.086652	0.358476	43474	15584	178359	0.087377	2.497	341830	7.863	75
80	0.134577	0.499495	27890	13931	103516	0.134577	2.421	163471	5.861	80
85	0.232825	1.000000	13959	13959	59955	0.171382	4.295	59955	4.295	85

TABLE 3 — FEMALE LIFE TABLE

x	nM_x	nq_x	l_x	nd_x	nL_x	nm_x	na_x	T_x	$\overset{\circ}{e}_x$	x
0	0.011922	0.011794	100000	1179	98927	0.011922	0.090	7695776	76.958	0
1	0.000596	0.002380	98821	235	394694	0.000596	1.500	7596849	76.875	1
5	0.000276	0.001377	98585	136	492588	0.000276	2.500	7202154	73.055	5
10	0.000241	0.001203	98450	118	491979	0.000241	2.721	6709566	68.152	10
15	0.000533	0.002661	98331	262	491038	0.000533	2.636	6217588	63.231	15
20	0.000589	0.002943	98070	289	489639	0.000589	2.541	5726550	58.393	20
25	0.000652	0.003258	97781	319	488134	0.000653	2.581	5236911	53.558	25
30	0.000843	0.004226	97462	412	486339	0.000847	2.638	4748777	48.724	30
35	0.001222	0.006092	97051	591	483887	0.001222	2.690	4262438	43.920	35
40	0.001978	0.009847	96459	950	480101	0.001978	2.689	3778551	39.172	40
45	0.003061	0.015194	95510	1451	474158	0.003061	2.664	3298449	34.535	45
50	0.004469	0.022240	94058	2092	465363	0.004495	2.644	2824292	30.027	50
55	0.006371	0.031494	91966	2896	453024	0.006393	2.649	2358928	25.650	55
60	0.009563	0.046777	89070	4166	435683	0.009563	2.680	1905905	21.398	60
65	0.015847	0.076440	84904	6490	409551	0.015847	2.694	1470221	17.316	65
70	0.027659	0.130125	78414	10204	368466	0.027692	2.687	1060670	13.527	70
75	0.051192	0.229319	68210	15642	303956	0.051461	2.628	692204	10.148	75
80	0.092624	0.377595	52568	19850	214302	0.092624	2.555	388248	7.386	80
85	0.188097	1.000000	32719	32719	173946	0.119837	5.316	173946	5.316	85

TABLE 4 — OBSERVED VITAL RATES AND RATIOS

CRUDE RATES Per Thousand	BOTH SEXES	MALES	FEMALES	RATES STANDARDIZED ON USA 1980 Per Thousand	BOTH SEXES	MALES	FEMALES	VITAL STATISTICS	
BIRTH RATE	14.14	14.79	13.51	BIRTH RATE	16.65		15.79	GFR x 1000	59.936
DEATH RATE	10.63	11.28	10.01	DEATH RATE	9.74	10.79	8.74	TFR	1.935
RATE OF INCREASE	3.51	3.51	3.50	RATE OF INCREASE	6.91		7.05	GRR	0.943
								NRR	0.921
								μ	26.646
PERCENT OF POPULATION IN AGE GROUP				RATES STANDARDIZED ON MEXICO 1980				σ^2	32.061
								GENERATION	26.695
UNDER 15	23.93	24.99	22.92	BIRTH RATE	15.02		14.76	POP. SEX RATIO	1.042
15 - 64	62.60	64.31	60.95	DEATH RATE	3.91	4.84	2.96	SEX RATIO AT BIRTH	1.051
65 AND OLDER	13.47	10.70	16.13	RATE OF INCREASE	11.12		11.80	DEP. RATIO x 100	59.757

AGE AT LAST BIRTHDAY	ESTIMATED MID-YEAR POPULATION BOTH SEXES	MALES Number	MALES Percent	FEMALES Number	FEMALES Percent	BIRTHS BY AGE OF MOTHER AND SEX	DEATHS BOTH SEXES	DEATHS MALES	DEATHS FEMALES	AGE AT LAST BIRTHDAY	
0	757142	387842	1.5	369300	1.3		8010	4728	3282	0	
1-4	2875403	1472200	5.6	1403203	5.1		1699	962	737	1-4	
5-9	4178143	2138208	8.1	2039935	7.4		1344	829	515	5-9	
10-14	4245471	2179304	8.3	2066167	7.5	153	1250	761	489	10-14	
15-19	4343016	2208810	8.4	2134206	7.7	52166	3995	2892	1103	15-19	
20-24	4214171	2120851	8.1	2093320	7.6	273280	5126	3906	1220	20-24	
25-29	4250335	2151301	8.2	2099034	7.6	290841	4595	3344	1251	25-29	
30-34	4276522	2191112	8.3	2085410	7.6	143336	5242	3595	1647	30-34	
35-39	2996133	1537994	5.8	1458139	5.3	33514	5211	3562	1649	35-39	TABLE 1
40-44	3021507	1535843	5.8	1485664	5.4	6600	8558	5925	2633	40-44	
45-49	3222213	1618421	6.2	1603792	5.8	461	14986	10652	4334	45-49	DATA
50-54	3177793	1567468	6.0	1610325	5.8	25	22391	15943	6448	50-54	
55-59	3068555	1467374	5.6	1601181	5.8		30063	20999	9064	55-59	
60-64	1750156	816125	3.1	934031	3.4		24128	16655	7473	60-64	
65-69	2304287	1018165	3.9	1286122	4.7		49338	32430	16908	65-69	
70-74	2080027	860503	3.3	1219524	4.4		71484	43002	28482	70-74	
75-79	1597433	603120	2.3	994313	3.6		91012	47460	43552	75-79	
80-84	945996	300140	1.1	645856	2.3	410547 M	90751	37672	53079	80-84	
85+	575716	137606	0.5	438110	1.6	389829 F	107924	30164	77760	85+	
TOTAL	53880019	26312387		27567632		800376	547107	285481	261626	TOTAL	

x	nM_x	nq_x	l_x	nd_x	nL_x	nm_x	na_x	T_x	$\overset{\circ}{e}_x$	x	
0	0.012191	0.012057	100000	1206	98904	0.012191	0.091	7018623	70.186	0	
1	0.000653	0.002610	98794	258	394533	0.000653	1.500	6919719	70.042	1	
5	0.000388	0.001937	98537	191	492205	0.000388	2.500	6525187	66.221	5	
10	0.000349	0.001745	98346	172	491393	0.000349	3.046	6032981	61.345	10	
15	0.001309	0.006529	98174	641	489419	0.001310	2.735	5541588	56.447	15	
20	0.001842	0.009167	97533	894	485453	0.001842	2.525	5052170	51.800	20	
25	0.001554	0.007742	96639	748	481302	0.001554	2.470	4566717	47.255	25	TABLE 2
30	0.001641	0.008186	95891	785	477566	0.001644	2.594	4085415	42.605	30	
35	0.002316	0.011595	95106	1103	472984	0.002331	2.691	3607850	37.935	35	MALE
40	0.003858	0.019124	94003	1798	465915	0.003858	2.719	3134866	33.349	40	LIFE
45	0.006582	0.032414	92205	2989	454104	0.006582	2.684	2668952	28.946	45	TABLE
50	0.010171	0.049662	89217	4431	435613	0.010171	2.637	2214848	24.825	50	
55	0.014311	0.069574	84786	5899	409865	0.014392	2.616	1779235	20.985	55	
60	0.020407	0.097693	78887	7707	376135	0.020489	2.625	1369369	17.359	60	
65	0.031851	0.148013	71180	10536	330773	0.031851	2.615	993235	13.954	65	
70	0.049973	0.222886	60645	13517	270483	0.049973	2.578	662461	10.924	70	
75	0.078691	0.330573	47128	15579	196999	0.079083	2.520	391979	8.317	75	
80	0.125515	0.475246	31549	14993	119455	0.125515	2.446	194979	6.180	80	
85	0.219206	1.000000	16555	16555	75524	0.155136	4.562	75524	4.562	85	

x	nM_x	nq_x	l_x	nd_x	nL_x	nm_x	na_x	T_x	$\overset{\circ}{e}_x$	x	
0	0.008887	0.008815	100000	882	99193	0.008887	0.085	7849852	78.499	0	
1	0.000525	0.002098	99118	208	395954	0.000525	1.500	7750658	78.196	1	
5	0.000252	0.001261	98910	125	494241	0.000252	2.500	7354704	74.357	5	
10	0.000237	0.001183	98786	117	493664	0.000237	2.732	6860464	69.448	10	
15	0.000517	0.002581	98669	255	492743	0.000517	2.639	6366800	64.527	15	
20	0.000583	0.002910	98414	286	491363	0.000583	2.527	5874057	59.687	20	
25	0.000596	0.002976	98128	292	489930	0.000596	2.572	5382694	54.854	25	TABLE 3
30	0.000790	0.003955	97836	387	488266	0.000792	2.640	4892764	50.010	30	
35	0.001131	0.005673	97449	553	485960	0.001138	2.676	4404498	45.198	35	FEMALE
40	0.001772	0.008825	96896	855	482496	0.001772	2.679	3918538	40.441	40	LIFE
45	0.002702	0.013427	96041	1290	477195	0.002702	2.665	3436041	35.777	45	TABLE
50	0.004004	0.019834	94751	1879	469334	0.004004	2.646	2958846	31.227	50	
55	0.005661	0.028084	92872	2608	458190	0.005692	2.634	2489512	26.806	55	
60	0.008001	0.039430	90264	3559	443031	0.008034	2.671	2031322	22.504	60	
65	0.013146	0.063807	86705	5532	420826	0.013147	2.705	1588291	18.318	65	
70	0.023355	0.110835	81172	8997	385216	0.023355	2.705	1167465	14.383	70	
75	0.043801	0.199381	72176	14390	327158	0.043986	2.657	782249	10.838	75	
80	0.082184	0.343055	57785	19824	241209	0.082184	2.593	455091	7.876	80	
85	0.177490	1.000000	37962	37962	213881	0.108622	5.634	213881	5.634	85	

CRUDE RATES

Per Thousand	BOTH SEXES	MALES	FEMALES
BIRTH RATE	14.85	15.60	14.14
DEATH RATE	10.15	10.85	9.49
RATE OF INCREASE	4.70	4.75	4.65

RATES STANDARDIZED ON USA 1980

Per Thousand	BOTH SEXES	MALES	FEMALES
BIRTH RATE	16.81		15.92
DEATH RATE	8.80	9.90	7.75
RATE OF INCREASE	8.01		8.17

VITAL STATISTICS

GFR x 1000	61.759	TABLE 4
TFR	1.950	
GRR	0.950	OBSERVED
NRR	0.931	VITAL
μ	26.835	RATES
σ^2	27.360	AND
GENERATION	26.871	RATIOS
POP. SEX RATIO	1.048	
SEX RATIO AT BIRTH	1.053	
DEP. RATIO x 100	56.991	

PERCENT OF POPULATION IN AGE GROUP

UNDER 15	22.38	23.48	21.32
15 - 64	63.70	65.43	62.05
65 AND OLDER	13.93	11.10	16.63

RATES STANDARDIZED ON MEXICO 1980

	BOTH SEXES	MALES	FEMALES
BIRTH RATE	14.97		14.69
DEATH RATE	3.51	4.43	2.58
RATE OF INCREASE	11.45		12.11

TABLE 1 — DATA

AGE AT LAST BIRTHDAY	ESTIMATED MID-YEAR POPULATION BOTH SEXES	MALES Number	MALES Percent	FEMALES Number	FEMALES Percent	BIRTHS BY AGE OF MOTHER AND SEX	DEATHS BOTH SEXES	DEATHS MALES	DEATHS FEMALES	AGE AT LAST BIRTHDAY
0	742224	379985	1.4	362239	1.3		6389	3741	2648	0
1-4	3045648	1559722	5.8	1485926	5.3		1384	770	614	1-4
5-9	3702045	1896295	7.0	1805750	6.4		910	532	378	5-9
10-14	4208154	2160190	8.0	2047964	7.2	162	1067	673	394	10-14
15-19	4265077	2179837	8.1	2085240	7.4	33544	3011	2138	873	15-19
20-24	4296254	2159556	8.0	2136698	7.6	228753	4567	3432	1135	20-24
25-29	4207309	2106750	7.8	2100559	7.4	291334	4529	3291	1238	25-29
30-34	4269483	2147845	8.0	2121638	7.5	154636	5250	3657	1593	30-34
35-39	4256349	2165387	8.0	2090962	7.4	52366	7192	4956	2236	35-39
40-44	2974973	1516952	5.6	1458021	5.2	7166	7436	5269	2167	40-44
45-49	2969457	1498630	5.6	1470827	5.2	424	12116	8654	3462	45-49
50-54	3130082	1552746	5.8	1577336	5.6	46	20175	14490	5685	50-54
55-59	3054312	1476770	5.5	1577542	5.6		28980	20831	8149	55-59
60-64	2904494	1350479	5.0	1554015	5.5		38487	26805	11682	60-64
65-69	1613924	722430	2.7	891494	3.2		30493	20233	10260	65-69
70-74	2030147	842589	3.1	1187558	4.2		63365	38315	25050	70-74
75-79	1686177	636848	2.4	1049329	3.7		88309	46903	41406	75-79
80-84	1114350	372059	1.4	742291	2.6	394112 M	100805	44443	56362	80-84
85+	699997	175169	0.7	524828	1.9	374319 F	128031	37759	90272	85+
TOTAL	55170456	26900239		28270217		768431	552496	286892	265604	TOTAL

TABLE 2 — MALE LIFE TABLE

x	nM_x	nq_x	l_x	nd_x	nL_x	nm_x	na_x	T_x	$\overset{\circ}{e}_x$	x
0	0.009845	0.009757	100000	976	99109	0.009845	0.087	7129093	71.291	0
1	0.000494	0.001972	99024	195	395609	0.000494	1.500	7029984	70.993	1
5	0.000281	0.001402	98829	139	493798	0.000281	2.500	6634375	67.130	5
10	0.000312	0.001557	98690	154	493140	0.000312	2.966	6140577	62.221	10
15	0.000981	0.004893	98537	482	491608	0.000981	2.769	5647437	57.313	15
20	0.001589	0.007917	98055	776	488390	0.001589	2.574	5155829	52.581	20
25	0.001562	0.007780	97278	757	484508	0.001562	2.512	4667440	47.980	25
30	0.001703	0.008478	96521	818	480632	0.001703	2.586	4182931	43.337	30
35	0.002289	0.011425	95703	1093	475954	0.002297	2.657	3702300	38.685	35
40	0.003473	0.017356	94610	1642	469268	0.003499	2.697	3226346	34.102	40
45	0.005775	0.028502	92968	2650	458731	0.005776	2.695	2757078	29.656	45
50	0.009332	0.045664	90318	4124	441952	0.009332	2.663	2298347	25.447	50
55	0.014106	0.068243	86194	5882	416997	0.014106	2.625	1856395	21.537	55
60	0.019849	0.095244	80312	7649	383205	0.019961	2.601	1439397	17.923	60
65	0.028007	0.131812	72662	9578	340468	0.028131	2.615	1056192	14.536	65
70	0.045473	0.204975	63085	12931	284361	0.045473	2.598	715724	11.345	70
75	0.073649	0.312033	50154	15650	212247	0.073733	2.538	431363	8.601	75
80	0.119451	0.458483	34504	15820	132435	0.119452	2.466	219116	6.350	80
85	0.215558	1.000000	18685	18685	86680	0.150828	4.639	86680	4.639	85

TABLE 3 — FEMALE LIFE TABLE

x	nM_x	nq_x	l_x	nd_x	nL_x	nm_x	na_x	T_x	$\overset{\circ}{e}_x$	x
0	0.007310	0.007261	100000	726	99334	0.007310	0.082	7956907	79.569	0
1	0.000413	0.001651	99274	164	396686	0.000413	1.500	7857573	79.150	1
5	0.000209	0.001046	99110	104	495291	0.000209	2.500	7460888	75.279	5
10	0.000192	0.000962	99006	95	494815	0.000192	2.726	6965597	70.355	10
15	0.000419	0.002091	98911	207	494073	0.000419	2.668	6470782	65.420	15
20	0.000531	0.002652	98704	262	492884	0.000531	2.566	5976709	60.552	20
25	0.000589	0.002943	98442	290	491510	0.000589	2.576	5483825	55.706	25
30	0.000751	0.003748	98153	368	489893	0.000751	2.632	4992315	50.863	30
35	0.001069	0.005354	97785	524	487690	0.001073	2.642	4502422	46.044	35
40	0.001486	0.007449	97261	725	484622	0.001495	2.674	4014732	41.278	40
45	0.002354	0.011705	96537	1130	480063	0.002354	2.681	3530110	36.567	45
50	0.003604	0.017870	95407	1705	473035	0.003604	2.654	3050047	31.969	50
55	0.005166	0.025518	93702	2391	462884	0.005166	2.647	2577012	27.502	55
60	0.007517	0.037173	91311	3394	448603	0.007566	2.657	2114128	23.153	60
65	0.011509	0.056351	87917	4954	428229	0.011569	2.708	1665525	18.944	65
70	0.021094	0.100615	82962	8347	395724	0.021094	2.713	1237296	14.914	70
75	0.039460	0.180906	74615	13498	341685	0.039505	2.674	841572	11.279	75
80	0.075930	0.321545	61117	19652	258815	0.075930	2.620	499887	8.179	80
85	0.172003	1.000000	41465	41465	241072	0.102993	5.814	241072	5.814	85

TABLE 4 — OBSERVED VITAL RATES AND RATIOS

CRUDE RATES

Per Thousand	BOTH SEXES	MALES	FEMALES
BIRTH RATE	13.93	14.65	13.24
DEATH RATE	10.01	10.67	9.40
RATE OF INCREASE	3.91	3.99	3.85

RATES STANDARDIZED ON USA 1980

Per Thousand	BOTH SEXES	MALES	FEMALES
BIRTH RATE	15.57		14.75
DEATH RATE	8.17	9.24	7.16
RATE OF INCREASE	7.40		7.58

VITAL STATISTICS

GFR x 1000	57.073
TFR	1.825
GRR	0.889
NRR	0.874
μ	27.475
σ^2	26.963
GENERATION	27.542
POP. SEX RATIO	1.051
SEX RATIO AT BIRTH	1.053
DEP. RATIO x 100	51.868

PERCENT OF POPULATION IN AGE GROUP

	BOTH SEXES	MALES	FEMALES
UNDER 15	21.20	22.29	20.17
15 - 64	65.85	67.49	64.28
65 AND OLDER	12.95	10.22	15.55

RATES STANDARDIZED ON MEXICO 1980

	BOTH SEXES	MALES	FEMALES
BIRTH RATE	13.63		13.38
DEATH RATE	3.19	4.05	2.32
RATE OF INCREASE	10.44		11.06

PROJECTED POPULATION

AGE GROUP	1990 BOTH SEXES	1990 MALES	1990 FEMALES	1995 BOTH SEXES	1995 MALES	1995 FEMALES
0-4	3803	1948	1855	3766	1929	1837
5-9	3781	1936	1845	3798	1945	1853
10-14	3698	1894	1804	3778	1934	1844
15-19	4198	2153	2045	3689	1888	1801
20-24	4246	2166	2080	4179	2139	2040
25-29	4273	2142	2131	4222	2148	2074
30-34	4184	2090	2094	4249	2125	2124
35-39	4239	2127	2112	4154	2070	2084
40-44	4213	2135	2078	4196	2097	2099
45-49	2927	1483	1444	4145	2087	2058
50-54	2893	1444	1449	2852	1429	1423
55-59	3008	1465	1543	2780	1362	1418
60-64	2886	1357	1529	2842	1346	1496
65-69	2683	1200	1483	2665	1206	1459
70-74	1427	603	824	2373	1002	1371
75-79	1654	629	1025	1161	450	711
80-84	1192	397	795	1169	392	777
85+	935	244	691	1000	260	740
TOTAL	56240	27413	28827	57018	27809	29209

STABLE EQUIVALENT TO ORIGINAL POPULATION

	MALES Number	MALES Percent	FEMALES Number	FEMALES Percent	AGE GROUP	
	1980	5.8	1886	5.1	0-4	
	2025	5.9	1930	5.2	5-9	TABLE 5
	2073	6.1	1975	5.4	10-14	
	2118	6.2	2021	5.5	15-19	POPULATION
	2156	6.3	2066	5.6	20-24	PROJECTED
	2192	6.4	2112	5.7	25-29	WITH
	2228	6.5	2157	5.9	30-34	FIXED
	2261	6.6	2201	6.0	35-39	AGE-
	2285	6.7	2241	6.1	40-44	SPECIFIC
	2289	6.7	2275	6.2	45-49	BIRTH
	2260	6.6	2297	6.2	50-54	AND
	2185	6.4	2303	6.3	55-59	DEATH
	2058	6.0	2288	6.2	60-64	RATES
	1873	5.5	2238	6.1	65-69	(female
	1603	4.7	2119	5.8	70-74	dominant,
	1226	3.6	1875	5.1	75-79	in 000s)
	784	2.3	1456	4.0	80-84	
	526	1.5	1389	3.8	85+	
	34122		36829		TOTAL	

VITAL RATES OF PROJECTED POPULATION

Per Thousand	1990 BOTH SEXES	1990 MALES	1990 FEMALES	1995 BOTH SEXES	1995 MALES	1995 FEMALES
BIRTH RATE	13.64	14.36	12.97	13.21	13.89	12.56
DEATH RATE	10.74	11.21	10.28	10.86	11.39	10.36
RATE OF INCREASE	2.91	3.15	2.69	2.35	2.50	2.20

AGE STRUCTURE OF PROJECTED POPULATION

	BOTH SEXES	MALES	FEMALES	BOTH SEXES	MALES	FEMALES
% UNDER 15	20.06	21.08	19.10	19.89	20.88	18.94
% 15-64	65.91	67.71	64.19	65.43	67.21	63.74
% 65 AND OLDER	14.03	11.21	16.72	14.68	11.90	17.32
DEPEND. RATIO x 100	51.73	47.69	55.79	52.83	48.78	56.89

VITAL RATES OF STABLE POPULATION

Per Thousand	MALES	FEMALES	
BIRTH RATE	11.59	10.20	TABLE 6
DEATH RATE	16.42	15.09	PROJECTED
RATE OF INCREASE		-4.90	VITAL RATES

STABLE AGE STRUCTURE

	MALES	FEMALES	
% UNDER 15	17.81	15.72	(female
% 15-64	64.56	59.63	dominant)
% 65 AND OLDER	17.62	24.65	
DEPEND. RATIO x 100	54.89	67.70	

AND RATIOS (female dominant)

MATRIX PARAMETERS

AGE GROUP	FEMALE BIRTH RATES	NET MATERNITY FUNCTION	COEFF. OF MATRIX EQUATION	ORIGINAL MATRIX SUB-DIAGONAL	ORIGINAL MATRIX FIRST ROW	STABLE MATRIX FISHER VALUES	STABLE MATRIX REPRODUCTIVE VALUES		
0-4	0.0000	0.0000	0.0000	0.99853	0.00000	0.996	1840317	λ_1 0.97582	
5-9	0.0000	0.0000	0.0001	0.99904	0.00010	0.973	1757181	λ_2 0.36536-0.74885i	TABLE 7
10-14	0.0000	0.0002	0.0195	0.99850	0.01950	0.950	1946362	λ_4 -0.32075+0.42733i	
15-19	0.0078	0.0387	0.1479	0.99759	0.14846	0.909	1896216	λ_6 -0.39221+0.02857i	LESLIE
20-24	0.0522	0.2570	0.2946	0.99721	0.29643	0.741	1583963	r_1 -0.00490	MATRIX
25-29	0.0676	0.3321	0.2530	0.99671	0.25532	0.429	902009	r_2 -0.03649-0.22338i	AND ITS
30-34	0.0355	0.1739	0.1167	0.99550	0.11817	0.165	350786	r_4 -0.12535+0.44294i	ANALYSIS
35-39	0.0122	0.0595	0.0355	0.99371	0.03616	0.044	91720	r_6 -0.18666+0.61377i	(females)
40-44	0.0024	0.0116	0.0061	0.99059	0.00628	0.007	9980	c_1 368291	
45-49	0.0001	0.0007	0.0004	0.98536	0.00038	0.000	628	$2\pi/y$ 28.1283	
50-54	0.0000	0.0001	0.0000	0.97854	0.00004	0.000	57	Δ 13.0469	

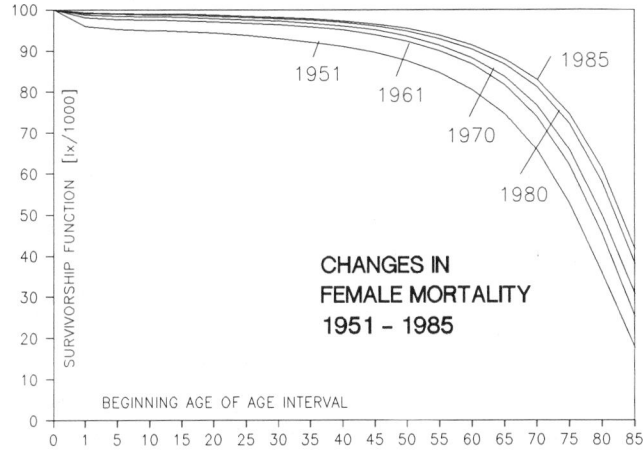

CHANGES IN FEMALE MORTALITY 1951 - 1985

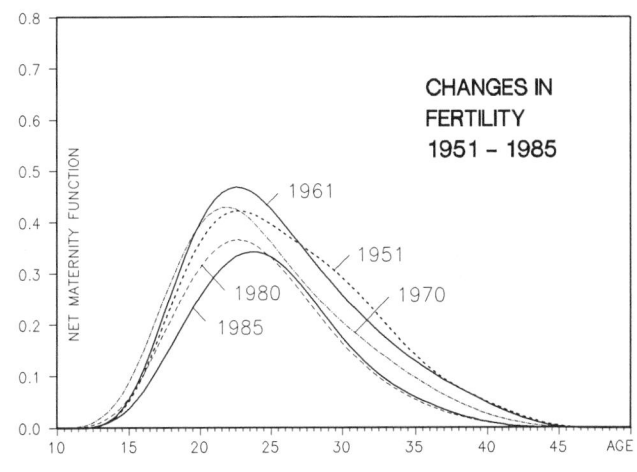

CHANGES IN FERTILITY 1951 - 1985

TABLE 1 — DATA

AGE AT LAST BIRTHDAY	ESTIMATED MID-YEAR POPULATION BOTH SEXES	MALES Number	MALES Percent	FEMALES Number	FEMALES Percent	BIRTHS BY AGE OF MOTHER AND SEX	DEATHS BOTH SEXES	DEATHS MALES	FEMALES	AGE AT LAST BIRTHDAY
0	234897	120485	1.5	114412	1.2		4382	2493	1889	0
1-4	1002472	514385	6.6	488087	5.3		859	494	365	1-4
5-9	1430051	732485	9.3	697566	7.6		587	365	222	5-9
10-14	1317268	674905	8.6	642363	7.0	22	472	304	168	10-14
15-19	1306432	670757	8.5	635675	6.9	36940	1071	740	331	15-19
20-24	924964	472562	6.0	452402	4.9	78786	967	695	272	20-24
25-29	1166862	585992	7.5	580870	6.3	70369	1311	912	399	25-29
30-34	1316325	662452	8.4	653873	7.1	35629	1673	1071	602	30-34
35-39	1062751	534454	6.8	528297	5.7	12971	1951	1217	734	35-39
40-44	989917	453423	5.8	536494	5.8	2113	2862	1658	1204	40-44
45-49	914073	351114	4.5	562959	6.1	99	3877	1868	2009	45-49
50-54	618767	233318	3.0	385449	4.2		4025	2025	2000	50-54
55-59	1009204	383803	4.9	625401	6.8		10912	5769	5143	55-59
60-64	1113964	447876	5.7	666088	7.2		20580	11412	9168	60-64
65-69	1014788	424714	5.4	590074	6.4		33005	18621	14384	65-69
70-74	761033	286474	3.6	474559	5.2		41011	19891	21120	70-74
75-79	490574	168538	2.1	322036	3.5		43192	17595	25597	75-79
80-84	265933	92273	1.2	173660	1.9	121601 M	38352	14686	23666	80-84
85+	117953	40824	0.5	77129	0.8	115328 F	29732	10905	18827	85+
TOTAL	17058228	7850834		9207394		236929	240821	112721	128100	TOTAL

TABLE 2 — MALE LIFE TABLE

x	nM_x	nq_x	l_x	nd_x	nL_x	nm_x	na_x	T_x	$\mathring{e}_x$	x
0	0.020691	0.020315	100000	2032	98182	0.020691	0.105	6814697	68.147	0
1	0.000960	0.003832	97968	375	390935	0.000960	1.500	6716515	68.558	1
5	0.000498	0.002488	97593	243	487358	0.000498	2.500	6325579	64.816	5
10	0.000450	0.002255	97350	220	486264	0.000451	2.780	5838221	59.971	10
15	0.001103	0.005542	97131	538	484410	0.001111	2.689	5351958	55.101	15
20	0.001471	0.007338	96592	709	481233	0.001473	2.560	4867548	50.393	20
25	0.001556	0.007752	95884	743	477572	0.001556	2.516	4386316	45.746	25
30	0.001617	0.008058	95140	767	473855	0.001618	2.590	3908744	41.084	30
35	0.002277	0.011395	94374	1075	469375	0.002291	2.681	3434889	36.397	35
40	0.003657	0.018249	93298	1703	462516	0.003681	2.665	2965514	31.785	40
45	0.005320	0.026457	91596	2423	452356	0.005357	2.680	2502998	27.327	45
50	0.008679	0.042549	89172	3794	437164	0.008679	2.707	2050641	22.996	50
55	0.015031	0.072636	85378	6202	412580	0.015031	2.692	1613477	18.898	55
60	0.025480	0.120252	79177	9521	373668	0.025480	2.667	1200897	15.167	60
65	0.043844	0.198401	69656	13820	315205	0.043844	2.607	827229	11.876	65
70	0.069434	0.297449	55836	16608	238154	0.069738	2.530	512024	9.170	70
75	0.104398	0.413003	39228	16201	154866	0.104614	2.453	273870	6.982	75
80	0.159158	0.560962	23026	12917	81158	0.159158	2.370	119004	5.168	80
85	0.267122	1.000000	10109	10109	37846	0.214764	3.744	37846	3.744	85

TABLE 3 — FEMALE LIFE TABLE

x	nM_x	nq_x	l_x	nd_x	nL_x	nm_x	na_x	T_x	$\mathring{e}_x$	x
0	0.016511	0.016268	100000	1627	98533	0.016511	0.098	7336068	73.361	0
1	0.000748	0.002986	98373	294	392758	0.000748	1.500	7237536	73.572	1
5	0.000318	0.001590	98079	156	490007	0.000318	2.500	6844777	69.788	5
10	0.000262	0.001307	97924	128	489318	0.000262	2.662	6354770	64.895	10
15	0.000521	0.002611	97796	255	488374	0.000523	2.635	5865451	59.977	15
20	0.000601	0.003004	97540	293	486984	0.000602	2.555	5377078	55.127	20
25	0.000687	0.003429	97247	333	485434	0.000687	2.595	4890093	50.285	25
30	0.000921	0.004596	96914	445	483525	0.000921	2.658	4404660	45.449	30
35	0.001389	0.006950	96468	670	480795	0.001394	2.694	3921135	40.647	35
40	0.002244	0.011163	95798	1069	476527	0.002244	2.698	3440339	35.913	40
45	0.003569	0.017783	94728	1685	469705	0.003586	2.663	2963813	31.287	45
50	0.005189	0.025634	93044	2385	459668	0.005189	2.672	2494108	26.806	50
55	0.008224	0.040353	90659	3658	444860	0.008224	2.695	2034440	22.441	55
60	0.013764	0.066713	87000	5804	421684	0.013764	2.705	1589580	18.271	60
65	0.024377	0.115527	81196	9380	384341	0.024406	2.693	1167896	14.384	65
70	0.044504	0.201788	71816	14492	324887	0.044605	2.640	783555	10.911	70
75	0.079485	0.334110	57324	19153	239742	0.079889	2.552	458668	8.001	75
80	0.136278	0.505543	38172	19297	141604	0.136278	2.448	218927	5.735	80
85	0.244098	1.000000	18874	18874	77323	0.184927	4.097	77323	4.097	85

TABLE 4 — OBSERVED VITAL RATES AND RATIOS

CRUDE RATES

Per Thousand	BOTH SEXES	MALES	FEMALES
BIRTH RATE	13.89	15.49	12.53
DEATH RATE	14.12	14.36	13.91
RATE OF INCREASE	-0.23	1.13	-1.39

PERCENT OF POPULATION IN AGE GROUP

	BOTH SEXES	MALES	FEMALES
UNDER 15	23.36	26.01	21.10
15 - 64	61.10	61.09	61.12
65 AND OLDER	15.54	12.90	17.78

RATES STANDARDIZED ON USA 1980

Per Thousand	BOTH SEXES	MALES	FEMALES
BIRTH RATE	19.13		18.11
DEATH RATE	12.21	12.09	12.32
RATE OF INCREASE	6.92		5.79

RATES STANDARDIZED ON MEXICO 1980

	BOTH SEXES	MALES	FEMALES
BIRTH RATE	17.78		17.44
DEATH RATE	4.69	5.32	4.05
RATE OF INCREASE	13.08		13.38

VITAL STATISTICS

GFR x 1000	59.973
TFR	2.183
GRR	1.063
NRR	1.033
μ	25.480
σ^2	30.128
GENERATION	25.461
POP. SEX RATIO	1.173
SEX RATIO AT BIRTH	1.054
DEP. RATIO x 100	63.655

PROJECTED POPULATION

STABLE EQUIVALENT TO ORIGINAL POPULATION

AGE GROUP	1975 BOTH SEXES	1975 MALES	1975 FEMALES	1980 BOTH SEXES	1980 MALES	1980 FEMALES	MALES Number	MALES Percent	FEMALES Number	FEMALES Percent	AGE GROUP	
0-4	1199	614	585	1279	655	624	657	7.5	626	7.0	0-4	
5-9	1234	633	601	1194	611	583	651	7.4	620	6.9	5-9	TABLE 5
10-14	1428	731	697	1231	631	600	645	7.4	616	6.9	10-14	
15-19	1313	672	641	1423	728	695	639	7.3	611	6.8	15-19	POPULATION
20-24	1300	666	634	1307	668	639	630	7.2	605	6.8	20-24	PROJECTED
25-29	920	469	451	1293	661	632	622	7.1	599	6.7	25-29	WITH
30-34	1160	581	579	914	465	449	613	7.0	593	6.6	30-34	FIXED
35-39	1306	656	650	1151	576	575	603	6.9	586	6.6	35-39	AGE-
40-44	1051	527	524	1291	647	644	591	6.7	577	6.5	40-44	SPECIFIC
45-49	972	443	529	1031	515	516	574	6.5	566	6.3	45-49	BIRTH
50-54	890	339	551	947	429	518	551	6.3	550	6.2	50-54	AND
55-59	593	220	373	853	320	533	517	5.9	529	5.9	55-59	DEATH
60-64	941	348	593	553	199	354	465	5.3	498	5.6	60-64	RATES
65-69	985	378	607	833	293	540	390	4.4	451	5.0	65-69	(female
70-74	820	321	499	798	285	513	293	3.3	379	4.2	70-74	dominant,
75-79	536	186	350	577	209	368	189	2.2	278	3.1	75-79	in 000s)
80-84	278	88	190	305	98	207	99	1.1	163	1.8	80-84	
85+	138	43	95	145	41	104	46	0.5	89	1.0	85+	
TOTAL	17064	7915	9149	17125	8031	9094	8775		8936		TOTAL	

VITAL RATES OF PROJECTED POPULATION

VITAL RATES OF STABLE POPULATION

Per Thousand	1975 BOTH SEXES	1975 MALES	1975 FEMALES	1980 BOTH SEXES	1980 MALES	1980 FEMALES		MALES	FEMALES	
BIRTH RATE	14.77	16.34	13.41	15.74	17.22	14.43	BIRTH RATE	15.36	14.30	TABLE 6
DEATH RATE	14.52	14.11	14.88	14.44	13.48	15.29	DEATH RATE	14.06	13.04	PROJECTED
RATE OF INCREASE	0.25	2.23	-1.47	1.29	3.74	-0.87	RATE OF INCREASE		1.26	VITAL RATES

AGE STRUCTURE OF PROJECTED POPULATION

STABLE AGE STRUCTURE

	1975 BOTH SEXES	1975 MALES	1975 FEMALES	1980 BOTH SEXES	1980 MALES	1980 FEMALES		MALES	FEMALES	AND RATIOS (female
% UNDER 15	22.62	24.98	20.58	21.63	23.62	19.86	% UNDER 15	22.25	20.84	dominant)
% 15-64	61.22	62.19	60.39	62.85	64.85	61.09	% 15-64	66.16	63.95	
% 65 AND OLDER	16.16	12.84	19.03	15.52	11.53	19.05	% 65 AND OLDER	11.59	15.22	
DEPEND. RATIO x 100	63.34	60.81	65.59	59.11	54.21	63.70	DEPEND. RATIO x 100	51.14	56.38	

AGE GROUP	FEMALE BIRTH RATES	NET MATERNITY FUNCTION	COEFF. OF MATRIX EQUATION	ORIGINAL MATRIX SUB-DIAGONAL	ORIGINAL MATRIX FIRST ROW	STABLE MATRIX FISHER VALUES	STABLE MATRIX REPRODUCTIVE VALUES	MATRIX PARAMETERS		
0-4	0.0000	0.0000	0.0000	0.99739	0.00000	1.021	615109	λ_1	1.00631	
5-9	0.0000	0.0000	0.0000	0.99859	0.00004	1.030	718536	λ_2	0.27464+0.74778i	TABLE 7
10-14	0.0000	0.0001	0.0691	0.99807	0.06939	1.038	666759	λ_4	-0.43530-0.35456i	
15-19	0.0283	0.1381	0.2755	0.99716	0.27713	0.976	620143	λ_6	-0.45807+0.00000i	LESLIE
20-24	0.0848	0.4128	0.3495	0.99682	0.35263	0.701	317038	r_1	0.00126	MATRIX
25-29	0.0590	0.2863	0.2072	0.99607	0.20975	0.346	201160	r_2	-0.04547+0.24376i	AND ITS
30-34	0.0265	0.1282	0.0929	0.99435	0.09435	0.135	88196	r_4	-0.11545-0.49161i	ANALYSIS
35-39	0.0120	0.0575	0.0333	0.99112	0.03403	0.040	20941	r_6	-0.15615+0.62832i	(females)
40-44	0.0019	0.0091	0.0048	0.98568	0.00492	0.005	2788	c_1	89364	
45-49	0.0001	0.0004	0.0002	0.97863	0.00021	0.000	120	$2\pi/y$	25.7757	
50-54	0.0000	0.0000	0.0000	0.00000	0.00000	0.000	0	Δ	6.5072	

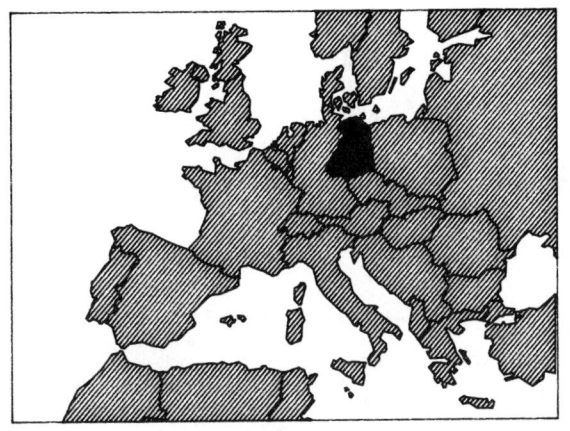

EDUCATION [1984]

% of primary school-age children enrolled:	98
secondary school-age children enrolled:	87
ca. 20-24 year olds in higher education:	30

LABOR FORCE

Average annual labor force growth (%) 1980-85:	0.9
% of the 1980 labor force in agriculture:	11
in industry:	50
in services:	39

TABLE 8

SOCIO-ECONOMIC INDICATORS

GNP & INCOME DISTRIBUTION

GNP per capita (in US Dollars) 1979:	5310
GNP growth rate (%) 1979:	2.3
% share of total household income	
Lowest 20% of households:	na
Highest 10% of households:	na

HEALTH & NUTRITION

Population per physician 1981:	490
Daily calorie supply per capita 1985:	3791

	AGE AT LAST BIRTHDAY	ESTIMATED MID-YEAR POPULATION					BIRTHS BY AGE OF MOTHER AND SEX	DEATHS			AGE AT LAST BIRTHDAY
		BOTH SEXES	MALES Number	Percent	FEMALES Number	Percent		BOTH SEXES	MALES	FEMALES	
	0	180042	92377	1.2	87665	1.0		2885	1684	1201	0
	1-4	806012	413333	5.3	392679	4.3		594	325	269	1-4
	5-9	1231001	630506	8.1	600495	6.7		499	300	199	5-9
	10-14	1428902	731672	9.4	697230	7.7	19	499	326	173	10-14
	15-19	1321820	678242	8.7	643578	7.1	30156	1056	782	274	15-19
	20-24	1310834	672456	8.6	638378	7.1	91740	1351	1013	338	20-24
	25-29	915337	465373	5.9	449964	5.0	35802	865	592	273	25-29
	30-34	1165016	585714	7.5	579302	6.4	16051	1411	922	489	30-34
TABLE 1	35-39	1310399	659268	8.4	651131	7.2	6689	2244	1428	816	35-39
	40-44	1052446	528241	6.8	524205	5.8	1278	2996	1941	1055	40-44
DATA	45-49	973943	444616	5.7	529327	5.9	63	4068	2427	1641	45-49
	50-54	890014	339737	4.3	550277	6.1		5761	2984	2777	50-54
	55-59	593348	221175	2.8	372173	4.1		5984	3114	2870	55-59
	60-64	934311	349463	4.5	584848	6.5		16032	8422	7610	60-64
	65-69	975492	377812	4.8	597680	6.6		28916	15438	13478	65-69
	70-74	816767	320371	4.1	496396	5.5		42874	22033	20841	70-74
	75-79	535908	184874	2.4	351034	3.9		47324	20163	27161	75-79
	80-84	276655	86157	1.1	190498	2.1	93655 M	40797	14515	26282	80-84
	85+	131878	41552	0.5	90326	1.0	88143 F	34233	11708	22525	85+
	TOTAL	16850125	7822939		9027186		181798	240389	110117	130272	TOTAL

x	nM_x	nq_x	l_x	nd_x	nL_x	nm_x	na_x	T_x	$\overset{\circ}{e}_x$	x
0	0.018230	0.017936	100000	1794	98388	0.018230	0.101	6855767	68.558	0
1	0.000786	0.003139	98206	308	392055	0.000786	1.500	6757379	68.808	1
5	0.000476	0.002376	97898	233	488909	0.000476	2.500	6365324	65.020	5
10	0.000446	0.002226	97666	217	487853	0.000446	2.815	5876415	60.169	10
15	0.001153	0.005758	97448	561	485944	0.001155	2.689	5388562	55.297	15
20	0.001506	0.007511	96887	728	482626	0.001508	2.514	4902618	50.601	20
TABLE 2										
25	0.001272	0.006339	96159	610	479277	0.001272	2.507	4419992	45.965	25
30	0.001574	0.007841	95550	749	475962	0.001574	2.615	3940714	41.243	30
MALE	35	0.002166	0.010793	94800	1023	471647	0.002169	2.698	3464753	36.548	35
LIFE	40	0.003674	0.018342	93777	1720	464894	0.003700	2.679	2993106	31.917	40
TABLE	45	0.005459	0.027140	92057	2498	454491	0.005497	2.680	2528212	27.463	45
	50	0.008783	0.043361	89559	3883	438782	0.008850	2.679	2073722	23.155	50
	55	0.014079	0.068176	85675	5841	414863	0.014079	2.686	1634940	19.083	55
	60	0.024100	0.114086	79834	9108	377929	0.024100	2.668	1220076	15.283	60
	65	0.040862	0.186227	70726	13171	322336	0.040862	2.624	842147	11.907	65
	70	0.068773	0.294367	57555	16942	246302	0.068787	2.552	519811	9.032	70
	75	0.109063	0.428478	40613	17402	158848	0.109549	2.459	273509	6.735	75
	80	0.168472	0.582756	23211	13526	80289	0.168472	2.356	114661	4.940	80
	85	0.281767	1.000000	9685	9685	34371	0.233885	3.549	34371	3.549	85

x	nM_x	nq_x	l_x	nd_x	nL_x	nm_x	na_x	T_x	$\overset{\circ}{e}_x$	x
0	0.013700	0.013532	100000	1353	98773	0.013700	0.093	7408611	74.086	0
1	0.000685	0.002735	98647	270	393913	0.000685	1.500	7309838	74.101	1
5	0.000331	0.001656	98377	163	491478	0.000331	2.500	6915925	70.300	5
10	0.000248	0.001240	98214	122	490776	0.000248	2.578	6424448	65.413	10
15	0.000426	0.002127	98092	209	489969	0.000426	2.637	5933672	60.491	15
20	0.000529	0.002649	97884	259	488789	0.000530	2.570	5443703	55.614	20
TABLE 3	25	0.000607	0.003034	97624	296	487413	0.000608	2.606	4954915	50.755	25
	30	0.000844	0.004212	97328	410	485681	0.000844	2.657	4467502	45.901	30
FEMALE	35	0.001253	0.006252	96918	606	483193	0.001254	2.692	3981821	41.084	35
LIFE	40	0.002013	0.010052	96312	968	479321	0.002020	2.685	3498628	36.326	40
TABLE	45	0.003100	0.015391	95344	1467	473341	0.003100	2.697	3019307	31.667	45
	50	0.005047	0.025078	93877	2354	463915	0.005075	2.677	2545966	27.120	50
	55	0.007711	0.037883	91523	3467	449613	0.007711	2.693	2082052	22.749	55
	60	0.013012	0.063170	88055	5562	427490	0.013012	2.701	1632439	18.539	60
	65	0.022551	0.107195	82493	8843	392134	0.022551	2.701	1204948	14.607	65
	70	0.041985	0.191319	73650	14091	335235	0.042032	2.657	812814	11.036	70
	75	0.077374	0.326723	59559	19459	250478	0.077689	2.568	477579	8.019	75
	80	0.137965	0.510572	40100	20474	148400	0.137965	2.455	227101	5.663	80
	85	0.249374	1.000000	19626	19626	78701	0.191437	4.010	78701	4.010	85

CRUDE RATES

TABLE 4	Per Thousand	BOTH SEXES	MALES	FEMALES
	BIRTH RATE	10.79	11.97	9.76
OBSERVED	DEATH RATE	14.27	14.08	14.43
VITAL	RATE OF INCREASE	-3.48	-2.10	-4.67

RATES
AND
RATIOS

PERCENT OF POPULATION IN AGE GROUP

UNDER 15	21.64	23.88	19.70
15 - 64	62.12	63.20	61.18
65 AND OLDER	16.24	12.92	19.12

RATES STANDARDIZED ON USA 1980

Per Thousand	BOTH SEXES	MALES	FEMALES
BIRTH RATE	13.84		13.05
DEATH RATE	12.03	12.05	12.02
RATE OF INCREASE	1.80		1.03

RATES STANDARDIZED ON MEXICO 1980

	BOTH SEXES	MALES	FEMALES
BIRTH RATE	13.10		12.80
DEATH RATE	4.53	5.21	3.83
RATE OF INCREASE	8.57		8.97

VITAL STATISTICS

GFR x 1000	45.270
TFR	1.553
GRR	0.753
NRR	0.735
μ	24.563
σ^2	25.487
GENERATION	24.721
POP. SEX RATIO	1.154
SEX RATIO AT BIRTH	1.063
DEP. RATIO x 100	60.976

AGE AT LAST BIRTHDAY	ESTIMATED MID-YEAR POPULATION BOTH SEXES	MALES Number	Percent	FEMALES Number	Percent	BIRTHS BY AGE OF MOTHER AND SEX	DEATHS BOTH SEXES	MALES	FEMALES	AGE AT LAST BIRTHDAY	
0	239764	123152	1.6	116612	1.3		2958	1753	1205	0	
1-4	845079	434135	5.5	410944	4.6		567	331	236	1-4	
5-9	978896	501924	6.4	476972	5.4		332	208	124	5-9	
10-14	1226305	627872	8.0	598433	6.7	23	362	230	132	10-14	
15-19	1426011	730102	9.3	695909	7.8	37364	1184	851	333	15-19	
20-24	1322869	679652	8.7	643217	7.2	118564	1327	959	368	20-24	
25-29	1302260	669153	8.5	633107	7.1	66069	1267	914	353	25-29	
30-34	906959	460512	5.9	446447	5.0	16668	1091	758	333	30-34	
35-39	1152241	577892	7.4	574349	6.5	5182	2035	1307	728	35-39	TABLE 1
40-44	1293206	648390	8.3	644816	7.3	1180	3656	2400	1256	40-44	
45-49	1031860	515116	6.6	516744	5.8	82	4737	3147	1590	45-49	DATA
50-54	946209	428154	5.5	518055	5.8		6750	4134	2616	50-54	
55-59	852512	320219	4.1	532293	6.0		9000	4807	4193	55-59	
60-64	551359	201274	2.6	350085	3.9		9331	4768	4563	60-64	
65-69	826404	296410	3.8	529994	6.0		23779	12001	11778	65-69	
70-74	799283	288914	3.7	510369	5.7		39832	19516	20316	70-74	
75-79	584164	209338	2.7	374826	4.2		49959	22573	27386	75-79	
80-84	309562	95519	1.2	214043	2.4	125668 M	43549	15975	27574	80-84	
85+	142261	39049	0.5	103212	1.2	119464 F	36538	11277	25261	85+	
TOTAL	16737204	7846777		8890427		245132	238254	107909	130345	TOTAL	

x	nM_x	nq_x	l_x	nd_x	nL_x	nm_x	na_x	T_x	$\mathring{e}_x$	x	
0	0.014234	0.014053	100000	1405	98727	0.014234	0.094	6868806	68.688	0	
1	0.000762	0.003044	98595	300	393628	0.000762	1.500	6770079	68.666	1	
5	0.000414	0.002070	98295	203	490964	0.000414	2.500	6376451	64.871	5	
10	0.000366	0.001830	98091	180	490083	0.000366	2.924	5885487	60.000	10	
15	0.001166	0.005812	97912	569	488240	0.001166	2.685	5395404	55.105	15	
20	0.001411	0.007031	97342	684	485020	0.001411	2.527	4907163	50.411	20	
25	0.001366	0.006810	96658	658	481667	0.001366	2.533	4422143	45.750	25	TABLE 2
30	0.001646	0.008216	96000	789	478114	0.001650	2.609	3940477	41.047	30	
35	0.002262	0.011249	95211	1071	473574	0.002262	2.683	3462363	36.365	35	MALE
40	0.003701	0.018355	94140	1728	466740	0.003702	2.708	2988789	31.748	40	LIFE
45	0.006109	0.030275	92412	2798	455594	0.006141	2.688	2522049	27.291	45	TABLE
50	0.009655	0.047503	89614	4257	438145	0.009716	2.668	2066455	23.059	50	
55	0.015012	0.073013	85357	6232	412170	0.015120	2.655	1628310	19.076	55	
60	0.023689	0.112220	79125	8879	374832	0.023689	2.658	1216140	15.370	60	
65	0.040488	0.184674	70246	12973	320406	0.040488	2.624	841308	11.977	65	
70	0.067550	0.289844	57273	16600	245750	0.067550	2.553	520902	9.095	70	
75	0.107830	0.423382	40673	17220	159691	0.107834	2.464	275152	6.765	75	
80	0.167244	0.580313	23453	13610	81378	0.167244	2.363	115461	4.923	80	
85	0.288791	1.000000	9843	9843	34083	0.243120	3.463	34083	3.463	85	

x	nM_x	nq_x	l_x	nd_x	nL_x	nm_x	na_x	T_x	$\mathring{e}_x$	x	
0	0.010333	0.010237	100000	1024	99066	0.010333	0.088	7464750	74.647	0	
1	0.000574	0.002294	98976	227	395338	0.000574	1.500	7365684	74.419	1	
5	0.000260	0.001299	98749	128	493426	0.000260	2.500	6970346	70.586	5	
10	0.000221	0.001102	98621	109	492856	0.000221	2.705	6476921	65.675	10	
15	0.000479	0.002390	98512	235	492009	0.000479	2.652	5984065	60.744	15	
20	0.000572	0.002857	98277	281	490690	0.000572	2.528	5492057	55.884	20	
25	0.000558	0.002786	97996	273	489316	0.000558	2.564	5001367	51.036	25	TABLE 3
30	0.000746	0.003736	97723	365	487774	0.000748	2.695	4512051	46.172	30	
35	0.001268	0.006319	97358	615	485372	0.001268	2.694	4024277	41.335	35	FEMALE
40	0.001948	0.009703	96743	939	481546	0.001949	2.690	3538905	36.581	40	LIFE
45	0.003077	0.015340	95804	1470	475642	0.003090	2.701	3057359	31.913	45	TABLE
50	0.005050	0.024957	94335	2354	466227	0.005050	2.687	2581717	27.368	50	
55	0.007877	0.038912	91980	3579	451628	0.007925	2.689	2115491	22.999	55	
60	0.013034	0.063267	88401	5593	429101	0.013034	2.693	1663863	18.822	60	
65	0.022223	0.105684	82808	8752	393806	0.022223	2.688	1234762	14.911	65	
70	0.039806	0.182046	74057	13482	338681	0.039807	2.656	840956	11.356	70	
75	0.073063	0.311035	60575	18841	257189	0.073257	2.575	502274	8.292	75	
80	0.128825	0.485961	41734	20281	157432	0.128825	2.474	245085	5.873	80	
85	0.244749	1.000000	21453	21453	87653	0.185639	4.086	87653	4.086	85	

CRUDE RATES

Per Thousand	BOTH SEXES	MALES	FEMALES
BIRTH RATE	14.65	16.02	13.44
DEATH RATE	14.23	13.75	14.66
RATE OF INCREASE	0.41	2.26	-1.22

RATES STANDARDIZED ON USA 1980

Per Thousand	BOTH SEXES	MALES	FEMALES
BIRTH RATE	17.46		16.55
DEATH RATE	11.80	12.06	11.55
RATE OF INCREASE	5.66		5.00

VITAL STATISTICS

GFR x 1000	59.003	TABLE 4
TFR	1.954	
GRR	0.952	OBSERVED
NRR	0.933	VITAL
μ	24.538	RATES
σ^2	22.712	AND
GENERATION	24.571	RATIOS
POP. SEX RATIO	1.133	
SEX RATIO AT BIRTH	1.052	
DEP. RATIO x 100	55.183	

PERCENT OF POPULATION IN AGE GROUP

	BOTH SEXES	MALES	FEMALES
UNDER 15	19.66	21.50	18.03
15 - 64	64.44	66.66	62.48
65 AND OLDER	15.90	11.84	19.49

RATES STANDARDIZED ON MEXICO 1980

	BOTH SEXES	MALES	FEMALES
BIRTH RATE	16.46		16.17
DEATH RATE	4.37	5.12	3.61
RATE OF INCREASE	12.08		12.56

TABLE 1 — DATA

AGE AT LAST BIRTHDAY	ESTIMATED MID-YEAR POPULATION BOTH SEXES	MALES Number	MALES Percent	FEMALES Number	FEMALES Percent	BIRTHS BY AGE OF MOTHER AND SEX	DEATHS BOTH SEXES	MALES	FEMALES	AGE AT LAST BIRTHDAY
0	227608	117011	1.5	110597	1.3		2175	1255	920	0
1-4	930609	476337	6.1	454272	5.2		557	330	227	1-4
5-9	1071750	548962	7.0	522788	6.0		304	183	121	5-9
10-14	976004	499787	6.4	476217	5.4	18	252	169	83	10-14
15-19	1226417	628666	8.0	597751	6.8	26172	824	573	251	15-19
20-24	1417243	725518	9.2	691725	7.9	111264	1341	978	363	20-24
25-29	1291526	660099	8.4	631427	7.2	63235	1248	904	344	25-29
30-34	1268706	645912	8.2	622794	7.1	21623	1535	1085	450	30-34
35-39	887430	447815	5.7	439615	5.0	4591	1460	952	508	35-39
40-44	1128826	562795	7.2	566031	6.5	711	2920	1922	998	40-44
45-49	1264623	629539	8.0	635084	7.2	34	5278	3510	1768	45-49
50-54	999470	493396	6.3	506074	5.8		6966	4613	2353	50-54
55-59	903776	402055	5.1	501721	5.7		9414	5822	3592	55-59
60-64	793378	290457	3.7	502921	5.7		13021	6718	6303	60-64
65-69	490592	171959	2.2	318633	3.6		12691	6289	6402	65-69
70-74	684101	229138	2.9	454963	5.2		31604	14405	17199	70-74
75-79	580478	190578	2.4	389900	4.4		46856	19968	26888	75-79
80-84	340045	108017	1.4	232028	2.6	117195 M	46761	17871	28890	80-84
85+	161726	42098	0.5	119628	1.4	110453 F	40146	11823	28323	85+
TOTAL	16644308	7870139		8774169		227648	225353	99370	125983	TOTAL

TABLE 2 — MALE LIFE TABLE

x	$_nM_x$	$_nq_x$	l_x	$_nd_x$	$_nL_x$	$_nm_x$	$_na_x$	T_x	$\overset{\circ}{e}_x$	x
0	0.010725	0.010622	100000	1062	99032	0.010726	0.088	6954659	69.547	0
1	0.000693	0.002766	98938	274	395067	0.000693	1.500	6855628	69.292	1
5	0.000333	0.001665	98664	164	492910	0.000333	2.500	6460561	65.480	5
10	0.000338	0.001689	98500	166	492142	0.000338	2.854	5967651	60.585	10
15	0.000911	0.004548	98333	447	490651	0.000911	2.729	5475509	55.683	15
20	0.001348	0.006718	97886	658	487832	0.001348	2.569	4984857	50.925	20
25	0.001369	0.006825	97229	664	484516	0.001370	2.548	4497025	46.252	25
30	0.001680	0.008388	96565	810	480874	0.001684	2.591	4012509	41.552	30
35	0.002126	0.010609	95755	1016	476401	0.002132	2.663	3531635	36.882	35
40	0.003415	0.016942	94739	1605	470006	0.003415	2.701	3055234	32.249	40
45	0.005576	0.027528	93134	2564	459794	0.005576	2.708	2585228	27.758	45
50	0.009349	0.045982	90570	4165	443174	0.009397	2.676	2125434	23.467	50
55	0.014481	0.070463	86406	6088	417788	0.014573	2.661	1682260	19.469	55
60	0.023129	0.110609	80317	8870	380646	0.023304	2.639	1264472	15.743	60
65	0.036573	0.168262	71447	12022	328708	0.036573	2.627	883826	12.370	65
70	0.062866	0.272760	59425	16209	257830	0.062866	2.576	555118	9.341	70
75	0.104776	0.414489	43216	17913	170962	0.104776	2.481	297287	6.879	75
80	0.165446	0.576477	25304	14587	88167	0.165446	2.371	126326	4.992	80
85	0.280845	1.000000	10717	10717	38159	0.232530	3.561	38159	3.561	85

TABLE 3 — FEMALE LIFE TABLE

x	$_nM_x$	$_nq_x$	l_x	$_nd_x$	$_nL_x$	$_nm_x$	$_na_x$	T_x	$\overset{\circ}{e}_x$	x
0	0.008318	0.008256	100000	826	99244	0.008319	0.084	7545341	75.453	0
1	0.000500	0.001996	99174	198	396203	0.000500	1.500	7446097	75.081	1
5	0.000231	0.001157	98976	114	494596	0.000231	2.500	7049894	71.228	5
10	0.000174	0.000871	98862	86	494114	0.000174	2.724	6555298	66.308	10
15	0.000420	0.002097	98776	207	493397	0.000420	2.673	6061184	61.363	15
20	0.000525	0.002620	98569	258	492210	0.000525	2.549	5567787	56.486	20
25	0.000545	0.002721	98310	267	490903	0.000545	2.576	5075577	51.628	25
30	0.000723	0.003625	98043	355	489388	0.000726	2.674	4584674	46.762	30
35	0.001156	0.005781	97688	565	487130	0.001159	2.683	4095285	41.922	35
40	0.001763	0.008780	97123	853	483642	0.001763	2.688	3608156	37.150	40
45	0.002784	0.013842	96270	1333	478298	0.002786	2.709	3124514	32.456	45
50	0.004650	0.023091	94938	2192	469610	0.004668	2.684	2646216	27.873	50
55	0.007159	0.035219	92745	3266	456246	0.007159	2.710	2176606	23.469	55
60	0.012533	0.061299	89479	5485	434682	0.012618	2.682	1720359	19.226	60
65	0.020092	0.096021	83994	8065	401411	0.020092	2.699	1285678	15.307	65
70	0.037803	0.173688	75929	13188	348857	0.037803	2.666	884267	11.646	70
75	0.068961	0.295620	62741	18547	268954	0.068961	2.587	535409	8.534	75
80	0.124511	0.474193	44193	20956	168308	0.124511	2.487	266455	6.029	80
85	0.236759	1.000000	23237	23237	98147	0.175852	4.224	98147	4.224	85

TABLE 4 — OBSERVED VITAL RATES AND RATIOS

CRUDE RATES

Per Thousand	BOTH SEXES	MALES	FEMALES
BIRTH RATE	13.68	14.89	12.59
DEATH RATE	13.54	12.63	14.36
RATE OF INCREASE	0.14	2.26	-1.77

PERCENT OF POPULATION IN AGE GROUP

UNDER 15	19.26	20.86	17.82
15 - 64	67.18	69.71	64.91
65 AND OLDER	13.56	9.43	17.27

RATES STANDARDIZED ON USA 1980

Per Thousand	BOTH SEXES	MALES	FEMALES
BIRTH RATE	15.64		14.76
DEATH RATE	11.20	11.47	10.95
RATE OF INCREASE	4.44		3.81

RATES STANDARDIZED ON MEXICO 1980

	BOTH SEXES	MALES	FEMALES
BIRTH RATE	14.64		14.31
DEATH RATE	4.07	4.78	3.35
RATE OF INCREASE	10.57		10.96

VITAL STATISTICS

GFR x 1000	54.404
TFR	1.756
GRR	0.852
NRR	0.838
μ	24.797
σ^2	22.950
GENERATION	24.879
POP. SEX RATIO	1.115
SEX RATIO AT BIRTH	1.061
DEP. RATIO x 100	48.857

PROJECTED POPULATION

AGE GROUP	1990 BOTH SEXES	1990 MALES	1990 FEMALES	1995 BOTH SEXES	1995 MALES	1995 FEMALES
0-4	1095	563	532	1001	515	486
5-9	1156	592	564	1092	561	531
10-14	1070	548	522	1154	591	563
15-19	974	498	476	1068	546	522
20-24	1221	625	596	969	495	474
25-29	1411	721	690	1216	621	595
30-34	1284	655	629	1403	715	688
35-39	1260	640	620	1276	649	627
40-44	878	442	436	1246	631	615
45-49	1111	551	560	864	432	432
50-54	1231	607	624	1081	531	550
55-59	957	465	492	1178	572	606
60-64	844	366	478	892	424	468
65-69	715	251	464	757	316	441
70-74	412	135	277	601	197	404
75-79	503	152	351	302	89	213
80-84	342	98	244	298	78	220
85+	182	47	135	185	43	142
TOTAL	16646	7956	8690	16583	8006	8577

STABLE EQUIVALENT TO ORIGINAL POPULATION

MALES Number	MALES Percent	FEMALES Number	FEMALES Percent	AGE GROUP
556	5.5	526	5.0	0-4
575	5.7	544	5.2	5-9
595	5.9	563	5.3	10-14
614	6.1	582	5.5	15-19
633	6.3	602	5.7	20-24
651	6.4	622	5.9	25-29
670	6.6	643	6.1	30-34
688	6.8	663	6.3	35-39
703	7.0	682	6.5	40-44
713	7.1	699	6.6	45-49
712	7.0	711	6.7	50-54
695	6.9	716	6.8	55-59
656	6.5	706	6.7	60-64
587	5.8	676	6.4	65-69
477	4.7	609	5.8	70-74
328	3.2	486	4.6	75-79
175	1.7	315	3.0	80-84
79	0.8	191	1.8	85+
10107		10536		TOTAL

TABLE 5

POPULATION PROJECTED WITH FIXED AGE-SPECIFIC BIRTH AND DEATH RATES (female dominant, in 000s)

VITAL RATES OF PROJECTED POPULATION

Per Thousand	1990 BOTH SEXES	1990 MALES	1990 FEMALES	1995 BOTH SEXES	1995 MALES	1995 FEMALES
BIRTH RATE	12.90	13.90	11.99	11.45	12.21	10.74
DEATH RATE	13.19	11.95	14.33	12.68	11.51	13.77
RATE OF INCREASE	-0.29	1.95	-2.34	-1.23	0.70	-3.03

VITAL RATES OF STABLE POPULATION

Per Thousand	MALES	FEMALES
BIRTH RATE	10.94	9.89
DEATH RATE	18.00	17.00
RATE OF INCREASE		-7.11

TABLE 6

PROJECTED VITAL RATES AND RATIOS (female dominant)

AGE STRUCTURE OF PROJECTED POPULATION

	1990 BOTH SEXES	1990 MALES	1990 FEMALES	1995 BOTH SEXES	1995 MALES	1995 FEMALES
% UNDER 15	19.95	21.40	18.62	19.58	20.82	18.43
% 15-64	67.11	70.01	64.45	67.49	70.15	65.01
% 65 AND OLDER	12.94	8.58	16.93	12.93	9.03	16.56
DEPEND. RATIO x 100	49.01	42.83	55.16	48.17	42.56	53.82

STABLE AGE STRUCTURE

	MALES	FEMALES
% UNDER 15	17.07	15.49
% 15-64	66.64	62.89
% 65 AND OLDER	16.29	21.61
DEPEND. RATIO x 100	50.07	59.00

AGE GROUP	FEMALE BIRTH RATES	NET MATERNITY FUNCTION	COEFF. OF MATRIX EQUATION	ORIGINAL MATRIX SUB-DIAGONAL	ORIGINAL MATRIX FIRST ROW	STABLE MATRIX FISHER VALUES	STABLE MATRIX REPRODUCTIVE VALUES
0-4	0.0000	0.0000	0.0000	0.99828	0.00000	0.991	560008
5-9	0.0000	0.0000	0.0000	0.99903	0.00005	0.958	501051
10-14	0.0000	0.0001	0.0525	0.99855	0.05259	0.926	440888
15-19	0.0212	0.1048	0.2445	0.99759	0.24549	0.843	503644
20-24	0.0780	0.3841	0.3113	0.99735	0.31338	0.571	395071
25-29	0.0486	0.2385	0.1605	0.99691	0.16197	0.241	152269
30-34	0.0168	0.0824	0.0536	0.99538	0.05422	0.072	45076
35-39	0.0051	0.0247	0.0138	0.99284	0.01405	0.016	7107
40-44	0.0006	0.0029	0.0015	0.98895	0.00157	0.002	953
45-49	0.0000	0.0001	0.0001	0.98184	0.00006	0.000	42
50-54	0.0000	0.0000	0.0000	0.00000	0.00000	0.000	0

MATRIX PARAMETERS

λ_1	0.96508
λ_2	0.25479+0.75615i
λ_4	-0.41900+0.33525i
λ_6	-0.38933-0.00000i
r_1	-0.00711
r_2	-0.04515+0.24916i
r_4	-0.12450+0.49336i
r_6	-0.18866-0.62832i
c_1	105340
$2\pi/y$	25.2177
Δ	8.6779

TABLE 7

LESLIE MATRIX AND ITS ANALYSIS (females)

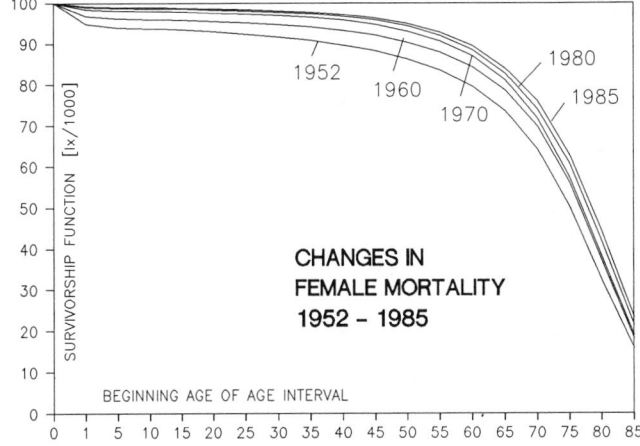

CHANGES IN FEMALE MORTALITY 1952 - 1985

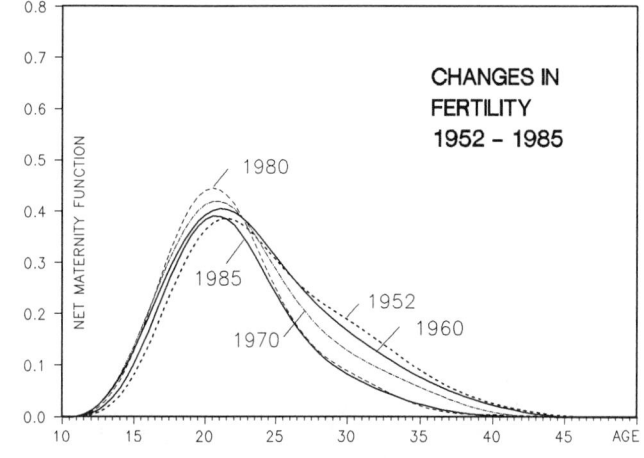

CHANGES IN FERTILITY 1952 - 1985

TABLE 1 — DATA

AGE AT LAST BIRTHDAY	ESTIMATED MID-YEAR POPULATION BOTH SEXES	MALES Number	MALES Percent	FEMALES Number	FEMALES Percent	BIRTHS BY AGE OF MOTHER AND SEX	DEATHS BOTH SEXES	DEATHS MALES	DEATHS FEMALES	AGE AT LAST BIRTHDAY
0	824736	422579	1.5	402157	1.3		19165	11201	7964	0
1-4	3890740	1993117	6.9	1897623	6.0		3786	2156	1630	1-4
5-9	4990118	2556431	8.9	2433687	7.7		2604	1608	996	5-9
10-14	4352676	2234486	7.7	2118190	6.7	99	1789	1131	658	10-14
15-19	3995827	2044088	7.1	1951739	6.1	69931	4168	3048	1120	15-19
20-24	3725104	1905018	6.6	1820086	5.7	236484	4546	3419	1127	20-24
25-29	4292609	2226671	7.7	2065938	6.5	223470	5094	3633	1461	25-29
30-34	4954605	2587687	9.0	2366918	7.4	182646	6951	4825	2126	30-34
35-39	3928896	2047343	7.1	1881553	5.9	74692	7789	5089	2700	35-39
40-44	3925465	1947470	6.7	1977995	6.2	21738	11705	7284	4421	40-44
45-49	3782082	1610333	5.6	2171749	6.8	1728	17377	9452	7925	45-49
50-54	2556402	1068094	3.7	1488308	4.7	20	17653	9776	7877	50-54
55-59	3753567	1573790	5.5	2179777	6.9		41003	24070	16933	55-59
60-64	3687161	1562809	5.4	2124352	6.7		68836	41590	27246	60-64
65-69	3158704	1346376	4.7	1812328	5.7		100854	59872	40982	65-69
70-74	2272505	861103	3.0	1411402	4.4		116520	59502	57018	70-74
75-79	1422933	485911	1.7	937022	2.9		117354	49947	67407	75-79
80-84	761827	262099	0.9	499728	1.6	416321 M	101605	39886	61719	80-84
85+	374609	131306	0.5	243303	0.8	394487 F	86033	32478	53555	85+
TOTAL	60650566	28866711		31783855		810808	734832	369967	364865	TOTAL

TABLE 2 — MALE LIFE TABLE

x	$_nM_x$	$_nq_x$	l_x	$_nd_x$	$_nL_x$	$_nm_x$	$_na_x$	T_x	$\overset{\circ}{e}_x$	x
0	0.026506	0.025899	100000	2590	97708	0.026506	0.115	6727165	67.272	0
1	0.001082	0.004315	97410	420	388590	0.001082	1.500	6629457	68.057	1
5	0.000629	0.003140	96990	305	484187	0.000629	2.500	6240868	64.346	5
10	0.000506	0.002541	96685	246	482898	0.000509	2.852	5756680	59.540	10
15	0.001491	0.007457	96440	719	480527	0.001497	2.677	5273782	54.685	15
20	0.001795	0.008934	95720	855	476475	0.001795	2.513	4793255	50.076	20
25	0.001632	0.008125	94865	771	472403	0.001632	2.505	4316780	45.504	25
30	0.001865	0.009282	94095	873	468369	0.001865	2.592	3844376	40.857	30
35	0.002486	0.012396	93221	1156	463391	0.002494	2.651	3376007	36.215	35
40	0.003740	0.018591	92066	1712	456357	0.003751	2.680	2912616	31.636	40
45	0.005870	0.029159	90354	2635	445646	0.005912	2.676	2456259	27.185	45
50	0.009153	0.044837	87719	3933	429505	0.009157	2.688	2010613	22.921	50
55	0.015294	0.073867	83786	6189	404664	0.015294	2.695	1581108	18.871	55
60	0.026612	0.125261	77597	9720	365241	0.026612	2.660	1176444	15.161	60
65	0.044469	0.201121	67877	13652	306581	0.044528	2.597	811203	11.951	65
70	0.069100	0.296405	54226	16073	231349	0.069474	2.525	504621	9.306	70
75	0.102790	0.408427	38153	15583	151015	0.103187	2.449	273272	7.163	75
80	0.152179	0.543384	22570	12264	80591	0.152179	2.370	122258	5.417	80
85	0.247346	1.000000	10306	10306	41666	0.189765	4.043	41666	4.043	85

TABLE 3 — FEMALE LIFE TABLE

x	$_nM_x$	$_nq_x$	l_x	$_nd_x$	$_nL_x$	$_nm_x$	$_na_x$	T_x	$\overset{\circ}{e}_x$	x
0	0.019803	0.019458	100000	1946	98256	0.019803	0.104	7363440	73.634	0
1	0.000859	0.003429	98054	336	391376	0.000859	1.500	7265184	74.094	1
5	0.000409	0.002044	97718	200	488091	0.000409	2.500	6873807	70.343	5
10	0.000311	0.001554	97518	152	487229	0.000311	2.610	6385716	65.482	10
15	0.000574	0.002872	97367	280	486166	0.000575	2.611	5898487	60.580	15
20	0.000619	0.003091	97087	300	484698	0.000619	2.543	5412322	55.747	20
25	0.000707	0.003530	96787	342	483108	0.000707	2.581	4927624	50.912	25
30	0.000898	0.004485	96445	433	481218	0.000899	2.667	4444515	46.083	30
35	0.001435	0.007175	96013	689	478473	0.001440	2.690	3963298	41.279	35
40	0.002235	0.011118	95324	1060	474183	0.002235	2.701	3484825	36.558	40
45	0.003649	0.018168	94264	1713	467322	0.003665	2.665	3010642	31.938	45
50	0.005293	0.026139	92551	2419	457069	0.005293	2.649	2543320	27.480	50
55	0.007768	0.038154	90132	3439	442686	0.007768	2.681	2086251	23.147	55
60	0.012826	0.062317	86693	5402	421069	0.012830	2.705	1643565	18.958	60
65	0.022613	0.107761	81291	8760	386227	0.022681	2.691	1222496	15.039	65
70	0.040398	0.185194	72531	13432	331044	0.040575	2.647	836269	11.530	70
75	0.071937	0.308269	59099	18218	251156	0.072538	2.566	505224	8.549	75
80	0.123505	0.470452	40880	19232	155720	0.123505	2.469	254069	6.215	80
85	0.220116	1.000000	21648	21648	98348	0.155903	4.543	98348	4.543	85

TABLE 4 — OBSERVED VITAL RATES AND RATIOS

CRUDE RATES

Per Thousand	BOTH SEXES	MALES	FEMALES
BIRTH RATE	13.37	14.42	12.41
DEATH RATE	12.12	12.82	11.48
RATE OF INCREASE	1.25	1.61	0.93

PERCENT OF POPULATION IN AGE GROUP

	BOTH SEXES	MALES	FEMALES
UNDER 15	23.18	24.97	21.56
15 - 64	63.65	64.34	63.01
65 AND OLDER	13.17	10.69	15.43

RATES STANDARDIZED ON USA 1980

Per Thousand	BOTH SEXES	MALES	FEMALES
BIRTH RATE	17.03		16.11
DEATH RATE	11.80	12.23	11.40
RATE OF INCREASE	5.22		4.71

RATES STANDARDIZED ON MEXICO 1980

	BOTH SEXES	MALES	FEMALES
BIRTH RATE	15.26		14.97
DEATH RATE	4.80	5.64	3.96
RATE OF INCREASE	10.46		11.01

VITAL STATISTICS

GFR x 1000	56.955
TFR	2.013
GRR	0.979
NRR	0.946
μ	27.356
σ^2	38.429
GENERATION	27.395
POP. SEX RATIO	1.101
SEX RATIO AT BIRTH	1.055
DEP. RATIO x 100	57.119

PROJECTED POPULATION / STABLE EQUIVALENT TO ORIGINAL POPULATION

AGE GROUP	1975 BOTH SEXES	MALES	FEMALES	1980 BOTH SEXES	MALES	FEMALES	MALES Number	Percent	FEMALES Number	Percent	AGE GROUP	
0-4	3928	2010	1918	3946	2019	1927	2206	6.7	2105	6.2	0-4	
5-9	4698	2405	2293	3913	2001	1912	2219	6.8	2119	6.2	5-9	TABLE 5
10-14	4979	2550	2429	4687	2399	2288	2235	6.8	2137	6.3	10-14	
15-19	4338	2224	2114	4961	2537	2424	2247	6.9	2154	6.3	15-19	POPULATION
20-24	3973	2027	1946	4312	2205	2107	2251	6.9	2170	6.4	20-24	PROJECTED
25-29	3703	1889	1814	3949	2010	1939	2255	6.9	2185	6.4	25-29	WITH
30-34	4266	2208	2058	3680	1873	1807	2258	6.9	2198	6.4	30-34	FIXED
35-39	4913	2560	2353	4230	2184	2046	2257	6.9	2208	6.5	35-39	AGE-
40-44	3881	2016	1865	4853	2521	2332	2246	6.9	2211	6.5	40-44	SPECIFIC
45-49	3851	1902	1949	3807	1969	1838	2215	6.8	2201	6.5	45-49	BIRTH
50-54	3676	1552	2124	3740	1833	1907	2157	6.6	2175	6.4	50-54	AND
55-59	2447	1006	1441	3519	1462	2057	2053	6.3	2128	6.2	55-59	DEATH
60-64	3493	1420	2073	2279	908	1371	1872	5.7	2045	6.0	60-64	RATES
65-69	3261	1312	1949	3094	1192	1902	1587	4.9	1895	5.6	65-69	(female
70-74	2569	1016	1553	2660	990	1670	1210	3.7	1641	4.8	70-74	dominant,
75-79	1633	562	1071	1842	663	1179	798	2.4	1257	3.7	75-79	in 000s)
80-84	840	259	581	964	300	664	430	1.3	788	2.3	80-84	
85+	452	136	316	501	134	367	225	0.7	502	1.5	85+	
TOTAL	60901	29054	31847	60937	29200	31737	32721		34119		TOTAL	

VITAL RATES OF PROJECTED POPULATION / VITAL RATES OF STABLE POPULATION

Per Thousand	1975 BOTH SEXES	MALES	FEMALES	1980 BOTH SEXES	MALES	FEMALES	STABLE MALES	STABLE FEMALES	
BIRTH RATE	13.12	14.12	12.21	13.43	14.39	12.55	13.79	12.53	TABLE 6
DEATH RATE	12.87	13.07	12.69	13.42	13.23	13.60	15.75	14.57	
RATE OF INCREASE	0.25	1.05	-0.48	0.00	1.16	-1.06		-2.03	PROJECTED VITAL RATES

AGE STRUCTURE OF PROJECTED POPULATION / STABLE AGE STRUCTURE

	1975 BOTH SEXES	MALES	FEMALES	1980 BOTH SEXES	MALES	FEMALES	STABLE MALES	STABLE FEMALES	
% UNDER 15	22.34	23.97	20.85	20.59	21.98	19.30	20.35	18.64	AND RATIOS
% 15-64	63.29	64.72	61.98	64.54	66.79	62.48	66.66	63.53	(female
% 65 AND OLDER	14.37	11.31	17.17	14.87	11.23	18.22	12.99	17.83	dominant)
DEPEND. RATIO x 100	58.01	54.51	61.35	54.94	49.73	60.05	50.02	57.41	

MATRIX PARAMETERS

AGE GROUP	FEMALE BIRTH RATES	NET MATERNITY FUNCTION	COEFF. OF MATRIX EQUATION	ORIGINAL MATRIX SUB-DIAGONAL	FIRST ROW	STABLE MATRIX FISHER VALUES	REPRODUCTIVE VALUES	MATRIX PARAMETERS		
0-4	0.0000	0.0000	0.0000	0.99685	0.00000	1.016	2336568	λ_1	0.98988	
5-9	0.0000	0.0000	0.0001	0.99823	0.00006	1.009	2455329	λ_2	0.36027+0.69714i	TABLE 7
10-14	0.0000	0.0001	0.0424	0.99782	0.04264	1.000	2119025	λ_4	-0.02579+0.55725i	
15-19	0.0174	0.0848	0.1956	0.99698	0.19697	0.949	1852242	λ_6	-0.38126+0.32946i	LESLIE
20-24	0.0632	0.3064	0.2803	0.99672	0.28318	0.742	1349654	r_1	-0.00203	MATRIX
25-29	0.0526	0.2543	0.2175	0.99609	0.22040	0.448	925102	r_2	-0.04848+0.21876i	AND ITS
30-34	0.0375	0.1807	0.1365	0.99430	0.13893	0.220	521188	r_4	-0.11673+0.32341i	ANALYSIS
35-39	0.0193	0.0924	0.0589	0.99104	0.06026	0.077	145367	r_6	-0.13708+0.48579i	(females)
40-44	0.0053	0.0254	0.0136	0.98553	0.01402	0.015	30451	c_1	341191	
45-49	0.0004	0.0018	0.0009	0.97806	0.00096	0.001	2183	$2\pi/y$	28.7216	
50-54	0.0000	0.0000	0.0000	0.96853	0.00002	0.000	24	Δ	5.8557	

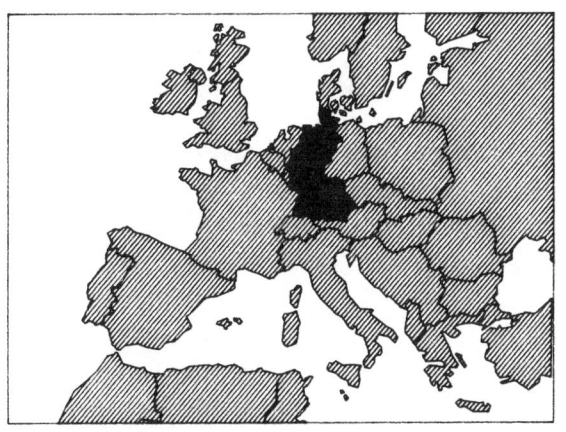

EDUCATION [1984]

% of primary school-age children enrolled:	99
secondary school-age children enrolled:	74
ca. 20-24 year olds in higher education:	29

LABOR FORCE

Average annual labor force growth (%) 1980-85:	0.7	
% of the 1980 labor force in agriculture:	6	TABLE 8
in industry:	44	
in services:	50	SOCIO-ECONOMIC INDICATORS

GNP & INCOME DISTRIBUTION

GNP per capita (in US Dollars) 1985:	10940
GNP average annual growth rate (%) 1965-85:	2.7
% share of total household income 1978	
Lowest 20% of households:	7.9
Highest 10% of households:	24.0

HEALTH & NUTRITION

Population per physician 1981:	420
Daily calorie supply per capita 1985:	3474

TABLE 1 — DATA

AGE AT LAST BIRTHDAY	ESTIMATED MID-YEAR POPULATION BOTH SEXES	MALES Number	MALES Percent	FEMALES Number	FEMALES Percent	BIRTHS BY AGE OF MOTHER AND SEX	DEATHS BOTH SEXES	DEATHS MALES	DEATHS FEMALES	AGE AT LAST BIRTHDAY
0	601274	308105	1.0	293169	0.9		11875	6873	5002	0
1-4	2779576	1422393	4.8	1357183	4.2		2197	1229	968	1-4
5-9	4808201	2464623	8.4	2343578	7.2		1959	1163	796	5-9
10-14	5097320	2612251	8.9	2485069	7.7	91	1643	1027	616	10-14
15-19	4519675	2321544	7.9	2198131	6.8	47008	4648	3373	1275	15-19
20-24	4239910	2139316	7.3	2100594	6.5	183729	4633	3423	1210	20-24
25-29	4031142	2085582	7.1	1945560	6.0	199006	3985	2811	1174	25-29
30-34	4380258	2283546	7.7	2096712	6.5	104050	5843	3994	1849	30-34
35-39	4978024	2592691	8.8	2385333	7.4	52995	9129	6110	3019	35-39
40-44	3922280	2029796	6.9	1892484	5.9	12663	11660	7830	3830	40-44
45-49	3875448	1908678	6.5	1966770	6.1	947	17605	11305	6300	45-49
50-54	3718252	1563903	5.3	2154349	6.7	23	25613	14754	10859	50-54
55-59	2477180	1016044	3.4	1461386	4.5		25350	14775	10575	55-59
60-64	3463470	1402809	4.8	2060661	6.4		58156	34317	23839	60-64
65-69	3317355	1331940	4.5	1985415	6.1		95123	55176	39947	65-69
70-74	2635399	1043333	3.5	1592066	4.9		127383	69279	58104	70-74
75-79	1678106	573652	1.9	1104454	3.4		132735	59078	73657	75-79
80-84	869381	263704	0.9	605677	1.9	309135 M	111435	40776	70659	80-84
85+	436869	135455	0.5	301414	0.9	291377 F	98269	33767	64502	85+
TOTAL	61829370	29499365		32330005		600512	749241	371060	378181	TOTAL

TABLE 2 — MALE LIFE TABLE

x	nM_x	nq_x	l_x	nd_x	nL_x	nm_x	na_x	T_x	$\mathring{e}_x$	x
0	0.022307	0.021872	100000	2187	98049	0.022307	0.108	6809409	68.094	0
1	0.000864	0.003449	97813	337	390408	0.000864	1.500	6711360	68.614	1
5	0.000472	0.002357	97475	230	486803	0.000472	2.500	6320952	64.847	5
10	0.000393	0.001965	97246	191	485850	0.000393	3.018	5834149	59.994	10
15	0.001453	0.007261	97055	705	483632	0.001457	2.670	5348299	55.106	15
20	0.001600	0.007967	96350	768	479817	0.001600	2.483	4864667	50.490	20
25	0.001348	0.006717	95582	642	476319	0.001348	2.519	4384850	45.875	25
30	0.001749	0.008709	94940	827	472730	0.001749	2.616	3908531	41.168	30
35	0.002357	0.011726	94113	1104	468008	0.002358	2.681	3435801	36.507	35
40	0.003858	0.019199	93010	1786	460912	0.003874	2.683	2967793	31.908	40
45	0.005923	0.029297	91224	2673	449925	0.005940	2.682	2506881	27.480	45
50	0.009434	0.046483	88552	4116	433149	0.009503	2.666	2056956	23.229	50
55	0.014542	0.070400	84436	5944	408352	0.014557	2.674	1623806	19.231	55
60	0.024463	0.115703	78491	9082	371239	0.024463	2.664	1215455	15.485	60
65	0.041425	0.188480	69410	13082	315805	0.041425	2.612	844215	12.163	65
70	0.066402	0.285847	56327	16101	242099	0.066506	2.544	528410	9.381	70
75	0.102986	0.410567	40226	16516	159203	0.103740	2.461	286311	7.117	75
80	0.154628	0.549476	23711	13028	84257	0.154628	2.368	127108	5.361	80
85	0.249286	1.000000	10682	10682	42851	0.192135	4.011	42851	4.011	85

TABLE 3 — FEMALE LIFE TABLE

x	nM_x	nq_x	l_x	nd_x	nL_x	nm_x	na_x	T_x	$\mathring{e}_x$	x
0	0.017062	0.016804	100000	1680	98486	0.017062	0.099	7472593	74.726	0
1	0.000713	0.002848	98320	280	392579	0.000713	1.500	7374107	75.001	1
5	0.000340	0.001697	98040	166	489782	0.000340	2.500	6981529	71.211	5
10	0.000248	0.001239	97873	121	489088	0.000248	2.701	6491746	66.328	10
15	0.000580	0.002901	97752	284	488084	0.000581	2.617	6002659	61.407	15
20	0.000576	0.002876	97468	280	486643	0.000576	2.507	5514575	56.578	20
25	0.000603	0.003014	97188	293	485239	0.000604	2.604	5027932	51.734	25
30	0.000882	0.004400	96895	426	483476	0.000882	2.655	4542693	46.883	30
35	0.001266	0.006315	96469	609	480934	0.001267	2.686	4059217	42.078	35
40	0.002024	0.010107	95860	969	477063	0.002031	2.693	3578283	37.328	40
45	0.003203	0.015898	94891	1509	470967	0.003203	2.689	3101219	32.682	45
50	0.005041	0.025006	93382	2335	461434	0.005060	2.655	2630252	28.167	50
55	0.007236	0.035598	91047	3241	447677	0.007240	2.668	2168818	23.821	55
60	0.011569	0.056343	87806	4947	427647	0.011569	2.699	1721141	19.602	60
65	0.020120	0.096171	82859	7969	395972	0.020124	2.701	1293495	15.611	65
70	0.036496	0.168608	74890	12627	344973	0.036603	2.665	897523	11.985	70
75	0.066691	0.289073	62263	17999	267848	0.067197	2.585	552550	8.874	75
80	0.116661	0.451125	44265	19969	171169	0.116661	2.488	284702	6.432	80
85	0.213998	1.000000	24296	24296	113532	0.148767	4.673	113532	4.673	85

TABLE 4 — OBSERVED VITAL RATES AND RATIOS

CRUDE RATES

Per Thousand	BOTH SEXES	MALES	FEMALES
BIRTH RATE	9.71	10.48	9.01
DEATH RATE	12.12	12.58	11.70
RATE OF INCREASE	-2.41	-2.10	-2.68

PERCENT OF POPULATION IN AGE GROUP

UNDER 15	21.49	23.08	20.04
15 - 64	64.06	65.57	62.67
65 AND OLDER	14.45	11.35	17.29

RATES STANDARDIZED ON USA 1980

Per Thousand	BOTH SEXES	MALES	FEMALES
BIRTH RATE	12.36		11.66
DEATH RATE	11.20	11.82	10.62
RATE OF INCREASE	1.16		1.04

RATES STANDARDIZED ON MEXICO 1980

	BOTH SEXES	MALES	FEMALES
BIRTH RATE	10.99		10.75
DEATH RATE	4.47	5.31	3.61
RATE OF INCREASE	6.53		7.14

VITAL STATISTICS

GFR x 1000	41.172
TFR	1.451
GRR	0.704
NRR	0.683
μ	27.229
σ^2	32.552
GENERATION	27.455
POP. SEX RATIO	1.096
SEX RATIO AT BIRTH	1.061
DEP. RATIO x 100	56.112

AGE AT LAST BIRTHDAY	ESTIMATED MID-YEAR POPULATION BOTH SEXES	MALES Number	MALES Percent	FEMALES Number	FEMALES Percent	BIRTHS BY AGE OF MOTHER AND SEX	DEATHS BOTH SEXES	DEATHS MALES	DEATHS FEMALES	AGE AT LAST BIRTHDAY	
0	598037	306402	1.0	291635	0.9		7821	4455	3366	0	
1-4	2333277	1196068	4.1	1137209	3.5		1448	801	647	1-4	
5-9	3385730	1729712	5.9	1656018	5.2		1081	677	404	5-9	
10-14	4869580	2497598	8.5	2371982	7.4	76	1317	830	487	10-14	
15-19	5218067	2687054	9.1	2531013	7.9	38524	4261	3114	1147	15-19	
20-24	4662065	2409419	8.2	2252646	7.0	184039	4620	3562	1058	20-24	
25-29	4302079	2196528	7.5	2105551	6.5	224911	4066	2848	1218	25-29	
30-34	3968108	2045496	7.0	1922612	6.0	124605	4435	2963	1472	30-34	
35-39	4294961	2213829	7.5	2081123	6.5	38101	7108	4732	2376	35-39	TABLE 1
40-44	4884698	2514717	8.5	2369981	7.4	9711	12575	8564	4011	40-44	
45-49	3829290	1957348	6.7	1871942	5.8	641	16140	10903	5237	45-49	DATA
50-54	3761436	1827669	6.2	1933767	6.0	49	24201	16020	8181	50-54	
55-59	3571260	1471906	5.0	2099354	6.5		34190	20380	13810	55-59	
60-64	2336604	927795	3.2	1408809	4.4		33933	19751	14182	60-64	
65-69	3153125	1215962	4.1	1937163	6.0		76394	43560	32834	65-69	
70-74	2814123	1048020	3.6	1766103	5.5		115593	61700	53893	70-74	
75-79	1986223	708908	2.4	1277315	4.0		138017	66049	71968	75-79	
80-84	1057289	316945	1.1	740344	2.3	318480 M	118920	44658	74262	80-84	
85+	540386	145758	0.5	394628	1.2	302177 F	107987	32443	75544	85+	
TOTAL	61566338	29417134		32149204		620657	714107	348010	366097	TOTAL	

x	nM_x	nq_x	l_x	nd_x	nL_x	nm_x	na_x	T_x	$\overset{\circ}{e}_x$	x	
0	0.014540	0.014351	100000	1435	98701	0.014540	0.095	6991265	69.913	0	
1	0.000670	0.002674	98565	264	393601	0.000670	1.500	6892564	69.929	1	
5	0.000391	0.001955	98301	192	491026	0.000391	2.500	6498964	66.113	5	
10	0.000332	0.001660	98109	163	490216	0.000332	2.978	6007938	61.237	10	
15	0.001159	0.005779	97946	566	488432	0.001159	2.704	5517721	56.334	15	
20	0.001478	0.007368	97380	717	485119	0.001479	2.517	5029290	51.646	20	
25	0.001297	0.006460	96663	624	481747	0.001296	2.492	4544170	47.011	25	TABLE 2
30	0.001449	0.007220	96038	693	478539	0.001449	2.617	4062423	42.300	30	
35	0.002137	0.010635	95345	1014	474377	0.002137	2.685	3583884	37.589	35	MALE
40	0.003406	0.016906	94331	1595	467990	0.003408	2.702	3109507	32.964	40	LIFE
45	0.005570	0.027616	92736	2561	457755	0.005595	2.686	2641517	28.484	45	TABLE
50	0.008765	0.043068	90175	3884	441847	0.008790	2.675	2183761	24.217	50	
55	0.013846	0.067521	86292	5826	417784	0.013946	2.653	1741914	20.186	55	
60	0.021288	0.101497	80465	8167	383181	0.021314	2.656	1324130	16.456	60	
65	0.035823	0.165093	72298	11936	333187	0.035823	2.629	940949	13.015	65	
70	0.058873	0.257493	60362	15543	264007	0.058873	2.568	607762	10.069	70	
75	0.093170	0.379059	44819	16989	181373	0.093670	2.485	343755	7.670	75	
80	0.140901	0.515278	27830	14340	101775	0.140901	2.394	162382	5.835	80	
85	0.222581	1.000000	13490	13490	60607	0.159553	4.493	60607	4.493	85	

x	nM_x	nq_x	l_x	nd_x	nL_x	nm_x	na_x	T_x	$\overset{\circ}{e}_x$	x	
0	0.011542	0.011422	100000	1142	98960	0.011542	0.090	7672987	76.730	0	
1	0.000569	0.002273	98858	225	394870	0.000569	1.500	7574027	76.615	1	
5	0.000244	0.001219	98633	120	492865	0.000244	2.500	7179157	72.786	5	
10	0.000205	0.001026	98513	101	492333	0.000205	2.711	6686292	67.872	10	
15	0.000453	0.002264	98412	223	491529	0.000453	2.621	6193959	62.939	15	
20	0.000470	0.002347	98189	230	490382	0.000470	2.555	5702430	58.076	20	
25	0.000578	0.002893	97959	283	489114	0.000579	2.605	5212048	53.207	25	TABLE 3
30	0.000766	0.003824	97675	374	487498	0.000766	2.651	4722934	48.353	30	
35	0.001142	0.005693	97302	554	485216	0.001142	2.666	4235436	43.529	35	FEMALE
40	0.001692	0.008436	96748	816	481861	0.001694	2.700	3750220	38.763	40	LIFE
45	0.002798	0.013945	95932	1338	476556	0.002807	2.681	3268359	34.070	45	TABLE
50	0.004231	0.020947	94594	1981	468364	0.004231	2.676	2791803	29.514	50	
55	0.006578	0.032531	92612	3013	456035	0.006606	2.668	2323439	25.088	55	
60	0.010067	0.049220	89600	4410	437792	0.010073	2.686	1867403	20.842	60	
65	0.016950	0.081571	85189	6949	409980	0.016950	2.702	1429611	16.782	65	
70	0.030515	0.142563	78240	11154	365361	0.030529	2.683	1019631	13.032	70	
75	0.056343	0.249261	67086	16762	295415	0.056741	2.613	654270	9.753	75	
80	0.100307	0.401863	50324	20223	201614	0.100307	2.527	358854	7.131	80	
85	0.191431	1.000000	30101	30101	157241	0.123449	5.224	157241	5.224	85	

CRUDE RATES

Per Thousand	BOTH SEXES	MALES	FEMALES
BIRTH RATE	10.08	10.83	9.40
DEATH RATE	11.60	11.83	11.39
RATE OF INCREASE	-1.52	-1.00	-1.99

RATES STANDARDIZED ON USA 1980

Per Thousand	BOTH SEXES	MALES	FEMALES
BIRTH RATE	12.40		11.74
DEATH RATE	9.79	10.49	9.13
RATE OF INCREASE	2.61		2.61

VITAL STATISTICS

GFR x 1000	41.008	TABLE 4
TFR	1.457	
GRR	0.709	OBSERVED
NRR	0.693	VITAL
μ	27.532	RATES
σ^2	27.720	AND
GENERATION	27.715	RATIOS
POP. SEX RATIO	1.093	
SEX RATIO AT BIRTH	1.054	
DEP. RATIO x 100	50.792	

PERCENT OF POPULATION IN AGE GROUP

UNDER 15	18.17	19.48	16.97
15 - 64	66.32	68.84	64.00
65 AND OLDER	15.51	11.68	19.02

RATES STANDARDIZED ON MEXICO 1980

	BOTH SEXES	MALES	FEMALES
BIRTH RATE	10.86		10.66
DEATH RATE	3.80	4.58	3.00
RATE OF INCREASE	7.06		7.65

TABLE 1 DATA

AGE AT LAST BIRTHDAY	ESTIMATED MID-YEAR POPULATION BOTH SEXES	MALES Number	MALES Percent	FEMALES Number	FEMALES Percent	BIRTHS BY AGE OF MOTHER AND SEX	DEATHS BOTH SEXES	DEATHS MALES	DEATHS FEMALES	AGE AT LAST BIRTHDAY
0	582220	298322	1.0	283898	0.9		5244	3001	2243	0
1-4	2403907	1232046	4.2	1171861	3.7		1070	575	495	1-4
5-9	2880540	1471637	5.0	1408903	4.4		670	359	311	5-9
10-14	3365615	1716547	5.9	1649068	5.2	53	662	389	273	10-14
15-19	4902119	2518121	8.6	2383998	7.5	20564	2908	2099	809	15-19
20-24	5293134	2724882	9.3	2568252	8.1	148928	3847	2881	966	20-24
25-29	4694053	2425025	8.3	2269028	7.1	232017	3543	2497	1046	25-29
30-34	4271828	2175598	7.5	2096230	6.6	134128	4082	2742	1340	30-34
35-39	3889877	1991804	6.8	1898073	6.0	43102	5315	3453	1862	35-39
40-44	4210512	2147438	7.4	2063074	6.5	6778	9494	6298	3196	40-44
45-49	4777130	2430057	8.3	2347073	7.4	549	17293	11689	5604	45-49
50-54	3714790	1871187	6.4	1843603	5.8	36	22024	15088	6936	50-54
55-59	3613467	1723999	5.9	1889468	5.9		33144	22032	11112	55-59
60-64	3372841	1346722	4.6	2026119	6.4		46222	27339	18883	60-64
65-69	2141628	811348	2.8	1330280	4.2		45660	25682	19978	65-69
70-74	2729439	981617	3.4	1747822	5.5		98927	51874	47053	70-74
75-79	2186802	733044	2.5	1453758	4.6		135357	63524	71833	75-79
80-84	1294418	403910	1.4	890508	2.8	300053 M	135368	54320	81048	80-84
85+	699756	177826	0.6	521930	1.6	286102 F	133461	38537	94924	85+
TOTAL	61024076	29181130		31842946		586155	704291	334379	369912	TOTAL

TABLE 2 — MALE LIFE TABLE

x	nM_x	nq_x	l_x	nd_x	nL_x	nm_x	na_x	T_x	$\overset{\circ}{e}_x$	x
0	0.010060	0.009968	100000	997	99090	0.010060	0.087	7154926	71.549	0
1	0.000467	0.001865	99003	185	395551	0.000467	1.500	7055836	71.269	1
5	0.000244	0.001219	98819	120	493792	0.000244	2.500	6660284	67.399	5
10	0.000227	0.001133	98698	112	493272	0.000227	3.040	6166492	62.478	10
15	0.000834	0.004160	98586	410	491991	0.000834	2.706	5673221	57.546	15
20	0.001057	0.005273	98176	518	489606	0.001057	2.537	5181230	52.775	20
25	0.001030	0.005138	97659	502	487058	0.001030	2.539	4691624	48.041	25
30	0.001260	0.006297	97157	612	484324	0.001263	2.613	4204566	43.276	30
35	0.001734	0.008642	96545	834	480802	0.001735	2.695	3720242	38.534	35
40	0.002933	0.014566	95711	1394	475362	0.002933	2.711	3239439	33.846	40
45	0.004810	0.023804	94317	2245	466442	0.004813	2.710	2764077	29.306	45
50	0.008063	0.039751	92071	3660	451886	0.008099	2.685	2297635	24.955	50
55	0.012780	0.062219	88412	5501	429228	0.012816	2.668	1845750	20.877	55
60	0.020300	0.097553	82911	8088	395485	0.020451	2.642	1416522	17.085	60
65	0.031653	0.147425	74822	11031	347965	0.031701	2.630	1021037	13.646	65
70	0.052845	0.234365	63792	14951	282911	0.052845	2.589	673072	10.551	70
75	0.086658	0.356371	48841	17406	200846	0.086662	2.509	390161	7.988	75
80	0.134485	0.499019	31436	15687	116645	0.134485	2.416	189315	6.022	80
85	0.216712	1.000000	15749	15749	72671	0.152576	4.614	72671	4.614	85

TABLE 3 — FEMALE LIFE TABLE

x	nM_x	nq_x	l_x	nd_x	nL_x	nm_x	na_x	T_x	$\overset{\circ}{e}_x$	x
0	0.007901	0.007844	100000	784	99281	0.007901	0.083	7819306	78.193	0
1	0.000422	0.001688	99216	167	396444	0.000422	1.500	7720025	77.811	1
5	0.000221	0.001103	99048	109	494968	0.000221	2.500	7323581	73.940	5
10	0.000166	0.000827	98939	82	494502	0.000166	2.648	6828613	69.018	10
15	0.000339	0.001695	98857	168	493888	0.000339	2.629	6334111	64.073	15
20	0.000376	0.001879	98689	185	492996	0.000376	2.567	5840224	59.178	20
25	0.000461	0.002307	98504	227	491979	0.000462	2.619	5347228	54.284	25
30	0.000639	0.003203	98277	315	490650	0.000641	2.667	4855249	49.404	30
35	0.000981	0.004899	97962	480	488701	0.000982	2.690	4364599	44.554	35
40	0.001549	0.007718	97482	752	485669	0.001549	2.685	3875898	39.760	40
45	0.002388	0.011883	96730	1149	480991	0.002390	2.688	3390229	35.048	45
50	0.003762	0.018717	95580	1789	473756	0.003776	2.683	2909238	30.438	50
55	0.005881	0.029010	93791	2721	462651	0.005881	2.683	2435482	25.967	55
60	0.009320	0.045832	91070	4174	445666	0.009366	2.679	1972831	21.663	60
65	0.015018	0.072659	86896	6314	419956	0.015034	2.699	1527165	17.575	65
70	0.026921	0.126240	80583	10212	379322	0.026921	2.690	1107209	13.740	70
75	0.049412	0.221940	70371	15618	314929	0.049593	2.636	727887	10.344	75
80	0.091013	0.372346	54753	20387	224000	0.091013	2.559	412957	7.542	80
85	0.181871	1.000000	34366	34366	188957	0.113235	5.498	188957	5.498	85

TABLE 4 — OBSERVED VITAL RATES AND RATIOS

CRUDE RATES

Per Thousand	BOTH SEXES	MALES	FEMALES
BIRTH RATE	9.61	10.28	8.98
DEATH RATE	11.54	11.46	11.62
RATE OF INCREASE	-1.94	-1.18	-2.63

PERCENT OF POPULATION IN AGE GROUP

UNDER 15	15.13	16.17	14.17
15 - 64	70.04	73.18	67.16
65 AND OLDER	14.83	10.65	18.67

RATES STANDARDIZED ON USA 1980

Per Thousand	BOTH SEXES	MALES	FEMALES
BIRTH RATE	10.87		10.32
DEATH RATE	8.87	9.55	8.24
RATE OF INCREASE	2.00		2.08

RATES STANDARDIZED ON MEXICO 1980

	BOTH SEXES	MALES	FEMALES
BIRTH RATE	9.32		9.17
DEATH RATE	3.31	4.00	2.60
RATE OF INCREASE	6.01		6.57

VITAL STATISTICS

GFR x 1000	37.512
TFR	1.296
GRR	0.632
NRR	0.622
μ	28.352
σ^2	26.347
GENERATION	28.572
POP. SEX RATIO	1.091
SEX RATIO AT BIRTH	1.049
DEP. RATIO x 100	42.781

PROJECTED POPULATION

AGE GROUP	1990 BOTH SEXES	1990 MALES	1990 FEMALES	1995 BOTH SEXES	1995 MALES	1995 FEMALES
0-4	2969	1518	1451	2935	1501	1434
5-9	2982	1528	1454	2965	1516	1449
10-14	2878	1470	1408	2978	1526	1452
15-19	3359	1712	1647	2872	1466	1406
20-24	4886	2506	2380	3348	1704	1644
25-29	5274	2711	2563	4868	2493	2375
30-34	4674	2411	2263	5251	2695	2556
35-39	4248	2160	2088	4648	2394	2254
40-44	3855	1969	1886	4210	2135	2075
45-49	4150	2107	2043	3800	1932	1868
50-54	4666	2354	2312	4053	2041	2012
55-59	3577	1777	1800	4494	2236	2258
60-64	3408	1588	1820	3372	1638	1734
65-69	3094	1185	1909	3113	1398	1715
70-74	1862	660	1202	2688	963	1725
75-79	2148	697	1451	1466	468	998
80-84	1460	426	1034	1437	405	1032
85+	1003	252	751	1137	265	872
TOTAL	60493	29031	31462	59635	28776	30859

STABLE EQUIVALENT TO ORIGINAL POPULATION

MALES Number	MALES Percent	FEMALES Number	FEMALES Percent	AGE GROUP	
1613	3.6	1542	3.1	0-4	
1750	3.9	1673	3.4	5-9	TABLE 5
1899	4.2	1816	3.7	10-14	
2059	4.6	1970	4.0	15-19	POPULATION
2226	5.0	2137	4.3	20-24	PROJECTED
2406	5.4	2317	4.7	25-29	WITH
2599	5.8	2511	5.1	30-34	FIXED
2804	6.2	2717	5.5	35-39	AGE-
3012	6.7	2934	5.9	40-44	SPECIFIC
3211	7.2	3158	6.4	45-49	BIRTH
3381	7.5	3379	6.8	50-54	AND
3489	7.8	3586	7.2	55-59	DEATH
3493	7.8	3753	7.6	60-64	RATES
3339	7.4	3843	7.8	65-69	(female
2950	6.6	3771	7.6	70-74	dominant,
2275	5.1	3402	6.9	75-79	in 000s)
1436	3.2	2629	5.3	80-84	
972	2.2	2410	4.9	85+	
44914		49548		TOTAL	

VITAL RATES OF PROJECTED POPULATION

Per Thousand	1990 BOTH SEXES	1990 MALES	1990 FEMALES	1995 BOTH SEXES	1995 MALES	1995 FEMALES
BIRTH RATE	10.14	10.81	9.51	9.60	10.18	9.05
DEATH RATE	12.72	12.14	13.25	13.19	12.47	13.87
RATE OF INCREASE	-2.58	-1.32	-3.74	-3.60	-2.29	-4.82

AGE STRUCTURE OF PROJECTED POPULATION

	1990 BOTH SEXES	1990 MALES	1990 FEMALES	1995 BOTH SEXES	1995 MALES	1995 FEMALES
% UNDER 15	14.59	15.56	13.71	14.89	15.79	14.05
% 15-64	69.59	73.36	66.12	68.61	72.05	65.40
% 65 AND OLDER	15.81	11.09	20.17	16.50	12.16	20.55
DEPEND. RATIO x 100	43.69	36.32	51.24	45.75	38.79	52.90

VITAL RATES OF STABLE POPULATION

Per Thousand	MALES	FEMALES	
BIRTH RATE	6.96	6.02	TABLE 6
DEATH RATE	23.35	22.62	PROJECTED
RATE OF INCREASE		-16.60	VITAL RATES

STABLE AGE STRUCTURE

	MALES	FEMALES	
% UNDER 15	11.72	10.15	AND RATIOS (female dominant)
% 15-64	63.85	57.45	
% 65 AND OLDER	24.43	32.40	
DEPEND. RATIO x 100	56.61	74.08	

MATRIX

AGE GROUP	FEMALE BIRTH RATES	NET MATERNITY FUNCTION	COEFF. OF MATRIX EQUATION	ORIGINAL MATRIX SUB-DIAGONAL	ORIGINAL MATRIX FIRST ROW	STABLE MATRIX FISHER VALUES	STABLE MATRIX REPRODUCTIVE VALUES
0-4	0.0000	0.0000	0.0000	0.99847	0.00000	0.967	1408442
5-9	0.0000	0.0000	0.0000	0.99906	0.00004	0.892	1256445
10-14	0.0000	0.0001	0.0104	0.99876	0.01046	0.821	1354687
15-19	0.0042	0.0208	0.0802	0.99819	0.08046	0.747	1780499
20-24	0.0283	0.1395	0.1925	0.99794	0.19361	0.611	1568213
25-29	0.0499	0.2455	0.1994	0.99730	0.20091	0.375	851870
30-34	0.0312	0.1532	0.1037	0.99603	0.10477	0.152	317699
35-39	0.0111	0.0542	0.0310	0.99379	0.03142	0.038	72635
40-44	0.0016	0.0078	0.0042	0.99037	0.00425	0.005	10002
45-49	0.0001	0.0005	0.0003	0.98496	0.00031	0.000	818
50-54	0.0000	0.0000	0.0000	0.97656	0.00002	0.000	46

MATRIX PARAMETERS

λ_1	0.92034	
λ_2	$0.39081+0.70376i$	TABLE 7
λ_4	$-0.21344+0.49402i$	
λ_6	$-0.46586-0.00000i$	LESLIE MATRIX
r_1	-0.01660	AND ITS
r_2	$-0.04338+0.21278i$	ANALYSIS
r_4	$-0.12392+0.39572i$	(females)
r_6	$-0.15277-0.62832i$	
c_1	495486	
$2\pi/y$	29.5294	
Δ	17.2808	

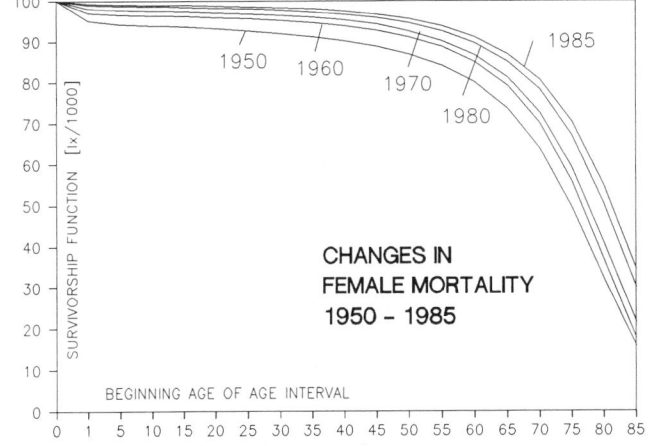

CHANGES IN FEMALE MORTALITY 1950 – 1985

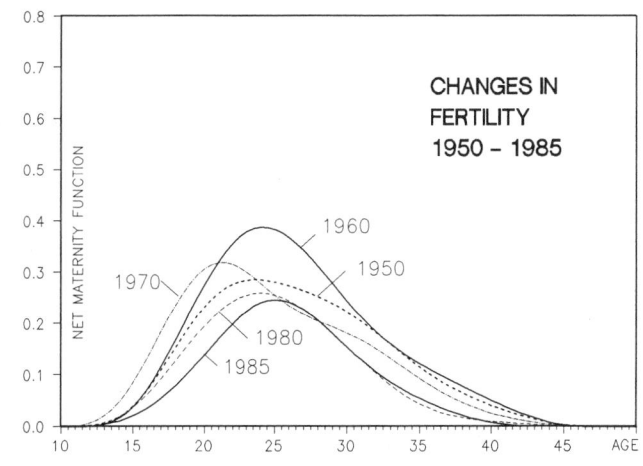

CHANGES IN FERTILITY 1950 – 1985

TABLE 1 — DATA

AGE AT LAST BIRTHDAY	ESTIMATED MID-YEAR POPULATION BOTH SEXES	MALES Number	MALES Percent	FEMALES Number	FEMALES Percent	BIRTHS BY AGE OF MOTHER AND SEX	DEATHS BOTH SEXES	DEATHS MALES	DEATHS FEMALES	AGE AT LAST BIRTHDAY
0	147769	75236	1.8	72533	1.6		5476	3093	2383	0
1-4	601475	304977	7.1	296498	6.6		607	323	284	1-4
5-9	702608	361803	8.4	340805	7.6		299	177	122	5-9
10-14	714783	367989	8.6	346794	7.7	39	286	183	103	10-14
15-19	660122	337914	7.9	322208	7.2	11881	403	295	108	15-19
20-24	638519	327851	7.6	310668	6.9	44635	490	364	126	20-24
25-29	509122	247357	5.8	261765	5.8	39956	440	292	148	25-29
30-34	617916	292571	6.8	325345	7.2	30387	558	315	243	30-34
35-39	666573	322511	7.5	344062	7.6	14567	825	490	335	35-39
40-44	656879	319158	7.4	337721	7.5	3141	1227	724	503	40-44
45-49	511648	242656	5.7	268992	6.0	287	1550	937	613	45-49
50-54	442057	205442	4.8	236615	5.3	35	2441	1481	960	50-54
55-59	507595	245011	5.7	262584	5.8		4083	2559	1524	55-59
60-64	443056	216619	5.0	226437	5.0		6095	3756	2339	60-64
65-69	377163	174963	4.1	202200	4.5		8378	4918	3460	65-69
70-74	263158	114940	2.7	148218	3.3		10290	5231	5059	70-74
75-79	156398	67226	1.6	89172	2.0		10037	4781	5256	75-79
80-84	104270	41539	1.0	62731	1.4	75024 M	10445	4546	5899	80-84
85+	71695	28711	0.7	42984	1.0	69904 F	13099	5528	7571	85+
TOTAL	8792806	4294474		4498332		144928	77029	39993	37036	TOTAL

TABLE 2 — MALE LIFE TABLE

x	nM_x	nq_x	l_x	nd_x	nL_x	nm_x	na_x	T_x	$\overset{\circ}{e}_x$	x
0	0.041111	0.039707	100000	3971	96585	0.041111	0.140	7065648	70.656	0
1	0.001059	0.004225	96029	406	383103	0.001059	1.500	6969063	72.572	1
5	0.000489	0.002443	95624	234	477534	0.000489	2.500	6585960	68.874	5
10	0.000497	0.002486	95390	237	476395	0.000498	2.659	6108426	64.036	10
15	0.000873	0.004360	95153	415	474787	0.000874	2.645	5632031	59.189	15
20	0.001110	0.005545	94738	525	472406	0.001112	2.555	5157243	54.437	20
25	0.001180	0.005885	94213	554	469673	0.001180	2.492	4684837	49.726	25
30	0.001077	0.005369	93658	503	467066	0.001077	2.562	4215165	45.006	30
35	0.001519	0.007570	93155	705	464127	0.001519	2.661	3748099	40.235	35
40	0.002268	0.011321	92450	1047	459856	0.002276	2.711	3283971	35.521	40
45	0.003861	0.019321	91404	1766	453047	0.003898	2.752	2824116	30.897	45
50	0.007209	0.035461	89638	3179	440792	0.007211	2.673	2371069	26.452	50
55	0.010444	0.050983	86459	4408	422040	0.010444	2.673	1930277	22.326	55
60	0.017339	0.083480	82051	6850	394288	0.017372	2.669	1508238	18.382	60
65	0.028109	0.132452	75201	9961	352486	0.028258	2.639	1113950	14.813	65
70	0.045511	0.206538	65241	13475	293724	0.045875	2.590	761464	11.672	70
75	0.071118	0.304327	51766	15754	219853	0.071656	2.526	467740	9.036	75
80	0.109439	0.428442	36012	15429	140984	0.109439	2.467	247887	6.883	80
85	0.192539	1.000000	20583	20583	106903	0.124701	5.194	106903	5.194	85

TABLE 3 — FEMALE LIFE TABLE

x	nM_x	nq_x	l_x	nd_x	nL_x	nm_x	na_x	T_x	$\overset{\circ}{e}_x$	x
0	0.032854	0.031937	100000	3194	97208	0.032854	0.126	7521344	75.213	0
1	0.000958	0.003822	96806	370	386300	0.000958	1.500	7424136	76.691	1
5	0.000358	0.001788	96436	172	481750	0.000358	2.500	7037836	72.979	5
10	0.000297	0.001484	96264	143	480960	0.000297	2.483	6556085	68.105	10
15	0.000335	0.001675	96121	161	480213	0.000335	2.567	6075126	63.203	15
20	0.000406	0.002031	95960	195	479336	0.000407	2.617	5594912	58.305	20
25	0.000565	0.002823	95765	270	478183	0.000565	2.624	5115577	53.418	25
30	0.000747	0.003728	95495	356	476624	0.000747	2.612	4637393	48.562	30
35	0.000974	0.004857	95139	462	474611	0.000974	2.657	4160769	43.734	35
40	0.001489	0.007439	94677	704	471750	0.001493	2.681	3686158	38.934	40
45	0.002279	0.011417	93972	1073	467422	0.002295	2.726	3214408	34.206	45
50	0.004057	0.020122	92899	1869	460144	0.004062	2.671	2746986	29.569	50
55	0.005804	0.028638	91030	2607	449176	0.005804	2.708	2286843	25.122	55
60	0.010330	0.050572	88423	4472	431840	0.010355	2.702	1837667	20.783	60
65	0.017112	0.082683	83951	6941	404032	0.017180	2.735	1405827	16.746	65
70	0.034132	0.159575	77010	12289	356383	0.034482	2.667	1001795	13.009	70
75	0.058942	0.259621	64721	16803	282843	0.059408	2.574	645412	9.972	75
80	0.094036	0.381095	47918	18261	194195	0.094036	2.514	362570	7.566	80
85	0.176135	1.000000	29657	29657	168375	0.107127	5.677	168375	5.677	85

TABLE 4 — OBSERVED VITAL RATES AND RATIOS

CRUDE RATES

Per Thousand	BOTH SEXES	MALES	FEMALES
BIRTH RATE	16.48	17.47	15.54
DEATH RATE	8.76	9.31	8.23
RATE OF INCREASE	7.72	8.16	7.31

PERCENT OF POPULATION IN AGE GROUP

	BOTH SEXES	MALES	FEMALES
UNDER 15	24.64	25.85	23.49
15 - 64	64.30	64.20	64.39
65 AND OLDER	11.06	9.95	12.12

RATES STANDARDIZED ON USA 1980

Per Thousand	BOTH SEXES	MALES	FEMALES
BIRTH RATE	20.34		19.08
DEATH RATE	9.04	8.80	9.27
RATE OF INCREASE	11.29		9.81

RATES STANDARDIZED ON MEXICO 1980

	BOTH SEXES	MALES	FEMALES
BIRTH RATE	18.07		17.57
DEATH RATE	4.09	4.56	3.61
RATE OF INCREASE	13.98		13.96

VITAL STATISTICS

GFR x 1000	66.764
TFR	2.398
GRR	1.157
NRR	1.105
μ	27.407
σ^2	34.270
GENERATION	27.345
POP. SEX RATIO	1.047
SEX RATIO AT BIRTH	1.073
DEP. RATIO x 100	55.529

PROJECTED POPULATION

AGE GROUP	1975 BOTH SEXES	1975 MALES	1975 FEMALES	1980 BOTH SEXES	1980 MALES	1980 FEMALES
0-4	706	364	342	729	376	353
5-9	747	379	368	702	362	340
10-14	701	361	340	745	378	367
15-19	713	367	346	700	360	340
20-24	658	336	322	711	365	346
25-29	636	326	310	655	334	321
30-34	507	246	261	633	324	309
35-39	615	291	324	504	244	260
40-44	662	320	342	610	288	322
45-49	649	314	335	654	315	339
50-54	501	236	265	635	306	329
55-59	428	197	231	484	226	258
60-64	481	229	252	406	184	222
65-69	406	194	212	441	205	236
70-74	324	146	178	348	161	187
75-79	204	86	118	251	109	142
80-84	104	43	61	136	55	81
85+	85	31	54	86	33	53
TOTAL	9127	4466	4661	9430	4625	4805

STABLE EQUIVALENT TO ORIGINAL POPULATION

MALES Number	MALES Percent	FEMALES Number	FEMALES Percent	AGE GROUP	
371	7.7	349	7.4	0-4	
363	7.5	341	7.2	5-9	TABLE 5
355	7.4	334	7.0	10-14	
348	7.2	328	6.9	15-19	POPULATION
340	7.1	321	6.8	20-24	PROJECTED
332	6.9	315	6.6	25-29	WITH
324	6.7	308	6.5	30-34	FIXED
316	6.6	301	6.3	35-39	AGE-
307	6.4	294	6.2	40-44	SPECIFIC
297	6.2	286	6.0	45-49	BIRTH
284	5.9	276	5.8	50-54	AND
267	5.5	265	5.6	55-59	DEATH
245	5.1	250	5.3	60-64	RATES
215	4.5	230	4.8	65-69	(female
176	3.7	199	4.2	70-74	dominant,
129	2.7	155	3.3	75-79	in 000s)
81	1.7	104	2.2	80-84	
61	1.3	89	1.9	85+	
4811		4745		TOTAL	

VITAL RATES OF PROJECTED POPULATION

Per Thousand	1975 BOTH SEXES	1975 MALES	1975 FEMALES	1980 BOTH SEXES	1980 MALES	1980 FEMALES
BIRTH RATE	16.22	17.16	15.32	16.38	17.29	15.51
DEATH RATE	9.42	9.87	8.99	9.99	10.46	9.53
RATE OF INCREASE	6.80	7.29	6.32	6.39	6.83	5.98

VITAL RATES OF STABLE POPULATION

Per Thousand	MALES	FEMALES	
BIRTH RATE	16.23	15.34	TABLE 6
DEATH RATE	12.54	11.67	PROJECTED
RATE OF INCREASE		3.67	VITAL RATES

AGE STRUCTURE OF PROJECTED POPULATION

	BOTH SEXES	MALES	FEMALES	BOTH SEXES	MALES	FEMALES
% UNDER 15	23.59	24.71	22.52	23.07	24.12	22.07
% 15-64	64.10	64.09	64.10	63.55	63.71	63.40
% 65 AND OLDER	12.31	11.20	13.38	13.38	12.17	14.54
DEPEND. RATIO x 100	56.01	56.03	56.00	57.36	56.96	57.74

STABLE AGE STRUCTURE

	MALES	FEMALES	
% UNDER 15	22.65	21.59	AND RATIOS
% 15-64	63.59	62.04	(female
% 65 AND OLDER	13.76	16.37	dominant)
DEPEND. RATIO x 100	57.25	61.19	

MATRIX TABLE

AGE GROUP	FEMALE BIRTH RATES	NET MATERNITY FUNCTION	COEFF. OF MATRIX EQUATION	ORIGINAL MATRIX SUB-DIAGONAL	ORIGINAL MATRIX FIRST ROW	STABLE MATRIX FISHER VALUES	STABLE MATRIX REPRODUCTIVE VALUES
0-4	0.0000	0.0000	0.0000	0.99636	0.00000	1.044	385127
5-9	0.0000	0.0000	0.0001	0.99836	0.00013	1.067	363574
10-14	0.0001	0.0003	0.0428	0.99845	0.04306	1.088	377381
15-19	0.0178	0.0854	0.2088	0.99817	0.21022	1.065	343168
20-24	0.0693	0.3322	0.3421	0.99760	0.34510	0.867	269335
25-29	0.0736	0.3521	0.2834	0.99674	0.28654	0.524	137194
30-34	0.0450	0.2147	0.1558	0.99578	0.15807	0.236	76630
35-39	0.0204	0.0969	0.0590	0.99397	0.06015	0.075	25890
40-44	0.0045	0.0212	0.0118	0.99083	0.01208	0.014	4712
45-49	0.0005	0.0024	0.0014	0.98443	0.00141	0.002	436
50-54	0.0001	0.0003	0.0002	0.97616	0.00017	0.000	42

MATRIX PARAMETERS

λ_1	1.01851	
λ_2	0.36444+0.74856i	TABLE 7
λ_4	-0.39160-0.36088i	
λ_6	-0.08970+0.49588i	LESLIE
r_1	0.00367	MATRIX
r_2	-0.03665+0.22354i	AND ITS
r_4	-0.12602-0.47940i	ANALYSIS
r_6	-0.13706+0.34995i	(females)
c_1	47429	
$2\pi/y$	28.1071	
Δ	5.9047	

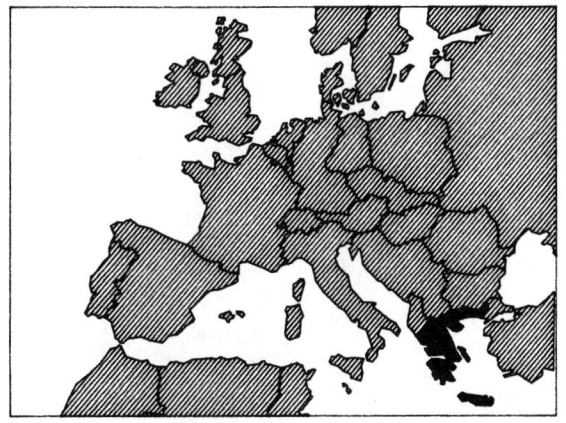

EDUCATION [1984]

% of primary school-age children enrolled:	105
secondary school-age children enrolled:	82
ca. 20-24 year olds in higher education:	17

LABOR FORCE

Average annual labor force growth (%) 1980-85:	0.6
% of the 1980 labor force in agriculture:	31
in industry:	29
in services:	40

GNP & INCOME DISTRIBUTION

GNP per capita (in US Dollars) 1985:	3550
GNP average annual growth rate (%) 1965-85:	3.6
% share of total household income	
Lowest 20% of households:	na
Highest 10% of households:	na

HEALTH & NUTRITION

Population per physician 1981:	400
Daily calorie supply per capita 1985:	3721

TABLE 8

SOCIO-ECONOMIC INDICATORS

TABLE 1 — DATA

AGE AT LAST BIRTHDAY	ESTIMATED MID-YEAR POPULATION BOTH SEXES	MALES Number	MALES Percent	FEMALES Number	FEMALES Percent	BIRTHS BY AGE OF MOTHER AND SEX	DEATHS BOTH SEXES	DEATHS MALES	DEATHS FEMALES	AGE AT LAST BIRTHDAY
0	140420	72271	1.6	68149	1.5		4190	2388	1802	0
1-4	549625	283788	6.4	265837	5.8		417	221	196	1-4
5-9	759301	391286	8.8	368015	8.0		291	184	107	5-9
10-14	711107	366210	8.3	344897	7.5	119	273	167	106	10-14
15-19	704654	361397	8.2	343257	7.4	15341	447	318	129	15-19
20-24	638526	332670	7.5	305856	6.6	47110	524	372	152	20-24
25-29	614310	303497	6.8	310813	6.7	43200	544	362	182	25-29
30-34	519424	250012	5.6	269412	5.8	21720	486	316	170	30-34
35-39	615894	291222	6.6	324672	7.0	11521	759	459	300	35-39
40-44	656003	317799	7.2	338204	7.3	2943	1183	732	451	40-44
45-49	636596	308332	7.0	328264	7.1	266	1954	1182	772	45-49
50-54	499616	240811	5.4	258805	5.6	50	2422	1511	911	50-54
55-59	429304	200783	4.5	228521	5.0		3587	2289	1298	55-59
60-64	465070	219377	5.0	245693	5.3		6358	3850	2508	60-64
65-69	401618	189400	4.3	212218	4.6		9194	5479	3715	65-69
70-74	315542	142126	3.2	173416	3.8		11905	6435	5470	70-74
75-79	200947	85411	1.9	115536	2.5		13529	6422	7107	75-79
80-84	106620	44149	1.0	62471	1.4	73312 M	11534	5011	6523	80-84
85+	81965	31056	0.7	50909	1.1	68958 F	15996	6534	9462	85+
TOTAL	9046542	4431597		4614945		142270	85593	44232	41361	TOTAL

TABLE 2 — MALE LIFE TABLE

x	nM_x	nq_x	l_x	nd_x	nL_x	nm_x	na_x	T_x	$\mathring{e}_x$	x
0	0.033042	0.032115	100000	3212	97194	0.033042	0.126	7104113	71.041	0
1	0.000779	0.003109	96789	301	386402	0.000779	1.500	7006919	72.394	1
5	0.000470	0.002348	96488	227	481871	0.000470	2.500	6620518	68.615	5
10	0.000456	0.002280	96261	219	480797	0.000456	2.686	6138646	63.771	10
15	0.000880	0.004396	96042	422	479218	0.000881	2.655	5657849	58.910	15
20	0.001118	0.005580	95619	534	476793	0.001119	2.556	5178632	54.159	20
25	0.001193	0.005950	95086	566	474028	0.001193	2.523	4701839	49.448	25
30	0.001264	0.006304	94520	596	471146	0.001265	2.560	4227812	44.729	30
35	0.001576	0.007851	93924	737	467876	0.001576	2.633	3756665	39.997	35
40	0.002303	0.011456	93187	1068	463477	0.002303	2.699	3288790	35.292	40
45	0.003834	0.019059	92119	1756	456572	0.003845	2.708	2825313	30.670	45
50	0.006275	0.031192	90364	2819	445420	0.006328	2.730	2368741	26.213	50
55	0.011400	0.055609	87545	4868	426419	0.011417	2.678	1923321	21.970	55
60	0.017550	0.084289	82677	6969	397085	0.017550	2.661	1496903	18.106	60
65	0.028928	0.135561	75708	10263	354226	0.028973	2.631	1099817	14.527	65
70	0.045277	0.205066	65445	13421	294997	0.045494	2.599	745591	11.393	70
75	0.075189	0.319438	52024	16619	219029	0.075874	2.527	450594	8.661	75
80	0.113502	0.440512	35406	15597	137413	0.113502	2.460	231565	6.540	80
85	0.210394	1.000000	19809	19809	94152	0.144689	4.753	94152	4.753	85

TABLE 3 — FEMALE LIFE TABLE

x	nM_x	nq_x	l_x	nd_x	nL_x	nm_x	na_x	T_x	$\mathring{e}_x$	x
0	0.026442	0.025837	100000	2584	97713	0.026442	0.115	7568094	75.681	0
1	0.000737	0.002944	97416	287	388948	0.000737	1.500	7470380	76.685	1
5	0.000291	0.001453	97129	141	485295	0.000291	2.500	7081432	72.907	5
10	0.000307	0.001536	96988	149	484578	0.000307	2.557	6596138	68.010	10
15	0.000376	0.001879	96839	182	483761	0.000376	2.604	6111560	63.110	15
20	0.000497	0.002484	96657	240	482708	0.000497	2.587	5627799	58.224	20
25	0.000586	0.002926	96417	282	481395	0.000586	2.546	5145091	53.363	25
30	0.000631	0.003150	96135	303	479953	0.000631	2.610	4663696	48.512	30
35	0.000924	0.004610	95832	442	478127	0.000924	2.656	4183743	43.657	35
40	0.001334	0.006647	95391	634	475508	0.001334	2.720	3705617	38.847	40
45	0.002352	0.011732	94757	1112	471214	0.002359	2.689	3230109	34.089	45
50	0.003520	0.017566	93645	1645	464419	0.003542	2.686	2758895	29.461	50
55	0.005680	0.028086	92000	2584	454126	0.005690	2.727	2294476	24.940	55
60	0.010208	0.049876	89416	4460	436886	0.010208	2.714	1840350	20.582	60
65	0.017506	0.084364	84956	7167	408328	0.017553	2.704	1403464	16.520	65
70	0.031543	0.147703	77789	11490	362465	0.031699	2.695	995136	12.793	70
75	0.061513	0.270534	66299	17936	288434	0.062185	2.599	632671	9.543	75
80	0.104416	0.413995	48363	20022	191752	0.104416	2.500	344237	7.118	80
85	0.185861	1.000000	28341	28341	152485	0.117374	5.380	152485	5.380	85

TABLE 4 — OBSERVED VITAL RATES AND RATIOS

CRUDE RATES

Per Thousand	BOTH SEXES	MALES	FEMALES
BIRTH RATE	15.73	16.54	14.94
DEATH RATE	9.46	9.98	8.96
RATE OF INCREASE	6.27	6.56	5.98

PERCENT OF POPULATION IN AGE GROUP

	BOTH SEXES	MALES	FEMALES
UNDER 15	23.88	25.13	22.68
15 - 64	63.89	63.77	64.00
65 AND OLDER	12.23	11.11	13.32

RATES STANDARDIZED ON USA 1980

Per Thousand	BOTH SEXES	MALES	FEMALES
BIRTH RATE	19.86		18.72
DEATH RATE	9.17	8.92	9.41
RATE OF INCREASE	10.69		9.31

RATES STANDARDIZED ON MEXICO 1980

	BOTH SEXES	MALES	FEMALES
BIRTH RATE	17.94		17.52
DEATH RATE	3.90	4.37	3.43
RATE OF INCREASE	14.03		14.09

VITAL STATISTICS

GFR x 1000	64.072
TFR	2.319
GRR	1.124
NRR	1.082
μ	26.804
σ^2	34.722
GENERATION	26.753
POP. SEX RATIO	1.041
SEX RATIO AT BIRTH	1.063
DEP. RATIO x 100	56.531

AGE AT LAST BIRTHDAY	ESTIMATED MID-YEAR POPULATION BOTH SEXES	MALES Number	Percent	FEMALES Number	Percent	BIRTHS BY AGE OF MOTHER AND SEX	DEATHS BOTH SEXES	MALES	FEMALES	AGE AT LAST BIRTHDAY	
0	146939	75949	1.6	70990	1.4		3037	1741	1296	0	
1-4	570650	295075	6.2	275575	5.6		363	216	147	1-4	
5-9	703239	363202	7.7	340037	6.9		209	117	92	5-9	
10-14	778954	402246	8.5	376708	7.7	187	244	159	85	10-14	
15-19	724776	373789	7.9	350987	7.1	18456	418	311	107	15-19	
20-24	697711	354478	7.5	343233	7.0	54145	578	407	171	20-24	
25-29	649570	329364	7.0	320206	6.5	43002	460	334	126	25-29	
30-34	657205	323836	6.8	333369	6.8	22044	545	356	189	30-34	
35-39	563773	272892	5.8	290881	5.9	7701	624	387	237	35-39	TABLE 1
40-44	652024	311472	6.6	340552	6.9	2288	1178	745	433	40-44	
45-49	681162	329093	7.0	352069	7.2	270	1910	1215	695	45-49	DATA
50-54	645043	311053	6.6	333990	6.8	41	3122	1981	1141	50-54	
55-59	488406	235616	5.0	252790	5.1		3902	2548	1354	55-59	
60-64	415963	191470	4.0	224493	4.6		5600	3484	2116	60-64	
65-69	438139	202284	4.3	235855	4.8		9562	5637	3925	65-69	
70-74	353432	162720	3.4	190712	3.9		13375	7284	6091	70-74	
75-79	254247	110066	2.3	144181	2.9		16173	7964	8209	75-79	
80-84	136550	55818	1.2	80732	1.6	76698 M	15074	6658	8416	80-84	
85+	84722	32914	0.7	51808	1.1	71436 F	18119	7117	11002	85+	
TOTAL	9642505	4733337		4909168		148134	94493	48661	45832	TOTAL	

x	$_nM_x$	$_nq_x$	l_x	$_nd_x$	$_nL_x$	$_nm_x$	$_na_x$	T_x	$\overset{\circ}{e}_x$	x	
0	0.022923	0.022464	100000	2246	97998	0.022923	0.109	7198633	71.986	0	
1	0.000732	0.002923	97754	286	390300	0.000732	1.500	7100634	72.638	1	
5	0.000322	0.001609	97468	157	486947	0.000322	2.500	6710334	68.847	5	
10	0.000395	0.001975	97311	192	486126	0.000395	2.768	6223387	63.954	10	
15	0.000832	0.004159	97119	404	484660	0.000833	2.687	5737261	59.075	15	
20	0.001148	0.005727	96715	554	482207	0.001149	2.531	5252601	54.310	20	
25	0.001014	0.005057	96161	486	479583	0.001014	2.488	4770394	49.608	25	TABLE 2
30	0.001099	0.005489	95675	525	477100	0.001101	2.574	4290811	44.848	30	
35	0.001418	0.007076	95150	673	474189	0.001420	2.685	3813711	40.081	35	MALE
40	0.002392	0.011894	94476	1124	469788	0.002392	2.692	3339522	35.348	40	LIFE
45	0.003692	0.018305	93353	1709	462858	0.003692	2.715	2869734	30.741	45	TABLE
50	0.006369	0.031505	91644	2887	451628	0.006393	2.717	2406876	26.263	50	
55	0.010814	0.053191	88756	4721	432908	0.010905	2.697	1955248	22.029	55	
60	0.018196	0.087353	84035	7341	402930	0.018218	2.650	1522340	18.115	60	
65	0.027867	0.130694	76695	10024	359696	0.027867	2.628	1119410	14.596	65	
70	0.044764	0.202319	66671	13489	300969	0.044818	2.599	759714	11.395	70	
75	0.072357	0.309032	53182	16435	225521	0.072876	2.542	458745	8.626	75	
80	0.119281	0.458112	36747	16834	141133	0.119281	2.469	233224	6.347	80	
85	0.216230	1.000000	19913	19913	92091	0.151463	4.625	92091	4.625	85	

x	$_nM_x$	$_nq_x$	l_x	$_nd_x$	$_nL_x$	$_nm_x$	$_na_x$	T_x	$\overset{\circ}{e}_x$	x	
0	0.018256	0.017961	100000	1796	98385	0.018256	0.101	7663503	76.635	0	
1	0.000533	0.002131	98204	209	392292	0.000533	1.500	7565118	77.035	1	
5	0.000271	0.001352	97995	132	489642	0.000271	2.500	7172825	73.196	5	
10	0.000226	0.001128	97862	110	489038	0.000226	2.531	6683183	68.292	10	
15	0.000305	0.001525	97752	149	488414	0.000305	2.685	6194145	63.366	15	
20	0.000498	0.002489	97603	243	487415	0.000498	2.536	5705731	58.459	20	
25	0.000393	0.001966	97360	191	486327	0.000394	2.535	5218316	53.598	25	TABLE 3
30	0.000567	0.002835	97168	275	485195	0.000568	2.653	4731989	48.699	30	
35	0.000815	0.004066	96893	394	483550	0.000815	2.678	4246793	43.830	35	FEMALE
40	0.001271	0.006339	96499	612	481080	0.001271	2.687	3763243	38.998	40	LIFE
45	0.001974	0.009826	95887	942	477290	0.001974	2.722	3282164	34.229	45	TABLE
50	0.003416	0.017016	94945	1616	471008	0.003430	2.699	2804874	29.542	50	
55	0.005356	0.026661	93329	2488	460964	0.005398	2.716	2333865	25.007	55	
60	0.009426	0.046205	90841	4197	444642	0.009440	2.721	1872901	20.617	60	
65	0.016642	0.080179	86644	6947	417451	0.016642	2.730	1428259	16.484	65	
70	0.031938	0.148965	79697	11872	370919	0.032007	2.678	1010808	12.683	70	
75	0.056935	0.252074	67825	17097	298291	0.057316	2.612	639889	9.434	75	
80	0.104246	0.414637	50728	21034	201769	0.104246	2.534	341599	6.734	80	
85	0.212361	1.000000	29694	29694	139829	0.146773	4.709	139829	4.709	85	

CRUDE RATES

Per Thousand	BOTH SEXES	MALES	FEMALES
BIRTH RATE	15.36	16.20	14.55
DEATH RATE	9.80	10.28	9.34
RATE OF INCREASE	5.56	5.92	5.22

PERCENT OF POPULATION IN AGE GROUP

UNDER 15	22.81	24.01	21.66
15 - 64	64.05	64.08	64.01
65 AND OLDER	13.14	11.91	14.33

RATES STANDARDIZED ON USA 1980

Per Thousand	BOTH SEXES	MALES	FEMALES
BIRTH RATE	19.30		18.10
DEATH RATE	9.04	8.68	9.37
RATE OF INCREASE	10.26		8.73

RATES STANDARDIZED ON MEXICO 1980

	BOTH SEXES	MALES	FEMALES
BIRTH RATE	17.69		17.20
DEATH RATE	3.56	4.00	3.11
RATE OF INCREASE	14.14		14.09

VITAL STATISTICS

GFR x 1000	63.541	TABLE 4
TFR	2.227	
GRR	1.074	OBSERVED
NRR	1.045	VITAL
μ	26.119	RATES
σ^2	32.879	AND
GENERATION	26.091	RATIOS
POP. SEX RATIO	1.037	
SEX RATIO AT BIRTH	1.074	
DEP. RATIO x 100	56.138	

ESTIMATED MID-YEAR POPULATION / BIRTHS / DEATHS

AGE AT LAST BIRTHDAY	BOTH SEXES	MALES Number	MALES Percent	FEMALES Number	FEMALES Percent	BIRTHS BY AGE OF MOTHER AND SEX	DEATHS BOTH SEXES	DEATHS MALES	DEATHS FEMALES	AGE AT LAST BIRTHDAY
0	119577	61883	1.3	57694	1.1		1881	1096	785	0
1-4	529279	278686	5.7	250593	5.0		246	152	94	1-4
5-9	713785	369136	7.6	344649	6.8		175	106	69	5-9
10-14	701931	361921	7.4	340010	6.7	93	179	110	69	10-14
15-19	771927	401314	8.2	370613	7.4	13396	507	374	133	15-19
20-24	724500	374588	7.7	349912	6.9	41304	648	493	155	20-24
25-29	696702	345719	7.1	350983	7.0	35970	601	461	140	25-29
30-34	665303	337200	6.9	328103	6.5	17853	597	412	185	30-34
35-39	666436	331798	6.8	334638	6.6	6421	774	511	263	35-39
40-44	569237	275839	5.6	293398	5.8	1287	943	611	332	40-44
45-49	657352	314257	6.4	343095	6.8	131	1927	1241	686	45-49
50-54	682841	327009	6.7	355832	7.1	26	3068	1979	1089	50-54
55-59	629913	303411	6.2	326502	6.5		4927	3234	1693	55-59
60-64	467493	222567	4.6	244926	4.9		5972	3898	2074	60-64
65-69	389233	175467	3.6	213766	4.2		8205	4781	3424	65-69
70-74	387626	172763	3.5	214863	4.3		13980	7780	6200	70-74
75-79	281985	124269	2.5	157716	3.1		17874	9189	8685	75-79
80-84	175788	72738	1.5	103050	2.0	60422 M	17931	8266	9665	80-84
85+	93386	36315	0.7	57071	1.1	56059 F	20766	8101	12665	85+
TOTAL	9924294	4886880		5037414		116481	101201	52795	48406	TOTAL

TABLE 1 — DATA

TABLE 2 — MALE LIFE TABLE

x	nM_x	nq_x	l_x	nd_x	nL_x	nm_x	na_x	T_x	$\overset{\circ}{e}_x$	x
0	0.017711	0.017433	100000	1743	98431	0.017711	0.100	7235911	72.359	0
1	0.000545	0.002179	98257	214	392492	0.000545	1.500	7137480	72.641	1
5	0.000287	0.001435	98043	141	489862	0.000287	2.500	6744988	68.796	5
10	0.000304	0.001519	97902	149	489204	0.000304	2.940	6255127	63.892	10
15	0.000932	0.004650	97753	455	487732	0.000932	2.725	5765923	58.984	15
20	0.001316	0.006564	97299	639	484936	0.001317	2.561	5278191	54.247	20
25	0.001333	0.006644	96660	642	481683	0.001333	2.483	4793255	49.589	25
30	0.001222	0.006091	96018	585	478646	0.001222	2.533	4311572	44.904	30
35	0.001540	0.007689	95433	734	475426	0.001543	2.631	3832926	40.164	35
40	0.002215	0.011038	94699	1045	471112	0.002219	2.719	3357499	35.454	40
45	0.003949	0.019567	93654	1833	464041	0.003949	2.693	2886387	30.820	45
50	0.006052	0.029846	91821	2741	452843	0.006052	2.714	2422346	26.381	50
55	0.010659	0.052213	89081	4651	434696	0.010700	2.698	1969503	22.109	55
60	0.017514	0.084731	84430	7154	405358	0.017648	2.653	1534807	18.179	60
65	0.027247	0.128141	77276	9902	362987	0.027280	2.638	1129449	14.616	65
70	0.045033	0.203245	67374	13693	304076	0.045033	2.605	766462	11.376	70
75	0.073944	0.313301	53680	16818	226894	0.074123	2.532	462386	8.614	75
80	0.113641	0.441444	36862	16273	143194	0.113641	2.473	235492	6.388	80
85	0.223076	1.000000	20590	20590	92299	0.159539	4.483	92299	4.483	85

TABLE 3 — FEMALE LIFE TABLE

x	nM_x	nq_x	l_x	nd_x	nL_x	nm_x	na_x	T_x	$\overset{\circ}{e}_x$	x
0	0.013606	0.013440	100000	1344	98781	0.013606	0.093	7751553	77.516	0
1	0.000375	0.001499	98656	148	394254	0.000375	1.500	7652772	77.570	1
5	0.000200	0.001001	98508	99	492294	0.000200	2.500	7258518	73.685	5
10	0.000203	0.001014	98410	100	491814	0.000203	2.662	6766224	68.756	10
15	0.000359	0.001793	98310	176	491132	0.000359	2.639	6274410	63.823	15
20	0.000443	0.002213	98133	217	490128	0.000443	2.518	5783278	58.933	20
25	0.000399	0.001993	97916	195	489106	0.000399	2.562	5293149	54.058	25
30	0.000564	0.002817	97721	275	487957	0.000564	2.642	4804043	49.161	30
35	0.000786	0.003929	97446	383	486329	0.000787	2.648	4316087	44.292	35
40	0.001132	0.005643	97063	548	484066	0.001132	2.720	3829757	39.456	40
45	0.001999	0.009951	96515	960	480364	0.001999	2.696	3345691	34.665	45
50	0.003060	0.015196	95555	1452	474449	0.003060	2.710	2865328	29.986	50
55	0.005185	0.025752	94103	2423	464954	0.005212	2.706	2390879	25.407	55
60	0.008468	0.041922	91679	3843	449700	0.008547	2.737	1925925	21.007	60
65	0.016018	0.077375	87836	6796	423673	0.016041	2.718	1476226	16.807	65
70	0.028856	0.135284	81040	10963	379940	0.028856	2.696	1052553	12.988	70
75	0.055067	0.244257	70076	17117	309518	0.055301	2.613	672613	9.598	75
80	0.093789	0.381722	52960	20216	215546	0.093789	2.564	363096	6.856	80
85	0.221917	1.000000	32744	32744	147550	0.157872	4.506	147550	4.506	85

TABLE 4 — OBSERVED VITAL RATES AND RATIOS

CRUDE RATES

Per Thousand	BOTH SEXES	MALES	FEMALES
BIRTH RATE	11.74	12.36	11.13
DEATH RATE	10.20	10.80	9.61
RATE OF INCREASE	1.54	1.56	1.52

RATES STANDARDIZED ON USA 1980

Per Thousand	BOTH SEXES	MALES	FEMALES
BIRTH RATE	14.53		13.60
DEATH RATE	8.80	8.60	8.98
RATE OF INCREASE	5.73		4.61

VITAL STATISTICS

GFR x 1000	49.133
TFR	1.677
GRR	0.807
NRR	0.790
μ	26.242
σ^2	31.459
GENERATION	26.383
POP. SEX RATIO	1.031
SEX RATIO AT BIRTH	1.078
DEP. RATIO x 100	51.940

PERCENT OF POPULATION IN AGE GROUP

	BOTH SEXES	MALES	FEMALES
UNDER 15	20.80	21.93	19.71
15 - 64	65.82	66.17	65.47
65 AND OLDER	13.38	11.90	14.82

RATES STANDARDIZED ON MEXICO 1980

	BOTH SEXES	MALES	FEMALES
BIRTH RATE	13.24		12.85
DEATH RATE	3.34	3.84	2.83
RATE OF INCREASE	9.90		10.01

PROJECTED POPULATION

AGE GROUP	1990 BOTH SEXES	1990 MALES	1990 FEMALES	1995 BOTH SEXES	1995 MALES	1995 FEMALES
0-4	578	299	279	581	301	280
5-9	648	340	308	578	299	279
10-14	713	369	344	647	339	308
15-19	701	361	340	712	368	344
20-24	769	399	370	698	359	339
25-29	721	372	349	765	396	369
30-34	694	344	350	718	370	348
35-39	662	335	327	690	341	349
40-44	662	329	333	657	332	325
45-49	563	272	291	655	324	331
50-54	646	307	339	553	265	288
55-59	663	314	349	626	294	332
60-64	599	283	316	630	293	337
65-69	430	199	231	551	253	298
70-74	339	147	192	374	167	207
75-79	304	129	175	266	110	156
80-84	188	78	110	203	81	122
85+	118	47	71	126	51	75
TOTAL	9998	4924	5074	10030	4943	5087

STABLE EQUIVALENT TO ORIGINAL POPULATION

	MALES Number	MALES Percent	FEMALES Number	FEMALES Percent	AGE GROUP	
	332	4.8	310	4.4	0-4	
	347	5.0	323	4.6	5-9	TABLE 5
	362	5.3	338	4.8	10-14	
	378	5.5	353	5.1	15-19	POPULATION
	393	5.7	368	5.3	20-24	PROJECTED
	408	5.9	384	5.5	25-29	WITH
	424	6.1	401	5.7	30-34	FIXED
	440	6.4	418	6.0	35-39	AGE-
	456	6.6	435	6.2	40-44	SPECIFIC
	470	6.8	451	6.5	45-49	BIRTH
	479	7.0	466	6.7	50-54	AND
	481	7.0	478	6.8	55-59	DEATH
	469	6.8	483	6.9	60-64	RATES
	439	6.4	476	6.8	65-69	(female
	385	5.6	446	6.4	70-74	dominant,
	300	4.4	380	5.4	75-79	in 000s)
	198	2.9	277	4.0	80-84	
	134	1.9	198	2.8	85+	
	6895		6985		TOTAL	

VITAL RATES OF PROJECTED POPULATION

Per Thousand	1990 BOTH SEXES	1990 MALES	1990 FEMALES	1995 BOTH SEXES	1995 MALES	1995 FEMALES
BIRTH RATE	11.88	12.51	11.27	11.72	12.34	11.12
DEATH RATE	10.97	11.48	10.47	11.40	11.85	10.96
RATE OF INCREASE	0.91	1.03	0.80	0.33	0.49	0.16

VITAL RATES OF STABLE POPULATION

Per Thousand	MALES	FEMALES		
BIRTH RATE	9.60	8.79		TABLE 6
DEATH RATE	18.42	17.73		PROJECTED
RATE OF INCREASE		-8.94		VITAL RATES AND RATIOS (female dominant)

AGE STRUCTURE OF PROJECTED POPULATION

	1990 BOTH SEXES	1990 MALES	1990 FEMALES	1995 BOTH SEXES	1995 MALES	1995 FEMALES
% UNDER 15	19.40	20.48	18.36	18.00	19.00	17.04
% 15-64	66.81	67.33	66.31	66.84	67.61	66.10
% 65 AND OLDER	13.79	12.20	15.34	15.15	13.39	16.86
DEPEND. RATIO x 100	49.68	48.53	50.81	49.60	47.91	51.28

STABLE AGE STRUCTURE

	MALES	FEMALES
% UNDER 15	15.10	13.90
% 15-64	63.78	60.65
% 65 AND OLDER	21.12	25.44
DEPEND. RATIO x 100	56.80	64.87

AGE GROUP	FEMALE BIRTH RATES	NET MATERNITY FUNCTION	COEFF. OF MATRIX EQUATION	ORIGINAL MATRIX SUB-DIAGONAL	ORIGINAL MATRIX FIRST ROW	STABLE MATRIX FISHER VALUES	STABLE MATRIX REPRODUCTIVE VALUES	MATRIX PARAMETERS	
0-4	0.0000	0.0000	0.0000	0.99850	0.00000	0.992	305724	λ_1 0.95629	
5-9	0.0000	0.0000	0.0003	0.99903	0.00032	0.950	327338	λ_2 0.31570+0.70957i	TABLE 7
10-14	0.0001	0.0006	0.0430	0.99861	0.04315	0.909	309010	λ_4 -0.31958+0.33482i	
15-19	0.0174	0.0854	0.1819	0.99796	0.18264	0.827	306668	λ_6 -0.39737+0.13887i	LESLIE
20-24	0.0568	0.2784	0.2598	0.99791	0.26138	0.611	213944	r_1 -0.00894	MATRIX
25-29	0.0493	0.2412	0.1845	0.99765	0.18599	0.326	114481	r_2 -0.05056+0.23043i	AND ITS
30-34	0.0262	0.1278	0.0863	0.99666	0.08725	0.128	41922	r_4 -0.15407+0.46658i	ANALYSIS
35-39	0.0092	0.0449	0.0276	0.99535	0.02794	0.036	11975	r_6 -0.17305+0.56108i	(females)
40-44	0.0021	0.0102	0.0056	0.99235	0.00565	0.007	1919	c_1 69850	
45-49	0.0002	0.0009	0.0005	0.98769	0.00054	0.001	223	$2\pi/y$ 27.2667	
50-54	0.0000	0.0002	0.0001	0.97999	0.00009	0.000	32	Δ 13.4357	

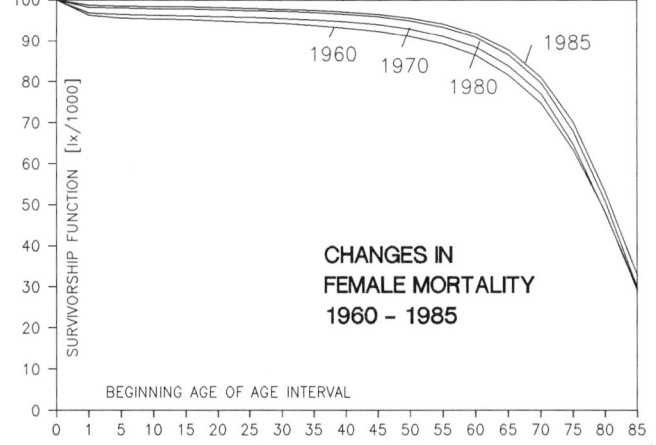

CHANGES IN FEMALE MORTALITY 1960 - 1985

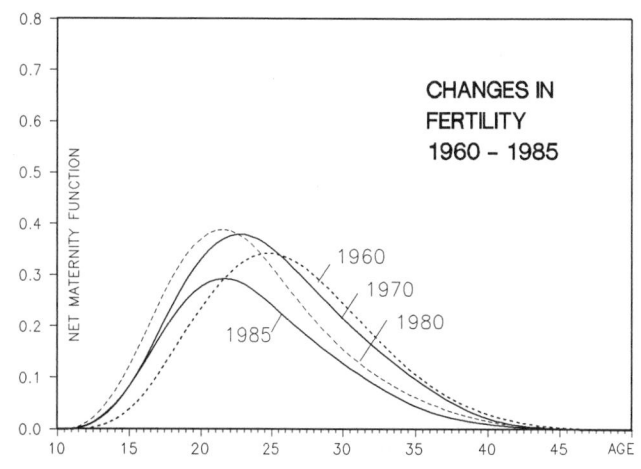

CHANGES IN FERTILITY 1960 - 1985

AGE AT LAST BIRTHDAY	ESTIMATED MID-YEAR POPULATION					BIRTHS BY AGE OF MOTHER AND SEX	DEATHS			AGE AT LAST BIRTHDAY
	BOTH SEXES	MALES		FEMALES			BOTH SEXES	MALES	FEMALES	
		Number	Percent	Number	Percent					
0	148504	76639	1.5	71865	1.3		5449	3147	2302	0
1-4	563729	290588	5.8	273141	5.1		592	334	258	1-4
5-9	643256	330680	6.6	312576	5.9		258	153	105	5-9
10-14	795992	408615	8.2	387377	7.3	181	292	188	104	10-14
15-19	926607	474883	9.5	451724	8.5	22571	726	539	187	15-19
20-24	796724	404936	8.1	391788	7.4	62401	799	587	212	20-24
25-29	737670	370691	7.4	366979	6.9	40481	895	637	258	25-29
30-34	676209	328975	6.6	347234	6.5	17852	967	656	311	30-34
35-39	703982	344743	6.9	359239	6.7	6617	1525	1004	521	35-39
40-44	734779	357543	7.1	377236	7.1	1609	2394	1522	872	40-44
45-49	734131	348390	7.0	385741	7.2	99	3571	2168	1403	45-49
50-54	453798	211817	4.2	241981	4.5	8	3283	1968	1315	50-54
55-59	643937	298821	6.0	345116	6.5		7474	4551	2923	55-59
60-64	584229	267860	5.3	316369	5.9		11459	6993	4466	60-64
65-69	473621	212473	4.2	261148	4.9		15659	9232	6427	65-69
70-74	355830	148328	3.0	207502	3.9		19064	9815	9249	70-74
75-79	210109	79897	1.6	130212	2.4		18519	8230	10289	75-79
80-84	106171	38750	0.8	67421	1.3	78366 M	15247	6239	9008	80-84
85+	48632	16932	0.3	31700	0.6	73453 F	12024	4582	7442	85+
TOTAL	10337910	5011561		5326349		151819	120197	62545	57652	TOTAL

TABLE 1 — DATA

x	nM_x	nq_x	l_x	nd_x	nL_x	nm_x	na_x	T_x	$\overset{\circ}{e}_x$	x
0	0.041063	0.039662	100000	3966	96588	0.041063	0.140	6635443	66.354	0
1	0.001149	0.004584	96034	440	383035	0.001149	1.500	6538854	68.089	1
5	0.000463	0.002311	95594	221	477416	0.000463	2.500	6155820	64.396	5
10	0.000460	0.002298	95373	219	476382	0.000460	2.802	5678404	59.539	10
15	0.001135	0.005660	95154	539	474518	0.001135	2.680	5202023	54.670	15
20	0.001450	0.007234	94615	684	471419	0.001452	2.581	4727505	49.966	20
25	0.001718	0.008568	93930	805	467691	0.001721	2.562	4256086	45.311	25
30	0.001994	0.009935	93126	925	463426	0.001997	2.619	3788395	40.680	30
35	0.002912	0.014463	92200	1333	457875	0.002912	2.655	3324970	36.062	35
40	0.004257	0.021074	90867	1915	449842	0.004257	2.654	2867095	31.553	40
45	0.006223	0.030857	88952	2745	438318	0.006262	2.653	2417253	27.175	45
50	0.009291	0.045601	86207	3931	421897	0.009318	2.675	1978935	22.956	50
55	0.015230	0.073559	82276	6052	397386	0.015230	2.688	1557037	18.925	55
60	0.026107	0.123119	76224	9385	359141	0.026131	2.658	1159651	15.214	60
65	0.043450	0.197054	66839	13171	302507	0.043539	2.594	800510	11.977	65
70	0.066171	0.285575	53668	15326	230563	0.066473	2.535	498003	9.279	70
75	0.103008	0.410784	38342	15750	151804	0.103754	2.466	267439	6.975	75
80	0.161006	0.565724	22592	12781	79380	0.161006	2.373	115635	5.118	80
85	0.270612	1.000000	9811	9811	36255	0.219026	3.695	36255	3.695	85

TABLE 2 — MALE LIFE TABLE

x	nM_x	nq_x	l_x	nd_x	nL_x	nm_x	na_x	T_x	$\overset{\circ}{e}_x$	x
0	0.032032	0.031158	100000	3116	97272	0.032032	0.124	7216266	72.163	0
1	0.000945	0.003769	96884	365	386624	0.000945	1.500	7118994	73.479	1
5	0.000336	0.001678	96519	162	482190	0.000336	2.500	6732371	69.752	5
10	0.000268	0.001341	96357	129	481469	0.000268	2.560	6250181	64.865	10
15	0.000414	0.002068	96228	199	480668	0.000414	2.637	5768711	59.949	15
20	0.000541	0.002707	96029	260	479523	0.000542	2.610	5288043	55.067	20
25	0.000703	0.003514	95769	337	478037	0.000704	2.603	4808520	50.210	25
30	0.000896	0.004472	95432	427	476167	0.000896	2.671	4330483	45.378	30
35	0.001450	0.007227	95005	687	473448	0.001450	2.699	3854316	40.569	35
40	0.002312	0.011496	94319	1084	469093	0.002312	2.693	3380868	35.845	40
45	0.003637	0.018146	93234	1692	462230	0.003660	2.670	2911776	31.231	45
50	0.005434	0.026900	91543	2462	451975	0.005448	2.670	2449546	26.759	50
55	0.008470	0.041536	89080	3700	436856	0.008470	2.691	1997571	22.424	55
60	0.014116	0.068502	85380	5849	413443	0.014146	2.699	1560714	18.280	60
65	0.024611	0.116762	79531	9286	376185	0.024685	2.688	1147272	14.425	65
70	0.044573	0.202364	70245	14215	317646	0.044752	2.638	771087	10.977	70
75	0.079017	0.333422	56030	18682	234360	0.079713	2.549	453441	8.093	75
80	0.133608	0.498072	37348	18602	139230	0.133608	2.446	219081	5.866	80
85	0.234763	1.000000	18746	18746	79852	0.173421	4.260	79852	4.260	85

TABLE 3 — FEMALE LIFE TABLE

TABLE 4 — OBSERVED VITAL RATES AND RATIOS

CRUDE RATES

Per Thousand	BOTH SEXES	MALES	FEMALES
BIRTH RATE	14.69	15.64	13.79
DEATH RATE	11.63	12.48	10.82
RATE OF INCREASE	3.06	3.16	2.97

PERCENT OF POPULATION IN AGE GROUP

	BOTH SEXES	MALES	FEMALES
UNDER 15	20.81	22.08	19.62
15 - 64	67.64	68.02	67.28
65 AND OLDER	11.55	9.90	13.10

RATES STANDARDIZED ON USA 1980

Per Thousand	BOTH SEXES	MALES	FEMALES
BIRTH RATE	17.30		16.28
DEATH RATE	12.50	12.58	12.43
RATE OF INCREASE	4.80		3.84

RATES STANDARDIZED ON MEXICO 1980

	BOTH SEXES	MALES	FEMALES
BIRTH RATE	16.06		15.66
DEATH RATE	5.28	6.06	4.50
RATE OF INCREASE	10.77		11.16

VITAL STATISTICS

GFR x 1000	56.650
TFR	1.972
GRR	0.954
NRR	0.913
μ	25.470
σ^2	29.547
GENERATION	25.522
POP. SEX RATIO	1.063
SEX RATIO AT BIRTH	1.067
DEP. RATIO x 100	47.852

PROJECTED POPULATION

AGE GROUP	1975			1980			STABLE EQUIVALENT TO ORIGINAL POPULATION				AGE GROUP
							MALES		FEMALES		
	BOTH SEXES	MALES	FEMALES	BOTH SEXES	MALES	FEMALES	Number	Percent	Number	Percent	
0-4	753	387	366	761	391	370	382	6.4	361	5.9	0-4
5-9	710	366	344	751	386	365	387	6.5	367	6.0	5-9
10-14	642	330	312	708	365	343	393	6.6	373	6.1	10-14
15-19	794	407	387	641	329	312	399	6.7	379	6.2	15-19
20-24	923	472	451	790	404	386	403	6.7	385	6.3	20-24
25-29	793	402	391	917	468	449	407	6.8	390	6.3	25-29
30-34	733	367	366	787	398	389	411	6.9	396	6.4	30-34
35-39	670	325	345	726	363	363	413	6.9	401	6.5	35-39
40-44	695	339	356	661	319	342	413	6.9	404	6.6	40-44
45-49	720	348	372	681	330	351	410	6.9	405	6.6	45-49
50-54	712	335	377	698	335	363	402	6.7	404	6.6	50-54
55-59	434	200	234	681	316	365	385	6.4	397	6.5	55-59
60-64	597	270	327	401	180	221	355	5.9	383	6.2	60-64
65-69	514	226	288	524	227	297	304	5.1	354	5.8	65-69
70-74	383	162	221	415	172	243	236	3.9	305	5.0	70-74
75-79	251	98	153	270	107	163	158	2.6	229	3.7	75-79
80-84	119	42	77	142	51	91	84	1.4	138	2.2	80-84
85+	57	18	39	63	19	44	39	0.7	81	1.3	85+
TOTAL	10500	5094	5406	10617	5160	5457	5981		6152		TOTAL

TABLE 5 — POPULATION PROJECTED WITH FIXED AGE-SPECIFIC BIRTH AND DEATH RATES (female dominant, in 000s)

VITAL RATES OF PROJECTED POPULATION

Per Thousand	1975			1980			VITAL RATES OF STABLE POPULATION	
	BOTH SEXES	MALES	FEMALES	BOTH SEXES	MALES	FEMALES	MALES	FEMALES
BIRTH RATE	15.35	16.33	14.42	14.60	15.50	13.74	13.20	12.04
DEATH RATE	12.39	13.04	11.78	12.96	13.44	12.52	16.74	15.60
RATE OF INCREASE	2.96	3.29	2.64	1.63	2.06	1.22	-3.57	

TABLE 6 — PROJECTED VITAL RATES AND RATIOS (female dominant)

AGE STRUCTURE OF PROJECTED POPULATION

	BOTH SEXES	MALES	FEMALES	BOTH SEXES	MALES	FEMALES	STABLE AGE STRUCTURE	
							MALES	FEMALES
% UNDER 15	20.06	21.26	18.92	20.91	22.12	19.76	19.43	17.90
% 15-64	67.35	68.04	66.70	65.77	66.71	64.88	66.84	64.11
% 65 AND OLDER	12.60	10.70	14.39	13.32	11.17	15.36	13.72	18.00
DEPEND. RATIO x 100	48.48	46.97	49.93	52.04	49.89	54.12	49.61	55.99

MATRIX PARAMETERS

AGE GROUP	FEMALE BIRTH RATES	NET MATERNITY FUNCTION	COEFF. OF MATRIX EQUATION	ORIGINAL MATRIX		STABLE MATRIX			
				SUB-DIAGONAL	FIRST ROW	FISHER VALUES	REPRODUCTIVE VALUES		
0-4	0.0000	0.0000	0.0000	0.99648	0.00000	1.024	353322	λ_1	0.98231
5-9	0.0000	0.0000	0.0005	0.99851	0.00055	1.010	315561	λ_2	$0.27612+0.73637i$
10-14	0.0002	0.0011	0.0586	0.99834	0.05894	0.993	384516	λ_4	$-0.37501+0.32176i$
15-19	0.0242	0.1162	0.2429	0.99762	0.24449	0.916	413879	λ_6	$-0.37110+0.15301i$
20-24	0.0771	0.3695	0.3123	0.99690	0.31517	0.651	255127	r_1	-0.00357
25-29	0.0534	0.2551	0.1868	0.99609	0.18907	0.318	116658	r_2	$-0.04805+0.24241i$
30-34	0.0249	0.1184	0.0803	0.99429	0.08162	0.119	41355	r_4	$-0.14099+0.48649i$
35-39	0.0089	0.0422	0.0259	0.99080	0.02651	0.034	12069	r_6	$-0.18256+0.55010i$
40-44	0.0021	0.0097	0.0051	0.98537	0.00529	0.006	2229	c_1	61503
45-49	0.0001	0.0006	0.0003	0.97781	0.00034	0.000	152	$2\pi/\gamma$	25.9198
50-54	0.0000	0.0001	0.0000	0.96655	0.00004	0.000	10	Δ	7.2819

TABLE 7 — LESLIE MATRIX AND ITS ANALYSIS (females)

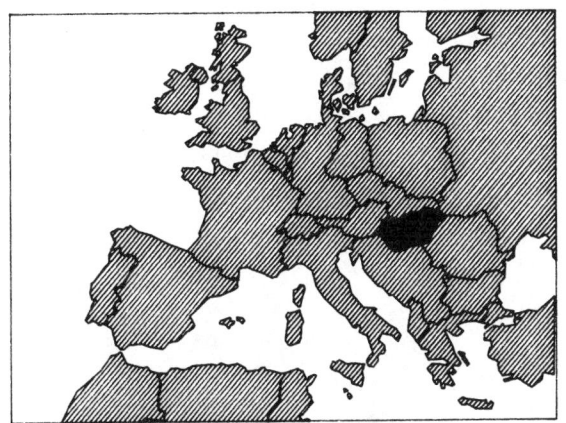

EDUCATION [1984]

% of primary school-age children enrolled:	99
secondary school-age children enrolled:	73
ca. 20-24 year olds in higher education:	15

LABOR FORCE

Average annual labor force growth (%) 1980-85:	0.0
% of the 1980 labor force in agriculture:	18
in industry:	44
in services:	38

GNP & INCOME DISTRIBUTION

GNP per capita (in US Dollars) 1985:	1950
GNP average annual growth rate (%) 1965-85:	5.8
% share of total household income 1982	
Lowest 20% of households:	6.9
Highest 10% of households:	20.5

HEALTH & NUTRITION

Population per physician 1981:	300
Daily calorie supply per capita 1985:	3482

TABLE 8 — SOCIO-ECONOMIC INDICATORS

TABLE 1 — DATA

AGE AT LAST BIRTHDAY	ESTIMATED MID-YEAR POPULATION BOTH SEXES	MALES Number	MALES Percent	FEMALES Number	FEMALES Percent	BIRTHS BY AGE OF MOTHER AND SEX	DEATHS BOTH SEXES	DEATHS MALES	DEATHS FEMALES	AGE AT LAST BIRTHDAY
0	184329	94536	1.8	89793	1.7		6380	3632	2748	0
1-4	606401	311647	6.1	294754	5.4		450	259	191	1-4
5-9	709813	365834	7.2	343979	6.3		245	153	92	5-9
10-14	642133	329986	6.5	312147	5.8	194	226	147	79	10-14
15-19	793942	407240	8.0	386702	7.1	27865	600	426	174	15-19
20-24	922343	471705	9.2	450638	8.3	82673	928	684	244	20-24
25-29	792492	401834	7.9	390658	7.2	52284	846	580	266	25-29
30-34	732765	367282	7.2	365483	6.7	22678	1162	823	339	30-34
35-39	670133	324950	6.4	345183	6.4	6974	1438	958	480	35-39
40-44	694293	338489	6.6	355804	6.6	1494	2476	1622	854	40-44
45-49	719153	347603	6.8	371550	6.8	76	4068	2604	1464	45-49
50-54	711178	334271	6.5	376907	6.9	2	5894	3649	2245	50-54
55-59	432851	199175	3.9	233676	4.3		5085	3071	2014	55-59
60-64	596902	270502	5.3	326400	6.0		11778	7213	4565	60-64
65-69	516158	227572	4.5	288586	5.3		16338	9460	6878	65-69
70-74	384923	162710	3.2	222213	4.1		20445	11005	9440	70-74
75-79	253202	97639	1.9	155563	2.9		22178	10334	11844	75-79
80-84	121008	41872	0.8	79136	1.5	99907 M	17109	6898	10211	80-84
85+	56506	18221	0.4	38285	0.7	94333 F	13456	4711	8745	85+
TOTAL	10540525	5113068		5427457		194240	131102	68229	62873	TOTAL

TABLE 2 — MALE LIFE TABLE

x	nM_x	nq_x	l_x	nd_x	nL_x	nm_x	na_x	T_x	$\overset{\circ}{e}_x$	x
0	0.038419	0.037184	100000	3718	96785	0.038419	0.135	6627396	66.274	0
1	0.000831	0.003317	96282	319	384328	0.000831	1.500	6530612	67.828	1
5	0.000418	0.002089	95962	200	479310	0.000418	2.500	6146284	64.049	5
10	0.000445	0.002225	95762	213	478338	0.000445	2.791	5666974	59.178	10
15	0.001046	0.005218	95549	499	476596	0.001046	2.698	5188636	54.304	15
20	0.001450	0.007225	95050	687	473572	0.001450	2.555	4712040	49.574	20
25	0.001443	0.007205	94363	680	470192	0.001446	2.610	4238469	44.916	25
30	0.002241	0.011178	93684	1047	465941	0.002247	2.635	3768276	40.223	30
35	0.002948	0.014665	92636	1359	460018	0.002953	2.671	3302335	35.648	35
40	0.004792	0.023697	91278	2163	451382	0.004792	2.685	2842317	31.139	40
45	0.007491	0.036810	89115	3280	437880	0.007491	2.654	2390935	26.830	45
50	0.010916	0.053510	85835	4593	418270	0.010981	2.626	1953056	22.754	50
55	0.015419	0.074604	81242	6061	392063	0.015459	2.666	1534786	18.892	55
60	0.026665	0.125435	75181	9430	353656	0.026665	2.641	1142723	15.200	60
65	0.041569	0.189167	65750	12438	298919	0.041609	2.601	789067	12.001	65
70	0.067636	0.290549	53312	15490	228550	0.067775	2.546	490148	9.194	70
75	0.105839	0.419248	37823	15857	148870	0.106516	2.462	261598	6.916	75
80	0.164740	0.574038	21966	12609	76539	0.164740	2.360	112728	5.132	80
85	0.258548	1.000000	9356	9356	36189	0.203926	3.868	36189	3.868	85

TABLE 3 — FEMALE LIFE TABLE

x	nM_x	nq_x	l_x	nd_x	nL_x	nm_x	na_x	T_x	$\overset{\circ}{e}_x$	x
0	0.030604	0.029803	100000	2980	97383	0.030604	0.122	7246744	72.467	0
1	0.000648	0.002588	97020	251	387451	0.000648	1.500	7149360	73.690	1
5	0.000267	0.001336	96769	129	483520	0.000267	2.500	6761909	69.877	5
10	0.000253	0.001265	96639	122	482909	0.000253	2.649	6278389	64.967	10
15	0.000450	0.002247	96517	217	482072	0.000450	2.633	5795480	60.046	15
20	0.000541	0.002704	96300	260	480873	0.000541	2.588	5313408	55.175	20
25	0.000681	0.003405	96040	327	479420	0.000682	2.617	4832535	50.318	25
30	0.000928	0.004638	95713	444	477524	0.000930	2.657	4353116	45.481	30
35	0.001391	0.006938	95269	661	474835	0.001392	2.716	3875592	40.681	35
40	0.002400	0.011936	94608	1129	470459	0.002400	2.715	3400757	35.946	40
45	0.003940	0.019523	93479	1825	463160	0.003940	2.680	2930298	31.347	45
50	0.005956	0.029539	91654	2707	451905	0.005991	2.649	2467138	26.918	50
55	0.008619	0.042351	88946	3767	435952	0.008641	2.669	2015234	22.657	55
60	0.013986	0.067740	85179	5770	412559	0.013986	2.688	1579281	18.541	60
65	0.023833	0.113161	79409	8986	376219	0.023885	2.682	1166722	14.693	65
70	0.042482	0.193564	70423	13631	319986	0.042600	2.643	790503	11.225	70
75	0.076136	0.322853	56792	18335	239172	0.076662	2.557	470518	8.285	75
80	0.129031	0.485699	38456	18678	144758	0.129031	2.456	231345	6.016	80
85	0.228418	1.000000	19778	19778	86587	0.165821	4.378	86587	4.378	85

TABLE 4 — OBSERVED VITAL RATES AND RATIOS

CRUDE RATES

Per Thousand	BOTH SEXES	MALES	FEMALES
BIRTH RATE	18.43	19.54	17.38
DEATH RATE	12.44	13.34	11.58
RATE OF INCREASE	5.99	6.20	5.80

PERCENT OF POPULATION IN AGE GROUP

UNDER 15	20.33	21.55	19.17
15 - 64	67.04	67.73	66.38
65 AND OLDER	12.64	10.72	14.44

RATES STANDARDIZED ON USA 1980

Per Thousand	BOTH SEXES	MALES	FEMALES
BIRTH RATE	20.95		19.78
DEATH RATE	12.38	12.68	12.10
RATE OF INCREASE	8.56		7.68

RATES STANDARDIZED ON MEXICO 1980

	BOTH SEXES	MALES	FEMALES
BIRTH RATE	19.59		19.18
DEATH RATE	5.21	6.04	4.36
RATE OF INCREASE	14.38		14.82

VITAL STATISTICS

GFR x 1000	72.858
TFR	2.383
GRR	1.157
NRR	1.111
μ	25.238
σ^2	29.559
GENERATION	25.177
POP. SEX RATIO	1.061
SEX RATIO AT BIRTH	1.059
DEP. RATIO x 100	49.171

AGE AT LAST BIRTHDAY	ESTIMATED MID-YEAR POPULATION					BIRTHS BY AGE OF MOTHER AND SEX	DEATHS			AGE AT LAST BIRTHDAY	
	BOTH SEXES	MALES		FEMALES			BOTH SEXES	MALES	FEMALES		
		Number	Percent	Number	Percent						
0	152807	78466	1.5	74341	1.3		3443	1968	1475	0	
1-4	691518	355557	6.9	335961	6.1		418	249	169	1-4	
5-9	792841	407925	7.9	384916	7.0		259	169	90	5-9	
10-14	711572	366935	7.1	344637	6.2	236	246	153	93	10-14	
15-19	645711	332550	6.4	313161	5.7	21286	471	333	138	15-19	
20-24	786667	401256	7.7	385411	7.0	61115	840	630	210	20-24	
25-29	901431	457285	8.8	444146	8.0	44419	1123	813	310	25-29	
30-34	773345	390420	7.5	382925	6.9	15663	1273	876	397	30-34	
35-39	716301	356885	6.9	359416	6.5	4910	2010	1396	614	35-39	TABLE 1
40-44	655899	315681	6.1	340218	6.2	990	2890	1949	941	40-44	
45-49	676710	326503	6.3	350207	6.3	51	4535	2995	1540	45-49	DATA
50-54	691607	329443	6.3	362164	6.6	3	7001	4672	2329	50-54	
55-59	675226	310056	6.0	365170	6.6		10046	6480	3566	55-59	
60-64	400865	178844	3.4	222021	4.0		8765	5361	3404	60-64	
65-69	528408	229141	4.4	299267	5.4		17835	10371	7464	65-69	
70-74	422215	174876	3.4	247339	4.5		23069	12446	10623	70-74	
75-79	273572	105659	2.0	167913	3.0		24468	11996	12472	75-79	
80-84	148354	51223	1.0	97131	1.8	76115 M	20801	8451	12350	80-84	
85+	66073	19697	0.4	46376	0.8	72558 F	15862	5421	10441	85+	
TOTAL	10711122	5188402		5522720		148673	145355	76729	68626	TOTAL	

x	$_nM_x$	$_nq_x$	l_x	$_nd_x$	$_nL_x$	$_nm_x$	$_na_x$	T_x	$\overset{\circ}{e}_x$	x	
0	0.025081	0.024535	100000	2453	97823	0.025081	0.113	6555991	65.560	0	
1	0.000700	0.002796	97547	273	389504	0.000700	1.500	6458168	66.206	1	
5	0.000414	0.002069	97274	201	485866	0.000414	2.500	6068664	62.387	5	
10	0.000417	0.002093	97072	203	484913	0.000419	2.790	5582798	57.512	10	
15	0.001001	0.004995	96869	484	483251	0.001001	2.737	5097885	52.626	15	
20	0.001570	0.007821	96385	754	480118	0.001570	2.600	4614634	47.877	20	
25	0.001778	0.008851	95632	846	476106	0.001778	2.576	4134517	43.234	25	TABLE 2
30	0.002244	0.011195	94785	1061	471476	0.002251	2.692	3658411	38.597	30	
35	0.003912	0.019460	93724	1824	464422	0.003927	2.699	3186935	34.003	35	MALE
40	0.006174	0.030470	91900	2800	452954	0.006182	2.662	2722512	29.625	40	LIFE
45	0.009173	0.044900	89100	4001	436131	0.009173	2.658	2269559	25.472	45	TABLE
50	0.014182	0.068612	85099	5839	411719	0.014182	2.640	1833428	21.545	50	
55	0.020899	0.100079	79260	7932	377335	0.021022	2.609	1421709	17.937	55	
60	0.029976	0.139970	71328	9984	332636	0.030014	2.596	1044374	14.642	60	
65	0.045260	0.203962	61344	12512	276443	0.045260	2.580	711738	11.602	65	
70	0.071170	0.302814	48832	14787	207714	0.071190	2.535	435296	8.914	70	
75	0.113535	0.440782	34045	15007	131904	0.113769	2.446	227581	6.685	75	
80	0.164984	0.573360	19039	10916	66164	0.164985	2.341	95678	5.025	80	
85	0.275220	1.000000	8123	8123	29513	0.225568	3.633	29513	3.633	85	

x	$_nM_x$	$_nq_x$	l_x	$_nd_x$	$_nL_x$	$_nm_x$	$_na_x$	T_x	$\overset{\circ}{e}_x$	x	
0	0.019841	0.019494	100000	1949	98253	0.019841	0.104	7282570	72.826	0	
1	0.000503	0.002010	98051	197	391710	0.000503	1.500	7184317	73.272	1	
5	0.000234	0.001168	97854	114	488982	0.000234	2.500	6792607	69.416	5	
10	0.000270	0.001352	97739	132	488386	0.000271	2.658	6303626	64.494	10	
15	0.000441	0.002201	97607	215	487526	0.000441	2.629	5815239	59.578	15	
20	0.000545	0.002721	97392	265	486324	0.000545	2.597	5327714	54.704	20	
25	0.000698	0.003484	97127	338	484839	0.000698	2.646	4841390	49.846	25	TABLE 3
30	0.001037	0.005188	96789	502	482789	0.001040	2.700	4356550	45.011	30	
35	0.001708	0.008531	96287	821	479549	0.001713	2.706	3873761	40.232	35	FEMALE
40	0.002766	0.013750	95465	1313	474300	0.002768	2.695	3394212	35.554	40	LIFE
45	0.004397	0.021763	94153	2049	465974	0.004397	2.663	2919912	31.013	45	TABLE
50	0.006431	0.031677	92103	2918	453689	0.006431	2.660	2453938	26.643	50	
55	0.009765	0.048033	89186	4284	435924	0.009827	2.664	2000249	22.428	55	
60	0.015332	0.074182	84902	6298	409802	0.015369	2.665	1564355	18.425	60	
65	0.024941	0.117836	78604	9262	371371	0.024941	2.663	1154523	14.688	65	
70	0.042949	0.195212	69342	13536	314605	0.043026	2.628	783152	11.294	70	
75	0.074277	0.315469	55805	17605	236019	0.074591	2.557	468547	8.396	75	
80	0.127148	0.480647	38200	18361	144406	0.127148	2.462	232527	6.087	80	
85	0.225138	1.000000	19840	19840	88122	0.161981	4.442	88122	4.442	85	

CRUDE RATES

Per Thousand	BOTH SEXES	MALES	FEMALES
BIRTH RATE	13.88	14.67	13.14
DEATH RATE	13.57	14.79	12.43
RATE OF INCREASE	0.31	-0.12	0.71

RATES STANDARDIZED ON USA 1980

Per Thousand	BOTH SEXES	MALES	FEMALES
BIRTH RATE	17.06		16.19
DEATH RATE	12.89	13.74	12.09
RATE OF INCREASE	4.16		4.10

VITAL STATISTICS

GFR x 1000	57.726	TABLE 4
TFR	1.924	
GRR	0.939	OBSERVED
NRR	0.912	VITAL
μ	24.633	RATES
σ^2	28.210	AND
GENERATION	24.686	RATIOS
POP. SEX RATIO	1.064	
SEX RATIO AT BIRTH	1.049	
DEP. RATIO x 100	54.701	

PERCENT OF POPULATION IN AGE GROUP

UNDER 15	21.93	23.30	20.64
15 - 64	64.64	65.51	63.82
65 AND OLDER	13.43	11.19	15.54

RATES STANDARDIZED ON MEXICO 1980

	BOTH SEXES	MALES	FEMALES
BIRTH RATE	16.21		15.94
DEATH RATE	5.19	6.22	4.14
RATE OF INCREASE	11.02		11.80

TABLE 1 — DATA

AGE AT LAST BIRTHDAY	ESTIMATED MID-YEAR POPULATION BOTH SEXES	MALES Number	MALES Percent	FEMALES Number	FEMALES Percent	BIRTHS BY AGE OF MOTHER AND SEX	DEATHS BOTH SEXES	DEATHS MALES	DEATHS FEMALES	AGE AT LAST BIRTHDAY
0	125417	64100	1.2	61317	1.1		2651	1493	1158	0
1-4	528938	270121	5.3	258817	4.7		288	165	123	1-4
5-9	842479	432944	8.4	409535	7.4		225	131	94	5-9
10-14	791726	407230	7.9	384496	7.0	198	194	122	72	10-14
15-19	709881	365806	7.1	344075	6.3	17736	493	354	139	15-19
20-24	642745	330315	6.4	312430	5.7	47644	646	494	152	20-24
25-29	782154	397941	7.7	384213	7.0	39519	1050	782	268	25-29
30-34	894533	452378	8.8	442155	8.0	18992	1817	1287	530	30-34
35-39	764188	384035	7.5	380153	6.9	5163	2390	1682	708	35-39
40-44	702840	347450	6.8	355405	6.5	913	3436	2416	1020	40-44
45-49	636933	302603	5.9	334330	6.1	35	4771	3295	1476	45-49
50-54	647632	306754	6.0	340878	6.2		7038	4773	2265	50-54
55-59	647809	299953	5.8	347856	6.3		10388	6933	3455	55-59
60-64	615059	271687	5.3	343372	6.2		13869	8789	5080	60-64
65-69	350556	148466	2.9	202090	3.7		11237	6517	4720	65-69
70-74	426921	172287	3.3	254634	4.6		22497	12133	10364	70-74
75-79	300104	112437	2.2	187667	3.4		25073	11899	13174	75-79
80-84	158036	53753	1.0	104283	1.9	66826 M	21190	8667	12523	80-84
85+	80762	23483	0.5	57279	1.0	63374 F	18361	6102	12259	85+
TOTAL	10648713	5143728		5504985		130200	147614	78034	69580	TOTAL

TABLE 2 — MALE LIFE TABLE

x	nM_x	nq_x	l_x	nd_x	nL_x	nm_x	na_x	T_x	$\overset{\circ}{e}_x$	x
0	0.023292	0.022819	100000	2282	97968	0.023292	0.110	6509865	65.099	0
1	0.000611	0.002440	97718	238	390277	0.000611	1.500	6411897	65.616	1
5	0.000303	0.001512	97480	147	487030	0.000303	2.500	6021620	61.773	5
10	0.000300	0.001504	97332	146	486364	0.000301	2.962	5534590	56.863	10
15	0.000968	0.004859	97186	472	484869	0.000974	2.753	5048226	51.944	15
20	0.001496	0.007451	96714	721	481864	0.001496	2.635	4563357	47.184	20
25	0.001965	0.009780	95993	939	477748	0.001965	2.638	4081493	42.519	25
30	0.002845	0.014131	95054	1343	472142	0.002845	2.671	3603745	37.912	30
35	0.004380	0.021752	93711	2038	463836	0.004395	2.685	3131602	33.418	35
40	0.006954	0.034353	91673	3149	451046	0.006982	2.676	2667767	29.101	40
45	0.010889	0.053138	88523	4704	431511	0.010901	2.639	2216721	25.041	45
50	0.015560	0.075026	83819	6289	404164	0.015560	2.625	1785210	21.298	50
55	0.023114	0.109496	77531	8489	367287	0.023114	2.601	1381045	17.813	55
60	0.032350	0.150652	69041	10401	319861	0.032518	2.563	1013758	14.683	60
65	0.043896	0.198503	58640	11640	264871	0.043947	2.566	693897	11.833	65
70	0.070423	0.299957	47000	14098	200190	0.070423	2.531	429026	9.128	70
75	0.105828	0.417212	32902	13727	129515	0.105989	2.451	228837	6.955	75
80	0.161238	0.565671	19175	10847	67271	0.161238	2.363	99322	5.180	80
85	0.259848	1.000000	8328	8328	32050	0.205697	3.848	32050	3.848	85

TABLE 3 — FEMALE LIFE TABLE

x	nM_x	nq_x	l_x	nd_x	nL_x	nm_x	na_x	T_x	$\overset{\circ}{e}_x$	x
0	0.018885	0.018571	100000	1857	98333	0.018885	0.102	7319660	73.197	0
1	0.000475	0.001899	98143	186	392106	0.000475	1.500	7221327	73.580	1
5	0.000230	0.001147	97957	112	489502	0.000230	2.500	6829221	69.717	5
10	0.000187	0.000938	97844	92	489010	0.000188	2.694	6339719	64.794	10
15	0.000404	0.002026	97752	198	488298	0.000406	2.653	5850710	59.852	15
20	0.000487	0.002430	97554	237	487209	0.000487	2.624	5362412	54.968	20
25	0.000698	0.003482	97317	339	485811	0.000698	2.711	4875203	50.096	25
30	0.001199	0.005977	96979	580	483560	0.001199	2.700	4389392	45.261	30
35	0.001862	0.009302	96399	897	479917	0.001868	2.682	3905832	40.517	35
40	0.002870	0.014293	95502	1365	474341	0.002878	2.677	3425915	35.873	40
45	0.004415	0.021861	94137	2058	465885	0.004417	2.667	2951574	31.354	45
50	0.006645	0.032714	92079	3012	453338	0.006645	2.657	2485690	26.995	50
55	0.009932	0.048528	89067	4322	435172	0.009932	2.649	2032352	22.818	55
60	0.014794	0.071943	84745	6097	409401	0.014892	2.651	1597180	18.847	60
65	0.023356	0.111048	78648	8734	372840	0.023425	2.664	1187778	15.102	65
70	0.040702	0.185636	69914	12979	318872	0.040702	2.635	814939	11.656	70
75	0.070199	0.300716	56936	17122	242993	0.070461	2.565	496066	8.713	75
80	0.120087	0.460742	39814	18344	152757	0.120087	2.475	253074	6.356	80
85	0.214023	1.000000	21470	21470	100317	0.148946	4.672	100317	4.672	85

TABLE 4 — OBSERVED VITAL RATES AND RATIOS

CRUDE RATES

Per Thousand	BOTH SEXES	MALES	FEMALES
BIRTH RATE	12.23	12.99	11.51
DEATH RATE	13.86	15.17	12.64
RATE OF INCREASE	-1.64	-2.18	-1.13

RATES STANDARDIZED ON USA 1980

Per Thousand	BOTH SEXES	MALES	FEMALES
BIRTH RATE	16.20		15.33
DEATH RATE	12.68	13.85	11.57
RATE OF INCREASE	3.52		3.76

VITAL STATISTICS

GFR x 1000	51.004
TFR	1.833
GRR	0.892
NRR	0.868
μ	25.039
σ^2	27.020
GENERATION	25.115
POP. SEX RATIO	1.070
SEX RATIO AT BIRTH	1.054
DEP. RATIO x 100	51.179

PERCENT OF POPULATION IN AGE GROUP

	BOTH SEXES	MALES	FEMALES
UNDER 15	21.49	22.83	20.24
15 - 64	66.15	67.25	65.12
65 AND OLDER	12.36	9.92	14.64

RATES STANDARDIZED ON MEXICO 1980

	BOTH SEXES	MALES	FEMALES
BIRTH RATE	15.17		14.88
DEATH RATE	5.15	6.29	3.99
RATE OF INCREASE	10.02		10.89

PROJECTED POPULATION

AGE GROUP	1990 BOTH SEXES	1990 MALES	1990 FEMALES	1995 BOTH SEXES	1995 MALES	1995 FEMALES
0-4	631	323	308	642	329	313
5-9	653	333	320	629	322	307
10-14	841	432	409	652	333	319
15-19	790	406	384	840	431	409
20-24	707	364	343	786	403	383
25-29	639	327	312	702	360	342
30-34	775	393	382	634	324	310
35-39	883	444	439	766	386	380
40-44	749	373	376	866	432	434
45-49	681	332	349	726	357	369
50-54	608	283	325	651	311	340
55-59	606	279	327	570	258	312
60-64	588	261	327	551	243	308
65-69	538	225	313	514	216	298
70-74	285	112	173	437	170	267
75-79	305	111	194	205	73	132
80-84	176	58	118	180	58	122
85+	94	26	68	105	28	77
TOTAL	10549	5082	5467	10456	5034	5422

STABLE EQUIVALENT TO ORIGINAL POPULATION

MALES Number	MALES Percent	FEMALES Number	FEMALES Percent	AGE GROUP	
358	6.2	341	5.4	0-4	
367	6.4	350	5.6	5-9	TABLE 5
377	6.5	360	5.7	10-14	
387	6.7	370	5.9	15-19	POPULATION
396	6.8	379	6.0	20-24	PROJECTED
404	7.0	389	6.2	25-29	WITH
410	7.1	399	6.3	30-34	FIXED
415	7.2	407	6.5	35-39	AGE-
415	7.2	414	6.6	40-44	SPECIFIC
408	7.1	418	6.6	45-49	BIRTH
393	6.8	418	6.6	50-54	AND
368	6.4	413	6.6	55-59	DEATH
329	5.7	400	6.3	60-64	RATES
281	4.8	374	5.9	65-69	(female
218	3.8	329	5.2	70-74	dominant,
145	2.5	258	4.1	75-79	in 000s)
78	1.3	167	2.7	80-84	
38	0.7	113	1.8	85+	
5787		6299		TOTAL	

VITAL RATES OF PROJECTED POPULATION

Per Thousand	1990 BOTH SEXES	1990 MALES	1990 FEMALES	1995 BOTH SEXES	1995 MALES	1995 FEMALES
BIRTH RATE	12.11	12.90	11.38	12.86	13.71	12.07
DEATH RATE	14.26	15.27	13.33	14.50	15.38	13.68
RATE OF INCREASE	-2.15	-2.37	-1.95	-1.64	-1.67	-1.61

AGE STRUCTURE OF PROJECTED POPULATION

	1990 BOTH SEXES	1990 MALES	1990 FEMALES	1995 BOTH SEXES	1995 MALES	1995 FEMALES
% UNDER 15	20.14	21.41	18.96	18.39	19.54	17.33
% 15-64	66.60	68.11	65.20	67.82	69.64	66.14
% 65 AND OLDER	13.25	10.47	15.84	13.78	10.82	16.54
DEPEND. RATIO x 100	50.14	46.82	53.37	47.45	43.60	51.20

VITAL RATES OF STABLE POPULATION

Per Thousand	MALES	FEMALES	
BIRTH RATE	12.50	10.89	TABLE 6
DEATH RATE	18.10	16.54	PROJECTED
RATE OF INCREASE		-5.65	VITAL RATES AND RATIOS

STABLE AGE STRUCTURE

	MALES	FEMALES	(female dominant)
% UNDER 15	19.06	16.69	
% 15-64	67.82	63.60	
% 65 AND OLDER	13.12	19.71	
DEPEND. RATIO x 100	47.46	57.24	

AGE GROUP	FEMALE BIRTH RATES	NET MATERNITY FUNCTION	COEFF. OF MATRIX EQUATION	ORIGINAL MATRIX SUB-DIAGONAL	ORIGINAL MATRIX FIRST ROW	STABLE MATRIX FISHER VALUES	STABLE MATRIX REPRODUCTIVE VALUES	MATRIX PARAMETERS		
0-4	0.0000	0.0000	0.0000	0.99809	0.00000	1.005	321794	λ_1	0.97214	
5-9	0.0000	0.0000	0.0006	0.99899	0.00061	0.979	400955	λ_2	$0.26445+0.73967i$	TABLE 7
10-14	0.0003	0.0012	0.0619	0.99854	0.06205	0.952	366083	λ_4	$-0.37639-0.31791i$	
15-19	0.0251	0.1225	0.2421	0.99777	0.24314	0.864	297443	λ_6	$-0.02279+0.35877i$	LESLIE
20-24	0.0742	0.3616	0.3024	0.99713	0.30443	0.597	186621	r_1	-0.00565	MATRIX
25-29	0.0501	0.2432	0.1722	0.99537	0.17380	0.275	105835	r_2	$-0.04828+0.24549i$	AND ITS
30-34	0.0209	0.1011	0.0664	0.99247	0.06736	0.094	41348	r_4	$-0.14158-0.48805i$	ANALYSIS
35-39	0.0066	0.0317	0.0188	0.98838	0.01924	0.023	8888	r_6	$-0.20461+0.32685i$	(females)
40-44	0.0013	0.0059	0.0031	0.98217	0.00319	0.003	1218	c_1	62995	
45-49	0.0001	0.0002	0.0001	0.97307	0.00012	0.000	43	$2\pi/y$	25.5947	
50-54	0.0000	0.0000	0.0000	0.00000	0.00000	0.000	0	Δ	6.8865	

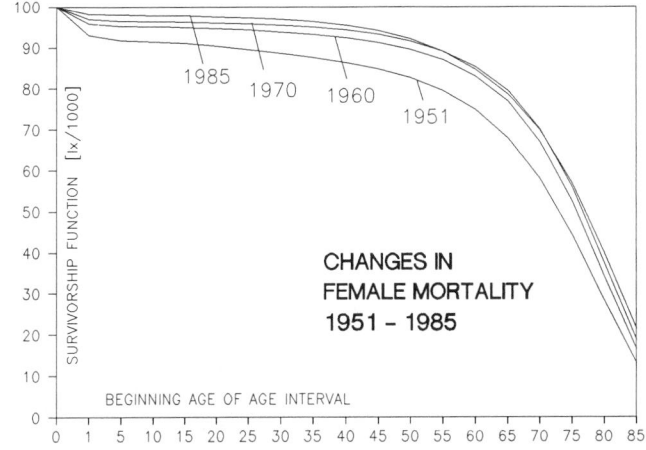

CHANGES IN
FEMALE MORTALITY
1951 – 1985

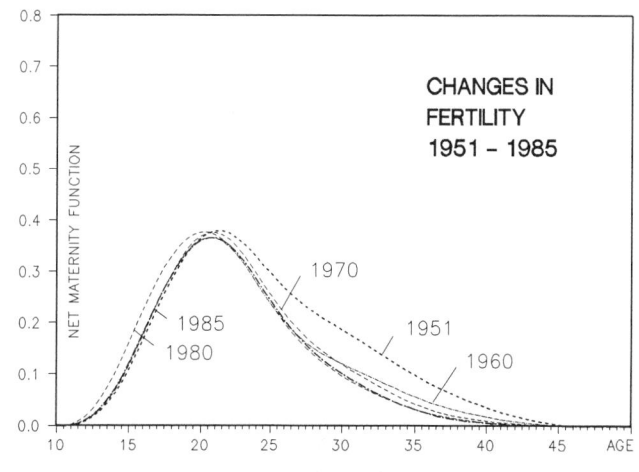

CHANGES IN
FERTILITY
1951 – 1985

Table 1 — DATA

AGE AT LAST BIRTHDAY	ESTIMATED MID-YEAR POPULATION BOTH SEXES	MALES Number	MALES Percent	FEMALES Number	FEMALES Percent	BIRTHS BY AGE OF MOTHER AND SEX	DEATHS BOTH SEXES	DEATHS MALES	DEATHS FEMALES	AGE AT LAST BIRTHDAY
0	4018	2055	2.0	1963	1.9		53	35	18	0
1-4	17198	8812	8.5	8386	8.3		11	6	5	1-4
5-9	22899	11670	11.3	11229	11.1		9	5	4	5-9
10-14	22515	11570	11.2	10945	10.8	1	5	2	3	10-14
15-19	20036	10324	10.0	9712	9.6	717	16	12	4	15-19
20-24	17147	8935	8.7	8212	8.1	1368	19	15	4	20-24
25-29	13528	6892	6.7	6636	6.6	942	16	14	2	25-29
30-34	10976	5568	5.4	5408	5.4	545	14	13	1	30-34
35-39	11479	5829	5.6	5650	5.6	322	21	16	5	35-39
40-44	11322	5774	5.6	5548	5.5	121	31	23	8	40-44
45-49	10464	5322	5.2	5142	5.1	7	44	26	18	45-49
50-54	9137	4601	4.5	4536	4.5		40	31	9	50-54
55-59	8251	4040	3.9	4211	4.2		85	60	25	55-59
60-64	7169	3536	3.4	3633	3.6		117	79	38	60-64
65-69	6075	2961	2.9	3114	3.1		140	82	58	65-69
70-74	5000	2303	2.2	2697	2.7		180	103	77	70-74
75-79	3833	1730	1.7	2103	2.1		219	116	103	75-79
80-84	1967	846	0.8	1121	1.1	2071 M	206	94	112	80-84
85+	1090	417	0.4	673	0.7	1952 F	231	85	146	85+
TOTAL	204104	103185		100919		4023	1457	817	640	TOTAL

Table 2 — MALE LIFE TABLE

x	$_nM_x$	$_nq_x$	l_x	$_nd_x$	$_nL_x$	$_nm_x$	$_na_x$	T_x	$\overset{\circ}{e}_x$	x
0	0.017032	0.016774	100000	1677	98489	0.017032	0.099	7069225	70.692	0
1	0.000681	0.002719	98323	267	392622	0.000681	1.500	6970737	70.897	1
5	0.000428	0.002140	98055	210	489752	0.000428	2.500	6578115	67.086	5
10	0.000173	0.000869	97845	85	489089	0.000174	3.381	6088363	62.224	10
15	0.001162	0.005825	97760	569	487530	0.001168	2.767	5599274	57.275	15
20	0.001679	0.008390	97191	815	484001	0.001685	2.604	5111743	52.595	20
25	0.002031	0.010129	96375	976	479498	0.002036	2.563	4627742	48.018	25
30	0.002335	0.011625	95399	1109	474288	0.002338	2.558	4148244	43.483	30
35	0.002745	0.013635	94290	1286	468389	0.002745	2.618	3673956	38.964	35
40	0.003983	0.019732	93005	1835	460626	0.003984	2.604	3205567	34.467	40
45	0.004885	0.024178	91169	2204	450572	0.004892	2.607	2744941	30.108	45
50	0.006738	0.033354	88965	2967	438238	0.006771	2.780	2294369	25.790	50
55	0.014851	0.072006	85998	6192	415654	0.014898	2.685	1856131	21.583	55
60	0.022342	0.106093	79805	8467	378503	0.022369	2.576	1440477	18.050	60
65	0.027693	0.130031	71339	9276	334350	0.027744	2.591	1061975	14.886	65
70	0.044724	0.201950	62062	12533	280029	0.044758	2.584	727625	11.724	70
75	0.067052	0.289116	49529	14320	212425	0.067410	2.540	447596	9.037	75
80	0.111111	0.434950	35209	15314	137568	0.111322	2.487	235171	6.679	80
85	0.203837	1.000000	19895	19895	97603	0.137227	4.906	97603	4.906	85

Table 3 — FEMALE LIFE TABLE

x	$_nM_x$	$_nq_x$	l_x	$_nd_x$	$_nL_x$	$_nm_x$	$_na_x$	T_x	$\overset{\circ}{e}_x$	x
0	0.009170	0.009093	100000	909	99168	0.009170	0.086	7733670	77.337	0
1	0.000596	0.002381	99091	236	395773	0.000596	1.500	7634501	77.046	1
5	0.000356	0.001780	98855	176	493834	0.000356	2.500	7238729	73.226	5
10	0.000274	0.001370	98679	135	493062	0.000274	2.542	6744895	68.352	10
15	0.000412	0.002062	98544	203	492232	0.000413	2.606	6251834	63.442	15
20	0.000487	0.002429	98340	239	491093	0.000486	2.450	5759602	58.568	20
25	0.000301	0.001487	98102	146	490113	0.000298	2.290	5268509	53.705	25
30	0.000185	0.000935	97956	92	489609	0.000187	3.152	4778397	48.781	30
35	0.000885	0.004419	97864	432	488366	0.000885	2.794	4288787	43.824	35
40	0.001442	0.007198	97432	701	485665	0.001444	2.871	3800421	39.006	40
45	0.003501	0.017368	96730	1680	479501	0.003504	2.530	3314756	34.268	45
50	0.001984	0.009903	95050	941	473125	0.001989	2.741	2835255	29.829	50
55	0.005937	0.029426	94109	2769	464402	0.005963	2.782	2362130	25.100	55
60	0.010460	0.051305	91340	4686	446022	0.010507	2.722	1897728	20.777	60
65	0.018626	0.089484	86654	7754	415106	0.018680	2.658	1451706	16.753	65
70	0.028550	0.133846	78899	10560	369631	0.028570	2.645	1036600	13.138	70
75	0.048978	0.221253	68339	15120	306151	0.049388	2.649	666969	9.760	75
80	0.099911	0.401959	53219	21392	214109	0.099911	2.570	360818	6.780	80
85	0.216939	1.000000	31827	31827	146709	0.151951	4.610	146709	4.610	85

Table 4 — OBSERVED VITAL RATES AND RATIOS

CRUDE RATES

Per Thousand	BOTH SEXES	MALES	FEMALES
BIRTH RATE	19.71	20.07	19.34
DEATH RATE	7.14	7.92	6.34
RATE OF INCREASE	12.57	12.15	13.00

RATES STANDARDIZED ON USA 1980

Per Thousand	BOTH SEXES	MALES	FEMALES
BIRTH RATE	23.73		22.39
DEATH RATE	9.14	9.22	9.07
RATE OF INCREASE	14.59		13.32

RATES STANDARDIZED ON MEXICO 1980

Per Thousand	BOTH SEXES	MALES	FEMALES
BIRTH RATE	21.60		21.12
DEATH RATE	3.57	4.29	2.84
RATE OF INCREASE	18.02		18.28

PERCENT OF POPULATION IN AGE GROUP

	BOTH SEXES	MALES	FEMALES
UNDER 15	32.65	33.05	32.23
15 - 64	58.55	58.94	58.15
65 AND OLDER	8.80	8.00	9.62

VITAL STATISTICS

GFR x 1000	86.875
TFR	2.817
GRR	1.367
NRR	1.340
μ	27.224
σ^2	44.642
GENERATION	26.982
POP. SEX RATIO	0.978
SEX RATIO AT BIRTH	1.061
DEP. RATIO x 100	70.785

PROJECTED POPULATION

STABLE EQUIVALENT TO ORIGINAL POPULATION

AGE GROUP	1975 BOTH SEXES	MALES	FEMALES	1980 BOTH SEXES	MALES	FEMALES	MALES Number	Percent	FEMALES Number	Percent	AGE GROUP	
0-4	21	11	10	25	13	12	11	9.9	11	9.3	0-4	
5-9	21	11	10	21	11	10	11	9.3	10	8.8	5-9	TABLE 5
10-14	23	12	11	21	11	10	10	8.8	10	8.3	10-14	
15-19	23	12	11	23	12	11	10	8.3	9	7.9	15-19	POPULATION
20-24	20	10	10	22	11	11	9	7.8	9	7.4	20-24	PROJECTED
25-29	17	9	8	20	10	10	9	7.4	8	7.0	25-29	WITH
30-34	14	7	7	17	9	8	8	6.9	8	6.7	30-34	FIXED
35-39	10	5	5	14	7	7	7	6.4	7	6.3	35-39	AGE-
40-44	12	6	6	10	5	5	7	6.0	7	5.9	40-44	SPECIFIC
45-49	11	6	6	12	6	6	6	5.6	6	5.5	45-49	BIRTH
50-54	10	5	5	10	5	5	6	5.1	6	5.2	50-54	AND
55-59	8	4	4	10	5	5	5	4.6	6	4.8	55-59	DEATH
60-64	8	4	4	8	4	4	5	4.0	5	4.4	60-64	RATES
65-69	6	3	3	7	3	4	4	3.3	5	3.9	65-69	(female
70-74	5	2	3	6	3	3	3	2.6	4	3.3	70-74	dominant,
75-79	4	2	2	4	2	2	2	1.9	3	2.6	75-79	in 000s)
80-84	2	1	1	3	1	2	1	1.2	2	1.7	80-84	
85+	2	1	1	2	1	1	1	0.8	1	1.1	85+	
TOTAL	217	111	106	235	119	116	115		117		TOTAL	

VITAL RATES OF PROJECTED POPULATION

VITAL RATES OF STABLE POPULATION

Per Thousand	1975 BOTH SEXES	MALES	FEMALES	1980 BOTH SEXES	MALES	FEMALES		MALES	FEMALES	
BIRTH RATE	21.49	21.93	21.05	22.75	23.26	22.24	BIRTH RATE	20.68	19.34	TABLE 6
DEATH RATE	7.52	8.37	6.65	7.77	8.58	6.94	DEATH RATE	9.82	8.47	PROJECTED
RATE OF INCREASE	13.98	13.56	14.40	14.98	14.67	15.30	RATE OF INCREASE		10.86	VITAL RATES AND

AGE STRUCTURE OF PROJECTED POPULATION

STABLE AGE STRUCTURE

										RATIOS
% UNDER 15	30.01	30.43	29.59	28.65	29.16	28.13	% UNDER 15	28.06	26.45	(female
% 15-64	60.96	61.34	60.58	62.27	62.66	61.88	% 15-64	62.15	61.10	dominant)
% 65 AND OLDER	9.03	8.24	9.83	9.08	8.18	9.99	% 65 AND OLDER	9.79	12.45	
DEPEND. RATIO x 100	64.04	63.03	65.08	60.59	59.60	61.60	DEPEND. RATIO x 100	60.91	63.66	

AGE GROUP	FEMALE BIRTH RATES	NET MATERNITY FUNCTION	COEFF. OF MATRIX EQUATION	ORIGINAL MATRIX SUB-DIAGONAL	FIRST ROW	STABLE MATRIX FISHER VALUES	REPRODUCTIVE VALUES	MATRIX PARAMETERS		
0-4	0.0000	0.0000	0.0000	0.99776	0.00000	1.038	10742	λ_1	1.05581	
5-9	0.0000	0.0000	0.0001	0.99844	0.00011	1.098	12333	λ_2	0.35804+0.70661i	TABLE 7
10-14	0.0000	0.0002	0.0883	0.99832	0.08861	1.161	12711	λ_4	0.01926+0.61240i	
15-19	0.0358	0.1763	0.2866	0.99769	0.28821	1.136	11034	λ_6	-0.36709+0.41477i	LESLIE
20-24	0.0808	0.3969	0.3673	0.99800	0.37014	0.902	7411	r_1	0.01086	MATRIX
25-29	0.0689	0.3376	0.2885	0.99897	0.29133	0.570	3781	r_2	-0.04660+0.22036i	AND ITS
30-34	0.0489	0.2394	0.1872	0.99746	0.18927	0.299	1620	r_4	-0.09797+0.30787i	ANALYSIS
35-39	0.0277	0.1350	0.0932	0.99447	0.09448	0.120	678	r_6	-0.11816+0.45906i	(females)
40-44	0.0106	0.0514	0.0273	0.98731	0.02780	0.029	160	c_1	1172	
45-49	0.0007	0.0032	0.0016	0.98670	0.00163	0.002	8	$2\pi/y$	28.5133	
50-54	0.0000	0.0000	0.0000	0.00000	0.00000	0.000	0	Δ	8.2268	

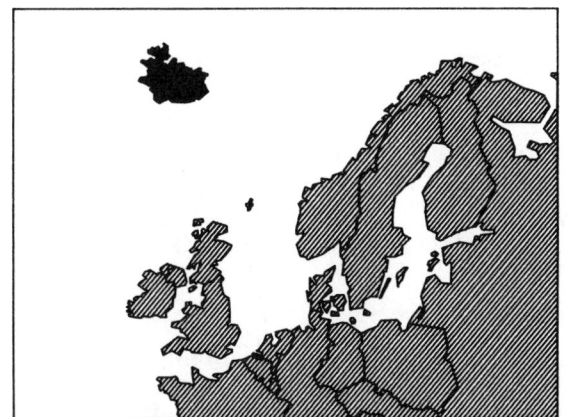

EDUCATION [1984]

% of primary school-age children enrolled:	na
secondary school-age children enrolled:	na
ca. 20-24 year olds in higher education:	na

LABOR FORCE

Average annual labor force growth (%) 1980-85:	na	
% of the 1980 labor force in agriculture:	10	TABLE 8
in industry		
and services:	90	SOCIO-

GNP & INCOME DISTRIBUTION

GNP per capita (in US Dollars) 1985:	10710	ECONOMIC
GNP average annual growth rate (%) 1965-85:	2.4	INDICATORS
% share of total household income		
Lowest 20% of households:	na	
Highest 10% of households:	na	

HEALTH & NUTRITION

Population per physician 1981:	na
Daily calorie supply per capita 1985:	na

TABLE 1 — DATA

AGE AT LAST BIRTHDAY	ESTIMATED MID-YEAR POPULATION BOTH SEXES	MALES Number	MALES Percent	FEMALES Number	FEMALES Percent	BIRTHS BY AGE OF MOTHER AND SEX	DEATHS BOTH SEXES	DEATHS MALES	DEATHS FEMALES	AGE AT LAST BIRTHDAY
0	3992	2006	1.7	1986	1.7		22	11	11	0
1-4	17303	8867	7.3	8436	7.0		9	5	4	1-4
5-9	20860	10637	8.8	10223	8.5		3	2	1	5-9
10-14	21090	10843	8.9	10247	8.5		4	3	1	10-14
15-19	21028	10729	8.8	10299	8.6	358	14	10	4	15-19
20-24	22145	11249	9.3	10896	9.1	1221	17	15	2	20-24
25-29	21027	10758	8.9	10269	8.6	1206	17	16	1	25-29
30-34	18743	9682	8.0	9061	7.5	737	16	13	3	30-34
35-39	16422	8553	7.0	7869	6.6	292	16	12	4	35-39
40-44	12986	6566	5.4	6420	5.3	40	15	14	1	40-44
45-49	10456	5239	4.3	5217	4.3	2	34	16	18	45-49
50-54	10922	5456	4.5	5466	4.6		42	29	13	50-54
55-59	10540	5257	4.3	5283	4.4		59	37	22	55-59
60-64	9383	4619	3.8	4764	4.0		109	74	35	60-64
65-69	7636	3646	3.0	3990	3.3		141	83	58	65-69
70-74	6303	2860	2.4	3443	2.9		204	119	85	70-74
75-79	4718	2091	1.7	2627	2.2		246	130	116	75-79
80-84	3281	1389	1.1	1892	1.6	1904 M	253	129	124	80-84
85+	2568	918	0.8	1650	1.4	1952 F	436	172	264	85+
TOTAL	241403	121365		120038		3856	1657	890	767	TOTAL

TABLE 2 — MALE LIFE TABLE

x	nM_x	nq_x	l_x	nd_x	nL_x	nm_x	na_x	T_x	$\overset{\circ}{e}_x$	x
0	0.005484	0.005456	100000	546	99498	0.005484	0.079	7486027	74.860	0
1	0.000564	0.002252	99454	224	397258	0.000564	1.500	7386529	74.271	1
5	0.000188	0.000940	99230	93	495919	0.000188	2.500	6989272	70.435	5
10	0.000277	0.001383	99137	137	495420	0.000277	3.058	6493353	65.499	10
15	0.000932	0.004650	99000	460	493957	0.000932	2.734	5997933	60.585	15
20	0.001333	0.006646	98540	655	491116	0.001333	2.584	5503976	55.855	20
25	0.001487	0.007409	97885	725	487610	0.001487	2.499	5012859	51.212	25
30	0.001343	0.006689	97160	650	484163	0.001342	2.484	4525249	46.575	30
35	0.001403	0.007011	96510	677	480934	0.001407	2.615	4041086	41.872	35
40	0.002132	0.010671	95833	1023	476769	0.002145	2.656	3560152	37.150	40
45	0.003054	0.015238	94810	1445	470738	0.003069	2.706	3083383	32.522	45
50	0.005315	0.026248	93366	2451	461058	0.005315	2.645	2612645	27.983	50
55	0.007038	0.034690	90915	3154	447597	0.007046	2.787	2151588	23.666	55
60	0.016021	0.077504	87761	6802	422975	0.016081	2.673	1703991	19.416	60
65	0.022765	0.108524	80959	8786	384269	0.022864	2.664	1281016	15.823	65
70	0.041608	0.189814	72173	13700	328077	0.041757	2.606	896747	12.425	70
75	0.062171	0.270006	58474	15788	253399	0.062306	2.532	568670	9.725	75
80	0.092873	0.377274	42686	16104	173400	0.092873	2.514	315271	7.386	80
85	0.187364	1.000000	26581	26581	141871	0.119165	5.337	141871	5.337	85

TABLE 3 — FEMALE LIFE TABLE

x	nM_x	nq_x	l_x	nd_x	nL_x	nm_x	na_x	T_x	$\overset{\circ}{e}_x$	x
0	0.005539	0.005511	100000	551	99493	0.005539	0.079	8040021	80.400	0
1	0.000474	0.001894	99449	188	397325	0.000474	1.500	7940528	79.845	1
5	0.000098	0.000489	99261	49	496181	0.000098	2.500	7543204	75.994	5
10	0.000098	0.000488	99212	48	495969	0.000098	3.119	7047022	71.030	10
15	0.000388	0.001940	99164	192	495346	0.000388	2.546	6551053	66.063	15
20	0.000184	0.000917	98971	91	494599	0.000184	2.169	6055707	61.187	20
25	0.000097	0.000488	98880	48	494297	0.000098	2.818	5561108	56.241	25
30	0.000331	0.001663	98832	164	493792	0.000333	2.756	5066811	51.267	30
35	0.000508	0.002536	98668	250	492697	0.000508	2.433	4573019	46.348	35
40	0.000156	0.000855	98418	84	492177	0.000171	6.063	4080323	41.459	40
45	0.003450	0.017188	98333	1690	487662	0.003466	2.630	3588145	36.490	45
50	0.002378	0.011823	96643	1143	480418	0.002378	2.551	3100484	32.082	50
55	0.004164	0.020652	95501	1972	473041	0.004169	2.738	2620066	27.435	55
60	0.007347	0.036298	93528	3395	460070	0.007379	2.770	2147024	22.956	60
65	0.014536	0.070621	90133	6365	436090	0.014596	2.710	1686954	18.716	65
70	0.024688	0.117107	83768	9810	396077	0.024768	2.680	1250864	14.932	70
75	0.044157	0.200373	73958	14819	334191	0.044344	2.598	854787	11.558	75
80	0.065539	0.283403	59139	16760	255728	0.065539	2.615	520596	8.803	80
85	0.160000	1.000000	42379	42379	264868	0.090987	6.250	264868	6.250	85

TABLE 4 — OBSERVED VITAL RATES AND RATIOS

CRUDE RATES Per Thousand	BOTH SEXES	MALES	FEMALES	RATES STANDARDIZED ON USA 1980 Per Thousand	BOTH SEXES	MALES	FEMALES	VITAL STATISTICS	
BIRTH RATE	15.97	15.69	16.26	BIRTH RATE	16.48		16.23	GFR x 1000	64.233
DEATH RATE	6.86	7.33	6.39	DEATH RATE	7.04	7.22	6.88	TFR	1.947
RATE OF INCREASE	9.11	8.35	9.87	RATE OF INCREASE	9.44		9.35	GRR	0.985
								NRR	0.974
PERCENT OF POPULATION IN AGE GROUP				RATES STANDARDIZED ON MEXICO 1980				μ	27.417
								σ^2	34.841
								GENERATION	27.434
UNDER 15	26.20	26.66	25.74	BIRTH RATE	14.69		14.99	POP. SEX RATIO	0.989
15 - 64	63.65	64.36	62.93	DEATH RATE	2.58	3.06	2.09	SEX RATIO AT BIRTH	0.975
65 AND OLDER	10.15	8.98	11.33	RATE OF INCREASE	12.11		12.90	DEP. RATIO x 100	57.110

PROJECTED POPULATION

AGE GROUP	1990 BOTH SEXES	MALES	FEMALES	1995 BOTH SEXES	MALES	FEMALES
0-4	20	10	10	20	10	10
5-9	21	11	10	20	10	10
10-14	21	11	10	21	11	10
15-19	21	11	10	21	11	10
20-24	21	11	10	21	11	10
25-29	22	11	11	21	11	10
30-34	21	11	10	22	11	11
35-39	19	10	9	21	11	10
40-44	16	8	8	19	10	9
45-49	12	6	6	16	8	8
50-54	10	5	5	12	6	6
55-59	10	5	5	10	5	5
60-64	10	5	5	10	5	5
65-69	9	4	5	10	5	5
70-74	7	3	4	8	4	4
75-79	5	2	3	5	2	3
80-84	3	1	2	4	2	2
85+	3	1	2	3	1	2
TOTAL	251	126	125	264	134	130

STABLE EQUIVALENT TO ORIGINAL POPULATION

MALES Number	Percent	FEMALES Number	Percent	AGE GROUP	
10	6.4	10	6.0	0-4	
10	6.4	10	6.0	5-9	TABLE 5
10	6.4	10	6.0	10-14	
10	6.5	10	6.0	15-19	POPULATION
10	6.5	10	6.0	20-24	PROJECTED
10	6.4	10	6.1	25-29	WITH
10	6.4	10	6.1	30-34	FIXED
10	6.4	10	6.1	35-39	AGE-
10	6.4	11	6.1	40-44	SPECIFIC
10	6.3	10	6.1	45-49	BIRTH
10	6.2	10	6.0	50-54	AND
9	6.1	10	6.0	55-59	DEATH
9	5.8	10	5.8	60-64	RATES
8	5.3	10	5.6	65-69	(female
7	4.5	9	5.1	70-74	dominant,
5	3.5	7	4.3	75-79	in 000s)
4	2.4	6	3.3	80-84	
3	2.0	6	3.4	85+	
155		169		TOTAL	

VITAL RATES OF PROJECTED POPULATION

Per Thousand	1990 BOTH SEXES	MALES	FEMALES	1995 BOTH SEXES	MALES	FEMALES
BIRTH RATE	15.87	15.64	16.09	15.31	15.15	15.47
DEATH RATE	7.26	7.73	6.78	7.47	7.95	6.98
RATE OF INCREASE	8.61	7.91	9.31	7.84	7.19	8.49

VITAL RATES OF STABLE POPULATION

Per Thousand	MALES	FEMALES	
BIRTH RATE	12.86	11.95	TABLE 6
DEATH RATE	13.78	12.91	PROJECTED
RATE OF INCREASE		-.96	VITAL RATES AND

AGE STRUCTURE OF PROJECTED POPULATION

	BOTH SEXES	MALES	FEMALES	BOTH SEXES	MALES	FEMALES
% UNDER 15	24.40	24.60	24.20	23.06	23.08	23.04
% 15-64	64.87	65.84	63.90	65.73	66.88	64.58
% 65 AND OLDER	10.73	9.55	11.91	11.21	10.03	12.38
DEPEND. RATIO x 100	54.15	51.87	56.50	52.14	49.52	54.84

STABLE AGE STRUCTURE

	MALES	FEMALES	
% UNDER 15	19.28	17.92	RATIOS
% 15-64	63.01	60.39	(female
% 65 AND OLDER	17.71	21.69	dominant)
DEPEND. RATIO x 100	58.69	65.59	

AGE GROUP	FEMALE BIRTH RATES	NET MATERNITY FUNCTION	COEFF. OF MATRIX EQUATION	ORIGINAL MATRIX SUB-DIAGONAL	ORIGINAL MATRIX FIRST ROW	STABLE MATRIX FISHER VALUES	STABLE MATRIX REPRODUCTIVE VALUES	MATRIX PARAMETERS		
0-4	0.0000	0.0000	0.0000	0.99872	0.00000	1.004	10464	λ_1	0.99520	
5-9	0.0000	0.0000	0.0000	0.99957	0.00000	1.000	10228	λ_2	0.37485+0.72439i	TABLE 7
10-14	0.0000	0.0000	0.0436	0.99874	0.04366	0.996	10207	λ_4	-0.10768-0.55047i	
15-19	0.0176	0.0872	0.1839	0.99849	0.18441	0.949	9770	λ_6	-0.41107-0.32982i	LESLIE
20-24	0.0567	0.2806	0.2872	0.99939	0.28851	0.760	8282	r_1	-0.00096	MATRIX
25-29	0.0595	0.2939	0.2486	0.99898	0.24986	0.467	4796	r_2	-0.04076+0.21865i	AND ITS
30-34	0.0412	0.2033	0.1479	0.99778	0.14884	0.214	1941	r_4	-0.11564-0.35279i	ANALYSIS
35-39	0.0188	0.0926	0.0540	0.99895	0.05449	0.064	503	r_6	-0.12810-0.49308i	(females)
40-44	0.0032	0.0155	0.0082	0.99083	0.00831	0.009	57	c_1	1715	
45-49	0.0002	0.0009	0.0005	0.98515	0.00048	0.000	3	$2\pi/\gamma$	28.7357	
50-54	0.0000	0.0000	0.0000	0.00000	0.00000	0.000	0	Δ	17.8155	

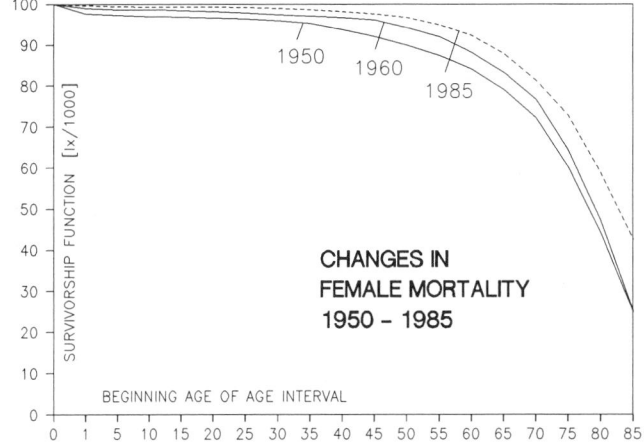

CHANGES IN FEMALE MORTALITY 1950 – 1985

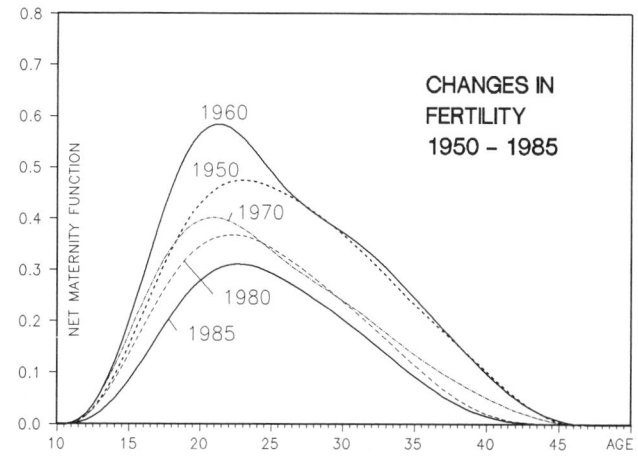

CHANGES IN FERTILITY 1950 – 1985

TABLE 1 — DATA

AGE AT LAST BIRTHDAY	ESTIMATED MID-YEAR POPULATION BOTH SEXES	MALES Number	MALES Percent	FEMALES Number	FEMALES Percent	BIRTHS BY AGE OF MOTHER AND SEX	DEATHS BOTH SEXES	DEATHS MALES	DEATHS FEMALES	AGE AT LAST BIRTHDAY
0	64886	33276	2.2	31610	2.1		1214	703	511	0
1-4	250769	128570	8.6	122199	8.2		202	116	86	1-4
5-9	316940	161828	10.8	155112	10.5		123	82	41	5-9
10-14	298557	152112	10.2	146445	9.9	19	87	60	27	10-14
15-19	267727	136773	9.1	130954	8.8	2477	160	106	54	15-19
20-24	215251	109961	7.4	105290	7.1	15823	186	129	57	20-24
25-29	172993	87736	5.9	85257	5.8	20774	151	91	60	25-29
30-34	151351	76823	5.1	74528	5.0	14936	175	103	72	30-34
35-39	149107	75488	5.0	73619	5.0	9695	191	110	81	35-39
40-44	152729	76424	5.1	76305	5.1	3559	378	245	133	40-44
45-49	160124	79533	5.3	80591	5.4	265	742	454	288	45-49
50-54	159082	80039	5.4	79043	5.3	3	1234	737	497	50-54
55-59	154847	78429	5.2	76418	5.2		1867	1150	717	55-59
60-64	134066	68131	4.6	65935	4.4		2669	1700	969	60-64
65-69	111751	54493	3.6	57258	3.9		3486	2167	1319	65-69
70-74	98986	44593	3.0	54393	3.7		4658	2562	2096	70-74
75-79	61775	27774	1.9	34001	2.3		4960	2650	2310	75-79
80-84	36375	15663	1.0	20712	1.4	34751 M	4622	2209	2413	80-84
85+	20932	8114	0.5	12818	0.9	32800 F	4785	1983	2802	85+
TOTAL	2978248	1495760		1482488		67551	31890	17357	14533	TOTAL

TABLE 2 — MALE LIFE TABLE

x	nM_x	nq_x	l_x	nd_x	nL_x	nm_x	na_x	T_x	$\overset{\circ}{e}_x$	x
0	0.021126	0.020735	100000	2073	98146	0.021126	0.106	6922794	69.228	0
1	0.000902	0.003601	97927	353	390825	0.000902	1.500	6824648	69.692	1
5	0.000507	0.002530	97574	247	487252	0.000507	2.500	6433824	65.938	5
10	0.000394	0.001973	97327	192	486182	0.000395	2.642	5946571	61.099	10
15	0.000775	0.003887	97135	378	484809	0.000779	2.707	5460389	56.214	15
20	0.001173	0.005862	96757	567	482394	0.001176	2.544	4975580	51.423	20
25	0.001037	0.005169	96190	497	479724	0.001037	2.531	4493186	46.711	25
30	0.001341	0.006692	95693	640	476905	0.001343	2.563	4013462	41.941	30
35	0.001457	0.007270	95053	691	473715	0.001459	2.760	3536558	37.206	35
40	0.003206	0.015915	94362	1502	468454	0.003206	2.767	3062843	32.459	40
45	0.005708	0.028172	92860	2616	458293	0.005708	2.704	2594388	27.939	45
50	0.009208	0.045077	90244	4068	441777	0.009208	2.679	2136095	23.670	50
55	0.014663	0.070906	86176	6110	416725	0.014663	2.684	1694318	19.661	55
60	0.024952	0.118063	80065	9453	378092	0.025001	2.648	1277593	15.957	60
65	0.039767	0.181499	70613	12816	322089	0.039791	2.583	899501	12.739	65
70	0.057453	0.252053	57797	14568	253366	0.057497	2.555	577412	9.990	70
75	0.095413	0.385587	43229	16668	174292	0.095636	2.489	324046	7.496	75
80	0.141033	0.515715	26560	13698	97123	0.141033	2.395	149755	5.638	80
85	0.244392	1.000000	12863	12863	52632	0.185848	4.092	52632	4.092	85

TABLE 3 — FEMALE LIFE TABLE

x	nM_x	nq_x	l_x	nd_x	nL_x	nm_x	na_x	T_x	$\overset{\circ}{e}_x$	x
0	0.016166	0.015933	100000	1593	98562	0.016166	0.097	7402894	74.029	0
1	0.000704	0.002810	98407	277	392935	0.000704	1.500	7304332	74.226	1
5	0.000264	0.001321	98130	130	490327	0.000264	2.500	6911396	70.431	5
10	0.000184	0.000923	98001	90	489792	0.000185	2.668	6421070	65.521	10
15	0.000412	0.002069	97910	203	489080	0.000414	2.679	5931278	60.579	15
20	0.000541	0.002711	97708	265	487905	0.000543	2.611	5442198	55.699	20
25	0.000704	0.003525	97443	343	486397	0.000706	2.624	4954293	50.843	25
30	0.000966	0.004829	97099	469	484363	0.000968	2.583	4467896	46.014	30
35	0.001100	0.005489	96630	530	481902	0.001101	2.644	3983534	41.224	35
40	0.001743	0.008682	96100	834	478655	0.001743	2.789	3501632	36.437	40
45	0.003574	0.017726	95266	1689	472537	0.003574	2.755	3022977	31.732	45
50	0.006288	0.030986	93577	2900	461152	0.006288	2.678	2550440	27.255	50
55	0.009383	0.045943	90677	4166	443651	0.009390	2.663	2089289	23.041	55
60	0.014696	0.071221	86511	6161	418115	0.014736	2.656	1645637	19.022	60
65	0.023036	0.109275	80350	8780	381151	0.023036	2.654	1227522	15.277	65
70	0.038534	0.176767	71570	12651	327991	0.038572	2.640	846371	11.826	70
75	0.067939	0.293253	58919	17278	252671	0.068382	2.574	518380	8.798	75
80	0.116503	0.450604	41641	18763	161055	0.116503	2.487	265709	6.381	80
85	0.218599	1.000000	22877	22877	104654	0.154151	4.575	104654	4.575	85

TABLE 4 — OBSERVED VITAL RATES AND RATIOS

CRUDE RATES

Per Thousand	BOTH SEXES	MALES	FEMALES
BIRTH RATE	22.68	23.23	22.12
DEATH RATE	10.71	11.60	9.80
RATE OF INCREASE	11.97	11.63	12.32

RATES STANDARDIZED ON USA 1980

Per Thousand	BOTH SEXES	MALES	FEMALES
BIRTH RATE	31.80		30.03
DEATH RATE	11.09	10.98	11.20
RATE OF INCREASE	20.71		18.83

VITAL STATISTICS

GFR x 1000	107.815
TFR	3.975
GRR	1.930
NRR	1.872
μ	30.162
σ^2	37.526
GENERATION	29.766
POP. SEX RATIO	0.991
SEX RATIO AT BIRTH	1.059
DEP. RATIO x 100	73.429

PERCENT OF POPULATION IN AGE GROUP

	BOTH SEXES	MALES	FEMALES
UNDER 15	31.27	31.81	30.72
15 - 64	57.66	58.12	57.20
65 AND OLDER	11.07	10.07	12.09

RATES STANDARDIZED ON MEXICO 1980

	BOTH SEXES	MALES	FEMALES
BIRTH RATE	26.79		26.22
DEATH RATE	4.32	4.86	3.76
RATE OF INCREASE	22.47		22.46

PROJECTED POPULATION

STABLE EQUIVALENT TO ORIGINAL POPULATION

AGE GROUP	1976 BOTH SEXES	1976 MALES	1976 FEMALES	1981 BOTH SEXES	1981 MALES	1981 FEMALES	MALES Number	MALES Percent	FEMALES Number	FEMALES Percent	AGE GROUP	
0-4	358	184	174	419	215	204	175	13.1	166	12.7	0-4	
5-9	314	161	153	357	183	174	157	11.8	149	11.4	5-9	TABLE 5
10-14	316	161	155	314	161	153	141	10.6	134	10.3	10-14	
15-19	298	152	146	316	161	155	127	9.5	121	9.2	15-19	POPULATION
20-24	267	136	131	297	151	146	113	8.5	108	8.3	20-24	PROJECTED
25-29	214	109	105	265	135	130	101	7.6	97	7.4	25-29	WITH
30-34	172	87	85	214	109	105	91	6.8	87	6.7	30-34	FIXED
35-39	150	76	74	171	87	84	81	6.1	78	6.0	35-39	AGE-
40-44	148	75	73	149	75	74	72	5.4	70	5.3	40-44	SPECIFIC
45-49	150	75	75	145	73	72	64	4.8	62	4.7	45-49	BIRTH
50-54	156	77	79	146	72	74	55	4.1	54	4.2	50-54	AND
55-59	152	76	76	148	72	76	47	3.5	47	3.6	55-59	DEATH
60-64	143	71	72	141	69	72	38	2.9	40	3.1	60-64	RATES
65-69	118	58	60	127	61	66	29	2.2	33	2.5	65-69	(female
70-74	92	43	49	98	46	52	21	1.6	25	1.9	70-74	dominant,
75-79	73	31	42	67	29	38	13	1.0	18	1.3	75-79	in 000s)
80-84	37	15	22	44	17	27	6	0.5	10	0.8	80-84	
85+	21	8	13	22	8	14	3	0.2	6	0.5	85+	
TOTAL	3179	1595	1584	3440	1724	1716	1334		1305		TOTAL	

VITAL RATES OF PROJECTED POPULATION

VITAL RATES OF STABLE POPULATION

Per Thousand	1976 BOTH SEXES	1976 MALES	1976 FEMALES	1981 BOTH SEXES	1981 MALES	1981 FEMALES		MALES	FEMALES	
BIRTH RATE	24.66	25.29	24.03	26.87	27.56	26.17	BIRTH RATE	28.27	27.30	TABLE 6
DEATH RATE	10.46	11.22	9.70	10.05	10.65	9.44	DEATH RATE	7.18	6.19	PROJECTED
RATE OF INCREASE	14.20	14.07	14.33	16.82	16.91	16.73	RATE OF INCREASE	21.11		VITAL RATES AND RATIOS

AGE STRUCTURE OF PROJECTED POPULATION

STABLE AGE STRUCTURE

										(female dominant)
% UNDER 15	31.10	31.74	30.45	31.70	32.41	30.98	% UNDER 15	35.47	34.48	
% 15-64	58.15	58.51	57.79	57.91	58.24	57.57	% 15-64	59.10	58.51	
% 65 AND OLDER	10.75	9.75	11.76	10.40	9.35	11.45	% 65 AND OLDER	5.42	7.01	
DEPEND. RATIO x 100	71.96	70.91	73.03	72.69	71.71	73.69	DEPEND. RATIO x 100	69.19	70.91	

AGE GROUP	FEMALE BIRTH RATES	NET MATERNITY FUNCTION	COEFF. OF MATRIX EQUATION	ORIGINAL MATRIX SUB-DIAGONAL	ORIGINAL MATRIX FIRST ROW	STABLE MATRIX FISHER VALUES	STABLE MATRIX REPRODUCTIVE VALUES	MATRIX PARAMETERS		
0-4	0.0000	0.0000	0.0000	0.99762	0.00000	1.072	164909	λ_1	1.11134	
5-9	0.0000	0.0000	0.0002	0.99891	0.00015	1.194	185263	λ_2	$0.47473-0.80474i$	TABLE 7
10-14	0.0001	0.0003	0.0226	0.99855	0.02269	1.329	194573	λ_4	$-0.05701-0.63636i$	
15-19	0.0092	0.0449	0.2005	0.99760	0.20146	1.454	190453	λ_6	$-0.42645-0.46886i$	LESLIE
20-24	0.0730	0.3560	0.4657	0.99691	0.46918	1.404	147790	r_1	0.02111	MATRIX
25-29	0.1183	0.5755	0.5234	0.99582	0.52889	1.060	90386	r_2	$-0.01359-0.20756i$	AND ITS
30-34	0.0973	0.4713	0.3897	0.99492	0.39548	0.614	45738	r_4	$-0.08960-0.33203i$	ANALYSIS
35-39	0.0639	0.3081	0.2083	0.99326	0.21242	0.259	19092	r_6	$-0.09121-0.46177i$	(females)
40-44	0.0226	0.1084	0.0580	0.98722	0.05953	0.061	4644	c_1	13047	
45-49	0.0016	0.0075	0.0038	0.97591	0.00397	0.004	312	$2\pi/y$	30.2710	
50-54	0.0000	0.0001	0.0000	0.96205	0.00005	0.000	3	Δ	9.8833	

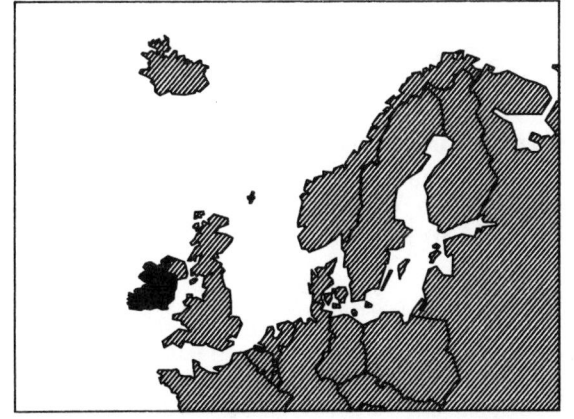

EDUCATION [1984]

% of primary school-age children enrolled:	97
secondary school-age children enrolled:	93
ca. 20-24 year olds in higher education:	22

LABOR FORCE

Average annual labor force growth (%) 1980-85:	1.6	
% of the 1980 labor force in agriculture:	19	TABLE 8
in industry:	34	
in services:	48	SOCIO- ECONOMIC INDICATORS

GNP & INCOME DISTRIBUTION

GNP per capita (in US Dollars) 1985:	4850
GNP average annual growth rate (%) 1965-85:	2.2
% share of total household income 1973	
Lowest 20% of households:	7.2
Highest 10% of households:	25.1

HEALTH & NUTRITION

Population per physician 1981:	780
Daily calorie supply per capita 1985:	3831

AGE AT LAST BIRTHDAY	ESTIMATED MID-YEAR POPULATION BOTH SEXES	MALES Number	Percent	FEMALES Number	Percent	BIRTHS BY AGE OF MOTHER AND SEX	DEATHS BOTH SEXES	MALES	FEMALES	AGE AT LAST BIRTHDAY
0	70297	35837	2.3	34460	2.2		1176	667	509	0
1-4	270103	138463	8.8	131640	8.4		221	133	88	1-4
5-9	319300	163400	10.4	155900	10.0		105	62	43	5-9
10-14	313500	159900	10.2	153600	9.9	8	107	74	33	10-14
15-19	287500	146500	9.3	141000	9.0	3254	149	119	30	15-19
20-24	239200	122200	7.8	117000	7.5	16321	219	165	54	20-24
25-29	203100	103500	6.6	99600	6.4	21856	182	127	55	25-29
30-34	171300	86800	5.5	84500	5.4	14665	166	103	63	30-34
35-39	152200	77100	4.9	75100	4.8	8026	244	150	94	35-39
40-44	149200	75200	4.8	74000	4.7	2848	373	231	142	40-44
45-49	152600	76000	4.8	76600	4.9	195	697	417	280	45-49
50-54	156400	77500	4.9	78900	5.1	5	1226	759	467	50-54
55-59	152700	76300	4.9	76400	4.9		1775	1103	672	55-59
60-64	141300	70500	4.5	70800	4.5		2762	1775	987	60-64
65-69	120400	59100	3.8	61300	3.9		3739	2344	1395	65-69
70-74	98700	45900	2.9	52800	3.4		4842	2786	2056	70-74
75-79	69800	30000	1.9	39800	2.6		5335	2749	2586	75-79
80-84	37700	15800	1.0	21900	1.4	34532 M	4860	2298	2562	80-84
85+	22000	8400	0.5	13600	0.9	32646 F	4994	2015	2979	85+
TOTAL	3127300	1568400		1558900		67178	33172	18077	15095	TOTAL

TABLE 1 DATA

TABLE 2 — MALE LIFE TABLE

x	$_nM_x$	$_nq_x$	l_x	$_nd_x$	$_nL_x$	$_nm_x$	$_na_x$	T_x	$\overset{\circ}{e}_x$	x
0	0.018612	0.018306	100000	1831	98355	0.018612	0.102	6921899	69.219	0
1	0.000961	0.003833	98169	376	391737	0.000961	1.500	6823543	69.508	1
5	0.000379	0.001895	97793	185	488502	0.000379	2.500	6431806	65.770	5
10	0.000463	0.002314	97608	226	487518	0.000463	2.695	5943304	60.890	10
15	0.000812	0.004071	97382	396	486008	0.000816	2.725	5455786	56.025	15
20	0.001350	0.006745	96985	654	483332	0.001353	2.561	4969778	51.242	20
25	0.001227	0.006108	96331	588	480168	0.001225	2.469	4486446	46.573	25
30	0.001187	0.005932	95743	568	477365	0.001190	2.624	4006279	41.844	30
35	0.001946	0.009721	95175	925	473743	0.001953	2.696	3528914	37.078	35
40	0.003072	0.015264	94250	1439	467983	0.003074	2.730	3055171	32.416	40
45	0.005487	0.027098	92811	2515	458369	0.005487	2.739	2587188	27.876	45
50	0.009794	0.047875	90296	4323	441402	0.009794	2.669	2128819	23.576	50
55	0.014456	0.069935	85973	6012	415914	0.014456	2.679	1687417	19.627	55
60	0.025177	0.118848	79961	9503	377451	0.025177	2.648	1271503	15.902	60
65	0.039662	0.181071	70458	12758	321589	0.039671	2.594	894052	12.689	65
70	0.060697	0.264202	57700	15244	251029	0.060727	2.542	572463	9.921	70
75	0.091633	0.373047	42455	15838	172434	0.091849	2.484	321434	7.571	75
80	0.145443	0.527967	26617	14053	96623	0.145443	2.405	149000	5.598	80
85	0.239881	1.000000	12564	12564	52377	0.180351	4.169	52377	4.169	85

TABLE 3 — FEMALE LIFE TABLE

x	$_nM_x$	$_nq_x$	l_x	$_nd_x$	$_nL_x$	$_nm_x$	$_na_x$	T_x	$\overset{\circ}{e}_x$	x
0	0.014771	0.014576	100000	1458	98681	0.014771	0.095	7442868	74.429	0
1	0.000668	0.002670	98542	263	393512	0.000668	1.500	7344187	74.528	1
5	0.000276	0.001378	98279	135	491058	0.000276	2.500	6950675	70.724	5
10	0.000215	0.001073	98144	105	490450	0.000215	2.439	6459617	65.818	10
15	0.000213	0.001067	98039	105	489957	0.000214	2.742	5969167	60.886	15
20	0.000462	0.002316	97934	227	489137	0.000464	2.652	5479211	55.948	20
25	0.000552	0.002765	97707	270	487889	0.000554	2.606	4990074	51.072	25
30	0.000746	0.003740	97437	364	486344	0.000749	2.693	4502185	46.206	30
35	0.001252	0.006264	97073	608	483959	0.001256	2.691	4015840	41.369	35
40	0.001919	0.009556	96465	922	480252	0.001919	2.754	3531882	36.613	40
45	0.003655	0.018126	95543	1732	473763	0.003655	2.719	3051629	31.940	45
50	0.005919	0.029191	93811	2738	462666	0.005919	2.667	2577867	27.479	50
55	0.008796	0.043095	91073	3925	446207	0.008796	2.667	2115201	23.225	55
60	0.013941	0.067588	87148	5890	422027	0.013957	2.672	1668994	19.151	60
65	0.022757	0.108189	81258	8791	385774	0.022788	2.667	1246967	15.346	65
70	0.038939	0.178240	72466	12916	331705	0.038939	2.629	861193	11.884	70
75	0.064975	0.281751	59550	16778	257145	0.065248	2.580	529487	8.891	75
80	0.116986	0.452465	42772	19353	165427	0.116986	2.497	272342	6.367	80
85	0.219044	1.000000	23419	23419	106915	0.154694	4.565	106915	4.565	85

TABLE 4 — OBSERVED VITAL RATES AND RATIOS

CRUDE RATES

Per Thousand	BOTH SEXES	MALES	FEMALES
BIRTH RATE	21.48	22.02	20.94
DEATH RATE	10.61	11.53	9.68
RATE OF INCREASE	10.87	10.49	11.26

PERCENT OF POPULATION IN AGE GROUP

UNDER 15	31.12	31.73	30.51
15 - 64	57.73	58.12	57.34
65 AND OLDER	11.15	10.15	12.15

RATES STANDARDIZED ON USA 1980

Per Thousand	BOTH SEXES	MALES	FEMALES
BIRTH RATE	28.37		26.81
DEATH RATE	11.02	11.03	11.00
RATE OF INCREASE	17.35		15.81

RATES STANDARDIZED ON MEXICO 1980

	BOTH SEXES	MALES	FEMALES
BIRTH RATE	24.08		23.58
DEATH RATE	4.25	4.85	3.63
RATE OF INCREASE	19.83		19.95

VITAL STATISTICS

GFR x 1000	100.596
TFR	3.518
GRR	1.710
NRR	1.664
μ	29.797
σ^2	37.891
GENERATION	29.470
POP. SEX RATIO	0.994
SEX RATIO AT BIRTH	1.058
DEP. RATIO x 100	73.210

AGE AT LAST BIRTHDAY	ESTIMATED MID-YEAR POPULATION					BIRTHS BY AGE OF MOTHER AND SEX	DEATHS			AGE AT LAST BIRTHDAY
	BOTH SEXES	MALES		FEMALES			BOTH SEXES	MALES	FEMALES	
		Number	Percent	Number	Percent					
0	73379	37717	2.2	35662	2.1		746	418	328	0
1-4	279625	143313	8.3	136312	8.0		170	102	68	1-4
5-9	349487	179108	10.4	170379	9.9		105	63	42	5-9
10-14	341238	175271	10.1	165967	9.7	18	99	69	30	10-14
15-19	326429	166729	9.6	159752	9.3	3527	229	163	66	15-19
20-24	276127	140446	8.1	135681	7.9	15931	237	188	49	20-24
25-29	246053	124378	7.2	121675	7.1	23157	174	126	48	25-29
30-34	231958	118287	6.8	113671	6.6	18363	206	135	71	30-34
35-39	193829	99286	5.7	94543	5.5	8846	233	148	85	35-39
40-44	165924	85320	4.9	80604	4.7	2135	376	247	129	40-44
45-49	151850	77781	4.5	74069	4.3	180	578	353	225	45-49
50-54	149680	75320	4.4	74360	4.3	1	1039	662	377	50-54
55-59	149606	73289	4.2	76317	4.5		1696	1088	608	55-59
60-64	139266	67978	3.9	71288	4.2		2534	1587	947	60-64
65-69	133919	64306	3.7	69613	4.1		3886	2423	1463	65-69
70-74	103138	48380	2.8	54758	3.2		4950	3003	1947	70-74
75-79	68451	29172	1.7	39279	2.3		5382	2913	2469	75-79
80-84	40462	15415	0.9	25047	1.5	37075 M	5015	2316	2699	80-84
85+	22984	7910	0.5	15074	0.9	35083 F	5274	2064	3210	85+
TOTAL	3443405	1729354		1714051		72158	32929	18068	14861	TOTAL

TABLE 1 DATA

x	nM_x	nq_x	l_x	nd_x	nL_x	nm_x	na_x	T_x	$\overset{\circ}{e}_x$	x
0	0.011083	0.010972	100000	1097	99000	0.011083	0.089	7010684	70.107	0
1	0.000712	0.002842	98903	281	394909	0.000712	1.500	6911684	69.884	1
5	0.000352	0.001757	98622	173	492676	0.000352	2.500	6516775	66.078	5
10	0.000394	0.001968	98448	194	491822	0.000394	2.830	6024100	61.190	10
15	0.000981	0.004893	98255	481	490167	0.000981	2.699	5532278	56.305	15
20	0.001339	0.006675	97774	653	487240	0.001339	2.503	5042111	51.569	20
25	0.001013	0.005047	97121	490	484360	0.001012	2.457	4554871	46.899	25
30	0.001141	0.005699	96631	551	481826	0.001143	2.586	4070511	42.124	30
35	0.001491	0.007473	96080	718	478780	0.001500	2.740	3588685	37.351	35
40	0.002895	0.014458	95362	1379	473657	0.002911	2.712	3109905	32.611	40
45	0.004538	0.022540	93984	2118	465160	0.004554	2.754	2636248	28.050	45
50	0.008789	0.043087	91865	3958	450303	0.008790	2.720	2171088	23.633	50
55	0.014845	0.071742	87907	6307	424825	0.014845	2.667	1720785	19.575	55
60	0.023346	0.110643	81600	9029	386731	0.023346	2.644	1295960	15.882	60
65	0.037679	0.172888	72572	12547	332989	0.037679	2.619	909229	12.529	65
70	0.062071	0.270132	60025	16215	260625	0.062215	2.564	576240	9.600	70
75	0.099856	0.399890	43810	17519	174829	0.100208	2.476	315615	7.204	75
80	0.150243	0.539237	26291	14177	94361	0.150243	2.384	140786	5.355	80
85	0.260936	1.000000	12114	12114	46425	0.206613	3.832	46425	3.832	85

TABLE 2 MALE LIFE TABLE

x	nM_x	nq_x	l_x	nd_x	nL_x	nm_x	na_x	T_x	$\overset{\circ}{e}_x$	x
0	0.009197	0.009121	100000	912	99166	0.009197	0.086	7576114	75.761	0
1	0.000499	0.001993	99088	197	395858	0.000499	1.500	7476948	75.458	1
5	0.000247	0.001232	98890	122	494148	0.000247	2.500	7081090	71.605	5
10	0.000181	0.000904	98769	89	493637	0.000181	2.691	6586942	66.691	10
15	0.000413	0.002067	98679	204	492905	0.000414	2.590	6093305	61.749	15
20	0.000361	0.001803	98475	178	491931	0.000361	2.488	5600400	56.871	20
25	0.000394	0.001975	98298	194	491031	0.000395	2.639	5108468	51.969	25
30	0.000625	0.003129	98104	307	489803	0.000627	2.668	4617437	47.067	30
35	0.000899	0.004513	97797	441	487980	0.000905	2.724	4127634	42.206	35
40	0.001600	0.008030	97355	782	485035	0.001612	2.772	3639654	37.385	40
45	0.003038	0.015126	96574	1461	479550	0.003046	2.728	3154619	32.665	45
50	0.005070	0.025056	95113	2383	470058	0.005070	2.689	2675069	28.125	50
55	0.007967	0.039115	92730	3627	455280	0.007967	2.693	2205011	23.779	55
60	0.013284	0.064428	89103	5741	432145	0.013284	2.671	1749731	19.637	60
65	0.021016	0.100165	83362	8350	397311	0.021016	2.665	1317586	15.806	65
70	0.035556	0.164573	75012	12345	346032	0.035676	2.649	920275	12.268	70
75	0.062858	0.273778	62667	17157	271899	0.063100	2.585	574243	9.163	75
80	0.107757	0.424827	45510	19334	179421	0.107757	2.511	302343	6.643	80
85	0.212949	1.000000	26176	26176	122922	0.147576	4.696	122922	4.696	85

TABLE 3 FEMALE LIFE TABLE

CRUDE RATES

Per Thousand	BOTH SEXES	MALES	FEMALES
BIRTH RATE	20.96	21.44	20.47
DEATH RATE	9.56	10.45	8.67
RATE OF INCREASE	11.39	10.99	11.80

PERCENT OF POPULATION IN AGE GROUP

UNDER 15	30.31	30.96	29.66
15 - 64	58.97	59.49	58.46
65 AND OLDER	10.71	9.55	11.89

RATES STANDARDIZED ON USA 1980

Per Thousand	BOTH SEXES	MALES	FEMALES
BIRTH RATE	24.82		23.46
DEATH RATE	10.59	10.96	10.23
RATE OF INCREASE	14.23		13.24

RATES STANDARDIZED ON MEXICO 1980

	BOTH SEXES	MALES	FEMALES
BIRTH RATE	21.06		20.63
DEATH RATE	3.89	4.56	3.21
RATE OF INCREASE	17.16		17.42

VITAL STATISTICS

GFR x 1000	92.511	
TFR	3.070	
GRR	1.493	
NRR	1.463	
μ	29.726	
σ^2	36.410	
GENERATION	29.491	
POP. SEX RATIO	0.991	
SEX RATIO AT BIRTH	1.057	
DEP. RATIO x 100	69.566	

TABLE 4

OBSERVED VITAL RATES AND RATIOS

AGE AT LAST BIRTHDAY	ESTIMATED MID–YEAR POPULATION						BIRTHS BY AGE OF MOTHER AND SEX	DEATHS			AGE AT LAST BIRTHDAY
	BOTH SEXES	MALES			FEMALES			BOTH SEXES	MALES	FEMALES	
		Number	Percent		Number	Percent					
0	61172	31315	1.8		29857	1.7		534	295	239	0
1-4	262906	135103	7.6		127803	7.2		113	65	48	1-4
5-9	350650	179847	10.2		170803	9.6		84	56	28	5-9
10-14	349973	179381	10.1		170592	9.6	2	94	59	35	10-14
15-19	331100	169887	9.6		161213	9.1	2642	178	144	34	15-19
20-24	286424	144112	8.1		142312	8.0	11768	198	160	38	20-24
25-29	258439	129086	7.3		129353	7.3	19921	167	126	41	25-29
30-34	242689	122198	6.9		120491	6.8	16674	205	135	70	30-34
35-39	229740	116410	6.6		113330	6.4	8309	244	156	88	35-39
40-44	191751	97962	5.5		93789	5.3	1991	324	207	117	40-44
45-49	161740	82769	4.7		78971	4.5	114	551	321	230	45-49
50-54	147511	75156	4.2		72355	4.1	4	869	554	315	50-54
55-59	142215	70514	4.0		71701	4.0		1504	944	560	55-59
60-64	139978	67219	3.8		72759	4.1		2543	1603	940	60-64
65-69	129498	61080	3.5		68418	3.9		3661	2334	1327	65-69
70-74	110996	50881	2.9		60115	3.4		5279	3179	2100	70-74
75-79	75519	32635	1.8		42884	2.4		5788	3239	2549	75-79
80-84	42884	16126	0.9		26758	1.5	31756 M	5309	2507	2802	80-84
85+	25458	8009	0.5		17449	1.0	29669 F	5982	2187	3795	85+
TOTAL	3540643	1769690			1770953		61425	33627	18271	15356	TOTAL

TABLE 1 — DATA

TABLE 2 — MALE LIFE TABLE

x	$_nM_x$	$_nq_x$	l_x	$_nd_x$	$_nL_x$	$_nm_x$	$_na_x$	T_x	$\overset{\circ}{e}_x$	x
0	0.009420	0.009340	100000	934	99146	0.009420	0.086	7079886	70.799	0
1	0.000481	0.001922	99066	190	395788	0.000481	1.500	6980740	70.466	1
5	0.000311	0.001556	98876	154	493993	0.000311	2.500	6584952	66.598	5
10	0.000329	0.001643	98722	162	493258	0.000329	2.839	6090958	61.698	10
15	0.000848	0.004243	98560	418	491832	0.000850	2.690	5597700	56.795	15
20	0.001110	0.005541	98141	544	489359	0.001111	2.522	5105868	52.026	20
25	0.000976	0.004867	97597	475	486798	0.000976	2.496	4616510	47.302	25
30	0.001105	0.005513	97122	535	484309	0.001105	2.567	4129712	42.521	30
35	0.001340	0.006695	96587	647	481419	0.001343	2.655	3645402	37.742	35
40	0.002113	0.010592	95940	1016	477410	0.002128	2.744	3163984	32.979	40
45	0.003878	0.019372	94924	1839	470518	0.003908	2.769	2686574	28.302	45
50	0.007371	0.036396	93085	3388	457787	0.007401	2.745	2216056	23.807	50
55	0.013387	0.064958	89697	5827	435188	0.013389	2.718	1758269	19.602	55
60	0.023847	0.112931	83871	9472	397175	0.023847	2.658	1323081	15.775	60
65	0.038212	0.175100	74399	13027	340920	0.038212	2.615	925906	12.445	65
70	0.062479	0.271067	61372	16636	266264	0.062479	2.560	584986	9.532	70
75	0.099249	0.397860	44736	17799	178820	0.099534	2.480	318722	7.125	75
80	0.155463	0.552836	26937	14892	95791	0.155463	2.388	139902	5.194	80
85	0.273068	1.000000	12045	12045	44111	0.222183	3.662	44111	3.662	85

TABLE 3 — FEMALE LIFE TABLE

x	$_nM_x$	$_nq_x$	l_x	$_nd_x$	$_nL_x$	$_nm_x$	$_na_x$	T_x	$\overset{\circ}{e}_x$	x
0	0.008005	0.007947	100000	795	99272	0.008005	0.084	7645232	76.452	0
1	0.000376	0.001501	99205	149	396449	0.000376	1.500	7545960	76.064	1
5	0.000164	0.000819	99056	81	495079	0.000164	2.500	7149511	72.176	5
10	0.000205	0.001025	98975	101	494628	0.000205	2.547	6654431	67.233	10
15	0.000211	0.001055	98874	104	494115	0.000211	2.561	6159804	62.300	15
20	0.000267	0.001336	98770	132	493529	0.000267	2.583	5665689	57.363	20
25	0.000317	0.001589	98638	157	492828	0.000318	2.705	5172161	52.436	25
30	0.000581	0.002907	98481	286	491735	0.000582	2.664	4679333	47.515	30
35	0.000776	0.003887	98195	382	490087	0.000779	2.679	4187597	42.646	35
40	0.001247	0.006281	97813	614	487743	0.001260	2.850	3697511	37.802	40
45	0.002912	0.014557	97198	1415	482758	0.002931	2.714	3209767	33.023	45
50	0.004354	0.021610	95784	2070	474197	0.004365	2.719	2727009	28.471	50
55	0.007810	0.038364	93714	3595	460326	0.007810	2.707	2252812	24.039	55
60	0.012919	0.062699	90118	5650	437350	0.012919	2.656	1792486	19.890	60
65	0.019395	0.092800	84468	7839	404147	0.019395	2.679	1355136	16.043	65
70	0.034933	0.161599	76629	12383	354049	0.034976	2.650	950989	12.410	70
75	0.059439	0.260982	64246	16767	280848	0.059702	2.592	596940	9.291	75
80	0.104716	0.415939	47479	19748	188590	0.104716	2.529	316092	6.658	80
85	0.217491	1.000000	27731	27731	127503	0.152779	4.598	127503	4.598	85

TABLE 4 — OBSERVED VITAL RATES AND RATIOS

CRUDE RATES

Per Thousand	BOTH SEXES	MALES	FEMALES
BIRTH RATE	17.35	17.94	16.75
DEATH RATE	9.50	10.32	8.67
RATE OF INCREASE	7.85	7.62	8.08

PERCENT OF POPULATION IN AGE GROUP

	BOTH SEXES	MALES	FEMALES
UNDER 15	28.94	29.70	28.18
15 - 64	60.20	60.76	59.64
65 AND OLDER	10.86	9.53	12.18

RATES STANDARDIZED ON USA 1980

Per Thousand	BOTH SEXES	MALES	FEMALES
BIRTH RATE	19.64		18.45
DEATH RATE	10.34	10.81	9.90
RATE OF INCREASE	9.29		8.54

RATES STANDARDIZED ON MEXICO 1980

	BOTH SEXES	MALES	FEMALES
BIRTH RATE	16.55		16.11
DEATH RATE	3.68	4.35	3.01
RATE OF INCREASE	12.87		13.11

VITAL STATISTICS

GFR x 1000	73.172
TFR	2.438
GRR	1.177
NRR	1.159
μ	29.936
σ^2	34.715
GENERATION	29.850
POP. SEX RATIO	1.001
SEX RATIO AT BIRTH	1.070
DEP. RATIO x 100	66.104

PROJECTED POPULATION

AGE GROUP	1991 BOTH SEXES	1991 MALES	1991 FEMALES	1996 BOTH SEXES	1996 MALES	1996 FEMALES
0-4	319	165	154	348	180	168
5-9	323	166	157	318	164	154
10-14	351	180	171	323	166	157
15-19	349	179	170	349	179	170
20-24	330	169	161	348	178	170
25-29	285	143	142	329	168	161
30-34	257	128	129	285	143	142
35-39	241	121	120	257	128	129
40-44	228	115	113	240	120	120
45-49	190	97	93	226	114	112
50-54	159	81	78	185	94	91
55-59	141	71	70	152	77	75
60-64	132	64	68	132	65	67
65-69	125	58	67	118	55	63
70-74	108	48	60	104	45	59
75-79	82	34	48	80	32	48
80-84	46	17	29	50	18	32
85+	25	7	18	27	8	19
TOTAL	3691	1843	1848	3871	1934	1937

STABLE EQUIVALENT TO ORIGINAL POPULATION

MALES Number	MALES Percent	FEMALES Number	FEMALES Percent	AGE GROUP	
176	8.2	164	7.7	0-4	
171	8.0	160	7.5	5-9	TABLE 5
167	7.8	156	7.3	10-14	
162	7.6	152	7.2	15-19	POPULATION
157	7.4	148	7.0	20-24	PROJECTED
153	7.2	145	6.8	25-29	WITH
148	7.0	141	6.6	30-34	FIXED
144	6.7	137	6.4	35-39	AGE-
139	6.5	133	6.2	40-44	SPECIFIC
134	6.3	128	6.0	45-49	BIRTH
127	6.0	123	5.8	50-54	AND
118	5.5	116	5.5	55-59	DEATH
105	4.9	108	5.1	60-64	RATES
88	4.1	97	4.6	65-69	(female
67	3.1	83	3.9	70-74	dominant,
44	2.1	64	3.0	75-79	in 000s)
23	1.1	42	2.0	80-84	
10	0.5	28	1.3	85+	
2133		2125		TOTAL	

VITAL RATES OF PROJECTED POPULATION

Per Thousand	1991 BOTH SEXES	1991 MALES	1991 FEMALES	1996 BOTH SEXES	1996 MALES	1996 FEMALES
BIRTH RATE	18.20	18.84	17.56	18.96	19.62	18.30
DEATH RATE	9.28	9.91	8.65	9.08	9.54	8.62
RATE OF INCREASE	8.92	8.93	8.91	9.88	10.08	9.69

VITAL RATES OF STABLE POPULATION

Per Thousand	MALES	FEMALES	
BIRTH RATE	16.86	15.79	TABLE 6
DEATH RATE	11.91	10.86	PROJECTED
RATE OF INCREASE		4.93	VITAL RATES AND RATIOS (female dominant)

AGE STRUCTURE OF PROJECTED POPULATION

	1991 BOTH SEXES	1991 MALES	1991 FEMALES	1996 BOTH SEXES	1996 MALES	1996 FEMALES
% UNDER 15	26.88	27.67	26.09	25.56	26.37	24.76
% 15-64	62.66	63.41	61.92	64.63	65.43	63.84
% 65 AND OLDER	10.46	8.92	12.00	9.81	8.21	11.41
DEPEND. RATIO x 100	59.58	57.69	61.51	54.72	52.84	56.65

STABLE AGE STRUCTURE

	MALES	FEMALES
% UNDER 15	24.08	22.61
% 15-64	65.05	62.59
% 65 AND OLDER	10.87	14.80
DEPEND. RATIO x 100	53.74	59.78

AGE GROUP	FEMALE BIRTH RATES	NET MATERNITY FUNCTION	COEFF. OF MATRIX EQUATION	ORIGINAL MATRIX SUB-DIAGONAL	ORIGINAL MATRIX FIRST ROW	STABLE MATRIX FISHER VALUES	STABLE MATRIX REPRODUCTIVE VALUES
0-4	0.0000	0.0000	0.0000	0.99871	0.00000	1.021	160992
5-9	0.0000	0.0000	0.0000	0.99909	0.00001	1.048	179001
10-14	0.0000	0.0000	0.0196	0.99896	0.01961	1.075	183410
15-19	0.0079	0.0391	0.1181	0.99881	0.11850	1.083	174608
20-24	0.0399	0.1971	0.2819	0.99858	0.28311	0.990	140933
25-29	0.0744	0.3666	0.3476	0.99778	0.34968	0.727	94038
30-34	0.0668	0.3287	0.2511	0.99665	0.25315	0.389	46863
35-39	0.0354	0.1736	0.1118	0.99522	0.11307	0.141	15936
40-44	0.0103	0.0500	0.0267	0.98978	0.02713	0.029	2702
45-49	0.0007	0.0034	0.0017	0.98227	0.00179	0.002	146
50-54	0.0000	0.0001	0.0001	0.97075	0.00007	0.000	5

MATRIX PARAMETERS

λ_1	1.02498	
λ_2	$0.46170+0.75211i$	TABLE 7
λ_4	$-0.13030+0.58843i$	
λ_6	$-0.33541+0.40051i$	LESLIE
r_1	0.00493	MATRIX
r_2	$-0.02499+0.20405i$	AND ITS
r_4	$-0.10127+0.35774i$	ANALYSIS
r_6	$-0.12986+0.45359i$	(females)
c_1	21265	
$2\pi/\gamma$	30.7927	
Δ	9.2680	

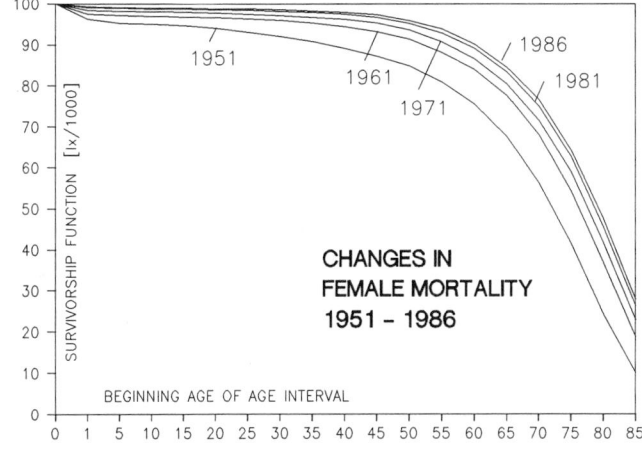

CHANGES IN FEMALE MORTALITY 1951 – 1986

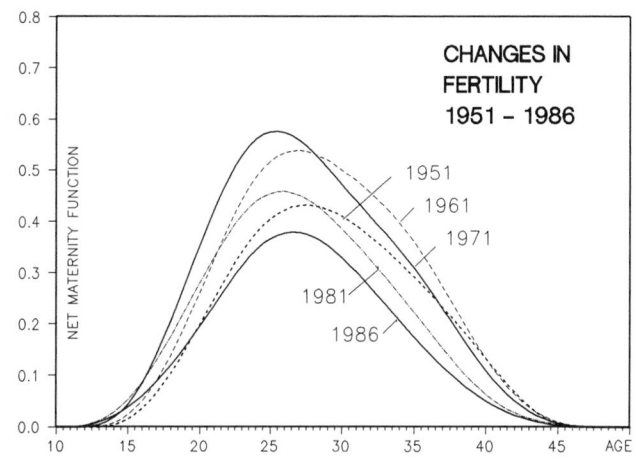

CHANGES IN FERTILITY 1951 – 1986

TABLE 1 — DATA

AGE AT LAST BIRTHDAY	ESTIMATED MID-YEAR POPULATION BOTH SEXES	MALES Number	MALES Percent	FEMALES Number	FEMALES Percent	BIRTHS BY AGE OF MOTHER AND SEX	DEATHS BOTH SEXES	DEATHS MALES	DEATHS FEMALES	AGE AT LAST BIRTHDAY
0	904600	463750	1.8	440850	1.6		26639	15094	11545	0
1-4	3685150	1887700	7.2	1797450	6.5		3646	1960	1686	1-4
5-9	4556250	2334600	8.9	2221650	8.1		1938	1215	723	5-9
10-14	4080050	2085200	7.9	1994850	7.3	485	1686	1070	616	10-14
15-19	3856500	1966400	7.5	1890100	6.9	49770	2992	2152	840	15-19
20-24	4096500	2077350	7.9	2019150	7.3	259677	3406	2377	1029	20-24
25-29	3534650	1766850	6.7	1767800	6.4	268514	3195	2127	1068	25-29
30-34	3859450	1918400	7.3	1941050	7.1	192643	4235	2714	1521	30-34
35-39	3695600	1831900	7.0	1863700	6.8	98239	5899	3639	2260	35-39
40-44	3703000	1828600	6.9	1874400	6.8	29905	9514	6094	3420	40-44
45-49	3625450	1745000	6.6	1880450	6.8	2208	14967	9371	5596	45-49
50-54	2384900	1136000	4.3	1248900	4.5	31	15619	9843	5776	50-54
55-59	3159850	1511400	5.7	1648450	6.0		32557	21066	11491	55-59
60-64	2817550	1325450	5.0	1492100	5.4		46541	29789	16752	60-64
65-69	2228700	1005100	3.8	1223600	4.5		58026	35308	22718	65-69
70-74	1604150	660900	2.5	943250	3.4		70527	37503	33024	70-74
75-79	1075850	418350	1.6	657500	2.4		78470	36613	41857	75-79
80-84	608463	234443	0.9	374020	1.4	463592 M	73178	31281	41897	80-84
85+	345787	128557	0.5	217230	0.8	437880 F	68061	27447	40614	85+
TOTAL	53822450	26325950		27496500		901472	521096	276663	244433	TOTAL

TABLE 2 — MALE LIFE TABLE

x	nM_x	nq_x	l_x	nd_x	nL_x	nm_x	na_x	T_x	$\overset{\circ}{e}_x$	x
0	0.032548	0.031647	100000	3165	97232	0.032548	0.125	6881985	68.820	0
1	0.001038	0.004142	96835	401	386338	0.001038	1.500	6784753	70.065	1
5	0.000520	0.002599	96434	251	481544	0.000520	2.500	6398414	66.350	5
10	0.000513	0.002571	96184	247	480357	0.000515	2.730	5916870	61.516	10
15	0.001094	0.005459	95936	524	478434	0.001095	2.618	5436513	56.668	15
20	0.001144	0.005706	95413	544	475711	0.001144	2.518	4958079	51.965	20
25	0.001204	0.006004	94868	570	472942	0.001204	2.544	4482368	47.248	25
30	0.001415	0.007050	94299	665	469905	0.001415	2.612	4009426	42.518	30
35	0.001986	0.009892	93634	926	466034	0.001988	2.695	3539520	37.802	35
40	0.003333	0.016537	92708	1533	460020	0.003333	2.705	3073486	33.152	40
45	0.005370	0.026717	91175	2436	450251	0.005410	2.692	2613466	28.664	45
50	0.008665	0.042590	88739	3779	434932	0.008690	2.682	2163215	24.377	50
55	0.013938	0.067499	84959	5735	411437	0.013938	2.670	1728284	20.343	55
60	0.022475	0.106928	79225	8471	376150	0.022521	2.642	1316847	16.622	60
65	0.035129	0.162871	70753	11524	326285	0.035318	2.615	940696	13.295	65
70	0.056745	0.250644	59230	14846	259962	0.057106	2.563	614412	10.373	70
75	0.087518	0.360018	44384	15979	181814	0.087887	2.490	354449	7.986	75
80	0.133427	0.495856	28405	14085	105562	0.133427	2.411	172635	6.078	80
85	0.213501	1.000000	14320	14320	67073	0.148693	4.684	67073	4.684	85

TABLE 3 — FEMALE LIFE TABLE

x	nM_x	nq_x	l_x	nd_x	nL_x	nm_x	na_x	T_x	$\overset{\circ}{e}_x$	x
0	0.026188	0.025595	100000	2559	97734	0.026188	0.115	7464292	74.643	0
1	0.000938	0.003743	97441	365	388850	0.000938	1.500	7366558	75.601	1
5	0.000325	0.001626	97076	158	484984	0.000325	2.500	6977708	71.879	5
10	0.000309	0.001544	96918	150	484228	0.000309	2.579	6492723	66.992	10
15	0.000444	0.002220	96768	215	483324	0.000444	2.593	6008496	62.092	15
20	0.000510	0.002546	96553	246	482169	0.000510	2.564	5525171	57.224	20
25	0.000604	0.003018	96308	291	480839	0.000604	2.593	5043003	52.363	25
30	0.000784	0.003911	96017	376	479206	0.000784	2.660	4562164	47.514	30
35	0.001213	0.006049	95642	578	476863	0.001213	2.676	4082957	42.690	35
40	0.001825	0.009085	95063	864	473328	0.001825	2.698	3606094	37.934	40
45	0.002976	0.014870	94199	1401	467759	0.002995	2.688	3132766	33.257	45
50	0.004625	0.022943	92799	2129	459027	0.004638	2.667	2665007	28.718	50
55	0.006971	0.034299	90670	3110	446130	0.006971	2.679	2205981	24.330	55
60	0.011227	0.054851	87560	4803	426687	0.011256	2.686	1759851	20.099	60
65	0.018567	0.089510	82757	7408	396820	0.018667	2.710	1333164	16.109	65
70	0.035011	0.162731	75349	12262	348201	0.035214	2.672	936344	12.427	70
75	0.063661	0.277847	63088	17529	273210	0.064158	2.591	588143	9.323	75
80	0.112018	0.437053	45559	19912	177754	0.112018	2.487	314932	6.913	80
85	0.186963	1.000000	25647	25647	137178	0.118623	5.349	137178	5.349	85

TABLE 4 — OBSERVED VITAL RATES AND RATIOS

CRUDE RATES

Per Thousand	BOTH SEXES	MALES	FEMALES
BIRTH RATE	16.75	17.61	15.92
DEATH RATE	9.68	10.51	8.89
RATE OF INCREASE	7.07	7.10	7.04

PERCENT OF POPULATION IN AGE GROUP

	BOTH SEXES	MALES	FEMALES
UNDER 15	24.57	25.72	23.47
15 - 64	64.53	64.98	64.10
65 AND OLDER	10.89	9.30	12.42

RATES STANDARDIZED ON USA 1980

Per Thousand	BOTH SEXES	MALES	FEMALES
BIRTH RATE	19.85		18.75
DEATH RATE	10.27	10.51	10.04
RATE OF INCREASE	9.58		8.70

RATES STANDARDIZED ON MEXICO 1980

	BOTH SEXES	MALES	FEMALES
BIRTH RATE	17.35		16.98
DEATH RATE	4.38	5.06	3.70
RATE OF INCREASE	12.96		13.28

VITAL STATISTICS

GFR x 1000	68.104
TFR	2.381
GRR	1.157
NRR	1.111
μ	28.264
σ^2	36.488
GENERATION	28.195
POP. SEX RATIO	1.044
SEX RATIO AT BIRTH	1.059
DEP. RATIO x 100	54.959

PROJECTED POPULATION

AGE GROUP	1975 BOTH SEXES	1975 MALES	1975 FEMALES	1980 BOTH SEXES	1980 MALES	1980 FEMALES
0-4	4392	2252	2140	4447	2280	2167
5-9	4573	2342	2231	4376	2243	2133
10-14	4547	2329	2218	4563	2336	2227
15-19	4068	2077	1991	4534	2320	2214
20-24	3841	1955	1886	4051	2065	1986
25-29	4079	2065	2014	3824	1944	1880
30-34	3518	1756	1762	4059	2052	2007
35-39	3835	1903	1932	3494	1741	1753
40-44	3658	1808	1850	3795	1878	1917
45-49	3642	1790	1852	3598	1770	1828
50-54	3531	1686	1845	3547	1729	1818
55-59	2289	1075	1214	3389	1595	1794
60-64	2959	1382	1577	2143	982	1161
65-69	2538	1150	1388	2665	1199	1466
70-74	1875	801	1074	2134	916	1218
75-79	1202	462	740	1402	560	842
80-84	671	243	428	750	268	482
85+	438	149	289	484	154	330
TOTAL	55656	27225	28431	57255	28032	29223

STABLE EQUIVALENT TO ORIGINAL POPULATION

MALES Number	MALES Percent	FEMALES Number	FEMALES Percent	AGE GROUP
2256	8.0	2144	7.5	0-4
2205	7.8	2097	7.3	5-9
2159	7.6	2055	7.1	10-14
2110	7.5	2014	7.0	15-19
2059	7.3	1972	6.9	20-24
2010	7.1	1930	6.7	25-29
1960	6.9	1888	6.6	30-34
1908	6.7	1844	6.4	35-39
1848	6.5	1796	6.2	40-44
1776	6.3	1742	6.1	45-49
1684	5.9	1678	5.8	50-54
1563	5.5	1601	5.6	55-59
1403	5.0	1503	5.2	60-64
1194	4.2	1372	4.8	65-69
934	3.3	1182	4.1	70-74
641	2.3	910	3.2	75-79
365	1.3	581	2.0	80-84
228	0.8	440	1.5	85+
28303		28749		TOTAL

TABLE 5 — POPULATION PROJECTED WITH FIXED AGE-SPECIFIC BIRTH AND DEATH RATES (female dominant, in 000s)

VITAL RATES OF PROJECTED POPULATION

Per Thousand	1975 BOTH SEXES	1975 MALES	1975 FEMALES	1980 BOTH SEXES	1980 MALES	1980 FEMALES
BIRTH RATE	16.35	17.19	15.54	16.14	16.96	15.36
DEATH RATE	10.34	10.98	9.74	10.87	11.39	10.37
RATE OF INCREASE	6.00	6.21	5.81	5.27	5.56	4.99

VITAL RATES OF STABLE POPULATION

Per Thousand	MALES	FEMALES
BIRTH RATE	16.64	15.47
DEATH RATE	12.87	11.74
RATE OF INCREASE		3.73

TABLE 6 — PROJECTED VITAL RATES AND RATIOS (female dominant)

AGE STRUCTURE OF PROJECTED POPULATION

	1975 BOTH SEXES	1975 MALES	1975 FEMALES	1980 BOTH SEXES	1980 MALES	1980 FEMALES
% UNDER 15	24.28	25.43	23.18	23.38	24.47	22.34
% 15-64	63.64	64.27	63.04	63.63	64.48	62.82
% 65 AND OLDER	12.08	10.30	13.78	12.99	11.05	14.84
DEPEND. RATIO x 100	57.13	55.60	58.63	57.15	55.08	59.19

STABLE AGE STRUCTURE

	MALES	FEMALES
% UNDER 15	23.39	21.90
% 15-64	64.73	62.50
% 65 AND OLDER	11.88	15.60
DEPEND. RATIO x 100	54.48	60.00

MATRIX PARAMETERS / LESLIE MATRIX

AGE GROUP	FEMALE BIRTH RATES	NET MATERNITY FUNCTION	COEFF. OF MATRIX EQUATION	ORIGINAL MATRIX SUB-DIAGONAL	ORIGINAL MATRIX FIRST ROW	STABLE MATRIX FISHER VALUES	STABLE MATRIX REPRODUCTIVE VALUES
0-4	0.0000	0.0000	0.0000	0.99671	0.00000	1.037	2321532
5-9	0.0000	0.0000	0.0003	0.99844	0.00029	1.060	2355394
10-14	0.0001	0.0006	0.0312	0.99813	0.03135	1.082	2157537
15-19	0.0128	0.0618	0.1815	0.99761	0.18274	1.071	2025060
20-24	0.0625	0.3012	0.3280	0.99724	0.33099	0.904	1825730
25-29	0.0738	0.3548	0.2929	0.99661	0.29639	0.580	1024502
30-34	0.0482	0.2310	0.1766	0.99511	0.17927	0.284	551262
35-39	0.0256	0.1221	0.0794	0.99259	0.08101	0.104	193669
40-44	0.0077	0.0367	0.0197	0.98824	0.02023	0.022	41268
45-49	0.0006	0.0027	0.0014	0.98133	0.00142	0.001	2766
50-54	0.0000	0.0001	0.0000	0.97190	0.00003	0.000	37

Matrix parameters:

λ_1 1.01883
λ_2 0.39254 − 0.73800i
λ_4 −0.38192 − 0.41547i
λ_6 −0.03370 + 0.53731i
r_1 0.00373
r_2 −0.03585 − 0.21639i
r_4 −0.11442 − 0.46283i
r_6 −0.12384 + 0.32669i
c_1 287487
$2\pi/y$ 29.0360
Δ 4.8869

TABLE 7 — LESLIE MATRIX AND ITS ANALYSIS (females)

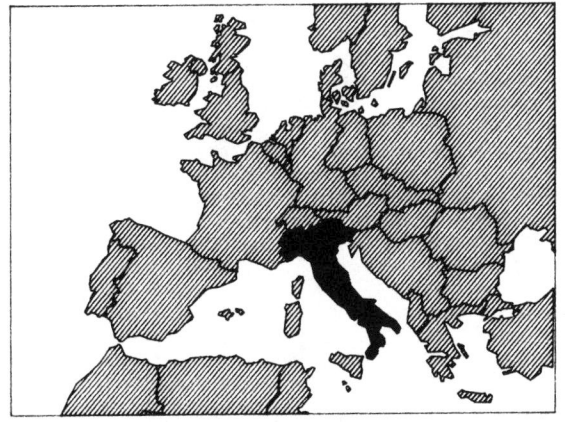

EDUCATION [1984]
% of primary school-age children enrolled:	99
secondary school-age children enrolled:	74
ca. 20-24 year olds in higher education:	26

LABOR FORCE
Average annual labor force growth (%) 1980-85:	0.7
% of the 1980 labor force in agriculture:	12
in industry:	41
in services:	48

GNP & INCOME DISTRIBUTION
GNP per capita (in US Dollars) 1985:	6520
GNP average annual growth rate (%) 1965-85:	2.6
% share of total household income 1977	
Lowest 20% of households:	6.2
Highest 10% of households:	28.1

HEALTH & NUTRITION
Population per physician 1981:	750
Daily calorie supply per capita 1985:	3538

TABLE 8 — SOCIO-ECONOMIC INDICATORS

AGE AT LAST BIRTHDAY	ESTIMATED MID-YEAR POPULATION BOTH SEXES	MALES Number	MALES Percent	FEMALES Number	FEMALES Percent	BIRTHS BY AGE OF MOTHER AND SEX	DEATHS BOTH SEXES	DEATHS MALES	DEATHS FEMALES	AGE AT LAST BIRTHDAY
0	846805	434824	1.6	411981	1.5		17526	9984	7542	0
1-4	3471694	1782896	6.6	1688798	6.0		2148	1223	925	1-4
5-9	4563334	2335511	8.6	2227823	7.9		1540	964	576	5-9
10-14	4554906	2328854	8.6	2226052	7.8	589	1528	961	567	10-14
15-19	4057680	2065255	7.6	1992425	7.0	62890	2847	2031	816	15-19
20-24	3818300	1933559	7.1	1884741	6.6	240319	2974	2184	790	20-24
25-29	4045364	2038081	7.5	2007283	7.1	277166	3043	2054	989	25-29
30-34	3500821	1742857	6.4	1757964	6.2	145509	3327	2146	1181	30-34
35-39	3806679	1884584	7.0	1922095	6.8	76809	5355	3418	1937	35-39
40-44	3654046	1803663	6.7	1850383	6.5	22846	8701	5651	3050	40-44
45-49	3642792	1787829	6.6	1854963	6.5	1670	14547	9729	4818	45-49
50-54	3536352	1686278	6.2	1850074	6.5	54	22883	15037	7846	50-54
55-59	2293280	1076679	4.0	1216601	4.3		23191	15206	7985	55-59
60-64	2970778	1388128	5.1	1582650	5.6		47418	31043	16375	60-64
65-69	2527443	1145482	4.2	1381961	4.9		65228	40988	24240	65-69
70-74	1871304	798079	2.9	1073225	3.8		78236	44500	33736	70-74
75-79	1210530	462027	1.7	748503	2.6		87877	42411	45466	75-79
80-84	681176	243775	0.9	437401	1.5	426160 M	82313	34225	48088	80-84
85+	387716	133674	0.5	254042	0.9	401692 F	83664	31186	52478	85+
TOTAL	55441000	27072035		28368965		827852	554346	294941	259405	TOTAL

TABLE 1 DATA

x	$_nM_x$	$_nq_x$	l_x	$_nd_x$	$_nL_x$	$_nm_x$	$_na_x$	T_x	$\overset{\circ}{e}_x$	x
0	0.022961	0.022501	100000	2250	97995	0.022961	0.109	6960399	69.604	0
1	0.000686	0.002739	97750	268	390330	0.000686	1.500	6862403	70.204	1
5	0.000413	0.002062	97482	201	486908	0.000413	2.500	6472073	66.392	5
10	0.000413	0.002065	97281	201	485961	0.000413	2.787	5985164	61.524	10
15	0.000983	0.004921	97080	478	484279	0.000986	2.650	5499203	56.646	15
20	0.001130	0.005632	96603	544	481654	0.001130	2.502	5014924	51.913	20
25	0.001008	0.005027	96059	483	479094	0.001008	2.519	4533270	47.193	25
30	0.001231	0.006145	95576	587	476488	0.001233	2.633	4054176	42.418	30
35	0.001814	0.009031	94988	858	472980	0.001814	2.713	3577688	37.665	35
40	0.003133	0.015562	94130	1465	467330	0.003135	2.732	3104708	32.983	40
45	0.005442	0.026874	92666	2490	457624	0.005442	2.709	2637378	28.461	45
50	0.008917	0.043997	90175	3967	441670	0.008983	2.679	2179754	24.172	50
55	0.014123	0.068531	86208	5908	417220	0.014160	2.661	1738084	20.162	55
60	0.022363	0.106222	80300	8530	381414	0.022363	2.645	1320864	16.449	60
65	0.035782	0.165138	71770	11852	330524	0.035858	2.610	939450	13.090	65
70	0.055759	0.246684	59918	14781	263701	0.056052	2.572	608927	10.163	70
75	0.091793	0.375441	45137	16946	183263	0.092471	2.497	345226	7.648	75
80	0.140396	0.514343	28191	14500	103278	0.140396	2.402	161963	5.745	80
85	0.233299	1.000000	13691	13691	58685	0.172044	4.286	58685	4.286	85

TABLE 2 MALE LIFE TABLE

x	$_nM_x$	$_nq_x$	l_x	$_nd_x$	$_nL_x$	$_nm_x$	$_na_x$	T_x	$\overset{\circ}{e}_x$	x
0	0.018307	0.018010	100000	1801	98381	0.018307	0.101	7590389	75.904	0
1	0.000548	0.002188	98199	215	392259	0.000548	1.500	7492008	76.294	1
5	0.000259	0.001292	97984	127	489604	0.000259	2.500	7099750	72.458	5
10	0.000255	0.001274	97858	125	488991	0.000255	2.623	6610146	67.549	10
15	0.000410	0.002049	97733	200	488190	0.000410	2.583	6121154	62.631	15
20	0.000419	0.002094	97533	204	487161	0.000419	2.540	5632974	57.755	20
25	0.000493	0.002462	97328	240	486068	0.000493	2.606	5145813	52.871	25
30	0.000672	0.003356	97089	326	484681	0.000672	2.658	4659744	47.995	30
35	0.001008	0.005027	96763	486	482695	0.001008	2.699	4175063	43.147	35
40	0.001648	0.008213	96277	791	479561	0.001649	2.697	3692368	38.352	40
45	0.002597	0.012910	95486	1233	474597	0.002597	2.703	3212807	33.647	45
50	0.004241	0.021129	94253	1991	466653	0.004268	2.684	2738210	29.052	50
55	0.006563	0.032424	92262	2991	454354	0.006584	2.675	2271557	24.621	55
60	0.010347	0.050527	89270	4511	435944	0.010347	2.693	1817203	20.356	60
65	0.017540	0.084560	84760	7167	407321	0.017596	2.701	1381259	16.296	65
70	0.031434	0.147289	77592	11429	361580	0.031607	2.692	973938	12.552	70
75	0.060743	0.267177	66164	17677	288604	0.061252	2.612	612358	9.255	75
80	0.109940	0.431568	48486	20925	190332	0.109940	2.510	323754	6.677	80
85	0.206572	1.000000	27561	27561	133422	0.140151	4.841	133422	4.841	85

TABLE 3 FEMALE LIFE TABLE

CRUDE RATES

Per Thousand	BOTH SEXES	MALES	FEMALES
BIRTH RATE	14.93	15.74	14.16
DEATH RATE	10.00	10.89	9.14
RATE OF INCREASE	4.93	4.85	5.02

PERCENT OF POPULATION IN AGE GROUP

UNDER 15	24.24	25.42	23.11
15 - 64	63.72	64.30	63.16
65 AND OLDER	12.05	10.28	13.73

RATES STANDARDIZED ON USA 1980

Per Thousand	BOTH SEXES	MALES	FEMALES
BIRTH RATE	18.29		17.26
DEATH RATE	10.12	10.53	9.73
RATE OF INCREASE	8.17		7.52

RATES STANDARDIZED ON MEXICO 1980

	BOTH SEXES	MALES	FEMALES
BIRTH RATE	16.21		15.86
DEATH RATE	4.02	4.73	3.29
RATE OF INCREASE	12.20		12.57

VITAL STATISTICS

GFR x 1000	62.386
TFR	2.167
GRR	1.052
NRR	1.022
μ	27.617
σ^2	35.925
GENERATION	27.603
POP. SEX RATIO	1.048
SEX RATIO AT BIRTH	1.061
DEP. RATIO x 100	56.941

TABLE 4 OBSERVED VITAL RATES AND RATIOS

AGE AT LAST BIRTHDAY	ESTIMATED MID-YEAR POPULATION					BIRTHS BY AGE OF MOTHER AND SEX	DEATHS			AGE AT LAST BIRTHDAY
	BOTH SEXES	MALES		FEMALES			BOTH SEXES	MALES	FEMALES	
		Number	Percent	Number	Percent					
0	657020	337689	1.2	319331	1.1		9320	5431	3889	0
1-4	2959593	1520002	5.5	1439591	5.0		1548	832	716	1-4
5-9	4338987	2225616	8.1	2113371	7.3		1383	796	587	5-9
10-14	4614266	2356798	8.6	2257468	7.8	110	1524	935	589	10-14
15-19	4569470	2327433	8.5	2242037	7.7	44519	3142	2351	791	15-19
20-24	4042522	2044373	7.4	1998149	6.9	195846	3152	2336	816	20-24
25-29	3790506	1901446	6.9	1889060	6.5	210198	2784	1952	832	25-29
30-34	4017563	2008879	7.3	2008684	6.9	130597	3589	2332	1257	30-34
35-39	3502601	1739110	6.3	1763491	6.1	46001	4632	2981	1651	35-39
40-44	3760348	1855719	6.8	1904629	6.6	12216	7770	5049	2721	40-44
45-49	3611700	1771821	6.4	1839879	6.4	869	12941	8631	4310	45-49
50-54	3566787	1731933	6.3	1834854	6.3	45	21378	14742	6636	50-54
55-59	3413403	1600129	5.8	1813274	6.3		32433	21897	10536	55-59
60-64	2169325	992929	3.6	1176396	4.1		32369	21326	11043	60-64
65-69	2708380	1216544	4.4	1491836	5.2		63693	40381	23312	65-69
70-74	2119265	903213	3.3	1216052	4.2		82921	47976	34945	70-74
75-79	1393594	542476	2.0	851118	2.9		90811	46274	44537	75-79
80-84	764289	261742	1.0	502547	1.7	330978 M	86700	36308	50392	80-84
85+	434263	134348	0.5	299915	1.0	309423 F	92420	31925	60495	85+
TOTAL	56433882	27472200		28961682		640401	554510	294455	260055	TOTAL

TABLE 1 DATA

x	nM_x	nq_x	l_x	nd_x	nL_x	nm_x	na_x	T_x	$\overset{\circ}{e}_x$	x
0	0.016083	0.015853	100000	1585	98569	0.016083	0.097	7066049	70.660	0
1	0.000547	0.002186	98415	215	393121	0.000547	1.500	6967480	70.797	1
5	0.000358	0.001787	98200	175	490559	0.000358	2.500	6574359	66.949	5
10	0.000397	0.001982	98024	194	489701	0.000397	2.841	6083800	62.064	10
15	0.001010	0.005045	97830	494	487990	0.001011	2.652	5594099	57.182	15
20	0.001143	0.005698	97336	555	485295	0.001143	2.501	5106108	52.458	20
25	0.001027	0.005120	96782	496	482670	0.001027	2.501	4620813	47.745	25
30	0.001161	0.005793	96286	558	480104	0.001162	2.621	4138143	42.978	30
35	0.001714	0.008549	95728	818	476747	0.001717	2.685	3658039	38.213	35
40	0.002721	0.013521	94910	1283	471642	0.002721	2.733	3181292	33.519	40
45	0.004871	0.024101	93627	2256	463020	0.004873	2.734	2709651	28.941	45
50	0.008512	0.041741	91370	3814	448065	0.008512	2.696	2246631	24.588	50
55	0.013685	0.066761	87556	5845	424118	0.013782	2.662	1798566	20.542	55
60	0.021478	0.102450	81711	8371	388759	0.021533	2.635	1374448	16.821	60
65	0.033193	0.153795	73340	11279	339808	0.033193	2.616	985689	13.440	65
70	0.053117	0.236000	62060	14646	274837	0.053291	2.579	645881	10.407	70
75	0.085301	0.354355	47414	16801	195275	0.086040	2.512	371044	7.826	75
80	0.138717	0.511032	30613	15644	112777	0.138717	2.425	175769	5.742	80
85	0.237629	1.000000	14969	14969	62992	0.177100	4.208	62992	4.208	85

TABLE 2 MALE LIFE TABLE

x	nM_x	nq_x	l_x	nd_x	nL_x	nm_x	na_x	T_x	$\overset{\circ}{e}_x$	x
0	0.012179	0.012045	100000	1205	98905	0.012179	0.091	7733064	77.331	0
1	0.000497	0.001987	98795	196	394691	0.000497	1.500	7634160	77.272	1
5	0.000278	0.001388	98599	137	492654	0.000278	2.500	7239469	73.423	5
10	0.000261	0.001304	98462	128	491998	0.000261	2.559	6746815	68.522	10
15	0.000353	0.001764	98334	173	491251	0.000353	2.586	6254816	63.608	15
20	0.000408	0.002041	98161	200	490310	0.000409	2.544	5763565	58.716	20
25	0.000440	0.002200	97960	216	489284	0.000441	2.602	5273254	53.831	25
30	0.000626	0.003127	97745	306	488009	0.000626	2.664	4783970	48.944	30
35	0.000936	0.004676	97439	456	486136	0.000937	2.676	4295961	44.089	35
40	0.001429	0.007120	96983	690	483329	0.001431	2.701	3809825	39.283	40
45	0.002343	0.011653	96293	1122	478871	0.002343	2.689	3326496	34.546	45
50	0.003617	0.017933	95171	1707	471915	0.003617	2.692	2847625	29.921	50
55	0.005810	0.028855	93464	2697	461094	0.005849	2.691	2375709	25.418	55
60	0.009387	0.046105	90767	4185	444173	0.009422	2.691	1914615	21.094	60
65	0.015626	0.075435	86582	6531	417967	0.015626	2.712	1470442	16.983	65
70	0.028736	0.135223	80051	10826	375215	0.028852	2.687	1052475	13.148	70
75	0.052328	0.234698	69225	16247	307694	0.052802	2.635	677260	9.783	75
80	0.100273	0.402414	52978	21319	212611	0.100273	2.548	369566	6.976	80
85	0.201707	1.000000	31659	31659	156955	0.134630	4.958	156955	4.958	85

TABLE 3 FEMALE LIFE TABLE

CRUDE RATES

Per Thousand	BOTH SEXES	MALES	FEMALES
BIRTH RATE	11.35	12.05	10.68
DEATH RATE	9.83	10.72	8.98
RATE OF INCREASE	1.52	1.33	1.70

PERCENT OF POPULATION IN AGE GROUP

UNDER 15	22.27	23.44	21.17
15 - 64	64.58	65.43	63.78
65 AND OLDER	13.15	11.13	15.06

RATES STANDARDIZED ON USA 1980

Per Thousand	BOTH SEXES	MALES	FEMALES
BIRTH RATE	13.90		13.06
DEATH RATE	9.42	10.01	8.88
RATE OF INCREASE	4.47		4.18

RATES STANDARDIZED ON MEXICO 1980

	BOTH SEXES	MALES	FEMALES
BIRTH RATE	12.26		11.94
DEATH RATE	3.61	4.35	2.87
RATE OF INCREASE	8.65		9.07

VITAL STATISTICS

GFR x 1000	46.930	TABLE 4
TFR	1.636	
GRR	0.790	OBSERVED
NRR	0.773	VITAL
μ	27.491	RATES
σ^2	31.487	AND
GENERATION	27.638	RATIOS
POP. SEX RATIO	1.054	
SEX RATIO AT BIRTH	1.070	
DEP. RATIO x 100	54.850	

TABLE 1 — DATA

AGE AT LAST BIRTHDAY	ESTIMATED MID-YEAR POPULATION BOTH SEXES	MALES Number	MALES Percent	FEMALES Number	FEMALES Percent	BIRTHS BY AGE OF MOTHER AND SEX	DEATHS BOTH SEXES	DEATHS MALES	DEATHS FEMALES	AGE AT LAST BIRTHDAY
0	614611	315573	1.1	299038	1.0		7397	4121	3276	0
1-4	2561573	1315438	4.8	1246135	4.3		1167	651	516	1-4
5-9	3972920	2038716	7.4	1934204	6.6		885	508	377	5-9
10-14	4488358	2298005	8.3	2190353	7.5	21	1150	762	388	10-14
15-19	4765148	2426086	8.8	2339062	8.0	35265	2835	2154	681	15-19
20-24	4369229	2216351	8.0	2152878	7.4	180080	3078	2366	712	20-24
25-29	3939696	1976918	7.2	1962778	6.7	204816	2803	2018	785	25-29
30-34	3857921	1926600	7.0	1931321	6.6	123231	3110	2050	1060	30-34
35-39	3757259	1870977	6.8	1886282	6.5	48309	4378	2799	1579	35-39
40-44	3705726	1831788	6.6	1873938	6.4	9558	7208	4712	2496	40-44
45-49	3601788	1767860	6.4	1833928	6.3	580	11721	7768	3953	45-49
50-54	3567555	1733545	6.3	1834010	6.3	68	20402	13954	6448	50-54
55-59	3436221	1635691	5.9	1800530	6.2		31494	21718	9776	55-59
60-64	2863427	1301884	4.7	1561543	5.3		40334	26599	13735	60-64
65-69	2208556	980111	3.5	1228445	4.2		50847	32190	18657	65-69
70-74	2285342	973432	3.5	1311910	4.5		84773	49709	35064	70-74
75-79	1512346	588992	2.1	923354	3.2		96375	49254	47121	75-79
80-84	848832	293331	1.1	555501	1.9	309913 M	92747	38962	53785	80-84
85+	479277	140607	0.5	338670	1.2	292015 F	101626	33558	68068	85+
TOTAL	56835785	27631905		29203880		601928	564330	295853	268477	TOTAL

TABLE 2 — MALE LIFE TABLE

x	nM_x	nq_x	l_x	nd_x	nL_x	nm_x	na_x	T_x	$\overset{\circ}{e}_x$	x
0	0.013059	0.012906	100000	1291	98828	0.013059	0.092	7140319	71.403	0
1	0.000495	0.001977	98709	195	394350	0.000495	1.500	7041490	71.336	1
5	0.000249	0.001245	98514	123	492265	0.000249	2.500	6647140	67.474	5
10	0.000332	0.001657	98392	163	491616	0.000332	2.899	6154876	62.555	10
15	0.000888	0.004430	98229	435	490130	0.000888	2.671	5663260	57.654	15
20	0.001068	0.005326	97793	521	487677	0.001068	2.524	5173131	52.899	20
25	0.001021	0.005091	97273	495	485123	0.001021	2.497	4685453	48.168	25
30	0.001064	0.005310	96777	514	482649	0.001065	2.590	4200330	43.402	30
35	0.001496	0.007461	96264	718	479670	0.001497	2.706	3717681	38.620	35
40	0.002572	0.012798	95545	1223	474948	0.002575	2.727	3238011	33.890	40
45	0.004394	0.021764	94323	2053	466986	0.004396	2.746	2763064	29.294	45
50	0.008049	0.039518	92270	3646	452996	0.008049	2.709	2296078	24.884	50
55	0.013278	0.064479	88623	5714	429764	0.013296	2.663	1843083	20.797	55
60	0.020431	0.097992	82909	8124	395417	0.020547	2.646	1413319	17.047	60
65	0.032843	0.152358	74785	11394	346747	0.032860	2.615	1017901	13.611	65
70	0.051066	0.227267	63391	14407	282119	0.051066	2.582	671155	10.588	70
75	0.083624	0.348465	48984	17069	202539	0.084276	2.517	389036	7.942	75
80	0.132826	0.495296	31915	15807	119007	0.132826	2.434	186497	5.844	80
85	0.238665	1.000000	16108	16108	67490	0.178339	4.190	67490	4.190	85

TABLE 3 — FEMALE LIFE TABLE

x	nM_x	nq_x	l_x	nd_x	nL_x	nm_x	na_x	T_x	$\overset{\circ}{e}_x$	x
0	0.010955	0.010847	100000	1085	99011	0.010955	0.089	7795314	77.953	0
1	0.000414	0.001655	98915	164	395252	0.000414	1.500	7696302	77.807	1
5	0.000195	0.000974	98752	96	493518	0.000195	2.500	7301050	73.933	5
10	0.000177	0.000885	98655	87	493069	0.000177	2.612	6807532	69.003	10
15	0.000291	0.001455	98568	143	492498	0.000291	2.610	6314464	64.062	15
20	0.000331	0.001654	98425	163	491728	0.000331	2.568	5821966	59.151	20
25	0.000400	0.002000	98262	197	490840	0.000400	2.613	5330238	54.245	25
30	0.000549	0.002743	98065	269	489699	0.000549	2.664	4839397	49.349	30
35	0.000837	0.004180	97796	409	488039	0.000838	2.693	4349699	44.477	35
40	0.001332	0.006642	97388	647	485452	0.001333	2.702	3861660	39.652	40
45	0.002155	0.010725	96741	1038	481322	0.002156	2.705	3376426	34.900	45
50	0.003516	0.017437	95703	1669	474653	0.003516	2.685	2894886	30.249	50
55	0.005430	0.026830	94034	2523	464343	0.005433	2.690	2420233	25.738	55
60	0.008796	0.043356	91511	3968	448453	0.008847	2.705	1955889	21.373	60
65	0.015187	0.073507	87544	6435	422932	0.015216	2.702	1507436	17.219	65
70	0.026727	0.125900	81109	10212	382063	0.026727	2.701	1084504	13.371	70
75	0.051032	0.229447	70897	16267	316146	0.051454	2.643	702442	9.908	75
80	0.096823	0.391513	54630	21388	220903	0.096823	2.557	386295	7.071	80
85	0.200986	1.000000	33242	33242	165393	0.133865	4.975	165393	4.975	85

TABLE 4 — OBSERVED VITAL RATES AND RATIOS

CRUDE RATES

Per Thousand	BOTH SEXES	MALES	FEMALES
BIRTH RATE	10.59	11.22	10.00
DEATH RATE	9.93	10.71	9.19
RATE OF INCREASE	0.66	0.51	0.81

RATES STANDARDIZED ON USA 1980

Per Thousand	BOTH SEXES	MALES	FEMALES
BIRTH RATE	12.60		11.88
DEATH RATE	9.08	9.64	8.56
RATE OF INCREASE	3.51		3.32

VITAL STATISTICS

GFR x 1000	43.056
TFR	1.490
GRR	0.723
NRR	0.709
μ	27.786
σ^2	30.238
GENERATION	27.972
POP. SEX RATIO	1.057
SEX RATIO AT BIRTH	1.061
DEP. RATIO x 100	50.105

PERCENT OF POPULATION IN AGE GROUP

	BOTH SEXES	MALES	FEMALES
UNDER 15	20.48	21.60	19.41
15 - 64	66.62	67.63	65.66
65 AND OLDER	12.90	10.77	14.92

RATES STANDARDIZED ON MEXICO 1980

	BOTH SEXES	MALES	FEMALES
BIRTH RATE	11.02		10.77
DEATH RATE	3.39	4.08	2.69
RATE OF INCREASE	7.63		8.08

PROJECTED POPULATION

AGE GROUP	1988			1993								AGE GROUP	

AGE GROUP	BOTH SEXES	MALES	FEMALES	BOTH SEXES	MALES	FEMALES
0-4	3058	1573	1485	3183	1637	1546
5-9	3171	1628	1543	3053	1570	1483
10-14	3968	2036	1932	3167	1626	1541
15-19	4479	2291	2188	3960	2030	1930
20-24	4749	2414	2335	4464	2280	2184
25-29	4354	2205	2149	4732	2401	2331
30-34	3925	1967	1958	4337	2193	2144
35-39	3840	1915	1925	3907	1955	1952
40-44	3729	1853	1876	3811	1896	1915
45-49	3659	1801	1858	3682	1822	1860
50-54	3524	1715	1809	3579	1747	1832
55-59	3439	1645	1794	3396	1627	1769
60-64	3244	1505	1739	3246	1513	1733
65-69	2615	1142	1473	2960	1320	1640
70-74	1907	797	1110	2259	929	1330
75-79	1785	699	1086	1490	572	918
80-84	991	346	645	1170	411	759
85+	582	166	416	679	196	483
TOTAL	57019	27698	29321	57075	27725	29350

STABLE EQUIVALENT TO ORIGINAL POPULATION

	MALES		FEMALES		AGE GROUP	
	Number	Percent	Number	Percent		
0-4	1838	4.3	1735	3.8	0-4	
5-9	1950	4.6	1843	4.0	5-9	TABLE 5
10-14	2071	4.9	1957	4.3	10-14	
15-19	2196	5.2	2079	4.6	15-19	POPULATION
20-24	2323	5.5	2207	4.8	20-24	PROJECTED
25-29	2457	5.8	2342	5.1	25-29	WITH
30-34	2599	6.1	2485	5.5	30-34	FIXED
35-39	2746	6.5	2633	5.8	35-39	AGE-
40-44	2891	6.8	2785	6.1	40-44	SPECIFIC
45-49	3023	7.1	2936	6.4	45-49	BIRTH
50-54	3118	7.3	3078	6.8	50-54	AND
55-59	3145	7.4	3202	7.0	55-59	DEATH
60-64	3077	7.2	3288	7.2	60-64	RATES
65-69	2869	6.7	3297	7.2	65-69	(female
70-74	2482	5.8	3167	7.0	70-74	dominant,
75-79	1894	4.4	2786	6.1	75-79	in 000s)
80-84	1184	2.8	2070	4.5	80-84	
85+	714	1.7	1648	3.6	85+	
TOTAL	42577		45538		TOTAL	

VITAL RATES OF PROJECTED POPULATION

Per Thousand	1988			1993		
	BOTH SEXES	MALES	FEMALES	BOTH SEXES	MALES	FEMALES
BIRTH RATE	11.17	11.84	10.54	11.43	12.11	10.78
DEATH RATE	10.87	11.51	10.25	11.60	12.16	11.08
RATE OF INCREASE	0.31	0.33	0.29	-0.17	-0.05	-0.29

AGE STRUCTURE OF PROJECTED POPULATION

	BOTH SEXES	MALES	FEMALES	BOTH SEXES	MALES	FEMALES
% UNDER 15	17.89	18.91	16.92	16.48	17.43	15.57
% 15-64	68.30	69.72	66.95	68.53	70.20	66.95
% 65 AND OLDER	13.82	11.37	16.13	14.99	12.36	17.48
DEPEND. RATIO x 100	46.42	43.44	49.36	45.92	42.44	49.37

VITAL RATES OF STABLE POPULATION

Per Thousand	MALES	FEMALES	
BIRTH RATE	8.48	7.47	TABLE 6
DEATH RATE	20.62	19.74	PROJECTED
RATE OF INCREASE		-12.27	VITAL RATES

STABLE AGE STRUCTURE

	MALES	FEMALES	
% UNDER 15	13.76	12.16	AND RATIOS (female
% 15-64	64.76	59.37	dominant)
% 65 AND OLDER	21.47	28.48	
DEPEND. RATIO x 100	54.40	68.45	

AGE GROUP	FEMALE BIRTH RATES	NET MATERNITY FUNCTION	COEFF. OF MATRIX EQUATION	ORIGINAL MATRIX		STABLE MATRIX		MATRIX PARAMETERS			
				SUB-DIAGONAL	FIRST ROW	FISHER VALUES	REPRODUCTIVE VALUES				
0-4	0.0000	0.0000	0.0000	0.99849	0.00000	0.981	1515785	λ_1	0.94049		
5-9	0.0000	0.0000	0.0000	0.99909	0.00001	0.924	1787200	λ_2	0.37277+0.70424i	TABLE 7	
10-14	0.0000	0.0000	0.0180	0.99884	0.01807	0.870	1905151	λ_4	-0.32905+0.35290i		
15-19	0.0073	0.0360	0.1178	0.99844	0.11820	0.801	1874142	λ_6	-0.12344+0.46519i	LESLIE
20-24	0.0406	0.1995	0.2240	0.99820	0.22517	0.639	1374825	r_1	-0.01227	MATRIX
25-29	0.0506	0.2485	0.2000	0.99767	0.20143	0.380	746639	r_2	-0.04543+0.21679i	AND ITS
30-34	0.0310	0.1516	0.1061	0.99661	0.10710	0.161	310052	r_4	-0.14575+0.46425i	ANALYSIS
35-39	0.0124	0.0606	0.0363	0.99470	0.03679	0.046	86917	r_6	-0.14626+0.36604i	(females)
40-44	0.0025	0.0120	0.0064	0.99149	0.00649	0.007	13655	c_1	455372	
45-49	0.0002	0.0007	0.0004	0.98614	0.00042	0.000	898	$2\pi/y$	28.9822	
50-54	0.0000	0.0001	0.0000	0.97828	0.00004	0.000	85	Δ	16.9420	

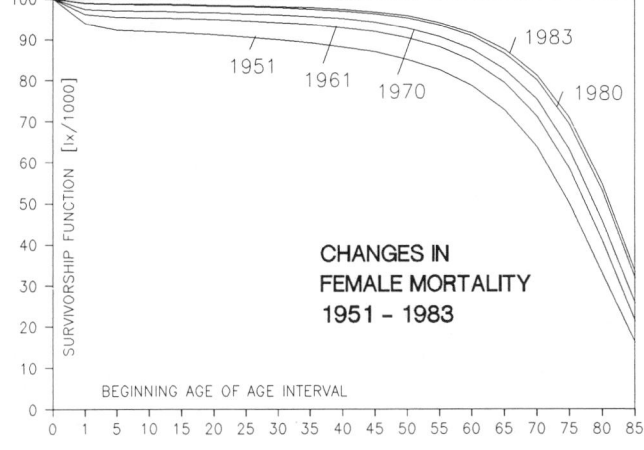

CHANGES IN FEMALE MORTALITY 1951 - 1983

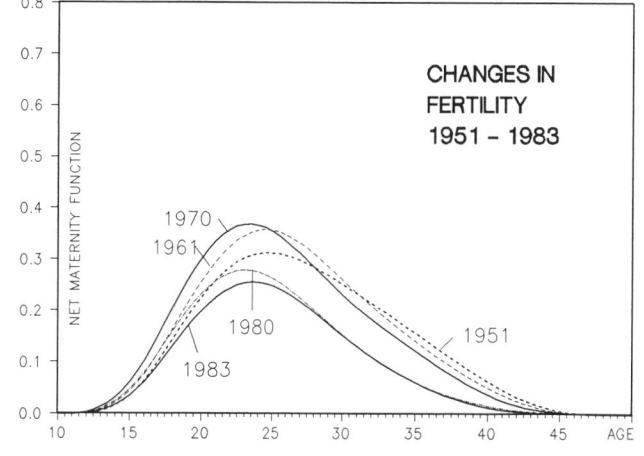

CHANGES IN FERTILITY 1951 - 1983

TABLE 1 DATA

AGE AT LAST BIRTHDAY	ESTIMATED MID-YEAR POPULATION BOTH SEXES	MALES Number	MALES Percent	FEMALES Number	FEMALES Percent	BIRTHS BY AGE OF MOTHER AND SEX	DEATHS BOTH SEXES	DEATHS MALES	DEATHS FEMALES	AGE AT LAST BIRTHDAY
0	4384	2228	1.3	2156	1.2		110	63	47	0
1-4	19187	9815	5.9	9372	5.4		11	3	8	1-4
5-9	25785	13129	7.9	12656	7.3		13	10	3	5-9
10-14	25254	12885	7.7	12369	7.2		10	6	4	10-14
15-19	24186	12350	7.4	11836	6.9	332	26	18	8	15-19
20-24	23279	11892	7.1	11387	6.6	1492	34	22	12	20-24
25-29	22405	11648	7.0	10757	6.2	1355	34	24	10	25-29
30-34	23139	11930	7.2	11209	6.5	730	41	27	14	30-34
35-39	23986	12397	7.4	11589	6.7	380	44	26	18	35-39
40-44	25055	12728	7.6	12327	7.1	116	97	62	35	40-44
45-49	21257	9650	5.8	11607	6.7	6	96	54	42	45-49
50-54	17529	8455	5.1	9074	5.3		160	109	51	50-54
55-59	20886	10046	6.0	10840	6.3		304	205	99	55-59
60-64	20081	9361	5.6	10720	6.2		393	253	140	60-64
65-69	16925	7536	4.5	9389	5.4		573	326	247	65-69
70-74	12172	5078	3.1	7094	4.1		619	360	259	70-74
75-79	7447	2963	1.8	4484	2.6		609	288	321	75-79
80-84	3961	1526	0.9	2435	1.4	2225 M	521	238	283	80-84
85+	2127	819	0.5	1308	0.8	2186 F	459	194	265	85+
TOTAL	339045	166436		172609		4411	4154	2288	1866	TOTAL

TABLE 2 MALE LIFE TABLE

x	nM_x	nq_x	l_x	nd_x	nL_x	nm_x	na_x	T_x	$\overset{\circ}{e}_x$	x
0	0.028276	0.027589	100000	2759	97567	0.028277	0.118	6647902	66.479	0
1	0.000306	0.001222	97241	119	388668	0.000306	1.500	6550335	67.362	1
5	0.000762	0.003801	97122	369	484689	0.000762	2.500	6161667	63.442	5
10	0.000466	0.002328	96753	225	483272	0.000466	2.808	5676978	58.675	10
15	0.001457	0.007272	96528	702	481022	0.001459	2.695	5193706	53.805	15
20	0.001850	0.009212	95826	883	476979	0.001851	2.564	4712685	49.180	20
25	0.002060	0.010250	94943	973	472319	0.002060	2.537	4235705	44.613	25
30	0.002263	0.011252	93970	1057	467206	0.002263	2.499	3763386	40.049	30
35	0.002097	0.010437	92913	970	462381	0.002097	2.749	3296180	35.476	35
40	0.004871	0.024123	91943	2218	454488	0.004880	2.644	2833799	30.821	40
45	0.005596	0.027852	89725	2499	443053	0.005641	2.770	2379311	26.518	45
50	0.012892	0.062609	87226	5461	423613	0.012892	2.708	1936258	22.198	50
55	0.020406	0.097271	81765	7953	389754	0.020406	2.602	1512646	18.500	55
60	0.027027	0.126918	73811	9368	346616	0.027027	2.605	1122891	15.213	60
65	0.043259	0.196346	64443	12653	291896	0.043348	2.604	776275	12.046	65
70	0.070894	0.302530	51790	15668	220083	0.071192	2.519	484379	9.353	70
75	0.097199	0.390429	36122	14103	144629	0.097512	2.449	264296	7.317	75
80	0.155963	0.553874	22019	12196	78196	0.155963	2.384	119667	5.435	80
85	0.236874	1.000000	9823	9823	41470	0.176958	4.222	41470	4.222	85

TABLE 3 FEMALE LIFE TABLE

x	nM_x	nq_x	l_x	nd_x	nL_x	nm_x	na_x	T_x	$\overset{\circ}{e}_x$	x
0	0.021800	0.021383	100000	2138	98091	0.021800	0.107	7307678	73.077	0
1	0.000854	0.003407	97862	333	390613	0.000854	1.500	7209588	73.671	1
5	0.000237	0.001185	97528	116	487352	0.000237	2.500	6818975	69.918	5
10	0.000323	0.001618	97413	158	486714	0.000324	2.782	6331622	64.998	10
15	0.000679	0.003379	97255	329	485527	0.000677	2.723	5844908	60.099	15
20	0.001054	0.005258	96926	510	483383	0.001054	2.548	5359381	55.293	20
25	0.000930	0.004638	96417	447	480984	0.000930	2.541	4875998	50.572	25
30	0.001249	0.006226	95970	598	478415	0.001249	2.601	4395014	45.796	30
35	0.001553	0.007738	95372	738	475169	0.001553	2.708	3916599	41.067	35
40	0.002839	0.014102	94634	1335	470030	0.002839	2.647	3441430	36.366	40
45	0.003619	0.018005	93299	1680	462550	0.003632	2.650	2971400	31.848	45
50	0.005620	0.027780	91620	2545	452215	0.005628	2.688	2508850	27.383	50
55	0.009133	0.044704	89074	3982	436011	0.009133	2.649	2056635	23.089	55
60	0.013060	0.063417	85092	5396	413202	0.013060	2.728	1620624	19.045	60
65	0.026307	0.124075	79696	9888	375091	0.026362	2.635	1207422	15.150	65
70	0.036510	0.168810	69808	11784	321241	0.036684	2.641	832331	11.923	70
75	0.071588	0.307904	58024	17866	246754	0.072403	2.573	511091	8.808	75
80	0.116222	0.448862	40158	18025	155094	0.116222	2.465	264337	6.582	80
85	0.202599	1.000000	22133	22133	109243	0.135790	4.936	109243	4.936	85

TABLE 4 OBSERVED VITAL RATES AND RATIOS

CRUDE RATES

Per Thousand	BOTH SEXES	MALES	FEMALES
BIRTH RATE	13.01	13.37	12.66
DEATH RATE	12.25	13.75	10.81
RATE OF INCREASE	0.76	-0.38	1.85

PERCENT OF POPULATION IN AGE GROUP

	BOTH SEXES	MALES	FEMALES
UNDER 15	22.01	22.87	21.18
15 - 64	65.42	66.37	64.51
65 AND OLDER	12.57	10.77	14.32

RATES STANDARDIZED ON USA 1980

Per Thousand	BOTH SEXES	MALES	FEMALES
BIRTH RATE	16.75		16.15
DEATH RATE	11.96	12.66	11.31
RATE OF INCREASE	4.79		4.84

RATES STANDARDIZED ON MEXICO 1980

	BOTH SEXES	MALES	FEMALES
BIRTH RATE	14.96		14.94
DEATH RATE	4.99	5.87	4.09
RATE OF INCREASE	9.97		10.85

VITAL STATISTICS

GFR x 1000	54.651
TFR	1.964
GRR	0.974
NRR	0.936
μ	27.129
σ^2	33.593
GENERATION	27.170
POP. SEX RATIO	1.037
SEX RATIO AT BIRTH	1.018
DEP. RATIO x 100	52.859

PROJECTED POPULATION

AGE GROUP	1975 BOTH SEXES	1975 MALES	1975 FEMALES	1980 BOTH SEXES	1980 MALES	1980 FEMALES
0-4	22	11	11	22	11	11
5-9	23	12	11	22	11	11
10-14	26	13	13	23	12	11
15-19	25	13	12	26	13	13
20-24	24	12	12	25	13	12
25-29	23	12	11	24	12	12
30-34	23	12	11	23	12	11
35-39	23	12	11	22	11	11
40-44	23	12	11	23	12	11
45-49	24	12	12	23	12	11
50-54	20	9	11	24	12	12
55-59	17	8	9	19	8	11
60-64	19	9	10	15	7	8
65-69	18	8	10	17	8	9
70-74	14	6	8	14	6	8
75-79	8	3	5	10	4	6
80-84	5	2	3	5	2	3
85+	3	1	2	3	1	2
TOTAL	340	167	173	340	167	173

STABLE EQUIVALENT TO ORIGINAL POPULATION

MALES Number	MALES Percent	FEMALES Number	FEMALES Percent	AGE GROUP	
12	6.7	12	6.1	0-4	
12	6.8	12	6.2	5-9	TABLE 5
12	6.9	12	6.2	10-14	
12	6.9	12	6.3	15-19	POPULATION
12	6.9	12	6.3	20-24	PROJECTED
12	7.0	12	6.4	25-29	WITH
12	7.0	12	6.4	30-34	FIXED
12	7.0	12	6.5	35-39	AGE-
12	6.9	12	6.5	40-44	SPECIFIC
12	6.8	12	6.5	45-49	BIRTH
12	6.6	12	6.4	50-54	AND
11	6.2	12	6.2	55-59	DEATH
10	5.6	11	6.0	60-64	RATES
8	4.7	10	5.5	65-69	(female
6	3.6	9	4.8	70-74	dominant,
4	2.4	7	3.7	75-79	in 000s)
2	1.3	4	2.4	80-84	
1	0.7	3	1.7	85+	
174		188		TOTAL	

VITAL RATES OF PROJECTED POPULATION

Per Thousand	1975 BOTH SEXES	1975 MALES	1975 FEMALES	1980 BOTH SEXES	1980 MALES	1980 FEMALES
BIRTH RATE	13.22	13.65	12.80	13.62	14.11	13.16
DEATH RATE	13.06	14.15	12.01	13.77	14.62	12.96
RATE OF INCREASE	0.16	-0.50	0.79	-0.15	-0.51	0.20

VITAL RATES OF STABLE POPULATION

Per Thousand	MALES	FEMALES	
BIRTH RATE	13.77	12.44	TABLE 6
DEATH RATE	16.13	14.86	PROJECTED
RATE OF INCREASE		-2.42	VITAL RATES AND RATIOS

AGE STRUCTURE OF PROJECTED POPULATION

	BOTH SEXES	MALES	FEMALES	BOTH SEXES	MALES	FEMALES
% UNDER 15	20.87	21.69	20.08	19.80	20.56	19.08
% 15-64	65.29	66.68	63.96	65.76	67.45	64.15
% 65 AND OLDER	13.85	11.63	15.96	14.44	11.99	16.77
DEPEND. RATIO x 100	53.16	49.98	56.34	52.08	48.26	55.88

STABLE AGE STRUCTURE

	MALES	FEMALES	
% UNDER 15	20.39	18.53	(female
% 15-64	66.85	63.48	dominant)
% 65 AND OLDER	12.77	17.99	
DEPEND. RATIO x 100	49.60	57.53	

AGE GROUP	FEMALE BIRTH RATES	NET MATERNITY FUNCTION	COEFF. OF MATRIX EQUATION	ORIGINAL MATRIX SUB-DIAGONAL	ORIGINAL MATRIX FIRST ROW	STABLE MATRIX FISHER VALUES	STABLE MATRIX REPRODUCTIVE VALUES	MATRIX PARAMETERS		
0-4	0.0000	0.0000	0.0000	0.99723	0.00000	1.017	11723	λ_1	0.98797	
5-9	0.0000	0.0000	0.0000	0.99869	0.00000	1.008	12751	λ_2	0.33893+0.72340i	TABLE 7
10-14	0.0000	0.0000	0.0337	0.99756	0.03388	0.997	12328	λ_4	-0.39300+0.40612i	
15-19	0.0139	0.0675	0.1907	0.99558	0.19193	0.953	11275	λ_6	0.01065+0.48852i	LESLIE
20-24	0.0649	0.3139	0.3071	0.99504	0.31045	0.749	8532	r_1	-0.00242	MATRIX
25-29	0.0624	0.3003	0.2273	0.99466	0.23098	0.427	4589	r_2	-0.04491+0.22653i	AND ITS
30-34	0.0323	0.1544	0.1158	0.99322	0.11830	0.188	2103	r_4	-0.11414+0.46796i	ANALYSIS
35-39	0.0162	0.0772	0.0496	0.98919	0.05098	0.065	759	r_6	-0.14323+0.30980i	(females)
40-44	0.0047	0.0219	0.0116	0.98409	0.01201	0.013	160	c_1	1897	
45-49	0.0003	0.0012	0.0006	0.97766	0.00063	0.001	7	$2\pi/y$	27.7367	
50-54	0.0000	0.0000	0.0000	0.00000	0.00000	0.000	0	Δ	4.9669	

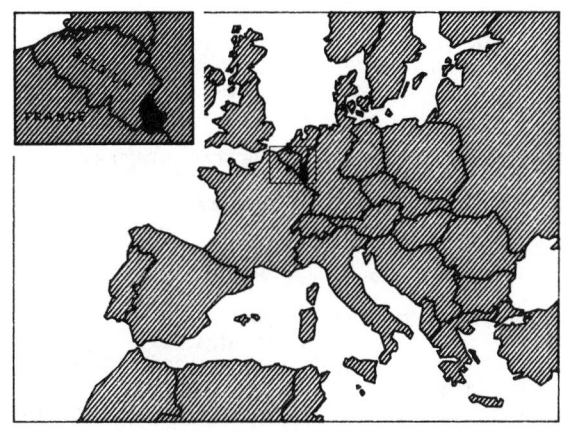

EDUCATION [1984]

% of primary school-age children enrolled:	na
secondary school-age children enrolled:	na
ca. 20-24 year olds in higher education:	na

LABOR FORCE

Average annual labor force growth (%) 1980-85:	0.4	
% of the 1980 labor force in agriculture:	6	TABLE 8
in industry		
and services:	94	SOCIO-ECONOMIC INDICATORS

GNP & INCOME DISTRIBUTION

GNP per capita (in US Dollars) 1985:	14260
GNP average annual growth rate (%) 1965-85:	4.0
% share of total household income	
Lowest 20% of households:	na
Highest 10% of households:	na

HEALTH & NUTRITION

Population per physician 1981:	na
Daily calorie supply per capita 1985:	na

AGE AT LAST BIRTHDAY	ESTIMATED MID-YEAR POPULATION					BIRTHS BY AGE OF MOTHER AND SEX	DEATHS			AGE AT LAST BIRTHDAY
	BOTH SEXES	MALES		FEMALES			BOTH SEXES	MALES	FEMALES	
		Number	Percent	Number	Percent					
0	4148	2158	1.2	1990	1.1		37	20	17	0
1-4	16995	8700	4.9	8295	4.4		13	10	3	1-4
5-9	20502	10500	5.9	10002	5.3		3	1	2	5-9
10-14	21423	11027	6.2	10396	5.5		8	5	3	10-14
15-19	25987	13199	7.4	12788	6.8	138	23	16	7	15-19
20-24	29694	14786	8.3	14908	7.9	1087	33	28	5	20-24
25-29	30529	15153	8.5	15376	8.2	1619	35	23	12	25-29
30-34	29506	14920	8.4	14586	7.7	970	34	16	18	30-34
35-39	27600	14400	8.1	13200	7.0	256	38	28	10	35-39
40-44	23887	12303	6.9	11584	6.1	31	76	41	35	40-44
45-49	23518	11934	6.7	11584	6.1	3	83	62	21	45-49
50-54	23164	11647	6.5	11517	6.1		141	93	48	50-54
55-59	22970	11286	6.3	11684	6.2		239	160	79	55-59
60-64	18190	7619	4.3	10571	5.6		272	165	107	60-64
65-69	13437	5797	3.3	7640	4.1		346	214	132	65-69
70-74	14411	5816	3.3	8595	4.6		596	323	273	70-74
75-79	11123	4070	2.3	7053	3.7		727	387	340	75-79
80-84	6444	2067	1.2	4377	2.3	2122 M	678	277	401	80-84
85+	3147	893	0.5	2254	1.2	1982 F	645	225	420	85+
TOTAL	366675	178275		188400		4104	4027	2094	1933	TOTAL

TABLE 1 DATA

TABLE 2 — MALE LIFE TABLE

x	nM_x	nq_x	l_x	nd_x	nL_x	nm_x	na_x	T_x	$\overset{\circ}{e}_x$	x
0	0.009268	0.009190	100000	919	99160	0.009268	0.086	7021380	70.214	0
1	0.001149	0.004585	99081	454	395188	0.001149	1.500	6922220	69.864	1
5	0.000095	0.000476	98627	47	493016	0.000095	2.500	6527031	66.179	5
10	0.000453	0.002265	98580	223	492455	0.000453	3.011	6034015	61.209	10
15	0.001212	0.006044	98357	595	490442	0.001212	2.745	5541560	56.342	15
20	0.001894	0.009424	97762	921	486535	0.001894	2.531	5051118	51.668	20
25	0.001518	0.007559	96841	732	482288	0.001518	2.384	4564583	47.135	25
30	0.001072	0.005348	96109	514	479299	0.001072	2.579	4082295	42.476	30
35	0.001944	0.009708	95595	928	475873	0.001950	2.737	3602996	37.690	35
40	0.003333	0.016594	94667	1571	469710	0.003344	2.694	3127123	33.033	40
45	0.005195	0.025689	93096	2392	459913	0.005200	2.673	2657413	28.545	45
50	0.007985	0.039208	90704	3556	445382	0.007985	2.711	2197500	24.227	50
55	0.014177	0.068864	87148	6001	421749	0.014230	2.669	1752118	20.105	55
60	0.021656	0.103801	81146	8423	385994	0.021822	2.657	1330369	16.395	60
65	0.036916	0.169598	72723	12334	334106	0.036916	2.607	944375	12.986	65
70	0.055536	0.244705	60390	14778	266089	0.055536	2.573	610269	10.106	70
75	0.095086	0.384565	45612	17541	184036	0.095312	2.490	344180	7.546	75
80	0.134011	0.496979	28071	13951	104102	0.134011	2.401	160144	5.705	80
85	0.251960	1.000000	14120	14120	56042	0.195053	3.969	56042	3.969	85

TABLE 3 — FEMALE LIFE TABLE

x	nM_x	nq_x	l_x	nd_x	nL_x	nm_x	na_x	T_x	$\overset{\circ}{e}_x$	x
0	0.008543	0.008476	100000	848	99224	0.008543	0.085	7713461	77.135	0
1	0.000362	0.001445	99152	143	396251	0.000362	1.500	7614237	76.793	1
5	0.000200	0.000999	99009	99	494798	0.000200	2.500	7217986	72.902	5
10	0.000289	0.001442	98910	143	494230	0.000289	2.750	6723188	67.973	10
15	0.000547	0.002733	98767	270	493167	0.000547	2.517	6228958	63.067	15
20	0.000335	0.001676	98498	165	492099	0.000335	2.643	5735791	58.233	20
25	0.000780	0.003895	98332	383	490796	0.000780	2.738	5243692	53.326	25
30	0.001234	0.006152	97949	603	488238	0.001234	2.496	4752896	48.524	30
35	0.000758	0.003812	97347	371	485985	0.000764	2.980	4264658	43.809	35
40	0.003021	0.015026	96976	1457	481338	0.003027	2.570	3778673	38.965	40
45	0.001813	0.009027	95519	862	475541	0.001813	2.620	3297335	34.520	45
50	0.004168	0.020644	94656	1954	468860	0.004168	2.737	2821794	29.811	50
55	0.006761	0.033282	92702	3085	456320	0.006761	2.669	2352934	25.382	55
60	0.010122	0.049751	89617	4459	437773	0.010185	2.687	1896614	21.164	60
65	0.017277	0.083282	85158	7092	409535	0.017318	2.708	1458842	17.131	65
70	0.031763	0.147706	78066	11531	363031	0.031763	2.632	1049307	13.441	70
75	0.048206	0.216744	66535	14421	298288	0.048346	2.615	686276	10.314	75
80	0.091615	0.374563	52114	19520	213066	0.091615	2.566	387988	7.445	80
85	0.186335	1.000000	32594	32594	174922	0.117972	5.367	174922	5.367	85

TABLE 4 — OBSERVED VITAL RATES AND RATIOS

CRUDE RATES					RATES STANDARDIZED ON USA 1980				VITAL STATISTICS	
Per Thousand	BOTH SEXES	MALES	FEMALES		Per Thousand	BOTH SEXES	MALES	FEMALES	GFR x 1000	43.648
BIRTH RATE	11.19	11.90	10.52		BIRTH RATE	11.78		11.06	TFR	1.389
DEATH RATE	10.98	11.75	10.26		DEATH RATE	9.62	10.52	8.77	GRR	0.671
RATE OF INCREASE	0.21	0.16	0.26		RATE OF INCREASE	2.16		2.29	NRR	0.658
									μ	27.836
PERCENT OF POPULATION IN AGE GROUP					RATES STANDARDIZED ON MEXICO 1980				σ^2	25.753
									GENERATION	28.028
UNDER 15	17.20	18.17	16.29		BIRTH RATE	10.21		9.93	POP. SEX RATIO	1.057
15 - 64	69.56	71.38	67.83		DEATH RATE	3.68	4.48	2.86	SEX RATIO AT BIRTH	1.071
65 AND OLDER	13.24	10.46	15.88		RATE OF INCREASE	6.53		7.07	DEP. RATIO x 100	43.769

PROJECTED POPULATION

AGE GROUP	1990 BOTH SEXES	1990 MALES	1990 FEMALES	1995 BOTH SEXES	1995 MALES	1995 FEMALES
0-4	20	10	10	19	10	9
5-9	21	11	10	20	10	10
10-14	20	10	10	21	11	10
15-19	21	11	10	20	10	10
20-24	26	13	13	21	11	10
25-29	30	15	15	26	13	13
30-34	30	15	15	30	15	15
35-39	30	15	15	30	15	15
40-44	27	14	13	29	15	14
45-49	23	12	11	27	14	13
50-54	23	12	11	23	12	11
55-59	22	11	11	22	11	11
60-64	21	10	11	21	10	11
65-69	17	7	10	19	9	10
70-74	12	5	7	14	5	9
75-79	11	4	7	9	3	6
80-84	7	2	5	7	2	5
85+	5	1	4	5	1	4
TOTAL	366	178	188	363	177	186

STABLE EQUIVALENT TO ORIGINAL POPULATION

AGE GROUP	MALES Number	MALES Percent	FEMALES Number	FEMALES Percent	AGE GROUP
0-4	11	4.0	10	3.4	0-4
5-9	11	4.3	11	3.7	5-9
10-14	12	4.6	12	4.0	10-14
15-19	13	4.9	12	4.3	15-19
20-24	14	5.3	13	4.6	20-24
25-29	15	5.6	14	4.9	25-29
30-34	16	6.0	15	5.3	30-34
35-39	17	6.4	17	5.7	35-39
40-44	18	6.8	18	6.1	40-44
45-49	19	7.2	19	6.4	45-49
50-54	20	7.5	20	6.9	50-54
55-59	21	7.7	21	7.2	55-59
60-64	20	7.6	22	7.4	60-64
65-69	19	7.1	22	7.5	65-69
70-74	16	6.1	21	7.1	70-74
75-79	12	4.5	18	6.3	75-79
80-84	7	2.8	14	4.9	80-84
85+	4	1.6	13	4.3	85+
TOTAL	265		292		TOTAL

TABLE 5

POPULATION PROJECTED WITH FIXED AGE-SPECIFIC BIRTH AND DEATH RATES (female dominant, in 000s)

VITAL RATES OF PROJECTED POPULATION

Per Thousand	1990 BOTH SEXES	1990 MALES	1990 FEMALES	1995 BOTH SEXES	1995 MALES	1995 FEMALES
BIRTH RATE	10.76	11.46	10.11	9.71	10.32	9.13
DEATH RATE	12.07	12.32	11.83	12.65	12.80	12.50
RATE OF INCREASE	-1.30	-0.86	-1.72	-2.94	-2.48	-3.37

VITAL RATES OF STABLE POPULATION

Per Thousand	MALES	FEMALES
BIRTH RATE	7.73	6.67
DEATH RATE	22.52	21.59
RATE OF INCREASE		-14.92

TABLE 6

PROJECTED VITAL RATES AND RATIOS (female dominant)

AGE STRUCTURE OF PROJECTED POPULATION

	1990 BOTH SEXES	1990 MALES	1990 FEMALES	1995 BOTH SEXES	1995 MALES	1995 FEMALES
% UNDER 15	16.78	17.75	15.86	16.38	17.34	15.46
% 15-64	69.30	71.77	66.96	68.50	70.83	66.29
% 65 AND OLDER	13.92	10.48	17.17	15.13	11.84	18.25
DEPEND. RATIO x 100	44.30	39.33	49.33	45.99	41.19	50.85

STABLE AGE STRUCTURE

	MALES	FEMALES
% UNDER 15	12.82	11.10
% 15-64	65.16	58.75
% 65 AND OLDER	22.02	30.15
DEPEND. RATIO x 100	53.48	70.21

MATRIX PARAMETERS / LESLIE MATRIX AND ITS ANALYSIS

AGE GROUP	FEMALE BIRTH RATES	NET MATERNITY FUNCTION	COEFF. OF MATRIX EQUATION	ORIGINAL MATRIX SUB-DIAGONAL	ORIGINAL MATRIX FIRST ROW	STABLE MATRIX FISHER VALUES	STABLE MATRIX REPRODUCTIVE VALUES
0-4	0.0000	0.0000	0.0000	0.99863	0.00000	0.972	9998
5-9	0.0000	0.0000	0.0000	0.99885	0.00000	0.903	9036
10-14	0.0000	0.0000	0.0129	0.99785	0.01288	0.839	8727
15-19	0.0052	0.0257	0.0995	0.99783	0.09996	0.768	9824
20-24	0.0352	0.1733	0.2114	0.99735	0.21288	0.617	9200
25-29	0.0509	0.2496	0.2032	0.99479	0.20513	0.367	5640
30-34	0.0321	0.1568	0.1012	0.99538	0.10266	0.142	2068
35-39	0.0094	0.0455	0.0259	0.99044	0.02637	0.032	421
40-44	0.0013	0.0062	0.0034	0.98796	0.00351	0.004	47
45-49	0.0001	0.0006	0.0003	0.98595	0.00031	0.000	4
50-54	0.0000	0.0000	0.0000	0.00000	0.00000	0.000	0

λ_1 0.92810
λ_2 0.37711+0.71342i
λ_4 -0.23003-0.50754i
λ_6 -0.36231-0.20149i
r_1 -0.01492
r_2 -0.04290+0.21691i
r_4 -0.11695-0.39927i
r_6 -0.17610-0.52681i
c_1 2908
$2\pi/y$ 28.9673
Δ 18.1043

TABLE 7

LESLIE MATRIX AND ITS ANALYSIS (females)

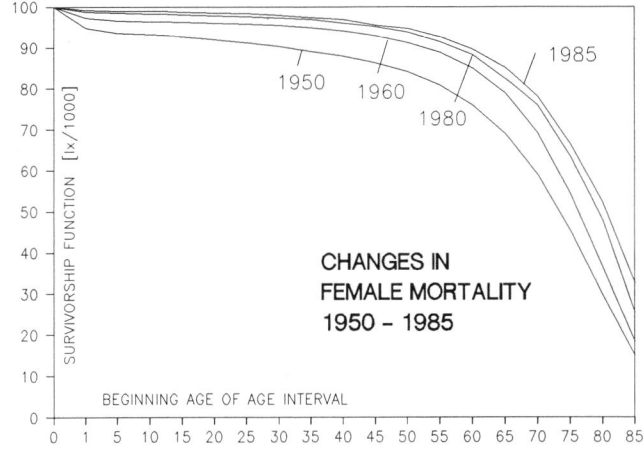

CHANGES IN FEMALE MORTALITY 1950 – 1985

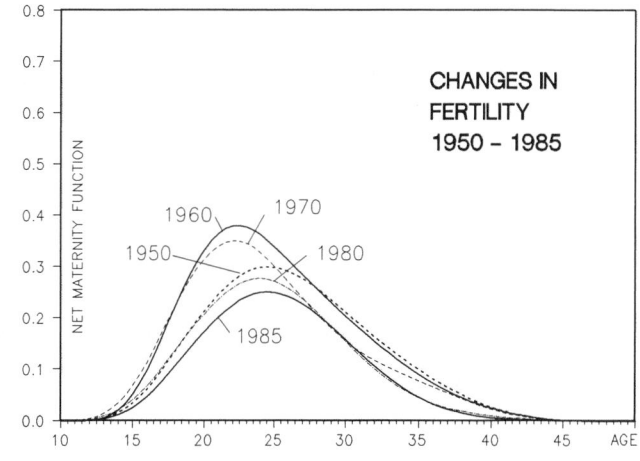

CHANGES IN FERTILITY 1950 – 1985

TABLE 1 — DATA

AGE AT LAST BIRTHDAY	ESTIMATED MID-YEAR POPULATION BOTH SEXES	MALES Number	MALES Percent	FEMALES Number	FEMALES Percent	BIRTHS BY AGE OF MOTHER AND SEX	DEATHS BOTH SEXES	DEATHS MALES	DEATHS FEMALES	AGE AT LAST BIRTHDAY
0	5138	2664	1.7	2474	1.5		148	86	62	0
1-4	25210	12962	8.3	12248	7.2		7	3	4	1-4
5-9	24888	12851	8.2	12037	7.1		6	5	1	5-9
10-14	34834	17671	11.3	17163	10.1		14	7	7	10-14
15-19	34082	17093	11.0	16989	10.0	227	23	17	6	15-19
20-24	32899	15573	10.0	17326	10.2	1766	17	14	3	20-24
25-29	22174	9898	6.4	12276	7.2	1614	17	15	2	25-29
30-34	20072	8944	5.7	11128	6.6	984	13	8	5	30-34
35-39	18962	8353	5.4	10609	6.3	548	23	16	7	35-39
40-44	18037	8283	5.3	9754	5.7	162	44	26	18	40-44
45-49	17797	8467	5.4	9330	5.5	13	69	46	23	45-49
50-54	14262	6838	4.4	7424	4.4		93	58	35	50-54
55-59	13667	6524	4.2	7143	4.2		176	114	62	55-59
60-64	14097	6641	4.3	7456	4.4		320	181	139	60-64
65-69	11872	5417	3.5	6455	3.8		431	247	184	65-69
70-74	8104	3658	2.3	4446	2.6		457	235	222	70-74
75-79	5529	2361	1.5	3168	1.9		501	235	266	75-79
80-84	2486	1046	0.7	1440	0.8	2782 N	393	185	208	80-84
85+	1459	609	0.4	850	0.5	2532 F	318	121	197	85+
TOTAL	325569	155853		169716		5314	3070	1619	1451	TOTAL

TABLE 2 — MALE LIFE TABLE

x	$_nM_x$	$_nq_x$	l_x	$_nd_x$	$_nL_x$	$_nm_x$	$_na_x$	T_x	$\overset{\circ}{e}_x$	x
0	0.032282	0.031395	100000	3140	97253	0.032282	0.125	6793900	67.939	0
1	0.000231	0.000925	96860	90	387218	0.000231	1.500	6696647	69.137	1
5	0.000389	0.001943	96771	188	483384	0.000389	2.500	6309429	65.200	5
10	0.000396	0.001979	96583	191	482497	0.000396	2.816	5826045	60.322	10
15	0.000995	0.004962	96392	478	480812	0.000995	2.604	5343549	55.436	15
20	0.000899	0.004493	95913	431	478540	0.000901	2.618	4862736	50.699	20
25	0.001515	0.007559	95482	722	475606	0.001518	2.498	4384196	45.916	25
30	0.000894	0.004465	94761	423	472783	0.000895	2.589	3908590	41.247	30
35	0.001915	0.009562	94338	902	469648	0.001921	2.739	3435807	36.420	35
40	0.003139	0.015583	93435	1456	463864	0.003139	2.725	2966160	31.746	40
45	0.005433	0.026875	91979	2472	454193	0.005443	2.693	2502295	27.205	45
50	0.008482	0.041818	89507	3743	439165	0.008523	2.763	2048102	22.882	50
55	0.017474	0.083970	85764	7202	412134	0.017474	2.683	1608937	18.760	55
60	0.027255	0.128047	78563	10060	369099	0.027255	2.643	1196803	15.234	60
65	0.045597	0.205669	68503	14089	308345	0.045691	2.575	827704	12.083	65
70	0.064243	0.277594	54414	15105	234647	0.064374	2.522	519359	9.545	70
75	0.099534	0.399619	39309	15709	157092	0.099997	2.488	284712	7.243	75
80	0.176864	0.602988	23601	14231	80462	0.176864	2.362	127620	5.408	80
85	0.198686	1.000000	9370	9370	47158	0.133233	5.033	47158	5.033	85

TABLE 3 — FEMALE LIFE TABLE

x	$_nM_x$	$_nq_x$	l_x	$_nd_x$	$_nL_x$	$_nm_x$	$_na_x$	T_x	$\overset{\circ}{e}_x$	x
0	0.025061	0.024515	100000	2452	97825	0.025061	0.113	7285127	72.851	0
1	0.000327	0.001305	97548	127	389876	0.000327	1.500	7187303	73.679	1
5	0.000083	0.000415	97421	40	487004	0.000083	2.500	6797427	69.774	5
10	0.000408	0.002037	97381	198	486435	0.000408	2.638	6310423	64.802	10
15	0.000353	0.001764	97182	171	485459	0.000353	2.360	5823988	59.929	15
20	0.000173	0.000860	97011	83	484826	0.000172	2.269	5338529	55.030	20
25	0.000163	0.000818	96927	79	484467	0.000164	2.855	4853703	50.076	25
30	0.000449	0.002255	96848	218	483745	0.000451	2.730	4369236	45.114	30
35	0.000660	0.003315	96630	320	482487	0.000664	2.935	3885491	40.210	35
40	0.001845	0.009205	96309	887	479509	0.001849	2.701	3403003	35.334	40
45	0.002465	0.012310	95423	1175	474454	0.002476	2.735	2923494	30.637	45
50	0.004714	0.023485	94248	2213	466279	0.004747	2.758	2449040	25.985	50
55	0.008680	0.042586	92035	3919	451555	0.008680	2.801	1982761	21.544	55
60	0.018643	0.089350	88115	7873	422317	0.018643	2.681	1531206	17.377	60
65	0.028505	0.133982	80242	10751	375933	0.028598	2.649	1108889	13.819	65
70	0.049933	0.223744	69491	15548	310276	0.050111	2.609	732956	10.547	70
75	0.083965	0.349712	53943	18864	223161	0.084533	2.532	422680	7.836	75
80	0.144444	0.526407	35078	18466	127838	0.144444	2.425	199519	5.688	80
85	0.231765	1.000000	16613	16613	71680	0.170085	4.315	71680	4.315	85

TABLE 4 — OBSERVED VITAL RATES AND RATIOS

CRUDE RATES

Per Thousand	BOTH SEXES	MALES	FEMALES
BIRTH RATE	16.32	17.85	14.92
DEATH RATE	9.43	10.39	8.55
RATE OF INCREASE	6.89	7.46	6.37

RATES STANDARDIZED ON USA 1980

Per Thousand	BOTH SEXES	MALES	FEMALES
BIRTH RATE	16.66		15.44
DEATH RATE	12.34	11.83	12.83
RATE OF INCREASE	4.32		2.61

VITAL STATISTICS

GFR x 1000	60.793
TFR	2.024
GRR	0.965
NRR	0.934
μ	28.949
σ^2	36.192
GENERATION	28.992
POP. SEX RATIO	1.089
SEX RATIO AT BIRTH	1.099
DEP. RATIO x 100	58.006

PERCENT OF POPULATION IN AGE GROUP

	BOTH SEXES	MALES	FEMALES
UNDER 15	27.67	29.61	25.88
15 - 64	63.29	61.99	64.48
65 AND OLDER	9.05	8.40	9.64

RATES STANDARDIZED ON MEXICO 1980

	BOTH SEXES	MALES	FEMALES
BIRTH RATE	14.34		13.77
DEATH RATE	4.82	5.38	4.24
RATE OF INCREASE	9.52		9.52

PROJECTED POPULATION

AGE GROUP	1975			1980			STABLE EQUIVALENT TO ORIGINAL POPULATION				AGE GROUP	
							MALES		FEMALES			
	BOTH SEXES	MALES	FEMALES	BOTH SEXES	MALES	FEMALES	Number	Percent	Number	Percent		
0-4	27	14	13	31	16	15	16	6.6	15	6.1	0-4	
5-9	31	16	15	27	14	13	16	6.6	15	6.2	5-9	TABLE 5
10-14	25	13	12	31	16	15	16	6.7	15	6.3	10-14	
15-19	35	18	17	25	13	12	16	6.8	15	6.3	15-19	POPULATION
20-24	34	17	17	35	18	17	16	6.8	15	6.4	20-24	PROJECTED
25-29	32	15	17	34	17	17	17	6.8	15	6.5	25-29	WITH
30-34	22	10	12	32	15	17	17	6.9	15	6.5	30-34	FIXED
35-39	20	9	11	22	10	12	17	6.9	16	6.6	35-39	AGE-
40-44	19	8	11	20	9	11	17	6.9	16	6.6	40-44	SPECIFIC
45-49	18	8	10	18	8	10	17	6.9	16	6.6	45-49	BIRTH
50-54	17	8	9	17	8	9	16	6.7	16	6.6	50-54	AND
55-59	13	6	7	17	8	9	15	6.4	15	6.5	55-59	DEATH
60-64	13	6	7	13	6	7	14	5.8	15	6.1	60-64	RATES
65-69	13	6	7	11	5	6	12	4.9	13	5.5	65-69	(female
70-74	9	4	5	9	4	5	9	3.8	11	4.6	70-74	dominant,
75-79	5	2	3	7	3	4	6	2.5	8	3.4	75-79	in 000s)
80-84	3	1	2	3	1	2	3	1.3	5	1.9	80-84	
85+	2	1	1	2	1	1	2	0.8	3	1.1	85+	
TOTAL	338	162	176	354	172	182	242		239		TOTAL	

VITAL RATES OF PROJECTED POPULATION

Per Thousand	1975			1980			VITAL RATES OF STABLE POPULATION			
	BOTH SEXES	MALES	FEMALES	BOTH SEXES	MALES	FEMALES	MALES	FEMALES		
BIRTH RATE	17.98	19.60	16.48	18.39	19.96	16.92	13.48	12.51		TABLE 6
DEATH RATE	9.52	10.36	8.74	9.65	10.27	9.07	15.75	14.89		PROJECTED
RATE OF INCREASE	8.46	9.23	7.74	8.74	9.69	7.86		-2.37		VITAL RATES

AGE STRUCTURE OF PROJECTED POPULATION

	BOTH SEXES	MALES	FEMALES	BOTH SEXES	MALES	FEMALES	STABLE AGE STRUCTURE			AND RATIOS
							MALES	FEMALES		(female
% UNDER 15	24.49	26.39	22.74	25.05	26.97	23.26	19.90	18.62		dominant)
% 15-64	66.13	65.03	67.14	65.90	64.91	66.83	66.82	64.84		
% 65 AND OLDER	9.38	8.58	10.12	9.05	8.12	9.91	13.28	16.54		
DEPEND. RATIO x 100	51.23	53.78	48.94	51.74	54.07	49.63	49.66	54.21		

AGE GROUP	FEMALE BIRTH RATES	NET MATERNITY FUNCTION	COEFF. OF MATRIX EQUATION	ORIGINAL MATRIX		STABLE MATRIX		MATRIX PARAMETERS		
				SUB-DIAGONAL	FIRST ROW	FISHER VALUES	REPRODUCTIVE VALUES			
0-4	0.0000	0.0000	0.0000	0.99857	0.00000	1.019	15004	λ_1	0.98821	
5-9	0.0000	0.0000	0.0000	0.99883	0.00000	1.009	12140	λ_2	0.41018+0.71366i	TABLE 7
10-14	0.0000	0.0000	0.0155	0.99799	0.01549	0.998	17126	λ_4	-0.38514-0.42178i	
15-19	0.0064	0.0309	0.1332	0.99870	0.13380	0.972	16518	λ_6	-0.02552+0.55371i	LESLIE
20-24	0.0486	0.2355	0.2695	0.99926	0.27108	0.826	14303	r_1	-0.00237	MATRIX
25-29	0.0626	0.3035	0.2537	0.99851	0.25535	0.540	6628	r_2	-0.03893+0.20983i	AND ITS
30-34	0.0421	0.2038	0.1613	0.99740	0.16260	0.274	3046	r_4	-0.11202-0.46216i	ANALYSIS
35-39	0.0246	0.1188	0.0783	0.99383	0.07919	0.105	1114	r_6	-0.11801+0.32337i	(females)
40-44	0.0079	0.0379	0.0205	0.98946	0.02090	0.023	227	c_1	2369	
45-49	0.0007	0.0031	0.0016	0.98277	0.00162	0.002	16	$2\pi/y$	29.9441	
50-54	0.0000	0.0000	0.0000	0.00000	0.00000	0.000	0	Δ	15.5290	

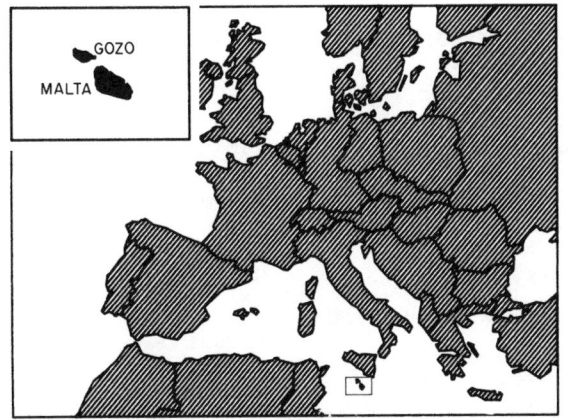

EDUCATION [1984]

% of primary school-age children enrolled:	na
secondary school-age children enrolled:	na
ca. 20-24 year olds in higher education:	na

LABOR FORCE

Average annual labor force growth (%) 1980-85:	1.1	
% of the 1980 labor force in agriculture:	5	TABLE 8
in industry		
and services:	95	SOCIO-

GNP & INCOME DISTRIBUTION

GNP per capita (in US Dollars) 1985:	3310	INDICATORS
GNP average annual growth rate (%) 1965-85:	8.1	
% share of total household income		
Lowest 20% of households:	na	
Highest 10% of households:	na	

HEALTH & NUTRITION

Population per physician 1981:	na
Daily calorie supply per capita 1985:	na

Table 1 — DATA

AGE AT LAST BIRTHDAY	ESTIMATED MID-YEAR POPULATION BOTH SEXES	MALES Number	MALES Percent	FEMALES Number	FEMALES Percent	BIRTHS BY AGE OF MOTHER AND SEX	DEATHS BOTH SEXES	DEATHS MALES	DEATHS FEMALES	AGE AT LAST BIRTHDAY
0	5323	2722	1.6	2601	1.5		53	27	26	0
1-4	22412	11458	6.8	10954	6.3		10	6	4	1-4
5-9	28321	14634	8.6	13687	7.8		10	9	1	5-9
10-14	26953	13898	8.2	13055	7.5		5	4	1	10-14
15-19	23994	12341	7.3	11653	6.7	147	8	6	2	15-19
20-24	26467	13634	8.0	12833	7.3	1070	17	12	5	20-24
25-29	28770	14552	8.6	14218	8.1	2000	21	14	7	25-29
30-34	27603	13873	8.2	13730	7.8	1275	13	10	3	30-34
35-39	29709	14781	8.7	14928	8.5	624	27	16	11	35-39
40-44	23023	11287	6.7	11736	6.7	123	34	19	15	40-44
45-49	18447	8770	5.2	9677	5.5	6	51	30	21	45-49
50-54	18020	8314	4.9	9706	5.5		67	46	21	50-54
55-59	16073	7393	4.4	8680	5.0		155	95	60	55-59
60-64	15335	7116	4.2	8219	4.7		214	136	78	60-64
65-69	11653	5406	3.2	6247	3.6		303	181	122	65-69
70-74	9210	4122	2.4	5088	2.9		407	207	200	70-74
75-79	7340	3131	1.8	4209	2.4		530	284	246	75-79
80-84	3869	1482	0.9	2387	1.4	2778 M	445	194	251	80-84
85+	2003	679	0.4	1324	0.8	2467 F	454	158	296	85+
TOTAL	344525	169593		174932		5245	2824	1454	1370	TOTAL

Table 2 — MALE LIFE TABLE

x	$_nM_x$	$_nq_x$	l_x	$_nd_x$	$_nL_x$	$_nm_x$	$_na_x$	T_x	$\overset{\circ}{e}_x$	x
0	0.009919	0.009830	100000	983	99102	0.009919	0.087	7238520	72.385	0
1	0.000524	0.002092	99017	207	395550	0.000524	1.500	7139418	72.103	1
5	0.000615	0.003070	98810	303	493291	0.000615	2.500	6743868	68.251	5
10	0.000288	0.001435	98506	141	492166	0.000287	2.405	6250577	63.453	10
15	0.000486	0.002431	98365	239	491288	0.000487	2.752	5758411	58.541	15
20	0.000880	0.004392	98126	431	489600	0.000880	2.611	5267123	53.677	20
25	0.000962	0.004799	97695	469	487286	0.000962	2.464	4777523	48.902	25
30	0.000721	0.003598	97226	350	485268	0.000721	2.533	4290236	44.126	30
35	0.001082	0.005408	96876	524	483169	0.001084	2.685	3804968	39.277	35
40	0.001683	0.008466	96352	816	479954	0.001700	2.783	3321799	34.475	40
45	0.003421	0.017099	95537	1634	473967	0.003447	2.725	2841844	29.746	45
50	0.005533	0.027481	93903	2581	463913	0.005563	2.829	2367877	25.216	50
55	0.012850	0.062480	91323	5706	443445	0.012867	2.692	1903964	20.849	55
60	0.019112	0.091602	85617	7843	409811	0.019137	2.670	1460520	17.059	60
65	0.033481	0.155695	77774	12109	360030	0.033633	2.618	1050709	13.510	65
70	0.050218	0.224118	65665	14717	292949	0.050236	2.596	690679	10.518	70
75	0.090706	0.371030	50948	18903	207680	0.091022	2.510	397730	7.807	75
80	0.130904	0.488750	32045	15662	119645	0.130904	2.409	190050	5.931	80
85	0.232695	1.000000	16383	16383	70405	0.171323	4.297	70405	4.297	85

Table 3 — FEMALE LIFE TABLE

x	$_nM_x$	$_nq_x$	l_x	$_nd_x$	$_nL_x$	$_nm_x$	$_na_x$	T_x	$\overset{\circ}{e}_x$	x
0	0.009996	0.009906	100000	991	99096	0.009996	0.087	7694422	76.944	0
1	0.000365	0.001459	99009	144	395676	0.000365	1.500	7595327	76.713	1
5	0.000073	0.000365	98865	36	494234	0.000073	2.500	7199650	72.823	5
10	0.000077	0.000384	98829	38	494059	0.000077	2.767	6705416	67.849	10
15	0.000172	0.000859	98791	85	493774	0.000172	2.878	6211356	62.874	15
20	0.000390	0.001946	98706	192	493082	0.000390	2.670	5717582	57.925	20
25	0.000492	0.002459	98514	242	491946	0.000492	2.427	5224500	53.033	25
30	0.000218	0.001092	98272	107	491115	0.000218	2.732	4732554	48.158	30
35	0.000737	0.003685	98164	362	490026	0.000738	2.800	4241439	43.208	35
40	0.001278	0.006422	97803	628	487586	0.001288	2.729	3751413	38.357	40
45	0.002170	0.010820	97175	1051	483330	0.002175	2.582	3263827	33.587	45
50	0.002164	0.010818	96123	1040	478472	0.002173	2.939	2780497	28.926	50
55	0.006912	0.034094	95083	3242	467988	0.006927	2.708	2302025	24.211	55
60	0.009490	0.046642	91841	4284	449543	0.009529	2.744	1834037	19.970	60
65	0.019529	0.094292	87558	8256	419229	0.019693	2.752	1384494	15.812	65
70	0.039308	0.179924	79302	14268	362593	0.039351	2.623	965265	12.172	70
75	0.058446	0.256504	65033	16681	284698	0.058593	2.574	602672	9.267	75
80	0.105153	0.417561	48352	20190	192005	0.105153	2.536	317974	6.576	80
85	0.223565	1.000000	28162	28162	125969	0.159848	4.473	125969	4.473	85

Table 4 — OBSERVED VITAL RATES AND RATIOS

CRUDE RATES

Per Thousand	BOTH SEXES	MALES	FEMALES
BIRTH RATE	15.22	16.38	14.10
DEATH RATE	8.20	8.57	7.83
RATE OF INCREASE	7.03	7.81	6.27

RATES STANDARDIZED ON USA 1980

Per Thousand	BOTH SEXES	MALES	FEMALES
BIRTH RATE	15.84		14.49
DEATH RATE	9.52	9.26	9.77
RATE OF INCREASE	6.32		4.72

VITAL STATISTICS

GFR x 1000	59.082
TFR	1.912
GRR	0.899
NRR	0.884
μ	28.817
σ^2	30.752
GENERATION	28.882
POP. SEX RATIO	1.031
SEX RATIO AT BIRTH	1.126
DEP. RATIO x 100	51.479

PERCENT OF POPULATION IN AGE GROUP

	BOTH SEXES	MALES	FEMALES
UNDER 15	24.09	25.19	23.04
15 - 64	66.02	66.08	65.96
65 AND OLDER	9.89	8.74	11.01

RATES STANDARDIZED ON MEXICO 1980

	BOTH SEXES	MALES	FEMALES
BIRTH RATE	13.54		12.84
DEATH RATE	3.36	3.80	2.92
RATE OF INCREASE	10.19		9.92

PROJECTED POPULATION

AGE GROUP	1991 BOTH SEXES	1991 MALES	1991 FEMALES	1996 BOTH SEXES	1996 MALES	1996 FEMALES
0-4	25	13	12	24	13	11
5-9	28	14	14	25	13	12
10-14	29	15	14	28	14	14
15-19	27	14	13	29	15	14
20-24	24	12	12	27	14	13
25-29	27	14	13	24	12	12
30-34	28	14	14	27	14	13
35-39	28	14	14	28	14	14
40-44	30	15	15	28	14	14
45-49	23	11	12	30	15	15
50-54	19	9	10	23	11	12
55-59	17	8	9	17	8	9
60-64	15	7	8	16	7	9
65-69	14	6	8	14	6	8
70-74	9	4	5	12	5	7
75-79	7	3	4	7	3	4
80-84	5	2	3	5	2	3
85+	3	1	2	3	1	2
TOTAL	358	176	182	367	181	186

STABLE EQUIVALENT TO ORIGINAL POPULATION

MALES Number	MALES Percent	FEMALES Number	FEMALES Percent	AGE GROUP	
14	5.9	13	5.5	0-4	
14	6.0	13	5.6	5-9	TABLE 5
15	6.1	13	5.7	10-14	
15	6.2	13	5.8	15-19	POPULATION
15	6.3	14	5.9	20-24	PROJECTED
15	6.4	14	6.0	25-29	WITH
16	6.5	14	6.2	30-34	FIXED
16	6.6	14	6.3	35-39	AGE-
16	6.7	15	6.4	40-44	SPECIFIC
16	6.8	15	6.5	45-49	BIRTH
16	6.8	15	6.5	50-54	AND
16	6.6	15	6.5	55-59	DEATH
15	6.3	15	6.4	60-64	RATES
14	5.6	14	6.1	65-69	(female
11	4.7	12	5.4	70-74	dominant,
8	3.4	10	4.3	75-79	in 000s)
5	2.0	7	3.0	80-84	
3	1.2	5	2.0	85+	
240		231		TOTAL	

VITAL RATES OF PROJECTED POPULATION

Per Thousand	1991 BOTH SEXES	1991 MALES	1991 FEMALES	1996 BOTH SEXES	1996 MALES	1996 FEMALES
BIRTH RATE	14.03	15.05	13.05	13.24	14.15	12.35
DEATH RATE	8.68	8.98	8.39	9.12	9.33	8.92
RATE OF INCREASE	5.35	6.06	4.66	4.12	4.82	3.43

VITAL RATES OF STABLE POPULATION

Per Thousand	MALES	FEMALES	
BIRTH RATE	11.71	10.92	TABLE 6
DEATH RATE	15.90	15.17	PROJECTED
RATE OF INCREASE		-4.25	VITAL

AGE STRUCTURE OF PROJECTED POPULATION

	1991 BOTH SEXES	1991 MALES	1991 FEMALES	1996 BOTH SEXES	1996 MALES	1996 FEMALES
% UNDER 15	22.86	24.00	21.75	21.19	22.34	20.06
% 15-64	66.53	66.75	66.31	67.78	68.27	67.30
% 65 AND OLDER	10.61	9.25	11.93	11.03	9.39	12.63
DEPEND. RATIO x 100	50.31	49.81	50.80	47.53	46.47	48.58

STABLE AGE STRUCTURE

	MALES	FEMALES	
% UNDER 15	17.89	16.72	RATES AND RATIOS
% 15-64	65.26	62.50	(female
% 65 AND OLDER	16.85	20.78	dominant)
DEPEND. RATIO x 100	53.22	60.01	

AGE GROUP	FEMALE BIRTH RATES	NET MATERNITY FUNCTION	COEFF. OF MATRIX EQUATION	ORIGINAL MATRIX SUB-DIAGONAL	ORIGINAL MATRIX FIRST ROW	STABLE MATRIX FISHER VALUES	STABLE MATRIX REPRODUCTIVE VALUES	MATRIX PARAMETERS	
0-4	0.0000	0.0000	0.0000	0.99891	0.00000	1.000	13553	λ_1 0.97898	
5-9	0.0000	0.0000	0.0000	0.99965	0.00000	0.980	13412	λ_2 0.41157+0.73268i	TABLE 7
10-14	0.0000	0.0000	0.0146	0.99942	0.01467	0.960	12528	λ_4 -0.32585-0.42714i	
15-19	0.0059	0.0293	0.1113	0.99860	0.11156	0.925	10783	λ_6 -0.11110+0.47692i	LESLIE
20-24	0.0392	0.1934	0.2594	0.99770	0.26032	0.795	10208	r_1 -0.00425	MATRIX
25-29	0.0662	0.3255	0.2700	0.99831	0.27155	0.520	7389	r_2 -0.03478+0.21180i	AND ITS
30-34	0.0437	0.2145	0.1554	0.99778	0.15658	0.238	3263	r_4 -0.12426-0.44450i	ANALYSIS
35-39	0.0197	0.0963	0.0602	0.99502	0.06077	0.076	1138	r_6 -0.14280+0.35993i	(females)
40-44	0.0049	0.0240	0.0127	0.99127	0.01291	0.014	164	c_1 2290	
45-49	0.0003	0.0014	0.0007	0.98995	0.00072	0.001	7	$2\pi/y$ 29.6660	
50-54	0.0000	0.0000	0.0000	0.00000	0.00000	0.000	0	Δ 14.9486	

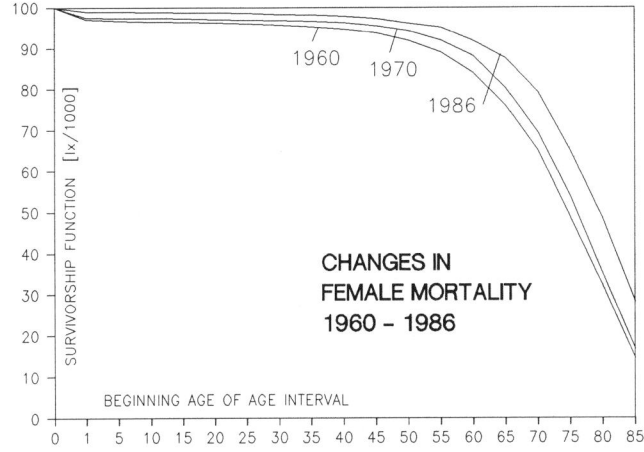

CHANGES IN FEMALE MORTALITY 1960 - 1986

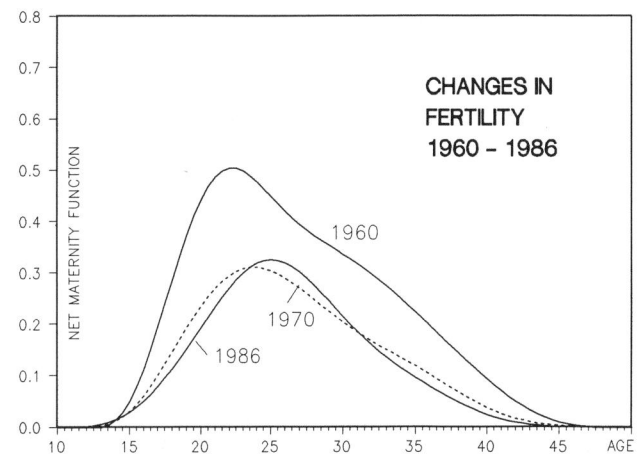

CHANGES IN FERTILITY 1960 - 1986

TABLE 1 — DATA

AGE AT LAST BIRTHDAY	ESTIMATED MID-YEAR POPULATION BOTH SEXES	MALES Number	MALES Percent	FEMALES Number	FEMALES Percent	BIRTHS BY AGE OF MOTHER AND SEX	DEATHS BOTH SEXES	DEATHS MALES	DEATHS FEMALES	AGE AT LAST BIRTHDAY
0	240408	123024	1.9	117384	1.8		3045	1756	1289	0
1-4	947800	484995	7.5	462805	7.1		776	453	323	1-4
5-9	1214303	621419	9.5	592884	9.1		544	357	187	5-9
10-14	1154999	590893	9.1	564106	8.6		417	268	149	10-14
15-19	1110708	568674	8.7	542034	8.3	12243	821	573	248	15-19
20-24	1185091	608467	9.4	576624	8.8	78881	932	667	265	20-24
25-29	916784	477220	7.3	439564	6.7	81339	679	454	225	25-29
30-34	813019	423009	6.5	390010	6.0	42218	730	462	268	30-34
35-39	775510	397161	6.1	378349	5.8	18469	1006	610	396	35-39
40-44	754307	376757	5.8	377550	5.8	5321	1581	961	620	40-44
45-49	754386	369407	5.7	384979	5.9	441	2735	1643	1092	45-49
50-54	649651	316732	4.9	332919	5.1		3929	2521	1408	50-54
55-59	627087	300783	4.6	326304	5.0		6168	4114	2054	55-59
60-64	569112	265992	4.1	303120	4.6		9162	6034	3128	60-64
65-69	479701	217561	3.3	262140	4.0		12314	7706	4608	65-69
70-74	366851	160519	2.5	206332	3.2		15228	8602	6626	70-74
75-79	253816	109016	1.7	144800	2.2		17064	8844	8220	75-79
80-84	145263	62460	1.0	82803	1.3	122330 M	16105	7735	8370	80-84
85+	79730	33300	0.5	46430	0.7	116582 F	16383	7292	9091	85+
TOTAL	13038526	6507389		6531137		238912	109619	61052	48567	TOTAL

TABLE 2 — MALE LIFE TABLE

x	$_nM_x$	$_nq_x$	l_x	$_nd_x$	$_nL_x$	$_nm_x$	$_na_x$	T_x	$\overset{\circ}{e}_x$	x
0	0.014274	0.014091	100000	1409	98724	0.014274	0.094	7083899	70.839	0
1	0.000934	0.003727	98591	367	393445	0.000934	1.500	6985176	70.850	1
5	0.000574	0.002868	98223	282	490412	0.000574	2.500	6591731	67.110	5
10	0.000454	0.002269	97942	222	489196	0.000454	2.696	6101319	62.295	10
15	0.001008	0.005026	97719	491	487434	0.001008	2.631	5612123	57.431	15
20	0.001096	0.005466	97228	531	484806	0.001096	2.487	5124689	52.708	20
25	0.000951	0.004741	96697	458	482337	0.000951	2.497	4639883	47.984	25
30	0.001092	0.005458	96238	525	479936	0.001095	2.609	4157546	43.200	30
35	0.001536	0.007673	95713	734	476871	0.001540	2.693	3677610	38.423	35
40	0.002551	0.012696	94979	1206	472157	0.002554	2.731	3200739	33.700	40
45	0.004448	0.022071	93773	2070	464188	0.004459	2.741	2728582	29.098	45
50	0.007959	0.039207	91703	3595	450314	0.007984	2.719	2264394	24.693	50
55	0.013678	0.066357	88108	5847	427021	0.013691	2.688	1814079	20.589	55
60	0.022685	0.107808	82261	8868	390418	0.022715	2.645	1387058	16.862	60
65	0.035420	0.163541	73393	12003	338146	0.035496	2.599	996640	13.580	65
70	0.053589	0.237386	61390	14573	271313	0.053713	2.555	658495	10.726	70
75	0.081126	0.337990	46817	15824	194525	0.081345	2.500	387181	8.270	75
80	0.123839	0.470143	30993	14571	117663	0.123839	2.440	192656	6.216	80
85	0.218979	1.000000	16422	16422	74994	0.154961	4.567	74994	4.567	85

TABLE 3 — FEMALE LIFE TABLE

x	$_nM_x$	$_nq_x$	l_x	$_nd_x$	$_nL_x$	$_nm_x$	$_na_x$	T_x	$\overset{\circ}{e}_x$	x
0	0.010981	0.010872	100000	1087	99009	0.010981	0.089	7658733	76.587	0
1	0.000698	0.002787	98913	276	394962	0.000698	1.500	7559724	76.428	1
5	0.000315	0.001576	98637	155	492797	0.000315	2.500	7164762	72.638	5
10	0.000264	0.001321	98482	130	492098	0.000264	2.611	6671965	67.748	10
15	0.000458	0.002285	98352	225	491216	0.000458	2.588	6179868	62.834	15
20	0.000460	0.002296	98127	225	490077	0.000460	2.524	5688652	57.972	20
25	0.000512	0.002561	97902	251	488904	0.000513	2.592	5198575	53.100	25
30	0.000687	0.003441	97651	336	487468	0.000689	2.660	4709671	48.230	30
35	0.001047	0.005228	97315	509	485397	0.001048	2.687	4222203	43.387	35
40	0.001642	0.008180	96806	792	482227	0.001642	2.722	3736806	38.601	40
45	0.002837	0.014107	96014	1354	476933	0.002840	2.684	3254579	33.897	45
50	0.004229	0.020983	94660	1986	468650	0.004238	2.660	2777646	29.343	50
55	0.006295	0.031044	92673	2877	456705	0.006299	2.684	2308996	24.915	55
60	0.010319	0.050484	89796	4533	438556	0.010337	2.700	1852290	20.628	60
65	0.017578	0.084779	85263	7229	409739	0.017642	2.707	1413735	16.581	65
70	0.032113	0.150034	78035	11708	362877	0.032264	2.669	1003995	12.866	70
75	0.056768	0.251776	66327	16699	291627	0.057263	2.604	641118	9.666	75
80	0.101083	0.404355	49627	20067	198520	0.101083	2.527	349492	7.042	80
85	0.195800	1.000000	29560	29560	150972	0.128124	5.107	150972	5.107	85

TABLE 4 — OBSERVED VITAL RATES AND RATIOS

CRUDE RATES

Per Thousand	BOTH SEXES	MALES	FEMALES
BIRTH RATE	18.32	18.80	17.85
DEATH RATE	8.41	9.38	7.44
RATE OF INCREASE	9.92	9.42	10.41

PERCENT OF POPULATION IN AGE GROUP

UNDER 15	27.28	27.97	26.60
15 - 64	62.55	63.07	62.03
65 AND OLDER	10.16	8.96	11.37

RATES STANDARDIZED ON USA 1980

Per Thousand	BOTH SEXES	MALES	FEMALES
BIRTH RATE	21.67		20.56
DEATH RATE	9.51	9.75	9.28
RATE OF INCREASE	12.15		11.28

RATES STANDARDIZED ON MEXICO 1980

	BOTH SEXES	MALES	FEMALES
BIRTH RATE	18.83		18.52
DEATH RATE	3.66	4.27	3.04
RATE OF INCREASE	15.16		15.47

VITAL STATISTICS

GFR x 1000	77.340
TFR	2.584
GRR	1.261
NRR	1.232
μ	28.164
σ^2	32.133
GENERATION	28.044
POP. SEX RATIO	1.004
SEX RATIO AT BIRTH	1.049
DEP. RATIO x 100	59.871

PROJECTED POPULATION

AGE GROUP	1975 BOTH SEXES	1975 MALES	1975 FEMALES	1980 BOTH SEXES	1980 MALES	1980 FEMALES	STABLE EQUIVALENT TO ORIGINAL POPULATION MALES Number	MALES Percent	FEMALES Number	FEMALES Percent	AGE GROUP
0-4	1243	635	608	1342	686	656	630	8.9	602	8.4	0-4
5-9	1185	606	579	1239	633	606	605	8.5	579	8.1	5-9
10-14	1212	620	592	1182	604	578	581	8.2	557	7.8	10-14
15-19	1152	589	563	1209	618	591	558	7.9	536	7.5	15-19
20-24	1107	566	541	1148	586	562	535	7.5	515	7.2	20-24
25-29	1180	605	575	1102	563	539	513	7.2	495	6.9	25-29
30-34	913	475	438	1176	602	574	491	6.9	476	6.6	30-34
35-39	808	420	388	908	472	436	470	6.6	456	6.4	35-39
40-44	769	393	376	802	416	386	449	6.3	437	6.1	40-44
45-49	743	370	373	759	387	372	425	6.0	416	5.8	45-49
50-54	736	358	378	726	359	367	397	5.6	394	5.5	50-54
55-59	624	300	324	709	340	369	363	5.1	370	5.2	55-59
60-64	588	275	313	587	275	312	320	4.5	342	4.8	60-64
65-69	513	230	283	531	238	293	267	3.8	308	4.3	65-69
70-74	407	175	232	436	185	251	206	2.9	263	3.7	70-74
75-79	281	115	166	312	125	187	143	2.0	204	2.8	75-79
80-84	165	66	99	183	70	113	83	1.2	134	1.9	80-84
85+	103	40	63	117	42	75	51	0.7	98	1.4	85+
TOTAL	13729	6838	6891	14468	7201	7267	7087		7182		TOTAL

TABLE 5

POPULATION PROJECTED WITH FIXED AGE-SPECIFIC BIRTH AND DEATH RATES (female dominant, in 000s)

VITAL RATES OF PROJECTED POPULATION

Per Thousand	1975 BOTH SEXES	1975 MALES	1975 FEMALES	1980 BOTH SEXES	1980 MALES	1980 FEMALES
BIRTH RATE	19.32	19.86	18.78	19.31	19.86	18.76
DEATH RATE	8.86	9.57	8.16	9.10	9.60	8.60
RATE OF INCREASE	10.46	10.29	10.62	10.21	10.26	10.16

VITAL RATES OF STABLE POPULATION

Per Thousand	MALES	FEMALES
BIRTH RATE	18.39	17.30
DEATH RATE	10.97	9.86
RATE OF INCREASE		7.44

TABLE 6

PROJECTED VITAL RATES AND RATIOS (female dominant)

AGE STRUCTURE OF PROJECTED POPULATION

	1975 BOTH SEXES	1975 MALES	1975 FEMALES	1980 BOTH SEXES	1980 MALES	1980 FEMALES
% UNDER 15	26.51	27.21	25.80	26.02	26.72	25.33
% 15-64	62.80	63.64	61.97	63.07	64.12	62.03
% 65 AND OLDER	10.69	9.15	12.23	10.91	9.16	12.63
DEPEND. RATIO x 100	59.23	57.14	61.37	58.55	55.96	61.21

STABLE AGE STRUCTURE

	MALES	FEMALES
% UNDER 15	25.62	24.21
% 15-64	63.80	61.78
% 65 AND OLDER	10.58	14.01
DEPEND. RATIO x 100	56.75	61.86

AGE GROUP	FEMALE BIRTH RATES	NET MATERNITY FUNCTION	COEFF. OF MATRIX EQUATION	ORIGINAL MATRIX SUB-DIAGONAL	ORIGINAL MATRIX FIRST ROW	STABLE MATRIX FISHER VALUES	STABLE MATRIX REPRODUCTIVE VALUES	MATRIX PARAMETERS		
0-4	0.0000	0.0000	0.0000	0.99762	0.00000	1.031	598269	λ_1	1.03788	
5-9	0.0000	0.0000	0.0000	0.99858	0.00000	1.073	636032	λ_2	0.39031+0.77689i	TABLE 7
10-14	0.0000	0.0000	0.0271	0.99821	0.02717	1.115	628977	λ_4	-0.36928+0.45282i	
15-19	0.0110	0.0541	0.1906	0.99768	0.19171	1.131	613173	λ_6	-0.04496+0.46054i	LESLIE
20-24	0.0668	0.3271	0.3843	0.99761	0.38736	0.979	564333	r_1	0.00744	MATRIX
25-29	0.0903	0.4415	0.3495	0.99706	0.35310	0.618	271567	r_2	-0.02798+0.22104i	AND ITS
30-34	0.0528	0.2575	0.1866	0.99575	0.18905	0.278	108395	r_4	-0.10747+0.45099i	ANALYSIS
35-39	0.0238	0.1156	0.0744	0.99347	0.07571	0.094	35535	r_6	-0.15412+0.33362i	(females)
40-44	0.0069	0.0332	0.0179	0.98902	0.01835	0.020	7377	c_1	71826	
45-49	0.0006	0.0027	0.0013	0.98263	0.00138	0.001	528	$2\pi/\gamma$	28.4249	
50-54	0.0000	0.0000	0.0000	0.00000	0.00000	0.000	0	Δ	4.9856	

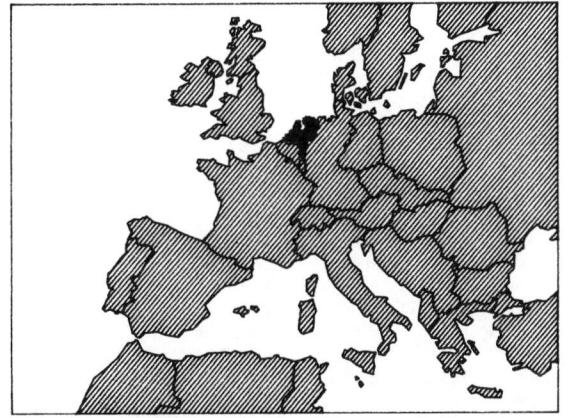

EDUCATION [1984]

% of primary school-age children enrolled:	95
secondary school-age children enrolled:	102
ca. 20-24 year olds in higher education:	31

LABOR FORCE

Average annual labor force growth (%) 1980-85:	1.4
% of the 1980 labor force in agriculture:	6
in industry:	32
in services:	63

TABLE 8

SOCIO-ECONOMIC INDICATORS

GNP & INCOME DISTRIBUTION

GNP per capita (in US Dollars) 1985:	9290
GNP average annual growth rate (%) 1965-85:	2.0
% share of total household income 1981	
Lowest 20% of households:	8.3
Highest 10% of households:	21.5

HEALTH & NUTRITION

Population per physician 1981:	480
Daily calorie supply per capita 1985:	3343

TABLE 1 — DATA

AGE AT LAST BIRTHDAY	ESTIMATED MID-YEAR POPULATION BOTH SEXES	MALES Number	MALES Percent	FEMALES Number	FEMALES Percent	BIRTHS BY AGE OF MOTHER AND SEX	DEATHS BOTH SEXES	DEATHS MALES	DEATHS FEMALES	AGE AT LAST BIRTHDAY
0	180839	92565	1.4	88274	1.3		1894	1097	797	0
1-4	847403	433327	6.4	414076	6.0		585	340	245	1-4
5-9	1204076	615893	9.1	588183	8.6		390	232	158	5-9
10-14	1230891	629600	9.3	601291	8.8		364	231	133	10-14
15-19	1171962	598803	8.8	573159	8.4	7230	688	489	199	15-19
20-24	1130673	577355	8.5	553318	8.1	54165	727	543	184	20-24
25-29	1200625	620005	9.1	580620	8.5	79905	740	490	250	25-29
30-34	924864	482333	7.1	442531	6.4	26795	772	481	291	30-34
35-39	817795	424560	6.2	393235	5.7	7842	944	571	373	35-39
40-44	774472	394130	5.8	380342	5.5	1797	1518	910	608	40-44
45-49	747071	370670	5.4	376401	5.5	142	2599	1640	959	45-49
50-54	740661	359802	5.3	380859	5.6		4215	2741	1474	50-54
55-59	627519	301545	4.4	325974	4.8		5759	3911	1848	55-59
60-64	592696	277202	4.1	315494	4.6		8814	5881	2933	60-64
65-69	516904	231639	3.4	285265	4.2		12623	8213	4410	65-69
70-74	411049	175590	2.6	235459	3.4		16109	9478	6631	70-74
75-79	283499	114946	1.7	168553	2.5		18076	9487	8589	75-79
80-84	166651	66068	1.0	100583	1.5	91090 M	17600	8325	9275	80-84
85+	96685	38211	0.6	58474	0.9	86786 F	19320	8466	10854	85+
TOTAL	13666335	6804244		6862091		177876	113737	63526	50211	TOTAL

TABLE 2 — MALE LIFE TABLE

x	nM_x	nq_x	l_x	nd_x	nL_x	nm_x	na_x	T_x	$\overset{\circ}{e}_x$	x
0	0.011851	0.011725	100000	1172	98933	0.011851	0.090	7148050	71.480	0
1	0.000785	0.003132	98828	310	394536	0.000785	1.500	7049117	71.327	1
5	0.000377	0.001882	98518	185	492126	0.000377	2.500	6654581	67.547	5
10	0.000367	0.001833	98333	180	491257	0.000367	2.749	6162455	62.669	10
15	0.000817	0.004080	98152	400	489818	0.000818	2.645	5671198	57.780	15
20	0.000940	0.004691	97752	459	487609	0.000940	2.492	5181379	53.005	20
25	0.000790	0.003944	97293	384	485512	0.000790	2.514	4693770	48.244	25
30	0.000997	0.004991	96910	484	483394	0.001000	2.614	4208258	43.425	30
35	0.001345	0.006732	96426	649	480636	0.001351	2.699	3724864	38.629	35
40	0.002309	0.011532	95777	1105	476420	0.002318	2.769	3244228	33.873	40
45	0.004424	0.021932	94672	2076	468664	0.004430	2.738	2767808	29.236	45
50	0.007618	0.037522	92596	3474	455033	0.007636	2.713	2299144	24.830	50
55	0.012970	0.063133	89121	5627	432577	0.013007	2.684	1844111	20.692	55
60	0.021216	0.101176	83495	8448	397742	0.021239	2.664	1411534	16.906	60
65	0.035456	0.163655	75047	12282	345895	0.035507	2.611	1013792	13.509	65
70	0.053978	0.238901	62765	14995	277194	0.054095	2.557	667897	10.641	70
75	0.082534	0.342954	47771	16383	197885	0.082791	2.499	390703	8.179	75
80	0.126007	0.476144	31388	14945	118605	0.126007	2.435	192818	6.143	80
85	0.221559	1.000000	16443	16443	74213	0.158003	4.513	74213	4.513	85

TABLE 3 — FEMALE LIFE TABLE

x	nM_x	nq_x	l_x	nd_x	nL_x	nm_x	na_x	T_x	$\overset{\circ}{e}_x$	x
0	0.009029	0.008955	100000	895	99181	0.009029	0.085	7782228	77.822	0
1	0.000592	0.002363	99105	234	395833	0.000592	1.500	7683047	77.525	1
5	0.000269	0.001342	98870	133	494020	0.000269	2.500	7287214	73.705	5
10	0.000221	0.001105	98738	109	493423	0.000221	2.573	6793194	68.800	10
15	0.000347	0.001736	98628	171	492726	0.000347	2.566	6299771	63.874	15
20	0.000333	0.001661	98457	164	491886	0.000333	2.552	5807045	58.980	20
25	0.000431	0.002155	98294	212	490972	0.000431	2.657	5315159	54.074	25
30	0.000658	0.003299	98082	324	489653	0.000661	2.663	4824187	49.185	30
35	0.000949	0.004752	97758	465	487725	0.000952	2.703	4334534	44.339	35
40	0.001599	0.007976	97294	776	484687	0.001601	2.703	3846809	39.538	40
45	0.002548	0.012664	96518	1222	479752	0.002548	2.680	3362122	34.834	45
50	0.003870	0.019200	95295	1830	472195	0.003875	2.659	2882370	30.247	50
55	0.005669	0.028048	93466	2622	461256	0.005684	2.683	2410175	25.787	55
60	0.009297	0.045552	90844	4138	444681	0.009306	2.695	1948919	21.453	60
65	0.015459	0.074821	86706	6487	418667	0.015495	2.709	1504238	17.349	65
70	0.028162	0.132694	80219	10645	376450	0.028276	2.685	1085571	13.533	70
75	0.050957	0.229020	69574	15934	310022	0.051396	2.625	709121	10.192	75
80	0.092212	0.376192	53640	20179	218832	0.092212	2.553	399099	7.440	80
85	0.185621	1.000000	33461	33461	180267	0.117097	5.387	180267	5.387	85

TABLE 4 — OBSERVED VITAL RATES AND RATIOS

CRUDE RATES

Per Thousand	BOTH SEXES	MALES	FEMALES
BIRTH RATE	13.02	13.39	12.65
DEATH RATE	8.32	9.34	7.32
RATE OF INCREASE	4.69	4.05	5.33

PERCENT OF POPULATION IN AGE GROUP

UNDER 15	25.34	26.03	24.65
15 - 64	63.87	64.76	62.98
65 AND OLDER	10.79	9.21	12.36

RATES STANDARDIZED ON USA 1980

Per Thousand	BOTH SEXES	MALES	FEMALES
BIRTH RATE	14.28		13.55
DEATH RATE	8.98	9.56	8.44
RATE OF INCREASE	5.30		5.11

RATES STANDARDIZED ON MEXICO 1980

	BOTH SEXES	MALES	FEMALES
BIRTH RATE	12.48		12.27
DEATH RATE	3.38	4.04	2.71
RATE OF INCREASE	9.10		9.57

VITAL STATISTICS

GFR x 1000	53.908
TFR	1.669
GRR	0.814
NRR	0.799
μ	27.381
σ^2	25.183
GENERATION	27.484
POP. SEX RATIO	1.009
SEX RATIO AT BIRTH	1.050
DEP. RATIO x 100	56.574

AGE AT LAST BIRTHDAY	ESTIMATED MID-YEAR POPULATION						BIRTHS BY AGE OF MOTHER AND SEX	DEATHS			AGE AT LAST BIRTHDAY	
	BOTH SEXES	MALES			FEMALES			BOTH SEXES	MALES	FEMALES		
		Number	Percent		Number	Percent						
0	177672	90945	1.3		86727	1.2		1557	902	655	0	
1-4	707301	362230	5.2		345071	4.8		368	197	171	1-4	
5-9	1050936	537130	7.6		513806	7.2		305	190	115	5-9	
10-14	1223263	625741	8.9		597522	8.4		270	164	106	10-14	
15-19	1254620	641795	9.1		612825	8.6	5631	654	462	192	15-19	
20-24	1201013	611838	8.7		589175	8.3	47220	823	589	234	20-24	
25-29	1151398	588928	8.4		562470	7.9	80222	741	519	222	25-29	
30-34	1206468	622944	8.9		583524	8.2	38893	864	562	302	30-34	
35-39	924494	479895	6.8		444599	6.2	7797	1036	624	412	35-39	TABLE 1
40-44	815100	419703	6.0		395397	5.5	1381	1435	898	537	40-44	
45-49	765776	387168	5.5		378608	5.3	150	2437	1568	869	45-49	DATA
50-54	732310	360670	5.1		371640	5.2		3797	2501	1296	50-54	
55-59	716926	343840	4.9		373086	5.2		5893	3929	1964	55-59	
60-64	593855	278534	4.0		315321	4.4		8185	5492	2693	60-64	
65-69	541192	242707	3.5		298485	4.2		11864	7824	4040	65-69	
70-74	445944	186769	2.7		259175	3.6		16056	9778	6278	70-74	
75-79	324045	126281	1.8		197764	2.8		18731	10061	8670	75-79	
80-84	193313	70166	1.0		123147	1.7	92986 M	17929	8297	9632	80-84	
85+	124169	44090	0.6		80079	1.1	88308 F	21334	8744	12590	85+	
TOTAL	14149795	7021374			7128421		181294	114279	63301	50978	TOTAL	

x	nM_x	nq_x	l_x	nd_x	nL_x	nm_x	na_x	T_x	$\overset{\circ}{e}_x$	x	
0	0.009918	0.009829	100000	983	99102	0.009918	0.087	7248833	72.488	0	
1	0.000544	0.002172	99017	215	395531	0.000544	1.500	7149731	72.207	1	
5	0.000354	0.001767	98802	175	493573	0.000354	2.500	6754200	68.361	5	
10	0.000262	0.001310	98627	129	492851	0.000262	2.789	6260627	63.478	10	
15	0.000720	0.003593	98498	354	491678	0.000720	2.701	5767775	58.557	15	
20	0.000963	0.004803	98144	471	489559	0.000963	2.533	5276098	53.759	20	
25	0.000881	0.004397	97673	429	487284	0.000881	2.484	4786539	49.006	25	TABLE 2
30	0.000902	0.004505	97243	438	485164	0.000903	2.596	4299255	44.211	30	
35	0.001300	0.006521	96805	631	482572	0.001308	2.695	3814091	39.400	35	MALE
40	0.002140	0.010708	96174	1030	478564	0.002152	2.760	3331519	34.641	40	LIFE
45	0.004050	0.020140	95144	1916	471380	0.004065	2.734	2852956	29.986	45	TABLE
50	0.006934	0.034168	93228	3185	458824	0.006943	2.703	2381576	25.546	50	
55	0.011427	0.055801	90043	5024	438663	0.011454	2.701	1922752	21.354	55	
60	0.019718	0.094540	85018	8038	406354	0.019780	2.669	1484090	17.456	60	
65	0.032236	0.149946	76980	11543	357541	0.032284	2.630	1077735	14.000	65	
70	0.052353	0.232594	65438	15220	290218	0.052445	2.571	720194	11.006	70	
75	0.079672	0.333177	50217	16731	209252	0.079957	2.500	429976	8.562	75	
80	0.118248	0.453723	33486	15193	128487	0.118248	2.437	220724	6.592	80	
85	0.198322	1.000000	18293	18293	92237	0.131454	5.042	92237	5.042	85	

x	nM_x	nq_x	l_x	nd_x	nL_x	nm_x	na_x	T_x	$\overset{\circ}{e}_x$	x	
0	0.007552	0.007500	100000	750	99312	0.007552	0.083	7939466	79.395	0	
1	0.000496	0.001980	99250	196	396509	0.000496	1.500	7840154	78.994	1	
5	0.000224	0.001118	99053	111	494990	0.000224	2.500	7443645	75.148	5	
10	0.000177	0.000887	98943	88	494503	0.000177	2.604	6948655	70.229	10	
15	0.000313	0.001565	98855	155	493910	0.000313	2.645	6454152	65.289	15	
20	0.000397	0.001985	98700	196	493020	0.000397	2.542	5960241	60.387	20	
25	0.000395	0.001972	98504	194	492048	0.000395	2.563	5467222	55.502	25	TABLE 3
30	0.000518	0.002592	98310	255	490968	0.000519	2.714	4975173	50.607	30	
35	0.000927	0.004653	98055	456	489221	0.000933	2.687	4484205	45.731	35	FEMALE
40	0.001358	0.006797	97599	663	486473	0.001364	2.705	3994984	40.933	40	LIFE
45	0.002295	0.011436	96936	1109	482114	0.002299	2.687	3508511	36.194	45	TABLE
50	0.003487	0.017296	95827	1657	475272	0.003487	2.669	3026397	31.582	50	
55	0.005264	0.026040	94170	2452	465175	0.005271	2.686	2551125	27.091	55	
60	0.008541	0.041984	91718	3851	449653	0.008564	2.680	2085949	22.743	60	
65	0.013535	0.065713	87867	5774	426063	0.013552	2.701	1636296	18.622	65	
70	0.024223	0.114934	82093	9435	388700	0.024274	2.693	1210233	14.742	70	
75	0.043840	0.199949	72658	14528	328985	0.044160	2.639	821532	11.307	75	
80	0.078215	0.328842	58130	19116	244395	0.078215	2.580	492547	8.473	80	
85	0.157220	1.000000	39014	39014	248151	0.088237	6.361	248151	6.361	85	

CRUDE RATES

Per Thousand	BOTH SEXES	MALES	FEMALES
BIRTH RATE	12.81	13.24	12.39
DEATH RATE	8.08	9.02	7.15
RATE OF INCREASE	4.74	4.23	5.24

PERCENT OF POPULATION IN AGE GROUP

UNDER 15	22.33	23.02	21.65
15 - 64	66.16	67.44	64.90
65 AND OLDER	11.51	9.54	13.45

RATES STANDARDIZED ON USA 1980

Per Thousand	BOTH SEXES	MALES	FEMALES
BIRTH RATE	13.64		12.92
DEATH RATE	8.05	8.87	7.29
RATE OF INCREASE	5.58		5.63

RATES STANDARDIZED ON MEXICO 1980

	BOTH SEXES	MALES	FEMALES
BIRTH RATE	11.77		11.55
DEATH RATE	3.04	3.71	2.36
RATE OF INCREASE	8.73		9.20

VITAL STATISTICS

GFR x 1000	50.831	TABLE 4
TFR	1.600	
GRR	0.779	OBSERVED
NRR	0.767	VITAL
μ	27.727	RATES
σ^2	22.667	AND
GENERATION	27.835	RATIOS
POP. SEX RATIO	1.015	
SEX RATIO AT BIRTH	1.053	
DEP. RATIO x 100	51.141	

TABLE 1 — DATA

AGE AT LAST BIRTHDAY	ESTIMATED MID-YEAR POPULATION BOTH SEXES	MALES Number	MALES Percent	FEMALES Number	FEMALES Percent	BIRTHS BY AGE OF MOTHER AND SEX	DEATHS BOTH SEXES	DEATHS MALES	DEATHS FEMALES	AGE AT LAST BIRTHDAY
0	175620	89780	1.3	85840	1.2		1430	808	622	0
1-4	697709	356411	5.0	341298	4.7		290	162	128	1-4
5-9	889460	455307	6.4	434153	5.9		156	97	59	5-9
10-14	1056428	539748	7.5	516680	7.1		193	120	73	10-14
15-19	1232350	629980	8.8	602370	8.2	4116	529	379	150	15-19
20-24	1271964	648162	9.0	623802	8.5	37820	702	513	189	20-24
25-29	1210024	615649	8.6	594375	8.1	78075	682	465	217	25-29
30-34	1149385	587222	8.2	562163	7.7	45309	847	519	328	30-34
35-39	1198543	616499	8.6	582044	7.9	11208	1217	739	478	35-39
40-44	916278	473024	6.6	443254	6.1	1426	1518	982	536	40-44
45-49	804112	411364	5.7	392748	5.4	182	2195	1367	828	45-49
50-54	751280	377012	5.3	374268	5.1		3737	2372	1365	50-54
55-59	709269	345278	4.8	363991	5.0		5761	3824	1937	55-59
60-64	679754	318916	4.4	360838	4.9		8854	5924	2930	60-64
65-69	544590	245527	3.4	299063	4.1		11622	7684	3938	65-69
70-74	471650	198287	2.8	273363	3.7		16121	9848	6273	70-74
75-79	356677	135040	1.9	221637	3.0		19895	10857	9038	75-79
80-84	226044	77339	1.1	148705	2.0	91366 M	20503	9285	11218	80-84
85+	150512	46538	0.6	103974	1.4	86770 F	26452	9902	16550	85+
TOTAL	14491649	7167083		7324566		178136	122704	65847	56857	TOTAL

TABLE 2 — MALE LIFE TABLE

x	nM_x	nq_x	l_x	nd_x	nL_x	nm_x	na_x	T_x	$\overset{\circ}{e}_x$	x
0	0.009000	0.008926	100000	893	99184	0.009000	0.085	7307484	73.075	0
1	0.000455	0.001816	99107	180	395980	0.000455	1.500	7208301	72.732	1
5	0.000213	0.001065	98927	105	494374	0.000213	2.500	6812321	68.862	5
10	0.000222	0.001111	98822	110	493876	0.000222	2.863	6317948	63.933	10
15	0.000602	0.003004	98712	297	492878	0.000602	2.696	5824072	59.000	15
20	0.000791	0.003950	98416	389	491122	0.000791	2.539	5331194	54.170	20
25	0.000755	0.003770	98027	370	489220	0.000755	2.524	4840072	49.375	25
30	0.000884	0.004410	97657	431	487255	0.000884	2.603	4350852	44.552	30
35	0.001199	0.005991	97227	583	484798	0.001202	2.706	3863597	39.738	35
40	0.002076	0.010405	96644	1006	480917	0.002091	2.708	3378800	34.961	40
45	0.003323	0.016587	95639	1586	474628	0.003342	2.752	2897883	30.300	45
50	0.006292	0.031132	94052	2928	463638	0.006315	2.738	2423255	25.765	50
55	0.011075	0.054072	91124	4927	444297	0.011090	2.701	1959617	21.505	55
60	0.018575	0.089257	86197	7694	413114	0.018624	2.677	1515320	17.580	60
65	0.031296	0.146123	78503	11471	365337	0.031399	2.631	1102206	14.040	65
70	0.049665	0.222046	67032	14884	299210	0.049745	2.585	736869	10.993	70
75	0.080398	0.335868	52148	17515	217165	0.080652	2.512	437659	8.393	75
80	0.120056	0.459197	34633	15903	132467	0.120056	2.441	220494	6.367	80
85	0.212772	1.000000	18730	18730	88027	0.147706	4.700	88027	4.700	85

TABLE 3 — FEMALE LIFE TABLE

x	nM_x	nq_x	l_x	nd_x	nL_x	nm_x	na_x	T_x	$\overset{\circ}{e}_x$	x
0	0.007246	0.007198	100000	720	99339	0.007246	0.082	7984856	79.849	0
1	0.000375	0.001499	99280	149	396749	0.000375	1.500	7885516	79.427	1
5	0.000136	0.000679	99131	67	495489	0.000136	2.500	7488768	75.544	5
10	0.000141	0.000706	99064	70	495157	0.000141	2.666	6993279	70.594	10
15	0.000249	0.001244	98994	123	494679	0.000249	2.635	6498122	65.642	15
20	0.000303	0.001514	98871	150	493992	0.000303	2.579	6003443	60.720	20
25	0.000365	0.001827	98721	180	493184	0.000366	2.659	5509451	55.808	25
30	0.000583	0.002913	98541	287	492033	0.000583	2.662	5016267	50.905	30
35	0.000821	0.004107	98254	404	490324	0.000823	2.658	4524234	46.046	35
40	0.001209	0.006070	97850	594	487896	0.001217	2.718	4033910	41.225	40
45	0.002108	0.010542	97256	1025	483958	0.002118	2.733	3546014	36.460	45
50	0.003647	0.018114	96231	1743	477101	0.003653	2.674	3062056	31.820	50
55	0.005322	0.026281	94488	2483	466634	0.005322	2.662	2584955	27.357	55
60	0.008120	0.039905	92005	3671	451507	0.008132	2.680	2118321	23.024	60
65	0.013168	0.064090	88333	5661	428627	0.013208	2.697	1666814	18.870	65
70	0.022948	0.109056	82672	9016	392508	0.022970	2.687	1238187	14.977	70
75	0.040778	0.186828	73656	13761	335985	0.040957	2.653	845679	11.481	75
80	0.075438	0.319401	59895	19131	253593	0.075438	2.602	509693	8.510	80
85	0.159174	1.000000	40765	40765	256100	0.090173	6.282	256100	6.282	85

TABLE 4 — OBSERVED VITAL RATES AND RATIOS

CRUDE RATES

Per Thousand	BOTH SEXES	MALES	FEMALES
BIRTH RATE	12.29	12.75	11.85
DEATH RATE	8.47	9.19	7.76
RATE OF INCREASE	3.83	3.56	4.08

RATES STANDARDIZED ON USA 1980

Per Thousand	BOTH SEXES	MALES	FEMALES
BIRTH RATE	12.72		12.05
DEATH RATE	7.84	8.67	7.07
RATE OF INCREASE	4.87		4.98

VITAL STATISTICS

GFR x 1000	46.869
TFR	1.512
GRR	0.736
NRR	0.726
μ	28.421
σ^2	22.408
GENERATION	28.546
POP. SEX RATIO	1.022
SEX RATIO AT BIRTH	1.053
DEP. RATIO x 100	46.042

PERCENT OF POPULATION IN AGE GROUP

	BOTH SEXES	MALES	FEMALES
UNDER 15	19.45	20.11	18.81
15 - 64	68.47	70.09	66.90
65 AND OLDER	12.07	9.80	14.29

RATES STANDARDIZED ON MEXICO 1980

	BOTH SEXES	MALES	FEMALES
BIRTH RATE	10.80		10.60
DEATH RATE	2.89	3.53	2.24
RATE OF INCREASE	7.91		8.37

PROJECTED POPULATION

AGE GROUP	1990 BOTH SEXES	1990 MALES	1990 FEMALES	1995 BOTH SEXES	1995 MALES	1995 FEMALES
0-4	894	458	436	890	456	434
5-9	872	445	427	892	457	435
10-14	889	455	434	871	445	426
15-19	1055	539	516	887	454	433
20-24	1230	628	602	1052	537	515
25-29	1269	646	623	1226	625	601
30-34	1206	613	593	1264	643	621
35-39	1144	584	560	1201	610	591
40-44	1191	612	579	1137	580	557
45-49	907	467	440	1178	604	574
50-54	789	402	387	889	456	433
55-59	727	361	366	764	385	379
60-64	673	321	352	690	336	354
65-69	625	282	343	618	284	334
70-74	475	201	274	545	231	314
75-79	378	144	234	380	146	234
80-84	249	82	167	265	88	177
85+	201	51	150	224	55	169
TOTAL	14774	7291	7483	14973	7392	7581

STABLE EQUIVALENT TO ORIGINAL POPULATION

MALES Number	MALES Percent	FEMALES Number	FEMALES Percent	AGE GROUP	
481	4.4	457	3.9	0-4	
508	4.6	483	4.1	5-9	TABLE 5
536	4.9	511	4.3	10-14	
566	5.2	540	4.6	15-19	POPULATION
597	5.5	570	4.8	20-24	PROJECTED
629	5.7	602	5.1	25-29	WITH
662	6.1	635	5.4	30-34	FIXED
697	6.4	669	5.7	35-39	AGE-
731	6.7	704	6.0	40-44	SPECIFIC
763	7.0	739	6.3	45-49	BIRTH
788	7.2	771	6.5	50-54	AND
799	7.3	797	6.7	55-59	DEATH
786	7.2	816	6.9	60-64	RATES
735	6.7	819	6.9	65-69	(female
637	5.8	793	6.7	70-74	dominant,
489	4.5	718	6.1	75-79	in 000s)
315	2.9	573	4.9	80-84	
222	2.0	612	5.2	85+	
10941		11809		TOTAL	

VITAL RATES OF PROJECTED POPULATION

Per Thousand	1990 BOTH SEXES	1990 MALES	1990 FEMALES	1995 BOTH SEXES	1995 MALES	1995 FEMALES
BIRTH RATE	12.35	12.83	11.88	11.79	12.26	11.34
DEATH RATE	9.29	9.64	8.95	9.78	10.08	9.49
RATE OF INCREASE	3.06	3.20	2.93	2.01	2.17	1.86

AGE STRUCTURE OF PROJECTED POPULATION

	1990 BOTH SEXES	1990 MALES	1990 FEMALES	1995 BOTH SEXES	1995 MALES	1995 FEMALES
% UNDER 15	17.97	18.63	17.32	17.72	18.38	17.08
% 15-64	68.98	70.94	67.07	68.71	70.75	66.73
% 65 AND OLDER	13.06	10.43	15.61	13.57	10.87	16.19
DEPEND. RATIO x 100	44.98	40.97	49.10	45.53	41.33	49.87

VITAL RATES OF STABLE POPULATION

Per Thousand	MALES	FEMALES	
BIRTH RATE	8.62	7.59	TABLE 6
DEATH RATE	19.69	18.80	PROJECTED
RATE OF INCREASE		-11.21	VITAL RATES AND RATIOS (female dominant)

STABLE AGE STRUCTURE

	MALES	FEMALES	
% UNDER 15	13.94	12.29	
% 15-64	64.15	57.94	
% 65 AND OLDER	21.92	29.77	
DEPEND. RATIO x 100	55.89	72.60	

MATRIX / TABLE 7

AGE GROUP	FEMALE BIRTH RATES	NET MATERNITY FUNCTION	COEFF. OF MATRIX EQUATION	ORIGINAL MATRIX SUB-DIAGONAL	ORIGINAL MATRIX FIRST ROW	STABLE MATRIX FISHER VALUES	STABLE MATRIX REPRODUCTIVE VALUES	MATRIX PARAMETERS	
0-4	0.0000	0.0000	0.0000	0.99879	0.00000	0.980	418583	λ_1	0.94548
5-9	0.0000	0.0000	0.0000	0.99933	0.00000	0.928	402748	λ_2	$0.39861+0.74073i$
10-14	0.0000	0.0000	0.0082	0.99903	0.00825	0.878	453477	λ_4	$-0.29444+0.55287i$
15-19	0.0033	0.0165	0.0812	0.99861	0.08141	0.823	495471	λ_6	$-0.42105+0.13230i$
20-24	0.0295	0.1459	0.2307	0.99836	0.23170	0.699	435966	r_1	-0.01121
25-29	0.0640	0.3156	0.2544	0.99767	0.25586	0.434	258217	r_2	$-0.03459+0.21542i$
30-34	0.0393	0.1932	0.1196	0.99653	0.12056	0.160	90164	r_4	$-0.09356+0.41203i$
35-39	0.0094	0.0460	0.0268	0.99505	0.02713	0.034	19562	r_6	$-0.16359+0.56743i$
40-44	0.0016	0.0076	0.0044	0.99193	0.00444	0.005	2311	c_1	118100
45-49	0.0002	0.0011	0.0005	0.98583	0.00056	0.001	228	$2\pi/y$	29.1668
50-54	0.0000	0.0000	0.0000	0.00000	0.00000	0.000	0	Δ	21.5538

LESLIE MATRIX AND ITS ANALYSIS (females)

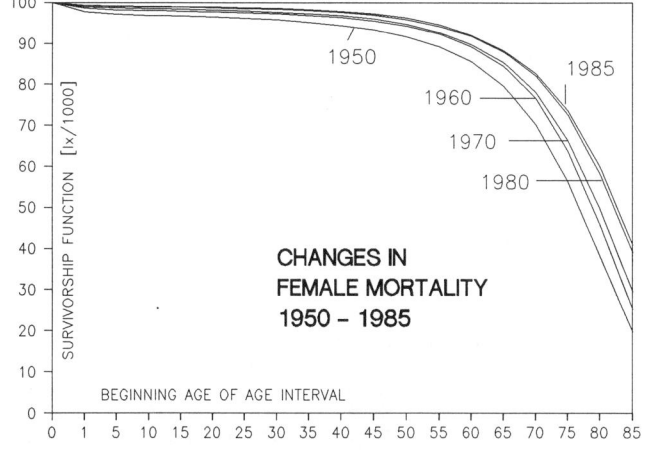

CHANGES IN FEMALE MORTALITY 1950 – 1985

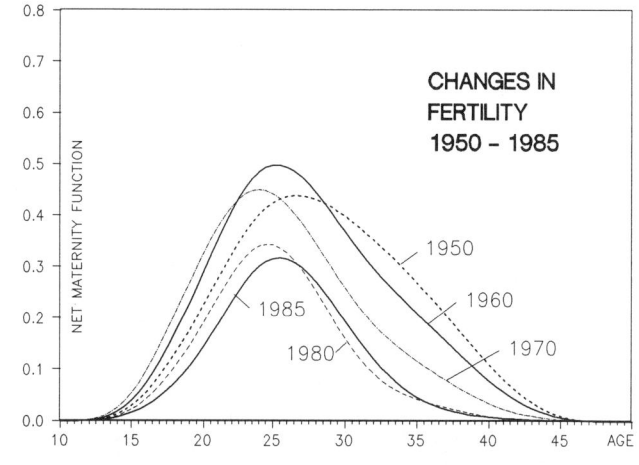

CHANGES IN FERTILITY 1950 – 1985

TABLE 1 — DATA

AGE AT LAST BIRTHDAY	ESTIMATED MID-YEAR POPULATION BOTH SEXES	MALES Number	MALES Percent	FEMALES Number	FEMALES Percent	BIRTHS BY AGE OF MOTHER AND SEX	DEATHS BOTH SEXES	DEATHS MALES	DEATHS FEMALES	AGE AT LAST BIRTHDAY
0	64260	33049	1.7	31211	1.6		823	499	324	0
1-4	264556	135961	7.0	128595	6.6		226	141	85	1-4
5-9	311931	160110	8.3	151821	7.8		134	91	43	5-9
10-14	307574	157372	8.2	150202	7.7	11	80	51	29	10-14
15-19	302749	155056	8.0	147693	7.6	6563	201	153	48	15-19
20-24	312010	161128	8.4	150882	7.7	25374	245	188	57	20-24
25-29	255252	131422	6.8	123830	6.4	18528	177	130	47	25-29
30-34	203436	103349	5.4	100087	5.1	8881	203	152	51	30-34
35-39	199341	101155	5.2	98186	5.0	3975	283	184	99	35-39
40-44	222032	112434	5.8	109598	5.6	1133	512	345	167	40-44
45-49	253334	127168	6.6	126166	6.5	86	913	614	299	45-49
50-54	246484	122158	6.3	124326	6.4		1385	948	437	50-54
55-59	230116	113123	5.9	116993	6.0		2080	1394	686	55-59
60-64	204289	97430	5.1	106859	5.5		2879	1923	956	60-64
65-69	176062	80535	4.2	95527	4.9		4270	2645	1625	65-69
70-74	141197	62066	3.2	79131	4.1		5686	3244	2442	70-74
75-79	96088	40908	2.1	55180	2.8		6214	3236	2978	75-79
80-84	54092	21880	1.1	32212	1.7	33271 M	5973	2721	3252	80-84
85+	32210	12243	0.6	19967	1.0	31280 F	6439	2686	3753	85+
TOTAL	3877013	1928547		1948466		64551	38723	21345	17378	TOTAL

TABLE 2 — MALE LIFE TABLE

x	$_nM_x$	$_nq_x$	l_x	$_nd_x$	$_nL_x$	$_nm_x$	$_na_x$	T_x	$\overset{\circ}{e}_x$	x
0	0.015099	0.014895	100000	1490	98653	0.015099	0.096	7100069	71.001	0
1	0.001037	0.004137	98510	408	393023	0.001037	1.500	7001416	71.073	1
5	0.000568	0.002838	98103	278	489818	0.000568	2.500	6608393	67.362	5
10	0.000324	0.001620	97824	159	488768	0.000324	2.766	6118575	62.546	10
15	0.000987	0.004922	97666	481	487213	0.000987	2.676	5629806	57.643	15
20	0.001167	0.005817	97185	565	484512	0.001167	2.499	5142593	52.915	20
25	0.000989	0.004935	96620	477	481937	0.000989	2.562	4658081	48.210	25
30	0.001471	0.007357	96143	707	479028	0.001477	2.614	4176144	43.437	30
35	0.001819	0.009057	95436	864	475171	0.001819	2.677	3697116	38.739	35
40	0.003068	0.015235	94571	1441	469538	0.003068	2.697	3221946	34.069	40
45	0.004828	0.023875	93131	2223	460516	0.004828	2.690	2752407	29.554	45
50	0.007760	0.038130	90907	3466	446499	0.007763	2.682	2291891	25.211	50
55	0.012323	0.059972	87441	5244	424991	0.012339	2.671	1845391	21.104	55
60	0.019737	0.094552	82197	7772	392829	0.019784	2.664	1420400	17.280	60
65	0.032843	0.152644	74425	11361	345156	0.032914	2.626	1027571	13.807	65
70	0.052267	0.232265	63065	14648	279682	0.052373	2.567	682415	10.821	70
75	0.079104	0.331706	48417	16060	202063	0.079481	2.508	402732	8.318	75
80	0.124360	0.471912	32357	15269	122784	0.124360	2.446	200669	6.202	80
85	0.219391	1.000000	17087	17087	77885	0.155350	4.558	77885	4.558	85

TABLE 3 — FEMALE LIFE TABLE

x	$_nM_x$	$_nq_x$	l_x	$_nd_x$	$_nL_x$	$_nm_x$	$_na_x$	T_x	$\overset{\circ}{e}_x$	x
0	0.010381	0.010284	100000	1028	99062	0.010381	0.088	7739181	77.392	0
1	0.000661	0.002640	98972	261	395233	0.000661	1.500	7640119	77.195	1
5	0.000283	0.001415	98710	140	493203	0.000283	2.500	7244886	73.395	5
10	0.000193	0.000965	98571	95	492620	0.000193	2.544	6751683	68.496	10
15	0.000325	0.001624	98476	160	491997	0.000325	2.618	6259063	63.560	15
20	0.000378	0.001888	98316	186	491120	0.000378	2.529	5767066	58.659	20
25	0.000380	0.001897	98130	186	490199	0.000380	2.573	5275946	53.765	25
30	0.000510	0.002561	97944	251	489156	0.000513	2.753	4785747	48.862	30
35	0.001008	0.005030	97693	491	487338	0.001008	2.706	4296591	43.981	35
40	0.001524	0.007592	97202	738	484298	0.001524	2.682	3809253	39.189	40
45	0.002370	0.011784	96464	1137	479669	0.002370	2.669	3324955	34.468	45
50	0.003515	0.017440	95327	1663	472807	0.003516	2.697	2845285	29.848	50
55	0.005864	0.028964	93664	2713	462026	0.005872	2.679	2372478	25.330	55
60	0.008946	0.043940	90952	3996	445689	0.008967	2.731	1910452	21.005	60
65	0.017011	0.082086	86955	7138	418501	0.017056	2.720	1464764	16.845	65
70	0.030860	0.144467	79817	11531	372200	0.030981	2.668	1046263	13.108	70
75	0.053969	0.240942	68286	16453	302260	0.054433	2.619	674063	9.871	75
80	0.100956	0.404092	51833	20945	207470	0.100956	2.532	371803	7.173	80
85	0.187960	1.000000	30888	30888	164332	0.119617	5.320	164332	5.320	85

TABLE 4 — OBSERVED VITAL RATES AND RATIOS

CRUDE RATES

Per Thousand	BOTH SEXES	MALES	FEMALES
BIRTH RATE	16.65	17.25	16.05
DEATH RATE	9.99	11.07	8.92
RATE OF INCREASE	6.66	6.18	7.13

PERCENT OF POPULATION IN AGE GROUP

	BOTH SEXES	MALES	FEMALES
UNDER 15	24.46	25.23	23.70
15 - 64	62.65	63.49	61.82
65 AND OLDER	12.89	11.28	14.47

RATES STANDARDIZED ON USA 1980

Per Thousand	BOTH SEXES	MALES	FEMALES
BIRTH RATE	21.48		20.24
DEATH RATE	9.15	9.51	8.82
RATE OF INCREASE	12.32		11.42

RATES STANDARDIZED ON MEXICO 1980

	BOTH SEXES	MALES	FEMALES
BIRTH RATE	19.32		18.87
DEATH RATE	3.54	4.24	2.83
RATE OF INCREASE	15.78		16.04

VITAL STATISTICS

GFR x 1000	75.371
TFR	2.513
GRR	1.218
NRR	1.194
μ	26.947
σ^2	34.507
GENERATION	26.833
POP. SEX RATIO	1.010
SEX RATIO AT BIRTH	1.064
DEP. RATIO x 100	59.611

PROJECTED POPULATION

AGE GROUP	1975			1980		
	BOTH SEXES	MALES	FEMALES	BOTH SEXES	MALES	FEMALES
0-4	332	171	161	354	182	172
5-9	327	168	159	331	170	161
10-14	312	160	152	327	168	159
15-19	307	157	150	310	159	151
20-24	301	154	147	306	156	150
25-29	311	160	151	300	153	147
30-34	255	131	124	309	159	150
35-39	203	103	100	253	130	123
40-44	198	100	98	200	101	99
45-49	219	110	109	195	98	97
50-54	247	123	124	214	107	107
55-59	237	116	121	239	117	122
60-64	218	105	113	224	107	117
65-69	186	86	100	198	92	106
70-74	150	65	85	158	69	89
75-79	109	45	64	116	47	69
80-84	63	25	38	71	27	44
85+	40	14	26	46	16	30
TOTAL	4015	1993	2022	4151	2058	2093

STABLE EQUIVALENT TO ORIGINAL POPULATION

MALES		FEMALES		AGE GROUP	
Number	Percent	Number	Percent		
169	8.6	160	8.1	0-4	
163	8.3	154	7.8	5-9	TABLE 5
157	8.0	149	7.5	10-14	
152	7.8	144	7.3	15-19	POPULATION
146	7.5	139	7.0	20-24	PROJECTED
140	7.2	134	6.8	25-29	WITH
135	6.9	130	6.6	30-34	FIXED
129	6.6	125	6.3	35-39	AGE-
124	6.3	120	6.1	40-44	SPECIFIC
117	6.0	115	5.8	45-49	BIRTH
110	5.6	110	5.6	50-54	AND
102	5.2	104	5.3	55-59	DEATH
91	4.6	97	4.9	60-64	RATES
77	3.9	88	4.5	65-69	(female
61	3.1	76	3.8	70-74	dominant,
42	2.2	59	3.0	75-79	in 000s)
25	1.3	40	2.0	80-84	
15	0.8	30	1.5	85+	
1955		1974		TOTAL	

VITAL RATES OF PROJECTED POPULATION

Per Thousand	1975			1980		
	BOTH SEXES	MALES	FEMALES	BOTH SEXES	MALES	FEMALES
BIRTH RATE	17.46	18.13	16.80	17.66	18.36	16.98
DEATH RATE	10.63	11.48	9.79	11.07	11.75	10.40
RATE OF INCREASE	6.83	6.66	7.01	6.59	6.61	6.58

AGE STRUCTURE OF PROJECTED POPULATION

	BOTH SEXES	MALES	FEMALES	BOTH SEXES	MALES	FEMALES
% UNDER 15	24.20	25.04	23.37	24.36	25.23	23.50
% 15-64	62.17	63.19	61.15	61.44	62.56	60.34
% 65 AND OLDER	13.64	11.77	15.48	14.20	12.21	16.16
DEPEND. RATIO x 100	60.86	58.24	63.53	62.76	59.84	65.73

VITAL RATES OF STABLE POPULATION

Per Thousand	MALES	FEMALES	
BIRTH RATE	17.86	16.64	TABLE 6
DEATH RATE	11.26	10.04	
RATE OF INCREASE		6.60	PROJECTED VITAL RATES AND RATIOS

STABLE AGE STRUCTURE

	MALES	FEMALES	(female dominant)
% UNDER 15	25.00	23.45	
% 15-64	63.74	61.70	
% 65 AND OLDER	11.26	14.85	
DEPEND. RATIO x 100	56.89	62.08	

AGE GROUP	FEMALE BIRTH RATES	NET MATERNITY FUNCTION	COEFF. OF MATRIX EQUATION	ORIGINAL MATRIX		STABLE MATRIX		MATRIX PARAMETERS		
				SUB-DIAGONAL	FIRST ROW	FISHER VALUES	REPRODUCTIVE VALUES			
0-4	0.0000	0.0000	0.0000	0.99779	0.00000	1.028	164334	λ_1	1.03354	
5-9	0.0000	0.0000	0.0001	0.99882	0.00009	1.065	161717	λ_2	$0.34027+0.75366i$	TABLE 7
10-14	0.0000	0.0002	0.0531	0.99874	0.05324	1.102	165541	λ_4	$-0.38874-0.35986i$	
15-19	0.0215	0.1059	0.2531	0.99822	0.25427	1.086	160352	λ_6	$-0.02704+0.49947i$	LESLIE
20-24	0.0815	0.4002	0.3778	0.99812	0.38026	0.862	130090	r_1	0.00660	MATRIX
25-29	0.0725	0.3554	0.2829	0.99787	0.28524	0.501	62041	r_2	$-0.03801+0.22934i$	AND ITS
30-34	0.0430	0.2103	0.1530	0.99628	0.15457	0.225	22518	r_4	$-0.12708-0.47895i$	ANALYSIS
35-39	0.0196	0.0956	0.0599	0.99376	0.06079	0.074	7251	r_6	$-0.13855+0.32498i$	(females)
40-44	0.0050	0.0243	0.0129	0.99044	0.01319	0.014	1524	c_1	19721	
45-49	0.0003	0.0016	0.0008	0.98569	0.00082	0.001	102	$2\pi/\gamma$	27.3966	
50-54	0.0000	0.0000	0.0000	0.00000	0.00000	0.000	0	Δ	4.6979	

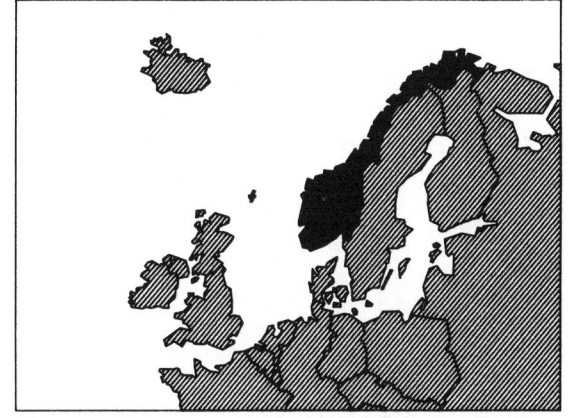

EDUCATION [1984]
% of primary school-age children enrolled:	97
secondary school-age children enrolled:	96
ca. 20-24 year olds in higher education:	29

LABOR FORCE
Average annual labor force growth (%) 1980-85:	0.8
% of the 1980 labor force in agriculture:	8
in industry:	29
in services:	62

GNP & INCOME DISTRIBUTION
GNP per capita (in US Dollars) 1985:	14370
GNP average annual growth rate (%) 1965-85:	3.3
% share of total household income 1982	
Lowest 20% of households:	6.0
Highest 10% of households:	22.8

HEALTH & NUTRITION
Population per physician 1981:	460
Daily calorie supply per capita 1985:	3239

TABLE 8

SOCIO-ECONOMIC INDICATORS

TABLE 1 — DATA

AGE AT LAST BIRTHDAY	ESTIMATED MID-YEAR POPULATION BOTH SEXES	MALES Number	Percent	FEMALES Number	Percent	BIRTHS BY AGE OF MOTHER AND SEX	DEATHS BOTH SEXES	MALES	FEMALES	AGE AT LAST BIRTHDAY
0	57499	29314	1.5	28185	1.4		625	364	261	0
1-4	252017	128944	6.5	123073	6.1		162	100	62	1-4
5-9	331373	170140	8.5	161233	8.0		109	78	31	5-9
10-14	312593	160414	8.1	152179	7.5	11	115	69	46	10-14
15-19	308585	157821	7.9	150764	7.5	6059	231	171	60	15-19
20-24	302089	155187	7.8	146902	7.3	19780	223	171	52	20-24
25-29	315242	163095	8.2	152147	7.5	19655	249	188	61	25-29
30-34	253245	130481	6.6	122764	6.1	7850	187	130	57	30-34
35-39	203799	103391	5.2	100408	5.0	2435	252	176	76	35-39
40-44	197926	100204	5.0	97722	4.8	519	419	279	140	40-44
45-49	219200	110550	5.6	108650	5.4	34	737	502	235	45-49
50-54	250033	124597	6.3	125436	6.2	2	1376	908	468	50-54
55-59	237112	115974	5.8	121138	6.0		2053	1385	668	55-59
60-64	218104	105078	5.3	113026	5.6		3049	2040	1009	60-64
65-69	187309	86325	4.3	100984	5.0		4162	2637	1525	65-69
70-74	151931	65844	3.3	86087	4.3		5593	3309	2284	70-74
75-79	109743	45114	2.3	64629	3.2		6855	3508	3347	75-79
80-84	63205	24782	1.2	38423	1.9	28849 M	6603	3092	3511	80-84
85+	36308	13286	0.7	23022	1.1	27496 F	7061	2787	4274	85+
TOTAL	4007313	1990541		2016772		56345	40061	21894	18167	TOTAL

TABLE 2 — MALE LIFE TABLE

x	nM_x	nq_x	l_x	nd_x	nL_x	nm_x	na_x	T_x	$\overset{\circ}{e}_x$	x
0	0.012417	0.012279	100000	1228	98884	0.012417	0.091	7172389	71.724	0
1	0.000776	0.003096	98772	306	394324	0.000776	1.500	7073505	71.614	1
5	0.000458	0.002290	98466	225	491768	0.000458	2.500	6679181	67.832	5
10	0.000430	0.002152	98241	211	490739	0.000431	2.800	6187413	62.982	10
15	0.001084	0.005406	98029	530	488890	0.001084	2.627	5696674	58.112	15
20	0.001102	0.005494	97499	536	486164	0.001102	2.511	5207784	53.413	20
25	0.001153	0.005746	96964	557	483414	0.001153	2.479	4721621	48.695	25
30	0.000996	0.004978	96407	480	480887	0.000998	2.614	4238207	43.962	30
35	0.001702	0.008537	95927	819	477760	0.001714	2.713	3757319	39.169	35
40	0.002784	0.013833	95108	1316	472518	0.002784	2.704	3279559	34.483	40
45	0.004541	0.022469	93792	2107	464102	0.004541	2.695	2807041	29.928	45
50	0.007287	0.035835	91685	3286	450841	0.007287	2.692	2342939	25.554	50
55	0.011942	0.058135	88399	5139	430076	0.011949	2.681	1892098	21.404	55
60	0.019414	0.092950	83260	7739	398128	0.019439	2.652	1462022	17.560	60
65	0.030547	0.142758	75521	10781	352068	0.030623	2.631	1063894	14.087	65
70	0.050255	0.224498	64740	14534	288538	0.050371	2.581	711826	10.995	70
75	0.077759	0.326974	50206	16416	210292	0.078063	2.518	423288	8.431	75
80	0.124768	0.473071	33790	15985	128118	0.124768	2.446	212996	6.304	80
85	0.209770	1.000000	17805	17805	84878	0.144270	4.767	84878	4.767	85

TABLE 3 — FEMALE LIFE TABLE

x	nM_x	nq_x	l_x	nd_x	nL_x	nm_x	na_x	T_x	$\overset{\circ}{e}_x$	x
0	0.009260	0.009182	100000	918	99160	0.009260	0.086	7814997	78.150	0
1	0.000504	0.002013	99082	199	395829	0.000504	1.500	7715836	77.873	1
5	0.000192	0.000961	98882	95	494174	0.000192	2.500	7320008	74.027	5
10	0.000302	0.001511	98787	149	493584	0.000303	2.641	6825834	69.096	10
15	0.000398	0.001988	98638	196	492705	0.000398	2.526	6332249	64.197	15
20	0.000354	0.001768	98442	174	491774	0.000354	2.501	5839544	59.320	20
25	0.000401	0.002004	98268	197	490858	0.000401	2.557	5347770	54.420	25
30	0.000464	0.002328	98071	228	489821	0.000466	2.660	4856912	49.524	30
35	0.000757	0.003805	97843	372	488380	0.000762	2.762	4367091	44.634	35
40	0.001433	0.007140	97470	696	485751	0.001433	2.700	3878711	39.794	40
45	0.002163	0.010761	96774	1041	481492	0.002163	2.715	3392960	35.061	45
50	0.003731	0.018495	95733	1771	474555	0.003731	2.679	2911468	30.412	50
55	0.005514	0.027238	93962	2559	463879	0.005517	2.682	2436913	25.935	55
60	0.008927	0.043800	91403	4003	447805	0.008940	2.699	1973034	21.586	60
65	0.015101	0.073127	87400	6391	422301	0.015134	2.700	1525228	17.451	65
70	0.026531	0.125347	81008	10154	381752	0.026599	2.706	1102927	13.615	70
75	0.051788	0.232189	70854	16452	315258	0.052185	2.629	721175	10.178	75
80	0.091378	0.373367	54403	20312	222288	0.091378	2.552	405917	7.461	80
85	0.185649	1.000000	34090	34090	183629	0.117166	5.387	183629	5.387	85

TABLE 4 — OBSERVED VITAL RATES AND RATIOS

CRUDE RATES

Per Thousand	BOTH SEXES	MALES	FEMALES
BIRTH RATE	14.06	14.49	13.63
DEATH RATE	10.00	11.00	9.01
RATE OF INCREASE	4.06	3.49	4.63

RATES STANDARDIZED ON USA 1980

Per Thousand	BOTH SEXES	MALES	FEMALES
BIRTH RATE	17.20		16.32
DEATH RATE	8.70	9.12	8.29
RATE OF INCREASE	8.50		8.03

VITAL STATISTICS

GFR x 1000	64.075
TFR	1.990
GRR	0.971
NRR	0.953
μ	26.411
σ^2	30.839
GENERATION	26.439
POP. SEX RATIO	1.013
SEX RATIO AT BIRTH	1.049
DEP. RATIO x 100	59.951

PERCENT OF POPULATION IN AGE GROUP

	BOTH SEXES	MALES	FEMALES
UNDER 15	23.79	24.56	23.04
15 - 64	62.52	63.62	61.43
65 AND OLDER	13.69	11.82	15.53

RATES STANDARDIZED ON MEXICO 1980

	BOTH SEXES	MALES	FEMALES
BIRTH RATE	15.59		15.33
DEATH RATE	3.32	4.00	2.64
RATE OF INCREASE	12.27		12.70

AGE AT LAST BIRTHDAY	ESTIMATED MID-YEAR POPULATION BOTH SEXES	MALES Number	MALES Percent	FEMALES Number	FEMALES Percent	BIRTHS BY AGE OF MOTHER AND SEX	DEATHS BOTH SEXES	DEATHS MALES	DEATHS FEMALES	AGE AT LAST BIRTHDAY	
0	51003	26231	1.3	24772	1.2		411	236	175	0	
1-4	210010	107479	5.3	102531	5.0		90	63	27	1-4	
5-9	311866	159374	7.9	152492	7.4		82	57	25	5-9	
10-14	332807	170945	8.4	161862	7.9	5	75	46	29	10-14	
15-19	313895	161069	8.0	152826	7.4	3855	223	165	58	15-19	
20-24	309593	158260	7.8	151333	7.3	16390	252	203	49	20-24	
25-29	303556	155849	7.7	147707	7.2	18076	233	166	67	25-29	
30-34	316117	163370	8.1	152747	7.4	9589	281	207	74	30-34	
35-39	253328	130217	6.4	123111	6.0	2692	308	210	98	35-39	TABLE 1
40-44	203111	102795	5.1	100316	4.9	415	373	256	117	40-44	
45-49	195970	98787	4.9	97183	4.7	17	631	429	202	45-49	DATA
50-54	214869	107583	5.3	107286	5.2		1110	752	358	50-54	
55-59	241686	118874	5.9	122812	6.0		2002	1385	617	55-59	
60-64	224868	107615	5.3	117253	5.7		3062	2082	980	60-64	
65-69	200142	93256	4.6	106886	5.2		4357	2890	1467	65-69	
70-74	163033	71270	3.5	91763	4.5		5622	3327	2295	70-74	
75-79	120238	48161	2.4	72077	3.5		6995	3693	3302	75-79	
80-84	74317	27851	1.4	46466	2.3	26348 N	7143	3279	3864	80-84	
85+	45211	15734	0.8	29477	1.4	24691 F	8090	3160	4930	85+	
TOTAL	4085620	2024720		2060900		51039	41340	22606	18734	TOTAL	

x	nM_x	nq_x	l_x	nd_x	nL_x	nm_x	na_x	T_x	$\overset{\circ}{e}_x$	x	
0	0.008997	0.008924	100000	892	99184	0.008997	0.085	7237711	72.377	0	
1	0.000586	0.002341	99108	232	395851	0.000586	1.500	7138527	72.028	1	
5	0.000358	0.001787	98876	177	493936	0.000358	2.500	6742676	68.194	5	
10	0.000269	0.001345	98699	133	493231	0.000269	3.014	6248740	63.311	10	
15	0.001024	0.005116	98566	504	491673	0.001026	2.704	5755509	58.392	15	
20	0.001283	0.006393	98062	627	488745	0.001283	2.504	5263835	53.679	20	
25	0.001065	0.005311	97435	518	485878	0.001065	2.494	4775090	49.008	25	TABLE 2
30	0.001267	0.006320	96917	613	483110	0.001268	2.588	4289212	44.256	30	
35	0.001613	0.008073	96305	777	479702	0.001621	2.655	3806102	39.521	35	MALE
40	0.002490	0.012468	95528	1191	474921	0.002508	2.719	3326400	34.821	40	LIFE
45	0.004343	0.021499	94336	2028	467025	0.004343	2.704	2851479	30.227	45	TABLE
50	0.006990	0.034396	92308	3175	454235	0.006990	2.699	2384454	25.831	50	
55	0.011651	0.056728	89133	5056	433986	0.011651	2.690	1930219	21.655	55	
60	0.019347	0.092589	84077	7785	402165	0.019357	2.660	1496233	17.796	60	
65	0.030990	0.144427	76292	11019	355152	0.031025	2.612	1094068	14.340	65	
70	0.046682	0.210225	65274	13722	293241	0.046795	2.586	738916	11.320	70	
75	0.076680	0.323395	51552	16672	216510	0.077001	2.526	445675	8.645	75	
80	0.117734	0.452675	34880	15789	134111	0.117734	2.448	229165	6.570	80	
85	0.200839	1.000000	19091	19091	95055	0.134166	4.979	95055	4.979	85	

x	nM_x	nq_x	l_x	nd_x	nL_x	nm_x	na_x	T_x	$\overset{\circ}{e}_x$	x	
0	0.007064	0.007019	100000	702	99356	0.007064	0.082	7934117	79.341	0	
1	0.000263	0.001053	99298	105	396931	0.000263	1.500	7834761	78.901	1	
5	0.000164	0.000819	99194	81	495765	0.000164	2.500	7437830	74.983	5	
10	0.000179	0.000895	99112	89	495362	0.000179	2.750	6942066	70.042	10	
15	0.000380	0.001897	99024	188	494663	0.000380	2.579	6446704	65.103	15	
20	0.000324	0.001618	98836	160	493786	0.000324	2.546	5952041	60.222	20	
25	0.000454	0.002265	98676	224	492837	0.000454	2.573	5458254	55.315	25	TABLE 3
30	0.000484	0.002422	98452	238	491700	0.000485	2.647	4965418	50.435	30	
35	0.000796	0.003995	98214	392	490158	0.000801	2.677	4473717	45.551	35	FEMALE
40	0.001166	0.005852	97821	572	487804	0.001174	2.723	3983559	40.723	40	LIFE
45	0.002079	0.010344	97249	1006	483943	0.002079	2.711	3495756	35.946	45	TABLE
50	0.003337	0.016556	96243	1593	477512	0.003337	2.676	3011813	31.294	50	
55	0.005024	0.024832	94650	2350	467829	0.005024	2.694	2534302	26.776	55	
60	0.008358	0.041028	92299	3787	452769	0.008364	2.695	2066472	22.389	60	
65	0.013725	0.066650	88512	5899	429064	0.013749	2.712	1613704	18.231	65	
70	0.025010	0.118478	82613	9788	390518	0.025064	2.696	1184640	14.340	70	
75	0.045812	0.207699	72825	15126	328432	0.046054	2.640	794121	10.904	75	
80	0.083158	0.345971	57700	19962	240055	0.083158	2.573	465689	8.071	80	
85	0.167249	1.000000	37737	37737	225635	0.098154	5.979	225635	5.979	85	

CRUDE RATES

Per Thousand	BOTH SEXES	MALES	FEMALES
BIRTH RATE	12.49	13.01	11.98
DEATH RATE	10.12	11.17	9.09
RATE OF INCREASE	2.37	1.85	2.89

PERCENT OF POPULATION IN AGE GROUP

	BOTH SEXES	MALES	FEMALES
UNDER 15	22.17	22.92	21.43
15 - 64	63.07	64.42	61.75
65 AND OLDER	14.76	12.66	16.82

RATES STANDARDIZED ON USA 1980

Per Thousand	BOTH SEXES	MALES	FEMALES
BIRTH RATE	14.82		13.94
DEATH RATE	8.13	8.78	7.51
RATE OF INCREASE	6.69		6.43

RATES STANDARDIZED ON MEXICO 1980

	BOTH SEXES	MALES	FEMALES
BIRTH RATE	13.20		12.87
DEATH RATE	3.05	3.75	2.34
RATE OF INCREASE	10.15		10.54

VITAL STATISTICS

GFR x 1000	55.164	TABLE 4
TFR	1.724	
GRR	0.834	OBSERVED
NRR	0.822	VITAL
μ	26.918	RATES
σ^2	28.605	AND
GENERATION	27.022	RATIOS
POP. SEX RATIO	1.018	
SEX RATIO AT BIRTH	1.067	
DEP. RATIO x 100	58.542	

AGE AT LAST BIRTHDAY	ESTIMATED MID-YEAR POPULATION BOTH SEXES	MALES Number	MALES Percent	FEMALES Number	FEMALES Percent	BIRTHS BY AGE OF MOTHER AND SEX	DEATHS BOTH SEXES	DEATHS MALES	DEATHS FEMALES	AGE AT LAST BIRTHDAY
0	50510	25902	1.3	24608	1.2		434	268	166	0
1-4	203674	104431	5.1	99243	4.7		97	56	41	1-4
5-9	260882	133728	6.5	127154	6.0		65	35	30	5-9
10-14	309339	157992	7.7	151347	7.2	3	64	46	18	10-14
15-19	334436	171472	8.3	162964	7.7	2904	225	165	60	15-19
20-24	318690	163253	7.9	155437	7.4	14498	238	177	61	20-24
25-29	312635	159732	7.8	152903	7.3	19187	232	168	64	25-29
30-34	306722	157336	7.7	149386	7.1	10546	260	181	79	30-34
35-39	316815	163700	8.0	153115	7.3	3472	377	261	116	35-39
40-44	260887	133954	6.5	126933	6.0	511	483	319	164	40-44
45-49	204460	103324	5.0	101136	4.8	16	614	402	212	45-49
50-54	189738	94877	4.6	94861	4.5		991	674	317	50-54
55-59	206030	101947	5.0	104083	4.9		1665	1134	531	55-59
60-64	224653	108376	5.3	116277	5.5		2997	2012	985	60-64
65-69	210603	97410	4.7	113193	5.4		4131	2733	1398	65-69
70-74	175236	77063	3.7	98173	4.7		6084	3732	2352	70-74
75-79	132189	53339	2.6	78850	3.7		7520	4154	3366	75-79
80-84	84341	30281	1.5	54060	2.6	26307 M	7725	3537	4188	80-84
85+	57347	18282	0.9	39065	1.9	24830 F	10170	3729	6441	85+
TOTAL	4159187	2056399		2102788		51137	44372	23783	20589	TOTAL

TABLE 1 DATA

TABLE 2 — MALE LIFE TABLE

x	$_nM_x$	$_nq_x$	l_x	$_nd_x$	$_nL_x$	$_nm_x$	$_na_x$	T_x	$\overset{\circ}{e}_x$	x
0	0.010347	0.010250	100000	1025	99065	0.010347	0.088	7263319	72.633	0
1	0.000536	0.002142	98975	212	395370	0.000536	1.500	7164254	72.384	1
5	0.000262	0.001308	98763	129	493492	0.000262	2.500	6768884	68.537	5
10	0.000291	0.001455	98634	144	492882	0.000291	2.999	6275392	63.623	10
15	0.000962	0.004801	98490	473	491350	0.000962	2.670	5782510	58.711	15
20	0.001084	0.005407	98018	530	488771	0.001084	2.515	5291160	53.982	20
25	0.001052	0.005245	97488	511	486165	0.001052	2.511	4802389	49.262	25
30	0.001150	0.005736	96976	556	483543	0.001150	2.595	4316224	44.508	30
35	0.001594	0.007948	96420	766	480305	0.001596	2.659	3832681	39.750	35
40	0.002381	0.011918	95654	1140	475641	0.002397	2.696	3352376	35.047	40
45	0.003891	0.019477	94514	1838	468411	0.003924	2.738	2876735	30.437	45
50	0.007104	0.034975	92676	3241	455902	0.007110	2.694	2408324	25.987	50
55	0.011123	0.054220	89434	4849	435941	0.011123	2.684	1952422	21.831	55
60	0.018565	0.088939	84585	7523	405222	0.018565	2.647	1516481	17.928	60
65	0.028057	0.131634	77062	10144	361412	0.028068	2.644	1111260	14.420	65
70	0.048428	0.217205	66918	14535	299711	0.048497	2.600	749848	11.205	70
75	0.077879	0.327193	52383	17139	219342	0.078140	2.516	450137	8.593	75
80	0.116806	0.449867	35244	15855	135738	0.116806	2.447	230795	6.549	80
85	0.203971	1.000000	19389	19389	95057	0.137714	4.903	95057	4.903	85

TABLE 3 — FEMALE LIFE TABLE

x	$_nM_x$	$_nq_x$	l_x	$_nd_x$	$_nL_x$	$_nm_x$	$_na_x$	T_x	$\overset{\circ}{e}_x$	x
0	0.006746	0.006704	100000	670	99384	0.006746	0.081	7964273	79.643	0
1	0.000413	0.001651	99330	164	396908	0.000413	1.500	7864889	79.180	1
5	0.000236	0.001179	99166	117	495536	0.000236	2.500	7467981	75.308	5
10	0.000119	0.000594	99049	59	495110	0.000119	2.730	6972445	70.394	10
15	0.000368	0.001839	98990	182	494522	0.000368	2.654	6477335	65.434	15
20	0.000392	0.001960	98808	194	493559	0.000392	2.526	5982813	60.550	20
25	0.000419	0.002091	98614	206	492568	0.000419	2.567	5489254	55.664	25
30	0.000529	0.002641	98408	260	491424	0.000529	2.632	4996685	50.775	30
35	0.000758	0.003786	98148	372	489888	0.000759	2.710	4505262	45.903	35
40	0.001292	0.006484	97776	634	487432	0.001301	2.713	4015373	41.067	40
45	0.002096	0.010498	97142	1020	483362	0.002110	2.696	3527942	36.317	45
50	0.003342	0.016588	96123	1594	476911	0.003343	2.678	3044580	31.674	50
55	0.005102	0.025212	94528	2383	467147	0.005102	2.695	2567669	27.163	55
60	0.008471	0.041532	92145	3827	451766	0.008471	2.659	2100522	22.796	60
65	0.012351	0.060075	88318	5306	429494	0.012353	2.720	1648756	18.668	65
70	0.023958	0.113715	83012	9440	393339	0.023999	2.699	1219262	14.688	70
75	0.042689	0.194603	73572	14317	334133	0.042849	2.644	825923	11.226	75
80	0.077469	0.326525	59255	19348	249753	0.077469	2.596	491790	8.300	80
85	0.164879	1.000000	39907	39907	242037	0.095814	6.065	242037	6.065	85

TABLE 4 — OBSERVED VITAL RATES AND RATIOS

CRUDE RATES Per Thousand	BOTH SEXES	MALES	FEMALES	RATES STANDARDIZED ON USA 1980 Per Thousand	BOTH SEXES	MALES	FEMALES	VITAL STATISTICS	
BIRTH RATE	12.29	12.79	11.81	BIRTH RATE	14.23		13.44	GFR x 1000	51.041
DEATH RATE	10.67	11.57	9.79	DEATH RATE	7.92	8.65	7.23	TFR	1.670
RATE OF INCREASE	1.63	1.23	2.02	RATE OF INCREASE	6.31		6.21	GRR	0.811
								NRR	0.799
								μ	27.482
PERCENT OF POPULATION IN AGE GROUP				RATES STANDARDIZED ON MEXICO 1980				σ^2	27.260
								GENERATION	27.593
UNDER 15	19.82	20.52	19.13	BIRTH RATE	12.47		12.21	POP. SEX RATIO	1.023
15 - 64	64.32	66.04	62.64	DEATH RATE	2.99	3.69	2.28	SEX RATIO AT BIRTH	1.059
65 AND OLDER	15.86	13.44	18.23	RATE OF INCREASE	9.48		9.92	DEP. RATIO x 100	55.480

PROJECTED POPULATION

AGE GROUP	1990			1995			STABLE EQUIVALENT TO ORIGINAL POPULATION				AGE GROUP
							MALES		FEMALES		
	BOTH SEXES	MALES	FEMALES	BOTH SEXES	MALES	FEMALES	Number	Percent	Number	Percent	
0-4	255	131	124	257	132	125	139	5.0	131	4.5	0-4
5-9	254	130	124	255	131	124	144	5.2	137	4.6	5-9
10-14	261	134	127	254	130	124	150	5.4	142	4.8	10-14
15-19	309	158	151	260	133	127	156	5.6	148	5.0	15-19
20-24	334	171	163	308	157	151	161	5.8	154	5.2	20-24
25-29	317	162	155	332	170	162	167	6.0	160	5.4	25-29
30-34	312	159	153	317	162	155	173	6.2	166	5.6	30-34
35-39	305	156	149	310	158	152	179	6.5	172	5.9	35-39
40-44	314	162	152	303	155	148	185	6.7	179	6.1	40-44
45-49	258	132	126	311	160	151	189	6.8	184	6.3	45-49
50-54	201	101	100	252	128	124	192	6.9	190	6.4	50-54
55-59	184	91	93	194	96	98	191	6.9	193	6.6	55-59
60-64	196	95	101	174	84	90	185	6.7	195	6.6	60-64
65-69	208	97	111	181	85	96	172	6.2	193	6.5	65-69
70-74	185	81	104	181	80	101	148	5.4	184	6.2	70-74
75-79	139	56	83	147	59	88	113	4.1	163	5.5	75-79
80-84	92	33	59	97	35	62	73	2.6	127	4.3	80-84
85+	73	21	52	80	23	57	53	1.9	128	4.3	85+
TOTAL	4197	2070	2127	4213	2078	2135	2770		2946		TOTAL

TABLE 5

POPULATION PROJECTED WITH FIXED AGE-SPECIFIC BIRTH AND DEATH RATES (female dominant, in 000s)

VITAL RATES OF PROJECTED POPULATION

Per Thousand	1990			1995			VITAL RATES OF STABLE POPULATION	
	BOTH SEXES	MALES	FEMALES	BOTH SEXES	MALES	FEMALES	MALES	FEMALES
BIRTH RATE	12.42	12.96	11.90	12.27	12.81	11.76	9.91	8.80
DEATH RATE	11.51	12.05	10.99	11.85	12.28	11.44	17.95	16.94
RATE OF INCREASE	0.91	0.91	0.91	0.42	0.53	0.32		-8.13

TABLE 6

PROJECTED VITAL RATES AND RATIOS (female dominant)

AGE STRUCTURE OF PROJECTED POPULATION / STABLE AGE STRUCTURE

	BOTH SEXES	MALES	FEMALES	BOTH SEXES	MALES	FEMALES	MALES	FEMALES
% UNDER 15	18.36	19.09	17.64	18.18	18.92	17.46	15.61	13.93
% 15-64	65.03	66.98	63.12	65.53	67.51	63.60	64.18	59.10
% 65 AND OLDER	16.62	13.92	19.23	16.29	13.57	18.94	20.20	26.97
DEPEND. RATIO x 100	53.78	49.29	58.42	52.61	48.13	57.24	55.81	69.19

AGE GROUP	FEMALE BIRTH RATES	NET MATERNITY FUNCTION	COEFF. OF MATRIX EQUATION	ORIGINAL MATRIX		STABLE MATRIX		MATRIX PARAMETERS	
				SUB-DIAGONAL	FIRST ROW	FISHER VALUES	REPRODUCTIVE VALUES		
0-4	0.0000	0.0000	0.0000	0.99848	0.00000	0.987	122261	λ_1	0.96014
5-9	0.0000	0.0000	0.0000	0.99914	0.00002	0.949	120703	λ_2	0.36864+0.73436i
10-14	0.0000	0.0000	0.0214	0.99881	0.02147	0.912	138057	λ_4	-0.26196+0.44540i
15-19	0.0087	0.0428	0.1332	0.99805	0.13364	0.856	139441	λ_6	-0.38580+0.07773i
20-24	0.0453	0.2235	0.2618	0.99799	0.26328	0.691	107403	r_1	-0.00813
25-29	0.0609	0.3001	0.2343	0.99768	0.23606	0.404	61826	r_2	-0.03928+0.22111i
30-34	0.0343	0.1685	0.1112	0.99688	0.11230	0.156	23240	r_4	-0.13205+0.42049i
35-39	0.0110	0.0539	0.0317	0.99499	0.03215	0.039	5915	r_6	-0.18651+0.58855i
40-44	0.0020	0.0095	0.0049	0.99165	0.00504	0.005	683	c_1	29439
45-49	0.0001	0.0004	0.0002	0.98665	0.00019	0.000	20	$2\pi/y$	28.4161
50-54	0.0000	0.0000	0.0000	0.00000	0.00000	0.000	0	Δ	14.8521

TABLE 7

LESLIE MATRIX AND ITS ANALYSIS (females)

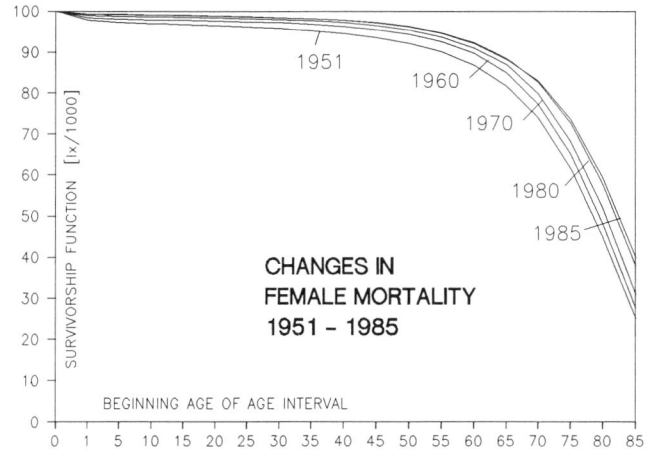

CHANGES IN FEMALE MORTALITY 1951 – 1985

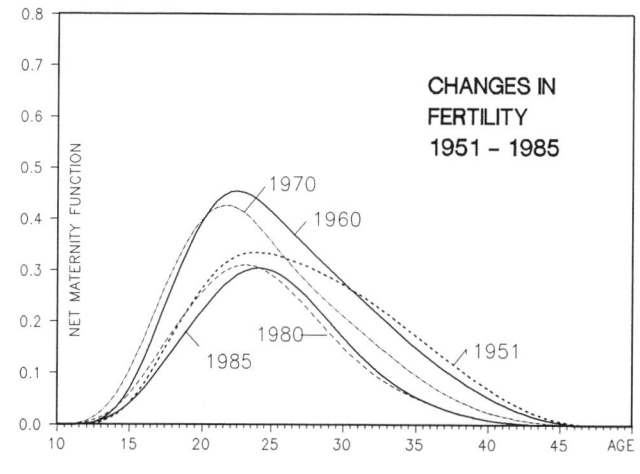

CHANGES IN FERTILITY 1951 – 1985

TABLE 1 — DATA

AGE AT LAST BIRTHDAY	ESTIMATED MID-YEAR POPULATION BOTH SEXES	MALES Number	MALES Percent	FEMALES Number	FEMALES Percent	BIRTHS BY AGE OF MOTHER AND SEX	DEATHS BOTH SEXES	DEATHS MALES	DEATHS FEMALES	AGE AT LAST BIRTHDAY
0	508500	261300	1.7	247200	1.5		18123	10509	7614	0
1-4	2029500	1038200	6.6	991300	5.9		2137	1214	923	1-4
5-9	2792100	1427700	9.0	1364400	8.2		1244	746	498	5-9
10-14	3440700	1755800	11.1	1684900	10.1	349	1325	822	503	10-14
15-19	3450900	1757400	11.1	1693500	10.1	50380	2475	1753	722	15-19
20-24	2833100	1431900	9.1	1401200	8.4	236592	3118	2312	806	20-24
25-29	1910000	959000	6.1	951000	5.7	123662	2448	1823	625	25-29
30-34	2172700	1084700	6.9	1088000	6.5	79216	3400	2413	987	30-34
35-39	2280300	1139900	7.2	1140400	6.8	41738	5032	3478	1554	35-39
40-44	2233500	1079500	6.8	1154000	6.9	13068	7177	4767	2410	40-44
45-49	1940200	894700	5.7	1045500	6.2	960	9131	5690	3441	45-49
50-54	1236400	564400	3.6	672000	4.0	8	8734	5403	3331	50-54
55-59	1538700	691300	4.4	847400	5.1		17573	10987	6586	55-59
60-64	1478900	665500	4.2	813400	4.9		27476	17041	10435	60-64
65-69	1150200	489400	3.1	660800	3.9		34438	19952	14486	65-69
70-74	781300	300600	1.9	480700	2.9		39044	19608	19436	70-74
75-79	467200	163400	1.0	303800	1.8		34600	15101	19499	75-79
80-84	191972	64394	0.4	127578	0.8	281814 M	27436	10155	17281	80-84
85+	89628	26506	0.2	63122	0.4	264159 F	21888	6961	14927	85+
TOTAL	32525800	15795600		16730200		545973	266799	140735	126064	TOTAL

TABLE 2 — MALE LIFE TABLE

x	nM_x	nq_x	l_x	nd_x	nL_x	nm_x	na_x	T_x	$\overset{\circ}{e}_x$	x
0	0.040218	0.038871	100000	3887	96651	0.040218	0.138	6641832	66.418	0
1	0.001169	0.004664	96113	448	383331	0.001169	1.500	6545182	68.099	1
5	0.000523	0.002609	95665	250	477699	0.000523	2.500	6161851	64.411	5
10	0.000468	0.002338	95415	223	476564	0.000468	2.710	5684152	59.573	10
15	0.000997	0.004988	95192	475	474886	0.001000	2.738	5207587	54.706	15
20	0.001615	0.008080	94717	765	471759	0.001622	2.613	4732702	49.967	20
25	0.001901	0.009480	93952	891	467588	0.001905	2.562	4260943	45.352	25
30	0.002225	0.011064	93061	1030	462837	0.002225	2.602	3793355	40.762	30
35	0.003051	0.015147	92032	1394	456872	0.003051	2.643	3330519	36.189	35
40	0.004416	0.021886	90638	1984	448520	0.004423	2.647	2873647	31.705	40
45	0.006360	0.031524	88654	2795	436711	0.006399	2.653	2425127	27.355	45
50	0.009573	0.047045	85859	4039	419922	0.009619	2.679	1988416	23.159	50
55	0.015893	0.076627	81820	6270	394484	0.015893	2.669	1568494	19.170	55
60	0.025606	0.120754	75550	9123	356220	0.025611	2.640	1174010	15.539	60
65	0.040768	0.186610	66427	12396	302430	0.040988	2.604	817790	12.311	65
70	0.065230	0.282847	54031	15283	232408	0.065758	2.530	515360	9.538	70
75	0.092417	0.376619	38749	14593	156897	0.093013	2.475	282952	7.302	75
80	0.157701	0.560572	24155	13541	85638	0.158116	2.405	126056	5.219	80
85	0.262620	1.000000	10614	10614	40418	0.208313	3.808	40418	3.808	85

TABLE 3 — FEMALE LIFE TABLE

x	nM_x	nq_x	l_x	nd_x	nL_x	nm_x	na_x	T_x	$\overset{\circ}{e}_x$	x
0	0.030801	0.029990	100000	2999	97368	0.030801	0.122	7303110	73.031	0
1	0.000931	0.003716	97001	360	387103	0.000931	1.500	7205742	74.285	1
5	0.000365	0.001823	96641	176	482762	0.000365	2.500	6818639	70.557	5
10	0.000299	0.001492	96464	144	481968	0.000299	2.542	6335877	65.681	10
15	0.000426	0.002132	96320	205	481117	0.000427	2.635	5853909	60.775	15
20	0.000575	0.002878	96115	277	479907	0.000576	2.583	5372792	55.900	20
25	0.000657	0.003289	95839	315	478437	0.000659	2.603	4892885	51.053	25
30	0.000907	0.004526	95523	432	476605	0.000907	2.659	4414448	46.213	30
35	0.001363	0.006792	95091	646	473955	0.001363	2.677	3937844	41.411	35
40	0.002088	0.010392	94445	981	469957	0.002088	2.689	3463889	36.676	40
45	0.003291	0.016442	93464	1537	463743	0.003314	2.674	2993932	32.033	45
50	0.004957	0.024612	91927	2263	454371	0.004979	2.674	2530188	27.524	50
55	0.007772	0.038175	89664	3423	440414	0.007772	2.690	2075817	23.151	55
60	0.012829	0.062378	86241	5380	418812	0.012845	2.696	1635403	18.963	60
65	0.021922	0.104840	80862	8478	384795	0.022031	2.698	1216592	15.045	65
70	0.040433	0.185700	72384	13442	329993	0.040734	2.625	831796	11.491	70
75	0.064184	0.280246	58943	16518	255094	0.064754	2.602	501804	8.513	75
80	0.135454	0.506545	42424	21490	158184	0.135853	2.490	246710	5.815	80
85	0.236479	1.000000	20934	20934	88526	0.175080	4.229	88526	4.229	85

TABLE 4 — OBSERVED VITAL RATES AND RATIOS

CRUDE RATES

Per Thousand	BOTH SEXES	MALES	FEMALES
BIRTH RATE	16.79	17.84	15.79
DEATH RATE	8.20	8.91	7.54
RATE OF INCREASE	8.58	8.93	8.25

PERCENT OF POPULATION IN AGE GROUP

UNDER 15	26.97	28.38	25.63
15 - 64	64.79	65.01	64.59
65 AND OLDER	8.24	6.61	9.78

RATES STANDARDIZED ON USA 1980

Per Thousand	BOTH SEXES	MALES	FEMALES
BIRTH RATE	19.28		18.14
DEATH RATE	11.98	12.28	11.69
RATE OF INCREASE	7.30		6.45

RATES STANDARDIZED ON MEXICO 1980

	BOTH SEXES	MALES	FEMALES
BIRTH RATE	17.29		16.87
DEATH RATE	5.11	5.98	4.23
RATE OF INCREASE	12.18		12.63

VITAL STATISTICS

GFR x 1000	64.432
TFR	2.253
GRR	1.090
NRR	1.042
μ	26.969
σ^2	34.309
GENERATION	26.943
POP. SEX RATIO	1.059
SEX RATIO AT BIRTH	1.067
DEP. RATIO x 100	54.336

PROJECTED POPULATION

AGE GROUP	1975 BOTH SEXES	MALES	FEMALES	1980 BOTH SEXES	MALES	FEMALES	STABLE EQUIVALENT TO ORIGINAL POPULATION MALES Number	Percent	FEMALES Number	Percent	AGE GROUP	
0-4	2859	1469	1390	3211	1650	1561	1538	7.6	1455	7.0	0-4	
5-9	2527	1293	1234	2847	1462	1385	1518	7.5	1438	6.9	5-9	TABLE 5
10-14	2786	1424	1362	2522	1290	1232	1503	7.4	1425	6.9	10-14	
15-19	3432	1750	1682	2779	1419	1360	1486	7.4	1412	6.8	15-19	POPULATION
20-24	3435	1746	1689	3416	1738	1678	1465	7.3	1397	6.7	20-24	PROJECTED
25-29	2816	1419	1397	3414	1730	1684	1441	7.1	1382	6.7	25-29	WITH
30-34	1896	949	947	2797	1405	1392	1416	7.0	1366	6.6	30-34	FIXED
35-39	2153	1071	1082	1879	937	942	1387	6.9	1348	6.5	35-39	AGE-
40-44	2250	1119	1131	2124	1051	1073	1351	6.7	1327	6.4	40-44	SPECIFIC
45-49	2190	1051	1139	2206	1090	1116	1305	6.5	1299	6.3	45-49	BIRTH
50-54	1884	860	1024	2127	1011	1116	1245	6.2	1263	6.1	50-54	AND
55-59	1181	530	651	1801	808	993	1161	5.7	1215	5.9	55-59	DEATH
60-64	1430	624	806	1098	479	619	1040	5.1	1146	5.5	60-64	RATES
65-69	1312	565	747	1270	530	740	876	4.3	1045	5.0	65-69	(female
70-74	943	376	567	1075	434	641	668	3.3	889	4.3	70-74	dominant,
75-79	575	203	372	692	254	438	448	2.2	682	3.3	75-79	in 000s)
80-84	277	89	188	341	111	230	242	1.2	420	2.0	80-84	
85+	101	30	71	147	42	105	114	0.6	233	1.1	85+	
TOTAL	34047	16568	17479	35746	17441	18305	20204		20742		TOTAL	

VITAL RATES OF PROJECTED POPULATION

Per Thousand	1975 BOTH SEXES	MALES	FEMALES	1980 BOTH SEXES	MALES	FEMALES
BIRTH RATE	18.79	19.93	17.70	19.36	20.48	18.29
DEATH RATE	9.03	9.65	8.44	9.75	10.21	9.31
RATE OF INCREASE	9.76	10.28	9.27	9.61	10.27	8.98

VITAL RATES OF STABLE POPULATION

Per Thousand	MALES	FEMALES	
BIRTH RATE	15.92	14.53	TABLE 6
DEATH RATE	14.32	12.99	PROJECTED
RATE OF INCREASE		1.54	VITAL RATES AND RATIOS

AGE STRUCTURE OF PROJECTED POPULATION

	BOTH SEXES	MALES	FEMALES	BOTH SEXES	MALES	FEMALES
% UNDER 15	24.00	25.27	22.80	24.00	25.24	22.82
% 15-64	66.57	67.11	66.07	66.14	66.90	65.40
% 65 AND OLDER	9.42	7.63	11.13	9.86	7.86	11.77
DEPEND. RATIO x 100	50.21	49.01	51.36	51.21	49.47	52.90

STABLE AGE STRUCTURE

	MALES	FEMALES	
% UNDER 15	22.57	20.82	(female dominant)
% 15-64	65.81	63.42	
% 65 AND OLDER	11.62	15.76	
DEPEND. RATIO x 100	51.95	57.68	

AGE GROUP	FEMALE BIRTH RATES	NET MATERNITY FUNCTION	COEFF. OF MATRIX EQUATION	ORIGINAL MATRIX SUB-DIAGONAL	FIRST ROW	STABLE MATRIX FISHER VALUES	REPRODUCTIVE VALUES	MATRIX PARAMETERS		
0-4	0.0000	0.0000	0.0000	0.99647	0.00000	1.036	1283134	λ_1	1.00775	
5-9	0.0000	0.0000	0.0002	0.99835	0.00024	1.048	1429564	λ_2	0.32198+0.73324i	TABLE 7
10-14	0.0001	0.0005	0.0349	0.99823	0.03505	1.057	1781556	λ_4	-0.40593+0.36299i	
15-19	0.0144	0.0692	0.2307	0.99749	0.23226	1.031	1746115	λ_6	0.03813+0.50245i	LESLIE
20-24	0.0817	0.3921	0.3465	0.99694	0.34983	0.800	1121571	r_1	0.00154	MATRIX
25-29	0.0629	0.3010	0.2345	0.99617	0.23741	0.446	423734	r_2	-0.04442+0.23140i	AND ITS
30-34	0.0352	0.1679	0.1259	0.99444	0.12799	0.204	221775	r_4	-0.12156+0.48240i	ANALYSIS
35-39	0.0177	0.0839	0.0548	0.99157	0.05605	0.073	83502	r_6	-0.13708+0.29901i	(females)
40-44	0.0055	0.0257	0.0139	0.98678	0.01433	0.016	18288	c_1	207431	
45-49	0.0004	0.0021	0.0010	0.97979	0.00109	0.001	1186	$2\pi/y$	27.1524	
50-54	0.0000	0.0000	0.0000	0.96928	0.00001	0.000	10	Δ	10.5876	

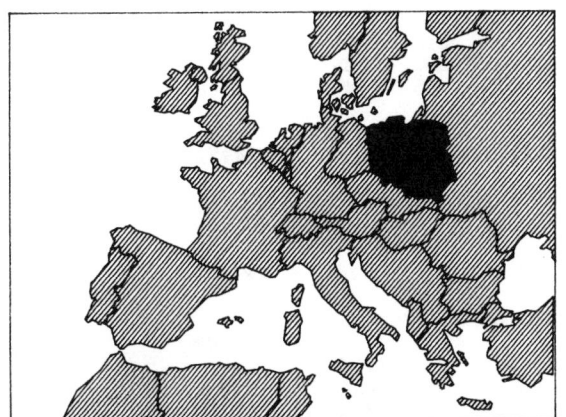

EDUCATION [1984]

% of primary school-age children enrolled:	101
secondary school-age children enrolled:	77
ca. 20-24 year olds in higher education:	16

LABOR FORCE

Average annual labor force growth (%) 1980-85:	0.7	
% of the 1980 labor force in agriculture:	29	TABLE 8
in industry:	39	
in services:	33	SOCIO-ECONOMIC INDICATORS

GNP & INCOME DISTRIBUTION

GNP per capita (in US Dollars) 1985:	2050
GNP growth rate (%) 1979:	-0.1
% share of total household income	
Lowest 20% of households:	na
Highest 10% of households:	na

HEALTH & NUTRITION

Population per physician 1981:	550
Daily calorie supply per capita 1985:	3280

TABLE 1 — DATA

AGE AT LAST BIRTHDAY	ESTIMATED MID-YEAR POPULATION BOTH SEXES	MALES Number	MALES Percent	FEMALES Number	FEMALES Percent	BIRTHS BY AGE OF MOTHER AND SEX	DEATHS BOTH SEXES	DEATHS MALES	DEATHS FEMALES	AGE AT LAST BIRTHDAY
0	627959	325012	2.0	302947	1.7		16001	9375	6626	0
1-4	2238487	1148059	6.9	1090428	6.2		2067	1148	919	1-4
5-9	2534159	1294639	7.8	1239520	7.1		1081	677	404	5-9
10-14	2775030	1419073	8.6	1355957	7.8		979	626	353	10-14
15-19	3422467	1746509	10.6	1675958	9.6	52549	2469	1777	692	15-19
20-24	3423603	1740489	10.5	1683114	9.6	286290	3887	3027	860	20-24
25-29	2799405	1415026	8.5	1384379	7.9	189005	3485	2648	837	25-29
30-34	1888963	946155	5.7	942808	5.4	67305	3052	2245	807	30-34
35-39	2143234	1065921	6.4	1077313	6.2	36485	4847	3494	1353	35-39
40-44	2241853	1113024	6.7	1128829	6.5	11296	7449	5261	2188	40-44
45-49	2184590	1047386	6.3	1137204	6.5	842	11366	7742	3624	45-49
50-54	1879614	857523	5.2	1022091	5.9		14139	9151	4988	50-54
55-59	1179884	529773	3.2	650111	3.7		13118	8214	4904	55-59
60-64	1438219	629811	3.8	808408	4.6		25584	15737	9847	60-64
65-69	1314114	567340	3.4	746774	4.3		37548	22383	15165	65-69
70-74	957711	382823	2.3	574888	3.3		44735	23727	21008	70-74
75-79	568312	201255	1.2	367057	2.1		44421	19939	24482	75-79
80-84	260817	82580	0.5	178237	1.0	332629 M	32982	12171	20811	80-84
85+	143709	39645	0.2	104064	0.6	311143 F	27686	8493	19193	85+
TOTAL	34022130	16552043		17470087		643772	296896	157835	139061	TOTAL

TABLE 2 — MALE LIFE TABLE

x	nM_x	nq_x	l_x	nd_x	nL_x	nm_x	na_x	T_x	$\overset{\circ}{e}_x$	x
0	0.028845	0.028130	100000	2813	97522	0.028845	0.119	6710870	67.109	0
1	0.001000	0.003990	97187	388	387779	0.001000	1.500	6613348	68.048	1
5	0.000523	0.002611	96799	253	483364	0.000523	2.500	6225569	64.314	5
10	0.000441	0.002203	96546	213	482250	0.000441	2.731	5742205	59.476	10
15	0.001017	0.005076	96334	489	480575	0.001017	2.763	5259956	54.601	15
20	0.001739	0.008669	95845	831	477229	0.001741	2.600	4779381	49.866	20
25	0.001871	0.009331	95014	887	472912	0.001875	2.567	4302151	45.279	25
30	0.002373	0.011843	94127	1115	467980	0.002382	2.617	3829239	40.681	30
35	0.003278	0.016264	93013	1513	461495	0.003278	2.641	3361259	36.138	35
40	0.004727	0.023376	91500	2139	452514	0.004727	2.669	2899764	31.691	40
45	0.007392	0.036381	89361	3251	439171	0.007403	2.652	2447250	27.386	45
50	0.010671	0.052349	86110	4508	419880	0.010736	2.633	2008079	23.320	50
55	0.015505	0.075101	81602	6128	393606	0.015570	2.649	1588199	19.463	55
60	0.024987	0.117970	75474	8904	356333	0.024987	2.637	1194593	15.828	60
65	0.039453	0.180271	66570	12001	304070	0.039467	2.602	838260	12.592	65
70	0.061979	0.270541	54569	14763	236748	0.062358	2.555	534190	9.789	70
75	0.099073	0.399056	39806	15885	158889	0.099975	2.473	297442	7.472	75
80	0.147384	0.530969	23921	12701	86179	0.147384	2.368	138553	5.792	80
85	0.214226	1.000000	11220	11220	52374	0.149909	4.668	52374	4.668	85

TABLE 3 — FEMALE LIFE TABLE

x	nM_x	nq_x	l_x	nd_x	nL_x	nm_x	na_x	T_x	$\overset{\circ}{e}_x$	x
0	0.021872	0.021453	100000	2145	98085	0.021872	0.107	7452174	74.522	0
1	0.000843	0.003364	97855	329	390596	0.000843	1.500	7354090	75.153	1
5	0.000326	0.001628	97526	159	487231	0.000326	2.500	6963494	71.402	5
10	0.000260	0.001301	97367	127	486526	0.000260	2.568	6476263	66.514	10
15	0.000413	0.002062	97240	201	485724	0.000413	2.626	5989738	61.597	15
20	0.000511	0.002553	97040	248	484597	0.000511	2.578	5504014	56.719	20
25	0.000605	0.003026	96792	293	483261	0.000606	2.618	5019416	51.858	25
30	0.000856	0.004291	96499	414	481523	0.000860	2.655	4536155	47.007	30
35	0.001256	0.006261	96085	602	479025	0.001256	2.676	4054632	42.199	35
40	0.001938	0.009648	95483	921	475299	0.001938	2.702	3575607	37.448	40
45	0.003187	0.015817	94562	1496	469349	0.003187	2.687	3100308	32.786	45
50	0.004880	0.024293	93066	2261	460071	0.004914	2.674	2630959	28.270	50
55	0.007543	0.037242	90805	3382	446180	0.007579	2.680	2170888	23.907	55
60	0.012181	0.059234	87423	5178	425131	0.012181	2.685	1724708	19.728	60
65	0.020307	0.097132	82245	7989	392793	0.020338	2.693	1299577	15.801	65
70	0.036543	0.169247	74256	12568	341923	0.036756	2.664	906784	12.212	70
75	0.066698	0.289771	61689	17876	265250	0.067392	2.584	564861	9.157	75
80	0.116760	0.450713	43813	19747	169126	0.116760	2.471	299611	6.838	80
85	0.184435	1.000000	24066	24066	130485	0.115947	5.422	130485	5.422	85

TABLE 4 — OBSERVED VITAL RATES AND RATIOS

CRUDE RATES

Per Thousand	BOTH SEXES	MALES	FEMALES
BIRTH RATE	18.92	20.10	17.81
DEATH RATE	8.73	9.54	7.96
RATE OF INCREASE	10.20	10.56	9.85

PERCENT OF POPULATION IN AGE GROUP

	BOTH SEXES	MALES	FEMALES
UNDER 15	24.03	25.29	22.83
15 - 64	66.43	67.01	65.89
65 AND OLDER	9.54	7.69	11.28

RATES STANDARDIZED ON USA 1980

Per Thousand	BOTH SEXES	MALES	FEMALES
BIRTH RATE	19.50		18.33
DEATH RATE	11.03	11.78	10.33
RATE OF INCREASE	8.47		8.00

RATES STANDARDIZED ON MEXICO 1980

	BOTH SEXES	MALES	FEMALES
BIRTH RATE	17.52		17.07
DEATH RATE	4.65	5.60	3.69
RATE OF INCREASE	12.87		13.38

VITAL STATISTICS

GFR x 1000	71.296
TFR	2.270
GRR	1.097
NRR	1.060
μ	26.807
σ^2	32.685
GENERATION	26.771
POP. SEX RATIO	1.055
SEX RATIO AT BIRTH	1.069
DEP. RATIO x 100	50.528

AGE AT LAST BIRTHDAY	ESTIMATED MID-YEAR POPULATION					BIRTHS BY AGE OF MOTHER AND SEX	DEATHS			AGE AT LAST BIRTHDAY
	BOTH SEXES	MALES		FEMALES			BOTH SEXES	MALES	FEMALES	
		Number	Percent	Number	Percent					
0	689146	353283	2.0	335863	1.8		14739	8654	6085	0
1-4	2563590	1310940	7.6	1252650	6.9		2048	1179	869	1-4
5-9	2864552	1465120	8.5	1399432	7.7		1145	698	447	5-9
10-14	2521832	1289626	7.4	1232206	6.8		809	526	283	10-14
15-19	2772184	1424292	8.2	1347892	7.4	44317	1962	1472	490	15-19
20-24	3339363	1709286	9.9	1630077	8.9	292837	3873	3095	778	20-24
25-29	3349985	1699060	9.8	1650925	9.0	225194	4594	3642	952	25-29
30-34	2768706	1395934	8.1	1372772	7.5	94799	4812	3637	1175	30-34
35-39	1854654	923469	5.3	931185	5.1	26959	4849	3601	1248	35-39
40-44	2101275	1037352	6.0	1063923	5.8	8026	8472	6238	2234	40-44
45-49	2171983	1067459	6.2	1104524	6.1	656	13252	9543	3709	45-49
50-54	2104181	995356	5.7	1108825	6.1	10	18764	13003	5761	50-54
55-59	1782976	796979	4.6	985997	5.4		22679	14867	7812	55-59
60-64	1096166	478299	2.8	617867	3.4		20504	12746	7758	60-64
65-69	1286123	537809	3.1	748314	4.1		38649	22991	15658	65-69
70-74	1089627	440196	2.5	649431	3.6		52793	29121	23672	70-74
75-79	708157	256578	1.5	451579	2.5		55888	26472	29416	75-79
80-84	343878	108329	0.6	235549	1.3	355496 M	44982	17153	27829	80-84
85+	169578	45943	0.3	123635	0.7	337302 F	35389	10574	24815	85+
TOTAL	35577956	17335310		18242646		692798	350203	189212	160991	TOTAL

TABLE 1

DATA

x	$_nM_x$	$_nq_x$	l_x	$_nd_x$	$_nL_x$	$_nm_x$	$_na_x$	T_x	$\overset{\circ}{e}_x$	x
0	0.024496	0.023974	100000	2397	97870	0.024496	0.112	6609158	66.092	0
1	0.000899	0.003589	97603	350	389535	0.000899	1.500	6511288	66.712	1
5	0.000476	0.002379	97252	231	485683	0.000476	2.500	6121754	62.947	5
10	0.000408	0.002039	97021	198	484666	0.000408	2.782	5636071	58.091	10
15	0.001033	0.005156	96823	499	483007	0.001033	2.780	5151405	53.204	15
20	0.001811	0.009015	96324	868	479557	0.001811	2.625	4668398	48.466	20
25	0.002144	0.010669	95456	1018	474807	0.002145	2.574	4188841	43.883	25
30	0.002605	0.013006	94437	1228	469280	0.002617	2.635	3714035	39.328	30
35	0.003899	0.019436	93209	1812	461824	0.003923	2.670	3244754	34.812	35
40	0.006013	0.029650	91397	2710	450643	0.006013	2.659	2782930	30.449	40
45	0.008940	0.043777	88687	3882	434286	0.008940	2.643	2332287	26.298	45
50	0.013064	0.063411	84805	5378	411257	0.013076	2.626	1898001	22.381	50
55	0.018654	0.089789	79427	7132	380080	0.018764	2.608	1486743	18.718	55
60	0.026649	0.125693	72296	9087	339826	0.026740	2.617	1106664	15.307	60
65	0.042749	0.193797	63208	12250	286545	0.042749	2.592	766837	12.132	65
70	0.066155	0.284470	50959	14496	219126	0.066155	2.540	480292	9.425	70
75	0.103173	0.411347	36463	14999	144293	0.103947	2.465	261166	7.163	75
80	0.158342	0.558336	21464	11984	75684	0.158342	2.360	116873	5.445	80
85	0.230155	1.000000	9480	9480	41189	0.169001	4.345	41189	4.345	85

TABLE 2

MALE LIFE TABLE

x	$_nM_x$	$_nq_x$	l_x	$_nd_x$	$_nL_x$	$_nm_x$	$_na_x$	T_x	$\overset{\circ}{e}_x$	x
0	0.018118	0.017827	100000	1783	98397	0.018118	0.101	7460223	74.602	0
1	0.000694	0.002770	98217	272	392189	0.000694	1.500	7361826	74.954	1
5	0.000319	0.001596	97945	156	489335	0.000319	2.500	6969637	71.159	5
10	0.000230	0.001148	97789	112	488668	0.000230	2.539	6480301	66.268	10
15	0.000364	0.001816	97677	177	487965	0.000364	2.641	5991633	61.341	15
20	0.000477	0.002384	97499	232	486937	0.000477	2.592	5503668	56.448	20
25	0.000577	0.002882	97267	280	485672	0.000577	2.637	5016731	51.577	25
30	0.000856	0.004297	96987	417	483968	0.000861	2.684	4531059	46.718	30
35	0.001340	0.006720	96570	649	481349	0.001348	2.688	4047091	41.908	35
40	0.002100	0.010448	95921	1002	477293	0.002100	2.694	3565742	37.174	40
45	0.003358	0.016660	94919	1581	470930	0.003358	2.684	3088449	32.538	45
50	0.005196	0.025667	93337	2396	461110	0.005196	2.672	2617519	28.044	50
55	0.007923	0.039172	90942	3562	446418	0.007980	2.673	2156409	23.712	55
60	0.012556	0.061288	87379	5355	424470	0.012616	2.680	1709991	19.570	60
65	0.020924	0.099777	82024	8184	391128	0.020924	2.680	1285521	15.673	65
70	0.036450	0.168026	73840	12407	340105	0.036480	2.655	894392	12.113	70
75	0.065140	0.283545	61433	17419	265207	0.065680	2.591	554287	9.023	75
80	0.118145	0.455405	44014	20044	169657	0.118145	2.485	289080	6.568	80
85	0.200712	1.000000	23970	23970	119423	0.133714	4.982	119423	4.982	85

TABLE 3

FEMALE LIFE TABLE

CRUDE RATES

Per Thousand	BOTH SEXES	MALES	FEMALES
BIRTH RATE	19.47	20.51	18.49
DEATH RATE	9.84	10.91	8.82
RATE OF INCREASE	9.63	9.59	9.66

RATES STANDARDIZED ON USA 1980

Per Thousand	BOTH SEXES	MALES	FEMALES
BIRTH RATE	19.70		18.65
DEATH RATE	11.63	12.77	10.55
RATE OF INCREASE	8.07		8.10

VITAL STATISTICS

GFR x 1000	76.121	TABLE 4
TFR	2.275	
GRR	1.108	OBSERVED
NRR	1.076	VITAL
μ	26.452	RATES
σ^2	30.325	AND
GENERATION	26.410	RATIOS
POP. SEX RATIO	1.052	
SEX RATIO AT BIRTH	1.054	
DEP. RATIO x 100	52.424	

PERCENT OF POPULATION IN AGE GROUP

UNDER 15	24.28	25.49	23.13
15 - 64	65.61	66.50	64.76
65 AND OLDER	10.11	8.01	12.11

RATES STANDARDIZED ON MEXICO 1980

BIRTH RATE	17.80		17.46
DEATH RATE	4.79	5.94	3.62
RATE OF INCREASE	13.00		13.84

TABLE 1 — DATA

AGE AT LAST BIRTHDAY	ESTIMATED MID-YEAR POPULATION BOTH SEXES	MALES Number	MALES Percent	FEMALES Number	FEMALES Percent	BIRTHS BY AGE OF MOTHER AND SEX	DEATHS BOTH SEXES	DEATHS MALES	DEATHS FEMALES	AGE AT LAST BIRTHDAY
0	686550	352352	1.9	334198	1.8		12523	7259	5264	0
1-4	2736354	1402572	7.7	1333782	7.0		1761	998	763	1-4
5-9	3223911	1648841	9.1	1575070	8.3		974	588	386	5-9
10-14	2852291	1458221	8.0	1394070	7.3		826	536	290	10-14
15-19	2509134	1282065	7.1	1227069	6.4	43041	1565	1161	404	15-19
20-24	2750337	1410386	7.8	1339951	7.0	244649	2675	2127	548	20-24
25-29	3305099	1687849	9.3	1617250	8.5	227551	3979	3068	911	25-29
30-34	3310313	1673845	9.2	1636468	8.6	114424	5340	4117	1223	30-34
35-39	2731293	1371361	7.6	1359932	7.1	41027	6637	4832	1805	35-39
40-44	1819784	900082	5.0	919702	4.8	6341	7115	5122	1993	40-44
45-49	2046651	999944	5.5	1046707	5.5	533	12336	8861	3475	45-49
50-54	2090692	1011579	5.6	1079113	5.7	10	19354	13751	5603	50-54
55-59	1990954	919319	5.1	1071635	5.6		27048	18323	8725	55-59
60-64	1647242	710906	3.9	936336	4.9		32805	20685	12120	60-64
65-69	975981	406079	2.2	569902	3.0		29026	16946	12080	65-69
70-74	1074251	419347	2.3	654904	3.4		51027	27335	23692	70-74
75-79	810233	297030	1.6	513203	2.7		63205	30193	33012	75-79
80-84	439537	139244	0.8	300293	1.6	348199 M	55611	22095	33516	80-84
85+	202374	52790	0.3	149584	0.8	329377 F	47651	14083	33568	85+
TOTAL	37202981	18143812		19059169		677576	381458	202080	179378	TOTAL

TABLE 2 — MALE LIFE TABLE

x	nM_x	nq_x	l_x	nd_x	nL_x	nm_x	na_x	T_x	$\overset{\circ}{e}_x$	x
0	0.020602	0.020229	100000	2023	98190	0.020602	0.105	6649939	66.499	0
1	0.000712	0.002841	97977	278	391213	0.000712	1.500	6551750	66.870	1
5	0.000357	0.001781	97699	174	488059	0.000357	2.500	6160537	63.056	5
10	0.000368	0.001847	97525	180	487229	0.000370	2.808	5672478	58.165	10
15	0.000906	0.004529	97345	441	485735	0.000908	2.759	5185249	53.267	15
20	0.001508	0.007514	96904	728	482788	0.001508	2.623	4699514	48.497	20
25	0.001818	0.009049	96176	870	478794	0.001818	2.605	4216726	43.844	25
30	0.002460	0.012242	95305	1167	473774	0.002463	2.640	3737932	39.221	30
35	0.003524	0.017592	94139	1656	466855	0.003547	2.682	3264159	34.674	35
40	0.005691	0.028265	92483	2614	456345	0.005728	2.679	2797304	30.247	40
45	0.008861	0.043408	89894	3901	440225	0.008862	2.663	2340959	26.049	45
50	0.013594	0.065853	85967	5661	416464	0.013594	2.638	1900734	22.110	50
55	0.019931	0.095210	80306	7646	383307	0.019947	2.616	1484269	18.483	55
60	0.029097	0.136739	72660	9935	339353	0.029278	2.590	1100963	15.152	60
65	0.041731	0.190001	62725	11918	284733	0.041856	2.576	761610	12.142	65
70	0.065185	0.280912	50807	14272	218952	0.065185	2.542	476877	9.386	70
75	0.101650	0.404682	36535	14785	145277	0.101771	2.471	257925	7.060	75
80	0.158678	0.560317	21750	12187	76802	0.158678	2.379	112649	5.179	80
85	0.266774	1.000000	9563	9563	35847	0.214227	3.748	35847	3.748	85

TABLE 3 — FEMALE LIFE TABLE

x	nM_x	nq_x	l_x	nd_x	nL_x	nm_x	na_x	T_x	$\overset{\circ}{e}_x$	x
0	0.015751	0.015530	100000	1553	98597	0.015751	0.097	7479508	74.795	0
1	0.000572	0.002285	98447	225	393226	0.000572	1.500	7380911	74.973	1
5	0.000245	0.001225	98222	120	490809	0.000245	2.500	6987685	71.142	5
10	0.000208	0.001041	98102	102	490262	0.000208	2.584	6496876	66.226	10
15	0.000329	0.001647	98000	161	489615	0.000330	2.626	6006614	61.292	15
20	0.000409	0.002043	97838	200	488715	0.000409	2.618	5516999	56.389	20
25	0.000563	0.002813	97638	275	487539	0.000563	2.624	5028284	51.499	25
30	0.000747	0.003736	97364	364	485987	0.000748	2.713	4540744	46.637	30
35	0.001327	0.006669	97000	647	483525	0.001338	2.719	4054757	41.802	35
40	0.002167	0.010846	96353	1045	479345	0.002180	2.684	3571232	37.064	40
45	0.003320	0.016473	95308	1570	472898	0.003320	2.680	3091887	32.441	45
50	0.005192	0.025652	93738	2405	463112	0.005192	2.680	2618988	27.939	50
55	0.008142	0.039954	91333	3649	448200	0.008142	2.680	2155876	23.604	55
60	0.012944	0.063307	87684	5551	425520	0.013045	2.676	1707676	19.475	60
65	0.021197	0.101454	82133	8333	391241	0.021298	2.669	1282157	15.611	65
70	0.036176	0.166706	73801	12303	340084	0.036176	2.649	890915	12.072	70
75	0.064325	0.279008	61498	17158	266062	0.064490	2.586	550831	8.957	75
80	0.111611	0.436621	44339	19359	173455	0.111611	2.508	284769	6.422	80
85	0.224409	1.000000	24980	24980	111314	0.160923	4.456	111314	4.456	85

TABLE 4 — OBSERVED VITAL RATES AND RATIOS

CRUDE RATES

Per Thousand	BOTH SEXES	MALES	FEMALES
BIRTH RATE	18.21	19.19	17.28
DEATH RATE	10.25	11.14	9.41
RATE OF INCREASE	7.96	8.05	7.87

PERCENT OF POPULATION IN AGE GROUP

UNDER 15	25.53	26.80	24.33
15 - 64	65.05	65.96	64.19
65 AND OLDER	9.41	7.24	11.48

RATES STANDARDIZED ON USA 1980

Per Thousand	BOTH SEXES	MALES	FEMALES
BIRTH RATE	20.18		19.08
DEATH RATE	11.77	12.90	10.70
RATE OF INCREASE	8.41		8.37

RATES STANDARDIZED ON MEXICO 1980

	BOTH SEXES	MALES	FEMALES
BIRTH RATE	18.25		17.88
DEATH RATE	4.67	5.78	3.54
RATE OF INCREASE	13.58		14.34

VITAL STATISTICS

GFR x 1000	74.076
TFR	2.329
GRR	1.132
NRR	1.104
μ	26.410
σ^2	30.068
GENERATION	26.353
POP. SEX RATIO	1.050
SEX RATIO AT BIRTH	1.057
DEP. RATIO x 100	53.722

PROJECTED POPULATION

AGE GROUP	1990 BOTH SEXES	1990 MALES	1990 FEMALES	1995 BOTH SEXES	1995 MALES	1995 FEMALES
0-4	3213	1647	1566	3106	1592	1514
5-9	3415	1750	1665	3204	1642	1562
10-14	3219	1646	1573	3410	1747	1663
15-19	2846	1454	1392	3212	1641	1571
20-24	2499	1274	1225	2835	1445	1390
25-29	2736	1399	1337	2486	1264	1222
30-34	3282	1670	1612	2716	1384	1332
35-39	3277	1649	1628	3250	1646	1604
40-44	2688	1340	1348	3226	1612	1614
45-49	1775	868	907	2623	1293	1330
50-54	1971	946	1025	1710	821	889
55-59	1975	931	1044	1863	871	992
60-64	1831	814	1017	1816	824	992
65-69	1457	596	861	1618	683	935
70-74	807	312	495	1207	459	748
75-79	790	278	512	595	207	388
80-84	492	157	335	481	147	334
85+	258	65	193	288	73	215
TOTAL	38531	18796	19735	39646	19351	20295

STABLE EQUIVALENT TO ORIGINAL POPULATION

MALES Number	MALES Percent	FEMALES Number	FEMALES Percent	AGE GROUP	
1612	8.3	1532	7.5	0-4	
1577	8.1	1500	7.4	5-9	TABLE 5
1545	8.0	1471	7.2	10-14	
1512	7.8	1442	7.1	15-19	POPULATION
1475	7.6	1412	6.9	20-24	PROJECTED
1435	7.4	1382	6.8	25-29	WITH
1394	7.2	1352	6.6	30-34	FIXED
1348	7.0	1321	6.5	35-39	AGE-
1293	6.7	1285	6.3	40-44	SPECIFIC
1224	6.3	1244	6.1	45-49	BIRTH
1136	5.9	1195	5.9	50-54	AND
1027	5.3	1135	5.6	55-59	DEATH
892	4.6	1058	5.2	60-64	RATES
734	3.8	955	4.7	65-69	(female
554	2.9	814	4.0	70-74	dominant,
361	1.9	625	3.1	75-79	in 000s)
187	1.0	400	2.0	80-84	
86	0.4	252	1.2	85+	
19392		20375		TOTAL	

VITAL RATES OF PROJECTED POPULATION

Per Thousand	1990 BOTH SEXES	1990 MALES	1990 FEMALES	1995 BOTH SEXES	1995 MALES	1995 FEMALES
BIRTH RATE	16.40	17.28	15.57	15.99	16.84	15.19
DEATH RATE	10.51	11.22	9.84	10.62	11.34	9.95
RATE OF INCREASE	5.89	6.06	5.73	5.37	5.50	5.24

VITAL RATES OF STABLE POPULATION

Per Thousand	MALES	FEMALES	
BIRTH RATE	17.14	15.43	TABLE 6
DEATH RATE	13.37	11.67	PROJECTED
RATE OF INCREASE		3.76	VITAL RATES AND RATIOS (female dominant)

AGE STRUCTURE OF PROJECTED POPULATION

	1990 BOTH SEXES	1990 MALES	1990 FEMALES	1995 BOTH SEXES	1995 MALES	1995 FEMALES
% UNDER 15	25.55	26.83	24.34	24.52	25.74	23.35
% 15-64	64.57	65.68	63.52	64.92	66.15	63.74
% 65 AND OLDER	9.87	7.50	12.14	10.57	8.11	12.91
DEPEND. RATIO x 100	54.86	52.26	57.43	54.05	51.18	56.89

STABLE AGE STRUCTURE

	MALES	FEMALES
% UNDER 15	24.41	22.10
% 15-64	65.67	62.95
% 65 AND OLDER	9.91	14.95
DEPEND. RATIO x 100	52.27	58.86

MATRIX PARAMETERS

AGE GROUP	FEMALE BIRTH RATES	NET MATERNITY FUNCTION	COEFF. OF MATRIX EQUATION	ORIGINAL MATRIX SUB-DIAGONAL	ORIGINAL MATRIX FIRST ROW	STABLE MATRIX FISHER VALUES	STABLE MATRIX REPRODUCTIVE VALUES
0-4	0.0000	0.0000	0.0000	0.99794	0.00000	1.026	1711698
5-9	0.0000	0.0000	0.0000	0.99888	0.00000	1.048	1650411
10-14	0.0000	0.0000	0.0417	0.99868	0.04187	1.069	1490121
15-19	0.0171	0.0835	0.2586	0.99816	0.25979	1.048	1285457
20-24	0.0888	0.4338	0.3836	0.99759	0.38605	0.802	1075086
25-29	0.0684	0.3335	0.2493	0.99682	0.25151	0.422	683125
30-34	0.0340	0.1652	0.1180	0.99493	0.11946	0.173	282872
35-39	0.0147	0.0709	0.0435	0.99136	0.04423	0.054	73178
40-44	0.0034	0.0161	0.0086	0.98655	0.00884	0.010	8755
45-49	0.0002	0.0012	0.0006	0.97931	0.00062	0.001	664
50-54	0.0000	0.0000	0.0000	0.96780	0.00001	0.000	12

λ_1	1.01897	
λ_2	0.30926+0.76675i	TABLE 7
λ_4	-0.42710+0.35565i	
λ_6	-0.00194+0.44378i	LESLIE
r_1	0.00376	MATRIX
r_2	-0.03805+0.23748i	AND ITS
r_4	-0.11747+0.48944i	ANALYSIS
r_6	-0.16248+0.31504i	(females)
c_1	203756	
$2\pi/y$	26.4574	
Δ	6.6835	

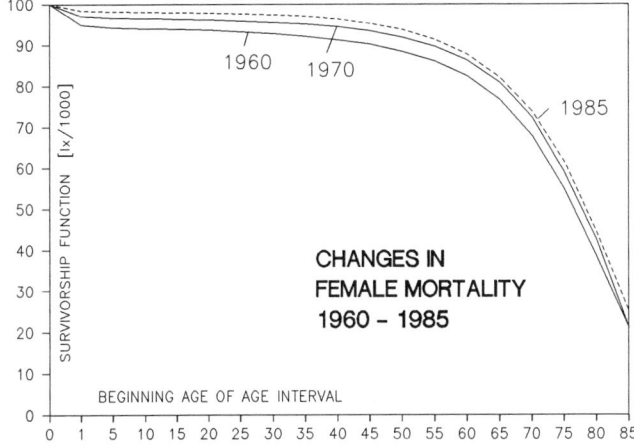

CHANGES IN FEMALE MORTALITY 1960 - 1985

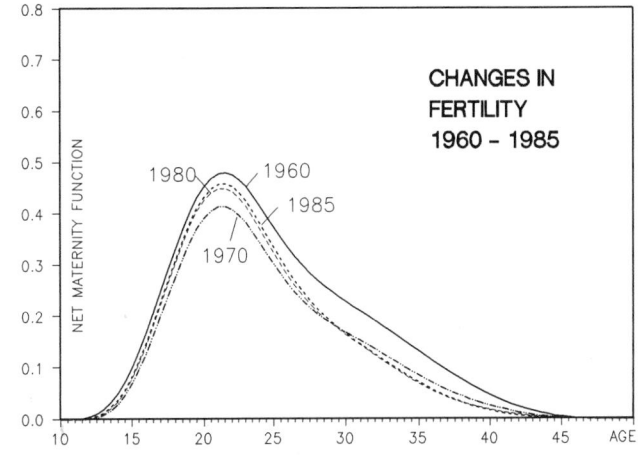

CHANGES IN FERTILITY 1960 - 1985

AGE AT LAST BIRTHDAY	ESTIMATED MID-YEAR POPULATION					BIRTHS BY AGE OF MOTHER AND SEX	DEATHS			AGE AT LAST BIRTHDAY
	BOTH SEXES	MALES		FEMALES			BOTH SEXES	MALES	FEMALES	
		Number	Percent	Number	Percent					
0	112731	43045	1.1	69686	1.5		10034	5583	4451	0
1-4	643248	327237	8.1	316011	7.0		2332	1234	1098	1-4
5-9	846151	430415	10.7	415736	9.2		727	425	302	5-9
10-14	809237	408936	10.1	400301	8.9	57	475	292	183	10-14
15-19	727788	353821	8.8	373967	8.3	10998	677	487	190	15-19
20-24	625372	296546	7.3	328826	7.3	47531	728	490	238	20-24
25-29	516536	240207	5.9	276329	6.1	47418	708	451	257	25-29
30-34	531720	249180	6.2	282540	6.3	34190	890	583	307	30-34
35-39	553381	261324	6.5	291949	6.5	22677	1256	807	449	35-39
40-44	549044	259815	6.4	289229	6.4	9153	1819	1175	644	40-44
45-49	511051	241645	6.0	269406	6.0	841	2445	1564	881	45-49
50-54	442714	208298	5.2	234416	5.2	26	3072	1958	1114	50-54
55-59	437884	205217	5.1	232667	5.2		4821	3105	1716	55-59
60-64	408417	183191	4.5	225226	5.0		7080	4311	2769	60-64
65-69	324876	139407	3.5	185469	4.1		9281	5262	4019	65-69
70-74	232742	93808	2.3	138934	3.1		11537	5878	5659	70-74
75-79	145998	56434	1.4	89564	2.0		13117	5903	7214	75-79
80-84	82139	28396	0.7	53743	1.2	89246 M	11920	4777	7143	80-84
85+	43521	12939	0.3	30582	0.7	83645 F	10174	3079	7095	85+
TOTAL	8544550	4039969		4504581		172891	93093	47364	45729	TOTAL

TABLE 1 DATA

TABLE 2 — MALE LIFE TABLE

x	$_nM_x$	$_nq_x$	l_x	$_nd_x$	$_nL_x$	$_nm_x$	$_na_x$	T_x	$\mathring{e}_x$	x
0	0.129701	0.118772	100000	11877	91573	0.129702	0.290	6019300	60.193	0
1	0.003771	0.014943	88123	1317	349199	0.003771	1.500	5927727	67.267	1
5	0.000987	0.004925	86806	428	432961	0.000987	2.500	5578528	64.264	5
10	0.000714	0.003568	86379	308	431156	0.000715	2.612	5145566	59.570	10
15	0.001376	0.006886	86070	593	428952	0.001382	2.639	4714410	54.774	15
20	0.001652	0.008245	85478	705	425668	0.001656	2.559	4285457	50.135	20
25	0.001878	0.009361	84773	794	421937	0.001881	2.571	3859789	45.531	25
30	0.002340	0.011633	83979	977	417554	0.002340	2.602	3437852	40.937	30
35	0.003087	0.015323	83002	1272	412010	0.003087	2.640	3020299	36.388	35
40	0.004522	0.022374	81731	1829	404348	0.004522	2.646	2608289	31.913	40
45	0.006472	0.031938	79902	2552	393491	0.006485	2.642	2203941	27.583	45
50	0.009400	0.046069	77350	3563	378433	0.009416	2.666	1810450	23.406	50
55	0.015130	0.073062	73787	5391	356304	0.015130	2.657	1432017	19.408	55
60	0.023533	0.111646	68396	7636	323966	0.023571	2.641	1075713	15.728	60
65	0.037746	0.173913	60759	10567	278647	0.037922	2.620	751747	12.373	65
70	0.062660	0.273265	50193	13716	217629	0.063024	2.570	473101	9.426	70
75	0.104600	0.415410	36477	15153	144231	0.105059	2.482	255472	7.004	75
80	0.168228	0.582312	21324	12417	73812	0.168228	2.358	111241	5.217	80
85	0.237963	1.000000	8907	8907	37429	0.178492	4.202	37429	4.202	85

TABLE 3 — FEMALE LIFE TABLE

x	$_nM_x$	$_nq_x$	l_x	$_nd_x$	$_nL_x$	$_nm_x$	$_na_x$	T_x	$\mathring{e}_x$	x
0	0.063872	0.060688	100000	6069	95015	0.063872	0.179	6953324	69.533	0
1	0.003475	0.013779	93931	1294	372489	0.003475	1.500	6858309	73.014	1
5	0.000726	0.003626	92637	336	462345	0.000726	2.500	6485820	70.013	5
10	0.000457	0.002282	92301	211	460958	0.000457	2.399	6023475	65.259	10
15	0.000508	0.002541	92091	234	459893	0.000509	2.609	5562518	60.403	15
20	0.000724	0.003624	91857	333	458490	0.000726	2.620	5102625	55.550	20
25	0.000930	0.004648	91524	425	456588	0.000932	2.579	4644135	50.742	25
30	0.001087	0.005419	91098	494	454313	0.001087	2.613	4187547	45.967	30
35	0.001538	0.007662	90605	694	451392	0.001538	2.651	3733234	41.204	35
40	0.002227	0.011079	89910	996	447218	0.002227	2.657	3281842	36.501	40
45	0.003270	0.016264	88914	1446	441178	0.003278	2.653	2834624	31.880	45
50	0.004752	0.023554	87468	2060	432534	0.004763	2.667	2393446	27.364	50
55	0.007375	0.036260	85408	3097	419894	0.007375	2.693	1960913	22.959	55
60	0.012294	0.059853	82311	4927	400265	0.012308	2.708	1541018	18.722	60
65	0.021669	0.103693	77384	8024	368542	0.021773	2.709	1140753	14.741	65
70	0.040732	0.187313	69360	12992	316620	0.041034	2.677	772211	11.133	70
75	0.080546	0.338153	56368	19061	235335	0.080995	2.560	455591	8.082	75
80	0.132910	0.495874	37307	18500	139189	0.132910	2.441	220256	5.904	80
85	0.231999	1.000000	18807	18807	81067	0.170139	4.310	81067	4.310	85

TABLE 4 — OBSERVED VITAL RATES AND RATIOS

CRUDE RATES

Per Thousand	BOTH SEXES	MALES	FEMALES
BIRTH RATE	20.23	22.09	18.57
DEATH RATE	10.90	11.72	10.15
RATE OF INCREASE	9.34	10.37	8.42

PERCENT OF POPULATION IN AGE GROUP

	BOTH SEXES	MALES	FEMALES
UNDER 15	28.22	29.94	26.68
15 - 64	62.07	61.87	62.26
65 AND OLDER	9.71	8.19	11.06

RATES STANDARDIZED ON USA 1980

Per Thousand	BOTH SEXES	MALES	FEMALES
BIRTH RATE	23.69		22.29
DEATH RATE	13.26	13.86	12.68
RATE OF INCREASE	10.43		9.60

RATES STANDARDIZED ON MEXICO 1980

	BOTH SEXES	MALES	FEMALES
BIRTH RATE	20.54		20.03
DEATH RATE	7.37	9.02	5.69
RATE OF INCREASE	13.17		14.34

VITAL STATISTICS

GFR x 1000	81.852
TFR	2.896
GRR	1.401
NRR	1.276
μ	29.012
σ^2	41.946
GENERATION	28.835
POP. SEX RATIO	1.115
SEX RATIO AT BIRTH	1.067
DEP. RATIO x 100	61.099

PROJECTED POPULATION

AGE GROUP	1975 BOTH SEXES	MALES	FEMALES	1980 BOTH SEXES	MALES	FEMALES
0-4	816	409	407	887	445	442
5-9	745	364	381	805	402	403
10-14	843	429	414	742	362	380
15-19	806	407	399	840	426	414
20-24	724	351	373	802	404	398
25-29	621	294	327	719	348	371
30-34	513	238	275	617	291	326
35-39	527	246	281	508	235	273
40-44	546	257	289	519	241	278
45-49	538	253	285	535	250	285
50-54	496	232	264	523	243	280
55-59	424	196	228	475	219	256
60-64	409	187	222	395	178	217
65-69	365	158	207	364	160	204
70-74	268	109	159	301	123	178
75-79	165	62	103	190	72	118
80-84	82	29	53	93	32	61
85+	45	14	31	46	15	31
TOTAL	8933	4235	4698	9361	4446	4915

STABLE EQUIVALENT TO ORIGINAL POPULATION

MALES Number	Percent	FEMALES Number	Percent	AGE GROUP
413	9.6	411	9.0	0-4
389	9.0	390	8.5	5-9
372	8.6	372	8.1	10-14
354	8.2	356	7.8	15-19
337	7.8	340	7.4	20-24
320	7.4	325	7.1	25-29
304	7.0	310	6.8	30-34
287	6.7	295	6.4	35-39
270	6.3	280	6.1	40-44
252	5.8	265	5.8	45-49
232	5.4	249	5.4	50-54
210	4.9	232	5.1	55-59
183	4.2	212	4.6	60-64
151	3.5	187	4.1	65-69
113	2.6	154	3.4	70-74
72	1.7	110	2.4	75-79
35	0.8	62	1.4	80-84
17	0.4	35	0.8	85+
4311		4585		TOTAL

TABLE 5

POPULATION PROJECTED WITH FIXED AGE-SPECIFIC BIRTH AND DEATH RATES (female dominant, in 000s)

VITAL RATES OF PROJECTED POPULATION

Per Thousand	1975 BOTH SEXES	MALES	FEMALES	1980 BOTH SEXES	MALES	FEMALES
BIRTH RATE	20.93	22.80	19.25	21.77	23.67	20.06
DEATH RATE	11.17	12.07	10.35	11.45	12.33	10.65
RATE OF INCREASE	9.77	10.73	8.90	10.32	11.34	9.41

VITAL RATES OF STABLE POPULATION

Per Thousand	MALES	FEMALES
BIRTH RATE	22.22	19.59
DEATH RATE	12.58	11.12
RATE OF INCREASE		8.47

AGE STRUCTURE OF PROJECTED POPULATION

	BOTH SEXES	MALES	FEMALES	BOTH SEXES	MALES	FEMALES
% UNDER 15	26.92	28.39	25.59	26.00	27.19	24.92
% 15-64	62.72	62.83	62.62	63.38	63.76	63.03
% 65 AND OLDER	10.37	8.78	11.79	10.63	9.05	12.06
DEPEND. RATIO x 100	59.44	59.16	59.70	57.79	56.84	58.66

STABLE AGE STRUCTURE

	MALES	FEMALES
% UNDER 15	27.23	25.59
% 15-64	63.78	62.47
% 65 AND OLDER	8.99	11.94
DEPEND. RATIO x 100	56.79	60.07

TABLE 6

PROJECTED VITAL RATES AND RATIOS (female dominant)

Leslie Matrix

AGE GROUP	FEMALE BIRTH RATES	NET MATERNITY FUNCTION	COEFF. OF MATRIX EQUATION	ORIGINAL MATRIX SUB-DIAGONAL	FIRST ROW	STABLE MATRIX FISHER VALUES	REPRODUCTIVE VALUES
0-4	0.0000	0.0000	0.0000	0.98896	0.00000	1.092	421292
5-9	0.0000	0.0000	0.0002	0.99700	0.00016	1.152	479037
10-14	0.0001	0.0003	0.0329	0.99769	0.03334	1.206	482587
15-19	0.0142	0.0654	0.1930	0.99695	0.19623	1.224	457784
20-24	0.0699	0.3206	0.3498	0.99585	0.35672	1.066	350531
25-29	0.0830	0.3791	0.3225	0.99502	0.33023	0.725	200475
30-34	0.0585	0.2660	0.2178	0.99357	0.22413	0.398	112497
35-39	0.0376	0.1696	0.1191	0.99075	0.12330	0.172	50123
40-44	0.0153	0.0685	0.0376	0.98649	0.03927	0.045	12972
45-49	0.0015	0.0067	0.0034	0.98041	0.00365	0.004	1064
50-54	0.0001	0.0002	0.0001	0.97078	0.00013	0.000	31

MATRIX PARAMETERS

λ_1	1.04327
λ_2	$0.41712 + 0.73122i$
λ_4	$0.01058 + 0.60310i$
λ_6	$-0.39940 + 0.45192i$
r_1	0.00847
r_2	$-0.03444 + 0.21048i$
r_4	$-0.10110 + 0.31065i$
r_6	$-0.10113 + 0.45892i$
c_1	45829
$2\pi/y$	29.8519
Δ	3.1113

TABLE 7

LESLIE MATRIX AND ITS ANALYSIS (females)

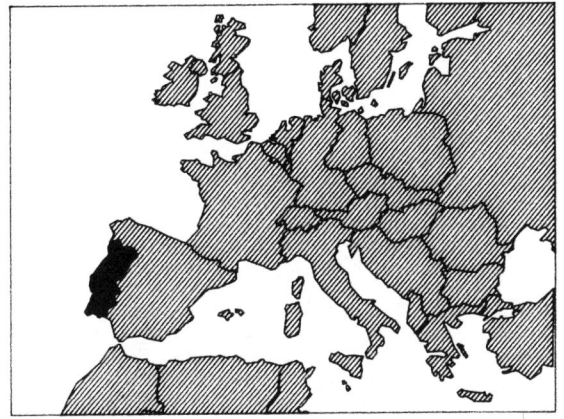

EDUCATION [1984]
% of primary school-age children enrolled:	120
secondary school-age children enrolled:	47
ca. 20-24 year olds in higher education:	12

LABOR FORCE
Average annual labor force growth (%) 1980-85:	1.0
% of the 1980 labor force in agriculture:	26
in industry:	37
in services:	38

GNP & INCOME DISTRIBUTION
GNP per capita (in US Dollars) 1985:	1970
GNP average annual growth rate (%) 1965-85:	3.3
% share of total household income 1973-74	
Lowest 20% of households:	5.2
Highest 10% of households:	33.4

HEALTH & NUTRITION
Population per physician 1981:	500
Daily calorie supply per capita 1985:	3161

TABLE 8

SOCIO-ECONOMIC INDICATORS

AGE AT LAST BIRTHDAY	ESTIMATED MID-YEAR POPULATION					BIRTHS BY AGE OF MOTHER AND SEX	DEATHS			AGE AT LAST BIRTHDAY
	BOTH SEXES	MALES		FEMALES			BOTH SEXES	MALES	FEMALES	
		Number	Percent	Number	Percent					
0	184700	94200	2.1	90500	1.8		6991	3990	3001	0
1-4	692600	352000	7.9	340600	6.8		1315	719	596	1-4
5-9	834700	421200	9.5	413500	8.3		603	361	242	5-9
10-14	891600	448600	10.1	443000	8.8	115	460	301	159	10-14
15-19	845100	423800	9.5	421300	8.4	15445	871	661	210	15-19
20-24	754000	361000	8.1	393000	7.8	55874	1080	829	251	20-24
25-29	620400	282800	6.4	337600	6.7	51712	842	593	249	25-29
30-34	518700	230400	5.2	288300	5.8	29299	887	595	292	30-34
35-39	550600	250200	5.6	300400	6.0	18467	1311	882	429	35-39
40-44	581200	267900	6.0	313300	6.3	7955	2032	1364	668	40-44
45-49	569600	264400	6.0	305200	6.1	742	2944	1960	984	45-49
50-54	537300	249200	5.6	288100	5.8	39	3961	2601	1360	50-54
55-59	445600	205500	4.6	240100	4.8		4799	3105	1694	55-59
60-64	450700	203500	4.6	247200	4.9		7764	4991	2773	60-64
65-69	384400	164300	3.7	220100	4.4		10497	6178	4319	65-69
70-74	292400	116800	2.6	175600	3.5		13011	6832	6179	70-74
75-79	168900	64300	1.4	104600	2.1		14058	6506	7552	75-79
80-84	84600	29000	0.7	55600	1.1	93099 M	12858	5172	7686	80-84
85+	41700	10700	0.2	31000	0.6	86549 F	11652	3621	8031	85+
TOTAL	9448800	4439800		5009000		179648	97936	51261	46675	TOTAL

TABLE 1 DATA

TABLE 2 — MALE LIFE TABLE

x	nM_x	nq_x	l_x	nd_x	nL_x	nm_x	na_x	T_x	$\overset{\circ}{e}_x$	x
0	0.042357	0.040871	100000	4087	96493	0.042357	0.142	6527850	65.279	0
1	0.002043	0.008129	95913	780	381702	0.002043	1.500	6431357	67.054	1
5	0.000857	0.004276	95133	407	474649	0.000857	2.500	6049654	63.591	5
10	0.000671	0.003350	94726	317	472907	0.000671	2.716	5575005	58.854	10
15	0.001560	0.007792	94409	736	470363	0.001564	2.714	5102098	54.042	15
20	0.002296	0.011442	93673	1072	465736	0.002301	2.545	4631735	49.446	20
25	0.002097	0.010427	92602	966	460617	0.002096	2.523	4165999	44.988	25
30	0.002582	0.012860	91636	1178	455363	0.002588	2.609	3705383	40.436	30
35	0.003525	0.017480	90458	1581	448555	0.003525	2.639	3250020	35.929	35
40	0.005091	0.025156	88876	2236	439121	0.005091	2.647	2801464	31.521	40
45	0.007413	0.036426	86641	3156	425735	0.007413	2.634	2362344	27.266	45
50	0.010437	0.051020	83485	4259	407323	0.010457	2.629	1936609	23.197	50
55	0.015109	0.073053	79225	5788	382543	0.015129	2.653	1529286	19.303	55
60	0.024526	0.115900	73438	8511	347041	0.024526	2.633	1146742	15.615	60
65	0.037602	0.172742	64926	11216	297698	0.037674	2.599	799702	12.317	65
70	0.058493	0.257294	53711	13819	235054	0.058793	2.576	502004	9.346	70
75	0.101182	0.407354	39891	16250	158949	0.102233	2.507	266950	6.692	75
80	0.178345	0.608314	23641	14381	80638	0.178345	2.388	108001	4.568	80
85	0.338411	1.000000	9260	9260	27363	0.310488	2.955	27363	2.955	85

TABLE 3 — FEMALE LIFE TABLE

x	nM_x	nq_x	l_x	nd_x	nL_x	nm_x	na_x	T_x	$\overset{\circ}{e}_x$	x
0	0.033160	0.032227	100000	3223	97185	0.033160	0.126	7271919	72.719	0
1	0.001750	0.006969	96777	674	385423	0.001750	1.500	7174734	74.137	1
5	0.000585	0.002922	96103	281	479812	0.000585	2.500	6789311	70.646	5
10	0.000359	0.001793	95822	172	478672	0.000359	2.448	6309498	65.846	10
15	0.000498	0.002492	95650	238	477683	0.000499	2.616	5830826	60.960	15
20	0.000639	0.003193	95412	305	476322	0.000640	2.577	5353143	56.106	20
25	0.000738	0.003691	95107	351	474696	0.000739	2.604	4876821	51.277	25
30	0.001013	0.005064	94756	480	472649	0.001015	2.639	4402125	46.457	30
35	0.001428	0.007117	94276	671	469812	0.001428	2.659	3929476	41.680	35
40	0.002132	0.010608	93606	993	465714	0.002132	2.670	3459665	36.960	40
45	0.003224	0.016003	92613	1482	459595	0.003225	2.660	2993950	32.328	45
50	0.004721	0.023407	91130	2133	450656	0.004733	2.658	2534355	27.810	50
55	0.007055	0.034782	88997	3095	437782	0.007071	2.673	2083700	23.413	55
60	0.011218	0.054678	85902	4697	418713	0.011218	2.701	1645917	19.160	60
65	0.019623	0.094026	81205	7635	388469	0.019655	2.701	1227204	15.112	65
70	0.035188	0.163833	73570	12053	340110	0.035439	2.699	838735	11.401	70
75	0.072199	0.310984	61516	19131	261768	0.073083	2.605	498625	8.106	75
80	0.138237	0.512197	42386	21710	157048	0.138237	2.472	236858	5.588	80
85	0.259065	1.000000	20676	20676	79810	0.203224	3.860	79810	3.860	85

TABLE 4 — OBSERVED VITAL RATES AND RATIOS

CRUDE RATES

Per Thousand	BOTH SEXES	MALES	FEMALES
BIRTH RATE	19.01	20.97	17.28
DEATH RATE	10.36	11.55	9.32
RATE OF INCREASE	8.65	9.42	7.96

PERCENT OF POPULATION IN AGE GROUP

UNDER 15	27.55	29.64	25.71
15 - 64	62.16	61.69	62.58
65 AND OLDER	10.29	8.67	11.72

RATES STANDARDIZED ON USA 1980

Per Thousand	BOTH SEXES	MALES	FEMALES
BIRTH RATE	21.67		20.30
DEATH RATE	12.55	13.17	11.97
RATE OF INCREASE	9.11		8.33

RATES STANDARDIZED ON MEXICO 1980

	BOTH SEXES	MALES	FEMALES
BIRTH RATE	19.07		18.52
DEATH RATE	5.53	6.60	4.45
RATE OF INCREASE	13.54		14.07

VITAL STATISTICS

GFR x 1000	76.151
TFR	2.617
GRR	1.261
NRR	1.195
μ	28.366
σ^2	42.426
GENERATION	28.232
POP. SEX RATIO	1.128
SEX RATIO AT BIRTH	1.076
DEP. RATIO x 100	60.880

AGE AT LAST BIRTHDAY	ESTIMATED MID-YEAR POPULATION					BIRTHS BY AGE OF MOTHER AND SEX	DEATHS			AGE AT LAST BIRTHDAY
	BOTH SEXES	MALES		FEMALES			BOTH SEXES	MALES	FEMALES	
		Number	Percent	Number	Percent					
0	157599	80093	1.7	77506	1.5		3852	2224	1628	0
1-4	688501	348007	7.4	340494	6.5		856	492	364	1-4
5-9	841100	427600	9.1	413500	8.0		498	314	184	5-9
10-14	872700	445100	9.5	427600	8.2	185	430	277	153	10-14
15-19	915100	465400	9.9	449700	8.6	17792	961	715	246	15-19
20-24	828700	417700	8.9	411000	7.9	55055	975	733	242	20-24
25-29	762000	374500	8.0	387500	7.5	44740	848	613	235	25-29
30-34	660400	305600	6.5	354800	6.8	24397	911	620	291	30-34
35-39	541700	239500	5.1	302200	5.8	10999	1048	681	367	35-39
40-44	547200	242000	5.2	305200	5.9	4596	1713	1114	599	40-44
45-49	567200	254400	5.4	312800	6.0	568	2528	1692	836	45-49
50-54	551900	246800	5.3	305100	5.9	20	3737	2484	1253	50-54
55-59	504800	228000	4.9	276800	5.3		5107	3362	1745	55-59
60-64	406200	182800	3.9	223400	4.3		6384	4102	2282	60-64
65-69	380200	168600	3.6	211600	4.1		10085	6061	4024	65-69
70-74	315700	134100	2.9	181600	3.5		13280	7229	6051	70-74
75-79	199562	80246	1.7	119316	2.3		15551	7442	8109	75-79
80-84	98217	34794	0.7	63423	1.2	81642 M	13401	5381	8020	80-84
85+	45121	9760	0.2	35361	0.7	76710 F	12806	4062	8744	85+
TOTAL	9883900	4685000		5198900		158352	94971	49598	45373	TOTAL

TABLE 1 DATA

x	nM_x	nq_x	l_x	nd_x	nL_x	nm_x	na_x	T_x	$\overset{\circ}{e}_x$	x
0	0.027768	0.027103	100000	2710	97607	0.027768	0.117	6741669	67.417	0
1	0.001414	0.005635	97290	548	387788	0.001414	1.500	6644061	68.292	1
5	0.000734	0.003665	96741	355	482821	0.000734	2.500	6256273	64.670	5
10	0.000622	0.003107	96387	300	481265	0.000622	2.765	5773453	59.899	10
15	0.001536	0.007656	96087	736	478709	0.001537	2.651	5292188	55.077	15
20	0.001755	0.008738	95352	833	474683	0.001755	2.509	4813479	50.481	20
25	0.001637	0.008155	94519	771	470690	0.001638	2.532	4338796	45.904	25
30	0.002029	0.010136	93748	950	466477	0.002037	2.620	3868106	41.261	30
35	0.002843	0.014196	92797	1317	460930	0.002858	2.679	3401629	36.656	35
40	0.004603	0.022771	91480	2083	452528	0.004603	2.661	2940699	32.146	40
45	0.006651	0.032744	89397	2927	440118	0.006651	2.654	2488171	27.833	45
50	0.010065	0.049159	86470	4251	422335	0.010065	2.644	2048052	23.685	50
55	0.014746	0.071388	82219	5869	397234	0.014776	2.638	1625717	19.773	55
60	0.022440	0.106730	76350	8149	362504	0.022479	2.638	1228484	16.090	60
65	0.035949	0.165471	68201	11285	313924	0.035949	2.600	865979	12.697	65
70	0.053908	0.238784	56916	13590	251676	0.054000	2.579	552055	9.700	70
75	0.092740	0.379580	43325	16445	175804	0.093543	2.518	300379	6.933	75
80	0.154653	0.557799	26880	14993	96015	0.156158	2.440	124574	4.635	80
85	0.416189	1.000000	11886	11886	28560	0.424516	2.403	28560	2.403	85

TABLE 2 MALE LIFE TABLE

x	nM_x	nq_x	l_x	nd_x	nL_x	nm_x	na_x	T_x	$\overset{\circ}{e}_x$	x
0	0.021005	0.020617	100000	2062	98156	0.021005	0.106	7458683	74.587	0
1	0.001069	0.004265	97938	418	390709	0.001069	1.500	7360527	75.155	1
5	0.000445	0.002222	97521	217	487061	0.000445	2.500	6969818	71.470	5
10	0.000358	0.001787	97304	174	486094	0.000358	2.558	6482757	66.624	10
15	0.000547	0.002732	97130	265	485009	0.000547	2.587	5996662	61.739	15
20	0.000589	0.002941	96865	285	483617	0.000589	2.520	5511653	56.901	20
25	0.000606	0.003030	96580	293	482190	0.000607	2.579	5028036	52.061	25
30	0.000820	0.004106	96287	395	480507	0.000823	2.653	4545846	47.211	30
35	0.001214	0.006077	95892	583	478113	0.001219	2.691	4065339	42.395	35
40	0.001963	0.009768	95309	931	474357	0.001963	2.650	3587226	37.638	40
45	0.002673	0.013280	94378	1253	468957	0.002673	2.660	3112868	32.983	45
50	0.004107	0.020352	93125	1895	461217	0.004109	2.675	2643911	28.391	50
55	0.006304	0.031188	91229	2845	449562	0.006329	2.686	2182694	23.925	55
60	0.010215	0.050144	88384	4432	431843	0.010263	2.726	1733132	19.609	60
65	0.019017	0.091167	83952	7654	402171	0.019031	2.702	1301289	15.500	65
70	0.033320	0.155199	76299	11841	354256	0.033426	2.700	899118	11.784	70
75	0.067962	0.295015	64457	19016	276823	0.068693	2.609	544862	8.453	75
80	0.126453	0.479952	45441	21810	172473	0.126453	2.490	268040	5.899	80
85	0.247278	1.000000	23632	23632	95567	0.188449	4.044	95567	4.044	85

TABLE 3 FEMALE LIFE TABLE

CRUDE RATES

Per Thousand	BOTH SEXES	MALES	FEMALES
BIRTH RATE	16.02	17.43	14.76
DEATH RATE	9.61	10.59	8.73
RATE OF INCREASE	6.41	6.84	6.03

RATES STANDARDIZED ON USA 1980

Per Thousand	BOTH SEXES	MALES	FEMALES
BIRTH RATE	17.42		16.41
DEATH RATE	11.71	12.46	11.00
RATE OF INCREASE	5.71		5.41

VITAL STATISTICS

GFR x 1000	62.758	TABLE 4
TFR	2.058	
GRR	0.997	OBSERVED
NRR	0.961	VITAL
μ	27.224	RATES
σ^2	40.861	AND
GENERATION	27.254	RATIOS
POP. SEX RATIO	1.110	
SEX RATIO AT BIRTH	1.064	
DEP. RATIO x 100	57.257	

PERCENT OF POPULATION IN AGE GROUP

	BOTH SEXES	MALES	FEMALES
UNDER 15	25.90	27.77	24.22
15 - 64	63.59	63.11	64.02
65 AND OLDER	10.51	9.12	11.76

RATES STANDARDIZED ON MEXICO 1980

	BOTH SEXES	MALES	FEMALES
BIRTH RATE	15.71		15.34
DEATH RATE	4.77	5.76	3.77
RATE OF INCREASE	10.94		11.57

TABLE 1 — DATA

AGE AT LAST BIRTHDAY	ESTIMATED MID-YEAR POPULATION BOTH SEXES	MALES Number	MALES Percent	FEMALES Number	FEMALES Percent	BIRTHS BY AGE OF MOTHER AND SEX	DEATHS BOTH SEXES	DEATHS MALES	DEATHS FEMALES	AGE AT LAST BIRTHDAY
0	132688	68737	1.4	63951	1.2		2327	1368	959	0
1-4	579612	298663	6.1	280949	5.3		559	344	215	1-4
5-9	810100	414300	8.5	395800	7.5		330	218	112	5-9
10-14	867100	442200	9.0	424900	8.1	107	357	234	123	10-14
15-19	859900	437400	8.9	422500	8.0	13575	785	569	216	15-19
20-24	854800	430200	8.8	424600	8.1	44269	974	748	226	20-24
25-29	757400	378500	7.7	378900	7.2	39551	888	657	231	25-29
30-34	676600	334100	6.8	342500	6.5	21072	880	619	261	30-34
35-39	627100	303700	6.2	323400	6.2	8982	1143	733	410	35-39
40-44	560000	265500	5.4	294500	5.6	2615	1477	966	511	40-44
45-49	577000	273000	5.6	304000	5.8	285	2392	1585	807	45-49
50-54	578800	271800	5.5	307000	5.8	36	3629	2403	1226	50-54
55-59	553200	256400	5.2	296800	5.6		5070	3352	1718	55-59
60-64	505400	231900	4.7	273500	5.2		7006	4477	2529	60-64
65-69	394100	176000	3.6	218100	4.2		8583	5314	3269	65-69
70-74	359200	152400	3.1	206800	3.9		13475	7746	5729	70-74
75-79	265719	103239	2.1	162480	3.1		17729	8665	9064	75-79
80-84	132928	46560	0.9	86368	1.6	67358 M	15231	6265	8966	80-84
85+	65353	17201	0.4	48152	0.9	63134 F	14504	4730	9774	85+
TOTAL	10157000	4901800		5255200		130492	97339	50993	46346	TOTAL

TABLE 2 — MALE LIFE TABLE

x	nM_x	nq_x	l_x	nd_x	nL_x	nm_x	na_x	T_x	$\overset{\circ}{e}_x$	x
0	0.019902	0.019553	100000	1955	98248	0.019902	0.104	6954973	69.550	0
1	0.001152	0.004594	98045	450	391053	0.001152	1.500	6856726	69.935	1
5	0.000526	0.002628	97594	256	487330	0.000526	2.500	6465673	66.251	5
10	0.000529	0.002643	97338	257	486124	0.000529	2.802	5978343	61.418	10
15	0.001301	0.006485	97081	630	483950	0.001301	2.691	5492219	56.574	15
20	0.001739	0.008660	96451	835	480208	0.001739	2.549	5008269	51.926	20
25	0.001736	0.008643	95616	826	476021	0.001736	2.510	4528061	47.357	25
30	0.001853	0.009234	94789	875	471822	0.001855	2.572	4052040	42.748	30
35	0.002414	0.012037	93914	1130	466911	0.002421	2.648	3580219	38.122	35
40	0.003638	0.018082	92784	1678	460032	0.003647	2.684	3113308	33.555	40
45	0.005806	0.028642	91106	2609	449454	0.005806	2.672	2653276	29.123	45
50	0.008841	0.043306	88496	3832	433476	0.008841	2.650	2203822	24.903	50
55	0.013073	0.063407	84664	5368	410629	0.013073	2.636	1770346	20.910	55
60	0.019306	0.092529	79296	7337	379135	0.019352	2.636	1359716	17.147	60
65	0.030193	0.141254	71959	10164	335769	0.030272	2.636	980582	13.627	65
70	0.050827	0.226475	61794	13995	275343	0.050827	2.597	644813	10.435	70
75	0.083931	0.349160	47799	16690	197615	0.084455	2.521	369470	7.730	75
80	0.134558	0.502720	31110	15639	115596	0.135294	2.445	171854	5.524	80
85	0.274984	1.000000	15470	15470	56259	0.223788	3.637	56259	3.637	85

TABLE 3 — FEMALE LIFE TABLE

x	nM_x	nq_x	l_x	nd_x	nL_x	nm_x	na_x	T_x	$\overset{\circ}{e}_x$	x
0	0.014996	0.014795	100000	1480	98662	0.014996	0.095	7661597	76.616	0
1	0.000765	0.003055	98520	301	393329	0.000765	1.500	7562935	76.765	1
5	0.000283	0.001414	98219	139	490750	0.000283	2.500	7169605	72.996	5
10	0.000289	0.001446	98081	142	490072	0.000289	2.663	6678855	68.096	10
15	0.000511	0.002553	97939	250	489093	0.000511	2.598	6188784	63.190	15
20	0.000532	0.002658	97689	260	487804	0.000532	2.538	5699691	58.345	20
25	0.000610	0.003048	97429	297	486426	0.000610	2.578	5211887	53.494	25
30	0.000762	0.003813	97132	370	484800	0.000764	2.678	4725461	48.650	30
35	0.001268	0.006336	96762	613	482372	0.001271	2.657	4240661	43.826	35
40	0.001735	0.008652	96149	832	478798	0.001738	2.661	3758289	39.088	40
45	0.002655	0.013191	95317	1257	473654	0.002655	2.670	3279492	34.406	45
50	0.003993	0.019782	94059	1861	465932	0.003993	2.654	2805837	29.831	50
55	0.005788	0.028561	92199	2633	454870	0.005789	2.675	2339906	25.379	55
60	0.009247	0.045413	89565	4067	438405	0.009278	2.684	1885036	21.046	60
65	0.014989	0.072712	85498	6217	413252	0.015043	2.710	1446631	16.920	65
70	0.027703	0.130285	79281	10329	372852	0.027703	2.720	1033379	13.034	70
75	0.055785	0.248120	68952	17108	304300	0.056222	2.635	660526	9.579	75
80	0.103812	0.413196	51844	21422	206351	0.103812	2.532	356226	6.871	80
85	0.202982	1.000000	30422	30422	149876	0.136129	4.927	149876	4.927	85

TABLE 4 — OBSERVED VITAL RATES AND RATIOS

CRUDE RATES

Per Thousand	BOTH SEXES	MALES	FEMALES
BIRTH RATE	12.85	13.74	12.01
DEATH RATE	9.58	10.40	8.82
RATE OF INCREASE	3.26	3.34	3.19

PERCENT OF POPULATION IN AGE GROUP

	BOTH SEXES	MALES	FEMALES
UNDER 15	23.53	24.97	22.18
15 - 64	64.49	64.93	64.08
65 AND OLDER	11.98	10.11	13.74

RATES STANDARDIZED ON USA 1980

Per Thousand	BOTH SEXES	MALES	FEMALES
BIRTH RATE	14.46		13.60
DEATH RATE	9.74	10.37	9.15
RATE OF INCREASE	4.72		4.45

RATES STANDARDIZED ON MEXICO 1980

	BOTH SEXES	MALES	FEMALES
BIRTH RATE	12.98		12.66
DEATH RATE	3.96	4.80	3.10
RATE OF INCREASE	9.02		9.56

VITAL STATISTICS

GFR x 1000	52.398
TFR	1.701
GRR	0.823
NRR	0.800
μ	27.161
σ^2	36.903
GENERATION	27.311
POP. SEX RATIO	1.072
SEX RATIO AT BIRTH	1.067
DEP. RATIO x 100	55.064

PROJECTED POPULATION

AGE GROUP	1990			1995			STABLE EQUIVALENT TO ORIGINAL POPULATION				AGE GROUP
							MALES		FEMALES		
	BOTH SEXES	MALES	FEMALES	BOTH SEXES	MALES	FEMALES	Number	Percent	Number	Percent	
0-4	658	339	319	682	351	331	383	5.2	361	4.6	0-4
5-9	710	366	344	655	337	318	397	5.4	375	4.8	5-9
10-14	808	413	395	709	365	344	413	5.6	390	5.0	10-14
15-19	864	440	424	805	411	394	428	5.8	405	5.2	15-19
20-24	855	434	421	860	437	423	442	6.0	421	5.4	20-24
25-29	849	426	423	850	430	420	457	6.2	437	5.6	25-29
30-34	753	375	378	845	423	422	471	6.4	454	5.8	30-34
35-39	672	331	341	747	371	376	486	6.6	470	6.0	35-39
40-44	620	299	321	664	326	338	499	6.8	486	6.3	40-44
45-49	550	259	291	610	292	318	507	6.9	501	6.4	45-49
50-54	562	263	299	537	250	287	510	6.9	513	6.6	50-54
55-59	557	257	300	541	249	292	503	6.8	522	6.7	55-59
60-64	523	237	286	527	238	289	484	6.6	524	6.7	60-64
65-69	463	205	258	480	210	270	446	6.1	515	6.6	65-69
70-74	341	144	197	401	168	233	381	5.2	484	6.2	70-74
75-79	278	109	169	265	104	161	285	3.9	411	5.3	75-79
80-84	170	60	110	178	64	114	174	2.4	290	3.7	80-84
85+	86	23	63	109	29	80	88	1.2	220	2.8	85+
TOTAL	10319	4980	5339	10465	5055	5410	7354		7779		TOTAL

TABLE 5

POPULATION PROJECTED WITH FIXED AGE-SPECIFIC BIRTH AND DEATH RATES (female dominant, in 000s)

VITAL RATES OF PROJECTED POPULATION

Per Thousand	1990			1995			VITAL RATES OF STABLE POPULATION		
	BOTH SEXES	MALES	FEMALES	BOTH SEXES	MALES	FEMALES	Per Thousand	MALES	FEMALES
BIRTH RATE	13.34	14.27	12.48	13.42	14.34	12.56	BIRTH RATE	10.43	9.24
DEATH RATE	10.46	11.14	9.84	11.11	11.66	10.59	DEATH RATE	18.47	17.38
RATE OF INCREASE	2.88	3.13	2.64	2.31	2.68	1.97	RATE OF INCREASE		-8.14

TABLE 6

PROJECTED VITAL RATES AND RATIOS (female dominant)

AGE STRUCTURE OF PROJECTED POPULATION / STABLE AGE STRUCTURE

	1990			1995				MALES	FEMALES
% UNDER 15	21.09	22.44	19.82	19.56	20.84	18.36	% UNDER 15	16.22	14.47
% 15-64	65.95	66.68	65.26	66.76	67.79	65.79	% 15-64	65.10	60.86
% 65 AND OLDER	12.97	10.88	14.91	13.69	11.37	15.85	% 65 AND OLDER	18.68	24.67
DEPEND. RATIO x 100	51.63	49.96	53.23	49.80	47.51	52.00	DEPEND. RATIO x 100	53.62	64.30

AGE GROUP	FEMALE BIRTH RATES	NET MATERNITY FUNCTION	COEFF. OF MATRIX EQUATION	ORIGINAL MATRIX		STABLE MATRIX		MATRIX PARAMETERS		
				SUB-DIAGONAL	FIRST ROW	FISHER VALUES	REPRODUCTIVE VALUES			
0-4	0.0000	0.0000	0.0000	0.99748	0.00000	0.996	343444	λ_1	0.96011	
5-9	0.0000	0.0000	0.0003	0.99862	0.00030	0.958	379364	λ_2	0.34613+0.68975i	TABLE 7
10-14	0.0001	0.0006	0.0383	0.99800	0.03846	0.921	391424	λ_4	-0.33227-0.39478i	
15-19	0.0155	0.0760	0.1610	0.99736	0.16200	0.848	358220	λ_6	-0.01265+0.46809i	LESLIE
20-24	0.0504	0.2461	0.2459	0.99717	0.24797	0.654	277876	r_1	-0.00814	MATRIX
25-29	0.0505	0.2457	0.1950	0.99666	0.19721	0.382	144927	r_2	-0.05183+0.22114i	AND ITS
30-34	0.0298	0.1443	0.1046	0.99499	0.10611	0.171	58714	r_4	-0.13233-0.45409i	ANALYSIS
35-39	0.0134	0.0648	0.0427	0.99259	0.04354	0.059	19152	r_6	-0.15175+0.31956i	(females)
40-44	0.0043	0.0206	0.0114	0.98926	0.01167	0.014	4004	c_1	77806	
45-49	0.0005	0.0021	0.0012	0.98370	0.00125	0.001	440	$2\pi/y$	28.4127	
50-54	0.0001	0.0003	0.0001	0.97626	0.00014	0.000	44	Δ	15.5865	

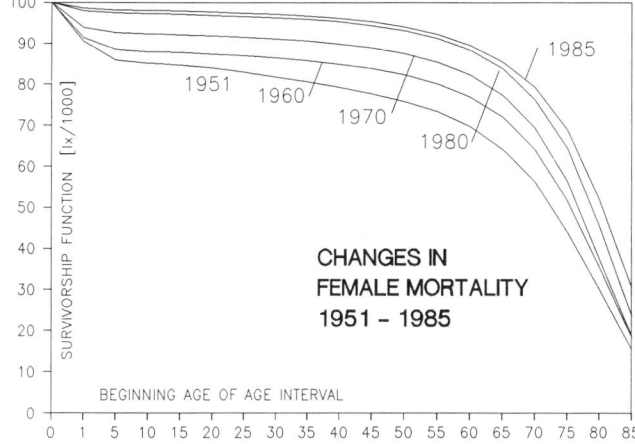

CHANGES IN FEMALE MORTALITY 1951 – 1985

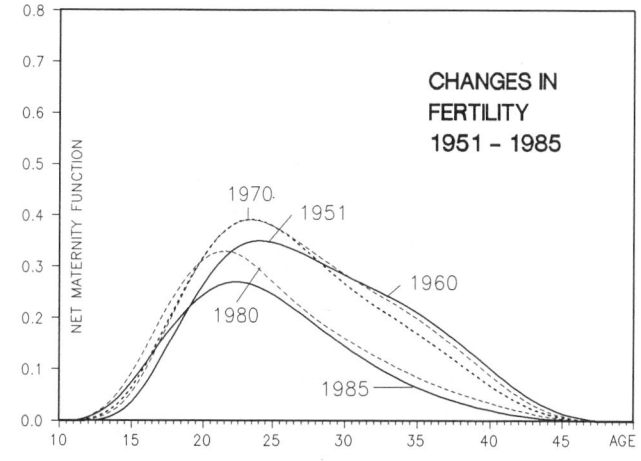

CHANGES IN FERTILITY 1951 – 1985

	AGE AT LAST BIRTHDAY	ESTIMATED MID-YEAR POPULATION					BIRTHS BY AGE OF MOTHER AND SEX	DEATHS			AGE AT LAST BIRTHDAY
		BOTH SEXES	MALES		FEMALES			BOTH SEXES	MALES	FEMALES	
			Number	Percent	Number	Percent					
	0	434223	222334	2.2	211889	2.1		21110	11890	9220	0
	1-4	1605368	820681	8.3	784687	7.6		3858	2037	1821	1-4
	5-9	1419194	727795	7.3	691399	6.7		1044	641	403	5-9
	10-14	1793106	915940	9.2	877166	8.5	281	1051	679	372	10-14
	15-19	1807304	921751	9.3	885553	8.6	58148	1609	1043	566	15-19
	20-24	1502029	764937	7.7	737092	7.2	148428	1842	1191	651	20-24
	25-29	1282600	644720	6.5	637880	6.2	96728	1725	1098	627	25-29
	30-34	1573178	786109	7.9	787069	7.6	74729	2747	1749	998	30-34
TABLE 1	35-39	1553111	779261	7.8	773850	7.5	37753	3392	2050	1342	35-39
DATA	40-44	1485727	739793	7.4	745934	7.2	10316	4464	2796	1668	40-44
	45-49	1302709	613604	6.2	689105	6.7	628	5706	3261	2445	45-49
	50-54	749284	335109	3.4	414175	4.0	23	5344	2996	2348	50-54
	55-59	1065901	490004	4.9	575897	5.6		11856	6932	4924	55-59
	60-64	938508	439763	4.4	498745	4.8		17450	10326	7124	60-64
	65-69	740444	340740	3.4	399704	3.9		22761	12799	9962	65-69
	70-74	494788	209731	2.1	285057	2.8		26137	12852	13285	70-74
	75-79	291093	114244	1.1	176849	1.7		25571	11245	14326	75-79
	80-84	149534	56186	0.6	93348	0.9	219483 M	21238	8431	12807	80-84
	85+	64440	22325	0.2	42115	0.4	207551 F	14350	5282	9068	85+
	TOTAL	20252541	9945027		10307514		427034	193255	99298	93957	TOTAL

	x	$_nM_x$	$_nq_x$	l_x	$_nd_x$	$_nL_x$	$_nm_x$	$_na_x$	T_x	$\overset{\circ}{e}_x$	x
	0	0.053478	0.051181	100000	5118	95705	0.053478	0.161	6582840	65.828	0
	1	0.002482	0.009867	94882	936	377187	0.002482	1.500	6487134	68.371	1
	5	0.000881	0.004394	93946	413	468696	0.000881	2.500	6109947	65.037	5
	10	0.000741	0.003700	93533	346	466823	0.000741	2.568	5641251	60.313	10
	15	0.001132	0.005650	93187	526	464696	0.001133	2.648	5174428	55.527	15
	20	0.001557	0.007777	92660	721	461553	0.001561	2.573	4709732	50.828	20
TABLE 2	25	0.001703	0.008483	91940	780	457809	0.001704	2.577	4248179	46.206	25
	30	0.002225	0.011065	91160	1009	453360	0.002225	2.582	3790371	41.579	30
MALE	35	0.002631	0.013073	90151	1179	447947	0.002631	2.617	3337010	37.016	35
LIFE	40	0.003779	0.018759	88973	1669	440925	0.003785	2.641	2889064	32.471	40
TABLE	45	0.005315	0.026432	87304	2308	431180	0.005352	2.687	2448138	28.042	45
	50	0.008940	0.043991	84996	3739	416311	0.008981	2.681	2016958	23.730	50
	55	0.014147	0.068482	81257	5565	393350	0.014147	2.676	1600648	19.699	55
	60	0.023481	0.111387	75692	8431	358651	0.023508	2.650	1207297	15.950	60
	65	0.037562	0.173215	67261	11651	308534	0.037761	2.616	848646	12.617	65
	70	0.061278	0.268564	55610	14935	241653	0.061803	2.563	540112	9.712	70
	75	0.098430	0.397143	40675	16154	162632	0.099329	2.478	298459	7.338	75
	80	0.150055	0.538437	24522	13203	87990	0.150055	2.378	135827	5.539	80
	85	0.236596	1.000000	11318	11318	47838	0.176166	4.227	47838	4.227	85

	x	$_nM_x$	$_nq_x$	l_x	$_nd_x$	$_nL_x$	$_nm_x$	$_na_x$	T_x	$\overset{\circ}{e}_x$	x
	0	0.043513	0.041951	100000	4195	96409	0.043513	0.144	7043142	70.431	0
	1	0.002321	0.009229	95805	884	381009	0.002321	1.500	6946733	72.509	1
	5	0.000583	0.002910	94921	276	473913	0.000583	2.500	6565724	69.171	5
	10	0.000424	0.002118	94644	200	472727	0.000424	2.526	6091811	64.365	10
	15	0.000639	0.003195	94444	302	471511	0.000640	2.649	5619085	59.496	15
	20	0.000883	0.004418	94142	416	469704	0.000885	2.579	5147574	54.679	20
TABLE 3	25	0.000983	0.004903	93726	460	467519	0.000983	2.579	4677870	49.910	25
	30	0.001268	0.006321	93267	590	464931	0.001268	2.621	4210351	45.143	30
FEMALE	35	0.001734	0.008639	92677	801	461475	0.001735	2.613	3745420	40.414	35
LIFE	40	0.002236	0.011123	91877	1022	456997	0.002236	2.665	3283945	35.743	40
TABLE	45	0.003548	0.017727	90855	1611	450556	0.003575	2.692	2826948	31.115	45
	50	0.005669	0.028084	89244	2506	440377	0.005691	2.668	2376392	26.628	50
	55	0.008550	0.041922	86738	3636	425278	0.008550	2.687	1936015	22.320	55
	60	0.014284	0.069375	83102	5765	402247	0.014332	2.700	1510737	18.179	60
	65	0.024923	0.118530	77336	9167	365566	0.025075	2.696	1108490	14.333	65
	70	0.046605	0.211317	68170	14405	306735	0.046964	2.632	742924	10.898	70
	75	0.081007	0.340158	53764	18288	223848	0.081700	2.541	436189	8.113	75
	80	0.137196	0.507146	35476	17991	131137	0.137196	2.430	212341	5.985	80
	85	0.215315	1.000000	17484	17484	81204	0.150485	4.644	81204	4.644	85

CRUDE RATES / RATES STANDARDIZED ON USA 1980 / VITAL STATISTICS

		BOTH SEXES	MALES	FEMALES	Per Thousand	BOTH SEXES	MALES	FEMALES		
TABLE 4	Per Thousand								GFR x 1000	81.239
	BIRTH RATE	21.09	22.07	20.14	BIRTH RATE	24.71		23.36	TFR	2.888
OBSERVED	DEATH RATE	9.54	9.98	9.12	DEATH RATE	12.37	11.95	12.77	GRR	1.403
VITAL	RATE OF INCREASE	11.54	12.08	11.02	RATE OF INCREASE	12.34		10.59	NRR	1.312
RATES									μ	26.628
AND									σ^2	37.948
RATIOS	PERCENT OF POPULATION IN AGE GROUP				RATES STANDARDIZED ON MEXICO 1980				GENERATION	26.433
	UNDER 15	25.93	27.02	24.89	BIRTH RATE	22.55		22.09	POP. SEX RATIO	1.036
	15 - 64	65.47	65.51	65.44	DEATH RATE	5.77	6.35	5.18	SEX RATIO AT BIRTH	1.057
	65 AND OLDER	8.59	7.47	9.67	RATE OF INCREASE	16.78		16.90	DEP. RATIO x 100	52.730

PROJECTED POPULATION

AGE GROUP	1975 BOTH SEXES	1975 MALES	1975 FEMALES	1980 BOTH SEXES	1980 MALES	1980 FEMALES
0-4	2098	1073	1025	2189	1120	1069
5-9	2023	1034	989	2081	1064	1017
10-14	1415	725	690	2017	1030	987
15-19	1787	912	875	1410	722	688
20-24	1798	916	882	1778	906	872
25-29	1493	759	734	1786	908	878
30-34	1272	638	634	1481	751	730
35-39	1558	777	781	1261	631	630
40-44	1533	767	766	1539	765	774
45-49	1458	723	735	1506	750	756
50-54	1266	592	674	1417	698	719
55-59	717	317	400	1210	560	650
60-64	992	447	545	667	289	378
65-69	831	378	453	879	384	495
70-74	602	267	335	676	296	380
75-79	349	141	208	425	180	245
80-84	166	62	104	198	76	122
85+	89	31	58	98	34	64
TOTAL	21447	10559	10888	22618	11164	11454

STABLE EQUIVALENT TO ORIGINAL POPULATION

AGE GROUP	MALES Number	MALES Percent	FEMALES Number	FEMALES Percent
0-4	981	10.0	937	9.5
5-9	924	9.4	883	9.0
10-14	874	8.9	837	8.5
15-19	826	8.4	793	8.1
20-24	780	7.9	750	7.6
25-29	734	7.5	709	7.2
30-34	691	7.0	670	6.8
35-39	648	6.6	632	6.4
40-44	606	6.1	594	6.1
45-49	563	5.7	556	5.7
50-54	516	5.2	516	5.3
55-59	463	4.7	474	4.8
60-64	401	4.1	426	4.3
65-69	328	3.3	367	3.7
70-74	244	2.5	293	3.0
75-79	156	1.6	203	2.1
80-84	80	0.8	113	1.2
85+	41	0.4	66	0.7
TOTAL	9856		9819	

TABLE 5

POPULATION PROJECTED WITH FIXED AGE-SPECIFIC BIRTH AND DEATH RATES (female dominant, in 000s)

VITAL RATES OF PROJECTED POPULATION

Per Thousand	1975 BOTH SEXES	1975 MALES	1975 FEMALES	1980 BOTH SEXES	1980 MALES	1980 FEMALES
BIRTH RATE	21.27	22.21	20.36	20.59	21.44	19.76
DEATH RATE	10.13	10.51	9.76	10.53	10.86	10.20
RATE OF INCREASE	11.15	11.70	10.61	10.06	10.57	9.56

AGE STRUCTURE OF PROJECTED POPULATION

	1975 BOTH SEXES	1975 MALES	1975 FEMALES	1980 BOTH SEXES	1980 MALES	1980 FEMALES
% UNDER 15	25.81	26.82	24.83	27.80	28.79	26.84
% 15-64	64.69	64.85	64.53	62.14	62.52	61.76
% 65 AND OLDER	9.50	8.32	10.64	10.07	8.69	11.40
DEPEND. RATIO x 100	54.58	54.19	54.96	60.94	59.95	61.92

VITAL RATES OF STABLE POPULATION

Per Thousand	MALES	FEMALES
BIRTH RATE	21.59	20.50
DEATH RATE	11.31	10.20
RATE OF INCREASE		10.29

STABLE AGE STRUCTURE

	MALES	FEMALES
% UNDER 15	28.19	27.06
% 15-64	63.19	62.33
% 65 AND OLDER	8.62	10.62
DEPEND. RATIO x 100	58.24	60.45

TABLE 6

PROJECTED VITAL RATES AND RATIOS (female dominant)

MATRIX

AGE GROUP	FEMALE BIRTH RATES	NET MATERNITY FUNCTION	COEFF. OF MATRIX EQUATION	ORIGINAL MATRIX SUB-DIAGONAL	ORIGINAL MATRIX FIRST ROW	STABLE MATRIX FISHER VALUES	STABLE MATRIX REPRODUCTIVE VALUES
0-4	0.0000	0.0000	0.0000	0.99266	0.00000	1.074	1070810
5-9	0.0000	0.0000	0.0004	0.99750	0.00037	1.140	787920
10-14	0.0002	0.0007	0.0756	0.99743	0.07636	1.202	1054706
15-19	0.0319	0.1505	0.3051	0.99617	0.30892	1.187	1051074
20-24	0.0979	0.4597	0.4021	0.99535	0.40874	0.921	679009
25-29	0.0737	0.3446	0.2796	0.99446	0.28548	0.533	340082
30-34	0.0461	0.2145	0.1620	0.99257	0.16634	0.256	201470
35-39	0.0237	0.1094	0.0701	0.99030	0.07249	0.091	70767
40-44	0.0067	0.0307	0.0164	0.98591	0.01709	0.019	13850
45-49	0.0004	0.0020	0.0011	0.97741	0.00112	0.001	830
50-54	0.0000	0.0001	0.0001	0.96571	0.00006	0.000	27

MATRIX PARAMETERS

λ_1	1.05281
λ_2	0.31849+0.74121i
λ_4	0.01506+0.54963i
λ_6	-0.41121+0.34692i
r_1	0.01029
r_2	-0.04295+0.23299i
r_4	-0.11963+0.30868i
r_6	-0.12398+0.48816i
c_1	98194
$2\pi/y$	26.9672
Δ	6.1443

TABLE 7

LESLIE MATRIX AND ITS ANALYSIS (females)

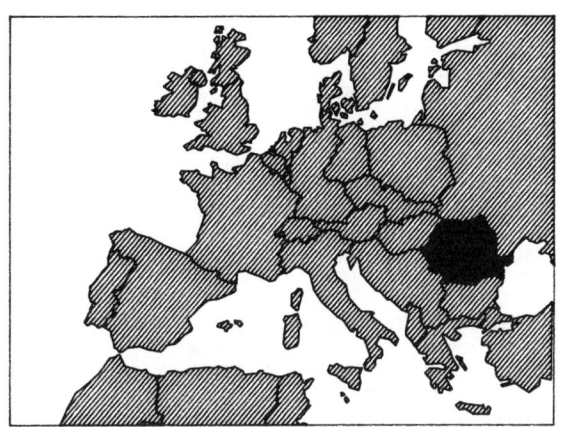

EDUCATION [1984]

% of primary school-age children enrolled:	98
secondary school-age children enrolled:	73
ca. 20-24 year olds in higher education:	12

LABOR FORCE

Average annual labor force growth (%) 1980-85:	0.7
% of the 1980 labor force in agriculture:	31
in industry:	44
in services:	26

GNP & INCOME DISTRIBUTION

GNP per capita (in US Dollars) 1979:	3580
GNP growth rate (%) 1979:	4.5
% share of total household income	
Lowest 20% of households:	na
Highest 10% of households:	na

HEALTH & NUTRITION

Population per physician 1981:	700
Daily calorie supply per capita 1985:	3385

TABLE 8

SOCIO-ECONOMIC INDICATORS

TABLE 1 — DATA

AGE AT LAST BIRTHDAY	ESTIMATED MID-YEAR POPULATION BOTH SEXES	MALES Number	MALES Percent	FEMALES Number	FEMALES Percent	BIRTHS BY AGE OF MOTHER AND SEX	DEATHS BOTH SEXES	DEATHS MALES	DEATHS FEMALES	AGE AT LAST BIRTHDAY
0	393913	201896	1.8	192017	1.7		11779	6671	5108	0
1-4	1613029	825715	7.5	787314	7.0		2568	1443	1125	1-4
5-9	1909338	977263	8.9	932075	8.3		1294	806	488	5-9
10-14	2007979	1024933	9.4	983046	8.7	405	942	625	317	10-14
15-19	1429972	731839	6.7	698133	6.2	50494	1114	737	377	15-19
20-24	1756936	894572	8.2	862364	7.7	172782	1903	1273	630	20-24
25-29	1774252	898861	8.2	875391	7.8	110989	2311	1470	841	25-29
30-34	1487708	750746	6.9	736962	6.6	42969	2405	1607	798	30-34
35-39	1259445	628917	5.7	630528	5.6	15784	3096	2063	1033	35-39
40-44	1543931	766731	7.0	777200	6.9	5083	5732	3905	1827	40-44
45-49	1491741	743692	6.8	748049	6.7	379	8290	5524	2766	45-49
50-54	1400731	689697	6.3	711034	6.3	19	11365	7324	4041	50-54
55-59	1188754	549091	5.0	639663	5.7		14468	8818	5650	55-59
60-64	661893	288339	2.6	373554	3.3		12106	6924	5182	60-64
65-69	888371	391077	3.6	497294	4.4		26804	14631	12173	65-69
70-74	681348	299714	2.7	381634	3.4		35073	18265	16808	70-74
75-79	437310	186389	1.7	250921	2.2		38148	18054	20094	75-79
80-84	193069	75031	0.7	118038	1.0	205176 M	29860	12246	17614	80-84
85+	81667	29134	0.3	52533	0.5	193728 F	22618	8052	14566	85+
TOTAL	22201387	10953637		11247750		398904	231876	120438	111438	TOTAL

TABLE 2 — MALE LIFE TABLE

x	$_nM_x$	$_nq_x$	l_x	$_nd_x$	$_nL_x$	$_nm_x$	$_na_x$	T_x	$\overset{\circ}{e}_x$	x
0	0.033042	0.032115	100000	3211	97194	0.033042	0.126	6657219	66.572	0
1	0.001748	0.006960	96789	674	385470	0.001748	1.500	6560025	67.777	1
5	0.000825	0.004115	96115	396	479586	0.000825	2.500	6174555	64.241	5
10	0.000610	0.003046	95719	292	477886	0.000610	2.561	5694970	59.497	10
15	0.001007	0.005039	95428	481	476016	0.001010	2.665	5217084	54.670	15
20	0.001423	0.007091	94947	673	473112	0.001423	2.589	4741068	49.934	20
25	0.001635	0.008150	94274	768	469516	0.001636	2.589	4267956	45.272	25
30	0.002141	0.010700	93505	1001	465180	0.002151	2.654	3798440	40.623	30
35	0.003280	0.016286	92505	1507	459027	0.003282	2.678	3333261	36.033	35
40	0.005093	0.025165	90998	2290	449627	0.005093	2.658	2874234	31.586	40
45	0.007428	0.036501	88708	3238	435894	0.007428	2.638	2424606	27.332	45
50	0.010619	0.051879	85470	4434	416907	0.010636	2.644	1988713	23.268	50
55	0.016059	0.077856	81036	6309	390259	0.016167	2.635	1571806	19.396	55
60	0.024013	0.113929	74727	8514	353406	0.024090	2.624	1181548	15.811	60
65	0.037412	0.171712	66214	11370	303903	0.037412	2.611	828142	12.507	65
70	0.060941	0.265421	54844	14557	238751	0.060970	2.563	524239	9.559	70
75	0.096862	0.392215	40287	15801	161824	0.097645	2.493	285488	7.086	75
80	0.163213	0.573074	24486	14032	85840	0.163470	2.392	123664	5.050	80
85	0.276378	1.000000	10454	10454	37824	0.226247	3.618	37824	3.618	85

TABLE 3 — FEMALE LIFE TABLE

x	$_nM_x$	$_nq_x$	l_x	$_nd_x$	$_nL_x$	$_nm_x$	$_na_x$	T_x	$\overset{\circ}{e}_x$	x
0	0.026602	0.025990	100000	2599	97700	0.026602	0.115	7185113	71.851	0
1	0.001429	0.005695	97401	555	388217	0.001429	1.500	7087412	72.765	1
5	0.000524	0.002614	96846	253	483598	0.000524	2.500	6699195	69.174	5
10	0.000322	0.001609	96593	155	482578	0.000322	2.510	6215597	64.348	10
15	0.000540	0.002704	96438	261	481577	0.000542	2.656	5733018	59.448	15
20	0.000731	0.003646	96177	351	480049	0.000731	2.618	5251441	54.602	20
25	0.000961	0.004795	95826	459	478017	0.000961	2.575	4771393	49.792	25
30	0.001083	0.005418	95367	517	475607	0.001086	2.627	4293376	45.020	30
35	0.001638	0.008162	94850	774	472436	0.001639	2.657	3817769	40.251	35
40	0.002351	0.011690	94076	1100	467824	0.002351	2.676	3345333	35.560	40
45	0.003698	0.018347	92976	1706	460920	0.003701	2.678	2877509	30.949	45
50	0.005683	0.028049	91270	2560	450401	0.005684	2.676	2416589	26.477	50
55	0.008833	0.043582	88710	3866	434545	0.008897	2.671	1966188	22.164	55
60	0.013872	0.067485	84844	5726	411010	0.013931	2.693	1531643	18.052	60
65	0.024478	0.115837	79118	9165	374403	0.024478	2.688	1120633	14.164	65
70	0.044042	0.200076	69954	13996	316806	0.044179	2.645	746230	10.667	70
75	0.080081	0.337739	55958	18899	233796	0.080836	2.566	429424	7.674	75
80	0.149223	0.540365	37058	20025	134196	0.149223	2.448	195628	5.279	80
85	0.277273	1.000000	17033	17033	61432	0.226866	3.607	61432	3.607	85

TABLE 4 — OBSERVED VITAL RATES AND RATIOS

CRUDE RATES

Per Thousand	BOTH SEXES	MALES	FEMALES
BIRTH RATE	17.97	18.73	17.22
DEATH RATE	10.44	11.00	9.91
RATE OF INCREASE	7.52	7.74	7.32

PERCENT OF POPULATION IN AGE GROUP

	BOTH SEXES	MALES	FEMALES
UNDER 15	26.68	27.66	25.73
15 - 64	63.04	63.38	62.70
65 AND OLDER	10.28	8.96	11.56

RATES STANDARDIZED ON USA 1980

Per Thousand	BOTH SEXES	MALES	FEMALES
BIRTH RATE	21.52		20.32
DEATH RATE	12.81	12.26	13.33
RATE OF INCREASE	8.71		6.99

RATES STANDARDIZED ON MEXICO 1980

	BOTH SEXES	MALES	FEMALES
BIRTH RATE	20.16		19.74
DEATH RATE	5.31	5.94	4.68
RATE OF INCREASE	14.85		15.06

VITAL STATISTICS

GFR x 1000	74.861
TFR	2.451
GRR	1.191
NRR	1.140
μ	25.265
σ^2	31.642
GENERATION	25.183
POP. SEX RATIO	1.027
SEX RATIO AT BIRTH	1.059
DEP. RATIO x 100	58.634

PROJECTED POPULATION

AGE GROUP	1985			1990		
	BOTH SEXES	MALES	FEMALES	BOTH SEXES	MALES	FEMALES
0-4	1918	983	935	1988	1019	969
5-9	1996	1021	975	1907	977	930
10-14	1904	974	930	1990	1017	973
15-19	2002	1021	981	1898	970	928
20-24	1423	727	696	1993	1015	978
25-29	1747	888	859	1415	722	693
30-34	1762	891	871	1734	880	854
35-39	1473	741	732	1744	879	865
40-44	1240	616	624	1451	726	725
45-49	1509	743	766	1212	597	615
50-54	1442	711	731	1459	711	748
55-59	1332	646	686	1371	666	705
60-64	1102	497	605	1234	585	649
65-69	588	248	340	979	428	551
70-74	728	307	421	483	195	288
75-79	485	203	282	519	208	311
80-84	243	99	144	270	108	162
85+	87	33	54	110	44	66
TOTAL	22981	11349	11632	23757	11747	12010

STABLE EQUIVALENT TO ORIGINAL POPULATION

	MALES		FEMALES		AGE GROUP	
	Number	Percent	Number	Percent		
	994	8.6	945	8.1	0-4	
	963	8.3	917	7.8	5-9	TABLE 5
	935	8.1	891	7.6	10-14	
	907	7.8	867	7.4	15-19	POPULATION
	879	7.6	842	7.2	20-24	PROJECTED
	849	7.3	817	7.0	25-29	WITH
	820	7.1	792	6.8	30-34	FIXED
	788	6.8	766	6.6	35-39	AGE-
	752	6.5	739	6.3	40-44	SPECIFIC
	711	6.1	710	6.1	45-49	BIRTH
	662	5.7	676	5.8	50-54	AND
	604	5.2	635	5.4	55-59	DEATH
	533	4.6	585	5.0	60-64	RATES
	447	3.9	520	4.4	65-69	(female
	342	3.0	428	3.7	70-74	dominant,
	226	1.9	308	2.6	75-79	in 000s)
	117	1.0	172	1.5	80-84	
	50	0.4	77	0.7	85+	
	11579		11687		TOTAL	

VITAL RATES OF PROJECTED POPULATION

Per Thousand	1985			1990		
	BOTH SEXES	MALES	FEMALES	BOTH SEXES	MALES	FEMALES
BIRTH RATE	17.11	17.82	16.42	18.01	18.74	17.30
DEATH RATE	10.80	11.32	10.28	11.11	11.57	10.67
RATE OF INCREASE	6.32	6.50	6.14	6.90	7.17	6.64

VITAL RATES OF STABLE POPULATION

Per Thousand	MALES	FEMALES	
BIRTH RATE	18.02	16.86	TABLE 6
DEATH RATE	12.79	11.67	PROJECTED
RATE OF INCREASE		5.20	VITAL RATES

AGE STRUCTURE OF PROJECTED POPULATION

% UNDER 15	25.32	26.24	24.41	24.78	25.66	23.91
% 15-64	65.41	65.92	64.92	65.29	65.98	64.62
% 65 AND OLDER	9.27	7.84	10.67	9.93	8.36	11.47
DEPEND. RATIO x 100	52.88	51.71	54.04	53.16	51.56	54.75

STABLE AGE STRUCTURE

	MALES	FEMALES	
% UNDER 15	24.97	23.56	AND RATIOS
% 15-64	64.83	63.56	(female
% 65 AND OLDER	10.20	12.88	dominant)
DEPEND. RATIO x 100	54.26	57.33	

AGE GROUP	FEMALE BIRTH RATES	NET MATERNITY FUNCTION	COEFF. OF MATRIX EQUATION	ORIGINAL MATRIX		STABLE MATRIX		MATRIX PARAMETERS		
				SUB-DIAGONAL	FIRST ROW	FISHER VALUES	REPRODUCTIVE VALUES			
0-4	0.0000	0.0000	0.0000	0.99523	0.00000	1.042	1020863	λ_1	1.02632	
5-9	0.0000	0.0000	0.0005	0.99789	0.00049	1.075	1001962	λ_2	0.25231+0.76105i	TABLE 7
10-14	0.0002	0.0010	0.0851	0.99792	0.08565	1.105	1086367	λ_4	-0.41499-0.33130i	
15-19	0.0351	0.1692	0.3181	0.99683	0.32100	1.047	731005	λ_6	0.05152+0.43076i	LESLIE
20-24	0.0973	0.4671	0.3807	0.99577	0.38538	0.742	640212	r_1	0.00520	MATRIX
25-29	0.0616	0.2943	0.2145	0.99496	0.21805	0.362	316669	r_2	-0.04418+0.25014i	AND ITS
30-34	0.0283	0.1347	0.0961	0.99333	0.09814	0.145	106638	r_4	-0.12659-0.49357i	ANALYSIS
35-39	0.0122	0.0574	0.0361	0.99024	0.03718	0.047	29332	r_6	-0.16702+0.29035i	(females)
40-44	0.0032	0.0149	0.0080	0.98524	0.00831	0.009	7056	c_1	116861	
45-49	0.0002	0.0011	0.0006	0.97718	0.00063	0.001	500	$2\pi/y$	25.1191	
50-54	0.0000	0.0001	0.0000	0.96480	0.00003	0.000	23	Δ	5.3867	

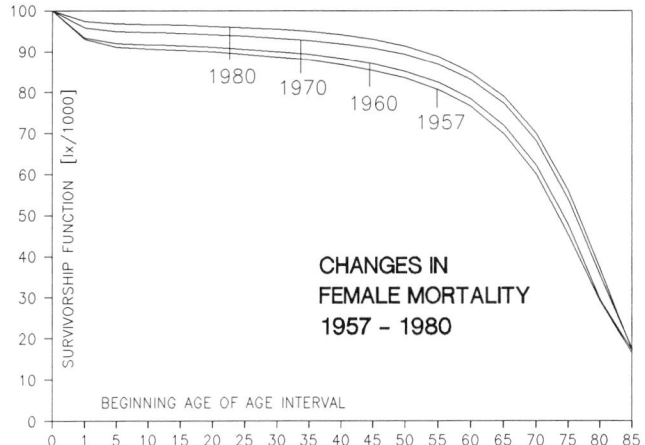

CHANGES IN FEMALE MORTALITY 1957 - 1980

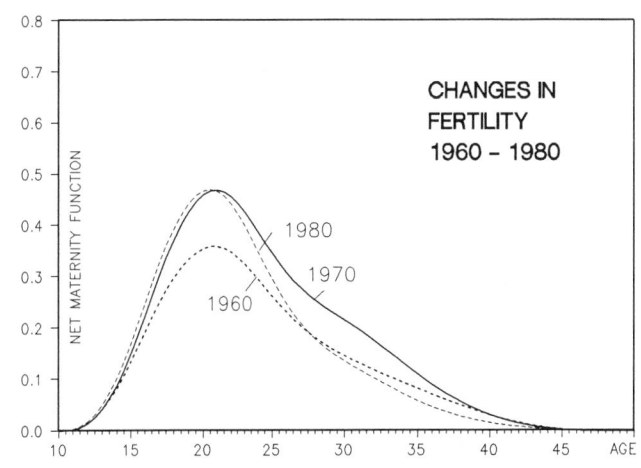

CHANGES IN FERTILITY 1960 - 1980

TABLE 1 — DATA

AGE AT LAST BIRTHDAY	ESTIMATED MID-YEAR POPULATION BOTH SEXES	MALES Number	MALES Percent	FEMALES Number	FEMALES Percent	BIRTHS BY AGE OF MOTHER AND SEX	DEATHS BOTH SEXES	DEATHS MALES	DEATHS FEMALES	AGE AT LAST BIRTHDAY
0	643860	330774	2.0	313086	1.8		18595	10706	7889	0
1-4	2547869	1305037	7.9	1242832	7.2		2422	1363	1059	1-4
5-9	3202134	1638777	9.9	1563357	9.0		1466	895	571	5-9
10-14	3013427	1538212	9.3	1475215	8.5	115	1119	671	448	10-14
15-19	2694347	1364150	8.2	1330197	7.7	18525	1701	1186	515	15-19
20-24	2534655	1280184	7.7	1254471	7.2	154369	2250	1594	656	20-24
25-29	2227101	1114404	6.7	1112697	6.4	222315	2328	1528	800	25-29
30-34	2062526	1020273	6.2	1042253	6.0	138651	2598	1667	931	30-34
35-39	2376565	1180630	7.1	1195935	6.9	93298	4256	2641	1615	35-39
40-44	2312554	1141888	6.9	1170666	6.8	30542	5735	3617	2118	40-44
45-49	2121782	1044132	6.3	1077650	6.2	2857	8233	5280	2953	45-49
50-54	1717935	802629	4.9	915306	5.3	393	10225	6271	3954	50-54
55-59	1621913	747578	4.5	874335	5.1		15148	9323	5825	55-59
60-64	1503368	688272	4.2	815096	4.7		22546	13870	8676	60-64
65-69	1261782	558567	3.4	703215	4.1		31518	18333	13185	65-69
70-74	907785	377770	2.3	530015	3.1		37614	19943	17671	70-74
75-79	582269	229478	1.4	352791	2.0		41276	19440	21836	75-79
80-84	334564	121275	0.7	213289	1.2	340073 M	38892	16199	22693	80-84
85+	186244	61178	0.4	125066	0.7	320992 F	37211	12463	24748	85+
TOTAL	33852680	16545208		17307472		661065	285133	146990	138143	TOTAL

TABLE 2 — MALE LIFE TABLE

x	nM_x	nq_x	l_x	nd_x	nL_x	nm_x	na_x	T_x	$\dot{e}_x$	x
0	0.032367	0.031475	100000	3148	97246	0.032367	0.125	6941196	69.412	0
1	0.001044	0.004167	96852	404	386401	0.001044	1.500	6843950	70.664	1
5	0.000546	0.002727	96449	263	481587	0.000546	2.500	6457549	66.953	5
10	0.000436	0.002183	96186	210	480437	0.000437	2.653	5975962	62.129	10
15	0.000869	0.004352	95976	418	478916	0.000872	2.692	5495525	57.259	15
20	0.001245	0.006216	95558	594	476355	0.001247	2.581	5016609	52.498	20
25	0.001371	0.006842	94964	650	473234	0.001373	2.556	4540254	47.810	25
30	0.001634	0.008138	94315	767	469736	0.001634	2.606	4067020	43.122	30
35	0.002237	0.011126	93547	1041	465277	0.002237	2.638	3597285	38.454	35
40	0.003168	0.015729	92506	1455	459153	0.003169	2.678	3132008	33.857	40
45	0.005057	0.025094	91051	2285	449954	0.005078	2.679	2672855	29.355	45
50	0.007813	0.038570	88766	3424	435876	0.007855	2.676	2222900	25.042	50
55	0.012471	0.060695	85343	5180	414659	0.012492	2.673	1787024	20.939	55
60	0.020152	0.096316	80163	7721	382739	0.020173	2.659	1372364	17.120	60
65	0.032821	0.152764	72442	11067	335944	0.032942	2.627	989626	13.661	65
70	0.052791	0.235302	61375	14442	271907	0.053113	2.579	653682	10.651	70
75	0.084714	0.351852	46934	16514	193521	0.085333	2.508	381775	8.134	75
80	0.133572	0.496436	30420	15102	113059	0.133572	2.415	188253	6.188	80
85	0.203717	1.000000	15318	15318	75194	0.137464	4.909	75194	4.909	85

TABLE 3 — FEMALE LIFE TABLE

x	nM_x	nq_x	l_x	nd_x	nL_x	nm_x	na_x	T_x	$\dot{e}_x$	x
0	0.025198	0.024647	100000	2465	97813	0.025198	0.113	7489080	74.891	0
1	0.000852	0.003401	97535	332	389312	0.000852	1.500	7391267	75.780	1
5	0.000365	0.001825	97204	177	485575	0.000365	2.500	7001955	72.034	5
10	0.000304	0.001517	97026	147	484765	0.000304	2.515	6516380	67.161	10
15	0.000387	0.001937	96879	188	483948	0.000388	2.617	6031615	62.259	15
20	0.000523	0.002616	96691	253	482858	0.000524	2.631	5547667	57.375	20
25	0.000719	0.003597	96438	347	481361	0.000721	2.605	5064809	52.519	25
30	0.000893	0.004457	96091	428	479449	0.000893	2.644	4583448	47.699	30
35	0.001350	0.006731	95663	644	476796	0.001350	2.638	4104000	42.900	35
40	0.001809	0.009013	95019	856	473090	0.001810	2.656	3627204	38.173	40
45	0.002740	0.013658	94163	1286	467834	0.002749	2.684	3154115	33.496	45
50	0.004320	0.021458	92877	1993	459756	0.004335	2.678	2686278	28.923	50
55	0.006662	0.032851	90884	2986	447493	0.006672	2.680	2226522	24.499	55
60	0.010644	0.052038	87898	4574	429000	0.010662	2.706	1779029	20.240	60
65	0.018750	0.090207	83324	7516	399336	0.018822	2.700	1350028	16.202	65
70	0.033341	0.155682	75808	11802	351587	0.033568	2.674	950693	12.541	70
75	0.061895	0.271365	64006	17369	278233	0.062426	2.594	599106	9.360	75
80	0.106396	0.420376	46637	19605	184265	0.106396	2.505	320873	6.880	80
85	0.197880	1.000000	27032	27032	136608	0.130432	5.054	136608	5.054	85

TABLE 4 — OBSERVED VITAL RATES AND RATIOS

CRUDE RATES

Per Thousand	BOTH SEXES	MALES	FEMALES
BIRTH RATE	19.53	20.55	18.55
DEATH RATE	8.42	8.88	7.98
RATE OF INCREASE	11.10	11.67	10.56

RATES STANDARDIZED ON USA 1980

Per Thousand	BOTH SEXES	MALES	FEMALES
BIRTH RATE	23.52		22.21
DEATH RATE	9.97	10.01	9.94
RATE OF INCREASE	13.54		12.27

VITAL STATISTICS

GFR x 1000	80.777
TFR	2.885
GRR	1.401
NRR	1.346
μ	29.451
σ^2	35.448
GENERATION	29.271
POP. SEX RATIO	1.046
SEX RATIO AT BIRTH	1.059
DEP. RATIO x 100	59.888

PERCENT OF POPULATION IN AGE GROUP

	BOTH SEXES	MALES	FEMALES
UNDER 15	27.79	29.09	26.55
15 - 64	62.54	62.76	62.33
65 AND OLDER	9.67	8.15	11.12

RATES STANDARDIZED ON MEXICO 1980

	BOTH SEXES	MALES	FEMALES
BIRTH RATE	19.98		19.55
DEATH RATE	4.25	4.87	3.63
RATE OF INCREASE	15.72		15.92

PROJECTED POPULATION

AGE GROUP	1975			1980			STABLE EQUIVALENT TO ORIGINAL POPULATION				AGE GROUP	
							MALES		FEMALES			
	BOTH SEXES	MALES	FEMALES	BOTH SEXES	MALES	FEMALES	Number	Percent	Number	Percent		
0-4	3295	1689	1606	3508	1798	1710	1657	9.7	1575	9.2	0-4	
5-9	3180	1629	1551	3283	1682	1601	1568	9.2	1492	8.7	5-9	TABLE 5
10-14	3196	1635	1561	3173	1625	1548	1487	8.7	1416	8.3	10-14	
15-19	3006	1533	1473	3188	1630	1558	1409	8.2	1344	7.9	15-19	POPULATION
20-24	2684	1357	1327	2994	1525	1469	1332	7.8	1274	7.5	20-24	PROJECTED
25-29	2523	1272	1251	2671	1348	1323	1258	7.4	1208	7.1	25-29	WITH
30-34	2214	1106	1108	2508	1262	1246	1187	6.9	1143	6.7	30-34	FIXED
35-39	2047	1011	1036	2198	1096	1102	1117	6.5	1081	6.3	35-39	AGE-
40-44	2352	1165	1187	2025	997	1028	1048	6.1	1019	6.0	40-44	SPECIFIC
45-49	2277	1119	1158	2315	1142	1173	976	5.7	958	5.6	45-49	BIRTH
50-54	2070	1011	1059	2222	1084	1138	899	5.3	895	5.2	50-54	AND
55-59	1655	764	891	1993	962	1031	813	4.8	828	4.8	55-59	DEATH
60-64	1528	690	838	1559	705	854	713	4.2	754	4.4	60-64	RATES
65-69	1363	604	759	1386	606	780	595	3.5	667	3.9	65-69	(female
70-74	1071	452	619	1157	489	668	458	2.7	559	3.3	70-74	dominant,
75-79	688	269	419	812	322	490	310	1.8	420	2.5	75-79	in 000s)
80-84	368	134	234	435	157	278	172	1.0	264	1.5	80-84	
85+	239	81	158	262	89	173	109	0.6	186	1.1	85+	
TOTAL	35756	17521	18235	37689	18519	19170	17108		17083		TOTAL	

VITAL RATES OF PROJECTED POPULATION

Per Thousand	1975			1980			VITAL RATES OF STABLE POPULATION		
	BOTH SEXES	MALES	FEMALES	BOTH SEXES	MALES	FEMALES	MALES	FEMALES	TABLE 6
BIRTH RATE	19.48	20.45	18.55	19.88	20.81	18.97	20.54	19.41	
DEATH RATE	8.98	9.38	8.59	9.37	9.73	9.01	10.38	9.25	PROJECTED
RATE OF INCREASE	10.51	11.07	9.96	10.51	11.07	9.96		10.15	VITAL RATES

AGE STRUCTURE OF PROJECTED POPULATION / STABLE AGE STRUCTURE

	1975 both	males	females	1980 both	males	females	STABLE MALES	STABLE FEMALES	
% UNDER 15	27.05	28.27	25.87	26.44	27.57	25.34	27.55	26.24	AND RATIOS
% 15-64	62.53	62.94	62.12	62.81	63.45	62.19	62.85	61.48	(female
% 65 AND OLDER	10.43	8.79	12.01	10.75	8.98	12.46	9.60	12.27	dominant)
DEPEND. RATIO x 100	59.94	58.87	60.97	59.20	57.59	60.79	59.11	62.65	

MATRIX PARAMETERS

AGE GROUP	FEMALE BIRTH RATES	NET MATERNITY FUNCTION	COEFF. OF MATRIX EQUATION	ORIGINAL MATRIX SUB-DIAGONAL	ORIGINAL MATRIX FIRST ROW	STABLE MATRIX FISHER VALUES	STABLE MATRIX REPRODUCTIVE VALUES			
0-4	0.0000	0.0000	0.0000	0.99682	0.00000	1.053	1637976	λ_1	1.05207	
5-9	0.0000	0.0000	0.0001	0.99833	0.00009	1.111	1737041	λ_2	0.43379+0.77217i	TABLE 7
10-14	0.0000	0.0002	0.0165	0.99831	0.01653	1.171	1727198	λ_4	-0.40747-0.46633i	
15-19	0.0068	0.0327	0.1606	0.99775	0.16168	1.216	1618083	λ_6	-0.04373+0.54779i	LESLIE
20-24	0.0598	0.2885	0.3778	0.99690	0.38109	1.112	1395062	r_1	0.01015	MATRIX
25-29	0.0970	0.4670	0.3883	0.99603	0.39300	0.771	858087	r_2	-0.02428+0.21179i	AND ITS
30-34	0.0646	0.3097	0.2452	0.99447	0.24908	0.399	416064	r_4	-0.09584-0.45779i	ANALYSIS
35-39	0.0379	0.1806	0.1203	0.99223	0.12288	0.159	189728	r_6	-0.11974+0.33009i	(females)
40-44	0.0127	0.0599	0.0330	0.98890	0.03396	0.038	44300	c_1	170847	
45-49	0.0013	0.0060	0.0035	0.98273	0.00363	0.004	4431	$2\pi/\gamma$	29.6669	
50-54	0.0002	0.0010	0.0005	0.97333	0.00051	0.001	465	Δ	3.2416	

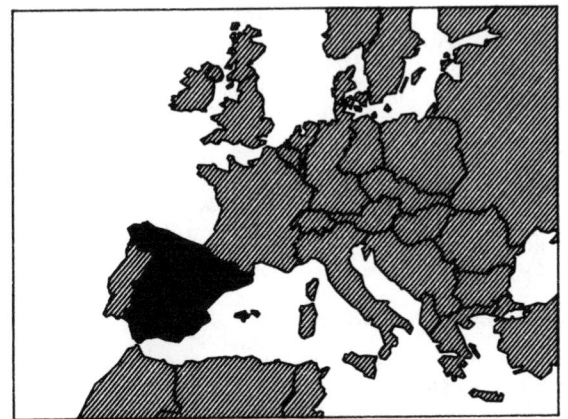

EDUCATION [1984]

% of primary school-age children enrolled:	108
secondary school-age children enrolled:	89
ca. 20-24 year olds in higher education:	26

LABOR FORCE

Average annual labor force growth (%) 1980-85:	1.3
% of the 1980 labor force in agriculture:	17
in industry:	37
in services:	46

TABLE 8

SOCIO-ECONOMIC INDICATORS

GNP & INCOME DISTRIBUTION

GNP per capita (in US Dollars) 1985:	4290
GNP average annual growth rate (%) 1965-85:	2.6
% share of total household income 1980-81	
Lowest 20% of households:	6.9
Highest 10% of households:	24.5

HEALTH & NUTRITION

Population per physician 1981:	360
Daily calorie supply per capita 1985:	3358

TABLE 1 — DATA

AGE AT LAST BIRTHDAY	ESTIMATED MID-YEAR POPULATION — BOTH SEXES	MALES Number	MALES Percent	FEMALES Number	FEMALES Percent	BIRTHS BY AGE OF MOTHER AND SEX	DEATHS BOTH SEXES	DEATHS MALES	DEATHS FEMALES	AGE AT LAST BIRTHDAY
0	652362	334868	1.9	317494	1.8		12631	7219	5412	0
1-4	2614649	1337764	7.7	1276885	7.0		2043	1171	872	1-4
5-9	3222932	1649918	9.5	1573014	8.7		1227	717	510	5-9
10-14	3170630	1621940	9.3	1548690	8.5	246	1093	648	445	10-14
15-19	2993750	1517432	8.7	1476318	8.1	31625	1721	1233	488	15-19
20-24	2578125	1307532	7.5	1270593	7.0	171296	2005	1473	532	20-24
25-29	2459473	1232993	7.1	1226480	6.8	231620	2066	1427	639	25-29
30-34	2226814	1111221	6.4	1115593	6.2	136513	2316	1506	810	30-34
35-39	2068923	1027098	5.9	1041825	5.7	67058	3277	2099	1178	35-39
40-44	2375642	1170826	6.7	1204816	6.6	27703	5576	3608	1968	40-44
45-49	2259962	1111600	6.4	1148362	6.3	2374	8277	5321	2956	45-49
50-54	2048840	995397	5.7	1053443	5.8	161	11905	7798	4107	50-54
55-59	1652551	768955	4.4	883596	4.9		14900	9405	5495	55-59
60-64	1535016	690188	4.0	844828	4.7		22270	13942	8328	60-64
65-69	1358163	599995	3.5	758168	4.2		31928	19244	12684	65-69
70-74	1067849	448023	2.6	619826	3.4		42485	23306	19179	70-74
75-79	653843	257049	1.5	396794	2.2		46237	22138	24099	75-79
80-84	363400	132504	0.8	230896	1.3	345982 M	42102	17714	24388	80-84
85+	212261	65537	0.4	146724	0.8	322614 F	43277	14891	28386	85+
TOTAL	35515185	17380840		18134345		668596	297336	154860	142476	TOTAL

TABLE 2 — MALE LIFE TABLE

x	$_nM_x$	$_nq_x$	l_x	$_nd_x$	$_nL_x$	$_nm_x$	$_na_x$	T_x	$\overset{\circ}{e}_x$	x
0	0.021558	0.021150	100000	2115	98111	0.021558	0.107	7043292	70.433	0
1	0.000875	0.003494	97885	342	390685	0.000875	1.500	6945182	70.952	1
5	0.000435	0.002170	97543	212	487186	0.000435	2.500	6554497	67.196	5
10	0.000400	0.001997	97331	194	486209	0.000400	2.697	6067311	62.337	10
15	0.000813	0.004068	97137	395	484769	0.000815	2.684	5581103	57.456	15
20	0.001127	0.005625	96742	544	482381	0.001128	2.561	5096333	52.680	20
25	0.001157	0.005774	96197	555	479621	0.001158	2.539	4613952	47.963	25
30	0.001355	0.006772	95642	648	476677	0.001359	2.632	4134331	43.227	30
35	0.002044	0.010170	94994	966	472722	0.002044	2.671	3657654	38.504	35
40	0.003082	0.015298	94028	1438	466802	0.003082	2.678	3184932	33.872	40
45	0.004787	0.023699	92590	2194	457892	0.004792	2.695	2718131	29.357	45
50	0.007834	0.038643	90396	3493	443870	0.007870	2.679	2260239	25.004	50
55	0.012231	0.059770	86902	5194	422444	0.012295	2.676	1816369	20.901	55
60	0.020200	0.096591	81708	7892	390023	0.020235	2.654	1393925	17.060	60
65	0.032074	0.149198	73816	11013	342940	0.032114	2.626	1003902	13.600	65
70	0.052020	0.232090	62803	14576	278869	0.052268	2.589	660963	10.524	70
75	0.086124	0.357256	48227	17229	198234	0.086914	2.510	382093	7.923	75
80	0.133687	0.496994	30998	15406	115237	0.133687	2.420	183859	5.931	80
85	0.227215	1.000000	15592	15592	68622	0.164546	4.401	68622	4.401	85

TABLE 3 — FEMALE LIFE TABLE

x	$_nM_x$	$_nq_x$	l_x	$_nd_x$	$_nL_x$	$_nm_x$	$_na_x$	T_x	$\overset{\circ}{e}_x$	x
0	0.017046	0.016788	100000	1679	98487	0.017046	0.099	7623375	76.234	0
1	0.000683	0.002727	98321	268	392614	0.000683	1.500	7524888	76.534	1
5	0.000324	0.001620	98053	159	489868	0.000324	2.500	7132273	72.739	5
10	0.000287	0.001436	97894	141	489120	0.000287	2.504	6642405	67.853	10
15	0.000331	0.001653	97754	162	488378	0.000331	2.582	6153285	62.947	15
20	0.000419	0.002095	97592	204	487468	0.000419	2.594	5664907	58.047	20
25	0.000521	0.002606	97388	254	486335	0.000522	2.622	5177439	53.163	25
30	0.000726	0.003635	97134	353	484847	0.000728	2.672	4691104	48.295	30
35	0.001131	0.005639	96781	546	482629	0.001131	2.664	4206257	43.462	35
40	0.001633	0.008136	96235	783	479359	0.001633	2.680	3723628	38.693	40
45	0.002574	0.012809	95452	1223	474421	0.002577	2.678	3244270	33.988	45
50	0.003899	0.019387	94229	1827	466917	0.003913	2.685	2769849	29.395	50
55	0.006219	0.030760	92403	2842	455427	0.006241	2.683	2302931	24.923	55
60	0.009858	0.048267	89560	4323	437836	0.009873	2.695	1847504	20.629	60
65	0.016730	0.080740	85238	6882	410453	0.016767	2.714	1409668	16.538	65
70	0.030943	0.145269	78355	11383	365621	0.031132	2.702	999215	12.752	70
75	0.060734	0.267667	66973	17926	291948	0.061403	2.606	633594	9.460	75
80	0.105623	0.418006	49046	20502	194102	0.105623	2.506	341646	6.966	80
85	0.193465	1.000000	28545	28545	147544	0.125546	5.169	147544	5.169	85

TABLE 4 — OBSERVED VITAL RATES AND RATIOS

CRUDE RATES

Per Thousand	BOTH SEXES	MALES	FEMALES
BIRTH RATE	18.83	19.91	17.79
DEATH RATE	8.37	8.91	7.86
RATE OF INCREASE	10.45	11.00	9.93

RATES STANDARDIZED ON USA 1980

Per Thousand	BOTH SEXES	MALES	FEMALES
BIRTH RATE	22.99		21.58
DEATH RATE	9.60	9.84	9.38
RATE OF INCREASE	13.39		12.20

VITAL STATISTICS

GFR x 1000	78.807
TFR	2.786
GRR	1.344
NRR	1.306
μ	28.829
σ^2	35.980
GENERATION	28.662
POP. SEX RATIO	1.043
SEX RATIO AT BIRTH	1.072
DEP. RATIO x 100	59.985

PERCENT OF POPULATION IN AGE GROUP

	BOTH SEXES	MALES	FEMALES
UNDER 15	27.20	28.45	26.01
15 - 64	62.51	62.90	62.12
65 AND OLDER	10.29	8.65	11.87

RATES STANDARDIZED ON MEXICO 1980

	BOTH SEXES	MALES	FEMALES
BIRTH RATE	19.81		19.27
DEATH RATE	3.83	4.46	3.20
RATE OF INCREASE	15.98		16.07

AGE AT LAST BIRTHDAY	ESTIMATED MID-YEAR POPULATION					BIRTHS BY AGE OF MOTHER AND SEX	DEATHS			AGE AT LAST BIRTHDAY
	BOTH SEXES	MALES Number	MALES Percent	FEMALES Number	FEMALES Percent		BOTH SEXES	MALES	FEMALES	
0	604645	309009	1.7	295636	1.6		7039	4111	2928	0
1-4	2564465	1316353	7.2	1248112	6.6		1638	926	712	1-4
5-9	3280462	1679430	9.2	1601032	8.4		1158	701	457	5-9
10-14	3228287	1653519	9.0	1574768	8.3	469	992	611	381	10-14
15-19	3176309	1624302	8.9	1552007	8.2	40646	1766	1255	511	15-19
20-24	2994091	1515865	8.3	1478226	7.8	166541	2148	1612	536	20-24
25-29	2573556	1303420	7.1	1270136	6.7	183481	2011	1446	565	25-29
30-34	2458487	1230117	6.7	1228370	6.5	112081	2395	1625	770	30-34
35-39	2230284	1112372	6.1	1117912	5.9	50629	2845	1878	967	35-39
40-44	2071927	1029299	5.6	1042628	5.5	15126	4275	2851	1424	40-44
45-49	2364347	1163355	6.3	1200992	6.3	1544	7437	4981	2456	45-49
50-54	2225350	1087951	5.9	1137399	6.0	129	11439	7676	3763	50-54
55-59	1985971	953432	5.2	1032539	5.4		15927	10815	5112	55-59
60-64	1570312	716197	3.9	854115	4.5		19248	12216	7032	60-64
65-69	1408095	611181	3.3	796914	4.2		28118	16977	11141	65-69
70-74	1171268	491336	2.7	679932	3.6		40137	22811	17326	70-74
75-79	826362	322852	1.8	503510	2.6		47877	24002	23875	75-79
80-84	417603	151032	0.8	266571	1.4	296018 M	44283	18834	25449	80-84
85+	234261	75524	0.4	158737	0.8	274628 F	47693	16243	31450	85+
TOTAL	37386082	18346546		19039536		570646	288426	151571	136855	TOTAL

TABLE 1 DATA

x	$_nM_x$	$_nq_x$	l_x	$_nd_x$	$_nL_x$	$_nm_x$	$_na_x$	T_x	$\overset{\circ}{e}_x$	x
0	0.013304	0.013145	100000	1315	98807	0.013304	0.093	7227262	72.273	0
1	0.000703	0.002809	98685	277	394049	0.000703	1.500	7128455	72.234	1
5	0.000417	0.002085	98408	205	491529	0.000417	2.500	6734406	68.433	5
10	0.000370	0.001847	98203	181	490598	0.000370	2.699	6242877	63.571	10
15	0.000773	0.003860	98022	378	489233	0.000773	2.686	5752279	58.684	15
20	0.001063	0.005310	97643	518	486954	0.001065	2.564	5263045	53.901	20
25	0.001109	0.005537	97125	538	484305	0.001110	2.546	4776091	49.175	25
30	0.001321	0.006593	96587	637	481401	0.001323	2.589	4291786	44.434	30
35	0.001688	0.008435	95950	809	477869	0.001694	2.673	3810385	39.712	35
40	0.002770	0.013761	95141	1309	472678	0.002770	2.688	3332516	35.027	40
45	0.004282	0.021199	93832	1989	464579	0.004282	2.697	2859838	30.478	45
50	0.007055	0.034759	91843	3192	451843	0.007065	2.691	2395259	26.080	50
55	0.011343	0.055490	88650	4919	431726	0.011394	2.657	1943416	21.922	55
60	0.017057	0.082424	83731	6901	402469	0.017148	2.655	1511690	18.054	60
65	0.027777	0.130694	76830	10041	360519	0.027862	2.647	1109221	14.437	65
70	0.046426	0.209235	66788	13974	300397	0.046520	2.600	748702	11.210	70
75	0.074344	0.316539	52814	16718	222926	0.074992	2.539	448305	8.488	75
80	0.124702	0.473572	36096	17094	137026	0.124751	2.458	225379	6.244	80
85	0.215071	1.000000	19002	19002	88353	0.150089	4.650	88353	4.650	85

TABLE 2 MALE LIFE TABLE

x	$_nM_x$	$_nq_x$	l_x	$_nd_x$	$_nL_x$	$_nm_x$	$_na_x$	T_x	$\overset{\circ}{e}_x$	x
0	0.009904	0.009815	100000	982	99104	0.009904	0.087	7828865	78.289	0
1	0.000570	0.002279	99018	226	395510	0.000570	1.500	7729762	78.064	1
5	0.000285	0.001426	98793	141	493612	0.000285	2.500	7334252	74.239	5
10	0.000242	0.001209	98652	119	492966	0.000242	2.537	6840640	69.341	10
15	0.000329	0.001645	98533	162	492270	0.000329	2.576	6347674	64.422	15
20	0.000363	0.001813	98371	178	491419	0.000363	2.566	5855403	59.524	20
25	0.000445	0.002227	98192	219	490441	0.000446	2.623	5363985	54.627	25
30	0.000627	0.003135	97974	307	489142	0.000628	2.638	4873544	49.743	30
35	0.000865	0.004330	97666	423	487349	0.000868	2.675	4384401	44.892	35
40	0.001366	0.006807	97244	662	484680	0.001366	2.676	3897052	40.075	40
45	0.002045	0.010177	96582	983	480640	0.002045	2.693	3412373	35.332	45
50	0.003308	0.016437	95599	1571	474342	0.003313	2.676	2931732	30.667	50
55	0.004951	0.024571	94027	2310	464809	0.004971	2.694	2457391	26.135	55
60	0.008233	0.040572	91717	3721	450046	0.008268	2.705	1992582	21.725	60
65	0.013980	0.067893	87996	5974	426331	0.014013	2.715	1542536	17.530	65
70	0.025482	0.120685	82022	9899	387354	0.025555	2.701	1116205	13.609	70
75	0.047417	0.215452	72123	15539	324272	0.047920	2.661	728851	10.106	75
80	0.095468	0.387439	56584	21923	229635	0.095468	2.569	404579	7.150	80
85	0.198126	1.000000	34661	34661	174944	0.130608	5.047	174944	5.047	85

TABLE 3 FEMALE LIFE TABLE

CRUDE RATES

Per Thousand	BOTH SEXES	MALES	FEMALES
BIRTH RATE	15.26	16.13	14.42
DEATH RATE	7.71	8.26	7.19
RATE OF INCREASE	7.55	7.87	7.24

PERCENT OF POPULATION IN AGE GROUP

UNDER 15	25.89	27.03	24.79
15 - 64	63.26	63.97	62.58
65 AND OLDER	10.85	9.00	12.64

RATES STANDARDIZED ON USA 1980

Per Thousand	BOTH SEXES	MALES	FEMALES
BIRTH RATE	18.19		17.02
DEATH RATE	8.50	8.74	8.27
RATE OF INCREASE	9.69		8.75

RATES STANDARDIZED ON MEXICO 1980

	BOTH SEXES	MALES	FEMALES
BIRTH RATE	15.91		15.43
DEATH RATE	3.23	3.83	2.62
RATE OF INCREASE	12.67		12.81

VITAL STATISTICS

GFR x 1000	64.188	TABLE 4
TFR	2.180	
GRR	1.049	OBSERVED
NRR	1.028	VITAL
μ	28.226	RATES
σ^2	36.412	AND
GENERATION	28.208	RATIOS
POP. SEX RATIO	1.038	
SEX RATIO AT BIRTH	1.078	
DEP. RATIO x 100	58.076	

AGE AT LAST BIRTHDAY	ESTIMATED MID-YEAR POPULATION BOTH SEXES	MALES Number	MALES Percent	FEMALES Number	FEMALES Percent	BIRTHS BY AGE OF MOTHER AND SEX	DEATHS BOTH SEXES	DEATHS MALES	DEATHS FEMALES	AGE AT LAST BIRTHDAY
0	491060	253639	1.4	237421	1.2		5285	2989	2296	0
1-4	2247020	1157746	6.2	1089274	5.6		1299	739	560	1-4
5-9	3245943	1672213	8.9	1573730	8.1		896	563	333	5-9
10-14	3290835	1692003	9.0	1598832	8.2	334	869	561	308	10-14
15-19	3320905	1699709	9.1	1621196	8.3	32300	1848	1284	564	15-19
20-24	3097445	1565310	8.4	1532135	7.9	131772	2313	1757	556	20-24
25-29	2708668	1364764	7.3	1343904	6.9	166767	2156	1572	584	25-29
30-34	2477721	1245544	6.6	1232177	6.3	96535	2276	1569	707	30-34
35-39	2386843	1194069	6.4	1192774	6.1	44852	3062	2052	1010	35-39
40-44	2067006	1031582	5.5	1035424	5.3	11634	3798	2590	1208	40-44
45-49	2216354	1090730	5.8	1125624	5.8	1035	6923	4693	2230	45-49
50-54	2312146	1134193	6.1	1177953	6.1	123	11184	7610	3574	50-54
55-59	2106158	1017284	5.4	1088874	5.6		15946	10863	5083	55-59
60-64	1773228	826861	4.4	946367	4.9		21135	14072	7063	60-64
65-69	1434557	624078	3.3	810479	4.2		26866	16411	10455	65-69
70-74	1251963	524278	2.8	727185	3.7		39959	22692	17267	70-74
75-79	913839	360171	1.9	553668	2.8		50588	25652	24936	75-79
80-84	530651	191742	1.0	338909	1.7	251585 M	50736	21859	28877	80-84
85+	299745	94620	0.5	205125	1.1	233767 F	55430	18847	36583	85+
TOTAL	38172087	18741036		19431051		485352	302569	158375	144194	TOTAL

TABLE 1 DATA

TABLE 2 — MALE LIFE TABLE

x	nM_x	nq_x	l_x	nd_x	nL_x	nm_x	na_x	T_x	$\mathring{e}_x$	x
0	0.011784	0.011659	100000	1166	98939	0.011784	0.090	7294732	72.947	0
1	0.000638	0.002549	98834	252	394706	0.000638	1.500	7195793	72.807	1
5	0.000337	0.001682	98582	166	492496	0.000337	2.500	6801087	68.989	5
10	0.000332	0.001657	98416	163	491717	0.000332	2.762	6308591	64.101	10
15	0.000755	0.003773	98253	371	490420	0.000756	2.717	5816874	59.203	15
20	0.001122	0.005604	97883	549	488081	0.001124	2.572	5326454	54.417	20
25	0.001152	0.005745	97334	559	485284	0.001152	2.522	4838374	49.709	25
30	0.001260	0.006287	96775	608	482408	0.001261	2.591	4353090	44.982	30
35	0.001718	0.008580	96166	825	478891	0.001723	2.647	3870682	40.250	35
40	0.002511	0.012509	95341	1193	473971	0.002516	2.706	3391791	35.575	40
45	0.004303	0.021302	94149	2006	466115	0.004303	2.692	2917820	30.992	45
50	0.006710	0.033034	92143	3044	453658	0.006710	2.681	2451705	26.608	50
55	0.010678	0.052230	89099	4654	434675	0.010706	2.675	1998048	22.425	55
60	0.017019	0.082245	84446	6945	405902	0.017111	2.649	1563373	18.513	60
65	0.026296	0.124294	77500	9633	364748	0.026410	2.638	1157471	14.935	65
70	0.043241	0.196259	67868	13320	307495	0.043317	2.609	792723	11.680	70
75	0.071222	0.304745	54548	16623	231901	0.071682	2.543	485228	8.895	75
80	0.114002	0.442321	37925	16775	147146	0.114002	2.468	253327	6.680	80
85	0.199186	1.000000	21150	21150	106181	0.132109	5.020	106181	5.020	85

TABLE 3 — FEMALE LIFE TABLE

x	nM_x	nq_x	l_x	nd_x	nL_x	nm_x	na_x	T_x	$\mathring{e}_x$	x
0	0.009671	0.009586	100000	959	99124	0.009671	0.086	7915361	79.154	0
1	0.000514	0.002054	99041	203	395657	0.000514	1.500	7816236	78.919	1
5	0.000212	0.001057	98838	105	493929	0.000212	2.500	7420579	75.078	5
10	0.000193	0.000963	98733	95	493444	0.000193	2.647	6926650	70.155	10
15	0.000348	0.001738	98638	171	492781	0.000348	2.602	6433206	65.220	15
20	0.000363	0.001814	98467	179	491897	0.000363	2.549	5940425	60.329	20
25	0.000435	0.002175	98288	214	490929	0.000435	2.600	5448528	55.434	25
30	0.000574	0.002870	98075	281	489711	0.000575	2.648	4957599	50.549	30
35	0.000847	0.004236	97793	414	487990	0.000849	2.644	4467887	45.687	35
40	0.001167	0.005828	97379	568	485588	0.001169	2.698	3979897	40.870	40
45	0.001981	0.009861	96811	955	481853	0.001981	2.691	3494309	36.094	45
50	0.003034	0.015064	95857	1444	475930	0.003034	2.677	3012455	31.427	50
55	0.004668	0.023141	94413	2185	467009	0.004678	2.686	2536525	26.866	55
60	0.007463	0.036846	92228	3398	453353	0.007496	2.708	2069516	22.439	60
65	0.012900	0.062878	88830	5585	431434	0.012946	2.724	1616163	18.194	65
70	0.023745	0.112834	83244	9393	394732	0.023795	2.712	1184730	14.232	70
75	0.045038	0.205127	73852	15149	333748	0.045390	2.656	789998	10.697	75
80	0.085206	0.353246	58703	20736	243369	0.085206	2.582	456249	7.772	80
85	0.178345	1.000000	37966	37966	212880	0.109432	5.607	212880	5.607	85

TABLE 4 — OBSERVED VITAL RATES AND RATIOS

CRUDE RATES

Per Thousand	BOTH SEXES	MALES	FEMALES
BIRTH RATE	12.71	13.42	12.03
DEATH RATE	7.93	8.45	7.42
RATE OF INCREASE	4.79	4.97	4.61

PERCENT OF POPULATION IN AGE GROUP

	BOTH SEXES	MALES	FEMALES
UNDER 15	24.30	25.48	23.15
15 - 64	64.10	64.94	63.28
65 AND OLDER	11.61	9.58	13.56

RATES STANDARDIZED ON USA 1980

Per Thousand	BOTH SEXES	MALES	FEMALES
BIRTH RATE	14.92		13.97
DEATH RATE	7.90	8.25	7.58
RATE OF INCREASE	7.01		6.40

RATES STANDARDIZED ON MEXICO 1980

	BOTH SEXES	MALES	FEMALES
BIRTH RATE	12.97		12.59
DEATH RATE	3.02	3.61	2.42
RATE OF INCREASE	9.95		10.17

VITAL STATISTICS

GFR x 1000	53.434
TFR	1.792
GRR	0.863
NRR	0.847
μ	28.387
σ^2	35.005
GENERATION	28.490
POP. SEX RATIO	1.037
SEX RATIO AT BIRTH	1.076
DEP. RATIO x 100	56.018

PROJECTED POPULATION

AGE GROUP	1988 BOTH SEXES	1988 MALES	1988 FEMALES	1993 BOTH SEXES	1993 MALES	1993 FEMALES
0-4	2501	1295	1206	2669	1382	1287
5-9	2732	1408	1324	2496	1292	1204
10-14	3242	1670	1572	2729	1406	1323
15-19	3285	1688	1597	3235	1665	1570
20-24	3310	1692	1618	3273	1679	1594
25-29	3085	1556	1529	3297	1682	1615
30-34	2698	1357	1341	3072	1547	1525
35-39	2464	1236	1228	2683	1347	1336
40-44	2369	1182	1187	2446	1224	1222
45-49	2041	1014	1027	2340	1162	1178
50-54	2174	1062	1112	2002	987	1015
55-59	2243	1087	1156	2108	1017	1091
60-64	2007	950	1057	2137	1015	1122
65-69	1644	743	901	1860	854	1006
70-74	1268	526	742	1450	626	824
75-79	1011	396	615	1024	397	627
80-84	633	229	404	699	251	448
85+	434	138	296	518	165	353
TOTAL	39141	19229	19912	40038	19698	20340

STABLE EQUIVALENT TO ORIGINAL POPULATION

MALES Number	MALES Percent	FEMALES Number	FEMALES Percent	AGE GROUP	
1497	5.4	1394	4.9	0-4	
1538	5.6	1433	5.1	5-9	TABLE 5
1581	5.7	1474	5.2	10-14	
1623	5.9	1516	5.4	15-19	POPULATION
1663	6.0	1558	5.5	20-24	PROJECTED
1703	6.2	1601	5.7	25-29	WITH
1743	6.3	1644	5.8	30-34	FIXED
1781	6.5	1687	6.0	35-39	AGE-
1815	6.6	1728	6.1	40-44	SPECIFIC
1838	6.7	1765	6.3	45-49	BIRTH
1842	6.7	1795	6.4	50-54	AND
1817	6.6	1814	6.4	55-59	DEATH
1747	6.3	1813	6.4	60-64	RATES
1616	5.9	1776	6.3	65-69	(female
1403	5.1	1673	5.9	70-74	dominant,
1089	4.0	1457	5.2	75-79	in 000s)
712	2.6	1094	3.9	80-84	
529	1.9	985	3.5	85+	
27537		28207		TOTAL	

VITAL RATES OF PROJECTED POPULATION

Per Thousand	1988 BOTH SEXES	1988 MALES	1988 FEMALES	1993 BOTH SEXES	1993 MALES	1993 FEMALES
BIRTH RATE	13.46	14.20	12.74	13.83	14.57	13.11
DEATH RATE	8.96	9.34	8.59	9.63	9.95	9.31
RATE OF INCREASE	4.50	4.86	4.15	4.20	4.62	3.80

AGE STRUCTURE OF PROJECTED POPULATION

	BOTH SEXES	MALES	FEMALES	BOTH SEXES	MALES	FEMALES
% UNDER 15	21.65	22.74	20.60	19.72	20.71	18.75
% 15-64	65.60	66.69	64.54	66.42	67.65	65.23
% 65 AND OLDER	12.75	10.57	14.85	13.86	11.64	16.02
DEPEND. RATIO x 100	52.44	49.94	54.93	50.56	47.82	53.31

VITAL RATES OF STABLE POPULATION

Per Thousand	MALES	FEMALES	
BIRTH RATE	10.85	9.84	TABLE 6
DEATH RATE	16.58	15.68	PROJECTED
RATE OF INCREASE		-5.83	VITAL RATES AND RATIOS

STABLE AGE STRUCTURE

	MALES	FEMALES	(female dominant)
% UNDER 15	16.76	15.25	
% 15-64	63.81	59.99	
% 65 AND OLDER	19.42	24.76	
DEPEND. RATIO x 100	56.71	66.70	

AGE GROUP	FEMALE BIRTH RATES	NET MATERNITY FUNCTION	COEFF. OF MATRIX EQUATION	ORIGINAL MATRIX SUB-DIAGONAL	ORIGINAL MATRIX FIRST ROW	STABLE MATRIX FISHER VALUES	STABLE MATRIX REPRODUCTIVE VALUES	MATRIX PARAMETERS		
0-4	0.0000	0.0000	0.0000	0.99828	0.00000	0.996	1321262	λ_1	0.97125	
5-9	0.0000	0.0000	0.0002	0.99902	0.00025	0.969	1524859	λ_2	0.39439-0.71157i	TABLE 7
10-14	0.0001	0.0005	0.0239	0.99866	0.02396	0.942	1505731	λ_4	-0.34336-0.43136i	
15-19	0.0096	0.0473	0.1255	0.99821	0.12604	0.892	1446166	λ_6	-0.05818-0.48687i	LESLIE
20-24	0.0414	0.2038	0.2486	0.99803	0.25005	0.742	1137159	r_1	-0.00583	MATRIX
25-29	0.0598	0.2934	0.2391	0.99752	0.24098	0.473	635365	r_2	-0.04127-0.21294i	AND ITS
30-34	0.0377	0.1848	0.1366	0.99648	0.13800	0.220	270755	r_4	-0.11908-0.44862i	ANALYSIS
35-39	0.0181	0.0884	0.0573	0.99508	0.05813	0.076	90954	r_6	-0.14253-0.33795i	(females)
40-44	0.0054	0.0263	0.0142	0.99231	0.01448	0.016	16827	c_1	282059	
45-49	0.0004	0.0021	0.0012	0.98771	0.00122	0.001	1552	$2\pi/\gamma$	29.5072	
50-54	0.0001	0.0002	0.0001	0.98126	0.00012	0.000	150	Δ	15.1514	

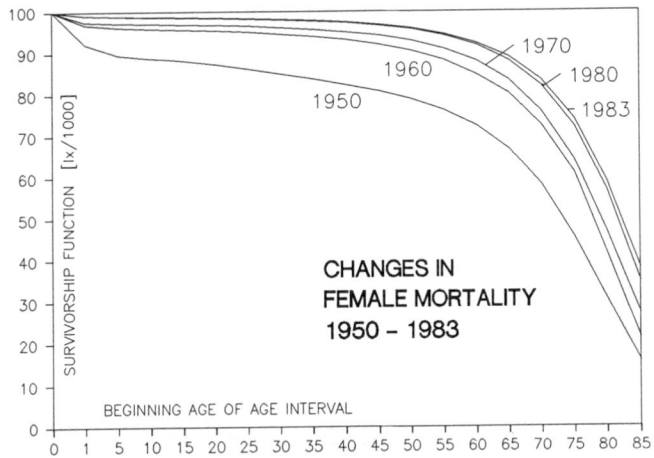

CHANGES IN FEMALE MORTALITY 1950 – 1983

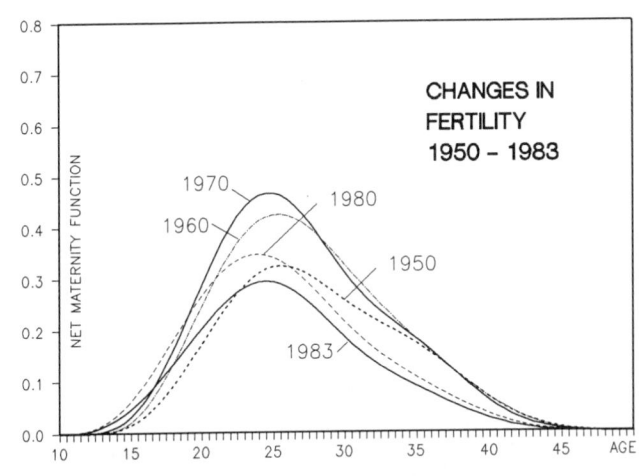

CHANGES IN FERTILITY 1950 – 1983

TABLE 1 — DATA

AGE AT LAST BIRTHDAY	ESTIMATED MID-YEAR POPULATION BOTH SEXES	MALES Number	MALES Percent	FEMALES Number	FEMALES Percent	BIRTHS BY AGE OF MOTHER AND SEX	DEATHS BOTH SEXES	DEATHS MALES	DEATHS FEMALES	AGE AT LAST BIRTHDAY
0	107091	55035	1.4	52056	1.3		1212	711	501	0
1-4	474364	243725	6.1	230639	5.7		251	157	94	1-4
5-9	563606	289078	7.2	274528	6.8		229	130	99	5-9
10-14	531380	273222	6.8	258158	6.4	18	151	96	55	10-14
15-19	553066	282984	7.0	270082	6.7	9162	393	267	126	15-19
20-24	661604	338219	8.4	323385	8.0	38912	519	366	153	20-24
25-29	612734	318217	7.9	294517	7.3	38098	511	358	153	25-29
30-34	482794	248912	6.2	233882	5.8	16383	504	351	153	30-34
35-39	446334	226310	5.6	220024	5.5	6027	637	390	247	35-39
40-44	475288	238780	5.9	236508	5.9	1446	1055	653	402	40-44
45-49	538092	269948	6.7	268144	6.7	103	1831	1125	706	45-49
50-54	511546	256152	6.4	255394	6.3	1	2745	1698	1047	50-54
55-59	509966	253756	6.3	256210	6.4		4158	2657	1501	55-59
60-64	475540	231805	5.8	243735	6.1		6478	4113	2365	60-64
65-69	396218	186072	4.6	210146	5.2		8836	5386	3450	65-69
70-74	305972	138199	3.4	167773	4.2		11494	6579	4915	70-74
75-79	210353	89968	2.2	120385	3.0		13342	6795	6547	75-79
80-84	121222	50050	1.2	71172	1.8	56542 M	12880	6007	6873	80-84
85+	65648	25898	0.6	39750	1.0	53608 F	12800	5578	7222	85+
TOTAL	8042818	4016330		4026488		110150	80026	43417	36609	TOTAL

TABLE 2 — MALE LIFE TABLE

x	nM_x	nq_x	l_x	nd_x	nL_x	nm_x	na_x	T_x	$\overset{\circ}{e}_x$	x
0	0.012919	0.012769	100000	1277	98841	0.012919	0.092	7226383	72.264	0
1	0.000644	0.002573	98723	254	394257	0.000644	1.500	7127542	72.197	1
5	0.000450	0.002246	98469	221	491793	0.000450	2.500	6733285	68.380	5
10	0.000351	0.001756	98248	173	490858	0.000352	2.790	6241492	63.528	10
15	0.000944	0.004707	98075	462	489297	0.000944	2.660	5750634	58.635	15
20	0.001082	0.005396	97614	527	486769	0.001082	2.533	5261337	53.900	20
25	0.001125	0.005616	97087	545	484104	0.001126	2.559	4774568	49.178	25
30	0.001410	0.007046	96542	680	481066	0.001414	2.585	4290464	44.442	30
35	0.001723	0.008596	95862	824	477375	0.001726	2.654	3809398	39.739	35
40	0.002735	0.013587	95038	1291	472191	0.002735	2.679	3332023	35.060	40
45	0.004167	0.020638	93746	1935	464250	0.004167	2.684	2859832	30.506	45
50	0.006629	0.032643	91811	2997	452108	0.006629	2.681	2395583	26.092	50
55	0.010471	0.051118	88815	4540	433596	0.010471	2.692	1943475	21.882	55
60	0.017743	0.085333	84274	7191	404631	0.017773	2.672	1509879	17.916	60
65	0.028946	0.135918	77083	10477	360699	0.029046	2.641	1105248	14.338	65
70	0.047605	0.214334	66606	14276	298644	0.047802	2.591	744549	11.178	70
75	0.075527	0.319772	52330	16734	220252	0.075975	2.526	445905	8.521	75
80	0.120020	0.459818	35596	16368	136376	0.120020	2.458	225652	6.339	80
85	0.215383	1.000000	19229	19229	89276	0.150534	4.643	89276	4.643	85

TABLE 3 — FEMALE LIFE TABLE

x	nM_x	nq_x	l_x	nd_x	nL_x	nm_x	na_x	T_x	$\overset{\circ}{e}_x$	x
0	0.009624	0.009540	100000	954	99128	0.009624	0.086	7732913	77.329	0
1	0.000408	0.001629	99046	161	395781	0.000408	1.500	7633785	77.073	1
5	0.000361	0.001801	98885	178	493978	0.000361	2.500	7238004	73.196	5
10	0.000213	0.001065	98707	105	493281	0.000213	2.602	6744026	68.324	10
15	0.000467	0.002330	98601	230	492459	0.000467	2.615	6250746	63.394	15
20	0.000473	0.002363	98372	232	491282	0.000473	2.523	5758287	58.536	20
25	0.000519	0.002598	98139	255	490077	0.000520	2.573	5267004	53.669	25
30	0.000654	0.003282	97884	321	488699	0.000657	2.689	4776927	48.802	30
35	0.001123	0.005605	97563	547	486552	0.001124	2.690	4288248	43.954	35
40	0.001700	0.008465	97016	821	483176	0.001700	2.681	3801696	39.186	40
45	0.002633	0.013085	96195	1259	478058	0.002633	2.683	3318520	34.498	45
50	0.004100	0.020304	94936	1928	470160	0.004100	2.654	2840462	29.920	50
55	0.005858	0.028900	93009	2688	458816	0.005858	2.683	2370302	25.485	55
60	0.009703	0.047513	90321	4291	441737	0.009715	2.701	1911486	21.163	60
65	0.016417	0.079367	86029	6828	414455	0.016474	2.702	1469749	17.084	65
70	0.029296	0.137770	79201	10912	370755	0.029431	2.686	1055294	13.324	70
75	0.054384	0.242508	68290	16561	301975	0.054842	2.616	684538	10.024	75
80	0.096569	0.389903	51729	20169	208859	0.096569	2.532	382563	7.396	80
85	0.181686	1.000000	31560	31560	173705	0.112949	5.504	173705	5.504	85

TABLE 4 — OBSERVED VITAL RATES AND RATIOS

CRUDE RATES

Per Thousand	BOTH SEXES	MALES	FEMALES
BIRTH RATE	13.70	14.08	13.31
DEATH RATE	9.95	10.81	9.09
RATE OF INCREASE	3.75	3.27	4.22

PERCENT OF POPULATION IN AGE GROUP

UNDER 15	20.84	21.44	20.25
15 - 64	65.49	66.36	64.62
65 AND OLDER	13.67	12.20	15.13

RATES STANDARDIZED ON USA 1980

Per Thousand	BOTH SEXES	MALES	FEMALES
BIRTH RATE	16.60		15.71
DEATH RATE	8.74	8.76	8.72
RATE OF INCREASE	7.86		7.00

RATES STANDARDIZED ON MEXICO 1980

	BOTH SEXES	MALES	FEMALES
BIRTH RATE	14.88		14.59
DEATH RATE	3.34	3.84	2.84
RATE OF INCREASE	11.53		11.75

VITAL STATISTICS

GFR x 1000	59.652
TFR	1.938
GRR	0.943
NRR	0.924
μ	26.917
σ^2	31.690
GENERATION	26.964
POP. SEX RATIO	1.003
SEX RATIO AT BIRTH	1.055
DEP. RATIO x 100	52.703

PROJECTED POPULATION

AGE GROUP	1975			1980			STABLE EQUIVALENT TO ORIGINAL POPULATION				AGE GROUP	
	BOTH SEXES	MALES	FEMALES	BOTH SEXES	MALES	FEMALES	MALES Number	Percent	FEMALES Number	Percent		
0-4	547	280	267	539	276	263	284	6.1	271	5.7	0-4	
5-9	580	298	282	546	280	266	288	6.2	274	5.8	5-9	TABLE 5
10-14	563	289	274	579	297	282	291	6.3	278	5.9	10-14	
15-19	530	272	258	562	288	274	295	6.4	281	5.9	15-19	POPULATION
20-24	551	282	269	528	271	257	298	6.4	285	6.0	20-24	PROJECTED
25-29	659	336	323	549	280	269	300	6.5	288	6.1	25-29	WITH
30-34	610	316	294	656	334	322	303	6.5	292	6.2	30-34	FIXED
35-39	480	247	233	606	314	292	305	6.6	295	6.2	35-39	AGE-
40-44	442	224	218	475	244	231	306	6.6	297	6.3	40-44	SPECIFIC
45-49	469	235	234	436	220	216	305	6.6	298	6.3	45-49	BIRTH
50-54	527	263	264	459	229	230	302	6.5	297	6.3	50-54	AND
55-59	495	246	249	509	252	257	293	6.3	294	6.2	55-59	DEATH
60-64	484	237	247	469	229	240	278	6.0	288	6.1	60-64	RATES
65-69	436	207	229	442	211	231	251	5.4	274	5.8	65-69	(female
70-74	342	154	188	376	171	205	211	4.6	249	5.3	70-74	dominant,
75-79	239	102	137	267	114	153	158	3.4	205	4.3	75-79	in 000s)
80-84	139	56	83	158	63	95	99	2.1	144	3.0	80-84	
85+	92	33	59	105	36	69	66	1.4	122	2.6	85+	
TOTAL	8185	4077	4108	8261	4109	4152	4633		4732		TOTAL	

VITAL RATES OF PROJECTED POPULATION

Per Thousand	1975 BOTH SEXES	MALES	FEMALES	1980 BOTH SEXES	MALES	FEMALES	VITAL RATES OF STABLE POPULATION Per Thousand	MALES	FEMALES	
BIRTH RATE	13.60	14.02	13.19	12.96	13.37	12.55	BIRTH RATE	12.35	11.47	TABLE 6
DEATH RATE	11.09	11.71	10.47	11.89	12.41	11.37	DEATH RATE	15.20	14.39	PROJECTED
RATE OF INCREASE	2.51	2.31	2.72	1.07	0.96	1.18	RATE OF INCREASE		-2.91	VITAL RATES

AGE STRUCTURE OF PROJECTED POPULATION

							STABLE AGE STRUCTURE			AND RATIOS
% UNDER 15	20.65	21.27	20.04	20.14	20.76	19.53	% UNDER 15	18.64	17.38	(female
% 15-64	64.11	65.21	63.02	63.54	64.75	62.34	% 15-64	64.41	61.61	dominant)
% 65 AND OLDER	15.24	13.52	16.94	16.32	14.49	18.13	% 65 AND OLDER	16.96	21.00	
DEPEND. RATIO x 100	55.98	53.35	58.68	57.38	54.44	60.41	DEPEND. RATIO x 100	55.27	62.30	

AGE GROUP	FEMALE BIRTH RATES	NET MATERNITY FUNCTION	COEFF. OF MATRIX EQUATION	ORIGINAL MATRIX SUB-DIAGONAL	FIRST ROW	STABLE MATRIX FISHER VALUES	REPRODUCTIVE VALUES	MATRIX PARAMETERS		
0-4	0.0000	0.0000	0.0000	0.99812	0.00000	1.003	283530	λ_1	0.98554	
5-9	0.0000	0.0000	0.0001	0.99859	0.00008	0.990	271870	λ_2	0.34613+0.73394i	TABLE 7
10-14	0.0000	0.0002	0.0407	0.99833	0.04087	0.977	252297	λ_4	-0.33674+0.38692i	
15-19	0.0165	0.0813	0.1845	0.99761	0.18542	0.924	249478	λ_6	-0.07472+0.42802i	LESLIE
20-24	0.0586	0.2877	0.2981	0.99755	0.30032	0.726	234818	r_1	-0.00291	MATRIX
25-29	0.0630	0.3085	0.2376	0.99715	0.23991	0.415	122355	r_2	-0.04178+0.22603i	AND ITS
30-34	0.0341	0.1666	0.1157	0.99565	0.11721	0.169	39597	r_4	-0.13352+0.45739i	ANALYSIS
35-39	0.0133	0.0649	0.0396	0.99306	0.04030	0.050	10895	r_6	-0.16672+0.34873i	(females)
40-44	0.0030	0.0144	0.0076	0.98941	0.00782	0.008	1996	c_1	47303	
45-49	0.0002	0.0009	0.0005	0.98348	0.00047	0.000	129	$2\pi/y$	27.7986	
50-54	0.0000	0.0000	0.0000	0.97587	0.00000	0.000	1	Δ	7.4199	

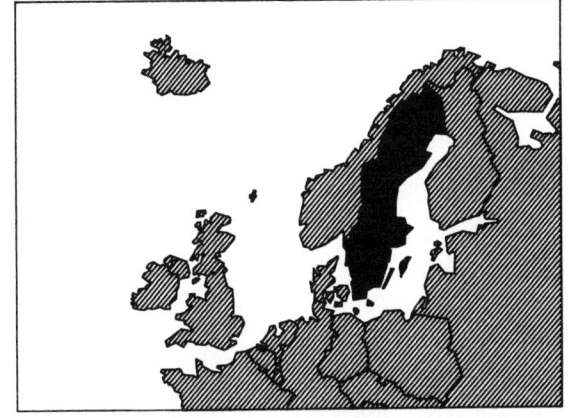

EDUCATION [1984]

% of primary school-age children enrolled:	98
secondary school-age children enrolled:	83
ca. 20-24 year olds in higher education:	38

LABOR FORCE

Average annual labor force growth (%) 1980-85:	0.3	
% of the 1980 labor force in agriculture:	6	TABLE 8
in industry:	33	
in services:	62	SOCIO-ECONOMIC

GNP & INCOME DISTRIBUTION

GNP per capita (in US Dollars) 1985:	11890	INDICATORS
GNP average annual growth rate (%) 1965-85:	1.8	
% share of total household income 1981		
Lowest 20% of households:	7.4	
Highest 10% of households:	28.1	

HEALTH & NUTRITION

Population per physician 1981:	410
Daily calorie supply per capita 1985:	3097

TABLE 1 — DATA

AGE AT LAST BIRTHDAY	ESTIMATED MID-YEAR POPULATION BOTH SEXES	MALES Number	Percent	FEMALES Number	Percent	BIRTHS BY AGE OF MOTHER AND SEX	DEATHS BOTH SEXES	MALES	FEMALES	AGE AT LAST BIRTHDAY
0	106202	54502	1.3	51700	1.3		894	522	372	0
1-4	444666	227950	5.6	216716	5.3		195	111	84	1-4
5-9	581224	298336	7.3	282888	6.9		184	113	71	5-9
10-14	563176	288767	7.1	274409	6.7	17	153	82	71	10-14
15-19	535531	274666	6.7	260865	6.3	7503	357	243	114	15-19
20-24	564882	287826	7.1	277056	6.7	31861	467	369	98	20-24
25-29	662894	339582	8.3	323312	7.9	39867	552	384	168	25-29
30-34	605401	313552	7.7	291849	7.1	18719	627	416	211	30-34
35-39	476724	244347	6.0	232377	5.6	4817	705	477	228	35-39
40-44	441120	222437	5.5	218683	5.3	809	1020	654	366	40-44
45-49	468207	233799	5.7	234408	5.7	39	1674	1060	614	45-49
50-54	526216	262139	6.4	264077	6.4		2822	1797	1025	50-54
55-59	494529	245144	6.0	249385	6.1		4064	2647	1417	55-59
60-64	483831	236558	5.8	247273	6.0		6439	4230	2209	60-64
65-69	435572	206202	5.1	229370	5.6		9705	6176	3529	65-69
70-74	342640	153638	3.8	189002	4.6		12575	7421	5154	70-74
75-79	238703	100898	2.5	137805	3.3		15235	8075	7160	75-79
80-84	139179	54386	1.3	84793	2.1	53242 M	14568	6899	7669	80-84
85+	81869	29807	0.7	52062	1.3	50390 F	15972	6651	9321	85+
TOTAL	8192566	4074536		4118030		103632	88208	48327	39881	TOTAL

TABLE 2 — MALE LIFE TABLE

x	nM_x	nq_x	l_x	nd_x	nL_x	nm_x	na_x	T_x	$\overset{o}{e}_x$	x
0	0.009578	0.009495	100000	949	99132	0.009578	0.086	7217677	72.177	0
1	0.000487	0.001945	99051	193	395720	0.000487	1.500	7118544	71.868	1
5	0.000379	0.001892	98858	187	493822	0.000379	2.500	6722824	68.005	5
10	0.000284	0.001423	98671	140	493055	0.000285	2.868	6229002	63.129	10
15	0.000885	0.004416	98530	435	491666	0.000885	2.733	5735947	58.215	15
20	0.001282	0.006390	98095	627	488933	0.001282	2.538	5244282	53.461	20
25	0.001131	0.005638	97469	550	485972	0.001131	2.506	4755348	48.789	25
30	0.001327	0.006630	96919	643	483070	0.001330	2.627	4269376	44.051	30
35	0.001952	0.009770	96276	941	479187	0.001963	2.667	3786306	39.327	35
40	0.002940	0.014627	95336	1394	473436	0.002945	2.674	3307119	34.689	40
45	0.004534	0.022432	93941	2107	464793	0.004534	2.668	2833683	30.164	45
50	0.006855	0.033737	91834	3098	451959	0.006855	2.673	2368890	25.795	50
55	0.010798	0.052671	88736	4674	432852	0.010798	2.684	1916931	21.603	55
60	0.017881	0.085840	84062	7216	403539	0.017881	2.676	1484079	17.655	60
65	0.029951	0.140064	76846	10763	358806	0.029998	2.638	1080540	14.061	65
70	0.048302	0.217010	66083	14341	295938	0.048458	2.596	721733	10.922	70
75	0.080031	0.335626	51742	17366	215738	0.080496	2.525	425796	8.229	75
80	0.126852	0.478896	34376	16463	129777	0.126853	2.442	210058	6.111	80
85	0.223136	1.000000	17914	17914	80281	0.159705	4.482	80281	4.482	85

TABLE 3 — FEMALE LIFE TABLE

x	nM_x	nq_x	l_x	nd_x	nL_x	nm_x	na_x	T_x	$\overset{o}{e}_x$	x
0	0.007195	0.007148	100000	715	99344	0.007195	0.082	7806045	78.060	0
1	0.000388	0.001549	99285	154	396756	0.000388	1.500	7706701	77.622	1
5	0.000251	0.001254	99131	124	495346	0.000251	2.500	7309944	73.740	5
10	0.000259	0.001294	99007	128	494734	0.000259	2.649	6814598	68.829	10
15	0.000437	0.002183	98879	216	493865	0.000437	2.545	6319864	63.915	15
20	0.000354	0.001767	98663	174	492888	0.000354	2.547	5825999	59.049	20
25	0.000520	0.002595	98489	256	491843	0.000520	2.648	5333111	54.149	25
30	0.000723	0.003620	98233	356	490324	0.000725	2.632	4841269	49.283	30
35	0.000981	0.004922	97878	482	488279	0.000987	2.698	4350945	44.453	35
40	0.001674	0.008345	97396	813	485109	0.001676	2.699	3862666	39.659	40
45	0.002619	0.013017	96583	1257	479985	0.002619	2.669	3377556	34.970	45
50	0.003881	0.019232	95326	1833	472330	0.003881	2.655	2897571	30.396	50
55	0.005682	0.028042	93493	2622	461355	0.005683	2.670	2425241	25.940	55
60	0.008933	0.043768	90871	3977	445212	0.008933	2.701	1963886	21.612	60
65	0.015386	0.074409	86894	6466	419632	0.015408	2.705	1518675	17.477	65
70	0.027270	0.128735	80428	10354	378306	0.027369	2.698	1099043	13.665	70
75	0.051957	0.232774	70074	16311	311580	0.052351	2.622	720737	10.285	75
80	0.090444	0.370120	53763	19899	220011	0.090444	2.547	409156	7.610	80
85	0.179037	1.000000	33864	33864	189146	0.110197	5.585	189146	5.585	85

TABLE 4 — OBSERVED VITAL RATES AND RATIOS

CRUDE RATES

Per Thousand	BOTH SEXES	MALES	FEMALES
BIRTH RATE	12.65	13.07	12.24
DEATH RATE	10.77	11.86	9.68
RATE OF INCREASE	1.88	1.21	2.55

PERCENT OF POPULATION IN AGE GROUP

	BOTH SEXES	MALES	FEMALES
UNDER 15	20.69	21.34	20.05
15 - 64	64.20	65.28	63.12
65 AND OLDER	15.11	13.37	16.83

RATES STANDARDIZED ON USA 1980

Per Thousand	BOTH SEXES	MALES	FEMALES
BIRTH RATE	15.34		14.51
DEATH RATE	8.64	9.01	8.29
RATE OF INCREASE	6.70		6.22

RATES STANDARDIZED ON MEXICO 1980

	BOTH SEXES	MALES	FEMALES
BIRTH RATE	13.74		13.47
DEATH RATE	3.24	3.83	2.63
RATE OF INCREASE	10.50		10.83

VITAL STATISTICS

GFR x 1000	56.366
TFR	1.779
GRR	0.865
NRR	0.851
μ	26.706
σ^2	28.388
GENERATION	26.792
POP. SEX RATIO	1.011
SEX RATIO AT BIRTH	1.057
DEP. RATIO x 100	55.772

TABLE 1 DATA

AGE AT LAST BIRTHDAY	ESTIMATED MID-YEAR POPULATION BOTH SEXES	MALES Number	MALES Percent	FEMALES Number	FEMALES Percent	BIRTHS BY AGE OF MOTHER AND SEX	DEATHS BOTH SEXES	DEATHS MALES	DEATHS FEMALES	AGE AT LAST BIRTHDAY
0	96351	49380	1.2	46971	1.1		671	402	269	0
1-4	391132	200283	4.9	190849	4.6		141	75	66	1-4
5-9	556826	285039	6.9	271787	6.5		116	72	44	5-9
10-14	584040	299627	7.3	284413	6.8	15	124	68	56	10-14
15-19	569010	291189	7.1	277821	6.6	4370	263	184	79	15-19
20-24	556089	284043	6.9	272046	6.5	25997	386	283	103	20-24
25-29	583417	298517	7.2	284900	6.8	35394	508	370	138	25-29
30-34	667598	342107	8.3	325491	7.8	23012	663	451	212	30-34
35-39	603762	311693	7.6	292069	7.0	7258	825	548	277	35-39
40-44	473824	241839	5.9	231985	5.5	987	1047	660	387	40-44
45-49	436272	218793	5.3	217479	5.2	31	1478	972	506	45-49
50-54	459188	227583	5.5	231605	5.5		2374	1552	822	50-54
55-59	509404	250806	6.1	258598	6.2		4145	2693	1452	55-59
60-64	469819	228618	5.6	241201	5.8		6178	4088	2090	60-64
65-69	444706	210739	5.1	233967	5.6		9254	5977	3277	65-69
70-74	379198	170782	4.1	208420	5.0		13168	8021	5147	70-74
75-79	271007	112624	2.7	158383	3.8		15831	8550	7281	75-79
80-84	160367	61195	1.5	99172	2.4	49860 M	15924	7572	8352	80-84
85+	98464	32819	0.8	65645	1.6	47204 F	18704	7287	11417	85+
TOTAL	8310474	4117672		4192802		97064	91800	49825	41975	TOTAL

TABLE 2 MALE LIFE TABLE

x	nM_x	nq_x	l_x	nd_x	nL_x	nm_x	na_x	T_x	$\mathring{e}_x$	x
0	0.008141	0.008081	100000	808	99260	0.008141	0.084	7278285	72.783	0
1	0.000374	0.001496	99192	148	396397	0.000374	1.500	7179026	72.375	1
5	0.000253	0.001262	99043	125	494905	0.000253	2.500	6782629	68.481	5
10	0.000227	0.001134	98918	112	494351	0.000227	2.847	6287724	63.565	10
15	0.000632	0.003159	98806	312	493330	0.000633	2.752	5793373	58.634	15
20	0.000996	0.004970	98494	490	491308	0.000996	2.625	5300043	53.811	20
25	0.001239	0.006179	98005	606	488541	0.001239	2.552	4808735	49.066	25
30	0.001318	0.006570	97399	640	485447	0.001318	2.580	4320194	44.356	30
35	0.001758	0.008786	96759	850	481810	0.001765	2.664	3834747	39.632	35
40	0.002729	0.013650	95909	1309	476529	0.002747	2.696	3352937	34.960	40
45	0.004443	0.022029	94600	2084	468164	0.004451	2.680	2876408	30.406	45
50	0.006819	0.033565	92516	3105	455358	0.006819	2.674	2408244	26.031	50
55	0.010737	0.052385	89411	4684	436212	0.010737	2.685	1952886	21.842	55
60	0.017881	0.085817	84727	7271	406626	0.017881	2.661	1516674	17.901	60
65	0.028362	0.132914	77456	10295	362984	0.028362	2.640	1110049	14.331	65
70	0.046967	0.211332	67161	14193	301721	0.047041	2.599	747065	11.124	70
75	0.075916	0.321208	52968	17014	222872	0.076338	2.533	445344	8.408	75
80	0.123736	0.470629	35954	16921	136751	0.123736	2.458	222471	6.188	80
85	0.222036	1.000000	19033	19033	85720	0.158366	4.504	85720	4.504	85

TABLE 3 FEMALE LIFE TABLE

x	nM_x	nq_x	l_x	nd_x	nL_x	nm_x	na_x	T_x	$\mathring{e}_x$	x
0	0.005727	0.005697	100000	570	99476	0.005727	0.080	7898099	78.981	0
1	0.000346	0.001382	99430	137	397378	0.000346	1.500	7798623	78.433	1
5	0.000162	0.000809	99293	80	496264	0.000162	2.500	7401246	74.540	5
10	0.000197	0.000984	99213	98	495831	0.000197	2.629	6904982	69.598	10
15	0.000284	0.001422	99115	141	495241	0.000285	2.632	6409151	64.664	15
20	0.000379	0.001891	98974	187	494423	0.000379	2.609	5913910	59.752	20
25	0.000484	0.002419	98787	239	493364	0.000484	2.616	5419487	54.860	25
30	0.000651	0.003252	98548	320	491986	0.000651	2.648	4926123	49.987	30
35	0.000948	0.004755	98227	467	490073	0.000953	2.721	4434137	45.142	35
40	0.001668	0.008354	97760	817	486896	0.001677	2.667	3944064	40.344	40
45	0.002327	0.011581	96944	1123	482092	0.002329	2.661	3457168	35.662	45
50	0.003549	0.017601	95821	1687	475197	0.003549	2.684	2975076	31.048	50
55	0.005615	0.027713	94134	2609	464608	0.005615	2.676	2499879	26.557	55
60	0.008665	0.042479	91526	3888	448603	0.008667	2.679	2035270	22.237	60
65	0.014006	0.067844	87638	5946	424505	0.014006	2.699	1586667	18.105	65
70	0.024695	0.116986	81692	9557	386465	0.024729	2.698	1162162	14.226	70
75	0.045971	0.208648	72135	15051	325217	0.046280	2.644	775697	10.753	75
80	0.084217	0.349713	57084	19963	237043	0.084217	2.577	450481	7.892	80
85	0.173920	1.000000	37121	37121	213438	0.104916	5.750	213438	5.750	85

TABLE 4 OBSERVED VITAL RATES AND RATIOS

CRUDE RATES

Per Thousand	BOTH SEXES	MALES	FEMALES
BIRTH RATE	11.68	12.11	11.26
DEATH RATE	11.05	12.10	10.01
RATE OF INCREASE	0.63	0.01	1.25

RATES STANDARDIZED ON USA 1980

Per Thousand	BOTH SEXES	MALES	FEMALES
BIRTH RATE	14.27		13.50
DEATH RATE	8.19	8.70	7.72
RATE OF INCREASE	6.08		5.78

VITAL STATISTICS

GFR x 1000	51.038
TFR	1.678
GRR	0.816
NRR	0.805
μ	27.582
σ^2	27.475
GENERATION	27.690
POP. SEX RATIO	1.018
SEX RATIO AT BIRTH	1.056
DEP. RATIO x 100	55.966

PERCENT OF POPULATION IN AGE GROUP

	BOTH	MALES	FEMALES
UNDER 15	19.59	20.26	18.94
15 - 64	64.12	65.45	62.80
65 AND OLDER	16.29	14.28	18.26

RATES STANDARDIZED ON MEXICO 1980

	BOTH SEXES	MALES	FEMALES
BIRTH RATE	12.48		12.23
DEATH RATE	3.01	3.61	2.40
RATE OF INCREASE	9.47		9.83

TABLE 1 — DATA

AGE AT LAST BIRTHDAY	ESTIMATED MID-YEAR POPULATION BOTH SEXES	MALES Number	MALES Percent	FEMALES Number	FEMALES Percent	BIRTHS BY AGE OF MOTHER AND SEX	DEATHS BOTH SEXES	DEATHS MALES	DEATHS FEMALES	AGE AT LAST BIRTHDAY
0	95913	49349	1.2	46564	1.1		666	366	300	0
1-4	376594	193236	4.7	183358	4.3		110	58	52	1-4
5-9	488102	249918	6.1	238184	5.6		74	49	25	5-9
10-14	555955	284405	6.9	271550	6.4	9	91	49	42	10-14
15-19	585464	300175	7.3	285289	6.7	3128	273	185	88	15-19
20-24	578212	295397	7.2	282815	6.7	23147	363	270	93	20-24
25-29	562452	287631	7.0	274821	6.5	36235	385	266	119	25-29
30-34	582082	297435	7.2	284647	6.7	24457	547	355	192	30-34
35-39	661789	337725	8.2	324064	7.7	9805	809	511	298	35-39
40-44	598122	307540	7.5	290582	6.9	1628	1040	682	358	40-44
45-49	467833	237513	5.8	230320	5.4	53	1299	864	435	45-49
50-54	427854	213003	5.2	214851	5.1	1	1989	1277	712	50-54
55-59	445480	218367	5.3	227113	5.4		3366	2201	1165	55-59
60-64	485160	234475	5.7	250685	5.9		5782	3825	1957	60-64
65-69	434196	204972	5.0	229224	5.4		8533	5547	2986	65-69
70-74	391033	176725	4.3	214308	5.1		12507	7719	4788	70-74
75-79	305475	127827	3.1	177648	4.2		16760	9240	7520	75-79
80-84	188728	70184	1.7	118544	2.8	50748 M	17299	8343	8956	80-84
85+	119935	37950	0.9	81985	1.9	47715 F	22139	8237	13902	85+
TOTAL	8350379	4123827		4226552		98463	94032	50044	43988	TOTAL

TABLE 2 — MALE LIFE TABLE

x	$_nM_x$	$_nq_x$	l_x	$_nd_x$	$_nL_x$	$_nm_x$	$_na_x$	T_x	$\overset{\circ}{e}_x$	x
0	0.007417	0.007366	100000	737	99324	0.007417	0.083	7378918	73.789	0
1	0.000300	0.001200	99263	119	396756	0.000300	1.500	7279594	73.336	1
5	0.000196	0.000980	99144	97	495479	0.000196	2.500	6882839	69.422	5
10	0.000172	0.000861	99047	85	495066	0.000172	3.006	6387360	64.488	10
15	0.000616	0.003077	98962	305	494124	0.000616	2.749	5892295	59.541	15
20	0.000914	0.004561	98657	450	492192	0.000914	2.569	5398171	54.716	20
25	0.000925	0.004614	98207	453	489931	0.000925	2.561	4905978	49.955	25
30	0.001194	0.005951	97754	582	487375	0.001194	2.600	4416047	45.175	30
35	0.001513	0.007538	97173	733	484133	0.001513	2.638	3928672	40.430	35
40	0.002218	0.011080	96440	1069	479737	0.002227	2.695	3444539	35.717	40
45	0.003638	0.018170	95371	1733	472881	0.003664	2.705	2964802	31.087	45
50	0.005995	0.029643	93639	2776	461825	0.006010	2.706	2491921	26.612	50
55	0.010079	0.049249	90863	4475	443963	0.010079	2.687	2030096	22.342	55
60	0.016313	0.078583	86388	6789	416146	0.016313	2.673	1586133	18.361	60
65	0.027062	0.127198	79599	10125	374132	0.027062	2.643	1169987	14.698	65
70	0.043678	0.197722	69475	13737	314498	0.043678	2.607	795855	11.455	70
75	0.072285	0.307996	55738	17167	236582	0.072563	2.547	481357	8.636	75
80	0.118873	0.456985	38571	17626	148278	0.118873	2.471	244775	6.346	80
85	0.217049	1.000000	20945	20945	96497	0.152521	4.607	96497	4.607	85

TABLE 3 — FEMALE LIFE TABLE

x	$_nM_x$	$_nq_x$	l_x	$_nd_x$	$_nL_x$	$_nm_x$	$_na_x$	T_x	$\overset{\circ}{e}_x$	x
0	0.006443	0.006405	100000	640	99411	0.006443	0.081	7983014	79.830	0
1	0.000284	0.001134	99360	113	397156	0.000284	1.500	7883603	79.344	1
5	0.000105	0.000525	99247	52	496104	0.000105	2.500	7486446	75.433	5
10	0.000155	0.000773	99195	77	495803	0.000155	2.773	6990342	70.471	10
15	0.000308	0.001541	99118	153	495227	0.000308	2.617	6494539	65.523	15
20	0.000329	0.001643	98965	163	494433	0.000329	2.578	5999312	60.620	20
25	0.000433	0.002163	98803	214	493515	0.000433	2.665	5504879	55.716	25
30	0.000675	0.003367	98589	332	492165	0.000675	2.649	5011365	50.831	30
35	0.000920	0.004588	98257	451	490215	0.000920	2.625	4519200	45.994	35
40	0.001232	0.006165	97806	603	487622	0.001237	2.662	4028985	41.194	40
45	0.001889	0.009467	97203	920	483921	0.001902	2.722	3541363	36.433	45
50	0.003314	0.016467	96283	1585	477760	0.003319	2.694	3057443	31.755	50
55	0.005130	0.025345	94698	2400	467895	0.005130	2.670	2579683	27.241	55
60	0.007807	0.038341	92297	3539	453310	0.007807	2.689	2111788	22.880	60
65	0.013027	0.063257	88759	5615	430860	0.013031	2.697	1658478	18.685	65
70	0.022342	0.106262	83144	8835	395453	0.022342	2.706	1227618	14.765	70
75	0.042331	0.193149	74309	14353	337818	0.042486	2.650	832165	11.199	75
80	0.075550	0.319906	59956	19180	253877	0.075550	2.607	494347	8.245	80
85	0.169568	1.000000	40776	40776	240470	0.100534	5.897	240470	5.897	85

TABLE 4 — OBSERVED VITAL RATES AND RATIOS

CRUDE RATES

Per Thousand	BOTH SEXES	MALES	FEMALES
BIRTH RATE	11.79	12.31	11.29
DEATH RATE	11.26	12.14	10.41
RATE OF INCREASE	0.53	0.17	0.88

PERCENT OF POPULATION IN AGE GROUP

	BOTH SEXES	MALES	FEMALES
UNDER 15	18.16	18.84	17.50
15 - 64	64.60	66.18	63.06
65 AND OLDER	17.24	14.98	19.44

RATES STANDARDIZED ON USA 1980

Per Thousand	BOTH SEXES	MALES	FEMALES
BIRTH RATE	14.54		13.70
DEATH RATE	7.64	8.13	7.18
RATE OF INCREASE	6.90		6.52

RATES STANDARDIZED ON MEXICO 1980

	BOTH SEXES	MALES	FEMALES
BIRTH RATE	12.48		12.19
DEATH RATE	2.77	3.32	2.22
RATE OF INCREASE	9.70		9.97

VITAL STATISTICS

GFR x 1000	49.917
TFR	1.734
GRR	0.840
NRR	0.828
μ	28.355
σ^2	27.110
GENERATION	28.445
POP. SEX RATIO	1.025
SEX RATIO AT BIRTH	1.064
DEP. RATIO x 100	54.796

PROJECTED POPULATION

AGE GROUP	1990			1995		
	BOTH SEXES	MALES	FEMALES	BOTH SEXES	MALES	FEMALES
0-4	487	251	236	481	248	233
5-9	472	242	230	486	250	236
10-14	488	250	238	472	242	230
15-19	555	284	271	487	249	238
20-24	584	299	285	554	283	271
25-29	576	294	282	582	298	284
30-34	560	286	274	575	293	282
35-39	579	295	284	557	284	273
40-44	657	335	322	575	293	282
45-49	591	303	288	650	330	320
50-54	459	232	227	581	296	285
55-59	415	205	210	446	223	223
60-64	425	205	220	396	192	204
65-69	449	211	238	393	184	209
70-74	382	172	210	396	177	219
75-79	316	133	183	310	130	180
80-84	214	80	134	221	83	138
85+	158	46	112	178	52	126
TOTAL	8367	4123	4244	8340	4107	4233

STABLE EQUIVALENT TO ORIGINAL POPULATION

	MALES		FEMALES		AGE GROUP	
	Number	Percent	Number	Percent		
0-4	258	*5.2*	243	*4.8*	0-4	
5-9	267	*5.4*	251	*4.9*	5-9	TABLE 5
10-14	276	*5.6*	259	*5.1*	10-14	
15-19	284	*5.8*	268	*5.2*	15-19	POPULATION
20-24	293	*5.9*	276	*5.4*	20-24	PROJECTED
25-29	301	*6.1*	285	*5.6*	25-29	WITH
30-34	310	*6.3*	294	*5.7*	30-34	FIXED
35-39	318	*6.4*	303	*5.9*	35-39	AGE-
40-44	326	*6.6*	311	*6.1*	40-44	SPECIFIC
45-49	332	*6.7*	319	*6.2*	45-49	BIRTH
50-54	335	*6.8*	326	*6.4*	50-54	AND
55-59	333	*6.7*	330	*6.4*	55-59	DEATH
60-64	322	*6.5*	330	*6.5*	60-64	RATES
65-69	300	*6.1*	324	*6.3*	65-69	(female
70-74	260	*5.3*	308	*6.0*	70-74	dominant,
75-79	202	*4.1*	272	*5.3*	75-79	in 000s)
80-84	131	*2.7*	211	*4.1*	80-84	
85+	88	*1.8*	207	*4.0*	85+	
TOTAL	4936		5117		TOTAL	

VITAL RATES OF PROJECTED POPULATION

Per Thousand	1990			1995		
	BOTH SEXES	MALES	FEMALES	BOTH SEXES	MALES	FEMALES
BIRTH RATE	11.65	12.19	11.13	11.56	12.09	11.04
DEATH RATE	12.34	12.85	11.86	12.85	13.22	12.49
RATE OF INCREASE	-0.69	-0.65	-0.73	-1.29	-1.13	-1.45

AGE STRUCTURE OF PROJECTED POPULATION

% UNDER 15	17.28	18.01	16.57	17.26	18.02	16.51
% 15-64	64.56	66.42	62.76	64.78	66.72	62.89
% 65 AND OLDER	18.16	15.57	20.67	17.97	15.25	20.60
DEPEND. RATIO x 100	54.89	50.57	59.34	54.37	49.87	59.01

VITAL RATES OF STABLE POPULATION

Per Thousand	MALES	FEMALES	
BIRTH RATE	10.38	9.41	TABLE 6
DEATH RATE	16.92	16.03	PROJECTED
RATE OF INCREASE		-6.61	VITAL RATES AND RATIOS (female dominant)

STABLE AGE STRUCTURE

	MALES	FEMALES	
% UNDER 15	16.23	14.73	
% 15-64	63.89	59.45	
% 65 AND OLDER	19.89	25.82	
DEPEND. RATIO x 100	56.53	68.22	

AGE GROUP	FEMALE BIRTH RATES	NET MATERNITY FUNCTION	COEFF. OF MATRIX EQUATION	ORIGINAL MATRIX		STABLE MATRIX		MATRIX PARAMETERS		
				SUB-DIAGONAL	FIRST ROW	FISHER VALUES	REPRODUCTIVE VALUES			
0-4	0.0000	0.0000	0.0000	0.99907	0.00000	0.990	227711	λ_1	0.96747	
5-9	0.0000	0.0000	0.0000	0.99939	0.00004	0.959	228434	λ_2	$0.39878-0.73864i$	TABLE 7
10-14	0.0000	0.0001	0.0132	0.99884	0.01322	0.928	252106	λ_4	$-0.23172+0.48963i$	
15-19	0.0053	0.0263	0.1112	0.99840	0.11151	0.886	252806	λ_6	$-0.39936-0.09356i$	LESLIE
20-24	0.0397	0.1961	0.2557	0.99814	0.25682	0.748	211568	r_1	-0.00661	MATRIX
25-29	0.0639	0.3153	0.2601	0.99726	0.26173	0.470	129241	r_2	$-0.03501-0.21515i$	AND ITS
30-34	0.0416	0.2049	0.1384	0.99604	0.13964	0.196	55876	r_4	$-0.12261+0.40256i$	ANALYSIS
35-39	0.0147	0.0719	0.0426	0.99471	0.04311	0.052	16795	r_6	$-0.17823-0.58230i$	(females)
40-44	0.0027	0.0132	0.0069	0.99241	0.00702	0.007	2175	c_1	51176	
45-49	0.0001	0.0005	0.0003	0.98727	0.00028	0.000	68	$2\pi/y$	29.2037	
50-54	0.0000	0.0000	0.0000	0.97935	0.00001	0.000	1	Δ	10.0423	

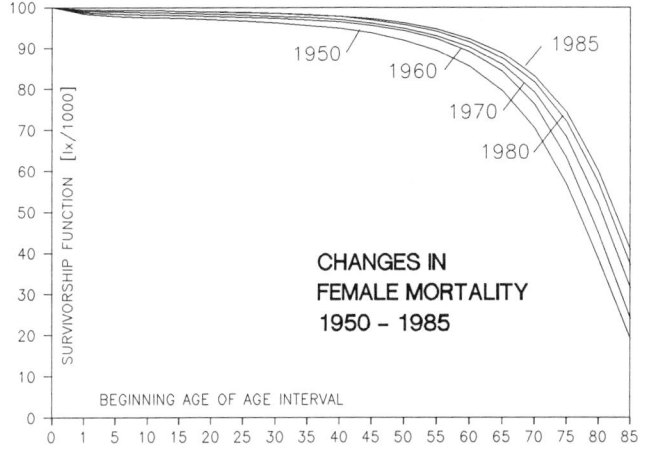

CHANGES IN FEMALE MORTALITY 1950 - 1985

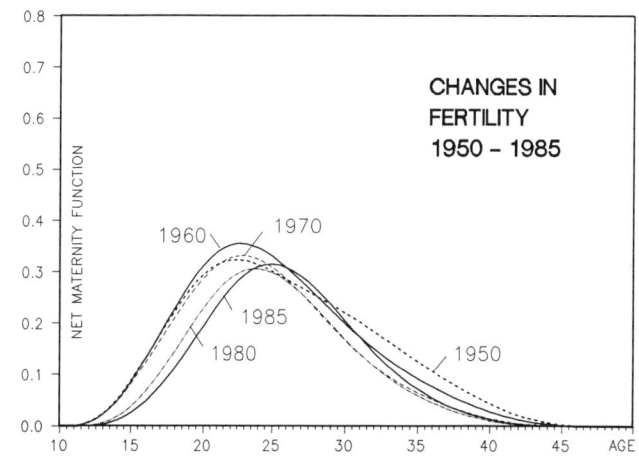

CHANGES IN FERTILITY 1950 - 1985

TABLE 1 — DATA

AGE AT LAST BIRTHDAY	ESTIMATED MID-YEAR POPULATION BOTH SEXES	MALES Number	MALES Percent	FEMALES Number	FEMALES Percent	BIRTHS BY AGE OF MOTHER AND SEX	DEATHS BOTH SEXES	DEATHS MALES	DEATHS FEMALES	AGE AT LAST BIRTHDAY
0	48000	24600	0.8	23400	0.7		1293	767	526	0
1-4	400900	204500	6.8	196400	6.2		483	274	209	1-4
5-9	510900	260500	8.6	250400	7.9		284	176	108	5-9
10-14	465300	237300	7.9	228000	7.2		161	101	60	10-14
15-19	447200	227200	7.5	220000	7.0	3562	343	251	92	15-19
20-24	496500	247200	8.2	249300	7.9	29262	537	429	108	20-24
25-29	505000	256500	8.5	248500	7.9	35565	435	322	113	25-29
30-34	440100	224500	7.4	215600	6.8	19609	479	331	148	30-34
35-39	413600	209000	6.9	204600	6.5	8569	540	352	188	35-39
40-44	388900	191400	6.3	197500	6.2	2423	858	552	306	40-44
45-49	374000	182200	6.0	191800	6.1	224	1354	841	513	45-49
50-54	316200	154700	5.1	161500	5.1	2	1812	1153	659	50-54
55-59	326700	156500	5.2	170200	5.4		3011	1959	1052	55-59
60-64	316600	145900	4.8	170700	5.4		4588	2945	1643	60-64
65-69	269700	118400	3.9	151300	4.8		6431	3895	2536	65-69
70-74	205700	84200	2.8	121500	3.8		8226	4501	3725	70-74
75-79	137200	53000	1.8	84200	2.7		8948	4261	4687	75-79
80-84	75900	27700	0.9	48200	1.5	51235 M	8532	3569	4963	80-84
85+	42500	14400	0.5	28100	0.9	47981 F	8776	3275	5501	85+
TOTAL	6180900	3019700		3161200		99216	57091	29954	27137	TOTAL

TABLE 2 — MALE LIFE TABLE

x	$_nM_x$	$_nq_x$	l_x	$_nd_x$	$_nL_x$	$_nm_x$	$_na_x$	T_x	$\overset{\circ}{e}_x$	x
0	0.031179	0.030349	100000	3035	97338	0.031179	0.123	6947109	69.471	0
1	0.001340	0.005341	96965	518	386566	0.001340	1.500	6849771	70.642	1
5	0.000676	0.003372	96447	325	481423	0.000676	2.500	6463205	67.013	5
10	0.000426	0.002131	96122	205	480140	0.000427	2.707	5981783	62.231	10
15	0.001105	0.005510	95917	529	478393	0.001105	2.744	5501643	57.358	15
20	0.001735	0.008640	95389	824	474896	0.001735	2.516	5023249	52.661	20
25	0.001255	0.006256	94564	592	471316	0.001255	2.453	4548353	48.098	25
30	0.001474	0.007353	93973	691	468177	0.001476	2.558	4077038	43.385	30
35	0.001684	0.008408	93282	784	464582	0.001688	2.669	3608860	38.688	35
40	0.002884	0.014355	92498	1328	459440	0.002890	2.705	3144279	33.993	40
45	0.004616	0.022908	91170	2089	451033	0.004630	2.694	2684838	29.449	45
50	0.007453	0.036724	89081	3271	437881	0.007471	2.699	2233805	25.076	50
55	0.012518	0.060821	85810	5219	416940	0.012518	2.680	1795924	20.929	55
60	0.020185	0.096423	80591	7771	384761	0.020197	2.659	1378985	17.111	60
65	0.032897	0.153003	72820	11142	337678	0.032995	2.628	994224	13.653	65
70	0.053456	0.237400	61678	14642	272762	0.053682	2.567	656546	10.645	70
75	0.080396	0.336559	47036	15830	195703	0.080889	2.506	383784	8.159	75
80	0.128845	0.484551	31206	15121	117356	0.128845	2.442	188080	6.027	80
85	0.227431	1.000000	16085	16085	70724	0.164773	4.397	70724	4.397	85

TABLE 3 — FEMALE LIFE TABLE

x	$_nM_x$	$_nq_x$	l_x	$_nd_x$	$_nL_x$	$_nm_x$	$_na_x$	T_x	$\overset{\circ}{e}_x$	x
0	0.022479	0.022037	100000	2204	98035	0.022479	0.108	7587809	75.878	0
1	0.001064	0.004245	97796	415	390147	0.001064	1.500	7489774	76.585	1
5	0.000431	0.002154	97381	210	486381	0.000431	2.500	7099626	72.906	5
10	0.000263	0.001314	97171	128	485536	0.000263	2.488	6613245	68.058	10
15	0.000418	0.002089	97044	203	484728	0.000418	2.584	6127709	63.144	15
20	0.000433	0.002164	96841	210	483684	0.000433	2.517	5642981	58.271	20
25	0.000455	0.002273	96631	220	482633	0.000455	2.615	5159296	53.392	25
30	0.000686	0.003435	96412	331	481277	0.000688	2.639	4676663	48.507	30
35	0.000919	0.004594	96081	441	479384	0.000921	2.692	4195386	43.665	35
40	0.001549	0.007726	95639	739	476520	0.001551	2.732	3716002	38.854	40
45	0.002675	0.013330	94900	1265	471580	0.002683	2.691	3239482	34.136	45
50	0.004080	0.020250	93635	1896	463754	0.004089	2.668	2767903	29.561	50
55	0.006181	0.030466	91739	2795	452185	0.006181	2.671	2304149	25.116	55
60	0.009625	0.047084	88944	4188	435097	0.009625	2.702	1851963	20.822	60
65	0.016761	0.080910	84756	6858	408097	0.016804	2.713	1416866	16.717	65
70	0.030658	0.143716	77899	11195	363520	0.030797	2.680	1008769	12.950	70
75	0.055665	0.247795	66703	16529	294152	0.056191	2.618	645250	9.673	75
80	0.102967	0.410399	50175	20592	199983	0.102967	2.529	351097	6.998	80
85	0.195765	1.000000	29583	29583	151115	0.128077	5.108	151115	5.108	85

TABLE 4 — OBSERVED VITAL RATES AND RATIOS

CRUDE RATES

Per Thousand	BOTH SEXES	MALES	FEMALES
BIRTH RATE	16.05	16.97	15.18
DEATH RATE	9.24	9.92	8.58
RATE OF INCREASE	6.82	7.05	6.59

PERCENT OF POPULATION IN AGE GROUP

	BOTH SEXES	MALES	FEMALES
UNDER 15	23.06	24.07	22.09
15 - 64	65.12	66.07	64.21
65 AND OLDER	11.83	9.86	13.71

RATES STANDARDIZED ON USA 1980

Per Thousand	BOTH SEXES	MALES	FEMALES
BIRTH RATE	17.70		16.64
DEATH RATE	9.66	10.03	9.32
RATE OF INCREASE	8.03		7.32

RATES STANDARDIZED ON MEXICO 1980

	BOTH SEXES	MALES	FEMALES
BIRTH RATE	15.36		14.97
DEATH RATE	4.13	4.88	3.36
RATE OF INCREASE	11.23		11.61

VITAL STATISTICS

GFR x 1000	64.962
TFR	2.115
GRR	1.023
NRR	0.986
μ	28.266
σ^2	32.979
GENERATION	28.274
POP. SEX RATIO	1.047
SEX RATIO AT BIRTH	1.068
DEP. RATIO x 100	53.570

PROJECTED POPULATION

AGE GROUP	1975 BOTH SEXES	1975 MALES	1975 FEMALES	1980 BOTH SEXES	1980 MALES	1980 FEMALES
0-4	482	248	234	479	246	233
5-9	447	228	219	480	247	233
10-14	510	260	250	446	227	219
15-19	464	236	228	509	259	250
20-24	446	226	220	462	235	227
25-29	494	245	249	443	224	219
30-34	503	255	248	492	244	248
35-39	438	223	215	500	253	247
40-44	410	207	203	433	220	213
45-49	383	188	195	404	203	201
50-54	366	177	189	374	182	192
55-59	304	147	157	352	168	184
60-64	308	144	164	288	136	152
65-69	288	128	160	281	127	154
70-74	231	96	135	246	103	143
75-79	158	60	98	178	69	109
80-84	89	32	57	103	36	67
85+	53	17	36	62	19	43
TOTAL	6374	3117	3257	6532	3198	3334

STABLE EQUIVALENT TO ORIGINAL POPULATION

MALES Number	MALES Percent	FEMALES Number	FEMALES Percent	AGE GROUP	
247	6.8	233	6.3	0-4	
246	6.8	233	6.3	5-9	TABLE 5
246	6.8	233	6.3	10-14	
246	6.8	233	6.3	15-19	POPULATION
245	6.8	233	6.3	20-24	PROJECTED
243	6.8	233	6.3	25-29	WITH
242	6.7	233	6.3	30-34	FIXED
241	6.7	233	6.3	35-39	AGE-
239	6.6	232	6.3	40-44	SPECIFIC
235	6.5	230	6.2	45-49	BIRTH
229	6.3	227	6.1	50-54	AND
218	6.1	222	6.0	55-59	DEATH
202	5.6	214	5.8	60-64	RATES
178	4.9	201	5.5	65-69	(female
144	4.0	180	4.9	70-74	dominant,
104	2.9	146	3.9	75-79	in 000s)
62	1.7	99	2.7	80-84	
38	1.0	75	2.0	85+	
3605		3690		TOTAL	

VITAL RATES OF PROJECTED POPULATION

Per Thousand	1975 BOTH SEXES	1975 MALES	1975 FEMALES	1980 BOTH SEXES	1980 MALES	1980 FEMALES
BIRTH RATE	15.58	16.46	14.74	14.97	15.79	14.19
DEATH RATE	10.01	10.50	9.54	10.63	10.99	10.28
RATE OF INCREASE	5.57	5.96	5.20	4.35	4.80	3.91

AGE STRUCTURE OF PROJECTED POPULATION

% UNDER 15	22.58	23.61	21.59	21.51	22.52	20.54
% 15-64	64.57	65.72	63.46	65.17	66.40	63.99
% 65 AND OLDER	12.86	10.67	14.95	13.31	11.07	15.46
DEPEND. RATIO x 100	54.88	52.16	57.58	53.44	50.59	56.27

VITAL RATES OF STABLE POPULATION

Per Thousand	MALES	FEMALES	
BIRTH RATE	14.13	12.92	TABLE 6
DEATH RATE	14.39	13.41	PROJECTED
RATE OF INCREASE		-.49	VITAL RATES AND RATIOS

STABLE AGE STRUCTURE

	MALES	FEMALES	(female dominant)
% UNDER 15	20.50	18.94	
% 15-64	64.93	62.07	
% 65 AND OLDER	14.57	18.99	
DEPEND. RATIO x 100	54.01	61.11	

MATRIX

AGE GROUP	FEMALE BIRTH RATES	NET MATERNITY FUNCTION	COEFF. OF MATRIX EQUATION	ORIGINAL MATRIX SUB-DIAGONAL	ORIGINAL MATRIX FIRST ROW	STABLE MATRIX FISHER VALUES	STABLE MATRIX REPRODUCTIVE VALUES
0-4	0.0000	0.0000	0.0000	0.99631	0.00000	1.023	224847
5-9	0.0000	0.0000	0.0000	0.99826	0.00000	1.024	256471
10-14	0.0000	0.0000	0.0190	0.99834	0.01908	1.024	233364
15-19	0.0078	0.0380	0.1563	0.99785	0.15737	1.003	220700
20-24	0.0568	0.2746	0.3043	0.99783	0.30713	0.842	209803
25-29	0.0692	0.3340	0.2729	0.99719	0.27600	0.526	130831
30-34	0.0440	0.2117	0.1544	0.99607	0.15660	0.244	52508
35-39	0.0203	0.0971	0.0627	0.99403	0.06383	0.083	16998
40-44	0.0059	0.0283	0.0155	0.98963	0.01585	0.018	3492
45-49	0.0006	0.0027	0.0013	0.98341	0.00139	0.001	277
50-54	0.0000	0.0000	0.0000	0.97505	0.00001	0.000	2

MATRIX PARAMETERS

λ_1	0.99756	
λ_2	$0.38736+0.73799i$	TABLE 7
λ_4	$-0.34579+0.40957i$	
λ_6	$-0.04742+0.47853i$	LESLIE MATRIX
r_1	-0.00049	AND ITS
r_2	$-0.03643+0.21749i$	ANALYSIS
r_4	$-0.12472+0.45439i$	(females)
r_6	$-0.14643+0.33392i$	
c_1	36914	
$2\pi/y$	28.8899	
Δ	7.5597	

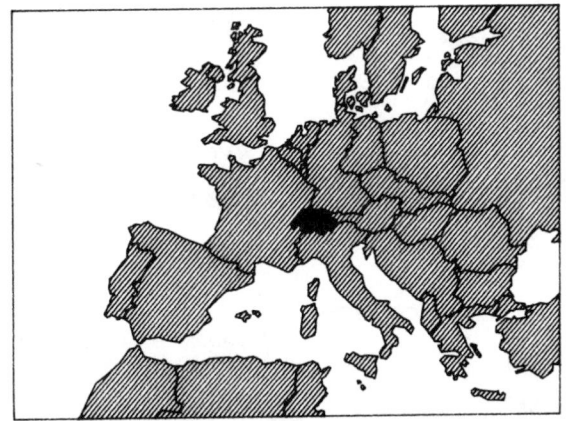

EDUCATION [1984]

% of primary school-age children enrolled:	na
secondary school-age children enrolled:	na
ca. 20-24 year olds in higher education:	21

LABOR FORCE

Average annual labor force growth (%) 1980-85:	0.7
% of the 1980 labor force in agriculture:	6
in industry:	39
in services:	55

TABLE 8

SOCIO-ECONOMIC INDICATORS

GNP & INCOME DISTRIBUTION

GNP per capita (in US Dollars) 1985:	16370
GNP average annual growth rate (%) 1965-85:	1.4
% share of total household income 1978	
Lowest 20% of households:	6.6
Highest 10% of households:	23.7

HEALTH & NUTRITION

Population per physician 1981:	390
Daily calorie supply per capita 1985:	3432

TABLE 1 — DATA

AGE AT LAST BIRTHDAY	ESTIMATED MID-YEAR POPULATION BOTH SEXES	MALES Number	MALES Percent	FEMALES Number	FEMALES Percent	BIRTHS BY AGE OF MOTHER AND SEX	DEATHS BOTH SEXES	DEATHS MALES	DEATHS FEMALES	AGE AT LAST BIRTHDAY
0	37400	19200	0.6	18200	0.6		743	444	299	0
1-4	339100	174300	5.6	164800	5.1		304	177	127	1-4
5-9	488300	249900	8.1	238400	7.3		185	110	75	5-9
10-14	509500	260400	8.4	249100	7.7		157	92	65	10-14
15-19	468000	236700	7.7	231300	7.1	2521	349	246	103	15-19
20-24	459000	224800	7.3	234200	7.2	20121	515	395	120	20-24
25-29	512800	256000	8.3	256800	7.9	31783	431	314	117	25-29
30-34	500500	256000	8.3	244500	7.5	17135	444	300	144	30-34
35-39	428200	217300	7.0	210900	6.5	5436	512	320	192	35-39
40-44	406500	204100	6.6	202400	6.2	1366	820	535	285	40-44
45-49	382400	186900	6.0	195500	6.0	102	1228	798	430	45-49
50-54	365100	176200	5.7	188900	5.8		1842	1190	652	50-54
55-59	305400	147700	4.8	157700	4.9		2545	1687	858	55-59
60-64	308600	144300	4.7	164300	5.1		3912	2594	1318	60-64
65-69	289000	128300	4.2	160700	4.9		6202	3922	2280	65-69
70-74	233800	97200	3.1	136600	4.2		7922	4580	3342	70-74
75-79	162000	61600	2.0	100400	3.1		9406	4629	4777	75-79
80-84	91600	32300	1.0	59300	1.8	40409 M	8833	3843	4990	80-84
85+	51500	16600	0.5	34900	1.1	38055 F	9574	3513	6061	85+
TOTAL	6338700	3089800		3248900		78464	55924	29689	26235	TOTAL

TABLE 2 — MALE LIFE TABLE

x	nM_x	nq_x	l_x	nd_x	nL_x	nm_x	na_x	T_x	$\overset{\circ}{e}_x$	x
0	0.023125	0.022658	100000	2266	97982	0.023125	0.109	7117912	71.179	0
1	0.001015	0.004052	97734	396	389947	0.001015	1.500	7019930	71.827	1
5	0.000440	0.002198	97338	214	486156	0.000440	2.500	6629983	68.113	5
10	0.000353	0.001766	97124	172	485253	0.000353	2.853	6143827	63.257	10
15	0.001039	0.005205	96953	505	483642	0.001043	2.777	5658575	58.364	15
20	0.001757	0.008747	96448	844	480148	0.001757	2.520	5174933	53.655	20
25	0.001227	0.006113	95604	584	476501	0.001227	2.397	4694785	49.106	25
30	0.001172	0.005845	95020	555	473734	0.001172	2.542	4218285	44.394	30
35	0.001473	0.007365	94465	696	470723	0.001478	2.701	3744550	39.640	35
40	0.002621	0.013070	93769	1226	466043	0.002630	2.715	3273828	34.914	40
45	0.004270	0.021182	92543	1960	458190	0.004278	2.691	2807784	30.340	45
50	0.006754	0.033361	90583	3022	445969	0.006776	2.701	2349595	25.939	50
55	0.011422	0.055763	87561	4883	426455	0.011449	2.675	1903626	21.741	55
60	0.017976	0.086272	82678	7133	396787	0.017976	2.672	1477171	17.866	60
65	0.030569	0.142626	75546	10775	352167	0.030596	2.628	1080384	14.301	65
70	0.047119	0.212112	64771	13739	290653	0.047268	2.583	728216	11.243	70
75	0.075146	0.318930	51032	16276	214917	0.075730	2.527	437563	8.574	75
80	0.118978	0.456734	34756	15874	133423	0.118978	2.458	222646	6.406	80
85	0.211626	1.000000	18882	18882	89223	0.146196	4.725	89223	4.725	85

TABLE 3 — FEMALE LIFE TABLE

x	nM_x	nq_x	l_x	nd_x	nL_x	nm_x	na_x	T_x	$\overset{\circ}{e}_x$	x
0	0.016429	0.016189	100000	1619	98540	0.016429	0.098	7799388	77.994	0
1	0.000771	0.003077	98381	303	392768	0.000771	1.500	7700849	78.276	1
5	0.000315	0.001572	98078	154	490007	0.000315	2.500	7308081	74.513	5
10	0.000261	0.001304	97924	128	489315	0.000261	2.604	6818074	69.626	10
15	0.000445	0.002226	97797	218	488464	0.000446	2.617	6328758	64.713	15
20	0.000512	0.002559	97579	250	487271	0.000512	2.503	5840294	59.852	20
25	0.000456	0.002275	97329	221	486100	0.000456	2.534	5353023	54.999	25
30	0.000589	0.002947	97108	286	484869	0.000590	2.660	4866923	50.119	30
35	0.000910	0.004558	96822	441	483086	0.000913	2.685	4382054	45.259	35
40	0.001408	0.007031	96380	678	480334	0.001411	2.686	3898967	40.454	40
45	0.002199	0.010948	95703	1048	476092	0.002201	2.688	3418633	35.721	45
50	0.003452	0.017170	94655	1625	469515	0.003462	2.687	2942542	31.087	50
55	0.005441	0.026918	93030	2504	459292	0.005452	2.661	2473027	26.583	55
60	0.008022	0.039384	90526	3565	444438	0.008022	2.703	2013734	22.245	60
65	0.014188	0.068708	86960	5975	421081	0.014189	2.704	1569297	18.046	65
70	0.024466	0.116133	80985	9405	383386	0.024532	2.710	1148216	14.178	70
75	0.047580	0.215685	71580	15439	321431	0.048031	2.638	764829	10.685	75
80	0.084148	0.349308	56142	19611	233049	0.084148	2.570	443398	7.898	80
85	0.173668	1.000000	36531	36531	210350	0.104602	5.758	210350	5.758	85

TABLE 4 — OBSERVED VITAL RATES AND RATIOS

CRUDE RATES

Per Thousand	BOTH SEXES	MALES	FEMALES
BIRTH RATE	12.38	13.08	11.71
DEATH RATE	8.82	9.61	8.08
RATE OF INCREASE	3.56	3.47	3.64

PERCENT OF POPULATION IN AGE GROUP

	BOTH SEXES	MALES	FEMALES
UNDER 15	21.68	22.78	20.64
15 - 64	65.26	66.35	64.22
65 AND OLDER	13.06	10.87	15.14

RATES STANDARDIZED ON USA 1980

Per Thousand	BOTH SEXES	MALES	FEMALES
BIRTH RATE	13.65		12.88
DEATH RATE	8.47	9.07	7.91
RATE OF INCREASE	5.18		4.97

RATES STANDARDIZED ON MEXICO 1980

	BOTH SEXES	MALES	FEMALES
BIRTH RATE	11.81		11.55
DEATH RATE	3.53	4.26	2.78
RATE OF INCREASE	8.28		8.76

VITAL STATISTICS

GFR x 1000	49.799
TFR	1.619
GRR	0.785
NRR	0.763
μ	28.043
σ^2	28.333
GENERATION	28.180
POP. SEX RATIO	1.051
SEX RATIO AT BIRTH	1.062
DEP. RATIO x 100	53.238

AGE AT LAST BIRTHDAY	ESTIMATED MID-YEAR POPULATION					BIRTHS BY AGE OF MOTHER AND SEX	DEATHS			AGE AT LAST BIRTHDAY
	BOTH SEXES	MALES		FEMALES			BOTH SEXES	MALES	FEMALES	
		Number	Percent	Number	Percent					
0	36600	18700	0.6	17900	0.6		596	350	246	0
1-4	283100	144900	4.7	138200	4.3		192	118	74	1-4
5-9	398900	204800	6.7	194100	6.0		122	78	44	5-9
10-14	477500	244100	7.9	233400	7.2		126	76	50	10-14
15-19	508800	260200	8.5	248600	7.7	1746	331	237	94	15-19
20-24	466600	233300	7.6	233300	7.2	16671	548	408	140	20-24
25-29	459700	226700	7.4	233000	7.2	29333	418	306	112	25-29
30-34	501900	252900	8.2	249000	7.7	19197	449	290	159	30-34
35-39	481000	245100	8.0	235900	7.3	5660	590	405	185	35-39
40-44	409700	205900	6.7	203800	6.3	972	751	491	260	40-44
45-49	391600	195000	6.3	196600	6.1	79	1152	718	434	45-49
50-54	367900	178100	5.8	189800	5.8	3	1693	1088	605	50-54
55-59	348100	165600	5.4	182500	5.6		2751	1832	919	55-59
60-64	286100	135200	4.4	150900	4.6		3534	2346	1188	60-64
65-69	281400	126500	4.1	154900	4.8		5551	3549	2002	65-69
70-74	252500	106000	3.4	146500	4.5		8143	4823	3320	70-74
75-79	188400	72500	2.4	115900	3.6		9952	5065	4887	75-79
80-84	113000	38500	1.3	74500	2.3	37717 M	10142	4523	5619	80-84
85+	66600	20100	0.7	46500	1.4	35944 F	12056	4144	7912	85+
TOTAL	6319400	3074100		3245300		73661	59097	30847	28250	TOTAL

TABLE 1 DATA

x	$_nM_x$	$_nq_x$	l_x	$_nd_x$	$_nL_x$	$_nm_x$	$_na_x$	T_x	$\overset{\circ}{e}_x$	x
0	0.018717	0.018407	100000	1841	98347	0.018717	0.102	7210916	72.109	0
1	0.000814	0.003251	98159	319	391839	0.000814	1.500	7112569	72.459	1
5	0.000381	0.001902	97840	186	488736	0.000381	2.500	6720730	68.691	5
10	0.000311	0.001556	97654	152	487944	0.000311	2.852	6231994	63.817	10
15	0.000911	0.004546	97502	443	486547	0.000911	2.826	5744050	58.912	15
20	0.001749	0.008714	97059	846	483223	0.001750	2.550	5257503	54.168	20
25	0.001350	0.006725	96213	647	479386	0.001350	2.404	4774281	49.622	25
30	0.001147	0.005717	95566	546	476493	0.001147	2.552	4294895	44.942	30
35	0.001652	0.008247	95020	784	473259	0.001656	2.653	3818403	40.185	35
40	0.002385	0.011897	94236	1121	468569	0.002393	2.671	3345144	35.497	40
45	0.003682	0.018304	93115	1704	461655	0.003692	2.700	2876575	30.893	45
50	0.006109	0.030189	91411	2760	450798	0.006122	2.733	2414922	26.418	50
55	0.011063	0.054099	88651	4796	432149	0.011098	2.685	1964122	22.156	55
60	0.017352	0.083564	83855	7007	402864	0.017394	2.658	1531973	18.269	60
65	0.028055	0.131557	76848	10110	360355	0.028055	2.638	1129109	14.693	65
70	0.045500	0.205081	66738	13687	300677	0.045519	2.588	768754	11.519	70
75	0.069862	0.299510	53051	15889	226188	0.070248	2.541	468077	8.823	75
80	0.117481	0.452987	37162	16834	143290	0.117481	2.474	241889	6.509	80
85	0.206169	1.000000	20328	20328	98599	0.140002	4.850	98599	4.850	85

TABLE 2 MALE LIFE TABLE

x	$_nM_x$	$_nq_x$	l_x	$_nd_x$	$_nL_x$	$_nm_x$	$_na_x$	T_x	$\overset{\circ}{e}_x$	x
0	0.013743	0.013574	100000	1357	98769	0.013743	0.093	7898811	78.988	0
1	0.000535	0.002139	98643	211	394043	0.000535	1.500	7800042	79.074	1
5	0.000227	0.001133	98432	112	491879	0.000227	2.500	7405999	75.240	5
10	0.000214	0.001071	98320	105	491353	0.000214	2.646	6914119	70.323	10
15	0.000378	0.001889	98215	186	490650	0.000378	2.712	6422766	65.395	15
20	0.000600	0.002997	98029	294	489422	0.000600	2.535	5932116	60.514	20
25	0.000481	0.002401	97736	235	488095	0.000481	2.515	5442694	55.688	25
30	0.000639	0.003188	97501	311	486758	0.000639	2.598	4954599	50.816	30
35	0.000784	0.003923	97190	381	485061	0.000786	2.668	4467841	45.970	35
40	0.001276	0.006386	96809	618	482640	0.001281	2.728	3982779	41.141	40
45	0.002208	0.010999	96191	1058	478493	0.002211	2.675	3500140	36.388	45
50	0.003188	0.015826	95133	1506	472166	0.003189	2.677	3021646	31.762	50
55	0.005036	0.024957	93627	2337	462717	0.005050	2.681	2549481	27.230	55
60	0.007873	0.038749	91290	3537	448269	0.007891	2.687	2086764	22.859	60
65	0.012924	0.062758	87753	5507	426105	0.012924	2.701	1638495	18.672	65
70	0.022662	0.107705	82246	8858	390884	0.022662	2.703	1212389	14.741	70
75	0.042166	0.192806	73388	14150	333661	0.042407	2.648	821506	11.194	75
80	0.075423	0.319475	59238	18925	250919	0.075423	2.608	487844	8.235	80
85	0.170151	1.000000	40313	40313	236925	0.101088	5.877	236925	5.877	85

TABLE 3 FEMALE LIFE TABLE

CRUDE RATES

Per Thousand	BOTH SEXES	MALES	FEMALES
BIRTH RATE	11.66	12.27	11.08
DEATH RATE	9.35	10.03	8.70
RATE OF INCREASE	2.30	2.23	2.37

PERCENT OF POPULATION IN AGE GROUP

	BOTH SEXES	MALES	FEMALES
UNDER 15	18.93	19.92	17.98
15 - 64	66.80	68.25	65.43
65 AND OLDER	14.27	11.83	16.59

RATES STANDARDIZED ON USA 1980

Per Thousand	BOTH SEXES	MALES	FEMALES
BIRTH RATE	13.05		12.38
DEATH RATE	7.96	8.60	7.35
RATE OF INCREASE	5.09		5.03

RATES STANDARDIZED ON MEXICO 1980

	BOTH SEXES	MALES	FEMALES
BIRTH RATE	11.14		10.96
DEATH RATE	3.24	3.95	2.52
RATE OF INCREASE	7.91		8.44

VITAL STATISTICS

GFR x 1000	46.032	TABLE 4
TFR	1.553	
GRR	0.758	OBSERVED
NRR	0.739	VITAL
μ	28.379	RATES
σ^2	25.098	AND
GENERATION	28.512	RATIOS
POP. SEX RATIO	1.056	
SEX RATIO AT BIRTH	1.049	
DEP. RATIO x 100	49.699	

TABLE 1 — DATA

AGE AT LAST BIRTHDAY	ESTIMATED MID-YEAR POPULATION BOTH SEXES	MALES Number	MALES Percent	FEMALES Number	FEMALES Percent	BIRTHS BY AGE OF MOTHER AND SEX	DEATHS BOTH SEXES	DEATHS MALES	DEATHS FEMALES	AGE AT LAST BIRTHDAY
0	37800	19200	0.6	18600	0.6		438	242	196	0
1-4	294800	150700	4.8	144100	4.3		215	123	92	1-4
5-9	365300	187100	5.9	178200	5.3		64	39	25	5-9
10-14	387600	198600	6.3	189000	5.7		102	58	44	10-14
15-19	470800	241300	7.6	229500	6.9	1006	304	224	80	15-19
20-24	524100	265900	8.4	258200	7.7	14329	522	399	123	20-24
25-29	502300	251800	7.9	250500	7.5	31735	480	337	143	25-29
30-34	488400	245500	7.7	242900	7.3	21526	423	277	146	30-34
35-39	501200	253400	8.0	247800	7.4	6647	557	376	181	35-39
40-44	493800	251200	7.9	242600	7.3	1034	809	520	289	40-44
45-49	412700	207000	6.5	205700	6.2	40	1060	689	371	45-49
50-54	386000	191500	6.0	194500	5.8	3	1559	1054	505	50-54
55-59	355300	171000	5.4	184300	5.5		2397	1596	801	55-59
60-64	326600	151400	4.8	175200	5.3		3477	2310	1167	60-64
65-69	273400	124000	3.9	149400	4.5		4840	3233	1607	65-69
70-74	244100	104900	3.3	139200	4.2		6849	4185	2664	70-74
75-79	209200	81200	2.6	128000	3.8		9599	5169	4430	75-79
80-84	138500	48200	1.5	90300	2.7	38904 M	11058	5025	6033	80-84
85+	92200	26200	0.8	66000	2.0	37416 F	15352	5024	10328	85+
TOTAL	6504100	3170100		3334000		76320	60105	30880	29225	TOTAL

TABLE 2 — MALE LIFE TABLE

x	nM_x	nq_x	l_x	nd_x	nL_x	nm_x	na_x	T_x	$\dot{e}_x$	x
0	0.012604	0.012461	100000	1246	98868	0.012604	0.091	7377134	73.771	0
1	0.000816	0.003258	98754	322	394211	0.000816	1.500	7278266	73.701	1
5	0.000208	0.001042	98432	103	491904	0.000208	2.500	6884055	69.937	5
10	0.000292	0.001459	98330	144	491362	0.000292	3.011	6392151	65.007	10
15	0.000928	0.004632	98186	455	489916	0.000928	2.769	5900789	60.098	15
20	0.001501	0.007475	97731	731	486870	0.001501	2.555	5410873	55.365	20
25	0.001338	0.006666	97001	647	483348	0.001338	2.439	4924003	50.763	25
30	0.001128	0.005626	96354	542	480428	0.001128	2.524	4440656	46.087	30
35	0.001484	0.007393	95812	708	477381	0.001484	2.629	3960228	41.333	35
40	0.002070	0.010324	95104	982	473241	0.002075	2.681	3482847	36.622	40
45	0.003329	0.016593	94122	1562	467026	0.003344	2.706	3009606	31.976	45
50	0.005504	0.027268	92560	2524	457024	0.005522	2.712	2542580	27.470	50
55	0.009333	0.045810	90036	4125	440666	0.009360	2.693	2085556	23.164	55
60	0.015258	0.073924	85912	6351	414861	0.015309	2.686	1644889	19.146	60
65	0.026073	0.123100	79561	9794	374641	0.026142	2.635	1230028	15.460	65
70	0.039895	0.182067	69767	12702	318319	0.039904	2.598	855386	12.261	70
75	0.063658	0.276032	57065	15752	246856	0.063809	2.558	537067	9.412	75
80	0.104253	0.413459	41313	17081	163844	0.104253	2.499	290211	7.025	80
85	0.191756	1.000000	24232	24232	126368	0.123970	5.215	126368	5.215	85

TABLE 3 — FEMALE LIFE TABLE

x	nM_x	nq_x	l_x	nd_x	nL_x	nm_x	na_x	T_x	$\dot{e}_x$	x
0	0.010538	0.010437	100000	1044	99048	0.010538	0.088	8064647	80.646	0
1	0.000638	0.002550	98956	252	395194	0.000638	1.500	7965599	80.496	1
5	0.000140	0.000701	98704	69	493347	0.000140	2.500	7570404	76.698	5
10	0.000233	0.001163	98635	115	492908	0.000233	2.686	7077058	71.750	10
15	0.000349	0.001741	98520	172	492196	0.000349	2.645	6584150	66.831	15
20	0.000476	0.002379	98348	234	491180	0.000476	2.596	6091954	61.943	20
25	0.000571	0.002851	98114	280	489885	0.000571	2.544	5600774	57.084	25
30	0.000601	0.003001	97835	294	488455	0.000601	2.554	5110889	52.240	30
35	0.000730	0.003646	97541	356	486876	0.000730	2.667	4622433	47.390	35
40	0.001191	0.005953	97185	579	484588	0.001194	2.685	4135557	42.553	40
45	0.001804	0.009008	96607	870	480996	0.001809	2.658	3650969	37.792	45
50	0.002596	0.012934	95737	1238	475830	0.002602	2.696	3169972	33.111	50
55	0.004346	0.021538	94498	2035	467779	0.004351	2.684	2694142	28.510	55
60	0.006661	0.032871	92463	3039	455274	0.006676	2.683	2226363	24.078	60
65	0.010756	0.052653	89424	4708	436333	0.010791	2.709	1771089	19.806	65
70	0.019138	0.091663	84715	7765	405755	0.019138	2.705	1334756	15.756	70
75	0.034609	0.160421	76950	12344	356158	0.034660	2.684	929002	12.073	75
80	0.066811	0.288714	64606	18653	279185	0.066811	2.649	572844	8.867	80
85	0.156485	1.000000	45953	45953	293659	0.087613	6.390	293659	6.390	85

TABLE 4 — OBSERVED VITAL RATES AND RATIOS

CRUDE RATES

Per Thousand	BOTH SEXES	MALES	FEMALES
BIRTH RATE	11.73	12.27	11.22
DEATH RATE	9.24	9.74	8.77
RATE OF INCREASE	2.49	2.53	2.46

PERCENT OF POPULATION IN AGE GROUP

UNDER 15	16.69	17.53	15.89
15 - 64	68.59	70.34	66.92
65 AND OLDER	14.72	12.13	17.18

RATES STANDARDIZED ON USA 1980

Per Thousand	BOTH SEXES	MALES	FEMALES
BIRTH RATE	12.73		12.14
DEATH RATE	7.03	7.68	6.42
RATE OF INCREASE	5.70		5.72

RATES STANDARDIZED ON MEXICO 1980

	BOTH SEXES	MALES	FEMALES
BIRTH RATE	10.70		10.58
DEATH RATE	2.80	3.43	2.17
RATE OF INCREASE	7.90		8.40

VITAL STATISTICS

GFR x 1000	45.504
TFR	1.532
GRR	0.751
NRR	0.735
μ	28.981
σ^2	23.088
GENERATION	29.103
POP. SEX RATIO	1.052
SEX RATIO AT BIRTH	1.040
DEP. RATIO x 100	45.793

PROJECTED POPULATION

AGE GROUP	1991 BOTH SEXES	1991 MALES	1991 FEMALES	1996 BOTH SEXES	1996 MALES	1996 FEMALES
0-4	375	191	184	362	184	178
5-9	331	169	162	375	191	184
10-14	365	187	178	331	169	162
15-19	387	198	189	364	186	178
20-24	469	240	229	385	197	188
25-29	522	264	258	466	238	228
30-34	500	250	250	519	262	257
35-39	486	244	242	498	249	249
40-44	498	251	247	483	242	241
45-49	489	248	241	493	248	245
50-54	406	203	203	481	243	238
55-59	376	185	191	395	195	200
60-64	340	161	179	360	174	186
65-69	305	137	168	317	145	172
70-74	244	105	139	272	116	156
75-79	203	81	122	204	82	122
80-84	154	54	100	150	54	96
85+	132	37	95	148	42	106
TOTAL	6582	3205	3377	6603	3217	3386

STABLE EQUIVALENT TO ORIGINAL POPULATION

MALES Number	MALES Percent	FEMALES Number	FEMALES Percent	AGE GROUP	
189	4.4	182	3.9	0-4	
199	4.6	192	4.1	5-9	TABLE 5
210	4.9	202	4.3	10-14	
220	5.1	213	4.6	15-19	POPULATION
231	5.4	224	4.8	20-24	PROJECTED
242	5.6	235	5.0	25-29	WITH
253	5.9	248	5.3	30-34	FIXED
265	6.2	260	5.6	35-39	AGE-
277	6.5	273	5.8	40-44	SPECIFIC
288	6.7	286	6.1	45-49	BIRTH
297	6.9	298	6.4	50-54	AND
302	7.0	309	6.6	55-59	DEATH
300	7.0	317	6.8	60-64	RATES
286	6.7	320	6.9	65-69	(female
256	6.0	314	6.7	70-74	dominant,
209	4.9	290	6.2	75-79	in 000s)
146	3.4	240	5.1	80-84	
119	2.8	266	5.7	85+	
4289		4669		TOTAL	

VITAL RATES OF PROJECTED POPULATION

Per Thousand	1991 BOTH SEXES	1991 MALES	1991 FEMALES	1996 BOTH SEXES	1996 MALES	1996 FEMALES
BIRTH RATE	11.53	12.07	11.01	10.71	11.20	10.23
DEATH RATE	10.47	10.72	10.24	11.01	11.28	10.76
RATE OF INCREASE	1.05	1.34	0.78	-0.31	-0.08	-0.52

VITAL RATES OF STABLE POPULATION

Per Thousand	MALES	FEMALES	
BIRTH RATE	8.71	7.70	TABLE 6
DEATH RATE	19.03	18.25	PROJECTED
RATE OF INCREASE		-10.55	VITAL RATES

AGE STRUCTURE OF PROJECTED POPULATION

	1991 BOTH SEXES	1991 MALES	1991 FEMALES	1996 BOTH SEXES	1996 MALES	1996 FEMALES
% UNDER 15	16.29	17.09	15.54	16.18	16.92	15.47
% 15-64	67.93	69.98	65.98	67.31	69.44	65.29
% 65 AND OLDER	15.78	12.93	18.48	16.51	13.64	19.24
DEPEND. RATIO x 100	47.21	42.89	51.56	48.57	44.01	53.17

STABLE AGE STRUCTURE

	MALES	FEMALES	
% UNDER 15	13.94	12.36	AND RATIOS
% 15-64	62.38	57.02	(female
% 65 AND OLDER	23.68	30.62	dominant)
DEPEND. RATIO x 100	60.30	75.38	

AGE GROUP	FEMALE BIRTH RATES	NET MATERNITY FUNCTION	COEFF. OF MATRIX EQUATION	ORIGINAL MATRIX SUB-DIAGONAL	ORIGINAL MATRIX FIRST ROW	STABLE MATRIX FISHER VALUES	STABLE MATRIX REPRODUCTIVE VALUES	MATRIX PARAMETERS		
0-4	0.0000	0.0000	0.0000	0.99819	0.00000	0.985	160303	λ_1	0.94861	
5-9	0.0000	0.0000	0.0000	0.99911	0.00000	0.936	166855	λ_2	0.41624-0.73576i	TABLE 7
10-14	0.0000	0.0000	0.0053	0.99855	0.00530	0.889	168023	λ_4	-0.26438-0.55158i	
15-19	0.0021	0.0106	0.0721	0.99794	0.07241	0.839	192622	λ_6	-0.42085-0.12349i	LESLIE
20-24	0.0272	0.1336	0.2189	0.99736	0.22031	0.726	187541	r_1	-0.01055	MATRIX
25-29	0.0621	0.3043	0.2582	0.99708	0.26053	0.473	118535	r_2	-0.03360-0.21119i	AND ITS
30-34	0.0434	0.2122	0.1381	0.99677	0.13976	0.193	46817	r_4	-0.09831-0.40355i	ANALYSIS
35-39	0.0132	0.0640	0.0371	0.99530	0.03764	0.045	11222	r_6	-0.16483-0.57123i	(females)
40-44	0.0021	0.0101	0.0053	0.99259	0.00540	0.006	1432	c_1	46673	
45-49	0.0001	0.0005	0.0002	0.98926	0.00025	0.000	58	$2\pi/\gamma$	29.7510	
50-54	0.0000	0.0000	0.0000	0.98308	0.00002	0.000	4	Δ	16.5965	

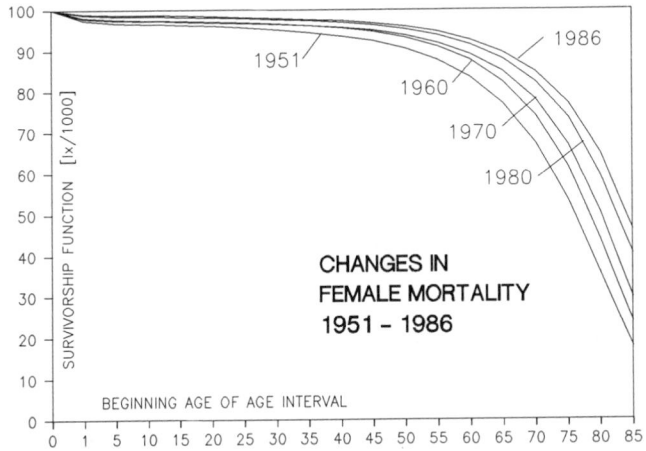

CHANGES IN FEMALE MORTALITY 1951 - 1986

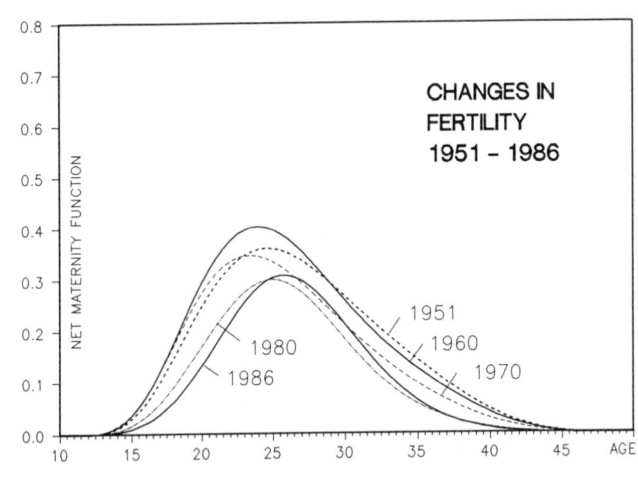

CHANGES IN FERTILITY 1951 - 1986

TABLE 1 — DATA

AGE AT LAST BIRTHDAY	ESTIMATED MID-YEAR POPULATION BOTH SEXES	MALES Number	Percent	FEMALES Number	Percent	BIRTHS BY AGE OF MOTHER AND SEX	DEATHS BOTH SEXES	MALES	FEMALES	AGE AT LAST BIRTHDAY
0	883700	453600	1.7	430100	1.5		16715	9713	7002	0
1-4	3734100	1900000	7.0	1834100	6.4		2737	1556	1181	1-4
5-9	4676800	2386700	8.8	2290100	8.0		1626	978	648	5-9
10-14	4111100	2123800	7.9	1987300	6.9		1240	773	467	10-14
15-19	3848000	1965100	7.3	1882900	6.6	92423	2414	1752	662	15-19
20-24	4255000	2142700	7.9	2112300	7.4	330985	3088	2131	957	20-24
25-29	3543300	1788700	6.6	1754600	6.1	272591	2583	1665	918	25-29
30-34	3301500	1674200	6.2	1627300	5.7	133727	3120	1920	1200	30-34
35-39	3207700	1618600	6.0	1589100	5.5	57659	4631	2720	1911	35-39
40-44	3361100	1674200	6.2	1686900	5.9	15443	8705	5116	3589	40-44
45-49	3636800	1791800	6.6	1845000	6.4	1079	16544	9871	6673	45-49
50-54	3182600	1547200	5.7	1635400	5.7		23382	14528	8854	50-54
55-59	3427200	1645700	6.1	1781500	6.2		41141	26552	14589	55-59
60-64	3209600	1499700	5.6	1709900	6.0		62168	40105	22063	60-64
65-69	2697100	1185200	4.4	1511800	5.3		84222	52011	32211	65-69
70-74	1962200	756100	2.8	1206100	4.2		95400	51578	43822	70-74
75-79	1328800	462800	1.7	866000	3.0		99826	46559	53267	75-79
80-84	818600	257200	1.0	561400	2.0	464948 M	90655	35437	55218	80-84
85+	444000	116800	0.4	327200	1.1	438959 F	95188	29390	65798	85+
TOTAL	55629100	26990100		28639000		903907	655385	334355	321030	TOTAL

TABLE 2 — MALE LIFE TABLE

x	$_nM_x$	$_nq_x$	l_x	$_nd_x$	$_nL_x$	$_nm_x$	$_na_x$	T_x	$\overset{\circ}{e}_x$	x
0	0.021413	0.021011	100000	2101	98122	0.021413	0.106	6869233	68.692	0
1	0.000819	0.003269	97899	320	390795	0.000819	1.500	6771110	69.164	1
5	0.000410	0.002047	97579	200	487395	0.000410	2.500	6380315	65.386	5
10	0.000364	0.001826	97379	178	486500	0.000365	2.773	5892920	60.515	10
15	0.000892	0.004450	97201	433	484988	0.000892	2.646	5406420	55.621	15
20	0.000995	0.004961	96769	480	482647	0.000995	2.506	4921432	50.858	20
25	0.000931	0.004646	96289	447	480340	0.000931	2.532	4438785	46.099	25
30	0.001147	0.005729	95841	549	477908	0.001149	2.633	3958445	41.302	30
35	0.001680	0.008373	95292	798	474652	0.001681	2.731	3480538	36.525	35
40	0.003056	0.015175	94494	1434	469249	0.003056	2.752	3005886	31.810	40
45	0.005509	0.027217	93061	2533	459539	0.005512	2.724	2536637	27.258	45
50	0.009390	0.045961	90528	4161	443108	0.009390	2.709	2077098	22.944	50
55	0.016134	0.077762	86367	6716	416266	0.016134	2.682	1633990	18.919	55
60	0.026742	0.125818	79651	10021	374690	0.026746	2.649	1217724	15.288	60
65	0.043884	0.199101	69629	13863	314406	0.044038	2.595	843035	12.107	65
70	0.068216	0.293050	55766	16342	238379	0.068556	2.525	528229	9.472	70
75	0.100603	0.400822	39424	15802	156701	0.100841	2.442	289850	7.352	75
80	0.137780	0.506283	23622	11959	86801	0.137780	2.382	133149	5.637	80
85	0.251627	1.000000	11663	11663	46349	0.194861	3.974	46349	3.974	85

TABLE 3 — FEMALE LIFE TABLE

x	$_nM_x$	$_nq_x$	l_x	$_nd_x$	$_nL_x$	$_nm_x$	$_na_x$	T_x	$\overset{\circ}{e}_x$	x
0	0.016280	0.016044	100000	1604	98552	0.016280	0.098	7499127	74.991	0
1	0.000644	0.002571	98396	253	392950	0.000644	1.500	7400574	75.212	1
5	0.000283	0.001414	98143	139	490366	0.000283	2.500	7007624	71.403	5
10	0.000235	0.001175	98004	115	489738	0.000235	2.560	6517258	66.500	10
15	0.000352	0.001756	97889	172	489035	0.000352	2.628	6027520	61.575	15
20	0.000453	0.002263	97717	221	488048	0.000453	2.579	5538485	56.679	20
25	0.000523	0.002618	97496	255	486868	0.000524	2.612	5050437	51.802	25
30	0.000737	0.003691	97240	359	485372	0.000739	2.689	4563568	46.931	30
35	0.001203	0.005997	96881	581	483092	0.001203	2.737	4078196	42.095	35
40	0.002128	0.010587	96300	1020	479188	0.002128	2.730	3595104	37.332	40
45	0.003617	0.017934	95281	1709	472442	0.003617	2.681	3115915	32.702	45
50	0.005414	0.026732	93572	2501	462014	0.005414	2.662	2643474	28.251	50
55	0.008189	0.040179	91071	3659	446826	0.008189	2.669	2181460	23.953	55
60	0.012903	0.062647	87412	5476	424342	0.012905	2.678	1734634	19.844	60
65	0.021306	0.101664	81936	8330	390286	0.021343	2.672	1310292	15.992	65
70	0.036334	0.167800	73606	12351	338841	0.036451	2.637	920006	12.499	70
75	0.061509	0.268394	61255	16440	266290	0.061739	2.568	581165	9.488	75
80	0.098358	0.395328	44814	17716	180122	0.098358	2.519	314874	7.026	80
85	0.201094	1.000000	27098	27098	134753	0.134159	4.973	134753	4.973	85

TABLE 4 — OBSERVED VITAL RATES AND RATIOS

CRUDE RATES

Per Thousand	BOTH SEXES	MALES	FEMALES
BIRTH RATE	16.25	17.23	15.33
DEATH RATE	11.78	12.39	11.21
RATE OF INCREASE	4.47	4.84	4.12

PERCENT OF POPULATION IN AGE GROUP

	BOTH SEXES	MALES	FEMALES
UNDER 15	24.10	25.43	22.84
15 - 64	62.87	64.28	61.54
65 AND OLDER	13.03	10.29	15.62

RATES STANDARDIZED ON USA 1980

Per Thousand	BOTH SEXES	MALES	FEMALES
BIRTH RATE	20.97		19.81
DEATH RATE	10.86	11.62	10.15
RATE OF INCREASE	10.11		9.66

RATES STANDARDIZED ON MEXICO 1980

Per Thousand	BOTH SEXES	MALES	FEMALES
BIRTH RATE	18.94		18.53
DEATH RATE	4.27	5.05	3.47
RATE OF INCREASE	14.67		15.07

VITAL STATISTICS

GFR x 1000	72.324
TFR	2.447
GRR	1.188
NRR	1.157
μ	26.760
σ^2	33.709
GENERATION	26.668
POP. SEX RATIO	1.061
SEX RATIO AT BIRTH	1.059
DEP. RATIO x 100	59.064

PROJECTED POPULATION

STABLE EQUIVALENT TO ORIGINAL POPULATION

AGE GROUP	1975 BOTH SEXES	MALES	FEMALES	1980 BOTH SEXES	MALES	FEMALES	MALES Number	Percent	FEMALES Number	Percent	AGE GROUP	
0-4	4512	2315	2197	4662	2392	2270	2316	8.5	2199	8.0	0-4	
5-9	4605	2346	2259	4500	2308	2192	2247	8.3	2134	7.7	5-9	TABLE 5
10-14	4669	2382	2287	4598	2342	2256	2182	8.0	2074	7.5	10-14	
15-19	4101	2117	1984	4659	2375	2284	2117	7.8	2015	7.3	15-19	POPULATION
20-24	3835	1956	1879	4087	2107	1980	2050	7.5	1957	7.1	20-24	PROJECTED
25-29	4239	2132	2107	3821	1946	1875	1985	7.3	1900	6.9	25-29	WITH
30-34	3529	1780	1749	4223	2122	2101	1922	7.1	1843	6.7	30-34	FIXED
35-39	3283	1663	1620	3509	1768	1741	1857	6.8	1785	6.5	35-39	AGE-
40-44	3176	1600	1576	3251	1644	1607	1787	6.6	1723	6.2	40-44	SPECIFIC
45-49	3303	1640	1663	3121	1567	1554	1703	6.3	1653	6.0	45-49	BIRTH
50-54	3532	1728	1804	3207	1581	1626	1598	5.9	1573	5.7	50-54	AND
55-59	3035	1453	1582	3368	1623	1745	1460	5.4	1480	5.4	55-59	DEATH
60-64	3173	1481	1692	2810	1308	1502	1279	4.7	1368	4.9	60-64	RATES
65-69	2833	1260	1573	2801	1245	1556	1046	3.8	1224	4.4	65-69	(female
70-74	2210	897	1313	2319	954	1365	770	2.8	1034	3.7	70-74	dominant,
75-79	1445	497	948	1621	590	1031	493	1.8	791	2.9	75-79	in 000s)
80-84	842	256	586	916	275	641	266	1.0	520	1.9	80-84	
85+	557	137	420	575	137	438	138	0.5	379	1.4	85+	
TOTAL	56879	27640	29239	58048	28284	29764	27216		27652		TOTAL	

VITAL RATES OF PROJECTED POPULATION

VITAL RATES OF STABLE POPULATION

Per Thousand	1975 BOTH SEXES	MALES	FEMALES	1980 BOTH SEXES	MALES	FEMALES	MALES	FEMALES	
BIRTH RATE	16.48	17.44	15.56	16.63	17.55	15.75	17.65	16.40	TABLE 6
DEATH RATE	12.37	12.78	11.99	12.58	12.93	12.25	12.16	10.93	PROJECTED
RATE OF INCREASE	4.10	4.66	3.58	4.04	4.62	3.50		5.46	VITAL RATES

AGE STRUCTURE OF PROJECTED POPULATION

STABLE AGE STRUCTURE

	BOTH SEXES	MALES	FEMALES	BOTH SEXES	MALES	FEMALES	MALES	FEMALES	AND RATIOS
% UNDER 15	24.24	25.48	23.06	23.70	24.90	22.57	24.79	23.17	(female
% 15-64	61.90	63.49	60.39	62.11	63.79	60.52	65.25	62.55	dominant)
% 65 AND OLDER	13.87	11.03	16.55	14.18	11.32	16.91	9.97	14.28	
DEPEND. RATIO x 100	61.56	57.50	65.60	61.00	56.77	65.23	53.26	59.87	

AGE GROUP	FEMALE BIRTH RATES	NET MATERNITY FUNCTION	COEFF. OF MATRIX EQUATION	ORIGINAL MATRIX SUB-DIAGONAL	FIRST ROW	STABLE MATRIX FISHER VALUES	REPRODUCTIVE VALUES	MATRIX PARAMETERS		
0-4	0.0000	0.0000	0.0000	0.99769	0.00000	1.031	2334972	λ_1	1.02769	
5-9	0.0000	0.0000	0.0000	0.99872	0.00000	1.062	2432707	λ_2	0.33621+0.75578i	TABLE 7
10-14	0.0000	0.0000	0.0583	0.99857	0.05850	1.093	2172295	λ_4	-0.37655-0.40007i	
15-19	0.0238	0.1166	0.2440	0.99798	0.24521	1.065	2004464	λ_6	-0.02727+0.46386i	LESLIE
20-24	0.0761	0.3714	0.3693	0.99758	0.37196	0.843	1780406	r_1	0.00546	MATRIX
25-29	0.0754	0.3673	0.2805	0.99693	0.28318	0.484	848871	r_2	-0.03795+0.23045i	AND ITS
30-34	0.0399	0.1937	0.1394	0.99530	0.14117	0.206	334894	r_4	-0.11979-0.46518i	ANALYSIS
35-39	0.0176	0.0851	0.0532	0.99192	0.05414	0.066	105236	r_6	-0.15329+0.32590i	(females)
40-44	0.0044	0.0213	0.0113	0.98592	0.01161	0.012	20792	c_1	276506	
45-49	0.0003	0.0013	0.0007	0.97793	0.00070	0.001	1292	$2\pi/y$	27.2652	
50-54	0.0000	0.0000	0.0000	0.00000	0.00000	0.000	0	Δ	4.5223	

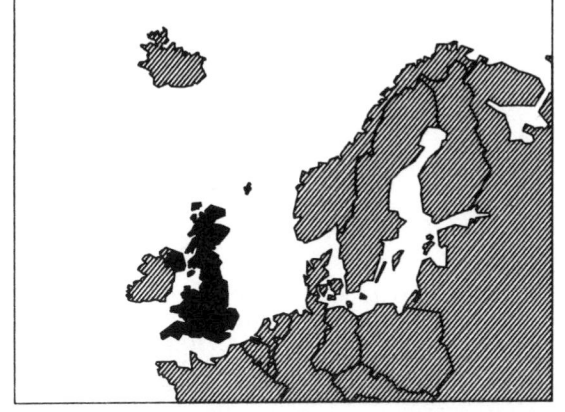

EDUCATION [1984]

% of primary school-age children enrolled:	101
secondary school-age children enrolled:	83
ca. 20-24 year olds in higher education:	20

LABOR FORCE

Average annual labor force growth (%) 1980-85:	0.5	
% of the 1980 labor force in agriculture:	3	TABLE 8
in industry:	38	
in services:	59	SOCIO-ECONOMIC

GNP & INCOME DISTRIBUTION

GNP per capita (in US Dollars) 1985:	8460	INDICATORS
GNP average annual growth rate (%) 1965-85:	1.6	
% share of total household income 1979		
Lowest 20% of households:	7.0	
Highest 10% of households:	23.4	

HEALTH & NUTRITION

Population per physician 1981:	680
Daily calorie supply per capita 1985:	3131

TABLE 1 — DATA

AGE AT LAST BIRTHDAY	ESTIMATED MID-YEAR POPULATION BOTH SEXES	MALES Number	MALES Percent	FEMALES Number	FEMALES Percent	BIRTHS BY AGE OF MOTHER AND SEX	DEATHS BOTH SEXES	DEATHS MALES	DEATHS FEMALES	AGE AT LAST BIRTHDAY
0	706900	363100	1.3	343800	1.2		11190	6392	4798	0
1-4	3233000	1662000	6.1	1571000	5.4		1999	1139	860	1-4
5-9	4539000	2328700	8.5	2210300	7.7		1369	829	540	5-9
10-14	4658500	2389700	8.7	2268800	7.9		1247	842	405	10-14
15-19	4125500	2108300	7.7	2017200	7.0	74087	2622	1871	751	15-19
20-24	3866600	1967000	7.2	1899600	6.6	220526	2831	2018	813	20-24
25-29	4224200	2136600	7.8	2087600	7.2	258228	2930	1883	1047	25-29
30-34	3496000	1771600	6.5	1724400	6.0	102377	3126	1962	1164	30-34
35-39	3260100	1652000	6.0	1608100	5.6	33583	4385	2576	1809	35-39
40-44	3160300	1593100	5.8	1567200	5.4	8049	7518	4430	3088	40-44
45-49	3297600	1639700	6.0	1657900	5.7	668	14136	8627	5509	45-49
50-54	3530600	1732300	6.3	1798300	6.2		25548	16003	9545	50-54
55-59	3039200	1458200	5.3	1581000	5.5		34336	21634	12702	55-59
60-64	3187300	1492700	5.5	1694600	5.9		58149	36947	21202	60-64
65-69	2847100	1272600	4.6	1574900	5.5		82804	51451	31353	65-69
70-74	2230100	908400	3.3	1321700	4.6		102781	58675	44106	70-74
75-79	1454800	500900	1.8	953900	3.3		104217	49459	54758	75-79
80-84	839800	253500	0.9	586300	2.0	359244 M	95274	37194	58080	80-84
85+	529100	131100	0.5	398000	1.4	338274 F	106015	31074	74941	85+
TOTAL	56225700	27361100		28864600		697518	662477	335006	327471	TOTAL

TABLE 2 — MALE LIFE TABLE

x	nM_x	nq_x	l_x	nd_x	nL_x	nm_x	na_x	T_x	$\overset{\circ}{e}_x$	x
0	0.017604	0.017329	100000	1733	98440	0.017604	0.100	6952409	69.524	0
1	0.000685	0.002737	98267	269	392396	0.000685	1.500	6853969	69.748	1
5	0.000356	0.001778	97998	174	489555	0.000356	2.500	6461573	65.936	5
10	0.000352	0.001763	97824	172	488742	0.000353	2.813	5972018	61.049	10
15	0.000887	0.004443	97651	434	487240	0.000890	2.656	5483276	56.152	15
20	0.001026	0.005117	97218	497	484843	0.001026	2.496	4996036	51.390	20
25	0.000881	0.004397	96720	425	482545	0.000881	2.518	4511193	46.642	25
30	0.001107	0.005538	96295	533	480208	0.001110	2.625	4028648	41.837	30
35	0.001559	0.007792	95762	746	477105	0.001564	2.718	3548440	37.055	35
40	0.002781	0.013823	95015	1313	472146	0.002782	2.768	3071335	32.325	40
45	0.005261	0.025998	93702	2436	463007	0.005261	2.741	2599189	27.739	45
50	0.009238	0.045247	91266	4130	446801	0.009242	2.692	2136182	23.406	50
55	0.014836	0.071710	87137	6249	421172	0.014836	2.678	1689381	19.388	55
60	0.024752	0.116963	80888	9461	382231	0.024752	2.653	1268209	15.679	60
65	0.040443	0.184475	71427	13177	325618	0.040466	2.608	885978	12.404	65
70	0.064592	0.279752	58251	16296	251237	0.064862	2.544	560360	9.620	70
75	0.098740	0.396860	41955	16650	167547	0.099376	2.464	309123	7.368	75
80	0.146722	0.529866	25305	13408	91384	0.146722	2.379	141575	5.595	80
85	0.237025	1.000000	11897	11897	50191	0.176927	4.219	50191	4.219	85

TABLE 3 — FEMALE LIFE TABLE

x	nM_x	nq_x	l_x	nd_x	nL_x	nm_x	na_x	T_x	$\overset{\circ}{e}_x$	x
0	0.013956	0.013781	100000	1378	98751	0.013956	0.094	7575853	75.759	0
1	0.000547	0.002187	98622	216	393948	0.000547	1.500	7477102	75.816	1
5	0.000244	0.001221	98406	120	491731	0.000244	2.500	7083154	71.979	5
10	0.000179	0.000893	98286	88	491224	0.000179	2.649	6591424	67.064	10
15	0.000372	0.001865	98198	183	490559	0.000373	2.638	6100200	62.121	15
20	0.000428	0.002138	98015	210	489565	0.000428	2.561	5609641	57.232	20
25	0.000502	0.002506	97806	245	488441	0.000502	2.602	5120076	52.349	25
30	0.000675	0.003383	97561	330	487041	0.000678	2.691	4631635	47.474	30
35	0.001125	0.005628	97231	547	484913	0.001129	2.735	4144595	42.626	35
40	0.001970	0.009808	96683	948	481260	0.001970	2.727	3659681	37.852	40
45	0.003323	0.016488	95735	1579	475045	0.003323	2.701	3178421	33.200	45
50	0.005308	0.026215	94156	2468	465036	0.005308	2.672	2703376	28.712	50
55	0.008034	0.039431	91688	3615	450003	0.008034	2.666	2238340	24.413	55
60	0.012512	0.060782	88073	5353	427867	0.012512	2.666	1788336	20.305	60
65	0.019908	0.095150	82720	7871	395222	0.019915	2.665	1360469	16.447	65
70	0.033371	0.155005	74849	11602	346938	0.033441	2.646	965247	12.896	70
75	0.057404	0.253364	63247	16024	277669	0.057711	2.593	618309	9.776	75
80	0.099062	0.397734	47222	18782	189598	0.099062	2.523	340640	7.214	80
85	0.188294	1.000000	28440	28440	151042	0.120112	5.311	151042	5.311	85

TABLE 4 — OBSERVED VITAL RATES AND RATIOS

CRUDE RATES

Per Thousand	BOTH SEXES	MALES	FEMALES
BIRTH RATE	12.41	13.13	11.72
DEATH RATE	11.78	12.24	11.35
RATE OF INCREASE	0.62	0.89	0.37

PERCENT OF POPULATION IN AGE GROUP

UNDER 15	23.37	24.65	22.15
15 - 64	62.58	64.15	61.10
65 AND OLDER	14.05	11.21	16.75

RATES STANDARDIZED ON USA 1980

Per Thousand	BOTH SEXES	MALES	FEMALES
BIRTH RATE	15.64		14.75
DEATH RATE	10.33	11.09	9.61
RATE OF INCREASE	5.31		5.14

RATES STANDARDIZED ON MEXICO 1980

	BOTH SEXES	MALES	FEMALES
BIRTH RATE	14.13		13.82
DEATH RATE	4.00	4.75	3.24
RATE OF INCREASE	10.14		10.58

VITAL STATISTICS

GFR x 1000	55.526
TFR	1.812
GRR	0.879
NRR	0.858
μ	26.497
σ^2	30.584
GENERATION	26.584
POP. SEX RATIO	1.055
SEX RATIO AT BIRTH	1.062
DEP. RATIO x 100	59.789

AGE AT LAST BIRTHDAY	ESTIMATED MID-YEAR POPULATION BOTH SEXES	MALES Number	MALES Percent	FEMALES Number	FEMALES Percent	BIRTHS BY AGE OF MOTHER AND SEX	DEATHS BOTH SEXES	MALES	FEMALES	AGE AT LAST BIRTHDAY	
0	734100	376600	1.4	357500	1.2		9147	5178	3969	0	
1-4	2669500	1369800	5.0	1299700	4.5		1379	789	590	1-4	
5-9	3892100	1999900	7.3	1892200	6.5		1022	609	413	5-9	
10-14	4532300	2325900	8.5	2206400	7.6		1090	655	435	10-14	
15-19	4695700	2400600	8.8	2295100	7.9	70115	2795	2031	764	15-19	
20-24	4165200	2116700	7.7	2048500	7.1	232606	2749	1941	808	20-24	
25-29	3831900	1936600	7.1	1895300	6.6	255731	2589	1709	880	25-29	
30-34	4179400	2107200	7.7	2072200	7.2	147881	3321	2059	1262	30-34	
35-39	3460700	1746300	6.4	1714400	5.9	39526	4351	2605	1746	35-39	TABLE 1
40-44	3220600	1624000	5.9	1596600	5.5	7156	6821	4124	2697	40-44	
45-49	3114600	1562000	5.7	1552600	5.4	693	11773	7206	4567	45-49	DATA
50-54	3207800	1584100	5.8	1623700	5.6		21487	13425	8062	50-54	
55-59	3370200	1631700	6.0	1738500	6.0		37817	23966	13851	55-59	
60-64	2832400	1327000	4.8	1505400	5.2		49689	31222	18467	60-64	
65-69	2846600	1278400	4.7	1568200	5.4		77843	47756	30087	65-69	
70-74	2380800	995000	3.6	1385800	4.8		102876	59284	43592	70-74	
75-79	1676700	612900	2.2	1063800	3.7		114348	57424	56924	75-79	
80-84	930800	275700	1.0	655100	2.3	386035 M	98374	38839	59535	80-84	
85+	588100	140700	0.5	447400	1.5	367673 F	112024	31538	80486	85+	
TOTAL	56329500	27411100		28918400		753708	661495	332360	329135	TOTAL	

x	nM_x	nq_x	l_x	nd_x	nL_x	nm_x	na_x	T_x	$\overset{\circ}{e}_x$	x	
0	0.013749	0.013580	100000	1358	98769	0.013749	0.093	7054335	70.543	0	
1	0.000576	0.002301	98642	227	394001	0.000576	1.500	6955566	70.513	1	
5	0.000305	0.001521	98415	150	491701	0.000305	2.500	6561565	66.672	5	
10	0.000282	0.001407	98265	138	491036	0.000282	2.899	6069864	61.770	10	
15	0.000846	0.004224	98127	414	489663	0.000846	2.655	5578828	56.853	15	
20	0.000917	0.004576	97713	447	487448	0.000917	2.506	5089165	52.083	20	
25	0.000882	0.004403	97265	428	485262	0.000882	2.512	4601717	47.311	25	TABLE 2
30	0.000977	0.004877	96837	472	483066	0.000978	2.628	4116455	42.509	30	
35	0.001492	0.007466	96365	720	480180	0.001498	2.714	3633388	37.704	35	MALE
40	0.002539	0.012667	95645	1212	475498	0.002548	2.747	3153208	32.968	40	LIFE
45	0.004613	0.022837	94434	2157	467325	0.004615	2.754	2677710	28.355	45	TABLE
50	0.008475	0.041572	92277	3836	452656	0.008475	2.724	2210385	23.954	50	
55	0.014688	0.071054	88441	6284	427605	0.014695	2.676	1757729	19.875	55	
60	0.023528	0.111470	82157	9158	389191	0.023531	2.642	1330123	16.190	60	
65	0.037356	0.171469	72999	12517	335076	0.037356	2.610	940932	12.890	65	
70	0.059582	0.260269	60482	15742	264003	0.059627	2.560	605856	10.017	70	
75	0.093692	0.381272	44741	17058	180748	0.094376	2.482	341853	7.641	75	
80	0.140874	0.515116	27682	14260	101222	0.140874	2.392	161105	5.820	80	
85	0.224151	1.000000	13423	13423	59882	0.161396	4.461	59882	4.461	85	

x	nM_x	nq_x	l_x	nd_x	nL_x	nm_x	na_x	T_x	$\overset{\circ}{e}_x$	x	
0	0.011102	0.010991	100000	1099	98999	0.011102	0.089	7663994	76.640	0	
1	0.000454	0.001814	98901	179	395155	0.000454	1.500	7564996	76.491	1	
5	0.000218	0.001091	98722	108	493338	0.000218	2.500	7169841	72.627	5	
10	0.000197	0.000985	98614	97	492838	0.000197	2.620	6676502	67.703	10	
15	0.000333	0.001664	98517	164	492194	0.000333	2.623	6183664	62.768	15	
20	0.000394	0.001973	98353	194	491292	0.000395	2.568	5691470	57.868	20	
25	0.000464	0.002319	98159	228	490246	0.000464	2.595	5200178	52.977	25	TABLE 3
30	0.000609	0.003043	97931	298	488967	0.000609	2.689	4709932	48.094	30	
35	0.001018	0.005104	97633	498	487028	0.001023	2.718	4220965	43.233	35	FEMALE
40	0.001689	0.008440	97135	820	483814	0.001694	2.731	3733936	38.441	40	LIFE
45	0.002942	0.014610	96315	1407	478372	0.002942	2.724	3250122	33.745	45	TABLE
50	0.004965	0.024545	94908	2330	469176	0.004965	2.698	2771751	29.205	50	
55	0.007967	0.039110	92578	3621	454459	0.007967	2.671	2302574	24.872	55	
60	0.012267	0.059624	88958	5304	432373	0.012267	2.659	1848115	20.775	60	
65	0.019186	0.091803	83654	7680	400281	0.019186	2.658	1415742	16.924	65	
70	0.031456	0.146456	75974	11127	353667	0.031461	2.645	1015461	13.366	70	
75	0.053510	0.237966	64847	15431	287163	0.053737	2.598	661794	10.205	75	
80	0.090879	0.371449	49416	18355	201976	0.090879	2.543	374631	7.581	80	
85	0.179897	1.000000	31060	31060	172656	0.111220	5.559	172656	5.559	85	

CRUDE RATES

Per Thousand	BOTH SEXES	MALES	FEMALES
BIRTH RATE	13.38	14.08	12.71
DEATH RATE	11.74	12.13	11.38
RATE OF INCREASE	1.64	1.96	1.33

PERCENT OF POPULATION IN AGE GROUP

	BOTH SEXES	MALES	FEMALES
UNDER 15	21.00	22.15	19.90
15 - 64	64.05	65.80	62.39
65 AND OLDER	14.95	12.05	17.71

RATES STANDARDIZED ON USA 1980

Per Thousand	BOTH SEXES	MALES	FEMALES
BIRTH RATE	16.24		15.41
DEATH RATE	9.69	10.38	9.04
RATE OF INCREASE	6.55		6.37

RATES STANDARDIZED ON MEXICO 1980

	BOTH SEXES	MALES	FEMALES
BIRTH RATE	14.48		14.24
DEATH RATE	3.68	4.36	2.98
RATE OF INCREASE	10.80		11.26

VITAL STATISTICS

GFR x 1000	57.209	TABLE 4
TFR	1.892	
GRR	0.923	OBSERVED
NRR	0.905	VITAL
μ	26.930	RATES
σ^2	29.149	AND
GENERATION	26.984	RATIOS
POP. SEX RATIO	1.055	
SEX RATIO AT BIRTH	1.050	
DEP. RATIO x 100	56.130	

TABLE 1 — DATA

AGE AT LAST BIRTHDAY	ESTIMATED MID-YEAR POPULATION					BIRTHS BY AGE OF MOTHER AND SEX	DEATHS			AGE AT LAST BIRTHDAY
	BOTH SEXES	MALES Number	Percent	FEMALES Number	Percent		BOTH SEXES	MALES	FEMALES	
0	741900	380100	1.4	361800	1.2		7030	4003	3027	0
1-4	2868400	1470000	5.3	1398400	4.8		1302	728	574	1-4
5-9	3398300	1745600	6.3	1652700	5.7		707	393	314	5-9
10-14	3887900	1997300	7.2	1890600	6.5		938	583	355	10-14
15-19	4540100	2328000	8.4	2212100	7.6	65435	2238	1612	626	15-19
20-24	4747000	2411800	8.7	2335200	8.0	222614	2760	2031	729	20-24
25-29	4102800	2073200	7.5	2029600	7.0	260192	2428	1648	780	25-29
30-34	3769600	1899300	6.9	1870300	6.4	143385	2876	1804	1072	30-34
35-39	4144200	2075400	7.5	2068800	7.1	50590	4704	2826	1878	35-39
40-44	3423600	1722400	6.2	1701200	5.9	7884	6421	3902	2519	40-44
45-49	3171000	1588800	5.8	1582200	5.4	628	10356	6343	4013	45-49
50-54	3040000	1514300	5.5	1526400	5.3		17541	10973	6568	50-54
55-59	3079100	1506600	5.5	1572500	5.4		31009	19312	11697	55-59
60-64	3145600	1494300	5.4	1651300	5.7		53503	33190	20313	60-64
65-69	2540200	1149700	4.2	1390500	4.8		66178	40138	26040	65-69
70-74	2400200	1015600	3.7	1384600	4.8		99785	57320	42465	70-74
75-79	1825900	691200	2.5	1134700	3.9		118556	61400	57156	75-79
80-84	1108000	351500	1.3	756500	2.6	385139 M	113130	47841	65289	80-84
85+	683400	158800	0.6	524600	1.8	365589 F	129194	35515	93679	85+
TOTAL	56617900	27573900		29044000		750728	670656	331562	339094	TOTAL

TABLE 2 — MALE LIFE TABLE

x	nM_x	nq_x	l_x	nd_x	nL_x	nm_x	na_x	T_x	$\bar{e}_x$	x
0	0.010531	0.010431	100000	1043	99049	0.010531	0.088	7165398	71.654	0
1	0.000495	0.001979	98957	196	395338	0.000495	1.500	7066350	71.408	1
5	0.000225	0.001125	98761	111	493528	0.000225	2.500	6671012	67.547	5
10	0.000292	0.001459	98650	144	492938	0.000292	2.832	6177484	62.620	10
15	0.000692	0.003457	98506	341	491735	0.000692	2.664	5684546	57.708	15
20	0.000842	0.004202	98166	413	489807	0.000842	2.524	5192811	52.898	20
25	0.000795	0.003968	97753	388	487806	0.000795	2.526	4703005	48.111	25
30	0.000950	0.004740	97365	462	485728	0.000950	2.622	4215199	43.293	30
35	0.001362	0.006792	96904	658	483004	0.001363	2.699	3729470	38.486	35
40	0.002265	0.011332	96246	1091	478757	0.002278	2.735	3246466	33.731	40
45	0.003992	0.019857	95155	1889	471516	0.004007	2.746	2767709	29.086	45
50	0.007246	0.035657	93265	3326	458786	0.007249	2.732	2296193	24.620	50
55	0.012818	0.062262	89940	5600	436863	0.012818	2.708	1837407	20.429	55
60	0.022211	0.105632	84340	8909	400795	0.022228	2.653	1400544	16.606	60
65	0.034912	0.161238	75431	12162	348164	0.034933	2.616	999749	13.254	65
70	0.056440	0.248145	63269	15700	278170	0.056440	2.569	651585	10.299	70
75	0.088831	0.364243	47569	17327	194427	0.089116	2.494	373415	7.850	75
80	0.136105	0.503188	30242	15218	111807	0.136105	2.411	178988	5.918	80
85	0.223646	1.000000	15025	15025	67181	0.160728	4.471	67181	4.471	85

TABLE 3 — FEMALE LIFE TABLE

x	nM_x	nq_x	l_x	nd_x	nL_x	nm_x	na_x	T_x	$\bar{e}_x$	x
0	0.008367	0.008303	100000	830	99240	0.008367	0.084	7742056	77.421	0
1	0.000410	0.001640	99170	163	396272	0.000410	1.500	7642816	77.068	1
5	0.000190	0.000950	99007	94	494800	0.000190	2.500	7246544	73.192	5
10	0.000188	0.000938	98913	93	494343	0.000188	2.602	6751744	68.259	10
15	0.000283	0.001414	98820	140	493765	0.000283	2.591	6257401	63.321	15
20	0.000312	0.001560	98681	154	493028	0.000312	2.568	5763637	58.407	20
25	0.000384	0.001925	98527	190	492185	0.000385	2.640	5270609	53.494	25
30	0.000573	0.002863	98337	282	491033	0.000573	2.688	4778424	48.592	30
35	0.000908	0.004532	98055	444	489258	0.000908	2.707	4287390	43.724	35
40	0.001481	0.007419	97611	724	486407	0.001489	2.725	3798132	38.911	40
45	0.002536	0.012651	96887	1226	481643	0.002545	2.723	3311725	34.181	45
50	0.004303	0.021306	95661	2038	473668	0.004303	2.725	2830082	29.584	50
55	0.007438	0.036568	93623	3424	460254	0.007438	2.704	2356415	25.169	55
60	0.012301	0.059786	90199	5393	438386	0.012301	2.662	1896161	21.022	60
65	0.018727	0.089696	84807	7607	406192	0.018727	2.655	1457774	17.189	65
70	0.030670	0.142987	77200	11039	359919	0.030670	2.637	1051582	13.622	70
75	0.050371	0.225020	66161	14888	295096	0.050450	2.601	691663	10.454	75
80	0.086304	0.356500	51274	18279	211798	0.086304	2.562	396567	7.734	80
85	0.178572	1.000000	32995	32995	184769	0.109862	5.600	184769	5.600	85

TABLE 4 — OBSERVED VITAL RATES AND RATIOS

CRUDE RATES

Per Thousand	BOTH SEXES	MALES	FEMALES
BIRTH RATE	13.26	13.97	12.59
DEATH RATE	11.85	12.02	11.68
RATE OF INCREASE	1.41	1.94	0.91

RATES STANDARDIZED ON USA 1980

Per Thousand	BOTH SEXES	MALES	FEMALES
BIRTH RATE	15.30		14.49
DEATH RATE	9.17	9.73	8.65
RATE OF INCREASE	6.13		5.84

VITAL STATISTICS

GFR x 1000	54.403
TFR	1.796
GRR	0.875
NRR	0.861
μ	27.299
σ^2	30.266
GENERATION	27.382
POP. SEX RATIO	1.053
SEX RATIO AT BIRTH	1.053
DEP. RATIO x 100	52.347

PERCENT OF POPULATION IN AGE GROUP

	BOTH SEXES	MALES	FEMALES
UNDER 15	19.25	20.28	18.26
15 - 64	65.64	67.51	63.87
65 AND OLDER	15.11	12.21	17.87

RATES STANDARDIZED ON MEXICO 1980

	BOTH SEXES	MALES	FEMALES
BIRTH RATE	13.55		13.30
DEATH RATE	3.38	3.98	2.76
RATE OF INCREASE	10.18		10.55

PROJECTED POPULATION

AGE GROUP	1990 BOTH SEXES	MALES	FEMALES	1995 BOTH SEXES	MALES	FEMALES
0-4	3778	1936	1842	3772	1933	1839
5-9	3605	1847	1758	3773	1933	1840
10-14	3395	1744	1651	3601	1845	1756
15-19	3880	1992	1888	3388	1739	1649
20-24	4528	2319	2209	3871	1985	1886
25-29	4733	2402	2331	4514	2309	2205
30-34	4089	2064	2025	4718	2392	2326
35-39	3753	1889	1864	4071	2053	2018
40-44	4114	2057	2057	3725	1872	1853
45-49	3381	1696	1685	4063	2026	2037
50-54	3102	1546	1556	3308	1651	1657
55-59	2925	1442	1483	2984	1472	1512
60-64	2880	1382	1498	2736	1323	1413
65-69	2828	1298	1530	2589	1201	1388
70-74	2151	919	1232	2393	1037	1356
75-79	1845	710	1135	1652	642	1010
80-84	1211	397	814	1223	408	815
85+	871	211	660	949	239	710
TOTAL	57069	27851	29218	57330	28060	29270

STABLE EQUIVALENT TO ORIGINAL POPULATION

MALES Number	Percent	FEMALES Number	Percent	AGE GROUP	
1928	5.7	1834	5.2	0-4	
1978	5.8	1882	5.3	5-9	TABLE 5
2030	6.0	1932	5.4	10-14	
2081	6.1	1984	5.6	15-19	POPULATION
2131	6.2	2036	5.7	20-24	PROJECTED
2181	6.4	2089	5.9	25-29	WITH
2232	6.5	2142	6.0	30-34	FIXED
2281	6.7	2193	6.2	35-39	AGE-
2323	6.8	2241	6.3	40-44	SPECIFIC
2352	6.9	2280	6.4	45-49	BIRTH
2352	6.9	2305	6.5	50-54	AND
2301	6.7	2302	6.5	55-59	DEATH
2170	6.4	2253	6.3	60-64	RATES
1937	5.7	2145	6.0	65-69	(female
1591	4.7	1954	5.5	70-74	dominant,
1143	3.4	1646	4.6	75-79	in 000s)
675	2.0	1214	3.4	80-84	
417	1.2	1089	3.1	85+	
34103		35521		TOTAL	

VITAL RATES OF PROJECTED POPULATION

Per Thousand	1990 BOTH SEXES	MALES	FEMALES	1995 BOTH SEXES	MALES	FEMALES
BIRTH RATE	13.60	14.30	12.94	13.05	13.68	12.45
DEATH RATE	12.50	12.53	12.48	12.62	12.64	12.60
RATE OF INCREASE	1.10	1.77	0.46	0.43	1.04	-0.15

AGE STRUCTURE OF PROJECTED POPULATION

% UNDER 15	18.89	19.84	17.97	19.44	20.35	18.57
% 15-64	65.51	67.46	63.64	65.20	67.08	63.39
% 65 AND OLDER	15.61	12.69	18.38	15.36	12.57	18.04
DEPEND. RATIO x 100	52.66	48.23	57.13	53.38	49.08	57.75

VITAL RATES OF STABLE POPULATION

Per Thousand	MALES	FEMALES	
BIRTH RATE	11.28	10.28	TABLE 6
DEATH RATE	16.70	15.75	PROJECTED
RATE OF INCREASE		-5.47	VITAL RATES

STABLE AGE STRUCTURE

	MALES	FEMALES	
% UNDER 15	17.40	15.90	AND RATIOS
% 15-64	65.70	61.44	(female
% 65 AND OLDER	16.90	22.66	dominant)
DEPEND. RATIO x 100	52.22	62.77	

AGE GROUP	FEMALE BIRTH RATES	NET MATERNITY FUNCTION	COEFF. OF MATRIX EQUATION	ORIGINAL MATRIX SUB-DIAGONAL	FIRST ROW	STABLE MATRIX FISHER VALUES	REPRODUCTIVE VALUES	MATRIX PARAMETERS		
0-4	0.0000	0.0000	0.0000	0.99856	0.00000	0.995	1751992	λ_1	0.97301	
5-9	0.0000	0.0000	0.0000	0.99908	0.00000	0.970	1602900	λ_2	0.36877+0.73403i	TABLE 7
10-14	0.0000	0.0000	0.0356	0.99883	0.03565	0.945	1785795	λ_4	-0.24357+0.48826i	
15-19	0.0144	0.0711	0.1500	0.99851	0.15054	0.885	1956881	λ_6	-0.36779+0.10847i	LESLIE
20-24	0.0464	0.2289	0.2681	0.99829	0.26943	0.712	1662617	r_1	-0.00547	MATRIX
25-29	0.0624	0.3073	0.2453	0.99766	0.24695	0.425	863232	r_2	-0.03933+0.22105i	AND ITS
30-34	0.0373	0.1833	0.1208	0.99638	0.12189	0.168	315021	r_4	-0.12116+0.40671i	ANALYSIS
35-39	0.0119	0.0583	0.0346	0.99417	0.03506	0.043	88372	r_6	-0.19171+0.57096i	(females)
40-44	0.0023	0.0110	0.0060	0.99021	0.00607	0.007	11404	c_1	355196	
45-49	0.0002	0.0009	0.0005	0.98344	0.00048	0.000	775	$2x/y$	28.4246	
50-54	0.0000	0.0000	0.0000	0.00000	0.00000	0.000	0	Δ	9.1660	

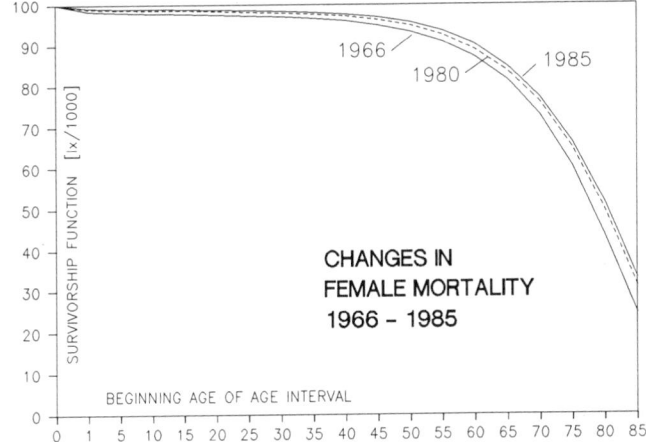

CHANGES IN FEMALE MORTALITY 1966 - 1985

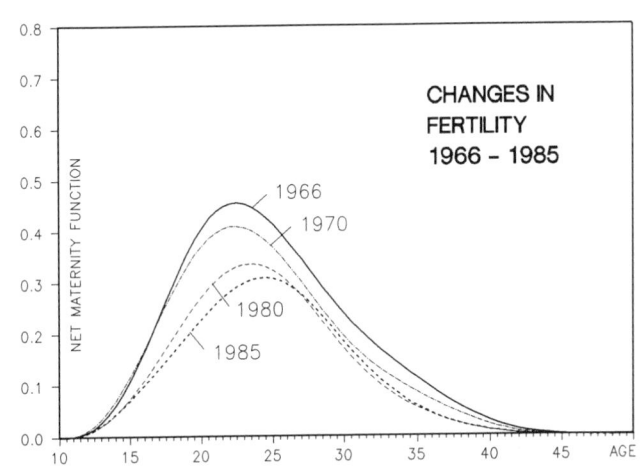

CHANGES IN FERTILITY 1966 - 1985

TABLE 1 — DATA

AGE AT LAST BIRTHDAY	ESTIMATED MID-YEAR POPULATION BOTH SEXES	MALES Number	MALES Percent	FEMALES Number	FEMALES Percent	BIRTHS BY AGE OF MOTHER AND SEX	DEATHS BOTH SEXES	DEATHS MALES	DEATHS FEMALES	AGE AT LAST BIRTHDAY
0	766300	393200	1.7	373100	1.5		14267	8269	5998	0
1-4	3242300	1647000	6.9	1595300	6.3		2326	1315	1011	1-4
5-9	4050900	2065400	8.7	1985500	7.9		1354	816	538	5-9
10-14	3534100	1828100	7.7	1706000	6.8		1050	649	401	10-14
15-19	3335200	1704200	7.2	1631000	6.5	80975	2121	1551	570	15-19
20-24	3760100	1894100	8.0	1866000	7.4	289209	2685	1836	849	20-24
25-29	3135700	1586100	6.7	1549600	6.2	238228	2231	1435	796	25-29
30-34	2912700	1482600	6.2	1430100	5.7	114086	2660	1654	1006	30-34
35-39	2821700	1429200	6.0	1392500	5.5	48323	3920	2297	1623	35-39
40-44	2963100	1480600	6.2	1482500	5.9	12756	7512	4420	3092	40-44
45-49	3222000	1590700	6.7	1631300	6.5	909	14269	8549	5720	45-49
50-54	2814700	1372600	5.8	1442100	5.7		20185	12613	7572	50-54
55-59	3034400	1461200	6.2	1573200	6.3		35671	23139	12532	55-59
60-64	2845500	1333100	5.6	1512400	6.0		54005	34960	19045	60-64
65-69	2392500	1054000	4.4	1338500	5.3		73742	45721	28021	65-69
70-74	1740800	671100	2.8	1069700	4.3		83514	45316	38198	70-74
75-79	1184800	411700	1.7	773100	3.1		88000	41195	46805	75-79
80-84	735500	230100	1.0	505400	2.0	403371 M	80542	31430	49112	80-84
85+	398800	103100	0.4	295700	1.2	381115 F	85140	25888	59252	85+
TOTAL	48891100	23738100		25153000		784486	575194	293053	282141	TOTAL

TABLE 2 — MALE LIFE TABLE

x	$_nM_x$	$_nq_x$	l_x	$_nd_x$	$_nL_x$	$_nm_x$	$_na_x$	T_x	$\overset{\circ}{e}_x$	x
0	0.021030	0.020642	100000	2064	98154	0.021030	0.106	6888976	68.890	0
1	0.000798	0.003187	97936	312	390963	0.000798	1.500	6790822	69.340	1
5	0.000395	0.001973	97624	193	487637	0.000395	2.500	6399859	65.556	5
10	0.000355	0.001782	97431	174	486773	0.000357	2.799	5912223	60.681	10
15	0.000910	0.004541	97257	442	485244	0.000910	2.639	5425450	55.784	15
20	0.000969	0.004835	96816	468	482907	0.000969	2.497	4940206	51.027	20
25	0.000905	0.004516	96348	435	480665	0.000905	2.532	4457299	46.263	25
30	0.001116	0.005573	95913	535	478295	0.001118	2.628	3976634	41.461	30
35	0.001607	0.008010	95378	764	475161	0.001608	2.737	3498339	36.679	35
40	0.002985	0.014827	94614	1403	469920	0.002985	2.754	3023177	31.953	40
45	0.005374	0.026559	93211	2476	460426	0.005377	2.726	2553257	27.392	45
50	0.009189	0.044999	90736	4083	444333	0.009189	2.711	2092832	23.065	50
55	0.015836	0.076375	86653	6618	417927	0.015836	2.683	1648498	19.024	55
60	0.026225	0.123539	80034	9887	376955	0.026230	2.652	1230572	15.376	60
65	0.043379	0.197074	70147	13824	317525	0.043537	2.598	853616	12.169	65
70	0.067525	0.290584	56323	16367	241141	0.067871	2.527	536092	9.518	70
75	0.100061	0.399173	39956	15949	159015	0.100302	2.444	294951	7.382	75
80	0.136593	0.503168	24007	12079	88434	0.136593	2.384	135936	5.662	80
85	0.251096	1.000000	11927	11927	47501	0.194163	3.983	47501	3.983	85

TABLE 3 — FEMALE LIFE TABLE

x	$_nM_x$	$_nq_x$	l_x	$_nd_x$	$_nL_x$	$_nm_x$	$_na_x$	T_x	$\overset{\circ}{e}_x$	x
0	0.016076	0.015846	100000	1585	98570	0.016076	0.097	7520243	75.202	0
1	0.000634	0.002531	98415	249	393039	0.000634	1.500	7421673	75.412	1
5	0.000271	0.001354	98166	133	490499	0.000271	2.500	7028634	71.599	5
10	0.000235	0.001176	98033	115	489887	0.000235	2.569	6538135	66.693	10
15	0.000349	0.001746	97918	171	489186	0.000349	2.630	6048248	61.768	15
20	0.000455	0.002272	97747	222	488197	0.000455	2.575	5559063	56.872	20
25	0.000514	0.002570	97525	251	487024	0.000515	2.600	5070866	51.996	25
30	0.000703	0.003521	97274	343	485581	0.000705	2.690	4583842	47.123	30
35	0.001166	0.005812	96932	563	483388	0.001166	2.743	4098261	42.280	35
40	0.002086	0.010379	96368	1000	479570	0.002086	2.728	3614874	37.511	40
45	0.003506	0.017391	95368	1659	472993	0.003506	2.680	3135304	32.876	45
50	0.005251	0.025935	93710	2430	462871	0.005251	2.664	2662311	28.410	50
55	0.007966	0.039104	91279	3569	448085	0.007966	2.671	2199440	24.096	55
60	0.012593	0.061184	87710	5366	426105	0.012594	2.681	1751355	19.968	60
65	0.020935	0.099980	82343	8233	392567	0.020972	2.674	1325251	16.094	65
70	0.035709	0.165151	74111	12239	341652	0.035824	2.639	932683	12.585	70
75	0.060542	0.264730	61871	16379	269570	0.060760	2.571	591031	9.553	75
80	0.097175	0.391637	45492	17816	183344	0.097175	2.524	321461	7.066	80
85	0.200379	1.000000	27676	27676	138117	0.133355	4.991	138117	4.991	85

TABLE 4 — OBSERVED VITAL RATES AND RATIOS

CRUDE RATES

Per Thousand	BOTH SEXES	MALES	FEMALES
BIRTH RATE	16.05	16.99	15.15
DEATH RATE	11.76	12.35	11.22
RATE OF INCREASE	4.28	4.65	3.93

PERCENT OF POPULATION IN AGE GROUP

	BOTH SEXES	MALES	FEMALES
UNDER 15	23.71	25.00	22.50
15 - 64	63.09	64.60	61.67
65 AND OLDER	13.20	10.41	15.83

RATES STANDARDIZED ON USA 1980

Per Thousand	BOTH SEXES	MALES	FEMALES
BIRTH RATE	20.69		19.55
DEATH RATE	10.72	11.48	10.00
RATE OF INCREASE	9.97		9.54

RATES STANDARDIZED ON MEXICO 1980

	BOTH SEXES	MALES	FEMALES
BIRTH RATE	18.71		18.32
DEATH RATE	4.20	4.98	3.41
RATE OF INCREASE	14.51		14.91

VITAL STATISTICS

GFR x 1000	71.427
TFR	2.410
GRR	1.171
NRR	1.140
μ	26.679
σ^2	33.409
GENERATION	26.597
POP. SEX RATIO	1.060
SEX RATIO AT BIRTH	1.058
DEP. RATIO x 100	58.505

PROJECTED POPULATION

AGE GROUP	1975 BOTH SEXES	1975 MALES	1975 FEMALES	1980 BOTH SEXES	1980 MALES	1980 FEMALES
0-4	3905	2003	1902	4006	2055	1951
5-9	3998	2034	1964	3895	1997	1898
10-14	4045	2062	1983	3992	2030	1962
15-19	3526	1822	1704	4035	2055	1980
20-24	3324	1696	1628	3514	1814	1700
25-29	3747	1885	1862	3312	1688	1624
30-34	3123	1578	1545	3732	1876	1856
35-39	2897	1473	1424	3106	1568	1538
40-44	2795	1413	1382	2869	1457	1412
45-49	2913	1451	1462	2748	1385	1363
50-54	3131	1535	1596	2831	1400	1431
55-59	2687	1291	1396	2989	1444	1545
60-64	2814	1318	1496	2492	1164	1328
65-69	2516	1123	1393	2488	1110	1378
70-74	1965	800	1165	2066	853	1213
75-79	1287	443	844	1447	528	919
80-84	755	229	526	820	246	574
85+	505	124	381	519	123	396
TOTAL	49933	24280	25653	50861	24793	26068

STABLE EQUIVALENT TO ORIGINAL POPULATION

MALES Number	MALES Percent	FEMALES Number	FEMALES Percent	AGE GROUP	
2002	8.4	1901	7.8	0-4	
1947	8.1	1851	7.6	5-9	TABLE 5
1896	7.9	1803	7.4	10-14	
1844	7.7	1757	7.2	15-19	POPULATION
1791	7.5	1710	7.0	20-24	PROJECTED
1739	7.3	1665	6.8	25-29	WITH
1688	7.0	1619	6.6	30-34	FIXED
1636	6.8	1572	6.4	35-39	AGE-
1578	6.6	1522	6.2	40-44	SPECIFIC
1509	6.3	1464	6.0	45-49	BIRTH
1421	5.9	1398	5.7	50-54	AND
1304	5.4	1320	5.4	55-59	DEATH
1147	4.8	1225	5.0	60-64	RATES
943	3.9	1101	4.5	65-69	(female
698	2.9	935	3.8	70-74	dominant,
449	1.9	720	3.0	75-79	in 000s)
244	1.0	478	2.0	80-84	
128	0.5	351	1.4	85+	
23964		24392		TOTAL	

VITAL RATES OF PROJECTED POPULATION

Per Thousand	1975 BOTH SEXES	1975 MALES	1975 FEMALES	1980 BOTH SEXES	1980 MALES	1980 FEMALES
BIRTH RATE	16.19	17.12	15.31	16.24	17.13	15.39
DEATH RATE	12.40	12.79	12.02	12.63	12.99	12.30
RATE OF INCREASE	3.79	4.33	3.29	3.60	4.14	3.09

AGE STRUCTURE OF PROJECTED POPULATION

	1975 BOTH SEXES	1975 MALES	1975 FEMALES	1980 BOTH SEXES	1980 MALES	1980 FEMALES
% UNDER 15	23.93	25.12	22.80	23.38	24.53	22.29
% 15-64	62.00	63.69	60.40	62.18	63.93	60.52
% 65 AND OLDER	14.07	11.20	16.80	14.43	11.54	17.19
DEPEND. RATIO x 100	61.30	57.02	65.56	60.81	56.42	65.23

VITAL RATES OF STABLE POPULATION

Per Thousand	MALES	FEMALES	
BIRTH RATE	17.29	16.05	TABLE 6
DEATH RATE	12.32	11.11	PROJECTED
RATE OF INCREASE		4.94	VITAL RATES

STABLE AGE STRUCTURE

			AND RATIOS
% UNDER 15	24.39	22.77	(female
% 15-64	65.33	62.53	dominant)
% 65 AND OLDER	10.27	14.69	
DEPEND. RATIO x 100	53.06	59.91	

AGE GROUP	FEMALE BIRTH RATES	NET MATERNITY FUNCTION	COEFF. OF MATRIX EQUATION	ORIGINAL MATRIX SUB-DIAGONAL	ORIGINAL MATRIX FIRST ROW	STABLE MATRIX FISHER VALUES	STABLE MATRIX REPRODUCTIVE VALUES
0-4	0.0000	0.0000	0.0000	0.99774	0.00000	1.030	2026842
5-9	0.0000	0.0000	0.0000	0.99875	0.00000	1.058	2100318
10-14	0.0000	0.0000	0.0590	0.99857	0.05920	1.086	1852101
15-19	0.0241	0.1180	0.2428	0.99798	0.24399	1.053	1717995
20-24	0.0753	0.3676	0.3657	0.99760	0.36822	0.830	1549006
25-29	0.0747	0.3637	0.2760	0.99704	0.27856	0.473	732749
30-34	0.0388	0.1882	0.1348	0.99548	0.13652	0.198	283792
35-39	0.0169	0.0815	0.0508	0.99210	0.05163	0.063	87896
40-44	0.0042	0.0200	0.0107	0.98629	0.01093	0.012	17233
45-49	0.0003	0.0013	0.0006	0.97860	0.00067	0.001	1090
50-54	0.0000	0.0000	0.0000	0.00000	0.00000	0.000	0

MATRIX PARAMETERS

λ_1	1.02501	
λ_2	$0.33345+0.75523i$	TABLE 7
λ_4	$-0.37485+0.40073i$	
λ_6	$-0.02828+0.45583i$	LESLIE
r_1	0.00494	MATRIX
r_2	$-0.03834+0.23100i$	AND ITS
r_4	$-0.12003+0.46457i$	ANALYSIS
r_6	$-0.15674+0.32655i$	(females)
c_1	243921	
$2\pi/y$	27.1995	
Δ	4.4619	

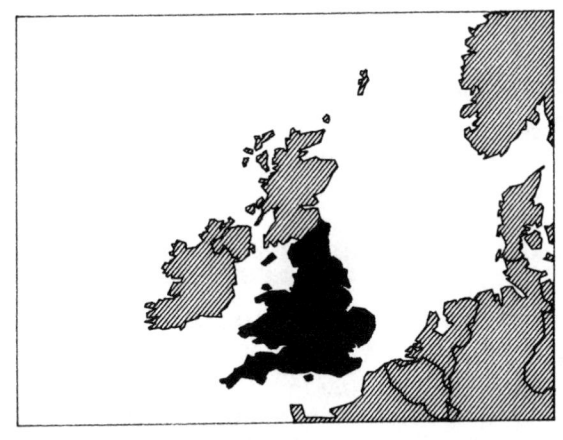

TABLE 1 — DATA

AGE AT LAST BIRTHDAY	ESTIMATED MID-YEAR POPULATION — BOTH SEXES	MALES Number	MALES Percent	FEMALES Number	FEMALES Percent	BIRTHS BY AGE OF MOTHER AND SEX	DEATHS BOTH SEXES	DEATHS MALES	DEATHS FEMALES	AGE AT LAST BIRTHDAY
0	649000	332500	1.4	316500	1.2		6141	3510	2631	0
1-4	2501600	1282200	5.3	1219400	4.8		1135	638	497	1-4
5-9	2959700	1520700	6.3	1439000	5.6		588	328	260	5-9
10-14	3388500	1741200	7.2	1647300	6.4		811	503	308	10-14
15-19	3964600	2032600	8.4	1932000	7.5	56929	1918	1374	544	15-19
20-24	4164400	2112100	8.7	2052300	8.0	193958	2368	1738	630	20-24
25-29	3601200	1818800	7.5	1782400	7.0	227486	2054	1405	649	25-29
30-34	3328900	1678300	6.9	1650600	6.4	126185	2482	1548	934	30-34
35-39	3689500	1847500	7.6	1842000	7.2	44393	4046	2418	1628	35-39
40-44	3034900	1529700	6.3	1505200	5.9	6882	5533	3358	2175	40-44
45-49	2802200	1408300	5.8	1393900	5.4	584	8896	5432	3464	45-49
50-54	2682400	1341000	5.5	1341400	5.2		15053	9406	5647	50-54
55-59	2724100	1338100	5.5	1386000	5.4		26693	16688	10005	55-59
60-64	2798800	1333800	5.5	1465000	5.7		46675	29016	17659	60-64
65-69	2258000	1026600	4.2	1231400	4.8		57632	35148	22484	65-69
70-74	2137900	907900	3.7	1230000	4.8		87348	50547	36801	70-74
75-79	1629900	619400	2.5	1010500	3.9		104655	54444	50211	75-79
80-84	993000	316300	1.3	676700	2.6	336835 M	100806	42918	57888	80-84
85+	614900	143000	0.6	471900	1.8	319582 F	115900	31908	83992	85+
TOTAL	49923500	24330000		25593500		656417	590734	292327	298407	TOTAL

TABLE 2 — MALE LIFE TABLE

x	nM_x	nq_x	l_x	nd_x	nL_x	nm_x	na_x	T_x	$\overset{\circ}{e}_x$	x
0	0.010556	0.010456	100000	1046	99046	0.010556	0.088	7185606	71.856	0
1	0.000498	0.001988	98954	197	395326	0.000498	1.500	7086559	71.614	1
5	0.000216	0.001078	98758	106	493522	0.000216	2.500	6691233	67.754	5
10	0.000289	0.001444	98651	142	492947	0.000289	2.830	6197711	62.824	10
15	0.000676	0.003375	98509	332	491768	0.000676	2.663	5704763	57.911	15
20	0.000823	0.004107	98176	403	489884	0.000823	2.523	5212996	53.098	20
25	0.000772	0.003856	97773	377	487933	0.000773	2.525	4723112	48.307	25
30	0.000922	0.004603	97396	448	485914	0.000923	2.619	4235179	43.484	30
35	0.001309	0.006528	96948	633	483285	0.001309	2.701	3749265	38.673	35
40	0.002195	0.010983	96315	1058	479180	0.002208	2.735	3265980	33.909	40
45	0.003857	0.019193	95257	1828	472168	0.003872	2.747	2786800	29.256	45
50	0.007014	0.034535	93429	3227	459837	0.007017	2.735	2314633	24.774	50
55	0.012471	0.060627	90202	5469	438497	0.012471	2.711	1854796	20.563	55
60	0.021754	0.103568	84734	8776	403097	0.021771	2.656	1416299	16.715	60
65	0.034237	0.158388	75958	12031	351151	0.034261	2.619	1013202	13.339	65
70	0.055675	0.245221	63927	15676	281570	0.055675	2.572	662051	10.356	70
75	0.087898	0.361211	48251	17429	197642	0.088184	2.498	380481	7.885	75
80	0.135688	0.502196	30822	15479	114076	0.135688	2.414	182840	5.932	80
85	0.223133	1.000000	15343	15343	68763	0.160093	4.482	68763	4.482	85

TABLE 3 — FEMALE LIFE TABLE

x	nM_x	nq_x	l_x	nd_x	nL_x	nm_x	na_x	T_x	$\overset{\circ}{e}_x$	x
0	0.008313	0.008250	100000	825	99244	0.008313	0.084	7761068	77.611	0
1	0.000408	0.001629	99175	162	396296	0.000408	1.500	7661824	77.256	1
5	0.000181	0.000903	99013	89	494844	0.000181	2.500	7265528	73.379	5
10	0.000187	0.000934	98924	92	494400	0.000187	2.612	6770684	68.443	10
15	0.000282	0.001407	98832	139	493823	0.000282	2.588	6276284	63.505	15
20	0.000307	0.001534	98693	151	493093	0.000307	2.556	5782461	58.591	20
25	0.000364	0.001824	98541	180	492283	0.000365	2.647	5289368	53.677	25
30	0.000566	0.002826	98361	278	491165	0.000566	2.690	4797085	48.770	30
35	0.000884	0.004412	98083	433	489425	0.000884	2.707	4305920	43.901	35
40	0.001445	0.007242	97651	707	486646	0.001453	2.727	3816495	39.083	40
45	0.002485	0.012399	96944	1202	481981	0.002494	2.723	3329849	34.348	45
50	0.004210	0.020849	95741	1996	474160	0.004210	2.722	2847868	29.745	50
55	0.007219	0.035505	93745	3328	461094	0.007219	2.707	2373708	25.321	55
60	0.012054	0.058618	90417	5300	439693	0.012054	2.662	1912614	21.153	60
65	0.018259	0.087546	85117	7452	408112	0.018259	2.655	1472921	17.305	65
70	0.029920	0.139740	77665	10853	362736	0.029920	2.642	1064809	13.710	70
75	0.049689	0.222348	66812	14856	298493	0.049769	2.606	702073	10.508	75
80	0.085545	0.353989	51957	18392	215000	0.085545	2.565	403579	7.768	80
85	0.177987	1.000000	33565	33565	188579	0.109246	5.618	188579	5.618	85

TABLE 4 — OBSERVED VITAL RATES AND RATIOS

CRUDE RATES

Per Thousand	BOTH SEXES	MALES	FEMALES
BIRTH RATE	13.15	13.84	12.49
DEATH RATE	11.83	12.02	11.66
RATE OF INCREASE	1.32	1.83	0.83

PERCENT OF POPULATION IN AGE GROUP

	BOTH SEXES	MALES	FEMALES
UNDER 15	19.03	20.04	18.06
15 - 64	65.68	67.57	63.89
65 AND OLDER	15.29	12.38	18.05

RATES STANDARDIZED ON USA 1980

Per Thousand	BOTH SEXES	MALES	FEMALES
BIRTH RATE	15.21		14.40
DEATH RATE	9.05	9.59	8.53
RATE OF INCREASE	6.17		5.87

RATES STANDARDIZED ON MEXICO 1980

Per Thousand	BOTH SEXES	MALES	FEMALES
BIRTH RATE	13.47		13.22
DEATH RATE	3.32	3.92	2.71
RATE OF INCREASE	10.15		10.51

VITAL STATISTICS

GFR x 1000	53.989
TFR	1.786
GRR	0.869
NRR	0.856
μ	27.299
σ^2	30.228
GENERATION	27.384
POP. SEX RATIO	1.052
SEX RATIO AT BIRTH	1.054
DEP. RATIO x 100	52.248

PROJECTED POPULATION

AGE GROUP	1990 BOTH SEXES	1990 MALES	1990 FEMALES	1995 BOTH SEXES	1995 MALES	1995 FEMALES
0-4	3299	1691	1608	3285	1684	1601
5-9	3146	1612	1534	3294	1688	1606
10-14	2957	1519	1438	3142	1610	1532
15-19	3382	1737	1645	2951	1515	1436
20-24	3954	2025	1929	3373	1730	1643
25-29	4153	2104	2049	3943	2017	1926
30-34	3589	1811	1778	4139	2095	2044
35-39	3314	1669	1645	3573	1801	1772
40-44	3664	1832	1832	3290	1655	1635
45-49	2998	1507	1491	3619	1805	1814
50-54	2743	1372	1371	2935	1468	1467
55-59	2583	1279	1304	2641	1308	1333
60-64	2552	1230	1322	2420	1176	1244
65-69	2522	1162	1360	2299	1072	1227
70-74	1917	823	1094	2141	932	1209
75-79	1649	637	1012	1479	578	901
80-84	1086	358	728	1097	368	729
85+	785	191	594	854	216	638
TOTAL	50293	24559	25734	50475	24718	25757

STABLE EQUIVALENT TO ORIGINAL POPULATION

MALES Number	MALES Percent	FEMALES Number	FEMALES Percent	AGE GROUP	
1681	5.6	1599	5.1	0-4	
1727	5.7	1643	5.2	5-9	TABLE 5
1774	5.9	1689	5.4	10-14	
1821	6.1	1735	5.5	15-19	POPULATION
1867	6.2	1783	5.7	20-24	PROJECTED
1913	6.4	1831	5.8	25-29	WITH
1960	6.5	1880	6.0	30-34	FIXED
2006	6.7	1927	6.2	35-39	AGE-
2046	6.8	1971	6.3	40-44	SPECIFIC
2074	6.9	2009	6.4	45-49	BIRTH
2078	6.9	2033	6.5	50-54	AND
2039	6.8	2034	6.5	55-59	DEATH
1928	6.4	1996	6.4	60-64	RATES
1728	5.7	1906	6.1	65-69	(female
1426	4.7	1743	5.6	70-74	dominant,
1030	3.4	1476	4.7	75-79	in 000s)
611	2.0	1093	3.5	80-84	
379	1.3	987	3.1	85+	
30088		31335		TOTAL	

VITAL RATES OF PROJECTED POPULATION

Per Thousand	1990 BOTH SEXES	1990 MALES	1990 FEMALES	1995 BOTH SEXES	1995 MALES	1995 FEMALES
BIRTH RATE	13.46	14.14	12.81	12.89	13.51	12.30
DEATH RATE	12.52	12.55	12.49	12.65	12.69	12.62
RATE OF INCREASE	0.94	1.59	0.32	0.24	0.82	-0.33

VITAL RATES OF STABLE POPULATION

Per Thousand	MALES	FEMALES	
BIRTH RATE	11.14	10.15	TABLE 6
DEATH RATE	16.78	15.84	PROJECTED
RATE OF INCREASE		-5.69	VITAL

AGE STRUCTURE OF PROJECTED POPULATION

	1990 BOTH SEXES	1990 MALES	1990 FEMALES	1995 BOTH SEXES	1995 MALES	1995 FEMALES
% UNDER 15	18.69	19.64	17.80	19.26	20.16	18.40
% 15-64	65.48	67.45	63.60	65.15	67.04	63.34
% 65 AND OLDER	15.82	12.91	18.61	15.59	12.80	18.26
DEPEND. RATIO x 100	52.72	48.25	57.24	53.49	49.16	57.88

STABLE AGE STRUCTURE

	MALES	FEMALES	
% UNDER 15	17.22	15.73	RATES
% 15-64	65.58	61.27	AND
% 65 AND OLDER	17.20	22.99	RATIOS
DEPEND. RATIO x 100	52.49	63.20	(female dominant)

AGE GROUP	FEMALE BIRTH RATES	NET MATERNITY FUNCTION	COEFF. OF MATRIX EQUATION	ORIGINAL MATRIX SUB-DIAGONAL	ORIGINAL MATRIX FIRST ROW	STABLE MATRIX FISHER VALUES	STABLE MATRIX REPRODUCTIVE VALUES	MATRIX PARAMETERS	
0-4	0.0000	0.0000	0.0000	0.99859	0.00000	0.995	1527820	λ_1	0.97196
5-9	0.0000	0.0000	0.0000	0.99910	0.00000	0.968	1393250	λ_2	0.36877+0.73356i
10-14	0.0000	0.0000	0.0354	0.99883	0.03550	0.942	1551598	λ_4	-0.24513-0.49224i
15-19	0.0143	0.0708	0.1489	0.99852	0.14938	0.881	1702484	λ_6	-0.36671-0.11725i
20-24	0.0460	0.2269	0.2664	0.99836	0.26771	0.709	1454971	r_1	-0.00569
25-29	0.0621	0.3059	0.2443	0.99773	0.24597	0.423	754780	r_2	-0.03944+0.22100i
30-34	0.0372	0.1828	0.1201	0.99646	0.12119	0.167	276138	r_4	-0.11960-0.40657i
35-39	0.0117	0.0574	0.0341	0.99432	0.03456	0.042	77739	r_6	-0.19091-0.56643i
40-44	0.0022	0.0108	0.0059	0.99041	0.00602	0.007	10061	c_1	313332
45-49	0.0002	0.0010	0.0005	0.98377	0.00051	0.001	721	$2\pi/y$	28.4310
50-54	0.0000	0.0000	0.0000	0.00000	0.00000	0.000	0	Δ	9.2841

Right margin labels for matrix section: TABLE 7 / LESLIE MATRIX AND ITS ANALYSIS (females)

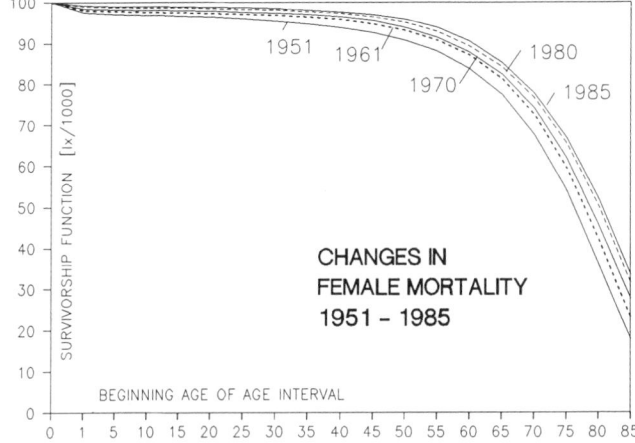

CHANGES IN FEMALE MORTALITY 1951 - 1985

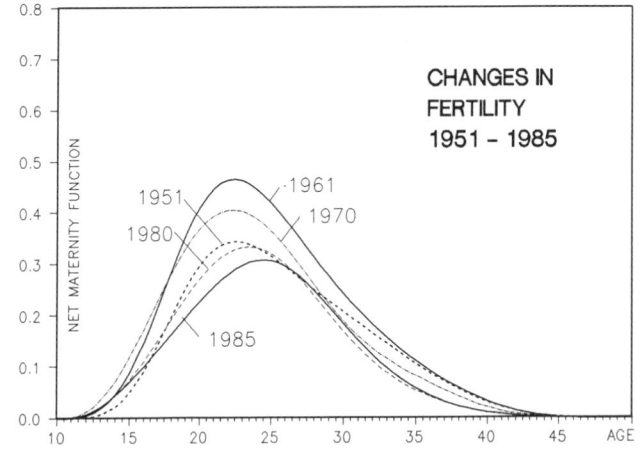

CHANGES IN FERTILITY 1951 - 1985

TABLE 1 — DATA

AGE AT LAST BIRTHDAY	ESTIMATED MID-YEAR POPULATION BOTH SEXES	MALES Number	MALES Percent	FEMALES Number	FEMALES Percent	BIRTHS BY AGE OF MOTHER AND SEX	DEATHS BOTH SEXES	DEATHS MALES	DEATHS FEMALES	AGE AT LAST BIRTHDAY
0	31300	16100	2.2	15200	2.0		734	434	300	0
1-4	128700	66300	8.9	62400	8.0		96	55	41	1-4
5-9	156900	80900	10.9	76000	9.8		65	37	28	5-9
10-14	140600	72000	9.7	68600	8.8		50	34	16	10-14
15-19	127400	65300	8.8	62100	8.0	2410	55	40	15	15-19
20-24	114000	57100	7.7	56900	7.3	10285	79	63	16	20-24
25-29	94000	46300	6.2	47700	6.1	8478	79	50	29	25-29
30-34	85100	42000	5.6	43100	5.5	6235	86	43	43	30-34
35-39	82100	40300	5.4	41800	5.4	3461	138	84	54	35-39
40-44	84200	40700	5.5	43500	5.6	1149	244	144	100	40-44
45-49	86900	42100	5.7	44800	5.8	68	437	264	173	45-49
50-54	79100	38300	5.1	40800	5.2		627	369	258	50-54
55-59	79500	37900	5.1	41600	5.3		1057	668	389	55-59
60-64	71200	33000	4.4	38200	4.9		1545	967	578	60-64
65-69	59500	26000	3.5	33500	4.3		2037	1219	818	65-69
70-74	46700	19200	2.6	27500	3.5		2528	1346	1182	70-74
75-79	29800	11700	1.6	18100	2.3		2420	1160	1260	75-79
80-84	17500	6500	0.9	11000	1.4	16539 M	2095	945	1150	80-84
85+	9600	3400	0.5	6200	0.8	15547 F	2179	842	1337	85+
TOTAL	1524100	745100		779000		32086	16551	8764	7787	TOTAL

TABLE 2 — MALE LIFE TABLE

x	$_nM_x$	$_nq_x$	l_x	$_nd_x$	$_nL_x$	$_nm_x$	$_na_x$	T_x	$\overset{\circ}{e}_x$	x
0	0.026957	0.026329	100000	2633	97672	0.026957	0.116	6770181	67.702	0
1	0.000830	0.003311	97367	322	388662	0.000830	1.500	6672509	68.529	1
5	0.000457	0.002284	97045	222	484669	0.000457	2.500	6283846	64.752	5
10	0.000472	0.002361	96823	229	483559	0.000473	2.568	5799177	59.895	10
15	0.000613	0.003069	96594	296	482294	0.000615	2.713	5315618	55.030	15
20	0.001103	0.005519	96298	531	480207	0.001107	2.586	4833324	50.191	20
25	0.001080	0.005381	95767	515	477535	0.001079	2.482	4353117	45.456	25
30	0.001024	0.005124	95251	488	475134	0.001027	2.700	3875582	40.688	30
35	0.002084	0.010389	94763	984	471596	0.002088	2.745	3400448	35.884	35
40	0.003538	0.017550	93779	1646	465167	0.003538	2.736	2928852	31.232	40
45	0.006271	0.030906	92133	2847	454080	0.006271	2.687	2463684	26.741	45
50	0.009634	0.047135	89286	4208	436814	0.009634	2.716	2009604	22.508	50
55	0.017625	0.084675	85077	7204	408724	0.017625	2.687	1572790	18.487	55
60	0.029303	0.137170	77873	10682	364109	0.029337	2.636	1164066	14.948	60
65	0.046885	0.210691	67191	14157	301640	0.046932	2.576	799957	11.906	65
70	0.070104	0.298743	53035	15844	225682	0.070204	2.507	498317	9.396	70
75	0.099145	0.395916	37191	14724	148308	0.099283	2.443	272634	7.331	75
80	0.145385	0.526659	22466	11832	81385	0.145385	2.385	124327	5.534	80
85	0.247647	1.000000	10634	10634	42941	0.190141	4.038	42941	4.038	85

TABLE 3 — FEMALE LIFE TABLE

x	$_nM_x$	$_nq_x$	l_x	$_nd_x$	$_nL_x$	$_nm_x$	$_na_x$	T_x	$\overset{\circ}{e}_x$	x
0	0.019737	0.019394	100000	1939	98261	0.019737	0.104	7353519	73.535	0
1	0.000657	0.002624	98061	257	391599	0.000657	1.500	7255257	73.987	1
5	0.000368	0.001840	97803	180	488567	0.000368	2.500	6863658	70.178	5
10	0.000233	0.001163	97623	114	487820	0.000233	2.386	6375091	65.303	10
15	0.000242	0.001208	97510	118	487260	0.000242	2.542	5887271	60.376	15
20	0.000281	0.001413	97392	138	486654	0.000283	2.771	5400012	55.446	20
25	0.000608	0.003056	97254	297	485601	0.000612	2.743	4913358	50.521	25
30	0.000998	0.004990	96957	484	483644	0.001000	2.640	4427757	45.667	30
35	0.001292	0.006443	96473	622	480941	0.001292	2.705	3944112	40.883	35
40	0.002299	0.011434	95852	1096	476768	0.002299	2.727	3463172	36.130	40
45	0.003862	0.019147	94756	1814	469619	0.003863	2.707	2986404	31.517	45
50	0.006324	0.031166	92942	2897	457947	0.006325	2.666	2516785	27.079	50
55	0.009351	0.045758	90045	4120	440630	0.009351	2.671	2058838	22.865	55
60	0.015131	0.073146	85925	6285	414971	0.015146	2.669	1618208	18.833	60
65	0.024418	0.115633	79640	9209	376734	0.024444	2.669	1203238	15.109	65
70	0.042982	0.195433	70431	13764	319345	0.043102	2.616	826504	11.735	70
75	0.069613	0.298333	56666	16905	241630	0.069964	2.533	507158	8.950	75
80	0.104545	0.414144	39761	16467	157508	0.104545	2.492	265528	6.678	80
85	0.215645	1.000000	23294	23294	108020	0.150747	4.637	108020	4.637	85

TABLE 4 — OBSERVED VITAL RATES AND RATIOS

CRUDE RATES

Per Thousand	BOTH SEXES	MALES	FEMALES
BIRTH RATE	21.05	22.20	19.96
DEATH RATE	10.86	11.76	10.00
RATE OF INCREASE	10.19	10.43	9.96

RATES STANDARDIZED ON USA 1980

Per Thousand	BOTH SEXES	MALES	FEMALES
BIRTH RATE	26.99		25.43
DEATH RATE	11.72	12.17	11.30
RATE OF INCREASE	15.27		14.13

PERCENT OF POPULATION IN AGE GROUP

	BOTH SEXES	MALES	FEMALES
UNDER 15	30.02	31.58	28.52
15 - 64	59.28	59.46	59.11
65 AND OLDER	10.70	8.97	12.36

RATES STANDARDIZED ON MEXICO 1980

	BOTH SEXES	MALES	FEMALES
BIRTH RATE	23.61		23.06
DEATH RATE	4.67	5.42	3.90
RATE OF INCREASE	18.94		19.16

VITAL STATISTICS

GFR x 1000	94.398
TFR	3.263
GRR	1.581
NRR	1.532
μ	28.519
σ^2	39.875
GENERATION	28.217
POP. SEX RATIO	1.045
SEX RATIO AT BIRTH	1.064
DEP. RATIO x 100	68.688

PROJECTED POPULATION

AGE GROUP	1975 BOTH SEXES	1975 MALES	1975 FEMALES	1980 BOTH SEXES	1980 MALES	1980 FEMALES
0-4	165	85	80	183	94	89
5-9	159	82	77	164	84	80
10-14	157	81	76	159	82	77
15-19	141	72	69	157	81	76
20-24	127	65	62	140	72	68
25-29	114	57	57	127	65	62
30-34	94	46	48	113	56	57
35-39	85	42	43	93	46	47
40-44	81	40	41	83	41	42
45-49	83	40	43	80	39	41
50-54	85	41	44	80	38	42
55-59	75	36	39	80	38	42
60-64	73	34	39	69	32	37
65-69	62	27	35	64	28	36
70-74	47	19	28	49	20	29
75-79	34	13	21	34	13	21
80-84	18	6	12	21	7	14
85+	11	3	8	11	3	8
TOTAL	1611	789	822	1707	839	868

STABLE EQUIVALENT TO ORIGINAL POPULATION

MALES Number	MALES Percent	FEMALES Number	FEMALES Percent	AGE GROUP	
82	11.4	78	10.9	0-4	
76	10.5	72	10.0	5-9	TABLE 5
70	9.7	67	9.3	10-14	
65	9.0	62	8.6	15-19	POPULATION
60	8.3	57	8.0	20-24	PROJECTED
55	7.6	53	7.4	25-29	WITH
51	7.0	49	6.8	30-34	FIXED
47	6.5	45	6.3	35-39	AGE-
43	5.9	41	5.8	40-44	SPECIFIC
39	5.4	38	5.3	45-49	BIRTH
35	4.8	34	4.8	50-54	AND
30	4.1	30	4.2	55-59	DEATH
25	3.4	27	3.7	60-64	RATES
19	2.6	22	3.1	65-69	(female
13	1.8	18	2.5	70-74	dominant,
8	1.1	12	1.7	75-79	in 000s)
4	0.6	7	1.0	80-84	
2	0.3	5	0.7	85+	
724		717		TOTAL	

VITAL RATES OF PROJECTED POPULATION

Per Thousand	1975 BOTH SEXES	1975 MALES	1975 FEMALES	1980 BOTH SEXES	1980 MALES	1980 FEMALES
BIRTH RATE	22.09	23.26	20.98	23.18	24.32	22.08
DEATH RATE	10.82	11.39	10.29	10.60	10.97	10.24
RATE OF INCREASE	11.27	11.87	10.69	12.58	13.35	11.84

AGE STRUCTURE OF PROJECTED POPULATION

	1975 BOTH SEXES	1975 MALES	1975 FEMALES	1980 BOTH SEXES	1980 MALES	1980 FEMALES
% UNDER 15	29.91	31.43	28.45	29.70	31.06	28.38
% 15-64	59.37	59.78	58.97	59.78	60.41	59.18
% 65 AND OLDER	10.72	8.79	12.58	10.52	8.52	12.45
DEPEND. RATIO x 100	68.44	67.28	69.57	67.27	65.52	68.99

VITAL RATES OF STABLE POPULATION

Per Thousand	MALES	FEMALES	
BIRTH RATE	24.23	23.02	TABLE 6
DEATH RATE	9.07	7.87	PROJECTED
RATE OF INCREASE		15.15	VITAL RATES AND RATIOS

STABLE AGE STRUCTURE

	MALES	FEMALES	
% UNDER 15	31.55	30.21	(female dominant)
% 15-64	62.04	60.80	
% 65 AND OLDER	6.41	8.99	
DEPEND. RATIO x 100	61.18	64.48	

AGE GROUP	FEMALE BIRTH RATES	NET MATERNITY FUNCTION	COEFF. OF MATRIX EQUATION	ORIGINAL MATRIX SUB-DIAGONAL	ORIGINAL MATRIX FIRST ROW	STABLE MATRIX FISHER VALUES	STABLE MATRIX REPRODUCTIVE VALUES	MATRIX PARAMETERS	
0-4	0.0000	0.0000	0.0000	0.99736	0.00000	1.060	82253	λ_1	1.07871
5-9	0.0000	0.0000	0.0000	0.99847	0.00000	1.146	87127	λ_2	$0.40998+0.76333i$
10-14	0.0000	0.0000	0.0458	0.99885	0.04600	1.239	84964	λ_4	$-0.03727+0.61795i$
15-19	0.0188	0.0916	0.2589	0.99876	0.26031	1.289	80031	λ_6	$-0.40010+0.38305i$
20-24	0.0876	0.4262	0.4222	0.99784	0.42500	1.116	63480	r_1	0.01515
25-29	0.0861	0.4182	0.3786	0.99597	0.38193	0.755	35994	r_2	$-0.02867+0.21558i$
30-34	0.0701	0.3390	0.2660	0.99441	0.26940	0.411	17706	r_4	$-0.09591+0.32621i$
35-39	0.0401	0.1930	0.1270	0.99132	0.12934	0.158	6625	r_6	$-0.11815+0.47559i$
40-44	0.0128	0.0610	0.0322	0.98501	0.03312	0.034	1486	c_1	7172
45-49	0.0007	0.0035	0.0017	0.97515	0.00180	0.002	79	$2\pi/y$	29.1452
50-54	0.0000	0.0000	0.0000	0.00000	0.00000	0.000	0	Δ	6.6163

TABLE 7

LESLIE MATRIX AND ITS ANALYSIS (females)

TABLE 1 — DATA

AGE AT LAST BIRTHDAY	ESTIMATED MID-YEAR POPULATION BOTH SEXES	MALES Number	Percent	FEMALES Number	Percent	BIRTHS BY AGE OF MOTHER AND SEX	DEATHS BOTH SEXES	MALES	FEMALES	AGE AT LAST BIRTHDAY
0	27600	14300	1.9	13300	1.7		265	151	114	0
1-4	107200	54700	7.2	52500	6.6		55	33	22	1-4
5-9	128000	65300	8.6	62700	7.9		33	16	17	5-9
10-14	135800	70000	9.2	65800	8.3		35	22	13	10-14
15-19	143500	74500	9.8	69000	8.7	1978	83	64	19	15-19
20-24	135300	70900	9.3	64400	8.1	7847	108	85	23	20-24
25-29	113900	57400	7.5	56500	7.1	9195	88	58	30	25-29
30-34	98000	48900	6.4	49100	6.2	5600	83	51	32	30-34
35-39	96800	48400	6.3	48400	6.1	2505	117	70	47	35-39
40-44	89200	44200	5.8	45000	5.7	490	189	123	66	40-44
45-49	78900	38900	5.1	40000	5.0	20	294	178	116	45-49
50-54	74000	35700	4.7	38300	4.8		516	341	175	50-54
55-59	72400	34200	4.5	38200	4.8		812	506	306	55-59
60-64	70500	32600	4.3	37900	4.8		1283	806	477	60-64
65-69	59000	26000	3.4	33000	4.2		1756	1078	678	65-69
70-74	53600	22300	2.9	31300	3.9		2439	1346	1093	70-74
75-79	38900	14600	1.9	24300	3.1		2667	1320	1347	75-79
80-84	21800	7000	0.9	14800	1.9	14184 M	2385	990	1395	80-84
85+	13500	3600	0.5	9900	1.2	13451 F	2747	850	1897	85+
TOTAL	1557900	763500		794400		27635	15955	8088	7867	TOTAL

TABLE 2 — MALE LIFE TABLE

x	$_nM_x$	$_nq_x$	l_x	$_nd_x$	$_nL_x$	$_nm_x$	$_na_x$	T_x	$\overset{\circ}{e}_x$	x
0	0.010559	0.010459	100000	1046	99046	0.010559	0.088	7028580	70.286	0
1	0.000603	0.002409	98954	238	395220	0.000603	1.500	6929534	70.028	1
5	0.000245	0.001224	98716	121	493276	0.000245	2.500	6534313	66.193	5
10	0.000314	0.001570	98595	155	492650	0.000314	2.905	6041037	61.271	10
15	0.000859	0.004287	98440	422	491235	0.000859	2.713	5548387	56.363	15
20	0.001199	0.005980	98018	586	488639	0.001200	2.524	5057152	51.594	20
25	0.001010	0.005026	97432	490	485918	0.001008	2.465	4568513	46.889	25
30	0.001043	0.005211	96942	505	483491	0.001045	2.585	4082595	42.114	30
35	0.001446	0.007225	96437	697	480615	0.001450	2.746	3599104	37.321	35
40	0.002783	0.013884	95740	1329	475681	0.002795	2.728	3118489	32.572	40
45	0.004576	0.022779	94411	2151	467301	0.004602	2.790	2642808	27.993	45
50	0.009552	0.046819	92260	4320	451365	0.009570	2.700	2175507	23.580	50
55	0.014795	0.071515	87941	6289	425070	0.014795	2.673	1724142	19.606	55
60	0.024724	0.116890	81652	9544	385919	0.024731	2.659	1299072	15.910	60
65	0.041462	0.188470	72107	13590	327776	0.041462	2.589	913152	12.664	65
70	0.060359	0.262664	58517	15370	254651	0.060359	2.532	585376	10.003	70
75	0.090411	0.369548	43147	15945	175603	0.090801	2.483	330725	7.665	75
80	0.141429	0.517483	27202	14077	99532	0.141429	2.409	155122	5.703	80
85	0.236111	1.000000	13125	13125	55590	0.175670	4.235	55590	4.235	85

TABLE 3 — FEMALE LIFE TABLE

x	$_nM_x$	$_nq_x$	l_x	$_nd_x$	$_nL_x$	$_nm_x$	$_na_x$	T_x	$\overset{\circ}{e}_x$	x
0	0.008571	0.008505	100000	850	99221	0.008571	0.085	7648221	76.482	0
1	0.000419	0.001674	99150	166	396183	0.000419	1.500	7548999	76.138	1
5	0.000271	0.001355	98984	134	494582	0.000271	2.500	7152816	72.263	5
10	0.000198	0.000987	98849	98	494003	0.000198	2.504	6658234	67.357	10
15	0.000275	0.001376	98752	136	493436	0.000275	2.621	6164230	62.421	15
20	0.000357	0.001788	98616	176	492665	0.000358	2.649	5670795	57.504	20
25	0.000531	0.002660	98440	262	491574	0.000533	2.614	5178130	52.602	25
30	0.000652	0.003262	98178	320	490133	0.000653	2.638	4686556	47.735	30
35	0.000971	0.004852	97858	475	488183	0.000973	2.673	4196424	42.883	35
40	0.001467	0.007341	97383	715	485319	0.001473	2.769	3708241	38.079	40
45	0.002900	0.014462	96668	1398	480145	0.002912	2.715	3222922	33.340	45
50	0.004569	0.022630	95270	2156	471431	0.004573	2.719	2742777	28.790	50
55	0.008010	0.039324	93114	3662	457106	0.008010	2.689	2271346	24.393	55
60	0.012586	0.061156	89452	5471	434537	0.012589	2.674	1814241	20.282	60
65	0.020545	0.098035	83982	8233	400730	0.020545	2.671	1379703	16.429	65
70	0.034920	0.161230	75749	12213	349739	0.034920	2.625	978973	12.924	70
75	0.055432	0.245123	63536	15574	280021	0.055617	2.582	629234	9.904	75
80	0.094257	0.382584	47962	18349	194674	0.094257	2.540	349213	7.281	80
85	0.191616	1.000000	29612	29612	154539	0.123739	5.219	154539	5.219	85

TABLE 4 — OBSERVED VITAL RATES AND RATIOS

CRUDE RATES

Per Thousand	BOTH SEXES	MALES	FEMALES
BIRTH RATE	17.74	18.58	16.93
DEATH RATE	10.24	10.59	9.90
RATE OF INCREASE	7.50	7.98	7.03

PERCENT OF POPULATION IN AGE GROUP

	BOTH SEXES	MALES	FEMALES
UNDER 15	25.59	26.76	24.46
15 - 64	62.42	63.61	61.28
65 AND OLDER	11.99	9.63	14.26

RATES STANDARDIZED ON USA 1980

Per Thousand	BOTH SEXES	MALES	FEMALES
BIRTH RATE	20.50		19.40
DEATH RATE	10.03	10.68	9.42
RATE OF INCREASE	10.46		9.98

RATES STANDARDIZED ON MEXICO 1980

	BOTH SEXES	MALES	FEMALES
BIRTH RATE	17.85		17.51
DEATH RATE	3.71	4.42	3.00
RATE OF INCREASE	14.14		14.52

VITAL STATISTICS

GFR x 1000	74.208
TFR	2.452
GRR	1.194
NRR	1.172
μ	28.225
σ^2	33.204
GENERATION	28.131
POP. SEX RATIO	1.040
SEX RATIO AT BIRTH	1.054
DEP. RATIO x 100	60.195

PROJECTED POPULATION

AGE GROUP	1990 BOTH SEXES	1990 MALES	1990 FEMALES	1995 BOTH SEXES	1995 MALES	1995 FEMALES
0-4	143	73	70	154	79	75
5-9	135	69	66	143	73	70
10-14	128	65	63	135	69	66
15-19	136	70	66	128	65	63
20-24	143	74	69	135	69	66
25-29	135	71	64	143	74	69
30-34	113	57	56	134	70	64
35-39	98	49	49	113	57	56
40-44	96	48	48	97	48	49
45-49	88	43	45	95	47	48
50-54	77	38	39	86	42	44
55-59	71	34	37	73	35	38
60-64	67	31	36	66	31	35
65-69	63	28	35	59	26	33
70-74	49	20	29	53	22	31
75-79	40	15	25	37	14	23
80-84	25	8	17	26	9	17
85+	16	4	12	18	5	13
TOTAL	1623	797	826	1695	835	860

STABLE EQUIVALENT TO ORIGINAL POPULATION

	MALES Number	MALES Percent	FEMALES Number	FEMALES Percent	AGE GROUP	
	72	8.5	69	7.9	0-4	
	70	8.2	67	7.7	5-9	TABLE 5
	68	8.0	65	7.5	10-14	
	66	7.7	63	7.3	15-19	POPULATION
	64	7.5	61	7.0	20-24	PROJECTED
	62	7.2	59	6.8	25-29	WITH
	60	7.0	57	6.6	30-34	FIXED
	58	6.8	55	6.4	35-39	AGE-
	55	6.5	54	6.2	40-44	SPECIFIC
	53	6.2	51	6.0	45-49	BIRTH
	50	5.8	49	5.7	50-54	AND
	45	5.3	46	5.4	55-59	DEATH
	40	4.7	43	5.0	60-64	RATES
	33	3.9	38	4.4	65-69	(female
	25	2.9	33	3.8	70-74	dominant,
	17	2.0	25	2.9	75-79	in 000s)
	9	1.1	17	2.0	80-84	
	5	0.6	13	1.5	85+	
	852		865		TOTAL	

VITAL RATES OF PROJECTED POPULATION

Per Thousand	1990 BOTH SEXES	1990 MALES	1990 FEMALES	1995 BOTH SEXES	1995 MALES	1995 FEMALES
BIRTH RATE	18.65	19.48	17.84	18.76	19.54	18.00
DEATH RATE	10.37	10.53	10.21	10.27	10.34	10.21
RATE OF INCREASE	8.28	8.95	7.63	8.48	9.20	7.79

VITAL RATES OF STABLE POPULATION

Per Thousand	MALES	FEMALES	
BIRTH RATE	17.40	16.22	TABLE 6
DEATH RATE	11.75	10.57	PROJECTED
RATE OF INCREASE		5.66	VITAL RATES

AGE STRUCTURE OF PROJECTED POPULATION

	BOTH SEXES	MALES	FEMALES	BOTH SEXES	MALES	FEMALES
% UNDER 15	25.01	26.05	24.01	25.45	26.46	24.47
% 15-64	63.09	64.48	61.75	63.14	64.53	61.80
% 65 AND OLDER	11.90	9.47	14.24	11.41	9.01	13.73
DEPEND. RATIO x 100	58.49	55.08	61.94	58.37	54.97	61.82

STABLE AGE STRUCTURE

	MALES	FEMALES	
% UNDER 15	24.69	23.08	AND RATIOS
% 15-64	64.83	62.27	(female
% 65 AND OLDER	10.48	14.64	dominant)
DEPEND. RATIO x 100	54.24	60.58	

AGE GROUP	FEMALE BIRTH RATES	NET MATERNITY FUNCTION	COEFF. OF MATRIX EQUATION	ORIGINAL MATRIX SUB-DIAGONAL	ORIGINAL MATRIX FIRST ROW	STABLE MATRIX FISHER VALUES	STABLE MATRIX REPRODUCTIVE VALUES
0-4	0.0000	0.0000	0.0000	0.99834	0.00000	1.024	67355
5-9	0.0000	0.0000	0.0000	0.99883	0.00000	1.055	66133
10-14	0.0000	0.0000	0.0344	0.99885	0.03452	1.086	71477
15-19	0.0140	0.0688	0.1805	0.99844	0.18124	1.083	74752
20-24	0.0593	0.2922	0.3408	0.99778	0.34269	0.930	59916
25-29	0.0792	0.3894	0.3307	0.99707	0.33332	0.608	34331
30-34	0.0555	0.2721	0.1975	0.99602	0.19966	0.285	13979
35-39	0.0252	0.1230	0.0744	0.99413	0.07545	0.089	4300
40-44	0.0053	0.0257	0.0134	0.98934	0.01372	0.014	641
45-49	0.0002	0.0012	0.0006	0.98185	0.00060	0.001	24
50-54	0.0000	0.0000	0.0000	0.00000	0.00000	0.000	0

MATRIX PARAMETERS

λ_1	1.02869	
λ_2	$0.40450+0.76147i$	TABLE 7
λ_4	$-0.12943-0.53587i$	
λ_6	$-0.36512-0.36508i$	LESLIE
r_1	0.00566	MATRIX
r_2	$-0.02964+0.21650i$	AND ITS
r_4	$-0.11910-0.36156i$	ANALYSIS
r_6	$-0.13220-0.47125i$	(females)
c_1	8648	
$2x/y$	29.0217	
Δ	4.4682	

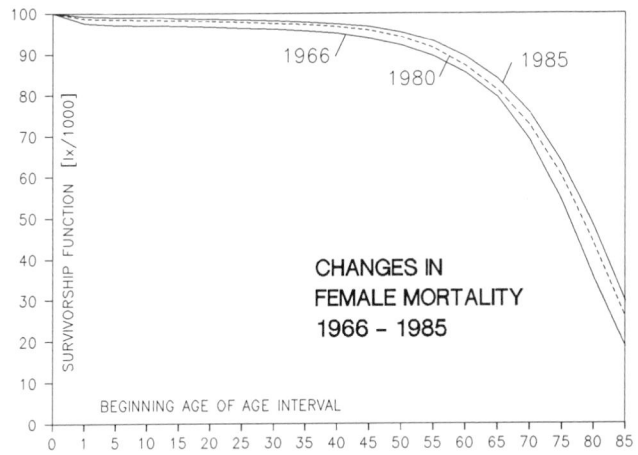

CHANGES IN FEMALE MORTALITY 1966 – 1985

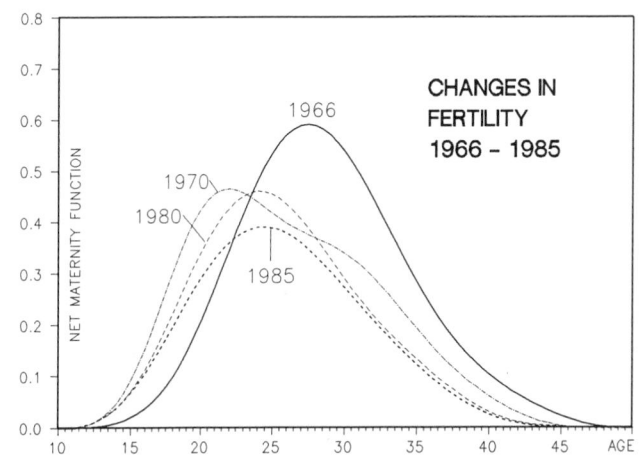

CHANGES IN FERTILITY 1966 – 1985

TABLE 1 — DATA

AGE AT LAST BIRTHDAY	ESTIMATED MID-YEAR POPULATION BOTH SEXES	MALES Number	MALES Percent	FEMALES Number	FEMALES Percent	BIRTHS BY AGE OF MOTHER AND SEX	DEATHS BOTH SEXES	DEATHS MALES	DEATHS FEMALES	AGE AT LAST BIRTHDAY
0	86100	44300	1.8	41800	1.5		1714	1010	704	0
1-4	363100	186700	7.4	176400	6.5		315	186	129	1-4
5-9	469000	240400	9.6	228600	8.4		207	125	82	5-9
10-14	436400	223700	8.9	212700	7.9		140	90	50	10-14
15-19	385400	195600	7.8	189800	7.0	9038	238	161	77	15-19
20-24	380900	191500	7.6	189400	7.0	31491	324	232	92	20-24
25-29	313600	156300	6.2	157300	5.8	25885	273	180	93	25-29
30-34	303700	149600	6.0	154100	5.7	13406	374	223	151	30-34
35-39	303900	149100	5.9	154800	5.7	5875	573	339	234	35-39
40-44	313800	152900	6.1	160900	5.9	1538	949	552	397	40-44
45-49	327900	159000	6.3	168900	6.2	102	1838	1058	780	45-49
50-54	288800	136300	5.4	152500	5.6		2570	1546	1024	50-54
55-59	313300	146600	5.8	166700	6.2		4413	2745	1668	55-59
60-64	292900	133600	5.3	159300	5.9		6618	4178	2440	60-64
65-69	245000	105200	4.2	139800	5.2		8443	5071	3372	65-69
70-74	174700	65800	2.6	108900	4.0		9358	4916	4442	70-74
75-79	114200	39400	1.6	74800	2.8		9406	4204	5202	75-79
80-84	65600	20600	0.8	45000	1.7	45038 M	8018	3062	4956	80-84
85+	35600	10300	0.4	25300	0.9	42297 F	7869	2660	5209	85+
TOTAL	5213900	2506900		2707000		87335	63640	32538	31102	TOTAL

TABLE 2 — MALE LIFE TABLE

x	nM_x	nq_x	l_x	nd_x	nL_x	nm_x	na_x	T_x	$\overset{\circ}{e}_x$	x
0	0.022799	0.022345	100000	2235	98009	0.022799	0.109	6712959	67.130	0
1	0.000996	0.003975	97765	389	390090	0.000996	1.500	6614951	67.661	1
5	0.000520	0.002596	97377	253	486252	0.000520	2.500	6224860	63.925	5
10	0.000402	0.002014	97124	196	485162	0.000403	2.656	5738608	59.085	10
15	0.000823	0.004120	96928	399	483725	0.000826	2.702	5253447	54.199	15
20	0.001211	0.006047	96529	584	481218	0.001213	2.554	4769722	49.412	20
25	0.001152	0.005747	95945	551	478375	0.001153	2.548	4288505	44.697	25
30	0.001491	0.007438	95394	710	475304	0.001493	2.652	3810130	39.941	30
35	0.002274	0.011309	94684	1071	470947	0.002274	2.688	3334826	35.220	35
40	0.003610	0.017905	93614	1676	464284	0.003610	2.742	2863879	30.593	40
45	0.006654	0.032809	91938	3016	452822	0.006661	2.724	2399595	26.100	45
50	0.011343	0.055266	88921	4914	433262	0.011343	2.692	1946773	21.893	50
55	0.018724	0.089711	84007	7536	402488	0.018724	2.672	1513512	18.017	55
60	0.031272	0.145546	76471	11130	355903	0.031272	2.624	1111023	14.529	60
65	0.048203	0.216308	65341	14136	292417	0.048341	2.575	755121	11.557	65
70	0.074711	0.316112	51205	16186	215672	0.075051	2.507	462703	9.036	70
75	0.106701	0.419237	35018	14681	137279	0.106943	2.424	247031	7.054	75
80	0.148641	0.533847	20337	10857	73042	0.148641	2.362	109752	5.397	80
85	0.258252	1.000000	9480	9480	36710	0.203518	3.872	36710	3.872	85

TABLE 3 — FEMALE LIFE TABLE

x	nM_x	nq_x	l_x	nd_x	nL_x	nm_x	na_x	T_x	$\overset{\circ}{e}_x$	x
0	0.016842	0.016590	100000	1659	98505	0.016842	0.099	7343613	73.436	0
1	0.000731	0.002920	98341	287	392646	0.000731	1.500	7245109	73.673	1
5	0.000359	0.001792	98054	176	489830	0.000359	2.500	6852463	69.885	5
10	0.000235	0.001175	97878	115	489108	0.000235	2.541	6362633	65.006	10
15	0.000406	0.002029	97763	198	488345	0.000406	2.628	5873525	60.079	15
20	0.000486	0.002429	97565	237	487250	0.000486	2.579	5385180	55.196	20
25	0.000591	0.002962	97328	288	485968	0.000593	2.672	4897930	50.324	25
30	0.000980	0.004894	97039	475	484102	0.000981	2.693	4411962	45.466	30
35	0.001512	0.007532	96565	727	481151	0.001512	2.701	3927860	40.676	35
40	0.002467	0.012269	95837	1176	476546	0.002467	2.754	3446709	35.964	40
45	0.004618	0.022849	94661	2163	468292	0.004619	2.681	2970164	31.377	45
50	0.006715	0.033052	92498	3057	455309	0.006715	2.651	2501872	27.048	50
55	0.010006	0.048883	89441	4372	436949	0.010006	2.654	2046562	22.882	55
60	0.015317	0.073928	85069	6289	410588	0.015317	2.654	1609614	18.921	60
65	0.024120	0.114319	78780	9006	372787	0.024159	2.656	1199025	15.220	65
70	0.040790	0.186532	69774	13015	317984	0.040930	2.627	826239	11.842	70
75	0.069545	0.298342	56759	16934	242326	0.069879	2.551	508255	8.955	75
80	0.110133	0.431074	39825	17168	155881	0.110133	2.481	265929	6.677	80
85	0.205889	1.000000	22658	22658	110048	0.139627	4.857	110048	4.857	85

TABLE 4 — OBSERVED VITAL RATES AND RATIOS

CRUDE RATES

Per Thousand	BOTH SEXES	MALES	FEMALES
BIRTH RATE	16.75	17.97	15.63
DEATH RATE	12.21	12.98	11.49
RATE OF INCREASE	4.54	4.99	4.14

PERCENT OF POPULATION IN AGE GROUP

	BOTH SEXES	MALES	FEMALES
UNDER 15	25.98	27.73	24.36
15 - 64	61.84	62.65	61.09
65 AND OLDER	12.18	9.63	14.55

RATES STANDARDIZED ON USA 1980

Per Thousand	BOTH SEXES	MALES	FEMALES
BIRTH RATE	22.01		20.73
DEATH RATE	12.04	12.83	11.29
RATE OF INCREASE	9.97		9.44

RATES STANDARDIZED ON MEXICO 1980

	BOTH SEXES	MALES	FEMALES
BIRTH RATE	19.81		19.34
DEATH RATE	4.78	5.64	3.91
RATE OF INCREASE	15.03		15.43

VITAL STATISTICS

GFR x 1000	74.315
TFR	2.568
GRR	1.244
NRR	1.208
μ	26.817
σ^2	33.078
GENERATION	26.700
POP. SEX RATIO	1.080
SEX RATIO AT BIRTH	1.065
DEP. RATIO x 100	61.711

PROJECTED POPULATION

AGE GROUP	1975 BOTH SEXES	MALES	FEMALES	1980 BOTH SEXES	MALES	FEMALES	STABLE EQUIVALENT TO ORIGINAL POPULATION MALES Number	Percent	FEMALES Number	Percent	AGE GROUP	
0-4	443	228	215	477	245	232	233	9.1	220	8.5	0-4	
5-9	448	230	218	442	227	215	224	8.8	212	8.2	5-9	TABLE 5
10-14	468	240	228	447	230	217	216	8.4	204	7.9	10-14	
15-19	435	223	212	467	239	228	207	8.1	197	7.6	15-19	POPULATION
20-24	384	195	189	434	222	212	199	7.8	189	7.3	20-24	PROJECTED
25-29	379	190	189	382	193	189	191	7.5	182	7.1	25-29	WITH
30-34	312	155	157	377	189	188	183	7.2	175	6.8	30-34	FIXED
35-39	301	148	153	310	154	156	175	6.9	168	6.5	35-39	AGE-
40-44	300	147	153	298	146	152	167	6.5	161	6.2	40-44	SPECIFIC
45-49	307	149	158	294	143	151	157	6.1	153	5.9	45-49	BIRTH
50-54	316	152	164	297	143	154	145	5.7	143	5.5	50-54	AND
55-59	273	127	146	299	141	158	130	5.1	133	5.1	55-59	DEATH
60-64	287	130	157	250	112	138	111	4.3	120	4.7	60-64	RATES
65-69	255	110	145	249	107	142	88	3.4	105	4.1	65-69	(female
70-74	197	78	119	204	81	123	63	2.4	87	3.4	70-74	dominant,
75-79	125	42	83	140	49	91	38	1.5	64	2.5	75-79	in 000s)
80-84	69	21	48	75	22	53	20	0.8	40	1.5	80-84	
85+	42	10	32	45	11	34	10	0.4	27	1.0	85+	
TOTAL	5341	2575	2766	5487	2654	2833	2557		2580		TOTAL	

VITAL RATES OF PROJECTED POPULATION

Per Thousand	1975 BOTH SEXES	MALES	FEMALES	1980 BOTH SEXES	MALES	FEMALES	VITAL RATES OF STABLE POPULATION Per Thousand	MALES	FEMALES	TABLE 6
BIRTH RATE	17.54	18.77	16.40	18.41	19.62	17.28	BIRTH RATE	18.99	17.67	
DEATH RATE	12.60	13.06	12.17	12.71	13.01	12.43	DEATH RATE	11.87	10.59	PROJECTED
RATE OF INCREASE	4.94	5.71	4.23	5.70	6.61	4.85	RATE OF INCREASE		7.09	VITAL RATES AND RATIOS

AGE STRUCTURE OF PROJECTED POPULATION

							STABLE AGE STRUCTURE			(female dominant)
% UNDER 15	25.44	27.11	23.89	24.89	26.43	23.44	% UNDER 15	26.29	24.65	
% 15-64	61.69	62.77	60.68	62.11	63.41	60.89	% 15-64	65.16	62.85	
% 65 AND OLDER	12.87	10.12	15.42	13.01	10.16	15.68	% 65 AND OLDER	8.54	12.50	
DEPEND. RATIO x 100	62.10	59.30	64.79	61.02	57.71	64.24	DEPEND. RATIO x 100	53.46	59.12	

AGE GROUP	FEMALE BIRTH RATES	NET MATERNITY FUNCTION	COEFF. OF MATRIX EQUATION	ORIGINAL MATRIX SUB-DIAGONAL	FIRST ROW	STABLE MATRIX FISHER VALUES	REPRODUCTIVE VALUES	MATRIX PARAMETERS		
0-4	0.0000	0.0000	0.0000	0.99731	0.00000	1.036	226094	λ_1	1.03607	
5-9	0.0000	0.0000	0.0000	0.99853	0.00000	1.076	246075	λ_2	0.33792+0.76635i	TABLE 7
10-14	0.0000	0.0000	0.0563	0.99844	0.05655	1.117	237568	λ_4	-0.38097+0.40101i	
15-19	0.0231	0.1126	0.2525	0.99776	0.25394	1.100	208842	λ_6	-0.02838+0.45956i	LESLIE
20-24	0.0805	0.3924	0.3898	0.99737	0.39295	0.879	166456	r_1	0.00709	MATRIX
25-29	0.0797	0.3873	0.2956	0.99616	0.29879	0.505	79393	r_2	-0.03546+0.23110i	AND ITS
30-34	0.0421	0.2040	0.1462	0.99390	0.14833	0.214	33001	r_4	-0.11843+0.46611i	ANALYSIS
35-39	0.0184	0.0884	0.0552	0.99043	0.05640	0.069	10619	r_6	-0.15511+0.32650i	(females)
40-44	0.0046	0.0221	0.0117	0.98268	0.01207	0.013	2053	c_1	25798	
45-49	0.0003	0.0014	0.0007	0.97228	0.00072	0.001	121	$2\pi/y$	27.1884	
50-54	0.0000	0.0000	0.0000	0.00000	0.00000	0.000	0	Δ	5.0490	

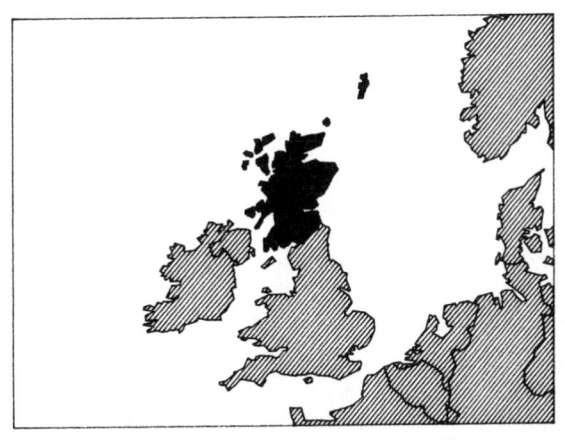

TABLE 1 — DATA

AGE AT LAST BIRTHDAY	ESTIMATED MID-YEAR POPULATION BOTH SEXES	MALES Number	MALES Percent	FEMALES Number	FEMALES Percent	BIRTHS BY AGE OF MOTHER AND SEX	DEATHS BOTH SEXES	DEATHS MALES	DEATHS FEMALES	AGE AT LAST BIRTHDAY
0	65300	33300	1.3	32000	1.2		624	342	282	0
1-4	259600	133100	5.4	126500	4.8		112	57	55	1-4
5-9	310600	159600	6.4	151000	5.7		86	49	37	5-9
10-14	363600	186100	7.5	177500	6.7		92	58	34	10-14
15-19	432000	220900	8.9	211100	7.9	6528	237	174	63	15-19
20-24	447300	228800	9.2	218500	8.2	20809	284	208	76	20-24
25-29	387700	197000	7.9	190700	7.2	23511	286	185	101	25-29
30-34	342700	172100	6.9	170600	6.4	11600	311	205	106	30-34
35-39	357900	179500	7.2	178400	6.7	3692	541	338	203	35-39
40-44	299500	148500	6.0	151000	5.7	512	699	421	278	40-44
45-49	289900	141600	5.7	148300	5.6	24	1166	733	433	45-49
50-54	284300	137600	5.5	146700	5.5		1972	1226	746	50-54
55-59	282600	134300	5.4	148300	5.6		3504	2118	1386	55-59
60-64	276300	127900	5.2	148400	5.6		5545	3368	2177	60-64
65-69	223200	97100	3.9	126100	4.7		6790	3912	2878	65-69
70-74	208700	85400	3.4	123300	4.6		9998	5427	4571	70-74
75-79	157100	57200	2.3	99900	3.8		11234	5636	5598	75-79
80-84	93200	28200	1.1	65000	2.4	34120 M	9939	3933	6006	80-84
85+	55000	12200	0.5	42800	1.6	32556 F	10547	2757	7790	85+
TOTAL	5136500	2480400		2656100		66676	63967	31147	32820	TOTAL

TABLE 2 — MALE LIFE TABLE

x	$_nM_x$	$_nq_x$	l_x	$_nd_x$	$_nL_x$	$_nm_x$	$_na_x$	T_x	$\overset{\circ}{e}_x$	x
0	0.010270	0.010175	100000	1017	99072	0.010270	0.087	7007398	70.074	0
1	0.000428	0.001711	98983	169	395507	0.000428	1.500	6908327	69.793	1
5	0.000307	0.001534	98813	152	493687	0.000307	2.500	6512820	65.910	5
10	0.000312	0.001557	98662	154	492973	0.000312	2.819	6019133	61.008	10
15	0.000788	0.003931	98508	387	491632	0.000788	2.657	5526160	56.099	15
20	0.000909	0.004536	98121	445	489505	0.000909	2.533	5034528	51.310	20
25	0.000939	0.004691	97676	458	487260	0.000940	2.561	4545023	46.532	25
30	0.001191	0.005951	97217	579	484735	0.001193	2.662	4057762	41.739	30
35	0.001883	0.009393	96639	908	481087	0.001887	2.678	3573028	36.973	35
40	0.002835	0.014159	95731	1355	475582	0.002850	2.732	3091941	32.298	40
45	0.005177	0.025631	94376	2419	466385	0.005186	2.729	2616359	27.723	45
50	0.008910	0.043663	91957	4015	450636	0.008910	2.722	2149973	23.380	50
55	0.015771	0.076080	87942	6691	424245	0.015771	2.689	1699337	19.323	55
60	0.026333	0.124061	81251	10080	382384	0.026361	2.632	1275092	15.693	60
65	0.040288	0.183640	71171	13070	324408	0.040288	2.594	892707	12.543	65
70	0.063548	0.274882	58101	15971	251322	0.063548	2.547	568300	9.781	70
75	0.098531	0.394920	42130	16638	168440	0.098777	2.463	316978	7.524	75
80	0.139468	0.510640	25492	13017	93335	0.139468	2.378	148538	5.827	80
85	0.225984	1.000000	12475	12475	55202	0.163846	4.425	55202	4.425	85

TABLE 3 — FEMALE LIFE TABLE

x	$_nM_x$	$_nq_x$	l_x	$_nd_x$	$_nL_x$	$_nm_x$	$_na_x$	T_x	$\overset{\circ}{e}_x$	x
0	0.008813	0.008742	100000	874	99200	0.008813	0.085	7588714	75.887	0
1	0.000435	0.001737	99126	172	396073	0.000435	1.500	7489514	75.556	1
5	0.000245	0.001224	98954	121	494465	0.000245	2.500	7093441	71.685	5
10	0.000192	0.000957	98832	95	493931	0.000192	2.557	6598976	66.769	10
15	0.000298	0.001491	98738	147	493337	0.000298	2.609	6105045	61.831	15
20	0.000348	0.001739	98591	171	492548	0.000348	2.638	5611708	56.919	20
25	0.000530	0.002652	98419	261	491471	0.000531	2.607	5119160	52.014	25
30	0.000621	0.003108	98158	305	490090	0.000623	2.702	4627689	47.145	30
35	0.001138	0.005687	97853	557	487997	0.001140	2.721	4137599	42.284	35
40	0.001841	0.009202	97297	895	484420	0.001848	2.696	3649602	37.510	40
45	0.002920	0.014517	96401	1399	478819	0.002923	2.722	3165181	32.833	45
50	0.005085	0.025138	95002	2388	469630	0.005085	2.747	2686363	28.277	50
55	0.009346	0.045742	92614	4236	453286	0.009346	2.691	2216733	23.935	55
60	0.014670	0.070923	88377	6268	427186	0.014673	2.655	1763447	19.954	60
65	0.022823	0.108295	82109	8892	389607	0.022823	2.645	1336261	16.274	65
70	0.037072	0.170228	73217	12464	336198	0.037072	2.602	946654	12.929	70
75	0.056036	0.246756	60754	14991	267281	0.056088	2.566	610456	10.048	75
80	0.092400	0.376267	45762	17219	186351	0.092400	2.534	343175	7.499	80
85	0.182009	1.000000	28543	28543	156824	0.113541	5.494	156824	5.494	85

TABLE 4 — OBSERVED VITAL RATES AND RATIOS

CRUDE RATES

Per Thousand	BOTH SEXES	MALES	FEMALES
BIRTH RATE	12.98	13.76	12.26
DEATH RATE	12.45	12.56	12.36
RATE OF INCREASE	0.53	1.20	-0.10

RATES STANDARDIZED ON USA 1980

Per Thousand	BOTH SEXES	MALES	FEMALES
BIRTH RATE	14.65		13.91
DEATH RATE	10.26	10.88	9.67
RATE OF INCREASE	4.39		4.25

VITAL STATISTICS

GFR x 1000	52.559
TFR	1.708
GRR	0.834
NRR	0.820
μ	26.944
σ^2	29.125
GENERATION	27.051
POP. SEX RATIO	1.071
SEX RATIO AT BIRTH	1.048
DEP. RATIO x 100	51.065

PERCENT OF POPULATION IN AGE GROUP

	BOTH SEXES	MALES	FEMALES
UNDER 15	19.45	20.65	18.34
15 - 64	66.20	68.06	64.46
65 AND OLDER	14.35	11.29	17.21

RATES STANDARDIZED ON MEXICO 1980

Per Thousand	BOTH SEXES	MALES	FEMALES
BIRTH RATE	13.07		12.86
DEATH RATE	3.81	4.48	3.13
RATE OF INCREASE	9.26		9.73

PROJECTED POPULATION

AGE GROUP	1990 BOTH SEXES	1990 MALES	1990 FEMALES	1995 BOTH SEXES	1995 MALES	1995 FEMALES
0-4	337	172	165	337	172	165
5-9	324	166	158	336	172	164
10-14	310	159	151	324	166	158
15-19	363	186	177	310	159	151
20-24	431	220	211	362	185	177
25-29	446	228	218	429	219	210
30-34	386	196	190	444	227	217
35-39	341	171	170	384	195	189
40-44	354	177	177	338	169	169
45-49	295	146	149	349	174	175
50-54	282	137	145	287	141	146
55-59	272	130	142	269	129	140
60-64	261	121	140	250	117	133
65-69	244	109	135	230	103	127
70-74	184	75	109	201	84	117
75-79	155	57	98	137	50	87
80-84	102	32	70	100	32	68
85+	72	17	55	78	19	59
TOTAL	5159	2499	2660	5165	2513	2652

STABLE EQUIVALENT TO ORIGINAL POPULATION

	MALES Number	MALES Percent	FEMALES Number	FEMALES Percent	AGE GROUP	
	174	5.4	167	4.9	0-4	
	181	5.6	173	5.1	5-9	TABLE 5
	187	5.8	179	5.3	10-14	
	194	6.0	185	5.4	15-19	POPULATION
	200	6.2	192	5.6	20-24	PROJECTED
	206	6.4	199	5.8	25-29	WITH
	213	6.6	206	6.0	30-34	FIXED
	219	6.8	212	6.2	35-39	AGE-
	225	7.0	219	6.4	40-44	SPECIFIC
	229	7.1	224	6.6	45-49	BIRTH
	229	7.1	228	6.7	50-54	AND
	224	7.0	228	6.7	55-59	DEATH
	209	6.5	223	6.6	60-64	RATES
	184	5.7	211	6.2	65-69	(female
	148	4.6	189	5.6	70-74	dominant,
	103	3.2	156	4.6	75-79	in 000s)
	59	1.8	113	3.3	80-84	
	36	1.1	98	2.9	85+	
	3220		3402		TOTAL	

VITAL RATES OF PROJECTED POPULATION

Per Thousand	1990 BOTH SEXES	1990 MALES	1990 FEMALES	1995 BOTH SEXES	1995 MALES	1995 FEMALES
BIRTH RATE	13.48	14.24	12.76	12.92	13.60	12.28
DEATH RATE	13.02	12.94	13.11	13.05	12.94	13.15
RATE OF INCREASE	0.45	1.30	-0.34	-0.13	0.66	-0.87

VITAL RATES OF STABLE POPULATION

Per Thousand	MALES	FEMALES	
BIRTH RATE	10.74	9.71	TABLE 6
DEATH RATE	18.03	17.05	PROJECTED
RATE OF INCREASE		-7.34	VITAL RATES AND

AGE STRUCTURE OF PROJECTED POPULATION

	BOTH SEXES	MALES	FEMALES	BOTH SEXES	MALES	FEMALES
% UNDER 15	18.84	19.93	17.81	19.32	20.32	18.36
% 15-64	66.50	68.49	64.65	66.25	68.22	64.39
% 65 AND OLDER	14.66	11.58	17.54	14.43	11.46	17.25
DEPEND. RATIO x 100	50.36	46.02	54.69	50.94	46.58	55.30

STABLE AGE STRUCTURE

	MALES	FEMALES	
% UNDER 15	16.83	15.23	RATIOS
% 15-64	66.69	62.21	(female
% 65 AND OLDER	16.48	22.56	dominant)
DEPEND. RATIO x 100	49.94	60.75	

AGE GROUP	FEMALE BIRTH RATES	NET MATERNITY FUNCTION	COEFF. OF MATRIX EQUATION	ORIGINAL MATRIX SUB-DIAGONAL	ORIGINAL MATRIX FIRST ROW	STABLE MATRIX FISHER VALUES	STABLE MATRIX REPRODUCTIVE VALUES	MATRIX PARAMETERS		
0-4	0.0000	0.0000	0.0000	0.99837	0.00000	0.991	157101	λ_1	0.96397	
5-9	0.0000	0.0000	0.0000	0.99892	0.00000	0.957	144510	λ_2	0.35655+0.73085i	TABLE 7
10-14	0.0000	0.0000	0.0372	0.99880	0.03735	0.924	163928	λ_4	-0.24976-0.46736i	
15-19	0.0151	0.0745	0.1518	0.99840	0.15236	0.854	180338	λ_6	-0.36766-0.05094i	LESLIE
20-24	0.0465	0.2290	0.2624	0.99781	0.26390	0.674	147173	r_1	-0.00734	MATRIX
25-29	0.0602	0.2959	0.2293	0.99719	0.23106	0.389	74101	r_2	-0.04136+0.22338i	AND ITS
30-34	0.0332	0.1627	0.1060	0.99573	0.10713	0.146	24902	r_4	-0.12701-0.41232i	ANALYSIS
35-39	0.0101	0.0493	0.0287	0.99267	0.02909	0.035	6186	r_6	-0.19822-0.60078i	(females)
40-44	0.0017	0.0080	0.0042	0.98844	0.00429	0.005	698	c_1	34027	
45-49	0.0001	0.0004	0.0002	0.98081	0.00020	0.000	30	$2\pi/y$	28.1275	
50-54	0.0000	0.0000	0.0000	0.00000	0.00000	0.000	0	Δ	10.3863	

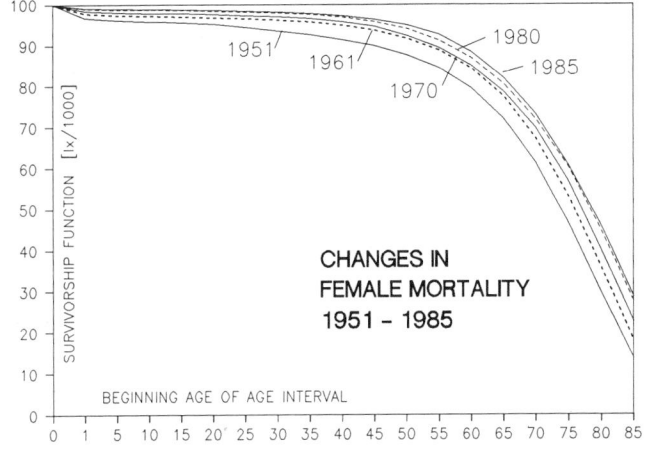

CHANGES IN FEMALE MORTALITY 1951 - 1985

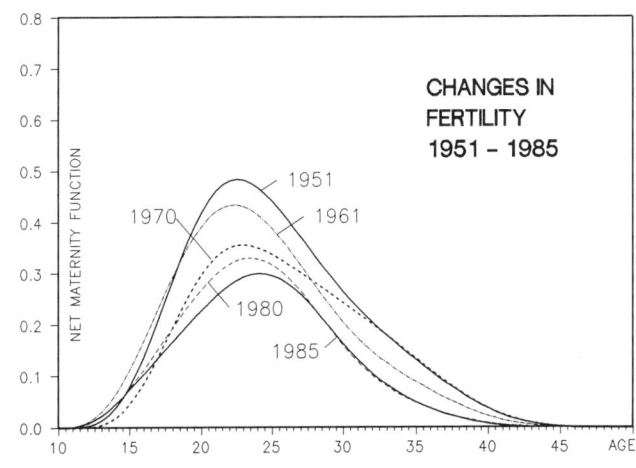

CHANGES IN FERTILITY 1951 - 1985

TABLE 1 — DATA

AGE AT LAST BIRTHDAY	ESTIMATED MID-YEAR POPULATION — BOTH SEXES	MALES Number	MALES Percent	FEMALES Number	FEMALES Percent	BIRTHS BY AGE OF MOTHER AND SEX	DEATHS BOTH SEXES	DEATHS MALES	DEATHS FEMALES	AGE AT LAST BIRTHDAY
0	352935	182025	1.8	170910	1.6		20180	10713	9467	0
1-4	1441464	743195	7.4	698269	6.7		3554	1757	1797	1-4
5-9	1843005	945667	9.5	897338	8.7		1039	620	419	5-9
10-14	1875479	958847	9.6	916632	8.8	215	866	531	335	10-14
15-19	1963540	1002612	10.0	960928	9.3	49558	1481	967	514	15-19
20-24	1687937	859402	8.6	828535	8.0	134202	1853	1291	562	20-24
25-29	1389264	698829	7.0	690435	6.7	86357	1725	1119	606	25-29
30-34	1554849	780736	7.8	774113	7.5	55874	2464	1609	855	30-34
35-39	1610447	803684	8.0	806763	7.8	27572	3526	2281	1245	35-39
40-44	1466638	708143	7.1	758495	7.3	8222	4750	2962	1788	40-44
45-49	1174735	526255	5.3	648480	6.3	967	5796	3476	2320	45-49
50-54	643519	288402	2.9	355117	3.4	311	4732	2805	1927	50-54
55-59	911456	415327	4.2	496129	4.8		10877	6451	4426	55-59
60-64	862052	407823	4.1	454229	4.4		17017	10157	6860	60-64
65-69	703588	319543	3.2	384045	3.7		22305	12734	9571	65-69
70-74	438070	186270	1.9	251800	2.4		24242	12183	12059	70-74
75-79	237895	92541	0.9	145354	1.4		21200	9616	11584	75-79
80-84	135733	49921	0.5	85812	0.8	187396 M	18518	7561	10957	80-84
85+	78353	28536	0.3	49817	0.5	175882 F	15717	6069	9648	85+
TOTAL	20370959	9997758		10373201		363278	181842	94902	86940	TOTAL

TABLE 2 — MALE LIFE TABLE

x	nM_x	nq_x	l_x	nd_x	nL_x	nm_x	na_x	T_x	$\overset{\circ}{e}_x$	x
0	0.058855	0.056114	100000	5611	95343	0.058855	0.170	6510137	65.101	0
1	0.002364	0.009401	94389	887	375336	0.002364	1.500	6414794	67.962	1
5	0.000656	0.003273	93501	306	466742	0.000656	2.500	6039458	64.592	5
10	0.000554	0.002765	93195	258	465362	0.000554	2.614	5572716	59.796	10
15	0.000964	0.004813	92938	447	463661	0.000965	2.703	5107355	54.955	15
20	0.001502	0.007507	92490	694	460775	0.001507	2.586	4643694	50.207	20
25	0.001601	0.007983	91796	733	457198	0.001603	2.568	4182919	45.568	25
30	0.002061	0.010254	91063	934	453093	0.002061	2.620	3725721	40.914	30
35	0.002838	0.014097	90129	1271	447661	0.002838	2.650	3272628	36.310	35
40	0.004183	0.020815	88859	1850	439999	0.004204	2.678	2824966	31.792	40
45	0.006605	0.032741	87009	2849	428376	0.006650	2.659	2384967	27.411	45
50	0.009726	0.047740	84161	4018	411416	0.009766	2.664	1956591	23.248	50
55	0.015532	0.074942	80143	6006	386678	0.015532	2.663	1545175	19.280	55
60	0.024905	0.117620	74137	8720	350124	0.024905	2.642	1158497	15.627	60
65	0.039851	0.182846	65417	11961	298527	0.040067	2.613	808373	12.357	65
70	0.065405	0.284026	53456	15183	230127	0.065976	2.553	509846	9.538	70
75	0.103911	0.413644	38273	15831	151149	0.104739	2.460	279719	7.309	75
80	0.151459	0.540491	22441	12129	80084	0.151459	2.352	128570	5.729	80
85	0.212679	1.000000	10312	10312	48487	0.148288	4.702	48487	4.702	85

TABLE 3 — FEMALE LIFE TABLE

x	nM_x	nq_x	l_x	nd_x	nL_x	nm_x	na_x	T_x	$\overset{\circ}{e}_x$	x
0	0.055392	0.052941	100000	5294	95575	0.055392	0.164	6984010	69.840	0
1	0.002574	0.010228	94706	969	376402	0.002574	1.500	6888435	72.735	1
5	0.000467	0.002332	93737	219	468140	0.000467	2.500	6512033	69.471	5
10	0.000365	0.001826	93519	171	467173	0.000365	2.538	6043893	64.628	10
15	0.000535	0.002672	93348	249	466146	0.000535	2.621	5576720	59.741	15
20	0.000678	0.003395	93099	316	464735	0.000680	2.604	5110573	54.894	20
25	0.000878	0.004385	92782	407	462935	0.000879	2.599	4645838	50.072	25
30	0.001104	0.005508	92376	509	460668	0.001104	2.623	4182903	45.281	30
35	0.001543	0.007688	91867	706	457685	0.001543	2.666	3722235	40.518	35
40	0.002357	0.011742	91160	1070	453314	0.002361	2.676	3264550	35.811	40
45	0.003578	0.017857	90090	1609	446702	0.003601	2.670	2811236	31.205	45
50	0.005426	0.026950	88481	2385	436894	0.005458	2.688	2364534	26.724	50
55	0.008921	0.043709	86097	3763	421831	0.008921	2.701	1927640	22.389	55
60	0.015103	0.073027	82334	6013	397736	0.015117	2.683	1505808	18.289	60
65	0.024922	0.118451	76321	9040	360793	0.025057	2.698	1108073	14.519	65
70	0.047891	0.216943	67281	14596	301707	0.048378	2.623	747280	11.107	70
75	0.079695	0.335054	52685	17652	219759	0.080325	2.526	445573	8.457	75
80	0.127686	0.480607	35032	16837	131861	0.127686	2.428	225813	6.446	80
85	0.193669	1.000000	18196	18196	93952	0.126110	5.163	93952	5.163	85

TABLE 4 — OBSERVED VITAL RATES AND RATIOS

CRUDE RATES

Per Thousand	BOTH SEXES	MALES	FEMALES
BIRTH RATE	17.83	18.74	16.96
DEATH RATE	8.93	9.49	8.38
RATE OF INCREASE	8.91	9.25	8.57

PERCENT OF POPULATION IN AGE GROUP

	BOTH SEXES	MALES	FEMALES
UNDER 15	27.06	28.30	25.87
15 - 64	65.11	64.93	65.30
65 AND OLDER	7.82	6.77	8.84

RATES STANDARDIZED ON USA 1980

Per Thousand	BOTH SEXES	MALES	FEMALES
BIRTH RATE	19.67		18.52
DEATH RATE	12.44	12.37	12.51
RATE OF INCREASE	7.23		6.01

RATES STANDARDIZED ON MEXICO 1980

	BOTH SEXES	MALES	FEMALES
BIRTH RATE	17.95		17.51
DEATH RATE	6.01	6.59	5.41
RATE OF INCREASE	11.94		12.10

VITAL STATISTICS

GFR x 1000	66.440
TFR	2.292
GRR	1.110
NRR	1.027
μ	26.561
σ^2	38.317
GENERATION	26.542
POP. SEX RATIO	1.038
SEX RATIO AT BIRTH	1.065
DEP. RATIO x 100	53.576

PROJECTED POPULATION

AGE GROUP	1975 BOTH SEXES	1975 MALES	1975 FEMALES	1980 BOTH SEXES	1980 MALES	1980 FEMALES
0-4	1780	917	863	1881	969	912
5-9	1779	917	862	1765	909	856
10-14	1838	943	895	1775	915	860
15-19	1870	955	915	1833	939	894
20-24	1954	996	958	1861	949	912
25-29	1678	853	825	1943	989	954
30-34	1380	693	687	1666	845	821
35-39	1540	771	769	1367	684	683
40-44	1589	790	799	1520	758	762
45-49	1436	689	747	1556	769	787
50-54	1139	505	634	1393	662	731
55-59	614	271	343	1087	475	612
60-64	844	376	468	568	245	323
65-69	760	348	412	745	321	424
70-74	567	246	321	613	268	345
75-79	305	122	183	396	162	234
80-84	136	49	87	175	65	110
85+	91	30	61	92	30	62
TOTAL	21300	10471	10829	22236	10954	11282

STABLE EQUIVALENT TO ORIGINAL POPULATION

MALES Number	MALES Percent	FEMALES Number	FEMALES Percent	AGE GROUP	
952	7.5	896	7.0	0-4	
939	7.4	884	6.9	5-9	TABLE 5
932	7.3	878	6.9	10-14	
924	7.3	871	6.8	15-19	POPULATION
913	7.2	864	6.8	20-24	PROJECTED
902	7.1	857	6.7	25-29	WITH
889	7.0	848	6.6	30-34	FIXED
874	6.9	838	6.6	35-39	AGE-
855	6.7	826	6.5	40-44	SPECIFIC
828	6.5	810	6.3	45-49	BIRTH
791	6.2	788	6.2	50-54	AND
740	5.8	757	5.9	55-59	DEATH
666	5.2	710	5.6	60-64	RATES
565	4.4	641	5.0	65-69	(female
434	3.4	533	4.2	70-74	dominant,
283	2.2	387	3.0	75-79	in 000s)
149	1.2	231	1.8	80-84	
90	0.7	164	1.3	85+	
12726		12783		TOTAL	

VITAL RATES OF PROJECTED POPULATION

Per Thousand	1975 BOTH SEXES	1975 MALES	1975 FEMALES	1980 BOTH SEXES	1980 MALES	1980 FEMALES
BIRTH RATE	18.40	19.31	17.52	18.26	19.12	17.42
DEATH RATE	9.43	9.91	8.96	9.91	10.33	9.50
RATE OF INCREASE	8.97	9.40	8.56	8.35	8.79	7.93

AGE STRUCTURE OF PROJECTED POPULATION

	BOTH SEXES	MALES	FEMALES	BOTH SEXES	MALES	FEMALES
% UNDER 15	25.34	26.52	24.19	24.38	25.49	23.29
% 15-64	65.93	65.89	65.97	66.54	66.79	66.29
% 65 AND OLDER	8.73	7.60	9.83	9.08	7.71	10.41
DEPEND. RATIO x 100	51.68	51.78	51.58	50.29	49.72	50.85

VITAL RATES OF STABLE POPULATION

Per Thousand	MALES	FEMALES	
BIRTH RATE	15.93	14.88	TABLE 6
DEATH RATE	14.84	13.87	PROJECTED
RATE OF INCREASE		1.01	VITAL RATES AND RATIOS

STABLE AGE STRUCTURE

	MALES	FEMALES	
% UNDER 15	22.18	20.79	(female dominant)
% 15-64	65.86	63.92	
% 65 AND OLDER	11.96	15.30	
DEPEND. RATIO x 100	51.84	56.46	

AGE GROUP	FEMALE BIRTH RATES	NET MATERNITY FUNCTION	COEFF. OF MATRIX EQUATION	ORIGINAL MATRIX SUB-DIAGONAL	ORIGINAL MATRIX FIRST ROW	STABLE MATRIX FISHER VALUES	STABLE MATRIX REPRODUCTIVE VALUES
0-4	0.0000	0.0000	0.0000	0.99187	0.00000	1.062	923117
5-9	0.0000	0.0000	0.0003	0.99793	0.00027	1.076	965721
10-14	0.0001	0.0005	0.0585	0.99780	0.05906	1.084	993293
15-19	0.0250	0.1164	0.2404	0.99697	0.24343	1.029	988483
20-24	0.0784	0.3644	0.3224	0.99613	0.32742	0.778	644374
25-29	0.0606	0.2803	0.2207	0.99510	0.22497	0.436	300778
30-34	0.0349	0.1610	0.1184	0.99352	0.12126	0.200	154745
35-39	0.0165	0.0757	0.0498	0.99045	0.05131	0.073	58571
40-44	0.0052	0.0238	0.0135	0.98541	0.01406	0.019	14145
45-49	0.0007	0.0032	0.0025	0.97804	0.00268	0.004	2505
50-54	0.0004	0.0019	0.0009	0.96552	0.00100	0.001	375

MATRIX PARAMETERS

λ_1	1.00508	
λ_2	0.30816+0.71765i	TABLE 7
λ_4	-0.39624-0.37365i	
λ_6	-0.47496-0.15018i	LESLIE
r_1	0.00101	MATRIX
r_2	-0.04943+0.23304i	AND ITS
r_4	-0.12153-0.47711i	ANALYSIS
r_6	-0.13938-0.56707i	(females)
c_1	127853	
$2\pi/y$	26.9618	
Δ	11.6473	

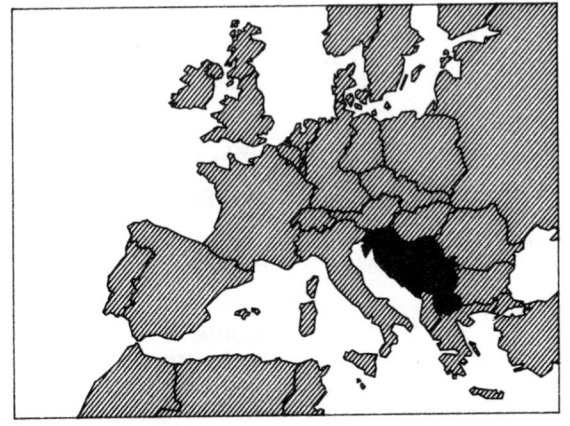

EDUCATION [1984]

% of primary school-age children enrolled:	98
secondary school-age children enrolled:	82
ca. 20-24 year olds in higher education:	20

LABOR FORCE

Average annual labor force growth (%) 1980-85:	1.0
% of the 1980 labor force in agriculture:	32
in industry:	33
in services:	34

GNP & INCOME DISTRIBUTION

GNP per capita (in US Dollars) 1985:	2070
GNP average annual growth rate (%) 1965-85:	4.1
% share of total household income 1978	
Lowest 20% of households:	6.6
Highest 10% of households:	22.9

HEALTH & NUTRITION

Population per physician 1981:	700
Daily calorie supply per capita 1985:	3602

TABLE 8

SOCIO-ECONOMIC INDICATORS

TABLE 1 — DATA

AGE AT LAST BIRTHDAY	ESTIMATED MID-YEAR POPULATION BOTH SEXES	MALES Number	MALES Percent	FEMALES Number	FEMALES Percent	BIRTHS BY AGE OF MOTHER AND SEX	DEATHS BOTH SEXES	DEATHS MALES	DEATHS FEMALES	AGE AT LAST BIRTHDAY
0	373097	192552	1.8	180545	1.7		15426	8370	7056	0
1-4	1438888	742251	7.1	696637	6.4		2457	1282	1175	1-4
5-9	1810537	926071	8.8	884466	8.2		928	525	403	5-9
10-14	1850788	947696	9.0	903092	8.3	282	697	427	270	10-14
15-19	1900702	971836	9.3	928866	8.6	50799	1245	815	430	15-19
20-24	1974214	1008600	9.6	965614	8.9	158193	1890	1340	550	20-24
25-29	1629988	832432	7.9	797556	7.4	101479	1821	1255	566	25-29
30-34	1329523	666871	6.3	662652	6.1	45048	1892	1261	631	30-34
35-39	1532007	764185	7.3	767822	7.1	23782	3017	1961	1056	35-39
40-44	1588596	792563	7.5	796033	7.3	7547	4835	3118	1717	40-44
45-49	1434763	690028	6.6	744735	6.9	792	6678	4220	2458	45-49
50-54	1147647	508769	4.8	638878	5.9	115	7936	4717	3219	50-54
55-59	619210	273191	2.6	346019	3.2		6760	3917	2843	55-59
60-64	854675	380043	3.6	474632	4.4		15257	8801	6456	60-64
65-69	766265	351629	3.3	414636	3.8		22792	12927	9865	65-69
70-74	572700	250291	2.4	322409	3.0		27998	14740	13258	70-74
75-79	307477	124599	1.2	182878	1.7		26644	12273	14371	75-79
80-84	134123	49413	0.5	84710	0.8	200476 N	18888	7778	11110	80-84
85+	86713	30289	0.3	56424	0.5	187561 F	17746	6397	11349	85+
TOTAL	21351913	10503309		10848604		388037	184907	96124	88783	TOTAL

TABLE 2 — MALE LIFE TABLE

x	nM_x	nq_x	l_x	nd_x	nL_x	nm_x	na_x	T_x	$\overset{\circ}{e}_x$	x
0	0.043469	0.041909	100000	4191	96412	0.043469	0.144	6704140	67.041	0
1	0.001727	0.006879	95809	659	381589	0.001727	1.500	6607728	68.968	1
5	0.000567	0.002831	95150	269	475077	0.000567	2.500	6226139	65.435	5
10	0.000451	0.002250	94881	214	473896	0.000451	2.624	5751063	60.614	10
15	0.000839	0.004185	94667	396	472431	0.000839	2.716	5277167	55.744	15
20	0.001329	0.006625	94271	625	469858	0.001329	2.603	4804736	50.967	20
25	0.001508	0.007527	93646	705	466522	0.001511	2.574	4334878	46.290	25
30	0.001891	0.009429	92942	876	462615	0.001894	2.612	3868355	41.621	30
35	0.002566	0.012754	92065	1174	457577	0.002566	2.659	3405740	36.993	35
40	0.003934	0.019492	90891	1772	450344	0.003934	2.679	2948163	32.436	40
45	0.006116	0.030297	89119	2700	439300	0.006146	2.668	2497819	28.028	45
50	0.009271	0.045680	86419	3948	422862	0.009335	2.661	2058519	23.820	50
55	0.014338	0.069664	82472	5745	398928	0.014402	2.662	1635657	19.833	55
60	0.023158	0.109797	76726	8424	363779	0.023158	2.643	1236729	16.119	60
65	0.036763	0.168989	68302	11542	313964	0.036763	2.613	872951	12.781	65
70	0.058891	0.259182	56760	14711	248104	0.059294	2.574	558986	9.848	70
75	0.098500	0.398110	42049	16740	168262	0.099487	2.492	310883	7.393	75
80	0.157408	0.556461	25309	14083	89470	0.157408	2.368	142621	5.635	80
85	0.211199	1.000000	11225	11225	53151	0.146506	4.735	53151	4.735	85

TABLE 3 — FEMALE LIFE TABLE

x	nM_x	nq_x	l_x	nd_x	nL_x	nm_x	na_x	T_x	$\overset{\circ}{e}_x$	x
0	0.039082	0.037806	100000	3781	96735	0.039082	0.136	7186432	71.864	0
1	0.001687	0.006718	96219	646	383262	0.001687	1.500	7089697	73.683	1
5	0.000456	0.002276	95573	217	477321	0.000456	2.500	6706436	70.171	5
10	0.000299	0.001494	95356	142	476422	0.000299	2.504	6229115	65.325	10
15	0.000463	0.002312	95213	220	475542	0.000463	2.621	5752693	60.419	15
20	0.000570	0.002846	94993	270	474313	0.000570	2.590	5277151	55.553	20
25	0.000710	0.003553	94723	337	472809	0.000712	2.611	4802838	50.704	25
30	0.000952	0.004758	94386	449	470872	0.000954	2.643	4330029	45.876	30
35	0.001375	0.006855	93937	644	468190	0.001375	2.679	3859157	41.082	35
40	0.002157	0.010731	93293	1001	464144	0.002157	2.681	3390967	36.347	40
45	0.003301	0.016403	92292	1514	457941	0.003306	2.676	2926824	31.713	45
50	0.005039	0.025086	90778	2277	448630	0.005076	2.690	2468883	27.197	50
55	0.008216	0.040565	88501	3590	434221	0.008268	2.693	2020253	22.827	55
60	0.013602	0.065947	84911	5600	411672	0.013602	2.700	1586031	18.679	60
65	0.023792	0.112898	79311	8954	375771	0.023829	2.679	1174359	14.807	65
70	0.041122	0.188741	70357	13279	320680	0.041410	2.658	798588	11.351	70
75	0.078582	0.332829	57078	18997	239022	0.079479	2.559	477909	8.373	75
80	0.131153	0.490578	38081	18682	142440	0.131153	2.433	238887	6.273	80
85	0.201138	1.000000	19399	19399	96447	0.134299	4.972	96447	4.972	85

TABLE 4 — OBSERVED VITAL RATES AND RATIOS

CRUDE RATES

Per Thousand	BOTH SEXES	MALES	FEMALES
BIRTH RATE	18.17	19.09	17.29
DEATH RATE	8.66	9.15	8.18
RATE OF INCREASE	9.51	9.94	9.11

PERCENT OF POPULATION IN AGE GROUP

UNDER 15	25.63	26.74	24.56
15 - 64	65.62	65.58	65.66
65 AND OLDER	8.75	7.68	9.78

RATES STANDARDIZED ON USA 1980

Per Thousand	BOTH SEXES	MALES	FEMALES
BIRTH RATE	19.66		18.48
DEATH RATE	11.67	11.48	11.86
RATE OF INCREASE	7.99		6.62

RATES STANDARDIZED ON MEXICO 1980

	BOTH SEXES	MALES	FEMALES
BIRTH RATE	18.04		17.58
DEATH RATE	5.22	5.78	4.65
RATE OF INCREASE	12.82		12.92

VITAL STATISTICS

GFR x 1000	68.518
TFR	2.279
GRR	1.101
NRR	1.042
μ	26.256
σ^2	35.867
GENERATION	26.228
POP. SEX RATIO	1.033
SEX RATIO AT BIRTH	1.069
DEP. RATIO x 100	52.390

AGE AT LAST BIRTHDAY	ESTIMATED MID-YEAR POPULATION					BIRTHS BY AGE OF MOTHER AND SEX	DEATHS			AGE AT LAST BIRTHDAY
	BOTH SEXES	MALES		FEMALES			BOTH SEXES	MALES	FEMALES	
		Number	Percent	Number	Percent					
0	368537	190284	1.7	178253	1.6		12021	6505	5516	0
1-4	1477535	763192	6.9	714343	6.3		1576	857	719	1-4
5-9	1793403	924921	8.4	868482	7.7		816	469	347	5-9
10-14	1797507	919003	8.4	878504	7.8	281	623	397	226	10-14
15-19	1837068	939992	8.6	897076	7.9	42949	1135	778	357	15-19
20-24	1885629	962676	8.8	922953	8.2	149423	1702	1220	482	20-24
25-29	1961596	1000095	9.1	961501	8.5	115969	1953	1428	525	25-29
30-34	1619728	825527	7.5	794201	7.0	49806	2022	1391	631	30-34
35-39	1318290	659518	6.0	658772	5.8	17193	2448	1685	763	35-39
40-44	1512942	751685	6.8	761257	6.7	5717	4448	3014	1434	40-44
45-49	1559759	773122	7.0	786637	7.0	686	7628	5151	2477	45-49
50-54	1395875	664553	6.0	731322	6.5	96	10516	6831	3685	50-54
55-59	1101805	480781	4.4	621024	5.5		12228	7358	4870	55-59
60-64	580095	250407	2.3	329688	2.9		9889	5755	4134	60-64
65-69	766061	329610	3.0	436451	3.9		21655	12006	9649	65-69
70-74	636668	279695	2.5	356973	3.2		30778	16456	14322	70-74
75-79	425094	175265	1.6	249829	2.2		32131	15549	16582	75-79
80-84	181387	68486	0.6	112901	1.0	197371 M	24362	10219	14143	80-84
85+	85477	29024	0.3	56453	0.5	184749 F	19430	6853	12577	85+
TOTAL	22304456	10987836		11316620		382120	197361	103922	93439	TOTAL

TABLE 1 DATA

x	$_nM_x$	$_nq_x$	l_x	$_nd_x$	$_nL_x$	$_nm_x$	$_na_x$	T_x	$\overset{\circ}{e}_x$	x
0	0.034186	0.033196	100000	3320	97106	0.034186	0.128	6778398	67.784	0
1	0.001123	0.004479	96680	433	385639	0.001123	1.500	6681293	69.107	1
5	0.000507	0.002532	96247	244	480627	0.000507	2.500	6295654	65.411	5
10	0.000432	0.002158	96004	207	479532	0.000432	2.653	5815026	60.571	10
15	0.000828	0.004131	95796	396	478076	0.000828	2.708	5335494	55.696	15
20	0.001267	0.006317	95401	603	475555	0.001267	2.596	4857419	50.916	20
25	0.001428	0.007116	94798	675	472344	0.001428	2.559	4381863	46.223	25
30	0.001685	0.008425	94124	793	468742	0.001692	2.635	3909520	41.536	30
35	0.002555	0.012737	93330	1189	463897	0.002563	2.682	3440778	36.867	35
40	0.004010	0.019865	92142	1830	456502	0.004010	2.702	2976881	32.308	40
45	0.006663	0.032806	90311	2963	444686	0.006663	2.681	2520379	27.908	45
50	0.010279	0.050413	87349	4404	426401	0.010327	2.651	2075693	23.763	50
55	0.015304	0.074315	82945	6164	400147	0.015405	2.635	1649293	19.884	55
60	0.022983	0.109404	76781	8400	364007	0.023077	2.631	1249146	16.269	60
65	0.036425	0.167559	68381	11458	314559	0.036425	2.613	885139	12.944	65
70	0.058836	0.257205	56923	14641	248844	0.058836	2.557	570579	10.024	70
75	0.088717	0.365359	42282	15448	172757	0.089421	2.498	321735	7.609	75
80	0.149213	0.539644	26834	14481	96660	0.149811	2.410	148979	5.552	80
85	0.236115	1.000000	12353	12353	52318	0.175332	4.235	52318	4.235	85

TABLE 2 MALE LIFE TABLE

x	$_nM_x$	$_nq_x$	l_x	$_nd_x$	$_nL_x$	$_nm_x$	$_na_x$	T_x	$\overset{\circ}{e}_x$	x
0	0.030945	0.030127	100000	3013	97357	0.030945	0.123	7327455	73.275	0
1	0.001007	0.004016	96987	390	386976	0.001007	1.500	7230098	74.547	1
5	0.000400	0.001996	96598	193	482507	0.000400	2.500	6843123	70.841	5
10	0.000257	0.001285	96405	124	481715	0.000257	2.498	6360616	65.978	10
15	0.000398	0.001988	96281	191	480953	0.000398	2.638	5878901	61.060	15
20	0.000522	0.002608	96090	251	479837	0.000522	2.558	5397947	56.176	20
25	0.000546	0.002728	95839	261	478569	0.000546	2.604	4918111	51.316	25
30	0.000795	0.003984	95578	381	476997	0.000798	2.658	4439542	46.450	30
35	0.001158	0.005789	95197	551	474712	0.001161	2.692	3962545	41.625	35
40	0.001884	0.009378	94646	888	471200	0.001884	2.715	3487833	36.851	40
45	0.003149	0.015631	93758	1466	465421	0.003149	2.701	3016632	32.175	45
50	0.005039	0.024944	92293	2302	456129	0.005047	2.683	2551211	27.643	50
55	0.007842	0.038790	89990	3491	441851	0.007900	2.679	2095081	23.281	55
60	0.012539	0.061334	86500	5305	420287	0.012623	2.698	1653230	19.113	60
65	0.022108	0.105181	81194	8540	386292	0.022108	2.696	1232943	15.185	65
70	0.040121	0.183402	72654	13325	331743	0.040166	2.634	846651	11.653	70
75	0.066373	0.288281	59329	17104	255309	0.066992	2.583	514908	8.679	75
80	0.125269	0.477065	42226	20144	160485	0.125522	2.486	259599	6.148	80
85	0.222787	1.000000	22081	22081	99114	0.158875	4.489	99114	4.489	85

TABLE 3 FEMALE LIFE TABLE

CRUDE RATES

Per Thousand	BOTH SEXES	MALES	FEMALES
BIRTH RATE	17.13	17.96	16.33
DEATH RATE	8.85	9.46	8.26
RATE OF INCREASE	8.28	8.50	8.07

PERCENT OF POPULATION IN AGE GROUP

UNDER 15	24.38	25.46	23.32
15 - 64	66.23	66.51	65.96
65 AND OLDER	9.39	8.03	10.72

RATES STANDARDIZED ON USA 1980

Per Thousand	BOTH SEXES	MALES	FEMALES
BIRTH RATE	18.55		17.45
DEATH RATE	11.30	11.27	11.34
RATE OF INCREASE	7.25		6.11

RATES STANDARDIZED ON MEXICO 1980

	BOTH SEXES	MALES	FEMALES
BIRTH RATE	17.02		16.59
DEATH RATE	4.79	5.42	4.14
RATE OF INCREASE	12.23		12.44

VITAL STATISTICS

GFR x 1000	66.083	
TFR	2.140	
GRR	1.035	
NRR	0.991	
μ	26.110	
σ^2	33.511	
GENERATION	26.116	
POP. SEX RATIO	1.030	
SEX RATIO AT BIRTH	1.068	
DEP. RATIO x 100	50.983	

TABLE 4 OBSERVED VITAL RATES AND RATIOS

TABLE 1 — DATA

AGE AT LAST BIRTHDAY	ESTIMATED MID-YEAR POPULATION BOTH SEXES	MALES Number	Percent	FEMALES Number	Percent	BIRTHS BY AGE OF MOTHER AND SEX	DEATHS BOTH SEXES	MALES	FEMALES	AGE AT LAST BIRTHDAY
0	363202	187125	1.6	176077	1.5		10361	5778	4583	0
1-4	1458017	752463	6.6	705554	6.0		1573	829	744	1-4
5-9	1866113	959611	8.4	906502	7.8		788	452	336	5-9
10-14	1823585	937357	8.2	886228	7.6	200	583	388	195	10-14
15-19	1805667	926710	8.1	878957	7.5	38458	1065	690	375	15-19
20-24	1857191	949607	8.3	907584	7.8	140296	1539	1095	444	20-24
25-29	1857392	949527	8.3	907865	7.8	111762	1717	1260	457	25-29
30-34	1887414	967616	8.5	919798	7.9	53663	2341	1657	684	30-34
35-39	1581047	804400	7.0	776647	6.6	17994	2868	1966	902	35-39
40-44	1301628	651507	5.7	650121	5.6	3722	3810	2557	1253	40-44
45-49	1486669	738027	6.5	748642	6.4	440	7094	4825	2269	45-49
50-54	1508026	741569	6.5	766457	6.6	94	11656	8009	3647	50-54
55-59	1333730	626180	5.5	707550	6.1		15547	10111	5436	55-59
60-64	1033246	439655	3.8	593591	5.1		17936	10482	7454	60-64
65-69	520830	217821	1.9	303009	2.6		14241	7762	6479	65-69
70-74	631606	261637	2.3	369969	3.2		29338	15045	14293	70-74
75-79	457957	190546	1.7	267411	2.3		36750	17981	18769	75-79
80-84	241334	93545	0.8	147789	1.3	189083 M	30002	13114	16888	80-84
85+	109414	38302	0.3	71112	0.6	177546 F	23674	8439	15235	85+
TOTAL	23124068	11433205		11690863		366629	212883	112440	100443	TOTAL

TABLE 2 — MALE LIFE TABLE

x	nM_x	nq_x	l_x	nd_x	nL_x	nm_x	na_x	T_x	$\overset{\circ}{e}_x$	x
0	0.030878	0.030063	100000	3006	97362	0.030878	0.122	6805710	68.057	0
1	0.001102	0.004395	96994	426	386909	0.001102	1.500	6708348	69.163	1
5	0.000471	0.002352	96567	227	482269	0.000471	2.500	6321439	65.461	5
10	0.000414	0.002069	96340	199	481230	0.000414	2.636	5839170	60.610	10
15	0.000745	0.003716	96141	357	479885	0.000745	2.705	5357940	55.730	15
20	0.001153	0.005750	95784	551	477598	0.001153	2.603	4878055	50.928	20
25	0.001327	0.006614	95233	630	474644	0.001327	2.585	4400457	46.207	25
30	0.001712	0.008534	94603	807	471105	0.001714	2.633	3925813	41.498	30
35	0.002444	0.012223	93796	1146	466321	0.002458	2.682	3454708	36.832	35
40	0.003925	0.019501	92649	1807	459101	0.003935	2.705	2988387	32.255	40
45	0.006538	0.032204	90843	2926	447487	0.006538	2.701	2529287	27.843	45
50	0.010800	0.052670	87917	4631	428754	0.010800	2.661	2081799	23.679	50
55	0.016147	0.078080	83286	6503	401025	0.016216	2.631	1653045	19.848	55
60	0.023841	0.113480	76783	8713	363116	0.023996	2.613	1252020	16.306	60
65	0.035635	0.164802	68070	11218	313478	0.035786	2.605	888904	13.059	65
70	0.057503	0.252304	56852	14344	249445	0.057503	2.573	575426	10.121	70
75	0.094366	0.381979	42508	16237	171767	0.094530	2.489	325981	7.669	75
80	0.140189	0.513172	26271	13481	96166	0.140189	2.390	154213	5.870	80
85	0.220328	1.000000	12789	12789	58047	0.156969	4.539	58047	4.539	85

TABLE 3 — FEMALE LIFE TABLE

x	nM_x	nq_x	l_x	nd_x	nL_x	nm_x	na_x	T_x	$\overset{\circ}{e}_x$	x
0	0.026028	0.025442	100000	2544	97746	0.026028	0.114	7386775	73.868	0
1	0.001054	0.004207	97456	410	388798	0.001054	1.500	7289028	74.793	1
5	0.000371	0.001852	97046	180	484780	0.000371	2.500	6900230	71.103	5
10	0.000220	0.001100	96866	107	484070	0.000220	2.552	6415450	66.230	10
15	0.000427	0.002131	96760	206	483310	0.000427	2.631	5931380	61.300	15
20	0.000489	0.002443	96553	236	482185	0.000489	2.532	5448070	56.425	20
25	0.000503	0.002514	96318	242	481008	0.000503	2.604	4965885	51.557	25
30	0.000744	0.003716	96075	357	479550	0.000744	2.684	4484878	46.681	30
35	0.001161	0.005828	95718	558	477314	0.001169	2.708	4005327	41.845	35
40	0.001927	0.009614	95161	915	473695	0.001931	2.696	3528014	37.074	40
45	0.003031	0.015049	94246	1418	467947	0.003031	2.686	3054319	32.408	45
50	0.004758	0.023533	92827	2184	459094	0.004758	2.692	2586371	27.862	50
55	0.007683	0.037805	90643	3427	445310	0.007695	2.693	2127277	23.469	55
60	0.012557	0.061516	87216	5365	423704	0.012663	2.693	1681967	19.285	60
65	0.021382	0.102624	81851	8400	389848	0.021547	2.690	1258263	15.373	65
70	0.038633	0.177130	73451	13010	336770	0.038633	2.657	868415	11.823	70
75	0.070188	0.300998	60441	18193	257916	0.070537	2.566	531645	8.796	75
80	0.114271	0.443597	42248	18741	164006	0.114271	2.480	273729	6.479	80
85	0.214240	1.000000	23507	23507	109723	0.149098	4.668	109723	4.668	85

TABLE 4 — OBSERVED VITAL RATES AND RATIOS

CRUDE RATES

Per Thousand	BOTH SEXES	MALES	FEMALES
BIRTH RATE	15.85	16.54	15.19
DEATH RATE	9.21	9.83	8.59
RATE OF INCREASE	6.65	6.70	6.60

PERCENT OF POPULATION IN AGE GROUP

UNDER 15	23.83	24.81	22.88
15 - 64	67.69	68.18	67.21
65 AND OLDER	8.48	7.01	9.92

RATES STANDARDIZED ON USA 1980

Per Thousand	BOTH SEXES	MALES	FEMALES
BIRTH RATE	17.81		16.77
DEATH RATE	11.03	11.13	10.95
RATE OF INCREASE	6.77		5.82

RATES STANDARDIZED ON MEXICO 1980

	BOTH SEXES	MALES	FEMALES
BIRTH RATE	16.30		15.91
DEATH RATE	4.60	5.28	3.92
RATE OF INCREASE	11.70		11.99

VITAL STATISTICS

GFR x 1000	63.325
TFR	2.048
GRR	0.992
NRR	0.954
μ	26.040
σ^2	31.171
GENERATION	26.068
POP. SEX RATIO	1.023
SEX RATIO AT BIRTH	1.065
DEP. RATIO x 100	47.739

PROJECTED POPULATION

AGE GROUP	1990			1995		
	BOTH SEXES	MALES	FEMALES	BOTH SEXES	MALES	FEMALES
0-4	1775	913	862	1767	909	858
5-9	1814	936	878	1769	910	859
10-14	1863	958	905	1811	934	877
15-19	1820	935	885	1859	955	904
20-24	1799	922	877	1813	930	883
25-29	1849	944	905	1792	917	875
30-34	1847	942	905	1840	937	903
35-39	1874	958	916	1834	933	901
40-44	1563	792	771	1852	943	909
45-49	1277	635	642	1533	772	761
50-54	1441	707	734	1238	608	630
55-59	1437	694	743	1373	661	712
60-64	1240	567	673	1335	628	707
65-69	926	380	546	1108	489	619
70-74	435	173	262	774	302	472
75-79	463	180	283	319	119	200
80-84	277	107	170	281	101	180
85+	155	56	99	178	64	114
TOTAL	23855	11799	12056	24476	12112	12364

STABLE EQUIVALENT TO ORIGINAL POPULATION

	MALES		FEMALES		AGE GROUP	
	Number	Percent	Number	Percent		
	932	6.7	879	6.2	0-4	
	936	6.7	884	6.2	5-9	TABLE 5
	943	6.8	890	6.2	10-14	
	948	6.8	897	6.3	15-19	POPULATION
	952	6.8	903	6.3	20-24	PROJECTED
	955	6.9	909	6.4	25-29	WITH
	956	6.9	914	6.4	30-34	FIXED
	955	6.9	918	6.4	35-39	AGE-
	949	6.8	919	6.4	40-44	SPECIFIC
	933	6.7	916	6.4	45-49	BIRTH
	902	6.5	907	6.4	50-54	AND
	851	6.1	888	6.2	55-59	DEATH
	778	5.6	852	6.0	60-64	RATES
	677	4.9	791	5.5	65-69	(female
	544	3.9	690	4.8	70-74	dominant,
	378	2.7	533	3.7	75-79	in 000s)
	213	1.5	342	2.4	80-84	
	130	0.9	231	1.6	85+	
	13932		14263		TOTAL	

VITAL RATES OF PROJECTED POPULATION

Per Thousand	1990			1995		
	BOTH SEXES	MALES	FEMALES	BOTH SEXES	MALES	FEMALES
BIRTH RATE	15.29	15.95	14.65	14.84	15.46	14.22
DEATH RATE	9.80	10.32	9.30	10.22	10.69	9.75
RATE OF INCREASE	5.49	5.63	5.35	4.62	4.77	4.47

VITAL RATES OF STABLE POPULATION

Per Thousand	MALES	FEMALES	TABLE 6
BIRTH RATE	13.75	12.61	PROJECTED
DEATH RATE	15.50	14.40	VITAL RATES
RATE OF INCREASE		-1.79	AND RATIOS

AGE STRUCTURE OF PROJECTED POPULATION

% UNDER 15	22.85	23.79	21.94	21.84	22.72	20.98
% 15-64	67.69	68.62	66.78	67.28	68.39	66.20
% 65 AND OLDER	9.46	7.60	11.28	10.87	8.88	12.82
DEPEND. RATIO x 100	47.74	45.74	49.75	48.62	46.22	51.06

STABLE AGE STRUCTURE

% UNDER 15	20.17	18.60	(female dominant)
% 15-64	65.89	63.27	
% 65 AND OLDER	13.94	18.13	
DEPEND. RATIO x 100	51.78	58.06	

AGE GROUP	FEMALE BIRTH RATES	NET MATERNITY FUNCTION	COEFF. OF MATRIX EQUATION	ORIGINAL MATRIX		STABLE MATRIX		MATRIX PARAMETERS		
				SUB-DIAGONAL	FIRST ROW	FISHER VALUES	REPRODUCTIVE VALUES			
0-4	0.0000	0.0000	0.0000	0.99637	0.00000	1.023	901971	λ_1	0.99110	
5-9	0.0000	0.0000	0.0003	0.99854	0.00027	1.018	922504	λ_2	0.29813+0.74015i	TABLE 7
10-14	0.0001	0.0005	0.0515	0.99843	0.05173	1.010	894911	λ_4	-0.38250-0.36075i	
15-19	0.0212	0.1024	0.2317	0.99767	0.23323	0.949	834457	λ_6	-0.39284-0.10412i	LESLIE
20-24	0.0749	0.3610	0.3239	0.99756	0.32678	0.704	638887	r_1	-0.00179	MATRIX
25-29	0.0596	0.2868	0.2111	0.99697	0.21355	0.364	330681	r_2	-0.04515+0.23758i	AND ITS
30-34	0.0283	0.1355	0.0945	0.99534	0.09590	0.143	131486	r_4	-0.12857-0.47709i	ANALYSIS
35-39	0.0112	0.0536	0.0333	0.99242	0.03399	0.044	33994	r_6	-0.18008-0.57650i	(females)
40-44	0.0028	0.0131	0.0072	0.98787	0.00743	0.009	5639	c_1	142620	
45-49	0.0003	0.0013	0.0008	0.98108	0.00083	0.001	755	$2\pi/y$	26.4471	
50-54	0.0001	0.0003	0.0001	0.96998	0.00014	0.000	114	Δ	10.1921	

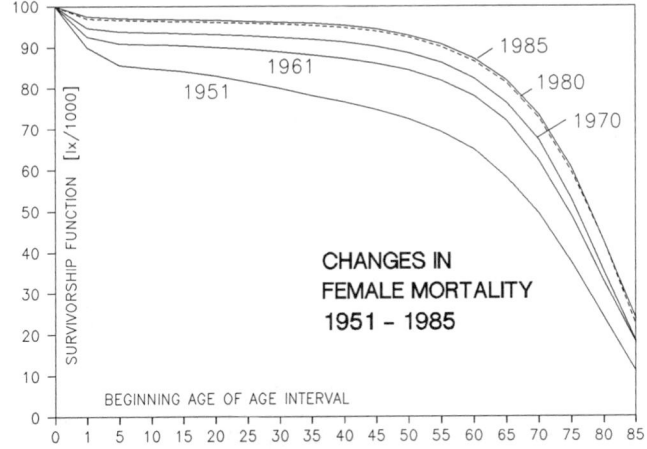

CHANGES IN FEMALE MORTALITY 1951 - 1985

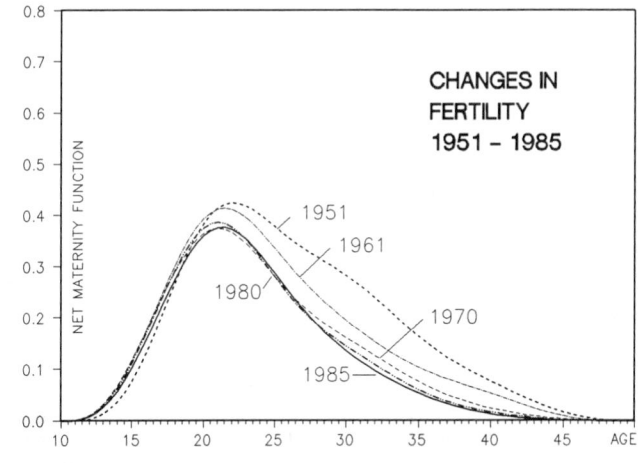

CHANGES IN FERTILITY 1951 - 1985

TABLE 1 — DATA

AGE AT LAST BIRTHDAY	ESTIMATED MID-YEAR POPULATION BOTH SEXES	MALES Number	MALES Percent	FEMALES Number	FEMALES Percent	BIRTHS BY AGE OF MOTHER AND SEX	DEATHS BOTH SEXES	DEATHS MALES	DEATHS FEMALES	AGE AT LAST BIRTHDAY
0	261629	133347	2.0	128282	2.0		4778	2685	2093	0
1-4	988136	505594	7.7	482542	7.4		842	467	375	1-4
5-9	1246436	638899	9.7	607537	9.3		481	292	189	5-9
10-14	1251076	640774	9.8	610302	9.4	156	419	287	132	10-14
15-19	1136296	577771	8.8	558525	8.6	30347	1281	907	374	15-19
20-24	1140607	531547	8.9	559060	8.6	98469	1423	1070	353	20-24
25-29	962394	497534	7.6	464860	7.2	87467	1007	705	302	25-29
30-34	823969	425822	6.5	398147	6.1	39604	1021	653	368	30-34
35-39	754860	388710	5.9	366150	5.6	15719	1374	883	491	35-39
40-44	803426	415976	6.3	387450	6.0	4301	2236	1376	860	40-44
45-49	797844	407574	6.2	390270	6.0	297	3862	2423	1439	45-49
50-54	677510	339272	5.2	338238	5.2	2	5146	3321	1825	50-54
55-59	616496	306569	4.7	309927	4.8		7619	5053	2566	55-59
60-64	516213	249170	3.8	267043	4.1		9787	6433	3354	60-64
65-69	399031	189631	2.9	209400	3.2		11897	7678	4219	65-69
70-74	298986	127045	1.9	171941	2.6		14005	7942	6063	70-74
75-79	203537	77825	1.2	125712	1.9		15355	7604	7751	75-79
80-84	121889	43819	0.7	78070	1.2	141114 M	14215	6323	7892	80-84
85+	66930	21057	0.3	45873	0.7	135248 F	13902	4972	8930	85+
TOTAL	13067265	6567936		6499329		276362	110650	61074	49576	TOTAL

TABLE 2 — MALE LIFE TABLE

x	$_nM_x$	$_nq_x$	l_x	$_nd_x$	$_nL_x$	$_nm_x$	$_na_x$	T_x	$\overset{\circ}{e}_x$	x
0	0.020135	0.019779	100000	1978	98228	0.020135	0.104	6822610	68.226	0
1	0.000924	0.003686	98022	361	391185	0.000924	1.500	6724381	68.601	1
5	0.000457	0.002283	97661	223	487747	0.000457	2.500	6333196	64.849	5
10	0.000448	0.002245	97438	219	486755	0.000449	3.013	5845449	59.992	10
15	0.001570	0.007833	97219	761	484330	0.001572	2.682	5358695	55.120	15
20	0.001840	0.009156	96458	883	480062	0.001840	2.479	4874365	50.534	20
25	0.001417	0.007048	95574	674	476156	0.001415	2.452	4394303	45.978	25
30	0.001534	0.007660	94901	727	472769	0.001538	2.612	3918147	41.287	30
35	0.002272	0.011310	94174	1065	468374	0.002274	2.657	3445379	36.585	35
40	0.003308	0.016416	93109	1528	462062	0.003308	2.722	2977005	31.973	40
45	0.005945	0.029390	91580	2692	451744	0.005958	2.712	2514943	27.462	45
50	0.009789	0.048035	88889	4270	434612	0.009824	2.697	2063199	23.211	50
55	0.016482	0.079559	84619	6732	407356	0.016527	2.662	1628587	19.246	55
60	0.025818	0.122045	77887	9506	366906	0.025908	2.630	1221231	15.680	60
65	0.040489	0.185218	68381	12665	311421	0.040670	2.593	854325	12.494	65
70	0.062513	0.272182	55716	15165	241345	0.062835	2.545	542904	9.744	70
75	0.097706	0.392610	40551	15921	162481	0.097985	2.470	301559	7.437	75
80	0.144298	0.523768	24630	12901	89402	0.144298	2.384	139078	5.647	80
85	0.236121	1.000000	11730	11730	49677	0.175754	4.235	49677	4.235	85

TABLE 3 — FEMALE LIFE TABLE

x	$_nM_x$	$_nq_x$	l_x	$_nd_x$	$_nL_x$	$_nm_x$	$_na_x$	T_x	$\overset{\circ}{e}_x$	x
0	0.016316	0.016079	100000	1608	98549	0.016316	0.098	7480589	74.806	0
1	0.000777	0.003103	98392	305	392805	0.000777	1.500	7382040	75.027	1
5	0.000311	0.001554	98087	152	490053	0.000311	2.500	6989234	71.256	5
10	0.000216	0.001083	97934	106	489443	0.000217	2.843	6499181	66.363	10
15	0.000670	0.003346	97828	327	488365	0.000670	2.628	6009738	61.431	15
20	0.000631	0.003152	97501	307	486734	0.000631	2.492	5521373	56.629	20
25	0.000650	0.003250	97194	316	485208	0.000651	2.593	5034639	51.800	25
30	0.000924	0.004630	96878	449	483337	0.000928	2.653	4549430	46.960	30
35	0.001341	0.006695	96429	646	480659	0.001343	2.697	4066094	42.167	35
40	0.002220	0.011042	95784	1058	476501	0.002220	2.714	3585434	37.433	40
45	0.003687	0.018298	94726	1733	469594	0.003691	2.671	3108933	32.820	45
50	0.005396	0.026712	92993	2484	459160	0.005410	2.664	2639339	28.382	50
55	0.008279	0.040703	90509	3684	443924	0.008299	2.660	2180179	24.088	55
60	0.012560	0.061266	86825	5319	421700	0.012614	2.664	1736255	19.997	60
65	0.020148	0.096712	81505	7883	389217	0.020252	2.677	1314555	16.128	65
70	0.035262	0.163338	73623	12025	339863	0.035383	2.651	925338	12.569	70
75	0.061657	0.269240	61597	16584	267807	0.061927	2.577	585475	9.505	75
80	0.101089	0.403821	45013	18177	179814	0.101089	2.511	317668	7.057	80
85	0.194668	1.000000	26836	26836	137854	0.127001	5.137	137854	5.137	85

TABLE 4 — OBSERVED VITAL RATES AND RATIOS

CRUDE RATES

Per Thousand	BOTH SEXES	MALES	FEMALES
BIRTH RATE	21.15	21.49	20.81
DEATH RATE	8.47	9.30	7.63
RATE OF INCREASE	12.68	12.19	13.18

PERCENT OF POPULATION IN AGE GROUP

UNDER 15	28.68	29.21	28.14
15 - 64	62.98	63.79	62.16
65 AND OLDER	8.34	6.99	9.71

RATES STANDARDIZED ON USA 1980

Per Thousand	BOTH SEXES	MALES	FEMALES
BIRTH RATE	24.50		23.32
DEATH RATE	10.81	11.55	10.11
RATE OF INCREASE	13.69		13.21

RATES STANDARDIZED ON MEXICO 1980

	BOTH SEXES	MALES	FEMALES
BIRTH RATE	22.02		21.72
DEATH RATE	4.38	5.21	3.54
RATE OF INCREASE	17.64		18.19

VITAL STATISTICS

GFR x 1000	88.451
TFR	2.866
GRR	1.402
NRR	1.361
μ	26.915
σ^2	33.555
GENERATION	26.722
POP. SEX RATIO	0.990
SEX RATIO AT BIRTH	1.043
DEP. RATIO x 100	58.783

PROJECTED POPULATION

AGE GROUP	1976 BOTH SEXES	1976 MALES	1976 FEMALES	1981 BOTH SEXES	1981 MALES	1981 FEMALES	STABLE EQUIVALENT TO ORIGINAL POPULATION MALES Number	MALES Percent	FEMALES Number	FEMALES Percent	AGE GROUP	
0-4	1422	725	697	1538	784	754	681	10.3	656	9.7	0-4	
5-9	1246	637	609	1417	722	695	641	9.7	617	9.1	5-9	TABLE 5
10-14	1245	638	607	1243	635	608	604	9.1	582	8.6	10-14	
15-19	1247	638	609	1239	634	605	567	8.6	548	8.1	15-19	POPULATION
20-24	1130	573	557	1239	632	607	531	8.0	516	7.6	20-24	PROJECTED
25-29	1134	577	557	1123	568	555	497	7.5	485	7.2	25-29	WITH
30-34	957	494	463	1128	573	555	466	7.0	456	6.7	30-34	FIXED
35-39	818	422	396	950	489	461	435	6.6	428	6.3	35-39	AGE-
40-44	746	383	363	809	416	393	405	6.1	401	5.9	40-44	SPECIFIC
45-49	789	407	382	733	375	358	374	5.6	373	5.5	45-49	BIRTH
50-54	774	392	382	764	391	373	340	5.1	344	5.1	50-54	AND
55-59	645	318	327	737	368	369	301	4.5	314	4.6	55-59	DEATH
60-64	570	276	294	597	286	311	256	3.9	281	4.2	60-64	RATES
65-69	457	211	246	506	234	272	205	3.1	245	3.6	65-69	(female
70-74	330	147	183	379	164	215	150	2.3	202	3.0	70-74	dominant,
75-79	221	86	135	243	99	144	95	1.4	150	2.2	75-79	in 000s)
80-84	127	43	84	138	47	91	49	0.7	95	1.4	80-84	
85+	84	24	60	89	24	65	26	0.4	69	1.0	85+	
TOTAL	13942	6991	6951	14872	7441	7431	6623		6762		TOTAL	

VITAL RATES OF PROJECTED POPULATION

Per Thousand	1976 BOTH SEXES	1976 MALES	1976 FEMALES	1981 BOTH SEXES	1981 MALES	1981 FEMALES
BIRTH RATE	21.77	22.17	21.37	21.78	22.23	21.34
DEATH RATE	8.79	9.54	8.03	8.92	9.69	8.15
RATE OF INCREASE	12.98	12.64	13.33	12.86	12.54	13.18

VITAL RATES OF STABLE POPULATION

Per Thousand	MALES	FEMALES	
BIRTH RATE	21.63	20.30	TABLE 6
DEATH RATE	10.10	8.76	PROJECTED
RATE OF INCREASE		11.54	VITAL RATES AND RATIOS (female dominant)

AGE STRUCTURE OF PROJECTED POPULATION

	BOTH SEXES	MALES	FEMALES	BOTH SEXES	MALES	FEMALES
% UNDER 15	28.06	28.60	27.52	28.24	28.78	27.70
% 15-64	63.19	64.09	62.28	62.65	63.59	61.71
% 65 AND OLDER	8.75	7.31	10.20	9.11	7.63	10.59
DEPEND. RATIO x 100	58.26	56.04	60.56	59.61	57.25	62.04

STABLE AGE STRUCTURE

	MALES	FEMALES
% UNDER 15	29.09	27.42
% 15-64	62.98	61.31
% 65 AND OLDER	7.93	11.27
DEPEND. RATIO x 100	58.77	63.11

AGE GROUP	FEMALE BIRTH RATES	NET MATERNITY FUNCTION	COEFF. OF MATRIX EQUATION	ORIGINAL MATRIX SUB-DIAGONAL	ORIGINAL MATRIX FIRST ROW	STABLE MATRIX FISHER VALUES	STABLE MATRIX REPRODUCTIVE VALUES	MATRIX PARAMETERS		
0-4	0.0000	0.0000	0.0000	0.99735	0.00000	1.047	639715	λ_1	1.05941	
5-9	0.0000	0.0000	0.0003	0.99876	0.00031	1.112	675861	λ_2	0.34553+0.78452i	TABLE 7
10-14	0.0001	0.0006	0.0652	0.99780	0.06549	1.180	719970	λ_4	-0.37827+0.42304i	
15-19	0.0266	0.1299	0.2747	0.99666	0.27639	1.184	661180	λ_6	-0.03440+0.45258i	LESLIE
20-24	0.0862	0.4196	0.4332	0.99686	0.43728	0.968	541111	r_1	0.01154	MATRIX
25-29	0.0921	0.4468	0.3410	0.99614	0.34536	0.569	264604	r_2	-0.03081+0.23118i	AND ITS
30-34	0.0487	0.2353	0.1681	0.99446	0.17092	0.242	96459	r_4	-0.11330+0.46008i	ANALYSIS
35-39	0.0210	0.1010	0.0634	0.99135	0.06485	0.078	28591	r_6	-0.15798+0.32933i	(females)
40-44	0.0054	0.0259	0.0138	0.98550	0.01425	0.015	5788	c_1	67623	
45-49	0.0004	0.0017	0.0009	0.97778	0.00092	0.001	358	$2\pi/y$	27.1782	
50-54	0.0000	0.0000	0.0000	0.96682	0.00001	0.000	2	Δ	3.2481	

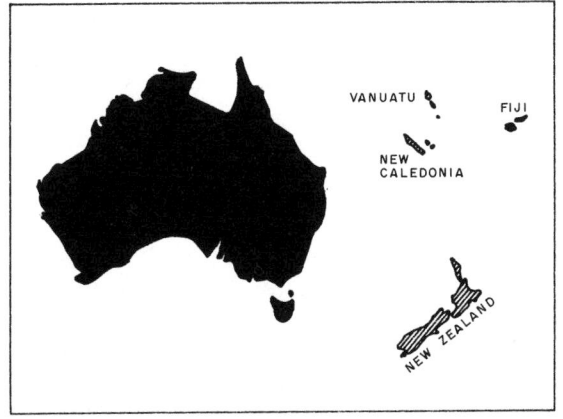

EDUCATION [1984]

% of primary school-age children enrolled:	107
secondary school-age children enrolled:	94
ca. 20-24 year olds in higher education:	27

LABOR FORCE

Average annual labor force growth (%) 1980-85:	1.8
% of the 1980 labor force in agriculture:	7
in industry:	32
in services:	61

TABLE 8

SOCIO-ECONOMIC INDICATORS

GNP & INCOME DISTRIBUTION

GNP per capita (in US Dollars) 1985:	10830
GNP average annual growth rate (%) 1965-85:	2.0
% share of total household income 1975-76	
Lowest 20% of households:	5.4
Highest 10% of households:	30.5

HEALTH & NUTRITION

Population per physician 1981:	500
Daily calorie supply per capita 1985:	3389

TABLE 1 — DATA

AGE AT LAST BIRTHDAY	ESTIMATED MID-YEAR POPULATION BOTH SEXES	MALES Number	MALES Percent	FEMALES Number	FEMALES Percent	BIRTHS BY AGE OF MOTHER AND SEX	DEATHS BOTH SEXES	DEATHS MALES	DEATHS FEMALES	AGE AT LAST BIRTHDAY
0	235581	120678	1.7	114903	1.7		3325	1952	1373	0
1-4	1045015	533878	7.7	511137	7.4		779	446	333	1-4
5-9	1248172	639744	9.2	608428	8.8		391	231	160	5-9
10-14	1290856	664094	9.5	626762	9.1	165	394	252	142	10-14
15-19	1233710	629462	9.0	604248	8.7	24053	1288	968	320	15-19
20-24	1164852	588423	8.4	576429	8.3	77175	1273	992	281	20-24
25-29	1159522	591783	8.5	567739	8.2	84913	1061	769	292	25-29
30-34	943941	486844	7.0	457097	6.6	33874	1046	698	348	30-34
35-39	827478	424988	6.1	402490	5.8	10461	1387	869	518	35-39
40-44	753354	388606	5.6	364748	5.3	2232	2017	1285	732	40-44
45-49	804081	415784	6.0	388297	5.6	135	3643	2399	1244	45-49
50-54	766223	387405	5.6	378818	5.5	4	5571	3713	1858	50-54
55-59	629724	309767	4.4	319957	4.6		7170	4747	2423	55-59
60-64	578918	279030	4.0	299888	4.3		10176	6662	3514	60-64
65-69	451354	211570	3.0	239784	3.5		12351	7865	4486	65-69
70-74	330110	145386	2.1	184724	2.7		14161	8452	5709	70-74
75-79	219710	83760	1.2	135950	2.0		14284	7274	7010	75-79
80-84	130528	44053	0.6	86475	1.2	119850 M	13606	5849	7757	80-84
85+	79866	23926	0.3	55940	0.8	113162 F	15098	5315	9783	85+
TOTAL	13892995	6969181		6923814		233012	109021	60738	48283	TOTAL

TABLE 2 — MALE LIFE TABLE

x	nM_x	nq_x	l_x	nd_x	nL_x	nm_x	na_x	T_x	$\overset{\circ}{e}_x$	x
0	0.016175	0.015943	100000	1594	98561	0.016175	0.097	6935091	69.351	0
1	0.000835	0.003335	98406	328	392803	0.000835	1.500	6836530	69.473	1
5	0.000361	0.001804	98078	177	489946	0.000361	2.500	6443728	65.700	5
10	0.000379	0.001896	97901	186	489159	0.000379	3.143	5953782	60.815	10
15	0.001538	0.007676	97715	750	486831	0.001541	2.674	5464623	55.924	15
20	0.001686	0.008393	96965	814	482764	0.001686	2.467	4977792	51.336	20
25	0.001299	0.006473	96151	622	479173	0.001299	2.457	4495028	46.750	25
30	0.001434	0.007162	95529	684	476006	0.001437	2.606	4015855	42.038	30
35	0.002045	0.010222	94845	969	471979	0.002054	2.684	3539849	37.323	35
40	0.003307	0.016430	93875	1542	465866	0.003311	2.724	3067870	32.680	40
45	0.005770	0.028473	92333	2629	455649	0.005770	2.712	2602005	28.181	45
50	0.009584	0.047018	89704	4218	438749	0.009613	2.683	2146356	23.927	50
55	0.015324	0.074197	85486	6343	412562	0.015374	2.656	1707607	19.975	55
60	0.023876	0.113219	79143	8961	374498	0.023927	2.632	1295045	16.363	60
65	0.037174	0.171276	70183	12021	322094	0.037320	2.602	920547	13.116	65
70	0.058135	0.255659	58162	14870	254365	0.058458	2.549	598453	10.289	70
75	0.086843	0.358374	43293	15515	177438	0.087438	2.485	344088	7.948	75
80	0.132772	0.494320	27778	13731	103418	0.132772	2.417	166650	5.999	80
85	0.222143	1.000000	14047	14047	63232	0.158651	4.502	63232	4.502	85

TABLE 3 — FEMALE LIFE TABLE

x	nM_x	nq_x	l_x	nd_x	nL_x	nm_x	na_x	T_x	$\overset{\circ}{e}_x$	x
0	0.011949	0.011821	100000	1182	98925	0.011949	0.090	7645424	76.454	0
1	0.000651	0.002602	98818	257	394629	0.000651	1.500	7546504	76.368	1
5	0.000263	0.001314	98561	130	492480	0.000263	2.500	7151871	72.563	5
10	0.000227	0.001132	98431	111	491905	0.000227	2.744	6659390	67.655	10
15	0.000530	0.002646	98320	260	490975	0.000530	2.602	6167485	62.729	15
20	0.000487	0.002434	98060	239	489700	0.000487	2.492	5676509	57.888	20
25	0.000514	0.002573	97821	252	488504	0.000515	2.611	5186809	53.023	25
30	0.000761	0.003822	97569	373	486992	0.000766	2.710	4698306	48.154	30
35	0.001287	0.006449	97196	627	484538	0.001294	2.697	4211313	43.328	35
40	0.002007	0.010004	96570	966	480619	0.002010	2.693	3726775	38.592	40
45	0.003204	0.015901	95604	1520	474492	0.003204	2.681	3246156	33.954	45
50	0.004905	0.024293	94083	2286	465100	0.004914	2.674	2771664	29.460	50
55	0.007573	0.037305	91798	3425	451004	0.007593	2.668	2306564	25.127	55
60	0.011718	0.057176	88373	5053	430085	0.011749	2.668	1855560	20.997	60
65	0.018709	0.090078	83320	7505	399072	0.018807	2.664	1425475	17.108	65
70	0.030906	0.144706	75815	10971	353201	0.031061	2.642	1026404	13.538	70
75	0.051563	0.230665	64844	14957	288363	0.051870	2.603	673203	10.382	75
80	0.089702	0.367621	49887	18339	204448	0.089702	2.547	384839	7.714	80
85	0.174884	1.000000	31547	31547	180391	0.105865	5.718	180391	5.718	85

TABLE 4 — OBSERVED VITAL RATES AND RATIOS

CRUDE RATES

Per Thousand	BOTH SEXES	MALES	FEMALES
BIRTH RATE	16.77	17.20	16.34
DEATH RATE	7.85	8.72	6.97
RATE OF INCREASE	8.92	8.48	9.37

RATES STANDARDIZED ON USA 1980

Per Thousand	BOTH SEXES	MALES	FEMALES
BIRTH RATE	18.51		17.48
DEATH RATE	9.77	10.65	8.93
RATE OF INCREASE	8.74		8.55

VITAL STATISTICS

GFR x 1000	69.327
TFR	2.150
GRR	1.044
NRR	1.020
μ	26.685
σ^2	30.345
GENERATION	26.673
POP. SEX RATIO	0.993
SEX RATIO AT BIRTH	1.059
DEP. RATIO x 100	56.774

PERCENT OF POPULATION IN AGE GROUP

	BOTH SEXES	MALES	FEMALES
UNDER 15	27.49	28.10	26.88
15 - 64	63.79	64.60	62.97
65 AND OLDER	8.72	7.30	10.15

RATES STANDARDIZED ON MEXICO 1980

	BOTH SEXES	MALES	FEMALES
BIRTH RATE	16.64		16.29
DEATH RATE	3.91	4.75	3.06
RATE OF INCREASE	12.73		13.23

| AGE AT LAST BIRTHDAY | ESTIMATED MID-YEAR POPULATION | | | | | BIRTHS BY AGE OF MOTHER AND SEX | DEATHS | | | AGE AT LAST BIRTHDAY |
| | BOTH SEXES | MALES | | FEMALES | | | BOTH SEXES | MALES | FEMALES | |
		Number	Percent	Number	Percent					
0	222568	114488	1.6	108080	1.5		2418	1384	1034	0
1-4	909621	465408	6.3	444213	6.0		523	308	215	1-4
5-9	1306585	667240	9.1	639345	8.7		355	211	144	5-9
10-14	1272220	650465	8.9	621755	8.5	106	360	224	136	10-14
15-19	1307557	666525	9.1	641032	8.7	17589	1138	859	279	15-19
20-24	1269148	644044	8.8	625104	8.5	66873	1370	1031	339	20-24
25-29	1209909	610553	8.3	599356	8.1	84500	1095	829	266	25-29
30-34	1180485	599835	8.2	580650	7.9	43620	1121	738	383	30-34
35-39	950531	485326	6.6	465205	6.3	11015	1262	834	428	35-39
40-44	809836	414661	5.7	395175	5.4	1723	1779	1150	629	40-44
45-49	741528	380108	5.2	361420	4.9	99	2787	1870	917	45-49
50-54	774536	396506	5.4	378030	5.1	2	4827	3280	1547	50-54
55-59	736844	365862	5.0	370982	5.0		7104	4745	2359	55-59
60-64	590711	282288	3.8	308423	4.2		8925	5912	3013	60-64
65-69	528613	245779	3.3	282834	3.8		12708	8234	4474	65-69
70-74	385075	170110	2.3	214965	2.9		14546	8886	5660	70-74
75-79	254037	102370	1.4	151667	2.1		15335	8426	6909	75-79
80-84	146861	49205	0.7	97656	1.3	115948 N	13858	6062	7796	80-84
85+	98691	27287	0.4	71404	1.0	109579 F	17184	5535	11649	85+
TOTAL	14695356	7338060		7357296		225527	108695	60518	48177	TOTAL

TABLE 1 DATA

x	nM_x	nq_x	l_x	nd_x	nL_x	nm_x	na_x	T_x	$\overset{\circ}{e}_x$	x
0	0.012089	0.011957	100000	1196	98913	0.012089	0.091	7101766	71.018	0
1	0.000662	0.002643	98804	261	394564	0.000662	1.500	7002853	70.876	1
5	0.000316	0.001580	98543	156	492327	0.000316	2.500	6608289	67.060	5
10	0.000344	0.001721	98387	169	491613	0.000344	3.085	6115962	62.162	10
15	0.001289	0.006425	98218	631	489640	0.001289	2.701	5624349	57.264	15
20	0.001601	0.007973	97587	778	485996	0.001601	2.506	5134709	52.617	20
25	0.001358	0.006764	96809	655	482369	0.001357	2.440	4648714	48.019	25
30	0.001230	0.006138	96154	590	479331	0.001231	2.559	4166344	43.330	30
35	0.001718	0.008604	95564	822	475916	0.001728	2.683	3687013	38.582	35
40	0.002773	0.013864	94742	1314	470728	0.002790	2.731	3211098	33.893	40
45	0.004920	0.024358	93428	2276	461949	0.004926	2.718	2740369	29.331	45
50	0.008272	0.040583	91153	3699	447191	0.008272	2.683	2278420	24.996	50
55	0.012969	0.063132	87453	5521	424403	0.013009	2.670	1831229	20.939	55
60	0.020943	0.100151	81932	8206	390385	0.021019	2.651	1406826	17.171	60
65	0.033502	0.155498	73727	11464	341283	0.033592	2.614	1016441	13.787	65
70	0.052237	0.232860	62262	14498	276098	0.052512	2.571	675157	10.844	70
75	0.082309	0.343741	47764	16418	197807	0.083002	2.502	399060	8.355	75
80	0.123199	0.467688	31346	14660	118994	0.123199	2.426	201252	6.420	80
85	0.202844	1.000000	16686	16686	82258	0.136346	4.930	82258	4.930	85

TABLE 2 MALE LIFE TABLE

x	nM_x	nq_x	l_x	nd_x	nL_x	nm_x	na_x	T_x	$\overset{\circ}{e}_x$	x
0	0.009567	0.009484	100000	948	99133	0.009567	0.086	7826078	78.261	0
1	0.000484	0.001934	99052	192	395728	0.000484	1.500	7726944	78.009	1
5	0.000225	0.001125	98860	111	494022	0.000225	2.500	7331217	74.158	5
10	0.000219	0.001093	98749	108	493496	0.000219	2.699	6837195	69.238	10
15	0.000435	0.002174	98641	214	492701	0.000435	2.654	6343699	64.311	15
20	0.000542	0.002708	98426	267	491466	0.000542	2.502	5850998	59.445	20
25	0.000444	0.002217	98160	218	490267	0.000444	2.554	5359532	54.600	25
30	0.000660	0.003301	97942	323	488952	0.000661	2.650	4869265	49.716	30
35	0.000920	0.004618	97619	451	487062	0.000926	2.709	4380313	44.872	35
40	0.001592	0.007977	97168	775	484063	0.001601	2.706	3893251	40.067	40
45	0.002537	0.012636	96393	1218	479161	0.002542	2.697	3409188	35.368	45
50	0.004092	0.020269	95175	1929	471408	0.004092	2.685	2930028	30.786	50
55	0.006359	0.031386	93246	2927	459413	0.006370	2.671	2458619	26.367	55
60	0.009769	0.047895	90319	4326	441543	0.009797	2.676	1999207	22.135	60
65	0.015818	0.076511	85994	6579	414681	0.015866	2.677	1557663	18.114	65
70	0.026330	0.124732	79414	9906	373935	0.026490	2.664	1142982	14.393	70
75	0.045554	0.207120	69509	14397	313328	0.045947	2.623	769047	11.064	75
80	0.079831	0.334440	55112	18432	230883	0.079831	2.576	455719	8.269	80
85	0.163142	1.000000	36680	36680	224837	0.093962	6.130	224837	6.130	85

TABLE 3 FEMALE LIFE TABLE

CRUDE RATES

Per Thousand	BOTH SEXES	MALES	FEMALES
BIRTH RATE	15.35	15.80	14.89
DEATH RATE	7.40	8.25	6.55
RATE OF INCREASE	7.95	7.55	8.35

PERCENT OF POPULATION IN AGE GROUP

UNDER 15	25.25	25.86	24.65
15 - 64	65.13	66.04	64.23
65 AND OLDER	9.62	8.11	11.13

RATES STANDARDIZED ON USA 1980

Per Thousand	BOTH SEXES	MALES	FEMALES
BIRTH RATE	16.22		15.32
DEATH RATE	8.68	9.56	7.84
RATE OF INCREASE	7.54		7.48

RATES STANDARDIZED ON MEXICO 1980

BIRTH RATE	14.36		14.07
DEATH RATE	3.41	4.18	2.62
RATE OF INCREASE	10.96		11.45

VITAL STATISTICS

GFR x 1000	61.486	TABLE 4
TFR	1.895	
GRR	0.921	OBSERVED
NRR	0.903	VITAL
μ	27.145	RATES
σ^2	28.321	AND
GENERATION	27.198	RATIOS
POP. SEX RATIO	1.003	
SEX RATIO AT BIRTH	1.058	
DEP. RATIO x 100	53.539	

AGE AT LAST BIRTHDAY	ESTIMATED MID-YEAR POPULATION					BIRTHS BY AGE OF MOTHER AND SEX	DEATHS			AGE AT LAST BIRTHDAY
	BOTH SEXES	MALES		FEMALES			BOTH SEXES	MALES	FEMALES	
		Number	Percent	Number	Percent					
0	241022	123187	1.6	117835	1.5		2453	1399	1054	0
1-4	958534	490986	6.2	467548	5.9		487	277	210	1-4
5-9	1175131	602564	7.6	572567	7.2		292	178	114	5-9
10-14	1350854	691162	8.8	659692	8.3		303	198	105	10-14
15-19	1304706	666977	8.5	637729	8.1	14560	1013	746	267	15-19
20-24	1349451	686549	8.7	662902	8.4	63478	1440	1087	353	20-24
25-29	1319507	667059	8.5	652448	8.3	95239	1241	894	347	25-29
30-34	1252655	627449	8.0	625206	7.9	55632	1172	809	363	30-34
35-39	1227636	624620	7.9	603016	7.6	16242	1389	890	499	35-39
40-44	968517	496034	6.3	472483	6.0	2104	1714	1111	603	40-44
45-49	818658	420166	5.3	398492	5.0	93	2517	1581	936	45-49
50-54	733043	375001	4.8	358042	4.5		3875	2511	1364	50-54
55-59	759024	385087	4.9	373937	4.7		6705	4447	2258	55-59
60-64	708545	344686	4.4	363859	4.6		9857	6494	3363	60-64
65-69	546339	253908	3.2	292431	3.7		11989	7632	4357	65-69
70-74	464339	205141	2.6	259198	3.3		16560	9841	6719	70-74
75-79	310310	126330	1.6	183980	2.3		17626	9596	8030	75-79
80-84	178823	63415	0.8	115408	1.5	126813 M	16638	7663	8975	80-84
85+	121218	32407	0.4	88811	1.1	120535 F	21537	6802	14735	85+
TOTAL	15788312	7882728		7905584		247348	118808	64156	54652	TOTAL

TABLE 1 DATA

TABLE 2 — MALE LIFE TABLE

x	nM_x	nq_x	l_x	nd_x	nL_x	nm_x	na_x	T_x	$\dot{e}_x$	x
0	0.011357	0.011240	100000	1124	98976	0.011357	0.089	7221848	72.218	0
1	0.000564	0.002254	98876	223	394947	0.000564	1.500	7122871	72.038	1
5	0.000295	0.001476	98653	146	492902	0.000295	2.500	6727925	68.198	5
10	0.000286	0.001432	98508	141	492269	0.000286	3.095	6235023	63.295	10
15	0.001118	0.005578	98367	549	490592	0.001118	2.739	5742754	58.381	15
20	0.001583	0.007886	97818	771	487181	0.001583	2.527	5252162	53.693	20
25	0.001340	0.006676	97046	648	483581	0.001340	2.451	4764981	49.100	25
30	0.001289	0.006426	96399	620	480451	0.001289	2.511	4281400	44.414	30
35	0.001425	0.007114	95779	681	477285	0.001428	2.637	3800949	39.685	35
40	0.002240	0.011217	95098	1067	473048	0.002255	2.712	3323664	34.950	40
45	0.003763	0.018781	94031	1766	466153	0.003788	2.734	2850616	30.316	45
50	0.006696	0.033044	92265	3049	454381	0.006710	2.722	2384463	25.844	50
55	0.011548	0.056240	89216	5018	434490	0.011548	2.690	1930083	21.634	55
60	0.018840	0.090511	84199	7621	403143	0.018904	2.658	1495593	17.763	60
65	0.030058	0.140815	76578	10783	357298	0.030180	2.627	1092450	14.266	65
70	0.047972	0.215557	65795	14182	294732	0.048120	2.586	735152	11.173	70
75	0.075960	0.321970	51612	16618	216930	0.076603	2.525	440420	8.533	75
80	0.120839	0.461981	34995	16167	133788	0.120839	2.453	223490	6.386	80
85	0.209893	1.000000	18828	18828	89702	0.144183	4.764	89702	4.764	85

TABLE 3 — FEMALE LIFE TABLE

x	nM_x	nq_x	l_x	nd_x	nL_x	nm_x	na_x	T_x	$\dot{e}_x$	x
0	0.008945	0.008872	100000	887	99188	0.008945	0.085	7872294	78.723	0
1	0.000449	0.001795	99113	178	396007	0.000449	1.500	7773105	78.427	1
5	0.000199	0.000995	98935	98	494429	0.000199	2.500	7377099	74.565	5
10	0.000159	0.000796	98836	79	494008	0.000159	2.786	6882670	69.637	10
15	0.000419	0.002091	98758	207	493311	0.000419	2.685	6388662	64.690	15
20	0.000533	0.002659	98551	262	492113	0.000533	2.543	5895351	59.820	20
25	0.000532	0.002656	98289	261	490798	0.000532	2.518	5403238	54.973	25
30	0.000581	0.002900	98028	284	489460	0.000581	2.605	4912439	50.113	30
35	0.000828	0.004142	97744	405	487778	0.000830	2.675	4422979	45.251	35
40	0.001276	0.006412	97339	624	485288	0.001286	2.745	3935200	40.428	40
45	0.002349	0.011761	96715	1137	480978	0.002365	2.717	3449913	35.671	45
50	0.003810	0.018921	95577	1808	473711	0.003817	2.691	2968935	31.063	50
55	0.006038	0.029774	93769	2792	462348	0.006038	2.673	2495224	26.610	55
60	0.009243	0.045331	90977	4124	445302	0.009261	2.676	2032876	22.345	60
65	0.014899	0.072261	86853	6276	419773	0.014951	2.691	1587574	18.279	65
70	0.025922	0.122549	80577	9875	379826	0.025998	2.665	1167801	14.493	70
75	0.043646	0.199272	70702	14089	320094	0.044015	2.628	787975	11.145	75
80	0.077768	0.327489	56613	18540	238406	0.077768	2.591	467880	8.264	80
85	0.165914	1.000000	38073	38073	229475	0.096745	6.027	229475	6.027	85

TABLE 4 — OBSERVED VITAL RATES AND RATIOS

CRUDE RATES

Per Thousand	BOTH SEXES	MALES	FEMALES
BIRTH RATE	15.67	16.09	15.25
DEATH RATE	7.53	8.14	6.91
RATE OF INCREASE	8.14	7.95	8.33

PERCENT OF POPULATION IN AGE GROUP

UNDER 15	23.60	24.20	22.99
15 - 64	66.14	67.15	65.12
65 AND OLDER	10.27	8.64	11.89

RATES STANDARDIZED ON USA 1980

Per Thousand	BOTH SEXES	MALES	FEMALES
BIRTH RATE	16.34		15.48
DEATH RATE	8.23	8.86	7.64
RATE OF INCREASE	8.10		7.84

RATES STANDARDIZED ON MEXICO 1980

	BOTH SEXES	MALES	FEMALES
BIRTH RATE	14.26		14.01
DEATH RATE	3.17	3.83	2.50
RATE OF INCREASE	11.09		11.50

VITAL STATISTICS

GFR x 1000	61.039
TFR	1.926
GRR	0.938
NRR	0.921
μ	27.688
σ^2	27.681
GENERATION	27.729
POP. SEX RATIO	1.003
SEX RATIO AT BIRTH	1.052
DEP. RATIO x 100	51.204

PROJECTED POPULATION

AGE GROUP	1990			1995		
	BOTH SEXES	MALES	FEMALES	BOTH SEXES	MALES	FEMALES
0-4	1230	630	600	1230	630	600
5-9	1197	613	584	1227	628	599
10-14	1174	602	572	1196	612	584
15-19	1348	689	659	1171	600	571
20-24	1298	662	636	1341	684	657
25-29	1342	681	661	1291	657	634
30-34	1314	663	651	1336	677	659
35-39	1246	623	623	1306	658	648
40-44	1219	619	600	1238	618	620
45-49	957	489	468	1205	610	595
50-54	802	410	392	937	476	461
55-59	708	359	349	775	392	383
60-64	717	357	360	670	333	337
65-69	648	305	343	657	317	340
70-74	474	209	265	562	252	310
75-79	369	151	218	377	154	223
80-84	215	78	137	256	93	163
85+	154	43	111	184	52	132
TOTAL	16412	8183	8229	16959	8443	8516

STABLE EQUIVALENT TO ORIGINAL POPULATION

MALES		FEMALES		AGE GROUP	
Number	Percent	Number	Percent		
634	6.1	605	5.6	0-4	
643	6.2	613	5.7	5-9	TABLE 5
651	6.3	621	5.8	10-14	
659	6.4	630	5.8	15-19	POPULATION
664	6.4	638	5.9	20-24	PROJECTED
669	6.5	645	6.0	25-29	WITH
675	6.5	653	6.0	30-34	FIXED
680	6.6	661	6.1	35-39	AGE-
684	6.6	667	6.2	40-44	SPECIFIC
684	6.6	671	6.2	45-49	BIRTH
677	6.6	671	6.2	50-54	AND
657	6.4	665	6.2	55-59	DEATH
619	6.0	650	6.0	60-64	RATES
557	5.4	622	5.8	65-69	(female
466	4.5	571	5.3	70-74	dominant,
348	3.4	488	4.5	75-79	in 000s)
218	2.1	369	3.4	80-84	
148	1.4	361	3.3	85+	
10333		10801		TOTAL	

VITAL RATES OF PROJECTED POPULATION

Per Thousand	1990			1995		
	BOTH SEXES	MALES	FEMALES	BOTH SEXES	MALES	FEMALES
BIRTH RATE	15.23	15.66	14.80	14.60	15.03	14.17
DEATH RATE	8.24	8.85	7.62	8.83	9.44	8.23
RATE OF INCREASE	6.99	6.81	7.17	5.77	5.59	5.94

VITAL RATES OF STABLE POPULATION

Per Thousand	MALES	FEMALES	TABLE 6
BIRTH RATE	12.34	11.22	PROJECTED
DEATH RATE	15.24	14.19	VITAL
RATE OF INCREASE		-2.97	RATES

AGE STRUCTURE OF PROJECTED POPULATION

% UNDER 15	21.94	22.54	21.34	21.54	22.15	20.94	
% 15-64	66.73	67.85	65.61	66.46	67.57	65.35	
% 65 AND OLDER	11.34	9.61	13.05	12.00	10.28	13.71	
DEPEND. RATIO x 100	49.87	47.38	52.42	50.48	48.00	53.01	

STABLE AGE STRUCTURE

% UNDER 15	18.66	17.03	AND
% 15-64	64.53	60.65	RATIOS
% 65 AND OLDER	16.81	22.32	(female
DEPEND. RATIO x 100	54.97	64.87	dominant)

AGE GROUP	FEMALE BIRTH RATES	NET MATERNITY FUNCTION	COEFF. OF MATRIX EQUATION	ORIGINAL MATRIX		STABLE MATRIX		MATRIX PARAMETERS		
				SUB-DIAGONAL	FIRST ROW	FISHER VALUES	REPRODUCTIVE VALUES			
0-4	0.0000	0.0000	0.0000	0.99845	0.00000	1.002	586693	λ_1	0.98527	
5-9	0.0000	0.0000	0.0000	0.99915	0.00000	0.989	566274	λ_2	0.38467+0.75400i	TABLE 7
10-14	0.0000	0.0000	0.0274	0.99859	0.02751	0.975	643379	λ_4	-0.26318+0.51329i	
15-19	0.0111	0.0549	0.1423	0.99757	0.14280	0.935	596058	λ_6	-0.39528-0.10541i	LESLIE
20-24	0.0467	0.2296	0.2894	0.99733	0.29119	0.780	516839	r_1	-0.00297	MATRIX
25-29	0.0711	0.3491	0.2807	0.99727	0.28319	0.478	311616	r_2	-0.03334+0.21981i	AND ITS
30-34	0.0434	0.2122	0.1381	0.99656	0.13975	0.187	117075	r_4	-0.11004+0.40892i	ANALYSIS
35-39	0.0131	0.0640	0.0373	0.99489	0.03784	0.045	26890	r_6	-0.17876-0.57620i	(females)
40-44	0.0022	0.0105	0.0055	0.99112	0.00565	0.006	2853	c_1	107989	
45-49	0.0001	0.0005	0.0003	0.98489	0.00028	0.000	114	$2\pi/y$	28.5849	
50-54	0.0000	0.0000	0.0000	0.00000	0.00000	0.000	0	Δ	16.3277	

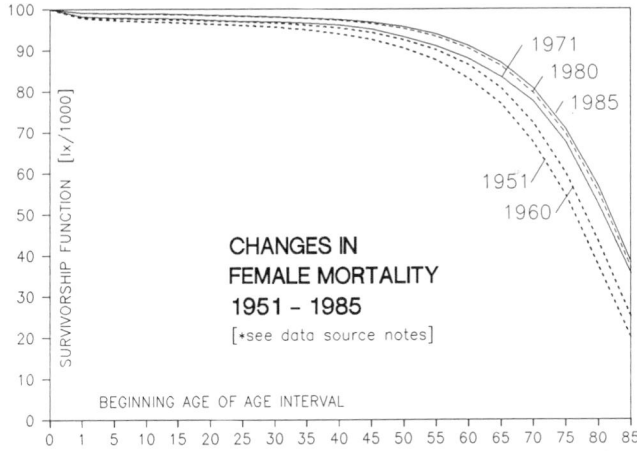

CHANGES IN FEMALE MORTALITY 1951 - 1985

[*see data source notes]

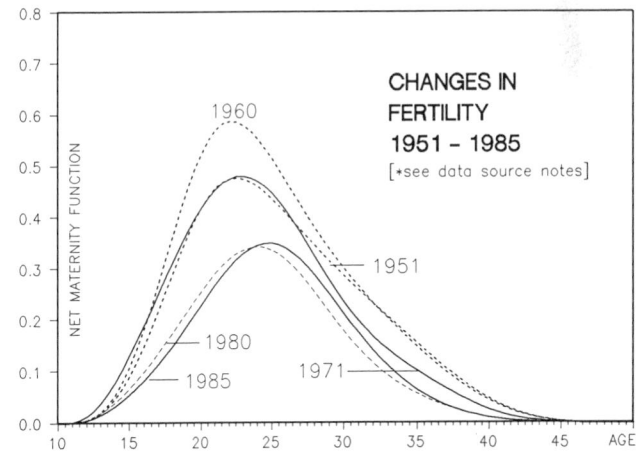

CHANGES IN FERTILITY 1951 - 1985

[*see data source notes]

TABLE 1 — DATA

AGE AT LAST BIRTHDAY	ESTIMATED MID-YEAR POPULATION BOTH SEXES	MALES Number	MALES Percent	FEMALES Number	FEMALES Percent	BIRTHS BY AGE OF MOTHER AND SEX	DEATHS BOTH SEXES	DEATHS MALES	DEATHS FEMALES	AGE AT LAST BIRTHDAY
0	15923	8256	2.8	7667	2.7		681	356	325	0
1-4	60951	31621	10.9	29330	10.4		193	125	68	1-4
5-9	73766	37529	12.9	36237	12.8		82	58	24	5-9
10-14	73018	37059	12.8	35959	12.7		85	52	33	10-14
15-19	66631	33675	11.6	32956	11.6	1566	112	70	42	15-19
20-24	57398	28864	9.9	28534	10.1	6308	145	81	64	20-24
25-29	48021	23942	8.3	24079	8.5	4758	130	68	62	25-29
30-34	39733	19698	6.8	20035	7.1	2281	116	75	41	30-34
35-39	32475	16275	5.6	16200	5.7	1116	134	76	58	35-39
40-44	26455	13354	4.6	13101	4.6	346	173	99	74	40-44
45-49	21387	10855	3.7	10532	3.7	127	206	135	71	45-49
50-54	17305	8829	3.0	8476	3.0		274	158	116	50-54
55-59	13673	6979	2.4	6694	2.4		274	178	96	55-59
60-64	10200	5213	1.8	4987	1.8		282	179	103	60-64
65-69	7218	3625	1.2	3593	1.3		266	171	95	65-69
70-74	4598	2236	0.8	2362	0.8		280	170	110	70-74
75-79	2111	1076	0.4	1035	0.4		171	100	71	75-79
80-84	1029	489	0.2	540	0.2	8551 M	149	86	63	80-84
85+	1208	582	0.2	626	0.2	7951 F	194	127	67	85+
TOTAL	573100	290157		282943		16502	3947	2364	1583	TOTAL

TABLE 2 — MALE LIFE TABLE

x	$_nM_x$	$_nq_x$	l_x	$_nd_x$	$_nL_x$	$_nm_x$	$_na_x$	T_x	$\mathring{e}_x$	x
0	0.043120	0.041584	100000	4158	96438	0.043120	0.143	6087179	60.872	0
1	0.003953	0.015658	95842	1501	379615	0.003953	1.500	5990742	62.507	1
5	0.001545	0.007698	94341	726	469889	0.001545	2.500	5611127	59.477	5
10	0.001403	0.006995	93615	655	466486	0.001404	2.576	5141237	54.919	10
15	0.002079	0.010367	92960	964	462522	0.002084	2.636	4674751	50.288	15
20	0.002806	0.013960	91996	1284	456837	0.002811	2.552	4212230	45.787	20
25	0.002840	0.014127	90712	1281	450442	0.002845	2.566	3755393	41.399	25
30	0.003807	0.018929	89431	1693	443078	0.003821	2.593	3304951	36.956	30
35	0.004670	0.023200	87738	2035	433902	0.004691	2.649	2861873	32.619	35
40	0.007414	0.036683	85702	3144	421272	0.007463	2.697	2427971	28.330	40
45	0.012437	0.060730	82558	5014	400994	0.012503	2.647	2006699	24.306	45
50	0.017896	0.086127	77545	6679	371761	0.017965	2.610	1605705	20.707	50
55	0.025505	0.120512	70866	8540	333651	0.025596	2.579	1233944	17.412	55
60	0.034337	0.158918	62326	9905	287408	0.034462	2.555	900293	14.445	60
65	0.047172	0.212455	52421	11137	234964	0.047399	2.563	612885	11.692	65
70	0.076029	0.321474	41284	13272	173117	0.076664	2.491	377921	9.154	70
75	0.092937	0.376368	28012	10543	113132	0.093191	2.446	204804	7.311	75
80	0.175869	0.602617	17469	10527	59859	0.175869	2.389	91672	5.248	80
85	0.218213	1.000000	6942	6942	31813	0.154928	4.583	31813	4.583	85

TABLE 3 — FEMALE LIFE TABLE

x	$_nM_x$	$_nq_x$	l_x	$_nd_x$	$_nL_x$	$_nm_x$	$_na_x$	T_x	$\mathring{e}_x$	x
0	0.042389	0.040902	100000	4090	96491	0.042389	0.142	6757987	67.580	0
1	0.002318	0.009220	95910	884	381428	0.002318	1.500	6661496	69.456	1
5	0.000662	0.003306	95025	314	474342	0.000662	2.500	6280068	66.088	5
10	0.000918	0.004581	94711	434	472532	0.000918	2.638	5805726	61.299	10
15	0.001274	0.006374	94277	601	470013	0.001279	2.713	5333194	56.569	15
20	0.002243	0.011192	93676	1048	465883	0.002250	2.616	4863181	51.915	20
25	0.002575	0.012790	92628	1185	460154	0.002575	2.480	4397298	47.473	25
30	0.002046	0.010195	91443	932	454977	0.002049	2.597	3937144	43.056	30
35	0.003580	0.017890	90511	1619	448832	0.003608	2.700	3482167	38.472	35
40	0.005648	0.028001	88892	2489	438501	0.005676	2.606	3033336	34.124	40
45	0.006741	0.033420	86403	2888	425435	0.006787	2.722	2594835	30.032	45
50	0.013686	0.066586	83515	5561	404200	0.013758	2.595	2169400	25.976	50
55	0.014341	0.069434	77954	5413	376575	0.014373	2.562	1765200	22.644	55
60	0.020654	0.098855	72542	7171	345356	0.020764	2.580	1388625	19.142	60
65	0.026440	0.125077	65370	8176	307432	0.026596	2.625	1043270	15.959	65
70	0.046571	0.210997	57194	12068	256873	0.046980	2.589	735838	12.866	70
75	0.068599	0.295163	45126	13320	192788	0.069090	2.534	478965	10.614	75
80	0.116667	0.448097	31807	14252	122164	0.116667	2.413	286178	8.997	80
85	0.107029	1.000000	17554	17554	164014	0.044978	9.343	164014	9.343	85

TABLE 4 — OBSERVED VITAL RATES AND RATIOS

CRUDE RATES

Per Thousand	BOTH SEXES	MALES	FEMALES
BIRTH RATE	28.79	29.47	28.10
DEATH RATE	6.89	8.15	5.59
RATE OF INCREASE	21.91	21.32	22.51

PERCENT OF POPULATION IN AGE GROUP

	BOTH SEXES	MALES	FEMALES
UNDER 15	39.03	39.45	38.59
15 - 64	58.15	57.79	58.53
65 AND OLDER	2.82	2.76	2.88

RATES STANDARDIZED ON USA 1980

Per Thousand	BOTH SEXES	MALES	FEMALES
BIRTH RATE	28.77		26.95
DEATH RATE	13.92	15.32	12.60
RATE OF INCREASE	14.85		14.35

RATES STANDARDIZED ON MEXICO 1980

	BOTH SEXES	MALES	FEMALES
BIRTH RATE	25.56		24.82
DEATH RATE	7.13	8.22	6.02
RATE OF INCREASE	18.42		18.80

VITAL STATISTICS

GFR x 1000	113.465
TFR	3.437
GRR	1.656
NRR	1.521
μ	27.836
σ^2	43.769
GENERATION	27.503
POP. SEX RATIO	0.975
SEX RATIO AT BIRTH	1.075
DEP. RATIO x 100	71.959

PROJECTED POPULATION

AGE GROUP	1980 BOTH SEXES	1980 MALES	1980 FEMALES	1985 BOTH SEXES	1985 MALES	1985 FEMALES
0-4	85	44	41	97	50	47
5-9	76	39	37	84	43	41
10-14	73	37	36	76	39	37
15-19	73	37	36	73	37	36
20-24	66	33	33	71	36	35
25-29	56	28	28	65	33	32
30-34	48	24	24	56	28	28
35-39	39	19	20	46	23	23
40-44	32	16	16	38	19	19
45-49	26	13	13	30	15	15
50-54	20	10	10	24	12	12
55-59	16	8	8	18	9	9
60-64	12	6	6	14	7	7
65-69	8	4	4	10	5	5
70-74	6	3	3	7	3	4
75-79	3	1	2	4	2	2
80-84	2	1	1	2	1	1
85+	1	0	1	1	0	1
TOTAL	642	323	319	716	362	354

STABLE EQUIVALENT TO ORIGINAL POPULATION

MALES Number	MALES Percent	FEMALES Number	FEMALES Percent	AGE GROUP
42	12.1	39	11.4	0-4
39	11.1	36	10.5	5-9
35	10.2	33	9.7	10-14
33	9.4	31	8.9	15-19
30	8.6	28	8.2	20-24
27	7.8	26	7.5	25-29
25	7.1	24	6.9	30-34
23	6.5	22	6.3	35-39
20	5.8	20	5.7	40-44
18	5.1	18	5.1	45-49
15	4.4	16	4.5	50-54
13	3.7	13	3.9	55-59
10	2.9	11	3.3	60-64
8	2.2	9	2.7	65-69
5	1.5	7	2.1	70-74
3	0.9	5	1.5	75-79
2	0.4	3	0.9	80-84
1	0.2	4	1.1	85+
349		345		TOTAL

TABLE 5

POPULATION PROJECTED WITH FIXED AGE-SPECIFIC BIRTH AND DEATH RATES (female dominant, in 000s)

VITAL RATES OF PROJECTED POPULATION

Per Thousand	1980 BOTH SEXES	1980 MALES	1980 FEMALES	1985 BOTH SEXES	1985 MALES	1985 FEMALES
BIRTH RATE	29.86	30.64	29.06	29.83	30.65	29.00
DEATH RATE	7.06	8.14	5.96	7.40	8.42	6.37
RATE OF INCREASE	22.80	22.50	23.11	22.43	22.23	22.63

VITAL RATES OF STABLE POPULATION

Per Thousand	MALES	FEMALES
BIRTH RATE	26.42	24.77
DEATH RATE	11.12	9.50
RATE OF INCREASE		15.27

TABLE 6

PROJECTED VITAL RATES AND RATIOS (female dominant)

AGE STRUCTURE OF PROJECTED POPULATION

	1980 BOTH SEXES	1980 MALES	1980 FEMALES	1985 BOTH SEXES	1985 MALES	1985 FEMALES
% UNDER 15	36.58	37.26	35.89	35.74	36.61	34.86
% 15-64	60.33	59.89	60.77	60.87	60.39	61.37
% 65 AND OLDER	3.09	2.85	3.34	3.39	3.01	3.78
DEPEND. RATIO x 100	65.76	66.97	64.56	64.28	65.60	62.95

STABLE AGE STRUCTURE

	MALES	FEMALES
% UNDER 15	33.38	31.57
% 15-64	61.30	60.21
% 65 AND OLDER	5.31	8.22
DEPEND. RATIO x 100	63.12	66.08

AGE GROUP	FEMALE BIRTH RATES	NET MATERNITY FUNCTION	COEFF. OF MATRIX EQUATION	ORIGINAL MATRIX SUB-DIAGONAL	ORIGINAL MATRIX FIRST ROW	STABLE MATRIX FISHER VALUES	STABLE MATRIX REPRODUCTIVE VALUES
0-4	0.0000	0.0000	0.0000	0.99251	0.00000	1.087	40205
5-9	0.0000	0.0000	0.0000	0.99618	0.00000	1.182	42824
10-14	0.0000	0.0000	0.0538	0.99467	0.05442	1.280	46043
15-19	0.0229	0.1076	0.3019	0.99121	0.30700	1.330	43831
20-24	0.1065	0.4962	0.4672	0.98770	0.47924	1.112	31720
25-29	0.0952	0.4381	0.3438	0.98875	0.35712	0.688	16555
30-34	0.0549	0.2496	0.1993	0.98649	0.20933	0.358	7173
35-39	0.0332	0.1490	0.1024	0.97698	0.10902	0.161	2610
40-44	0.0127	0.0558	0.0403	0.97020	0.04388	0.057	743
45-49	0.0058	0.0247	0.0124	0.95009	0.01388	0.014	147
50-54	0.0000	0.0000	0.0000	0.00000	0.00000	0.000	0

MATRIX PARAMETERS

λ_1	1.07935
λ_2	0.32543+0.76540i
λ_4	-0.49862+0.35162i
λ_6	-0.56520-0.00000i
r_1	0.01527
r_2	-0.03685+0.23376i
r_4	-0.09882+0.50548i
r_6	-0.11412-0.62832i
c_1	3452
$2\pi/y$	26.8792
Δ	12.8670

TABLE 7

LESLIE MATRIX AND ITS ANALYSIS (females)

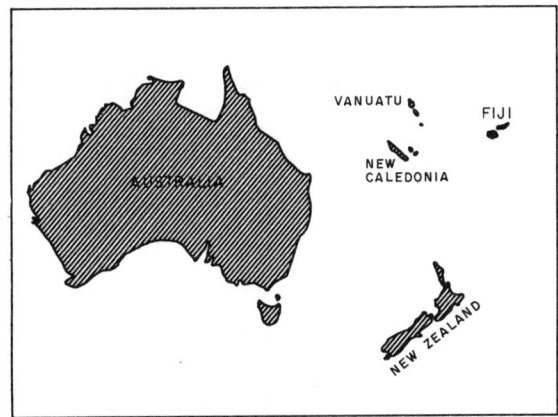

EDUCATION [1984]

% of primary school-age children enrolled:	na
secondary school-age children enrolled:	na
ca. 20-24 year olds in higher education:	na

LABOR FORCE

Average annual labor force growth (%) 1980-85:	2.3
% of the 1980 labor force in agriculture:	46
in industry and services:	54

GNP & INCOME DISTRIBUTION

GNP per capita (in US Dollars) 1985:	1710
GNP average annual growth rate (%) 1965-85:	2.9
% share of total household income	
Lowest 20% of households:	na
Highest 10% of households:	na

HEALTH & NUTRITION

Population per physician 1981:	na
Daily calorie supply per capita 1985:	na

TABLE 8

SOCIO-ECONOMIC INDICATORS

TABLE 1 — DATA

AGE AT LAST BIRTHDAY	ESTIMATED MID-YEAR POPULATION BOTH SEXES	MALES Number	MALES Percent	FEMALES Number	FEMALES Percent	BIRTHS BY AGE OF MOTHER AND SEX	DEATHS BOTH SEXES	DEATHS MALES	DEATHS FEMALES	AGE AT LAST BIRTHDAY
0	18003	9198	2.9	8805	2.8		726	379	347	0
1-4	66798	34477	10.8	32321	10.3		192	105	87	1-4
5-9	78108	39879	12.4	38229	12.2		81	39	42	5-9
10-14	78267	39718	12.4	38549	12.3	1	59	27	32	10-14
15-19	75242	38082	11.9	37160	11.8	1955	130	78	52	15-19
20-24	65811	32886	10.3	32925	10.5	7354	106	67	39	20-24
25-29	53697	26557	8.3	27140	8.6	5284	98	58	40	25-29
30-34	43389	21600	6.7	21789	6.9	2633	108	62	46	30-34
35-39	35902	17885	5.6	18017	5.7	1196	134	83	51	35-39
40-44	29646	14920	4.7	14726	4.7	355	162	95	67	40-44
45-49	24118	12223	3.8	11895	3.8	32	212	137	75	45-49
50-54	19253	9824	3.1	9429	3.0	3	256	164	92	50-54
55-59	15129	7712	2.4	7417	2.4		284	179	105	55-59
60-64	11574	5951	1.9	5623	1.8		372	221	151	60-64
65-69	8103	4128	1.3	3975	1.3		277	161	116	65-69
70-74	5074	2505	0.8	2569	0.8		274	160	114	70-74
75-79	2919	1400	0.4	1519	0.5		196	115	81	75-79
80-84	1440	647	0.2	793	0.3	9614 N	171	99	72	80-84
85+	1678	759	0.2	919	0.3	9199 F	220	145	75	85+
TOTAL	634151	320351		313800		18813	4058	2374	1684	TOTAL

TABLE 2 — MALE LIFE TABLE

x	$_nM_x$	$_nq_x$	l_x	$_nd_x$	$_nL_x$	$_nm_x$	$_na_x$	T_x	$\overset{\circ}{e}_x$	x
0	0.041205	0.039795	100000	3979	96578	0.041205	0.140	6295310	62.953	0
1	0.003046	0.012090	96021	1161	381180	0.003046	1.500	6198732	64.556	1
5	0.000978	0.004878	94860	463	473142	0.000978	2.500	5817552	61.328	5
10	0.000680	0.003395	94397	320	471287	0.000680	2.823	5344410	56.616	10
15	0.002048	0.010207	94076	960	468111	0.002051	2.635	4873123	51.800	15
20	0.002037	0.010137	93116	944	463230	0.002038	2.509	4405012	47.307	20
25	0.002184	0.010885	92172	1003	458429	0.002189	2.575	3941782	42.765	25
30	0.002870	0.014337	91169	1307	452800	0.002887	2.671	3483353	38.208	30
35	0.004641	0.023074	89862	2073	444431	0.004665	2.647	3030553	33.725	35
40	0.006367	0.031555	87788	2770	432558	0.006404	2.695	2586123	29.459	40
45	0.011208	0.054923	85018	4669	414190	0.011274	2.665	2153565	25.331	45
50	0.016694	0.080616	80349	6477	386277	0.016769	2.612	1739375	21.648	50
55	0.023211	0.110411	73871	8156	349953	0.023307	2.621	1353098	18.317	55
60	0.037137	0.170634	65715	11213	300867	0.037270	2.529	1003145	15.265	60
65	0.039002	0.178169	54502	9711	248488	0.039078	2.526	702278	12.885	65
70	0.063872	0.277695	44791	12438	193141	0.064400	2.523	453790	10.131	70
75	0.082143	0.341667	32353	11054	133971	0.082510	2.486	260649	8.056	75
80	0.153014	0.548162	21299	11675	76302	0.153014	2.414	126678	5.948	80
85	0.191041	1.000000	9624	9624	50375	0.123721	5.234	50375	5.234	85

TABLE 3 — FEMALE LIFE TABLE

x	$_nM_x$	$_nq_x$	l_x	$_nd_x$	$_nL_x$	$_nm_x$	$_na_x$	T_x	$\overset{\circ}{e}_x$	x
0	0.039409	0.038113	100000	3811	96711	0.039409	0.137	6958620	69.586	0
1	0.002692	0.010695	96189	1029	382183	0.002692	1.500	6861909	71.338	1
5	0.001099	0.005478	95160	521	474496	0.001099	2.500	6479726	68.093	5
10	0.000830	0.004142	94639	392	472242	0.000830	2.572	6005230	63.454	10
15	0.001399	0.006977	94247	658	469623	0.001400	2.551	5532988	58.708	15
20	0.001185	0.005905	93589	553	466570	0.001184	2.511	5063366	54.102	20
25	0.001474	0.007372	93036	686	463556	0.001480	2.628	4596796	49.409	25
30	0.002111	0.010554	92351	975	459443	0.002121	2.630	4133240	44.756	30
35	0.002831	0.014140	91376	1292	453871	0.002847	2.672	3673797	40.205	35
40	0.004550	0.022638	90084	2039	445625	0.004576	2.649	3219926	35.744	40
45	0.006305	0.031244	88045	2751	433773	0.006342	2.655	2774301	31.510	45
50	0.009757	0.047981	85294	4092	416832	0.009818	2.645	2340527	27.441	50
55	0.014157	0.069042	81201	5606	393136	0.014261	2.704	1923695	23.690	55
60	0.026854	0.126840	75595	9588	354712	0.027032	2.574	1530559	20.247	60
65	0.029182	0.136481	66006	9009	307901	0.029258	2.543	1175847	17.814	65
70	0.044375	0.201117	56998	11463	256696	0.044657	2.532	867946	15.228	70
75	0.053325	0.236345	45535	10762	201050	0.053528	2.526	611250	13.424	75
80	0.090794	0.368491	34773	12813	141126	0.090794	2.445	410200	11.797	80
85	0.081610	1.000000	21959	21959	269074	0.027433	12.253	269074	12.253	85

TABLE 4 — OBSERVED VITAL RATES AND RATIOS

CRUDE RATES

Per Thousand	BOTH SEXES	MALES	FEMALES
BIRTH RATE	29.67	30.01	29.31
DEATH RATE	6.40	7.41	5.37
RATE OF INCREASE	23.27	22.60	23.95

PERCENT OF POPULATION IN AGE GROUP

	BOTH SEXES	MALES	FEMALES
UNDER 15	38.03	38.48	37.57
15 - 64	58.94	58.57	59.31
65 AND OLDER	3.03	2.95	3.12

RATES STANDARDIZED ON USA 1980

Per Thousand	BOTH SEXES	MALES	FEMALES
BIRTH RATE	28.89		27.47
DEATH RATE	12.39	13.58	11.27
RATE OF INCREASE	16.50		16.21

RATES STANDARDIZED ON MEXICO 1980

	BOTH SEXES	MALES	FEMALES
BIRTH RATE	25.79		25.42
DEATH RATE	6.37	7.19	5.53
RATE OF INCREASE	19.42		19.88

VITAL STATISTICS

GFR x 1000	114.957
TFR	3.425
GRR	1.675
NRR	1.549
μ	27.495
σ^2	39.279
GENERATION	27.178
POP. SEX RATIO	0.980
SEX RATIO AT BIRTH	1.045
DEP. RATIO x 100	69.668

PROJECTED POPULATION

AGE GROUP	1985 BOTH SEXES	1985 MALES	1985 FEMALES	1990 BOTH SEXES	1990 MALES	1990 FEMALES
0-4	98	50	48	109	56	53
5-9	84	43	41	96	49	47
10-14	78	40	38	84	43	41
15-19	77	39	38	77	39	38
20-24	75	38	37	77	39	38
25-29	66	33	33	74	37	37
30-34	53	26	27	64	32	32
35-39	43	21	22	53	26	27
40-44	35	17	18	42	21	21
45-49	28	14	14	34	17	17
50-54	22	11	11	27	13	14
55-59	18	9	9	21	10	11
60-64	14	7	7	16	8	8
65-69	10	5	5	11	5	6
70-74	6	3	3	8	4	4
75-79	4	2	2	5	2	3
80-84	2	1	1	2	1	1
85+	2	0	2	3	1	2
TOTAL	715	359	356	803	403	400

STABLE EQUIVALENT TO ORIGINAL POPULATION

MALES Number	MALES Percent	FEMALES Number	FEMALES Percent	AGE GROUP	
46	12.1	44	11.5	0-4	
42	11.1	40	10.5	5-9	TABLE 5
38	10.2	37	9.7	10-14	
35	9.3	34	8.9	15-19	POPULATION
32	8.5	31	8.1	20-24	PROJECTED
29	7.8	28	7.4	25-29	WITH
27	7.1	26	6.8	30-34	FIXED
24	6.4	24	6.2	35-39	AGE-
22	5.8	21	5.6	40-44	SPECIFIC
19	5.1	19	5.0	45-49	BIRTH
17	4.4	17	4.5	50-54	AND
14	3.7	15	3.9	55-59	DEATH
11	2.9	12	3.2	60-64	RATES
8	2.2	10	2.6	65-69	(female
6	1.6	8	2.0	70-74	dominant,
4	1.0	6	1.4	75-79	in 000s)
2	0.5	4	0.9	80-84	
1	0.3	6	1.6	85+	
377		382		TOTAL	

VITAL RATES OF PROJECTED POPULATION

Per Thousand	1985 BOTH SEXES	1985 MALES	1985 FEMALES	1990 BOTH SEXES	1990 MALES	1990 FEMALES
BIRTH RATE	30.51	30.97	30.04	29.75	30.27	29.23
DEATH RATE	6.62	7.45	5.77	6.90	7.70	6.09
RATE OF INCREASE	23.89	23.52	24.27	22.85	22.57	23.13

VITAL RATES OF STABLE POPULATION

Per Thousand	MALES	FEMALES	
BIRTH RATE	26.42	25.01	TABLE 6
DEATH RATE	10.30	8.87	PROJECTED
RATE OF INCREASE		16.14	VITAL

AGE STRUCTURE OF PROJECTED POPULATION

	BOTH SEXES	MALES	FEMALES	BOTH SEXES	MALES	FEMALES
% UNDER 15	36.26	36.88	35.63	36.00	36.68	35.32
% 15-64	60.40	60.03	60.76	60.39	60.09	60.70
% 65 AND OLDER	3.34	3.08	3.61	3.61	3.23	3.98
DEPEND. RATIO x 100	65.57	66.57	64.57	65.59	66.43	64.75

STABLE AGE STRUCTURE

	MALES	FEMALES	
% UNDER 15	33.41	31.70	RATES
% 15-64	60.93	59.70	AND
% 65 AND OLDER	5.67	8.60	RATIOS
DEPEND. RATIO x 100	64.14	67.50	(female dominant)

AGE GROUP	FEMALE BIRTH RATES	NET MATERNITY FUNCTION	COEFF. OF MATRIX EQUATION	ORIGINAL MATRIX SUB-DIAGONAL	ORIGINAL MATRIX FIRST ROW	STABLE MATRIX FISHER VALUES	STABLE MATRIX REPRODUCTIVE VALUES	MATRIX PARAMETERS		
0-4	0.0000	0.0000	0.0000	0.99082	0.00000	1.087	44697	λ_1	1.08403	
5-9	0.0000	0.0000	0.0000	0.99525	0.00003	1.189	45457	λ_2	0.34397+0.77247i	TABLE 7
10-14	0.0000	0.0001	0.0604	0.99445	0.06129	1.295	49925	λ_4	-0.41091+0.40048i	
15-19	0.0257	0.1208	0.3152	0.99350	0.32141	1.345	49973	λ_6	0.03953+0.54627i	LESLIE
20-24	0.1092	0.5096	0.4754	0.99354	0.48799	1.116	36736	r_1	0.01614	MATRIX
25-29	0.0952	0.4413	0.3564	0.99113	0.36818	0.684	18552	r_2	-0.03354+0.23037i	AND ITS
30-34	0.0591	0.2715	0.2094	0.98787	0.21826	0.344	7493	r_4	-0.11110+0.47381i	ANALYSIS
35-39	0.0325	0.1473	0.0999	0.98183	0.10543	0.137	2473	r_6	-0.12041+0.29971i	(females)
40-44	0.0118	0.0525	0.0291	0.97340	0.03129	0.035	513	c_1	3818	
45-49	0.0013	0.0057	0.0032	0.96094	0.00351	0.004	46	$2\pi/y$	27.2738	
50-54	0.0002	0.0006	0.0003	0.94315	0.00037	0.000	4	Δ	12.5673	

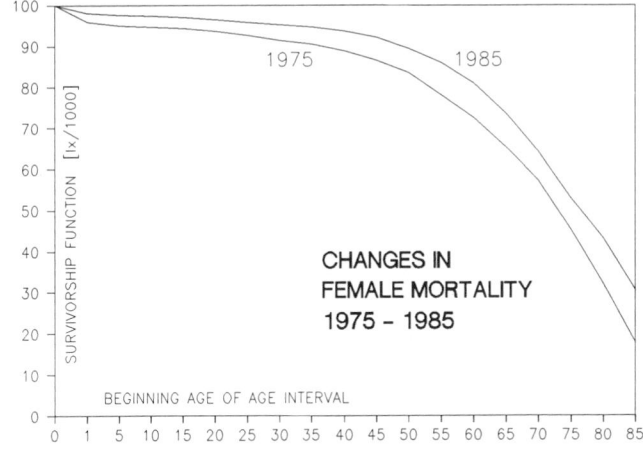

CHANGES IN FEMALE MORTALITY 1975 - 1985

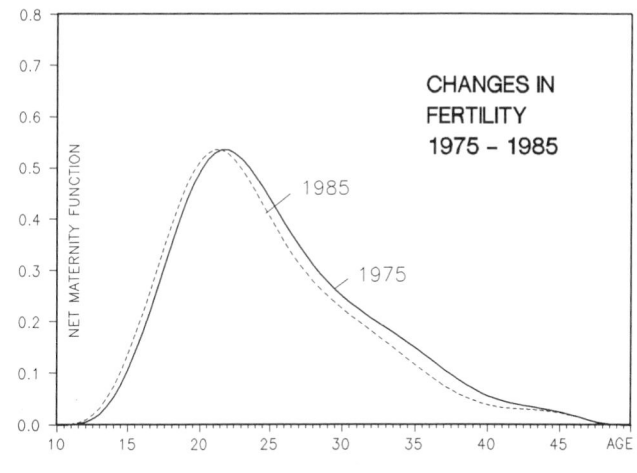

CHANGES IN FERTILITY 1975 - 1985

	AGE AT LAST BIRTHDAY	ESTIMATED MID-YEAR POPULATION					BIRTHS BY AGE OF MOTHER AND SEX	DEATHS			AGE AT LAST BIRTHDAY
		BOTH SEXES	MALES		FEMALES			BOTH SEXES	MALES	FEMALES	
			Number	Percent	Number	Percent					
	0	2539	1273	2.7	1266	3.3		62	38	24	0
	1-4	9183	4728	9.9	4455	11.7		12	7	5	1-4
	5-9	11850	6094	12.8	5756	15.2		4	2	2	5-9
	10-14	10381	5397	11.3	4984	13.1	2	5	2	3	10-14
	15-19	8109	4175	8.8	3934	10.4	372	17	15	2	15-19
	20-24	10345	6686	14.0	3659	9.6	1017	14	10	4	20-24
	25-29	6454	3593	7.5	2861	7.5	756	11	8	3	25-29
	30-34	6216	3561	7.5	2655	7.0	425	12	11	1	30-34
TABLE 1	35-39	5515	3289	6.9	2226	5.9	227	9	5	4	35-39
	40-44	4827	3058	6.4	1769	4.7	72	27	24	3	40-44
DATA	45-49	3555	2206	4.6	1349	3.6	3	19	15	4	45-49
	50-54	2322	1343	2.8	979	2.6	1	20	14	6	50-54
	55-59	1761	1022	2.1	739	1.9		23	15	8	55-59
	60-64	1078	581	1.2	497	1.3		38	27	11	60-64
	65-69	694	326	0.7	368	1.0		17	10	7	65-69
	70-74	354	161	0.3	193	0.5		22	15	7	70-74
	75-79	248	105	0.2	143	0.4		18	10	8	75-79
	80-84	106	42	0.1	64	0.2	1487 M	15	7	8	80-84
	85+	89	34	0.1	55	0.1	1388 F	10	4	6	85+
	TOTAL	85626	47674		37952		2875	355	239	116	TOTAL

x	$_nM_x$	$_nq_x$	l_x	$_nd_x$	$_nL_x$	$_nm_x$	$_na_x$	T_x	$\overset{\circ}{e}_x$	x
0	0.029851	0.029087	100000	2909	97442	0.029851	0.121	6514505	65.145	0
1	0.001481	0.005900	97091	573	386933	0.001481	1.500	6417062	66.093	1
5	0.000328	0.001640	96518	158	482196	0.000328	2.500	6030129	62.476	5
10	0.000371	0.001943	96360	187	481656	0.000389	4.229	5547933	57.575	10
15	0.003593	0.017808	96173	1713	476690	0.003593	2.563	5066276	52.679	15
20	0.001496	0.007444	94460	703	470404	0.001495	2.302	4589586	48.588	20
TABLE 2 25	0.002227	0.011136	93757	1044	466325	0.002239	2.643	4119182	43.935	25
30	0.003089	0.015319	92713	1420	459942	0.003088	2.449	3652858	39.400	30
MALE 35	0.001520	0.007618	91293	695	455160	0.001528	3.126	3192916	34.974	35
LIFE 40	0.007848	0.038727	90597	3509	444677	0.007890	2.632	2737755	30.219	40
TABLE 45	0.006800	0.033465	87089	2914	428324	0.006804	2.557	2293078	26.330	45
50	0.010424	0.051189	84174	4309	410693	0.010491	2.638	1864753	22.153	50
55	0.014677	0.072128	79866	5761	387280	0.014874	2.909	1454061	18.206	55
60	0.046472	0.210571	74105	15604	332049	0.046994	2.534	1066781	14.396	60
65	0.030675	0.142354	58501	8328	272444	0.030567	2.591	734732	12.559	65
70	0.093168	0.383800	50173	19256	203433	0.094657	2.537	462288	9.214	70
75	0.095238	0.379612	30916	11736	123540	0.095000	2.355	258854	8.373	75
80	0.166667	0.578038	19180	11087	66521	0.166667	2.350	135315	7.055	80
85	0.117647	1.000000	8093	8093	68793	0.054600	8.500	68793	8.500	85

x	$_nM_x$	$_nq_x$	l_x	$_nd_x$	$_nL_x$	$_nm_x$	$_na_x$	T_x	$\overset{\circ}{e}_x$	x
0	0.018957	0.018640	100000	1864	98327	0.018957	0.102	7418015	74.180	0
1	0.001122	0.004477	98136	439	391446	0.001122	1.500	7319689	74.587	1
5	0.000347	0.001736	97697	170	488059	0.000347	2.500	6928243	70.916	5
10	0.000602	0.003012	97527	294	486917	0.000603	2.555	6440184	66.035	10
15	0.000508	0.002549	97233	248	485597	0.000510	2.699	5953266	61.227	15
20	0.001093	0.005474	96986	531	483653	0.001098	2.600	5467670	56.376	20
TABLE 3 25	0.001049	0.005205	96455	502	480945	0.001044	2.355	4984016	51.672	25
30	0.000377	0.001891	95953	181	479385	0.000378	2.915	4503071	46.930	30
FEMALE 35	0.001797	0.009014	95771	863	476827	0.001810	2.650	4023686	42.014	35
LIFE 40	0.001696	0.008472	94908	804	472641	0.001701	2.639	3546859	37.372	40
TABLE 45	0.002965	0.014889	94104	1401	467439	0.002998	2.801	3074217	32.668	45
50	0.006129	0.030533	92703	2830	457145	0.006192	2.750	2606779	28.120	50
55	0.010825	0.053395	89872	4799	438647	0.010940	2.767	2149634	23.919	55
60	0.022133	0.105618	85074	8985	403347	0.022277	2.549	1710987	20.112	60
65	0.019022	0.091021	76088	6926	363683	0.019043	2.580	1307640	17.186	65
70	0.036269	0.168456	69163	11651	318225	0.036612	2.632	943957	13.648	70
75	0.055944	0.248840	57512	14311	253620	0.056428	2.629	625732	10.880	75
80	0.125000	0.474056	43201	20480	163836	0.125000	2.453	372112	8.614	80
85	0.109091	1.000000	22721	22721	208276	0.046402	9.167	208276	9.167	85

CRUDE RATES

	Per Thousand	BOTH SEXES	MALES	FEMALES
TABLE 4	BIRTH RATE	33.58	31.19	36.57
OBSERVED	DEATH RATE	4.15	5.01	3.06
VITAL	RATE OF INCREASE	29.43	26.18	33.52

RATES
AND
RATIOS

PERCENT OF POPULATION IN AGE GROUP

	BOTH SEXES	MALES	FEMALES
UNDER 15	39.65	36.69	43.37
15 - 64	58.61	61.91	54.46
65 AND OLDER	1.74	1.40	2.17

RATES STANDARDIZED ON USA 1980

Per Thousand	BOTH SEXES	MALES	FEMALES
BIRTH RATE	39.51		37.10
DEATH RATE	11.41	13.02	9.89
RATE OF INCREASE	28.11		27.21

RATES STANDARDIZED ON MEXICO 1980

	BOTH SEXES	MALES	FEMALES
BIRTH RATE	35.48		34.52
DEATH RATE	5.12	6.39	3.84
RATE OF INCREASE	30.35		30.69

VITAL STATISTICS

GFR x 1000	155.801
TFR	4.716
GRR	2.277
NRR	2.191
μ	27.625
σ^2	43.652
GENERATION	26.991
POP. SEX RATIO	0.796
SEX RATIO AT BIRTH	1.071
DEP. RATIO x 100	70.631

PROJECTED POPULATION

AGE GROUP	1975			1980			STABLE EQUIVALENT TO ORIGINAL POPULATION				AGE GROUP	
							MALES		FEMALES			
	BOTH SEXES	MALES	FEMALES	BOTH SEXES	MALES	FEMALES	Number	Percent	Number	Percent		
0-4	15	8	7	18	9	9	7	16.2	6	15.5	0-4	
5-9	12	6	6	15	8	7	6	13.9	5	13.4	5-9	TABLE 5
10-14	12	6	6	12	6	6	5	12.0	5	11.5	10-14	
15-19	10	5	5	12	6	6	4	10.3	4	9.9	15-19	POPULATION
20-24	8	4	4	10	5	5	4	8.8	3	8.5	20-24	PROJECTED
25-29	11	7	4	8	4	4	3	7.5	3	7.3	25-29	WITH
30-34	7	4	3	11	7	4	3	6.4	3	6.3	30-34	FIXED
35-39	7	4	3	7	4	3	2	5.5	2	5.4	35-39	AGE-
40-44	5	3	2	6	3	3	2	4.6	2	4.7	40-44	SPECIFIC
45-49	5	3	2	5	3	2	2	3.9	2	4.0	45-49	BIRTH
50-54	3	2	1	5	3	2	1	3.2	1	3.4	50-54	AND
55-59	2	1	1	3	2	1	1	2.6	1	2.8	55-59	DEATH
60-64	2	1	1	2	1	1	1	1.9	1	2.2	60-64	RATES
65-69	0	0	0	2	1	1	1	1.4	1	1.7	65-69	(female
70-74	0	0	0	0	0	0	0	0.9	1	1.3	70-74	dominant,
75-79	0	0	0	0	0	0	0	0.5	0	0.9	75-79	in 000s)
80-84	0	0	0	0	0	0	0	0.2	0	0.5	80-84	
85+	0	0	0	0	0	0	0	0.2	0	0.6	85+	
TOTAL	99	54	45	116	62	54	42		40		TOTAL	

VITAL RATES OF PROJECTED POPULATION

Per Thousand	1975			1980			VITAL RATES OF STABLE POPULATION			
	BOTH SEXES	MALES	FEMALES	BOTH SEXES	MALES	FEMALES	Per Thousand	MALES	FEMALES	TABLE 6
BIRTH RATE	33.72	31.82	36.03	34.25	32.79	35.97	BIRTH RATE	35.85	33.94	
DEATH RATE	4.61	5.65	3.36	4.94	6.12	3.56	DEATH RATE	6.77	4.81	PROJECTED
RATE OF INCREASE	29.11	26.18	32.67	29.31	26.67	32.41	RATE OF INCREASE		29.13	VITAL RATES AND RATIOS

AGE STRUCTURE OF PROJECTED POPULATION

	1975			1980			STABLE AGE STRUCTURE			
% UNDER 15	38.98	36.53	41.95	38.72	36.81	40.96	% UNDER 15	42.14	40.36	(female
% 15-64	58.99	61.78	55.60	58.83	61.04	56.24	% 15-64	54.73	54.63	dominant)
% 65 AND OLDER	2.03	1.69	2.45	2.45	2.15	2.80	% 65 AND OLDER	3.13	5.00	
DEPEND. RATIO x 100	69.52	61.86	79.85	69.98	63.83	77.82	DEPEND. RATIO x 100	82.73	83.03	

AGE GROUP	FEMALE BIRTH RATES	NET MATERNITY FUNCTION	COEFF. OF MATRIX EQUATION	ORIGINAL MATRIX		STABLE MATRIX		MATRIX PARAMETERS		
				SUB-DIAGONAL	FIRST ROW	FISHER VALUES	REPRODUCTIVE VALUES			
0-4	0.0000	0.0000	0.0000	0.99650	0.00000	1.097	6279	λ_1	1.15679	
5-9	0.0000	0.0000	0.0005	0.99766	0.00047	1.274	7333	λ_2	0.34677+0.79923i	TABLE 7
10-14	0.0002	0.0009	0.1113	0.99729	0.11197	1.477	7360	λ_4	-0.44896+0.46304i	
15-19	0.0457	0.2217	0.4353	0.99600	0.43909	1.590	6254	λ_6	0.05376+0.61639i	LESLIE
20-24	0.1342	0.6490	0.6313	0.99440	0.63926	1.362	4985	r_1	0.02913	MATRIX
25-29	0.1276	0.6136	0.4920	0.99676	0.50104	0.879	2516	r_2	-0.02757+0.23229i	AND ITS
30-34	0.0773	0.3705	0.3026	0.99467	0.30917	0.469	1245	r_4	-0.08771+0.46815i	ANALYSIS
35-39	0.0492	0.2348	0.1638	0.99122	0.16826	0.204	455	r_6	-0.09602+0.29676i	(females)
40-44	0.0196	0.0929	0.0489	0.98899	0.05072	0.052	92	c_1	409	
45-49	0.0011	0.0050	0.0036	0.97798	0.00381	0.005	6	$2\pi/y$	27.0494	
50-54	0.0005	0.0023	0.0011	0.95953	0.00121	0.001	1	Δ	6.2489	

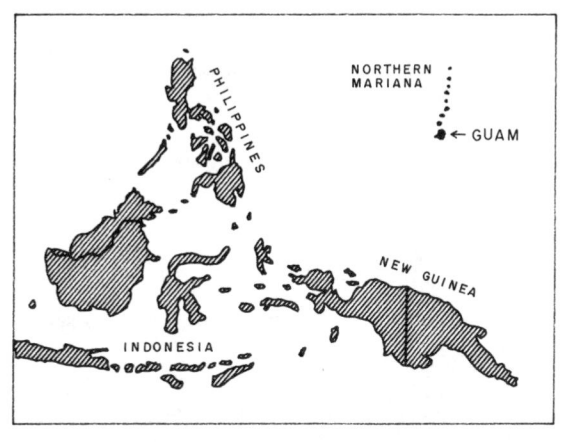

TABLE 1 — DATA

AGE AT LAST BIRTHDAY	ESTIMATED MID-YEAR POPULATION BOTH SEXES	MALES Number	MALES Percent	FEMALES Number	FEMALES Percent	BIRTHS BY AGE OF MOTHER AND SEX	DEATHS BOTH SEXES	DEATHS MALES	DEATHS FEMALES	AGE AT LAST BIRTHDAY
0	2875	1429	2.6	1446	2.8		49	30	19	0
1-4	10206	5229	9.4	4977	9.8		5	2	3	1-4
5-9	12709	6495	11.7	6214	12.2		6	4	2	5-9
10-14	11407	5869	10.5	5538	10.9	5	6	5	1	10-14
15-19	11060	5883	10.6	5177	10.2	379	9	7	2	15-19
20-24	11176	6054	10.9	5122	10.0	988	15	13	2	20-24
25-29	10387	5224	9.4	5163	10.1	895	19	14	5	25-29
30-34	9345	4882	8.8	4463	8.8	518	14	13	1	30-34
35-39	6284	3406	6.1	2878	5.6	153	11	7	4	35-39
40-44	5079	2665	4.8	2414	4.7	60	14	10	4	40-44
45-49	4215	2184	3.9	2031	4.0	5	17	13	4	45-49
50-54	4007	2251	4.0	1756	3.4		31	21	10	50-54
55-59	2931	1643	3.0	1288	2.5		37	26	11	55-59
60-64	1939	1014	1.8	925	1.8		41	26	15	60-64
65-69	1426	733	1.3	693	1.4		47	27	20	65-69
70-74	814	394	0.7	420	0.8		35	19	16	70-74
75-79	459	186	0.3	273	0.5		30	13	17	75-79
80-84	181	68	0.1	113	0.2	1545 M	12	5	7	80-84
85+	123	31	0.1	92	0.2	1458 F	24	8	16	85+
TOTAL	106623	55640		50983		3003	422	263	159	TOTAL

TABLE 2 — MALE LIFE TABLE

x	$_nM_x$	$_nq_x$	l_x	$_nd_x$	$_nL_x$	$_nm_x$	$_na_x$	T_x	$\mathring{e}_x$	x
0	0.020994	0.020607	100000	2061	98157	0.020994	0.106	6892250	68.923	0
1	0.000382	0.001528	97939	150	391383	0.000382	1.500	6794093	69.370	1
5	0.000616	0.003075	97790	301	488197	0.000616	2.500	6402710	65.474	5
10	0.000852	0.004256	97489	415	486465	0.000853	2.638	5914514	60.669	10
15	0.001190	0.005933	97074	576	484059	0.001190	2.723	5428049	55.917	15
20	0.002147	0.010690	96498	1032	480056	0.002149	2.640	4943990	51.234	20
25	0.002680	0.013318	95467	1271	474198	0.002681	2.535	4463934	46.759	25
30	0.002663	0.013205	94195	1244	467799	0.002659	2.446	3989736	42.356	30
35	0.002055	0.010236	92951	951	462478	0.002057	2.605	3521937	37.890	35
40	0.003752	0.018756	92000	1726	456041	0.003784	2.706	3059459	33.255	40
45	0.005952	0.029440	90274	2658	445203	0.005970	2.679	2603418	28.839	45
50	0.009329	0.045783	87617	4011	428841	0.009354	2.696	2158215	24.632	50
55	0.015825	0.076922	83605	6431	403068	0.015955	2.674	1729374	20.685	55
60	0.025641	0.121625	77174	9386	363463	0.025825	2.613	1326306	17.186	60
65	0.036835	0.169810	67788	11511	310743	0.037044	2.551	962843	14.204	65
70	0.048223	0.216373	56277	12177	251284	0.048458	2.528	652100	11.587	70
75	0.069892	0.298326	44100	13156	187086	0.070321	2.460	400816	9.089	75
80	0.073529	0.312387	30944	9666	131280	0.073633	2.575	213729	6.907	80
85	0.258065	1.000000	21277	21277	82450	0.201873	3.875	82450	3.875	85

TABLE 3 — FEMALE LIFE TABLE

x	$_nM_x$	$_nq_x$	l_x	$_nd_x$	$_nL_x$	$_nm_x$	$_na_x$	T_x	$\mathring{e}_x$	x
0	0.013140	0.012985	100000	1298	98821	0.013140	0.092	7531103	75.311	0
1	0.000603	0.002407	98702	238	394212	0.000603	1.500	7432282	75.301	1
5	0.000322	0.001608	98464	158	491924	0.000322	2.500	7038070	71.479	5
10	0.000181	0.000903	98306	89	491313	0.000181	2.574	6546146	66.590	10
15	0.000386	0.001933	98217	190	490631	0.000387	2.612	6054834	61.648	15
20	0.000390	0.001952	98027	191	489716	0.000391	2.808	5564203	56.762	20
25	0.000968	0.004830	97836	473	487980	0.000968	2.463	5074487	51.867	25
30	0.000224	0.001109	97363	108	486589	0.000222	2.901	4586507	47.107	30
35	0.001390	0.006996	97255	680	484719	0.001404	2.711	4099918	42.156	35
40	0.001657	0.008270	96575	799	480933	0.001661	2.570	3615199	37.434	40
45	0.001969	0.009902	95776	948	476904	0.001989	2.916	3134266	32.725	45
50	0.005695	0.028379	94828	2691	468024	0.005750	2.728	2657363	28.023	50
55	0.008540	0.042246	92137	3892	451842	0.008615	2.729	2189338	23.762	55
60	0.016216	0.078921	88244	6964	425301	0.016375	2.714	1737496	19.690	60
65	0.028860	0.135925	81280	11048	379893	0.029082	2.601	1312195	16.144	65
70	0.038095	0.175272	70232	12310	321354	0.038306	2.579	932302	13.275	70
75	0.062271	0.270994	57922	15697	250173	0.062743	2.487	610948	10.548	75
80	0.061947	0.269130	42226	11364	183322	0.061990	2.553	360776	8.544	80
85	0.173913	1.000000	30861	30861	177453	0.104805	5.750	177453	5.750	85

TABLE 4 — OBSERVED VITAL RATES AND RATIOS

CRUDE RATES

Per Thousand	BOTH SEXES	MALES	FEMALES
BIRTH RATE	28.16	27.77	28.60
DEATH RATE	3.96	4.73	3.12
RATE OF INCREASE	24.21	23.04	25.48

RATES STANDARDIZED ON USA 1980

Per Thousand	BOTH SEXES	MALES	FEMALES
BIRTH RATE	26.92		25.42
DEATH RATE	9.92	10.23	9.62
RATE OF INCREASE	17.00		15.80

VITAL STATISTICS

GFR x 1000	110.210
TFR	3.184
GRR	1.546
NRR	1.509
μ	27.193
σ^2	42.383
GENERATION	26.869
POP. SEX RATIO	0.916
SEX RATIO AT BIRTH	1.060
DEP. RATIO x 100	60.521

PERCENT OF POPULATION IN AGE GROUP

	BOTH SEXES	MALES	FEMALES
UNDER 15	34.89	34.19	35.65
15 - 64	62.30	63.27	61.23
65 AND OLDER	2.82	2.54	3.12

RATES STANDARDIZED ON MEXICO 1980

	BOTH SEXES	MALES	FEMALES
BIRTH RATE	24.38		23.86
DEATH RATE	4.08	4.85	3.30
RATE OF INCREASE	20.30		20.56

PROJECTED POPULATION

AGE GROUP	1985			1990		
	BOTH SEXES	MALES	FEMALES	BOTH SEXES	MALES	FEMALES
0-4	15	8	7	16	8	8
5-9	13	7	6	15	8	7
10-14	12	6	6	13	7	6
15-19	12	6	6	12	6	6
20-24	11	6	5	12	6	6
25-29	11	6	5	11	6	5
30-34	10	5	5	11	6	5
35-39	9	5	4	10	5	5
40-44	6	3	3	9	5	4
45-49	5	3	2	6	3	3
50-54	4	2	2	5	3	2
55-59	4	2	2	4	2	2
60-64	2	1	1	4	2	2
65-69	2	1	1	2	1	1
70-74	2	1	1	2	1	1
75-79	0	0	0	0	0	0
80-84	0	0	0	0	0	0
85+	0	0	0	0	0	0
TOTAL	118	62	56	132	69	63

STABLE EQUIVALENT TO ORIGINAL POPULATION

	MALES		FEMALES		AGE GROUP	
	Number	Percent	Number	Percent		
	7	11.4	7	10.8	0-4	
	6	10.5	6	10.0	5-9	TABLE 5
	6	9.7	6	9.3	10-14	
	6	9.0	5	8.6	15-19	POPULATION
	5	8.2	5	7.9	20-24	PROJECTED
	5	7.5	5	7.3	25-29	WITH
	4	6.9	4	6.7	30-34	FIXED
	4	6.3	4	6.2	35-39	AGE-
	4	5.8	4	5.7	40-44	SPECIFIC
	3	5.2	3	5.3	45-49	BIRTH
	3	4.6	3	4.8	50-54	AND
	2	4.0	3	4.3	55-59	DEATH
	2	3.4	2	3.7	60-64	RATES
	2	2.7	2	3.1	65-69	(female
	1	2.0	1	2.4	70-74	dominant,
	1	1.4	1	1.7	75-79	in 000s)
	1	0.9	1	1.2	80-84	
	0	0.5	1	1.1	85+	
TOTAL	62		63		TOTAL	

VITAL RATES OF PROJECTED POPULATION

Per Thousand	1985			1990		
	BOTH SEXES	MALES	FEMALES	BOTH SEXES	MALES	FEMALES
BIRTH RATE	26.74	26.51	26.98	25.46	25.39	25.54
DEATH RATE	4.38	5.26	3.43	4.89	5.82	3.90
RATE OF INCREASE	22.35	21.25	23.54	20.57	19.57	21.64

AGE STRUCTURE OF PROJECTED POPULATION

	BOTH SEXES	MALES	FEMALES	BOTH SEXES	MALES	FEMALES
% UNDER 15	34.20	33.67	34.77	33.30	33.01	33.62
% 15-64	62.48	63.23	61.67	62.67	63.08	62.24
% 65 AND OLDER	3.32	3.10	3.55	4.02	3.92	4.14
DEPEND. RATIO x 100	60.05	58.16	62.15	59.56	58.54	60.66

VITAL RATES OF STABLE POPULATION

Per Thousand	MALES	FEMALES	
			TABLE 6
BIRTH RATE	24.18	22.79	
DEATH RATE	8.87	7.46	PROJECTED
RATE OF INCREASE		15.34	VITAL RATES

STABLE AGE STRUCTURE

	MALES	FEMALES	AND
			RATIOS
% UNDER 15	31.65	30.08	(female
% 15-64	60.88	60.46	dominant)
% 65 AND OLDER	7.47	9.47	
DEPEND. RATIO x 100	64.25	65.40	

LESLIE MATRIX TABLE

AGE GROUP	FEMALE BIRTH RATES	NET MATERNITY FUNCTION	COEFF. OF MATRIX EQUATION	ORIGINAL MATRIX SUB-DIAGONAL	ORIGINAL MATRIX FIRST ROW	STABLE MATRIX FISHER VALUES	STABLE MATRIX REPRODUCTIVE VALUES	MATRIX PARAMETERS	
0-4	0.0000	0.0000	0.0000	0.99775	0.00000	1.054	6767	λ_1 1.07969	
5-9	0.0000	0.0000	0.0011	0.99876	0.00108	1.140	7085	λ_2 0.33946+0.74897i	TABLE 7
10-14	0.0004	0.0022	0.0883	0.99861	0.08858	1.231	6820	λ_4 -0.34040-0.46218i	
15-19	0.0355	0.1744	0.3165	0.99813	0.31806	1.238	6409	λ_6 -0.53253+0.19000i	LESLIE
20-24	0.0937	0.4586	0.4347	0.99646	0.43761	1.003	5139	r_1 0.01534	MATRIX
25-29	0.0842	0.4107	0.3425	0.99715	0.34600	0.624	3224	r_2 -0.03913+0.22905i	AND ITS
30-34	0.0564	0.2742	0.1997	0.99616	0.20230	0.311	1386	r_4 -0.11102-0.44112i	ANALYSIS
35-39	0.0258	0.1251	0.0916	0.99219	0.09314	0.123	353	r_6 -0.11404+0.55978i	(females)
40-44	0.0121	0.0580	0.0319	0.99162	0.03267	0.035	83	c_1 618	
45-49	0.0012	0.0057	0.0029	0.98138	0.00295	0.003	6	$2\pi/y$ 27.4314	
50-54	0.0000	0.0000	0.0000	0.00000	0.00000	0.000	0	Δ 14.1438	

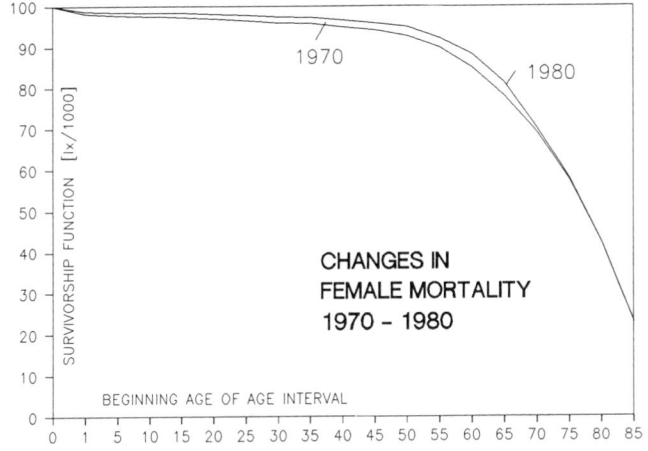

CHANGES IN FEMALE MORTALITY 1970 - 1980

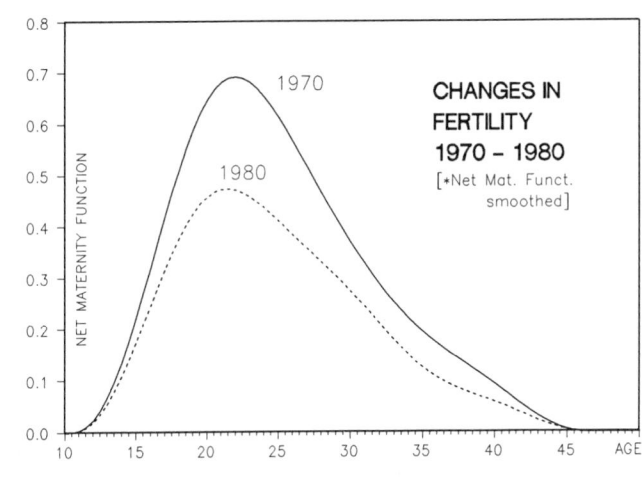

CHANGES IN FERTILITY 1970 - 1980

[*Net Mat. Funct. smoothed]

TABLE 1 — DATA

AGE AT LAST BIRTHDAY	ESTIMATED MID-YEAR POPULATION BOTH SEXES	MALES Number	MALES Percent	FEMALES Number	FEMALES Percent	BIRTHS BY AGE OF MOTHER AND SEX	DEATHS BOTH SEXES	MALES	FEMALES	AGE AT LAST BIRTHDAY
0	61194	31243	2.2	29951	2.1		1040	590	450	0
1-4	235915	120440	8.5	115475	8.2		233	136	97	1-4
5-9	311878	159303	11.3	152575	10.8		148	90	58	5-9
10-14	295786	151236	10.7	144550	10.2	56	133	87	46	10-14
15-19	258910	132451	9.4	126459	8.9	8130	274	200	74	15-19
20-24	227364	115262	8.2	112102	7.9	23377	254	186	68	20-24
25-29	184180	92822	6.6	91358	6.5	18232	203	147	56	25-29
30-34	160913	81066	5.7	79847	5.6	7998	209	142	67	30-34
35-39	152152	77381	5.5	74771	5.3	3364	315	188	127	35-39
40-44	161860	83333	5.9	78527	5.5	976	496	309	187	40-44
45-49	157660	79499	5.6	78161	5.5	74	782	480	302	45-49
50-54	138779	68008	4.8	70771	5.0		1029	606	423	50-54
55-59	131181	64950	4.6	66231	4.7		1603	1037	566	55-59
60-64	112036	54814	3.9	57222	4.0		2175	1424	751	60-64
65-69	88514	41880	3.0	46634	3.3		2788	1779	1009	65-69
70-74	64404	27548	1.9	36856	2.6		2987	1669	1318	70-74
75-79	43168	16711	1.2	26457	1.9		3326	1664	1662	75-79
80-84	36767	13491	1.0	23276	1.6	31924 M	3169	1431	1738	80-84
85+	6630	2330	0.2	4300	0.3	30283 F	3676	1450	2226	85+
TOTAL	2829291	1413768		1415523		62207	24840	13615	11225	TOTAL

TABLE 2 — MALE LIFE TABLE

x	nM_x	nq_x	l_x	nd_x	nL_x	nm_x	na_x	T_x	$\overset{\circ}{e}_x$	x
0	0.018884	0.018569	100000	1857	98333	0.018884	0.102	6797122	67.971	0
1	0.001129	0.004504	98143	442	391467	0.001129	1.500	6698790	68.255	1
5	0.000565	0.002821	97701	276	487816	0.000565	2.500	6307323	64.557	5
10	0.000575	0.002884	97425	281	486520	0.000577	2.839	5819507	59.733	10
15	0.001510	0.007548	97144	733	483992	0.001515	2.640	5332987	54.897	15
20	0.001614	0.008038	96411	775	480123	0.001614	2.506	4848995	50.295	20
25	0.001584	0.007888	95636	754	476307	0.001584	2.515	4368872	45.682	25
30	0.001752	0.008740	94882	829	472416	0.001755	2.596	3892565	41.025	30
35	0.002430	0.012081	94053	1136	467606	0.002430	2.661	3420149	36.364	35
40	0.003708	0.018383	92916	1708	460642	0.003708	2.693	2952543	31.776	40
45	0.006038	0.029827	91208	2721	449691	0.006050	2.666	2491902	27.321	45
50	0.008911	0.043769	88488	3873	433548	0.008933	2.704	2042210	23.079	50
55	0.015966	0.077061	84615	6521	407961	0.015983	2.682	1608662	19.012	55
60	0.025979	0.122678	78094	9580	367920	0.026040	2.646	1200701	15.375	60
65	0.042479	0.193270	68514	13242	310519	0.042644	2.580	832781	12.155	65
70	0.060585	0.264863	55272	14640	240362	0.060906	2.541	522262	9.449	70
75	0.099575	0.396856	40633	16125	161941	0.099575	2.444	281900	6.938	75
80	0.106071	0.419378	24507	10278	97093	0.105855	2.524	119959	4.895	80
85	0.622318	1.000000	14229	14229	22865	0.758035	1.607	22865	1.607	85

TABLE 3 — FEMALE LIFE TABLE

x	nM_x	nq_x	l_x	nd_x	nL_x	nm_x	na_x	T_x	$\overset{\circ}{e}_x$	x
0	0.015025	0.014823	100000	1482	98659	0.015025	0.096	7385745	73.857	0
1	0.000840	0.003353	98518	330	393245	0.000840	1.500	7287085	73.967	1
5	0.000380	0.001899	98187	186	490471	0.000380	2.500	6893840	70.211	5
10	0.000318	0.001592	98001	156	489635	0.000319	2.634	6403370	65.340	10
15	0.000585	0.002929	97845	287	488537	0.000587	2.601	5913734	60.440	15
20	0.000607	0.003028	97558	295	487055	0.000607	2.508	5425197	55.610	20
25	0.000613	0.003065	97263	298	485593	0.000614	2.579	4938142	50.771	25
30	0.000839	0.004213	96965	409	483911	0.000844	2.765	4452550	45.919	30
35	0.001699	0.008469	96556	818	480888	0.001701	2.685	3968639	41.102	35
40	0.002381	0.011841	95739	1134	476066	0.002381	2.683	3487751	36.430	40
45	0.003864	0.019163	94605	1813	468826	0.003867	2.684	3011685	31.834	45
50	0.005977	0.029515	92792	2739	457522	0.005986	2.650	2542859	27.404	50
55	0.008546	0.041960	90053	3779	441397	0.008561	2.653	2085337	23.157	55
60	0.013124	0.063903	86275	5513	418542	0.013172	2.673	1643940	19.055	60
65	0.021637	0.103380	80761	8349	384284	0.021726	2.662	1225398	15.173	65
70	0.035761	0.165638	72412	11994	333758	0.035937	2.640	841114	11.616	70
75	0.062819	0.271864	60418	16425	261474	0.062819	2.527	507355	8.397	75
80	0.074669	0.321436	43993	14141	188217	0.075130	2.755	245882	5.589	80
85	0.517674	1.000000	29852	29852	57665	0.584984	1.932	57665	1.932	85

TABLE 4 — OBSERVED VITAL RATES AND RATIOS

CRUDE RATES

Per Thousand	BOTH SEXES	MALES	FEMALES
BIRTH RATE	21.99	22.58	21.39
DEATH RATE	8.78	9.63	7.93
RATE OF INCREASE	13.21	12.95	13.46

PERCENT OF POPULATION IN AGE GROUP

	BOTH SEXES	MALES	FEMALES
UNDER 15	31.98	32.69	31.26
15 - 64	59.56	60.09	59.02
65 AND OLDER	8.46	7.21	9.72

RATES STANDARDIZED ON USA 1980

Per Thousand	BOTH SEXES	MALES	FEMALES
BIRTH RATE	27.12		25.67
DEATH RATE	13.92	13.63	14.19
RATE OF INCREASE	13.20		11.48

RATES STANDARDIZED ON MEXICO 1980

	BOTH SEXES	MALES	FEMALES
BIRTH RATE	24.56		24.10
DEATH RATE	4.93	5.69	4.15
RATE OF INCREASE	19.64		19.95

VITAL STATISTICS

GFR x 1000	97.013
TFR	3.157
GRR	1.537
NRR	1.492
μ	26.624
σ^2	33.835
GENERATION	26.368
POP. SEX RATIO	1.001
SEX RATIO AT BIRTH	1.054
DEP. RATIO x 100	67.907

PROJECTED POPULATION

AGE GROUP	1975 BOTH SEXES	1975 MALES	1975 FEMALES	1980 BOTH SEXES	1980 MALES	1980 FEMALES
0-4	328	168	160	375	192	183
5-9	296	151	145	328	168	160
10-14	311	159	152	296	151	145
15-19	294	150	144	310	158	152
20-24	257	131	126	293	149	144
25-29	226	114	112	256	130	126
30-34	183	92	91	224	113	111
35-39	159	80	79	181	91	90
40-44	150	76	74	158	79	79
45-49	158	81	77	147	74	73
50-54	153	77	76	153	78	75
55-59	132	64	68	146	72	74
60-64	122	59	63	123	58	65
65-69	99	46	53	107	49	58
70-74	73	32	41	82	36	46
75-79	48	19	29	54	22	32
80-84	29	10	19	32	11	21
85+	10	3	7	8	2	6
TOTAL	3028	1512	1516	3273	1633	1640

STABLE EQUIVALENT TO ORIGINAL POPULATION

MALES Number	MALES Percent	FEMALES Number	FEMALES Percent	AGE GROUP	
164	11.4	156	10.9	0-4	
151	10.5	144	10.1	5-9	TABLE 5
140	9.7	133	9.3	10-14	
129	9.0	123	8.6	15-19	POPULATION
119	8.3	114	8.0	20-24	PROJECTED
109	7.6	105	7.3	25-29	WITH
100	7.0	97	6.8	30-34	FIXED
92	6.4	90	6.3	35-39	AGE-
84	5.8	82	5.7	40-44	SPECIFIC
76	5.3	75	5.2	45-49	BIRTH
68	4.7	68	4.7	50-54	AND
59	4.1	61	4.2	55-59	DEATH
49	3.4	53	3.7	60-64	RATES
39	2.7	45	3.2	65-69	(female
28	1.9	37	2.5	70-74	dominant,
17	1.2	27	1.8	75-79	in 000s)
10	0.7	18	1.2	80-84	
2	0.1	5	0.4	85+	
1436		1433		TOTAL	

VITAL RATES OF PROJECTED POPULATION

Per Thousand	1975 BOTH SEXES	1975 MALES	1975 FEMALES	1980 BOTH SEXES	1980 MALES	1980 FEMALES
BIRTH RATE	23.63	24.28	22.98	24.80	25.48	24.13
DEATH RATE	9.16	9.76	8.57	8.72	9.42	8.02
RATE OF INCREASE	14.46	14.51	14.41	16.09	16.07	16.11

VITAL RATES OF STABLE POPULATION

Per Thousand	MALES	FEMALES	
BIRTH RATE	24.20	22.97	TABLE 6
DEATH RATE	8.98	7.77	PROJECTED
RATE OF INCREASE		15.21	VITAL RATES AND RATIOS (female dominant)

AGE STRUCTURE OF PROJECTED POPULATION

	BOTH SEXES	MALES	FEMALES	BOTH SEXES	MALES	FEMALES
% UNDER 15	30.87	31.58	30.16	30.49	31.21	29.76
% 15-64	60.60	61.12	60.07	60.89	61.41	60.37
% 65 AND OLDER	8.53	7.30	9.76	8.62	7.38	9.87
DEPEND. RATIO x 100	65.03	63.61	66.47	64.23	62.83	65.66

STABLE AGE STRUCTURE

	MALES	FEMALES
% UNDER 15	31.70	30.25
% 15-64	61.64	60.60
% 65 AND OLDER	6.65	9.15
DEPEND. RATIO x 100	62.22	65.02

AGE GROUP	FEMALE BIRTH RATES	NET MATERNITY FUNCTION	COEFF. OF MATRIX EQUATION	ORIGINAL MATRIX SUB-DIAGONAL	ORIGINAL MATRIX FIRST ROW	STABLE MATRIX FISHER VALUES	STABLE MATRIX REPRODUCTIVE VALUES
0-4	0.0000	0.0000	0.0000	0.99709	0.00000	1.056	153526
5-9	0.0000	0.0000	0.0005	0.99830	0.00046	1.142	174306
10-14	0.0002	0.0009	0.0769	0.99776	0.07727	1.234	178417
15-19	0.0313	0.1529	0.3237	0.99697	0.32590	1.253	158458
20-24	0.1015	0.4944	0.4831	0.99700	0.48791	1.011	113340
25-29	0.0972	0.4718	0.3539	0.99654	0.35846	0.578	52765
30-34	0.0488	0.2360	0.1706	0.99375	0.17346	0.246	19612
35-39	0.0219	0.1053	0.0671	0.98997	0.06860	0.082	6162
40-44	0.0061	0.0288	0.0155	0.98479	0.01600	0.017	1309
45-49	0.0005	0.0022	0.0011	0.97589	0.00113	0.001	87
50-54	0.0000	0.0000	0.0000	0.00000	0.00000	0.000	0

MATRIX PARAMETERS

λ_1	1.07900
λ_2	$0.32613+0.79855i$
λ_4	$-0.39984+0.41764i$
λ_6	$0.00231+0.45749i$
r_1	0.01521
r_2	$-0.02956+0.23661i$
r_4	$-0.10957+0.46689i$
r_6	$-0.15640+0.31315i$
c_1	14341
$2\pi/y$	26.5547
Δ	3.8875

TABLE 7

LESLIE MATRIX AND ITS ANALYSIS (females)

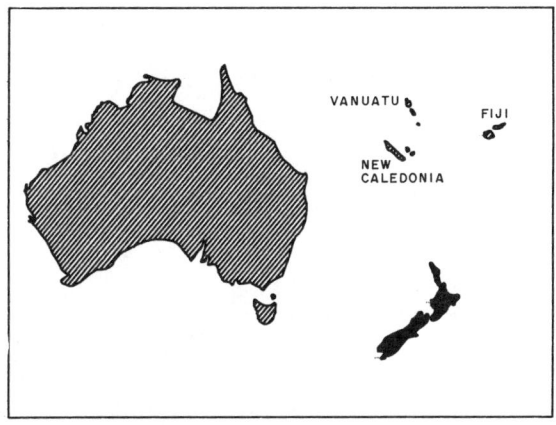

EDUCATION [1984]

% of primary school-age children enrolled:	106
secondary school-age children enrolled:	85
ca. 20-24 year olds in higher education:	29

LABOR FORCE

Average annual labor force growth (%) 1980-85:	1.8
% of the 1980 labor force in agriculture:	11
in industry:	33
in services:	56

GNP & INCOME DISTRIBUTION

GNP per capita (in US Dollars) 1985:	7010
GNP average annual growth rate (%) 1965-85:	1.4
% share of total household income 1981-82	
Lowest 20% of households:	5.1
Highest 10% of households:	28.7

HEALTH & NUTRITION

Population per physician 1981:	610
Daily calorie supply per capita 1985:	3386

TABLE 8

SOCIO-ECONOMIC INDICATORS

TABLE 1 — DATA

AGE AT LAST BIRTHDAY	ESTIMATED MID-YEAR POPULATION BOTH SEXES	MALES Number	MALES Percent	FEMALES Number	FEMALES Percent	BIRTHS BY AGE OF MOTHER AND SEX	DEATHS BOTH SEXES	DEATHS MALES	DEATHS FEMALES	AGE AT LAST BIRTHDAY
0	56420	28820	1.9	27600	1.8		904	534	370	0
1-4	246290	125550	8.1	120740	7.8		240	131	109	1-4
5-9	307900	157100	10.2	150800	9.7		142	94	48	5-9
10-14	321270	164110	10.6	157160	10.1	73	110	66	44	10-14
15-19	295590	150790	9.7	144800	9.3	7922	302	231	71	15-19
20-24	257710	131220	8.5	126490	8.1	20041	286	209	77	20-24
25-29	244100	122960	7.9	121140	7.8	19078	246	157	89	25-29
30-34	198720	100590	6.5	98130	6.3	6854	233	136	97	30-34
35-39	169350	85740	5.5	83610	5.4	2096	296	175	121	35-39
40-44	155930	79520	5.1	76410	4.9	529	412	251	161	40-44
45-49	160750	82790	5.3	77960	5.0	46	739	487	252	45-49
50-54	156060	78210	5.1	77850	5.0		1153	737	416	50-54
55-59	133120	64430	4.2	68690	4.4		1473	941	532	55-59
60-64	125400	60220	3.9	65180	4.2		2387	1521	866	60-64
65-69	103040	48340	3.1	54700	3.5		2812	1793	1019	65-69
70-74	74940	33190	2.1	41750	2.7		3382	1974	1408	70-74
75-79	48010	18950	1.2	29060	1.9		3158	1640	1518	75-79
80-84	28030	9710	0.6	18320	1.2	28874 M	2979	1291	1688	80-84
85+	17470	5360	0.3	12110	0.8	27765 F	3860	1435	2425	85+
TOTAL	3100100	1547600		1552500		56639	25114	13803	11311	TOTAL

TABLE 2 — MALE LIFE TABLE

x	$_nM_x$	$_nq_x$	l_x	$_nd_x$	$_nL_x$	$_nm_x$	$_na_x$	T_x	$\overset{\circ}{e}_x$	x
0	0.018529	0.018225	100000	1823	98362	0.018529	0.101	6897453	68.975	0
1	0.001043	0.004163	98177	409	391688	0.001043	1.500	6799090	69.253	1
5	0.000598	0.002987	97769	292	488114	0.000598	2.500	6407402	65.536	5
10	0.000402	0.002009	97477	196	486988	0.000402	2.981	5919289	60.725	10
15	0.001532	0.007656	97281	745	484661	0.001537	2.659	5432301	55.841	15
20	0.001593	0.007928	96536	765	480739	0.001592	2.463	4947640	51.252	20
25	0.001277	0.006356	95771	609	477307	0.001275	2.458	4466901	46.642	25
30	0.001352	0.006758	95162	643	474277	0.001356	2.615	3989594	41.924	30
35	0.002041	0.010206	94519	965	470355	0.002051	2.678	3515317	37.192	35
40	0.003156	0.015696	93554	1468	464456	0.003162	2.742	3044962	32.548	40
45	0.005882	0.029020	92086	2672	454303	0.005882	2.708	2580506	28.023	45
50	0.009423	0.046207	89413	4132	437440	0.009445	2.670	2126203	23.779	50
55	0.014605	0.070811	85282	6039	412420	0.014643	2.683	1688763	19.802	55
60	0.025257	0.119218	79243	9447	373821	0.025272	2.630	1276343	16.107	60
65	0.037091	0.170689	69796	11913	320372	0.037186	2.599	902522	12.931	65
70	0.059476	0.260777	57882	15094	252379	0.059809	2.547	582150	10.057	70
75	0.086544	0.357248	42788	15286	175421	0.087138	2.480	329771	7.707	75
80	0.132956	0.495786	27502	13635	102554	0.132956	2.436	154350	5.612	80
85	0.267724	1.000000	13867	13867	51796	0.214634	3.735	51796	3.735	85

TABLE 3 — FEMALE LIFE TABLE

x	$_nM_x$	$_nq_x$	l_x	$_nd_x$	$_nL_x$	$_nm_x$	$_na_x$	T_x	$\overset{\circ}{e}_x$	x
0	0.013406	0.013245	100000	1324	98798	0.013406	0.093	7548032	75.480	0
1	0.000903	0.003603	98676	356	393813	0.000903	1.500	7449234	75.492	1
5	0.000318	0.001590	98320	156	491209	0.000318	2.500	7055420	71.760	5
10	0.000280	0.001399	98164	137	490493	0.000280	2.628	6564211	66.870	10
15	0.000490	0.002455	98026	241	489563	0.000492	2.639	6073719	61.960	15
20	0.000609	0.003043	97786	298	488209	0.000610	2.582	5584155	57.106	20
25	0.000735	0.003674	97488	358	486583	0.000736	2.607	5095946	52.272	25
30	0.000988	0.004952	97130	481	484518	0.000993	2.648	4609363	47.456	30
35	0.001447	0.007243	96649	700	481604	0.001454	2.657	4124844	42.679	35
40	0.002107	0.010506	95949	1008	477396	0.002111	2.670	3643240	37.971	40
45	0.003232	0.016043	94941	1523	471201	0.003232	2.700	3165844	33.345	45
50	0.005344	0.026412	93418	2467	461325	0.005348	2.664	2694643	28.845	50
55	0.007745	0.038110	90950	3466	446748	0.007759	2.691	2233318	24.555	55
60	0.013286	0.064487	87484	5642	424123	0.013302	2.643	1786570	20.422	60
65	0.018629	0.089572	81843	7331	392147	0.018694	2.672	1362447	16.647	65
70	0.033725	0.156931	74512	11693	344633	0.033908	2.631	970300	13.022	70
75	0.052237	0.233326	62819	14657	278788	0.052575	2.591	625447	9.956	75
80	0.092140	0.376163	48161	18117	196621	0.092140	2.561	346659	7.198	80
85	0.200248	1.000000	30045	30045	150038	0.133036	4.994	150038	4.994	85

TABLE 4 — OBSERVED VITAL RATES AND RATIOS

CRUDE RATES

Per Thousand	BOTH SEXES	MALES	FEMALES
BIRTH RATE	18.27	18.66	17.88
DEATH RATE	8.10	8.92	7.29
RATE OF INCREASE	10.17	9.74	10.60

PERCENT OF POPULATION IN AGE GROUP

	BOTH SEXES	MALES	FEMALES
UNDER 15	30.06	30.73	29.39
15 - 64	61.18	61.80	60.56
65 AND OLDER	8.76	7.47	10.04

RATES STANDARDIZED ON USA 1980

Per Thousand	BOTH SEXES	MALES	FEMALES
BIRTH RATE	20.53		19.57
DEATH RATE	10.31	11.03	9.62
RATE OF INCREASE	10.22		9.95

RATES STANDARDIZED ON MEXICO 1980

	BOTH SEXES	MALES	FEMALES
BIRTH RATE	18.75		18.53
DEATH RATE	4.15	4.95	3.33
RATE OF INCREASE	14.60		15.20

VITAL STATISTICS

GFR x 1000	77.743
TFR	2.368
GRR	1.161
NRR	1.130
μ	26.142
σ^2	31.007
GENERATION	26.070
POP. SEX RATIO	1.003
SEX RATIO AT BIRTH	1.040
DEP. RATIO x 100	63.444

AGE AT LAST BIRTHDAY	ESTIMATED MID-YEAR POPULATION					BIRTHS BY AGE OF MOTHER AND SEX	DEATHS			AGE AT LAST BIRTHDAY	
	BOTH SEXES	MALES		FEMALES			BOTH SEXES	MALES	FEMALES		
		Number	Percent	Number	Percent						
0	50760	25930	1.7	24830	1.6		650	360	290	0	
1-4	203800	103800	6.6	100000	6.4		138	75	63	1-4	
5-9	294280	150010	9.6	144270	9.2		96	58	38	5-9	
10-14	301480	154410	9.9	147070	9.4	48	96	56	40	10-14	
15-19	314000	161270	10.3	152730	9.7	5869	306	207	99	15-19	
20-24	266680	136770	8.8	129910	8.3	16618	342	242	100	20-24	
25-29	236290	117830	7.5	118460	7.6	17493	287	207	80	25-29	
30-34	235780	117450	7.5	118330	7.5	8124	253	155	98	30-34	
35-39	190560	96560	6.2	93500	6.0	1998	272	165	107	35-39	TABLE 1
40-44	164350	81990	5.2	82360	5.3	361	368	211	157	40-44	
45-49	147690	76010	4.9	71680	4.6	31	632	347	285	45-49	DATA
50-54	156210	80290	5.1	75920	4.8		1003	633	370	50-54	
55-59	144560	72170	4.6	72390	4.6		1590	994	596	55-59	
60-64	121920	58670	3.8	63250	4.0		2157	1354	803	60-64	
65-69	110550	51810	3.3	58740	3.7		3186	1908	1278	65-69	
70-74	85970	38150	2.4	47820	3.0		3708	2175	1533	70-74	
75-79	56120	23310	1.5	32810	2.1		4004	2174	1830	75-79	
80-84	31060	10560	0.7	20500	1.3	25938 M	3415	1548	1867	80-84	
85+	19620	5440	0.3	14180	0.9	24604 F	4173	1451	2722	85+	
TOTAL	3131180	1562430		1568750		50542	26676	14320	12356	TOTAL	

x	$_nM_x$	$_nq_x$	l_x	$_nd_x$	$_nL_x$	$_nm_x$	$_na_x$	T_x	$\overset{\circ}{e}_x$	x	
0	0.013884	0.013711	100000	1371	98757	0.013884	0.094	6993697	69.937	0	
1	0.000723	0.002885	98629	285	393804	0.000723	1.500	6894940	69.908	1	
5	0.000387	0.001931	98344	190	491247	0.000387	2.500	6501136	66.106	5	
10	0.000363	0.001812	98154	178	490419	0.000363	3.013	6009889	61.229	10	
15	0.001284	0.006406	97977	628	488456	0.001285	2.726	5519471	56.335	15	
20	0.001769	0.008824	97349	859	484642	0.001773	2.552	5031015	51.680	20	
25	0.001757	0.008738	96490	843	480294	0.001755	2.443	4546373	47.118	25	TABLE 2
30	0.001320	0.006574	95647	629	476656	0.001319	2.490	4066079	42.511	30	
35	0.001709	0.008546	95018	812	473181	0.001716	2.650	3589424	37.776	35	MALE
40	0.002573	0.012866	94206	1212	468269	0.002588	2.722	3116242	33.079	40	LIFE
45	0.004565	0.022613	92994	2103	460193	0.004570	2.729	2647974	28.475	45	TABLE
50	0.007884	0.038724	90891	3520	446436	0.007884	2.722	2187781	24.070	50	
55	0.013773	0.066944	87371	5849	423364	0.013816	2.693	1741344	19.930	55	
60	0.023078	0.109696	81522	8943	386597	0.023132	2.650	1317980	16.167	60	
65	0.036827	0.169359	72580	12292	333456	0.036862	2.605	931383	12.833	65	
70	0.057012	0.250898	60288	15126	264643	0.057156	2.567	597927	9.918	70	
75	0.093265	0.380639	45162	17190	182776	0.094051	2.497	333283	7.380	75	
80	0.146591	0.531040	27971	14854	101329	0.146591	2.406	150508	5.381	80	
85	0.266728	1.000000	13117	13117	49179	0.213591	3.749	49179	3.749	85	

x	$_nM_x$	$_nq_x$	l_x	$_nd_x$	$_nL_x$	$_nm_x$	$_na_x$	T_x	$\overset{\circ}{e}_x$	x	
0	0.011679	0.011557	100000	1156	98948	0.011679	0.090	7558893	75.589	0	
1	0.000630	0.002516	98844	249	394756	0.000630	1.500	7459945	75.472	1	
5	0.000263	0.001316	98596	130	492654	0.000263	2.500	7065189	71.658	5	
10	0.000272	0.001359	98466	134	492034	0.000272	2.794	6572535	66.749	10	
15	0.000648	0.003239	98332	319	490915	0.000649	2.659	6080501	61.836	15	
20	0.000770	0.003843	98014	377	489128	0.000770	2.506	5589587	57.029	20	
25	0.000675	0.003371	97637	329	487367	0.000675	2.517	5100458	52.239	25	TABLE 3
30	0.000828	0.004141	97308	403	485579	0.000830	2.617	4613091	47.407	30	
35	0.001144	0.005739	96905	556	483242	0.001151	2.694	4127513	42.593	35	FEMALE
40	0.001906	0.009568	96349	922	479715	0.001922	2.800	3644271	37.824	40	LIFE
45	0.003976	0.019733	95427	1883	472704	0.003984	2.647	3164556	33.162	45	TABLE
50	0.004874	0.024094	93544	2254	462461	0.004874	2.667	2691852	28.776	50	
55	0.008233	0.040454	91290	3693	447875	0.008246	2.678	2229391	24.421	55	
60	0.012696	0.061770	87597	5411	425461	0.012718	2.685	1781516	20.338	60	
65	0.021757	0.103547	82186	8510	390821	0.021775	2.637	1356055	16.500	65	
70	0.032058	0.149429	73676	11009	342313	0.032161	2.632	965234	13.101	70	
75	0.055776	0.247369	62667	15502	275942	0.056178	2.588	622921	9.940	75	
80	0.091073	0.372103	47165	17550	192704	0.091073	2.543	346979	7.357	80	
85	0.191961	1.000000	29615	29615	154275	0.123985	5.209	154275	5.209	85	

CRUDE RATES

Per Thousand	BOTH SEXES	MALES	FEMALES
BIRTH RATE	16.14	16.60	15.68
DEATH RATE	8.52	9.17	7.88
RATE OF INCREASE	7.62	7.44	7.81

PERCENT OF POPULATION IN AGE GROUP

UNDER 15	27.16	27.79	26.53
15 - 64	63.16	63.94	62.38
65 AND OLDER	9.69	8.27	11.09

RATES STANDARDIZED ON USA 1980

Per Thousand	BOTH SEXES	MALES	FEMALES
BIRTH RATE	17.68		16.74
DEATH RATE	10.18	10.78	9.61
RATE OF INCREASE	7.51		7.13

RATES STANDARDIZED ON MEXICO 1980

	BOTH SEXES	MALES	FEMALES
BIRTH RATE	15.92		15.63
DEATH RATE	3.96	4.64	3.27
RATE OF INCREASE	11.96		12.35

VITAL STATISTICS

GFR x 1000	65.898	TABLE 4
TFR	2.046	
GRR	0.996	OBSERVED
NRR	0.971	VITAL
μ	26.506	RATES
σ^2	28.620	AND
GENERATION	26.521	RATIOS
POP. SEX RATIO	1.004	
SEX RATIO AT BIRTH	1.054	
DEP. RATIO x 100	58.337	

TABLE 1 — DATA

AGE AT LAST BIRTHDAY	ESTIMATED MID-YEAR POPULATION BOTH SEXES	MALES Number	MALES Percent	FEMALES Number	FEMALES Percent	BIRTHS BY AGE OF MOTHER AND SEX	DEATHS BOTH SEXES	DEATHS MALES	DEATHS FEMALES	AGE AT LAST BIRTHDAY
0	51360	26390	1.6	24970	1.5		560	321	239	0
1-4	201440	103550	6.4	97890	5.9		113	56	57	1-4
5-9	256050	130860	8.0	125190	7.6		85	46	39	5-9
10-14	298950	151900	9.3	147050	8.9	38	95	55	40	10-14
15-19	304040	155940	9.6	148100	9.0	4497	307	230	77	15-19
20-24	293000	149510	9.2	143490	8.7	14934	326	237	89	20-24
25-29	266410	133320	8.2	133090	8.1	19316	289	201	88	25-29
30-34	248100	122140	7.5	125960	7.6	9964	241	151	90	30-34
35-39	238070	119140	7.3	118930	7.2	2666	302	164	138	35-39
40-44	190470	95930	5.9	94540	5.7	361	409	251	158	40-44
45-49	161910	81760	5.0	80150	4.9	22	607	357	250	45-49
50-54	145450	74360	4.6	71090	4.3		886	554	332	50-54
55-59	147520	74630	4.6	72890	4.4		1494	960	534	55-59
60-64	139700	67660	4.2	72040	4.4		2248	1414	834	60-64
65-69	112350	51150	3.1	61200	3.7		2812	1717	1095	65-69
70-74	95580	42340	2.6	53240	3.2		3799	2212	1587	70-74
75-79	66100	26960	1.7	39140	2.4		4252	2308	1944	75-79
80-84	38330	13450	0.8	24880	1.5	26557 M	3805	1799	2006	80-84
85+	23990	6450	0.4	17540	1.1	25241 F	4850	1495	3355	85+
TOTAL	3278820	1627440		1651380		51798	27480	14528	12952	TOTAL

TABLE 2 — MALE LIFE TABLE

x	nM_x	nq_x	l_x	nd_x	nL_x	nm_x	na_x	T_x	$\overset{\circ}{e}_x$	x
0	0.012164	0.012031	100000	1203	98906	0.012164	0.091	7099069	70.991	0
1	0.000541	0.002160	98797	213	394654	0.000541	1.500	7000163	70.854	1
5	0.000352	0.001756	98584	173	492485	0.000352	2.500	6605509	67.004	5
10	0.000362	0.001809	98410	178	491721	0.000362	3.142	6113025	62.118	10
15	0.001475	0.007349	98232	722	489480	0.001475	2.671	5621304	57.225	15
20	0.001585	0.007895	97510	770	485628	0.001585	2.501	5131824	52.628	20
25	0.001508	0.007503	96741	726	481851	0.001506	2.449	4646196	48.027	25
30	0.001236	0.006160	96015	591	478580	0.001236	2.476	4164345	43.372	30
35	0.001377	0.006881	95423	657	475610	0.001381	2.706	3685765	38.625	35
40	0.002616	0.013099	94767	1241	471016	0.002635	2.731	3210155	33.874	40
45	0.004366	0.021741	93525	2033	462984	0.004392	2.717	2739139	29.288	45
50	0.007450	0.036694	91492	3357	449790	0.007464	2.715	2276155	24.878	50
55	0.012863	0.062458	88135	5505	427931	0.012863	2.685	1826365	20.722	55
60	0.020899	0.099842	82630	8250	393792	0.020950	2.654	1398433	16.924	60
65	0.033568	0.155761	74380	11586	344254	0.033654	2.614	1004641	13.507	65
70	0.052244	0.232095	62795	14574	278687	0.052296	2.579	660387	10.517	70
75	0.085608	0.354746	48220	17106	198524	0.086165	2.511	381700	7.916	75
80	0.133755	0.497406	31114	15476	115708	0.133755	2.424	183175	5.887	80
85	0.231783	1.000000	15638	15638	67468	0.170106	4.314	67468	4.314	85

TABLE 3 — FEMALE LIFE TABLE

x	nM_x	nq_x	l_x	nd_x	nL_x	nm_x	na_x	T_x	$\overset{\circ}{e}_x$	x
0	0.009571	0.009489	100000	949	99133	0.009572	0.086	7685065	76.851	0
1	0.000582	0.002326	99051	230	395629	0.000582	1.500	7585932	76.586	1
5	0.000312	0.001556	98821	154	493719	0.000312	2.500	7190303	72.761	5
10	0.000272	0.001359	98667	134	493021	0.000272	2.658	6696584	67.871	10
15	0.000520	0.002596	98533	256	492060	0.000520	2.639	6203563	62.959	15
20	0.000620	0.003098	98277	304	490638	0.000620	2.546	5711503	58.116	20
25	0.000661	0.003302	97973	323	489064	0.000661	2.528	5220865	53.289	25
30	0.000715	0.003570	97649	349	487424	0.000715	2.644	4731801	48.457	30
35	0.001160	0.005805	97300	565	485187	0.001164	2.671	4244377	43.621	35
40	0.001671	0.008385	96736	811	481844	0.001683	2.739	3759190	38.860	40
45	0.003119	0.015579	95925	1494	476173	0.003138	2.692	3277346	34.166	45
50	0.004670	0.023151	94430	2186	467066	0.004681	2.674	2801173	29.664	50
55	0.007326	0.036018	92244	3322	453503	0.007326	2.677	2334107	25.304	55
60	0.011577	0.056392	88922	5014	432883	0.011584	2.662	1880604	21.149	60
65	0.017892	0.086021	83907	7218	402675	0.017925	2.664	1447721	17.254	65
70	0.029808	0.139500	76689	10698	358263	0.029861	2.646	1045045	13.627	70
75	0.049668	0.222963	65991	14714	294548	0.049953	2.594	686782	10.407	75
80	0.080627	0.337465	51278	17304	214622	0.080627	2.586	392235	7.649	80
85	0.191277	1.000000	33973	33973	177612	0.123254	5.228	177612	5.228	85

TABLE 4 — OBSERVED VITAL RATES AND RATIOS

CRUDE RATES

Per Thousand	BOTH SEXES	MALES	FEMALES
BIRTH RATE	15.80	16.32	15.28
DEATH RATE	8.38	8.93	7.84
RATE OF INCREASE	7.42	7.39	7.44

RATES STANDARDIZED ON USA 1980

Per Thousand	BOTH SEXES	MALES	FEMALES
BIRTH RATE	16.50		15.64
DEATH RATE	9.30	9.82	8.81
RATE OF INCREASE	7.20		6.83

VITAL STATISTICS

GFR x 1000	61.353
TFR	1.927
GRR	0.939
NRR	0.919
μ	27.103
σ^2	28.048
GENERATION	27.147
POP. SEX RATIO	1.015
SEX RATIO AT BIRTH	1.052
DEP. RATIO x 100	53.598

PERCENT OF POPULATION IN AGE GROUP

	BOTH SEXES	MALES	FEMALES
UNDER 15	24.64	25.36	23.93
15 - 64	65.10	66.02	64.21
65 AND OLDER	10.26	8.62	11.87

RATES STANDARDIZED ON MEXICO 1980

	BOTH SEXES	MALES	FEMALES
BIRTH RATE	14.63		14.36
DEATH RATE	3.59	4.24	2.94
RATE OF INCREASE	11.03		11.43

PROJECTED POPULATION

AGE GROUP	1990 BOTH SEXES	1990 MALES	1990 FEMALES	1995 BOTH SEXES	1995 MALES	1995 FEMALES
0-4	262	134	128	271	139	132
5-9	253	130	123	262	134	128
10-14	256	131	125	251	129	122
15-19	298	151	147	255	130	125
20-24	303	155	148	296	150	146
25-29	291	148	143	301	154	147
30-34	265	132	133	290	147	143
35-39	246	121	125	264	132	132
40-44	236	118	118	245	120	125
45-49	187	94	93	233	116	117
50-54	158	79	79	184	92	92
55-59	140	71	69	152	76	76
60-64	139	69	70	131	65	66
65-69	126	59	67	125	60	65
70-74	95	41	54	108	48	60
75-79	74	30	44	74	29	45
80-84	45	16	29	50	18	32
85+	29	8	21	33	9	24
TOTAL	3403	1687	1716	3525	1748	1777

STABLE EQUIVALENT TO ORIGINAL POPULATION

MALES Number	MALES Percent	FEMALES Number	FEMALES Percent	AGE GROUP	
138	6.2	132	5.7	0-4	
140	6.3	134	5.8	5-9	TABLE 5
142	6.4	135	5.9	10-14	
144	6.5	137	5.9	15-19	POPULATION
145	6.5	139	6.0	20-24	PROJECTED
146	6.6	141	6.1	25-29	WITH
147	6.6	143	6.2	30-34	FIXED
149	6.7	144	6.2	35-39	AGE-
150	6.7	145	6.3	40-44	SPECIFIC
149	6.7	146	6.3	45-49	BIRTH
147	6.6	145	6.3	50-54	AND
142	6.4	143	6.2	55-59	DEATH
133	6.0	139	6.0	60-64	RATES
118	5.3	131	5.7	65-69	(female
97	4.4	119	5.1	70-74	dominant,
70	3.2	99	4.3	75-79	in 000s)
42	1.9	73	3.2	80-84	
25	1.1	62	2.7	85+	
2224		2307		TOTAL	

VITAL RATES OF PROJECTED POPULATION

Per Thousand	1990 BOTH SEXES	1990 MALES	1990 FEMALES	1995 BOTH SEXES	1995 MALES	1995 FEMALES
BIRTH RATE	15.99	16.52	15.46	15.66	16.18	15.14
DEATH RATE	8.85	9.37	8.33	9.18	9.66	8.71
RATE OF INCREASE	7.14	7.15	7.13	6.48	6.53	6.43

VITAL RATES OF STABLE POPULATION

Per Thousand	MALES	FEMALES	
BIRTH RATE	12.50	11.45	TABLE 6
DEATH RATE	15.58	14.57	PROJECTED
RATE OF INCREASE		-3.12	VITAL RATES

AGE STRUCTURE OF PROJECTED POPULATION

	1990 BOTH SEXES	1990 MALES	1990 FEMALES	1995 BOTH SEXES	1995 MALES	1995 FEMALES
% UNDER 15	22.64	23.38	21.91	22.27	23.02	21.54
% 15-64	66.53	67.48	65.58	66.69	67.59	65.81
% 65 AND OLDER	10.83	9.14	12.50	11.04	9.40	12.65
DEPEND. RATIO x 100	50.32	48.19	52.48	49.94	47.95	51.96

STABLE AGE STRUCTURE

	MALES	FEMALES	
% UNDER 15	18.91	17.36	AND RATIOS
% 15-64	65.27	61.65	(female
% 65 AND OLDER	15.82	20.98	dominant)
DEPEND. RATIO x 100	53.20	62.19	

AGE GROUP	FEMALE BIRTH RATES	NET MATERNITY FUNCTION	COEFF. OF MATRIX EQUATION	ORIGINAL MATRIX SUB-DIAGONAL	ORIGINAL MATRIX FIRST ROW	STABLE MATRIX FISHER VALUES	STABLE MATRIX REPRODUCTIVE VALUES	MATRIX PARAMETERS		
0-4	0.0000	0.0000	0.0000	0.99789	0.00000	1.003	123194	λ_1	0.98450	
5-9	0.0000	0.0000	0.0003	0.99859	0.00031	0.989	123845	λ_2	0.36454+0.75344i	TABLE 7
10-14	0.0001	0.0006	0.0367	0.99805	0.03684	0.975	143372	λ_4	-0.28184+0.49618i	
15-19	0.0148	0.0728	0.1608	0.99711	0.16170	0.925	136953	λ_6	-0.37950+0.07177i	LESLIE
20-24	0.0507	0.2488	0.2974	0.99679	0.29986	0.750	107678	r_1	-0.00312	MATRIX
25-29	0.0707	0.3459	0.2669	0.99665	0.27000	0.440	58496	r_2	-0.03559+0.22403i	AND ITS
30-34	0.0385	0.1879	0.1204	0.99541	0.12226	0.163	20471	r_4	-0.11220+0.41748i	ANALYSIS
35-39	0.0109	0.0530	0.0310	0.99311	0.03159	0.038	4470	r_6	-0.19026+0.59094i	(females)
40-44	0.0019	0.0090	0.0048	0.98823	0.00493	0.005	507	c_1	23084	
45-49	0.0001	0.0006	0.0003	0.98087	0.00033	0.000	27	$2\pi/y$	28.0459	
50-54	0.0000	0.0000	0.0000	0.00000	0.00000	0.000	0	Δ	16.6136	

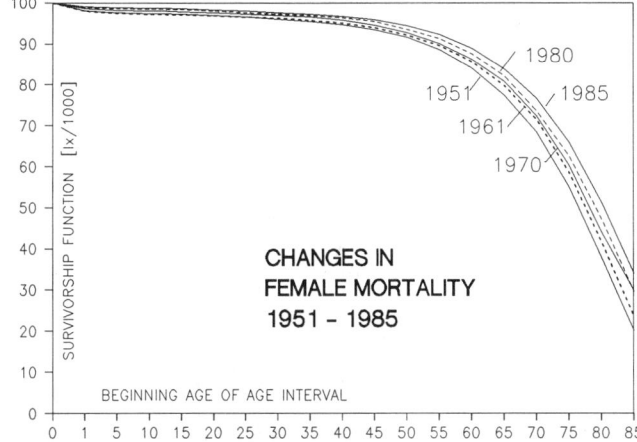

CHANGES IN FEMALE MORTALITY 1951 - 1985

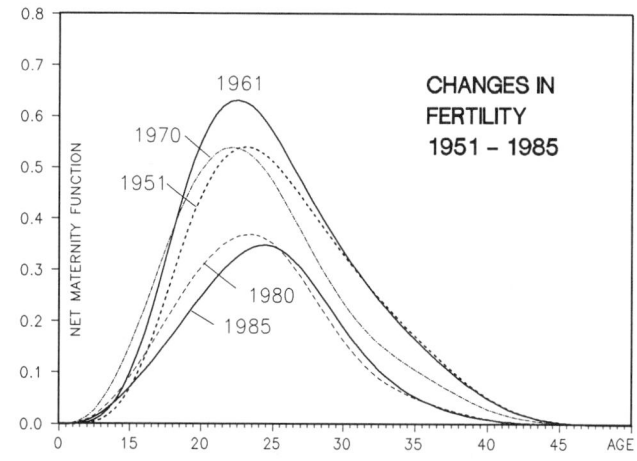

CHANGES IN FERTILITY 1951 - 1985

AGE AT LAST BIRTHDAY	ESTIMATED MID-YEAR POPULATION						BIRTHS BY AGE OF MOTHER AND SEX	DEATHS			AGE AT LAST BIRTHDAY
	BOTH SEXES	MALES		FEMALES				BOTH SEXES	MALES	FEMALES	
		Number	Percent	Number	Percent						
0	4683198	2370435	1.9	2312763	1.6			121821	65898	55923	0
1-4	17963575	9113628	7.5	8849947	6.3			61907	37458	24449	1-4
5-9	21349470	10828948	8.9	10520522	7.5			13924	8664	5260	5-9
10-14	20952859	10626782	8.7	10326077	7.4			11569	7438	4131	10-14
15-19	24743339	12704902	10.4	12038437	8.6	483777		26281	19058	7223	15-19
20-24	23884641	12045888	9.9	11838753	8.4	2085223		41996	32524	9472	20-24
25-29	21287022	10675474	8.8	10611548	7.6	1326487		50111	39499	10612	25-29
30-34	14519256	7226202	5.9	7293054	5.2	506681		43083	33602	9481	30-34
35-39	15756156	7649391	6.3	8106765	5.8	249192		68253	51634	16619	35-39
40-44	19086588	9236007	7.6	9850581	7.0	103393		105565	78968	26597	40-44
45-49	16542401	7871920	6.5	8670481	6.2	13001		130920	94070	36850	45-49
50-54	17095795	7360873	6.0	9734922	6.9			177893	118510	59383	50-54
55-59	10432784	3695284	3.0	6737500	4.8			142520	82220	60300	55-59
60-64	8812122	3005131	2.5	5806991	4.1			178824	97817	81007	60-64
65-69	9735791	3173384	2.6	6562407	4.7			286465	144389	142076	65-69
70-74	6231338	1941334	1.6	4290004	3.1			324358	142834	181524	70-74
75-79	5119818	1371876	1.1	3747942	2.7			322618	116430	206188	75-79
80-84	2605237	679467	0.6	1925770	1.4	2442674	N	258191	79733	178458	80-84
85+	1283264	291201	0.2	992063	0.7	2325080	F	266514	72898	193616	85+
TOTAL	262084654	121868127		140216527		4767754		2632813	1323644	1309169	TOTAL

TABLE 1 — DATA

x	$_nM_x$	$_nq_x$	l_x	$_nd_x$	$_nL_x$	$_nm_x$	$_na_x$	T_x	$\overset{\circ}{e}_x$	x
0	0.027800	0.027134	100000	2713	97605	0.027800	0.117	6233189	62.332	0
1	0.004110	0.016273	97287	1583	385188	0.004110	1.500	6135584	63.067	1
5	0.000800	0.003992	95703	382	477562	0.000800	2.500	5750396	60.086	5
10	0.000700	0.003494	95321	333	475842	0.000700	2.705	5272834	55.316	10
15	0.001500	0.007475	94988	710	473361	0.001500	2.774	4796991	50.501	15
20	0.002700	0.013427	94278	1266	468435	0.002702	2.665	4323631	45.860	20
25	0.003700	0.018414	93012	1713	460956	0.003716	2.603	3855195	41.448	25
30	0.004650	0.023097	91300	2109	451486	0.004671	2.623	3394240	37.177	30
35	0.006750	0.033214	89191	2962	438861	0.006750	2.606	2942754	32.994	35
40	0.008550	0.041893	86228	3612	422494	0.008550	2.606	2503892	29.038	40
45	0.011950	0.058096	82616	4800	401592	0.011952	2.606	2081398	25.194	45
50	0.016100	0.077881	77816	6060	374519	0.016182	2.597	1679807	21.587	50
55	0.022250	0.106172	71756	7618	340487	0.022375	2.599	1305288	18.191	55
60	0.032550	0.150849	64138	9675	297238	0.032550	2.576	964801	15.043	60
65	0.045500	0.204858	54463	11157	245210	0.045500	2.571	667563	12.257	65
70	0.073575	0.311001	43305	13468	182696	0.073718	2.488	422353	9.753	70
75	0.084869	0.348035	29837	10384	122252	0.084943	2.406	239656	8.032	75
80	0.117346	0.452079	19453	8794	74827	0.117529	2.449	117404	6.035	80
85	0.250336	1.000000	10659	10659	42578	0.192878	3.995	42578	3.995	85

TABLE 2 — MALE LIFE TABLE

x	$_nM_x$	$_nq_x$	l_x	$_nd_x$	$_nL_x$	$_nm_x$	$_na_x$	T_x	$\overset{\circ}{e}_x$	x
0	0.024180	0.023671	100000	2367	97896	0.024180	0.111	7272233	72.722	0
1	0.002763	0.010975	97633	1071	387853	0.002763	1.500	7174337	73.483	1
5	0.000500	0.002497	96561	241	482204	0.000500	2.500	6786485	70.282	5
10	0.000400	0.001998	96320	192	481130	0.000400	2.551	6304281	65.451	10
15	0.000600	0.002996	96128	288	479959	0.000600	2.638	5823151	60.577	15
20	0.000800	0.003994	95840	383	478282	0.000800	2.603	5343192	55.751	20
25	0.001000	0.005003	95457	478	476141	0.001003	2.603	4864910	50.964	25
30	0.001300	0.006512	94979	619	473452	0.001306	2.663	4388770	46.208	30
35	0.002050	0.010201	94361	963	469531	0.002050	2.637	3915318	41.493	35
40	0.002700	0.013416	93398	1253	464063	0.002700	2.662	3445787	36.893	40
45	0.004250	0.021041	92145	1939	456185	0.004250	2.657	2981724	32.359	45
50	0.006100	0.030111	90207	2716	444643	0.006109	2.647	2525539	27.997	50
55	0.008950	0.044118	87490	3860	428413	0.009010	2.658	2080897	23.784	55
60	0.013950	0.067540	83630	5648	404904	0.013950	2.654	1652484	19.759	60
65	0.021650	0.103195	77982	8047	371419	0.021667	2.702	1247580	15.998	65
70	0.042313	0.192413	69935	13456	317214	0.042421	2.588	876161	12.528	70
75	0.055014	0.242889	56478	13718	248665	0.055166	2.541	558947	9.897	75
80	0.092668	0.378459	42760	16183	174103	0.092951	2.547	310282	7.256	80
85	0.195165	1.000000	26577	26577	136179	0.127481	5.124	136179	5.124	85

TABLE 3 — FEMALE LIFE TABLE

TABLE 4 — OBSERVED VITAL RATES AND RATIOS

CRUDE RATES

Per Thousand	BOTH SEXES	MALES	FEMALES
BIRTH RATE	18.19	20.04	16.58
DEATH RATE	10.05	10.86	9.34
RATE OF INCREASE	8.15	9.18	7.25

PERCENT OF POPULATION IN AGE GROUP

	BOTH SEXES	MALES	FEMALES
UNDER 15	24.78	27.03	22.83
15 - 64	65.69	66.85	64.68
65 AND OLDER	9.53	6.12	12.49

RATES STANDARDIZED ON USA 1980

Per Thousand	BOTH SEXES	MALES	FEMALES
BIRTH RATE	19.55		18.54
DEATH RATE	12.41	14.27	10.66
RATE OF INCREASE	7.14		7.88

RATES STANDARDIZED ON MEXICO 1980

	BOTH SEXES	MALES	FEMALES
BIRTH RATE	17.76		17.46
DEATH RATE	5.83	7.38	4.26
RATE OF INCREASE	11.93		13.20

VITAL STATISTICS

GFR x 1000	69.694
TFR	2.268
GRR	1.106
NRR	1.053
μ	26.488
σ^2	34.496
GENERATION	26.454
POP. SEX RATIO	1.151
SEX RATIO AT BIRTH	1.051
DEP. RATIO x 100	52.233

PROJECTED POPULATION

AGE GROUP	1984 BOTH SEXES	MALES	FEMALES	1989 BOTH SEXES	MALES	FEMALES
0-4	23780	12147	11633	24209	12366	11843
5-9	22441	11360	11081	23564	12016	11548
10-14	21287	10790	10497	22376	11319	11057
15-19	20872	10571	10301	21206	10734	10472
20-24	24569	12573	11996	20726	10461	10265
25-29	23640	11854	11786	24315	12372	11943
30-34	21008	10456	10552	23329	11610	11719
35-39	14257	7024	7233	20628	10164	10464
40-44	15376	7364	8012	13910	6762	7148
45-49	18462	8779	9683	14876	7000	7876
50-54	15792	7341	8451	17625	8187	9438
55-59	16072	6692	9380	14817	6674	8143
60-64	9594	3226	6368	14707	5842	8865
65-69	7806	2479	5327	8502	2661	5841
70-74	7969	2364	5605	6396	1847	4549
75-79	4662	1299	3363	5976	1582	4394
80-84	3464	840	2624	3150	795	2355
85+	1893	387	1506	2531	478	2053
TOTAL	272944	127546	145398	282843	132870	149973

STABLE EQUIVALENT TO ORIGINAL POPULATION

MALES Number	Percent	FEMALES Number	Percent	AGE GROUP	
11794	8.2	11295	7.2	0-4	
11553	8.1	11103	7.0	5-9	TABLE 5
11399	8.0	10971	7.0	10-14	
11229	7.8	10838	6.9	15-19	POPULATION
11005	7.7	10695	6.8	20-24	PROJECTED
10724	7.5	10544	6.7	25-29	WITH
10401	7.3	10382	6.6	30-34	FIXED
10012	7.0	10196	6.5	35-39	AGE-
9545	6.7	9979	6.3	40-44	SPECIFIC
8985	6.3	9715	6.2	45-49	BIRTH
8298	5.8	9377	6.0	50-54	AND
7470	5.2	8947	5.7	55-59	DEATH
6458	4.5	8374	5.3	60-64	RATES
5276	3.7	7607	4.8	65-69	(female
3893	2.7	6433	4.1	70-74	dominant,
2579	1.8	4994	3.2	75-79	in 000s)
1563	1.1	3463	2.2	80-84	
881	0.6	2682	1.7	85+	
143065		157595		TOTAL	

VITAL RATES OF PROJECTED POPULATION

Per Thousand	1984 BOTH SEXES	MALES	FEMALES	1989 BOTH SEXES	MALES	FEMALES
BIRTH RATE	18.52	20.30	16.95	17.48	19.07	16.08
DEATH RATE	10.84	11.35	10.39	11.32	11.72	10.97
RATE OF INCREASE	7.68	8.95	6.56	6.16	7.34	5.11

VITAL RATES OF STABLE POPULATION

Per Thousand	MALES	FEMALES	
BIRTH RATE	17.16	14.83	TABLE 6
DEATH RATE	15.20	12.87	PROJECTED
RATE OF INCREASE		1.95	VITAL RATES AND RATIOS (female dominant)

AGE STRUCTURE OF PROJECTED POPULATION

	1984			1989		
% UNDER 15	24.73	26.89	22.84	24.80	26.87	22.97
% 15-64	65.82	67.33	64.49	65.81	67.59	64.23
% 65 AND OLDER	9.45	5.78	12.67	9.39	5.54	12.80
DEPEND. RATIO x 100	51.94	48.52	55.07	51.95	47.95	55.68

STABLE AGE STRUCTURE

	MALES	FEMALES
% UNDER 15	24.29	21.17
% 15-64	65.79	62.85
% 65 AND OLDER	9.92	15.98
DEPEND. RATIO x 100	51.99	59.11

AGE GROUP	FEMALE BIRTH RATES	NET MATERNITY FUNCTION	COEFF. OF MATRIX EQUATION	ORIGINAL MATRIX SUB-DIAGONAL	FIRST ROW	STABLE MATRIX FISHER VALUES	REPRODUCTIVE VALUES	MATRIX PARAMETERS	
0-4	0.0000	0.0000	0.0000	0.99270	0.00000	1.034	11546356	λ_1 1.00981	
5-9	0.0000	0.0000	0.0000	0.99777	0.00000	1.052	11069676	λ_2 0.29781+0.73786i	TABLE 7
10-14	0.0000	0.0000	0.0470	0.99757	0.04748	1.065	10996214	λ_4 -0.41733+0.24765i	
15-19	0.0196	0.0941	0.2524	0.99651	0.25549	1.029	12384428	λ_6 0.06532+0.45888i	LESLIE
20-24	0.0859	0.4108	0.3505	0.99552	0.35601	0.777	9202094	r_1 0.00195	MATRIX
25-29	0.0610	0.2903	0.2253	0.99435	0.22988	0.419	4441361	r_2 -0.04571+0.23744i	AND ITS
30-34	0.0339	0.1604	0.1154	0.99172	0.11839	0.186	1355908	r_4 -0.14461+0.52120i	ANALYSIS
35-39	0.0150	0.0704	0.0471	0.98836	0.04869	0.066	533634	r_6 -0.15379+0.28588i	(females)
40-44	0.0051	0.0238	0.0135	0.98302	0.01418	0.016	160498	c_1 1575939	
45-49	0.0007	0.0033	0.0017	0.97470	0.00178	0.002	15773	2π/y 26.4626	
50-54	0.0000	0.0000	0.0000	0.00000	0.00000	0.000	0	Δ 7.6022	

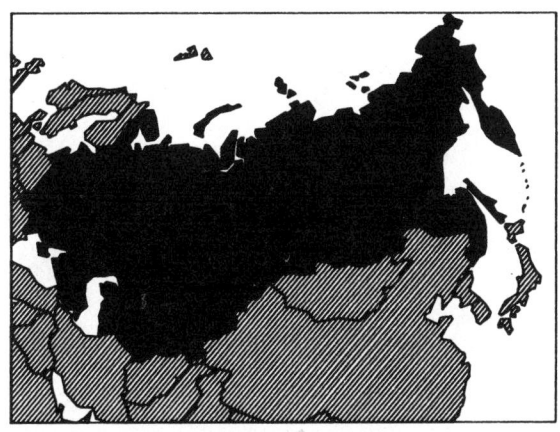

EDUCATION [1984]

% of primary school-age children enrolled:	106
secondary school-age children enrolled:	100
ca. 20-24 year olds in higher education:	21

LABOR FORCE

Average annual labor force growth (%) 1980-85:	0.9	
% of the 1980 labor force in agriculture:	20	TABLE 8
in industry:	39	
in services:	41	SOCIO-

GNP & INCOME DISTRIBUTION

GNP per capita (in US Dollars) 1979:	5210	ECONOMIC
GNP growth rate (%) 1979:	3.5	INDICATORS
% share of total household income		
Lowest 20% of households:	na	
Highest 10% of households:	na	

HEALTH & NUTRITION

Population per physician 1981:	270
Daily calorie supply per capita 1985:	3440

TABLE 1 DATA

AGE AT LAST BIRTHDAY	ESTIMATED MID-YEAR POPULATION BOTH SEXES	MALES Number	MALES Percent	FEMALES Number	FEMALES Percent	BIRTHS BY AGE OF MOTHER AND SEX	DEATHS BOTH SEXES	DEATHS MALES	DEATHS FEMALES	AGE AT LAST BIRTHDAY
0	5252983	2679933	2.0	2573050	1.7		126869	68821	58048	0
1-4	20889862	10660344	8.1	10229518	6.9		64404	39235	25169	1-4
5-9	23226189	11812417	8.9	11413772	7.6		12835	8269	4566	5-9
10-14	22262212	11275206	8.5	10987006	7.4		10061	6765	3296	10-14
15-19	20635971	10441517	7.9	10194454	6.8	452634	16583	11486	5097	15-19
20-24	22166892	11220015	8.5	10946877	7.3	2108369	27859	20196	7663	20-24
25-29	24676706	12554221	9.5	12122485	8.1	1768671	38573	28875	9698	25-29
30-34	22227719	11047694	8.4	11180025	7.5	885458	44323	33143	11180	30-34
35-39	19449811	9610903	7.3	9838908	6.6	332555	54163	39405	14758	35-39
40-44	11038637	5344836	4.0	5693801	3.8	49536	46234	33138	13096	40-44
45-49	19572889	9231397	7.0	10341492	6.9	5654	118132	84006	34126	45-49
50-54	15123737	7046118	5.3	8077619	5.4		137229	94418	42811	50-54
55-59	16567674	7402169	5.6	9165505	6.1		228171	150264	77907	55-59
60-64	12745156	4593216	3.5	8151940	5.5		242647	135041	107606	60-64
65-69	7366485	2352824	1.8	5013661	3.4		210940	101642	109298	65-69
70-74	6533197	1885954	1.4	4647243	3.1		344768	142688	202080	70-74
75-79	5845412	1581014	1.2	4264398	2.9		395355	141115	254240	75-79
80-84	3806753	912589	0.7	2894164	1.9	2870534 M	332122	96362	235760	80-84
85+	1949506	391110	0.3	1558396	1.0	2732343 F	318848	75434	243414	85+
TOTAL	281337791	132043477		149294314		5602877	2770116	1310303	1459813	TOTAL

TABLE 2 MALE LIFE TABLE

x	nM_x	nq_x	l_x	nd_x	nL_x	nm_x	na_x	T_x	$\overset{\circ}{e}_x$	x
0	0.025680	0.025109	100000	2511	97775	0.025680	0.114	6501822	65.018	0
1	0.003680	0.014588	97489	1422	386401	0.003680	1.500	6404048	65.690	1
5	0.000700	0.003494	96067	336	479496	0.000700	2.500	6017647	62.640	5
10	0.000600	0.003000	95731	287	477978	0.000601	2.637	5538151	57.851	10
15	0.001100	0.005489	95444	524	476029	0.001101	2.724	5060173	53.017	15
20	0.001800	0.008962	94920	851	472590	0.001801	2.635	4584144	48.295	20
25	0.002300	0.011437	94070	1076	467770	0.002300	2.604	4111554	43.708	25
30	0.003000	0.014919	92994	1387	461666	0.003005	2.619	3643784	39.183	30
35	0.004100	0.020420	91606	1871	453638	0.004124	2.651	3182118	34.737	35
40	0.006200	0.030592	89736	2745	442233	0.006208	2.652	2728480	30.406	40
45	0.009100	0.044545	86991	3875	425819	0.009100	2.643	2286246	26.282	45
50	0.013400	0.064996	83116	5402	402836	0.013410	2.641	1860428	22.384	50
55	0.020300	0.097015	77713	7539	370612	0.020343	2.618	1457592	18.756	55
60	0.029400	0.138093	70174	9691	327555	0.029585	2.594	1086980	15.490	60
65	0.043200	0.196993	60483	11915	273831	0.043512	2.601	759424	12.556	65
70	0.075658	0.318138	48569	15452	204228	0.075658	2.501	485593	9.998	70
75	0.089256	0.361792	33117	11982	134238	0.089256	2.384	281365	8.496	75
80	0.105592	0.414480	21136	8760	82964	0.105592	2.407	147127	6.961	80
85	0.192872	1.000000	12375	12375	64164	0.125857	5.185	64164	5.185	85

TABLE 3 FEMALE LIFE TABLE

x	nM_x	nq_x	l_x	nd_x	nL_x	nm_x	na_x	T_x	$\overset{\circ}{e}_x$	x
0	0.022560	0.022115	100000	2212	98028	0.022560	0.108	7396969	73.970	0
1	0.002460	0.009782	97788	957	388763	0.002460	1.500	7298941	74.640	1
5	0.000400	0.001998	96832	193	483676	0.000400	2.500	6910178	71.363	5
10	0.000300	0.001500	96638	145	482840	0.000300	2.568	6426502	66.500	10
15	0.000500	0.002498	96494	241	481905	0.000500	2.665	5943662	61.596	15
20	0.000700	0.003494	96252	336	480451	0.000700	2.588	5461757	56.744	20
25	0.000800	0.003992	95916	383	478653	0.000800	2.577	4981306	51.934	25
30	0.001000	0.004995	95533	477	476542	0.001001	2.645	4502653	47.132	30
35	0.001500	0.007520	95056	715	473618	0.001509	2.676	4026111	42.355	35
40	0.002300	0.011443	94341	1080	469176	0.002301	2.657	3552492	37.656	40
45	0.003300	0.016374	93262	1527	462766	0.003300	2.681	3083316	33.061	45
50	0.005300	0.026213	91735	2405	453118	0.005307	2.690	2620550	28.567	50
55	0.008500	0.041676	89330	3723	437991	0.008500	2.674	2167431	24.263	55
60	0.013200	0.064504	85607	5522	415202	0.013299	2.676	1729440	20.202	60
65	0.021800	0.104760	80085	8390	381241	0.022006	2.713	1314238	16.411	65
70	0.043484	0.196848	71695	14113	324559	0.043484	2.597	932997	13.013	70
75	0.059619	0.259490	57582	14942	250624	0.059619	2.505	608438	10.566	75
80	0.081460	0.338670	42640	14441	177275	0.081460	2.512	357814	8.391	80
85	0.156195	1.000000	28199	28199	180539	0.087464	6.402	180539	6.402	85

TABLE 4 OBSERVED VITAL RATES AND RATIOS

CRUDE RATES

Per Thousand	BOTH SEXES	MALES	FEMALES
BIRTH RATE	19.92	21.74	18.30
DEATH RATE	9.85	9.92	9.78
RATE OF INCREASE	10.07	11.82	8.52

PERCENT OF POPULATION IN AGE GROUP

	BOTH SEXES	MALES	FEMALES
UNDER 15	25.46	27.59	23.58
15 - 64	65.47	67.02	64.11
65 AND OLDER	9.06	5.39	12.31

RATES STANDARDIZED ON USA 1980

Per Thousand	BOTH SEXES	MALES	FEMALES
BIRTH RATE	21.83		20.70
DEATH RATE	11.16	12.60	9.80
RATE OF INCREASE	10.67		10.90

RATES STANDARDIZED ON MEXICO 1980

	BOTH SEXES	MALES	FEMALES
BIRTH RATE	19.80		19.47
DEATH RATE	5.12	6.32	3.89
RATE OF INCREASE	14.69		15.57

VITAL STATISTICS

GFR x 1000	79.679
TFR	2.526
GRR	1.232
NRR	1.179
μ	26.419
σ^2	31.979
GENERATION	26.318
POP. SEX RATIO	1.131
SEX RATIO AT BIRTH	1.051
DEP. RATIO x 100	52.731

PROJECTED POPULATION

AGE GROUP	1992 BOTH SEXES	1992 MALES	1992 FEMALES	1997 BOTH SEXES	1997 MALES	1997 FEMALES
0-4	26840	13715	13125	26480	13531	12949
5-9	25932	13211	12721	26623	13582	13041
10-14	23169	11775	11394	25869	13170	12699
15-19	22195	11229	10966	23099	11727	11372
20-24	20530	10366	10164	22081	11148	10933
25-29	22012	11106	10906	20386	10260	10126
30-34	24459	12390	12069	21819	10961	10858
35-39	21967	10856	11111	24170	12175	11995
40-44	19116	9369	9747	21590	10583	11007
45-49	10762	5146	5616	18635	9022	9613
50-54	18859	8733	10126	10368	4869	5499
55-59	14290	6482	7808	17823	8035	9788
60-64	15231	6542	8689	13131	5729	7402
65-69	11325	3840	7485	13447	5469	7978
70-74	6023	1755	4268	9236	2864	6372
75-79	4829	1240	3589	4449	1153	3296
80-84	3993	977	3016	3304	766	2538
85+	3653	706	2947	3828	756	3072
TOTAL	295185	139438	155747	306338	145800	160538

STABLE EQUIVALENT TO ORIGINAL POPULATION

MALES Number	MALES Percent	FEMALES Number	FEMALES Percent	AGE GROUP	
12811	9.1	12260	8.2	0-4	
12295	8.7	11805	7.9	5-9	TABLE 5
11878	8.4	11421	7.6	10-14	
11464	8.1	11047	7.4	15-19	POPULATION
11029	7.8	10673	7.1	20-24	PROJECTED
10580	7.5	10305	6.9	25-29	WITH
10119	7.2	9942	6.7	30-34	FIXED
9636	6.8	9576	6.4	35-39	AGE-
9104	6.5	9193	6.2	40-44	SPECIFIC
8495	6.0	8788	5.9	45-49	BIRTH
7788	5.5	8339	5.6	50-54	AND
6944	4.9	7811	5.2	55-59	DEATH
5948	4.2	7176	4.8	60-64	RATES
4818	3.4	6386	4.3	65-69	(female
3483	2.5	5268	3.5	70-74	dominant,
2218	1.6	3943	2.6	75-79	in 000s)
1329	0.9	2703	1.8	80-84	
996	0.7	2667	1.8	85+	
140935		149303		TOTAL	

VITAL RATES OF PROJECTED POPULATION

Per Thousand	1992 BOTH SEXES	1992 MALES	1992 FEMALES	1997 BOTH SEXES	1997 MALES	1997 FEMALES
BIRTH RATE	18.48	20.04	17.08	17.80	19.17	16.57
DEATH RATE	10.67	10.47	10.84	10.90	10.93	10.87
RATE OF INCREASE	7.81	9.57	6.24	6.91	8.24	5.70

VITAL RATES OF STABLE POPULATION

Per Thousand	MALES	FEMALES	
BIRTH RATE	19.07	17.13	TABLE 6
DEATH RATE	12.79	10.86	PROJECTED
RATE OF INCREASE		6.28	VITAL RATES

AGE STRUCTURE OF PROJECTED POPULATION

	BOTH SEXES	MALES	FEMALES	BOTH SEXES	MALES	FEMALES
% UNDER 15	25.73	27.75	23.91	25.78	27.63	24.10
% 15-64	64.17	66.14	62.41	63.04	64.82	61.41
% 65 AND OLDER	10.10	6.11	13.68	11.19	7.55	14.49
DEPEND. RATIO x 100	55.84	51.20	60.23	58.64	54.27	62.83

STABLE AGE STRUCTURE

	MALES	FEMALES	
% UNDER 15	26.24	23.77	AND RATIOS
% 15-64	64.64	62.19	(female
% 65 AND OLDER	9.11	14.04	dominant)
DEPEND. RATIO x 100	54.69	60.80	

AGE GROUP	FEMALE BIRTH RATES	NET MATERNITY FUNCTION	COEFF. OF MATRIX EQUATION	ORIGINAL MATRIX SUB-DIAGONAL	ORIGINAL MATRIX FIRST ROW	STABLE MATRIX FISHER VALUES	STABLE MATRIX REPRODUCTIVE VALUES
0-4	0.0000	0.0000	0.0000	0.99360	0.00000	1.043	13357344
5-9	0.0000	0.0000	0.0000	0.99827	0.00000	1.084	12367062
10-14	0.0000	0.0000	0.0522	0.99806	0.05260	1.120	12305374
15-19	0.0217	0.1043	0.2778	0.99698	0.28062	1.103	11243964
20-24	0.0939	0.4513	0.3959	0.99626	0.40114	0.848	9281660
25-29	0.0712	0.3406	0.2623	0.99559	0.26677	0.458	5553324
30-34	0.0386	0.1841	0.1311	0.99386	0.13388	0.195	2182710
35-39	0.0165	0.0781	0.0490	0.99062	0.05035	0.062	611541
40-44	0.0042	0.0199	0.0106	0.98634	0.01097	0.012	66706
45-49	0.0003	0.0012	0.0006	0.97915	0.00065	0.001	6786
50-54	0.0000	0.0000	0.0000	0.00000	0.00000	0.000	0

MATRIX PARAMETERS

λ_1	1.03187	
λ_2	$0.30976+0.76534i$	TABLE 7
λ_4	$-0.40695+0.33632i$	
λ_6	$0.00296+0.46518i$	LESLIE
r_1	0.00628	MATRIX
r_2	$-0.03832+0.23724i$	AND ITS
r_4	$-0.12776+0.49019i$	ANALYSIS
r_6	$-0.15306+0.31289i$	(females)
c_1	1493020	
$2\pi/y$	26.4842	
Δ	5.7178	

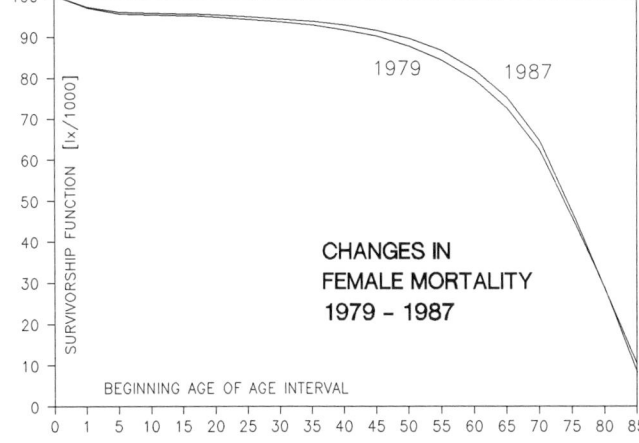

CHANGES IN FEMALE MORTALITY 1979 - 1987

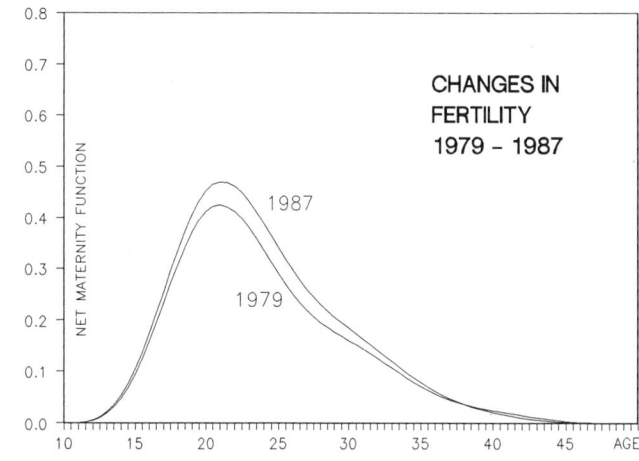

CHANGES IN FERTILITY 1979 - 1987

Appendixes

APPENDIX A:
Country/Territory Groupings Defined

The country/territory groupings listed below, with the exception of the European Community, are identical with those for which the United Nations Population Division provided extensive data and estimates in the course of the eleventh round of its Global Demographic Assessments. The tables for the European Community included in the UN-based tabulations were prepared from UN-assembled data for the individual EC member countries.

For countries or territories with populations of generally less than 300,000 in 1985, for which the United Nations did not prepare specific tabulations, total populations figures for the year 1985 as estimated by the United Nations Population Division during the tenth round of its Global Demographic Assessments can be found in Appendix B of this volume. These countries/territories are included in the UN tabulations for the regions in which they are located.

In the UN-based tabulations, the population of the Republic of China (Taiwan) is included in the population of the People's Republic of China.

In the following listing, names of continents, regions, countries, and territories with separate UN-based tabulations in the tabular section of this volume are printed in **bold** letters.

TOTAL WORLD POPULATION
is divided into: national populations in the **More Developed Regions** and the **Less Developed Regions** of the world.

MORE DEVELOPED REGIONS
include: **Northern America, Japan,** all of **Europe, Australia, New Zealand,** and the **Union of Soviet Socialist Republics.**

LESS DEVELOPED REGIONS
include: **Africa, Latin America, Asia** with the exceptions of Japan and the Asian parts of the USSR. **Melanesia, Micronesia,** and **Polynesia.**

AFRICA
Regions: **Central Africa, Eastern Africa, Northern Africa, Southern Africa,** and **Western Africa.**

CENTRAL AFRICA
includes: **Angola, Cameroon, Central African Republic, Chad, Congo, Equatorial Guinea, Gabon,** São Tomé and Principe, and **Zaire.**

EASTERN AFRICA
includes: the British Indian Ocean Territories, **Burundi, Comoros, Djibouti, Ethiopia, Kenya, Madagascar, Malawi, Mauritius** with Agalesa, Rodrigues, and St. Brandon, **Mozambique, Réunion, Rwanda,** Seychelles, **Somalia, Tanzania, Uganda, Zambia,** and **Zimbabwe.**

NORTHERN AFRICA
includes: **Algeria, Egypt, Libya, Morocco, Sudan, Tunisia,** and the Western Sahara.

SOUTHERN AFRICA
includes: **Botswana, Lesotho, Namibia, Republic of South Africa,** and **Swaziland.**

WESTERN AFRICA
includes: **Benin, Burkina Faso, Cape Verde, Gambia, Ghana, Guinea, Guinea-Bissau, Ivory Coast, Liberia, Mali, Mauritania, Niger, Nigeria,** St. Helena with Ascension and Tristan da Cunha, **Senegal, Sierra Leone,** and **Togo.**

THE AMERICAS
Subcontinents: **Latin America, Northern America.**

LATIN AMERICA
Regions: **Caribbean, Central America,** and **South America.**

CARIBBEAN
includes: Anguilla, Antigua and Barbuda, the Bahamas, **Barbados,** the British Virgin Islands, Cayman Islands, **Cuba,** Dominica, **Dominican Republic,**

Grenada, **Guadeloupe, Haiti, Jamaica, Martinique,** Montserrat, the Netherlands Antilles, **Puerto Rico,** St. Christopher and Nevis, St. Lucia, St. Vincent and the Grenadines, **Trinidad and Tobago,** Turks and Caicos Islands, and the U.S. Virgin Islands.

CENTRAL AMERICA

includes: Belize, **Costa Rica, El Salvador, Guatemala, Honduras, Mexico, Nicaragua,** and **Panama.**

SOUTH AMERICA

includes: **Argentina, Bolivia, Brazil, Chile, Colombia, Ecuador,** Falkland Islands, French Guiana, **Guyana, Paraguay, Peru, Suriname, Uruguay,** and **Venezuela.**

NORTHERN AMERICA

includes: The Bermudas, **Canada,** Greenland, St. Pierre and Miquelon, and the **United States of America.**

ASIA

Regions: **Eastern Asia, Southeastern Asia, Southern Asia,** and **Western Asia.** Excluded are the Asian parts of the USSR.

EASTERN ASIA

includes: the **People's Republic of China,** the Republic of China (Taiwan), **Hong Kong, Japan, Democratic People's Republic of Korea** (North Korea), **Republic of Korea** (South Korea), Macao, and **Mongolia.**

SOUTHEASTERN ASIA

includes: Brunei, **Burma, Kampuchea, East Timor, Indonesia, Laos, Malaysia, Philippines, Singapore, Thailand,** and **Vietnam.**

SOUTHERN ASIA

includes: **Afghanistan, Bangladesh, Bhutan, India, Iran,** the Maldives, **Nepal, Pakistan,** and **Sri Lanka.**

WESTERN ASIA

includes: **Bahrain, Cyprus,** Gaza Strip, **Iraq, Israel, Jordan, Kuwait, Lebanon, Oman, Qatar, Saudi Arabia, Syria, Turkey,** the **United Arab Emirates, Yemen,** and **Democratic Yemen** (South Yemen).

EUROPE

Regions: **Eastern Europe** (excl. the European parts of the USSR), **Northern Europe, Southern Europe,** and **Western Europe.**

EASTERN EUROPE (COMECON)

includes: **Bulgaria, Czechoslovakia, German Democratic Republic** (East Germany), **Hungary, Poland,** and **Romania.**

NORTHERN EUROPE

includes: Channel Islands, **Denmark,** the Faeroe Islands, **Finland, Iceland, Ireland,** Isle of Man, **Norway, Sweden,** and the **United Kingdom of Great Britain and Northern Ireland.**

SOUTHERN EUROPE

includes: **Albania,** Andorra, Gibraltar, **Greece, Italy, Malta, Portugal,** San Marino, **Spain,** the Vatican State, and **Yugoslavia.**

WESTERN EUROPE

includes: **Austria, Belgium, France,** the **Federal Republic of Germany** (West Germany), Liechtenstein, **Luxembourg,** Monaco, the **Netherlands,** and **Switzerland.**

EUROPEAN COMMUNITY

includes: **Belgium, Denmark, France,** the **Federal Republic of Germany, Greece, Ireland, Italy, Luxembourg,** the **Netherlands, Portugal, Spain,** and the **United Kingdom of Great Britain and Northern Ireland.**

OCEANIA

Regions: **Australia–New Zealand, Melanesia, Micronesia,** and **Polynesia.**

AUSTRALIA–NEW ZEALAND

includes: **Australia** with the Cocos (Keeling) Islands, Christmas Island and Norfolk Island, and **New Zealand.**

MELANESIA

includes: Fiji, New Caledonia, **Papua New Guinea,** Solomon Islands, and Vanuatu.

MICRONESIA

includes: Guam, Kiribati with Canton and Enderbury Islands, Johnston Island, Midway Islands, Nauru, the Pacific Islands comprising the Federated States of Micronesia, Marshall Islands, Northern Mariana and Palau, and Wake Islands.

POLYNESIA

includes: American Samoa, Cook Islands, French Polynesia, Niue, Pitcairn, Samoa, Tokelau, Tonga, Tuvalu, and Wallis and Futuna Islands.

UNION OF SOVIET SOCIALIST REPUBLICS

includes: all Republics of the USSR in Asia and Europe: Armenian SSR, Azerbaijan SSR, Estonia SSR, Georgian SSR, Kazakh SSR, Kirgiz SSR, Latvian SSR, Lithuanian SSR, Moldavian SSR, Russian SFSR, Ukrainian SSR, Uzbek SSR, Tadzhik SSR, Turkmen SSR, and White Russian SSR.

APPENDIX B:

Land Areas and Estimated 1985 Populations of Countries and Territories Not Separately Listed Among UN-Based Tabulations

CONTINENT/REGION	COUNTRY/TERRITORY	AREA (km²)	1985 POPULATION
AFRICA			
CENTRAL AFRICA	São Tomé and Principe	963	97,000
EASTERN AFRICA	British Indian Ocean Territories	75	2,000
	Seychelles	375	76,000
NORTHERN AFRICA	Western Sahara	266,000	155,000
WESTERN AFRICA	St. Helena with Ascension and Tristan da Cunha	420	6,000
THE AMERICAS			
CARIBBEAN	Anguilla	91	7,000
	Antigua and Barbuda	443	80,000
	Bahamas	13,939	230,000
	British Virgin Islands	153	13,000
	Cayman Islands	259	20,000
	Dominica	751	76,000
	Grenada	344	112,000
	Montserrat	104	12,000
	Netherlands Antilles	1,010	264,000
	St. Christopher and Nevis[1]	269	46,000
	St. Lucia[2]	616	130,000
	St. Vincent–The Grenadines	388	104,000
	Turks and Caicos Islands	430	8,000
	U.S. Virgin Islands	342	105,000
CENTRAL AMERICA	Belize	22,966	163,000
SOUTH AMERICA	Falkland Islands & Dependencies	16,053	2,000
	French Guiana	91,000	82,000
NORTHERN AMERICA	Bermuda	54	79,000
	Greenland[1]	2,175,600	54,000
	St. Pierre and Miquelon	242	6,000
ASIA			
EASTERN ASIA	Republic of China (Taiwan)[1]	36,185	19,135,000[3]
	Macao	16	394,000
SOUTHEASTERN ASIA	Brunei	5,765	232,000

CONTINENT/REGION	COUNTRY/TERRITORY	AREA (km²)	1985 POPULATION
SOUTHERN ASIA	Maldives	298	183,000
WESTERN ASIA	Gaza Strip (Palestine)	*na*	490,000
EUROPE			
NORTHERN EUROPE	Channel Islands	194	138,000
	Faeroe Islands	1,399	42,000
	Isle of Man	588	69,000
SOUTHERN EUROPE	Andorra	487	40,000
	Gibraltar	6	31,000
	San Marino	60	22,000
	Vatican State	0.44	1,000
WESTERN EUROPE	Liechtenstein	158	28,000
	Monaco	1.5	27,000
OCEANIA			
MELANESIA	New Caledonia	18,998	153,000
	Solomon Islands	29,785	270,000
	Vanuatu	14,763	142,000
MICRONESIA	Guam[1]	541	114,000
	Johnston Island	*na*	*na*
	Kiribati with Canton and Enderbury Islands	754	64,000
	Midway Islands	4.9	*na*
	Nauru	20	6,000
	Pacific Islands	1,380	154,000
	Wake Islands	7.6	*na*
POLYNESIA	American Samoa	199	35,000
	Cook Islands	236	20,000
	French Polynesia	4,000	163,000
	Niue	259	3,000
	Pitcairn Islands	47	*na*
	Samoa	2,934	163,000
	Tokelau	10	*na*
	Tonga	699	109,000
	Tuvalu	25	8,000
	Wallis & Futuna Islands	275	12,000

1. See Detailed Country Tabulations
2. See Summary Table
3. Source: Department of Population, Statistics and Census Division, Republic of China.
na–not available

Sources: **Area:** *The Hammond Ambassador World Atlas.* Maplewood, NJ: Hammond Inc., 1988. Copyright © 1988 by Hammond, Inc. Reprinted by permission of Hammond, Inc.
Population: *World Population Prospects: Estimates and Projections as Assessed in 1984.* Population Studies No. 98. New York: United Nations, 1986, 48–53.

APPENDIX C:
Data—Sources, Adjustments, Qualifications

A. United Nations Data and Estimates

All tabulations in this section are based on data and estimates obtained by the United Nations in the course of the *eleventh* round of its *global demographic assessments*. No changes were made on the UN figures. UN data tape: courtesy of Population Division, United Nations Department of International Economic and Social Affairs. New York: United Nations 1988.

B. Detailed Country Tabulations

In the source notes to the Detailed Country Tabulations, references are given in full every time except when the same source has been quoted before in the same paragraph. The abbreviation *DYB 19nn* stands for *Demographic Yearbook 19nn*, New York: United Nations; the year of publication of the various volumes is not indicated. The abbreviation *DYB HS 1979* refers to the *Demographic Yearbook Historical Supplement 1979*, New York: United Nations 1979.

ARGENTINA

1970 POPULATION: Midyear estimate based on a sample of returns from the 30 September 1970 Census and 1984 United Nations population estimates. Cf. *DYB HS 1979*, Tab. 3, pp. 240–43, and *World Population Prospects: Estimates and Projections as Assessed in 1984*. New York: United Nations 1986, p. 231. BIRTHS BY AGE OF MOTHER: *DYB HS 1979*, Tab. 5, p. 420. BIRTHS BY SEX: *DYB HS 1979*, Tab. 20, p. 476. DEATHS: *DYB HS 1979*, Tab. 9, pp. 650–51.

AUSTRALIA

1970–1985 Courtesy of Demographic Section, Australian Bureau of Statistics. Belconnen A.C.T., December 1987.

After the 1981 Census, Australia adopted a new procedure of estimating its population: resident population including the estimated number of Australian residents overseas. The new population estimates, which are backdated to 1971, are adjusted for census underenumeration and based on a revised definition of the overseas migration component. Because of this new estimation procedure, the data from 1971 onward are not directly comparable to those published for earlier years.

AUSTRIA

1970 POPULATION: Midyear estimate. *Demographisches Jahrbuch Österreichs 1985*, Tab. 9.03, p. 202. Österreichisches Statistisches Zentralamt, Vienna 1986. Age groups under 1 and 1–4 estimated. BIRTHS BY AGE OF MOTHER & SEX: *DYB HS 1979*, Tab. 5, p. 432. DEATHS: *DYB HS 1979*, Tab. 9, pp. 700–703.

1975 POPULATION: Midyear estimate. *DYB 1976*, Tab. 7, pp. 188–89. Individual age groups of males adjusted to male total shown in source. BIRTHS BY AGE OF MOTHER & SEX: *DYB HS 1979*, Tab. 5, p. 432. DEATHS: *DYB HS 1979*, Tab. 9, pp. 700–703.

1980 POPULATION: Midyear estimate. *DYB 1981*, Tab. 7, pp. 226–27. BIRTHS BY AGE OF MOTHER: *DYB 1981*, Tab. 23, p. 583. BIRTHS BY SEX: *DYB 1981*, Tab. 20, p. 483. DEATHS: *DYB 1981*, Tab. 13, pp. 346–47.

1985 POPULATION: Midyear estimate. *Demographisches Jahrbuch Österreichs 1985*, Tab. 9.03, p. 203. Österreichisches Statistisches Zentralamt, Vienna 1986. Age groups under 1 and 1–4 estimated. BIRTHS BY AGE OF MOTHER & SEX: *Statistisches Handbuch für die Republik Österreich*, 37. Jahrgang, Tab. 2.26, p. 45. Österreichisches Statistisches Zentralamt, Vienna 1986. DEATHS: op. cit., Tab. 2.30, p. 47.

BARBADOS
1970 POPULATION: Midyear estimate based on 7 April 1970 population; cf. *DYB HS 1979,* Tab. 3, pp. 228–29. **BIRTH BY AGE OF MOTHER:** *DYB HS 1979,* Tab. 5, p. 408. **BIRTHS BY SEX:** *DYB 1981,* Tab. 20, p. 472. **DEATHS:** *DYB HS 1979,* Tab. 9, pp. 598–99.

Births and deaths recorded by year of registration rather than occurrence.

BELGIUM
1970 POPULATION: Midyear estimate based on populations of 1 July 1969 and 31 December 1970; cf. *DYB 1972,* Tab. 6, pp. 190–91, and *DYB 1973,* Tab. 6, pp. 166–67. **BIRTHS & DEATHS:** Courtesy of Nationaal Instituut voor de Statistiek, Ministerie van Economische Zaken. Brussels: October 1987.

1975 POPULATION: Midyear estimate. *DYB 1977,* Tab. 7, pp. 210–11. Ages under 1 and 1–4 estimated. **BIRTHS & DEATHS:** Courtesy of Nationaal Instituut voor de Statistiek, Ministerie van Economische Zaken, Brussels: October 1987.

1980, 1984 Courtesy of Nationaal Instituut voor de Statistiek, Ministerie van Economische Zaken. Brussels: October 1987.

BULGARIA
1970–1985 Courtesy of Ministry of Foreign Affairs, Bulgaria. Sofia: October 1987.

1985 population age groups under 1 and 1–4 estimated.

CANADA
1970–1985 Courtesy of Social and Economic Studies Division, Statistics Canada. Ottawa: July 1987.

CHILE
1970 POPULATION: Midyear estimate based on 22 April 1970 Census and 1984 United Nations population estimates. Cf. *DYB HS 1979,* Tab. 3, pp. 242–43, and *World Population Prospects: Estimates and Projections as Assessed in 1984,* New York: United Nations 1986, p. 236. **BIRTHS BY AGE OF MOTHER & SEX:** *DYB HS 1979,* Tab. 5, p. 421. **DEATHS:** *DYB HS 1979,* Tab. 9, pp. 652–53.

1980 POPULATION: Midyear estimate. *DYB 1980,* Tab. 7, pp. 188–89. Population age groups 80 and older extrapolated. **BIRTHS BY AGE OF MOTHER & SEX:** *DYB 1981,* Tab. 23, pp. 575–76. **DEATHS:** *DYB 1981,* Tab. 31, pp. 342–43.

CHINA, PEOPLE'S REPUBLIC
1981 Courtesy of State Statistical Bureau of the People's Republic of China. Beijing: November 1987.

All tabulations exclude the Republic of China (Taiwan), Hong Kong, and Macao.

CHINA, REPUBLIC OF (TAIWAN)
1970–1985 Courtesy of Department of Population, Statistics and Census Division, Ministry of Interior, Republic of China. Taipei: December 1987.

COMECON COUNTRIES (EASTERN EUROPE)
1970–1980 Cf. source notes for *Bulgaria, Czechoslovakia, German Democratic Republic, Hungary, Poland,* and *Romania.*

The European COMECON countries are the original member countries of the *Council for Mutual Economic Assistance,* which was established in 1949. The founding countries are identical with those comprising the Eastern European Region (cf. UN-Based Data and Tabulations).

CYPRUS, REPUBLIC OF
1980, 1985 Courtesy of Department of Statistics and Research, Ministry of Finance, Republic of Cyprus. Nicosia: September 1987.

1980 figures for total population, total deaths and births by age of mother revised on the basis of the 1982 Census of Housing. 1980 population age groups under 1 and 1–4 estimated. Population and deaths for age groups 70 and older in 1980 and 75 and older in 1985 extrapolated.

CZECHOSLOVAKIA
1970–1985 Courtesy of Federální Statisticky Urad CSSR. Prague: August and September 1987.

DENMARK
1970–1985 Courtesy of Danmarks Statistik. Copenhagen: October 1987.

ENGLAND AND WALES (U.K.)
1970–1985 Cf. source notes for the *United Kingdom of Great Britain and Northern Ireland.*

EUROPEAN COMMUNITY
1970–1980 Cf. source notes for *Belgium, Denmark, France, Federal Republic of Germany, Greece, Ireland, Italy, Luxembourg,* the *Netherlands, Portugal, Spain,* and *U.K.*

The European Community was originally founded in 1950 as the European Economic Community. The first member countries were Belgium, the Netherlands, Luxembourg, France, Italy, and West Germany. Since then, the membership in the Community has been expanded to twelve. All twelve of the present member countries are included in the tabulations. regardless of the time at which they joined the Community.

FIJI
1975, 1980   Courtesy of Bureau of Statistics, Fiji. Suva: September 1987.

1980 population estimate based on total population figure reported by Bureau of Statistics and age structure of 31 December 1980 population reported in *DYB 1982*, Tab. 7, pp. 204–5. 1980 population and deaths for age groups 75 and older extrapolated.

FINLAND
1970–1985   Courtesy of Central Statistical Office of Finland. Helsinki: August 1987.

1985 deaths under 1 and 1–4 estimated.

FRANCE
1970–1985   Courtesy of the Département des Population et Ménages, Institut National de la Statistique et des Etudes Economiques, France. Paris: September 1987.

GERMAN DEMOCRATIC REPUBLIC
1970–1985   Courtesy of Staatliche Zentralverwaltung für Statistik, Ministerrat der Deutschen Demokratischen Republik. Berlin: December 1987.

1970 distribution of births by age of mother at time of birth of child estimated from distribution of births by age of mother at beginning of 1970.

GERMANY, FEDERAL REPUBLIC
1970–1985   Courtesy of Statistisches Bundesamt, Federal Republic of Germany. Wiesbaden: August 1987.

All data include West Berlin.

GREECE
1970–1985   Courtesy of National Statistical Service of Greece. Athens: August 1987.

1970–85 deaths adjusted for probable undercount on the basis of 1984 United Nations estimates of the crude death and infant mortality rates for the periods 1965–70 to 1980–85; cf. *World Population Prospects: Estimates and Projections as Assessed in 1984.* New York: United Nations 1986, p. 310.

GREENLAND
1970, 1975   Courtesy of Danmarks Statistik. Kopenhagen: October 1987.

1980   POPULATION: Midyear estimate. *DYB 1981*, Tab. 7, pp. 214–15. BIRTHS BY AGE OF MOTHER & SEX: *DYB 1981*, Tab. 23, p. 570. DEATHS: *DYB 1981*, Tab. 13, pp. 338–39.

1985   Courtesy of Danmarks Statistik. Kopenhagen: October 1987.

GUAM
1970   POPULATION: Midyear estimate based on 1 April 1970 population; cf. *DYB HS 1979*, Tab. 3, pp. 278–79. BIRTHS BY AGE OF MOTHER: *DYB HS 1979*, Tab. 5, p. 455. BIRTHS BY SEX: *DYB 1981*, Tab. 20, p. 489. DEATHS: *DYB HS 1979*, Tab. 9, pp. 774–77.

1980   POPULATION: Midyear estimate based on 1 April 1980 population; cf. *DYB 1982*, Tab. 7, pp. 206–7. BIRTHS BY AGE OF MOTHER & SEX: *DYB 1982*, Tab. 10, p. 289. DEATHS: *DYB 1982*, Tab. 18, pp. 374–75.
The population figures refer to the de jure population plus the armed forces stationed in the area. The births and deaths include U.S. military personnel, their dependents, and contract employees.

GUATEMALA
1985   Courtesy of Instituto Nacional de Estadística Guatemala. Guatemala: September 1987.

Population: CELADE estimate. Ages under 1 and 1–4 estimated, ages 80 and older extrapolated.

HONG KONG
1970–1980   Courtesy of the Census and Statistics Department. Hong Kong, September 1987.

The 1980 data exclude Vietnamese refugees. The 1970 deaths refer to *registered* deaths, the 1975 and 1980 deaths to *known* deaths.

HUNGARY
1970–1985   Courtesy of Hungarian Central Statistical Office. Budapest: September 1987.

ICELAND
1970–1985   Courtesy of Statistical Bureau of Iceland. Reykjavik: August 1987.

IRELAND
1971–1986   Courtesy of Central Statistics Office. Dublin, January 1988 with the exception of the 1975 population: Midyear estimate, *DYB 1976*, Tab. 7, pp. 190–91. 1975 age groups under 1 and 1–4 estimated.

ISRAEL
1970–1985   Courtesy of Central Bureau of Statistics, Prime Minister's Office, State of Israel. Jerusalem: September 1987.

Data refer to Jewish population only; they include East Jerusalem and Israeli residents in territories occupied by Israel since 1967. 1970 deaths 75 and older, 1975 population 75 and older, and 1980 population 80 and older extrapolated.

ITALY
1970–1983   Courtesy of Istituto Centrale di Statistica, Italy. Rome: July 1987.

JAPAN
1970   POPULATION: Midyear estimate based on population of 1 October 1970; cf. *DYB HS 1979*, Tab. 3, pp. 250–51. BIRTHS BY AGE OF MOTHER: *1985 Vital Statistics*. Ministry of Health and Welfare, Tab. 4.5, p. 86. BIRTHS BY SEX: *DYB HS 1979*, Tab. 5, pp. 426–27. DEATHS: *DYB HS 1979*, Tab. 9, pp. 680–81.

1975   POPULATION: Midyear estimate based on population of 1 October 1975; cf. *DYB HS 1979*, Tab. 3, pp. 250–51. BIRTHS BY AGE OF MOTHER: *1985 Vital Statistics*. Ministry of Health and Welfare, Tab. 4.5, p. 86. BIRTHS BY SEX: *DYB 1981*, Tab. 23, p. 579. DEATHS: *DYB 1980*, Tab. 26, pp. 506–7.

1980   POPULATION: Midyear estimate based on 1 October 1980 population; cf. *DYB 1981*, Tab. 7, pp. 222–23. BIRTHS BY AGE OF MOTHER: *1985 Vital Statistics*. Ministry of Health and Welfare, Tab. 4.5, p. 87. BIRTHS BY SEX: *DYB 1981*, Tab. 20, p. 480. DEATHS: *DYB 1981*, Tab. 13, pp. 344–45.
Data refer to Japanese nationals in Japan only. Data for 1970 exclude Okinawa.

KUWAIT
1970–1980   Courtesy of Central Statistical Office, Ministry of Planning. Kuwait: September 1987.
1970, 1975, and 1980 population data adjusted from census date (21 April) to midyear.

LUXEMBOURG
1970   POPULATION: Midyear estimate based on populations of 1 July 1969 and 31 December 1970; cf. *DYB 1970*, Tab. 6, pp. 340–41, and *DYB 1971*, Tab. 7, p. 279. BIRTHS BY AGE OF MOTHER & SEX: *DYB HS 1979*, Tab. 5, p. 443. DEATHS: *DYB HS 1979*, Tab. 9, pp. 738–39.

1975   POPULATION: Midyear estimate based on populations of 31 December 1974 and 15 October 1978; cf. *DYB 1976*, Tab. 7, pp. 192–93, and *DYB 1979*, Tab. 7, pp. 230–31. BIRTHS BY AGE OF MOTHER & SEX: *DYB HS 1979*, Tab. 5, p. 443. DEATHS: *DYB HS 1979*, Tab. 9, pp. 738–39.

1980   POPULATION: Midyear estimate based on populations of 15 October 1979 and 31 March 1981; cf. *DYB 1983*, Tab. 7, pp. 200–201, and *DYB 1984*, Tab. 7, pp. 212–13. BIRTHS BY AGE OF MOTHER & SEX: *DYB 1982*, Tab. 10, p. 287. DEATHS: *DYB 1982*, Tab. 18, pp. 370–71.

1985   Courtesy of Service Central de la Statistique et des Etudes Economiques. Luxembourg: August 1987.
Population age groups 80 and older extrapolated.

MALAYSIA (PENINSULAR)
1970–1985   Courtesy of Department of Statistics, Malaysia. Kuala Lumpur: September 1987.
1975 population age groups under 1 and 1–4 estimated, 1970 and 1975 age groups 75 and older extrapolated.

MALTA
1970   POPULATION: Midyear estimate. *DYB 1971*, Tab. 7, p. 281. BIRTHS BY AGE OF MOTHER: *DYB HS 1979*, Tab. 5, p. 443. BIRTHS BY SEX: *DYB 1981*, Tab. 20, p. 484. DEATHS: *DYB HS 1979*, Tab. 9, pp. 740–41. Data refer to Maltese population and other residents.

1986   POPULATION: Midyear estimate based on population of 31 December 1985 and 31 December 1986; cf. *Demographic Review of the Maltese Islands 1986*. Valletta, Central Office of Statistics, Tabs. 2 & 3, pp. 2–3; BIRTHS BY AGE OF MOTHER: ibid., Tab. 11, p. 12. BIRTHS BY SEX: ibid., Tab. 9, p. 9; DEATHS: ibid., Tabs. 18 and 19, pp. 20–21. All data refer to the Maltese population only.

MAURITIUS
1970–1980   Courtesy of Central Statistical Office, Mauritius. Port Louis: September 1987.

MEXICO
1970–1983   Courtesy of Direccion General de Estadística, Direccion de Estadísticas Demograficas y Sociales, Mexico. Mexico, D.F.: April 1988.
1970 population under 1 and 80 and older estimated. Births to mothers aged 40 and older for 1970, 1980, and 1983 extrapolated following 1973 pattern; cf. *DYB HS 1979*, Tab. 5, p. 414.

THE NETHERLANDS
1970–1985   Courtesy of Department for Population Statistics, Netherlands Central Bureau of Statistics. Voorburg: September 1978.

NEW ZEALAND
1970–1985   Courtesy of Department of Statistics, New Zealand. Wellington: November 1987.

NORTHERN IRELAND (U.K.)
1970–1985   Cf. source notes for the *United Kingdom of Great Britain and Northern Ireland*.

NORWAY
1970–1985   Courtesy of Central Bureau of Statistics, Norway. Oslo: August 1987.

PANAMA

1970 POPULATION: Midyear estimate based on population of 10 May 1970; cf. *DYB HS 1979*, Tab. 3, pp. 236–37. Age groups 75 and older extrapolated. BIRTHS BY AGE OF MOTHER & SEX: *DYB HS 1979*, Tab. 5, pp. 415–16. DEATHS: *DYB HS 1979*, Tab. 9, pp. 632–33.

1980 POPULATION: Midyear estimate. *DYB 1981*, Tab. 7, pp. 216–17. Age classification based on year of birth rather than on exact date of birth. Age groups 80 and older extrapolated. BIRTHS BY AGE OF MOTHER & SEX: *DYB 1982*, Tab. 10, p. 282. DEATHS: *DYB 1982*, Tab. 18, pp. 360–61.

All data exclude the former Panama Canal Zone.

POLAND

1970–1985 Courtesy of International Statistics Division, Central Statistical Office, Polish People's Republic. Warsaw: August 1987.

PORTUGAL

1970 POPULATION: Midyear estimate based on 15 December 1970 population; cf. *DYB HS 1979*, Tab. 3, pp. 270–71. BIRTHS BY AGE OF MOTHER: *DYB HS 1979*, Tab. 5, p. 446. Age-specific births adjusted to total for same year shown in *DYB 1981*, Tab. 20, p. 486. BIRTHS BY SEX: *DYB 1981*, Tab. 20, p. 486. DEATHS: *DYB HS 179*, Tab. 9, pp. 748–49.

1975 POPULATION: Midyear estimate. *DYB 1977*, Tab. 7, pp. 216–17. BIRTHS BY AGE OF MOTHER & SEX: *DYB HS 1979*, Tab. 5, pp. 446–47. DEATHS: *DYB 1980*, Tab. 26, pp. 528–29.

1980, 1985 Courtesy of National Statistical Institute, Portugal. Lisbon: September 1987.

1980 and 1985 population age groups under 1 and 1–4 estimated, age groups 75 and older extrapolated.

PUERTO RICO

1970–1985 Courtesy of Department of Health, Commonwealth of Puerto Rico. San Juan, September 1987.

ROMANIA

1970 POPULATION: Midyear estimate. *DYB 1972*, Tab. 6, pp. 198–99. BIRTHS BY AGE OF MOTHER: *DYB HS 1979*, Tab. 5, p. 447. BIRTHS BY SEX: *DYB 1981*, Tab. 20, p. 486. DEATHS: *DYB HS 1979*, Tab. 9, pp. 750–51.

1975 POPULATION: Midyear estimate. *DYB 1976*, Tab. 7, pp. 192–93. BIRTHS BY AGE OF MOTHER: *DYB HS 1979*, Tab. 7, pp. 192–93. BIRTHS BY AGE OF MOTHER: *DYB HS 1979*, Tab. 5, p. 447. BIRTHS BY SEX: Estimated on the basis of 1971–74 sex ratios at birth; cf. *DYB 1981*, Tab. 20, p. 487. DEATHS: *DYB HS 1979*, Tab. 9, pp. 750–51. Age groups under 1 and 1–4 estimated.

1980 POPULATION: Midyear estimate. *DYB 1981*, Tab. 7, pp. 230–31. BIRTHS BY AGE OF MOTHER: *DYB 1981*, Tab. 23, p. 592. BIRTHS BY SEX: cf. Births by Sex 1975. DEATHS: *DYB 1981*, Tab. 13, pp. 350–51. Age groups under 1 and 1–4 estimated.

SCOTLAND (U.K.)

1970–1985 Cf. source notes for the *United Kingdom of Great Britain and Northern Ireland*.

SPAIN

1970–1983 Courtesy of Instituto Nacional de Estadística, Spain. Madrid: February 1988.

Census population 31 December 1970 adjusted to midyear.

ST. CHRISTOPHER AND NEVIS

1970 POPULATION: Midyear estimate based on 1 April 1970 population; cf. *DYB HS 1979*, Tab. 3, pp. 238–39. BIRTHS BY AGE OF MOTHER: *DYB HS 1979*, Tab. 5, p. 417. BIRTHS BY SEX: *DYB 1981*, Tab. 20, p. 474. DEATHS: *DYB HS 1979*, Tab. 9, pp. 638–39.

1980 POPULATION: Midyear estimate based on 12 May 1980 population; cf. *DYB 1984*, Tab. 7, pp. 198–99. Age groups under 1 and 1–4 estimated. BIRTHS BY AGE OF MOTHER: *DYB 1982*, Tab. 10, p. 282. BIRTHS BY SEX: *DYB 1981*, Tab. 20, p. 475. DEATHS: *DYB 1982*, Tab. 18, pp. 362–63.

Births and deaths recorded by year of registration rather than occurrence.

Until 1967, St. Christopher and Nevis (St. Kitts and Neville) formed an administrative unit with the island of Anguilla. The 1970 and 1980 data exclude the island of Anguilla.

SINGAPORE

1970–1985 Courtesy of Department of Statistics, Republic of Singapore. Singapore: September 1987.

The 1970 population is the census population of 22 June, the 1980 population the census population of 24 June.

SOUTH AFRICA, REPUBLIC OF

1970–1985 Courtesy of Central Statistical Service, Republic of South Africa. Pretoria: October and December 1987.

All data sets include only the white, colored, and Asian populations; they exclude the black population because of the unavailability of reliable vital statistics. Blacks numbered 15.3 million in 1970

(*Census Report 02-05-05*) and 17 million in 1980 (*Census Report 02-80-04*).

The 1970 data include the Republics of Transkei, Bophuthatswana, Venda, and Ciskei; the 1980 data exclude the Republics of Transkei, Bophuthatswana, and Venda, and the 1985 data exclude the Republics of Transkei, Bophuthatswana, Venda, and Ciskei. All population figures are based on censuses taken in the respective years. The 1985 census is not adjusted for possible undercounts.

SWEDEN
1970–1985 Courtesy of Statistics Sweden. Stockholm: August 1987.

SWITZERLAND
1970–1986 Courtesy of Bundesamt für Statistik. Bern: January 1988.

Age of mother at time of childbirth calculated as difference between years of birth of mother and child, age at death as difference between year of birth and year of death.

TRINIDAD AND TOBAGO
1970 POPULATION: Midyear population based on 7 April 1970 population and 1984 United Nations estimates. Cf. *DYB HS 1979*, Tab. 3, pp. 272–73, and *World Population Prospects: Estimates and Projections as Assessed in 1984.* New York: United Nations 1986, p. 257. BIRTHS BY AGE OF MOTHER & SEX: *DYB HS 1979*, Tab. 5, p. 418. DEATHS: *DYB HS 1979*, Tab. 9, pp. 642–44.

UNITED KINGDOM OF GREAT BRITAIN AND NORTHERN IRELAND
1970–1985 Courtesy of Central Statistical Office, Great Britain. London: August 1987.

UNITED STATES OF AMERICA
1970 POPULATION: Midyear estimate based on 1 April 1970 census population. Cf. U.S. Bureau of the Census, *1980 Census of Population,* vol. I: *Characteristics of the Population;* Part B: General Population Characteristics, No. 1: U.S. Summary. Washington, D.C., 1983, Tab. 44, pp. 37–38. BIRTHS BY AGE OF MOTHER & SEX: U.S. National Center for Health Statistics, *Vital Statistics of the United States, 1970,* vol. I: *Natality.* Rockville, Maryland, 1975, Tab. 1–52, pp. 37–38. Based on a 50 percent sample of births. DEATHS: U.S. National Center for Health Statistics, op. cit., vol. II: *Mortality;* Part A, Tab. 1–26, pp. 184–85.

1975 POPULATION: Midyear estimate of resident population. U.S. Bureau of the Census, *Current Population Reports,* P-25: Population Estimates and Projections, No. 643. Washington, D.C., 1977, Tab. 2, p. 11. BIRTHS BY AGE OF MOTHER & SEX:

U.S. National Center for Health Statistics, *Vital Statistics of the United States, 1975,* vol. I: *Natality.* Hyattsville, Maryland, 1978, Tab. 1–52, p. 73. Based on 100 percent of births in selected states and on a 50 percent sample in all other states. DEATHS: U.S. National Center for Health Statistics, op. cit., vol. II: *Mortality;* Part A, Tab. 1–26, pp. 186–87.

1980 POPULATION: Midyear estimate based on 1 April 1980 census population. See 1970 population. BIRTHS BY AGE OF MOTHER & SEX: U.S. National Center for Health Statistics, *Vital Statistics of the United States, 1980,* vol. I: *Natality.* Hyattsville, Maryland, 1984, Tab. 1–54, p. 85. Based on 100 percent of births in selected states and on a 50 percent sample in all other states. DEATHS: U.S. National Center for Health Statistics, op. cit., vol. II: *Mortality,* Part A, Tab. 1–25, pp. 242–43.

1985 POPULATION: Midyear estimate of resident population. U.S. Bureau of the Census, *Current Population Reports,* P-25: Population Estimates and Projections, No. 1000. Washington, D.C., 1985, Tab. 2, pp. 23–24. BIRTHS BY AGE OF MOTHER: U.S. National Center for Health Statistics, *Monthly Vital Statistics Report,* Advanced Report of Final Natality Statistics 1985. Hyattsville, Maryland, 1987, Tab. 2, p. 14. BIRTHS BY SEX: Op. cit., Tab. 7, p. 20. DEATHS: U.S. National Center for Health Statistics, *Vital Statistics of the United States, 1985,* vol. II: *Mortality,* Part B. Hyattsville, Maryland, 1988, Tab. 8.5, pp. 170–71.

UNION OF SOVIET SOCIALIST REPUBLICS
1970 POPULATION, BIRTHS, AND AGE-SPECIFIC DEATH RATES: Courtesy of State Committee of the USSR on Statistics, Scientific Research Institute of Statistics, Department of Demography. Moscow: April 1988.

1979 POPULATION: State Committee for Statistics, *Population of the USSR 1987,* Statistical Collection, Moscow 1988, p. 49. BIRTHS BY AGE OF MOTHER: Obtained from average annual rates for the period 1978–81; op. cit., p. 209. BIRTHS BY SEX: Estimates based on sex ratios for the years 1971–73; cf. *DYB 1981,* Tab. 25, p. 491. DEATHS: Obtained from average annual rates for the period 1978–81; op. cit., p. 321.

1987 POPULATION: State Committee for Statistics, *Population of the USSR 1987.* Statistical Collection, Moscow 1987, p. 49. BIRTHS BY AGE OF MOTHER: Obtained from average annual rates for the years 1986–87; op. cit., p. 20–29. BIRTHS BY SEX: See 1979. DEATHS: Obtained from average annual rates for the years 1986–87; op. cit., p. 321.

1979 and 1987 population and deaths under 1 and 1–4 estimated, 65 and older extrapolated.

VENEZUELA

1970–1985 Courtesy of Oficina Central de Estadística e Informatica, Republica de Venezuela. Caracas: October 1987.

Population under 1 and 1–4 estimated, 75 and older extrapolated. Births and deaths recorded by year of registration rather than occurrence. All data exclude Indian jungle population estimated at 32,000 in 1961.

YUGOSLAVIA

1970–1985 Courtesy of International Division, Federal Statistical Office. Beograd: January 1988.

C. Social & Economic Indicators *

Most social and economic indicators shown in this volume are taken from *World Development Report 1987,* compiled by the International Bank for Reconstruction and Development/The World Bank, Washington, D.C. Other sources of socioeconomic indicators used are quoted below.

EDUCATION: op. cit., Table 31, pp. 262–63.
The primary source supplying the original data was UNESCO. The reference date, if quoted as "c. 1984," is "generally not more than three years distant from 1984" (p. 282). Enrollment figures represent estimated ratios (expressed in percent) of all pupils enrolled to the population of school age. Most countries consider primary-school age to be 6–11 years, and secondary-school age 12–17 years. In the estimation of the enrollment ratios, existing differences between countries in terms of standard age and duration of schooling are taken into account. For some countries, enrollment ratios exceed 100 percent "because some pupils are younger or older than the country's primary school age" (ibid.). The ratios for those in higher education normally use the 20–24 age cohort as denominator (cf. ibid.).

LABOR FORCE: op. cit., Table 32, pp. 264–65.
Labor Force is defined as "economically active persons 10 years and older, including the armed forces and the unemployed, but excluding housewives, students, and other economically inactive groups" (p. 282). Main source of the labor force data is the International Labor Organization (ILO).

The *Agricultural Sector* is composed of agriculture, forestry, hunting, and fishing; *Industry* comprises mining, manufacturing, construction, electricity, gas, and water. All other economic activities are classified as *Services* (p. 272).

Labor-force information for Barbados, Cyprus, Fiji, Iceland, Luxembourg, Malta, and Puerto Rico is taken from: UN Department of International Economic and Social Affairs, *World Demographic Estimates and Projections, 1950–2025.* United Nations, New York, 1988; for the Republic of China (Taiwan) from the *Handbook of the Nations/1981,* Second Edition. Detroit: Grand River Books, 1981.

GNP: op. cit., Table 1, pp. 202–3.
"Gross National Product (GNP) measures the total domestic and foreign output claimed by residents and is calculated without making deductions for depreciation. It comprises gross domestic product adjusted by income residents receive from abroad for labor and capital less similar payments made to nonresidents who contributed to the domestic economy" (p. 268).

The 1985 GNP per capita figures are calculated according to the World Bank's *Atlas* method "on the basis of the 1983–85 base period" (pp. 268–69).

GNP data for countries with populations of less than 1 million inhabitants are taken from the *World Development Report 1987,* Box A1, p. 269; for Bulgaria, the Republic of China (Taiwan), Czechoslovakia, the German Democratic Republic, Poland, Romania, and the USSR from the *Handbook of the Nations/1981,* Second Edition. Detroit: Grand River Books, 1981.

INCOME DISTRIBUTION: op. cit., Table 26, pp. 252–53.
The Income Distribution figures "refer to the total disposable household income accruing to percentile groups of households ranked by total household income" (p. 280). Sources from which the base information was obtained include the Economic Commission for Latin America and the Caribbean (ECLAC), the Economic & Social Commission for Asia and the Pacific (ESCAP), the International Labor Organization (ILO), the Organization for International Cooperation and Development (OECD), the United Nations, the World Bank, and national sources. Because of differences among countries in official statistical systems and concepts applied as well as the use of information from surveys originally designed for other purposes, the estimates, while "considered the best available . . . should be interpreted with extreme caution" (*World Development Report 1987,* 252–53).

HEALTH AND NUTRITION: op. cit., Table 30, pp. 260–61.
Estimates of Population per Physician are based on World Health Organization (WHO) information.

*From *World Development Report 1987.* Copyright © 1987 by The International Bank for Reconstruction and Development/The World Bank. Reprinted with permission of Oxford University Press, Inc.

The Daily Calorie Supply per capita estimates, derived from data supplied by the Food and Agriculture Organization (FAO), are "calculated by dividing the calorie equivalent of the food supplies in an economy by the population. 'Food Supplies' comprise domestic production, imports less exports, and changes in stocks; they exclude animal feed, seeds for use in agriculture, and food lost in processing and distribution" (p. 282).

APPENDIX D:
VANPRO—A Demographic Software Package

All demographic parameters assembled in the Detailed Country Tabulations of this volume were generated by means of a number of specifically designed computer programs. The prototypes of these programs were developed for the University of Chicago's mainframe computer some 20 years ago. In 1971, all programs were rewritten with some modifications and made "portable," so that they could be used on computers of different makes. In preparation for this volume, the routines were rewritten once again, this time in MICROSOFT FORTRAN 4.01, and adapted for use on the PC. To make the programs truly portable, they were combined in a software package named VANPRO, an abbreviation derived from VITAL ANALYSIS PROGRAMS. The user of VANPRO can easily recalculate our figures or extend the computations to additional populations. To facilitate the generation of new data files, VANPRO includes a menu selection CREATE DATA FILE. Another selection, COMBINE DATA SETS, makes it possible to combine up to 30 existing data files into a new one for a larger population unit. The only input required for any of the demographic routines included in VANPRO—eight in all—is the original data file containing age-sex specific population, birth, and death information.

Aside from the two data-file creation options mentioned, VANPRO incorporates the following demographic routines:

Selection 8: POPULATION DATA AND RATES
9: DIRECT STANDARDIZATION
10: LIFE TABLES
11: POPULATION PROJECTION
12: LOTKA EQUATION
13: LESLIE MATRIX
14: COMPLEX ROOTS
15: INTRINSIC RATES

These routines are either identical or expanded versions of those published under similar names and in the form of FORTRAN IV source codes in *Population: Facts and Methods of Demography* (1971) except that they have been adapted to MICROSOFT FORTRAN 4.01. The expanded routines include (1) POPULATION DATA AND RATES, (2) POPULATION PROJECTION, and (3) LESLIE MATRIX. The routine POPULATION DATA AND RATES calculates a host of vital rates and age-sex ratios for the observed population as does POPULATION PROJECTION for the projected populations. LESLIE MATRIX in its present form incorporates a partial spectral decomposition of the projection matrix and a procedure for calculating the contributions of the principal pair of complex roots and all other roots of the matrix taken together to the difference between the observed population and its stable equivalent.

The printed output of all VANPRO selections exceeds that displayed in the tables of the Detailed Country Tabulations. Selections LIFE TABLES and LOTKA EQUATION show intermediate parameters that have to be calculated before the final ones appearing in the printed tables can be obtained; LESLIE MATRIX extends the calculations beyond those whose results are presented in the book; DIRECT STANDARDIZATION not only produces standardized rates but decomposes the difference between two crude rates, and COMPLEX ROOTS as well as INTRINSIC RATES use procedures for approximating the values of the dominant and complex roots of the projection matrix that differ from those employed in obtaining the results presented in the printed tables. For a summary of the printed and disk output produced by any one of the eight VANPRO selections, see the listing on the following pages of this Appendix.

The README file of VANPRO does not contain detailed mathematical explanations of the procedures applied to the data. For such explanations, the reader is referred to the just cited earlier population volume or to the Demographic Data and Parameters chapter of this book.

VANPRO is entirely menu-driven and its operation does not require any special manual. All information needed for the running of the package not immediately obvious from the program prompts can be found in the README menu selection. To activate the package, you just insert the VANPRO diskette into a floppy drive of an IBM PC, IBM compatible or clone and type VANPRO and ⟨ENTER⟩. The compiled version of VANPRO occupies less than 140 KB of memory and, therefore, can be run on a PC of minimal configuration. What is needed in many instances is a printer. If the output is directed toward a disk file (a user option), a printer is not required except for the two data-file creation routines. The menu selections SET INPUT/OUTPUT DIRECTORIES and SET OUTPUT DEVICE make it possible to specify the input and output directories and output device and, if desired, to save these specifications for future use.

Readers interested in obtaining a copy of VANPRO on a floppy disk can do so at the price of a blank diskette and mailing charges by writing to:

Office of Population Studies
University of San Carlos
Cebu City 6000
PHILIPPINES.

VANPRO Output*

MENU SELECTION	PRINTED OUTPUT	DISK OUTPUT
POPULATION DATA AND RATES	Distributions of population, births, and deaths, by age and sex;	
	Crude rates of birth, death, and natural increase, by sex;	Crude rates of birth, death, and natural increase, by sex;
	Infant mortality rate, by sex;	Infant mortality rate, by sex;
	General fertility rate;	General fertility rate;
	Percent of population <15, 15–64, 65+, by sex;	Percent of population <15, 15–64, 65+, by sex;
	Youth, old age, total dependency ratios, by sex;	Youth, old age, total dependency ratios, by sex;
	Child/woman ratio;	Child/woman ratio;
	Sex ratio at birth;	Sex ratio at birth;
	Age-specific and total population sex ratios.	Age-specific and total population sex ratios.
DIRECT STANDARD-IZATION	*Age distributions of given and standard populations, given events and rates, and expected events;*	
	Crude rates of standard and given population, standardized rate;	Crude rates of standard and given population, standardized rate;
	Ratio of standardized to standard rate;	Ratio of standardized to standard rate;
	Rate- and age-structural components of difference between crude rates of given and standard populations using three different age-structural weights.	Rate- and age-structural components of difference between crude rates of given and standard populations using three different age-structural weights.
LIFE TABLES	Male and/or female life-table columns (19 age groups): $_nP_x, _nD_x, _nM_x, _nq_x, l_x, _nd_x, _nL_x, _nm_x, _na_x, T_x, r_x, e_x.$	Male and/or female life-table columns (19 age groups): $_nM_x, _nq_x, l_x, _nd_x, _nL_x, _nm_x, _na_x, T_x, e_x.$
POPULATION PROJECTION	*Projected populations by age and sex in five-year intervals.* Projection period specified by user (maximum: 500 years);	Projected populations by age and sex in five-year intervals. Projection period specified by user (maximum: 500 years);

*Optional printed output is shown in italics. For specifications of the disk output files, see VANPRO menu selection README.

MENU SELECTION	PRINTED OUTPUT	DISK OUTPUT
	Percent of projected populations <15, 15–64, 65+, by sex;	
	Dependency ratios of projected populations, by sex;	
	Birth, death, and growth rates of projected populations, by sex;	
	Stable equivalent of observed population by age and sex (absolute numbers and percent);	Stable equivalent of observed population by age and sex (absolute numbers and percent);
	Intrinsic rates of birth, death, and increase for females; female dominant stable rates of birth and death for males;	Intrinsic rates of birth, death, and increase for females;
	Index of dissimilarity between observed and stable age structure.	Index of dissimilarity between observed and stable age structure.
LOTKA EQUATION	Female population in childbearing age groups;	
	Births by age of mother;	
	Age-specific birth rates;	
	Age-specific female birth rates;	Age-specific female birth rates;
	Life-table population ($_nL_x$);	
	Net maternity function;	Net maternity function;
	First and second moments of net maternity function;	First and second moments of net maternity function;
	Sex ratio at birth;	
	TFR, GRR, NRR, μ, σ^2, r, T.	*TFR, GRR, NRR, μ, σ^2, r, T.*
LESLIE MATRIX	Assembled abbreviated projection matrix;	First row and subdiagonal of abbreviated projection matrix;
	First column and row of first stable matrix (actual and normalized values);	First column and row of first (abbreviated) stable matrix, normalized;
	Fisher values;	Fisher values;
	Age-specific and total reproductive values;	Age-specific and total reproductive values;
	Dominant root and corresponding r;	Dominant root and corresponding r.
	First column and row of first spectral component (18×18 matrix);	
	First column and row of first deflated matrix (18×18);	
	Stable equivalent to total population c_1;	
	First column and row of second stable matrix (18×18);	
	First column and row of second spectral component (18×18 matrix);	
	Principal pair of complex roots with corresponding rs;	
	Stable equivalents c_2 and c_3;	
	Contributions of 1) dominant root, 2) principal pair of complex roots, and 3) all other complex roots taken together to observed population, by age.	
COMPLEX ROOTS	Coefficients of Lotka's characteristic equation;	Coefficients of Lotka's characteristic equation;

MENU SELECTION	PRINTED OUTPUT	DISK OUTPUT
	Roots of the projection matrix, corresponding annual values r and absolute roots, in order of magnitude.	Roots of the projection matrix, corresponding annual values r and absolute roots, in order of magnitude.
INTRINSIC RATES	Net maternity function; Three estimates of intrinsic rate obtained through iterative process from 1) Lotka's integral equation, 2) LaPlace transform, 3) Matrix equation; Number of cycles to achieve convergence in iterative process.	Three estimates of intrinsic rate obtained through iterative process from 1) Lotka's integral equation, 2) LaPlace transform, 3) Matrix equation.

Cooperating National Statistical Agencies and Correspondents

We would like to express our sincere appreciation and gratitude to the national statistical agencies all over the world for providing us with most of the data for the Detailed Country Tabulations in this volume, and to our correspondents in these agencies who shared with us their expertise and time.

EGYPT: A. Shalaby, Central Agency for Public Mobilisation & Statistics; MALAWI: W. R. M'manga, National Statistical Office; MAURITIUS: H. Y. Wong Man Wan, Central Statistical Office; LESOTHO: M. Africa, Bureau of Statistics; SENEGAL: The Director, Direction de la Statistique, Ministère de l'Economie et des Finances; SEYCHELLES: M. T. Gopal, Information Systems Division, President's Office; SOUTH AFRICA, REPUBLIC: M. S. Kruger, Central Statistical Service.

CANADA: Dhruva N. Nagnur, Social and Economic Studies Division, Statistics Canada; COLOMBIA: Oscar Cleves C., Departamento Administrativo Nacional de Estadística; ECUADOR: Gualberto Andrade P., Instituto Nacional de Estadística y Censos; EL SALVADOR: Ana Ide Lopez, Direccion General de Estadística y Censos; GUATEMALA: Aura M. Calderon, Instituto Nacional de Estadística; MEXICO: Ma. Elena Figueroa Marquez, Direccion General de Estadística; PUERTO RICO: Jose A. Saliceti, Department of Health; UNITED STATES OF AMERICA: Thomas W. Pullum, Population Research Center, the University of Texas at Austin; Nancy L. Boone, U.S. Department of the Interior; URUGUAY: Orual Andina, Direccion General de Estadística y Censos; VENEZUELA: Yajaira Garcia Valles, Oficina Central de Estadística e Informatica.

CHINA, PEOPLE'S REPUBLIC: Zhang Sai, State Statistical Bureau of the People's Republic of China; CHINA, REPUBLIC OF (TAIWAN): Tseng, Chin-Yueh, Department of Population, Ministry of Interior; CYPRUS, REPUBLIC OF: I. Chappa, Department of Statistics and Research, Ministry of Finance; HONG KONG: Joseph Lee, Census and Statistics Department; INDIA: M. G. Sardana, Central Statistical Organization, Dept. of Statistics, Ministry of Planning; INDONESIA: Sri Poedjastoeti, Central Bureau of Statistics; ISRAEL: Z. Eisenbach, Central Bureau of Statistics; JAPAN: Joji Sawada, Management and Coordination Agency, Statistics Bureau; KUWAIT: Musa'ad H. Al-Omaim, Central Statistical Office, Ministry of Planning; MALAYSIA: Kwok Kwan Kit, Jabatan Perangkaan Malaysia; SINGAPORE: Kenneth Goh, Dept. of Statistics; SRI LANKA: The Director, Dept. of Census and Statistics; THAILAND: Niyom Purakam, National Statistical Office.

BELGIUM: L. Diels, Nationaal Instituut voor de Statistiek; BULGARIA: D. Popov, Ministère des Affaires Etrangères; CZECHOSLOVAKIA: Vladimir Micka, Federalni Statisticky Urad CSSR; DENMARK: Bodil Stenvig, Danmarks Statistik; FINLAND: Eero Heikkonen, Central Statistical Office of Finland; FRANCE: C. Seibel, Institut National de la Statistique et des Etudes Economiques; GERMAN DEMOCRATIC REPUBLIC: Herr Koch, Staatliche Zentralverwaltung für Statistik; GERMANY, FEDERAL REPUBLIC: Herr Bosse, Statistisches Bundesamt; GREECE: George Siampos, National Statistical Service of Greece; HUNGARY: The President, Hungarian Central Statistical Office; ICELAND: Gudni Baldursson, Statistical Bureau of Iceland; IRELAND: Margaret O'Beirne, Central Statistics Office; ITALY: The Director General, Istituto Central Statistica; LUXEMBOURG: G. Als, Service Central de la Statistique et des Etudes Economiques; MALTA: A. Briffa, Central Office of Statistics; NETHERLANDS: P. Verhoef, Centraal Bureau voor de Statistiek; NORWAY: Eva Jemblie Monssen, Statistisk Sentralbyra; POLAND: T. Kania, Central Statistical Office; PORTUGAL: Manuel J. Rosa, National Statistical Institute; SPAIN: Carmen Arribas, Instituto Nacional de Estadística; SWEDEN: Hans Lundström, Statistics Sweden; SWITZERLAND: W. Zingg, Bundesamt für Statistik; UNITED KINGDOM OF GREAT BRITAIN AND NORTHERN IRELAND: K. A. Burrows, Central Statistical Office; YUGOSLAVIA: Margita Jakic, International Division, Federal Statistical Office.

AUSTRALIA: C. Y. Choi, Demographic Section, Australian Bureau of Statistics; FIJI: V. Lewai, Bureau of Statistics; NEW ZEALAND: B. Haines, Department of Statistics.

UNION OF SOVIET SOCIALIST REPUBLICS: A. G. Volkov, Department of Demography, Scientific Research Institute of Statistics, State Committee of the USSR on Statistics; Sergej Sherbov, International Institute for Applied Systems Analysis, Laxenburg, Austria.

Region-Country-Territory Index

The numbers or the letter B after the territorial names indicate the pages on which demographic information for the population of the territory can be found. When three numbers are shown, the first refers to the Summary Table, the second to UN-Based Information, and the third to Detailed Country Tabulations. The letter *B* refers to Appendix B. The names of geographical regions are printed in capital letters.

For good measure, A and C, for Appendixes A (country/territory grouping) and C (data sources), are also listed here.

A

Afghanistan 80–81, 208
AFRICA 64–65, 109, A
Agalesa, Rodrigues, and St. Brandon *see* Mauritius
Albania 90–91, 255
Algeria 64–65, 115
American Samoa, *see* Samoa, American
Andorra *B*
Angola 64–65, 116
Anguilla *B*
Antigua *B*
Antilles, Netherlands *B*
Argentina 74–75, 171, 302–3, C
Ascension, *see* St. Helena, Ascension, and Tristan da Cunha
ASIA 80–81, 203, A
Australia, 100–101, 288, 560–65, C
AUSTRALIA–NEW ZEALAND 98–99, 284, A
Austria 90–91, 256, 400–405, C

B

Bahamas *B*
Bahrain 82–83, 209
Bangladesh 82–83, 210
Barbados 74–75, 172, 304–5, C
Barbuda *B*
Belgium 90–91, 257, 406–11, C

Belize *B*
Benin 64–65, 117
Bermuda *B*
Bhutan 82–83, 211
Bolivia 74–75, 173
Botswana 66–67, 118
Brazil 74–75, 174
British Indian Ocean Territories *B*
British Virgin Islands, *see* Virgin Islands, British
Brunei *B*
Bulgaria 90–91, 258, 412–17, C
Burkina Faso 66–67, 119
Burma 82–83, 212
Burundi 66–67, 120

C

Caicos Islands, *see* Turks and Caicos Islands
Cameroon 66–67, 121
Canada 80–81, 200, 334–39, C
Canton, *see* Kiribati, Canton, and Enderbury
Cape Verde 66–67, 122
CARIBBEAN 74–75, 168, A
Cayman Islands *B*
CENTRAL AFRICA 64–65, 110, A
Central African Republic 66–67, 123
CENTRAL AMERICA 74–75, 169, A
Chad 66–67, 124
Channel Islands *B*
Chile 74–75, 175, 306–9, C
China, People's Republic 82–83, 213, 350–51, C
China, Republic of (Taiwan) 82–83, 352–57, B, C
Christmas Island, *see* Australia
Cocos Islands, *see* Australia
Colombia 74–75, 176
COMECON, *see* EASTERN EUROPE
Comoros 66–67, 125
Congo 66–67, 126
Cook Islands *B*
Costa Rica 74–75, 177